THE NEW GROVE

DICTIONARY OF MUSIC AND MUSICIANS

Volume Nineteen

THE NEW GROVE

Dictionary of Music and Musicians

SECOND EDITION

Edited by

Stanley Sadie

Executive editor

John Tyrrell

VOLUME 19

Paliashvili to Pohle

GROVE

An imprint of Oxford University Press

Oxford University Press

Oxford   New York

Auckland   Bangkok   Buenos Aires   Cape Town   Chennai
Dar es Salaam   Delhi   Hong Kong   Istanbul   Karachi   Kolkata
Kuala Lumpur   Madrid   Melbourne   Mexico City   Mumbai   Nairobi
São Paulo   Shanghai   Taipei   Tokyo   Toronto

ISBN-13 978-0-19-517067-2
ISBN 0-19-517067-9

———

First Edition of *A Dictionary of Music and Musicians*, planned and edited by
Sir George Grove, DCL, in four volumes, with an Appendix edited by J. A. Fuller Maitland,
and an index by Mrs Edmond Wodehouse, 1878, 1880, 1883, 1889
Reprinted 1890, 1900

Second Edition, edited by J. A. Fuller Maitland, in five volumes, 1904–10

Third Edition, edited by H. C. Colles, in five volumes, 1927

Fourth Edition, edited by H. C. Colles, in five volumes, with Supplementary Volume, 1940

Fifth Edition, edited by Eric Blom, in nine volumes, 1954; with Supplementary Volume 1961
Reprinted 1961, 1973, 1975

American Supplement, edited by Waldo Selden Pratt, in one volume, 1920
Reprinted with new material, 1928; many later reprints

The New Grove Dictionary of Music and Musicians™ first edition
edited by Stanley Sadie in twenty volumes, 1980
Reprinted 1981, 1984, 1985, 1986, 1987, 1988, 1989, 1990, 1991, 1992, 1993, 1994, 1995
Reprinted in paperback 1995, 1996, 1997, 1998

The New Grove Dictionary of Music and Musicians, second edition
edited by Stanley Sadie / executive editor John Tyrrell
published in twenty-nine volumes by Macmillan Publishers Limited in the year 2001

———

Text keyboarded by Alden Bookset, Oxford, England
Database management by Semantico, Brighton, England
Pagination by Clowes Group, Suffolk, England
Printed in the United States of America
3 5 7 9 8 6 4 2

Contents

THE DICTIONARY, VOLUME NINETEEN

Paliashvili – Pohle   1

General Abbreviations

A	alto, contralto [voice]		BFA	Bachelor of Fine Arts
a	alto [instrument]		BFE	British Forum for Ethnomusicology
AA	Associate of the Arts		bk(s)	book(s)
AB	Alberta; Bachelor of Arts		BLitt	Bachelor of Letters/Literature
ABC	American Broadcasting Company; Australian Broadcasting Commission		blq(s)	burlesque(s)
			blt(s)	burletta(s)
Abt.	Abteilung [section]		BM	Bachelor of Music
ACA	American Composers Alliance		BME, BMEd	Bachelor of Music Education
acc.	accompaniment, accompanied by		BMI	Broadcast Music Inc.
accdn	accordion		BMus	Bachelor of Music
addl	additional		bn	bassoon
addn(s)	addition(s)		BRD	Federal Republic of Germany (Bundesrepublik Deutschland [West Germany])
ad lib	ad libitum			
aft(s)	afterpiece(s)		Bros.	Brothers
Ag	Agnus Dei		BRTN	Belgische Radio en Televisie Nederlands
AGMA	American Guild of Musical Artists		BS, BSc	Bachelor of Science
AIDS	Acquired Immune Deficiency Syndrome		Bs	Benedictus
AK	Alaska		BSM	Bachelor of Sacred Music
AL	Alabama		Bte	Benedicite
all(s)	alleluia(s)		Bucks.	Buckinghamshire
AM	Master of Arts		Bulg.	Bulgarian
a.m.	ante meridiem [before noon]		bur.	buried
AMC	American Music Center		BVM	Blessed Virgin Mary
Amer.	American		BWV	Bach-Werke-Verzeichnis [Schmieder, catalogue of J.S. Bach's works]
amp	amplified			
AMS	American Musicological Society			
Anh.	Anhang [appendix]		C	contralto
anon.	anonymous(ly)		c	circa [about]
ant(s)	antiphon(s)		¢	cent
appx(s)	appendix(es)		CA	California
AR	Arkansas		Cambs.	Cambridgeshire
arr(s).	arrangement(s), arranged by/for		Can.	Canadian
a-s	all-sung		CanD	Cantate Domino
ASCAP	American Society of Composers, Authors and Publishers		cant(s).	cantata(s)
			cap.	capacity
ASOL	American Symphony Orchestra League		carn.	Carnival
attrib(s).	attribution(s), attributed to; ascription(s), ascribed to		cb	contrabass [instrument]
			CBC	Canadian Broadcasting Corporation
Aug	August		CBE	Commander of the Order of the British Empire
aut.	autumn		CBS	Columbia Broadcasting System
AZ	Arizona		CBSO	City of Birmingham Symphony Orchestra
aztl	azione teatrale		CD(s)	compact disc(s)
			CE	Common Era [AD]
B	bass [voice], bassus		CeBeDeM	Centre Belge de Documentation Musicale
B	Brainard catalogue [Tartini], Benton catalogue [Pleyel]		cel	celesta
			CEMA	Council for the Encouragement of Music and the Arts
b	bass [instrument]			
b	born		cf	confer [compare]
BA	Bachelor of Arts		c.f.	cantus firmus
bal(s)	ballad opera(s)		CFE	Composers Facsimile Edition
bap.	baptized		CG	Covent Garden, London
Bar	baritone [voice]		CH	Companion of Honour
bar	baritone [instrument]		chap(s).	chapter(s)
B-Bar	bass-baritone		chbr	chamber
BBC	British Broadcasting Corporation		Chin.	Chinese
BC	British Columbia		chit	chitarrone
BCE	before Common Era [BC]		choreog(s).	choreography, choreographer(s), choreographed by
bc	basso continuo		Cie	Compagnie
Bd.	Band [volume]		cimb	cimbalom
BEd	Bachelor of Education		cl	clarinet
Beds.	Bedfordshire		clvd	clavichord
Berks.	Berkshire		cm	centimetre(s); comédie en musique
Berwicks.	Berwickshire		cmda	comédie mêlée d'ariettes

CNRS	Centre National de la Recherche Scientifique	ens	ensemble
CO	Colorado	ENSA	Entertainments National Service Association
Co.	Company; County	EP	extended-play (record)
Cod.	Codex	esp.	especially
col(s).	column(s)	etc.	et cetera
coll.	collected by	EU	European Union
collab.	in collaboration with	ex., exx.	example, examples
com	*componimento*		
comm(s)	communion(s)	f, ff	following page, following pages
comp(s).	composer(s), composed (by)	f., ff.	folio, folios
conc(s).	concerto(s)	*f*	forte
cond(s).	conductor(s), conducted by	fa(s)	farsa(s)
cont	continuo	facs.	facsimile(s)
contrib(s).	contribution(s)	fasc(s).	fascicle(s)
Corp.	Corporation	Feb	February
c.p.s.	cycles per second	*ff*	fortissimo
cptr(s)	computer(s)	*fff*	fortissississimo
Cr	Credo, Creed	fig(s).	figure(s) [illustration(s)]
CRI	Composers Recordings, Inc.	FL	Florida
CSc	Candidate of Historical Sciences	fl	flute
CT	Connecticut	*fl*	floruit [he/she flourished]
Ct	Contratenor, countertenor	Flem.	Flemish
CUNY	City University of New York	*fp*	fortepiano [dynamic marking]
CVO	Commander of the Royal Victorian Order	Fr.	French
Cz.	Czech	frag(s).	fragment(s)
		FRAM	Fellow of the Royal Academy of Music, London
D	Deutsch catalogue [Schubert]; Dounias catalogue [Tartini]	FRCM	Fellow of the Royal College of Music, London
		FRCO	Fellow of the Royal College of Organists, London
d.	denarius, denarii [penny, pence]	FRS	Fellow of the Royal Society, London
d	died	fs	full score
DA	Doctor of Arts		
Dan.	Danish	GA	Georgia
db	double bass	Gael.	Gaelic
DBE	Dame Commander of the Order of the British Empire	GEDOK	Gemeinschaft Deutscher Organisationen von Künstlerinnen und Kunstfreundinnen
dbn	double bassoon	GEMA	Gesellschaft für Musikalische Aufführungs- und Mechanische Vervielfaltingungsrechte
DC	District of Columbia		
Dc	Discantus	Ger.	German
DD	Doctor of Divinity	Gk.	Greek
DDR	German Democratic Republic (Deutsche Demokratische Republik [East Germany])	Gl	Gloria
		Glam.	Glamorgan
DE	Delaware	glock	glockenspiel
Dec	December	Glos.	Gloucestershire
ded(s).	dedication(s), dedicated to	GmbH	Gesellschaft mit Beschränkter Haftung [limited-liability company]
DeM	Deus misereatur		
Dept(s)	Department(s)	grad(s)	gradual(s)
Derbys.	Derbyshire	GSM	Guildhall School of Music, London (to 1934)
DFA	Doctor of Fine Arts	GSMD	Guildhall School of Music and Drama, London (1935–)
dg	*dramma giocoso*		
dir(s).	director(s), directed by	gui	guitar
diss.	dissertation		
dl	*drame lyrique*	H	Hoboken catalogue [Haydn]; Helm catalogue [C.P.E. Bach]
DLitt	Doctor of Letters/Literature		
DM	Doctor of Music	Hants.	Hampshire
dm	*dramma per musica*	Heb.	Hebrew
DMA	Doctor of Musical Arts	Herts.	Hertfordshire
DME, DMEd	Doctor of Musical Education	HI	Hawaii
DMus	Doctor of Music	hmn	harmonium
DMusEd	Doctor of Music Education	HMS	His/Her Majesty's Ship
DPhil	Doctor of Philosophy	HMV	His Master's Voice
Dr	Doctor	hn	horn
DSc	Doctor of Science/Historical Sciences	Hon.	Honorary; Honourable
DSM	Doctor of Sacred Music	hp	harp
Dut.	Dutch	hpd	harpsichord
		HRH	His/Her Royal Highness
E.	East, Eastern	Hung.	Hungarian
EBU	European Broadcasting Union	Hunts.	Huntingdonshire
ed(s).	editor(s), edited (by)	Hz	Hertz [c.p.s.]
EdD	Doctor of Education		
edn(s)	edition(s)	IA	Iowa
EdS	Education Specialist	IAML	International Association of Music Libraries
EEC	European Economic Community	IAWM	International Alliance for Women in Music
e.g.	exempli gratia [for example]	ibid.	ibidem [in the same place]
el-ac	electro-acoustic	ICTM	International Council for Traditional Music
elec	electric, electronic	ID	Idaho
EMI	Electrical and Musical Industries	i.e.	id est [that is]
Eng.	English	IFMC	International Folk Music Council
eng hn	english horn	IL	Illinois
ENO	English National Opera	ILWC	International League of Women Composers

IMC	International Music Council
IMS	International Musicological Society
IN	Indiana
Inc.	Incorporated
inc.	incomplete
incid	incidental
incl.	includes, including
inst(s)	instrument(s), instrumental
int(s)	intermezzo(s), introit(s)
IPEM	Instituut voor Psychoakoestiek en Elektronische Muziek, Ghent
IRCAM	Institut de Recherche et Coordination Acoustique/Musique
ISAM	Institute for Studies in American Music
ISCM	International Society for Contemporary Music
ISDN	Integrated Services Digital Network
ISM	Incorporated Society of Musicians
ISME	International Society for Music Education
It.	Italian
Jan	January
Jap.	Japanese
Jb	Jahrbuch [yearbook]
JD	Doctor of Jurisprudence
Jg.	Jahrgang [year of publication/volume]
jr	junior
Jub	Jubilate
ĸ	Kirkpatrick catalogue [D. Scarlatti]; Köchel catalogue [Mozart: no. after '/' is from 6th edn; also Fux]
kbd	keyboard
KBE	Knight Commander of the Order of the British Empire
KCVO	Knight Commander of the Royal Victorian Order
kg	kilogram(s)
Kgl	Königlich(e, er, es) [Royal]
kHz	kilohertz [1000 c.p.s.]
km	kilometre(s)
KS	Kansas
KY	Kentucky
Ky	Kyrie
£	libra(e) [pound(s) sterling]
L.	no. of song in R.W. Linker: *A Bibliography of Old French Lyrics* (University, MS, 1979)
L	Longo catalogue [A. Scarlatti]
LA	Louisiana
Lanarks.	Lanarkshire
Lancs.	Lancashire
Lat.	Latin
Leics.	Leicestershire
LH	left hand
lib(s)	libretto(s)
Lincs.	Lincolnshire
lit(s)	litany (litanies)
Lith.	Lithuanian
LittD	Doctor of Letters/Literature
LLB	Bachelor of Laws
LLD	Doctor of Laws
loc. cit.	loco citato [in the place cited]
LP	long-playing record
LPO	London Philharmonic Orchestra
LSO	London Symphony Orchestra
Ltd	Limited
Ltée	Limitée
M, MM.	Monsieur, Messieurs
m	metre(s)
MA	Massachusetts; Master of Arts
Mag	Magnificat
MALS	Master of Arts in Library Sciences
mand	mandolin
mar	marimba
MAT	Master of Arts and Teaching
MB	Bachelor of Music; Manitoba
MBE	Member of the Order of the British Empire
MD	Maryland
ME	Maine

MEd	Master of Education
mel	*melodramma, mélodrame*
mels	*melodramma serio*
melss	*melodramma semiserio*
Met	Metropolitan Opera House, New York
Mez	mezzo-soprano
mf	mezzo-forte
MFA	Master of Fine Arts
MGM	Metro-Goldwyn-Mayer
MHz	megahertz [megacycles]
MI	Michigan
mic	microphone
Middx	Middlesex
MIDI	Musical Instrument Digital Interface
MIT	Massachusetts Institute of Technology
MLitt	Master of Letters/Literature
Mlle, Mlles	Mademoiselle, Mesdemoiselles
MM	Master of Music
M.M.	Metronome Maelzel
mm	millimetre(s)
MMA	Master of Musical Arts
MME, MMEd	Master of Music Education
Mme, Mmes	Madame, Mesdames
MMT	Master of Music in Teaching
MMus	Master of Music
MN	Minnesota
MO	Missouri
mod	modulator
Mon.	Monmouthshire
movt(s)	movement(s)
MP(s)	Member(s) of Parliament
mp	mezzo-piano
MPhil	Master of Philosophy
Mr	Mister
Mrs	Mistress; Messieurs
MS	Master of Science(s); Mississippi
MS(S)	manuscript(s)
MSc	Master of Science(s)
MSLS	Master of Science in Library and Information Science
MSM	Master of Sacred Music
MT	Montana
Mt	Mount
mt(s)	music-theatre piece(s)
MTNA	Music Teachers National Association
MusB, MusBac	Bachelor of Music
muscm(s)	musical comedy (comedies)
MusD, MusDoc	Doctor of Music
musl(s)	musical(s)
MusM	Master of Music
N.	North, Northern
n(n).	footnote(s)
nar(s)	narrator(s)
NB	New Brunswick
NBC	National Broadcasting Company
NC	North Carolina
ND	North Dakota
n.d.	no date of publication
NDR	Norddeutscher Rundfunk
NE	Nebraska
NEA	National Endowment for the Arts
NEH	National Endowment for the Humanities
NET	National Educational Television
NF	Newfoundland and Labrador
NH	New Hampshire
NHK	Nippon Hōsō Kyōkai [Japanese broadcasting system]
NJ	New Jersey
NM	New Mexico
no(s).	number(s)
Nor.	Norwegian
Northants.	Northamptonshire
Notts.	Nottinghamshire
Nov	November
n.p.	no place of publication
nr	near
NRK	Norsk Rikskringkasting [Norwegian broadcasting system]

NS	Nova Scotia
NSW	New South Wales
NT	North West Territories
Nunc	Nunc dimittis
NV	Nevada
NY	New York [State]
NZ	New Zealand
ob	*opera buffa*; oboe
obbl	obbligato
OBE	Officer of the Order of the British Empire
obl	*opéra-ballet*
OC	Opéra-Comique, Paris [the company]
oc	*opéra comique* [genre]
Oct	October
off(s)	offertory (offertories)
OH	Ohio
OK	Oklahoma
OM	Order of Merit
ON	Ontario
op(s)	opera(s)
op., opp.	opus, opera [plural of opus]
op. cit.	opere citato [in the work cited]
opt.	optional
OR	Oregon
orat(s)	oratorio(s)
orch	orchestra(tion), orchestral
orchd	orchestrated (by)
org	organ
orig.	original(ly)
ORTF	Office de Radiodiffusion-Télévision Française
os	*opera seria*
oss	*opera semiseria*
OUP	Oxford University Press
ov(s).	overture(s)
Oxon.	Oxfordshire
P	Pincherle catalogue [Vivaldi]
p.	*pars*
p., pp.	page, pages
p	piano [dynamic marking]
PA	Pennsylvania
p.a.	per annum [annually]
pan(s)	pantomime(s)
PBS	Public Broadcasting System
PC	no. of chanson in A. Pillet and H. Carstens: *Bibliographie der Troubadours* (Halle, 1933)
PE	Prince Edward Island
perc	percussion
perf(s).	performance(s), performed (by)
pf	piano [instrument]
pfmr(s)	performer(s)
PhB	Bachelor of Philosophy
PhD	Doctor of Philosophy
PhDEd	Doctor of Philosophy in Education
pic	piccolo
pl(s).	plate(s); plural
p.m.	post meridiem [after noon]
PO	Philharmonic Orchestra
Pol.	Polish
pop.	population
Port.	Portuguese
posth.	posthumous(ly)
POW(s)	prisoner(s) of war
pp	pianissimo
ppp	pianississimo
PQ	Province of Quebec
PR	Puerto Rico
pr.	printed
prep pf	prepared piano
PRO	Public Record Office, London
prol(s)	prologue(s)
PRS	Performing Right Society
Ps(s)	Psalm(s)
ps(s)	psalm(s)
pseud(s).	pseudonym(s)
pt(s)	part(s)
ptbk(s)	partbook(s)
pubd	published

pubn(s)	publication(s)
PWM	Polskie Wydawnictwo Muzyczne
QC	Queen's Counsel
qnt(s)	quintet(s)
qt(s)	quartet(s)
R	[in signature] editorial revision
R	photographic reprint [edn of score or early printed source]
R.	no. of chanson in G. Raynaud, *Bibliographie des chansonniers français des XIIIe et XIVe siècles* (Paris, 1884)
ʀ	Ryom catalogue [Vivaldi]
r	recto
R	response
RAF	Royal Air Force
RAI	Radio Audizioni Italiane
RAM	Royal Academy of Music, London
RCA	Radio Corporation of America
RCM	Royal College of Music, London
re(s)	response(s) [type of piece]
rec	recorder
rec.	recorded [in discographic context]
recit(s)	recitative(s)
red(s).	reduction(s), reduced for
reorchd	reorchestrated (by)
repr.	reprinted
resp(s)	respond(s)
Rev.	Reverend
rev(s).	revision(s); revised (by/for)
RH	right hand
RI	Rhode Island
RIAS	Radio im Amerikanischen Sektor
RIdIM	Répertoire International d'Iconographie Musicale
RILM	Répertoire International de Littérature Musicale
RIPM	Répertoire International de la Presse Musicale
RISM	Répertoire International des Sources Musicales
RKO	Radio-Keith-Orpheum
RMCM	Royal Manchester College of Music
rms	root mean square
RNCM	Royal Northern College of Music, Manchester
RO	Radio Orchestra
Rom.	Romanian
r.p.m.	revolutions per minute
RPO	Royal Philharmonic Orchestra
RSFSR	Russian Soviet Federated Socialist Republic
RSO	Radio Symphony Orchestra
RTÉ	Radio Telefís Éireann
RTF	Radiodiffusion-Télévision Française
Rt Hon.	Right Honourable
RTVB	Radio-Télévision Belge de la Communauté Française
Russ.	Russian
ʀv	Ryom catalogue [Vivaldi]
S	San, Santa, Santo, São [Saint]; soprano [voice]
S	sound recording
S.	South, Southern
$	dollars
s	soprano [instrument]
s.	solidus, solidi [shilling, shillings]
SACEM	Société d'Auteurs, Compositeurs et Editeurs de Musique
San	Sanctus
sax	saxophone
SC	South Carolina
SD	South Dakota
sd	*scherzo drammatico*
SDR	Süddeutscher Rundfunk
Sept	September
seq(s)	sequence(s)
ser(s)	serenata(s)
ser.	series
Serb.	Serbian
sf, *sfz*	sforzando, sforzato
sing.	singular
SJ	Societas Jesu [Society of Jesus]
SK	Saskatchewan
SO	Symphony Orchestra

SOCAN	Society of Composers, Authors and Music Publishers of Canada		unperf.	unperformed
Sp.	Spanish		unpubd	unpublished
spkr(s)	speaker(s)		UP	University Press
Spl	Singspiel		US	United States [adjective]
SPNM	Society for the Promotion of New Music		USA	United States of America
spr.	spring		USSR	Union of Soviet Socialist Republics
sq	square		UT	Utah
sr	senior			
SS	Saints (It., Sp.); Santissima, Santissimo [Most Holy]		v, vv	voice, voices
SS	steamship		v., vv.	verse, verses
SSR	Soviet Socialist Republic		*v*	verso
St(s)	Saint(s)/Holy, Sankt, Sint, Szent		*v.*	versus
Staffs.	Staffordshire		V	versicle
STB	Bachelor of Sacred Theology		VA	Virginia
Ste	Sainte		va	viola
str	string(s)		vc	cello
sum.	summer		vcle(s)	versicle(s)
SUNY	State University of New York		VEB	Volkseigener Betrieb [people's own industry]
Sup	superius		Ven	Venite
suppl(s).	supplement(s), supplementary		VHF	very high frequency
Swed.	Swedish		VI	Virgin Islands
SWF	Südwestfunk		vib	vibraphone
sym(s).	symphony (symphonies), symphonic		viz	videlicet [namely]
synth	synthesizer, synthesized		vle	violone
			vn	violin
T	tenor [voice]		vol(s).	volume(s)
t	tenor [instrument]		vs	vocal score, piano vocal score
tc	*tragicommedia*		VT	Vermont
td(s)	*tonadilla*(s)			
TeD	Te Deum		W.	West, Western
ThM	Master of Theology		WA	Washington [State]
timp	timpani		Warwicks.	Warwickshire
tm	*tragédie en musique*		WDR	Westdeutscher Rundfunk
TN	Tennessee		WI	Wisconsin
tpt	trumpet		Wilts.	Wiltshire
Tr	treble [voice]		wint.	winter
tr(s)	tract(s); treble [instrument]		WNO	Welsh National Opera
trad.	traditional		woo	Werke ohne Opuszahl
trans.	translation, translated by		Worcs.	Worcestershire
transcr(s).	transcription(s), transcribed by/for		WPA	Works Progress Administration
trbn	trombone		WQ	Wotquenne catalogue [C.P.E. Bach]
TV	television		WV	West Virginia
TWV	Menke catalogue [Telemann]		ww	woodwind
TX	Texas		WY	Wyoming
U.	University		xyl	xylophone
UCLA	University of California at Los Angeles			
UHF	ultra-high frequency		YMCA	Young Men's Christian Association
UK	United Kingdom of Great Britain and Northern Ireland		Yorks.	Yorkshire
Ukr.	Ukrainian		YT	Yukon Territory
unacc.	unaccompanied		YWCA	Young Women's Christian Association
unattrib.	unattributed		YYS	(Zhongguo yishu yanjiuyuan) Yinyue yanjiusuo and variants (Music Research Institute (of the Chinese Academy of Arts))
UNESCO	United Nations Educational, Scientific and Cultural Organization			
UNICEF	United Nations International Children's Emergency Fund		z	Zimmermann catalogue [Purcell]
			zar(s)	zarzuela(s)
unorchd	unorchestrated		zargc	*zarzuela género chico*

Bibliographical Abbreviations

All bibliographical abbreviations used in this dictionary are listed below, following the typography used in the text of the dictionary. Broadly, *italic* type is used for periodicals and for reference works; roman type is used for anthologies, series etc. (titles of individual volumes are italicized).

Full bibliographical information is not normally supplied in the list below if it is available elsewhere in the dictionary. Its availability is indicated as follows: D – in the list of 'Dictionaries and encyclopedias of music'; E – in the list of 'Editions, historical'; and P – in the list of 'Periodicals'; these lists are located in vol.28. For other items, in particular national (non-musical) biographical dictionaries, basic bibliographical information is given here; and in some cases extra information is supplied to clarify the abbreviation used.

Festschriften and congress reports are not generally covered in this list. Although Festschrift titles are sometimes shortened in the dictionary, sufficient information is always given for unambiguous identification (dedicatee; occasion, if the same person is dedicatee of more than one Festschrift; place and date of publication; and name(s) of editor(s) if known). For fuller information on musical Festschriften up to 1967 see W. Gerboth: *An Index to Musical Festschriften and Similar Publications* (New York, 1969). The published titles of congress reports are generally reduced to their essentials, but sufficient information is always given for purposes of identification (society or topic; place and date of occurrence; journal issue if published in a periodical; editor(s) and publication details in unfamiliar cases). A comprehensive list of musical and music-related 'Congress reports' appears in vol.28. Further information can be found in J. Tyrrell and R. Wise: *A Guide to International Congress Reports in Music, 1900–1975* (London, 1979).

19CM	*19th Century Music* P	*ApelG*	W. Apel: *Geschichte der Orgel- und Klaviermusik bis 1700* (Kassel, 1967; Eng. trans., rev., 1972)
ACAB	*American Composers Alliance Bulletin* P	*AR*	*Antiphonale sacrosanctae romanae ecclesiae pro diurnis horis* (Paris, Tournai and Rome, 1949)
AcM	*Acta musicologica* P	*AS*	W.H. Frere, ed.: *Antiphonale sarisburiense* (London, 1901–25/R)
ADB	*Allgemeine deutsche Biographie* (Leipzig, 1875–1912)	*AshbeeR*	A. Ashbee: *Records of English Court Music* (Snodland/Aldershot, 1986–95)
AdlerHM	G. Adler, ed.: *Handbuch der Musikgeschichte* (Frankfurt, 1924, 2/1930/R)	*AsM*	*Asian Music* P
AfM	*African Music* P	*AudaM*	A. Auda: *La musique et les musiciens de l'ancien pays de Liège* D
AH	Analecta hymnica medii aevi E	*AusDB*	*Australian Dictionary of Biography* (Melbourne, 1966–96)
AllacciD	L. Allacci: *Drammaturgia* D	*Baker5[–8]*	*Baker's Biographical Dictionary of Musicians* D
AM	*Antiphonale monasticum pro diurnis horis* (Tournai, 1934)	*BAMS*	*Bulletin of the American Musicological Society* P
AmbrosGM	A.W. Ambros: *Geschichte der Musik* (Leipzig, 1862–82/R)	*BDA*	*A Biographical Dictionary of Actors, Actresses, Musicians, Dancers, Managers & Other Stage Personnel in London, 1660–1800* (Carbondale, IL, 1973–93)
AMe, AMeS	*Algemene muziekencyclopedie* and suppl. D		
AMf	*Archiv für Musikforschung* P		
AMI	L'arte musicale in Italia E		
AMMM	Archivium musices metropolitanum mediolanense E		
AMP	Antiquitates musicae in Polonia E	*BDECM*	A. Ashbee and D. Lasocki, eds.: *A Biographical Dictionary of English Court Musicians, 1485–1714* (Aldershot, 1998)
AMw	*Archiv für Musikwissenschaft* P		
AMZ	*Allgemeine musikalische Zeitung* (1798–1848, 1863–5, 1866–82) P	*BDRSC*	A. Ho and D. Feofanov, eds.: *Biographical Dictionary of Russian/Soviet Composers* D
AMz	*Allgemeine (deutsche) Musik-Zeitung/Musikzeitung* (1874–1943) P	*BeckEP*	J.H. Beck: *Encyclopedia of Percussion* D
		BeJb	*Beethoven-Jahrbuch* P
Anderson2	E.R. Anderson: *Contemporary American Composers: a Biographical Dictionary* D	*BenoitMC*	M. Benoit: *Musiques de cour: chapelle, chambre, écurie, 1661–1733* (Paris, 1971)
AnM	*Anuario musical* P	*BenzingB*	J. Benzing: *Die Buchdrucker des 16. und 17. Jahrhunderts* (Wiesbaden, 1963, 2/1982)
AnMc, AnMc	*Analecta musicologica* P		
AnnM	*Annales musicologiques* P	*BerliozM*	H. Berlioz: *Mémoires* (Paris, 1870; ed. and trans. D. Cairns, 1969, 2/1970); ed. P. Citron (Paris, 1969, 2/1991)
AnthonyFB	J.R. Anthony: *French Baroque Music from Beaujoyeulx to Rameau* (London, 1973, 3/1997)		
AntMI	Antiquae musicae italicae E	*BertolottiM*	A. Bertolotti: *Musici alla corte dei Gonzaga in Mantova dal secolo XV al XVIII* (Milan, 1890/R)
AÖAW	*Anzeiger der Österreichischen Akademie der Wissenschaften, philosophisch-historische Klasse* (1948–)		

BicknellH	S. Bicknell: *The History of the English Organ* (Cambridge, 1996)
BJb	*Bach-Jahrbuch* P
BladesPI	J. Blades: *Percussion Instruments and their History* (London, 1970, 2/1974)
BlumeEK	F. Blume: *Die evangelische Kirchenmusik* (Potsdam, 1931–4/R, enlarged 2/1965 as *Geschichte der evangelischen Kirchenmusik*; Eng. trans., enlarged, 1974, as *Protestant Church Music: a History*)
BMB	Bibliotheca musica bononiensis (Bologna, 1967–)
BMw	*Beiträge zur Musikwissenschaft* P
BNB	Biographie nationale [*belge*] (Brussels, 1866–1986)
BoalchM	D.H. Boalch: *Makers of the Harpsichord and Clavichord 1440 to 1840* D
BoetticherOL	W. Boetticher: *Orlando di Lasso und seine Zeit* (Kassel, 1958)
Bouwsteenen: JVNM	*Bouwsteenen: jaarboek der Vereeniging voor Nederlandsche muziekgeschiedenis* P
BoydenH	D.D. Boyden: *A History of Violin Playing from its Origins to 1761* (London, 1965)
BPM	*Black Perspective in Music* P
BrenetC	M. Brenet: *Les concerts en France sous l'ancien régime* (Paris, 1900/R)
BrenetM	M. Brenet: *Les musiciens de la Sainte-Chapelle du Palais* (Paris, 1910/R)
BrookB	B.S. Brook, ed.: *The Breitkopf Thematic Catalogue, 1762–1787* (New York, 1966)
BrookSF	B.S. Brook: *La symphonie française dans la seconde moitié du XVIIIe siècle* (Paris, 1962)
BrownI	H.M. Brown: *Instrumental Music Printed Before 1600: a Bibliography* (Cambridge, MA, 1965)
Brown-Stratton BMB	J.D. Brown and S.S. Stratton: *British Musical Biography* D
BSIM	*Bulletin français de la S.I.M.* [also *Mercure musical* and other titles] P
BUCEM	E.B. Schnapper, ed.: *British Union-Catalogue of Early Music* (London, 1957)
BurneyFI	C. Burney: *The Present State of Music in France and Italy* (London, 1771, 2/1773)
BurneyGN	C. Burney: *The Present State of Music in Germany, the Netherlands, and the United Provinces* (London, 1773, 2/1775)
BurneyH	C. Burney: *A General History of Music from the Earliest Ages to the Present Period* (London, 1776–89); ed. F. Mercer (London, 1935/R) [p. nos. refer to this edn]
BWQ	*Brass and Woodwind Quarterly* P
CaffiS	F. Caffi: *Storia della musica sacra nella già cappella ducale di San Marco in Venezia dal 1318 al 1797* (Venice, 1854–5/R); ed. E. Surian (Florence, 1987)
CaM	Catalogus musicus (Kassel, 1963–)
CampbellGC	M. Campbell: *The Great Cellists* D
CampbellGV	M. Campbell: *The Great Violinists* D
CAO	Corpus antiphonalium officii (Rome, 1963–79)
CBY	*Current Biography Yearbook* (1955–)
CC	B. Morton and P. Collins, eds.: *Contemporary Composers* D
CeBeDeM directory	*CeBeDeM et ses compositeurs affiliés*, ed. D. von Volborth-Danys (Brussels, 1977–80)
CEKM	Corpus of Early Keyboard Music E
CEMF	Corpus of Early Music (in Facsimile) (Brussels, 1970–72)
CHM	*Collectanea historiae musicae* (1953–66)
Choron-FayolleD	A.-E. Choron and F.J.M. Fayolle: *Dictionnaire historique des musiciens*
ClinkscaleMP	M.N. Clinkscale: *Makers of the Piano* D
CM	Le choeur des muses E
CMc	*Current Musicology* P
CMI	I classici musicali italiani (Milan, 1941–56)
CMM	Corpus mensurabilis musicae E
ČMm	*Časopis Moravského musea* [*muzea*, 1977–] P
CMR	*Contemporary Music Review* P
CMz	*Cercetări de muzicologie* P
CohenE	A.I. Cohen: *International Encyclopedia of Women Composers* D
CohenWE	Y.W. Cohen: *Werden und Entwicklung der Musik in Israel* (Kassel, 1976)
COJ	*Cambridge Opera Journal* P
CooverMA	J.B. Coover: *Music at Auction: Puttick and Simpson* (Warren, MI, 1988)
CoussemakerS	C.-E.-H. de Coussemaker: *Scriptorum de musica medii aevi nova series* (Paris, 1864–76/R, 2/1908, ed. U. Moser)
CroceN	B. Croce: *I teatri di Napoli* (Naples, 1891/R, 5/1966)
ČSHS	*Československy hudební slovník* D
CSM	Corpus scriptorum de musica (Rome, later Stuttgart, 1950–)
CSPD	Calendar of State Papers (Domestic) (London, 1856–1972)
Cw	Das Chorwerk E
DAB	*Dictionary of American Biography* (New York, 1928–37, suppls., 1944–)
DAM	*Dansk aarbog for musikforskning* P
Day-Murrie ESB	C.L. Day and E.B. Murrie: *English Song-Books* (London, 1940)
DBF	*Dictionnaire de biographie française* (Paris, 1933–)
DBI	*Dizionario biografico degli italiani* (Rome, 1960–)
DBL, DBL2, DBL3	*Dansk biografisk leksikon* (Copenhagen, 1887–1905, 2/1933–45, 3/1979–84)
DBNM, DBNM	*Darmstädter Beiträge zur neuen Musik* P
DBP	E. Vieira, ed.: *Diccionário biográphico de musicos portuguezes* (Lisbon, 1900)
DČHP	*Dějiny české hudby v příkladech* (Prague, 1958)
DDT	Denkmäler deutscher Tonkunst E
DEMF	A. Devriès and F. Lesure: *Dictionnaire des éditeurs de musique français* D
DEUMM	*Dizionario enciclopedico universale della musica e dei musicisti* D
DeutschMPN	O.E. Deutsch: *Music Publishers' Numbers* (London, 1946)
DHM	Documenta historica musicae E
Dichter-ShapiroSM	H. Dichter and E. Shapiro: *Early American Sheet Music*
DJbM	*Deutsches Jahrbuch der Musikwissenschaft* P
DlabaczKL	G.J. Dlabacž: *Allgemeines historisches Künstler-Lexikon*
DM	Documenta musicologica (Kassel, 1951–)
DMt	*Dansk musiktidsskrift* P
DMV	Drammaturgia musicale veneta (Milan, 1983–)
DNB	*Dictionary of National Biography* (Oxford, 1885–1901, suppls., 1901–96)
DoddI	G. Dodd, ed.: *Thematic Index of Music for Viols* (London, 1980–)
DTB	Denkmäler der Tonkunst in Bayern E
DTÖ	Denkmäler der Tonkunst in Österreich E
DugganIMI	M.K. Duggan: *Italian Music Incunabula: Printers and Type* (Berkeley, 1991)
DVLG	*Deutsche Vierteljahrsschrift für Literaturwissenschaft und Geistesgeschichte* (1923–)
ECCS	The Eighteenth-Century Continuo Sonata E
ECFC	The Eighteenth-Century French Cantata E
EDM	Das Erbe deutscher Musik E
EECM	Early English Church Music E
EG	*Etudes grégoriennes* P
EI	*The Encyclopaedia of Islam* (Leiden, 1928–38, 2/1960–)
EinsteinIM	A. Einstein: *The Italian Madrigal* (Princeton, NJ, 1949/R)
EIT	*Yezhegodnik imperatorskikh teatrov* P
EitnerQ	R. Eitner: *Biographisch-bibliographisches Quellen-Lexikon* D
EitnerS	R. Eitner: *Bibliographie der Musik-Sammelwerke des XVI. und XVII. Jahrhunderts* (Berlin, 1877/R)
EKM	Early Keyboard Music E
EL	The English School of Lutenist Songwriters, rev. as The English Lute-Songs E
EM	The English Madrigal School, rev. as The English Madrigalists E
EMc	*Early Music* P
EMC1, 2	*Encyclopedia of Music in Canada* (Toronto, 1981, 2/1992) D

EMDC	A. Lavignac and L. de La Laurencie, eds.: *Encyclopédie de la musique et dictionnaire du Conservatoire* D	
EMH	*Early Music History* P	
EMN	*Exempla musica neerlandica* E	
EMS	see EM	
EMuz	*Encyklopedia muzyczne* D	
ERO	*Early Romantic Opera* E	
ES	*English Song 1600–1675* (New York, 1986–9)	
ES	*Enciclopedia dello spettacolo* D	
ESLS	see EL	
EthM	*Ethnomusicology* P	
EthM Newsletter	*Ethno[-]musicology Newsletter* P	
EwenD	D. Ewen: *American Composers: a Biographical Dictionary* D	
FAM	*Fontes artis musicae* P	
FasquelleE	*Encyclopédie de la musique* D	
FCVR	*Florilège du concert vocal de la Renaissance* E	
FellererG	K.G. Fellerer: *Geschichte der katholischen Kirchenmusik* (Düsseldorf, 1939, enlarged 2/1949; Eng. trans., 1961/R)	
FellererP	K.G. Fellerer: *Der Palestrinastil und seine Bedeutung in der vokalen Kirchenmusik des 18. Jahrhunderts* (Augsburg, 1929/R)	
FenlonMM	I. Fenlon: *Music and Patronage in Sixteenth-Century Mantua* (Cambridge, 1980–82)	
FétisB, FétisBS	F.-J. Fétis: *Biographie universelle des musiciens* and suppl. D	
FisherMP	W.A. Fisher: *One Hundred and Fifty Years of Music Publishing in the United States* (Boston, 1933)	
FiskeETM	R. Fiske: *English Theatre Music in the Eighteenth Century* (London, 1973, 2/1986)	
FlorimoN	F. Florimo: *La scuola musicale di Napoli e i suoi conservatorii* (Naples, 1880–83/R)	
FO	*French Opera in the 17th and 18th Centuries* (New York, 1983–)	
FortuneISS	N. Fortune: *Italian Secular Song from 1600 to 1635: the Origins and Development of Accompanied Monody* (diss., U. of Cambridge, 1954)	
Friedlaender DL	M. Friedlaender: *Das deutsche Lied im 18. Jahrhundert* (Stuttgart and Berlin, 1902/R)	
FrotscherG	G. Frotscher: *Geschichte des Orgelspiels und der Orgelkomposition* (Berlin, 1935–6/R, music suppl. 1966)	
FuldWFM	J.J. Fuld: *The Book of World-Famous Music* D	
FullerPG	S. Fuller: *The Pandora Guide to Women Composers: Britain and the United States (1629 – Present)* D	
FürstenauG	M. Fürstenau: *Zur Geschichte der Musik und des Theaters am Hofe zu Dresden* (Dresden, 1861–2/R)	
GänzlBMT	K. Gänzl: *The British Musical Theatre* (London, 1986)	
GänzlEMT	K. Gänzl and A. Lamb: *Encyclopedia of Musical Theatre* D	
GaspariC	G. Gaspari: *Catalogo della Biblioteca del Liceo musicale di Bologna*, i–iv (Bologna, 1890–1905/R); v, ed. U. Sesini (Bologna, 1943/R)	
GerberL	E.L. Gerber: *Historisch-biographisches Lexikon der Tonkünstler* D	
GerberNL	E.L. Gerber: *Neues historisch-biographisches Lexikon der Tonkünstler* D	
GerbertS	M. Gerbert: *Scriptores ecclesiastici de musica sacra potissimum* (St Blasien, 1784/R, 3/1931)	
GEWM	*The Garland Encyclopedia of World Music* D	
GfMKB	*Gesellschaft für Musikforschung: Kongress-Bericht* [1950–]	
GiacomoC	S. di Giacomo: *I quattro antichi conservatorii musicali di Napoli* (Milan, 1924–8)	
GLMT	*Greek and Latin Music Theory* (Lincoln, NE, 1984–)	
GMB	*Geschichte der Musik in Beispielen* E	
GMM	*Gazzetta musicale di Milano* P	
GOB	*German Opera 1770–1800*, ed. T. Bauman (New York, 1985–6)	
GöhlerV	A. Göhler: *Verzeichnis der in den Frankfurter und Leipziger Messkatalogen der Jahre 1564 bis 1759 angezeigten Musikalien* (Leipzig, 1902/R)	

GoovaertsH	A. Goovaerts: *Histoire et bibliographie de la typographie musicale dans les Pays-Bas* (Antwerp, 1880/R)	
GR	*Graduale sacrosanctae romanae ecclesiae* (Tournai, 1938)	
Grove1[–5]	G. Grove, ed.: *A Dictionary of Music and Musicians* D	
Grove6	*The New Grove Dictionary of Music and Musicians* D	
GroveA	*The New Grove Dictionary of American Music* D	
GroveI	*The New Grove Dictionary of Musical Instruments* D	
GroveJ	*The New Grove Dictionary of Jazz* D	
GroveJapan	*The New Grove Dictionary of Music and Musicians*, Jap. trans. D	
GroveO	*The New Grove Dictionary of Opera* D	
GroveW	*The New Grove Dictionary of Women Composers* D	
GS	W.H. Frere, ed.: *Graduale sarisburiense* (London, 1894/R)	
GSJ	*Galpin Society Journal* P	
GSL	K.J. Kutsch and L. Riemann: *Grosses Sängerlexikon* D	
GV	R. Celletti: *Le grandi voci: dizionario critico-biografico dei cantanti* D	
HAM	*Historical Anthology of Music* E	
Harrison MMB	F.Ll. Harrison: *Music in Medieval Britain* (London, 1958, 4/1980)	
HawkinsH	J. Hawkins: *A General History of the Science and Practice of Music* (London, 1776)	
HBSJ	*Historical Brass Society Journal* P	
HDM	W. Apel: *Harvard Dictionary of Music* D	
HJb	*Händel-Jahrbuch* P	
HJbMw	*Hamburger Jahrbuch für Musikwissenschaft* P	
HM	*Hortus musicus* E	
HMC	*Historical Manuscripts Commission [Publications]*	
HMT	*Handwörterbuch der musikalischen Terminologie* D	
HMw	*Handbuch der Musikwissenschaft* (Potsdam, 1927–34)	
HMYB	*Hinrichsen's Musical Year Book* P	
HoneggerD	M. Honegger: *Dictionnaire de la musique* D	
HopkinsonD	C. Hopkinson: *A Dictionary of Parisian Music Publishers 1700–1950* D	
Hopkins-RimbaultO	E.J. Hopkins and E.F. Rimbault: *The Organ: its History and Construction* (London, 1855, 3/1887/R)	
HPM	*Harvard Publications in Music* E	
HR	*Hudební revue* P	
HRo	*Hudební rozhledy* P	
Humphries-SmithMP	C. Humphries and W.C. Smith: *Music Publishing in the British Isles* D	
HV	*Hudební věda* P	
ICSC	*The Italian Cantata in the Seventeenth Century* (New York, 1985–6)	
IIM	*Italian Instrumental Music of the Sixteenth and Early Seventeenth Centuries* E	
IIM	*Izvestiya na Instituta za muzika* P	
IMa	*Instituta et monumenta* E	
IMi	*Istituzioni e monumenti dell'arte musicale italiana* (Milan, 1931–9, new ser., 1956–64)	
IMSCR	*International Musicological Society: Congress Report* [1930–]	
IMusSCR	*International Musical Society: Congress Report* [II–IV, 1906–11]	
IO	*The Italian Oratorio 1650–1800* E	
IOB	*Italian Opera 1640–1770*, ed. H.M. Brown E	
IOG	*Italian Opera 1810–1840*, ed. P. Gossett E	
IRASM	*International Review of the Aesthetics and Sociology of Music* P	
IRMAS	*International Review of Music Aesthetics and Sociology* P	
IRMO	S.L. Ginzburg: *Istoriya russkoy muzïki v notnïkh obraztsakh* (Leningrad, 1940–52, 2/1968–70)	
ISS	*Italian Secular Song 1606–1636* (New York, 1986)	
IZ	*Instrumentenbau-Zeitschrift* P	
JAMIS	*Journal of the American Musical Instrument Society* P	
JAMS	*Journal of the American Musicological Society* P	
JASA	*Journal of the Acoustical Society of America* P	
JazzM	*Jazz Monthly* P	
JBIOS	*Journal of the British Institute of Organ Studies* P	

JbLH	Jahrbuch für Liturgik und Hymnologie P
JbMP	Jahrbuch der Musikbibliothek Peters P
JbO	Jahrbuch für Opernforschung P
JbSIM	Jahrbuch des Staatlichen Instituts für Musikforschung Preussischer Kulturbesitz P
JEFDSS	Journal of the English Folk Dance and Song Society P
JFSS	Journal of the Folk-Song Society P
JIFMC	Journal of the International Folk Music Council P
JJ	Jazz Journal P
JJI	Jazz Journal International P
JJS	Journal of Jazz Studies P
JLSA	Journal of the Lute Society of America P
JM	Journal of Musicology P
JMR	Journal of Musicological Research P
JMT	Journal of Music Theory P
JoãoIL	[João IV:] Primeira parte do index da livraria de musica do muyto alto, e poderoso Rey Dom João o IV. nosso senhor (Lisbon, 1649); ed. J. de Vasconcellos (Oporto, 1874–6)
Johansson FMP	C. Johansson: French Music Publishers' Catalogues (Stockholm, 1955)
JohanssonH	C. Johansson: J.J. & B. Hummel: Music Publishing and Thematic Catalogues (Stockholm, 1972)
JR	Jazz Review P
JRBM	Journal of Renaissance and Baroque Music P
JRMA	Journal of the Royal Musical Association P
JRME	Journal of Research in Music Education P
JT	Jazz Times P
JVdGSA	Journal of the Viola da Gamba Society of America P
JVNM	see Bouwsteenen: JVNM
KdG	Komponisten der Gegenwart, ed. H.-W. Heister and W.-W. Sparrer D
KermanEM	J. Kerman: The Elizabethan Madrigal: a Comparative Study (New York, 1962)
KidsonBMP	F. Kidson: British Music Publishers, Printers and Engravers D
KingMP	A.H. King: Four Hundred Years of Music Printing (London, 1964)
KJb	Kirchenmusikalisches Jahrbuch P
KM	Kwartalnik muzyczny P
KöchelKHM	L. von Köchel: Die kaiserliche Hof-Musikkapelle in Wien von 1543 bis 1867 (Vienna, 1869/R)
KretzschmarG	H. Kretzschmar: Geschichte des neuen deutschen Liedes (Leipzig, 1911/R)
KrummelEMP	D.W. Krummel: English Music Printing (London, 1975)
LaborD	Diccionario de la música Labor D
La BordeE	J.-B. de La Borde: Essai sur la musique ancienne et moderne D
LabordeMP	L.E.S.J. de Laborde: Musiciens de Paris, 1535–1792 D
LafontaineKM	H.C. de Lafontaine: The King's Musick (London, 1909/R)
La Laurencie EF	L. de La Laurencie: L'école française de violon de Lully à Viotti (Paris, 1922–4/R)
LAMR	Latin American Music Review P
LaMusicaD	La musica: dizionario D
LaMusicaE	La musica: enciclopedia storica D
Langwill7	see Waterhouse-Langwill7
LedeburTLB	C. von Ledebur: Tonkünstler-Lexicon Berlin's (Berlin, 1861/R)
Le HurayMR	P. Le Huray: Music and the Reformation in England, 1549–1660 (London, 1967, 2/1978)
LipowskyBL	F.J. Lipowsky: Baierisches Musik-Lexikon D
LM	Lucrări de muzicologie P
Lockwood MRF	L. Lockwood: Music in Renaissance Ferrara (Oxford, 1984)
LoewenbergA	A. Loewenberg: Annals of Opera, 1597–1940 D
LPS	The London Pianoforte School 1766–1860 P
LS	The London Stage, 1660–1800 (Carbondale, IL, 1960–68)
LSJ	Lute Society Journal P
LU	Liber usualis missae et officii pro dominicis et festis duplicibus cum cantu gregoriano (Solesmes, 1896, and later edns incl. Tournai, 1963)
Lütgendorff GL	W.L. von Lütgendorff: Die Geigen- und Lauten-macher vom Mittelalter bis zur Gegenwart D
LZMÖ	Lexikon zeitgenössischer Musik aus Österreich (Vienna, 1997)
MA	Musical Antiquary P
MAB	Musica antiqua bohemica E
MAk	Muzïkal'naya akademiya P
MAM	Musik alter Meister E
MAMS	Monumenta artis musicae Sloveniae E
MAn	Music Analysis P
MAP	Musica antiqua polonica E
MAS	Musical Antiquarian Society [Publications] E
Mattheson GEP	J. Mattheson: Grundlage einer Ehren-Pforte (Hamburg, 1740); ed. Max Schneider (Berlin, 1910/R)
MB	Musica britannica E
MC	Musica da camera E
McCarthyJR	A. McCarthy: Jazz on Record (London, 1968)
MCL	H. Mendel and A. Reissmann, eds.: Musikalisches Conversations-Lexikon (Berlin, 1870–80, 3/1890–91/R)
MD	Musica disciplina P
ME	Muzïkal'naya entsiklopediya D
MEM	Mestres de l'Escolanía de Montserrat E
MersenneHU	M. Mersenne: Harmonie universelle D
MeyerECM	E.H. Meyer: English Chamber Music (London, 1946/R, rev. 3/1982 with D. Poulton as Early English Chamber Music)
MeyerMS	E.H. Meyer: Die mehrstimmige Spielmusik des 17. Jahrhunderts (Kassel, 1934)
MF	Music in Facsimile (New York, 1983–91)
Mf	Die Musikforschung P
MG	Musik und Gesellschaft P
MGG1, 2	Die Musik in Geschichte und Gegenwart D
MGH	Monumenta Germaniae historica
MH	Música hispana E
MischiatiI	O. Mischiati: Indici, cataloghi e avvisi degli editori e librai musicali italiani (Florence, 1984)
MISM	Mitteilungen der Internationalen Stiftung Mozarteum P
MJb	Mozart-Jahrbuch [Salzburg, 1950–] P
ML	Music & Letters P
MLE	Music for London Entertainment 1660–1800 E
MLMI	Monumenta lyrica medii aevi italica E
MM	Modern Music P
MMA	Miscellanea musicologica [Australia] P
MMB	Monumenta musicae byzantinae E
MMBel	Monumenta musicae belgicae E
MMC	Miscellanea musicologica [Czechoslovakia] P
MME	Monumentos de la música española E
MMFTR	Monuments de la musique française au temps de la Renaissance E
MMg	Monatshefte für Musikgeschichte P
MMI	Monumenti di musica italiana E
MMMA	Monumenta monodica medii aevi E
MMN	Monumenta musica neerlandica E
MMP	Monumenta musicae in Polonia E
MMR	Monthly Musical Record P
MMRF	Les maîtres musiciens de la Renaissance française E
MMS	Monumenta musicae svecicae E
MNAN	Music of the New American Nation E
MO	Musical Opinion P
MooserA	R.-A. Mooser: Annales de la musique et des musiciens en Russie au XVIIIme siècle D
MoserGV	A. Moser: Geschichte des Violinspiels (Berlin, 1923, rev. 2/1966–7 by H.J. Nösselt)
MQ	Musical Quarterly P
MR	Music Review P
MRM	Monuments of Renaissance Music E
MRS	Musiche rinascimentali siciliane E
MS	Muzïkal'nïy sovremennik P
MSD	Musicological Studies and Documents E
MT	Musical Times P
MusAm	Musical America P
MVH	Musica viva historica E
MVSSP	Musiche vocali e strumentali sacre e profane E
Mw	Das Musikwerk E
MZ	Muzikološki zbornik P
NA	Note d'archivio per la storia musicale P
NBeJb	Neues Beethoven-Jahrbuch P
NBL	Norsk biografisk leksikon (Oslo, 1923–83)
NDB	Neue deutsche Biographie (Berlin, 1953–)

Neighbour-TysonPN	O.W. Neighbour and A. Tyson: *English Music Publishers' Plate Numbers* (London, 1965)	
NericiS	L. Nerici: *Storia della musica in Lucca* (Lucca, 1879/R)	
NewcombMF	A. Newcomb: *The Madrigal at Ferrara, 1579–1597* (Princeton, NJ, 1980)	
NewmanSBE	W.S. Newman: *The Sonata in the Baroque Era* (Chapel Hill, NC, 1959, 4/1983)	
NewmanSCE	W.S. Newman: *The Sonata in the Classic Era* (Chapel Hill, NC, 1963, 3/1983)	
NewmanSSB	W.S. Newman: *The Sonata since Beethoven* (Chapel Hill, NC, 1969, 3/1983)	
NicollH	A. Nicoll: *The History of English Drama, 1660–1900* (Cambridge, 1952–9)	
NM	Nagels Musik-Archiv E	
NMÅ	*Norsk musikkgranskning årbok* P	
NNBW	*Nieuw Nederlandsch biografisch woordenboek* (Leiden, 1911–37)	
NÖB	*Neue österreichische Biographie* (Vienna, 1923–35)	
NOHM, NOHM	*The New Oxford History of Music* (Oxford, 1954–90)	
NRMI	*Nuova rivista musicale italiana* P	
NZM	*Neue Zeitschrift für Musik* P	
OHM, OHM	*The Oxford History of Music* (Oxford, 1901–5, 2/1929–38)	
OM	*Opus musicum* P	
ÖMz	*Österreichische Musikzeitschrift* P	
ON	*Opera News* P	
OQ	*Opera Quarterly* P	
OW	*Opernwelt* P	
PalMus	Paléographie musicale E	
PAMS	*Papers of the American Musicological Society* P	
PÄMw	Publikation älterer praktischer und theoretischer Musikwerke E	
PazdírekH	B. Pazdírek: *Universal-Handbuch der Musikliteratur aller Zeiten und Völker* (Vienna, 1904–10/R)	
PBC	Publicaciones del departamento de música E	
PEM	C. Dahlhaus and S. Döhring, eds.: *Pipers Enzyklopädie des Musiktheaters* (Munich and Zürich, 1986–97)	
PG	*Patrologiae cursus completus*, ii: Series graeca, ed. J.-P. Migne (Paris, 1857–1912)	
PGfM	see PÄMw	
PierreH	C. Pierre: *Histoire du Concert spirituel 1725–1790* (Paris, 1975)	
PIISM	Pubblicazioni dell'Istituto italiano per la storia della musica E	
PirroHM	A. Pirro: *Histoire de la musique de la fin du XIVe siècle à la fin du XVIe* (Paris, 1940)	
PirrottaDO	N. Pirrotta and E. Povoledo: *Li due Orfei: da Poliziano a Monteverdi* (Turin, 1969, enlarged 2/1975; Eng. trans., 1982, as *Music and Theatre from Poliziano to Monteverdi*)	
PitoniN	G.O. Pitoni: *Notitia de contrapuntisti e de compositori di musica* (MS, c1725, I-Rvat C.G.I/1–2); ed. C. Ruini (Florence, 1988)	
PL	*Patrologiae cursus completus*, i: Series latina, ed. J.-P. Migne (Paris, 1844–64)	
PM	Portugaliae musica E	
PMA	*Proceedings of the Musical Association* P	
PMFC	Polyphonic Music of the Fourteenth Century E	
PMM	*Plainsong and Medieval Music* P	
PNM	*Perspectives of New Music* P	
PraetoriusSM	M. Praetorius: *Syntagma musicum*, i (Wittenberg and Wolfenbüttel, 1614–15, 2/1615/R); ii (Wolfenbüttel, 1618, 2/1619/R; Eng. trans., 1986, 2/1991); iii (Wolfenbüttel, 1618, 2/1619/R)	
PraetoriusTI	M. Praetorius: *Theatrum instrumentorum* [pt ii/2 of *PraetoriusSM*]	
PRM	*Polski rocznik muzykologiczny* P	
PRMA	*Proceedings of the Royal Musical Association* P	
Przywecka-SameckaDM	M. Przywecka-Samecka: *Drukarstwo muzyczne w Polsce do końca XVIII wieku* (Kraków, 1969)	
PSB	*Polskich słownik biograficzny* (Kraków, 1935)	
PSFM	Publications [Société française de musicologie] E	
Quaderni della RaM	*Quaderni della Rassegna musicale* P	
Rad JAZU	*Rad Jugoslavenske akademije znanosti i umjetnosti* P	
RaM	*Rassegna musicale* P	
RBM	*Revue belge de musicologie* P	
RdM	*Revue de musicologie* P	
RdMc	*Revista de musicología* P	
ReeseMMA	G. Reese: *Music in the Middle Ages* (New York, 1940)	
ReeseMR	G. Reese: *Music in the Renaissance* (New York, 1954, 2/1959)	
RefardtHBM	E. Refardt: *Historisch-biographisches Musikerlexikon der Schweiz* D	
ReM	*Revue musicale* P	
RFS	Romantic French Song 1830–1870 E	
RGMP	*Revue et gazette musicale de Paris* P	
RHCM	*Revue d'histoire et de critique musicales* P	
RicciTB	C. Ricci: *I teatri di Bologna nei secoli XVII e XVIII: storia aneddotica* (Bologna, 1888/R)	
RicordiE	C. Sartori and R. Allorto: *Enciclopedia della musica* D	
RiemannG	H. Riemann: *Geschichte der Musiktheorie im IX.–XIX. Jahrhundert* (Berlin, 2/1921/R; Eng. trans. of pts i–ii, 1962/R, and pt iii, 1977)	
RiemannL11, 12	*Hugo Riemanns Musiklexikon* (11/1929, 12/1959–75) D	
RIM	*Rivista italiana di musicologia* P	
RIMS	*Rivista internazionale di musica sacra* P	
RM	*Ruch muzyczny* P	
RMARC	*R.M.A. [Royal Musical Association] Research Chronicle* P	
RMC	*Revista musical chilena* P	
RMF	Renaissance Music in Facsimile (New York, 1986–8)	
RMFC	*Recherches sur la musique française classique* P	
RMG	*Russkaya muzikal'naya gazeta* P	
RMI	*Rivista musicale italiana* P	
RMS	Renaissance Manuscript Studies (Stuttgart, 1975–)	
RN	*Renaissance News* P	
RosaM	C. de Rosa, Marchese di Villarosa: *Memorie dei compositori di musica del regno di Napoli* (Naples, 1840)	
RRAM	Recent Researches in American Music E	
RRMBE	Recent Researches in the Music of the Baroque Era E	
RRMCE	Recent Researches in the Music of the Classical Era E	
RRMMA	Recent Researches in the Music of the Middle Ages and Early Renaissance E	
RRMNETC	Recent Researches in the Music of the Nineteenth and Early Twentieth Centuries E	
RRMR	Recent Researches in the Music of the Renaissance E	
SachsH	C. Sachs: *The History of Musical Instruments* (New York, 1940)	
SainsburyD	J.H. Sainsbury: *A Dictionary of Musicians* D	
SartoriB	C. Sartori: *Bibliografia della musica strumentale italiana stampata in Italia fino al 1700* (Florence, 1952–68)	
SartoriD	C. Sartori: *Dizionario degli editori musicali italiani* D	
SartoriL	C. Sartori: *I libretti italiani a stampa dalle origini al 1800* (Cuneo, 1990–94)	
SBL	*Svenskt biografiskt lexikon* (Stockholm, 1918–)	
SCC	The Sixteenth-Century Chanson E	
ScheringGIK	A. Schering: *Geschichte des Instrumental-Konzerts* (Leipzig, 1905, 2/1927/R)	
ScheringGO	A. Schering: *Geschichte des Oratoriums* (Leipzig, 1911/R)	
SchillingE	G. Schilling: *Encyclopädie der gesammten musikalischen Wissenschaften, oder Universal-Lexicon der Tonkunst* D	
SČHK	*Slovník české hudební kultury* (Prague, 1997)	
SchmidlD, SchmidlDS	C. Schmidl: *Dizionario universale dei musicisti* and suppl. D	
SchmitzG	E. Schmitz: *Geschichte der weltlichen Solokantate* (Leipzig, 1914, 2/1955)	
SchullerEJ	G. Schuller: *Early Jazz* (New York, 1968/R)	
SchullerSE	G. Schuller: *The Swing Era* (New York, 1989)	
SchwarzGM	B. Schwarz: *Great Masters of the Violin* D	
SCISM	Seventeenth-Century Italian Sacred Music E	
SCKM	Seventeenth-Century Keyboard Music (New York, 1987–8)	
SCMA	Smith College Music Archives E	
SCMad	Sixteenth-Century Madrigal E	

SCMot	Sixteenth-Century Motet E	
SeegerL	H. Seeger: *Musiklexikon* D	
SEM	Series of Early Music [University of California] E	
SennMT	W. Senn: *Musik und Theater am Hof zu Innsbruck* (Innsbruck, 1954)	
SH	*Slovenská hudba* P	
SIMG	*Sammelbände der Internationalen Musik-Gesellschaft* P	
SKM	*Sovetskiye kompozitorï i muzïkovedï* (Moscow, 1978–89)	
SM	see *SMH*	
SMA	*Studies in Music* [Australia] P	
SMC	*Studies in Music from the University of Western Ontario* [Canada] P	
SMd	Schweizerische Musikdenkmäler E	
SMH	*Studia musicologica Academiae scientiarum hungaricae* P	
SmitherHO	H. Smither: *A History of the Oratorio* (Chapel Hill, NC, 1977–)	
SML	*Schweizer Musikerlexikon* D	
SMM	Summa musicae medii aevi E	
SMN	*Studia musicologica norvegica* P	
SMP	*Słownik muzyków polskich* D	
SMSC	Solo Motets from the Seventeenth Century (New York, 1987–8)	
SMw	*Studien zur Musikwissenschaft* P	
SMz	*Schweizerische Musikzeitung/Revue musicale suisse* P	
SOB	Süddeutsche Orgelmeister des Barock E	
SOI	L. Bianconi and G. Pestelli, eds.: *Storia dell'opera italiana* (Turin, 1987–; Eng. trans., 1998–)	
SolertiMBD	A. Solerti: *Musica, ballo e drammatica alla corte medicea dal 1600 al 1637* (Florence, 1905/R)	
SouthernB	E. Southern: *Biographical Dictionary of Afro-American and African Musicians* D	
SovM	*Sovetskaya muzïka* P	
SpataroC	B.J. Blackburn, E.E. Lowinsky and C.A. Miller: *A Correspondence of Renaissance Musicians* (Oxford, 1991)	
SPFFBU	*Sborník prací filosofické [filozofické] fakulty brněnské university [univerzity]* P	
SpinkES	I. Spink: *English Song: Dowland to Purcell* (London, 1974, repr. 1986 with corrections)	
StevensonRB	R. Stevenson: *Renaissance and Baroque Musical Sources in the Americas* (Washington DC, 1970)	
Stevenson SCM	R. Stevenson: *Spanish Cathedral Music in the Golden Age* (Berkeley, 1961/R)	
StevensonSM	R. Stevenson: *Spanish Music in the Age of Columbus* (The Hague, 1960/R)	
StiegerO	F. Stieger: *Opernlexikon* D	
STMf	*Svensk tidskrift för musikforskning* P	
StrohmM	R. Strohm: *Music in Late Medieval Bruges* (Oxford, 1985)	
StrohmR	R. Strohm: *The Rise of European Music* (Cambridge, 1993)	
StrunkSR1, 2	O. Strunk: *Source Readings in Music History* (New York, 1950/R, rev. 2/1998 by L. Treitler)	
SubiráHME	J. Subirá: *Historia de la música española e hispanoamericana* (Barcelona, 1953)	
TCM	Tudor Church Music E	
TCMS	Three Centuries of Music in Score (New York, 1988–90)	
Thompson1 [–11]	O. Thompson: *The International Cyclopedia of Music and Musicians*, 1st–11th edns D	
TM	Thesauri musici E	
TSM	Tesoro sacro musical P	
TVNM	*Tijdschrift van de Vereniging voor Nederlandse muziekgeschiedenis* [and earlier variants] P	

UVNM	Uitgave van oudere Noord-Nederlandsche Meesterwerken E	
Vander Straeten MPB	E. Vander Straeten: *La musique aux Pays-Bas avant le XIXe siècle* D	
VannesD	R. Vannes, with A. Souris: *Dictionnaire des musiciens (compositeurs)* D	
VannesE	R. Vannes: *Essai d'un dictionnaire universel des luthiers* D	
VintonD	J. Vinton: *Dictionary of Contemporary Music* D	
VirdungMG	S. Virdung: *Musica getutscht* (Basle, 1511/R)	
VMw	*Vierteljahrsschrift für Musikwissenschaft* P	
VogelB	E. Vogel: *Bibliothek der gedruckten weltlichen Vocalmusik Italiens, aus den Jahren 1500 bis 1700* (Berlin, 1892/R)	
WalterG	F. Walter: *Geschichte des Theaters und der Musik am kurpfalzischen Hofe* (Leipzig, 1898/R)	
WaltherML	J.G. Walther: *Musicalisches Lexicon, oder Musicalische Bibliothec* D	
Waterhouse-LangwillI	W. Waterhouse: *The New Langwill Index: a Dictionary of Musical Wind-Instrument Makers and Inventors* D	
WDMP	Wydawnictwo dawnej muzyki polskiej E	
WE	The Wellesley Edition E	
WECIS	Wellesley Edition Cantata Index Series (Wellesley, MA, 1964–72)	
Weinmann WM	A. Weinmann: *Wiener Musikverleger und Musikalienhändler von Mozarts Zeit bis gegen 1860* (Vienna, 1956)	
WilliamsNH	P. Williams: *A New History of the Organ: from the Greeks to the Present Day* (London, 1980)	
WinterfeldEK	C. von Winterfeld: *Der evangelische Kirchengesang und sein Verhältniss zur Kunst des Tonsatzes* (Leipzig, 1843–7/R)	
WolfeMEP	R.J. Wolfe: *Early American Music Engraving and Printing* (Urbana, IL, 1980)	
WolfH	J. Wolf: *Handbuch der Notationskunde* (Leipzig, 1913–19/R)	
WurzbachL	C. von Wurzbach: *Biographisches Lexikon des Kaiserthums Oesterreich* (Vienna, 1856–91)	
YIAMR	*Yearbook, Inter-American Institute for Musical Research*, later *Yearbook for Inter-American Musical Research* P	
YIFMC	*Yearbook of the International Folk Music Council* P	
YoungHI	P.T. Young: *4900 Historical Woodwind Instruments* (London, 1993) [enlarged 2nd edn of *Twenty Five Hundred Historical Woodwind Instruments* (New York, 1982)]	
YTM	*Yearbook for Traditional Music* P	
ZahnM	J. Zahn: *Die Melodien der deutschen evangelischen Kirchenlieder* (Gütersloh, 1889–93/R)	
ZDADL	*Zeitschrift für deutsches Altertum und deutsche Literatur* (1876–)	
ZfM	*Zeitschrift für Musik* P	
ŹHMP	*Źródła do historii muzyki polskiej* E	
ZI	*Zeitschrift für Instrumentenbau* P	
ZIMG	*Zeitschrift der Internationalen Musik-Gesellschaft* P	
ZL	*Zenei lexikon* D	
ZMw	*Zeitschrift für Musikwissenschaft* P	
ZT	*Zenetudományi tanulmányok* P	

Discographical Abbreviations

20C	20th Century
20CF	20th Century-Fox
AAFS	Archive of American Folksong (Library of Congress)
A&M Hor.	A&M Horizon
ABC-Para.	ABC-Paramount
AH	Artists House
AIMP	Archives Internationales de Musique Populaire (Musée d'Ethnographie, Geneva), pubd by VDE-Gallo
Ala.	Aladdin
AM	American Music
Amer.	America
AN	Arista Novus
Ant.	Antilles
Ari.	Arista
Asy.	Asylum
Atl.	Atlantic
Aut.	Autograph
Bak.	Bakton
Ban.	Banner
Bay.	Baystate
BB	Black and Blue
Bb	Bluebird
Beth.	Bethlehem
BH	Bee Hive
BL	Black Lion
BN	Blue Note
Bruns.	Brunswick
BS	Black Saint
BStar	Blue Star
Cad.	Cadence
Can.	Canyon
Cand.	Candid
Cap.	Capitol
Car.	Caroline
Cas.	Casablanca
Cat.	Catalyst
Cen.	Century
Chi.	Chiaroscuro
Cir.	Circle
CJ	Classic Jazz
Cob.	Cobblestone
Col.	Columbia
Com.	Commodore
Conc.	Concord
Cont.	Contemporary
Contl	Continental
Cot.	Cotillion
CP	Charlie Parker
CW	Creative World
Del.	Delmark
DG	Deutsche Grammophon
Dis.	Discovery
Dra.	Dragon
EB	Electric Bird
Elec.	Electrola
Elek.	Elektra
Elek. Mus.	Elektra Musician
EmA	EmArcy
ES	Elite Special
Eso.	Esoteric
Ev.	Everest
EW	East Wind
Ewd	Eastworld
FaD	Famous Door
Fan.	Fantasy
FD	Flying Dutchman
FDisk	Flying Disk
Fel.	Felsted
Fon.	Fontana
Fre.	Freedom
FW	Folkways
Gal.	Galaxy
Gen.	Gennett
GM	Groove Merchant
Gram.	Gramavision
GTJ	Good Time Jazz
HA	Hat Art
Hal.	Halcyon
Har.	Harmony
Harl.	Harlequin
HH	Hat Hut
Hick.	Hickory
HM	Harmonia Mundi
Hor.	Horizon
Hyp.	Hyperion
IC	Inner City
IH	Indian House
ImA	Improvising Artists
Imp.	Impulse!
Imper.	Imperial
IndN	India Navigation
Isl.	Island
JAM	Jazz America Marketing
Jlgy	Jazzology
Jlnd	Jazzland
Jub.	Jubilee
Jwl	Jewell
Jzt.	Jazztone
Key.	Keynote
Kt.	Keytone
Lib.	Liberty
Lml.	Limelight
Lon.	London
Mdsv.	Moodsville
Mer.	Mercury
Met.	Metronome
Metro.	Metrojazz
MJR	Master Jazz Recordings
Mlst.	Milestone
Mlt.	Melotone
Moers	Moers Music
MonE	Monmouth-Evergreen
Mstr.	Mainstream
Musi.	Musicraft

Nat.	National		SE	Strata-East
NewJ	New Jazz		Sig.	Signature
Norg.	Norgran		Slnd	Southland
NW	New World		SN	Soul Note
			SolS	Solid State
OK	Okeh		Son.	Sonora
OL	Oiseau-Lyre		Spot.	Spotlite
Omni.	Omnisound		Ste.	Steeplechase
			Sto.	Storyville
PAct	Pathé Actuelle		Sup.	Supraphon
PAlt	Palo Alto			
Para.	Paramount		Tak.	Takoma
Parl.	Parlophone		Tan.	Tangent
Per.	Perfect		TE	Toshiba Express
Phi.	Philips		Tei.	Teichiku
Phon.	Phontastic		Tel.	Telefunken
PJ	Pacific Jazz		The.	Theresa
PL	Pablo Live		Tim.	Timeless
Pol.	Polydor		TL	Time-Life
Prog.	Progressive		Tran.	Transition
Prst.	Prestige			
PT	Pablo Today		UA	United Artists
PW	Paddle Wheel		Upt.	Uptown
Qual.	Qualiton		Van.	Vanguard
			Var.	Variety
Reg.	Regent		Vars.	Varsity
Rep.	Reprise		Vic.	Victor
Rev.	Revelation		VJ	Vee-Jay
Riv.	Riverside		Voc.	Vocalion
Roul.	Roulette			
RR	Red Records		WB	Warner Bros.
RT	Real Time		WP	World Pacific
Sack.	Sackville		Xan.	Xanadu
Sat.	Saturn			

Library Sigla

The system of library sigla in this dictionary follows that used by Répertoire International des Sources Musicales, Kassel, as listed in its publication *RISM-Bibliothekssigel* (Kassel, 1999). Below are listed the sigla to be found; a few of them are additional to those published in the RISM list, but have been established in consultation with the RISM organization. Some original RISM sigla that have now been changed are retained here.

More information on individual libraries is available in the libraries list in volume 28.

In the dictionary, sigla are always printed in *italic*. In any listing of sources a national sigillum applies without repetition until it is contradicted.

Within each national list, entries are alphabetized by sigillum, first by capital letters (showing the city or town) and then by lower-case ones (showing the institution or collection).

A: AUSTRIA

A	Admont, Benediktinerstift, Archiv und Bibliothek
DO	Dorfbeuren, Pfarramt
Ed	Eisenstadt, Domarchiv, Musikarchiv
Ee	——, Esterházy-Archiv
Eh	——, Haydn-Museum
Ek	——, Stadtpfarrkirche
El	——, Burgenländisches Landesmuseum
ETgoëss	Ebenthal (nr Klagenfurt), Goëss private collection
F	Fiecht, St Georgenberg, Benediktinerstift, Bibliothek
FB	Fischbach (Oststeiermark), Pfarrkirche
FK	Feldkirch, Domarchiv
Gd	Graz, Diözesanarchiv
Gk	——, Universität für Musik und Darstellende Kunst
Gl	——, Steiermärkische Landesbibliothek am Joanneum
Gmi	——, Institut für Musikwissenschaft
Gu	——, Universitätsbibliothek
GÖ	Göttweig, Benediktinerstift, Musikarchiv
GÜ	Güssing, Franziskaner Kloster
H	Herzogenburg, Augustiner-Chorherrenstift, Musikarchiv
HE	Heiligenkreuz, Zisterzienserkloster
Ik	Innsbruck, Tiroler Landeskonservatorium
Imf	——, Tiroler Landesmuseum Ferdinandeum
Imi	——, Musikwissenschaftliches Institut der Universität
Iu	——, Universitätsbibliothek
Kk	Klagenfurt, Kärntner Landeskonservatorium, Stiftsbibliothek
Kla	——, Landesarchiv
Kse	——, Schlossbibliothek Ebental
KN	Klosterneuburg, Augustiner-Chorherrenstift, Stiftsbibliothek
KR	Kremsmünster, Benediktinerstift, Musikarchiv
L	Lilienfeld, Zisterzienser-Stift, Musikarchiv und Bibliothek
LA	Lambach, Benediktinerstift
LIm	Linz, Oberösterreichisches Landesmuseum
LIs	——, Bundesstaatliche Studienbibliothek
M	Melk, Benediktiner-Superiorat Mariazell
MB	Michaelbeuern, Benediktinerabtei
MS	Mattsee, Stiftsarchiv
MT	Maria Taferl (Niederösterreich), Pfarre
MZ	Mariazell, Benediktiner-Priorat, Bibliothek und Archiv
N	Neuburg, Pfarrarchiv
R	Rein, Zisterzienserstift
RB	Reichersberg, Stift

Sca	Salzburg, Carolino Augusteum: Salzburger Museum für Kunst und Kulturgeschichte, Bibliothek
Sd	——, Dom, Konsistorialarchiv, Dommusikarchiv
Sk	——, Kapitelbibliothek
Sl	——, Landesarchiv
Sm	——, Internationale Stiftung Mozarteum, Bibliotheca Mozartiana
Smi	——, Universität Salzburg, Institut für Musikwissenschaft, Bibliothek
Sn	——, Nonnberg (Benediktiner-Frauenstift), Bibliothek
Sp	——, Bibliothek des Priesterseminars
Ssp	——, Erzabtei St Peter, Musikarchiv
Sst	——, Bundesstaatliche Studienbibliothek [in *Su*]
Su	——, Universitätsbibliothek
SB	Schlierbach, Stift
SCH	Schlägl, Prämonstratenser-Stift, Bibliothek
SE	Seckau, Benediktinerabtei
SEI	Seitenstetten, Benediktinerstift, Musikarchiv
SF	St Florian, Augustiner-Chorherrenstift, Stiftsbibliothek, Musikarchiv
SL	St Lambrecht, Benediktiner-Abtei, Bibliothek
SPL	St Paul, Benediktinerstift St Paul im Lavanttal
ST	Stams, Zisterzienserstift, Musikarchiv
STEp	Steyr, Stadtpfarre
TU	Tulln, Pfarrkirche St Stephan
VOR	Vorau, Stift
Wa	Vienna, St Augustin, Musikarchiv
Waf	——, Pfarrarchiv Altlerchenfeld
Wdo	——, Zentralarchiv des Deutschen Orden
Wdtö	——, Gesellschaft zur Herausgabe von Denkmälern der Tonkunst in Österreich
Wgm	——, Gesellschaft der Musikfreunde
Wh	——, Pfarrarchiv Hernals
Whh	——, Haus-, Hof- und Staatsarchiv
Whk	——, Hofburgkapelle [in *Wn*]
Wk	——, St Karl Borromäus
Wkm	——, Kunsthistorisches Museum
Wlic	——, Pfarrkirche Wien-Lichtental
Wm	——, Minoritenkonvent
Wmi	——, Institut für Musikwissenschaft der Universität
Wn	——, Österreichische Nationalbibliothek, Musiksammlung
Wp	——, Musikarchiv, Piaristenkirche Maria Treu
Ws	——, Schottenabtei, Musikarchiv
Wsa	——, Stadtarchiv
Wsfl	——, Schottenfeld, Pfarrarchiv St Laurenz

Wsp	——, St Peter, Musikarchiv
Wst	——, Stadt- und Landesbibliothek, Musiksammlung
Wu	——, Universitätsbibliothek
Wwessely	——, Othmar Wessely, private collection
WAIp	Waidhofen (Ybbs), Stadtpfarre
WIL	Wilhering, Zisterzienserstift, Bibliothek und Musikarchiv
Z	Zwettl, Zisterzienserstift, Stiftsbibliothek

AUS: AUSTRALIA

CAnl	Canberra, National Library of Australia
Msl	Melbourne, State Library of Victoria
Pml	Perth, Central Music Library
PVgm	Parkville, Grainger Museum, University of Melbourne
Sb	Sydney, Symphony Australia National Music Library
Scm	——, New South Wales State Conservatorium of Music
Sfl	——, University of Sydney, Fisher Library
Smc	——, Australia Music Centre Ltd, Library
Sml	——, Music Branch Library, University of Sydney
Sp	——, Public Library
Ssl	——, State Library of New South Wales, Mitchell Library

B: BELGIUM

Aa	Antwerp, Stadsarchief
Aac	——, Archief en Museum voor het Vlaamse Culturleven
Ac	——, Koninklijk Vlaams Muziekconservatorium
Ak	——, Onze-Lieve-Vrouw-Kathedraal, Archief
Amp	——, Museum Plantin-Moretus
As	——, Stadsbibliotheek
Asj	——, Collegiale en Parochiale Kerk St-Jacob, Bibliotheek en Archief
Ba	Brussels, Archives de la Ville
Bc	——, Conservatoire Royal, Bibliothèque, Koninklijk Conservatorium, Bibliotheek
Bcdm	——, Centre Belge de Documentation Musicale [CeBeDeM]
Bg	——, Cathédrale St-Michel et Ste-Gudule [in *Bc* and *Br*]
Bmichotte	——, Michotte private collection [in *Bc*]
Br	——, Bibliothèque Royale Albert 1er/Koninlijke Bibliotheek Albert I, Section de la Musique
Brtb	——, Radiodiffusion-Télévision Belge
Bsp	——, Société Philharmonique
BRc	Bruges, Stedelijk Muziekconservatorium, Bibliotheek
BRs	——, Stadsbibliotheek
D	Diest, St Sulpitiuskerk
Gc	Ghent, Koninklijk Muziekconservatorium, Bibliotheek
Gcd	——, Culturele Dienst Province Oost-Vlaanderen
Geb	——, St Baafsarchief
Gu	——, Universiteit, Centrale Bibliotheek, Handskriftenzaal
La	Liège, Archives de l'État, Fonds de la Cathédrale St Lambert
Lc	——, Conservatoire Royal de Musique, Bibliothèque
Lg	——, Musée Grétry
Lu	——, Université de Liège, Bibliothèque
LVu	Leuven, Katholieke Universiteit van Leuven
MA	Morlanwelz-Mariemont, Musée de Mariemont, Bibliothèque
MEa	Mechelen, Archief en Stadsbibliotheek
Tc	Tournai, Chapitre de la Cathédrale, Archives
Tv	——, Bibliothèque de la Ville

BR: BRAZIL

Rem	Rio de Janeiro, Universidade Federal do Rio de Janeiro, Escola de Música, Biblioteca Alberto Nepomuceno
Rn	——, Fundação Biblioteca Nacional, Divisão de Música e Arquivo Sonoro

BY: BELARUS

MI	Minsk, Biblioteka Belorusskoj Gosudarstvennoj Konservatorii

C: CUBA

HABn	Havana, Biblioteca Nacional José Martí

CDN: CANADA

Cu	Calgary, University of Calgary, Library
E	Edmonton (AB), University of Alberta
HNu	Hamilton (ON), McMaster University, Mills Memorial Library, Music Section
Lu	London (ON), University of Western Ontario, Music Library
Mc	Montreal, Conservatoire de Musique, Centre de Documentation
Mcm	——, Centre de Musique Canadienne
Mm	——, McGill University, Faculty and Conservatorium of Music Library
Mn	——, Bibliothèque Nationale
On	Ottawa, National Library of Canada, Music Division
Qmu	Quebec, Monastère des Ursulines, Archives
Qsl	——, Musée de l'Amérique Francçaise
Qul	——, Université Laval, Bibliothèque des Sciences Humaines et Sociales
Tcm	Toronto, Canadian Music Centre
Tu	——, University of Toronto, Faculty of Music Library
Vcm	Vancouver, Canadian Music Centre
VIu	Victoria, University of Victoria

CH: SWITZERLAND

A	Aarau, Aargauische Kantonsbibliothek
Bab	Basle, Archiv der Evangelischen Brüdersozietät
Bps	——, Paul Sacher Stiftung, Bibliothek
Bu	——, Universität Basel, Öffentliche Bibliothek, Musikabteilung
BEb	Berne, Burgerbibliothek/Bibliothèque de la Bourgeoisie
BEl	——, Schweizerische Landesbibliothek/Bibliothèque Nationale Suisse/Biblioteca Nationale Svizzera/Biblioteca Naziunala Svizra
BEsu	——, Stadt- und Universitätsbibliothek
BM	Beromünster, Musikbibliothek des Stifts
BU	Burgdorf, Stadtbibliothek
CObodmer	Cologny-Geneva, Fondation Martin Bodmer, Bibliotheca Bodmeriana
D	Disentis, Stift, Musikbibliothek
E	Einsiedeln, Benedikterkloster, Musikbibliothek
EN	Engelberg, Kloster, Musikbibliothek
Fcu	Fribourg, Bibliothèque Cantonale et Universitaire
FF	Frauenfeld, Thurgauische Kantonsbibliothek
Gc	Geneva, Conservatoire de Musique, Bibliothèque
Gpu	——, Bibliothèque Publique et Universitaire
Lmg	Lucerne, Allgemeine Musikalische Gesellschaft
Lz	——, Zentralbibliothek
LAac	Lausanne, Archives Cantonales Vaudoises
LAcu	——, Bibliothèque Cantonale et Universitaire
LU	Lugano, Biblioteca Cantonale
MSbk	Mariastein, Benediktinerkloster
MÜ	Müstair, Frauenkloster St Johann
N	Neuchâtel, Bibliothèque Publique et Universitaire
OB	Oberbüren, Kloster Glattburg
P	Porrentruy, Bibliothèque Cantonale Jurasienne (incl. Bibliothèque du Lycée Cantonal)
R	Rheinfelden, Christkatholisches Pfarramt
S	Sion, Bibliothèque Cantonale du Valais
SAf	Sarnen, Benediktinerinnen-Abtei St Andreas
SAM	Samedan, Biblioteca Fundaziun Planta
SGd	St Gallen, Domchorarchiv
SGs	——, Stiftsbibliothek, Handschriftenabteilung
SGv	——, Kantonsbibliothek (Vadiana)
SH	Schaffhausen, Stadtbibliothek
SO	Solothurn, Zentralbibliothek, Musiksammlung
SObo	——, Bischöfliches Ordinariat der Diözese Basel, Diözesanarchiv des Bistums Basel
W	Winterthur, Stadtbibliothek
Zi	Zürich, Israelitische Kultusgemeinde
Zma	——, Schweizerisches Musik-Archiv [in *Nf*]
Zz	——, Zentralbibliothek
ZGm	Zug, Pfarrarchiv St Michael

CO: COLOMBIA

B	Bogotá, Archivo de la Catedral

CZ: CZECH REPUBLIC

Bam	Brno, Archiv města Brna
Bb	——, Klášter Milosrdných Bratří [in *Bm*]
Bm	——, Moravské Zemské Muzeum, Oddělení Dějin Hudby
Bsa	——, Státní Oblastní Archiv
Bu	——, Moravská Zemeská Knihovna, Hudební Oddělení
BER	Beroun, Statní Okresní Archiv
BROb	Broumov, Knihovna Benediktinů [in *HK*]
CH	Cheb, Okresní Archiv
CHRm	Chrudim, Okresní Muzeum
D	Dačice, Knihovna Františkánů [in *Bu*]
H	Hronov, Muzeum
HK	Hradec Králové, Státní Vědecká Knihovna
HKm	——, Muzeum Východních Čech
HŘ	Hradiště u Znojma, Knihovna Křižovníků [in *Bu*]
Jla	Jindřichův Hradec, Státní Oblastní Archiv Třeboni
K	Český Krumlov, Státní Oblastní Archiv v Třeboni, Hudební Sbírka
KA	Kadaň, Děkanský Kostel
KL	Klatovy, Státní Oblastní Archiv v Plzni, Pobočka Klatovy
KR	Kroměříž, Knihovna Arcibiskupského Zámku
KRa	——, Státní y Zámek a Zahrady, Historicko-Umělecké Fondy, Hudební Archív
KRA	Králíky, Kostel Sv. Michala [in *UO*]
KU	Kutná Hora, Okresní Muzeum [in *Pnm*]
LIa	Česká Lípa, Okresní Archív
LIT	Litoměřice, Státní Oblastní Archiv
LO	Loukov, Farní Kostel
LUa	Louny, Okresní Archív
ME	Mělník, Okresní Muzeum [on loan to *Pnm*]
MH	Mnichovo Hradiště, Vlastivědné Muzeum
MHa	——, Státní Oblatní Archiv v Praze – Pobočka v Mnichovoě Hradišti
MT	Moravská Třebová, Knihovna Františkánů [in *Bu*]
NR	Nová Říše, Klášter Premonstrátů, Knihovna a Hudební Sbírka
OLa	Olomouc, Zemeský Archiv Opava, Pracoviště Olomouc
OP	Opava, Slezské Muzeum
OS	Ostrava, Česky Rozhlas, Hudební Archiv
OSE	Osek, Knihovna Cisterciáků [in *Pnm*]
Pa	Prague, Státní Ústřední Archiv
Pak	——, Pražská Metropolitní Kapitula
Pdobrovského	——, Národní Muzeum, Dobrovského (Nostická) Knihovna
Pk	——, Konservatoř, Archiv a Knihovna
Pn	——, Knihovna Národního Muzea
Pnd	——, Národní Divadlo, Hudební Archiv
Pnm	——, Národní Muzeum
Pr	——, Česky Rozhlas, Archívní a Programové Fondy, Fond Hudebnin
Ps	——, Památník Národního Písemnictví, Knihovna
Psj	——, Kostel Sv. Jakuba, Farní Rad
Pst	——, Knihovna Kláštera Premonstrátů (Strahovská Knihovna) [in *Pnm*]
Pu	——, Národní Knihovna, Hudební Oddělení
Puk	——, Karlova Univerzita, Filozofická Fakulta, Ústav Hudební Vědy, Knihovna
PLa	Plzeň, Městský Archiv
PLm	——, Západočeské Muzeum, Uměleckoprůmyslové Oddělení
POa	Poděbrady, Okresní Archiv Nymburk, Pobočka Poděbrady
POm	——, Muzeum
R	Rajhrad, Knihovna Benediktinského Kláštera [in *Bm*]
RO	Rokycany, Okresní Muzeum
ROk	——, Děkanský Úřad, Kostel
SE	Semily, Okresní Archiv v Semilech se Sídlem v Bystré nad Jizerou
SO	Sokolov, Okresní Archiv se Sídlem Jindřchovice, Zámek
TC	Třebíč, Městsky Archiv
TU	Turnov, Muzeum, Hudební Sbírka [in *SE*]
VB	Vyšší Brod, Knihovna Cisterciáckého Kláštera
Z	Žatec, Muzeum
ZI	Žitenice, Státní Oblastní Archiv v Litoměřicích
ZL	Zlonice, Památník Antonína Dvořáka

D: GERMANY

Aa	Augsburg, Kantoreiarchiv St Annen
Aab	——, Archiv des Bistums Augsburg
Af	——, Fuggersche Domänenkanzlei, Bibliothek
Ahk	——, Heilig-Kreuz-Kirche, Dominikanerkloster, Biliothek [in *Asa*]
As	——, Staats- und Stadtbibliothek
Asa	——, Stadtarchiv
Au	——, Universität Augsburg, Universitätsbibliothek
AAm	Aachen, Domarchiv (Stiftsarchiv)
AAst	——, Öffentliche Bibliothek, Musikbibliothek
AB	Amorbach, Fürstlich Leiningische Bibliothek
ABG	Annaberg-Buchholz, Kirchenbibliothek St Annen
ABGa	——, Kantoreiarchiv St Annen
AG	Augustusburg, Evangelisch-Lutherisches Pfarramt der Stadtkirche St Petri, Musiksammlung
AIC	Aichach, Stadtpfarrkirche [on loan to *FS*]
ALa	Altenburg, Thüringisches Hauptstaadtsarchiv Weimar, Aussenstelle Altenburg
AM	Amberg, Staatliche Bibliothek
AN	Ansbach, Staatliche Bibliothek
ANsv	——, Sing- und Orchesterverein (Ansbacher Kantorei), Archiv [in *AN*]
AÖhk	Altötting, Kapuziner-Kloster St Konrad, Bibliothek
ARk	Arnstadt, Evangelisch-Lutherisches Pfarramt, Bibliothek
ARsk	——, Stadt- und Kreisbibliothek
ASh	Aschaffenburg, Schloss Johannisburg, Hofbibliothek
ASsb	——, Schloss Johannisburg, Stiftsbibliothek
Ba	Berlin, Amerika-Gedenkbibliothek, Musikabteilung [in *Bz*]
Bda	——, Akademie der Künste, Stiftung Archiv
Bdhm	——, Hochschule für Musik Hanns Eisler
Bga	——, Geheimes Staatsarchiv, Stiftung Preussischer Kulturbesitz
Bgk	——, Bibliothek zum Grauen Kloster [in *Bs*]
Bhbk	——, Staatliche Hochschule für Bildende Kunst, Bibliothek
Bhm	——, Hochschule der Künste, Hochschulbibliothek, Abteilung Musik und Darstellende Kunst
Bim	——, Staatliches Institut für Musikforschung, Bibliothek
Bk	——, Staatliche Museen Preussischer Kulturbesitz, Kunstbibliothek
Bkk	——, Staatliche Museen Preussischer Kulturbesitz, Kupferstichkabinett
Br	——, Deutsches, Rundfunkarchiv Frankfurt am Main – Berlin, Historische Archive, Bibliothek
Bs	——, Stadtbibliothek, Musikbibliothek [in *Bz*]
Bsb	——, Staatsbibliothek zu Berlin Preussischer Kulturbesitz
Bsommer	——, Sommer private collection
Bsp	——, Evangelische Kirche Berlin-Brandenburg, Sprachenkonvikt, Bibliothek
Bst	——, Stadtbücherei Wilmersdorf, Hauptstelle
BAa	Bamberg, Staatsarchiv
BAs	——, Staatsbibliothek
BAL	Ballenstedt, Stadtbibliothek
BAR	Bartenstein, Fürst zu Hohenlohe-Bartensteinsches Archiv [on loan to *NEhz*]
BAUd	Bautzen, Domstift und Bischöfliches Ordinariat, Bibliothek und Archiv
BAUk	Bautzen, Stadtbibliothek
BAUm	——, Stadtmuseum
BB	Benediktbeuern, Pfarrkirche, Bibliothek
BDk	Brandenburg, Dom St Peter und Paul, Domstiftsarchiv und -bibliothek
BDH	Bad Homburg vor der Höhe, Stadtbibliothek
BDS	Bad Schwalbach, Evangelisches Pfarrarchiv
BE	Bad Berleburg, Fürstlich Sayn-Wittgenstein-Berleburgsche Bibliothek

BEU	Beuron, Bibliothek der Benediktiner-Erzabtei
BFb	Burgsteinfurt, Fürst zu Bentheimsche Musikaliensammlung [on loan to *MÜu*]
BG	Beuerberg, Stiftskirche
BGD	Berchtesgaden, Stiftkirche, Bibliothek [on loan to *FS*]
BH	Bayreuth, Stadtbücherei
BIB	Bibra, Pfarrarchiv
BIT	Bitterfeld, Kreis-Museum
BKÖs	Bad Köstritz, Forschungs- und Gedenkstätte Heinrich-Schütz-Haus
BMs	Bremen, Staats- und Universitätsbibliothek
BNba	Bonn, Beethoven-Haus, Beethoven-Archiv
BNms	——, Musikwissenschaftliches Seminar der Rheinischen Friedrich-Wilhelm-Universität
BNsa	——, Stadtarchiv und Wissenschaftliche Stadtbibliothek
BNu	——, Universitäts- und Landesbibliothek
BO	Bollstedt, Evangelische Kirchengemeinde, Pfarrarchiv
BOCHmi	Bochum, Ruhr-Universität, Fakultät für Geschichtswissenschaft, Musikwissenschaftliches Institut
BS	Brunswick, Stadtarchiv und Stadtbibliothek
BUCH	Buchen (Odenwald), Bezirksmuseum, Kraus-Sammlung
Cl	Coburg, Landesbibliothek, Musiksammlung
Cs	——, Staatsarchiv
Cv	——, Kunstsammlung der Veste Coburg, Bibliothek
CEbm	Celle, Bomann-Museum, Museum für Volkskunde Landes- und Stadtgeschichte
CR	Crimmitschau, Stadtkirche St Laurentius, Notenarchiv
CZ	Clausthal-Zellerfeld, Kirchenbibliothek [in *CZu*]
CZu	——, Technische Universität, Universitätsbibliothek
Dhm	Dresden, Hochschule für Musik Carl Maria von Weber, Bibliothek [in *Dl*]
Dl	——, Sächsische Landesbibliothek – Staats- und Universitäts-Bibliothek, Musikabteilung
Dla	——, Sächsisches Hauptstaatsarchiv
Dmb	——, Städtische Bibliotheken, Haupt- und Musikbibliothek [in *Dl*]
Ds	——, Sächsische Staatsoper, Notenbibliothek [in *Dl*]
DB	Dettelbach, Franziskanerkloster, Bibliothek
DEl	Dessau, Anhaltische Landesbücherei
DEsa	——, Stadtarchiv
DGs	Duisburg, Stadtbibliothek, Musikbibliothek
DI	Dillingen an der Donau, Kreis- und Studienbibliothek
DL	Delitzsch, Museum, Bibliothek
DM	Dortmund, Stadt- und Landesbibliothek, Musikabteilung
DO	Donaueschingen, Fürstlich Fürstenbergische Hofbibliothek
DS	Darmstadt, Hessische Landes- und Hochschulbibliothek, Musikabteilung
DSim	——, Internationales Musikinstitut, Informationszentrum für Zeitgenössische Musik, Bibliothek
DSsa	Darmstadt, Hessisches Staatsarchiv
DT	Detmold, Lippische Landesbibliothek, Musikabteilung
DTF	Dietfurt, Franziskanerkloster [in *Ma*]
DÜha	——, Nordrhein-Westfälisches Hauptstaatsarchiv
DÜk	Düsseldorf, Goethe-Museum, Bibliothek
DÜl	——, Universitäts- und Landesbibliothek, Heinrich Heine Universität
DWc	Donauwörth, Cassianeum
Ed	Eichstätt, Dom [in *Eu*]
Es	——, Staats- und Seminarbibliothek [in *Eu*]
Eu	——, Katholische Universität, Universitätsbibliothek
Ew	——, Benediktinerinnen-Abtei St Walburg, Bibliothek
EB	Ebrach, Katholisches Pfarramt, Bibliothek
EC	Eckartsberga, Pfarrarchiv
EF	Erfurt, Statd- und Regionalbibliothek, Abteilung Wissenschaftliche Sondersammlungen
EIa	Eisenach, Stadtarchiv, Bibliothek
EIb	——, Bachmuseum

EN	Engelberg, Franziskanerkloster, Bibliothek
ERu	Erlangen, Universitätsbibliothek
ERP	Landesberg am Lech-Erpfting, Katholische Pfarrkirche [on loan to *Aab*]
EW	Ellwangen (Jagst), Stiftskirche
F	Frankfurt, Stadt- und Universitätsbibliothek
Ff	——, Freies Deutsches Hochstift, Frankfurter Goethe-Museum, Bibliothek
Frl	——, Musikverlag Robert Lienau
Fsa	——, Stadtarchiv
FBa	Freiberg (Lower Saxony), Stadtarchiv
FBo	——, Geschwister-Scholl-Gymnasium, Andreas-Möller-Bibliothek
FLa	Flensburg, Stadtarchiv
FLs	Flensburg, Landeszentralbibliothek Schleswig-Holstein
FRu	Freiburg, Albert-Ludwigs-Universität, Universitätsbibliothek, Abteilung Handschriften, Alte Drucke und Rara
FRva	——, Deutsches Volksliedarchiv
FRIts	Friedberg, Bibliothek des Theologischen Seminars der Evangelischen Kirche in Hessen und Nassau
FS	Freising, Erzbistum München und Freising, Dombibliothek
FUl	Fulda, Hessische Landesbibliothek
FÜS	Füssen, Katholisches Stadtpfarramt St Mang
FW	Frauenchiemsee, Benediktinerinnenabtei Frauenwörth, Archiv
Ga	Göttingen, Staatliches Archivlager
Gb	——, Johann-Sebastian-Bach-Institut
Gms	——, Musikwissenschaftliches Seminar der Georg-August-Universität
Gs	——, Niedersächsische Staats- und Universitätsbibliothek
GBR	Grossbreitenbach (nr Arnstadt), Pfarramt, Archiv
GD	Goch-Gaesdonck, Collegium Augustinianum
GI	Giessen, Justus-Liebig-Universität, Bibliothek
GLAU	Glauchau, St Georgen, Musikarchiv
GM	Grimma, Göschenhaus-Seume-Gedenkstätte
GMl	——, Landesschule [in *Dl*]
GOa	Gotha, Augustinerkirche, Notenbibliothek
GOl	——, Forschungs- und Landesbibliothek, Musiksammlung
GÖs	Görlitz, Oberlausitzische Bibliothek der Wissenschaften bei den Städtischen Sammlungen
GOL	Goldbach (nr Gotha), Pfarrbibliothek
GRu	Greifswald, Universitätsbibliothek
GRH	Gerolzhofen, Katholische Pfarrei [on loan to *WÜd*]
GÜ	Güstrow, Museum der Stadt
GZsa	Greiz, Thüringisches Staatsarchiv Rudolstadt, Aussenstelle Greiz
Ha	Hamburg, Staatsarchiv
Hkm	——, Kunstgewerbemuseum, Bibliothek
Hmb	——, Öffentlichen Bücherhallen, Musikbücherei
Hs	——, Staats- und Universitätsbibliothek Carl von Ossietzky, Musiksammlung
HAf	Halle, Hauptbibliothek und Archiv der Franckeschen Stiftungen
HAh	——, Händel-Haus
HAmi	——, Martin-Luther-Universität, Universitäts- und Landesbibliothek Sachsen-Anhalt, Institut für Musikwissenschaft, Bibliothek
HAmk	——, Marktkirche Unser Lieben Frauen, Marienbibliothek
HAu	——, Martin-Luther-Universität, Universitäts- und Landesbibliothek Sachsen-Anhalt
HAR	Hartha (Kurort), Kantoreiarchiv
HB	Heilbronn, Stadtarchiv
HEms	Heidelberg, Musikwissenschaftliches Seminar der Rupert-Karls-Universität
HEu	——, Ruprecht-Karls-Universität, Universitätsbibliothek, Abteilung Handschriften und Alte Drucke
HER	Herrnhut, Evangelische Brüder-Unität, Archiv
HGm	Havelberg, Prignitz-Museum, Bibliothek
HL	Haltenbergstetten, Schloss (über Niederstetten, Baden-Württemburg), Fürst zu Hohenlohe-Jagstberg'sche Bibliothek [in *Mbs*]

HOE	Hohenstein-Ernstthal, Kantoreiarchiv der Christophorikirche
HR	Harburg (nr Donauwörth), Fürstlich Oettingen-Wallerstein'sche Bibliothek Schloss Harburg [in *Au*]
HRD	Arnsberg-Herdringen, Schlossbibliothek (Bibliotheca Fürstenbergiana) [in *Au*]
HSj	Helmstedt, Ehemalige Universitätsbibliothek
HSk	——, Kantorat St Stephani [in *W*]
HVkm	Hanover, Bibliothek des Kestner-Museums
HVl	——, Niedersächsische Landesbibliothek
HVs	——, Stadtbibliothek, Musikbibliothek
HVsa	——, Staatsarchiv
IN	Markt Indersdorf, Katholisches Pfarramt, Bibliothek [on loan to *FS*]
ISL	Iserlohn, Evangelische Kirchengemeinde, Varnhagen-Bibliothek
Jmb	Jena, Ernst-Abbe-Bücherei und Lesehalle der Carl-Zeiss-Stiftung, Musikbibliothek
Jmi	Jena, Friedrich-Schiller-Universität, Sektion Literatur- und Kunstwissenschaften, Bibliothek des ehem. Musikwissenschaftlichen Instituts [in *Ju*]
Ju	——, Friedrich-Schiller-Universität, Thüringer Universitäts- und Landesbibliothek
JE	Jever, Marien-Gymnasium, Bibliothek
Kdma	Kassel, Deutsches Musikgeschichtliches Archiv
Kl	——, Gesamthochschul-Bibliothek, Landesbibliothek und Murhardsche Bibliothek, Musiksammlung
Km	——, Musikakademie, Bibliothek
Ksp	——, Louis Spohr-Gedenk- und Forschungsstätte, Archiv
KA	Karlsruhe, Badische Landesbibliothek
KAsp	——, Pfarramt St Peter
KAu	——, Universitätsbibliothek
KBs	Koblenz, Stadtbibliothek
KFp	Kaufbeuren, Protestantisches Kirchenarchiv
KIl	Kiel, Schleswig-Holsteinische Landesbibliothek
KIu	——, Universitätsbibliothek
KMs	Kamenz, Stadtarchiv
KNa	Cologne, Historisches Archiv der Stadt
KNd	——, Kölner Dom, Erzbischöfliche Diözesan- und Dombibliothek
KNh	——, Staatliche Hochschule für Musik, Bibliothek
KNmi	——, Musikwissenschaftliches Institut der Universität
KNu	——, Universitäts- und Stadtbibliothek
KPs	Kempten, Stadtbücherei
KPsl	——, Stadtpfarrkirche St Lorenz, Musikarchiv
KR	Kleinröhrsdorf (nr Bischofswerda), Pfarrkirchenbibliothek
KZa	Konstanz, Stadtarchiv
Lm	Lüneburg, Michaelisschule
Lr	——, Ratsbücherei, Musikabteilung
LA	Landshut, Historischer Verein für Niederbayern, Bibliothek
LB	Langenburg, Fürstlich Hohenlohe-Langenburg'sche Schlossbibliothek [on loan to *NEhz*]
LEb	Leipzig, Bach-Archiv
LEbh	——, Breitkopf & Härtel, Verlagsarchiv
LEdb	——, Deutsche Bücherei, Musikaliensammlung
LEm	——, Leipziger Städtische Bibliotheken, Musikbibliothek
LEmi	——, Universität, Zweigbibliothek Musikwissenschaft und Musikpädagogik [in *LEu*]
LEsm	——, Stadtgeschichtliches Museum, Bibliothek, Musik- und Theatergeschichtliche Sammlungen
LEst	——, Stadtbibliothek [in *LEu* and *LEm*]
LEt	——, Thomanerchor, Bibliothek [in *LEb*]
LEu	——, Karl-Marx-Universität, Universitätsbibliothek, Bibliotheca Albertina
LFN	Laufen, Stiftsarchiv
LI	Lindau, Stadtbibliothek
LIM	Limbach am Main, Pfarrkirche Maria Limbach
LST	Lichtenstein, Stadtkirche St Laurentius, Kantoreiarchiv
LÜh	Lübeck, Bibliothek der Hansestadt, Musikabteilung
LUC	Luckau, Stadtkirche St Nikolai, Kantoreiarchiv
Ma	Munich, Franziskanerkloster St Anna, Bibliothek
Mb	——, Benediktinerabtei St Bonifaz, Bibliothek
Mbm	——, Bibliothek des Metropolitankapitels
Mbn	——, Bayerisches Nationalmuseum, Bibliothek
Mbs	——, Bayerische Staatsbibliothek
Mf	——, Frauenkirche [on loan to *FS*]
Mh	——, Staatliche Hochschule für Musik, Bibliothek
Mhsa	——, Bayerisches Hauptstaatsarchiv
Mk	——, Theatinerkirche St Kajetan
Mm	——, Bibliothek St Michael
Mo	——, Opernarchiv
Msa	——, Staatsarchiv
Mth	——, Theatermuseum der Clara-Ziegler-Stiftung
Mu	——, Ludwig-Maximilians-Universität, Universitätsbibliothek, Abteilung Handschriften, Nachlässe, Alte Drucke
MAl	Magdeburg, Landeshauptarchiv Sachsen-Anhalt [in *WERa*]
MAs	——, Stadtbibliothek Wilhelm Weitling, Musikabteilung
ME	Meissen, Stadt- und Kreisbibliothek
MEIk	Meiningen, Bibliothek der Evangelisch-Lutherischen Kirchengemeinde
MEIl	——, Thüringisches Staatsarchiv
MEIr	——, Meininger Museen, Abteilung Musikgeschichte/Max-Reger-Archiv
MERa	Merseburg, Domstift, Stiftsarchiv
MG	Marburg, Westdeutsche Bibliothek [in *Bsb*]
MGmi	——, Musikwissenschaftliches Institut der Philipps-Universität, Abteilung Hessisches Musikarchiv
MGs	——, Staatsarchiv und Archivschule
MGu	——, Philipps-Universität, Universitätsbibliothek
MGB	Mönchen-Gladbach, Bibliothek Wissenschaft und Weisheit, Johannes-Duns-Skotus-Akademie der Kölnischen Ordens-Provinz der Franziskaner
MH	Mannheim, Wissenschaftliche Stadtbibliothek
MHrm	——, Städtisches Reiss-Museum
MHst	——, Stadtbücherei, Musikbücherei
MLHb	Mühlhausen, Blasiuskirche, Pfarrarchiv Divi Blasii [on loan to *MLHm*]
MLHm	——, Marienkirche
MLHr	——, Stadtarchiv
MMm	Memmingen, Evangelisch-Lutherisches Pfarramt St Martin, Bibliothek
MR	Marienberg, Kirchenbibliothek
MT	Metten, Abtei, Bibliothek
MÜd	Münster, Bischöfliches Diözesanarchiv
MÜp	——, Bischöfliches Priesterseminar, Bibliothek
MÜs	——, Santini-Bibliothek [in *MÜp*]
MÜu	——, Westfälische Wilhelms-Universität, Universitäts- und Landesbibliothek, Musiksammlung
MÜG	Mügeln, Evangelisch-Lutherisches Pfarramt St Johannis, Musikarchiv
MY	Mylau, Kirchenbibliothek
MZmi	Mainz, Musikwissenschaftliches Institut der Johannes-Gutenberg-Universität
MZp	——, Bischöfliches Priesterseminar, Bibliothek
MZs	——, Stadtbibliothek
MZsch	——, Musikverlag B. Schott's Söhne, Verlagsarchiv
MZu	——, Johannes-Gutenberg-Universität, Universitätsbibliothek, Musikabteilung
Ngm	Nuremberg, Germanisches National-Museum, Bibliothek
Nla	——, Bibliothek beim Landeskirchlichen Archiv
Nst	——, Bibliothek Egidienplatz
NA	Neustadt an der Orla, Evangelisch-Lutherische Kirchengemeinde, Pfarrarchiv
NAUs	Naumburg, Stadtarchiv
NAUw	——, St Wenzel, Bibliothek
NEhz	Neuenstein, Hohenlohe-Zentralarchiv
NH	Neresheim, Bibliothek der Benediktinerabtei
NL	Nördlingen, Stadtarchiv, Stadtbibliothek und Volksbücherei
NLk	——, Evangelisch-Lutherisches Pfarramt St Georg, Musikarchiv
NM	Neumünster, Schleswig-Holsteinische Musiksammlung der Stadt Neumünster [in *KIl*]

NNFw	Neunhof (nr Nürnberg), Freiherrliche Welser'sche Familienstiftung
NO	Nordhausen, Wilhelm-von-Humboldt-Gymnasium, Bibliothek
NS	Neustadt an der Aisch, Evangelische Kirchenbibliothek
NT	Neumarkt-St Veit, Pfarrkirche
NTRE	Niedertrebra, Evangelisch-Lutherische Kirchgemeinde, Pfarrarchiv
OB	Ottobeuren, Benediktinerabtei
OBS	Gessertshausen-Oberschönenfeld, Abtei
OF	Offenbach am Main, Verlagsarchiv André
OLH	Olbernhau, Evangelisch-Lutherisches Pfarramt, Pfarrarchiv
ORB	Oranienbaum, Landesarchiv
Pg	Passau, Gymnasialbibliothek
Po	——, Bistum, Archiv
PA	Paderborn, Erzbischöfliche Akademische Bibliothek [in *HRD*]
PE	Perleberg, Pfarrbibliothek
PI	Pirna, Stadtarchiv
PL	Plauen, Stadtkirche St Johannis, Pfarrarchiv
PO	Pommersfelden, Graf von Schönbornsche Schlossbibliothek
POL	Polling, Katholisches Pfarramt
POTh	Potsdam, Fachhochschule Potsdam, Hochschulbibliothek
Rp	Regensburg, Bischöfliche Zentralbibliothek, Proske-Musikbibliothek
Rs	——, Staatliche Bibliothek
Rtt	——, Fürst Thurn und Taxis Hofbibliothek
Ru	——, Universität Regensburg, Universitätsbibliothek
RAd	Ratzeburg, Domarchiv
RB	Rothenburg ob der Tauber, Stadtarchiv und Rats- und Konsistorialbibliothek
RH	Rheda, Fürst zu Bentheim-Tecklenburgische Musikbibliothek [on loan to *MÜu*]
ROmi	Rostock, Universitätsbibliothek, Fachbibliothek Musikwissenschaften
ROs	——, Stadtbibliothek, Musikabteilung
ROu	——, Universität, Universitätsbibliothek
RT	Rastatt, Bibliothek des Friedrich-Wilhelm-Gymnasiums
RUh	Rudolstadt, Hofkapellarchiv [in *RUl*]
RUl	——, Thüringisches Staatsarchiv
Sl	Stuttgart, Württembergische Landesbibliothek
SBj	Straubing, Kirchenbibliothek St Jakob [in *Rp*]
SCHOT	Schotten, Liebfrauenkirche
SHk	Sondershausen, Stadtkirche/Superintendentur, Bibliothek
SHm	——, Schlossmuseum
SHs	——, Schlossmuseum, Bibliothek [in *SHm*]
SI	Sigmaringen, Fürstlich Hohenzollernsche Hofbibliothek
SNed	Schmalkalden, Evangelisches Dekanat, Bibliothek
SPlb	Speyer, Pfälzische Landesbibliothek, Musikabteilung
STBp	Steinbach (nr Bad Salzungen), Evangelische-Lutherisches Pfarramt, Pfarrarchiv
STOm	Stolberg (Harz), Pfarramt St Martini, Pfarrarchiv
SUH	Suhl, Wissenschaftliche Allgemeinbibliothek, Musikabteilung
SÜN	Sünching, Schloss
SWl	Schwerin, Landesbibliothek Mecklenburg-Vorpommern, Musiksammlung
SWs	——, Stadtbibliothek, Musikabteilung [in *SWl*]
SWth	——, Mecklenburgisches Staatstheater, Bibliothek
Tl	Tübingen, Schwäbisches Landesmusikarchiv [in *Tmi*]
Tmi	——, Bibliothek des Musikwissenschaftlichen Institut
Tu	——, Eberhard-Karls-Universität, Universitätsbibliothek
TEG	Tegernsee, Pfarrkirche
TEGha	——, Herzogliches Archiv
TEI	Teisendorf, Katholisches Pfarramt, Pfarrbibliothek
TIT	Tittmoning, Pfarrkirche [in *Fs*]
TO	Torgau, Evangelische Kirchengemeinde, Johann-Walter-Kantorei
TRb	Trier, Bistumarchiv

TRs	——, Stadtbibliothek
TZ	Bad Tölz, Katholisches Pfarramt Maria Himmelfahrt [in *FS*]
Us	Ulm, Stadtbibliothek
Usch	——, Von Schermar'sche Familienstiftung, Bibliothek
UDa	Udestedt, Evangelisch-Lutherisches Pfarramt [in *Dl*]
URS	Ursberg, St Josef-Kongregation, Orden der Franziskanerinnen
W	Wolfenbüttel, Herzog August Bibliothek, Handschriftensammlung
Wa	——, Niedersächsisches Staatsarchiv
WA	Waldheim, Stadtkirche St Nikolai, Bibliothek
WAB	Waldenburg, St Bartholomäus, Kantoreiarchiv
WD	Wiesentheid, Musiksammlung des Grafen von Schönborn-Wiesentheid
WERhb	Wernigerode, Harzmuseum, Harzbücherei
WEY	Weyarn, Pfarrkirche, Bibliothek [on loan to *FS*]
WF	Weissenfels, Schuh- und Stadtmuseum Weissenfels (mit Heinrich-Schütz-Gedenkstätte) [on loan to *BKÖs*]
WFe	——, Ephoralbibliothek
WFmk	——, Marienkirche, Pfarrarchiv [in *HAmk*]
WGl	Wittenberg, Lutherhalle, Reformationsgeschichtliches Museum
WGH	Waigolshausen, Katholische Pfarrei [on loan to *WÜd*]
WH	Bad Windsheim, Stadtbibliothek
WIl	Wiesbaden, Hessische Landesbibliothek
WINtj	Winhöring, Gräflich Toerring-Jettenbachsche Bibliothek [on loan to *Mbs*]
WO	Worms, Stadtbibliothek und Öffentliche Büchereien
WRdn	Weimar, Deutsches Nationaltheater und Staatskappelle, Archiv
WRgm	——, Goethe-National-Museum (Goethes Wohnhaus)
WRgs	——, Stiftung Weimarer Klassik, Goethe–Schiller-Archiv
WRh	——, Hochschule für Musik Franz Liszt
WRiv	——, Hochschule für Musik Franz Liszt, Institut für Volksmusikforschung
WRl	——, Thüringisches Hauptstaatsarchiv Weimar
WRtl	——, Thüringische Landesbibliothek, Musiksammlung [in *WRz*]
WRz	——, Stiftung Weimarer Klassik, Herzogin Anna Amalia Bibliothek
WS	Wasserburg am Inn, Chorarchiv St Jakob, Pfarramt [on loan to *FS*]
WÜd	Würzburg, Diözesanarchiv
WÜst	——, Staatsarchiv
WÜu	——, Bayerische Julius-Maximilians-Universität, Universitätsbibliothek
Z	Zwickau, Ratsschulbibliothek, Wissenschaftliche Bibliothek
Zsa	——, Stadtarchiv
Zsch	——, Robert-Schumann-Haus
ZE	Zerbst, Stadtarchiv
ZEo	——, Gymnasium Francisceum, Bibliothek
ZGh	Zörbig, Heimatmuseum
ZI	Zittau, Christian-Weise-Bibliothek, Altbestand [in *Dl*]
ZL	Zeil, Fürstlich Waldburg-Zeil'sches Archiv
ZZs	Zeitz, Stiftsbibliothek

DK: DENMARK

A	Århus, Statsbiblioteket
Ch	Christiansfeld, Brødremenigheden (Herrnhutgemeinde)
Kar	Copenhagen, Det Arnamagnaeanske Institut
Kc	——, Carl Claudius Musikhistoriske Samling [in *Km*]
Kk	——, Kongelige Bibliotek
Kmk	——, Kongelige Danske Musikkonservatorium
Ku	——, Det Kongelige Bibliotek Fiolstraede
Kv	——, Københavns Universitet, Musikvidenskabeligt Institut, Bibliotek
Ol	Odense, Landsarkivet for Fyen

Ou	——, Universitetsbibliotek, Musikafdelingen
Sa	Sorø, Sorø Akademi, Biblioteket
Tv	Tåsinge, Valdemars Slot

E: SPAIN

Ac	Avila, S Apostólica Iglesia Catedral de el Salvador, Archivo Catedralicio
Asa	——, Monasterio de S Ana
AL	Alquézar, Colegiata
ALB	Albarracín, Catedral, Archivo
AR	Aránzazu, Archivo Musical del Monasterio de Aránzazu
AS	Astorga, Catedral
Bac	Barcelona, Archivo de la Corona de Aragón/Arixiu de la Corona d'Aragó
Bbc	——, Biblioteca de Catalunya, Sección de Música
Bc	——, S.E. Catedra Basiclica, Arixiu
Bcd	——, Centro de Documentació Musical de la Generalitat de Catalunya 'El Jardi Dels Tarongers'
Bih	——, Arixiu Històric de la Ciutat
Bim	——, Consejo Superior de Investigaciones Científicas, Departamento de Musicología, Biblioteca
Bit	——, Institut del Teatre, Centre d'Investigació, Documentació i Difusió
Boc	——, Orfeó Català, Biblioteca
Bu	——, Universitat Autónoma
BA	Badajoz, Catedral, Archivo Capitular
BUa	Burgos, Catedral, Archivo
BUlh	——, Cistercian Monasterio de Las Huelgas
C	Córdoba, S Iglesia Catedral, Archivo de Música
CA	Calahorra, Catedral
CAL	Calatayud, Colegiata de S María
CU	Cuenca, Catedral, Archivo Capitular
CUi	——, Instituto de Música Religiosa
CZ	Cádiz, Archivo Capitular
E	San Lorenzo de El Escorial, Monasterio, Real Biblioteca
G	Gerona, Catedral, Archivo/Arxiu Capitular
Gp	——, Biblioteca Pública
GRc	Granada, Catedral Metropolitana, Archivo Capitular [in *GRcr*]
GRcr	——, Capilla Real, Archivo de Música
GRmf	——, Archivo Manuel de Falla
GU	Guadalupe, Real Monasterio de S María, Archivo de Música
H	Huesca, Catedral
J	Jaca, Catedral, Archivo Musical
JA	Jaén, Catedral, Archivo Capitular
JEc	Jerez de la Frontera, Colegiata
L	León, Catedral, Archivo Histórico
Lc	——, Real Basilica de S Isidoro
LEc	Lérida, Catedral
LPA	Las Palmas de Gran Canaria, Catedral de Canarias
Mah	Madrid, Archivo Histórico Nacional
Mba	——, Archivo de Música, Real Academia de Bellas Artes de S Fernando
Mc	——, Real Conservatorio Superior de Música, Biblioteca
Mca	——, Casa de Alba
Mcns	——, Congregación de Nuestra Señora
Md	——, Centro de Documentación Musical del Ministerio de Cultura
Mdr	——, Convento de las Descalzas Reales
Mm	——, Biblioteca Histórica Municipal
Mmc	——, Casa Ducal de Medinaceli, Biblioteca
Mn	——, Biblioteca Nacional
Mp	——, Patrimonio Nacional
Msa	——, Sociedad General de Autores y Editores
MA	Málaga, Catedral, Archivo Capitular
MO	Montserrat, Abadía
MON	Mondoñedo, Catedral, Archivo
OL	Olot, Biblioteca Popular
ORI	Orihuela, Catedral, Archivo
OV	Oviedo, Catedral Metropolitana, Archivo
P	Plasencia, Catedral, Archivo de Música
PAc	Palma de Mallorca, Catedral, Archivo
PAp	——, Biblioteca Provincial
PAL	Palencia, Catedral de S Antolín, Archivo de Música
PAMc	Pamplona, Catedral, Archivo
PAS	Pastrana, Museo Parroquial
RO	Roncesvalles, Monasterio S María, Biblioteca
Sc	Seville, Institución Colombina
SA	Salamanca, Catedral, Archivo Catedralicio
SAc	——, Conservatorio Superior de Música de Salamanca, Biblioteca
SAu	——, Biblioteca Universitaria
SAN	Santander, Biblioteca de la Universidad Menéndez, Sección de Música
SC	Santiago de Compostela, Catedral Metropolitana
SCu	——, Biblioteca de la Universidad
SD	Santo Domingo de la Calzada, Catedral Archivo
SE	Segovia, Catedral, Archivo Capitular
SEG	Segorbe, Archivo de la Catedral
SI	Silos, Abadía de S Domingo, Archivo
SU	Seu de Urgel, Catedral
Tc	Toledo, Catedral, Archivo y Biblioteca Capitulares
Tp	——, Biblioteca Pública Provincial y Museo de la S Cruz
TAc	Tarragona, Catedral
TE	Teruel, Catedral, Archivo Capitular
TO	Tortosa, Catedral
TUY	Tuy, Catedral
TZ	Tarazona, Catedral, Archivo Capitular
V	Valladolid, Catedral Metropolitana, Archivo de Música
Vp	——, Parroquia de Santiago
VAa	Valencia, Archivo Municipal
VAc	——, Catedral Metropolitana, Archivo y Biblioteca, Archivo de Música
VAcp	——, Real Colegio: Seminario de Corpus Christi, Archivo Musical del Patriarca
VAu	——, Biblioteca Universitaria
VI	Vich, Museu Episcopal
Zac	Zaragoza, Catedrale de La Seo y Basílica del Pilar, Archivo de Música de las Catedrales
Zcc	——, Colegio de las Escuelas Pías de S José de Calasanz, Biblioteca
Zs	——, La Seo, Biblioteca Capitular [in *Zac*]
Zvp	——, Iglesia Metropolitana [in *Zac*]
ZAc	Zamora, Catedral

ET: EGYPT

Cn	Cairo, National Library (Dar al-Kutub)
MSsc	Mount Sinai, St Catherine's Monastery

EV: ESTONIA

TALg	Tallinn, National Library of Estonia

F: FRANCE

A	Avignon, Médiathèque Ceccano
Ac	——, Bibliothèque du Conservatoire
AB	Abbeville, Bibliothèque Nationale
AG	Agen, Archives Départementales de Lot-et-Garonne
AI	Albi, Bibliothèque Municipale
AIXc	Aix-en-Provence, Bibliothèque du Conservatoire
AIXm	——, Bibliothèque Méjanes
AIXmc	——, Bibliothèque de la Maîtrise de la Cathédrale
AL	Alençon, Bibliothèque Municipale
AM	Amiens, Bibliothèque Municipale
AN	Angers, Bibliothèque Municipale
APT	Apt, Basilique Ste Anne
AS	Arras, Médiathèque Municipale
ASOlang	Asnières-sur-Oise, Collection François Lang
AUT	Autun, Bibliothèque Municipale
AVR	Avranches, Bibliothèque Nationale
B	Besançon, Bibliothèque Municipale
Ba	——, Bibliothèque de l'Archevêché
BE	Beauvais, Bibliothèque Municipale
BG	Bourg-en-Bresse, Bibliothèque Municipale
BO	Bordeaux, Bibliothèque Municipale
BS	Bourges, Bibliothèque Municipale
C	Carpentras, Bibliothèque Municipale (Inguimbertine)

CA	Cambrai, Médiathèque Municipale
CAc	——, Cathédrale
CC	Carcassonne, Bibliothèque Municipale
CF	Clermont-Ferrand, Bibliothèque Municipale et Interuniversitaire, Département Patrimoine
CH	Chantilly, Musée Condé
CHd	——, Musée Dobrie
CHRm	Chartres, Bibliothèque Municipale
CLO	Clermont-de-l'Oise, Bibliothèque
CO	Colmar, Bibliothèque de la Ville
COM	Compiègne, Bibliothèque Municipale
CSM	Châlons-en-Champagne, Bibliothèque Municipale
Dc	Dijon, Conservatoire Jean-Philippe Rameau, Bibliothèque
Dm	——, Bibliothèque Municipale
DI	Dieppe, Fonds Anciens et Local, Médiathèque Jean Renoir
DO	Dôle, Bibliothèque Municipale
DOU	Douai, Bibliothèque Nationale
E	Epinal, Bibliothèque Nationale
EMc	Embrun, Trésor de la Cathédrale
EV	Evreux, Bibliothèque Municipale
F	Foix, Bibliothèque Municipale
G	Grenoble, Bibliothèque Municipale
Lad	Lille, Archives Départementales du Nord
Lc	——, Bibliothèque du Conservatoire
Lm	——, Bibliothèque Municipale Jean Levy
LA	Laon, Bibliothèque Municipale
LG	Limoges, Bibliothèque Francophone Municipale
LH	Le Havre, Bibliothèque Municipale
LM	Le Mans, Bibliothèque Municipale Classée, Médiathèque Louis Aragon
LYc	Lyons, Conservatoire National de Musique
LYm	——, Bibliothèque Municipale
Mc	Marseilles, Conservatoire de Musique et de Déclamation
MD	Montbéliard, Bibliothèque Municipale
ME	Metz, Médiathèque
MH	Mulhouse, Bibliothèque Municipale
ML	Moulins, Bibliothèque Municipale
MO	Montpellier, Bibliothèque de l'Université
MOf	——, Bibliothèque Inter-Universitaire, Section Médecine
MON	Montauban, Bibliothèque Municipale Antonin Perbosc
Nm	Nantes, Bibliothèque Municipale, Médiathèque
NAc	Nancy, Bibliothèque du Conservatoire
O	Orléans, Médiathèque
Pa	Paris, Bibliothèque de l'Arsenal
Pan	——, Archives Nationales
Pc	——, Conservatoire [in *Pn*]
Pcf	——, Bibliothèque de la Comédie Française
Pcnrs	——, Centre National de la Recherche Scientifique, Bibliothèque
Pd	——, Centre de Documentation de la Musique Contemporaine
Pe	——, Schola Cantorum
Peb	——, Ecole Normale Supérieure des Beaux-Arts, Bibliothèque
Pgm	——, Gustav Mahler, Bibliothèque Musicale
Phanson	——, Collection Hanson
Pi	——, Bibliothèque de l'Institut de France
Pim	——, Bibliothèque Pierre Aubry
Pm	——, Bibliothèque Mazarine
Pmeyer	——, André Meyer, private collection
Pn	——, Bibliothèque Nationale de France
Po	——, Bibliothèque-Musée de l'Opéra
Ppincherle	——, Marc Pincherle, private collection
Ppo	——, Bibliothèque Polonaise de Paris
Prothschild	——, Germaine, Baronne Edouard de Rothschild, private collection
Prt	——, Radio France, Documentation Musicale
Ps	——, Bibliothèque de la Sorbonne
Psal	——, Editions Salabert
Pse	——, Société des Auteurs, Compositeurs et Editeurs de Musique
Psg	——, Bibliothèque Ste-Geneviève
Pshp	——, Société d'Histoire du Protestantisme Français, Bibliothèque

Pthibault	——, Geneviève Thibault, private collection [in *Pn*]
R	Rouen, Bibliothèque Municipale
Rc	——, Bibliothèque du Conservatoire
RS	Reims, Bibliothèque Municipale
RSc	——, Maîtrise de la Cathédrale
Sc	Strasbourg, Bibliothèque du Conservatoire
Sgs	——, Union Sainte Cécile, Bibliothèque Musicale du Grand Séminaire
Sim	——, Université des Sciences Humaines, Institut de Musicologie
Sm	——, Bibliothèque Municipale
Sn	——, Bibliothèque Nationale et Universitaire
Ssp	——, Bibliothèque du Séminaire Protestant
SDI	St Dié, Bibliothèque Municipale
SEm	Sens, Bibliothèque Municipale
SERc	Serrant, Château
SO	Solesmes, Abbaye de St-Pierre
SOM	St Omer, Bibliothèque Municipale
SQ	St Quentin, Bibliothèque Municipale
T	Troyes, Bibliothèque Municipale
TLm	Toulouse, Bibliothèque Municipale
TOm	Tours, Bibliothèque Municipale
V	Versailles, Bibliothèque
VA	Vannes, Bibliothèque Municipale
VAL	Valenciennes, Bibliothèque Municipale
VN	Verdun, Bibliothèque Municipale

FIN: FINLAND

A	Turku, Åbo Akademi, Sibelius Museum, Bibliotek ja Arkiv
Hy	Helsinki, Helsingin Yliopiston Kirjasto/Helsinki University Library/Suomen Kansalliskikjasto
Hyf	——, Helsingin Yliopiston Kirjasto, Department of Finnish Music

GB: GREAT BRITAIN

A	Aberdeen, University, Queen Mother Library
AB	Aberystwyth, Llyfryell Genedlaethol Cymru/National Library of Wales
ABu	——, University College of Wales
ALb	Aldeburgh, Britten-Pears Library
AM	Ampleforth, Abbey and College Library, St Lawrence Abbey
AR	Arundel Castle, Archive
Bp	Birmingham, Public Libraries
Bu	——, Birmingham University
BA	Bath, Municipal Library
BEcr	Bedford, Bedfordshire County Record Office
BEL	Belton (Lincs.), Belton House
BENcoke	Bentley (Hants.), Gerald Coke, private collection
BEV	Beverley, East Yorkshire County Record Office
BO	Bournemouth, Central Library
BRp	Bristol, Central Library
BRu	——, University of Bristol Library
Ccc	Cambridge, Corpus Christi College, Parker Library
Ccl	——, Central Library
Cclc	——, Clare College Archives
Ce	——, Emmanuel College
Cfm	——, Fitzwilliam Museum, Dept of Manuscripts and Printed Books
Cgc	——, Gonville and Caius College
Cjc	——, St John's College
Ckc	——, King's College, Rowe Music Library
Cmc	——, Magdalene College, Pepys Library
Cp	——, Peterhouse College Library
Cpc	——, Pembroke College Library
Cpl	——, Pendlebury Library of Music
Cssc	——, Sidney Sussex College
Ctc	——, Trinity College, Library
Cu	——, University Library
CA	Canterbury, Cathedral Library
CDp	Cardiff, Public Libraries, Central Library
CDu	——, University of Wales/Prifysgol Cymru
CF	Chelmsford, Essex County Record Office
CH	Chichester, Diocesan Record Office
CHc	——, Cathedral
CL	Carlisle, Cathedral Library
DRc	Durham, Cathedral Church, Dean and Chapter Library

DRu	——, University Library
DU	Dundee, Central Library
En	Edinburgh, National Library of Scotland, Music Dept
Ep	——, City Libraries, Music Library
Er	——, Reid Music Library of the University of Edinburgh
Es	——, Signet Library
Eu	——, University Library, Main Library
EL	Ely, Cathedral Library [in *Cu*]
EXcl	Exeter, Cathedral Library
Ge	Glasgow, Euing Music Library
Gm	——, Mitchell Library, Arts Dept
Gsma	——, Scottish Music Archive
Gu	——, University Library
GL	Gloucester, Cathedral Library
GLr	——, Record Office
H	Hereford, Cathedral Library
HAdolmetsch	Haslemere, Carl Dolmetsch, private collection
HFr	Hertford, Hertfordshire Record Office
Ir	Ipswich, Suffolk Record Office
KNt	Knutsford, Tatton Park (National Trust)
Lam	London, Royal Academy of Music, Library
Lbbc	——, British Broadcasting Corporation, Music Library
Lbc	——, British Council Music Library
Lbl	——, British Library
Lcm	——, Royal College of Music, Library
Lcml	——, Central Music Library
Lco	——, Royal College of Organists
Lcs	——, English Folk Dance and Song Society, Vaughan Williams Memorial Library
Ldc	——, Dulwich College Library
Lfm	——, Faber Music
Lgc	——, Guildhall Library
Lk	——, King's Music Library [in *Lbl*]
Lkc	——, King's College Library
Llp	——, Lambeth Palace Library
Lmic	——, British Music Information Centre
Lmt	——, Minet Library
Lpro	——, Public Record Office
Lrcp	——, Royal College of Physicians
Lsp	——, St Paul's Cathedral Library
Lspencer	——, Woodford Green: Robert Spencer, private collection
Lst	——, Savoy Theatre Collection
Lu	——, University of London Library, Music Collection
Lue	——, Universal Edition
Lv	——, Victoria and Albert Museum, Theatre Museum
Lwa	——, Westminster Abbey Library
Lwcm	——, Westminster Central Music Library
LA	Lancaster, District Central Library
LEbc	Leeds, University of Leeds, Brotherton Library
LEc	——, Leeds Central Library, Music and Audio Dept
LF	Lichfield, Cathedral Library
LI	Lincoln, Cathedral Library
LVp	Liverpool, Libraries and Information Services, Humanities Reference Library
LVu	——, University, Music Department
Mch	Manchester, Chetham's Library
Mp	——, Central Library, Henry Watson Music Library
Mr	——, John Rylands Library, Deansgate
MA	Maidstone, Kent County Record Office
NH	Northampton, Record Office
NO	Nottingham, University of Nottingham, Department of Music
NTp	Newcastle upon Tyne, Public Libraries
NW	Norwich, Central Library
NWhamond	——, Anthony Hamond, private collection
NWr	——, Record Office
Oas	Oxford, All Souls College Library
Ob	——, Bodleian Library
Oc	——, Coke Collection
Occc	——, Corpus Christi College Library
Och	——, Christ Church Library
Ojc	——, St John's College Library
Olc	——, Lincoln College Library

Omc	——, Magdalen College Library
Onc	——, New College Library
Ouf	——, Faculty of Music Library
Owc	——, Worcester College
P	Perth, Sandeman Public Library
PB	Peterborough, Cathedral Library
PM	Parkminster, St Hugh's Charterhouse
R	Reading, University, Music Library
SA	St Andrews, University of St Andrews Library
SB	Salisbury, Cathedral Library
SC	Sutton Coldfield, Oscott College, Old Library
SH	Sherborne, Sherborne School Library
SHR	Shrewsbury, Salop Record Office
SHRs	——, Library of Shrewsbury School
SOp	Southampton, Public Library
SRfa	Studley Royal, Fountains Abbey [in *LEc*]
STb	Stratford-on-Avon, Shakespeare's Birthplace Trust Library
STm	——, Shakespeare Memorial Library
T	Tenbury Wells, St Michael's College Library [in *Ob*]
W	Wells, Cathedral Library
WA	Whalley, Stonyhurst College Library
WB	Wimborne, Minster Chain Library
WC	Winchester, Chapter Library
WCc	——, Winchester College, Warden and Fellows' Library
WCr	——, Hampshire Record Office
WMl	Warminster, Longleat House Old Library
WO	Worcester, Cathedral Library
WOr	——, Record Office
WRch	Windsor, St George's Chapel Library
WRec	——, Eton College, College Library
Y	York, Minster Library
Ybi	——, Borthwick Institute of Historical Research

GCA: GUATEMALA

Gc	Guatemala City, Cathedral, Archivo Capitular

GR: GREECE

Aels	Athens, Ethniki Lyriki Skini
Akounadis	——, Panayis Kounadis, private collection
Aleotsakos	——, George Leotsakos, private collection
Am	——, Mousseio ke Kendro Meletis Ellinikou Theatrou
An	——, Ethnikē Bibliotēkē tēs Hellados
AOd	Mt Athos, Mone Dionysiou
AOdo	——, Mone Dohiariou
AOh	——, Mone Hilandariou
AOi	——, Mone ton Iveron
AOk	——, Mone Koutloumousi
AOml	——, Mone Megistis Lávras
AOpk	——, Mone Pantokrátoros
AOva	——, Vatopedi Monastery
P	Patmos
THpi	Thessaloniki, Patriarhikó Idryma Paterikon Meleton, Vivliotheke

H: HUNGARY

Ba	Budapest, Magyar Tudományos Akadémia Könyvtára
Bami	——, Magyar Tudományos Akadémia Zenetudományi Intézet, Könyvtár
Bb	——, Bartók Béla Zeneművészeti Szakközépiskola, Könyvtár [in *Bl*]
Bl	——, Liszt Ferenc Zeneművészeti Főiskola, Könyvtár
Bn	——, Országos Széchényi Könyvtár
Bo	——, Állami Operaház
Br	——, Ráday Gyűjtemény
Bs	——, Központi Szemináriumi Könyvtár
Bu	——, Eötvös Loránd Tudományegyetem, Egyetemi Könyvtár
BA	Bártfá, St Aegidius [in *Bn*]
Efko	Esztergom, Főszékesegyházi Kottártár
Efkö	——, Főszékesegyházi Könyvtár
Gc	Győr, Püspöki Papnevelő Intézet Könyvtára
Gk	——, Káptalan Magánlevéltár Kottatára
GYm	Gyula, Múzeum

K	Kalocsa, Érseki Könyvtár
KE	Keszthely, Helikon Kastélymúzeum, Könyvtár
P	Pécs, Székesegyházi Kottatár
PH	Pannonhalma, Főapátság, Könyvtár
Se	Sopron, Evangélikus Egyházközség Könyvtára
SFm	Székesfehérvár, István Király Múzeum
VEs	Veszprém, Székesegyházi Kottatár

HR: CROATIA

Dsmb	Dubrovnik, Franjevački Samostan Male Braće, Knjižnica
KIf	Kloštar Ivanić, Franjevački Samostan
OMf	Omiš, Franjevački Samostan
R	Rab, Župna Crkva
Sk	Split, Glazbeni Arhiv Katedrale Sv. Dujma
SMm	Samobor, Samoborski Muzej
Vu	Varaždin, Uršulinski Samostan
Zaa	Zagreb, Hrvatska Akademija Znanosti i Umjetnosti, Arhiv
Zh	——, Hrvatski Glazbeni Zavod, Knjižnica i Arhiv
Zha	——, Zbirka Don Nikole Udina-Algarotti [on loan to *Zh*]
Zhk	——, Arhiv Hrvatsko Pjevačko Društvo Kolo [in *Zh*]
Zs	——, Glazbeni Arhiv Nadbiskupskog Bogoslovnog Sjemeništa
Zu	——, Nacionalna i Sveučilišna Knjižnica, Zbirka Muzikalija i Audiomaterijala
ZAzk	Zadar, Znanstvena Knjižnica

I: ITALY

Ac	Assisi, Biblioteca Comunale [in *Af*]
Ad	——, Cattedrale S Rufino, Biblioteca dell'Archivio Capitolare
Af	——, Sacro Convento di S Francesco, Biblioteca-Centro di Documentazione Francescana
ALTsm	Altamura, Associazione Amici della Musica Saverio Mercadante, Biblioteca
AN	Ancona, Biblioteca Comunale Luciano Benincasa
AO	Aosta, Seminario Maggiore
AOc	——, Cattedrale, Biblioteca Capitolare
AP	Ascoli Piceno, Biblioteca Comunale Giulio Gabrielli
APa	——, Archivio di Stato
AT	Atri, Basilica Cattedrale di S Maria Assunta, Biblioteca Capitolare e Museo
Baf	Bologna, Accademia Filarmonica, Archivio
Bam	——, Collezioni d'Arte e di Storia della Casa di Risparmio (Biblioteca Ambrosini)
Bas	——, Archivio di Stato, Biblioteca
Bc	——, Civico Museo Bibliografico Musicale
Bca	——, Biblioteca Comunale dell'Archiginnasio
Bl	——, Conservatorio Statale di Musica G.B. Martini, Biblioteca
Bof	——, Congregazione dell'Oratorio (Padri Filippini), Biblioteca
Bpm	——, Università degli Studi, Facoltà di Magistero, Cattedra di Storia della Musica, Biblioteca
Bsf	——, Convento di S Francesco, Biblioteca
Bsm	——, Biblioteca del Convento di S Maria dei Servi e della Cappella Musicale Arcivescovile
Bsp	——, Basilica di S Petronio, Archivio Musicale
Bu	——, Biblioteca Universitaria, sezione Musicale
BAca	Bari, Biblioteca Capitolare
BAcp	——, Conservatorio di Musica Niccolò Piccinni, Biblioteca
BAn	——, Biblioteca Nazionale Sagarriga Visconti-Volpi
BAR	Barletta, Biblioteca Comunale Sabino Loffredo
BDG	Bassano del Grappa, Biblioteca Archivo Museo (Biblioteca Civica)
BE	Belluno, Biblioteche Lolliniana e Gregoriana
BGc	Bergamo, Biblioteca Civica Angelo Mai
BGi	——, Civico Istituto Musicale Gaetano Donizetti, Biblioteca
BI	Bitonto, Biblioteca Comunale E. Bogadeo (ex Vitale Giordano)
BRc	Brescia, Conservatorio Statale di Musica A. Venturi, Biblioteca
BRd	——, Archivio e Biblioteca Capitolari
BRq	——, Biblioteca Civica Queriniana

BRs	——, Seminario Vescovile Diocasano, Archivio Musicale
BRsmg	——, Chiesa della Madonna delle Grazie (S Maria), Archivio
BV	Benevento, Biblioteca Capitolare
BZa	Bolzano, Archivio di Stato, Biblioteca
BZf	——, Convento dei Minori Francescani, Biblioteca
BZtoggenburg	——, Count Toggenburg, private collection
CAcon	Cagliari, Conservatorio di Musica Giovanni Pierluigi da Palestrina, Biblioteca
CARc	Castell'Arquato, Archivio Capitolare (Parrocchiale)
CARcc	——, Chiesa Collegiata dell'Assunta, Archivio Musicale
CAS	Cascia, Monastero di S Rita, Archivio
CATa	Catania, Archivio di Stato
CATc	——, Biblioteche Riunite Civica e Antonio Ursino Recupero
CATm	——, Museo Civico Belliniano, Biblioteca
CATus	——, Università degli Studi di Catania, Facoltà di Lettere e Filosofia, Dipartimento di Scienze Storiche, Storia della Musica, Biblioteca
CC	Città di Castello, Duomo, Archivio Capitolare [in *CCsg*]
CCc	——, Biblioteca Comunale Giosuè Carducci
CCsg	——, Biblioteca Stori Guerri e Archivi Storico
CDO	Codogno, Biblioteca Civica Luigi Ricca
CEc	Cesena, Biblioteca Comunale Malatestiana
CF	Cividale del Friuli, Duomo (Parrocchia di S Maria Assunta), Archivio Capitolare
CFm	——, Museo Archeologico Nazionale, Biblioteca
CFVd	Castelfranco Veneto, Duomo, Archivio
CHc	Chioggia, Biblioteca Comunale Cristoforo Sabbadino
CHf	——, Archivio dei Padri Filippini [in *CHc*]
CHTd	Chieti, Biblioteca della Curia Arcivescovile e Archivio Capitolare
CMac	Casale Monferrato, Duomo di Sant'Evasio, Archivio Capitolare
CMbc	——, Biblioteca Civica Giovanni Canna
CMs	——, Seminario Vescovile, Biblioteca
COc	Como, Biblioteca Comunale
COd	——, Duomo, Archivio Musicale
CORc	Correggio, Biblioteca Comunale
CRas	Cremona, Archivio di Stato
CRd	——, Biblioteca Capitolare [in *CRsd*]
CRg	——, Biblioteca Statale
CRsd	——, Archivio Storico Diocesano
CRE	Crema, Biblioteca Comunale
CT	Cortona, Biblioteca Comunale e dell'Accademia Etrusca
DO	Domodossola, Biblioteca e Archivio dei Rosminiani di Monte Calvario [in *ST*]
E	Enna, Biblioteca e Discoteca Comunale
Fa	Florence, Ss Annunziata, Archivio
Fas	——, Archivio di Stato, Biblioteca
Fbecherini	——, Becherini private collection
Fc	——, Conservatorio Statale di Musica Luigi Cherubini
Fd	——, Opera del Duomo (S Maria del Fiore), Biblioteca e Archivio
Ffabbri	——, Mario Fabbri, private collection
Fl	——, Biblioteca Medicea Laurenziana
Fm	——, Biblioteca Marucelliana
Fn	——, Biblioteca Nazionale Centrale, Dipartimento Musica
Folschki	——, Olschki private collection
Fr	——, Biblioteca Riccardiana
Fs	——, Seminario Arcivescovile Maggiore, Biblioteca
Fsa	——, Biblioteca Domenicana di S Maria Novella
Fsl	——, Parrocchia di S Lorenzo, Biblioteca
Fsm	——, Convento di S Marco, Biblioteca
FA	Fabriano, Biblioteca Comunale
FAd	——, Duomo (S Venanzio), Biblioteca Capitolare
FAN	Fano, Biblioteca Comunale Federiciana
FBR	Fossombrone, Biblioteca Civica Passionei
FEc	Ferrara, Biblioteca Comunale Ariostea
FEd	——, Duomo, Archivio Capitolare
FELc	Feltre, Museo Civico, Biblioteca

FEM	Finale Emilia, Biblioteca Comunale
FERaa	Fermo, Archivio Storico Arcivescovile con Archivio della Pietà
FERas	——, Archivio di Stato di Ascoli Piceno, sezione di Fermo
FERc	——, Biblioteca Comunale
FERd	——, Metropolitana (Duomo), Archivio Capitolare [in *FERaa*]
FERvitali	——, Gualberto Vitali-Rosati, private collection
FOc	Forlì, Biblioteca Comunale Aurelio Saffi
FOLc	Foligno, Biblioteca Comunale
FOLd	——, Duomo, Archivio
FRa	Fara in Sabina, Monumento Nazionale di Farfa, Biblioteca
FZac	Faenza, Basilica Cattedrale, Archivio Capitolare
FZc	——, Biblioteca Comunale Manfrediana, Raccolte Musicali
Gc	Genoa, Biblioteca Civica Berio
Gim	——, Civico Istituto Mazziniano, Biblioteca
Gl	——, Conservatorio di Musica Nicolò Paganini, Biblioteca
Gremondini	——, P.C. Remondini, private collection
Gsl	——, S Lorenzo (Duomo), Archivio Capitolare
Gu	——, Biblioteca Universitaria
GO	Gorizia, Seminario Teologico Centrale, Biblioteca
GR	Grottaferrata, Biblioteca del Monumento Nazionale
GUBd	Gubbio, Biblioteca Vescovile Fonti e Archivio Diocesano (con Archivio del Capitolo della Cattedrale)
I	Imola, Biblioteca Comunale
IBborromeo	Isola Bella, Borromeo private collection
IE	Iesi, Biblioteca Comunale
IV	Ivrea, Cattedrale, Biblioteca Capitolare
La	Lucca, Archivio di Stato
Las	——, Biblioteca-Archivio Storico Comunale
Lc	——, Biblioteca Capitolare Feliniana e Biblioteca Arcivescovile
Lg	——, Biblioteca Statale
Li	——, Istituto Musicale L. Boccherini, Biblioteca
Ls	——, Seminario Arcivescovile, Biblioteca
LA	L'Aquila, Biblioteca Provinciale Salvatore Tommasi
LANc	Lanciano, Biblioteca Diocesano (con Archivio della Cattedrale)
LT	Loreto, Santuario della S Casa, Archivio Storico
LU	Lugo, Biblioteca Comunale Fabrizio Trisi
LUi	——, Istituto Musicale Pareggiato G.L. Malerbi
Ma	Milan, Biblioteca Ambrosiana
Malfieri	——, Famiglia Trecani degli Alfieri, private collection
Mas	——, Archivio di Stato
Mb	——, Biblioteca Nazionale Braidense
Mc	——, Conservatorio di Musica Giuseppe Verdi, Biblioteca
Mcap	——, Archivio Capitolare di S Ambrogio, Biblioteca
Mcom	——, Biblioteca Comunale Sormani
Md	——, Capitolo Metropolitano, Biblioteca e Archivio
Mgallini	——, Natale Gallini, private collection
Mr	——, Biblioteca della Casa Ricordi
Ms	——, Biblioteca Teatrale Livia Simoni
Msartori	——, Claudio Sartori, private collection [in *Mc*]
Msc	——, Chiesa di S Maria presso S Celso, Archivio
Mt	——, Biblioteca Trivulziana e Archivio Storico Civico
Mu	——, Università degli Studi di Milano, Facoltà di Giurisprudenza, Biblioteca
Muc	——, Università Cattolica del Sacro Cuore, Biblioteca
MAa	Mantua, Archivio di Stato
MAad	——, Archivio Storico Diocesano
MAav	——, Accademia Nazionale Virgiliana di Scienze, Lettere ed Arti, Archivio Musicale
MAc	——, Biblioteca Comunale
MAC	Macerata, Biblioteca Comunale Mozzi-Borgetti
MC	Montecassino, Monumento Nazionale di Montecassino, Biblioteca
MDAegidi	Montefiore dell'Aso, Francesco Egidi, private collection
ME	Messina, Biblioteca Regionale Universitaria
MEs	——, Biblioteca Painiana (del Seminario Arcivescovile S Pio X)
MOd	Modena, Duomo, Biblioteca e Archivio Capitolare
MOe	——, Biblioteca Estense e Universitaria
MOs	——, Archivio di Stato [in *MOe*]
MTc	Montecatini Terme, Biblioteca Comunale
MTventuri	——, Antonio Venturi, private collection [in *MTc*]
MZ	Monza, Parrocchia di S Giovanni Battista, Biblioteca Capitolare
Na	Naples, Archivio di Stato
Nc	——, Conservatorio di Musica S Pietro a Majella, Biblioteca
Nf	——, Biblioteca Oratoriana dei Gerolamini (Filippini)
Ng	——, Monastero di S Gregorio Armeno, Archivio
Nlp	——, Biblioteca Lucchesi Palli [in *Nn*]
Nn	——, Biblioteca Nazionale Vittorio Emanuele III
NON	Nonantola, Seminario Abbaziale, Biblioteca
NOVd	Novara, S Maria (Duomo), Biblioteca Capitolare
NOVg	——, Seminario Teologico e Filosofico di S Gaudenzio, Biblioteca
NOVi	——, Istituto Civico Musicale Brera, Biblioteca
NT	Noto, Biblioteca Comunale Principe di Villadorata
Od	Orvieto, Opera del Duomo, Biblioteca
OFma	Offida, Parrocchia di Maria Ss Assunta, Archivio
OS	Ostiglia, Opera Pia G. Greggiati Biblioteca Musicale
Pas	Padua, Archivio di Stato
Pc	——, Duomo, Biblioteca Capitolare, Curia Vescovile
Pca	——, Basilica del Santo, Biblioteca Antoniana
Pci	——, Biblioteca Civica
Pl	——, Conservatorio Cesare Pollini
Ps	——, Seminario Vescovile, Biblioteca
Pu	——, Biblioteca Universitaria
PAac	Parma, Duomo, Archivio Capitolare con Archivio della Fabbriceria
PAas	——, Archivio di Stato
PAc	——, Biblioteca Palatina, sezione Musicale
PAcom	——, Biblioteca Comunale
PAp	——, Biblioteca Nazionale Palatina
PAt	——, Archivio Storico del Teatro Regio [in *PAcom*]
PAVc	Pavia, Chiesa di S Maria del Carmine, Archivio
PAVs	——, Seminario Vescovile, Biblioteca
PAVu	——, Biblioteca Universitaria
PCc	Piacenza, Biblioteca Comunale Passerini Landi
PCcon	——, Conservatorio di Musica G. Nicolini, Biblioteca
PCd	——, Duomo, Biblioteca e Archivio Capitolare
PCsa	——, Basilica di S Antonino, Biblioteca e Archivio Capitolari
PEas	Perugia, Archivio di Stato
PEc	——, Biblioteca Comunale Augusta
PEd	——, Biblioteca Domincini
PEl	——, Conservatorio di Musica Francesco Morlacchi, Biblioteca
PEsf	——, Congregazione dell' Oratorio di S Filippo Neri, Biblioteca e Archivio
PEsl	——, Duomo (S Lorenzo), Archivio
PEsp	——, Basilica Benedettina di S Pietro, Archivio e Museo della Badia
PEA	Pescia, Biblioteca Comunale Carlo Magnani
PESc	Pesaro, Conservatorio di Musica G. Rossini, Biblioteca
PESd	——, Duomo, Archivio Capitolare [in *PESdi*]
PESdi	——, Biblioteca Diocesana
PESo	——, Ente Olivieri, Biblioteca e Musei Oliveriana
PESr	——, Fondazione G. Rossini, Biblioteca
PIa	Pisa, Archivio di Stato
PIp	——, Opera della Primaziale Pisana, Archivio Musicale
PIraffaelli	——, Raffaelli private collection
PIst	——, Chiesa dei Cavalieri di S Stefano, Archivio
PIt	——, Teatro Verdi
PIu	——, Biblioteca Universitaria
PLa	Palermo, Archivio di Stato
PLcom	——, Biblioteca Comunale
PLcon	——, Conservatorio di Musica Vincenzo Bellini, Biblioteca

PLi	——, Università degli Studi, Facoltà di Lettere e Filosofia, Istituto di Storia della Musica, Biblioteca	*Smo*	Asciano (nr Siena), Abbazia Benedettina di Monte Oliveto Maggiore, Biblioteca
PLn	——, Biblioteca Centrale della Regione Sicilia tex (Nazionale)	*SA*	Savona, Biblioteca Civica Anton Giulio Barrili
PLpagano	——, Roberto Pagano, private collection	*SAa*	——, Seminario Vescovile, Biblioteca
PO	Potenza, Biblioteca Provinciale	*SE*	Senigallia, Biblioteca Comunale Antonelliana
PR	Prato, Archivio Storico Diocesano, Biblioteca (con Archivio del Duomo)	*SO*	Sant'Oreste, Collegiata di S Lorenzo sul Monte Soratte, Biblioteca
PS	Pistoia, Basilica di S Zeno, Archivio Capitolare	*SPc*	Spoleto, Biblioteca Comunale Giosuè Carducci
PSc	——, Biblioteca Comunale Forteguerriana	*SPd*	——, Biblioteca Capitolare (Duomo di S Lorenzo)
PSrospigliosi	——, Rospigliosi private collection	*SPE*	Spello, Collegiata di S Maria Maggiore, Archivio
Ra	Rome, Biblioteca Angelica	*SPEbc*	——, Biblioteca Comunale Giacomo Prampolini
Raf	——, Accademia Filarmonica Romana	*ST*	Stresa, Biblioteca Rosminiana
Ras	——, Archivio di Stato, Biblioteca	*STE*	Vipiteno, Convento dei Cappuccini (Kapuzinerkloster), Biblioteca
Rbompiani	——, Bompiani private collection	*Ta*	Turin, Archivio di Stato
Rc	——, Biblioteca Casanatense, sezione Musica	*Tci*	——, Civica Biblioteca Musicale Andrea della Corte
Rcg	——, Curia Generalizia dei Padre Gesuiti, Biblioteca	*Tco*	——, Conservatorio di Musica Giuseppe Verdi, Biblioteca
Rchg	——, Chiesa del Gesù, Archivio	*Td*	——, Cattedrale Metropolitana di S Giovanni Battista, Archivio Capitolare, Fondo Musicale della Cappella dei Cantori del Duomo e della Cappella Regia Sabauda
Rcsg	——, Congregazione dell'Oratorio di S Girolamo della Carità, Archivio [in *Ras*]		
Rdp	——, Archivio Doria Pamphili	*Tf*	——, Accademia Filarmonica, Archivio
Rf	——, Congregazione dell'Oratorio S Filippo Neri	*Tfanan*	——, Giorgio Fanan, private collection
Ria	——, Istituto di Archeologia e Storia dell'Arte, Biblioteca	*Tn*	——, Biblioteca Nazionale Universitaria, sezione Musicale
Ribimus	——, Istituto di Bibliografia Musicale, Biblioteca [in *Rn*]	*Tr*	——, Biblioteca Reale
		Trt	——, RAI – Radiotelevisione Italiana, Biblioteca
Rig	——, Istituto Storico Germanico di Roma, sezione Storia della Musica, Biblioteca	*TAc*	Taranto, Biblioteca Civica Pietro Acclavio
Rims	——, Pontificio Istituto di Musica Sacra, Biblioteca	*TE*	Terni, Istituto Musicale Pareggiato Giulio Briccialdi, Biblioteca
Rli	——, Accademia Nazionale dei Lincei e Corsiniana, Biblioteca	*TEd*	——, Duomo, Archivio Capitolare
Rlib	——, Basilica Liberiana, Archivio	*TLp*	Torre del Lago Puccini, Museo di Casa Puccini
Rmalvezzi	——, Lionello Malvezzi, private collection	*TOL*	Tolentino, Biblioteca Comunale Filelfica
Rmassimo	——, Massimo princes, private collection	*TRa*	Trent, Archivio di Stato
Rn	——, Biblioteca Nazionale Centrale Vittorio Emanuele II	*TRbc*	——, Castello del Buon Consiglio, Biblioteca [in *TRmp*]
Rp	——, Biblioteca Pasqualini [in *Rsc*]	*TRc*	——, Biblioteca Comunale
Rps	——, Chiesa di S Pantaleo (Padri Scolipi), Archivio	*TRcap*	——, Biblioteca Capitolare con Annesso Archivio
Rrai	——, RAI-Radiotelevisione Italiana, Archivio Musica	*TRfeininger*	——, Biblioteca Musicale Laurence K.J. Feininger [in *TRmp*]
Rrostirolla	——, Giancarlo Rostirolla, private collection [in *Fn* and *Ribimus*]	*TRmd*	——, Museo Diocesano, Biblioteca
		TRmp	——, Castello del Buonconsiglio: Monumenti e Collezioni Provinciali, Biblioteca
Rsc	——, Conservatorio di Musica S Cecilia		
Rscg	——, Abbazia di S Croce in Gerusalemme, Biblioteca	*TRmr*	——, Museo Trentino del Risorgimento e della Lotta per la Libertà, Biblioteca
Rsg	——, Basilica di S Giovanni in Laterano, Archivio Musicale	*TRE*	Tremezzo, Count Gian Ludovico Sola-Cabiati, private collection
Rslf	——, Chiesa di S Luigi dei Francesi, Archivio	*TRP*	Trapani, Biblioteca Fardelliana
Rsm	——, Basilica di S Maria Maggiore, Archivio Capitolare [in *Rvat*]	*TSci*	Trieste, Biblioteca Comunale Attilio Hortis
Rsmm	——, S Maria di Monserrato, Archivio	*TScon*	——, Conservatorio di Musica Giuseppe Tartini, Biblioteca
Rsmt	——, Basilica di S Maria in Trastevere, Archivio Capitolare [in *Rvic*]	*TSmt*	——, Civico Museo Teatrale di Fondazione Carlo Schmidl, Biblioteca
Rsp	——, Chiesa di S Spirito in Sassia, Archivio	*TVco*	Treviso, Biblioteca Comunale
Rss	——, Curia Generalizia dei Domenicani (S Sabina), Biblioteca	*TVd*	——, Biblioteca Capitolare della Cattedrale
		Us	Urbino, Cappella del Ss Sacramento (Duomo), Archivio
Ru	——, Biblioteca Universitaria Alessandrina		
Rv	——, Biblioteca Vallicelliana	*UD*	Udine, Duomo, Archivio Capitolare [in *UDs*]
Rvat	——, Biblioteca Apostolica Vaticana	*UDa*	——, Archivio di Stato
Rvic	——, Vicariato, Archivio	*UDc*	——, Biblioteca Comunale Vincenzo Joppi
RA	Ravenna, Duomo (Basilica Ursiana), Archivio Capitolare [in *RAs*]	*UDs*	——, Seminario Arcivescovile, Biblioteca
		URBcap	Urbania, Biblioteca Capitolare [in *URBdi*]
RAc	——, Biblioteca Comunale Classense	*URBdi*	——, Biblioteca Diocesana
RAs	——, Seminario Arcivescovile dei Ss Angeli Custodi, Biblioteca	*Vas*	Venice, Archivio di Stato
REm	Reggio nell'Emilia, Biblioteca Panizzi	*Vc*	——, Conservatorio di Musica Benedetto Marcello, Biblioteca
REsp	——, Basilica di S Prospero, Archivio Capitolare	*Vcg*	——, Casa di Goldoni, Biblioteca
RI	Rieti, Biblioteca Diocesana, sezione dell'Archivio Musicale del Duomo	*Vgc*	——, Fondazione Giorgio Cini, Istituto per le Lettere, il Teatro ed il Melodramma, Biblioteca
RIM	Rimini, Biblioteca Civica Gambalunga	*Vlevi*	——, Fondazione Ugo e Olga Levi, Biblioteca
RPTd	Ripatransone, Duomo, Archivio	*Vmarcello*	——, Andrighetti Marcello, private collection
RVE	Rovereto, Biblioteca Civica Girolamo Tartarotti	*Vmc*	——, Museo Civico Correr, Biblioteca d'Arte e Storia Veneziana
RVI	Rovigo, Accademia dei Concordi, Biblioteca	*Vnm*	——, Biblioteca Nazionale Marciana
Sac	Siena, Accademia Musicale Chigiana, Biblioteca	*Vqs*	——, Fondazione Querini-Stampalia, Biblioteca
Sas	——, Archivio di Stato	*Vs*	——, Seminario Patriarcale, Archivio
Sc	——, Biblioteca Comunale degli Intronati	*Vsf*	——, Biblioteca S Francesco della Vigna
Sco	——, Convento dell'Osservanza, Biblioteca		
Sd	——, Opera del Duomo, Archivio Musicale		

Vsm ——, Procuratoria di S Marco [in *Vlevi*]
Vsmc ——, S Maria della Consolazione detta Della Fava
Vt ——, Teatro La Fenice, Archivio Storico-Musicale
VCd Vercelli, Biblioteca Capitolare
VEaf Verona, Accademia Filarmonica, Biblioteca e Archivio
VEas ——, Archivio di Stato
VEc ——, Biblioteca Civica
VEcap ——, Biblioteca Capitolare
VEss ——, Chiesa di S Stefano, Archivio
VIb Vicenza, Biblioteca Civica Bertoliana
VId ——, Biblioteca Capitolare
VIs ——, Seminario Vescovile, Biblioteca
VIGsa Vigévano, Biblioteca del Capitolo della Cattedrale
VRNs Chiusi della Verna, Santuario della Verna, Biblioteca

IL: ISRAEL
J Jerusalem, Jewish National and University Library, Music Dept
Jgp ——, Greek Orthodox Patriarchate, Library (Hierosolymitike Bibliotheke)
Jp ——, Patriarchal Library
Ta Tel-Aviv, American for Music Library in Israel, Felicja Blumental Music Center and Library
Tmi ——, Israel Music Institute

IRL: IRELAND
C Cork, Boole Library, University College
Da Dublin, Royal Irish Academy Library
Dam ——, Royal Irish Academy of Music, Monteagle Library
Dc ——, Contemporary Music Centre
Dcb ——, Chester Beatty Library
Dcc ——, Christ Church Cathedral, Library
Dm ——, Archbishop Marsh's Library
Dmh ——, Mercer's Hospital [in *Dtc*]
Dn ——, National Library of Ireland
Dpc ——, St Patrick's Cathedral
Dtc ——, Trinity College Library, University of Dublin

J: JAPAN
Tma Tokyo, Musashino Ongaku Daigaku, Ioshokan
Tn ——, Nanki Ongaku Bunko

LT: LITHUANIA
V Vilnius, Lietuvos Muzikos Akademijos Biblioteka
Va ——, Lietuvos Mokslų Akademijos Biblioteka

LV: LATVIA
J Jelgava, Muzei
R Riga, Latvijas Mūzikas Akademijas Biblioteka

M: MALTA
Vnl Valletta, National Library

MD: MOLDOVA
KI Chişinău, Biblioteka Gosudarstvennoj Konservatorii im. G. Muzyčesku

MEX: MEXICO
Mc Mexico City, Catedral Metropolitana, Archivo Musical
Pc Puebla, Catedral Metropolitana, Archivo del Cabildo

N: NORWAY
Bo Bergen, Offentlige Bibliotek, Griegsamlingen
Ou Oslo, Universitetsbiblioteket
Oum ——, Nasjonalbiblioteket, Avdeling Oslo, Norsk Musikksamling
T Trondheim, Norges Teknisk-Naturvitenskapelige Universitet, Gunnerusbiblioteket

NL: THE NETHERLANDS
At Amsterdam, Toonkunst-Bibliotheek
Au ——, Universiteitsbibliotheek
DEta Delden, Huisarchief Twickel
DHa The Hague, Koninklijk Huisarchief

DHgm ——, Haags Gemeentemuseum, Muziekafdeling
DHk ——, Koninklijke Bibliotheek
E Enkhuizen, Archief Collegium Musicum
L Leiden, Gemeentearchief
Lml ——, Museum Lakenhal
Lt ——, Bibliotheca Thysiana [in *Lu*]
Lu ——, Rijksuniversiteit, Bibliotheek
LE Leeuwarden, Provinciale Bibliotheek van Friesland
R Rotterdam, Gemeentebibliotheek
SH 's-Hertogenbosch, Illustre Lieve Vrouwe Broederschap
Uim Utrecht, Letterenbibliotheek, Universiteit
Uu ——, Universiteit Utrecht, Universiteitsbibliotheek

NZ: NEW ZEALAND
Aua Auckland, University of Auckland, Archive of Maori and Pacific Music
Wt Wellington, Alexander Turnbull Library

P: PORTUGAL
AR Arouca, Mosteirode de S Maria, Museu de Arte Sacra, Fundo Musical
BRp Braga, Arquivo Distrital
BRs ——, Arquivo da Sé
Cmn Coimbra, Museu Nacional de Machado de Castro
Cs ——, Arquivo da Sé Nova
Cug ——, Universidade de Coimbra, Biblioteca Geral, Impressos e Manuscritos Musicais
Cul ——, Faculdade de Letras da Universidade
Em Elvas, Biblioteca Municipal
EVc Évora, Arquivo da Sé, Museu Regional
EVp ——, Biblioteca Pública e Arquivo Distrital
F Figueira da Foz, Biblioteca Pública Municipal Pedro Fernandes Tomás
G Guimarães, Arquivo Municipal Alfredo Pimenta
La Lisbon, Biblioteca da Ajuda
Lac ——, Academia das Ciências, Biblioteca
Lant ——, Arquivo Nacional da Torre do Tombo
Lc ——, Biblioteca do Conservatório Nacional
Lcg ——, Fundação Calouste Gulbenkian, Biblioteca Geral de Arte, Serviço de Música
Lf ——, Fabrica da Sé Patriarcal
Ln ——, Biblioteca Nacional, Centro de Estudos Musicológicos
Lt ——, Teatro Nacional de S Carlos
LA Lamego, Arquivo da Sé
Mp Mafra, Palácio Nacional, Biblioteca
Pm Porto, Biblioteca Pública Municipal
Va Viseu, Arquivo Distrital
Vs ——, Arquivo da Sé
VV Vila Viçosa, Fundaçao da Casa de Bragança, Biblioteca do Paço Ducal, Arquivo Musical

PL: POLAND
B Bydgoszcz, Wojewódzka i Miejska Biblioteka Publiczna, Dział Zbiórów Specjalnych
BA Barczewo, Kościoła Parafialny, Archiwum
CZ Częstochowa, Klasztor Ojców Paulinów: Jasna Góra Archiwum
GD Gdańsk, Polska Akademia Nauk, Biblioteka Gdańska
GDp ——, Wojewódzka Biblioteka Publiczna
GNd Gniezno, Archiwum Archidiecezjalne
GR Grodzisk Wielkopolski, Kościół Parafialny św. Jadwigi [in *Pa*]
Kc Kraków, Muzeum Narodowe, Biblioteka Czartoryskich
Kcz ——, Muzeum Narodowe, Biblioteka Czapskich
Kd ——, Biblioteka Studium OO. Dominikanów
Kj ——, Uniwersytet Jagielloński, Biblioteka Jagiellońska
Kk ——, Archiwum i Biblioteka Krakowskiej Kapituły Katedralnej
Kn ——, Muzeum Narodowe
Kp ——, Biblioteka Polskiej Akademii Nauk
Kpa ——, Archiwum Państwowe
Kz ——, Biblioteka Czartoryskich
KA Katowice, Biblioteka Śląska

KO	Kórnik, Polska Akademia Nauk, Biblioteka Kórnicka
KRZ	Krzeszów, Cysterski Kościół Parafialny [in *KRZk*]
KRZk	——, Klasztor Ss Benedyktynek
Lw	Lublin, Wojewódzka Biblioteka Publiczna im. H. Lopacińskiego
LA	Łańcut, Biblioteka-Muzeum Zamku
LEtpn	Legnica, Towarzystwa Przyaciół Nauk, Biblioteka
LZu	Łódź, Biblioteka Uniwersytecka
MO	Mogiła, Opactwo Cystersów, Archiwumi Biblioteka
OB	Obra, Klasztor OO. Cystersów
Pa	Poznań, Archiwum Archidiecezjalna
Pm	——, Biblioteka Zakładu Muzykologii Uniwersytetu Poznańskiego
Pr	——, Miejska Biblioteka Publiczna im. Edwarda Raczyńskiego
Pu	——, Uniwersytet im. Adama Mickiewicza, Biblioteka Uniwersytecka, Sekcja Zbiorów Muzycznych
PE	Pelplin, Wyższe Seminarium Duchowne, Biblioteka
R	Raków, Kościół Parafialny, Archiwum
SA	Sandomierz, Wyższe Seminarium Duchowne, Biblioteca
SZ	Szalowa, Archiwum Parafialne
Tm	Toruń, Ksiąznica Miejska im. M. Kopernika
Tu	——, Uniwersytet Mikołaja Kopernika, Biblioteka Głowna, Oddział Zbiorów Muzycznych
Wm	Warsaw, Muzeum Narodowe, Biblioteka
Wn	——, Biblioteka Narodowa
Wtm	——, Warszawskie Towarzystwo Muzyczne im Stanisława Moniuszki, Biblioteka, Muzeum i Archiwum
Wu	——, Uniwersytet Warszawski, Biblioteka Uniwersytecka, Gabinet Zbiorów Muzycznych
WL	Wilanów, Biblioteka [in *Wn* and *Wm*]
WRk	Wrocław, Biblioteka Kapitulna
WRu	——, Uniwersytet Wrocławski, Biblioteka Uniwersytecka
WRzno	——, Zakład Narodowy im. Ossolińskich, Biblioteka

RO: ROMANIA

Ba	Bucharest, Academiei Române, Biblioteca
BRm	Braşov, Biblioteca Judeteana
Cu	Cluj-Napoca, Universitatea Babes Bolyai, Biblioteca Centrală Universitară Lucian Blaga
J	Iaşi, Biblioteca Centrală Universitară Mihai Eminescu, Departmentul Colecţii Speciale
Sa	Sibiu, Direcţia Judeţeană a Arhivelor Naţionale
Sb	——, Muzeul Naţional Bruckenthal, Biblioteca

RUS: RUSSIAN FEDERATION

KA	Kaliningrad, Oblastnaya Universal'naya Nauchnaya Biblioteka
KAg	——, Gosudarstvennaya Biblioteka
KAu	——, Nauchnaya Biblioteka Kalingradskogo Gosudarstvennogo Universiteta
Mcl	Moscow, Rossiyskiy Gosudarstvennïy Arkhiv Literaturï i Iskusstva (RGALI)
Mcm	——, Gosudarstvennïy Tsentral'nïy Muzey Musïkal'noy Kul'turï imeni M.I. Glinki
Mim	——, Gosudarstvennïy Istorichesküy Muzey
Mk	——, Moskovskaya Gosudarstvennaya Konservatoriya im. P.I. Chaykovskogo, Nauchnaya Muzikal'naya Biblioteka imeni S.I. Taneyeva
Mm	——, Gosudarstvennaya Publichnaya Istoricheskaya Bibliotheka
Mrg	——, Rossiyskaya Gosudarstvennaya Biblioteka
Mt	——, Gosudarstvennïy Tsentral'nïy Teatral'nïy Musey im. A. Bakhrushina
SPan	St Petersburg, Rossiyskaya Akademiya Nauk, Biblioteka
SPia	——, Gosudarstvennïy Tsentral'nïy Istorichesküy Arkhiv
SPil	——, Biblioteka Instituta Russkoy Literaturï Rossiyskoy Akademii Nauk (Pushkinskiy Dom)
SPit	——, Rossiyskiy Institut Istorii Iskusstv
SPk	——, Biblioteka Gosudarstvennoy Konservatorii im. N.A. Rimskogo-Korsakova

SPph	——, Gosurdarstvennaya Filarmoniya im D.D. Shostakovicha
SPsc	——, Rossiyskaya Natsional'naya Biblioteka
SPtob	——, Gosudarstvennïy Akademichesky Mariinsky Teatr, Tsentral'naya Muzikal'naya Biblioteka

S: SWEDEN

A	Arvika, Ingesunds Musikhögskola
B	Bålsta, Skoklosters Slott
Gu	Göteborg, Universitetsbiblioteket
Hfryklund	Helsingborg, Daniel Fryklund, private collection [in *Skma*]
HÄ	Härnösand, Länsmuseet-Murberget
HÖ	Höör, Biblioteket
J	Jönköping, Per Brahegymnasiet
K	Kalmar, Stadtsbibliotek, Stifts och Gymnasiebiblioteket
Klm	——, Länsmuseet
L	Lund, Universitet, Universitetsbiblioteket, Handskriftsavdelningen
LB	Leufsta Bruk, De Geer private collection [in *Uu*]
LI	Linköping, Linköpings Stadsbiblotek, Stiftsbiblioteket
N	Norrköping, Stadsbiblioteket
Sdt	Stockholm, Drottningholms Teatermuseum
Sfo	——, Frimurare Orden, Biblioteket
Sic	——, Svensk Musik
Sk	——, Kungliga Biblioteket: Sveriges Nationalbibliotek
Skma	——, Statens Musikbibliothek
Sm	——, Musikmuseet, Arkiv
Smf	——, Stiftelsen Musikkulturens Främjande
Sn	——, Nordiska Museet, Arkivet
Ssr	——, Sveriges Radio Förvaltning, Musikbiblioteket
St	——, Kung. Teatern [in *Skma*]
Sva	——, Svenskt Visarkiv
STr	Strängnäs, Roggebiblioteket
Uu	Uppsala, Universitetsbiblioteket
V	Västerås, Stadsbibliotek, Stiftsavdelningen
Vll	Visby, Landsarkivet
VX	Växjö, Landsbiblioteket

SI: SLOVENIA

Lf	Ljubljana, Frančiškanski Samostan, Knjižnica
Ln	——, Narodna in Univerzitetna Knjižnica, Glavni Knjižni Fond
Lna	——, Nadškofijski Arhiv
Lng	——, Narodna in Univerzitetna Knjižnica, Glasbena Zbirka
Lnr	——, Narodna in Univerzitetna Knjižnica, Rokopisna Zbirka
Ls	——, Katedral, Glazbeni Arhiv
Nf	Novo Mesto, Frančiškanski Samostan, Knjižnica
Nk	——, Kolegiatni Kapitelj, Knjižnica
Pk	Ptuj, Knjižnica Ivana Potrča

SK: SLOVAKIA

BRa	Bratislava, Štátny Oblastny Archív
BRhs	——, Knižnica Hudobného Seminára Filozofickej Fakulty Univerzity Komenského
BRm	——, Archív Mesta Bratislavy
BRmp	——, Miestne Pracovisko Matice Slovenskej [in *Mms*]
BRnm	——, Slovenské Národné Múzeum, Hudobné Múzeum
BRsa	——, Slovenský Národný Archív
BRsav	——, Ústav Hudobnej Vedy Slovenská Akadémia Vied
BRu	——, Univerzitná Knižnica, Národné Knižničné Centrum, Hudobñy Kabinet
BSk	Banská Štiavnica, Farský Rímsko-Katolícky Kostol, Archív Chóru
J	Júr pri Bratislave, Okresny Archív, Bratislava-Vidiek [in *MO*]
KRE	Kremnica, Štátny Okresny Archív Žiar nad Hronom
Le	Levoča, Evanjelická a.v. Cirkevná Knižnica
Mms	Martin, Matica Slovenská
Mnm	——, Slovenské Národné Múzeum, Archív

MO	Modra, Štátny Okresny Archív Pezinok
NM	Nové Mesto nad Váhom, Rímskokatolícky Farsky Kostol
TN	Trenčín, Štátny Okresny Archív
TR	Trnava, Štátny Okresny Archív

TR: TURKEY

Ino	Istanbul, Nuruosmania Kütüphanesi
Itks	——, Topkapi Sarayi Müzesi
Iü	——, Üniversite Kütüphanesi

UA: UKRAINE

Kan	Kiev, Natsional'na Akademiya Nauk Ukraïni, Natsional'na Biblioteka Ukraïni im V.I. Vernads'kyy
Km	——, Spilka Kompozytoriv Ukrainy, Centr. 'Muz. Inform'
LV	L'viv, Biblioteka Vyshchoho Muzychnoho Instytutu im. M. Lyssenka

US: UNITED STATES OF AMERICA

AAu	Ann Arbor, University of Michigan, Music Library
AB	Albany (NY), New York State Library
AKu	Akron (OH), University of Akron, Bierce Library
ATet	Atlanta (GA), Emory University, Pitts Theology Library
ATu	——, Emory University Library
ATS	Athens (GA), University of Georgia Libraries
AU	Aurora (NY), Wells College Library
AUS	Austin, University of Texas at Austin, The Harry Ransom Humanities Research Center
AUSm	——, University of Texas at Austin, Fine Arts Library
Ba	Boston, Athenaeum Library
Bc	——, New England Conservatory of Music, Harriet M. Spaulding Library
Bfa	——, Museum of Fine Arts
Bgm	——, Isabella Stewart Gardner Museum, Library
Bh	——, Harvard Musical Association, Library
Bhs	——, Massachusetts Historical Society Library
Bp	——, Public Library, Music Department
Bu	——, Boston University, Mugar Memorial Library, Department of Special Collections
BAep	Baltimore, Enoch Pratt Free Library
BAhs	——, Maryland Historical Society Library
BApi	——, Arthur Friedheim Library, Johns Hopkins University
BAu	——, Johns Hopkins University Libraries
BAue	——, Milton S. Eisenhower Library, Johns Hopkins University
BAw	——, Walters Art Gallery Library
BAR	Baraboo (WI), Circus World Museum Library
BEm	Berkeley, University of California at Berkeley, Music Library
BER	Berea (OH), Riemenschneider Bach Institute Library
BETm	Bethlehem (PA), Moravian Archives
BL	Bloomington (IN), Indiana University Library
BLl	——, Indiana University, Lilly Library
BLu	——, Indiana University, Cook Music Library
BO	Boulder (CO), University of Colorado at Boulder, Music Library
BU	Buffalo (NY), Buffalo and Erie County Public Library
Cn	Chicago, Newberry Library
Cp	——, Chicago Public Library, Music Information Center
Cu	——, University, Joseph Regenstein Library, Music Collection
Cum	——, University of Chicago, Music Collection
CA	Cambridge (MA), Harvard University, Harvard College Library
CAe	——, Harvard University, Eda Kuhn Loeb Music Library
CAh	——, Harvard University, Houghton Library
CAt	——, Harvard University Library, Theatre Collection
CAward	——, John Milton Ward, private collection [on loan to CA]

CF	Cedar Falls (IA), University of Northern Iowa, Library
CHua	Charlottesville (VA), University of Virginia, Alderman Library
CHum	——, University of Virginia, Music Library
CHAhs	Charleston (SC), The South Carolina Historical Society
CHH	Chapel Hill (NC), University of North Carolina at Chapel Hill
CIhc	Cincinnati, Hebrew Union College Library: Jewish Institute of Religion, Klau Library
CIp	——, Public Library
CIu	——, University of Cincinnati College – Conservatory of Music, Music Library
CLp	Cleveland, Public Library, Fine Arts Department
CLwr	——, Western Reserve University, Freiberger Library and Music House Library
CLAc	Claremont (CA), Claremont College Libraries
COhs	Columbus (OH), Ohio Historical Society Library
COu	——, Ohio State University, Music Library
CP	College Park (MD), University of Maryland, McKeldin Library
CR	Cedar Rapids (IA), Iowa Masonic Library
Dp	Detroit, Public Library, Main Library, Music and Performing Arts Department
DAu	Dallas, Southern Methodist University, Music Library
DAVu	Davis (CA), University of California at Davis, Peter J. Shields Library
DMu	Durham (NC), Duke University Libraries
DN	Denton (TX), University of North Texas, Music Library
DO	Dover (NH), Public Library
E	Evanston (IL), Garrett Biblical Institute
Eu	——, Northwestern University
EDu	Edwardsville (IL), Southern Illinois University
EU	Eugene (OR), University of Oregon
FAy	Farmington (CT), Yale University, Lewis Walpole Library
FW	Fort Worth (TX), Southwestern Baptist Theological Seminary
G	Gainesville (FL), University of Florida Library, Music Library
GB	Gettysburg (PA), Lutheran Theological Seminary
GR	Granville (OH), Denison University Library
GRB	Greensboro (NC), University of North Carolina at Greensboro, Walter C. Jackson Library
Hhc	Hartford (CT), Hartt College of Music Library, The University of Hartford
Hm	——, Case Memorial Library, Hartford Seminary Foundation [in ATet]
Hs	——, Connecticut State Library
Hw	——, Trinity College, Watkinson Library
HA	Hanover (NH), Dartmouth College, Baker Library
HG	Harrisburg (PA), Pennsylvania State Library
HO	Hopkinton (NH), New Hampshire Antiquarian Society
I	Ithaca (NY), Cornell University
IDt	Independence (MO), Harry S. Truman Library
IO	Iowa City (IA), University of Iowa, Rita Benton Music Library
K	Kent (OH), Kent State University, Music Library
KC	Kansas City (MO), University of Missouri: Kansas City, Miller Nichols Library
KCm	——, Kansas City Museum, Library and Archives
KN	Knoxville (TN), University of Tennessee, Knoxville, Music Library
Lu	Lawrence (KS), University of Kansas Libraries
LAcs	Los Angeles, California State University, John F. Kennedy Memorial Library
LApiatigorsky	——, Gregor Piatigorsky, private collection [in STEdrachman]
LAs	——, The Arnold Schoenberg Institute Archives
LAuc	——, University of California at Los Angeles, William Andrews Clark Memorial Library
LAum	——, University of California at Los Angeles, Music Library

LAur	——, University of California at Los Angeles, Special Collections Dept, University Research Library
LAusc	——, University of Southern California, School of Music Library
LBH	Long Beach (CA), California State University
LEX	Lexington (KY), University of Kentucky, Margaret I. King Library
LOu	Louisville, University of Louisville, Dwight Anderson Music Library
LT	Latrobe (PA), St Vincent College Library
M	Milwaukee, Public Library, Art and Music Department
Mc	——, Wisconsin Conservatory of Music Library
MAhs	Madison (WI), Wisconsin Historical Society
MAu	——, University of Wisconsin
MB	Middlebury (VT), Middlebury College, Christian A. Johnson Memorial Music Library
MED	Medford (MA), Tufts University Library
MG	Montgomery (AL), Alabama State Department of Archives and History Library
MT	Morristown (NJ), National Historical Park Museum
Nf	Northampton (MA), Forbes Library
Nsc	——, Smith College, Werner Josten Library
NA	Nashville (TN), Fisk University Library
NAu	——, Vanderbilt University Library
NBu	New Brunswick (NJ), Rutgers – The State University of New Jersey, Music Library, Mabel Smith Douglass Library
NEij	Newark (NJ), Rutgers – The State University of New Jersey, Rutgers Institute of Jazz Studies Library
NH	New Haven (CT), Yale University, Irving S. Gilmore Music Library
NHoh	——, Yale University, Oral History Archive
NHub	——, Yale University, Beinecke Rare Book and Manuscript Library
NO	Normal (IL), Illinois State University, Milner Library, Humanities/Fine Arts Division
NORsm	New Orleans, Louisiana State Museum Library
NORtu	——, Tulane University, Howard Tilton Memorial Library
NYamc	New York, American Music Center Library
NYbroude	——, Broude private collection
NYcc	——, City College Library, Music Library
NYcu	——, Columbia University, Gabe M. Wiener Music & Arts Library
NYcub	——, Columbia University, Rare Book and Manuscript Library of Butler Memorial Library
NYgo	——, University, Gould Memorial Library [in *NYu*]
NYgr	——, The Grolier Club Library
NYgs	——, G. Schirmer, Inc.
NYhs	——, New York Historical Society Library
NYhsa	——, Hispanic Society of America, Library
NYj	——, The Juilliard School, Lila Acheson Wallace Library
NYkallir	——, Rudolf F. Kallir, private collection
NYlehman	——, Robert O. Lehman, private collection [in *NYpm*]
NYlibin	——, Laurence Libin, private collection
NYma	——, Mannes College of Music, Clara Damrosch Mannes Memorial Library
NYp	——, Public Library at Lincoln Center, Music Division
NYpl	——, Public Library, Center for the Humanities
NYpm	——, Pierpont Morgan Library
NYpsc	——, New York Public Library, Schomburg Center for Research in Black Culture in Harlem
NYq	——, Queens College of the City University, Paul Klapper Library, Music Library
NYu	——, University Bobst Library
NYw	——, Wildenstein Collection
NYyellin	——, Victor Yellin, private collection
OAm	Oakland (CA), Mills College, Margaret Prall Music Library
OB	Oberlin (OH), Oberlin College Conservatory of Music, Conservatory Library
OX	Oxford (OH), Miami University, Amos Music Library
Pc	Pittsburgh, Carnegie Library, Music and Art Dept
Ps	——, Theological Seminary, Clifford E. Barbour Library
Pu	——, University of Pittsburgh
Puf	——, University of Pittsburgh, Foster Hall Collection, Stephen Foster Memorial
PHci	Philadelphia, Curtis Institute of Music, Library
PHf	——, Free Library of Philadelphia, Music Dept
PHff	——, Free Library of Philadelphia, Edwin A. Fleisher Collection of Orchestral Music
PHgc	——, Gratz College
PHhs	——, Historical Society of Pennsylvania Library
PHlc	——, Library Company of Philadelphia
PHmf	——, Musical Fund Society [on loan to *PHf*]
PHphs	——, The Presbyterian Historical Society Library [in *PHlc*]
PHps	——, American Philosophical Society Library
PHu	——, University of Pennsylvania, Van Pelt-Dietrich Library Center
PO	Poughkeepsie (NY), Vassar College, George Sherman Dickinson Music Library
PRs	Princeton (NJ), Theological Seminary, Speer Library
PRu	——, Princeton University, Firestone Memorial Library
PRw	——, Westminster Choir College
PROhs	Providence (RI), Rhode Island Historical Society Library
PROu	——, Brown University
PRV	Provo (UT), Brigham Young University
R	Rochester (NY), Sibley Music Library, University of Rochester, Eastman School of Music
Su	Seattle, University of Washington, Music Library
SA	Salem (MA), Peabody and Essex Museums, James Duncan Phillips Library
SBm	Santa Barbara (CA), Mission Santa Barbara
SFp	San Francisco, Public Library, Fine Arts Department, Music Division
SFs	——, Sutro Library
SFsc	——, San Francisco State University, Frank V. de Bellis Collection
SJb	San Jose (CA), Ira F. Brilliant Center for Beethoven Studies, San José State University
SL	St Louis, St Louis University, Pius XII Memorial Library
SLug	——, Washington University, Gaylord Music Library
SLC	Salt Lake City, University of Utah Library
SM	San Marino (CA), Huntington Library
SPma	Spokane (WA), Moldenhauer Archives
SR	San Rafael (CA), American Music Research Center, Dominican College
STu	Palo Alto (CA), University, Memorial Library of Music, Department of Special Collections of the Cecil H. Green Library
STEdrachmann	Stevenson (MD), Mrs Jephta Drachman, private collection; Mrs P.C. Drachman, private collection
STO	Stony Brook (NY), State University of New York at Stony Brook, Frank Melville jr Memorial Library
SY	Syracuse (NY), University Music Library
SYkrasner	——, Louis Krasner, private collection [in *CAh* and *SY*]
TA	Tallahassee (FL), Florida State University, Robert Manning Strozier Library
U	Urbana (IL), University of Illinois, Music Library
Uplamenac	——, Dragan Plamenac, private collection [in *NH*]
V	Villanova (PA), Villanova University, Falvey Memorial Library
Wc	Washington, DC, Library of Congress, Music Division
Wca	——, Cathedral Library
Wcf	——, Library of Congress, American Folklife Center and the Archive of Folk Culture
Wcg	——, General Collections, Library of Congress
Wcm	——, Library of Congress, Motion Picture, Broadcasting and Recorded Sound Division
Wcu	——, Catholic University of America, Music Library

Wdo   ——, Dumbarton Oaks
Wgu   ——, Georgetown University Libraries
Whu   ——, Howard University, College of Fine Arts
          Library
Ws   ——, Folger Shakespeare Library
WB   Wilkes-Barre (PA), Wilkes College Library
WC   Waco (TX), Baylor University, Music Library
WGc   Williamsburg (VA), College of William and Mary,
          Earl Gregg Swenn Library
WI   Williamstown (MA), Williams College Library
WOa   Worcester (MA), American Antiquarian Society
          Library

WS   Winston-Salem (NC), Moravian Music
          Foundation, Peter Memorial Library
Y   York (PA), Historical Society of York County,
          Library and Archives

YU: YUGOSLAVIA (REPUBLICS OF MONTENEGRO AND SERBIA)
Bn   Belgrade, Narodna Biblioteka Srbije, Odelenje
          Posebnih Fondova

ZA: SOUTH AFRICA
Csa   Cape Town, South African Library

A Note on the Use of the Dictionary

This note is intended as a short guide to the basic procedures and organization of the dictionary. A fuller account will be found in the Introduction, vol. l, pp.xv–xxv.

Abbreviations in general use in the dictionary are listed on pp.vii–xi; bibliographical ones (periodicals, reference works, editions etc.) are listed on pp.xiii–xviii and discographical abbrevations on pp.xix–xx.

Alphabetization of headings is based on the principle that words are read continuously, ignoring spaces, hyphens, accents, bracketed matter etc., up to the first comma; the same principle applies thereafter. 'Mc' and 'M'' are listed as 'Mac', 'St' as 'Saint'.

Bibliographies are arranged chronologically (within section, where divided), in order of year of first publication, and alphabetically by author within years.

Cross-references are shown in small capitals, with a large capital at the beginning of the first word of the entry referred to. Thus 'The instrument is related to the BASS TUBA' would mean that the entry referred to is not 'Bass tuba' but 'Tuba, bass'.

Signatures where the article was compiled by the editors or in the few cases where an author has wished to remain anonymous are indicated by a square box (□).

Work-lists are normally arranged chronologically (within section, where divided). Italic symbols used in them (like *D-Dl* or *GB-Lbl*) refer to the libraries holding sources, and are explained on pp.xxi–xxxvii; each national sigillum stands until contradicted.

P

[continued]

Paliashvili, Zakharia (*b* Kutaisi, 4/16 Aug 1871; *d* Tbilisi, 6 Oct 1933). Georgian composer and folklorist. Brought up in a Catholic family in which music occupied an important place, he sang in the church choir at the age of eight and at an early stage learnt to play the organ. In 1887 he moved to Tbilisi, joining a choir founded by the folk-music enthusiast L. Agniashvili. A few years later he entered the Tbilisi Music School, where he studied the horn and started to compose; he then went on to study with Sergey Taneyev at the Moscow Conservatory (1900–03). Returning to Tbilisi (1903), he taught at the Music School and the Georgian Grammar School, and helped to establish the Georgian Philharmonic Society (1905), under whose auspices he later founded a choir and orchestra. He also directed the society's music school (1908–17) and became a member of the governing body of the Association for the Staging of Operas in the Georgian Language. During an eight-year period he travelled throughout almost the whole of Georgia, notating approximately 300 traditional songs. He took an active part in the country's musical life, and from 1919 was a professor at the Tibilisi Conservatory, at various times serving as its director (1919, 1923, 1929–32). In 1925 Paliashvili was named 'People's Artist', the first Georgian composer on whom this Soviet title was conferred. His operas were staged by the leading opera theatres of the former Soviet Union and were also performed in Europe and America. The Opera and Ballet Theatre in Tbilisi was named after him, and a monument in his honour was erected in front of the building. The Z. Paliashvili Prize of the Georgian Republic was established in 1971.

Paliashvili's strikingly original work constitutes the first significant body of Georgian music composed in the Western art music tradition. He succeeded in creating a cogent and highly original fusion of national tradition with the styles and genres of European music. Although his musical language remained traditional, often resembling that of the 19th-century national schools, his understanding of vernacular sources and their potential for integration into the professional sphere opened up enormous possibilities for Georgian musical art. He recognized the importance of mastering European musical traditions and addressed this task rapidly and purposefully, testing his strengths in almost every vocal genre. He selected and cultivated in his music those aspects of folk and church tradition that were in harmony with the aesthetic and social needs of early 20th-century Georgia. His works often reflect an interest in mythical and historical subject-matter.

Paliashvili produced a significant corpus of chamber-vocal music but is known principally for his operas, in which he laid the foundations for a Georgian national musical language. His finest achievement in the genre was *Abesalom da Eteri* ('Abesalom and Eteri', 1918), an exceptionally integrated conception combining folk-epic and lyric-dramatic elements and displaying the thematic, dramatic and stylistic tendencies evident elsewhere in his operatic output. Characteristic of this monumental operatic tragedy is a broad canvas of well-rounded numbers, oratorio-like choruses and a fluid beauty of melodic material reminiscent of bel canto. The chorus plays an active role in the drama, drawing together each strand of the action. Although the foundation of the music lies in rural Georgian folk traditions, Paliashvili also draws on Georgian urban songs and ancient religious melodies. Their influence is evident in the severe diatonicism, in the originality of the polyphonic texture, and in the harmony with its combination of 4ths and 5ths. His later opera *Daisi* ('Twilight'), with its introspective concentration and elements of psychological drama, reveals a new direction. The story unfolds against the lively and colourful backdrop of the *Khatoba* festival, and the musical language is richly melodious, closely linked with everyday genres and with folksong. Particular prominence is given to solo numbers based on monodic urban song and the romance, while the various choral episodes display stylistic affinities with the Georgian folk tradition of polyphonic choral music.

Throughout his life Paliashvili tirelessly studied the works of Bach, Palestrina, Handel and the composers of the polyphonic schools. However, the fundamental source of his artistic inspiration remained old Georgian church music, to which he devoted many years of careful study. Although this was evident in works as early as his six-part Mass (1900), the most interesting example of a synthesis between the Western and Eastern Church traditions remains his *Kartuli Liturgia* ('Georgian Liturgy', 1911), a set of canticles for the Liturgy of St John Chrysostom.

WORKS
(selective list)

Ops: Abesalom da Eteri (4, P. Mirianashvili, after Eteriani), 1909–18, Tbilisi, 1919; Daisi [Twilight] (3, V. Gunia), 1923, Tbilisi, 1923; Latavra (4, after S. Shanshiashvili), 1927, Tbilisi, 1928

Vocal: Mass, E♭, chorus, org, 1900; Dges mertskhali [Today a Swallow] (A. Tsereteli), chorus, 1908; Mravalzhamieri [Many Years of Life] (P. Mirianashvili), T, chorus, orch, 1908; Sazejmo kantata [Triumphal Cant.], solo vv, chorus, orch, 1927; Iavnana [Lullaby] (Tsereteli), a cappella chorus

Orch: Kartuli suita [Georgian Suite], 1928

Songs (1v, pf; all dated 1908): Akhalagnago sulo [In love with youthful spirit] (D. Tumanishvili); Miqvarda [I loved] (I. Grishashvili); Nana shvilo [Lullaby] (I. Chavchavadze); Nu tvaltmaktsob [Don't tempt [me]] (Grishashvili); Ristvis miqvarkhar [Why do I love you] (Chavchavadze)

Other works: arrs. of traditional songs; incid music; Kartuli Liturgia [Georgian Liturgy], choral arr. of 22 church anthems for the Liturgy of St John Chrysostom, 1911

Principal publishers: Muzfond Gruzii (Tbilisi), Muzgiz, Muzïka, Sovetskiy kompozïtor (Moscow and Leningrad)

BIBLIOGRAPHY

I. Maralidze: 'Musika da kartveli musikosni' [Music and Georgian musicians], Teatri da tskhovreba (1914), no.15, pp.7–8

M. Ippolitov-Ivanov: 50 let russkoy muzïki v moikh vospominaniyakh [50 years of Russian music in my recollections] (Moscow, 1934)

I. Zurabishvili: 'Zakharia Paliashvilis opera "Abesalom da Eteri"', Teatraluri portretebi (Tbilisi, 1941, 2/1972), 48–112

Sh. Kashmadze: Z. Paliashvili (Tbilisi, 1948)

K. Tbileli: 'O narodnosti muzïkal'nogo yazïka operï Z. Paliashvili Daisi' [On the folk quality of the musical language of Paliashvili's opera Daisi], SovM (1951), no.8, pp.77–81

V. Donadze: Zakhariy Paliashvili (Moscow, 1958, 2/1971)

N. Chiaureli: 'Abesalom da Eteris intonatsiuri analizistvis', Sabchota khelovneba (1961), no.10, pp.44–8

L. Danilevich: 'Operï Z. Paliashvili i A. Spendiarova' [The operas of Z. Paliashvili and A. Spendiarian], O sovetskoy muzike (Moscow, 1962), 72–92

Z. Paliashvili: Biografichesky spravochnik [Biographical reference book] (Tbilisi, 1964)

L. Zambakhidze: Zakharia Paliashvili bibliografia (Tbilisi, 1966)

Sh. Aslanishvili: Gza 'Abesalomisaken' [The way to Abesalom] (Tbilisi, 1971)

S. Nasidze: 'Poliponiuri kherkhebi operashi "Abesalom da Eteri"' [Polyphonic devices in Abesalom da Eteri], Sabchota khelovneba (1971), no.10, pp.14–18

O. Taktakishvili: 'Neugasimïy fakel gruzinskoy muzïki' [The inextinguishable torch of Georgian music], SovM (1971), no.8, pp.46–9

A. Tsulukidze: Zakharia Paliashvili (Tbilisi, 1971) [in Georgian, Russ. and Fr.]

P. Khuchua: Z. Paliashvili: tskhovreba da mogvatseoba [Paliashvili: life and work] (Tbilisi, 1974)

V. Donadze: 'Zakharia Paliashvili', Muzika respublik Zakavkaz'ya (Tbilisi, 1975), 45–63

S. Ginzburg: 'Z.P. Paliashvili', Muzikal'naya literatura narodov SSSR (Moscow, 1979), 178–215

N. Dimitriadi: 'O khudozhestvennoy kontseptsii Z.P. Paliashvili i osnovnïkh esteticheskikh problemakh gruzinskoy muzïkal'noy klassiki' [The artistic concepts of Z.P. Paliashvili and the fundamental aesthetic issues of the Georgian classical music], Nauchniye trudï Tbilisskoy Goskonservatorii (Tbilisi, 1982), 86–94

V. Donadze: 'Z. Paliashvili', Kartuli musikis istoria, i (Tbilisi, 1990), 157–243

LEAH DOLIDZE

Palindrome. A piece or passage in which a RETROGRADE follows the original (or 'model') from which it is derived (see MIRROR FORMS). The retrograde normally follows the original directly. The term 'palindrome' may be applied exclusively to the retrograde itself, provided that the original preceded it. In the simplest kind of palindrome a melodic line is followed by its 'cancrizans', while the harmony (if present) is freely treated. The finale of Beethoven's Hammerklavier Sonata op.106 provides an example. Unlike the 'crab canon', known also as 'canon cancrizans' or 'canon al rovescio', in which the original is present with the retrograde, a palindrome does not present both directional forms simultaneously.

Much rarer than any of these phenomena is the true palindrome, where the entire fabric of the model is reversed, so that the harmonic progressions emerge backwards too. Byrd's eight-voice motet Diliges Dominum is a polyphonic example in which at the halfway point the two voices of each pair exchange parts and present them backwards. It may be that the text's exhortation to 'love thy neighbour as thyself' suggested to Byrd the reflexive reprise to bring the music back to its starting-point.

The two known examples in 18th-century music are both minuets. C.P.E. Bach's Minuet in C for keyboard (H216) has two eight-bar sections, the second a reversal of the first. The minuet of Haydn's Symphony no.47 (which appears also in the Piano Sonata HXVI:26 and the Violin Sonata HVI:4), composed in 1772, only a year or two after C.P.E. Bach's, is so exactly and proudly palindromic that Haydn wrote out only the first section, followed by the instruction 'Menuet al reverso'. Minuets, with their tendency to less sophisticated textures and harmonic rhythm than other genres of the Classical period, lent themselves more readily to such contrivances; hence, paradoxically, a tradition of simplicity and relaxation co-existed with one of intellectual devices in this context.

When it is observed that only one 19th-century composer is known to have written a true palindrome, the reader's guesswork may begin with Brahms, or even Schumann, but probably not with Schubert. The true palindrome in Schubert's opera-melodrama Die Zauberharfe (1820) is not only a surprise but constitutes a technical tour de force. The harmonic thinking is far more venturesome than that in the Haydn minuet, as ex.1 reveals (the example shows part of the original and the equivalent part of the retrograde); and the orchestra is now a Romantic one complete with trombones. A further innovation is the structural separation of the retrograde from the original, with 309 bars of music between them. In forming his retrograde, Schubert was compelled to allow himself some licence in the ordering of pitches and rhythms within a bar or half-bar. (A detailed commentary on this example appears in B. Newbould: 'A Schubert Palindrome', 19CM, xv, 1991–2, pp.207–14.)

With the abandonment of tonality by the composers of the Second Viennese School, the stringent harmonic demands of the palindrome were considerably eased. Berg's Lyrische Suite, Kammerkonzert and the film music in Lulu all make use of palindrome, and in Webern's Symphony op.21 the development of the first movement is a palindrome, with the succession of instrumental timbres reversed accordingly. In the music of these and later serialists, palindromic excursions have become, if not commonplace, less infrequent and less awesome as technical feats. A more remarkable 20th-century example is found in Hindemith's Ludus tonalis (1942), where the substantial Postludium is not merely a palindrome (or horizontal mirror image) of the equally lengthy Praeludium, but a vertical mirror image too, in which each strand within the texture appears in melodic inversion while the texture itself is also inverted so that the topmost strand becomes the lowest and the others migrate accordingly. Part of an extended multi-movement work which displays other symmetrical features too, this

Ex.1

framing 'mirror palindrome' is a substantial example embracing several sections in different tempos.

BRIAN NEWBOULD

Paling. Dutch family of musicians. Jan Hendrik Paling (*b* Woerden, 14 Dec 1796; *d* Rotterdam, 23 Feb 1879) was a carillonneur, organist and piano maker. In 1826 he opened a piano factory in Rotterdam and quickly gained a wide reputation for the quality of tone produced by his instruments. He was also active as a music publisher. His son Willem Hendrik Paling (*b* Rotterdam, 1 Sept 1825; *d* Sydney, 27 Aug 1895) studied the violin and piano under Bartholomeus Tours and taught at the Rotterdam music school for three years (1844–7). In 1855 he emigrated to Australia and, after considerable success as a violinist and teacher, he started the firm of W.H. Paling & Co., piano manufacturers. Willem's brother Anton Adriaan Paling (*b* Rotterdam, 14 Sept 1835; *d* Nijmegen, 12 Oct 1922) was a pupil of his father and joined him in the piano factory, becoming head of the firm in 1879. After his death the business was incorporated into that of C. Quispel.

BIBLIOGRAPHY

NNBW (J.W. Enschedé)
'Paling, William Henry', *The Australian Encyclopedia*, ed. A.H. Chisholm (Sydney, 1958)

HERBERT ANTCLIFFE/JAN TEN BOKUM

Palisca, Claude V(ictor) (*b* Fiume [now Rijeka, Croatia], 24 Nov 1921). American musicologist. He studied music at Queens College, New York (BA 1943), musicology with Kinkeldey at Harvard University (MA 1948), where he took the doctorate in 1954 with a dissertation on the origins of Baroque music in 16th-century theory and polemics, and composition with Piston, Rathaus and Randall Thompson. After teaching at the University of Illinois (1953–9), he joined the faculty of Yale University, where he was appointed professor of music history (1964) and chairman of the music department (1969–75, 1992); he was named Henry L. and Lucy G. Moses Professor of

Music in 1980 and retired in 1992. He has also held appointments as visiting lecturer at the universities of California at Berkeley, Princeton, Michigan, Western Australia, Zagreb, Granada and Barcelona.

Palisca is one of the leading scholars of his generation, admired for his searching work in his own subject areas and for his breadth of knowledge. His main interests are late Renaissance and Baroque music and the history of music theory. His monograph on Baroque music (1968) emphasizes stylistic development; his discussion of the music is supported with citations from writers of the period and shows how Baroque practices grew from those of the Renaissance. As co-translator of Zarlino's *Istitutioni harmoniche*, he has been praised for an accurate and idiomatic text. His other writings include a lucid explanation of the theoretical basis of the Artusi–Monteverdi dispute and a discussion of the relationship between 17th-century scientific empiricism and contemporary developments in harmonic theory and musical temperament.

Palisca has also pursued an interest in musicology as a discipline and its relation to music education in the USA. His contribution to the volume *Musicology* (1963) traces the development of musical scholarship in America, stressing the humanistic aspects. As director of the seminar on music education, sponsored by the American Office of Education and Yale University, he was responsible for the preparation of its report; he is also director of research for the Yale Music Curriculum Project. His educational concerns include the music education syllabus of state schools, undergraduate training for musicological research, and the direction that research might most profitably take at graduate and postgraduate levels. Palisca has served as president of the AMS (1970–72) and the National Council of the Arts in Education (1967–9); as senior fellow of the National Endowment for the Humanities (1972–3); on the council of the Renaissance Society of America (1973–4); and with the IMS as a director (1972–7) and as vice-president (1977–82).

WRITINGS

Studies in the History of Italian Music and Music Theory (Oxford, 1994) [S]

'Girolamo Mei: Mentor to the Florentine Camerata', *MQ*, xl (1954), 1–20

The Beginnings of Baroque Music: its Roots in Sixteenth Century Theory and Polemics (diss., Harvard U., 1954)

'Vincenzo Galilei's Counterpoint Treatise: a Code for the *seconda pratica*', *JAMS*, ix (1956), 81–96; repr. in *S*, 30–53

'A Clarification of "Musica Reservata" in Jean Taisnier's "Astrologiae", 1559', *AcM*, xxxi (1959), 133–61

Girolamo Mei (1519–1594): Letters on Ancient and Modern Music to Vincenzo Galilei and Giovanni Bardi: a Study with Annotated Text, MSD (1960, 2/1977)

'Vincenzo Galilei and some Links between "Pseudo-Monody" and Monody', *MQ*, xlvi (1960), 344–60; repr. in *S*, 346–63

'Scientific Empiricism in Musical Thought', *Seventeenth Century Science and the Arts*, ed. H.H. Rhys (Princeton, NJ, 1961), 91–137; repr. in *S*, 200–35

'Musical Asides in the Diplomatic Correspondence of Emilio de' Cavalieri', *MQ*, xlix (1963), 339–55

with F.Ll. Harrison and M. Hood: *Musicology* (Englewood Cliffs, NJ,1963)

'The First Performance of "Euridice"', *The Department of Music, Queens College of the City University of New York: Twenty-Fifth Anniversary Festschrift*, ed. A. Mell (Flushing, NY, 1964), 1–23; repr. in *S*, 432–51

'The *Musica* of Erasmus of Höritz', *Aspects of Medieval and Renaissance Music: a Birthday Offering to Gustave Reese*, ed. J. LaRue and others (New York, 1966/R), 628–48; repr. in *S*, 146–67

Baroque Music (Englewood Cliffs, NJ, 1968, 3/1991)

'The Alterati of Florence, Pioneers in the Theory of Dramatic Music', *New Looks at Italian Opera: Essays in Honor of Donald J. Grout*, ed. W.W. Austin (Ithaca, NY, 1968), 9–38; repr. in *S*, 408–31

with G.A. Marco: *The Art of Counterpoint* (New Haven, CT, 1968) [trans. of G. Zarlino: *Le istitutioni harmoniche*, iii (Venice, 1558)]

'The Artusi–Monteverdi Controversy', *The Monteverdi Companion*, ed. D. Arnold and N. Fortune (London, 1968, 2/1985 as *The New Monteverdi Companion*), 127–58; repr. in *S*, 54–87

'Vincenzo Galilei's Arrangements for Voice and Lute', *Essays in Musicology in Honor of Dragan Plamenac*, ed. G. Reese and R.J. Snow (Pittsburgh, 1969), 207–32

'Stylistic Change and the History of Ideas', *Musicology and the Computer; Musicology 1966–2000: New York 1965 and 1966*, 211–15

'Marco Scacchi's Defense of Modern Music (1649)', *Words and Music: the Scholar's View … in Honor of A. Tillman Merritt* (Cambridge, MA, 1972), 189–235; repr. in *S*, 88–145

'The "Camerata Fiorentina": a Reappraisal', *Studi musicali*, i (1972), 203–36

'*Ut oratoria musica*: the Rhetorical Basis of Musical Mannerism', *The Meaning of Mannerism: Hanover, NH, 1970*, ed. F.W. Robinson and S.G. Nichols (Hanover, 1972), 37–65; repr. in *S*, 282–311

'Music and Science', *Dictionary of the History of Ideas*, ed. P.P. Wiener, iii (New York, 1973), 260–64

'Towards an Intrinsically Musical Definition of Mannerism in the Sixteenth Century', *Mannerisms in arte e musica: Rome 1973* [*Studi musicali*, iii (1974)], 313–46; repr. in *S*, 312–45

'The Musical Humanism of Giovanni Bardi', *Poesia e musica nell'estetica del XVI e XVII secolo: Florence 1976*, 47–72

ed.: *Hucbald, Guido, and John on Music: Three Medieval Treatises* (New Haven, CT, 1978)

ed.: *Norton Anthology of Western Music* (New York, 1980, 3/1996)

ed.: D.J. Grout: *A History of Western Music* (New York, 3/1980, 5/1996)

'Peri and the Theory of Recitative', *SMA*, xv (1981), 51–61; repr. in *S*, 452–66

ed., with D.K. Holoman: *Musicology in the 1980s: Boston 1981* [incl. 'Reflections on Musical Scholarship in the 1960s', 15–30]

'A Discourse on the Performance of Tragedy by Giovanni de' Bardi (?)', *MD*, xxxvii (1983), 327–43

'Introductory Notes on the Historiography of the Greek Modes', *JM*, iii (1984), 221–8

Humanism in Italian Renaissance Musical Thought (New Haven, CT, 1985)

'The Science of Sound and Musical Practice', *Science and the Arts in the Renaissance: Washington DC 1978*, ed. J.W. Shirley and F.D. Hoeniger (Washington DC and London, 1985), 59–73

'The Recitative of Lully's *Alceste*: French Declamation or Italian Melody?', *Actes de Baton Rouge: Baton Rouge, LA, 1985*, ed. S.A. Zebouni (Paris, 1986), 21–34; repr. in *S*, 491–507

'Humanism and Music', *Renaissance Humanism: Foundations, Forms, and Legacy*, ed. A. Rabil (Philadelphia, 1988), iii, 450–85

'"Baroque" as a Music-Critical Term', *French Musical Thought, 1600-1800*, ed. G. Cowart (Ann Arbor, 1989), 7–21

ed.: *The Florentine Camerata: Documentary Studies and Translations* (New Haven, CT, 1989)

'Die Jahrzehnte um 1600 in Italien', *Italienische Musiktheorie im 16. und 17. Jahrhundert: Antikenrezeption und Satzlehre*, ed. F. Zaminer (Darmstadt, 1989), 221–306

'Boethius in the Renaissance', *Music Theory and its Sources: Antiquity and the Middle Ages*, ed. A. Barbera (Notre Dame, IN, 1990), 259–80; repr. in *S*, 168–88

'Interdisciplinary Trends in American Musicology', *Tendenze e metodi nella ricerca musicologica: Latina 1990*, 1–10

'An Introduction to the Musica of Johannes dictus Cotto vel Affligemensis', *Beyond the Moon: Festschrift Luther Dittmer*, ed. B. Gillingham and P. Merkley (Ottawa, 1990), 144–62

'Mode Ethos in the Renaissance', *Essays in Musicology: a Tribute to Alvin Johnson*, ed. L. Lockwood and E.H. Roesner (Philadelphia, 1990), 126–39

'Francisco de Salinas et l'humanisme italien', *Musique et humanisme à la Renaissance* (Paris, 1993), 37–45

'Aria in Early Opera', *Festa musicologica: Essays in Honor of George J. Buelow*, ed. T.J. Mathiesen and B.V. Rivera (Stuyvesant, NY, 1995), 257–69

'Mersenne pro Galilei contra Zarlino', *Essays in Honour of David Evatt Tunley*, ed. F. Callaway (Perth, 1995), 61–72

'Bernardino Cirillo's Critique of Polyphonic Church Music of 1549: its Background and Resonance', *Music in Renaissance Cities and Courts: Studies in Honor of Lewis Lockwood*, ed. J.A. Owens and A. Cummings (Warren, MI, 1996), 281–92

'Giovanni Battista Doni's Interpretation of the Greek Modal System', *JM*, xv (1997), 3–18

PAULA MORGAN

Palladius, David (*b* Magdeburg; *fl* 1572–99). German composer and writer on music. He may have been a pupil of Gallus Dressler, who was Kantor of the Lateinschule at Magdeburg from 1558. From 1572 to 1599 he was Kantor at the Martineum, Brunswick, and as such was responsible for the music at the church of St Martin, where Johann Zanger had been appointed pastor in 1571. He is not heard of after 1599 unless he was the David Palladius who was Kantor at Stade from 1605 to 1625. He was a typical German composer of the Lassus school. His principal work is the *Nuptiales cantiones*, a collection of 22 wedding pieces, mostly for six voices. The 16 motets based on biblical texts bear witness to his solid, workmanlike training, while the settings of the six metrical texts, which include an ode by Horace, show in addition one or two individual features. Compared with earlier composers of humanist odes Palladius loosened the musical fabric: instead of having all the voices declaim the text homophonically, he added counterpoints, set one group of voices against another, inserted polyphonic sections and created lively rhythms by means of syncopation.

His *Isagoge musicae* is in the tradition of school song compendia but differs from them in both content and form. Using as examples the openings of several motets, especially by Lassus, Palladius explained how to use the key signature to find the first note and which solmization syllables are to be chosen. For the practising of solmization he wrote, instead of the notes, only the solmization syllables between the lines of the staff. A treatise announced in the preface from which the pupils were to learn the correct method of setting a text evidently never appeared.

WORKS

VOCAL

Ein newe Lied dem Hochwirden ... Herrn Hinrico Julio ... und der löblichen Stadt Brunswig zu Ehren ... gemacht, 6vv (Magdeburg, 1590)

Nuptiales cantiones, 4–7vv (Wittenberg, 1590–92)

Der 122. Psalm neben 2 anderen Sprüchen aus dem 41. Psalm und aus dem 4. Buch Mosis (Helmstedt, 1595)

Motet, 4vv, 1597[8]; ed. in *Handbuch der deutschen evangelischen Kirchenmusik*, i/2 (Göttingen, 1942), 115

4 motets (incl. one in 1597[8]), 4vv, *D-Lr* KN 144

Motet, 6vv, formerly Biblioteca Rudolfina, Liegnitz (now ?*PL-WRu*)

Several other works, *D-ZGh* (see *BoetticherOL*, i, 837)

THEORETICAL WORKS

Isagoge musicae (Helmstedt, 1588)

BIBLIOGRAPHY

BoetticherOL

F. Welter: *Katalog der Musikalien der Ratsbücherei Lüneburg* (Lippstadt, 1950)

K.G. Hartmann: 'Die Handschrift KN 144 der Ratsbücherei zu Lüneburg', *Mf*, xiii (1960), 1–27

K.W. Niemöller: *Untersuchungen zu Musikpflege und Musikunterricht an den deutschen Lateinschulen vom ausgehenden Mittelalter bis um 1600* (Regensburg, 1969)

B.K.F. Wilson: *Choral Pedagogy: Crossroads of Theory and Practice in Sixteenth-Century Germany* (diss., Boston U., 1995)

MARTIN RUHNKE

Pallandios, Menelaos G. (*b* Piraeus, 11 Feb 1914). Greek composer. He studied the piano at the Piraeus League Conservatory (1925–30) and was a pupil of Economides in harmony, counterpoint and composition. His education was continued at the Athens Conservatory (1930–36), where he studied form with Mitropoulos, and with Casella in Rome (1939–40). From 1936 he taught harmony and counterpoint at the Athens Conservatory where he was appointed director in 1962 and chairman of the administrative board in 1986. He was general director of the National State Opera, Athens (1964–7), and in 1969 was elected to the Athens Academy, later becoming its president (1983–4) and its general secretary (1984–90). Pallandios is a composer of the national school, and some of his best work has been suggested by ancient Greek subjects. Until the mid-1950s he employed a chromatic style influenced by Franck, Wagner and early Schoenberg; thereafter his music was freely diatonic, colourfully orchestrated and reminiscent of Prokofiev and Les Six. For many years his administrative work has left him little opportunity for composition. He has, however, found time for literary writing, publishing a series of philosophical reflections on music, art and other matters.

WORKS

(*selective list*)

Dramatic: Antigone (op, Sophocles, trans. Pallandios), 1942; Pombi ston Aheronta [Procession towards Acheron], ballet, 1942; Prosefhi se archaeo nao [Prayer in an Ancient Temple], ballet, 1942; Electra, ballet, 1944; Penthesilea, ballet, 1944; 3 Archaic Suites, ballet, 1949; Greek Triptych, ballet, 1960; incid music for 8 Gk. plays, 10 film scores

Vocal: Thus Spoke the Prophets (orat., Bible, trans. Pallandios), nar, Mez, T, chorus, orch, 1948; Cycle (Pallandios), 1v, orch, 1971, inc.; *c*45 songs on text by modern Gk. poets, incl. 3 Songs (I. Tsatsos), Mez, pf, 1986

Orch: Phos sti zoi [Light to Life], 1940; Miroloi ke horos [Lament and Dance], 1941; Prelude, 1941; Suite in Ancient Style, str, 1941; Prosefhi stin Akropoli [Prayer on the Acropolis], 1942; Narcissus, 1942; Greek Classical Ov., 1944; 6 Pieces, 1945; Sym., B, 1948; Divertimento, 1952; Tragic Poem, str, 1953; Chaconne, 1957; Pf Conc., e, 1958

Other inst: Jouets au piano, pf, 1939, orchd as Little Suite, 1940; Sonata, vn, pf, 1940; Pf Sonatina, 1942; Habanera, vn, pf, 1942; Cretan Dance, pf, 1942; 4 Preludes, pf, 1946; 5 Characteristic Pieces, ob, cl, bn, 1961; Dialoghoi [Dialogues], vn, vc, 1981; Pf Sonata, 1983; Elliniki suita [Hellenic Suite], pf, 1986

Principal publishers: Greek Ministry of Education, Pallandios

WRITINGS

only those on music

ed.: Menelaos G. Pallandios, moussourgos (Athens, 1968)

Speeches at the Athens Academy, *Praktika tis Akadhimias Athenon* [Athens Academy reports], xlv (1970), 270–84 [on Beethoven]; lii (1977), 60–73 [on Bach and Handel]; lx (1985), 537–49

BIBLIOGRAPHY

A.S. Theodoropoulo: 'Synchronoi hellenes moussikoi: 5. Menelaos Pallandios', *Anglohelleniki epitheorissi*, iii/3 (1947), 152–3

M. Dounias: *Moussikokritika* (Athens, 1963), 111, 141, 160f, 174, 317

D.A.H.: 'Menelaos Pallandios', *Néa estia*, lxxxvii (1970), 47 only

G. Leotsakos: 'Pallandios, Menelaos', *Pangosmio viografiko lexico* [Universal biographical dictionary], viii (Athens, 1988) 111–12

GEORGE LEOTSAKOS

Pałłasz, Edward (*b* Starogard Gdański, 30 Aug 1936). Polish composer. He studied musicology with Lissa at Warsaw University (1959–64) and is self-taught as a composer. He taught at the Warsaw Drama School (1969–75), was president of the association of Polish authors (1988–93) and in 1995 was appointed director of Polish Radio's Second Programme. He has won many prizes, especially in Poland for his folk music arrangements and pieces for children.

Pałasz's many masterly folksong and carol settings belong to an antiquated if honourable Polish tradition, though sometimes the chosen material is developed to create a more abstract form, as in *Łado, łado*. Here and elsewhere, there is a strong natural lyricism, allied to an amalgam of pre-war styles and modernist ideas of a less radical nature. His orchestral writing eschews grandiose statements, preferring to weave delicate filigrees of short motifs – textures which are especially subtle in fast tempi, as in the outer movements of *Symphony '1976'*. Several of his works point to his ability to blend and mobilize a wide range of harmonic idioms.

WORKS
(selective list)

Op: Gdzie diabeł nie może, czyli Czerwone buciki [When the Devil can do Nothing, or The Little Red Shoes] (TV op, E. Fiszer), 1972, Polish TV, Warsaw, 13 June 1976

Orch: 9 zdarzeń [9 Events], orch, 1973; 3 bajki kaszubskie [3 Kashubian Folktales], orch, 1975; Sym. '1976'; Vn Conc., 1978; Dziewczyna o płowych włosach [The Girl with the Flaxen Hair], orch, 1985

Choral: Łado, łado (folk texts), 24vv, lute, 1973; Consolare, munde tristis, solo vv, chorus, orch, 1981; Supplicatio, S, B, children's chorus, chorus, orch, 1983; De Beata Virgine Maria Claromontana (J. Wojtczak), chorus, 1984; 3 pieśni żałobne [3 Funereal Songs] (E. Michalska, T. Nowak, W. Dąbrowski), chorus, 1984; 2 pieśni [2 Songs] (O. Mandelstam), chorus, 1989; Kolędy kaszubskie [Kashubian Carols] (folk texts), chorus, 1994

Solo vocal: Fragmenty (Sappho), S, fl, hp, va, perc, 1967; Pod borem czarna chmara [A Black Cloud at the Edge of the Forest] (folk texts), S, chbr orch, 1974; Ballady Franciszka Villona [Ballads of François Villon], B-Bar, str, 1990; folksong arrs.

Chbr and solo inst: Miniatury, pf, 1970; Bajki [Fairytales], wind qnt, 1972; Muzyka na dziedziniec Zamku Królewskiego [Music for the Courtyard of the Royal Castle], brass, timp, 1974; 2 Reminiscences from Childhood, b cl, mar, 1983; 2 Dreams of Life and Death, 17 str, 1987; Apostrofa, pf, str trio, 1988; Quodlibet, 2 pf, 1994

Music for children, radio and film scores, light music

Principal publishers: PWM, Agencja Autorska

BIBLIOGRAPHY
E. Szczepańska: 'Edward Pałasz: Symfonia 1976', *RM*, xxviii/25 (1984), 5–7

ADRIAN THOMAS

Pallavicini, Vincenzo [Vicenzo] (*b* Brescia; *d* after 1766). Italian composer. His birthplace is known only from a superscription on his composition exercise for admission to the Accademia Filarmonica of Bologna in 1743 (*I-Bc*). Gerber's suggestion that he may have been a son of the more illustrious Brescian composer Carlo Pallavicino (*d* 1688) seems unlikely on both temporal and stylistic grounds. His motet *Ave maris stella* (also 1743) was cited by Feller as a prime example of the modern 'mixed' style which employed so much declamatory and harmonic freedom that it obscured the contrapuntal structure. He was a friend of Padre Martini (four of his letters, from 1750 to 1766, survive in *Bc*). A serious opera of his, *Il Demetrio*, was performed at Brescia in 1751. Gerber's assertion that about this time he was *maestro di cappella* of Venice's Ospedale degli Incurabili has not been substantiated. He did, however, live in Venice between 1756 and 1766. Before that (1743–56) he had been *maestro di cappella* of S Clemente, Brescia. During the 1750s and 60s, according to his letters to Martini, he had hoped to be appointed *maestro* in Udine and in Iesi. Pallavicini's principal claim to historical notice derives from the fact that he set the first act of Goldoni's libretto *Lo speziale* (Domenico Fischietti wrote acts 2 and 3), first performed in Venice at the Teatro S Samuele on 26 December 1754 (scores, *A-Wn*, *B-Bc*; one aria, *I-Gl*). This work was both a critical and a popular success, achieving performances throughout north Italy as well as in Dresden, Vienna, Munich, London and St Petersburg (sometimes under the title *Il botanico novellista* or, in German, *Der Apotheker*). The libretto, according to its preface, had been written three years earlier; Ortolani suggested that Pallavicini might at that time have been commissioned to write the whole opera but left it unfinished, and that completion was left to Fischietti. The Breitkopf supplement for 1767 lists a 'sinfonia accomodata per il cembalo solo' by Pallavicini.

BIBLIOGRAPHY
FellererP; *FétisB*; *GerberL*

G. Ortolani, ed.: *Tutte le opere di Carlo Goldoni* (Verona, 1935–56), xi, 1277

A. Schnoebelen: *Padre Martini's Collections of Letters in the Civico Museo Bibliografico Musicale in Bologna: an Annotated Index* (New York, 1979), 450

R. Del Silenzio: 'Celebrazioni per la festa annuale della Beata Vergine del Santo Rosario nella chiesa di S. Clemente in Brescia', *Civiltà Bresciana*, iv/2 (1995), 69–72

C. Valder-Knechtges: 'Musiker am Ospedale degl'Incurabili in Venedig 1765–1768', *Mf*, xxxiv (1981), 50–56

JAMES L. JACKMAN (with MARCO BIZZARINI)

Pallavicino, Benedetto (*b* Cremona, *c*1551; *d* Mantua, 26 Nov 1601). Italian composer.

1. LIFE.   According to Giuseppe Bresciani (1599–1670), Pallavicino was an organist in his youth in various churches in the district of Cremona; he may have studied there with Marc' Antonio Ingegneri. His first publication, a book of four-voice madrigals, was dedicated to the Accademia Filarmonica of Verona in 1579, and from this year until at least 1581 he seems to have been in the service of Vespasiano Gonzaga at the ducal court of Sabbioneta. By 1583 he had joined the nearby court of the Gonzagas of Mantua, where he was to remain for the rest of his life in the company of such musicians as Giaches de Wert, Giovanni Giacomo Gastoldi, Salamone Rossi and Claudio Monteverdi. The earliest known record of his presence in Mantua is a letter of 29 October 1583 (in *I-MAc*), in which he is described as a singer and composer; the following year he was sent to Venice to report on the abilities of a singer in S Marco. He was in Venice again in 1586, to supervise the printing of Guglielmo Gonzaga's *Magnificat* settings; the dedication of Pallavicino's 1587 book of madrigals for six voices, addressed to Guglielmo, declares his admiration for these works.

Guglielmo Gonzaga died in August, 1587, and was succeeded by his son Vincenzo. In 1588 Pallavicino dedicated his fourth book of five-voice madrigals to the new duke in enthusiastic terms, but it seems he was not immediately appreciated, for a payroll of around 1588–9 (*I-MAc*) shows that he was receiving less money than most of the other musicians at the court. Perhaps for this reason he applied in 1589 for the newly vacant position of *maestro* of the Scuola degli Accoliti and the cathedral choir of Verona; the post was given to the Veronese musician Giammateo Asola. Pallavicino may have been reconciled to his continuing employment at Mantua by a gift of 50 gold scudi made by Duke Vincenzo in January 1590 in recognition of his faithful services to the Gonzaga family.

Little documentation survives of the last decade of Pallavicino's life. A payroll of around 1592–3 shows that his salary was by then double that of four years earlier, although it was still considerably inferior to many others, and especially to that of Monteverdi, who had joined the Mantuan court around 1590. Nonetheless, on the death of Wert in 1596, it was Pallavicino and not Monteverdi who was appointed Wert's successor. This appointment is not surprising, for by that date he had been employed at the court for at least 13 years, and had produced seven books of madrigals. The preface of his sixth book of five-voice madrigals, addressed in 1600 to Count Alessandro Bevilacqua, suggests that he also found frequent patronage from the Accademia Filarmonica of Verona. A letter of 7 September 1601 requests that he be excused from a debt of 80 scudi, pleading other debts and children to support. A little over two months later he died of fever at the age of 50, and was succeeded in his position by Monteverdi. Pallavicino's son Bernardino, who had entered the Camaldolense order of S Marco in Mantua with the assistance of Vincenzo Gonzaga, published posthumous editions of his father's seventh and eighth books of five-voice madrigals in 1604 and 1612, along with two collections of sacred music. A similarity of name between father and son has lead some scholars to suppose that Pallavicino was still alive in 1612, but the discovery of his death notice (*I-MAc*) leaves no doubt of the exact date of his decease.

2. WORKS. Pallavicino was a prolific composer of madrigals, producing ten books (including the two published posthumously) of four-, five- and six-voice works. His early five-voice works are written in a dense imitative style and show considerable mastery of counterpoint; purely structural techniques, such as the simultaneous development of two or more motives, seem to have taken primacy over depiction of the text through word painting or expressive devices. The six-voice *Tirsi morir volea*, published in his first book for five voices, is an example of Pallavicino's ability to combine and develop a number of motives simultaneously and to unify a multipartite composition by the use of recurring motivic cells. At the same time it ignores the latent dramatic possibilities of the text, making little textural distinction between narrative and dialogue passages; from this point of view it is conservative compared to the setting by Wert, published in the same year.

Pallavicino's second book, published in 1584 shortly after he moved to Mantua, reflects the influence of composers at the courts of Mantua and nearby Ferrara. In some madrigals of this book the emerging luxuriant style is apparent in Pallavicino's new use of extensive melismatic passages on key words of the text. His approach to diminution at times seems indebted to Wert, whose diminution figures are thematically conceived and worked. Wert's influence is heard in the two-part setting of Petrarch's sonnet *Passa la nave mia*, where descriptive words such as 'vento', 'dolci' and 'onde' (with its rapid succession of parallel 6-4 chords), call into play the florid word painting typical of Wert's pastoral settings. The diminution in madrigals such as *Deh, cara vita mia* and *In dir che sete bella*, show the influence of Ferrarese composers such as Lelio Bertani and Paolo Virchi; in these works the diminution is often restricted to a single voice or pair of voices, with no clearly defined melodic shape, and found mostly in the final measures of the madrigals, for structural emphasis.

By the publication of Pallavicino's fourth book of madrigals in 1588, his musical style had undergone a considerable change. Taken as a whole, the fourth book is representative of the main trends of the madrigal at Mantua in the late 1580's. The influence of Wert is very much apparent in these compositions, above all in their new concern with the expressive possibilities of the texts. *Hor lieto il pesce* is full of the musical impressionism characteristic of Wert's pastoral madrigal *Vezzosi augelli* (1586), while others, such as the setting of Guarini's *Con che soavità*, show that Pallavicino had learnt the expressive and dramatic possibilities of parlando homophony. Another technique perhaps derived from Wert is the use of sudden contrasts of rhythm and texture to achieve expressive effect: the opening passage of *Arsi, piansi e cantai*, in which each word is set separately with appropriate imagery and texture, has precedent in Wert's *Giunto a la tomba* (1581). Other madrigals show the influence of Ferrarese composers; the setting of Guarini's *Tutt'eri fuoco, Amore*, with its diminution on key words of the text, written out ornamentation at places of structural importance and concertante exchanges of voices within repeated sections, is similar in form and concept to some of Luzzaschi's *Madrigali* composed for the *concerto di donne* of Ferrara.

Pallavicino's fifth book of madrigals, published in 1593, is surprisingly conservative. There are few if any new elements of style to be found in these works. The texts, which are light lyric pieces, are set in an unexceptional manner; the music has an easy lyrical quality, while the frequent use of sequential passages creates a strong sense of tonal direction. Some features, such as the sustained bass notes supporting duets in the upper voices outlined in parallel thirds, resemble the madrigals of Monteverdi's second book for five voices. Pallavicino's setting of Tasso's *Dolcemente dormiva la mia Clori*, for example, is closely related to Monteverdi's madrigal on the same text.

Pallavicino's sixth book of madrigals, published in 1600 but composed over some five years prior to its publication, shows once again a radical change of style. A new seriousness of mood prevails throughout this book. The poetic texts, mostly by Guarini, are epigrammatic works full of evocative imagery and witty conceits; Pallavicino's settings belong to the tradition of the *seconda pratica* and are as up-to-date as any of the madrigals by his contemporaries at the Mantuan court. For the most part the madrigals are in a declamatory homophonic style which carefully mirrors the natural rhythms of the texts. The poetic imagery is conveyed through a wide range of expressive techniques: false relations, harmonic and melodic diminished intervals and wide leaps in the melodic line, are now all fundamental features of his style. His use of dissonance is the most important innovation in this publication: the major 7th that opens the fine setting of Guarini's *Cruda Amarilli*, for example, is an effective gesture that was later quoted by Sigismondo d'India in his madrigal on the same text.

The contents of the seventh book of madrigals, published posthumously in 1604, are varied in style and would seem to have been composed over the last twelve years of the composer's life. There are some examples of the canzonetta-madrigal popular at Mantua during the early 1590s. Others must have been written quite late in the decade: *Una farfalla*, for example, with its spectacular contrast of florid concertante trio sections, together with the clear-cut sequential movement of the parts, has no precedence in Pallavicino's works but has a counterpart in Monteverdi's *Io mi son giovinetta* (1603). A few pieces in this book recall the madrigals of the sixth book in their expressive intensity, but are distinguished by their brevity and discontinuity of style and form. They rely for effect on abrupt contrasts of tempo and texture, juxtaposing declamatory passages which exaggerate the natural rhythms of the text with rapid imitation at close rhythmic intervals. A good example is the setting of Guarini's *Tu parti, a pena giunta*, which was cited by Banchieri in his *Conclusioni nel suono dell'organo* (Bologna, 1609). It is certainly these works that Banchieri had in mind when he placed Pallavicino in the company of Gesualdo, Fontanelli and Cavalieri, among those precursors of Monteverdi who were concerned with subjecting music to the expression of the words.

Most of the madrigals of the posthumous *Ottavo libro de madrigali a cinque voci* seem to have been composed around 1589–93, for they share many features of the fourth and fifth madrigal collections. Only *Deh, valoroso un tempo*, *Perché mi lasci in vita* and *Voi ch'a pianto mai* would seem to date from the late 1590's. This book concludes with five eight-voice madrigals for two choirs of approximately equal range. Almost entirely homophonic and with little melodic interest, they rely on the sonorities achieved by antiphonal exchange between choirs, making much use of echo effects. Pallavicino showed slight interest in the lighter forms, and he seems to have written little music for theatrical performance beyond the *Mascherata da Orbi* published in his first book of five voice madrigals, and a long comic madrigal in six parts entitled *Cinque compagni* in his second book of 1584. It is possible that some of the eight-voice works were also intended for some kind of staged performance.

Pallavicino's secular publications enjoyed considerable success: most of his five-voice madrigal books were reprinted in Venice at least twice, while the Antwerp publisher Phalèse brought out a collection of 44 works from his second, fourth and fifth books in 1604, as well as editions of his sixth and seventh books and the six voice madrigals. He is also represented in some 31 secular anthologies published between 1583 and 1624. His music was clearly appreciated in England, since around 20 manuscripts of English origin contain his madrigals, some given English texts but mostly copied without text. The most important single source is the so-called Tregian Manuscript (*GB-Lbl* Egerton 3665), in which Pallavicino is represented by no fewer than 100 madrigals, a contribution second only to that of Marenzio.

Although it is chiefly for his madrigals that Pallavicino is remembered, his output was not confined to secular music alone: his masses were published posthumously in 1603, and the *Sacrae Dei laudes*, a collection of 14 polychoral psalms, in 1605. A number of psalm settings for eight voices have also survived in manuscripts (*I-Bc*). There is no evidence to show that any of these works were written for the ducal chapel of S Barbara. The inventories of music in S Barbara drawn up in 1610 and 1611 include no music by Pallavicino, and there are no manuscript sources of his music to be found in the archive of S Barbara. An inventory of 1623 lists his masses, and the same date on the cover of the cantus partbook suggests that they were purchased that year. It is likely that Pallavicino's appointment as *maestro di cappella* 'et della camera et della chiesa' in 1596 did not involve more than nominal supervision of the music of S Barbara, since

Gastoldi was made permanent director of its music in 1592 and held the position until 1609. The dedications of Pallavicino's sacred works suggest rather that they may have been composed for the use of the Mantuan churches of S Andrea and S Marco.

The masses, in the *prima pratica* style and perhaps early works, include parodies of motets by Wert and Lassus. The polychoral motets of the *Sacrae Dei laudes* are predominantly homophonic and make effective use of the sonorities obtained from the antiphonal exchange and combination of musical material. In the preface to his *Salmi a quattro chori* (Venice, 1612), Viadana cited Pallavicino's 16-voice settings of *Jubilate* and *Laudate* for their use of extensive passages of doubling at the octave between choirs, a distinguishing feature of the polychoral style of the early 17th century whose origins are generally attributed to Viadana himself. The antiphonal psalms for two four-voice choirs (*I-Bc*) are strictly homophonic, the settings of *Miserere mei Deus* and *Confitebor* employing extensive passages of *falsobordone*.

Pallavicino's music was esteemed by many of his contemporaries and was praised by such theorists as Artusi, Cerone and Banchieri. While Banchieri listed him among progressive composers, Artusi placed him in a conservative context which indicates that he cannot have known Pallavicino's later madrigals at the time of writing. The omission of his name from Giulio Cesare Monteverdi's response to Artusi's attack on his brother's madrigals was certainly due to personal animosity between Claudio Monteverdi and Pallavicino. It would seem that there was lively rivalry between the two composers; their practice of reworking each other's madrigals, which can be traced back to 1587 and continued on Monteverdi's part for some years after Pallavicino's death, is more competitive than complimentary. His rival's animosity may have influenced modern scholarly opinion of Pallavicino's music: Monteverdi scholars dismissed him as a conventional if not mediocre composer until as late as 1957, when Denis Arnold examined his later madrigals in relation to Wert and Monteverdi. More recent scholarship has shown him to be an interesting composer whose compositions make use of many innovative techniques; his later madrigals are among the finest examples of the genre to be written at the Mantuan court towards the end of the century.

WORKS

Edition: *Benedetto Pallavicino: Opera omnia*, ed. P. Flanders and K. Bosi Monteath, CMM, lxxxix (1982–1996) [P i–vii]

SECULAR VOCAL

Il primo libro de madrigali, 4vv (Venice, 1579) [1579]
Il primo libro de madrigali, 5vv (Venice, 1581) [1581]
Il secondo libro de madrigali, 5vv (Venice, 1584, 2/1607) [1584, 1607a]
Il terzo libro de madrigali, 5vv (Venice, 1585, 2/1607) [1585, 1607b]
Il primo libro de madrigali, 6vv (Venice, 1587) [1587]
Il quarto libro de madrigali, 5vv (Venice, 1588) [1588]
Il quinto libro de madrigali, 5vv (Venice, 1593) [1593]
Il sesto libro de madrigali, 5vv (Venice, 1600) [1600]
Il settimo libro de madrigali, 5vv (Venice, 1604) [1604]
L'ottavo libro de madrigali, 5, 8vv (Venice, 1612) [1612]
1583[10] (attrib. Wert), 1586[9], 1587[6], 1588[18], 1593[3], 1594[6], 1595[5], 1597[24], 1600[11], 1604[8], 1606[6], 1609[14], 1624[16]

A chi creder degg'io (Tasso), 5vv, 1593, P iii; Ahi, come a un vago sol (Guarini), 5vv, 1600, P iii; Ahi disperata vita, 5vv, 1604, P iv; Ahimè, quell'occhi suoi, 5vv, 1584, P i; Amatemi, ben mio (Tasso), 5vv, 1585, P ii; Amor, ecco si parte, 5vv, 1585, P ii; Amor, io parto (Guarini), 5vv, 1600, P iii; Amorosette ninfe, 5vv, 1593, P iii; Amor, s'avvien giammai, 5vv, 1585, P ii; Amor, se non consenti,

5vv, 1600, P iii; Amor, se pur degg'io, 5vv, 1593, P iii; Anima del cor mio, 5vv, 1600, P iii; Anime pellegrine (Guarini), 5vv, 1604, P iv; A poco a poco io sento, 5vv, 1600, P iii; Ardor felice e caro, 5vv, 1604, P iv; Arsi, piansi e cantai, 5vv, 1588, P ii; Arte mi siano i crini, 5vv, 1588, P ii; Avventurose spoglie (Manfredi), 6vv, 1587, P v; Avventurose stille, 5vv, 1604, P iv; Baci amorosi e cari (Rossi), 5vv, 1593, P iii; Bella è la donna mia, 5vv, 1612, P iv; Bene mio, tu m'hai lasciato, 6vv, 1587, P v; Ben è ragion ch'io t'ami, 5vv, 1588, P ii; Ben l'alme si partiro, 5vv, 1593[3], P vii; Ben si vedrà se la nemica mia (Martelli), 5vv, 1581, P i

Cara e dolce mia vita, 5vv, 1586[9], P vii; Ch'io non t'ami (Guarini), 5vv, 1600, P iii; Chi vi bascia e vi morde, 6vv, 1587 (1624[16] as Edles Bild, Jungfrau schone), P v; Chi vuol veder Amore, 4vv, 1588[18] (Mascherata da Orbi), 5vv, 1581, P i; Ciechi noi siamo (Mascherata da Orbi), 5vv, 1581, P i; Cinque compagni, 7vv, 1584, P i; Come cantar poss'io (Guarini), 5vv, 1604, P iv; Come poss'io, Madonna, 5vv, 1584, P i; Come vivrò nelle mie pene (Tasso), 5vv, 1600, P iii; Con che soavità (Guarini), 5vv, 1588, P ii; Con che non languire (Guarini), 5vv, 1600, P iii; Cruda Amarilli (Guarini), 5vv, 1600, P iii; Crudelissima doglia, 5vv, 1600, P iii; Crudel, perché mi fuggi? (Guarini), 6vv, 1587, P v (1597[24] as Cruell, why dost thou flye mee); Dammi la mano, 5vv, 1585, P ii; Deh, cara vita mia, 5vv, 1584, P i; Deh, com'invan chiedete (Guarini), 5vv, 1612, P iv; Deh, dolce anima mia (Guarini), 5vv, 1600, P iii

Deh, mia vezzosa Fillide, 5vv, 1585, P ii; Deh, perché lagrimar, 6vv, 1587, P v (1624[16] as Tag und Nach weinen); Deh, scema il foco, 6vv, 1587, P v (1597[24] as Love quench this heat; 1624[16] as Sie thut wol mir gefallen); Deh, valoroso un tempo, 5vv, 1612, P iv; Destossi fra il mio gelo, 5vv, 1584, P i; Dimmi per grazia, Amore, 5vv, 1604, P iv; Di tre catene, O donna, 5vv, 1612, P iv; Dolce, grave et acuto (Rinaldi), 5vv, 1593, P iii; Dolcemente dormiva (Tasso), 5vv, 1593, P iii; Dolce mia caro mano, 5vv, 1584, P i; Dolci mi son gl'affanni, 5vv, 1607a, P i; Dolce spirto d'amore (Guarini), 5vv, 1600, P iii; Donna gentile e bella (Tasso), 6vv, 1587, P v; Donna importuna, 5vv, 1607a, P i; Donna, la bella mano, 5vv, 1581, P i; Donna, se quel Ohimè, 5vv, 1593, P iii (GB-Lbl Add. 29366–8 as Cruell unkind adieu); Donna, se voi m'odiate (Rinaldi), 5vv, 1593, P iii

Donna, s'io resto vivo (Parabosco), 5vv, 1585, P ii; Donna, son senza core, 5vv, 1612, P iv; E mira e tocca (Rinaldi), 5vv, 1612, P iv; Era l'anima mia (Guarini), 5vv, 1600, P iii; Felice chi vi mira (Guarini), 5vv, 1604, P iv; Filla cara ed amata (Parma), 5vv, 1588, P ii; Filli, tu pur sei quella, 5vv, 1593, P iii; Fulminava d'amor questa rubella (Goselini), 5vv, 1585, P ii; Gentil pastor che miri, 6vv, 1587, P v; Gentil pastor che miri, 8vv, 1612, P iv; Giunto che m'hebb' Amor, 5vv, 1588, P ii; Il cantar nuovo (Petrarch), 4vv, 1579, P v; I lieti amanti (Sanazzaro), 6vv, 1587, P v; In boschi Ninfa, 6vv, 1587, P v; In dir che sarei bella (Tansillo), 6vv, 1584, P i; Io amai sempre (Petrarch), 5vv, 1581, P i; Io disleale? Ah cruda (Guarini), 5vv, 1600, P iii; Io già cantando (Barignano), 5vv, 1581, P i; Io mi sento morir (Guarini), 5vv, 1604, P iv; Io morirò, cor mio, 5vv, 1612, P iv

Io non posso gioire (Tasso), 5vv, 1612, P iv; Io son bella e delicata, 5vv, 1581, P i; L'almo splendor, 5vv, 1585, P ii; La tua cara Amarilli, 5vv, 1588, P ii; Laura soave, vita di mia vita (Cassola), 5vv, 1585, P ii; Levò con la sua mano, 5vv, 1593, P iii; Lidia gentil, 4vv, 1579, P v; Lunge da voi, ben mio (Tasso), 5vv, 1600, P iii; Mentre che qui d'intorno, 5vv, 1588, P ii; Mentr'i crin d'oro, 4vv, 1579, P v; Mia Filli, s'egli è vero, 5vv, 1593, P iii; Mirami, vita mia, 5vv, 1584, P i; Misero te non vedi, 5vv, 1584, P i; Negatemi pur, cruda (Guarini), 5vv, 1612, P iv; Nel bel fiorito maggio, 4vv, 1579, P v; Nel dolce seno (Tasso), 6vv, 1587, P v; Ne veder fuor de l'onde, 5vv, 1604, P iv; Ninfe leggiadre, 6vv, 1583[10] (attr. Wert), 1584, P i; Ninfe leggiadre, 8vv, 1612, P iv; Non ardo e son nel fuoco, 4vv, 1579, P v; Non dispiegate (Martelli), 5vv, 1584, P i; Non è questo la mano (Tasso), 4vv, 1579, P v; Non ha sì belle perle, 5vv, 1585, P ii; Non mi ferir più, Amore, 5vv, 1588, P ii

Non mirar, non mirare (Alberti), 5vv, 1588, P ii; Non son in queste rive (Tasso), 5vv, 1604, P iv; Nuova angioletta (Petrarch), 4vv, 1579, P v; O che dolce gioire (Rinaldi), 5vv, 1593, P iii; O che soave bacio (Guarini), 5vv, 1604, P iv; Occhi leggiadri e belli (Tasso), 6vv, 1587, P v; Occhi, un tempo mia vita (Guarini), 5vv, 1588, P ii; O come vaneggiate (Guarini), 5vv, 1600, P iii; O come vanneggiate (Guarini), 5vv, 1604, P iv; O dolce vita mia, 5vv, 1581, P i; O dolorosa sorte (Quirini), 5vv, 1604, P iv; O gran felicità, 5vv, 1581, P i; Oggi nacqui, ben mio (Guarini), 5vv, 1600, P iii; Ohimè, e come puoi tu senza me morire, 6vv, 1587, P v; Ohimè, se tanto amate (Guarini), 5vv, 1600, P iii; Ond'avviene ch'io t'amo, 8vv, 1593, P iii; Onde ne vieni, Amore?, 8vv, 1593, P iii; Or che

alla bella Clori, 5vv, 1588, P ii; Or che 'l donar (Rinaldi), 5vv, 1593, P iii

Or che soave l'aura, 5vv, 1586[9], P vii; Or che soave l'aura, 8vv, 1612, P iv; Or lieto il pesce, 5vv, 1588, P ii; Or veggio chiar, 5vv, 1584, P i; O saette d'amore (Parabosco), 5vv, 1584, P i; Parlo misero o taccio? (Guarini), 5vv, 1604, P iv; Parte la vita mia, 6vv, 1587, P v; Parte la vita mia, 8vv, 1612, P iv; Partomi donna, 4vv, 1579, P v; Partomi donna, 6vv, 1587, P v; Passa la nave mia (Petrarch), 5vv, 1584, P i; Passa la nave tua (Tasso), 5vv, 1588, P ii; Perché mi lasci in vita, 5vv, 1612, P iv; Perfida, pur potesti (Celiano), 5vv, 1588, P ii; Poiché stella nemica, 6vv, 1584, P i; Qual nube spinta d'importuno vento, 5vv, 1581, P i; Quand'io penso al martire (Bembo), 5vv, 1607b, P ii; Quando benigno stella (Bonacorso da Montemagno), 4vv, 1579, P v; Quel dì ch'io persi il core, 5vv, 1585, P ii; Quercia ch'in queste belle selve, 4vv, 1579, P v

Romperan questi miei preghi, 5vv, 1604, P iv; Rosa grata e gentile, 5vv, 1585, P ii; Rose gittomi al viso, 6vv, 1587, P v; Se alle rose, 5vv, 1585, P ii; Se ben al vincer nacqui, 5vv, 1604, P iv; Sedea fra gigli e rose (Lazzaroni), 6vv, 1594[6], P vii; Se per haver furato, 5vv, 1593, P iii; Se sì poca mercede (Grillo), 5vv, 1604[8], P vii; Se specchio amor vi fa, 5vv, 1585, P ii; Se v'ho donato il core, 5vv, 1593, P iii; Se voi sète il mio core (Celiano), 5vv, 1588, P ii; S'il Sol si rende bello, 5vv, 1585, P ii; Si, mi dicesti (Guarini), 5vv, 1588, P ii; S'io miro in te (Rinaldi), 5vv, 1593, P iii; Spargete, ninfe d'Arno (Guidiccioni), 5vv, 1581, P i; Stiam'Amor a veder (Petrarch), 4vv, 1579, P v; Stillando perle (Parabosco), 5vv, 1604, P iv; Stringiti pur al petto (Rinaldi), 5vv, 1612, P iv; Taci, prendi in man l'arco (Alberti), 4vv, 1595[5], P vii; T'amo mia vita (Guarini), 5vv, 1593, P iii (1600[11] as Gaudent in coelis); Tante piagh'ha 'l mio core (Celiano), 3vv, 1587[6], P vii

Temprati i sdegni, 5vv, 1600, P iii; Tirsi morir volea (Guarini), 6vv, 1581, P i (GB-Lcm 684 as Thirsis to die; 1609[14] as Omnes morti vicini); Tra le purpuree rose (Ariosto), 5vv, 1581, P i; Tra più soavi fiori, 5vv, 1581, P i; Tu ninfa di beltà, 5vv, 1584, P i; Tu parti a pena giunto (Guarini), 5vv, 1604, P iv; Tu pur ti parti (Borgogni), 5vv, 1593, P iii; Tutt'eri foco, Amore (Guarini), 5vv, 1588, P ii (1606[6] as Qui super thronum); Una farfalla (Guarini), 5vv, 1604, P iv; Va carolando intorno (Rinaldi), 5vv, 1593, P iii; Vaga scopre Diana, 6vv, 1587, P v (1624[16] as Schons lieb thut doch nich wenden); Vaghi boschetti (Ariosto), 5vv, 1581, P v; Vago candido fiore, 5vv, 1585, P ii; Viva la donna mia, 5vv, 1585, P ii; Viva sempre scolpita, 8vv, 1612, P iv; Vivrò io mai (Guarini), 5vv, 1600, P iii; Voi ch'a pianto mai (Parabosco), 5vv, 1612, P iv; Voi mi chiedete il core (Tasso), 5vv, 1604, P iv; Voi, nemico crudele, 5vv, 1604, P iv; Vorrei mostrar, 6vv, 1587, P v (1624[16] as Amor, ich thu dir klagen)

SACRED VOCAL

Liber primus missarum, 4–6vv (Venice, 1603) [1603]
Sacrae Dei laudes, 8, 12, 16vv (Venice, 1605) [1605]

Masses (all 1603, P vii): Benedicam Domino, Hoc est preceptum meum, 5vv; Omnia quae fecisti nobis, 6vv; Ut re mi fa sol la, 4vv

Motets: Beatus vir, 8vv, I-Bc, P vii; Benedicite omnia opera, 8vv, 1605, P vi; Cantate Domino, 8vv, 1605, P vi; Canite tuba, 8vv, 1605, P vi; Confitebor, 8vv, Bc, P vii; Deus misereatur nostri, 8vv, 1605, P vi; Dixit Dominus, 8vv, Bc, P vii; Dum complerentur, 8vv, 1605, P vi; In te Domine speravi, 8vv, 1605, P vi; Jubilate Deo, 8vv, 1605, P vi; Jubilate Deo, 16vv, 1605, P vi; Laudate Dominum, 8vv, 1605, P vi; Laudate Dominum, 16vv, 1605, P vi; Laudate pueri, 8vv, Bc, P vii; Miserere mei Deus, 8vv, Bc, P vii; Misericordia Domini, 8vv, 1605, P vi; Omnes gentes, 8vv, 1605, P vi; O sacrum convivium, 8vv, 1605, P vi; Quis est iste, 12vv, 1605, P vi

BIBLIOGRAPHY

EinsteinIM; FenlonMM

G.M. Artusi: L'Artusi, overo Delle imperfettioni della moderna musica (Venice, 1600/R), 3

A. Banchieri: Conclusioni nel suono dell'organo (Bologna, 1609/R), 60

P. Cerone: El melopeo y maestro (Naples, 1613/R), 89

G. Bresciani: Uomini insegni di Cremona (MS, I-CRg)

D. Arnold: '"Seconda pratica": a Background to Monteverdi's Madrigals', ML, xxxviii (1957), 341–52

T.W. Bridges: The Madrigals of Benedetto Pallavicino (diss., U. of California, Berkeley, 1959)

G. Pontirolli: 'Notizie di musicisti cremonesi dei secoli XVI e XVII', Bollettino storico cremonese, xxii (1961–4), 149–92

D. Arnold: *Monteverdi* (London, 1963, rev. 3/1990 by T. Carter) ·

P. Flanders: *The Madrigals of Benedetto Pallavicino* (diss., New York U., 1971)

P. Flanders: *A Thematic Index to the Works of Benedetto Pallavicino* (Hackensack, NJ, 1974)

K.L. Bosi Monteath: *The Five-Part Madrigals of Benedetto Pallavicino* (diss., U. of Otago, 1981)

A. Delfino: *L'Opera Sacra di Benedetto Pallavicino* (diss., U. of Pavia, 1983–4)

K. Fischer: 'Nuove tecniche della policoralità lombarda nel primo Seicento: il loro influsso sulle opere di compositori di altri aree', *La musica sacra in Lombardia nella prima metà del Seicento: Como 1985*, 41–60

G.E. Watkins and T. La May: 'Imitatio and Emulatio: Changing Concepts of Originality in the Madrigals of Gesualdo and Monteverdi in the 1590s', *Claudio Monteverdi: Festschrift Reinhold Hammerstein zum 70. Geburtstag*, ed. L. Finscher (Laaber, 1986), 453–87

L. Sirch: 'Era l'anima mia: Monteverdi, Fontanelli, Pecci e Pallavicino. Note sulla Seconda pratica', *Rassegna veneta di studi musicali*, v–vi (1989/90), 103–35

K. Bosi: 'The Ferrara Connection: Diminution in the Early Madrigals of Benedetto Pallavicino', *Altro Polo: Essays on Italian music in the Cinquecento*, ed. R. Charteris (Sydney, 1990), 131–58

S. Parisi: 'Musicians at the Court of Mantua during Monteverdi's Time: Evidence from the Payrolls', *Musicologia humana: Studies in honor of Warren and Ursula Kirkendale*, ed. S. Gmeinwieser, D. Hiley and J. Riedlbauer (Florence, 1994), 183–208

A. Newcomb: 'A New Context for Monteverdi's Mass of 1610', *Studien zur Musikgeschichte: Eine Festschrift für Ludwig Finscher*, ed. A. Laubenthal and K. Kusav-Windweh (Kassel, 1995), 163–73

S. Patuzzi: *Benedetto Pallavicino 'Maestro di Capella' del Duca Vincenzo* (diss., U. of Parma, 1995–6)

S. Patuzzi: '"Poter metter fine allo infinito": i "madrigali di musica" di Benedetto Pallavicino', *Atti e memorie dell'Accademia nazionale virgiliana di scienze, lettere ed arti*, new ser., lxiv (1996), 135–65

H. Schick: *Musikalische Einheit im Madrigal von Rore bis Monteverdi* (Tutzing, 1998)

K. BOSI MONTEATH

Pallavicino [Pallavicini], **Carlo** (*b* Salò, *c*1640; *d* Dresden, 29 Jan 1688). Italian composer. By 1665 he was organist at the basilica of S Antonio, Padua. Towards the end of 1666 he moved to Dresden, where he served under Johann Georg II, Elector of Saxony, as vice-Kapellmeister, replacing Heinrich Schütz on his death in 1672 as Kapellmeister. From June 1673, he again served as organist at S Antonio in Padua, but moved to Venice one year later, where he served as *maestro di coro* (1674–85) at the Ospedale degli Incurabili. During Carnival 1685, Johann Georg III, the son of Pallavicino's earlier employer, visited Venice and offered him the position of *camerae ac teatralis musicae praefectus*. Sources indicate that Pallavicino did not leave for Dresden until the beginning of 1687. In August and September of that year, he again visited Venice and then returned to Dresden; he was reportedly about to return to Venice, to supervise the Ospedale degli Incurabili, when he died.

Pallavicino's first operatic productions in Venice, *Demetrio* and *Aureliano*, were for the small Teatro S Moisè in 1666, before his first departure for Dresden. His association with theatres owned by the Grimani brothers began with his third opera, *Il tiranno humiliato d'amore*, written for the Teatro di SS Giovanni e Paolo and produced in his absence in 1667. After his return in 1673, he contributed to this theatre on a regular basis, and in 1678, when the Grimanis opened the Teatro Grimani a S Giovanni Grisostomo, the most luxurious Venetian opera house of their day, Pallavicino received the commission for the inaugural opera, *Vespasiano*, an emblematic choice since Vespasian, the founder of the Colosseum, was a touchstone for regal theatricality. During the next two decades, *Vespasiano* was often restaged for the opening of theatres; Pallavicino may have supervised the Genoese production at the Teatro del Falcone in 1680, since he signed the dedication of the libretto. In 1679 Pallavicino's *Le amazoni nell'isole fortunate* inaugurated the private theatre of the Procurator Marco Contarini in Piazzola, where Domenico Freschi later became house composer; the *Mercure galant* (December 1679 and February 1680) provides a description and an engraving of this work. For Carnival 1680 he also provided an opera, *Messalina*, for the Teatro S Salvador, where Sartorio was house composer.

After becoming the house composer of the S Giovanni Grisostomo, Pallavicino monopolized seven seasons and provided ten scores during the first ten years. He also continued to write for the SS Giovanni e Paolo. His operas focus on the rapid interaction of characters engaged in lively stage action, and several involve a great deal of spectacle, particularly those for the S Giovanni Grisostomo. Along with Legrenzi and Sartorio, Pallavicino created a style that responded to the audience's insatiable desire for tunefully ingratiating pieces. Their operas are packed with many short arias and recitative is minimal. The arias usually comprise two strophes in da capo form: settings often establish a constant rhythmic and motivic background against which Pallavicino highlighted certain details with word-painting or melismas. The declamatory pattern of the voice and the accompaniment is usually the same. Motto arias are frequent. Recitatives and the vast majority of arias are supported by continuo alone. Upper melodic instruments are used in a strictly compartmentalized manner in arias, mostly in homorhythmic ritornellos after the singer has concluded, thereby prolonging the mood of the aria and covering the singer's exit. Less often, ritornellos precede rather than follow the aria. When upper melodic instruments actually accompany an aria they nearly always alternate with the voice, anticipating and echoing vocal phrases and joining the voice only to add weight to the closing vocal phrase. The use of instruments simultaneously with the voice is limited to certain well-defined situations that invoke a shadowy atmosphere, such as oncoming sleep, foreboding, night and incantation. Pallavicino usually called for five-part strings (two violins, two *violette* and cello) with basso continuo (at least two harpsichords, as well as lutes and several theorbos). Certain scores call for one or two trumpets.

WORKS

OPERAS

drammi per musica in three acts, first performed in Venice, unless otherwise stated

VGG – S Giovanni Grisostomo
VGP – SS Giovanni e Paolo

Demetrio (G. dall'Angelo), S Moisè, ded. 1 Jan 1666, *I-Vnm*

Aureliano (prol., 3, dall'Angelo), S Moisè, ded. 25 Feb 1666

Il tiranno humiliato d'amore, ovvero Il Meraspe (prol., 3, G. Faustini, rev. N. Beregan), VGP, 12 Dec 1667

Diocleziano (M. Noris), VGP, ded. 10 Dec 1674, *MOe*, *Vnm*, arias *Vqs*

Enea in Italia (G.F. Bussani), VGP, carn. 1675, *Vnm*, arias *Nc*

Galieno (Noris), VGP, ded. 23 Dec 1675, *A-Wn* (?autograph), *I-Nc*, *Vnm*, arias *Vqs*

Vespasiano (G.C. Corradi), VGG, carn. 1678, *MOe*; carn. 1680, *Vnm*, arias *B-Bc*, *I-MOe*, *Rvat* and *Vqs*

Nerone (Corradi), VGG, carn. 1679, arias, *GB-Ob*, *I-MOe*, *Rvat*, *Vqs* and *Mercure galant* (April 1679)

Le amazoni nell'isole fortunate (prol., 3, F.M. Piccioli), Piazzola sul Brenta, Contarini, 1679, *Vnm*

Messalina (Piccioli), S Salvador, ded. 28 Dec 1679, *I-Vnm* (facs. in DMV, viii, forthcoming), arias *MOe*, *Tn* and *Vqs*

Bassiano, ovvero Il maggior impossibile (Noris), VGP, carn. 1682, MOe, arias *Tn* and *Vqs*

Carlo re d'Italia (Noris), VGG, carn. 1682, arias *Tn* and *Vqs*

Il re infante (Noris), VGG, 10 Jan 1683, arias *B-Bc, F-Pn, GB-Lbl, I-Vqs* and *Mercure galant* (April 1683)

Licinio imperatore (Noris), VGG, 18–25 Dec 1683

Ricimero re de' vandali (Noris), VGG, carn. 1684

Massimo Puppieno (Aureli), VGP, 6 Jan 1685, *Nc, PESc*

Penelope la casta (Noris), VGG, ded. 28 Jan 1685

Amore inamorato (Noris), VGG, 19 Jan 1686, arias *MOe*

Didone delirante (A. Franceschi), VGP, carn. 1686

L'amazone corsara, ovvero L'Avilda regina de' Goti (Corradi), VGP, *c*1 Feb 1686; carn. 1688, *D-Mbs* (facs. in IOB, xiii, 1978), *I-Nc*, arias *GB-Lbl* and *I-MOe*

Elmiro re di Corinto (V. Grimani and G. Frisari), VGG, 26 Dec 1686, arias *GB-Lbl, Ob* and *Pallade veneta* (Jan 1687)

La Gierusalemme liberata (Corradi, after T. Tasso), VGP, 4 Jan 1687; as Armida (Ger. trans. G. Fiedler, retains Pallavicino's arias), Hamburg, Gänsemarkt, 1695, *B-Bc* (19th-century copy), *D-Dl, F-Pn* (19th-century copy), *US-LAum*, ed. in DDT, 1v (1916/R), arias *F-Pn, I-Rvat* and *Pallade veneta* (Jan 1687)

ORATORIOS

S Francesco Xaverio (C. Badoer), Venice, Ospedale degli Incurabili 1677, lost

Il trionfo dell'innocenza (Piccioli), Venice, Ospedale degli Incurabili 1686, lost

Il trionfo della castità (G.M. Giannini), Modena, 1688, *I-MOe*

OTHER VOCAL

1 sacred aria, 1v, bc, 1670[1]

2 masses, 2 ps, sacred aria, 1, 4–5vv, insts, *D-Bsb, Dkh, Dl, S-Uu*

1 canzonet, 1670[3]

Arias, cantatas, *D-Mbs, I-MOe, Nc, Tn*

Antiope (S.B. Pallavicino), Dresden, Hof, 14 Feb 1689, Acts 1 and 2 *D-Dl* [completed by N.A. Strungk]

BIBLIOGRAPHY

FürstenauG

Mercure galant (April 1679, Dec 1679, Feb 1680, March 1683, April 1683)

J. Smith: 'Carlo Pallavicino', *PRMA*, xcvi (1969–70), 57–71

H.C. Wolff: 'Italian Opera from the Later Monteverdi to Scarlatti', *NOHM*, v (1975), 1–72, esp. 42–4

C. Sartori: 'I ricuperi dell'Ufficio Ricerche Fondi Musicali: Domenico Gabrieli, Carlo Pallavicino, Freschi, Legrenzi, Sartorio e Marcantonio Ziani', *NRMI*, xiv (1980), 548–54

R. Walton: 'Massimo Puppiero: The Original Setting', *South African Journal of Musicology*, iii (1983), 37–46

H.S. Saunders: *The Repertoire of a Venetian Opera House (1678–1714): the Teatro Grimani di San Giovanni Grisostomo* (diss., Harvard U., 1985)

B. Glixon: *Recitative in Seventeenth-Century Venetian Opera: its Dramatic Function and Musical Language* (diss., Rutgers U., 1985)

E. Rosand: *Opera in Seventeenth-Century Venice: the Creation of a Genre* (Berkeley and Los Angeles, 1991)

HARRIS S. SAUNDERS

Pallavicino, Germano (*b* Cremona, *c*1545–50; *d* after 1610). Italian organist and composer. According to Santoro he was the brother of Benedetto Pallavicino. Giuseppe Bresciani (1599–1670) said that he was renowned in the district of Cremona as an organist and teacher. Documents (in *I-CRd* and *CRas*) record that in 1568 he received the sum of 26 scudi for his duties as assistant organist at the cathedral. The following year he was witness to Graziadio Antegnati's contract for the new organ of the collegiate church of S Agata in Cremona.

According to the preface of Placido Falconio's *Psalmodia vespertina* (Brescia, 1579), he was responsible, together with Falconio and Costanzo Antegnati, for bringing a music printer to Brescia from Venice: presumably the firm of Vincenzo Sabbio, the publisher of Falconio's psalms. In 1599, Pallavicino was organist at Pizzeghettone, near Cremona; he was called to testify in a

dispute between the Carmelite brothers of S Bartolomeo in Cremona and the organ builder Lorenzo Stanga regarding an instrument made for that church. His name is listed among the colleagues of Costanzo Antegnati, in the preface to the latter's *L'arte organica* (Brescia, 1608). In 1610 he was organist at Toscolano, having at some stage been organist at Maderno. The little of his music that survives comprises an incomplete *Secondo libro delle fantasie, over ricercari a quattro voci … con duo motetti nel fine sopra il canto fermo* (Venice, 1610), three four-part madrigals published in Lindner's *Liber secundus gemmae musicalis* (RISM 1589[8]) and five instrumental works (two ricercars, two fantasias and a toccata, all for four parts, some from the incomplete *Secondo libro*) in a German tablature manuscript (*D-Brd*, ed. A. Carideo: *Anonimi, G. Pallavicino e F. Stivori: opere per organo*, Bologna, 1999).

BIBLIOGRAPHY

G. Cesari and G. Pannain, eds.: *La musica in Cremona nella seconda metà del secolo XVI*, IMi, vi (1939), xv

G. Pontiroli: 'Notizie di musicisti cremonesi nel secoli xvi e xvii', *Bollettino storico cremonese*, xxii (1961–4), 149–92

E. Santoro: *La famiglia e la formazione di Claudio Monteverdi: note biografiche con documenti inediti* (Cremona, 1967), 21

O. Mischiati: 'Documenti sull'organaria padana rinascimentale, II: organari a Cremona', *L'Organo*, xxiii (1985), 59–231

A. Delfino: 'Ingegneri didatta: alcune ipotesi per una ricerca', *Marc'Antonio Ingegneri: Cremona 1992*, 25–45

O. Mischiati: *Bibliografia delle opere dei musicisti bresciani pubblicate a stampa dal 1497 al 1740* (Florence, 1992), i, 262–3; ii, 717–9

O. Mischiati: 'Gli Antegnati nella prospettiva storiografica', *Gli Antegnati: studi e documenti su una stirpe di organari bresciani del rinascimento*, ed. O. Mischiati (Bologna, 1995), 73–163

M. Sala: 'La fortuna critica degli Antegnati', *Gli Antegnati: studi e documenti su una stirpe di organari bresciani del rinascimento*, ed. O. Mischiati (Bologna, 1995), 63–72

A. Carideo: 'Wiederentdekte Kompositionen von Francesco Stivori und Germano Pallavicino', *Basler Jb für historische Musikpraxis*, xxii (1998), 53–67

K. BOSI MONTEATH

Pallavicino [Pallavicini], Stefano Benedetto (*b* Padua, 21 March 1672; *d* Dresden, 16 April 1742). Italian librettist and poet, son of CARLO PALLAVICINO. He was educated at the college of the Padri Somaschi at Salò and after completing his studies he went early in 1687 with his father to Dresden, where in 1688, at the age of only 16, he was employed as court poet. From 1695 to 1716 he was court poet and private secretary to the Elector Palatine Johann Wilhelm at Düsseldorf. On the elector's death he returned via Kassel to Dresden, where he again entered the service of the Saxon electoral court. He remained there until his death. From 1701 he was a member of the Arcadian Society. He wrote numerous opera, oratorio and cantata texts and was also the author of a highly regarded translation of Horace. He was one of the leading reformers of the opera libretto at the beginning of the 18th century. At the age of 15 he wrote a libretto, *Antiope*, for his father, who died before completing the score (it was finished by N.A. Strungk). Several other composers set his opera librettos, among them Lotti, Steffani, Wilderer and above all Hasse, who also set three oratorio texts by him. The last of these, *I pellegrini al sepolcro di Nostro Redentore* (1742), was for Johann Georg Sulzer in every respect the ideal oratorio text. A four-volume edition of Pallavicino's works was published two years after his death: *Opere del Sig. Stefano Benedetto Pallavicino*, ed. F. Algarotti (Venice, 1744).

BIBLIOGRAPHY

FürstenauG; OG (S. Dahms) [incl. work-list]

M. Fürstenau: 'Die Oper "Antiope" und die Bestallungen des kurfürstlich sächsischen Vice-Kapellmeisters Nicolaus Adam Strunk und des Hofpoeten Stefano Pallavicini', *MMg*, xiii (1881), 1–6

I. Becker-Glauch: *Die Bedeutung der Musik für die Dresdener Hoffeste bis in die Zeit Augusts des Starken* (Kassel, 1951)

G. Croll: 'Musikgeschichtliches aus Rapparinis Johann-Wilhelm-Manuskript (1709)', *Mf*, xi (1958), 257–64

G. Steffen: *Johann Hugo von Wilderer (1670 bis 1724), Kapellmeister am kurpfälzischen Hofe zu Düsseldorf und Mannheim* (Cologne, 1960)

H. Riemenschneider: *Tanz und Hofoper in der Residenz Düsseldorf* (Cologne, 1972)

W. Dean: 'The Genesis and Early History of Ottone', *Göttinger Händel-Beitrage*, ii (1986), 129–40

L. Bianconi and G. La Face Bianconi, eds.: *L libretti italiani di Georg Friedrich Händel e le loro fonti* (Florence, 1992)

SIBYLLE DAHMS

Pallet [valve] (Ger. *Ventil*). In the wind-chest of an organ, the pallet is the valve which, when brought into play by pulling or pushing away from the mortise it otherwise closes, admits wind to the channel or groove of a particular key and hence, if the stop mechanism allows it, to the foot-hole of the pipe(s) of that stop. The 'pallet box' is strictly the substructure of the WIND-CHEST in which the row of pallets, one for each key in the compass, is housed. The word itself (usually spelt 'palat') was used to mean any of the several kinds of valve found in an organ (bellows pallet, key pallet etc) by James Talbot in his manuscript treatise of *c*1695, probably under the influence of his French sources.

As a tight seal between pallet and grid is crucial to the good working of the key action and the proper speech of the pipework, much technical attention has been paid to the shape and material of the springs (usually of brass alloy until the 19th century, when steel 'piano wire' was introduced) and the covering of the pallet and its opening in the grid. Some early Scandinavian and 17th-century Dutch pallets were made with a self-sealing, inflating leather covering. Most classical organs relied on one or more layers of leather on the pallet together with leather on the grid; Romantic organs came to use pallets with a thick layer of felt between leather and wood. As soundboards became larger and used heavier wind pressures, pallets became more difficult to open; at first, smaller double pallets were used, but by the middle of the 19th century, several methods of alleviating the touch (usually by 'back on back' or 'broken' pallets) were used.

PETER WILLIAMS, MARTIN RENSHAW

Palló, Imre (*b* Matisfalva, 23 Oct 1891; *d* Budapest, 25 Jan 1978). Hungarian baritone. After studying at the Budapest Academy of Music under Georg Anthes, and later in Italy with Sammarco, he made his Royal Hungarian Opera début in 1917, as Alfio, and was soon its leading interpreter of lyric baritone roles. He sang with refined diction and velvety tone, his voice showing good balance in all registers, and he also possessed an imposing stage presence; all these qualities were notably displayed in his Verdi roles, especially Posa, Luna, Falstaff (the first in Hungary) and Simon Boccanegra. His peasant origins were advantageous in Kodály – he created the title role in *Háry János* (1926) and the Suitor in *Székely fonó* ('The Spinning Room', 1932). In 1935 he took part in Rocca's *Il dibuk* in Rome. From 1957 to 1959 he was Intendant of the Hungarian State Opera. (A. Németh: *Palló Imre*, Budapest, 1970)

PÉTER P. VÁRNAI

Pallota [Pallotta], Matteo. *See* PALOTTA, MATTEO.

Palm, Siegfried (*b* Wuppertal, 25 April 1927). German cellist and educationist. He studied (1933–45) with his father, Siegfried Palm (a cellist in the Wuppertal city orchestra), then (1950–53) in Enrico Mainardi's masterclass at Salzburg. He was principal cellist in the Lübeck city orchestra (1945–7), the Hamburg Radio SO (1947–62) and the Cologne RSO (1962–7). In 1962 he became a professor with a masterclass at the Staatliche Hochschule für Musik in Cologne, and in 1972 was appointed director there. From 1977 to 1981 he was Intendant of the Deutsche Oper, Berlin. In 1982 he was elected president of the ISCM, a post he held until 1987, and in 1988 he became president of the Deutsche Gesellschaft für Neue Musik.

Palm has played a leading part in the development and extension of cello technique. In the 1950s and 60s he was the first to perform works by Penderecki (Sonata for Cello and Orchestra), Xenakis (*Nomos alpha*) and Zillig (Cello Concerto) which had been considered technically unplayable. He has built an international reputation as a cellist specializing in avant-garde music, and has toured throughout the world. A friend of Zimmermann and Penderecki, he has given first performances of the former's *Canto di speranza* and *Pas de trois*, Sonata and Four Short Pieces for solo cello, and *Intercommunicazione*; and of the latter's Cello Concerto and *Capriccio per Siegfried Palm*. Among his other first performances are concertos by Blacher, Delas, Feldman, Ligeti, Halffter and Medek, and works by Becker, Benguerel, Engelmann, Fortner, Kagel, Kelemen (whose cello concerto he has recorded), Sinopoli, Liebermann, Yun and Rihm.

As a chamber musician, Palm played with the Hamann Quartet, specializing in new music (1950–62); in 1965 he formed a duo with Aloys Kontarsky, and in 1967 succeeded Cassadó as cellist of the Cologne Trio, with Max Rostal and Heinz Schröter. Since the late 1980s he has played in a trio with Bruno Canino and Saschko Gawriloff. He plays a 1708 cello by Giovanni Grancino. He began to teach at the Darmstadt summer courses in 1962, and has also taught at the Royal Swedish Academy of Music (from 1966), Dartmouth College, USA (1969 and 1972), Marlboro, USA (from 1970), the Sibelius Academy, Helsinki (1971), and at the courses at Breukelen, the Netherlands (1972). He is widely sought after as an adjudicator at international festivals, and has published *Pro musica nova: Studien zum Spielen neuer Musik für Cello* (Cologne, 1974), which contains original contributions by leading contemporary composers.

BIBLIOGRAPHY

R. Lück: *Werkstattgespräche mit Interpreten neuer Musik* (Cologne, 1971), 81ff [with discography]

RUDOLF LÜCK/TULLY POTTER

Palma, Athos (*b* Buenos Aires, 7 June 1891; *d* Miramar, 10 Jan 1951). Argentine composer. His initial studies were at the National Conservatory in Buenos Aires with Troiani (piano), Cattaneo (sight-singing) and García Jacot (violin). After a ten-year stay in Europe (1904–14) he returned to Argentina, where he continued studies with Troiani. He also studied medicine for several years and completed the course in philosophy and letters at Buenos

Aires University. Thereafter he devoted himself to composing and teaching music. Isabel Aretz, Carlos Suffern and Abraham Jurafsky were among his students. Palma held positions as vice-president of the board of directors of the Teatro Colón (1932), professor of harmony at the National Conservatory and inspector of the National Council of Education. He wrote two pedagogical works, the five-volume *Teoría razonada de la música* and a *Tratado completo de armonía* (Buenos Aires, 1941).

WORKS
(selective list)

Ops: Nazdah (G. di San Leo), 1924; Los hijos de sol, 1928
Orch: Cantares de mi tierra, suite, str, 1914; Jardines, sym. poem, 1926; Los hijos de sol, sym. poem, 1929
Chbr: Sonata, vc, pf, 1912; Sonata, vn, pf, 1924

BIBLIOGRAPHY

N. Lamuraglia: *Athos Palma: vida, arte, educación* (Buenos Aires, 1954)
R. Arizaga: *Enciclopedia de la música argentina* (Buenos Aires, 1972)

JOHN M. SCHECHTER

Palma [De Palma, Di Palma], **Silvestro** (*b* Barano d'Ischia, 15 March 1754; *d* Naples, 8 Aug 1834). Italian composer. According to Rosa's *Memorie*, he owed his initial musical education to a patroness, Carlotta di Sangro, daughter of the Prince of Sansevero, and entered the Conservatorio di S Maria di Loreto in Naples at the age of 16. In the late 1780s he studied with Paisiello, whose music he took as a model; contemporary documents often refer to him as 'pupil of Paisiello'. He became well known as a composer of opera, especially comic opera, because of his talent for witty, effervescent and lightly textured music. The Naples *Monitore* (2 May 1810) praised his opera *Lo scavamento* for the naturalness and simplicity of its music and for its avoidance of the contemporary fault of too many notes and too prominent accompaniment. He was, it says, the 'support of the good Neapolitan school', a reference to the close affinity between his music and that of the previous generation of Neapolitan composers. After 1813 his operas disappeared from the repertory. This may have been caused by changing tastes among Neapolitan audiences; Rosa provided another explanation in saying that Palma fell ill, which forced him to cancel contracts for new music and wrecked his chances of a more prosperous livelihood.

WORKS
OPERAS
unless otherwise stated, all are commedie per musica, first performed in Naples, Teatro dei Fiorentini

La finta matta (2, D. Piccinni), 1789
Gli amanti della dote (dg, 2, S. Zini), Florence, S Maria, sum. 1791; arias, *I-Tf, Rsc*
Le nozze in villa (int, 2), Rome, Valle, carn. 1792
Chi mal fa, mal aspetti, ovvero Lo scroccatore smascherato (dramma tragicomico, 2), Venice, S Moisè, aut. 1792
L'ingaggiatore di campagna (int), Florence, Palla a Corda, 1792, *I-Fc*
La pietra simpatica (2, G. Lorenzi), aut. 1795, *Nc*; as L'anello incantato (farsetta per musica), Rome, Valle, carn. 1796, *Bc, Rsc, Rvat*
Gli amanti ridicoli (2, Lorenzi), aut. 1797, *Nc*
Il pallone aerostatico (2, G. Palomba), spr. 1802, *Nc*
Le seguaci di Diana (2, Lorenzi), sum. 1805; also as Le ninfe di Diana, *Nc*
L'erede senza eredità (2, Palomba), 29 Sept 1808, *Nc*
Lo scavamento (2, Palomba), 29 April 1810, *Nc*
I furbi amanti (2, Palomba), aut. 1810, *Nc*
Il palazzo delle fate (2, Palomba), aut. 1812, *Nc*
I vampiri (2, Palomba), Naples, Nuovo, 1812, *Nc*
Le miniere di Polonia (melodramma, 3, G. Giannetti), wint. 1813, *Nc*
8 arias in G. Paisiello's Le vane gelosie (3, Lorenzi), spr. 1790, *Nc*

I viaggiatori (op), inc., *Fc*
Other arias and duets: *D-Hs, I-Bc, CMac, Nc, PEsp, Rc, Rrai, Rrostirolla, Rsc, Vnm; S-St; US-LAum, SFsc*
Doubtful: La schiava fortunata, Naples, 1801; Il naturalista immaginario, Florence, 1806; La sposa contrastata, Naples, 1813; Il geloso di sé stesso, 1814; I giudici di Agrigento

OTHER WORKS

Sacred: Magnificat, Salve regina, Miserere, Litanie, Veni Creator Spiritus: all S, org, *I-Mc* [attrib. only to 'Palma' in MSS]; Le sette stazioni della vergine addolorata, 2 S, bc, *Mc*; Sancta Maria, sancta Dei Genitrix, *S-Smf**
Inst: Sinfonia, B♭, *I-Mc, Nc*; Sonata, D, pf, *Mc*; 3 Pieces, hp, *US-BEm*

BIBLIOGRAPHY

FlorimoN; RosaM
R. Zanetti: *La musica italiana nel Settecento* (Busto Arsizio, 1978), 1512–13

MICHAEL F. ROBINSON/LUISELLA MOLINA

Palma Ociosa. *See* PETRUS FRATER DICTUS PALMA OCIOSA.

Palmer, Felicity (Joan) (*b* Cheltenham, 6 April 1944). English mezzo-soprano. The daughter of a music master, she studied at the GSM in London (1962–7) and then for a year with Marianne Schech at the Musikhochschule, Munich. In 1970 she won a Kathleen Ferrier Scholarship, and made her Queen Elizabeth Hall début, in Purcell's *Dioclesian*; subsequent appearances in oratorio confirmed her reputation as a singer of quick musicianship and confident projection. After a decade as a soprano (début role, Purcell's Dido with Kent Opera, 1971) and wide experience as Countess Almaviva, Donna Elvira and Pamina, she retrained as a mezzo-soprano. She has won international renown for her magnetic presence and powerful musical command in shaping phrases and projecting words, amply compensating for occasionally edgy tone. Palmer's mezzo-soprano repertory includes the title role in Handel's *Tamerlano*, Juno in *Semele*, Gluck's Orpheus, Fricka, Mistress Quickly, the Countess (*Queen of Spades*), Herodias, Clytemnestra, Kabanicha (*Kát'a Kabanová*) and the title role in the stage première of Gerhard's *The Duenna* (1992, Madrid). In 1997 she sang Strauss's Clytemnestra at Covent Garden. Her many recordings reflect her two vocal 'identities' and her versatility, and include Gluck's *Armide*, Electra (*Idomeneo*), Marcellina (*Le nozze di Figaro*), many works by Handel and *The Dream of Gerontius*. She was made a CBE in 1993.

BIBLIOGRAPHY

E. Forbes: 'Felicity Palmer', *Opera*, xlv (1994), 1033–8

MAX LOPPERT

Palmer, Frederik. Pseudonym of Emma Sophie Amalia Zinn, Danish songwriter and wife of Johan Peter Emilius Hartmann. *See* HARTMANN family.

Palmer, Geoffrey Molyneux (*b* Staines, Middlesex, 8 Oct 1882; *d* Dublin, 29 Nov 1957). Irish composer. He studied at Oxford, where in 1901 he was the youngest BMus in college history. From 1904 to 1907 he studied composition with Stanford at the RCM. He moved to Ireland *c*1910 where he was active as an organist near Dublin. A victim of multiple sclerosis, he became increasingly dependent on the care of his two sisters.

Palmer was chiefly known for his many folksong arrangements and sentimental ballads, several of which were published in England. His largest scores include the opera *Srúth na Maoile* [Sea of Moyle] (1923). 32 settings of Joyce poems (from the 36 poems in the *Chamber Music* collection) written between 1907 and 1949 remained unknown and unperformed until the early 1980s. They were discovered in the library of Southern Illinois University, Carbondale, and published in 1993. The songs display a remarkable formal melodic and harmonic freedom that is not characteristic of any of his other works. Palmer appears to have been the first composer to set Joyce's poetry, an effort which gained the praise of the writer. As late as 1934 Joyce wrote: "30 or 40 composers at least have set my little poems to music. The best is Molyneux Palmer. After him are Moeran and Bliss." (Joyce's *Letters*, vol. III, 340).

WORKS
(*selective list*)

STAGE

Ops: Finn Varra Maa [The Irish Santa Claus] (T.H. Nally), *c*1917; Srúth na Maoile [Sea of Moyle] (T. O'Kelly) 1923; Gráinne Goes (O'Kelly), *c*1924

VOCAL

Choral (SATB): Choral Works, op.1, 1906; The Abbot of Inisfalen (W. Allingham), 1909; Anthems, op.13, 1911; Choral Works, op.14, 1912; The Fields in May (W. Allingham), 1928; Four Ducks in a Pond (W. Allingham), 1928; On Music, 1935; The Robin, 1938; Duain Chroí Iosa [Hymn to the Sacred Heart], 1953
Choral (other): Folk Songs, op.15, 1913; Good-bye to Summer, 1915; By that Dim Lake, 1920; Serenade no.1, 1920; Serenade no.2, 1931; Folk Songs, op.20, 1953
Songs: The Heart Beat (H. Heine, trans. G. MacDonald), 1904; 32 Poems from Chbr Music (J. Joyce), 1907–49; Folk Songs, op.12, 1911; The Man for Galway, 1911; Husho my Lanna (C. Rossetti), 1914; When you are Old (W.B. Yeats), *c*1950

INSTRUMENTAL

Dolás/Dolour, vc, pf, 1913; Knickerbocker Lane, orch, 1941

Principal publishers: Banks & Son, Breitkopf & Härtel, Curwen, H.W.F. Deane & Sons, Novello, Pigott, Stainer & Bell

BIBLIOGRAPHY

A. Fleischmann, ed.: *Music in Ireland: Cork 1952*
S. Gilbert and R. Ellmann: *Letters of James Joyce*, i–iii (New York, 1957–66)
M. Teicher Russel: *James Joyce's Chamber Music: The Lost Song Settings* (Bloomington, IN, 1993) [with cassette]
A. Klein: *Die Musik Irlands im 20. Jahrhundert* (Hildesheim, 1996)

AXEL KLEIN

Palmer, Henry (*b* ?1590–1600; *d* Durham, 1640). English music copyist, composer and singer. He was sworn in as a lay clerk at Durham Cathedral on 20 July 1627. In 1628 he assumed responsibility for training and supervising the cathedral choristers during the temporary suspension from duty of the organist Richard Hutchinson. He was still at the cathedral in 1639, since he was described as 'laici cler. hujus ecclesiae' at the baptism of his son William on 25 March of that year. He is primarily remembered today as a copyist. He played a significant role in copying the unique and comprehensive collection of church music that was formerly in daily use in cathedral services at Durham and which is now in the cathedral library there. Specimens of his handwriting in the cathedral treasurers' books clearly show that over 150 compositions in three organbooks copied during the 1630s (*GB-DRc* A1, A5 and A6) are predominantly in his hand. He may also have copied some items in the related vocal partbooks. All of his compositions are in manuscripts formerly associated with Durham Cathedral (including the Dunnington-Jefferson bass partbook, Y). The verse anthem *Lord, what is man* (*Cu*) is entirely in the composer's hand.

WORKS

Ky, 4vv, Cr, verse (inc.): *GB-Cu*, *DRc*
Preces, 4vv, Ps cxviii.24–9, verse (inc.): *Cu*, *DRc*
9 anthems, 3 full, 6 verse, *Cu*, *DRc*, *Lbl*, *Y* (all inc.)

BIBLIOGRAPHY

W.K. Ford: 'An English Liturgical Partbook of the 17th Century', *JAMS*, xii (1959), 144–60
J. Morehen: *The Sources of English Cathedral Music c.1617–c.1644* (diss., U. of Cambridge, 1969), 22ff, 156ff
R.T. Daniel and P. le Huray: *The Sources of English Church Music, 1549–1660*, EECM, suppl. i (London, 1972)

JOHN MOREHEN

Palmer, Robert (Moffett) (*b* Syracuse, NY, 2 June 1915). American composer and teacher. He won a scholarship to the Eastman School of Music as a pianist, but gradually shifted his emphasis to composition, studying with Bernard Rogers and Howard Hanson (BM 1938, MM 1940). He went on to study composition with Roy Harris, Aaron Copland and, most important, Quincy Porter. He taught at the University of Kansas (1940–43) and Cornell University (1943–80). His honours include an American Academy of Arts and Letters award (1946), Guggenheim Fellowships (1952–3, 1960–61) and a Fulbright Senior Fellowship (1960–61). He has received commissions from the Koussevitzky Foundation (1943, for the String Quartet no.2), the Elizabeth Sprague Coolidge Foundation (1950, for the Piano Quintet), the National Association of Educational Broadcasters (1960, for the *Memorial Music*), the Lincoln Center (1965, for the *Centennial Overture*) and Cornell University.

Palmer's distinctive style can be seen as an outgrowth of the styles of his teachers, though it is also connected with the work of Milhaud, Hindemith, Tippett, Petrassi and Bartók. His best-known piece, the *Toccata ostinato* for piano (1945), is an exciting treatment in 13/8 time of a boogie-woogie inspiration, familiar to Palmer from his experience playing jazz duets. The Piano Concerto (1971) is noteworthy for its culmination in a swinging long-breathed tune that incorporates motifs from the first movement, which have been developed fugally and combined with contrasting motifs.

WORKS

Orch: Poem, vn, chbr orch, 1938; Conc., small orch, 1940; K 19, sym. elegy, 1945; Variations, Chorale and Fugue, 1947, rev. 1954; Chbr Conc., vn, ob, str, 1949; Sym. no.1, 1953; Memorial Music, 1960; Centennial Ov., 1965; Sym. no.2, 1966; Choric Song and Toccata, band, 1968; Pf Conc., 1971; Symphonia concertante, 9 insts, 1972; Ov. on a Southern Hymn, sym. band, 1979; Conc., 2 pf, 2 perc, str, brass, 1984; incid music
Vocal: 2 Songs (W. Whitman), 1v, pf, 1940; Abraham Lincoln walks at midnight (V. Lindsay), chorus, orch, 1948; Carmina amoris (Sappho, others), S, cl, vn, pf, 1951, arr. with chbr orch; Slow, slow, fresh Fount (B. Jonson), SATB, 1953, rev. 1959; Of Night and the Sea (chbr cant., Whitman, E. Dickinson, others), S, B, orch, 1956; And in that day (Bible: *Isaiah*), anthem, chorus, 1963; Nabuchodonosor (Bible: *Daniel*), T, B, TTBB, wind, perc, 2 pf, 1964; Portents of Aquarius, nar, SATB, org, 1975
Chbr and solo inst: Str Qt no.1, 1939; Conc., 5 insts, 1943; Str Qt no.2, 1943, rev. 1947; Pf Qt no.1, 1947; Pf Qnt, 1950; Sonata, va, pf, 1951; Qnt, cl, str trio, pf, 1952, rev. 1953; Str Qt no.3, 1954; Sonata, vn, pf, 1956; Pf Trio, 1958; Str Qt no.4, 1960; Organon I, fl, cl, 1962; Epithalamium, org, 1968; Sonata, tpt, pf, 1972; Pf Qnt no.2, 1974; Organon II, vn, va, 1975; Sonata no.1, vc, pf, 1978; Sonata no.2, vc, pf, 1983
Pf: Sonata no.1, 1938, rev. 1946; 3 Preludes, 1941; Sonata no.2, 1942, rev. 1948; Sonata, 2 pf, 1944; Toccata ostinato, 1945; Sonata, pf 4 hands, 1952; Evening Music, 1956; 7 Epigrams, 1957; Morning Music, 1973; Sonata no.3, 1979

MSS and scores in *US-I*

Principal publishers: Elkan-Vogel, Peer, Peters, G. Schirmer, Valley

BIBLIOGRAPHY

AG (W.W. Austin) [incl. further bibliography]; *EwenD*

W.W. Austin: 'The Music of Robert Palmer', *MQ*, xlii (1956), 35–50

R. Salvatore: 'The Piano Music of Robert Palmer', *Clavier*, xxviii/4 (1989), 22–30

WILLIAM W. AUSTIN

Palmerini, Giovanni Battista (*fl* 1722–8). Italian bass. He was a member of the Elector Palatine's chapel at Düsseldorf in 1723, and probably the Palmerini from Mantua who had sung in Pietro Torri's *Adelaide* at Munich the previous October. In 1726 he performed one of his own motets at a Paris Concert Spirituel (February) and appeared at the Hamburg opera. He sang at the King's Theatre in London during the last two seasons of the Royal Academy between January 1727 and June 1728. Handel wrote small parts for him in *Admeto* (Meraspes, in which he made his début on 31 January 1727), *Riccardo Primo* (Berardo) and *Siroe* (Arasse); he also sang in revivals and in Ariosti's *Teuzzone*. He is said to have been an aging singer whose powers were on the decline, but he may have been the Abate Giambattista Palmerini who sang in a serenata in honour of Maria Theresa at Mantua in 1739. It appears from the few arias Handel composed for him that he was a baritone with a high tessitura and a compass from *G* to *f'*. Another bass singer of this name, Andrea Palmerini of Genoa, sang at the festival of S Croce at Lucca in September 1741.

WINTON DEAN

Palmerini, Luigi (*b* Bologna, 26 Dec 1768; *d* Bologna, 27 Jan 1842). Italian organist, composer and teacher. A pupil of Mattei in Bologna from 1786 to 1790, he was appointed organist at S Petronio in 1817. On 13 June 1838 he succeeded Giuseppe Pilotti as temporary *maestro di cappella* there, and held both positions until his death. He was a member of the Accademia Filarmonica and served as its *principe* in 1804.

According to Fétis, the traditional contrapuntal style of organ playing in Italy ended with Palmerini; this opinion must have been founded on his improvisations, as his only surviving music specifically designated for the organ, a concerto (*I-Bc*), is highly pianistic. 16 sonatas for an unspecified keyboard instrument also survive (*Bc*). Fétis stated that some Bolognese musicians preferred Palmerini's figured bass method, the *Metodo d'accompagnamento numerico* (MS, *Bc*), to Mattei's. Of Palmerini's sacred music, a *Pange lingua*, an *O salutaris*, a *Profezia di Nabucodonosor* for tenor solo and a *Passio in Dominica Palmarum* are extant at S Petronio. The Bologna Conservatory library possesses a *Dies irae* dated 1824, a *Tantum ergo* and a secular aria, *Celebrarla io pur vorrei*.

BIBLIOGRAPHY

EitnerQ; *FétisB*

E. Succi: *Catalogo con brevi cenni biografici e succinte descrizioni degli autografi e documenti di celebri a distinti musicisti posseduti da Emilia Succi* (Bologna, 1888)

G. Masutto: *Della musica sacra in Italia* (Venice, 1889)

MILTON SUTTER

Palmgren, Selim (*b* Björneborg [now Pori], 16 Feb 1878; *d* Helsinki, 16 Dec 1951). Finnish composer, pianist and conductor. He was a pupil of Wegelius (harmony and counterpoint) and of Petzet, Melcer-Szczawiński and Ekman (piano) at the Helsinki Music Institute (1895–9), and then studied in Germany and Italy with Conrad Ansorge, Wilhelm Berger and Busoni. Back in Finland he held appointments as conductor of the Helsinki University Chorus (1902–4, 1927–8), for whom he composed several partsongs. From 1909 to 1912 he conducted the orchestra of the Turku Musical Society, after which he worked solely as a composer and pianist. He undertook several extensive European tours, on some of which he was accompanied by his first wife, the singer Maikki Järnefelt (he married the singer Minna Talvik in 1930). In 1920–21 he toured the USA and in 1923 he was appointed to teach composition at the Eastman School. He was professor of harmony and composition at the Sibelius Academy, Helsinki (1936–51), and in 1950 he received an honorary doctorate from Helsinki University.

Palmgren's music for the piano is distinguished by a real understanding of the instrument, a remarkable faculty for suggesting definite and widely contrasted moods and an agreeably proportioned mixture of melodic, harmonic and rhythmic invention. His five piano concertos are in the tradition of Liszt and Rachmaninoff, and the second, *Virta* ('The River', 1913), became an international success following its performance in Berlin by Ignacy Friedman under the composer's baton. Palmgren's gift in catching the essence of an impression or a picture is displayed at its best in character pieces, such as the 24 Preludes (1907). In addition to piano music, Palmgren wrote a large number of partsongs, sometimes with a strong national flavour, though this is not necessary to the expression of his frequently fanciful and individual tone.

WORKS
(selective list)

Opera: Daniel Hjort (3, Palmgren, after J.J. Wecksell), 1910, Turku, 21 April 1910; rev. 1937

Pf Concs.: no.1, g, op.13, 1904; no.2 'Virta' [The River], op.33, 1913; no.3 'Metamorphoses', op.41, 1916; no.4 'April', op.85, 1927; no.5, A, op.99, 1940

Other orch: Vuodenajat [The Seasons], op.24, 1908; Pastorale, op.50, 1918; Concert Fantasy, op.104, vn, orch, 1945

Pf: Sonata, d, op.11, 1900; Fantasy, op.6, ?1901; En route, op.9, ?1901; Toukokuu [May], op.27, 1906–7; 24 Preludes, op.17, 1907; 24 Etudes, op.77, 1921–2; Sonatine, F, op.93, 1935; *c*250 other pieces

Other works: *c*100 songs, *c*100 partsongs, cant, incid music

Principal publishers: Fazer, Gehrman, Hansen

BIBLIOGRAPHY

S. Palmgren: *Minusta tuli muusikko* [I became a musician] (Porvoo, 1948)

K. Maasalo: 'Selim Palmgren', *Suomalaisia sävellyksiä* [Finnish compositions], ii (1969), 55–81

B.B. Hong: *The Five Piano Concertos of Selim Palmgren* (diss., Indiana U., 1992)

E. Salmenhaara, ed.: *Suomalaisia säveltäjiä* (Helsinki, 1994)

E. Salmenhaara: *Kansallisromantiikan valtavirta* [The mainstream of national Romanticism], Suomen musiikin historia [A history of Finnish music], ii (Porvoo, 1996)

ILKKA ORAMO

Palmieri, Eddie [Edward] (*b* East Harlem, New York, 15 Dec 1936). American pianist, percussionist, bandleader, composer and arranger. Following his older brother Charlie, he took up the piano when he was eight, but at 13 he began playing the timbales in his uncle's band, Chino y sus Almas Tropicales. Returning to the piano in 1951, he formed a nine-piece band with timbalero Joey Quijano. He replaced his brother Charlie in Johnny Segui's band in 1955, then joined Tito Rodríguez in 1958. In 1961 he formed the ensemble La Perfecta. Modifying the flute-and-violin *charanga* format popular at the time, Palmieri used trombones in place of violins and coined the 'trombanga' sound that became his trademark and influenced later salsa bands. In his band were such leading musicians as the timbalero Manny Oquendo, the trombonist Barry Rogers and the vocalist Ismael Quintana. Complementing the group's dynamic swing, Palmieri forged a percussive piano style, incorporating modal jazz influences from contemporary pianist McCoy Tyner. Among his representative tunes from this period are *Azucar*, *Tirándote flores*, *Viejo socarrón*, *Muñeca*, *Café*, *Bomba de corazón* and *Cuidate compai*.

In addition to transforming Latin dance music, Palmieri also began experimental forays into Latin jazz, recording with the vibraphone player Cal Tjader (1966–7). La Perfecta disbanded in 1968, but Palmieri continued to develop his rugged brand of salsa with such classics as *Justicia*, *Lindo yambú*, *Vamonos pa'l monte*, *Palo pa' rumba* and *La verdad*. Dubbed 'El Loco' ('the Crazy Man') and also the 'Sun of Latin Music', Palmieri has been at the vanguard of Latin music from the 1950s. Between 1974 and 1994 he won five Grammy Awards, the only Latin bandleader to have done so. He also helped launch the careers of the vocalists Lalo Rodríguez in the mid-1970s and La India in the early 90s. Palmieri has also recorded notable Latin jazz albums such as *Palmas* (Elek., 1994).

LISE WAXER

Palmo's Opera House. New York theatre opened in 1844. *See* NEW YORK, §4.

Palm wine. Form of West African guitar band HIGHLIFE music from Sierra Leone. Palm wine music (known in Sierra Leone as *maringa*) takes its name from the alcoholic beverage made from fermented palm sap served in coastal bars, a fairly cheap alternative to bottled beer. Palm wine was first made famous by Ebenezer Calender and his Maringar Band, who were known for their calypso-influenced style that drew heavily on the music of freed Caribbean slaves who had returned to Sierra Leone. Calender recorded extensively in the 1950s and 1960s, singing in the Krio language. The Kru-speaking sailors of Liberia who traded all along the west coast of Africa were accomplished guitarists, and their music may have influenced both Trinidadian calypso and Freetown *maringa* (Ashcroft and Trillo, 634). S.E. Rogie (*d* 1994) helped to popularize a form of palm wine internationally, and bands of expatriate musicians in London continued to maintain the palm wine music tradition.

BIBLIOGRAPHY

AND OTHER RESOURCES

Sierra Leone Music: West African Gramophone Records Recorded at Freetown in the 1950s and early 60s, Zensor Musikproduktion ZS 41 (1988) [incl. notes by W. Bender]
African Elegant: Sierra Leone's Kru/Krio Calypso Connection, Original Music OMCDO15 (1992)
Dead Men Don't Smoke Marijuana, perf. S.E. Rogie, RealWorld 8 39639 2 (1994)
E. Ashcroft and R. Trillo: 'Palm-Wine Sounds', *The Rough Guide to World Music*, i (London, 1999), 634–7

GREGORY F. BARZ

Palo Alto. Town in California, USA, near San Francisco. It is the seat of Stanford University. *See* SAN FRANCISCO, §5.

Pálóczi Horváth, Ádám (*b* Kömlőd, 11 May 1760; *d* Nagybajom, 28 Jan 1820). Hungarian poet and folksong collector. The son of a clergyman, he studied at the Reformed College in Debrecen from 1773 until 1780 and, after a short career as a public servant, devoted himself to farming. He was in close contact with the leading Hungarian poets and language reformers of his day and maintained an intense and many-sided literary activity, writing lyric and epic works, a comedy, and historical, linguistic, philosophical and scientific essays.

In the 18th and 19th centuries the Protestant colleges of Hungary fostered national traditions and opposed the centralizing, German-orientated tendencies of the imperial court in Vienna. Under this influence at the college in Debrecen, Pálóczi Horváth developed a sense of history that later expressed itself in activities as a collector of folksongs and historical and sacred songs. His manuscript collection *Ó es Új, mint-egy ötödfél-száz énekek, ki magam tsinálmányja, ki másé* ('About 450 songs, old and new, composed partly by me, partly by others'), introduced a new era in the history of Hungarian folklore and musicology. Completed in 1813 and recopied in 1814, the manuscript contains 357 melodies, among them 45 of Pálóczi Horváth's own compositions, 23 psalms and mourning songs, 148 old Hungarian folksongs, historical songs and texted Ungaresca dances with text and some fashionable patriotic and sentimental songs from the 1790s. His notation was primitive, giving neither clef, key signature nor tempo indication. To indicate rhythm he used only two symbols; the intervals, on the other hand, were reliably established. As the collection was compiled from oral tradition and contains almost all the popular Hungarian musical genres of its time, it presents a faithful picture of popular national musical culture in upper-middle-class Hungary around 1800.

BIBLIOGRAPHY
I. Bartalus: *Magyar Orpheus* (Pest, 1869)
A. Herrmann: 'Horváth Ádám énekeinek kéziratai' [The MSS of Horváth's songs], *Magyar zenetudomány*, i (1907), 24
B. Sztankó: 'Pálóczi Horváth Ádám dallamai' [Pálóczi Horváth's melodies], *Magyar zenetudomány*, i (1907), 5
B. Szabolcsi: 'Pálóczi Horváth Ádám ötödfélszáz énekének töredékes kézirata' [The MS fragment of Pálóczi Horváth's 450 songs], *Irodalomtörténeti közlemények*, xxxvii (1927), 99–108
D. Bartha: *Horváth Ádám népdal-feljegyzéseinek ritmusáról* [Horváth's rhythmic notation of folksong], *Zenetudományi tanulmányok*, i (1953), 267–78
D. Bartha and J. Kiss, eds.: *Ötödfélszáz énekek* (Budapest, 1953) [critical edn of Pálóczi Horváth's 450 songs]

FERENC BÓNIS

Palol [Palon], Berenguier de. *See* BERENGUIER DE PALAZOL.

Palomares, Juan de (*b* Seville, *c*1573; *d* before 1609). Spanish composer and guitarist. The 19th-century writer Baltasar Saldoni mistakenly created a second Palomares with the forename Pedro. Lope de Vega rated Juan de Palomares second only to Juan Blas de Castro as a composer of courtly love laments. In 1623 Hurtado de Mendoza praised Castro for his sweetness, Palomares for his novelty. Palomares's three extant songs are in four manuscript sources. *En el campo florido*, a three-part canción which is a setting of an autobiographical lament of the exiled Lope de Vega, is in three sources (the Turin cancionero, *I-Tn* R.I–14, ed. M. Querol Gavaldá, Madrid, 1986; *E-Mmc* olim 13231; and, as a sacred contrafactum, *Lo mejor de mi vida*, in *E-Mn* 1370–72; ed., after first and third sources, in MME, xviii, 1956, and after the second by J. Bal y Gay, *Treinta canciones de Lope de Vega*, Madrid, 1935). The long melismas closing each of the seven strophes are as expressive as a protracted Andalusian 'ay'. *Sobre moradas violetas* is a three-part romance in the Sablonara cancionero of 1625 (in *D-Mbs* ed. in Aroca); it is reduced to a duet in the Turin cancionero. *Hermosa Galatea* is a four-part sonnet setting (in *E-Mmc* olim 13231).

BIBLIOGRAPHY

L. de Vega Carpio: *La Dorotea*, Biblioteca de Autores Españoles, xxxiv (1855), 68–9; *Laurel de Apolo*, ibid., xxxviii (1856), 201*a*; *El jardin de Lope* (1621), ibid., 424*a*; *La bella mal maridada* (1609), *Obras dramáticas*, iii (Madrid, 1917), 639*a*

J. Aroca, ed.: *Cancionero musical y poético del siglo XVII recogido por Claudio de la Sablonara* (Madrid, 1916), 335–6

J.F. Montesinos: 'Contribución al estudio de la lírica de Lope de Vega', *Revista de filología española*, xii (1925), 284–90

R. Benítez Claros, ed.: *Antonio Hurtado de Mendoza: Obras poéticas*, i (Madrid, 1947), 25

R.A. Pelinski: *Die weltliche Vokalmusik Spaniens am Anfang des 17. Jahrhunderts: der Cancionero Claudio de la Sablonara* (diss., U. of Munich, 1969)

G.A. Davies: *A Poet at Court: Antonio Hurtado de Mendoza (1586–1644)* (Oxford, 1971), 196, n.18

ROBERT STEVENSON/R

Palomino, José (*b* Madrid, 1755; *d* Las Palmas, 9 April 1810). Spanish composer. His skill as a violinist earned him a place in the Spanish royal chapel at an early age. A pupil of Rodríguez de Hita, he had early success composing *tonadillas*, including the popular *El canapé* (1767); these apparently attracted the Madrid nobility and some were listed among the music of the 12th Duke of Alba. In 1774 Palomino emigrated to Lisbon, where he became a member of the S Cecilia brotherhood on 21 March. By 1785 he was a 'virtuoso instrumentalist of the royal chapel'; the fine Portuguese violinist Inácio José María de Freitas was among his students. On 15 June 1785 his *serenata Il ritorno di Astrea in terra*, celebrating the double marriages of the Portuguese and Spanish *infantes*, was produced at the Spanish embassy under the auspices of the ambassador, Count Fernán Nuñez, grandee of Spain. It so delighted his audience that he was given an elegant box containing 4000 duros as well as special pensions. His intermezzos and Portuguese *entremeses* were produced in the theatres for national music, the Teatro do Salitre and Teatro de Rua dos Condes. Despite the insanity of Maria I in 1792, Palomino remained at the court, petitioning for Portuguese citizenship after '28 years of service'. According to contemporaries, he played in one of the best court orchestras in Europe; but in addition he served as orchestral leader at both theatres for national music. He left Lisbon about 1807–8 when the royal family fled the Napoleonic invasion. He accepted the post of *maestro de capilla* in Las Palmas for a salary equivalent to 20,000 reales, and died two years later.

Palomino's vocal writing is characterized by a melodic focus with little polyphony. Frequently, melodies are strung together by small rhythmic motifs. There are prominent ensemble sets, possibly influenced by his comic works such as the popular *Os amantes astutós* (*P-Ln*) and *O enganno aparente* (both 1793, for the Salitre theatre). Another *entremés* (for the Rua dos Condes), *As Regatieras zelozas* (1801; *Ln*), featured a fashionable Brazilian *modinha* (a sentimental art song).

In addition to his *serenata* (*P-Ln*, *La*), his most significant remaining work, three songs were published in the *Jornal de modhinas*, and three duets and six *modhinas* survive in manuscript (in *E-Mn* 2261). Three *tonadillas*, including *El canapé* (ed. in J. Subirá: *La tonadilla escénica*, iii, Madrid, 1930), are identified as his among manuscripts in the Biblioteca Municipal, Madrid, as well as two by

Antonio Palomino and five others ascribed merely to 'Palomino'. A four-voice motet, at Lisbon Cathedral, is his only extant sacred work. Of his instrumental works, only a concerto or quintet for keyboard and strings, an incomplete duet for violin and keyboard (both 1785; *P-Ln*) and a piano sonata (*La*) have survived.

BIBLIOGRAPHY

DBP; *GroveO* (E. Russell)

[J. Vasconcellos:]*Catalogue des livres rares composant la bibliothèque musicale d'un amateur* (Oporto, 1898), 189

J. Subirá: *La tonadilla escénica: sus obras y sus autores* (Barcelona, 1933), 51, 122–4

J. Subirá: *El Teatro del Real Palacio, 1849–1851* (Madrid, 1950), 68, 74

M.C. de Brito: *Opera in Portugal in the Eighteenth Century* (Cambridge, 1989), 72, 159

ELEANOR RUSSELL

Palotta [Pallota, Pallotta], **Matteo** ['Il Palermitano' or 'Panormitano'] (*b* ?Palermo, *c*1688; *d* Vienna, 28 March 1758). Italian composer. He probably studied music in Naples and had made a name for himself as a composer by 1720. He obtained the doctorate of theology, and became a minor canon in Palermo by 1730. In 1733 he applied for the post of composer at the imperial court in Vienna and stayed there until 1741, when he was dismissed; he was reappointed in 1749 and held the position for the rest of his life. The works composed in Vienna between 1732 and 1750, in the *stylus antiquus*, indicate that J.J. Fux and A. Caldara were his models in both choice of medium and treatment of text. Palotta wrote interestingly on liturgical composition and solmization in his *Gregoriani cantus enucleata praxis et cognitio … cum notis autographis ipsius in margine adjectis*. The treatise survives only in manuscript (*A-Wgm*) as do the masses, litanies, *Ave regina*, complines, vespers, hymns and sequences of the Vienna period (*A-Wn*, *Wgm*, *D-Bsb*). A four-part *Miserere* appears in *Sammlung ausgezeichneter Kompositionen für die Kirche*, ii (Trier, 1859).

BIBLIOGRAPHY

KöchelKHM; *WurzbachL*

F.W. Riedel: *Kirchenmusik am Hofe Karls VI. (1711–1740): Untersuchungen zum Verhältnis von Zeremoniell und musikalischem Stil im Barockzeitalter* (Munich, 1977)

R. Flotzinger and G.Grüber: *Musikgeschichte Österreichs*, ii: *Vom Barock zum Vormärz* (Vienna, 2/1995)

RENATE FEDERHOFER-KÖNIGS

Palsa, Johann (*b* Jarmeritz [now Jaroměřice], 20 June 1752; *d* Berlin, 24 Jan 1792). Bohemian horn player who specialized in *cor alto* playing. He was presumably a pupil of Joseph Matiegka (1728–1804), an eminent horn teacher in Prague (Dlabacž). In Paris in 1770, while still a teenager, Palsa formed a duo with the *cor basse* player CARL TÜRRSCHMIDT thus initiating what would become a lifelong horn-playing partnership. Between 1773 and 1781 Palsa and Türrschmidt played at the Concert Spirituel on at least 14 occasions (Pierre). In 1781 Joseph Raoux made one of his four silver *cors solo* for Palsa.

Palsa was noted for his mastery of cantabile style in the high register and praised for the beauty and purity of his tone. Forkel wrote 'One can not hear anything more beautiful than the little duets that Palsa and his partner Türrschmidt play with each other on two silver horns, especially those that are in minor keys'. As a horn duo the fame of Palsa and Türrschmidt was matched only by that of the brothers Böck. Together with Türrschmidt, Palsa wrote two sets of six horn duos opp.1–2 (Paris, by 1784) and a set of 50 op.3 (Berlin, 1795); two additional horn duets by Palsa found in *A-Sca* have been edited by J. Brand (Munich, 1990). Upon his death Palsa was replaced by Jean Lebrun (1759–c1809) as first horn (*cor alto*) in the duo.

BIBLIOGRAPHY
FétisB; DlabačžKL; GerberL; GerberNL; PierreH
J.N. Forkel: *Musikalischer Almanach für Deutschland auf das Jahr 1784* (Leipzig, 1783/R), 148–9
H.A. Eschstruth: *Musikalische Bibliothek*, i (Marburg and Giessen, 1784–5/R), 61
C.F. Ledebur: *Tonkünstler-Lexikon Berlin's* (Berlin, 1861/R), 408–9
G. Bereths: *Die Musikpflege am kurtrierischen Hofe zu Koblenz-Ehrenbreitstein* (Mainz, 1964), 98–9, 166
H. Fitzpatrick: *The Horn and Horn-Playing and the Austro-Bohemian Tradition from 1680 to 1830* (London, 1970)
R. Morley-Pegge: *The French Horn* (London, 1963, 2/1973)
S. Murray: 'The Double Horn Concerto: a Specialty of the Oettingen-Wallerstein Court', *JM*, iv (1985–6), 507–34
HORACE FITZPATRICK/THOMAS HIEBERT

Palschau, Johann Gottfried Wilhelm (*b* ?Copenhagen, 21 Dec 1741; *d* St Petersburg, 3 June/5 July 1815). German pianist and composer. The son of a musician from Holstein who played in the Royal Opera orchestra in Copenhagen, he travelled abroad on concert tours from an early age, performing in London (1754) and Hamburg (1761), and about 1771 he studied with J.G. Müthel in Riga. In 1777 he settled in St Petersburg, where he quickly found favour at court and pursued a highly successful career as a concert artist with the violinist L.P. Yershov; he was (from 1778) one of the few professional musicians in the New Music Society. As a composer he concentrated entirely on writing for the keyboard; his works include two sonatas (Nuremberg, 1762), two concertos for harpsichord and strings (Riga, 1771) and several sets of variations on Russian folktunes.

BIBLIOGRAPHY
EitnerQ; GerberL; GerberNL; MooserA
R. Kaiser: 'Palschaus Bach-Spiel in London: zur Bach-Pflege in England um 1750', *BJb 1993*, 255–9
E. Stöckl: *Musikgeschichte der Russlanddeutschen* (Dülmen, 1993), 47
GEOFFREY NORRIS/KLAUS-PETER KOCH

Pålson-Wettergren, Gertrud. *See* WETTERGREN, GERTRUD.

Pálsson, Páll P(ampichler) (*b* Graz, 9 May 1928). Icelandic composer and conductor of Austrian birth. He was a pupil of Franz Mixa, Michl and Brugger in Graz and studied conducting at the Hamburg Hochschule für Musik (1959–60). In 1949 he moved to Iceland to conduct the Reykjavík city band and play first trumpet in the Iceland SO, of which he later became assistant conductor; he was made the orchestra's permanent conductor in 1971, a position he relinquished in the late 1980s. He became director of the Reykjavík Male Choir in 1964 and in 1975 toured the USA and Canada with the Iceland Singers. He has also served as conductor and artistic director of the Reykjavík Chamber Ensemble, founded in 1974.

Recognized as an outstanding conductor, he has also distinguished himself as a prolific composer. His works, which reveal a broad range of stylistic and technical interests, include numerous Icelandic folksong arrangements for male chorus, and he shows a predilection for aleatory writing with quasi-improvisatory passages. In 1991 he was awarded the Knight's Cross of the Order of the Falcon; he is also the recipient of the Grand Honorary Medal of the District of Styria (Austria).

WORKS
(*selective list*)
Choral: Requiem, mixed chorus, 1970; Songs, male vv, 1973; 2 Limericks (Th. Valdimarsson), 1974
Orch: Suite arctica, brass band, 1969; Cl Conc., 1982; Hendur [Hands], str, 1983; Sinfonietta concertante, hn, tpt, tbn, small orch, 1988; Concerto di Giubileo, 1989; Ljáðu mér vaengi [Lend me Wings], Mez, orch, 1993; Vn Conc., 1998
Chbr: Hringspil [Rounds] I, cl, bn, vn, va, 1964; Hringspil II, 2 tpt, hn, trbn, 1965; Kristallar [Crystals], str qt, ww qnt, 1970; Mixed Things, fl, pf, 1976

BIBLIOGRAPHY
A. Burt: *Iceland's Twentieth-Century Composers and a Listing of their Works* (Annandale, VA, 1975, 2/1977)
G. Bergendal: *New Music in Iceland* (Reykjavík, 1991)
M. Podhajski: *Dictionary of Icelandic Composers* (Warsaw, 1997)
AMANDA M. BURT/R

Palumbo, Costantino (*b* Torre Annunziata, nr Naples, 30 Nov 1843; *d* Naples, 15 Jan 1926). Italian pianist and composer. With Beniamino Cesi and Giuseppe Martucci he represented the international success of the Neapolitan piano school. In 1854 he entered the Naples Conservatory, where he studied composition with Mercadante and the piano with Francesco Lanza and Michelangelo Russo.

When still very young he embarked on a brilliant concert career and appeared in the principal cities in Italy and abroad. In Paris he met Rossini and was a regular visitor to his salon, receiving the older man's praise and affection. After returning to Italy he won success for his original style of playing, and as a result was appointed to teach the piano at the Naples Conservatory from 1873, and to be the principal pianist involved in the celebrations in Florence in honour of Bartolomeo Cristofori (1876). He had contacts with the leading musicians of his day, including Francesco Florimo, Thalberg and Boito (who provided the libretto for his opera *Pier Luigi Farnese*), and held an important position in Neapolitan musical life until the end of the century, when he withdrew from public appearances.

His main significance lies in having contributed, through the broadening of his own concert repertory, to a modernization of taste in instrumental music. His repertory ranged from works written for the harpsichord (his transcriptions for piano include an otherwise forgotten concerto by Francesco Durante) to the music of the Romantic school – at the time still a novelty for Neapolitan audiences – and the fashionable fantasias on opera themes and salon music. While he owed his popularity to the latter, at the same time he attempted to revitalize his own idiom in compositions involving other forces by taking his inspiration from music from the past or choosing unusual instrumental combinations.

WORKS
(*selective list*)
printed works published in Naples unless otherwise stated

OPERAS
Maria Stuart (E. Golisciani), Naples, S Carlo, 23 April 1874
Pier Luigi Farnese (A. Boito), 1891, unperf.

PIANO SOLO
Tarantella, op.7 (1864); Ballata, op.10 (c1864; previously pubd as op.15); Toccata, op.21 (c1865); Mazurka, op.23 (c1867); 3 nocturnes, opp.35–8 (1871); 3 preludes and fugues, opp.49–51 (1873); Barcarola, op.71 (1876); Serenata, op.76 (1879)
Fantasias and variations: Carnevale di Napoli, op.1 (c1863); on Verdi's La traviata, op.5 (c1865); on F. Halévy's La Juive, op.16 (c1865); on Meyerbeer's L'Africaine, opp.20, 22 (c1865); Brezze

di Napoli, op.27 (c1870); on Verdi's Aida, opp.46–7 (1872); Saluto a Napoli, op.52 (c1873); on Gounod's Faust, op.60 (c1875) Transcrs. (in *I-Nc*): L. Leo: Arietta; F. Durante: pf conc.

OTHER WORKS

Vocal: Studio sulla Divina Commedia, sonata-fantasia, pf, chorus, tpt, trbn, cimb, timp (Milan, 1892); Mater dolorosa, preghiera meditazione, solo vv, choruses, orch, *I-Nc*; Qui tollis, A, chorus, orch, *Nc*

Inst: Rama, sym. poem, orch (c1900); Pf Conc., *Nc*; Sonata, vn, pf, *Nc*

BIBLIOGRAPHY

DEUMM; *FétisB*; *FlorimoN*; *SchmidlD*

M.C. Caputo: *Annuario con note biografico-storiche* (Naples, 1875)

A. Longo: 'Costantino Palumbo', *Arte pianistica*, i/7 (1914), 1–2

G. Napoli: 'Costantino Palumbo', *Vita musicale italiana*, xv/2 (1928), 5–6

V. Vitale: *Il pianoforte a Napoli nell'Ottocento* (Naples, 1983)

F. Esposito and G. Olivieri: 'L'attività pianistica a Napoli al tempo di Alessandro Longo: Costantino Palumbo', *Alessandro Longo: Amantea 1995* (forthcoming)

FRANCESCO ESPOSITO

Paluselli, Stefan [Johann Anton] (*b* Kurtatsch, South Tyrol, 9 Jan 1748; *d* Stams, Oberinntal, 27 Feb 1805). Austrian composer and choirmaster. A member of the Cistercian order. His musical talent led him to be accepted as a boarder at the St Nikolaihaus in Innsbruck around 1760, where the students were maintained free of charge and performed as choristers or instrumentalists in the university church choir. At the same time he attended the Innsbruck Gymnasium; after concluding his studies there, in 1768 he probably studied philosophy at the University of Innsbruck. In 1770 his Singspiel *Das alte deutsche Wörtlein Tut* was performed at the Gymnasium theatre. In the same year he entered the abbey of Stams, notable for its cultivation of music. He devoted himself to the study of theology and in 1774 he was ordained a priest in Bressanone. He became violin teacher to the abbey school in 1785 and was promoted to head music instructor and choirmaster in 1791.

About 1790 he developed a solmization system for teaching the choirboys at Stams which resembled the system constructed by Agnes Hundoegger in Germany a century later. However, like his work as a whole, it did not have wide influence.

Paluselli was one of the most notable musical personalities of 18th-century Tyrol. Even his early works exhibit the strong personal style that elevates his music above that of other monastic composers. In his secular and sacred works alike he sometimes followed traditional models but at other times displayed unique approaches to the sequence of movements, internal form and text setting. Both in melodic construction and form he prefers an aggregation of small units to large-scale thematic design and development. His music is occasionally reminiscent of Vivaldi. Other characteristics include passages in a folk idiom, finely nuanced rhythmic writing and a certain musical playfulness for which he had a special gift. He also contributed to the development of programmatic music, in particular with his *Soggetti diversi*.

WORKS
all MSS in A-ST, unless otherwise stated

VOCAL

Secular: Das alte deutsche Wörtlein Tut (Spl), Innsbruck, Gymnasium, 1770, lib *A- Imf*; Die Freude der Herde (Musica, V. Siller), Stams, 1775 rev. 1792; Der Zoll (Operetta), Stams, 1778; Das Opfer der Gärtner (Spl), Stams, 1780; Die Weintraube in der Torkel (Spl/orat), Stams, 1781; Der Musikfreund, Stams, 1783; Pastorum candidati (cant.), Stams, 1789; Die Hirtenfeier (Spl),

Stams, 1783; Das frohlockende Stams (T. Voglsanger), Stams, 1790; Diana et Ursus (Musica, Voglsanger), Stams, 1802; Freudengefühle des Stiftes Stams, Stams, 1804; other occasional cants.

Sacred: 6 masses, 1 lost: c100 other works, incl. grads, offs, ants, hymns, resps, seqs; Christmas cant., c1773, *Imf*, *ST*, *CH-E*; Lieder, duets; chorus in Edmund Angerer: Der wieder aufblühende Garten und Weinberg (orat), c1780

INSTRUMENTAL

Orch: divertimento, D; divertimento, F, ob, str, ed. in DTÖ, lxxxvi (1949/R); partita, D; Partita gran rumore, D; Musica seu parthia; serenata for 13 insts, D; sonata for 6 insts, B♭; Synphonia, B♭; scherzo, D; La simplicità, D; Balletto pastorale, dances

Chbr: Quadro, 2 vn, va, vc, c1775; Bourlesca, La confusione, La curiosità, Fantasia, Fuga ariosa, all 2 vn, b, c1775; divertimento da camera, E♭; Galanterie, 2 vn, va, 2 hn, b, c1770; Cassatio, 2 fl, 2 va, b, c1770; divertimento, C, 2 fl, 2 ob, 2 hn, b, c1790

Hpd: [70] Soggetti diversi, c1800

BIBLIOGRAPHY

Registrum Musicalum Stamsensius, 1791 -after 1800, *A-ST*

W. Senn: Introduction to DTÖ, lxxxvi (1949/R), pp.xivff

H. Post: *Schuelmayster, Cantores und Singknaben im Landt im Geping* (Innsbruck, 1993)

H. Herrmann-Schneider: 'Registrum Musicalium Stamsesnium 1791', *Eines Fürsten Traum, Meinhard II.: das Werden Tirols*, Tiroler Landesausstellung, 1995 (Innsbruck, 1995), 569–70 [exhibition catalogue]

H. Herrmann-Schneider: *Die Musikhandschriften der Zisterzienser-Abtei Stams: Thematischer Katalog* (forthcoming)

WALTER SENN, HILDEGARD HERRMANN-SCHNEIDER

Paluskar, Vishnu Digambar (*b* Kurundwad, 1872; *d* 1931). North Indian (Hindustani) classical music vocalist. He was the son of a *kīrtankār* (performer of religious discourses) in Kurundwad and was educated in an English-medium school. In 1887 his eyesight was damaged by firecrackers and he was removed from school to begin musical training with Balkrishna Buwa of the Gwalior *gharānā*. He became sensitized to the difference between his social status and that of his teacher and was determined to improve the status of musicians.

In 1897 Paluskar advocated public performance in order to make classical music widely accessible and to provide a means for musicians to earn a livelihood independent of rich patrons. In 1901 he founded the Gandharva Mahāvidyālaya, the first Indian music institution underwritten by public sources. To support it Paluskar lectured and gave concerts, tailoring performances to include patriotic songs, folksongs and devotional compositions along with classical vocal music. He also introduced *tablā taraṅg*, the use of a set of *tablā* drums tuned to a series of pitches.

In 1908 the main school shifted to Bombay and regular syllabuses, texts, examinations and performances were instituted, the latter including public appearances by female students from middle- and upper-class families. Opening music training to 'respectable' females effectively revolutionized the reception of classical music in India. In 1911 Paluskar received the consent of the Governor of Bombay to confer the degrees of *Saṅgīt Praveśikā* after four years and *Saṅgīt Pravīṇ* after five years. The school has grown to incorporate more than 25 branches.

Paluskar's legacy was and is continued by important musicians and teachers such as Narayan Rao Vyas, Vinayak Rao Patwardhan, B.R. Deodhar, Omkarnath Thakur and Vinay Chandra Maudgalya.

BIBLIOGRAPHY

V.R. Athavale: *Pandit Vishnu Digambar* (New Delhi, 1967)

G.M. Ranade: *Music in Maharashtra* (New Delhi, 1967)

V.R. Athavale: 'The Source of Inspiration behind Pandit Paluskar's Contribution to Music', *Journal of the Indian Musicological Society*, vii/1 (1976), 14–21

B.C. Wade: *Khyāl: Creativity within North India's Classical Vocal Tradition* (Cambridge, 1984)

BONNIE C. WADE

Paminger [Päminger, Panninger], **Leonhard** (*b* Aschach an der Donau, 25 March 1495; *d* Passau, 3 May 1567). Austrian composer, poet and theologian. He was the son of a court official of the Count of Schaumburg. From 1505 he received a humanist education in Vienna, and after staying briefly in Aschach and Salzburg he matriculated at Vienna University in the summer of 1513. During his three years' study he earned a living as a bass in the Stadtkantorei of the Stephansdom and taught himself composition. In 1516 he settled in Passau, where he became schoolmaster of St Nikola in about 1517 and Rektor in 1529. At about this time, he copied the choirbook *D-Bsb* Mus.ms.40024. He apparently lost the position of Rektor in 1557 because he had adopted Lutheran beliefs, but he remained as secretary until his death. He was held in high esteem by his contemporaries and was closely associated with influential figures of the Reformation including Martin Luther and Philipp Melanchthon. At Passau he came into contact with theologians, physicians and philosophers. In this milieu he established a reputation not only as a composer, but also as an author. Three of his sons – Balthasar (*b* ?Passau, *c*1523; *d* ?Passau, 23 Jan 1546), Sophonias (*b* Passau, 5 Feb 1526; *d* Nuremberg, July 1603) and Sigismund (*b* Passau, 1539; *d* Seitenstetten, Lower Austria, 24 Feb 1571) – were also writers and composers.

Paminger was one of the most important of the early Lutheran composers who combined the style of Josquin's successors with the native German style. He won international recognition early in his career and his works were included in French and Italian anthologies. Apart from a few German secular songs, his works consist mainly of settings of Latin antiphons, responsories, psalms, hymns and Propers, and German Protestant hymns. Most numerous among his works are the cantus firmus free motets, in which passages of free counterpoint alternate with imitative polyphony. The use of paired imitation anticipates *cori spezzati* techniques. Traces of the technical virtuosity of composers such as Ockeghem and Josquin are found in, for example, the 16-voice canon in *In profunditatem*. Several motets on biblical texts include quodlibets, a compositional practice that evidently formed part of the Lutheran liturgical tradition. The five-voice setting of the Gospel narrative of the Nativity *Exiit edictum a Caesare Augusto*, for example, incorporates five Christmas hymns. In the cantus firmus motets, canonic techniques and imitation are less widely used; a notable exception is the double crab canon on *Vexilla regis prodeunt*. The adoption of portions of the Proper into the Lutheran liturgy accounts for Paminger's settings of introits, alleluias, sequences and *prosae*. Here too canonic techniques are evident. In the songs, the replacement of the original Latin texts with German texts is indicative of Paminger's stance towards the Reformation. Four volumes of his projected ten-volume edition of Protestant hymns were published after his death; they contain over 680 works. The remaining six volumes were to have included masses, *Magnificat* settings, biblical stories, dedicatory pieces, bicinia and tricinia; these unpublished compositions are lost.

WORKS

Primus tomus ecclesiasticarum cantionum, a prima dominica adventus, usque ad passionem … Jesu Christi, 4–6 and more vv (Nuremberg, 1573)

Secundus tomus ecclesiasticarum cantionum, a passione … Jesu Christi, usque ad primam dominicam post festum Santa Trinitatis, 4–6 and more vv (Nuremberg, 1573)

Tertius tomus ecclesiasticarum cantionum, a prima dominica post festum Santa Trinitatis, usque ad primam dominicam adventus … Jesu Christi, 4–6 and more vv (Nuremberg, 1576)

Quartus tomus ecclesiasticarum cantionum, 4–6 and more vv (Nuremberg, 1580)

12 motets, 1537[1], 1538[2], 1538[3], 1538[6], 1539[6], 1542[6], 1553[4], 1553[5], 1558[4], 1559[1], 1559[2], 1560[2], 1564[5], 1568[7]

9 Ger. hymns, 1560[2]

3 Ger. songs, 1544[19], 1544[20], 1556[29]

WRITINGS

Trans. of 13 comedies by Plautus, Terence, Macropedius and others, lost

Criticisms of Papists, Anti-Papists, Sacramentarians and the Adversaries of the 'Pure Doctrine' of the Sun of God, lost

Ein schön Gebet Leonharten Paemingerzu Gott dem Heiligen Geist 'O Herre Gott, heiliger Geist', incl. in *Ein schön kurzweilig und nützes Hochzeitsgespräch* (see below)

Epitaphia secundum Germanicum et Latinum in obitu Rosinae coniugis filii Sophoniae

Dialogus oder Gesprech eines Christen mit einem Widertauffer (1567)

Kurtzer Bericht von den Coruptelen und Irthumen, die Gegenwertigkeit, des waren leibes und bluts, unsers HERRN und Hailandes Jesu Christi im heiligen Abendmal belangende (Regensburg, 1567)

Ein schön kurzweilig und nützes Hochzeitsgespräch vierer Ehefrauen, wie man den hlg. Ehestand mit Gottesfurcht anfangen, christlich und einig darinnen leben sol. (1578)

BIBLIOGRAPHY

C.C. Hirsch: *De vita Pamingerorum commentarius* (Oettingen, 1764–7)

K. Weinmann: 'Leonhard Paminger', *KJb*, xx (1907), 122–35

K. Schiffmann: 'Leonhard Paminger aus Aschach an der Donau', *Linzer Tages-Post: Unterhaltungsbeilage*, viii (1909), 50

I. Roth: *Leonhard Paminger: ein Beitrag zur deutschen Musikgeschichte des 16. Jahrhunderts* (Munich, 1935)

G. Pätzig: 'Das Chorbuch Mus. ms. 40024 der Deutschen Staatsbibliothek Berlin: eine wichtige Quelle zum Schaffen Isaacs aus der Hand Leonhard Pämingers', *Festschrift Walter Gestenberg*, ed. G. von Dadelsen and A. Holschneider (Wolfenbüttel, 1964), 122–42

C. Meyer: '*Vexilla regis prodeunt*: un canon énigmatique de Leonhard Paminger', *Festschrift Christoph-Hellmut Mahling*, ed. A. Beer, K. Pfarr and W. Ruf (Tutzing, 1977), 909–17

OTHMAR WESSELY/WALTER KREYSZIG

Pampani, Antonio Gaetano (*b* Modena, *c*1705; *d* Urbino, Dec 1775). Italian composer. Until the late 1730s librettos and other sources often identified him as Pampino or Pampini. While Eitner's belief that these spellings designate two composers is probably incorrect, the existence of an older Antonio Pampini might explain the occurrence of a Pampini in Fermo as late as 1748 (according to Paolucci) when the composer under consideration was already engaged at the Ospedaletto in Venice. On the other hand, Fétis's statement that Pampani died in Venice in 1769 is without foundation. That his birthplace was Florence (Paolucci) or Romagna (*La BordeE*) may be rejected; printed librettos of several Venetian works indicate Modena.

The earliest reference to Pampani relates that when elected *maestro di cappella* of Fano Cathedral on 18 July 1726 he was unable to assume duties promptly because he was engaged at the opera in Urbino. How long he had been in Urbino is not told, but the Fano documents mention that he studied with [?Filippo] Salviati there.

Some time after coming to Fano, he began directing the orchestra of the Teatro del Sole in Pesaro and providing occasional arias (e.g. for Bononcini's *Crispo*, 1730) as well as intermezzos (*Delbo mal maritato*, 1730). After his resignation from Fano Cathedral in late July 1734, he conducted in Pesaro at least until autumn 1737, and composed two operas for Venice (1735, 1737) and three oratorios for Fermo and Macerata (1739, 1740). Between 1740 and 1746, when he again wrote an oratorio for Fermo, he seems to have stopped composing: no known works belong to the intervening years while he was, possibly, *maestro di cappella* of Fermo Cathedral (as an aria of 1738 in *I-Tn* and the libretto of 1746 indicate).

Pampani's acceptance as member of the Accademia Filarmonica of Bologna in 1746 marked a turning-point in his career. A considerable number of major works appeared during the ensuing decade. For the opera houses of Venice and major theatres of Rome, Milan and Turin he wrote an *opera seria* annually. As director of the celebrated chorus and orchestra of the Poveri Derelitti (also known as the Ospedaletto) in Venice he composed oratorios, groups of solo motets (for solo soprano and solo alto with orchestral accompaniment), and other sacred music for women's chorus, along with violin and cello concertos for performance at vesper services (often marked specifically for the Assumption) between 1749 and 1764. The libretto for a revival in 1765 of his oratorio *L'innocenza rispettata* at the oratorio of S Filippo Neri in Venice still identifies Pampani as *maestro* of the Ospedaletto, but in the following year Tommaso Traetta directed his own oratorio (*Rex Salomon*, 15 August 1766) as the institution's new *maestro*. On 27 December 1767 Pampani was named *maestro di cappella* of Urbino Cathedral but was excused from duties until 1 July 1768 in order to supervise the production in May of *Demetrio*, his last opera for Venice. Giuseppe Gazzaniga assumed his position at Urbino in late December 1775, shortly after Pampani's death.

Almost nothing is known about Pampani's personal life. The manuscript score of a symphony (*B-Bc*) identifies him as 'abbate' but no other source so names him. A certain Teresa Fortunata Pampino, who appeared in his first opera for Venice (*L'Anagilda*, 1735), may prove to be a relative, perhaps his wife.

WORKS

DRAMATIC

opere serie unless otherwise stated

Delbo mal maritato (int), Pesaro, Sole, 1730
L'Anagilda (A. Zaniboni), Venice, S Cassiano, carn. 1735, *D-Wa*
Sedecia, Ascoli, 1736, lib *I-AP*
Artaserse Longimano (P. Metastasio: *Temistocle*), Venice, S Angelo, carn. 1737
Siroe (?pasticcio, ?Metastasio), Ferrara, 1738
Semiramide riconosciuta, Fermo, 1741, lib *FERc*, arias *Fc*
La caduta d'Amulio (C. Gandini), Venice, S Angelo, carn. 1746
La clemenza di Tito (Metastasio), Venice, S Cassiano, carn. 1748, arias *F-Pn*
Adriano in Siria (Metastasio), Milan, Ducal, carn. 1750
Artaserse (Metastasio), Venice, S Giovanni Grisostomo, carn. 1750, arias *GB-Lbl, I-MAav, MOe, Nc, Vc*
Venceslao (A. Zeno), Venice, S Cassiano, carn. 1752
Andromaca (A. Salvi), Rome, Argentina, carn. 1753, arias *GB-Lbl, I-Rsc*, pasticcio collab. A. Aurisicchio
Madama Dulcinea, o Tiberio cuoco del maestro del bosco (int), Pesaro, Sole, carn. 1753
Eurione (A. Papi), Rome, Capranica, 8 Jan 1754, arias *GB-Lbl*
Astianatte (Salvi), Venice, S Moisè, carn. 1755, aria *I-MOe*
Antigono (Metastasio), Turin, Regio, 26 Dec 1757, arias *Tf*

Demofoonte (Metastasio), Rome, Dame, carn. 1757, scores *P-La*, arias *D-RH, GB-Lbl, I-Rc*
L'olimpiade [Act 2] (Metastasio), Venice, S Benedetto, 26 Dec 1766, score *P-La*, arias *I-Fc* [Act 1 by P.A. Guglielmi, Act 3 by Brusa]
Il Demetrio (Metastasio), Venice, S Benedetto, Ascension 1768, score *P-La*, arias *I-Tf*
Insertion arias in G. Bononcini's Crispo, Pesaro, Sole, carn. 1730
Insertion aria in Vivaldi's Rosmira fedele, Venice, 1738, *Tn*
Arias from unidentified ops in *CH-E, EN; D-Bsb, Dl, DS, EB, Mbs, SWl; F-Pn; GB-Lam, Lbl, Lcm; I-Af, Fc, MAav, MOe, Nc, Vc; US-BEm*

ORATORIOS

S Maurizio e compagni martiri, Perugia, S. Marianuova, 1738, score and parts *I-Vsmc*
Assalonne (O. Turchi), Fermo, 1739
L'obbedienza di Gionata, 1739, score *D-Mbs*
Ester (G.C. Cordara), Mandola, 1740, lib *I-Vgc*
Il Giefte, Fermo, S Filippo, 1746, 'con intermezzi'
La vocazione di S Francesco d'Assisi (A. Scardarilla), Gubbio, 1749, lib *Ma*
L'innocenza rispettata, Venice, Oratorio di S Filippo Neri, 1749, score and parts *Vsmc*
Messiae praeconium carmine complexum, Venice, Poveri Derelitti, 1754
Sofonea id est Joseph pro Rex Aegypti, Venice, Poveri Derelitti, 1755
Triumphus Judith, Venice, Poveri Derelitti, 1757 [lib incl. motet texts]
La morte di Abele (Metastasio), Venice, Accademia Filarmonica, 22 March 1758
Prophetiae evangelicae ac mors Isaiae, Venice, Poveri Derelitti, 1760 [lib incl. motet texts]
Pro solemni die BMV, Venice, Poveri Derelitti, 1764 [lib incl. motet texts]
Amor divino e Urbana (cant. a 2), ?Urbino, 1768, *URBcap**

MOTETS FOR SOLO SOPRANO OR ALTO AND ORCHESTRA
all composed for the Poveri Derelitti; published librettos dated 1747–61 give groups of texts

Ab impio venatore; Ad solem eja; Affectus ardentes; Affectus fallaces; Affectus terrenus; Agitatae furibundae; Ah tu barbara, crudelis; Aquilo, surge et veni; Aquila volitando; A somno cessate; A venatoris telo Gemebunda; Barbara gens ingrata; Canite buccina; Canoro concentu; Carae venite ad fontem; Coeli laetantes chori mundi; Coelo tonante pavet afflictum cor; Columba adorata; De matutino; De monte virenti; Dente rabido lethali
Dum fugat astra Aurora, Dum Philomela in ramo; Dum vivo, maris unda; Ecce furiae debaccando; Ecce Ramus a decora; Ecce signum; Excitata, sum comprehensa; Exeant ab imo; Exit ursa rapta prole; Fluctus inter agitata; Fugendo a reo crudeli; Fuge sol, atro, pallore; Fulgura, o Deus, a coelo; Hoc est regnum umbrae mortis; Horti clausi folia; Imagines laetae; In scuto potenti; In vertice fumante; In voce laetabunda; In voce modulata; Laeta ridens maris unda; Laeta sum jucunda nimis
Lux serena; Mare fremit in procella; Me jactat haec unda in ventre; Modo in uno; Montes alti; Morde terram; Oh fulgida Aurora; O Jesu clemens; O quam laeta; Pede tremente fugio; Placida surge aurora; Properate vos micando; Pueri omnes; Pugnat, exardet aether; Puro affectu; Qualis excitat; Quid hoc est rei?; Quot ver explicuit flores; Recede sol ab axe; Recessit aura rigida; Reflorente amoeno aprili
Sacra tempora dilecti rosae; Scandit astra, virgo excelsa; Sibilant venti in mari; Sit avernus in furore; Sole petente occasum nimbo; Squallida, inculta; Strident venti; Sum agitata in mente; Sum navis agitata; Surge, o pastor; Tace, non audio te; Tubae sono; Tu rapida è coelo; Unda fremit; Vade repente; Video lucentes vias; Vocat agnus; Vos detestor
Fra l'orror ovunque io miro, cant., S, orch, org, *D-F*; Mira in quanto horrore, 2vv, orch; Sagittas hostis mei, 2vv, orch

OTHER SACRED WORKS
PD – *Venice, Poveri Derelitti*

Messa a più voci, 1764, *I-URBcap*
Mag, PD, 1748, 1749, 1753, 1756, 1757, 1761, 1764 [*D-Dl*, n.d.], undated, *Bsb**
Pss: Confitebor tibi à 4, PD, 17 May 1756, *CH-E* [*I-URBcap**]; De profundis, *D-DS*; Dixit Dominus, PD, 1753, *Dl*; In convertendo Dominus à 4, *Bsb*; Lauda Jerusalem, PD, 1764; Laudate pueri, PD, 1742 [*I-Rrostirolla**] 1748, 1749, 24 Sept 1753 [*I-URBcap**],

1754, 1756, 1761, 1764; Laetatus sum, PD, 1761; Nisi Dominus, PD, 1748, 1753, 1761, 1764, *I-Rrostirolla*
Hymns: Pange lingua à 3, *P-La*; Sicut erat à 4, 1746; Tantum ergo à 8, *D-DS*; Tantum ergo à 5, *I-Rrostirolla*
Ants: 8 Salve regina, 1v, orch, PD; Domine probasti à 4, PD, 14 Aug 1764, *I-URBcap**
Sicut erat in principio, 4vv, bc, *Baf**
Pietà mio Dio, canone, 3vv, *BGi*

INSTRUMENTAL

Sonata, hpd, in J.U. Haffner, Raccolta musicale, ii (Nuremberg, *c*1750)
2 sonatas, e, D, hpd, *I-Bsf*; Sonata, G, hpd, *Bc*; 3 sonatas, F, G, G, hpd, *Fc*; Sonata, hpd, *D-Dl*, according to Eitner
Conc., G, hpd, orch, *I-Bc*; 3 concs., *D-DS*, according to Eitner; concs. 3 for vn, vc and va d'amore, lost, cited in printed libs of the Poveri Derelitti dated 1747, 1748, 1749, 1753, 1754, 1755, 1757, 1758
Allegro, E♭, F, hpd, *GB-Lbl*; Toccata, D, org, *I-Bc*; Sym., D, *B-Bc*, *I-BGc*; Sym., G, *Vlevi*; Fuga à 4, 1746, *Baf*; Capriccio, F, hpd, *Fc*

BIBLIOGRAPHY

EitnerQ; FétisB; GerberNL; La BordeE; MGG1 (P. Kast); *ScheringGO; SmitherHO*, i
Salmi che si cantano in tutti li vesperi (Venice, 1752)
G.B. Martini: *Serie cronologica de' principi dell' Accademia de' Filarmonici di Bologna* (Bologna, 1776/R), 31
Raccolta di cose sacre chi si soglio cantare … Poveri Derelitti (Venice, 1777)
C. Baccili: *Il teatro di Fermo* (Recanati, 2/1886), 36
C. Cinelli: *Memorie cronistoriche del Teatro di Pesaro dall'anno 1637 al 1897* (Pesaro, 1898), 51, 53, 56
B. Ligi: *La cappella musicale del duomo di Urbino*, NA, ii (1925)
R. Paolucci: 'La cappella musicale del duomo di Fano', *NA*, iii (1926), 81–168, esp. 130; iv (1927), 100–15

SVEN HANSELL (with LUISELLA MOLINA)

Pampanini, Rosetta (*b* Milan, 2 Sept 1896; *d* Corbola, nr Rovigo, 2 Aug 1973). Italian soprano. A pupil of Emma Molajoli, she made her début in 1920 at the Teatro Nazionale, Rome, as Micaëla in *Carmen*. She was then heard at the S Carlo, Naples (1923), at the Comunale, Bologna (1923–4) and at La Scala (1925) in *Madama Butterfly*, conducted by Toscanini; she returned there until 1930 and again between 1934 and 1937. She sang in the leading Italian theatres and appeared at the Colón, Buenos Aires (1926), at Covent Garden (1928) in *Madama Butterfly* and *Pagliacci* and as Liù in *Turandot*, returning there in 1929 and 1933, at the Berlin Städtische Oper (1929), at the Chicago Civic Opera (1931–2) and at the Paris Opéra (1935). Pampanini's pure, natural voice was full of warmth and brilliance, with a strong, resonant top register; she was considered one of the world's leading Puccini sopranos between 1925 and 1940, partly because of the variety of colour and inflection she brought to the utterances of Mimì, Cio-Cio-San and Manon, partly because of the grace and simplicity of her bearing. She was also admired in *Andrea Chénier*, *Iris* and *Tosca*. After she retired in 1946 she taught singing in Milan; Amy Shuard and Victoria Elliott were among her pupils.

BIBLIOGRAPHY

ES (R. Celletti); *GV* (R. Celletti; R. Vegeto)
W. Moran, ed.: *Herman Klein and the Gramophone* (Portland, OR, 1990)

RODOLFO CELLETTI/R

Pamphili, Benedetto (*b* Rome, 25 April 1653; *d* Rome, 22 March 1730). Italian patron and librettist. His immense wealth was largely derived from a pension granted by his great-uncle, Pope Innocent X, his salary as Grand Prior in Rome of the Knights of Malta from 1678, and his benefices as a cardinal from 1 September 1681. His literary gifts are reflected in his post as *principe* of the Accademia degli Umoristi in Rome (by 1677) and his 'acclamation' as Fenicio Larisseo in the Arcadian Academy (12 May 1695). His fascination with oratorios is manifested by his protectorship of two organizations that produced them, the Collegio Clementino (1689–1730) and the Arciconfraternita del SS Crocifisso (1694–1724). Pamphili's *maestri di musica* were Alessandro Melani (*c*1676–*c*1681), Lulier (1681–90) and Cesarini (1690–1730). From 1684 to 1690 his most highly paid instrumentalist was Corelli, who (like Lulier) chose not to follow him to Bologna, where he was papal legate from August 1690 to October 1693. Pamphili's financial records name many other instrumentalists and composers whom he regularly employed, including Pasquini (1677–*c*1710), Amadei (1685–1708) and Handel (1707). His musicians played for the occasional oratorios and weekly 'academies' that he began to sponsor in 1677.

During Pamphili's creative years all the popes except Alexander VIII (who sent him to Bologna) successfully restricted or banned public opera performances in Rome. This may well explain why Pamphili wrote mainly oratorios and cantatas. His oratorio productions in Rome were sumptuous, as witnessed by the number of instrumentalists: 32 for Scarlatti's *Il trionfo della gratia* (1685) and 60 for Lulier's *S Maria Maddalena de' pazzi* (1687). The same was true for oratorios he sponsored. He is never named as librettist in Roman editions, but those printed elsewhere between 1678 and 1729 sometimes do name him. His 88 cantata texts (in *I-Rvat* Vat.lat.10205–6) range widely in subject matter and were undoubtedly written for his weekly academies. Among the composers who set his cantata and oratorio texts are G.M. Bononcini, D.F. Bottari, C.F. Cesarini, V. Chicheri, Severo De Luca, C. Foschi, Francesco Gasparini, G.F. Handel, G.L. Lulier, Alessandro Melani, F.A. Messi, Bernado Pasquini, N. Romaldi, C. Rotondi, D.N. Sarri and Alessandro Scarlatti.

BIBLIOGRAPHY

SartoriL
P. Mandosio: *Bibliotheca romana seu romanorum scriptorum centuriae*, i (Rome, 1682), 325–6
L. Zambarelli: *Il nobile pontificio Collegio Clementino di Roma* (Rome, 1936)
L. Montalto: *Un mecenate in Roma barocca: il cardinale Benedetto Pamphili (1653–1730)* (Florence, 1955)
R.L. Weaver: 'Materiali per le biografie dei fratelli Melani', *RIM*, xii (1977), 252–95
R. Bossa: 'Corelli e il cardinal Benedetto Pamphilj: alcune notizie', *Nuovissimi studi corelliani: Fusignano 1980*, 211–23
C. Annibaldi: 'L'archivio musicale Doria Pamphili: saggio sulla cultura aristocratica a Roma fra 16° e 19° secolo', *Studi musicali*, xi (1982), 91–120, 277–344
H.J. Marx: 'Die "Giustificazioni della Casa Pamphilij" als musikgeschichtliche Quelle', *Studi musicali*, xii (1983), 121–87
H.J. Marx: 'Händel in Rom: seine Beziehung zu Benedetto Card. Pamphilj', *HJb*, xxix (1983), 107–18
A. Morelli: 'Il *Theatro spirituale* ed altre raccolte di testi per oratori romani del Seicento', *RIM*, xxi (1986), 61–143
S. Franchi: *Drammaturgia romana: repertorio bibliografico cronologico dei testi drammatici pubblicati a Roma e nel Lazio, secolo XVII* (Rome, 1988)
G. Staffieri: *Colligite fragmenta: la vita musicale romana negli 'Avvisi Marescotti' (1683–1707)* (Lucca, 1990)
A. Morelli: '*Il tempio armonico*: musica nell'Oratorio dei Filippini in Roma (1575–1705)', AnMc, no.27 (1991)

LOWELL LINDGREN

Pamphilon, Edward (*b* before 1615; *fl c*1660–90). English violin maker. Although most authorities place his workshop on London Bridge, there is no clear evidence of this. The Pamphilon family, which includes four other violin makers, was active in the Essex villages of Widdington, Little Hadham and Clavering in the 17th and 18th centuries. Edward Pamphilon's instruments certainly found their way to the shop of the music seller John Miller on London Bridge, where they were labelled and sold. Original labels are rare, and do not specify the place of origin; one gives a date of 1684, and another is very precise, specifying a date of 3 April 1685. Most labels were presumably removed by later dealers to facilitate the resale of Pamphilon's violins as more valuable Brescian instruments. The instruments do, in fact, bear a close resemblance to earlier Brescian work, having a high build and rather crude workmanship, but they differ in several features: the ribs are set into a slot cut around the inner edge of the back, the belly and the sides of the neck root; and the neck root protrudes into the soundbox. This construction method is also characteristic of Flemish makers of the time. The scroll is distinctive, decorated with small punch marks around the turns of the volute. The instruments sometimes have a very high-quality varnish, at first glance easily mistaken for Italian.

JOHN DILWORTH

Pan. God of the Greeks and Romans. He was native to Arcadia, a mountainous rural region in the Peloponnese, where shepherding was a major occupation. His father was Hermes, the only other important Arcadian god and the mythological inventor of the lyre. He had the torso and head of a man and the legs, tail and horns of a goat. His attributes were primarily musical and amorous, the latter association stemming from the shepherd's desire for flock fertility. In the 5th century BCE his cult spread to Athens, and subsequently to other urban areas of Greece and Rome, where he symbolized pastoral love, revelry and musicality. Pictorially he was shown in the company of nymphs, satyrs, Dionysus and the Muses, sometimes dancing and at other times playing the aulos or more often the syrinx. Cassiodorus and Isidore of Seville attributed to him the invention of a wind instrument called the pandoura.

In mythology he was the subject of two musical myths, both of which are related in Ovid's *Metamorphoses*: the story of his invention of the panpipes (i.689–712; *see* SYRINX) and the story of his musical contest with Phoebus Apollo (xi.153–79). In the latter, a variant of the musical contest between Apollo and Marsyas (*see* AULOS), Pan with his syrinx brashly challenges Apollo with his kithara. Apollo's art is superior, but Midas, one of the judges, prefers Pan's and as a punishment is made to grow ass's ears. Bach celebrated the myth in his *dramma per musica Der Streit zwischen Phoebus und Pan* BWV201.

BIBLIOGRAPHY

M. Jost: 'Pan', *The Oxford Classical Dictionary*, ed. S. Hornblower and A. Spawforth (Oxford, 3/1996)
G. Wille: *Musica romana* (Amsterdam, 1967), 525–8

JAMES W. McKINNON

Pan playing the panpipes, with a sackbut and recorder (right) and racket, cornett and bass recorder (left): ivory carving (1618–24) by Christoph Angermaier (Bayerisches Nationalmuseum, Munich)

Pan-African Orchestra. Orchestra founded in 1988 in Accra, Ghana, under the leadership of its conductor and founder Nana Danso Abiam. The orchestra of approximately 28 instrumentalists is guided by a creative and practical philosophy that calls for a return to indigenous traditions and resources. The leader integrates music, musical instruments and performers from various ethnic groups and from various African countries; financial limitations constrain the hiring and use of musicians and musical instruments from several African countries, however. The Ghanaian government, especially the Commission on Culture, actively supports both the ideals of the former President Kwame Nkrumah, a leader in the Pan-African and African Personality movement, and the related philosophy and objectives of the Pan-African Orchestra. Abiam composes and arranges most of the music, which is closely related to indigenous practices. Instruments of the orchestra include a variety of original African instruments: KORA (21-string plucked chordophone), *gyilli* (xylophone), *axatse* (shakers), *adawuro* and *gankogui* (bells), *gonje* (one-string, bowed chordophone), assorted drums, flutes (*atentenben*, *wia*), animal horns and others. Minimal notation is used, and the leader has devised a form of notation for players who cannot read musical notation. The conductor employs a fly swatter in place of a baton and a pair of strung concussion toy instruments found in several West African societies, which he plays in the traditional manner as a time regulator. The orchestra has performed in the UK, Germany and in the USA. The 1995 compact disc recording titled *The Pan African Orchestra, Opus 1*, Real World Records, CAR2350 (1995) was the first commercial release of the orchestra (all selections composed or arranged by Abiam).

The creative musical interests of the conductor had been nurtured at the Institute of African Studies, University of Ghana, where he had helped redesign and mass-produce the vertical *atentenben* bamboo flute. He had then spent several years in Germany and the UK, returning to Ghana and assuming leadership of the Ghana National Symphony Orchestra. Due to internal problems, Abiam had resigned and began to explore the possibilities of an orchestra of indigenous African instruments with a repertory deriving from indigenous musical traditions; the Pan-African Orchestra was the product of this effort.

DANIEL AVORGBEDOR

Panagiotes the New Chrysaphes [Panagiotēs Chrysaphēs ho Neos] (*b* ?1620–25; *d* after 1682). Romaic (Greek) composer, cantor and hymnographer. As *prōtopsaltēs* of the Ecumenical Patriarchate of Constantinople from about 1655 to 1682, he helped bring to fruition the revival of Byzantine chanting initiated by his predecessor, Theophanes Karykes. He was a student of the patriarchal *prōtopsaltēs* Georgios Raidestinos, at whose suggestion he claims to have embarked on the recomposition of the late medieval stichērarion popularly attributed to Manuel Chrysaphes. This task, described by Panagiotes as 'beau-tification' (*kallopismos*), was accomplished through the incorporation of novel melodic formulae (*theseis*) hitherto transmitted orally in the patriarchal chapel. He also revised in similar manner the entire anastasimatarion and excerpts from the heirmologion. Among his other chants for the Divine Office are a modally ordered series of eight *kekragaria* for Hesperinos, responsories, acclamations, *troparia*, *idiomela* and *megalynaria* for Orthros, and a modally ordered series of eight *pasapnoaria* for Lauds ('Hoi ainoi'). For the eucharistic liturgies, he wrote Cherubic Hymns, and numerous communion verses for Sundays, weekdays and feasts of the liturgical year. His miscellaneous chants include several kalophonic *stichēra*, and a didactic song, *Ho thelōn mousikōn mathein* ('He who wishes to learn music'), that illustrates the perform-ance of common *theseis*. (For a fuller list of works see Stathis, 1995.)

Panagiotes' musical achievements, which his contem-poraries regarded as comparable to those of late Byzantine masters, led to his becoming known during his own lifetime as 'the New Chrysaphes'. Nearly all musical manuscripts transmitting his works – including his eight surviving autographs – employ this sobriquet to the exclusion of his Christian name, which is attested only by his student Dionysios the Hieromonk. Whereas Panagi-otes' Stichērarion was soon overtaken in popularity by that of his pupil GERMANOS OF NEW PATRAS, his Anastasimatarion remained in widespread use until it was replaced a century later by the collections of PETROS PELOPONNESIOS and PETROS BYZANTIOS. The few works later printed in Chrysanthine editions include an Easter Sunday *doxastikon* (ed. Phōkaeus) and four kalophonic hymns transcribed by Gregorios the Protopsaltes (ed. Lampadarios and Stephanos the First Domestikos).

Critical assessment of Panagiotes' works is complicated by scholarly disagreements over their realization in performance. According to Stathēs, his *theseis* were interpreted melismatically in a manner congruent with the transcriptions made by CHOURMOUZIOS THE ARCHIVIST of his Stichērarion (*GR-An* MPT 761–5) and Anastasimatarion (*An* MPT 758). However, this view has been challenged by Karas and Arvanitis, who generally favour a less florid approach to their realization.

BIBLIOGRAPHY

CHRYSANTHINE MUSIC EDITIONS

T. Phōkaeus, ed.: *Tameion anthologias* [Treasury of an anthology] (Constantinople, 1824), ii, 357–65 [transcr. Chourmouzios the Archivist]

I. Lampadarios and Stephanos the First Domestikos, eds.: *Pandektē* (Constantinople, 1850–51), i, 337–41, 344–50; iii, 45–54, 254–68, 294–306 [transcr. Gregorios the Protopsaltes]

STUDIES

S.I. Karas: 'Hē orthē hermēneia kai metagraphē tōn byzantinōn mousikōn cheirographōn' [The correct interpretation and transcription of Byzantine musical MSS], *Hellēnika*, ix (1955), 140–49 [repr., with an afterword, Athens, 1990]

C.G. Patrinelis: 'Protopsaltae, Lampadarioi and Domestikoi of the Great Church during the Post-Byzantine Period (1453–1821)', *Studies in Eastern Chant*, iii, ed. M. Velimirović (London, 1973), 141–70

G.T. Stathēs: *Ta cheirographa byzantinēs mousikēs: Hagion Oros* [The MSS of Byzantine Music: Holy Mountain] (Athens, 1975–93)

G.T. Stathēs: *Hē dekapentasyllabos hymnographia en tē byzantinē melopoiïa* [15-syllable hymnography in Byzantine composition] (Athens, 1977) [with Fr. summary]

M. Chatzēgiakoumēs: *Cheirographa ekklēsiastikēs mousikēs (1453–1820)* [MSS of ecclesiastical music] (Athens, 1980)

G.T. Stathis: 'The "Abridgements" of Byzantine and Post-Byzantine Compositions', *Cahiers de l'Institut du Moyen-Age grec et latin*, no.44 (1983), 16–38

A. Şirli: *The Anastasimatarion: the Thematic Repertory of Byzantine and Post-Byzantine Musical Manuscripts (the 14th-19th centuries)*, i (Bucharest, 1986)

G.T. Stathēs: 'Panagiōtēs Chrysaphēs ho Neos kai Prōtopsaltēs', *Melourgoi tou iz aiōna* [Composers of the 17th century], ed. E. Spanopoulou (Athens, 1995), 7–16, 23–7

ALEXANDER LINGAS

Panama (Sp. República de Panamá). Country in Central America. The most southerly state of Central America, it is bordered by Costa Rica to the east and Colombia to the west. It has the Caribbean Sea to the north and the Pacific Ocean to the south, connected by the Panama Canal. Panama covers an area of 75,517 km² and has a population of 2.86 million (2000 estimate).

I. Art music. II. Traditional music.

I. Art music

Little documentation of musical activities in the Cathe-dral of Panama City during the colonial period is available. It is known that Juan de Araujo (1646–1712), who ended up as *maestro de capilla* in La Plata (today Sucre, Bolivia) Cathedral, was active at Panama Cathedral from 1676 to, presumably, 1680, the year he was appointed at La Plata. No work composed in Panama during the colonial period or the 19th century is extant.

Only in the 20th century did the cultivation of art music develop in Panama, mostly centred in and around the National Conservatory (beginning in 1911), first known as Escuela Nacional de Música (founded in 1904). Narciso Garay (1876–1953) directed the institution from 1904 to 1918; in 1921 it closed due to lack of official support. During its early existence the conservatory trained a good number of musicians who contributed to an incipient music education in various institutions. In 1941 the central government reopened the National Conservatory under the direction of the renowned Panamanian violinist Alfredo de Saint-Malo (1898–1984), who sponsored the publication of the conserva-tory's journal *Armonía*. At the same period, the National SO was founded under the conductor Herbert de Castro, who was succeeded by the cellist Walter Myers in 1944. Through regular concerts in both the capital and various cities and towns, the orchestra contributed to the knowledge and cultivation of classical music. In 1952 it was reorganized as the National Orchestra, with Herbert de Castro returning as its main conductor. The conservatory changed its name to the National Institute of Music in 1953, and inaugurated a mixed chorus and an orchestra made up of students and teachers.

The main venue for concerts, operas and other performances by local and visiting groups in the capital city has been the Teatro Nacional, inaugurated in 1908. Larger concert halls followed, such as Teatro Central, Teatro Presidente and Teatro Bellavista. The state also sponsored the Banda Republicana (founded in 1904) and the Banda del Cuerpo de Bomberos (the Firemen's Band, 1909) that gave weekly concerts in the main public squares of Panama City. Beginning in 1909, music has been taught in elementary and secondary schools, and in 1953 the government created a department of musical culture and education in the ministry of education. Among the few private initiatives supporting art music have been the Unión Musical, whose orchestral ensemble was organized in 1934 by Pedro Rebolledo, a band director and composition student of Julián Carrillo in Mexico, the Sociedad de Conciertos Daniel, and the Sociedad Pro-Arte Musical de Panama. A number of choral groups have developed in the capital and other cities.

The most important composers in Panama have been Santos Jorge (1870–1941), organist at Panama Cathedral and author of the country's national anthem, Alberto Galimany (1889–1974), composer of the popular *Marcha Panamá* and the orchestral suite *Vasco Nuñez de Balboa* (1941), Carlos Arias Quintero (*b* 1903), composer of sacred works and piano pieces, and Ricardo Fábrega (1905–73), composer of works of popular character. The most significant Panamanian composer of the 20th century is Roque Cordero (*b* 1917), who has won international recognition for his original and substantial creative output. Prominent among the subsequent generation of composers are José Luis Cajar and Marina Saiz Salazar.

BIBLIOGRAPHY

R. Cordero: 'El folklore en la creación musical panameña', *Revista Universidad*, no.31 (1952), 103

R. Cordero: 'Actualidad musical de Panama', *Buenos Aires Musical*, no.197 (1957), 5

R. Cordero: 'Relaciones de la educación musical con los conservatorios de música', *RMC*, nos.87–8 (1964), 63–7

R. Cordero: 'La música en Centro América y Panamá', *Journal of Interamerican Studies*, no.8 (1966), 411–18

II. Traditional music

The traditional music of Panama is the result of a mixture of three cultures. During the colonial period African slaves were brought to Panama, and their music and dances were added to the music already developing from a mixture of Spanish and Amerindian music. These three elements combined to form a new music that is rich in rhythmic and melodic variety. Although today only popular international music is heard in the ballrooms and night clubs of the principal cities of Panama, traditional music is still an important part of the national heritage. Since the 1940s folklore groups have been formed in secondary schools and their activities encouraged through competitions. Other groups have been organized to perform national dances as part of the tourist industry. In inland towns performances of the songs and dances described here take place during national and regional celebrations, social activities and religious observances, especially those honouring patron saints.

Recordings of Panamanian traditional music have been made by Myron Schaeffer and are in the Library of Congress, Washington, DC.

1. Instruments. 2. Songs and dances. 3. Popular music.

1. INSTRUMENTS.   Panamanian traditional folkdances are accompanied by string instruments and drums. The most important string instruments are the *mejoranera* and the *bocona*, simple guitars of small and medium size respectively with five gut or nylon strings, used to accompany the dances *mejorana*, *cumbia* and *punto*. The *mejoranera* is tuned e′–b–a–a′–d′, although the third and fourth strings are sometimes tuned to g, g′. Because of this tuning, the tonic chord is usually played in its 6-4 inversion, and the subdominant in a 6-3 inversion. Only the dominant appears in root position. Originally, the melodies for these dances were played on a regional three-string fiddle called a *rabel* (perhaps a descendant of the Arab *rabāb*), but this has been replaced by a standard violin. Sometimes, especially in the *cumbia*, the melody is played on an accordion.

The three native drums most widely used are the *caja* or *tambora* (large), *pujador* (medium) and *repicador* (small). The *tambora* is a double-headed drum made from a cylindrical hollow log 35 to 45 cm long, with a skin 30 to 35 cm in diameter on each end. It is placed on the ground or on a small bench in a horizontal position and the drumheads and body of the instrument are struck with two simple wooden drumsticks. The *pujador* is about 70 cm high, and the *repicador* is about 55 cm high; each has only one skin about 20 cm in diameter on the upper end, and the body tapers down to the other end, which is open. These two drums rest on the ground, held firmly between the knees, and are struck with the flat of the fingers and the palms and ball of the hands. The player of the *pujador* sometimes presses his left elbow on to the centre of the drumhead while striking it with the extended fingers of his right hand, which produces a change in sonority. Other variations in sound are produced by raising the *pujador* or the *repicador* off the floor with the knees.

The *guáchara* or *güiro* is a large hollow gourd with a series of transverse grooves carved on its surface, which are rasped with a small hardwood rod or a piece of heavy wire to accompany the rhythm of the dance. Flutes and double basses, as well as Cuban maracas and claves, have been added to the folk orchestra, but these instruments are not indigenous to Panama.

The Panamanian Indians have a great number of flutes, among which may be mentioned a unique type of panpipe played by the Cuna Indians of the San Blas Islands, called the *kamu-purui*. It is similar to the *antara* of Peru, the *capador* of Colombia and the *rondador* of Ecuador, but although each of these has tubes tied together to form a single body, the *kamu-purui* has its seven bamboo tubes tied to form two groups, of three and four tubes. The tuning of the tubes is also distinctive, as is the manner in which they are played. The group of four tubes is tuned in ascending perfect 5ths and the group of three in descending perfect 5ths, with the higher notes of each group separated by an interval of a major 2nd, or a major or minor 3rd (ex.1*a*). The performer holds the group of four tubes in his left hand and the group of three in his right, with the smallest tube of each group touching in the

Ex.1

(a) *Kamu-purui* tunings; transcr. R. Cordero

(b) *Kamu-purui* melody; rec. and transcr. R. Cordero

centre to form a solid row of tubes (see illustration). Sound is produced by blowing between two tubes and producing two notes simultaneously in an interval of a perfect 5th. The space between the two groups is not used, as it does not produce a perfect 5th.

The *kamu-purui* are constructed in pairs, as are nearly all flutes of the Cuna Indians. They are designated male and female, with the female tuned a major 2nd, minor 2nd, or, occasionally, a minor 3rd higher than the male. The male and female instruments are played alternately, thereby producing a composite melodic line in parallel 5ths (ex.1*b*).

Three or more pairs of musician–dancers (usually men, but sometimes mixed pairs) play the *kamu-purui* while dancing. The instruments are not perfectly tuned to each other, so that unusual sonorities are produced. Several women join the dance, each shaking a *nasis* or *nasisi* to accompany the music. These are dried gourds, into which small seeds have been inserted, with handles of deer bone wrapped with waxed braided cord.

The *kamu-purui* is the only flute of the Cuna Indians in which the female instrument has as many notes as the male instrument. Contrary to Narciso Garay's statements, other female instruments of the Cunas, such as the *suppe* and *tolo* , have only one or two notes and are used to accompany melodies played on male instruments with up to four finger-holes. Music performed on the *kamu-purui* , as well as all music of the Cuna Indians, is handed down orally from generation to generation by the *kantule* (sometimes called *kamoturo*) or official musician, whose function it is to perform and teach the traditional songs of the tribe. In his work the *kantule* is helped by his assistant, the *kansueti* , who is the only person authorized to cut, in a special ceremony, the bamboo cane from which the different flutes of the tribe are made.

Differing from the music of the Cuna Indians, in which there are few traces of polyphonic music, that of the Guaymi Indians of the central provinces combines several instruments of individual timbres and specific melodic patterns to form polyphonic combinations. Some of the Guaymi instruments are: small drums (not found among the Cunas); the *tólero* or *toleró*, a vertical flute made from the leg bone of a deer or jaguar; the *drúbulo*, or shell trumpet; the *niví-grotu*, a trumpet made from a bull's horn; and ocarinas of different shapes.

These instruments are used, along with singing, in ceremonial dances such as the *chichada del cacao*, celebrating a girl's puberty, in which participants consume a fermented drink made with roasted cacao nuts, or in a game with dancing called *juego de balsería* in which two men try, in turn, to hit the other's legs with a long piece of light balsa wood.

2. SONGS AND DANCES.   The two most important folkdances of Panama are the *tamborito* and the *mejorana*. The former is considered the national dance of the country *par excellence*. Its antiphonally arranged melody, its intricate contrapuntal rhythm on the drums and its precise dance movements reflect both African and Spanish origin. The *tonada* or melody of the *tamborito*, sung exclusively by women, is divided into two parts. The first of these is solo, intoned by the *cantadora-alante* ('front' singer), and allows for improvisation in each repetition. The second part is sung in unison, with little variation, by women clapping their hands in the line of participants encircling the drummers and dancers. The melody is symmetrically distributed between soloist and chorus, with phrases of either two or four bars. The *cantadora-alante* usually has the first phrase and the chorus the second, although this order is sometimes reversed. The two melodic sections are repeated an indefinite number of times. Most *tamborito* melodies are in major keys, although many are in minor keys and there are even some in other modes. The second (choral) phrases sometimes end on the dominant.

The *tonada* is in moderate 2/4 metre, accompanied by the *tambora*, the *pujador* and the *repicador*. Participants of both sexes clap a combination of three rhythms simultaneously in each bar: two crotchets, four quavers and two syncopated quavers. The *repicador* and the *pujador* sustain an interesting contrapuntal rhythm, while the *tambora* establishes rhythmic symmetry with accents

Kamu-purui (panpipes) played by Cuna Indians

Ex.2 *Y orelé, tamborito tonada*; transcr. R. Cordero

struck on the right-hand drumhead in an unvarying four-bar pattern. The left-hand drumhead and the wood, however, are struck in a variety of rhythms. The *tonada* is repeated many times; but when singing is suspended the drums continue to play and the *repicador* and the *pujador* have an animated rhythmic dialogue until the new *tonada* begins.

A further melodic characteristic of the *tamborito* is the syncopated anticipation of the first beat by a semiquaver. This almost always occurs at the end of a phrase or motif, but sometimes appears in almost every bar (see ex.2). The melodic phrase of the *cantadora-alante* is nearly always in a different rhythm from that of the chorus (as shown in ex.2). However, there are infrequent examples in which the two phrases are rhythmically equal. In a few rare cases, instead of changing the rhythm of its phrase, the chorus varies the melodic line, and sometimes there is soloist–chorus overlapping (ex.3; in this case the chorus initiates the *tonada*).

The *tamborito* is danced by one mixed couple at a time; they dance separately into the centre of the circle, present themselves to the drummers with a specific pattern of steps, and then (still separated) demonstrate their choreographic ability for several minutes. When a second man enters the circle dancing and chooses his partner by bowing before her, the first couple retires dancing to join the circle of participants clapping to the music. This pattern is repeated indefinitely.

In certain regions of the country, a type of *tamborito* that gradually accelerates is called *tambor norte*. In other regions, however, the *norte* is more subdued; the livelier version is called *tambor corriente*. When the dance is performed in a house and not in the open air, as is customary, it is called *tambor de orden*.

The *mejorana* is performed in two different forms, one instrumental and the other vocal. The instrumental *mejorana* is danced with the melody played on the *rabel* or violin, and is simply called *mejorana*. The vocal form, called *socavón*, is sung exclusively by men and is not danced. In both, the accompaniment and certain melodic interludes are played on the *mejoranera* or on the *bocona*. The *mejoranera* alternates the tonic chord (in 6-4 position)

with the dominant from one bar to the next, occasionally with the subdominant in between.

The *mejorana* is in moderate tempo. The metre is 6/8, maintained in the accompaniment while the melody constantly changes back and forth from 6/8 to 2/4. Another type of instrumental *mejorana*, called *mejorana-poncho*, employs a 3/2 metre in an equally moderate tempo.

The sung *mejorana*, or *socavón*, has an improvisational character; the text comments on local, national and international incidents (political or civil). The *mejorana* singer accompanies himself, or is accompanied by another musician, on the *mejoranera*. Two singers may alternate, improvising questions and answers, a form called *desafío* (duel, or challenge). The literary style of the *mejorana* is of Spanish origin and is common to almost all Latin America. It begins with a *cuarteta* or *redondilla* (quatrain), followed by four *décimas* (ten-line stanzas) of the same metre, each of which ends with a line from the initial quatrain taken in sequence. Before beginning the *cuarteta*, and between one *décima* and the next, the singer improvises a melismatic phrase without words, using falsetto, called *bujeo*. The sung *mejorana* may take one of three different forms: the *zapatero*, which starts and finishes on the tonic (or harmony of the tonic); the *mesano*, which starts and finishes on the dominant (or harmony of the dominant); and the *gallino*, which is in a minor key. The *mejorana-gallino*, in turn, is either *cantar a lo divino*, when texts have religious themes, or *cantar a lo humano*, when they deal with secular subjects.

The *mejorana* is a collective dance in which men stand in a row facing an equal number of women. The two rows of dancers advance until they meet and then recede to their point of departure; this movement is repeated several times. At a predetermined moment, the two rows cross through each other to occupy opposite sides. The dance is divided into *paseo* (strolling) and *zapateado* (foot-stamping in an intricate pattern).

Other important folkdances are the *cumbia* and the *punto*. The *cumbia* is a dance of definite African origin. It is in 2/4 metre, and has a vocal and an instrumental version, both danced; the melody is played on the *rabel* or the violin, although occasionally the accordion is used. The melody usually consists of short phrases, constantly repeated, using the chords only of the tonic and dominant.

Ex.3 *Arriba monteriano, tamborito tonada*; transcr. R. Cordero

It is accompanied by the *mejoranera* or the *bocona* in a constant rhythm of quavers, against semiquavers (with an occasional quaver) which are beaten on the two heads and the wood of the *tambora*. While the more European influenced version of the folk *cumbia* (found especially in the Central Provinces) relies primarily upon string instruments, the more Afro-Panamanian traditional *cumbia* may include more than one drum together with a *churuca* or *guáchara* (scraper) and features an alternation between female solo and chorus singing similar to a call and response pattern. The dance is performed by separate mixed pairs revolving around the orchestra, and each woman carries a lighted bundle of candles.

Like the *mejorana* and the *cumbia*, the *punto* exists in both vocal and instrumental versions, and like those of the *cumbia* both are danced. The melody of the *punto* is also played on the *rabel* or the violin and accompanied by the *mejoranera* or the *bocona*. It is in 6/8 metre with a sustained rhythm of three quavers to a beat in the accompaniment, while in the melody some beats are divided into two quavers. However this does not entail a change to 2/4 metre such as occurs in the *mejorana*. The *punto* is danced collectively by couples, with *paseo* and *zapateado* steps like those of the *mejorana*. It differs from the latter in having a more stylized melodic line with various periods of two phrases, the first ending on the dominant and the second on the tonic. The initial period returns frequently, giving a rondo character to this dance. When the *punto* is in a minor key it is called *coco*.

The *congo* dance and music complex is centred in communities of higher African ethnicity and cultural retention in the Caribbean coastal region. A *congo* performance group includes three or four drummers on *congos*, single-headed wedge-hoop drums; a female chorus; and dancers that act out historical recreations of the slavery period and subsequent emancipation. The *revellín* (lead singer, called *cantalante* outside the *congo* community) engages the chorus in call and response vocals. The *revellín* usually begins a performance, followed by the chorus who also add *palmadas* (hand-clapping) on the downbeats of phrases, and the drums enter one at a time to create the full complement of musicians to accompany the dance drama. Common themes include passage on slave ships and stories of escaped slaves, as well as more general Christian-derived themes. Although the dancers follow the rhythmic foundation of the musical accompaniment, often two distinct storylines are given simultaneously as the verses may not always exactly coincide with dancers' historical portrayal. Although becoming less common, traditionally *congo* groups pay visits to other *congo* groups' *palacios* (palaces), houses constructed as performance spaces.

Another dance drama, involving different types of devil figures, is one of the most important contemporary public performances. The dances and processions of the *diablos sucios*, found in the interior, are accompanied by various combinations of a *pito* (transverse cane flute), guitar and button accordion. The dancers play castanets and *vejigas*, inflated animal bladders struck by a stick. Their performances on Corpus Christi have elevated their bright red striped costumes and grotesque masks to prominent national symbols of Panamanian cultural identity. A related tradition is the *diablos de los espejos* ('devils with mirrors'), or *gran diablos* ('great devils'), where dancers

enact liturgical dramas to an accompaniment that can include accordion and drums similar to *congo* drums.

Other Afro-Panamanian musical traditions include the *bullerengue* and the *bunde*. The accompaniment to both dances consists of several drums, hand clapping and responsorial female singing. The *bullerengue* is found principally in Darién and the dance is closely related to the *tamborito*. Calypso, somewhat modified from its Trinidadian and Jamaican form, is still performed but with Spanish lyrics by descendants of Afro-Caribbean immigrant canal contract workers known as *Antillanos*. In this community, centred in the canal zone and Colón, many former traditional music practices (such as contradance and cuadrille) have fallen into disuse, and are now relegated to folklore presentations.

The *grito* (field holler or shout), found especially on the Azuero peninsula, probably developed as a means of communication during agricultural work. At present it is also commonly performed by both men and women on social occasions, as a vocal duel.

3. POPULAR MUSIC. The principal form of Panamanian popular music is generally known simply as *música típica*. The earlier rural instrumentation consisted of a two or three row button (diatonic) accordion, a triangle, one or more *tambores* and a *caja* (double-headed drum played with hand and a stick). Extensive urbanization in the latter half of the 20th century brought *música típica* to the attention of urban dwellers. In the 1950s and 60s Yin Carrizo, Victorio Vergara and Sandra and Sammy Sandoval helped to establish *música típica* as a national genre. Related to, and influenced by, the Colombian *cumbia* and *vallenato*, *música típica* has tended to eschew the *cumbia*'s integration of brass sections and other influences from *salsa* and other Caribbean music. In general, *música típica* performers in Panama retain a more folk-rooted style and instrumentation, typically incorporating drum kit, bass, guitar and the indispensable button accordion. The widespread acceptance of the genre is illustrated in the stature of *música típica* performers such as Osvaldo Ayala, who has recorded with the national symphony orchestra as well as with several international artists.

Many Caribbean styles have significantly influenced musical culture in Panama, substantiating the country's claim as the 'crossroads of the Americas'. One important example is the popularity of the Haitian *konpas* band Tabou Combo, who resided in Panama for much of the 1970s and 80s. During the same two decades, Euro-Panamanian Rubén Blades became one of the most influential singer-songwriters and band leaders of *salsa*. While most of his contributions to *salsa* have taken place in New York, more recently his creative activity has been centred on Panama. His Grammy-winning album *La rosa de los vientos* (1996) featured compositions and performances by other Panamanian musicians. Similarly, jazz pianist and composer Danilo Pérez lives primarily in New York but his 1998 album *Central Avenue*, named after Panama City's major thoroughfare, contains some elements of Panamanian music. Also maintaining a residence in New York is Afro-Panamanian 'El General' (Edgardo A. Franco) who has been at the forefront of the type of Spanish-language rap sometimes labelled 'dancehall reggaespañol', an off-shoot of the Jamaican reggae dancehall style. El General's broad bilingual appeal was aided by his recordings of separate versions of the same song in

English and Spanish as well as occasionally mixing both languages in the same song. *Rock panameño* (or *rock nacional*) grew in importance in the 1990s (an international festival has been held since 1996). Spearheaded by the band Equinox, some of the most innovative developments have been in the more experimental style of *rock progresivo*.

BIBLIOGRAPHY
AND OTHER RESOURCES

GEWM, ii ('Panama'; R.R. Smith)

F. Densmore: *Music of the Tule Indians of Panama* (Washington DC, 1926)

N. Garay: *Tradiciones y cantares de Panamá* (Brussels, 1930, 2/1982)

M. Schaeffer and others: 'Catorce tamboritos panameños', *Boletín del Instituto de investigaciones folklóricas*, i (1944)

M.F. and D.P.Zárate: *La décima y la copla en Panamá* (Panamá, 1953)

M.F. Zárate: *Brevario de folklore* (Panamá, 1958)

M.F. with D.P.Zárate: *Tambor y socavón: un estudio comprensivo de dos temas del folklore panameño y de sus implicaciones históricas y culturales* (Panamá, 1968)

S.S. McCosker: *The Lullabies of the San Blas Cuna Indians of Panama* (Göteborg, 1974)

R.R. Smith: *The Society of Los Congos of Panama: an Ethnomusicological Study of the Music and Dance-theater of an Afro-Panamanian Group* (diss., Indiana, U., 1976)

L.R. and R.A. Cheville: *Festivals and Dances of Panama* (Panamá, 1977)

R. Velasquez and M. Brandt: *Culturas aborígenes de Latinoamérica*, i: *Guaymíes: Panamá* (Caracas, 1980) [incl. sound cassette and slides]

G.M. Lopez and L.G. Joly: 'Singing a Lullaby in Kuna: a Female Verbal Art', *Journal of American Folklore*, xciv (1981), 351–8

J. Sherzer and S.A. Wicks: 'The Intersection of Music and Language in Kuna Discourse', *LAMR*, iii (1982), 147–64

S. Smith: *Panpipes for Power, Panpipes for Play: the Social Management of Cultural Expression in Kuna Society* (diss., U. of California, Berkeley, 1984)

Street Music of Panama: Cumbias, Tamboritos and Mejoranas, coll. M. Blaise, Vogue PIP OMCD 008 (1985) [incl. notes by J. Storm Roberts]

R. Smith: 'They Sing with the Voice of the Drum: Afro-Panamanian Musical Traditions', *More than Drumming: Essays on African and Afro-Latin American Music and Musicians*, ed. I.V. Jackson (Westport, 1985), 163–98

B. Janson Perez: 'El autobus en dos canciones panameñas: notas sobre la situación de consumo e identificación popular', *Caravelle*, no.48 (1987), 107–18

Panama: tamboritos y mejoranas, coll. E. Llerenas and E. Ramírez de Arellano, Música Traditional MT 09 (1987)

S.I. Carmona Maya: *La música, un fenómeno cosmogónico en la cultura kuna* (Medellín, 1989)

B. Janson Perez: 'Arms of Criticism and Criticism of Arms in Panama: the Songs of Pedro Altamiranda', *Studies in Latin American Popular Culture*, viii (1989), 93–105

GERARD BÉHAGUE (I), ROQUE CORDERO/T.M. SCRUGGS (II, 1–2), T.M. SCRUGGS (II, 3)

Pan American Association of Composers. Organization dedicated to the promotion of experimental contemporary music and its performance in the USA, Latin America and Europe. It was founded by Edgard Varèse in New York in 1928 after the discontinuation of the INTERNATIONAL COMPOSERS' GUILD (1921–7). The association was one of the first to encourage cooperation among composers throughout the Americas and to stimulate performances of American music outside the USA. Henry Cowell was acting president from 1929 to 1933; other composer-members were Antheil, Carlos Chávez, Ives (who gave considerable financial support), Riegger and Salzedo. Membership was small and concerts were managed by the composers themselves. Slonimsky, the regular conductor for the association from 1931, directed the premières of several significant American works, and in 1933 the association sponsored a series of weekly concerts on radio station WEVD, New York. Although it achieved greater success and recognition than the International Composers' Guild, the Pan American Association fell victim to the Depression and was disbanded in 1934.

VIVIAN PERLIS

Panassié, Hugues (*b* Paris, 27 Feb 1912; *d* Montauban, 8 Dec 1974). French writer on jazz. After studying the saxophone he first wrote about jazz at the age of 18. He was one of the founders (in 1932) and then president of the Hot Club de France, and from 1935 to 1946 he was the editor of the journal *Jazz-hot*. With his unrivalled enthusiasm for communication, Panassié wrote hundreds of articles for this and other periodicals and was the author of several books, notably *Le jazz hot*, an important study that was among the first to treat jazz seriously. In 1938 Count Basie dedicated to him and recorded a composition called *Panassié Stomp*. The same year, in New York, Panassié organized a series of small-group recording sessions with Mezz Mezzrow which also included (at various times) Tommy Ladnier and Sidney Bechet; these were highly influential and contributed considerably to the New Orleans revival movement. In 1939 he recorded a swing septet under the leadership of Frankie Newton. However, Panassié's reputation as an articulate advocate of jazz has to some extent been tarnished by his extreme conservatism: from the mid-1940s he expressed the opinion that bop was not jazz, thus denying the evolution of the genre. His private collection is now in the Discothèque Municipale at Villefranche-de-Rouergue.

WRITINGS

Le jazz hot (Paris, 1934; Eng. trans., rev. 1936/R)

The Real Jazz (New York, 1942, enlarged 2/1960/R; Fr. orig. pubd as *La véritable musique de jazz*, Paris, 1945, enlarged 2/1952)

La musique de jazz et le swing (Paris, 1943, 2/1945)

Douze années de jazz (1927-1938): souvenirs (Paris, 1946)

Cinq mois à New-York (Paris, 1947)

Louis Armstrong (Paris, 1947/R)

Jazz panorama (Paris, 1950)

Discographie critique des meilleurs disques de jazz (Paris, 1951, 2/1958)

with M. Gautier: *Dictionnaire du jazz* (Paris, 1954/R, enlarged 4/1987; Eng. trans., 1956, 2/1956 as *Guide to Jazz*, ed. A.A. Gurwitch)

Petit guide pour une discothèque de jazz (Paris, 1955)

Histoire du vrai jazz (Paris, 1959)

La bataille du jazz (Paris, 1965)

Louis Armstrong (Paris, 1969; Eng. trans., New York, 1971)

Monsieur Jazz: entretiens avec Pierre Casalta (Paris, 1975)

ANDRÉ CLERGEAT

Panderete (Sp.). *See* TAMBOURINE.

Pandiatonicism [pandiatonism]. A term coined by Slonimsky (*Music since 1900*, 1938, rev. 4/1972; *Thesaurus of Scales and Melodic Patterns*, 1947) to denote the free use of several diatonic degrees in a single chord, the 6th, 7th or 9th being the most usual additions to the triad. Such added notes are usually placed in the treble, so that their positions as natural harmonics are emphasized. Pandiatonicism differs from polytonality in avoiding the superposition of different keys.

☐

Pandolfi Mealli, Giovanni Antonio (*fl* 1660–69). Italian composer and violinist. He was among the instrumentalists of Archduke Ferdinand of Austria at Innsbruck when his opp.3 and 4 were published in 1660. The 1669 volume is attributed only to 'D. Gio. Antonio Pandolfi' but there is little doubt that it is by the same composer. The 1660 sonatas are characterized by rhapsodical, improvisatory outpourings over simple continuo accompaniments. While requiring considerable manual dexterity they never exceed fifth position. The designation 'per chiesa e camera' suggests an all-purpose style, and all 12 sonatas bear dedications, some to such famous musicians as Antonio Cesti, then *maestro di cappella della camera* at Innsbruck. The 1669 collection is remarkable in its choice of instrumentation: besides the 'terza parte della viola a beneplacito' (actually essential), the specified continuo is organ, a common chamber instrument but hardly ever mentioned, as here, in connection with dances. The dedication refers to performances at an academy.

WORKS

[6] Sonate … per chiesa e camera, vn, bc, op.3 (Innsbruck, 1660)
[6] Sonate … per chiesa e camera, vn, bc, op.4 (Innsbruck, 1660)
Sonate, cioe balletti, etc., 1–2 vn, opt. basso di viola, bc (org) (Rome, 1669)
opp.1 and 2 not known

ROBIN BOWMAN/PETER ALLSOP

Pandolfini, Angelica (*b* Spoleto, 21 Aug 1871; *d* Lenno, Como, 15 July 1959). Italian soprano. As the daughter of Francesco Pandolfini, she was brought up with a singing career in view, though she first studied the piano in Paris. She trained as a singer under Jules Massart and made her début in *Faust* at Modena in 1894. Later that year in Malta she became associated with the new *verismo* operas, and was soon known throughout Italy as an outstanding Mimì. 1897 brought her début at La Scala where, in 1902, she created the title role in Cilea's *Adriana Lecouvreur*. Her repertory also included Eva in *Die Meistersinger* (sung in Italian), Desdemona and the heroines of *La traviata* and *Aida*, both of which revealed weaknesses and presaged her early retirement in 1909. She made only five records, all extremely rare in their original form. Among them is Adriana's first aria, sung with tenderness and some endearing personal touches. (*GV*, R. Celletti)

J.B. STEANE

Pandolfini, Francesco (*b* Termini Imerese, Palermo, 22 Nov 1833; *d* Milan, 15 Feb 1916). Italian baritone. He studied in Florence with Ronconi and made his début in 1859 at Pisa as the Count of Vergy in Donizetti's *Gemma di Vergy*. After singing in Genoa, Turin and Rome, in 1871 he was engaged at La Scala, where he sang Don Carlo (*La forza del destino*) and, in 1872, Amonasro in the first Italian performance of *Aida*. He created Arnoldo in Ponchielli's *I lituani* (1874). At Covent Garden in 1877 he sang Rigoletto, Antonio (*Linda di Chamounix*) and Ford (*Die lustigen Weiber von Windsor*), returning in 1882 for Nélusko and Amonasro. He sang at Monte Carlo (1884) as Alphonse (*La favorite*) and Valentin (*Faust*). In 1887 he was engaged at the S Carlo. His repertory included Severo (*Poliuto*), Alfonso (*Lucrezia Borgia*), Riccardo (*I puritani*), Thomas' Hamlet, Macbeth, Don Carlo (*Ernani*) and Alfio (*Cavalleria rusticana*), which he sang at his farewell in Rome (1890).

ELIZABETH FORBES

Pandora [pandore]. *See* BANDORA.

Pandoura (Gk.; Lat. *pandura*). An instrument generally identified with the Greco-Roman LUTE (it is generally

classified as a CHORDOPHONE). Lutes made a late entry into the Greco-Roman world, not appearing until after Alexander's Persian conquest. They are represented chiefly on a fairly small number of Greek terracottas and Roman sarcophagi. Organologists distinguish two types among these lutes: one with a roughly rectangular soundbox that is clearly demarcated from the neck, and one with an almond-shaped soundbox that merges with the neck. The instruments are generally pictured played by a female figure (or by Eros) stopping the strings with her left hand and plucking them, often by plectrum, with her right. Pollux referred to the pandoura as *trichordon* ('three-string'), but the sculpted lutes show varying, if small, numbers of strings. Perhaps it is best simply to say that the instruments had fewer strings than either the kithara or the harp.

There was considerable confusion, particularly among later authors, about the identification of the pandoura. Cassiodorus and Isidore of Seville described it as a wind instrument invented by the god Pan, and the *Suda* identified it with the PĒKTIS, a type of harp. More helpfully, Pollux vaguely associated it with the mono-chord, and Nicomachus actually confused the two instruments; in fact the monochord, with its long narrow fingerboard, is closely related to the lute. 'Pandoura' and the related 'tanbur' are names for lutes found today from the Balkans to the Middle East, and the term 'bandurria' is also derived from 'pandoura'.

See also GREECE, §I, 5(iii)(b).

BIBLIOGRAPHY

G. Fleischhauer: *Etrurien und Rom*, Musikgeschichte in Bildern, ii/5 (Leipzig, 1964, 2/1978)
R.A. Higgins and R.P. Winnington-Ingram: 'Lute-Players in Greek Art', *Journal of Hellenic Studies*, lxxxv (1965), 62–71
G. Wille: *Musica romana* (Amsterdam, 1967)
M. Maas and J.M. Snyder: *Stringed Instruments of Ancient Greece* (New Haven, CT, 1989), 185–6
M.L. West: *Ancient Greek Music* (Oxford, 1992), 79–80
T.J. Mathiesen: *Apollo's Lyre: Greek Music and Music Theory in Antiquity and the Middle Ages* (Lincoln, NE, 1999), 283–5

JAMES W. McKINNON

Pandurina (Ger.). *See* MANDORE.

Pane, Domenico dal. *See* DAL PANE, DOMENICO.

Panenka, Jan (*b* Prague, 8 July 1922; *d* Prague, 12 July 1999). Czech pianist. He studied with František Maxián in Prague and with Serebryakov in Leningrad, made his début in Prague in 1944 and in 1951 won the international piano competition there. He was a distinguished chamber musician: he was a member of the Suk Trio (from 1957) and played with Josef Suk, Josef Chuchro, the Smetana Quartet and other groups. In 1959 he was appointed a soloist with the Czech PO. His technique was brilliant, but his playing was devoid of superfluous effects or ostentation. Panenka performed in music centres of Europe, South Africa, Australia, New Zealand, Japan, India and China, and made numerous recordings. His performance of Beethoven's piano concertos won him a state award (1972), and his recording with Suk of Janáček's and Debussy's sonatas a Grand Prix du Disque (1959). He taught at the Prague Academy (AMU) from 1965.

BIBLIOGRAPHY

ČSHS
J. Kozák: *Instrumentalisté. Čestí koncertní umělci* [Czech concert artists: instrumentalists] (Prague, 1983), 19–20
Obituary, *HRo*, lii/9 (1999), 26 only

ALENA NĚMCOVÁ

Panerai, Rolando (*b* Campi Bisenzio, nr Florence, 17 Oct 1924). Italian baritone. He studied in Florence and Milan, making his début in 1946 in Florence as Enrico Ashton (*Lucia di Lammermoor*). At Naples (1947–8) he sang Pharaoh (*Mosè in Egitto*), Luna, Germont and Rossini's Figaro. In 1951 he made his La Scala début as the High Priest (*Samson et Dalila*), returning as Enrico Ashton, Apollo (*Alceste*), the Husband (*Amelia al ballo*) and in the title role of *Mathis der Maler* (Italian première, 1957). In 1955 he created Ruprecht in the stage première of *The Fiery Angel* in Venice and sang Mozart's Figaro in Aix-en-Provence. He made his Salzburg début in 1957 as Ford, then sang Masetto, Paolo (*Boccanegra*) and Guglielmo, returning as Ford in 1980. At San Francisco (1958) he sang both Figaros and Marcello. In 1962 he created the title role of Turchi's *Il buon soldato Švejk* (Milan). He sang all over Italy, in Vienna, Munich, Paris and at the Metropolitan. Having made his Covent Garden début in 1960 as Rossini's Figaro, he returned in the 1980s as Don Alfonso, Don Pasquale, Falstaff and Dulcamara. He had a dark-toned, vibrant voice and incisive diction, heard to advantage on his recordings of such roles as Guglielmo, Luna, Ford, Silvio and Marcello.

ALAN BLYTH

Panharmonicon. A MECHANICAL INSTRUMENT of the Orchestrion type. It was invented by JOHANN NEPOMUK MAELZEL and first exhibited by him in Vienna in 1804. The instrument was designed to play orchestral music, and various accounts describe it as capable of imitating the sounds of the french horn, clarinet, trumpet, oboe, bassoon, German flute, flageolet, drum, cymbal and triangle. The sounds were actually produced by various flue, reed and free-reed organ pipes, as well as air-driven percussion devices. The Panharmonicon achieved popularity in a period when such mechanical curiosities had great public appeal and were frequently taken on tour; Maelzel's instrument had many imitators, including a virtually identical instrument (made by a fellow Viennese, Joseph J. Gurk) exhibited in Germany and England in 1810 and 1811.

Maelzel's Panharmonicon was taken to the USA in 1811 and was exhibited throughout the eastern states between June that year and June 1812 by the Boston organ builder William M. Goodrich, after which it was shipped back to Europe. In 1824 Goodrich built a replica of the instrument for a Boston museum, which again was exhibited in various places for a year.

The repertory of the Panharmonicon consisted largely of popular marches and overtures, as well as pastorales, rondos and similar pieces. Music by Haydn, Mozart and Cherubini (as well as many lesser composers) was also performed on the instrument, the most remarkable example being Beethoven's 'Battle Symphony' (*Wellingtons Sieg*, 1813), originally written for Maelzel's instrument and later transcribed for orchestra.

The Panharmonicon was a tour de force of musical instrument technology which later resulted in the ORCHESTRION. Another instrument of this genre was the APOLLONICON.

BIBLIOGRAPHY

A.W.J.G. Ord-Hume: *Clockwork Music* (London and New York, 1973)

B. Owen: *The Organ in New England* (Winston-Salem, NC, 1979)

BARBARA OWEN, ARTHUR W.J.G. ORD-HUME

Panhormitano, Bartolomeo Lieto. *See* LIETO PANHORMITANO, BARTOLOMEO.

Pan Huanglong [Pan Hwang-Long] (*b* Puli, 9 Sept 1945). Taiwanese composer and music educator. He graduated from the National Taiwan University (1967–71) then studied composition with Lehmann at the Musikhochschule and Musikakademie in Zürich (1974–6); he continued his studies with Helmut Lachenmann at the Hochschule für Musik and Theater in Hanover (1976–8) and with Isang Yun at the Hochschule der Künste in Berlin (1978–80). Upon his return to Taiwan he became professor of music and composition at the National Institute of the Arts in Taibei and founded the Modern Music Centre there in 1984. This organization became the kernel of the Taiwan branch of the ISCM, which Pan co-founded with Wen Longxin and Zeng Xingkui in 1989.

While making use of the entire array of modernist and avant-garde techniques, Pan's music is often inspired by Chinese philosophical or mythical concepts. *Hudiemeng* (1979) and *Du, ein sterblicher, unnützer Mensch* (1981) are based on texts by the Daoist philosopher Zhuangzi. *Yijing* (1995–6) makes use of the *Classic of Changes* (also an inspiration to Cage), while *Penglai* (1978) is a sonic depiction of a Chinese paradise. His compositions series *Yin-Yang* (1992–5) and *Wuxing shengke* (1979–86) are based on the Chinese philosophy of change in which all parts of the cosmos are said to be in constant flux. These works depict the permutations of the five primary elements as they successively produce and destroy each other: movement generates new movement, or is destroyed by new movement. Each motif is subjected to constant metamorphosis: change may occur in sound colour, texture, structure, dynamics or metre.

WORKS
(*selective list*)

INSTRUMENTAL

Orch: Fengqiao yebo [Night-Mooring near a Maple Bridge], 1974; Metempsychose, 5 solo str, orch, 1977, rev. 1979; Penglai [Paradise], 1978; Liyun Datong [Harmony of the World]: I, 1987, arr. sym. band, 1987–8, III, 1990; Conc., vc, chbr orch, 1996–7; Conc., vc, 13 insts, 1996–7

Chbr: Lässt mich allein, hp, timp, db, pf, 1976; Niaokan [Bird's-Eye View], mar, vib, 1977; Str Qt no.2, 1977; Hudiemeng [Transformation], fl, cl, perc, 2 vc, 1979; Yinguo [Cause and Effect], fl, (vc/b cl), pf, 1979; Yinguo, ww ens, 1979; Enlightenment, 2 fl, hp, vc, db, 1979; Qidai [Expectation], ob, cl, bn, 1980; Rondo, pf trio, 1980; Cl Qt, 1980–81; Str Qt no.3, 1981, rev. 1983; Bachcap, fl, 1984–5; Zhuangyan de xixi [Majestic Game], perc ens, 1985; [5] Dialogues, 6 trad. Chin. insts, 1991; Yijing [Classic of Changes], bamboo fl, pipa, huqin, perc, 1995–6; Totem and Taboo, 6 perc, 1996; East and West, Chin. wind inst, ob, va, zheng, hp, 1998

Solo inst: Liuyue moli [White Jasmine in June], pf, 1976; Guodu [Interim], vn, 1978; Pictures from Childhood, pf, 1983–4; Solo I, hp, 1998

VOCAL

Farewell, chorus, 1971; Du, ein sterblicher, unnützer Mensch, was weisst du denn? (Zhuangzi), Bar, vc, hp, perc, pf, 1981; Suoyi yi daole wanshang [And So Comes the Night] (Ya Xun), 1v, orch/chbr orch/pf, 1986

COMPOSITIONAL SERIES

Qian huai [Expelling Yearnings]: I, fl, pf, 1975; II, db, 1976; III, vc, 1976; IV, org/(trbn, pf), 1976

Wuxing shengke [Elements of Change]: I, 8 pfmrs, 1979–80; II, orch, 1981–2; III, 16 insts, 5 assistant insts, 1986

Yuan, Juese, Wanhuatong [Kaleidoscope], pfmr(s): I, 1986–7; II, 1988; III, 1995

Taiwan fengqing [Formosa Landscape]: cl, vc, pf, 1987, rev. 1993; fl ens, I, 1987, rev. 1988, II, 1987, rev. 1992; orch, 1987, rev. 1995; str/str qt, 1987, rev. 1990; wind qnt, 1987

Labyrinth Promenade: I, hp(s), 1988; II, trbn(s), 1989; III, zheng(s), 1992; pipa, zheng, 1992, rev. 1994; huqin, (pipa, yangqin)/(bamboo fls)/(bamboo fls, yangqin), 1992, rev. 1997; 5 trad. Chin. insts, 1992, rev. 1997; IV, pipa(s), 1994; V, huqin(s), 1997; VI, di(s)/xiao(s), 1997; VII, yangqin(s), 1997; VIII, fl(s), 1998; IX, cl(s), 1998; X, vn(s), 1998; XI, vc(s), 1998; (fl, vc)/(cl, vn)/(fl, vc, hp)/(cl, hp, vn, vc), 1998

Yin-Yang: I (Pan), nar, chorus, 14 insts, 1992; II (Pan, Zhao Yuanren), nar, chorus, wind qnt, 1992; III, pf qt, 1993; IV (Zhao), nar, chorus, tubular bells, 1993; V (Pan, Zhao), nar, chorus, 14 insts, 1994; VI (Pan, Zhao), female chorus, 3 perc, 1995; VII, 14 insts, 1995; VIII (Pan, Zhao), nar, chorus, 1995; IX (Pan) nar, chorus, 14 insts, 1995

MSS in C.C. Liu Collection, Institute of Chinese Studies, U. of Heidelberg

Principal publishers: Bote & Bock, Bosse, Council for Cultural Affairs (Taibei)

WRITINGS

Modern Music's Focus (Taipei, 1987)
Let's Appreciate Contemporary Music (Taipei, 1990)
Fresh Inspiration from Chinese Culture for my Musical Composition (Taipei, 1993)

BIBLIOGRAPHY

KdG (Schu-chi Lee)
Zhao Ronglin: 'Reushi women de znoqujia: Pan Huanglong' [Get to know our composers: Pan Huanglong], *Yinyue yu yinxiang*, no.169 (1987), 90–93
Liang Maochun: 'Zheli zhi hua: Taiwan zuoqujia Pan Huanglong de yinyue' [A philosophical flower: the music of Taiwanese composer Pan], *Music from China Radio*, no.3 (1996), 16–17
Luo Zhongrong, ed.: *Xiandai yinyue xinshang cidian* [Dictionary for the appreciation of new music] (Beijing, 1997), 395–6
B. Mittler: *Dangerous Tunes: the Politics of Chinese Music in Hong Kong, Taiwan and the People's Republic of China since 1949* (Wiesbaden, 1997), esp. 327–8
Liu Ching-chih: *Zhongguo xin yinyue shilun* [Essays on Chinese new music], ii (Taipei, 1998), 710–11

BARBARA MITTLER

Paniagua y Vasques, Cenobio (*b* Tlalpujahua, Michoacan, 30 Oct 1821; *d* Córdoba, Veracruz, 2 Nov 1882). Mexican composer. He began his career as a violinist in the Morelia cathedral orchestra, which was conducted by his uncle. When the uncle moved to Mexico City Paniagua joined him, becoming a member of the orchestra of the metropolitan cathedral. He also taught himself composition by reading an Italian translation of Reicha's *Cours de composition musicale*. Through his contacts with Bottesini and other foreign musicians then resident in Mexico, he eventually succeeded in having his opera *Catalina de Guisa* (composed in 1845, to a libretto by Felice Romani) produced in Mexico City on 29 September 1859. Though sung in Italian, it was the first Mexican opera ever staged, and its enormous success brought him a host of followers, thus establishing a true operatic school in Mexico. He also wrote a one-act comic skit, *Una riña de aguadores*, produced in 1859. His second opera, *Pietro d'Abano*, with a libretto by Antonio Boni, produced in 1863, was less enthusiastically received. At that time he had organized a Mexican troupe through which he intended to promote not only his works but also his daughter's career as a singer. The enterprise failed, seriously damaging his career, and in 1868 he moved from the capital to the small town of Córdoba. His later works, which added nothing to his reputation, consisted mostly of religious music, including a cantata *Siete palabras* (1869), an oratorio *Tobias* (1870), a requiem (1882), and about 70 masses. He also wrote dances, marches and other salon pieces for the piano. Paniagua's most important pupil was Melesio Morales.

BIBLIOGRAPHY

GroveO (R. Stevenson)
M.G. Revilla: 'Cenobio Paniagua', *Revista musical mexicana*, ii (1942), 178–252
R. Stevenson: *Music in Mexico* (New York, 1952/R), 196–7

JUAN A. ORREGO-SALAS/R

Panisorhythm. *See* ISORHYTHM.

Panizza, Héctor [Ettore] (*b* Buenos Aires, 12 Aug 1875; *d* Milan, 27 Nov 1967). Argentine conductor and composer. He began his musical studies with his father Giovanni Grazioso Panizza, an Italian cellist and composer, and continued them at the Milan Conservatory with Giuseppe Frugatta (piano), Amintore Galli (harmony), Michele Saladino (counterpoint) and Vincenzo Ferroni (composition). After graduating with the first prize in composition (1898), he launched an impressive conducting career, becoming the first Argentine opera director to achieve international acclaim. He conducted musical seasons at Covent Garden (1907–14) and at La Scala (1916–17, 1921–32), where he shared the podium with Toscanini (1921–9). At the Metropolitan Opera he succeeded Tullio Serafin (1934–42), and at the Teatro Colón he intermittently directed 20 operatic seasons (1921–55). He was best known for his performances of the Italian lyric repertory, but his interpretations of Wagner and Strauss were also admired.

As a composer, Panizza stands as one of the first in Argentina to write operas and symphonic music with a solid sense of technical mastery. Unlike many native musicians of his day he remained remote from the prevailing nationalist current, preferring to align himself aesthetically with *verismo*. His popular opera *Aurora* (1907), set during the Argentine revolutionary period, initially provoked sharp controversy because of its Italian text (by Luigi Illica, one of Puccini's principal librettists) and its lack of a specifically Argentine musical content. Many, however, acknowledged the work as artistically effective, and it later earned a permanent place in the repertory of the Teatro Colón, where it was performed in a revised, Spanish version.

WORKS

Stage: Il fidanzato del mare (op, 1, R. Carugati), 1896, Buenos Aires, Teatro de la Opera, 15 Aug 1897; Medioevo latino (triptych, 3, L. Illica), 1899, Genoa, Politeama Genovese, 17 Nov 1900; Aurora, 1907 (op, 3, Illica after H. Quesada), Buenos Aires, Colón, 5 Sept 1908, version in Sp., 1945; Bizancio, 1939 (poema dramático, 3, G. Macchi after A. Bailly), Buenos Aires, Colón, 25 July 1939
Orch: Bodas campestres, suite, *c*1892; Theme with Variations, *c*1916
Chbr music; songs; It. trans. of Berlioz's Grand traité d'instrumentation et d'orchestration modernes (Milan, 1912)

Principal publishers: Ricordi, Ricordi Americana (Buenos Aires), Suvini and Zerboni

BIBLIOGRAPHY

E. de la Guardia and R. Herrera: *El arte lírico en el Teatro Colón: con motivo de las Bodas de Plata (1908–1933)* (Buenos Aires, 1933)
H. Panizza: *Medio siglo de vida musical* (Buenos Aires, 1952) [autobiographical essay]
C.J. Luten: 'The Impassioned Argentine', *ON*, xxxviii/14 (1974), 26–7
M. Kuss: *Nativistic Strains in Argentine Operas Premiered at the Teatro Colón (1908–1972)* (diss., UCLA, 1976) [incl. catalogue of works]

DEBORAH SCHWARTZ-KATES

Pankiewicz, Eugeniusz (*b* Siedlce, 15 Dec 1857; *d* Tworki, nr Warsaw, 24 Dec 1898). Polish pianist and composer. He was the brother of the painter Józef Pankiewicz. He studied the piano at Lublin, at the Warsaw Music Institute (?1875–7) under Józef Wieniawski and at St Petersburg (1878–80) under Leschetizky; he was probably at the Moscow Conservatory in 1880, and studied composition in Warsaw with Władysław Żeleński (1880–81) and Zygmunt Noskowski (1881–3). He taught the piano at the Warsaw Music Institute in the 1880s and 90s (with frequent interruptions, occasioned by travel or illness); these were his most creative years as a composer. He also worked at the Marian Institute and as a private tutor. He performed as a solo pianist, chamber music player and accompanist in Warsaw and elsewhere in Poland, but his chief activity was as a composer. From 1895 to 1898 he underwent treatment in a mental hospital.

Pankiewicz is best known for his solo songs, a field in which he was among the most important composers before Szymanowski. In his vocal compositions he made particular use of variation form and used an extensive range of harmonic as well as polyphonic devices; he also greatly extended the accompanist's role. Some of his songs are no more than modern arrangements of Polish folksongs, notably those of the Tatra mountains, whose original tonal characteristics he managed to preserve; many are declamatory in character and some of these contain elements of recitative. In his original songs, he drew on texts by well-known Polish and foreign poets. He composed 48 solo songs, which were reprinted several times, many of them in the collection *Eugeniusz Pankiewicz: Pieśni zebrane* (Kraków, 1956–7). His instrumental works include a Theme and Variations for string quartet (now lost) and about 40 piano miniatures in which Chopin's influence is apparent; among these works the Variations on an Original Theme in D is the most significant. He left many sketches and unfinished works.

WORKS

MSS of extant unpublished works in family's private collection

Choral: 2 songs, TTBB, op.15: no.1 [Hej do pracy (Hey to Work)] (Warsaw, 1890), no.2 [Krakowiak] in Poźniak; 5 songs, SS, pf, op.16: no.3 (Warsaw, 1898), 3 in Poźniak; Barkarola, S/T, male vv, pf, op.17 (Kraków, 1955); 6 pieśni weselnych ludowych polskich [6 Polish Wedding Folksongs], SA, pf, op.18 (Warsaw, 1917); Ballada (A. Oppmann), S, A, vv, pf, op.21; 3 songs, TTBB, 1 in Poźniak, 2 pubd singly (Warsaw, 1890, 1913)

1v, pf: 6 songs (A. Asnyk, H. Heine, S. Grochowski), opp.5, 6 (Warsaw, 1887); 8 pieśni ludowych polskich [8 Polish Folksongs], op.14, ed. (Kraków, 1956); Z miłosnych dziejów [From the History of Love] (M. Bałucki), cycle of 6 songs, op. 19 (Warsaw, 1930); 28 others, incl. 22 pubd in *Eugeniusz Pankiewicz: Pieśni zebrane* [Selected songs], i–ii (Kraków, 1956–7), 4 in Poźniak

Pf: Krakowiak-fantasia, op.9, pubd in *Echo muzyczne, teatralne i artystyczne*, v (1888); Preludium on Gdy się Chrystus rodzi, op.8, pubd in *Kłosy* (1888); Variations sur un thème original, D, op.10 (Warsaw, 1931); 7 mazurkas, opp.1–3, 1874; 3 waltzes, 1874–5; Humoresque and Menuet, op.1 (Warsaw, 1881); 2 Mazurkas, op.3 (Warsaw, 1883); 3 feuilles d'album, op.2 (Warsaw, 1885); Chaconne, Menuet, Gavotte, op.4 (Warsaw, 1887); Burlesque and Menuet, op.12 (St Petersburg, 1891); Improvisation, op.11, no.1, pubd in *Echo muzyczne*, iv (1887); Improvisation, op.11, no.2, in Poźniak

Lost: Theme and variations, str qt, 1882; Variations et fugue, pf, op.7; Krakowiak and A la cracovienne, pf, op.9; 12 further single works for pf, incl. 4 dances; 3 choral works: op.16, no.1, Nokturn and Serenada, male vv; solo songs

BIBLIOGRAPHY

SMP

M. Malcz: 'Eugeniusz Pankiewicz', *Tygodnik ilustrowany*, xl (1899), 56

W. Poźniak: *Eugeniusz Pankiewicz* (Kraków, 1958) [incl. thematic catalogue of works]

A. Nowak-Romanowicz and others, eds.: *Z dziejów polskiej kultury muzycznej* [History of Polish musical culture], ii (Kraków, 1966)

KATARZYNA MORAWSKA

Pann, Anton (*b* Sliven, Bulgaria, 1796; *d* Bucharest, 2 Nov 1854). Romanian printer and publisher. He studied music in Bucharest (1812–18) with Dionisie Fotino and Petru Efesiu. As a psalm reader and teacher of psalmody, he founded in 1843 the first printing shop in Bucharest to publish traditional church service music in the Romanian language in place of Greek; he also published folklore collections, calendars, almanacs and folk writings. His first printed book, *Bazul teoretic şi practic al muzicii bisericeşti* ('The theoretical and practical basis of church music', 1846), was followed by a number of church service books. He also published a book of carols (1830–54) and collected folk music, which he transcribed into church modes and published in six booklets: *Spitalul amorului sau Cîntătorul dorului* ('Love hospice or the singer of longing', 1850, 2/1852). After his death his printing shop (equipped with music printing presses) became the property of the Bucharest Metropolitan Church.

BIBLIOGRAPHY

G. Dem Teodorescu: *Operele lui Anton Pann* (Bucharest, 1891)

G. Dem Teodorescu: *Viaţa şi activitatea lui Anton Pann* [Life and activity of Anton Pann] (Bucharest, 1893)

I. Manole: *Anton Pann* (Bucharest, 1954)

G. Ciobanu: *Anton Pann: Cîntece de lume* [Songs of the world] (Bucharest, 1955)

V. Cosma: *Muzicieni români: compozitori şi muzicologi* (Bucharest, 1970), 344–6

T. Moisescu: *Prolegomene bizantine* (Bucharest, 1985)

VIOREL COSMA

Pannain, Guido (*b* Naples, 17 Nov 1891; *d* Naples, 6 Sept 1977). Italian musicologist and composer. He studied the piano with his father and counterpoint and harmony with his grandfather; he continued both subjects at the Naples Conservatory with Camillo de Nardis and took an arts degree at Naples University (1914). Subsequently he was professor of music history at Naples Conservatory (1915–47) and at the Accademia Nazionale d'arte drammatica in Rome. He began his active career as a music critic for the *Corriere del mattino* (1920) and continued at other Neapolitan dailies, including *Battaglia del mezzogiorno* (1922), *Roma* (1928–30) and *Il mattino* (1932–43); he then moved to the Rome daily *Il tempo* (1947) and next to the weekly *Epoca* (1950–57).

Pannain's chief musicological work was the study of Neapolitan music, resulting in surveys of the musical environment created by the oratorio of Filippo Neri and his followers, the various 15th- to 18th-century schools (including a special study of Domenico Scarlatti), Bellini, and the conservatory and its history. Two early articles deal with manuscripts in the Naples Biblioteca Nazionale. With Prota-Giurleo he provided the first penetrating studies of the city's music. Another lifelong interest was the music of Monteverdi, represented by numerous articles in *Rassegna musicale* (1958–68) and by an analysis of the madrigals and sacred polyphony in *Claudio Monteverdi* (1967). His early compositions were influenced by Impressionism but in later works (the operas *Beatrice Cenci*, 1942, and *Madame Bovary*, 1955) he returned to a post-Puccini Italian style. He wrote on contemporary music, an interest probably stimulated by Pannain's own composing. The concern to arrive at an aesthetic judgment which characterizes his research shows his adherence to Croce's views. He was a member of the Accademia Nazionale di S Cecilia and the Lincei Academy.

WORKS
(selective list)

Ops: L'intrusa (1, R. Giani, after M. Maeterlinck), Genoa, 1926; Beatrice Cenci (3, V. Viviani), Naples, 1942; Madame Bovary (3, after G. Flaubert), Naples, 1955

Mimodramas: Capri, 1930–31; Il sogno di Agave (R. Forges Davanzati), 1935

Choral: Requiem, 1912; Paolo Uccello, S, female vv, orch, 1930; Ps li, S, vv, orch, 1946, rev. 1950; Stabat mater, T, vv, orch, 1969

Orch: Preludio, str, 1910; Ouverture, 1911; Intermezzo, vc, orch, 1911; Amleto, sym. poem, 1915; Fuga, 1924; Sinfonietta, 1927; 2 vn concs., 1930, 1960; Va Conc., 1954; Hp Conc., 1959; Pf Conc., 1969

Other works: chbr music, songs

Principal publishers: Curci, Ricordi, Suvini Zerboni

WRITINGS

La teoria musicale di Giovanni Tinctoris (Naples, 1913)

Le origini della scuola musicale napoletana (Naples, 1914)

Le origini e lo sviluppo dell'arte pianistica in Italia dal 1500 fino al 1730 circa (Naples, 1917)

'Note di archeologia musicale', *RMI*, xxvi (1919), 486–517

'Liber musicae', *RMI*, xxvii (1920), 407–40

Lineamenti di storia della musica (Naples, 1922, 10/1974)

Musicisti dei tempi nuovi (Milan, 1932, 2/1954; Eng. trans., 1932/R)

with A. Della Corte: *Vincenzo Bellini: il carattere morale, i caratteri artistici* (Turin, 3/1952) [incl. 'Saggio critico', 77–123]

with A. Della Corte: *Storia della musica* (Turin, 1936, 4/1964)

Il Conservatorio di musica di S. Pietro a Maiella (Florence, 1942)

La vita del linguaggio musicale (Milan, 1947, 2/1956)

L'arte della fuga di G.S. Bach (Rome, 1948)

Ottocento musicale italiano: saggi e note (Milan, 1952)

Da Monteverdi a Wagner (Milan, 1955)

L'opera e le opere ed altri scritti di letteratura musicale (Milan, 1958)

'Studi monteverdiani', *RaM*, xxviii (1958), 7–15, 97–108, 187–95, 281–92; xxix (1959), 42–50, 95–105, 234–46, 310–21; xxx (1960), 24–32, 230–40, 312–24; xxxi (1961), 14–26, xxxii (1962), 1–20

'L'opera' [*Un ballo in maschera*], *Verdi: Bollettino dell'Istituto di studi verdiani*, i (1960), 73–89, 609–74; Eng. and Ger. transs. in *Quaderni della RaM*, no.3 (1965), 13–24, 894–927

'L'opera' [*La forza del destino*], *Verdi: Bollettino dell'Istituto di studi verdiani*, ii (1961–6), 755–92, Eng. trans., 1103–54

'Serghei Prokofiev', *Approdo musicale*, no.13 (1961), 5–67

Giuseppe Verdi (Turin, 1964)

Richard Wagner: vita di un artista (Milan, 1964)

with G. Barblan and C. Gallico: *Claudio Monteverdi nel quarto centenario della nascita* (Turin, 1967) [incl. 'Polifonia profana e sacra', 251–359]

Un libro su Carlo Gesualdo (Naples, 1968)

'Note sui Responsori di Carlo Gesualdo da Venosa', *Chigiana*, new ser., v (1968), 231–7

Saggi wagneriani (Venice, 1968)

'L'opera' [*Rigoletto*], *Verdi: Bollettino dell'Istituto di studi verdiani*, iii/7 (1969), 89–123; Eng. and Ger. transs., 466–509

Introduzione al teatro di Riccardo Wagner (Venice, 1971)

'La musica a Napoli dal '500 a tutto il '700', *Storia di Napoli*, viii (Naples, 1971), 715–87

'L'arte pianistica di D. Scarlatti', *Studi musicali*, i (1972), 133–45

EDITIONS

L'oratorio dei Filippini e la scuola musicale di Napoli, IMi, v (1934)

CAROLYN GIANTURCO

Pannell, Raymond (*b* London, ON, 25 Jan 1935). Canadian composer. He studied the piano with Steuermann, and composition with Bernard Wagenaar and Vittorio Giannini at the Juilliard School (1954–9). Beginning in the mid-1960s he became increasingly involved with opera. In 1966 he directed an opera workshop at the Stratford Festival, Ontario and during the period 1968–70 served as the assistant director and resident composer of the Atlanta Municipal Theater. He co-founded Toronto's Co-Opera Theatre in 1975 and became its general director, a post he held until 1984. His own opera, *The Luck of Ginger Coffey* (1967) was commissioned by the CBC for Canada's centennial year. The work juxtaposes elements from jazz, serial and popular musics within a traditional operatic structure. *Exiles* (1973) combines an eclectic mix of musical materials with poetry and photography. Pannell's video opera, *Aberfan* (1976), inspired by the Welsh disaster in which a slag heap buried schoolchildren alive, won the Salzburg TV Opera Prize in 1977 and an ACTRA Award in 1978. In the 1980s Pannell turned his creative energies to writing fiction (*EMC2*).

WORKS
(selective list)

Stage: Aria da capo (chbr op, E. St Vincent Millay), 1963; The Luck of Ginger Coffey (op, R. Hambleton after B. Moore), 1967; The Exiles (B. Pannell), 1973; Go (children's op, R. Pannell), 1975; Midway (R. and B. Pannell), 1975; Aberfan (video op, R. and B. Pannell), 1976; Circe (masque, 1, M. Atwood), 1977; N–E–W–S (radio op, R. and B. Pannell), 1977; Souvenirs (B. Pannell), 1978, rev. as As Long as a Child Remembers, 1984; The Downsview Anniversary Song Spectacle Celebration Pageant (R. Pannell), 1979; Refugees (vaudeville op), 1979; Harvest (TV op, R. Pannell), 1980; Thank You, Mr. Ludwig van, 1988; The Animals of Limbo (pageant), 1990; The Forbidden Christmas (musical, Atwood, R. Pannell), 1990

Orch: Double Conc. no.1, pf, v, orch, 1957; Pf Conc. no.2, 1961; Ballad, pf, orch, 1968; Give Us This Day, children's chorus, orch, 1970; Don Quixote's Christmas Conc., nar, pf, orch, 1981; Chorale and Toccata, 1989

WRITINGS

'Aria da capo', *Opera Canada*, iv/Feb (1963), 5–6

'Building a Tradition', *Opera Canada*, xviii/Sept (1977), 14–15

'Opera in the 1980s', *Opera Canada*, xxi/spr. (1980), 36, 70

'Goodnight Co-Opera, Sweet Dreams', *Canadian Theatre Review*, xl/Fall (1984), 23–8

ELAINE KEILLOR

Panni, Marcello (*b* Rome, 24 Jan 1940). Italian conductor and composer. He studied at the Rome Conservatory (conducting with Ferrara, 1963; composition with Petrassi, 1964), and then studied conducting with Manuel Rosenthal at the Paris Conservatoire (1965–8). In 1971 he founded the Ensemble Teatromusica, with whom he performed his musical pantomime, *Klangfarbenspiel*, at the Piccola Scala, Milan (1972), and the 'azione scenica' *La partenza dell'Argonauta* at the Maggio Musicale Fiorentino. He has conducted rarely performed works, such as Pergolesi's *Il Flaminio* (Naples, 1982), for which he also provided a new critical edition, and has given the European premières of works by Berio, Bussotti, Cage, Feldman, Glass and others. He has also appeared as a guest conductor at La Scala, the Metropolitan Opera, the Vienna Staatsoper, the Paris Opéra and elsewhere. Panni held the Milhaud Chair in Composition at Mills College, Oakland, California (1980–84), and in 1993 was appointed principal conductor of the Bonn Opera, becoming musical director in 1995. In 1994 he was appointed artistic director of the Pomeriggi Musicali in Milan. He has recorded Pergolesi's opera *Adriano in Siria* and oratorio *La morte di San Giuseppe*, Paisiello's *Nina, pazza per amore*, Handel's *Giulio Cesare*, Donizetti's *La fille du régiment*, Petrassi's *Il Cordovano* and Berio's *Passaggio*.

Panni's compositions include choral, orchestral and chamber music, works of music theatre and two operas, *Hanjo* and *Il giudizio di Paride*.

RENATO MEUCCI

Panninger, Leonhard. *See* PAMINGER, LEONHARD.

Panny, Joseph (*b* Kolmitzberg, Lower Austria, 23 Oct 1794; *d* Mainz, 7 Sept 1838). Austrian violinist and composer. He studied the violin with his father and the organ and harmony with his grandfather, Joseph Breinesberger. At the age of 19 he became a schoolteacher in Greinberg, where Joseph Eybler chanced to hear a cantata of his; impressed by Panny's talent, he offered to teach him, and by 1815 Panny was in Vienna studying with Eybler. He made his début on 13 April 1825 in a programme of his own works, an overture, choruses, an Adagio and Polonaise for oboe and bassoon, and excerpts from an opera, *Das Mädchen von Rügen*. Undaunted by a review in the *Allgemeine musikalische Zeitung* that found his music full of gaucheries and lacking in originality, he continued to give similar concerts, in June 1827 and February 1828, to audiences comprising mainly complimentary-ticket holders.

As a violinist Panny is remembered less for his own prowess than for his brief association with Paganini, whom he met in Venice and in Trieste in 1824. Paganini played Panny's dramatic sonata 'The Tempest' at his farewell concert in Vienna on 24 July 1828, but before the end of the year had found both sonata and composer unsympathetic. Panny's talent as a performer did not match his ambition, persistence or advance publicity. In 1829 he made an extensive tour of Germany, and in 1830 he toured northern Germany. He was active as a conductor in Bergen during the winter of 1831–2 and in Altona the following year. In 1834 he founded a music school at Weisserling, Alsace. His final tour took him to Berlin, Scandinavia and England where, according to the *Allgemeine musikalische Zeitung*, he did not arouse enthusiasm. In 1836 he settled in Mainz (where Schott had already published many of his works), married, founded a music school and continued to compose. But his health failed in 1837.

BIBLIOGRAPHY
FétisB; PazdírekH [with list of pubd works]
J.G. Hornmeyer: Obituary, *Mainzer Gazette* (1838), nos.111–13
Obituary, *AMZ*, xl (1838), 883
E. van der Straeten: *The History of the Violin* (London, 1933/R), ii, 109
G.I.C. de Courcy: *Paganini, the Genoese* (Norman, OK, 1957/R), i, 260, 268, 275
ALBERT MELL

Panocha Quartet. Czech string quartet. It was formed at the Prague Conservatory in 1968 from a trio consisting of Jiří Panocha (*b* Kladno, 3 June 1950), Jaroslav Hlůže and Jaroslav Kulhan (*b* České Budějovice, 7 Dec 1950). At the suggestion of their teacher, Josef Micka, they recruited Pavel Zejfart (*b* Prague, 7 May 1952) to make up a quartet. In 1971 Hlůže was replaced on the viola by Miroslav Sehnoutka (*b* Prague, 17 Jan 1952). Having won prizes in several national competitions, they made their US début in 1975 and their German and Irish débuts the following year. In 1980 they toured Japan with the Smetana Quartet, whose members had been among their teachers. Since then they have enjoyed an international reputation. Their repertory, founded on the Czech masters and the Viennese classics, includes the complete cycles by Dvořák and Martinů (both of which they have recorded) and a large number of quartets by Haydn, as well as many 20th-century works. Their playing is admired for its fine tone, stylistic sensitivity, technical address and polish. They have collaborated on record and in concert with the

pianists Rudolf Firkušný, Jan Panenka and András Schiff. Jiří Panocha plays a 1743 violin by Carlo Antonio Testore of Milan.
TULLY POTTER

Panofka, Heinrich (*b* Breslau, 3 Oct 1807; *d* Florence, 18 Nov 1887). German singing teacher, violinist, composer and critic. He studied singing with the Kantors Strauch and Förster, and learnt the violin with Joseph Mayseder. His initial career was as a violinist. About 1834 he settled in Paris, as a performer, critic and composer, and editor of and contributor to the new *Gazette et revue musicale*; he was also a correspondent for the *Neue Zeitschrift für Musik*. He was a prolific composer for the violin and of solo songs. After 1840 Panofka's interest turned towards the art and techniques of the great singers he heard in Paris. He studied the methods of Marco Bordogni, and went to London in 1847 and directed the chorus of the Royal Italian Opera under Lumley. He met Jenny Lind there and studied her vocal techniques, as well as those of Lablache, Fraschini and Staudigl. In London he was esteemed more as a singing teacher than as a violinist. His first didactic work, the *Practical Singing Tutor* (London, 1852), was published shortly before he returned to Paris, and his *L'art de chanter* op.81 (Paris, 1854) brought him fame which he could never have achieved as a violinist or a composer. His *Abécédaire vocal* (Paris, 1858), intended for beginners, was equally successful and innovatory, by-passing the interminable *solfège* exercises found in other singing tutors of the time. The *Voix et chanteurs* (Paris, c1870), which includes biographical notices of famous contemporary singers, is the product of Panofka's stay in Florence in the late 1860s. Panofka's vocal studies were enormously influential in Europe and America during the second half of the 19th century. They still provide useful practice material; the *Vademecum du chanteur* (the second part of *L'art de chanter*) and two sets of vocalises (opp.85–6) are available in modern editions.

BIBLIOGRAPHY
ADB (R. Eitner); *DEUMM* (P. Mioli); *PazdírekH* [with list of published works]
E. van der Straeten: *The History of the Violin* (London, 1933/R), ii, 221–2
ALBERT MELL/R

Panormitano. *See* PALOTTA, MATTEO.

Panormitano, Bartolomeo Lieto. *See* LIETO PANHORMITANO, BARTOLOMEO.

Panormitano, Mauro. *See* CIAULA, MAURO.

Panormo. Sicilian-English family, makers of violins, bows and guitars. Vincenzo Panormo (*b* Monreale, nr Palermo, 30 Nov 1734; *d* London, 19 March 1813) is thought to have made violins before leaving his native Sicily, but it is doubtful whether any instruments have survived from that period. According to his eldest son Francis, Vincenzo taught himself from an early age to make musical instruments of various kinds. However, since he rarely labelled his instruments, most accounts of his life are vague; the story becomes clearer after his arrival in England. He went to France, where he apparently worked profitably until the Revolution drove him to London in 1789. He is believed to have been working in Dublin around 1791, but was resident in London again by 1793, where his shop was first in Bloomsbury and finally in Soho. A printed label shows that in Paris he worked in the rue de l'Arbre Sec in the 1770s; reproductions of this label have been inserted into all sorts of violins, mostly by other makers. From London only manuscript labels are known, and these are rarely seen, implying that his work was mostly sold unsigned. Sometimes he branded his surname at the top of the back or on the lower rib of an instrument.

Whether or not he had formal instruction in Italy, Panormo's French-period violins are much more akin to those of the contemporary Paris makers than to any of the Italians, although he took most of his ideas from Stradivari. In London he both aided as well as learnt from the leading dealer of the day, John Betts, and one of his first pupils was almost certainly the fine Scottish maker Matthew Hardie. A comparison of Panormo's instruments with those of his London contemporaries shows him to have been the most important maker of his time, perhaps better than the others because of an innate Italian flair for woodworking. His varnish was also superior at times, although not always, for cheaper instruments were also much in demand. Panormo is also famed for his double basses.

Joseph Panormo (*b* Naples, 1767; *d* London, 20 July 1837), Vincenzo's second son, was an able assistant to his father; he continued to make instruments after his father's death, but finally died in St Anne's Workhouse 'in the greatest destitution'. As he apparently never signed his instruments there are some doubts about what he made, but most of those attributed to him come close to those of Vincenzo in quality. With the help of the eminent Spanish guitarist Fernando Sor, Joseph began making guitars, copying Sor's own Spanish-made instrument and incorporating various improvements suggested by Sor. The guitars were made lighter than before, with improved internal bracing, and to a larger model with deeper sides. Despite the success of these improvements, which made the name of Panormo synonymous with the guitar in 19th-century London, many of Joseph's instruments were labelled and sold by dealers rather than himself.

George Panormo (*b* 1776; *d* 3 Jan 1852) was the third son of Vincenzo. He made violins, cellos and bows, in which he was assisted by his son, George Louis [Lewis] (1815–77). Louis Panormo (*b* Paris, 1784; *d* Auckland, NZ, 11 Aug 1862), became the most successful of the family in making and selling guitars of high quality in his workshops in Bloomsbury. He also made instruments and bows of the violin family, the bows stamped L. PANORMO being held in particularly high esteem. In 1854 he emigrated to New Zealand, but his nephew George Louis continued the manufacture of instruments thereafter labelled 'G.L. PANORMO'.

BIBLIOGRAPHY

*Lütgendorff*GL; *Vannes*E

W. Sandys and S.A. Forster: *The History of the Violin* (London, 1864)

W.M. Morris: *British Violin Makers* (London, 1904, 2/1920)

A.P. Sharpe: *The Story of the Spanish Guitar* (London, 1954)

CHARLES BEARE, JOHN DILWORTH, PHILIP J. KASS

Pan-Pacific pop. A term for neo-Polynesian acculturated music with local language texts mostly about love, the beauties of the islands, activities of island life and sad farewells. Western or Western-style tunes are used and the songs are accompanied by guitar, electric guitar, ukelele and often by percussion instruments of island and foreign origin.

In the 1990s, the term 'Pacific Beat' was used by record producers to distinguish groups who pursued popular styles such as rap and techno, in English as well as vernacular languages. Hawaiian adaptations of Jamaican reggae (sometimes called 'Jawaiian') have achieved popularity elsewhere in the Pacific.

See also POLYNESIA, §I, 2(i), (ii), 3(v)

AMY STILLMAN

Panperdut. *See* MARCABRU.

Panpipes. Instrument consisting of a number of pipes of graduated lengths, joined together either in the form of a bundle or more commonly in the form of a raft. It is classified by Hornbostel and Sachs as a set of end-blown flutes (*see* AEROPHONE). The pipes lack mouthpieces and are blown across their tops while the lower ends are stopped. The instrument is found in central Europe and in areas bordering the Pacific. In European art music the panpipes have traditionally been regarded as a pastoral instrument. Telemann specified 'flûte pastorelle' in a concert suite in E♭ (ed. A. Hoffmann in NM, no.177) and 'flauto pastorale' in a short piece in E in *Der getreue Music-Meister* (1728–9); these are often played on a recorder, but Hunt ('Fitting the Instrument to the Music', *Recorder and Music Magazine*, 1983, March, p.228) has suggested that panpipes were intended. In *Die Zauberflöte*, Mozart gave Papageno, as a 'child of nature', a set of panpipes to attract birds into his cage.

1. Early panpipes and distribution. 2. South American, Andean. 3. South American, non-Andean. 4. Oceania. 5. Central Europe and Asia. 6. China.

1. EARLY PANPIPES AND DISTRIBUTION. Though the instrument may appear as early as the 6th millenium BCE in drawings of animal dances from Çatal Hüyük in Anatolia, its earliest extant European representations appear on three bronze urns from the Illyrian Hallstatt culture of north-east Italy, dating from the 6th and 5th centuries BCE (fig.1). They show it functioning prominently in scenes from the aristocratic feudal culture of the period, such as offertory processions and festive meals. Panpipes later gained considerable popularity among the Etruscans, who enjoyed a wide variety of wind instruments. In Greece, where it was called the SYRINX, and originally had pipes of the same length stopped at various points with wax, it was an instrument of low status with

1. *Panpipes: detail from a bronze urn (c500 BCE), Illyrian Hallstatt culture, in the Museo Civico, Bologna*

rustic connotations. Presumably both the Illyrian and Greek instruments had a common ancestor in the Indo-European Iron Age culture of the Danube Basin; today the panpipes are an important feature of Romanian folk music (see §5 below).

The Greek instrument may be the source of the large panpipes on bronze statuettes from Parthia in the early centuries CE. The same may be the case with Sassanid panpipes (the *mushtaq*) which appear in the court orchestra of Khosrow Parviz (Khosrow II, 590–628 CE) in cave reliefs at Taq-e Bostan and on silver cups from Kālār Dasht of the 6th century. But the Sassanid *mushtaq* may equally well be of Chinese origin.

The instrument appeared very early in China (see §6 below), and is also found in Myanmar (formerly Burma), where, among the Kachin and Shan, they are played with *hnyìn* (small bamboo free-reed mouth organs) for dance music, often at times of mourning.

Panpipes are also found in the central Pacific islands and western Latin America (particularly Peru and Bolivia, where, among other names, they are called *antara*, and Ecuador, where they are called *rondador*). They are often strikingly similar to Chinese panpipes in that they are a double instrument in which each half produces a whole-tone scale. An interesting version of the instrument has the two wings entirely separated, bound together only by a cord and blown by two players. Citing such evidence Sachs (1940) argued that Pacific panpipes were all derived from those of ancient China, having spread southwards to Myanmar and eastwards across the Pacific with the aid of the ocean currents.

2. SOUTH AMERICAN, ANDEAN. One- and two-rank panpipes are played throughout the length of the Andean chain, from Colombia, through Ecuador, Peru, Bolivia, northern Chile and north-western Argentina. The Colombian *castrapuercas* or *capador* (the predominant name) receives its name from the 17th-century Spanish gelder who announced his presence with a panpipe. It is a ten-pipe panpipe in a series of five. In Ecuador, the syrinx is made of cane or, more rarely, the thin feathers of a condor or vulture. It appears in three sizes played by Quechuas: eight-tube (highlands; played with a small double-headed drum in pipe-and-tabor fashion); 15-tube (Chimborazo, at Carnival); and 20- to 43-tube (solo or in folk groups with other instruments). The tubes of the Ecuadorian *rondador* are closed at the bottom, and are arranged not in strict staircase fashion, as with south Andean instruments, but in 'zigzag' style, gradually becoming longer (*see* ECUADOR, §II, 1(ii)). In Argentina and the Bolivian altiplano, the widely accepted term for panpipe is the Aymara word, *siku*; in most instances this is a two-rank instrument, of which the second rank, of open tubes, is the same length or half as long as the first, of closed tubes. The open-pipe rank is blown softly to support the closed, melody pipes and to modify the tone colour. Both ranks resemble a raft in shape, with pipes arranged by size in a staircase pattern. The *zampoña* of Gral, Bilbao Province, Potosí Department, on the Bolivian altiplano, has its pipes ranked in joined pairs, one pair having two ranks with eight pipes in each, and the other two ranks with seven pipes in each. One rank in each linked pair is closed. The tubes of the other rank are open and cut, at an angle, to half the length of the closed tubes; they sound two octaves higher. The open pipes sound indirectly when the closed pipes are blown and amplify their sonority. *Zampoñas*

elsewhere may have the open tubes the same length as the matching closed pipes, producing notes one octave higher. The Spanish *fusa* prevails in some regions, especially north-west Argentina.

Panpipes, with other native aerophones, play a major role in the festival cycle in the altiplano high plateau zone of Bolivia and Peru. Here the agricultural cycle and the cycle of saints' days determine the choice of musical instruments. The *jula-jula* panpipes (three- and four-tube) are connected with a ritual battle, part of Carnival. The *sikuri* (two-rank, 17-tube panpipes) and *lakita* (single- or double-rank, seven- or eight-tube) are linked to the agricultural cycle. Panpipes of the altiplano generally perform in pairs which share the melodic line; this practice of hocketing has been explained as necessitated by the impossibility of sustained playing at an altitude of 4000 metres. The leading panpipe is called *ira*, the follower *arca*. The number of pipes in the *arca* often differs by one from that of the *ira*. Melody proceeds in parallel organum fashion: some ensembles produce from two to four parallel octaves, other types perform in parallel 5ths and octaves. Panpipes on the altiplano are commonly played in ensembles, rarely as solo instruments. Strings and wind are rarely mixed. All flutes, including panpipes, are typically performed by men; women may dance to panpipe music. Ensembles consisting exclusively of panpipes include the *maizu* (Chipayas), *jula-jula* (Aymaras, Quechuas), and *chirihuano* (Aymaras, Quechuas, Chipayas).

2. *Rondador (panpipes) player, Cuenca, Ecuador, 1980*

3. Lawa-Sikus (panpipe ensemble) of the Altiplano region, department of La Paz

The *maizu* ensemble comprises four panpipes, one with three stopped tubes and three with two stopped tubes. The three-pipe instrument (*lutaqa* or *ira*) is considered masculine and the two-pipe one (*mataqa* or *arca*) feminine. They are played in hocketing pairs, as described above; the three two-pipe instruments are played in unison, each by a different performer. The instruments of the *chirihuano* ensemble are made from the *tokoro* reed, harder than the *caña-hueca* reed used for the similar *jula-jula*. Each rank of the typical pair has three or four pipes and there are up to 12 players in an ensemble: two on the lowest panpipes, the *jilawiri* (or *kilawiri*); four on the next highest, the *liku*; two on the next highest again, the *orqo*; and four on the highest, the *sanja*. There is one octave difference in pitch between one size and the next. The ensemble, using hocket technique (*ira* and *arca*), performs duple-metre *wayñus* (dance-songs), the musicians dancing as they play in keeping with traditional practice. The *siku* is a panpipe group with drum(s).

See also BOLIVIA, §II, 1 and PERU, §II, 3.

3. SOUTH AMERICAN, NON-ANDEAN. Among pre-Columbian Peruvian coastal societies, the Paracas Culture (400 BCE–400 CE) had panpipes, each in pairs of six tubes, or (from the Pisco Valley) of three to seven tubes. The south-coast Nazca (400–1000 CE) had clay panpipes (*antaras*) with three to 15 tubes which could produce untempered semitones and which show other evidence of clear tuning intentionality in manufacture. The northcoast Mochica (400–1000) and Chimú (*c*120–1460) had panpipes of three to seven tubes. The Yunca culture from coastal Trujillo and Chimbote had, among other types, two-rank panpipes of six tubes each. Today the Ocaina Indians of the Peruvian tropical forest region play a four-tube panpipe, the Bora of this region a three-tube instrument. To the south, the Orejones play ten-tube

instruments and the Yaguas 22- to 32-tube (single row) syrinxes. The Conibo play bamboo panpipes. In Colombia, the coastal Motilón Indians play panpipes of bamboo and feather quills. The Cuna of the San Blas Islands off Panama play pairs of panpipes (*kamu-purui*), each of seven bamboo tubes bound into groups of three and four; the 'male' and 'female' instruments play in hocket, producing composite melodies in parallel 5ths. In the early 20th century, the Uitoto (Witoto) of the Colombian Amazon had panpipes with varying numbers of tubes. The Tucano Indians of the south-eastern Colombian Amazon play cane and bamboo panpipes. Large groups of Tucano men play antiphonally, and men play panpipes as women pound cocoa leaves.

See also PERU, §II, 2.

4. OCEANIA. Panpipes have reached a remarkable peak of development in the Solomon Islands, where there are elaborate ensembles played by men and boys. In Malaita there are seven extant types of ensemble, the best known of which are those of the 'Are'are people ('au keto, 'au paina, 'au tahana, 'au taka'iori). These panpipes play 'programme music' based upon the sounds and events of nature and of daily activities including the calls of parrots, the swinging motion of a spider, raindrops falling on a leaf, or 'the satisfied cry of the pig when it is fed in the morning'. Some ensembles make use of equiheptatonic scales in which the octave is divided into seven equal steps. The melodic intervals produced by such panpipes are steps of one, two, three or more equiheptatonic units. Each ensemble of panpipes is characterized by a different number of musicians, a different organization of the scale, a particular type of polyphony and a distinctive repertory. Northwards, panpipes are found throughout New Guinea and offshore island groups including the Bismarck archipelago. The distribution of panpipes in New Guinea and the Bismarck archipelago is similar to that of rattles

4. Rondador (panpipes) player, Cuenca, Ecuador, 1980

and jew's harps, with a central belt of concentration from the Highlands to Morobe and another area of concentration in southern New Ireland. Both raft and bundle panpipes are found, with the raft form most common. The southern limit of expansion is marked by the Polynesian islands of Tonga (where the instrument is known as *mimiha*) and Samoa (*fa'aili'ofe*), where it is now all but forgotten.

5. CENTRAL EUROPE AND ASIA.   Various types of panpipes are found in Russia, Georgia and Romania. In Russia, the *kuviklï* (*kugiklï*) is a woman's instrument, played in the south-western oblasts (*see* RUSSIAN FEDERATION, §II, 4). These panpipes, consisting of two to five stopped reed pipes, may be used for playing dance music, or as accompanying instruments in an ensemble that includes singers. In Georgia, an ancient type of panpipe known as *soinari* or *larchemi* is played in Guri and Megrelia (though its use is dying out); it consists of six reed pipes of various lengths fastened in a row. They are tuned in 3rds from the bass pipes, which are positioned in the middle and are a 2nd apart. The tuning varies according to the piece being performed. Sometimes the pieces are performed by two players who can divide the instrument into two, taking three pipes each.

The earliest evidence for the existence of panpipes (*nai*) in Romania is from archaeological sources; the earliest documentary sources date from the 16th and 17th centuries. From the second half of the 18th century the *nai* appeared frequently in the *taraf* ensembles of the *lăutari* (professional folk musicians) in Romanian principalities. The oldest native names for the instrument are *fluierar*, *fluierici*, *fluierător*, *şuieras* etc.; in addition the term 'muscal' is found, like the *nai*, of oriental origin. These terms, and the fact that both early and contemporary pipes are made of bamboo stems, have led to the hypothesis that a fusion occurred between an ancient, rural instrument and an oriental professional one, the older type giving way to the new.

The 'classical' Romanian *nai* consists of a concave row of 20 pipes, of different lengths and diameters, in order

of size. The pipes are open at the upper end and glued together; they rest on a slightly curved stick or, more recently, are set into a curved pipe. The lower ends of the pipes are stopped with cork and filled with beeswax; the tuning is regulated by the quantity of wax. The *nai* produces a diatonic scale from *b'* to *g''''*, with F♯s. Intermediate notes can be obtained by slightly modifying the angle of the instrument during performance. This leads to the characteristic portamento effects in slow melodies. The *nai* is played by *lăutari*, who have recently introduced additional pipes. Such modified instruments may have 25, 28 or 30 pipes, expanding the lower register.

Between the two World Wars the *nai* almost disappeared but was successfully revived, largely owing to the work of Fănică Luca (1894–1968), who trained many successful young *nai* players.

6. CHINA.   The presence of panpipe-type instruments in ancient China is attested by the post-15th century BCE oracle bone pictographs showing two and three tubes bound together with a cord and invention legends ascribed to an even earlier period. When mentioned in the classic texts of the 3rd–2nd centuries BCE, the Chinese panpipe (*paixìao*) was simply known as *xiao* (a name later applied to vertical flutes with finger-holes). The *Zhouli* states that a large one had 24 pipes, a small one had 16 pipes; other sources, however, cite different numbers. While it seems that, most normally, pipes were closed at their lower ends (*dixiao*), a note in the *Erya* states that on some the lower ends were left open (*dongxiao*). Two panpipes with closed ends have been found at different tomb sites in central China dating to the 5th century BCE, one of a white stone (possibly jade), the other of lacquered bamboo. On both there are only 13 pipes, tuned pentatonically. According to the 2nd century CE *Fengsu Tungyi*, their profile

5. Stone panpipes from Peru

6. Paixiao (panpipes)

filled to varying depths with wax to govern vibrating lengths. According to Chen Yang's early 12th-century music treatise *Yueshu* (*c*1100), pipe numbers varied widely from one type to another (e.g. 10, 12, 13, 16, 17, 18, 21, 24), some tuned diatonically, others tuned chromatically. An 18-pipe Chinese instrument dating to about the 8th century, preserved at the Shōsōin Repository in Japan, is an example of this style of panpipe, with pipes of similar lengths, bevelled at their blowing ends and closed at their bottoms. As shown by Hayashi Kenzō (1975), this panpipe was tuned diatonically (though including the equivalents of both *fa* and *fa♯*) with a compass of more than two octaves. A detailed line drawing of an 18-pipe panpipe also appears in the *Yueshu* (fig.7*a*). Identified as *fengxiao* ('phoenix *xiao*'), both ends of the frame on this instrument are decorated with carved phoenix heads.

Sometime before the 14th century the Chinese panpipe was called *paixiao* ('row *xiao*'), in an attempt to distinguish it from the popular vertical flute which became known by the borrowed name *dongxiao* ('open *xiao*') or *xiao*. This new panpipe style, which has been pictured in 18th century sources and survives in museum collections, typically has 16 notched bamboo pipes of varying lengths, arranged in a double-wing shape (long pipes at both ends, short pipes in the middle) and enclosed in a red-lacquered wooden case (fig.7*b*). Its pipes are tuned chromatically with a compass of little more than one octave. As shown by Chuang Pen-li (1963), U-shaped notches usually appear at the blowing ends of open-ended pipes as a way to facilitate tone production (a feature not needed on closed pipes which respond readily without notches). As preserved at the Taibei Confucian shrine, the *paixiao* of today is constructed in this same external form; but instead of U-shaped notches at the blowing ends, the pipes are provided with ducts for more consistent tone production.

'resembles a (single) wing of the phoenix'. Single-wing panpipes (long pipes at one end) are also pictured in the 4th–6th century CE paintings and stone reliefs at Dunhuang, Yungang and Gongxian, suggesting that this shape was the prevailing design for the early period. Morphological, decorative and musical associations with the mythical phoenix would remain a constant theme in the development of the Chinese panpipe.

By the Tang dynasty (618–907), panpipes with pipes of similar lengths appeared more frequently, their bottoms

BIBLIOGRAPHY

SachsH

Chen Yang: *Yueshu* [Treatise on music] (*c*1100/*R*)

(a)

(b)

7. (a) Paixiao (marked 'Fengxiao') from 'Yueshu', 12th century; (b) Paixiao from 'Lülü Zhengyi', 18th century

Chuang Pen-li: *Zhongguo gudai zhi paixiao* [Panpipes of ancient China] (Taibei, 1963) [with Eng. summary]

Zhongguo yinyue shi cankao tupian [Illustrations for reference on Chinese music history], Minzu yinyue yanjiusuo, ix (Shanghai and Beijing, 1964)

R. Stevenson: *Music in Aztec and Inca Territory* (Berkeley, 1968)

H. Zemp: 'Instruments de musique de Malaita II', *Journal de la Société des Oceanistes*, no.34 (1972), 7–48

M. McLean: 'Recordings from Musée de l'Homme', *Journal of the Polynesian Society*, lxxxiii (1974), 490–91

K. Hayashi: 'Restoration of a Panpipe in the Shōsōin', *AsM*, vi (1975), 15–27

C.A. Coba Andrade: 'Instrumentos musicales ecuatorianos', *Sarance*, no.7 (1979), 70–95

C. Ziegler: *Les instruments de musique égyptiens au Musée du Louvre* (Paris, 1979)

H.C. Buechler: *The Masked Media: Aymara Fiestas and Social Interaction in the Bolivian Highlands* (The Hague, 1980)

M.P. Baumann: 'Music, Dance, and Song of the Chipayas (Bolivia)', *LAMR*, ii (1981), 171–222

M.P. Baumann: 'Music of the Indios in Bolivia's Andean Highlands (Survey)', *The World of Music*, xxv/2 (1982), 80–96

Tong Kin-woon: *Shang Musical Instruments* (diss., Wesleyan U., IL, 1983): repr. in *AsM*, xiv/2 (1982–3), pp.17–182; xv (1983–4), no.1, pp.103–84; no.2, pp.67–143

A. Valencia-Chacon: *El siku bipolar altiplano estudio de los conjuntos orquestales de sikus bipolares del Altiplano Peruano* (diss., Escuele Nacional de Música, Lima, 1983)

M.P. Baumann: 'The Kantu Ensemble of the Kallawaya at Charazani (Bolivia)', *YTM*, xvii (1985), 146–66

B. Broere: 'Some Considerations Concerning Panpipe Music of the Kuna Indians in Colombia', *AnM*, xli (1986), 6–16

Liu Dongsheng and others, eds.: *Zhongguo yueqi tuzhi* [Pictorial record of Chinese musical instruments] (Beijing, 1987) [YYS pubn]

C. Bolaños: *Les antaras Nasca: historia y análisis* (Lima, 1988)

G. Borras: 'Analyse d'une "medida" servant à la fabrication de syrinx aymaras', *Journal de la Société des Américanistes*, lxxviii (1992), 45–56

Liu Dongsheng, ed.: *Zhongguo yueqi tujian* [Pictorial guide to Chinese instruments] (Ji'nan, 1992), 116–19

T. Turino: *Moving Away from Silence: Music of the Peruvian Altiplano and the Experience of Urban Migration* (Chicago, 1993)

M. McLean: *Diffusion of Musical Instruments and their Relation to Language Migrations in New Guinea* (Boroko, 1994), 17–19

Zhongguo yueqi zhi [Monograph on Chinese musical instruments] (Ji'nan, n.d. [c1995])

Zhongguo yinyue wenwu daxi [Compendium of Chinese musical relics] (1998–)

JAMES W. McKINNON, ROBERT ANDERSON/R (1), JOHN M. SCHECHTER/R (2, 3), MERVYN McLEAN (4), TIBERIU ALEXANDRU, GRIGOL CHKHIKVADZE/R (5), ALAN R. THRASHER (6)

Pans. The individual instruments of a steel band, made from oildrums whose ends are hammered into a concave shape and tuned. *See* STEEL BAND *and* TRINIDAD AND TOBAGO.

Pan Shiji [Chew Shyh-Ji] (*b* Taibei, 29 July 1957). Taiwanese composer and teacher. She studied composition with Hsu Tsang-houei and took piano lessons before her family emigrated to Canada in 1974. Pan pursued further composition studies with Robert Turner at the University of Manitoba (1976–80) and with Chou Wen-chung at Columbia University, New York (1980–88). Her interest and expertise in traditional Asian music, stemming from her contact with Chou's music and her work at the Columbia Center for Ethnomusicology, distinguishes her from her contemporaries in Taiwan, where training in ethnomusicology is rare. After her return to Taiwan in 1988, Pan became a professor of composition at the National Academy of the Arts. Asian influence is evident in many of her compositions, for example in her use of Chinese instruments in the series *Configuration – Transformation – Shape* or of Asian poetry in *Paiju sanshou*

(1991) and *Three Songs* (1996). Repetitive patterns and restraint in the use of musical material, typical features of Asian music, combine in *Dubai de nigu* (1990). Pan has developed an Asian variety of serialism based on 'linear cells', which she employs in her series of quartets for violin, viola, cello and guitar. The subject of her impressionistic sound painting *In the Dark* (1998) is the massacre in 1947 of Taiwanese indigenous people by Nationalists from mainland China.

WORKS
(selective list)

Orch: Dream World, 1979; Music for Orch, 1980; 3 Pieces, 1982; Raining Night, 1997–9

Vocal: The Lodge Amid the Bamboos, S, chbr ens, 1980; Paiju sanshou [3 Haiku], Mez, pf, 1991; 3 Songs (Pan), 1996; In the Dark (Pan), S, pf, 1998; Qiu Lu, chorus, 1998

Chbr and solo inst: Music for Hn and Pf, 1979; Music for Pf, 1979; Wind Qnt, 1979; Brass Qnt, 1980; Str Qt in 1 Movt, 1980; Ensemble, brass, perc, 1981; Hudson River Caprice, fl, cl, hn, va, vc, perc, 1981; Str Qt, 1981; Piece, hn, pf, 1984; Str Qt no.1, vn, va, vc, gui, 1985; Str Qt no.2, vn, va, vc, gui, 1986; Str Qt no.3, vn, va, vc, gui, 1988; Dubai de nigu [The Soliloquy of Pandora], 2 vn, 2 va, 2 vc, db, 1990; Configuration – Transformation – Shape, (qin, cptr)/(xiao, erhu, qin, pipa, zheng); Shapes, cl, 1996; Si, wind qnt, tpt, pf, str trio, db, 1997; Str Qt no.4, vn, va, vc, gui, 1998

MSS in C.C. Liu Collection, Institute of Chinese Studies, U. of Heidelberg

WRITINGS

'Wei'erdi de geju yu guojia yishi' [Nationalism in Verdi's operas], *Lishi yuekan*, xiii/2 (1989)

'Genji monogatari de yinyue shenghuo: shitan yazhou yinyue wenhua jiaoliu' [Musical life in the Tale of Genji: a study in Asian musical exchange], *Yishu pinglun* (1990), no.10

'Anuo Xunbaike xunzhao shi'eryin zuopin hesheng ji qushi de tongyixing' [Schoenberg in search of harmonic and formal unity], *Yishu pinglun* (1993), no.10; (1995), no.10

'Ershi shiji yinyue xin shengsi' [New ideas on 20th-century music] *Biaoyan yishu zazhi* (1994), no.9

BIBLIOGRAPHY

B. Mittler: 'Mirrors and Double Mirrors: the Politics of Identity in New Music from Hong Kong and Taiwan', *CHIME*, no.9 (1996), 4–44, esp. 24

B. Mittler: *Dangerous Tunes: the Politics of Chinese Music in Hong Kong, Taiwan and the People's Republic of China since 1949* (Wiesbaden, 1997), 221–8

BARBARA MITTLER

Panseron, Auguste (Mathieu) (*b* Paris, 26 April 1795; *d* Paris, 29 July 1859). French teacher and composer. He studied music with his father, a teacher and friend of Grétry. In 1804 he entered the Conservatoire, and nine years later won the Prix de Rome with his cantata *Herminie*. He remained in Italy for several years, studying counterpoint with Mattei in Bologna and then singing in Naples and Rome with García and Siboni. At this time he composed a number of small pieces, some masses and an Italian opera, *I Bramini*. The 19th-century writer Georges Bénédit described how Panseron, Rossini and García, all in Rome in 1816, would sing through the ensembles of *Il barbiere* which Rossini was composing at the time. Panseron then travelled in Austria and Germany, meeting Salieri in Vienna and Winter in Munich, and wrote a mass for Prince Esterházy, who also invited him to become the honorary director of his chapel; he also visited Russia.

In the summer of 1818 he returned to Paris where he took up a post as an accompanist at the Opéra-Comique. His opera *La grille du parc* (a collaboration with Ancelot) was performed in 1820 with some success, and published; two more operas followed. However, he feared that he was embarking on a career of 'deception and pitfalls', and thus turned instead to teaching, acquiring a brilliant reputation. He was appointed professor at the Conservatoire in 1826, and published a number of didactic works which were used in conservatories all over France and, in translation, abroad. He continued to compose, but concentrated on *romances* and chamber pieces which were popular in salons and at concerts. His style was described by the critic Jules Lovy as representing the echo of the distant past (*Le ménestrel*, 7 August 1859). A Pie Jesu improvised on the *jour de service* of his teacher Gossec was admired for its feeling and grace, and was sung at many funeral occasions during the 19th century, including his own. In 1843 he was awarded the Légion d'Honneur, and he also received the Couronne de Chêne in the Netherlands. He died of a respiratory infection; at his funeral his coffin was carried by Auber, Halévy, Thomas, Monnais and Baron Taylor, who also gave a long oration at the ceremony (*FétisB*).

WORKS
(selective list)

many works published in Paris

VOCAL

Herminie (cant.), 1813; Requiem, 1818; Pie Jesu; De profundis; masses, motets
Ops: I Bramini, c1814; La grille du parc, 1820, collab. Ancelot; Les deux cousines, 1821; Ecole de Rome, Odéon, 4 Nov 1827
More than 500 romances, lv, pf, incl. Le songe de Tartini, La fête de la madonne, Malvina, Cinq mars, Adieu donc mes amis
200 nocturnes, 2/3vv, pf
More than 100 works for girls' boarding schools and orphéons
Albums lyriques, incl. 12 romances, chansonettes, nocturnes (1830)

INSTRUMENTAL

Transcriptions and arrs. of op airs by Bellini, Donizetti, Halévy, Onslow and others
Romances, hn, ob, fl, cl, vn, vc

DIDACTIC

ABC musical, ou Solfège (1841); Suite de l'ABC (1841); Solfège à deux voix (1842); Solfège d'artiste (1842); 12 études spéciales (1847); Traité de l'harmonie pratique et des modulations (1855); 36 exercices à changements de clefs (1855); 25 vocalises (1858)

SARAH HIBBERD

P'ansori. Korean operatic form probably dating from the early 18th century. *See* KOREA, §9(i).

Pantaleon (i) [pantalon]. A large DULCIMER invented by and named after PANTALEON HEBENSTREIT (1668–1750). It had 185 double strings of metal and gut and was capable of flexible dynamic variation. For illustration *see* HELLENDAAL, PIETER.

Pantaleon (ii). A term used by several German writers of the second half of the 18th century to designate a small square piano.

Pantaleoni, Romilda (*b* Udine, 1847; *d* Milan, 20 May 1917). Italian soprano. She studied in Milan, making her début there in 1868 at the Teatro Carcano in Foroni's *Margherita*. After singing in Rome, Genoa, Modena, Naples, Turin, Vienna and Brescia, in 1883 she made her début at La Scala as La Gioconda. She sang Anna in the first Milan performance of Puccini's *Le villi* (1884) and created the title role in Ponchielli's *Marion Delorme* (1885). She sang Desdemona in the first performance of Verdi's *Otello* (1887) and created Tigrana in Puccini's *Edgar* (1889). Her repertory included Mathilde (*Guillaume Tell*), Paolina (*Poliuto*), Valentine (*Les Huguenots*), Sélika (*L'Africaine*), Marguerite (*Faust*) and Margherita (*Mefistofele*), as well as many Verdi roles: Leonora (*Il trovatore* and *La forza del destino*), Amelia (*Un ballo in maschera*), Elisabeth de Valois (*Don Carlos*) and Aida. She also sang Santuzza and Elsa. A magnificent singing actress, she retired in 1891 after the death of the conductor Franco Faccio with whom she had a liaison. Her brother, Adriano Pantaleoni (1837–1908), was a baritone who sang regularly at La Scala.

ELIZABETH FORBES

Pantaloncina, La. The Italian dancer Giovanna Cortini, wife of JEAN–BAPTISTE DENIS.

Pantalon stop (Ger. *Pantalonzug, Pantaleonzug, Cälestin, Cölestin*). A device occasionally applied to unfretted clavichords in Germany and Scandinavia from about 1725 to 1800. It was named after the pantaleon or pantalon, a large dulcimer invented by Pantaleon Hebenstreit (1667–1750), the tone of which was characterized by the resonance of undamped strings. The pantalon stop consists of a series of tangent-like brass blades set in a movable bar so that all of them can be raised at once by the action of a stop-knob. When raised, these blades touch the strings immediately to the right or left of the point at which they are struck by the tangents carried by the keys. When the keys are released the strings rest on the pantalon-stop blades, which continue to separate the sounding part of the strings from the cloth damping woven between them at their left-hand end: hence the strings continue to sound instead of having their vibrations damped out as soon as the key is released. In addition, the strings vibrate sympathetically with other notes being played. The effect produced by the stop is essentially that of a hand-operated damper-lifting mechanism like that on many early square pianos, and it is likely that this device on pianos was sometimes also called by the same name.

The first known use of the pantalon stop was not in a conventional clavichord but in a type of CEMBAL D'AMOUR made about 1727 by Johann Ernst Hähnel of Meissen, an associate of Hebenstreit. From 1732 onwards, Jakob Adlung made clavichords with the device and suggested that the blades could be covered with leather or cloth to make the sound die away more quickly. In the several surviving clavichords equipped with a pantalon stop (the earliest dating from 1752, made by Christian Kintzing of Neuwied), it is usually divided so that it may be used in only the treble or bass. While Adlung favoured the 'beautiful and almost heavenly' sound of the stop (a quality reflected in its alternative name, *Cälestin*), D.G. Türk (*Clavierschule*, 1789) wrote that it caused students to acquire a 'hacking' manner of playing. Another disadvantage is that, since the pantalon-stop blades cannot touch the strings at exactly the same point as the tangents do, there may be a detectable change in the pitch of a note after the key is released.

BIBLIOGRAPHY

J. Adlung: *Anleitung zu der musikalischen Gelahrtheit* (Erfurt, 1758/R, 2/1783), 568–71
B. Brauchli: *The Clavichord* (Cambridge, 1998), 152–7

EDWIN M. RIPIN/JOHN KOSTER

Pantheon. London auditorium, built in 1772 and converted into an opera house in 1791. *See* LONDON (i), §V, 1.

Pantomime (from Gk. *pantomimos*: 'one who does everything by imitation'). A musical-dramatic genre, taking different forms in different periods and places. The Latin *pantomimus* originally referred to a Roman actor who specialized in dumb show, supported by instrumental music and a chorus; by extension the word denotes a dramatic representation in dumb show. Normal modern English usage is confined to a theatrical entertainment, usually presented in the Christmas season, which, whilst no longer in dumb show, continues to use music and other spectacular elements to support a children's tale that is often no more than a flimsy backcloth for buffoonery, dancing, topical songs and allusions and, until comparatively recent times, a harlequinade.

1. Ancient Rome. 2. England. 3. Mainland Europe.

1. ANCIENT ROME.   The origins of pantomime are of great antiquity, but it was made fashionable in Rome in 22 BCE by Pylades of Cilicia and Bathyllus of Alexandria. As Horace wrote (*Satires*, i, 5, 64), to dance the shepherd Cyclops in tragic mask and buskins was nothing new. According to Macrobius (*Saturnalia*, ii, 7) Pylades was responsible for introducing instruments and chorus; Bathyllus seems to have specialized in light, satyric themes, and Pylades was in style closer to the tragedy. Pantomime usually took its subject matter from mythology, but also from history and the themes of tragic drama; unlike straight mime, it was not coarse.

The performance took place on a public stage or in a private house. The *pantomimus*, sometimes supported by a speaking actor, wore a graceful silk costume and a fine mask with closed lips. The chorus and instrumentalists stood behind him. The *pantomimus* sometimes appeared in as many as five roles in turn, each with its own mask. There are tributes to the eloquence and directness of a good dancer who could undertake to retell a whole tale with several parts, and to the expressiveness of one performer whose powers of mime, Lucian wrote, were rich enough to overcome the language barrier for a foreign visitor – unable to comprehend the narrative songs, he nevertheless so highly prized the actor's miming that he wished to take him home to his own country to act as an interpreter (a similar tribute was paid to 'Kasperl' Laroche – himself originally a dancer – in Vienna at the beginning of the 19th century, by the Turkish minister Ismael Effendi who, largely ignorant of German, claimed to understand what Laroche was saying, thanks to his mimetic powers; see *Ueberblick des Ueberblicks des neuesten Zustandes der Literatur des Theaters und des Geschmacks in Wien*, by C** X**, 1802, p.78).

The use of steps, posture and especially of gesture ('manus loquacissimae, digiti clamosi') was aided by conventions not unlike those familiar from modern ballet. The role of the songs seems to have been minor; those fragments that survive are in Greek rather than Latin. Lucan and Statius were among poets who were not afraid to abase their talents by earning good money writing pantomimes, for it became a highly popular form of entertainment, not without importance in its effects on morality (especially after females began to appear in pantomimes), and even on the political scene the historian Zosimus attributed the moral decline of Rome to the vast popularity of the *pantomimi*.

2. ENGLAND.   The renewal of interest in ancient forms of drama during the Renaissance led to the birth of various kinds of pantomime, the boundaries between which are often hard to distinguish. In England the title denotes a new form, which, in the early 18th century, looked to many sources for its success. The characters of the *commedia dell'arte* were familiar to audiences; their popularity had increased during the previous century, and the influx of actors from the Paris fairgrounds and the Théâtre Italien provided a new impetus to interval entertainment in dancing and mime. In the second decade of the century visiting foreign troupes and the published scenarios of Gherardi's collections provided a framework for *lazzi*, involving Harlequin and other *commedia* characters, as well as introducing a mythological constituent. By 1715 a pattern assembled from these elements provided a more extended type of 'afterpiece' entertainment. The playhouse managers frequently advertised these as 'Entertainments' and promoted what was clearly beginning to be a popular form which might enliven their stock repertory. The farcical (or 'grotesque') parts, which appear to have had continuous musical accompaniment (the 'Comic Tunes'), began to be interspersed with masque-like interludes sung in the style of Italian *opera seria* (the 'Serious' or 'Vocal' parts), which supplied a foil to the clowning and which scaled down the operatic conventions that might have become tedious for the largely middle-class playhouse audiences. 'Descriptions' were published, providing a libretto for the 'serious' parts but not detailing the buffoonery, which was improvised. The devisers of these afterpieces looked to contemporary Italian opera for recitative and aria in the 'serious' parts, to the French *ballet de cour* for the dances, to the English masque for the scenes, machines and decorations, and to the *commedia dell'arte* for the knockabout. The serious parts are sometimes referred to as 'masque' interludes in playbills and contemporary writing, but continental French influences were strong.

John Weaver developed the first 'Entertainments' in dancing of any length with a story in mime. *The Tavern Bilkers* (1703) was not, as he claimed, the first of its kind but was probably the first to appear in which the dance element was to the fore. His *Loves of Mars and Venus* (1717), which he believed was similar to the Roman pantomimes, was in fact akin to the later *ballet d'action*. It was John Rich, owner and actor-manager of the theatre in Lincoln's Inn Fields, who seized upon disparate elements and moulded them into what became the pantomime tradition. Rich's first pantomimes, always performed as afterpieces, appeared in 1717 in competition with Drury Lane. Often identified by the inclusion of the word 'Harlequin' in the title (e.g. *Harlequin Dr. Faustus*, 1712; see illustration), the pantomimes produced from 1723 to 1728 saw the success of the form as a popular afterpiece. Rich's most successful pantomimes were all devised by Lewis Theobald, and in these he worked closely with the composer John Ernest Galliard, whose familiarity with da capo aria, use of motto openings and predictability of phrase structure and tonality led to a fairly formalized type of melody and harmony, ideal for the easygoing playhouse audiences. In his pantomime music of 1723–6 he favoured a straightforward binary form with little use of ritornello and a shortwinded vocal line; *The Rape of Proserpine* (1727) marks a change in his pantomime style, with more da capo arias, arioso, with fewer binary airs and more use of ritornello.

The 'grotesque' sections, with continuous music, were given titles such as 'Wedding Dance', 'Jigg', 'Clodpole', 'Gardener's Dance', 'The Birth of Harlequin', or 'Quaker's Dance', which indicate the action that accompanied them.

John Rich as Harlequin in John Thurmond's pantomime 'Harlequin Dr. Faustus', performed at Lincoln's Inn Fields Theatre in December 1723: watercolour by an unknown artist in the British Museum, London

They were published as 'Comic Tunes', whether they were for knockabout or dance; some quickly came to be regarded as traditional. The most developed pantomimes consisted of an overture, possibly a dozen airs and a concluding chorus, with recitative and airs in alternation. Most of the airs deal with pastoral subjects, nature and love or joy and sorrow.

In the course of time the pantomime changed in character, becoming a more fully integrated comic play, the characters and action of which were close to the stock elements of the Italian comedy, with young lovers and their resourceful servants outwitting jealous parents and guardians, often with supernatural assistance. Vocal rather than instrumental music dominated, and some of the leading composers provided scores for the pantomimes (Galliard and Pepusch in the early years, and later the Arnes, Dibdin, Linley, Boyce, Shield and others). Suitable instrumental music accompanied the elaborate transformation scenes, though as the emphasis shifted more strongly towards the spectacular elements of the age of the British melodrama, reputable musicians more rarely wrote pantomime scores. In the 20th century, popular songs of the moment were introduced without relevance or apology, and under the influence of the music hall and variety turn little remains but the name and the framework of a moral fairytale.

3. MAINLAND EUROPE.   On the Continent too the pantomime was a popular form of entertainment in the 18th and 19th centuries, though the phenomenon varied widely between different centres and periods. In France, where Noverre demonstrated the virtues of Garrick's realistic approach to stage characterization, pantomime tended to be a dignified form of danced entertainment. Rousseau's *Dictionnaire de musique* (1768, p.359) defines the pantomime as an 'Air to which two or more dancers execute in dance an action (which is itself also known

under the same term). The pantomime airs ... speak, as it were, and form images, in the situations in which the dancer is to put on a particular expression'. The French tradition of pantomimic scenes and characters in the lyric theatre lived on in the famous mute title-role of Auber's *La muette de Portici* (also known as *Masaniello*, 1828); and though Wagner (who greatly admired *La muette*) had in fact completed the second act of *Rienzi* before he moved to Paris in autumn 1839, the ballet sequence in that act is often referred to as a pantomime because of the thematic and even dramatic relevance of the dances to the story. Adam's *La poupée de Nuremberg* (1852) and the Olympia act of Offenbach's *Les contes d'Hoffmann* (1881) are further French operatic scores that contain important pantomimic elements. Wagner may be held to have written the most successful of all pantomimic scenes in opera, that in Act 3 of *Die Meistersinger von Nürnberg* in which Beckmesser, painfully reminded at every turn of his beating of the night before, finds and misappropriates Walther's Prize Song when he visits Sachs's temporarily deserted workshop.

There was a strong pantomime tradition in 18th-century Vienna, where the presence of a vital popular theatre (including native elements, above all the character of Hanswurst, and elements derived from the *commedia dell'arte*, such as Harlequin, Pantaloon and Columbine) was combined with a marked south German tendency to use music in the theatre. The appellation 'Pantomime' was used in Vienna at least as early as the 1720s. Among authors of pantomime scenarios Kurz-Bernardon is the most important, and Haydn's lost music for Kurz's *Der (neue) krumme Teufel* (*c*1758) includes a pantomime, *Arlequin der neue Abgott Ram in America*. Mozart, with the assistance of distinguished friends, gave a pantomime of his own composition (K446/416*d*; only a fragment survives) at a public rout during Carnival 1783; he gave an account of it in his letter to his father of 12 March that year. The pantomime tradition continued to be strong in Vienna roughly until the advent of the operetta; elements of its more elevated aspect live on in the Kessler–Richard Strauss collaboration *Josephslegende* (1912–14).

BIBLIOGRAPHY

MGG2

E. Gherardi: *Le Théâtre Italien* (Paris, 1694, 5/1721)

J. Weaver: *A History of the Mimes and Pantomimes* (London, 1728)

C. Cibber: *An Apology for the Life of Mr Colley Cibber* (London, 1740)

[J.C. Strodtmann]: *Abhandlung von den Pantomimen* (Hamburg, 1749)

J.-J. Rousseau: *Dictionnaire de la musique* (Paris, 1768/R1969)

T. Davies: *Memoirs of the Life of David Garrick Esq.* (London, 1780/R, 2/1808/R)

P. Sawyer: *John Rich v. Drury Lane* (diss., Columbia U., 1934)

W. Beare: 'Pantomimus', *The Oxford Classical Dictionary*, ed. N.G.L. Hammond and H.H. Scullard (Oxford, 1949, 2/1970), 776–7

P. Hartnoll, ed.: *The Oxford Companion to the Theatre* (London, 1951, 2/1978)

R. Southern: *Changeable Scenery* (London, 1952)

F.L. Miesle: *Pantomime and Spectacle on the London Stage 1714–1761* (diss., Ohio State U., 1955)

A. Nicoll: *Early Eighteenth Century Drama* (London, 1955)

S. Rosenfeld: *The Theatre of the London Fairs in the 18th Century* (Cambridge, 1960)

A. Nicoll: *The World of Harlequin* (Cambridge, 1963)

R.J. Broadbent: *A History of Pantomime* (New York, 1964)

E. Stadler: 'Das abendländische Theater im Altertum und im Mittelalter', *Das Atlantisbuch des Theaters*, ed. M. Hürlimann (Zürich and Freiburg, 1966), esp. 512

A.M. Heiss: *Die Pantomime im Alt-Wiener Volkstheater* (diss., U. of Vienna, 1969)

K. Richards and P. Thompson, eds.: *Essays on the Eighteenth-Century English Stage* (London, 1972)

R. Fiske: *English Theatre Music in the Eighteenth Century* (London, 1973, 2/1986)

V. Korda: 'Körperbewegung, Tanz, Pantomime, Movement', *Musikerziehung*, xxxiii (1979), 75–6

C. Chapman: *English Pantomime and its Music* (diss., U. of London, 1981)

J. Hera: *Der verzauberte Palast: aus der Geschichte der Pantomime* (Berlin, 1981)

A.D. Shapiro: 'Action Music in American Pantomime and Melodrama, 1730–1913', *American Music*, ii/4 (1984), 49–72

A. von Wangenheim: *Béla Bartók: der wunderbare Mandarin: Von der Pantomime zum Tanztheater* (diss., U. of Cologne, 1984)

R. Ralph: *The Life and Works of John Weaver* (New York, 1985)

B.D. Chesley: *The Faces of Harlequin in Eighteenth-Century English Pantomime* (diss., Indiana U., 1986)

J. House: *Music Hall Memories: Recollections of Scottish Music Hall and Pantomime* (Glasgow, 1986)

M.E. Smith: *Music for the Ballet-Pantomime at the Paris Opéra 1825–1850* (diss., Yale U., 1988)

M.E. Kenley: *Sixteenth-Century Matachines Dances: Morescas of Mock Combat and Comic Pantomime* (diss., Stanford U., 1993)

G. Kroó: 'Pantomime: the Miraculous Mandarin', *The Bartók Companion*, ed. M.G.W. Gillies (London, 1993), 372–384

D. Pickering and J. Morley, eds.: *Encyclopedia of Pantomime* (Andover, 1993)

H.L. Power: 'Pantomime Songs and the Limits of Narative in Ulysses', *Picking up Airs: Hearing the Music in Joyce's Text*, ed. R.H. Bauerle (Urbana, UL, 1993), 53–66

F. Becker: '"Erfindet mir Tänze, dichtet mir Pantomimen": Frank Wedekinds Tanzlieder', *Musiktheorie*, x/l (1995), 21–36

M. Burden: 'The Independent Masque 1700–1800: a Catalogue', *RMARC*, no.28 (1995), 59–159

PETER BRANSCOMBE (1, 3), CLIVE CHAPMAN (2)

Pantonality. A term coined by Rudolph Réti (in *Tonality, Atonality, Pantonality*, London, 1958) to explain the continued extension of tonal language in the late 19th century as it had been developed by Wagner, Debussy and others. This harmonic extension had taken some music beyond the point at which it could be said to be in a single key, or to waver among or shift in and out of a number of clearly discernible key centres, without falling into categories defined as bitonal or polytonal (presenting two or more keys simultaneously), or strictly non-tonal or 12-note serial (as in Schoenberg and Webern). Put more positively, pantonality is characterized chiefly by the notion of 'movable tonics'; that is, it recognizes and makes use of tonal relationships in intervals, melodic figures and chord progressions without defining, or even implying, a key centre in any large-scale sense. It may thus be applied to much of the music of Bartók and Berg, and of Stravinsky and Hindemith up to about 1920; a vast repertory of 'pantonal' music followed later in the 20th century from the developments of these composers.

WILLIAM DRABKIN

Pantoum [pantum] (Fr., from Malayan *pantun*). A Malayan verse form consisting of four-line stanzas from each of which the second and fourth lines are repeated to form the first and third of the next; the last line of the final stanza repeats the opening line of the poem. The scheme was made known in France by Ernest Fouinet and adopted by Victor Hugo in his *Orientales* and subsequently by other French and English poets. The second movement of Ravel's Piano Trio is entitled 'Pantoum', and in it Ravel attempted an ingenious synthesis of a musical equivalent of the verse form with that of the traditional scherzo and trio. He may have been prompted to this by Debussy's setting of the pantoum 'Harmonie du soir', the second of the *Cinq poèmes de Baudelaire*.

BIBLIOGRAPHY

B. Newbould: 'Ravel's Pantoum', *MT*, cxvi (1975), 228–31

MICHAEL TILMOUTH/R

Panufnik, Sir **Andrzej** (*b* Warsaw, 24 Sept 1914; *d* London, 27 Oct 1991). Polish composer and conductor, active in England.

1. LIFE. He was the younger son of a celebrated violin maker and writer on violin making, Tomasz Panufnik, and a violinist of partly English descent, Matylda Thonnes. He began his formal musical training in 1932 at the Warsaw Conservatory, taking classes in percussion before transferring to theory and composition, the latter under Kazimierz Sikorski; other influential teachers included Jerzy Lefeld and Maliszewski. His first acknowledged work, the Piano Trio, was composed in 1934. After graduating in 1936, he studied conducting with Weingartner in Vienna (1937–8) before following the well-trodden path of inter-war Polish composers to Paris. There he took lessons from Philippe Gaubert in conducting Debussy and heard much new music, including Berg's Lyric Suite and Bartók's Sonata for two pianos and percussion. He spent the spring and summer of 1939 in London, returning to Warsaw shortly before the German invasion of Poland on 1 September.

During World War II Panufnik stayed in Warsaw and participated in its severely restricted musical life, notably as a duo-pianist with Lutosławski in café concerts and underground events, but also conducting the premières of his *Uwertura tragiczna* (or *Tragic Overture*) and second wartime symphony. In 1944–5 all his manuscripts were inadvertently destroyed by an occupant of a friend's Warsaw apartment. After the war, Panufnik reconstructed several of these lost scores and in the process persuaded the publishers PWM to adopt clearer score layouts – since

Andrzej Panufnik, 1983

universally familiar – which left pages blank of all but the active playing parts. Between 1945 and 1947 he worked mainly as a conductor, firstly of the Kraków PO and then of the Warsaw PO (1946–7). He was also engaged by several leading orchestras abroad (in Berlin, London, Paris and Zürich) and presently became one of Poland's most respected conductors, alongside Grzegorz Fitelberg.

Panufnik was soon acknowledged as an innovatory composer thanks largely to *Krąg kwintowy* ('Circle of 5ths') and the orchestral *Kołysanka* (or *Lullaby*) and Nocturne, all composed in 1947. In the same year he was awarded the Szymanowski Prize for the Nocturne, while in 1949 his *Sinfonia rustica* took the Chopin Prize. His subsequent troubles with the Stalinist dogmas of the Polish United Workers' Party were no different in nature from those experienced by other composers. His arm was twisted to compose socialist-realist mass songs, all of his other music was subject to official scrutiny and partial bans were placed on several works, especially the Nocturne and *Sinfonia rustica*; yet, like other Polish composers, he was awarded state prizes. His own position was exacerbated by the ways in which he was manipulated, as a non-member of the Party, into becoming an acceptable face of the new Polish state. Articles praising the communist system and condemning Western capitalist imperialism appeared under his name; and he was compelled to participate in cultural delegations, including that which he led to China in 1953, accompanied by the folk troupe Mazowsze. On the positive side, his dubiously privileged position allowed him occasionally to conduct abroad, and it was during one of these visits, to Zürich in July 1954, that his escape to the West was engineered. His music was immediately banned in Poland and for over 20 years his name rarely appeared there in print.

Although there was a flurry of Western interest in Panufnik's defection and his open condemnation of the communist system, he soon found himself deprived of critical attention as he settled in England (he became a British citizen in 1961). As he ruefully commented: 'I had leapt from my Polish position of Number One to no one at all in England'. Although he received some financial and moral support (notably from a few British composers, including Vaughan Williams), after the sensation of his defection had subsided he quickly found that he needed

to re-establish himself as a conductor, rather than as a composer, in order to make ends meet. Following appearances as a conductor in Birmingham, he was appointed musical director of the CBSO in 1957, the same year in which Stokowski conducted the première of *Sinfonia elegiaca* in Houston, and in which *Rhapsody*, the first of two BBC commissions, was performed in London. From 1959, after resigning from the CBSO, Panufnik concentrated solely on composition. He retained his strong ties with Polish history and culture; indeed, prominent works from the period 1963–7 reinforce the impression of exile. With *Katyń Epitaph* (1967) he even returned to the political fray. He composed this tribute to the 15,000 Polish POWs murdered on Soviet soil in 1943 at a time when the USSR had still not acknowledged that its forces, and not those of the retreating Nazis, had been responsible for the crime.

Winning the Prince Rainier Competition in 1963 for *Sinfonia sacra* marked a turning-point in Panufnik's career. (He would receive the award again 20 years later, this time for his entire output.) In 1970 Stokowski gave the première of *Universal Prayer* in New York and a recording of selected works by Panufnik was released by the LSO under Jascha Horenstein. Others who became associated with his music include Menuhin, who commissioned the Violin Concerto, David Atherton, and the Boston SO under Seiji Ozawa.

In Poland, the ban on Panufnik's music was lifted in 1977, and *Universal Prayer* received its Polish première at the Warsaw Autumn Festival that year. Although many Polish premières of his music were given at subsequent Warsaw Autumns, it was not until a democratically elected government took office that Panufnik accepted an invitation to return to Poland. At the 1990 Festival, 11 of his works were performed in his presence and he himself directed the European première of *Harmony*. That same year he also conducted the première of Symphony no.10 in Chicago. He was knighted in 1991 and posthumously awarded the Knight's Cross of the Order of Polonia Restituta by President Lech Wałęsa. Shortly before his death he completed the Cello Concerto for Rostropovich.

2. WORKS.   Many traits of Panufnik's mature style are apparent in works he reconstructed in 1945. The Piano

Trio has Ravelian impulses, both harmonically and rhythmically, *Pięć pieśni ludowych* ('Five Polish Peasant Songs') is permeated with bittersweet juxtapositions and superimpositions of major and minor triads, while the *Tragic Overture* is characterized by nervous energy, tight motivic control and sharply delineated textures and dynamics. In the postwar works Panufnik indulged his fascination for abstract patterns and schematic ideas. For instance, the *Circle of 5ths* contains several early instances of symmetrical procedures (especially in pitch, register and dynamics), while *Lullaby* employs strict contrapuntal layering (the latter is also remarkable for its glissandos articulated by quarter-tones). The Nocturne is the most persuasive of these exploratory pieces and combines acute orchestral textures (anticipating Polish 'sonorism' of the late 1950s and the 60s) with expressive lyricism and subtle realization of arch form. Arguably the most appealing composition of the late 1940s, however, is *Sinfonia rustica*, which draws on the Classical symphonic tradition as well as Polish folk music. Like the much later Third Quartet, the *Sinfonia* was inspired by semi-abstract palindromic papercuts, the kind found in Polish folk art. These patterns have a bearing on orchestration and harmony, as well as form – a symmetrical four-movement model – and the layout of the orchestra.

The years 1949–54 were rather barren for Panufnik, especially with regard to his evolution as a composer. His *Uwertura bohaterska* ('Heroic Overture') especially is narrative (i.e. socialist realist) rather than abstract (or 'formalist'), and to all appearance more bombastic than subtle. That Panufnik later recycled, with minimal changes, the musical content of *Symfonia pokoju* ('Symphony of Peace', 1951) to produce *Sinfonia elegiaca* and *Invocation for Peace* suggests that he was content with its musical aspect. What he discarded in this process, however, were the work's socialist-realist texts and the politically charged context in which it had been written and officially promoted as a worthy example of Polish cultural policy. Nor did his new life in the West produce a stylistic rebirth of the kind experienced by his colleagues in Poland during the late 1950s. Both the *Rhapsody* and *Polonia* are picturesque rather than adventurous, and even when he began to develop in new directions in the early 1960s the BBC Third Programme, which at his stage was thoroughly enamoured of the European avant garde, deliberately ignored his music. But signs that he was regaining confidence are apparent in the characteristically melancholic *Landscape* and *Autumn Music* (both 1962) which combine the sound world and symmetrical shape of the Nocturne with developments in motivic design and sequencing first heard in the *Tragic Overture*.

Sinfonia sacra (1963), written to commemorate 1000 years of Polish Christianity, reinforces this synthesis. Each of the three Visions of the symphony is based on one of three consecutive intervals from the opening of the medieval hymn *Bogurodzica* (a source he would return to for *Sinfonia votiva*), while the first two phrases of the hymn are reserved for the climax of the concluding movement. The symphony's intervallic integrity, cool archaisms, detached formal rituals and directly emotional devices – brass fanfares, militaristic percussion, expansive string cantilenas – are still rooted in his music of the postwar decade. But the intricate formal and motivic designs that were to serve him faithfully throughout his output are also increasingly in evidence.

At the centre of Panufnik's revitalized abstractionism was his development of thematic-cells in works from *Reflections* (1968) onwards. Panufnik's reliance on these three-note cells (the most common is F–B–E) was undoubtedly related to the intensive analytical studies he made, when a student in Vienna, of all the published scores by Schoenberg, Berg and Webern; he was drawn to the latter's music in particular. In his setting of Alexander Pope's poem *Universal Prayer*, Panufnik's focus on limited intervallic content, combined with an extended structural palindrome, slow tempos and alternating textures, is unrelenting to the point of ascetic meditation. Here and in subsequent works, Panufnik invested the organization of pitch, rhythm, dynamics and texture with mystical and alchemical properties in his search for a spiritual dimension. He was in many ways a 20th-century reflection of the medieval belief in the Quadrivium as well as of Pope's dictum: 'Order is Heav'n's first Law'.

Despite his almost hermetic compositional world, Panufnik's aesthetic remained firmly rooted in 18th- and 19th-century practices, drawing on tonal, rhythmic and gestural conventions as a counterweight to his deployment of pitch cells. If some of his more severe works appear over-formulated, others demonstrate a keen ability to harness geometric designs to progressive effect. The pre-compositional planning for *Sinfonia di sfere*, for example, allowed for three overarching, expanding regions of activity, as well as six parametric spheres of influence governing harmony, rhythm, melody, dynamics, tempo and form. Musically, this result is both complex and compelling. From the early 1980s the style becomes gradually more relaxed. Fast sections are less prone to rhythmic or registral sequencing and forms can accommodate passionate lyricism. Sometimes the structures are pared down, as in the slow–fast, two-movement schemes of the *Sinfonia votiva* and Cello Concerto, while Panufnik's love of nature is conjured-up in *Arbor cosmica* in the form of 12 unusually variegated 'evocations', each of which represent a branch of what he calls 'the cosmic tree' (his structural diagram for this work is but one of many which evince his fascination with symbols and symmetries). *Sinfonia votiva* in particular demonstrates Panufnik's command of long-term goals (the work lasts for 40 minutes) and effectively initiates a neo-romantic phase which culminates in the last two symphonies and the final chamber works for strings.

Certain abiding concerns underlie the distinctive linguistic and formal achievements of Panufnik's last three decades. Perhaps unsurprisingly, these stem from music written during periods of crisis in the composer's career: World War II, socialist realism in Poland and the cultural isolation he sometimes experienced in England. The impression formed is of a career dominated by the need to find and secure a compositional world that was safe from outside interference, hence the search for geometric rationale and highly controlled forms derived from cells. The nature of his music was nevertheless programmatic and communicative. There are few works without descriptive titles or subtitles, and many later compositions revisit earlier musical and extra-musical concerns; the Bassoon Concerto (1985), for example, recalls folklike major–minor inflections in its commemoration of the murder of Father Jerzy Popiełuszko by the perpetrators of Polish martial law. The ever-present lyricism is almost invariably set against nervy, aggressive rhythmic impulses (often articulated by drums), a contrast through which he not infrequently seems to be exorcizing demons from the past in an attempt to evoke a sense of hope, compassion and heightened contemplation. His musical world serves as a powerful testament to his struggle for both abstract perfection and human expressivity.

WORKS

VOCAL

Choral: 5 pieśni ludowych [5 Polish Peasant Songs], unison S/Tr, 2 fl, 2 cl, b cl, 1940, reconstructed 1945, rev. 1959; Symfonia pokoju [Sym. of Peace] (J. Iwaszkiewicz), chorus, orch, 1951, withdrawn; Song to the Virgin Mary, chorus/6 solo vv, 1964, rev. 1969, arr. str sextet, 1987; Universal Prayer (cant., A. Pope), S, A, T, B, chorus, 3 hp, org, 1968–9; Winter Solstice (C. Jessel), S, Bar, chorus, 3 tpt, 3 trbn, timp, glock, 1972

Solo vocal: 4 pieśni walki podziemnej [4 Songs of the Underground Struggle] (Z. Zawadzka, S.R. Dobrowolski, W. Lebiedew-Kumacz), 1v, pf, 1943–4; Pieśń Zjednoczonej Partii [Song of the United Party] (L. Lewin), 1v, pf, 1948 arr. chorus; Warzawski wiatr [Warsaw Wind] (K.I. Gałczyński), 1v, pf, 1949; Suita polska (Hommage à Chopin), 5 vocalises, S, pf, 1949, rev. 1955, arr. fl, str, 1966; Pieśń zwycięstwa [Song of Victory] (S. Wygodzki), 1v, pf, c1950; Pokój nad światem [Peace to the World] (Dobrowolski), 1v, pf, 1951; Ślubowanie młodych [Youth Pledge] (W. Broniewski), 1v, pf, 1952 [from film Ślubujemy]; Nowy czas [New Time] (J. Ficowski), 1v, pf, 1954; Love Song (P. Sidney), Mez, hp/pf, 1976, arr. Mez, hp/pf, str, 1991; Dreamscape, vocalise, Mez, pf, 1977; Modlitwa do Matki Boskiej Skępskiej [Prayer to the Mother of God at Skępe] (J. Pietrkiewicz), 1v/unison vv, org/pf/insts, 1990

ORCHESTRAL

Syms.: 2 syms., 1939, 1941, destroyed, 1st reconstructed 1945, withdrawn; Sinfonia rustica (Sym. no.1), 1948, rev. 1955; Sinfonia elegiaca (Sym. no.2), 1957, rev. 1966 [after Symfonia pokoju]; Sinfonia sacra (Sym. no.3), 1963; Sinfonia concertante (Sym. no.4), fl, hp, str, 1973; Sinfonia di sfere (Sym. no.5), 1974–5; Sinfonia mistica (Sym. no.6), 1977; Metasinfonia (Sym. no.7), org, str, timp, 1978; Sinfonia votiva (Sym. no.8), 1981, rev. 1984; no.9 (Sinfonia della speranza), 1986, rev. 1987; no.10, 1988, rev. 1990

Other: Uwertura tragiczna (Tragic Ov.), 1942, reconstructed 1945, rev. 1955; Nocturne, 1947, rev. 1955; Kołysanka (Lullaby), 29 str, 2 hp, 1947, rev. 1955; Uwertura bohaterska [Heroic Ov.], 1950–52, rev. 1969; Rhapsody, 1956; Polonia, suite, 1959; Autumn Music, 1962, rev. 1965; Landscape, str, 1962, rev. 1965; Pf Conc., 1962, rev. 1970, 1972, 1982; Katyń Epitaph, 1967, rev. 1969; Vn Conc., str, 1971; Conc. festivo, 1979; Concertino, perc, str, 1979–80; Arbor cosmica, str orch/12 str, 1983; A Procession for Peace, 1983; Bn Conc., 1985; Harmony, 1989; Vc Conc., 1991

CHAMBER AND SOLO PIANO

Pf Trio, 1934, reconstructed 1945, rev. 1977; Wind Qnt, fl, ob, 2 cl, bn, 1953, rev. as Quintetto accademico, 1956; Triangles, 3 fl, 3 vc, 1972; Str Qt no.1, 1976; Paean, 6 hn, 6 tpt, 6 trbn, org ad lib, 1980, red. 4 hn, 3 tpt, 3 trbn, tuba, org ad lib; Str Qt no.2 'Messages', 1980; Sextet 'Trains of Thought', 2 vn, 2 va, 2 vc, 1987; Str Qt no.3 'Wycinanki' [Papercuts], 1990

Krąg kwintowy [Circle of 5ths], 1947, rev. as 12 Miniature Studies, nos.1–6, 1955, 7–12, 1964; Reflections, 1968; Pentasonata, 1984

OTHER WORKS

Ballet: Miss Julie (2, choreog. K. Macmillan), chorus, insts, Stuttgart, 8 March 1970; others choreog. to existing works

Film scores: Strachy [Ghosts] (E. Cękalski, K. Szołowski), 1938; Wir Stwosz, 1951; Ślubujemy [We Pledge], 1952

Works for young people: 2 Lyric Pieces, 1963: no.1, 2 cl, b cl/bn, hn/tpt, tpt, trbn, no.2, str; Thames Pageant (cant., C. Jessel), 2 Tr choruses, wind, brass, perc, str, 1969; Invocation for Peace (Jessel), Tr vv, 2 tpt, 2 trbn, 1972, arr. chorus/5vv [from Symfonia pokoju]

Works after old Polish music: Divertimento, str, 1947, rev. 1955 [after F. Janiewicz: str trios]; Suita staropolska [Old Polish Suite], str, 1950, rev. 1955; Koncert gotycki [Gothic Conc.], tpt, timp, hp, hpd ad lib, str, 1951, rev. as Conc. in modo antico, 1955 [from film Wit Stwosz]; Jagiellonian Triptych, str orch, 1966

MSS in *GB-Lbl*

Principal publishers: Boosey & Hawkes, PWM

WRITINGS

'Życie muzyczne w dziesiejszej Polsce' [Musical life in today's Poland], *Kultura*, nos.87–8 (1955), 7–19; abbreviated Eng. version: 'Composers and Commissars', *Encounter*, iv/3 (1955), 3–8

'About my Autumn Music and Universal Prayer',*Tempo*, no.96 (1971), 11–15

Impulse and Design in my Music (London, 1974)

Composing Myself (London, 1987)

BIBLIOGRAPHY

KdG(M. Homma)

Z. Mycielski: 'I Symfonia Panufnika', *RM*, i/6 (1945), 7–8

Z. Mycielski: 'Pięć pieśni ludowych', *RM*, ii/17–18 (1946), 40–42

F. Wrobel: 'Z zagadnień muzyki ćwierćtonowej (Na marginesie Kołysanki A. Panufnika)' [Issues concerning quarter-tone music (on the margins of Panufnik's Lullaby)], *RM*, iv/18 (1948), 13–16

A. Moskalukówna: 'Kołysanka Andrzeja Panufnika: Próba analizy kolorystycznej' [An attempt at a colouristic analysis], *RM*, v/13 (1949), 25–6

H. Truscott: 'Andrzej Panufnik', *Tempo*, nos.55–6 (1960), 13–18

B. Hall: 'Andrzej Panufnik and his Sinfonia sacra', *Tempo*, no.71 (1964–5), 14–22

P. French: 'The Music of Andrzej Panufnik', *Tempo*, no.84 (1968), 6–14

S. Walsh: 'The Music of Andrzej Panufnik', *Tempo*, no.111 (1974), 7–14

C. Macdonald: 'O muzyce Andrzeja Panufnika', *RM*, xxvii/20 (1983), 3–6, 11

N. Osborne: 'Panufnik at 70', *Tempo*, no.150 (1984), 2–10

T. Kaczyński: 'Obecność Panufnika' [The presence of Panufnik], *Przemiany techniki dźwiękowej, stylu i estetyki w polskiej muzyce lat 70*, ed. L. Polony (Kraków, 1986), 193–207

H. Truscott: 'The Achievement of Andrzej Panufnik', *Tempo*, no.163 (1987), 7–12

M. Homma: 'Composing Myself – Composing my Style: O 'Arbor cosmica' Andrzeja Panufnika', *Muzyka źle obecna*, ed. K. Tarnawska-Kaczorowska, ii (Warsaw, 1989), 396–423

A. Tuchowski: 'Sinfonia sacra Andrzeja Panufnika a wartość muzyki' [Panufnik's Sinfonia sacra and the meaning of music], ibid., 424–33

H. Truscott: 'The Symphonies of Andrzej Panufnik', *MT*, cxxx (1989), 390–93

K. Stasiak: *An Analytical Study of the Music of Andrzej Panufnik* (diss., Queen's U., Belfast, 1990)

K. Tarnawska-Kaczorowska: 'Andrzej Panufnik i fletnia Marsjasza' [Andrzej Panufnik and the Flute of Marsyas], *Kultura Niezależna*, no.65 (1990), 3–15

T. Potter: 'All my Children: a Portrait of Andrzej Panufnik', *MT*, cxxxii (1991), 186–91

M. Głowiński: 'Pochwała bohaterskiego oportunizmu: episod socrealistyczny w biografii Andrzeja Panufnika' [In praise of heroic time-serving: the socialist-realist episode in Panufnik's biography], *Rytuał i demagogia: trzynaście szkiców o sztuce zdegradowanej* (Warsaw, 1992), 95–103

T. Kaczyński: *Andrzej Panufnik i jego muzyka* (Warsaw, 1994)

M. Dąbrowski: *Wielka podróż 'Mazowsza'* [Mazowsze's great journey] (Poznań, 1996)

B. Jacobson: *A Polish Renaissance* (London, 1996)

E. Siemdaj: 'Pomiędzy uczciem a intelektem: geneza autorefleksji muzycznej Andrzeja Panufnika' [Between emotion and intellect: the genesis of Panufnik's self-image and his perception of music], *Muzyka polska 1945–1995*, ed. H. Oleszko (Kraków, 1996), 175–82

K. Jaraczewska-Mockałło: *Andrzej Panufnik: Katalog dzieł i bibliografia* [Catalogue of works and bibliography] (Warsaw, 1997)

ADRIAN THOMAS

Panzacchi [Pansacchi], **Domenico** (*b* Bologna, *c*1730; *d* Bologna, 1805). Italian tenor. He is said to have been a pupil of Bernacchi and sang in *opera seria* from 1746. In Vienna in 1748–9 he first worked with Anton Raaff, who was to overshadow him in parts of his later career. In 1751–7 he was at Madrid (Raaff arriving at a higher salary in 1755) and from 1760 until his pensioning in 1782 he was in the service of the Munich court (which Raaff joined after 1778), with occasional operatic engagements in Italy. He sang the title roles in Bernasconi's *Agelmondo* (1760), *Temistocle* (1762) and *Demofoonte* (1766), but he is best remembered for creating Arbaces in *Idomeneo* (1781); he was a great favourite with the Munich audiences and Mozart found his singing and acting worthy of respect.

BIBLIOGRAPHY

LipowskyBL; SartoriL

E. Anderson, ed.: *The Letters of Mozart and his Family* (London, 1938, 3/1985)

DENNIS LIBBY/PAUL CORNEILSON

Panzéra, Charles (Auguste Louis) (*b* Geneva, 16 Feb 1896; *d* Paris, 6 June 1976). Swiss baritone. He volunteered for the French Army during World War I, then made France his home. A student at the Paris Conservatoire, he made his début as Albert in *Werther* in 1919 at the Opéra-Comique. There he sang a range of secondary roles, his only significant stage appearance being Pelléas, which he also performed in Amsterdam and Florence; his interpretation was highly praised by Debussy's widow. A born recitalist, Panzéra was one of the foremost interpreters of *mélodies* of his time. In 1922 he gave the first performance of Fauré's last song cycle *L'horizon chimérique*, dedicated to him and suiting to perfection his keen but reserved style, as his recording confirms. Through Europe and the USA, with triumphant success, he championed the art of French song, together with his wife and accompanist, the talented pianist Madeleine Baillot. Panzéra's voice was a perfect example of the baryton Martin, the timbre tenor-like with no heavy overtones. A prolific recording artist, he left superb interpretations of Duparc's songs showing words and tone finely wedded, the expression restrained, never exaggerated. He retired in the early 1950s and taught at the Conservatoire.

WRITINGS

L'art de chanter (Paris, 1945)

L'amour de chanter (Paris, 1957)

L'art vocal: 30 leçons de chant (Paris, 1959)

50 mélodies françaises: leçons de style et d'interprétation/50 French Songs (Brussels and New York, 1964)

Votre voix: directives générales (Paris, 1967)

ANDRÉ TUBEUF/ALAN BLYTH

Paoli, Giovanni. *See* PABLOS, JUAN.

Paolo, Giampaolo de. *See* DOMENICO, GIANPAOLO DI.

Paolo Aretino. *See* ARETINO, PAOLO.

Paolo da Ferrara. *See* FERRARESE, PAOLO.

Paolo [di Marco] da Firenze [Don Paolo Tenorista da Firenze; Magister Dominus Paulus Abbas de Florentia] (*b* Florence, *c*1355; *d* Florence, after 20 September 1436). Italian music theorist and composer of more known pieces than any other Trecento composer apart from Landini.

Most earlier views on his life were superseded by the discovery of an antiphoner (*F-DOU* 1171), dated 1417, with an inscription crediting its organization to Dominus Paulus, abbot of the Benedictine monastery of S Martino al Pino, near Arezzo, and rector of the church of S Maria Annunziata Virgine (generally known by the name of the hospice it occupied and served, Orbatello) in Florence.

This antiphoner is beautifully illuminated in the style of S Maria degli Angeli in Florence, namely the style found both in the Squarcialupi Codex and the manuscript *I-Fl* Ashb.999, which contains Paolo's *Gaudeamus omnes*. Further evidence that this is the correct Paolo comes from his will, bequeathing three books of music and 'unum Boetium musicale'.

The will, made in Florence and dated 21 September 1436, names his father, Marco, and three brothers: Domenico, Antonio and Nicolo. Since the act of resignation of Paolo's abbacy, dated 16 June 1433, says he was around 78 years old, a birthdate of around 1355 seems certain. So he is likely to have entered the Benedictine order in about 1380. On 8 March 1401 he was appointed abbot of S Martino al Pino. According to the 18th-century Arezzo chronicler Hieronymus Aliotti, Paolo supported the election of Pope Alexander V at the Council of Pisa in 1409, a detail that would fit well with the text of his madrigal *Girand' un bel falcon*, almost certainly reflecting Florentine antipathy to Pope Gregory XII in that year.

It is not clear how long before 1417 he became rector at Orbatello in Florence, but several documents report his residence there from February 1420 until January 1427. In 1419 and 1423 he acted as papal legate for S Maria degli Angeli. Moreover, the text of *Godi, Firenze* suggests that he was resident in Florence in 1406.

The above documentation (all first presented in Günther, 1987) eliminates earlier identifications of the composer as a singer at S Reparata, Florence, in 1408 and as the Camaldolite Paolo at the Badia del Sasso, near Arezzo, in 1419. (His portrait in the Squarcialupi Codex, see illustration, has him in the black of a Benedictine, not the white of a Camaldolite; since this was done at the Camaldolite monastery S Maria degli Angeli, it can hardly be wrong.) Moreover, no evidence has been found to support earlier theories that he could have been related to the affluent Capponi or Leoni families of Florence; details of his will and reports on the poverty of his brother, Domenico di Marco, suggest that Paolo was from a humble family.

Paolo da Firenze: miniature from the Squarcialupi Codex (I-Fl Med.Pal.87, f.55v)

Far harder to construe is the Paolo, abbot of S Andrea de Pozzo in the diocese of Arezzo (and near to S Martino al Pino), who witnessed a document of Cardinal Angelo Acciaiuoli in Rome on 16 July 1404. The composer was abbot of S Martino al Pino from 1401 to 1433 and seems unlikely to have held another abbacy at the same time; but a document of May 1419 shows him appointing a new rector to S Andrea de Pozzo – in fact the man who eventually became his successor as abbot of S Martino al Pino. Moreover, in 1404 Cardinal Acciaiuoli received a decorated missal from the monastery of S Maria degli Angeli.

That Paolo's name has the suffix 'tenorista' the first time it appears in *F-Pn* it.568 suggests that he was at some stage active as a professional singer, perhaps before he became abbot. The prefix 'Don' (or 'Dominus'), otherwise used only for the Benedictine Donato, endorses the view that he was a Benedictine.

Most of his music survives in *F-Pn* it.568, sometimes with the ascription erased (though in most cases endorsed by other sources) and sometimes with indications in the original index that almost certainly imply his authorship (fully argued in Nádas, 1989). But the other main Trecento sources almost entirely overlook him, which is odd for the second most prolific composer in that repertory. There is nothing in *I-Fn* Panciatichiano 26; just one piece in *GB-Lbl* Add.29987; two at the very end of *I-La* 184; and one in *F-Pn* n.a.fr.6771 (Codex Reina) – a *unicum* (*Perch' i' non seppi*) often doubted on the grounds of its style and the manuscript's non-Florentine origin, though the ascription is one of only four in the entire original layer of the manuscript and should therefore not be taken lightly. Most puzzling of all, two gatherings (16 folios) of *I-Fl* Pal.87 (the Squarcialupi codex) are laid out for his music, each opening headed 'Magister Dominus Paulus Abbas de Florentia', and preceded by a marvellous portrait (see illustration), but no music was entered. An added puzzle in this last case is the coat of arms at the foot of the portrait page as well as on the first page of the manuscript, once identified as that of the Leoni family, but now considered unidentifiable. While the earlier view that Paolo was largely responsible for the Squarcialupi codex was based on much evidence now shown to be untenable, the placing of those arms, and Paolo's demonstrable contacts with S Maria degli Angeli, where it was illuminated, strongly point to some kind of contact yet to be defined.

More recently discovered sources clarify the picture. The 'Lowinsky' fragment (now *US-Cn* Case ML 096.P36, facs. and edn in Pirrotta, 1961) is entirely of his work, though without any ascriptions. The fully ascribed 'Ciliberti' fragment (owned by Galliano Ciliberti; facs. and partial edn in Brumana, 1987) is also devoted to Paolo, this time with ascriptions on each page and adding several new works; it was from a larger manuscript evidently organized by composer. The almost illegible palimpsest manuscript *I-Fsl* 2211, devotes its 14th gathering to his work, endorsing tentative ascriptions elsewhere.

Marrocco's edition of Paolo (PMFC, ix, 1977) contains only 33 of the 61 works listed below, cautiously avoiding those in *F-Pn* it.568 with erased ascriptions (which he put among the anonymous works in PMFC, viii and xi); but although those erasures have not been explained there are now enough supporting ascriptions elsewhere (as also for the erased ascriptions to Landini in the same manuscript) for confidence that these works are indeed by Paolo. What can perhaps be said is that most of them lack the quality and individuality of Paolo's best work, so it is just possible that he later preferred to suppress them; if so, perhaps it was a similar attitude that delayed his decision on which pieces to have copied into the Squarcialupi codex.

The dates of 1406 for *Godi, Firenze* (Günther, 1967) and of 1409 for *Girand' un bel falcon* (convincingly argued in Günther, 1987) must stand as a basis for a chronology, supported by the more tentative date 1397–1402 for *Sofrir m'estuet* (Nádas, 1989). All three are works of high individuality.

The madrigals ascribed with the 'PA' monogram in *F-Pn* it.568 (that is, those in the added gathering 6) seem to show the influence of the Ciconia generation (perhaps after 1400) and to be in a later style than the others, which draw more heavily on the styles of Landini and even Jacopo da Bologna. Similarly, the ballatas ascribed 'PA' (in the added gathering 8) show the most ambitious style, with unexpected textures (*La vaga luce, Lena virtù*), notational ambition (*Amor da po', Amor tu solo*), metrical irregularity and unpredictable tonal schemes (*Chi l'agg' i' fatto*), whereas the remainder show strong influence from the later works of Landini.

On such a model, it looks very unlikely that any of his known music could be later than about 1410, despite his having lived a further quarter-century.

WORKS

Editions: *Paolo Tenorista in a New Fragment of the Italian Ars Nova*, ed. N. Pirrotta (Palm Springs, CA, 1961) [P]
Italian Secular Music, ed. W.T. Marrocco, PMFC, viii (1972), ix (1975), xi (1978) [M viii, M ix, M xi]
Italian Sacred Music, ed. K. von Fischer and F.A. Gallo, PMFC, xii (1976) [F]

Because of the unusual situation both of source distribution and authorship for Paolo's music, all sources and ascriptions are given here. The ascription 'PA' in *F-Pn* it.568 is a ligatured sign; ascriptions given as 'implied' are for works only at the bottom of an opening that is headed with an ascription. 'Lw' indicates the Lowinsky fragment, now *US-Cn* Case ML 096.P36; 'Cil' is the fragment owned by Galliano Ciliberti (Perugia).

MADRIGALS

Corse per l'onde già di speme piena, 2vv, M ix, 116; *F-Pn* 568 ('PA'), *I-Fsl* 2211 ('P. Abbas')

Era Venus al termin del suo giorno, 2vv, M ix, 124; *F-Pn* 568 ('PA'), *I-Fsl* 2211 ('P. Abbas')

Fra duri scogli sanz' alcun governo, 2vv, M ix, 127; *F-Pn* 568 ('PA')

Girand' un bel falcon gentil e bianco, 2vv, M viii, 32; *F-Pn* 568 ('Don Paolo': ascription erased), *I-Fsl* 2211 ('P. Abbas'); probably intended to be the first work in the Paolo section of the Squarcialupi Codex and evidently a Florentine invective against Pope Gregory XII, perhaps in February 1409 (Günther, 1987)

Godi, Firenze, poi che se' sì grande, 3vv, M ix, 130; *F-Pn* 568 ('PA'); celebrating the Florentine victory over Pisa, 9 October 1406 (Günther, 1967)

Nell' ora ch'a segar la bionda spiga, 2vv (verto and chiuso endings for the ritornello imply missing text), M ix, 144; *F-Pn* 568 ('PA')

Non più 'nfelice alle suo membra nacque, 2vv, M ix, 150; *Pn* 568 ('Don Paolo Tenorista Da firenze': name written out fully as it is the first work by him in the MS)

Se non ti piacque in ingrat' abitare, 2vv, M ix, 167; *Pn* 568 ('Don Paolo'), *GB-Lbl* Add.29987 ('M[adrigale] di don paghollo')

Tra verdi frond' in' isola 'n sul fonte, 2vv, M ix, 174; *F-Pn* 568 ('Don Paolo'); appears again later in the MS, textless and anon.; Senhal: ORSA

Una fera gentil più ch'altra fera, 2vv, M ix, 180; *Pn* 568 ('D.P.')

Una smaniosa e insensata vecchia, 2vv, M viii, 96; *Pn* 568 (anon.), *I-Fsl* 2211 ('P. Abbas')

Un pellegrin uccel gentil e bello, 2vv, M ix, 183; *F-Pn* 568 ('Don Pa.')

Ventilla con tumulto la gran fama, 2vv, M ix, 189; *Pn* 568 ('PA'), *I-Fsl* 2211 ('P. Abbas')

BALLATAS

Amor, da po' che tu ti maravigli, 3vv, M ix, 102; *F-Pn 568* ('PA')

Amor, de' dimmi se sperar merzede, 3vv, M ix, 105, P 81; *Pn 568* ('Don Paolo'), *I-Fsl* 2211 ('Abbas Paulus'; 2vv), Lw (2vv)

Amor mi stringe assai più che non sole, 2vv (but empty stave for Contratenor in *F-Pn 568*), M xi, 9; *Pn 568* ('PA': implied), *I-Fsl* 2211 ('Abbas Paulus')

Amor, tu solo 'l sai, 3vv, M ix, 108, P 78 (preferable); *F-Pn 568* ('PA'), Lw (2vv)

Astio non morì mai, 2vv, M xi, 11; *Pn 568* (anon.), *I-Fsl* 2211 ('Abbas Paulus'), Cil ('D.P.')

Benchè partito da te 'l corpo sia, 3vv (text inc.), M ix, 110; *F-Pn 568* ('Don Paolo')

Ben posson pianger gli ochi e star dolente, 2vv (inc.), ed. in Brumana (1987), 29; Cil ('D.P.')

Che l'agg' i' fatto a questa donna altera, 3vv, M ix, 112; *Pn 568* ('PA')

Chi vuol veder l'angelica belleza, 3vv, M ix, 114; *Pn 568* ('PA')

Da tanto disonesto et reo fervore, 2vv (inc.), ed. in Brumana (1987), 30; Cil ('D.P.': implied)

De', dolze morte, cavami di pena, 3vv, M xi, 43; *Pn 568* ('DP': ascription erased); Senhal: LENA

De', fa per quella speme e fede ch'io, 3vv, M xi, 45; *Pn 568* ('DP': ascription erased), Cil ('D.P.')

De', passa temp' amaro, 2vv, M xi, 49; *Pn 568* ('DP': ascription erased), Cil ('D.P.': implied)

Doglia continua per la suo partita, 2vv, M ix, 120, P 75; *Pn 568* ('Pa.'), Lw (in same hand that copied Ciconia's *Con lagrime* into *Pn 568*); Senhal: ALESANDRA

Dolze mie donna grazios' e pia, 3vv (form unclear; perhaps a sonnet), M xi, 56, P 72; Lw (anon., but from context surely by Paolo)

Donna, perchè mi veggi altra mirare, 2vv, M ix, 122; *Pn 568* ('Don Paolo')

Donne et fanciulle, chi ha gentil cuore, 2vv, M xi, 65; *Pn 568* ('DP': ascription erased)

Fatto m'à sdegno partir vie d'amore, 3vv, M xi, 72; *Pn 568* ('DP': ascription erased), Cil ('D.P.')

In quella parte che si lieva 'l giorno, 3vv, M xi, 83; *Pn 568* ('Do. Pa.': ascription erased)

Lasso, grev' è 'l partir anima mia, 2vv, M ix, 134; *Pn 568* ('PA')

La vaga luce che fa invidi' al sole, 3vv, M ix, 136; *Pn 568* ('PA'), *I-La* 184 (2vv, with more florid discantus); Senhal: NENCIO LISA

Lena, virtù e speranza, ogni cor duro, 3vv, M ix, 138; *F-Pn 568* ('PA'); Senhal: LENA

Ma' ri' aver di me pietà non veggio, 3vv, M ix, 142; *Pn 568* ('PA'); Senhal: MARIA

Merzè, per Dio, perchè, 2vv, M xi, 91; *Pn 568* ('DP': ascription erased)

Mort' è la fe' e lo sperar va giù, 2vv, M xi, 96; *Pn 568* ('Franciscus': ascription erased), Cil ('D.P.'); Senhal: SARA

Non c'è rimasa fe', 3vv (text of three stanzas), M ix, 148; *Pn 568* ('PA')

Ome, s'io gli piango, 2vv (form very unclear), M xi, 116; *Pn 568* ('DP': ascription erased)

Or sie che può com' a vo' piace sia, 2vv, M ix, 154; *I-Fsl* 2211 ('P. Abbas')

Perchè vendetta far or non si po', 2vv, M ix, 156; *F-Pn 568* ('Don Paolo')

Perch' i' non seppi passar caut' al varco, 3vv, M ix, 158; *Pn* n.a.fr.6771 ('Dompni pauli': ascription sometimes questioned, but the first ascription to appear in the MS and one of only four composer ascriptions in the main body of the MS)

Po' c'ànno di mirar gli occhi mie stanchi, 2vv, M ix, 162; *Pn 568* ('Don Paolo'), *I-Fsl* 2211 ('Abbas Paulus')

S'Amor in cor gentil à signoria, 3vv, M ix, 164, P 69; *F-Pn 568* ('PA'; Contratenor added in a different hand), Lw (2vv)

Se già seguir altra che te non volli, 3vv, M xi, 126; *Pn 568* ('DP': ascription erased), Cil ('[D.] P.'; incomplete); Senhal: SANDRA

Se le n'arà pietà, Amor, ti prego, 3vv, M xi, 128; *Pn 568* ('DP': ascription erased); Senhal: LENA

Se partir mi convien dal tuo bel viso, 3vv, M xi, 136; *Pn 568* ('DP': ascription erased), Cil ('D.P.'); Senhal: MADALENA (cf. the 'Lena' of Lena, virtù e speranza)

Se per virtù, Amor, donna m'accese, 3vv, M ix, 170; *Pn 568* ('PA'); Senhal: NENCIO LISA

Sie mille mille volte benedetta, 2vv, M xi, 141; *Pn 568* ('DP': ascription erased), *I-Fsl* 2211 ('Abbas Paulus'), Cil ('D.P.': implied)

Sofrir m'estuet et plus non puys durer, 3vv (text partly in French), M ix, 172; *F-Pn 568* ('PA'); text in *I-Fr* 2735; apparently against the Visconti, who invaded Tuscany, 1397–1402 (see Nádas, 1989)

Tra speranza e fortuna i' pur m'aggiro, 3vv, M xi, 150; *F-Pn 568* ('Do. Pa.': ascription erased), *I-La* 184 (2vv only, but facing page is lost; immediately after La vaga luce and in same hand)

Uom c'osa di veder tutta beleza, 3vv, M ix, 178; *F-Pn 568* ('Don Paolo'), *I-Fsl* 2211 ('Abbas Paulus'); Senhal: COSA

Vago e benigno Amor, fammi contento, 3vv, M ix, 186; *F-Pn 568* ('PA')

. . . dio/Donna da te torra ma' il cor mi[o], 3vv, ed. in Brumana (1987), 31; Cil ('D.P.': implied; fragmentary)

. . . il benigna col nobil aspetto, only 1 inc. voice survives, ed. in Brumana (1987), 33; Cil ('D.P.': implied; fragmentary)

3 unidentified pieces in *I-Fsl* 2211

OTHER SECULAR WORKS ATTRIBUTABLE TO PAOLO
all in *F-Pn it.568; see* Nádas (1989)

Achurr' uom' soccorri tu, 2vv, M xi, 1

Altro che sospirar non so nè voglio, 3vv, M xi, 2

Amor, merzè, 2vv, M xi, 7

Già la speranza in te giovana perse, 3vv, M xi, 78; Senhal: GIOVANA

Se 'l mie fallir mi t'avie, donna, tolto, 3vv, M xi, 131

SACRED WORKS

Benedicamus Domino, 3vv, F 105; *F-Pn 568* ('DP': erased, but in index 'PA')

Gaudeamus omnes in Domino, 2vv, F 110; *I-Fl* Ashb.999 ('PAU')

THEORETICAL WORKS

Ars ad adiscendum contrapunctum, ed. in Seay from *I-Fl*; *I-Fl* Ashb.1119 ('secundum paulum de Florentia'), *I-Sc* I.V. 36, ('secundum magistrum paulum de florentia'; with better readings)

BIBLIOGRAPHY

N. Pirrotta and E.Li Gotti: 'Paolo Tenorista, Fiorentino "extra moenia"', *Estudios dedicados a Menéndez Pidal*, iii (Madrid, 1952), 577–606

N. Pirrotta: 'Paolo da Firenze in un nuovo frammento dell'Ars Nova', *MD*, x (1956), 61–6

A. Seay: 'Paolo da Firenze: a Trecento Theorist', *L'Ars Nova Italiana del Trecento I: Certaldo 1959*, 118–40

N. Pirrotta: *Paolo Tenorista in a New Fragment of the Italian Ars Nova* (Palm Springs, CA, 1961)

U. Günther: 'Die "anonymen" Kompositionen des Manuskripts Paris, BN, fonds ital. 568 (Pit)', *AMw*, xxiii (1966), 73–92

U. Günther: 'Zur Datierung des Madrigals "Godi, Firenze" und der Handschrift Paris, B.N., fonds it. 568 (Pit)', *AMw*, xxiv (1967), 99–119

K. von Fischer: 'Paolo da Firenze und der Squarcialupi-Kodex (I-Fl 87)', *Quadrivium*, ix (1968), 5–24

G. Corsi, ed.: *Poesie musicali del Trecento* (Bologna, 1970), 267ff

K.-J. Sachs: *Der Contrapunctus im 14. und 15. Jahrhundert* (Wiesbaden, 1974)

M. Fabbri and J.Nádas: 'A Newly Discovered Trecento Fragment: Scribal Concordances in Late-Medieval Florentine Manuscripts', *EMH*, iii (1983), 67–81

F.A. D'Accone: 'Una nuova fonte dell'Ars Nova italiana: il codice di San Lorenzo, 2211', *Studi musicali*, xiii (1984), 2–31

J. Nádas: 'Manuscript San Lorenzo 2211: Some Further Observations', *L'Europa e la musica del Trecento: Congresso IV: Certaldo 1984* [*L'Ars Nova italiana del Trecento*, vi (Certaldo, 1992)], 145–68

J.L. Nádas: *The Transmission of Trecento Secular Polyphony* (diss., New York U., 1985)

B. Brumana and G.Ciliberti: 'Le ballate di Paolo da Firenze nel frammento "Cil"', *Esercizi: arte, musica, spettacolo*, ix (1986), 5–37

B. Brumana and G.Ciliberti: 'Nuove fonti per lo studio dell'opera di Paolo da Firenze', *RIM*, xxii (1987), 3–33

U. Günther, J. Nádas and J.A. Stinson: 'Magister Dominus Paulus Abbas de Florentia: New Documentary Evidence', *MD*, xli (1987), 203–46

J. Nádas: 'The Songs of Don Paolo Tenorista: the Manuscript Tradition', *In cantu et sermone: for Nino Pirrotta*, ed. F. Della Seta and F. Piperno (Florence, 1989), 41–64

G. Carsaniga: 'I testi di Paolo Tenorista (nuove proposte di lettura)', *Studi e problemi di critica testuale*, xl (1990), 5–22

DAVID FALLOWS

Paolo Tenorista. *See* PAOLO DA FIRENZE.

Paolucci, Giuseppe (*b* Siena, 25 May 1726; *d* Assisi, 24 April 1776). Italian composer and theorist. He studied in Bologna with Martini during the 1750s and like him was a member of the Franciscan order. Eight sacred works from this period (1752–6) are in the Bologna Conservatory library. About 150 letters from Paolucci to Martini (also in *I-Bc*) are evidence of their close friendship. Between 1756 and 1769 he was *maestro di cappella* at S Maria Gloriosa dei Frari in Venice, and from August 1770 until January 1772 at S Martino in Senigallia. He then worked at S Francesco in Assisi until his death.

Paolucci is best known for his treatise *Arte pratica di contrappunto* (Venice, 1765–72), which served as a model for Martini's *Esemplare ossia Saggio fondamentale pratico di contrappunto* (Bologna, 1774–5). While Martini concentrated almost exclusively on the 16th century, Paolucci used a number of examples from the 18th, including one by Handel, as well as a passing reference to J.S. Bach. There is no detailed study of Paolucci's music, which includes more than 200 sacred works (primarily for chorus, soloists and orchestra) and a few instrumental pieces (in *I-Af*). He published *Preces octo vocibus concinendae in oratione quadraginta horarum* (Venice, 1767).

BIBLIOGRAPHY

FellererP
R. Morrocchi: *La musica in Siena* (Siena, 1886/R), 117
G. Radiciotti: *Teatro musica e musicisti in Sinigaglia* (Tivoli, 1893/R), 127–30
G. Tebaldini: *L'archivio musicale della Cappella Antoniana in Padova* (Padua, 1895), 24–5, 149
F. Vatielli: *Lettere di musicisti brevemente illustrati* (Pesaro, 1917), 49–53
D. Sparacio: 'Musicisti minori conventuali', *Miscellanea francescana*, xxv (1925), 92–4

HOWARD BROFSKY

Papadikē. The usual term for a short elementary manual of Middle Byzantine musical notation, included as an introduction to the AKOLOUTHIAI manuscripts of the 14th century onwards. The adjective *papadikos* (from *papas* presumably not in the sense of 'priest' but rather as an equivalent to *psaltēs*, the soloist or precentor) is also used in other contexts: (1) *hē papadikē*, for the whole collection of the soloist's repertory, corresponding to the earlier psaltikon; (2) *to papadikon genos*, the most melismatic of the three musical styles in modern Greek (neo-Byzantine) chant; (3) *hē papadikē* or *hē papadikē technē*), as an general expression denoting Byzantine chant; similarly the expressions *hē psaltikē technē* or *hē mousikē technē* ('the psaltic art' or 'the art of music') may also be found.

From a typological point of view the elementary papadikē occupies a position between the post-medieval treatises on music theory and the early lists of neumes, of which the oldest known specimen is a table in *GR-AOml* γ 67 (10th century). Alongside the didactic poems of JOANNES GLYKYS and JOANNES KOUKOUZELES it has functioned as a basis for the teachers' oral instruction, surviving even the reform of the 'Three Teachers' in the early 19th century (*see* CHRYSANTHOS OF MADYTOS). It has been commented upon in manuscripts such as *I-Rvat* gr.872, ff.240*v* ff (14th-century; ed. Tardo, pp.164ff). Over the centuries the text has undergone many modifications, according to the needs of the scribes and teachers. (In the absence of a critical edition, however, a full study of the various textual types has not yet been possible.)

The earliest version is found in a stichērarion from the year 1289, *F-Pn* gr.261. Under the rubric 'Here begin the signs of the "papadic" art', the manuscript provides no less than three different lists of neumes (single and grouped neumes; neumes with interval values; and *melē*, rhythmical and group signs), tables of neumes combined into ascending and descending intervals, and a diagram relating the Byzantine modes to those of ancient Greece. Although this version antedates the earliest papadikai of the akolouthiai manuscripts, it already includes a major part of the elements listed below.

In the 15th century there already existed at least four different versions of the papadikē, varying in completeness and order of contents. A papadikē normally consists of lists showing: (*a*) the ascending and descending interval signs, sometimes called *sēmadia phōnētika* ('phonetic signs'), divided into *sōmata* ('bodies' or steps) and *pneumata* ('spirits' or leaps), and their interval value; (*b*) the 'great hypostaseis' (subsidiary, cheironomic signs, called *aphōna sēmadia* or *megalai hypostaseis* or *ta megala sēmadia ta dia cheironomias*); (*c*) the *phthorai*, modulation signs of the modes; (*d*) examples to illustrate how all intervals can be expressed by combinations of *sōmata* and *pneumata*; (*e*) further examples to illustrate how ascending *sōmata* in specific combinations lose their interval value: they are 'dominated' (*kyrieuontai* or *hypotassontai*) by descending *sōmata*, by *pneumata* and by the *ison*.

The most complete type of papadikē includes in addition to these items, a series of paragraphs on the modes (including the 'middle modes', *mesoi*, of the four authentic modes and sometimes the *diphōnoi*, or *mesoi*, of the four plagal modes), giving their ancient and medieval names: Dorian, Lydian etc., *ananes*, *neanes* etc.

After these lists of neumes and neume combinations there may be various diagrams. These were probably intended for use when teachers introduced their pupils to the problems of modulation and orientation within the modal system. Many papadikai also include a list of modal intonations (*enēchēmata*), combined with the incipits of well-known *troparia* from which one could learn how to adapt intonations to melodic incipits by means of a suitable *cauda*.

The core of the papadikē thus consists of lists and diagrams. But many sources also include a varying number of short melodies, made ad hoc, to serve as a bridge between the lists and their application to actual singing.

EDITIONS

GerbertS, iii, 397ff
W. Christ: 'Beiträge zur kirchlichen Litteratur der Byzantiner', *Sitzungsberichte der bayerischen Akademie der Wissenschaften, Philosophisch-historische Klasse* (1870), 267–9
V. Gardthausen: 'Beiträge zur griechischen Palaeographie', VI, *Bericht über die Verhandlungen der Königlichen sächsischen Gesellschaft der Wissenschaften zu Leipzig* (1880), 81–8
O. Fleischer: *Neumen-Studien*, iii: *Die spätgriechische Tonschrift* (Berlin, 1904), 15–83
J.-B. Thibaut: *Monuments de la notation ekphonétique et hagiopolite de l'église grecque* (St Petersburg, 1913), pls.xxiv–xxviii
L. Tardo: *L'antica melurgia bizantina* (Grottaferrata, 1938), 151–63
E. Wellesz: *A History of Byzantine Music and Hymnography* (Oxford, 2/1961), 411–15
D. Stefanović: 'Crkvenoslovenski prevod priručnika vizatijske neumske notacije u rukopisu 311 monastira Hilandara' [A Church Slavonic translation of a manual of neumatic notation in *GR-AOh* 311], *Hilandarski zbornik*, ii (1971), 113–30
H. Seppälä: *Elementartheorie der byzantinischen Musik* (Helsinki, 1976)

BIBLIOGRAPHY

H. Riemann: 'Die Metrophonie der Papadiken', *SIMG*, ix (1907–8), 1–31

H.J.W. Tillyard: 'Fragment of a Byzantine Musical Handbook in the Monastery of Laura on Mt. Athos', *Annual of the British School at Athens*, xix (1912–13), 95–117

E. Wellesz: 'Die Rhythmik der byzantinischen Neumen', *ZMw*, ii (1919–20), 617 only, 628–33

H.J.W. Tillyard: 'A Byzantine Musical Handbook of Milan', *Journal of Hellenic Studies*, xlvi (1926), 219–22

J. Milojkovič-Djurič: 'A Papadike from Skoplje', *Studies in Eastern Chant*, i, ed. M. Velimirović (London, 1966), 50

C. Hannick: 'Die Lehrschriften der Byzantinischen Kirchenmusik', *Die hochsprachliche Profane Literatur der Byzantiner*, ed. H. Hunger, ii (Munich, 1978), 196–218

C. Troelsgård: 'The Development of a Didactic Poem: some Remarks on the "Ison, oligon oxeia" by Ioannes Glykys', *Byzantine Chant: Athens 1993*, 69–85

JØRGEN RAASTED/CHRISTIAN TROELSGÅRD

Papadopoulos, Joannes. See KOUKOUZELES, JOANNES.

Papaioannou, Iōhannēs [John] G(eōrgios) (*b* Athens, 23 Jan 1915). Greek architect, pianist, writer on music and administrator. Graduating from Athens Technical University as an architect in 1935, he has had a distinguished career in a number of postwar reconstruction programmes and from 1959 to 1972 as director of research at the Athens Centre of Ekistics (Settlements). His musical training included harmony, counterpoint and composition studies with Felix Petyrek and Petros Petridis in Athens in the late 1920s. As a pianist he has performed complete cycles of Haydn and Schubert sonatas and Mozart piano works and has given premières of many contemporary works. He has also taught music history at the Athenaeon (1952–67) and at the Pierce College in Athens (1966–8). In 1961 he toured the USA in a cultural exchange programme and on his return became co-director of the Studio for New Music of the Athens Goethe Institute and general secretary of the Society of the Friends of Skalkottas. He was appointed general secretary of the Hellenic Association for Contemporary Music in 1965 and of the Greek section of the ISCM in 1965 and 1990; he was also vice-president of the ISCM executive committee, 1978–84.

Papaioannou has devoted much energy to promoting the music both of Skalkottas (whose works as president of the Skalkottas committee he has edited) and of Jani Christou. He has also played extensively in chamber music ensembles, as a soloist in concertos for piano, and as a harpsichordist, organist and percussionist. He has organized many concerts and festivals (42 for the Greek section of the ISCM), and mixed media performances and acted as a producer and programme author for several series of recordings of contemporary music. He has been awarded the Order of the Phoenix in Greece (1985) and the Verdienstkreuz in Germany (1980), and was made a Chevalier des Arts et des Lettres (1985).

WRITINGS

'Nikos Skalkottas', *European Music in the Twentieth Century*, ed. H. Hartog (London, 1957/R), 336–45

'La Grèce byzantine: la musique', 'La Grèce moderne: la musique', *La civilisation grecque de l'antiquité à nos jours*, ed. C. Delvoye and G. Roux, ii (Brussels, 1969), 553–61, 599–605

A Complete Discography of Serious Greek Music (Athens, 1976)

'Die neue griechische Schule: der Weg zur Selbständigkeit', *NZM*, Jg.140 (1979), 33–9

Towards a Definition of Contemporary Music: a Historic Approach (Athens, 1980)

Introduction to *Nikos Skalkottas: Complete Works* (Newton Centre, MA, 1998)

DIMITRI CONOMOS

Papaioannou, Yannis Andreou (*b* Cavala, 6 Jan 1910; *d* Athens, 11 May 1989). Greek composer and teacher. Although he studied the piano with Marika Laspopoulou and composition with Alekos Kontis at the Hellenic Conservatory, Athens (1922–34), as well as the piano and orchestration with Riadis in Thessaloniki (1928–9), he considered himself essentially self-taught, especially in 20th-century compositional techniques. In 1949 a one-year UNESCO scholarship enabled him to visit the major European music centres and to become familiar with new compositional developments; in Paris he took lessons with Honegger. For ten years (1951–61) he taught music at the aristocratic National Lyceum of Anavryta, Athens, and from 1953 he was professor of counterpoint and composition at the Hellenic Conservatory. He was the first president of both the Greek section of the ISCM (1964–75) and the Hellenic Association for Contemporary Music (1965–75).

Papaioannou exerted considerable influence as a teacher; alone in Greece before the mid-1970s in teaching atonality, 12-note and serial techniques, he numbered among his many pupils Adamis, Antoniou, Aperghis, Kounadis and Tezzakis. He acknowledged various phases in his creative career. Early Impressionist (1932–8) and nationalist (1939–43) periods were followed by an interest in Hindemithian neo-classicism (as in one of his best pieces, the Suite for violin and piano or orchestra) and the use of Byzantine modes in the First Symphony. Then Papaioannou began to use 12-note (1953–62) and more recent serial procedures until in 1966 he adopted what he described as 'an entirely personal technique'. Though from the late 1950s, stimulated by the example of Skalkottas, he increasingly sought an austere and ascetic but well-wrought atonal counterpoint, his early works reveal him as a spontaneous melodist. That lyrical quality resurfaced in a few of the later works, such as *Paean eis tin eirinin* ('Paean to Peace', 1980).

WORKS
(*selective list*)

STAGE

Agnos (dramatic idyll, prol, 2 pts, M. Alexandropoulos), 1937; Sklavas lytrossi [Liberation of a Slave Woman] (choreographic tableau), 1945; Pirates (ballet), 1952; Himoniatiki fantasia [Winter Fantasy] (ballet), 1951; Antigone (ballet, 4 scenes, H. Freund, after Sophocles), 1965; incid music

ORCHESTRAL

5 Syms.: 1946, 1947, 1953, 1963, 1964

32 works, incl.: Idhyllio [Idyll], 1938; O koursaros [The Corsair], 1939; Choreographic Prelude, 1940; Pf Conc no.1, 1940; Poiema tou dhasous [Forest Poem], 1942; Vassilis Arvanitis, 1945; Triptych, str, 1947; Orthros ton psychon [Matin of Souls], 1947; Pygmalion, 1950; Koursarikoi horoi [Corsair Dances], pf/orch, 1952; Pf Conc. no.2, 1952; Conc. for Orch, 1954; Hellas (P.B. Shelley), nar, orch, 1956; Images d'Asie, suite, 1961; India, suite, 1961; Concertino, pf, str, 1962; Tableau symphonique, 1968; Conc., vn, chbr orch, 1971; Conc., vn, pf, orch, 1973; Meteorissi [Suspended in the Air], vc, orch, 1979; Pf Conc. no.3, 1989, inc.

VOCAL

8 Choral, acc., incl.: Dafnis ke Chloi (G. Drossinis), chorus, orch/pf, 1933; I kidheia tou Sarpidhonos [The Funeral of Sarpedon] (cant., C. Cavafy), Mez, nar, chorus, chbr orch, 1966; Vimata [The Steps] (Cavafy), chorus, 10 insts, 1967; O fotofraktis [The Aperture] (A. Embeirikos: Octana), solo vv, chorus, ens, 1982; Encomium (Kotsiras), solo vv, chorus, ens, 1984–5, inc.

32 Choral, unacc. (mixed chorus unless otherwise stated), incl.: 3 tragoudhia tis nychtas [3 Songs of the Night] (Y. Koutsoheras), 3-pt female chorus, 1954; Eros anikate machan [Love Unconquerable] (Sophocles: *Antigone*), 1965; Ionikon [Ionian] (Cavafy), 1967; Trihelicton [Triply Wound] (Embeirikos), 1976; I Karyatides (Embeirikos), 1978; Enorassi ton proïnon oron [Vision of Matins Hours] (Embeirikos), 1979; Paean eis tin eirinin [Paean to Peace] (Bacchylides), 1980; Ateliofo spiti [Unfinished House] (G. Kotsiras), 1984; Monemvassia (Kotsiras), male chorus, 1984; 2 Songs (Kotsiras), 1984; I logosteméni psychi [The Exhausted Soul] (O. Votsi), 1986; Katathessi [Testimony] (Votsi), 1986; I lampsi [Shining] (Kotsiras), 1986; O foteinos o vrahos [The Sunny Rock] (A. Mavrikios), 1986; Voreioanatoliki palami [North-Eastern Palm] (Embeirikos), female chorus, 1986; Horos ton myston [Chorus of the Initiated] (Aristophanes: *The Frogs*), 1987

56 Solo vocal (1v, pf unless otherwise stated), incl.: 7 Songs (Y. Gryparis), 1938–46; Apostamenos erotas [Tired Love], 1943; Synnefa tis trellis notias [Clouds of the Mad South Wind] (L. Porphyras), 1943; Yassemia [Jasmines] (Palamas), 1944; Kapoia perpatimata [Some Walks] (Palamas), 1945; Dhouléftres aspromandilousses [White-Kerchiefed Working Girls] (Palamas), 1945; To kardhiochtypi [The Heartbeat] (Palamas), 1959; Ekomissa is tin téchin [I brought to art], Teliomena [Things Fulfilled], Apoleipein o theos Antonion [God Abandons Antony] (Cavafy), Mez/Bar, fl, ob, pf, va, vc, perc, 1966; 3 Byzantine Odes, S, ens, 1968; Monologues of Electra (Sophocles), S, ens, 1968; Orphei hymni, nar, ens, 1971; Prometheus (Aeschylus), 1974; 3 Songs (Cavafy), 1974; 4 Lieder (Kotsiras, Votsi), lyric S, fl, pf, 1984; Énas poiitis sti thalassa [A Poet at Sea] (A. Zakythinos), S, cl, vn, vc, pf, 1986; 2 Songs (G. Byron), 1989

CHAMBER AND SOLO INSTRUMENTAL

51 works, incl.: Nocturno, 1935; Burlesca, vn, pf, 1936; Fantasia, vn, pf, 1936; Sonata vn, pf, 1936; Romanesca, fl, va, hp, 1938; Pastorale, 1938; Sonata no.2, vn, pf, 1946; Suite, 7 movts, vn, pf/str/orch, 1954; Str Qt, 1959; Suite, gui, 1960; Sonatina, fl, gui, 1962; Qt, fl, cl, gui, vc, 1962; Trio, ob, cl, bn, 1962; Str Trio, 1963; Trio, fl, va, gui, 1967; Qt, ob, cl, va, pf, 1968; I parlata tou Arlekinou (La parlata d'Arlecchino) [the Harlequin's Speech], tuba, 1971; Portrait, tuba, 1972; Syneirmoi [Associations], ob, cl, hn, pf, perc, vn, va, db, 1973; 5 haraktires [5 Characters], brass qnt, 1970; Ichomorfés [Soundforms], vn, 1974; Puck, vc, 1976; Pf Trio, 1977; Halkografia [Engraving], hn, pf, 1977; Dioyssiakon [Dionysiac], db, 1978; Erotiki exomologhissi tou Minotavrou [Love Confession of the Minotaur], tuba, pf, 1978; Satyricon, vn, va, 1978; Duo, vn, vc, 1982; Pegasus, fl, 1984, arr. fl, pf, 1987; Polymorphon, vn, hp, 1985; Metope, cl, hp, 1986; Proanakrousma s'éna taxidi [Prelude to a Journey], fl, cl, perc, pf, vn, va/vc, 1986; Aétoma, 4 fl, 1987; Caryatid, canon, org, 1987; Sonata, vc, pf, 1988

32 Pf, incl.: Odalisque, 1937; 24 Preludes, 1939; Partita in modo antico, pf/hpd, 1953; 12 Inventions and Toccata, 1958; Sonata, 1958; 6 Miniatures, 1959; 2 suites, 1959, 1960; Oraculum, 1965; 7 Pieces, 1969; Enigma, 1969; 8 Anaglypha [8 Bas-Reliefs], 1986; Erotic, 1986

MSS in Benakis Museum, Athens

Principal publishers: Modern, Gerig, Greek Ministry of Education, Nakas, Nomos, Nomos-Nakas, U. of Thessaloniki

BIBLIOGRAPHY

A.S. Theodoropoulou: 'Synchronoi hellenes moussikoi: 7. Yannis Papaioannou', *Anglohelleniki epitheorissi*, iii (1947), 213–4

M. Dounias: *Moussikokritika* (Athens, 1963), 91, 140, 176, 212, 285

B. Schiffer: 'Neue griechische Musik', *Orbis musicae*, i (1971–2), 193–201, esp. 198–9

G. Leotsakos: 'Papaïoannou, Yannis Andréou', *Pangosmio viografiko lexico* [Universal biographical dictionary], viii (Athens, 1988), 141–2

K. Moschos and H. Xanthoudakis, eds.: *Yannis A. Papaïoannou: pleres katalogos ergon* [Complete catalogue of works] (Athens, 1990/R)

GEORGE LEOTSAKOS

Papalia, Giovanni Maria (*b* Seminara, Calabria, *fl* Messina, 1589; *d* ?before 1598). Italian composer. According to Paolo Gualtieri (see Martire), Papalia was a Franciscan friar and the author of 'several books of music'. Only one of his publications survives, *Il primo libro de madrigali a cinque voci* (Messina, 1589, inc.). Printed by Fausto Bufalini, it was among the first music books printed in Messina. The volume is dedicated to Cesare Gaetani, who was governor of Messina and several times major of Palermo; his mother's family, the Moncada, counts of Caltanissetta, were patrons of some of the earliest Sicilian madrigalists. Papalia is not represented among the composers in the Sicilian-dominated anthology *Le risa a vicenda* (RISM 1598[8]), suggesting that he may have been dead, or at least no longer active as a composer, by that year.

Of the texts of his 21 madrigals, ten are anonymous, nine are from Sannazaro's *Arcadia* and two are from Petrarch's *Canzoniere*. His music shows the influence of Giovannelli, Macque and Marenzio.

BIBLIOGRAPHY

EitnerQ; SchmidlD

D. Martire: *Calabria sacra e profana* (MS, 17th century, Rome, Curia Generalizia dei Minimi, San Francesco di Paola ai Monti, FC 83)

G. Pitarresi: 'Alcune perdute edizioni napoletane di opere di polifonisti calabresi della prima metà del Seicento', *NA*, new ser., v (1987), 35–51

G. Pitarresi: 'Il primo libro de madrigali a cinque voci di Giovanni Maria Papalia (1589)', *Ceciliana per Nino Pirrotta*, ed. M.A. Balsano and G. Collisani (Palermo, 1994), 59–96 [incl. edn of 1 madrigal]

P.E. Carapezza: '"Quel frutto stramaturo e succoso": il madrigale napoletano del primo Seicento', *La musica a Napoli durante il Seicento: Naples 1985*, 17–27, esp. 17–18

P.E. Carapezza: 'The Madrigal in Venice around the Year 1600', *Heinrich Schütz und die Musik in Dänemark: Copenhagen 1985*, 197–204, esp. 197–8

PAOLO EMILIO CARAPEZZA, GIUSEPPE COLLISANI

Papandopulo, Boris (*b* Honnef am Rhein, 25 Feb 1906; *d* Zagreb, 16 Oct 1991). Croatian composer and conductor. He studied composition with Bersa at the Zagreb Academy of Music, graduating in 1929, and conducting with Fock at the New Vienna Conservatory (1925–8). Afterwards he lived in Zagreb, except for three years when he was conductor of the Zvonimir music society in Split (1935–8). He directed the choral society Kolo, the orchestra of the Croatian Music Institute, the Zagreb Opera (1940–45, of which he was director, 1943–5) and the Radio Zagreb SO (1942–5). After the war he conducted opera in Rijeka (where he was director of the Opera, 1953–9), Sarajevo (1948–53), Zagreb (1959–65) and Split (1968–74), and for a number of years was resident conductor at Cairo. Between 1931 and 1938 Papandopulo wrote reviews for the daily press. In 1965 he became a full member of the Yugoslav (now Croatian) Academy of Sciences and Arts.

When he started composing Papandopulo declared himself to be a follower of a national style, but he was one of the first Yugoslav composers to take an interest in neo-classicism. However, he quickly found a means of synthesizing such techniques with the rhythms and melodies of folk music. Papandopulo employed different styles almost concurrently, and so it is difficult to describe his evolution in terms of periods; yet there is a distinct change separating his pre-war and postwar work. In his earlier music a youthful temperament gave rise to an enthusiastic virtuosity in the use of expressive means, involving contrapuntal play, colourful timbres and exterior decorativeness, although at the same time there are pieces of a more solemn and profound character. In the later phase, when his music became richer and more complex, he did not entirely reject the earlier features.

The works couched in a national style range from folksong harmonizations to ritual pieces after the Stravinskian manner that combine traditional with cosmopolitan traits. In such ritual and sacred works, which were particularly important to Papandopulo's development before 1940, the harmony and sometimes the melodic motives are based on folk models. The form of these works relies on the repetition or variation of short, simple themes, as in the chorus *Dodolice* (1932), or their deployment in canonic formations. In the oratorio *Muka gospodina našega Isukrsta* ('The Passion of Our Lord Jesus Christ', 1936) he makes dramatically effective use of the free style of Dalmatian church singing, which contains elements of both Gregorian chant and the traditional folk idiom.

A fine example of his neo-classical style is the *Concerto da camera* (1929), the first of Papandopulo's major works. The use of folk ideas is evident in the central part of the opening Capriccio, while the middle movement is a fugue on a grotesque theme and the fifth a colourful finale of accented rhythms. Other neo-classical works include the Sinfonietta for strings (1938), formed on early Baroque models, the *Hommage à Bach* (1973) and the two concerti grossi (1971, 1990). The Piano Sonata no.1 (1929) is stylistically reminiscent of Prokofiev's first sonata; additionally it is an outstanding example of Expressionism found in the Croatian repertory for piano.

For the remainder of his career Papandopulo divided his time between writing cantatas, concertos, opera, ballet and chamber music. The language of these works includes virtuoso writing, novel technical devices and even 12-note rows, while elsewhere it employs elements of folk, jazz or popular styles.

WORKS
(selective list)

STAGE

Zlato [Gold] (pantomime-ballet with singing, B. Pečić), Zagreb, 31 May 1930; Amfitrion (comic op, M. Štimac and E. Golisciani, after Molière), Zagreb, 17 Feb 1940; Sunčanica [The Sun-Flower Girl] (romantic op, M. Šoljačić, after I. Gundulić), Zagreb, 13 June 1942; Žetva [Harvest] (ballet, N. Kirsanova), Sarajevo, 25 March 1950; Intermezzo (ballet, F. Horvat), Sarajevo, 25 May 1953; Rona (op, F. Delak, after A. Leskovac), Rijeka, 25 May 1955; Beatrice Cenci (ballet, F. Reyna), Zagreb, 11 March 1963; Džentlemen i lopov [Gentleman and Thee] (comic op, A. Aranicki, after B. Nušić), Split, 12 April 1974; Gitanella (ballet, N. Turkalj), 1966, unperf.; Dr Atom (Q+H³+H²=He⁴+n+Q) (ballet, N. Fabrio), Rijeka, 29 Oct 1966; Menschen im Hotel/Ljudi u hotelu (ballet, P. Struck, after V. Baum), Vienna, 27 May 1967; Marulova pisan [Marul's Song] (festive music tableau, V. Rabadan), Split, 15 Aug 1970; Madame Buffault (fantastic op, P. Struck), 1972, unperf.; Kentervilski duh [The Canterville Ghost] (comic chbr op, N. Turkalj, after O. Wilde), Osijek, 5 June 1979; Teuta (ballet, F. Horvat, after D. Demeter), Novi Sad, 10 April 1979; 3 kavalira gospodice Melanije [Miss Melanija's 3 Gallants] (ballet, B. Rakić, after M. Krleža), Zagreb, 19 April 1976; Požar u operi [Fire at the Opera] (comic op, F. Hadžić), Zagreb, April 1983; Kraljevo [Royal Fair] (ballet, J. Lešić, after Krleža), Zagreb, 13 Jan 1990; incid music, film scores

ORCHESTRAL

Dozivanje kiše [Call for the Rain], sym. poem, 1925; Phantasy, pf, orch, ?1930; Sym. no.1, 1930; Sinfonietta, str, 1938; Vn Conc., 1943; Pf Conc. no.1, 1944; Sym. no.2, 1946; Pf Conc. no.2, 1947; Kolo druga Tita [Comrade Tito's Reel-Dance], sym. variations, 1948; Praeludium, 1949; Concertino, tpt, timp, str, 1950; Koncertna uvertira [Ov. Concertante], 1951; Poema o Neretvi [The Poem of the Neretva], sym. poem, 1951; Divertimento, str, 1953; Bn Conc., 1958; Vrzino kolo [Witch's Reel-Dance], sym. scherzo, pf, orch, 1958; Pf Conc. no.3, 1959; Hpd Conc., 1962; Boje i kontrasti [Colours and Contrasts], variations, 1963;

Concert Music, fl, hp, str, perc, 1965; Db Conc., 1968; Marche arabe symphonique, 1968; 4 Timp Conc., 1969; U početku bijaše ritam [In the Beginning there was Rhythm], 1969; Conc. grosso I, wind qnt, perc, str, 1971; Hommage à Bach, 1973; Pintarichiana, str, 1974; Pop-Conc., 2 pf, orch, 1974; Per aspera ad astra, org, orch, 1976; Mali concert [Little Conc.], pic, orch, 1977; Double Conc., vn, vc, orch, 1978; Concertino, ob, orch, 1981; Cl Conc., 1982; Trbn Conc., 1983; Xyl Conc., 1983; Mali concert, pf, str, 1983; Sinfonia brevis, 1984; Svečana uvertira [Solemn Ov.], 1985; Triple Conc., ob, cl, bn, str, 1986; Double Conc., ob, xyl, str, 1987; Sax Conc., 1987; Conc. grosso II, wind qnt, str, 1990

VOCAL

Cants.: Slavoslovje [Laudamus] (Bible), S, A, T, B, SATB, orch, 1926–7; Stojanka, Majka Knežopojka [Stojanka, Mother of Knežpolje] (S. Kulenović), S, SATB, orch, 1950; Ustanici [Rebels] (H. Humo), SATB, orch, 1951; Oranje Kraljevića Marka [Prince Marko's Ploughing] (A. Muradbegović), S, A, T, B, SATB, orch, 1956; Legende o drugu Titu [Legends about Comrade Tito] (V. Nazor), S, Mez, A, Bar, spkr, SATB, 2 fl, 3 trp, perc, 1960; Konjanik [Horserider] (J. Kaštelan), Bar, chbr ens, 1961; Borbena kantata [Warriors' Cant.] (P. Cindrić), spkr, S, A, T, B, SATB, orch, 1961; Srce od ognja [Heart of Fire] (Kaštelan), Mez, Bar, SATB, orch, 1965; Ruke prema noći [Hands Extended to the Night] (N. Turkalj), children's chorus, SATB, orch, 1968; Gospi od Zdravlja [To Virgin Mary of the Health], S, T, SATB, orch, 1971; Istarske freske iz Berma [Istrian Frescoes from Beram] (V. Fajdetić), SATB, orch, 1973; Libertas (S. Stražičić) B, SATB, orch, 1974; Credo: Legenda o mojoj zemlji [Credo: a Legend about my Homeland] (I. Krajač), S, A, T, B, spkr, children's chorus, 2 SATB, orch, 1975; Podnevna simfonija [Midday Sym.] (M. Krleža), S, A, T, B, SATB, 1980; Non bene pro toto libertas venditur auro (L. Paljetak), S, SATB, orch, 1981; Varaždinska rapsodija [Varaždin Rhapsody] (G. Krklec, Z. Milković), A, B, SATB, orch, 1981; Pohvala Dubrovniku [Praise to Dubrovnik] (L. Paljetak), B, SATB, orch, 1983; Oda Križaniću [Ode to Krizanić] (I. Golub), T, SATB, 1983; Ep o slobodi [Epos about the Freedom] (B. Karakaš), S, A, T, B, children's chorus, orch, 1985; Mile Gojsalica (J. Marušić), S, B, SATB, org, str, 1985; Jubilate, T, SATB, orch, 1985; Carmen Boscovichianum (V. Rabadan), S, A, T, Bar, B, org, 1987; Himna suncu [Hymn to the Sun] (L. Paljetak), Bar, SATB, orch, 1987; Pri sv. Kralju [At the Tri Kralja] (A.G. Matoš), T, SATB, orch, 1990

Sacred: Pokoj vječni I [Requiem I], TB, 1930; Pokoj vječni II, TB, 1935; Muka gospodina našega Isukrsta (po Ivanu) [Passion of our Lord Jesus (according to St John)] S, A, T, B, TB, 1936; Ps ii, T, TB, 1936; Hrvatska misa [Croatian Mass], d, S, A, T, B, SATB, 1939; Osorski requiem [Osor Requiem] (medieval Croatian), S, A, T, B, SATB, org, perc, sopele, elec gui, 1977; Osorski misterij [Osor Misterium] (songbook from Osor, 1530), S, A, T, B, SATB, orch, 1977–8; Poljička pučka misa [The Poljice Mass] (trad. text), SATB, org, 1983; Ps cv, SATB, 1987

Choruses: Svatovske [Wedding Songs] (traditional ritual, folk texts), S, SATB, 1924; Utva zlatokrila [Gold-winged Swan] (V. Nazor), S, A, T, B, SATB, 1932; Dodolice (trad. ritual, folk texts), S, SA, pf, 1932; Ljubavne pjesme [Songs of Love] TB, before 1934; Ps cxxxxviii, SA, 1936

Other: Conc. da camera, S, vn, 7 wind insts, pf, 1929; Pjesma ljubavi [Song of Love], cycle, S, pf, 1930; Čakavska suita [Čakavian suite] (D. Gervais), lv, pf, 1955; Hochzeitsgesang (H. Heine), Bar, org, 1978; 3 balade Petrice Kerempuha, S, eng hn, hp, 1978; Poema o Mostaru [The Poem about Mostar] (H. Humo and A. Šantić), sym. poem, B, orch, 1980

CHAMBER AND SOLO INSTRUMENTAL

6 str qts: op.7, 1927; op.20, ?1931; op.126, 1945; 1950; 1970; 1983

Other chbr: Introduzione, arioso e danza, op.78, vc, pf, 1938; Qnt, op.90, cl, str qt, 1940; Mala suita [Little Suite], wind trio, 1949; Phantasy, vn, pf, 1950; 3 Studies, vn, pf, 1950; 3 Movts, wind qnt, 1954; Sonata, va, pf, 1956; 3 Movts hp, 1960; Elegy, bn, pf, 1965; Razgover ugodni [A Pleasant Conversation], fl, hpd, 1969; Mali koncert [Little Conc.], wind qnt, 1971; 5 Studies, 2 vn, 1972; Sextet, 2 vn, va, vc, db, pf, 1974; 3 Dialogues, vn, db, 1974; In modo antico preludium and fugue, pf trio, 1975; Monologue, vn, 1976; Passacaglia, org, 1977; Toccata cromatica, org, 1977; Qt, gui, vn, va, vc, 1977; Scherzo, bn, pf, 1978; Sonata, ob, cl, bn, gui, 1982; Prelude, hn, org, 1982; Wind Octet, 1985; Suite, hpd, 1986; Chbr Conc., vn, wind qnt, 1986; Papandopulijada, vn, va, pf, 1986; Meditation, vn, pf, 1987; Trio, tpt, hn, trbn, 1987; Rapsodia concertante, vc, pf, 1987; Trio, fl, bn, pf, 1987; Sonata, vn, pf, 1988; Preludij, org, 1990; Legenda, hn, hp, 1990; Igra u 2 [A Game for 2], ob, vib, 1990

Pf: Sonata no.1, 1929; 2 Preludes, 1930; Partita, 1930; Contradanza, 1931; Igra (Scherzo fantastico), 1932; Hrvatski tanac [Croatian Dance], c1934; Sonatina, 1942; Mali koncert [Little Conc.], 1945; Sonata no.2, a, 1951–2; 8 Studies, 1956; Dodekafonski koncert, 2 pf, 1960; Plesna suita [Dance Suite], pf 4-hands, 1968; '10×1', 1989

Principal publishers: H. Gerig, M. Reift, International Music Co., Hrvatska akademija znanosti i umjetnosti, Društvo hrvatskih skladatelja

BIBLIOGRAPHY

K. Kovačević: *Hrvatski kompozitori i njihova djela* [Croatian composers and their works] (Zagreb, 1960), 358–81 [incl. Eng. summary]

Z. Hudovsky: 'Boris Papandopulo kao muzički pisac i kritičar' [Papandopulo as writer and critic], *Arti musices*, iv (1973), 133–46 [incl. Eng. summary]

E. Krpan: 'Stvaralaštvo za zbor Borisa Papandopula do godine 1940' [The choral music of Papandopulo before 1940], *Arti musices*, xix (1988), 113–36 [incl. Eng. and Ger. summary]

M. Riman: *Dodekafonski postupci u djelima Borisa Papandopula* [12-note procedures in the works of Papandopulo) (Rijeka, 1988)

T. Gaćeša: 'Prva sonata za klavir B. Papandopula' [Papandopulo's first piano sonata], *Tonovi*, vii/2:18 (1992), 15–20

I. Supičić, ed.: *Boris Papandopulo, 1906–1991* (Zagreb, 1994) [incl. complete list of works and writings, compiled by Erika Krpan]

I. Paulus: 'Boris Papandopulo, skladatelj filmske glazbe' [Papandopulo, a composer of film music], *Hrvatski filmski ljetopis*, ii/5 (1996), 56–61 [incl. Eng. summary]

M. Bergamo: 'Kozmopolitizam s folklornim likom: bilješke uz *Dodolice* Borisa Papandopula' [Cosmopolitan with a pretence of folklore: notes on *Dodolice* by Papandopulo], *Cantus*, no.99 (1998), 8–10

ZDRAVKO BLAŽEKOVIĆ, KREŠIMIR KOVAČEVIĆ

Papavoine (i) [first name unknown] (*b* ?Normandy, *c*1720; *d* ?Marseilles, 1793). French composer and violinist. His first names may have been Louis-Auguste. Gregoir's use of the initial 'J' for Papavoine's first name is most probably based on the name Jean-Noël Papavoine (possibly his son), a *maître des pantomimes et répétiteur* active in Lille and The Hague. Papavoine is first mentioned early in 1752 in a request for a privilege to publish *Six simphonies* op.1, dedicated to 'le Marquis de la Bourdonnaye, Conseiller d'État, Intendant de Rouen'; the work's title-page called him 'premier violon de l'Académie de musique de Rouen', living in Paris. About 1754 Papavoine married Mlle Pellecier, a musician and composer whose *Six cantatilles* were advertised in the *Mercure de France* in January 1755. During the next three years he composed three collections of orchestral and chamber music. On 19 May 1757 a symphony of his was performed at the Concert Spirituel. From 1760 to 1762 he was leader of the second violins in the orchestra of the Comédie-Italienne, for which he composed two *comédies mêlées d'ariettes*, now lost. From 1764 to 1765 he returned briefly to instrumental composition with two violin sonatas, two violin duos 'à la grecque' and two symphonies for large orchestra. About 1767 he joined N.-M. Audinot in forming the Théâtre de l'Ambigu-Comique, devoted primarily to marionette and pantomime productions with music. He was associated with that theatre as late as 1789. In the *Almanach des spectacles* for 1790 he is listed among the living composers, and according to Gerber he was in that year orchestra director and first violinist at the Marseilles opera. The date and place of his death was supplied by Fétis. He published virtually all of his and his wife's music himself. They appear to have had two children, both of whom he trained as engravers:

Angélique (*b* Paris, 1759) and a son (*d* Paris, 1796), possibly the Jean-Noël mentioned above.

Papavoine was one of the first French symphonists to write in the Classical style. The *Six simphonies* op.1 (1752) resemble Sammartini's sinfonias but have more violinistic leaps and embroidery characteristic of the *style galant*. The Symphony in D (*c*1765) shows Mannheim influences. Two of Papavoine's chamber works represent a particular pre-Romantic tendency to idealize the past: the missing *Duos à la grecque*, which employed quarter-tones (see La Laurencie), and two *airs* in imitation of troubadour songs (see Chailley). His op.4 (1757) is lost: its full title, *Grandes symphonies en concerto pour deux violons, alto et violoncelle obligés et deux autres violons et basse que l'on peut supprimer*, indicates that it may have been an early symphonie concertante.

WORKS
all printed works published in Paris

OPERAS
all performed in Paris; music unpublished and lost

Barbacole, ou Le manuscrit volé (cmda, 1, A.-J. Labbet de Morambert, J. de Lagrange and A.-F. Sticotti), Comédie-Italienne (Hôtel de Bourgogne), 15 Sept, 1760, lib F-Pn
Le vieux coquet, ou Les deux amies (oc, 3, A. Bret, after W. Shakespeare: *The Merry Wives of Windsor*), Comédie-Italienne (Hôtel de Bourgogne), 7 Nov 1761; also known as Les deux amies, ou Le vieux garçon, lib Pn
Le répertoire (comédie, 1, J.-F. Mussot [Arnould]), Ambigu-Comique, 1771
Zélie (pièce mêlée de musique), Ambigu-Comique, 1775

Also music for a large number of plays and pantomimes at Ambigu-Comique, inc. Alceste, ou La force de l'amour et de l'amitié, Les filets de Vulcain, Le fort pris d'assaut, La curiosité punie, Le magicien de village, ou L'âne perdu et retrouvé

INSTRUMENTAL
Syms. [thematic catalogue in Brook]: 6 simphonies, str, bc, op.1 (1752); 6 symphonies, str, bc, op.3 (1755), lost; [6] Grandes symphonies en concerto, 2 vn, va, vc obbl, 2 vn, b, op.4 (1757), lost; Symphonie, obs, fls, hns, str (1764), lost; 2ème symphonie, fls/obs, hns, str (1765), lost; Symphonie, D, 2 ob, 2 hn, str, c1765, F-Pc, ?identical with 2ème symphonie
Chamber: Pièces de clavecin en trio, vn acc., op.2 (1754), lost; [2] Sonates, vn, b (1764), lost; [2] Duos à la grecque, 2 vn (1764), lost; 2 airs in Recueil de romances historiques, tendres et burlesques, i (1767); Recueil d'airs choisis de l'Ambigu-Comique, 2 vn/mand, op.5 (1770), lost

BIBLIOGRAPHY
BrookSF; FétisB; GerberNL; La LaurencieEF
Almanach des spectacles (Paris, 1791)
E.G.J. Gregoir: *Littérature musicale: documents historiques relatifs à l'art musical et aux artistes-musiciens*, i–iv (Brussels, 1872–6)
C.D. Brenner: *A Bibliographical List of Plays in the French Language 1700–1789* (Berkeley, 1947)
J. Chailley: 'La musique médiévale vue par le XVIIIe et le XIXe siècle', *Mélanges d'histoire et d'esthétique musicales … offerts à Paul-Marie Masson* (Paris, 1955), i, 95–103

BARRY S. BROOK, RICHARD VIANO/JULIE ANNE SADIE

Papavoine (ii) [Pellecier], Mme [first name unknown] (*b* *c*1735; *fl* 1755–61). French composer. By 1755, she was married to the violinist Papavoine (*d* 1793), the composer of symphonies and comic operas. The *Mercure de France* of January 1755 contains a 'Catalogue des oeuvres de M. et Mme Papavoine', ascribing six *cantatilles* to her as Mlle Pellecier (*Les arrets d'amour*, *La tourterelle*, *Les charmes de la voix*, *La fête de l'amour*, *Issé* and *Le joli rien*) and two as Mme Papavoine (*Le triomphe des plaisirs* and *Le Cabriolet* (F-Pn), which requires two violins and contains a tempest movement). The issue also includes a short, 12-bar unaccompanied *air gaiment* (*Nous voici donc au jour* *l'an*) by her, and the following year a modest little chanson (*Vous fuyez sans vouloir m'entendre*) appeared in the July issue; lastly, a 'pastorale' melody (*Reviens, aimable Thémire*) appeared in May 1761. At least one more *cantatille*, *La France sauvée ou Le triomphe de la vertù* (*US-Cn*), has been attributed to her. (*SchmidlD*)

JULIE ANNE SADIE

Pape, Andy [Andrew] **(Jacob)** (*b* Los Angeles, 1 Sept 1955). Danish composer of American birth. He moved to Denmark in 1971 and studied musicology at the University of Copenhagen (1975–7), also undertaking private composition studies with Abrahamsen and Aaquist. In 1985 he took the final examination at the Royal Danish Conservatory, where Nørholm was his teacher. Alongside his studies he taught music at the Bernadotte School in Copenhagen. From 1987 to 1993 he was head of the music department at the College of Art in Holback, and he has since composed full-time. He has twice been awarded the three-year scholarship from the Government Art Fund (1985 and 1993).

He has identified himself as a musical dramatist with the operas *Houdini den store* ('Houdini the Great', 1988) and *Bokseren* ('The Boxer', 1994–5), both written in collaboration with the Danish film director, actor and writer Erik Clausen. These operas, the first of which was performed both at the Royal Theatre in Copenhagen and as street theatre, combine entertainment and social criticism, borrowing stylistic features from popular music. Pape's music reflects a strong awareness of his relationship with the audience, and several of his works are best characterized as instrumental theatre, e.g. *Variations on 'Nearer my God to Thee'* (1990), in which brutality, sentimentality, powerlessness and madness are exposed in the interaction between a drunken pianist and a spiteful page turner. Pape likes to confront taboos of the classical concert environment and feels no obligation to the European musical tradition. This is characteristic of *Concerto grosso* for recorder, cello, tuba and orchestra (1996); its title is that of a historic form, but its instrumentation, in a work which emphasizes joy in creating music, avoids the well-proved and well-balanced in favour of the grotesque. In addition to a large amount of percussion music, Pape has composed music for films, including Clausen's *Min fynske barndom* ('My Childhood Symphony', 1993), based on Carl Nielsen's childhood memoirs.

WORKS
(selective list)

Stage: Houdini den store [Houdini the Great] (street op, 8 scenes, E. Clausen), 1988, Copenhagen, 1989; Bokseren [The Boxer] (op, prelude, 5 scenes, Clausen), 1994–5, Århus, 1995; Leonora Christine - dronning af blaataarn [The Queen of the Blue Tower] (op, 2, N. Malinovski), 1998, Copenhagen, 1999

Film: Min fynske barndom [My Childhood Sym.] (dir. Clausen), 1993; En loppe kan også gø [Flees Bark Too] (dir. S. Olsson), 1996

Inst theatre: Duet for Solo Cello, vc, performing cellist, 1987; Variations on 'Nearer my God to Thee', pf, page turner, 1990; And Man Created God, cl, vc, pf, 1992; En lille natmusik, cl, vc, performer, 1992; Byens orkester [The Town Orchestra] (H. Laurens), conductor/nar, fl, cl, bn, tpt, pf, hp, vn, va, vc, 1994–5; In Search of . . . (the Unanswered Question), perc, 1997

Orch: Clarino Conc., pic tpt, orch, 1990; Scherzo animalesco, 2 pf, 2 tpt, hn, orch, 1994; Conc. grosso 'In maggiore e in minore', rec, vc, tuba, orch, 1996; Days of a Snare Drum, snare drum, orch, 1998; Traces of Time Lost, bn, orch, 1998

Vocal: Jabberwockey, pf, SATB, 1976; Wind Song, pf, 1v, 1978; Trae [Tree], SATB, bass drums, 1986; Scat, SATB, 1986; . . . jeg

har aldrig set en sommerfugl her . . . [. . . I have never seen butterfly here . . .'), song cycle, S, vn, accdn, 1990–92; Leonorasange (L.C. Ulfeldt, Malinovski), Mez, pic, vc, accdn, 1998

Chbr: Str Qt, op.11, 1979; As Times Go By, 2 pf, 1981–2; Piece of Mind, 2 pf, 1983–4; Louisiana Mix, 3 unspecified insts, 1985; Just One Note, 2 pf, perc, 1988; CaDance for 4, 4 perc, 1984, rev. 1989; CaDance for 2, 2 perc, 1989; Trio, op.42, vn, pf, perc, 1989–91; Sax Qt, 1992; Talking Drums II, 2 talking drums, 1992; Marrrrimba Rrrock, mar, perc, 1992; Divertimento subito, 2 accdn, perc, 1993; HIT'N'RUN, 4 perc, 1997

Solo inst: Shepherd's Song, ob, 2 digital delays, 1982; Marrrrimba, mar, vib ad lib, 1991–2

Principal publishers: Hansen, Samfundet til Udgivelse af Dansk Musik

BIBLIOGRAPHY

N. Rosing-Schouw: 'Uden for båsene: et portraet af komponisten Andy Pape', *DMt*, lxi (1986–7), 124–32

THOMAS MICHELSEN

Pape, Heinrich (*b* Ratzeburg, nr Lübeck, 27 July 1609; *d* Stockholm, 25 April 1663). German organist and composer. In 1625 he was in Hamburg as an organ student of Jacob Praetorius (ii). His first position as organist was in nearby Mittelnkirchen. He was then organist at Altona from 1630 to 1662, when he became organist at the Jacobskyrka, Stockholm. He married the sister of Johann Rist.

Pape was one of the most prolific composers of the mid-17th-century Hamburg school of songwriters. He set many sacred and secular verses by Rist, to whom he remained loyal when most members of the Hamburg school abandoned setting his poems: there are 36 settings by him in Rist's *Des edlen Daphnis aus Cimbrien Galathee* (Hamburg, 1642) and a further 23 in three collections published between 1648 and 1652. Two composers called Heinrich Pape, 'the elder' and 'the younger', are distinguished in the 15 melodies they contributed to Jacob Schwieger's second set of *Liebes-Grillen* (Hamburg, 1656). Pape's father was also called Heinrich, but since he died in 1637 'the elder' must refer to Pape himself and 'the younger' to a son of his, who is also represented by eight songs in Schwieger's *Des Flüchtigen Flüchtige Feld-Rosen* (Hamburg, 1655) and of whom nothing further is known. One song 'by Heinrich Pape' is in Georg Heinrich Schrieber's *Neu ausgeschlagener Liebes- und Frühlingsknospen* (Frankfurt, 1664). Pape's settings of Rist's sacred poems are inferior to his secular songs, among which those published in 1642 are particularly notable; it has been suggested that the sacred songs may have been the work of another composer.

BIBLIOGRAPHY

W. Krabbe: *Johann Rist und das deutsche Lied* (diss., U. of Berlin, 1910), 141ff

W. Vetter: *Das frühdeutsche Lied* (Münster, 1928), i

JOHN H. BARON

Pape, Jean Henri [Johann Heinrich] (*b* Sarstedt, nr Hanover, 1 July 1789; *d* Asnières, nr Paris, 2 Feb 1875). French piano maker. He arrived in Paris in 1811 and after visiting London helped Ignace Pleyel to organize his new piano factory. By 1819 he was running his own business at 7 rue Montesquieu. Pape's great interest was inventing; hence some of his 137 patents were design achievements but were never put into regular practical use. For instance, he designed a square piano with the keyboard in the middle, although its normal place, near the left, is perfectly satisfactory. Towards the end of his career he built pianos in all kinds of shapes, including round, hexagonal and oval, for drawing-rooms, but these more unusual instruments were not popular, with the result that Pape, who had once employed over 300 men, died poor.

However, Pape brilliantly solved technical problems in the piano. He designed the down-striking French grand action, and it is largely owing to his influence that interest in this type of action spread through Europe and America. His action avoided the unseating effect on the strings of the more common up-striking actions, and resolved the problem of weakness across the action gap. It took less space and obviated the need for iron braces as the strings were placed lower, in the strongest part of the instrument. Pape is also known for his experiments using felt hammer coverings, first patented by him in 1826, and for his early use of tempered steel wire. Probably his most famous invention was the 'pianino' (patented in 1828; possibly inspired by Robert Wornum), a small upright one metre high in which the earliest use of overstringing is found. The bass strings cross over the treble, giving a longer speaking-length and helping to brace the case. This was the first of a series of pianinos built by Pape, and the type of small inexpensive upright piano which became the domestic instrument *par excellence* in France and England by the mid-century. He also designed a chromatic harp, patented in 1845, in which the strings were arranged in two planes that crossed centrally and distributed the tension. This was further developed by the Pleyel company (see HARP, §V, 7(ii)).

After Erard and Pleyel, Pape was the most famous French piano maker during the first half of the 19th century; he was described in the *Musical World* (1836) as the 'Broadwood of the French capital'. Cherubini composed at an 1817 square piano by Pape, and Moscheles, Boieldieu and Auber purchased instruments by him. Bechstein was among Pape's pupils. The mother-of-pearl and ivory square piano made for Queen Victoria is preserved at Osborne House, Isle of Wight.

BIBLIOGRAPHY

Notice sur les inventions et les perfectionnements de H. Pape (Paris, 1845/R 1939)

R.E.M. Harding: *The Piano-Forte: its History Traced to the Great Exhibition of 1851* (Cambridge, 1933/R, 2/1978/R)

F.J. Hirt: *Meisterwerke des Klavierbaus: Geschichte der Saitenklaviere von 1440 bis 1880* (Olten, 1955; Eng. trans., 1968/R as *Stringed Keyboard Instruments, 1440–1880*)

C. Michaud-Pradelles: *Jean-Henri Pape: un facteur de pianos allemand à Paris (1789–1875)* (diss., Paris Conservatoire, 1975)

MARGARET CRANMER

Pape, René (*b* Dresden, 4 Sept 1964). German bass. He was a member of the Dresden Kreuzchor (1974–81) and made his stage début in 1988 at the Berlin Staatsoper, where he has since been a member of the regular ensemble, singing Sarastro, Rocco, Ramfis, Fasolt, Hunding, King Mark and Pogner, among others. His first appearance at the Salzburg Festival was as Don Fernando (*Fidelio*) and in Bach's *St Matthew Passion* in 1990, returning the following year to undertake Sarastro in the Johannes Schaaf-Solti staging. He sang Fasolt at Bayreuth each year from 1994 to 1998. His début at La Scala was in 1991 as Sarastro, and he first appeared at the Vienna Staatsoper as Hunding (1996), at Covent Garden as Heinrich der Vogler (1997) and at the Metropolitan as Fasolt (1997). He is also a notable concert artist. His well-formed, compact bass and refined, shapely phrasing can be heard on disc as Pogner and in *The Creation*, *The Seasons* and Mozart's Requiem, all with Solti.

ALAN BLYTH

Papineau-Couture, Jean (*b* Montreal, 12 Nov 1916). Canadian composer, grandson of GUILLAUME COUTURE. He studied in Montreal with Françoise d'Amour, Léo-Pol Morin and Gabriel Cusson, at the New England Conservatory (BMus 1941), where his teachers included Quincy Porter (composition), Beveridge Webster (piano) and Francis Findlay (conducting), and at the Longy School, Cambridge, Massachusetts (1941–3) with Boulanger, whom he followed to the University of Wisconsin, Madison, and to Montecito, California. In 1946 he was appointed a professor at the Montreal section of the Quebec Province Conservatory, moving from there in 1951 to teach composition at the University of Montreal, where he held the posts of professor (from 1951), secretary (1952) and dean (1968–73). He also served as president of the Montreal centre of the Jeunesses Musicales (1956–70), the Canadian League of Composers (1957–9, 1963–6), the Quebec Academy of Music (1961–3), the Société de Musique Contemporaine du Québec (1966–73), the Canadian Music Council (1967–8) and the CMC (1973–4).

Papineau-Couture has composed extensively in most genres apart from opera. His preference, however, has been for small orchestral and chamber ensembles, as such groups enable him both to expose the contrapuntal writing that has always been an important feature of his style, and to express the intimate nature of his personality. His music makes much use of mirror structures or fan-like expansions and contractions, as indicated by the subtitles of the *Pièces concertantes*, and his liking for counterpoint is evident in his frequent use of such devices as imitation, inversion, retrograde and augmentation. An intellectual fascination with a problem to be solved often serves as the stimulus for a composition. Nevertheless, he has remarked on the necessity for a musical structure to be perceptible to the ear, without requiring consultation of a gloss or score.

Papineau-Couture's early studies with d'Amour brought him into contact with 20th-century French music, in particular with the work of Milhaud and Honegger. This, coupled with the influence of Boulanger, who introduced him to the music of Stravinsky and Hindemith, led him to adopt a neo-classical style in his earliest works (up to 1948), which are often cast in the conventional forms of sonata, suite and so on. Later he replaced tonality with a system of polarity lacking a fixed harmonic hierarchy. In the second movement of *Papotages* (or *Tittle-tattle*), for example, polar pitches act as anchorage points. He then explored atonality on a Hindemithian pattern, often using chords of superimposed 4ths. At the same time he was influenced by Schoenberg's 12-note method, notably in the Violin Suite (1956), marked at once the end of a period of research and the beginning of his maturity. In subsequent works he has built on Hindemith's chord formations and Stravinsky's rhythmic impulse. This phase of consolidation has also seen innovations, sometimes under the influence of Varèse, as in the timbre-orientated, neo-Impressionist tendency of *Viole d'amour* for chorus (1966), the Sextet (1967) and *Paysage* for voices and instruments (1968). In general, however, his music has been firmly planned and classical in conception. His honours include the Quebec prize

(1981), membership in the Order of Canada (1993) and the Canadian Governor's prize for the arts (1994).

WORKS

STAGE AND ORCHESTRAL

Stage: Papotages (Tittle-tattle) (ballet), orch, 1949; Eclosion (ballet, M. Racine), vn, pf, tape, 1961; Le rossignol (music for marionette play), fl, vc, pf, 1962

Orch: Concerto grosso, chbr orch, 1943, rev. 1955; Sym. no.1, C, 1948, rev. 1956; Aria, 1949; Conc., vn, chbr orch, 1951–2; Marche de Guillaumet, 1952; Ostinato, str, hp, pf, 1952; Poème, 1952; Prelude, 1953; Pièce concertante no.1 'Repliement', pf, str, 1957; Pièce concertante no.2 'Eventails', vc, chbr orch, 1959; Pièce concertante no.3 'Variations', fl, cl, vn, vc, hp, str, 1959; Pièce concertante no.4 'Additions', ob, str, 1959; 3 Pieces, 1961; Pièce concertante no.5 'Miroirs', 1963; Pf Conc., 1965; Suite Lapitsky, 1965; Oscillations, chbr orch, 1969; Clair-obscur, dbn, db, orch, 1986

VOCAL

Choral: Ps cl, S, T, chorus, fl, bn, brass, org, 1954; Te mater, 3vv, 1958; Viole d'amour (R. Lasnier), SATB, 1966

Solo vocal: Eglogues (P. Baillargeon), A, fl, pf, 1942; Pater, Mez/Bar, org, 1944; Ave Maria, Mez/Bar, org, 1945; Complainte populaire, S, B, pf, 1946; Quatrains (F. Jammes), S, pf, 1947; Mort (F. Villon), A, pf, 1956; Paysage (St Denys Garneau), 8 spkrs, 8 solo vv, wind qnt, hp, pf, perc, str qnt, 1968; Contraste, 1v, orch, 1970; Chanson de Rahit (H. Suyin), 1v, cl, pf, 1972; Nuit polaire (J. Papineau-Couture), 10 insts, 1986; Glanures (I. Papineau-Coutrure), S, chbr orch, 1994

CHAMBER AND SOLO INSTRUMENTAL

For 4 or more insts: Suite, fl, cl, bn, hn, pf, 1947; Rondo, 4 rec, 1953; Str Qt no.1, 1953; Fantaisie, wind qnt, 1963; Canons, 2 tpt, hn, trbn, tuba, 1964; Sextet, ob, cl, bn, str trio, 1967; Str Qt no.2, 1967; Nocturnes, fl, cl, gui, hpd, perc, vn, vc, 1969; Obsession, 16 insts, 1973; Arcadie, 4 fl, 1986; Les arabesques d'Isabelle, fl, eng hn, cl, bn, pf, 1989; Celebrations, 5 wind, 4 brass, perc, cel, pf, str, 1991; Automne, fl, ob, cl, bn, hn, str qt, db, 1992; Vents capricieux, fl, ob, cl, bn, pf, 1993; Chocs sonores, perc ens, 1994; Str Qt no.3, 1996; Appel, ob, bn, hn, tpt, pf trio, 1997; Pf Trio, 1997; Septet, fl, ob, cl, bn, vn, va, vc, 1997; Qnt, ob, vn, vc, pf, 1998

For 1–3 insts: Sonata, G, vn, pf, 1944, rev. 1953; Suite, fl, pf, 1944–5; Aria, vn, 1946; Suite, vn, 1956; 3 caprices, vn, pf, 1962; Dialogues, vn, pf, 1967; Dyarchie, hpd, 1971; Départ, a fl, 1974; Trio à 4 mouvements, va, cl, pf, 1974; Verségères, b fl, 1975, rev. 1988; J'aime les tierces mineures, fl, 1976; Slano, vn, va, vc, 1976; Le débat du coeur et du corps, nar, vc, perc, 1977, rev. 1984; Exploration, gui, 1983; Prouesse, va, 1985; Courbes, org, 1987; Vers l'extinction, org, 1987; Quasa passacaille, org, 1988; Thrène, vn, pf, 1988; Autour du Dies irae, org, 1991; C'est bref, org, 1991; Tournants, org, 1992; Fantasques, vc, pf, 1995; Discussion animée, vn, pf, 1997

Pf: Suite, 1942–3; Mouvement perpétuel, 1943; 2 valses, 1943–4; Etude, bb, 1944–5; Rondo, 4 hands, 1945; Aria, 1960; Complémentarité, 1971, rev. 1984; Nuit, 1978; Idée, 1982; Méandres, 1998

Principal publishers: Berandol, CMC, Peer

WRITINGS

'Que sera la musique canadienne', Amérique française, ii/2 (1942), 24–6

'L'année musicale au Canada en 1957', Livre de l'année (1958), 220–24

'L'année musicale', Livre de l'année (1959), 300–03

Notes sur la 'Pièce concertante no.1' (Toronto, 1961)

with H. Sutermeister and A. de la Vega: 'Training of Composers', The Modern Composer and his World: Stratford, ON, 1960, 17–34

'Le danger de la spirale de l'inflation devant la nouveauté', Journal des Jeunesses musicales du Canada (1967)

with I. Papineau-Couture: 'Souvenirs', Cahiers canadiens de musique/ Canada Music Book no.4 (1972), 59–63 [on Stravinsky]

BIBLIOGRAPHY

J. Beckwith: 'Composers in Toronto and Montreal', University of Toronto Quarterly, xxvi (1956–7), 47–69

J. Beckwith: 'Jean Papineau-Couture', Canadian Music Journal, iii/2 (1958–9), 4–20

Y. Rivard: 'Retour de Jean Papineau-Couture à la couleur', Scène musicale, no.254 (1970)

R. Duguay: 'Jean Papineau-Couture', Musiques du Kébèk, ed. Duguay (Montreal, 1971), 145ff [interview]

G. Potuin: 'J. Papineau-Couture', Le Devoir (24 Oct 1981)

L. Bail-Milot: 'Jean Papineau-Couture', Variations, i/1 (1977), 32–4

L. Bail Milot: Jean Papineau-Couture: la vie, la carrière et l'oeuvre (Montreal, 1986)

LYSE RICHER/MARIE-THÉRÈSE LEFEBVRE

Papini, Guido (b Camaiore, nr Lucca, 1 Aug 1847; d London, 3 Oct 1912). Italian violinist and composer. He studied with Ferdinando Giorgetti at the Istituto Musicale at Florence. He made a successful début at the age of 13, but subsequently considered giving up music as a career. He returned to Florence at the invitation of Basevi to lead the quartet of the Società del Quartetto. Concerts in Italy and France earned him a reputation as a violinist with an expressive and beautiful tone and brilliant technique. He was court violinist to the Queen of Italy; at Lisbon he received the Cross of Merit. From 1874 he lived in England. In London in that year he played the viola in John Ella's Musical Union concerts, alternating with Sarasate and later with Wieniawski as leader of the quartet. He was soloist at the Philharmonic concerts in 1875, 1877 and 1878 and, in 1876, with the Pasdeloup Orchestra and the Bordeaux PO. Among the distinguished musicians he toured with were Rubinstein, von Bülow and Bottesini. From 1893 to 1896, when illness caused his resignation, he was principal violin professor of the Royal Irish Academy of Music at Dublin and inaugurated important chamber concerts there. During his remaining years in London, despite poor health, he devoted himself to composition and private teaching. He was an examiner of the College of Violinists, which he served for several years as president.

Ephemeral fantasies, transcriptions and salon pieces for violin and piano make up the bulk of Papini's more than 200 works, but he did write a few pieces in the larger forms, such as the Violin Concerto in D minor op.36. His trios (for two violins and piano) and a quartet (for three violins and piano) Cobbett found to be 'light and graceful, but of no permanent interest'. The pedagogical works and editions are of more lasting value: a violin method in four parts, op.57, L'archet: a Technical Work for the Practice of the Different Bowings Most in Use op.118, several sets of études and an edition of four Boccherini cello concertos.

BIBLIOGRAPHY

T. Phipson: Guido Papini and the Italian School of Violinists (London, 1886)

B. Henderson: 'Guido Papini', The Strad, xvii (1906–7), 234–5 [with photograph]

Cobbett's Cyclopedic Survey of Chamber Music, ii (London, 1929–30, rev. 2/1963/R by C. Mason), 206

E. HERON-ALLEN/ALBERT MELL

Papp, Géza (b Budapest, 29 April 1915). Hungarian musicologist and educationist. He studied theory with Bárdos, music history with Bartha and composition with Kodály at the Budapest Academy, where he took diplomas in church choir conducting (1937) and music teaching (1940). He taught in various secondary schools (1941–60) before becoming an editor with a publisher of school textbooks. He worked in a freelance capacity for the Hungarian music history section of the Institute of Musicology, and took the CSc in 1970 with a collected edition of Hungarian 17th-century songs. His principal areas of research were 17th- and 18th-century Hungarian music history, music education and principles of school textbooks. He edited numerous schoolbooks and collaborated in writing several music educational works.

WRITINGS

A magyar katolikus egyházi népének kezdetei [The sources of the Hungarian Catholic hymn] (Budapest, 1942)

'Kájoni János orgonakönyve' [Ioan Caianui's organ book], *Magyar zenei szemle*, ii (1942), 133–55

'Ismeretlen Kochanowski-fordítások a XVI–XVII. századból' [Unknown Kochanowski translations from the 16th and 17th centuries], *Irodalomtörténeti közlemények*, lxv (1961), 328–40

'Über die Verbreitung des Quintwechsels', *SMH*, viii (1966), 189–209

'Le psautier de Genève dans la Hongrie du XVIIe siècle', *SMH*, ix (1967), 281–99

'Przyczynki do związków muzyki polskiej z węgierską w XVII wieku' [Notes on the connection between Polish and Hungarian music in the 17th century], *Studia Hieronymo Feicht septuagenario dedicata*, ed. Z. Lissa (Kraków, 1967), 235–51; Ger. trans. in *SMH*, x (1968), 37–54

'Szőlősy Benedek és énekeskönyveinek nyomdahelye' [Benedek Szőlősy and the printing house of his songbooks], *Magyar könyvszemle* (1967), 78

'Die Haupttypen des ungarischen Liedes im XVI–XVII. Jahrhundert', *Musica antiqua II: Bydgoszcz 1969*, 283–313

'Przyczynki do związków dawnej poezji węgierskiej z polską' [Remarks on the connection between Hungarian and Polish Poetry], *Studia z dziejów polsko-węgierskich stosunków literackich i kulturalnych*, ed. J. Reychman and others (Warsaw, 1969), 132–50

A XVII. század énekelt dallamai [Tunes sung in the 17th century] (diss., Hungarian Academy of Sciences, 1970; Budapest, 1970, as *Régi magyar dallamok tára* [Collection of old Hungarian songs], ii)

'Egy prozódiai jelenség Kodály kórusműveiben' [A prosodical phenomenon in the choruses of Kodály], *Kóta* (1972), no.3

'Stilelemente des frühen Werbungstanzes in der Gebrauchsmusik des 18. Jahrhunderts', *Musica antiqua III: Bydgoszcz 1972*, 639–79

'Zur Geschichte der ungarischen Tanzmusik: Probleme des Werbungstanzes', *Studia instrumentorum musicae popularis IV: Balatonalmádi 1973*, 142–7

'Tankönyv és módszer' [Schoolbook and method], *Az ének-zene tanítása* (1974), 111–14, 171–8, 259–75; (1975), 55–63, 111–19, 197–203; (1976), 23–8

'Die Quellen der "Verbunkos-Musik": ein bibliographischer Versuch', *SMH*, xxi (1979), 151–217; xxiv (1982), 35–97; xxvi (1984), 59–132; xxxii (1990), 55–224

'A verbunkos kéziratos emlékei I' [Manuscript records of the verbunkos I], *Magyar zene*, xxiv (1983), 248–68; II, *Zenetudományi dolgozatok* (1986), 301–28

'További adatok a verbunkoskiadványok megjelenési idejéhez' [More comments on the chronology of the publication of the verbunkos], *Magyar zene*, xxv (1984), 245–67

'Unbekannte "Verbunkos" – Transkriptionen von Ferenc Liszt: "Ungarischer Romanzero"', *SMH*, xxix (1987), 181–218

ed. K. Bárdos: *Magyarország zenetörténete*, ii: *1541–1686* (Budapest, 1990)

'A Liszt-rapszódiák forrásaihoz' [On the sources of the rhapsodies of Liszt], *Magyar zene*, xxxiv (1993), 163–71

'A nagy potpourri: témyek, fölvetések, ellentmondások, következtetések' [The great potpourri: facts, propositions, contradictions, conclusions], *Zenetudományi dolgozatok* (1995–6), 167–76

ANTAL BORONKAY

Pappano, Antonio (*b* Epping, Essex, 30 Dec 1959). American conductor. After early music lessons with his father, he studied the piano, composition and conducting in the USA with, respectively, Norma Verrilli, Arnold Franchetti (a pupil of Richard Strauss) and Gustav Meier. His first engagement was as répétiteur and assistant conductor at the New York City Opera, and he subsequently worked at the Liceu in Barcelona, the Lyric Opera of Chicago, Frankfurt Opera and Bayreuth (as Barenboim's assistant) before being appointed music director of the Norwegian National Opera in 1990. Pappano made his Covent Garden début conducting *La bohème* the same year, and in 1992 became music director of La Monnaie in Brussels. The following year he made an acclaimed début with *Siegfried* at the Vienna Staatsoper, returning there for *I vespri siciliani* in 1998. He has also appeared at the Metropolitan Opera (where he conducted *Yevgeny Onegin* in the 1997–8 season), San Francisco Opera, the ENO, the Berlin Staatsoper, the Théâtre du Châtelet and the Teatro Comunale in Florence, and has worked with many of the world's leading symphony orchestras, including the Berlin PO, Chicago SO, Cleveland Orchestra, LSO and Israel PO, of which he became principal guest conductor in 1997. Pappano's conducting combines refinement of detail with a powerful dramatic sweep, as can be heard in his recordings of Puccini's *La rondine* (which won a 1997 *Gramophone* award) and *Trittico*, and of Massenet's *Werther*. In 1999 he was appointed music director of Covent Garden with effect from the 2002–3 season.

RICHARD WIGMORE

Papua New Guinea. *See* MELANESIA, §III.

Pâque, (Marie Joseph Léon) Désiré (*b* Liège, 21 May 1867; *d* Bessancourt, Val-d'Oise, 20 Nov 1939). Belgian composer who adopted French nationality. An orphan from an early age, he studied at the Liège Conservatory, where he was appointed assistant professor of solfège in 1889. His early compositions, influenced by Russians such as Cui and Borodin, won several prizes, including those of the Belgian Royal Academy (String Quartet op.23), and the Paris Pro Musica (Piano Trio op.46). After a short time spent researching Bulgarian folksong in Sofia, Pâque became professor of piano and composition at the conservatory in Athens (1900–02). Following a brief period working in Brussels and Paris he resided in Lisbon, where he taught composition and organ at the conservatory (1906–9). Before World War I he visited England and taught and conducted in Hamburg, Bremen, Rostock, Berlin and Geneva. While in Berlin he was engaged by the publisher Simrock as a resident composer, receiving an annual salary. From 1914 Pâque lived in Paris and became organist of St Louis d'Antin. He married four times, and a daughter from his third marriage, Désirée Pâque-Sweertz, pursued a career as a concert violinist. During Pâque's final years, spent in Paris and Bessancourt, he became a recluse, making no contact with any noted French composer. Instead he devoted himself to composition and to the writing of many articles concerning his revolutionary musical ideas.

An unrecognized and brilliantly original composer, Pâque formulated theories of composition that anticipated those of Schoenberg. He advocated principles of atonality, referring to the 'mode chromatique moderne', and proposed the abandonment of several musical conventions such as the regular time signature and the traditional approach to development. The latter he replaced with his own system known as 'adjonction constante', whereby development occurs either by attaching new motifs to unchangeable main themes or by juxtaposing material differently against these unaltered themes. Pâque's lack of recognition is a result of his publishing almost nothing about his theories until later in his life. However, he spent much time in correspondence with Charles Lalo, reader in aesthetics at the Sorbonne, concerning his theories, and in 1910 he dedicated to Lalo his *Esthétique musicale d'un* musicien (published 18 years later in instalments under the title 'Essai sur la mélodie'). The series of articles he wrote for the *Revue musicale* during the 1930s under the general heading *Notre esthétique musicale* define his philosophies established almost 40 years earlier.

Even by 1893 Pâque had published *Vingt leçons de lecture musicale*, exercises that deliberately avoid a definite key, and in 1895 – four years before the *Verklärte Nacht* sextet – he wrote a Sonata for piano trio 'without a fixed and pre-established tonality'. His Symphony no.1 for organ and his first three piano sonatas, dating from the same year as Schoenberg's *Harmonielehre* (1911), make very clear use of 'adjonction constante' and are, to a degree, atonal, foreshadowing works such as Berg's Piano Sonata. The evolvement of his expressive freedom can be seen in the 12 books of *Effusions lyriques* for piano, which were written throughout his life, and his style is at its most focussed in his late works for chamber combinations.

WORKS
(selective list)

STAGE AND ORCHESTRAL

Op: Vaïma, op.47, 1903, Ostend, 1904
Syms.: [no.1], op.33, 1895; [no.2] 'La Parisienne', op.52, 1905; [no.3], op.76, 1912; [no.4], op.86, 1916–17; [no.5], op.95, org, orch, 1919; [no.6], op.109, 1925–7; [no.7], op.125, 1934; [no.8], op.129, 1935–6
Pièces de musique symphonique: op.92, 1918; op.132, 1936; op.137, 1937
Concs.: Pf Conc. no.1, op.4, 1888; Vc Conc., op.28, 1893; Conc., op.118, ww, str, 1931–2; Pf Conc. no.2, op.127, 1935
Other: Le Dieu et la Bayadère, op.60, 1908; Jeanne d'Arc, op.65, 1909

CHAMBER AND SOLO INSTRUMENTAL

Str qts: [no.1], op.23, 1892; [no.2], op.30, 1894; [no.3], op.37, 1897; [no.4], op.38, 1899; [no.5], op.44, 1902; [no.6], op.90, 1917; [no.7], op.96, 1921; [no.8], op.122, 1933; [no.9], op.138, 1937; [no.10], op.144, 1939
Pf: Effusions lyriques, 12 books, I, op.12, 1890–92; II, op.55, 1896–1905; III, op.56, 1896–8; IV, op.79, 1906–13; V, op.81, 1913–14; VI, op.84, 1915–16; VII, op.91, 1918; VIII, op.104, 1925–6; IX, op.116, 1930–33; X, op.123, 1934–5; XI, op.133, 1936–7; XII, op.142, 1938–9; 5 Sonatas, opp.68–70, 73, 1911, op.117, 1930–31; 50 miscellaneous pieces
Other: Sonata, op.7, vn, pf, 1890; Sonata, pf trio, 1895; Pf Qnt, op.35, 1896; Sonata, op.43, vn, pf, 1902; Pf Trio, op.46, 1903; Sym. no.1, op.67, org, 1910; Sonata, op.85, va, pf, 1915; Pf Trio, op.98, 1923; Pf Qnt, op.102, 1924; Pf Trio, op.115, 1930; Sonata, op.126, vn, pf, 1934; Pf Qnt, op.141, 1938; 26 other chamber works; 23 pieces, org

VOCAL

20 leçons musicale, op.21, 1892–3; Requiem, op.41, solo vv, chorus, orch, org, 1900; 4 Motets, op.83, 1914–15; Messe brève, op.114, chorus, org (1929); Messe chromatique, op.119 (1931–2); 4 Cantates concertantes, op.121, SSA, orch, 1933; Polyphonie mystique, op.136, 1937; Interludes, op.140, vv, str, 1937–8; Messe brève, op.143, chorus, org (1939); 44 mélodies, 1v, pf; 2 duos; 18 secular choral pieces

Principal publishers: Simrock, Senart/Salabert, Coppenrath, Breitkopf & Härtel, Schneider, Editions Combre

WRITINGS

'Essai sur la mélodie', *Guide du concert*, xiv (1927–8), 825–7, 857–9, 888–90, 920–22, 953–4
'Notre esthétique', *ReM*, no.101 (1930), 119–31
'L'atonalité ou mode chromatique unique', *ReM*, no.107 (1930), 135–40
'Musique pure, libre et disciplinée', *ReM*, no.138 (1933), 105–9

BIBLIOGRAPHY

C. Coeuroy: 'Désiré Pâque', *ReM*, iii/1 (1921), 73–
L. Lavoye: 'Un grand méconnu: Désiré Pâque', *Revue musicale belge* (1938, 20 Jan, 5 and 20 Feb)
P. Gilson: 'Désiré Pâque: compositeur liégeois méconnu', *Bulletin de la Société Liégeoise de Musicologie*, lxx/July (1990), 2–18
P. Gilson: 'Neuf lettres de Désiré Pâque à Sylvain Dupuis', *RBM* xlvii (1993), 251–8

JOHN SCOTT WHITELEY

Pär, Joseph. See BEER, JOSEPH.

Parabosco, Girolamo (*b* Piacenza, *c*1524; *d* Venice, 21 April 1557). Italian composer. He was the son of the Brescian organist Vincenzo Parabosco (*d* 1556) and, according to Zarlino, the pupil of Adrian Willaert by 5 December 1541. Parabosco described himself as a 'discipulo di M. Adriano' in his 1546 madrigal collection and eulogized Willaert in his comedy, *La notte* (1546). He probably studied with Willaert before 1540 when his two ricercares appeared in the anthology *Musica nova* (RISM 1540²²). Significantly, perhaps in view of his youth and his student relationship with Willaert, Parabosco's name (like that of his fellow pupil, Girolamo Cavazzoni) appears in lower-case letters in the running heads of *Musica nova*. In or shortly before 1546 Parabosco visited Florence briefly as a guest of Francesco Corteccia. Between 1548 and 1551 he made trips to Urbino, Ferrara, Piacenza, Brescia, Padua and Verona. Returning to Venice, he was elected first organist at S Marco on 16 June 1551, retaining this post until his death. Active in literary and musical academies in Venice, he knew Antonfrancesco Doni, Andrea Calmo, Pietro Aretino and Titian. Notwithstanding Parabosco's acquaintance with Titian, the suggestion first made by Molmenti and accepted by others that Titian's *Venus and the Organist with Lapdog* (*c*1545–8; Prado) portrays Parabosco, is probably incorrect. A better case can be made for a 17th-century copy (in *I-Ma*) of a lost 16th-century portrait of Parabosco which bears some resemblance to an engraving in the 1795 edition of his *I diporti*.

The two youthful instrumental works from *Musica nova* differ strikingly. Although using successive points of imitation, the first (no.18) incorporates considerable sequential repetition. The ricercare 'Da pacem' is exceptional, because it is based on a cantus firmus from the antiphon for peace. Each of the antiphon's four phrases appears in the tenor with anticipations by one of the other voices. This work may refer to the war between Venice and the sultan which ended in October 1540, the year in which *Musica nova* was published. Parabosco's motet-like madrigals show his study with Willaert. Their imitative polyphony is often dense and rarely relieved by harmonic episodes; voices are often in contrasting groups. Harmonies are rich, text repetition is frequent and the declamation excellent.

WORKS

Editions: *Girolamo Parabosco: Composizioni*, ed. F. Bussi (Piacenza, 1961) [B]
   A. Doni: *Dialogo della musica*, ed. G.F. Malipiero (Vienna, 1965) [M]

[21] Madrigali, 5vv (Venice, 1546); 3 in B, 1 in M, 1 in *EinsteinIM*, iii
4 other madrigals, 1541¹³, 1544²²; B, M
Instrumental: Benedictus a 2, 1543¹⁹, B; Ricercare a 4, 1540²², B, ed. in MRM, i (1964); Ricercare 'Da pacem' a 4, 1540²², B, ed. in MRM, i (1964)

Ipsa te rogat pietatis, motet, lost

BIBLIOGRAPHY

EinsteinIM
G. Zarlino: *Sopplimenti musicali* (Venice, 1588/R)

G. Bianchini: *Girolamo Parabosco, scrittore e organista del secolo XVI* (Venice, 1899)
H.C. Slim: *The Keyboard Ricercar and Fantasia in Italy, ca. 1500–1550, with Reference to Parallel Forms in European Lute Music of the Same Period* (diss., Harvard U., 1961)
F. Bussi: *Umanità e arte di Gerolamo Parabosco* (Piacenza, 1961) [see also review by H.C. Slim, *JAMS*, xvii (1964), 401–4]
M. Feldman: 'The Academy of Domenico Venier, Music's Literary Muse in Mid-Cinquecento Venice', *Renaissance Quarterly*, xliv (1991), 476–512

H. COLIN SLIM

Parabovi, Filippo [Francesco] **Maria.** *See* PERABOVI, FILIPPO MARIA.

Parać, Ivo (*b* Split, 24 June 1890; *d* Split, 4 Dec 1954). Croatian composer. Drawn to Italian art and culture from a young age, he graduated in composition from Pesaro Conservatory in 1923. He also studied privately with Pizzetti, Perosi and Alaleona. After returning to Split he taught briefly in Belgrade; from 1925 until his death (which occurred on the day of the Split première of his only opera) he lived in Split, conducting and teaching (from 1948) at the music school.

Parać's post-Romantic, lyrical musical language grew out of the Italian tradition, although he never used the typical Italian bel canto style. After 1924 his work underwent a change: he discovered the national Croatian tradition and tried to include elements of it in his own musical idiom. His artistic interest was nevertheless always focussed on vocal forms. His opera, *Adelova pjesma* ('Adel's Song'), a romantic lyrical tragedy, occupies an exceptional position among Croatian operas of the time; its musical language shows an individual use of Wagnerian technique, with leitmotifs in the orchestral texture and predominantly declamatory vocal writing. The summit of his vocal works is the cycle of 12 songs, *Musiche Pascoliane* (1930), with its rich vocal nuances and Impressionist-sounding piano accompaniment. As well as a composer, Parać was a gifted and prolific poet.

WORKS

Op: Adelova pjesma [Adel's Song] (3, epilogue, V. Desnica, after L. Botić), Zagreb 1930–34, 7 June 1941, rev. 1951
Orch: Fantasia marinaresca, 1917; Marcia funebre, 1917; Saš ume i smora [From the Woods and from the Sea], suite, 1917
Solo vocal: Canoni dal mare (Parać), song cycle, 1v, pf; Idillio maremmano (G. Carducci), T, orch; La novella di nonna Lucia (Carducci), T, orch; Musiche Pascoliane (Pascoli), song cycle, 1v, pf, 1930
Choral: Amor, 3 motets, chorus; 3 canti corali (Carducci), mixed chorus, orch; Exultatio, 3 motets, chorus; Madrigali dell'estate (G. d'Annunzio), choral cycle (1930)
Other inst: Andante amoroso, str qt; Minuetto appassionato, pf; Proljetna suita [Spring Suite], pf; Serenatella, fl, va, vc, pf

BIBLIOGRAPHY

J. Andreis: *Music in Croatia* (Zagreb, 1974, enlarged 2/1982)
J. Andreis: 'Ivo Parać: život i djela' [Ivo Parać: life and works], *Rad JAZU*, no.377 (1978), 5–127
J. Andreis: 'Luka Botić dva puta na opernoj pozornici' [Luka Botić twice on the operatic stage], *Zvuk*, no.3 (1979), 5–18
M. Škunca: 'Tragovi impresionizma u skladateljskom opusu Ive Paraća "Musiche Pascoliane"/Les éléments d'impressionnisme dans le cycle d'Ivo Parać "Musiche Pascoliane"', *Recepcija glazbe Claudea Debussyja u Hrvatskoj/La réception de la musique de Claude Debussy en Croatie*, ed. S. Majer-Bobetko and Z. Weber (Zagreb, 1996), 109–52

KORALJKA KOS

Paradeiser, Marian (Carl) [Karl] (*b* Riedenthal, 11 Oct 1747; *d* Melk, 16 Nov 1775). Austrian composer and violinist. From the age of 12 or 13, when he began serving as a choirboy, he spent his life almost entirely at Melk Abbey. He sang soprano and studied the violin under the *regens chori* Marian Gurtler (1703–66) and after 1761 composition with Robert Kimmerling and perhaps with the organist J.G. Albrechtsberger. He took his vows on 11 November 1767 and, after a period of study in Vienna, was ordained on 29 September 1771. Having taught in the lower school at Melk for three years, before taking up his appointment as professor of theology he died at the age of 28.

During his brief 13-year creative span Paradeiser developed a respectable reputation built around a small but valuable corpus of approximately 65 works. This was established early on through the success of large-scale vocal-orchestral works composed for Melk in the 1760s and through his own virtuoso violin playing well displayed in the concertos and the occasional symphonic movement. Later, as he specialized in composing chamber music for strings, he became known for his trios and quartets, as shown by their dissemination, and reports (*AMZ*, Maximilian Stadler) that they were favoured by the imperial director of chamber music in Vienna, Franz Kreibich (1728–97). It has been suggested that Haydn's opp.1, 2 and 9 may have influenced Paradeiser in his divertimento quartet writing (Finscher), but even closer parallels can be found between Paradeiser's and Albrechtsberger's chamber music composed at Melk in 1759–60.

WORKS
in MS at A-M, unless otherwise stated

Cants.: Die nöthigen Sorgen sind glücklich vertrieben (B. Schuster, E. Müller, G. Winnerl), Singgedicht, 4 S, 2 A, 4vv, orch, perf. Melk, 17 Feb 1765; Ecloga Seladon (Schuster), 4 S, A, T, 7vv, orch, perf. Melk, 29 June 1772; Er kömmt heran, der Hochgeweihte, doubtful attrib.
Church music: Mass, *D-Bsb*; Kyrie, Alma Redemptoris mater, Ave regina, 2 Salve regina; Benedictus quem tentavit, motet; O Jesu care, S, A, orch, listed in Melk catalogue
Inst: 3 syms., ed. in The Symphony 1720–1840, ser. B, vi (New York, 1982); 9 orch minuets; 3 vn concs.; Concertino, org/hpd, vn, vc, orch; Concertino, vn, va, vc, orch; Concertino, 2 vn, va, vc, bc; Concertino, 2 vn, str orch, 1775; 17 str qts (divertimentos), 10 trios, 2 vn, b, *A-KR*, *SEI*, *Wn*, *CH-Gc* (London, n.d.) *CZ-Bm*, *Pnm*, *D-MÜs*, *I-MOe*; Sonata, vn, b; Capricio, vn; 2 further str qts listed in *Kleine Quartbuch* (*A-Wn*); 6 str qts, 1 trio, listed in Traeg catalogue (1799)

BIBLIOGRAPHY

EitnerQ; *FétisB*; *GerberNL*; *MGG1* (F. Heller); *SchillingE*
'Bericht über den Musikzustand des löbl. Stiftes Mölk in alter und neuer Zeit', *Allgemeine musikalische Zeitung* [Vienna], ii (1818), 349–52, 357–60, esp. 358, 365–7; repr. in *Musicologia austriaca*, iii (1982), 31–5, esp. 33
S. Molitor: *Biographische und kunsthistorische Stoffsammlungen zur Musik in Österreich* (MS, *A-Wn*, *c*1838)
B. Wind: *Die Streichquartette des Karl Marian Paradeisers, eines österreichischen Kleinmeisters aus der Frühzeit der Wiener Klassik* (diss., U. of Innsbruck, 1969)
L. Finscher: *Studien zur Geschichte des Streichquartetts*, i (Kassel, 1974)
K. Wagner, ed.: *Abbé Maximilian Stadler: seine Materialien zur Geschichte der Musik unter den österreichischen Regenten* (Kassel, 1974)
R.N. Freeman: *The Practice of Music at Melk Abbey: Based upon the Documents 1681–1826* (Vienna, 1989)
R.N. Freeman: *The String Concertos of Marian Carl Paradeiser* (forthcoming)

ROBERT N. FREEMAN

Parademarsch (Ger.). Slow march. *See* MARCH, §1.

Paradiddle. A rudiment of the art of side-drumming. *See* DRUM, §II, 2.

Paradies [Paradisi], (Pietro) Domenico (*b* Naples, 1707; *d* Venice, 25 Aug 1791). Italian composer and teacher. He is believed to have studied with Nicola Porpora in Naples, but little is known about his early life. The first documented performance of his music was of the opera *Alessandro in Persia* (Lucca, 1738), on a libretto of the Florentine Francesco Vanneschi. The poor reception of this work marked the beginning of a generally unsuccessful career as a composer for the stage. During the 1739–40 season Paradies moved to Venice, where he was employed by the Conservatorio dei Mendicanti, one of the city's four famous schools for orphaned girls. There his reputation as an opera composer suffered further when his *serenata* of 1740, *Il decreto del fato*, proved unpopular. During this period, however, he was exposed to the vibrant Venetian musical life of the era and the progressive keyboard music of composers such as his contemporary Baldassare Galuppi.

Paradies emigrated to London in 1746 and, shortly thereafter, changed the spelling of his name (from the Italian form 'Paradisi'). He was one of numerous Italian composers, including Galuppi, who worked there during the mid-18th century. His series of operatic failures continued in January of 1747, when his setting of Vanneschi's *Fetonte* encountered negative reaction during its nine performances at the King's Theatre, Haymarket. Charles Burney described the arias as 'ill-phrased' and lacking in '*estro* or grace'. Although Paradies continued to supply arias for pasticcio productions at the King's Theatre, where Vanneschi had become impresario, he never met with success as a composer of opera. He achieved some renown in England, however, as a teacher of harpsichord and composition. His most distinguished student was the elder Thomas Linley, who later became a highly regarded composer of English opera. In 1770, anticipating retirement, Paradies sold his manuscript collection to Richard (later Viscount) Fitzwilliam. He returned to Venice, where he spent the rest of his life.

Although Paradies published a concerto for organ or harpsichord and orchestra and composed numerous other instrumental works, his most enduring fame rests on his 12 *Sonate di gravicembalo*. This collection, published by John Johnson under the protection of a royal privilege in 1754, was reprinted several times in England during the composer's life, as well as by Le Clerc and Imbault in Paris and Roger in Amsterdam. These sonatas quickly achieved widespread popularity in England and on the continent. The letters of Leopold Mozart indicate that they were studied and performed in his household. Although Burney attributed Paradies's failure as an opera composer to inexperience, the sonatas consistently display refined craftsmanship. Several of them appeared in 19th- and 20th-century collections of keyboard music, and the entire set exists in two modern editions. The second movement of the sixth sonata, often published separately, entitled 'Toccata', has remained popular among harpsichordists and pianists.

The 12 sonatas are all in two movements. They display some of the more progressive features of the time along with many that are still firmly rooted in Baroque style. Their most modern attribute is the appearance of Classical formal procedure within many individual movements. The opening movements of the sonatas are the most complex and innovative, with 11 of the 12 recognizable as various versions of sonata form. Five of the closing movements are lively, quasi-contrapuntal studies, characterized by rhythmic regularity and broken-chord figuration. Their binary structures sometimes approximate sonata forms except for the lack of rhythmic differentiation (e.g. the 'Toccata' from Sonata no.6). Three are *gigas* and one is a minuet, all in binary form. The remaining three finales are lyrical rondos in slow or moderate tempos. Although many passages approach the cantabile style of Classical pianoforte music, this music was obviously conceived for harpsichord. Dynamic markings are non-existent. The textures exemplify the transitional state of keyboard composition of the mid-century. Much of the writing, especially in the finales, is in two parts in a style that resembles counterpoint, but in which one voice is normally more harmonic than melodic. Some movements begin with brief canonic passages, but quickly abandon imitative style. The first movements tend to be dominated by the melody in the right hand with various patterns outlining the harmony in the left. The true Alberti bass is used only occasionally. Many passages show the influence of the graceful keyboard idiom of Paradies's Neapolitan predecessor Domenico Scarlatti. In his manipulation of form, Paradies is inconsistent. Of the 11 first movements that resemble sonata form, seven omit all or part of the principal thematic area in the recapitulation in the manner of Scarlatti. Four, however, contain convincing thematic differentiation in the expositions and full recapitulations. Similarly, some of the sections after the central double bar are perfunctory transpositions of opening material, while others contain relatively sophisticated thematic development.

The other instrumental works are less progressive than the sonatas. The two keyboard concertos are in the Baroque style and show little differentiation between solo and tutti material. The sinfonias are typical tripartite Italian overtures. Of the dramatic works, *Fetonte* is unusual in its use of ballet music for chorus. Several excerpts from the operas were published in song collections. Paradies's style in these is competent, but facile and uninspired.

WORKS

DRAMATIC
all MSS autograph

Alessandro in Persia (opera, F. Vanneschi), Lucca, 1738, *A-Wgm*
Il decreto del fato (serenata), Venice, 1740, *GB-Cfm*
Le muse in gara (serenata, G. Belli), Venice, 1740, *Cfm*
Fetonte (opera, F. Vanneschi), London, King's Theatre in the Haymarket, 17 Jan 1747, *Cfm*; favourite songs (London, 1747)
La forza d'amore (pasticcio), London, Little Theatre in the Haymarket, 19 Jan 1751, *Cfm*, *Lbl*; favourite songs (London, 1751)
Antioco (opera),? not perf., frags., *Cfm*

OTHER WORKS
[12] Sonate di gravicembalo (London, 1754; ed H. Ruf and H. Bemmann, Mainz, 1971); 6 ed. in Le tresor des pianistes, xiv (Paris, *c*1870)
A Favourite Concerto (B♭), org/hpd, insts (London, *c*1768); pubd as Concerto in B (Mainz, 1965)
A Favourite Minuet with Variations (C), kbd (London, *c*1770)
Concerto (G minor), org/hpd, insts, *Cfm*
Allegro (G), kbd, frags., *Cfm*
Several symphony-overtures; other kbd works; solfeggi for S; cantatas; arias: *B-Bc*, *GB-Cfm* (autographs), *Lbm*, *Lcm*, *US-Wc*

BIBLIOGRAPHY
BurneyH
F. Torrefranca: *Le origine italiane del romanticismo musicale* (Turin, 1930)
L. Hoffmann-Erbrecht: *Deutsche und italienische Klaviermusik zur Bachzeit* (Leipzig and Wiesbaden, 1954)

W.S. Newman: *The Sonata in the Classic Era* (Chapel Hill, NC, 1963, 3/1983)

G. Giachin: 'Contributo alla conoscenza di Paradisi', *NRMI*, ix (1975), 358–66

D.C. Sanders: *The Keyboard Sonatas of Giustini, Paradisi, and Rutini: Formal and Stylistic Innovation in Mid-Eighteenth-Century Italian Keyboard Music* (diss., U. of Kansas, 1983)

D.E. Freeman: 'Johann Christian Bach and the Early Italian Masters', *Eighteenth-Century Keyboard Music*, ed. R.L. Marshall (New York, 1994), 230–69

DONALD C. SANDERS

Paradis [Paradies], **Maria Theresia** (*b* Vienna, bap. 15 May 1759; *d* Vienna, 1 Feb 1824). Austrian composer, pianist, organist and singer. She was the daughter of the Imperial Secretary and Court Councillor to Empress Maria Theresa, after whom she was named (the empress was not however her godmother, as was formerly believed). Some time between her second and fifth year she became blind; Anton Mesmer was able to improve her condition only temporarily, in 1777–8. She received a broad education from Leopold Kozeluch (piano), Vincenzo Righini (singing), Salieri (singing, dramatic composition), Abbé Vogler (theory and composition) and Carl Friberth (theory). By 1775 she was performing as a pianist and singer in Viennese concert rooms and salons. Composers who wrote for her include Salieri (an organ concerto, 1773), Mozart (a piano concerto, probably K456) and possibly Haydn (a piano concerto, HXVIII:4).

On 18 August 1783 she set out on an extended tour towards Paris and London, in the company of her mother and Johann Riedinger, her amanuensis and librettist. She visited Mozart and his family in Salzburg on 27 August. After concerts in Frankfurt (5 October 1783), Koblenz (30 October 1783) and elsewhere, she reached Paris in early March of the following year. On 1 April she appeared at the Concert Spirituel; the *Journal de Paris* (4 April 1784) wrote of her: 'one must have heard her to form an idea of the touch, the precision, the fluency and vividness of her playing'. Before leaving Paris at the end of October she made 14 public appearances. She also assisted Valentin Haüy, 'father and apostle of the blind', in establishing the first school for the blind, which he opened in Paris in 1785. In November 1784 Paradis went to London, where she performed at court, in the palace of the Prince of Wales (Carlton House) and in the Professional Concert in the Hanover Square Rooms, among other places; her performances were less well received than they had been in Paris, however. After many concerts in other west European cities she returned in 1786 by way of Berlin and Prague to Vienna. Plans to tour Russia and Italy did not materialize, but she returned to Prague in 1797 for the production of her opera *Rinaldo und Alcina*.

During her journey Paradis began composing solo piano music as well as pieces for voice and keyboard. The earliest music attributed to her was a set of four sonatas of about 1777, but these are probably the work of Pietro Domenico Paradies, with whom she is often confused (the Toccata in A sometimes ascribed to her is from a sonata by him). Similarly, the famous *Sicilienne* is spurious, probably the work (after a Weber violin sonata op.10 no.1) of its purported discoverer, Samuel Dushkin. Many of her authentic works of this period are lost. Her earliest extant major work is the collection *Zwölf Lieder auf ihrer Reise in Musik gesetzt*, composed 1784–6. By 1789 she was devoting more time to composition than performance; between then and 1797 she wrote at least five operas and three cantatas. After the failure of *Rinaldo und Alcina*, she increasingly devoted her energy to teaching; in 1808 she founded her own music school where she taught the piano, singing and theory, primarily to young girls. A Sunday concert series at the school featured the work of her outstanding students. She continued to teach up to the time of her death.

Paradis apparently had exceptionally accurate hearing, as well as ready comprehension and a good memory (she is said to have played over 60 concertos by heart). When composing she used a composition board invented by Riedinger, and for correspondence a hand printing machine constructed by Wolfgang von Kempelen. Her songs are representative of operatic style, with coloratura and trills; the influence of Salieri's dramatically composed scenes is especially apparent. Her stage works owe much to Viennese Singspiel, and in her piano style she is indebted to her teacher Kozeluch.

WORKS

STAGE

Ariadne und Bacchus (melodrama, 1, J. Riedinger), Laxenburg, Schlosstheater, 20 June 1791, lost

Der Schulkandidat (ländliches Spl, 3, ?Riedinger), Vienna, Theater in der Leopoldstadt, 5 Dec 1792; *A-LIm* (Act 3 and pt of Act 2 lost); ov. ed. H. Matsushita (Fayetteville, AR, 1992)

Rinaldo und Alcina [Die Insel der Verführung] (Zauberoper, 3, L. von Baczko), Prague, Nostitzsches Nationaltheater, 30 June 1797, lost

Grosse militärische Oper (F. von Niederstradon), ?1805, lost

Zwei ländliche Opern, lost

OTHER WORKS

Cantatas: Trauerkantate auf den Tod Leopolds II (Riedinger) (1792), lost, lib *Wgm*; Deutsches Monument Ludwigs des Unglücklichen (Riedinger), *KR* (orch pts), vs (Vienna, 1793); Kantate auf Wiedergenesung meines Vaters, lost

Other vocal: Lied auf die Blindheit des Frl. M. Th. v. Paradis (Ich war ein kleines Würmchen) (G.K. Pfeffel), in *Wiener Musenalmanach* (1785); 12 Lieder auf ihrer Reise in Musik gesetzt (Leipzig, 1786), 2 ed. in DTÖ, liv, Jg.xxvii/2 (1920), ed. H. Matsushita (Fayetteville, AR, 1987); Leonore (G.A. Bürger), ballade (Vienna, 1790), ed. H. Matsushita (Fayetteville, AR, 1989); Auf die Damen, welche statt Gold, nun Leinwand für die verwundeten Krieger zupfen (?Burger) (Vienna, 1794), ed. H. Matsushita (Fayetteville, AR, 1997); Da eben seinen Lauf (Mlle Jerusalem), rev. as aria (Vienna, 1813); Auf Brüder, auf, geniesst des Lebens Wonne (Riedinger), chorus (Vienna, 1813), lost; other lieder, lost

Inst: 2 pf concs., g, C, lost; 12 pf sonatas, opp.1–2 (Paris, 1792), probably by D. Paradies, lost; Pf Trio (Vienna, 1800), lost; Fantasie, G, pf (Vienna, 1807), ed. H. Matsushita; Fantasie, C, 1811; Variations, kbd; An meine entfernten Lieben, pf, lost

BIBLIOGRAPHY

Choron-FayolleD; DlabaczKL; FétisB; GerberL; Grove1 (C.F. Pohl); *SainsburyD; SchillingE; SchmidlD*

C. Burney: 'An Account of Mademoiselle Theresa Paradis of Vienna', *London Magazine*, iv (1785), 30–32

J. Riedinger: 'Notenschrift für Blinde', *AMZ*, xii (1810), 905–10

L. Frankl: *Biographie der M. Th. Paradis* (Linz, 1876)

H. Ullrich: 'Maria Theresia Paradis and Mozart', *ML*, xxvii (1946), 224–33

O. Brües: *Mozart und das Frl. von Paradis* (Tübingen, 1952)

E. Komorzynski: 'Mozart und Maria Theresia Paradis', *MJb 1952*, 110–16

H. Ullrich: 'Maria Theresia Paradis' grosse Kunstreise', *ÖMz*, xv (1960), 470–80; xvii (1962), 11–26; xviii (1963), 475–83; xix (1964), 430–35; xx (1965), 589–97 [see also *BMw*, vi (1964), 129ff; *Sächsische Heimatblätter 1964*, 393ff]

H. Ullrich: 'Maria Theresia Paradis (1759–1824) als Musikpädagogin', *Musikerziehung*, xiv (1960–61), 9–13

H. Ullrich: 'Das Stammbuch der Maria Theresia Paradis', *Jb des Bonner Heimat-und Geschichtsvereins*, xv (1961), 340–84

H. Ullrich: 'Die Bildnisse der blinden Musikerin Maria Theresia Paradis', *Musikerziehung*, xv (1961–2), 69–72

H. Ullrich: 'Maria Theresia Paradis in London', *ML*, xliii (1962), 16–24

H. Ullrich: 'Maria Theresia Paradis und Dr. Franz Anton Mesmer', *Jb des Vereines für Geschichte der Stadt Wien*, xvii–xviii (1962), 149–88

H. Ullrich: 'Die erste öffentliche Musikschule der Maria Theresia Paradis in Wien (1808–1824)', *Musikerziehung*, xvi (1962–3), 187–91; xvii (1963–4), 56–61

H. Ullrich: 'Drei wiederaufgefundene Werke von Maria Theresia Paradis', *ÖMz*, xvii (1962), 458–71 [see also xxi (1966), 400]

H. Ullrich: 'Maria Theresia Paradis: Werkverzeichnis', *BMw*, v (1963), 117–54 [see also viii (1966), 256–8]

E. Badura-Skoda: 'Zur Entstehung des Klavierkonzertes in B-Dur KV 456', *MJb 1964*, 193–7

H. Ullrich: 'Maria Theresia Paradis' zweite Reise nach Prag 1797: die Uraufführung von "Rinaldo und Alcina"', *Mf*, xix (1966), 152–63

H. Matsushita: *The Musical Career and Composition of Marie Theresia von Paradis 1759–1824* (diss., Brigham Young U., 1989)

S. Evers: 'Der Fall der Maria Theresia Paradis (1759–1824)', *Klinische Monatsblätter für Augenheilkunde*, cxcix/2 (1991), 122–7

E. Ostleitner: 'Neue Forschungsergebnisse über Maria Theresia Paradis', *Off-Mozart: Musical Culture and the 'Kleinmeister' of Central Europe 1750–1820: Zagreb 1992*, 77–83

RUDOLPH ANGERMÜLLER, HIDEMI MATSUSHITA/RON RABIN

Paradon. *See* BARYTON (i).

Paradossi, Giuseppe. *See* TROILI, GIUSEPPE.

Paraguay (Sp. República del Paraguay). Country in South America. It has an area of 406,752 km² and a population of 5·5 million (2000 estimate). The river Paraguay marks the divide between two geographically and culturally distinct areas, populated since ancient times by indigenous peoples. To the east is sub-tropical jungle, inhabited by horticulturalists belonging to the Tupí-Guaraní linguistic group. To the west is the northern Chaco, whose inhabitants are hunter-gatherers belonging to the Maskoy, Mataco-Mak'á, Guaycurú and Zamuco groups. The population of both regions also includes peasants of creole and foreign descent. The only common link between the indigenous cultures of the two areas is that they exist in the same country, where Guaraní-Spanish bilingualism is well established both in practice and, since 1992, by law, according Paraguay singular status in Latin America. The spread of Guaraní was encouraged by the mingling of races in the early days of the Spanish conquest. It was also later adopted by the Jesuits in order to avoid contact between the Spaniards and the natives living in 'reductions', as the stable communities established by the missionaries were known. Sources of information about musical activity in Paraguay are sparse and unfortunately imprecise. Juan Max Boettner's book (*c*1957) remains unsurpassed, although it contains several obvious errors as regards indigenous music. Various researchers have collected indigenous music *in situ*, including Carlos Vega and Isabel Aretz, who also documented creole music; and Jorge Novati and Irma Ruiz, ethnomusicologists at the Instituto Nacional de Musicología of Argentina, whose archives also contain recordings made by Vega of a Mak'á group from Paraguay brought for other purposes to Buenos Aires in 1939.

For various historical and cultural reasons, art music was a late development. During the colonial period the antagonistic relationship between Paraguayans and Jesuits meant that no evidence could be found in the cities of 159 years of teaching and the successful practice of European music within the protected atmosphere of the Guaraní reductions. Moreover, contrary to what occurred in Moxos and Chiquitos, the expulsion of the Jesuits marked the beginning of the end of the musical practices imposed under their harsh regime. The political vicissitudes of the two ensuing centuries also resulted in the arrested development of art music, to the extent that, according to Szarán (2000), the first Paraguayan opera, *Juana de Lara* by Florentín Giménez, with libretto by Milcíades Jiménez y Velázquez, did not appear until 1987. It is significant that academically trained composers of the last 50 years have their roots in popular folk music: the symphonic poem based on folk tunes has become the principal genre, a further indication of the unfailing vitality of creole music. From the 19th century onwards folksongs and dances based on the European heptatonic scale from the colonial centres were re-created and given a distinctive local style. The guitar, harp and violin played, and continue to play, an important role. Indigenous music, unknown beyond native communities, exhibits features of inter-ethnic cross-culturalization, with little if any Western influence.

I. Art music. II. Traditional and popular music.

I. Art music

Documents dating from the early days of the Spanish conquest mention a choir at Asunción Cathedral, the members of which included Gregorio de Acosta, Juan de Xara, Antonio Coto, Antonio de Tomás and Antonio Romero, who were active in this and other churches until at least the 1570s. Records also refer to numerous military bands, playing a strong repertory of popular and patriotic music, a tradition which persisted in Paraguay for centuries. In 1540 Father Juan Gabriel Lezcano founded a school on the outskirts of Asunción, where the children were taught music. The Jesuits merit special attention as far as music teaching is concerned. The Jesuit province of Paraguay (1609–1768) embraced a large territory including part of present-day Argentina and Uruguay. The Belgian Jean Vaisseau-Vaseo (1584–1623), first music master in Guayrá, was succeeded by the Frenchman Louis Berger (1588–1639). The missions achieving the most success in the practice of academic music brought from Europe or composed by Jesuits were San Ignacio Guazú (Paraguay) and Yapeyú (now Argentina), the latter under the charge of Antonio Sepp. The excellence of Guaraní musicians earned repeated praise from distinguished visitors. A great variety of European musical instruments, including organs, were manufactured in the missions. The Jesuit practice of replacing religious and secular Guaraní music, initially tolerated on their arrival, has deprived succeeding generations of these traditions. The missions' objective was to instil European cultural beliefs by converting the native population to Christianity. Music played a substantial role in achieving this aim, since it embraced practically every aspect of everyday life, including fiestas and ceremonies. The Jesuits' *Cartas Anuas* and other documents describe musical practices transplanted from Europe. These have been classified in two groups: communal religious and missionary music (the only European music found during the early years), and festive music, which included ceremonial music. In the first type, the entire community participated, requiring no support in terms of either teaching or performance. Communal music included *cantaricos*, community songs with Guaraní texts of a religious, doctrinal nature, hymns, litanies and other para-liturgical genres, dedicated to Jesus, the

Virgin Mary and various saints honoured by specific ceremonies. The second type required a complex and expensive infrastucture, which included training professional musicians, importing musical scores and instruments, organizing workshops for the manufacture of instruments, and the copying of music for distribution to towns and other missions. Festive and ceremonial music followed four European traditions: (1) martial music (with various combinations of trumpets, *chirimías* (oboes), drums, bassoons, horns, etc.), used by the army and at ceremonies welcoming distinguished visitors; (2) open-air music, recreational and processional pieces combining religious music and music derived from urban traditions including litanies and hymns, wind and fife and drum bands; (3) 'indoor' music intended for the religious liturgy of the church; and (4) dances, including those fashionable in Europe at the time (such as *españoleta*, *pavane*, *canario* etc.) and symbolic dances for ceremonial use. For a century and a half this, broadly speaking, was the musical scene in the missions. When these were disbanded, Catholic, Guaraní-speaking villages were established, laying the ground for strong popular religious activities and creating a very particular cultural situation. At the same time Indian villages in the jungle also repopulated.

In towns with European and mestizo populations, some Jesuits attempted to form choirs and bands, but with little success. In 1811, Paraguay gained independence from Spain under Rodríguez Francia. As 'Supreme Dictator' (1814–40) he closed the frontiers, resulting in cultural stagnation. However, during the subsequent peacetime regime (1840–65) Carlos Antonio López and his son Francisco Solano López, who succeeded him, showed a measure of interest in art music. Concerts with foreign conductors were held in the cathedral, the cathedral organ was restored and choirs were organized. The appointment in 1853 of a Frenchman, Francisco Sauvaget de Dupuis, to instruct military bandsmen indicates the importance attached to this form of music. Cantalicio Guerrero, trained by Dupuis, formed an orchestra in 1863, but the most intense musical activity came from a different direction, from the ballroom orchestras that played dances such as the lancers, quadrille, cotillion, waltz, mazurka, schottische and polka. It was not until ten years after the War of the Triple Alliance (1865–70) that there was any formal interest in culture. In 1881, the Sociedad Filarmónica La Lira and other similar groups were created to give

concerts and organize musical soirées. Choirs were formed, while zarzuela companies arrived and instruments were imported from Europe. In 1887, the Compañia Italiana de Opera Bufa, under the direction of Guillermo Januski, introduced opera to Paraguay, but despite the creation of the Centro Lírico in 1974, no stable Paraguayan opera company has ever been formed. The Teatro Nacional opened in 1891, while in 1895 the Instituto Paraguayo, which would train future musicians, was founded. Soon afterwards Gustavo Sosa Escalada introduced the concert guitar. With the outbreak of World War I many artistic ensembles arrived and European maestros such as Lefranck, Ochoa, Segalés and Malinverni settled in Paraguay. They taught the first generation of musicians who then went abroad for further training, gaining an international reputation. Fernando Centurión (1886–1938), who founded the Cuarteto Haydn in 1911, composed the country's first symphonic works: *Marcha heroica*, *Serenata Guaraní* and *Capricho sobre un tema Paraguayo*. From 1940 onwards, successive dictatorships forced numerous composers into exile, notably José Asunción Flores (1904–72), Carlos Lara Bareiro (1914–88), Francisco Alvarenga (1910–57) and Emilio Bigi (1910–47). Among those who remained in Paraguay were Remberto Giménez (1899–1977) and Juan Carlos Moreno González (1916–82), composer of the *Zarzuela Paraguaya* as well as chamber and symphonic works. Later composers included Luis Cañete (1905–85), Florentin Giménez (*b* 1925) and Nicolás Pérez González (*b* 1935). The Asunción group of composers, concentrating on contemporary music, emerged in the 1970s. At the beginning of the 21st century there are still no professional choirs, although there is lively amateur activity.

II. Traditional and popular music

1. Indigenous music. 2. Creole and popular music.

1. INDIGENOUS MUSIC. The Chaco region is home to 11 Amerindian nations, belonging to four linguistic families: Mascoy (Angaité, Guaná, Lengua, Sanapaná, Toba Maskoy); Mataco-Mak'á (Chorote, Nivaklé and Mak'á); Guaycurú (Emok-Toba) and Zamuco (Ayoreo and Chamacoco). Apart from these there are enclaves of Chiriguano (sometimes incorrectly known as Guarayo) and Tapieté, who belong to the Tupí-Guaraní group and who arrived in the area during the 20th century. Because of their cultural affinity and inter-ethnic cross-culturalization, the musical conventions, instruments and forms of

Ex.1 *Nivaklé* song-dance with kettle-drum with water (*tojkisham*); rec. and transcr. I. Ruiz

1. *An elderly Nivaklé woman using a stick rattle made with animal hooves (Photo I. Ruiz)*

expression of the first three are similar to those of the Chaqueño Amerindians of Argentina, although the Mascoy are found only in Paraguay. Music documented for these ethnic groups includes nocturnal dances for boys, songs for men and women and an important collection of shamanic songs. The first, in the form of round dances, were very much alive in the 1970s and were still the only form of entertainment available in remote villages, while retaining their essential function as courtship dances. The lead singer, standing in the centre of the circle, marks the rhythm by beating a *tambor de agua* (a kettledrum filled with water) with a stick (ex.1). For some tribes this instrument – which the Zamuco did not have – was linked to male initiation rites. Songs for women deal with a wide range of subjects, including the souls and blood of those killed in war; various types of birdsong and lullabies; other songs accompanying the ritual dances which mark a young girl's entry into puberty (with a *palo-sonajero de uñas* – a stick rattle of animal hooves, fig.1). Outstanding among the musical customs of adult males are songs accompanied by the *maraca* (a gourd rattle), an instrument presented to boys during their rite of passage to puberty. Shamanic songs – with or without *maracas* according to the tribe – are intended to summon various benevolent forces and beings of the natural world and to exorcize the forces of evil. Shamanic medicine involving the recovery of lost souls is supported by a wide range of songs.

The Chamacoco and Ayoreo of the northern Chaco show notable musical differences from other tribes. Although they share use of the *maraca* with other groups, including the Guaraní, it is used in different ways with distinctive symbolic meanings. In contrast with the emphatic style of most songs in regular duple rhythm sung by men of the Chaco tribes, Ayoreo singing consists of continuous vibrato male voices with the uninterrupted shaking of a gourd rattle and with musical phrases continuing until the singers run out of breath. A bizarre stance is adopted for singing (fig.2). Another oddity is that the Ayoreo have no dances. Ayoreo songs for solo female voice usually tell the stories of incidents that have happened in the community.

The Tupí-Guaraní tribes of the eastern region are the Paĩtavyterã, Avá or Chiripá, Mbyá and Aché-Guayakí.

The first three represent the '*monteses*' (or 'wild ones') who escaped Spanish and creole oppression for centuries. They conserve their own religious traditions and rituals, notably musical performances of various types, which reveal a certain degree of Western influence. In search of seclusion, and in the case of Mbyá, 'a land without evil', some groups migrated to the jungles of Argentina and Brazil. Their two sacred musical instruments are the *mbaraká* played only by men, which the Mbyá replaced with a five-string guitar, and the *takuapú* (rhythm tube played by women). Among the Aché-Guayakí, who became horticulturalists, the men reclaim their original role as hunters through the improvised texts of solitary nocturnal songs, while the women sing in plaintive style at religious ceremonies. Other musical instruments used by these groups include wooden whistles (by the Nivaklé and Ayoreo); vertical and transverse flutes by the Chiriguano; vertical flutes and panpipes by the Mbyá; and musical bows called *gualambáu* and *guyrapa'í* by the Paĩtavyterã and Chiripá, although some of these are no longer used. There are also examples of rustic fiddles with a single string used by the Mak'á, Lengua and Toba and various two-headed drums, both instruments adopted more recently.

2. CREOLE AND POPULAR MUSIC.   Although originally of European origin, creole traditions are the most representative of Paraguayan music since, in creole hands and with the consolidation of the nation state, they have acquired a character of their own. Forerunners are the

2. *Ayoreo Indian singing with a gourd rattle (Photo J. Novati)*

aforementioned European dances, which in the 18th and 19th centuries were danced in the salons of the nobility, in public and private ballrooms and at open-air band concerts. Dances based on the cotillion include *La golondrina* (now obsolete), and *El Santa Fe*, also called *Cielito de Santa Fe* or *Chopí*, a single tune without lyrics. Boettner (*c*1957) indicates that the *Chopí* was still danced at popular festivals in the 1950s, describing how it was choreographed for three couples and consisted of four figures: a greeting, a chain, a *toreo* and a waltz. Boettner also mentions *La palomita*, popular during the war of 1865–70. Special attention is given to the polka or *polca*, the most widespread of all dances. All that remains of the dance that arrived from Europe around 1850 is the name. In lively tempo, usually sung in 3rds by two singers, it is traditionally played by guitars, harp or violin (fig.3). A double bass was added at a later stage to provide a ground bass in 3/4 time, in counterpoint to the usually syncopated 6/8 rhythm of both guitars and singers. The oldest polkas such as *Campamento Cerro León* (ex.2), which has

Ex.2 *Campamento Cerro León, polca* (Bottner, 1957)

become a kind of 'popular anthem', are by anonymous composers. *Campamento Cerro Léon* (*Cerro Corá a* Guaraní *purajheí* or song by Giménez and Fernández) and *India* (a *guarania* by Flores and Ortíz Guerrero) were officially declared *Canciones Populares Nacionales* in 1944 by the Paraguayan government. This gesture, indicative of the power of popular music, enshrined the *polca*, the *purajheí* and the *guarania* (a genre created in 1928 by Flores) as the three most representative genres. Both the *purajheí* and *guarania* are derivations of the *polca* although they are purely vocal and their tempo is slower than that of the dance version. The songs tell of military, political and patriotic exploits or explore romantic themes. Also popular are the *galopa* and 'onomatopoeic' pieces such as *Guyrá campana* ('Bell-Bird'), *Polka burro* ('Donkey Polka') and *Tren lechero* ('Milk Train'). These show off the virtues of the diatonic, pedalless harp with characteristic techniques of lavish glissandi and ornamentation, on occasion using techniques of the violin.

A striking feature of Paraguayan creole music is the continuity between oral and popular urban traditions and

3. *Paraguayan creole group with violin, harp and guitar (Photo E. Hossman 1944)*

their influence on academic music. Szarán describes attempts to 'modernize' creole music, through the creation of a *nuevo cancionero*, a movement inspired by similar endeavours in Argentina and Chile.

BIBLIOGRAPHY
I.D. Strelnikov: 'Les Kaa-îwuá du Paraguay', *Atti del XXII congresso internazionale degli americanisti: Rome 1926*, 333–66
F. Müller: 'Beiträge zür Ethnographie der Guaraní-Indianer im östlichen Waldgebiet von Paraguay', *Anthropos*, xxix (1934), 177–208, 441–60, 696–702; xxx (1935), 151–64, 433–50, 767–83
J.M. Boettner: *Música y músicos del Paraguay* (Asunción, *c*1957)
P. Clastres: 'L'arc et le panier', *L'homme*, ii/1 (1966), 13–31
I. Ruiz: 'La ceremonia ñemongaraí de los Mbiá de la provincia de Misiones', *Temas de ethnomusicología*, i (1984), 45–102
I. Ruiz: 'Los instrumentos musicales de los indígenas del Chaco central',*Revista del Instituto de Investigación Musicológica Carlos Vega*, vi (1985), 35–78
B. Susnik: *Guía del Museo Etnográfico 'Andrés Barbero'* (Asunción, 1987)
B. Illari: 'Lo urbano, lo rural y las instituciones musicales en las reducciones jesuíticas de guaraníes', *Ciudad/campo en las artes en Argentina y Latinoamérica* (Buenos Aires, 1991), 155–63
B. Súsnik and M. Chase-Sardi: *Los indios del Paraguay* (Madrid, 1995)
L. Szarán: 'Paraguay', *Diccionario de la música española e hispanoamericana* (Madrid, 2000)
IRMA RUIZ

Paraklitikē kai teleia. Pair of signs used in Byzantine EKPHONETIC NOTATION.

Parallagē. A term used by the 15th-century composer MANUEL CHRYSAPHES to describe a particular style of singing Byzantine chant. In his treatise *On the Theory of the Art of Chanting* (ed. D.E. Conomos, MMB, *Corpus scriptorum*, ii, 1985), Chrysaphes reproached singers who were content to read the neumes drily and ignore the vocal flourishes (*theseis*) prescribed by the great composers of the past. This practice, which he called singing 'by parallagē', is a falsification of the true manner of chanting. However, at the heart of this condemnation lies a conflict of neumatic interpretation, which had begun in the early 14th century when a conservative group rejected the kalophonic innovations of JOANNES KOUKOUZELES and his followers (*see* KALOPHONIC CHANT).

DIMITRI CONOMOS

Parallel fifths, parallel octaves. CONSECUTIVE FIFTHS, CONSECUTIVE OCTAVES.

Parallel key. A minor key having the same tonic as a given major key, or vice versa; C major and C minor are parallel keys.

Parallelklang (Ger.). *See under* KLANG (ii).

Parallel motion. In PART-WRITING, the simultaneous melodic movement of two or more parts in the same direction and at a distance of the same interval or intervals. *See also* CONSECUTIVE FIFTHS, CONSECUTIVE OCTAVES.

Paralleltonart (Ger.). *See* RELATIVE KEY.

Parameter. A term associated, in musical parlance, with SERIALISM, where it refers to the aspects of a musical context: pitch or pitch class, rhythm, loudness and timbre are all different parameters. In serialism its use arises when a composer attempts to serialize the different aspects of a musical composition. Many mathematical terms have found their way into musical terminology, but it is difficult to see how the musical application of 'parameter' is an interpretation of the mathematical meaning. In the mathematics of functions a parameter generally is a constant which may be assigned different values. While in synthesized music certain parameters of a note must be specified, the extension of the term to less quantifiable areas is unhelpful.

PAUL LANSKY, GEORGE PERLE

Paramount. American record label. Established in 1916, it was the main label of the New York Recording Laboratories of Port Washington, Wisconsin. A race series began in August 1922 and proved extremely successful; by the time it was discontinued in 1932 more than 1100 releases had been made. The work of jazz and blues singers predominated, including that of Ma Rainey, Ida Cox, Alberta Hunter, Charley Patton and Blind Lemon Jefferson. Many discs in the race catalogue are now acknowledged to be classics, including recordings by King Oliver, Lovie Austin's Blues Serenaders and Jimmy O'Bryant's Original Washboard Band. Paramount's General Series contained a smaller proportion of jazz, but included some discs by Fletcher Henderson and the Original Memphis Five and a considerable amount of hot dance music.

During the early 1920s Paramount was closely associated with the Bridgeport Die & Machine Co. and also exchanged many masters with Plaza (later part of ARC). In 1929 it moved to Grafton, Wisconsin; operations ceased in 1932. Thereafter, however, a small number of race issues appeared in a Paramount series produced by ARC. The collector John Steiner revived the label in the late 1940s, putting out both reissues and new material; LPs of the latter were released until the early 1950s.

BIBLIOGRAPHY

M. Wyler: *A Glimpse of the Past: an Illustrated History of some Early Record Companies that Made Jazz History* (West Moors, Dorset, 1957)
R.M.W. Dixon and J. Godrich: *Recording the Blues* (London, 1970)
M.E. Vreede: *Paramount 12/13000 Series* (London, 1971) [discography]
C. Hillman: 'Paramount Serenaders 1923–1926', *Storyville*, no.67 (1976), 8–13; no.68 (1976), 52–4; no.69 (1977), 91–4; no.70 (1977), 149–52; no.72 (1977), 226–7; no.73 (1977), 29–30; no.74 (1977), 67–8; no.75 (1978), 84–5 [incl. discography]
B. Rust: *The American Record Label Book* (New Rochelle, NY, 1978), 226

HOWARD RYE/BARRY KERNFELD

Paraphonia (Lat., from Gk.: 'sounding beside'). A term used in the writings of a number of Greek theorists (notably Thrasyllus, Pseudo-Longinus and Bryennius) to designate the intervals of the 4th and 5th. In 1928, Peter Wagner called attention to the appearance of a similar term in the *Ordines romani I–III* (7th–8th centuries). Of the seven members of the Schola Cantorum listed in the *Ordines*, the fourth is called *archiparaphonista* and the last three *paraphonistae*. Wagner also found references to *paraphonistae* in French sources and in a sequence text. He concluded that the designation *paraphonista* described a singer who sang in paraphonic intervals, that is, in parallel 4ths and 5ths. He thus suggested that organum-like polyphony existed in the Church well before it was first described, and that, owing to the word's Greek origin, the practice came from Byzantine music.

Wagner's theories were disputed by Gastoué on philological grounds. Gastoué argued that *paraphonista* did not come from *paraphonia*, but instead was the result of adding the prefix *para* ('beside') to *phonista* ('singer'). Thus the term would mean 'singer standing beside', referring to the physical placement of the *paraphonistae*

beside the boys' choir (also mentioned in the *Ordines*). In Gastoué's view, the *paraphonistae* sang in support of the boys' choir, and occasionally sang solos.

Gastoué was answered in turn by both Wagner and Moberg who argued that his combination *para-phonista* was philologically impossible. Moberg went on to interpret a passage in Pseudo-Longinus so as to demonstrate that there was indeed a Byzantine practice of singing in polyphonic 4ths and 5ths.

Subsequently Handschin, who discussed the subject at some length, agreeing with Gastoué that the *paraphonistae* did not sing in parallel 4ths and 5ths, put forward yet another interpretation: that *para* meant 'inferior' ('untergeordnet'), and that the *paraphonista* was a singer in the chorus, or one in an inferior position to the cantor, the word itself being a paraphase of the Latin *succentor*. Tomasello, however, has defined the *paraphonistae* as 'adult singers who were cantors or song leaders at the patriarchal churches [of Rome]' in the 12th century, who sometimes took the place of the *primicerius* of the papal Schola in ceremonies.

Reese and Ludwig also disagreed with Wagner and Moberg, but did not go into detail. Later, Eggebrecht tended to favour Wagner's theories; he did not consider, however, that the use of the word reflected a very early beginning of organized polyphony (*diaphonia*), but rather some sort of improvisatory practice.

BIBLIOGRAPHY

RiemannL12 (H.H. Eggebrecht)
A. Gastoué: 'Paraphonie et paraphonistes', *RdM*, ix (1928), 61–3
P. Wagner: 'La paraphonie', *RdM*, ix (1928), 15–19
P. Wagner: 'A propos de la paraphonie', *RdM*, x (1929), 4 only
C.-A. Moberg: 'Eine vergessene Pseudo-Longinus-Stelle über die Musik', *ZMw*, xii (1929–30), 220–25
F. Ludwig: 'Weltliche und mehrstimmige kirchliche Musik bis 1030', *AdlerH*
G. Reese: *Music in the Middle Ages* (New York, 1940), 252
J. Handschin: *Musikgeschichte im Überblick* (Lucerne, 1948), 129–32
A. Tomasello: 'Ritual, Tradition, and Polyphony at the Court of Rome', *JM*, iv (1985–6), 447–71

RICHARD SHERR

Paraphrase. (1) A compositional technique, popular particularly in the 15th and 16th centuries, whereby a pre-existing melody (usually chant) is used in a polyphonic work; it may be subjected to rhythmic and melodic ornamentation but is not obscured. Examples can be found in settings of the Mass Ordinary from the 14th and 15th centuries. In early 15th-century settings of hymns, antiphons and sequences based on chant, the borrowed melody usually appears in the upper voice and was not subject to much alteration. In cyclic masses, however, borrowed melodies (mainly restricted to the tenor) could be extensively paraphrased (e.g. Du Fay's *Missa 'Ave regina celorum'*). In masses of the late 15th century and the 16th, paraphrased melodies appear within an imitative texture, moving from voice to voice (as in Josquin's *Missa 'Pange lingua'* or Palestrina's masses based on hymns). It has been suggested that 15th- and 16th-century composers consciously included in their works short citations or paraphrases of sections of well-known chants or even of works by other composers for interpretative or symbolic purposes. Paraphrases of popular tunes are also found in the music of Charles Ives, notably in his Second Symphony (1902).

(2) In the 19th century the 'Paraphrase de Concert', sometimes called 'Réminiscences' or 'Fantaisie', was a

virtuoso work based on well-known tunes, usually taken from popular operas. Liszt in particular wrote such paraphrases for piano, including 'Grande paraphrase de la marche de Donizctti' (1847) and *Totentanz: Paraphrase über das Dies irae* (1849).

See also BORROWING; PARAPHRASES, SCOTTISH; PARODY (i); PSALMS, METRICAL.

BIBLIOGRAPHY
J. Handschin: 'Zur Frage der melodischen Paraphrasierung im Mittelalter', *ZMw*, x (1927–8), 513–59
R.L. Marshall: 'The Paraphrase Technique of Palestrina in his Masses based on Hymns', *JAMS*, xvi (1963), 347–72
E.H. Sparks: *Cantus Firmus in Mass and Motet, 1420–1520* (Berkeley, 1963/R)
I. Godt: 'Renaissance Paraphrase Technique: a Descriptive Tool', *Music Theory Spectrum*, ii (1980), 110–18
S. Döhring: 'Réminiscences: Liszts Konzeption der Klavierparaphrase', *Festschrift Heinz Becker*, ed. J. Schläder and R. Quandt (Laaber, 1982), 131–51
J.P. Burkholder: 'Quotation and Paraphrase in Ives's Second Symphony', *19CM*, xi (1987–8), 3–25
G. Boyd: 'The Development of Paraphrase Technique in the Fifteenth Century', *Indiana Theory Review*, ix (1988), 23–62
C. Reynolds: 'The Counterpoint of Allusion in Fifteenth-Century Masses', *JAMS*, xlv (1992), 228–60
M. Fromson: 'Themes of Exile in Willaert's *Musica Nova*', *JAMS*, xlvii (1994), 442–88

RICHARD SHERR

Paraphrases, Scottish. Metrical versions of passages from the scriptures sung to psalm tunes in the Church of Scotland.

The Scottish Psalter of 1575 contained in an appendix five paraphrases; the edition of 1595 contained ten and that of 1635 had 14. When the present psalter was published in 1650 these all disappeared, but it seems that the Church had intended to use paraphrases, for in 1647 the General Assembly had recommended that Zachary Boyd, minister at the Barony Parish Church, Glasgow, should 'be at the paines to translate the other Scripturall Songs in meeter, and to report his travels also to the Commission of Assembly'. Nothing came of this because Boyd's verses were doggerel. Other efforts were equally unsuccessful and interest in the matter was lost for nearly 100 years. In 1741 a committee was appointed to consider the possibility of paraphrases and in 1745 it produced 45 paraphrases of scripture. These were sent by the General Assembly for consideration by the presbyteries, but the 1745 rebellion proved too great a distraction and nothing was done. In 1775 another committee was appointed, enlarged in 1777, and in 1781 it submitted to the Assembly the *Translations and Paraphrases in Verse, of Several Passages of Sacred Scripture*. They were not formally authorized, but the Assembly allowed their temporary use, pending a final decision, in congregations where the minister might find them useful for instruction. Final approval was never given, but with tacit consent the custom arose of printing them with the metrical psalms and so they passed into use. They comprise the original 45 paraphrases of the 1745 edition, though much revised, along with 22 new ones. The main authors were John Morison, John Logan, Philip Doddridge, Isaac Watts, Nahum Tate and William Cameron, but the committee took great liberties in revision and in some cases left only fragments of the original versions.

Many of the paraphrases are now obsolete, although the 1929 edition of the Scottish Psalter recommended 42 as being suitable for singing in public worship. The 1927 *Revised Church Hymnary* contains 13 paraphrases (numbered among the hymns) while *The Church Hymnary: Third Edition* (1973) contains 22. Some of the best-known paraphrases are found in the hymnbooks of other churchcs, including 'O God of Bethel' (*Genesis* xxviii.20–22), 'While humble shepherds watched their flocks' (*Luke* ii.8–15) and 'I'm not ashamed to own my Lord' (2 *Timothy* i.12). (D.J. Maclagan: *The Scottish Paraphrases*, Edinburgh, 1889)

See also PSALMS, METRICAL, §IV, 1.

G.V.R. GRANT

Pararol [Pararols], **Berenguier de.** *See* BERENGUIER DE PALAZOL.

Paratico, Giuliano (*b* Brescia, *c*1550; *d* Brescia, ?1617). Italian composer and lutenist. He practised as a notary in the episcopal chancery at Brescia. Although Marenzio and Bertani advised him to further his musical career by travel, he is not known to have left Brescia. Gaspari considered him 'outstanding in his compositions, especially in the more affective pieces, in which he revealed himself unique and original' and commented on the sweet quality of his voice. He was still living in 1613, and, according to Fétis, died in 1617 at the age of 66. Of a first book of *Canzonette a tre voci*, dedicated to Countess Barbara Maggia Gambara, only the bass partbook survives. It contains 22 compositions, of which one is by the 'count of Villachiara' and two are by Lelio Bertani. His *Canzonette a tre voci, libro secondo* (Brescia, 1588²⁵), dedicated to Francesco Morosino, contains 22 compositions, each bearing its own dedication; one work is by Andrea Picenni. The canzonetta *Di pianti e di sospir* is intabulated for lute in Terzi's *Secondo libro de intavolatura* (RISM 1599¹⁹).

BIBLIOGRAPHY
FétisB; GaspariC; MischiatiI
O. Rossi: *Elogi historici di bresciani illustri* (Brescia, 1620), 499
L. Cozzando: *Libraria bresciana* (Brescia, 1694/R), 141–2
G. Gaspari: *Miscellanea musicale* (MS, *I-Bc* UU.12), i, 348, 351; ii, 317
E. Caccia: 'Cultura e letteratura nei secoli XV e XVI', *Storia di Brescia: La dominazione veneta (1426–1575)* (Brescia, 1963), 482
O. Mischiati: *Bibliografia delle opere dei musicisti bresciani pubblicate a stampa dal 1497 al 1740*, i (Brescia, 1982), 159; ii (Florence, 1992), 720–22

PIER PAOLO SCATTOLIN

Paray, Paul (M.A. Charles) (*b* Le Tréport, 24 May 1886; *d* Monte Carlo, 10 Oct 1979). French conductor and composer. He studied with his father, an organist, and in Rouen, where he became an organist at 17. A year later he entered the Paris Conservatoire, won a *premier prix* in harmony and, in 1911, the Prix de Rome. Conscripted into the French army in 1914, he was taken prisoner until 1918. He made his début at a test concert with the Lamoureux Orchestra in 1920, and as a result was appointed assistant conductor of the Concerts Lamoureux, succeeding Camille Chevillard as principal in 1923. Five years later Paray became conductor of the Monte Carlo PO, and from 1933 he was principal conductor of the Concerts Colonne in Paris.

During World War II Paray conducted in Marseilles and Monte Carlo, and returned to Paris in 1944 to reorganize the Colonne Orchestra after the liberation. He remained with the Concerts Colonne until his appointment as principal conductor of the Detroit SO (1952–63). At Detroit he inaugurated the Henry and Edsel Ford Auditorium in 1956 with his *Mass of Joan of Arc*, originally composed in 1931 for the quincentenary commemoration at Rouen and first performed there. He also recorded the mass and made several discs of French works, notably by Berlioz, Bizet, Chabrier, Ravel and Roussel. Paray acquired a reputation as a reliable conductor in a wide range of the classical repertory. As a composer he tended towards academic propriety. His works include the symphonic poem *Adonis troublé* (1921, staged at the Paris Opéra in 1922 as the ballet *Artémis troublée*), two symphonies, a *Fantaisie* for piano and orchestra, and various chamber and piano works.

BIBLIOGRAPHY

L'art musical (7 Jan 1938) [Paray issue]
W.L. Landowski: *Paul Paray, musicien de France et du monde* (Lyons, 1956)
H. Stoddard: *Symphony Conductors of the U.S.A.* (New York, 1957)

NOËL GOODWIN

Parazol, Berenguier de. *See* BERENGUIER DE PALAZOL.

Parč, František Xaver. *See* PARTSCH, FRANZ XAVER.

Pardessus (Fr.). A 'descant' instrument, that is, one with a high range, a 4th or 5th above the treble size (called 'DESSUS' in French).

The 'pardessus de viole', a descant VIOL, was initially shaped like a small treble viol and had six strings, tuned g–c′–e′–a′–d″–g″. It emerged about 1690: the earliest surviving instrument, by Michel Collichon, dates from about that time and the estate inventory of Jean Rousseau (1644–99) lists a pardessus. It was first mentioned in print in Joseph Sauveur's *Principes d'acoustique et de musique* (Paris, 1701/R) and the first music verifiably composed for it was Thomas Marc's *Suitte de pièces de dessus et de pardessus de viole et trois sonates avec les basses continües* (Paris, 1724). By the 1720s the *dessus* was disappearing, and by the 1730s 'dessus' and 'pardessus' were often used interchangeably. Among the composers who published music for this instrument were Barrière, Boismortier and Dollé.

A five-string pardessus, tuned g–d′–a′–d″–g″, emerged in the 1730s. Although the early models of this instrument retained features of the treble viol body, some later ones resembled violins and were called 'quintons' (*see* QUINTON). Composers who wrote for the five-string pardessus include Blainville, Dollé, Lendormy and Vibert. The *VI sonates pour deux pardessus de violes* op.1 by Barthélemy de Caix (Paris and Lyons, 1748) are among the most difficult and interesting works for the instrument. In addition, a 'Mr de Villeneuve' made idiomatic transcriptions of a large portion of the works of Marin Marais. Louis de Caix d'Hervelois and others wrote many works of a melodic nature intended for either the five- or six-string pardessus, and the instrument was listed as an alternative on over 100 publications. The method by Michel Corrette (1748) is the only one to survive.

The pardessus was played by cultivated amateurs and is often considered a lady's instrument. However, many gentlemen played it, especially in the provinces where instruction on the violin may have been limited. The most notable virtuoso was Mlle Lévi, who played concertos at the Concert Spirituel in 1745. After about 1760 the instrument began to decline, and it had largely disappeared by 1790.

BIBLIOGRAPHY

M. Corrette: *Méthode pour apprendre facilement à jouer du pardessus de viole à 5 et à 6 cordes* (Paris, 1738/R; Eng. trans., 1990)
A. Rose: 'The Solo Repertoire for *Dessus* and *Pardessus de Violes*', *Chelys*, ix (1980), 14–22
R. Green: 'Charles Dollé's First Work for Pardessus de Viole', *JVdGSA*, xviii (1981), 67–75
R. Green: 'The *Pardessus de Viole* and its Literature', *EMc*, x (1982), 300–07
H. Miloradovitch: 'Eighteenth-Century Transcriptions for Viols of Music by Corelli & Marais in the Bibliothèque Nationale, Paris: Sonatas and "Pièces de Viole"', *Chelys*, xii (1983), 47–73
R. Green: 'The Treble Viol in 17th-Century France and the Origins of the Pardessus de Viole', *JVdGSA*, xxiii (1986), 64–71
C. Dubuquoy-Portois: 'Le Pardessus de viole au XVIIIe siècle: un nouvel instrument de divertissement', *Instrumentistes et luthiers parisiens: XVIIIe–XIXe siècles*, ed. F. Gétreau (Paris, 1988), 134–48
S. Milliot: 'Du nouveau sur Jean Rousseau, maître de musique et de viole (1644–1699)', *RMFC*, xxvii (1991–2), 35–42
R. Green: 'Recent Research and Conclusions Concerning the "Pardessus de Viole" in Eighteenth Century France', *A Viol Miscellany*, ed. J. Boer and G. van Oorschot (Utrecht, 1994), 103–14

ROBERT A. GREEN

Pardon, Walter (*b* Knapton, Norfolk, 4 March 1914; *d* Knapton, 9 June 1996). English traditional singer. A village carpenter, he had a repertory of over 150 songs including traditional, popular, music hall and rare Agricultural Union songs. Most of his repertory was learnt from his uncle Billy Gee (*b* 1863), passed on from Pardon's grandfather, who had acquired them in turn from itinerant broadside sellers at a cost of one penny each. Pardon performed within the context of the family rather than the public house until he was 'discovered' by members of the Folk Revival during the early 1970s. In 1976 he represented England at the American Bicentennial Celebrations at the Smithsonian Institute of Folklife in Washington, DC, and in 1983 he was awarded the Gold Badge of the ENGLISH FOLK DANCE AND SONG SOCIETY, its highest honour for services to folk music. Pardon was admired for his introspective vocal style and quality of phrasing, sense of pitch and enunciation.

BIBLIOGRAPHY
AND OTHER RESOURCES

W. Pardon: 'Walter Pardon: an Autobiography', rec. P. Bellamy, *Folk Review* (1974)
A Proper Sort, perf. W. Pardon, Leader LED2063 (1975)
M. Yates: '"Stand up ye Men of Labour": the Socio-Political Songs of Walter Pardon', *Musical Traditions*, i (1983), 22–7
The Voice of the People: the Traditional Music of England, Ireland, Scotland and Wales, ed. R. Hall, iv: *Farewell, my Own Dear Native Land: Songs of Exile and Emigration*, various pfmrs, Topic TSCD 654 (1999)

DAVE ARTHUR

Paredes, Juan. *See* BONET DE PAREDES, JUAN.

Parenti, Paolo Francesco (*b* Naples, 15 Sept 1764; *d* Paris, 1821). Italian composer and singing master. He studied at the Pietà dei Turchini conservatory in Naples, learning counterpoint from Sala, harmony and accompaniment from Taranino, probably voice from La Barbera, and, in Villarosa's description, taking Traetta's music as his guide (Traetta had left Naples by this time). In the next few years he is said to have written a good deal of sacred music; the little that has survived was praised by Prota-Giurleo and Paduano for its contrapuntal skill and invention. During this period he was probably often away from Naples. According to Gervasoni and the *Biografia* he composed four serious operas and three comic ones; oddly, except for *Nitteti*, no production records have been located for these works, although Florimo said that *La vendemmia* was his first opera, written for Naples, and

Villarosa reported that *Il matrimonio per fanatismo* was greatly applauded in Rome.

In 1790 Parenti went to Paris, where, according to Fétis, he was first employed by the Opéra-Comique to add pieces to a revival of Gluck's *La rencontre imprévue* on 1 May. This was given as *Les fous de Médine* and not, as previously thought, in translation as *I pazzi di Medina* (Brenner). Loewenberg, however, maintained that the new musical arrangement was by J.P. Solié. He subsequently wrote four comic works for the Théâtre Italien. Villarosa claimed that Parenti served as director of the Italian comic opera in Paris for the year 1802, though this fact has not been substantiated. Otherwise, he supported himself as a singing teacher of the Italian style, for which he had a high reputation.

WORKS
music lost unless otherwise indicated

La vendemmia (ob), Naples, ?before 1783; aria, *B-Bc*
La Nitteti (os, P. Metastasio), Florence, Pergola, carn. 1783
Il matrimonio per fanatismo (ob), Rome, ?before 1790
Les deux portraits (oc, 2, C.-J.L. d'Avrigny), Paris, OC (Favart), 20 Aug 1790
L'homme et le malheur (oc, 1, d'Avrigny), Paris, OC (Favart), 22 Oct 1793
Le cri de la patrie (oc, 3, ? G. Moussard), Paris, OC (Favart), 28 Dec 1793

?Unperf.: I viaggiatori felici (ob); Antigono (os, Metastasio), *F-Pn**; Il re pastore (os, ?Metastasio), 1810, *Pn**; Artaserse (os, ?Metastasio); Pezzi sciolti, *Pn**; Philomedia, ou L'art di chanter, *Pn* (possibly autograph); Pimmalione, *Pn*

Cr, 2 lits, Mag: all 4vv, insts, *I-Nc*

BIBLIOGRAPHY
FétisB; FlorimoN; LoewenbergA; MGG1 (U. Prota-Giurleo and L. Paduano); *RosaM*
C. Gervasoni: *Nuova teoria di musica* (Parma, 1812/R), 227
D. Martuscelli, ed.: *Biografia degli uomini illustri del Regno di Napoli*, iii (Naples, 1816), 52
C. Brenner: *The Théâtre Italien: its Repertory, 1716–1793, with a Historical Introduction* (Berkeley, 1961), 473

JAMES L. JACKMAN/R

Parepa(-Rosa), Euphrosyne [De Boyescu, Parepa] (*b* Edinburgh, 7 May 1836; *d* London, 21 Jan 1874). Scottish soprano. Her father was Baron Georgiades de Boyescu, a Walachian magnate, and her mother the soprano Elizabeth Seguin, with whom she studied. She made her début in Malta under the name of Euphrosyne Parepa in 1855 as Amina in *La sonnambula*. After appearances in Italy, Spain and Portugal she was engaged by Frederick Gye for the 1857 season of the Royal Italian Opera at the Lyceum (Covent Garden having burnt down the previous year), where she made her début as Elvira in *I puritani*. Between 1859 and 1865 she appeared at both Covent Garden and Her Majesty's, in a repertory that included Leonora (*Il trovatore*), Zerlina (*Fra Diavolo*) and Elvira (*La muette de Portici*). She also sang in the Handel festivals of 1862 and 1865, and in Germany. In 1865 she went to the USA on a concert tour with Carl Rosa, whom she married there in February 1867 (her first husband, Captain H. de Wolfe Carvell, having died in 1865) and in the same year she and her husband formed an opera company, in which she sang leading roles. In 1871–2 she toured America again, and appeared in New York in Italian opera with Wachtel and Santley. In 1872 she appeared at the Lower Rhine Festival, Düsseldorf, and returned to Covent Garden as Donna Anna and Norma. On her death her husband abandoned the Drury Lane season and founded the Parepa-Rosa Scholarship at the RAM in her memory.

He also decided to spend the rest of his life giving opera in English.

Her voice combined power and sweetness, and had a compass of two and a half octaves, extending to *d''*; despite her many stage appearances she was more successful in oratorio than in opera.

BIBLIOGRAPHY
DNB (R.H. Legge)
Obituary, *New York Times* (23 Jan 1874)
G.P. Upton: *Musical Memories* (Chicago, 1908)
E.B. Marks: *They All Had Glamour* (New York, 1944)

HAROLD ROSENTHAL/ELIZABETH FORBES

Pareto, Graziella [Graciela] (*b* Barcelona, 15 May 1889; *d* Rome, 1 Sept 1973). Spanish soprano. She studied with Vidal in Milan, and made her début as Amina at Madrid in 1908, taking the role in Parma shortly afterwards. For two seasons from 1909 she appeared at the Teatro Colón, Buenos Aires, as Gilda, Adina, Rosina and Ophelia (Thomas' *Hamlet*), parts she sang there later on her 1926 return. In Italy she sang at Rome, Naples, as Meyerbeer's Marguerite de Valois at Turin, 1912, and reached La Scala in 1914, as Gilda. At Covent Garden in 1920 she played Norina, Violetta, and Leïla (*Les pêcheurs de perles*) under Beecham, who considered her the best *soprano leggero* of her day (in *A Mingled Chime* he described her voice as being 'of exquisite beauty, haunting pathos and flawless purity'). She appeared at Chicago (1923–5), and as Carolina (*Il matrimonio segreto*) at the 1931 Salzburg Festival. Her records, which include extracts from her leading roles, offer proof of a pure, limpid soprano, capable, as in 'Dite alla giovine' from *La traviata*, of considerable pathos.

BIBLIOGRAPHY
GV (R. Celletti; J.P. Kenyon)
G. Fraser: 'Graziella Pareto', *Record Collector*, xvii (1966–8), 75–89

ALAN BLYTH

Parfaict, François (*b* Paris, 10 May 1698; *d* Paris, 25 Oct 1753). French theatre historian and dramatist. Parfaict and his brother Claude (*b* Paris, 1705; *d* Paris, 26 June 1777) came from an upper middle-class family whose origins go back to Jean Parfaict (*b* 1440). François, even as a young man, was closely associated with the theatre. In 1724 he collaborated with Marivaux on comedies for both the French and Italian theatres, including *La fausse suivante ou Le fourbe puni*. He married Marie-Jacqueline Tiphaigne, and one child, Gabrielle-Philippe, was born to them on 21 February 1742.

His most important works, written in collaboration with his brother Claude, deal with the history of French theatre which, from its origins up to 1721, is the subject of the *Histoire du théâtre françois*. The *Dictionnaire des théâtres de Paris* treats alphabetically all plays (including operas) which 'from the year 1552 up to the present have been performed on the stages of the different theatres of Paris' (preface). Cast lists, revival dates, cross-references to the *Mercure de France* and the *Recueil général des opéra*, and anecdotes concerning authors, composers, actors and actresses, dancers and stage designers make this a valuable source for any study of French opera of the period. Equally important is the manuscript *Histoire de l'Académie royale de musique* which, although receiving a privilege dated 1741, was never printed. It is a chronological discussion of important events in French opera from 1645 (*La finta pazza*) to 1741. Its descriptions are striking. The singer Du Mény, for example, 'never knew his music and often sang out of tune. Added to this he was extremely addicted to drink'. Lully is described as having a 'lively and strange countenance, without nobility, dark complexioned, with small eyes, protruding nose and large mouth'. After François's death, Claude Parfaict edited a second edition of the *Dictionnaire des théâtres* and began a *Dramaturgie générale* which was never completed.

WRITINGS

with C. Parfaict: *Histoire du théâtre françois depuis son origine jusqu'à présent* (Paris, 1734–49/R)
Agendas historiques et chronologiques des théâtres de Paris (Paris, 1735–7; repr. 1876 as *Agendas des théâtres de Paris, 1735, 1736 et 1737*)
Histoire de l'Académie royale de musique depuis son établissement jusqu'à présent (MS,1741, F-Pn; 1835 copy with annotations by Beffara, Pn fr.12.355)
Mémoires pour servir à l'histoire des spectacles de la foire, par un acteur forain (Paris, 1743/R)
Histoire de l'ancien théâtre italien, depuis son origine en France, jusqu'à sa suppression en l'année 1697 (Paris, 1753, 2/1767/R)
with C. Parfaict: *Dictionnaire des théâtres de Paris, contenant toutes les pièces qui ont été representées jusqu'à présent sur les differens théâtres françois, et sur celui de l'Académie royale de musique* (Paris, 1756/R, 2/1767, with G. d'Abguerbe)

BIBLIOGRAPHY

ES (M. Spaziani) [with complete list of writings]
J.G. Prod'homme: 'Les frères Parfaict, historiens de l'Opéra', *ReM*, nos.100–05 (1930), 110–18
P. Mélèse: *Répertoire analytique des documents contemporains ... concernant les théâtres sous Louis XIV* (Paris, 1934)
H. Finke: *Les frères Parfaict: ein Beitrag zur Kenntnis des literarischen Geschmacks in der ersten Hälfte des XVIII Jahrhunderts* (diss., U. of Dresden, 1936)
P. Vendrix: *Aux origines d'une discipline historique: la musique et son histoire en France aux XVIIe et XVIIIe siècles* (Geneva, 1993)
JAMES R. ANTHONY

Parhalling. See HALLING.

Pari, Claudio [Paris, Claude] (*b* Salines [now Salins-les-Bains], Burgundy, 1574; *fl* Palermo, 1598–1619). Italian composer of Burgundian birth. In the auto-da-fé celebrated at the monastery of S Domenico, Palermo, on 22 December 1598, he was sentenced to row in the galleys for five years for heresy. From 6 September 1611 to 18 March 1619, the dates of the dedications of his second and fourth books of five-part madrigals, he was active in Sicily, particularly in Palermo. In the dedication of the third book he refers to his ultramontane origin, and on all the title-pages he is described as Burgundian. The dedication and postscript of the second book state that, as well as the lost first book, he had already published a collection of six-part madrigals, which is also lost. In 1615, according to an uncatalogued document in the Archivio di Stato, Palermo, he received a three-year appointment as director of music at the house of the Jesuits at Salemi, in western Sicily.

Pari's predilection for madrigal cycles is noteworthy. His second book is entitled *Il pastor fido* and consists only of settings of texts from Guarini's dramatic pastoral. The bulk of the third book is made up of three cycles of madrigals to other texts from the same work. *Il lamento d'Arianna*, which gives its name to the fourth book, opens the volume and accounts for the first 12 of its 20 madrigals. Only the first is a setting of Rinuccini's text, thus corresponding to the first madrigal of Monteverdi's famous cycle (in his book 6, 1614); the other madrigals are settings of Ariadne's lament as interpolated by G.A.

dell'Anguillara into his translation in ottavas of Ovid's *Metamorphoses*, imitating the lament of Olympia in Ariosto's *Orlando Furioso* and, indirectly, the lament of Ariadne in Ovid's *Heroides*. To judge from Ayello's reference to it (see below), the lost book of six-part madrigals may also have been composed to a single extended text divided into several sections.

In a postscript to the second book Don Giovanni Battista di Ayello, a gentleman of Palermo, perceptively defined Pari's style:

> He has used many new and elaborate sorts of counterpoint, including various canons and many imitative entries using double subjects – as may be seen in his first two collections of madrigals, for five and six voices – making each voice clear and distinct and without confusing the words ... [In] the sixth part of the first [book] for six voices, which begins 'Fra sì contrarie tempre', it may be seen with what artifice the six voices are worked out, with two contrary-motion entries that form an uninterrupted double canon using natural tones and semitones, that is without relying on any accidentals. It is true that in the present *Pastor fido* he has ceased using so much counterpoint, in order to vary his style, and has preferred to ensure only that the words be articulated gracefully in every voice ... Everyone can be sure that he has worked everything into his music with great industry, particularly the new and extraordinary dissonances, which he has used, not wantonly or haphazardly, but with every justification, with great art and with due regard for the words.

The title-page of the third book, which is indeed a manifesto of *musica reservata*, proclaims that its contents are 'created out of several styles and new kinds of invention never before used by anybody and with much use of imitation, strict counterpoint and close interpretation of the words'. They thus contain all the ingredients of musical mannerism – recourse to archaic stylistic procedures, novelties of style and experiments in harmony and structure, as well as strict counterpoint and great care in interpreting the words – and were clearly intended for cognoscenti.

These features are also found in *Il lamento d'Arianna*. The 12 madrigals are rigorously based on a few distinctive rhythmic and melodic elements, all derived from Monteverdi's cycle and clearly announced in the first madrigal. The vast majority of sections consist of double and triple fugues, with consequent overlapping of lines of text, against which the few short passages of syllabic declamation stand out in sharp relief. From this kind of writing and from the continual absence of cadences stems the objection of 'length, velocity and continuity of utterance' that Ayello, in the postscript cited above, had already accepted without refuting and that bring Gombert to mind as Pari's possible stylistic model. Moreover, he took advantage of such structures to insert the 'new and extraordinary dissonances' to which Ayello referred, often neither prepared nor resolved and having the effect of maintaining the harmonic tension and breaking the monotony that might otherwise have accrued from long stretches of polytextual imitation. The scoring for the five voices is resourceful and effective. In the last part, obviously to convey the resigned state of the desolate Ariadne, the harmonic tension slackens and the texture clears: instead of complex polyphony there are two passages of free declamation (*falsobordone*), dissonance is used sparingly and the soprano part stands out at times from the texture of the other parts. The remaining madrigals in the book (settings of verses by Alessandro Aligeri, Isabella Andreini, Francesco Contarini and F. Scaglia) confirm Pari's ability in handling the virtuoso concertante style, with appropriate exploitation of double and triple fugues. He may be considered a worthy follower of Giovanni de Macque's chromatic style and is indeed worthy to stand alongside the best Sicilian madrigalists of the day, such as Antonio Il Verso (who also published a *Lamento d'Arianna* in 1619), Sigismondo d'India and Giuseppe Palazzotto e Tagliavia.

WORKS

Il pastor fido, secondo libro de' madrigali, 5vv (Palermo, 1611)
Il terzo libro de' madrigali, 5vv (Palermo, 1617)
Il lamento d'Arianna, quarto libro de' madrigali, 5vv (Palermo, 1619); ed. in MRS, i (1970)
Il primo libro di madrigali, 5vv, lost
Il primo libro di madrigali, 6vv, lost

BIBLIOGRAPHY

P.E. Carapezza: 'L'ultimo oltramontano o vero l'antimonteverdi: un esempio di *musica reservata* tra manierismo e barocco', *NRMI*, iv (1970), 213–43, 411–44; repr. with Eng. trans. as introduction to MRS, i (1970)
P.E. Carapezza: 'Il madrigale napoletano del primo Seicento', *La musica a Napoli durante il Seicento*, ed. D.A. D'Alessandro and A. Ziino (Rome, 1987), 17–27, esp. 26
P.E. Carapezza: 'Madrigalisti siciliani', *Nuove effemeridi*, no.11 (1990), 97–106, esp. 103–06
F. Renda: *L'Inquisizione in Sicilia: i fatti, le persone* (Palermo, 1996), 342

PAOLO EMILIO CARAPEZZA/GIUSEPPE COLLISANI

Pariati, Pietro (*b* Reggio nell'Emilia, 27 March 1665; *d* Vienna, 14 Oct 1733). Italian poet and librettist. Secretary to Rinaldo, Duke of Modena, he was in Madrid in 1695 and after his return to Italy spent three years in prison. He then lived in Venice from the end of 1699 until summer 1714, when he was appointed court poet in Vienna by Charles VI, for whom he had already written laudatory theatrical works staged in Barcelona.

In Venice Pariati started to work as a librettist with Apostolo Zeno, contributing to the versification and drafting of his librettos. The extent of their collaboration is not as great as has been thought, however; Pariati alone was responsible for *Artaserse*, *Anfitrione*, *La Svanvita*, *Il falso Tiberino*, *Sesostri re di Egitto* and *Costantino* (for an alternative view *see* ZENO, APOSTOLO). He began by revising 'in the modern style' 17th-century works such as *Sidonio* and turning into *dramma musicale* form recent tragedies such as Giulio Agosti's *Artaserse*. Very soon he began to turn out prose works on his own account for the Milan and Bologna stages. Established at the same time in Venetian theatrical circles, where he met composers including Albinoni and Gasparini and the *buffo* singers Giovanni Battista Cavana and Santa Marchesini, he devoted himself to writing comic scenes, *tragicommedie* (*Anfitrione*) and intermezzos, particularly for the Teatro S Cassiano. Drawing on Plautus, Molière and Cervantes, together with a wide theatrical experience, he refined the features that became characteristic of his comic style: rapid pace, brightness of dialogue and a taste for lexical extremes.

In Vienna, where he was joined by Zeno in 1718 and replaced by Metastasio in 1729, Pariati wrote oratorios (13), cantatas and chamber works (15), pastoral dramas and theatrical pieces (14) for the festive celebrations of the imperial family. The most famous such piece was the *festa teatrale Costanza e Fortezza*, set by Fux in 1723. For the court theatre he revived earlier works, wrote two new librettos and continued to collaborate with Zeno. He also found a new expressive freedom in the fantasy intermezzo and comic scene, using comedy not only as a source of laughter and entertainment, but also as an instrument with which to provoke, deride and debunk. Between 1716 and 1724 Pariati wrote alone four intermezzos and four *tragicommedie*; with *Don Chisciotte in Sierra Morena* and *Alessandro in Sidone* he even involved Zeno in his chosen field, dragging him beyond the confines of serious works into the territory of literary parody and social criticism. He exploited his favourite devices fully, varying and intertwining them: dual identity in *Il finto Policare* and *Penelope*, the philosopher's ironic situation in *Alessandro in Sidone* and in *Creso*, mental imbalance in *Don Chisciotte* and *Archelao*. Avoiding generic forms, Pariati flung his darts at diverse targets, including personal enemies and court intrigue, the very foundations of *opera seria*. He thus effected a twofold distortion: corrosive parody undermines the drama's heroic virtue and progressively erodes credibility, while an explosive stylistic mixture gives rise to the transformation into tragicomedy.

LIBRETTOS

OPERAS

dm – *dramma per musica*

Artaserse (dm, after G. Agosti), Giannettini, 1705 (Orlandini, 1706; Sandoni, 1709; Ariosti, 1724); *Antioco* (dm, with A. Zeno), F. Gasparini, 1705; *Ambleto* (dm, with Zeno), Gasparini, 1706 (Carcani, 1742); *Statira* (dm, with Zeno), Gasparini, 1706 (Albinoni, 1726); *Sidonio* (dm), Lotti, 1706; *Florinetta e Frappolone* (int), ?Gasparini, 1706; *Anfitrione* (tragicommedia), Gasparini, 1707; *La Svanvita* (dm), A. Fiorè, 1707 (Schürmann, 1715, as Regnero)
Flavio Anicio Olibrio (dm, with Zeno), Gasparini, 1708 (Porpora, 1711; G. Porta, 1726, as Il trionfo di Flavio Olibrio; Vinci, 1728; E. Duni, 1736, as La tirannide debellata; Jommelli, 1740, as Ricimero re dei Goti); *L'Engelberta* (dm, with Zeno), Fiorè, 1708; *Astarto* (dm, with Zeno), Albinoni, 1708 (F. Conti, 1718; Caldara, 1725); *Pollastrella e Parpagnacco* (int), Gasparini, 1708; *Vespetta e Pimpinone* (int), Albinoni, 1708 (Conti, 1717, as Grilletta e Pimpinone); *Zenobia in Palmira* (dm, with Zeno), ?Chelleri, 1709 (Leo, 1725; Brusa, 1725, as L'amore eroico)
Il falso Tiberino (dm), C.F. Pollarolo, 1709; *Brunetta e Burlotto* (int), 1709; *Ciro* (dm), Albinoni, 1710 (Conti, 1715); *Sesostri re di Egitto* (dm), Gasparini, 1710 (A.M. Bononcini, 1716; Conti, 1717; Fiorè, 1717; Sellitto, 1742; Terradellas, 1751; Cocchi, 1752; Bertoni, 1754; Sarti, 1755; Galuppi, 1757; Sciroli, 1759; C. Monza, 1760; P. Guglielmi, 1766); *Bertolda e Volpone* (int), 1710; *Galantina e Tulipano* (int), ?Albinoni, 1710; *Il Giustino* (dm, after N. Beregan), Albinoni, 1711 (Vivaldi, 1724; Handel, 1737)
Costantino (dm), Gasparini, 1711 (Lotti and Caldara, 1716; Orlandini, 1731, as Massimiano); *Dorimena e Tuberone* (int), Conti, 1714; *Teseo in Creta* (dm), Conti, 1715 (Leo and others, 1721, as Arianna e Teseo; Porpora, 1728, as Arianna e Teseo; Broschi, 1732, as Arianna e Teseo; Handel, 1734, as Arianna in Creta; Lampugnani, 1737, as Arianna e Teseo; P. Chiarini, 1739, as Arianna e Teseo; G. de Majo, 1747, as Arianna e Teseo; Abos, 1748, as Arianna e Teseo; Pescetti, 1750, as Arianna e Teseo; Sarti, 1756, as Arianna e Teseo; Mazzoni, 1758, as Arianna e Teseo; Carcani, 1759, as Arianna e Teseo; Ponzo, 1762, as Arianna e Teseo; Galuppi, 1763, as Arianna e Teseo; Insanguine, 1773, as Arianna e Teseo; Fischietti, 1777, as Arianna e Teseo; Winter, 1792, as I sacrifizi di Creta)
Bagatella, Mamalucca e Pattatocco (int), Conti, 1715; *Galantina e Pampalugo* (int), Conti, 1715; *Il finto Policare* (tragicommedia), Conti, 1716; *Cajo Marzio Coriolano* (dm), Caldara, 1717; *Farfalletta, Lirone e Terremoto* (int), Conti, 1718; *Don Chisciotte in Sierra Morena* (tragicommedia, with Zeno), Conti, 1719; *Alessandro in Sidone* (tragicommedia, with Zeno), Conti, 1721; *Archelao re di Cappadocia* (tragicommedia), Conti, 1722; *Costanza e Fortezza* (festa teatrale), Fux, 1723; *Creso* (tragicommedia), Conti, 1723; *Penelope* (tragicommedia), Conti, 1724
Doubtful: comic scenes for *Alba Cornelia*, 1704 (Conti, 1714) [lib. also attrib. S. Stampiglia]; *Erighetta e Don Chilone* (int), ? Gasparini, 1707 [lib. also attrib. A. Salvi]

OTHER LIBRETTOS

Da la virtude ha la bellezza onore (serenata), Pollarolo, 1704; *Il voto crudele* (orat), A. Lotti, 1712; *L'Umiltà coronata in Esther* (orat),

Lotti, 1714; *I satiri in Arcadia* (favola pastorale), Conti, 1714, rev. as *Cloris und Thyrsis* (favola pastorale), Conti, 1721; *La Fede sacrilega nella morte di S Giovanni Battista* (orat), J.J. Fux, 1714; *Dafne in lauro* (componimento per camera), Fux, 1714; *La donna forte nella madre dei sette Maccabei* (orat), Fux, 1715; *La più bella* (festa teatrale), G. Reinhardt, 1715; *Angelica vincitrice di Alcina* (festa teatrale), Fux, 1716; *Il fonte della salute aperto dalla grazia nel Calvario* (componimento sacro), Fux, 1716; *Caio Marzio Coriolano*, A. Caldara, 1717; *Diana placata* (festa teatrale), Fux, 1717; *Gesù Cristo condannato* (componimento per musica), Caldara, 1717; *Alceste* (festa teatrale), G. Porsile, 1718; *Cristo nell'orto* (componimento per musica), Fux, 1718; *Amore in Tessaglia* (serenata), Conti, 1718; *La colpa originale* (orat), Conti, 1718; *Elisa* (componimento teatrale), Fux, 1719; *Galatea vendicata* (festa teatrale), Conti, 1719; *Gesù Cristo negato da Pietro* (componimento per musica), Fux, 1719; *Apollo in cielo* (componimento da camera), Caldara, 1720; *Cantata allegorica* (cant.), Conti, 1720; *La cena di Signore* (componimento sacro), Fux, 1720; *Il giudicio di Enone* (festa teatrale), Reinhardt, 1721; *La via del saggio*, Conti, 1721; *Il rè del dolore in Gesù Cristo Signor nostro coronato di spine* (componimento sacro), Caldara, 1722; *Le nozze di Aurora*, Fux, 1722; *Trionfo d'amore* (componimento poetico), Albinoni, 1722; *La concordia de' planeti*, Caldara, 1723; *Il giorno felice* (componimento per musica), Porsile, 1723; *Meleagro* (festa teatrale), Conti, 1724; *La corona d'Arianna* (festa teatrale), Fux, 1726; *Il Testamento di nostro Signor Gesù Cristo sul Calvario* (componimento sacro), Fux, 1726; *Il sacrifizio in Aulide* (festa teatrale), G. Reutter, 1735

BIBLIOGRAPHY

A. Zeno: *Poesie drammatiche*, ed. G. Gozzi (Venice, 1744)
N. Campanini: *Un precursore del Metastasio* (Reggio nell'Emilia, 1889, 2/1904)
O. Wessely: *Pietro Pariatis Libretto zu Johann Joseph Fuxens 'Costanza e fortezza'* (Graz, 1969)
G. Gronda: 'Per una ricognizione dei libretti di Pietro Pariati', *Civiltà teatrale e Settecento emiliano: Reggio nell'Emilia 1985*, 115–36
E. Kanduth: 'Das Libretto im Zeichen der Arcadia, Paradigmatisches in den Musikdramen Zenos (Pariatis) und Metastasios', *Opern als Text: Romanistische Beiträge zur Libretto-Forschung*, ed. A. Gier (Heidelberg, 1986), 33–53
G. Gronda, ed.: *La carriera di un librettista: Pietro Pariati da Reggio di Lombardia* (Bologna, 1990) [incl. essays by B. Dooley, H. Seifert and R. Strohm]
R. Bossard: 'Von San Luca nach Covent Garden: die Wege des Giustino zu Händel', *Göttinger Händel-Beiträge*, iv (1991), 146–73
G. Gronda: 'La Betulia liberata e la tradizione viennese dei componimenti sacri', *Mozart, Padova e la 'Betulia liberata': Padua 1989*, 27–42
L. Bianconi and G. La Face Bianconi, eds.: *I libretti italiani di Georg Friedrich Händel e le loro fonti* (Florence, 1992–)
B. Brumana: 'Figure di Don Chisciotte nell'opera italiana tra Seicento e Settecento', *Europäische Mythen der Neuzeit: Faust und Don Juan: Salzburg 1992*, 699–712
A. Sommer-Mathis: 'Von Barcelona nach Wien: die Einrichtung des musik- und Theaterbetriebes am Wiener Hof durch Kaiser Karl VI', *Musica Conservata: Günther Brosche zum 60. Beburtstag*, ed. J. Gmeiner and others (Tutzing, 1999), 355–80

GIOVANNA GRONDA

Paridon. *See* BARYTON (i).

Parigi, Francesco da. *See* FRANCESCO DA MILANO.

Parík, Ivan (*b* Bratislava, 17 Aug 1936). Slovak composer. He took private lessons with Albrecht (1951–3), attended the Bratislava Conservatory (1953–8), where his teachers included Očeňaš (composition) and Kornel Schimpl (conducting), and then studied composition with Moyzes at the Bratislava Academy of Music and Dramatic Art (until 1962). From 1959 he was a producer at Czechoslovak television, Bratislava, and between 1968 and 1997 he taught theory and composition at the Academy of Music, becoming professor in 1990 and rector in 1994. He was one of the principal organizers of the Smolenice New Music Days from 1968 to 1971.

At the beginning of his career Parík was influenced by Debussy, Hindemith and Bartók. His works from this period possess an introverted personal style combined with postwar avant-garde techniques. When developing his own musical language he was inspired primarily by the achievements of the Second Viennese School, in particular those of Webern, with whom he shared a preoccupation with detail. Distinguishing features of this earlier style include economy of expression, fragile construction, sound transparency and an interest in timbre and expressivity, all of which can be heard in *Dve piesne* ('Two Songs', 1959), the Flute Sonata (1962), *Piesne o padajúcom lístí* ('Songs about Falling Leaves', 1962) for piano and *Hudba pre troch* ('Music for Three', 1964). During the second half of the 1960s – and perhaps influenced by fine art – Parík placed greater emphasis on timbral considerations, structural detail and compositional unity, as exemplified by *Hudba k baletu* ('Music to Ballet'), or *Fragmenty*. These priorities were explored further at the Experimental Music Studio of Czechoslovak Radio, where he realized a series of works since considered a mainstay of the Slovak electro-acoustic tradition. In *Hommage to William Croft* (1969), *In memoriam Ockeghem* (1971) and *Pocta Hummelovi* ('Homage to Hummel', 1980) Parík juxtaposes music of the past with electro-acoustic means.

WORKS
(selective list)

INSTRUMENTAL

Orch.: Ov., 1962; Hudba k baletu [Music to Ballet], 1968; Fragmenty, 1969; Introdukcia k Haydnovej symfónii č.102, 1971; Hudba pre dychy [Music for Winds], brass, 8 db, perc, 1981; Musica pastoralis, 1984; Hudba pre flautu, violu a orch 1987; Ako sa pije zo studničky [How is it drunken from a well] (M. Rúfus), spkr, chbr orch, 1990

Chbr: Meditácia, va, pf, 1956; Hudba pre 4 sláčikové nástroje [4 str insts], str qt, 1958; Epitaf na spôsob improvizácií [Epitaph in the Style of Improvisations], fl, va, vc, 1961; Hudba pre 3, fl, ob, cl, 1964; Vezová hudba [Tower Music], 4 hn, 4 tpt, 4 trbn, bells, tape, 1968; Hudba k vernisázi II [Music for a Private Viewing II], fl, tape, 1970; Epitaf II, fl, gui, 1976; Hudba pre Milosa Urbáska, str qt, 1987; Quadrofónia, 4 vc, 1987; Meditácia, after Jacopone da Todi, fl, org, 1997; other duos

Solo inst: 3 kusy [3 Pieces], pf, 1960; Piesne o padajúcom lístí [Songs about Falling Leaves], pf, 1962; Sonata, fl, 1962; Hudba k vernisázi [Music for a Private Viewing], fl, 1967; Sonata, vc, 1967; Pastorale, org, 1979; Pospevovanie [Chant], fl, 1991; Listy priatel'ke [Letters], pf, 1992; Kyrie na pamät' Konstantína filozofa [Kyrie in Memory of the Philosopher Constantine], org, 1997; other works, incl. sonatas

El-ac: Hommage to William Croft, 1969; Variácie na obrazy Milosa Urbáska [Variations to Paintings by Milos Urbásek], 1970; In memoriam Ockeghem, 1971; Sonata-Canon, vc, elecs, 1971; Sonata pastoralis '44, 1974; Vonku predo dvermi [Outside the Door], 1974; Cantica feralia, 1975; Pocta Hummelovi [Homage to Hummel], 1980; Conc. grosso, 1991

Vocal: Missa brevis, SATB, 1957, rev. 1997; 2 piesne [2 Songs] (Jap. poetry), S, cl, gui, claves, cimb, 1959; Citácie [Quotations], SATB, 1964; Medzi horami [Among the Mountains] (ballad), SATB, 1973; Cas odchodov [Time of Departures] (M. Rúfus), S/T, pf, 1976, rev. 1978; Videné zblízka nad jazerom [Looking closer over the lake] (M. Hal'amová), spkr, fl, ob, cl, hn, bn, str qt, 1979; Sená [Haymaking] (Rúfus), SATB, 1982; 2 árie [2 Arias] (Stabat Mater), 1v, orch, 1989, arr. 1v, pf/org

Film scores, incid music

MSS in *SK-Mms*

Principal recording companies: Opus, Slovak Radio, Supraphon

Principal publishers: Opus, Slovenský hudobný fond

BIBLIOGRAPHY
I. Hrušovský: *Slovenská hudba* (Bratislava, 1964), 382ff

KATARÍNA LAKOTOVÁ

Parikian, Manoug (*b* Mersin, Turkey, 15 Sept 1920; *d* London, 24 Dec 1987). British violinist of Armenian parentage. He studied with Louis Pecskai at Trinity College of Music, London, from 1936 to 1939. He made his début as a concerto soloist in 1947 at Liverpool and in 1949 at the Royal Albert Hall, London. He led the Liverpool PO (1947–8) and the Philharmonia Orchestra (1949–57). He also led various chamber ensembles and formed duo partnerships with George Malcolm (1950–55), Lamar Crowson (1956–65) and in 1966 with Malcolm Binns. From 1957 he enjoyed considerable success as a soloist in all European countries (including the USSR), the Middle East and Canada. In 1976 he formed a piano trio for the Wigmore Hall 75th anniversary series, with Bernard Roberts (who was replaced by Hamish Milne in 1984) and Amaryllis Fleming; the trio went on to achieve international recognition. Parikian was an artist of wide musical sympathies with many first performances to his credit (Rawsthorne, Seiber and Skalkottas), and concertos by Gordon Crosse, Alexander Goehr and Hugh Wood were dedicated to him, as well as works by Elizabeth Maconchy and Thea Musgrave; he also inspired many younger English composers to write major works for his instrument. An exceptionally stylish violinist, he produced a tone of remarkable purity and displayed a polished technique. He made many important recordings. He taught at the RCM, 1954–6, and from 1959 at the RAM. He played a Stradivari of 1687.

BIBLIOGRAPHY

*Campbell*IIGV

J. Creighton: *Discopaedia of the Violin, 1889–1971* (Toronto, 1974)

J. Ford: Interview, *The Strad*, xciv (1983–4), 340–43

WATSON FORBES/MARGARET CAMPBELL

Paris. Capital city of France. It is situated on the River Seine, downstream from its junction with the River Marne. The city proper has a population of approximately 2.2 million, with approximately 10 million in the greater Paris area.

I. To 1450. II. 1450–1600. III. 1600–1723. IV. 1723–89. V. Music at court outside Paris. VI. 1789–1870. VII. After 1870.

I. To 1450

The importance of Paris as a musical centre in medieval times lies chiefly in the period from the mid-12th century to the early 14th, when it led the European musical world in its institutions and in new methods of composition. Although there were other centres of great musical importance – the Benedictine abbeys of St Maur-des-Fossés and St Denis, the royal Ste Chapelle and the Augustinian abbey of St Victor, for example – the most celebrated activity occurred at Notre Dame. The cathedral nurtured some of the first recognized composers of stature, and they in turn realized some remarkable achievements: the earliest inclusive corpus of polyphonic liturgical music for the celebration of the Mass and Office; the first system of musical notation that clearly specified rhythmic values as well as pitches; and the development of major new musical genres. At Notre Dame not only organum but monophonic and polyphonic conductus attained their richest forms; and the creation of the motet from the discant sections of organum became a landmark in musical history. Moreover the most important musical theorists from about 1240 to 1350 all worked at, or had contact with, Parisian institutions.

1. Urban development. 2. The university. 3. Music theory. 4. Practical music.

1. URBAN DEVELOPMENT.   The physical growth of medieval Paris was closely linked with the spread of Christianity and the city's rise in political importance under Merovingian leadership late in the 5th century. Originally a Gallic settlement on what is now the Ile de la Cité, Paris, then called Lutetia, expanded to the left bank of the Seine soon after the Roman conquest in 53 BCE. The early cathedral, evident already by the mid-5th century and first dedicated to St Stephen in the mid-7th, stood within the eastern quarter of the Ile de la Cité, just to the west of the present site of Notre Dame. Early in the 6th century Paris became the residence of the Merovingian king Clovis (ruled 482–511), a convert to Christianity, and thereafter saw many of its first major ecclesiastical foundations. Churches rose amid the vineyards on the left bank, among them basilicas dedicated to the Holy Apostles (later Ste Geneviève), to Vincent (later the abbey of St Germain-des-Prés) and to St Julien. By the middle of the 8th century there were many more, both in the south on the left bank and to the north, where St Germain-le-Rond (later St Germain-l'Auxerrois), St Martin (later the priory of St Martin-des-Champs) and the abbey of St Denis lay (founded in the 7th century by King Dagobert I).

During the Carolingian period the centre of the Holy Roman Empire moved east and Paris temporarily lost importance. Charlemagne (ruled 768–814), assisted by such scholars as Alcuin (*c*735–804) and Theodolphus of Orléans (*c*760–821), brought the liturgical and musical traditions of Rome north, displacing and absorbing the earlier Gallican liturgy and essentially condemning its music to oblivion, although occasional traces remain. Despite disruption and invasion in the 9th and 10th centuries, Paris continued to grow, as did the number and importance of its abbeys and churches. By the end of the 12th century the city had assumed the physical character it was to retain for the remainder of the Middle Ages: the Right Bank, principally the commercial quarter, became known as the Ville and acquired city walls in the 13th century; the cathedral and the royal palace dominated the Ile de la Cité; while the growing university and its ancillary institutions overwhelmed the Left Bank (hence the later name 'Latin Quarter').

With the reigns of Louis VII (ruled 1137–80) and his son Philip II Augustus (ruled 1180–1223), who expanded the kingdom to its largest extent and made Paris the seat of his government, new churches had appeared and continued to proliferate. On the Ile construction proceeded on Notre Dame (begun 1150s, high altar consecrated 1182), which together with the chevet of St Denis (1140–44) and the Ste Chapelle (1241–6; fig.1) comprised important witnesses to the new style of Gothic architecture. Along with the building of such edifices there was equal attention devoted to the Parisian liturgy and its chant. The flourishing state of liturgical music is amply demonstrated by numerous chant manuscripts that have survived from Parisian centres, whose comparison reveals a rich complex of interrelationships in liturgical practice and music for many of the city's institutions. By the 13th century an enormous increase in the demand for books, caused primarily by the university, led to a substantial growth in the profession of lay copying and manuscript illumination. Thus the central source of the polyphonic

1. *Interior of the Ste Chapelle, 1241–6*

Notre Dame repertory, the Florence manuscript (*I-Fl* Plut.29.1; *c*1250), has been traced to an atelier with no monastic or collegiate connections, the professional shop of Johannes Grusch. Copying continued in the religious houses as well: liturgical manuscripts survive from Notre Dame itself, the Ste Chapelle, the churches of Ste Geneviève, St Germain-des-Prés, St Germain-l'Auxerrois, St Eustache, Notre Dame de l'Annonciation, St Magloire, St Denis, the Sorbonne, the Collège de Laon, the abbey of St Victor and many other places. In his capital Philip Augustus created an atmosphere in which peace reigned and the arts flourished, and Paris became an intellectual centre in which the monarch was pre-eminent.

The Black Death, the Hundred Years War and revolutionary agitation interrupted the prosperity of Paris in the 14th century. Further disturbances and loss of prestige occurred in the 15th century during the Anglo-Burgundian alliance, which culminated in 1422 with the English occupation of the city. It was not until 1436 that Paris once again became the seat of a French king, the weak and timorous Charles VII, at the beginning of whose reign the city's economy was in ruins, its population depleted and its university overcome by intellectual stagnation. The rapid decline in the fortunes of Paris is reflected in its music, which after a spectacular ascendancy in the 'Notre Dame epoch' lost impetus during the next two centuries.

2. THE UNIVERSITY.   The early development of the University of Paris remains obscure, although the tradition of ecclesiastical education suggests that the city's churches and monasteries would have encouraged learning from their earliest times. By the mid-12th century two important classes of schools were well established and together formed the *stadium* at Paris: the foremost consisted of those instructors who practised in the environs of the cathedral and were administered by the chancellor, who controlled the *licentia docendi*; the other group comprised the schools of ecclesiastical institutions, the most prominent of which were St Victor and Mont-Ste-Geneviève. At this time the university was a loose association of teaching masters (*magistri*) and students (*scolares parisienses*) who for the most part became organized into separate political and cultural 'nations' within the *studium*.

The growing independence of the schools from the chancellor's control informs much of the history of the University of Paris in the first quarter of the 13th century. The largest strides occurred early in the tenure of Philip the Chancellor (1217–36), himself a prolific author of conductus and motet texts. By 1231, after numerous legal wranglings and several teaching strikes by the masters, the university was able to ally itself effectively with the papacy and check the chancellor's power. *Bulla fulminante* and *Aurelianis civitas*, two conductus from around this time and both ascribable to Philip, paint vivid pictures of the crises that attended the University of Paris and neighbouring schools.

Continuing in the tradition established in the 12th century, the university attracted the most celebrated teachers of Europe during the 13th and 14th. The ranks of its masters opened to admit Dominicans and Franciscans beginning in 1229, and from their midst came such lights as Bonaventura (*d* 1274), Albertus Magnus (*d* 1280) and Thomas Aquinas (*d* 1274). Among all this activity the teaching of music held an important place as one of the foundational liberal arts; university statutes of 1215 made provision for 'extraordinary' lectures (on religious holidays) when '[students] shall study nothing except philosophy, rhetoric and the Quadrivium'. Although medieval records are not precise on how the teaching of music was effected at this time, numerous indirect sources suggest that it was practised both as a science and as a craft at the University of Paris, which became renowned for its teaching of the seven liberal arts. A former student at Paris, Guy da Basoches, left a description of Paris of about 1175, which is the earliest of many similar documents: 'On this island, the seven sisters, to wit, the liberal arts, have secured an eternal abiding place for themselves'. Practical music-making, too, was mentioned by Matthew Paris, who related that in 1254 Henry III of England was welcomed in Paris with 'special songs and instrumental music' performed by the *scolares parisienses* 'mostly from the English-German nation'. Books used by Parisian scholars often contain sections devoted to music, inventories of the various *nations* of the university include chant books, and instruction in chanting was given in some colleges and *nations*. In 1413 the English-German *nation* appointed a Parisian bachelor of medicine, Henri de Saxe, as organist of its church, St Mathurin; two years later he had gained the same post at Notre Dame. Many choirmasters of the grammar schools and singers in the royal chapel held ties to the university; and, before their matriculation, many scholars received musical training in the choir schools, including the *maîtrise* of Notre Dame.

3. MUSIC THEORY.   The writings of professors and students of the university were highly esteemed during the 12th and 13th centuries; no centre in the medieval world of learning was as important as Paris. The study of music theory, if only as a philosophical branch of mathematics, is attested by several treatises written by former students that have portions devoted to music: the *De eodem et diverso* by Adelard of Bath (*fl c*1120) and chapter 13 of

Gossouin's *Image du monde* (1245), for example. Robert Grosseteste (*c*1170–1253) and Robert Kilwardby (*d* 1279), both alumni of the university, included sections on music in their philosophical writings. Alain de Lille (*d* 1202), sometime teacher at Paris and the author of a conductus preserved in the Florence codex, discussed the psychological effects of music as well as musical Intervals in the allegorical poem *Anticlaudianus*.

But by far the most important treatises are those which discuss the exciting new art of polyphony, its diverse genres and styles, and its methods of rhythmical notation. The latter topic in particular was to become the focus of the most progressive theoretical treatises throughout the later development of the Notre Dame school (after *c*1250) and during the important changes which occurred early in the 14th century with the French Ars Nova. Although these works are not directly specified by the university curriculum, they provide many oblique associations with it in their organization, terminology and methods of argument; and many, if not all, of their known authors or compilers evince some contact with the city and its schools. Examples include the *Tractatus de musica* (late 13th century) assembled 'for the use of students' by Hieronymus de Moravia, who taught at the Dominican monastery of St Jacques in Paris. He included a unique chapter on the playing of string instruments with the bow and four treatises on mensural notation. Among these, the first, the *Discantus positio vulgaris* (*c*1220s–40s?), is probably the earliest extant treatise to discuss the rhythmic practices associated with Notre Dame polyphony; the second is the seminal *De mensurabili musica* (1240s–60s?) ascribed to a Johannes de Garlandia, who included a chapter on modal combinations and a discussion of melodic figures; the third is the pivotal *Ars cantus mensurabilis* of Franco of Cologne (*c*1280), which laid the foundations of later rhythmic notations.

Situated chronologically between the Garlandian and Franconian works is the *Tractatus de musica* of Lambertus, who expanded the number of rhythmic modes beyond Garlandia's conventional six, and who was vigorously attacked for it by the St Emmeram Anonymus (1279). Garlandian principles continue to be the focus in the fruitful work of an English student of Paris, Coussemaker's Anonymus 4. His tract presents an amplified discussion of both regular and irregular modes and gives invaluable historical information about Notre Dame music and its great composers, Leoninus and Perotinus. Similarly Johannes de Grocheio, possibly a Paris teacher, supplied a unique sociological view of Parisian music at the turn of the century in his *De musica*. But the summa of all Ars Antiqua theory comes from a writer who had also been a student at Paris: in his *Speculum musice* Jacobus of Liège dealt with both *musica speculativa* and *musica practica*, and showed that he had first-hand knowledge of each.

That Paris was in the forefront of the latest trends is demonstrated by the treatises of Johannes de Muris, a musician, mathematician, astronomer and teacher at the Sorbonne, whose *Notitia artis musice* (*c*1321) shows that he had links with Philippe de Vitry (1291–1361). Muris's treatises found a wide dissemination throughout western Europe and his mathematical work, *Musica speculativa secundum Boetium*, superseded Boethius's original as the standard musical text for students of the universities well into the Renaissance. All aspects of music come under Muris's keen scrutiny – speculative theory, rhythm, notation, prolation, alteration, isorhythmic motet and ballade forms – and many later musical tracts are clearly based on his teaching. His universal fame is an indication of the great interest in music of all kinds at the University of Paris in the Middle Ages. It points to the high position that the city held when it was designated 'the mother of all learning' and sustained the study of music through its cathedral and university.

4. PRACTICAL MUSIC.   Musical activity in Paris during the Middle Ages is attested by a variety of witnesses. Liturgical documents describe the melodic content of Parisian ceremony, both the chant that sounded within church walls and that of outside stational processions. In the greater establishments on major feasts – particularly at Notre Dame – highly skilled solo singers also spun out organa, conductus and possibly motets, and the organ accompanied or elaborated specific choral chants. Notre Dame first acquired such an instrument by 1332, and they also appear at St Séverin (*c*1350), St Germain-l'Auxerrois (1402) and St Jacques-de-la-Boucherie (1427) during this period.

Numerous sources of polyphony suggest a thriving interest in the most novel musical forms within the city, particularly in the diverse species of motets that came to populate the 'new' musical repertory of the 13th and early 14th centuries. Principal manuscripts such as the Florence codex, one of the Wolfenbüttel sources (*D-W* 1099), and the Bamberg (*D-Bs* Lit. 115), Montpellier (*F-MO*fH 196) and La Clayette (*F-Pn* n.a.l.13521) manuscripts all claim Parisian origin. Their widespread geographical dissemination and that of numerous other small sources indicates the allure that the new *musica mensurabilis* of Paris once exerted in musical centres as far afield as Spain, Poland and England. Some of the works in these manuscripts even point to events in the city's history, as they mourn the loss of kings and clerics, celebrate their coronations and investiture or castigate all levels of society for corrupt behaviour. This last issue is particularly well represented in the first great musical monument of the Ars Nova, Gervès du Bus's ROMAN DE FAUVEL (*F-Pn* fr.146), a vivid allegorical satire on political intrigue in the royal court, compiled in Paris about 1317 by Chaillou de Pesstain. A vibrant impression of Parisian city life appears in the texts of a 13th-century motet *On parole de batre/A Paris soir/Frese nouvele* from the Montpellier manuscript, which was taken over and expanded into a larger piece in the mid-14th century, *Je comence ma chanson/Et je servi/Soules viex (I-IV)*.

Knowledge of specific composers and poets points to several illustrious individuals with ties to the schools, churches and courts of Paris. Many more must have lived or worked in the city, yet relatively few are named, and details of their lives are often sparser still. Of particular interest is the renowned philosopher Peter Abelard (1079–1142), who created hymns, planctus and a lost repertory of secular song, the latter almost certainly while teaching within the cathedral close. The poets Alain de Lille, Walter of Châtillon and Peter of Blois were also connected at one point to the schools of Paris and have left several of their songs in Parisian manuscripts. Notre Dame in particular owes its early musical fame to Adam of St Victor (*d* 1146), who wrote many sequences in his capacity as cantor of the cathedral before he retired to the abbey whose name he familiarly bears; while the great

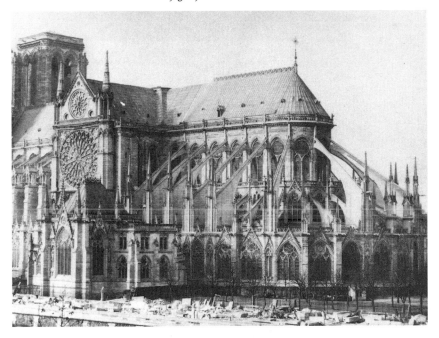

2. East end of the cathedral of Notre Dame, reconstruction with flying buttresses completed mid-14th century

composers of polyphonic music Leoninus (*d c*1201) and Perotinus (Petrus Succentor?; *d* 1238), said to be the authors of the *Magnus liber organi* of Notre Dame, are now nearly legendary. Other lights of Notre Dame include cantor Albertus Parisiensis (*d* 1177), Adam's successor and the author of a conductus in the Codex Calixtinus; Philip the Chancellor (*d* 1236), mentioned above, whose poetic activities may also include the first examples of the medieval motet; and the religious and secular music of the later composers Aubert Billard, Guillaume Benoît and Etienne Grossin.

In other milieux, Parisian vernacular composition is represented by Li Moine de St Denis (*fl* 1230s), who contributed a motet to the Montpellier codex; by the chansons of the trouvère Moniot de Paris; and by Jehannot de L'Escurel. The polymath Philippe de Vitry, perhaps responsible for the musical manuscript of the *Roman de Fauvel* and the creation of the isorhythmic motet, spent long periods in Paris in the service of the court and even had a three-month stint as a canon at Notre Dame. Franco of Cologne and Petrus de Cruce likewise give evidence of at least a fleeting connection to the city; and it seems likely that some of the surviving French secular music from the later 14th century (ed. W. Apel, CMM, liii, 1970–71) comes from Parisian composers, although only Pierre des Molins and Jehan Vaillant are actually described as having lived there. In the early 15th century Nicolas Grenon was at Paris from about 1399 to 1403 and, according to Martin le Franc (*Le champion des dames*, *c*1440), Johannes Carmen, Johannes Cesaris and Johannes Tapissier 'astounded all Paris' with their new methods of composition.

References in sermons, literature, non-musical treatises and written records can often illuminate the music enjoyed in lay and public circles of Paris during the Middle Ages; the preaching of the clergy, the texts of romances, chansons and motets, and the injunctions of civic documents are altogether replete with references to urban music-making, dance and minstrelsy. From them we learn that citizens from many walks of life often took part in *caroles*, where refrain songs and, possibly, instrumental pieces such as *ductiae* and *estampies* formed the musical framework for public dancing in the open air. Paris was also a focal point for professional singers and players of secular music. In September 1321 a group of 37 'menestreus et menestrelles, jongleurs et jongleresses' petitioned the provost of Paris to enact a set of legal statutes that would regulate the behaviour of their members and set rules for those who sought to join their enterprise. The successive names given to a certain street in Paris demonstrate that an association of minstrels had formed part of the city's population for some time: 'Vicus viellarotum' (1225), 'Vicus ioculatorum' (1236) and finally 'Rue aus Jongleurs', where the 1321 statutes indicate that potential customers could hire entertainment for their feasts and celebrations. From such evidence we may infer that popular and dance music were assiduously practised in Paris at all times throughout the Middle Ages.

II. 1450–1600

1. Ile de la Cité. 2. The Ville. 3. The university. 4. Music publishing.

1. ILE DE LA CITÉ.   The musical history of Renaissance Paris aptly reflects the principal institutions that dominated cultural and political life there. On the Ile de la Cité, historically the centre of ecclesiastical and secular governance, the cathedral of Notre Dame and the Ste Chapelle du Palais (parish church of the nearby royal residence in Paris) continued to be important centres of musical production. In the late 15th century the royal courts of Charles VIII and Louis XI spent considerable parts of the year travelling among various châteaux of the Loire valley, but by about 1500 Paris had become a more regular place of royal residence and a centre of artistic patronage.

A musician working in the royal *maison* of King François I (1515–47), for instance, would by ancient convention have belonged to one of three separate departments of this suitably vast (but surprisingly mobile) juggernaut of official attendants: a staff of domestic

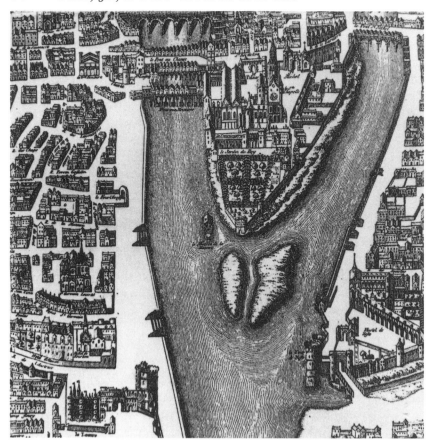

3. Map of Paris looking east, c1540, showing the old Palais Royal at the western end of the Ile de la Cité, the Ste Chapelle in the centre of the island, the south-east defensive tower of the Louvre on the Right Bank (bottom left) and the Hôtel de Bourbon, directly above the Louvre: engraving

servants (the *chambre*), clerics and singers charged with the observance of sacred liturgy (the *chapelle*), and officials for public ceremony and military protection (the *écurie*). Each of these administrative divisions carried with it an implied set of social circumstances, constraints whose operation can at times be detected in the music of those who sang and played at court.

The royal *chambre* of the 1530s and 40s included a small vocal ensemble and several instrumentalists, musicians who were above all prized as interpreters of the French chansons, dance music and instrumental solos that served as private musical entertainment for the king and his guests. Among this group were several Italian players, including the famous Mantuan lutenist Alberto da Ripa, whose contrapuntal skill and extraordinary feeling for the sonorous qualities of his instrument were held in high regard by the princes and prelates for whom he played. But if Ripa enjoyed a pre-eminent reputation among patrons and *literati* of the early 16th century, it was not until after both his death and the death of his royal patron that his music was made available to the general public, edited (with permission of the new king, Henri II, who ruled between 1547 and 1559) by Guillaume Morlaye, one of the great lutenist's pupils, in collaboration with the printing firm of Fezandat. In a dedicatory epistle to Henri, Morlaye justified the patent commercialism of the venture by offering lavish praise for French monarchs – including two of 'the most noble, virtuous and magnanimous kings in Europe', namely François I and Henri II, who had until now carefully guarded Albert's music as a private domain. Appropriating this formerly secret and

socially restricted art as an object of profit and commodity for public enjoyment, Morlaye's print hints at the growing interdependence of aristocratic Patronage and bourgeois commerce. If printers came to rely on princes for protection from competition, rulers looked to the press for the ready means to promote the princely virtue of their sponsorship of private music.

Whereas music in the royal *chambre* was directed principally at the creation of personal and private meanings for aristocratic audiences, that of the *écurie* was aimed at the ceremonial and political requirements of the monarchy as it faced a wide French public. The subtle blend of a small vocal ensemble and the quiet resonance of the lute had no place in the *écurie*, where the musical forces consisted of outdoor instrumentalists: drummers and pipers attached to the military guard plus trumpeters and shawm players (including some Italian instrumentalists) who played during large social dances and public processions. Complementing gesture and visual spectacle, their playing called attention in sound to the sort of flamboyant display that accompanied elevated status. When Henri II and Catherine de' Medici made their official entry into the city of Paris as King and Queen of France in 1549, for example, the accompanying spectacle would have been the envy of any aristocratic couple. The procession from the Porte St Denis to Notre Dame and the nearby royal palace involved thousands of participants – cavalry, merchants, civic officials, scholars, courtiers and princes.

In addition to their ensembles of public and private musicians, French monarchs seem to have had several church choirs in their direct service. By the 1530s François' own *chapelle* was by far the largest of his musical organizations, an institution boasting nearly three dozen adult singers (plus choirboys) divided between two specialist choirs – one for liturgical plainchant and another for *musique*, or polyphonic compositions. The Ste Chapelle du Palais, not far from the royal Parisian residence, also had its own professional choir, an organization that, like the king's chapel, was very much at the centre of musical life under the French monarchs. Many of the composers active in these establishments were also the same composers who figured prominently in the early production of the royal music printer, Pierre Attaingnant. Claudin de Sermisy (*c*1490–1562) had been a minor cleric at the Ste Chapelle long before his appointment to the rank of *sous-maître* in the royal chapel (in practice he was the musical director, although the titular leadership of the group was in the hands of an aristocrat, Cardinal François de Tournon), where from the 1530s until his death he held a prestigious canonical post. Pierre Certon, a close contemporary of Sermisy, began musical service in Paris at Notre Dame, but later joined the Ste Chapelle as a *clerc* and then as *maître des enfants*, a post he held from 1536 until his death in 1572. Like Sermisy, Certon enjoyed the favour of several French monarchs, who conferred upon him the title of *chantre de la chapelle du Roy* and *compositeur de musique de la chapelle du Roy*. Either or both of these positions may have been purely honorific, but the distinction suggests the prestige and enduring protection that French rulers lavished on their favourite composers and singers, among whom are counted not only Sermisy and Certon, but a series of other important French musicians of the 16th century: Jean Conseil, Antonius Divitis, Mathieu Gascongne, Jean Richafort, Pierre Sandrin [Regnault], Antoine Mornable, Nicolas de La Grotte, Jean Maillard, Guillaume Costeley and Eustache Du Caurroy. Indeed, the pursuit of ecclesiastical offices for musicians prompted François I, like other French kings before him, to intercede with ecclesiastical authorities on behalf of his singers in order to obtain for them benefices or other canonical appointments, not only in Paris, but throughout the kingdom. Notre Dame de Paris serves as a case in point, for although it was to an unusual degree a cathedral built and maintained through the beneficence of a clerical élite, royal patronage was also important there. Royal foundations for the construction and maintenance of buildings and of services, such that, in Craig Wright's view, the sanctuary of Notre Dame was increasingly appropriated as 'a stage from which to project to his numerous subjects a positive image of the most Christian King' (Wright, 1989). The abbey of St Denis, just beyond the confines of the city of Paris itself, was yet another locus to enjoy royal musical and ecclesiastical patronage.

2. THE VILLE. Elsewhere in Paris, too, were important centres of aristocratic musical patronage. The Hôtel (now Musée) de Cluny on the left bank of the Seine, Parisian residence of the powerful Cardinal Jean de Lorraine, doubtless served as a locus of musical activity. A prodigious patron of music and the other arts, Jean is known to have a band of Italian instrumentalists in his service, and for a time to have been a protector of Alberto da Ripa. Indeed, throughout the 16th century members of the Lorraine-Guise family collaborated with each other and with the royal household as patrons of music and

musicians. Jacques Arcadelt, the northern composer who had worked in the Italian peninsula during the 1540s, returned to Paris in the entourage of Cardinal Charles de Lorraine (nephew of Jean), and eventually became a member of the royal musical household there. Pierre Clereau and Pierre Sandrin, too, enjoyed the protection of the powerful and widely travelled Guise clan, and it seems significant that these two composers, along with Arcadelt, were among the first to pursue the implications of Ronsard's classicizing poetics. Another important venue for the nascent *air de cour* was the Parisian musical and literary salon of Catherine de Clermont, the Comtesse de Retz, which boasted an impressive range of musical visitors as well as an equally impressive collection of instruments.

In addition to the various observances endowed by the ruling élite, many other religious communities in Paris also used music for devotional purposes. In the late 16th century, for instance, a Jesuit college there legislated against overly complex sacred polyphony and the use of instruments in the liturgy. French Protestants, too, directed vocal music towards pious aims. Claude Goudimel, a composer central to the development of the Huguenot polyphonic psalter, was active in Paris through the 1550s and 1560s, at first as a member of the university community and then as an editor to the Du Chemin publishing firm. He was killed in the anti-Protestant violence that shook Paris in 1572. Claude Le Jeune, too, wrote music for Protestant audiences in late 16th-century Paris. According to Mersenne, Le Jeune's *Dodecacorde* (a collection of psalm settings organized according to Zarlino's disposition of the 12 melodic modes that was first printed in 1598) was still in manuscript form when the composer fled Paris in the anti-Huguenot riots of 1590, and was saved for later publication by Jacques Mauduit, a friend of the composer.

Elsewhere in Paris citizens might encounter music to entertain rather than edify or inspire. The parish church of St Merry on the right bank of the Seine, for instance, was the site of the Confrérie de St Julien-des-Ménétriers, the religious organization of the minstrels of Paris. Founded during the 14th century, the corporation and its confraternity periodically chose from among their ranks a leader, the *roi* or *maître des ménétriers*, whose title was summarily approved by the King of France. This chief minstrel, by authority of his guild and the throne, oversaw the rules of conduct and contract by which all members of this popular band of Parisian players were obliged to abide. Musical standards, too, were enforced by the organization, and no doubt some of the dance tunes, arrangements and variation techniques promoted in printed books and manuals by musicians such as Claude Gervaise (for the royal printer Attaingnant) and Jean d'Estrée (for the printer Du Chemin) derived from the traditions of the *ménétriers* whose administrative locus was in the parish of St Merry. With so much performing in evidence, it should not be surprising that instrument making flourished in the city; some 70 builders are known by name from the period 1540–1610. Inventories reveal that a single builder might have as many as 600 instruments of all kinds, either finished or in construction, including some that were imported, mainly from Italy.

The Ville was also the centre of theatrical enterprise. As early as the beginning of the 15th century the Confrérie de la Passion used a hall next to the Trinité, near the Porte

St Denis, to perform its mystery and morality plays interspersed with farces and *sotties*; Arnoul Greban's *Vray mistère de la Passion* (*c*1452) is the best-known example. By the 16th century this offshoot of medieval liturgical drama was no longer controlled by the clergy and had become a popular spectacle of dubious moral character, performed by lay actors. Yet the guild did not loosen its control on the revenues but enjoyed a legal monopoly. In 1548 it erected the first Parisian theatre specifically designed as such since Roman times. This playhouse was at the heart of the most populous quarter, near Les Halles and St Eustache, and was known as the Hôtel de Bourgogne. It was occasionally leased out to other companies, particularly the Enfants sans Souci, an amateur group from the milieu of the law courts.

Many of these theatrical performances, which alternatively range among the conventions of moral allegory and political farce, allude to the *timbres* and texts of monophonic chansons that apparently enjoyed wide circulation among aristocratic and popular urban audiences alike. The texts and tunes of these chansons are known through two important courtly manuscripts of the early 16th century and through later collections of printed poems. Composers such as Antoine de Févin and Jean Mouton, and others closely linked with the Paris and with the French royal court, acknowledged the currency of these tunes, arranging a considerable number of them for three and four voices.

Elsewhere in the city of Paris, music took yet other forms, quite different from either the theatrical chansons of the urban farces or the polyphonic chansons or solo

4. *Entrance of Charles V into Paris: miniature by Jean Fouquet from the 'Grandes Chroniques de France', c1460 (F-Pn fr.6465, f.417r)*

airs of the aristocratic salons and courts. By the 14th century it was customary for sovereigns and other dignitaries to make their formal entrance into Paris via the Porte St Denis, then traverse the length of the rue St Denis to the Châtelet before crossing to the Ile. Certain fixed stations along this route came to be the traditional sites for pageants, *tableaux vivants* and architectural monuments; the stations were the Porte St Denis, the fountain of the Ponceau, the Trinité, the Porte aux Peintres, the Holy Innocents (near which the fountain decorated by Goujon as a memorial to Henri II's entry in 1549 still stands), and at the Châtelet. A final pageant station was traditional before the entrance to the Palais Royal on the Ile. These events constituted street theatre in several senses. The populace marvelled at the majesty of the sovereign, who was preceded by trumpets and followed by a magnificent retinue, an awesome sight that Jean Fouquet captured in his fine miniatures (fig.4). Before every pageant station the nobility stopped to witness a spectacle that often included theatrical machinery, speeches, inscriptions and instrumentally accompanied songs and dances, in which the minstrels' guild participated. Such entertainments were locally planned and financed, being organized at the Hôtel de Ville by the civil authorities of Paris; they were often allegorical jumbles of ancient history, myth, superstition and folklore.

The last two generations of Valois preferred the various Italian troupes of comedians that visited Paris, such as the famous Venetian group known as I Gelosi, invited by Henri III in 1577. They played in the Salle du Petit-Bourbon, which fell into royal hands after the treason of Charles de Bourbon in 1524. Attempts by the guild to exercise its privileges and force the Italians to play in the Hôtel de Bourgogne were foiled by royal opposition. The performances of I Gelosi were the first in which female players appeared in Paris, and they caused as much surprise and delight as the dancing and the almost continuous sounding of music, during the acts and the entr'actes. The all-night performance of the *Balet comique de la Royne* to an audience of over 9000, staged in the same hall in 1581 (fig.5) probably also employed such spectacles (see McGowan, 1963).

3. THE UNIVERSITY.   During the 13th to 15th centuries several colleges were founded in the university, the most notable being the one endowed by Robert de Sorbonne in 1257. The university colleges were mostly charitable institutions, and the focus of their teaching was religious doctrine. Many dioceses throughout France established scholarships for several years' training in one of the Parisian colleges. Each college had a chapel where the students were required to attend daily services and sing chant, in which they were given instruction. But music otherwise had little place in the university, unless it was studied in connection with mathematics. Some of the most learned men of the French Renaissance echoed a largely medieval theoretical heritage when they presented geometric and proportional justifications for elemental intervals of sound. Jacques Le Febvre d'Etaples, professor in the Collège de Cardinal Lemoine (he was also teacher of the Swiss music theorist Heinrich Glarean), published just such a speculative treatise, *Musica libris quatuor demonstrata*, at Paris in 1496, while Oronce Finé, first professor of mathematics at the Collège de France, wrote a similarly abstract consideration of sound and proportions, the *Protomathesis*, that appeared in 1532. Not all

5. 'Circé, ou le Balet comique de la Royne', Salle du Petit-Bourbon, 15 October 1581: engraving by Jacques Patin; performed for the wedding celebrations of the Duke of Joyeuse and Marguerite de Vaudemont

musical activity in the university community was so abstract, however. Janequin was enrolled as a student there during the years around 1550 (when he was already in his sixth decade), as was Claude Goudimel. Maximilian Guilliaud, whose *Rudiments de musique practique* was one of several books addressed to young students that the Du Chemin enterprise issued during the 1550s, was himself a member of the Collège de Navarre.

4. MUSIC PUBLISHING. The concentration of learning on the Left Bank made the university an unparalleled centre for the diffusion and extension of knowledge. Long before the introduction of the printing press the scriptoria around the colleges supported a vast industry of paper and parchment makers, scribes, illuminators, binders and book-sellers, all organized into guilds, and all subject to the governance of the university. The rector of the Sorbonne introduced printing into France in 1470, importing three German printers; immediately printing presses were so rapidly established throughout the quarter that by 1500 Paris became one of the leading European publishing centres, both in quality and quantity.

The impetus for early printing at the Sorbonne had come from scholars who wished to produce better texts in order to restore the ancient languages and literatures, pagan as well as Judeo-Christian, a peculiarly Renaissance phenomenon. Soon the printing industry was turned to other uses, such as the publication of liturgical service books; Parisian printers were the chief suppliers to the dioceses of northern France and England. The first plainchant printed in France (1494) was inscribed 'to the masters of the Sorbonne to use in their chapel'. This branch of Parisian printing led to the development of the printing of mensural music. Michel Toulouze, a neighbour of Guerson in the Clos Bruneau, printed chant books and also made some attempts at printing mensural notes in the last years of the 15th century. His edition of Guerson's *Regulae* (*c*1500) was the first of 15 brought out by various publishers until the middle of the 16th century. Pierre Attaingnant began as a liturgical printer in the 1520s with a business and premises in the rue de la Harpe inherited from his father-in-law, Philippe Pigouchet. By 1528 he perfected a method of printing mensural notes from type with a single impression, which made mass-production possible.

Exactly who bought and used any of these books will remain something of a topic for continuing investigation. Among the books issued by Attaingnant, for instance, were volumes of sacred music conceived with audiences at court and in French regional churches clearly in mind. But in addition to these ceremonial or public uses of printed music, it is also evident that the new medium was destined in many instances for private domestic enjoyment. Indeed, not long after its advent in France, printed music books were already to be counted among the most prized personal possessions of urban bureaucrats and merchants. At the time of his death in 1544, for instance, the personal library of Jean de Badonvillier, an official in the Paris *chambre des comptes*, contained a printed collection of masses, two of Attaingnant's chanson anthologies, and printed books of motets by Claudin de Sermisy and Johannes Lupi.

François I gave Attaingnant a monopoly on music printing, but at his death (1547) this was broken. Du Chemin set up a shop in the rue St Jean de Latran, followed a few years later by the partnership of Adrian Le Roy and Robert Ballard in the nearby rue St Jean de Beauvais. Issuing dozens of volumes of sacred and secular music, from Arcadelt in the 1550s to Lassus in the 1570s and Le Jeune in the 1580s, the Ballards eventually eliminated all competition and founded a publishing dynasty that was to last for several generations.

The next generation of academically inclined poets and musicians was preoccupied less with the new chanson than with humanist notions of reviving ancient song. Jean Dorat, professor of Greek, gathered around him at the Collège de Coqueret a group of disciples that included Ronsard, Du Bellay, Tyard, Baïf and Etienne Jodelle, the 'Pléiade'. Ronsard's *Amours* (1552) were produced in collaboration with Goudimel, Janequin and Certon, master of the children at the Ste Chapelle. Humanist experiment became more and more apparent in the chansons of the third quarter of the century, leading to the radical solution of *musique mesurée*. Baïf and the composer J.T. de Courville, its creators, founded an Académie de Poésie et de Musique to propagate the new style in Baïf's house in the rue des Fossés St Victor (1571). Lassus was sufficiently impressed by the style to attempt it during his visits to Paris (1572–4), when he also wrote the music for the *Ballet des polonais*, in collaboration with Dorat. After the death of Charles IX (1574) the Académie was increasingly controlled by Henri III, holding its meetings in the Louvre.

The revival of ancient theatre attempted by Jodelle, Baïf, Garnier and Du Bellay (c1550) (erudite attempts to provide the French language with an equivalent to Greek tragedy) aroused no interest at the Hôtel de Bourgogne across the Seine, and its performances eventually took place on improvised stages in the various colleges, or in the provinces. There is perhaps no clearer example of the difference in atmosphere that separated the Ville from the university. Until the late 16th century only a few narrow bridges crossed the Seine; however, Henri III built a great stone bridge of unprecedented width, linking the Ile, Ville and university – the Pont Neuf – and the tripartite division of Paris subsequently became less significant. The religious wars split Paris; after Henri III's flight to Chartres in 1588 the Guises and the Sainte-Ligues controlled the capital until Henri de Navarre abjured Protestantism in 1593.

III. 1600–1723

1. General. 2. Religious institutions. 3. Theatres. 4. Orchestras. 5. Private concerts.

1. GENERAL.   During the 17th century the population of Paris increased from a quarter to over half a million. By 1702 the city had been divided into 20 quarters, whose boundaries remained relatively stable until the Revolution. After Mazarin's death the medieval face of Paris was changed. 'It may very well be', wrote Martin Lister, 'that Paris is in a manner a new city within this 40 years. 'Tis certain since this King came to the Crown, 'tis so much altered for the better' (*A Journey to Paris in the Year 1698*, London, 1699). Perrault's colonnade of the Louvre (1667–74), Le Nôtre's Tuileries gardens (1667), Porte St Denis (1672) and Porte St Martin (1674), the Place des Victoires (1686) and the Place Vendôme (1699) all reflect the spirit of the *grand siècle*.

Colbert, complying with Louis XIV's passion for order, completed the plans for royal academies that would centralize the artistic and intellectual life of the regime. In 1661 only the Académie Française (established by Richelieu in 1635) and the Académie Royale de Peinture et de Sculpture (1648) existed; Colbert founded five additional academies: the Académie Royale de Danse (1661), Académie des Inscriptions, Médailles et Belles-lettres (1663), Académie des Sciences (1666), Académies d'Opéra (1669, becoming the Académie Royale de Musique in 1672) and Académie Royale d'Architecture (1671).

The quarters of Paris bordering the Right Bank (St Jacques-de-la-Boucherie, Ste Opportune, the Louvre, Les Halles, St Eustache, La Grève, St Martin-des-Champs) were little affected by the city's rebuilding. They were noisy, crowded and malodorous, with narrow, winding streets and houses built so high that Montesquieu's Persian deemed them occupied 'only by astrologers'. Shops of *luthiers* and harpsichord builders were found there, and many dancing masters and instrumentalists belonging to the Confrérie de St Julien-des-Ménétriers lived there, especially along the streets bordering the rue St Martin. In the nearby parishes of St Merry, St Nicolas-des-Champs and St Jacques-de-la-Boucherie were the homes of most of the organ makers of Paris.

The Marais was the most fashionable quarter during the first half of the 17th century. Here was the *salon précieux* of Mlle de Scudéry, and in the Hôtel Carnavelet Mme de Sévigné found 'bel air, une belle cour, un beau jardin'. In the spacious town houses of the nobility music

was an adornment and a mark of distinction; divertissements were performed in the *salles* or courtyards of the *hôtels*. Such was the divertissement composed by André Campra in 1697 for the Duke of Sully to honour the Duke of Chartres. Marie de Lorraine, Duchess of Guise, employed 12 singers and several instrumentalists at the Hôtel du Marais (now the Musée des Archives Nationales) on the rue de Chaume. For the last 16 years of her life her composer-in-residence was Marc-Antoine Charpentier, who wrote eight dramatic works for her and many *petits motets* for performance in her chapel, which adjoined the Grande Salle of her *hôtel*.

The Marais' claim to fashionable society was challenged by other quarters. A pleasing stylistic unity characterized Christophe Marie's development of the Ile St Louis between 1614 and 1646. As early as 1624 Catherine de Vivonne had established her Hôtel de Rambouillet, the headquarters of *préciosité*, on the rue de l'Oratoire-du-Louvre. With the completion of Richelieu's Palais du Cardinal in 1634 (known as the Palais Royal from 1643, when Anne of Austria made it her residence) the Marais had a serious rival, and later in the century two more in the neighbouring quarters of St Honoré and Butte St Roch. Describing the Palais Royal section in 1643 Corneille wrote: 'We must presume from these superb roofs that all the inhabitants are gods or kings' (*Le menteur*) – a conceit flattering to the élite who lived there. Men of influence in government, letters and the arts preferred these quarters.

Mazarin's sumptuous palace, one section of which, the Hôtel de Nevers, was converted into the Bibliothèque Nationale in 1721, set the tone for the rue de Richelieu, which soon became 'one of the most beautiful and straight streets of Paris' (G. Brice, *A New Description of Paris*, 1687). During the reign of Louis XIV this and nearby streets were inhabited by such members of the 'vile bourgeoisie' (Saint-Simon) as Colbert and Louvois. Many of this class, prototypes of the 18th-century middle-class entrepreneur, found it distinctly advantageous socially to present concerts in their salons. Monsieur Jourdain (*Le bourgeois gentilhomme*, Act 2 scene i) was advised to have a concert at his home 'every Wednesday or Thursday' if he wanted to be considered a person of quality. From 1715 to 1725 Antoine Crozat, the wealthy treasurer of the Etats du Languedoc, held two weekly concerts at his home on the rue de Richelieu (see fig.8 below).

Because of their central location and proximity to the Opéra these quarters were favoured by both composers and performers. Four of Lully's houses were in the Palais Royal quarter, and Lalande maintained a large dwelling in the rue Ste Anne, as did the king's harpsichordist, D'Anglebert. Destouches lived next to the church of St Roch, and Mouret resided in the Place du Palais Royal next to the Café de la Régence from 1717 to 1734. From 1724 until his death François Couperin (ii) lived at the corner of the rue Neuve des Bons Enfants (now rue Radziwill) and the rue des Petits Champs; he may have been acquainted with Rameau, who at the time of his marriage (1726) also lived in the rue des Petits Champs.

2. RELIGIOUS INSTITUTIONS.   In addition to the Chapelle Royale (see §V, 1 below), the churches of Paris frequented by the royalty during the period of Louis XIII and Louis XIV were Notre Dame, St Germain-l'Auxerrois (the parish church of the Louvre), the Ste Chapelle, the chapel of the Tuileries palace, the convent of the Feuillants in the

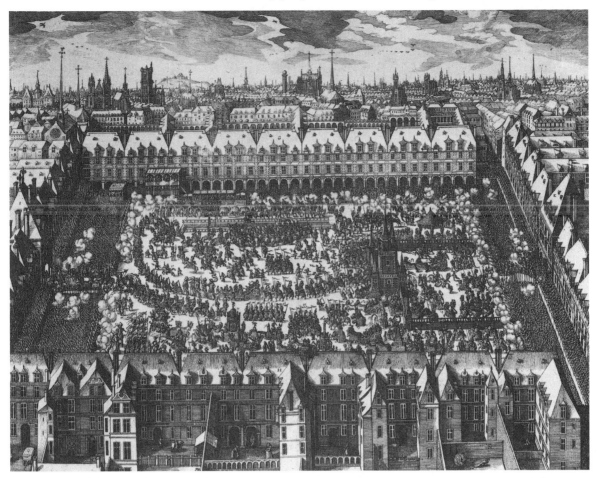

6. Carrousel in the Place Royale (now Place des Vosges), 1612: engraving; 150 musicians accompanied a gigantic equestrian ballet before 10,000 spectators

rue de Vauguard and the convent of the Théatins, established on the Quai Malaquais by Mazarin in 1648. The *maîtrises* of these churches produced conservative music throughout much of this period. However, the two conventual chapels, together with the Augustinians' chapel in the Place des Victoires and that of the Jesuits in the Faubourg St Antoine, were generally more responsive to secular influences stemming from the *air de cour* and from opera. Italian influence was especially strong in the chapel of the Théatins, whose priests were called 'pères du chant' and whose music was under Lorenzani's direction from 1685 to at least 1687. The aristocracy flocked to hear his *petits motets* at regular Wednesday performances, and in November 1685 the *Mercure galant* complained that the Théatins, 'under the pretext of devotion to the souls in Purgatory, sang a veritable opera in their church . . . where seats could be rented for ten sols'.

Many Parisian convents were also known for their musical activities. Antoine Boësset taught the nuns of the abbey of Montmartre and the sweetness of the nuns' voices at the convent of the Assumption 'attracted many of the *beau monde* every Saturday to their litanies' (Sauval, i, p.470).

The nuns of the abbey of Longchamp were permitted to use singers from the Opéra for the annual Good Friday Tenebrae service. The origin of the 'Promenades de Longchamp' may be traced to the great number of fashionable Parisians in attendance at this service for which François Couperin composed his *Leçons de ténèbres* (*c*1714).

The *Ceremoniale parisiense* (1662) gave ecclesiastical sanction to the conservative bias of the Paris churches. The stern voice of the Council of Trent is heard in this document, which warns against using any instrument but the organ in church. Undoubtedly it made some composers reluctant to use obbligato instruments, particularly in masses. Plainchant had been accompanied by the serpent at the Ste Chapelle since 1651, but it was not until the end of the century that Campra was permitted to introduce violins at Notre Dame. The repressive measures of the *Ceremoniale* were evidently relaxed for special occasions; for the celebration of the birth of the Duke of Burgundy a 'concert of trumpets, oboes and violins' began the Vespers at Notre Dame (*Mercure galant*, October 1682). It is clear from an ordinance of the Archbishop of Paris (1674) that the secularization of religious music, attacked so vehemently by Le Cerf de la Viéville (*Comparaison de la musique italienne et de la musique française*, 1705), was already in evidence. The ordinance condemned singing profane or secular music in any chapel or church, and 'inviting others, through tickets or publicity to come and hear the music as though it were a spectacle or theatre performance'.

According to a document (in *BrenetM*, p.243) given to François Chaperon, his duties as *maître de musique* at the Ste Chapelle (1679–98) included teaching music to the choirboys, and composing and conducting all music performed. Some of Chaperon's important predecessors at the Ste Chapelle had been the conservative and quarrelsome Artus Aux-Cousteaux (*maître de musique*, *c*1643–51) and three composers who were important to the development of the double chorus motet in France: Formé (canon, 1626–38), Veillot (canon, 1651–8) and Thomas Gobert (canon, 1651–72). From Chaperon's death in 1698 until his own death in 1704 Charpentier was in control of the considerable musical forces of the Ste Chapelle; he was succeeded by Nicolas Bernier, who remained there until 1726.

Except for Veillot (*maître de musique*, 1640–43), Campra (1694–1700) and Lallouette (1700–16; 1718–27), those in charge of music at Notre Dame were among the most conservative of French composers; they generally wrote *a cappella* masses in Renaissance style. Frémart (1625–40) preceded Veillot, who was followed by Cosset (1643–6). The surviving music of Pierre Robert dates from his tenure at the Chapelle Royale rather than his ten-year service at Notre Dame (1653–63). Mignon (*maître de chapelle* at Notre Dame, 1664–94) wrote six masses, which, with their Lullian homophony and occasional madrigalisms, are generally less conservative than those of his predecessors.

The *maîtrise* at St Germain-l'Auxerrois was led by the conservative Péchon in the 1640s. More important was Chaperon, who used his position there as a stepping-stone to the Ste Chapelle, and who numbered among his singers Lalande and Marais, both of whom left the *maîtrise* in 1672. Chaperon was followed by Minoret (who left in 1683), Jean-Baptist Fossart and, finally, Nicolas Bernier (1698–1704) who, like Chaperon, went directly from St Germain to the Ste Chapelle.

Certain Paris churches were important in the development of the French classical organ. Parisian and Norman organ builders such as Valeran Héman, Claude de Villiers, Delaunay, Pierre and Alexandre Thierry, Etienne Enoc, Pierre Desenclos and Robert Clicquot created a type of organ which became standardized by the late 1660s and remained so for a century. The typical four-manual classical French organ is exemplified by those at Notre Dame, St Louis-des-Invalides, St Paul, St Germain-des-Prés, St Merry and St Gervais. Among the more important Paris organists, who composed music ideally suited to the unique colour combinations of this instrument, are: Louis Couperin (St Gervais, 1653–61); Du Mont (St Paul, 1643–84); Etienne Richard (St Nicolas-des-Champs and, after 1652, St Jacques-de-la-Boucherie); Nivers (St Sulpice, 1654–1714); Lebègue (St Merry, 1664–1702); Gigault (St Honoré, St Martin-des-Champs, St Nicolas-des-Champs and the Hôpital du Saint Esprit); Raison (abbey of Ste Geneviève, 1666–1714, and the convent of the Jacobins, rue St Jacques, 1687–1719); François Couperin (ii) (St Gervais, 1685–1723); Louis Marchand (Jesuit College, 1689, St Benoît, St Honoré, 1703–7, and the convent of the Cordeliers, 1717–32); Louis Nicolas Clérambault (St Sulpice, 1714, and the convent of the Jacobins, rue St Jacques, 1719), Jean-François Dandrieu (St Merry, 1704); Dagincourt (Ste Madeleine-en-la-Cité, 1701–6); Dornel

(Ste Madeleine-en-la-Cité, 1706–16, and the abbey of Ste Geneviève, 1716) and Daquin (Petit St Antoine, 1706, St Paul, 1727, and the convent of the Cordeliers, 1732). The *Ceremoniale parisiense*, in the hierarchical spirit of the age, lay down careful rules for Parisian organists (see Dufourcq, 1955) which partly explain the uniform style of the organ music by many of these composers.

The Jesuit institutions in Paris played a leading role in the musical life of the city from 1603, the date of their recall, until the suppression of the order in 1761. The Jesuit church of St Louis in the Marais quarter had a sumptuous gallery, and was an ideal place to hear the masses and motets of Charpentier (appointed musical director *c*1684). The Collège de Clermont (founded in 1561 and known as the Collège Louis-le-Grand after 1683) was a Jesuit school in the rue St Jacques for the sons of wealthy Parisians. One of the two annual spectacles performed there marked the completion of a year's work early in August; it included a Latin tragedy and French *intermèdes* that often related to the tragedy, and beginning in 1684, sacred *tragédies en musique* were composed for the occasion. The most important of these is Charpentier's *David et Jonathas* (1688). Among other composers serving this college were Lalande, Collasse, Campra, Lallouette, Desmarets, Clérambault, Beauchamps and Royer.

3. THEATRES.   Parisian theatres were in a precarious position during the 17th century because of changes in taste, lack of royal support, jealous rivalries, repressive patents and poor financial management. However, at various times between the establishment of Molière's company in Paris (1658) and that of Lully's Académie Royale de Musique (1672) Parisians were offered a wide variety of entertainment at a number of theatres: the Hôtel de Bourgogne (now 29 rue Etienne Marcel); the Petit Bourbon, located approximately where the colonnade of the Louvre now stands; two theatres in the Palais Royal; the Théâtre du Marais (now 90 rue Vieille du Temple); the Salle des Machines in the Tuileries palace; and the Académie d'Opéra, erected on the Bouteille tennis court which extended from the rue de Seine (now no.42) to the rue des Fossés-de-Nesles (now 43 rue Mazarine), opposite the rue de Guénégaud.

At the Hôtel de Bourgogne a permanent company was formed in 1629 to play tragedies. In the same year the king awarded the company an annual grant of 12,000 livres, double the amount later given to the Marais and the Palais Royal. The king granted the Petit Bourbon to Molière and his comedians in 1658 and later (1661) also the larger of the theatres in the Palais Royal.

Molière's Palais Royal company achieved its greatest success in elaborate performances of the Molière–Lully *comédies-ballets* for the court at Versailles, St Germain-en-Laye, Fontainebleau and Chambord. Molière's final *comédie-ballet*, *Le malade imaginaire*, had music by Charpentier, being written after Molière's break with Lully; though planned for the court, it was performed at the Palais Royal. On Molière's death (1673) his Palais Royal company merged with that of the Théâtre du Marais to form the Théâtre Guénégaud, in the same theatre that had housed the Académie d'Opéra.

Charpentier provided music for the Théâtre Guénégaud and its successor the Comédie-Française, formed by an amalgamation with the Hôtel de Bourgogne company at the command of Louis XIV in 1680. Between his 1673 and 1685 versions of *Le malade imaginaire* Charpentier composed music for 14 productions of plays by Thomas and Pierre Corneille, Donneau de Visé, Poisson, Baron and Dancourt. Other composers who worked for the Comédie-Française were Gillier, Grandval, Raison, Lalande, Mouret and Jean-Baptiste Quinault.

Sauval found the Petit Bourbon theatre, dating from the days of the Valois kings, the 'highest and longest [hall] in the realm'. Until its demolition in 1660, to make way for Perrault's colonnade, this hall served both Molière's company and the Comédie-Italienne. The court ballets, balls and masquerades of Louis XIII and the young Louis XIV took place there, as well as in the Grande Salle of the Louvre, the Grande Salle of the Tuileries Palace, the Palais Royal (See fig.7) and the *salles* of the Hôtel de Ville and the Arsenal. The *Ballet comique de la reine* (1581) and two of the seven Italian operas introduced to Paris by Mazarin were performed at the Petit Bourbon (Sacrati's *La finta pazza*, 1645, and Caproli's *Le nozze di Peleo e di Theti*, 1654).

From 1634 to 1673 the Théâtre du Marais (capacity 1500) responded to the French taste for elaborate mises-en-scène in productions of *pièces à machines*. In Corneille's *Andromède* Dassoucy's music functions only to 'satisfy the ears of the spectators while the eyes are engaged watching the descent or ascent of a machine' (preface). Closer to opera is Claude Boyer's *Les amours de Jupiter et de Sémélé* (1666), in which spoken drama is subordinated to dance, machine and Mollier's music.

Another theatre designed to support huge machinery was known as the Théâtre des Machines. The septuagenarian architect Gaspare Vigarani and his two sons built it between 1659 and 1662 in the Tuileries palace for Mazarin, who died before its completion. Cavalli's *Ercole amante* was performed there in 1662 as a posthumous finale to Mazarin's ill-fated efforts to win the French over to Italian opera. This hall, according to Sauval, could accommodate 7000 people, and its stage machinery could elevate more than 100 performers at once. It was an immense failure; in 1665 Bernini expressed the general complaint that no-one could hear anything at all. After great expense, three years of construction and six years of use, it ceased regular performances.

Perrin's short-lived Académie d'Opéra opened on 3 March 1671 with his and Cambert's *Pomone*, usually considered the first French opera. The theatre was fashioned from the Bouteille tennis court in the rue des Fossés de Nesles (today 42 rue Mazarine). After a series of misadventures had led him to a debtors' prison Perrin sold his privilege (which he had held since 1669) to Lully, and on 1 April 1672 the Académie d'Opéra was forced to close.

The first two productions of Lully's new Académie Royale de Musique (*Les fêtes de l'Amour et de Bacchus*, 15 November 1672, and *Cadmus et Hermione*, 27 April 1673) were performed in a theatre built hastily by Carlo Vigarani at the Bel Air tennis court on the rue de Vaugirard (now between the Odéon theatre and the Luxembourg gardens). After Molière's death Lully was given the theatre of the Palais Royal free of charge (28 April 1673). With the 3000 *livres* given to him by the king, Lully instructed Vigarani to prepare the Palais Royal for the production of operas. This was completed early in 1674. The Palais Royal is the most important theatre in the history of the French lyric stage during the *grand siècle*. Cavalli's *Egisto* ('we were only 20 or 30 and we almost died of boredom and the cold', Mme de Motteville) and Luigi Rossi's *Orfeo* were performed there in 1646 and 1647 respectively. In 1651 Louis XIV made his début as a dancer there, in the *Ballet de Cassandre*, and from 1661 to 1673 the theatre served Molière's company and the Comédie-Italienne alternately. It was the home of French opera from 1673 until it burnt down in 1763; from 1673 until the death of the Regent Philippe, Duke of Orléans, in 1723, over 100 stage works were performed there, including the 13 *tragédies en musique* by Lully and works in the same genre by Collasse, Campra, Destouches, Mouret and others. From 1697 (*L'Europe galante*) popular *opéras-ballets* by Campra, Montéclair and Mouret challenged the supremacy of the *tragédie en musique* and, in spite of some opposition from aestheticians, returned the comic muse to the stage of the Palais Royal.

Built by Le Mercier and opened in 1641, the theatre was much longer than it was wide (fig.7). By Lully's time it had a parterre, an amphitheatre, a double balcony and three rows of boxes (the king's box was first on the right facing the stage, and the queen's first on the left; *see* OPERA, fig.35). The theatre was cramped. Lagrave (p.86) estimated that its capacity was between 1300 and 1400, although it contained only 1270 seats. Its stage was small. Riccoboni wrote: 'The Decorations of the Stage of the Opera are very handsome, but not to be compared with those of Italy, the Smallness of the Stage not admitting of their being either so large or so magnificent as those of the vast Theatres of Venice, Milan, etc'. (1741, p.152). The price of admission was double that of the other theatres (see Lagrave, pp.46ff). Performances began at 5.15 on Tuesdays, Thursdays (only in winter), Fridays and Sundays, and it was closed for 23 days during the Easter season and for 11 days for other religious feasts. The printed libretto (*livret*) was sold at the door of the theatre before each performance. It cost 30 sols.

In 1712 Louis XIV ordered the construction of an annexe to the Académie Royale de Musique, rue St Nicaise. Known as the Magasin de l'Opéra, it contained a school of singing, a school of dance, administrative offices, a library, rehearsal halls and a ballroom. The rules governing all the activities of the Académie Royale de Musique are fully described in two royal ordinances of 1713 and 1714 (in Durey de Noinville, i, pp.105–46); they reveal an administration generally sensitive to the needs of the singers, dancers, instrumentalists, conductors, stage designers, machinists and tailors employed by the Opéra. There were six sopranos, three *hautes-contres*, two tenors and three basses among the solo singers. It is not possible to fix the exact number of choristers at the Paris Opéra during Lully's tenure. The names of the chorus members did not appear in the librettos until 1699. The fluctuating numbers in the first decade of the 18th century (30 in 1701, 22 in 1704, 32 in 1706) reflect the economic woes of the Opéra under the direction of Jean-Nicolas de Francine, Lully's son-in-law (see La Gorce 1979, p.177). The dancers consisted of 12 men and 10 women (for details concerning the Opéra orchestra, see below).

Lully's original privilege (March 1672) gave him administrative control of the Académie Royale de Musique for his lifetime and extended this to his heirs. His son-in-law Francine shared the privilege with Hyacinthe

7. Richelieu's theatre in the Palais Royale during the performance of a play: engraving by Michel van Lochon, 1643; seated (from left to right) are Cardinal Richelieu, Louis XIII, Anne of Austria and the dauphin (Louis XIV); note the musicians playing in the upper right gallery

Gaureault du Mont in 1698. Problems of finance and discipline plagued the opera in the early 18th century, and in 1713 Destouches was appointed inspecteur-général to maintain order and discipline. When Francine retired in 1728 Destouches took over as director of the opera. In 1715, with the permission of the regent, the Académie Royale de Musique sponsored all-night public masked balls at the Palais Royal; these rapidly became a favourite pastime in Paris (see Durey de Noinville, i, p.164).

The Comédie-Italienne had been popular since its arrival in the city during the reign of Henri III. The troupe, led by Scaramouche, alternated with Molière's company at the Petit Bourbon and, after 1660, at the Palais Royal. On the creation of the Comédie-Française (1680) the Italians took over the Hôtel de Bourgogne, where they performed until they were deported in May 1697 for having satirized Mme de Maintenon in *La fausse prude* (8 January 1696). The repertory of this so-called Ancien Théâtre Italien (see Gherardi) included many parodies of Lully's operas. Of the 55 plays mentioned in Gherardi 43 use music extensively, despite the fact that Lully's patent of 22 April 1673 had reduced the number of musicians who might appear in any performance outside the Académie Royale de Musique to two vocalists and six instrumentalists. Among the identified composers who wrote for the Ancien Théâtre Italien are Lully, Cambert, Masse and Gillier.

By 1680 Paris had only three regular theatre companies: the Opéra, the Comédie-Française and the Comédie-Italienne. Each competed for public favour and jealously guarded its monopolies. Nowhere may the arrogance of power be better observed than in the attempts of the Opéra and the Comédie-Française to suppress the popular entertainments at the Théâtres de la Foire.

The Foire St Germain (3 February to Palm Sunday) and the Foire St Laurent (17 June to the end of September) had been the scene of farces and acrobatic displays since the Middle Ages; however, they became a threat to the Opéra and the Comédie-Française only in 1697, when they adopted the repertory of the expelled Comédie-Italienne (*see* THÉÂTRES DE LA FOIRE). The early years of the 18th century saw the Opéra and the Comédie-Française involved in a series of legal battles aimed at preventing the *forains* from speaking or singing on their stages. It is a tribute to the imagination of creative men and women that the Théâtres de la Foire (who took the name of Opéra-Comique in 1715) found ways of circumventing the repressive edicts of their powerful rivals.

Philippe of Orléans became regent in 1715, and lost no time in calling the Italians back to Paris. In 1716 the Nouveau Théâtre Italien was established at the Palais Royal under the direction of Luigi Riccoboni (known as Lélio). French plays by Autreau, Marivaux, Fuzelier and others were introduced into the repertory side by side with comedies by Riccoboni and parodies by Dominique and Romagnesi. From 1717 until the year before his death in 1738 Mouret was the chief composer of the Nouveau Théâtre Italien.

4. ORCHESTRAS. The most important orchestra in Paris from the foundation of the Académie Royale de Musique to the death of the regent was the orchestra of the Opéra. Precise information concerning its membership under the direction of Lully is lacking. The earliest known source that gives information about the Opéra orchestra is an archival document of 1704 (La Gorce, 1979). The orchestra, like the chorus, was divided into a *grand* and *petit choeur*. The *grand choeur* consisted of nine violins, eight violas (divided into three parts), eight *basses de violons* (after 1700 usually violoncellos), eight winds (oboes, transverse flutes or, more usually, recorders and bassoons) and one set of kettledrums. The *petit choeur* consisted of two violins, two *basses de violons*, two bass viols and (after 1700) one double bass, one harpsichord and two theorbos. According to the Royal Ordinances of 1713 and 1714, two transverse flutes were added to the *petit choeur*. Supernumeraries must have been hired to play the trumpet, musette and cromorne parts occasionally called for in Lully's operas. A *batteur de mesure* directed the orchestra. According to the Royal Ordinance of 1713, the Opéra orchestra had 48 members (Durey de Noinville, i, 121ff), a number that hardly varied for half a century. Members of the Opéra orchestra were often used in concerts independent of the opera performances at the Palais Royal. 30 members gathered half an hour before dancing began at the public masked balls to present a concert of 'important *morceaux de Symphonie* by the best masters'. Once a year, on St Louis Eve (24 August), free public concerts for the city of Paris were given in the Tuileries gardens by vocalists and instrumentalists from the Académie and were attended by the king. The repertory was largely made up of overtures, dances and large choral sections from Lully's operas (see *BrenetC*, p.169). After Lully's death the Opéra orchestra was conducted by Marais (1695–1710), Lacoste (1710–14), Mouret (1714–18) and Jean-Féry Rebel (1718–33).

Hidden in the notarial contracts of the Minutier Central are references to two Paris chamber orchestras dating from the first years of Louis XIV's reign (see Dufourcq, 1954). The first, founded in 1656, was a string orchestra of 12 players under the direction of Léonard de Lorge, which gave a concert lasting an hour every Saturday. The second was a string orchestra of 11 players, dating from 1667, whose concerts were given on Wednesdays under the direction of Henry Mathieu.

From the Middle Ages the street musicians of Paris had been organized in various guilds. In the 17th century the minstrels' guild, the Confrérie de St Julien-des-Ménétriers, was the powerful and paternalistic protector of the 'dancing-masters and players of instruments both high and low and the oboes' of Paris. The articles governing the syndicate assured a remarkable degree of protection for its members, who were hired to perform for weddings, engagement parties, banquets, masquerades, street serenades and formal concerts. The leader of the Confrérie was known as the *roi des ménétriers*, and later as the *roi des violons*. By the middle of the 17th century many of the Confrérie's better players were absorbed into the 24 Violons, the Petits Violons, the Ecurie or the Opéra

orchestra and its influence began to decline, although as late as 1660 Guillaume Dumanoir (i), then *roi des violons*, had 200 performers under his command. In that year the dancing-masters declared their independence from the Confrérie and a year later established their own Académie Royale de Danse. Guillaume Michel Dumanoir, who took control of the Confrérie in 1668, tried in vain to bring 'composers, organists and masters of the harpsichord' under the jurisdiction of his syndicate. The king's organists Lebègue, Nivers, Buterne and François Couperin, with the authority of the king behind them, removed the threat of control by the Confrérie (*Lettres patentes*, 25 June 1707); the syndicate became the butt of musical jokes, such as Couperin's 'Les fastes de la grande et ancienne Mxnxstrxndxsx' (*Ordre* no.11).

5. PRIVATE CONCERTS. The journals, gazettes, almanachs, letters and memoirs of the 17th and early 18th centuries document the active concert life of the *haut monde* of Parisian society, embracing both the nobility and the middle class. Jacques de Gouy, unfamiliar with either the earlier concerts of Mauduit at Baïf's Académie de Poésie et de Musique or the concerts of voices and instruments, of viols and harpsichord and of lutes described by Mersenne, believed the 'first concerts' to have been some *concerts spirituels* given before 1650 in the home of the king's organist, Pierre Chabanceau de La Barre (iii). At the end of the 17th century another series of *concerts spirituels*, organized weekly by Abbé Mathieu in his presbytery at St André-des-Arts, helped to popularize the music of Luigi Rossi, Cavalli, Carissimi, Corelli, Cazzati and other Italian composers.

In 1641 Chambonnières began the popular series of midday concerts given by the 'Assemblée des Honestes Curieux' on Wednesdays and Saturdays at his home. Titon du Tillet recorded that Sainte-Colombe, violist and teacher of Marais, gave family concerts in which he and his two daughters played viols. Christian Huygens wrote to his father in glowing terms about the concerts given by 'Monsieur Lambert and Mlle Hilaire, his sister-in-law, who sings like an angel'. Some concerts seem to have been particularly ambitious. In December 1678 the *Mercure galant* described the concerts 'in the manner of small operas' given by Mollier at his home every Thursday, and Dangeau stated that the music-loving Princess of Conti had a performance of *Alceste* mounted in her home.

Towards the end of the reign of Louis XIV Paris took the place of Versailles as a musical centre; the town house or country château substituted for the centralized court. By the end of the regency (1723), according to Nemeitz, one could hear a concert every day in Paris; he specifically mentioned concerts 'at the homes of the Duke of Aumont, Ambassador to England . . . Abbé Grave, Mlle de Maes, who ordinarily gave one a week; and then at the home of Mons Clérambault, who gave one about every 15 days or three weeks'.

IV. 1723–89

During the 18th century French became established as the universal language of Europe's educated classes, and Paris provided the lead in most cultural matters. The one exception was music, where the influence of Italian and German musicians proved increasingly crucial across Europe as the century progressed. In addition to its reputation for taste and elegance, 18th-century Paris was one of the most active intellectual centres of Europe, matched only by London and Amsterdam. Home to the Encyclopedists – Diderot, D'Alembert, Rousseau, Grimm and d'Holbach – the French capital provided ample scope for the discussion and dissemination of ideas through its numerous salons frequented by a cosmopolitan society. Here the revolution in beliefs took place. The second half of the century witnessed the rapid growth of pamphlets and periodicals and of music publishing and engraving. Firms like Sieber, Boivin, La Chevardière and, later, Pleyel issued music of French, German and Italian origin and developed close links with publishing firms in other European cities. The capital's expansion, evident in the growth in population and in a vast array of new buildings, meant that Paris gradually replaced Versailles as a focus for intellectual and cultural activities. As these transferred from the court to Parisian town houses or to country mansions, so musical patronage shifted away from the king, eroding the power of royal authority established so pervasively by Louis XIV.

1. Religious institutions. 2. Concert life. 3. Theatres.

1. RELIGIOUS INSTITUTIONS.   Sacred choral music continued to be written in Paris through the 18th century, although after 1725 it developed principally at the Concert Spirituel rather than in the churches. The noble *grand motet Versaillais*, embodied in the works of Lalande, endured for another 50 years, but after 1740, stimulated by paying audiences and the influence of opera and instrumental music, Mondonville and others began to introduce tuneful melodies, crowd-pleasing virtuosity and colourful instrumental effects into the genre. With this new popular element motets flourished in churches and on stage for much of the century, although they were out of favour in Paris by the time of the Revolution.

Few churches actually had the resources for choral music, chant generally being considered sufficient. Many visitors remarked on this, including William Jones, in 1777:

'In the services of their church, they seldom practise more than the plain song, accompanied in the unison or octave by a leathern serpent .... I asked, how it happened that they did not affect harmony more, and sing in parts, as we do in the services of the choir? They answered, that it was purposely avoided, lest the people should bestow all their attention to the music, and forget their errand to the church.'

Churches that continued a tradition of choral music – notably Notre Dame, the Ste Chapelle and St Germain l'Auxerrois, and the Holy Innocents – continued to celebrate major feast days with motets and masses, but they could no longer boast *maîtres* like Charpentier, Campra and Bernier. Two of the *maîtres* who held posts at these churches in the second half of the century are important: François Giroust, maître at the Saints-Innocents, converted his popularity at the Concert Spirituel into a post at the Chapelle Royale; Jean-François Le Sueur achieved notoriety at Notre Dame before moving to the world of opera.

Churches invariably drew large audiences for special musical events, which were always well advertised. Mrs Cradock writes of paying about a shilling each to get good seats for Pentecost Mass at Notre Dame, and sending a servant to hold them in advance. Mercier says that Vespers, the most popular service, was dubbed *l'opéra des gueux* (beggars' opera). It was so fashionable at the Saints-Innocents under Abbé Roze that in 1778 the poor were excluded, and the archbishop had to intervene. Le Sueur created a storm of controversy in 1787 when he

tried to convert major church feasts at Notre Dame into spectacular musical productions. He drew in huge crowds but subsequently lost his job. A popular annual event was St Cecilia's day at St Mathurin, which the city's musicians turned into a musical extravaganza.

By the middle of the century the severe liturgical organ tradition of Lebègue, Nivers, Couperin and Grigny had been supplanted by a more decorative style, associated with Marchand, Dandrieu, Clérambault and Du Mage. After an organ was installed at the Concert Spirituel in 1748, the trend towards concert use of the instrument increased, and a new generation of virtuosos emerged. They filled their masses and Vespers with dances, theatrical airs and elaborate variations, especially on the *Magnificat* and *Te Deum*. Although this development is lamented by modern scholars (as it was by English and German visitors at the time), organists have rarely enjoyed such popularity. Daquin was renowned for his noëls, as was G.-A. Calvière for his sonic effects. Balbastre attracted so many listeners to St Roch that his *messes de minuit* and *Te Deums* were forbidden by the archbishop; a similar ban was imposed at St Germain-des-Prés.

2. CONCERT LIFE.   Paris cultivated an active concert life from the earliest years of the 18th century, although many events were patronized by the upper echelons of society only. About 1730 the German traveller Nemitz referred, in his *Séjour de Paris* (in *F-Pn*), to private events organized at the homes of several illustrious patrons, including the *premier gentilhomme* and English ambassador the Duc d'Aumont, the Prince de Conti Louis-Armand de Bourbon, and Antoine Crozat, *grand trésorier* of the Ordre du Saint-Esprit, and his brother Pierre (fig.8). The Concert Italien, which developed from the Crozats' private concerts, was established in 1724 by Mme de Prie and offered twice-weekly subscription concerts, initially in the Salle du Louvre and from 1726 at the Palais des Tuileries. These, however, were eclipsed by a venture established at a similar time and destined to become the century's most famous concert institution, the Concert Spirituel.

Founded by Anne Danican Philidor, the Concert Spirituel presented its inaugural concert on 18 March 1725 and quickly established a reputation as an important forum for new music and platform for virtuosos of all nationalities. Philidor was granted the privilege by the Opéra to stage concerts of instrumental and sacred music (to Latin texts) on religious feast days when theatres were closed, using the Opéra's own orchestra and soloists; other singers were drawn from the Chapelle Royale and from Parisian churches. The use of French and the performance of operatic scenes were not allowed. Various infringements occurred, particularly from the beginning of 1728 when concerts incorporating secular French music were staged twice a week. This was also the year when Philidor transferred his privilege to Jean-Joseph Mouret, Michel de Lanny and Pierre Simard, who carried out their duties until the Opéra assumed control in 1734.

Concerts were given until 1784 in the specially prepared Salle des Suisses at the Tuileries. The return of Louis XVI to the palace necessitated a move to the Salle des Machines where the acoustics and décor were far inferior. Others occurred in 1789, one year before the Concert Spirituel was disbanded, first to the Salle Favart and then to the Opéra's new home at the Théâtre de la Porte-St-Martin.

Marie Antier and Catherine Lemaure were among the Opéra's soloists to appear during the early years of the

8. *Concert at the home of Monsieur Pierre Crozat: painting by Nicolas Lancret, c1735 (Alte Pinakothek, Munich)*

enterprise; they were followed by Marie Fel, Pierre Jélyotte and, later, by Joseph Legros (who took over the directorship in 1777), Sophie Arnould and Rosalie Levasseur. The vocal repertory of the Concert Spirituel included motets (*grands motets* by Lalande were particularly popular), cantatas, *airs italiens* and, from the mid-century, French oratorios. Italian singers appeared as early as 1726: first Giovanni Battista Palmerini then Domenico Annibali, Maria Monza and, most notably, Caffarelli, who sang two Italian *ariettes* on 5 November 1753. The German tenor Anton Raaff appeared in nine concerts in 1778. Native and foreign instrumentalists contracted by the Concert Spirituel included a host of talented violinists, among them Jean-Baptiste Anet and Jean-Pierre Guignon (who indulged in a contest in 1725) and Jean-Marie Leclair. Parisian audiences were introduced to a variety of Italian sonatas and concertos, and these not only encouraged the dissemination of Italian music in the French capital but also accelerated the transition to the Italian-style violin. Works were often executed by their composers; failing that, Vivaldi's concertos provided an admirable showpiece. Other instrumentalists included the cellists Jean-Pierre and Jean-Louis Duport, and the flautists Michel Blavet and Pierre-Gabriel Buffardin. The installation of a new organ in 1748 (under Joseph-Nicolas-Pancrace Royer's directorship) led to the popularization of the organ concerto, spearheaded by Claude Balbastre between 1755 and 1762; and in the 1760s the Germans Christian Hochbrucker and Philippe-Jacques Meyer created a new vogue for the harp.

From the middle of the century, instrumental works by German and Austrian composers were incorporated with greater frequency into the repertory of the Concert Spirituel. Symphonies by Johann Stamitz, which were the first to include clarinets in Paris, encouraged the orchestra to expand and led to an interest in the French symphony by composers such as François-Joseph Gossec, Simon Leduc and Joseph Boulogne de Saint-Georges. On 15

August 1762 the orchestra dispensed with their *batteur de mesure*, Gaviniès leading the first violins and Nicolas Capron the seconds; by 1775, when the directorship was in the hands of Gaviniès, Gossec and Leduc, the orchestra comprised 58 players (there was also a choir of 44 to support 11 soloists) and rehearsals were efficient and well planned. In the intervening period, Mondonville had served as director (1755–62), programming many of his own compositions, followed by the triumvirate Antoine Dauvergne, Gabriel Capperan and Nicolas-René Joliveau. Symphonies by Haydn were heard from 1777 (fig.9), and in 1778 Mozart's Symphony no.31, K297/300a, received its première. Distinguished soloists in later years included Viotti, Boccherini and Kreutzer.

In 1769 a subscription series known as the Concert des Amateurs was established in Paris. Backed financially by the *fermier général* La Haye and the *intendant général* Claude-François-Marie Rigoley, Comte d'Ogny, concerts

9. *Handbill for a Concert Spirituel, Palais des Tuileries, 2 February 1779*

were given weekly between December and March at the Hôtel de Soubise, conducted by Gossec, and these quickly acquired a high reputation. After Gossec moved to the Concert Spirituel, Saint-Georges became *chef d'orchestre* until the society was disbanded in 1781. It was replaced by the Concert de la Loge Olympique, whose venue until 1786 was the Palais Royal and thereafter was the Salle des Gardes at the Tuileries. Haydn's 'Paris' symphonies (nos.82–7) were commissioned by d'Ogny and performed by the society during their 1787 season; in 1788, the year before the enterprise ceased, its orchestra numbered 74 and was comparable in size to that of the Opéra.

Throughout the century concert life continued to flourish in the homes of musically inclined members of the aristocracy. Between 1731 and 1762 concerts organized by the *fermier général* La Riche de La Pouplinière (initially at his Parisian town house and from 1747 at his château in Passy) were well patronized and introduced some of the century's most important works and performers to the Parisian musical world. La Pouplinière engaged a succession of notable music directors – Rameau, Stamitz and Gossec – and provided opportunities to celebrated and lesser-known musicians of all nationalities. Rameau's *Hippolyte et Aricie* was first performed by La Pouplinière's musicians; and Gossec recounts how, on the advice of Stamitz, this orchestra was the first to introduce horns on a regular basis. Indeed, many important instrumental works performed at the Concert Spirituel were heard first at La Pouplinière's. Another notable patron was Louis-François de Bourbon, Prince de Conti, who, from about 1761 to 1771, held gatherings of writers, politicians, philosophers, artists and musicians, and earned the reputation, after La Pouplinière's death, of hosting the most famous concerts in Paris. Musicians in his employment included Johann Schobert, Jean Joseph Rodolphe, Pierre Vachon, Josef Kohaut and, as *chef d'orchestre*, Jean-Claude Trial.

Until 1789 Parisian concert life, though one of the richest in Europe, remained mainly the pleasure of a social élite. Occasional open-air celebrations enticed a wider public, but it was not until the Revolution that entertainment for the masses began to develop on any significant scale.

3. THEATRES.   For much of the 18th century the main Parisian theatres were engaged in a bitter rivalry born of the monopolies established by Louis XIV and the subvention of these by enterprising entrepreneurs. Of the four public theatres, the Opéra enjoyed the highest status and wielded the greatest power. Royal subsidies were also provided for the Comédie-Française and, from 1723, for the Comédie-Italienne (recalled in 1716 after 19 years' absence): members of both troupes were allowed to style themselves *comédiens ordinaires du roi*. The unofficial Opéra-Comique, while probably the most popular theatre among Parisians, led the most precarious existence (operating seasonally at the fairs of St Germain and St Laurent) until its merger with the Comédie-Italienne in 1762. It had to contend with the jealousies of its official rivals, was entirely dependent on box-office receipts and was surpressed entirely for certain periods.

Although the impression created by the Paris Opéra was of an illustrious and luxurious theatre, the institution was in reality plagued by financial difficulties for much of the 18th century and pursued the least adventurous

programming policy of any Parisian theatre. Far many more old works than new sustained the repertory. At least one opera by Lully was revived each year until 1779, an indication that while Rameau was partially successful in breaking away from the grip of the past, it was Gluck's impact on the *tragédie lyrique* in the 1770s and 80s that proved more significant. Once Gluck's works were established in the Opéra's repertory, the challenge from an influx of Italian composers – premières by Piccinni and Sacchini were given alongside performances of works by Paisiello and Anfossi – proved irresistible. The more varied programming and competition this engendered, manifest in the public controversy between Gluckists and Piccinnists, certainly provided a much-needed boost to the Opéra's revenues, as had the earlier Querelle des Bouffons (1752–4).

For the visitor the Opéra retained much of its splendour and it continued to provide a public setting for the aristocracy. Performances were staged four times a week throughout the year except during Lent. Visitors (though not *habitués*) were impressed by the machinery and decorations, although some were critical of the theatre's small capacity (under 1300). When, in 1763, the old rectangular Palais Royal was razed by fire, the company moved temporarily to the enormous Salle des Machines (cap. 8000) at the Tuileries palace. A new theatre, designed by P.-L. Moreau, was built on the original site and opened in 1770. Architectural improvements, including a rounded interior, allowed for better lines of vision to the stage and increased the capacity to 2000. However, fire again destroyed the building, on 8 June 1781; within a few months a new theatre had been constructed near Porte-St-Martin, and this was to remain the Opéra's home until 1794.

Like the Opéra, the Comédie-Italienne experienced financial problems throughout the 18th century, caused

10. *Interior of the Hôtel de Bourgogne during a performance by the Opéra-Comique: drawing by Pierre-Alexandre Wille, 1767 (F-Pn)*

primarily by continual expansion (without a corresponding increase in revenue) but also by the success of the Opéra-Comique. Initial ploys – recruiting playwrights such as Le Sage and Fuzelier from their rivals and relocating to the fairgrounds once their petitions had forced the regular theatres to close (1721–3) – made little difference to long-term fortunes. However, the repertory it presented at the Hôtel de Bourgogne (fig.10) was perhaps the most diverse of all the Parisian theatres, including Italian farces, French plays, ballets, vaudeville comedies and parodies. Particularly successful were Pierre Baurans' parodies, staged in the 1750s, of Italian pieces heard at the Opéra during the Querelle des Bouffons.

The Opéra-Comique, having survived half a century of vicissitudes, reopened after a seven-year closure in 1752, under the direction of Jean Monnet. The involvement of such figures as Favart, Noverre, Vadé, Dauvergne, Duni and Sedaine brought great success to the venture, prompting sustained machinations by the Comédie-Italienne which led to the merger of the two companies in 1762. The long-term advantage to the Opéra-Comique of playing to audiences throughout the year was offset by the fact that only five of its players were integrated into the new troupe: Laruette, Audinot, Clairval and Mlles Deschamps and Nessel. Attendance revived (most notably on nights when *opéras comiques* were presented) and the varied repertory continued with certain restrictions: opera in Italian, choruses and recitative were all forbidden. On 28 April 1783 the company moved to a new theatre, the Salle Favart (cap. 1282) designed by J.F. Heurtier. The design was less than perfect and various faults were corrected the following year by C. de Wailly.

The centre of Parisian marketplace entertainment shifted after 1762 to the fashionable Boulevard du Temple which, by 1789, boasted several theatres including the Ambigu-Comique. Many of these theatres maintained the ethos of the fair theatres, performing farces, pantomimes, marionette plays and occasional *opéras comiques* and providing rigorous competition for the official establishments.

V. Music at court outside Paris

1. Versailles: (i) 1664–1715 (ii) 1715–89. 2. Fontainebleau. 3. Saint-Cyr. 4. Sceaux. 5. Saint Germain-en-Laye.

1. VERSAILLES.

(i) 1664–1715. During the reign of Louis XIII Versailles was no more than a village in the midst of marshy woodland. Between 1631 and 1634 Louis had a hunting-lodge built there; designed by Philibert de Roy, this small palace had a central building and two wings, which today form three sides of the marble court. Louis XIV ordered that construction begin on a new palace at Versailles soon after he reached the age of majority (23) in 1661. The architect Le Vau (Jules Hardouin-Mansart after 1678), the decorator Le Brun and the landscape architect Le Nôtre laboured for half a century enveloping the hunting-lodge within the most magnificent palace in Europe (fig.11). In 1682 Louis XIV moved permanently to Versailles from Saint Germain-en-Laye. The town that sprang up around the palace housed about 24,000 people by the time of his death.

The king's musicians were known as Officiers du Roy. To be an *officier*, one had to fulfil three conditions: to be

11. *Château de Versailles: engraving by Gabriel or Adam Pérelle, 1660s*

12. Divertissement in the gardens at Versailles, the first day (7 May 1664) of a three-day 'grand divertissement' (known collectively as Les Plaisirs de l'Ile Enchantée) given by Louis XIV to honour his mother, Anne of Austria, and his queen, Marie-Thérèse: engraving by Israël Silvestre, 1664

of good moral character; to profess and practise the Roman Catholic religion; and to possess funds sufficient to buy the post. Succession upon retirement or death was usually accomplished by what was called a *survivance*, in which the *officier* gave the right to inherit the post to a designated relative, or the right to purchase the post to a friend or possibly a student. At Versailles this was one way of building family dynasties of musicians such as the Hotteterre, Philidor, Rebel or Boesset families.

By the end of the reign of Louis XIV, there were between 150 and 200 Officiers du Roy of whom some were housed in the Grande Ecurie. Lully maintained a small apartment there in order to be near the king, and for the same reason Lalande took an apartment bordering the Grand Commun. Musicians of status sought dwellings in the 'Parc-aux-Cerfs' (Lalande, Jacques Danican Philidor), in the rue Dauphine (André Danican Philidor) and in the Avenue de Saint Cloud; others lived in the parish of Notre Dame de Versailles (completed by Mansart in 1686). A small colony of Italian singers, including the castratos Antonio Favalli and Antonio Bagniera, grew up behind the Grande Ecurie in the Avenue de Paris.

The musical history of Versailles began 18 years before Louis XIV finally settled there. In May 1664 he ordered divertissements lasting three days to honour his mother, Anne of Austria, and his queen, Marie-Thérèse. Known collectively as Les Plaisirs de l'Ile Enchantée, they included a carousel, concerts, ballets and the Molière–Lully *comédie-ballet, La princesse d'Elide*; this was the first of the *grands divertissements* of Versailles (fig.12). The second, known as the Fête de Versailles, celebrated the

Peace of Aix-la-Chapelle for a single day (18 July 1668). Its principal divertissement was the Molière–Lully *comédie-ballet, George Dandin*. The third and most ambitious of the Versailles divertissements (4 July to 31 August 1674) celebrated the conquest of the Franche-Comté. Lully's *Alceste* was performed in the marble court on 4 July (fig.13); his *Eglogue de Versailles* on 11 July in a salon constructed in a grove adjacent to the Trianon palace; and his *Les fêtes de l'Amour et de Bacchus* on 28 July in a theatre built next to the 'grotto of the dragon'.

During Louis XIV's lifetime Versailles had no permanent theatre suitable for elaborate stage productions. The Salle des Comédies, a small theatre built in 1682, seated only 350. Vigarani's project of 1685 for a large Salle des Ballets in the north wing of the palace was abandoned. Performances in the palace were held in temporary theatres, such as one built in 1700 in the vestibule between the 'court of the princes' and the gardens; others were built in the Salon de Mars and in the *grands appartements*. More elaborate productions took place on hastily constructed stages in the marble court (*Alceste*, 1674), in the two pavilions flanking the fountain of the Renommée, on the Grand Canal after its completion in 1672, at the Trianon and in wooded glades. After 1681 the riding-school in the Grande Ecurie was often converted into a theatre.

Although stage productions comparable to the *grands divertissements* were rare in the 1680s and 1690s, Versailles saw the first performances of Lully's *Phaëton* (6 January 1683) and *Roland* (8 January 1685, in the Grande Ecurie). Among other large-scale stage works performed either in their entirety or in selected acts at Versailles were Lully's *Persée* (1682, in the Grande Ecurie), *Atys* (1682), *Temple de la paix* (1685), *Thésée* (1688), *Acis et Galatée* (1695) and *Armide* (1710); Lalande's *Les fontaines de Versailles* (1683), *Epithalame* (1685, music lost), *Le ballet de la jeunesse* (1686), Desmarets' ballet or serenade (1691); Desmarets' *Endymion* (1686, music lost); Lorenzani's *Nicandre e Fileno* (1681); Collasse's *Thétis et Pélée* (1689) and *Enée et Lavinie* (1690); and André Danican Philidor's *Le canal de Versailles* (1687) and *Le mariage de la grosse Cathos* (1688).

The later years of Louis XIV's reign (1690–1715) were marked by military defeats, economic and social crises and personal tragedies. Under the pious eye of Mme de Maintenon the monarch withdrew more and more from active social life ('The king never attends public concerts or the theatre', Dangeau's *Journal*, 9 October 1704), and the town houses of Paris and country châteaux gradually replaced Versailles as centres of aristocratic entertainment. Music, however, continued to play an important role in the daily life of the king, as indicated by the *Journal* of the Marquis de Dangeau (1684–1720). In addition to the ever-present ceremonial music the king heard private performances of chamber and solo works and favourite comedies. Three evenings a week were set aside for musical entertainments under the generic title of *appartements*. Among the king's favourite musicians for his *appartements* were Germain Pinel (lute), Marie-Anne and Jeanne de Lalande, Anne de La Barre, Mlle Hilaire (singers), Robert de Visée (guitar), Decoteaux and Philibert Rebillé (flutes), Antoine Forqueray and Marais (viols), Jacquet de La Guerre and François Couperin (harpsichord) and Jean-Féry Rebel (violin).

Dangeau recorded that normally the king took his supper in bed at 10 o'clock. 'Ordinarily he would order Vize [Robert de Visée] to come and play his guitar at about 9 o'clock' (11 May 1686). On festive days the king's dinner was always accompanied by music, mostly orchestral extracts chosen from Lully's operas and from Lalande's *Sinphonies pour les soupers du Roi*.

François Couperin's *Concerts royaux* were performed for Louis XIV at Versailles on selected Sundays in 1714 and 1715. In the published edition (1722) Couperin supplied the names of his musicians for these *petits concerts de chambre*: they were François Duval (violin), André Danican Philidor (oboe and bassoon), Hilaire Verloge (viol), Dubois (oboe and bassoon) and Couperin himself (harpsichord).

On St Louis' Day (25 August) in 1715, just seven days before his death, the ailing king heard the oboes and drums of the musicians of the Grande Ecurie playing under his window for his *reveil*, and on the same day he even 'wished to hear the 24 Violons perform in his antechamber during dinner' (Dangeau, 25 August 1715).

For administrative purposes music at the court of Louis XIV was organized into three large groups: Musique de la Chambre, Musique de la Grande Ecurie and Musique de la Chapelle Royale. These divisions continued until 1761, when for economic reasons the Chapelle and the Chambre were combined.

(a) Musique de la Chambre.   During the 17th and 18th centuries two men, each serving a six-month term, were

13. *Performance of Lully's tragédie lyrique 'Alceste', Cour de Marbre, Versailles, 4 July 1674: engraving by Jean Le Pautre from 'Les divertissements de Versailles, 1674' (Paris, 1676)*

appointed to the position of *surintendant* of the Musique de la Chambre. They were responsible for the choice of secular music at court performances, for distributing parts to performers, for overseeing the many rehearsals and for administrative details. Among the most important *surintendants* were J.B. Boësset, Lully, Collasse, Lalande, Collin de Blamont and Destouches.

Aiding the *surintendant* and attending to the musical education of the Chambre's young musicians (known as *pages*) was the *maître de musique de la chambre*. The third administrative division was that of *compositeur de la chambre*, whose specific tasks were often reflected in special titles: *compositeur de la musique instrumentale* (Lazarini, Lully) or *compositeur des entrées des ballets* (Beauchamps, Ballon).

The musicians of the Chambre numbered about eight solo singers, a harpsichordist, two lutenists, one theorbist, four flautists, three viol players and four violinists.

Financed as part of the Chambre and technically *officiers* of the Chambre, the 24 Violons du Roi (actually 25 by 1663) were an autonomous group (fig.15). The *Etat de la France* for various years give a profile of this famous string orchestra, which played for royal ballets, for coronations and marriages, and for the king's dinner on festive days such as New Year's Day, May Day and St Louis' Day. The distribution of parts within the typical five-part texture of French 17th-century instrumental music were as follows: six first violins, six bass violins and four each of the three inner voices, all tuned as the modern viola.

The Petits Violons came under the jurisdiction of the Cabinet rather than the Chambre. Reserved for those musicians whose presence the king deemed indispensable, the Cabinet functioned as an administrative annexe to the Chambre. At some time after March 1653 the king assigned the Petits Violons to Lully, who first directed them in the court ballet *La galanterie du temps*. In 1702 the *Etat de la France* detailed the tasks of the Petits Violons (by then called the Violons du Cabinet): 'They

number 21, and they follow the king on all of his travels. They are usually used in all of the divertissements of His Majesty such as serenades, balls, ballets, comedies, operas, *appartements* and other private concerts'. The Petits Violons were suppressed about 1715; the 24 Violons continued in existence until 1761.

(b) Musique de la Grande Ecurie.   The musicians of the Grande Ecurie provided music to accompany the pomp and ceremony for the *grand siècle*. Under Louis XIV they were divided into five categories consisting of about 40 instrumentalists: trumpets (12 players), fifes and drums (eight), violins, oboes, sackbuts and cornetts (12), six additional oboes and musettes, and six players of crumhorns and trumpets marine. The four best trumpet players were always available to precede the royal coach on horseback. The famous 12 Grands Hautbois du Roi (ten oboes and two bassoons) had only three annual official duties (the *levers* of the king on New Year's Day, May Day and on St Louis' Day); at other times they combined with the 24 Violons or the Petits Violons in court entertainments.

All the musicians of the Grande Ecurie were available for the many ceremonies attending foreign dignitaries, such as the envoys from Siam (1686) and the ambassadors from Persia (1715). They were the chief source of music for parades and outdoor *fêtes*, they accompanied the king to *parlement* and their fanfares were heard both on the battlefield and during the hunt.

For ceremonial music the king also had at his disposal the four trumpets and drums of his Gardes du Corps, the six trumpets of his Gendarmerie Françoise, the fifes and drums of his Swiss Guards and the four oboes and drums of his Musketeers.

(c) Musique de la Chapelle Royale.   Louis XIV took an active interest in the music of his Chapelle Royale long before his permanent move to Versailles. In 1663 he chose four *sous-maîtres* (Du Mont, Expilly, Robert, Gobert), rather than the customary two; each took a quarter of the

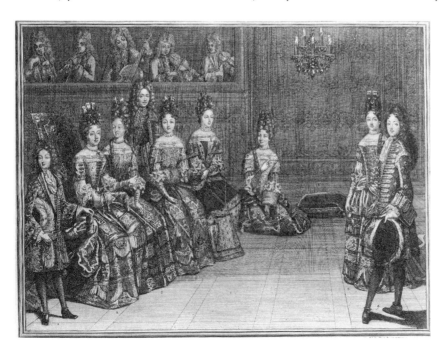

14. *Music room of the fourth chamber of the queen's apartments at Versailles: engraving by Antoine Trouvain, 1696*

15. One of the 24 Violons du Roi, dressed in characteristic uniform: engraving by Nicolas Arnoult, 1688

year's work. In 1678 he apointed four organists (Nivers, Lebègue, Thomelin, Buterne). After the death of two *sous-maîtres* and the retirement of Robert and Du Mont in 1683 he announced a solemn competition for four replacements; there were 35 competitors. He himself intervened to assure a position for Lalande; Minoret, Goupillet and Collasse obtained the others. By virtue of his talent and the death of his colleagues Lalande had charge of the entire year at the Chapelle Royale by 1714. Between 1684 and 1686 50 motets composed for soloists, chorus and orchestra by Du Mont, Lully and Robert were printed at the order of the king, establishing the *grand motet* as the favoured religious genre of the period.

A *sous-maître* had authority comparable to that of the *surintendant* of the Musique de la Chambre. He trained the choir and chose or composed the music for the king's Mass (a *Messe basse solennelle*) and other religious ceremonies. His superior, the *maître*, was normally a highly-placed ecclesiastic, not a musician.

The *Etat de la France* for 1708 summarizes the singers under the *sous-maître*: 11 sopranos, 18 *hautes-contres*, 23 tenors, 24 baritones and 14 basses. The sopranos were male falsettists (*dessus mues*), castratos (*dessus italiens*) and boy sopranos (*pages*); women were used on occasion towards the end of the reign of Louis XIV, and Mlle Hortense Desjardins was given a post in 1722. Cornetts lent support to the sopranos when necessary. In 1708 the orchestra of the Chapelle comprised six violins and violas, four bass violins, two flutes, two oboes, a bassoon, a crumhorn and two serpents.

Curiously Versailles did not have a setting worthy of the *grands motets* until late in the king's life. The first chapel (1664) was only a little larger than a salon; the second (1670–73) was a large single-storey salon in the queen's wing; the third (1673–82) was built in the king's wing on the site of the Salon de Sacre; the fourth (from 1682), on two levels, was on the site of the Salon d'Hercule (see Himelfarb, 1984). The splendid final chapel that still stands was begun by Mansart and completed in 1710 by Robert de Cotte (fig.16).

Some of the music heard at Versailles during the reign of Louis XIV survives thanks to copies made from about 1680 to 1730 by the king's librarian, André Danican Philidor *l'aîné*, and his *atelier*. Separate parts as well as full scores exist for the most popular operas, divertissements, *concerts* and *grands motets*. There is also selected music from the reigns of earlier monarchs from François I to Louis XIII. The 'Collection Philidor' is dispersed; the most important holdings are now at the Bibliothèque Municipale of Versailles (*F-V*) and the Bibliothèque Nationale (*F-Pn*).

(ii) 1715–89. After a regency spent mainly in Paris, Louis XV reinstated the château of Versailles, one of several royal palaces, as his court's official residence in 1725. The young king maintained the musical structure of the Chambre, the Grand Ecurie and the Chapelle, but throughout his reign displayed a greater passion for architecture and science than for music. Louis XV's consort Marie Leczinska, his mistress Mme de Pompadour and, later, Louis XVI's consort Marie Antoinette were all to animate musical and theatrical life at Versailles.

Marie Leczinksa and her children played several instruments – Mme Henriette was painted by Nattier performing on the bass viol (*see* VIOL, fig.12) – and the queen established concerts (the Concerts de la Reine) that took place in her Grand Cabinet. Programmes included cantatas, motets and instrumental music by Lalande, Leclair, Destouches and Campra, among others, as well as individual acts of operas. Italian musicians were well received, the memoirs of the Duc de Luynes recounting visits by Bordoni, Cuzzoni and Farinelli. More spectacular were the lavish productions staged to celebrate important royal occasions: a hastily erected theatre in the Grande Ecurie served, in 1745, as the venue for Rameau's *La princesse de Navarre*, commissioned in honour of the dauphin's marriage to Maria Teresa of Spain. Other operas by Rameau received their premières under such circumstances at Versailles.

Mme de Pompadour's arrival at court highlighted the vogue for amateur theatricals among the aristocracy in the 18th century. In 1747 she launched her Théâtre des Petits Cabinets, initially intended as a social diversion for an intimate gathering of friends in her private apartments (fig.17). In less than two years the growth of her project necessitated a move to a larger venue; with the Duc de la Vallière as director, the librettist Paradis de Moncrif served as *sous-directeur*, François Rebel as *chef d'orchestre* and Dehesse as *maître de ballet*. The company's repertory began by mixing plays with operas, but musical works came to predominate, particularly those with a pastoral emphasis. In all, 33 different operas were staged, around one third newly commissioned, with Mme de Pompadour generally taking the leading role. Notable premières included Rameau's *Les surprises de l'Amour* (1748). Excessive costs led the king to intervene and

16. Interior of the royal chapel at Versailles, begun by Jules Hardouin Mansart, 1699, and completed by Robert de Cotte, 1710

abandon the enterprise in 1750 – performances continued until 1753 at Bellevue – and in 1761 he ordered that the Chambre be merged with the Chapelle.

The construction of a permanent theatre at Versailles, a project first planned by Louis XIV, was finally realized in 1770 under the direction of the architect A.-J. Gabriel (visiting troupes up until this time had performed in either the Cour des Princes or the Grand Ecurie). The inaugural performance on 16 May of Lully's *Persée* celebrated the dauphin's marriage to Marie Antoinette. After the death of Louis XV in 1774 the new queen resurrected the fashion for amateur performance at her private theatre in the Trianon. Here *opéras comiques* by important composers of the day were staged, Marie Antoinette taking such leading roles as Jenny (Monsigny's *Le roi et le fermier*) and Colette (Rousseau's *Le devin du village*).

2. FONTAINEBLEAU.   The château of Fontainebleau, situated some 70 km south of Paris, originated in the 12th

century but was enlarged during the reign of François I (1515–47). The building programme continued during subsequent reigns, and the interior of the château was much enriched by Louis XIII (reigned 1610–43). While the abundant hunting attracted the French court to the area (and had done so since the 12th century), there were also evening entertainments in the château. During the reign of Louis XIV concerts, operas and plays were performed by the king's royal musicians, members of the Académie Royale de Musique and the leading theatrical troupes in Paris. Indeed, when the country's finances permitted, the annual *voyage* to Fontainebleau, usually in the early autumn, resulted in a showcase for the performing arts symbolic of the wealth, power and magnificence of both the court and the country at large.

A variety of the larger rooms and galleries served as performance venues in the château; however, it was in the Salle de la Belle Cheminée that the majority of theatrical

17. *Théâtre des Petits Cabinets, with Mme de Pompadour in a performance of Lully's 'Acis et Galatée', 1749: engraving after Charles-Nicolas Cochin II*

and operatic performances were given. A stage equipped with machinery was installed by 1682, although no fixed seating was introduced at this time. The theatre was renovated for the wedding of Louis XV in 1725, and stage boxes and balconies were installed to increase the seating area. At the same time, a partitioned area for an orchestra was introduced. A subsequent renovation, completed for the *voyage* of 1754, increased the available seating and corrected problems with the stage itself. The theatre's maximum capacity appears to have been around 700. While the narrow width of the building created problems which were never fully resolved, this theatre was probably the court's finest until the construction of the Versailles opera house in 1770.

Many operatic works were performed at the château. Louis XIV supervised the rehearsals of Destouches' new works there, including *Issé* (1697), *Amadis de Grèce* (1698) and *Omphale* (1700). A renewed emphasis on opera during the second half of the 18th century resulted in premières of works by Rameau, Mondonville, La Borde, Francœur, Grétry and others. Rousseau left an amusing account of the first performance of his *Le devin du village* (1752) in his *Confessions*. During the reign of Louis XVI, works by foreign-born composers (notably Gluck, Piccinni, Salieri and Sacchini) were presented. The triumphant première of Piccinni's *Didon* took place at the château in 1783.

Louis XVI's court did not return to Fontainebleau after 1786. Restored by Napoleon, the château remained popular with the court during the Restoration and the Second Empire, although the association with music, and opera in particular, declined. Fire destroyed the theatre in 1856, and a new, smaller theatre was installed in the Louis XV wing in the following year.

3. SAINT-CYR.   Mme de Maintenon established the Maison Royale St-Louis de Saint-Cyr in the village of Saint-Cyr, just west of Versailles, in June 1686 with the approval of her husband Louis XIV. The school was designed to house about 250 daughters of impoverished army officers and noblemen and to educate them in the pious and simple virtues. Its importance lies in the amount of music composed for the 'usage de l'église et communauté des dames et demoiselles . . . à Saint-Cyr'.

In 1688 Mme de Maintenon commissioned Racine to write a tragedy combining piety with diversion. *Esther*, with incidental music by Jean-Baptiste Moreau, was given its first complete performance on 26 January 1689 before an audience including Louis XIV and Bossuet. There were four revivals the following month, one of which was attended by the recently exiled James II and Queen Mary of England. Although Mme de Maintenon found her young charges more eager to sing the melodies of *Esther* than the psalms, she permitted a second Racine–Moreau tragedy, *Athalie*, to be performed (5 January 1691) – this time without décor and costumes. Recognizing the power of music to distract her charges, Mme de Maintenon exercised considerable control over the music performed at Saint-Cyr. She found, for example, too many ornaments and extended vocal melismas in certain motets by Nivers and went so far as to forbid the performance of one of these, *Adjuro vos*, which she deemed 'trop tendre'.

Two other composers contributed to the musical life of Saint-Cyr: Nivers, who was organist and singing teacher from 1686 to his death in 1714, and his successor Louis-Nicolas Clérambault, who held the position until 1721, when he was replaced by his son, César-François-Nicolas.

Between them Nivers and Clérambault composed almost 100 motets for one or two solo voices alternating with a two-part chorus; many are without continuo. The extensive music section of the Saint-Cyr library (now in *F-Pn* and *F-V*) also included motets by Lalande, Campra and Mondonville; Racine's *cantiques spirituelles* in musical settings by Lalande, Moreau, Collasse and Marchand; sacred cantatas by Clérambault; *airs spirituels* by L'Affilard, Nivers and Clérambault; and noëls by Pellegrin and Colletet. Besides Moreau's incidental music for *Esther* and *Athalie* the library had simplified versions of *Jephté* by Nivers and *Iphigénie* by Campra and Desmarets, in addition to arrangements of Lully's operatic prologues and three manuscript collections of dances. The Maison Royale was closed in 1793.

4. SCEAUX.   The château at Sceaux, designed by Perrault and decorated by Lebrun, was a favourite site for court entertainments throughout the reign of Louis XIV. On 16 July 1685, for example, the Marquis de Seignlay provided a divertissement for the king and the court that included

a performance of the pastorale *Idylle sur la paix* by Racine with music by Lully.

Louis-Auguste de Bourbon, the Duke of Maine, purchased the château in 1699 for his talented wife Anne-Louise de Bourbon. The duchess soon surrounded herself with a *pléiade* of well-known musicians and poets. In *Les divertissemens de Sceaux* of 1712, Abbé Genest described her divertissements as 'pure amusement, unrehearsed . . . a type of impromptu entertainment'. During this early period, from 1702 to 1714, the divertissements often took place not at Sceaux but at the nearby château of Châtenay, owned by Nicolas de Malezieu. The only composer mentioned during this period is Matho. In 1714 the duchess initiated her famous Grandes Nuits de Sceaux – diversions on a grand scale. The most important of these took place on 16 evenings between 31 July 1714 and 15 May 1715. Despite the disapproval of Saint-Simon ('Sceaux was more than ever the theatre of the follies of the Duchess of Maine . . . [and] of the ruin of her husband'), the Grandes Nuits became the most fashionable aristocratic entertainment at the close of the reign of *le roi soleil*.

Many of the productions called for music; among the composers employed were Mouret, Bernier, Bourgeois, Collin de Blamont, Courbois and Marchand (probably one of the 'Versailles Marchands', perhaps Pierre-Nicolas, rather than Louis). Most of the music was composed by Mouret, who was *surintendant* of the duchess's music from 1709 to about 1730.

Lyric comedies (e.g. Mouret's *Les amours de Ragonde*), plays, dramatic divertissements, ballets *en action* (long before Cahusac and Noverre) and cantatas (e.g. Bernier's *Les nuits de Sceaux*, 1715) were performed in a garden setting designed by Le Nôtre. The Grandes Nuits de Sceaux ended abruptly with the death of Louis XIV.

5. SAINT GERMAIN-EN-LAYE.   French kings began using Saint Germain-en-Laye as a residence in the Middle Ages. By the mid-17th century the town had a population of about 10,000 and boasted two châteaux. François I had the *château vieux* almost completely reconstructed, retaining only the 13th-century chapel and the 14th-century keep. Louis XIV had a commodious *salle des comédies* with loges constructed in the west wing. It accommodated the large, elaborate machines of C. Vigarani (see Massip, 1976, pp.118–19) and had a rehearsal hall. The *château neuf* was built for Henri II, enlarged by Henri IV and demolished by Charles X. Louis XIV was born in the *château neuf* in 1638, just five years before Louis XIII died there.

As the favoured royal residence of Louis XIV before his move to Versailles, Saint Germain-en-Laye witnessed all manner of court entertainments. The following Lully ballets were first performed there: *Les muses* (1666); *La pastorale comique* (1667); *Le Sicilien* (1667); *Les amants magnifiques* (1670, when Louis XIV appeared as dancer for the last time); *Ballet des ballets* (1671); and *Le triomphe de l'amour* (1681). Some of Lully's operas were first performed there too; *Thésée* (1675); *Atys* (1676; see fig.18); *Isis* (1677); and *Proserpine* (1680).

The court's move to Versailles in 1682–3 naturally diminished the number of *fêtes* performed at Saint Germain-en-Laye. However, a second flowering occurred when Louis XIV invited the exiled English King James II to settle there (1690–1701) with his son, who continued the Stuart court as James III (1701–12). An Italian,

18. *Set by Carlo Vigarani for Lully's 'Atys' (Act 5 scene vi), Saint Germain-en-Laye, 10 January 1676: engraving by Lalouette after François Chauveau from the libretto*

Innocenzo Fede (*b* 1661), was their *maître de musique*. During the later period, this court must have been a 'centre of intense musical activity' (Corp, 1995, p.222). Besides Fede's music for the royal chapel, the repertory included Italian arias, sonatas and cantatas. The Bibliothèque Nationale preserves these today in a collection of seven volumes copied under Philidor's direction.

VI. 1789–1870

The period from the Revolution to the fall of the Second Empire was one of extreme instability in French society and politics. There was an enormous growth in industry and in urban living, great advances were made in pure and applied science, and by 1830 the government was controlled by a wealthy middle class. The social changes of the period are an essential background feature of French Romanticism, and the impact of these changes created crises of conscience in many artists.

From the fall of the Bastille (14 July 1789) to the fall of Robespierre (27 July 1794) the Revolution took its most radical course; the Directory (1795–9) was a period of consolidation. On 9 November 1799 Napoleon's *coup d'état* of Brumaire established the Consulate, and in 1804 he crowned himself emperor in Paris. The period ended with Napoleon's abdication (1814) and defeat at Waterloo (18 June 1815).

The Bourbon Restoration saw first the moderate but weak Louis XVIII (king from 1814), who was followed by the right-wing, pro-clerical Charles X in 1824. Charles' repressive measures prompted the Revolution of 1830. Louis-Philippe's constitutional 'July Monarchy' (1830–48) oversaw the prosperity of the commercial class and the increasing and sometimes active discontent of the working class. Socialist theory and organization became firmly established. In 1848 the monarchy was overthrown and the Second Republic founded with Louis Napoleon, nephew of Napoleon I, as president; in 1852 he was elected emperor, thus becoming Napoleon III. This Second Empire lasted until 3 September 1870.

1. Religious institutions. 2. Patronage. 3. Opera companies, theatres. 4. Concert life. 5. Education. 6. Criticism, publishing and instrument making.

1. RELIGIOUS INSTITUTIONS.   The Chapelle Royale in the Tuileries had 35 instrumentalists when it was closed down in 1792. Napoleon reinstituted the Chapelle a decade later, bringing the orchestra up to 50 and the choir to 34 by 1810; he also had a new building constructed by early 1806. Paisiello was the initial director of music, with responsibility for composition, and was succeeded in 1804 by Le Sueur. J.P.E. Martini was co-director in 1814, and he was replaced on his death in 1816 by Cherubini. C.-H. Plantade was the *maître de musique* from about 1814 until the dissolution of the new Chapelle Royale in the July Revolution of 1830; by that time 115 persons were attached to it, including 54 singers. Napoleon III re-established the Chapelle; in 1862 Auber was *maître de chapelle* and Tilmant conductor.

Immediately before the Revolution, in 1786–7, Le Sueur had mounted his own large-scale orchestral and choral music at Notre Dame. Other churches saw large forces, often augmented by amateur musicians, on special occasions; normally, however, the organ and small ensembles or a serpent sufficed. By the end of 1792 organized Christian worship had ceased in Paris, but the situation was alleviated by Napoleon's Concordat of 1801. Meanwhile some churches were converted between 1793 and 1794 for the practice of 'natural' religion, particularly the Culte de l'Etre Suprême, and it seems probable that singing was accompanied by groups of orchestral instruments.

From 1802 recovery in Christian worship was slow; the Church was impoverished and its music at a low ebb. By 1813 cathedrals and parishes in France were reduced musically to plainchant, and competent organists were few. A handful of *maîtrises* were re-established with state help from 1813. Paris was one such privileged diocese (see §5 below), but lack of consistent funds meant that little distinctive musical activity was carried on before the mid-19th century. By then the poor level of musical taste in worship had become a cause for public concern. The government responded in 1853 by giving support to Niedermeyer's Ecole de Musique Religieuse et Classique, with the intention that this school should train personnel to revivify church music and the *maîtrises* throughout France.

Important events in the history of the organ in Paris were the appointment of François Benoist as organ professor at the Conservatoire (1819) and that of the virtuoso Boëly, one of the earlier French exponents of Bach's music, to St Germain-l'Auxerrois (1837). Noted organists of the succeeding generation appointed to important Parisian churches in the late 1850s and early 1860s were Antoine Batiste and Bazille (both at St Eustache), Louis Lefébure-Wély (St Sulpice, 1863), Charles Chauvet (St Merry, 1866; Trinité, 1869), Gigout (St Augustin, 1863), Saint-Saëns (Madeleine, 1857) and Franck (Ste Clotilde, 1859). Technique in general, and especially pedal technique, was probably not highly developed, for much of the inherited repertory consisted of arrangements of opera pieces requiring little or no pedal work. Credit for reforming that situation is due to Franck and his epoch-making *Six pièces* (1860–62), to the inspiration afforded by the model playing of the Belgian J.N. Lemmens (and his teacher Adolf Friedrich Hesse), and most profoundly to the builder Cavaillé-Coll, who systematically rebuilt many Parisian instruments (including those of Notre Dame, Ste Clotilde, St Sulpice and the Trinité), providing the means for the later achievements of the composer-performers Widor and Guilmant. His first design (1833), for the abbey church of St Denis, was realized in 1841.

2. PATRONAGE.   The Revolution temporarily stopped aristocratic and bourgeois patronage, substituting little by direct means. The foundation of the Conservatoire by the state in 1795 (see §5 below), however, created many new salaried teaching posts, which were relatively secure and carried prestige. During the Napoleonic era, the Bourbon restoration and the July monarchy the state commissioned a few works from composers for ceremonies, for example Berlioz's *Grande messe des morts* (1837) and *Symphonie funèbre et triomphale* (1840, for the tenth anniversary of the 1830 Revolution).

Napoleon's amnesty for the exiles led to an early return of private patronage. A press report of May 1803 notes that 'M. and Mme Ladurner entertained a brilliant circle where, among others, amateurs and distinguished virtuosos were heard'. Thus musical salons continued from the old century to the new. The fortunes made by industrialists, bankers and others made Paris immensely wealthy. Fashionable pianists such as Liszt, Chopin and Sigismund Thalberg were patronized as expensive teachers. Chopin gave as few as seven public recitals in Paris, but gave eight or nine piano lessons a day at 20 francs a lesson. Charles Hallé was asked to educate a banker's family simply by playing the piano to them one evening a week. Wealthy publishers also became patrons: Armand Bertin of the *Journal des débats* ran a salon and was rumoured to have been the source of Paganini's gift of 20,000 francs to Berlioz in 1838; Maurice Schlesinger, the music publisher who also ran the *Gazette musicale*, sponsored concerts and supported the young Richard Wagner (1840–42) with commissions and with money; and the Erard family of music publishers and manufacturers were also powerful patrons. A successful début in the theatre was of great consequence for a composing career, and the directors of the various opera houses wielded great influence since they could commission or refuse operas for production. As 'commercial patrons', however, they could not afford to allow conflicts of taste between the composer and the public.

From time to time a number of awards for composition were instituted, often biassed towards opera: the Prix Cressent (opera, *opéra comique*); Prix Rossini (lyrical or sacred composition); Prix Mombinne (*opéra comique*); Prix de Saussay (librettos); Prix Nicolo (vocal composition); and the Prix Chartier (instituted 1861 for chamber music). The music Prix de Rome was founded in 1803 and awarded annually until 1968 by the Académie des Beaux-Arts to composition students; winners spent four years at the Villa Medici, sending their work back to Paris. This prize immediately gave a certain degree of recognition to young composers, some of whom began writing stage works in Italy.

3. OPERA COMPANIES, THEATRES. The story of opera and theatre life in Paris is particularly complex because of the way in which companies and theatres were named. The Opéra commonly means the Académie Royale (or Impériale) de Musique, but it can also refer to the building used at any one time by that company; this practice was also common among other companies and theatres. A building might also be known by the name of a previous patron or company, and theatres quite often burnt down and were rebuilt elsewhere, to be christened with the name of an old or new company, or an old or new patron. Only the most important of the Parisian companies and theatres are discussed below.

Laws passed in 1791–2 that made it possible for anybody to open a public theatre profoundly changed the status quo; the resulting abundance of new spectacles included *opéra comique*, melodrama and vaudeville. Under the Empire an evident increase in the number of debased entertainments led Napoleon in 1807 to reduce the total number of theatres to eight: the Opéra, Opéra-Comique, Théâtre Italien (Théâtre de l'imperatrice, later Odéon), Théâtre Français, Vaudeville, Variétés, Gaîté and Ambigu-Comique. The first three were the 'official' musical theatres, but the others all possessed small orchestras. Under the Restoration the Théâtre de la Porte-St-Martin and the Gymnase opened, performing lighter pieces, and the Théâtre Italien became a strong rival to the Opéra and the Opéra-Comique. The immense variety and vitality of the Parisian musical stage is seen especially in companies like the Ambigu-Comique, whose repertory is forgotten, but which achieved high standards and originality within the limits of its activity.

(i) The Opéra. The principal opera company of Paris underwent several changes of title as the result of political events. The main ones were, from 1791, Théâtre de l'Opéra; from 1794, Théâtre des Arts; from 1804, Académie Impériale de Musique; and from 1814, Académie Royale de Musique, except for the Hundred Days. The company also occupied several theatres: from 1781, Théâtre de la Porte-St-Martin; from 1794, Théâtre Montansier (cap. 1650); during 1820–21, the first Salle Favart and the Salle Louvois (Broignart, 1791); and from 16 August 1821, the new permanent premises in the rue Le Peletier (built by Debret, cap. 1954; fig.19). Gas lighting, which revolutionized stage effects, was introduced in 1822.

The Opéra was administered by the City of Paris during much of the 1790s, but Napoleon gradually arrogated it. In 1802 he retained the right to determine expenses for new works; his Minister of the Interior had the power of veto. In the reforms of 1807, when Picard became director, Napoleon sought to make the Opéra the privileged state showpiece it had traditionally been; he exercised influence over the selection of the repertory and in 1811 imposed dues payable to the Opéra by smaller theatres, fully restoring the position under the *ancien régime*, arrangements that persisted until the July Monarchy. Directorships, including those of Viotti (from 1819) and Habeneck (from 1821), tended to be of short duration; conductors during this period were Jean-Baptiste Rey (i) (until his death in 1810), Persuis (until 1817), Rodolphe Kreutzer (until 1824) and Habeneck and Valentino (until 1831). The orchestra was large, with an average of 70 players, and maintained a high standard, owing its fame not least to soloists like Baillot, Gustave

Vogt and Dauprat. Conversely the French style of dramatic singing was often censured. Gradually the impact of Italian singing was felt, particularly through the influence of Rossini. Famous female singers at the Opéra included Branchu, Gavaudan, Dorus-Gras, Malibran, Viardot and Cinti-Damoreau, and male singers Lays, Adolphe and Louis Nourrit, Derivis, Lainez and later Lafont, Duprez and Faure.

Important premières at the Opéra included Le Sueur's *Ossian* (1804), Spontini's *La vestale* (1807) and *Fernand Cortez* (1809) and Kreutzer's *Abel* (1810). Earlier works were constantly revived, for example Gluck's *Orphée* (1800) and *Alceste* (1803) and Rousseau's *Le devin du village* (1810). Famous works were imported from elsewhere; Mozart's *Le nozze di Figaro* was seen in 1793, *Die Zauberflöte* (as *Les mystères d'Isis*) in 1801 and *Don Giovanni* in 1805, though all three in mutilated form. Rossini appeared with *Le siège de Corinthe* in 1826, *Moïse* (1827) and *Le comte Ory* (1828), three scores revised from earlier works. His only original work for the Parisian stage was *Guillaume Tell* (1829), which, with Auber's revolution-inciting *La muette de Portici* (1828), established the style of French grand opera which became current during the reign of Louis-Philippe. This almost always involved a historical or semi-historical plot; there were large casts, sumptuous costumes, highly realistic scenery and complex stage machinery. Under the directorship of Véron (1831–5) this formula was exploited with signal acumen in Meyerbeer's *Robert le diable* (1831); his librettist, Eugène Scribe (fig.20), became a specialist in providing texts for these sometimes bloodcurdling spectacles, such as Auber's *Gustave III* (1833) and Halévy's *La Juive* (1835). It would be hard to overestimate the role played by Ciceri, the Opéra's chief designer from 1824 to 1847, whose designs corresponded to the intentions of grand opera. Following the staggering reception accorded Meyerbeer's *Les Huguenots* (1836) this species declined in quality, if not quantity. The directorships of Duponchel (1835–41) and Pillet (1841–7) were notable mainly for the tragic failure of Berlioz's *Benvenuto Cellini* (1838), the commissioning of Donizetti's *La favorite* (1840) and an authentic version of Weber's *Der Freischütz* (1841), given in French with recitatives by Berlioz.

Conductors from the July Monarchy on were Habeneck (1831–46), Girard (1846–60), Dietsch (1860–63) and Hainl (1863–72). The early part of the Second Empire and the directorships of Roqueplan (1847–54), Crosnier (1854–6) and Royer (1856–62) were largely uneventful. Meyerbeer's position as the leading figure in grand opera was confirmed with *Le prophète* (1849), and he exerted a strong influence on Verdi's French opera, *Les vêpres siciliennes*, which had its première at the Opéra in 1855. Gounod's early *Sapho* (1851) and *La Nonne sanglante* (1854), an avowedly Meyerbeerian piece, made an inauspicious beginning. The first performance of the Opéra version of Wagner's *Tannhäuser*, with the obligatory ballet, took place on 13 March 1861. Meyerbeer's reputation was reaffirmed after his death (1864) with *L'Africaine* (1865) and by his pervasive influence on Verdi's second Opéra commission, *Don Carlos* (1867). Gounod's *Faust* (Théâtre Lyrique, 1859) quickly established itself as a classic in its Opéra version (1869). Before this time, as far back as 1852, few memorable new French works had been staged: the two by Gounod above and his artfully Meyerbeerian *La reine de Saba* (1862),

19. *Interior of the Opéra in the rue Le Peletier during a performance of Meyerbeer's 'Robert le diable', first performed 21 November 1831: colour lithograph by Jules Arnout*

Herculanum by Félicien David (1859) and *Hamlet* by Ambroise Thomas (1868).

Ballet was at least as popular as opera, and ballets were normally worked into operatic evenings (as in *Tannhäuser*) if they did not actually round off the opera itself. Several ballets, now forgotten, remained very popular; in the period up to 1830 at least, that could be said of few new operas. Notable ballets included Catel's *Alexandre chez Apelles* (1808) on account of its large measure of original music, Sor's *Cendrillon* (1823), and *La fille mal gardée* (1828) with music arranged and composed by Hérold. There followed Adolphe Adam's second ballet *Giselle* (1841) and Burgmüller's sequel *La péri* (1843; fig.21), both with choreography by Jean Coralli. Adam remained the foremost writer of ballet music until his *Le corsair* (1856). No comparable figure appeared until Delibes, who first collaborated with Minkus on *La source* (1866), and whose *Coppélia* (1870) was the last important work to be given in the old Opéra building before it burnt down on 29 October 1873. The outstanding dancers and choreographers came from the Vestris and Gardel families; Louis Antoine Duport was a rival of Auguste Vestris. Later male dancers included Jules Perrot, the greatest before Nizhinsky, and Lucien and Marius Petipa. Notable ballerinas were Maria Taglioni (the Sylphide) and Carlotta Grisi (Giselle), with some competition from Fanny Elssler.

(ii) Théâtre Italien (Comédie-Italienne, Théâtre Favart, later Opéra-Comique). This well-established company did not present Italian works during the period under consideration but was a French company in which *opéra comique* as a form matured with the works of Grétry and Dalayrac. It moved to the Salle Favart in 1783. In the

1790s it was forced into competition with the Feydeau company (see below), and gave new works by Méhul (*Euphrosine*, 1790), Dalayrac (*Marianne*, 1796), Henri-Montan Berton (*Le délire*, *Montano et Stéphanie*, 1799),

20. *Eugène Scribe: caricature by Benjamin [Roubaud], lithograph from the series 'Panthéon charivarique' in the journal 'Le charivari' (1841)*

21. Carlotta Grisi leaps into the arms of Lucien Petipa in Act 1 of the ballet 'La péri' (music Friedrich Burgmüller, choreography Jean Coralli), first performed at the Opéra in 1843: lithograph after Marie-Alexandre Menut-Alophe

Rodolphe Kreutzer and the young Boieldieu (*Le calife de Bagdad*, 1800). As in other theatres of the time both serious *opéras comiques* (revolutionary, classical or historical) and comedies were played. The company disbanded in 1801 and later the same year combined with the Feydeau company.

(iii) Théâtre de Monsieur (later Théâtre Feydeau). Founded just before the Revolution by L. Autié and Viotti, the company adopted the name of its patron, Monsieur, Comte de Provence, later Louis XVIII. Performances in 1789 were in the Tuileries, in 1790 in the Foire St Germain and from 1791 in the newly built Salle Feydeau, a neo-classical theatre in the rue Feydeau designed by Le Grand and Molinos (see fig.23). Italian opera (Pergolesi, Sarti, Paisiello etc.) and plays were given. The first important French opera given was Cherubini's *Lodoïska* (1791, famed for its final conflagration scene), which established it as a second Opéra-Comique company in competition with that at the Favart. *Lodoïska* was followed by Le Sueur's *Paul et Virginie* (1794), Pierre Gaveaux's *Léonore* (1798; libretto the source of Beethoven's *Fidelio*) and Cherubini's *Médée* (1797) and *Les deux journées* (1800). It merged with the Favart company in 1801 and was called the Opéra-Comique. The excellent orchestra of the theatre gave many concerts there; other ensembles also used the building for concerts until its demolition in 1829.

(iv) Théâtre (National) de l'Opéra-Comique. This new company, comprising the Favart and Feydeau companies, was formally created by act of government on 16 September 1801 and given official status in 1807. It occupied various theatres until 1805, when it moved to the Salle Feydeau. Its beginning was secure and high standards were maintained. Spontini's first French works were given there and subsequently many famous *opéras comiques* by Méhul (*Joseph*, 1807), Boieldieu, whose *La dame blanche* (1825) came to symbolize the genre as well

as the institution (despite the influence of Rossini), Isouard, Auber and Hérold. The company remained at the Salle Feydeau until 1829, when it moved to the Salle Ventadour. In 1832 it moved to the first Théâtre des Nouveautés in the Place de la Bourse (opened 1827) and in 1840 to the second Salle Favart (rebuilt by Charpentier) where it remained, except for the 1853 season, until the building burnt down in 1887, having been restored by Crépinet in 1879.

As Boieldieu's career drew to a close in the 1830s younger men produced a brilliant stream of more robust entertainment pieces: Auber's *Fra Diavolo* (1830), *Le cheval de bronze* (1835), *Le domino noir* (1837) and *Les diamants de la couronne* (1841); Hérold's *Zampa* (1831) and *Le pré aux clercs* (1832); and Adam's *Le chalet* (1834) and *Le postillon de Longjumeau* (1836). The only other noteworthy event of the period was the première of Donizetti's *La fille du régiment* in 1840.

The type of *opéra comique* prevalent in the 1830s was later cultivated by Thomas in *Le Caïd* (1849) and *Raymond* (1851) but otherwise the Second Empire saw the establishment of a more frivolous and deliberately sentimental type, sometimes called operetta, typified in Adam's *Si j'étais roi* (1852) and, particularly, Massé's *Les noces de Jeannette* (1853). The term 'opéra comique' ceases to have real meaning from that time onwards, when the company suffered intense competition from Offenbach's genuine operettas at the Bouffes-Parisiens, except in the academic sense of musical numbers with spoken dialogue. In 1846 the Opéra-Comique let its hall and singers for an unfortunate performance of *La damnation de Faust*, conducted by Berlioz himself. Emile Perrin, the new impresario of the Opéra-Comique, dedicated himself to renewing the repertory, and by 1862 Meyerbeer, Auber, Halévy and Ambroise Thomas dominated it. The first Meyerbeer opera for the Opéra-Comique was *L'étoile du nord* (1854); it had had 100

22. *The different theatres of the Opéra-Comique: (1) Salle de la Foire St Laurent; (2) Hôtel de Bourgogne; (3) Salle Favart (i); (4) Salle Feydeau; (5) Salle Ventadour; (6) Salle de la Bourse; (7) Salle Favart (ii): engraving after Guiaud marking the centenary (28 April 1883) of the first Salle Favart*

performances by February 1855. In that same month the first of the many settings of *Manon Lescaut* (this one by Auber) was mounted, without great success.

(v) Théâtre Italien   (known also as Opéra-Bouffe). The beginnings of this new troupe lay in Napoleon's preference for Italian music and the imaginative speculations of the aging Mlle Montansier. It primarily gave Italian opera and had no relationship with the Comédie-Italienne. Financial difficulties beset the company from its first performance on 31 May 1801 at the Salle Olympique and at the Salle Favart (1802), but it prospered from 1804, when Picard brought it under the wing of the Théâtre Louvois; it was called the Théâtre de l'Impératrice from then until 1809. It later performed at the Odéon (1808–15) and then until 1841 in different theatres, including the Salle Favart (1825–38). Its directors included Spontini (1810–12) and Rossini (1824–6). According to Spohr, in 1820 Parisians preferred its orchestra to that of the Opéra. Mozart's *Le nozze di Figaro* was given in 1807, *Così fan tutte* in 1809 and *Don Giovanni* in 1811. Before Rossini's advent Zingarelli, Paisiello, Cimarosa and Salieri were the composers most often performed.

The first of the many Rossini operas to be given were *L'italiana in Algeri* (1817) and *Il barbiere di Siviglia* (1819). Rossini, as director, produced Meyerbeer's *Il crociato in Egitto* in 1825, the first work by this composer to be given in Paris. Bellini's *I puritani* and *Norma* were both given in 1835, the former (which was specially commissioned) with a cast including Giulia Grisi, Lablache, and Mario and Antonio Tamburini – artists whose

names became inseparably linked with the Théâtre Italien in this period. Donizetti's *Anna Bolena* (1831; his first work given in Paris), *L'elisir d'amore* (1839) and *Lucia di Lammermoor* (1837) were included in the repertory.

The company's sojourn at the Salle Ventadour (1841–76; fig.23) began well with a lavish production of Rossini's *Semiramide* and continued with the success of *Don Pasquale* (1843), commissioned from Donizetti. The last major events at the theatre, and in the company's history, were productions of Verdi's *Nabucco* in 1845 and *Ernani* in 1846, after which the institution lost its distinctive character.

(vi) Théâtre Lyrique.   The most important rival company to the Opéra and Opéra-Comique in the second half of the century opened in 1851 as the Opéra-National at the Théâtre Historique under the direction of Edmond Seveste. Under his brother Jules Seveste (1852–4) it was known as the Théâtre Lyrique. Emile Perrin ran it briefly before the directorship went to the 30-year-old Léon Carvalho and his wife, Marie Miolan, in 1855. From then the theatre acquired an enviable artistic reputation, due largely to Gounod's *Le médecin malgré lui* (1858), *Faust* (with spoken dialogue, 1859), *Philémon et Baucis* (1860), *Mireille* (1864) and *Roméo et Juliette* (1867; fig.24). In 1862 the company moved to the building in the Place du Châtelet (cap. 1243) that subsequently became the Théâtre des Nations, then the Théâtre Sarah Bernhardt and finally the Théâtre de la Ville. Apart from a short break in 1860–61 Carvalho remained in control until 1868; during that last period he gave the important premières of Bizet's *Les*

23. *Performance by the Théâtre Italien at the Salle Ventadour: engraving by Charles Mottram after Eugène Lami from Jules Janin's 'Un hiver à Paris' (1843)*

pêcheurs de perles (1863) and *La jolie fille de Perth* (1867), as well as the last three acts (abridged) of Berlioz's *Les Troyens* (1863). Carvalho tended to alter the works he presented to bring them in line with his own idea of dramaturgy; nevertheless, he was successful and energetic, and his resignation in 1868 marked the end of the Théâtre Lyrique's period of eminence. He was succeeded by Pasdeloup (1868–70), who mounted Wagner's *Rienzi* in 1869 but who, like many later impresarios, failed to revive the company, which performed in a succession of different theatres for one or two seasons at a time.

(vii) Other theatres.   Two well-known companies that were suppressed in 1807 were the Théâtre des Associés and the Théâtre des Jeunes Artistes, a troupe of child actors who gave comedies, pantomimes and vaudevilles. Of those that survived, the Ambigu-Comique was perhaps the most distinguished secondary theatre. For 20 years before the Revolution a topical repertory of pantomime with music was performed; declamation and singing were legally prohibited, although these restrictions could be disregarded in the 1780s when enthusiasm and semi-official support for the lesser theatres permitted. The orchestra was small, but its music was essential, since it expressed the mimed emotions and enhanced all manner of stage effects. As far as is known music was arranged more often than composed. When this company rose to new eminence after 1800 with Pixérécourt's melodramas in dialogue, music had a less crucial, though still important, role to play. Overtures, dances, speeches and effects all required music. Quaisain and Louis Alexandre Piccinni were the principal composer-arrangers.

When the Théâtre Italien left the Odéon in 1815 the latter theatre presented a mixture of plays, vaudevilles

ROMÉO & JULIETTE
OPÉRA EN 5 ACTES   DE CHARLES GOUNOD

24. *Gounod's 'Roméo et Juliette', first performed at the Théâtre Lyrique, 1867: poster by Leray and Lamy*

and *opéras comiques*. There in 1824 and 1826 Castil-Blaze put on his notorious arrangements of Weber's *Der Freischütz* and *Euryanthe*, given as *Robin des bois* and *La forêt de Sénart* respectively.

The Théâtre de la Porte-St-Martin was another interesting company that survived the decree of 1807. It opened in September 1802, and though forced to shut in 1807, it reopened as the Théâtre des Jeux-Gymniques on 1 January 1810. It made a speciality of melodrama, pantomime and ballet, and the popularity of its ballets *Les chevaliers de la table ronde* (1811) – with Franconi's horses – and *Lise et Colin dans leur ménage* (1812) was such that the Opéra successfully applied for an injunction, on the grounds that it had infringed the older theatre's sole right to give ballets 'of a noble and gracious style, such as those whose subjects derive from mythology or history'. However, the company again reopened (under its original name) in December 1814, with an official licence to present ballet, and its reputation was sustained and admired. Chief choreographers were Jean Aumer (from 1802), Frédéric Blache (from 1814), Jean Coralli (1825–9) and then Petit. Older ballets such as *Les six ingénus*, *Annette et Lubin* and *Le déserteur* were given, but also newer creations than helped to pave the way of the Romantic style, such as *La laitière polonaise* (1817) with its skating dance and *Rosine et Almaviva*. The great acrobat-dancer Mazurier appeared here from 1823 to his death in 1828. Towards the 1840s a series of fairy plays and reviews were given, featuring a *corps de ballet* and brilliant soloists. Such were *La biche au bois* (1845) and *La belle aux cheveux d'or* (1847). With the arrival of the ballerina as romantic heroine and the necessity for a new style of group choreography, the Porte-St-Martin found regular ballet performances too costly to maintain, and the drama company predominated after 1850.

Information on the many small boulevard theatres is in Brazier (1838), Beaulieu (1905) and Cain (1906).

4. CONCERT LIFE. Theatres were most commonly used for concerts up to 1810, especially the Opéra and the Salle Feydeau. The first true concert hall of the period was that built for the Conservatoire, designed by Delannoy and opened in 1811 (fig.25). At this time the Conservatoire buildings stood on the gardens of the old Menus-Plaisirs, near the junction of today's rue Bergère and rue du Faubourg Poissonnière. The hall (which still exists) was U-shaped, with the orchestra at the straight end, and had a capacity of 1055. Little natural light entered, and oil was used instead of gas lighting to lessen the risk of fire. This hall was used by students and great virtuosos, by Conservatoire and other orchestras, and by chamber groups.

The Concert Spirituel ceased in 1790 with the abolition of royal privileges, but the great momentum of concert life generated in the final two decades of the *ancien régime* could not simply cease. The new Feydeau theatre orchestra gave highly popular concerts; and overtures, concertos and symphonies were performed during theatrical evenings at the Feydeau, the Favart and the Opéra. Military music could be heard at concerts during the years 1793–5. Under the Directory the Feydeau concerts rose to new heights, and brilliant soloists became the attraction: Punto, Baillot, Rode, J.X. Lefèvre and Ozi. Napoleon had his personal 'Band of the First Consul', with 27 musicians, and doubtless he was imitated. But the taste for larger orchestral groups led in 1798 to the founding of a subscription society, the Concerts de la rue de Cléry. Its greatest popularity was during 1800–03; in the 1802–3 season it gave 12 concerts, at which one or two Haydn symphonies were almost invariably played. J.F. Reichardt wished that Haydn could hear these performances himself. After 1803 the society declined until it ceased in 1805. The Concerts de la rue Grenelle were begun in 1803 as part of a musical 'academy' for professionals and amateurs; the venture and its orchestra lasted only three years.

The newly formed Conservatoire had given annual prizewinners' concerts since 1797, but on 6 November 1800 the first pupils' concert proper took place; thereafter between five and 12 concerts were given each year, running (like the Cléry concerts) from winter to early

25. Concert hall of the Conservatoire, designed by Delannoy and opened in 1811: engraving by P.S. Germain from 'L'illustration' (15 April 1843)

summer. The orchestra comprised about 60 players, both teachers and pupils, and the performances soon became valued for their excellence and the eclectic planning of their programmes: music for orchestra by Haydn, Méhul and Cherubini; for voices by Cimarosa, Winter, Salieri, Gluck and Rameau; compositions by senior students; symphonies and opera excerpts by Mozart; and Beethoven's first three symphonies. The young prizewinner Habeneck directed these concerts from 1806 until 1815, when financial difficulties diminished the number of concerts; they ceased in 1824.

The promulgation of the Concordat (1802) prompted the revival of *concerts spirituels* from 1805 at various theatres, but they were dull reflections of the original series. The Société Académique des Enfants d'Apollon, dormant since 1789, was revived in 1807.

New ventures during the Restoration included the appearance of a Concert des Amateurs series in 1825 at the Tivoli d'Hiver; Théophile Tilmant first performed there as a conductor. Other important developments owed their existence to Habeneck; from 1818 he directed a new series of three annual Holy Week concerts at the Opéra. Some works by Beethoven were given, including the Second Symphony and the popular Allegretto of the Seventh. On 5 February 1828, having become inspector general of the Conservatoire, Habeneck, with the Minister of Arts and others, formally initiated a new concert series, the Société des Concerts du Conservatoire; the orchestra consisted of past and present pupils (76 string players and 25 wind). The first of the six annual concerts was on 9 March 1828 and began with Beethoven's 'Eroica'; Habeneck's enthusiastic followers had already been preparing for over a year. The second concert was devoted entirely to Beethoven and included the Third Piano Concerto and the Violin Concerto; the third concert included the Fifth Symphony and *Egmont* Overture. These and subsequent concerts finally established Beethoven in France (fig.26).

Habeneck's successors were the violinist Narcisse Girard (14 January 1849), another violinist (and Habeneck's sub-conductor) Théophile Tilmant (13 January 1861) and François Hainl (10 January 1864), already conductor of the Opéra, who was elected in preference to Deldevez and Berlioz. Hainl's successful regime saw the redecoration of the Conservatoire concert hall in 1865 and the tentative inclusion of Wagner in the programmes.

The initiative of Habeneck was undoubtedly responsible for the proliferation of concert series in the late 1820s and early 1830s, such as L'Athénée Musical (1829–44) founded by Chelard. Most of these, like Fétis's Concerts Historiques (four concerts in 1832–3) and later Berlioz's Société Philharmonique (1850–51), were similarly short-lived. The Société Ste Cécile (1850–55), founded by François Seghers, presented some works by Mendelssohn and Schubert. Schumann was also performed; at the time he was considered avant-garde, and exercised considerable influence over the younger generation.

Of far greater importance was the Société des Jeunes Artistes du Conservatoire, founded by Pasdeloup in 1852 to present recognized masterpieces alongside music by young composers. It gave its first performance on 20 February 1853; the orchestra was drawn from the best of the Conservatoire students and comprised 62 players (including the 17-year-old Lamoureux) and a choir of 40 conducted by Antoine Batiste. From its inception the society was an important influence in French musical life,

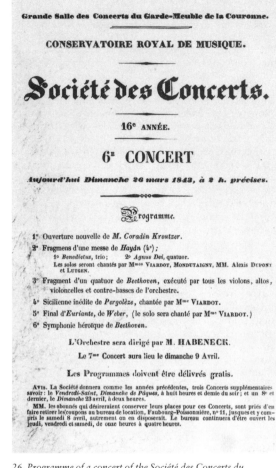

26. Programme of a concert of the Société des Concerts du Conservatoire, 26 March 1843, conducted by Habeneck (who had initiated the series in 1828) and featuring Pauline Viardot

and continued Habeneck's work by firmly establishing the French reputation of the Viennese Classics and of Mendelssohn and Schumann. Indeed, some of the earliest French works presented, such as the curious symphonies of Gounod and the Second Symphony of Saint-Saëns, were among the earliest works in 'classical' forms by Frenchmen. In 1856 when Auber, the director of the Conservatoire, became patron, its name was changed to Société des Jeunes Artistes du Conservatoire Impérial de Musique; but by 1861 it had a large deficit, and Pasdeloup initiated the series Concerts Populaires de Musique Classique at the Cirque Napoléon (Cirque d'Hiver after 1870). In spite of the inexpensive seats (5 francs maximum, compared with 12 at the Conservatoire) the enterprise repaid itself after only three of the six Sunday afternoon concerts in the first season, and Pasdeloup booked the theatre for a year. The orchestra consisted of 56 strings and 25 wind, and included 44 Conservatoire *premier prix* winners. Until the war of 1870 the series was an unquestionable artistic and financial success.

Under Louis-Philippe a distinct public demand brought about many light classical concerts, typically with a promenade audience and dancing during the quadrilles. Promenade concerts were extremely popular; when Henri Valentino started his Concerts Valentino in October 1837

In 1813 some money was voted for the setting up of *maîtrises* in major dioceses, including Paris, but funds were often insufficient and variable. Central treasury support from 1826 was severely cut in 1830, and the depressed condition of the *maîtrises* persisted. In about 1853 official support was given to Niedermeyer's new Ecole de Musique Religieuse et Classique, conceived as a continuation of Choron's work. (The government hoped it would provide competent musicians for churches and *maîtrises*.) The curriculum included the study of the organ, 16th-century counterpoint and the ecclesiastical modes. Saint-Saëns was appointed professor of piano on Niedermeyer's death in 1861 and among his first pupils were Fauré, Gigout and Messager.

6. CRITICISM, PUBLISHING AND INSTRUMENT MAKING. The first specifically musical journal of the period was the *Correspondance des amateurs musiciens* (1802–5). Before this, notices of musical events appeared in the *Journal des spectacles* and *Courrier des spectacles*; retrospective information formed the substance of the annual *Almanach des spectacles*. The *Tablettes de polymnie* (1810–11) stands as forerunner of the many periodicals that proliferated with French Romanticism, beginning with Fétis's *La revue musicale* (1827–35). This was combined in 1835 with the short-lived *Gazette musicale de Paris* to become *La revue et gazette musicale de Paris*, which ran until 1880.

The *Journal des débats*, founded in 1791, had a long tradition of musical criticism before Berlioz joined the staff in 1835. The other principal music critics were Comettant (*Le siècle*), Escudier and the vituperative Scudo (*Revue des deux mondes*). These and other writers produced an enormous quantity of occasional writing about music.

Music publishing was not adversely affected during the troubled decade of 1789–99, and the intense activity of the *ancien régime* continued. Royal privileges vanished, and musical education and commercial and domestic music-making were catered for in a vast output of engraved music. All genres were published, and the trend towards keyboard arrangements was well under way before 1800, but full scores of operas rather than vocal scores continued to be issued at the beginning of the 19th century. As music periodicals became more common the custom of including piano music or songs to attract subscribers was established. Lithography was introduced to Paris in 1802 but took time to make its impact. Few composers published their own music (Dalayrac and Pleyel are exceptions), although Cherubini, Méhul, Kreutzer, Rode, Isouard and Boieldieu set up a joint venture from 1802 to 1811. Principal houses in the earlier period were Erard, Gaveau, Imbault, Leduc (which survives), Sieber and Pleyel; and later Choudens, Costallat, Durand, Hamelle and Schlesinger.

Paris was an important European centre of instrument making. Among the most important makers were Cousineau (harps), Erard (harps, pianos), Pleyel (pianos), Triébert (woodwind), Buffet (woodwind), Savary (woodwind), Courtois (brass) and Sax (brass). Moreover, many string instruments from 19th-century Paris are increasingly valued, especially those by Lupot, F.L. Pique and Vuillaume.

VII. After 1870

1. Introduction. 2. 1870–1918. 3. 1918–44. 4. After 1945.

1. INTRODUCTION.   Since the Third Republic, whose leaders believed that music should serve the public good, Paris's function as the centre of musical life in France has changed and expanded. Just as the country's social, financial, and political élite all live in Paris, so too is much of the French musical world based in the city. A majority of the country's patrons, producers, composers, musical instrument manufacturers, performers, publishers, critics and teachers, together with a large potential public, form

30. *Fête de l'Etre Suprème on the Champs de Mars, 8 June 1794, showing the specially erected mountain, Tree of Liberty and the Statue of Hercules (on the pillar); painting attributed to Pierre-Antoine Demachy (Musée Carnavalet, Paris)*

an interactive network of overlapping forces. A large range of performance venues – not only prestigious theatres, concert halls, museums, cultural centres and private homes, but also brasseries, jazz clubs, parks and even the metro – makes an intense concentration of creative activity possible. The symbolism of place embedded in Paris's geography gives meaning to every musical event. Some spaces – such as the Palais Garnier (Théâtre National de l'Opéra) and the great Champs de Mars – remind listeners of the socio-political contexts in which music earlier thrived. Others – such as the adjustable hall (*espace de projection*) of IRCAM – imply new relationships between composer, performer and public. Great musical instruments abound, not only in the Conservatoire's museum, but also in the 19th-century halls of the major piano manufacturers (the Salle Pleyel, Salle Erard and Salle Gaveau), the multitude of Parisian churches and the studios of musical research. The Conservatoire has drawn to the capital the country's finest and assured a continual succession of highly trained musicians. Always receptive to a wide range of musicians from around the world, including Stravinsky, Falla, Enescu, Sidney Bechet, Elliott Carter and Xenakis, partly, in recent years, because of its recording studios, it has also attracted some of the best musicians of world beat from Africa, the Arab world and the Antilles. Unremitting vitality and ferocious competition have fed Parisians' ceaseless search for distinction, thereby assuring constant change in their musical tastes and activity.

What makes Paris distinct as a musical centre is what links the musical world with the world of politics. Because republican (and later socialist) leaders have believed that music can have a healthy moral influence, shape people's identity and behaviour and, as a collaborative medium, promote respect for social institutions, they have subsidized it with significant state funding. They have also looked to it as a means of enhancing national pride and exhibiting France's prestige abroad. This support has ranged from hundreds of thousands of francs – 80% of both the Opéra's annual budget in the 19th century and the Ensemble InterContemporain's budget from 1977 – to a few thousand for smaller organizations serving some national priority. It has also made possible music's extensive role in the city's Universal Exhibitions of 1878, 1889, 1900, 1931 and 1937 and in numerous international congresses, such as those devoted to music history in 1900 and radio art in 1937.

For the most important musical institutions in the country – the Opéra, Opéra-Comique and the Paris Conservatoire – the rhythm of existence has depended on the goodwill of the Chambre des Députés. So, too, after 1879 and, especially, 1920 certain smaller concert societies and amateur music groups looked to the state for help. Even though the arts budget has never been more than 0·3% of the state's total, each year during the annual budget discussions the nation's deputies review the subsidies of these organizations and their *cahiers de charge*, and what is expected in return for this support. During times of political turmoil the largest budget item, the Opéra, has provoked heated debate. Some have thought it should turn a profit, and its receipts are regularly published in the press and followed avidly by the general public; others, more concerned about the Opéra's utility as a reflection of larger political issues, have forced changes in its repertory. In 1879, for example,

those who argued for musical museums as guardians of national traditions prevailed; those who insisted that the leading institutions serve as outlets for new work by living French composers forced changes in 1891 at the Opéra and in 1898 at the Opéra-Comique; those wanting more popular works performed there have influenced decisions made shortly after World War II and also more recently. From the internal conflicts between those in the Chambre des Députés who have demanded that music be more accessible to *les classes populaires* and those who have preferred to protect élitist traditions and the international reputation of French music have also come various attempts to 'return art to the people'. This has included four versions of an Opéra Populaire in Paris (1874; 1879–80; summer seasons in 1879–82 and 1883–4; 1900–01; and again in the late 1930s). It has also resulted in recurring efforts at decentralization, especially after 1901; the expansion of radio in the late 1930s; and the Jeunesses Musicales around the country in the 1940s and 50s.

Because of the state's perspective on music's role in society, control of much of the musical world emanates from Paris. The continuity of French traditions can be linked to this centralization of power, a relic of France's monarchical past. In 1870 music was placed under the Ministry of Public Instruction and Fine Arts, which in 1932 changed its name to the Ministry of National Education. Except for two short periods when there was a separate arts minister, from November 1881 to January 1882 and later in the 1930s under the Popular Front, the arts were confined to a division, department or under-secretary of state. This changed in the Fifth Republic. In 1959 the government created a Ministry of Cultural Affairs to take control of the arts. A separate music section was created in 1970. Despite these changes, however, the administration of the arts has remained at the Palais Royal. Close geographical proximity to their most expensive responsibilities – the Opéra, Comédie Française, Opéra-Comique and, more recently, IRCAM – has assured not only institutional accountability but also the government's continued support. A similar relationship with the orchestras of Colonne and Lamoureux led to instigating *cahiers de charge* for such associations, beginning in 1897. Until 1940 this meant regular state review of their performances of new French music, their ticket prices and the number of their concerts at reduced prices or seats available to the blind or poor. Other branches of government have also had direct influence on the musical world. For many years, the requirement that performing organizations get permission from the Préfecture de la Police before holding public concerts meant that the government was involved in overseeing the activities of private concert societies and amateur music groups. Riots outside the Opéra's first production of *Lohengrin* in 1891 (*see* FRANCE, fig.17) and continued threats by anti-German patriots at other concerts made maintenance of social order one of the main criteria for censuring repertory.

One of the results of this relationship to the state has been a concentration of educational institutions and important competitions in Paris. Arguably the most important step toward a career for any musician has been entrance into the Paris Conservatoire, never an easy task. According to Pistone (1979), in 1900 210 singers competed for 21 places, 195 pianists for 27 places and

131 violinists for 14. Although there have always been other music schools in Paris – the most important being the Ecole Niedermeyer (founded 1853), the Schola Cantorum (founded 1894) and the Ecole Normale de Musique (founded 1919) – a *premier prix* from the Paris Conservatoire virtually assures a musician of a career. Not only has study with teachers from Massenet and Fauré to Messiaen had a major impact on composers from Ravel and Schmitt to Boulez and Grisey, the pre-eminent composition competition at the Conservatoire, the PRIX DE ROME (ended in 1968), exposed a composer's work to the review of the six most powerful musicians in the country, those at the Académie des Beaux-Arts, all of whom had to live in Paris. This group not only chose the winner, it also sponsored Parisian performances of the winner's work composed during three subsequent years in Rome. Since the 1870s the Académie has also awarded other composition prizes, including the Cressent, Rossini, Monbinne and Nicolo prizes. In 1876 the City of Paris began to offer its own composition prize, the music equivalent of the annual salon for painters. This prize included 10,000 francs for a Parisian première.

Another effect of state support has been technological innovation in Paris, as symbolized by the Eiffel Tower of 1889. In the 19th century the great Parisian exhibitions encouraged a race for new patents, resulting in the double-keyboard piano, the chromatic harp and hundreds of other new instruments. The installation of Cavaillé-Coll organs in St Sulpice, Ste Madeleine-en-la-Cité, La Trinité, Notre Dame, the Princesse de Polignac's salon and elsewhere helped stimulate a new way of writing for the instrument. In 1881 the Opéra's use of electric lighting and the *théâtrephone* to transmit music to listeners outside the hall transformed the public's experience of theatre. In the 20th century the film and radio industries based in Paris have provided new opportunities for musicians. Since 1948 music research has been an integral part of work at the radio. The GROUPES DE RECHERCHES MUSICALES (founded 1958), directed by Pierre Schaeffer and later François Bayle, invented electro-acoustic music there. Music research and creation became departments of the Maison de la Radio in 1975. They have also been priorities at the computer research facilities of IRCAM in the 1980s and 90s.

More indirectly, Paris has also proved immensely stimulating for musicians seeking inspiration, fame and fortune. Cafés, journal headquarters, bookstores and private homes have provided important contexts for discussing ideas, performing music and building bonds. In the early 1880s Debussy, who came from the working class, visited daily the bourgeois home of Mme Vasnier for whom he wrote some of his best songs and whose encouragement was an important part of his early career. He met Satie at the Auberge du Clou and Proust at the Café Wéber. In the early 1890s he discussed occultist and symbolist ideas with poets and other writers at the Revue Blanche and at the bookstore, the Librairie de l'Art Indépendent. He also attended Mallarmé's Tuesday salon. In the 1920s Adrienne Monnier's bookstore and Jean Wiener's Gaya bar similarly attracted composers such as Ravel, Auric and Poulenc and singers such as Maurice Chevalier, together with Cocteau, Picasso, Tzara, Paul Poiret and others for jazz performances.

As a centre of innovation and intellectual life, Paris has long been an arbiter of taste and fashion. As part of *la vie mondaine*, musical performances have provided élite audiences with numerous opportunities to see and be seen. Before World War I especially, the huge ornate staircase and numerous boxes of the Palais Garnier, completed in 1875, served as a backdrop to the theatre's elegant public (fig.31). Some have asserted that the Opéra was a 'neutral terrain for the privileged', a momentary escape from listeners' fierce political differences. Others point to the allure of *snobisme*, or the élite public's desire to stay abreast of the most recent trends, whether represented by Wagner, the Ballets Russes or, more recently, computer music. Such an appeal grew increasingly important after 1900 as producers used 'scandals' to draw crowds and generate interest. Linking fashion, luxury and music between 1905 and 1913, Gabriel Astruc attracted aristocrats, wealthy industrialists and financiers to over 1000 performances he presented. This strategy contributed to the success of his annual spring series of Italian operas, his succession of foreign visitors (Caruso in 1905, the New York Metropolitan Opera in 1910 and Toscanini in 1911) and his Théâtre des Champs-Elysées, which opened in 1913 with Debussy's *Jeux* and Stravinsky's *The Rite of Spring*.

From the late 19th century, however, increasing numbers of bourgeois listeners were drawn to concerts, replacing the wealthy élite as the largest component of the Parsian musical public. Concert series conducted by Pasdeloup (founded 1861 as the Concerts Populaires), Colonne (founded 1873 as the Concert National; fig.32) and Lamoureux (founded 1881), all still functioning, eventually built huge audiences of two to three thousand

31. *Staircase of the Opéra (Palais Garnier) during the opening ceremony on 5 January 1875: painting by Edouard Detaille, 1878 (Musée de Versailles et de Trianon)*

32. Handbill of the first Concert National at the Théâtre de l'Odéon, 2 March 1873, conducted by Edouard Colonne (after whom the series was later named), with Saint-Saëns and Pauline Viardot

people who came Sunday after Sunday for 24 weeks per season. Some paid only one franc or less. By the 1890s arts director Gustave Larroumet credited these associations with spreading the taste for music more than the opera houses or the most prestigious Parisian orchestra, the Société des Concerts du Conservatoire (founded 1828), whose subscription seats rarely changed hands. Some critics, such as Camille Mauclair, thought these concerts helped people 'forget their misery, flee from who they were and find who they wanted to be'. They helped to make music an integral part of city life.

The tactics used by the orchestral associations set important precedents for their successors. As with other forms of bourgeois diversion, like reading and drawing, organizers understood that concerts needed to nourish and educate as well as entertain. In 1885–6 Colonne decided that his concerts that season would 'form a complete summary of the history of music' and be accompanied by programmes with extensive notes written by Charles Malherbe, archivist at the Opéra. By 1900 such notes were a major part of a Parisian listener's experience. Concert repertory also reflected a desire to teach. Not only the major orchestras but also soloists such as Marie Jaëll and Edouard Risler occasionally performed works in series, such as the symphonies or sonatas of Beethoven in chronological order. At the end of the 19th century they also dug up neglected works from the past and combined old and new on concert programmes. The juxtaposition of old works and classics of modern music with premières of new works has characterized a number of concert programmes since then, including Boulez's Domaine Musical (1954–73).

Paris has also been the site of many specialized music societies. Some, including the Association des Chanteurs de St Gervais (1892) and Les Arts Florissants (1979), have focussed on early music, others on individual composers or single genres. Some have arisen out of political divisions, such as those created by the Boulanger and Dreyfus affairs, or attempts to bridge such divisions. In an effort to solidify the *ralliement* ideology of the 1890s, for example, Comtesse Greffuhle's Société des Grandes Auditions Musicales (1890–1913) used music to bring republicans together with *ancien régime* sympathizers. Antagonisms between composers have generated numerous new initiatives advocating various approaches to musical progress: the Société Nationale de Musique (1871–1939), the Société Musicale Indépendante (1909–35), Triton (1932–9), Ars Nova (founded 1963), Itinéraire (founded 1973) and the Ensemble Inter-Contemporain (founded 1976). The proliferation of *petites chapelles* in Paris, each with its own aesthetic beliefs, has made the city an ideological battlefield among those seeking to shape the future.

Certain private musical venues have served to define and promote the interests of such groups. In the late 19th century, for example, the Friday evening concerts of Mme de Saint-Marceaux, attended by painters, sculptors and writers as well as musicians, served as testing grounds for members of the Société Nationale, including Fauré, Saint-Saëns and d'Indy. The salons of Chausson and Chabrier performed a similar function. From the turn of the century until the 1930s the Princesse de Polignac sponsored in her home premières of new works by such composers as Poulenc and Stravinsky. In 1945 it was at René Leibowitz's home that Boulez first heard Schoenberg's Wind Quintet, initiating his lifelong interest in serialism, and in private classes at Messiaen's home that he, Barraqué, Berio, Maderna, Stockhausen and others found support for a new way of writing. Similarly, in the late 1940s and early 1950s Boulez was supported by Suzanne Tézenas and her friends, who funded the concerts at Théâtre Marigny which evolved into the Domaine Musical concerts and publications. In addition to aristocrats and members of the *haute bourgeoisie*, Tézenas's circle included painters, art gallery directors and writers, who, it has been suggested, supported serial music because they saw a link between it and the abstract painting they were collecting.

Amateur musical groups, many of them choruses, have also thrived in Paris, though perhaps less so than in the provinces. Guillot de Sainbris' Société chorale d'Amateurs performed regularly in the late 19th century and was reviewed frequently in the press because it often gave the premières of works by contemporary composers. Other amateur groups were formed by workers at factories and department stores. The Bon Marché, for example, which had a choral society and wind band from 1872 to the turn of the century, offered its musicians regular solfège classes and hired retired directors of the National Guard band to conduct. Their ensembles performed each summer in the park outside the store. The attempt to bring music education to the lower classes, sponsored by groups such as the Association Galiniste, eventually led to the creation of a number of schools. The most famous, Gustave Charpentier's Conservatoire Populaire Mimi Pinson, was founded for working-class girls in 1902. Subsidies from both the Minister of Public Instruction and the City of Paris allowed them to perform concerts at the Palais du

33. Interior of the Palais du Trocadéro, built for the 1878 Exposition Universelle, with the organ by Cavaillé-Coll

Trocadéro. The Jeunesses Musicales created in Paris in 1941 for girls left behind during the war continued this spirit. As they expanded to 40,000 members, they were given the major halls of Paris for their conference concerts, including the Opéra (beginning in 1942) and the Salle Pleyel. By 1944 they had played for 300,000 listeners and their activities spread throughout the country.

At less formal venues such as skating rinks, the Jardin Zoologique d'Acclimatation and the kiosks of the Tuileries, Palais Royal and Luxembourg Gardens, part-time orchestras, amateur wind groups (*orphéons*) and the military bands of the various French regiments have animated public spaces with cheap or free concerts. By performing transcriptions of popular operas, such groups helped to spread the taste for classical music among the masses in the late 19th and early 20th centuries. When the socialists came to power in 1981, the minister of culture Jack Lang revived this activity. His annual Fête de la Musique on the summer solstice has come to involve the entire city in a wide range of popular as well as classical music-making, all free to the public.

As music became an increasingly important part of culture, music criticism and musicology blossomed in Paris. In 1902, for example, it was not uncommon for new works at the Opéra to receive four dozen reviews in as many different print media in the first two weeks of performances. Critics based in Paris but writing as foreign correspondents also have helped promote French musicians abroad. They have educated audiences by writing programme notes for concerts, lecturing at concerts and

developing radio programmes. The Sorbonne offered its first musicology course in 1895 and created the Institut de Musicologie in 1951. The Ecole Pratique des Hautes Etudes, the CNRS and the ethnomusicology division of the Museum of Man have also been important centres of research, but none more so than the music department of the Bibliothèque Nationale, the Opéra library and the Archives Nationales.

2. 1870–1918. Between 1861 and 1896, the population of Paris rose by nearly 50%, with most of this growth coming after 1870. Between 1876 and 1881 more than a quarter of a million of these newcomers were poor people seeking jobs in Paris's growing industries. Wanting the state to be seen as representing popular sovereignty, the republicans who came to power in the late 1870s aimed to make music accessible to the largest number of listeners. Paris was their proving ground. They forced the Opéra and other state-funded institutions to provide free or reduced-price concerts to a broader public. The Opéra, for example, began performances for a wider public on Sundays, and in 1892 started a Saturday subscription series for families. The government also sponsored huge festivals at the Hippodrome, many of them devoted to contemporary French music; and it built the colossal Palais du Trocadéro for the 1878 Exhibition and installed in it one of Cavaillé-Coll's great organs (fig.33).

Because republicans also understood musical progress as a way of demonstrating the country's regeneration after the Franco-Prussian war, they maintained support for the country's élite institutions. In spite of constant debates over the Opéra's utility, from 1876 to 1914 they subsidized the Opéra with over 800,000 francs a year, while after 1880 the Opéra-Comique received a subsidy of 300,000 francs a year. More than 800,000 listeners attended the Palais Garnier in an average year. Expenses and receipts stayed almost constant during this period and the repertory changed only gradually. Preference at the Opéra for Meyerbeer and Gounod (1000 performances of *Les Huguenots* by 1903 and of *Faust* by 1905) only gradually ceded to Wagner (nine works produced between *Lohengrin* in 1891 and *Parsifal* in 1914) and Saint-Saëns (100 performances of *Samson et Dalila* between 1892 and 1898). The Opéra also performed 77 new works between 1875 and 1914, two or three per year in the 1890s. At the Opéra-Comique, Bizet's *Carmen*, Thomas's *Mignon*, Massenet's *Manon* and Gounod's *Mireille* remained popular despite more performances of new works. After a fire in 1887, the Opéra-Comique moved to the Théâtre Lyrique and the Château-d'Eau before finally, in 1898, at huge public expense, occupying the Salle Favart. The Eden-Théâtre also performed opera and operetta (1883–94), as did other theatres like the Théâtre Italien, Théâtre Lyrique, Théâtre des Bouffes-Parisiens, Théâtre de la Gaîté, Théâtre de la Renaissance, Théâtre de la République and Théâtre des Variétés.

Musical life exploded at the end of the century in part because in the 1880s the government, which had previously focussed on individual arts initiatives, turned to economic liberalism and the encouragement of large business interests. Not only did the theatres on the right bank boulevards thrive, so did three circuses. Montmartre became a centre of night life with the opening of Rudolphe Salis' 'Le Chat Noir' (1881; see CABARET), Aristide Bruant's 'Le Mirliton' (1885), 'Le Divan Japonais' (1886; fig.34), frequented by the famous singer Yvette Guilbert (fig.35), and 'La Cigale' (1887). Their appeal spread to all social classes. The cabaret 'Chat Noir', for example, attracted well-off snobs and foreign aristocrats on the 'chic day', Friday evening, as well as bourgeois and working class on other days. It offered theatrical sketches, songs, and, after 1886, nightly shadow puppet shows. Satie played the piano there from 1888 to 1891, after which he moved to the Auberge du Clou and the Café de la Nouvelle Athènes. According to guides of the time, there were around 200 such café-concerts in Paris in 1890, earning over 100,000 francs a month. While some attacked such venues for their politically satirical songs and 'vulgar' entertainment, others praised them for liberating both composers and the public from narrow views about music.

Other cabarets and music halls, such as the Folies-Bergère (see CAFÉ-CONCERT), the Casino de Paris and Olympia, made their reputations in the 1890s with *revues à grand spectacle*. The Folies-Bergère and Olympia were the first to incorporate film (Lumière Cinématographe in 1898) and others soon followed. Unlike the café-concerts, music halls were international in nature. Along with operettas, musical plays, ballets and circus acts, they included foreign groups – exotic dancers like Loïe Fuller or soloists from Java, women's orchestras from Austria and eastern Europe, ragtime and American popular dance. Although café-concerts tended to disappear by 1918, music halls thrived until the mid-1930s when cinema claimed much of their public.

Classical music groups were also formed in increasing numbers. In 1900 there were 162 music societies in Paris, although the increasing popularity of sports clubs and other activities led to a decline thereafter. Orchestras tended to present the same formula of about five works, each in a different genre, and many during this period gave premières of new works as well as featuring distinguished singers from the Opéra. In addition to the major orchestras, orchestral music was presented by, among others, the Société des Grands Concerts de Broustet (founded 1881), the Concerts Modernes de Godard (founded 1884), the Concerts Chaigneau (founded 1887), Eugène d'Harcourt's Concerts Eclectiques Populaires (founded 1893), Le Rey's Société Philharmonique (founded 1900) and the Concerts Séchiari (founded 1906). With an orchestra of 14, many of them Prix de Rome winners, the Concerts Rouge (founded 1889) gave nightly concerts of symphonies and operas in a brasserie on the rue de Tournon. Their competitor, the Concerts Touche, did the same in another brasserie after 1906.

Chamber music also thrived. Besides groups dedicated to new music, audiences heard the Nouvelle Société de Musique de Chambre (1873), the Quatuor Ste-Cécile, a women's ensemble directed by Marie Tayau (1875), the Société des Quatuors Populaires (1877), the Société des Instruments à Vent (1879), the Société de Musique Française d'Edouard Nadaud (1880), the Société des Quatuors Modernes (1881), the Quatuor Parent (1890), the Quatuor Capet (1893), the Société de Musique d'Ensemble de René Lenormand (1894), the Société Moderne des Instruments à Vent (1895), the Double Quintette de Paris (1897) and many others.

The success of these concerts linked music to family life, led many to taking piano or singing lessons, contributed to the growth of the musical instrument industry and created demand for easily available and inexpensive musical scores. This resulted in the production of a great number of regular music publications, all based in Paris. Especially before World War I this included weekly musical scores in newspapers such as *Le Figaro* and *L'Echo de Paris*, innumerable monthly journals of music transcribed for piano, monthly music supplements to family magazines such as *Illustration* and cheap sheet music.

The war interrupted musical life. The Opéra closed after *Les Huguenots* on 29 July 1914, moved for a brief period to the Trocadéro and returned to the Palais Garnier in December 1915. Performances continued under the new leadership of Jacques Rouché. In spring 1915 the Opéra-Comique gave the premières of works by Bruneau, Leroux, Messager and Casadesus and gave 32 performances of Paul Vidal's *Soldats de France*. Just as the Union-Sacrée, the coalition controlling the Chambre des Députés, embraced a politics of national unity, so the previously competitive Concerts Lamoureux and Concerts Colonne merged during the war. Some hoped, in vain, that the two most important groups promoting new music, the Société Nationale and the Société Musicale Indépendante, would bury their differences and do the same.

3. 1918–44.   After the war Paris was lively again, but also full of fascist leagues. Like the conservative coalition that came to power in the Chambre des Députés, musical producers sought works that represented a French identity on which many could agree. On 17 January 1919 the Opéra reopened with Rameau's *Castor et Pollux*. Three

34. *Programme for a Sunday matinée, Le Divan Japonais, 3 December 1897*

days later the Société Musicale Indépendante gave the première of Lili Boulanger's *Clairières dans le ciel*. Performing French music became a priority for many organizations. Between 1919 and 1939 the Opéra, under Jacques Rouché, gave the premières of 71 operas and 73 ballets, many of them by French composers such as Schmitt, d'Indy, Ravel, Bruneau, Hahn and Roussel. The Opéra-Comique, criticized for becoming a place to try out new works, mounted even more premières of French works as well as making 60 recordings. From 1937 the state itself began to commission French composers as part of the politics of the Popular Front.

35. Yvette Guilbert taking a bow: wash drawing by Henri de Toulouse-Lautrec, 1894

New institutions and musical organizations were also created. In 1919 Alfred Cortot and Alfred Mangeot founded the Ecole Normale de Musique with the explicit purpose of preparing students for careers, including teaching music. The American Conservatory in Fontainebleau, south-east of Paris, opened in 1921, attracting numerous Americans to the classes of Nadia Boulanger. Many orchestras and new music groups also began, the most important being the revived Concerts Pasdeloup (1918), the Concerts Koussevitzky (1921–9), the Concerts Wiéner (1921–4), the Concerts Siohan (1924–32), the Concerts Straram (1926), the Orchestre Symphonique de Paris (1928) and, in the 1930s, the Société Philharmonique de Paris, the Concerts Poulet and the Orchestre Féminin Jane Evrard. A new Salle Pleyel opened in October 1927 with Stravinsky conducting his *Firebird* and Ravel his *Valse*; and the Montparnasse boulevard on the left bank became a favourite night spot.

Despite this productivity and attempts to expose audiences to new music, tastes were becoming more conservative. In 1929 an Opéra subscriber interviewed by Rouché said he would rather hear *Faust* 100 times than the same modern work twice. A few years later, Jacques Ibert told an interviewer that students, who previously filled the top floor at premières, were no longer going to the Opéra-Comique. Renewed spirituality and interest in Catholicism played a role. In 1923 another school for sacred music opened, the Institut Grégorien of the Institut Catholique. In the 1930s composers began to write works based on religious figures, especially Joan of Arc (Paray, Rosenthal, Rivier and Honegger). Some also turned to ancient Greece or wrote new works for the harpsichord. Wanda Landowska presented Sunday Concerts champêtres of early music, while Nadia Boulanger put on concerts of Monteverdi, Purcell and Bach (1933–8). Forced by their *cahiers de charge* to give so many minutes of new French works, orchestras drew audiences with endless festivals of Beethoven or Wagner. The two societies devoted to new music, Sérénade and Triton, were formed in the early 1930s but came to an end in 1939, as did the Société Nationale and, in 1935, the Société Musicale Indépendante.

Audiences, too, began to shrink, as did the number of music publishers, piano makers, amateur singing societies and music teachers. According to the *Guide musical* the number of concerts in Paris declined from 1810 in 1924–5 to 1025 in 1938–9, although the popularity of orchestral concerts increased to 1930. Some blame the advent of radio, sound films and the rising popularity of the phonograph and pianola. The first radio transmission in France came from the Radio Tour-Eiffel, a state-owned station, in 1921; Radio Paris, the first private station, was created in 1922. Daily broadcasts began in 1925 and by 1935 music on the radio ran from early morning until after midnight. Radio became an important part of the musical world of Paris, stimulating the government in 1935 to create a Conseil Supérieur de la Radiodiffusion to involve the participation of authorities from the arts, sciences and literature. Radio broadcast both recordings and live performances, the first one coming from the Opéra after the victory of the Left in the legislative elections of 1932. Its popularity also generated a new orchestra, the Orchestre National de la Radiodiffusion, formed in 1934, the first orchestra with musicians paid monthly as state employees. It began to pay musicians broadcast rights; and its programmes, some of them explicit in their pedagogical role, reached five million by 1939. That year, from Radio Paris and Paris-PTT alone, audiences each week could have heard 52 variety programmes, including two operettas, as well as 75 classical concerts, including three by the radio orchestra. New publications like *Mon programme* published by the newspaper *Le petit parisien*, became integral parts of the listening experience.

Meanwhile the popularity of jazz transformed the city, going beyond what Oriental exoticism had represented for composers and audiences before the war. At cinemas and music halls, blues, ragtime and dixieland were played by black orchestras such as the Charleston Jazzband. At first this attracted intellectuals and aficionados. Sartre dreamed of becoming a jazz musician after the Hot Club opened in 1932. Django Reinhardt, among others, performed there. Later, big bands such as those of Count Basie, Duke Ellington and Benny Goodman attracted the mass public. Indeed, some black Americans gained more recognition in Paris than in the USA. The sound of American ballroom and swing on records, as well as popular singers like Edith Piaf, helped drive the craze for recordings in the 1930s. New journals sprang up to feed this interest, among them *Bulletin du Hot Club*, *Jazz Hot* and, later, *Jazz Magazine*.

The new forces contributed to crisis at the Opéra. It adapted to the public's increasing taste for spectacle by presenting mixed genres often involving dance (Roussel's *Padmâvatî*, Schmitt's music for the film *Salammbô* and the productions featuring Ida Rubenstein). However, Rouché was forced to spend his private fortune to keep it afloat in part because the state subsidy never rose and in 1928 taxes were over one million francs. Between 1931 and 1937 the Opéra's receipts fell by 38%. On 14 January 1939 the state made it a public institution, assuming total responsibility and creating the Réunion des Théâtres Lyriques Nationaux. Subscribers were then divested of their quasi-permanent seats and only a few evenings were reserved for them. The Opéra closed with the war on 1 September 1939, reopened and then closed again when German troops entered Paris on 14 June 1940.

During the occupation military bands performed German music before the Opéra and Notre Dame, in the Tuileries Gardens, and at the Place de la République. Meanwhile, musical life returned to a kind of normal. The Conservatoire reopened on 24 June, as did cinemas, theatres, cabarets, music halls, circuses, followed in August by the Opéra, Opéra-Comique and Comédie Française. Without necessarily collaborating with the Vichy regime, many composers and playwrights were content to have their works performed during this period, including Poulenc (*Les animaux modèles*), Honegger (*Antigone*) and Schmitt (*La tragédie de Salomé*), Claudel (*L'annonce faite à Marie*), Giono (*Le bout de la route*) and Sartre (*Huis clos*). In addition to some Wagner, the opera houses continued presenting their repertory of late 19th-century French masterpieces. Major orchestras also continued to perform. Radio stations were perhaps the only aspect of the musical world directly reflecting Paris's political condition. A 'war of the waves' took place between the communist Radio Liberté, the German-influenced Radio Paris, and Radio Vichy. This propagandistic use of the medium contributed to a dramatic increase in the number of radios in the city.

4. AFTER 1945.   After the liberation of Paris, musical leaders changed their orientation. Responding to the increased popularity of radio, Manuel Rosenthal reorganized the Orchestre National de la Radiodiffusion, increased its size, and added a lyric orchestra, a chamber orchestra and six provincial orchestras. Henry Barraud programmed more non-French composers, including Stravinsky, Bartók, Hindemith and Prokofiev. In 1947, the Conservatoire initiated new classes in analysis (Messiaen), aesthetics (Beaufils) and musicology (Dufourcq). In 1951 the Prix de Rome competition changed to accommodate post-tonality and allowed composers to include earlier works and a wider variety of genres; and in 1952 Bernard Gavoty introduced analysis lectures to accompany the contemporary music concerts of the Jeunesses Musicales.

Under the Fourth Republic mass culture became a major phenomenon, with the number of radios growing to over ten million in the 1950s. After 1945 radio also became a state monopoly, with Radiodiffusion Française

(RDF) the most important national station; this later became Office de Radiodiffusion-Télévision Française (ORTF) with the creation of the second television channel in 1964. Along with cinema and television, the popularity of radio contributed to a standardization of taste and repertory. This, however, was accompanied by a widespread crisis. The Jeunesses Musicales became one of the most important cultural movements in the world, spreading to almost 200 provincial towns. But from 1949 to 1963 there was a further decline in the musical public. While the Société des Concerts du Conservatoire maintained high attendance at its concerts, the Concerts Pasdeloup often played to a hall two-thirds full, Colonne to somewhat less, and Lamoureux to even fewer listeners. At the same time, although 60% of the country's musicians resided in Paris, the number of orchestral musicians in the city declined from 7000 in 1930 to 2000 in 1964. By 1963 only 23 associations were receiving state subsidies, and subsidies of the most important orchestras had decreased substantially. Instrumental production also declined, especially in pianos. Whereas in 1929 20,000 instruments were built in Paris, by 1962 only 2000 were made there. The French lute industry almost disappeared. Only the production of wind instruments maintained previous levels; and while the record industry grew substantially, the music publishing business stalled.

Some saw the problems of the 1950s and 60s as a product of French protectionism and sought to address this by looking beyond French frontiers. In 1952 Nicolas Nabokov founded the Oeuvre du XXe Siècle to present the works of Schoenberg and Webern; the society gave the Parisian première of Berg's *Wozzeck*. Boulez's Domaine Musical also revealed new works coming from abroad, as did the Opéra-Comique, whose 1954 Festival de Paris became known as the Théâtre des Nations from 1957 to 1963.

In 1959, with the erosion of private patronage of music, the government decided to take charge of the situation and attributed to culture a ministry of its own under the leadership of André Malraux. He believed that culture is not inherited but 'conquered'. It is an existential struggle to 'protect the imaginary' and 'resurrect nobility' in a world of imagery provided by machines. Acknowledging the need for new visions of musical life, in 1966 he appointed Marcel Landowski as director of music. Their politics consisted of rethinking the role and nature of orchestras and music pedagogy, funding festivals (96 of them by 1974) and commissioning composers. In 1967 this resulted in the creation of a new orchestra of 110 salaried musicians, the Orchestre de Paris, replacing the Société des Concerts du Conservatoire. Funding was provided by the state (50%) the City of Paris (33%) and the Conseil Général de la Seine (17%). At its inaugural concert on 14 November 1967, Charles Münch conducted the première of Stravinsky's *Requiem Canticles* together with Debussy's *La mer* and Berlioz's *Symphonie fantastique*. In 1973 the orchestra moved to the Palais des Congrès and later the Salle Pleyel. The state and City of Paris also shared funding for various new music initiatives, including the Journées de Musique Contemporaine (1968), which formed part of the Semaines Musicales Internationales de Paris (founded 1968), the Festival d'Automne (1972) and the research centre IRCAM (1975); see INSTITUT DE RECHERCHE ET COORDINATION ACOUSTIQUE/MUSIQUE, created to encourage collective work and reputedly as a condition of Boulez's return to France from New York. All this was part of a conscious effort to recognize and support the city as a European, not merely a French, centre of musical and artistic life.

Malraux's concept of culture took hold, and whereas in 1960 people's spending on cultural events constituted one sixth of their spending on food, this increased to one third by 1979. Moreover culture became a focal point in the debates about national identity and national heritage. When the socialists came to power in 1981, it became even more important. Because they doubled the Ministry of Culture's budget, spending was increased on musical production, musical centres and new music associations. The musical landscape changed radically. In 1980 the Théâtre Musical de Paris at the Théâtre du Châtelet, supported by the city as a public service to 'inform, instruct, and elevate' its citizens, added an important venue for operas and new music as well as foreign orchestras, singers and dance groups. This strengthened the importance of Paris as an international creative centre. So did the Maison de la Culture in Bobigny, which began to offer major premières such as that of Boulez's *Répons* and later operas directed by foreigners like Robert Wilson and Peter Sellars. Meanwhile IRCAM, which expanded its research programmes in the 1980s and its pedagogical programmes in the 1990s, continued to function as a place of international exchange funded entirely by the state, although for some its excessive cost and Boulez's tight control limited other kinds of growth in the musical world. By the mid-1980s, however, there were six orchestras performing in Paris and the state supported 11 centres of music research in the suburban area. The radio orchestra gave 350 concerts per season and performed 150 new works each year, over 40 of them commissions. The public stations France-Musique, France-Culture and France-Inter broadcast over 10,000 hours of music per year, while the extremely successful Festival d'Automne brought music from all over the world.

Besides favouring innovation, research and new projects over established institutions, the socialists also sought to make music available to a diverse public including the young and working class and to support popular along with élite genres. In the spirit of integrating the traditional sections of Paris in the midst of sociological transformation, plans began for a Cité de la Musique in the working-class neighbourhood of La Villette – eventually to contain a new building for the Conservatoire, a concert hall, a musical instrument museum, a pedagogical institute and a research centre. Expansion into the Bercy area led to the construction of the Palais des Sports, completed in 1983. Its 13,000 seats made operas such as *Aïda*, *Turandot*, *Carmen* and *Faust* available to the masses. In 1982 President Mitterrand announced his plan to build a new opera house, the Opéra Bastille, in the Marais district. Opera performances at the old house, the Palais Garnier, ceased in 1987 and it is now used mainly for ballet. The Opéra Bastille (fig.36) was virtually completed for its inaugural operatic concert on 13 July 1990; a short operatic season had already opened on 17 March 1990 with P.L. Pizzi's production of *Les Troyens*. From the beginning the house has been treated as a political football. Daniel Barenboim, appointed artistic director in 1987, was dismissed in 1989 by the newly appointed president of the board, Pierre Bergé, who took overall artistic control and appointed Myung-Whun Chung as his musical director. But controversy, both financial and practical, has continued to dog the Opéra Bastille, as exemplified by the resignation of Chung in 1994 after disagreements with Bergé and his successor, Hugues Gall.

The state has taken explicit steps to help popular musicians in Paris, and for huge rock concerts it helped build 'Zénith'. Paris also developed as a centre for African musicians including Manu Dibango, Salif Keïta, Ray Lema, Mory Kanté, Alpha Blondy and the group Xalam, especially after the annual African festival at the Porte de la Villette (founded 1978). Jack Lang subsidized some of

36. *Opéra Bastille, designed by Carlos Ott, opened 1990*

these concerts, and at La Villette each July he also supported a festival of jazz. In the mid-1980s the state lowered the tax on recordings, funded the creation of an Orchestre National de Jazz, and founded centres for the study of jazz (1984), rock (1986) and traditional music (1992), and a studio to record popular music. State support for jazz and popular music grew 350% from 1980 to 1990.

In 1987 and 1990 laws passed to attract private foundations to the support of music further transformed the musical world. It became possible for any corporate foundation 'recognized of public utility' to deduct its contributions to non-profit organizations from its taxes, and so private enterprise became a major factor. This represented a substantial change from the long tradition of state control. Corporate foundations who close to support music in Paris include: France Télécom (vocal music); the Société Générale (young performers, musical practice, musicological conferences and contemporary music); the Caisse des Dépôts (the Théâtre des Champs-Elysées, jazz, and Baroque music); the BNP (comic opera); Le Crédit Local de France (opera); Hewlett Packard France (the Festival d'Art Sacré de la Ville de Paris); and Moët Hennessy and Louis Vuitton (IRCAM). Of all foundation money supporting the arts, a majority has gone to music, and a third of this to music in Paris.

In the early twenty-first century Paris remains musically vibrant. On any day, on average 20 classical concerts are presented in over 80 venues, together with performances in over 70 venues for jazz, folk and popular music, as well as ballet, and traditional music and dance from around the world. France-Musique broadcasts around 400 concerts per year, the majority by its four ensembles, although at low frequency for a limited public. France-Culture and France-Classique also programme classical music. Popular music, however, is the norm on the radio as well as in restaurants and stores. Although the city shares in the worldwide crisis concerning both the role of serious music and the notion of a distinct national music, the centralization of government in Paris and its commitment to arts organizations as public services assure a continuation of support for musical developments that reflect evolving concepts of progress.

BIBLIOGRAPHY

A General. B To 1600: (i) Sacred (ii) Secular. C 1600–1789: (i) Stage (ii) Sacred (iii) Other. D 1789–1870. E After 1870.

A: GENERAL

BrenetM; *ES* (L. Chancerel and others) [incl. comprehensive list of theatres];*HopkinsonD*; *LabordeMP*; *MGG2* (B. Schilling-Wang and others)

H. Sauval: *Histoire et recherches des antiquités de la ville de Paris* (Paris, 1724/R)

Castil-Blaze: *L'opéra italien de 1548 à 1856* (Paris, 1856)

A. de Lasalle and E.Thoinan: *La musique à Paris* (Paris, 1863)

E. Noel and E. Stoullig: *Les annales du théâtre et de la musique* (Paris, 1876–1918)

T. de Lajarte: *Bibliothèque musicale du Théâtre de l'Opéra* (Paris, 1878/R)

A. Soubies and C. Malherbe: *Précis de l'histoire de l'Opéra-comique* (Paris, 1887)

L. de Fourcaud, A. Pougin and L. Pradet: *La Salle Pleyel* (Paris, 1893)

C. Pierre: *Les facteurs d'instruments de musique* (Paris, 1893)

La maison Erard 1780–1903, ses origines, ses inventions (Paris, 1903)

L.H. Lecomte: *Histoire des théâtres de Paris* (Paris, 1905–12)

M. Poëte: *Une vie de cité: Paris de sa naissance à nos jours* (Paris, 1925–7)

J.-G. Prod'homme: *L'Opéra (1669–1925)* (Paris, 1925)

F. Raugel: *Les grandes orgues des églises de Paris et du département de la Seine* (Paris, 1927)

M.-D. Calvocoressi: *Musicians Gallery: Music and Ballet in Paris and London* (London, 1933)

R. Héron de Villefosse: *Histoire de Paris* (Paris, 1948, 2/1955)

B. Gavoty: *Deux capitales romantiques: Vienne, Paris* (Paris, 1953)

A. Lejeune and S. Wolff: *Les quinze salles de l'Opéra de Paris (1669–1955)* (Paris, 1955)

A. Boll: *De l'Académie royale à la Salle Garnier: l'Opéra 1669–1960* (Paris, 1960)

D. Cayre: *Paris, capitale culturelle, l'exemple de la musique classique* (Paris, 1970)

J. Gourret: *Histoire de l'Opéra de Paris, 1669–1971: portraits de chanteurs* (Paris, 1977)

S. Pitou: *The Paris Opera: an Encyclopedia of Operas, Ballets, Composers and Performers* (Westport, CT, and London, 1983)

J. Siegel: *Bohemian Paris: Culture, Politics and the Boundaries of Bourgeois Life (1830–1930)* (New York, 1985)

J.-P. Babelon: *Paris au XVIe siècle* (Paris, 1986)

N. Salinger, ed.: *Orchestre de Paris* (Paris, 1987)

B. Marchand: *Paris, histoire d'une ville, XIX–XX siècle* (Paris, 1993)

E. Hondre, ed.: *Le Conservatoire de musique de Paris* (Paris, 1995)

A. Bongrain and Y.Gérard, eds.: *Le Conservatoire de Paris, des menus-plaisirs à la Cité de la musique (1795–1995)* (Paris, 1996)

F. Gétreau: *Les collections instrumentales du Conservatoire de Paris 1793–1993* (Paris, 1996)

B: TO 1600

(i) Sacred

G. Dubois: *Historia ecclesiae parisiensis* (Paris, 1690–1710)

B.E.C. Guérard: *Cartulaire de l'Eglise Notre-Dame de Paris* (Paris, 1850)

F.L. Chartier: *L'ancien chapitre de Notre-Dame de Paris et sa maîtrise* (Paris, 1897/R)

A. Gastoué: *Histoire du chant liturgique à Paris* (Paris, 1904) [orig. pubd in *Revue du chant grégorien*, xi–xii (1902–4)]

J. Handschin: 'Zur Geschichte von Notre Dame', *AcM*, iv (1932), 5–17, 49–55, 104–5

Y. Rokseth, ed.: *Polyphonies du XIIIe siècle: le manuscrit H 196 de la Faculté de médecine de Montpeller*, iv: *Etudes et commentaires* (Paris, 1948)

F.A. Yates: 'Dramatic Religious Processions in Paris in the Late Sixteenth Century', *AnnM*, ii (1954), 215–70

E.F. Flindell: *The Achievements of the Notre Dame School* (diss., U. of Pennsylvania, 1959)

G. Birkner: 'Notre Dame-Cantoren und -Succentoren vom Ende des 10. bis zum Beginn des 14. Jahrhunderts', *In memoriam Jacques Handschin*, ed. H. Anglès and others (Strasbourg, 1962), 107–26

H. Husmann: 'St. Germain und Notre-Dame', *Natalicia musicologica Knud Jeppesen septuagenario collegis oblata*, ed. B. Hjelmborg and S. Sørenson (Copenhagen, 1962), 31–6

H. Husmann: 'The Enlargement of the *Magnus Liber Organi* and the Paris Churches St. Germain l'Auxerrois and Ste. Geneviève-du-Mont', *JAMS*, xvi (1963), 176–203

H. Husmann: 'The Origin and Destination of the *Magnus Liber Organi*', *MQ*, xlix (1963), 311–30

H. Husmann: 'Notre Dame und Saint Victor: Repertoire-Studien zur Geschichte der gereimten Prosen', *AcM*, xxxvi (1964), 98–123, 191–221

M. Huglo: 'Les Debuts de la polyphonie à Paris: les premiers *organa* Parisiens', *Forum Musicologicum*, iii (1982), 93–117

M. Haas: 'Die Musiklehre im 13. Jahrhundert von Johannes de Garlandia bis Franco', *Die Mittelalterliche Lehre von der Mehrstimmkeit*, *Geschichte der Musiktheorie*, ed. F. Zaminer, v (Darmstadt, 1984), 89–159

A.W. Robertson: 'The Reconstruction of the Abbey Church at St. Denis (1231–81): the Interplay of Music and Ceremony with Architecture and Politics', *EMH*, v (1985), 187–238

C. Wright: 'Education in the Maîtrise of Notre-Dame of Paris at the End of the Middle Ages', *L'enseignement de la musique au Moyen Age et à la Renaissance: Royaumont 1985*, 130–33

M.E. Fassler: 'The Role of the Parisian Sequence in the Evolution of Notre-Dame Polyphony', *Speculum*, lxii (1987), 345–74

N.E. Smith: 'The Parisian Sanctorale ca. 1225', *Capella Antiqua München: Festschrift zum 25jährigen Bestehen*, ed. T. Drescher (Tutzing, 1988), 247–61

C.M. Wright: *Music and Ceremony at Notre Dame of Paris, 500–1500* (Cambridge, 1989)

R.A. Baltzer: 'How Long was Notre Dame Organum Performed?', *Beyond the Moon: Festschrift Luther Dittmer*, ed. B. Gillingham and P. Merkley (Ottawa, 1990), 118–43

J.T. Brobeck: *The Motet at the Court of Francis I* (diss., U. of Pennsylvania, 1991)

A.W. Robertson: *The Service-Books of the Royal Abbey of Saint Denis: Images of Ritual and Music in the Middle Ages* (Oxford, 1991)

R.A. Baltzer: 'The Geography of the Liturgy at Notre-Dame of Paris', *Plainsong in the Age of Polyphony*, ed. T.F. Kelly, Cambridge Studies in Performance Practice, ii (Cambridge, 1992), 32–44 [incl. list of Parisian plainchant sources]

M.E. Fassler: *Gothic Song: Victorine Sequences and Augustinian Reform in Twelfth-Century Paris* (Cambridge, 1993)

J.T. Brobeck: 'Musical Patronage in the Royal Chapel of France under Francis I (r. 1515–1547)', *JAMS*, xlviii (1995), 187–239

(ii) Secular

H. Prunières: 'La musique de la chambre et de l'écurie sous le règne de François Ier (1516–1547)', *Année musicale*, i (1911), 215–51

A. Pirro: *La musique à Paris sous le règne de Charles VI, 1380–1422* (Strasbourg, 1930, 2/1958)

F.A. Yates: *The French Academies in the Sixteenth Century* (London, 1947)

F.A. Yates: 'Poésie et musique pour les "Magnificences" du mariage du duc de Joyeuse, Paris, 1581', *Musique et poésie au XVIe siècle: Paris 1953*, 241–64

F. Lesure: 'La facture instrumentale à Paris au seizième siècle', *GSJ*, vii (1954), 11–52

F. Lesure: 'Les orchestres populaires à Paris vers la fin du XVIe siècle' *RdM*, xxxvi (1954), 39–54

N.C. Carpenter: *Music in the Medieval and Renaissance Universities* (Norman, OK, 1958)

D. Heartz: 'Parisian Music Publishing under Henri II: a propos of Four Recently Discovered Guitar Books', *MQ*, xlvi (1960), 448–67

M. Le Moël: 'La chapelle de musique sous Henri IV et Louis XIII', *RMFC*, vi (1966), 5–26

N. Pirrotta: 'Dante Musicus: Gothicism, Scholasticism, and Music', *Speculum*, xliii (1968), 245–57

S.W. Deierkauf-Holsboer: *Le Théâtre de l'Hôtel de Bourgogne*, i (Paris, 1968–70)

S. Bonime: 'The Musicians of the Royal Stable under Charles VIII and Louis XII (1485–1514)', *CMc*, no.25 (1978), 7–21

L.L. Perkins: 'Musical Patronage at the Royal Court of France under Charles VII and Louis XI (1422–83)', *JAMS*, xxxvii (1984), 507–66

M.E. Everist: 'The Rondeau Motet: Paris and Artois in the Thirteenth Century', *ML*, lxix (1988), 1–22

R. Sherr: 'The Membership of the Chapels of Louis XII and Anne de Bretagne in the Years Preceeding Their Deaths', *JM*, vi (1988), 60–82

M.E. Everist: *Polyphonic Music in Thirteenth-Century France: Aspects of Sources and Distribution* (New York and London, 1989)

R. Freedman: 'Paris and the French Court under François I', *The Renaissance: from the 1470s to the end of the 16th Century*, ed. I. Fenlon (London, 1989), 174–96

M. Huglo: 'The Study of Ancient Sources of Music Theory in the Medieval University', *Music Theory and its Sources: Antiquity and the Middle Ages*, ed. A. Barbera (Notre Dame, 1990), 150–72

E.H. Roesner, F.Avril and N. Regalado: *The Roman de Fauvel in the Edition of Mesire Chaillou de Pesstain: a Reproduction in Facsimile of the Complete Manuscript Paris, Bibliothèque Nationale, fonds français, 146* (New York, 1990)

c: 1600–1789

(i) Stage

E. Gherardi: Preface to *Recueil général de toutes les comédies et scènes françoises jouées par les comédiens italiens du Roy* (Paris, 1700)

C.-C. Genest: *Les divertissements de Sceaux* (Paris, 1712)

L. Riccoboni: *Réflexions historiques et critiques sur les diférens théâtres de l'Europe* (Paris, 1738; Eng. trans., 1741)

C. and F. Parfaict: *Histoire de l'Académie royale de musique* (MS, c1741, *F-Pn* n. a. fr. [6532])

J.B. Durey de Noinville and L. Travenol: *Histoire du théâtre de l'Académie royale de Musique* (Paris, 1753, 2/1757/*R*)

[C. and F. Parfaict]: *Dictionnaire des théâtres de Paris* (Paris, 1756/ *R*, rev. 2/1767 with G. d'Abguerbe)

L.-F. Beffara: *Dictionnaire de l'Académie royale de musique* (autograph MS, 1783–4, *F-Po* Rés. 602)

J. Vatout: *Le Palais de Fontainebleau* (Paris, 1840)

A. Jullien: *Les grandes nuits de Sceaux* (Paris, 1876)

A. d'Auriac: *Le théâtre de la foire* (Paris, 1878)

E. Campardon: *L'Académie royale de musique au XVIIIe siècle* (Paris, 1884/*R*)

E. Bourges: *Quelques notes sur le théâtre de la cour à Fontainebleau* (Paris, 1892)

M. Brenet: *Les concerts en France Sour l'ancien régime* (Paris, 1900)

N.M. Bernardin: *La comédie Italienne en France et les Théâtres de la Foire et du Boulevard (1570–1791)* (Paris, 1902)

L. de La Laurencie: 'La grande saison italienne de 1752: les Bouffons', *BSIM*, viii/6 (1912), 18–33; viii/7–8, 13–22

G. Cucuel: 'Notes sur la comédie Italienne de 1717 à 1789', *SIMG*, xv (1913–14), 154–66

P. Mélèse: *Le théâtre et le public à Paris sous Louis XIV, 1659–1715* (Paris, 1934)

P. Mélèse: *Répertoire analytique des documents contemporains ... concernant le théâtre à Paris sous Louis XIV, 1659–1715* (Paris, 1934)

R. Viollier: 'La musique à la cour de la duchesse du Maine, de Châtenay aux grandes nuits de Sceaux, 1700–1715', *ReM*, nos.192–4 (1939), 96–105, 133–8

M. Barthélemy: 'La musique dramatique à Versailles de 1660 à 1715', *XVIIe siècle*, no.34 (1957), 7–18

J. Lough: *Paris Theatre Archives in the 17th and 18th Centuries* (London, 1957)

M.M. McGowan: *L'art du ballet de cour en France: 1581–1643* (Paris, 1963)

C.R. Barnes: 'Instruments and Instrumental Music at the "Théâtres de la Foire" (1697–1762)', *RMFC*, v (1965), 142–68

R. Lowe: *Marc-Antoine Charpentier et l'opéra de collège* (Paris, 1966)

C.R. Barnes: 'Vocal Music at the "Théâtres de la Foire" 1697–1762, I: Vaudeville', *RMFC*, viii (1968), 141–60

H. Turrentine: 'The Prince de Conti: a Royal Patron of Music', *MQ*, liv (1968), 309–15

A. Ducrot: 'Les représentations de l'Académie royale de musique à Paris au temps de Louis XIV (1671–1715)', *RMFC*, x (1970), 19–55

W.H. Kaehler: *The Operatic Repertoire of Madame de Pompadour's Théâtre des Petits Cabinets (1747–1753)* (diss., U. of Michigan, 1971)

B. Lossky: *The National Museum of the Château de Fontainebleau* (Paris, 1971)

H. Lagrave: *Le théâtre et le public à Paris de 1715 à 1750* (Paris, 1972)

G. Sadler: 'Rameau, Piron and the Parisian Fair Theatres', *Soundings*, iv (1974), 13–29

C. Massip: 'Musique et musiciens à Saint-Germain-en-Laye (1651–1683)', *RMFC*, xvi (1976), 261–31

E. Giuliani: 'Le public de l'Opéra de Paris de 1750 à 1760: mesure et définition', *IRASM*, viii (1977), 159–81

J. de La Gorce: *L'opéra sous le règne de Louis XIV: le merveilleux ou les puissances surnaturelles, 1671–1715* (diss., U. of Paris-Sorbonne, 1978)

J. de La Gorce: 'L'Académie royale de musique en 1704', *RdM*, lxv (1979), 160–91

J. de La Gorce: 'L'opéra et son public au temps de Louis XIV', *Bulletin de la Société de l'histoire de Paris et de l'Ile de France* (1981), 27–46

J. de La Gorce: 'L'opéra français à la cour de Louis XIV', *Revue d'histoire du théâtre*, xxxv (1983), 387–401

G. Sadler: 'Rameau's Singers and Players at the Paris Opéra: a Little-Known Inventory of 1738', *EMc*, xi (1983), 453–67

R. Fajon: *L'opéra à Paris du Roi-soleil à Louis le Bien-aimé* (Geneva, 1984)

P.F. Rice: 'The Court Theatre at Fontainebleau', *Theatre Research International*, ix/2 (1984), 127–39

L. Rosow: 'From Destouches to Berton: Editorial Responsibility at the Paris Opéra', *JAMS*, xl (1987), 285–309

P.F. Rice: *The Performing Arts at Fontainebleau from Louis XIV to Louis XVI* (Ann Arbor, 1989)

B. Coeyman: 'Theatres for Opera and Ballet During the Reigns of Louis XIV and Louis XV', *EMc*, xviii (1990), 22–37

J. de La Gorce: *L'opéra à Paris au temps de Louis XIV: histoire d'un théâtre* (Paris, 1992)

P.F. Rice: 'The Performing Arts at the Court of Louis XIV', *Man and Nature/L'homme et la nature*, xi (1992), 59–75

E.T. Corp: 'The Exiled Court of James II and James III: a Century of Italian Music in France, 1689–1712', *JRMA*, cxx (1995), 216–31

J. Gribenski, ed.: *D'un opéra l'autre: hommage à Jean Mongrédien* (Paris, 1996)

D. Charlton: *French Opera: 1730–1830: Meaning and media* (Aldershot, 1999)

(ii) Sacred

BrenetM

M. Sonnet: *Ceremoniale parisiense* (Paris, 1662)

F.L. Chartier: *L'ancien chapitre de Notre-Dame de Paris et sa maîtrise* (Paris, 1897/R)

M. Brenet: *La musique sacrée sous Louis XIV* (Paris, 1899)

M. Brenet: 'La musique dans les églises de Paris, de 1716 à 1738 d'après les almanachs du temps', *Tribune de Saint-Gervais*, viii (1902), 274–81; ix (1903), 71–5

N. Dufourcq: *Le grand orgue et les organistes de Saint-Merry de Paris* (Paris, 1947)

N. Dufourcq: 'De l'emploi du temps des organistes parisiens sous les règnes de Louis XIII et Louis XIV, et de leur participation à l'office', *ReM*, no.226 (1955), 35–47

M. Benoit and N. Dufourcq: *Dix années à la Chapelle royale de musique, d'après une correspondance inédite, 1718–1728* (Paris, 1957)

F. Raugel: 'La musique à la chapelle du Château de Versailles sous Louis XIV', *XVIIe siècle*, no.34 (1957), 19–25

M. Bert: 'La musique à la maison royale Saint-Louis de Saint-Cyr', *RMFC*, iii (1963), 55–71; iv (1964), 127–31; v (1965), 91–127

M. Le Moël: 'La chapelle de musique sous Henri IV et Louis XIII', *RMFC*, vi (1966), 5–26

A.-M. Yvon-Briand: 'La maîtrise de Notre-Dame aux XVIIe et XVIIIe siècles', *Huitième centenaire de Notre-Dame de Paris: Paris 1964* (Paris, 1967), 359–99

J.E. Morby: *Musicians at the Royal Chapel of Versailles, 1683–1792* (diss., U. of California, Berkeley, 1971)

D.H. Foster: 'The Oratorio in Paris in the 18th Century', *AcM*, xlvii (1975), 67–133

B. Gérard: 'La musique dans les églises de la Cité aux XVIIe et XVIIIe siècles', *RMFC*, xvi (1976), 153–86

H. Himelfarb: 'Lieux eminents du grand motet: décor symbolique et occupation de l'espace dans les deux dernières chapelles royales de Versailles (1682 et 1710)', *Le grand motet français: Paris 1984*, 17–27

J. Eby: 'Music at the Church of the SS Innocents, Paris, in the Late Eighteenth Century', *JRMA*, cxvii (1992), 247–69

J. Lionnet: 'Innocenzo Fede et la musique à la cour des Jacobites à Saint-Germain-en-Laye', *Revue de la Bibliothèque nationale*, xlvi (1992), 14–18

(iii) Other

AnthonyFB; BenoitMC; BrenetC; BurneyFI; PierreH

J.C. Nemeitz: *Le séjour de Paris* (Leiden, 1727)

W. Jones: *Observations in a Journey to Paris by way of Flanders* (London, 1777)

Le Chevalier de Jaucourt: 'Paris', *Encyclopédie ou dictionnaire raisonné des sciences*, xxiv (Berne and Lausanne, 1780), 116–37

L.S. Mercier: *Tableau de Paris* (Amsterdam, 1782–3; partial Eng. trans., 1929, as *The Picture of Paris, Before and After the Revolution*)

A. Elwart: *Histoire des concerts populaires de musique classique* (Paris, 1864)

J. Ecorcheville: 'Quelques documents sur la musique de la Grande Ecurie du roi', *SIMG*, ii (1900–01), 608–42

G. Capon and R. Yve-Plessis: *Paris galant au dix-huitième siècle: vie privée du prince de Conty* (Paris, 1907)

G. Cucuel: *La Pouplinière et la musique de chambre au XVIIIe siècle* (Paris, 1913/R)

P. Loubet de Sceaury: *Musiciens et facteurs d'instruments de musique sous l'ancien régime: statutes corporatifs* (Paris, 1949)

N. Dufourcq: 'Concerts parisiens et associations de "Symphonistes"', *RBM*, viii (1954), 46–55

H. Burton: 'Les académies de musique en France au XVIIIe siècle', *RdM*, xxxvii (1955), 122–47

B. Bardet: *Les violons de la musique de chambre sous Louis XIV, 1634–1715* (diss., Ecole des Chartes, 1956)

E. Borrel: 'Notes sur la musique de la Grande écurie de 1650 à 1789', *XVIIe siècle*, no.34 (1957), 33–41

P. Citron: 'Notes sur la musique de chambre à Versailles', ibid., 26–32

M. Benoit and N. Dufourcq: 'Les musiciens de Versailles à travers les minutes notariales de LAMY versées aux Archives départementales de Seine-et-Oise', *RMFC*, iii (1963), 189–206

N. Dufourcq and M. Benoit: 'Documents des musiciens de Versailles des minutes du Bailliage de Versailles conservées aux Archives départementales de Seine-et-Oise', *RMFC*, vi (1966), 197–226

M. Jurgens: *Documents du minutier central concernant l'histoire de la musique (1600–1650)* (Paris, 1967–74)

N. Dufourcq, ed.: *La musique à la cour de Louis XIV et de Louis XV, d'après les 'Mémoires' de Sourches et Luynes, 1681–1758* (Paris, 1970)

M. Benoit: *Versailles et les musiciens du roi, 1661–1733* (Paris, 1971)

N. Dufourcq: 'Les fêtes de Versailles: la musique', *XVIIe siècle*, nos 98–9 (1973), 67–75

M. Benoit and N. Dufourcq: 'Les musiciens de Versailles à travers les minutes notariales de Maître Gayot, versées aux Archives départementales des Yvelines (1661–1733)', *RMFC*, xv (1975), 155–90

A. Chastel: 'Etude sur la vie musicale à Paris, à travers la presse, pendant le règne de Louis XVI', *RMFC*, xvi (1976), 37–70

A. Devriès: *Edition et commerce de la musique gravée à Paris dans la première moitié du XVIIIe siècle: les Boivin, les Leclerc* (Geneva, 1976)

C. Massip: *La vie des musiciens de Paris au temps de Mazarin (1643–1661)* (Paris, 1976)

L. Lindgren: 'Parisian Patronage of Performers from the Royal Academy of Musick (1719–28)', *ML*, lviii (1977), 4–28

B. Brévan: *Les changements de la vie musicale parisienne de 1774 à 1799* (Paris, 1980)

R.M. Isherwood: *Farce and Fantasy: Popular Entertainment in Eighteenth-Century Paris* (New York, 1986)

B.R. Hanning: 'The Iconography of a Salon Concert: a Reappraisal', *French Musical Thought, 1600–1800*, ed. G. Cowart (Ann Arbor, 1989), 129–48

J. Mongrédien: 'Paris: the End of the Ancien Régime', *Man & Music: the Classical Era*, ed. N. Zaslaw (London, 1989), 61–98

M. Benoit: 'Paris, 1661–87: the Age of Lully', *Man & Music: the Early Baroque Era*, ed. C. Price (London, 1993), 239–69

D. Heartz: 'The Concert Spirituel in the Tuileries Palace', *EMc*, xxi (1993), 241–8

C. Massip: 'Paris, 1600–61', *Man & Music: the Early Baroque Era*, ed. C. Price (London, 1993), 218–37

D: 1789–1870

BerliozM

J.F. Reichardt: *Vertraute Briefe aus Paris geschrieben in den Jahren 1802 und 1803* (Hamburg, 1804, 2/1805; ed. R. Weber, 1981)

J. Pinkerton: *Recollections of Paris in the Years 1802–3–4–5* (London, 1806)

F.-J. Fétis: *Curiosités historiques de la musique* (Paris, 1830)

Castil-Blaze: *Chapelle-musique des rois de France* (Paris, 1832)

N. Brazier: *Chroniques des petits théâtres de Paris*, 1837, 2/1838 as *Histoire des petits théâtres de Paris, depuis leur origine*

A. Elwart: *Histoire de la Société des concerts du Conservatoire impérial de musique* (Paris, 1860, enlarged 2/1864)

A. Elwart: *Histoire des Concerts populaires de musique classique* (Paris, 1864)

T. de Lajarte: *Bibliothèque musicale du Théâtre de l'Opéra* (Paris, 1878/R)

E. Deldevez: *La Société des concerts, 1860 à 1885* (Paris, 1887)

A. Dandelot: *La Société des concerts du Conservatoire de 1823 à 1897* (Paris, 1898)

C. Pierre, ed.: *Le Conservatoire national de musique et de déclamation* (Paris, 1900)

M. Albert: *Les théâtres des boulevards (1789–1848)* (Paris, 1902)

H.R. Beaulien: *Les théâtres du boulevard du Crime* (Paris, 1905)

G. Cain: *Anciens théâtres de Paris: le boulevard du Temple, les théâtres du boulevard* (Paris, 1906, 3/1920)

J. Tiersot: *Les fêtes et les chants de la Révolution française* (Paris, 1908)

H. de Curzon: 'History and Glory of the Concert-Hall of the Paris Conservatory', *MQ*, iii (1917), 304–18

A.W. Locke: *Music and the Romantic Movement in France* (London, 1920)

A. Dandelot: *La Société des concerts du Conservatoire* (Paris, 1923)

J.-G. Prod'homme and E. de Crauzat: *Les menus plaisirs du roi: l'Ecole royale et le Conservatoire de musique* (Paris, 1929)

M.H. Winter: *Le théâtre du merveilleux* (Paris, 1962; Eng. trans., 1964)

W. Kolneder: 'Die Gründung des Pariser Konservatoriums', *Mf*, xx (1967), 56–7

A.B. Perris: *Music in France during the Reign of Louis-Philippe: Art as 'a Substitute for the Heroic Experience'* (diss., Northwestern U., 1967)

E. Bernard: 'Jules Pasdeloup et les Concerts populaires', *RdM*, lvii (1971), 150–78

D.P. Charlton: *Orchestration and Orchestral Practice in Paris, 1789 to 1810* (diss., U. of Cambridge, 1974)

B. François-Sappey: 'La vie musicale à Paris à travers les Mémoires d'Eugène Sauzay (1809–1901)', *RdM*, lx (1974), 159–210

M.H. Winter: *The Pre-Romantic Ballet* (London, 1974)

H.R. Cohen, ed.: *Les gravures musicales dans L'Illustration, 1843–1899* (Quebec and New York, 1983)

M. Haine: *Les facteurs d'instruments de musique à Paris au 19e siècle* (Brussels, 1985)

J.-M. Fauquet: *Les sociétés de musique de chambre à Paris de la Restauration à 1870* (Paris, 1986)

J. Mongrédien: *La musique en France des Lumières au Romantisme (1789–1830)* (Paris, 1986)

J. Fulcher: *The Nation's Image: French Grand Opera as Politics and Politicized Art* (Cambridge, 1987)

S. Huebner: 'Opera Audiences in Paris, 1830–1870', *ML*, lxx (1989), 206–25

N. Wild: *Dictionnaire des théâtres parisiens au XIXe siècle* (Paris, 1989)

R.P. Locke: 'Paris: Centre of Intellectual Ferment (1789–1852)', *Man & Music: the Early Romantic Era, Between Revolutions: 1789 and 1848*, ed. A. Ringer (London, 1990), 32–83

J. Johnson: *Listening in Paris: a Cultural History* (Berkeley, 1995)

H. Berlioz: *Critique musicale*, ed. H.R. Cohen and Y. Gérard, i: *1823–1834* (Paris, 1996), ii: *1835–1836* (Paris, 1998)

E: AFTER 1870

J. Tiersot: *Musique pittoresques et promenades à l'Exposition universelle de 1889* (Paris, 1889)

O. Comettant: *Histoire de cent mille pianos et d'une salle de concert* (Paris, 1890)

V. d'Indy and others: *La Schola cantorum, son histoire depuis sa fondation jusqu'en 1925* (Paris, 1927)

P. Coppola: *Dix-sept ans de musique à Paris* (Geneva and Paris, 1944)

R. Dumensil: *La musique en France entre les deux guerres* (Paris, 1946)

H. Panassié: *Douze années de jazz (1927–1938): souvenirs* (Paris, 1946)

S. Wolff: *Un demi-siècle d'opéra comique 1900–1950* (Paris, 1953)

C. Hopkinson: *A Dictionary of Parisian Music Publishers, 1700–1950* (London, 1954)

M. d'Ollone: *Le théâtre lyrique et son public* (Paris, 1955)

R. Shattuck: *The Banquet Years: the Origins of the Avant Garde in France 1885 to World War I* (New York, 1955)

G. de Lioncourt: *Un témoignage sur la musique et sur la vie au XXme siècle* (Reims, 1956)

S. Wolff: *L'Opéra au Palais Garnier (1875–1962)* (Paris, 1962)

Situation de la musique en France, ed. Chambre syndicale des éditeurs de musique en France (Paris, 1963–1966)

Situation artistique et sociale du musicien en 1964, ed. Institut de France Académie des Beaux-Arts (Paris, 1965)

J. Feschotte: *Histoire du music-hall* (Paris, 1967)

M. Herbert: *La chanson à Montmartre* (Paris, 1967) [history of cabaret from 1878]

E. Bernard: 'Jules Pasdeloup et les Concerts populaires', *RdM*, lvii (1971), 150–78

P. Miquel: *Histoire de la radio et de la télévision*, (Paris, 1972)

E. Bernard: *La vie symphonique à Paris entre 1861 et 1914* (thesis, U. of Paris I, 1976)

A. Halimi: *Chantons sous l'occupation* (Paris, 1976)

N. Wild, ed.: *Affiches illustrés (1850–1950), Les arts du spectacle on France*, ii (Paris, 1976)

Y. Rivière and C. Pouillon, eds.: *Passage du XXe siècle*, IRCAM, Jan–July 1977 (Paris, 1977)

P.-M. Menger: *La condition du compositeur et le marché de la musique contemporain* (Paris, 1978)

D. Pistone: *La musqiue en France de la Révolution à 1900* (Paris, 1979)

A. Devriès and F. Lesure: *Dictionnaire des éditeurs de musique française* (Geneva, 1979–88)

F. Caradec and A.Weill: *Le café-concert* (Paris, 1980)

X. Dupuis: *Analyse économique de la production lyrique* (Paris, 1980)

J. Gourret: *Le miracle Liebermann: sept saisons à l'Opera de Paris (1973–1980)* (Paris, 1980)

M. Landowski: *Balailles pour la musique* (Paris, 1980)

P. Albert and A.J. Tudesq: *Histoire de la radio-télévision* (Paris, 1981)

M. Delahaye and D. Pistone: *Musique et musicologie dans les universités françaises: histoire, méthodes, programmes* (Paris, 1982)

A. Larquie, ed.: *Gestion et politique des grands théâtres lyriques européens* (Paris, 1982)

J.-P. Leonardi, M. Collin and J. Markovitz: *Festival d'automne à Paris 1972–1982* (Paris, 1982)

'La musique à Paris en 1900', *Revue internationale de musique française*, no.12 (Geneva, 1983)

A. Hennion: *Les conservatoires et leurs élèves* (Paris, 1983)

P.-M. Menger: *Le paradox du musicien; Le compositeur, le mélomane, et l'Etat dans la société contemporaine* (Paris, 1983)

P. Gumplowicz and M.Rostain: *Histoire des institutions de diffusion musicale en France* (Paris, 1976–84)

C. Dupechez: *Histoire de l'Opéra de Paris: un siècle au Palais Garnier, 1875–1980* (Paris, 1984)

S. Gut: *Le groupe Jeune France* (Paris, 1984)

M. Oberthür: *Cafés and Cabarets of Montmartre* (Salt Lake City, 1984)

H. Eck, ed.: *La guerre des ondes* (Paris, 1985)

M. Haine: *Les facteurs d'instruments de musique à Paris au 19e siècle* (Bruxelles, 1985)

P. Olivier: *La musique au quotidien* (Paris, 1985)

C. Rearick: *Pleasures of the Belle Epoque: Entertainment and Festivity in Turn-of-the-Century France* (New Haven, CT, 1985)

C. Mead: *Charles Garnier's Paris Opera: Architectural Empathy and the Renaissance of French Classicism* (Cambridge, MA, 1986)

V. Montjardet-Robin: *Le ministère Malraux (1959–1969): Les musiciens et les débuts de la politique musicale en France* (thesis, U. of Paris VII, 1986)

E. Brody: *Paris. The Musical Kaleidoscope 1870–1925* (New York, 1987)

J.-M. Nectoux: *1913 Le Théâtre des Champs-Elysées: les dossiers du Musée d'Orsay* (Paris, 1987)

J. Pasler: 'Pelléas and Power: Forces Behind the Reception of Debussy's Opera', *19th Century Music* (1987), 243–64

D. Pistone, ed.: *Le théâtre lyrique français 1945–1985* (Paris, 1987)

M. Haine: 'Concerts historiques dans la seconde moitié du 19e siècle', *Musique et société: hommages à Robert Wangermée*, ed. H. Vanhulst and M. Haine (Brussels, 1988), 121–42

'Les années vingt', *Revue internationale de musique française*, no.29 (Geneva, 1989)

L. Garafola: *Diaghilev's Ballets Russes* (New York, 1989)

P.-M. Menger: *Les laboratoires de la création musicale: auteurs, organisations et politique de la recherche musicale* (Paris, 1989)

D. Pistone, ed.: 'Paris et la musique 1890–1900', *Revue internationale de musique française*, no.28 (1989), 7–55

N. Wild: *Dictionnaire des théâtres parisiennes au XIXe siècle* (Paris, 1989)

M. Chimènes: 'Les institutions musicales en France: repères chronologiques' *InHarmoniques*, no.6 (1990), 161–83

P. Urfalino: *Quatre voix pour un Opéra* (Paris, 1990)

'L'Itinéraire', *ReM*, nos.421–5 (1991)

La musique et la danse, la politique culturelle 1981–1991, ed. Ministère de la culture, de la communication et des grand travaux (Paris, 1991)

J. Gribenski: 'La recherche musicologique en France depuis 1958', *AcM*, lxiii (1991), 211–37

J. Pasler: 'Paris: Conflicting Notions of Progress', *Man & Music: the Late Romantic Era*, ed. J. Samson (London, 1991), 389–416

F. Patureau: *Le Palais Garnier dans la société parisienne* (Liège, 1991)

N. Perloff: *Art and the Everyday: Popular Entertainment and the Circle of Erik Satie*, (Oxford, 1991)

Musique, Etat et culture Ministère de la culture et de la communication, ed. (Paris, 1992)

J. Aguila: *Le Domaine musical, Pierre Boulez et vingt ans de création contemporaine* (Paris, 1992)

G. Scarpetta: *Le festival d'automne de Michel Guy* (Paris, 1992)

M. Oberthür: *Le chat noir 1881–1897: les dossiers du Musée d'Orsay* (Paris, 1992)

J. Brooks: 'Nadia Boulanger and the Salon of the Princesse de Polignac', *JAMS*, xlvi (1993), 415–68

J. Pasler: 'Concert Programs and their Narratives as Emblems of Ideology', *International Journal of Musicology*, ii (1993), 249–308

M. Dibango: *Three Kilos of Coffee: an Autobiography* (Chicago, 1994)

Répertoire du Mécénat d'entreprise, 10th ed. (Paris, 1995)

J. Boivin: *La classe de Messiaen* (Paris, 1995)

Lire l'IRCAM (Paris, 1996)

M. Chimènes: '*L'Information musicale*: une parenthèse de *La revue musicale*', *Des revues sous l'occupation: La Revue des revues*, no.24 (1997) 91–110

M. Duchesneau: *L'avant-garde musicale et ses sociétés à Paris de 1871 à 1939* (Liège, 1997)

M.E. Poole: 'Gustave Charpentier and the Conservatoire Populaire de Mimi Pinson', *19th Century Music*, xx/3 (1997) 231–52

A. Veitl: *Politique de la musique contemporaine: le compositeur, la 'recherche musicale', et l'Etat en France de 1958 à 1991*, (Paris, 1997)

M.C. Strasser: *Ars Gallica: the Société Nationale and its role in French musical life, 1871–1891* (diss. U. of Illinois 1998)

J. Pasler: 'Building a public for orchestral music: Les Concerts Colonne', *Concert et public: mutation de la vie musicale en Europe de 1780 à 1914*, ed. H.E. Bödeker, P. Veit and M. Werner (Paris, 2000)

GORDON A. ANDERSON/THOMAS B. PAYNE (I), DANIEL HEARTZ/RICHARD FREEDMAN (II), JAMES R. ANTHONY (III; V, 1(i), 3–5), ELISABETH COOK (IV, introduction, 2, 3; V, 1(ii)), JOHN EBY (IV, 1), PAUL F. RICE (V, 2), DAVID CHARLTON, JOHN TREVITT/GUY GOSSELIN (VI), JANN PASLER (VII)

Paris, Aimé (*b* 1798; *d* 1866). French educationist. A former pupil of Pierre Galin, he abandoned a legal career to perfect and propagate Galin's method of teaching sightsinging. Cooperating with his sister Nanine and her husband Emile Chevé he produced the GALIN-PARIS-CHEVÉ METHOD. He devised the 'langue des durées', which forms an essential part of that teaching method.

BERNARR RAINBOW

Paris, Anton Ferdinand (*b* Salzburg, 19 Feb 1744; *d* Salzburg, 2 June 1809). Austrian composer and organist. The son of the former cathedral organist Georg Joseph Paris (1700–60), he was active in a similar capacity at the Salzburg court from 1762. He was a friend of the Mozart family and apparently figured in Leopold Mozart's negotiations with Archbishop Colloredo concerning the terms of Mozart's last appointment in Salzburg. According to Leopold's letters of 31 August and 3 September 1778, Paris was given additional pay to take over some of Wolfgang's duties as court and cathedral organist, and Wolfgang was required to play the cathedral organ only for major feasts, with Paris doing duty at other times.

Paris was an active composer, mostly of church music. For the most part his compositions are written in a modern if conservative, shortwinded and uninventive style, including his two surviving orchestral works, a symphony and a keyboard concerto. His pedagogical keyboard works, composed as part of his duties at the Kapellhaus, are lost. Paris was also active as a copyist, not only of his own works but also of works by Mozart, Hafeneder and Romanus Hofstetter, among others. He is said to have been a passionate hunter.

WORKS

Sacred: masses, *D-LFN*, *TEI*; lits, *A-Wn*, *D-LFN*, *FW*; offs, *CH-E* (incl. autographs), *D-LFN*; Regina caeli, Vespers, Ave Regina, Tantum ergo, ants, hymns, sacred arias, *A-MB*, *Sn*, *Ssp*, *D-LFN*, *TZ* (incl. autographs), *WS*

Inst: Sym., F, *A-MB*, ed. in RRMCE, xl (1994); Conc., C, kbd, *Ssp*; numerous cadenzas, preludes and versettes for organ, *Sn*; pedagogical kbd works, lost (see Pillwein)

BIBLIOGRAPHY

B. Pillwein: *Biographische Schilderungen oder Lexikon salzburgischer theils verstorbener theils lebender Künstler* (Salzburg, 1821), 181–2

E. Hintermaier: *Die Salzburger Hofkapelle von 1700 bis 1806: Organisation und Personal* (diss., U. of Salzburg, 1972), 309–12

C. Eisen: Preface to *Orchestral Music in Salzburg, 1750–1780*, RRMCE, xl (1994)

H. Schuler: *Mozarts Salzburger Freunde und Bekannte: Biographien und Kommentar* (Wilhelmshaven, 1996), 163–5

CLIFF EISEN

Paris, Claude. *See* PARI, CLAUDIO.

Paris, Guillaume-Alexis [Alexandre] (*b* Liège, ?1756; *d* St Petersburg, 18/30 Jan 1840). Flemish conductor and composer. In 1776 he was on the staff of the theatre at Maastricht. He directed the orchestra of the Théâtre de la Monnaie in Brussels from 1780, was musical director and conductor of a theatre at Ghent in 1782–3, was in Lyons in 1784 and by January 1786 was conducting in a Liège theatre, where his opera *Le nouveau sorcier* was given. In 1787–8 he conducted French operas in Amsterdam, and from 1790 to at least 1792 he did the same at La Monnaie. When the French invaded Brussels in 1794 he and his company fled to Hamburg, encountering C.-F.-H. Duquesnoy, with whom he probably collaborated in mounting French operas for émigrés. In 1799 he was engaged to direct the French theatre at the St Petersburg court. This was the beginning of a remarkable career as a conductor and a composer of operas and ballets. Apart from his theatrical post, he conducted the St Petersburg Philharmonic Society (founded in 1802); during his 20 years in that position, he conducted several performances of the *Messiah*, Haydn's *Creation* and *The Seasons*, and Mozart's *Requiem*. His talent was such that Boieldieu, who succeeded him at the theatre in 1804, preferred to leave the conducting of his own new works to Paris; his authority and impartiality were particularly lauded. In 1824 he retired with a generous pension, remaining in Russia until his death. His compositions, mostly works for the stage, remain little known.

WORKS

Le nouveau sorcier (op, P. Dubuisson), Liège, 9 Jan 1786

Les lois et les rois (scène lyrique), Brussels, Monnaie, 15 April 1793

Les amants protées (vaudeville), Moscow, Jan 1806, perf. St Petersburg, 1808, in Russ., as Le revirement, ou Les disputes jusqu'aux larmes

Ballets: Le retour de Thétis (P. Chevalier), Gatchina, Palace Theatre, 15 Sept 1799, *RUS-SPan*; L'arrivée de Thétis (Chevalier), Gatchina, Palace Theatre, 1 Nov 1799; La famille des simples d'esprit, Gatchina, Palace Theatre, 1823; La forêt noire (3), 1824

Inst: Chaconne concertante, orch, 1795

BIBLIOGRAPHY

AudaM; *EitnerQ*; *MooserA*, iii; *VannesD*

R.-A. Mooser: 'Un musicien belge en Russie au début du XIXe siècle: Guillaume-Alexis Paris (1756–1840)', *RBM*, i (1946–7), 21–6

R.A. Mooser: *L'opéra-comique français en Russie au XVIIIe siècle* (Conches, 1932, enlarged 2/1954)

H. Schuler: *Mozarts Salzburger Freunde und Bekannte: Biographien und Kommentar* (Wilhelmshaven, 1996), 163–5

PHILIPPE MERCIER

Paris, Juan (*b* 1759; *d* Santiago de Cuba, 10 June 1845). Spanish composer and choirmaster. He was a priest. Nothing is known about his life or musical training prior to 1805, by which date he was choirmaster in Santiago de Cuba Cathedral, replacing Francisco José Hierrezuelo, who worked there for two years as Esteban Salas y Castro's successor. París occupied his post for forty years, during which time he trained a generation of musicians and contributed to the cultural development of the cathedral within the city. He reformed the choir in 1807, changing the members and including flute, oboe and violin in the orchestra.

París composed a great deal of music, carols in particular. Indeed his first compositions, written while he was working as choirmaster, were four carols: *Cautivos de Israel*, *Albricias pastores*, *Vamos* and *A qué fin van los pastores con tanta prisa a Belén*. The scores and the individual parts of the first-mentioned have survived. Almost all his works of this type are for four voices and follow the ternary form Allegro–Lento–Allegro, with some variations, such as the inclusion of a recitative or a sung and accompanied pastourelle. From 1806 he broadened the carols out into four movements or sections: Adagio–Recitado–Andante–Allegretto, or other combinations; on occasions he substituted the brief introductory piece with a true prelude. *Hasta cuándo … santo cielo?*, *Qué raro portento* and other works date from this period. Between 1808 and 1829 he composed nearly 30 carols. In 1806 and in 1824 pamphlets with the lyrics to some of the carols appeared, but the music itself remained unpublished. Virtually all París's work can be found in the archives of the Museo Eclesiástico de Cuba, situated in Santiago de Cuba Cathedral.

BIBLIOGRAPHY

A. Carpentier: *La música en Cuba* (Mexico City, 1946, 3/1988)

P. Hernández Balaguer: 'La capilla de música de la catedral de Santiago de Cuba', *RMC*, no.90, (1964), 14–61

V. Feliu: 'Juan París sucesor de Esteban salos en la Capilla de Música de la Catedralde Santiago de Cuba (1805–1845)', *Revista Biblioteca Nacional José Martí* (La Habana, 1985), 5–26

VICTORIA ELI RODRÍGUEZ

Parish Alvars, Elias [Parish, Eli] (*b* Teignmouth, 28 Feb 1808; *d* Vienna, 25 Jan 1849). English harpist and composer. He studied with François Dizi and also worked with Théodore Labarre in London. For some time in the 1820s he was employed by the harp manufacturers Schwieso and Grosjean at their Soho Square premises, where he may have met the shadowy figure known as A. Alvars, who dedicated a harp piece to Frederick Grosjean, and who may well be the person whose surname Eli Parish appears to have adopted; at the same time he changed his name from Eli to Elias. It is as Elias Parish Alvars that his name appears on his earliest published compositions (Artaria, 1836).

From the early 1830s he was based mainly in Vienna, though he is known to have given concerts in Germany in 1830 and in Italy in 1833, when he shared a concert in Milan with John Field. In 1836 he was appointed first harp at the Imperial and Royal Opera of Vienna, but two years later he was back in London, dedicating his Concertino op.34 to Queen Victoria, and his Fantasia op.35 to Sigismond Thalberg, who is said to have developed his famous 'three-handed' piano technique in imitation of Parish Alvars's writing for the harp. A *Grande fantaisie brillante* for harp and piano based on *Anna Bolena*, *La sonnambula* and *Lucia di Lammermoor* and composed jointly with Carl Czerny can be dated to 1838. From 1839 until 1842 he made a leisurely tour of the Eastern Mediterranean, commemorated in his *Voyage d'un harpiste en Orient* op.62.

In May 1842 Parish Alvars bought his first new 'Gothic' model double-action harp from Pierre Erard. The acquisition of this more robustly constructed, mechanically superior instrument appears to have been significant; already unsurpassed as a virtuoso, he developed many innovative techniques, integrating pedal and manual skills in a completely unprecedented way, seizing brilliantly on the advantages and possibilities presented by the new harp, and engendering the enthusiasm of his contemporaries, among them Berlioz, Liszt and Mendelssohn. His innovations include chordal glissandi, double, triple and quadruple harmonics, the combination of harmonics with glissandi, the use of enharmonic effects (as in *La danse des fées* op.76), glissandi both with the pedals and with the tuning-key (*Sérénade* op.83), the pre-setting of pedals in such a way as to give an impression of brilliant virtuosity (*Grand Study in Imitation of the Mandoline* op.84) and the use of scordatura (*Last Grand Fantasia*).

Parish Alvars was in London again in 1846, this time with the intention of settling there permanently, but finding the musical establishment unsympathetic to the harp as a solo instrument, he returned to Vienna, where in 1847 he was appointed chamber musician to the emperor. His last important public appearance was at a concert of his own compositions in Vienna on 2 January 1848.

Parish Alvars's published compositions for the harp include over 80 works for solo harp, many of which are of phenomenal difficulty; three concertos, two concertinos (one for solo harp and one for two harps) and duos for harp and piano. His unpublished works include the fantasia *Sounds of Ossian*, among the most demanding solos ever written for the harp, a symphony, an overture inspired by Byron's *Manfred*, an opera *The Legend of Teignmouth* and two piano concertos. (H.-J. Zingel: *Harfenmusik im 19. Jahrhundert: Versuch einer historischen Darstellung* (Wilhelmshaven, 1976; Eng. trans., 1992)

ANN GRIFFITHS

Parish clerk. A subordinate official who for many centuries played an important role in the music of an English parish church, in addition to other duties. A similar role was played in German churches by the Küster (Lat. *custos*). In the Middle Ages parish clerks usually belonged to minor priestly orders, and assisted the parish priest in various functions. Their musical importance was greatest in the century before the Reformation, when in the richer churches they were often at the head of a staff of full-time musicians ('clerks' or 'conducts') and sometimes were also expected to train the choristers. Something of this organization survived in some churches until about 1570, but from then on the parish clerk was left to lead the congregation alone. He was no longer in orders, he was ill-paid and his standing rapidly sank to that of a menial. The Canons of 1603 still required incumbents to appoint as parish clerk a man who had 'competent skill in singing (if it may be)', but this was seldom observed, and John Playford in 1671 lamented that few London parish clerks could even lead a common psalm tune properly (*see* PLAYFORD family, (1)). With the introduction of lining out the parish clerk had to read out each line of the metrical psalm before it was sung, and in some places this developed into a curious kind of chant. As time went on he was often left to choose the psalms and the tunes as well. He would announce the psalm in the traditional form, 'Let us sing to the glory of God the –th psalm', and in many cases the choir would have had no previous warning of his choice. Increasingly the parish clerk became a figure of fun, as Caleb Quotem in many an 18th-century farce, or as Davy Diggs in Hewlett's *The Parish Clerk* (1841). Nevertheless, some parish clerks became notable church musicians – Abraham Barber at Wakefield, WILLIAM KNAPP at Poole, JOHN ARNOLD at Great Warley, Essex, Michael Broome and James Kempson at Birmingham, all of whom published collections of church music. The parish clerk had disappeared in all but the most remote country places long before the end of the 19th century.

The Company of Parish Clerks of London, also known before the Reformation as the Fraternity of St Nicholas, dates back at least to 1233. It was incorporated by charter in 1442; the fraternity was suppressed in 1547, but the company remained, obtaining its last charter in 1640. Its powers included the right to examine every London parish clerk in the ability to sing psalms. Before the Reformation clerks had played an important part in pageants and other entertainments, and they continued to sing at the Lord Mayor's election. Soon after 1660 the Company acquired an organ, and began fortnightly practices of psalmody which continued to 1822, when the last organist resigned. For most of this period they used Playford's *Psalms and Hymns in Solemn Musick* on these occasions. The Company's hall in Silver Street was destroyed in World War II with most of the surviving records, which are, however, described by Ebblewhite.

See also ANGLICAN AND EPISCOPALIAN CHURCH MUSIC.

BIBLIOGRAPHY
B. P[ayne]: *The Parish-Clerk's Guide* (London, 2/1694)
J. Fox: *The Parish Clerk's Vade Mecum* (London, 1752)
L. Milbourne: *Psalmody Recommended, in a Sermon Preach'd to the Company of Parish Clerks* (London, 1713)
J.T.J. Hewlett: *The Parish Clerk* (London, 1841) [a novel]
J. Christie: *Some Account of Parish Clerks* (London, 1893)
J. Wickham Legg, ed.: *The Clerk's Book of 1549* (London, 1903)
P.H. Ditchfield: *The Parish Clerk* (London, 1907)
E.A. Ebblewhite: *The Parish Clerks' Company and its Charters* (London, 1932)
H. Baillie: *London Churches, their Music and Musicians (1485–1560)* (diss., U. of Cambridge, 1958)
R.H. Adams: *The Parish Clerks of London* (Chichester, 1971)
N. Temperley: 'John Playford and the Metrical Psalms', *JAMS*, xxv (1972), 331–78
N. Temperley: *The Music of the English Parish Church* (Cambridge, 1979), i, 7, 44–5, 88ff, 119–20
N. Temperley: 'The Old Way of Singing: its Origins and Development', *JAMS*, xxxiv (1981), 511–44
NICHOLAS TEMPERLEY

Pariton. *See* BARYTON (i).

Parizot [Parisot]. French family of organ builders. Originally from the Lorraine region, they were active in the 18th century. Claude Parizot (*b* Etain, before 1700; *d* ?Etain, *c*1752) was the son of a carpenter, he was recruited by Christophe Moucherel while building the organ at Etain (1720–21). He followed his master to Paris and then worked for François Thierry. He became a master organ builder, probably in Paris around 1730. Asked to work for the Premonstratensian order with the Alsatian builder Georges Daniel Faul, his work can be found at Abbeville (St Georges, 1736, and St Sépulchre, 1738). However, it seems that he lost his position to Charles Dallery, and went to work in Rouen for Charles Lefèvre. He worked on the organ at St Rémy, Dieppe, in 1737. After he finished building the organ at Séry-aux-Prés Abbey, Amiens (1739), he moved to Caen to build instruments at Mondaye Abbey (1740; surviving), Sées Cathedral, Ardenne Abbey, and particularly Notre Dame de Guibray at Falaise (1746–52; surviving). The organ at Gouffern Abbey (1754) has been mis-attributed to him: it is actually by one of his nephews. He returned to Etain and died there.

Henri Parizot (*b* Etain, 1736; *d* Le Mans, 1795), a nephew and pupil of Claude, moved to Alençon in 1755, where he married Julienne Pavillon in 1759. He later moved to Le Mans. Examples of his prolific output include organs at La Ferté-Bernard (1758), St Jean, Caen (1769–72), St Sulpice, Fougères (1772), Mortain (1774), St Lô (1780 and 1792), St Gervais Falaise, St Pierre, Coutances (1782), Fontaine-Daniel Abbey (1784), La Trinité, Cherbourg (1785) and probably Gouffern Abbey (1788).

Nicolas Parizot (*b* Etain, *c*1735; *d* Le Mans, 1792), brother of Henri, and nephew and pupil of Claude, settled in Le Mans in 1754. He married there in 1759 and worked locally: at Mamers (1760), Abbaye de Perseigne (1762), Notre Dame, Vire (1762), Torcé (1763) and St Suzanne, Courcité (1777). His son became a carpenter and Nicolas himself seems to have given up organ-building in favour of his brother.

BIBLIOGRAPHY
M. Vanmackelberg: *Les orgues d'Abbeville* (Abbeville, 1966)
F. Sabatier: 'Le grand orgue de la Cathédrale de Sées', *L'orgue*, no.149 (1974), 6–19
M. Vanmackelberg: 'Autour des Parizot facteurs d'orgues au Mans (seconde moitié du XVIIIe s.)', *La Province du Maine*, xiv/53–4 (1985), 63–6
J.-F. Détrée: 'Le grand orgue de la cathédrale de Coutances', *L'orgue*, no.197 (1986), 14–18
PIERRE HARDOUIN

Park, John (*b* Greenock, 14 Jan 1804; *d* St Andrews, 8 April 1865). Scottish composer. He came from a musical family and was a parish minister of the Church of Scotland. He was educated in the local schools of Greenock and Paisley, then at the universities of Glasgow and Aberdeen, and gained the DD. His first Scottish charge was that of Glencairn, Dumfriesshire, where he was appointed in 1843; after 11 years there he accepted a call to the First Charge of the Collegiate Parish Church (Holy Trinity) in the university town of St Andrews, Fife, where he remained until his death. Highly gifted in painting, verse and music, he played several instruments and excelled as a composer. 'Music was his native element', wrote J.C. Shairp, principal of St Andrews University, in his foreword to Park's *Songs*.

Park's compositions include a small number of works for solo piano and piano duet (1831, *GB-Er*), of which Sonata no.4 for solo piano is perhaps the most interesting; although he followed the normal conventions of a four-movement sonata, the simplicity of his style can reveal delicate subtleties, and the clarity of his textures is refreshingly undemonstrative. His songs (*c*100 in total) are only occasionally overtly Scottish, but his setting of Lady Grizel Baillie's 'There was ance a May' is a beautiful contribution to the genre. Some, such as his treatment of Shelley's 'Hymn of Pan', are extended and varied, while others are tiny vignettes. Many are settings of his own verses, often pious, and disarmingly unpretentious, while some hint at disappointed love (Park never married). He also wrote the words for the ever-popular *I wish I were where Gadie rins*, setting them to a traditional tune he collected himself.

Park refused to publish any of his works during his lifetime, but told his relatives 'When I am gone, you may do what you will with them'. In 1876 a selection of 64 of his finest songs was successfully published and they are still sung today. Three volumes of songs in manuscript completed by 1849, and three music sketchbooks are held in the Reid Music Library at the University of Edinburgh. Of a gentle, slightly melancholy disposition, he appears to have been held in deep affection, despite the fact that he avoided much in the way of pastoral duties. He suffered a stroke just after hearing the 'Alleluia' chorus from Handel's *Messiah* and never regained consciousness.

BIBLIOGRAPHY

Brown-StrattonBMB; DNB (J.C. Hadden)

Obituary, *Glasgow Herald* (11 April 1865)

J.C. Shairp: Foreword to *Songs Composed and in part Written by the Late Rev. John Park* (Leeds, 1876)

J.D. Brown: *Biographical Dictionary of Musicians* (Paisley and London, 1886/R)

D. Baptie: *Musical Scotland* (Edinburgh and Glasgow, 1894)

H. Scott : *Fasti Ecclesiae Scoticanae*, v (Edinburgh, 1925)

H.G. Farmer: *History of Music in Scotland* (London, 1947/R)

JEAN MARY ALLAN/JOHN PURSER

Park [née Reynolds], **Maria Hester** (*b* 29 Sept 1760; *d* Hampstead, 7 June 1813). English composer and teacher. She played the harpischord and piano in public concerts and taught music to members of the nobility, including the Duchess of Devonshire and her daughters. In April 1787 she married the engraver and man of letters Thomas Park (1759–1834). On 22 October 1794 Haydn wrote to thank Park for sending him two charming prints, enclosing 'for the Mistris Park a little Sonat' with the promise of visiting her within a few days. Although she suffered from ill-health for many years, her family life was a happy one; her husband wrote several touching poems to her. Her surviving music, spanning a quarter of a century, is that of a very competent, professional composer. Her sonatas are varied and spirited, while the concerto for keyboard and strings reveals an individual voice, particularly in the final rondo.

Earlier reference works confuse her with the singer and composer Maria F. Parke, to the extent of calling the singer Maria Hester Parke; the British Library *Catalogue of Printed Music* clearly distinguishes the two. Her keyboard sonatas opp.1 and 2 were published under her maiden name.

WORKS
published in London

op.
1	Sonatas, hpd/pf, vn acc. (1785), ded. Countess of Uxbridge
2	3 Sonatas, hpd/pf (*c*1786)
3	A Set of Glees with the Dirge in Cymbeline (?1790)
4	2 Sonatas, pf/hpd (1790)
6	Concerto, pf/hpd, str (?1795)
7	Sonata, pf (?1796)
13	2 Sonatas, pf, vn acc. (?1801)
—	Waltz, pf (?1800)
—	Divertimento, pf, vn acc. (?1811)

Possibly lost, advertised in op.13: 6 Divertimentos, hp, pf, op.8; 6 Duets, hp, pf, op.9; Sonata with the Berlin Favourite; Sonata with Prince Adolphus Fancy

BIBLIOGRAPHY

A. Seward: *Letters* (Edinburgh, 1811)

Gentleman's Magazine, lxxxiii (1813), 596

T. Park: *Morning Thoughts and Midnight Musings* (London, 1818)

'Thomas Park, Esq.', *Annual Biography*, xx (1835), 257–63

H.C.R. Landon: *Haydn in England 1791–1795* (London, 1976)

Calendar of London Concerts 1750–1800 (Goldsmiths College, U. of London; S. McVeigh) [restricted-access database]

OLIVE BALDWIN, THELMA WILSON

Park Choon-suk [Pak Ch'unsŭk] (*b* Seoul, 1933). Korean composer of popular music. He was the son of a rich businessman and had the opportunity to learn the piano during childhood. He showed musical talent from an early age and entered the College of Music at Seoul National University, but he was inclined to the world of popular music and soon gave up his career as a classical musician. He subsequently composed many songs which were performed by some of the most well-known singers in the Korean mainstream popular music market, and he also discovered several new singers and helped them to establish their careers. Park composed around 2500 songs and more than 200 film soundtracks. His music covers a wide range of genres including pop, jazz and ballad, but he is principally noted for his contribution to *t'ŭrot'ŭ* ('trot') music, which developed during the 1930s under the influence of Japanese popular music while Korea was under the Japanese colonial regime (1910–45). Although *t'ŭrot'ŭ* was at one time subject to criticism as being part of the legacy of Japanese colonialism, it gained widespread popularity among Koreans, and Park has had more hits than any other composer of *t'ŭrot'ŭ* songs.

KIM CHANG-NAM

Parke [Park]. English family of musicians.

(1) **John Parke** (*b* London, 1745; *d* London, 2 Aug 1829). Oboist. He studied with Simpson, but preferred to develop the soft sweet tone that J.C. Fischer introduced into England. In the late 1760s he was principal oboist at the oratorios and a performer at Ranelagh and Marylebone Gardens. After one season at the King's Theatre, he was replaced by Fischer in 1769, but by 1771 he was playing at Vauxhall Gardens. In that year he became first oboe at Drury Lane where he remained for most of his career. He was especially praised for his obbligatos – 'his accompanying a voice is particularly delicate' (*ABC Dario Musico*, 1780) – and Thomas Linley the younger wrote several fine arias with oboe obbligato for him. He often played concertos of his own in oratorio intervals, as also in the pleasure gardens, but none seems to have survived. Parke also played in the Queen's band, for the Prince of Wales at Carlton House, in the Concert of Ancient Music, and (with his brother) in the Professional Concert and probably in most or all of the famous Haydn concerts in Hanover Square Rooms. Parke retired about 1815. His son Henry (1793–1835) was a pupil of Sir John Soane and became an architect; some of his drawings and watercolours can be seen in the Soane Museum, London.

(2) **William Thomas Parke** (*b* London, 15 Feb 1761; *d* London, 26 Aug 1847). Oboist and composer, brother of (1) John Parke. At ten he was learning the flute and at 11 the oboe from his brother; also, at 13, the piano from Charles Rousseau Burney, the historian's nephew. In 1775 he sang in the Drury Lane chorus as a treble in Dibdin's *A Christmas Tale*, and in 1776 he was, significantly, judged good enough after 'rather more than

three months' practice' to play the viola at Vauxhall Gardens and Drury Lane. On his own he worked hard at the oboe, and in 1783, on the recommendation of William Shield, he succeeded Sharp as first oboe at Covent Garden. In 1787 he joined the Professional Concert.

According to Sainsbury, 'his tone [was] remarkably sweet, his execution rapid and articulate, his shakes brilliant, his cantabiles and cadenzas varied and fanciful, and … his judicious style of playing adagio movements evince[d] the greatest feeling and expression'. Shield so admired his playing that he wrote long soprano arias with a difficult concertante oboe part in his *Robin Hood*, *Fontainbleau*, *The Choleric Fathers* and *Marian*. Mrs Billington, who sang the one in *Marian*, inspired a similar aria that Shield added to Grétry's *Richard Coeur-de-lion* in which Parke played the concertante part on a flute. There are also concertante parts for Parke in the overtures to Hook's *The Fair Peruvian*, Shield's *The Woodman* and Mazzinghi's *The Magician No Conjurer* and *The Exile*.

After studying composition with Baumgarten, the leader of the Covent Garden orchestra, Parke was able to play an oboe concerto of his own in an oratorio interval at Drury Lane in 1786, and in 1791–2 he published two sets of duets for two flutes or two oboes. He was already extending the upper range of the oboe, and at a Hanover Square Rooms concert in 1796 he first demonstrated his high G, presumably in another concerto of his own. Only one was ever published, *A Grand Concerto for the Oboe, German Flute, or Clarinet* (c1805). In his memoirs he mentions concertos by himself that included variations on *Rule, Britannia, God Save the King* and *The Bridge of Lodi*.

Shield, who disliked writing overtures to his own operas, got Parke to compose those in *Netley Abbey* and *Lock and Key*, as also the Act 2 finale in *The Lad of the Hills*. Parke also composed a pantomime-ballet, *The Tithe Pig* (11 April 1795), but the music is lost. After Shield's retirement from Covent Garden in 1797 Parke was not asked for any more theatre music.

In 1786 he had adapted Dalayrac's *Nina* for the benefit performance of Covent Garden's singing actress Elizabeth Martyr who, two years earlier, had been the first English Chérubin in Beaumarchais' comedy. Petite and 'a good breeches figure', she was Parke's mistress until her death in 1807, when she bequeathed her farm at Yalding in Kent to the two sons she had had by him. Mrs Martyr specialized in the cheerful sailor-boy songs Parke wrote for her. Later in life he composed little else but songs – about 150 for Vauxhall Gardens between 1808 and 1821. He also wrote elegies on the deaths of Sir John Moore (1809) and the Princess Amelia (1810), and an *Ode to Peace* (1814).

Parke's garrulous *Musical Memoirs* were published in 1830; they are a useful source of information about Shield and on contemporary performing practice. His *New Preceptor for the German Flute* had appeared in 1806.

(3) Maria Frances Parke (*b* London, 26 Aug 1772; *d* London, 31 July 1822). English soprano, composer and pianist, eldest daughter of (1) John Parke. She was taught by her father and played the harpsichord at his 1781 benefit concert when she was eight years old. The following year at his benefit she made her début as a singer and played a piano concerto by J.S. Schroeter. In 1784 the *Public Advertiser* praised the taste and spirit of her playing and a year later wrote that she 'certainly will be one of the best Piano Forte performers in England'. However, as an adult performer she was primarily a singer. She had sung among the trebles in the Handel Commemoration concerts in 1784 and by the age of 20 was a leading soprano soloist in concerts and oratorios in London and the provinces. Her uncle W.T. Parke remembered her singing in *Messiah* 'with great taste and judgement'. She sang at Haydn's benefit concert at the Hanover Square Room on 2 May 1794 and both sang and played at her own benefit on the 19th, when Haydn 'presided at the piano-forte'. She retired on her marriage to John Beardmore in 1815.

She has been confused with the composer Maria Hester Park (née Reynolds), but her published compositions are all attributed to 'Miss Parke' and often signed 'MFP' on the title-page. Miss F. Parke, her younger sister Francesca Margaretta, sang at her benefit concerts in 1798 and 1799.

WORKS
published in London

Inst: 3 Grand Sonatas, pf, op.1 (1799); 2 Grand Sonatas, pf, vn acc. ad lib, op.2 (?1800); Divertimento and Military Rondo, pf (?1807)

Vocal: I have often been told (1787); God of Slaughter, duet (?1806); What is beauty, duet (?1810)

BIBLIOGRAPHY
BDA; SainsburyD
W.T. Parke: *Musical Memoirs* (London, 1830)
H.C.R. Landon: *Haydn in England 1791–1795* (London, 1976)
S. McVeigh: *Concert Life in London from Mozart to Haydn* (Cambridge, 1993)
Calendar of London Concerts 1750–1800 (Goldsmith's College, U. of London; S. McVeigh) [restricted-access database]
ROGER FISKE/JANET K. PAGE (1, 2), OLIVE BALDWIN, THELMA WILSON (3)

Parke, Thomas. See PACK, THOMAS.

Parkening, Christopher (William) (*b* Los Angeles, 14 Dec 1947). American guitarist. Inspired by the guitar transcriptions of his cousin Jack Marshall, he took up the instrument at the age of 11. After several years' study with Celedonio Romero and Pepe Romero, he participated in the masterclasses of Segovia at the University of California, Berkeley, and subsequently studied privately with him. In 1964–5 he spent a year at UCLA but then transferred to the University of Southern California as a cello student of Gabor Rejto (the guitar was not yet taught at the university); asked to found a guitar department there, he eventually became its head (1971–5). Meanwhile, he made his recording début in 1967 and his concert début a year later. For the next decade he enjoyed a highly successful career as a performer, and his recordings from this period are notable for their energy and bravura. By 1977, however, he had become disenchanted with his increasingly stressful career and happily realized his long-standing dream of retiring at 30. Abandoning the concert stage, he moved to a ranch in Montana, where he taught the guitar, and appeared only rarely as a recitalist (for example, in Washington DC, 1979). About 1981, after becoming a committed Christian, he resumed his performing career, with the intention of playing 'only for God's glory' (quoting J.S. Bach); since that time his recordings (various reissues apart) have usually included a number of overtly religious works. In performance, he gradually recaptured the successful formula of his earlier recitals, which were centred on colourful shorter pieces, and critics have drawn particular attention to his greater subtlety of expression. Since the mid-1980s he has often been joined in concerts by guitarists such as David Brandon. Parkening has published *The Christopher Parkening Guitar Method* (Chicago, 1972–), several volumes of transcriptions, including one of works by Bach (Chicago, 1973–), and *Music for Guitar*, an edition of 19 pieces by Rodrigo (Mainz, 1995).

BIBLIOGRAPHY
C. Cooper: Interview, *Classical Guitar*, v/6 (1986–7), 12–15
L. Valdez: 'Christopher Parkening: Poet of the Guitar', *Ovation*, vii/Jan (1987), 12–15
                                                    THOMAS F. HECK

Parker, monk of Stratford. Composer, possibly identifiable with WILLIAM STRATFORD.

Parker, Alice (*b* Boston, 16 Dec 1925). American composer, organist and conductor. She studied at Smith College (BA 1947) and the Juilliard School of Music (MS 1949), where her teachers included Robert Shaw, Julius Herford and Vincent Persichetti. She worked as an arranger for the Robert Shaw Chorale (1949–67), taught at Westminster Choir College, and founded and directed Melodious Accord, Inc. Her more than 400 compositions include operas, cantatas, choral pieces, and song cycles on Amerindian texts and poems by Ogden Nash, Robert Frost and Emily Dickinson. Her association with Shaw produced numerous choral settings of American folksongs, hymns and spirituals. Her many honours include a MacDowell Colony Fellowship, ASCAP awards, honorary doctorates, grants from the NEA and AMC, and commissions from Chanticleer, the Vancouver Chamber Singers and the Atlanta SO. She is the author of *Musical Reference Grammar* (New York, 1964), *Creative Hymn Singing* (Chapel Hill, NC, 1976), *Folk Song Transformations* (New York, 1985) and *Melodious Accord* (Chicago, 1991).

WORKS
(selective list)

Ops: The Martyrs' Mirror (2), Lansdale, PA, 1971; The Family Reunion (1), Norman, OK, 1975; Singers Glen (prol, 2), Lancaster, PA, 1978; The Ponder Heart (2), Jackson MS, 1982

Choral-orch: Pilgrims and Strangers, 1975; Guadete: 6 Latin Christmas Hymns, 1976; Commentaries, SSA, SSAA, orch, 1978; Songs from the Dragon Quilt, nar, SATB, orch, 1984; Earth, Sky, Spirit, children's vv, orch, 1986; The World's One Song, 1990; That Sturdy Vine (J. Janzen, trad. hymns), SATB, children's vv, S, orch, 1991; Singing in the Dark, male vv, orch, 1995

Cants.: A Sermon from the Mountain (M.L. King), nar, SATB, str, ad lib jazz inst, 1969; The Feast of Ingathering, SATB, org, 1972; Melodious Accord, SSATB, brass qt, hp, 1974; In Praise of Singing, SATB, str qnt, 1981; Sacred Syms., SATB, fl, vn, vc, org, 1983; Elinor Wylie: Incantations, SSA, cl, pf, 1984; Kentucky Psalms, SATB, str qnt, 1984; The Babe of Bethlehem, SSAA, handbells/pf, 1986; A Gift from the Sea, 5 groups: children's vv, (fl, hp, db), (banjo, db), orch, pf, 1989; Angels and Challengers, SATB, ob, 2 cl, bn, pf, 1990; Listen, Lord (J.W. Johnson, spirituals), SATB, A, db, perc, pf, 1991; Clearings (W. Berry), SATB, S, B, chbr ens; Harmonious Herbst (trad. Moravian), SATB, S fl, ob, bn, str insts

Other choral: Psalms of Praise, TB, perc, 1964; Street Corner Spirituals, SATB, tpt, drum, gui, 1964; 5 American Folk Songs, SATB, 1968; Away, Melancholy, SSA/SSAA, tambourine, 1971; Carols to Play and Sing, SATB, perc, org, 1971; 6 Hymns to Dr Watts, (SATB)/(Bar, ww qt), 1975; There and Back Again, SATB, ww qt, 1977; Play-Party, Songs, SATB, pf, 1982; 3 Folksongs, SAB, pf, 1983; SongStream, SATB, pf 4 hands, 1983; Millay Madrigals, SATB, 1985; Stars and Stones, SATB, ob, vn, pf, 1987; Dem Bells, chorus, handbells, 1988; Women on the Plains, SSA, pf, 1988; American Dances, SA, pf, 1989; Anniversary hymns, SATB, 1989; Roll Round with the Year, TTBB, gui/pf, 1989; Sacred Madrigals, SSATB, 1989; Three Seas, SSAA, fl, bn, hp, 1989;

Water Songs, unison/SA, pf, 1989; Wren Songs, SATB, 1991; Great Trees (Berry), SATB, kbd, 1991; Hollering Sun (N. Wood, Amerindian), SATB, 1992; Zimre Chayim (trad. Hebrew), SATB, Mez, 1994; Sweet Manna, SATB, 1998; Sing Now of Peace (Bible, W. Shakespeare, Amerindian), SATB, vibraphones, perc, 1999

Song cycles: Astrometaphysical: 4 Songs to Robert Frost, S, pf, 1968; A Gnasherie (O. Nash), Mez, pf, 1971; Songs for Eve (A. MacLeish), 4vv, str qt, 1975; Echoes from the Hills (E. Dickinson), S, fl, cl, hn, str, 1979; Of Irlaunde, Bar, fl, pf, 1979; 3 Mountain Hymns, S, pf, 1982; Songs of the Turtle (Amerindian), S, str qt, 1994

Principal publishers: Carl Fischer, Jaymar, ECS, G. Schirmer, Hal Leonard

Principal recording companies: Musical Heritage Society, GIA

BIBLIOGRAPHY
J.A. Latta: *Alice Parker: Choral Composer, Arranger and Teacher* (diss., U. of Illinois, Urbana, 1986)
A. Meier: 'Alice Parker: Working Toward a Musical Society', *Music Educators Journal*, lxxiii/5 (1986–7), 36–41
                    SHARON PRADO HOWARD (text, bibliography),
                              CHRISTINE AMMER (work-list)

Parker, Charlie [Charles, jr; Bird; Chan, Charlie; Yardbird] (*b* Kansas City, KS, 29 Aug 1920; *d* New York, 12 March 1955). American jazz alto saxophonist. He was one of the most important and influential improvising soloists in jazz, and a central figure in the development of bop in the 1940s. A legendary figure in his own lifetime, he was idolized by those who worked with him, and he inspired a generation of jazz performers and composers.

l. Life. 2. Style. 3. Influence.

1. LIFE. Parker was the only child of Charles and Addie Parker. In 1927 the family moved to Kansas City, Missouri, an important centre of African American music in the 1920s and 1930s. Parker had his first music lessons in the local public schools; he began playing the alto saxophone in 1933 and worked occasionally in semi-professional groups before leaving school in 1935 to become a full-time musician. From 1935 to 1939 he worked mainly in Kansas City with a wide variety of local blues and jazz groups. Like most jazz musicians of his time, he developed his craft largely through practical experience: listening to older local jazz masters, acquiring a traditional repertory and learning through the process of trial and error in the competitive Kansas City bands and jam sessions.

In 1939 Parker first visited New York (then the principal centre of jazz musical and business activity), and stayed for nearly a year. Although he worked only sporadically as a professional musician, he often participated in jam sessions. By his own later account (Levin and Wilson, 1949), he was bored with the stereotyped changes that were being used then: 'I kept thinking there's bound to be something else … I could hear it sometimes, but I couldn't play it'. While working over *Cherokee* in a jam session with the guitarist Biddy Fleet, Parker suddenly found that, by using the higher intervals of a chord as a melody line and backing them with appropriately related changes, he could play what he had been 'hearing'. Yet it was not until 1944–5 that his conceptions of rhythm and phrasing had evolved sufficiently to form his mature style.

Parker's name first appeared in the music press in 1940; from this date his career is more fully documented. From 1940 to 1942 he played in Jay McShann's band, with which he toured the Southwest, Chicago and New York, and took part in his first recording sessions in Dallas (1941). These recordings, as well as several made for broadcasting from the same period, document his early, swing-based style, and at the same time reveal his extraordinary gift for improvisation. In December 1942 he joined Earl Hines's big band, which then included several other young modernists such as Dizzy Gillespie. By May 1944 they, with Parker, formed the nucleus of Billy Eckstine's band.

During these years Parker regularly participated in after-hours jam sessions at Minton's Playhouse and Monroe's Uptown House in New York, where the informal atmosphere and small groups favoured the development of his personal style, and of the new bop music generally. Unfortunately a strike by the American Federation of Musicians silenced most of the recording industry from August 1942, causing this crucial stage in Parker's musical evolution to remain poorly documented (there are 9 privately-recorded acetates from February 1943 with Parker playing tenor saxophone and 4 more from late 1943–early 1944 with Parker on alto). When the recording ban ended, Parker recorded as a sideman (from 15 September 1944) and as a leader (from 26 November 1945), which introduced his music to a wider public and to other musicians.

The year 1945 marked a turning-point in Parker's career: in New York he led his own group for the first time and worked extensively with Gillespie in small ensembles. In December 1945 he and Gillespie took the new jazz style to Hollywood, where they fulfilled a six-week night-club engagement. Parker continued to work in Los Angeles, recording and performing in concerts and night clubs, until 29 June 1946, when a nervous breakdown and addiction to heroin and alcohol caused his confinement at the Camarillo State Hospital. He was released in January 1947 and resumed work in Los Angeles.

Parker returned to New York in April 1947. He formed a quintet (with Miles Davis, Duke Jordan, Tommy Potter and Max Roach), which recorded many of his most famous pieces. The years from 1947 to 1951 were Parker's most fertile period. He worked in a wide variety of settings (night clubs, concerts, radio and recording studios) with his own small ensembles, a string group and Afro-Cuban bands, and as a guest soloist with local musicians when travelling without his own group. He recorded slightly over half his surviving work and visited Europe (1949 and 1950). Though still beset by problems associated with drugs and alcohol, he attracted a very large following in the jazz world and enjoyed a measure of financial success.

In July 1951 Parker's New York cabaret licence was revoked at the request of the narcotics squad: this banned him from night-club employment in the city and forced him to adopt a more peripatetic life until the licence was reinstated (probably in autumn 1953). Sporadically employed, badly in debt and in failing physical and mental health, he twice attempted suicide in 1954 and voluntarily committed himself to Bellevue Hospital, New York. His last public engagement was on 5 March 1955 at Birdland, a New York night club named in his honour. He died seven days later in the Manhattan apartment of his friend the Baroness Pannonica de Koenigswarter, sister of Lord Rothschild.

2. STYLE. Parker was among the supremely creative improvisers in jazz, one whose performances, like Armstrong's before him, changed the nature of the music. The force and originality of his style was such that many listeners rejected his music as no longer part of the jazz tradition, and as other jazz musicians took up and elaborated his innovations the music sank to what was then its lowest ebb in popular acceptance. Only decades after his death did Parker shed the élite aura attached to him by fellow musicians and admiring jazz fans and begin to assume a classical status in the popular imagination.

Although Parker was an innovator, his music is rooted firmly in tradition. Like the Kansas City music he heard when young, Parker's repertory was built on a very limited number of models: the 12-bar blues, a number of popular songs, several jazz standards and newly invented jazz melodies using the underlying harmonies of popular songs. This last-named category and blues account for about half the pieces he recorded. Although the device of composing new melodic themes to borrowed chord progressions was not new to jazz, bop musicians of the 1940s employed this technique much more extensively, partly for financial reasons (to avoid paying copyright royalties) and partly to frighten the uninitiated (who could not always recognize the underlying chord patterns), but also to invent themes that were more consistent with the new jazz style than the original melodies. Thus, by restricting himself to a few harmonic sources, Parker was able to improvise over a few familiar patterns, against which he constantly tested his ingenuity and powers of imagination. A number of Parker's newly composed melodic themes (based on existing harmonic and metric structures) themselves became jazz standards, among them *Anthropology* (1950, Sonet; based on the chord progressions of George Gershwin's *I got rhythm*, and written in collaboration with Gillespie), *Now's the Time* (1945, Savoy; blues), *Ornithology* (1946, Dial; based on Morgan Lewis's *How High the Moon*, probably written in collaboration with Little Benny Harris) and *Scrapple from the Apple* (1947, Dial; the A section from *I got rhythm* and the bridge from Fats Waller's *Honeysuckle Rose*).

Parker's outstanding achievement was not his composition but his brilliant improvisation. His improvised line combined drive and a complex organization of pitch and rhythm with a clarity rarely achieved by earlier soloists. In contrast to the rich timbres of Johnny Hodges and Benny Carter, the two most important predecessors on his instrument, Parker developed a penetrating tone with a slow, narrow vibrato. This suited the aggressive nature of the new music, and allowed him to concentrate on line and rhythm. Parker's improvisations are usually based on the harmonic structure of the original. Melodic ornamentation or paraphrase occasionally occur, but characteristically these are reserved for thematic statements of popular melodies in the opening or closing chorus (ex.1).

His organization of rhythm and pitch often has an oblique relationship to the principal elements of jazz variation – the pulse (beat) and chord progressions. His solo on Dizzy Gillespie's *Groovin' High* (1945, Guild; ex.2) disturbs the crotchet pulse, steadfastly maintained by the accompanying double bass, resulting in an ever-changing succession of varied subdivisions. This rhythmic complexity is often used in conjunction with highly syncopated lines and persistently contrasting phrase lengths and accents, all helping to obscure the beat, metre and harmonic rhythm. His occasional derivation of pitches from the theme is often hidden by this kind of

Ex.1 Parker's opening thematic statement on *Out of Nowhere* (1948, Le Jazz Cool); transcr. J. Patrick

chords within the given progression. Despite this harmonic complexity, Parker's best work has a clear and coherent line. Sometimes this is achieved by motivic development, as in ex.3, the first ten bars of his solo on *Klactoveedsedstene* (1947, Dial; based on the chord progressions of Juan Tizol's *Perdido*). This passage is constructed from three short ideas, developed and combined, with silences of subtly varied length throughout.

In his improvisations, Parker most often drew from a corpus of formulae and arranged them into ever-new patterns, a technique sometimes known as *cento*. This aspect of Parker's art has been exhaustively investigated by Owens (*Charlie Parker*, 1974), who codified Parker's improvisational work according to about 100 formulae. Many of these are specific to certain keys (where they may be easier to finger) or to particular pieces. Some occur in earlier swing music, particularly in the work of Lester Young, but others originated with Parker himself, and later became common property among musicians working in the bop style. Although it is based on a limited number of such formulae, Parker's work is neither haphazard nor 'formulaic' in a restricted sense: the arrangement of the formulae was subject to constant variation and redisposition, and his performances of a piece were never identical. The overriding criterion was always the coherence and expressiveness of the musical line.

Closely related to this approach is Parker's use of musical quotations. Probably no jazz musician before him was as fond of this device, or as wide-ranging in his choice of material, as Parker, particularly in private performances in a relaxed atmosphere. His improvisations contain snatches of melody from popular songs and light classics; from earlier jazz performances such as Armstrong's *West End Blues*; from his own jazz compositions; and even quotations from Wagner, Bizet and Stravinsky. He retained this device throughout his career, and it is another measure of his authority in jazz that witty quotations became characteristic of the bop style as a whole.

3. INFLUENCE.   Although Parker was not solely responsible for the development of the bop style, he was its most

treatment. This can be seen in his solo on *Groovin' High*, notably in bars 5 and 15.

Parker's line typically includes pitches outside the given harmony: in addition to those produced by passing notes, suspensions and other familiar devices, these result from free use of chord extensions beyond the 7th (particularly the flattened 9th and raised 11th), chromatic interpolations suggesting passing chords, the interchange of major, minor, augmented and diminished triads with others on the same root and the anticipation or prolongation of

Ex.2 Parker's improvisation on D. Gillespie, *Groovin' High* (1945, Guild): transcr. J. Patrick

Ex.3 *Klactoveedsedstene* (1947, Dial); transcr. J. Patrick

important representative and a source of inspiration to all musicians who took part in its early growth. His influence was not limited to performers on his own instrument: his lines, rhythmic devices and favourite motifs were transferred to instruments other than reeds, such as the trombone, vibraphone, piano and guitar, and many innovations of bop drummers were made in response to the increased rhythmic complexity of his music.

Parker's influence was immediate and intense. His most famous early solos were learnt note-for-note by thousands of aspiring young bop musicians on all instruments; as early as 1948 published transcriptions of them were available for study purposes. Some were even given texts by bop singers and performed as independent pieces. Parker's impact was naturally strongest on alto saxophonists such as Sonny Stitt, Cannonball Adderley, Phil Woods and many others; only Lee Konitz and West Coast musicians such as Paul Desmond managed to create viable independent styles on alto saxophone. Despite the differences in timbre and mobility of the lower-pitched, bulkier instrument, many tenor saxophonists also came under Parker's sway, most notably Sonny Rollins and John Coltrane. Only in the early 1960s did Parker's influence gradually wane as the modal style led to the abandonment of bop's formulaic approach and the smoothing out of its erratic rhythms, and the free-jazz style dispensed with preset harmonic patterns; nor did Parker's music play a role in the emergence of jazz-rock in the early 1970s. Nevertheless, his work remained available on disc in more or less complete reissue series, and recordings of his performances were discovered on private tapes, matrices or radio recordings, and issued posthumously.

With the revival of bop in the mid-1970s Parker's music once again became a vital force in the evolution and teaching of jazz. The Fine Arts Library at the University of Texas, Austin, holds the world's largest collection of recordings by Parker, and hundreds of his solos are now available to the student in published transcriptions. The group Supersax, based in Los Angeles, achieved some popular success playing Parker's solos in harmonized arrangements for saxophone chorus. His work has been the subject of several university dissertations. Although the evanescent, hieratic and emotionally disturbing nature of Parker's music precludes popularity on a par with that of Armstrong or Ellington, his place beside them as a creative force in jazz history is assured.

WORKS
(selective list)

Anthropology [originally issued as Thrivin' on a Riff] (1945, Savoy); Koko (1945, Savoy); Now's the Time (1945, Savoy); Moose the Mooche (1946, Dial); Ornithology (1946, Dial); Yardbird Suite (1946, Dial); Cool Blues (1947, Dial); Donna Lee (1947, Savoy); Embraceable you (1947, Dial); Klactoveedsedstene (1947, Dial); Scrapple from the Apple (1947, Dial); Ah-leu-cha (1948, Savoy); Parker's Mood (1948, Savoy); Bloomdido (1950, Mercury/Clef); Au Privave (1951, Mercury/Clef); Blues for Alice (1951, from Charlie Parker 1951–3, Clef); My Little Suede Shoes (1951, Mercury/Clef)

BIBLIOGRAPHY
TRANSCRIPTIONS

[M. Feldman, ed.]: *Charles Parker's Bebop for Alto Sax: 4 Solos* (New York, 1948)

P. Pinkerton, ed.: *Charlie Parker: Nine Solos Transcribed from Historic Recordings* (New York, 1961)

W.D. Stuart: *Famous Transcribed Recorded Jazz Solos: Charlie 'Bird' Parker* (New York, 1961)

Charlie Parker: Sketch Orks, Designed for Small Groups (New York, 1967)

T. Owens: *Charlie Parker: Techniques of Improvisation*, ii (diss., UCLA, 1974) [190 pieces]

S. Watanabe, ed.: *Jazz Improvisation: Transcriptions of Charlie Parker's Great Alto Solos* (Tokyo, c1975) [25 pieces]

J. Aebersbold and K. Stone, eds: *Charlie Parker Omnibook* (New York, 1978) [60 pieces]

A. White, ed.: *The Charlie Parker Collection: 308 Transcribed Alto Saxophone and Tenor Saxophone Solos* (Washington DC, 1978–9)

DOCUMENTS AND SOURCES

N. Hentoff and R. Sanjek: *Charlie Parker* (New York, 1960) [list of compositions]

R. Reisner: *Bird: the Legend of Charlie Parker* (New York, 1961, 2/1962/R)

G.R. Davies: 'Charlie Parker Chronology', *Discographical Forum*, nos.17–26 (1970–71)

D. Morgenstern and others: *Bird and Diz: a Bibliography* (New York, 1973)

P. Koster and D.M. Bakker: *Charlie Parker* (Alphen aan de Rijn, 1974–6) [incl. discography]

C. Parker and F. Paudras: *To Bird with Love* (Antigny, 1981) [photographs]

R. Bregman, L. Bukowski and N. Saks: *The Charlie Parker Discography* (Redwood, NY, 1993)

T. Hirschmann: *Charlie Parker: kritische Beiträge zur Bibliographie sowie zu Leben und Werk* (Tutzing, 1994)

Bird - The Chan Parker Collection, Christie's, 8 Sept 1994 (London, 1994) [auction catalogue]

K. Vale: *Bird's Diary – The Life of Charlie Parker 1945–1955* (London, 1996) [reprints of collected source material]

Charlie Parker sessionography (College Park, MD, University of Maryland; P. Losin) [on-line database: Parker recording sessions, with notes and biographical information; initially inaugurated by J. Burton, Aug 29 1995]

BIOGRAPHICAL STUDIES

L. Feather: *Inside Be-bop* (New York, 1949/R1977 as *Inside Jazz*), 11–18

M. Levin and J.S. Wilson: '"No Bop Roots in Jazz": Parker', *Down Beat*, xvi/17 (1949), 1 only, 12–13; rev. as 'The Chili Parlor Interview', *Down Beat*, xxxii/6 (1965), 13–15

M. Harrison: *Charlie Parker* (London, 1960); repr. in *Kings of Jazz*, ed. S. Green (New York, 1978)

I. Gitler: 'Charlie Parker and the Alto and Baritone Saxophonists', *Jazz Masters of the Forties* (New York, 1966/R1983 with discography), 15–57

J. Burns: 'Bird in California', *Jazz Journal*, xxii/7 (1969), 10 only

D. Amram: 'Bird in Washington', *Jazz Journal*, xxiii/8 (1970), 4–5

R. Russell: *Jazz Style in Kansas City and the Southwest* (Berkeley, 1971/R, 2/1973), 179ff

R. Russell: *Bird Lives: the High Life and Hard Times of Charlie 'Yardbird' Parker* (New York, 1973)

R. Russell: 'West Coast Bop', *Jazz & Blues*, iii/2 (1973), 8–11

N.T. Davis: *Charlie Parker's Kansas City Environment and its Effects on his Later Life* (diss., Wesleyan U., 1974)

J. Patrick: 'Al Tinney, Monroe's Uptown House, and the Emergence of Modern Jazz in Harlem', *Annual Review of Jazz Studies*, ii (1983), 150–79

B. Priestley: *Charlie Parker* (Tunbridge Wells, 1984) [incl. discography]

I. Gitler: *Swing to Bop: an Oral History of the Transition in Jazz in the 1940s* (New York, 1985)

G. Giddins: *Celebrating Bird: the Triumph of Charlie Parker* (New York, 1987)

P.N. Wilson and U. Goeman: *Charlie Parker: sein Leben, seine Musik, seine Schallplatten* (Schaftlach, 1988)

E. Komera: 'The Dial Recordings of Charlie Parker', *The Bebop Revolution in Words and Music*, ed. D. Oliphant (Austin, TX, 1994), 79ff

C. Woideck: *Charlie Parker: His Music and Life* (Ann Arbor, MI, 1997)

ANALYTICAL STUDIES

A. Hodeir: *Hommes et problèmes du jazz, suivi de la religion du jazz* (Paris, 1954; Eng. trans., enlarged, 1956/R, 2/1979 as *Jazz: its Evolution and Essence*), 99

A. Morgan: 'Charlie Parker: the Dial Recordings', *JazzM*, i/7 (1955–6), 7–10 [includes discography]

L. Feather: 'The Anatomy of Improvisation', *The Book of Jazz: a Guide to the Entire Field* (New York, 1957, 2/1965), 209–44

R. Russell: *The Art of Jazz: Essays on the Nature and Development of Jazz*, ed. M. Williams (New York, 1959/R), 195ff

M. James: *Ten Modern Jazzmen: an Appraisal of the Recorded Work of Ten Modern Jazzmen* (London, 1960), 111–24

J.F. Mehegan: *Jazz Improvisation*, ii (New York, 1962), 101

D. Heckman: 'Bird in Flight: Parker the Improviser', *Down Beat*, xxxii/6 (1965), 22–4

J. Siddons: 'Parker's Mood', *Down Beat*, xxxii/6 (1965), 25 only

F. Tirro: 'The Silent Theme Tradition in Jazz', *MQ*, liii (1967), 313–34

D. Baker: 'Charlie Parker's "Now's the Time" Solo', *Down Beat*, xxxviii/19 (1971), 32–3

O. Peterson: 'Early Bird', *Jazz Journal*, xxiv/4 (1971), 34–6

R. Wang: 'Jazz Circa 1945: a Confluence of Styles', *MQ*, lix (1973), 531

T. Owens: 'Applying the Melograph to "Parker's Mood"', *Selected Reports*, ii/1 (1974–5), 166–75

T. Owens: *Charlie Parker: Techniques of Improvisation* (diss., UCLA, 1974)

L.O. Koch: 'Ornithology: a Study of Charlie Parker's Music', *Journal of Jazz Studies*, ii/1 (1974), 61–87; ii/12 (1975), 61–95

L. Koch: 'A Numerical Listing of Charlie Parker's Recordings', *Journal of Jazz Studies*, ii/2 (1975), 86

J. Patrick: 'Charlie Parker and Harmonic Sources of Bebop Composition: Thoughts on the Repertory of New Jazz in the 1940s', *Journal of Jazz Studies*, ii/2 (1975), 3–23

J. Patrick: Disc notes, *Charlie Parker: the Complete Savoy Studio Recordings*, Savoy 5501 (1978)

T. Hirschmann: *Untersuchungen zu den Kompositionen von Charlie Parker* (diss., U. of Mainz, 1982)

L. Koch: *Yardbird Suite: a Compendium of the Music and Life of Charlie Parker* (Bowling Green, OH, 1988)

J. Patrick: disc notes, *The Complete Dean Benedetti Recordings of Charlie Parker*, Mosaic MD7-129 (1990)

S. Sandvik: 'Polyharmony, Polyrhythm and Motivic Development in Charlie Parker's *Klact-Oveeseds-Tene* (Take 1) Solo', *Jazzforschung*, xxiv (1992), 83–97

T. Owens: 'The Parker Style', *Bebop: The Music and Players* (New York, 1995), 28–45

H. Martin: *Charlie Parker and Thematic Improvisation* (Lanham, MD, 1996)

OTHER STUDIES

Down Beat, xxxii/6 (1965) [Parker issue]

J. Patrick: 'The Uses of Jazz Discography', *Notes*, xxix (1972–3), 17–25

J.S. Patrick: 'Discography as a Tool for Musical Research and Vice Versa', *Journal of Jazz Studies*, i/1 (1973), 65–83

J. Patrick: 'Musical Sources for the History of Jazz', *Black Perspective in Music*, iv (1976), 46–53

Coda, no.181 (1981) [Parker issue]

C. Woideck, ed.: *The Charlie Parker Companion: Six Decades of Commentary* (New York, 1998)

Oral history material in *US-AUSm*

JAMES PATRICK

Parker, Daniel (*fl* London, *c*1700–30). English violin maker. His most probable early instructor in the craft was the maker Barak Norman, whose reputation was already established at the end of the 17th century. However, his life has so far eluded research, and he remains a shadowy figure in the London trade of that time. His connections with other violin makers are intriguing. Work labelled by Edward Lewis sometimes seems to show Parker's hand, but violins attributed to him have also been found to bear the signature or label of Joseph Hare, a violin maker and music publisher with whom Parker was certainly closely associated. As is true of so many violin makers since Parker's time, his success had its basis in an appreciation of the work of Antonio Stradivari. In 1687 a set of Stradivari instruments are said to have been ordered for James II. More significant is the presence in London between 1702 and 1705 of the Cremonese violinist Gaspare Visconti, who was personally acquainted with Stradivari, and whose compositions were published by Hare. Parker might well have had a number of opportunities to study the great master's early work: his working life was to coincide with the best years of Stradivari's. Parker copied the Stradivari instruments with respect to form: outlines, archings, layout of scroll and pegbox, placing of soundholes, etc. In details of workmanship he followed the practices of English contemporaries such as Norman and Nathaniel Cross. His varnish, which varies in colour from a light orange-brown to a bright, clear red, was of the same fine quality that has allowed so many early English instruments to pass as Italian.

Parker was equally successful with his violas, which he made in various sizes, including in his output some remarkably elegant instruments based on Stradivari's 'long pattern'. Only a limited number of his instruments survive, but almost all of them are first rate tonally and have established his reputation as the finest early English maker of violins. One of his champions was Fritz Kreisler, who owned and often performed on an outstanding example of Parker's work.

BIBLIOGRAPHY

W. Sandys and S.A.Forster: *The History of the Violin* (London, 1864)

W.M. Morris: *British Violin Makers* (London, 1904, 2/1920)

The British Violin: Historical Aspects of Violin and Bow Making in the British Isles: London 1998

CHARLES BEARE/JOHN DILWORTH

Parker, Horatio (William) (*b* Auburndale, MA, 15 Sept 1863; *d* Cedarhurst, NY, 18 Dec 1919). American composer and church musician. At 14 he took piano and organ lessons with his mother; he later studied composition with George Chadwick, the piano with John Orth and theory with Stephen Emery in Boston. He was church organist in Dedham, Massachusetts, 1880–82. His first compositions were 50 songs on poems by Kate Greenaway, written shortly after his first year of musical study; within the next few years he composed keyboard, chamber and some short orchestral pieces. From 1882 to 1885 he studied at the Hochschule für Musik in Munich, including composition under Josef Rheinberger. During this time he wrote his first extensive compositions, including the *Ballad of a Knight and his Daughter*, the cantata *King Trojan* and the Symphony in C.

On returning to America, Parker spent several years in New York, where he taught at the cathedral schools of St Paul and St Mary (1886–90), at the General Theological Seminary (1892) and at the National Conservatory of Music (1892–3). He was organist and choirmaster at St

Luke's in Brooklyn from 1885 to 1887, St Andrew's in Harlem from 1887 to 1888, and at Holy Trinity in Manhattan from 1888 to 1893.

Parker's reputation as a composer was established during the early 1890s with performances of his student works, the publication of a considerable amount of church music, and major works including the overture *Count Robert of Paris*, heard at the first public concert of the New York Manuscript Society in 1890; the cantata *Dream-King and his Love*, which won the National Conservatory prize in 1893; and the oratorio *Hora novissima*, written for the Church Choral Society of New York in 1893. There followed a series of major vocal and choral compositions, including *Cáhal Mór of the Wine-Red Hand*, a rhapsody for baritone and orchestra first performed by the Boston SO (1895); the dramatic oratorio *The Legend of St Christopher*, a commission from the Oratorio Society of New York (1897); and the motet *Adstant angelorum chori*, which received a prize and performance by the Musical Art Society of New York (1899).

Frequent performances of *Hora novissima* during the 1890s brought Parker to national prominence. In autumn 1893 he left New York to become organist and choirmaster at the fashionable Trinity Church in Boston. The following year he received an honorary MMus from Yale University and accepted the Battell Professorship of the Theory of Music there, a position he retained until his death. In 1904 he was made dean of the School of Music, and under his guidance Yale gained a national reputation for training composers. Parker also became an important musical figure in the New Haven community by organizing and conducting the New Haven SO (from 1895 to 1918) and the Choral Society (from 1903 to 1914). He conducted various choral societies and glee clubs both in the vicinity of New Haven and as far away as Philadelphia. He continued in his post at Trinity Church in Boston until 1902, when he left to take up a similar post at the collegiate church of St Nicholas in New York; he served this Dutch Reformed church until 1910.

A performance of *Hora novissima* at the Three Choirs Festival in Worcester in 1899 was the first of a series of activities in England which included the commission of *A Wanderer's Psalm* for the Hereford Festival and the performance of *Hora novissima* in Chester (both in 1900) and of part iii of *St Christopher* at Worcester and *A Star Song* at Norwich (both in 1902). He received an honorary MusD from Cambridge University in 1902.

Significant vocal and choral compositions from his later years include *Crépuscule*, a prizewinning concert aria performed by the Philadelphia Orchestra in 1912; the cantata *King Gorm the Grim* (1908) and the morality *The Dream of Mary* (1918), both for the Norfolk (Connecticut) Festival; and the oratorio *Morven and the Grail* (1915), commissioned for the centennial celebration of the founding of the Handel and Haydn Society of Boston.

Parker's second area of composition was theatre music. After writing incidental music for two plays, *The Eternal Feminine* (1904) and *The Prince of India* (1906), he composed music for two grand operas: *Mona*, which won a prize offered by the Metropolitan Opera Company and received four performances in that house (1912); and *Fairyland*, which won a prize offered by the National Federation of Music Clubs and six performances in Los Angeles (1915).

Parker composed numerous songs, anthems and hymns. Apart from some character-pieces for organ and piano, his instrumental composition was infrequent after the early years; however, the symphonic poem *A Northern Ballad* (1899) and the Concerto for Organ and Orchestra were performed by major American orchestras. Parker performed his Concerto with the Boston SO (1902) and the Chicago SO (1903).

Parker's health, which had been uncertain since his youth, deteriorated rapidly during World War I, and he died of pneumonia contracted while on a recuperative trip to the West Indies in 1919. His last compositions, *The Red Cross Spirit Speaks* (1918) and *A.D. 1919*, are marked more by emotional fervour than by his creativity.

Parker composed steadily throughout his life, although his church, educational and conducting duties were extensive. He was capable of intense concentration and frequently used the time while commuting from New Haven to Boston or New York for composing. After 1907, many of his largest works were written during summers at his family's vacation home in Blue Hill, Maine.

His career as a composer can be divided into three periods. The first was strongly eclectic and included the student and New York cantatas as well as the oratorio *Hora novissima*. The latter contains flowing, balanced melodic lines, moderately chromatic harmony, colourful orchestration and stirring polyphonic effects.

The second period was marked by an increasing concern for dramatic expression in several of the larger choral works, and the fulfilment, with *Mona*, of a desire to write an opera. The contrasting, sectional structures of the first period gave way to an increasingly unified, highly expressive style. The key works are *Cáhal Mór of the Wine-Red Hand*, with its integration of solo voice and orchestra; *The Legend of St Christopher*, with its well-developed leading motif technique; *A Star Song*, with its long-phrased melodies, tonally evasive harmony and unified structure; and finally *Crépuscule* and *Mona*, with their pervading chromaticism, vacillating tonalities and sometimes angular, disjunctive melodies.

During this same period Parker wrote a number of cantatas and ceremonial pieces which had a more conservative cast and sustained his reputation as a traditionalist. They include *Adstant angelorum chori*, with its allusions to Renaissance polyphony; *A Wanderer's Psalm*, with its contrasting sections and unifying *tonus peregrinus*; *Hymnos Andron*, with its application of the rhythm and structure of Greek poetry; and the occasional pieces, *Union and Liberty* and *Spirit of Beauty*, with their balanced sections.

The third period, following *Mona*, was stylistically regressive: for example, *An Allegory of War and Peace*, *The Dream of Mary*, *The Red Cross Spirit Speaks* and *A.D. 1919* are marked by a return to diatonic harmony, more traditional key relationships, balanced structures and clearly defined melody. Parts of *Morven and the Grail* and *Fairyland* also show these tendencies. These works reflect Parker's concern, during his last few years, to communicate more directly with the American public.

During his lifetime Parker was considered a craftsman without equal and was one of America's most highly respected composers, but since his death, the number of performances of his major works has declined steadily. Even his more imaginative works, in which he attempted to follow such composers as Wagner, d'Indy, Strauss, Debussy and Elgar, are received no better than the more conservative pieces, which show the influence of Brahms, Dvořák and Gounod. Parker's inability to achieve a strongly individualistic style, and his reliance on chromatic formulae which are now considered too sentimental, have undoubtedly contributed to the neglect of his music. *Hora novissima*, *A Northern Ballad* and a few anthems are still occasionally heard, and several of his songs have a beauty which should rescue them from obscurity.

WORKS
printed works published in New York unless otherwise stated

CHORAL

op.

2	5 Part Songs, 1882; listed in Strunk
—	2 Gesänge für Gemischten Chor, 1882; listed in 9. *Jahresbericht der Königlichen Musikhochschule in München* (1882–3), 37
1	Mountain Shepherd's Song (Uhland), TTBB, pf, 1883 (Boston, 1884)
3	Psalm 23, S, women's chorus, org, hp, 1884; Munich, Königliche Musikhochschule, 23 Dec 1884 (pubd as The Lord is my Shepherd, 1904)
6	Ballade (F.L. Stolberg), f, chorus, orch, 1884; Munich, Königliche Musikhochschule, 7 July 1884 (pubd as The Ballad of a Knight and his Daughter, 1891)
8	König Trojan (A. Muth), ballad, T, Bar, SATB, orch, 1885; Munich, Königliche Musikhochschule, 15 July 1885 (pubd as King Trojan, Boston, 1886)
15	Idylle (cant., J.W. von Goethe), T, B, SATB, orch, 1886 (1891)
14	Blow, Blow, thou Winter Wind (W. Shakespeare), TTBB, pf, 1888 (1892)
16	Normannenzug (cant., H. Lingg), TTBB, orch, 1888 (pubd as The Norsemen's Raid, Cincinnati, 1911)
—	Ecclesia, SATB, SSA boys' chorus, org, 1889, *US-NH*
21	The Kobolds (cant., A. Bates), SATB, orch, 1890; Springfield, MA, Choral Festival, 7 May 1891 (London, 1891)
26	Harold Harfager, partsong, SATB, orch, 1891 (1891)
31	Dream-King and his Love (cant., Geibel, trans. E. Whitney), T, SATB, orch, 1891; New York, 30 March 1893 (1893)
27	2 Choruses for Women: The Fisher (Goethe), The Water Fay (H. Heine), SSAA, pf (1892)
30	Hora novissima (orat, B. de Morlaix), S,A,T,B, SATB, orch, 1893; New York, Church Choral Society, 3 May 1893 (London, 1893)
33	3 Choruses, male vv: My Love (L.E. Mitchell), Three Words (W.B. Dunham), Valentine (C.G. Blanden) (1893)
37	The Holy Child (Christmas cant., I. Parker), S,T, B, SATB, pf/org, 1893 (1893)
39	4 Choruses, male vv: Behold, how good and joyful; Blest are the departed; Lord dismiss us with thy blessing; Softly now the light of day, 1893 (1894)
42	Ode for Commencement Day at Yale University (E.C. Stedman), 1895 (1895)
—	In May, partsong, female chorus, hp, orch, 1897 (1897)
—	Laus Artium (cant.), solo v, SATB, orch, 1898, *NH*
43	The Legend of St Christopher (dramatic orat, I. Parker), solo vv, chorus, orch, 1897; New York, Oratorio Society, 15 April 1898 (London and New York, 1898)
45	Adstant angelorum chori (Thomas à Kempis), motet, 8vv, 1899; New York, Musical Art Society, 16 March 1899 (1899)
50	A Wanderer's Psalm (cant., after Ps cvii), solo vv, chorus, orch, 1900; Hereford, Three Choirs Festival, 13 Sept 1900 (London, 1900)
48	3 Part Songs, TTBB: Awake, my Lady Sweetlips (E. Higginson), The Lamp in the West (Higginson), The Night has a Thousand Eyes (F.W. Bourdillon) (Cincinnati, 1901)
53	Hymnos Andron (T.D. Goodell), solo vv, TTBB, orch, 1901; Yale U., 23 Oct 1901 (pubd as Greek Festival Hymn, 1901)
54	A Star Song (H.B. Carpenter), lyric rhapsody, solo vv, chorus, orch, 1901; Norwich (England) Festival, 23 Oct 1902 (Cincinnati, 1902)
54b	Come Away! (J. Dowland), SATB (London, 1901)
—	The Robbers (J. Baillie), SATB, pf; in W.L. Tomlin: *The Laurel Song Book* (Boston, 1901)
—	An Even Song (C. Thaxter), SA, pf (London, 1901)
60	Union and Liberty (O.W. Holmes), chorus, band/orch, 1905; commissioned for and perf. at inauguration of President T. Roosevelt (1905)
61	Spirit of Beauty (ode, A. Detmers), male chorus, band/orch, 1905; Buffalo, NY, ded. of Albright Art Gallery, 31 May 1905 (1905)
63	The Shepherds' Vision (Christmas cant., F. Van der Stucken, trans. A. Jennings), solo vv, chorus, org, (ob, str, hp ad lib), 1900 (1906)
64	King Gorm the Grim (T. Fontane, trans. M.P. Whitney), ballad, chorus, orch, 1907; Norfolk Festival, 4 June 1908 (1908) Piscatrix, TTBB (1908)
—	Songs for Parker daughters, trios, female vv, 1911: I Remember the black wharfs and ships (H.W. Longfellow), September Gale (C.H. Crandall), Rollicking Robin (L. Larcom), no.1 (Boston and New York, 1923)
66	School Songs, SATB, pf: no.1 unidentified, Springtime Reveries (N. Waterman), The Storm (Waterman), Freedom Our Queen (O.W. Holmes); nos.2–4 (Boston, 1912, 1919, 1911)
—	The Song of the Swords (from op, Mona), SATB, pf (New York and Boston, 1911)
73	A Song of Times (cant., J.L. Long), S, SATB, bugle corps, band/orch, org, 1911; Philadelphia, Wanamaker Dept Store, 1 Dec 1911 (1911)
—	A Song of a Pilgrim Soul (H. Van Dyke), partsong, vv, pf (1912)
74	7 Greek Pastoral Scenes (Meleager, Argentarius), SA, female chorus, ob, hp, str, 1912 (1913)
75	The Leap of Roushan Beg (Longfellow), ballad, T, TTBB, orch; Philadelphia, Orpheus Club, 1913–14 season (1913)
76	Alice Brand (cant., Scott), solo vv, SSA, pf (1913)
—	Gloriosa patria, patriotic hymn (1915)
79	Morven and the Grail (orat, B. Hooker), solo vv, chorus, orch, 1915; Boston, 13 April 1915 (Boston, 1915)
—	Ave virgo gloriosa (from op, Fairyland), female chorus, pf, 1915 (1915)
82	The Dream of Mary (J.J. Chapman), morality, solo vv, children's chorus, chorus, congregation, org, orch, 1918; Norfolk Festival, 4 June 1918 (1918)
—	Triumphal March (D.K. Stevens), SATB, pf; in G. Parsons: *High School Song Book* (Boston, 1919)
84	A.D. 1919 (cant., Hooker), S, chorus, orch, 1919; Yale U., June 1919 (New Haven, 1919)
—	I Remember (Longfellow), female vv, pf; in *A Book of Choruses for High Schools and Choral Societies* (Boston, 1923)

STAGE

—	The Eternal Feminine (incid music, F. Nathan), chorus, orch, 1903–4; New Haven, 7 Nov 1904; lost
—	The Prince of India (incid music, J.I.C. Clarke, after L.E. Wallace), 1v, chorus, orch, 1905; New York, Broadway Theatre, 24 Sept 1906, *NH*
71	Mona (op, 3, Hooker), 1910; New York, Metropolitan, 12 March 1912 (1911)
77	Fairyland (op, 3, Hooker), 1914; Los Angeles, 1 July 1915 (1915)
80	Cupid and Psyche (masque, 3, J.J. Chapman), 1916; New Haven, 16 June 1916, *NH*
81	An Allegory of War and Peace (F.H. Markoe), chorus, band, 1916; New Haven, 21 Oct 1916, *NH*

SONGS
1 voice, piano unless otherwise stated

—	Kate Greenaway Songs, 50 settings, 1878; see Kearns (1990) for individual listing, *NH*
—	La coquette, 1879, *NH*

— 3 Songs: Goldilocks, Slumber Song, Wedding Song, 1881 (Boston, 1882)

10 3 Love Songs: Love's Chase (T.L. Beddoes), Night Piece to Julia (R. Heink [Herrick]), Orsame's Song (Suckling), 1886 (Boston, 1886)

— 2 Sacred Songs: Rest, There is a Land of Pure Delight, 1890 (Boston, 1890)

22 3 Sacred Songs: Evening, Heaven's Hope, Morning (1891)

23 3 Songs: My Love, O Waving Trees, Violet, 1891(1891)

24 6 Songs: Cavalry Song (E.C. Stedman), Egyptian Serenade (G.W. Curtis), O Ask me Not (H. Hopfen), Pack, clouds, away! (T. Heywood), Spring Song (Curtis), The Light is Fading (E.A. Allen) (1891)

— Come see the Place (1893), also arr. as anthem

34 3 Songs: I know a Little Rose, My Lady Love, On the Lake (1893)

— In Glad Weather (C.B. Going) (1893)

— A Rose Song, unison chorus, pf (London, 1893)

— 2 Songs: Fickle Love (L.C. Moulton), Uncertainty (C. Swain) (Boston, 1893)

— 2 Songs: A Song of Three Little Birds, Love is a Rover (S.M. Peck), 1893 (Cincinnati, 1893)

— Divine Love (A. Jennings) (Boston, 1894)

— 2 Shakespeare Songs: A Poor Soul Sat Sighing, It was a Lover and his Lass (Boston, 1894)

40 Cáhal Mór of the Wine-Red Hand (J.C. Mangan), rhapsody, Bar, orch, 1893; Boston, 29 March 1895 (1910)

— Salve regina (1895)

— Spanish Cavalier's Song (I. Parker) (Boston, 1896)

47 6 Old English Songs: Come, O come, my life's delight (T. Campion), Love is a sickness (S. Daniel), He that loves a rosy cheek (T. Carew), Once I loved a maiden fair (Old English), The Complacent Lover (C. Selby), The Lark (W. Davenant), 1897–9 (Cincinnati, 1899)

– The Green is on the Grass Again, 1900, NH

51 4 Songs: A Spinning Song (I. Parker), At Twilight (E.A. Baker), June Night (E. Higginson), Love in May (Higginson), 1901 (Cincinnati, 1901)

— The Toedt Songs, S, vn, pf, 14 songs as Christmas gifts for children of close friends, 1903–16, microfilm of MS, NH (for individual listing see Kearns (1990), no.5 (1939)

59 4 Songs: Good-Bye (C. Rossetti), Serenade (N.H. Dole), Songs (R.L. Stevenson), The Blackbird (W.E. Henley) (1904)

— 2 Songs from Tennyson's Queen Mary: Lute Song, Milkmaid's Song (1904)

58 3 Sacred Songs, org acc.: Come, Holy Ghost (St Ambrose), Declining now, the sun's bright wheel (C. Coffin), Lo, now the shades of night (St Gregory) (London, 1905)

— Springtime of Love (F.D. Sherman), 1905 (1905)

— Last Night the Nightingale (T. Marzials); The Garden Pirate (G. Rogers); The Reason Why (G. Cooper); 1906, NH

62 Crépuscule (J. de Beaufort, trans. E. Whitney), concert aria, Mez, orch, 1907; Philadelphia, 27 March 1911 (1912)

— The First Christmas, 4 S, pf, 1907, NH

— The Wandering Knight's Song (Cincinnati, 1908)

— O, I will Walk with you; On the Hillside; The Presence Dwells among the Starlit Places; Lamentation (trans. G. Morris); 1909, NH

70 7 Songs (B. Hooker): A Man's Song, A Robin's Egg, A Woman's Song, I Shall Come Back, Offerings, Only a Little While, Together, 1910 (Cincinnati, 1910)

— A Christmas Song (J.G. Holland), 1911; in Century Illustrated Monthly Magazine (Dec 1911)

— Rollicking Robin (L. Larcom), 1911, NH

— 2 Songs: A Perfect Love (A.H. Hyatt), 1913, Her cheek is like a tinted rose (F.E. Coates), 1912 (Boston, 1914)

— 3 Songs: Across the Fields (W. Crane), 1906, Morning Song (M. Schütze), 1908, Nightfall (Schütze), 1908 (Boston, 1914)

78 The Progressive Music Series for Basal Use in Primary, Intermediate and Grammar Grades, 61 songs, 1914–19 (Boston and New York, 1914–19); for individual listings see Kearns (1990)

— It was a Lover and his Lass (W. Shakespeare), 2 S, vn, pf, 1916, NH

— Tomorrow (F.E. Coates), 1915; The Pearl (A. Hyatt), 1916; NH

83 The Red Cross Spirit Speaks (J. Finley), 1v, orch, 1918 (1918)

— Hymn for the Victorious Dead (H. Hagedorn); in The Outlook (18 Dec 1918)

ANTHEMS, SERVICES
for SATB, organ; solo voices as indicated

— Christ our Passover (1890)

— Bow down thine ear; Deus misereatur, E, 1890; Magnificat, E♭, with solo v; Nunc dimittis, E♭; The Lord is my light; There is a land of pure delight, with solo v (all pubd in 1890)

— Give unto the Lord, 1890; I will set his dominion in the sea (1891)

— The Riven Tomb, in New York Herald (29 March 1891); Te Deum, A (1891); Who shall Roll us away the Stone?, with S solo (1891)

— 12 Christmas Carols for Children, unison chorus, pf (1891)

— The Morning and Evening Service, E, together with the Office for The Holy Communion, 1890 (London, 1892)

— Let us Rise up and Build, 1892, NH

— Before the Heavens were Spread Abroad, with T solo (London, 1893)

— Come See the Place, arr. as anthem, 1v, chorus/qt, org (1893)

34b Magnificat and Nunc dimittis, E♭, 1893 (London, 1893)

— Te Deum, B♭ (1893)

— Rejoice in the Lord; Look ye Saints, the Sight is Glorious, 1894 (1976)

— Light's Glittering Morn, with B solo, 1894 (1894)

— Far from the World, with S/T solo (1896)

— O Lord, I will Exalt thee, 1897 (1897)

— Calm on the Listening Ear of Night, with S/T solo, 1898; in The Churchman (10 Dec 1898)

— Grant, we beseech thee, merciful Lord, 1899 (Boston, 1898)

— Behold, ye Despisers, with B solo (London, 1899)

— Now Sinks the Sun (from The Legend of St Christopher), a cappella, 1897 (London, 1900)

— In Heavenly Love Abiding, with S solo; While we have Time; 1900 (both pubd London, 1900)

— Thou Shalt Remember, with Bar solo, 1901 (London, 1901)

— Come, gentles, rise (D. Evans), unison chorus, org, 1903 (1905)

— God, that Makest Earth and Heaven (1903/R)

— Brightest and Best, with S solo, 1904 (1904)

57 The Office for the Holy Communion, B♭, 1904 (New York and London, 1904)

— It Came upon the Midnight Clear, solo vv, chorus, org, (vn, hp ad lib), 1904 (Boston, 1904)

— I Shall not Die but Live, with Bar solo, 1905 (Boston, 1905)

— To Whom then Will ye Liken God, with T solo, 1909 (1909)

— The Voice that breathed o'er Eden, unison chorus, kbd, 1916, NH

— He Faileth Not, with S/T solo, 1919 (1919)

— He who Hath Led Will Lead, NH

The following hymnals contain the majority of Parker's hymn settings (for individual listings see Kearns, 1990):

H. Parker, ed.: The Hymnal, Revised and Enlarged … of the Protestant Episcopal Church in the USA (1903)

H. Parker and H.B. Jepson, eds.: University Hymns for Use in the Battell Chapel at Yale with Tunes Arranged for Male Voices (1907)

The Hymnal … of the Protestant Episcopal Church in the USA (1918)

The Hymnal of the Protestant Episcopal Church in the USA (1943)

KEYBOARD
individual listings in Kearns (1990)

— Geschwindmarsch für zwei Orgelspielern, 1881 (Carol Stream, IL, 1975)

9	5 morceaux caractéristiques, pf (Boston, 1886)
19	4 Sketches, pf (Boston, 1890)
17	4 Compositions, org (1890)
23	6 Lyrics, pf (1891)
20	4 Compositions, org (1891)
28	4 Compositions, org (1891)
32	5 Sketches, org (1893)
36	4 Compositions, org (1893)
—	2 Compositions, pf; in *Famous Composers and their Works*, xiii (Boston, 1895), 1097–106
—	3 Compositions, org; in D. Buck: *Vox organi* (Boston, 1896)
49	3 morceaux caractéristiques, pf (Cincinnati, 1899)
—	Praesentir Marsch, pf 4 hands, 1906, *NH*
65	Organ Sonata, E♭ (1908)
67	4 Compositions, org (pubd as op.66, 1910)
68	5 Short Pieces, org (1908)
—	Introduction and Fugue, e, org, 1916, *NH*

ORCHESTRAL AND CHAMBER

4	Concert Overture, E♭, orch, 1884; Munich, Königliche Musikhochschule, 7 July 1884, *NH*
5	Regulus, ov. héroïque, orch, 1884, *NH*
12	Venetian Overture, B♭, orch, 1884, *NH*
13	Scherzo, g, orch, 1884, *NH*
7	Symphony, C, orch, 1885; Munich, Königliche Musikhochschule, 11 May 1885, *NH*
11	String Quartet, F, 1885; Detroit, MI, 29 Nov 1887; in J. Graziano, ed.: *Three Centuries of American Music*, viii (1991), 245–313
24b	Count Robert of Paris, ov., orch, 1890; New York, 10 Dec 1890, *NH*
35	Suite, pf, vn, vc, New York, 3 March 1893 (1904)
38	String Quintet, d, 1894; Boston, 21 Jan 1895, *NH*
41	Suite, e, pf, vn, 1894; Boston, 15 Jan 1895, *NH*
46	A Northern Ballad, sym. poem, 1899; Boston SO, 29 Dec 1899, *NH*
55	Organ Concerto, 1902; Boston SO, 26 Dec 1902 (London, 1903)
56	Vathek, sym. poem, 1903, *NH*
72	Collegiate Overture, with male chorus, 1911; Norfolk Festival, 7 June 1911, *NH*
77d	Fairyland Suite (prelude, int, ballet from op, Fairyland), 1915, *NH*

WRITINGS

'Concerning Contemporary Music', *Proceedings of the American Academy of Arts and Letters*, i (1909–10), 36–43; repr. in *North American Review*, cxci (1910), 517–26
'Some Orchestral Conditions', *Atlantic Monthly*, cxix (1917), 485–90
'Our Taste in Music', *Yale Review*, 2nd ser., vii (1917–18), 777–88

BIBLIOGRAPHY

R. Hughes: *Contemporary American Composers* (Boston, 1900, rev. 2/1914/R by A. Elson as *American Composers*)
J. van Broekhaven: '*Mona*: a Thematic Analysis', *Musical Observer*, vi/4 (1912), 22–8
G.W. Chadwick: *Horatio Parker* (New Haven, 1921/R)
E.E. Hipsher: *American Opera and its Composers* (Philadelphia, 1927, 2/1934/R)
D.S. Smith: 'A Study of Horatio Parker', *MQ*, xvi (1930), 153–69
O.W. Strunk: 'Works of Horatio W. Parker', *MQ*, xvi (1930), 164–9
J.T. Howard: *Our American Music: Three Hundred Years of it* (New York, 1931, enlarged 4/1965 as *Our American Music: a Comprehensive History from 1620 to the Present*)
I.P. Semler and P. Underwood: *Horatio Parker: a Memoir for his Grandchildren* (New York, 1942/R)
W.C. Rorick: 'The Horatio Parker Archives in the Yale University Music Library', *FAM*, xxvi (1979), 298–304
W.K. Kearns: 'Horatio Parker's *Mona*: its Place in the Composer's Career and in American Opera', *Sonneck Society Newsletter*, vi/3 (1980), 11–12
W.K. Kearns: 'Horatio Parker and the English Choral Societies', *American Music*, iv/1 (1986), 20–33
W.K. Kearns: *Horatio Parker, 1863–1919: his Life, Music, and Ideas* (Metuchen and London, 1990)
W.K. Kearns: 'Horatio Parker's Oratorios: a Measure of the Changing Genre at the Turn of the Twentieth Century', *Inter-American Music Review*, xi/2 (1990–91), 65–73
N.E. Tawa: *The Coming of Age of American Art Music: New England's Classical Romanticists* (New York, Westport, CT, and London, 1991)
S.E. Scroggins: *The Songs of Horatio Parker* (diss., U. of Maryland, 1995)
W.K. Kearns: 'Horatio Parker, Edward Elgar, and Choral Music at the Turn of the Twentieth Century', *Elgar Society Journal*, x/i (1997), 4–24

WILLIAM KEARNS

Parker, J(ames) C(utler) D(unn) (*b* Boston, 2 June 1828; *d* Brookline, MA, 27 Nov 1916). American composer, organist and teacher. A graduate of both the Boston Latin School and Harvard College (1848), he abandoned law in favour of music. From 1851 to 1854 he studied with Hauptmann, Moscheles, Plaidy, Richter and Rietz in Leipzig. When he returned to Boston he began teaching the piano, organ and harmony at the New England Conservatory (1871–97) and was organist at the fashionable Trinity Church (1864–91). His compositions, always thoroughly conservative, included a cantata, *St John*, written for the 75th anniversary of the Handel and Haydn Society (of which he was organist), and an Easter oratorio, *The Life of Man*, sung by the society in 1895. He published a *Manual of Harmony* (Boston, 1855), edited a large anthology of sacred choruses (Boston, 1861), and translated several works including practical manuals and the texts of some of Mendelssohn's partsongs (1856) and Gade's *Comala* (1875).

WORKS
(selective list)

all published in Boston

7 Part Songs (1875); Redemption Hymn, A, 4vv, vs (1877); The Blind King (after L. Uhland), ballad, Bar, male vv, orch, vs (1883); St John (cant.), solo vv, 4vv, orch, vs (1890); The Life of Man (orat), solo vv, 4vv, orch, vs (1894)

BIBLIOGRAPHY

DAB (F.W. Coburn); *GroveA* (R. Stevenson) [incl. further bibliography]
L.C. Elson and others: 'Passing of J.C.D. Parker', *New England Conservatory Magazine-Review*, vii/2 (1916–17), 45

ROBERT STEVENSON

Parker, Maceo. *See* JBS.

Parker, Roger (Leslie) (*b* London, 2 Aug 1951). English musicologist. He studied at London University (1974–81) under Margaret Bent and Pierluigi Petrobelli, completing his doctoral studies with a dissertation on early Verdi. He became a professor at Cornell University in 1982; in 1988 he was appointed co-director of the critical edition of Donizetti and the next year became founding co-editor of the *Cambridge Opera Journal*. His edition of *Nabucco* (1987) inaugurated the new critical edition of Verdi's operas. In 1993 he returned to England to take up the position of lecturer at Oxford University; in 1996 he became a reader in music and fellow of St Hugh's College and in 1999 was appointed Professor of Music at Cambridge University. He was awarded the Premio 'Giuseppe Verdi' (Parma, 1986), a John Simon Guggenheim Fellowship (1989) and the Dent Medal (1991). Parker's central interests lie in Italian opera of the 19th century, in which area his work has led to the re-examination of traditional assumptions and entrenched attitudes; but his knowledge and perceptions extend to many other areas, as his writing on analytical topics and his enterprising editing have demonstrated. His book *Leonora's Last Act* (1997) includes discussion of the possibilities of an 'authentic' staging of Verdi's operas, and the advantages and disadvantages of analysing them according to terms that his contemporaries might have understood.

WRITINGS

Studies in Early Verdi (1832–1844): New Information and Perspectives on the Milanese Musical Milieu and the Operas from Oberto to Ernani (diss., U. of London, 1981; New York, 1989)

ed., with C. Abbate: *Analyzing Opera: Verdi and Wagner: Ithaca, NY, 1984* [incl. 'Introduction: On Analyzing Opera', 1–26 [with C. Abbate]; 'Motives and Recurring Themes in *Aida*', 222–40]

with A. Groos: *Giacomo Puccini: La bohème* (Cambridge, 1986)

ed., with A. Groos: *Reading Opera: Ithaca, NY, 1986* [incl. 'On Reading 19th-Century Opera: Verdi Through the Looking Glass', 288–305]

ed.: *The Oxford Illustrated History of Opera* (Oxford, 1994; repr. 1996 as *The Oxford History of Opera*)

Leonora's Last Act: Essays in Verdian Discourse (Princeton, NJ, 1997)

EDITIONS

G. Verdi: *Nabucco* (Milan, 1987)
G. Puccini: *Tosca* (Milan, 1995)

ROSEMARY WILLIAMSON

Parkhurst, Susan McFarland [Parkhurst, Mrs E.A.] (*b* Leicester, MA, 5 June 1836; *d* Brooklyn, NY, 4 May 1918). American composer. She composed popular songs and parlour piano solos during the 1860s. A skilful writer, she gained most recognition for songs on such topical themes as temperance and abolition. *Father's a drunkard and mother is dead* (1866), which she and her daughter ('Little Effie') performed at concerts and temperance meetings in New York, became a standard of the period. Other successful songs include *New Emancipation Song*, *There are voices*, *Spirit Voices* and *Weep no more for Lilly* (all 1864).

Horace Waters, the New York publisher associated mainly with Stephen Foster, promoted Parkhurst's work, printing a *Select Catalogue of Mrs. E.A. Parkhurst's Compositions* in 1864. She contributed tunes to Waters's collections of 'Sunday school' hymns: *The Athenaeum* (1863), *The Golden Harp* (1863) and *Zion's Refreshing Showers* (1867). In the early 1860s Parkhurst worked at Waters's music store, where she encountered Foster. She published 'Personal Recollections of the Last Days of Stephen Foster' in the September 1916 issue of the magazine *The Etude*, describing herself as a 'lady who in her youth was known as a successful composer, and who, when a young girl, took a friendly interest in Stephen Foster'.

Writing in the standard song-and-chorus format of the period, Parkhurst infused popular song formulae with a more ambitious musical language. Her harmonic vocabulary was more expansive and richer than that found in most average songs of the period, and the piano postludes she often used to round off her songs were more imaginative. Original prints of about 60 songs are held in the Music Division of the New York Public Library; instrumental works are at the American Antiquarian Society, Worcester, Massachusetts.

BIBLIOGRAPHY

E.M. Smith, ed.: *Women in Sacred Song: a Library of Hymns, Religious Poems and Sacred Music by Women* (Boston, 1885)
M.R. Turner: *The Parlour Song Book* (London, 1972)
R. Crawford, ed.: *Civil War Songs* (New York, 1977)
J. Tick: *American Women Composers before 1870* (Ann Arbor, 1983, 2/1995)
K. Pendle, ed.: *Women and Music: a History* (Bloomington, IN, 1991)
J. Finson: *The Voices that are Gone: themes in 19th-century American popular song* (New York, 1994)

JUDITH TICK

Park Lane Group. London concert organization founded in 1956. *See* LONDON (i), §VI, 4(iii).

Parlamagni, Antonio (*b* 1759; *d* Florence, 9 Oct 1838). Italian bass. Having made his début about 1788, he sang very successfully as a *basso buffo* in Rome, Florence and Venice. At La Scala he sang Figaro in Paisiello's *Il barbiere di Siviglia* and appeared in operas by Palma and Paer (1797), Sarti and Mayr (1800), and in 1812 created Macrobio in Rossini's *La pietra del paragone*. In 1821 he sang Isidoro in the first performance of Rossini's *Matilde di Shabran* at the Teatro Apollo, Rome; his daughter Annetta Parlamagni sang the contralto role of Edoardo and was also a fine Rosina (*Barbiere*), a role she sang in Siena in 1835.

ELIZABETH FORBES

Parlando (It.: 'speaking'; gerund of *parlare*). A performance direction. 'Parlante' (present participle of *parlare*) is also used. In vocal music, as in Verdi's Requiem at the words 'fac eas, Domine', 'parlando' directs that the voice should approximate to speech. In instrumental music its use is more vague. Beethoven headed the sixth bagatelle of his op.33 *allegretto quasi andante: con una certa espressione parlante* – a context which suggests that *parlante* could be translated 'eloquent'. The second of Schumann's Abegg Variations op.1 has at the beginning *basso parlando*. The notion of musical eloquence was one that sprang naturally from 18th-century philosophical thought on music (*see* RHETORIC AND MUSIC, §I). *Quasi parlando* ('as though speaking') is also common.

DAVID FALLOWS

Parlante. *See* PARLANDO.

Parlasca [Perlasca], **Bernardino.** *See* BORLASCA, BERNARDINO.

Parley of Instruments. British Renaissance and Baroque string consort, founded by PETER HOLMAN in 1979. It takes its name from the public concerts given in London by John Banister in 1676. The core group consists of Judy Tarling and Theresa Caudle (violins), Mark Caudle (bass viol, bass violin and cello) and Peter Holman (harpsichord and chamber organ). The ensemble has pioneered the revival of Renaissance violins modelled on instruments by Gasparo da Salò and Andrea Amati from the late 16th century, which produce a more blended, viol-like sound than their 18th-century counterparts. With their short 'French' bows, the group has done much to revive the 17th-century orchestral repertory in recordings such as 'A High-Priz'd Noise', featuring dance music by Ferrabosco II, Stephen Nau and William Lawes. The Parley also fields a Classical orchestra and has moved into the 19th century with recordings of West-Gallery Music.

LUCY ROBINSON

Parliament. American funk-rock group led by GEORGE CLINTON.

Parlour organ. *See* REED ORGAN.

Parlow, Kathleen (*b* Calgary, 20 Sept 1890; *d* Oakville, ON, 19 Aug 1963). Canadian violinist. At the age of four she was taken to San Francisco where for ten years she studied the violin, first with a cousin and then with Henry

Holmes. In 1905 she travelled to London where she gave a recital in the Bechstein Hall and played Beethoven's Violin Concerto with the LSO. In 1906 she commenced studies in St Petersburg with Auer, who became not only her teacher but her financial and musical adviser for many years. Until 1926 she lived in England, touring Europe (she was Glazunov's choice to play his Concerto at the International Musical Festival at Ostend, 1907) and making regular visits to North America. In 1922 she made a successful tour of the Orient. Returning to the USA in 1926, Parlow made several tours (notably one of Mexico), taught at Mills College, Oakland (1929–36), and led the South Mountain Quartet in the Berkshires during the summers of 1935–41. Finally she settled in Toronto (1941) where she taught at the Conservatory, led her own highly influential quartet (1943–58), performed and made frequent radio broadcasts almost to the end of her life. She also played in a duo with Ernest MacMillan, and with MacMillan and Zara Nelsova formed the Canadian Trio.

Parlow's playing was in the Auer tradition: a big, pure tone, suave legato and effortless technique. She made many recordings before she became somewhat disenchanted with that medium in 1926. Her quartet recorded several works by Canadian composers. She owned the 1735 'Viotti' Guarneri, which she bequeathed to the University of Toronto.

BIBLIOGRAPHY

EMC2 (G. Ridout; with discography)

K. Parlow: 'Student Days in Russia', *Canadian Music Journal*, vi/1 (1961–2), 13–20

M.P. French: *Kathleen Parlow: a Portrait* (Toronto, 1967)

J. Creighton: *Discopaedia of the Violin, 1889–1971* (Toronto, 1974)

T. Potter: 'Reluctant Virtuoso', *The Strad*, cviii (1997), 610–15

GODFREY RIDOUT/TULLY POTTER

Parma. City in northern Italy. The earliest references to music in the city occur in the medieval statutes of Parma Cathedral, which indicate that it was traditional for the *primicerio* to instruct clerics in the art of choral singing. Valuable information may be found in the work of 15th-century theorists, notably Giorgio Anselmi, a teacher, doctor and mathematician; his treatise *De musica* (1434) was praised by Gaffurius. The presence in Parma of Johannes Legrense, who died there in 1473, was also of some importance; one of his pupils, Nicolaus Burtius of Parma, wrote *Musices opusculum* (1487), disputing the theories of Ramos de Pareia and affirming those of Guido of Arezzo. Burtius was still *guardacore* at the cathedral in 1518.

In the mid-16th century, when the Farnese family created a political stability that Parma had previously lacked, cultural development became more significant and continuous. Music, which played an increasingly conspicuous and clearly defined role in this period, was fostered by three important *cappelle*: at the cathedral, the Chiesa

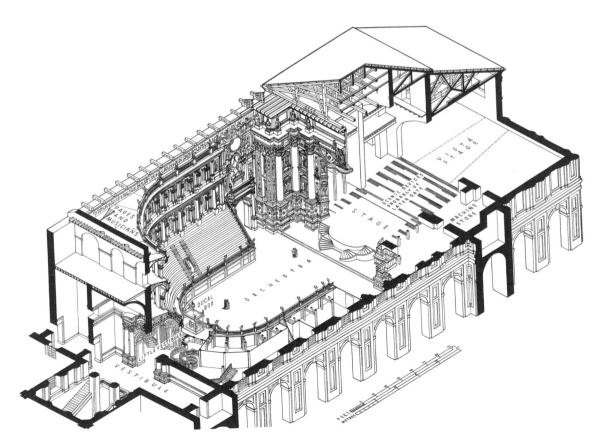

1. *Teatro Farnese, Parma, designed by Giovanni Battista Aleotti, 1618, showing the theatre arranged for the inaugural production, 1628; conjectural reconstruction from R. and H. Leacroft, 'Theatre and Playhouse' (London, 1984)*

2. Design by Domenico Mauro for Sabadini's 'Il favore degli dei', Act 1 scene xxvii, Teatro Farnese, Parma, 1690; engraving by Francesco Maria Francia

della Madonna della Steccata and the ducal palace. Musicians often served at more than one of these. The cathedral *cappella*, formally founded in 1564, continued a tradition that had been established by such Italian musicians as Archangelo da Correggio (*primicerio* in 1479) and by such foreigners as the Flemish Guglielmo Dillen. Musicians who worked there in the 17th century include Giacinto Merulo (nephew of Claudio Merulo), G.B. Chinelli, M. Dionigi, Marco Marazzoli ('dell'Arpa') and Giorgio Martinelli.

The Steccata *cappella* was established in 1528, the same year as the church. Its greatest period was under Giovanni Maria Lanfranco, *maestro* from 1540 until his death in 1545. Other 16th-century *maestri* included Stefano Alessandrini, Pietro Pontio, who was equally famous as composer and theorist, Raynaldo Caussin, his son Ernold, highly esteemed in his day as a composer, and Gottfried Palmartz, a Flemish organist and composer. The frequent movement of musicians in Parma is exemplified in the career of Claudio Merulo, who was appointed to the court in 1586, to the cathedral as organist in 1587 and to the Steccata as organist from 1591 to 1604; at the Steccata he built for his own use a 4' positive organ, now in Parma Conservatory. 17th-century developments included the cultivation of instrumental music; but even after 1694, when Duke Francesco granted

the musicians the freedom to perform at entertainments outside the church, the *cappella* continued to embellish the major feasts with customary splendour.

The ducal chapel was the central expression of the Farnese family's love of music in the 16th century. It was founded in 1545, before Pier Luigi Farnese had moved to Parma, and with the engagement of famous singers and players, especially from the Netherlands (Alessandro Farnese was governor of Flanders), it played an increasingly important part in the city's life. The most distinguished figures were Claudio Merulo and Cipriano de Rore. Rore was at Parma from 1561 to 1563 and from November 1564 until his death in December 1565; both he and Merulo were buried in the cathedral. Three other Flemish musicians who worked at the court were Baldoino Blondeau, Josquino Persoens and Jean d'Arras. Their colleagues included G.A. Veggio, Giulio Buonagiunta, Orazio Bassani and Santino Garsi; they acted both as composers and as instrumentalists. 17th-century court *maestri di cappella* included Francesco Manelli, who held the same post at the Steccata, F.A.M. Pistocchi, B. Sabadini and Francesco Corselli. Performances of music by the most important composers of the day enriched the court's musical life; among those who dedicated works to the duke of Parma were D'India (*Il quarto libro dei madrigali a cinque voci*), Paolo Quagliati (*Il primo libro dei madrigali*), Domenico Mazzocchi (*La catena d'Adone*) and Marco da Gagliano (*La Flora*).

Although instrumental music was followed attentively by the Farnese family, theatrical works became increasingly important in the 17th century. In 1618–19 Duke Ranuccio I commissioned Gian Battista Aleotti to construct the Teatro Farnese on the first floor of the Palazzo della Pilotta; it opened on 21 December 1628 (see fig.1) with the tourney *Mercurio e Marte* (libretto by Claudio Achillini, *intermedi* by Monteverdi), which concluded the festivities to mark the marriage of Odoardo Farnese and Margherita de' Medici (see Reiner). Operas by Manelli, Sabadini (fig.2) and Leonardo Vinci were performed there. The theatre was closed in 1732 and was almost completely destroyed in 1944; it was later reconstructed, but is not in use. There were also smaller theatres. The theatre at the Collegio dei Nobili was founded by Ranuccio I in 1600; the Teatro della Racchetta in Borgo del Leon d'Oro was administered by the Sanoitale family from 1688 to 1832, when it was closed. The Teatrino della Corte was built in 1689 by Ranuccio II and opened with G.F. Tosi's *L'idea di tutte le perfezioni*, performed for the duke's marriage to Dorothea of Neuburg (1690). The Teatro Ducale (1688, also built by Ranuccio II) assumed greater significance because it was more suitable for opera; it opened with A. Giannettini's *Teseo in Atene* (libretto by A. Aureli, settings by F. Galli-Bibiena).

The treaty of Aix-la-Chapelle in 1748 assigned the duchy of Parma to the Infante Philip of Bourbon, second son of Elizabeth Farnese, and during the Bourbon domination arts and letters flourished to such an extent that Parma became known as the 'Athens of Italy'. This was largely because of the general intendant of the royal household, Guillaume du Tillot, who was responsible for theatrical performances. The royal orchestra was employed on these occasions, and a Regia Scuola di Canto was established in 1769 to serve the Teatro Ducale; the school was directed by F.Z. Poncini, organist at the Steccata *cappella*. It was during this period that Carlo Innocenzo Frugoni, the refined Arcadian poet, and Tommaso Traetta, the southern composer whom Philip had appointed *maestro di cappella* in 1758, attempted their reform of opera. Their aim was to reconcile French taste and Neapolitan spectacle, and they produced several important works, including *Ippolito ed Aricia* (1759), *I tindaridi* and *Le feste d'Imeneo*. There were also performances of *opere buffe* by Paisiello to librettos by Goldoni (*Le virtuose ridicole*, *Il negligente* and *I bagni d'Abano*), which marked the beginning of the composer's fame. Others working at the ducal court during the 18th century were Alessandro Besozzi (ii), Gaspare Ghiretti, Giuseppe Colla, G.F. Fortunati and G.S. Mangot (Rameau's brother-in-law). In 1792, towards the end of the Bourbon period, Duke Ferdinand named Ferdinando Paer honorary *maestro di cappella*. Although he stayed only a few years in his native city before embarking on his illustrious career in Vienna, Dresden and Paris, Paer occasionally returned to Parma; a visit in 1809 was notable for the first performance of *Agnese* at the Teatrino in the Villa Douglas-Scotti.

In 1815 political events took Napoleon's second wife, Marie-Louise of Austria to Parma, and a new period of musical growth began. She instigated the Scuola Canto Corale at the Ospizio delle Arti, which later also provided instrumental tuition and formed the basis of the present conservatory (the Conservatorio di Musica A. Boito). The

3. Poster for the Verdi centenary season at the Teatro Regio, Parma, 1913

court orchestra, directed from 1835 to 1840 by Paganini, was also founded at her behest (1816). In 1821, feeling that the Teatro Ducale was no longer adequate, she commissioned the architect Nicola Bettoli to construct a new theatre; it opened in 1829 with Bellini's *Zaira*, a success which created bitter controversy. In a century when opera provided the most direct and widespread expression of popular involvement in the aesthetic and political ideals of the day, the new Teatro Ducale, after 1849 called the Teatro Regio, became the centre of Parma musical life. It staged opera performances of the highest calibre from 1829 to 1873 and remains an important centre of operatic activity. Besides Verdi, who was brought up near Parma, many notable composers worked there in the 19th century, among them Ferdinando Orlandi, Ferdinando Melchiorri, G.C. Ferrarini, Giovanni Rossi (ii), Gualtiero Sanelli, Ferdinando Provesi and Emilio Usiglio. Parma also produced such important conductors as Manlio and Gaetano Bavagnoli, Giovanni Bolzoni, Cleofonte Campanini, Giuseppe del Campo and Toscanini. Directors of the conservatory included Ferrarini, Giusto Dacci, Arrigo Boito, Giovanni Tebaldini, Guglielmo Zuelli and Luigi Trecate. The most important 20th-century composer from Parma was Ildebrando Pizzetti.

The music section of the Palatine library comprises some 100,000 printed books and 500 manuscripts, of which the most precious are the treatises of Aaron, Vicentino and Zarlino, and over 400 sonatas by D. Scarlatti. The collection of about 700 volumes and 150 handbills from the house of Bourbon and the music library of Marie-Louise is an invaluable source of information, especially about early 19th-century works for the theatre.

In 1963, under the auspices of UNESCO and the Italian ministry of education, the Istituto di Studi Verdiani was established at Parma; by its publications and research it has given the study of Verdi's works a new historical and musicological basis. Since 1989 a Verdi Festival has been held annually in September and October.

BIBLIOGRAPHY

GroveO (G.P. Minardi) [incl. further bibliography]
G. Negri: Cronologia del Nuovo teatro ducale di Parma (Parma, 1839)
P.E. Ferrari: Spettacoli drammatico-musicali e coreografici in Parma dal 1628 al 1883 (Parma, 1884)
G. Dacci: Cenni storici e stilistici intorno alla Reale Scuola di Musica in Parma (Parma, 1888)
L. Balestrieri: Feste e spettacoli alla corte dei Farnesi: contributo alla storia del melodramma (Parma, 1909)
G. Lombardi: Il Teatro farnesiano in Parma: note a appunti con documenti (Parma, 1909)
C. Alcari: Cinquant'anni di vita del Teatro Reinach di Parma (1871–1921) (Parma, 1921)
C. Alcari: Il Teatro regio di Parma nella sua storia dal 1883 al 1929 (Parma, 1929)
N. Pelicelli: 'Musicisti in Parma', NA, viii (1931), 132–42, 196–215, 278–90; ix (1932), 41–52, 112–29, 217–46; x (1933), 32–43, 116–26, 233–48, 314–25; xi (1934), 29–57, 248–81; xii (1935), 82–92, 317–42 [series covering 15th–19th centuries]
G. Drei: L'archivio di stato di Parma (Rome, 1941)
M. Ferrarini: Parma musicale ottocentesca (Parma, 1946)
M. Corradi Cervi: Cronologia del Teatro regio di Parma (1928–1948) (Parma, 1955)
L. Parigi: 'Una "schola cantorum" quattro-cinquecentesca nel duomo di Parma', RaM, xxv (1955), 118–27
L. Gambara: Il Conservatorio di musica 'A. Boito' di Parma (Parma, 1958)
M. Medici: 'Osservazioni sulla biblioteca musicale di Parma', Aurea Parma, xlviii (1964), 119–65
S. Reiner: 'Preparations in Parma: 1618, 1627–8', MR, xxv (1964), 273–301
I. Allodi, ed.: I teatri di Parma dal Farnese al Regio (Milan, 1969)
V. Cervetti, C. del Monte and V. Segreto, eds.: Teatro regio: cronologia degli spettacoli lirici (Parma, 1979–82)
M.G. Borazzo: Musica, scenotecnica, illusione nel grande apparato farnesiano dal 1628 a Parma (diss., U. of Parma, 1982)
N. Albarosa and R. Di Benedetto, eds.: Musica e spettacolo a Parma nel Settecento (Parma, 1984)
C. Gallico: Le capitali della musica, Parma (Milan, 1985)
L. Allegri and R. Di Benedetto, eds.: La Parma in festa: spettacolarità e teatro nel ducato di Parma nel Settecento (Modena, 1987)
P. Cirani: Musica e spettacolo a Colorno tra XVI e XIX secolo (Parma, 1995)
M. Cadossi: La vita musicale a Parma nel primo decennio del Novecento (diss., U. of Parma, 1995)

GIAN PAOLO MINARDI

Parma, Ildebrando da. See PIZZETTI, ILDEBRANDO.

Parma, Nicolo [Nicola] (b Mantua; fl 1575–1613). Italian composer. He probably spent his early career at Mantua in the service of the Gonzaga family, since he was one of seven composers who wrote cantus-firmus masses using chants from the Kyriale ad usum Ecclesiae S. Barbara, a revised liturgy devised for the ducal chapel of S Barbara at Mantua by Duke Guglielmo Gonzaga. Parma's mass is in a manuscript source believed to date from about 1575.

He also contributed madrigals to L'amorosa caccia (RISM 1588[14]), an anthology by native Mantuans many of whom were then employed either at S Barbara or at Mantua Cathedral (S Pietro), and also to the third volume of the Floridi virtuosi d'Italia (1586[9]), a collection with a strong Mantuan flavour dedicated to Duke Guglielmo. His own Secondo libro of 1592 is dated from Pavia, and the inclusion of his Gite felici in Lodovico Torti's Secondo libro delle canzoni a tre voci (1584[10]) suggests that he may have been there for some time. In his Madrigali a sei voci of 1606 (now lost) he was apparently described as 'maestro di Cappella dell'Incoronata', which Pitoni believed to be S Maria Incoronata at Lodi, near Pavia. From 1610 to 1613 he was maestro at Novara Cathedral, but was evidently dissatisfied there, because on 7 April 1613 he applied for a vacant canonry at S Barbara, Mantua. Although it is traditionally accepted that he was successful, since he appears in a list of Mantuan musicians in Cagnani's 'Lettera cronologica', his name does not appear in the surviving chapel records.

In his sacred works Parma handled a variety of styles with competence and fluency. The pieces for small forces are usually in the standard post-Tridentine polyphonic manner, and those for larger ensembles show his ability in a polychoral style. The Missa Beatae Mariae Virginis is designed for alternatim performance as specified in the S Barbara liturgy.

WORKS

SECULAR

Il primo libro de madrigali, 5vv, lost, MischiatiI
Il secondo libro de madrigali, 5, 6vv (Venice, 1592)
Madrigali, 6vv (1606), lost, mentioned in PitoniN
Madrigals, 1584[10], 1586[9], 1588[14]

SACRED

Cantiones sacrae, lost
Motetti lib.I, lost
Sacrae cantiones, 5–10vv, lib.II (Venice, 1586)
Motetti, 8–10vv, lib.II (1586), lost, MischiatiI
Canzoni sacrae (1590), lost
Motecta, 8, 12vv, bc (org) (Venice, 1606)
Psalm, 5vv, 1592[3]
Missa Beatae Mariae Virginis, c1575, I-Mc

BIBLIOGRAPHY

BertolottiM; MischiatiI; PitoniN
G. Draudius: Bibliotheca classica (Frankfurt, 1611)
E. Cagnani: 'Lettera cronologica: foreword to Raccolta d'alcune rime di scrittori mantovani (Mantua, 1612)
A. Göhler: Verzeichnis der in den Frankfurter und Leipziger Messkatalogen der Jahre 1564 bis 1759 angezeigten Musikalien (Leipzig, 1902/R)

IAIN FENLON

Parma, Santino Garsi da. See GARSI, SANTINO.

Parma, Viktor (b Trieste, 20 Feb 1858; d Maribor, Slovenia, 25 Dec 1924). Slovenian composer of Italian descent. He studied composition while a law student in Vienna, and attended Anton Bruckner's lectures. After World War I he became honorary Kapellmeister of the National Theatre in Maribor. At the end of the 19th century and the beginning of the 20th, Parma was the most prolific and popular operatic composer of Slovenia. Although cosmopolitan by inclination – his principal model was Verdi in his early and middle creative periods, and he also followed the verismo trend to some extent – he was devoted to the national Slovenian cause. As well as several operettas, he composed four operas, of which Urh, grof celjski ('Ulrich, Count of Cilli') was the first all-sung Slovenian opera. Zlatorog ('The Goat with the Golden

Horns') is his best opera in terms of musical technique and artistic achievement.

WORKS

Stage: Urh, grof celjski [Ulrich, Count of Cilli] (op, 3, A. Funtek), 1894; Ksenija (op, 1, F. Göstl and Funtek), 1896; Stara pesem [The Old Song] (dramatic romance, 1, G. Menasci, after H. Heine), 1897; Caričine Amazonke [The Empress's Amazons] (operetta, A.D. Borum), 1902; Nečak [The Nephew] (operetta, F.A. Hirsch), 1906; Venerin hram [The Temple of Venus] (operetta, R. Felden and B. Swowsky), 1908; Zaručnik v škripcih [The Fiancé in a Fix] (operetta, A. Grund), 1917; Zlatorog [The Goat with the Golden Horns] (prol., 3, R. Brauer, after R. Baumbach), 1919

Other vocal: Povodni mož [The Waterman] (ballad, F. Prešeren), 1v, chorus, orch, 1910; Sveti Senan [Holy Senan] (ballad, F. Prešeren), 1v, chorus, orch, 1922; choruses, songs

Inst works, incl. str qt (1923), pf pieces

MANICA ŠPENDAL

Parmegiani, Bernard (*b* Paris, 27 Oct 1927). French composer. After studying mime with Jacques Lecoq (1957–61), a discipline he has regarded as influential to his composing, he worked as a sound engineer for French television. In late 1959 he joined the Groupe de Recherches Musicales (GRM), founded the previous year by Pierre Schaeffer under the auspices of RTF; *Alternances* (1963) was composed for the famous and tempestuous Concert Collectif devised by Schaeffer. Subsequently he provided studio assistance to several composers, most notably Xenakis, and produced music for radio, television and the stage. As head of the Musique-Image section of the GRM, he also wrote many film scores. Among his wide range of functional compositions is a jingle written for Charles de Gaulle airport in 1971. After leaving GRM in 1992, he set up a studio at Saint Rémy in Provence.

Parmegiani began to write electro-acoustic works for the concert hall in the 1960s. *Violostries* (1965), a dense polyphonic work in four movements for violin and tape, is constructed out of nine basic violin tones (sound cells) suggested to the composer by violinist Devy Erlih. *L'instant mobile* (1966) shows the emergence of Parmegiani's preoccupation with the passing of time, an interest that led 25 years later to a series of works inspired by ideas of temporal perception. *Capture éphémère* (1967), one of his most successful pieces, alludes to the passing of time, as well as to the brevity and transience of sound; it is a dynamic composition in which the subject is perfectly illustrated through micro-montage. In 1971 with *Pour en finir avec le pouvoir d'Orphée*, a work that amounts to a confession of faith, he claims to have broken with the seductive power of repetition and the spellbinding musical fabric in which he had excelled. During this period he composed *Enfer* (1972), the first part of a *Divine Comedy* (after Dante) written in collaboration with Bayle.

It was only with the pivotal work *De natura sonorum* (1975) and subsequently with *Dedans-Dehors* (1977), however, that Parmegiani, out of a desire for rigour and abstraction, broke free of his tendency towards aural enchantment. What his music lost in charm and spontaneity it gained in meaning and compositional skill; nonetheless, the economy of his methods and the linearity of his subjects could not mask the lingering sensuality in his music. From this point on, his sound palette was modified and clarified. To some extent he abandoned massive orchestral textures in favour of a more agile kind of counterpoint. At times, however, he reverted to full-bodied and warm material, often situated in the middle or lower register. In *La création du monde* (1984), for

example, he turned back to progressive mutations of sound material. Later works include the four *Exercismes* (1985–9), compositions of almost pointillist refinement; *Litaniques* (1987), which takes up his fascination with incantatory music; *Rouge-Mort* (1987), after Mérimée's *Carmen*, as powerful and dramatic as its model; *Le présent composé* (1991), *Entre-Temps* (1992) and *Plain-Temps* (1993), highly wrought works that refer back to reflections on time; the resonant *Sonare* (1996); and *Sons/jeux* (1998). Other notable features of his music include: a sense of humour, often emphasized by punning titles; a generosity of inspiration in an almost popular vein, particularly evident in his early works; a frequent, but never banal, use of synthesized sound; and a love of the 'material' element.

WORKS

(*selective list*)

Tape: L'instant mobile, 1966; Bidule en ré, 1969; L'oeil écoute, 1970; Pour en finir avec le pouvoir d'Orphée I, 1971; La roue Ferris, 1971; Enfer, 1972 (after Dante: *Divine Comedy*); Ponomatopées, 1972; Paradis, 1974, collab. F. Bayle (after Dante: *Divine Comedy*); De natura sonorum, 1975; Dedans-Dehors, 1977; Des mots et des sons, 1978; Mess media sons/La table des matières, 1979; L'écho du miroir (Parmegiani), 1980; La création du monde, 1984; Exercisme 2, 1985; Exercisme 3, 1986; Litaniques, 1987; Rouge-Mort: Thanatos, 1987 (after Mérimée: *Carmen*); Exercisme 4, 1989; Le présent composé, 1991; Entre-Temps, 1992; Plain-Temps, 1993; Eclectic bolero, 1995; Sonare, 1996; Sons/jeux, 1998

Tape and insts: Violostries, vn, tape, 1965, collab. D. Erlih; Jazzex, jazz qt, tape, 1966; Et après, bandoneon, tape, 1973, collab. M. Portal; Tuba-Raga et tuba-ci tuba-là, tuba, tape, collab. C. Buquet; Exercisme 1, synth trio, tape, 1985, collab. Trio TM+

BIBLIOGRAPHY

M. Chion: *Les musiques électroacoustiques* (Aix-en-Provence, 1976), 65ff
P. Mion, J.J. Nattiez and J.C. Thomas: *L'envers d'une oeuvre* (Paris, 1982)
F. Bayle, M. Chion and F. Delalands: *Exposition acousmatique Bernard Parmegiani* (Arras, 1983) [catalogue]
R. Sutherland: 'Parmegiani', *London Magazine*, new ser., xxxi/11–12 (1991–2), 106–9
M. Ratté: 'Parmegiani: la nature musicale des sons', *Spirale*, no.24 (1993), 10 only
R. Khazam: 'Sound Thinking', *The Wire*, no.76 (1998), 36–9

FRANCIS DHOMONT

Parmerud, Åke (*b* Lidköping, 24 July 1953). Swedish composer. He studied at the Göteborg Conservatory from 1978 after having worked as a photographer. He also studied with Bodin and Rune Lindblad. Since 1987 he has been teaching computer music and composition at the Göteborg Conservatory; he also teaches at the Lindblad-studio of the University of Göteborg.

Parmerud has written instrumental and multimedia music, but it is above all his electro-acoustic music that has attracted attention and won prizes. He often combines tapes with instruments and also with voices. Examples include *Remain*, for orchestra and tape, *Alias* based on vocal sounds and quotations from Dowland and Gesualdo, and *Retur*, for saxophone quartet and tape. He occasionally collaborates with other composers, such as Anders Blomqvist, with whom he wrote the music for a two-hour documentary on Greta Garbo. This work gave rise to *Strings & Shadows*, in which the sounds of the harp are transformed.

Interactions and transformation processes between different sound sources, and also within the same material (a voice, instrument, chord or specific sound), are characteristic of Parmerud's work. His explorations in the world of sound culminated in *Grains of Voices*, based on different singing styles throughout the world. The various sections of the work are based on the Creation story in the Bible, nursery rhymes, prayers and poems.

WORKS

Stage: Floden av glas, multimedia, 1978–82; The Heart of Silence, multimedia, 1997–8

Other: Närheter, 1978; Time's Imaginary Eve, S, tape, slides, 1980; Remain, orch, tape, 1982; Yttringar, S, 6 insts, tape, 1983; Krén, tape, 1984; Maze, tape, 1985; Yàn, perc ens, tape, 1985; Isola, chbr orch, tape, 1985–6; Éxor, pf, 1986; Inori, hpd, synth, 1987; Alias, tape, 1990; Reed my Lips, wind qnt, cptr, 1991; Les objets obscurs, tape, 1991; Inside Looking Out, cptr, small orch, 1992; Retur, sax qt, cptr, 1992–3; Jeux imaginaires, tape, 1993; Strings & Shadows, hp, cptr, 1993; Renaissance, tape, 1994; Grains of Voices, tape, 1994–5; Mirage, cptr, chbr ens, 1995–6; Efterbild, cptr, orch, 1997–8

HANS-GUNNAR PETERSON

Parodi, Teresa (*b* Genoa, 27 Aug 1827; *d* after 1878). Italian soprano. She entered the musical institute in Genoa at the age of 12, and after studying with Felice Ronconi in Milan was heard by Pasta, who was so impressed that she accepted Parodi as a student and adopted her. Parodi's début was in Bergamo (1845, in *Gemma di Vergy*) and from there she went to Verona, La Spezia, Florence and Rome; her success throughout Italy was immediate. Her London début, as Norma, was at Her Majesty's Theatre (1849). She was engaged by Max Maretzek as the prima donna for his Astor Place Opera Company in 1850–51, with which she appeared to great acclaim in New York, Philadelphia and Boston. She and Maurice Strakosch then organized a concert troupe and embarked on an extended tour of the eastern USA. Parodi subsequently performed again with the Astor Place company and with Strakosch, and sang with the Paris Opéra. In the late 1850s she returned to the USA and (again with Strakosch) organized the Parodi Opera Company, with which she appeared all over the American South and Midwest (1859–60). The extent of Parodi's activities after 1860 is unknown, but as late as 1878 she appeared with James Henry Mapleson's company at the Academy of Music in New York, where her voice was described as 'rich, sweet, clear and sympathetic'.

BIBIBLIOGRAPHY

M. Maretzek: *Crotchets and Quavers* (New York, 1855); repr. in *Revelations of an Opera Manager in 19th Century America* (New York, 1968)

M. Maretzek: *Sharps and Flats* (New York, 1890); repr. in *Revelations of an Opera Manager in 19th Century America* (New York, 1968)

K.K. Preston: *Opera on the Road: Travelling Opera Troupes in the United States, 1825–1860* (Urbana, IL, 1993)

KATHERINE K. PRESTON

Parody (i). A term used to denote a technique of composition, primarily associated with the 16th century, involving the use of pre-existing material. Although the technique of parody was important, particularly in mass composition, throughout the 16th century, the term itself was not used until 1587 when it appeared in the form 'parodia' on the title-page of a mass by Jakob Paix. 'Missa ... ', 'Missa super ... ' or 'Missa ad imitationem ... ', followed by the title of the work on which the mass was based, had been the usual way in which borrowed material was acknowledged. The preference for Greek terms, seen earlier in Kotter's use of 'anabolē' for prelude, for example, was a product of humanistic influence which was strong in Germany by the time of Paix, and may

account for his adoption of 'parodia' from the Greeks as the equivalent of 'ad imitationem'. In 1603 Calvisius published a motet based on a piece of Josquin's labelled 'Parode ad Josquini', and in 1611 there appeared a treatise by Georg Quitschreiber entitled 'De parodia'. The term thus occurred in a mere handful of works of little significance and was unknown before Paix's use of it. Ambros's innocent reference in *Geschichte der Musik* (iii, 1868) to Paix's *Missa parodia* in his description of what has come to be termed 'parody technique' is the source of the general currency it has acquired, particularly since Peter Wagner's *Geschichte der Messe* (1913).

The technique of borrowing more than one voice from a model has a history that stretches back to the 14th century, but in early examples, such as Antonio Zachara da Teramo's Gloria 'Rosetta' (based on his ballata *Rosetta che non canci*), entire blocks of material are quoted in a manner that resembles more the technique of contrafactum than the parody of the 16th century. In the later 15th century, occasional use of the other voices of a polyphonic model can be found in mass settings, mostly in combination with a cantus firmus structure, as in Obrecht's *Missa 'Fortuna desperata'* and *Missa 'Rosa playsante'*, where substantial passages from the chanson models are introduced when the cantus firmus ceases in the tenor parts.

In Renaissance music the borrowing of material from one composition as the basis of another was commonplace. The essential feature of parody technique is that not merely a single part is appropriated to form a cantus firmus in the derived work, but the whole substance of the source – its themes, rhythms, chords and chord progressions – is absorbed into the new piece and subjected to free variation in such a way that a fusion of old and new elements is achieved.

By the early 16th century the principle was well established as Josquin's *Missa 'Mater Patris'* (printed 1514) and the *Missa 'Ave Maria'* by Antoine de Févin (*d* 1512) show, although there was now an increasing tendency to use motets as source material in addition to secular forms such as chansons and madrigals. Parody masses form a large proportion of the masses of such composers as Gombert, Crecquillon, Morales, Victoria, Lassus and Palestrina. Two of the best-known examples of composers using material from their own motets are Palestrina's *Missa 'Assumpta est Maria'* and Victoria's *Missa 'O quam gloriosum'*; the Sanctus of Monte's *Missa super 'Cara la vita'* and the madrigal of Wert on which it is based are printed in HAM (no.146). Occasionally a double parody appears, as in G.M. Nanino's mass based on Palestrina's madrigal and mass *Vestiva i colli*. The last significant example of the parody mass was Monteverdi's of 1610 based on Gombert's motet *In illo tempore*.

Brief allusions to the technique of parody (though not to the term itself) occur in theoretical writings by Vicentino (1555), Zarlino (1558) and Pietro Pontio (1588 and 1595) long after the method was well established. But the fullest account (an elaboration of Pontio) is found in Cerone's *Melopeo y maestro* (1613). Cerone suggested that the beginning of the model should be used, with varied contrapuntal treatment, at the beginnings of the five main movements of the mass and that their endings should similarly correspond to its close; subsidiary motifs from the model should be employed elsewhere in the mass, although the beginning of the second Kyrie and parts of the Agnus Dei might be freely invented. In practice there was a tendency to allow the beginning, middle (often the opening of the second part if the model was a motet in two parts) and end of the model to reappear at corresponding points in each main movement. Sub-sections such as the 'Qui tollis' and 'Osanna' were derived from the middle portion, and the whole was drawn together by newly composed sections, which might still be motivically related to the model. Later composers often broke the model down into more sections, but these usually reappeared in the derived mass in their original order.

It has been suggested (Lockwood, 1964) that parody technique of the 16th century and later can be distinguished from earlier examples of borrowing more than one voice from a model because 16th-century parody is based on the structural technique of points of imitation. In Lockwood's view, the change of polyphonic model from the 15th-century chanson with its easily extractable single lines to the motivically structured 16th-century motet, chanson and madrigal created parody technique. Others, however, have argued that there is no causal relationship between the rise of the imitative style in polyphonic models and this type of parody. Debates concerning parody technique have centred on its relationship to the concept of 'imitatio' in the Renaissance. Brown (1982) argued that the idea in the 15th and 16th centuries of creating, by a variety of means, entirely new musical works based on pre-existing models grew from the venerable rhetorical tradition of 'imitatio' as elaborated particularly by the humanists. Meconi (1994), however, argued that there is no real connection between the practice of polyphonic borrowing and rhetorical theories of 'imitatio'. The question of the relationship of parody technique to this important aspect of Renaissance thought therefore remains open.

Parody technique, though primarily associated with the mass, was not uncommon in other areas of 16th-century music. It is found in settings of the *Magnificat*, and chansons were written parodying other chansons. Keyboard and consort pieces, though often mere intabulations of vocal works, sometimes break the model into fragments and expand it by inserted material, as in Giulio Severino's *Fantasia … sopra 'Susane un jour'* in Molinaro's *Intavolatura* (Venice, 1599[18]), which is based on Lassus's well-known chanson, or Cabezós *Tiento sobre 'Malheur me bat'*, based on a chanson by Ockeghem in the *Odhecaton*. Other examples depart from the model to a greater extent, perhaps making significant use only of its opening section. Parody, whether vocal or instrumental, had its dangers, since it could become compilation rather than composition, and some parodies represent no more than a competent manipulation of scissors and paste. But handled with skill and imagination it could be a genuinely re-creative exercise in free variation.

Although the use of borrowed material persisted through the Baroque period, to employ the term 'parody' in connection with it is in many ways unfortunate since the particular techniques of 16th-century parody are often not in evidence. Purcell's Trumpet Tune 'Cibell' is a parody of a piece by Lully, but Francesco Durante's duet versions of some of Scarlatti's solo cantatas and most of Bach's or Handel's transformations of their own or others' music are perhaps better described as reworkings or arrangements when they are not simply contrafacta.

The type of borrowing implied in parody was discredited during the 19th century when originality was sought of a kind that would admit little more than symbolic quotation in major works. Mendelssohn's, Schumann's and later Busoni's arrangements of Bach, or Grieg's toying with Mozart, cannot usefully be compared with the parody mass, which had constituted a main stream in Renaissance music with a contemporaneity quite distinct from that of the Romantic era's intermittent manipulation of music from its remoter past. A creative engagement with earlier music, as opposed to mere pastiche, has been one of the concerns of 20th-century music. But again, works like Stravinsky's *The Fairy's Kiss* and *Pulcinella*, though exhibiting the kind of interaction of composer and model that was characteristic of 16th-century parody, at the same time indulge a stylistic dichotomy far removed from it. The remoteness in style of the model from that of the idiom in which it is placed in works like Peter Maxwell Davies's Taverner fantasias, which represent a preoccupation with music based on borrowed material, similarly engenders a conflict foreign to the total synthesis that was the aim of 16th-century parody.

See also BORROWING, §§5–6.

BIBLIOGRAPHY

ReeseMR

P.A. Pisk: 'Das Parodieverfahren in den Messen des Jacobus Gallus', *SMw*, v (1918), 35–48

A. Schering: 'Über Bachs Parodieverfahren', *BJb 1921*, 49–95

J. Schmidt[-Görg]: 'Die Messen des Clemens non Papa', *ZMw*, ix (1926–7), 129–58

A. Tessier: 'Quelques parodies de Couperin', *RdM*, x (1929), 40–44

J. Schmidt-Görg: 'Vier Messen aus dem XVI. Jahrhundert über die Motette "Panis quem ego dabo" des Lupus Hellinck', *KJb*, xxv (1930), 77–93

W. Steinecke: *Die Parodie in der Musik* (Wolfenbüttel, 1934/R)

J. Schmidt-Görg: 'Die "Introites de taverne": eine französische Introiten-Parodie des 16. Jahrhunderts', *KJb*, xxx (1935), 51–6

C. Van den Borren: 'De quelques aspects de la parodie musicale', *Académie royale de Belgique: bulletin de la classe des beaux-arts*, xx (1938), 146–63

W.H. Rubsamen: 'Some First Elaborations of Masses from Motets', *BAMS*, iv (1940), 6–12

J. Daniskas: 'Een bijdrage tot de geschiedenis der parodie-techniek', *TVNM*, xvii/1 (1948), 21–43

F. Ghisi: 'L'ordinarium missae nel XV. secolo ed i primordi della parodia', *Congresso internazionale di musica sacra [I]: Rome 1950*, 308–11

R.B. Lenaerts: 'The 16th-Century Parody Mass in the Netherlands', *MQ*, xxxvi (1950), 410–21

N. Pirrotta: 'Considerazioni sui primi esempi di missa parodia', *Congresso internazionale di musica sacra [I]: Rome 1950*, 315–18

F.H. Denker: *A Study of the Transition from the Cantus-Firmus Mass to the Parody Mass* (diss., U. of Rochester, 1951)

J.M. Ward: 'The Use of Borrowed Material in 16th-Century Instrumental Music', *JAMS*, v (1952), 88–98

R.D. Wilder: *The Masses of Orlando di Lasso with Emphasis on his Parody Technique* (diss., Harvard U., 1952)

J. Klassen: 'Untersuchungen zur Parodiemesse Palestrinas', *KJb*, xxxvii (1953), 53–63

J. Klassen: 'Das Parodieverfahren in der Messe Palestrinas', *KJb*, xxxviii (1954), 24–54

J. Klassen: 'Zur Modellbehandlung in Palestrinas Parodiemessen', *KJb*, xxxix (1955), 41–55

M. Reimann: 'Pasticcios und Parodien in norddeutschen Klaviertabulaturen', *Mf*, viii (1955), 265–71

L. Schrade: 'A Fourteenth Century Parody Mass', *AcM*, xxvii (1955), 13–39 [see also xxviii (1956), 54–5]

M. Heise: *Zum Wesen und Begriff der Parodiemesse des 16. Jahrhunderts* (diss., U. of Innsbruck, 1956)

K. von Fischer: 'Kontrafakturen und Parodien italienischer Werke des Trecento und frühen Quattrocento', *AnnM*, v (1957), 43–59

R. Jackson: 'Musical Interrelations between Fourteenth Century Mass Movements (a Preliminary Study)', *AcM*, xxix (1957), 54–64

E.T. Ferand: 'Embellished "Parody Cantatas" in the Early Eighteenth Century', *MQ*, xliv (1958), 40–64

H.C. Wolff: 'Die ästhetische Auffassung der Parodiemesse des 16. Jahrhunderts', *Miscelánea en homenaje a Monseñor Higinio Anglés* (Barcelona, 1958–61), 1011–17

S. Clercx-Lejeune: 'Les débuts de la messe unitaire et de la "missa parodia" au XIV siècle et principalement dans l'oeuvre de Johannes Ciconia', *L'ars nova italiana del trecento I: Certaldo 1959*, ed. B. Becherini (Certaldo, 1962), 97–104

G.A. Michael: *The Parody Mass Technique of Philippe de Monte* (diss., New York U., 1959)

L. Richter: 'Parodieverfahren im Berliner Gassenlied', *DJbM*, iv (1959), 48–81

W. Blankenburg: 'Das Parodieverfahren im Weihnachtsoratorium Johann Sebastian Bachs', *Musik und Kirche*, xxxii (1962), 245–54; repr. in *Johann Sebastian Bach* (Darmstadt, 1970), 493–506

W. Braun: 'Zur Parodie im 17. Jahrhundert', *GfMKB: Kassel 1962*, 154–6

H.M. Brown: 'The *chanson spirituelle*, Jacques Buus, and Parody Technique', *JAMS*, xv (1962), 145–73

R.C. Davis: *Self Parody among the Cantatas of Johann Sebastian Bach* (diss., Boston U., 1962)

A. Clarkson: *The Rationale and Technique of Borrowing in Franco-Flemish Parody-Compositions of the High Renaissance* (diss., Columbia U., 1963)

W. Elders: 'Enkele aspecten van de parodie-techniek in de madrigaalmissen van Philippus de Monte', *TVNM*, xix/3–4 (1962–3), 131–42

G. Gruber: *Beiträge zur Geschichte und Kompositionstechnik des Parodiemagnificat in der 2. Hälfte des 16. Jahrhunderts* (diss., U. of Graz, 1964)

R.B. Lenaerts: 'Parodia, reservata-kunst en muzikaal symbolisme', *Liber amicorum Charles van den Borren* (Antwerp, 1964), 107–12

L. Lockwood: 'A View of the Early 16th-Century Parody Mass', *The Department of Music, of the City University of New York: Queens College Twenty-Fifth Anniversary Festschrift (1937–1962)*, ed. A. Mell (Flushing, NY, 1964), 53–77

J. Ward: 'Parody Technique in 16th-Century Instrumental Music', *The Commonwealth of Music, in Honor of Curt Sachs*, ed. G. Reese and R. Brandel (New York, 1965), 202–28

W. Elders: 'Parodie en declamatie-techniek in de 16e eeuw', *TVNM*, xx/3 (1966), 140–53

P. Gossett: 'Techniques of Unification in Early Cyclic Masses and Mass Pairs', *JAMS*, xix (1966), 222–31

O.W. Johnson: 'A Preliminary Study of the Parody Technique of Archangelo Crivelli', *Paul A. Pisk: Essays in his Honor*, ed. J. Glowacki (Austin, 1966), 66–73

L. Lockwood: 'On "Parody" as Term and Concept in 16th-Century Music', *Aspects of Medieval and Renaissance Music: a Birthday Offering to Gustave Reese*, ed. J. LaRue and others (New York, 1966/R), 560–75

P. Brainard: 'Bach's Parody Procedure and the St. Matthew Passion', *JAMS*, xxii (1969), 241–60

P.G. Swing: *Parody and Form in Five Polyphonic Masses by Mathieu Gascongne* (diss., U. of Chicago, 1969)

F. Dobbins: '"Doulce mémoire": a Study of the Parody Chanson', *PRMA*, xcvi (1969–70), 85–101

Q.W. Quereau: 'Sixteenth-Century Parody: an Approach to Analysis', *JAMS*, xxxi (1978), 407–41

H.M. Brown: 'Emulation, Competition, and Homage: Imitation and Theories of Imitation in the Renaissance', *JAMS*, xxxv (1982), 1–48

S. Curtis: 'La technique de la parodie dans les chansons à cinq et six voix de Nicolas de La Grotte', *RdM*, lxx (1984), 173–97

L. Perkins: 'The L'homme armé Masses of Busnoys and Okeghem: a Comparison', *JM*, iii (1984), 363–96

J.P. Burkholder: 'Johannes Martini and the Imitation Mass of the Late Fifteenth Century', *JAMS*, xxxviii (1985), 470–523

J.P. Burkholder: '"Quotation" and Emulation: Charles Ives's Uses of his Models', *MQ*, lxxi (1985), 1–26

R. Orlich: *Die Parodiemessen von Orlando di Lassus* (Munich, 1985)

C. Reardon: 'Two Parody Magnificats on Palestrina's *Vestiva i colli*', *Studi musicali*, xv (1986), 67–99

G.J. Buelow: 'The Case for Handel's Borrowings: the Judgment of Three Centuries', *Handel Tercentenary Collection*, ed. S. Sadie and A. Hicks (Basingstoke, 1987), 61–82

J.H. Roberts: 'Why did Handel Borrow?', ibid., 83–92

D. Flanagan: 'Some Aspects of the Sixteenth-Century Parody Mass in England', *MR*, xlix (1988), 1–11

A. Mann: 'Bach's Parody Technique and its Frontiers', *Bach Studies*, ed. D.O. Franklin (Cambridge, 1989), 115–24

R. Strohm: 'Messzyklen über deutsche Lieder in den Trienter Codices', *Liedstudien: Wolfgang Osthoff zum 60. Geburtstag*, ed. M. Just and R. Wiesend (Tutzing, 1989), 77–106

R. Wegman: 'Another "Imitation" of Busnoy's *Missa L'homme armé* – Some Observations on *imitatio* in Renaissance Music', *JRMA*, cxiv (1989), 189–202

V.M. Franke: *Palestrina's Fifteen Five-Part Imitation Masses Modelled upon Motets* (diss., U. of Oxford, 1990)

D.J. Sibley: *Parody Technique in the Masses of Palestrina* (diss., U. of Nottingham, 1990)

F. Heidlberger: 'Handels *Israel in Egypt* und das Problem der Entlehnung', *Von Isacc bis Bach: Festschrift Martin Just*, ed. F. Heidlberger, W. Osthoff and R. Wiesend (Kassel, 1991), 241–55

D. Crook: *Orlando di Lasso's Imitation Magnificats for Counter-Reformation Munich* (Princeton, NJ, 1994)

H. Meconi: 'Does Imitatio Exist?', *JM*, xii (1994), 152–78

A.P. Leverett: 'Song Masses in the Trent Codices: the Austrian Connection', *EMH*, xiv (1995), 205–56

MICHAEL TILMOUTH/RICHARD SHERR

Parody (ii). A composition generally of humorous or satirical intent in which turns of phrase or other features characteristic of another composer or type of composition are employed and made to appear ridiculous, especially through their application to ludicrously inappropriate subjects. Parody, in the non-technical sense of the word, has been a frequent source of humour in music, often aimed at the correction of stylistic idiosyncrasies or exaggeration. Some composers have even been prepared to parody their own work: Cesti, himself the author of many cantatas, parodied the genre in *Aspettate, adesso canto*, and the humour of *Così fan tutte* and *Der Schauspieldirektor* owes a good deal to Mozart's treatment of the coloratura style in arias like 'Come scoglio'.

Opera, as the most extravagant kind of musical entertainment, has invited parody throughout its history, but such parodies, meaningless without a knowledge of the original, are often an indication of the success the original achieved. Lully's operas were parodied in performances at the Ancien Théâtre Italien, initially merely spoken, later with pointedly humorous texts allied to Lully's music or with his texts set to popular vaudeville melodies. A rash of parodies was provoked by the Querelle des Bouffons and the Gluck–Piccinni controversy, and many works now regarded as significant in the operatic repertory were at one time given a similar distinction; Mozart's *Die Zauberflöte*, for example, was parodied by Wenzel Müller in 1818, and J.N. Nestroy dealt suitably with the heroics and posturings of Wagner's *Tannhäuser* and *Lohengrin*. Popular theatre and puppet theatre in Vienna provided natural outlets for this kind of satire; from the time of *The Beggar's Opera* the popular theatre in London produced a spate of healthy antidotes to what were considered to be the unnatural features and excesses of serious opera, culminating perhaps in the commonplace words of Captain Corcoran set to high-flown recitative in Sullivan's *HMS Pinafore*. Parody of Italian opera lends dramatic point to the scene in Britten's *Midsummer Night's Dream* where the play within the play becomes a mock-Italian opera within the opera. The more sophisticated and 'artificial' kinds of composition have naturally provided a target for humorous imitation in popular or lighter forms. Einstein pointed out how the affectation and 'super-sensitivity' of the madrigal were mocked in frottolas, villanellas and canzoni, and how Andrea Gabrieli parodied a famous piece, Rore's *Ancor che col partire*, by having it sung as a three-voice *giustiniana* by three trembling and stuttering old men.

Bach's 'Peasant' Cantata *Mer hahn en neue Oberkeet* (BWV212) is subtitled 'Cantate burlesque' and satirizes among other things the italianate da capo aria so readily adopted by German composers (including Bach himself) at the time. Mozart, too, parodied the incompetent lesser composers of his day, their mechanical constructions and short-breathed paragraphs, in the sextet *Ein musikalischer Spass* K522 (1787), and Wagner presented Beckmesser in a similar light in *Die Meistersinger*.

There is an element of parody in the appropriation of features of popular music in serious works, though pastoral effects like that of simulated bagpipe drones in 18th-century music generally serve to remind the listener that the rustic idiom was merely assumed for the moment: a pleasant conceit like the rustic life depicted in so many paintings of the *fêtes champêtres*, when picnic baskets concealed an excellent bottle of champagne and other necessary appurtenances of civilization. This veneer and artificiality has gone in Beethoven's humorous view of the village band in the scherzo of the Pastoral Symphony; Mahler's street bands are not so much parodies as realities in his all-embracing symphonic world.

Towards the close of the 19th century, parody, especially in French music, became a tool, often sharp-edged, to overthrow the inflated idioms of late Romanticism. The pleasantries of Chabrier's quadrilles on themes from Wagner's *Tristan und Isolde* and similar pieces by Fauré and Messager based on the *Ring* were followed by works of more acid intent such as Debussy's 'Golliwogg's Cake-Walk' with its quotation from *Tristan und Isolde* and the satires and caricatures of Satie. Ravel's piano pieces in the manner of Borodin and Chabrier (the latter once described as a parody of Chabrier parodying Gounod) are comparatively innocent, but Bartók's parody of Shostakovich in the interruption to the intermezzo of the Concerto for Orchestra is more vitriolic in intent. The neo-classical movement saw the production of many works by Stravinsky, Hindemith, Prokofiev and others which imitate certain features of earlier styles, but they were not often primarily intended to display the models in a maliciously humorous light: the urbanity and wit of Haydn and his contemporaries are what Prokofiev sought to mirror in his Classical Symphony.

BIBLIOGRAPHY

FiskeETM

C. Sallier: 'Discours sur la Parodie', *Histoire de l'Académie royale des inscriptions et belles lettres*, vii (Paris, 1733), 398
A. Font: *Favart, l'opéra-comique et la comédie-vaudeville aux XVIIe et XVIIIe siècles* (Paris, 1894)
A. Arnheim: 'Le devin du village von Jean-Jacques Rousseau und die Parodie "Les amours de Bastien et Bastienne"', *SIMG*, iv (1902–3), 686–727
G. Calmus: *Zwei Opernburlesken aus der Rokokozeit* (Berlin, 1912)
A. Einstein: 'Die Parodie in der Villanella', *ZMw*, ii (1919–20), 212–24; [Eng. trans. in *EinsteinIM*]
P.A. Merbach: 'Parodien und Nachwirkungen von Webers "Freischütz"', *ZMw*, ii (1919–20), 642–55
G. Cucuel: 'Les opéras de Gluck dans les parodies du XVIIIe siècle', *ReM*, iii/5 (1922), 201–21; iii/6 (1922), 51–68
R. Haas: 'Wiener deutsche Parodieopern um 1730', *ZMw*, viii (1925–6), 201–25

M. Chat: *Studien zur Technik der Parodie und des Komischen an Parodien Favarts* (diss., U. of Vienna, 1930)
V.B. Grannis: *Dramatic Parody in 18th-Century France* (New York, 1931)
M. Bührmann: *J.N. Nestroys Parodien* (diss., U. of Kiel, 1933)
R. Rüschka: *Wiener literarische Parodien von den Anfängen bis auf Nestroy* (diss., U. of Vienna, 1935)
F. Brukner: 'Die Alt-Wiener Parodie', *Jb deutscher Bibliophilen und Literaturfreunde*, xxi–xxii (1937)
D.J. Grout: 'Seventeenth-Century Parodies of French Opera', *MQ*, xxvii (1941), 211–19, 514–26
L. Frank: *Dramatic Parody by Marionettes in 18th-Century Paris* (New York, 1946)
S. Dörffelt: *Die musikalische Parodie bei Offenbach* (diss., U. of Frankfurt, 1954)
K. Hortschansky: *Parodie und Entlehnung im Schaffen Chr.W. Glucks* (diss., U. of Kiel, 1966)
D.J. Keahey: 'Così fan tutte: Parody or Irony?', *Paul A. Pisk: Essays in his Honor*, ed. J. Glowacki (Austin, 1966), 116–30
M. See: 'Opernparodie und Parodieoper', *NZM*, Jg.127 (1966), 372–88
F. Moureau: 'Lully en visite chez l'Arlequin: parodies italiennes avant 1697', *Jean-Baptiste Lully: St Germain-en-Laye and Heidelberg 1987*, 235–50
M. Hunter: 'Some Representations of *opera seria* in *opera buffa*', *COJ*, iii (1991), 89–108

MICHAEL TILMOUTH

Parody mass. A musical setting of the five movements of the Ordinary of the Roman Catholic Mass that is unified by the presence of the entire texture of a pre-existing polyphonic work, represented by borrowed motifs and points of imitation. The relationship is usually clearest at the beginning, middle and end of each movement. The designation 'imitation mass', more in keeping with the terminology used in the 16th century to describe this type of composition, has been adopted by some scholars.

See also BORROWING IN MUSIC; MASS, §II, 6–9; PARODY (i).

Paroisse-Pougin, Arthur. *See* POUGIN, ARTHUR.

Parra, Violeta (*b* San Carlos, Nuble, 4 October 1917; *d* Santiago, 5 February 1967). Chilean traditional singer, collector, *cantautor* (singer-songwriter), poet and artist. Parra inherited a folkloric repertory from her parents, singing with members of her family in circuses, theatres and bars in Santiago. From 1953 she dedicated her life to the subject of Chilean folklore: collecting, broadcasting on radio, recording and teaching. During the periods 1954–6 and 1961–4 she lived in France, based in Paris, performing in festivals, theatres, clubs, radio and television and recording Chilean music. In 1964 her art was exhibited at the Louvre's Musée des Arts Decoratifs. On her return to Chile she installed a tent in a suburb of Santiago called La Reina, and here she lived and worked with Chilean popular culture, performing until her premature death by suicide.

With intuitive and powerful talent, Parra consciously introduced an original aesthetic to popular urban song, bringing together distinctive aspects of different Latin American traditions in a manner which could be described as a kind of 'primitivism', while at the same time developing literary, musical and performing aspects of the tradition, establishing her own influential models of popular Chilean musics during the 1960s. She had seminal influence on the emerging, groundbreaking generation who were to forge Chile's *nueva canción* (new song) tradition, including her own children Angel and Isabel Parra, VÍCTOR JARA, Patricio Manns and the groups Inti Illimani and Quilapayún, whose music was to play an integral part in the political and social life of 20th-century

Chile from the late 1960s onwards; as well as on the repertory of other innovative popular musicians.

Of her 277 works registered with the Chilean Performing Rights Society the following, recorded for Odeon, France, can be singled out: *Casamiento de negros* (1953), *La jardinera* (1960), *Arriba quemando el sol* (1965), *La carta* (*c*1965), *La pericona se ha muerto* (1966); as can *Cantores que reflexionan*, *El rin del angelito*, *Gracias de la vida*, *Run Run se fue pa'l norte* and *Volver a los diecisiete*, recorded in 1966 for RCA Victor, Chile, issued as part of her final recording *Las últimas composiciones*. Self-taught and self-motivated, she is considered one of the key Latin American folklorists and popular musicians of the 20th century.

BIBLIOGRAPHY

AND OTHER RESOURCES

V. Parra: *Cantos folklóricos Chilenos* (Santiago, 1979)

B. Subercaseaux et al: *Gracias a la vida, Violeta Parra, testimonio* (Santiago, 1982)

I. Parra: *El libro mayor de Violeta Parra* (Madrid, 1985)

P. Manns: *Violeta Parra, la guitarra indócil* (Concepción, Chile, 1986)

M. Agosín and I. Dolz: *Violeta Parra o la expresión inefable, un analisis crítico de su poesía, prosa y pintura* (Santiago, 1992)

RECORDINGS

Cantos de Chile, Le Chant du Monde (1956)

La cueca presentada por Violeta Parra, Odeon LDC 36038 (1957)

Recordando a Chile, canciones de Violeta Parra, Odeon SLDC 36533 (1965)

Las últimas composiciones de Violeta Parra, RCA Victor CML 2456 (1966)

JUAN PABLO GONZALEZ

Parran, Antoine (*b* Nemours, 1587; *d* Bourges, 24 Oct 1650). French theorist and composer. He was a Jesuit who became a novice at Nancy in 1608 and later taught grammar and humanistic studies for many years at the college there. His *Traité de la musique théorique et pratique* (Paris, 1639, 2/1646/R) is a didactic manual devoted to a systematic presentation of the contrapuntal rules governing an older compositional style, exemplified especially by the music of Du Caurroy and Le Jeune, whose works he praised. He exhibited a historical awareness unusual for the time, as well as concern with the aesthetics and social function of music. He corresponded with Mersenne. He is known to have been a composer too, but except for the examples in his treatise, none of his music appears to have survived.

BIBLIOGRAPHY

H. Schneider: *Die französische Kompositionslehre in der ersten Hälfte des 17. Jahrhunderts* (Tutzing, 1972), 112–36

W. Seidel: 'Französische Musiktheorie im 16. und 17. Jahrhundert' in W. Seidel and B. Cooper: *Entstehung nationaler Traditionen: Frankreich*, Geschichte der Musiktheorie, ix (Darmstadt, 1986), 82–5

P. Vendrix: *Aux origines d'une discipline historique: La musique et son histoire en France aux XVIIe et XVIIIe siècles* (Geneva, 1993), 18–19, 209–10, 267–8

ALBERT COHEN

Parratt, Sir Walter (*b* Huddersfield, 10 Feb 1841; *d* Windsor, 27 March 1924). English organist, teacher and composer. He was a child prodigy, educated by his parents (his father, Thomas, 1793–1862, was organist of St Peter's, Huddersfield, from 1812 to 1862) and at the age of ten could play *Das wohltemperirte Clavier* from memory. From the age of 11, when he had lessons from George Cooper at St Sepulchre's, Holborn, London, he was organist of various churches in Huddersfield and London. In 1861 he became organist of St Michael's,

Great Witley, Worcestershire, and private organist to the Earl of Dudley, associating with Adolf von Holst and F.A.G. Ouseley at St Michael's College, Tenbury Wells. In 1864 he married Emma Gledhill, with whom he had five children. In 1868 he went to Wigan as parish church organist and, in 1872, succeeded Stainer at Magdalen College, Oxford. There he conducted the musical societies of Exeter, Trinity, Jesus and Pembroke Colleges, and the Oxford Choral Society, graduating BMus in 1873. His first significant composition, incidental music to *Agamemnon*, was produced at Balliol College in 1880.

In 1882 he received a royal command to succeed George Elvey as organist of St George's Chapel, Windsor, and from there his influence spread over the whole country. When the RCM opened in 1883, George Grove invited him to become chief professor of the organ. Many honours followed; he was knighted and made private organist to the queen in 1892 and became Master of the Queen's Music in 1893 (confirmed by Edward VII and George V) and honorary DMus at Oxford (1894), Cambridge (1910) and Durham (1912). He became dean of the Faculty of Music at London University in 1905 and was president of the Royal College of Organists from 1905 to 1909. In 1908 he succeeded Parry to the chair of music at Oxford, resigning in 1918. Edward VII awarded him the MVO (1901), and George V the CVO (1917) and KCVO (1921).

Parratt is best remembered for the part he played with Parry and Stanford in the renaissance of English music. His impeccable taste and style were founded on his early association with S.S. Wesley and the latter's promotion of J.S. Bach's works, which Parratt continued. He was the foremost exponent and teacher of the organ of his time, most of the leading organ appointments in the country

Walter Parratt: drawing by John Singer Sargent, charcoal, 1914 (Royal College of Music, London)

being filled by his pupils, and he succeeded in raising both the standard of organ playing and the status of the organist. He rejected his contemporaries' attempts to make the organ imitate the orchestra, advocating instead a style founded on technical accuracy, clarity of phrasing and simple registration. From his youth onwards Parratt was conscious of the general decline of taste in church music and, from his appointment to St George's Chapel, set a standard in his choice of works ranging from Tallis to Wesley: here also many works by the rising school of church composers led by Stanford received their first performances. He also promoted contemporary British music through his position as Master of the Music. Parratt had a strong, magnetic, highly strung personality and an engaging sense of humour, and possessed an exceptional memory, which he put to good use in his principal hobby, chess. His compositions include the *Obiit Service*, written for St George's Chapel, the anthem *Confortare* for the coronation of Edward VII (1902) and other sacred music, incidental music for plays and some 20 songs and partsongs. He also published the article 'Music' in T.H. Ward's *The Reign of Queen Victoria* (London, 1887) and contributed ten articles to the second edition of *Grove's Dictionary*.

BIBLIOGRAPHY

DNB (R.F.M. Akerman)
'Mr. Walter Parratt's Last Sunday in Wigan', *Wigan Observer* (5 Oct 1872), 4
'Sir Walter Parratt', *British Musician*, vii (1894), 37–8 [incl. portrait]
F.G. Shinn: *Musical Memory and its Cultivation* (London, 1899/R), 70
J.E. West: *Cathedral Organists, Past and Present* (London, 1899, 2/1921), 122, 134
F.G. Edwards: 'Sir Walter Parratt, Master of the King's Musick', *MT*, xliii (1902), 441–50 [6 illustrations]
Obituaries: *Huddersfield Daily Examiner* (27 March 1924); *Manchester Guardian* (28 March 1924); *Huddersfield Weekly Examiner* (29 March 1924); *Saturday Review* (5 April 1924); *MT*, lxvi (1924), 401–2
H. Whelbourn: *Celebrated Musicians, Past and Present* (London, 1930), 218
D.F. Tovey and G. Parratt: *Walter Parratt, Master of the Music* (London, 1941)
F. Knights: 'Three Magdalen Organists: Paul Benecke's Reminiscences of John Stainer, Walter Parratt and John Varley Roberts', *The Organ*, lxviii (1989), 137–45
FREDERICK HUDSON/ROSEMARY WILLIAMSON

Parr-Davies, Harry. *See* DAVIES, HARRY PARR.

Parreiras Neves, Ignacio. *See* NEVES, IGNACIO PARREIRAS.

Parrenin Quartet. French string quartet. Its members since 1980 have been Jacques Parrenin, John Cohen, Jean-Claude Dewaele and René Benedetti. When formed in 1944, the quartet included, besides Serge Collot as viola player, Marcel Charpentier as second violinist and Pierre Penassou as cellist. Collot was succeeded in 1958 by Michel Walès who in turn was replaced by Dénes Marton in 1964. After his death in a car accident in 1970, Marton was succeeded by Gérard Caussé and the same year Jacques Ghestem replaced Charpentier. Parrenin studied in Lorient and at the Paris Conservatoire (with Calvet) and formed the original quartet on completing his studies. After five years as resident ensemble at Radio Luxembourg, the quartet began extensive international touring in 1949 and by 1970 had built up a far-reaching reputation, winning particular acclaim in the USA, eastern Europe and the USSR. Its repertory emphasizes music of the Second Viennese School and a representative cross-section of pieces by the most prominent composers since 1945, and includes the standard Classical and Romantic works. The quartet's familiarity with such an extensive range of styles enriched its interpretations of the key works of the early 20th century, so that for many years and for many listeners its performances of Webern, for instance, were not only authoritative but definitive. Its recordings of the core French repertoire were also acclaimed. At no time did the quartet sacrifice a full ensemble tone even in the most refined, sparsely textured contemporary pieces. However, the later personnel changes seemed to disturb its corporate identity, and the ensemble has found it difficult to sustain the reputation it had enjoyed in the 1950s and 1960s. Among the Parrenin Quartet's many (more than 150) premières are the Quartet no.1 by Roberto Gerhard (1955), the Quartet no.2 by Henze (1952), the Quartet no.6 by Bacewicz (1960), the Quartet no.2 by Penderecki (1968) and works by Berio, Boulez, Ohana, Petrassi and Xenakis.

LESLIE EAST/R

Parris, Robert (*b* Philadelphia, 21 May 1924). American composer and music critic. After graduating from the University of Pennsylvania (BS 1945, MS 1946), he studied composition at the Juilliard School of Music (BS 1948) with Mennin and Bergsma, and at Tanglewood (1950–51) with Ibert and Copland. A Fulbright Fellowship (1952–3) enabled him to continue his studies with Arthur Honegger at the Ecole Normale, Paris. From 1961 to 1975 he served as music critic for the *Washington Post* and *Washington Star*. He joined the music department at George Washington University in 1963. He has received commissions from the Detroit SO (*The Phoenix*, 1969), the Albany SO, New York (*The Messengers*, 1974), the Contemporary Music Forum (*The Book of Imaginary Beings II*, 1983) and the National SO (*Symphonic Variations*, 1987).

Parris's music balances a keen sense of order with an imaginative exploration of extreme registers, wide-ranging textures, intricate rhythmic/metric schemes and virtuosic performance techniques. Together with a penchant for counterpoint, his music demonstrates a striking economy of means, an emboldened sense of contrast and a passionate lyricism. His works are often darkly introspective, even macabre, a feature enhanced by intense chromaticism and expressionistic orchestration. The mystical visions evoked in his preferred texts are often transmuted into musical imagery. (*EwenD*; *Baker 8*)

WORKS
(selective list)

INSTRUMENTAL

Orch: Harlequin's Carnival, 1949; Sym. no.1, 1952; Pf Conc., 1954; Conc., 5 timp, orch, 1955; Va Conc., 1956; Vn Conc., 1958; Conc., trbn, chbr orch, 1964; Fl Conc., 1964; Timp Conc. (The Phoenix), 1969; The Messengers (Angels), 1974; The Unquiet Heart, vn, orch, 1981; Chbr Music, 1984; Sym. Variations, 1987; 5 other orch works
Chbr: Str Qt no.1, 1951; Str Trio no.2, 1951; Str Qt no.2, 1952; Sinfonia, brass, 1963; Book of Imaginary Beings I, fl, vn, vc, pf, 2 perc, 1967; Conc., vn, vc, pf, perc, 1967, rev. 1977; Book of Imaginary Beings II, cl, vn, va, vc, 2 perc, 1983; Metamorphic Variations, fl, cl, vn, vc, perc, 1986; Sonata, vc, pf, before 1949; Variations, pf, 1952; Fantasy and Fugue, vc, 1955; Cadenza, Caprice and Ricercar, vc, pf, 1961; 3 Duets, elec gui, amp hpd, 1985; 22 other chbr works

VOCAL

Choral: The Hollow Men, T, male chorus, chbr ens, 1949; Hymn for the Nativity (Peter the Venerable), SATB, 8 brass, 3 timp, perc, 1962; Reflections on Immortality, brass, chorus, 1966; 6 other choral works
Solo: The Leaden Echo and the Golden Echo (Hopkins), Bar, orch, 1960; Cynthia's Revells (B. Jonson), Bar, pf, opt. gui, 1979; 10 other solo vocal works
Principal publishers: ACA, Peters

CECELIA H. PORTER

Parrish, Carl (*b* Plymouth, PA, 9 Oct 1904; *d* Valhalla, NY, 27 Nov 1965). American musicologist and composer. He studied at the American Conservatory in Fontainebleau (1932), the MacPhail School of Music (BM 1933), Cornell University (MA 1936) and Harvard University, where he took the doctorate in 1939 with a dissertation on the influence of the early piano on 18th-century keyboard technique and composition. Harvard awarded him the Knight prize in chamber music composition in 1938, and in 1945 he received the ABC composition prize. Later he won other honours: a Fulbright appointment for research in France in 1953 and a Guggenheim Fellowship in musicology for 1958–9. He taught at Wells College (1929–43), Fisk University (1943–6), Westminster Choir College (1946–9), Pomona College (1949–53) and Vassar College (1953–65), at the summer school sessions at Stanford University and at the universities of Minnesota, North Carolina and Southern California. Parrish's compositions include partsongs for chorus, choral arrangements of folksongs, pieces for piano and for orchestra, a set of organ preludes, a song cycle, a string quartet, and a *Magnificat* for soprano solo, women's voices and organ. He is best known for his writings, of which the most important are two anthologies of early music showing the styles of composition at different periods, and a standard work on the transcription of medieval music.

WRITINGS

The Early Piano and its Influences on Keyboard Technique and Composition in the Eighteenth Century (diss., Harvard U., 1939)
'Criticisms of the Piano when it was New', *MQ*, xxx (1944), 428–40
with J.F. Ohl: *Masterpieces of Music before 1750* (New York, 1951)
'A Curious Use of Coloration in the Pixérécourt Codex', *Essays on Music in Honor of Archibald Thompson Davidson* (Cambridge, MA, 1957), 83–90
The Notation of Medieval Music (New York, 1957, 2/1959/R)
A Treasury of Early Music (New York, 1958)
ed. and trans.: J. Tinctoris: *Terminorum musicae diffinitorium* (New York, 1963/R)
Thoroughbass Method (New York, 1965/R) [trans. of H. Keller: *Schule des Generalbass-Spiels*, Kassel, 1931, 4/1956]
'A Renaissance Music Manual for Choirboys', *Aspects of Medieval and Renaissance Music: a Birthday Offering to Gustave Reese*, ed. J. LaRue and others (New York, 1966/R), 649–64

BIBLIOGRAPHY

G. Haydon: 'Carl Parrish (1904–1965)', *JAMS*, xix (1966), 434 [obituary]

RAMONA H. MATTHEWS

Parrott, Andrew (Haden) (*b* Walsall, 10 March 1947). English conductor. Following undergraduate and research studies at Merton College, Oxford, he founded the Taverner Choir and then the Taverner Consort and Players, with whom he has made over 50 recordings, ranging from Machaut through much 16th-, 17th- and 18th-century music to Pärt and Tavener. In his refreshing and revealing Bach recordings he has adopted Joshua Rifkin's view that the choruses and orchestral music were usually intended to be performed one-to-a-part. In addition to his work with period-instrument ensembles, Parrott has conducted many orchestras in Britain, Europe and the USA, and in 2000 was appointed music director of the London Mozart Players. In the field of contemporary music he has conducted the London Sinfonietta and the Nash Ensemble, sung with Electric Phoenix, and acted as assistant to Tippett. He worked with Kent Opera from 1989 and has conducted at La Scala, Opera North, Covent Garden and Drottningholm. He has taught through symposia and in workshops at Cambridge, Cornell, the GSM, the RAM and Dartington International Summer School. His scholarly writings reflect his particular concern with performing practice and include many influential articles, notably in *Early Music*, and the book *The Essential Bach Choir* (London, 2000).

GEORGE PRATT

Parrott, (Horace) Ian (*b* London, 5 March 1916). British composer and writer. He studied at Harrow (1929–31), the RCM (1932–4), privately with Benjamin Dale, and at New College, Oxford (1934–7); he took the Oxford DMus in 1940. After teaching at Malvern College (1937–9) and completing military service, he was appointed to a lectureship at Birmingham University in 1946. From 1950 until 1983 he occupied the Gregynog Chair of Music at the University College of Wales, Aberystwyth. His honours include first prize from the Royal Philharmonic Society (1949) for the symphonic poem *Luxor* (1947), the Harriet Cohen Musicology Award (1966) and the Glyndwr Award (1994).

Following his move to Wales in 1950 Parrott identified himself closely with Welsh musical life; at Aberystwyth he fostered generations of young Welsh composers, including William Mathias and David Harries. His compositions also reflect his interest in the Welsh language and culture. His opera *The Black Ram* (1951–3), for example, incorporates Welsh folksongs. Among his most successful works are five symphonies and five string quartets. In addition to composing, he has written on a wide range of topics; his books include *Elgar* (London, 1971), *Cyril Scott and his Piano Music* (London, 1992) and *The Crying Curlew: Peter Warlock* (Llandysul, 1994).

WORKS

Stage: The Sergeant-Major's Daughter (op, K. Womersley), 1942–3, Cairo, 1943; Maid in Birmingham (ballet), 1949; The Black Ram (op, I. Bell), 1951–3, concert perf., BBC, 1957, staged, Aberystwyth, 1966; Once upon a Time (op, C.J. Price), 1958–9, Christchurch, 1960; The Lady of Flowers (op, A. Cooper), 1981, Colchester, 1982
Orch: El Alamein, sym. prelude, 1944; Sym no.1, 1946; Luxor, sym. poem, 1947; Pf Conc., 1948; Pensieri, str orch, 1950; Romeo and Juliet, ov., 1953; Variations on a Theme of Dufay, 1955; Eng Hn Conc., 1956; 4 Shakespeare Dances, 1956; Y Dair [The Three Ladies], 1958; Seithenin, ov., 1959; Sym no.2 'Round the World', 1960; Vc Conc., 1961; The Three Moorish Princesses, nar, orch, 1964; Suite, vn, orch, 1965; Sym. no.3, 1966; Trbn Conc., 1967; Homage to Two Masters, 1970; Reaching for the Light, 2 ob, bn, 2 hn, glock, str, hpd, pf, 1971; Concertino, 2 gui, orch, 1973; Sinfonietta (Sym. no.4), 1978; Sym. no.5, 1979; Arfordir Ceredigion [Ceredigion's Coastline], 1992; Fanfare Ov., 1993
Vocal: I heard a Linnet Courting (R. Bridges), high v, pf, 1940; Absence (J. Donne), low v, pf, 1943; In Phaeacia (J.E. Flecker), A Ship, an Isle (Flecker), high v, orch, 1945–6; Ps xci, SATB, orch, 1946; Three Kings Have Come (cant.), S, Bar, SATB, pf, str, 1951; Jubilate Deo, SATB, org, 1963; The Song of the Stones of St Davids, SATB, 1968; Flamingoes (J. Wilson), low v, pf, 1972; Welsh Folk Song Mass, SATB, 1972; Song for Dyfed, 2 nar, SATB, pf, 1973; Surely the Lord is in This Place, chorus, 1974; Master Hugues of Saxe-Gotha, male vv, 1975; Cymru Fach [Wales], male vv, 1976; 2 Thoughtful Songs (W. Blake, G.M. Hopkins), medium

v, pf, 1977; My Cousin Alice, SATB, tape, 1982; No Complaints, Bar, pf, 1984; Anthem of Dedication, SATB, org, 1985; Mag and Nunc, S, org; Mae 'Nghariad i'n Fenws [My Love is a Venus] (trad); Adam Lay ybounden (trad); Eastern Wisdom, medium v, orch, 1987; Arglwydd Ein Ior Ni [O Lord, our God], SATB, org, 1991; Aphorisms and Arias of Death and Life (various), S, Bar, pf, 1995; Songs of Renewal (various), S, rec, pf, 1995

Chbr and solo inst: Ob Qt, 1946; Str Qt no.1, 1946; Wind Qnt no.1, 1948; Fantasy-Trio, pf trio, 1950; Family Prelude and Fugue, str, pf, 1956; Str Qt no.2, 1956; Ceredigion, hp, 1957; Str Qt no.3, 1957; Sonatina, trbn, pf, 1958; Fantasy for James Blades, perc, 1959; Septet, fl, cl, str qt, pf, 1962; Str Qt no.4, 1963; Big Hat Guy, vn, pf, 1965; Partita, hp, 1967; Wind Qnt no.2 'Fresh about Cook Strait', 1970; Arabesque and Dance, rec, hpd, 1972; Fanfare and March, brass qt, 1973; Soliloquy and Dance, hp, 1973; Devils Bridge Jaunt, pf qt, 1974; Duo Fantastico no.1, vn, pf, 1976; Gleaming Brass, brass qnt, 1977; Arfon, hp, 1978; Fantasy-Sonata, cl, pf, 1979; Reflections, vn, pf, 1982; Suite, vc, pf, 1982; Autumn Landscapes, ob, pf, 1983; Duo, cl, tpt, 1983; Duo, 2 gui, 1988; Duo Fantastico no.2, vn, pf, 1990; Fun Fugato and Awkward Waltz, bn, pf, 1990; Fantasising on a Welsh Tune, fl, ob, pf, 1993; Str Qt no.5, 1994; Awel Dyfi, rec, 1995; The Wrexham Pipers Meet the Machynlleth Marchers, rec, gui, 1996; Portraits, rec, pf, 1999

Kbd: Theme and Six Variants, pf, 1945; Fantasy and Allegro, 2 pf, 1946; Fantasia, org, 1974; Aspects, pf, 1975; Fantasy, pf, 1976; Suite no.1, org, 1977; Hands Across the Years, org, 1980

Principal publishers: Chester, Curwen, Lengnick, Musica Rara, Guild for Promotion of Welsh Music, Thames, Oecumuse, Samuel King, Banks, Gwynn, Novello, Curiad, Forsyth

BIBLIOGRAPHY

CC1 (L. Davies)

H.F. Redlich: 'A New Welsh Folk Opera', *ML*, xxxvii (1956), 101–6

A.F.L. Thomas: 'Ian Parrott at 50', *MT*, cvii (1966), 210–11

MALCOLM BOYD/GERAINT LEWIS

Parry, Henry John. English music publisher, partner in the firm of EDWIN ASHDOWN.

Parry, Sir (**Charles**) **Hubert** (**Hastings**) (*b* Bournemouth, 27 Feb 1848; *d* Rustington, Sussex, 7 Oct 1918). English composer, scholar and teacher. Combining these three activities with a forceful personality and social position, he exercised a revitalizing influence on English musical life at a time in the 19th century when standards of composition, performance, criticism and education were low.

1. Life and works. 2. Style and influence.

1. LIFE AND WORKS. The sixth child from the first marriage of Thomas Gambier Parry, painter and art collector, Parry grew up at Highnam Court near Gloucester. While attending Twyford School, near Winchester, he became acquainted with S.S. Wesley at Winchester Cathedral. At Eton he received instruction from Sir George Elvey at St George's Chapel, Windsor, and obtained the BMus in 1866, before entering Exeter College, Oxford, to read law and modern history. During the summer of 1867 he studied in Stuttgart with Henry Hugo Pierson; this was the only formal musical training he received while at Oxford. After taking the BA in 1870 he worked at Lloyd's of London as an underwriter, a move in accordance with both his father's wishes and those of his future wife's family. In 1872 he married his childhood sweetheart, Maude Herbert, sister of George, 13th Earl of Pembroke; they had two children, Dorothea and Gwendolen, named after characters in George Eliot's novels.

In his first few years at Lloyd's Parry took some lessons with William Sterndale Bennett. Desiring more criticism than Bennett was prepared to give, he applied (through Joachim) to study with Brahms in Vienna. When this project failed to materialize, he began a course of study with Edward Dannreuther, a renowned pioneer, champion of Wagner and piano virtuoso. Under Dannreuther's tuition Parry improved his piano technique, but gradually emphasis shifted from the keyboard repertory to the discussion and study of contemporary music, particularly of instrumental works by Liszt, Tchaikovsky and Brahms. This had a profound effect on the development of Parry's musical language, a fact demonstrated in the scale and profusion of chamber works such as the *Grosses Duo* for two pianos (1875–7), the Piano Trio in E minor (no.1, 1877), the Nonet for wind instruments (1877), the Fantasie Sonata in B minor for violin and piano (1878) and the Piano Quartet (1879), all written for Dannreuther's series of semi-private concerts at his home, 12 Orme Square, Bayswater. Parry also became a fervent Wagnerite, attending *Der Ring des Nibelungen* at Bayreuth in 1876, assisting when Wagner was Dannreuther's guest in London in 1877 and again visiting Bayreuth, to hear *Parsifal* three times in 1882. His admiration for Wagner is evident in his concert overture *Guillem de Cabestanh* (1878), conducted by Manns at the Crystal Palace in 1879, and perhaps more controversially in his setting of Shelley's *Prometheus Unbound* for the Gloucester Three Choirs Festival in 1880, a year which also witnessed two performances of his Piano Concerto in F♯ major.

Parry gave up his work at Lloyd's in 1877, confident that he could make a living as a musician. Besides Dannreuther's encouragement, further support came from George Grove, who engaged Parry as sub-editor for his new *Dictionary of Music and Musicians*, an enterprise to which Parry contributed more than 100 articles. Within the province of musical scholarship and theory Parry showed himself to be versatile and original, attributes which, combined with his compositional abilities, persuaded Grove to enlist him in 1883 as Professor of Musical History at the newly founded RCM. That same year the University of Cambridge conferred on him an honorary doctorate, Oxford following suite in 1884 as well as appointing him choragus to the university.

Parry's first period of creative maturity was largely dominated by instrumental composition, and during the 1880s the production of no fewer than four symphonies and a symphonic suite (*Suite moderne*) suggests that orchestral music held a major attraction for him. In addition to the challenge of large-scale symphonic forms, he also turned his attention to opera, inspired by his vivid impressions of Wagner's music dramas and by the interest shown in indigenous opera by Carl Rosa. Unfortunately, however, Parry lacked experience of the stage and he failed to assimilate the necessary elements of Wagner's musico-dramatic technique, shortcomings which were not enhanced by Una Taylor's deficient libretto. *Guenever*, his one foray into operatic music, was abandoned after Rosa's refusal to perform it in 1886. To counter his disappointment, Parry enjoyed his first taste of national acclaim with the ode *Blest Pair of Sirens*, written for and dedicated to Stanford and the Bach Choir. Its success brought mixed blessings: his reputation as a composer rapidly became established, but the demands brought by commissions from provincial festivals signalled a shift from symphonic to choral music, a change of direction much lamented by Bernard Shaw.

In 1888 Parry's national renown was consolidated with *Judith*, the first of three oratorios. Other choral works followed in rapid succession, notably the *Ode on St Cecilia's Day* (1889) for Leeds, *L'Allegro ed Il Pensieroso* (1890) for Norwich, *The Lotos-Eaters* for Cambridge (1892), *Job* (1892) for Gloucester and *King Saul* (1894) for Birmingham. For the Purcell bicentenary in 1895 he worked with Robert Bridges on the ode *Invocation to Music*, and, two years later, composed a setting of the *Magnificat* in celebration of Queen Victoria's Diamond Jubilee. Such was Parry's esteem and popularity during the 1890s that he was regarded as the nation's unofficial composer laureate, a position he bore with some reservation. In 1895 he succeeded Grove as director of the RCM and in 1898 he was knighted in recognition of his services to British music. In 1900, after Stainer's resignation, he was appointed Heather Professor of Music at Oxford and in 1902 he was made a baronet. Suffering from worsening heart trouble he was forced to give up the chair at Oxford in 1908, but retained his directorship at the RCM until his death.

A Song of Darkness and Light (1898), his second collaboration with Bridges, marked a period of his output in which he was preoccupied with the expression of his own personal heterodoxy. Between 1898 and 1908 he produced a number of choral works (so-called ethical oratorios) such as *Voces clamantium* (1903), *The Love that Casteth out Fear* (1904) and *The Soul's Ransom* (1906), drawing on texts from the Bible and his own words in which he attempted to elucidate his humanitarian convictions. In 1907 this culminated in *The Vision of Life*, written for the Cardiff Festival and for which Parry

provided the entire text. The sentiments and symbols of *The Vision of Life*, with its main protagonist, The Dreamer, and the chorus of Dream Voices, deeply appealed to Elgar who, significantly perhaps, went on to explore a similar theme in *The Music Makers* of 1912. The unfocussed and at times obscure philosophical message of these ethical deliberations left audiences unmoved and, after the performance of *Beyond these voices there is peace* at Worcester in 1908, caused Parry to reconsider the best means of enunciating his artistic ideals. In his later choral works he wisely returned to the poetry of established authors, setting Dunbar's *Ode on the Nativity* (1912) and Bridges' naval ode *The Chivalry of the Sea* (1916), an achievement crowned by the supremely eloquent and poignantly valedictory *Songs of Farewell* (1914–15), a group of six motets which represent the summit of British *a cappella* music.

Thanks largely to the initiatives of the Philharmonic Society, Parry also turned his attention to orchestral composition. Between 1909 and 1910 he extensively revised his Fourth Symphony, composing a new scherzo as well as appending an ethical programme ('Finding the Way') to the entire work. Similar programmes, of an essentially autobiographical significance, informed his last two orchestral works, the Fifth Symphony (later renamed Symphonic Fantasia '1912'), written for the (by then 'Royal') Philharmonic Society's centenary celebrations, and his only symphonic poem, *From Death to Life* (1914).

2. STYLE AND INFLUENCE. Parry's musical style is a complex aggregate reflecting his assimilation of indigenous as well as continental traditions. Trained in the organ loft during his schooldays and educated through the degree system of the ancient universities, he had imbibed fully the aesthetics of Anglican church music and the oratorio-centred repertory of the provincial music festivals by the age of 18. His early works, sacred and secular, betray the influences of Sterndale Bennett, Stainer and, most of all, Mendelssohn, whose stylistic paradigms are clearly emulated in his Oxford exercise 'O Lord, Thou hast cast us out' (1866). His study with Pierson, however, disabused him of Mendelssohn and the years spent working with Dannreuther during the 1870s were crucial in awakening him to the music of Brahms and Wagner. Both these composers exerted a powerful influence on the development of his technique. The chamber works written between 1876 and 1890 exhibit a thorough understanding of Brahmsian generative procedures, the Piano Quartet in A♭ and the Piano Trio in B minor (no.2) being particularly fine examples. Other influences, notably those of Schumann and Liszt, are also evident in the more experimental Wind Nonet (1877) and Fantasie Sonata in one movement for violin and piano (1878), which show an interest in melodic transformation and cyclic design. An especially intriguing instance of the Liszt–Brahms fusion can be seen in the Piano Concerto in F♯ (1878–80), in its arresting tonal events, inventive structures and, perhaps most remarkably, in the lengthy virtuoso cadenza at the end of the finale.

Cyclic treatment remained an important component of Parry's orchestral music, but in these larger works his more mature lyrical style, infused with a diatonicism gleaned from his English heritage and allied with the Romantic sonority of larger orchestral forces, begins to take centre stage. The rhapsodic First Symphony (1880–82) and the melodically fertile Second (1882–3)

Hubert Parry (standing), with Alexander Mackenzie (left) and Charles Villiers Stanford, Bournemouth, 1910

have a confidence and energy which are consolidated in the shorter, more overtly Classical Third Symphony, the first version of the Fourth Symphony (both performed in 1889) and in the motivically discursive *Overture to an Unwritten Tragedy* (1893). Parry once again shows a predilection for original structural thinking, be it in the illusion of four symphonic movements in his Symphonic Variations (1897) or the deft manipulation of sonata principles in the *Elegy for Brahms* (1897), a work unperformed during his lifetime but which Stanford exhumed and conducted at the RCM memorial concert for Parry in November 1918. This inclination for formal intricacy continued in the considerably revised and expanded Fourth Symphony (1909–10), and, above all, in the cyclic involution and structural compression of the Symphonic Fantasia '1912', arguably his masterpiece.

The influence of Wagner is conspicuous in both the *Concertstück* for orchestra (1877) and the overture *Guillem de Cabestanh* (1878), but it was altogether more prominent in his first major choral commission, *Scenes from Prometheus Unbound* (1880), a work hailed by some as the beginning of the so-called English Musical Renaissance. The opening prelude and scenes in Part 2 for Jupiter and The Spirit of the Hour, in revealing a clear debt to *Tristan und Isolde* and the *Ring*, had a powerful sense of contemporaneity which struck a note of modernism in the ears of English audiences. In fact, while *Prometheus* displays a certain *étincelle électrique* (as described by Prosper Sainton: 'Charles Harford Lloyd', *MT*, xl, 1899, p.373), it bears all the symptoms of immaturity and inchoateness, and its most 'modern' traits are precisely those which Parry later chose to jettison. In *Blest Pair of Sirens* his earlier Wagnerian enthusiasms are more completely digested (as in the paraphrase of *Die Meistersinger von Nürnberg* in the introduction) within a muscular language of greater diatonic dissonance, a stylistic attribute linking him with his English predecessors such as Stainer, S.S. Wesley, Ouseley and Walmisley. This diatonic tendency remained a pronounced feature of Parry's music and was used to great effect, be it lyrically in *L'Allegro*, the *Invocation to Music* and *The Pied Piper of Hamelin*, grandiosely in the *Te Deum* (1873), the coronation anthem *I was glad* and the *Ode to Music*, or polyphonically in *De profundis* (a tour de force for 12-part chorus), the *Ode on the Nativity* and the *Songs of Farewell*.

Parry also showed a flair for miniature forms. His 12 volumes of *English Lyrics* were undoubtedly an important vernacular precedent to the outpouring of songs by the next generation, particularly those setting Shakespeare. In contrast to the Elizabethan lyrics of the earlier volumes, he evidently felt an increasing empathy with contemporary poetry, which he used more frequently in later songs (the ninth set is devoted entirely to the poems of Mary Coleridge). The quality of these settings is variable but a number, among them *Through the Ivory Gate* (set iii), *A Welsh Lullaby* (set v) and *From a City Window* (set x), are especially fine. Other small-scale compositions – the *12 Short Pieces* (1894) for violin and piano, the *Shulbrede Tunes* for piano, the late chorale preludes and fantasias for organ and some of the partsongs – show a high level of imagination and craftsmanship, but none perhaps more so than the elastic phraseology of the choral song *Jerusalem*, an immutable favourite with the English public.

Another important facet of Parry's creative energies was his contribution to musical scholarship. At Oxford he was deeply impressed by Ruskin's morality of art, to which he held a lifelong allegiance. In maintaining an interest in philosophy, the arts, social sciences and politics after leaving university, he was also drawn into the tide of evolutionist thought, particularly through the 'social Darwinism' of Herbert Spencer. This profoundly influenced his approach to the study of musical history, in which he believed that the principles of man's evolutionary past, as seen biologically, intellectually and socially, were, according to the natural laws of the universe, reflected in the growth and change in music. This stance in itself transformed the role of the music critic and historian into one analogous with the scientist. Parry remained a fervent exponent of musical evolutionism, espousing tenets of ethnocentrism (in which German music was venerated above that of other European nations), the importance of tradition and training, and the balance between expression and design. Such standpoints recur with conviction in his many articles, lectures and books, notably *The Art of Music* (1893, significantly renamed *The Evolution of the Art of Music* in later editions) and *Style in Musical Art* (1911), a compilation of his Oxford lectures. Moreover, at the end of his life Parry continued to pursue an essentially Darwinist philosophy outside music in his unpublished *Instinct and Character*, a somewhat over-amplified but nevertheless valuable summation of his moral aesthetic.

Parry's personality, as with many Victorians, embraced many apparent contradictions. One side of it reveals the idealist, the radical and even, perhaps, the political rebel (as a supporter of Gladstonian liberalism). And yet, as an establishment figure, he was also an ardent advocate of tradition, nervous of artistic extremes and therefore seemingly conservative and restrained. He was drawn towards hedonism (as is clear from *The Lotos-Eaters*) but this is consciously balanced by a puritanical zeal. As if to compound these apparent paradoxes, he was deeply religious but nevertheless developed a pathological loathing for organized religion. His musical style and sensibility, capable of passionate yearning and affecting melancholy, is also imbued with a natural reserve, a tempered respect for technique and a propensity for moderation. These attributes, combined with a profound sense of the composer's obligation to society, was his legacy to a younger generation of composers and admirers, among them Vaughan Williams, Holst, Howells, Bliss and, most notably, Finzi.

WORKS

fuller list in Dibble (Life and Music, 1992)

printed works first published in London unless otherwise stated

MSS in GB-Ctc, Lbl, Lcm, Lco, Ob, R; Old Rectory, Highnam; Shulbrede Priory, Sussex

STAGE

incidental music unless otherwise stated

The Birds (Aristophanes), Cambridge, 27 Nov 1883 (1885)
Guenever (op, U. Taylor, Ger. trans. by F. Althaus) 1884–6, unperf.
The Frogs (Aristophanes), Oxford, 24 Feb 1892 (Leipzig, 1892); rev., Oxford, 19 Feb 1909
Hypatia (S. Ogilvie), London, Haymarket, 2 Jan 1893; suite, orch, 5 movts, London, 9 March 1893
A Repentance (P.M.T. Craigie), London, St James's, 28 Feb 1899
Agamemnon (Aeschylus), Cambridge, 16 Nov 1900 (1900)
The Clouds (Aristophanes), Oxford, 1 March 1905 (Leipzig, 1905)
Proserpine (ballet, P.B. Shelley), London, Haymarket, 25 June 1912
The Acharnians (Aristophanes), Oxford, 21 Feb 1914 (1914)

ORATORIOS, SERVICES

Magnificat and Nunc dimittis, A, 1864

Te Deum, B♭, ?1864

Morning, Communion and Evening Service, D, chorus, org, 1866–9 (1868–9)

Kyrie eleison, fugue, 8vv, 1867

Te Deum, E♭, 1873

Evening Service ('The Great'), D, 1881, ed. Dibble (1984)

Judith (orat, Apocrypha and H. Parry), S, A, T, B, chorus, orch, Birmingham, 29 Aug 1888 (1888)

Job (orat, Bible and Parry), S, T, 2B, chorus, orch, Gloucester, 8 Sept 1892, vs (1892), fs (1898)

King Saul (orat, Bible and Parry), S, A, T, B, chorus, orch, Birmingham, 3 Oct 1894 (1894)

Magnificat, F, S, chorus, orch, Hereford, 15 Sept 1897 (1897)

Thanksgiving Te Deum, F, S, B, chorus, orch, Hereford, 11 Sept 1900 (1900); rev., with Eng. text, Gloucester, 11 Sept 1913 (1913)

Te Deum, D, for coronation of George V, chorus, orch, London, Westminster Abbey, 23 June 1911 (1911)

OTHER SACRED

Praise God from whom all blessings flow, chorale, 1864–5

Lobet den Herren, 5vv, 1867

O Lord, Thou hast cast us out (cant., Bible), Eton College, 8 Dec 1867 (1867)

Ode on St Cecilia's Day (A. Pope), S, B, chorus, orch, Leeds, 11 Oct 1889 (1889)

De profundis (Ps cxxx), S, 12vv, orch, Hereford, 10 Sept 1891 (1891)

Grace for a City Dinner (Benedictus), 4vv, 1897

Voces clamantium (Bible and Parry), S, B, chorus, orch, Hereford, 10 Sept 1903 (1903)

The Love that Casteth out Fear (sinfonia sacra, Bible and Parry), chorus, orch, Gloucester, 7 Sept 1904 (1904)

Praise God in His Holiness, ps, B, org, 1906

The Soul's Ransom (sinfonia sacra, Bible and Parry), S, B, chorus, orch, Hereford, 12 Sept 1906 (1906)

Beyond these voices there is peace (Bible and Parry), S, B, chorus, orch, Worcester, 9 Sept 1908 (1908)

Eton Memorial Ode (R. Bridges), Eton College, 18 Nov 1908 (1908)

Ode on the Nativity (W. Dunbar), S, chorus, orch, Hereford, 12 Sept 1912 (1912)

I believe it (R. Browning), soliloquy, B, org, 1912

God is our hope (Ps xlvi), B, double chorus, orch, London, St Paul's Cathedral, 24 April 1913 (1913)

motets

[6] Songs of Farewell: My soul, there is a country (H. Vaughan), 4vv (1916); I know my soul hath power to know all things (J. Davies), 4vv (1916); Never weather-beaten sail (T. Campion), 5vv (1916); There is an old belief (J.G. Lockhart), 6vv (1916); At the round earth's imagined corners (J. Donne), 7vv (1917); Lord, let me know mine end (Ps xxxix), 8vv (1918)

anthems

In my distress, 1863

Fear thou not, 1864

O sing unto the Lord a new song, 1864

Blessed is He, 1865 (1865)

Prevent us O Lord, 1865 (1865)

Why boastest though thyself, 1865

Blessed are they that dwell in Thy house, 1870

Lord, I have loved the habitation of Thy house, 1870

Hear my words, ye people (Bible), chorus, orch, Salisbury, 10 May 1894 (1894)

I was glad (Ps cxxii), coronation anthem for Edward VII, London, Westminster Abbey, 9 Aug 1902 (1902), rev. version, 23 June 1911 [for George V]

Hymn tunes and chants

SECULAR CHORAL
with orchestra

Scenes from Prometheus Unbound (dramatic cant., Shelley), S, A, T, B, chorus, orch, Gloucester, 7 Sept 1880 (1880)

The Glories of Our Blood and State (ode, J. Shirley: *The Contention of Ajax and Ulysses*), chorus, orch, Gloucester, 4 Sept 1883 (1885)

Blest Pair of Sirens (At a Solemn Music) (ode, J. Milton), chorus, orch, London, 17 May 1887 (1887)

L'Allegro ed Il Pensieroso (cant., Milton), S, B, chorus, orch, Norwich, 15 Oct 1890 (1890)

Eton (ode, A.C. Swinburne), chorus, orch, Eton College, 28 June 1891 (1891)

The Lotos-Eaters (A. Tennyson), choric song, S, chorus, orch, Cambridge, 13 June 1892 (1892)

Invocation to Music (ode, Bridges), S, T, B, chorus, orch, Leeds, 2 Oct 1895 (1895)

A Song of Darkness and Light (Bridges), S, chorus, orch, Gloucester, 15 Sept 1898 (1898)

Ode to Music (A.C. Benson), S, S, A, T, B, chorus, orch, London, RCM, 13 June 1901 (1901)

War and Peace (sym. ode, Benson and Parry), S, A, T, B, chorus, orch, London, Royal Albert Hall, 30 April 1903 (1903)

The Pied Piper of Hamelin (cant., Browning), T, B, chorus, orch, Norwich, 26 Oct 1905, vs (1905), fs (1906)

The Vision of Life (sym. poem, Parry), S, B, chorus, orch, Cardiff, 26 Sept 1907 (1907); rev. 1914 (1914) [rev. for Norwich Festival but not perf.]

The Chivalry of the Sea (naval ode, Bridges), chorus, orch, London, 12 Dec 1916 (1916)

partsongs

Tell me where is fancy bred (W. Shakespeare), 4vv, 1864; Fair daffodils (R. Herrick), madrigal, 5vv, 1865 (1866); Persicos odi (Horace), 4vv, 1865; Take, O take those lips away (Shakespeare), TTBB, 1865; Oft in the stilly night (T. Moore), 1866; Dost thou idly ask (W.C. Bryant), 1867; Pure spirit, O where art thou? (?Parry), 1867; There lived a sage (?Parry), 4 male vv, 1869; He is coming (Mrs H. Gladstone), carol (1874); 3 Trios, female vv (1875); 6 Lyrics from an Elizabethan Song Book, 4–6vv (1897); 6 Modern Lyrics, 4vv (1897); 8 Four-Part Songs (1898); Who can dwell with greatness (A. Dobson), 5vv, 1899, in *Choral Songs . . . in Honour of Queen Victoria* (1899); In Praise of Song (?Parry), 8vv (1904); 6 Partsongs (1909); 7 Partsongs, ATB (1910); La belle dame sans merci (Keats), 5vv, 1914–15, ed. P.M. Young (1979); When Christ was born of Mary free (Harleian MS) (1915); I know an Irish lass, 4vv, ?1916; 2 carols (1917)

unison and school songs

Rock-a-bye (1893); Land to the leeward ho! (M. Preston) (1895); The best school of all (H. Newbolt), 1908 (1916); 5 Unison Songs (1909); School Songs (1911); 3 Unison Songs (1913); School Songs (1914); Come join the merry chorus (H. Smith) (1915); A Hymn for Aviators (M.C.D. Hamilton) (1915); For all we have and are (R. Kipling), 1916; Jerusalem (W. Blake), choral song, unison vv, orch (1916); 3 Songs for 'Kookoorookoo' (C. Rossetti) (1916); 3 School Songs (1918); England (Shakespeare) (1919)

SOLO SONGS
for 1 voice and piano unless otherwise stated

[74] English Lyrics, 12 sets, 1874–1918 (1885–1920): i, 4 songs, 1881–5 (1885); ii (Shakespeare), 5 songs, 1874–85 (1886); iii, 6 songs (1895); iv, 6 songs, 1885–96 (1896); v, 7 songs, 1877–1901 (1902); vi, 6 songs (1903); vii, 6 songs, 1888–1906 (1907); viii, 6 songs, c1904–6 (1907); ix (M. Coleridge), 7 songs, 1908 (1909); x, 6 songs, 1909 (1918); xi, 8 songs, 1910–18, ed. E. Daymond, C. Wood and H.P. Greene (1920); xii, 7 songs, c1870–1918, ed. Daymond, Wood and Greene (1920)

Fair is my love (E. Spenser), 1864; Love not me (anon.), 1865; When stars are in the quiet skies (E. Bulwer-Lytton), 1865; Why does azure deck the sky (Moore), 1865 (1866); Autumn (T. Hood), 1865–6 (1867), orchd 1867; When the grey skies are flushed with rosy streaks, ?1866; Angel hosts, sweet love, befriend thee (Lord Hervey), 1866 (1867); Go, lovely rose (E. Waller), 1866; Love the Tyrant (?Parry), 1866; Sleep, my love, untouched by sorrow, 1867; Dainty form, so firm and slight, 1868; 3 Odes of Anacreon (trans. Moore), 1868–78 (1880), no.2 orchd; An Epigram (Fairest dreams may be forgotten) (?Parry), 1869; Ah! woe is me! poor silver wing!, 1869; A River of Life (Lord Pembroke) (1870); Not Unavailing (The flower of purest whiteness), ?1872

An Evening Cloud (J. Wilson), 1873; A Shadow (What lack the valleys) (A. Proctor), 1873; 3 Songs (1873); 4 Sonnets (Shakespeare, Ger. trans. F. Bodenstedt), 1873–82 (1887), Eng. and Ger. text; A Garland of [6] Shakespearian and Other Old-Fashioned Songs (1874, repr. separately, 1880–81); Sonnet (If thou survive my well-contented day) (Shakespeare), 1874; Twilight (Lord Pembroke), 1874 (1875); Absence, hear my protestation (J. Hoskins), 1881; And wilt though leave me thus? (T. Wyatt), 1881; My passion you regard with scorn, ?1881; I arise from dreams of thee (Shelley), 1883; The Maid of Elsinore (H. Boulton), in *12 New Songs by British Composers* (1891)

The North Wind (W.E. Henley), B, orch, 1899; The Soldier's Tent (from the Bard of Dimbovitza, trans. A. Strettell and C. Sylva), scena, Bar, orch, 1900 (1901); Von edler Art (from Nuremberg songbook, 1549, trans. P. England), 1900 (1906); Newfoundland (C. Boyle), 1st version (1904), 2nd version, ?1904; Fear no more the heat o' the sun (Shakespeare) (1906); The Laird of Cockpen (Lady Nairn), Bar, pf, 1906 (1907)

ORCHESTRAL

Allegretto scherzando, Eb, 1867
Intermezzo religioso, 1867, Gloucester, 3 Sept 1868 [from Sonata, f, pf duet, 1865]
Piano Concerto, g, 1869, inc.
Vivien, ov., 1873, ?unperf., lost
Concertstück, g, 1877
Guillem de Cabestanh, ov., 1878, London, 15 March 1879
Piano Concerto, F♯, 1878–80, rev. 1884 and 1895, London, 3 April 1880
Symphony no.1, G, 1880–82, Birmingham, 31 Aug 1882
Symphony no.2 'Cambridge', F, 1882–3, Cambridge, 12 June 1883; rev., London, 6 June 1887; rev., with new finale, 30 May 1895 (1906)
Suite moderne (Suite symphonique), 1886, Gloucester, 9 Sept 1886, rev. 1892
Symphony no.3 'English', C, 1887–9, London, 23 May 1889; rev., Leeds, 30 Jan 1895; rev., Bournemouth, 18 Dec 1902 (1907)
Symphony no.4, e, 1889, London, 1 July 1889; rev. as 'Finding the Way', 1909–10, London, 10 Feb 1910 (1921)
An English Suite, str, 1890–1918, London, 20 Oct 1922 (1921), arr. Daymond, pf (1923)
Overture to an Unwritten Tragedy, a, 1893, Worcester, 13 Sept 1893; rev., London, 19 April 1894; rev. 1905 (1906)
'Lady Radnor' Suite, str, 1894, London, 29 June 1894 (1902); arr. pf (1905), arr. vn, pf (1915), arr. small orch
Elegy for Brahms, a, 1897, London, 9 Nov 1918
Symphonic Variations, e, 1897, London, 3 June 1897 (1897)
Symphonic Fantasia '1912' (Symphony no.5), b, 1912, London, 5 Dec 1912 (1922)
From Death to Life, sym. poem, bb/Bb, 1914, Brighton, 12 Nov 1914; rev., London, 18 March 1915
Foolish Fantasia (To finish the frolic if it will do), wind band, perf. Oxford, date unknown

CHAMBER

Nonet, Bb, fl, ob, eng hn, 2 cl, 2 bn, 2 hn, 1877
Quintet, Eb, 2 vn, 2 va, vc, 1883–4, London, 18 May 1884; rev. 1896, 1902, score (1909)
3 str qts: g, 1867; C, 1868; G, 1878–80, London, 26 Feb 1880, ed. M. Allis (1995)
Piano Quartet, Ab, 1879, London, 13 Feb 1879 (1884)
Trios: Short Trios, F, vn, va, pf, 1868; Pf Trio [no.1], e, 1877, London, 31 Jan 1878 (Leipzig, 1879); Pf Trio [no.2], b, 1884, London, 25 Nov 1884 (1884); 2 Intermezzi, str trio, 1884, ed. (1950); Pf Trio [no.3], G, 1889–90, London, 13 Feb 1890, rev. 1893
Vn, pf: 3 movts, 1863; Allegretto pastorale, G, 1870; 6 pieces (Freundschaftslieder), 1872; Sonata, d, 1875; Fantasie sonata in 1 movt, b, 1878, London, 30 Jan 1879; Partita, d, London, 2 Dec 1886 (1886) [rev. of Suite de pièces, 1873–7, Cannes, 8 Feb 1877]; Sonata, D, 1888–9, London, 14 Feb 1889, rev. 1894; 12 Short Pieces, 1894 (1895); Piece, G, 1896; Romance, F (1896); Suite, D (1907); Suite, F (1907)
Vc, pf: 2 Duettinos, F, G, 1868; Sonata, A, 1879–80, London, 12 Feb 1880 (1883)

KEYBOARD

2 pf: Grosses Duo, e, 1875–7 (Leipzig, 1877)
Pf 4 hands: Ov., b, 1865; Sonata, f, 1865; Characteristic Popular Tunes of the British Isles, 2 bks, 1885 (1885)
Pf solo: Little Piano Piece, variations, 1862; Andante non troppo, Bb, 1865; 4 fugues, 1865: c, Eb, F, e; Piece, g, 1865; Andante, C, 1867; Sonnets and Songs without Words, 3 sets: i, 1868 (1869), ii, 1867–75 (1875), iii, 1870–77 (1877); A Little Forget-me-not, Bb, 1870; 7 Charackterbilder (1872); 2 Short Pieces, C, F, ?1873; Variations on an Air by [J.S.] Bach, 1873–5; 2 sonatas: [no.1], F (1877), [no.2], A, 1876–7 (1878); Theme and 19 Variations, d, 1878 (1885); Cosy (1892); [10] Shulbrede Tunes, 1911–14 (1914);

Hands Across the Centuries, suite, 1916–18 (1918); Sleepy, ?1917; 5 Miniatures, ed. (1926) [incl. Cosy and Sleepy]

Org: Grand Fugue with 3 Subjects, G, 1865; Fantasia and Fugue, G, 1877–1912 (1913); Chorale Preludes, set 1, 1911–12 (1912); 3 Chorale Fantasias, 1911–14 (1915); Toccata and Fugue 'The Wanderer', G/e, 1912–18 (1921); Elegy, Ab, 1913 (1922) [for funeral of the 14th Earl of Pembroke, 7 April 1913]; Chorale Preludes, set 2, 1915 (1916); For the Little Organ Book, ed. (1924)

EDITIONS AND ARRANGEMENTS

W. Boyce: [Trio] Sonatas nos.10 and 12 (1747), arr. as Suite, e, 2 vn, va, vc (1892)
ed., with W.B. Squire and L. Benson: *A Collection of Madrigals by Ancient Composers* (1899)
H. Purcell: Soul of the World (from Hail, bright Cecilia), addl orch, 1918

WRITINGS

123 articles in *Grove1*
'On some Bearings of the Historical Method upon Music', *PMA*, xi (1884–5), 1–9
Studies of Great Composers (London, 1886/R)
The Art of Music (London, 1893; enlarged as *The Evolution of the Art of Music*, London, 1896, 2/1934/R)
Summary of the History and Development of Mediaeval and Modern European Music (London, 1893, 2/1904)
'Purcell', *National Review*, xxvi (1895–6), 339–50
The Music of the Seventeenth Century, OHM, iii (1902, rev. 2/1938/ R by E.J. Dent)
Johann Sebastian Bach: the Story of the Development of a Great Personality (New York and London, 1909, 2/1934/R)
'How Modern Song grew up', *MT*, lii (1911), 11–15 [lecture, Reading U. College, 9 Nov 1910]
'The Meaning of Ugliness in Art', *IMusSCR IV [London 1911]*, ed. C. Maclean (London, 1912), 77–83; also pubd *MT*, lii (1911), 507–11
Style in Musical Art (London, 1911/R) [collected Oxford lectures]
'Things that Matter', *MQ*, i (1915), 313–28
'The Significance of Monteverde', *PMA*, xlii (1915–16), 51–67
Instinct and Character (MS, c1915–18, GB-Lbl, Lcm, Ob, Shulbrede Priory, Sussex)]
ed. H.C. Colles: *College Addresses delivered to Pupils of the Royal College of Music* (London, 1920)
Lectures for University of Oxford (*Ob*) and RCM (*Lcm*)

BIBLIOGRAPHY

LIFE AND WORKS, GENERAL ASSESSMENT

Grove3 (E. Daymond) [incl. catalogue of works]
J.A. Fuller Maitland: *English Music in the Nineteenth Century* (London, 1902)
H.C. Colles: *The Growth of Music* (Oxford, 1912–16)
H.C. Colles: 'Sir Hubert Parry', *Music Student*, viii (1915–16), 177–80
Obituaries: R.H. Legge, *MT*, lix (1918), 489–91; R. Vaughan Williams, *Music Student*, xi (1918–19), 79
W.H. Hadow: 'Sir Hubert Parry', *PMA*, xlv (1918–19), 135–47; repr. in *Collected Essays* (London, 1928/R), 148–61
C.V. Stanford: 'A Tribute', *RCM Magazine*, xv/1 (1918–19), 7 only
J.A. Fuller Maitland: 'Hubert Parry', *MQ*, v (1919), 299–307
A.C. Mackenzie: 'Hubert Hastings Parry: his Work and Place among British Composers', *RAM Club Magazine*, no.56 (1919), 7–12; repr. in *Proceedings of the Royal Institution of Great Britain*, xxii (1922), 542–9
R.O. Morris: 'Hubert Parry', *ML*, i (1920), 94–103
A. Brent-Smith: 'Charles Hubert Hastings Parry', *ML*, vii (1926), 221–8
C.L. Graves: *Hubert Parry: his Life and Works* (London, 1926)
H.P. Allen: 'Hubert Parry', *RCM Magazine* (1933), May, 7–10 [special Jubilee issue]
C. McNaught: 'Hubert Parry 1848–1918', *MT*, lxxxix (1948), 41–2
G. Finzi: 'Hubert Parry: a Revaluation', *Making Music*, no.10 (1949), 4–8
R. Vaughan Williams: *National Music and Other Essays*, ed. M. Kennedy (London, 1963, 2/1987)
F. Howes: *The English Musical Renaissance* (London, 1966)
H. Howells: 'Hubert Parry', *ML*, l (1969), 223–9; repr. in *RCM Magazine*, lxv/3 (1969), 19–23
N. Temperley, ed.: *Music in Britain: the Romantic Age 1800–1914* (London, 1981/R1988 as *The Blackwell History of Music in Britain: the Romantic Age, 1800–1914*)

S. Banfield: 'Renaissance Men', *The Listener* (12 Jan 1984)
J.C. Dibble: 'Parry and Elgar: a New Perspective', *MT*, cxxv (1984), 639–43
J.C. Dibble: *C. Hubert H. Parry: his Life and Music* (Oxford, 1992)
C. Palmer: *Herbert Howells: a Centenary Celebration* (London, 1992)
R. Stradling and M. Hughes: *The English Musical Renaissance, 1860–1940: Construction and Deconstruction* (London, 1993)
M. Saremba: 'Captain Parry: Hubert Parry (1848–1918)', *Elgar, Britten & Co.: eine Geschichte der britischen Musik in zwölf Portraits* (Zürich, 1994), 55–84
B. Benoliel: *Parry before 'Jerusalem': Studies of his Life and Music with Excerpts from his Published Writings* (Aldershot, 1997)

MEMOIRS, BIOGRAPHY

C.L. Graves: *The Life and Letters of Sir George Grove, C.B.* (London, 1903/R)
E. Gambier Parry: *Annals of an Eton House* (London, 1907)
C.V. Stanford: *Studies and Memories* (London, 1908)
C.V. Stanford: *Pages from an Unwritten Diary* (London, 1914)
C. Bailey: 'Sir Hubert Parry and OUDS', *Oxford Magazine* (25 Oct 1918)
'The Funeral of Sir Hubert Parry', *MT*, lix (1918), 491–2
H. Walford Davies: 'Sir Hubert as Teacher', *RCM Magazine*, xv/1 (1918–19), 8–11
G. Greene: *Two Witnesses: a Personal Recollection of Hubert Parry and Friedrich von Hügel* (London, 1930)
H. Greene: *Charles Villiers Stanford* (London, 1935)
H.C. Colles: *H. Walford Davies: a Biography* (London, 1942)
R. Elkin: *Queen's Hall 1893–1941* (London, 1944)
H. Darke: 'Memories of Parry', *RCM Magazine*, lxiv (1967–8), 77–8
W. Fox: *Douglas Fox: a Chronicle* (Bristol, 1976)
P.M. Young: *George Grove, 1820–1900* (London, 1980)
J.C. Dibble: 'Inner Loneliness', *The Listener* (19 March 1987)
C. Ehrlich: *First Philharmonic: a History of the Royal Philharmonic Society* (Oxford, 1995)
S. Lloyd: *Sir Dan Godfrey: Champion of British Composers* (London, 1995)
M. Musgrave: *The Musical Life of the Crystal Palace* (Cambridge, 1995)

MUSICAL AND LITERARY WORKS

J.A. Fuller Maitland: 'Mr C. Hubert Parry's "Scenes from Prometheus Unbound"', *MMR*, xi (1881), 153–4
C.V. Stanford: 'Mr Hubert Parry's "Judith"', *Fortnightly Review*, xliv (1888), 537–45
R. Boughton: 'Modern British Song Writers: II. C.H.H. Parry', *Music Student*, vi (1913–14), 39–40
K.H. Luce: 'Parry's Chorale Preludes: an Amateur's Impressions', *Music Student*, x (1917–18), 456
F.G. Webb: 'The Words of Sir Hubert Parry', *MT*, lix (1918), 492–4
E. Daymond: 'The Purpose of Life', *RCM Magazine*, xv/1 (1918–19), 11–13 [on Parry's ethical choral works]
J.A. Fuller Maitland: 'The Literary Work of Sir Hubert Parry', *RCM Magazine*, xv/1 (1918–19), 14–17
C.H. Lloyd: 'Parry at Play', *RCM Magazine*, xv/1 (1918–19), 17–19
D. Ponsonby: 'Pages from the Note-Books of Hubert Parry', *ML*, i (1920), 318–29
H.C. Colles: 'Parry as a Song-Writer', *MT*, lxii (1921), 82–7, 155–8, 235–8; repr. in *Essays and Lectures* (London, 1945/R), 55–75
A. Ponsonby: 'On Instinct and Character', *Times Literary Supplement* (2 March 1922)
E. Daymond: 'On an Early Manuscript Book of Sir Hubert Parry's', *RCM Magazine*, xix (1922–3), 75–9
E.J. Dent: 'Parry's Prometheus Unbound', *Cambridge Review*, xlviii (1926–7), 488
H.C. Colles: 'Parry', *Cyclopedic Survey of Chamber Music*, ed. W.W. Cobbett (Oxford, 1929/R, enlarged 2/1963 by C. Mason), 207–11
J.A. Fuller Maitland: *The Music of Parry and Stanford* (Cambridge, 1934)
D.F. Tovey: 'Symphonic Variations', 'Overture to an Unwritten Tragedy', 'At a Solemn Music' [Blest Pair of Sirens], *Essays in Musical Analysis* (Oxford, 1935–9/R), ii, pp.142–5; iv, pp.143–7; v, pp.232–5
W.G. Whittaker: 'A Neglected Masterpiece', *MT*, lxxiv (1938), 898–9 [on motet, *Beyond these voices there is peace*]
S. Baylis: 'The Lady Radnor of Parry's Suite', *The Strad*, l (1939–40), 251–2
A.E.F. Dickinson: 'The Neglected Parry', *MT*, xc (1949), 108–9

E. Barsham: 'Parry's Manuscripts: a Rediscovery', *MT*, ci (1960), 86–7
G. Beechey: 'Parry and his Organ Music', *MT*, cix (1968), 956–8, 1057–9
S. Banfield: 'British Chamber Music at the Turn of the Century', *MT*, cxv (1974), 211–13
J.C. Dibble: 'Structure and Tonality in Parry's Chamber Music', *British Music Society Journal*, iii (1981), 13–23
J.C. Dibble: 'Parry and English Diatonic Dissonance', *British Music Society Journal*, v (1983), 58–71
S. Banfield: *Sensibility and English Song* (Cambridge, 1985)
J.C. Dibble: 'Under a Bushel', *The Listener* (10 Oct 1985)
J.C. Dibble: *The Music of Hubert Parry: a Critical and Analytical Study* (diss., U. of Southampton, 1986)
J.C. Dibble: 'National Developments in Britain and Ireland: a Matter of Style and Morality', *Welttheater: die Künste im 19. Jahrhundert*, ed. P. Andraschke and E. Spaude (Freiburg, 1992), 58–65
J.C. Dibble: 'Parry's Choral Fantasia, "When I survey the wondrous Cross"', *JBIOS*, xvii (1993), 118–30
M.J. Allis: *The Creative Process of C. Hubert H. Parry* (diss., U. of London, 1994)

JEREMY DIBBLE

Parry, John (i) ['Parry Ddall'] (*b* Bryn Cynan, *c*1710; *d* Ruabon, 7 Oct 1782). Welsh harper. He was blind, and was taught to play the Welsh triple harp by a relative, Robert Parry of Llanllyfni, and by Stephan Shon Jones of Penrhyndeudraeth. With perseverance and (according to the report of another blind harper, Richard Roberts of Caernarvon, 1796–1855) 'earnest prayer for the gift of playing the harp', Parry became the most distinguished harper of his generation in Great Britain. From 1734 he was harper to the first Sir Watkin Williams Wynn of Wynnstay, Ruabon, and continued from 1749 to his death in the service of Sir Watkin Williams Wynn II. This Welsh baronet was an active patron of the arts and he numbered Sir Joshua Reynolds, David Garrick and Handel among his friends. It was probably in playing for Sir Watkin's circle in London that Parry so impressed Handel and also recommended himself to the attention of the Prince of Wales, who became his patron. A performance of Parry's at Cambridge in 1757 proved to be a source of inspiration for Thomas Gray's Pindaric Ode *The Bard*; Gray wrote to his friend William Mason:

Mr Parry has been here and scratched out such ravishing blind harmony, such tunes of a thousand years old, with names enough to choke you, as have set all this learned body a dancing, and inspired them with due respect to my old bard, his countryman, whenever he shall appear. Mr Parry, you must know, has set my Ode in motion again, and has brought it at last to a conclusion.

Parry's most important contribution lay in the fact that, in collaboration with Evan Williams, a Welsh organist and fellow harper in London, he published the first collection (supposedly entirely) of Welsh melodies. Of the 24 untitled tunes in *Antient British Music* at least half are indisputably Welsh: a few of Parry's florid arrangements, however, can be identified as tunes known in 16th-century England, such as *The Frog Galliard* (Aria II), *Monsieur's Almain* (Aria X) and *Mall Sims* (Aria XXIII). *Mock Nightingale* (Aria VI) is a variant of an early 18th-century country dance tune and Aria XV is derived from the 17th-century ballad *Methinks the Poor Town*. This kind of variety was typical of a professional Welsh harper's repertory passed on orally before the middle of the 18th century.

Parry's final volume, *British Harmony*, contains, among its traditional Welsh tunes, a May carol and a New Year *quête* song, while the piece *Erddigan tro'r Tant* has some of the characteristics of the harp music of the Robert ap

Huw period. As in his other collections no words are printed with the music. However, in 1745, shortly after the appearance of *Antient British Music*, Parry and Williams intended to bring out a volume of Welsh tunes with words. A specimen manuscript exists containing six tunes with Welsh words to be sung in *canu penillion* style, the earliest examples of this form of traditional Welsh singing.

WORKS

Antient British Music, or A Collection of Tunes, never before published, which are retained by the Cambro-Britons (more particularly in North Wales), hp/hpd/vn/fl, bc (London, 1742), collab. E. Williams
A Collection of Welsh, English & Scotch Airs with New Variations also 4 New Lessons, hp/hpd (London, 1761), also incl. 12 Airs, gui
Twelve Airs, gui/2 gui (London, c1765)
British Harmony, being a Collection of Antient Welsh Airs, the Traditional Remains of those originally sung by the Bards of Wales (Ruabon and London, 1781, 2/c1809 as Cambrian Harmony)

BIBLIOGRAPHY

Y Cerddor [The musician], xi/Sept (1889)
R. Griffith: *Llyfr Cerdd Dannau* [Book of music for the harp] (Caernarvon, 1913)
W.S. Gwynne Williams: *Welsh National Music and Dance* (London, 1932, 4/1971)
J.Ll. Williams: *Y Tri Thelynor* [The three harpists] (London, 1945)
R.D. Griffith: 'Parry, John', *The Dictionary of Welsh Biography down to 1940*, ed. J.E. Lloyd and R.T. Jenkins (London, 1959)
A. Rosser: *Telyn a Thelynor* [Harps and harpists] (Cardiff, 1981)
O. Ellis: *The Story of the Harp in Wales* (Cardiff, 1991)
S. McVeigh: *Concert Life in London from Mozart to Haydn* (Cambridge, 1993)

OWAIN EDWARDS/PHYLLIS KINNEY

Parry, John (ii) (*b* Denbigh, 18 Feb 1776; *d* London, 8 April 1851). Welsh instrumentalist and composer. After studying the harp and the clarinet he joined the band of the Denbighshire militia in 1793 and became master of it in 1795. In this position he became proficient on a large number of instruments, and he exhibited his talents at Covent Garden in 1805. He settled in London in 1807, as a teacher of the flageolet. In 1809 he was engaged to provide some music for Vauxhall Gardens; in 1814 he began composing and arranging music for various operatic farces and other stage productions. In several cases he was responsible for the libretto as well as the music. At least five dramatizations of Scott's *Ivanhoe* were presented in London in 1820: the one at Covent Garden was the most successful, partly because of Parry's song 'The Lullaby'. He was particularly skilled at composing ballads with a Celtic flavour, which he often sang himself. At his farewell concert in June 1837 he sang his own popular ballad *Jenny Jones* accompanied on the harp by his son, JOHN ORLANDO PARRY. The duet *Flow gently Deva* was also for many years a favourite.

Parry maintained his Welsh links, conducting the cymrodorion and eisteddfods held in various places in Wales. He was one of the promoters of the Cambrian Society, and at the Powys Eisteddfod of 1820 he received the title of 'Bardd Alaw' (Master of Song). He was treasurer of the Royal Society of Musicians from 1831 to 1849, and secretary of the Royal Musical Festival held at Westminster Abbey in 1834. He wrote several books on musical subjects and was an assiduous collector and arranger of Welsh melodies. From 1834 to 1849 he was music critic of *The Morning Post*.

WORKS
all performed in London; music lost by the composer unless otherwise stated
LCG – Covent Garden
LDL – Drury Lane Theatre

Fair Cheating, or The Wise Ones Outwitted (operatic farce), LDL, 15 June 1814, vs pubd
Harlequin Hoax, or A Pantomine Proposed (extravaganza, T. Dibdin), Lyceum, 16 Aug 1814, vs pubd
Oberon's Oath, or The Paladin and the Princess (musical drama, B. Thompson), LDL, 21 May 1816
High Notions, or A Trip to Exmouth (operatic farce), LCG, 11 Feb 1819, 2 songs pubd
Helpless Animals, or Bachelor's Fare (operatic farce), LCG, 17 Nov 1819, vs pubd
Ivanhoe, or The Knight Templar (musical drama, S. Beazley, after W. Scott), LCG, 2 March 1820, ov. pubd
Two Wives, or A Hint to Husbands (operatic farce), LDL, 2 June 1824
My Uncle Gabriel (operatic farce), LDL, 10 Dec 1824, 2 songs pubd
A Trip to Wales (operatic farce), LDL, 11 Nov 1826
Caswallon, or The Briton Chief (tragedy, C.E. Walker), LDL, 12 Jan 1829
The Sham Prince (burletta), St James's, 29 Sept 1836

Music in: The Merry Wives of Windsor (1824)

6 collections of Welsh airs (1804–48)
Numerous songs, ballads, catches, etc., pubd singly and in contemporary anthologies

WRITINGS

Articles in *Cambro-Britain* (1819–22)
Il puntello, or The Supporter (London, 1832) [incl. rudiments of music]
An Account of the Rise and Progress of the Harp (London, 1834)
An Account of the Royal Musical Festival held in Westminster Abbey, 1834 (London, 1834)

BIBLIOGRAPHY

DNB (J.C. Hadden); *MGG1* (C. Lloyd Davies); *NicollH*

PETER CROSSLEY-HOLLAND/NICHOLAS TEMPERLEY

Parry, John Orlando (*b* London, 3 Jan 1810; *d* East Molesey, Surrey, 20 Feb 1879). Welsh pianist and singer, son of JOHN PARRY (ii). He studied the harp under Bochsa and in May 1825 appeared as a performer on that instrument. His principal gifts, however, were as a pianist and, above all, as a baritone and entertainer. His voice was rich, though not powerful, and was at its best in a comic vein or in simple ballads. In 1833 he went to Italy, living for some time at Naples where he learnt from Lablache. At his benefit concert in June 1836 he gave the first public indication in England of the extraordinary nature of his comic talent, by joining Maria Malibran in Mazzinghi's duet *When a little farm we keep*, and mimicking Harley. In the same year he appeared in his father's *Sham Prince*, in Hullah's *Village Coquettes* and other pieces. In 1837 he gave his *Buffo Trio Italiano* (accompanying himself on the piano), in which he successfully imitated Grisi, Ivanov and Lablache. In 1840 he introduced *Wanted, a Governess* (with words by George Dubourg), the success of which induced him to abandon serious and devote himself to comic singing. In 1849 he gave up concert singing and produced an entertainment, *Notes, Vocal and Instrumental*, written by Albert Smith, in which he exhibited a large number of his own watercolour paintings, and which was very successful. He gave similar entertainments in 1850 and 1852. He had long been a victim of fits of nervous hysteria; in 1853 these became so bad that he was compelled to retire from public performance. He became organist of St Jude's, Southsea, and practised as a teacher. He made several brief returns to the stage, the last at the Gaiety Theatre on 7 February 1877. Parry composed or compiled a large number of songs, of which 34 are listed by Boase (*DNB*). He also wrote a few glees and a good deal of dance music for the piano.

BIBLIOGRAPHY

DNB (G.C. Boase)

C. Scott and C. Howard: *The Life and Reminiscences of E.L. Blanchard* (London, 1891), i, 260, 338; ii, 437, 457, 464–5, 484

C.B. Andrews and J.A. Orr-Ewing: *Victorian Swansdown: Extracts from the Early Travel Diaries of John Orlando Parry* (London,1935)

P.A. Scholes, ed.: *The Mirror of Music 1844–1944* (London, 1947/ R), 509–10

W.H. HUSK/NICHOLAS TEMPERLEY

Parry, Joseph (*b* Merthyr Tydfil, 21 May 1841; *d* Penarth, 17 Feb 1903). Welsh composer. He came from a musical family and showed talent at an early age, but owing to the poor circumstances of his parents he gave up school to work in a coal mine at the age of nine. In 1854 his family emigrated to Danville, Pennsylvania, where they lived in a Welsh community. He was employed in an iron works, but he also learnt music, including theory, from two emigré Welsh musicians, John Abel Jones and W.J. Price. During the next 20 years he travelled frequently between Wales and the USA, performing, studying and composing songs and glees with Welsh texts. He won several eisteddfod prizes in both countries. In 1865 he was inducted into the Gorsedd of Bards of the National Eisteddfod, taking the bardic title 'Pencerdd America'. In 1868 he had raised enough money to enter the RAM, where he studied under Sterndale Bennett, Manuel García and Steggall. He won a bronze medal (1870) and a silver medal (1871). In 1871 he received the MusB at Cambridge and then returned to Danville to run a music school. In 1873 he became the first professor of music at the University College of Wales (Aberystwyth), but he left acrimoniously in 1880. It seems that part of his dispute with college authorities stemmed from the success of his music class, which at one time accounted for more than a quarter of the college's students. In 1878 he took the MusD at Cambridge. He established a private school of music in Swansea (1881–8), and from 1888 until his death he was lecturer in music at the University College of South Wales and Monmouthshire in Cardiff.

Parry's compositions enjoyed much favour during his lifetime both in Britain and the USA. He wrote some orchestral and chamber music, but most of his work is choral or dramatic: his *Blodwen* is believed to be the first Welsh opera, and his oratorio *Saul of Tarsus* created a considerable stir at the Cardiff Festival of 1892. His standing among Welsh musicians became almost legendary. Young considered that his academic success undermined his vitality as a composer: 'in his major works he felt obliged to use a nondescript style thought to be proper to a Doctor of Music'. However, his hymn tune 'Aberystwyth' stands as a monument to his talents, and his partsong *Myfanwy* is the most popular and performed setting of a Welsh text for male choir. He was less at ease with instrumental idioms than with vocal, but his *Tydfil Overture* (unpublished) for the virtuoso Cyfarthfa Band (the private band of R.T. Crawshay of Merthyr Tydfil) is almost certainly the earliest original art music composition for brass band.

His son Joseph Haydn Parry (*b* Danville, PA, 27 May 1864; *d* London, 27 March 1894) composed three operas, *Cigarette* (Cardiff, 1892), *Miami* (London, 1893) and *Marigold Farm* (unperformed), as well as other works. In the early 1890s he taught composition at the GSM, London.

WORKS
STAGE
operas unless otherwise stated

Blodwen (3, R. Davies), concert perf., Aberystwyth, 1878; stage, Swansea, 20 June 1878 (Aberystwyth, 1878)

Virginia (E.R. Jones), Swansea, Royal, 1883, lost

Arianwen (3, D. Rowlands and J. Parry), Cardiff, Royal, 5 June 1890 (Cardiff, 1890)

Sylvia (3, D.M. Parry), Cardiff, Royal, 12 Aug 1895 (Cardiff, 1895)

Cap and Gown (operetta, 1, I.B. John), Cardiff, South Wales School of Music, 1898

King Arthur, 1896–9 (3, H.E. Lewis), unperf.

His Worship the Mayor, 1895–1900 (3, A. Mee), unperf.

Ceridwen (1, E. Rees), concert perf., Liverpool, 1900 (London, 1900)

Y ferch o'r Scer, 1900–02 (3, ?J. Parry), unperf.

The Maid of Cefn Ydfa (3, J. Bennett), Cardiff, Grand, Dec 1902

CHORAL

Orats: The Prodigal Son, Chester, 1866; Emmanuel, London, 1880; Saul of Tarsus, Rhyl and Cardiff, 1892

Cants.: The Birds, Wrexham, 1873; Jerusalem (MusD exercise), Cambridge, 1878; Joseph, Swansea, 1881; Nebuchadnezzar, London, 1884; Cambria, Llandudno, 1896

OTHER WORKS

Orch works, incl. syms. ovs., Ballad (Cardiff, 1892); str qt; *c*400 hymn tunes (incl. Aberystwyth, 1877), anthems; songs

Cambrian Minstrelsie, 6 vols. (Edinburgh, 1893) [collection of Welsh songs, ed. and harmonized by Parry]

BIBLIOGRAPHY

E.K. Evans and others: *Cofiant Dr Joseph Parry* (Cardiff and London, 1921)

P.M. Young: *A History of British Music* (London, 1967), 491–2

O.T. Edwards: *Joseph Parry, 1841–1903* (Cardiff, 1970)

D. Rhys: *Joseph Parry: Bachgen Bach o Ferthyr* [Little boy from Merthyr] (Cardiff, 1998)

PETER CROSSLEY-HOLLAND/NICHOLAS TEMPERLEY

Pars (Lat.: 'part'). A section or division of a work (e.g. the *prima* and *secunda pars* of a motet). *See also* PARTITA.

Parsch, Arnošt (*b* Bučovice, Moravia, 12 Feb 1936). Czech composer. After private composition study with Jaromír Podešva, he graduated from the Brno Academy (JAMU) as a pupil of Miloslav Ištvan in composition and of Jan Kapr, Ctirad Kohoutek and Alois Piňos in theory. Like other Czech composers of his generation, he has often shown an ironic attitude to the serial methods he employs, the tendency to humour becoming a predominant trait in his work at the end of the 1960s, when the importance of aleatory writing increased. In about 1970 he began to incorporate more diverse ideas and techniques in collage structures containing frequent sharp confrontations of style. Parsch has always been stimulated by ideas from pictorial art and by sound situations in life. Together with Piňos, R. Růžička and Miloš Štědroň, he was a founder-member of the Brno composers' group formed in 1967. He served as secretary to the Brno branch office of the Czech Composers' Union (1969–77) in addition to holding a number of teaching positions at the Janáček Academy of Performing Arts (assistant professor 1971–3 and 1990–91, lecturer in theory and composition, and vice rector for foreign relations and school development 1991–7, professor of composition from 1997). He has also had a long association with the Brno International Music Festival, firstly as secretary (1977–93) and from 1993 as president.

WORKS
(selective list)

Vocal: Znamení touhy [A Sign of Longing] (cant.), 1972; Viver lieto voglio, op.57, chorus, 1980 [from madrigal by G.G. Gastoldi]; Džbánky [Jugs] (P. Aujezdský), op.59, chorus, 1981; Jízda králů [The Kings' Ride] (cant.), op.66, T, B, chorus, chbr ens, 1984; Ústa [Mouths] (Aujezdský), op.64, chorus, 1984; Vyzvání lásky [Invitations to Love] (Aujezdský), 5 songs, T, pf, 1987; Vítání jara [The Welcoming of Spring], 15 scenes, op.76, Mez, T, B-Bar, chorus, children's chorus, orch, 1990; Uspávanky [Lullabies], op.78, female v, 2 dulcimer, db, bell, 1991; Etudes amoureuses, op.87, Mez, vn, mar, hpd, 1995; Popravy a vzkříšení [Executions and Resurrections] (L. Čačalová), op.89, 5 songs, female v, pf, 1996

Orch: Sonata, chbr orch, 1966; Samsàrah, sym. no.1, 1967; Sym. no.2, 1969–70; Pro futuro, op.58, 1980; Daleko provdaná [Married to a Faraway Place], op.60, jazz orch, 1982; Sym.-Conc., op.62, hn, orch, 1982; Rondeau, op.63, vn, orch, 1983; Poem-Conc., op.69, dulcimer, orch, 1986; Conc., op.73, b cl, pf, orch, 1989; Studánky [Fountains], op.81, folk orch, 1991; V samotě [Loneliness], op.83, 1993; Most [Bridge], op.88, 1996

Chbr and solo inst: Rota, vn, pf, 1965; Transposizioni I, wind qnt, 1967; Str Qt, 1969; 4 Pieces, 4 insts, 1972; 2 Rondeaux, op.65, str, 1984; Dialogue, op.67, hn, org, 1985; Bn Sonata, op.70, bn/(bn, pf), 1986; Zpívám si [Singing to Myself], fantasy, op.68, cl, gui, 1986; Metamorfosi del canto moravo, op.72, hpd, 1988; Kresby [Drawings], op.75, cl, vn, pf, 1989; Daleké obzory [Faraway Horizons], op.77, fl, b cl, pf, 1990; Musica per i montanari, op.79, 2 hn, 1991; Rapsodietta, op.80, 11 str, 1992; Meditace [Meditations], op.82, gui, 1993; Hlas řeky [Voice of the River], op.85, 9 players, 1994; Str Qt no.3, op.84, str qt, 1994; Úboči hory [Hillside], op.86, vn, perc, 1995; Růžová zahrada [The Rose Garden], op.90, small conc., pf, 8 players, 1997; Šťastná voda [Happy Water], op.91, eng hn, vc, 1998

El-ac: Poetica no.3, elecs, 1967; Transposizioni II, elecs, 1969; Kuře krákoře [Chicken Clucking], elecs, 1970, collab. M. Štědroň; Josefu Horákovi [To Josef Horák], b cl, pf, tape, c1970; Polyfonie no.1, b cl, pf, tape, c1970; Viva Che, elecs, 1972, collab. Štědroň; Rozednívání [Dawn], op.61, 1982; Proměny času [Metamorphoses of Time], op.74, 1989

WRITINGS

'Transpozice konkrétních zvukových dějů' [The transposition of concrete sound events], OM, ii (1970), 171–3

BIBLIOGRAPHY

M. Štědroň: 'Participación del racionalismo e irracionalismo en la nueva musica checa', Sonda, i/Oct (1967), 25–30
M. Štědroň: 'Arnošt Parsch: Rota' (Prague, 1971) [introduction to score]

MILOŠ ŠTĚDROŇ

Parsley, Osbert (b 1511; d Norwich, 1585). English composer and singer. He spent most of his life in Norwich where he was a 'singing-man' in the cathedral choir. A memorial tablet to Parsley in the north aisle of the nave of Norwich Cathedral provides most of the biographical information so far available:

OSBERTO PARSLEY

Musicae Scientissimo
Ei quondam Consociati
Musici posuerunt Anno 1585

Here lies the Man whose Name in Spight of Death.
Renowned lives by Blast of Golden Fame:
Whose Harmony survives his vital Breath.
Whose Skill no Pride did spot whose Life no Blame.
Whose low Estate was blest with quiet Mind:
As our sweet Cords with Discords mixed be:
Whose Life in *Seventy* and *Four* Years entwin'd.
As falleth mellowed Apples from the Tree.
Whose Deeds were Rules whose Words were Verity:
Who here a Singing-man did spend his Days.
Full *Fifty* Years in our Church Melody
His Memory shines bright whom thus we praise.

Parsley was thus one of several composers whose lives spanned the Reformation and who wrote church music for both Latin and English rites. On the evidence of his surviving output, Parsley's art found its most congenial expression in his Latin church music. The psalm *Conserva me, Domine,* in which flowing lines weave expressive webs of polyphony, is a particularly noteworthy contribution to the genre. His setting of the Lamentations follows contemporary practice in providing settings of the Hebrew letters which precede each section; however, the appearance of the liturgical chant in the upper voice throughout is unusual.

Parsley's surviving church music to English texts includes two four-part Morning Services (each of which consists of *Te Deum* and *Benedictus*) and a single anthem *This is the day*. It is markedly inferior in quality to his Latin church music, being marred by stiff points of imitation and an unimaginative approach to problems of texture. A setting of both *Magnificat* and *Nunc dimittis*, which in some 17th-century sources is associated with the First Service's *Te Deum* and *Benedictus*, is variously attributed to Parsley and Tye. On stylistic grounds it might equally well have been written by either composer, although the duplication of material between the morning and evening canticles would appear to favour Parsley as composer.

Parsley's instrumental ensemble music illustrates various aspects of his ingenuity. In all, five In Nomine settings have survived, though the two most interesting of these (both for five viols) exist only in a fragmentary state. One of the In Nomines gives five beats to each note of the plainsong cantus firmus. This feature can also be seen in the *Spes nostra* for five viols. Another five-part instrumental composition entitled *Perslis clocke*, which is described in one source as *The Songe upon the Dyaall*, is based on the hexachord. A three-part instrumental canon by Parsley on the plainsong *Salvator mundi* was printed as a musical example in Morley's *Plaine and Easie Introduction to Practicall Musicke* (London, 1597).

WORKS

Editions: *Hugh Aston (1480?–1522), John Merbecke (1523–1585?), Osbert Parsley (1511–1585)*, ed. E.H. Fellowes, TCM, x (1929/R) [F]
Elizabethan Consort Music, I, ed. Paul Doe, MB, xliv (1979) [D]

SACRED

Morning Service (TeD, Bs), 4vv, F 256
Te Deum, Benedictus, 4vv, F 271
Magnificat, Nunc dimittis, 4vv, F 290 (attrib. Parsley in 1936 edn, attrib. Tye in 1963 edn)
This is the day, 4vv, GB-Cu, Ob, US-NYp
Conserva me, Domine, 5vv, F 237
Lamentationes, 5vv, F 247
Jesus decus angelicum, inc.; ed. in TCM, appx (1948)

INSTRUMENTAL

Conserva me, Domine (arrs. in tablature of 3-pt sections of the psalm), GB-Lbl Add.29246
5 In Nomines, 3 a 5 (2 inc.), 2 a 4, Lbl Add.32377, Ob Mus.Sch.D.212–16, Ob Tenbury 1464; 3 ed. in D 29, 31, 104

Perslis clocke: 'The song upon the dial', 5 viols; D 78
Salvator mundi (3-part canon), in Morley (1597); D 3
Spes nostra, 5 viols; D 79
Super septem planetarium, inc., Ob Tenbury 1464

BIBLIOGRAPHY

Le HurayMR
T. Morley: *A Plaine and Easie Introduction to Practicall Musicke* (London, 1597/R); ed. R.A. Harman (London, 1952, 2/1963/R)

N. Boston: *The Musical History of Norwich Cathedral* (Norwich, 1963) [orig. pubd in Reports of the Friends of Norwich Cathedral, 1938–9]

R.T. Daniel and P. Le Huray: *The Sources of English Church Music, 1549–1660*, EECM, suppl.i (1972)

J. Morehen: 'The Instrumental Consort Music of Osbert Parsley', *The Consort*, no.30 (1974), 67–72

JOHN MOREHEN

Parsons. At least four English musicians of this name, apparently unrelated, composed church music between the 1550s and 1660s; *see* PARSONS, JOHN; PARSONS, ROBERT (i); PARSONS, ROBERT (ii); PARSONS, WILLIAM. Several works ascribed in the sources simply to 'Parsons' or 'Mr Parsons' may be attributed with some degree of certainty to Robert Parsons (i) or William Parsons.

BIBLIOGRAPHY

Le HurayMR

MSS of Wells Cathedral, 958–1812, HMC 12: Wells, ii (1914), 274, 276, 287

J.F. Chanter: *The Custos and College of Vicars Choral of the Cathedral Church of St. Peter, Exeter* (Exeter, 1933)

A.G. Matthews: *Walker Revised: being a Revision of John Walker's 'Sufferings of the Clergy during the Grand Rebellion 1642–60'* (Oxford, 1948/R)

M. Frost: *English & Scottish Psalm & Hymn Tunes c. 1543–1677* (London, 1953)

P. Oboussier: 'Turpyn's Book of Lute-Songs', *ML*, xxxiv (1953), 145–9

W.K. Ford: 'Concerning William Parsons', *ML*, xxxvii (1956), 333–5

Calendar of Patent Rolls: Elizabeth I, 1556–1559, iv (London, 1964)

A. Smith: 'The Gentlemen and Children of the Chapel Royal of Elizabeth I: an Annotated Register', *RMARC*, no.5 (1965), 13–46

M. Joiner: 'British Museum Add. MS 15117: a Commentary, Index and Bibliography', *RMARC*, no.7 (1969), 51–109

P. Doe: 'Tallis's "Spem in alium" and the Elizabethan Respond-Motet', *ML*, li (1970), 1–14

R. Daniel and P. le Huray: *Sources of English Church Music 1549–1660*, EECM, suppl. i (London, 1972)

W.A. Edwards: *The Sources of Elizabethan Consort Music* (diss., U. of Cambridge, 1974)

H. Benham: *Latin Church Music in England c. 1460–1575* (London, 1977, 2/1980), 167–8, 170, 212, 214, 219–21

G. Dodd: *Thematic Index of Music for Viols* (London, 1980–82)

D. Mateer: 'Oxford, Christ Church Music MSS 984–8: An Index and Commentary', *RMARC*, no.20 (1986–7), 1–18

D. Greer: 'Manuscript Additions in Early Printed Music', *ML*, lxxii (1991), 523–35

P. Holman: *Four and Twenty Fiddlers: the Violin at the English Court, 1540–1690* (Oxford, 1993, 2/1995)

P. Doe: Introduction to *Robert Parsons: Latin Sacred Music*, EECM, xl (1994)

PHILIPPE OBOUSSIER

Parsons, Geoffrey (Penwill) (*b* Sydney, 15 June 1929; *d* London, 26 Jan 1995). Australian pianist and accompanist. He studied with Winifred Burston at the Sydney Conservatory (1941–8), and with Friedrich Wührer in Munich (1956). His first significant concert performance was of a Mozart concerto in Sydney (1946); a 1948 tour of Australia with Essie Ackland decided him on a career as an accompanist. In Britain important early appearances included those with Peter Dawson (Southampton, 1950); Hüsch in *Winterreise* (London, 1955); and a first Royal Festival Hall recital (1961) with Schwarzkopf, whose principal accompanist he later became. Los Angeles, Streich, Gedda, Hotter, Popp, Baker, Bär, Hampson, Tortelier and Milstein are other musicians for whom he regularly played. After the retirement of Gerald Moore, Parsons became the leading accompanist in Britain, admired internationally for the subtle authority and quiet strength of his playing, less dramatic or flamboyant than Moore's but no less responsive. His repertory was extensive, and he was adept at matching his style to that of his partner. He made many recordings, of which his long series with Olaf Bär is perhaps his most significant achievement, with singer and pianist achieving a close interpretative rapport.

MAX LOPPERT/R

Parsons, Gram [Connor, Cecil Ingram, III] (*b* Winterhaven, FL, 5 Nov 1946; *d* Joshua Tree, CA, 19 Sept 1973). American country rock singer, songwriter and guitarist. Generally regarded as the principal architect of country rock, the earliest of his classic compositions in this style was the elegiac *Hickory Wind* (1968), which first appeared on the Byrds' album *Sweetheart of the Rodeo*. Often co-writing with Chris Hillman of the Byrds, Parsons contributed such songs as *Ooh Las Vegas*, *Sin City* and *My Uncle* to the repertory of the prototype country rock group, the Flying Burrito Brothers, between 1969 and 1971. He then worked briefly with the Rolling Stones on their album *Exile on Main St* before recording two solo albums of his own, *GP* (Rep., 1973) and the posthumously released *Grievous Angel* (Rep., 1974); these included further well-crafted ballads such as *Grievous Angel*, *In My Hour of Darkness*, *She* and *The New Soft Shoe*. His style combined the intense melancholy of the strand of country music associated with Hank Williams and George Jones and the kinetic energy of heavily amplified rock. Subsequent to his death, his compositions have been recorded by Emmylou Harris, Elvis Costello and Poco, one of the many country rock groups inspired by his pioneering efforts. For further information see B. Fong-Torres: *Hickory Wind: the Life and Times of Gram Parsons* (London, 1991).

DAVE LAING

Parsons, John (*b c*1575; *d* London, bur. 3 Aug 1623). English organist and composer. He was appointed parish clerk and one of the organists of St Margaret's, Westminster, in 1616, and Organist and Master of the Choristers of Westminster Abbey on 7 December 1621. His annual salary was £16, to which was added £36 13s. 4d. for looking after the choristers. Married in 1600, he had three children. He is buried in the cloisters of Westminster Abbey.

Very little of John Parsons's music survives in complete form. A late 17th-century score of his Burial Service (*GB-Ob* Tenbury 787), bound in black covers, and including Purcell's *Remember not O Lord, our offences* was probably used at the funeral of Charles II in 1685, when Parsons's service is known to have been performed. The verse anthem *Holy Lord God almighty* is dated 16 January 1622 in a note appended to the work by Adrian Batten in his organbook (*Ob* Tenbury 791). Camden's *Remains … concerning Britaine* (London, 7/1674) contains an interesting epitaph on the composer:

> Death passing by and hearing Parsons play,
> Stood much amazed at his depth of skill,
> And said, 'This artist must with me away'
> (For death bereaves us of the better still),
> But let the quire, while he keeps time, sing on,
> For Parsons rests, his service being done.

For bibliography *see* PARSONS.

PHILIPPE OBOUSSIER

Parsons, Michael (Edward) (*b* Bolton, 12 Dec 1938). English composer and performer. After reading classics at St John's College, Oxford (1957–61), he studied composition with Fricker at the RCM (1961–2). He was active as a writer on music in the 1960s, during which period he got to know Cardew, attending his workshops at Morley College and co-founding the SCRATCH ORCHESTRA with him in 1969, along with Skempton. Between 1970 and 1990 he was a visiting lecturer in the department of Fine Art, Portsmouth Polytechnic and at the Slade School of Art, University College London. During 1996–7 he was composer-in-residence at Kettle's Yard, Cambridge. He has been involved in long-term collaborations with Skempton and John White.

Parsons's music has a number of diverse, overlapping influences that continue to develop, creating a varied yet personal sound world. His early music was strongly influenced by Webern and the idea of structural ordering remains important. In contrast, along with Cardew, he explored some of the ideas of Cage, Wolff and Feldman. His 'Scratch' music closely followed the group's manifesto aims, aspects of which continue in his work with mixed media forms. At Portsmouth and Slade his association with the English 'Systems' artists (including Malcolm Hughes and Geoffrey Steele) began. Subsequent works have a strong constructional element, usually employing some form of permutational scheme applied to pitch and rhythm (such as the pendulum sequence applied to a pentatonic scale in *Pentatonic Music*, 1975). This period also illustrates his interest in folk musics and change-ringing patterns, as well as rhythms derived from numerical patterns and abstracts of dance rhythms. Later works, such as the *Four Oblique Pieces* (1996), are less rigidly systematized, engaging more directly with sound as colour and the chromatic worlds of Webern and Feldman. His affinity with Mondrian and interest in computer-generated sounds is seen in the series of *Levels*. Several works from the 1990s show renewed interest in large-scale choral writing. The meticulous calligraphy of his scores and his preference for transparent structures and audible processes emphasize the aesthetic of expression through clarity rather than grandiose statement.

WORKS
(selective list)

Songs: Luna (G. Reynolds), S, 1981; Sirian Air (Parsons), female v, 1982; Luna (Reynolds), S, 4 gamelan players, 1982; 3 Arctic Songs (F. Nansen), Bar, pf, 1984; 2 Arctic Songs (Nansen), S, pf, 1985; 3 Songs from Skopelos (trad. Gk.), S, hurdy-gurdy, 1992; 2 Greek Choral Odes (Sophocles), SATB, 1997–8

Other vocal: Mindfulness of Breathing (Buddhaghosa), low male vv, 1969; Mindfulness Occupied with the Body (Buddhaghosa), 40 or more vv, perc, 1970; Expedition to the North Pole (Nansen), S, B, SATB, pf, 1988; Lamentations (Vulgate), SSAATTBB, ob, cl, bn, vn, va, vc, db, 1997; 2 Greek Choral Odes (Sophocles), SATB, 1997–8

Pf (solo unless otherwise stated): Piano Piece, 1962; Piano Piece, 1967; Piano Piece March, 1968; Variations, 1971; Rhythm Studies I and II, 2 pf, 1971; Rhythm Studies 3 and 4, 1973; Canon, pf 4 hands, 1973; Arctic Rag, 1974; Fourths and Fifths, 1977; 3 Pieces, pf 4 hands, 1980; Bagatelle, 1983; Arctic Instrumental Music, pf 4 hands, 1988; Skopelos 1–4, 1992; Triptych, 1993; 4 Oblique Pieces, 1996; Fourth Bagatelle, 1996; Jive and Jive 2, 1996; Fourth Bagatelle, 1996; 2 Canons, 1997; krapp music, pf, tape, 1999

Other chbr and inst: Highland Variations, str, qt, 1972; 6 Studies in Counterrhythm, 2 perc, 1974; Piece for 4 Woodblocks, 2 perc, 1974; Echo Piece, 2 perc, 1974; Pentatonic Music, vn/va, 1975; Canon in Proportional Tempi, 3 melody insts, 3 woodblocks, 1978; 4 Pieces, tpt, hn, trbn, 1980; Changes for Gamelan, 12 players, 1981; Changes for October Dance and Epilogue, piano accdn, 1983; Arctic Instrumental Music, 2 va, 2 eʰ-cl, mar, pf 4 hands, 1987; Kucinata, cl, perc, 1988; Nani mi marice, cl, perc, 1989; Barcarolle, fl, 1989; Fourths and Fifths, fl, 1990; Syzygy, ob, cl, 2 trbn, 1991; Kucinata and Nani mi marice, fl, perc, 1992;

Talea, vc, 1997; Apartment House Suite, cl, trbn, vn, vc, pf, perc, 1998; Apartment House Suite 2, 2 cl, 2 vn, 2 vc, hp, pf, perc, 1999

Computer-controlled elecs: Levels I–VIII, 1988–92; Tenebrio, 1995; Levels IX–XII (Cambridge Levels), 4-channel installation, 1996

Photocopied scores in *GB-Lmic*

Principal publishers: Experimental Music Catalogue, Forward Music Ltd, Frog Peak Music

WRITINGS

'Systems in Art and Music', *MT*, cxvii (1976), 815–18
'Echo Piece at Muddusjarvi', *Contact*, no.16 (1977), 8–10
'The Music of Howard Skempton', *Contact*, no.21 (1980), 12–16
'Howard Skempton: Chorales, Landscapes and Melodies', *Contact*, no.30 (1987), 16–29
'Das London Scratch Orchestra', *Positionen*, no.26 (1996), 8–12
'Bildende Kunst und Musik', *MusikTexte*, no.75 (1998), 66–7
'Expedition to the North Pole', *Pix*, 3 (2000), 112–23

BIBLIOGRAPHY

K. Potter: 'Some aspects of an experimental attitude: an Interview with Michael Parsons', *Contact*, no.8 (1974), 20–25
H. Ehrler: 'Tönende Experimente: der englische Komponist Michael Parsons', *MusikTexte*, no.75 (1998), 62–6

MICHAEL NEWMAN

Parsons, Robert (i) (*b* c1535; *d* Newark-upon-Trent, 25 Jan 1571/2). English composer. He is first documented in the Teller's Roll for 1560–1 (PRO E405/126, 1ᵛ, 10ᵛ), where payments by Parsons to Richard Bower, Master of the Children of the Chapel Royal, are recorded. This confirms that Parsons was involved at the Chapel and the court before his appointment as a Gentleman of the Chapel Royal on 17 October 1563. A connection with the choirboy plays is suggested by a number of his songs, and it is possible that he acted as 'usher' to the children.

On 30 May 1567 he was granted a Crown lease for 21 years on three rectories near Lincoln. We know that he was still alive in November 1571, when the annual tax certificate issued to court servants refers to his residence in Greenwich (PRO E111/293/10). His death is recorded in the Cheque Book of the Chapel Royal: 'Robt. Parsons was drowned at Newark uppon Trent the 25th of Januarie, and Wm. Bird sworne gentleman in his place at the first the 22d of Februarie followinge, Aᵒ 14ᵒ [1571/2, from] Lincolne'. The date of his death would seem to be confirmed by an entry in *Index to Intestates, Prerogative Court of Canterbury*, vol.2, 1572–80, 3: '1571/2 Feb 7 Robert Parsons, East Greenwich, Kent, to relict Helen Parson'.

The fine anthem *Deliver me from mine enemies* and the 'great' First Service, based on the 1549 Prayer Book text and surely written for the Chapel Royal, both feature in Barnard's *The First Book of Selected Church Musick* (RISM 1641⁵). Elizabeth I's Act of Uniformity prescribing the 1552 text applied only from 24 June 1559. As the musical style of the service is clearly Elizabethan, it can be dated from 1558–9. But as in the case of Byrd, Parsons's Latin settings are more impressive. Doe dates the alternating *Magnificat* to Mary's reign. Using canon, and contrasting full sections with more elaborate writing for reduced forces, this setting testifies to Parsons's technical virtuosity. It is known that Latin texts continued to be set during Elizabeth's reign, and the motets *O bone Jesu* and the fine *Ave Maria* date from the late 1560s. These are unusual pieces, the first incorporating various psalm texts punctuated by invocations. Doe poses the possibility that these 'paraliturgical' motets may relate to the oppressed Catholics, and that the sub-text in *Ave Maria* points to Mary Queen of Scots, who fled to England in 1568 and who was regarded as the true monarch of English recusants. Perhaps Parsons, like his successor, Byrd, was a Catholic.

Parsons made a major contribution to early Elizabethan instrumental repertory. The five-part In Nomine survives in many sources and must have been among the most widely performed. The technical problems set by *De la court* and *The Songe called Trumpetts* suggest that they were written for professional court musicians, with violinists very likely to be playing the upper parts.

Parsons was a composer of considerable standing and his music is characterized by a rich harmonic texture with extensive passing and suspended dissonance. The lack of clear modulation to related keys places him between the Edwardian and later Elizabethan composers. Robert Dow's eulogy, written in the 1580s (*Och* 987), suggests that he died at the height of his powers and at a relatively early age:

Qui tantus primo Parsone in flore fuisti,
Quantus in autumno in morere fores.

(Parsons, you who were so great in the springtime of life, How great you would have been in the autumn, had not death intervened.)

WORKS

Editions: *Robert Parsons: Latin Sacred Music*, ed. P. Doe, EECM, xl (1994) [D]
Elizabethan Consort Music: I, ed. P. Doe, MB, xliv (1979) [E]

SACRED

Ave Maria, 5vv; D 132
Credo quod Redemptor, 6vv; D 69
Domine quis habitabit, inc., 6vv; D 94
Iam Christus astra ascenderat, inc., 6vv; D 33
Libera me, Domine, 5vv; D 45
Magnificat, inc., 6/7vv; D 1
Magnus es Domine, 3vv (attrib. Taverner in bassus); D 141
O bone Jesu, 5/6vv; D 105
Peccantem me quotidie, inc., 5vv; D 60
Retribuo servo tuo, 5vv; D 75
First Service, F (Ven, TeD, Bs, Ky, Cr, Mag, Nunc), 4–7vv, 1641⁵; Nunc ed. in *Treasury of English Church Music*, ii (London, 1965)
Service of v parts for meanes (Ven, TeD, Bs, Ky, Cr), 5vv, *GB-DRc*, *Ob*, *Och*
Deliver me from mine enemies, 6vv, 1641⁵ (also wrongly attrib. Byrd, in *Lbl*, and White, in *US-NYp*); ed. P. Oboussier (Oxford, 1954)
Holy Lord God almighty, 5vv, *BEm*, *NYp*, *GB-DRc*, *Lbl*, *Llp*, *Ob*, *Y*

doubtful

Second Service for meanes in F (Ven, TeD, Bs, Mag, Nunc), inc., ?5vv, *Lbl*, *Lcm*
First Magnificat and Nunc dimittis in medio chori in d, inc., ?5vv, *Ob*

SECULAR VOCAL

A wofull heart, inc., *Ob*
Ah, alas, you salt sea gods (Abradad), S, 4 viols, *Lbl*, *Ob* (attrib. 'Mr. B'), *Och* (attrib. Farrant); ed. in MB, xxii (1967), 15
Enforc'd by love and fear, A, 4 viols; ed. in MB, xxii (1967), 9
In youthfull yeeres (R. Edwards), A, b lute, *IRL-Dtc*, *GB-Lbl*
Pandolpho 1: Pour down, you pow'rs divine, Ct, 4 viols, *Lbl*; Ct, b lute, *Ckc*, *Ob* (attrib. N. Strogers)
Pandolpho 2: No grief is like to mine, Ct, b lute, *Ckc*; ed. in MB, xxii (1967); lute version ed. P. Oboussier, *The Turpyn Book of Lute Songs* (London, 1981)

doubtful

What bredde the wofull fall, inc., A only extant, *Ob*
When I look back: A only extant, 4 viols, *Ob*; arr. lute, *Lbl*

INSTRUMENTAL

De la Court, 5 pts; E 56
In Nomine, 4 pts; E 32
In Nomine, 4 pts; E 33

In Nomine, 5 pts; E 106; kbd arr. by Byrd, ed. in MB, xxviii (1971), 12; lute arrs., *GB-Cu*, *Lbl* Add.29246, *IRL-Dm*
In Nomine, 7 pts (also wrongly attrib. Byrd); E 148
In Nomine, 7 pts; E 150
A Songe of Mr R. Parsons, 5 pts; E 62
Mr. Parsons his Songe or The Songe called Trumpetts (also called Lusti gallant and Cante cantate), 6 pts; E 136
O quam glorifica, 3 pts, *GB-Och*
Ut re me fa sol, 4 pts; E 20

For bibliography see PARSONS.

PHILIPPE OBOUSSIER

Parsons, Robert (ii) (*b* ?Colyton, Devon, 1596; *d* Exeter, July 1676). English composer, priest and singer. His family is well documented in Exeter and Devon records, but there is no evidence to connect him with any other composers bearing his surname. His will, drawn up on 2 December 1675, shows him to have been a man of some substance, for his goods and property were valued at over £2000 when he died in the following year. He was admitted to Exeter Cathedral as a lay vicar in 1621 and married Grace Irish, daughter of the custos, in 1624. He was appointed a priest-vicar in 1640, and was custos of the College of Vicars Choral during the Visitation of Bishop Ward in 1665. He was also rector of St Martin's, Exeter, from 1634, and deputy librarian of St John's Hospital, whose books were placed in the Lady Chapel of the cathedral in 1657.

Little of his music survives. Most extensive is the short Morning and Evening Service, a competent work, if rather archaic in style. The dates of the manuscripts in which most of Parsons's works are found suggest that he stopped composing about 1640. Attributions are generally made to 'Mr. Parsons de Exon' or 'Mr. Robert Parsons of Exeter', to distinguish him from the earlier composer of the same name.

WORKS
SACRED

Morning and Evening Service in D (TeD, Bs, Ky, Cr, Mag, Nunc), 4vv, *GB-Cp*, *DRc*
4 verse anthems: 3/5vv, viols, org, *DRc*, *LbL*, *Ob*; 4vv, inc., *Cp*, *DRc*, *Lbl*; 3/6vv, org, *DRc*, *LbL*, *Och*, *Y*, *US-NYp*; ?3/5vv, inc., *GB-Cpc*, *Lbl*, *Och*

For bibliography see PARSONS.

PHILIPPE OBOUSSIER

Parsons, William (*fl* 1545–63). English composer. His name appears in the register of vicars-choral at Wells in 1555. On four occasions between 1552 and 1560 payments to Parsons are noted in the *Communar's Paper Book*, suggesting that he was also employed as composer and copyist to the cathedral: 'Paid William Parsons, Feb 11 (1552), by order of the president and chapter, for divers songs and books by him made and to be made. 16s. 4d.' In 1553 he was paid 5s. for '15 books containing 3 masses and a primer' and in 1560, 20s. for 'making and pricking off certayne songes in Englisshe'. There are no later references to Parsons in the surviving records at Wells.

Little of his music remains and most is incomplete. He probably wrote the *Flatt Service* by 'Mr. Parsons of Wells', the location distinguishing him from Robert Parsons (ii) of Exeter, whose music features in the same source. The setting is in a note-for-note style, similar to that found in Tallis's Short Service of *c*1550. Two Latin motets survive. The Easter antiphon *Christus resurgens*, in two sections and based on the Sarum plainchant, is a typical example of the ritual Marian motet. *Anima*

Christi, for three voices, is only one section of a much longer motet for six voices.

William Parsons is generally credited with being the composer of 81 out of 141 settings in John Day's *The Whole Psalmes in Foure Parts* (RISM 1563⁸). As the major contributor he may have been involved in an editorial capacity.

WORKS

Anima Christi, 3vv, *GB-Lcm, Ob*
Anima mea liquefacta est (attrib. 'W.P.'), 3vv, *Lbl*
Christus resurgens, 5vv, *Ob*
Salve regina misericordia (attrib. 'W.P.'), 3vv, *Lbl*
Almighty God ('A Prayer for the Quene'), 4vv, 1563⁸
Come, Holy Ghost, 4vv, 1563⁸
In trouble and in thrall, 4vv, 1563⁸; ed. in *Treasury of English Church Music*, ii (London, 1965)
Lord, save us, inc., 5vv, *GB-SHR*
O Lord, turn not thy face ('The Lamentation of a Sinner'), 4vv, *Lbl*
Out of the deep, inc., *GL, US-NYp* (also incorrectly attrib. Tallis)
Preserve us, Lord ('A Prayer'), 4vv, 1563⁸
Remember not, O Lord, 4vv, *US-BEm, GB-GL, Lcm, WB*
Wherewithall shall a younge man, inc., 4vv, *Y*
81 settings in 1563⁸

doubtful

The Flatt Service in g ('Mr Parsons of Wells'), inc., ?5vv, *DRc*
Have mercy on us, Lord, 4vv, *Lbl* (MS insert in 3437.g.19)
Laye not up for yourself, 5vv, *Lbl, SHR*
Litany for trebles, inc., 5vv, *US-NYp*
O Lord Almighty, inc., ?5vv, *GB-SHR*
Remember not, O Lord, inc., 4vv, *WB*

For bibliography *see* PARSONS.

PHILIPPE OBOUSSIER

Part (i) (Fr. *voix*; Ger. *Stimme*; It. *voce*). The line or lines of music read by an individual performer or performing section in the realization of a musical work; the written music itself, hence 'the piano part', 'the first violin part', 'the english horn part', 'the soprano part' etc. For performing purposes, the parts of a composition are usually copied separately, and these copies are also called 'parts'. Thus, for example, in a symphonic work the players in the first violin section read the first violin part, which contains the music of no other parts of the composition (except cues that may facilitate the players' correct placing of their part in the ensemble); one therefore contrasts the parts of a musical work with its score, the form of the work in which all the parts are shown simultaneously.

WILLIAM DRABKIN/R

Part (ii). In polyphonic music, one of the individual musical lines that contribute to one or more elements of the music, for example two-part counterpoint, four-part harmony, six-part texture; to avoid confusion with the third meaning of 'part' given below, the word 'voice' is sometimes used instead, e.g. four-voice fugue. Certain forms or genres are often described by the number of parts or voices their polyphonic structure consistently maintains, for instance, two-part invention, three-voice chanson (chanson à 3). One frequently distinguishes the outer (highest and lowest) parts (Ger. *Aussensatz*) from the inner (middle) part or parts.

In early polyphony parts were named not according to vocal range or timbre, but on the basis of their function in the contrapuntal design, and part names therefore reflected the hierarchies of parts characteristic of various COUNTERPOINT theories. Such theories initially disussed techniques of taking a pre-existing melody and supplying an additional part: the earliest designations for these two elements are 'vox principalis' and 'vox organalis' (*see* ORGANUM, §1), or simply 'cantus' and 'organum'. In the 12th century the upper parts in mensural organum were given numerical names: after the cantus, the second, third and fourth parts above were referred to as 'duplum', 'triplum' and 'quadruplum'.

In the early motet the name tenor (*see* TENOR, §2) was given to the part bearing the pre-existent plainsong melody, and the texted duplum was called the 'motetus' (in three- and four-part motets the names 'triplum' and 'quadruplum' were maintained). In the 14th and 15th centuries 'tenor' referred to the main lower part which 'held up' the harmony, and the tenor was often paired with a CONTRATENOR; the principal upper part (usually undesignated in musical sources) was referred to as the 'cantus' or 'discantus'. A fourth part would be added to this discantus–tenor–contratenor framework; when this was functionally an additional contratenor, as was often the case in the 15th century, the terms 'contratenor altus' and 'contratenor bassus' ('high' and 'low' contratenors) were used to distinguish the two.

With the introduction of such names as 'contratenor bassus', part names began to take on registral connotations. By about 1500 the word 'bassus' was in use as a noun meaning the lowest polyphonic part. In the 16th century the names used in the commonest type of setting, in four parts, were 'superius', 'altus', 'tenor' and 'bassus' (these are the ancestors of the modern names soprano, alto, tenor and bass). Sometimes the lowest part was designated by the Greek *basis*, which referred to its 'fundamental' importance rather than to its lowness. For compositions in five or six parts, the names 'quinta vox' (quintus) and 'sexta vox' (sextus) were used; occasionally a fifth part was called *vagans* (Lat.: 'wandering'), which implies a variable range.

WILLIAM DRABKIN/R

Part (iii) (Fr. *partie*; Ger. *Teil*; It. *parte*; Lat. *pars*). The primary division of certain large-scale works (especially oratorios), equivalent to the act in theatrical works; in smaller forms, one of the sections of a work by which its form is defined, e.g. three-part song form; *prima pars*, *secunda pars* of a motet.

WILLIAM DRABKIN/R

Pärt, Arvo (*b* Paide, 11 Sept 1935). Estonian composer. He studied at the music middle school in Tallinn under Harri Otsa and Tormis and then at the Tallinn Conservatory under Eller, from whose class he graduated in 1963. While still a student he found work as a recording engineer with Estonian radio, and as a composer of film and theatre music. He continued to support himself with such work during much of his early career.

His earliest works, mostly for piano, are neo-classical in style. In 1962 his children's cantata *Meie aed* ('Our Garden') received joint first prize at the All-Union Young Composers' Competition in Moscow. At this time he was studying serial composition from the few scores and textbooks that had found their way into the Soviet Union; the first of his works to use serial technique was the orchestral *Nekrolog*. This path earned him official rebuke, though he nevertheless continued to apply serial procedures throughout the 1960s. *Perpetuum mobile* (1963) applies serial technique to pitch, duration and rhythm throughout, while the First Symphony (1963–4) explores canonic procedures and is deservedly subtitled 'Polyphonic'. Both works are related through the use of different versions of the same all-interval row. In 1964 Pärt revealed his growing interest in J.S. Bach, employing rows that incorporate the B–A–C–H motif and writing often in imitation of the Baroque style. The works *Pro et contra* and the Second Symphony (both 1966) also make significant use of collage and frequently set in opposition the perceived turmoil of Modernist dissonance against the calm order of tonal (neo-Baroque) consonance. These processes receive their most climactic treatment in *Credo* (1968), a pivotal work of Pärt's career; here the tonal world of Bach's C major prelude from book 1 of *Das wohltemperirte Clavier* is slowly distorted through application of a chain of 5ths used as a 12-note row. Ultimately, the tonal impression dominates, but this work provoked an official scandal – not for its musical language but for its avowal of Christianity.

After *Credo* Pärt reached an impasse both musically and professionally. For several years (from 1968) he concentrated on exploring tonal monody and simple two-part counterpoint in exercises inspired by his studies of early music and Gregorian chant. During this period he produced two works (*Laul armastatule* – subsequently withdrawn – and the Third Symphony) which reveal the strength of these preoccupations. It was only in 1976, however, that he began to compose fluidly again, this time using a tonal technique of his own creation which he calls 'tintinnabuli' (after the bell-like resemblance of notes in a triad). The first piece to be written in this new style was the short piano solo *Für Alina*.

A two-part homophonic texture forms the basis of tintinnabuli technique: a melodic voice moves mostly by step around a central pitch (often but not always the tonic), and the tintinnabuli voice sounds the notes of the tonic triad. The relationship between these two voices follows a predetermined scheme (which varies in detail from work to work) and is never haphazard. Furthermore, the entire structure of a tintinnabuli work is predetermined either by some numerical pattern or by the syntax and prosody of a chosen text. Very often these two ideals are combined.

Typically, the melodic voice part can be reduced to ascending or descending modes, to or from a central pitch. To this the tintinnabuli voice is fitted note by note (ex.1), either by providing the pitch in the triad that is nearest to the melodic voice pitch (1st position), or the pitch that is nearest but one (2nd position). The tintinna-buli pitches may be applied above or below the pitches of the melodic voice, or alternate between these (ex.2).

Ex.1

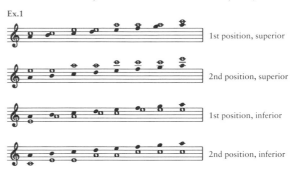

1st position, superior

2nd position, superior

1st position, inferior

2nd position, inferior

In 1976–7 Pärt laid the foundations of this new style and composed several of the works that would help to establish his international reputation – *Cantus in memoriam Benjamin Britten*, *Fratres*, *Summa* and *Tabula Rasa*. However, his position as a composer of overtly religious music in an austere and seemingly simple tonal style endeared him neither to the Soviet authorities nor to the academic establishment, and the development of his career as a composer inside the Soviet Union was continuously being frustrated. In 1980 he and his family emigrated, first to Vienna and then to Berlin. He took with him sketches of the *St John Passion*, which was completed in 1982 and has become the quintessential work of the tintinnabuli style. A strict, through-composed setting of the text, the Passion employs the tintinnabuli techniques described above but using a number of interconnected triads and pitch centres so that the whole work draws upon three sets of overlapping 5ths: D–A–E–B. The work lasts approximately 70 minutes, and comprises a short introduction (*exordium*) and conclusion flanking the main narrative section of the text. The Evangelist is represented by an SATB quartet and four instruments; the part of Christ is sung by a bass solo and that of Pilate by a tenor. Both solo voices are accompanied by the organ, as is the choir, who sing the remaining roles and also represent the turba. The words are set in a rhythmic scheme which employs three relative note values – short, medium and long – operating at three different speeds. Ex.3 shows the general scheme of the work and the relative range of the different voices. (Turba is here used for the choir's collective role. The tintinnabuli triad

Ex.2

alternating

Arvo Pärt, 1993

Ex.3

for each group is always fixed and is given in semibreves; a square white note denotes a pedal or drone pitch and the black note heads indicate the melodic scales employed. The underlying note value is shown in brackets.)

The majority of Pärt's works composed after 1980 are for chorus or small vocal ensemble; his choice of texts has ranged from Latin (which predominated at first) to German, Church Slavonic, Spanish, Italian and English. Among the larger works mention should be made of *Te Deum* which invokes – but does not in fact use – Gregorian chant; *Stabat mater*, in essence an extended piece of chamber music for double trio (three strings and three voices); *Miserere* which incorporates an earlier setting (here revised) of the *Dies irae* sequence; two *a cappella* choral works, the (Latin) *Magnificat* and the (German) Seven Magnificat Antiphons; and *Litany* (1994), the first work since the Third Symphony to employ something approaching a full orchestra; and *Kanon Pokajanen*, a large-scale *a cappella* setting of Russian Orthodox texts.

In later works, the underlying tintinnabuli concept has remained largely unchanged, though it has been subject to various technical refinements. The use of speech patterns to determine melodic contours and the combination of enharmonically related triads and chromatically inflected scales have enriched Pärt's musical vocabulary; later choral works have also shown a tendency to divide text and music more equally among vocal parts, creating a more fluid texture.

WORKS

VOCAL

Choral (acc.): Meie aed [Our Garden], op.3, children's chorus, orch, 1959; Maailma samm [Stride the World] (orat, E. Vetemaa), 1960, withdrawn; Credo, SATB, pf, orch, 1968; Laul armastatule [Song for the Beloved] (cant., S. Rustaveli), 2 solo vv, chorus, orch, 1973, withdrawn; An den Wassern zu Babel sassen wir und weinten . . . (Ps cxxxvii), SATB, pic, ob, cl, bn, hn, vn, va, vc, db, 1976–84, rev. 1994, arr. SATB, org; Missa syllabica, SATB/(S, A, T, B), org, 1977, rev. 1996, arr. unacc. SATB; De profundis (Ps cxxx), male chorus, perc ad lib, 1977–80; Cantate Domino (Ps xcv), SATB/(S, A, T, B), org, 1977, rev. 1996; St John Passion, T, B, vocal qt (SATB), SATB, ob, bn, vn, vc, org, 1982; Te Deum, 3 choruses, pf, str, tape, 1984–5, rev. 1992; Miserere, S, A, T, T, B,

SATB, 10 insts, org, 1989, rev. 1992; The Beatitudes, SATB/(S, A, T, B), org, 1990, rev. 1991; Beatus Petronius, 2 choruses (SATB), 2 org, 1990; Berliner Messe, SATB/(S, A, T, B), org, 1990–91, rev. 1997, arr. vv/chorus, str, 1991–2; Statuit ei dominus, 2 mixed choruses, 2 org, 1990; Litany 'Prayers of St John Chrysostom for Each Hour of the Day and Night', A/Ct, T, T, B, SATB, orch, 1994, rev. 1996

Choral (unacc.): Solfeggio, SATB, 1964–96; Summa, SATB/(S, A, T, B), 1977; 2 slawische Psalmen (Pss cxvii, cxxxi), 1984; 7 Magnificat Antiphons, SATB, 1988; Magnificat, SATB, 1989; Nynje k wam pribjegaju (Nun eile ich zu euch), SATB/solo vv, 1989, rev. 1997, withdrawn; Bogoróditse Dyévo [Mother of God and Virgin], SATB, 1990; Mementoi, SATB, 1994, rev. 1996, withdrawn; I am the True Vine, SATB, 1996; Dopo la vittoria, SATB, 1996–7; Kanon Pokajanen, SATB, 1997: Ode I, 1997, Ode III, 1997, Ode IV, 1997, Ode V, Ode VI - Kontakion - Ikos, 1997, Memento (Ode VII), 1994, 1997, Ode VIII, 1997, Ninye k vam (Ode IX), 1989, 1997, Gebet nach dem Kanon/Prayer after the Kanon, 1997; Tribute to Caesar (Bible: *Matthew*), SATB, 1997; The Woman with the Alabaster Box (*Matthew*), SATB, 1997; Triodion, SATB, 1998

Other vocal: Sarah was 90 Years Old, S, 2 T, perc, org, 1976, rev. 1990; Ein Wallfahrtslied (Ps cxxi), T/Bar, str qt, 1984, rev. 1996; Es sang vor langen Jahren (Motet für de la Motte) (C. von Brentano), A/Ct, vn, va, 1984; Stabat mater, S, A, T, str trio, 1985; And One of the Pharisees . . . (Bible: *Luke*), Ct/A, T, B, 1992

INSTRUMENTAL

Orch: Nekrolog, op.5, 1960; Perpetuum mobile, op.10, 1963; Sym. no.1 'Polyphonic', 1963–4; Pro et contra, conc., vc, orch, 1966; Sym. no.2, 1966; Sym. no.3, 1971; Wenn Bach Bienen gezüchtet hätte . . ., pf, wind qnt, str, 1976–84; Tabula Rasa, double conc., 2 vn/(vn, va), str, prep pf, 1977; Summa, str, 1991 [version of choral work]; Cantus in memoriam Benjamin Britten, str, bell, 1977; Psalom, str, 1995 [arr. of str qt]; Festina lente, str, hp ad lib, 1988; Mein Weg hat Gipfel und Wellentäler, 12 str, perc, 1990–98 [arr. of org work]; Silouans Song 'My soul yearns after the Lord', str, 1991; Fratres: vn, str, perc, 1992, trbn, str, perc, 1993 [both based on chbr work, 1977]; Trisagion, str, 1992, rev. 1994

Chbr: Collage über B-A-C-H, ob, hpd, pf, str, 1964; Quintettino, wind qnt, 1964; Musica sillabica, op.12, 12 insts, 1964, withdrawn; Concerto Piccolo über B-A-C-H, tpt, hpd, pf, str, 1964–94; Pari intervallo, 4 rec, 1976–80, arr. org; Arbos, 7 rec/8 rec, 3 triangles ad lib, 1977, arr. 4 tpt, 4 trbn, perc, 1986; Fratres, fl, ob, cl, bn, hn, str qt, db, perc, 1977, arr. vcs, 1983, arr. str qt, 1985, arr. wind octet, 1990, arr. str, perc, 1991; Fratres, vn, pf, 1980 [based on chbr work, 1977]; Summa, vn, 2 va, vc, 1990, arr. str qt, 1991 [versions of choral work]; Spiegel im Spiegel, va, pf, 1978, arr. vc, pf; Psalom, str qt, 1985–91, rev. 1993, arr. str orch; Darf ich . . ., vn, tubular bell (C♯) ad lib, str, 1995, rev. 1999

Kbd: Sonatine, op.1/1, pf, 1958; Sonatine, op.1/2, pf, 1959; Partita, op.2, pf, 1958; Diagramme, op.11, pf, 1964; Für Alina, pf, 1976; Trivium, org, 1976; Pari intervallo, org, 1980 [arr. of chbr work]; Variationen zur Gesundung von Arinuschka, pf, 1977; Annum per annum, org, 1980; Mein Weg hat Gipfel und Wellentäler, org, 1989, arr. str, perc; 4 leichte Tanzstücke 'musik für kindertheater', pf, 1956–7; Puzzle, org, 1997, withdrawn

Principal publishers: Universal Edition, Muzïka, Sikorski, Sovetsky kompozitor

BIBLIOGRAPHY

M. Vaitmaa: 'Arvo Pärt', *Kuus Eesti Tanase Muusika Loojat* [Six Estonian creators of modern music], ed. H. Tauk (Tallinn, 1970), 35–60

S. Bradshaw: 'Arvo Pärt', *Contact*, no.26 (1983), 25–8

L. Mattner: 'Arvo Pärt: Tabula rasa', *Melos*, xlvii/2 (1985), 82–99

M. Elste: 'An Interview with Arvo Pärt', *Fanfare*, xi/4 (1987–8), 337–41

W. Sandner: 'De stille Ton: zu den Orchesterwerken von Arvo Pärt', *Studien zur Instrumentalmusik: Lothar Hoffmann Erbrecht zum 60. Geburtstag*, ed. A. Bingmann and others (Tutzing, 1988), 509–13

J. McCarthy: 'An Interview with Arvo Pärt', *MT*, cxxx (1989), 130–33

R. Brotbeck and R. Wächter: 'Learning to Hear Silence: a Conversation with the Estonian Composer Arvo Pärt', *NZM*, Jg.151, no.3 (1990), 13–16

M. Vaitmaa: 'Tintinnabuli: elämänkatsomus, tyyli ja tekniikka, Arvo Pärtin sävellyksista' [Tintinnabuli – philosophy, style and technique: the compositions of Arvo Pärt], *Musiikkitiede*, ii/2 (1990), 61–82

D. Clarke: 'Parting Glances', *MT*, cxxxiv (1993), 680–84

J. Fisk: 'The New Simplicity; the Music of Górecki, Tavener and Pärt', *Hudson Review*, xlvii (1994), 394–412

F.M. Hess and C. Frink: 'Die tönende Stille der Glocken: Arvo Pärts Tintinnabuli Stil, Emanation oder Technik?', *NZM*, Jg.158, no.3 (1997), 38–41

P. Hillier: *Arvo Pärt* (Oxford, 1997)

H. de la Motte: 'Kreativität und musikalisches Handwerk', *Controlling Creative Processes in Music*, ed. R. Kopiez and W. Auhagen (New York, 1998)

G. Smith: 'Sources of Invention: Geoff Smith talks to Arvo Pärt', *MT*, cxl (1999)

PAUL D. HILLIER

Partart, Antonio. *See* PATART, ANTONIO.

Partbooks (Fr. *parties séparées*; Ger. *Stimmbücher*). Manuscripts or printed books that contain music for only a single voice (whether human or instrumental) of a composition, as opposed to those sources (scores, choirbooks, table-books etc.) that supply the complete music. The Shrewsbury fragment (Shrewsbury School, MS VI, *c*1430) is probably the lone survivor of a set of three partbooks (S. Rankin, *PRMA*, cii, 1975–6, pp.129–44), but otherwise the format seems to date from the late 15th century, becoming standard for the dissemination of ensemble music in the 16th and 17th centuries. Among the earliest surviving partbooks are the three known as the 'Glogauer Liederbuch' (*D-Bsb* Mus.ms.40098), which date from about 1480; the earliest printed partbooks extant are the four books comprising the *Motetti C* collection issued by the Venetian printer Ottaviano Petrucci in 1504 (see illustration). With the increasing use and availability of scores from the late 17th century onwards the role of partbooks was to some extent pre-empted, although the practice of performing from separate parts has survived for certain types of music (e.g. chamber and orchestral music) to the present day. This is partly because of the considerable expense involved in providing every performer with a score containing much material not strictly necessary for his individual need.

A basic set of early partbooks usually consisted of four books, although there might be as few as two or as many as ten. Although various designations are found, the most usual ones, in descending order of pitch, are: Cantus or Discantus or Superius or Medius, Altus or Contratenor, Tenor and Bassus. The fifth and sixth partbooks, if required, were called Quintus and Sextus respectively, whatever their pitch. Although these designations evolved in a period when the music in the partbooks was primarily (or even exclusively) vocal, the terms were retained in the 16th and 17th centuries for both vocal and instrumental sets of books. Additional partbooks to the four listed above, if for a voice in approximately the same range as one of them, may carry the qualification 'primus' or 'secundus' (e.g. 'Cantus primus', 'Bassus secundus'). English liturgical partbooks normally carried an additional qualification, 'Decani' or 'Cantoris', depending on the side of the choir for which they were intended. Slight variants of the above designations are sometimes found, as also are other names of limited application (e.g. 'Triplex', the highest of the original three voices of a motet, from which the word 'Treble' is indirectly derived).

The extent to which partbooks were used for performance in the Renaissance and early Baroque periods is still a matter of debate. Printed partbooks have never been cheap, and even manuscript books would have entailed considerable expense when a professional copyist was involved. Many sets of partbooks survive in such excellent condition that it seems unlikely that they were ever used in performance; in other examples the high incidence of undetected (or uncorrected) errors, some of which are in themselves relatively insignificant, strongly suggests that the books could not possibly have served as performing material. Furthermore, sets of English liturgical partbooks of the period 1550–1650 included only one boy's partbook for each side of the choir, although the full complement of boys would often have been between eight and twelve. In all these cases, at least, it is possible that sets of partbooks were master copies preserving a repertory of which only a fraction was performed, and that from memory. The loss of a partbook would have rendered the remaining members of the set useless for performance. Many surviving sets from the 16th century onwards lack at least one partbook, and in exceptional

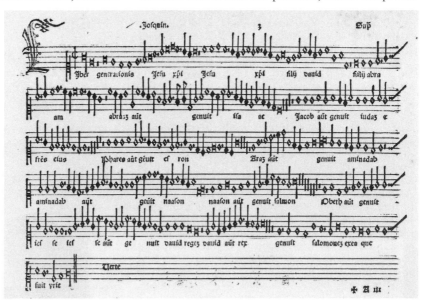

Opening of Josquin's motet 'Liber generationis Jesu Christi' from the superius partbook of Petrucci's 'Motetti C' (Venice, 1504)

cases only a single one survives from a set of as many as ten.

JOHN MOREHEN/RICHARD RASTALL

Partch, Harry (*b* Oakland, CA, 24 June 1901; *d* San Diego, 3 Sept 1974). American composer, theorist, instrument maker and performer. He dedicated most of his life to implementing an alternative to equal temperament, which he found incapable of the true consonance his ear and essentially tonal aesthetic demanded. He invented an approach to just intonation he called 'monophony'; realizing that traditional instruments and performers would be inimical to his system, he designed and constructed new and adapted instruments, developed notational systems, and trained performing groups wherever he was living and working. By the 1940s he had transformed a profound antipathy to the European concert tradition into the idea of 'corporeality', emphasizing a physical and communal quality in his music.

Growing up in the American Southwest, Partch had piano lessons and played well enough to accompany silent films in Albuquerque. By 1920 he had returned to California, where he spent the next 13 years as a proofreader, piano teacher and violist. During this period he began to research intonation, sparked by his discovery of Helmholtz's *On the Sensations of Tone* in 1923: he was particularly influenced by Helmholtz's preference for just intonation, and by the translator A.J. Ellis's discussions of 19th-century experimental keyboard instruments, most of them English. He experimented with just intonation on string instruments, and eventually developed the 'adapted viola' by attaching a cello fingerboard to a viola and indicating appropriate finger positions, an instrument he finished in 1930 in New Orleans during a one-year sojourn there. By 1928 he had completed the first draft of a theoretical treatise, *Exposition of Monophony*, which extended triadic consonance to include the 7th, 9th and 11th partials. He also posited a symmetrical 29-note-per-octave scale (more properly gamut) for the adapted viola. Acknowledging the text-setting principles of early opera, Gluck, Musorgsky, Debussy and the Schoenberg of *Pierrot lunaire*, his first 'monophonic' works featured an 'intoning' voice that used Sprechgesang in a non-expressionist manner and was accompanied (in 1930–33) by the adapted viola. From the outset he used pitches outside the chosen gamut, never restricting himself dogmatically.

Partch presented his first recitals in 1932–3. By 1933 his gamut had evolved to 37 tones (after flirtations with 39, 41 and even 55 tones), and the last draft of *Exposition of Monophony* was finished (though subsequently lost until the early 1980s). He went to New York, where he won a grant to do research in England (1934–5), where he studied the work and instruments he had read about in *On the Sensations of Tone*; he also met Yeats, Arnold Dolmetsch, Dulac, A.E. and (in Rapallo) Pound. In addition to the new adapted guitar, he had a first keyboard instrument (the Ptolemy) built in London; it was abandoned after being shipped to California. He returned to the USA in the spring of 1935; by June he had begun a nine-month transient existence in the western states, the subject of his socio-musical diary, *Bitter Music*. This narrative of life on the road and in Depression-era federal work camps mixes irony, nostalgia and homoeroticism with drawings and interpolations of voice-and-piano renderings of transcribed speech-music, along with more complex settings. Partch nearly published it in 1940, but later tried to destroy all copies; it resurfaced in the 1980s.

By 1941 Partch was in the Midwest, where he expanded his instrumentarium (adding notably two chordophones – the kithara and harmonic canon (see illustration) – and an adapted harmonium, the chromelodeon), set a final 43-tone gamut and began to compose for larger ensembles. During the early 1940s he concentrated on works with 'Americana' texts, including hitchhikers' inscriptions (*Barstow*), newsboys' cries (*San Francisco*) and a hobo's train journey (*US Highball*). He had his first semi-official university association at the University of Wisconsin in Madison from 1944 to 1947; his anti-academic views were reinforced by the music faculty's generally hostile attitude towards his music (see Wiecki).

He returned to California and composed smaller pieces suffused with the melancholy of his first 'monophonic' music. His treatise, *Genesis of a Music*, was finally published in 1949; in it the 'expanded tonality diamond', based on the consonant hexad and revealing an interlocking series of common tones, reached fruition. He worked with Ben Johnston (1950–51) and presented the original version of *King Oedipus* at Mills College, Oakland (1952). His Gate 5 Ensemble (1953–5) performed and recorded *Plectra and Percussion Dances* and the revised *Oedipus* for his private record label (later also called Gate 5). These large-ensemble works have a mixture of tragic solemnity and vigorous rhythm, the latter due to the new percussion instruments: the diamond marimba, bass marimba, marimba eroica, cloud-chamber bowls and spoils of war.

In 1956 he moved to Urbana, where Johnston taught at the University of Illinois, to produce *The Bewitched*, a mime drama featuring a coloratura witch leading a group of 'lost musicians' through a dramatic haze; the première (1957) barely survived the friction between composer and

Harry Partch with his Castor and Pollux (harmonic canon II, above) and gourd tree and cone gongs (below)

choreographer Alwin Nikolais (see Gilmore, 1995). In 1958 he collaborated with Madeline Tourtelot on three films (*Windsong*, *Music Studio* and the performing sections of *US Highball*), then returned to Urbana to compose and produce *Revelation in the Courthouse Park* and *Water! Water!*. Another major event at Urbana was his meeting Danlee Mitchell, a percussionist who became his foremost performer, conductor, assistant, amanuensis and friend for the rest of his life.

Partch returned to California for good in 1962. With the exception of a few smaller pieces, his music since the early 1950s had been truly 'corporeal': dramaturgically intense, musically eclectic, and with the instruments (now over 20) and their performers in full view of the audience. The culmination of his theatrical and musical theories was *Delusion of the Fury*, a two-act work in which he used two non-European myths: a Japanese noh tale of a pilgrim doing penance for a killing, and an African story of a quarrel judged by a deaf and near-sighted judge. The work has some of Partch's most beautiful as well as most invigorating music; the variety of textures allows the subtleties of his harmonies and instrumental timbres to come forward. (Tourtelot filmed the 1969 production.)

He was never in good health, and his physical and mental stability began to give way in the last decade of his life. He managed to compose the score for *The Dreamer that Remains*, an episodic but touching mesh of reminiscences and music in an earlier style. He died of a heart attack a year after the film's completion. By that time, his instrumentarium (excluding small hand instruments) comprised the following:

chordophones (plucked or struck with mallets unless otherwise stated): adapted guitars I and II, adapted viola (bowed), kithara I and II, surrogate kithara, harmonic canons I, II (Castor and Pollux) and III (blue rainbow), crychord, koto (a gift from Lou Harrison and not altered)

idiophones (all tuned unless otherwise stated): diamond marimba, quadrangularis reversum, bass marimba, marimba eroica and mbira bass dyad (all wood); boos I and II, eucal blossom (bamboo); gourd tree, cone gongs (metal); cloud-chamber bowls, mazda marimba (glass); zymo-xyl (glass and wood), spoils of war (metal and wood, includes whang gun)

aerophones: chromelodeons I and II (modified reed organs), bloboy (pipes and bellows)

As Johnston noted soon after Partch's death, the problems in preserving a music so intimately tied to its creator and a fragile and unique instrumentarium are immense. Dean Drummond, a Partch performer in the 1960s and the founder of the New York group Newband, has taken possession of the instruments that had belonged to him; they have been used in Partch performances and new works by Drummond and others, while copies have been made of some. They now reside at Montclair State University (New Jersey). But reproductions of the composer's tablature scores, transcriptions into expanded conventional notation, recordings and films remain the primary means by which to study and hear the music – a somewhat ironic situation given Partch's lifelong ambivalence about recording.

Nevertheless interest in Partch has increased greatly since his death, and overtaken the view held of him in life as quixotic or worse. His eclecticism, especially his unfettered use of traditional music from around the world, anticipated many post-serialist trends, and he has served as a model for developments in intonation, acoustic instruments and timbre, even as computer programs produce the fine tunings of his 'monophony'. He influenced the percussive motor-rhythm music of the minimalists of the 1960s and 70s, and his theatre works are precursors of numerous experiments since the mid-1950s. His life provides an example of curmudgeonly but humane courage.

WORKS
all in just intonation unless otherwise stated

Works in equal temperament, incl. pf conc., sym. poem, *c*50 songs, 1910s–20s, destroyed 1930

String Quartet, vn, 2 va, vc, *c*1925–7, lost

My Heart Keeps Beating Time, equal temperament (L. Yoell), 1v, pf, 1929, rev. 1935 (in *Bitter Music*)

17 Lyrics of Li Po (trans. S. Obata), 1v, adapted va, 1930–33; San Francisco, 9 Feb 1932

By the Rivers of Babylon (Ps cxxxvii), 1v, adapted va, 1931; San Francisco, 9 Feb 1932; final rev., 1v, vc, kithara II, chromelodeon, 1955

Potion Scene from Romeo and Juliet (W. Shakespeare), 1v, adapted va, 1931; San Francisco, 9 Feb 1932; rev. 1955, 1v, 2 S, vc, orig. insts

The Lord is My Shepherd (Ps xxiii), 1v, adapted va, 1932; San Francisco, 9 Feb 1932; rev., 1v, chromelodeon, kithara, 1943

Barstow: Eight Hitchhiker Inscriptions from a Highway Railing at Barstow, California, 1v, adapted gui, 1941; New York, 22 April 1944; final rev., 2 vv, orig. insts, 1968, facs. and transcr. ed. R. Kassel (Madison, forthcoming) [1st of 4 works in The Wayward cycle]

December, 1942: 3 Settings, 1v, adapted gui: Come Away, Death (Shakespeare: *Twelfth Night*), The Heron (Tsuryuki, trans. A. Waley), The Rose (E. Young); nos.2–3 rev., 1v, orig. insts, in Intrusions

Dark Brother (T. Wolfe: *God's Lonely Man*), Bar, adapted va, chromelodeon, kithara, Indian drum, 1942–3; Madison, WI, 3 May 1945; rev., addl bass mar, after 1951

Mad Scene from King Lear (Shakespeare), 1v, chromelodeon, kithara, *c*1942–3, lost

US Highball: a Musical Account of a Transcontinental Hobo Trip (Partch), vv, gui I, kithara, chromelodeon, 1943; New York, 22 April 1944; rev., 2 vv, large ens of orig. insts, 1955 [2nd of 4 works in The Wayward cycle]

San Francisco: a Setting of the Cries of Two Newsboys on a Foggy Night in the Twenties, 1v, adapted va, chromelodeon, kithara, 1943; 22 April 1944; rev., 1v, vc, kithara II, chromelodeon, 1955 [3rd of 4 works in The Wayward cycle]

The Letter: a Depression Message from a Hobo Friend, 1v, adapted gui, kithara, 1943; final rev., 1v, large ens of orig. insts, 1972 [4th of 4 works in The Wayward cycle]

2 Settings from Finnegans Wake (J. Joyce): Isobel, Annah the Allmaziful, S, double flageolet/2 fl, kithara, 1944; Madison, 7 March 1945

Y[ankee] D[oodle] Fantasy (Partch), S, tin fls, tin ob, flexatone, chromelodeon, 1944; New York, 22 April 1944

'I'm very happy to be able to tell you about this … ' (W. Ward, BBC transcr.), S, Bar, kithara, Indian drum, 1945; Madison, 3 May 1945; lost

Polyphonic Recidivism on a Japanese Theme (The Crane), equal temperament, SATB, 1945

Intrusions, incl. Study on Olympos' Pentatonic, Study on Archytas' Enharmonic, The Waterfall (Young), The Street (W. Motley: *Knock On Any Door*), Lover (G. Leite), Soldiers—War—Another War (G. Ungaretti, trans. W.F. Weaver), Vanity (Ungaretti, trans. Weaver), Cloud Chamber Music, 1v, orig. insts, last work with chorus, Indian deer-hoof rattle, 1946–50

Sonata Dementia (Partch), 1v, insts, 1949–50; rev. as Ring Around the Moon

The Wooden Bird (incid. music, W. Leach), 1v, insts, 1950, collab. B. Johnston; Charlottesville, VA, 10 Jan 1951

Plectra and Percussion Dances: Castor and Pollux, a Dance for the Twin Rhythms of Gemini, 1952, rev. 1968; Ring Around the Moon, a Dance Fantasm for Here and Now (Partch), 1952–3; Even Wild Horses, Dance Music for an Absent Drama (A. Rimbaud: *A Season in Hell*), vv, large ens of orig. insts, 1949–52; Berkeley, CA, 19 Nov 1953

King Oedipus (1, after W.B. Yeats, after Sophocles), 10 solo vv, chorus, large ens of orig. insts, 1951 (begun 1933); Oakland, CA, 14 March 1952; rev. as Oedipus (Partch and J. Churchill, after Sophocles), 1952–4; Oakland, 2 June 1954; final rev., 1967; New York, 24 April 1997

2 Settings from Lewis Carroll: O Frabjous Day!, The Mock Turtle Song, 1v, orig. insts, 1954; no.1, Mill Valley, CA, 13 Feb 1954

Ulysses at the Edge, vv, tpt, db, model skindrums, boo, 1955; final rev., vv, a sax, bar sax, orig. insts, 1961–2; added to The Wayward cycle

The Bewitched (dance satire, 1, Partch), S, chorus, dancers, large ens of orig. and trad. insts, 1955–6; Urbana, IL, 26 March 1957

Windsong (film score, dir. M. Tourtelot), large ens of orig. insts, 1958; rev. as Daphne of the Dunes (dance), 1967

Revelation in the Courthouse Park (1, after Euripides: Bacchae), 16 solo vv, 4 speakers, chorus, dancers, large ens of orig. and trad. insts, 1959–60; Urbana, 11 April 1961

Bless This Home (V. Prockelo), 1v, ob, orig. insts, 1961

Rotate the Body in all its Planes (ballad for gymnasts, based on Revelation in the Courthouse Park, Chorus 3), S, chorus, large ens of orig. and trad. insts, 1961; Urbana, 8 April 1962

Water! Water! (satirical 'intermission', 2, Partch), solo vv, choruses, large ens of orig. and trad. insts, 1961; Urbana, 9 March 1962

Jine the Calvary (trad.), 1v, orig. insts, 1963

Study, harmonic canon I and kithara I, 1963–4

And on the Seventh Day Petals Fell in Petaluma, large ens of orig. insts, 1963–6; Los Angeles, 8 May 1966

Delusion of the Fury: a Ritual of Dream and Delusion (2, Partch, after Jap. and African trad.), actors, chorus, dancers, large ens of orig. and small hand insts, 1965–6; Los Angeles, 9 Jan 1969

The Dreamer that Remains: a Study in Loving (film score, dir. S. Pouliot), vv, chorus, large ens of orig. insts, 1972; La Jolla, CA, 25 March 1973

recorded interviews in US-NHoh, US-U

WRITINGS

T. McGeary, ed.: Harry Partch: 'Bitter Music': Collected Journals, Essays, Introductions and Librettos (Urbana, IL, 1991) [BM]

Exposition of Monophony (c1927–1933), excerpts in Interval, iv/2 (1983), 6; iv/3 (1984), 8–9

'Ratio Keyboard Design, September 8, 1932', Interval, v/3 (1986–7), 14–17

Analysis and Transcription of California Indian Melodies from the Lummis Cylinder Collection at the Southwest Museum, Los Angeles (1933), excerpts in Kassel (1991)

'A New Instrument', MO, lviii (1934–5), 764–72

Bitter Music (1935–6, rev. 1940)

Preface to Patterns of Music (1940) [BM]

Review of J. Yasser: Theory of Evolving Tonality (c1942–4), Interval, iv/4 (1985), 5–6

'Show Horses in the Concert Ring', Circle, no.10 (1948), 43–50; repr. in Soundings [Los Angeles], no.1 (1972), 66–76 [BM]

Genesis of a Music: an Account of a Creative Work, its Roots and its Fulfillments (Madison, WI, 1949, enlarged 2/1974)

'The Rhythmic Motivations of Castor and Pollux and Even Wild Horses' (1952) [BM]

'Life in the Houses of Technituion' (c1953), Allos, ed. K. Gaburo (La Jolla, CA, 1980), 291–301

'Some New and Old Thoughts After and Before The Bewitched' (1955) [BM]

'Selected Correspondence to Lou Harrison 1955–1970', A Lou Harrison Reader (Santa Fe, 1987), 54–62

'The Ancient Magic', Music Journal, xvii/5 (1959), 16 only [BM]

Manual on the Maintenance and Repair of, and the Musical and Attitudinal Techniques for, Some Putative Musical Instruments (1963), Interval, i/2 (1978), 8–12; i/3 (1979), 7–14; i/4–5 (1979), 15–18, 31–4

'The University and the Creative Arts: Comment', Arts in Society, ii/3 (1963), 22 [BM]

Lecture, Source, i/1 (1967), 103 only [BM]

A Quarter-Saw Section of Motivations and Intonations (1967) [lecture] [excerpt, BM]

P. Blackburn, ed.: Enclosures, iii (St Paul, 1997) ['scrapbook' of Partch materials]

BIBLIOGRAPHY

GroveA (P. Earls)

S.N. Mayfield: 'Student Devises 29-Degree Octave Theory of Music', Times-Picayune [New Orleans] (16 Nov 1930)

J.M. Barbour: Review of Genesis of a Music, MQ, xxxvi (1950), 131–5

W. Leach: 'Music for Words Perhaps', Theatre Arts, xxxvii/1 (1953), 65–8

P.M. Schafer: 'New Records', Canadian Music Journal, iii/2 (1959), 55–8 [on US Highball]

M.J. Mandelbaum: Multiple Division of the Octave and the Tonal Resources of 19-Tone Temperament (Ann Arbor, 1961)

W. Mellers: 'An American Aboriginal', Tempo, no.64 (1963), 2–6

'Harry Isn't Kidding', Time (5 July 1963)

P. Earls: 'Harry Partch: Verses in Preparation for Delusion of the Fury', Yearbook, Inter-American Institute for Musical Research, iii (1967), 1–32

A. Woodbury: 'Harry Partch: Corporeality and Monophony', Source, i/2 (1967), 91–3

E. Friedman: 'Tonality in the Music of Harry Partch', Composer [Hamilton], ii/1 (1970), 17–24

A. Hiss: 'Hobo Concerto', New Yorker (7 Feb 1970)

S.L. Pouliot: 'Filming the Work of Harry Partch, or Get to Know Your Genius', American Cinematographer, lv (1974), 322–5, 333, 344–5

J. Cott: 'The Forgotten Visionary', Rolling Stone, no.158 (1974), 32–4, 36, 38

G. Kvistad and A. Otte: 'Harry Partch (1901–74): Genesis of a Music', Numus West, i/6 (1974), 29 only

B. Johnston: 'The Corporealism of Harry Partch', PNM, xiii/2 (1974–5), 85–97

W. Zimmerman: 'Ben Johnston on Harry Partch', Desert Plants: Conversations with 23 American Musicians (Vancouver, 1976), 347–71 [incl. score of The Letter]

R. Wernick: Review ofGenesis of a Music, JMT, xx (1976), 133–7

J. Fritsch: 'Die Tonalität des Harry Partch', Feedback Papers, no.14 (Cologne, 1977), 17; repr. in R. Brinkmann, ed.: Avantgarde Jazz Pop (Mainz, 1978), 31–41

G.A. Hackbarth: An Analysis of Harry Partch's 'Daphne of the Dunes' (Ann Arbor, 1979)

J. Smith: 'The Partch Reverberations: Notes on a Musical Rebel', San Diego Weekly Reader (25 Sept 1980); repr. in Interval, iii/1 (1981), 7–12; iii/2 (1981), 6–9, 12; Soundings, xii (1982), 46–59

M. Stahnke: 'Gedanken zu Harry Partch', Neuland: Ansätze zur Musik der Gegenwart, ii (1981–2), 242–51

W. Burt: The Music of Harry Partch (Melbourne, 1982)

P. Garland: Americas: Essays on American Musicians and Culture, 1973–80 (Santa Fe, 1982), 56–63, 267–90

W. Salmon: 'The Influence of Noh on Harry Partch's Delusion of the Fury', PNM, xxii/1–2 (1984), 233–45

K. Gaburo: 'In Search of The Bewitched: Concerning Physicality', The Percussionist, xxiii/3 (1985), 54–84

T. Kakinuma: The Musical Instruments of Harry Partch as an Apparatus of Production in Musical Theatre (diss., U. of California, 1989)

T. McGeary: The Music of Harry Partch (Brooklyn, 1991) [catalogue incl. bibliography (to 1974) and discography]

R. Kassel: 'Harry Partch in the Field', Musicworks, no.51 (1991), 6–15

W. Mellers: 'An Authentic American Composer', Times Literary Supplement (31 May 1991), 16 [on Bitter Music]

R.V. Wiecki: 'Relieving "12-Tone Paralysis": Harry Partch in Madison, Wisconsin, 1944–1947', American Music, ix/1 (1991), 43–66

R. Maltz: 'Microtonal Techniques in the Music of Harry Partch and Ben Johnston', Music Research Forum, vii (1992), 14–37

B. Gilmore: 'On Harry Partch's Seventeen Lyrics of Li Po', PNM, xxx/2 (1992), 22–58; erratum, PNM, xxxi/1 (1993), 332–3

J. Schneider: 'Bringing Back Barstow', Guitar Review, no.95 (1993), 1–13

'Remembering Harry Partch', 1/1 Just Intonation, viii/4 (1994) [Partch issue]

B. Gilmore: '"A Soul Tormented": Alwin Nikolais and Harry Partch's The Bewitched', MQ, lxxxi (1995), 80–107

R. Kassel: The Evolution of Harry Partch's Monophony (Ann Arbor, 1996)

B. Gilmore: Harry Partch: a Biography (New Haven, 1998)

RICHARD KASSEL

Part-crossing (Ger. *Stimmkreuzung, Stimmenkreuzung*). (1) In PART-WRITING, the rising of the lower of two parts above the higher or, conversely, the falling of the higher of two parts below the lower. It is sometimes used as a means of avoiding consecutive 5ths or octaves (ex.1) or

Ex.1
(a) avoidance of consecutive 5ths   (b) avoidance of consecutive octaves

other features regarded as bad part-writing. *See also* VOICE-EXCHANGE.

(2) The sounding of a voice or instrument higher (lower) than another which by nature lies above (below) it in register or tessitura, usually for emphasis or special effect; for instance, the tenors singing above the altos in a choir, or the cello in a string quartet taking the melodic line, accompanied below by the second violin and viola.

WILLIAM DRABKIN

Parte (i) (It.: 'part'). A vocal or instrumental part.

Parte (ii) (It.: 'part'). A section of a work or a variation (*see* PARTITA).

Partenio [Partenico], **Gian** [Giovanni] **Domenico** (*b* Spilimbergo, Friuli, before 1650; *d* Venice, 1701). Italian composer, singer, priest and probably a doctor of philosophy. He rose through the musical ranks at S Marco, Venice, beginning as a tenor in February 1666 and receiving an increase in salary from 80 to 100 ducats in January 1674. In July 1685 he succeeded Legrenzi as *vicemaestro di cappella* and in May 1692 succeeded Volpe as *maestro di cappella* after acting in this capacity since the previous December. He was energetic as *vicemaestro*, but his tenure as *maestro* coincided with a period of deteriorating musical standards. He served as *maestro di coro* at the Ospedale dei Mendicanti from 1685 to 1689. Enthusiastic comments in the Venetian monthly *Pallade Veneta* about his compositions for the Mendicanti indicate that many sacred vocal works (including settings of vespers psalms) are lost. In 1687 he was termed the 'Apollo of this virtuous Parnassus'. The singers who worked under his direction at the Mendicanti were highly praised for their ornamentation, intonation and naturalness (*franchezza*) of expression. His requiem mass may well have been composed for the funeral there in April 1688 of the Doge Marc'Antonio Giustiniani, when, according to *Pallade Veneta*, a 'chorus of innocent lambs … wept in song' in a mass concerted with stringed instruments. It is believed that Partenio was also closely associated with the Ospedale degli Incurabili.

Sporadically active as an opera composer, Partenio enjoyed the patronage of the Duchess Benedetta of Brunswick (in 1669), Counts Giovanni Antonio Mesmes (in 1673) and Carlo Vicenzo Iovanelli (in 1682), and Prince Eugenio of Savoy (in 1687). As a priest he served the parish church of S Martino, which he made the headquarters for the guild (*sovvegno*) of S Cecilia, a league of 100 performers and music teachers. Partenio was the society's principal founder, and Legrenzi and Volpe were among its chief supporters. Elaborate celebrations of the saint's feast on 22 November began in 1685 at S Martino.

Considering Partenio's importance at S Marco, surprisingly little of his music survives, a fact lending credence to Caffi's claim that many of his works once in the archives of the Ospedale dei Mendicanti were dispersed and then lost in the early 19th century. Although he was perhaps more important in his own day for his church music he is now remembered chiefly as an opera composer.

WORKS

OPERAS
all performed in Venice

Genserico (N. Beregan), SS Giovanni e Paolo, 1669, *I-Vnm* IV–427 (= 9951) [some music by A. Cesti]

Iphide greca (N. Minato), I Saloni, spr. 1671 (Act 1 by Partenio, 2 by D. Freschi, 3 by A. Sartorio), *Vnm* IV–421 (= 9945)

La costanza trionfante (C. Ivanovich), S Moisè, 1673 (lost)

Dionisio, overo La virtù trionfante del vitio (M. Noris), SS Giovanni e Paolo, 3 Jan 1681 (Act 1 by P. Franceschini), *Vc* (score), *Vqs* Cl.VIII, Cod.VI (arias)

Flavio Cuniberto (Noris), S Giovanni Grisostomo, 29 Nov 1681, revived Jan 1687, *Bc* (score), *MOe* (score and arias), *Vqs* Cl.VIII, Cod.VII (arias and duets)

OTHER WORKS

Missa pro defunctis, 4vv, *Vlevi*, *Vnm* IV–1178 (= 10995)

2 motets: Jesum Nazarenum, 3vv, *Vnm* IV–1822 (– 11645); Confitebor tibi, 2vv, 2 vn, bn, bc, *D-Bsb* 30, 257

A volume of motets, op.1, 2–3vv, published in Venice, lost

Cantata, Il fervido meriggio, S, bc, without text, *Kl*

BIBLIOGRAPHY

CaffiS

Charter of the St Cecilia Society (1687, *I-Vnm* VII–2447 [= 10056]), f.3

C. Sartori: 'Un catalogo di Giuseppe Sala del 1715', *FAM*, xiii (1966), 112–16

G. Ellero, J. Scarpa and M.C. Paolucci, eds.: *Arte e musica all'Ospedaletto: schede d'archivio sull'attività musicale degli ospedali dei Derelitti e dei Mendicanti di Venezia (sec. XVI–XVIII)* (Venice, 1978)

E. Selfridge-Field: *Pallade Veneta: Writings on Music in Venetian Society, 1650–1750* (Venice, 1985)

G. Pressacco: 'Legrenzi, i Savorgnan, e la Furlana', *Giovanni Legrenzi e la Cappella ducale di San Marco: Venice and Clusone 1990*, 133–84

N. Dubowy: 'Partenios Flavio', *Recercare X* (1998), 313–43

ELEANOR SELFRIDGE-FIELD

Partheneia [partheneusis, parthenia]. Dancing chorus of maidens. The maiden chorus is attested from the earliest days of ancient Greek musical culture. Reference is made to a dancing chorus of maidens and young men in the *Iliad* (xviii.590–606), and the *Homeric Hymn to Apollo* (156–64) refers to a chorus of maidens at Delos, who skilfully sang hymns to Apollo, Leto and Artemis. Scenes of dancing women appear on numerous vases, sometimes playing the crotala and dancing alone, at other times holding hands and dancing as a chorus. Pseudo-Plutarch (*On Music*, 1136f) referred specifically to *partheneia* composed by ALCMAN, PINDAR, Simonides and BACCHYLIDES. An extended excerpt from such a composition by Alcman is preserved in *PLouvre E3320* (1st century CE), running to more than 100 lines, organized in general in 14-line strophes. The text is rather fragmented until line 35, after which it is fairly well preserved until line 101. Although the text tends towards a style more intimate and personal than that of the other musical types, it does contain a few specific references to its musical nature. The chorus consisted of ten maidens led by an 'illustrious chorus-leader' (*ha klenna choragos*, 44), who is given the epithet *Hagēsichora* (53). Later, the poet introduced graceful similes to describe *Hagēsichora*'s role. Pseudo-Plutarch remarked that Alcman wrote Dorian *partheneia*, and although the context of the passage may lead to the assumption that he was referring to the *tonos*, he carefully distinguished between *Dōria partheneia*, a purely generic usage, and *Dōriou tropou* or *en tēi Dōristi*, which are specific references to musical modes.

A few fragments survive from the two books of *partheneia* composed by Pindar. Employing some of the same images encountered in the Homeric hymn and the Alcman fragment, the first antistrophe and epode and the second strophe of frag.104d refer additionally to the accompaniment of the aulos and the practice of carrying laurel branches in the dance. It would appear from this passage that the *partheneia* made use of vivid onomatopoeia. In the lines describing the aulos's sound and the Zephyr wind, for example, the poet stresses the long, open vowel omega (*auliskōn hupo lōtinōn*) and diphthongs based on alpha (*auliskōn, aoidais* and *aipsēras*), as well as the whistling sounds of the sigma and the zeta (*Zephurou te sigazei pnoas aipsēras*). The presence of the laurel branches indicates that frag.104d must come from the *daphnēphorika*, a subcategory of the *partheneia* dedicated to Apollo Ismenios and Chalazios held every ninth year in Boeotia. Proclus's *Useful Knowledge* provides a detailed description of the participants in the procession who carry a special branch (*kōppō*) decorated with brass spheres and garlands representing the sun, the moon, and other heavenly bodies, while the maiden chorus follows, holding out branches of olive in supplication and singing a hymn (cf Pollux, *Onomasticon*, iv.53).

The term was used much later as the title of the collection of keyboard music presented to Princess Elizabeth and Prince Frederick on the occasion of their marriage (1613): *Parthenia or the Maydenhead of the First Musicke that ever was printed for the Virginalls*, a whimsical reference both to the newness of the venture and the wedding; it reappeared in the title of its companion volume, *Parthenia In-Violata* (*c*1624), which has a part for bass viol.

BIBLIOGRAPHY

J. Sandys, ed. and trans.: *The Odes of Pindar, Including the Principal Fragments* (London and Cambridge, MA, 1915, 3/1937/R)

D.L. Page: *Alcman: The Partheneion* (Oxford, 1951/R)

B. Snell ed.: *Pindari carmina cum fragmentis*, pts i–ii (Leipzig, 1953, rev. 5/1971–5 by H. Maehler)

L. Lawler: *Dance in Ancient Greece* (Middletown, CT, 1964), 102–4

G. Prudhommeau: *La danse grecque antique* (Paris, 1965)

J.W. Fitton: 'Greek Dance', *Classical Quarterly*, new ser., xxiii (1973), 254–74

A.J. Neubecker: *Altgriechische Musik* (Darmstadt, 1977), 50–51

T.J. Mathiesen: *Apollo's Lyre: Greek Music and Music Theory in Antiquity and the Middle Ages* (Lincoln, NE, 1999), 83–8

THOMAS J. MATHIESEN

Parthia [parthie]. *See* PARTIE (i) and PARTITA.

Parthian Empire. Ancient state to the east of the Roman Empire, extending at the height of its power from Mesopotamia to the Indus, and independent from about 250 BCE until its overthrow by the Persians in 224 CE. Texts and pictorial representations illuminate the prominent role of minstrels (*gōsān* in the Parthian language) in the Parthian Empire and the subject of their songs is clear from a fragment of text written a few centuries after the fall of the empire, when the language was still spoken: 'like a *gōsān*, who proclaims the worthiness of kings and heroes of old' (Boyce, 11). The Greek writer Strabo (*c*64 BCE – 19 CE) noted that Parthians taught their young men songs about 'the deeds both of gods and of the noblest men' (*Geographica*, xv.3.18) and according to Plutarch (*c*46 – *c*120 CE) the *gōsān* praised Parthian heroes and ridiculed the Romans with equal gusto (*Crassus*, xxxii.3). The Parthian minstrels influenced the Armenians, whose courtly *gusanner* sang heroic tales to the accompaniment of drums, pipes, lyres and trumpets (see Boyce, 13–14). Parthian songs probably continued to be performed, at least in the north-eastern parts of greater Iran, long after the Empire had ceased and by being absorbed into the Iranian national epic, *Šāhnāme*, collected by Firdausi in about 1000.

To the bewilderment of the Romans, the Parthian army used large drums (Gk. *rhoptra*) to prepare for battle: 'they had rightly judged that, of all the senses, hearing is the one most apt to confound the soul, soonest rouses its emotions and most effectively unseats the judgement' (Plutarch, *Crassus*, xxiii.7). Many of the instruments mentioned in the surviving texts are also depicted in Parthian art, and the majority appear to have been patterned on Hellenistic models known in Greece, Rome and Egypt. The most magnificent depictions are those carved on ivory drinking horns (Gk. *rhuta*) of the 2nd century BCE found at the ancient Parthian capital of Nisa (modern Nessa, near Ashkhabad in Turkmenistan; see Colledge, fig.2 and Karomatov, 54–9) but probably made in Bactria (Boardman, 90). The carvings show auloi, kitharai and syrinxes played at Dionysian dances, ritual processions, and sacrificial offerings as well as at theatrical performances.

Musicians are also commonly shown on terracotta plaques, one of which, for example, portrays a female harp player (Colledge, pl.20d). Similar plaques from Babylon also depict harps, lutes, tambourines, syrinxes, lyres and clappers (Karvonen-Kannas, nos.277–336). Several bronze statuettes from Dura-Europus on the Euphrates (Qal'at as Sāliḥīyah, Syria) show a double aulos and unusually long panpipes; and bone tablets dating from the 1st or 2nd centuries CE and originating in Olbia, Ukraine, depict female dancers, musicians and acrobats. A temple at Hatra (Al Ḥaḍr, Iraq), dedicated to the Sun, the Moon and the goddess Atargatis, has a stone frieze dating from the 2nd century CE that shows a wedding procession. Among the celebrants is a singer surrounded by musicians playing tambourines, a 13-pipe syrinx, a transverse flute, double and single reed pipes and a trumpet (see Rashid, 156–65).

Christianity and with it the music of the East Syrian liturgy penetrated the area beyond the upper Tigris, via Edessa (now Urfa, Turkey) in Roman Syria, probably in the first half of the 2nd century (*see* SYRIAN CHURCH MUSIC). It coexisted with pagan minstrel traditions.

BIBLIOGRAPHY

M.I. Rostovtzeff and P.V.C. Baur, eds.: *The Excavations at Dura-Europos*, ix: *Preliminary Report of the Ninth Season of Work, 1935–1936*, i (New Haven, 1944)

M. Boyce: 'The Parthian Gōsān and Iranian Minstrel Tradition', *Journal of the Royal Asiatic Society of Great Britain and Ireland* (1957), 10–45

M.A.R. Colledge: *The Parthians* (New York, 1967)

S.A. Rashid: *Mesopotamien*, Musikgeschichte in Bildern, ii/2 (Leipzig, 1984)

F.M. Karomatov, V.A. Meskeris and T.S. Vyzgo: *Mittelasien*, Musikgeschichte in Bildern, ii/9 (Leipzig, 1987)

J. Boardman: *The Diffusion of Classical Art in Antiquity* (London, 1994)

K. Karvonen-Kannas: *The Seleucid and Parthian Terracotta Figurines from Babylon in the Iraq Museum, the British Museum and the Louvre* (Florence, 1995)

BO LAWERGREN

Partia. See PARTIE (i) and PARTITA.

Partial. One of the component vibrations at a particular frequency in a complex mixture. It need not be harmonic. The fundamental and all overtones may be described as partials; in this case, the fundamental is the first partial, the first overtone the second partial, and so on. *See also* SOUND, §5.

MURRAY CAMPBELL

Partial signature. A 'key' signature, usually a ♭, that is given in some but not all the voices of a polyphonic composition. Such signatures occur in 13th-century sources and were very common throughout the 14th and 15th centuries. For discussion of their significance *see* MUSICA FICTA, §III, (ii). □

Particella (It.; Ger. *Particell*). A SKETCH or draft in compressed short score used by some composers as part of their standard composition procedure.

Partie (i) [parthia, parthie, partia] (Ger., Fr.: 'part'). A term for a suite or other multi-movement genre in the 17th and 18th centuries (*see* PARTITA).

Partie (ii) (Fr.). (1) A term used, synonymously with 'mouvement', for a movement ('sonate en quatre parties').
(2) Voice part ('fugue à trois parties').

Parties séparées (Fr.). *See* PARTBOOKS.

Partimen. *See* JEU-PARTI and TENSO.

Partimento (It.: 'division'). A term used fairly frequently in the late 18th and early 19th centuries to denote exercises in figured-bass playing, not so much as accompaniments to a solo instrument as self-contained pieces. Composers using this term were very often Neapolitan or Milanese, though the significance of this is unknown. The word may or may not refer to the 17th century practice of divisions, i.e. performing variations on a repeating (figured) bass; more likely it reflects the common Italian practice *c*1700 of writing bass lines for keyboard players to work into fully-fledged pieces. The definition is attested to as early as 1634 by G.F. Cavalliere in *Il scolaro principiante di musica* (Naples). Examples are common in MSS, e.g. the 'Arpeggi per cembalo' exercises in *GB-Lbl* Add.14244 (?A. Scarlatti), the organ 'Versetti … per rispondere al coro' in *Lbl* Add.31501 (?B. Pasquini), and the complete solo and even duet figured-bass sonatas for harpsichord by Pasquini in *Lbl* Add.31501. Fugues were often intended by composers as realizations of their carefully planned figured basses (Keller, Handel, Pasquini); other instruments too were expected thus to develop their basses (Carulli's guitar tutors). Typical titles of the books devoted to such harmonic and contrapuntal instruction are F. Fenaroli: *Regole musicale per i principianti di cembalo* (Naples, 1775) and *Partimenti ossia basso* (Rome, *c*1800/*R*), G. Tritto: *Partimenti e regole generali* (Milan, 1816), and C. Cotumacci: *Regole dell'accompagnamento, e partimenti* (MS, Naples, listed by C.F. Becker: *Systematisch-chronologische Darstellung der musikalischen Literatur von der frühesten bis auf die neuste Zeit*, Leipzig,

1836–9/*R*). Other composers of *partimenti* include N. Sala and N. Zingarelli.

BIBLIOGRAPHY
A. Choron: *Principes de composition des écoles d'Italie* (Paris, 1808)
M. Panni: *Dechiffrage: Twelve Partimenti for One or More Performers* (London and New York, 1981)
R. Cafiero: 'La didattica del partimento a Napoli fra settecento e ottocento: note sulla fortuna delle "Regole" di Carlo Cotumacci', *Gli affetti convenienti all'idee: studi sulla musica vocale italiana*, ed. M. Caraci Vela, R. Cafiero and A. Romagnoli (Naples, 1993), 549–79

PETER WILLIAMS/ROSA CAFIERO

Partita [parte] (It.; Ger. *Partie, Parthie, Partia, Parthia*; Lat. *pars*). A term used at different times for a variation, a piece, a set of VARIATIONS and a SUITE or other multi-movement genres. Perhaps the earliest use of the term was in Vincenzo Galilei's manuscript *Libro d'intavolatura di liuto, nel quale si contengono i passamezzi, le romanesche, i saltarelli, et le gagliarde*, written in 1584 and probably composed over the preceding 20 years (Torrefranca), containing a *Romanesca undecima con cento parti*, a *Passemezzo sesto con* [5] *parti*, and *Aria del Gazzella con XII parti*. Shortly afterwards Prospero Luzi published a dance manual entitled *Opera bellissima nella quale si contengono molte partite et passaggi di gagliarda* (1589); to what extent 'partite' was consciously derived from 'parti' is unknown, but both seem to be equivalent in meaning to *mutanze* or *modi*, i.e. variations or elaborations on the bass of a traditional tune. 'Partite' or 'partite diversi' continued to be used by the Italians in this sense, though less and less frequently, throughout the 17th century; examples of pieces called 'partite sopra', *Ruggiero, zefiro, fidele, monica, folia*, then *ciaccona* and *passacagli* and finally miscellaneous tunes, exist by Mayone, Trabaci, Frescobaldi, Michelangelo Rossi, Gregorio Strozzi and Alessandro Scarlatti.

It may have been Frescobaldi's pupil Froberger who first used 'partite' in the sense of 'pieces' in his *Libro secondo di toccate … gigue et altre partite* (autograph, 1649, *A-Wn*). The older Italian meaning survived, with acknowledgment by Spiridion, in an appendix called 'Adjunctum Frescobaldicum' to the fourth part of his *Nova instructio* (1675), containing *Partite sopra passacagli*, by J.A. Reincken (*Partite diverse sopra … 'La Meyerin'*) and by Bach (*partite diverse* on various chorales), while the newer one reappeared with the first publications of Froberger's works in 1693.

In 1680 Biber divided the pieces of his *Mensa sonora* into six suites which he labelled *Pars I, Pars II* etc. He may have thought of 'pars' as a term for a group of pieces or simply as a division of a collection, but it was the former meaning that was taken up by Kuhnau as a designation for a suite in his *Neuer Clavier-Übung … bestehend in sieben Partien* (1689). Johann Krieger followed in 1697 with a collection of suites whose title was given in German and Italian: *Sechs musicalische Partien, Sei partite musicali*, thus establishing a new meaning for 'partita' by a process of folk etymology. Krieger was echoed by J.A. Schmierer the next year: *Zodiaci musici in XII partitas balleticas … Das ist, Dess in zwölff balletischen Parthyen … Himmel-Creyses* (1698). Both 'partita' in its new meaning of suite and 'partie' and its variants thus appear to be the arbitrary constructions of late 17th-century German composers. Both terms were used in their various meanings by Bach.

'Partita' as a term for variation died out in the early 18th century, but it retained its meaning of suite, though often restricted in its number of movements. The orchestral partita in particular was popular in western Austria (a large collection survives at Stift Lambach) and in Salzburg, where partitas were widely composed between about 1720 and 1750. Thereafter the genre apparently gave way to the symphony (the last known example of a Salzburg orchestral partita, by Michael Haydn, dates from 1770; its three movements are now better known as parts of the symphony Perger 12). Ferdinand Seidl's sole extant *Parthia* (A-LA, 239), possibly composed in the 1740s, is typical: each of its four movements (Intrada, Menuet, Intermezzo, Finale) is moderate or fast in tempo and largely based on dances; like most partitas of the time it is scored for two violins, two trumpets, timpani and basso (lacking violas, which are also missing from Eberlin's lost partita in G major and Leopold Mozart's only extant work of the type; see Eisen, 1994). Some partitas, however, including a considerable number of works from the Viennese orbit, were conceived one-to-a-part; by and large these represent a subset of the divertimento, which at the time was a catch-all term for soloistic ensemble music (Webster, 1974). The term largely disappeared well before the end of the century, except in the case of outdoor wind music, where *Feldpartita* or *Feldpartye* continued to be used. Schilling's *Encyclopädie* (1840) says that *Parthie*, *Parthia* and *Partita* all have the same meaning, that of the successor to the suite, in which prestos, allegros and the like are interpolated among the dances.

BIBLIOGRAPHY

ApelG; MGG2 (T. Schipperges)

F. Torrefranca: 'Origine e significato di repicco, partita, ricercare, sprezzatura', *IMSCR V: Utrecht 1952*, 404–14

F. Torrefranca: 'Documenti definitivi sulla partita', *GfMKB: Bamberg 1953*, 143–8

J. Webster: 'Towards a History of Viennese Chamber Music in the Early Classical Period', *JAMS*, xxvii (1974), 212–47

Gesellschaftsgebundene instrumentale Unterhaltungsmusik des 18. Jahrhunderts: Eichstätt 1988

T. Schipperges: 'Partita' (1993), *HMT*

C. Eisen: Introduction to *Orchestral Music in Salzburg: 1750–1780*, RRMCE, xl (1994)

DAVID FULLER/CLIFF EISEN

Partition (Fr.; Ger. *Partitur*). *See* SCORE.

Partitura (It., Lat.). In its strictest sense *partitura* means simply 'score', and as such is the equivalent of *partition* (Fr.), *Partitur* (Ger.) etc. It is more specifically used, however, to describe sources of keyboard music of the 16th to the 18th centuries notated in open score (usually four staves), as opposed to those in keyboard score (on two staves) or one of the types of keyboard tablature. In many of the earliest uses of this notation, most of which are Italian, the word 'partitura' and its most common derivatives (*spartiti*, *partite* etc.), were used on title-pages to describe music that had originally been written for voices or other instruments but had later been 'scored' for solo instrumental performance, usually on a keyboard instrument. Some scholars consider that early *partiturae* of this nature may have been issued for study purposes rather than for performance, although the two functions are not mutually exclusive. The use of the term 'partitura' was later extended to include collections of works conceived originally for keyboard instruments. The earliest surviving source in *partitura* notation is Rocco Rodio's

Libro di ricercate a quattro voci (Naples, 1575). Owing to its particular suitability for contrapuntal keyboard music the *partitura* became increasingly popular, and its use spread to other countries including Germany (where only tablature had previously been used for keyboard music) and Portugal. The earliest uses of the *partitura* in these countries include Samuel Scheidt's *Tabulatura nova* (Hamburg, 1624) and Manuel Rodrigues Coelho's *Flores de musica pera o instrumento de tecla & harpa* (Lisbon, 1620/R). The *partitura* was used for keyboard music as late as the 18th century, one of the last but most important instances being for J.S. Bach's *Art of Fugue* (published 1751). In some German publications this form of notation was loosely described as tablature (*Tabulatura*, *Tabulaturbuch* etc.).

See also INTAVOLATURA; ORGAN SCORE; and TABLATURE.

BIBLIOGRAPHY

WolfH

W. Apel: *The Notation of Polyphonic Music, 900–1600* (Cambridge, MA, 1942, 5/1961; Ger. trans., rev., 1970)

JOHN MOREHEN

Partiturophon. An electronic keyboard instrument constructed by JÖRG MAGER, assisted by Dr W. Janovsky, in Darmstadt in 1930–31, in versions with three and four monophonic manuals plus pedalboard.

Part names. *See* PART (ii).

Parton, Dolly (Rebecca) (*b* 19 Jan 1946, Pigeon Forge, TN). American country singer-songwriter. She was one of 12 children born to a sharecropper in a one-room cabin in the Tennessee Mountains. She learnt her first songs from her extended family and from the church. At an early age she began writing her own songs and playing a home-made guitar. By the time she was ten she was starring regularly on Cas Walker's 'Farm and Home Hour' television programme, earning $20 a week. In 1960 she made her first record and in 1964, having been the first in her family to graduate from high school, she moved to Nashville. By 1967 she had a recording contract and a spot on the long-running Porter Waggoner television show and was soon a regular on the famed 'Grand Ole Opry'. Her popularity increased consistently in the 1970s, with a number of crossover hits, including the title tracks from *Jolene* (RCA, 1974) and *Here you come again* (RCA, 1977), and a syndicated television show. Innumerable awards and increasing international success afforded her the opportunity to star with Jane Fonda in the Hollywood film *9 to 5*. Parton's title song (RCA, 1980) was a transatlantic hit and was nominated for an Academy Award. Since then she has starred in several other successful films. She has collaborated with a number of musicians, including Kenny Rogers and Smokey Robinson and on the bestselling album *Trio* (1987) with Linda Ronstadt and Emmylou Harris.

Parton is country music's most celebrated female practitioner and certainly its most successful. Her outrageous appearance is misleading, belying considerable talent. Her silvery voice with its affecting vibrato is most adaptable and is most striking on her own songs, which display a genuine gift for narrative verse and a sparkling wit. Like Loretta Lynn, Parton has often addressed the inequalities of the woman's lot, for example *Just because I'm a woman* (RCA, 1968). She has received some criticism from Nashville purists for her relocation to the mainstream, but in reality she has helped to broaden the

Dolly Parton

audience for country music and enabled other Nashville performers to expand their careers. She has paid tribute to her roots in such songs as 'Coat of Many Colors' (*Coat of many Colors*, 1974) and 'To Daddy'.

BIBLIOGRAPHY

C. Flippo: 'Dolly Parton', *Rolling Stone* (25 Aug 1977); repr. in *The Best of Rolling Stone*, ed. R. Love (London, 1994)

P. Carr, ed.: *The Illustrated History of Country Music* (New York, 1979)

M.A. Bufwack and R.K. Oermann: *Finding her Voice: the Saga of Women in Country Music* (New York, 1993)

D. Parton: *Dolly: My Life and other Unfinished Business* (London, 1994)

A. Vaughan: 'The Entertainer', *Country Music International*, i/6 (1994–5), 42–7

W. Parton: *Smoky Mountain Memories: Stories from the Parton Family* (Nashville, 1996)

M. Blake: 'Living Doll', *Country Music International*, iii/10 (1996–7), 50–53

LIZ THOMSON

Partos, Oedoen [Ödön] (*b* Budapest, 1 Oct 1907; *d* Tel-Aviv, 6 July 1977). Israeli composer, string player and teacher of Hungarian origin. Born to an assimilated Jewish upper middle class family, he was a child prodigy and studied the violin with Ormandy. Hubay heard him play the violin at the age of eight and took him as a pupil at the Budapest Academy of Music, where he also studied composition with Kodály. After graduating from the academy in 1924, he was leader of the Lucerne Stadtsorchester (1924–6) and the Budapest Konzertorchester (1926–7). In 1927 he moved to Germany, working as a soloist, and in 1933 he became first violinist of the Jewish Cultural Centre. At the end of that year he returned to

Hungary, moving then to Baku to teach the violin and composition at the conservatory (1935) and returning to Budapest as leader of the Konzertorchester (1937). During these years as a soloist in Europe he was very active in contemporary music and gave the premières of several works written for him, including Kadosa's Violin Concerto and Suite for violin and piano. In 1938 he was invited by Huberman to become first violist with the Palestine SO (later the Israel PO), after which he lived in Tel-Aviv. He stayed with the orchestra until 1956, also playing the viola in the Israel Quartet (1939–54) and appearing as a soloist in Israel and abroad. In 1951 he was appointed director of the Israel Academy of Music (later the Rubin Academy of Tel-Aviv University), and in 1961 he was made a professor. He travelled extensively as an adjudicator, lecturer and teacher, and received many honours, most notably the first award of the Israel State Prize (1954).

Partos arrived in Palestine steeped in contemporary European traditions, particularly those of Bartók and Kodály. From them he had come to see folk music as a source of inspiration and to develop his personal style by enlarging Western tonality through a mixture of modal, oriental and chromatic elements; the best example of his work under their influence is the Concertino for strings (1932). By building on these principles, Partos was able to acclimatize himself musically and, in a conscious effort to seek out his Jewish ancestry, he took a particular interest in the musics of the various Eastern Jewish communities. He soon began to make arrangements of their folksongs, first for the Palestinian singer Bracha Zefira (Four Folk Songs, 1939), then for unaccompanied chorus (Six Songs, 1941). The experience had a strong effect on his later instrumental works, including the Four Israeli Tunes for string instrument and piano (1948), *Hezionot* ('Visions') for flute, piano and strings (1957) and *Maqamat* for flute and string quartet (1959). He also used some folk elements of the Ashkenazi communities of eastern Europe, notably in *Yizkor* ('In memoriam') for strings (1947), a work written in response to the Holocaust. In all these works, he brought a Western technique to bear on Eastern material, whether whole tunes, fragmentary gestures or melismatic patterns.

In 1960 there came a change with Partos's turning towards 12-note technique; this is best exemplified in *Tehillim* ('Psalms') for string quartet or chamber orchestra and *Dmuyot* ('Images') for orchestra, both of which date from that year. It is important to stress, however, that his use of 12-note principles was never strict: fragments of three to six notes from the series were often cast as motifs or melodic cells and certain notes were also duplicated at the octave, thus implying a tonal hierarchy. Moreover, Partos always retained some connection with the music of his adopted environment, going as far as to affirm a connection between dissonant, serially-derived harmony and the clashes that result from heterophony. He found expressive force in the combination of serialism with an Eastern melos or biblical cantillation; the influence of *maqām* is still present, for example, in *Psalms*.

The size of Partos's output from the early 1960s bears witness to his stimulation by 12-note methods, but the genres he chose were dictated by his needs as a performer; the Sinfonia concertante for viola and orchestra comes from this period, as does as *Agada* ('Legend') for viola, piano and percussion: he gave the first performance of the latter at the 1962 ISCM Festival. Strings are, indeed, predominant in the vast majority of his works, and his writing for the medium includes Eastern practices, such as very long notes, richly varied embellishments and microtones, all to be found in *Maqamat*, *Psalms*, *Netivim* ('Paths') for orchestra (1969) and *Shiluvim* ('Fusions') for viola and chamber orchestra (1970). Partos employed a generalized serialism in such works as *Arpiliyot* ('Nebulae') for wind quintet (1966), though construction and ordering always remained a means to an expressive end. After 1970 he used a freer technique, involving proportional notation, microtones, clusters and some degree of aleatory writing, which he associated with Eastern improvisation principles.

WORKS
(selective list)

ORCHESTRAL

Yizkor [In memoriam], va, str, 1947; Va Conc. no.1 (Song of Praise), 1949: Ein gev, sym. fantasy, 1951–2; Mourning Music (Oriental Ballad), va, chbr orch, 1956; Hezionot [Visions], fl, pf, str, 1957; Va Conc. no.2, 1957; Vn Conc., 1958; Maqamat, fl, str, 1959; Dmuyot [Images], 1960; Sinfonia concertante (Va Conc. no.3), 1962; Sym. Movts, 1966; Netivim [Paths], elegy, 1970; Shiluvim [Fusions], va, chbr orch, 1970; Music for Chbr Orch, 1972; Arabesque, ob, chbr orch, 1975; Arr. of K. Stamitz: Va Conc., D

CHAMBER AND INSTRUMENTAL

Concertino (Str Qt no.1), 1932, rev. 1939; Improvisation and Niggun, hp, 1959; Tehilim [Psalms], str qt, 1960; Agada [Legend], va, pf, perc, 1960; Il tur [Improvisation], 12 hp, 1960; Arpiliyot [Nebulae], wind qnt, 1966; 3 Fantasies, 2 vn, 1972; Mizmor [Chant], hp, 1975; Fantasia, pf trio, 1977; Ballade, pf qt, 1977; Invenzione a tre (Homage to Debussy), fl, va, hp, 1977

VOCAL

Im nin'alu [If the Generous Doors have been Locked] (S. Shabazi), 1952; Rabat tsraruni [Many a time have they afflicted me] (Ps cxl, Ps xiii 5–6), chorus, 1965, arr. with chbr orch, 1966

Many song arrs.

Principal publisher: Israel Music Institute

BIBLIOGRAPHY

Y.W. Cohen: *Werden und Entwicklung der Musik in Israel* (Kassel, 1976) [pt.ii of rev. edn of M. Brod: *Die Musik Israels*]
W.Y. Elias: *Oedoen Partos* (Tel-Aviv, 1978)
A. Bahat: *Oedoen Partos* (Tel-Aviv, 1984) [Hebrew]

WILLIAM Y. ELIAS/R

Partridge, Ian (*b* London, 12 June 1938). English tenor. He studied at the RCM (1956–8) and subsequently at the GSM. After his début as a soloist in Bexhill (*Messiah*, 1958), he became one of Britain's most valuable oratorio tenors, prized internationally in Schütz, Handel and Bach (notably as the Evangelist) for his pleasing freshness of timbre, the natural musicality of his phrasing and the grace and clarity of his diction. He was also an admired recitalist, and with his sister Jennifer Partridge, recorded lieder (notably *Die schöne Müllerin* and *Dichterliebe*), *mélodies* and English song (including Vaughan Williams's *On Wenlock Edge* and songs by Delius, Gurney, Finzi and Britten). One of Partridge's rare operatic roles, later recorded, was Iopas in Covent Garden's second production of *Les Troyens* (1969).

MAX LOPPERT

Partsch [Bartsch, Parč], **Franz** [František] **Xaver** (*b* Dux [now Duchcov], 30 Jan 1760; *d* Prague, 6 April 1822). Bohemian composer. His father, a Kantor and organist at Dux, first taught him music; he then studied philosophy and law at Prague, but encouraged by Václav Praupner decided to make music his career. He completed his musical training and in 1790 was appointed music teacher for Prince Auersperg's family. At Prague he was also the assistant music director ('Flieglist') of Franz Spengler's German theatrical troupe (*c*1793–6), which first performed his Singspiel *Victor und Heloise*. Later he turned to sacred music and was Praupner's successor as choirmaster of the Týn Church in Prague from 1 July 1807 until his death. Partsch's musical idiom was a belated 'second' *galant* style. Some of his songs have hints of early Romantic expressivity, and his sacred works often have folklike pastoral and dance elements.

WORKS

Victor und Heloise, oder Das Hexengericht (Spl, 3, Illein, F. Hegrad), Prague, Nostitzsches Nationaltheater, 4 Dec 1794, lib pubd (lost)
Sacred (mostly CZ-Pnm): Mass, A, for S concertante; Vox clamantis, D, aria, S solo; Salve regina, E♭; 2 motets, G, C, pastorale, S solo; vocal qt, E♭, inc.; others
Other vocal: 12 Lieder für das schöne Geschlecht, 1v, pf (Prague, 1790); 6 Gesänge, 1v, pf (Prague, n.d.), 2 ed. M. Poštolka in *Songs*, ii (Prague, 1962); Die Feldflasche, 1v, pf (Prague, n.d.); unacc. vocal qts, Pnm
Inst: 11 leichte Variationen über ein Kosakenlied, pf (Prague, n.d.); Sonata, F, hpd, ed. in MVH, xxxi (1974); other works, incl. arrs., sonatas, hpd/pf, org, vc, some doubtful, Pnm

BIBLIOGRAPHY

J.F. von Schönfeld, ed.: *Jb der Tonkunst von Wien und Prag* (Vienna, 1796/R), 146, 152
G.J. Dlabacž: *Allgemeines historisches Künstler-Lexikon* (Prague, 1815/R), i, 94; ii, 426
A. Jelen: 'Životopis F.X. Parče' [Biography], *Čechoslav* (1825), 370–71, 388–90, 401–3
O. Teuber: *Geschichte des Prager Theaters*, ii (Prague, 1885), 312
V. Němec: *Pražské varhany* [Prague organs] (Prague, 1944), 257
T. Volek: 'Repertoir pražské Spenglerovy divadelní společnosti v sezóně 1793–94' [Repertory of the Spengler theatrical troupe for the season 1793–4], *MMC*, no.14 (1960), 23–36, esp. 26 [with Ger. summary]
T. Volek: 'Repertoir Nosticovského divadla v Praze z let 1794, 1796–8' [Repertory of the Nostic Theatre in Prague 1794, 1796–8], *MMC*, no.16 (1961), 5–191, esp. 49, 183 [with Ger. summary]
Z. Pilková: 'Doba osvícenského absolutismu (1740–1810)' [The age of enlightened absolutism (1740–1810)], *Hudba v českých dějinách: od středověku do nové doby* [Music in Czech history: from the Middle Ages to the modern era] (Prague, 1983, 2/1989), 211–84, esp. 266, 273
J. Berkovec: *Musicalia v pražském periodickém tisku 18. století* [Music references in 18th-century Prague periodicals] (Prague, 1989), 198

MILAN POŠTOLKA

Partsong. A piece of music in two or more voice-parts without independent accompaniment. In theory, the term encompasses forms such as the glee, madrigal and unaccompanied anthem. In practice, however, it usually refers to small-scale secular pieces for unaccompanied choral singing. No precise definition is possible: the supposition that partsongs differ from madrigals in moving homophonically with the melody in the top voice overlooks the textural variety of both madrigals and partsongs. Nor is the text definitive, since there are sacred examples such as Sullivan's *Five Sacred Partsongs* (1871). Partsongs are usually single entities, but there exist lengthy multi-sectional works, possibly intended as competitive showpieces, that are susceptible to no other definition. Other languages have no exact equivalent of the term: this may be a reflection of its breadth and inexactitude in all countries where partsongs flourish.

The partsong was cultivated in England from the early 17th century. Collections of rounds, catches and quodlibets, usually on topical, witty and sometimes bawdy texts, provided material for convivial music-making. These pieces were simpler than madrigals. Composers such as Weelkes and, later, William and Henry Lawes, Arne and Purcell wrote many examples. In the late 18th century the inception of men's singing clubs led to a formalization of partsinging. The GLEE, typically a short, predominantly homophonic piece, superseded earlier forms, but members of glee clubs sang a wider variety of music, including madrigals and arrangements, than their name suggests. Competitions were established for the composition and performance of glees and partsongs.

In the 19th century, interest in music of the past stimulated a revival of the madrigal as a distinct type within the partsong. Pearsall and other composers transcended pastiche with richly expressive madrigals. Sterndale Bennett, Barnby, Sullivan, Macfarren, Pearsall, Benedict and numerous others produced partsongs, varied as much in length, substance, mood and texture as in quality and originality. Except where archaism was intended, the musical language of the partsong typified its time, and it often miniaturized standard forms of the period, ternary or rounded binary form being frequent choices. Reciprocal influence between partsong and anthem, canticle, hymn and even Anglican psalm-chant is evident. The increase in musical literacy, the popularity of choral singing, and the accessibility of relatively cheap printed music were both causes and effects of the partsong's enormous popularity.

The late 19th-century festival movement stimulated demand for partsongs that were technically more challenging and of greater musical worth. Partsongs by Parry, Stanford, Elgar, Charles Wood and others met this demand, with imaginative use of textures, sensitivity towards texts and regard for the organization, balance and sentiment of each piece. Their early 20th-century successors extended this tradition, some, such as Holst and Vaughan Williams, incorporating folksong arrangements. These composers and others such as Finzi, Ireland, Moeran and Howells produced partsongs of great originality that transcended the reflective, lilting style that characterized some English music of this period. Most of the later repertory was by lesser composers, although Britten was a notable exception: his *Five Flower Songs* (1950) showed that English partsongs about nature could be energetic, colourful and witty. Later composers have incorporated modern choral techniques, including improvisation, into the partsong, challenging even the most expert choirs.

Similar developments occurred in Germany from the 19th century. The Liedertafel, a male-voice music society, was founded in Berlin in 1808 by Mendelssohn's teacher Zelter and first met the following year. Its aim was convivial as well as musical, and it provided a model for other choirs (the men's choir movement, often linked to local customs and the wearing of traditional costume, survives). Some composers, such as Marschner, Weber and Wagner, confined their partsong output to male voices only. Later in the 19th century, mixed choirs and competitive choral festivals were established. The partsongs of composers including Schubert, Schumann, Franz, Mendelssohn, Cornelius and Brahms set much German Romantic poetry, and show parallels with their lieder in both style and sentiment. Reciprocal influence is apparent between Mendelssohn's partsongs and contemporaneous smaller English choral forms. Some of Bruckner's and Brahms's partsongs show affinities with their unaccompanied church music. Towards the end of the 19th century, partsongs diversified in character. Composers such as Wolf and Schoenberg produced longer unaccompanied secular choral pieces for highly accomplished choirs. In the 20th century the partsong tradition continued in Germany, and its boundaries were extended by composers such as Pfitzner, Distler, Webern, Hindemith, Pepping and Richard Strauss.

In France, men's choral societies ('Orphéons') were established from the mid-19th century. They travelled widely to competitive festivals, and large choirs went abroad to give concerts. Gounod and others wrote specially for these societies and for mixed choirs. A few partsongs were written by Saint-Saëns, Delibes, Debussy and Ravel. Those by d'Indy are more numerous but hardly more diverse. There are some examples by later French composers, but unaccompanied settings of sacred texts form the stronger tradition. In the Latin countries the partsong has been largely neglected. In eastern Europe partsongs were written by Tchaikovsky and Rimsky-Korsakov in Russia, by Bartók and Kodály in Hungary, and by Dvořák and Janáček in Bohemia and Czechoslovakia; in all these countries folksong has been influential. In the USA the partsong has been cultivated as part of a wider tradition of choral singing, particularly involving college choirs, by composers including Macdowell, Horatio Parker, Randall Thompson and, most conspicuously, Elliott Carter.

See also BARBERSHOP; CATCH; QUODLIBET; and ROUND.

BIBLIOGRAPHY

M. Hurd: 'Glees, Madrigals and Partsongs', *Music in Britain: the Romantic Age, 1800–1914*, ed. N. Temperley (London, 1981), 242–65

J. Blezzard: 'Richard Strauss a Cappella', *Tempo*, no.176 (1991), 21–8

J. Blezzard: 'Peter Cornelius: the Later Mixed Partsongs and their Unknown Antecedents', *MR*, liii (1992), 191–209

J. Blezzard: 'Sing, Hear: the German Romantic Partsong', *MT*, cxxxiv (1993), 254–6

JUDITH BLEZZARD

Part-writing [voice-leading] (Fr. *conduite des voix*; Ger. *Stimmführung*; It. *condotta delle voci*). That aspect of counterpoint and polyphony which recognizes each part as an individual line (or 'voice'), not merely as an element of the resultant harmony; each line must therefore have a melodic shape as well as a rhythmic life of its own. In discussions of part-writing a distinction is made between linear or conjunct motion and movement by leap (i.e. by a 3rd or greater) in a single part, and between various types of relative motion between two or more parts: similar motion, two or more parts moving simultaneously in the same direction; parallel motion, two or more parts moving in the same direction and at the distance of the same interval or intervals; oblique motion, one part moving while another part remains stationary; and contrary motion, two parts moving in opposite directions. In good part-writing each part is shaped to a recognizable contour (such as an ascending or descending line, or an arc) having an identity in the polyphonic fabric of a composition or passage. Conjunct motion is generally preferred to movement by leap in all parts except the bass; similar motion among all the parts (except in two-part writing), hidden (covered) 5ths or octaves between the outer parts and consecutive (parallel) 5ths or octaves between any parts are usually avoided.

WILLIAM DRABKIN

Pasacalle (Sp.). In Spain, a term signifying music to accompany walking, including religious processions. In Latin America it denotes various couple-dances, usually in slow tempo. *See* PASSACAGLIA, §1.

Pasaribu, Amir (*b* Tapanuli, Sumatra, 21 May 1915). Indonesian composer. His family, from the Batak nobility, was familiar with Western classical music. After studying music at the Dutch high school in Bandung, Pasaribu trained to be a pianist. The first Indonesian to take up a classical music education abroad, in 1936 he continued his piano and cello studies at the Musashino music school in Japan. On his return in 1939 he worked as a cellist in the radio symphony orchestra Oshio Kioku Kangen Goku during the Japanese occupation of Indonesia; in 1942 he studied composition with the Dutch composer James Zwart in Indonesia. Pasaribu was one of the few composers with an academic background in Indonesia in the period after the 1945 revolution. Melodies inspired by the Malay music of his native region and the gamelan music of Java often appear in his technically masterful compositions, written mainly for piano and small ensemble. His style was influential on the composers of the 1950s, when his was the only Indonesian music included in the classical repertory.

In the 1950s Pasaribu was known as an authoritative critic and a teacher devoted to the development of formal music schools in Indonesia. It may be said that he is largely responsible for the emergence in the 1950s and 60s of a generation of Indonesian musicians with a classical background. Appointed by the newly independent Indonesian government to develop the infrastructure of modern musical life, he established the League of Composers (a copyright organization), headed the music department of Radio Republik Indonesia and developed the music high school in Yogyakarta and the music teachers' school in Jakarta. In the country's uncertain economic situation in 1968, Pasaribu went to Suriname to work for the Dutch-Indonesian Institute for Cultural Cooperation as a cellist; after Suriname's independence in 1975 he became the conductor of the Paramaribo SO. In 1995 he returned to Indonesia and settled in Medan.

FRANKI RADEN

Pasaribu, Ben (M.) (*b* Medan, Sumatra, 1956). Indonesian composer. Beginning his musical career as a drummer in a rock group, he studied ethnomusicology at the University of North Sumatra. He also studied music at Marymount College in Tarrytown, New York, and composition with Alvin Lucier at the Wesleyan University in Middletown, Conneticut. After studying in America he produced many works for electronic media alone and in combination with acoustic instruments. A member of the Batak people, he has studied and absorbed many elements of their traditional music into his own work. This bringing together of two very different musical worlds has made his compositions highly distinctive. His use of ritual forms is a characteristic feature: in *Nerhen Surasura* (1992) for tape and instruments the players are required to be in a state of trance before beginning to perform. A composition teacher and dean of the arts faculty at the Huria Kristen Batak Prostestant Nommensen University in Medan, Pasaribu is an active and influential figure in the contemporary music scene in north Sumatra. His percussion group Medan Percussion Ensemble appears annually at the popular International Jakarta Percussion Festival.

FRANKI RADEN

Pasatieri, Thomas (*b* New York, 20 Oct 1945). American composer. A prolific composer by the age of 15, he studied with Boulanger before entering the Juilliard School of Music, where his composition teachers included Vittorio Giannini. At 19 he received the first doctorate awarded by the school. He has taught at Juilliard, the Manhattan School of Music and the Cincinnati Conservatory; he has also directed the Atlanta Opera (1980–84). Early in 1984 he moved to California to work in films and television.

Primarily interested in composing for the voice, Pasatieri wrote two operas in 1964, *Flowers of Ice* and *The Trysting Place*. His first opera to be staged was *The Women* (1965), performed at Aspen, Colorado, where he was a pupil of Milhaud. Its success convinced him that opera was his natural medium. His next two operas, *La Divina*, a comedy about the last performance of an aging coloratura soprano, and *Padrevia*, a gothic horror story based on Boccaccio, were given their premières in college opera theatres in New York. From 1971 to 1972 six of his operas were produced in Seattle, including *Calvary*, based on the play by W.B. Yeats, and *Black Widow*, his first full-length opera, staged by Lotfi Mansouri in 1972. Derived from Miguel de Unamuno's novella *Dos madres*, the work presents in stark tableaux the tragedy of a barren woman obsessed with motherhood.

Highly emotional characters in strong theatrical situations became characteristic of many of Pasatieri's operas. *The Trial of Mary Lincoln*, with a libretto by the television writer Anne Howard Bailey, is a moving portrait of the first lady in her later years during the court trial that judged her insane. Tailored to the intimacy of television, the opera uses flashbacks, dissolves and voice-overs.

The Seagull, Pasatieri's most successful opera, is based on Chekhov's play of 1896. To make it effective as musical theatre, Pasatieri and his librettist, Kenward Elmslie, concentrated the action of the story and heightened the personal and dramatic relationships: they added an aria to expand the role of Masha; an overtly incestuous duet between Madam Arkadina and Konstantin; and a dramatic final aria that coincides with Konstantin's offstage suicide. The work's lush, romantic score and the excellent cast and creative production of the Houston Grand Opera afforded *The Seagull* a favourable critical reception. The *Three Sisters* (1979) was the first of Pasatieri's operas to be recorded in its entirety.

With the exception of a somewhat more dissonant score for *Before Breakfast* (1980), Pasatieri's style has evolved little over the years. His music is conservative and melodic, with dramatic, soaring lines in the manner of Giacomo Puccini and Richard Strauss. The lyrical, singable nature of his works has convinced many fine singers to take part in premières of his operas, including Evelyn Lear, Frederica Von Stade, Richard Stilwell, John Reardon, Lili Chookasian, James Morris, Jennie Tourel and Theodor Uppman.

In addition to his operas, Pasatieri has composed more than 400 songs, many with chamber ensemble accompaniments. His *Sieben Lehmannlieder* (1988), commissioned by the Music Academy of the West, is a song cycle that sets poems by Lotte Lehmann. The songs, closely reflecting the texts, progress in lyrical melismatic flourishes and often feature an especially high tessitura. *Canciones del barrio* for voice, string quartet and piano, was commissioned by UCLA for the Festival of American and Mexican Works, 1993.

In 1986 the Verdehr Trio commissioned Pasatieri to compose an 'opera for three instruments'. This request resulted in the neo-Romantic *Theatrepieces* for violin, clarinet and piano (1987), his first score in many years not to involve the human voice. In three movements, the work reflects Pasatieri's career in opera and film and his fascination with 'characters who sing without words' (disc notes, Crystal Records, 1990). *Theatrepieces* became the springboard for other instrumental works, such as the Concerto for Two Pianos and Strings (1994) and the Sonata for Viola and Piano (1995).

WORKS

OPERAS

Flowers of Ice (2, R. Rogers), 1964, unperf.
The Trysting Place (1, Pasatieri, after B. Tarkington), 1964, unperf.
The Women (chbr op, 1, Pasatieri), Aspen, CO, 20 Aug 1965
La Divina (comic op, 1, Pasatieri), New York, Juilliard School, 16 March 1966
Padrevia (1, Pasatieri, after G. Boccaccio), New York, Brooklyn College, 18 Nov 1967
The Penitentes (3, A.H. Bailey), 1967, Aspen, CO, 3 Aug 1974
Calvary (chbr op, 1, after W.B. Yeats), Seattle, St Thomas Episcopal Church, 7 April 1971
Black Widow (3, Pasatieri, after M. de Unamuno: *Dos madres*), Seattle, 2 March 1972
The Trial of Mary Lincoln (TV op, 17 scenes, Bailey), Boston, NET, 14 Feb 1972
The Seagull (3, K. Elmslie, after A.P. Chekhov), Houston, 5 March 1974
Signor Deluso (comic op, 1, Pasatieri, after Molière: *Sganarelle, ou Le cocu imaginaire*), Wolf Trap, VA, 27 July 1974
Ines de Castro (3, B. Stambler), Baltimore, 30 March 1976
Washington Square (chbr op, 2, Elmslie, after H. James), Detroit, 1 Oct 1976
Three Sisters (1, Elmslie, after Chekhov), 1979, Columbus, OH, 13 March 1986
Before Breakfast (1, F. Corsaro, after E. O'Neill), New York, City Opera, 9 Oct 1980

The Goose Girl (children's op, 1, Pasatieri, after J.L. and W.C. Grimm), Fort Worth, TX, 15 Feb 1981
Maria Elena (1, Pasatieri), Tucson, AZ, 6 April 1983

OTHER VOCAL

Choral: Permit Me Voyage (J. Agee), S, SATB, orch, 1976; Mass, S, Mez, T, Bar, chorus, orch, 1983; A Joyful Noise, SATB, brass sextet, org, perc, 1985; 3 Mysteries (W. Whitman, G. Meredith, P. Sidney), SATB, 1991; The Harvest Frost (C. Sandburg), SATB, chbr ens, 1993; Bang the Drum Loudly, children's chorus, 1994; Canticle of Praise, SATB, org, 1995; Morning's Innocent (gay and lesbian poets), male vv, ob, vc, hp, pf, 1995
Songs (1v, pf, unless otherwise stated): 3 American Songs (L. Phillips), 1971; 3 Coloratura Songs (Phillips, J. Fletcher), 1971; 2 Shakespeare Songs, 1971; 3 Poems (J. Agee), 1974; Rites de passage (Phillips), 1v, chbr orch/str qt, 1974; Far from Love (E. Dickinson), S, cl, vn, vc, pf, 1976; Day of Love (K. van Cleave), song cycle (1983); 3 Sonnets from the Portuguese (E.B. Browning), 1984; 7 Lehmannlieder (L. Lehmann), song cycle, 1v, pf/orch, 1988; Windsongs (R. Ramsay, R.H. Deutsch, R. Nixon), S, pf (1989); Alleluia (Latin, trans. Pasatieri) (1991), arr. SATB, pf; Canciones del barrio, 1v, str qt, 1993; various carols and christmas songs, Bar, chbr orch

INSTRUMENTAL

Invocations, orch, 1968; 2 Sonatas (Cameos), pf, 1975; Theatrepieces, cl, vn, pf, 1987; Pf Conc., 1993, unpubd; Conc., 2 pf, str, 1994, unpubd; Sonata, vn, pf, 1994; Qt, fl, str, 1995; Serenade, vn, chbr orch/pf, 1995; Sonata, va, pf, 1995; Sonata, fl, pf, 1997

Principal publishers: Presser, G. Schirmer, Belwin-Mills

BIBLIOGRAPHY

S. Fleming: 'Pasatieri's *The Seagull*', *High Fidelity/Musical America*, xxiv/6 (1974), 32–3
R. Jacobson: 'Thomas Pasatieri: Opera is the Plural of Opus', *After Dark*, vi/11 (1974), 45–9
H.C. Schonberg: '*Ines de Castro* in Baltimore', *New York Times* (1 April 1976)
A. Hughes: 'Pasatieri's *Washington Square* Opera States its Case', *New York Times* (15 Oct 1977)
J. Rockwell: 'Baltimore Opera's Three Portraits of Women', *New York Times* (3 Feb 1985)
R.H. Kornick: *Recent American Opera: a Production Guide* (New York, 1991), 222–32

ELISE KIRK

Pascal, Florian. The pseudonym of Joseph Benjamin Williams, English composer who headed the firm of JOSEPH WILLIAMS.

Pascale [Paschali], Francesco. *See* PASQUALI, FRANCESCO.

Paşcanu, Alexandru (*b* Bucharest, 3 May 1920; *d* Bucharest, 6 July 1989). Romanian composer. He studied composition with Negrea, aesthetics with Cuclin, folklore with Brăiloiu and conducting with Perlea at the Bucharest Academy (1938–46), also graduating in law from Bucharest University in 1944. Paşcanu taught in lyceums and at the Academy, where he developed a valuable course manual. In 1951–2 he was barred from teaching for political reasons and worked as artistic secretary for the Army Ensemble. His music includes impressionistic, modal, folk and occasionally jazz elements and is descriptive and highly charged with emotion. While a preoccupation with harmonic colouring is a feature of his chamber music, for instance *Noapte de vară* (1955), a neo-classical rigour informs *Scherzo simfonic* (1948) and *Preludiu şi toccata* (1956). In *Suita română* (1967) and his many choral arrangements for children Paşcanu incorporates the melodic character of Romanian folk music.

WORKS
(selective list)

Inst: Scherzo simfonic, 1948; Poemul Carpaţilor, orch, 1954; Noapte de vară [Summer Night], hn, pf, 1955; Preludiu şi toccata, orch, 1956; In memoriam, orch, 1957; Răsărit de soare [Sunrise], vn, pf, 1959; Marea Neagră [The Black Sea], orch, 1960; Pastorală, pf, 1963; Suita română, orch, 1967; Balada, cl, orch, 1977
Choral music for children: În tabără [On the Campsite] (G. Naum), 1965; Bocete străbune [Ancient Laments] (trad. text), 1971; Chindia, 1971; Ah, ce bucurie [Oh, what Joy], 1979; Festum hibernum, 1979; many arrs.

BIBLIOGRAPHY

V. Cosma: *Muzicieni români* (Bucharest, 1970)
C. Cazaban: 'Alexandru Paşcanu: *Bocete străbune*', *Muzica*, xxii/10 (1972), 10–12
Z. Vancea: *Creaţia muzicală românească în secolele XIX–XX*, ii (Bucharest, 1978)
A. Dogaru: 'Alexandru Paşcanu', *Muzica*, xxx/10–11 (1980), 86–96

OCTAVIAN COSMA

Pascarola, Giovanni Tommaso Benedictis da. *See* BENEDICTIS DA PASCAROLA, GIOVANNI TOMMASO.

Pasche [Passhe], William (*fl c*1513–37). English composer and church musician. In 1513 he was admitted to the Fraternity of St Nicholas (a guild of musicians and clerks of the collegiate and parish churches of London and its hinterland), and from *c*1519 to 1526 he occurs as one of the six lay vicars of the choir of St. Paul's Cathedral, London. He had left this employment by June 1534, and may well be identifiable with the singing-man of this name who in 1527 and 1528 was a clerk of the choir of the parish church of St Peter, West Cheap, London. In 1547 the possessions of this church included books of polyphony and vestments for men and boys of the choir, and during the 1540s its rector was the composer John Gwynneth; it may well have enjoyed a musical culture sufficiently ambitious to require the services of a prominent musician to lead it. In addition, Pasche received payments from the parish church of Kingston-upon-Thames, Middlesex, in 1514–15 for the 'oversight of the organs', and again in 1536–7. The death of his wife Embryth was notified to the Fraternity of St Nicholas in 1517.

The composer must be distinguished from other persons of the same name with whom he has been confused, including one who was a Fellow of New College, Oxford, 1494–1506; one whose will was proved before Commissaries of the Prerogative Court of Canterbury sitting in St Paul's Cathedral in July 1525; and a Mr Pashe who in 1516 was a long-deceased founder of one of the chantries established in St George's Chapel, Windsor. Flood's claim that in 1476 the composer was a gentleman of the household chapel of Anne Holland, Duchess of Exeter, is clearly based on yet further misunderstanding of the source of this last misidentification.

'M[aster] Pashe' headed the list of English composers whose authority Thomas Morley acknowledged in his *A Plaine and Easie Introduction to Practicall Musicke* (1597), but only three works have survived, all extended and ornate. Four out of five voices of a *Magnificat* setting and of a votive antiphon *Sancta Maria mater Dei* (ed. N. Sandon, Newton Abbot, 1994) survive in *GB-Cu* Peterhouse 471–4. Into the latter the composer worked both a particular five-note motif common to certain other contemporary compositions and a brief phrase reminiscent of chants for the litany, which had provided the starting-point for its lengthy prose text. A five-voice mass, *Christus resurgens* (*Cgc* 667) has survived complete. Suggestions that he was the W.P. whose initials were inscribed beside a *Salve regina* in *Lbl* Add.5665 seem unlikely.

BIBLIOGRAPHY

W.H.G. Flood: *Early Tudor Composers* (London, 1925)

H.B. Walters: *London churches at the Reformation* (London, 1939), 563–71

H. Baillie: 'Some Biographical Notes on English Church Musicians, Chiefly Working in London (1485–1569)', *RMARC*, no.2 (1962), 18–57

N. Sandon: 'F G A B-flat A: some Thoughts on a Tudor Motive', *EMc*, xii (1984), 56–63

ROGER BOWERS

Paschil, Josif (*b* Bucharest, 17 Sept 1877; *d* Bucharest, 29 March 1966). Romanian composer and pianist. After studying with Wachmann at the Bucharest Conservatory he studied composition and the organ with Fauré in Paris (1901–2). As well as sustaining a career as a concert pianist (1893–1935), Paschil worked in Bucharest as organist at the Choral Temple (1901–25), conductor for several opera companies (1903–06), conductor of the choirs of the German Societies (1903–43) and organist at the cathedral of St Iosif in his later years. Most active as a composer in his early years, he favoured the theatre and was attracted to specifically Romanian subject matter. Rich in folk imagery and highly accessible, his music is notable for the clarity of its dramatic argument. Paschil

wrote musical commentaries in German-language periodicals in Bucharest.

WORKS
(selective list)

Stage: Marioara (op, 2, after C. Sylva), 1904, Bucharest, Lyric, 3 May 1904; Lulli (operetta, 3, D. de Laforet), 1906; Amorul învingător [Love Triumphant] (ballet-pantomime), 1913; Eros învingător [Eros Triumphant] (ballet), 1913; Domnul codrilor [Lord of the Forests] (op, 3, E. Aslan), 1914–15

Orch: Curtea de Argeş, suite; Fantezie haiducească [Bandit's Fantasy]; Fantazie rapsodică; Floarea României [Flower of Romania], medley; Impresiuni de la mănăstire [Impressions from the Monastery]

Vocal-orch works, songs, didactic pieces

Principal publishers: T. Esanu, N. Mischonznicky, Moravetz

BIBLIOGRAPHY

V. Cosma: *Muzicieni români* (Bucharest, 1970)

O.L. Cosma: *Hronicul muzicii româneşti*, vii (Bucharest, 1986); viii (1988); ix (1991)

OCTAVIAN COSMA

Pascual Ramírez (y Arellano), Francisco (*b* province of Segovia, 1683; *d* Palencia, 26 Dec 1743). Spanish composer. In 1711 he worked as a professional musician at El Burgo de Osma Cathedral, and in October of the same year he unsuccessfully competed for the post of *maestro de capilla* of Sigenza Cathedral, for which he composed the eight-part villancico *De dulces consonancias*. In October 1719 he was appointed *maestro de capilla* of Astorga Cathedral, and was required to be present at processions both inside and outside the church and to attend to the special music for feast days and Rogation Days. As a result, in addition to the known villancicos, he composed music for various theatrical festivities in the city; for instance, for the panegyric play *El escándalo de Grecia*, performed at the Corpus Christi celebrations in San Bartolomé de Astorga in 1720. From May 1723 until his death he was *maestro de capilla* of Palencia Cathedral, where he upgraded the musical staff by admitting several cantors and instrumentalists; he even used occasional reinforcements, such as the musicians of the Prince's regiment for the Christmas festivities of 1738.

His music has survived almost in its entirety in the archive of Palencia Cathedral as part of the legacy bequeathed by the composer four days before his death. In his Latin works he uses the traditional polychoral and contrapuntal language of the time, very elaborate and with obbligato instruments such as the oboe and pairs of violins. Of equal interest are his Spanish works, in which the change in taste that took place at the beginning of the 18th century is evident in the mixture of the polychoral tradition of the 17th century, with works that alternate the choral refrain (*estribillo*) with the stanza for solo voices (*copla*), and the italianate style, with its alternation of recitatives and arias. These works were written for a variety of occasions, including Christmas, Corpus Christi and various Marian feasts, as well as canonizations and enshrinements of saints. His scant surviving output of incidental music for sacred plays for Christmas and Corpus Christi bears witness to the role music played in the celebration of traditional feasts in the urban environment at the start of the 18th century.

WORKS

Lat. works, most in *E-PAL*, 1 in *SE*: 1 mass, 1 requiem, 4 pss, 20 lamentations, 6 motets, 3 hymns, 1 verse, 1 res, 1 lesson for the dead, 1 invitatory for the dead, 1 sequence for the Resurrection

Sp. works, *PAL*: 239 villancicos, 2–15vv, 83 cants., 1v, 2 pieces of incid music for sacred plays, 27 other works, 1–4vv

PABLO L. RODRÍGUEZ

Pasculli, Antonino (*b* Palermo, 13 Oct 1842; *d* Palermo, 23 Feb 1924). Italian oboist and composer. Known as perhaps the greatest oboe virtuoso of all time, Pasculli's legendary abilities have often stimulated comparisons with Paganini. Beginning his career at the age of 14, he toured in Germany, Italy and Austria. He was one of the first oboists active in the Italian-Austrian regions to use a French-style oboe, and was famed for his light and effortless bravura style. His appointment to the staff of the Palermo Conservatory in 1860 signalled the end of his itinerant career. In 1879 he took over the directorship of the Palermo municipal musical corps, a position to which he dedicated much time and energy. He had all the wind players learn a string instrument, so as well as conventional band repertory he was able to introduce contemporary music unfamiliar to Sicilian audiences, including works by Wagner, Debussy, Grieg and Sibelius. However, his sight was deteriorating seriously, and medical advice attributed this to his oboe playing; in 1884 he gave his last public performance. At his retirement in 1913 the symphony band dissolved. Like so many other virtuosos of the 19th century, Pasculli composed music for his own use. As well as a large number of variations on popular operatic themes, he wrote some pedagogical material and compositions for the corps, including a symphonic poem, *Naiadi e Silfidi*, and *Di qui non si passa*, an elegy on the death of his son, who was killed in action in World War I.

BIBLIOGRAPHY
L. Rosset: 'Antonino Pasculli, the "Paganini of the Oboe"', *Double Reed*, x (1987), 44–5
O. Zoboli, ed.: Introduction, *Antonino Pasculli: Fantasia sull'opera Poliuto di Donizetti* (Montreux, 1989)

GEOFFREY BURGESS

Pas de Brabant (Fr.). *See* SALTARELLO.

Pas de charge (Fr.). Double-quick march. *See* MARCH, §1.

Pasdeloup, Jules Etienne (*b* Paris, 15 Sept 1819; *d* Fontainebleau, 13 Aug 1887). French conductor and administrator. He won *premiers prix* for solfège (1832) and piano (1834) at the Paris Conservatoire. The death of his father, François Pasdeloup, who was a conductor at the Opéra-Comique, forced him to earn a living, and at the age of 14 he was already giving music lessons. He was a lecturer in solfège at the Conservatoire from 1841 and in the piano from 1847 to 1850, and in 1855 he became professor of choral music; he subsequently abandoned official teaching posts. In the wake of the political events of 1848 Pasdeloup was appointed *régisseur* of the Château de Saint Cloud, a post which enabled him to meet the most distinguished personalities of the Second Empire and to be a kind of impresario for the regime. He was then engaged by Nieuverkerke, superintendent of fine arts, to organize concerts at the Louvre, and later by Haussmann to set up a series of concerts at the Hôtel de Ville. He was also asked to arrange musical soirées in the apartments of Princess Mathilde.

The Société des Jeunes Artistes was Pasdeloup's first major success as a conductor. It is said that after offering a scherzo he had composed to Habeneck, who refused it without so much as looking at it, he decided to form a symphonic society to perform the music of young composers who had been reduced to composing for the stage or not at all. Pasdeloup contacted his pupils from the Conservatoire and started sessions in orchestral technique. In December 1852 the statutes of the society were laid down, and the first concert was given in the Salle Herz on 20 February 1853. In 1856 Auber, the director of the Conservatoire, became patron of the society, which then became known as the Société des Jeunes Artistes du Conservatoire Impérial de Musique. This offered it such benefits as free use of rehearsal rooms and instruments. During its nine years' existence the society gave the first performances of numerous works, including symphonies by Gounod and Saint-Saëns, and performances of Schumann's Symphony no.1 (performed 1857, ten years before it was given at the Société des Concerts du Conservatoire) and the Wedding March from Wagner's *Lohengrin*. But after nine years its deficit, until then borne by Pasdeloup, rose to 77,000 francs. Pasdeloup decided on a change of plan, and in 1861 hired the Cirque Napoléon for six Concerts Populaires de Musique Classique. The hall seated almost 5000, and the orchestra numbered 110. The aim of these concerts was to bring classical music to a culturally deprived public, which until then had not been permitted to enter the Société des Concerts du Conservatoire. The first of these concerts was given on 27 October. After three concerts, public support was so great that Pasdeloup was able to book the Cirque Napoléon for a year. Until the war of 1870 the Concerts Populaires were an unquestionable artistic and financial success. All the famous soloists of the day played at these Sunday concerts. The works of the five 'greats' – Beethoven, Haydn, Mozart, Weber and Mendelssohn – were played frequently, but Pasdeloup also gave an important place to contemporary French composers and performed works of the German symphonists then unknown in France. The names of Schumann and especially Wagner provoked hostile reactions which grew with the rising nationalism in the 1870s and assumed such political significance that these composers' works had to be excluded from the programmes.

Pasdeloup shared the directorship of the Paris Orphéon with Bazin. In 1868 he founded the Société des Oratorios, which gave the first Paris performance of the first part of Bach's *St Matthew Passion* at the Panthéon. He also joined the Théâtre Lyrique in 1868 and produced *Rienzi* there the following year. The Théâtre Lyrique collapsed at the beginning of 1870, a few months before war broke out. But the war did not interrupt the Concerts Populaires for long; Pasdeloup, who fought bravely with the National Guard, resumed his concerts during the siege, only to have them interrupted again during the Commune until October 1871. It was at this time that the rivalry began which eventually overcame Pasdeloup. First, the Société Nationale (1871) and later the Concert National (1873) were conducted by Colonne, who gave six concerts at the Odéon before moving to the Châtelet in 1874. For some time Pasdeloup's popularity withstood the undeniable technical superiority of Colonne; in 1878 he requested and obtained a grant of 20,000 francs. But the arrival of Charles Lamoureux, who inaugurated the Nouveaux-Concerts in 1881, proved the death-blow to the Concerts Populaires; Pasdeloup tried in vain to save his institution by increasing his appeals for financial aid and for new ideas, and was forced to abandon the struggle in 1884. His friends organized a farewell festival which raised

100,000 francs and assured him a comfortable retirement. He was asked to start a musical season at Monaco, but this, too, was a failure. In October 1886 he tried once again to establish his concerts at the Cirque Napoléon; he succeeded in giving five concerts and a festival devoted to the music of Franck before he died.

Pasdeloup was a great stimulus to French musical life. In creating an orchestra devoted to playing new works, he inspired the writing of symphonic music by composers who might otherwise have ignored this form. His promotion of Classical, German Romantic and French symphonic music contributed to the creation of a new, larger and more diverse musical public. He also wrote music for the voice, for the piano and for orchestra, though none of his works was performed at any of his concerts or has since enjoyed any popularity.

BIBLIOGRAPHY

A. Elwart: *Histoire des Concerts populaires de musique classique* (Paris, 1864)
A. Jullien: 'Jules Pasdeloup et les Concerts populaires', *Musique: mélanges d'histoire et de critique* (Paris, 1896)
M. Griveau: 'Impressions musicales d'enfance et de jeunesse', *BSIM*, vi (1910), 662
C. Saint-Saëns: *Portraits et souvenirs* (Paris, 1920)
E. Bernard: 'Jules Pasdeloup et les Concerts populaires', *RdM*, lvii (1971), 150
T.J. Walsh: *Second Empire Opera: the Théâtre Lyrique, Paris, 1851–1870* (London and New York, 1981)

ELISABETH BERNARD

Paseo [passeo] (Sp.). A type of *ripresa* or ritornello similar to the Spanish *passacalle* (see PASSACAGLIA). It first appeared in J.C. Amat's *Guitarra española* (originally published in 1586/1596, though the earliest surviving copy dates from 1626). Sanz (1674) described Amat's *paseos* as *passacalles* and used the two terms interchangeably in the titles of his own compositions. Pablo Minguet y Yrol in the guitar portion of his *Reglas y advertencias generales* (Madrid, 1754/*R*) quoted extensively from Amat's book and substituted the word 'passacalle' for 'paseo'. Cabanilles wrote five sets of keyboard variations called *passacalles* and four others entitled *paseos* (see HAM, no.239). The term occurs with a choreographic meaning in Juan de Esquivel's *Discursos sobre el arte del dançado* (Seville, 1642), where it refers to a complete cycle of dance steps.

BIBLIOGRAPHY

R. Hudson: 'Further Remarks on the Passacaglia and Ciaccona', *JAMS*, xxiii (1970), 302–14
R. Hudson: *Passacaglio and Ciaccona: from Guitar Music to Italian Keyboard Variations in the 17th Century* (Ann Arbor, 1981)

RICHARD HUDSON

Pasero, (Giacinto Tommaso) Tancredi (*b* Turin, 11 Jan 1893; *d* Milan, 17 Feb 1983). Italian bass. He studied with Arturo Pessina and made his début at the Politeama Chiarella, Turin, as the King of Egypt (*Aida*) in 1917. In 1924 he appeared at the Teatro Costanzi, Rome, and at the Colón, Buenos Aires, where he returned until 1930. In 1926 he made his début at La Scala in *Don Carlos*, and sang there, almost continuously, until 1951. He was engaged at the Metropolitan (1929–33), at Covent Garden (1931) and at the Paris Opéra (1935). He retired in 1955. His voice was full, mellow and even across a wide range, and he sang with a fine sense of style in a repertory extending from Sarastro to Escamillo. He was outstanding in such Italian *basso cantante* roles as Oroveso (*Norma*), Zaccaria, Ramfis, Fiesco, Padre Guardiano and Philip II;

and in the latter part of his career he became a renowned Boris Godunov.

BIBLIOGRAPHY

ES (R. Celletti); *GV* (R. Celletti; R. Vegeto)
S. Winstanley: 'Tancredi Pasero', *Record Advertiser*, iii/4 (1972–3), 2 [with discography]
N. Linnell: 'Tancredi Pasero, 1893–1983: a Tribute', *Record Collector*, xxviii (1983–4), 141–3
C. Clerico: *Tancredi Pasero: Voce verdiana* (Turin, 1983)

RODOLFO CELLETTI/VALERIA PREGLIASCO GUALERZI

Pasetto, Giordano [Pasetus, Jordanus]. *See* PASSETTO, GIORDANO.

Pashchenko, Andrey Filippovich (*b* Rostov-na-Donu, 3/15 Aug 1885; *d* Moscow, 16 Nov 1972). Russian composer. As a child he sang in a church choir, received violin lessons, studied at a charitable music school and took correspondence courses. He directed amateur choirs and wrote reviews for the Moscow periodicals *Muzïkal'nïy truzhenik* and *Muzïka i zhizn'*. From 1911 he was librarian of the St Petersburg Court Orchestra and he took an active part in its reorganization as the State Orchestra (1917) and finally as the Petrograd (later Leningrad) Philharmonic Orchestra (1921), remaining in this post until 1931. Meanwhile he had received his formal compositional training as a mature student at the St Petersburg Conservatory under Witohl and later Steinberg (1914–17). The result of his library work was the *Muzïkal'nïye proizvedeniya P.I. Chaykovskogo: isto-riko-bibliograficheskiy ukazatel'* [The musical works of Tchaikovsky: a historical and bibliographic index] (1918–21). The manuscript was accepted for publication but lost. Together with Glazunov, Findeyzen and Steinberg he founded the Society for the Propagation of Contemporary Russian Music (1922–3). He became a member of the Artistic Council of the Leningrad Philharmonic Orchestra in 1926 and the State Academic Theatre of Opera and Ballet in 1928. In 1957 he received the title Honoured Representative of the Arts of the RSFSR, and in 1961 he settled in Moscow.

Pashchenko's name first appeared on concert programmes in 1914 with the scherzo-fantasy *Arlekina i Kolombina* ('Harlequin and Columbine') and the symphonic poem *Vakkhanki* ('The Bacchantes'). During the years of the Revolution and revolutionary construction Pashchenko enthusiastically immersed himself in the new socialist culture. Pashchenko's output is extensive, particularly in the field of choral music, where his epic, monumental style is most fully evident, its objective tone conveying mass feelings and impulses. His subjects may be taken from Greek mythology, pagan Slav legend (*Viriney*) or heroic contemporary events, as in the *Rekviyem pamyati geroicheskikh boytsov* ('Requiem in Memory of the Heroic Warriors') written during the Leningrad blockade of 1942. Both in original choral pieces and free folksong arrangements Pashchenko displayed a deep understanding of Russian peasant singing and polyphony: his choral writing employs a diversity of techniques, often to illustrative effect. Close links with Russian folk music are also apparent in the texture of Pashchenko's orchestral music, indigenous polyphony is combined with classical counterpoint, in which he was particularly interested: he wrote about 200 fugues at the beginning of the 1920s. But it is the broadly presented choral music that distinguishes his opera *Orliniy bunt* ('The Eagle Revolt'), concerning the Pugachyov uprising.

This work played an important role in shaping Soviet music drama, particularly in the portrayal of historical and revolutionary themes – for example, the theme of Vasily Chapayev, the hero of the Civil War, was embodied in the aria *Chyornïy yar* ('The Black Ravine'). However, Pashchenko's reputation as an opera composer was established later with his comic and satirical works: *Tsar' Maksimilian* is a 'buffoon play' based on ideas from folk tales and is linked with Rimsky-Korsakov's *Zolotoy petushok* ('The Golden Cockerel') and traditional Russian farce; it has all the mordancy of a political pamphlet. In general, Pashchenko's music is tonally simple and lapidary, with a somewhat rough energy, a winning straightforwardness and resoluteness of expression.

Pashchenko was a productive composer. His contemporaries noted his irascible temperament and his exceptional industriousness (he wrote several operas and his choral symphony, no.12, in the period 1966–7). Throughout his life Pashchenko was noted for his impulsive reaction to events taking place around him. When seriously ill, he completed his Symphony no.16 which he dedicated to the 50th anniversary of education in the USSR. For many decades (from the 1950s to the 90s) his works were not performed and as a whole were not advocated.

WORKS
(selective list)

Operas: Orlinïy bunt (Pugovshchina) [The Eagle Revolt (The Pugachyov Affair)] (S. Spassky), 1925; Tsar' Maksimilian (A. Remizov), 1926–9; Chyornïy yar [The Black Ravine] (I. Seyfullina), 1931; Pompadurï [The Pompadours] (A. Ivanovsky, V. Rozhdestvensky, after M. Saltïkov-Shchedrin), 1936; Svad'ba Krechinskogo [Krechinsky's Wedding] (Spassky, after Sukhovo-Kobïlin), 1947; Shut Balakirev [The Buffoon Balakirev] (A. Mareingof), 1949; Goryachiye serdtsa [Passionate Hearts] (N. Tokunova), 1952; Kapriznaya nevesta [The Capricious Bride], 1953; Radda i Loyko [Radda and Loyko] (after M. Gor'ky: Makar Chudra), 1957, rev. 1966; Nila Shnishko (after A.D. Salinsky), 1961; Velikiy soblaznitel' [The Great Seducer] (after A.K. Tolstoy), 1963–6; Alpiyskaya ballada [The Alpine Ballad] (D. Kulakov, after V.V. Bïkov), 1963–6; Afrikanskaya lyubov' [African Love] (Pashchenko, after P. Merimée), 1966; Zhenshchina, èto d'yavol [Woman, She is the Devil], 1966; Kon' v senatye [A Horse in the Senate] (after L. Andreyev), 1967; Portret [The Portrait] (after Gogol'), 1968; Master i Margarita [The Master and Margarita] (after M. Bulgakov), 1971

Choral: Russian folksongs, 2 suites, 1920, 1923; Viriney (S. Gorodetsky), suite, 1922; Osvobozhdyonnïy Prometey [Prometheus Unbound] (I. Sadofeyev), solo vv, chorus, orch, 1934; Pesn' solntsenostsa [Song of the Sun-Bearer] (N. Klyuyev), soli, chorus, orch, 1924, rev. 1941; Rekviyem pamyati geroicheskikh boytsov [Requiem in Memory of the Heroic Warriors] (Pashchenko), solo vv, chorus, orch, 1942; Lenin (orat, N. Khikmet, K. Seytliyev, V. Voyzhenin, A. Yashin), 1957; Vozvïs'te golos, chestnïye lyudi [Raise your Voices, Upstanding People] (cant., A.A. Surkov), 1962; Oda Sovetskomu Soyuzu [An Ode to the Soviet Union] (O. Orlinova), 1969

Other works: 16 symphonies (1915–72); 4 sinfoniettas, sym. poems, 9 str qts, over 60 songs

Principal publishers: Muzgiz, Sovetskiy kompozitor

WRITINGS

'Pashchenko o svoyey opere' [Pashchenko on his opera], *Rabochiy i teatr* (1925), no.44, p.10 only

'Yubiley velikogo orkestra' [The jubilee of a great orchestra], *Krasnaya gazeta* (4 May 1928)

'Protiv gruppovshchinï' [Against group interests], SovM (1933), no.3, pp.121–5 [about the group interests of critics]

BIBLIOGRAPHY
N. Malkov: 'Muzïkal'no-kharakteristicheskiye ètyudï [Musical and descriptive studies]: 2. A.F. Pashchenko', *Yezhenedel'nik Petrogradskikh akademicheskikh teatrov* (1922), no.5, pp.24–7

B. Asaf'yev: 'Orlinïy bunt' [The Eagle Revolt], *Zhizn' iskusstva* (1925), no.46; repr. in Izbrannïye trudï, v (Moscow, 1957)

Islamey (pseud. of N. Malkov): 'Kontsert iz prozvedeniy Pashchenko' [A concert of works by Pashchenko], *Rabochiy i teatr* (1933), no.11, p.23 only

'A.F. Pashchenko', *Sovetskiye kompozitorï*, i [Soviet composers] (Leningrad, 1938), 45–6

Yu. Kremlyov: 'A.F. Pashchenko: ocherk tvorchestva' [A.F. Pashchenko: an outline of his creative work], *Ocherki po istorii i teorii muziki* (Leningrad, 1939), 116–91

M. Druskin: 'Opera Pashchenko "Pompadori"' [Pashchenko's opera 'The Pompadours'], *Teatr* (1940), no.1; repr. in M. Druskin: ocherki, stat'i, zametki [Essays, articles, notes] (Leningrad, 1987), 275–81

E. Meylikh: *A.F. Pashchenko* (Leningrad, 1960)

GENRIKH ORLOV/LYUDMILA KOVNATSKAYA

Pashe, William. English composer, possibly identifiable with PASCHE, WILLIAM .

Pashkevich, Vasily Alekseyevich (*b c*1742; *d* St Petersburg, 9/20 March 1797). Composer and singer, possibly of Russian birth (the name is Polish). He probably received his training from Vincenzo Manfredini, the chief composer in the early 1760s at the court of Peter III and later at that of Catherine II. From 1763 he is listed as a member of the court orchestra, and he presumably also sang in the court chapel choir. In 1773–4 he taught singing at the Academy of Fine Arts. His first musical comedy, *Neschast'ye ot karetï* ('Misfortune from a Coach'), was produced at the Hermitage in 1779, Pashkevich himself appearing in one of the roles. The next year he was among those entrusted with the preparation of a grandiose 'theatrical festival' in honour of the empress's name-day, the others all being Italians (none of the music survives). After the success of his early operas in a privately owned enterprise, Pashkevich was re-employed by the court (1783) as a violinist in the 'first' orchestra; six years later he was put in charge of music for the royal balls, and was leader of the orchestra. At the same time he held the rank of soloist (*bol'shoy pevchiy*) in the chapel choir. Catherine II put him to work setting her own librettos and in 1790, after *Nachal'noye upravleniye Olega* ('The Early Reign of Oleg'), made him an award of 1600 rubles 'for divers composing of music and efforts beyond his obligation'. By the end of his career Pashkevich had attained the salary rank of Collegiate Assessor, the civilian equivalent of colonel (only Giuseppe Sarti equalled his standing, and not until the reign of Tsar Paul). His closeness to Catherine cost him dearly in the end, for on the accession of her son Paul he was dismissed without pension; he died shortly thereafter.

Pashkevich and Fomin were the most important native composers of opera in 18th-century Russia. Pashkevich's output can be divided into two groups. The earlier consists of five comedies (of which three survive) that formed the core repertory of Karl Knipper's 'free' (public) theatre on Tsaritsïn Lug (Queen's Meadow), where Pashkevich directed the music for the duration of its existence as a private enterprise (1779–83). This was primarily a dramatic theatre, and all of the musical plays written for it, though called comic operas, were of the type *comédie mêlée d'ariettes*, a spoken comedy interspersed with modest musical numbers that could be performed by actors. The first Russian specimen, *Anyuta* (1772; text by the court actor Mikhail Popov, music lost) has been attributed to Pashkevich; but while he may have taken part in the performance (at the Tsarskoye Selo palace, by members of the court chapel choir), it is more likely that

Anyuta, like many of its French prototypes, was made up of contrafacta to folk and popular tunes.

The libretto of *Misfortune from a Coach*, like that of *Skupoy* ('The Miser', 1781), Pashkevich's second opera, was by Knyazhnin, an outstanding neo-classical poet and playwright. One of the classics of 18th-century Russian drama, it is a typical satirical tale of rustic wit. Though it seems an indictment of serfdom (and was much touted as such by Soviet scholarship), it was not regarded so by contemporary audiences (indeed, the play was a great favourite of Catherine II). Pashkevich's music, in keeping with the literary style of the libretto, is devoid of the popular tone one might expect in an opera with peasant characters. Instead, the music sung by the peasant couple, especially in the duet in Act 2 through which they make their appeal to their master, is couched in a parodistically sentimental idiom, full of exaggerated appoggiaturas and *soupirs* (quaver rests). By contrast, Pashkevich's third surviving opera, *Sanktpeterburgskiy gostinnïy dvor* ('The St Petersburg Bazaar', 1782), to a libretto by Mikhail Matinsky, is a bench-mark of the emergent Russian national style. The music to a second libretto by Matinsky, *Tunisskiy pasha* ('The Pasha of Tunis', 1782), has not survived.

Three works to librettos by the Empress Catherine (written with the help of her literary secretary, Aleksandr Khrapovitsky) make up the second group of Pashkevich's operas. These were lavish court productions, in up to five acts, with choruses, ballets, large instrumental forces and singers capable of a decorative vocal idiom. Nevertheless, they all remained true to the simple conception of a play with musical numbers. Only the music of the first of them, *Fevey* (1786), was wholly by Pashkevich. The title character of this work – based on a fairy-tale by Catherine – is a Siberian prince (tenor), who pursues a dream vision of a beautiful princess to the ends of the earth. Curiously foreshadowing the technique of certain 19th-century Russian masters, Pashkevich based his score on the contrast between a selfconsciously Russian idiom and an 'oriental' one, in this case an imaginary Mongol style. His 'Kalmyk chorus', a concoction of Lombard rhythms and drone 5ths, attracted a great deal of favourable attention, many spectators taking it as authentic. Pashkevich's contribution to the other operas with texts by Catherine – *The Early Reign of Oleg* (mainly by Sarti) and the one-act *Fedul s det'mi* ('Fedul and his Children'; mainly by Martín y Soler) – was (apart from the attractive overture to *Fedul*) largely confined to interludes of local colour in the form of choral harmonizations of Russian folksongs. The wedding scene in Act 3 of *The Early Reign of Oleg*, with its three finely wrought choruses, a refinement on the bride's party in *The St Petersburg Bazaar*, is perhaps Pashkevich's most elegant and characteristic achievement in the national vein.

WORKS
all first performed in St Petersburg; all extant MSS in R U-SPtob

Neschast'ye ot kareti [Misfortune from a Coach] (comic op, 2, Ya.B. Knyazhnin), Hermitage, 7/18 Nov 1779, excerpt in *IRMO*
Skupoy [The Miser] (comic op, 1, Knyazhnin, after Molière and A. Sumarkov), Knipper's, sum. 1781; ed. Ye. Levashov (Moscow, 1973); excerpt in *IRMO*
Lzhets [The Liar] (Knyazhnin), 1 no. pubd (1781), music otherwise lost
Tunisskiy pasha [The Pasha of Tunis] (comic op, 2, M.A. Matinsky), Knipper's, 22 June/3 July 1782, music lost
Sanktpeterburgskiy gostinnïy dvor [The St Petersburg Bazaar] (comic op, 3, Matinsky), Knipper's, aut. 1782; rev. as Kak pozhivyosh',

tak i proslivyosh' [You'll be Known by the Way you Live], Bol'shoy, 2/13 Feb 1792; ed. Ye. Levashov (Moscow, 1980); excerpts in *IRMO*
Fevey (comic op, 4, Catherine II), Bol'shoy, 19/30 April 1786; vs arr. I. Pratsch (St Petersburg, 1789); excerpt in *IRMO*
Nachal'noye upravleniye Olega [The Early Reign of Oleg] (5, Catherine II), Hermitage, 15/26 Oct 1790 (St Petersburg, 1791), collab. G. Sarti and C. Canobbio
Fedul s det'mi [Fedul and his Children] (play with music, 1, Catherine II and A.V. Khrapovitsky), Hermitage, 16/27 Jan 1791; vs (Moscow, 1895); collab. V. Martín y Soler

BIBLIOGRAPHY

IRMO; *MooserA*
J. Grot, ed.: *Lettres de Grimm à l'impératrice Catherine II* (St Petersburg, 2/1866)
V.A. Prokof'yev: 'Mikhail Matinsky i yego opera "Sankt-Peterburgskiy gostinïy dvor"', *Muzïka i muzikal'nïy bït staroy Rossii* [Music and musical life in Old Russia], ed. B. Asaf'yev, i (Leningrad, 1927), 58–69
A.S. Rabinovich: *Russkaya opera do Glinki* [Russian opera before Glinka] (Moscow, 1948)
D. Lehmann: *Russlands Oper und Singspiel in der zweiten Hälfte des 18. Jahrhunderts* (Leipzig, 1958)
M. Whaples: 'Eighteenth-Century Russian opera in the Light of Soviet Scholarship', *Indiana Slavic Studies*, ii (1958), 113–34
Yu.V. Keldïsh: 'Nachalo russkoye operï: V. Pashkevich, Ye. Fomin' [The origins of Russian opera: Pashkevich, Fomin], *Russkaya muzïka XVIII veka* (Moscow, 1965), 244–380
O. Levashova: *Russkaya vokal'naya lirika XVIII veka*, Pamyatniki russkogo muzïkal'nogo iskusstva [Monuments of Russian art music], i (Moscow, 1972)
Ye. Levashov: 'Sushchestvoval li kompozitor Matinskiy?' [Did the composer Matinsky exist?], *SovM* (1973), no.5, pp.81–8
S. Karlinsky: 'The Age of Catherine: Comic Opera and Verse Comedy', *Russian Drama from its Beginnings to the Age of Pushkin* (Berkeley and Los Angeles, 1985), 116–49
Ye. Levashov: 'V.A. Pashkevich', *Istoriya russkoy muzïki v desyati tomakh* [The history of Russian music in ten volumes], ed. Yu.V. Keldïsh, iii (Moscow, 1985), 46–83

RICHARD TARUSKIN

Pashta. Sign used in Hebrew EKPHONETIC NOTATION. *See also* JEWISH MUSIC, §III, 2(ii).

Pasillo. A dance-music genre descended from the Austrian waltz and cultivated during the colonization of Colombia and Ecuador as a formal ballroom dance. The modern *pasillo* survives in folk tradition in two forms: the slow *pasillo* is known for its nostalgic texts and melancholy melodies; the faster instrumental *pasillo* is in rondo form, each section in a contrasting tonal area, and is characterized by syncopated melodies and both horizontal and vertical polyrhythmic effects created between the 3/4 and 6/8 alternation in the guitar and *tiple* (small 12-string guitar) accompaniment and the *bandola* (bandurria: flat-backed lute) melodies.

WILLIAM GRADANTE

Pasindén. Female singer in Sundanese gamelan. *See* PESINDHÈN. *See also* INDONESIA, §V, 1.

Pasino, Stefano [Ghizzolo] (*b* Brescia, ?early 17th century; *d* ?Lonato, nr Brescia, after 1679). Italian organist and composer. He worked for a time as a priest at the church at Cona, near Chioggia. In 1635 he had become town organist of Lonato. By 1651 he had moved a few miles north to Salò, where he was *maestro di cappella* of the cathedral. From the dedication of his sonatas (1679) it appears that he had to give up his musical activities for a time before returning to Lonato, presumably in old age. In this dedication, addressed to the town authorities of Lonato, he mentioned the composers G.A. Bertoli, G.M. Lanfranco and Pietro Verdina, but not Giovanni Ghizzolo, whose name he shared as a nickname. Though both came from Brescia, both were priests and both wrote masses *da concerto e cappella*, there is no evidence of any association between them. Pasino was clearly an inventive composer, whose surviving publications show that he was interested in writing in both *prima* and *seconda pratica* styles.

WORKS

Messe da concerto, e cappella & per li defunti, 4vv, op.4 (Venice, 1635)
Motetti concertati, 2–4vv, 2 vn, va, Laetatus, 5vv … con un Pater noster da cappella sopra il canto fermo, 5vv, op.6 (Venice, 1651)
Ricercari, op.7; lost, cited in *FétisB*
Sonate de quali, una è composta in canone, & un'altra ad imitatione di versi sogliono fave diversi animali bruti, a 2–4, op.8 (Venice, 1679)

JOHN HARPER

Paskalis, Kostas (*b* Levadia, Boeotia, 1 Sept 1929). Greek baritone. He studied in Athens, making his début there in 1951 as Rigoletto. In 1958 he sang Renato in Vienna, where he was a member of the Staatsoper for 20 years. He made his British début in 1964 as Macbeth at Glyndebourne, where he also sang Don Giovanni (1967), and his Metropolitan début in 1965 as Don Carlo (*La forza*), returning as Ford. At Salzburg he created Pentheus in Henze's *The Bassarids* in 1966 and at La Scala sang Valentin (1967). He made his Covent Garden début in 1969 as Macbeth, returning for Iago, Scarpia and Rigoletto. His repertory included William Tell, Escamillo (which he recorded), Barnaba (*La Gioconda*), Yevgeny Onegin and Harlequin (*Ariadne auf Naxos*), but it was in Verdi that he excelled, as Posa, Rigoletto, Amonasro, Boccanegra, Luna, Germont, Nabucco and, his finest roles, Iago and Macbeth (the latter preserved on video). He was an arresting actor and had a warm, resonant voice with a wide range, although his concern for powerful characterization sometimes caused him to distort his vocal line.

ALAN BLYTH

Paso doble (Sp.: 'double step'). Hispanic-derived dance genre, generally in 6/8 metre. See MEXICO, §II; PHILIPPINES, §III, 5(iv).

Pasoqa. Accent denoting a main pause in Syriac EKPHONETIC NOTATION.

Pas ordinaire (Fr.). Slow march. See MARCH, §1.

Pasoti, Giovanni Giacomo. Italian printer. *See under* DORICO, VALERIO.

Paspy. *See* PASSEPIED.

Pasquale [Pasquali], Bonifacio (*d* Padua, Feb 1585). Italian composer. He is recorded as a monk at the monastery of S Francesco, Bologna, on 18 November 1565, and as *maestro di cappella* there on 3 September 1567. He then moved to Padua where he was *maestro di cappella* of S Antonio from 16 Jan 1569 until his death. On 27 May 1576 he was paid 30 ducats for the publication of his psalms. In 1584 he was invited to take charge of the *cappella* of Piacenza Cathedral but he declined. Fétis's statement that he was appointed *maestro di cappella* of Parma Cathedral is not documented and conflicts with Pasquale's documented activities between 1567 and 1585; moreover, as Busi noted, it seems unlikely that Pasquale held the post at Parma before 1567, since the only document to refer to him before that date names him only

as a monk. Pasquale was also a member of the academy at Padua. His only known volume of compositions is *I salmi che si cantano tutto l'anno al Vespro … et un Magnificat* (Venice, 1576[7]), for five and eight voices, which ends with a *Magnificat* by Giulio Rinaldi. Martini quoted three extracts from this work and mentioned another of Pasquale's works, the *Completorium lib. 8*, of which no copies survive.

BIBLIOGRAPHY

FétisB; GaspariC
G.B. Martini: *Esemplare os sia saggio fondamentale pratico di contrappunto sopra il canto fermo*, i (Bologna, 1774/R), 108, 151, 206
L. Busi: *Il Padre G.B. Martini* (Bologna, 1891/R), 201ff
G. Gaspari: *Miscellanea musicale* (MS, *I-Bc*, UU.12), i, 11f, 14; iii, 72f
G. Tebaldini: *L'archivio musicale della Cappella Antoniana* in Padova (Padua, 1895), 9f, 12, 90, 110, 152

PIER PAOLO SCATTOLIN

Pasquali [Pascale, Paschali], Francesco (*b* Cosenza, late 16th century; *d* after 1634). Italian composer. He is described as 'nobile cossentino' in his 1615 publication. He studied in Rome and seems to have spent some time in or around that city. From 1622 to 1631 he was *maestro di cappella* of Viterbo Cathedral. He dedicated his *Madrigali* of 1627 and *Varie musiche* (1633) to Cardinal Tiberio Muti, Bishop of Viterbo and Toscanella, whom he served for many years. He may have been the Cecco Pasquali who was a singer at Assisi, probably about 1628–9, and the dedication of his *Varie musiche* was dated at Ancona on 20 December 1632. In 1635 he applied, unsuccessfully, for the position of *maestro* of Urbino Cathedral. He published at least six books of music. The secular ones, of which only that of 1627 survives complete, reflect the contemporary shift in interest from the polyphonic to the concertato madrigal, dialogue and solo song. The four-part dialogue *Che fai, Tirsi gentile* (1627) reveals Pasquali as a competent composer in the Roman style.

WORKS
all with bc

[Madrigali], 5vv, op.1 (Venice, 1615)
Sacrae cantiones, 2–5vv, op.2 (Venice, 1617)
Mottetti, 2–4vv, op.3 (Rome, 1618), lost
Madrigali, libro secondo, 5vv, op.4 (Venice, 1618)
Madrigali, libro terzo, 1–5vv, op.5 (Rome, 1627)
Varie musiche, 1–5vv, op.6 (Orvieto, 1633)

BIBLIOGRAPHY
PitoniN
C. Crivellati: *Discorsi musicali* (Viterbo, 1624)
B. Ligi: 'La cappella musicale del duomo di Urbino', *NA*, ii (1925) [whole issue]
A.V. Jones: *The Motets of Carissimi* (Ann Arbor, 1982)
J. Whenham: *Duet and Dialogue in the Age of Monteverdi*, i (Ann Arbor, 1982), 188–9
A. De Angelis: 'La cappella musicale di Viterbo nel secolo XVII', *RIM*, xix (1984), 21–35

COLIN TIMMS

Pasquali, Niccolo (*b* c1718; *d* Edinburgh, 13 Oct 1757). Italian composer, violinist, theoretician and impresario. It is assumed that Pasquali was born about 1718, since the Edinburgh burial records give the age at which he died as 39. According to Burney he came to London about 1743 and from then on was extremely active in the three main British musical centres. He spent the period 1748–9 in Dublin, where he produced an oratorio, *Noah*, and a masque, *The Temple of Peace*. By 1750 he was back in London, returning to Dublin in 1751. From

October 1752 onwards he lived in Edinburgh, where he led the orchestras at both the Canongate Theatre and the Musical Society, wrote and acted in a 'whimsical Farce' entitled *The Enraged Musician* (based on Hogarth's print), and composed, among other works, a *Stabat mater* which continued to be performed in Edinburgh after his death. His arrangement of Corelli's concerto grosso op.6 no.4, with additional parts for horns, trumpets and timpani, survived in the concert repertory until the 1770s (see Fiske, 260).

Much of Pasquali's music is no longer extant. He was a fluent, prolific writer, accustomed to working in the theatre; he probably learnt a great deal from Handel. Cudworth suspected that he had a valuable influence on Boyce. Several of his Twelve Overtures of 1751 have subtitles which show they belonged to theatrical productions for which the rest of Pasquali's music is lost.

Pasquali also wrote a figured bass instruction book, *Thorough-bass made Easy*, which was published in Edinburgh in 1757 at the end of his short, energetic career. It went through at least three British editions and – translated into French and Dutch – one in Amsterdam; it contains excellent advice which is still of value, e.g. on different ways to break chords when accompanying recitative. In restrospect it seems to be Pasquali's most important achievement.

WORKS

ORATORIOS

Noah, lost; David, lost, hpd part, *GB-Lcm*

MASQUES

The Temple of Peace, Apollo and Daphne, The Grand Festino, Venus and Adonis, The Nymphs of the Spring, The Triumphs of Hibernia; only ovs. survive

COMIC OPERA

The Enraged Musician, or The Tempest Rehearsed, advertised in *Edinburgh Evening Courant*, 13 Jan 1753; lost

CANTATAS

Pastora, S, vn, bc, in Thorough-bass made Easy (Edinburgh, 1757); Tweedside, listed in *GB-Eu* La.III.761, lost; Vineyard, listed in *Eu*, lost

OTHER WORKS

12 overtures (London, 1751, as Raccolta di overture); Overture Stabat mater, listed in *Eu*, lost
6 sonatas op.1, vn, bc (London, 1744); two sets of 3 sonatas, 2 vn, va, bc (London, c1750); many minuets
12 English songs in score (London, 1750); many single songs
Arr. of Corelli, concerto grosso, op.6 no.4 (Amsterdam, 1714), addl hns, tpts, timp, lost

WRITINGS

Thorough-bass made Easy (Edinburgh, 1757, later edn, 1763); ed. J. Churchill (London, 1974)
The Art of Fingering the Harpsichord (Edinburgh, ?1760)

BIBLIOGRAPHY

FiskeETM, 159, 203, 260, 384–6, 595; *MGG1* (C Cudworth and H.F. Redlich)
D. Fraser-Harris: *Saint Cecilia's Hall in the Niddry Wynd* (Edinburgh, 1899, 2/1911/R), 268–72
W.H.G. Flood: *A History of Irish Music* (Dublin, 1905, 3/1913/R, 4/1927), 293ff
D. Johnson: *Music and Society in Lowland Scotland in the Eighteenth Century* (London, 1972), 47–8, 54–5, 142
D. Johnson: *Scottish Fiddle Music in the 18th Century* (Edinburgh, 1984), 217

DAVID JOHNSON

Pasqualini, Marc'Antonio ['Malagigi'] (*b* Rome, bap. 25 April 1614; *d* Rome, 3 July 1691). Italian soprano castrato and composer. The son of a barber from Imola, he studied with Vincenzo Ugolini while employed as a boy soprano at S Luigi dei Francesi in Rome from 1623; in 1629 his contract of apprenticeship was bought out by the younger Cardinal Antonio Barberini, who remained his patron and promoter. Imposed upon the Cappella Sistina by Barberini in 1631, the boy became a full member of the choir in July 1634. Despite fulfilling the needs of his patron ahead of those of the choir, Pasqualini eventually served as *puntatore* (penalty scorer) for the choir in 1648 and as *maestro di cappella* in 1655; he retired in 1659 but returned occasionally to sing as a substitute.

Pasqualini was among the earliest singers with steady experience on the operatic stage. He sang in the 1628 Farnese wedding festivities in Parma, and in Rome he performed leading roles in the Barberini productions of *Sant' Alessio* (1632, 1634), *Erminia sul Giordano* (1633), *Didimo e Theodora* (1635, 1636), *Chi soffre speri* (1637, 1639) and *Il palazzo incanto* (1642), as well as singing in the French ambassador's production of *La Sincerità trionfante* (1638–9). After Cardinal Antonio had fled to Paris, Pompeo Colonna presented him in his own *Ratto di Proserpina* (1645, Rome). Pasqualini's final stage appearance was in *Orfeo* by Luigi Rossi, given in Paris in 1647. Short in stature, he specialized in unhappy characters (often women disguised as men), such as the lamenting Bradamante of Rossi's *Palazzo incantato*. Such roles provided poignant, triple-metre lyrical arias as well as distressed or vengeful recitative soliloquies.

The music he performed for the Barberini – by Stefano Landi, Marco Marazzoli and, after 1641, Luigi Rossi – influenced Pasqualini's own compositions. It appears that many of the manuscript scores that he owned remained in the Barberini collection (*I-Rvat*). These include anthologies (dated between 1638 and 1676) of secular and devotional vocal chamber music and undated scores and parts of oratorios in Italian. Much is in Pasqualini's own hand; some are compositional sketches. To complicate matters of authorship in the oratorios, some portions are contrafacta and arrangements of earlier, seemingly independent pieces. Over 40 chamber cantatas, however, are securely identified as his through attributions in concordant sources; he may well have composed over 100 others (see Murata, 1985). Most of the attributed works are among the Pasqualini autographs in the Barberini collection. In other sources Pasqualini's music appears from the mid-century, at the height of his fame as a singer and about the time that Andrea Sacchi painted the full-length portrait of him now in the New York Metropolitan Museum of Art.

BIBLIOGRAPHY

A. Cametti: 'Musicisti celebri del Seicento in Roma: M.A. Pasqualini', *Musica d'oggi*, iii (1921), 69–71, 97–9
H. Prunières: 'Les musiciens du Cardinal Antonio Barberini', *Mélanges de musicologie offerts à M. Lionel de la Laurencie* (Paris, 1933), 119–22
G. Rose: 'Pasqualini as Copyist', *AnMc*, no.14 (1974), 170–75
M. Murata: 'Further Remarks on Pasqualini and the Music of *MAP*', *AnMc*, no.19 (1979), 125–45
M. Murata: *Operas for the Papal Court, 1631–1668* (Ann Arbor, 1981)
T. Ford: 'Andrea Sacchi's "Apollo Crowning the Singer M.A. Pasqualini"', *EMc*, xii (1984), 79–84
J. Lionnet: *La musique à Saint-Louis des français de Rome au XVIIe siècle* (Venice, 1985), i, 57–8; ii, 53–4, 71–2
M. Murata: Introduction to *Cantatas by Marc' Antonio Pasqualini, 1614–1691*, ISCS, iii (1985)
F.T. Camiz: 'The Castrato Singer: from Informal to Formal Portraiture', *Artibus et historie*, no.18 (1988), 171–86

F. Hammond: *Music & Spectacle in Baroque Rome: Barberini Patronage under Urban VIII* (New Haven, CT, 1994)

MARGARET MURATA

Pasquin (*fl* 1469–74; *d* before 1497). Franco-Flemish composer. He joined the choir of Cambrai Cathedral in 1469, and was still active there in 1474. In 1472–3 Tinctoris criticized his (as yet unidentified) *Missa authenti prothi irregularis* for its contradictory use of minims (citing two excerpts from the 'Cum sancto'), and described the work generally as 'lacking in all art and melody'; this was the only work Tinctoris censured for its style as a whole, and its identification might shed interesting light on the early history of music criticism. Yet Pasquin was famous enough to be mentioned by Guillaume Cretin in his *Déploration* for Johannes Ockeghem (1497), where he is among the 13 deceased composers who pay musical tribute to Ockeghem in the underworld.

Pasquin's only surviving work is a four-part *Missa 'Da pacem'* (*I-Rvat* C.S.41), a setting whose style suggests a date in the 1470s. The plainchant cantus firmus, though rhythmicized differently in each movement, is treated like a traditional 'scaffold' tenor, in long note values with occasional *prolatio maior* augmentation. The setting strongly recalls the sacred music of Busnoys in its use of these and other mensural contrasts, its employment of the signature O2, the retention of plainchant text in the tenor, the introduction of three-part imitations around the long-held tenor notes, and especially the tendency for the outer voices to move in parallel tenths.

BIBLIOGRAPHY

E. Thoinan: *Déploration de Guillaume Cretin sur le trépas de Jean Okeghem* (Paris, 1864)

C. Wright: 'Musiciens à la cathédrale de Cambrai, 1475–1550', *RdM*, lxii (1976), 204–28

A. Seay, ed.: *Johannes Tinctoris: opera theoretica*, CSM, xxii/2a (1978)

R.C. Wegman: 'Sense and Sensibility in Late-Medieval Music: Thoughts on Aesthetics and "Authenticity"', *EMc*, xxiii (1995), 298–312

ROB C. WEGMAN

Pasquini, Bernardo (*b* Massa Valdinievole [now Massa e Cozzile, Pistoia], 7 Dec 1637; *d* Rome, 22 Nov 1710). Italian composer, harpsichordist and organist. Renowned in his day as a virtuoso keyboard player, he was the most important Italian composer of keyboard music between Frescobaldi and Domenico Scarlatti. He also made a significant contribution to the traditions of Roman opera and oratorio.

1. LIFE. Pasquini claimed to have attended the school at Uzzano, near his birthplace; according to G.B. Martini he was brought up by an uncle at Ferrara. He had reached Rome by 1650, and he lived there for the rest of his life. It has always been maintained that his teachers were Antonio Cesti and Loreto Vittori, but he made a detailed study of the works of Palestrina and Frescobaldi; he copied Frescobaldi's *Il primo libro delle fantasie* (1608, *D-Bsb*). He held a series of organist posts in Rome: at S Maria in Valicella from 1657 (following F. Fontana); then at Chiesa Nuova and S Luigi dei Francesi after the death of Mutii in 1661 (also at S Luigi, 1973–5); and at S Maria in Aracoeli from 8 February 1664 until his death, with the title 'organist of the Senate and Roman people'. In 1664 he played as a harpsichordist for Louis XIV while in the entourage of the papal legate, Cardinal Flavio Chigi. From 1664 to 1685 he was one of the organists in the oratorio performances at the oratory of S Marcello.

Pasquini's contemporary reputation rested largely on his outstanding virtuosity as a keyboard player and gained him the patronage of Queen Christina of Sweden, Prince Colonna, Cardinal Ottoboni, Cardinal Pamphili and, above all, Prince Giambattista Borghese. In November 1666 he became harpsichordist and musical director to Prince Giambattista and about 1669 he moved into an apartment on the third floor of the recently completed Palazzo Nuovo of the Borghese. The census records of the parish of S Lorenzo in Lucina confirm that he lived there from at least 1671 until his death, sharing the accommodation at first with two other musicians and later with his nephews, notably, from 1691 to 1710, Bernardo Felice Ricordati, who studied with him and eventually took his surname.

Outside the Borghese household Pasquini was involved in performances of secular music throughout Rome. His stature as a keyboard player was equal to that of Corelli as a violinist, and they performed together not only in oratorios but in operas and chamber concerts. Corelli led the orchestra for the performances of Pasquini's opera *Dov'è amore è pietà* at the Teatro Capranica in 1679 and of his cantata *Accademia per musica* at the palace of Queen Christina of Sweden in 1687. In the musicians' guild, the Congregazione di S Cecilia, each rose to become 'guardian' of his respective section – Pasquini of the organists and Corelli of the instrumentalists. On 26 April 1706, together with Alessandro Scarlatti, they became members of the Arcadian Academy (founded in 1690), where they were known respectively as Protico Azeriano, Arcomelo Erimanteo and Terpandro; their patron Cardinal Ottoboni also belonged to it. Here, and on other occasions, Pasquini must have met Handel during his stay in Rome. He apparently travelled to the court of the Emperor Leopold I at Vienna, where at least one of his oratorios was performed, and in 1664, in the company of Cardinal Flavio Chigi, nephew of Pope Alexander VII, he went to Paris, where he played to Louis XIV. He also visited Florence and other Italian cities. He attracted pupils to Rome from far and wide: in addition to the Italians G.M. Casini, T.B. Gaffi, Francesco Gasparini, Domenico Zipoli and possibly Francesco Durante and Domenico Scarlatti, he taught J.P. Krieger, Georg Muffat and pupils sent from Vienna by the emperor.

Pasquini's reputation was such that medallions bearing his portrait were struck after his death. He was buried in the church of S Lorenzo in Lucina, where there is a memorial bust carved by Pietro Papaleo. There is a portrait of him by Andrea Pozzo (in *I-Fc*; fig.1).

2. WORKS. Though Pasquini enjoyed a reputation as a keyboard player comparable to that of Frescobaldi earlier in the century, little of his music was published. Three pieces by him, ascribed to 'N.N. di Roma', were published by G.C. Arresti (in RISM *c*1697[8]), and he was represented in a collection of toccatas and suites issued in Amsterdam by Roger (RISM, 1698[4]/*R*). Most of his keyboard music survives in four autograph manuscripts compiled between 1691 and about 1705 (facs. in SCKM, vii–viii, 1988) and intended for the use of his nephew B.F. Ricordati, for whom he probably wrote his practical instruction manual *Saggi di contrappunto* (1695) and possibly also the lost *Regole per ben suonare il cembalo o organo*.

The better and larger part of Pasquini's keyboard output consists of dance suites, variation sets, arias and individual dances, but 11 contrapuntal pieces and 35 inventiveness, supported by an increasing balance of phrase, tonality and form that looks forward to the *galant* style. Following the Italian tradition of grouped dances found in Frescobaldi's ballettos (1637) and the instrumental music of Cazzati, G.B. Vitali, G.M. Bononcini and Corelli, he established the keyboard suite in Italy. Of his 17 suites, five have two dances, five have three, six have four, and one has five, each suite being in one key. The basic pattern is that of allemanda-corrente-giga (an arrangement found in several of Corelli's sonatas of 1685), but any one movement may be replaced by an aria, *bizzaria*, *tastata* or unspecified dance. Eight of the suites include the basic grouping, which in six of them is followed by an additional unspecified dance or dances. All the dances are in binary form. The influence of dance music is apparent in the 14 sets of variations, which range in length from a dance movement with a single variation to the 24 of the *Partite di bergamasca*. In most of them the individual sections are either bipartite or binary, and several are identified as dances. The most famous are the 14 variations on the folia, which typically illustrate the influence of violin figuration on keyboard music. The four passacaglias range from 12 to 24 sections.

He composed 28 sonatas written only in figured bass, the most curious and individual group in his output. Exactly half are for two harpsichords, almost all being in three movements, arranged Allegro-Andante-Allegro; the other half, for a single instrument, are in two to five movements. They have no obvious precedent.

In recent decades scholarly attention has been given to Pasquini's dramatic and vocal music, though the majority remains unpublished and much work still remains to be done. Scores for 12 of his 18 known operas and seven of his 13 oratorios survive. There are also cantatas, arias and solo motets. Most of the early operas are comedies. *L'Idalma* is a typical example both dramatically and musically. The late operas include a *festa teatrale*, *La caduta del regno dell'Amazzoni*, for the wedding of Carlos II of Spain to Marianna, Countess Palatine. It was probably the most extravagant production in Rome at that time. Pasquini's oratorios received performances in Florence, Modena, Naples and Vienna though most may have been intended for Rome in the first instance. In his dramatic music Pasquini made frequent use of the da capo principle in short arias, but ostinato bass and strophic procedures are often more important. Many of the arias have only continuo accompaniment, and where other instruments are used it is normally in refrains and short interjections. Vocal ensembles are generally through-composed. His arioso style, especially in the oratorios, is

1. Bernardo Pasquini: portrait by Andrea Pozzo, late 17th century) (Conservatorio Statale di Musica 'Luigi Cherubini', Florence)

toccatas recall the sterner influences of Frescobaldi and early Baroque music. Though Frescobaldi's techniques of thematic variation can be seen in the *Ricercare con fuga in più modi*, the two fugal sonatas in Arresti's print, on the other hand, display contrasting, lively subjects and are clearly tonal. The toccatas, sometimes called *tastatas*, are equally varied in style and structure. One is a long pedal-point toccata, recalling those 'sopra i pedali' in Frescobaldi's 1627 volume, while another is only 15 bars long. Some are in a single section, while one is divided into five sections with alternating common and triple metres. The passage-work is often brilliant, but sequences, parallel writing, scales and tonal figuration replace the angularity and rhetorical drama of the early Baroque toccata.

Pasquini's suites and variations were evidently conceived for the harpsichord. Here he showed great melodic

2. Autograph of the opening of the first of Pasquini's 14 sonatas for two harpsichords, 1704, written in figured bass only (GB-Lbl Add.31501, f.3v)

fluent, expressive and affective, and in his changes of metre he recalls fluid, less continuous style of the mid-17th century. There is also more formal dramatic writing, for example the bravura arias sung by the abandoned Idalma.

Pasquini was regarded as the leading dramatic composer in Rome in the 1670s. In the 1680s his popularity was equalled and then surpassed by his younger contemporaries, notably Alessandro Scarlatti. After 1690 he wrote only one opera, *Eudossia*, and a contemporary account suggests that he may have been stuggling to meet the current demands of taste and fashion.

WORKS

Editions: *B. Pasquini: Collected Works for Keyboard*, ed. M.B. Haynes, CEKM, v/1–7 (1964–8) [H 1–7]
Opere per cembalo e organo, ed. H. Illy, MVSSP, xxxviii (1971)

KEYBOARD

Toccatas: Prelude, 11 tastatas, 22 toccatas, Toccata con lo Scherzo del cucco (10 in *GB-Lbl* Add.36661, 1 in 1698[4], H 5–6

Dances: 17 suites, 3 allemandes, 22 arias, 4 bizzarias, corrente, 4 gigues, H 2

Variations: Partite del saltarello, Partite di bergamasca, Partite diversi di follia, Partite diversi sopra alemanda, Variationi capricciose, Variationi e inventione, Variationi fioritas, Variationi sopra la follia, 5 sets of variations, 4 movts with single variations, H 3–4

Sonatas: 4 for org (3 in *c*1697[8]), H 1, 6; 14 for hpd (figured bass only), H 7; 14 for 2 hpd (figured bass only), H 7, ed. W. Kolneder, *Vierzehn Sonaten* (Lottstetten, 1987)

Other works: 3 canzonas (2 in *Lbl* Add.36661), 2 capriccios, fantasia, fuga, 2 ricercars, H 1; 4 passacaglias, bergamasca, H 3–4; 10 accadenze, 10 untitled pieces, 4 frags., H 7; 5 doubtful pieces from minor sources, H 7

OPERAS
first performed in Rome unless otherwise stated
dm – *dramma per musica*

La sincerità con la sincerità, overo Il Tirinto (favola drammatica per musica, G.F. Apolloni and other Accademici Sfaccendati), Ariccia, Palazzo Chigi, 20 Oct 1672, *I-MOe*

La forza d'amore (componimento drammatico rusticale, Apolloni), ?1672, *B-Bc, GB-Cfm, Lcm, I-Fc*

L'Amor per vendetta, overo L'Alcasta (dm, Apolloni), Tordinona, 27 Jan 1673, *D-MÜs, I-MOe*, arias in *Nc*

La donna ancora è fedele (dm, D.F. Contini), Palazzo Colonna, carn. 1676, *I-MOe*, arias in *Bc, Nc* and *Rvat*

[Il Trespolo tutore balordo] (commedia per musica, G.C. Villifranchi, rev. Bertucci), Palazzo Colonna, 10 Feb 1677, *F-Pn*

Dov'è amore è pietà (drama musicale, C. Ivanovich, after G.A. Moniglia: *Ipermestra*), Capranica, 6 Jan 1679, 1 aria in *I-MOe*

L'Idalma, overo Chi la dura la vince (commedia per musica, G.D. De Totis), Palazzo Capranica, 6 Feb 1680, *F-Pn* (facs. in IOB, ii, 1977), arias in *Pc, I-Fbecherini, Folschki* (see Bonaventura, 1906–8) and *Vnm*

Il Lisimaco (dm, 'Comagio Baldosini' [Giacomo Sinibaldi]), ?Palazzo Riario, carn. 1681, formerly *D-Hs, WD*, arias in *I-Bsp* and *US-Su*

La Tessalonica (dm, N. Minato), Palazzo Colonna, 31 Jan 1683, *A-Wgm*, arias *D-MÜs, F-Pc, GB-Lbl, I-Nc, Rc, Rsc, Rvat, Vnm*

La vita e un sogno di notte (commedia, 3, J. Cicogini), Palazzo Pamphili, 12 Feb 1684

L'Arianna (dm), Palazzo Colonna, 3 Feb 1685, arias in *GB-Lbl, Ob, I-Bc* and *Rvat*

Il silentio d'Arpocrate (dm, Minato), Palazzo Colonna, 26 Jan 1686, arias in *F-Pn* and *I-Rvat*

Santa Dimna, figlia del re d'Irlanda [Act 2] (sacred op, 3, B. Pamphili), [Act 1 by Alessandro Melani, Act 3 by A. Scarlatti], arias in *GB-Lbl, I-Rvat*

I giochi Troiani (dm, C.S. Capece), Palazzo Colonna, Feb 1688, 2 arias *Rvat*, 1 aria *Bc*

La caduta del regno dell'Amazzoni (festa teatrale, De Totis), Palazzo Colonna, before 15 Jan 1690, *GB-Lbl, F-Pc* (inc.), arias in *I-Fc, MOe, Rli* and *Rvat*

Alessio, Seminario Romano, 1690

Il Colombo, overo L'India scoperta (dm, P. Ottoboni), Tordinona, 28 Dec 1690, *GB-Lbl*, arias in *D-MÜs, I-Bc, Rli* and *Rvat*

Eudossia (A. Pollioni), Seminario Romano, 6 Feb 1692, arias in *D-MÜs* and *I-Rsc*

ORATORIOS
(music lost unless otherwise indicated)

Caino e Abel, 5vv (Apolloni), Rome, Cappella del Principe Borghese, 1671, *I-Rvat*

L'Agar (F.B. Nencini), Rome, Oratorio della Pietà, 17 March 1675

Assuero (Nencini), Rome, Oratorio della Pietà, 15 April 1675

Sant'Alessio (G.F. Bernini), Rome, Oratorio dei Filippini, 1675, *A-Wn, I-MOe*

Sant'Agnese (B. Pamphili), Vienna, 1678, *A-Wn*; Modena, 1685, *I-MOe*

Sant'Eufrasia (Lazarini), Rome, lib pubd 1678

Salutazione angelica, Messina, lib pubd 1681

Divae Clarae triumphus (A.F. Noceto), Rome, Oratorio del Crocifisso, 20 March 1682

L'idolatria di Salomone (?L'Orsini), Rome, Collegio Clementino, 1686; renamed La caduta di Salomone, Florence, Congregazione dell'Oratorio, 1693

I fatti di Mosè nel deserto (G.B. Giardini), Modena, 1687, *MOe, B-Bc*

Il martirio dei santi, Vito, Modesto e Crescenzio (D.F. Contini), Modena, lib pubd 1687, *I-MOe*

L'Abramo, Congregazione dell'Oratorio, Palermo, 1688; renamed L'Ismaele, Florence, Oratorio di S Filippo Neri, 1693

La sete di Cristo, Modena, 1689, *MOe*

S maria di Soria, 5vv, Rome, Cappella del Principe Borghese, March 1694

David trionfante contro Goliath, Florence, Oratorio di S Filippo Neri, 1694

Fermate, onde del Tebro, in lode di San Filippo Neri (*MS*, Biblioteca Oratoriana Girolamini, Naples)

Oratorio a 5 [on Cain and Abel], *I-Rvat*

CANTATAS

Aplauso musicale, 5vv, *c*1679, *I-Fc*

Erminia in riva del Giordano (B. Pamphili), Rome, 1682; 1 aria ed. in Alte Meister des Bel Canto, i–ii (Leipzig, 1912)

Accademia per musica (A. Guidi), Rome, Palazzo Riaro, Feb 1687, to celebrate coronation of James II of England, music lost

Aplauso festivo (Guidi), Rome, probably Palazzo Pamphili, Feb 1687, music lost (mentioned in Montalto) [? = Accademia per musica]

Il colosso della costanza, 4vv, Rome, Seminario Romano, 15 April 1689, arias *F-Pc*

Sovra un'accesa pira, 1v, 2 vn, bc

Over 50 solo cants., some *I-MOe*

OTHER VOCAL

Solo motets, arias, *D-MÜs, F-Pn, GB-Lbl, Ob, I-Bc, Fc, MOe, Nc, Rvat*

WRITINGS

Saggi di contrappunto, 1695, *D-Bsb**

Regole per ben suonare il cembalo o organo, lost, partial copies, 1715, 1729, *I-Bc*

BIBLIOGRAPHY

ApelG; EitnerQ; FrotscherG; SartoriL

A. Bonaventura: 'Di un codice musicale del secolo XVII', *La bibliofilia*, viii (1906–7), 321–35; ix (1907–8), 327–9

A. Bonaventura: *Bernardo Pasquini* (Ascoli Piceno, 1923)

G. Roncaglia: '*Il Tirinto* di Bernardo Pasquini e i suoi intermezzi', *RaM*, iv (1931), 331–9

E. Dagnino: 'Marginalia', *NA*, ix (1932), 270–76; xi (1934), 68–9

R. Casimiri: 'Oratorii del Masini, Bernabei, Melani, Di Pio, Pasquini e Stradella, in Roma nell'anno santo 1675', *NA*, xiii (1936), 157–69

A. Cametti: *Il teatro di Tordinona poi di Apollo* (Tivoli, 1938)

E.J. Luin: *Bernardo Pasquini e il suo tricentenario* (Rome, 1939)

A. Damerini: 'Di alcuni maestri toscani – L'"Aplauso musicale" di Bernardo Pasquini', *Musicisti toscani*, ii, Chigiana, xii (1955), 27–38

L. Montalto: *Un mecenate in Roma barocca* (Florence, 1955)

A. Liess: 'Materialien zur römischen Musikgeschichte des Seicento: Musikerlisten des Oratorio San Marcello 1664–1725', *AcM*, xxix (1957), 137–71

W. Heimrich: *Die Orgel- und Cembalo-Werke Bernardo Pasquinis* (diss., Free U. of Berlin, 1958)

A. Liess: 'Die Sammlung der Oratorienlibretti (1679–1725) und der restliche Musikbestand des Fondo San Marcello der Biblioteca Vaticana in Rom', *AcM*, xxxi (1959), 63–80

M.B. Haynes: *The Keyboard Works of Bernardo Pasquini* (diss., Indiana U., 1960)

M. Borrelli: *Una interessante raccolta di libretti a stampa di oratori della fine del Seicento, presso la Biblioteca dell'Oratorio di Londra* (Naples, 1962)

G.F. Crain: *The Operas of Bernardo Pasquini* (diss., Yale U., 1965)

P. Bjurstrom: *Feast and Theatre in Queen Christina's Rome* (Stockholm, 1966)

C. Gianturco: '*Il Trespolo tutore* di Stradella e di Pasquini: due diversi concezioni dell'opera comica', *Venezia e il melodramma del Settecento: Venice 1973, i, 185–98*

C.M. Gianturco: 'Evidence for a Late Roman School of Opera', *ML*, lvi (1975), 4–17

A. Silbiger: *Italian Manuscript Sources of 17th Century Keyboard Music* (Ann Arbor, 1980)

A. Silbiger: 'The Roman Frescobaldi Tradition, c.1640–1670', *JAMS*, xxxiii (1980), 42–87

G. Morelli: 'L'Apolloni librettista di Cesti, Stradella e Pasquini', *Alessandro Stradella e il suo tempo: Siena 1982* [Chigiana, new ser., xix (1982)], 211–64

A. Silbiger: 'Keyboard Music by Corelli's Colleagues: Roman Composers in English Sources', *Nuovissimi studi Corelliani Fusignano 1980*, 253–68

F. Della Seta: 'I Borghese (1691–1731): la musica di una generazione', *NA*, new ser., i (1983), 139–208

H.J. Marx: 'Die "Giustificazioni della casa Pamphili" als musikgeschichtliche Quelle', *Studi musicali*, xii (1983), 121–87

E. Ozolins: *The Oratorios of Bernardo Pasquini* (diss., U. of California, LA, 1983)

R. Lefevre: '*Il Tirinto* de Bernardo Pasquini all'Ariccia (1672)', *Lunario romano, 1986: musica e musicisti nel Lazio* (Rome, 1985), 237–68

G. Oost: 'Improvisation in der Sonate für zwei cembali: Bernardo Pasquini als Vorbild für Mattheson und Händel?', *Der Einfluss der italienischen Musik in der ersten Hälfte des 18. Jahrhunderts: Blankenburg, Harz 1987*, 64–77

S. Franchi: *Drammaturgia romana: repertorio bibliografico cronologico dei testi drammatici pubblicati a Roma e nel Lazio, secolo XVII* (Rome, 1988)

F. Tasini: 'Bernardo Pasquini: La sete di Christo (1683)', *RIMS*, ix (1988), 19–44

F. Carboni, T.M. Gialdroni and A. Ziino: 'Cantate ed arie romane del tardo Seicento nel Fondo Caetani della Biblioteca Corsiniana: repertorio, forme e strutture', *Studi musicali*, xviii (1989), 49–192

M. Carnevali: *Gli oratori romani di Bernardo Pasquini* (diss., U. degli Studi di Roma, 1989–90)

L. Mancini: *Alcuni aspetti della produzione cembalo-organista di Bernardo Pasquini* (diss., U. degli Studi di Roma, 1990–91)

J. Herczog: 'Tendenze letterarie e sviluppo musicale dell'oratorio italiano nel Settecento tra Vienna e il paese d'origine', *NRMI*, xxv (1991), 217–31

A. Morelli: 'La circulazione dell'oratorio italiano nel Seicento', *Studi musicali*, xxvi (1997), 105–86

JOHN HARPER/LOWELL LINDGREN

Pasquini, Ercole (*b* Ferrara, mid-16th century; *d* Rome, 1608–19). Italian composer and organist. According to Superbi he studied with Alessandro Milleville and played 'i primi organi' for many years in Ferrara before moving to Rome in 1597. In the 1580s he taught the harpsichord, organ and composition to the daughters of G.B. Aleotti, court architect at Ferrara: in 1593 Aleotti referred to Pasquini as a 'buon vecchio' in the dedication of a book of four-part madrigals by his daughter Vittoria. Pasquini may be the 'organist Ercole' who is mentioned in the *ridotto* of Mario Bevilacqua of Verona in 1593. The same year his *favola boscareccia* entitled *I fidi amanti*, written for the forthcoming marriage of Leonora d'Este to Carlo Gesualdo, was published in Verona. Pasquini addressed Leonora as his patron in this work of which only the text survives. Pasquini succeeded Luzzaschi as organist of the Accademia della Morte, and was succeeded there by

Ex.1(a)

(b)

(c)

(d)

Frescobaldi. On 6 October 1597 he was elected organist of the Cappella Giulia, Rome. He was also organist of the nearby Santo Spirito in Sassia in 1604. During 1605 he was in hospital and on 19 May 1608 was dismissed from his post at S Pietro. According to Superbi, 'he had a very delicate and nimble hand; on occasion he played so splendidly that he enraptured the people and truly amazed them'. Superbi added that he died under unfortunate circumstances. Pietro della Valle and Luigi Battiferri (in his *Ricercari* op.3, of 1669) attested to Pasquini's fame well into the 17th century.

By virtue of the 30 keyboard compositions that have survived in manuscript, Pasquini must be counted among the important predecessors of Frescobaldi. The toccatas consist of several short sections containing novel figuration, 7th chords and experimental harmonies which generate great nervous tension. The *durezze e ligature* are among the earliest works of this type. Most of the canzonas are in three sections, with the central one in triple time. In several of them the opening subject reappears in varied form in one or more of the remaining sections; they are therefore among the earliest examples of the variation canzona. Ex.1 gives the subject of a *canzona francese* of 1600 (CEKM, xii, p.38) and its variants. The variations on the Ruggiero, *passamezzo antico* and romanesca employ the same type of nervous figuration found in the toccatas. The correntes are the earliest known examples in Italy; they consist of two or three sections of irregular length. Only five of Pasquini's vocal compositions have survived. The most impressive is the motet *Quem vidistis, pastores*, which is for two five-part choirs.

WORKS

2 motets, 5, 10vv, in R. Aleotti, Sacrae Cantiones (Venice, 1593); 1, 4vv, in 1618[3]

1 madrigal, 5vv, 1591[9] (contrafactum, in 1606[6]); 1 in 1604[8]

6 toccatas, 2 durezze e ligature, 12 canzanas, 1 intabulation of C. Rore, Anchor che col partire, 5 sets of variations, 4 dances, 1 untitled (doubtful); all ed. in CEKM, xii (1966)

1 mass, 10vv; Missa 'Vestiva i colli', 3 choirs; Cantiones, 16 vols.; Madrigali alla Sma. Vergine, 5vv: lost, cited in inventory of Archduke Siegmund Franz, Innsbruck, 1665

BIBLIOGRAPHY

ApelG; NewcombMF

A. Superbi: *Apparato de gli huomini illustri della città di Ferrara* (Ferrara, 1620), 132

M. Guarini: *Compendio historico dell'origine … delle chiese … diocesi di Ferrara* (Ferrara, 1621), 247

P. della Valle: *Della musica dell'età nostra* (MS, 1640); pr. in A. Solerti: *Le origini del melodramma* (Turin, 1903/R)

A. Cametti: 'Girolamo Frescobaldi in Roma', *RMI*, xv (1908), 701–52

F. Waldner: 'Zwei Inventarien aus dem XVI. und XVII. Jahrhundert über hinterlassene Musikinstrumente und Musikalien am Innsbrucker Hofe', *SMw*, iv (1916), 128–47

A. Allegra: 'La cappella musicale di S. Spirito in Saxia di Roma', *NA*, xvii (1940), 28–38, esp. 30

W. Apel: 'Die süditalienische Clavierschule des 17. Jahrhunderts', *AcM*, xxxiv (1962), 128–41

W.R. Shindle: *The Keyboard Works of Ercole Pasquini* (diss., Indiana U., 1963)

H.B. Lincoln: 'I manoscritti chigiani di musica organo-cembalistica della Biblioteca apostolica vaticana', *L'organo*, v (1964–7), 63–82

A. Silbiger: *Italian Manuscript Sources of 17th-Century Keyboard Music* (Ann Arbor, 1980)

J.L. Ladewig: *Frescobaldi's 'Recercari, et Canzoni Franzese' (1615): a Study of the Contrapuntal Keyboard Idiom in Ferrara, Naples, and Rome, 1580–1620* (diss., U. of California, Berkeley, 1978)

W.R. Shindle: 'The Vocal Compositions of Ercole Pasquini', *Frescobaldi Studies: Madison, WI, 1983*, 124–36

A. Newcomb: 'Frescobaldi's Toccatas and their Stylistic Ancestry', *PRMA*, cxi (1984–5), 28–44

J. Ladewig: 'The Origins of Frescobaldi's Variation Canzonas Reappraised', *Frescobaldi Studies: Madison, WI, 1983*, 235–68

R. Judd: 'Italy', *Keyboard Music before 1700*, ed. A. Silbiger (New York, 1995), 235–311

D. Schulenberg: 'Some Problems of Text, Attribution, and Performance in Early Italian Baroque Keyboard Music', *Journal of Seventeenth-Century Music*, iv/1 (1998), 1–15

W. RICHARD SHINDLE

Pas redoublé (Fr.). Quick march. See MARCH, §1.

Pass, Walter (*b* Feldkirch, 22 Jan 1942). Austrian musicologist. He studied the piano and singing at the Vienna Musikhochschule (1960–1964) and musicology from 1961 with Schenk, Graf and Wessely at the University of Vienna, where he took the doctorate in 1967 with a dissertation on Jacob Regnart and his Latin motets. He completed the *Habilitation* in 1973 with a study of music at the court of Maximilian II and joined the staff of the musicological institute in Vienna in 1964. In 1971 he began to work for Denkmäler der Tonkunst in Österreich and he was appointed chief editor of the series Thesauri Musici that same year. A board member of the International Schoenberg Society (from 1973), he organized, with Rudolf Stephan, the first international Schoenberg congress (in Vienna in 1974). Pass has concentrated on the works of Renaissance composers active in the regions of modern Austria; in his later writings he has examined Austrian music and politics during the 20th century.

WRITINGS

Jacob Regnart und seine lateinischen Motetten nebst einem thematischen Katalog sämtlicher Werke (diss., U. of Vienna, 1967)

Thematischer Katalog sämtlicher Werke Jacob Regnarts (ca.1540–1599) (Vienna, 1969)

'Grundzüge einer Musikgeschichte Voralbergs', *ÖMz*, xxv (1970), 434–48

'Der Kammermusikkreis Gottfried van Swietens und das "Kammermusikalische"', *Musica cameralis: Brno VI 1971*, 387–96

Musik und Musiker am Hof Maximilians II (Habilitationsschrift, U. of Vienna, 1973; Tutzing, 1980)

'Schönberg und die "Vereinigung schaffender Tonkünstler in Wien"', *ÖMz*, xxix (1974), 298–303

'Jacob Regnarts Mariale und die katholische Reform in Tirol', *Festschrift Walter Senn*, ed. E. Egg and E. Fässler (Munich, 1975), 158–73

'Jacob Vaets und Georg Prenners Vertonungen des "Salve Regina" in Joanellus' Sammelwerk von 1568', *De ratione in musica: Festschrift Erich Schenk*, ed. T. Antonicek, R. Flotzinger and O. Wessely (Kassel, 1975), 24–49

'Musikleben seit 1945', *Musikgeschichte Österreichs*, ed. R. Flotzinger and G. Gruber, ii (Vienna, 1979)

'Eine Handschrift aus dem Schottenstift zu Wein zur Erklärung der Trienter Codices', *ÖMz*, xxxv (1980), 1443–53

'Zwei unbekannte Wiener Visitatio-Sepulchri-Fragmente aus der ersten Hälfte des 18. Jahrhunderts', *Festschrift Othmar Wessely*, ed. M. Angerer and others (Tutzing, 1982), 447–55

ed.: *Musik im mittelalterlichen Wien* (Vienna, 1986) [exhibition catalogue]

'Das vierstimmige "Magnificat" des Arnold von Bruck in dem vor einigen Jahren wiederentdeckten Chorbuch Ws Sign.2a.19', *SMw*, xlii (1993), 467–74

ed., with M. Csáky: *Europa im Zeitalter Mozarts* (Vienna, 1995) [incl. 'Der Wiener musikalischer Stil', 339–58]

with G. Scheit and W. Svoboda: *Orpheus im Exil: die Vertreibung der österreichischen Musik von 1938 bis 1945* (Vienna, 1995)

ed.: *Bekenntnis zur österreichischen Musik in Lehre und Forschung: eine Festschrift für Eberhard Würzl* (Vienna, 1996) [incl. 'Erberhard Würzl und die Zeitschrift Musikerziehung', 161–76]

EDITIONS

H. Bildstein: *Orpheus christianus, seu symphoniarum sacrarum prodromus*, DTÖ, cxxii, cxxvi (1971–6)

Jacob Regnart: Collected Works, iv: *Sacrae aliquot cantiones: 1575*, CMM, lxii/4 (1975); v: *Aliquot cantiones: 1577*, CMM, lxii/5 (1975)

J.B. Staudt: *Ferdinandus Quintus Rex Hispaniae Maurorum Dormitor: Drama des Wiener Jesuitenkollegs anlässlich der Befreiung von Türken 1683*, DTÖ, cxxxii (1981)

BIBLIOGRAPHY

Mitteilungen der Österreichischen Gesellschaft für Musikwissenschaft, vi (1976) [incl. list of writings]

Passacaglia (It.; Fr. *passacaille*; Ger. *passacalia*; It. *passacaglio*, *passagallo*, *passacagli*, *passacaglie*; Sp. *pasacalle*, *passacalle*). In 19th- and 20th-century music, a set of ground-bass or ostinato variations, usually of a serious character; in the earliest sources, a short, improvised ritornello between the strophes of a song. The term is sometimes used interchangeably with 'chaconne' (the forms 'chaconne' and 'passacaglia' are used throughout this article regardless of the national tradition under discussion). This article concentrates on the early years of the passacaglia, when the term had a quite distinct meaning. Its subsequent history, which largely parallels that of the chaconne, is summarized here; the two genres and their close relationship are explored in greater detail in the article CHACONNE.

1. Beginnings in Spain and Italy. 2. Italy from 1627. 3. Later history in Spain. 4. France. 5. Germany. 6. England. 7. After 1800.

1. BEGINNINGS IN SPAIN AND ITALY. The passacaglia appears to have originated in early 17th-century Spain as the *pasacalle*, a brief improvisation (usually barely more than a few rhythmically strummed cadential chords) that guitarists played between the strophes of a song, somewhat in the nature of a vamp. The term comes from *pasar* (to walk) and *calle* (street), possibly deriving from outdoor performances or from a practice of popular musicians to take a few steps during these interludes. The first references to *pasacalles* appear in Spanish literature in about 1605; in certain contexts the term seems to have been used interchangeably with PASEO.

The term was soon exported to France and Italy, at first, again, to allude to ritornellos (or *riprese*) improvised between song strophes. As with the chaconne, the earliest written examples are found in Italy in *alfabeto* (chord) guitar tablatures, and take the form of brief, rhythmic chord progressions outlining a cadential formula, most commonly I–IV–V–I or an elaboration of it (ex.1*a*). The progressions usually appear in a range of keys, rhythms and strumming patterns, and in duple as well as triple

Ex.1 Passacaglia bass patterns (all transposed and reduced to equivalent note values)

(a) Sanseverino (1620): strumming formula (chords strummed in direction of arrows)

(b) Frescobaldi: *Cento partite* (1637)

(c) Louis Couperin: *Passacaille* for harpsichord

(d) Kerll: Passacaglia for harpsichord (*c*1670)

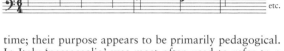

time; their purpose appears to be primarily pedagogical. In Italy 'passacaglio' was most often used to refer to a single statement of a chord scheme, and the plural 'passacagli' for a succession or collection of more than one statement; but both terms, as well as the feminine *passacaglia* and its plural *passacaglie*, as well as variants like *passagallo*, *passagalli*, *passachaglie* and numerous other spellings, were used with little distinction throughout the century.

2. ITALY FROM 1627.   No examples of notated compositions entitled *passacagli* (or one of its variants) other than the guitar-strumming formulae can be dated before 1627, when Frescobaldi published a *Partite sopra passacagli* for keyboard, along with a *Partite sopra la ciaccona*. It is not clear whether he should be credited with the creation of the passacaglia as an independent musical genre (as opposed to an improvised ritornello for another composition), but the 1627 set contains many of the characteristics of the numerous passacaglias for all kinds of instrumental and vocal combinations that appeared in subsequent years. The newer passacaglias are typically in the form of continuous (linked) variations over a bass that may itself be subject to considerable variation. The old I–IV–V–I strumming formula is expanded into innumerable variants, often in the form of elaborations of a descending tetrachord bass (e.g. i–v⁶–iv⁷⁶–V), usually with the metrical phrase remaining as four groups of three beats (ex.1*b*). Chromatic intermediary steps are frequent, as are other digressions, as well as ascending versions (e.g. i–VII⁶–i⁶–iv–V). The earlier notion of the passacaglia as an improvised ritornello, sometimes on a specified bass, survived for some time, and is encountered, for example, in Monteverdi's *L'incoronazione di Poppea* (1642). No doubt connected with this practice is a continuing tradition of presenting sets of passacaglias for the guitar in a full range of modes or keys, both major and minor, thus providing the player with models and exercises for improvising preludes and interludes of arbitrary length. A similar purpose may have been intended for a collection of 44 anonymous and untitled variation sets for keyboard on descending bass patterns (in *I-Rvat* Chigi Q IV 27, a manuscript probably associated with Frescobaldi and his pupils). The pieces are ordered by key, ascending by step from C, and include sets in both duple and triple time; those in triple time closely resemble Frescobaldi's passacaglias. Improvised guitar interludes continued to be

called 'passagalli' in the folk music of some areas of Italy into the 19th century (Hudson, 1981, p.281).

In its new guise as an independent variation chain, the passacaglia shared many features with the chaconne, including the linking of variations, cadential articulation and the use of triple metre. Yet Frescobaldi's passacaglias also show some distinctions (not necessarily in every instance), such as a less exuberant, more restrained character, slower tempo, minor rather than major key, smoother, often conjunct, melodic motion and more frequent dissonant suspensions on downbeats. The similarities, differences and ambiguities between the passacaglia and the chaconne are explored to the fullest in Frescobaldi's extraordinary *Cento partite sopra passacaglie* (1637), with its alternating sections marked 'passacaglie' and 'ciaccona', and sometimes a gradual, subtle metamorphosis from one into the other (see Silbiger, 1996).

Some of these distinctions between the two genres continued to be present in the works of later composers in Italy and elsewhere, particularly when a chaconne and a passacaglia appear side by side or in the same collection; however, when one or the other appears by itself, the distinctive features may be less evident or altogether absent (for Italian composers who published such chaconne-passacaglia pairs, *see* CHACONNE, §2). Composers such as Bernardo Storace also followed in Frescobaldi's footsteps by shifting key, mode and metre in some of their passacaglias.

In vocal settings, Italian passacaglias were sometimes interrupted by recitatives (e.g. Frescobaldi's *Così mi disprezzate*, 1630). Sections that resemble a passacaglia without being identified as such are found in operas, cantatas and sacred works. However, the present-day tendency to regard any lament with a descending tetrachord bass as a passacaglia does not appear to have historical precedence unless the piece also shows other genre markings. By the beginning of the 18th century the passacaglia was rapidly losing ground in Italy, but it continued to flourish in France, Germany and elsewhere for some time.

3. LATER HISTORY IN SPAIN.   In Spain an active and artistically significant passacaglia tradition survived independently of the chaconne; it remained rooted in the old ritornello practice and was relatively unaffected by the passacaglia developments in Italy and France. Like the early strumming exercises, the later passacaglias continued to be presented in sets covering a full range of commonly used keys, in major as well as minor modes and in duple as well as triple metre. The passacaglias of Francisco Guerau (1694), Antonio de Santa Cruz (*c*1700) and Santiago de Murcia (1732) were not simple chord formulae, however, but extended variation sets that took full advantage of the guitar's technical and expressive possibilities. Very similar passacaglias can be found in the contemporary keyboard repertory, including some wonderful examples by Cabanilles.

After Santiago de Murcia's *Passacalles y obras* (1732) the passacaglia vanished from the Spanish written tradition. The term 'passacalle' continued to be used in folk practice, however, to refer to instrumental preludes and interludes during dancing (for example for the *seguidillas* in La Mancha; see Russell, 1995, p.88) as well as to music accompanying actual dances (for example for stick dances in Castille; Russell, 80). In some areas of Latin America guitar ritornellos for popular dance music are still called 'passacalles' (Hudson, 1981, pp.280–81).

4. FRANCE.   In France the Hispanic-Italian passacaglia, like the chaconne, was transformed during the mid-17th century into a distinctive native genre, although before that the genre had already had some impact as an exotic Spanish import. A 'passacalle' (in the earlier sense of ritornello) occurs in an *air* to a Spanish text by De Bailly (1614), and in 1623 the Spanish expatriate Luis de Briçeño published in Paris a guitar method that included in chord tablature brief chaconnes and passacaglias similar to the early Italian examples. During the 1640s the promotion of Italian music and musicians by Cardinal Mazarin brought wider familiarity with the two genres in their newer incarnations. A harpsichord passacaglia by Luigi Rossi (who visited Paris in 1646 and whose *Orfeo* was performed there the following year) enjoyed wide manuscript circulation. Francesco Corbetta, who settled in Paris around 1648 and became guitar teacher to the future Louis XIV, was perhaps the greatest Italian guitar virtuoso of his time, and the composer of numerous chaconnes and passacaglias.

By the late 1650s the French passacaglia tradition was firmly in place, already showing many of the characteristics that would mark the genre during the later 17th century and the 18th. Like the chaconne, the passacaglia was cultivated both in chamber music, especially by guitarists, lutenists and keyboard players, and on the musical stage. Among the earliest surviving examples are two *passacailles* for harpsichord by Louis Couperin, which are based on ostinatos that outline descending tetrachords (ex.1c). French composers generally seem to have favoured the chaconne over the passacaglia (*see* CHACONNE, §4); Schneider (1986) lists 18 chaconnes but only five passacaglias in Lully's theatrical productions, for example. Nevertheless, Lully's lengthy and impressive *passacaille* from *Armide* (1686) became a much admired model of the genre, emulated by many, including Purcell and J.S. Bach. According to theorists such as Brossard (1703) and Rousseau (1767), the passacaglia was ordinarily in the minor and the chaconne in the major ('rules' often violated), and passacaglias were performed at more deliberate tempos than chaconnes (18th-century reports indicate *c*100 beats a minute compared to *c*120–160 for chaconnes; see Miehling, 1993).

A continuing favourite among French passacaglias is François Couperin's searingly chromatic *Passacaille* in B minor from his *Ordre* no.8 for harpsichord (1717), an extended rondeau structure. After 1740 the passacaglia fell largely out of fashion in instrumental solo and chamber music, but maintained a place on the musical stage throughout the final decades of the century, albeit still far outnumbered by the chaconne.

5. GERMANY.   Distinct German forms of the passacaglia developed only in the later years of the 17th century, most strikingly in solo organ music. The German organists, drawing on traditions of cantus-firmus improvisation and ground-bass divisions, created a series of majestic ostinato compositions, shaped by increasingly brilliant figurations. A passacaglia from well before 1675 by J.C. Kerll (who had studied in Rome) still used the traditional descending tetrachord as ground-bass formula (ex.1d); however, later composers such as Buxtehude and Pachelbel introduced bass formulae of their own devising, which were treated during at least the first part of the composition as rigorous ostinatos. These bass progressions assume a thematic significance not present in the traditional formulae, as various techniques borrowed from chorale improvisation were brought to bear on them. The busy passage-work and contrapuntal density largely obliterated any dance feeling, and relationships to the genre's origin became increasingly tenuous. Such is the case in the most famous passacaglia of this tradition, J.S. Bach's Passacaglia in C minor (BWV582), which concludes with a lengthy fugue on its ostinato subject (possibly derived from a short passacaglia in an organ mass of 1687 by André Raison).

Passacaglias written during the same period for instrumental ensemble more closely followed French models or combined the French and Germanic approaches, as did those conceived primarily for harpsichord. Bach also used the genre in some vocal works, although not indicated as such (BWV12, later reworked into the 'Crucifixus' of the Mass in B minor; BWV78). Some might argue that the opening chorus of BWV12 (like the 'Lamento der Freunde' in the keyboard Capriccio BWV992) should be classified as a lament rather than as a passacaglia, but there can be no such doubt about the magnificent opening of BWV78, which has all the musical hallmarks of a French operatic chaconne/passacaglia number; indeed, the passacaglia from Lully's *Armide* may have been its direct source of inspiration.

6. ENGLAND.   Pieces called 'passacaglia' or 'passacaille' are rarely encountered in English sources; compositions that might have been given such titles on the Continent are usually designated 'chaconne' or 'ground'. A notable exception is the *passacaille* 'How happy the Lover' in Purcell's *King Arthur* (1691). With its alternating instrumental, solo and vocal sections, this seems to be modelled on the passacaglia in Lully's *Armide* (to which there also is a textual reference).

7. AFTER 1800.   When 19th- and 20th-century composers returned to writing passacaglias, they found their models in a handful of 'rediscovered' pieces by the German masters, especially Bach's Passacaglia for organ and perhaps also the Passacaglia from Handel's Suite no.7 in G minor, works deserving of their canonic status, but atypical of the former mainstream genre traditions (Handel's passacaglia was in fact in duple metre). From Bach's passacaglia they took what now became the defining feature: the ostinato bass. The theme-and-variation idea, often incidental to earlier passacaglias (if present at all) became central to the revived genres. As with Bach, the ostinato theme is usually stated at the outset in bare form and in a low register. The association of the passacaglia with Bach and with the organ also contributed to a mood of gravity; most 19th- and 20th-century examples call for a slowish tempo. Some writers attempted to define a distinction between the passacaglia and the chaconne based primarily on the examples by Bach, but no consensus was ever reached and for the most part the terms continued to be used interchangebly. For a more detailed discussion of the modern revival of the chaconne and passacaglia, *see* CHACONNE, §7.

BIBLIOGRAPHY

L. Stein: 'The Passacaglia in the Twentieth Century', *ML*, xl (1959), 150–53

F. Mathiassen: 'Jeppesen's *Passacaglia*', *Natalicia musicologica Knud Jeppesen septuagenario collegis oblata*, ed. B. Hjelmborg and S. Sørenson (Copenhagen, 1962), 293–308

M. Schuler: 'Zur Frühgeschichte der Passacaglia', *Mf*, xvi (1963), 121–26

T. Walker: 'Ciaccona and Passacaglia: Remarks on their Origin and Early History', *JAMS*, xxi (1968), 300–20

D.D. Handel: *The Contemporary Passacaglia* (diss., U. of Rochester, 1969)

D.D. Handel: 'Britten's Use of the Passacaglia', *Tempo* no.92 (1970), 2–6

R. Hudson: 'Further Remarks on the Passacaglia and Ciaccona', *JAMS*, xxiii (1970), 302–14

R. Hudson: 'The Ripresa, the Ritornello, and the Passacaglia', *JAMS*, xxiv (1971), 364–94

R. Hudson: *Passacaglio and Ciaccona: from Guitar Music to Italian Keyboard Variations in the 17th Century* (Ann Arbor, 1981)

N.D. Pennington: *The Spanish Baroque Guitar with a Transcription of De Murcia's 'Passacalles y obras'* (Ann Arbor, 1981)

R. Hudson: *The Folia, the Saraband, the Passacaglia, and the Chaconne*, MSD, xxxv (1982)

H. Schneider: 'Chaconne und Passacaille bei Lully', *Studi corelliani IV: Fusignano 1986*, 319–34

H. Pimmer: *Die süddeutsch-österreichische Chaconne und Passacaglia 1670–1770* (Munich, 1992)

R. Harris-Warrick: 'Interpreting Pendulum Markings for French Baroque Dances', *Historical Performance*, vi (1993), 9–22

C.H. Russell: *Santiago de Murcia's Códice Saldivar no.4: a Treasure of Secular Guitar Music from Baroque Mexico*, i (Urbana, IL, 1995)

A. Silbiger: 'Passacaglia and Ciaccona: Genre Pairing and Ambiguity from Frescobaldi to Couperin', *Journal of Seventeenth-Century Music*, ii/1 (1996) <www.sscm-jscm.org>

M. Zenck: 'Reinterpreting Bach in the Nineteenth and Twentieth Centuries', *The Cambridge Companion to Bach*, ed. J. Butt (Cambridge, 1997), 226–50

J. Schwartz: 'The *Passacaille* in Lully's *Armide*: Phrase Structure in the Choreography and the Music', *EMc*, xxvi (1998), 300–320

For further bibliography see CHACONNE and OSTINATO.

ALEXANDER SILBIGER

Passage. A term used, much as in a literary reference (as, e.g. in 'a passage in Shakespeare'), to refer to part of a composition generally characterized by some particular treatment or technique but without implications as to its formal position, e.g. 'a passage in double counterpoint' or 'a scale passage'. The term 'passage-work' is often used pejoratively to describe transitional sections (especially of keyboard works) consisting of brilliant figuration or virtuoso display but with little if any thematic substance, a sense possibly deriving from the Italian passaggio (see PASSAGGIO (ii)).

MICHAEL TILMOUTH/R

Passaggio (i) (It.: 'passage'). A transition or modulation.

Passaggio (ii) (It.: 'passage'). In Italy from the late 16th century to the 18th, an improvised vocal or instrumental DIVISION moving primarily by step. In early Baroque music the term may also refer to ornamentation in general, including semi-formulaic ornaments such as the *trillo* and *gruppo* (see ORNAMENTS) as well as diminutions. Both meanings are evident in Rognoni's *Selva de varii passaggi* (1620); Rousseau (*Dictionnaire de musique*, 1767) gave 'passage' as the equivalent French term but noted that the practice of inserting these divisions was more common among Italian than among French singers.

MICHAEL TILMOUTH/STEWART A. CARTER

Passaggio (iii) (It.: 'passage'). In Baroque music a florid piece or section of a piece designed to show off the skill of the performer, though usually of negligible thematic content. The elder Matteis used a *passaggio* in the A minor and E minor suites of the second and fourth books respectively of his *Ayrs for the Violin* (1685), that in A

minor being marked '*passaggio rotto*', i.e. in broken-chord figurations.

MICHAEL TILMOUTH/STEWART A. CARTER

Passamezzo [pass'e mez(z)o, passo e mezzo, passomez(z)o] (It.). An Italian dance in duple metre popular from the mid-16th century to about 1650; its musical scheme was frequently used as a subject for instrumental variations until the 1680s. The meaning of the term is uncertain. Among the various etymologies proposed in modern times, the most widely accepted suggests a derivation from *passo e mezzo* ('a step and a half'), possibly referring to the step pattern of this dance. Mersenne proposed an analogous interpretation in his *Harmonie universelle* (1636–7), but he also subscribed to other hypotheses, providing an eloquent illustration of the uncertainty that, even in the early 17th century, surrounded the term.

A significant proportion of the pieces labelled 'passamezzo' are based on two different but related chord progressions known as the *passamezzo antico* (or *passamezzo per B molle*) and the *passamezzo moderno* (or *nuovo*, or *comune*, or *passamezzo per B quadro*). Although in the extant sources this distinction emerges only in the late 1550s, both types are already clearly defined in earlier examples simply entitled 'passamezzo'. The most common progression for the *passamezzo antico* takes the form i–VII–i–V–III–VII–i–V–I, while the *moderno* usually follows the scheme I–IV–I–V–I–IV–I–V–I. The framework chords are spaced at metrically equal intervals as the music unfolds in two phrases, the first leading to V, the second to I. The basic musical scheme was usually repeated a number of times in succession during a dance. Intermediary harmonies, relating as V or IV–V to I, may precede or follow any framework chord. Ex.1 shows a *passamezzo antico* for lute published in 1552 by Hans Gerle. Ex.2, from an Italian keyboard manuscript of the early 17th century, illustrates both melodic and chordal variation applied to the opening two framework chords of a *passamezzo moderno*. According to the Renaissance practice of grouping dances in duple and triple time into pairs or suites, the passamezzo is often followed by one or more triple dances, such as the saltarello, gagliarda or paduana, based on the same chordal scheme. The triple dance and occasionally the passamezzo itself were sometimes provided with smaller units called *riprese* or ritornellos, which occurred in pairs between repetitions of the main scheme and in longer chains at the end.

The chord progression of the *passamezzo antico* is virtually identical to that of the ROMANESCA, with the exception of the opening chord (usually III in the romanesca). This has generated some confusion about the nature of such formulae, confusion also fostered by the fact that there has been a tendency in modern scholarship to equate these genres with their bass progressions. In all probability the passamezzo, like many other Renaissance dances, was defined not by a single chord sequence but by a complex of elements including metric patterns, reference pitches, characteristic melodic and rhythmic gestures and stylistic conventions tied to performance practice. Although deceptively similar in their bass lines, the passamezzo and the romanesca must have differed in other respects, equally vital to the identification of the genre. A clue may be found in Galilei's *Primo libro della prattica del contrapunto* (1588–91), where the excited sound of the romanesca is compared with the quiet one

Ex.1 Rosseto: *Passemeso* (Hans Gerle: *Ein newes sehr künstlichs Lautenbuch*, 1552)

there any apparent vestige of what may once have been a step or step pattern generic to the passo e mezzo and different from other dances. What is certain is that all 'passo e mezzo' choreographies are elaborated variants of the pavana'. Although choreographically similar, the two dances did retain some individual features; and towards the end of the 16th century the passamezzo seems gradually to have superseded the pavana in popularity. The distinction between them probably rested in the music: although the two forms share many features, there are differences, particularly in the overall structure and in the presence of an ostinato bass controlling the harmonic design (*see* PAVAN). The histories of each dance do appear ambiguously intertwined, however. There are examples of pavanas constructed upon the chord progression characteristic of the passamezzo, yet it is not difficult to find passamezzos in which the same progression is altogether absent. Titles such as *pavana passamezzo* (Claude Gervaise, *Sixième livre de danceries*, 1555; Antony Holborne, *The Cittharn Schoole*, 1597) or *pavana in passo e mezzo* (I-Vnm Ital.IV.1227) further emphasize the indistinctness of the two dances, while at the same time suggesting that the passamezzo and the pavana did indeed differ in subtle ways that encouraged some musicians to create hybrid forms by artfully exploiting their inherent ambiguities.

The *passo e mezzo* in *Vnm* Ital.IV.1227 (*c*1530) is perhaps the earliest extant composition based on the formula of the *passamezzo antico*. Although the passamezzo developed mainly in Italy, both types appeared in lutebooks published in Nuremberg by Hans Neusidler: the *B molle* type in 1536, with the curious title *ein welscher Tantz Wascha mesa*, the *B quadro* type in 1540 (*Passa mesa, ein welscher Tantz*). Hundreds of passamezzos in both printed and manuscript sources followed these early examples. Settings and variations for lute include works by Abondante, Domenico Bianchini, Antonio Rotta, Gorzanis, Terzi, Vincenzo Galilei and Simone Molinaro in Italy; Hans Gerle, Wolff Heckel, Matthäus Waissel, Kargel and Reymann in Germany; Adriaenssen, Denss and Le Roy in France and the Low Countries; and Alison and Holborne in England; numerous passamezzos may be found also in Phalèse's collections. Keyboard

of the passamezzo. Other characteristics of the passamezzo include smooth rhythmic motion, suggestive of walking dance steps, and recurring figurations consisting principally of regularly moving scale segments (Silbiger). The analogies between the chord progressions of the passamezzo and the romanesca (progressions partly recognizable in the FOLIA as well) seem simply to point to a common musical idiom characterized by certain standard sequences which cannot be regarded as exclusive to any single genre.

There is some evidence that the passamezzo was closely related to the pavana. Francisco de Salinas reported that the two terms were confused ('pavana milanesa, sive passoemezzo vulgo vocatur', *De Musica*, 1577), and Arbeau mentioned the passamezzo in his *Orchésographie* (1588) as a pavana 'performed less heavily and to a lighter beat'. J.-B. Besard ignored this rhythmic distinction, stating in the preface to his *Thesaurus harmonicus* (1603) that 'pavana' is simply the Italian name for *paduana*, that is to say passamezzo; he added that most French composers called their passamezzos 'pavanas' ('cum Pavana Italicum nomen nil aliud sit quam Paduana, id est Passemezzo, et plerique Galli non aliter suas passemezas quam pavanas nominent'). The few extant choreographies, which appeared much later than the earliest musical examples, in Fabritio Caroso's *Il ballarino* (1581) and *Nobiltà di dame* (1600) and in Livio Lupi's *Libro di gagliarda, tordiglione, passa e mezzo, canari e passeggi* (1607), seem to confirm such a connection. Sutton (p.39) concluded that 'there is no simple choreography, nor is

Ex.2 *Pass'e mezo*, US-LAum 51/1

examples appear in Gardane's *Intavolatura nova di varie sorti de balli* (1551) as well as in works by Ammerbach, Bernhard Schmid (i) and Jacob Paix in Germany; Facoli, G.M. Radino, Valente and Andrea Gabrieli in Italy; Byrd, Morley, Philips and Bull in England; and Sweelinck from the Netherlands. Other 16th-century passamezzos were written for instrumental or vocal ensemble (examples by Bendusi and Mainerio and in the collections of Phalèse and Susato), guitar and cittern. Of particular interest are two manuscript collections from the second half of the 16th century, each containing a cycle of passamezzos composed on the 12 degrees of the chromatic scale. The first, compiled by Gorzanis (*D-Mbs* Mus.ms.1511a, 1567), contains 24 passamezzos, 12 *per b molle* and 12 *per b quadro*, paired with a saltarello. The second, completed by Vincenzo Galilei in 1584 (*I-Fn* Anteriori di Galilei, 6), extends the entire cycle to 24 passamezzo–romanesca–saltarello suites, 12 with a *passamezzo antico* and 12 with a *passamezzo moderno*, arranged according to the ascending series of semitones.

Passamezzos from the 17th century include works by Besard for lute, Kapsberger for chitarrone, Ercole Pasquini, Picchi, Scheidt, Martino Pesenti and Bernardo Storace for keyboard instruments, Biagio Marini, Gasparo Zanetti and G.B. Vitali for chamber ensemble, and a rare example for voices and instruments by Giovanni Valentini (1621). Most of these 16th- and 17th-century examples consist of sets of continuous variations on one of the harmonic grounds given above; many are very lengthy compositions. In addition to these variation forms, almost all the Italian guitar tablatures from the first half of the 17th century contain single statements of the passamezzo ground notated in the form of chord-strumming formulae. Several 16th-century passamezzos are not based on the musical structures of the *antico* and *moderno* types. Some bear descriptive names, such as *passamezzo della bataglia*, *ala bolognese*, *de Bruynswick*, *de hautbois*, *du roy*, *la paganina*. Other titles possibly refer to pre-existing popular tunes or vocal compositions, often French chansons, that provided the thematic material for the passamezzo. Examples are *pas'e mezo sopra una canzon francese*, *pass'e mezo sopra Je presigne*, *pas'e mezo detto Loisa core per el mondo* and *pass'e mezo sopra Gie vo deser d'un bois ah* in Gorzanis's *Opera nova de lauto* (*c*1575–8), *passo e mezo deto Caro fier homo* in Gorzanis's *Secondo libro de intabulatura di liuto* (1562), *Gitene Ninfe, pass'e mezo a 5* in Orazio Vecchi's *Selva di varia ricreatione* (1590), and *passemezo Il est jour* and *passemezo Tuti porti core mio* in Viaera's *Nova et elegantissima in cythara ludenda carmina* (1564). That such pieces were identified as passamezzos reinforces the hypothesis that other characteristic genre markings were as important to the definition of the genre as the chord progression traditionally associated with it. By the 1560s, however, an increasing number of passamezzos display the familiar chordal schemes, and the great popularity of the dance no doubt helped in consolidating a dual system of modality in Italian popular music.

In English sources the names 'passemeasure', 'passing-measure', 'passy-measures' or 'passemeasure(s) pavan' are usually associated with the chord progression of the *passamezzo antico*, whereas compositions entitled 'quadro pavan' or 'quadran(t) pavan' tend to exhibit the scheme typical of the *passamezzo moderno* (a chronological list of settings of both the 'passingmeasure' and the 'quadro pavan' may be found in Ward). The terms 'quadro' and 'quadran(t)', which appear from the 1570s, have been explained as a corruption of *B quadratum*, referring to the chord progression in the major mode underlying both the *passamezzo per B quadro* and the quadro pavan. However, it remains uncertain whether the quadro pavan may simply be equated with the *passamezzo moderno*. It is more likely that the English quadro pavan, like its continental counterpart, flourished in a stylistic climate that thrived on the ambivalence between the passamezzo and the pavana.

BIBLIOGRAPHY

BrownI; *MGG2* (S. Dahms)

M. Dolmetsch: *Dances of Spain and Italy from 1400 to 1600* (London, 1954)

I. Horsley: 'The 16th-Century Variation: a New Historical Survey', *JAMS*, xii (1959), 118–32

W. Apel: *Geschichte der Orgel- und Klaviermusik bis 1700* (Kassel, 1967; Eng. trans., rev., 1972)

K.H. Taubert: *Höfische Tänze, ihre Geschichte und Choreographie* (Mainz, 1968)

S.V. Martin: *The Passamezzo in Germany in the Sixteenth Century* (diss., U. of North Carolina, 1974)

E. Apfel: *Entwurf eines Verzeichnisses aller Ostinato-Stücke zu Grundlagen einer Geschichte der Satztechnik, iii: Untersuchungen zur Entstehung unf Frühgeschichte des Ostinato in der komponierten Mehrstimmigkeit* (Saarbrücken, 1977)

A. Silbiger: *Italian Manuscript Sources of the 17th Century Keyboard Music* (Ann Arbor, 1980), 39–44

J. Sutton and F.M.Walker, eds.: Fabritio Caroso: *Nobiltà di Dame* (Oxford, 1986)

J.M. Ward: *Music for Elizabethan Lutes* (Oxford, 1992)

GIUSEPPE GERBINO, ALEXANDER SILBIGER

Passarini [Passerini], **Francesco** [Camillo] (*b* Bologna, 10 Nov 1636; *d* Bologna, 23 Sept 1694). Italian composer. On 17 January 1652 he entered the S Francesco monastery, Bologna, receiving the tonsure on 28 January. It was presumably then that he changed his first name to Francesco. From 1662 to 1663 he was an organist at Ferrara; some authorities have him at Correggio in 1663, Bologna in 1664 and Ravenna in 1666, but he was certainly *maestro di cappella* of S Francesco, Bologna, from 1666 to 1672. In 1672 he was appointed *maestro di cappella* for the parish of S Giovanni in Persiceto. In 1673 he moved to Venice and was *maestro di cappella* of S Maria Gloriosa dei Frari there until 1680. In 1676 he wrote a *Te Deum* which was performed at Venice to celebrate the instalment of Pope Innocent XI. He returned to his former post of *maestro* at S Francesco, Bologna, in 1680; apart from a short time in Florence as *maestro di cappella* of S Croce (1691–2) and a visit to Pistoia (1692–3) he remained at S Francesco until his death. He may have had connections with Mantua, for his op.3 is dedicated to Isabella Gonzaga and his op.2 to a Mantuan ecclesiastical dignitary.

Passarini's extant music consists entirely of sacred vocal works, many of which are in the concertato style typical of the mid-17th century. In his works for double choir he showed a preference for lively, imitative part-writing and made prominent use of instruments, particularly trumpets and cornetts. Numerous extant manuscript copies of his music testify to his popularity and esteem; an autograph inventory of his works drawn up in 1694 (now in *I-Bc*) indicates that much of his music is lost.

WORKS

ORATORIOS

Il sacrifizio d'Abramo (G.B.F. Lutti), Vienna, 1685, *A-Wn*
Dio placato (Lutti), Vienna, 1687, *Wn*

Abrame sagrificante (T. Stanzani), Bologna, Arciconfraternita dei SS
    Sebastiano e Rocco, 27 March 1689, lost
Il martirio di S Sebastiano (?A. Navesi), Florence, Oratorio di S
    Filippo Neri, 20 Jan 1690, lost

OTHER WORKS

Salmi concertati, 3–6vv, some with vns, con letanie della Beata
    Virgine, 5vv, op.1 (Bologna, 1671)
Antifone della Beata Virgine, 1v, bc, op.2 (Bologna, 1671)
Compieta, 5vv, vns, op.3 (Bologna, 1672)
Messe brevi, 8vv, bc, op.4 (Bologna, 1690)
2 works, 1685[1], 1695[1]

Mass (Ky, Gl, Cr), *I-Bc*
Ky–Gl, *Bc* (inc.)
3 Ky, 4, 8vv, insts, bc, *Bc*
Psalms, vesper psalms, Mag, 8vv, bc, *Bc*
Motets, 4, 5, 8, 16vv, insts, bc, *Baf, Bc, Bsf, Pc*
Cantatas, 3vv, *Bsf*
Other works, *D-Bsb, Dkh, S-Uu*
Many lost works, listed in autograph inventory, 1694, *I-Bc*

BIBLIOGRAPHY

GaspariC
L. Busi: *Il Padre G.B. Martini* (Bologna, 1891/R), 225ff
G. Tebaldini: *L'archivio musicale della Cappella Antoniana in
    Padova* (Padua, 1895), 110
D. Sparacio: 'Il P.M. Giambattista Martini *Minore Conventuale*',
    Miscellanea francescana, xvii (1916), 138–55
R. Lustig: 'Saggio bibliografico degli oratorii stampati a Firenze dal
    1690 al 1725', *NA*, xiv (1937), 57–64, 109–16, 244–50, esp. 60
U. Rolandi: 'Oratorii stampati a Firenze dal 1690 al 1725', *NA*, xvi
    (1939), 32–9, esp. 33, 35
G. Zanotti, ed.: *Biblioteca del convento di S. Francesco di Bologna:
    catalogo del fondo musicale*, ii (Bologna, 1970)

JUDITH NAGLEY

Passau. City in Bavaria, Germany. A bishopric was set up
there in 739. The cultivation of music in the cathedral
school from the 9th century established a tradition that
came to maturity when a succession of Renaissance
prince-bishops gave distinguished musicians, including
Hofhaimer, his pupil Johann Schachinger (who was born
there) and Senfl, the opportunity to work at Passau. The
Kläglich Lied (1584) of M. Steinbach and the Passauer
Liedertisch (1590) indicate a broader interest in secular
music in the late 16th century. At this time too several
instrument makers worked at Passau. Urban Loth and
Georg Kopp were among the leading musicians there in
the earlier 17th century, but they were overshadowed by
Georg Muffat, who was Kapellmeister to the Bishop of
Passau from 1690 to 1704.

The city had fleeting associations with both Mozart
and Haydn: for instance, Joseph Friebert, the bishop's
director of music from 1763 to 1799, added words to
Haydn's *Die sieben letzten Worte* about 1792 and Haydn
heard this version at Passau in 1795. Burney, who visited
the city in 1772, admired the cathedral organ built by
Johann Egendacher in 1733. Edmund Holmes later
described the Passau organist Seytl as 'one of the remnants
of the Bach school of organ playing'.

During the 19th century a strong secular choral
tradition developed at Passau. At this period a more
general awareness of the 16th-century polyphonic tradition was much stimulated by the musicological and
practical endeavours of F.X. Haberl, and his disciple C.
Bachstefel continued his work. The five-manual organ in
the cathedral built by G.F. Steinmeyer & Co. in 1928 was
said at the time to be the largest in the world.

The Fürstbischöfliches Opernhaus, converted from an
existing ballroom into a theatre, was inaugurated in 1783.
After coming into state ownership in 1803 it was known
first as the Kurfürstliches and then as the Königliches

Theater. Throughout the 19th century it was threatened
with closure because of inadequate funds. In 1833 the
city acquired the building and set up a permanent opera
company, which continued until 1914. From 1914 to
1946 touring companies performed at the theatre. In
1952 the Südostbayerisches Stadttheater was founded,
combining the companies of Passau, Landshut and
Straubing.

BIBLIOGRAPHY

BurneyGN
E. Holmes: *A Ramble among the Musicians of Germany* (London,
    1828, 3/1838)
H. Kühberger: *Die Dom-Orgel zu Passau* (Passau, 1928)

PERCY M. YOUNG

Passecaille. *See* PASSACAGLIA.

Passenger, Aegidius. *See* BASSENGIUS, AEGIDIUS.

Passeo. *See* PASEO.

Passepied [passe-pied, paspy, passe-pié] (Fr.). A French
court dance and instrumental form that flourished in the
17th and 18th centuries. It was a faster version of the
minuet, usually written in 3/8 or 6/8 (dotted crotchet =
*c*46–54) with an upbeat, and having two sections, four-
bar phrases, and fairly constant movement in quavers and
semiquavers. It was frequently used in French opera and
ballet, often in pastoral scenes, as well as in orchestral
and keyboard suites of the mid- and late Baroque period.
These passepieds usually appeared in pairs, the first to be
repeated (da capo) after the second was played.

The passepied was first mentioned in 1548 by Noël du
Fail as a court dance common in Brittany. Both Rabelais
(*Voyages et navigations des îles inconnues*, 1557) and
Thoinot Arbeau (*Orchésographie*, 1588) mentioned the
dance as the characteristic BRANLE of Brittany. Examples
of the branle-passepied, a fast duple-metre dance with the
three-bar phrases characteristic of the *branle simple*,
appeared in Praetorius's *Terpsichore* (1612; ex.1) and
Mersenne's *Harmonie universelle* (1636–7). The one
passepied included in the Kassel Manuscript of early 17th-
century dances (Ecorcheville: *Vingt suites d'orchestre du
XVIIe siècle français*, Paris, 1906/R) is a branle-passepied.

Ex.1 M. Praetorius: from *Terpsichore* (1612)

It is difficult to see the relationship between these
passepieds and the dance as it was 'remodelled' for use in
the court of Louis XIV. The dance was written in triple
metre and constructed of two- and four-bar phrases rather
than the three-bar groups characteristic of the branle. The
steps of the passepied were identical with those of the

minuet, i.e. four steps were performed during two triple-time bars of music, the steps ordinarily coming on the first, third, fourth and fifth (or sixth) beats of the six-beat pattern (see MINUET, §1). Like the minuet, the passepied was usually performed at a ball by one couple at a time, while the rest of the company looked on; because of its faster tempo, however, the interest of the passepied was not so much in the elegance of individual steps as in the geometrical patterns described on the floor. Individual choreographies for the passepied were published in the Beauchamp-Feuillet notation beginning in 1700; 15 French choreographies and five English ones survive, and others in German and Spanish publications, all for social dancing (see Little and Marsh for sources). Some choreographies are set to two pieces of passepied music with various repeat schemes (e.g. Little and Marsh, no.6620), and others are one of a 'suite' of several different dances (e.g. *La Bourgogne*, Little and Marsh, no.1560). In a somewhat simplified form, with less intricate steps, the passepied was also performed by several couples as a CONTREDANSE.

The passepied was danced in many French operas and ballets, including Lully's *Persée* (1682), Campra's *L'Europe galante* (1697), Destouches' *Amadis de Grèce* (1699), Desmarets' *Iphigénie en Tauride* (1704), Destouches' *Callirhoé* (1712), Mouret's *Le triomphe de sens* (1732) and Rameau's *Platée* (1745). Usually pairs of passepieds appeared in these works, often linked with pairs of rigaudons; like the rigaudon, the passepied was often associated with pastoral and maritime scenes. No theatrical choreographies have survived.

Instrumental pieces entitled 'Passepied' showing the dance's characteristic rhythm and phrase structure appeared in many 17th- and 18th-century suites and overtures. The music is usually in 3/8 time, with an upbeat, long phrases in a length divisible by four measures, and strongly accented hemiolas in unexpected places. Ex.2 shows part of a keyboard passepied by François Couperin in which this possibility is exploited. In the pair of passepieds in Bach's Orchestral Suite in C major the idea of combining bars in a hemiola is the basis of the main rhythmic motif of both movements, as shown in the top voice in ex.3. Bach also set passepieds for keyboard in his Fifth English Suite, the Fifth Partita, and the Overture in the French Style. Other instrumental composers who favoured the passepied include Gaspard Le Roux (*Pièces de clavecin*, 1705), M.P. de Montéclair (*Concerts*), J.C.F. Fischer (*Blumen-Büschlein*, 1698), J.J. Fux

Ex.2 F. Couperin: from *Premier livre de pièces de clavecin, 2e ordre*

Ex.3 J. S. Bach: Orchestral Suite in C major BWV 1066

(DTÖ, lxxxv), Telemann (Werke, xii, xviii), and J.E. Pestel (*Andreas-Bach-Buch*). In the 20th century Debussy, Delibes, Lachaume and Percy Turnbull were among those who used the title 'passepied'.

BIBLIOGRAPHY

E. Galbrun: *La danse bretonne* (Carhaix, 1936)
L. Horst: *Pre-Classic Dance Forms* (New York, 1937/R)
J.-M. Guilcher: *La tradition populaire de danse en Basse-Bretagne* (Paris and The Hague, 1963)
M. Little and N. Jenne: *Dance and the Music of J.S. Bach* (Bloomington, IN, 1991) 83–91, 230
M. Little and C. Marsh: *La Danse Noble: an Inventory of Dances and Sources* (Williamstown, MA, 1992)

MEREDITH ELLIS LITTLE

Passereau, Pierre (*fl* 1509–47). French composer. His output consists almost entirely of chansons, a single motet representing his sole contribution to the sacred repertory. According to an unsubstantiated statement by Fétis, he was a priest at the church of St Jacques-de-la-Boucherie in Paris. In 1509 he sang tenor in the chapel of the Duke of Angoulême (later François I) and between 1525 and 1530 he may have sung at Cambrai Cathedral. Lesure asked in *MGG1* whether Passereau was a family name or a nickname, but later reported that the composer's identity and background had been uncovered in the archives of Bourges Cathedral (Lesure, 1972, p.72).

Most of Passereau's chansons were published by Pierre Attaingnant, the first royal printer of music. It is possible that François I recommended his former singer to Attaingnant, who published the work of several poets and musicians associated with the French court.

Although Passereau wrote music for a few doleful texts (his *Ce fut amour* could easily be taken for a piece by Sermisy, a master of the lyrical chanson), most of his works are narrative or descriptive songs of a more cheerful nature, with graceful melodies, syllabic settings in freely imitative polyphony occasionally alternating with chordal passages, and with lively rhythms and repeated notes. For these he usually chose unsophisticated literary texts of the sort found in *chanson rustique* collections, with indelicate subjects emphasized by blunt language and unsubtle puns.

Passereau has often been considered merely a minor master. Attaingnant, however, devoted a whole collection (RISM 1536[6]) to the work of Janequin and Passereau, an exceptional procedure for the time and a measure of their popularity. The ever popular *Il est bel et bon*, with its onomatopoeic imitation of the clucking of hens, was sung in the streets of Venice, according to Andrea Calmo. This and other chansons by Passereau enjoyed several editions and were transcribed for various instruments in France and elsewhere. Fragments of some of his works appear in three *fricassées*. The tune of *Je ne seray jamais bergere* was used in a farce entitled *Amoureux qui ont les botines*. The text of *Il s'est fait écosser le jonc*, an anonymous satirical song directed against Diane de Poitiers, official mistress of Henry II, has the lines 'Bon, bon, bon, mon compère' and 'O le joli jonc' in the refrain. These seem to refer to *Il est bel et bon* and *Sur le joly, joly jonc*. Rabelais paid a fitting tribute to Passereau by including him in his list of 'merry musicians'.

WORKS
all for 4 voices

Edition: *Passereau: Opera omnia*, ed. G. Dottin, CMM, xlv (1967) [contains all works except 'Il me convient']

CHANSONS

A ung Guillaume, apprenti, dist son maistre; Au joly son du sansonnet; Ce fut amour dont je fus abusée; Ce joly moys de may; Ce n'est pas jeu, mais c'est bien cas pour rire; Et gentil mareschal (also attrib. Janequin); Hellas, madame, faictes-luy quelque bien

Il est bel et bon, commere, mon mary; Il me convient (lute transcr. in 1582[15] attrib. 'Paserau'; not printed in Dottin; vocal model not known); Je ne seray jamais bergere; Je n'en diray mot, bergere, m'amye; Je n'en puis plus durer, Marquet; L'oeil est a vous, le cueur et la pensée; Marie monstroit a sa dame; Mon mari est allé au guet

Nostre dince, mon con, mon compere (Superius and T have 'Saincte Barbe, mon con, mon compere'; erroneously attrib. Janequin in 1538[13]); Perrin, Perrinette et Perrot; Pourquoy donc ne fringuerons nous; Si vous la baisez, comptez quinze; Sur la rousée fault aller; Sur le joly, joly, jonc, ma doulce amye

Tous amoureux qui hantes le commun; Ung compaignon gallin gallant; Ung petit coup m'amye, ung petit coup, hellas (erroneously attrib. Janequin in 1538[19]); Ung peu plus hault, ung peu plus bas; Va, mirelidrogue, va

Pourquoy voulez-vous, cousturier, attrib. Passereau in 1538[19] is by Janequin (1534[12])

MOTET

Unde veniet auxilium michi

BIBLIOGRAPHY

BrownI; FétisB; HoneggerD; MGG1 (F. Lesure); ReeseMR

H.M. Brown: *Music in the French Secular Theater, 1400–1550* (Cambridge, MA, 1963)

G. Breton: *La chanson satirique de Charlemagne à Charles de Gaulle*, i (Paris, 1967)

F. Lesure: 'Archival Research: Necessity and Opportunity', *Perspectives in Musicology*, ed. B.S. Brook, E.O. Downes and S. van Solkema (New York, 1972), 56–79

L.F. Bernstein: '*La courone et fleur des chansons a troys*: a Mirror of the French Chanson in Italy in the Years between Ottaviano Petrucci and Antonio Gardano', *JAMS*, xxvi (1973), 1–68

ISABELLE CAZEAUX

Passerini, Christina (*fl* 1750–76). Italian soprano. In 1750, on the recommendation of Telemann, she and her husband, Giuseppe Passerini, a violinist, conductor and composer, on their way from Russia to Scotland, met Handel at The Hague. He was immediately impressed by her and promised to further her career. They gave a concert at the Edinburgh Musical Society on 14 August 1751, when she took part in a Handel duet and sang 'several English and Scots tunes', and he promised to 'exhibit a new instrument, called the Viole d'Amour'. They moved to London about 1752 and were engaged in operas at the King's Theatre in 1753–4. Christina sang Thrasymedes in *Admeto* (1754), the last revival of a Handel opera for more than a century. Handel engaged her for his 1754 and 1755 oratorio seasons when she took leading parts in *Alexander Balus*, *Deborah*, *Saul*, *Joshua*, *Judas Maccabaeus Samson*, *Messiah*, *L'Allegro Alexander's Feast*, *Esther* and *Joseph*, and in *Messiah* at the Foundling Hospital. In 1755 she sang in J.C. Smith's *The Fairies* at Drury Lane. After appearing at the Musicians Fund benefit concert at the King's Theatre in March 1757, she rejoined the opera company at the King's Theatre for the closing weeks of the season. The Passerinis were very active in promoting performances of Handel's oratorios in the provinces; between 1754 and 1760 they performed at Salisbury, Oxford, Bath, Bristol and Birmingham. About 1762 they settled in Dublin, where they continued to present oratorios. Christina sang in Purcell's *King Arthur* (1763) at Crow Street Music Hall and as Arbaces in the first Dublin production of Arne's *Artaxerxes* at Smock Alley Theatre (1765). Her career came to an end after she and her husband were assaulted in September 1776. Their son, Francis (*d* 8 March 1809), also a singer, appeared in *King Arthur* (with his mother), and in operas by Giordani (1766) and Arne, Gazzaniga, Piccinni (*La buona figliuola*), Paisiello and Anfossi at Smock Alley (1776–8).

WINTON DEAN

Passerini, Francesco. See PASSARINI, FRANCESCO.

Passet (*fl* early 15th century). French composer. His rondeau *Si me fault faire departie* (ed. in CMM, xi/2, 1959, p.101) is ascribed 'Passet', to which a later hand added 'de Tonnaco', perhaps in error for 'de Tornaco' ('from Tournai'). The rondeau *Se vous scaviés* (ed. in CMM, xi/1, 1955, p.26) also appears with an ascription to Cesaris, which Reaney rejected on stylistic grounds (CMM, xi/1, p.xiv); its music was used for the *lauda Se vuoi gustare el dolz' amor Jesù* by Feo Belcari and was therefore evidently well known in Florence in the mid-15th century. Both works are in the simplest polyphonic song style of their time. (See also D. Fallows: *A Catalogue of Polyphonic Songs, 1415–1480*, Oxford, 1999)

DAVID FALLOWS

Passetto [Pasetto], **Giordano** [Frater Jordanus Pasetus; Fra Jordan] (*b* Venice, *c*1484; *d* Padua, 8 Nov 1557). Italian composer. He was a Dominican friar at the church of SS Giovanni e Paolo in Venice at a time when the *maestro di* *cappella* was Petrus Castellanus, Petrucci's editor. A Credo of his was sent to Ercole d'Este by the Ferrarese ambassador in Venice in 1504, with the remark that he was 'very gifted in these things'; the mass followed shortly thereafter. An organist, he was given permission to play at the nunnery of Santo Spirito in Venice in 1505, and in 1509 he became organist in SS Giovanni e Paolo. He was elected *maestro di cappella* at the Cathedral of Padua in 1520, and held this position until shortly before his death. He is chiefly remembered as the composer of a set of madrigals *a voce pare* printed in 1541 (dedicated to a cathedral canon, Benedetto Contarini): this is the only 16th-century print of secular works known to contain exclusively pieces for equal voices (in this case low, or men's, voices). Passetto's vesper psalms are all for double choir, with the second choir consisting of voices of low range.

A collection of 127 motets (*I-Pc* A 17) is signed 'Frater Jordanus Pasetus Venetus … scripsit hec manu propria … 1522'. One motet is ascribed to Mouton; the remainder bear no ascriptions, but a number have been identified with French and Flemish musicians of the same generation. The repertory is closely related to that of Petrucci's *Motetti de la Corona* and probably represents what was sung at Passetto's church in Venice; some of the unidentified compositions may be by him. He also copied another manuscript in the same library (MS D 27), containing works of the Gombert generation. Presumably Passetto copied both manuscripts in fulfilment of a promise made at the time of his appointment to provide the cathedral with 'good and new songs and motets'.

WORKS

[25] Madrigali nuovi a voce pare … 4vv, libro primo (Venice, 1541)
Audi bone persone (villotta alla padoana con quatro parte), 1552[23]
Su, su, su pastori, frottola ('Fra Jordan'), 1531[4]
[12] Vesper psalms, 8vv, *I-Pc* D 25–26
Nigra sum sed formosa, 8vv, *I-VEaf* 218

BIBLIOGRAPHY

SpataroC
R. Casimiri: 'Musica e musicisti nella cattedrale di Padova nei sec. XIV, XV, XVI: contributo per una storia', *NA*, xviii (1941), 101–214, esp. 101–3, 189–207
L. Lockwood: 'Josquin at Ferrara: New Documents and Letters', *Josquin des Prez: New York 1971*, 103–37, esp. 116 and 134–5
H.C. Slim: 'An Anonymous Twice-Texted Motet', *Words and Music: the Scholar's View … in Honor of A. Tillman Merritt*, ed. L. Berman (Cambridge, MA, 1972), 293–316
S. Boorman: 'Petrucci's Type-Setters and the Process of Stemmatics', *Formen und Probleme der Überlieferung mehrstimmiger Musik im Zeitalter Josquins Desprez: Wolfenbüttel 1976*, 245–80
F. Carey: 'Composition for Equal Voices in the Sixteenth Century', *JM*, ix (1991), 300–42
B.J. Blackburn: 'Petrucci's Venetian Editor: Petrus Castellanus and his Musical Garden', *MD*, xlix (1995), 15–45, esp. 37–8

FRANK CAREY/BONNIE J. BLACKBURN

Passhe, William. *See* PASCHE, WILLIAM.

Passing note (Ger. *Durchgang*). A NON-HARMONIC NOTE that leads from one note to another in a single direction and usually by conjunct motion.

Passion. The story of the Crucifixion as recorded in the Gospels of Matthew (xxvi–xxvii), Mark (xiv–xv), Luke (xxii–xxiii) and John (xviii–xix). In the Roman liturgy the Passion texts are recited as Gospel lessons during Mass on Palm Sunday (*Matthew*), Thursday of Holy Week (*Mark*), Wednesday of Holy Week (*Luke*) and Good Friday (*John*). At a very early date special lesson tones were developed for reciting the Passion, and polyphonic settings of its texts have been made since the 15th century.

1. Monophonic Passion. 2. Beginnings of the polyphonic Passion. 3. Catholic Passion after 1520. 4. Protestant Passion to 1600. 5. 17th century. 6. 18th century. 7. 19th and 20th centuries.

1. MONOPHONIC PASSION.   The earliest report of the use of the Passion in a religious ceremony is that of the pilgrim Egeria who visited Jerusalem in the 4th century and described the services held there during Holy Week. These readings were essentially commemorative in nature, while those in the Western Church (according to patristic theology) took on a didactic function as Gospel lessons. Indeed, Augustine emphasized the need for a solemn delivery ('Solemniter legitur passio, solemniter celebratur'). About the middle of the 5th century Pope Leo the Great decreed that the St Matthew Passion should be read during the Mass for Palm Sunday and the Mass for the Wednesday in Holy Week, while that of St John should be read on Good Friday. Some 200 years later the St Matthew Passion was replaced by that of St Luke for use during the Wednesday Mass, and from the 10th century it became the custom in the Roman Church to sing the Passion according to St Mark on the Tuesday of Holy Week. In the Gallican, Ambrosian, Mozarabic and southern Italian liturgies the texts were allotted somewhat differently and sometimes only single verses from the Passion were read.

Ex.1 *St John Passion, F-RS, 258 (12th century)*

Re-spon-dit Pi-la-tus: Numquid e-go Ju-dae-us sum?..

… Res-pon-dit Je-sus: Re-gnum me-um non est de hoc mun-do.

As indicated in the Roman Ordines, the Passion texts were originally chanted by a single singer (*diakon*), and there is no reliable evidence that they were sung by more than one until the 13th century. Manuscripts survive from as early as the 9th century in which pitch, tempo and volume are indicated by the so-called *litterae significativae* ('significative letters') but these should not be interpreted as evidence for the distribution of parts to different people.

But the letters do reveal an essentially dramatic approach to the Passion at an early stage of development and may be divided into three groups accordingly: letters for the narrative sections (Evangelist), letters for the words of Christ, and letters for the words of the turba (direct speech by groups or individuals). In the narrative portions of the text the letter *c* (*celeriter*, later interpreted as *cronista* or cantor) occurs especially frequently. There also occur the letters *m* (*mediocriter*), *d* (*tonus directaneus*) and especially in southern Italian sources *l* or *lec* (*lectio*). The words of Christ often bear the letter *t* (*tenere* or *trahere*), which was often transformed into a cross after the 12th century.

Other letters used for the words of Christ are *i* (*iusum, inferius*), *b* (*bassa voce*), *d* (*deprimatur* or *dulcius*), *l* (*lente, leniter*), *s* (*suaviter*) and, in the Jumièges manuscripts, *a* (*augere*). The words of Christ, sometimes distinguished by the colour red, are also prescribed in certain manuscripts to be delivered in the Gospel tone by

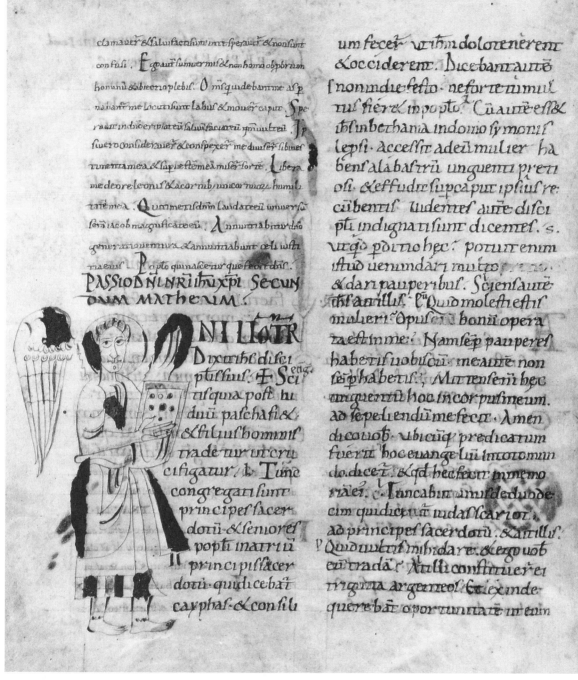

1. Significative letters in a monophonic setting of the St Matthew Passion, from a missal from central Italy, 11th century (I-Rvat Barb.lat.560, f.33v): Evg, ev – evangelium (a cross is added at the beginning to indicate the words of Christ); l – lectio (narration); s – sursum (turba); p – ?pressio (used here for the words of Judas)

the letters *evg* (see fig.1). Occasionally, as in the Sarum rite, the words of Christ on the cross are specially emphasized, either by a higher pitch or by a special use of neumes. The turba is most often marked by the letter *s* (*sursum*, later interpreted as *synagoga*), as well as by the letters *a* (*altius*), *l* (*levare*) and *f* (*fortiter*). In certain sources a distinction is made between the turba of the disciples (*lm* for *levare mediocriter*) and the turba of the Jews (*ls* for *levare sursum*).

From the 12th century there are sources in which the pitches of the Passion recitative are fixed exactly by means of Roman letters, but the *litterae significativae* continued to be used. The earliest manuscripts with precise pitch notation came from Corbie (fig.2) and Reims (12th century), and in these the recitation note for the words of Christ is *d* (alternating with *f*), while that for the Evangelist is *a* and that for the turba *d'*. In these sources the various formulae of melodic punctuation may also be determined

2. Opening of the melody of the Palm Sunday St Matthew Passion, in alphabetic notation, from a MS from Corbie, 12th century (F-Pn lat.11958, f.75)

(ex.1). From the 13th and 14th centuries, once again in France before elsewhere, Passions may be found in which lesson tones are written in neumes or square notes on the staff (fig.3). Here the recitation notes for Christ, Evangelist and turba (in that order) are most commonly *f/d, g, c'*; *f, a, d'*; or *f/e, a, c'*.

The English Sarum Gradual, on the other hand, has its own Passion tones: the recitation notes are *e/f, c'/b, f'/c'*; Christ's words on the cross *d'/eb'*. Spain also had its own tradition, and while hardly any Passion tones written down before the second half of the 15th century have survived (at least in southern Spain), towards the end of the 15th century and in the 16th there are, among others, tones with the recitation notes *eb, g, c'* (rite of Toledo Cathedral) and *f/d, a, c'/d'* (Escorial, chapel of Felipe II). In Hungary, alongside *f, c', f'* (somewhat rare), *e/d, a, d'* occurs particularly frequently. The Passion tone F Lydian (*f, c', f'*) appeared for the first time in German sources of the 14th century and was first used in Rome in the late 19th, succeeding *g, c', f'*, used in most Italian sources since Guidetti (1586).

The earliest definite distribution of the parts of the Passion lesson among several people is to be found in the *Gros livre* of the Dominicans dating from 1254. Here the words of Christ are recited on the notes *B, A* or *c*, the Evangelist sections on *f*, and the turba sections on *bb*. It is conceivable that the Passion text in the *Rationale divinorum officiorum* of Durandus, which indicates that the words of Christ are to be spoken softly and those of the Jews with loud cries and coarse voices, is related to Dominican practice.

In a Sarum Gradual at Parma (*I-PAc 98; c*1300) the Passion lesson is divided between five singers (recitation notes *e* and *d'/eb–c'–g* and *f'*) and the words of Christ on the cross are chanted by a special singer. Indeed, the division of the Passion lesson among three singers became universal in the course of the 14th and 15th centuries. The first indication of a choral (monophonic) presentation of the turba is found in the manuscript *PL-WRu I-F459*, written in 1348. These various elements of performing practice (the use of the *litterae significativae*, the division of the parts among several characters and the use of a chorus for the turba) increased the dramatic impact of the Passion text, and their presence suggests that a new element of *compassio* had infiltrated the older didactic Passion. The origin of this new attitude is to be sought on the one hand in the mysticism of suffering propagated by Bernard of Clairvaux and in Franciscan-Dominican piety on the other.

3. Opening of the melody of the St John Passion from a Spanish MS, 16th century (E-E Passionario N.2)

2. BEGINNINGS OF THE POLYPHONIC PASSION.   In the
15th century theological trends reached beyond *compassio* to an *imitatio Christi* in the sense of a tangible first-hand experience of the Passion. Passion plays became increasingly longer, and polyphony was introduced for the turba of the Passion proper in imitation of the older polyphonic lessons for Christmas. Indeed, those types of Passion that served as models far into the 17th century originated in the 15th and 16th centuries. Here two main groups may be distinguished: responsorial and through-composed.

In the responsorial Passion (which is referred to in the older literature as 'choral Passion' or, less happily, 'dramatic Passion') the narrative sections of the Evangelist are chanted monophonically while the words of Christ and the turba may be set polyphonically in one of four different ways: only those parts of the turba that are the speeches of groups of people are set polyphonically; all the turba is polyphonic, i.e. all direct speech apart from the words of Christ; the words of Christ as well are set polyphonically (only after about 1535–40); and in connection with any of the above, the title of the Passion (the so-called *exordium* 'Passio Domini nostri') and later also a *conclusio*, which is not taken from the Gospel accounts, are both included in the polyphonic setting.

The earliest extant example of a responsorial Passion is of English origin, a *St Luke Passion* and a fragmentary *St Matthew Passion* in the manuscript *GB-Lbl* Eg.3307 (ed. McPeek, 1963, pp.48, 54) compiled between 1430 and 1444. Written in three-part English discant style, the settings include the *exordium* and the words of the turba and individual characters, but not the words of Christ (ex.2). Closely related to these Passions are those of

Ex.2 Exordium, *St Luke Passion*, GB-Lbl Eg.3307

Pas - si - o Do - mi - ni no - stri Je - su [Christi]

another English source, a single surviving partbook (*GB-SHRs*, olim III, 42), which dates from the same period and contains settings of Passions according to St Matthew and St John. The next known Passion of English origin is the four-part *St Matthew Passion* by Richard Davy, found in the Eton Choirbook (*c*1490; ed. in MB, xii, 1961), which uses the Sarum Passion tone to some extent.

Apart from these early English sources there is a short treatise written in south Germany about the middle of the 15th century (*D-HR* ii.lat.2.2⁰6) that is specially important for the German Protestant Passion (ed. in Göllner, *Die mehrstimmigen liturgischen Lesungen*, 1969, ii, 130ff), as well as for the continental responsorial Passion as a whole.

Ex.3 shows how a three-part *turba judaeorum* originated by combining the three recitation notes *f*, *c′*, *f′*. Another example of a 15th-century responsorial Passion

Ex.3 Harburg MS

Re - us est mor - tis.

that remains unique comes from a manuscript compiled in northern Italy between about 1470 and 1480 (*I-MOe* α.M.1.12). Here the turba sections of the St Matthew and St John Passions are written in a three-part fauxbourdon style with the cantus firmus (recitation tone) in the upper voice (ex.4).

Ex.4 *St John Passion*, I-MOe α. M.1.12

Non scin - da - mus e - am   sed sor - tia mur de il - la,

The three turba sections of the disciples in the St Matthew Passion ('Ut quid perditio haec', 'Ubi vis paremus', 'Numquid ego sum') are written for six or even eight parts. Even more remarkable, however, is the fact that the monophonic choral sections for the words spoken by individual characters are differentiated according to male and female pitch registers, suggesting that these pieces are part of a Passion play and not liturgical. Both Passions have survived anonymously, but they are quite possibly the works of Johann Martini, Brebis or even Binchois, who is supposed to have written 'Passions en nouvelle manière'.

In the through-composed Passion (often referred to in literature as the 'motet Passion') the complete text including the narration is set polyphonically. From the 16th century onwards three types may be distinguished according to text: those setting the complete text according to one Evangelist; the so-called *summa Passionis* (Passion harmony), made up of sections taken from all four Gospels, including all seven words of Christ on the cross, an *exordium* and a *conclusio*; and the setting of a shortened version of the text from one Gospel (found only in Protestant Germany).

The earliest example of a polyphonic *summa Passionis* is of Italian origin. In the two oldest manuscripts in which it is recorded (*I-Rvat* C.S.42, 1507, and *I-Fn* II. I.232, 1514) Johannes a la Venture and Antoine de Longueval are named as the composer of the work (ed. in Kade, 1893, pp.246–73). The same composition appeared in Georg Rhau's collection of 1538 in Wittenberg where it is attributed to Obrecht (ed. in *Georg Rhau: Musikdrucke*, x, 1990, pp.34–56). The text is divided into three sections somewhat analogous to the stations of the *via crucis* that came into vogue at exactly that time. The tradition of the harmony of the Gospels or the Passion, however, is considerably older. It can be traced back to early Christian times and was popularized above all by the *Monotessaron* of Johannes Gerson (*c*1420). The Longueval Passion, which survives in more than 30 manuscripts, is written in a very loose *falsobordone* style of Italian stamp and the Passion tone is found mostly in the tenor part. The turba sections are mostly four-part; the words spoken by individual characters (including the words of Christ) are two-part with some exceptions, and the sections of the Evangelist are for two, three or four parts (ex.5). Since the *summa Passionis* could not be used as a Gospel lesson within the Mass itself, the Longueval Passion may have been written in 1502–4 to celebrate Good Friday in the private chapel of Ercole d'Este in Ferrara (Heyink, 1990). The work did not find widespread acceptance in Catholic areas, except for Bohemia, but was to be of

Ex.5 Longueval: Passion

great importance for the Protestant Passion in Germany (see §4 below; for the introduction of polyphony in the Spanish Passion in the late 15th century and the early 16th, see §3).

3. CATHOLIC PASSION AFTER 1520.   The responsorial Passion was the most widespread type in Italy. Settings of the texts from St Matthew and St John are most common, those from St Mark and St Luke being less frequent and less ambitious. Among the oldest are those of Corteccia (St John, 1527, and St Matthew, 1532), in which only the *exordium*, the turba sections and the final *evangelium* (the last section of the Evangelist's Passion narrative) are set polyphonically. Corteccia's Passions may have been written in imitation of works by Bernardo Pisano, which have not survived. Similar settings include those of P. Ferrarensis (St Mark and St Luke, 1565), Vincenzo Ruffo (St Matthew and St Luke, 1574–9), P.A. Giacobetti (1601) and Charles d'Argentille, who was active in Rome before 1543. Among the large number of Italian Passions in which the speeches of individuals (apart from Christ) are also set polyphonically are a fragment of an anonymous six-voice *St John Passion* written in the *falsobordone* style (I-MOd IX), the *St John Passion* of Jacquet of Mantua (c1540), in the style of Sermisy's Passion, and the works by Giovanni Contino (1561), Manfred Barbarini Lupus (1562–4, written for the monastery at St Gallen), Paolo Isnardi (before 1570), Floriano Canale (1579), G.M. Asola (1583), Francesco Rovigo (c1580) and a *St Mark Passion* written for Mantua in about 1580 by Giaches de Wert.

A most important innovation, setting the words of Christ polyphonically, was introduced in certain responsorial Passions no later than the 1540s. The earliest examples are a St Matthew Passion and two St John Passions (I-BGc 1207–8) by Gasparo Alberti, who was

active in Bergamo between 1508 and 1560 (ex.6). Hardly justifiable from a liturgical point of view, such settings

Ex.6 Gasparo Alberti: *St John Passion*

are basically chordal and reveal the same tendency to expressive declamation as the contemporary madrigal. The inclusion of the words of Christ among the polyphonic settings was prefigured in Longueval's *summa Passionis* and possibly too in the lost *Parole di Christo in cantu figurato* (c1534) of the Spaniard Juan Escribano, who was a singer in the papal chapel in Rome. Other Italian composers of responsorial Passions who set the words of Christ polyphonically were P. Ferrarensis (St Matthew and St John, 1565), Ruffo (St John, c1570), Placido Falconio (four Passions, 1580), Paolo Aretino (St John; ed. in Musica liturgica, i/6, 1958), Asola (St John, 1583), Francesco Soriano (four Passions, c1585, printed for the first time in 1619), Teodoro Clinio (four Passions, 1595) and Serafino Cantone (St Matthew and St John, 1604). In some of these works the contrast between the majestic utterances of Christ and the emotionally intense cries of the Jews is developed in a way reminiscent of the madrigal (ex.7). In some Italian Passions of this type the close of the Passion lesson (Evangelist) is included in the polyphonic setting as well, providing an opportunity for a dramatic multi-voiced conclusion. At the end of his *St Luke Passion* ('Et mulieres quae secutae'), for example, Clinio united the six turba parts, the four individual characters and the three parts of the *vox Christi* into a 13-part setting.

Ex.7 Paolo Aretino: *St John Passion*

In Italy, alongside the responsorial Passion, the type of setting in which the text of one Evangelist appears in its entirety in a simple note-against-note style appears only rarely. The only known examples are the *St Matthew Passion* by Jan Nasco (before 1550, printed in 1561), who was active in northern Italy (this work is also known in a divergent form in Spanish manuscripts from Valencia and Montserrat), and the *St John Passion* by Cipriano de Rore (*c*1550, printed in 1557). Ruffo also composed a *St John Passion* along these lines, the style of which was influenced by the reforms of the Council of Trent.

16th-century Catholic Passions of German origin are linked with the Italian responsorial type in which the *vox Christi* is not set polyphonically. Chief among these are the four Passions that Lassus composed for the Bavarian Hofkapelle between 1575 and 1582. In these works Lassus combined a polyphonic motet style with Italian *falsobordone* elements; the turba sections are set chordally for full chorus, but the words of the individual characters are composed as bicinia and tricinia. His St Mark, St Luke and St John Passions (1580–82) are distinguished from the older *St Matthew Passion* (1575) by a stricter liturgical attitude; verbal repetition is largely avoided and the Passion tone is usually clearly recognizable. To the tradition of Lassus belong an anonymous *St Matthew Passion* (*D-Mbs* Mus.76) and possibly also the three lost Passions by Jacob Reiner. Indeed, the settings of Lassus served as models for the responsorial Passion in Catholic areas far into the 17th and 18th centuries, a fact attested to by adaptations of his works from Freising (1707) and Weingarten (1745). Stylistic cross-references to Lassus's Passions also occur in late 16th-century Protestant works, particularly those of Leonhard Lechner. Other Catholic Passions of the responsorial type include a *St Matthew Passion* by Johannes Mangon (1574; in *D-AAm*), and four from the Austrian monastery at Rein, which show Italian influence; only their turba sections are set in polyphony. The only definitely new compositions for *summa* texts in the Catholic areas of Germany, apart from Longueval's work and a *summa* by Mangon, originated in Silesia, Moravia and Prague, which belonged to the German Empire in the 16th century. These include three Passions by Jacob Handl (1578, printed in 1586) and one by Jacob Regnart (*c*1580). One of the settings by Handl, for two choruses of contrasting register, is especially outstanding. The turba sections are in eight parts, the words of the Evangelist in four to eight parts; the *vox Christi* is sung by a deeper chorus and the individual parts by a higher one. New discoveries provide proof of the existence of Hussite Passions in late 16th-century Bohemia that translated the Longueval text into Czech.

The Catholic Passions composed in Spain, Portugal, Mexico and other Spanish- and Portuguese-speaking countries during this period (and indeed in the following centuries) may be divided into three broad groups: (1) Passions following the Roman rite and style; (2) Passions 'in the Spanish style' (*more hispano*); and (3) Passions in which the narrative words of the Evangelist (but not Christ's words) are set to polyphony, a type found exclusively in Aragon after 1550.

The influence of the Roman rite is seen in the earliest known Spanish reponsorial Passions, by Juan de Anchieta (*E-V*; ed in Preciado, 1995). Probably composed before 1523, these were written for four voices in chordal style

on the Toledan lesson tone. The Italian responsorial style is also found in Victoria's two Passion settings (Rome, 1585), in two Passions by Melchior Robledo (ed. P. Calahorra, *Opera polyphonica*, i, Zaragoza, 1986), and in a few works from the monastery of Montserrat (*E-MO* 750, 752).

The most important type of Iberian responsorial Passion, sometimes designated as *more hispano*, originated in the late 15th century and the early 16th. It was described in the diary of Johannes Burkhard, who was *clericus caeremoniarum* at the papal court of Alexander VI (himself a Spaniard) from 1483 to 1506. Burkhard reported that three Spaniards performed the Passion and, departing from the Roman rite, sang the Evangelist's narrative words 'Flevit amare', 'Emisit spiritum' and 'Contra sepulcrum', he also mentioned certain of Christ's words that were sung polyphonically. This practice is confirmed by a great number of Passions in 16th- and 17th-century manuscripts from Spain, Portugal, Mexico and Central and South America (ex.8). Three of the five Passions by Guerrero also show traces of the *more hispano*. In his five-voice Passions according to St Matthew and St Luke and the four-voice Passion according to St Mark, the Evangelist's words 'Flevit amare' and 'Et cepit flere' are set polyphonically in addition to the usual turba sections. Some of Christ's words are set in polyphony in other Iberian Passions: for example, in a Mexican Passion (Codex del Convento del Carmen, *c*1600; ed. in Bal y Gay, 1952) the following words of Christ are set in polyphony: 'Tristis est anima mea', 'Eli, Eli lamma', 'Mulier ecce filius tuus' and 'Consumatum est'. (For polyphonic settings of the various sentences of the Evangelist and Christ, probably following local traditions, see J.V. González-Valle, ed., MME, xlix, 1992, and R. Snow, ed., MRM, ix, 1996.) That such emotionally charged utterances received special treatment in the Spanish Passion may perhaps be explained by the fact that Iberian piety was closely linked with a mystique of suffering. It should also be pointed out, however, that in the Mozarabic rite, which was newly revived about 1500, the Passion lesson for Maundy Thursday closed with the words 'Et egressus foras, flevit amare'.

The third type of Iberian polyphonic Passion, from Aragon, was probably derived from an Italian model, Nasco's through-composed *St Matthew Passion*, transmitted by Ferdinand of Aragon from Italy to the cathedral of Valencia before 1550 as a 'cosa rara' (Fischer, 1995). Nasco's work was adapted to fit the liturgical use of Valencia, with the polyphonic words of Christ and other

Ex.8 *Matthew Passion, E-MA*

Et e-gres - sus fo - ras, fle-vit a-ma-

Et e-gres - sus fo - ras, fle-vit a -

- re.

- ma - re.

individuals omitted (see MME, xlix, 1992, where it is erroneously attributed to B.C. Comes, who also wrote several Passions of this type in the early 17th century). Another important Passion composer, one of the first to imitate Nasco, was Juan Oloron, *maestro de capilla* at Huesca Cathedral from 1551 to 1560. Polyphonic settings of the *processus*, the narrative sections of the Passion, also appeared in Spanish-dominated Naples, where G.M. Trabaci composed his four Passions (1635) based on the Aragonese lesson tone.

Very few Catholic Passions of French origin from this period are known, possibly because Calvinist influence was strong in France at exactly the time when the setting of the Passion was among the most important concerns of lesson composition in other countries. Apart from the Passions of Longueval and d'Argentille, who were active in Italy, and the Passions of Rore (St John, 1557) and Lassus (St Matthew, 1575), which were printed in Paris, there are only two other settings, one anonymous and the other by Claudin de Sermisy. Both are responsorial types and are contained in Attaingnant's *Liber decimus: Passiones* (Paris, 1534; RISM 1535²). The Reformation was apparently responsible for the almost total lack of Passion settings in England. Apart from an anonymous setting in the Gyffard Partbooks which is stylistically related to the Passion composed by Richard Davy about 1490, the only known setting is the three-part turba section of the *St John Passion* by Byrd (1607). The only documentary evidence for the polyphonic Passion in 16th-century Poland is the *Exclamationes Passionum* (turba sections and individual parts in polyphony, but not the *vox Christi*) by Wacław z Szamotuł, printed in Kraków in 1553.

4. PROTESTANT PASSION TO 1600.   The theological basis for the Protestant Passion, at least in the first half of the 16th century, was formed by Luther's *theologia crucis*: 'The Passion of Christ should not be acted out in words and pretence, but in real life'. In his *Deutsche Messe* (1526) Luther pronounced against the 'Vier-Passionen-Singen', referring apparently to the *summa Passionis*. The text of a Passion harmony by Luther's friend the Reformer Johann Bugenhagen, which appeared at the same time, was intended to be read, not sung. However, since Bugenhagen's text soon enjoyed great popularity, along with the responsorial Passion (which was never criticized by Luther), the monophonic and polyphonic *summa* in Latin and German soon came into vogue despite Luther's objections.

In the Lutheran rite the reading of the Passion was spread out over the entire Passion period. Both monophonic and polyphonic Passions as well as *summae* of various kinds were sung from the Sundays 'Laetere' and 'Judica' (i.e. two weeks and one week before Palm Sunday) through Palm Sunday until Good Friday, the *summa* texts being restricted mostly to Matins and Vespers. The *Psalmodia* of Lucas Lossius (1553), compiled for the church at Lüneburg, prescribes the monophonic Latin St Matthew Passion for Mass on Palm Sunday and the monophonic *summa* for Matins on Good Friday; a polyphonic Passion was to be provided for Matins on Wednesday of Holy Week. The monophonic Passion was performed according to Luther's Gospel tone (as well as pre-Reformation tradition) by three people on the recitation notes f, c', f'. Mention should also be made of a monophonic *Liedpassion*, which was used in the Protestant (not only Lutheran) sphere as early as the 1530s.

This is a text from Bugenhagen's *summa* put into verse and sung to Sebald Heyden's melody 'O Mensch, bewein dein Sünde gross'.

In Lutheran-Protestant Germany the polyphonic Passion occurs both as a responsorial Passion (particularly those of St Matthew and St John) in German and as a Latin or German *summa Passionis*. The models for the responsorial Passions are the so-called 'Walterian Passions' of Luther's friend Johann Walter (i), which are regarded not so much as compositions in their own right as examples of how Passions were to be sung (*St Matthew Passion*, ed. in Kade, 1893, pp.274–305, and in Handbuch der deutschen evangelischen Kirchenmusik, i, 1974, pp.26–38). Various types developed out of these models, the simplest of which had only the turba of the disciples and of the crowd in four parts; everything else was performed monophonically with the Passion notes f, c', f'. In use as early as 1530, its simple settings are closely related to the three-part versions of the Füssen Passion Treatise (ex.9). After about 1550–60 a polyphonic

Ex.9 Walter: *St Matthew Passion*

exordium ('Das Leiden unseres Herrn Jesu Christi') and a polyphonic *conclusio* were added to the turba sections (e.g. *PL-WRu* Mus.11), possibly in imitation of Longueval's *summa*, which achieved wide popularity in Germany. However, Longueval's *conclusio*, 'Qui passus est', was usually replaced by a specifically Lutheran thanksgiving, 'Dank sei unserem Herren', presumably borrowed from Heyden's *Liedpassion*. The polyphonic sections of Walter's prototype were often revised and composed anew, as in Johannes Keuchenthal's *Kirchen Gesenge latinisch und deudsch* (Wittenberg, 1573), where the *exordium* and *conclusio* are artfully revised and the turba section 'Herr, bin ich's' is set canonically. In the works of Keuchenthal and Jacob Meiland (1568–70) there is a gradual move away from the use of the cantus firmus, always clearly recognizable in Walter's prototype, and the use of more skilful techniques of composition.

The German responsorial Passion was further modified when the words of Christ were set polyphonically after the Italian fashion, leaving only the narrative portions of the text monophonic. The first work of this kind in German was Antonio Scandello's *St John Passion* (1561; ed. in Kade, 1893, pp.306–44). Scandello, who was active at Bergamo Cathedral from 1541 to 1547, probably borrowed this type of Passion chant from Alberti. With this development Passion music in Germany moved even further away from Luther's theology in a line of development that led to the Passion oratorios of the 17th century. Bartholomäus Gesius (St John, 1588) followed the pattern set by Scandello, and the two Passions by Rogier Michael, composed in Dresden before 1619 (now lost), also belong to this type.

The *summa Passionis* in both Latin and German was composed in Protestant Germany in monophonic and polyphonic form. Lossius's *Psalmodia* (1553) transmitted Longueval's Latin text with the exception of the *conclusio*, but the anonymous 'Auszug der Historien des Leidens unseres Herren Jesu Christi, durch die vier Evangelisten beschrieben, in eine action gestellet, gesangsweise' (1552) is a special case. In its design this work is based on the responsorial prototype of Walter, where *exordium*, *conclusio* and turba sections are sung in four parts. Like the other versions of Walter's original, this type of Passion was also handed down until the late 17th century, as in the so-called 'Glashütter Passion' (*c*1680; ed. in Ameln and Mahrenholz, 1932, i/4, 79–94).

Apart from the Walterian models themselves, the most widespread Passion in Germany was that of Longueval, which was published by Rhau in Wittenberg in 1538 under Obrecht's name; the work appears in over 30 sources in four- and six-part versions. Included in the same print is a four-part *summa* by Johannes Galliculus (identified in the source as a St Mark Passion) that was textually identical with Longueval's and was also through-composed; the use of the Passion tone as a cantus firmus is also similar to that of Longueval. Paulus Bucenus (1578) composed a Latin *summa* after the pattern of these two models, in which the part-writing is extended and a greater degree of independence from the liturgical cantus firmus is achieved. Johannes Herold (1594) also set a German translation of Longueval's *summa* text for six parts.

Apart from these *summae*, the texts of which are based on Longueval's model, through-composed works were written in Germany that were based on the text of only one Gospel (St John). In these works, however, the Latin text is shortened, the seven words of Christ on the cross completed (following Longueval's example) and the whole is divided into five sections. It is also characteristic for this type that the Passion tone furnishes the basis for the polyphonic setting. The Latin Passions by Balthasar Resinarius (1544) and Ludwig Daser (1578) belong in this category. That of Daser, presumably written for the Stuttgart Hofkapelle, is directly dependent on that of Resinarius, but the texts of the *exordium* and *conclusio* are different in each case; those of Daser coincide with Longueval's, but not those of Resinarius. There is a direct path from Daser's work to one of the most representative German Passions of the 16th century, Lechner's *St John Passion* (1594), which is also in five sections; the fifth section gives an exact translation into German of the third section of Longueval's Passion. In Lechner's setting the Passion notes *f*, *c'*, *f'* still form the basis of the four-part setting.

A final group of German Passions is based on the four-part German Passion of Joachim a Burck (Wittenberg, 1568). Burck's text is a greatly abridged version of St John's Gospel, but in contrast to the works mentioned above there are no additions from the other gospels (with the exception of the *conclusio* borrowed from *Mark* ix.24). Since the composer himself made mention of the Longueval Passion in his foreword, this work may also be included within the tradition of that model. A new feature in Burck's work, however, is the almost total abandonment of the Passion tone, which is represented only by the F-Ionian mode. Regrettably, the only surviving part of Burck's *St Luke Passion* (1597) is that of the tenor. Burck's *St John Passion* (ed. in PÄMw, xxii, 1898/R) itself became the model for later compositions, particularly the four-part *St John Passion* by Johann Steuerlein (1576) and the five-part *St Matthew Passion* by Johann Machold (1593), which uses the shortened version of the

St Matthew text and a verse of a song ('O Jesu Christe, Gottes Sohn') as a *conclusio*. The inclusion of the latter marked the beginning of the tradition of inserting song strophes into the Passion.

5. 17TH CENTURY. As an independent form occupying a position halfway between a biblical reading and an oratorio, Passion composition is concentrated after 1600 in German-speaking areas, particularly those dominated by Lutheranism. The essential ambiguity of the form is responsible for the juxtaposition of artlessness and artifice, of the archaic and the novel, and (in literature) of polemics and tranquil reflection. In Catholic parts of Germany and in other European countries much less appears to have been made of these inherent and explicit conflicts in the later history of the Passion, and the form either has comparatively little artistic or liturgical significance, or it developed fairly smoothly along its own lines, as in the Viennese *sepolcri*. Although many influences of Catholic south Germany can be detected in the Passion of central Germany, it alone represents the most vital evolution of the form throughout much of the 17th and 18th centuries.

The responsorial and through-composed types served as models well into the 17th century and even into the 18th. Scandello's German version of the figural Passion of north Italy remained important, particularly as it influenced the development of the Easter *historia* (see ORATORIO, §7) and the oratorio Passion of the second half of the century, but its only notable offspring among Passions proper in the first half was that of Ambrosius Beber (St Mark, 1610). In Beber's Passion the traditional recitation tone of the monophonic sections is replaced by a new one in G-Dorian, and the polyphonic sections appear to have been influenced by the settings of Lassus. The *summa Passionis* of Longueval is also represented in a six-part setting by Gesius, published in 1613, but by this time the Latin version was falling into disfavour. The most successful alternative to the text in Latin was not a straight translation into German, as in the Passion of Herold, but a reformulation of text and music, modelled on the setting of Burck. A specifically central German tradition was hereby established that based the text (divided once more into three parts) on a drastically abridged and in places free Lutheran translation of the Passion according to St John (together with the introduction 'Höret das Leiden unsers Herren Jesu Christi aus dem Evangelisten Johanne' and the conclusion 'Wir glauben, lieber Herr, mehre unsern Glauben, amen'). In this type of Passion the music is through-composed in a declamatory style with reminiscences of a cantus firmus and with varying, inconsistent groups of voices characterizing the protagonists. The texture seems rather stiff in comparison with the more melismatic polyphony of its Latin counterparts, but it is more in line with the expressive declamation of the contemporary motet. The style was intensified and perfected, harmonically and expressively, by the Freiberg Kantor J.C. Demantius in his six-part German Passion published in 1631.

The strongest tradition of Passion setting in the first half of the 17th century, however, was that based on the responsorial models of Walter. As in the preceding decades the composer whose name was printed was responsible only for the newly written polyphonic sections (pieces representing dramatic action or the utterances of the turba); it long remained standard practice to use the traditional recitation tone for the monologues, including the narrative of the Evangelist. The contrast between one voice and several was made even more dramatic by increasing the rhythmic and harmonic variety in the polyphonic settings, as in those of Melchior Vulpius (St Matthew, 1613) and Christoph Schultze (St Luke, 1653). With their copiously fugued turbae the three Dresden Passions of Schütz (St Matthew, St John and St Luke, c1665) belong to this tradition, in spite of the fact that he created his own highly expressive recitation tones. The style of Schütz was adopted by the slightly later Dresden Kapellmeister M.G. Peranda (St Mark, 1668), although in the monophonic sections he reverted to the old practice. All the surviving Dresden Passions of the 17th century remained in manuscript, being intended primarily for use at the electoral court of Saxony. In the original compositions of Passion choruses written for other places the number of voices was increased from four to five, as in the *St John Passion* by O.S. Harnisch (1621), or even, occasionally, to six (Vulpius and Schultze).

A new epoch in the history of the Passion began to develop about 1650, when musicians in the north German Hanseatic cities introduced fundamental and ornamental instruments to the delivery of the Passion. Such settings, called 'oratorio Passions', were broken up by the insertion of reflective episodes, sinfonias, parallel biblical texts, new madrigalian verses and hymns. The earliest instrumental accompanied Passions were those by Thomas Selle of Hamburg, who also fully exploited the heritage of the central German tradition of the Passion. His *St Matthew Passion* (1642) consists of the old Protestant type in the version of Grimm (1629), with the addition of continuo throughout and two melodic instruments for the parts of Christ and the Evangelist. In his *St John Passion*, which appeared in 1643 with three 'Intermedien' (motets), there are many relics of the old recitation tone, and the text is in the tradition of Burck and Demantius. Schütz's *Sieben Wortte Jesu Christi am Kreuz* (manuscript, undated) also included two sinfonias as well as two melodic instruments for the part of Christ and may represent a direct link with north Germany. It was not until somewhat later (about 1665), however, especially in the region of Brunswick and Lüneburg, that settings 'mit einer Stimm und Instrumenten' and the sinfonia became firmly established. This oratorio-like expansion, first found in the Wolfenbüttel *St Matthew Passion* of Martin Köler (text published in 1664), consisted of biblical sayings in connection with the Last Supper ('Kleine geistliche Konzerte'), sinfonias (some with chorale tunes), old chorales (chorale arias), Latin text (the motet *Ecce quomodo moritur justus*) and two hymns of Johann Rist (new or free arias). The troping of the Passion in Hamburg seems to have taken a different and somewhat less uniform course; there is a gap in extant settings between those of Selle and the printed texts (from 1676). The Königsberg *St Matthew Passion* by Johann Sebastiani (which appeared in manuscript in 1663, and in print in 1672) may have been influenced by practices in Hamburg, whereas the Riga Passions are closer in construction to the Brunswick-Lüneburg type; the Danzig *St Matthew Passion* of Thomas Strutz (1664, text alone) steered a somewhat different course with an aria for Jesus.

In addition to providing settings for the inserted material, composers wrote choruses (turbae, *exordium* and *conclusio*), and for court churches composers such as Sebastiani, Köler and Johann Theile (1673) also provided recitative. By contrast, in non-aristocratic circles the monophonic recitation tone was retained in spite of strong inroads made by the new Baroque styles. The completely original music of Theile's *St Matthew Passion* could have been performed by unaccompanied voices, the arias being replaced by German chorales 'where instrumental music is not customary during Lent' (preface of 1673).

6. 18TH CENTURY. In the 18th century there were basically four different types of Passion setting. The simple old type without instruments was by this time commonly embellished with hymns, but was more or less ignored by the best composers. A second type, the oratorio Passion, was more artistic, but still adhered to the biblical text; and a third was the Passion oratorio in operatic style with completely original text. Finally, there was the lyrical meditation on the Passion without direct dialogue. The only respect in which nomenclature has distinguished between these varieties is that the oratorio Passion, in contrast to the Passion proper and the Passion oratorio, is often called 'Passions-Music' (coupled with the name of the Gospel), while the textually freer Passion, generally based on all four Gospels, often has a poetic title. The former is the type most commonly found in the first third of the 18th century. By adhering closely to a single Gospel text (written in red ink in the autograph score of Bach's *St Matthew Passion*) it met the devotional requirements of orthodox Lutheranism. In its traditional form (e.g. J.V. Meder's *St Matthew Passion*, autograph score, 1700) it became established in north Germany, just as the old Protestant Passion had done long before in central Germany. Compositions of this type (for example the *St Matthew Passion* by J.G. Kühnhausen, c1680) competed with the older liturgical Passion (such as those by Thomas Mancinus, 1620), and compositions by well-known masters (such as Telemann) competed with local settings (for example the *St Matthew Passion* by J.T. Römhild of Danzig, c1750). Of the five Passions attributed to Bach after his death, it must be assumed that two have disappeared completely. The genre reached its highest achievements in his dramatic *St John Passion* (1724) and the *St Matthew Passion* (1727 or 1729) with its dialogue of double choir.

The oratorio Passion played practically no part in the Catholic parts of Europe during the 17th and 18th centuries (the Latin settings of the *St John Passion* by Alessandro Scarlatti, c1680, and Gaspare Gabellone, 1756, are untroped and are fairly isolated examples), but the Passion oratorio in Italian is one of the most important phenomena in the history of the oratorio proper, especially in Vienna (see ORATORIO, §6). The Protestant counterpart is found in Hamburg, where the roots of the operatic, German Passion oratorio with original text can clearly be traced. The type became fully established with the omission of the Evangelist in C.F. Hunold's *Der blutige und sterbende Jesus* (set by Keiser, 1704) and the substitution of expressive paraphrase in B.H. Brockes's *Der für die Sünden der Welt gemarterte und sterbende Jesus*, set by Keiser (1712), Telemann (1716), Handel (?1716), Mattheson (1718) and others. To conservative minds, these works contained 'the spirit of opera more than God's Word', with the effect of 'ear-tickling' rather than 'edification' (Hörner, 1933, 32–3), and they were little used in divine worship. In Danzig, churches were permitted only simple Passion formulae without madrigalistic arias. However, the cantata of later times, both sacred and secular examples, owed much to them for its development.

The lyrical passages and symbolic roles (including the all but indispensable 'daughter of Zion') found in the German Passion oratorio were models for the lyrical Passion meditation in oratorio form. It is represented in Italy and italianized Germany from 1730 onwards by Metastasio's *La Passione di Gesù Cristo* (set by Caldara, Jommelli, Paisiello and others). An increasing aversion to operatic qualities in sacred music, aesthetic objections to sung narratives and dialogues (J.A.P. Schulz, 1774), and the general excess of feeling in the age of sentiment favoured the development of this type in Evangelical parts of Germany. As early as 1720 it is discernible in several Passions by G.H. Stölzel, Kapellmeister of Gotha, but is best exemplified in C.H. Graun's *Tod Jesu* (text by K.W. Ramler, commissioned by Princess Anna Amalia of Prussia). After its first performance in Berlin on 26 March 1755, *Tod Jesu* enjoyed considerable success for two reasons: it presented the Passion story as it reflected the image of a sensitive and contemplative Christ, and it used the simplified musical language of pre-Classicism. As a 'Passion cantata' it could have been performed liturgically either in its entirety or in part, as was the case with Graun's 'Zweite Passion' of about 20 years earlier, *Ein Lämmlein geht und trägt die Schuld*. No other setting of Ramler's libretto was able to compete with Graun's, not even Telemann's (1755). Even though its influence has been very little researched, *Tod Jesu* seems to have marked an important departure in the history of the Passion similar to those initiated earlier by the works of Longueval, Walter, Burck and Scandello. Other Passion oratorios from the second half of the 18th century include that of J.E. Bach (1764), which won renown for its 'thoroughly German' choral writing. Even better known, however, were the *Passions-Kantate* of G.A. Homilius (Leipzig, 1775), edited by J.A. Hiller and celebrated as 'classical', and the Passion oratorios of J.H. Rolle (1753–83).

Classification of the 18th-century Passion is made difficult by a multitude of hybrid forms. Telemann's *St Luke Passion* of 1728, for example, combines elements of oratorio and Gospel history in turn, and each of the five principal sections is preceded with a 'poetical prelude' ('poetische Vorbereitung'). Parody and pasticcio are also important factors; pieces by various composers were transferred to 'new' works, where they either retained their original function (e.g. in a Hamburg Brockes Passion in manuscript form) or else took on a new one (cantata movements by Telemann and J.S. Bach are found in a manuscript Passion pasticcio based on Graun). The Passion oratorio yielded texts and modern musical forms ('free' recitatives, da capo arias etc.) for the oratorio Passion (J.S. Bach, Telemann), or even provided complete pieces (two arias by Graun were introduced into the *St Matthew Passion* of Meder long after the latter's death).

7. 19TH AND 20TH CENTURIES. The function of choral music altered radically in the first half of the 19th century with the advent of public concerts, choral societies and great music festivals. As a result, works such as Beethoven's *Christus am Ölberge* (1803) and Spohr's *Des Heilands letzte Stunden* (1834–5) belong more to the history of the oratorio than the Passion. Indeed, the church could offer no satisfactory liturgical alternative, and more traditional works such as Bach's 'newly discovered *St Matthew Passion*' or Graun's *Tod Jesu* were performed in public concert halls or in churches made to serve as concert halls. This situation began to change only with the revival of interest in the history of church music that took place around the middle of the century (Giuseppe Baini's *Passion turbae*, Rome, 1830; reprints, 1861, of early Passions) and with the musicological research that the Cecilian movement brought in its wake. Heinrich von Herzogenberg's *Die Passion* (1896) marked the return of the original composition of the liturgical Passion, but thenceforth composers were to base their works less on the old types of musical setting of the Passion than on the works of great historical figures, particularly Schütz (Hugo Distler's *Choral-Passion*, 1933) and Bach (dialogue of double choir in Ernst Pepping's *Passionsbericht des Matthäus*, 1950). A distinction must still be made between works intended specifically for liturgical use, such as Eberhard Wenzel's Passion of 1968, and those intended primarily for concert performance, such as Herbert Collum's *Johannespassion* (1953) or Penderecki's *Passio et mors Domini nostri Jesu Christi secundum Lucam* (1965). Penderecki's references to Bach were surpassed in Mauricio Kagel's *Sankt-Bach-Passion* (1985), which tells the 'passion story' of Bach's life and is based on the B–A–C–H motif. Arvo Pärt's *Passio Domini nostri Jesu Christi secundum Joannem* (1982) is another well-known example from the late 20th century.

BIBLIOGRAPHY

LITURGY AND MONOPHONIC PASSION

MGG1 ('Passion', §A; B. Stäblein); *MGG2* ('Passion', §A; K.H. Schlager)

H. Böckeler: 'Der Passions-, Evangelien- und Epistel-Gesang in der Stiftskirche zu Aachen', *Gregorius-Blatt*, iv (1879), 38–41

H. Böckeler: 'Ueber den Passionsgesang', *Gregorius-Blatt*, v (1880), 97–9, 121–4; vi (1881), 27–9, 52, 86–90

H. Böckeler: 'Ueber den Cantus Passionis', *Gregorius-Blatt*, viii (1883), 43

H.M. Bannister: *Monumenti Vaticani di paleografia musicale latina* (Leipzig, 1913), 1914

P. Wagner: *Einführung in die gregorianischen Melodien*, iii: *Gregorianische Formenlehre* (Leipzig, 1921/R), 243–51

H.A.P. Schmidt: *Hebdomada Sancta*, ii (Rome, 1957)

P. Eloi Chevallier: 'Cantus Passionis antiquior', *Revue grégorienne*, xxxix (1960), 150–59

G. Schmidt: 'Grundsätzliche Bemerkungen zur Geschichte der Passionshistorie', *AMw*, xvii (1960), 100–25

K. Bárdos: 'Die Variation in der ungarischen Passion des 16.–18. Jahrhunderts', *SM*, iv (1963), 289–323

M. Schuler: 'Spanische Musikeinflüsse in Rom um 1500', *AnM*, xxv (1970), 27–36

K. von Fischer: 'Die Passion von ihren Anfängen bis ins 16. Jahrhundert', *Gattungen der Musik in Einzeldarstellungen: Gedenkschrift Leo Schrade*, ed. W. Arlt and others (Berne, 1973), 574–89

G. Massenkeil: 'Eine unbekannte Quelle zur Geschichte der lateinischen choralen Passion in Frankreich', *Musicae scientiae collectanea: Festschrift Karl Gustav Fellerer zum sechzigsten Geburtstag*, ed. H. Hüschen (Cologne, 1973), 380–85

T. Göllner: 'Unknown Passion Tones in Sixteenth-Century Hispanic Sources', *JAMS*, xxviii (1975), 46–71

POLYPHONIC PASSION TO 1600

MGG1 ('Passion', §B; W. Blankenburg; §C; K. von Fischer); *MGG2* ('Passion', §B; K. von Fischer)

O. Kade: *Die ältere Passionskomposition bis zum Jahre 1631* (Gütersloh, 1893/R)

H.J. Moser: *Die mehrstimmige Vertonung des Evangeliums*, i (Leipzig, 1931/R), 9–14

K. Ameln, C. Mahrenholz and W. Thomas, eds.: *Handbuch der deutschen evangelischen Kirchenmusik* (Göttingen, 1932)

A. Schmitz: 'Zu Walters Choralpassion', *Festschrift Theodor Siebs* (Breslau, 1933/R), 445–61

A. Schmitz: 'Italienische Quellen zur Figural-Passion des 16. Jahrhunderts', *Festschrift Max Schneider zum 60. Geburtstag*, ed. H.J. Zingel (Halle and Eisleben, 1935/R), 92–102

A. Smijers: 'De Mattheus-Passie van Jacob Obrecht', *TVNM*, xiv/3 (1935), 182–4

W. Blankenburg: 'Die deutsche Liedpassion', *Musik und Kirche*, ix (1937), 12–22

K. Ameln: 'Die ältesten Passionsmusiken', *Musik und Kirche*, xi (1939), 12–16

K. Ameln and C. Gerhardt: 'Johann Walter und die älteste deutsche Passionskomposition', *Monatsschrift für Gottesdienst und kirchliche Kunst*, xliv (1939), 103–8

H.J. Moser: 'Die Klagenfurter deutsche Passion des Johannes Heroldt', *Musik und Kirche*, xi (1939), 71–7

H.H. Eggebrecht: 'Die Matthäus-Passion von Melchior Vulpius (1613)', *Mf*, iii (1950), 143–8

K. Ameln: 'Die Anfänge der deutschen Passionshistorie', *IMSCR IV: Basle 1949*, 39–45

J. Bal y Gay: *Tesoro de la música polifonica en Mexico* (Mexico City, 1952), 197–222

K. von Fischer: 'Zur Geschichte der Passionskomposition des 16. Jahrhunderts in Italien', *AMw*, xi (1954), 189–205

A. Schmitz: *Oberitalienische Figuralpassionen des 16. Jahrhunderts* (Mainz, 1955/R)

G. Schmidt: 'Zur Quellenlage der Passionen J. Meilands', *Jb für Liturgik und Hymnologie*, i (1955), 101–9; iii (1957), 124–6

P. Robertson: *A Critical Survey of the Motet Passion* (diss., U. of London, 1957)

B. Smallman: *The Background of Passion Music* (London, 1957, 2/1970)

K. von Fischer: 'Neues zur Passionskomposition des 16. Jahrhunderts', *IMSCR VII: Cologne 1958*, 107–8

A. Schmitz: 'Zur motettischen Passion des 16. Jahrhunderts', *AMw*, xvi (1959), 232–45

G. Schmidt: 'Grundsätzliche Bemerkungen zur Geschichte der Passionshistorie', *AMw*, xvii (1960), 100–25

A. Schmitz: 'Bemerkungen zu Vincenzo Ruffo's Passionskompositionen', *Miscelánea en homenaje a Monseñor Higinio Anglés* (Barcelona, 1961), 821–32

K. von Fischer: 'Zur katholischen Passions-Komposition des späten 16. und frühen 17. Jahrhunderts', *Mf*, xv (1962), 260–64

K. von Fischer: 'Ein singulärer Typus portugiesischer Passionen des 16. Jahrhunderts', *AMw*, xix–xx (1962–3), 180–85

G.S. McPeek: *The British Museum Manuscript Egerton 3307* (London, 1963), 48–50, 54–61

W. Blankenburg: 'Zu den Johannes-Passionen von Ludwig Daser (1578) und Leonhard Lechner (1593)', *Musa–mens–musici: im Gedenken an Walther Vetter* (Leipzig, 1969), 63–6

T. Göllner: *Die mehrstimmigen liturgischen Lesungen*, ii (Tutzing, 1969), 127–38

K. von Fischer: 'Die Passion von ihren Anfängen bis ins 16. Jahrhundert', *Gattungen der Musik in Einzeldarstellungen: Gedenkschrift Leo Schrade*, ed. W. Arlt and others, i (Berne and Munich, 1973), 589–620

J.-V. González-Valle: *Die Tradition des liturgischen Passionsvortrags in Spanien* (Munich, 1974)

A. Thiele: 'Eine unbekannte Passionshandschrift des 16. Jahrhunderts', *BMw*, xvi (1974), 195–217

K. Ameln, C. Mahrenholz and W. Thomas, eds.: 'Die biblischen Historien: Die mehrstimmigen Sätze', *Handbuch der deutschen evangelischen Kirchenmusik*, i/4 (Göttingen, 1974), 26–183

K. Bárdos: *Volksmusikartige Variierungstechnik in den Ungarischen Passionen (15. bis 18. Jahrhundert)* (Budapest, 1975)

E.C. Cramer: 'Some Observations Concerning the Lamentations and Passions of Wacław Szamotuł', *Journal of the Canadian Association of University Schools of Music*, v (1975), 22–31

A.E. Davidson: *The Quasi-Dramatic St. John Passions from Scandinavia and their Medieval Background* (Kalamazoo, MI, 1981)

I. Capelle: 'Zur Verwendung des Passionstones in den durchkomponierten Passionen des 16. Jahrhunderts, insbesondere in der "Johannes-Passion" Leonard Lechners', *Festschrift Arno Forchert zum 60. Geburtstag*, ed. G. Allroggen and D. Altenburg (Kassel, 1986), 61–76

G. Haberkamp: 'Die "verschollenen" Passionen von Jacob Reiner (vor 1560–1606)', *Questiones in musica: Festschrift F. Krautwurst zum 65. Geburtstag*, ed. F. Brusniak and H. Leuchtmann (Tutzing, 1989)

J.-V. González-Valle: *Polifonia Aragonesa*, vi (Zaragoza, 1990)

R. Heyink: 'Die Passionsmotette von Antoine de Longueval: Herkunft, Zuschreibung und Ueberlieferung', *AMw*, xlvii (1990), 217–48

E.C. Cramer: 'Some Aspects of Musical Style in a Recently Discovered Setting of Sixteenth-Century Spanish Passion', *Musica Antiqua ix* [Bydgoszcz 1991], i, ed. E. Harendarska (Bydgoszcz, 1991), 223–48

L. Finscher: *Die Musik des 15. und 16. Jahrhunderts*, Neues Handbuch der Musikwissenschaft, ed. C. Dahlhaus, iii/2 (Laaber, 1990), 414–24

K. von Fischer: 'Die Passions-Motetten des Jacobus Gallus und ihre Beziehungen zur Passion des Antoine de Longaval', *Gallus Carniolus in europska renesansa* (Ljubljana, 1991), 63–70

D. Preciado: 'Los pasiónes polifonicas del codex musical de Valladolid son de Juan de Anchieta, y las primeras completas conocidas cn España', *Revista Aragonesa de Musicologia*, viii (1992), 57–68

K. von Fischer: 'Zur mehrstimmigen Passionsvertonung des 16. Jahrhunderts in Spanien und Böhmen', *AMw*, lii (1995), 1–17

K. von Fischer: *Die Passion: Musik zwischen Kunst und Kirche* (Kassel, 1997)

G. Massenkeil: *Oratorium und Passion*, ii: *Passionsmusik* (Laaber, 1999)

M. Lütolf: *Geschichte der Passion in Italien* (forthcoming)

PASSION AFTER 1600

ScheringGO; WinterfeldEK, iii

J.T. Mosewius: *J.S. Bachs Matthäuspassion: musikalisch-ästhetisch dargestellt* (Berlin, 1852)

C.H. Bitter: *Beiträge zur Geschichte des Oratoriums* (Berlin,1872/R)

P. Spitta: *Die Passionen nach den vier Evangelisten von Heinrich Schütz* (Leipzig, 1886)

F. Zarncke: 'Chr. Reuter als Passionsdichter', *Berichte der Sächsischen Akademie der Wissenschaften zu Leipzig* (1887), 306–68

O. Kade: *Die ältere Passionskomposition bis zum Jahre 1631* (Gütersloh, 1893)

P. Spitta: *Die Passionsmusiken von J.S. Bach und H. Schütz* (Leipzig, 1893)

K. Knoke: *Die Passionen Christi von Thomas Mancinus* (Göttingen, 1897)

M. Schneider: 'Die alte Choralpassion in der Gegenwart', *ZIMG*, vi (1904–5), 491–504

F. Spitta: 'Die Passionen von Heinrich Schütz und ihre Wiederbelebung', *JbMP 1906*, 15–28

H.J. Moser: 'Aus der Frühgeschichte der deutschen General-basspassion', *JbMP 1920*, 18–30; repr. in H.J. Moser: *Musik in Zeit und Raum* (Berlin, 1960), 63–74

W. Lott: 'Zur Geschichte der Passionskomposition von 1650–1800', *AMw*, iii (1921), 285–320

W. Lott: 'Zur Geschichte der Passionsmusiken auf Danziger Boden mit Bevorzugung der oratorischen Passionen', *AMw*, vii (1925), 297–328

K.G. Fellerer: 'Ein Freisinger Mensuralkodex aus dem Jahre 1707 von Michael Wurmb', *ZMw*, viii (1925–6), 361–74

H.M. Adams: 'Passion Music before 1724', *ML*, vii (1926), 258–64

F. Smend: 'Die Johannes-Passion von Bach: auf ihren Bau untersucht', *BJb 1926*, 105–54

F. Smend: 'Bachs Matthäus-Passion: Untersuchungen zur Geschichte des Werkes bis 1750', *BJb 1928*, 1–95; repr. in F. Smend: *Bach-Studien: gesammelte Reden und Aufsätze*, ed. C. Wolff (Kassel, 1969), 11–83

R. Gerber: *Das Passionsrezitativ bei Heinrich Schütz und seine stilgeschichtlichen Grundlagen* (Gütersloh, 1929)

P. Epstein: 'Ein unbekanntes Passionsoratorium von Christian Flor (1667)', *BJb 1930*, 56–99

R. Gerber: 'Die deutsche Passion von Luther bis Bach', *Luther-Jb*, xiii (1931), 131

K. Nef: 'Schweizerische Passionsmusiken', *Schweizerisches Jb für Musikwissenschaft*, v (1931), 113–26

B. Grusnick: 'Hugo Distlers Choralpassion', *Musik und Kirche*, v (1933), 39

H. Hörner: *Georg Philipp Telemanns Passionsmusiken: ein Beitrag zur Geschichte der Passion in Hamburg* (Leipzig, 1933)

K. Nef: 'Beiträge zur Geschichte der Passion in Italien', *ZMw*, xvii (1935), 208–41

A. Adrio: 'Die Matthäuspassion von J.G. Kühnhausen (Celle um 1700)', *Festschrift Arnold Schering zum sechzigsten Geburtstag*, ed. H. Osthoff (Berlin, 1937/R), 24–36

B. Lundgren: 'En okänd Mattheuspassion från mitten av 1600-talet', *STMf*, xxviii (1946), 72–84

A. Dürr: 'Zu den verschollenen Passionen Bachs', *BJb 1949–50*, 81–5

M. Cooper: 'Jommelli and his "Passione"', *The Listener*, xliv (1950), 713

H.H. Eggebrecht: 'Die Matthäus-Passion von Melchior Vulpius (1613)', *Mf*, iii (1950), 143–8

P. Mies: 'Neuzeitliche Passionskompositionen', *Zeitschrift für Kirchenmusik*, lxxi (1951), 30–35

E. Hanley: 'Current Chronicle', *MQ*, xxxix (1953), 241–7 [discussion of A. Scarlatti's *St John Passion*]

H. Römhild: 'Die Matthäus-Passion von Johann Theodor Römhild', *Mf*, ix (1956), 26–33

J. Birke: *Die Passionsmusiken von Thomas Selle (1599 bis 1663): Beiträge zur Geschichte der Passion im 17. Jahrhundert* (diss., U. of Hamburg, 1957)

B. Smallman: *The Background of Passion Music: J.S. Bach and his Predecessors* (London, 1957, enlarged, 2/1970)

J. Birke: 'Eine unbekannte anonyme Matthäuspassion aus der zweiten Hälfte des 17. Jahrhunderts', *AMw*, xv (1958), 162–86

J. Birke: 'Zur Geschichte der Passionsaufführungen in Hamburg bis zum Tode des Kantors Thomas Selle', *Zeitschrift des Vereins für hamburgische Geschichte*, xliv (1958), 219–32

W. Braun: *Die mitteldeutsche Choralpassion im 18. Jahrhundert* (Berlin, 1960)

W. Braun: 'Andreas Unger und die biblische Historie in Naumburg an der Saale', *Jb für Liturgik und Hymnologie*, vii (1962), 172–86

W. Blankenburg: 'Die Aufführungen von Passionen und Passionskantaten in der Schlosskirche auf dem Friedenstein zu Gotha zwischen 1699 und 1770', *Festschrift Friedrich Blume*, ed. A.A. Abert and W. Pfannkuch (Kassel, 1963), 50–59

J. Chailley: *Les Passions de J.S. Bach* (Paris, 1963)

A. Dürr: 'Beobachtungen am Autograph der Matthäus-Passion', *BJb 1963–4*, 47–52

J.W. Grubbs: 'Ein Passions-Pasticcio des 18. Jahrhunderts', *BJb 1965*, 10–42

M. Geck: *Die Wiederentdeckung des Matthäuspassion im 19. Jahrhundert* (Regensburg, 1967)

M.J. Moser: *Die Passion von Schütz bis F. Martin* (Wolfenbüttel, 1967)

H. Becker: 'Die Brockes-Passion von G.F. Händel', *Musica*, xxii (1968), 135–737

A. Dürr: 'Eine Handschriftensammlung des 18. Jahrhunderts in Göttingen', *AMw*, xxv (1968), 314

A. Dürr: 'Neues über Bachs Pergolesi-Bearbeitung', *BJb 1968*, 89–100

D.G. Moe: *The Saint Mark Passion of R. Keiser: a Practical Edition, with an Account of its Historical Background* (diss., State U. of Iowa, 1968)

P. Brainard: 'Bach's Parody Procedure and the St. Matthew Passion', *JAMS*, xxii (1969), 241–60

W. Steude: 'Die Markuspassion in der Leipziger Passionen-Handschrift des J.Z. Grundig', *DJbM*, xiv (1969), 96–116

G. Grote: 'Der Weg zum "Passionsbericht des Matthäus" von Ernst Pepping: strukturelle Untersuchungen', *Festschrift Ernst Pepping zu seinem 70. Geburtstag* (Berlin, 1972), 57–84

I. König: *Studien zum Libretto des 'Tod Jesu' von K.W. Ramler und K.H. Graun* (Munich, 1972)

J.B. Haberlen: *A Critical Survey of the North German Oratorio Passion to 1700* (diss., U. of Illinois, 1974)

H. Friedrichs: *Das Verhältnis von Text und Musik in den Brockespassionen Keisers, Händels, Telemanns und Matthesons: mit einer Einführung in ihre Entstehungs- und Rezeptionsgeschichte sowie den Bestand ihrer literarischen und musikalischen Quellen* (Munich, 1975)

A. Glöckner: 'J.S. Bachs Aufführungen zeitgenössischer Passionsmusiken', *BJb 1977*, 75–119

S.A. Malinowski jr: *The Baroque Oratorio Passion* (diss., Cornell U., 1978)

R. Robinson and A. Winold: *A Study of the Penderecki St. Luke Passion* (Celle, 1983)

L. and I. Stieger: 'Die theologische Bedeutung der Doppelchörigkeit in J.S. Bachs "Matthäus-Passion"', *Bachiana et alia musicologica: Festschrift Alfred Dürr zum 65. Geburtstag*, ed. W. Rehm (Kassel, 1983), 275–86

E. Axmacher: *Aus Liebe will mein Heyland sterben*, Beiträge zur theologischen Bachforschung, ii (Stuttgart, 1984)

U. Prinz, ed.: *J.S. Bach, Matthäuspassion* BWV244: Vorträge des Sommerakademie J.S. Bach 1985 (Stuttgart, 1990)

M. Geck: *J.S. Bach Johannespassion* BWV245 (Munich, 1991)

J. Schmedes: *T. Selle und die biblischen Historien im 17. Jahrhundert* (diss., Munich U., 1992)

U. Prinz, ed.: *J.S. Bach, Johannespassion* BWV245: Vorträge des Meisterkurses 1986 und der Sommerakademie J.S. Bach 1990 (Stuttgart, 1993)

M. Lölkes: 'Beobachtungen zu einigen Sinfonien in den Matthäuspassionen von F. Funke und J.V. Meder', *Musik und Kirche*, lxiv (1994), 11–23

Passionmusik im Umfeld von J.S. Bach (Leipzig, 1994)

K. von Fischer: 'Der Passionsgesang in einer evangelisch-liturgischen Karwochenordnung aus der Mitte des 19. Jahrhunderts', *Telemannia et alia musicologica: Festschrift G. Fleischhauer zum 65. Geburtstag*, ed. D. Gutknecht, H. Krones and F. Zschoch (Oschersleben, 1995), 234–9

W. Reich: *M. Kagel, Sankt-Bach-Passion: Kompositionstechnik und didaktische Perspektiven* (Saarbrücken, 1995)

H.-J. Schulze: 'Eine rätselhafte Johannes-Passion "di Doles" [G. Gebel d.J.]', *R. Eller zum Achtzigsten*, (Rostock, 1995), 67–74

H. Lölkes: *Ramlers 'Der Tod Jesu' in den Vertonungen von Graun und Telemann* (Kassel, 1999)

W. Braun: *Choralpassionen der Bachzeit: J.C. Gerstner* (forthcoming)

KURT VON FISCHER (1–4), WERNER BRAUN (5–7)

Passionary. See LITURGY AND LITURGICAL BOOKS, §II, 3(v).

Passion play. The dramatic representation of Christ's Passion and Crucifixion. The subject is rare in medieval Latin church drama but is a regular feature of vernacular religious plays. The Passion plays in which music plays the largest part are those closely associated with the Complaint of Mary beneath the cross (*see* PLANCTUS; MARIENKLAGE; MEDIEVAL DRAMA, §III, 2(i)).

The term is used also for the vernacular civic plays of France and elsewhere that enact the story of the Passion. In these music often played a considerable part.

JOHN STEVENS/RICHARD RASTALL

Passy, Ludvig Anton Edmund (*b* Stockholm, 3 Sept 1789; *d* Drottningholm, 16 Aug 1870). Swedish pianist and composer of French parentage. He studied the piano with Luigi Piccinni, who was then living in Stockholm, and composition with J.N. Eggert. Subsequently he became a piano pupil of John Field in St Petersburg, and from 1817 he lived in Sweden. He was the most famous Swedish pianist of his time, and was very active as a concert soloist. He was also attached to the royal court, and was the pianist in the royal orchestra (1818–23), organist of the royal chapel (1833–66), and music teacher to Crown Prince Oscar and his wife. In 1840 he was elected to the Stockholm Academy of Music and given the title of professor.

Passy's compositions display a virtuoso pianistic style, in the tradition of Hummel and Clementi; most of them are superficial virtuoso music, though some do have more profound qualities. Among his works are two operas, *Den nordiska kvinnan* ('The Nordic Woman') and *Inbillning och verklighet* ('Fancy and Truth'); a movement of a symphony; Fantasy for piano on motifs from Meyerbeer's *Robert le diable*; Fantasy and Variations for piano on Swedish national melodies (op.6, Leipzig, 1826), a piano trio, four string quartets, fugues for organ, solo songs and choruses. Most of his works are unpublished (manuscripts in *S-Skma*).

BIBLIOGRAPHY

SchillingE

T. Uppström: *Pianister i Sverige* (Stockholm, 1973)

AXEL HELMER

Passy-measures. See PASSAMEZZO.

Pasta, Carlo Enrico (*b* Milan, 17 Nov 1817; *d* Milan, 31 Aug 1898). Italian composer. He studied at the Milan Conservatory and in Paris. Claiming to be a nephew of Giuditta Pasta, he succeeded in having his first opera, *I tredici*, produced at Turin in 1851. He went to Lima in November 1855, announcing himself as having been the Sardinian king's director of military bands for several years. In 1857 he joined the Lima fraternity of S Cecilia. The première of his zarzuela *La cola del diablo* at the Teatro Principal on 3 October 1865 was so successful that the work was repeated several times and his female pupils gave him a large gold medal inscribed 'Al eminente compositor Enrique Pasta, sus discípulas'. On 11 April 1867 Pasta directed the première of his one-act zarzuela *Rafael Sanzio*, the first of his works to a libretto by Juan Cossio (1833–81). In 1871 his four-act *La Fronda* was advertised as the first opera composed in independent Peru. After further stage successes, in 1873 he returned to Italy, where he composed the opera *Atahualpa* (first performed at Genoa in 1875). In 1876 he was back in Lima, where *Atahualpa* was produced to great acclaim on 11 January 1877; the first opera on an Inca subject to be presented there, it received eight more performances. He was rewarded by the dedicatee the banker Dionisio Derteano, and on his final departure from Lima, newspapers announced (February 1877) that his total profit from *Atahualpa* (including sales of the vocal score published by the composer, 1875) exceeded 5000 soles. *Atahualpa* was also performed in Milan at the Teatro Dal Verme in September 1877.

WORKS

one-act zarzuelas sung in Spanish at the Teatro Principal, Lima, unless otherwise stated

I tredici (4, G. Giachetti), Turin, Sutera, 14 Jan 1851
El loco de la guardilla, 13 Feb 1863
La cola del diablo, Lima, 3 Oct 1865
Rafael Sanzio (J. Cossio), 11 Apr 1867, *US-Wc*
Placeres y dolores (Cossio), 1867
El pobre indio (Cossio and J. Vicente Camacho), 8 March 1868
Por un inglés, 5 May 1870
La Fronda (4), 5 Sept 1871
Una taza de thé, 4 Sept 1872
Atahualpa (4, A. Ghislanzoni), Genoa, Paganini, 23 Nov 1875, vs *BEm*

BIBLIOGRAPHY

StiegerO
R. Barbacci : 'Apuntes para un diccionario biográfico musical peruano', *Fénix*, vi (1949), 414–510, esp. 483–4
A. Tauro : *Enciclopedia ilustrada del Perú* (Lima, 1987), ii, 595; iv, 1563

ROBERT STEVENSON

Pasta, Giovanni (*b* Milan, 1604; *d* Milan, ?1663/4). Italian composer, organist, author and cleric. He appears to have been most active as a musician in his early years. He was organist of S Alessandro in Colonna, Bergamo, from at least 1626 to early in 1634. He then became a canon at S Maria Fulcorina, Milan, and later chaplain of the Collegio Tuffo there. His two known volumes of music are *Affetti d'Erato: madrigali in concerto* for two to four voices and continuo, with the addition of four solo songs (Venice, 1626); and *Arie a voce sola* op.2 (Milan, 1634; referred to by Eitner but now apparently lost). His was a very ordinary talent, and music seems not to have lost by his subsequent devotion to the church and to writing; 16 literary works are listed by Calvi, including two for which he provided music – two sets of *Le due sorelle: musica e poesia concertate in arie musicali* (Venice, after 1634),

which are lost. Calvi also stated (in 1664) that Pasta had just died.

BIBLIOGRAPHY

D. Calvi: *Scena letteraria de gli scrittori bergamaschi* (Bergamo, 1664), 509ff [incl. portrait]
F. Picinelli: *Ateneo de' letterati milanesi* (Milan, 1670), 317

NIGEL FORTUNE

Pasta [née Negri], Giuditta (Angiola Maria Costanza) (*b* Saronno, nr Milan, 26 Oct 1797; *d* Como, 1 April 1865). Italian soprano. She studied in Milan with Giuseppe Scappa and Davide Banderali and later with Crescentini and Paer among others. In 1816 she made her début at the Teatro degli Accademici Filodrammatici, Milan, in the première of Scappa's *Le tre Eleonore*; soon after, she appeared in Paris at the Théâtre Italien as Donna Elvira, Giulietta in Zingarelli's *Giulietta e Romeo* and in two operas by Paer. Her London début at the King's Theatre in 1817 was as Telemachus in Cimarosa's *Penelope*. She also sang Cherubino and Despina.

After singing in all the main Italian centres from 1818 (her roles included Rossini's Cenerentola and Cimarosa's Curiazio), she achieved her first great triumph singing Rossini's Desdemona at the Théâtre Italien, Paris, in 1821, subsequently appearing there as Tancredi and Queen Elizabeth. In the following decade she established herself as Europe's greatest soprano, exerting a major influence on the styles of Bellini and Donizetti and becoming one of Rossini's favourite singers. Her great roles included Zingarelli's Romeo, Mayr's Medea and Paisiello's Nina. She made a triumphant return to London in 1824 as Desdemona and also sang Zerlina and Semiramide (one of her greatest interpretations). For the

Giuditta Pasta in the mad scene of Donizetti's 'Anna Bolena', Act 2: painting by Aleksandr Bryullov (Museo Teatrale alla Scala, Milan)

next few years she alternated between London and Paris, adding roles by Meyerbeer and Rossini (she created Corinna in *Il viaggio a Reims* in 1825) to her repertory. In 1826–7 she sang in Naples, creating the title role of Pacini's *Niobe* at the S Carlo.

Her first Bellini role was Imogene in *Il pirata* (1830, Vienna). Subsequently she created Amina in *La sonnambula* (1831, Teatro Carcano, Milan) and the title roles in *Norma* (her début at La Scala in 1831) and *Beatrice di Tenda* (1833, La Fenice). For Donizetti she created the title role in *Anna Bolena* (1830, Teatro Carcano; see illustration) and Bianca in *Ugo, conte di Parigi* (1832). After 1835, when she retired from the stage, Pasta's appearances were infrequent, though she performed in London in 1837 and Berlin and Russia in 1840–41. Her voice had begun to show signs of wear and she lost the desire to compete with the legend she had created.

Pasta's greatness lay in her naturalness, truth of expression and individual timbre, which enabled her, within a phrase, to achieve soul-stirring emotion. She could execute intricate *fioriture* but channelled her bravura to illuminate the drama, though she was often criticized for faulty intonation. An accomplished actress, her deportment and portrayal of dignity were without peer.

BIBLIOGRAPHY

Stendhal: 'Madame Pasta', *Vie de Rossini* (Paris, 1824 2/1854); ed. H. Prunières (Paris, 1922); Eng. trans., ed. R.N. Coe (London, 1956, 2/1970)
J. Ebers: *Seven Years of the King's Theatre* (London, 1828)
H.S. Edwards: *The Prima Donna: her History and Surroundings from the Seventeenth to the Nineteenth Century* (London, 1888)
M. Ferranti-Giulini: *Giuditta Pasta e i suoi tempi* (Milan, 1935)
L. Cambi, ed.: *Vincenzo Bellini: Epistolario* (Verona, 1943)
F. Pastura: *Bellini secondo la storia* (Parma, 1959)
K. Stern: 'The Theatre of Bel Canto', *ON*, xl/16 (1975–6), 10–16
V. Pini: *Giuditta Pasta – i suoi tempi e Saronno* (Milan, 1977)
K. Stern: 'Giuditta Pasta', *ON*, xlvi/12 (1981–2), 8–11
K. Stern: *Giuditta Pasta: a Documentary Biography* (diss., City U., New York, 1983)

KENNETH STERN

Pasta, La Piccola. *See* TACCHINARDI-PERSIANI, FANNY.

Pasterla, La. Pseudonym of Costanza Piantanida, wife of GIOVANNI PIANTANIDA.

Pasterwiz, Georg [Robert] (**von**) (*b* Bierhütten, nr Passau, 7 June 1730; *d* Kremsmünster, 26 Jan 1803). Austrian composer. He was educated at Niederaltaich and later in Kremsmünster, where he entered the Benedictine monastery in 1749. He received his theological training at the University of Salzburg, where he also attended courses in law and mathematics in order to qualify himself to teach at the monastery's Ritterakademie. His musical abilities brought him into contact with Johann Ernst Eberlin, who became his teacher. After his ordination in 1755 he was allowed four years to complete his education. In 1755 he composed the music for the comedy *Abul Granatae rex*, which was followed by a series of other stage works. In 1759 he began teaching philosophy, later mathematics and physics, finally political science and economics. From 1767 to 1783 he was the monastery's *regens chori*. During Joseph II's restrictions he had to give up these duties to act as treasurer at the monastery; when it was threatened with dissolution in 1785 he went to Vienna as its representative. He spent the last eight years of his life in Kremsmünster, where he remained dean of the Upper School until 1801.

In addition to 17 articles published in connection with his teaching at the Ritterakademie, Pasterwiz left over 500 musical compositions, mostly liturgical. Almost every year a new dramatic work was produced for the monastery, initially in Latin, after 1773 in Italian and eventually in German. The edition of *VIII fughe per l'organo o clavicembalo* opp.1–3 shows his mastery of counterpoint and of the organ. Several of these fugues were included in later collections, and a new edition was issued in 1972.

WORKS
MSS mainly at A-KR, also Wn, D-Bsb, Dl, B-Bc, GB-Lbl

Stage: Mardochäus (drama), 1751; Jephtias (drama), 1758; Joas (drama), 1759; Athamas (Spl), 1774; Samson (Spl), 1775; Il Giuseppe riconosciuto (P. Metastasio), 1777; Der wahre Vater, 1782; others
Sacred: Requiem (Munich, n.d.); Terra tremuit, 4vv, orch (Vienna, *c*1803); 14 masses, 83 grads, 85 offs, incl. Super flumina Babylonis (Altötting, 1992), 11 vespers, 38 Mag, 40 Marian ants, 4 lits, 4 TeD, 16 Advent arias, 24 Passion arias
Inst: [24] Fughe, org/hpd, opp.1–3 (Vienna, 1790–92), ed. R. Walter (Altötting, 1972); 300 Themata und Versetten, org/pf, op.4 (Vienna, 1803), ed. R. Walter (Altötting, 1984); Variations, hpd; 22 menuets, orch

BIBLIOGRAPHY
GerberL; WurzbachL
W. Kaas-Cornelius: *Georg von Pasterwiz als Kirchenkomponist* (diss., U. of Vienna, 1925)
K.G. Fellerer: *Der Palestrinastil und seine Bedeutung in der vokalen Kirchenmusik des 18. Jahrhunderts* (Augsburg, 1929/R)
M. Tremmel: 'Georg von Pasterwiz', *Monatshefte für katholische Kirchenmusik*, xii (1930)
A. Kellner: *Musikgeschichte des Stiftes Kremsmünster* (Kassel, 1956), 436–531
M. Kammermayer: 'Robert von Pasterwitz (7.6.1730–26.1.1803): Herkunft und Ausbildung', *Musik in Bayern*, xlviii (1994), 91–103

ALTMAN KELLNER

Pasticcio (It.: 'jumble', 'hotch-potch', 'pudding'; Fr. *pastiche*). An opera made up of various pieces from different composers or sources and adapted to a new or existing libretto. The practice began in the late 17th century but the term came into general use only after about 1730 to describe an *opera seria* or *buffa*, typically based on popular librettos of Metastasio or Goldoni. Arias were selected mainly by the singers in a given production, the recitatives and ensembles being supplied by the house composer, music director or even the theatre manager.

1. Definition. 2. Origins. 3. The early London pasticcios. 4. The composer as pasticheur. 5. The later pasticcio.

1. DEFINITION. As applied to opera, the term was at first somewhat pejorative. J.J. Quantz, during a visit to Florence in 1725 (though writing in 1755), heard several operas 'patched together with arias of various masters, which is called "pastry" by the Italians, "un pasticcio"'. The verb form was used more loosely to describe the process of revision. In 1735, when Vivaldi asked Goldoni to fit aria texts into an existing libretto, the poet said he had to 'accommodate or cook up the drama' to the composer's taste, 'for better or worse' ('accomodare o impasticciare il Dramma a suo gusto, per mettervi bene o male le Arie'). During the second half of the 18th century the pasticcio acquired a degree of respectability. In 1742 Horace Walpole wrote: 'Our operas begin tomorrow with a pasticcio, full of most of my favourite songs'. Later, the designation appears without stigma on the title-pages of

librettos and in composers' contracts. Most first-rank opera composers – including Vivaldi, Bononcini, Handel, Hasse, Gluck, Mozart and Haydn – arranged or at least willingly contributed to pasticcios. Nevertheless, 18th-century critics and modern historians have tended to dismiss such pieces as inartistic medleys. This attitude is unjustified, but no discussion should skirt the issues of originality and authorial integrity.

The term 'pasticcio' has been applied to several different kinds of work:

(*i*) Revival with substitutions: arias by various composers are substituted for pieces thought unsuitable for the available singers;

(*ii*) True pasticcio:

(*a*) a patchwork in which singers, librettist or impresario fill out an existing libretto entirely with *arie di bagaglio* ('suitcase' arias), or

(*b*) a composite original, in which diverse arias by several composers are fashioned into a new plot;

(*iii*) a composer patchwork: a composer incorporates his own arias, old or new, into another's score; and

(*iv*) a self-pastiche: an amalgam of a composer's own arias in a new context.

There is considerable overlapping among these various types. Parody, defined here as the adding of new words to old music, is a process common to those pasticcios in which care has been taken to fit the borrowed arias into the new dramatic context. Related to the pasticcio is the collaborative medley, a fairly rare type, in which two or more composers divide the labour of setting a new or specially adapted libretto, usually act by act. Examples are *Muzio Scevola* (1721, London: Act 1 by Filippo Amadei, Act 2 by Giovanni Bononcini, Act 3 by Handel) and *La virtù trionfante* (1724, Rome: Act 1 by Benedetto Micheli, Act 2 by Vivaldi, Act 3 by Romaldo). Though usually called a pasticcio, Haydn's *La Circe ossia L'isola incantata* (1789, Eszterháza), which incorporates parts of J.G. Naumann's *L'ipocondriaco* and an anonymous opera based on the Circe story, as well as large chunks of original music by Haydn, would be more accurately described as a 'collaborative medley' or a 'composer patchwork', type (*iii*).

2. ORIGINS.   The pasticcio arose from practical exigency. The opening of many new public and court theatres at Venice and then throughout Italy in the 1640s and 50s increased the demand for opera and caused companies to become ever more dependent on revivals. Because operas were almost always composed for specific singers and adapted to local conditions, revivals with new singers in different theatres required extensive changes; even a perennial favourite such as Cavalli's *Giasone* was revised from production to production. In works of this period, recitative, aria and ensemble are closely bound together; revisions accordingly tended not to be of the piecemeal kind characteristic of the later pasticcio. But when, by about 1670, the aria had acquired greater musical weight and detached itself from the recitative, it became easier for an impresario to allow singers to substitute arias they already knew than to hire someone to adjust the original music to suit new voices and characters.

Almost all revivals of Italian operas in the last 20 years of the 17th century were subjected to the pasticcio process,

in that they comprised diverse arias by more than one composer. The practice seems to have had only one major drawback, apart from the inevitable disturbance of the work's original integrity (assuming it had any): without the composer or an enlightened impresario to guide them, singers might make substitutions which were inappropriate to the dramatic context or might overlook the need for variety and contrast between arias.

Few 17th-century operas are of type (*ii*), that is, works assembled entirely from existing arias to old or new librettos. An exception is the Milan production of *Arione* (1694), the libretto of which lists 27 different local composers whose arias were assembled in a deliberate patchwork. When Italian opera was exported to northern European courts and cities in the early years of the 18th century, local companies without experienced or capable *opera seria* composers had to turn to the pasticcio. Such works were common in Hamburg, Brunswick, Brussels and especially London.

3. THE EARLY LONDON PASTICCIOS.   The first extended discussion of the pasticcio appears in the English translation of François Raguenet's *Paralèle des italiens et des françois, en ce qui regarde la musique et les opéra* (*A Comparison between the French and Italian Musick and Opera's*, 1709). Raguenet opined provocatively that Italian operas were 'poor, incoherent Rapsodies without any Connexion or Design … patch'd up with thin, insipid Scraps'. In a footnote the English translator qualified this sweeping remark, explaining that Raguenet meant revivals, in which for 'Convenience or Necessity … Airs are alter'd or omitted, according to the Fancy or Ability of the Singers, without the Approbation or Knowledge of the Composer'. Appended to the translation of Raguenet is the anonymous 'Critical Discourse on Opera's and Musick in England', an account of the London opera scene during 1705–9 which centres on the pasticcio (called here 'a patchwork' or 'medley'), the dominant kind of Italian opera heard in London before Handel arrived in 1710. Included is the following satirical recipe, which nevertheless describes how several of the London pasticcios were actually concocted:

Pick out about an hundred *Italian* Airs from several Authors, good, or bad, it signifies nothing. Among these, make use of fifty five, or fifty six, of such as please your Fancy best, and Marshall 'em in the manner you think most convenient. When this is done, you must employ a Poet to write some *English* Words, the Airs of which are to be adapted to the *Italian* Musick. In the next place you must agree with some Composer to provide the Recitative … When this is done, you must make a Bargain with some Mungril *Italian* Poet to Translate the Part of the *English* that is to be Perform'd in *Italian*; and then deliver it into the Hands of some Amanuensis, that understands Musick better than your self, to Transcribe the Score, and the Parts.

The principal target of this paragraph is *Thomyris, Queen of Scythia* (1707), produced by J.J. Heidegger, who helped choose the arias by Alessandro Scarlatti, Dieupart, Francesco Gasparini, Albinoni and Giovanni Bononcini. J.C. Pepusch arranged the music, composed fresh recitatives and directed from the harpsichord, while P.A. Motteux provided the libretto *post facto*. The castrato Valentino Urbani sang in Italian, the rest of the cast in English.

The author of the 'Critical Discourse' did not condemn the pasticcio *per se*; rather, he claimed that there was no Italian opera which 'will go down here without some Alterations'. Moreover, he praised the pasticcio version of Scarlatti's *Pyrrhus and Demetrius* (1708) in which the arranger Nicola Haym 'first consider'd what Places of Necessity required new Airs' and composed them himself according to 'the Taste of the *English*'. Perhaps with some knowledge of Handel's imminent arrival, the author concluded that no Italian operas ought to be produced in London that were not 'intire, and of one Author, or at least prepar'd by a Person that is capable of uniting different Styles so artfully as to make 'em pass for one'. The implied distinction between good and bad pasticcios resurfaces in criticism throughout the 18th century.

4. THE COMPOSER AS PASTICHEUR.   During the heyday of *opera seria*, the pasticcio became a genre in its own right, no longer simply the unwelcome by-product of a hasty revival or the last resort of an opera company without a resident composer. Even Handel and Vivaldi, who exceptionally for the time were their own impresarios, produced significant numbers of pasticcios. These works were generally mounted either early in the season, before a new opera was ready, or near the end to fill out the repertory or to appease certain star singers. Though a pasticcio required much less labour than an original opera, the composer-arranger could claim it as his own and be paid accordingly.

Elpidia (1725, London) will serve as an example of Handel's procedure. He took the dramatic skeleton from a 1697 libretto by Zeno, retaining only the text of two duets and some recitative. Eschewing the first setting by M.A. Ziani, he then selected most of the arias from recent works – Vinci's *Ifigenia* and *Rosmira fede* and Orlandini's *Berenice* – while composing himself only the secco recitative and perhaps the duets. The arias were chosen with reference to his singers (Cuzzoni, Senesino, Francesco Borosini and others), some of the pieces being already in their repertories. Naturally, the result is stylistically removed from Handel, but it is not less dramatic or coherent than many of his own operas; and (as Strohm has observed) the pasticcios allowed Handel to test the *galant* tastes of the fickle London audience more radically than he dared to do in his own operas.

Handel's *Oreste* (1734, London), consisting of arias borrowed from his own works with only the recitatives and ballet music newly composed (type (*iv*)), presents an aesthetic dilemma. Since most Italian operas contained significant amounts of previously composed music (the proportion increased with each revival), and since Handel was anyway a prodigious borrower and adapter of his own and others' music, there is only a fine line of distinction between this self-pastiche and, say, *Rinaldo* (1711), his first London opera and the supposed vanquisher of the despised polyglot pasticcios. Ironically, *Rinaldo* was constructed much like a pasticcio: several arias were taken with little change from earlier works; some were given parodied texts; a few were borrowed from other composers. As with *Oreste*, the only part of *Rinaldo* that is entirely new is the secco recitative.

5. THE LATER PASTICCIO.   London did not of course have a monopoly on pasticcios; all Italian opera houses indulged in the practice to some extent. But the King's Theatre continued to be the largest consumer till the end of the century. After Handel abandoned opera for oratorio in the 1730s, the Haymarket opera house, which was run as a commercial venture without government subvention, was left with no first-rank composer and tended to pander to the fickle tastes of the audience. Vast sums were spent

on singers, while virtually the entire repertory was imported. Later, even with reputable house composers such as J.C. Bach (1762–72), Sacchini (1772–81) and Anfossi (1782–6), the King's Theatre still relied on revivals and pasticcios for the bulk of its repertory.

Charles Burney, who chronicled this era from direct experience in his *General History of Music*, did not belittle the pasticcio; with its infinite capacity for substitution, it was an ideal showcase for the latest Italian music and singers. Neither did he make much distinction between the dramatic quality of one-composer operas and pasticcios. One of Burney's rare criticisms of the pasticcio as drama is directed at the popular 1770 revival of Gluck's *Orfeo*, to which J.C. Bach had added recitatives and arias as well as some pieces by P.A. Guglielmi, while the Haymarket house poet Giovanni Bottarelli made the necessary adjustments to Calzabigi's original libretto: 'the unity, simplicity, and dramatic excellence of this opera, which had gained the composer so much credit on the Continent, were greatly diminished here by the heterogeneous mixture of Music, of other composers, in a quite different style'. Burney expected less of true pasticcios (type (*ii*)), such as the 1786 *Didone abbandonata*, for which he complimented the prima donna Gertrud Mara on her choice of songs.

Other English critics identified 'a general defect of all pasticcios', namely, 'the want of proper light and shade in the disposition of the songs'. A reviewer of Antonio Andrei's 1784 *Silla* (music selected from Anfossi, Gluck, Alessandri, Martini, Sarti and Tommaso Giordani) elucidated this defect: 'the sole objection which can be urged against this opera, with regard to the music, lies in its superlative excellence … a feast, where the viands were entirely of sugar … where the singers, regardless of the necessary imposition of the shades, the chiaroscuro, have no other aim but to elevate and surprize'.

Opera seria, still essentially a succession of self-contained virtuoso arias, was better suited for pastiche treatment than *opera buffa*, with its much longer and more complicated librettos and greater reliance on secco recitative and through-composed finales. But, while serious pasticcios constitute the vast majority, comic opera was subjected to the same process. Even the early intermezzos, such as Alessandro Scarlatti's *Lesbina e Milo* (1701, Naples), were liable to be transformed by patchwork revivals. Full-length *buffo* pasticcios had become well established by the middle of the century, both reworkings of Goldoni classics (type (*iia*)) and those with new plots fashioned from diverse pieces (type (*iib*)). An example of the latter is *La donna di spirito* (1775, London), which includes arias and duets by 12 different composers; interestingly, the borrowed pieces are found only in the first few scenes of each act, the much longer finales being newly composed, presumably by the anonymous pasticheur.

By the third quarter of the century 'pasticcio' had lost its pejorative connotation. Two *drammi giocosi* (1759, Venice, and 1791, Udine) were actually titled 'Il Pasticcio', the latter being an adaptation of various works by Da Ponte and Vicente Martín y Soler. The adapter of the former explained in a preface that, with apologies to all composers concerned, he had selected the most popular arias from recent Goldoni operas and devised a plot ('una comica azione') to link them together. A further sign of acceptance if not respectability is Joseph Mazzinghi's contract as house composer at the King's Theatre, London, in 1790–92: he agreed to 'compose and select all such new Music' as required and to 'arrange all the Pasticcios'.

Related to the various types of Italian pasticcio are ballad opera, English comic opera, *opéra comique* and Singspiel – all of which incorporated diverse, existing music into a framework of spoken dialogue, or mixed traditional or popular tunes with newly composed ones (see illustration). Among the various types of national quasi-opera, perhaps the closest to the spirit of the Italian pasticcio is the late 18th-century English melodrama, such as Stephen Storace's *The Siege of Belgrade* (1791, London). Music of various composers (both vocal and instrumental – all but Mozart's 'Rondo alla turca' being clearly identified in the published score) had been fitted with parodied texts, rescored, arranged and abridged. Storace's pastiche technique resembles Grétry's plan (not implemented) to produce an *opéra comique* by selecting certain symphonic movements of Haydn, working out a vocal line from the texture and, finally, adding suitable words.

It is difficult to say exactly when the Italian pasticcio died out. In the 1790s few operas were so billed, but Da Ponte and Martín y Soler, both employees of the King's Theatre at the time, provided parodies, arrangements and substitute arias for works which are pasticcios in all but name. A growing awareness of the complexity and unity of contemporary opera, together with the establishment of the operatic canon, gradually rendered the pasticcio obsolete. In 1828 John Ebers, a former manager of the King's Theatre, acknowledged the existence of the canon, but also confirmed the late survival of the pasticcio in London: 'Experience sufficiently proves to us, that the operas imported from the continent are, both in music and poetry, such as to render nugatory here [in London] the employment either of a poet, or a composer (other than as a conductor and arranger)'.

BIBLIOGRAPHY

BurneyH; Grove6 (R. Strohm)
'A Critical Discourse on Opera's and Musick in England', in F. Raguenet: *A Comparison between the French and Italian Musick and Opera's Translated from the French* (London, 1709)
J. Ebers: *Seven Years of the King's Theatre* (London, 1828)
O.G. Sonneck: 'Ciampi's *Bertoldo, Bertoldino e Cacasenno* and Favart's *Ninette à la cour*: a Contribution to the History of *Pasticcio*', *SIMG*, xii (1910–11), 525–64
'The Life of Herr J.J. Quantz as Sketched by Himself', in P. Nettl: *Forgotten Musicians* (New York, 1951), 280–319
F. Walker: '*Orazio*: the History of a Pasticcio', *MQ*, xxxviii (1952), 369–83
W.S. Lewis and others, eds.: *Horace Walpole's Correspondence with Horace Mann* (New Haven, CT, 1954)
G. Ortolani, ed.: *C. Goldoni: Tutte le opere*, i (Verona, 4/1959)
K. Hortschansky: 'Gluck und Lampugnani in Italien: zum Pasticcio *Arsace*', *AnMc*, no.3 (1966), 49–64
K. Hortschansky: '*Arianna*: ein Pasticcio von Gluck', *Mf*, xxiv (1971), 407–11
H. Becker: 'Opern-Pasticcio und Parodie-Oper', *Musicae scientiae collectanea: Festschrift Karl Gustav Fellerer zum siebzigsten Geburtstag*, ed. H. Hüschen (Cologne, 1973), 40–46
R. Strohm: 'Händels Pasticci', *AnMc*, no.14 (1974), 209–67; Eng. version in *Essays on Handel and Italian Opera* (Cambridge, 1985), 164–211
G. Lazarevich: 'Eighteenth-Century Pasticcio: the Historian's Gordian Knot', *AnMc*, no.17 (1976), 121–45
R. Strohm: *Italienische Opernarien des frühen Settecento*, AnMc, no.16 (1976) [incl. sources for 61 pasticcios and similar works, *c*1715–40]
F.L. Millner: *The Operas of Johann Adolf Hass* (Ann Arbor, 1979)
F.C. Petty: *Italian Opera in London 1760–1800* (Ann Arbor, 1980)
B. Baselt: 'Georg Friedrich Händels Pasticcio "Jupiter in Argos" und seine quellenmässige Überlieferung', *HJb 1987*, 57–71
L. Lindgren: 'Venice, Vivaldi, Vico and Opera in London, 1705–17: Venetian Ingredients in English Pasticci', *Nuovi studi vivaldiani: Florence 1987*, 633–66
C. Price: 'Italian Opera and Arson in Late Eighteenth-Century London', *JAMS*, xl (1989), 55–107
C.A. Price: 'Unity, Originality, and the London Pasticcio', *Harvard Library Bulletin*, new ser., ii/4 (1991), 17–30
D. Burrows: 'Handel's 1738 "Oratorio": a Benefit Pasticcio', *Gedenkschrift Bernd Baselt*, ed. K. Hortschansky and K. Musketa (Kassel, 1995), 11–38
E. Cross: 'Vivaldi and the Pasticcio: Text and Music in *Tamerlano*', *Con che soavità: Studies in Italian Opera, Song, and Dance*, ed. I. Fenlon and T. Carter (Oxford, 1995), 275–311

CURTIS PRICE

Playbill for the original production of Arne's pasticcio 'Love in a Village', Covent Garden, London, 8 December 1762

Paston, Edward (*b* ?Norwich, ?1550; *d* Norfolk, 1630). English music collector and amateur musician. He was the second son of Sir Thomas Paston and the head of a junior branch of the Norfolk family that wrote the 'Paston' letters. A Roman Catholic country gentleman who, in the words of his epitaph in Blofield church, was 'most skillfull of liberall Sciences especially musicke and Poetry as also strange languages', he played the lute, translated Spanish poetry, and probably wrote the English verses set to Italian madrigals in some manuscripts of his collection (e.g. *GB-Lbl* Eg.2009–12). In his will (PCC, Scroope 43) his library, divided between his three Norfolk houses, is described in some detail. The surviving music manuscripts are in English and North American libraries. Some have his name stamped on their bindings (e.g. *Lbl* Add.31992, *Lcm* 2089 and *Ob* Tenbury 340–44); others have been identified by their contents, bindings and scribes. Many of the books are devoted to continental music, sacred and secular, from Gombert to Giovanni Gabrieli. Paston's taste in English music extended backwards even to Fayrfax and Taverner. His collection is most important, however, as the sole source of many compositions by Byrd, who appears moreover to have written songs celebrating events in the Paston family life (see Brett, 1970).

BIBLIOGRAPHY

J. Kerman: 'Byrd's Motets: Chronology and Canon', *JAMS*, xiv (1961), 359–82

P. Brett: 'Edward Paston (1550–1630): a Norfolk Gentleman and his Musical Collection', *Transactions of the Cambridge Bibliographical Society*, iv (1964), 51–69

O. Neighbour: 'New Consort Music by Byrd', *MT*, cviii (1967), 506–08

P. Brett, ed.: *Consort Songs*, The Collected Works of William Byrd, xv (London, 1970), p.v; nos.36, 38

J. Bernstein: 'Lassus in English Sources: Two Chansons Recovered', *JAMS*, xxvii (1974), 315–25

S. McCoy: 'Lost Lute Solos Revealed in a Paston Manuscript', *Lute*, xxvi (1986), 21–39

S. McCoy: 'Edward Paston and the Textless Lute-Song', *EMc*, xv (1987), 221 7

P. Brett: 'Pitch and Transposition in the Paston Manuscripts', *Sundry Sorts of Music Books: Essays on the British Library Collections, Presented to O.W. Neighbour*, ed. C. Banks, A. Searle and M. Turner (London, 1993), 89–118

PHILIP BRETT

Paston Manuscripts (*c*1590–*c*1620). *See* SOURCES OF INSTRUMENTAL ENSEMBLE MUSIC TO 1630, §7 and SOURCES, MS, §IX, 19.

Pastoral [pastorale] (Fr., It. *pastorale*; Ger. *Hirtenstück*, *Hirtenspiel*, *Schäferspiel* etc.). A literary, dramatic or musical genre that depicts the characters and scenes of rural life or is expressive of its atmosphere. The term has been used in musical titles as both an adjective (Beethoven's Pastoral Symphony) and a noun (Franck's *Pastorale*) and may be used both ways in referring to the type in general.

1. General. 2. Antiquity. 3. Secular vocal forms: (i) Up to 1700 (ii) After 1700. 4. Christmas and instrumental pastorals in Italy. 5. 17th- and 18th-century Christmas and instrumental pastorals outside Italy. 6. 19th and 20th centuries.

1. GENERAL.   In its long history, the pastoral tradition has served a variety of audiences and artistic purposes. Accounts of it often stress the literary aspects of the tradition at the expense of the musical and pastorals addressed to cultivated audiences at the expense of the more popular, and in consequence the tradition often appears essentially artificial and unreal. Yet it has proved vital and flexible, not only as a self-contained genre, but (as in German Romantic music) occasionally in its ability to colour a variety of music not necessarily considered pastoral either by its composers or by critics. Arcadia or its equivalent can be an eschatological religious symbol, where the wolf lies down with the kid or where Christ is the Good Shepherd (as in Bach's cantata no.104). Or it may be a symbol of Nature whose response to the sacred, or to art, is immediate and authentic (as in the Orpheus legend and in the popular pastoral tradition where animals speak on Christmas Eve). Or it may be a symbol of the ideal to which the artist vainly aspires. Moreover, within the pastoral setting, disruptive events may occur, and they are not always negligible or accountable in terms of *double entendre*: the idealized surroundings may only heighten the sense of loss (as in Schubert's *Die schöne Müllerin*).

Pastoral depends upon the projection of a philosophical opposition, generally one between art and nature or between country and city. In pastoral music this opposition is usually reinforced by the use of distinctive styles, with the 'natural' style falling appreciably short of the complexity of the conventional style of the day. Even when pastoral appears to deal purely with rural life, its implied audience is almost invariably a knowing one, for whom the confrontation with 'natural' values traditionally represents a moral challenge. Accordingly, pastoral is often associated with political and religious allegories; indeed, most Renaissance and Baroque courtly operas, and other musical entertainments seeking to celebrate the status of a ruler, drew on pastoral.

The form and character of pastoral works are often influenced by notions of rhetorical persuasiveness, and in consequence the history of pastoral is often understood as a parallel to the history of rhetoric. New attitudes to the rhetorical force of pastoral took root in the 18th century. These have been associated (Halperin, 1983) with the critical attitude crystallized in Schiller's essay *Über naive und sentimentalische Dichtung* (1800), in which the category of the idyll was first defined as a 'mode of experience' (*Empfindungsweise*) – that is, in terms of its psychological and expressive value rather than its subject matter (see §6 below). Indeed, pastoral is today often defined as a 'mode' rather than as genre or style (see Loughrey, 1984).

The philosophical oppositions in pastoral have been a preoccupation of the secondary literature, especially in English, since Empson (1935; see in particular Kermode, 5/1954), and encourage very general definitions of pastoral that often transcend limitations of subject matter, genre or medium. A distinction has also been drawn between 'hard' and 'soft' pastoral, following the definitions of hard and soft primitivism (Lovejoy and Boas, 1935), and reflecting the ease or lack of ease presupposed by the pastoral model; the parodies of pastoral so important in its history usually arise from the substitution of hard for soft pastoral or vice versa. The term 'pastoral oasis' has also been used (Poggioli, 1975) to describe a section featuring pastoral characteristics within a longer, non-pastoral work; such 'oases' can be shown to be subject to different constraints from those governing a work that is completely pastoral.

2. ANTIQUITY.   Shepherds playing the syrinx – for the ancient Greeks, a typically pastoral instrument – appear in Homer's *Iliad* (xviii, ll.525–6). Pastoral music, as a subject of interest in its own right, may have first appeared with Stesichorus (6th century BCE): according to Aelian, Stesichorus was the first to compose 'pastoral songs' (*boukolika melē*; see *Varia historia*, x, 18), and he may have composed a lament for Daphnis (C.M. Bowra: *Greek Lyric Poetry*, Oxford, 2/1961, pp.84–5). Other origins were also claimed for pastoral song in antiquity, some, like that of Diodorus Siculus quoted below, no doubt mythical.

The pastoral song was first elevated to a considerable literary genre by THEOCRITUS (3rd century BCE) in his *Idylls*, which were probably intended for semi-dramatic public recitation. The pastoral *Idylls* include laments, strophic songs with refrains and singing matches, and the protagonists often play the syrinx as a literary device.

1. Scene from Torquato Tasso's 'Aminta', Act 2: woodcut (Venice, 1583)

These motifs perhaps originated in popular Sicilian shepherd music: Diodorus Siculus, for example, attributed the invention of pastoral song (*boukolikon poiēma kai melos*) to Daphnis, who played the syrinx (iv, chap.84). Other Alexandrians imitated Theocritus, and pastoral features are occasionally found in other musical genres. Greek terms for pastoral song include *boukoliasmos* (linked by Hesychius with 'rustic' music and dance), *boukolika* and so on. The closest to pastoral drama in antiquity was the satyr play; Euripides' *Cyclops*, for example, makes use of pastoral subject matter.

In ancient Rome, pastoral poetry was completely separated from music. Nevertheless, Virgil's *Eclogues* (or *Bucolics*), partly in imitation of Theocritus, and set in a fictitious Greek 'Arcadia', were performed as sung mime in the 1st century BCE (for the importance of musical concepts in the poetry of the *Eclogues*, see VIRGIL). It is no doubt primarily to Virgil that the persistence of Latin, and later vernacular, pastoral poetry is due.

Ancient dramatic theory (Aristotle and Horace, for example) takes no account of pastoral, however, and there are no contemporary accounts of the music used in satyr plays (see Brommer, 1944). This embarrassed some later 'neo-classical' pastoralists, who sought to conform to ancient precedent, for the use of traditional pastoral is itself virtually a statement of loyalty to classical ideals.

3. SECULAR VOCAL FORMS.

(i) Up to 1700. The themes of pastoral poetry were revived in Carolingian times, especially in the works of Alcuin (?735–804), and they occur also in the repertory of the troubadours and trouvères in the PASTOURELLE, where the earliest musical settings of pastoral poetry survive. The 13th-century *Jeu de Robin et Marion*, ascribed to Adam de la Halle, is an entire pastoral play set to music; from the 14th century ecclesiastical dramas featuring shepherds and lowly characters were accorded similar treatment.

Between the late 15th and mid-18th centuries, Virgil's *Eclogues* and other classical models, in Italian translation,

inspired a series of notable original productions, the first of which was Jacopo Sannazaro's *Arcadia*, a set of 12 eclogues (written 1481, published 1502). Pastoral themes occur occasionally in chansons and frottolas around 1500 but became ubiquitous during the subsequent history of the Italian and English madrigal. As the polyphonic madrigal gave birth to the monodic madrigal in the early 17th century, and the latter was superseded in due course by the cantata, the pastoral language was carried forward, with frequent references to Filli, Lilla, Clori, Dorillo, Silvio, Damone and other stock figures and use of devices such as the echo (see ECHO, (2)). Cantatas with two or three pastoral characters were particularly common; as these works grew in proportions and acquired instrumental support they served as the chief point of departure for the later SERENATA.

Even in the late 15th century, however, pastoral poems had been drawn out to large theatrical dimensions and associated with music. Angelo Poliziano's *Favola d'Orfeo* (1471) included various instrumental episodes and dances; and throughout the 16th century dramatic and musical pastorals became increasingly popular in Italian courts and academies, and strongly influenced early opera. They generally took the form of elegant courtly entertainments with a classical veneer, especially for weddings. The most influential pastoral dramas of the Renaissance, Torquato Tasso's *Aminta* (1581; fig.1) and G.B. Guarini's *Il pastor fido* (1589), were produced in courts such as Mantua and Ferrara, from which emerged also many other musical versions of pastoral: *intermedi* and similar celebratory occasional pieces (see INTERMEDIO); a flood of semi-dramatic polyphonic madrigals setting Guarini and other poets (*Il pastor fido* provided the texts of well over 500 madrigals); and the earliest operas, notably Monteverdi's *Orfeo* (1607; on Tasso, Guarini and opera, see Abert, 1970). Related to these is Cavalieri's sacred allegorical pastoral *Rappresentatione di Anima et di Corpo* (1600). Pastoral tales formed the basis of most of the early operas of the late 16th and early 17th centuries, the two most popular being *Dafne* (libretto by Ottaviano Rinuccini, 1597), set by Peri, Gagliano and Schütz, among others, and *Euridice* (Rinuccini, 1600), based on the story of Orpheus, set by Peri and Caccini. The ORPHEUS legend has had lasting appeal for composers since Poliziano and Monteverdi, forming the subject of operas by Stefano Landi, Antonio Sartorio, Antonio Draghi and many others up to Birtwistle in the late 20th century.

Pastoral operas declined in popularity in Italy towards the middle of the 17th century, as interest shifted to historical themes in *opera seria* and to a *commedia dell'arte* spirit in *opera buffa*. Yet the use of pastoral 'oases', supplying a distinctive, affective colouring for the sake of variety, became part of the opera composers' stock in trade for centuries to come (see Bianconi, 1970, for an example). Late 17th-century Italian secular pastorals are usually small-scale, sometimes termed *favole boscareccie*, and often intended as occasional entertainments (e.g. *La Circe*, a two-act pastoral 'operetta' with text by G.F. Apolloni and music by Cesti and Stradella, performed in the garden of the Villa Aldobrandini, Frascati, on 10 May 1668 in honour of Cardinal Leopoldo de' Medici). At the end of the 17th century, however, literati patronized by Queen Christina of Sweden and other aristocrats in Rome, together with composers such as Alessandro Scarlatti, sought to reconstruct Italian literary culture according to the traditional Christian classical pattern of Petrarch. Pastoral operas as such once more took their place in the repertory of this circle (see Dent, 1951, for an example). (For 17th-century Italian sacred pastorals, *see* §4 below.)

Guarini's *Il pastor fido* remained the chief model for pastorals in the 17th century, and was translated into all the principal European languages and various dialects (Bergamasque, 1600; English, 1602; Spanish, 1604; French, 1622; Neapolitan, 1628; vernacular Greek, 1658; German, 1671 etc.). It eventually lent itself to parody, as in *Il pastor infido* (a 'scherzo drammatico', Padua, 1715).

Of the countries in which pastoral drama and prose were cultivated in the Renaissance, Spain was also influential; a well-known early example of Spanish dramatic pastoral is the *Diana* of Jorge de Montemayor (c1560), and the Spanish pastoral romance was burlesqued in Cervantes's *Don Quixote* (1605–15). The most characteristic pastoral genre of the 17th century in Spanish musical theatre was the ZARZUELA, with spoken dialogue and songs; the earliest such piece sung throughout was Lope de Vega's *La selva sin amor* (1627). This repertory persisted until the introduction of Italian opera to Spain in the early 18th century.

French pastoral dramas drawing on Italian and Spanish precedents, with music, choruses, dancing and machines, appeared first in the late 16th century. Although the pastoral drama retreated in France in the 17th century in the face of French classical tragedy, pastoral theory formulated at that time (notably by Rapin and Fontanelle) was influential in France, England and elsewhere (see Congleton, 1952). The first pastoral to be sung throughout in France was *Le triomphe de l'Amour* of Charles de Bey and Michel de La Guerre (first performed 1655); subsequent pastorals included the *Pastorale d'Issy* of Cambert and Perrin (1659), an important part of the establishment of opera in France, Lully's *Les fêtes de l'Amour et de Bacchus* (1672) and Destouches's *Issé* (1697). At the same

time a perhaps paradoxical subgenre, the PASTORALE-HÉROÏQUE, is found.

Italian pastoral opera was performed as early as 1618 in the Steintheater at Hellbrunn (Salzburg) and also in other places in central Europe, including Bohemia and Poland, in the early 17th century. The earliest German operas were also chiefly indebted to the pastoral opera of the Italian courts (for example Schütz's *Dafne*, 1627, now lost, and S.T. Staden's sacred pastoral *Seelewig*, 1644). Pastorals remained popular in German-and Slavonic-speaking areas, largely because musical institutions were centred on local aristocratic courts; later examples include J.S. Kusser's *Erindo* (1694).

Italianate pastoral drama was established in England by Lyly, Shakespeare and Fletcher, among others, about 1600; this tradition, together with court masques, which reached their peak in the early 17th century, and pastoral entertainments such as Henry Lawes's setting of Milton's *Comus* (1634), represented the chief manifestations of dramatic pastoral in England before pastoral operas such as Blow's *Venus and Adonis* (c1683) and, perhaps, Purcell's *Dido and Aeneas* (1689; see Harris, 1980). However, the traditional pastoral opera was never strongly established in England during the Baroque or later.

(ii) After 1700. During the 18th century traditional pastoral opera retained its usefulness as a vehicle for graceful entertainments before noble patrons (fig.2), especially in France and Germany; examples range from Fux's *Orfeo ed Euridice* (1715) and Caldara's *Dafne* (1719) to Haydn's 'dramma pastorale giocoso' *La fedeltà premiata* (1780). The expression of the polarity of 'art' and 'nature' continued to develop, however, in accordance with the evolution of the conception of 'naturalness'. In the early 18th century German composers could allude to pastoral by means of simple, 'folklike' aria structures, often with vernacular texts, probably first found in pastorellas and other non-operatic genres. One such is 'Mein Kätchen ist ein Mädchen' from Keiser's *Croesus* (1711). Similar pastoral touches occur also, for example, in Bumbalka's Czech aria 'Já jsem plná veselosti' from the vernacular intermezzos to František Antonín Míča's opera *L'origine di Jaromeriz in Moravia* (1730; see Helfert, 1925). They are of great importance for the later creation of national styles in central European and German opera.

In Germany and elsewhere, this simple pastoral style contributed to the rise of the BALLAD OPERA, and (particularly in theatres subject to commercial pressures) to the pastoral parody, a wide variety of which was manifested in the 18th and 19th centuries; this at first often presupposed a fairly sophisticated understanding of the pastoral tradition. Among the most inventive parodies of the early 18th century are those of the 'Scriblerus Club' in England (Swift, Pope, Gay and others), whose aim was to ridicule 'all the false tastes in learning'. Gay's absurd versions of pastoral include the enormously successful *Beggar's Opera* (1728). Another, rather different product was his pastoral 'serenata' *Acis and Galatea*, set by Handel (1718); here the parodistic element is absent, and the work perhaps stands as a manifesto of contemporary English neo-classical pastoral. In Scotland Allan Ramsay's *The Gentle Shepherd* (first published in 1725 and often reprinted) was transformed on several occasions into a ballad opera, on the model of *The Beggar's Opera*, first in Edinburgh (1729) and later in London. A version with

2. 'La representacion de la opera pastoral': engraving (Bassano: Remondini, c1780) showing characters conventionally associated with pastoral opera

music by Thomas Linley (i) was produced in 1781. Of later 18th-century parodies, this time of the traditional Italian Platonic love pastoral, Lorenzo da Ponte's libretto for Mozart's opera *Così fan tutte* (1790) particularly deserves mention, though Mozart's setting is scarcely pastoral in any distinctive sense.

The French equivalents to the simple melodies of German and British ballad operas were the vaudevilles (popular melodies to which new texts were added), from which so-called vaudeville comedies were constructed in the first half of the 18th century (*see* VAUDEVILLE). These became the basis of a tradition of soft pastoral, of which J.-J. Rousseau's *Le devin du village* (1752) is an early example: this comprises *opéras comiques* in rural settings, often with deliberately simplified music, whose plots reflect a mythical, idealized view of the peasantry along the lines of Rousseau's own thought. Analogous works were also produced in England (for example the pasticcio *Love in a Village*, 1762); the Singspiele composed by J.A. Hiller in Leipzig in the second half of the century (for example *Die Jagd*, 1770) also represented adaptations of French librettos of this type. All such works reflect a simplified musical style which was regarded as the 'natural' pastoral style of the period – a natural style comparable, perhaps, to the soft pastoral of Marie Antoinette's milkmaid disguise.

In the 19th century the eclectic approach of composers such as Meyerbeer ensured the survival of pastoral 'oases' among other means of creating local colour in French grand opera and elsewhere; among the most original of these should be counted the shepherd's 'alte Weise' in Act 3 of Wagner's *Tristan und Isolde* (1865). Otherwise, in the French repertory as in the Italian, pastoral traits are not very evident, even with subject matter that would in earlier times have virtually demanded their use.

The 'folk-based' pastoral style in 18th-century opera became the basis, however, for many new developments in national opera repertories. Since the common conception of 'nature' at this period comprised landscape, often a specifically national landscape, the SINGSPIEL pastoral idiom acquired powerful new ideological and psychological content. From the early 19th century it was able to symbolize national aspirations, both in German Romantic operas such as Weber's *Der Freischütz* (1821) and subsequently (through the rediscovery of equivalent

idioms: see especially Nejedlý, 1929, iii) in works of the Czech nationalist school, of which the most prominent example is Smetana's *The Bartered Bride* (1866).

Pastoral parody, normally comic, also continued throughout the century, principally in French operettas and their offshoots elsewhere; to an unexpected extent these returned to Renaissance and Baroque pastorals for their basic subject matter or style (for example, Offenbach's *Orphée aux enfers*, 1858, and Sullivan's *Iolanthe*, 1882). In addition a new form of pastoral, the 'pastoral of childhood' (see Empson, 1935), may be discerned later in the century in the MÄRCHENOPER ('fairy-tale opera') such as Humperdinck's *Hänsel und Gretel* (1893).

The new soft Mediterranean pastoral idiom which had been developed from the late 19th century in French orchestral music and ballet, as in Debussy's *Prélude à l'après-midi d'un faune* (1892–4) and Ravel's *Daphnis et Chloé* (1912), in turn suggested hard equivalents in the early 20th century, as in Stravinsky's *The Rite of Spring* (1913) and *The Wedding* (1923), or later in the crude primitivism of Carl Orff (*Der Mond*, 1939; *Die Kluge*, 1943). Other deliberately 'simple' and by that token pastoral styles were developed from various styles of commercial popular music, often drawn from jazz, either directly or via the Broadway or Hollywood American musical (for example, in Milhaud's ballet *La création du monde*, 1923; Krenek's *Jonny spielt auf*, 1927; Gershwin's *Porgy and Bess*, 1935, among many others); these form an obvious hard counterpart to the soft pastoral both of the continuing folksong tradition, exemplified in Vaughan Williams's *Hugh the Drover* (1924), and of the musical-comedy tradition itself (e.g. Rodgers and Hammerstein's *Oklahoma!*, 1943). Another source of 'simple' music has been found in the styles of past ages, as in a number of the works of Stravinsky.

In some works composers did not merely cultivate 'simple' idioms but also rejected 19th-century notions of realism in opera, at the same time succeeding in returning to a more profound, moral version of pastoral. With Brecht and Weill, the use of a 'hard' cabaret idiom at odds with conventional expectations of opera is seen in *Die Dreigroschenoper* (1928) as in *Aufstieg und Fall der Stadt Mahagonny* (1930). Stravinsky's *The Rake's Progress* (1951) appears to represent a different, religious conception of pastoral, both Auden's libretto and Stravinsky's music setting up a pastoral opposition between country and city against which the spiritual progress of the hero can be measured.

4. CHRISTMAS AND INSTRUMENTAL PASTORALS IN ITALY. It is generally assumed that 17th- and 18th-century Italian composers created a vocabulary of instrumental motifs, associated with music for Christmas Eve, which eventually became the common property of all European music. This assumption is adopted here, although the history of pastoral music is as yet imperfectly understood: explicitly pastoral sacred songs are attested in Germany before they are in Italy (see §5 below), and it is not known whether the Spanish and Latin-American VILLANCICO – another explicitly pastoral tradition – had any links with pastoral music elsewhere in Europe.

Reference to pastoral music for Christmas was made by Castaldo (*Vita del B. Gaetano Tiene*, Rome, 2/1616, p.85), and he is one of several who claimed that the custom had been instituted by St Cajetan (Gaetano) of Thiene after a vision he had had on Christmas Eve 1517.

The earliest surviving collection of Christmas pastorals in Italy is the *Pastorali concenti al presepe* of Francesco Fiamengo (1637), written for the domestic Christmas Eve celebrations of his patron at Messina. This collection contains prototypes of most later Italian pastorals, both vocal and instrumental, including a *Sonata pastorale* 'a 2 Violini, Viola, e Trombone ò Leuto', and it contains, intermittently, many of the pastoral motifs later popularized by Corelli. These motifs include lilting melodies in triple time (here 3/2, later usually 6/8 or 12/8) mainly in conjunct motion, prominent use of parallel 3rds, drone basses and symmetrical phrases (ex.1). Such features are prominent in the music-making of Italian shepherds (*pifferari*), who have been recorded playing the shawm (*piffero*) and bagpipe (*zampogna*) at Christmas in towns since the 19th century (ex.2); it has been reasonably suggested that this music may have been cultivated in the 17th century and that it was being imitated in these and later pastorals.

Picturesque motifs of the same sort occurred in art music as early as 1581, in a madrigal by Marenzio, and they occur also in Frescobaldi's *Capriccio fatto sopra la Pastorale*, published in his *Toccate d'intavolatura di cimbalo … libro primo* in the same year as Fiamengo's collection. Pastorals for organ similar to the latter were written in Italy and elsewhere from the 17th century by many composers, including Bernardo Pasquini, Zipoli and possibly Bach (BWV590: the authenticity of this work has been questioned). Harpsichord pieces were also occasionally pastoral, notably (outside Italy) in the musette (*see* MUSETTE, (3)).

Fiamengo's vocal pieces include a lullaby to the Christ child; its text, like those of other 17th-century Italian and German pastorals, was designed to heighten the emotional pitch of devotion. This piece seems to be the earliest example of the NINNA, a category of Italian vocal Christmas pastoral in the form of a lullaby: *ninne* were written by Francesco Durante, Paisiello and Cimarosa, and the tradition survived until at least the 19th century.

Fiamengo's pastorals and those of other 17th-century Italian composers sometimes contain echo effects: these continued as an occasional feature of the later pastoral outside Italy. Other pastoral devices, such as dialogues between allegorical characters, also occur in 17th-century Italian pastorals, and there are 17th-century Italian

Ex.1 F. Fiamengo: *Pastorali concenti al presepe* (1637)

Ex.2 Transcribed from a record (Baines, *Bagpipe*)

Christmas motets containing sections with drone basses and melodies harmonized in 3rds. Leichtentritt (*Geschichte der Motett*, Leipzig, 1908/R) described one such motet by Carissimi, dating from 1675.

In the early 18th century the conventions of pastoral music were applied to the oratorio and concerto grosso. At the Vatican, in the first and second decades of the century, vernacular cantatas were given at banquets on Christmas Eve after First Vespers of Christmas (A. Adami, *Osservazioni per ben regolare il coro dei cantori della cappella pontificia*, 1711; the relevant passage is reproduced in U. Kirkendale, *Antonio Caldara: sein Leben und seine venezianisch-römischen Oratorien*, Graz, 1966, p.71). Cantatas with allegorical characters and pastoral characteristics were written for this purpose by Alessandro and Domenico Scarlatti and by Caldara; Domenico Scarlatti composed similar cantatas in Lisbon in the 1720s for the king's name day, which fell in the Christmas season. Pastoral motifs were used also in liturgical music: Durante wrote a Gloria *in pastorale* as well as other pastoral music. Pastoral masses subsequently enjoyed a great vogue, particularly in Germany (see §5 below).

Christmas cantatas contained vocal and instrumental pastorals (for example, at the end of introductory instrumental sinfonias) in which the pastoral vocabulary of the previous century reached its classic expression (ex.3). These pastorals are in many respects almost indistinguishable from sicilianas. Their tempo is often *larghetto* (although opinion about the correct tempo of Italian pastorals – whether they should be fast or slow – was not unanimous even in the 18th century); the time signature is often 12/8 or 6/8; the melodies are harmonized predominantly in 3rds and 6ths; long drone basses, or at least pedal points, on tonic and dominant are frequent; a distinction between concertino and ripieno groups of players is often drawn. Such features are best known, however, from the pastoral concerti grossi which were published by Italian composers at this time, especially in Corelli's 'Christmas' Concerto, 'fatto per la notte di Natale', published posthumously in 1714 as op.6 no.8. In this work, the pastoral ('ad libitum', a phrase admitting of varying interpretations) is placed at the end of a substantial concerto grosso.

Numerous concertos and, later, symphonies incorporating pastoral motifs in this style, presumably in imitation of Corelli (though their chronology is not clear), were written by a number of his Italian contemporaries and successors, including Torelli (published 1709), Manfredini, Locatelli, Schiassi, Ferrandini, Giuseppe Valentini and Geminiani. They subsequently came to be written throughout Europe.

5. 17TH- AND 18TH-CENTURY CHRISTMAS AND INSTRUMENTAL PASTORALS OUTSIDE ITALY. In the 17th century Germany and the Slavonic countries possessed a distinctive tradition of Christmas pieces in which well-known Christmas songs were quoted, often in a deliberately simple and perhaps 'popular' style. A mass by Tomasz Szadek of 1578 quotes the well-known song *Dies est laetitiae* (WDMP, xxxiii, *c*1957); a mass, *Exultandi tempus est*, by Franz Sales is in a simple homophonic style, with unusually extensive use of triple time, and it has been described as the German prototype of the pastoral mass (P. Wagner, *Geschichte der Messe*, i, Leipzig, 1913/R, 219ff). This tradition persisted even after the introduction of explicitly pastoral imagery (see

Ex.3 Caldara: Cantata a 3 voci con stromenti per la notte del Ssmo Natale (performed 1713), 'Quel pargoletto', *GB-Lam*

below): instrumental pieces quoting Christmas songs include the *Concerto secundo* of Adam Jarzębski, copied in 1627 (WDMP, li, 1964–5, pp.10ff) and various works by Pavel Vejvanovský dating from the 1660s and 1670s (e.g. MAB, xlviii, 1982–4 nos.16, 21). In Poland the well-known Christmas songs were themselves termed pastorals and were published in collections.

In a *Pastorale nel nascimento di Christo sopra il Joseph lieber Joseph mein* (before 1628), Daniel Bollius of Mainz may have attempted to reconcile the German and Italian traditions: an ornamented version of *Joseph lieber* (i.e. *Resonet in laudibus*) is quoted, and some Italianate motifs occur within it. *Joseph lieber* was associated with the German and Slavonic custom of 'rocking the Christ child'; Schütz in his *Historia der ... Geburth Gottes* (1664) also alluded to this custom by adopting a 'rocking' motif in the bass (ex.4), resembling those used by Merula (*see*

Ex.4 Schütz: *Historia der ... Geburth Gottes* (1664), *Intermedium I*
('Der Engel zu den Hirten auf dem Felde ... Worunter bisweilen
des Christkindleins Wiege mit eingeführet wird')

NINNA) and by Monteverdi, in Arnalta's lullaby 'Oblivion soave' in Act 2 of *L'incoronazione di Poppea* (1642).

A more lasting influence was exerted through Catholic hymnbooks in Germany and Bohemia (*see* CANTIONAL). In the 17th century the Jesuits seized on the hymnbook as a weapon of the Counter-Reformation; and the new texts, many written to old melodies, in these collections included pastoral texts which, like those of 17th-century Italian pastorals, were intended to evoke intense religious emotion. The Jesuit Friedrich Spee von Langenfeld included a number of pastoral texts in his popular *Trutznachtigall* (1628), which was widely imitated and translated into Czech (1665). Many Czech songs in earlier hymnbooks had been responsorially performed; this quasi-dramatic style, together with the pastoral convention and with idyllic Christmas songs such as those of Adam Michna, contributed to the formation of the PASTORELLA.

In France, Charpentier introduced popular noëls (melodies with strong pastoral connotations) into his Christmas Midnight Mass setting (*see* NOËL). Other French composers arranged noëls either for organ (Le Bègue, Dandrieu, Daquin, Michel Corrette and others; the tradition survived in the work of Guilmant) or for orchestra as 'symphonies' or 'suites de noëls' (Lalande, Gossec). From the second half of the 17th century the French court indulged a taste for the pseudo-pastoral also in secular music: the bellows-blown bagpipe (musette) and hurdy-gurdy were cultivated in instrumental and operatic music. The musette in turn gave its name to a movement in many 18th-century instrumental suites coupled with the gavotte and using drone basses.

A lasting tradition of instrumental pastorals began in Germany in the late 17th and early 18th centuries, when composers in and near Vienna wrote instrumental pastorals using the Italian pastoral vocabulary of Corelli and his contemporaries. *Sonate pastorali* (pastoral trio sonatas) were written by Fux, J.H. Schmelzer and others (manuscripts in *A-Wn* and *Wsp*). Besides the Italian conventions, the style of Austrian peasant music was imitated, presumably for comic rather than idyllic effect

(e.g. in Heinrich Biber's *Bauernkirchfahrt*; later pieces in this tradition include the *Bauernhochzeit*, 1755, of Leopold Mozart, ed. in DTB, xxvii, Jg.ix, vol.ii, 1908). Animal and bird sounds were imitated; Sandberger showed that this was an old tradition in German music (an example from this period is Poglietti's *Capriccio über das Henner- und Hannergeschrei* for keyboard).

From the late 17th century, in Poland, Moravia, Austria and elsewhere, the pastoral tradition developed in the music of provincial church choirs into the pastorella, the pastoral mass and settings of other liturgical texts (e.g. the *Pange lingua* and *Alma Redemptoris mater*) in pastoral style. These categories enjoyed an enormous vogue in the second half of the 18th century. Tittel (1935) enumerated many characteristics of the pastoral mass, which besides italianate features included fanfare motifs (reminiscent of the alphorn or *tuba pastoralis*), occasional sections in unison, omission of sections of text not in accordance with the Christmas mood and the predominance of even-bar phrases. An independent echo chorus of soloists is occasionally found, as in the punning echo effect from the most celebrated of Abbé Vogler's pastoral masses (1775; ex.5). Though Tittel termed this the 'Viennese' pastoral mass tradition, it was diffused throughout central Europe. Pastoral masses and other pastoral music remained traditional in many places in Austria even after the rise of Cecilianism; modern Austrian composers have occasionally written pastoral masses or mass sections.

In the early 18th century a pastoral style of instrumentation was developed in both sacred and secular pastorals, especially in German areas. Wind instruments symbolized the fluting or playing of reed pipes by classical shepherds: for this purpose such instruments as the chalumeau, oboe d'amore and oboe da caccia were used (as for example in the sinfonia of the second section of Bach's *Christmas Oratorio*, whose pastoral conventions otherwise resemble those of Corelli). Flutes and oboes, often in pairs, eventually became more usual; but the 'Pifa' ('pastoral symphony') of Handel's *Messiah* is still a simple string setting. The Italian pastoral conventions of the early 18th century came to be adopted in the works of Bach, Handel and their contemporaries wherever the text referred to shepherds, in both sacred and secular music – for example, in pastoral pieces such as Handel's *Acis and Galatea*, in Christmas works and in sacred works where Christ was referred to as the Good Shepherd (e.g. Bach's cantata *Du Hirte Israel, höre*, BWV104).

Ex.5 Abbé Vogler: Pastoral Mass (1775), 'Et incarnatus est'
(vocal parts only)

At an early date the pastoral tradition entered that of the symphony and solo concerto in Austria, Germany and Bohemia, sometimes in works written for Christmas. These works, by composers such as Leopold Hofmann, Linek and G.J. Werner, were virtually instrumental pastorellas; they contain pedal points and alphorn-like fanfares, as do the pastoral symphonies and concertos of Mannheim composers (Cannabich, Toeschi and others). Other such works stand more directly in the line of descent from Corelli.

Some works of this period include picturesque nature motifs, such as those in Vivaldi's 'Four Seasons' and bird-calls (Boccherini, G.J. Werner), and programmatic representations of storms and the thanksgiving of Nature at their abatement (Steibelt; J.H. Knecht, *Le portrait musical de la nature*, c1785; organ improvisations representing storms had been performed by Abbé Vogler and Knecht). A wide variety of picturesque motifs of this type occur in Haydn's *Creation* (1796–8) and *Seasons* (1798–1801). (For pastoral Christmas pieces in the Iberian peninsula and Latin America, *see* VILLANCICO).

6. 19TH AND 20TH CENTURIES. Beethoven adopted many of the conventions of 18th-century pastoral music in his Pastoral Symphony op.68 (1808), but he carefully described the work as 'more the expression of feeling than [realistic] painting', thereby revealing a preoccupation with the subjective psychological effects of the pastoral scene that was more thorough-going than that of his predecessors. The pastoral qualities of the work are due in part to an avoidance of the dynamic drive often associated with the tonal design of Beethoven's forms, in part to an unusual emphasis within the formal scheme on the subdominant and to the adoption of a generally slow harmonic rhythm. The first movement, moreover, is constructed almost entirely from major triads.

The picturesque and idyllic motifs of Nature already adopted in some 18th-century music (see above) and unconnected with the Christmas pastoral tradition, such as motifs suggesting running water or hunting scenes in the forest, came to permeate much of the music of composers such as Schubert and Weber (e.g. in the piano accompaniment to Schubert's *Die Forelle*, or Weber's *Freischütz* overture). They are indicative of an idealization of Nature, but may be given an ironic twist (as in Schubert's *Schäfers Klagelied*).

Some 19th-century composers increasingly preferred to use the forbidding and irrational aspects of Nature as models, or to attempt to re-create the pastoral music of an archaic period when, some believed, it had possessed a power later lost under the constraints of civilization. No doubt it is in this light that one should consider the pastoral convention, perhaps invented by Berlioz, of a melody comprising irregular expressive arabesques on a solo instrument, with all accompaniment totally jettisoned. There is an example (ex.6) in the *ranz des vaches*,

Ex.6 Berlioz: *Symphonie fantastique*, 'Scene aux champs'

or pastoral alphorn melody, for oboe and english horn in the 'Scène aux champs' from Berlioz's *Symphonie fantastique* (1830, subsequently revised; see N. Temperley, ed., *New Edition of the Complete Works*, xvi, Kassel, 1972, esp. pp.x, 191). Expressive, unaccompanied, rhythmically free passages contrasted with their immediate contexts had occurred earlier (e.g. in the first movement of Beethoven's Piano Sonata op.31 no.2, 1802), but Berlioz invested his with new significance: he intended this example specifically to evoke a mood of unsatisfied passion in a romantic northern pastoral setting. (The effect may have been suggested to Berlioz by a passage in Chateaubriand's *René* of 1805.)

Similar symbolic, imaginative re-creations of archaic pastoral melodies occur in the works of many later composers. Examples may be seen in the sailor's song in Act 1, and the shepherd's piping in Act 3, of Wagner's *Tristan und Isolde* (1857–9) and in the passages for natural E♭ trumpet and wordless voice in Vaughan Williams's *Pastoral Symphony* (1922). Debussy used similar melodies (e.g. ex.7, from *L'après-midi d'un faune*,

Ex.7 Debussy: *Prélude à l'après-midi d'un faune*

1891–4) to suggest the pastoral music of Greek antiquity – in other words, to create a specifically Mediterranean pagan pastoral convention. The works of a number of early 20th-century composers, notably in France, reflect a vogue for ancient Greek pastoral imagery, sometimes coupled with the influence of Debussy: these include Roussel's *Le poème de la forêt* (1906) and other works, Ravel's *Daphnis et Chloé* (1906–11), Carl Orff's *Tanzende Faune* (1914), and Dukas' *La plainte au loin du faune* (1920).

Throughout the 19th century and well into the 20th, composers continued to cultivate the older italianate pastoral inherited ultimately from Corelli (e.g. 'How lovely are the messengers' from Mendelssohn's *St Paul*, 1836), whose conventions came to be thought particularly well suited to performance during church services. Non-italianate characteristics were occasionally added to this type of pastoral, as in Dohnányi's *Pastoral* for piano, subtitled 'Hungarian Christmas Song' (1921). Berlioz chose this type of pastoral for the 'Shepherds' Farewell' in *L'enfance du Christ* (c1850–54) to create an 'archaic' effect; a similar neo-classical intention lies behind the italianate pastoral conventions of the second *Interludium* from Hindemith's *Ludus tonalis* for piano (1943).

For further information *see* BERGERETTE (ii); BRUNETTE; CACCIA; KOLĘDA; PAN; PROGRAMME MUSIC; QUEMPAS; RANZ DES VACHES; SICILIANA; SYRINX.

BIBLIOGRAPHY

ANTIQUITY

G. Knaack: 'Bukolik', *Paulys Real-Encyclopädie der classischen Alterthumswissenschaaft* (Stuttgart, 1893–1972) [index (Munich, 1980)]

J.M. Edmonds, ed. and trans.: *The Greek Bucolic Poets* (London and New York., 1912/R)

A.S.F. Gow, ed.: *Theocritus* (Cambridge, 1950, 2/1952)

W. Schmid: 'Bukolik', *Reallexikon für Antike und Christentum*, ed. T. Klauser (Stuttgart, 1950–)

R. Merkelbach: '*Boukoliastai* (der Wettgesang der Hirten)', *Rheinisches Museum für Philologie*, 3rd ser., xcix (1956), 97–133

E.G. Schmidt: 'Bukolik', *Der kleine Pauly*, ed. K. Ziegler and W. Sontheimer, i (Stuttgart, 1964), 964

SECULAR VOCAL FORMS

AllacciD; EinsteinIM; ES (F. Angeli and others); *GroveO* (G. Chew); *PirrottaDO*

F. von Schiller: 'Über naive und sentimentalische Dichtung', *Kleinere prosaische Schriften*, ii (Leipzig, 1800), 3–216 [earlier version in *Die Horen*, iv (Tübingen, 1795), 43–76; v (1796), 1–55]

K. Bartsch, ed.: *Romances et pastourelles françaises des XIIe et XIIIe siècles* (Leipzig, 1870/*R*)

A. Arnheim: '*Le devin du village* von Jean-Jacques Rousseau und die Parodie *Les amours de Bastien et Bastienne*', *SIMG*, iv (1902–3), 686–727

A. Solerti: *Gli albori del melodramma* (Milan, 1904/*R*)

E.J. Dent: *Alessandro Scarlatti: his Life and Works* (London, 1905, rev. 2/1960 by F. Walker)

J. Marsan: *La pastorale dramatique en France à la fin du XVIe et au commencement du XVIIe siècle* (Paris, 1905)

W.W. Greg: *Pastoral Poetry & Pastoral Drama* (London, 1906/*R*)

E. Carrara: *La poesia pastorale* (Milan, 1909)

L. de La Laurencie: 'Les pastorales en musique au XVIIe siècle en France avant Lully et leur influence sur l'opéra', *IMusSCR IV: London 1911*, 139–46 [Eng. summary, p.63]

E.H. Fellowes: *The English Madrigal Composers* (Oxford, 1921, 2/1948/*R*)

V. Helfert: *Hudba na jaroměřickém zámku* [Music at the Castle of Jaroměřice] (Prague, 1925)

Z. Nejedlý: *Bedřich Smetana*, iii: *Praha a venkov* [Prague and the countryside] (Prague, 1929)

G.F. Schmidt: *Die frühdeutsche Oper und die musikdramatische Kunst Georg Caspar Schürmanns*, ii (Regensburg, 1933), 41

W. Empson: *Some Versions of Pastoral* (London, 1935)

A.O. Lovejoy and G. Boas: *Primitivism and Related Ideas in Antiquity* (Baltimore, 1935)

W.H. Rubsamen: *Literary Sources of Secular Music in Italy (ca. 1500)* (Berkeley, 1943/*R*)

F. Brommer: *Satyrspiele* (Berlin, 1944, 2/1959)

D.J. Grout: *A Short History of Opera* (New York, 1947, rev. 3/1988 by H.W. Williams)

W.H. Auden: 'The Ironic Hero', *Horizon*, xx (1949), 86–94

E.J. Dent: 'A Pastoral Opera by Alessandro Scarlatti' [*La fede riconosciuta*, 1710], *MR*, xii (1951), 7–14

J.E. Congleton: *Theories of Pastoral Poetry in England 1684–1798* (Gainesville, FL, 1952)

F. Kermode: *English Pastoral Poetry* (London, 1952)

A. Hartmann: 'Battista Guarini and *Il pastor fido*', *MQ*, xxxix (1953), 415–25

F. Kermode: Introduction to W. Shakespeare: *The Tempest* (London, 5/1954, 6/1958)

N. Burt: 'Opera in Arcadia', *MQ*, xli (1955), 145–70

H.C. Wolff: 'Orpheus als Opernthema', *Musica*, xv (1961), 423–5

A. Holschneider: 'Musik in Arkadien', *Festschrift Walter Gerstenberg*, ed. C. von Dadelsen and A. Holschneider (Wolfenbüttel, 1964), 59–67

W.V. Porter: 'Peri and Corsi's *Dafne*: some New Discoveries and Observations', *JAMS*, xviii (1965), 170–96

R. Cody: *The Landscape of the Mind: Pastoralism and Platonic Theory* (Oxford, 1969)

T.G. Rosenmeyer: *The Green Cabinet: Theocritus and the European Pastoral Lyric* (Berkeley, 1969)

A.A. Abert: 'Tasso, Guarini e l'opera', *NRMI*, iv (1970), 827–40

L. Bianconi: 'Die pastorale Szene in Metastasios *Olimpiade*', *GfMKB: Bonn 1970*, 185–91

J.A. Wilhelm: *Seven Troubadours* (University Park, PA, 1970)

P.V. Marinelli: *Pastoral* (London, 1971)

R. Poggioli: *The Oaten Flute: Essays on Pastoral Poetry and the Pastoral Idea* (Cambridge, MA, 1975)

H. Cooper: *Pastoral: Mediaeval into Renaissance* (Ipswich, 1977)

E.T. Harris: *Handel and the Pastoral Tradition* (London, 1980)

H. Jung: *Die Pastorale: Studien zur Geschichte eines musikalischen Topos* (Berne and Munich, 1980)

D.M. Halperin: *Before Pastoral* (New Haven, 1983)

G. Chew: 'Handel as Shepherd', *MT*, cxxv (1984), 498–500

B. Loughrey, ed.: *The Pastoral Mode* (London, 1984)

A. Patterson: *Pastoral and Ideology: Virgil to Valéry* (Berkeley and Los Angeles, 1987)

M.R. Wade: *The German Baroque Pastoral 'Singspiel'* (Berne, 1990)

CHRISTMAS AND INSTRUMENTAL PASTORALES

ApelG; FrotscherG

A. Sandberger: 'Zu den geschichtlichen Voraussetzungen der Pastoralsinfonie', *Ausgewählte Aufsätze zur Musikgeschichte*, ii: *Forschungen, Studien und Kritiken zu Beethoven und zur Beethovenliteratur* (Munich, 1924/*R*), 154–200 [comprehensive summary]

O. Ursprung: *Die katholische Kirchenmusik* (Potsdam, 1931/*R*), 230

H. Engel: *Das Instrumentalkonzert* (Leipzig, 1932, 2/1971–4)

J.R.H. de Smidt: *Les noëls et la tradition populaire* (Amsterdam, 1932)

E. Tittel: 'Die Wiener Pastoralmesse', *Musica divina*, xxiii (1935), 192–6

K.M. Klier: *Schatz österreichischer Weihnachtslieder aus den ältesten Quellen mit den Weisen herausgegeben* (Klosterneuburg, 1937–8)

A.A. Dimpfl: *Die Pastoralmesse* (diss., U. of Erlangen, 1945)

S. Struth: *Das weihnachtliche Hirtenlied* (diss., U. of Mainz, 1949)

E. Rosenfeld: *Friedrich Spee von Langenfeld: eine Stimme in der Wüste* (Berlin, 1958), 156ff

Z.M. Szweykowski: 'Rozkwit wielogłosowości w XVI wieku' [The development of polyphony in the 16th century], *Z dziejów polskiej kultury muzycznej*, i: *Kultura staropolska* [From the history of Polish musical culture, i: Early Polish culture] (Kraków, 1958), 79–156

A. Baines: *Bagpipes* (Oxford, 1960, 3/1995), 66ff, 95

E. Tittel: *Österreichische Kirchenmusik* (Vienna, 1961)

K. Pfannhauser: 'Weihnachten im Liede; Weihnachten in der Musik', *Josefstädter Heimatmuseum*, xliv (1965), 71

H.D. Johnstone: 'Tempi in Corelli's Christmas Concerto', *MT*, cvii (1966), 956–9

G.A. Chew: *The Christmas Pastorella in Austria, Bohemia and Moravia* (diss., U. of Manchester, 1968)

K. Ameln: '"Resonet in laudibus", "Joseph, lieber Joseph mein"', *JbLH*, xv (1970), 52–112

Z.M. Szweykowski: 'Tradition and Popular Elements in Polish Music of the Baroque Era', *MQ*, lvi (1970), 99–115

C. Cudworth: 'Per la notte di Natale', *MT*, cxii (1971), 1165–6

19TH CENTURY

A.H. King: 'Mountains, Music, and Musicians', *MQ*, xxxi (1945), 395–419

GEOFFREY CHEW/R (1–2, 4–6), OWEN JANDER/ GEOFFREY CHEW (3)

Pastorale-héroïque (Fr.). A type of BALLET-HÉROÏQUE whose plot often turns on the loves of nobles or gods (or goddesses), usually in disguise, for shepherdesses (or shepherds) in Arcadian settings. The tone is sentimental, rather than comic. It could be in several acts (e.g. Rameau's *Acante et Céphise*, 1751) or a single entrée or act in a larger work (e.g. Floquet's 'La cour d'amour' in *L'union de l'Amour et des arts*, 1773).

For bibliography *see* OPÉRA-BALLET.

Pastorella [pastorela, pastoritia] (It. or Lat., diminutive of *pastorale*). A church composition for Christmas, found in central Europe from the second half of the 17th century to the 20th century, in Roman Catholic areas. In one or more movements, it is usually for choir or soloists and small orchestra (less often purely instrumental), and usually represents events from a sequence based partly on *Luke* ii: the announcement of midnight, appearance of angels, awakening and dialogue of shepherds and their offering of gifts (or singing and playing, sometimes of a lullaby) to the Christ child. Some deal with the Magi; some were probably designed as edifying substitutes for an ancient ceremony of rocking the Christ child (*Kindelwiegen, kolébání*).

A 'pastorella', mentioned in 1669 in a letter to Karl Liechtenstein-Castelcorn, Prince Bishop of Olmütz, may be an offertory, *Venito, ocyus venito*, by J.H. Schmelzer, which formed the basis for a number of later pastorellas, such as a pastoral trio sonata attributed to Schmelzer in the Rost Codex (*F-Pn* Rés.Vm⁷ 673), and an anonymous Łowicz pastorella of 1699, *Parvule pupule*. There are early pastorellas by Gottfried Finger (attested in an English source), J.D. Zelenka (like the Schmelzer offertory, attested at Dresden), and Fux. Other early sources include Christmas plays with songs and arias, such as the anonymous (Jesuit?) Rakovník *Pastýřská hra o narození Páně* (after 1684) and other plays of religious orders; the *Harmonia caelestis*, a collection of church songs published by Pál Esterházy at Vienna in 1711 but compiled some 10 years earlier (pastorellas continued to be written by Esterházy court composers up to and including Haydn); and quasi-dramatic songs in CANTIONAL such as the *Slavíček rajský* of J.J. Božan (1719).

From the early 18th century, pastorellas with Latin and vernacular texts spread rapidly within Austria (including the Czech lands), Bavaria, Poland and elsewhere in Central Europe, mainly outside the cities. Baroque pastorellas are 'pastoral' by virtue of more or less emphatic allusions to a so-called *stylus rusticanus*, no doubt based on aspects of contemporary folk music; they are often comic in tone, and were often designed to appear to an unsophisticated audience. Some of the allusions are those used by Corelli or Bach (drone basses, melodies harmonized in 3rds and 6ths), but most are indigenous: they include Scotch snaps, fanfare motifs with duple time signatures (alluding to the *tuba pastoralis* or alphorn), melodies or harmonies in exotic scales, and sections entirely in unison for chorus and instruments. Many pastorellas feature folk (or toy) instruments such as the pastoral trumpet, hurdy-gurdy, bagpipes and cuckoo, and many pastorella texts are in dialect.

A great many pastorellas survive in manuscript from the second-half of the 18th century and the 19th century, a period regarded by Berkovec (1987) as the apogee of the genre. Many of these draw on the 'tuneful' style of church music used by composers such as F.X. Brixi. Some are symphonies – a pastoral symphony in this tradition was in effect an instrumental pastorella; some are contrafacta of well-known opera arias (e.g. by Mozart). From the mid-18th century, the Latin Mass Ordinary text was also set in pastoral style in Czech-speaking areas, then Czech vernacular pastorellas were interpolated, and after 1780 the Czech pastoral mass often consisted of a series of vernacular pastorellas entirely replacing the Ordinary, as in the best-known of the Czech Christmas Masses by J.J. Ryba. But the comic tone of Baroque pastorellas became increasingly unacceptable in the second half of the 18th century, and survived mainly only in rural productions; in places aspiring to good taste, the pastorella was often transformed in various ways (for example, by being sentimentalized), and the allusions to the *stylus rusticanus* were toned down.

The tradition remained popular in Bohemia and Moravia throughout the 19th and 20th centuries. Smetana quoted a well-known pastorella melody in *Hubička*, no doubt for its associations with the folk heritage; Czech historians have emphasized the role of the pastorella during the 17th and 18th centuries in preserving a sense of Czech nationality, through language and music, that nourished the Czech National Revival in the 19th century.

As liturgical music, pastorellas may usually have been intended for the offertory (or gradual) of the Christmas Midnight Mass; but practice varied widely, and it can only be said that pastorellas were almost always performed in church, and between Christmas Eve and the Purification.

See also PASTORAL, PASTOURELLE and WEIHNACHTSLIED.

BIBLIOGRAPHY

K.M. Klier, ed.: *Schatz österreichischer Weihnachtslieder aus den ältesten Quellen mit den Weisen herausgegeben* (Klosterneuburg, n.d.)

J. Berkovec, ed.: *České vánoční pastorely/Pastorelle boemiche*, MAB, xxiii (1955)

G.A. Chew: *The Christmas Pastorella in Austria, Bohemia and Moravia and its Antecedents* (diss., U. of Manchester, 1968)

A. and Z.M. Szweykowski, eds.: *Pastorele staropolskie na zespoły wokalno-instrumentalne* [Early Polish pastorellas in vocal-instrumental collections], ŽHMP, xii (1968)

J. Berkovec: *České pastorely* [Czech pastorellas] (Prague, 1987)

W.M. Marchiwica: *Pastorele gidelskie wobec tradycji pastorelli polskiej* (diss., U. of Kraków, 1988)

M. Germer: *The Austro-Bohemian Pastorella and Pastoral Mass to c1780* (diss., New York, U., 1989)

G.A. Chew: 'The Austrian Pastorella and the *Stylus Rusticanus*: Comic and Pastoral Elements in Austrian Music, 1750–1800', *Music in Eighteenth-Century Austria*, ed. D.W. Jones (New York, 1996), 133–93

G.A. Chew: 'Haydn's Pastorellas: Genre, Dating and Transmission in the Early Church Works', *Studies in Music History Presented to H.C. Robbins Landon*, ed. O. Biba and D. Wyn Jones (London, 1996), 21–43

GEOFFREY CHEW

Pastorita. *See* PASTOURELLE.

Pastorius, Jaco [John Francis] (*b* Norristown, PA, 1 Dec 1951; *d* Fort Lauderdale, FL, 12 Sept 1987). American bass guitarist. He grew up in Fort Lauderdale and as a teenager accompanied rhythm and blues and pop artists, including the Temptations and the Supremes. In 1975 he worked with Pat Metheny in Boston, and the following year he attracted widespread notice with his performances on the album *Heavy Weather* (Col.) by Weather Report, with whom he had a long association. From that time he was much in demand as a bass player and producer in a wide variety of settings, which included performances on a number of albums by Joni Mitchell in the late 1970s. From 1980 to about 1983 he toured with his own group, Word of Mouth. He died as a result of injuries sustained during a brawl at the Midnight Club in Fort Lauderdale.

Unlike many jazz and rock bass guitarists, Pastorius used a fretless instrument, and played with immaculate intonation and melodic clarity, as heard on *Donna Lee* (from his album *Jaco Pastorius*, c1975, Epic). Although sometimes faulted for his flamboyant stage personality and eclecticism, he won the admiration of jazz and rock bass players for his fleet technique, incorporating among other features an unprecedented facility for producing artificial harmonics on the instrument (*Portrait of Tracy*, from *Jaco Pastorius*), and the imaginative fusion of styles in his solos. In his own groups, he often preferred to omit chordal instruments from the line-up, thereby leaving space for his own chords and those he implied in his imaginative lines (for example the title track from *Invitation*, 1982, WB). Stanley Clarke should be credited with pioneering a new melodic role for the electric bass guitar in jazz fusion, but Pastorius soon proved to be the greater player, pursuing creative new paths as Clarke settled into a lightweight fusion style. Pastorius's performances set the standard for this style of bass playing.

BIBLIOGRAPHY

N. Tesser: 'Jaco Pastorius: the Florida Flash', *Down Beat*, xliv/2 (1977), 12–13, 44 [incl. discography]

D. Roerich: 'Jaco Pastorius: the Musician Interviewed', *Musician*, no.26 (1980), 38–42

C. Silvert: 'Jaco Pastorius: the Word is Out', *Down Beat*, xlviii/12 (1981), 17–19, 71

J. Mitchell: 'Jaco', *The Jazz Musician*, ed. M. Rowland and T. Scherman (New York, 1994), 191–200

B. Milkowski: *Jaco: the Extraordinary and Tragic Life of Jaco Pastorius, 'the World's Greatest Bass Player'* (San Francisco, 1995)

J. BRADFORD ROBINSON/BARRY KERNFELD

Pastourelle [pastorelle, pastorella, pastorita] A French medieval lyric characterized by its pastoral theme. Unlike the bergerette, its form is variable, but it generally includes a refrain and follows the pattern of a dialogue between a gallant knight and a shepherdess (*pastourelle*) whose favours he seeks. Its origins may be popular, but classical precursors are found in Ovid, Theocritus and Virgil. Latin goliard verses (10th–12th centuries) provided prototypes for the many examples found in the courtly repertory of the troubadours and trouvères. Pastourelles were no doubt played and danced by the jongleurs; the oldest ones surviving with monophonic music are probably those of Marcabru (*c*1100–50), but the heyday of the musically notated form was not reached until the late 13th century. Echoed in the jeu-parti and notably in Adam de la Halle's *Jeu de Robin et de Marion*, the genre survived for many centuries in both folksong and art song; there are examples with the common opening lines 'L'autre jour par un matin' and 'L'autrier me chevalchoie' in modern folksong as well as in numerous 15th- and 16th-century polyphonic settings. The tradition was essentially French and rural, but it was affected by Arcadian manners and consequently flourished in post-Renaissance Italy as the PASTORELLA (*see also* PASTORAL); the Italian type in turn influenced the cultivation of the French pastourelle in 18th-century society.

BIBLIOGRAPHY

K. Bartsch, ed.: *Romances et pastourelles françaises des XII et XIIIe siècles* (Leipzig, 1870/R)

J. Audiau, ed.: *La pastourelle dans la poésie occitane du Moyen-Age* (Paris, 1923)

M. Delbouille: *Les origines de la pastourelle* (Brussels, 1927)

E. Piguet: *L'évolution de la pastourelle du XIIe siècle à nos jours* (Basle, 1927)

W.P. Jones: *The Pastourelle: a Study of the Origins and Tradition of a Lyric Type* (Cambridge, MA, 1931/R)

M. Zink: *La pastourelle: poésie et folklore au Moyen Age* (Paris, 1972)

J.-C. Rivière: *Pastourelles* (Geneva, 1974–6)

M. Pascale: ' Le musiche nelle pastourelles francesi del XII e XIII secolo: le variazioni melodiche nella tradizione manoscritta', *Annali della Facoltà di lettere e filosofia* [U. of Perugia], xiii (1975–6), 575–631

W.D. Paden: *The Medieval Pastourelle* (New York, 1987)

R. Freedman: ' Pastourelle jolie: the Chanson at the Court of Lorraine, c.1500', *JRMA*, cxvi (1991), 161–200

FRANK DOBBINS

Pastrana, Pedro de (*b* Toledo, *c*1490; *d* after 1558). Spanish composer. He was appointed chaplain to Charles V in Valladolid on 12 July 1527. On 13 August 1529 Clement VII made him abbot of the Cistercian abbey of S Bernardo, near Valencia, and he took up the appointment on 3 December without resigning as chaplain to the emperor. He visited Rome in 1533 and at about that time acquired a third appointment, as chaplain and *maestro de capilla* to the Duke and Duchess of Calabria, Ferdinand of Aragon and Germaine de Foix. José de Sigüenza later reported that the Duke had 'assembled the best *capilla* of musicians in Spain, of singers and of players of all kinds of instruments': between 1546 and 1550 (the year the duke died) it employed about 20 singers, two organists, three sackbut players, three or four shawm players, a harpist and two music copyists (Pompeo de Russi and the composer Bartolomé Cárceres).

In 1544, in view of the state into which the monastery of S Bernardo had fallen, the duke contrived to have it transferred to the Hieronymites and converted into a family pantheon. Pastrana was relieved of his abbacy, and although he continued to enjoy the economic benefits he had derived from it, his relations with the duke were affected; in 1546 his place in the *capilla* was taken by Juan Cepa, and he probably returned to the imperial court to profit from his remaining post as chaplain.

A few months later – in about the middle of 1547 – he was appointed *maestro de capilla* to Don Philip, the future Philip II, on the death of Juan García de Basurto. From the time he entered the service of the prince until his death he must have been permanently in residence in the Spanish court. Due to his age he was not one of the singers who accompanied Philip during his stay in Flanders (1548–50), nor was he part of Philip's retinue when he went to Winchester for his second marriage, to Mary Tudor, in 1554. In 1558 he added to his considerable income a benefice of 400 ducats a year from the diocese of Córdoba. On 9 February 1559 he gave his approval for the publication of Martín de Tapia's *Vergel de música*; he probably died shortly after.

According to an inventory of 1597, made a few months before Philip II's death, the Spanish royal chapel library owned at least two books containing works by Pastrana, one of 'psalms . . . beginning with *Dixe Dominus*' and the other 'beginning with a Magnificat . . . and some motets': neither appears to have survived. Two other inventories, of works belonging to Tarazona Cathedral, indicate that in the last third of the 16th century it possessed seven books containing works by Pastrana: only two of these survive. An untitled piece, possibly for keyboard, once formed part of the repertory of S Miguel Acatán, Guatemala. Pastrana was clearly a composer of strong personality, and wrote the earliest known villancico with two alternating choruses, *Señores, el qu'es nascido* (the next villancico with this feature is *Soleta y verge* (E-Bc 1166), by Bartolomé Cárceres and Juan Cepa).

WORKS

Mass, ?5vv, *E-TZ* 17, inc.

Magnificat, 5vv, *Bc* 1967; 3 Magnificat, 4vv, *TZ* 5; Magnificat, 4vv, *V* 5

Motets and hymns: Benedicamus Domino, 4vv, *TZ* 5; Domine memento, 4vv, *Tc* 21; In te Domine speravi, 4vv, *TZ* 5; Miserere mei, Deus, 4vv, *TZ* 5; Pater dimitte illis, 4vv, *TZ* 5; Secundum multitudinem dolorum, 6vv, *TZ* 17, inc.; Sicut cervus, 3vv, *TZ* 5; Tibi soli peccavi, 5vv, *TZ* 5; Beata nobis gaudia, 4vv, *Bc* 454 [doubtful]; Exultet celum laudibus, 4vv, *Bc* 454 [doubtful]

Psalms: Beati omnes, 4vv, *Zcc* C-3-14, anon.; Credidi, 4vv, *Zcc* C-3-14, anon.; De profundis, 4vv, *Zcc* C-3-14, anon.; Dixit Dominus, 4vv, *Zcc* C-3-14; Domine probasti me, *Zcc* C-3-14, anon.; In convertendo, 4vv, *Zcc* C-3-14, anon.; Memento Domine David, 4vv, *Zcc* C-3-14, anon.

Sacred villancicos: Qué lindo es el zagal, donzellas, 4vv, *TZ* 17, inc.; Señores, el qu'es nascido, 5vv, *TZ* 17 (ed. Gómez), 1556[30], 3vv, anon. (ed. Mitjana and Querol Rosso)

Secular villancicos: Ay dime señora, di!, 4vv, *Bc* 454; Llenos de
lágrimas tristes, 3vv, *Bc* 454 (and in original index of *Mn* 2-1-3),
also in *P-Em* 11973, ed. Joaquim
8 Fauxbourdons, 4vv, *E-Bc* 454 [doubtful]
Lost works: Te Deum; Asperges me; Ave maris stella; Beata quoque
agmina; Benedictus dominus; Christus resurgens; Circundederunt;
Cor mundum crea in me; Deus, deus meus; Dulcis amica mea; Ecce
nos reliquimus; Et exultavit; Gaude quia deo plena; Hostis
Herodes; Ibant magi; Ignis vibrante; In passione; Jure te laudamus;
Maria, mater gratie; Montes Gelboe; Nobis natus, nobis datus;
Non ex virili; Nuncius celso; O crux, ave spes unica; Pange lingua;
Quare tristis est; Regina celi; Scandans tribunal dextere; Tota
pulchra inmaculata; Ubi patres precellentes; Vexilla regis; Vidi
aquam; Vidi dulcedo; Vita et audivi; Vivo ego; 5 'Salmos de
Nuestra Señora'; 3 'Gozos de Nuestra Señora'

BIBLIOGRAPHY

M. Joaquim: *O cancionero musical e poetico da Biblioteca Públia
Hortênsia* (Coimbra, 1940), 94
H. Anglés, ed.: *La música en la corte de Carlos V*, MME, ii/1 (1944/
R, 2/1965), 26, 98
N. Alvarez: 'Nuevas noticias de músicos de Felipe II de su época y
sobre impresión de música', *AnM*, xv (1960), 195–217, esp. 196
J. Moll: 'Notas para la historia musical de la corte del Duque de
Calabria', *AnM*, xviii (1963), 123–35, esp. 130
R. Mitjana and L.Querol Rosso, ed.: *Cancionero de Uppsala*
(Madrid, 1980), no.47
P. Calahorra: 'Los fondos musicales en el siglo XVI de la Catedral de
Tarazona I: Inventarios', *Nassarre*, viii/2 (1992), 9–56
M.C. Gómez: 'Una versión a 5 voces del villancico *Señores, el qu'es
nascido* del Cancionero de Uppsala', *Nassarre*, xi (1995), 157–71

MARICARMEN GÓMEZ

Pászthory, Casimir von (*b* Budapest, 1 April 1886; *d*
Wermelskirchen, 18 Feb 1966). Austrian composer of
Hungarian origin. His mother, Gisela von Pászthory, was
a pupil of Liszt, and his stepfather was August Göllerich,
a biographer of Bruckner. After initial training with his
mother he studied in Vienna, Paris and Brussels. His first
public success came with the melodrama *Die Weise von
Liebe und Tod des Cornets Christoph Rilke* (1914), which
received particular praise from Rilke himself. He taught
the cello at the Vienna Volkskonservatorium (1927–34)
and then lived as a freelance composer. Grounded in the
late Romanticism of Strauss or Pfitzner, Pászthory's works
are in an original harmonic style; his chamber music,
while being strongly expressive, retains a strictness and
classicism in form and the spirit of counterpoint. His
operas are characterized by an unusual vocality and keen
sense of dramaturgy, such as in *Die Prinzessin und der
Schweinehirt.*

WORKS
(*selective list*)

Operas: Die drei gerechten Kammacher (after G. Keller), Graz, 1932;
Die Prinzessin und der Schweinehirt (after H.C. Andersen),
Weimar, 1937; Tilman Riemenschneider (after L.G. Bachmann),
Basle, 1959
Ballets: Erlenhügel, Karlsruhe, 1936; Isbrand und Isigildis, Weimar,
1938; Arvalány, Dresden, 1939; Tristan-Legende
Melodramas: Die Weise von Liebe und Tod des Cornets Christoph
Rilke (after R.M. Rilke), 1914; Die wilden Schwäne (after
Andersen), 1937
Orch: Thijl Uilenspiegel, 1933
Vocal: Das Jahr (J. Weinheber), 1v, orch; Sabine (P. Verlaine), 1v,
orch; song cycles (H. Hesse, Rilke, T.W. Storm, Bierbaum), other
songs and folksong arrs., choral works
Chbr: Sonata, vc, pf (1936); Str Qt (1951); Pf Trio

Principal publishers: Kistner & Siegel, Litolff, Peters, Universal

BIBLIOGRAPHY

G. Brosche, ed.: *Casimir von Pászthory 1886–1966* (Vienna, 1986)
H. Krones: 'In Memoriam', *ÖMz*, xli (1986), 183 only

JOSEPH CLARK/MATTHIAS SCHMIDT

Patachich, Iván (*b* Budapest, 3 June 1922; *d* Budapest, 9
May 1993). Hungarian composer. He studied composition under Siklós, Viski and Farkas at the Liszt Academy
of Music (1941–7) and was a conducting pupil of
Ferencsik. Répétiteur at the Hungarian State Opera
(1943–7), he was afterwards conductor at the Comic
Opera and Madách Theatres, and in 1953 he was
appointed director of music to the Budapest Film Studios.
His Sextet for harp and wind took first prize at the
Moscow World Youth Festival (1957). After a period
influenced by Bartók and Kodály he began to adopt new
techniques, with which he came into contact at Darmstadt
summer courses. Patachich pioneered electronic music in
Hungary: he established the studio EXASTUD (Experi-
mentum auditorii studii) in Budapest in 1971, and his
electronic score for the film *Immortality* won first prize at
the San Francisco Film Festival. His *Metamorphosi* for
marimba and tape was awarded the electro-acoustic prize
at Bourges (1978) and *Ludi spaziali* the Grand Prix at
CIME (Confédération Internationale de Musique Electro-
nique, France, 1984). He experimented with electro-
acoustic and computer music in Stuttgart and Utrecht,
and realized works at Columbia University, New York
(1969), Stockholm (1974), Bourges (1980) and Paris
(1988).

WORKS
(*selective list*)

STAGE AND VOCAL

Fekete-fehér [Black and White] (ballet), 1958; Theomachia (op.1, S.
Weöres), 1962; Bakaruhában [Sunday Romance] (ballet), 1963;
Mgongo and Mlaba (ballet), 1965; Fuente Ovejuna (op, 3, L. de
Vega), 1969; Sudio sintetico (ballet), 1973; Möbius tér [Möbius
Space] (sci-fi pantomime, P. Greguss, G. Urbán), 1980; Brave New
World (op, 3, M. Hubay, after A. Huxley), 1988–9
Choral (acc.): Messa di Santa Marguerita, chorus, orch, 1967; Music
of the Bible (cant., Sir cha Sirim), T, chorus, orch, 1968; Canti
stravaganti (cant., C. Morgenstern), chorus, tape, 1981; Az
éjszaka csodái [Miracles of the Night] (cant., Weöres), 1985;
Canticum canticorum (Bible), chorus, insts, 1985; Miracle of the
Hermit Thrush (cant.), chorus, orch, tape, 1987
Songs, choruses, incid music, film scores

ORCHESTRAL

Hp Conc. no.1, 1956; Fl Conc., 1958; Va Conc., 1959; Ob Conc.,
1959; Serenade, str, 1960; Gui Conc., 1961; 3 pezzi, cl, orch,
1961; Conc. breve, vc, orch, 1962; Pf Conc. no.1, 1963;
Sinfonietta Savariensis, 1964; Vn Conc., 1964; Bn Conc., 1965;
Quadri di Picasso, 1965; Sym. no.1, 1965; Perc Conc., 1966; Sym.
no.2, 1966; Colori 67, 1967; Hp Conc. no.2, 1968; Pf Conc. no.2,
1968; Conc., vn, pf, orch, 1969; Divertimento, str, 1969; 3 Schizzi,
1969; Org Conc., 1971; Concertino, pf, wind, 1972; Conc.,
cimb/mar, orch, 1975; Coordinate, 1979; Naconxypan szigetén
[On the Island of Naconxypan], 5 sym. poems, 1986; DX7
Reports no.2, synth, orch, 1987; Trbn Conc., 1988; Tpt Conc.,
1988; Pour 24 cordes, 1989

INSTRUMENTAL AND TAPE

Sonata no.1, vn, pf, 1948; Sextet, hp, wind, 1957; Qnt, hp, fl, str,
1958; Hp Trio, 1958; Duet, vn, va, 1959; Wind Qnt, 1960; Duet,
vn, gui, 1961; Str Qt no.1, 1961; Petite Suite, 2 cl, 1962; Pf Trio
no.1, 1962; Sonata, va, 1962; Sonata, vc, 1963; Sonata no.2, vn,
pf, 1964; Sonata, vn, 1964; Sonata, pf, 1965; 16 pezzi, gui, 1966;
Str Qt no.2, 1966; Ritmi dispari, wind, 1966; Elementi, perc,
1966; 3 pezzi, org, 1966; Contrasti, 2 pf, 1967; Pf Trio no.2,
1967; 4 studii, perc, 1968; Costruzioni, perc, 1969; 4 disegni, vn,
pf, 1969; Table Music, wind insts, 1970; Verbunkos és friss, brass
insts, 1971; Quartettino, sax qt, 1972; Modelli, fl, va, gui, 1975;
Ja amidohele, 5 vc, 1976; Septetto, 3 tpt, 2 trbn, tuba, hp, 1976;
Quartettino, 4 hn, 1976; Hispanica, 6 wind insts, 1977; Gradus ad
fidulam I–III, vn pieces, 1987–8
Tape: Galaxis, 1968; Studio sintetico, 1972; Spettri, 1973; Funzione
acustica, 1975; Movimenti spaziale, 1976; Calling Sounds, 1977;
Hommage à l'électronique, 1978; Studio analitico, 1979; Pacem

mundo, 1980; Pantheos, 1980; Annales, 1982; Moog Fantasy, 1983; Studium digitale, 1984; Musique destinée, 1987; Chanson nocturne du poisson, 1988; Watermusic, 1989; Ad europam, 1990; Exehipo, 1991

Principal publisher: Editio Musica

BIBLIOGRAPHY

Contemporary Hungarian Composers (Budapest, 1970, 5/1989)

G. Kroó: *A magyar zeneszerzés 25 éve* [25 years of Hungarian composition] (Budapest, 1971)

G. Kroó: *A magyar zeneszerzés 30 éve* [30 years of Hungarian composition] (Budapest, 1975)

MELINDA BERLÁSZ

Pataky, Kálmán [Koloman von] (*b* Alsólendva, 14 Nov 1896; *d* Los Angeles, 3 March 1964). Hungarian tenor. After little serious study, he made his début at the Budapest Opera in 1922, as the Duke of Mantua, which led to an invitation to sing under Schalk at the Vienna Staatsoper in 1926. Until the Nazi invasion of Austria, Vienna remained his base, although he often sang in Budapest and abroad (usually as Koloman von Pataky), notably at the Paris Opéra (1928), Glyndebourne (1936), La Scala (1940), Stockholm and, frequently, at the Colón, Buenos Aires. He sang Florestan under Toscanini at Salzburg in 1936. He spent the war in Hungary, returning to the Colón for a few performances in 1946. Pataky was not an accomplished actor, but his classically beautiful voice and thorough understanding of style (developed largely during his years in Vienna), his wide cultural background and gift for musical characterization made him one of the leading Mozart tenors; he was an outstanding Don Ottavio, Belmonte and Tamino. Other roles included Puccini's Rodolfo and Des Grieux, and (though he was perhaps less well suited to these heroic roles) Radames, Cavaradossi and Turiddu. Pataky's sweet tone and refined technique are well displayed in his recording of Don Ottavio in Busch's Glyndebourne *Don Giovanni*.

BIBLIOGRAPHY

GV (E. Gara; T. Kaufmann and R. Vegeto)

V. Somogyi and I. Molnár: *Pataky Kálmán* (Budapest, 1968)

A. Blyth: 'Koloman von Pataky and Walter Widdop', *Opera*, xl (1989), 288–95

PÉTER P. VÁRNAI/ALAN BLYTH

Patanè, Giuseppe (*b* Naples, 1 Jan 1932; *d* Munich, 30 May 1989). Italian conductor. The son of the conductor Franco Patanè (1908–68), he studied the piano and composition at the Naples Conservatory and made his conducting début at the Teatro Mercadante there with *La traviata* in 1951. He was engaged as répétiteur and assistant conductor at the Teatro S Carlo, Naples, until 1956, and began to make appearances in other cities. During the 1960s he worked mainly in Austria and Germany, at the Linz Landestheater as principal conductor (1961–2), and as resident conductor at the Deutsche Oper, Berlin (1962–8). Patanè first appeared at La Scala in 1969, conducting *Rigoletto*, and later worked at Naples, Rome, Munich, Dresden, San Francisco and Covent Garden, where he made his début with *La forza del destino* in 1973. Patanè appeared at the Metropolitan Opera in 1978, and from 1982 to 1984 was co-principal conductor of the American SO in New York. He became musical director of the Arena di Verona (1983), and after a period at the Nationaltheater in Mannheim (1987), became chief conductor of the Munich RO in 1988. Patanè was appointed musical director at the Rome Opera in 1989, but died before he could take up the post. His opera recordings include *Madama Butterfly*, *Il trittico*, *Maria Stuarda*, *La Cenerentola* and Bellini's *I Capuleti ed i Montecchi*. Patanè was a dynamic conductor in both the operatic and symphonic repertory, with much of Toscanini's rhythmic ebullience and tensile line; some of his Beethoven performances in particular stood worthily in the Toscanini tradition.

BERNARD JACOBSON

Patart [Batardi, Partart, Patard, Patarto, Pätard, Pedardo, Pedart], **Antonio** (*fl* 1582–1605). Italian composer and instrumentalist, active in Austria, Bavaria and Poland. He was a trumpet and cornett player to the Archduke Karl II at Graz from 1 September 1582 to 1590; he then moved to Munich, where, until 1595, he served in the court chapel, which until 1594 was directed by Lassus. His last known appointment was as a wind player in the Italian chapel at the Warsaw court of Sigismund III. He is first mentioned in court records there in 1598, and he remained at Warsaw until at least 1605, when, on the occasion of the marriage of Sigismund to the Austrian archduchess Konstanza, he conducted his own compositions. His only surviving works are two six-voice motets (RISM 1604² and 1621²) and an incomplete mass for eight voices (in *PL-GD*). Like Alfonso Pagani, who worked at the Warsaw court around 1604, Patart created a direct link with the Munich tradition of Lassus, who remained popular in Poland until about 1630. At least seven other members of the Patart family were wind players at the courts of Graz, Munich and Warsaw in the late 16th century and early 17th: Antonio's father, Giovanni (*d* Graz, 1603), and his brothers Bernardo, Carlo, Giovanni Giacomo and Rinaldi; Simon (*c*1574), a cornett player whose relationship to Antonio is not known; and Sigismundus (*fl* 1626–36), who is mentioned in the records of the court and of the collegiate church of St John the Baptist in Warsaw and was probably Antonio's son. In Federhofer's opinion, the Patart family exerted a marked Italian influence on the wind music performed at German and Polish courts in the early 17th century.

BIBLIOGRAPHY

DEUMM

A. Sandberger: *Beiträge zur Geschichte der bayerischen Hofkapelle unter Orlando di Lasso*, iii (Leipzig, 1895/R), 193ff

Z. Jachimecki: *Wpływy włoskie w muzyce polskiej* [Italian influences in Polish music] (Kraków, 1911), 176

H. Feicht: 'Przyczynki do dziejów kapeli królewskiej w Warszawie za rządów kapelmistrzowskich Marka Scacchiego' [Contributions to the history of the royal chapel in Warsaw under the musical directorship of Marco Scacchi], *KM*, no.1 (1928), 20–34, 125–44; rep. in *Studia nad muzyka polskiego renesansu i baroku* (Kraków, 1980), 243–88

A. Chybiński: *Słownik muzyków dawnej Polski* [Dictionary of early Polish musicians] (Kraków, 1949), 96

H. Federhofer: 'Graz Court Musicians and their Contributions to the *Parnassus musicus Ferdinandaeus* (1615)', *MD*, ix (1955), 167–244

H. Federhofer: 'Musikalische Beziehungen zwischen den Höfen Erzherzog Ferdinands von Innerösterreich und König Sigismunds III von Polen', *The Works of Frederick Chopin: Warsaw 1960*, 522–6

O. Mortensen: 'The Polish-Dance in Denmark', *The Works of Frederick Chopin: Warsaw 1960*, 572–7

A. Szweykowska: 'Przeobrażenia w kapeli królewskiej na przełomie XVI i XVII wieku' [Changes in the royal chapel in the late 16th and 17th centuries], *Muzyka*, xiii/2 (1968), 3–21 [with Eng. summary]

A. Szweykowska: 'Notatki dotyczące kapeli królewskiej w XVII wieku' [Notes about the royal chapel in the 17th century], *Muzyka*, xvi/3 (1971), 91–8 [with Eng. summary]

MIROSŁAW PERZ

Patavinus, Antonius Stringarius. *See* STRINGARI, ANTONIO.

Patbrué [Patbru], **Cornelis Thymanszoon.** *See* PADBRUÉ, CORNELIS THYMANSZOON.

Patchable, Charles Theodore. *See* PACHELBEL family, (3).

Pate, John (*d* Hampstead [now in London], bur. 14 Jan 1704). English tenor-countertenor. Evelyn described him as 'reputed the most excellent singer, ever England had' (30 May 1698). Pate's first recorded appearance was in Purcell's *The Fairy Queen* (1692), in which he sang Mopsa 'in woman's habit' in the duet 'Now the maids and the men'. Purcell's autograph score *GB-Ob* Mus. Sch.C.26 names him as the singer of ''Tis Nature's voice' in his 1692 St Cecilia ode, although the *Gentleman's Journal* stated that it was sung 'with incredible Graces by Mr. Purcell himself'. In 1695 Pate was involved in a Jacobite riot and subsequently travelled to Italy. He returned in 1698 with Italian songs in his repertory and had two successful stage and concert seasons. In September 1700 he was reported to be imprisoned in the Bastille and condemned to death on the wheel for 'killing a man'. However, he sang in Richard Steele's *The Funeral* in December 1701 and performed songs in Italian and English at Drury Lane in February 1703.

BIBLIOGRAPHY

BDA; *LS*

J. Noble: 'Purcell and the Chapel Royal', *Henry Purcell 1659–1695: Essays on his Music*, ed. I. Holst (London, 1959), 52–66

O. Baldwin and T. Wilson: 'Alfred Deller, John Freeman and Mr. Pate', *ML*, l (1969), 103–10

O. Baldwin and T. Wilson: 'Purcell's Stage Singers', *Performing the Music of Henry Purcell*, ed. M. Burden (Oxford, 1996), 105–29

OLIVE BALDWIN, THELMA WILSON

Patent notes. Notes used in shape-note notation. *See* SHAPE-NOTE HYMNODY.

Patent voice flute. Alto flute in G, with an extra hole covered by a vibrating membrane. It was also known as the *flauto di voce*. *See* MIRLITON.

Pater a Monte Carmelo. *See* SPIRIDION.

Pater noster [Lord's Prayer]. The prayer that Christ taught his disciples (*Matthew* vi.9–13; *Luke* xi.2–4). Variants of the biblical texts reflect early Aramaic-Syriac and Greek oral traditions as well as liturgical and semi-liturgical accretions. The liturgical Latin text was established within the Roman rite by the early 7th century; Pope Gregory I moved it from its place after the Fraction in the Mass to its present position after the Eucharistic Prayer, as in the Eastern rites. In Gregory's reform it was recited only by the celebrant. The exordium introducing the prayer and a simple form of the concluding embolism (beginning 'Libera nos quesumus domine ab omnibus malis') may also date from Gregory's time; but similar accretions are found in Eastern and in other Latin rites (see Boe, 1998). The prayer also originally concluded each service of the

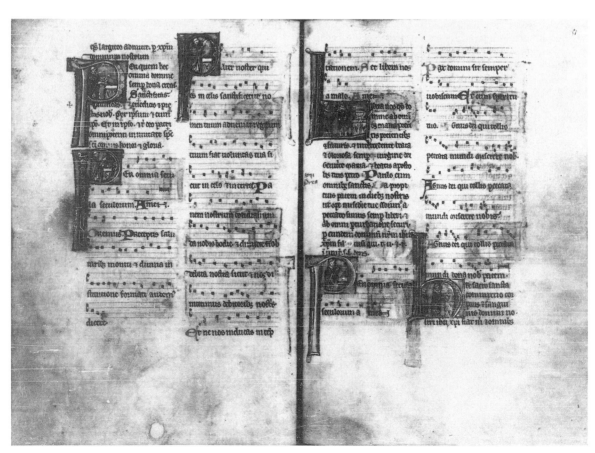

1. Pater noster, F-Pa 135, ff.150v–151

Ex.1 South Italian *Pater noster* melodies with exordia and embolisms

a) Everyday melody (*I-Rvat* 7231, f.57)

Per om-ni-a se-cu-la se-cu-lo-rum. A-men. O-re-mus.[P]re-cep-tis sa-lu-ta-ri-bus mo-ni-ti. et di-ui-na in-sti-tu-ti-o-ne for-ma-ti au-de-mus di-ce-re.

b) Sunday-festal melody (*I-BV* 40, f.27v–28)

Perom-ni-a se-cu-la se-cu-lo-rum. A-men. O-re-mus. Pre-cep-tis sa-lu-ta-ri-bus mo-ni-ti. et di-ui-na in-sti-tu-ti-o-ne for-ma-ti au-de-mus di-ce-re.

Pa-ter nos-ter qui es in ce-lis. Sanc-ti-fi-ce-tur no-men tu-um. Ad-ue-ni-at reg-num tu-um. Fi-at-uo-lun-tas tu-a. Sic-ut in ce-lo et in ter-ra.

Pa-ter nos-ter qui es in ce-lis. Sanc-ti-fi-ce-tur no-men tu-um. Ad-ue-ni-at reg-num tu-um. fi-at uo lun-tas tu-a. Sic-ut in ce-lo et in ter-ra.

Pa-nem nos-trum co-ti-di-a-num da no-bis ho-di-e. Et di-mit-te no-bis de-bi-ta nos-tra. Sic-ud et nos di-mit-ti-mus de-bi-to-ri-bus nos-tris.

Pa-nem nos-trum co-ti-di-a-num, da no-bis ho-di-e. et di-mit-te no-bis de-ui-ta nos-tra. sic-ut et nos di-mit-ti-mus de-bi-to-ri-bus nos-tris.

et ne nos in-du-cas in temp-ta-ti-o-nem. Sed li-be-ra nos a ma-lo. Li-be-ra nos que-su-mus do-mi-ne ab om-ni-bus ma-lis. Pre-te-ri-tis.

[sic]

et ne nos in-du-cas in temp-ta-ti-o-nem. Sed li-be-ra nos a ma-lo. Li-be-ra nos que-su-mus do-mi-ne ab om-ni-bus ma-lis pre-te-ri-tis.

Pre-sen-ti-bus et fu-tu-ris. Et in-ter-ce-den-te pro no-bis be-a-ta et glo-ri-o-sa sem-per-que uir-gi-nem de-i ge-ni-tri-ce ma-ri-a...

pre-sen-ti-bus et fu-tu-ris. et in-ter-ce-den-te pro no-bis be-a-ta et glo-ri-o-sa sem-per-que uir-gi-ne de-i ge-ni-tri-ce ma-ri-a...

Cum om-ni-bus sanc-tis... Da pro-pi-ti-us pa-cem in di-e-bus nos-tris...

cum om-ni-bus sanc-tis... Da pro-pi-ti-us pa-cem in di-e-bus nos-tris...

= anticipatory liquesence (uncommon)

or = lesser liquesence

or = greater liquesence

Divine Office, where it was prayed silently, the officiant raising his voice only at the phrase 'Et ne nos inducas in temptationem' so that all might answer 'Sed libera nos a malo'; but according to the Rule of St Benedict the prayer was to be sung aloud at the end of Lauds and Vespers by the senior monk present.

Before about 1050 the *Pater noster* was generally transmitted orally, the celebrant knowing only the local version of the melody, which would have been in so-called 'anaphoral chant' (for a description of anaphoral chant, see K. Levy, 'The Byzantine Sanctus and its Modal Tradition in East and West', *AnnM*, vi, 1958–63, pp.7–67). The embolisms of the melodies in ex.1 are different contemporary versions of an anaphoral chant formula using the pitches *ut*, *re* and *mi*. However, as early as the late 10th century, notation for the *Pater noster* began to be inserted in sacramentaries and missals in order to control or replace local versions, or simply to act as an aide-mémoire for the celebrant. Three separate melodic traditions dating from the late 10th century and

Ex.2 Northern *Pater noster* melodies with exordia

the 11th are identifiable: two were sung mainly in southern Italy and the third principally north of the Alps.

The first melodic formulation is found as the sole chant in votive missals for parish and chantry priests and in miscellaneous collections, especially those containing Masses for the Dead. The melody appears first in a votive missal from the Monte Cassino region (*I-MC 426, c*1000), and in later Cassinese manuscripts is given the rubric 'In cotidianis diebus' ('for daily use'). It appears in a number

of south Italian manuscripts from the 12th and 13th centuries; ex.1 shows the version from *I-Rvat* 7231 (13th century), which, as in other later manuscripts, has internal phrases that are notated one step higher than in the earlier manuscripts (*I-MC* 426, f.35*v*; *MC* 339, f.65*v*); these phrases are indicated by brackets above the staff. The earliest source for the second melody is a gradual (*I-BV* 40) probably copied at the abbey of S Sofia in Benevento in the first half of the 11th century; the melody is transcribed in ex.1 for comparison with the melody for daily use. This formulation was used for Sundays and feast days at Monte Cassino (*I-MC 339*: rubric 'In dominicis seu festis diebus'); it was also used in the churches of Salerno and adjoining areas, in regional monasteries and at the Lombard court.

The third melody appears in 11th-century manuscripts from all over northern Europe, but only occasionally in southern Italy, where it was given the rubric 'Francisca' ('Frankish' it may have been entered in Cassinese altarbooks as an alternative chant for use by northern clergy; for more detailed discussion see Boe, 1998). Ex.2 shows the versions of the melody from the abbey of Figeac in Aquitaine (*F-Pn* 2293; 11th century, melody in heighted Aquitanian neumes) and St Denis (*Pn* 9436, mid-11th century, melody in northern French neumes, slightly heighted), in contrast to a decorated southern Italian version (*I-Rc* 614; 12th century, Beneventan script and notation) and the 13th-century Franciscan festal version (*F-Pn* 10503; second half of 13th century, notated with F-clef on five-line staff), which is almost identical to the festal tone of the Vatican edition. This formulation also resembles the Sarum and Dominican chants (see below).

All three formulations arrange the pitches *ut re mi fa* in a repeated series of inflections generally moving by step. The first formulation (ex.1a) originally employed the initial pitches *ut re mi*, a medial cadence *út–re(re) re*, and a final cadence *ré–mi re*. It may derive from a Milanese chant resembling a psalm tone (see Cabrol, 1929; and Boe, 1981). In the second and third formulations (ex.1b and ex.2), each repeated member of the series begins with one or two similar forephrases and ends with a distinct afterphrase – in similar manner to the recitation tones for prefaces and readings. While the two south Italian formulations (though independent in origin) both use the initial *ut re mi mi*, the northern melody instead used the inverted form *mí re–ut re mi* for 'Páter noster' and 'Pánem nostrum'. But in the north after about 1200, this form came to be replaced (possibly owing to Cistercian reforms: see Choisselet and Vernet) by the rising inflection *ut re mi mi* found in the Dominican standard melody of 1255–6 and notably in the Franciscan festal and ferial chants, which were soon adopted by the Roman curia and eventually in the Vatican edition of 1907, as well as in Sarum books after about 1300. (See fig.1, from *F-Pa* 135, an early Sarum missal where the original inverted initial at these words was erased and replaced by the rising inflection.) Nevertheless, the northern melody remains distinct from the southern Italian ones in several respects: for example, the ecphonesis 'Per omnia secula seculorum' begins on *la* below *ut* in the northern melody but not in the southern formulations (see Boe, 1998). Conservative institutions like Cluny and some cathedrals long retained the old inverted form of the initial figure. Local variants of all melodies exist, especially where *mi*, when accented or climactic, was raised to *fa*: for example, the initials *ut re FÁ mi* or *FÁ re–ut re mi*.

In the 13th century a new penitential *Pater noster* chant appeared in response to the purgatorial aspects emphasized in the ever more numerous votive Masses for the Dead. This austere, unornamented ferial chant, supplied in Franciscan missals, was developed from the Franciscan festal melody (and is therefore related to the northern

chant); it should not be confused with the nearly syllabic reformed chant that was sung by the Cistercians at all masses.

In Masses of the Gallican rite, *Pater noster* seems to have immediately preceded the Communion and to have been recited by all; if sung, no source survives. The Mozarabic *Pater noster* formula found in a 1755 edition of Cardinal Ximenes's *Missale mixtum* of 1500 is well known: the 'Amen' interjections are authentically Mozarabic, but the oral tradition for the melody must have been slender at best. At Rome, the tradition for *Pater noster* was purely oral before northern pontificals arrived (cf *I-Rc* 614 in ex.2) and before Franciscan chants and notation were adopted in the 13th century. Thus the origins of the northern melody remain unclear: it may have gone north from Rome in the 8th century, or it may have been reshaped from anaphoral chant by Frankish celebrants.

Rare instances of tropes for *Pater noster* are found in some manuscripts of the 12th and 13th centuries, generally in unusual liturgical contexts. Later examples were non-liturgical. (See Stäblein, 1977.) The festal melody was used as a cantus firmus by Renaissance composers (there are settings by Willaert, Gombert, Lassus and Palestrina, among others); many settings of the text do not use the chant melody at all.

In the Anglican rite the Lord's Prayer, complete with exordium, was first set to English for the Communion service of 1549 by John Marbeck in his short-lived *Booke of Common Praier Noted* (1550). Marbeck freely adapted the northern *Pater noster* chant, using one note per syllable but notes of different lengths. At Mattins and Evensong, Marbeck treated the last two phrases of the Lord's Prayer as versicle and response, just as at the Latin lesser Hours, the rest of the text being either monotoned or possibly spoken. A few composers set the Lord's Prayer chorally, but most Tudor and Jacobean choral settings for the cathedral Office do not include it. The choral settings by Robert Stone and John Farmer (i) are now sometimes sung with such responses. During the late 19th and early 20th centuries, the Sarum and 1907 Vatican chants for *Pater noster* were more closely adapted to the English text for the Anglican Eucharist by G.W. Palmer and C.W. Douglas, among others. Following the Second Vatican Council, new chants have been composed and older chants (such as that of the Mozarabic *Pater noster*) have been fitted to the revised texts of the Anglican rite and the Roman rite in English.

BIBLIOGRAPHY

Grove6 (R. Steiner); *MGG1* (B. Stäblein); *MGG2* (K. Schlager)
P. Wagner: *Einführung in die gregorianischen Melodien*, iii: *Gregorianische Formenlehre: eine choralische Stilkunde* (Leipzig, 1921/R)
F. Cabrol: 'Le chant du Pater à la messe', *Revue grégorienne*, xiii (1928), 161–8; xiv (1929), 1–17
H. Leclercq: 'Messe', §25; 'Oraison dominicale', *Dictionnaire d'archéologie chrétienne et de liturgie*, ed. F. Cabrol and H. Marrou, xi (Paris, 1933); xii (Paris, 1936)
J. Claire: 'L'évolution modale dans les récitatifs liturgiques', *Revue grégorienne*, xli (1963), 127–51
B. Stäblein: 'Pater-Noster-Tropen', *Sacerdos et cantus gregoriani magister: Festschrift Ferdinand Haberl*, ed. F.A. Stein (Regensburg, 1977), 247–78
J. Boe: 'The Neumes and Pater Noster Chant of Montecassino Codex 426', *Monastica: scritti raccolti in memoria del XV centenario della nascita di S. Benedetto*, i, Miscellanea cassinese, xliv (Monte Cassino, 1981), 219–35

D. Choisselet and P.Vernet, eds.: *Les 'Ecclesiastica officia' cisterciens du XIIe siècle: texte latin selon les manuscrits édités de Trente 1711, Ljubljana 31 et Dijon 114* (Oelenberg, 1989)

J. Boe: 'The Frankish Pater Noster Chant: Tradition and Anaphoral Context', *Chant and its Peripheries: Essays in Honour of Terence Bailey*, ed. B. Gillingham and P. Merkeley (Ottawa, 1998), 179–203

J. Boe, ed.: *Ordinary Chants and Tropes for the Mass from Southern Italy, A.D. 1000–1250*, iv: *Pater Noster Chants and Agnus Dei, with Ite Missa Est* (Madison, WI, forthcoming)

JOHN BOE

Paterson, Robert Roy (*b* Edinburgh, 16 July 1830; *d* Edinburgh, 3 Dec 1903). Scottish musician and music publisher. He was the son of Robert Paterson, who founded the music dealers and publishersPATERSON & SONS. He received a thorough musical education both in Edinburgh, where he studied the violin and flute, and in 1847 at the Leipzig Conservatory, where he studied the piano with Moscheles and composition with Otto Richter. He later gained experience of the music trade in London at the piano makers Collard & Collard and Broadwood before entering the family firm. In 1859, at the death of his father, he undertook the direction of the firm, which expanded to become one of the most important of its kind in Scotland, with branches in numerous Scottish cities. At the same time he played an active part in Edinburgh's musical life, particularly in the city's Musical Association, then the most active in Scotland. In 1887 he took over the management of the Choral Union Orchestra concerts when they ran into financial difficulties; they then continued as Paterson's Concerts until 1931, except for a short interruption during World War I, and mostly engaged the Scottish Orchestra from its inception in 1893. Paterson composed songs and piano music which he published under the pseudonym of Alfred Stella. (Obituary, *MT*, xlv (1904), 31 only)

PETER WARD JONES

Paterson & Sons. Scottish music dealers, publishers and instrument makers. The firm was started in Edinburgh about 1819 by Robert Paterson (*d* 1859) and others as Robert Paterson, Mortimer & Co. In 1826 Peter Walker Roy (*d* Edinburgh, 7 Dec 1851) joined the firm, which became Paterson & Roy and later opened a London branch. After Roy's death the business traded as Paterson & Sons. Paterson was succeeded at his death by his son Robert Roy Paterson, under whose direction the firm expanded to become one of the most important of its kind in Scotland, with branches in Glasgow (1857, directed by Paterson's elder brother John Walker Paterson), Perth (1864), Ayr (1868), Dundee (1882), Dumfries (1886), Paisley (1887), Kilmarnock (1892), and later Aberdeen and Oban. Its 19th-century publications included Scottish music of all kinds, with many reprints of standard editions of Scottish songs. During the 20th century its publishing activities were gradually taken over by the London branch, which, as Paterson's Publications Ltd, concentrated largely on choral and piano music for school and amateur use. The Scottish branch of the business ceased in 1964; the London branch was bought by Novello & Co. in 1989.

BIBLIOGRAPHY

Humphries-SmithMP

A. Pearson: 'Prominent Music Publishers, XIV: Paterson & Sons', *MO*, xvii (1893–4), 585 only

J.A. Parkinson: *Victorian Music Publishers: an Annotated List* (Warren, MI, 1990)

PETER WARD JONES

Patey [née Whytock], **Janet** (**Monach**) (*b* London, 1 May 1842; *d* Sheffield, 28 Feb 1894). Scottish contralto. She studied under John Wass and made her début in Birmingham in 1860 (as Ellen Andrews); thereafter she studied under Mrs Sims Reeves and Ciro Pinsuti. In 1866 she married the baritone John (George) Patey (*b* Stonehouse, Devon, 1835; *d* Falmouth, 4 Dec 1901), who had studied opera singing in Paris and Milan. He had made his London début in 1858 and was well known as a singer of light roles at Covent Garden and Italian opera at the Lyceum Theatre. Mrs Patey, after the retirement of Sainton-Dolby in 1870, came to be regarded as the leading British contralto, being referred to as the 'English Alboni'. She and her husband toured widely abroad, in the USA, Australia and elsewhere. John Patey retired from singing in 1888 and joined the music publishing firm of Willis in London. (*DNB* (R.H. Legge))

JEAN MARY ALLAN

Pathet. An Indonesian term often translated as 'mode'. *See* INDONESIA, §III, 4; MODE, §V, 4(ii); SOUTH-EAST ASIA, §3(iii).

Pathie [Patie, Patye], **Rogier** [Roger] (*b* ?Cambrai, *c*1510; *d* ?Valladolid, after 1564). Franco-Flemish composer and organist. In May 1530 his father, Jean Pathie, a singer at the court of François I, was paid 35 livres to cover food and medical expenses for his son Rogier, 'petit organiste' to the king. Becker's biography of C. Marot claimed that 'Roger' fled from Paris in 1534. By 1536 Rogier Pathie had succeeded Sigismund Yver as organist to the Netherlandish chapel of Queen Mary of Hungary, a post he retained until her death. He is also mentioned in the accounts of her court between 1536 and 1565 as her *valet de chambre* and as her almoner or treasurer. (The inventory of her instruments and the catalogue of her library, which he compiled, are printed in *Vander StraetenMPB*, vii, 439–94.) He was a prebendary at St Baaf Cathedral, Ghent, from 1540 to 1542. Although Mary's court was based at Brussels or Lille, it travelled frequently; Pathie was called upon to enlist singers for Charles V from Tournai in 1541 and from Arras, Brussels, Ghent and Lille in 1542. He probably ended his days in Spain.

Only two motets and four chansons by Pathie have survived. The motet *O altitudo*, published in Paris in 1535, was reprinted in Ferrara with an ascription to Dominique Phinot. The second motet, a double canon by inversion, was published posthumously in Nuremberg. The chanson *D'amour me plains* was a resounding success, appearing in more than 26 editions between 1539 and 1644, and in at least 21 instrumental arrangements printed between 1545 and 1583. Its fame no doubt caused the misattribution to 'Rogier' of other popular pieces included in Phalèse's seventh book of chansons, notably *Doulce memoire* by Sandrin, *Ce moys de May* by Godard and *Si pur ti guardo* by Ferrabosco or Baldassare Donato, an error followed in many of the later instrumental transcriptions.

WORKS
all for four voices

O altitudo divitiarum sapientiae et scientiae Dei, 1535[5] ('Roger'; attrib. Phinot, 1538[5]), ed. A.T. Merritt, *Treize livres de motets parus chez Pierre Attaingnant*, xiii (Monaco, 1963)

Sicut lilium inter spinas, 1567[1] ('Rogier')

Cesse mon oeil de plus la regarder, 1534[14]; intabulation, lute, 1v or solo lute, 1553[33], ed. in PSFM, iv–v (1934/R)

D'amour me plains et non de vous m'amye, 1539[15-16] ('Rogier'), ed. in SCC, xxi (1991); lute intabulation, 1556[31]

En vous voyant j'ai liberté perdue, 1538[14] ('Rogier'), ed. in SCC, xxi (1991); lute intabulation, 1556[31]

Le doulx baiser que j'ai au départir, 1534[14] ('Rogier')

BIBLIOGRAPHY

BrownI; Vander StraetenMPB, vii

L. Cimber and F. Danjou: Archives curieuses de l'histoire de France depuis Louis XI jusqu'a Louis XVIII, 1st ser., iii (Paris, 1835), 82

P.A. Becker: Clement Marot: sein Leben (Munich, 1926)

H. Anglès: La música en la corte de Carlos V, i (Barcelona, 1944, 2/1965/R)

FRANK DOBBINS

Patinkin, Mandy [Mandel] (b Chicago, 30 Nov 1952). American actor and singer. He is the most versatile of performers, known for his work on Broadway, film and television. For Broadway he created the roles of Che Guevara in Lloyd Webber's Evita (1979), George Seurat in Sondheim's Sunday in the Park with George (1986), and Archibald Craven in Simon's The Secret Garden (1991), all of which received critical praise. He won a Tony award for his performance in Evita. He has released a number of solo albums, including Mandy Patinkin (1989), Dress Casual (1990), Oscar and Steve (1995) and the entirely Yiddish Mamaloshen (1998). In addition to his singing activities, Patinkin has appeared in a number of dramatic roles on both film and television. Film credits include Ragtime (1981), Yentl (1983), The Princess Bride (1987), and Dick Tracy (1990), although the last of these is the only one in which Patinkin utilized his musical talents. In the mid-1990s, Patinkin starred in the television series 'Chicago Hope', for which he won an Emmy Award in 1995; his character in this provided the opportunity for Patinkin to display his vocal abilities numerous times for television audiences. Perhaps the best way to describe his very distinctive sound is as a 'falsetto tenor'. His ability to create musical line and his exceedingly innate sense of musicianship have brought emotional life to every song he has sung and to every character he has portrayed.

WILLIAM A. EVERETT, LEE SNOOK

Patiño, Carlos (b S María del Campo Rus, Cuenca, bap. 9 Oct 1600; d Madrid, 5 Sept 1675). Spanish composer. He was a choirboy at Seville Cathedral from 22 June 1612, where he studied with Francisco Company, Juan de Vaca, and Alonso Lobo. He also had important contact with Francisco de Santiago. From 25 January 1622 until early 1625 he was married to Laura María de Vargas Texeda Lozano. After her death following childbirth he seems to have studied for the priesthood, a requirement for his subsequent positions.

Meanwhile, on 19 January 1623 he became maestro de canto de órgano at Seville Cathedral. In 1628 he competed unsuccessfully for the position of maestro de capilla at Salamanca Cathedral, but on 8 March of that year he was appointed maestro de capilla of the Monasterio de la Encarnación, Madrid, where he succeeded Gabriel Díaz Bessón. In that year he was entrusted with the final preparation for publication of López de Velasco's Libro de misas, motetes, salmos, Magnificas, y otras cosas tocantes al culto divino (Madrid, 1628). On 1 January 1634 Patiño succeeded Mateo Romero as maestro de capilla in the royal chapel; simultaneously he served as vice-maestro and rector of the college of choirboys until 7 February 1657. In 1660 he asked for retirement, pleading ill health; his request was denied, but he was provided with an assistant and substitute. In addition to his musical activities, he was a painter.

Patiño was one of the finest musicians in Spain in the 17th century and along with Romero established the Baroque style there. He is specially important for replacing the Italian madrigal style by a specifically Spanish one. A few of his sacred works are for a single chorus but most are for two or three choruses. Nearly all include continuo, often designated for organ, harp, clavichord, or bajoncillo (small dulcian); vocal parts are occasionally doubled by instruments. The polychoral works include imitative sections alongside more chordal ones featuring word-generated motives and the dramatic juxtaposition of quick and slow segments. In both melody and harmony Patiño can be quite bold, his style including leaps of a diminished 4th, false relations (sometimes simultaneous) and unprepared dissonances alongside mild chromaticism. While Patiño was principally a composer of Latin sacred music, he also composed sacred music in Spanish as well as theatre music (cuatros de empezar) to be sung as preludes to dramatic productions. The tonos humanos are characterized by lively rhythms with frequent hemiola; several of them were composed for court occasions involving the Spanish royal family. Patiño's works enjoyed wide circulation in the Spanish colonies of Latin America, as shown by the many well-used and incomplete manuscripts found there. Many sacred works were lost in the great Lisbon earthquake of 1755.

WORKS

Editions: Carlos Partiño: Obras musicales recopilades, ed. L. Siemens Hernández (Cuenca, 1986–) [SH]

Las obras humanas de Carlos Patiño, ed. D. Becker (Cuenca, 1987) [B]

Latin sacred, 4–12 vv, some with obbl insts, bc: 13 masses, 4–12vv, E-MO, V, 1 ed. in MME, xli (1982); 49 motets and other sacred Latin works; 6 litanies; 11 cantos evangelicos; 21 psalms: Mn, Zac, Mba, Bc

Spanish sacred, mostly for 4vv, some for 3–12vv: Missa de la bakella 'Escoutes', 12vv, ed. in MME, xli (1982); 2 eucharist hymns; 14 villancicos for the Holy Sacrament; 18 Christmas villancicos; 12 tonos humanos: Mn, Zac, Mba, Bc; 2 tonos humanos ed. in MME, xxxii (1970)

Theatre music: Cuatros de empezar

BIBLIOGRAPHY

StevensonRB

R. Stevenson: 'Sixteenth and Seventeenth Century Resources in Mexico, I', FAM, i (1954), 69–78

N. Álvarez Solar-Quintes: 'Panorama musical desde Felipe III a Carlos II', AnM, xii (1957), 167–200

J. Subirá: 'Necrologías musicales madrileñas (años 1611–1808)', AnM, xiii (1958), 201–23

J. Subirá: 'El "cuatro" escénico español', Miscelánea en homenaje a Monseñor Higinio Anglés (Barcelona, 1958–61), 895–921

R. Stevenson: 'The Bogotá Music Archive', JAMS, xv (1962), 292–315

J. López-Calo: 'Corresponsales de Miguel de Irízar', AnM, xviii (1963), 197–238

L. Siemens Hernandez: 'Dos cartas del Maestro Carlos Patiño al Duque de Braganza (1634 y 1638)', RdMc, ix (1986), 253–60

D. Becker: 'La Plática sobre la música en toscano y los principios del teatro musical barroco en España', RdMc, x (1987), 501–15

H. Daschner: 'Carlos Patiño (1600–75): ein bedeutender spanischer Komponist tritt aus der Anonymität heraus', Musica, xlii (1988), 155–64

M. Querol Gavaldá: 'Carlos Patiño, un compositor barroco', Saber leer: Revista crítica de libros, no.18 (1988), 4–5

BARTON HUDSON

Patiño Carpio, Adrián (b La Paz, 19 Feb 1895; d La Paz, 4 April 1951). Bolivian composer, woodwind player and band director. He studied at the La Paz Conservatory with Rosendo Torrico. He played in several orchestras and ensembles and taught woodwind instruments in schools and at the La Paz Conservatory. From 1926 he directed the 'Loa' and 'Perez' regimental bands, giving concerts in La Paz and other cities in Bolivia. During the Chaco War (1932–5) he was appointed general band director of the Bolivian army. After his retirement he maintained a youth chorus and orchestra, with whom he performed new works.

He was awarded several honours, including the French Palmes Académiques. He composed tone poems, suites and preludes for orchestra such as *Alborada andina*, *En los Andes bolivianos*, *La cancion del Kilko*, *La tristeza del Arachi* and *La huerta* (incidental music for a drama by Angel Salas), almost 100 military and funeral marches, *boleros de caballería*, and hymns, three masses, Christmas carols, religious hymns and several traditional dances such as *cuecas*, *hauyños* and *bailecitos*.

CARLOS SEOANE

Paton, Mary Anne. *See* WOOD, MARY ANNE.

Patouilles. An early XYLOPHONE, illustrated and described by Mersenne.

Patricio, Andrea [Patricij, Andrija] (*b* Cres; *fl* 1550). Croatian composer. He came from the same family as the philosopher and musician Francesco Patrizi (1529–97). He is known only by four pieces in Antonio Barges's *Il primo libro de villotte* (Venice, 1550[18]; all ed. M. Asić, *Zvuk*, lxxxi, 1968, and V.L. Županović, Spomenici hrvatske glazbene prošlosti, i, Zagreb, 1970). *Solea lontan'in sonno* is predominantly homophonic, *In quel ben nat'aventuroso giorno* and *Madonna, quel suav'honesto sguardo* show a greater concern for word-painting, and *Son quest'i bei crin d'oro* is both melodically and harmonically a richly expressive piece.

BIBLIOGRAPHY

D. Plamenac: 'O hrvatskoj muzici u vrijeme renesanse' [Croatian music up to the Renaissance], *Hrvatskg revija*, ix (1936), 145–50

D. Plamenac: 'Music of the 16th and 17th Centuries in Dalmatia', *PAMS 1939*, 21–51, esp. 35

L. Županović: 'La musique croate du XVIe siècle', *Musica antiqua II: Bydgoszcz 1969*, 79–126

L. Županović: Introduction to *Hrvatski skladatelji*, Spomenici hrvatske glazbene prošlosti, i (Zagreb, 1970)

L. Županović: *Stoljeća hrvatske glazbe* (Zagreb, 1980), 32–3, 38–41; Eng. trans. as *Centuries of Croatian Music*, i (Zagreb, 1984), 34–5, 40–43

LOVRO ŽUPANOVIĆ

Patrick, Nathaniel (bap. Worcester, 9 March 1569; *d* Worcester, bur. 23 March 1595). English cathedral musician and composer. He was the son of William Patrick, weaver. Nathanial was Master of the Choristers at Worcester Cathedral from Michaelmas 1590 until his death. On 23 September 1593 he married Alice Hassard, who became Thomas Tomkins's second wife in 1597. Patrick's will was proved on 25 May 1595, and is printed in Atkins, together with an inventory of his belongings. On 22 October 1597 a licence was granted by the Stationers' Company to Thomas East to print the 'Songes of sundrye natures, whereof somme are Divine, some are madrigalles, and the rest psalmes and hymnes in Latin composed for 5 and 6 voyces and One for 8 voyces by Nathanaell Patrick sometyme master of the Children of the Cathedrall Churche of Worcester and Organist of the same'. No copy of this publication has survived, if indeed it was ever printed.

Patrick's only extant compositions are the consort songs *Clime not to high*, *Prepare to die* and *Send forth thy sighs* (GB-Lbl; all ed. in MB, xxii, 1967), and a Short or Whole Service (in many MSS; ed. W. Shaw, London, 1963). Three anthems *I will lift up mine eyes*, *Look down, O Lord* and *O clap your hands* (GB-Ckc 416; Ob) may possibly be by Richard Patrick, a lay clerk at Westminster Abbey from *c*1616 to 1626.

BIBLIOGRAPHY

I. Atkins: *The Early Occupants of the Office of Organist and Master of the Choristers of the Cathedral Church of Christ and the Blessed Virgin Mary, Worcester* (Worcester, 1918)

R.T. Daniel and P. le Huray: *The Sources of English Church Music, 1549–1660*, EECM, suppl.i (1972)

W. Shaw: *The Succession of Organists of the Chapel Royal and the Cathedrals of England and Wales from c.1538* (Oxford, 1991)

E.H. FELLOWES/PETER LE HURAY

Patta, Serafino (*b* Milan; *fl* 1606–19). Italian composer and organist. He was a monk of the Benedictine order based at the monastery of Monte Cassino, near Naples. His career as organist took him to Cesena, where he was at the Madonna del Monte in 1606, to Reggio nell'Emilia, where he is known to have served at SS Pietro e Prospero between 1609 and 1611, and to Pavia, where he was at S Salvatore in 1613 and 1614. By 1619 he had returned to his former post at Cesena.

Patta's output, which is all of sacred music, includes settings of masses and vesper psalms in a conventional five- or six-part texture and also early examples of concertato motets for a small number of voices. Indeed his 1614 collection is one of the earliest volumes of sacred monody: it consists of 13 Latin settings alternating with 12 Italian ones – spiritual madrigals marked 'pietosi affetti' – all the texts being by the dedicatee, Angelo Grillo. The music is of high quality: the sensitive declamation is responsive to the words, and vocal line and bass are well integrated. That such music was intended primarily for domestic devotional use is suggested by the inclusion on the title-page of the harpsichord and chitarrone as suitable continuo instruments.

In his second motet book (1613) Patta shows craftsmanship in the use of refrain and dialogue forms. The *Veni, Sancte Spiritus* has a thrice-repeated triple-time refrain alternating with solo and duet sections. *Quem vidistis pastores* is suitably set as a dialogue between angels and shepherds (SA and TTB respectively); the shepherds' response is taken up by the tutti at the end. *Forte* and *piano* markings are found in the doxology of the *Magnificat* and in a two-part canzona also found in this publication. (J. Roche: *North Italian Church Music in the Age of Monteverdi*, Oxford, 1984)

WORKS
all published in Venice

Missa psalmi motecta ac Litaniae in honorem deiparae Virginis, 5vv, bc (org) (1606)

Sacra cantica concinenda, 1–3vv, cum Litaniis BMV, 5vv (1609; enlarged 2/1611[4] with bc (org))

[14] Sacrorum canticorum, 1–5vv, bc, insts ad lib, liber II (1613)

[13] Motetti et [12] madrigali cavati da le poesie sacre de … A. Grillo, 1v, bc (org/hpd/chit/other inst) (1614)

Psalmi integri cum 2 canticis BMV ad Vesperas totius anni, 5vv, bc (org) (1619)

1 motet in 1620[2]

JEROME ROCHE

Patterson, Annie (Wilson) (*b* Lurgan, 27 Oct 1868; *d* Cork, 16 Jan 1934). Irish folksong collector, composer, writer on music, organist and lecturer. She studied at the Royal

Irish Academy of Music and the Royal University of Ireland (BA, MusB 1887; MusD 1889). From 1887 to 1897 she worked in Dublin as an organist, conductor and music examiner. In 1897 she organized the first Feis Ceoil festival of Irish music and in the same year acted as music adviser for the first Oireachtas, the national Irish-language festival. After settling in Cork in 1909, Patterson became organist at St Anne's, Shandon, and held a lectureship in Irish music at University College, Cork (1924–34). She continued as a music examiner, contributed to various periodicals and broadcast frequently on the national radio station. Her deep interest in Irish traditional music stimulated the collection, arrangement and publication of folksongs and she composed art music inspired by Irish mythology. Her works, few of which were published, include three operas, *The Ardrigh's Daughter*, *Oisín* and *The Bard of Éire*, a choral work *The Bells of Shandon*, several cantatas including *Finola* (1888), Six Original Gaelic Songs (1896), symphonic poems, choral marching songs and many arrangements of Irish airs. She wrote a number of music appreciation books, including a volume on the oratorio, a monograph on Schumann, and a study of the native music of Ireland (London, 1926).

WILLIAM H. GRATTAN FLOOD/PATRICK F. DEVINE

Patterson, Paul (Leslie) (*b* Chesterfield, 15 June 1947). English composer. After studying composition with Stoker at the RAM (1964–8), he received private tuition from Bennett (1968–70) and Lutyens (1967–70). He has taught at the RAM as Manson Fellow and lecturer (1969–86) and head of composition and contemporary music (1985–97). He came to attention with a Stravinskian Trumpet Concerto (1969); however, friendships with Polish composers, in particular Penderecki, Lutosławski and Stachowski, led to a radical change in direction apparent in *Kyrie* (1972) and *Time Piece* (1973), in which he adopted the graphic notation and textural techniques of the Polish school. These formative influences dominate Patterson's music of the 1970s, exemplified by the Requiem (1975), Clarinet Concerto (1976), *Cracowian Counterpoints* (1977, rev. 1978) and the large-scale choral work *Voices of Sleep* (1979). During the 1980s he increasingly moved towards a language that may be summarized as a rapprochement between the textural configurations of his earlier works and the 20th-century English tradition of composers like Britten. This process is traceable through three major choral works, *Mass of the Sea* (1983), *Stabat mater* (1985–6) and *Te Deum* (1987–8). Such evident flair for handling choral forces has continued with *The End* (1989) and *Magnificat* (1994), while other works of the early 1990s, for example the Violin Concerto (1992), show neo-classical traits. Communication has been a major preoccupation for Patterson, which led him to undertake several residencies, including at the King's School, Canterbury (1981–3). Several works have been composed for young performers or listeners: a youth orchestra work, *Sonors* (1973), *The Canterbury Psalms* (1981) and *Little Red Riding Hood* (1992) based on Roald Dahl's eponymous poem.

WORKS
(selective list)

Orch: Tpt Conc., op.3, 1969; Partita, op.8, 1970; Hn Conc., op.11, 1971; Piccola sinfonia, op.10, 1971; Sonors, op.17, 1973; Chromascope, op.24, brass band, 1974; Strange Meeting, op.29, 1975; The Circular Ruins, op.31, 1975; Wildfire, op.33, 1976; Cl Conc., op.34, 1976; Conc. for Orch., op.45, 1981; Sinfonia, str, op.46, 1982; Europhony, op.55, 1985; White Shadows on the

Dark Horizon, op.67, 1989; The Mighty Voice, op.71, wind band, 1991; Vn Conc., op.72, 1992; Roald Dahl's Little Red Riding Hood, op.73, 1992; Festivo, op.74, 1993; Songs of the West, ov., op.78, 1995

Chorus: Kyrie, op.13, SATB, pf duet, 1972; Time Piece, op.16, 6 male vv, 1973; Requiem, op.19, SATB, orch, 1975; Gloria, op.21, SATB, pf duet, 1973; Spare Parts, op.36, SATB, 1977, rev. 1979; Voices of Sleep, op.40, S, SATB, orch, 1979; The Canterbury Psalms, op.44, SATB, orch, 1981; Mass of the Sea, op.47, S, B, SATB, orch, 1983; Missa brevis, op.54, SATB, 1985; Stabat mater, op.57, Mez, SATB, orch, 1985–6; Te Deum, op.65, S, SATB, boys' vv, orch, 1987–8; The End, op.68, ATB, 1989; Magnificat, op.75, SATB, brass, org, perc, 1994; The Little Red Riding Hood Songbook, op.77, girls' vv, pf, 1994

Chmbr and solo inst: Rebecca, op.1, spkr, 1 ww, trbn, vn/vns, vc, pf, perc, 1966; Trilogy, org: Jubilate, op.5, 1969; Intrada, op.7, 1969, Interludium, op.15, 1972; Monologue, op.6, ob, 1970; Comedy, op.14, 5 wind, 1972, Flouresence, op.22, org, 1973; Conversations, op.25, cl, pf, 1974; Diversions, op.32, sax qt, 1976; Games, op.37, org, 1977; Cracowian Counterpoints, op.38, 14 insts, 1977, rev. 1978

At the Still Point of the Turning World, op.41, chmbr ens, 1980; Deception Pass, op.43, brass ens, 1980; Spiders, op.48, hp, 1983; Luslawice Variations, op.50, vn, 1984; Duologue, op.49, ob, pf, 1984; Mean Time, op.53, brass qnt, 1985; Str Qt, op.58, 1986; A Tunnel of Time, op.66, pno, 1988; Tides of Mananan, op.64, va, 1988; The Royal Eurostar, op.76, brass ens, perc, 1994

MSS in *GB-Lmic*

Principal publishers: Weinberger, Universal

BIBLIOGRAPHY
H. Cole: 'Patterson's Progress', *MT*, cxx (1980), 434–7
A. Burn: 'Profile: Paul Patterson', *Composer*, no.92 (1987), 3–6
G. Parry-Jones: 'Repertoire Guide: Paul Patterson', *Classical Music* (20 Nov 1993), 13 only

ANDREW BURN

Patter song. A comic song in which the humour derives from having the greatest number of words uttered in the shortest possible time. The technique was foreshadowed by such composers as Alessandro Scarlatti (the duet 'Non ti voglio' from *Tiberio imperatore d'Oriente*, 1702) but was not in common use until the second half of the 18th century, when composers often introduced the idea in *buffo* solos (e.g. Bartolo's aria 'La vendetta' in Act 1 scene iii of Mozart's *Le nozze di Figaro*). Other examples are found in the works of Logroscino, Piccinni, Paisiello, Haydn, Rossini (notably the 'confusion' ensemble in the Act 1 finale of *Il barbiere di Siviglia*), Donizetti and Sullivan (whose patter song in *Ruddigore* includes the lines: 'this particularly rapid, unintelligible patter isn't generally heard and if it is it doesn't matter').

□

Patti. Italian family of singers.

(1) **Salvatore Patti** (*b* Catania, 1800; *d* Paris, 21 Aug 1869). Tenor. Engaged as second tenor at the Real Teatro Carolino, Palermo, for the 1825–6 season, which was directed by Donizetti, he sang Pippetto in *L'ajo nell'imbarazzo* and Ismaele in the first performance of *Alahor di Granata* (6 January 1826). For the next decade he appeared at other theatres in Sicily and Italy, then in 1836 at the Teatro Valle, Rome, he sang Ugo in Donizetti's *Parisina* and Tamas in *Gemma di Vergy*, repeating the latter role in Naples the following year. His career as a singer continued in Italy and Spain until 1844, when he went to New York to manage seasons of Italian opera first at Palmo's, then at the Astor Place Opera House.

(2) **Caterina Chiesa Barilli-Patti** (*b* Rome; *d* Rome, 6 Sept 1870). Soprano, wife of (1) Salvatore Patti. She studied singing with Barilli, her first husband, and sang Eleanora at the first performance of Donizetti's *L'assedio*

di Calais in 1836 at the S Carlo, Naples, also appearing there in *I puritani*, *Gemma di Vergy* and Coppola's *La pazza per amore*. She is said to have sung Norma in Madrid the night before the birth of her youngest child, (4) Adelina Patti. After singing for a time in New York, she retired to Rome. The children of her first marriage, Clotilde (a contralto), Ettore (a baritone), Antonio and Nicolo (basses) Barilli, all had successful careers. Her eldest daughter by Patti, Amalia (*b* Paris, 1831; *d* Paris, Dec 1915), appeared as a soprano in opera and on the concert platform in the USA until her marriage to the pianist and impresario Maurice Strakosch.

(3) **Carlotta Patti** (*b* Florence, 30 Oct 1835; *d* Paris, 27 June 1889). Soprano, daughter of (1) Salvatore Patti and (2) Caterina Chiesa Barilli-Patti. She first studied the piano with Henri Herz, then decided to be a singer, making her début in January 1861 at a concert in New York. The following year she appeared in opera at the Academy of Music but, owing to the lameness from which she had suffered since childhood and to a temperamental unsuitability for the stage, did not repeat the experiment. She first sang in London in 1863 at Covent Garden, in a concert after the opera, and for the next 15 years pursued a highly successful career on the concert platform. In 1879 she married the Belgian cellist Ernest de Munck. Her voice was of considerable size, extremely flexible and extended up to *g'''* and even *g♯'''*. After her retirement she taught singing in Paris.

(4) **Adelina** [Adela] (**Juana Maria**) **Patti** (*b* Madrid, 19 Feb 1843; *d* Craig-y-Nos Castle, nr Brecon, Wales, 27 Sept 1919). Italian soprano, daughter of (1) Salvatore Patti and (2) Caterina Chiesa Barilli-Patti. She received her first singing lessons from her half-brother, Ettore Barilli, and when she was seven sang in a charity concert at Tripler Hall, New York. Accompanied by her brother-in-law, Maurice Strakosch, and the violinist Ole Bull, she toured the USA as a child prodigy for three years, and in 1857 she went on another long tour, with the pianist Gottschalk. She made her stage début in 1859 at the New York Academy of Music, in the title role of *Lucia di Lammermoor*, which she had studied with the conductor Emmanuele Muzio. After a tour of Philadelphia, Boston, Baltimore and other cities, during the winter of 1860–61 she sang in New Orleans and in Cuba.

She made her European début at Covent Garden on 14 May 1861, as Amina in *La sonnambula*; by the final curtain, the audience had succumbed completely to the spell of the 18-year-old prima donna, and Patti's quarter-century reign at Covent Garden had begun. After a tour of the British Isles, she sang in Berlin, Brussels, Amsterdam and The Hague.

She made her Paris début at the Théâtre Italien in 1862 and her first appearance in Vienna at the Carltheater in 1863, on both occasions as Amina. In October that year she sang Marguerite in Gounod's *Faust* for the first time, at Hamburg. In the winter of 1865–6 she made her first visit to Italy, singing at Florence, Bologna, Rome and Turin. In November 1868 she sang a duet from the *Stabat mater*, with Marietta Alboni, at Rossini's funeral in Paris and she spent the following winter in St Petersburg and Moscow.

Patti was London's first Aida in 1876 at Covent Garden, and she made her début at La Scala in *La traviata* in 1877. Her partner on those and many other occasions was the

Adelina Patti as Marguerite in Gounod's 'Faust', Act 3, with Jean-Baptiste Faure (Mephistopheles) and Giovanni Mario (Faust), Covent Garden, London, 1864: photograph by Caldesi & Co

tenor Ernest Nicolini, whom she married in 1886, after obtaining a divorce from her first husband, the Marquis de Caux. Returning to New York after an absence of over 20 years in 1881, she embarked on a concert tour, and for the following three winters she was engaged by Mapleson for his operatic tours of the USA, during which her fee rose to £1000 a performance. In 1885, her 25th consecutive season at Covent Garden, she sang the title role of *Carmen*, one of the very few misjudgments of her career. After another tour of the USA, she gave six farewell performances at the Metropolitan in April 1887. In 1888, after singing in Madrid and Lisbon, she appeared in Buenos Aires and Montevideo, then sang *Roméo et Juliette* at the Paris Opéra, with Gounod conducting, and Jean and Edouard de Reszke in the cast.

In 1895 Patti gave six farewell performances at Covent Garden, two each of Violetta, Zerlina and Rosina, her last operatic appearances in London, though in 1897 she sang at Monte Carlo and at Nice, where she created her final operatic role, *Dolores* by André Pollonnais. Her final American tour opened at Carnegie Hall, New York, on 4 November 1903, and her official London farewell took place at the Albert Hall on 1 December 1906, but she continued to take part in charity concerts until 1914.

During the later stages of Patti's career, the legends that surrounded her tended to obscure the fact that at the zenith of her vocal powers, between 1863 and 1880, she was also a remarkable actress, especially in comedy. In the early years, when the compass of her perfectly placed and produced voice extended easily to *f'''*, Amina, Lucia, Violetta, Norina and Rosina were the roles in which she excelled, and her interpretations were marred only by an over-use of ornamentation. Later, her secure technique enabled her to continue to sing many of these parts, but she also became pre-eminent in a slightly heavier lyric repertory, in such roles as Semiramide, Marguerite (which at first she had found uncomfortably low), Leonora (*Il trovatore*) and Aida. Although she rarely chose to sing in works lying outside her vocal, histrionic or emotional range, *L'Africaine* and *Les Huguenots* both exceeded these limits; the other two Meyerbeer operas in which she appeared, *Dinorah* and *L'étoile du nord*, suited her talents much better. Her amazing purity of tone and vocal flexibility after singing for more than half a century are amply illustrated by the recordings she made when in her 60s and testify to her exemplary care for her phenomenal gifts.

BIBLIOGRAPHY

M. Strakosch: *Souvenirs d'un imprésario* (Paris, 1886, 2/1887)
J.H. Mapleson: *The Mapleson Memoirs* (London, 1888); ed. H. Rosenthal (London, 1966)
M. Maretzek: *Sharps and Flats* (New York, 1890/R1968 as *Revelations of an Opera Manager in 19th-Century America*)
L. Arditi: *My Reminiscences*, ed. M.A. Zedlitz (London, 1896/R)
H. Klein: *The Reign of Patti* (London, 1920/R)
H. Rosenthal: *Two Centuries of Opera at Covent Garden* (London, 1958)
J.F. Cone: *Adelina Patti: Queen of Hearts* (Portland, OR, 1993)

ELIZABETH FORBES

Pattiera, Tino (*b* Cavtat, nr Dubrovnik, 27 June 1890; *d* Cavtat, 24 April 1966). Croatian tenor. He studied in Vienna and after gaining experience in operetta made his début at the Dresden Hofoper in 1914 as Manrico in *Il trovatore*. His fine voice was matched by good looks, and he became the most popular tenor in Dresden, especially when paired in the 1920s with the soprano Meta Seinemeyer. With her, and under Fritz Busch, he sang in some notable productions, including *La forza del destino*, *Don Carlos*, *The Queen of Spades* and *Andrea Chénier*. Although he specialized in the Italian repertory, he also sang Tannhäuser, and Bacchus in *Ariadne auf Naxos*. He joined the Chicago Opera Company in the 1921–2 season, and was a guest artist in Berlin, Vienna, Budapest and Belgrade. He gave his last concert at Dresden in 1953 and taught for some years in Vienna. Although a highly gifted singer, he lacked the secure technique and stylistic discipline to make the best use of his voice. Recordings preserve its distinctive timbre, and his duets with Seinemeyer make it understandable that their performances together in Dresden created an enthusiasm comparable to the Melba-and-Caruso evenings in London.

BIBLIOGRAPHY

A. Vincenti and J. Dennis: 'Tino Pattiera', *Record Collector*, xvii (1966–8), 268–85

J.B. STEANE

Patto, Angelico (*fl* 1613). Italian anthologist and composer. He is known only for his anthology *Canoro pianto di Maria vergine sopra la faccia di Christo estinto: poesia del ... Abbate Grillo ... posta in musica da diversi autori ...* for one voice and continuo (Venice, 1613³). On the title-page he is called 'Academico Giustiniano', and since the dedication is signed from S Giorgio Maggiore, Venice, he was possibly a priest there. The collection consists of 24 madrigals and a dialogue. The better-known of the composers represented are Barbarino, Stefano Bernardi, Dognazzi, Franzoni, Amedeo Freddi and Girolamo Marinoni. Patto included three settings of his own, but they are negligible. At least two of the contents, both by Barbarino and one of them the dialogue – *Ferma, ferma, Signore* (in J. Racek: *Stilprobleme der italienischen Monodie*, Prague, 1965, pp. 246–8), a version of *Ferma, ferma, Caronte* (1607) – are spiritual contrafacta of previously published secular pieces.

NIGEL FORTUNE

Patton, Charley (*b* nr Bolton, MS, *c*1891; *d* Indianola, MS, 28 April 1934). American blues singer and guitarist. In 1912 he moved to the Dockery plantation near Drew, MS, where he performed with Tommy Johnson, Willie Brown and other Mississippi blues singers who exchanged songs and techniques. He claimed to have been a lay preacher and recorded a few gospel items, including *Prayer of Death* (1929). A professional musician and songster, Patton was noted for his clowning and entertaining, but the majority of his recordings, made from 1929 until his death, present a more serious artist. Generally regarded as the archetypal Mississippi black American blues singer, he travelled as far as Milwaukee to play, and his fame extended far beyond the Mississippi area. He had a rasping voice of the 'heavy' kind admired by many other singers. *Pony Blues* (1929, Para.), included in his first recording session, was his most celebrated blues item, though *Down the Dirt Road* (1929, Para.) and *Moon Going Down* (1930, Para.), the latter with Willie Brown playing the flat-pick guitar in accompaniment, are perhaps his best recorded blues. The themes of his blues were often autobiographical, though sometimes the stanzas were confused; *High Sheriff Blues* (1934, Voc.) is among the more consistent narratives. Patton's recordings are sombre, often with percussive accompaniment on a guitar in open G tuning. He also performed ballads, including *Elder Greene Blues* and *Frankie and Albert* (both 1929, Para.), ragtime or dance-songs, such as the spirited *A Spoonful Blues* (1929, Para.), and spirituals from the songster repertory. His blues influenced Bukka White, Howlin' Wolf and many later singers.

BIBLIOGRAPHY

SouthernB
P. Oliver: *The Story of the Blues* (London, 1969/R)
J. Fahey: *Charley Patton* (London, 1970)
G. Oakley: *The Devil's Music: a History of the Blues* (London, 1976)
J.T. Titon: *Early Downhome Blues: a Musical and Cultural Analysis* (Urbana, IL, 1977)
R. Sacre, ed.: *The Voice of the Delta: Charley Patton and the Mississippi Blues Tradition* (Liège, 1987)
S. Calt and G. Wardlow: *King of the Delta Blues: the Life and Music of Charlie Patton* (Newton, NJ, 1988)

PAUL OLIVER

Patye, Rogier. *See* PATHIE, ROGIER.

Patzak, Julius (*b* Vienna, 9 April 1898; *d* Rottach-Egern, Bavaria, 26 Jan 1974). Austrian tenor. After studying music and conducting under Guido Adler, Franz Schmidt and others he took up singing in earnest, being entirely self-taught. Provincial engagements led to an invitation to join the Staatsoper in Munich in 1928, where he stayed until he joined the Vienna company in 1945. For more than three decades he was much in demand, particularly for Mozart tenor roles, and as his voice grew larger he became an incomparable Florestan and Palestrina, the only two of his grandest roles to have been recorded completely (and these only semi-officially). His extensive repertory ranged from Singspiel and operetta through the lighter Wagner roles and Richard Strauss to Verdi, Puccini and Musorgsky. Late in his career he was still a marvellously subtle and stylish performer of lieder, old Viennese theatre songs and the *Heurigen* songs of his native city, and he also took up conducting again. He was much sought after as a soloist in oratorios (the Evangelist in Bach's Passions and in Franz Schmidt's *Das Buch mit sieben Siegeln*). Among his many lieder and oratorio recordings, the version of *Das Lied von der Erde* with Walter and Ferrier is one of his finest. He was the first Austrian artist to be engaged by the BBC after the war, and he appeared at Covent Garden (where he had sung Tamino in 1938) as Florestan and Herod during the 1947 Vienna Staatsoper season; he returned to sing Florestan and Hoffmann with the resident company. His advocacy for new music, both opera and song, deserves mention, and he taught both at the Vienna Music Academy and at the Mozarteum, Salzburg.

Although Patzak's voice was generally considered small it was so finely projected and allied to such intelligent phrasing, meticulous enunciation and effective stage deportment that it seldom failed to make its mark. His slightly nasal timbre was immediately recognizable. When well into his 50s he was able to stand in as Lohengrin or continue to sing in the Beethoven, Mozart and Pfitzner operas with no loss of impact. He recorded several smaller roles, notably Mime in Furtwängler's RAI *Ring* of 1953, and made memorable recordings of operatic excerpts.

BIBLIOGRAPHY
P. Branscombe: 'Julius Patzak', *Opera*, v (1954), 403–7
J. Dennis: 'Julius Patzak', *Record Collector*, xix (1970–71), 195–222 [with discography by D. Brew]

PETER BRANSCOMBE

Pauer, Ernst (*b* Vienna, 21 Dec 1826; *d* Jugenheim, nr Darmstadt, 9 May 1905). Austrian pianist, editor and teacher, father of MAX VON PAUER. His father was a Lutheran minister, and his mother a member of the great piano-making family of Streicher. He studied the piano under Theodor Dirzka (until 1839) and F.X.W. Mozart (1839–44), harmony and counterpoint under Simon Sechter (1839–44) and orchestration and composition under Franz Lachner in Munich (1845–7). In 1847 he became director of the musical societies at Mainz, where he was active until 1851 conducting and composing theatrical music. However, his début as a pianist in London (23 June 1851) and subsequent appearances there were so successful that he decided to remain. He succeeded Potter as professor of the piano at the RAM (1859–64) and in 1861 began the first of three series of historical chronological performances of harpsichord and piano music. He also gave concerts abroad and was appointed Austrian court pianist in 1866. From 1870 he lectured on the history of keyboard music, the oratorio, modern music, the practice of teaching and other subjects. He was for many years principal professor of the piano at the Royal College of Music, London, from its foundation in 1876 as the National Training School for Music. In 1896 he retired to Jugenheim.

An assiduous editor, Pauer produced attractive and inexpensive editions of much 17th- and 18th-century keyboard music: *Old English Composers for the Virginal and Harpsichord*, 12 books of *Alte Klaviermusik*, 65 numbers of *Alte Meister*, *Alte Tänze*, etc. He made good piano arrangements (for two, four and eight hands) of the

symphonies of Beethoven and Schumann, and edited much 19th-century piano and vocal music including Clementi sonatinas, Moscheles studies, Mendelssohn songs, Schubert songs as transcribed by Liszt, and Schumann ballads for declamation. Some of his dramatic music was published by Schott in the 1850s and 1860s, as were instrumental works including a Violin Sonata op.46 and a Symphony in C minor op.50; he also produced several books of studies for piano.

WRITINGS
The Art of Pianoforte Playing (London, 1877)
The Elements of the Beautiful in Music (London, 1877)
Musical Forms (London, 1878)
The Birthday Book of Musicians and Composers (London, 1881)
A Dictionary of Pianists and Composers for the Pianoforte, with an Appendix of Manufacturers of the Instrument (London, 1895)

BIBLIOGRAPHY
E. Hanslick: *Geschichte des Concertwesens in Wien*, i (Vienna, 1869/R)
G. Beechey: 'Domenico Scarletti and Ernst Pauer', *MO*, cix (1986), 160–62, 251–3, 283–5

A.J. HIPKINS/R

Pauer, Jiří (*b* Libušín, nr Kladno, 22 Feb 1919). Czech composer. He first studied composition privately with Otakar Šín, and then with Alois Hába at the Prague Conservatory (1943–6) and with Pavel Bořkovec at the Academy of Musical Arts (1946–50). From 1945 to 1949 he was the treasurer of the Přítomnost association for contemporary music; later he held various positions in the Union of Czechoslovak Composers, being secretary-general from 1963–5. He was principal of opera at the Prague National Theatre (1953–5, 1965–7), director of the Czech PO (1958–80), professor of composition at the Academy of Musical Arts (1965–89) and general manager of the Prague National Theatre (1979–90). As a composer Pauer has undergone several stages of development. In the 1940s he was influenced by Hába, writing a set of *Burlesques* for quarter-tone piano. The next decade saw him committed to socialist realism in the composition of many mass songs expressing Communist Party principles. His move to a romantic style in the late 1950s was prompted by strictures concerning the need for music to be comprehensible to the people, but in the 1960s his music grew more complicated and began to show a synthesis of his earlier styles. Several of his works, among them the Bassoon Concerto (1949) and the opera *Žvanivý slimejš* ('Prattling Slug', 1949–50), have won a permanent place in the repertory due to their melodiousness and vigorous musicianship. His numerous honours include the Gottwald State Prize and the titles Artist of Merit (1965) and National Artist (1979).

WORKS
(selective list)

Stage: Žvanivý slimejš [Prattling slug] (fairy tale op, M. Mellanová, after J. Hloucha), 1949–50; Zuzana 'Vojířová (op, after J. Bor), 1954–7; Červená Karkulka [Red Riding Hood] (op, l, Mellanová), 1959; Manželské kontrapunkty [Matrimonial counterpoints] (5 operatic grotesques, Pauer, after S. Grodzieńská), 1961; Zdravý nemocný [The Hypochondriac] (comic op, 3, Pauer, after Molière: *Le malade imaginaire*), 1965–8; Labutí píseň [Swan Song] (monodrama, 1, Pauer, after A.P. Chekhov), low male v, chbr orch, 1973; Ferda mravenec [Ferdy the Ant] (children's ballet, J. Rey, after O. Sekora), 1975

Orch: Bn Concs., 1949; Ob Conc., 1954; Hn Conc., 1958; Symfonie, 1962–4; Panychida, 1969; Canto Festivo, 1970–71; Delfin, wind, 1972; Tpt Conc., 1972; Iniciály [Initials], 1974; Furiant, wind, 1974; Aurora, wind, 1976, arr. orch, 1977; Symfony for Str 1978; Mar Conc., mar, str, 1986; Symfonické sondy [Symphonic Probes], 1990

Vocal: Canto triste, Mez/Bar, chbr orch, 1971; Tragedie o vose a nose [Tragedy of the Wasp and the Nose], low v, orch, 1976; Hymnus komunistické straně [Hymn to the Communist Party] (V. Nezval), SATB, orch, 1977; Písně o lásce [Songs of Love] (V. Šefl), male, v, pf, 1982

Chbr: Sonatina, vn, pf, 1953; Sonata, vc, pf, 1954; Str Qt no.1, 1960; Wind Qnt, 1960; Divertimento, 9 insts, 1961; Pf Trio, 1963; Str Qt no.2, 1969; Str Qt no.3, 1970; Trompetina, tpt, pf, 1972; Trombonetta, trbn, pf, 1974–5; Tubonetta, tuba, pf, 1976; Árie a rondo, b cl, pf, 1978; Epizody, str qt, 1980; Sonata, vn, pf, 1986; Trio, 3 hn, 1986; Fagotina, bn, pf, 1987; Nonetto no.2, 1991; Akvarely [Watercolours], vn, pf, 1995; 3 kusy [3 Pieces], fl, pf, 1995; 4 skladby [4 Compositions], vn, pf, 1995; Zelené kousky [Green Pieces], tpt, hn, trbn, 1997; Dua, fl, pf, 1998

Solo inst: Suita, hp, 1947; Monology všedního dne [Everyday Monologues], cl, 1964; Interpolace, fl, 1968; Rapsodie, vc, 1969; Pastorely, ob, 1976; Monolity, pf, 1978; Zkratky [Abbreviations], mar, 1981; Romantické nálady [Romantic Moods], pf, 1995; Návraty [Returns], pf, 1997; Hry a vzpomínky [Games and Memories], pf, 1998

Principal publishers: DILIA, Panton, State Publishing House

BIBLIOGRAPHY

ČSHS; GroveO (H. Havlíková)

J. Paclt: 'Masové písně Jiřího Pauera' [Pauer's mass songs], HRo, viii (1955), 802–7

J. Válek: 'Zápas o hudbu dneška' [The struggle for contemporary music], HRo, xiv (1961), 637–41

V. Pospíšil: 'Nad skladatelským dilem Jiřího Pauera' [On Pauer's compositional output], HRo, xvi (1963), 704–6, 751–3

M. Kuna: 'S Jiřím Pauerem nejubilejně', HRo, xxvii (1974), 36–9

L. Šíp: Česká opera a její tvůrci [Czech operas and their authors] (Prague, 1983), 299–309

J. Štilec: 'Kde je umění, tam není stáří' [Where there is art, there is no old age], OM, xcii (1985), 113–18

V. Pospíšil: 'O Jiřím Pauerovi: výňatek z připravované knihy' [About Pauer: extract from a prepared book], HRo, xlii (1989), 83–6

J. Pauer: Kontrapunkty života [Counterpoints of life] (Prague, 1995)

OLDŘICH PUKL/MOJMÍR SOBOTKA

Pauer, Max von (b London, 31 Oct 1866; d Jugenheim, nr Darmstadt, 12 May 1945). German pianist, teacher and music administrator, son of ERNST PAUER. He studied with his father until 1881, and then went to Karlsruhe, where for four years he was a composition pupil of Vincenz Lachner at the conservatory. Pauer made a successful début in London at the age of 19 and then for two years devoted himself to concert work, but without making the impact he had hoped for. From 1887 he was a teacher at the Cologne Conservatory and in 1897 moved to Stuttgart, where he took over Dionys Pruckner's class. He became director of the Stuttgart Conservatory in 1908 and in 1924 succeeded Stephan Krehl as head of the Leipzig Conservatory, which under his leadership was reorganized as a Hochschule für Musik. Pauer remained director for ten years, after which he retired from administration. Especially effective in large-scale works of the piano literature, he developed into a notable Beethoven and Brahms player, and introduced numerous works by contemporary composers such as Reger and Rachmaninoff. He can be heard as pianist in a recording of Schubert's 'Trout' Quintet dating from the late 1920s. Admired as a flexible and inventive teacher, Pauer numbered among his pupils Julian von Karolyi, the teacher Walter Georgii and the accompanist Hubert Giesen. He composed some piano pieces, edited a large quantity of music, brought out a new edition of the Lebert-Stark Klavierschule (Stuttgart, 1904) and wrote an autobiography, Unser seltsames Ich: Lebensschau eines Künstlers (Stuttgart, 1942). For his service to Swabian musical life he was ennobled by the King of Württemberg.

JAMES METHUEN-CAMPBELL

Pauk, György (b Budapest, 26 Oct 1936). British violinist of Hungarian birth. He began studying the violin at the age of five and entered the Franz Liszt Academy as a pupil of Zathureczky, Weiner and Kodály. At 14 he made his début with an orchestra and, while a student, toured throughout eastern Europe. He won three important competitions: the Paganini, Genoa (1956); the Munich Sonata (1957, with his regular duo partner Peter Frankl); and the Long-Thibaud, Paris (1959). He made his Royal Festival Hall début in December 1961, having that year chosen London as his home. A well-schooled virtuoso in the central European tradition, Pauk is at his best in the concertos and sonatas of Bartók (all of which he has recorded), to which he brings vigorous commitment and sure technique; his tone, not large but admirably pure and fine in focus, is also heard to advantage in Mozart, Beethoven and Brahms. His other recordings include the complete Mozart violin concertos and Brahms's three violin sonatas. He plays in a piano trio with Frankl and Ralph Kirshbaum, which celebrated its 25th anniversary in 1997. Pauk took part in the première of Tippett's Triple Concerto (1980) and is the dedicatee of concertos by István Láng and William Mathias. In 1987 he was appointed professor of violin at the RAM.

BIBLIOGRAPHY

J. Creighton: Discopaedia of the Violin (Toronto, 1974, 2/1994)

MAX LOPPERT/R

Pauke (i) (Ger.). Kettledrum. See also DRUM and TIMPANI.

Pauke (ii) (Ger.). See under ORGAN STOP.

Paul, Les [Lester Polfuss] (b Waukesha, WI, 9 June 1915). American guitarist and guitar maker. He was one of the pioneers of the solid-bodied electric guitar, creating his first prototype in 1941, a four-foot wooden board known as 'the Log'. He had previously enjoyed some success as a hillbilly performer and with a jazz-oriented trio which broadcast from New York radio stations. His subsequent inventions included the floating bridge, electrodynamic pickups, dual pickup guitars and the Les Paulveriser, a machine to be used during performances to record sounds, play them back and electronically modify them. In 1952 the guitar manufacturer Gibson introduced its Les Paul model which became one of the most popular instruments among professional guitarists. He was also an innovator in the recording studio, developing such techniques as multitracking, echo delay and close-miking (the differential positioning of microphones). These techniques were put to use on a series of recordings made by Paul with the singer Mary Ford in the early 1950s. Among them were Mocking Bird Hill, How High the Moon and Vaya Con Dios. In subsequent decades Paul collaborated on recordings with country music guitar virtuoso Chet Atkins and jazz guitarist Al Di Meola.

DAVE LAING

Paul, Oscar (b Freiwaldau [now Jesenik], Silesia, 8 April 1836; d Leipzig, 18 April 1898). German writer on music. He was educated at the University of Leipzig, where he first studied theology, but soon changed to classical philology. At the same time he studied the piano at the Leipzig Conservatory with Plaidy, and history and theory of music with E.F. Richter and Moritz Hauptmann, taking his PhD at the university in 1860 under Hauptmann's direction. After spending some time in various German towns and abroad in pursuit of a career as a pianist, Paul returned to Leipzig in 1866, and was appointed to the university with an *Habilitationsschrift* on ancient Greek music theory (*Die absolute Harmonik der Griechen*). In 1869 he also became a teacher of music history, piano and composition at the Conservatory. In 1872 he published his most important work, a commentary on Boethius's *De institutione musica* together with a translation of the work into German – the first vernacular translation of *De institutione musica* to be published. (Paul's translation relied on printed sources, though Gottfried Friedlein had published the standard critical edition of the work in Leipzig in 1867, and had used the manuscript sources as well.) Paul became associate professor at the university in 1872. He edited for a short time two musical periodicals, *Tonhalle* and its successor, the *Musikalisches Wochenblatt*, and was for many years music critic of the *Leipziger Tagblatt*.

Paul edited Hauptmann's *Die Lehre von der Harmonik* for publication, and completed the last three chapters of the manuscript (occasionally using Hauptmann's words from his *Die Natur der Harmonik und der Metrik* of 1853). The opening of Paul's own *Lehrbuch der Harmonik* (1880) describes it as an attempt to combine ideas of both of his teachers, Richter and Hauptmann (though the latter remains most prominent; an abridged translation of the *Lehrbuch* written by Paul's pupil Theodore Baker introduced Hauptmann's theory of harmony in diluted form to an American audience. Besides Hauptmann, Paul was influenced by Rudolf Westphal (likewise a classicist who had studied theology), who valued in Paul the 'skilled musician with philological training'; this type of grounding was also very influential on Paul's pupil Hermann Kretzschmar.

WRITINGS

ed.: *Moritz Hauptmann: Denkschrift zu Feier seines siebezigjährigen Geburtstages* (Leipzig, 1862)
Die absolute Harmonik der Griechen (Leipzig, 1866)
ed.: M. von Hauptmann: *Die Lehre von der Harmonik* (Leipzig, 1868, 2/1873)
Geschichte des Klaviers vom Ursprünge bis zu den modernsten Formen dieses Instrumentes (Leipzig, 1868/R)
ed.: *Handlexikon der Tonkunst* (Leipzig, 1870–73)
Boetius und die griechische Harmonik (Leipzig, 1872/R 1973 as *Fünf Bücher über die Musik*)
Musikalische Instrumente (Brunswick, 1874)
Lehrbuch der Harmonik (Leipzig, 1880; Eng. trans., abridged, 1885 as *A Manual of Harmony*)

ROBERT W. WASON

Paula, Innocentio di. *See* DI PAULA, INNOCENTIO.

Paulet, Angélique (*b* c1591; *d* 1650). French singer and lutenist. Her father, *secrétaire ordinaire* of the *Chambre des Comptes*, was a gentleman from the Languedoc. She lived at court, where she attracted attention for her beauty and good nature, her musical talent and her ability to dance gracefully. Her first great success at court was as Arion in the *Ballet de la reine*, performed on 31 January 1609 with Queen Marie de Médicis in the role of Amphitrite. From 1620 until her death she frequented the famous *chambre bleue* of the Hôtel de Rambouillet, where the Marquise of Rambouillet received poets, musicians and members of the aristocracy who disliked the vulgarity of the French court, and where she met Tallemant des Réaux, who wrote extravagant anecdotes about her. According to Mlle de Scudéry she was a pupil of Pierre Guédron. She exercised a wealth of imagination in entertaining her friends. During a performance of Jean de Mairet's play *Sophonisbe* she gave a musical *entr'acte*, dressed as a nymph and singing to her own accompaniment on the theorbo; the Abbé Arnaud wrote that 'her admirable voice left us feeling no regrets for even the best violin ensemble as generally employed to play in the intervals'. Jean Chapelain (1595–1674) wrote the '*Récit de Mlle Paulet*' for her to perform in the *Ballet des Dieux, représentant l'astre du lion* (now lost).

BIBLIOGRAPHY

V. Cousin: *La société française au XVIIème siècle d'après le Grand Cyrus de Mlle de Scudéry* (Paris, 1858)
E. Magne: *Voiture et les origines de l'Hôtel de Rambouillet* (Paris, 1911)
G. Mongrédien: *Les historiettes de Tallemant des Réaux* (Paris, 1932–4)
M. McGowan: *L'art du ballet de cour en France, 1581–1643* (Paris, 1963/R)
G. Durosoir: *L'air de cour en France 1571–1655* (Liege, 1991)

GEORGIE DUROSOIR

Pauli, Hansjörg (*b* Winterthur, 14 March 1931). Swiss music journalist and film maker. He studied music at the Winterthur Conservatory (1953) and musical analysis under Hans Keller in London. His career as a musicologist, journalist and film maker began in 1956 when he wrote his first music reviews for Swiss newspapers. From 1960 to 1965 he was editor-in-chief at Radio Zürich's department of new music. Subsequently he directed the music department of the North German television network in Hamburg (1965–8), but resigned to live as a freelance author and film-script writer at Bergamo. In 1969 he took up a lecturing post in audio-visual drama at the Munich Hochschule für Film und Fernsehen.

Pauli belongs to the generation of German-speaking music journalists who base their work on the prevailing social contexts and conditions of composition and performance; he draws largely on the doctrines of Marx and Adorno and aims in his combination of a visual medium with music at the fusion of the various media into an integrated whole. These principles were applied in Mauricio Kagel's first films under Pauli's editorial supervision in Hamburg, and later in his work on contemporary music. The films he has written and directed himself include *Webern, oder Ein Leben für die Kunst* (1971–3), *Strawinsky Weekend* (1972–3), *Klänge machen Leute: Funktion und Mechanik von Filmmusik* (1973); among his substantial radio programmes are 'Weberns Spätwerk und Goethes Metamorphosenlehre' (1962), 'Virtuosenstück oder sinfonisches Werk' (1970, on Beethoven's Violin Concerto), 'Webern, Revisited' (1973), 'Westlich von Sante Fé: über das politische Potential von Filmmusik' (1974), 'Luc Ferrari' (1974–5) and 'Filmmusik: Geschichte, Funktion und Aesthetik' (1975).

WRITINGS

'On Strawinsky's "Threni"', *Tempo*, no.49 (1958), 16–33
'Hans Werner Henze's Italian Music', *The Score*, no.25 (1959), 26–37
'Klaus Huber', *Musica*, xvii (1963), 10–17
'Das Hörbare und das Schaubare: Fernsehen und jüngste Musik', *Musik auf der Flucht vor sich selbst*, ed. U. Dibelius (Munich, 1969), 29–40; Eng. trans. in *World of Music*, xiii/4 (1971), 32–47
'Un certain sourire', *Beethoven '70* (Frankfurt, 1970), 20–30 [with Adorno, Kagel, Metzger, Schnebel and Wildberger]
Für wen komponieren Sie eigentlich? (Frankfurt, 1971)
'Von der Idee zur Realisation: Ausdrucksmittel des heutigen Komponisten', *Musica*, xxv (1971), 447–50
'Filmmusik', *SMz*, cxiv (1974), 265–70
'Musik im Film', *SMz*, cxiv (1974), 326–31

'Avant-Garde und Volkstümlichkeit', *Zeitschrift für Musiktheorie*, vi/1 (1975), 4–10
Filmmusik, Stummfilm (1981)
'Aus Gesprächen über Webern', *Anton Webern*, ii, Musik-Konzepte (1984), 283–93
'Rundfunk und Neue Musik: zur Theorie und Praxis offentlichen Mäzenatentums', *Musikszene heute*, ed. E. Jost (Mainz, 1988), 8–20
'Funktionen von Filmmusik', *Film und Musik: Darmstadt 1993*, 8–17
Hermann Scherchen, 1891–1966 (Zürich, 1993)
'Zum Verhältnis der Vertikale und Horizontale in der Filmmusik', *Zwischen Aufklärung & Kulturindustrie: Festschrift für Georg Knepler zum 85. Geburtstag*, ed. H.-W. Heister, K. Heister-Grech and G. Scheit, ii (Hamburg, 1993), 261–70

HANSPETER KRELLMANN

Paulin, Frédéric Hubert (*b* Paris, 1678; *d* Paris, 25 Jan 1761). French composer. The son of a Parisian furrier, he was orphaned at the age of ten and from 1688 until June 1693 sang as choirboy at the church of the Cimetière des Innocents under the direction of Pierre Ferrier. He then studied composition with André Campra before taking up a post as serpent player at Notre Dame, Paris, on 18 August 1698. On 30 August he was appointed to a similar post at St Honoré; he was made *maître des enfants de choeur* there on 3 July 1715 and remained at St Honoré for the rest of his life. He won some success with his compositions, notably at the Concert Spirituel, but only a few have survived. His motets are in an unmistakably French style, somewhat backward-looking but showing clear Italian influence here and there.

Paulin's son Nicolas Hubert (*b* Paris, 1713; *d* Versailles, 29 Aug 1785) worked as an organist successively at St Pierre-des-Arcis, Paris (from 20 August 1731), Ste Opportune, Paris (from 12 January 1741), and Notre Dame, Versailles (from 13 February 1743). On 21 April 1755 he was made one of the four organists of the royal chapel and in 1769 he became also *maître de clavecin* to the pages of the Musique du Roi.

WORKS

Te Deum, Paris, 6 July 1704, lost
Airs sérieux et à boire (Paris, 1705)
Ier livre de motets . . . à l'usage des dames religieuses, 1–2vv, bc (Paris, 1705)
Works perf. at Concert Spirituel, all lost: Le triomphe de Daphné (divertissement), 1728; Les titans vaincus (divertissement), 1729; Les amans constans (pastorale), 1729
Airs pubd in *Mercure de France* (1734–6, 1738)
Absterget Deus, motet, CtTB, bc, *F-LYm*

BIBLIOGRAPHY

BrenetC; EitnerQ; MGG1 (J. Bonfils); *PierreH*
E. Kocevar: *Collégiale Sainte-Opportune de Paris: Orgues et Organistes 1535–1790* (Dijon, 1996), 231–48
E. Kocevar: 'Frédéric Hubert Paulin (1678–1761): maître de musique de Saint-Honoré à Paris', *RMFC*, xxix (1996–8), 189–222

ÉRIK KOCEVAR

Paulirinus, Paulus (*b* Prague, 1413; *d* after 1471). Czech theorist. He was the author of an encyclopedic work, *Liber viginti artium*, which includes a discussion of music as one of the arts. He was also known as Paulus de Praga and as Paulus Žídek, the latter suggesting that he was of Jewish origin although he may have been brought up as a Christian. He studied in Vienna and in Padua but the claim of a stay in Bologna has not yet been documented. Between 1443 and 1447 Paulirinus taught liberal arts at Prague University. From 1451 to 1455 he was involved in studies as well as political events at Kraków and Breslau. After 1455 he apparently retired to Plzeň where,

between 1459 and 1463, he wrote his voluminous encyclopedia in which, besides the liberal arts, he discussed zoology, mineralogy, medicine and metaphysics. The only known copy of this large manuscript is now in the Biblioteka Jagiellónska, Kraków (*PL-Kj* 257). It consists of 359 folios covering only 15 of the 20 arts. The section on music is on ff.153–62 and is not complete. Of the five *partitiones* (1. general discussion; 2. notation; 3. musical instruments; 4. Gregorian chant and 5. liturgical prescriptions for church music) the last two are lost and the section dealing with instruments is incomplete, but does contain the earliest known reference to the virginal. Critical editions of the chapters on musical instruments and mensural notation, and some of Paulirinus's definitions, have been published by Růžena Mužíková, who has also published an authoritative account of his life (1988).

BIBLIOGRAPHY

MGG1 (H. Hüschen)
H. Seidl: *Der 'Tractatus de musica' des Pergament-Kodex Nr. 257 Krakau unter besonderer Berücksichtigung der Musikinstrumentenkunde* (diss., U. of Leipzig, 1957)
R. Mužíková: 'Musica instrumentalis v traktatu Pavla Žídka z Prahy', *MMC*, no.17 (1965), 1–32
R. Mužíková: 'Pauli Paulirini de Praga Musica mensuralis', *Acta Universitatis Carolinae: philosophica et historica*, ii (1965), 57–87
M. Velimirović: 'The Pre-English Use of the Term "Virginal"', *Essays in Musicology in Honor of Dragan Plamenac*, ed. G. Reese and R.J. Snow (Pittsburgh, 1969/R), 341–52
S. Howell: 'Paulus Paulirinus of Prague on Musical Instruments', *JAMIS*, v–vi (1979–80), 9–36
R. Mužíková: 'Musicus-Cantor', *MMC*, no.31 (1984), 9–36
R. Mužíková: 'Magister Paulus de Praga', *MMC*, no.32 (1988), 9–18

MILOŠ VELIMIROVIĆ

Paullet (*fl* ?1380–1414). French composer. He is known only from one extant work, the three-voice ballade *J'aim. Qui? Vous. Moy? Voyre douce figure* (ed. in CMM, xi/2, 1959) in the seventh fascicle of *GB-Ob* Canon.misc.213, where the ascription 'Paullet' is in a slightly later hand. He may be identical with the man variously named as Macé, Mahieu, Mahieu de St Pol or Mattheo de Sancto Paolo among the chaplains of the Ste Chapelle of the Bourges palace in 1405–14. It appears significant that fascicles V–VIII of the Oxford manuscript, generally acknowledged as its earliest layer, contain several other works by composers associated with the Bourges chapel at the same time: Guillaume Legrant, Nicolas Grenon, Pierre Fontaine, Johannes Cesaris, Jean Charité. The ballade also survives in the Cambrai fragments (*F-CA* 1328), possibly dating from the 1380s, with a virtually illegible top voice and the opening of what seems to be a different contratenor. The clever text is unusual in being a dialogue between a male and a female persona; it is complete only in the top voice, but is underlaid to the two lower voices at three points where all voices are in imitation.

BIBLIOGRAPHY

P. Higgins: 'Music and Musicians at the Sainte-Chapelle of the Bourges Palace, 1405–1515', *IMSCR XIV: Bologna 1987*, iii, 689–701, esp. 692–4
D. Fallows: Introduction to *Oxford, Bodleian Library, MS Canon.misc.213* (Chicago, 1995)
D. Fallows: *A Catalogue of Polyphonic Songs, 1415–1480* (Oxford, 1999), 188, 712

PAULA HIGGINS

Paulli, Holger Simon (*b* Copenhagen, 22 Feb 1810; *d* Copenhagen, 23 Dec 1891). Danish conductor, composer and violinist. He studied the violin with Claus Schall, conductor at the Royal Theatre, Copenhagen, and later with F.T. Wexschall, becoming an assistant in the Royal Orchestra in 1822 and a member in 1828. He never pursued a solo violin career, but always remained an enthusiastic quartet player (viola). From 1835, and permanently from 1842, he conducted the Royal Orchestra's ballet music rehearsals, and in 1849 he succeeded Wexschall as leader. He was a close collaborator with the ballet-master August Bournonville and composed music for more than ten of the latter's ballets, many of which are still in the Danish repertory (e.g. *Napoli*, 1842, composed with Helsted, Gade and Lumbye, *Conservatoriet*, 1849, *Kermessen i Brügge*, 1851, the second part of *Blomsterfesten i Genzano*, 1858). He also composed two Singspiels (1850 and 1851), a concert overture (1841), violin pieces and songs. As conductor of the Royal Orchestra from 1863 to 1883 he was in charge of opera performances and introduced to Denmark operas by Verdi (*Il trovatore*, 1865) and Wagner (*Lohengrin*, 1870, *Die Meistersinger von Nürnberg*, 1872). He was also conductor of the Caeciliaforening (1872–7) and chairman of the Chamber Music Society (1868–91). Upon the founding of the Copenhagen Conservatory in 1866, he was appointed director jointly with Gade and Hartmann.

BIBLIOGRAPHY

DBL (N. Schiørring)

K. Hendriksen: *Fra billedmagerens kalejdoskop* (Copenhagen, 1954), 73–83 [autobiographical sketch by Paulli]

N. Schiørring: 'H.S. Paulli og dansk musikliv i det 19. århundrede', *Fund og forskning*, iv (1957), 98–119

E.M. von Rosen: 'Om mitt arbete med *Napoli*'s 2:a akt' [My work with the second act of *Napoli*], *Bournonville: Tradition – Rekonstruktion*, ed. O. Nørlyng and H. Urup (Copenhagen, 1989), 134–45

TORBEN SCHOUSBOE

Paulus, Stephen (Harrison) (*b* Summit, NJ, 24 Aug 1949). American composer. He studied composition with Paul Fetler and Dominick Argento at the University of Minnesota (BA 1971, MA 1974, PhD 1978). From 1973 to 1984 he was one of the managing composers of the Minnesota Composers Forum, an organization which he co-founded. He has served as composer-in-residence with the Minnesota Orchestra (1983–) and the Atlanta SO (1988–), and has completed commissions for Thomas Hampson, Evelyn Lear, Håken Hagegård and many others. His awards include Guggenheim Fellowships and a Kennedy Center Friedheim prize (1988).

A prolific composer, most of Paulus's works show the influence of Romanticism, employing a melodic style that can be considered tonal. *Quartessence* (1990), described by the composer as 'lyrical with angularity attached', extends the string quartet tradition. Several other compositions reflect Paulus's spiritual ideology. A play of 'light and shadow' forms multi-layered textures in the First Violin Concerto (1987), while a mystical journey from darkness to light is suggested in the Concerto for String Quartet and Orchestra 'Three Places of Enlightenment' (1995). The Concerto for Violin, Cello and Orchestra 'The Veil of Illusion' (1994), inspired by Shakti Gawain's *Living in the Light*, draws the listener through a 'veil' of materialism into a world of spiritual truth.

Paulus's operas, four of which were commissioned and first performed by the Opera Theatre of St Louis, Missouri, focus on ordinary people in small communities who become involved in intense dramatic situations. *The Village Singer* (1979) is set in New England around 1900, *The Postman Always Rings Twice* (1982) takes place on the California Coast in 1934, and *The Woodlanders* (1985) is set in a hamlet in England in 1870. *The Woman at Otowi Crossing* (1995) tells the story of an American woman poised between ancient Pueblo Indian culture and the modern scientific world. Both eerie and poetic, the most powerful moments in the opera are the heroine's encounter with the Amerindian spirit world. Paulus's music provides clear characterizations, as well as dramatic and lyrical expressivity, which can be heard in *The Postman Always Rings Twice* (1982) his most successful opera. Coloured by a lush, symphonic score, the work combines a well-structured libretto with relentless cinematic flow.

WORKS
(*selective list*)

Op (first perf. at St Louis, MO, Op Theatre unless otherwise stated): The Village Singer (1, M.D. Browne, after M.W. Freeman), 1979; The Postman Always Rings Twice (2, C. Graham, after J.M. Cain), 1982; The Woodlanders (3, Graham, after T. Hardy), 1985; Harmoonia (children's op, 1, Browne), 1991, Muscatine, IA, Central Middle Auditorium, 1991; The Woman at Otowi Crossing (2, J.V. Thorne, after F. Walters), 1995; Summer (2, J.V. Thorne, after E. Wharton), 1999, Koussevitzky Arts Centre, MA, 1999

Orch: Spectra, small orch, 1980; Translucent Landscapes, 1982; Conc. for Orch, 1983; 7 Short Pieces, 1984; Ordway Ov., 1985; Sym. in 3 Movts 'Soliloquy', 1986; Vn Conc., 1987; Concertante, 1989; Ice Fields, gui, orch, 1990; Sinfonietta, 1991; Tpt Conc., 1991; Voices from the Gallery, 1991; Org. Conc., 1992; Vn Conc. no.2, 1992; Conc. 'The Veil of Illusion', vn, vc, orch, 1994; Conc. 'Three Places of Enlightenment', str qt, orch, 1995

Choral: North Shore (Browne), S, Mez, Bar, SATB, orch, 1977; Songs and Rituals for the Easter and the May (Browne), S, Mez, SATB, chbr orch, 1977; Letters for the Times (17th-century Amer. newspapers, diaries), S, T, Bar, SATB, chbr ens, 1980; Jesu Carols, SATB, hp, 1985; Love Letters (letters by famous women), S, A, SSA, fl, perc, 1986; Madrigali di Michelangelo (Michelangelo), SATB, 1987; For All Saints (Julian of Norwich), SATB, org, 1990; Love's Philosophy (P.B. Shelley), SATB, 1992; 3 Songs (W. Owen), SATB, 1993; Meditations of Li Po (Li Bai [Li Po]), SATB, 1994; In Praise (Pss cxlviii, cl), SATB, handbells, org, 1995; Visions from Hildegard III (Hildegard of Bingen), SATB, fl, ob, hn, 2 tpt, trbn, tuba, timp, perc, org, 1996

Chbr and solo inst: Colors, brass qnt, 1974; Duo, cl, pf, 1974; Exploration, ens, 1974; Landmark Fanfare, brass qnt, 1978; Music for Contrasts, str qt, 1980; Dance, pf, 1986; Partita, vn, pf, 1986; Str Qt no.2, 1987; American Vignettes, vc, pf, 1988; Fantasy in 3 Parts, fl, gui, 1989; 7 Miniatures, str trio, 1990; Quartessence, str qt, 1990; Conc., brass qnt, 1991; Music of the Night, pf trio, 1992; Preludes, pf, 1994; Meditations on the Spirit, org, 1995; Toccata, org, 1996

Solo vocal: 3 Elizabethan Songs (Elizabethan poets), S, pf, 1973; Mad Book, Shadow Book 'Michael Morley's Songs' (Browne), T, pf, 1977; Artsongs (7 20th-century poets), T, pf, 1983; Letters from Colette, S, pf, str qt, perc, 1986; Bittersuite (O. Nash), Bar, pf, 1988; Night Speech, Bar, orch, 1989; The Long Shadow of Lincoln (C. Sandburg), B-bar, pf trio, 1994

Recorded interviews in *US-NHoh*

Principal publishers: European American, Carl Fischer, Kalmus, Schott, Universal

BIBLIOGRAPHY

A. Porter: 'Musical Events', *New Yorker* (25 June 1979)

M.A. Feldman: 'Triple Header', *ON*, xlix/17 (1984–5), 24–6

B. Cartland: 'Stephen Paulus and his "Postman"', *Opera Monthly*, i/10 (1989), 24–32

R.H. Kornich: *Recent American Opera: a Production Guide* (New York, 1991)

R. Markow: 'Paulus: Music of the Night', *Classical Music Magazine*, xviii/3 (1995), 25 only

ELISE KIRK

Paulus Abbas de Florentia. *See* PAOLO DA FIRENZE.

Paulus de Praga. *See* PAULIRINUS, PAULUS.

Paulus de Roda [de Rhoda, de Broda] (*fl* late 15th century). Composer. Compositions are attributed to Paulus de Rhoda in the Casanatense Chansonnier of about 1480 (*I-Rc* 2856) and in the slightly later Apel manuscript (*D-LEu* Cod.1494) one in each source. The Glogauer Liederbuch of around 1475–85 (formerly *D-Bsb* Mus.40098; now in *PL-Kj*) ascribes two other pieces, both untexted, to a 'Paulus de Broda'. Although there are few stylistic similarities between these pieces and the two credited to Paulus de Roda, the attributions would all seem to refer to the same person. Bibliographical support for that view comes from the Nikolaus Leopold manuscript (*D-Mbs* Mus.3154), which transmits the piece in the Apel manuscript (with a different Latin text, suggesting the work was conceived for instrumental performance) and one of the two pieces in the Glogauer Liederbuch, though both are without attribution. Paulus was probably identifiable with the 'Pauwels van Rode' who appears in the account books of the Confraternity of Our Lady (Illustre Lieve Vrouwe Broederschap) at 's-Hertogenbosch and the Guild of Our Lady at Bergen op Zoom; this supposition is buttressed by the fact that the piece in the Casanatense source bears a Dutch incipit. Van Rode was associated with the confraternity at 's-Hertogenbosch as early as 1471, and regularly recruited musicians for it. He was the successor of record to Obrecht as choirmaster of the Guild of Our Lady at Bergen op Zoom, a position he held from 1486 (or even as early as 1484) until 1489. He composed a requiem (now lost) that the confraternity at 's-Hertogenbosch paid to have copied in 1496 or 1497, and the brotherhood there celebrated a requiem for him in 1514.

Stylistically, Paulus's four extant works form a diverse group. They range in quality from the rather perfunctory and unimaginative compositions in the Glogauer Liederbuch to the impressive canonic piece in the Apel and Leopold manuscripts. Although Paulus had a penchant for imitative writing, he also exploited non-imitative textures and often deployed voices in parallel 3rds or 10ths. He articulated formal divisions with clear cadences but rarely varied the number of voices from one section to another. The canonic *Ave, salve, gaude, vale* is exceptional in that respect; it is a large-scale work that contrasts four-voice sections with alternating duos. It has been argued that, because of stylistic similarities with that work, two anonymous, untexted pieces in the Leopold manuscript are also by Paulus.

WORKS

Ave, salve, gaude, vale, 4vv, *D-Mbs* Mus.3154, ed. in EDM, 1st ser., lxxx (1987); in *D-LEu* Cod.1494 as Vulnerasti cor meum, ed. in EDM, 1st ser., xxxiv (1975)
Carmen, 3vv, *PL-Kj* (formerly *D-Bsb* Mus.40098) and *D-Mbs* Mus.3154 (expanded version); ed. in EDM, 1st ser., iv (1936) and lxxx (1987)
Ghenochte drive, 3vv, *I-Rc* 2856; ed. in Noblitt
Phfawin schwantcz, 4vv, *PL-Kj* (formerly *D-Bsb* Mus.40098); ed. in EDM, 1st ser., iv (1936)
Requiem, lost
2 untexted pieces, 4vv, *D-Mbs* Mus.3154; ed. in EDM, 1st ser., lxxx (1987); anon. in source, attrib. in Noblitt

BIBLIOGRAPHY

MGG1 ('Paulus de Broda'; L. Finscher)
A. Smijers: 'De Illustre Lieve Vrouwe Broederschap te 's-Hertogenbosch', *TVNM*, xiii/1–2 (1929), 46–100; xiii/3–4 (1931–2), 181–237; xiv/1–2 (1932–4), 48–105

T. Noblitt: 'Additional Compositions by Paulus de Rhoda?', *TVNM*, xxxvii (1987), 49–63
R. Wegman: 'Music and Musicians at the Guild of Our Lady in Bergen op Zoom, *c*.1470–1510', *EMH*, ix (1989), 175–249
R. Strohm: 'Instrumentale Ensemblemusik vor 1500: das Zeugnis der mitteleuropäischen Quellen', *Musik und Tanz zur Zeit Kaiser Maximilian I.: Innsbruck 1989*, 89–106

MARTIN STAEHELIN/THOMAS NOBLITT

Pauly, Reinhard G(eorg) (*b* Breslau [now Wrocław], 9 Aug 1920). American musicologist of German birth. He studied at Columbia University, where he took the BA in 1942 and the MA in 1947. Continuing graduate studies at Yale, he worked with Schrade and received the MMus in 1948 and the PhD in 1956. He joined the faculty of Lewis and Clark College, Portland, Oregon, as professor of music in 1948; from 1972 until his retirement in 1989 he was director of the college's music school.

Pauly's principal fields of research are opera and the sacred music of the late 18th century, especially Michael Haydn's church music and the effects on it of Joseph II's reforms. His brief general survey of the Classical period in the Prentice-Hall History of Music gives a particularly lucid account of the transition from the Baroque to the pre-Classical era. He was general editor of Amadeus Press from its origins in 1987 until 1998; he was also active as a translator for many of the Press's publications.

WRITINGS

'Benedetto Marcello's Satire on Early 18th-Century Opera', *MQ*, xxxiv (1948), 222–33
'Il teatro alla moda', *MQ*, xxxiv (1948), 371–401; xxxv (1949), 85–105 [Eng. trans. of B. Marcello: *Il teatro alla moda* (Venice, 1720/R)]
'Alessandro Scarlatti's "Tigrane"', *ML*, xxxv (1954), 339–46
Michael Haydn's Latin Proprium Missae Compositions (diss., Yale U., 1956)
'The Motets of Michael Haydn and of Mozart', *JAMS*, ix (1956), 67–9
'The Reforms of Church Music under Joseph II', *MQ*, xliii (1957), 372–82
'Some Recently Discovered Michael Haydn Manuscripts', *JAMS*, x (1957), 97–103
'Johann Ernst Eberlin's Motets for Lent', *JAMS*, xv (1962), 182–92
Music in the Classic Period (Englewood Cliffs, NJ, 1965, 3/1988)
Music and the Theater (Englewood Cliffs, NJ, 1970)
with B.W. Pritchard: 'Antonio Caldara's Credo a 8 voci: a Composition for the Duke of Mantua?', *Antonio Caldara*, ed. B.W. Pritchard (Aldershot, 1987), 49–76
with S. Buettner: *Great Composers, Great Artists: Portraits* (Portland, OR, 1992)

EDITIONS

Michael Haydn: Te Deum in C (1770) (New Haven, CT, 1961); *Timete Dominum* (New York, 1964)
Johann Ernst Eberlin: Te Deum and Magnificat (Madison, WI, 1971)
Antonio Caldara: Credo (Boston, 1986)

PAULA MORGAN

Pauly [Pauly-Dresden; née Pollak], **Rose** (*b* Eperjeske, 15 March 1894; *d* Kfar Shmaryahn, nr Tel-Aviv, 14 Dec 1975). Hungarian soprano. She studied in Vienna with Rosa Papier-Paumgartner, making her début during the 1917–18 season at Hamburg in a minor role in *Martha*. After singing at Gera and Karlsruhe, she went to Cologne, where she sang the title role in the German première of *Kát'a Kabanová* in 1922. She made her first appearance at the Vienna Staatsoper in 1923, singing Sieglinde, the Empress (*Frau ohne Schatten*) and Rachel (*La Juive*); in 1931 she created Agave in Wellesz's *Die Bakchantinnen*. Engaged at the Kroll Oper, Berlin (1927–31), she sang Leonore, Donna Anna, Senta, Carmen and Maria in Krenek's *Der Diktator*. At the Berlin Staatsoper she was acclaimed as Marie (*Wozzeck*), Jenůfa and Electra. She appeared at Salzburg as the Dyer's Wife (1933) and as Electra (1934–7), the role of her débuts in 1938 at Covent Garden (where Newman praised her dramatic intensity), and at the Metropolitan. Pauly was a most versatile singer, with a rich, powerful voice, and excelled as Strauss's Electra, Salome and the Dyer's Wife. She made few recordings, but extracts from *Elektra* give an idea of her compelling interpretation of the title role. (*GV*, L. Riemens; J.P. Kenyon and R. Vegeto)

LEO RIEMENS/ELIZABETH FORBES

Paumann, Conrad (*b* Nuremberg, *c*1410; *d* Munich, 24 Jan 1473). German organist, lutenist and composer. He was born blind, probably the son of an established craftsman family in Nuremberg, a free imperial town with a flourishing cultural life. The patrician Ulrich Grundherr, and from 1423 onwards his son Paul Grundherr, sponsored the talented but heavily handicapped young musician. Nothing specific, however, is known about his musical training. From at least as early as 1446 Paumann occupied the post of organist at St Sebaldus in Nuremberg, where the main organ had been built by Heinrich Traxdorff of Mainz in 1440–41. In 1446 he became engaged to Margarete Weichsler of Nuremberg. He undertook at that time not to leave the town without the permission of the town council. He was appointed official town organist in 1447.

He had by then already acquired a reputation as Germany's foremost organist. Hans Rosenplüt's poem eulogizing the town of Nuremberg (1447) praises Paumann as 'master of all masters', instrumentalist and composer as well. In 1450 Paumann broke his promise and left Nuremberg secretly for Munich, where he accepted a post as court organist of Duke Albrecht III of Bavaria. He had a salary and a house in Munich. Only through the intervention of the duchess, Anna, in 1451, was he absolved from his Nuremberg civic duties. He remained in Munich for the rest of his life, from 1460 serving under Duke Sigismund, and from 1467 under Albrecht IV.

From 1450 onwards Paumann visited many towns and countries, but only a few of his travels are documented. In 1454 at Landshut he played various instruments before Philip the Good of Burgundy. Travelling through Italy in 1470, the 'cieco miracoloso' declined attractive offers from the courts at Milan and Naples. At the court of the Gonzagas in Mantua, where his playing on various instruments caused a sensation, he was knighted and received valuable presents from princes. In 1471 he visited the Imperial Diet at Regensburg, and played the organ of the Schottenkloster before Emperor Friedrich III, the German princes of his suite, and a large crowd of notable listeners. As an authority on the organ he was often asked to examine new instruments (e.g. Salzburg, before 1464; Nördlingen, 1466 and 1472).

Paumann was buried at the south side of the Munich Frauenkirche where an epitaph, now inside the church below the loft, shows him with his instruments: portable organ, lute, recorder, harp and fiddle (see illustration); the inscription reads 'Anno 1473, on the evening of St Paul's conversion died and was here buried the most ingenious master of all instruments and music, cunrad pauman, knight, born blind at Nuremberg, God have mercy upon him'. His son Paul Paumann (*b* Nuremberg; *d* Munich, 1517), who had studied with his father,

Conrad Paumann: detail from his epitaph, 1473 (Frauenkirche, Munich)

succeeded him at the Munich court of Albrecht IV. Besides him, only Sebald Grave of Nördlingen is known as a direct pupil of Conrad, but the number of his students must have been large. The organ pieces of the fourth fascicle of the Lochamer Liederbuch, and also the bulk of the compositions in the Buxheim Organbook, can be identified as products of the Nuremberg and Munich Paumann schools.

Only a few of Paumann's works have survived, in four manuscripts from these two schools. Presumably Paumann's creative output consisted mostly of improvisations rather than worked-out compositions. Since his blindness prohibited him from writing down his own compositions, they could be recorded only from dictation. For this reason Virdung's attribution to him of the invention of German lute tablature (*Musica getutscht*, 1511) seems quite plausible, for it would have been particularly suitable for dictating music. The transmission of the *Fundamenta* is especially complicated because the extant sources reflect various stages of Paumann's didactic practices. The Buxheim Organbook contains two further, anonymous *Fundamenta* (ff.106*v*–8*v*, 124*v*–42*v*) which include concordances with those listed below.

Despite his very limited surviving output, Paumann must be considered the leading figure in 15th-century German instrumental music, known internationally not only as a virtuoso but also as a composer. Even in the 17th and 18th centuries he was still remembered as 'the very best organist' (H. Canisius: *Lectiones antiquae*, 1601–4) and 'in all musical arts the most expert and the most famous' (J. Staindl: *Chronicon generale*, 1763). His sole surviving vocal work, with its elegant melodic declamation and sophisticated contrapuntal texture, is clearly superior to the polyphonic songs of Paumann's German contemporaries and suggests his familiarity with Franco-Flemish music. All the Lochamer Liederbuch, Schedel Liederbuch and Buxheim Organbook transmit Franco-Flemish repertories among their German material. Paumann's organ works, settings of secular cantus firmi, are obviously the first of their kind to reflect the stylistic influence of the Burgundian chanson, especially with respect to the skilful handling of the three-part texture.

Characteristic of his organ style is the balancing of a highly ornamented discant, often using standard virtuoso figuration, and a solid tenor-countertenor basis. He deserves credit for refining the practice of the *Fundamentum* as a method of teaching organists. Though his *Fundamenta,* like earlier examples, still rely on formulae for their ornamental discants to given tenor patterns, they cease to be improvisation and become composition in the mature three-part pieces (e.g. no.5).

WORKS
VOCAL
Tenorlied, Wiplich figur, 3vv; facs. in EDM, 1st ser., lxxxiv, 1978

INSTRUMENTAL
Con lacrime, ed. B. Wallner, *Das Buxheimer Orgelbuch*, EDM, 1st ser., xxxvii (1958), 36
Jeloymors [Je loue amors], EDM, 1st ser., xxxviii, 262
Ich begerr nit merr, EDM, 1st ser., xxxvii, 138
Fundamentum magistri Conradi Pauman Contrapuncti, EDM, 1st ser., xxxix, 345
Fundamentum m.P.C.P., EDM, xxxviii, 234
Fundamentum organisandi magistri Conradi Paumanns ceci de Nürenberga anno 1452, ed. W. Apel, *Keyboard Music of the Fourteenth and Fifteenth Centuries*, CEKM, i (1963), 32
Fundamentum bonum trium notarum magistri Conradi in Nuremberg, CEKM, i, 52

BIBLIOGRAPHY
BertolottiM
F.W. Arnold and H. Bellerman: 'Das Locheimer Liederbuch nebst der Ars organisandi von Conrad Paumann', *Jb für musikalische Wissenschaft*, ii (1867), 1–234; pubd separately (Leipzig, 1926/R)
L. Schrade: *Die handschriftliche Überlieferung der ältesten Instrumentalmusik* (Lahr, 1931, enlarged 2/1968 by H.J. Marx)
O.A. Baumann: *Das deutsche Lied und seine Bearbeitungen in den frühen Orgeltabulaturen* (Kassel, 1934)
B.A. Wallner: 'Konrad Paumann', *Münchner Charakterköpfe der Gotik*, ed. A.-H. Bolongaro Crevenna (Munich, 1938), 21–36
J. Marix: *Histoire de la musique et des musiciens de la cour de Bourgogne sous le règne de Philippe le Bon* (Strasbourg, 1939/R)
T. Göllner: *Formen früher Mehrstimmigkeit in deutschen Handschriften des späten Mittelalters* (Tutzing, 1961)
F. Krautwurst: 'Konrad Paumann in Nördlingen', *Festschrift Heinrich Besseler*, ed. E. Klemm (Leipzig, 1961), 203–10
F. Krautwurst: 'Neues zur Biographie Konrad Paumanns', *Jb für fränkische Landesforschung*, xxii (1962), 141–56
C. Wolff: 'Conrad Paumanns Fundamentum organisandi und seine verschiedenen Fassungen', *AMw*, xxv (1968), 196–222
F. Krautwurst: 'Konrad Paumann', *Fränkische Lebensbilder*, viii (1977), 33–48
H. Minamino: 'Conrad Paumann and the Evolution of Solo Lute Practice in the Fifteenth Century', *JMR*, vi (1986), 291–310
D. Fallows: *A Catalogue of Polyphonic Songs, 1415–1480* (Oxford, 1999)

CHRISTOPH WOLFF

Paumgartner, Bernhard (*b* Vienna, 14 Nov 1887; *d* Salzburg, 27 July 1971). Austrian musicologist, conductor and composer. His father, Hans Paumgartner, was a writer on music and a friend of Bruckner, and his mother was Rosa Papier, a singer at the Court Opera. At an early age Paumgartner came into contact with the giants of Viennese music, including Bruckner, Wolf and Mahler. After a secondary education in the humanities he first studied law, in which he took the doctorate in 1911. He had already been an active musician (as conductor, horn-player, violinist and pianist) at school, and now studied musicology privately with Adler and was particularly influenced by Mandyczewski. His first professional appointment was as répétiteur at the Vienna Opera (1911–12). During World War I he was able to realize a project of his own: based in a military department called

'Musikhistorische Zentrale', he collected the songs of soldiers in the imperial multilingual army. In the course of this work, the results of which are lost, Paumgartner came into contact with Bartók and Kodály.

Paumgartner was subsequently director of the Salzburg Mozarteum (1917–38, 1945–59) and during his tenure this private institute was raised to the status of a state academy (1922) and Hochschule (1953). He found time outside his administrative work to run the conducting department and to be professor of music theory and history; one of his pupils was Karajan. Paumgartner initiated the summer courses that took place at the Mozarteum regularly from 1930, and in 1952 he founded the Camerata Academica, composed of both teachers and pupils, with which he made numerous concert tours and gramophone recordings.

Paumgartner was closely connected with the Salzburg Festival from its first year (1920), when he wrote and conducted music for Hofmannsthal's mystery play *Jedermann*; he composed music for numerous plays, organized performances of unfamiliar works by Mozart, made translations and arrangements, conducted orchestral concerts, serenades, church music, chamber concerts, and as an organizer was a major influence on the character of the festivals. In 1960 he became president of the Salzburg Festival, an office he retained until his death.

Paumgartner's first book was his biography of Mozart (1927), which was translated into many languages and was substantially expanded in its sixth edition; in collaboration with Otto Erich Deutsch, he published the letters of Leopold Mozart to his daughter (1936). He also wrote biographies of Schubert (1943) and Bach (1950) and studies on instrumental ensemble and the town of Salzburg. Many of his 140 published articles concern problems of historical performing practice. During World War II he did research in Florence on the history of musical relations between Italy and Austria, subsequently published in contributions to the first edition of *Die Musik in Geschichte und Gegenwart* and other publications. From 1923 his research was concentrated on Mozart.

Paumgartner edited a considerable amount of music for publication, mostly works of the Classical Viennese and Italian Baroque schools. His adaptation of Mozart's *Idomeneo* was performed in 1956 at the Salzburg Festival, and his version of Cavalieri's *Rappresentatione di Anima et di Corpo* was heard in a series of festival performances from 1968. His compositions include the opera *Die Höhle von Salamanca* (text after Cervantes, Dresden, 1923), the comic opera *Rossini in Neapel* (text by Hans Adler, Zürich, 1935), music for the stage, orchestral works, ballets and songs. Paumgartner was also a distinguished translator of operas (*Idomeneo*) and plays (by Goldoni, Molière and Beaumarchais).

WRITINGS
'Das Soldaten-Volkslied und seine Aufsammlung in der Musikhistorischen Zentrale des k.u.k. Kriegsministeriums', *Historisches Konzert am 12. Jänner 1918 im grossen Saal des Wiener Konzerthauses*, 28–31
ed., with A. Rottauscher: *Das Taghorn* (Vienna, 1923)
'W.A. Mozart: Adagio für Englischhorn, 2 Violinen und Violoncello', *Mozart-Jb 1923*, 147–54
'Der erste Prager Don-Juan-Darsteller Luigi Bassi', *Der Auftakt*, vii (1927), 113 only
Mozart (Berlin, 1927, enlarged 6/1967, 10/1993)
Salzburg (Vienna and Leipzig, 1935)
ed., with O.E. Deutsch: *Leopold Mozarts Briefe an seine Tochter* (Salzburg, 1936)

'Zur Aufführungspraxis Mozartscher Werke', *SMz*, lxxxi (1941), 321–8
'Der Dichter des Liedes KV 307', *Neues Mozart-Jb 1943*, 239–47
Franz Schubert (Zürich, 1943, 4/1974)
Johann Sebastian Bach (Zürich, 1950)
'Zu Mozarts Oboen-Concert KV 314', *MJb 1950*, 24–40
'Von der sogenannten Appoggiatur in der älteren Gesangsmusik', *Jahresbericht 1954–55 der Akademie Mozarteum*, 7–21; repr. in *Musikerziehung*, xxvi/4 (1973), 157–65
'Zur Darstellung älterer Musik', *ÖMz*, ix (1954), 310–14
'Die beiden Fassungen des Idomeneo', *Musica*, ix (1955), 423–9
'Johann Sebastian Bach und die Wiener Klassik', *BJb 1956*, 5–17
'Mozart, Master Dramatist', *Musical America*, xxvi/4 (1956), 4–5, 114–22
'Gedanken zum Salzburger Programm', *ÖMz*, xv (1960), 356–66
'Zur Erstaufführung von Mozarts Idomeneo im Neuen Festspielhaus', *ÖMz*, xvi (1961), 338–42
'Festspielregie in der Mozartstadt Salzburg', *Maske und Kothurn*, viii (1962), 120–31
'Mozart: Dichtung und Wahrheit', *ÖMz*, xvii (1962), 213–19
'Richard Strauss in der Schweiz', *ÖMz*, xix (1964), 379–85
'Von der sogenannten Werktreue', *Mozartgemeinde Wien, 1913–1963: Forscher und Interpreten* (Vienna, 1964), 150–55
Das instrumentale Ensemble von der Antike bis zur Gegenwart (Zürich, 1966)
Salzburg (Salzburg, 1966)
'Zum Crucifixus der h-moll-Messe J.S. Bachs', *ÖMz*, xxi (1966), 500–03
'Gustav Mahlers Bearbeitung von Mozarts Cosi fan tutte für seine Aufführung an der Wiener Hofoper', *Musik und Verlag: Karl Vötterle zum 65. Geburtstag*, ed. R. Baum (Kassel, 1968), 476–82
Das Kleine Beethovenbuch (Salzburg, 1968/R)
Erinnerungen (Salzburg, 1969)
'Vom Werden der Festspieloper', *ÖMz*, xxv (1970), 354–7
Vorträge und Essays (Kassel, 1972)

BIBLIOGRAPHY

E. Preussner, ed.: *Wissenschaft und Praxis: eine Festschrift zum 70. Geburtstag von Bernhard Paumgartner* (Zürich, 1958)
R. Wagner: 'Bernhard Paumgartners 50jährige Tätigkeit am Mozarteum', *ÖMz*, xxii (1967), 473–88
E. Werba: 'Bernhard Paumgartner und die Salzburger Festspiele', *ÖMz*, xxii (1967), 488–93
G. Croll, ed.: *Bernhard Paumgartner: Künstler und Forscher* (Salzburg, 1971) [incl. list of writings]
Obituaries: R. Klein, *ÖMz*, xxvi (1971), 516 only; F. Weigend, *Musica*, xxv (1971), 498–9

RUDOLF KLEIN

Paur, Emil (*b* Czernowitz [now Chernovtsy, Ukraine], 29 Aug 1855; *d* Frýdek-Místek, 7 June 1932). Austrian conductor, violinist and composer. After early studies with his father, the director of the Vienna Musikverein, in 1886 he entered the Vienna Conservatory, studying composition with Dessoff and violin with Hellmesberger. He became a member of the court orchestra in 1870, and from 1876 held conducting posts in Kassel, Königsberg, the Mannheim Hofoper (1880) and the Leipzig Stadttheater (1891). In 1893 he went to the USA, succeeding Nikisch as conductor of the Boston SO.

In 1898 Paur was elected music director of the New York Philharmonic Society in succession to Seidl, and in 1899 he succeeded Dvořák as director of the National Conservatory of Music in New York. He left both posts in 1902, returning first to Austria and then touring as guest conductor with many leading European orchestras. He conducted German opera at Covent Garden (1900) and in Madrid (1903) as well as in Berlin. His period as conductor of the Pittsburgh Orchestra (1904–10) raised it to international standards and introduced much new European and American music including works by Smetana, Goldmark, Rubinstein, MacDowell and Amy Beach; Paur's own symphony *In der Natur* was performed in 1909. Upon returning to Europe, Paur succeeded Carl

Muck as director of the Berlin Opera (1912) but resigned after a few months, remaining in Berlin as a concert conductor. His other compositions include a Piano Concerto in A (1909), a Violin Concerto, and chamber music.

BIBLIOGRAPHY

E. Kenny: 'Some Letters to Emil Paur', *Notes*, viii (1950–51), 631–49
R.F. Schwartz: 'Paur and the Pittsburgh: Requiem for an Orchestra', *American Music*, xii/2 (1994), 125–47

J.A. FULLER MAITLAND/MALCOLM MILLER

Pausa (i) (Lat.). In 15th-century keyboard music, a form of conclusion consisting of formulaic counterpoint over the long-held final note (*ultima*) of a section of the cantus firmus, before reaching a closing consonance. Octaves and 5ths frequently constitute the salient features of the figuration. This procedure was a part of organ-playing practice in the 15th century, the most extensive collections of examples being in Conrad Paumann's *Fundamentum organisandi* of 1452 (*D-Bsb* Mus.ms. 40613) and from his circle of pupils (*D-Mbs* cim.3526), and served to give structure to the course of the musical treatment of the cantus firmus by providing tonal resting places.

See also ORGAN POINT.

KLAUS ARINGER

Pausa (ii) (It., Sp.). *See* FERMATA, PAUSE and REST.

Pausa lunga. *See* LUNGA.

Pause. The sign of the corona or point surmounted by a semicircle showing the end of a phrase or indicating the prolongation of a note or rest beyond its usual value (often called FERMATA in the USA). In French, *pause* means a semibreve rest; in German, *Pause* means any rest.

Historically and in the most general sense, the pause is a sign for one part to pay attention to the others rather than to the beat, and to wait until everybody is ready before releasing or going on to the next note. It is used to mark the ends of phrases, sections or whole pieces, as in chorales, da capo arias, variations, etc; in canons only one of whose parts is written down, it may show where a leading part is to end or it may direct one part to hold and wait for the rest to catch up; in music for a soloist, a pause in the solo part may indicate that an improvised cadenza is called for, while the corresponding pauses in the accompanying parts show that they are to wait for the soloist to finish; in any music it may indicate a suspension of the beat, as in the allegro theme of Beethoven's op.111 or at high notes for the tenor in Italian operas. 14th-century examples of the pause may be found in Jo Cuvelier: *Se galass* and Franciscus: *De Narcissus* (CMM, liii/1(1970), 33 and 51). *See also* ORGAN POINT.

DAVID FULLER

Pautza, Sabin (*b* Calnic, nr Reşiţa, 8 Feb 1943). Romanian composer and conductor, active in the USA. After studying with Ciortea, Ion Dumitrescu, Negrea, Niculescu and Stroe at the Bucharest Academy (1960–65), he received a bursary to study at the Academia Musicale Chigiana in Siena with Donatoni and Maderna. Between 1966 and 1984 Pautza taught at the Iaşi Academy, then took the opportunity provided by a further study grant to leave Romania for the USA, where he found work as a lecturer at the Altan Institute, New York University (1985–8). In 1988 he became musical director and conductor of the Plainfield Symphony, and he has developed a successful conducting career in Europe and the USA. Pautza's work can be split into his Romanian and American periods. In the former he extended his musical language through improvisation, modal-chromatic techniques and the assimilation of elements of Romanian popular song. In the latter he has formed a synthesis of avant-garde influences which tends towards a simplicity of material. His scores, rich in substance and tension, characteristically explore the natural resonance of sound.

WORKS
(selective list)

Op: Another Love Story, 1980
Vocal: 4 Christmas Carols, chorus, 1966; Offering to the Children of the World, triple chorus, 1973; Canti prophani, children's chorus, orch, 1975; Columns (cant.), chorus, orch, 1978; Nocturnes, S, orch, 1980; Havku, 3 songs, S, orch, 1981; Light (cant.), chorus, orch, 1981; Missa brevis, S, chorus, 1982; Ebony Mass, solo vv, chorus, org, 1983; Sinfonia sacra, S, chorus, orch, 1991–2; Rita Dove Triptych, nar, S, orch, 1995
Orch: Seykylos Hymn, chbr orch, tape, 1969; 5 Pieces, 1972; Jocuri [Games] I, str, 1976; Jocuri II, 1978; Jocuri III, va/vc, orch/ens, 1979; Jocuri IV, vn, orch, 1980; Sym. no.1, 1982; Sym. 'In memoriam', 1984-6; Double Conc., va/vc, pf, orch, 1988–90; Sinfonietta, large orch, 1995
Chbr: Musica per 2, fl, pf, 1970; Laude, 10 insts, 1974; Str Qt no.1, 1976; Str Qt no.2, 1977; Str Qt no.3, 1979; 2 preludes, cl, pf, 1988; Trio no.1, str trio, 1991

OCTAVIAN COSMA

Pauwels, Jean-Englebert (*b* Brussels, 24, 26 or 29 Nov 1768; *d* Brussels, 3/4 June 1804). Flemish composer, violinist and conductor. His father, Jean Pauwels, was a bass singer and his elder brother, Jean-Joseph Pauwels, was a bass and a violinist at the royal chapel of the Austrian governor of the southern Netherlands. Jean-Englebert was a chorister at the royal chapel by the end of 1780; there he studied the violin with van Maldere and composition with Ignaz Vitzthumb. In 1788 he went to Paris and continued his composition studies with Le Sueur. He played the violin in the Théâtre Feydeau orchestra, and in 1790 became orchestra director in the Strasbourg Theatre. By 1791 or 1792 he was playing first violin in the Brussels Théâtre de la Monnaie where, in 1794, he became director of the orchestra. With Lambert Godecharle he founded the Société Concert des Grands in 1799; this became the best concert organization in Brussels before the establishment of the Conservatory concerts. According to Gregoir, Pauwels was not only a brilliant conductor but a remarkable violinist who became the point of departure for the Belgian violin school, whose members later included Vieuxtemps, C.-A. de Bériot and Alexandre Artôt.

Pauwel's music has not been studied extensively, but his contemporaries evidently thought highly of both his instrumental music and his stage works. According to Vander Linden, his instrumental pieces display graceful virtuosity and harmonic compactness, and his chamber music avoids theatrical effects. Fétis commented that, in spite of many strong sections and good musical organization, Pauwels's operas are hindered by their weak librettos.

Marie-Anne-Jeanne (or Jeanne-Catherine) Pauwels (1795–1839), a pianist and composer active in Brussels, was apparently unrelated to this family.

WORKS
printed works published in Brussels, unless otherwise indicated

STAGE
all first performed at Brussels, Théâtre de la Monnaie

La maisonnette dans les bois (oc, 1), 3 Aug 1796
L'auteur malgré lui (oc, 1, Claparède), 2 Nov 1801
L'arrivée du héros (scène lyrique, A. Verteuil) (*c*1803)
Léontine et Fonrose (oc, 4, Verteuil), 13 April 1804, ov. (n.d.)

OTHER WORKS
Sacred vocal: Messe solennelle, B-Bc; other masses in MS mentioned by Fétis
Secular vocal: 3 polonaises, S, orch (n.d.); Les deux amis, T, Bar, pf (n.d.); Air guerrier, B, pf (n.d.); Fétis mentions other works, incl. L'amitié, S, T, orch (n.d.)
Inst: Ier conc., vn, orch (n.d.); Ier conc., hn, orch (n.d.); 6 duos, 2 vn (Paris, n.d.); 3 quatuors dialogués, 2 vn, va, bc, op.2 (n.d.); other vn concs. and several syms. in MS mentioned by Fétis; Fl Conc., Pf Conc. mentioned in *Choron-FayolleD*

BIBLIOGRAPHY
Choron-FayolleD; *FétisB*; *MGG1* (A. Vander Linden); *VannesD*
E. Fétis: *Les musiciens belges*, ii (Brussels, 1849, 2/1854), 169–73
F. Faber: *Histoire du théâtre français en Belgique*, ii (Brussels, 1879), 194, 197; iv (1880), 148, 287, 335
E.G.J. Gregoir: *Les artistes-musiciens belges au XVIIIme et au XIXme siècle* (Brussels, 1885–90, suppl. 1887)
J. Isnardon: *Le Théâtre de la Monnaie* (Brussels, 1890), 101, 107, 109
C. van den Borren: *Geschiedenis van de muziek in de Nederlanden*, ii (Antwerp, 1951)

PHILIPPE MERCIER

Pavan [pavane, paven, pavin] (It. *pavana, padovana*; Fr. *pavane*; Ger. *Paduana*). A court dance of the 16th and early 17th centuries. There are hundreds of examples in the contemporary sources of consort, keyboard and lute music, among them some of the most inventive and profound instrumental compositions of the late Renaissance period.

The pavan was almost certainly of Italian origin. The earliest surviving source for it, Dalza's *Intabulatura de lauto* printed by Petrucci in Venice in 1508, contains five *pavane alla venetiana* and four *pavane alla ferrarese*, collectively described on the title-page as *padoane diverse*; both 'pavana' and 'padoana' are adjectives meaning 'of Padua', so the town presumably gave the dance its name. Some scholars, however, have suggested a derivation from the Spanish *pavón* (peacock) based on a supposed resemblance between the dignified movements of the dance and the spread of a peacock's tail.

The pavan was similar choreographically to the 15th-century bassadanza; it was sedate in character and was often used as an introductory, processional dance. A useful source of information on the dance is Arbeau, who gave the earliest account (1588) of the basic choreography:

The pavane is easy to dance, consisting merely of two single steps [*simples*] and one double step [*double*] forward, [followed by] two single steps and one double step backward. It is played in duple time [*mesure binaire*]; note that the forward steps begin on the left foot and the backward steps begin on the right foot.

As suitable music for the pavan, Arbeau gave a four-part setting of the popular song *Belle qui tiens ma vie* (later printed in Morley's *First Booke of Consort Lessons*, 1599, as *La coranta*) to be accompanied throughout by a repetitive minim–crotchet–crotchet drum rhythm (see illustration). He remarked that 'if you wish, you can have it sung or played in four-part harmony without dancing it'; he suggested that it might be played on 'viols, spinets, transverse flutes and flutes with nine holes, haut boys', and noted that the pavan was often used as a wedding march or 'when musicians head a procession of ... some notable guild'. A more complex choreography was given by Fabritio Caroso (*Il ballarino*, 1581), apparently intended for professional dancers.

As Arbeau prescribed, the music of a pavan is almost invariably in duple metre (two or four beats to the bar in

'Belle qui tiens ma vie', suggested by Arbeau as suitable music for the pavan, from his 'Orchésographie' (1588)

modern transcriptions) and usually consists of two, three or four sections of regular metrical structure, each repeated. Morley described the pavan as

a kind of staid music, ordained for grave dancing, and most commonly made of three strains, whereof every strain is played or sung twice; a strain they make to contain 8, 12, or 16 semibreves as they list, yet fewer than eight I have not seen in any pavan. In this you may not so much insist in following the point as in a fantasy, but it shall be enough to touch it once and so away to some close. Also in this you must cast your music by four, so that if you keep that rule it is no matter how many fours you put in your strain for it will fall out well enough in the end.

Not all composers followed Morley's rule of 'casting by four', that is, making the length of each strain a multiple of four semibreves. In the early 17th century asymmetrical phrase structures were particularly common, as, for example, in a keyboard pavan by Gibbons (ed. in MB, xx, 1962, no.16), where the number of semibreves in the three strains, each having a varied repeat, is 14, 13; 14, 14; 19, 20.

In both printed and manuscript sources for the 16th-century dance, the pavan frequently appeared as the first dance in a group, to be followed by one or more after-dances in faster triple metre; often these after-dances, or at least the first, were based on the melodic or harmonic material of the pavan. Italian sources generally labelled such after-dances 'saltarello', as in Dalza's collection, where the editor apparently thought the grouping of thematically related dances in the order pavan–saltarello–piva important enough to be mentioned in the preface ('tutte le pavane hanno el suo saltarello e piva'). Such widely distributed lute collections as G.A. Casteliono's

Intabolatura de leuto de diversi autori (1536) and the joint *Intabulatura … del Francesco da Milano et … Pietro Paolo Borrono* (1546) contain longer suite-like groups (called 'ballo' by Casteliono) in which the opening pavan is followed by three saltarellos, the first of which is melodically similar to the pavan. The most usual pairing later in the 16th century, particularly in northern Europe, was that of pavan and galliard, but it is probably true to say that most existing pavans are not linked to any other dance. Other early sources for the pavan include Hans Judenkünig's *Ain schone kunstliche Underweisung* (1523), containing one *Pavana alla veneciana* taken from Dalza; the *Dixhuit basses dances* for lute issued by the Parisian printer Attaingnant in 1530; and Luis de Milán's vihuela tablature *El maestro* (1536, containing some triple-time pavans). Some tempo indications in Milán's publication and in Alonso Mudarra's *Tres libros de musica en cifras para vihuela* (1546) suggest that the pavan was a fast or moderately fast dance. There is no doubt that, like many other dances, it became slower as time went on.

Early Italian keyboard dances, all anonymous, survive in a small Venetian manuscript of about 1530 (*I-Vnm* ital.iv.1227, ed. K. Jeppesen, *Balli antichi veneziani*, Copenhagen, 1962), with a linked pavan and saltarello, and in two fascicles from the collection at Castell'Arquato (*I-CARcc*) dating from about 1540 (ed. H.C. Slim, CEKM, xxxvii/1, 1975). The latter include 15 pavans each followed by a 'saltarello de la pavana', the two dances normally consisting of two variations on the same harmonic ground (*passamezzo moderno*, romanesca or *passamezzo antico*). The keyboard writing of these pieces is uncomplicated, with a decorative single line in the right hand supported by reiterative left-hand chords. Similar textures are employed in the earliest Italian publication of keyboard dances, the *Intabolatura nova di varie sorte de balli* issued by Gardano (1551). The single pavan in this collection, *Fusi pavana piana*, has sections of four and seven breves in length, each with varied repeat, a structure that distinguishes it from the tripartite *passamezzo moderno* and *antico* settings in the same book.

Solo instruments at this period would probably not have been suitable for accompanying dancing; the dances published for them were decorated versions of ensemble pieces, comparable in nature and function to the contemporary intabulations of chansons and motets. Surviving ensemble settings come mainly from France and the Low Countries until about 1570, and are generally in a simple, homophonic style with the tune in the top part. Lute and keyboard arrangements are sometimes elaborately 'coloured', and display idiomatic figuration of a kind often associated with later instrumental styles. Ex.1 shows the first strain of a pavan for four-part ensemble (superius only) from Attaingnant's *Six gaillardes et six pavanes* (1529–30), the first few bars of a keyboard pavan modelled on the same dance (upper staff only) from Attaingnant's *Quatorze gaillardes neuf pavennes* (1531) and the first few bars of the *Gaillarde sur la pavane* (upper staff) which follows immediately in the latter Attaingnant print.

Of the relatively few Italian ensemble dances extant from before 1560 (listed in Cunningham), about a dozen are of the pavan type, though none has the unambiguous title 'Pavana'. *La paduana del re* (in *GB-Lbl* Roy.App.59–62) is a true pavan with strains of 16, eight and eight

Ex.1

(a)

(b)

(c)

breves. On the other hand, the *Cortesa padoana* in Francesco Bendusi's *Opera nova de balli … a quatro* (1553) is an example of the triple-time PADOANA. By the mid-16th century in Italy the pavan was already giving place to the passamezzo, a similar dance in which the steps were more lively (according to Arbeau), with music usually constructed over a ground bass, either the *passamezzo antico* or the *passamezzo moderno*. In northern Europe the pavan remained popular, and music for it was adapted from many sources. For example, Susato's *Het derde musyck boexken* (1551) includes a four-voice pavan in three sections derived from Josquin's chanson *Mille regretz* and another based on Janequin's *La bataille de Marignan*.

The earliest surviving English pavans are probably the two in *GB-Lbl* Roy.App.58 (*c*1540), *The Emperorse Pavyn* (in triple time) and *Kyng Harry the VIIIth Pavyn* (ed. in MB, lxvi, 1995, nos.39, 41), both apparently three-part keyboard reductions of four-part consort pieces. The early Elizabethan manuscripts *GB-Lbl* Roy.App.74–6 (dances ed. in MB, xliv, 1979, nos.76–111) contain several consort pavans in a simple, homophonic style similar to that of contemporary collections on the Continent. Towards the end of the century, when the pavan as a dance was dying out, it was given a new significance as a musical form by English composers. Ex.2 shows the first strain of an anonymous pavan from the Dublin Virginal Manuscript (*IRL-Dtc*, *c*1570) in which the texture is elaborated by true counterpoint rather than by decoration of a homophonic original. This technique was greatly extended by Byrd, whose ten keyboard pavans in *My Ladye Nevell's Booke* (1591) display a degree of craftsmanship and an emotional weight unparalleled in

any earlier source. Until about 1625 the pavan continued to attract English composers, and examples for lute, keyboard and ensemble abound. Arrangements from one medium to another still occurred, but generally keyboard and lute examples existed in their own right, often exploiting the technique of the instruments to a considerable degree. Pavans for solo instruments normally included written-out varied repeat sections, unlike those for 'whole consort' which tended to be more restrained.

Many pavans have descriptive titles, often referring to technical features of the music, such as Byrd's *Pavan: Canon 2 in 1*, William Tisdale's *Pavana chromatica*, and the *Four-Note Pavan* by Alfonso Ferrabosco (ii), the upper voice of which consists entirely of repetitions of a four-note motif at different pitches and in different rhythms. Pieces called *Passamezzo Pavan* and *Quadran Pavan* are sets of variations on the *passamezzo antico* and *passamezzo moderno* respectively, and thus lack the usual tripartite structure. Other titles are indicative of mood, usually rather sombre, as suggested by Morley's description, such as Bull's *Melancholy Pavan*, Philips's *Pavana dolorosa* and Holborne's *Pavan: The Funerals*. Some pavans were apparently written in memory of recently deceased people, like those by Byrd and Gibbons in *Parthenia* (1612–13) dedicated to the Earl of Salisbury (*d* May 1612), but this is not true of all named pavans.

Relatively few English pavans were printed, but among the publications that include them are John Dowland's *Lachrimae, or Seaven Teares Figured in Seaven Passionate Pavans … for the Lute, Viols, or Violins, in Five Parts* (1604), Robert Dowland's *Varietie of Lute-Lessons* (1610), and the keyboard book *Parthenia*. Some pavans arranged for mixed consort were included in Morley's *First Booke of Consort Lessons* (1599). Perhaps because of the influence of such expatriate English composers as William Brade and Thomas Simpson, the pavan regained favour in 17th-century Germany as the first movement of consort suites by Peuerl, Schein, Scheidt and others. In Schein's *Banchetto musicale* (1617), for example, all the suites open with movements entitled *Padovana*.

In France, following an isolated keyboard pavan by Jacques Cellier of Reims, dated 1594 (see Ledbetter, frontispiece), there is a handful of examples written by

Ex.2

harpsichordists, among which Chambonnières' *Pavane L'entretien des dieux* and Louis Couperin's only pavan, in F♯ minor, are works of intense eloquence. 17th-century English examples include ten pavans by Tomkins that bear dates between 1647 and 1654, but these belong essentially to the virginalist tradition. The pavans that open some of Locke's suites, and the few independent examples by Purcell, are scored for two or three violins, bass viol and continuo, and retain the structure of three repeated sections. Such examples were becoming rare, however; Thomas Mace (*Musick's Monument*, 1676) defined both the form and its decline: '*Pavines*, are *Lessons* of 2, 3 or 4 *Strains*, very *Grave*, and *Sober*; *Full of Art*, and *Profundity*, but seldom us'd, in These our *Light Days*'.

Like other dance forms of the Renaissance and Baroque periods, the pavan has occasionally been reinterpreted by more recent composers. Delibes (*Airs de danse*, 1882) and Warlock (*Capriol Suite*, 1926) both composed pavans that quote Arbeau's music. Also based on a pre-existing work (from *Parthenia*) is Peter Maxwell Davies's *St Thomas Wake: Foxtrot for Orchestra on a Pavan by John Bull* (1969). The same composer's *Sir Charles [Groves] his Pavan* (1992) revives the idea of a pavan as a memorial piece.

Pavans by Fauré (op.50, 1887) and Ravel (*Pavane pour une infante défunte*, 1899; 'Pavane de la belle au bois dormant' from *Ma mère l'oye*, 1908–10) are justly celebrated, and all three exist in alternative scorings made by the composers. But the delicate gravity of Howells's 'De la Mare's Pavane' from *Lambert's Clavichord* (1926–7) could not be effectively transferred to any other instrument. This piece is very much in the Elizabethan spirit, 'cast by four' with a modest use of varied repetition and an undercurrent of polyphony; the overall form, however, is *ABA* rather than *ABC*. 20th-century pavans designed for actual dancing include the 'Pavane of the Sons of the Morning' in Vaughan Williams's *Job* (1930), and the Pavane in Britten's *Gloriana* (1953), which is the first of a group of dances accompanied by an onstage orchestra and woven into the dramatic action.

BIBLIOGRAPHY

BrownI

T. Arbeau: *Orchésographie* (Langres, 1588/*R*, 2/1589/*R*; Eng. trans., 1948, 2/1967)

T. Morley: *A Plaine and Easie Introduction to Practicall Musicke* (London, 1597/*R*); ed. R.A. Harman (London, 1952, 2/1963/*R*)

C. Sachs: *Eine Weltgeschichte des Tanzes* (Berlin, 1933; Eng. trans., 1937/*R*)

L. Messedaglia: 'La pavana, danza non spagnuola, ma padovana', *Atti e memorie della Accademia di agricoltura, scienze e lettere di Verona*, 5th ser., xxi (1942–3), 91–103

L.H. Moe: *Dance Music in Printed Italian Lute Tablatures from 1507 to 1611* (diss., Harvard U., 1956)

H. Spohr: *Studien zur italienischen Tanzkomposition um 1600* (diss., U. of Freiburg, 1956)

B. Delli: *Pavane und Galliarde: zur Geschichte der Instrumentalmusik im 16. und 17. Jahrhundert* (diss., Free U. of Berlin, 1957)

I. Horsley: 'The 16th-Century Variation: a New Historical Survey', *JAMS*, xii (1959), 118–32

D. Heartz, ed.: *Preludes, Chansons and Dances for Lute Published by Pierre Attaingnant, Paris (1529–1530)* (Neuilly-sur-Seine, 1964)

D. Heartz, ed.: *Keyboard Dances from the Earlier Sixteenth Century*, CEKM, viii (1965)

W.A. Edwards: *The Sources of Elizabethan Consort Music* (diss., U. of Cambridge, 1974)

C.M. Cunningham: 'Ensemble Dances in Early Sixteenth-Century Italy: Relationships with *villotte* and Franco-Flemish *danceries*', *MD*, xxxiv (1980), 159–203

J. Sutton: 'Triple Pavans: Clues to some Mysteries in 16th-Century Dance', *EMc*, xiv (1986), 175–81

D. Ledbetter: *Harpsichord and Lute Music in 17th-Century France* (London, 1987)

A. Silbiger: *Keyboard Music before 1700* (New York, 1995)

ALAN BROWN

Pavaniglia (It.). An instrumental dance which originated in the 16th century and became popular in Italy during the first half of the 17th. Its music had the fairly fixed melodic and harmonic structure shown in the lute version in ex.1. The chord progression is similar to that used in the earlier type of folia (*see* FOLIA, ex.2), and both are related to one of the main chordal schemes of the Renaissance dance style (*see* GROUND, ex.1*c*). Occasionally the VII chord in ex.1 is preceded or interrupted by IV, or the i chord in the ninth bar replaced by III. Cesare Negri (*Le gratie d'amore*, 1602) provided two examples, one like ex.1 entitled *Pavaniglia alla romana* and another, entitled *Pavaniglia all'uso di Milano*, which has the same harmonic scheme but a different melody moving generally a 3rd higher.

The earliest pavaniglias are those of Caroso (1581 and 1600) and Negri, both of whom gave the choreography for the dance together with the lute accompaniment. Most 17th-century examples are in Italian tablatures for the five-course Spanish guitar (beginning with Girolamo Montesardo in 1606), where they are sometimes followed by a *rotta della pavaniglia* in triple metre. Other early 17th-century examples of the pavaniglia include several for lute (the Bentivoglio manuscript at *US-SFsc* and *I-Fn* Magl.XIX 105 and 179), for discant and bass (*I-Bc* Q34) and for keyboard (*I-Fn* Magl.XIX 115 and 138 and the Chigi manuscripts in *Rvat*, ed. in CEKM, xxxii/2, 1968); there is also an example for instrumental ensemble by Gasparo Zanetti (1645). In addition, one source (*I-Fn* Magl.XIX 143) gives a text with the instruction 'parole sopra la pavaniglia'.

Several sources refer to the pavaniglia as a Spanish dance, and a relationship to the pavan is indicated by the fact that the same music occurs in Bull's *Spanish Pavan* in the Fitzwilliam Virginal Book, the pieces called *Pavane d'Espagne* by Arbeau (1588), Michael Praetorius (1612), Nicolas Vallet (1615) and Adriaen Valerius (1626), the

Ex.1 Fabritio Caroso: *Il ballarino* (Venice, 1581), *Pavaniglia* (upper- and lower-case Roman numerals indicate major and minor triads)

Pavana hispanica written jointly by Sweelinck and Scheidt, and two sets of *diferencias* on the *Pavana italiana* by Antonio de Cabezón. Most of the pavaniglia pieces are single statements of the music of ex.1, whereas many of the above pavans consist of elaborate sets of variations on the same music. English lute manuscripts of the late 16th and 17th centuries contain numerous examples of the 'Spanish Pavan', whose tune was sometimes used for singing broadside ballads. The beginning of the melody of ex.1 has a resemblance to the opening phrase of the chanson *Jay mis mon coeur*, which first appeared in Kotter's keyboard tablature of 1513.

BIBLIOGRAPHY

M. Dolmetsch: *Dances of Spain and Italy from 1400 to 1600* (London, 1954/R), 90–108

L.H. Moe: *Dance Music in Printed Italian Lute Tablatures from 1507 to 1611* (diss., Harvard U., 1956), 166–7; 249–51

H. Spohr: *Studien zur italienischen Tanzkomposition um 1600* (diss., U. of Freiburg, 1956), 3, 22–30, 69–73

D. Poulton: 'Notes on the Spanish Pavan', *LSJ*, iii (1961), 5–16

C.M. Simpson: *The British Broadside Ballad and its Music* (New Brunswick, NJ, 1966), 678–81

J.M. Ward: 'Apropos *The British Broadside Ballad and its Music*', *JAMS*, xx (1967), 28–86, esp. 75

G. Reese: 'An Early Seventeenth-Century Italian Lute Manuscript at San Francisco', *Essays in Musicology in Honor of Dragan Plamenac*, ed. G. Reese and R.J. Snow (Pittsburgh, 1969/R), 253–80

R. Hudson: 'The Concept of Mode in Italian Guitar Music during the First Half of the 17th Century', *ACM*, xlii (1970), 163–83

R. Hudson: 'The Music in Italian Tablatures for the Five-Course Spanish Guitar', *JLSA*, iv (1971), 21–42

R. Hudson: 'The Folia Melodies', *ACM*, xlv (1973), 98–119, esp.102

A. Silbiger: *Italian Manuscript Sources of the 17th Century Keyboard Music* (Ann Arbor, 1980), 39–44

J.M. Ward: 'The Relationship of Folk Music and Art Music in 17th-Century Spain', *Studi musicali*, xii (1983), 281–300

J. Sutton and F.M. Walker, eds.: *Fabritio Caroso: Nobiltà di Dame* (Oxford, 1986), 37–8; Eng. trans. as *Courtly Dance of the Renaissance*, ed. J. Sutton and F.M. Walker (New York, 1995), 158–61

RICHARD HUDSON

Pavarotti, Luciano (*b* Modena, 12 Oct 1935). Italian tenor. He studied in Modena with Pola and in Mantua with Campogalliani, making his début in 1961 at Reggio nell'Emilia as Rodolfo (*La bohème*) and quickly making an impression for his eloquent lyrical singing. In 1963 he sang Edgardo (*Lucia*) in Amsterdam and made his Covent Garden début as Rodolfo, returning as Alfredo, Elvino, Tonio (*Fille du régiment*), Gustavus III, Cavaradossi, Rodolfo (*Luisa Miller*), Radames and Nemorino (1990). In 1964 he sang Idamantes at Glyndebourne; in 1965 he made his American début at Miami, toured Australia with the Sutherland-Williams company, as Edgardo, and made his La Scala début as Rodolfo, returning for the Duke, Bellini's Tebaldo and Massenet's Des Grieux. At La Scala he also sang in a remarkable performance of Verdi's Requiem to mark the centenary of Toscanini's birth. He first sang at San Francisco in 1967 as Rodolfo, and the following year made his Metropolitan début, again as Rodolfo, later singing Manrico, Fernand (*La favorite*), Ernani, Cavaradossi, Idomeneus, Arturo (*I puritani*), Radames, Rodolfo (*Luisa Miller*, 1991) and the Italian Singer (*Der Rosenkavalier*).

Pavarotti had a bright, incisive tenor with a typically free, open, Italianate production and penetrating high notes. He made it a practice never to sing beyond his own means; and even when he tackled more dramatic roles such as Otello late in his career he never forced his fundamentally lyric tenor. Above all he had a directness of manner that went straight to his listeners' hearts. His voice and style were ideally suited to Donizetti, the early and middle-period works of Verdi (he was particularly admired as Alfredo and Gustavus III) and to Puccini's Rodolfo and Cavaradossi. His impassioned singing of Calaf's 'Nessun dorma' (*Turandot*) turned the aria into a bestseller, though in this role and some of the other heavier parts he essayed he arguably lacked the true *spinto* power.

Pavarotti's art is liberally preserved on disc and video, which give a true reflection of his voice and personality: no opera singer has understood better than he the new power of the media. He has recorded most of his major roles, some of them twice, and was one of the 'Three Tenor' combination (the others were Domingo and Carreras) of the 1990s that brought opera to an unprecedentedly wide public. His genial looks and generous, outgoing personality were ideally suited to that kind of phenomenon; indeed, it might well have not existed without his enthusiastic participation. Despite his enormous popular acclaim, Pavarotti has been anxious to preserve his reputation as a serious artist, and his voice retained its colour and vibrancy into his 60s.

BIBLIOGRAPHY

G. Gualerzi: 'Luciano Pavarotti', *Opera*, xxxii (1981), 118–24

L. Pavarotti: *My Own Story* (London, 1981)

M. Mayer: *Grandissimo Pavarotti* (Garden City, NY, 1986)

J. Kesting: *Luciano Pavarotti: ein Essay über den Mythos der Tenorstimme* (Düsseldorf, 1991; Eng. trans., 1996)

ALAN BLYTH, STANLEY SADIE

Paven. *See* PAVAN.

Pavesi, Stefano (*b* Casaletto Vaprio, nr Crema, 22 Jan 1779; *d* Crema, 28 July 1850). Italian composer. From 1795 to 1797 he studied with Piccinni in Naples. In 1797 he entered the Conservatorio di S Onofrio, just before it became part of S Maria di Loreto, and studied there until 1799 under Fenaroli. Expelled in that year of revolution because of his republican and Francophile ideals, he was deported to Marseilles and then went to Dijon, where he enrolled in the Italian regiment of Napoleon's army as a cimbasso player and took part in the Italian campaign. He left the army at Crema and completed his musical studies under Giuseppe Gazzaniga, who was *maestro di cappella* of the cathedral there. In 1803 in Venice, thanks to the protection of Gazzaniga, he staged his opera *Un avvertimento ai gelosi*, which in the next 20 years was followed by nearly 70 more, both *seria* and *buffa*. In 1818, he succeeded Gazzaniga as *maestro di cappella* at Crema and held the post until his death. From 1826 to 1830 he spent six months of each year as music director of the Hofoper in Vienna, succeeding Salieri.

Among the many opera composers who flourished in Italy between the last great masters of the 18th century and the advent of Rossini, Pavesi stands out for his strikingly individual musical personality. During the Napoleonic period the *Allgemeine musikalische Zeitung* acclaimed Pavesi as one of the five best composers in Italy. He had an original and lively melodic invention, supported by a mastery of the orchestra and polished craftsmanship that were perhaps learnt from Gazzaniga, a musician who had formed his style from a complex variety of European sources. His early symphonies are similar in style to late Haydn and Mozart; his best works are characterized by sparkling orchestration, unusual phrase structure, modal interchange and extensive development sections. Pavesi's opera *Ser Marcantonio* (1810), similar in subject to Donizetti's *Don Pasquale*, had 54 successive performances at La Scala and was taken up by the principal opera houses of Italy. *La fiera* (Florence, 1804) and *La festa della rosa* (Venice, 1808) also enjoyed great success, as did his last opera, *Fenella, ovvero La muta di Portici* (Venice, 1831).

WORKS

*c*68 operas, incl. La festa della rosa (G. Rossi), Venice, Fenice, 21 May 1808, *I-Mr**; Ser Marcantonio (oc, A. Anelli), Milan, Scala, 26 Sept 1810, *Fc*, *Mr*; Fenella, ovvero La muta di Portici (3, Rossi, after Scribe), Venice, Fenice, 5 Feb 1831, *Mr**
Other works: 1 orat; at least 5 cants.; songs, incl. Il Parnasso italiano (texts by P. Metastasio); masses; other sacred works, incl. Salmi, cantici ed inni cristiani del Conte L. Tadini posti in musica popolare dai maestri G. Gazzaniga e S. Pavesi (Crema, 1818); several syms., incl. C, Venice, 1805, B♭, ?Crema, 1818 (both pubd New York, 1982); 6 cembalo sonatas, *Nc*

BIBLIOGRAPHY

ES (M. Morini) [with detailed list of works]; *FlorimoN*; *GiacomoC*; *GroveO* (G.C. Ballola) [with complete list of operas]
AMZ, xi (1808–9), 370; xxii (1820), 446–7; xxxiii (1831), 53
F. Sanseverino: *Notizie intorno alla vita e alle opere del Maestro S. Pavesi* (Milan, 1851)
F. Florimo: *La scuola musicale de Napoli*, iii (Naples, 1882/*R*1969), 88–92
R.M. Longyear, ed.: *The Northern Italian Symphony, 1800–1840* (New York, 1982)

GIOVANNI CARLI BALLOLA/ROBERTA MONTEMORRA MARVIN

Pavillon (Fr.). The bell of a wind instrument, particularly of a brass instrument. The term dates from the Renaissance and derives from the bell's tent-like shape. *See* BELL (ii).

Pavillon chinois. *See* TURKISH CRESCENT.

Pavillon d'amour (Fr.). *See* LIEBESFUSS.

Pavin. *See* PAVAN.

Pavlenko, Sergey Vasil'yevich (*b* Sumï, Ukraine, 5 May 1952). Russian composer. He attended the Moscow Conservatory where he studied composition with Sidel'nikov and orchestration with Denisov (1972–7) and then undertook postgraduate studies there (1977–80). He then worked as music director at Yury Lyubimov's Taganka Theatre in Moscow (1976–82) and since 1982 has worked as a composer. He won first prize at the International Competition for works written for a saxophone ensemble (1988, Paris), and first at the 'Musique sacrée' competition (1995, Fribourg).

Pavlenko writes principally for instrumental forces and he rarely has recourse to the human voice. He adheres to the type of composition-drama that was widespread in Soviet music, striving to embody in a work the uniqueness of his ideas, a uniqueness which is often related to the character of the forces he chooses (in particular his predilection for wind instruments and especially saxophones) and to the contrast between the musical material and the manner of the development in large-scale forms. His attraction to symphonic forms is combined with a neo-Romantic language (Symphony no.4); in his chamber works – and particularly in the Symphony no.3 'Symfoniya prichetov' ('Symphony of Lamentations'), written for the 100th anniversary of Stravinsky's birth – the forces are handled in a way that reflects Stravinsky's style, whilst the writing comes close to the polyphony of Russian folk music.

Pavlenko does not restrict himself to any one method of composition, using on equal terms serial or aleatory techniques and tonality while always being sensitive to timbre and texture. His evolution has progressed in favour of a more traditional and simple language that abounds in melodic textures.

WORKS

Stage: Skripka Rotshil'da [Rothchild's Violin] (1, choreographic fantasy, after Chekhov), 1987
Orch: Sax Conc., 1975; Fl Conc., 1977; Vc Conc., 1979; Adagio, d, 1982; Sym. no.2, d, 1982; Sym. no.3 'Simfoniya prichetov' [Symphony of Lamentations], chbr orch, 1982; Vn Conc., 1983; Sym. no.4, 1985; Printsessa gryoz [The Princess of Dreams], sym. poem. 1994
Chbr and solo inst: 3 p'yesï [3 Pieces], db, pf, 1973; 4 p'yesï, cl, pf, 1974; Str Qt no.1, 1974; Pf Sonata no.1, 1975; Sonata, sax, pf, 1975; Liricheskaya poema [Lyrical Poem], fl, pf, 1976; Qnt, fl, cl, pf, vn, vc, 1976; Chbr Conc., ob, cl, hn, vn, va, vc, hpd, 1977; 4 p'yesï, bn, pf, 1977; Sonata, fl, 1977; Portretï [Portraits], fl, pf, 1978; Homage, bn, str, 1979; Pas de trois, fl, vn, pf, 1979; Pf Trio, 1979; Str Qt no.2, 1979; Variations, tpt pf, 1979; Conc. breve, 12 sax, 1980; James, cl, trbn, pf, 1980; Kontsert-serenada pamyati Vladimira Vïsotskogo [Conc-Serenade in Memory of Vladimir Vïsotsky], cl, str, 1980; Message, cl, 1980; Sonata-Continuo, b cl, 1980; Qt, 4 cl, 1980; Rozhdestvenskoye kaprichchio [A Christmas Capriccio], bn, str, 1980; Duo à tre, b cl, vib, mar, 1981; Pf Sonata no.2 'Fantasia quasi una sonata', 1981; Sonata, vc, 1983; Proshchaniye [Farewell], str, 1983; Orgelwerk, double fantasy with fugue, 1984; Intermezzo, a sax, hp, perc, 1985; Conc., ob, str, 1986; Kruzheva [Pieces of Lace], ww qnt, 1987; Pastoral', sax qnt, 1988; Retrospektsiya [Retrospection], perc ens, 1988; Conc., ww, perc, 1989; Posvyashcheniye [Dedication], ob, a sax, vc, 1989; Quasi toccata, hpd, 1989; Sinfonia humana, str, 1989; Trio-nocturne 'k pamyati Shopena' [In Memory of Chopin], fl, b cl, pf, 1989; Katzenmusik, 6–12 hn, 1990; Lara, cl, perc, 1990 [after M. Jarre's music for the film *Doctor Zhivago*]; Re Marcus, perc ens, 1991; Siren' [Lilac], cl, va, pf, 1991, after M. Vrubel'; Triversiya [Treversium], perc ens, chbr orch, 1991; Res facta, 4 vc, 1993; Ayvz-kompozitsiya [An Ives Composition], concerto no.2, 1993; Stansï [Stanzas], concerto no.2, s sax, chbr orch, 1994; V manere Gogena [In the Gauguin Manner], cl, vn, vc, pf, 1994; V podrazhaniye Denisovu [In Imitation of Denisov], bn, pf, 1994
Vocal: Vologodskaya svad'ba [A Vologda Wedding] (song cycle, trad.), 1973; Kantata pamyati Marinï Tsvetayevoy [Cantata in Memory of Marina Tsvetayeva], S, chbr orch, 1976; Kantata pamyati Osipa Mandel'shtama [Cantata in Memory of Osip Mandel'shtam], S, chbr orch, 1978; Syuita vodï [Suite of Water] (F. García Lorca), B, org, 1986; 2 Sonnets (P. Sydney), S, vc, org, 1988; Jesu redemptor ominium, anthem, S, chbr orch, 1995; Pesni bez slov [Songs Without Words] (P. Verlaine), S, cl, pf, 1996; Laguna (I. Brodsky), S, va, pf, 1996

BIBLIOGRAPHY

V. Yekimovsky: 'Sergey Pavlenko', *Musïka v SSSR* (1984), no.3
V. Barsky: 'Sergey Pavlenko na puti k prostoy muzïke' [Pavlenko on the path towards simple music], *Muzïka iz bïvshego SSSR*, ed. V. Tsenova and V. Barsky, i (Moscow, 1994), 272–82

SVETLANA SAVENKO

Pavlova, Anna (*b* St Petersburg, 31 Jan/12 Feb 1881; *d* The Hague, 23 Jan 1931). Russian dancer. *See* BALLET, §3(i).

Paxman. English firm of horn makers. It was founded in London as Paxman Bros. in 1919 by Harry (Henry Charles) Paxman (1894–1965) and two younger brothers, Bertram and William. Before World War II the firm sold and repaired musical instruments. In 1944 Paxman Bros. moved to new premises on Gerrard Street, where they continued to repair instruments and also built up a reputation for adapting and converting brass instruments to customers' specifications; a letter of 1948 from Dennis Brain testifies to the good work they had done in adapting a Raoux horn for him. Harry Paxman's eldest son Robert (*b* 1929) joined the firm in 1945 and it began to make horns modelled on the German instruments favoured by

British professional players, producing the first British-made rotary valve horn the same year. In 1959 the Australian horn player Richard Merewether introduced the firm to his new ideas on the physics and construction of the instrument; his descant horn in B♭ and F alto quickly found favour. In 1968 he produced a double horn in B♭ alto and B♭ soprano, designed to allow the modern player to cope with the high tessitura of Baroque horn parts; this instrument incorporated a new control valve, in which the windway diverges close to the mouthpiece, then converges in a chamber with a larger tube diameter at the point where the tubing begins to expand into the bell. The new system eliminated the coupled twin control valve previously used and allowed the longer instrument to be given a leadpipe with proper taper proportions. It was also used for Paxman's triple horn in F basso/B♭ alto/F alto, introduced in 1986. Since 1989 Paxman horns have been built with the bores of the cylindrical sections matched to the individual pitch length of each component of the double or triple horn: the triple horn, for example, uses bore diameters of 12·7 mm (F basso), 12 mm (B♭ alto) and 11·5 mm (F alto). The firm also manufactures a compensating double Wagner tuba in F and B♭ and copies of French hand horns from the Classical period. On Harry Paxman's retirement in 1961 Paxman Musical Instruments Ltd. was formed with Robert Paxman as director. The latter retired in 1995 and the firm was then taken over by a management team. In the same year the firm moved to Union Street.

CHRISTOPHER LARKIN

Paxton, Stephen (bap. Durham, 27 Dec 1734; d London, 18 Aug 1787). English composer and cellist. Like his brother William (b Durham, 8 Feb 1725; bur. Durham, 7 May 1778) and their nephew George (1749–79), he received his early musical training as a Durham chorister under James Hesletine. His arrival in London may have owed much to Spencer Cowper, dean of Durham (1746–74), and his brother, the 2nd Earl Cowper. In London Paxton became a pupil of William Savage 'for singing' and an early member of the band called upon by the Sharp family for their private concerts. 'A zealous and good Roman Catholic' (Argent, 28), he had some influence at the Sardinian Embassy Chapel, where his masses were frequently sung and where his nephew George was organist (before 1769–75). George was also a cellist and played at one Sharp concert and in the Drury Lane Theatre band. Stephen was elected a member of the Society of Musicians in 1757 (George was elected in 1772) and from 1780 was a professional member of the Noblemen's and Gentlemen's Catch Club. The brothers were noted as composers of glees (Stephen won four Catch Club gold medals; William two, both posthumous), and produced attractive and polished examples of the genre.

Stephen was active in London as a cello soloist and ensemble player for 30 years. Some of his instrumental works have been misattributed to William. This error apparently originated in Sainsbury's *Dictionary* (1824), which led to the London cellist being incorrectly identified as William. (Apart from visiting London for three months in 1751 William served as a Durham lay clerk from 1742 to 1778, was well known as a concert performer in Durham and Newcastle, and sang at Handel performances in York in 1769.) Stephen was one of the four principal cellists at the Handel Commemoration in Westminster Abbey (1784) and at other festivals there in aid of the Society of Musicians (1786–7). Among his activities outside London, he played at Hertford in July 1757, played and sang at Newcastle in August 1772 and was called upon when a new concert room was opened in Manchester in September 1776.

As a cello composer Stephen ranked second in England only to James Cervetto. His fluent and graceful melodic style, recalling that of J.C. Bach, is particularly notable in his op.1 cello sonatas, which include some expressive slow movements with elaborate, finely worked, *galant* lines. Although the op.3 *Easy Solos* are technically more assured than op.1, their interest is diminished by the simplicity of style. This is also true of the op.4 solos, and the op.6 *Lessons* are light to the point of triviality. Several works in these later sets incorporate national airs or well-known movements by Handel. The ducts for violin and cello show a similar falling-off; the op.4 duets include nothing as striking as the sonorous scoring of no.3 or the rhythmic vitality of the C minor first movement of no.5 in op.2. This tendency towards a simpler, more popular style, to be seen in Paxton's instrumental works, is characteristic of the development of English instrumental music during the 1770s and 80s.

WORKS
all published in London

op.
1	6 Solos, vc, b (1772)
2	8 Duets, with a Scots air and variations (vn, vc)/2 vc (by 1775)
3	6 Easy Solos, vc/bn, b (c1778)
4	4 Duets, vn, vc; 2 Solos, vc, b (c1780)
5	A Collection of Glees, Catches etc., 3, 4vv (c1782), 19 items, 5 by William Paxton
6	12 Easy Lessons, vc, b (1786)
—	Cello Concerto (c1787)
7	A Selection of 2 Songs, 6 Glees and 2 Catches (c1789)
—	19 glees, odes and catches in A Collection of Catches, ed. E.T. Warren, 1763–95; others in anthologies, single editions and MSS (*GB-Lbl*, *A-Wn*)
—	2 masses, D (incl. Tantum ergo), G, and Domine salvum fac in A Collection of Masses, ed. S. Webbe (1792); Mass, lost

Hymn, Praise ye the Lord, *GB-DRc*; The moon in saffron drest (in W. Shield, *Rosina*, 1782); March, 2 vn, 2 ob, 2 hn, b, lost

BIBLIOGRAPHY

BDA; *EitnerQ*

E.E. Reynolds, ed.: *The Mawhood Diary: Selections form the Diary Notebooks of William Mawhood, Woollen-Draper of London, for the Years 1764–1790* (London, 1956)

S. Sadie: *British Chamber Music, 1720–1790* (diss., U. of Cambridge, 1958)

M. Argent, ed.: *Recollections of R.J.S. Stevens* (London, 1992)

Calendar of London Concerts 1750–1800 (Goldsmiths College, U. of London; S. McVeigh) [restricted-access database]

B. Crosby: 'Stephen and Other Paxtons: an Investigation into the Identities and Careers of Four 18th-Century Musicians', *ML* (forthcoming)

BRIAN CROSBY, STANLEY SADIE

Paxton, William. English composer, brother of STEPHEN PAXTON.

Pay, Antony (Charles) (b London, 21 Feb 1945). English clarinettist. He studied with Wilfred Kealey and John Davies, and made his début at the age of 16 playing Mozart's Clarinet Concerto on a European tour with the National Youth Orchestra. He was principal clarinet with the RPO from 1968 to 1978, and from 1968 to 1983 with the London Sinfonietta, with which he gave the first performance of Henze's *The Miracle of the Rose* (1982).

He was also principal clarinet with the Academy of St Martin-in-the-Fields, 1976–86, the Academy of Ancient Music, 1983–94, and, from 1986, the Orchestra of the Age of Enlightenment. From 1986 to 1993 he played with the Nash Ensemble. Pay has appeared frequently as a soloist, and in concertos often conducts from the clarinet. His extensive discography includes the concertos of Mozart, Weber and Crusell, which he plays on reconstructions of period instruments, much chamber music and Berio's Concertino, conducted by the composer. He taught at the GSM from 1982 to 1990, and gives masterclasses throughout the world.

PAMELA WESTON

Payen, Nicolas [Colin] (*b* Soignies, *c*1512; *d* Madrid, after 24 April 1559). South Netherlandish composer. According to Fétis, Payen received his earliest musical education at St Vincent's, Soignies, before becoming a choirboy in Charles V's chapel in Spain. Payen's name is mentioned there from 1525 and appears in the prebendal lists for Mons and Gorinchem. During the 1530s he may have interrupted his service with the emperor for university studies. From 1540 he was in Charles's chapel as *clerc d'oratoire*, *chapelain des hautes messes*, and from 1556 as *maestro de capilla*, succeeding Canis. In 1558 he was granted a canonry in the collegiate church of Tournai and at the time of his death he held numerous prebends. Very little research has been done on Payen's music. Most of his works are sacred, and the two extant state motets show his concern for expressing the emotional content of the texts. In negotiations with the Duke of Bavaria, the imperial vice-chancellor Dr Seld named Payen among the representatives of *musica reservata*.

WORKS
MOTETS

Benedictus Dominus, 5vv, 1554[11]; Carole cur defles, 4vv, 1545[2] (on death of Queen Isabella); Confitemur dilecta nostra, 4vv, 1548[2]; Convertemini ad me, 4vv, 1548[2]; Domine demonstrasti mihi, 4vv, 1548[2]; Domine Deus salutis, 4vv, 1548[2]; Eripe me de inimicis, 4vv, 1554[11]; In Gott gelaub ich das er hat, 4vv, 1544[21], ed. in DDT, xxxiv (1908/R); Nisi quia Dominus, 4vv, 1553[6]; Quis dabit capiti, 4vv, 1547[6] (state motet); Resurrectio Christi, 5vv, 1546[7]

CHANSONS

Avecque vous, 4vv, 1544[10]; Fringotes jeune fillettes, 4vv, 1538[19] (lute intabulation 1546[32]); Hau de par Dieu, 4vv, 1538[19]; Il y a de lagnon, 1538[19] (lute intabulation 1548[12]); Je ne me puis tenir, 4vv, 1543[13]

BIBLIOGRAPHY

AmbrosGM; FétisB

A. Sandberger: *Beiträge zur Geschichte der bayerischen Hofkapelle unter Orlando di Lasso*, iii (Leipzig, 1895/R)

A. Demeuldre: *Le chapitre de Saint-Vincent à Soignies* (Soignies, 1902)

J. Schmidt-Görg: *Nicolas Gombert* (Bonn, 1938/R)

M. van Crevel: *Adrianus Petit Coclico* (The Hague, 1940)

H. Anglès: *La musica en la corte de Carlos V* (Barcelona, 1944)

A. Dunning: *Die Staatsmotette 1480–1555* (Utrecht, 1970)

ALBERT DUNNING

Payne, Anthony (Edward) (*b* London, 2 Aug 1936). English composer and critic. He was educated at Dulwich College, London, and the University of Durham, and worked as a music critic first on the *Daily Telegraph*, later on *The Independent*. In 1983 he was visiting Milhaud Professor at Mills College, California, and has since taught composition at the London College of Music (1983–6), the New South Wales Conservatorium (1986) and the University of Western Australia (1996). Although he had written music as a child, the start of his professional composing career dates only from 1965. With remarkable surefootedness, he developed a technique loosely derived from various numerical systems that were increasingly linked to the more musical concept of interval size. All the works of this period embrace both the textural implications of widely spaced harmonies and the more reflective tensions of melodic lines set within a rhythmic framework that alternates the strictly defined and the proportionately indicated. The already more relaxed charm of *A Day in the Life of a Mayfly* (1981) marks a stylistic turning-point that enabled Payne to pick up the threads of an Englishness he had earlier forced himself to deny.

From this point on he began to evolve a kind of 'modernized nostalgia' which he has made recognizably his own and which enables the stylistic developments of the 1980s and 90s now to be understood as the reverse reflection of a period in which the works of the 1960s – such as the *Phoenix Mass* (1965, rev. 1972) and *Paraphrases and Cadenzas* (1969, rev. 1978) – were brought into line with the 1970s developments of a post-avant-garde modernism. Later, a quite different kind of rebirth saw the abandoned sketches for a work first conceived in the late 1950s being put to confident and touchingly autobiographical purpose in *The Spirit's Harvest* (1985), his first work for full symphony orchestra and the first openly to acknowledge his English heritage. But Payne is first and foremost a composer of chamber music, and it is his long list of works for variously-constituted chamber ensembles, both with and without voices, that most clearly trace the imaginative course of his musical journey over the last three decades. He married the soprano Jane Manning in 1966.

WORKS
ORCHESTRAL

Suite from a Forgotten Ballet, 1955, rev. 1985; Contrapuncti, solo str qt, str orch, 1958, rev. 1979; Conc. for Orch, 1974; Song of the Clouds, solo ob, 2 hn, perc, str orch, 1979–80; Spring's Shining Wake, 1980–81; Songs and Seascapes, str orch, 1984; The Spirit's Harvest, 1985; Half-Heard in the Stillness, 1987; Time's Arrow, 1989–90; Symphonies of Wind and Rain, 1991; Hidden Muisc, 1992; Orchestral Variations: the Seeds Long Hidden, 1992–4

BRASS

Fire on Whaleness, brass band, perc, 1975–6; Fanfares and Processional, hn, 4 tpt, 4 trbn, tuba, 1986; Echoes of Courtly Love, hn, tpt, flugel hn, trbn, tuba, 1987; River-race, 4 hn, 4 tpt, 4 trbn, tuba, perc, 1990

CHAMBER AND SOLO INSTRUMENTAL

Paraphrases and Cadenzas, cl, va, pf, 1969, rev. 1978; Sonatas and Ricercars, fl, ob, cl, bn, hn, 1970–71; Paean, pf, 1971; Str Qt, 1978; Footfalls Echo in the Memory, vn, pf, 1978; The Stones and Lonely Places Sing, fl + pic, cl + b cl, hn, pf, vn, va, vc, 1978–9; Miniature Variations on a Theme of E.L., pf, 1980; A Day in the Life of a Mayfly, fl + pic, cl, perc, pf, vn, vc, 1981; Reflections in the Sea of Glass, org, 1983; The Song Streams in the Firmament, cl, 2 vn, va, vc, db, 1986; Consort Music, 2 vn, 2 va, vc, 1987–8; A 1940s Childhood, fl, gui, 1986–7, arr. fl, hp, 1989; Sea-Change, fl, cl, hp, 2 vn, va, vc, 1988; Amid the Winds of Evening, va, 1987; The Enchantress Plays, bn, pf, 1990; Empty Landscape – Heart's Ease, ob, cl, hn, vn, va, vc, 1994–5; Engines and Islands, fl, cl, perc, pf, vn, va, vc, 1996

VOCAL AND CHORAL

Phoenix Mass, SATB, 3 tpt, 3 trbn, 1965, rev. 1972; Two Songs without Words, 5 male vv, 1970; A Little Passiontide Cant (14th-century Eng.), SATB, 1974, rev. 1984; First Sight of Her and After (T. Hardy), 16 solo vv, 1975; The World's Winter (A. Tennyson), S, fl + pic, ob, cl, 1976; The Sea of Glass (Bible: *Revelations*), SATB, org, 1977; A Little Ascension Cant (attr. Cynewulf), SATB, 1977, rev. 1984; A Little Whitsuntide Cant (E. Bronte), SATB, 1977, rev. 1984; Evening Land (P. Lagerkvist), S, pf, 1980–81; A Little Christmas Cant (trad. carol texts), SATB, 1893

Alleluias and Hockets (after Machaut), SATB, 2 ob, eng hn, 2 bn, 2 tpt, 3 trbn, 1987; Adlestrop (E. Thomas), S, pf, 1989; First Sight of Her and After (Hardy), SATB, ob, cl, bn, hn, perc, vn, va, vc, db, arr. 1988; Aspects of Love and Contentment (8 Songs of Peter Warlock), S, fl, ob, cl, hn, hp, str qt, 1991; Break, break, break (Tennyson), SATB, 1996

OTHER

Fresh Dances for the Late Tchaikovsky (ballet), 2 vn, 2 va, 2 vc, pf 4 hands, 1993; Completion of Elgar's Sym. no.3, 1993–7

Principal publisher: Chester

WRITINGS

Schoenberg (London, 1968)
'Frank Bridge', *Tempo*, no.106 (1973), 18–25; no.107 (1973–4), 11–18
with L. Foreman and J. Bishop: *The Music of Frank Bridge* (London, 1976)
'Bax, Arnold', 'Bridge, Frank', 'Delius, Frederick', *Grove6*
Frank Bridge: Radical and Conservative (London, 1984)
'Englands zweite Renaissance in der Musik', *ÖMz*, xli (1986), 149–54
'Britten and the String Quartet', *Tempo*, no.163 (1987), 2–6
Numerous articles and reviews in *Tempo* and other journals

BIBLIOGRAPHY

S. Bradshaw and R.R. Bennett: 'Anthony Payne and his "Paean"', *Tempo*, no.100 (1972), 40–44
B. Northcott: 'Anthony Payne', *MT*, cxvi (1975), 36–8
M. Oliver: 'Miscellany', *British Music Now*, ed. L. Foreman (London, 1975), 162–77, esp. 169–71
S. Bradshaw: 'Anthony Payne's String Quartet', *Tempo*, no.128 (1979), 33 only
B. Northcott: 'Payne's Pleasure', *The Independent* (2 Aug 1996)
S. Johnson: 'Elgar/Payne', *Tempo*, no. 204 (1998), 4 only

SUSAN BRADSHAW

Payne, Jack (*b* Leamington Spa, 22 Aug 1899; *d* Tonbridge, 4 Dec 1969). English pianist and dance bandleader. He formed his first band during his World War I service in the Royal Flying Corps, and subsequently led his own small jazz group, in which he played piano. He worked in various Birmingham bands until moving to London in 1925, where he took over the band at the Hotel Cecil. He broadcast with this group from 1925, and recorded from 1927, ultimately enlarging it to ten players, and becoming conductor and singer himself, with Bob Busby as pianist. In 1928, as Director of Dance Music, he took over the BBC Dance Orchestra, with whom he broadcast almost daily, and made numerous recordings for Columbia. The orchestra also undertook theatrical bookings after appearing at the London Palladium in 1930, changing its name in the process to Jack Payne and His Orchestra. Like Jack Hylton, Payne was one of the first bandleaders to acquire popularity through broadcasting, and on leaving the BBC in 1932 he led a successful show band for most of the 1930s and during World War II. He toured South Africa in 1936, and returned to the BBC to direct its dance band (1941–6). His broadcasts and recordings are characterized by his own lightweight vocals, those of his guitarist Billy Scott-Coomber and those of his close harmony trio. His band's arrangements were immensely popular in their day, but lacked the jazz feeling of those by Hylton or Lew Stone. Payne also became a theatrical agent, concentrating on this after the war, as well as having a career as a radio presenter. He did not return to bandleading after 1947, and his last years were beset by financial difficulties. He played himself in the 1932 film *Say it with Music* (the theme which became his signature tune), and his band was one of several groups that appeared in *Sunshine Ahead* (1936). Payne was married to the pianist Peggy Cochrane.

BIBLIOGRAPHY

J. Payne: *This is Jack Payne* (London, 1932)
J. Payne: *Signature Tune* (London, 1947)
A. McCarthy: *The Dance Band Era* (London, 1971)
B. Rust: *The Dance Bands* (London, 1972)
P. Cochrane: *We Said It With Music* (Bognor Regis, 1979)
J. Chilton: *Who's Who of British Jazz* (London, 1997)

ALYN SHIPTON

Payne, Maggi (*b* Temple, TX, 23 Dec 1945). American composer, flautist and video artist. She studied the flute with Walfrid Kujala and composition with Alan Stout, William Karlins and Theodore Ashford at Northwestern University (BMus 1968). After a brief period at Yale University (1969), she continued her studies at the University of Illinois (MM 1970) with Gordon Mumma, Ben Johnston, Salvatore Martirano and James Beauchamp. Further postgraduate study in electronic music and recording media at Mills College (MFA 1972) led to posts there as recording engineer, assistant professor and co-director of the college's Center for Contemporary Music. Her honours include grants from the NEA and the Mellon Foundation.

Payne composes primarily for electronic tape. Her music often draws on sound sources from the physical world, particularly urban sounds recorded in the San Francisco area (*Airwaves (realities*, 1987; *Resonant Places*, 1992; *Liquid Metal*, 1994). She also frequently combines tape music with visual elements, such as dance (in several collaborations with video artist Ed Tannenbaum) and electronically manipulated video images of natural phenomena, such as moving water or desert landscapes. Several other works are based on flute sounds that have been extensively transformed into unexpected timbres and textures. A great sensitivity to spatial effects is also characteristic of her work.

WORKS

STAGE

Dance scores (all for tape): House Party (choreog. C. Brown), 1974; Synergy II (choreog. Brown), 1974; Inventory (choreog. M. Sakamoto), 1980; Rondo (choreog. B. Kagan), 1984; The Living Room (choreog. N. Bryan), 1987
Other: The Winter's Tale (incid music, W. Shakespeare), 1975

TRADITIONAL MEDIA

Inflections, fl, 1968; Songs of Flight (G. Snyder), S, pf, 1988; Desertscapes (M. Payne), 2 choruses, 1991; Minutia 0–13, 1–3 pf, 1996

ELECTRO-ACOUSTIC AND MULTIMEDIA

Video scores (all for tape, dir. E. Tannenbaum): 3 Movts with 2 Movts, 1982; Maytricks, 1983; Dance, 1984; Hikari, 1984; Contest, 1985; Gamelan, 1985; Hands, 1985; Shimmer, 1985; Back to Forth, 1986; Flights of Fancy (Viscous Meanderings), 1987; Ahh-Ahh (Queue the Lizards), 1987; Heavy Water, 1991; Close-ups, 1999
Video scores (all for tape, dir. M. Payne): Circular Motions, 1981; Crystal, 1982; Io, 1982; Solar wind, tape, video/slide projections, 1983; Airwaves (realities), 1987; Liquid Metal, 1994; Apparent Horizon, 1996
Tape and slide projections: Farewell, 1975; Transparencies, 1976; Spheres, 1977; Spirals, 1977; Lunar Earthrise, 1978; Lunar Dusk, 1979; Blue Metallics, tape, slide projections/film, 1980; Rising, tape, slide projections, opt. dancers, 1980; Ling, 1981
Other (tape unless otherwise stated): Ametropia, 1970, HUM, fl, tape, 1973; Orion (film score), 1973; VDO (film score), 1973; Allusions, dancers, tape, 16mm film, lighting, 1974; Scirocco, fl, tape, 1983; White Night, 1984; Subterranean Network, 1986; Phase Transitions, 1989; Resonant Places, 1992; Aeolian Confluence, 1993; Moiré, 1995; Raw data, 1998

BIBLIOGRAPHY
B. Demetz: 'New Faces', *Ear*, xii/6 (1987), 23
K. Gann: 'Medium Rare', *Village Voice* (27 Oct 1987), 96
G. Borchert: 'American Women in Electronic Music, 1984–94',
    CMR, xvi/1–2 (1997), 89–97

GAVIN BORCHERT

Pāyvar, Farāmarz (*b* Tehran, 1932). Persian *santur* player and composer. He comes from a musical family and for six years, from the age of 17, studied the *santur* with Abolhasan Sabā, followed by further training with other masters of Persian traditional music. Pāyvar has combined a career as a virtuoso performer and composer with scholarship which has yielded a number of significant publications. They include original compositions as well as arrangements and books on the technique of *santur*. His recordings, published both in Persia and abroad, are numerous. They encompass recordings of some of the *dastgāh*s with the inclusion of all known *guše*s, also shorter renditions of *dastgāh*s, original compositions and ensemble pieces written or arranged by him. He has travelled widely and is known internationally for his many concerts and recordings.

Pāyvar has a thorough knowledge of the *radif* of Persian traditional music. He has advanced the technique of *santur* playing to levels not attained by any other *santur* player. His performances of any given *dastgān* generally display exceptional agility and smoothness of hammer action on the *santur*, use of a wide range of sound, and the interpolation of difficult and lengthy composed *čahārmesrāb*s. On the other hand, his performance style is peppered with features of western virtuoso displays such as rapid scale movements, arpeggio patterns and passages in parallel thirds, all of which are essentially alien to Persian music.

HORMOZ FARHAT

Paz, Juan Carlos (*b* Buenos Aires, 5 Aug 1901; *d* Buenos Aires, 25 Aug 1972). Argentine composer and theorist. He studied in Buenos Aires with Roberto Nery (piano) and with Gaito and Fornarini (composition); then, after organ lessons with Jules Beyer, he studied with d'Indy at the Schola Cantorum, Paris. But essentially he was self-taught in composition, and he remained an independent and isolated figure. An enthusiasm for new musical developments brought him, together with his contemporaries Juan José and José María Castro, Gilardi and Ficher, to form the Grupo Renovación (1929). Their aims were to seek out and utilize the latest compositional trends and to give wider currency to their work. Through this they gave a beneficial jolt to Argentine musical life, encouraging constructive criticism and throwing light on the confused musical landscape of the period. Paz worked actively with the group until 1937, when disagreements between him and the other members led to a separation. He then founded the Conciertos de la Nueva Música to present the most innovatory European music, particularly chamber music. In 1944 he was joined by other composers, among them Perceval, Devoto and Eitler, and a new group took shape as the Agrupación Nueva Música. The group grew steadily and remained a force for avant-garde ideas. At the time of his participation in the Grupo Renovación, Paz also took an active role in the work of the Asociación del Profesorado Orquestal, whose orchestra introduced new European works, above all those of the Paris school, as well as giving a hearing to pieces by the youngest and least known Argentine composers.

Throughout Paz's career, his music displays great attention to formal considerations and an extremely economic use of materials. His first period, from the 1920s until the early 1930s, is post-Romantic in style, with influences from Franck and Strauss, e.g. the *Cuatro fugas sobre un tema* (1924–5) and the orchestral *Canto de Navidad* (1927). Next he was drawn to neo-classical Stravinsky and jazz in such works as the *Octeto* for wind instruments (1930) and *Tres movimientos de jazz* (1932), which exhibit a contrapuntal polytonal (at times atonal) language. The pull of Scandinavian literature (Ibsen in particular) at this time on the culture of the River Plate as a whole also surfaces in *Tres comentarios líricos a 'El cartero del rey'* (1926) and in the incidental music to Ibsen's *The Emperor Julian* (1931). Meanwhile Paz was making a profound study of the worldwide musical currents of the 1930s, a period when Latin American composers were somewhat bemused by the diversity of prevailing techniques. It was then that Paz directed his gaze to ideas quite unknown in Argentina at the time: the 12-note theories of Schoenberg. For four years he studied the procedures of Schoenberg and his pupils, particularly Webern, and from 1934 he adopted serial writing, for instance in the Passcaglia for orchestra (1936). But in 1950 he abandoned the 12-note system, convinced that it had nothing fundamentally new to offer, but also convinced that it was much less well known and understood than it deserved. After a period of reflection he surprised the public with these views, expounded in his book *Arnold Schoenberg, o el fin de la era tonal* (1954). From this time he explored a newly experimental, though highly structured idiom, resulting in some of his most notable works, including orchestral compositons *Rítmca ostinada* (1952), *Seis superposiciones* (1954), *Transformaciones canónicas* (1955) and *Continuidad* (1960), and the piano series *Núcleos* (1962–4), at which point he gave up composing.

But this was not the end of his exploratory activity, for he now gave his attention to the theoretical problems which had occupied him almost throughout his life. The result was *Alturas, tensiones, ataques, intensidades* (1970). Of his other books, the *Introducción a la música de nuestro tiempo* (1952) was of great importance in its day, containing as it did the fruit of more than 20 years of research and active participation in new music. Paz was equally an untiring apologist for contemporary aesthetic ideas in his numerous essays, published in over 25 Argentine and foreign periodicals, and in the hundreds of lectures that he gave in cultural and educational institutions. His teaching left an indelible mark on a whole generation of Argentine composers.

WORKS
(*selective list*)

ORCHESTRAL
Canto de Navidad, 1927, orchd 1930; Movimiento sinfónico, 1930; Juliano Emperador (incid music, H. Ibsen), 1931; 3 piezas, 1931; Passacaglia, 1936, 2nd version 1952–3; Música para orquesta: Preludio y fuga, 1940; Passacaglia, str, 1944, rev. 1949; Rítmica ostinada, 1952; 6 superposiciones, 1954; Transformaciones canónicas, 1955; Música para fagot, cuerdas y batería, 1955–6; Continuidad, 1960; Música para piano y orquesta, 1964

CHAMBER AND SOLO INSTRUMENTAL
Tema y transformaciones, fl, ob, 2 cl, b cl, 2 bn, 2 hn, 2 tpt, 1929; Octeto, fl, ob, 2 bn, 2 hn, 2 tpt, 1930; Sonatina no.1, cl, pf, 1930; Sonata, vn, pf, 1931; Conc. no.1, wind, pf, 1932; Sonatina no.2, fl, cl, 1932; Primera composición dodecafónica, fl, eng hn, vc, 1934; Segunda composición dodecafónica, fl, pf, 1934–5; Conc. no.2,

ob, bn, 2 hn, tpt, pf, 1935; Ov., wind qnt, hn, tpt, trbn, str trio, db, 1936; 4 piezas, cl, 1936; Primera composición en trío, fl, cl, bn, 1937

Tercera composición dodecafónica, cl, pf, 1937; Cuarta composición dodecafónica, vn, 1938; Str Qt no.1, 1938; Segunda composición en trío, cl, a sax, tpt, 1938; Tercera composición en trío, fl, ob, b cl/bn, 1940, rev. 1945; 3 comentarios líricos a 'El cartero del rey', fl, ob, cl, pf trio, 1942, [arr. pf work]; Str Qt no.2, 1940–43; Música para fl, sax y pf, 1943; Dédalus 1950, fl, cl, pf trio, 1950–51; Continuidad 1953, perc, 1953–4; 3 contrapuntos, cl, tpt, trbn, elec gui, cel, vc, 1955; Invención, str qt, 1961; Concreción 1964, fl, cl, bn, hn, tpt, trbn, tuba, 1964; Galaxia 64, org, 1964

PIANO

Coral, eb, 1921; 3 piezas líricas, 1922; Fantasía, 1923; Fantasía y fuga, bb, 1923; Preludio, coral y fuga, 1923; Sonata no.1, 1923; 4 fugas sobre un tema, 1924–5; Coral, F, 1925; Sonata no.2, 1925; 2 leyendas, 1925–6; 3 comentarios líricos a 'El cartero del rey', 1926, arr. ens, 1942; 6 baladas, 1927–9; Tema con transformaciones, 1928; 3 movimientos de jazz, 1932; 3 invenciones a 2 voces, 1932; Sonatina no.3, 1933; Sonata no.3, 1935; 10 piezas sobre una serie dodecafónica, 1936; Canciones y baladas, 1936–7; 5 piezas de carácter, 1937; Música 1946, 1945–7; Núcleos, 1962–4

OTHER WORKS

Song: Abel (M. Machado), 1v, pf, 1929
Arrs. for band or org of works by Bach, Beethoven and others

WRITINGS

Introducción a la música de nuestro tiempo (Buenos Aires, 1952)
La música en los Estados Unidos (Buenos Aires, 1952)
Arnold Schoenberg, o el fin de la era tonal (Buenos Aires, 1954)
Alturas, tensiones, ataques, intensidades (Buenos Aires, 1970)

BIBLIOGRAPHY

Composers of the Americas, ii (Washington DC, 1956)
J. Romano: Juan Carlos Paz: tribulaciones de un músico (Buenos Aires, 1970)
R. Arizaga: Enciclopedia de la música argentina (Buenos Aires, 1971)
J. Vinton, ed.: Dictionary of Contemporary Music (New York, 1974)
G. Béhague: Music in Latin America: an Introduction (Englewood Cliffs, NJ, 1979)
R. García Morillo: Estudios sobre música argentina (Buenos Aires, 1984)
M. Fischer, M. Furman Schleifer and J.M. Furman: Latin American Classical Composers: a Biographical Dictionary (Lanham, MD, 1996)
B.A. Tenenbaum, ed.: Encyclopedia of Latin American History and Culture, iv (New York, 1996)
SUSANA SALGADO

Pazdírek. Czech family of publishers and musicians.

(1) **Bohumil Pazdírek** [Johann Peter Gotthard] (b Drahanovice, Moravia, 19 Jan 1839; d Vöslau, nr Vienna, 17 May 1919). Publisher and composer. He was the son of Josef Pazdírek (1813–96), a village teacher and musician. He settled in Vienna in 1855 and worked for various publishers (Spina, Gustave Lewy, Doblinger) until 1868 when he founded his own firm, which published many of Schubert's posthumous works. When his firm was taken over by Doblinger in 1880, he began teaching at the Theresian Academy (1882–1906). He composed five operas, six string quartets, songs, chamber music and sacred music. With his brother (2) František, he published the 34-volume Universal-Handbuch der Musikliteratur (Vienna, 1904–10/R), which cited all musical editions known by them to be in print and is still a valuable work of reference.

(2) **František Pazdírek** (b Citov, nr Přerov, Moravia, 18 Dec 1848; d Vienna, 14 Feb 1915). Publisher, brother of (1) Bohumil. After his schooling in Olomouc, he entered his brother's firm in Vienna and gained further experience in Berlin and in Moscow (with Jürgenson). On his return

he worked with his brother (3) Ludevít Raimund. He initiated the ambitious but incomplete Prager Conservatorium Ausgabe, published the Musikliterarische Blätter and worked with his brother Bohumil on the Universal-Handbuch.

(3) **Ludevít Raimund Pazdírek** (b Citov, nr Přerov, Moravia, 23 Aug 1850; d Brno, 30 April 1914). Publisher, brother of (1) Bohumil and (2) František. After training as a teacher in Olomouc, he taught in Citov and other small Moravian towns. In 1879 he founded a publishing business in Horní Moštěnice in which he worked full time from 1889, moving to Bučovice (1891), Olomouc (1897) and finally to Brno (1911). His first publication was the frequently reprinted Malý koledníček ('Little carol book'). He specialized in church music and teaching manuals (e.g. Kocián's violin tutor, 1888), and himself composed some church and organ music.

(4) **Oldřich Pazdírek** (b Horní Moštěnice, nr Přerov, Moravia, 18 Dec 1887; d Brno, 3 Aug 1944). Publisher, son of (3) Ludevít. He took over the family firm in Brno in 1919. He concentrated on the works of Moravian composers, teaching and educational literature (e.g. Ševčk's violin tutor, Černušák's music history). Notable publications included the first editions of Janáček's Zápisník Zmizelého (1921) and Suite for strings (1926), Pazdírkův hudební slovník ('Pazdírek's music dictionary'), which began appearing from 1929 but was stopped by German censorship in 1941, Helfert's Leoš Janáček, i (1939), and the historical series Musica Antiqua Bohemica. From 1937 he began collaborating with the Prague firm of Melantrich under the name of Melpa. After his death the family business was continued by his son Dušan until nationalized in 1948.

BIBLIOGRAPHY

ČSHS
L.K. Žižka: 'Rod Pazdírků' [The Pazdírek family], Hudba a národ, ed. V. Mikota (Prague, 1940), 132–3
N. Simeone: The First editions of Leoš Janáček (Tutzing, 1991)
JOHN TYRRELL

Pazovsky, Ary Moiseyevich (b Perm', 21 Jan/2 Feb 1887; d Moscow, 6 Jan 1953). Russian conductor. He learnt the violin as a boy and studied at the St Petersburg Conservatory from 1897, first with P. Krasnokutsky and later with Leopold Auer (1900–04). Having begun his career as a violinist, he turned to conducting in 1905, first with provincial opera companies, then with Zimin's opera company, Moscow (1908–10), and successively at Khar'kiv, Odessa and Kiev until 1916. He became musical director of the Petrograd People's Opera (1916–18), conducted at the Bol'shoy Theatre (1923–4, 1925–8), and from 1926 to 1936 was musical director of the opera houses at Baku, Sverdlovsk, Khar'kiv and Kiev. He was artistic director at the Kirov Theatre, Leningrad (1936–43), when he conducted the premières of Oles' Chishko's The Battleship 'Potyomkin' in 1937 and Marian Koval's Yemel'yan Pugachyov (1942), as well as memorable productions of operas by Bizet, Glinka, Rimsky-Korsakov and Tchaikovsky. In 1943 he took a similar post at the Bol'shoy, but became seriously ill and was forced to give up conducting in 1948. Pazovsky was an outstanding opera conductor whose attention to detail and painstaking rehearsals were the key to his success, and whose greatest performances were characterized by artistic restraint, a careful balance between music and production and a deeply personal interpretation that was based on precise concern for the score. He made a detailed study of opera conducting in his *Zapiski dirizhyora* ('The writings of a conductor', Moscow, 1966), which deals with all aspects of the art.

I.M. YAMPOL'SKY

Peabody Institute. Conservatory established in BALTIMORE in 1857 as the Peabody Conservatory.

Peace, Jakub Jan. *See* RYBA, JAKUB JAN.

Peacham, Henry (*b* North Mimms, Herts., 1578; *d* ?London, *c*1644). English author and musician. He graduated MA from Trinity College, Cambridge, in 1598, and spent most of his career as a schoolmaster in Huntingdonshire, Norfolk, Lincolnshire and London, except for a period between 1613 and 1615 when he travelled in France, Germany and the Low Countries. The last known reference to him is a poem that he contributed for an engraving by Wenceslaus Hollar in 1644.

Peacham's musical importance lies in his chapter on music in *The Compleat Gentleman* (1622), a compendium of knowledge intended for the education of children from noble households. Peacham advocated the inclusion of music in the curriculum, though he warned against allowing musical pursuits to distract a gentleman from 'his more weightie imployments': 'I desire no more in you then to sing your part sure, and at the first sight, withall, to play the same upon your Violl, or the exercise of the Lute, privately to your selfe'. Appealing to scripture and to the writings of the ancients, he pointed to music's therapeutic properties. Peacham related music to poetry, the topic of his preceding chapter, and to rhetoric: 'hath not Musicke her figures, the same which Rhetorique?'. Most of his material is derived from unacknowledged sources: he borrowed from Byrd's preface to *Psalmes, Sonets & Songs* (1588) and from Morley's *Plaine and Easie Introduction to Practicall Musicke* (1597). He listed composers in order of preference and tried to impress with his knowledge of continental composers. However, the works that he cited can be traced to sources available in England. For example, Marenzio's *Io partirò* appeared in Yonge's *Musica Transalpina* translated into English and divorced from its original companion madrigals: Peacham's criticism of consecutive fifths which occur only in Yonge's print and his lack of awareness that it is the second *parte* of a tripartite madrigal show that he did not know the original Marenzio print.

Peacham used musical imagery in some emblems in *Minerva Britanna* (1612), included epigrams 'To Maister William Bird, the glory of our Nation for Musique' and 'To Maister Doctor *Dowland*' in *Thalia's Banquet* (1620), and drew an analogy between harmonious music and political concord in *The Duty of All True Subjects* (1639). Peacham and John Dowland were neighbours in Fetter Lane, London, in 1608–9; in *Minerva Britanna* he described Dowland showing him compositions by Moritz Landgrave of Hessen-Kassel. He also contributed a dedicatory poem for Robert Dowland's *A Musicall Banquet* (RISM 1610²⁰).

Peacham's reference to 'mine own master, Horatio Vecchi' in *The Compleat Gentleman* suggests that he studied composition in Italy, perhaps between 1598 and 1600. A four-voice madrigal headed *King James his quier* survives in one of his manuscripts of emblems (*GB-Lbl* Harl.6855), and is the first work to adapt the Oriana

motive to take into account Elizabeth's death. Epigram 70 from *Thalia's Banquet* (1620) refers to 'A set of 4 and 5 partes of the Authors ready for the presse'. This set has not survived; it may be the same as 'my songs of 4. and 5. Parts' mentioned in *Graphice* (1612).

WRITINGS

The Art of Drawing with the Pen (London, 1606/R1970, 2/1612 as *Graphice*, 3/1634 as *The Gentleman's Exercise*)
Minerva Britanna (London, 1612/R1973)
Thalia's Banquet (London, 1620)
The Compleat Gentleman (London, 1622/R1968; enlarged 2/1627/R 1634, 1906; rev. 3/1661); ed. V.B. Heltzel (Ithaca, 1962)
The Duty of All True Subjects to their King (London, 1639)
Basilicon Doron [book of emblems], *GB-Ob* MS Rawlinson Poetry 146, *Lbl* MS Harleian 6855 art.13 [incl. madrigal, 4vv], *Lbl* MS Royal 12A LXVI

BIBLIOGRAPHY

A.R. Young: *Henry Peacham* (Boston, 1979)
A.R. Young: 'Henry Peacham, Ben Jonson and the Cult of Elizabeth-Oriana', *ML*, lx (1979), 305–11
G.G. Butler: 'Music and Rhetoric in Early Seventeenth-Century English Sources', *MQ*, lxvi (1980), 53–64
S. Hankey: 'The Compleat Gentleman's Music', *ML*, lxxii (1981), 146–54
R. Toft: 'Musicke a Sister to Poetrie: Rhetorical Artifice in the Passionate Airs of John Dowland', *EMc*, xii (1984), 191–200

DAVID J. SMITH

Peacock, Kenneth Howard (*b* Toronto, 7 April 1922). Canadian ethnomusicologist, pianist and composer. After studying the piano at Toronto Conservatory (associate 1935) and music at the university (MusB 1942), he was a piano pupil of E. Robert Schmidt and Reginald Godden and a composition pupil of Francis Judd Cooke in Boston and John Weinzweig in Toronto. Initially he worked as a piano teacher in Toronto (1937–47) and Ottawa (1947–54) and appeared as a pianist and composer in live and broadcast concerts; later he turned to ethnomusicology, working first from 1951 to 1972 as a research fellow at the National Museum of Man, Ottawa (now the Canadian Museum of Civilization), and subsequently in freelance field research. His work included an investigation of Anglo-Canadian, French-Canadian and Amerindian music (1951–61) and the organization of fieldwork on the music of Canada's minority cultures (1962–72). During 19 fieldtrips from Newfoundland to British Columbia he studied the music and folk art of 40 cultures and established an archive of over 500 tapes at the National Museum. Besides publishing the results of these projects he produced an edition of popular Newfoundland songs and two records, *Indian Music of the Canadian Plains* and *Songs and Ballads of Newfoundland*. One of the first Canadian folk music scholars with an extensive background in music, Peacock collaborated with the maritime song collector, Helen Creighton, providing transcriptions for *Maritime Folk Songs* (Toronto, 1962) and *Folk Songs from Southern New Brunswick* (Ottawa, 1971); he likewise contributed to Robert Klymasz's *The Ukrainian Winter Folksong Cycle in Canada* (Ottawa, 1970) and more recently *The Ukrainian Folk Ballad in Canada* (New York, 1989). A member of the Canadian League of Composers, Peacock's compositions include several pieces based on folk sources, such as the cantata *Songs of the Cedar*, the orchestral *Essay on Newfoundland Themes* and a series for piano *Idioms*.

WRITINGS

'Nine Songs from Newfoundland', *Journal of American Folklore*, lxvii (1954), 123–36

'The Native Songs of Newfoundland', *Contributions to Anthropology 1960*, ii, National Museum of Canada: Bulletin, no.190 (1963), 213–39
Songs of the Newfoundland Outports (Ottawa, 1965)
'The Music of the Doukhobors', *Alphabet*, no.11 (1965–6), 33–44
A Practical Guide for Folk Music Collectors (Kingston, ON, 1966)
'Folk and Aboriginal Music', *Aspects of Music in Canada*, ed. A. Walter (Toronto, 1969), 62–89
Songs of the Doukhobors: an Introductory Outline (Ottawa, 1970) [incl. discs]
A Garland of Rue (Ottawa, 1971) [incl. discs]

GORDON E. SMITH

Peaker, Charles (*b* Derby, 6 Dec 1899; *d* Toronto, 11 Aug 1978). Canadian organist, conductor and teacher. Leaving England in 1913, he lived in Saskatoon until a scholarship took him to Toronto to study with Willan and MacMillan. He gained the FRCO in 1929, after working with Harold Darke, and a DMus in 1936. In 1944 he was appointed to St Paul's in Toronto, and became university organist in 1964. He gave many recitals in Toronto, throughout Canada and the USA, and made two recital tours in England (1956 and 1957). He instituted a series of Advent and Lent recitals at St Paul's in 1945 which brought performances of major choral works with orchestra (including many Canadian compositions) and concerts by distinguished organists to a large public. He taught at both the Royal Conservatory of Music, Toronto, and the University of Toronto. He was president of the Royal Canadian College of Organists from 1941 to 1943, and in 1974 was made a member of the Order of Canada. He retired from St Paul's in 1975.

GILES BRYANT

Pearce [Pearse, Pierce, Perse, Peers], **Edward** (*b* c1560; bur. London, 15 June 1612). English church musician and composer. He was a chorister of Canterbury Cathedral from 1568 to 1575, and a singing-man from 1577 until at least 1581. On 16 March 1589 he was sworn a Gentleman of the Chapel Royal, but in August 1600 he 'yealded up his place for the M[aster]ship of the children of Poules', having effectively succeeded Thomas Giles in that post in May 1599. One of Pearce's pupils at St Paul's was Thomas Ravenscroft, who wrote warmly of him as a trainer of boys' voices and composer for the lute and other instruments. Immediately upon his appointment at St Paul's, Pearce revived the commercial presentation of plays (with music) by the 'Children of Paul's' (inhibited since 1591), mounting some 27 plays in eight years. However, the incipient rehabilitation of the repute of church music, evident since the 1590s, rendered so gross a misuse of cathedral choristers already obsolescent, and following the replacement of Dean Alexander Nowell by the more responsible John Overall the play-house closed in 1607.

No sacred music by Pearce is known, and only two secular pieces (a four-part hunting song and a song for voice and three instruments) have survived; they were included by Ravenscroft in his *Briefe Discourse* (RISM 1614²¹). Three lute pieces survive in *IRL-Dtc*, *GB-Cu* and *Lbl*.

BIBLIOGRAPHY

BDECM
H.N. Hillebrand: 'The Child Actors: a Chapter in Elizabethan Stage History', *University of Illinois Studies in Language and Literature*, xi (1926), 1–356
M. Shapiro: *Children of the Revels: the Boy Companies of Shakespeare's Time and their Plays* (New York, 1977)
W.R. Gair: *The Children of Paul's: the Story of a Theatre Company, 1553–1608* (Cambridge, 1982)
L.P. Austern: *Music in English Children's Drama of the Later Renaissance* (Philadelphia, 1992)

THURSTON DART, DAVID SCOTT/ROGER BOWERS

Pearl Jam. American grunge band. Formed in 1990, it consisted of Eddie Vedder (Eddie Mueller; *b* Evanston, IL, 23 Dec 1964; vocals), Stone Gossard (*b* Seattle, WA, 20 July 1966; guitar), Mike McCready (*b* Seattle, WA, 5 April 1965; guitar), Jeff Ament (*b* Big Sandy, MT, 10 March 1963; bass) and Dave Abbruzzese (drums), who was replaced by Jack Irons (*b* Los Angeles, 18 July 1962) in 1994. Along with Nirvana, they were a major force in popularizing grunge, and alternative music more generally. Vedder's impassioned vocals addressed child abuse and neglect, as in the song 'Jeremy' from *Ten* (Epic, 1981), along with more traditional topics. The band's music was based on distorted guitar riffs, in the fashion of Led Zeppelin, but avoided the guitar virtuosity that had been characteristic of 1980s heavy metal in favour of post-punk directness.

ROBERT WALSER

Pears, Sir Peter (Neville Luard) (*b* Farnham, 22 June 1910; *d* Aldeburgh, 3 April 1986). English tenor. He won a scholarship to the RCM, London, where he spent two terms in 1933–4. At the same time he joined the BBC Chorus and then the BBC Singers (1934–8), and took lessons with Elena Gerhardt and Dawson Freer. He met Benjamin Britten in 1936 and a year later they gave their first recital together (which included Britten's *On this Island*). In 1939 they went to the USA, and while there Pears studied with Therese Behr (Schnabel's wife) and Clytie Hine Mundy.

Returning with Britten to London in 1942, he made his stage début in the title role of *Les contes d'Hoffmann* at the Strand Theatre. The next year he joined the Sadler's Wells company, singing Rossini's Almaviva, Rodolfo, the Duke of Mantua, Tamino, Ferrando and Vašek, and, memorably, creating the title role in *Peter Grimes* (1945). These years also saw the notable first performances, given by Pears and the composer, of Britten's Michelangelo Sonnets and the *Serenade* for tenor, horn and strings.

In 1946 Pears was one of the founders of the English Opera Group, with which he sang the Male Chorus in the première of *The Rape of Lucretia* (1946) and the title role in *Albert Herring* (1947), both at Glyndebourne. His other creations in Britten's dramatic works included Captain Vere in *Billy Budd* (1951, Covent Garden), Essex in *Gloriana* (1953, Covent Garden), Quint in *The Turn of the Screw* (1954, Venice), Flute in *A Midsummer Night's Dream* (1960, Aldeburgh), the Madwoman in *Curlew River* (1964, Aldeburgh), Nebuchadnezzar in *The Burning Fiery Furnace* (1966, Aldeburgh), the Tempter in *The Prodigal Son* (1968, Aldeburgh), Sir Philip Wingrave in *Owen Wingrave* (1971, BBC television) and Aschenbach in *Death in Venice* (1973, Aldeburgh). For the English Opera Group he also sang Macheath in Britten's realization of *The Beggar's Opera*, Satyavān in Holst's *Sāvitri*, and Mozart's Idomeneus; and he created Boaz in Berkeley's *Ruth* (1956). At Covent Garden he created Pandarus in Walton's *Troilus and Cressida* (1954), and will be remembered for his acute portrayals of Tamino, Vašek and David (*Die Meistersinger*) during the 1950s. He later took part in the premières of Henze's *Novae de*

Peter Pears

infinito laudes (1963) and Lutosławski's *Paroles tissées* (1965). He was made a CBE in 1957, and was knighted in 1977.

Pears was one of the founders of the Aldeburgh Festival, inaugurated in 1948, and remained a director until his death. He was an eloquent interpreter of Schubert, probably the leading Evangelist of his day in Bach's Passions, an impassioned Gerontius and a noted exponent of British song. He collaborated with Britten on the libretto of *A Midsummer Night's Dream* and on realizations of several works by Purcell, including *The Fairy Queen* (1967).

Britten wrote all his major tenor roles, and many of his solo vocal works, with the particular characteristics of Pears's voice in mind. Clear, reedy and almost instrumental in quality, it was capable of great expressive variety and flexibility, if no wide range of colour. Its inward, reflective timbre, tinged with poetry, was artfully exploited by Britten, from the role of Peter Grimes to that of Aschenbach, but the voice could also be commanding, almost heroic, as was shown in the more vehement sections of Captain Vere's role or in the part of the Madwoman in *Curlew River*; Pears's cheeky vein of humour was given full range as Albert Herring and as Flute. His recital partnership with Britten produced evenings of extraordinary interpretative insights, when line and tone were perfectly matched to the texts of Schubert's and Schumann's song cycles.

Pears continued singing until he was well into his sixties, and after his retirement was active in teaching and promoting young singers at the Britten-Pears School in Aldeburgh. His recordings include virtually all the roles Britten created for him, and his eloquent accounts of the Evangelist in Bach's Passions and Gerontius.

BIBLIOGRAPHY

H. Keller: 'Peter Pears', *Opera*, ii (1950–51), 287–92
J.B. Steane: *The Grand Tradition* (London, 1974), 506–10
M. Thorpe, ed.: *Peter Pears: a Tribute on his 75th Birthday* (London, 1985) [incl. discography]
'Sir Peter Pears 1910–1986: Three Tributes', *Opera*, xxxvii (1986), 624–30
C. Headington: *Peter Pears: a Biography* (London, 1992)
P. Reed: *The Travel Diaries of Peter Pears* (London, 1995)

ALAN BLYTH

Pearsall, Robert Lucas (*b* Clifton, nr Bristol, 14 March 1795; *d* Wartensee, Switzerland, 5 Aug 1856). English composer and antiquarian. His father was an army officer and amateur musician, of an old Staffordshire family, resident in the Bristol area, which had made money through ownership of a steel business. His mother was Elizabeth Lucas; Robert was their only child to survive infancy (the prefix 'de' was added to the surname after the composer's death, and was never used by him: hence it is even less authentic than Beethoven's 'van' or Weber's 'von').

Pearsall's father moved to Bristol about 1802 and died in 1813. At his mother's desire he was educated for the Bar by private tutors, and practised as a barrister (1821–5) at Bristol. After a slight stroke in 1825 he gave up his profession and went to live abroad on medical advice. He was then able to devote himself to his interests in history, genealogy, heraldry, painting, and above all music. His earliest known composition, a Minuet and Trio in B♭, is dated 14 July 1825 at Willsbridge, the family house near Bristol.

Pearsall lived for four years (1825–9) at Mainz, where he took lessons in composition from Joseph Panny. In this period he was caught up in the Cecilian movement and composed a number of Latin motets in the style that was regarded as 'pure'. In 1829, leaving his family behind (he had married Harriet Hobday in 1817 and had three children by her), he returned to England for a year. From 1830 to 1842 his home was at Karlsruhe. From there, however, he made many journeys to other European centres where he pursued his antiquarian interests. At Munich in 1832 he met Kaspar Ett, who helped his study of early music by teaching him to transcribe the notation. His composing now included orchestral works, and in 1834 he built a small theatre at his home for which he wrote a 'ballet-opera' *Die Nacht eines Schwärmers* and other pieces. In May 1836 he inherited Willsbridge by the death of his mother, and returned to England again for a year, selling the property in July 1837. During this visit he began composing 'madrigals' in imitation of Morley's balletts (and using the same texts). In January 1837 the Bristol Madrigal Society was founded, with Pearsall as one of the original members, and he had thus an unexpected opportunity to have these pieces performed. Their great success stimulated him to considerable effort in this line, and during the next few years most of his madrigals were written. He visited the society again in 1839, 1840, 1845 (when he was elected its first honorary member) and 1851. He also composed many partsongs for the society; his works became a permanent part of their repertory, and were kept alive at Bristol when his music was little known elsewhere.

In 1842 or 1843 Pearsall separated from his wife and acquired Schloss Wartensee, above Rorschach on Lake Constance, where he went to live with his daughter Philippa (1824–1917). He became intimate with the monks of St Gallen and Einsiedeln nearby, especially with the Chancellor of St Gallen, Johann Oehler, and in this period composed a quantity of music for the Roman Catholic Church and helped Oehler to edit the St Gallen *Gesangbuch*. He also wrote Anglican cathedral music, most of which was never performed. In 1854 he made over the Schloss to his wife and son, and moved to a small house in St Gallen, but after an attack of apoplexy he returned to Wartensee, where his wife nursed him throughout his last illness. Three days before his death Pearsall was received into the Roman Church, having been until that time a staunch Anglican. Less than a year earlier he had written:

I can now well understand the feeling of Henry IV of France when he made a cross on his breast as he mounted the walls of a battery under a heavy fire, although he was then only known as a confirmed Calvinistic Protestant – and I like him all the better for having in that manner given way to the dictates of his heart.

The passage illustrates that spirit of romance which found musical expression in such pieces as *Sir Patrick Spens* and *The Song of the Franc-Companies*.

Pearsall was not alone in his interest in reviving Renaissance music, and his German teachers passed on to him a mastery of strict counterpoint which had come down from the 16th century as an ecclesiastical tradition. Nor was there anything new in the revival of the English madrigal; the Madrigal Society of London had performed madrigals consistently since 1741, and had in 1811 offered a prize for the composition of a madrigal in imitation of ancient models. Many composers had written pastiche madrigals, notably Lord Mornington, William Beale (winner of the 1811 prize) and Samuel Wesley. Pearsall, however, was far more successful than any of these in bringing the form to life again. He began by modelling himself rather closely on Morley's balletts, and confining himself to four parts. Then he gradually expanded his resources, and it was here that his German training came to his aid. At the same time he managed to recapture a good deal of the spirit of the Elizabethan composers. His madrigals are not exact copies; on the contrary, their vitality stems from their remarkable ability to extend the madrigal style. He used for special effect chords which, to Elizabethan ears, were quite ordinary, such as the triad on the flattened 7th. In spite of his close study of 16th-century dissonance treatment, Pearsall did not adhere to the strict 'rules', but freely developed the principle of suspension to lengths undreamt of by Wilbye or Monteverdi – as in a passage in *Great god of love* which combined all seven notes of the scale simultaneously. His larger madrigals, notably *Lay a garland*, had a long-breathed phrase structure not found in their models, but derived from Classical music. Hence the element of surprise and interest was retained, as it could not be in a pure copy. Fuller Maitland considered these two eight-part madrigals 'real masterpieces in a form that has seldom been successfully employed in modern times'; the six-part *O ye roses* (singled out by Walker) and *Light of my soul* are little inferior, while the simpler balletts, *Sing we and chaunt it* and *No, no, Nigella* (the early, four-part

version), rival the Morley originals for freshness and charm.

Similar qualities are found in Pearsall's well-known setting of the German macaronic carol *In dulci jubilo*, which should be sung in the original version (revived in Parratt's edition) for solo octet and five-part chorus. The partsongs span most of his composing career, from *Take O take those lips away* (1830) to *Laugh not youth at age* (1852). *O who will o'er the downs so free* is unfortunately the only popular example now, but *When Allen-a-dale* and *Why with toil* were once great favourites. Though they often have surprising touches of antique colouring, they are harmonically conceived, in the glee tradition. The church music, on the other hand, is rather austerely contrapuntal, for the most part. Of the English cathedral music the Evening Service in G minor is certainly worth reviving. The Latin church music remains almost unknown, at least in Britain. Pearsall himself considered the Requiem his finest work.

Pearsall was respected in Catholic German-speaking circles as a contrapuntist, and as a pioneer in the rediscovery of Renaissance musical techniques. He also devoted much time and thought to the reform of English church music, though his efforts in this direction were little heeded.

Like many Romantics, especially in Germany, Pearsall was irresistibly attracted to the ideals and manners of the age of chivalry. In music the style of the 16th century seemed as remote as did the Middle Ages in the visual arts. His madrigals are the nearest equivalent, in English music, to the Gothic revival and the pre-Raphaelite school in painting. But they escape the ridicule that was in store for much neo-medieval art, because they are founded on a strong technique, whose demands generally prevail over the fascinations of the sham-antique.

WORKS

printed works published in London unless otherwise stated; MSS in CH-E, GB-Lbl, Bristol Madrigal Society Library and E. Hunt's private collection, Chesham Bois, Bucks

Editions: *The Sacred Compositions of R.L. de Pearsall*, ed. W.F. Trimnell (London, c1880) [T]

Novello's Part-Song Book, 2nd ser., x–xi (London, 1887) [N]

SACRED

For 4vv, wind insts, org: Ecce quam bonum, 1846; Adeste fideles, 1847; Pange lingua, 1847; Te Deum, 1847; Tenebrae, 1849; Oratio Jeremiae, 1852; Requiem, 1853–6; Lamentatio III in sabbato sancto; Veni Creator

c47 other Lat. works, 4vv, org, or 4vv unacc., incl. 4 pubd (Mainz, 1830–37)

4 morning services: C, 1848, T; 4th tone, 1849; G, 1850; 1st tone, 1851

2 evening services, F, g, 1849, T

Burial Service, 1849–50

Lord's Prayer, G, 1849; Gloria Patri, 4 female vv, 1854; other service music

12 anthems: O give thanks, 1838, T; I heard a voice, 1847, T; Let God arise, 1847, T; I will cry unto God, 1849, T; O clap your hands, 1851, T; Blessed is every one, 1852, T; Bow down thine ear; How blest is he; I will arise, C, T; I will arise, F; Let your light so shine, T; My heart is fixed, T

In dulci jubilo, 8 solo vv, 5vv, 1834, op.10 (1836)

Hymns and chants

For 4vv, orch: Ich stand in All, 1839; In dulci jubilo, Weihnachtslied; Christus ist erstanden

Gesänge bei der heiligen Firmung (St Gallen, 1847)

Hymns in Katholisches Gesangbuch (St Gallen, 1863)

'MADRIGALS'

Two children of this aged stream (The River Spirit's Song, after H. Purcell: King Arthur), 4 male vv, op.20 (1836), N

No, no, Nigella (after T. Morley), 4vv, 1836
Sing we and chaunt it (after Morley), 4vv, 1836, N
My bonny lass she smileth (after Morley), 4vv, 1836 (1875)
Why weeps, alas, my lady-love? (after Morley), 5vv, 1837, N
Take heed, ye shepherd swains (Pearsall), 6vv, 1837 (1840), N
I saw lovely Phyllis (?Pearsall), 4vv, 1837 (1840), N
Let us all go maying (Pearsall), 4vv, 1837 (1864), N
Shoot, false love (after Morley), 4vv, 1837 (1864), N
Light of my soul (Bulwer), 6vv, 1838, N
It was upon a springtide day (?Pearsall), 5vv, 1838 (1840), N
Spring returns (?Pearsall), 5vv, 1838 (1840), N
O ye roses so blooming and fair (Pearsall), 6vv, 1838 (1863), N
Down in my garden fair (?Pearsall), 4vv, 1839, N
Sweet as a flower in May (Pearsall), 4vv, 1839, N
Why should the cuckoo's tuneful note (Pearsall), 5vv, 1839, N
Great god of love (Pearsall), 8vv, 1839 (1840), N
List, lady! be not coy (J. Milton), 6vv, 1839 (1864), N
Lay a garland on her hearse (F. Beaumont, J. Fletcher), 8vv, 1840
   (1883), N
No, no, Nigella (after Morley), 8vv, c1840, N
Sing we and chaunt it (after Morley), 8vv, c1840 (1863), N
Why do the roses whisper? (Pearsall), 4vv, 1842, N
Nymphs are sporting (T. Oliphant), 4vv, 1842 (1853), N

OTHER VOCAL

Sir Patrick Spens, ballad-dialogue, 10vv, 1838 (1862)
Who shall have my lady fair?, ante-madrigal, 4vv, 1839 (1853)
60 Eng. partsongs, incl. 5 for male vv; 8 Ger. partsongs, incl. 1 for
   male vv; 2 Lat. partsongs, incl. 1 for male vv
9 arrs. of old melodies, 4vv, incl. Sumer is icumen in
Die Nacht eines Schwärmers, ballet with songs, Karlsruhe, 1834; 3
   other dramatic pieces
8 Eng. duets, 2 S, pf
31 Eng. songs, 1v, pf; 6 Ger. songs, 1v, pf

INSTRUMENTAL
for orchestra unless otherwise stated

Symphony, lost
3 ovs.: Der Schwärmer, 1829; Macbeth (Mainz, 1839); Kenilworth
2 marches, E♭; Waltz, E
3 fugues, str: A, d, D; Sonata in Imitative Counterpoint, str
2 str qnts: C, g; Str Qt, B♭, 1834 (Mainz, c1847)
Cuckoo Waltz, pf 4 hands, fl, vc, pipe, cuckoo
For org, wind insts: March, C; Introitus, D
3 minuets, vn, pf; 3 minuets, vn, cl
Fugue, d, org; 5 pieces, pf 4 hands

EDITIONS

O. de Lassus: Magnificat sex vocum (London, 1833)
Katholisches Gesangbuch ... herausgegeben vom bischöflichen
   Ordinariate des Bisthums St Gallen (St Gallen, 1863)
Various madrigals and partsongs

WRITINGS

'Cobbett's Letters on Music', *Felix Farley's Bristol Journal* (1839)
'Über den Ursprung und die Geschichte des englischen Madrigals',
   Zeitschrift für Deutschlands Musik-Vereine und Dilettanten, ii
   (1842), 143–71
Musica gregoriana (MS, 1849–50, *GB-Lbl* Add.37490)
'Observations on Chanting' (MS, 1851); ed. W.B. Squire: 'Pearsall on
   Chanting', *SIMG*, viii (1906–7), 166–220
An Essay on Consecutive Fifths and Octaves in Counterpoint
   (London, 1876)
Psalmodia: an Essay on Psalm-Tunes (MS, *GB-Lbl* Add.38549–50)

BIBLIOGRAPHY

DNB (R.H. Legge); *Grove2* (J. Fuller Maitland); *SchillingES*
Letters of Pearsall in E. Hunt's private collection, Chesham Bois,
   Bucks.
Musical World, v (1837), 158
E. de Saint-Maurice Cabany: *Notice nécrologique sur ... R.L. de
   Pearsall* (Paris, 1856)
A. Schubiger: *Die Pflege des Kirchengesanges und der Kirchenmusik
   in der deutschen katholischen Schweiz* (Einsiedeln, 1873), 55
J. Marshall: 'Pearsall: a Memoir', *MT*, xxiii (1882), 375–6
'Robert Lucas Pearsall', *Musical Herald*, no.699 (1906), 227–31
E. Walker: *A History of Music in England* (Oxford, 1907, enlarged
   3/1952/R by J.A. Westrup)
[H.W. Hunt:] *Robert Lucas Pearsall and the Bristol Madrigal Society*
   (Bristol, 1916)
A.W. Hill: *Henry Nicholson Ellacombe: a Memoir* (London, 1919),
   32–9
W.B. Squire: 'Letters of Robert Lucas Pearsall', *MQ*, v (1919),
   264–97; vi (1920), 296–315; *MT*, lxi (1920), 662–5; lxiii (1922),
   318–19; lxiv (1923), 359–60; lxv (1924), 24–8
E. Hunt: 'Robert Lucas Pearsall', *PRMA*, lxxxii (1955–6), 75–87
N. Temperley: 'Domestic Music in England, 1800–1860', *PRMA*,
   lxxxv (1958–9), 31–47
E. Hunt: *Robert Lucas Pearsall: the 'Compleat Gentleman' and his
   Music* (Chesham Bois, 1971)
V. Opheim: *The English Romantic Madrigal* (diss., U. of Illinois,
   1971)
M. Hurd: 'Glees, Madrigals and Partsongs', *Music in Britain: the
   Romantic Age 1800–1914*, ed. N. Temperley (London, 1981/R),
   250–53

NICHOLAS TEMPERLEY

Pearson, Henry Hugh. *See* PIERSON, HENRY HUGO.

Pearson, Martin. *See* PEERSON, MARTIN.

Pearson, William (*b* ?London, *c*1671; *d* ?London, 1735).
English music printer. A former apprentice of John
Heptinstall, he set himself up in London in 1698, and in
1699 published *Twelve New Songs* in which he used for
the first time a fount which he called the 'new London
character'. It was a marked improvement on the older
founts in use, and Pearson established a business partnership with Henry Playford. Pearson printed several notable
publications for Playford, including *Mercurius musicus*,
John Blow's *Amphion Anglicus*, some editions of *An
Introduction to the Skill of Musick*, some parts of *Wit
and Mirth*, the second volume of Henry Purcell's *Orpheus
Britannicus* and parts of *Harmonia sacra*. The partnership
broke up in 1703 as the result of a lawsuit and Pearson
continued to print independently until 1735. After his
death his business was carried on by his widow, Alice
Pearson, who continued to use the 'new London character'
for a few musical publications, among them John Wesley's
'Foundry' hymnbook, *A Collection of Tunes, Set to Music
as They Are Commonly Sung at the Foundery* (1742).

Pearson used his 'new London character' with great
skill. It was one of the first used in London that could
print round note heads, and quavers, semiquavers etc. in
groups as well as separately, and Pearson drew attention
to these advantages in his preface to the *Twelve New
Songs*. His work is notable for its clear impression, and
the attractive layout of the pages gives it a strikingly
modern appearance. Pearson was responsible for most of
the typeset music produced in London, 1699–1735; his
was the only fount of the time which could seriously
compete with the work of engravers, who were steadily
taking over music printing at the turn of the century.

For illustration *see* PRINTING AND PUBLISHING OF MUSIC, fig.8.

BIBLIOGRAPHY

Humphries-SmithMP; *KrummelEMP*
C.L. Day and E.B. Murrie: *English Song-Books 1651–1702 and their
   Publishers* (London, 1936/R)
M. Tilmouth: 'A Note on the Cost of Music Printing in London in
   1702', *Brio*, viii/1 (1971), 1–3
M. Treadwell: 'London Printers and Printing Houses in 1705',
   Publishing History, vii (1980), 5–44, esp. 33–4
D.R. Harvey: *Henry Playford: a Bibliographical Study* (diss., Victoria
   U. of Wellington, 1985)

MIRIAM MILLER/D. ROSS HARVEY

Peart, Donald (*b* Fovant, Wilts., 9 Jan 1909; *d* Sydney, 26
Nov 1981). English music administrator. He was educated
at Cheltenham College and Oxford (MA, BMus) where
he was an open scholar of the Queen's College, and at the
RCM. After army service in Africa and India during the

war he was invited in 1947 to take up the newly created chair of music at the University of Sydney, a post he held until 1974. In 1950 he founded the Pro Musica Society of Sydney University, which has been responsible for many first performances in Australia of operas and orchestral and choral music, including newly commissioned works. In 1956 he reformed the ISCM in Sydney; this became the headquarters of the Australian section and has played a large part in the presentation of new works by younger Australian composers. He became the first president of the Musicological Society of Australia in 1964 and of the New South Wales chapter of the Australian Society for Music Education in 1968. In 1965 he was chairman of the music committee of the Australian National Advisory Committee for UNESCO. In 1957 he was elected FRCM. Peart has edited Jenkins's six-part consort music (MB, xxxix, 1977).

WRITINGS

'Alfonso Ferrabosco and the Lyra Viol', *Musicology*, ii (1965–7), 13–21
'The Australian Avant-Garde', *PRMA*, xciii (1966–7), 1–9
'"The Shepherds' Calendar" of Maxwell Davies', *MMA*, i (1966), 219–25
'Asian Music in an Australian University', *Hemisphere*, xi/3 (1967), 13–17
Articles in *The Listener*, *Music Now* (ISCM, Australian Section)

ANN CARR-BOYD

Peasable, James. *See* PAISIBLE, JAMES.

Peaslee, Richard Cutts (*b* New York City, 13 June 1930). American composer. He graduated from Yale University and the Juilliard School, and also studied privately with Boulanger and Russo. His compositional style is eclectic, encompassing jazz influences, folk-like idioms, extended instrumental techniques and electronic sound resources. His early works for jazz ensemble culminated in *Stonehenge* (1963) for the London Jazz Orchestra. Many of his compositions exploit the virtuosity of particular performers. *Chicago Concerto* (1967) was written for Gerry Mulligan (baritone saxophone), *Nightsongs* (1973) for Harold Lieberman (trumpet and flugelhorn), *The Devil's Herald* (1975) for Harvey Phillips (tuba) and *Arrows of Time* (1994–6) for Joseph Alessi (trombone).

In the mid-1960s Peaslee began composing extensively for the stage. An early success was *Marat/Sade* (1964), a score which juxtaposed diverse elements drawn from 18th century classicism and 20th century compositional techniques as well as folk music and popular idioms. Other musicals include *Animal Farm* (1984), *Miracolo d'amore* (1988) and *The Snow Queen* (1990). He has collaborated with the choreographers Twyla Tharp (*Happily Ever After*, 1976), David Parsons (*Ring Around the Rosie*, 1994; *Touch*, 1996), Elisa Monte (*Feu follet*, 1995) and has composed music for the Joffrey and New York City ballet companies. He has also written several film and television scores.

WORKS
(*selective list*)

DRAMATIC

Musical theatre: The Marat/Sade (P. Brook), 1964; The Serpent, 1970; The Fable, 1975; The Children's Crusade, 1981; Animal Farm (P. Hall, A. Mitchell), 1984; Garden of Earthly Delights, 1984; The Green Knight, 1986; Vienna Lusthaus, 1986; Miracolo d'amore (M. Clarke), 1988; The Snow Queen (Mitchell), 1990
Dance music: Happily Ever After (T. Tharp), 1976; Ring around the Rosie (D. Parsons), 1994; Feu follet (A Cajun Tale) (E. Monte), 1995; Touch (Parsons), 1996

Film and TV scores: The Marat/Sade, 1966; Wild Wild World of Animals, 1977; The Power of Myth (J. Campbell, B. Moyers), 1988; Blown Sideways Through Life, 1995
Incid music for over 40 productions in London, New York and Paris

OTHER

Orch: Stonehenge, jazz ens, 1963; Chicago Conc., jazz ens, 1967; Oct Piece, 1970; Afterlight, 1985; Tarentella, 1988
Choral: Missa brevis for St John the Divine, SATB, org, 1994
Chbr: Nightsongs, tpt, hp, str, 1973; The Devil's Herald, 4 hn, tuba, perc, 1975; Distant Dancing, brass qnt, 1992; Arrows of Time, trbn, pf, 1994, orchd 1996
Principal publishers: Boosey & Hawkes, E.C. Schirmer, Margun, European American, Galaxy, Boonin

JOSEPH BRUMBELOE

Peau de buffle. A register of jacks with plectra made from buff leather, occasionally found – especially as an extra fourth register – on French late 18th-century harpsichords.

EDWIN M. RIPIN

Peccatte. French family of bow makers.

(1) **Dominique Peccatte** (*b* Mirecourt, 15 July 1810; *d* Mirecourt, 13 Jan 1874). Peccatte went at an early age (in 1826, it is believed) to work for JEAN-BAPTISTE VUILLAUME in Paris and his earliest work indicates that he learnt from Jean Persoit. Of his considerable output for Vuillaume, Peccatte seems to have made violin and viola bows almost exclusively, many to Vuillaume's patented 'self-rehairing' design. In 1838 Peccatte took over the shop of the younger François Lupot. A few bows exist that were made by Peccatte but which bear Lupot's brand-stamp. In 1847, shortly after his mother's death – and having earlier bought out his younger brother François' share of her holdings – Peccatte moved back to Mirecourt. In 1852 he purchased a house on the rue des Cloîtres where he lived until his death.

Peccatte's perfect aptitude for his craft, married with a shrewd business sense, won him success and recognition within both the trade and the community. Today Peccatte is generally held to be second only to Tourte, and his bows with their inspired hatchet heads do seem to continue a tradition established by the latter. Their consistently excellent playing qualities have established them as the bows most in demand by players, despite their continually escalating prices. The vast majority of Peccatte bows are round though one occasionally encounters an octagonal cello bow with a head modelled after Tourte.

(2) **François Peccatte** (*b* Mirecourt, 10 March 1821; *d* Paris, 30 Oct 1855). Brother of (1) Dominique Peccatte. He went to Paris for a short period early in his working life, then returned to Mirecourt and opened a shop in 1842, employing several workers to assist in his commerical production. François had some association with his illustrious brother Dominique, presumably during his stay in Paris and again when Dominique returned to Mirecourt. Indeed, much of François' best work shows the strong influence of Dominique. He returned to Paris not long before his premature death.

(3) **Charles Peccatte** (*b* Mirecourt, 14 Oct 1850; *d* Paris, 22 Oct 1918). Son of (2) François Peccatte. He was probably trained by August Lenoble with whom he later had a partnership which lasted until 1881. The early work includes very individual bows which can be described as of the Peccatte school but many of which have heads modelled somewhat after the early type of bow by

François Tourte. Charles also made bows for J.-B. Vuillaume which closely resemble those made by F.N. Voirin for Vuillaume.

Peccatte won silver medals at the Antwerp and Paris Expositions Universelles in 1885 and 1889 respectively, and was established on his own at 8 rue de Valois, Paris, by 1885. His work is very uneven in quality, and he seems to have offered a commercial range as well, as there are bows from Mirecourt and Germany which bear his authentic brand-stamp.

BIBLIOGRAPHY

J. Roda: *Bows for Musical Instruments of the Violin Family* (Chicago, 1959)
W.C. Retford: *Bows and Bow Makers* (London, 1964)
E. Vatelot: *Les archets français* (Nancy, 1976) [in Fr., Ger. and Eng.]

PAUL CHILDS

Pecci, Desiderio (*b* Siena, bap. 23 May 1593; *d* Siena, bur. 21 Aug 1638). Italian composer, lawyer and writer, distant cousin of TOMASO PECCI. He cultivated the necessary skills of a nobleman and won praise from his contemporaries not only as an able composer, singer and instrumentalist, but also for his talents as a poet, playwright and author of legal texts. He was regarded as one of Tuscany's leading lawyers, taught at the University of Siena and filled several of the city's prominent governmental offices. He was a member (with the name Ghiribizzoso) of the Accademia degli Intronati, and the Sienese chronicler Isidoro Ugurgieri Azzolini reported that he held concerts and academy meetings in his home. Although less distinguished as a composer than his cousin Tomaso, Pecci skilfully mingled affective and declamatory styles in his arias and madrigals, assiduously attending to the expressive requirements of his texts.

WORKS

Arie del Signor Desiderio Ghiribizzoso intronato, 1–3vv (Rome, 1626)
1 madrigal, 5vv, in A. Gregori: Primo libro de madrigali (Venice, 1617)
Sacri modulatus ad concentium, 2–4vv (Venice, 1629)
Madrigal, *D-Bsb*; Sub tuum praesidium, motet, 3vv, *GB-Cfm*

BIBLIOGRAPHY

EitnerQ
S.A. Luciani: *La musica in Siena* (Siena, 1942)
A. Mazzeo: *Compositori senesi del 500 ed del 600* (Poggibonsi, 1981)

LAURA BUCH

Pecci, Tomaso (*b* Siena, bap. 8 Oct 1576; *d* Siena, bur. 3 Dec 1604). Italian composer, cousin of DESIDERIO PECCI. He was born to a Sienese family of social prominence and political power. As a nobleman he held no court or church post, but he found a forum for his musical and literary activities in three of Siena's renowned academies: the Accademia dei Filomeli, the Accademia dei Filomati and Ferdinando I de' Medici's Cento Huomini d'Arme. He composed several dozen canzonettas (including two collections dedicated to the Filomeli), two books of madrigals and, for the Compagnia di S Caterina, a set of responsories for Holy Week, gaining recognition as an exponent of the emerging *seconda pratica*. In 1603 Pecci killed a fellow *uomo d'arme* in a duel, and his resultant exile brought him to Rome, where he met the Modenese composer Alfonso Fontanelli. Pecci died the following year and was buried with spiritual privilege by the Compagnia di S Caterina.

Pecci's reputation in the 17th century extended beyond Siena. He was included in Giulio Cesare Monteverdi's list of notable *seconda pratica* composers (published in Claudio Monteverdi's *Scherzi musicali*, 1607) along with Rore, Gesualdo, Fontanelli and others. He was praised by Adriano Banchieri and Pietro della Valle, admired by Fontanelli and lauded in a poem by Marino. The *seconda pratica* informs not only Pecci's madrigals and responsories, but also his canzonettas. He usually chose the concise poetic form of the epigrammatic madrigal as the basis for his secular works, extensively rewriting the original texts for many of his canzonetta settings. He matched the affective *meraviglia* of the texts with unprepared and multiple dissonances, chromaticism, unexpected shifts of mode and of hexachord, expressive melodic intervals, juxtaposed 3rd-relations and unconventional cadential patterns. The madrigal *Era l'anima mia* (1612) and the canzonetta *Mori mi dici* (1603[7]) offer cogent illustration of these devices.

WORKS

all published in Venice

Canzonette, 3vv (1599[11]); ed. M. Givliani (Trent, 1996)
Madrigali, 5vv (1602[8])
Canzonette, libro primo, 3vv (1603[12])
Canzonette, libro secondo, 3vv (1603[7])
Musicae modi in responsoria divini officii feria, 4–6vv (1603)
Madrigal, 5vv, libro secondo (1612)
Works in 1607[25], 1615[2], 1615[14]

Works in *D-Bsb* Landsberg 217; *Dl* Grimma 52, 1–2; *GB-Lbl* Eg.3665; *Och* 510–14; *I-Bc* Q.27, Q61–77; *Sc* L.V.34

BIBLIOGRAPHY

W.T. Foxe: *Text Expression and Tonal Coherence in the Printed Madrigals of Tommaso Pecci (1576–1604): a Sienese Perspective on the Second Practice* (diss., U. of Durham, 1991)
L. Buch: *Seconda prattica and the Aesthetic of Meraviglia: the Canzonettas and Madrigals of Tommaso Pecci (1576–1604)* (diss., U. of Rochester, 1993)

For further bibliography *see* PECCI, DESIDERIO

LAURA BUCH

Pecelli, Asprilio. *See* PACELLI, ASPRILIO.

Pecháček, Franz Xaver (*b* Vienna, 4 July 1793; *d* Karlsruhe, 15 Sept 1840). Austrian violinist and composer. He studied with his father, Franz Martin Pecháček (1763–1816), a well-known composer of popular minuets and ländler. At the age of eight he played at the Viennese court and, according to Fétis, gave a concert with his father in Prague in 1803, which included a concerto by Fodor, an Adagio by Rode and some original variations. From 1805 he studied the violin with Johann Kletzinsky and Ignaz Schuppanzigh and composition with Aloys Förster; from 1809 to 1822 he played in the orchestra of the Theater an der Wien. He visited Paris in the autumn and winter of 1821, accompanied by the Danish virtuoso Weckshall, and there, according to the *Allgemeine musikalische Zeitung*, he had great success. From 1822 to 1826 he was leader at Württemberg, and from 1826 he held the same post at Karlsruhe, where he maintained an association with the Duke of Baden until his death. A second visit by Pecháček to Paris in 1832, mentioned by Fétis, has not been substantiated.

During his tenure in the orchestra of the Theater an der Wien, Pecháček appeared frequently in local concerts. A reviewer for the *Allgemeine musikalische Zeitung* (1815) praised his beautiful tone, brilliant staccato and intrepid security in double stopping and shifting, and accorded him 'a worthy place in the ranks of present-day virtuosos'. The earliest of his 37 published works also date from this same period. The predominant genre is the theme and variations, in accordance with popular taste and Pechá-ček's own technical skills; but a small number of works, among them a quartet (1817) and three overtures (1820–21), show a developing ability and the desire to be more than a writer of virtuoso violin music.

BIBLIOGRAPHY

FétisB; PazdírekH; WurzbachL

G.J. Dlabacž: *Allgemeines historisches Künstler-Lexikon* (Prague, 1815/R), ii, 437

Obituary, *AMZ*, xlii (1840), 895

E. van der Straeten: *The History of the Violin* (London, 1933/R), ii, 109

ALBERT MELL

Pechel [Peckel], Bartłomiej. See PĘKIEL, BARTŁOMIEJ.

Pechin [Pečin], Gregor. See PESCHIN, GREGOR.

Péchon, André (*b* Picardy, *c*1600; *d* after 1683). French composer. He was *maître de chapelle* at St Germain-l'Auxerrois, Paris, in the 1640s, and in 1647 he won a prize at the Le Mans *Puy de musique* with a motet in honour of St Cecilia. In 1652 he was appointed *maître de musique* and principal chaplain of Meaux Cathedral, which did not prevent his directing the music at St Germain-l'Auxerrois again on 12 November 1660. Péchon gave up his post at Meaux in advanced old age, some time before 1683. His only known works, in the Brossard collection, are seven *a cappella* motets on a liturgical cantus firmus; only *Pange lingua* has a continuo part. Brossard stated that Péchon was still remembered and revered in 1724 for his compositional skill.

WORKS

all in F-Pn Rés.Vma 571 and Vm¹1647

Ave regina caelorum, 5vv; Ecce panis angelorum, 4 equal vv; Pange lingua, 2vv, bc; Si quis diligit me, 5vv, ed. D. Launay, *Anthologie du motet latin polyphonique, 1609–1661* (Paris, 1963); Stabat mater, 5vv

2 works, a 5 (without text)

BIBLIOGRAPHY

S. de Brossard: *Catalogue des livres de musique, théorique et prattique, vocalle et instrumentalle qui sont dans le cabinet du Sr Sébastien de Brossard* (MS, F-Pn, 1724)

P.A. Anjubault: *La Sainte Cécile au Mans après 1633* (Le Mans, 1862)

T. L'Huillier: 'Orgues, organistes et facteurs d'orgue dans l'ancienne province de Brie', *Bulletin archéologique du Comité des travaux historiques et scientifiques*, vii (1889), 322–49

M. Brenet: *Sébastien de Brossard: prêtre, compositeur, écrivain et bibliographile, d'après ses papiers inédits* (Paris, 1896), orig. pubd in *Mémoires de la Société de l'histoire de Paris et de l'Ile de France*, xxiii (1896)

Y. de Brossard: *La collection Sébastien de Brossard 1655–1730* (Paris, 1994)

YOLANDE DE BROSSARD

Peçi, Aleksandër (*b* Tirana, 24 April 1951). Albanian composer. After early mandolin and guitar lessons (1961–5) in Shën Saranda, southern Albania, he studied theory, solfège. harmony and the piano at the Jordan Misja Art Lyceum, Tirana (1965–9), and then composition (Zadeja) and orchestration (Ibrahimi) at the Tirana Conservatory (1969–74). After graduation he was musical director (1974–7) in Përmeti (where he was struck by the folk music of the region), composer-in-residence at the Tirana Revue Theatre (1977–9) and director of the State Ensemble of Popular Songs and Dances (1979–86). From 1986 he was salaried by the state to devote himself full time to composition. After the collapse of communism he was able to travel more widely: he participated in the 1992 Amsterdam International Composers' Workshop (with Yuasa, Ton de Leeuw and others) and took further courses in 1993 with Manneke in Amsterdam and with de Leeuw, Charpentier and Méfano in Paris. In 1993 he became president of the Albanian Association for New Music.

Peçi is one of the most successful products of the Albanian music education system set up in the 1960s. After the sober neoclassicism of the early ballet *Kecat dhe ujku* ('The Kids and the Wolf', 1979), he turned in the following decade to symphonic frescoes which echo his experiences of Albanian folklore. In works such as the Rhapsody no.4 (1987) and the *Poema baladike* (1989), he elaborates his thematic material in short motifs, thus producing dense textures in which drama and lyricism alternate poignantly. As he became better acquainted with contemporary musical trends after 1991, Peçi expanded his vocabulary, but without rejecting the past. Rather than yielding completely to the fascination of novel materials, he deployed contrasting elements to highly dramatic and atmospheric effect, often skilfully exploiting female voices (*Dialogue liturgique*, 1993). *Alb-Postmortium 97*, a response to the tragic Otranto Channel incident in which around 80 Albanians drowned attempting to emigrate to Italy in March, 1997, blends echoes of folk dirges and liturgical chant with taped sounds and a soaring coloratura soprano and ranks among the finest achievements of late 20th-century Albanian music.

WORKS

(selective list)

Ballets: Kecat dhe ujku [The Kids and the Wolf] (1, R. Bogdani, choreog. G. Kaçeli), Tirana, 13 Jan 1979; Ajkuna dhe Omeri/Ajunka kujton Omeri i ri [Aïkuna and Homeri/Aokuna Remembers Young Omeri] (choreographic duet, choreog. L. Çakalli), Tirana, 1986; 7 other small-scale ballets

Vocal: Cant. no.1/Kantatë për brezin e ri [Cant. for the Young Generation] (F. Hysi), mixed chorus, orch, ?1977; Cants. no.2, no.3 (F. Hysi), T, mixed chorus, orch, 1977, 1978; Zunë fushat dritheroje [The Plains Start Trembling] (Gj. Zheji), 1 female v, orch, 1983; Sym. no.1, b (D. Agolli), T, Mez, Bar, orch, 1984; Në emër të jetës [In the Name of Life], 1v, orch, 1988; Toka e diellit [Land of the Sun] (Xh. Spahiu), 1v, orch, 1989; Toka ime [My Land] (B. Londo), 4vv, pf, 1990; Dialogue liturgique (P. Budi: Doktrina Kristiana), nar, S, cl, tape, 1993; Alb-postmortium 97 (Epic of Gilgamesh, liturgical texts), nar, S, female v, tape, 1997; Pika shiu varë mbi qelq [Raindrops on Glass] (I. Kadare), S, tape, 1997; Le paradis des enfants (C.P. Baudelaire), children's chorus, pf, perc, ens, 1997–8; other solo vocal works

Orch: Suite, fl, str, c1973–4 Vc Conc. no.1, c, 1974; Përshtypje nga Festivali Folklorik Kombëtar [Impressions from the National Festival of Folklore], 5 sketches, 1974; 3 Sketches, vn, orch, 1974; Variations, hn, orch, 1975; Kënga jonë, këngë e popullit [Our Songs, the Song of the People], 1976; Festa e korrjeve [The Feast of the Harvest], 3 sketches, fl, orch, 1977; Vallja jonë, vallja e popullit [Our Dance, the Dance of the People], rhapsody, 1977; Kuadro heroïzmi [A Picture of Heroism], suite, pf, orch, 1978; Fantasia, vc, orch, 1979; Dance, vn, orch, 1980; Pf Conc., 1980; Fantasia, str, 1981; Vc Conc. no.2, 1982; Scherzo, 1985, rev. 1986; Sym. no.2, e♭, 1985–8; Rhapsody no.3, a, 1987; Rhapsody no.4, c♯, 1987; Dance, vn, small ens, 1987 [based on central Albanian folk song]; Dance, bilbil, trad. insts, 1987; Poema baladike [Poem-Ballad], vc, orch, 1989; Suite, fl, str, 1990; Polycentrum, str, 1999

Chbr: 3 Albanian Dances, vn, pf, 1965, rev., transcr. bn, pf, 1995; Sonata, vn, pf, 1972; Theme and Variations, vc, pf, 1973; 4 Dances from Central Albania, vn, pf, 1975; Rondo, str qt, c1975; 3 Dances, vc, pf, 1976 [on folk themes of southern Albania]; Suite, vn, pf, before 1983 [on folk dances of Përmeti]; Suite, str qt, 1990 [based on film score Kur po xhirohej një film]; Pentacentre-polymodale, xyl, vib, glock, str qnt, 1992; Kënga e thyer [The Broken Song], vc, pf, 1992 [possibly version of Kënga e këputur, vc, pf, 2 perc, perf. Tirana, 1993]; Homothétie et quantité sonores, fl, pf, 1994; Meditation et scherzo, cl, pf, , 1994, arr. vc, pf; Rrënjët e tingujve [The Roots of Sounds], cl, 1994;

Hétéroondulation spatiale, 2 vc, tape, 1995; Double sinusoïde, 2 vc, 1996; Alb-pygmei DD, pf, 1997; Broken Dream, bn, 1998; Remodelage, pf, 1998

12 scores incl.: Kur po xhironhej një film [When a Film was being Shot] (dir. Xh. Keko), 1981; Dasma e Sakos [The Marriage of Sako] (V. Koreshi, dir. V. Prifti), 1998

Principal publishers: Aelfior, Emerson

BIBLIOGRAPHY

A. Peçi: *Aleksandër Peçi* (Tirana, 1997) [in Fr. and Albanian]

R.H. Bogdani: *Koreografi & art i kultivuar* [Choreography and cultivated art] (Tirana, 1998)

GEORGE LEOTSAKOS

Peckover, Alfred. *See* PICCAVER, ALFRED.

Pečman, Rudolf (*b* Staré Město u Frýdku [now Frýdek-Místek], Moravia, 12 April 1931). Czech musicologist and administrator. He studied musicology under Racek and Štědroň, and aesthetics under Mirko Novák at Brno University (1950–55), graduating in 1955 and taking the doctorate in 1967 with a dissertation on Slavonic elements in Beethoven's works and the CSc in 1968 with a dissertation on Mysliveček. He was awarded the DSc in 1989 for his dissertation on Beethoven's stage works. He was appointed assistant lecturer at Brno University in 1955 but although a productive scholar and administrator (head of musicology department 1972–89), he was barred, as a non-communist, from promotion until 1984, when he became lecturer. After the revolution he was made vice-dean of the Philosophy Faculty (1989–91) and was appointed professor of musicology in 1990.

In 1966 Pečman was co-founder of the Brno International Music Festival, an annual event which, in the communist era, became an important focus of east-west musicological relations. He was general secretary (1966–76), during which period he edited the carefully documented festival programmes; until 1985 he edited the conference reports of the 'Brno Colloquia' linked to the festival. Pečman was the long-term editor of the Brno University faculty journal (*SPFFBU*: philosophy series F1–9, 1957–65; music series H1–30, 1966–95) and edited individual conference reports on Černušák (1984), Moravia in Czech music (1986) and Helfert (1988). He was president of the Musicology Section of the Composers Union (1984–9) and president of the Circle of the Friends of Music, Brno (1994–).

Pečman's prolific output as writer and publicist was influenced by that of his teacher Racek, with its focus on history and aesthetics. It includes studies of Mysliveček, Handel, opera (with a particular interest in the role of the libretto) and a thoughtful examination of the hostility in the Czech lands towards Dvořák. His wide range of interests is exemplified by the 35 volumes of programme books which he wrote for the circle of Music Friends in Brno (1970–97).

WRITINGS

ed.: *The Stage Works of Bohuslav Martinů: Brno I 1966* [incl. 'On the Artistic Types to which Bohuslav Martinů and Leoš Janáček Belong'], 115–24

Slovanské prvky v díle L. v. Beethovena [Slavonic elements in Beethoven's works] (diss., U. of Brno, 1967)

Skladatel Josef Mysliveček a jeho jevištní epilog [The composer Mysliveček and his stage epilogue] (diss., U. of Brno, 1968; Brno, 1970, as *Josef Mysliveček und sein Opernepilog*)

ed.: *Leoš Janáček ac musica europaea*[: *Brno III 1968*] [incl. 'Leoš Janáček und einige Strömungen des modernen Theaters', 131–40]

'Benda's "The Village Market" as a Precursor of "Fidelio"', *SPFFBU*, H5 (1970), 141–50

'Ludwig van Beethoven und Jiří Antonín Benda', *Beethoven Congress: Berlin 1970*, 453–64

'Die Musik in der Auffassung Heinrich Christoph Kochs', *SPFFBU*, H6 (1971), 51–62

'Niveau général de la controverse du Baroque musical et du Classicisme', *SPFFBU*, H7 (1972), 63–93

'Zum Begriff des Rokokostils in der Musik', *MZ*, ix (1973), 5–34

'Alessandro Scarlatti: a Predecessor of Joseph Haydn in the Genre of the String Quartet', *Haydn Studies: Washington DC 1975*, 456–9

'Apostolo Zeno und sein Libretto "Il Venceslao" zu dem gleichnamigen Pasticcio von Georg Friedrich Händel', *G.F. Händel und seine italienischen Zeitgenossen: Halle 1978*, 66–93

Beethoven dramatik [Beethoven as stage composer] (Hradec Králové, 1978)

'Contribution au problème de la musique nationale en Europe aux 18e et 19e siècles', *Musica viva in schola* (Brno, 1980), 11–25

ed.: *The Musical Theatre: Brno XV 1980*[incl. 'Libretti legen ihre Zeugenschaft ab', 59–92]

'Bach und Zelenka: ein Beitrag zur Entfaltung des Vivaldischen Stils', *Bach-Studien*, vi (1981), 139–43

'Baron Friedrich Melchior Grimm und die Musik', *Der Einfluss der französischen Musik auf die Komponisten der ersten Hälfte des 18. Jahrhunderts: Blankenburg, Harz, 1981*, 39–42

Beethovens Opernpläne (Brno, 1981)

Josef Mysliveček (Prague, 1981)

'Methusalem und Emilia Marty: von Shaw zu Čapek und Janáček', *SPFFBU*, H17 (1982), 21–40

'Zum oratorischen Schaffen Joseph Haydns und Josef Myslivečeks', *Joseph Haydn: Vienna 1982*, 101–4

ed.: *Gracian Černušák a otázky české hudební historiografie: Brno 1982*

'Zur Frage der thematischen Übereinstimmungen in Georg Friedrich Händels Werk', *SPFFBU*, H18 (1983), 35–46

'Wagner und Janáček', *Der Einfluss der romantischen Musik ... im 20. Jahrhundert: Dresden 1984*, 29–38

ed.: *Morava v české hudbě: Brno 1984*

Georg Friedrich Händel (Prague, 1985)

'Generalbass in den Lehrbüchern F.X. Brixis und F.X. Richters', *Generalbassspiel im 17. und 18. Jahrhundert: Editionsfragen: Blankenburg, Harz, 1986*, 36–8

'Der junge Bach und die italienische Musik', *Bach-Studien*, ix (1986), 84–9

ed.: *Vladimír Helfert v českém a evropském kontextu: Brno 1986*

'Einige Probleme der Opernforschung', *Zbornik Matice srpske za scenske umetnosti i muziku*, no.2 (1987), 41–57

'Einige Probleme der Affektentheorie bei Johann Joachim Quantz und Carl Philipp Emanuel Bach', *Fragen der Aufführungspraxis und Interpretation von Werken Carl Philipp Emanuel Bachs: Blankenburg, Harz, 1988*, i, 36–40

Eseje o Martinů [Essays on Martinů] (Brno, 1989)

Jevištní dílo L.v. Beethovena [Beethoven's stage works] (diss., U. of Brno, 1989)

Franz Xaver Richter und seine 'Harmonische Belehrungen' (Michaelstein, nr Blankenburg, 1990)

'Sub olea pacis et palma virtutis', *HJb* 1990, 163–70

'Dramatisch-szenische Aspekte in Händels Oratorien der mittleren Schaffenszeit', *HJb* 1991, 153–61

Sloh a hudba 1600–1900 [Style and music] (Brno, 1991, 2/1996)

Útok na Antonína Dvořáka [The attack on Antonín Dvořák] (Brno, 1992)

'Die unter freiem Himmel aufzuführende Musik Händels', *Georg Friedrich Händel: ein Lebensinhalt: Gedenkschrift für Bernd Baselt (1934–1993)*, ed. K. Hortschansky and K. Musketa (Kassel, 1995), 131–8

'Miscellania Haendeliana', *Telemanniana et alia musicologica: Festschrift für Günter Fleischhauer zum 65. Geburtstag*, ed. D. Gutknecht, H. Krones and F. Zschoch (Michaelstein, nr Blankenburg, 1995), 165–71

JOHN TYRRELL

Pécour [Pécourt], Louis Guillaume (*b* ?1651; *d* 11 April 1729). French dancing-master and choreographer. He was one of the finest dancers working under the celebrated royal choreographer Pierre Beauchamp. He is said in one source to have made his début as a dancer in a repeat performance of Lully's *Cadmus et Hermione* in 1674. When, on Lully's death in 1687, Beauchamp left the Opéra, Pécour was appointed in his place. He gave up

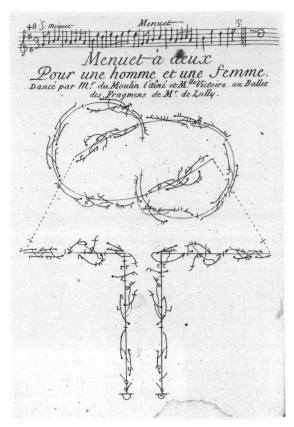

Choreography for a minuet by Lully from Pécour's 'Recüeil de dances' (Paris, 1704)

dancing in about 1703 but he held the post of ballet-master and choreographer at the Opéra until his death. His tutelage produced such outstanding dancers as La Fontaine, Subligny, Guiot, Prevost and Menese among the women and Blondy, Ballon, Dumoulin and Marcel among the men. He is credited with changing the 'S' figure of the MINUET to a 'Z', an innovation that helped keep the dancers in a proper relationship to each other and to the figure.

Many of his dances were recorded in the Beauchamp-Feuillet system of dance notation and can to a certain extent be re-created. Both the floor pattern and the steps are given in the notation. The style may be derived from a study of Pierre Rameau's *Le maître à danser* (Paris, 1725; Eng. trans., 1931/R), a didactic work that he personally approved. A total of 120 choreographies by him have so far come to light; most of them are for the theatre, but many are for social dancing. Many of the theatre dances include the names of the works for which they were created and of the performers who executed them. The choreographies may be found in *Recüeil de dances* (Paris, 1700/R, nine ball dances); *Recüeil de dances* (Paris, 1704/R, 35 theatre dances); *Recüeil* (Paris, 1712, nine ball and 30 theatre dances); annual collections published by Feuillet and Dezais (Paris, 1700–22, 26 ball dances); E. Pemberton: *An Essay for the Further Improvement of Dancing* (London, 1711, one jig); miscellaneous manuscript collections, four theatre dances (Little and Marsh contains a complete annotated inventory). Many of Pécour's works appeared in several prints and manu-

scripts; for example, 12 dances, all published previously, were put into a slightly revised version of the dance notation by Pierre Rameau in the second part of his *Abrégé de la nouvelle méthode* (Paris, 1725).

BIBLIOGRAPHY
A. Levinson: 'Les danseurs de Lully', *ReM*, vi/3 (1924–5), 44–55
W. Hilton: *Dance of Court and Theater* (Princeton, NJ, 1981)
A.L. Witherell: *Louis Pécour's 1700 'Recüeil de dances'* (Ann Arbor, 1983)
M. Little and C. Marsh: *La Danse Noble: an Inventory of Dances and Sources* (New York, 1992)
F. Lancelot: *La Belle Dance: Catalogue raisonné* (Paris, 1996)
MEREDITH ELLIS LITTLE

Pécsi, Sebestyén (*b* Budapest, 29 Oct 1910). Hungarian organist. He studied at the Budapest Academy of Music, obtaining his diploma in 1937. From 1938 he appeared as a concert organist both at home and in important European cities, becoming one of Hungary's foremost organists. In 1940 he was appointed a lecturer (later a professor) at the Liszt Academy of Music. His activity as a teacher resulted in a number of different pedagogical works, including an organ tutor (1956, 3/1974), an organ method (1965) and a technical study of the organ (1975). He edited organ music by Hungarian composers, and also composed lieder and works for orchestra and organ. In addition to his extensive recital work he made several recordings, mostly of Bach, Liszt and Kodály (including a work dedicated to him), and also works by contemporary Hungarian and French composers. He was awarded the Liszt Prize in 1957 and the Hungarian National Prize in 1974.

GERHARD WIENKE/R

Pedal (Fr. *pédale*; Ger. *Pedal*; It. *pedale*). Any of several types of lever, operated by the foot and used for a variety of purposes on musical instruments: (1) to change tuning, as in the pedal harp (*see* HARP, §V, 7 and TIMPANI, §V, 7).

(2) To operate the bellows of a chamber organ, REED ORGAN or the like; to operate the bellows and playing mechanism of a PLAYER PIANO, BARREL ORGAN or other MECHANICAL INSTRUMENT.

(3) To sound the bass drum and high-hat cymbals in the performance of popular music. See DRUM, §II, 1 and DRUM KIT.

(4) To produce expressive effects, to change the tone-colour, or to alter the volume, as on the PIANOFORTE, types of ORGAN and HARPSICHORD, the vibraphone and some electronic instruments. On the modern piano, the pedal at the right (the 'loud', 'sustaining' or 'damper' pedal) acts to move all the dampers away from the strings so that notes being played continue to sound even after the keys are no longer depressed; strings for other notes may also vibrate sympathetically with those being played. The pedal at the left (the 'soft' or 'una corda' pedal) on grand pianos acts to shift the entire action sideways so that the hammers do not strike all of the strings provided for each note (on upright pianos this pedal moves all the hammers closer to the strings so as to shorten their stroke, producing a sound of less volume). The middle pedal, where present, on grand pianos is a 'sostenuto' pedal. Notes already being produced when this pedal is depressed continue to sound after the fingers have left the keys. On upright pianos the middle pedal is sometimes a sostenuto pedal and sometimes a 'muffler' or a 'moderator' pedal that mutes the sound of the instrument by interposing a strip of cloth between the hammers and the strings. On

pianos of the 18th and early 19th centuries a variety of hand stops, knee levers and pedals were used (*see* PEDALLING). On some modern harpsichords the jack slides, buff battens and coupler are connected to individual pedals by means of which all changes of registration are effected without removing the hands from the keyboard. Pedal control of volume is found on both pipe and electronic organs.

Pedal-operated signal processor units may be used to enhance, distort or change the electrical signal produced by an ELECTRIC GUITAR or other electro-acoustic instruments (*see* ELECTRONIC INSTRUMENTS, §I, 5(i)).

See also COMPOSITION PEDAL; KNEE-LEVER; MACHINE STOP; SWELL.

(5) The term is used most widely for a series of pedals, arranged somewhat like the keys of a piano, to form a keyboard played by the feet rather than by the hands. This has been provided at various times for the harpsichord, clavichord, piano (*see* PEDAL CLAVICHORD; PEDAL HARPSICHORD; PEDAL PIANOFORTE), carillon and, above all, for the organ. On this instrument, the pedals are either keyboards for the feet (pedal keys, contained in a pedal-board) or levers operating an accessory device such as that to change stops (e.g. COMPOSITION PEDAL). Pedal-boards are sometimes also applied to the harpsichord and clavichord. The term is a direct equivalent of certain Latin phrases (for example, the keys 'pro tastandi cum pedibus' at S Maria Novella, Florence, 1379), although early vernacular usages are not at all clear (for example, the *pedalen* at Delft in 1483); the word does not seem to occur in England before *c*1525. Like 'organum' itself, *pes* (*pedes*) is a word belonging as much to medieval music as to medieval instruments (*see* PES(i)).

The early history of the pedal suggests that key levers for the feet could serve many musical purposes. Despite traditional stories, there seems to be no reason to think them a German invention. The protruding sticks for the feet at Halberstadt Cathedral (*c*1361) played a type of large BLOCKWERK, while the little positive organ at Norrelanda, Sweden (*c*1370), had them to play the bass pipes. Many 15th-century organs (e.g. those at Troyes, Haarlem, 's-Hertogenbosch and Utrecht) had a group of large open Bourdon pipes (usually ten) placed on a separate chest on the wall to the side of the organ supported by a pendentive or *trompe* (hence their name, *trompes*) and played in most instances by pedal keys which probably worked by admitting wind along conduits running to the pipes. The Ileborg organ MS of 1448 refers to 'pedale seu manuale'; and the Buxheim Organbook (1450–60) to playing the 'tenore inferius in pedali', probably at written pitch. From 1450 to 1550 pedals were of several types: pulldowns to manual keys or pallets with or without a rank or more of chorus or solo pipes (8′ Trumpet and 2′ Flute were common in the Netherlands by about 1540); pedal-boards playing transmitted stops from a manual; or a pedal organ with independent stops, often including reeds. The compass was ideally up to *c*′ and down to the lowest note of the main manual (*F* to *c*′ according to Schlick, 1511). By 1600 pedals in some areas had immense versatility, for example, the 26 stops on four chests at Grüningen Schlosskirche.

During the 17th century instruments like those at Grüningen and in the big Hanseatic town churches encouraged the development of alternate right–left toe-pedalling (Scheidemann, etc), and the writing of both bass and solo lines for the pedal. Praetorius noted that pedals were rare in England and Italy; but composers in northern France, the Netherlands and Germany developed the idea of pedals taking cantus firmus or solo lines, generally *en taille*, that is, with accompaniment above and below. Moreover many of Schlick's recommendations of 1511 are still valid: the pedal should have separate stops, a compass to *c*′, a tolerable length of key (*c*30 cm for naturals and 6 cm for sharps), a bench high enough to allow quick passage-work, and keys narrower than the space between them to make two- and even four-part playing easy.

While the 17th and 18th centuries saw variety in the shape, size and playing technique of the PEDAL-BOARD, nothing new could be added to the musical use of the department. French organists continued to emphasize *en taille* textures; Italian organists kept pedals for 'organ points'; in England pulldowns were rare before the 1790s; and in the Iberian peninsula pedals were largely reserved for pedal points in certain tonalities (C,D, E and F).

In the fully-fledged WERKPRINZIP organ of Hamburg (*c*1690), the pedal was very important and versatile, both aurally and visually; ideally it sounded an octave below the *Hauptwerk* Prinzipal, itself an octave below the *Rückpositiv*. 'German' pedals, that is, straight pedal-boards with independent stops and a compass of C to *c*′ became the norm from about 1820 in northern Europe, not least because J.S. Bach's organ works were then becoming increasingly available. On the grounds that organists' hands needed more than one keyboard for quick changes of sound, E.F. Walcker and others sometimes made double pedal-boards, more admired by such theorists as Töpfer than by players. The desire to extend the expressive powers of the instrument also led some builders (e.g. Walcker, Boston Music Hall, 1863) to practise, and some theorists (e.g. Audsley, *The Art of Organ Building*, 1905) to advocate, the enclosure of some of the Pedal registers in the swell box with the manual registers. Composers continued to exploit the traditional alternate-foot technique even in chromatic music, long after such travelling virtuosos as G.J. Vogler had introduced toe-and-heel pedalling.

See also PEDAL NOTE; PEDAL ORGAN; PEDAL POINT; ORGAN POINT.

EDWIN M. RIPIN, PETER WILLIAMS/DAVID ROWLAND (4),
NICHOLAS THISTLETHWAITE (5)

Pedal-board (i). A keyboard played by the feet, chiefly to be found in organs, but also in carillons, harpsichords, clavichords and pianos. It can be connected either to its own pipes (bells, strings) or to the manual keyboard(s) of the same instrument. Early types are for playing with the toes: short sticks protruding from the lower case-front either as simple strips of wood (Halberstadt, *c*1361) or as proto-keys (Norrlanda, *c*1370), small rectangular frames with short straight keys (16th-century Flanders and Italy), the same with longer keys but still for toe-pedalling (16th-century Netherlands and Germany), round or square studs into which the toe or ball of the foot presses (Iberian organs, 17th–18th centuries), flat, shallow, rectangular boxes through the upper board of which pass short separated pedal keys (France and Belgium, 18th century). Eventually, longer and thicker pedals designed for occasional playing with the heel were developed (18th-century Netherlands and Germany); these were called 'German pedals' in English sources from about 1810.

Romantic and modern organs have seen a great variety of pedal-board compasses (up to 32 notes, $C-g'$, in large Anglo-American organs) and styles (with concave, parallel or radiating forms, or combinations of these). Large Italian and German 19th-century organs possessed 'double' pedal-boards, the upper being placed at an angle to the lower. *See also* PEDAL.

PETER WILLIAMS/MARTIN RENSHAW

Pedal-board (ii). A rack of pedal-operated signal processor units for enhancing, distorting or changing the electrical signal produced by an ELECTRIC GUITAR or other electro-acoustic instrument. *See also* ELECTRONIC INSTRUMENTS, §I, 5(i).

PETER WILLIAMS/MARTIN RENSHAW

Pedalcembalo (Ger.). *See* PEDAL HARPSICHORD.

Pedal clarinet. A CONTRABASS CLARINET; a member of the clarinet family pitched two octaves below the soprano clarinet in B♭.

Pedal clavichord (Ger. *Pedalklavichord, Pedalclavier*). A clavichord equipped with a pedal-board like that of an organ. Instruments of this type are mentioned by Paulus Paulirinus of Prague (*c*1460) and Virdung (*Musica getutscht*, 1511), and a 15th-century drawing shows a clavichord with a two-and-a-half-octave compass B to f'', with a 12-note pedal-board B to b (with b♭ omitted, perhaps in error) beneath it. Such instruments were primarily used for practice purposes by organists, and this function is specifically cited by Paulirinus. Most of them presumably had pull-down pedals directly connected by cords to the bass notes of an ordinary clavichord, but Adlung (*Musica mechanica organoedi*, 1768) noted that such a system presents problems because the pedal keys must be more widely spaced than the manual and, accordingly, the cords must slant and therefore tend to drag the keys sideways as they are pulled down. This problem could be obviated by the use of a rollerboard, which, however, was noisy and vastly increased the cost of the instrument. A better system was to provide a completely separate instrument to be sounded by the pedal keys; this was set underneath an ordinary clavichord and could be strung with sub-octave as well as unison strings, thereby better approximating the resources of the pedal division of an organ.

The most elaborate pedal clavichords consisted of three separate instruments arranged one above the other and providing an approximation of an organ with two independent manuals and pedal. A single example of such an instrument survives, in the Musikinstrumenten-Museum of the University of Leipzig; it was made by Johan David Gerstenberg of Geringswalde, and comprises two double-strung, fret-free clavichords of normal size with a range of C to e''' and a much larger instrument set beneath them, also fret-free, which is quadruple-strung – with two strings tuned in unison and two tuned an octave lower – and has a two-octave range of C to c'. A pedal clavichord in pyramid form about 275 cm high and about 214 cm wide, with ten changes of tone, was made by H.N. Gerber in 1742, and a clavichord with pedal keyboard built into a single case made by Georg Gebel (i) of Breslau (who also made a similar pedal harpsichord) is reported by Mattheson in his *Grundlage einer Ehren-Pforte* (1740). An instrument of this kind is depicted in J. Verschuere Reynvaan's *Muzijkaal kunst-woordenboek* (1789), the

accompanying text for which (derived from Claas Douwes's *Grondig ondersoek van de toonen der muzijk*, 1699) states that on a pedal clavichord each course of strings can be struck by three or four tangents, so that only eight courses of strings would be required for its entire compass of two octaves and a note. Douwes claimed that the pedal-board on his instrument could be pushed into the instrument for ease in transporting it, an idea which to his knowledge had not been put into practice by anyone else. Music specially for pedal clavichord was composed by G.A. Sorge, H.N. Gerber, and F.W. Marpurg. The instrument continued to be used by organists until after 1800.

It is highly probable that J.S. Bach at one time owned a pedal clavichord of the kind with two independent manuals – he gave '3 Claviere nebst Pedal' to his son J.C. Bach sometime before his death (the implication derived from Forkel that he also owned a pedal harpsichord does not bear close scrutiny).

The universities of Nebraska, USA, and Göteburg, Sweden, have since 1993 and 1995, respectively, used copies of the Gerstenberg two-manual and pedal clavichord and have found them to be practical and effective training instruments for organists, demonstrating a constructive affinity between the clavichord action and that of the tracker organ. The fingers and the feet must use a positive and firm touch otherwise the clavichord does not speak clearly, and the dynamic sensitivity of the clavichord reveals any unevenness. Consequently, organists who prepare themselves by facing the extra difficulties of the pedal clavichord often find that their playing is more secure than if all their preparation had been on the organ.

BIBLIOGRAPHY

J. Adlung: *Musica mechanica organoedi*, ii, ed. J.L. Albrecht (Berlin, 1768/R), 158–62; ed. C. Mahrenholz (Kassel, 1931)
J. Handschin: 'Das Pedalklavier', *ZMw*, xvii (1935), 418–25
S. Jeans: 'The Pedal Clavichord and other Practice Instruments of Organists', *PRMA*, lxxvii (1950–51), 1–15
H. Henkel, ed.: *Clavichorde: Katalog*, Musikinstrumentem-Museum der Karl-Marx-Universität Leipzig, iv (Leipzig, 1981) [museum catalogue]
J. Potvlieghe: 'Het pedaalklavichord', *Orgelkunst viermaandelijks tijdschrift*, xi (1988), 113–25; repr. in *Het Clavichord*, ii (1989), 4–11
H. van Veen: 'Een tweeklaviers "pedaalclavicorde" in Alkmaar', *Het Clavichord*, ii/3 (1989), 12–14
J. Rass: 'Das Pedalclavichord und der Organist', *Het Clavichord*, vii/3 (1994), 55–62
J. Barnes and J. Speerstra: 'The Göteborg 1995 Pedal Clavichord', *Het Clavichord*, viii/1 (1995), 6–13
K. Ford: 'The Pedal Clavichord and the Pedal Harpsichord', *GSJ*, l (1997), 161
De clavicordio III: Magnano 1999 [incl. J. Speerstra: 'The Pedal Clavichord as a Pedagogical Tool for Organists', 109–18]

EDWIN M. RIPIN/JOHN BARNES

Pedalflügel (Ger.). *See* PEDAL PIANOFORTE.

Pedal harpsichord (Fr. *clavecin de pédale*; Ger. *Clavicymbelpedal, Pedalcembalo*). A harpsichord equipped with a pedal-board like that of an organ. Hardly any original examples survive, although a number of Italian harpsichords and virginals show clear evidence, in the form of attachments on the underside of the bass keys and holes in the bottom of the case, that at one time they were equipped with eight to 18 pedals connected to the lowest keys by cords. (Two Italian virginals in the Tagliavini collection, Bologna, of the 16th and early 19th centuries respectively, have been restored with reconstructions of their missing original pedal-boards.) Although this 'pull-down' system was also known in Germany, it seems that the more usual practice in Germany and France was to build a separate instrument with a pedal keyboard, to be placed on the floor underneath an ordinary two-manual harpsichord. The Weimar court organist J.C. Vogler (1696–1763), a pupil of J.S. Bach, possessed an extraordinary instrument (described in a contemporary advertisement, reprinted in Anthon, 1984) consisting of a two-manual harpsichord (with $2 \times 8'$, $1 \times 4'$, a buff stop, and a six-octave compass of C' to c''') and a pedal harpsichord in its own case underneath, disposed $1 \times 32'$, $1 \times 16'$, $2 \times 8'$, with two buff stops and a door in the lid to adjust the volume.

The *Encyclopédie méthodique* (i, 1791) mentions a different type of pedal harpsichord in which a second soundboard was applied to the underside of a harpsichord; heavy strings stretched beneath this soundboard were struck by pedal-operated hammers. This system was also employed in some pedal pianos. A large harpsichord made by Joachim Swanen (Paris, 1786; now in the Conservatoire des Arts et Métiers, Paris) has a pedal mechanism of this kind with a range of two octaves, but the mechanism now on the instrument does not appear to date from the 18th century.

Like the more common PEDAL CLAVICHORD, the pedal harpsichord seems to have been made and used primarily as a practice instrument for organists. While harpsichords and clavichords with pedals might be employed effectively in the literal performance of particular passages that J.S. Bach undoubtedly composed with stringed-keyboard instruments in mind (such as the cadenza in the first movement of the Brandenburg Concerto no.5, BWV1050 and the A minor fugue of *Das wohltemperirte Clavier*, i, BWV865) in which there are a few bass notes that cannot be played by the left hand, the belief, advanced by 19th- and early 20th-century scholars including Spitta and Schweitzer, that certain of his works, such as the Trio Sonatas BWV525–30 and the Passacaglia in C minor BWV582, were conceived specifically for the pedal harpsichord rather than the organ is untenable. Nevertheless, organ works of Bach and his contemporaries can be performed effectively on the pedal harpsichord, as surely they were, upon occasion, in their day. During the 20th century, several instrument builders constructed pedal harpsichords.

BIBLIOGRAPHY

F. Hubbard: *Three Centuries of Harpsichord Making* (Cambridge, MA, 1965, 2/1967), 110ff, 270ff

C.G. Anthon: 'An Unusual Harpsichord', *GSJ*, xxxvii (1984), 115–16

L.F. Tagliavini and J.H. van der Meer, eds.: *Clavicembali e spinette dal XVI al XIX secolo: collezione L.F. Tagliavini* (Bologna, 1986), 136–43, 164–9

K. Ford: 'The Pedal Clavichord and the Pedal Harpsichord', *GSJ*, l (1997), 161–79

EDWIN M. RIPIN/JOHN KOSTER

Pédalier (Fr.). (1) A pedal keyboard attached to a piano and capable of activating its hammers.

(2) An independent PEDAL PIANOFORTE made by Pleyel, Wolff & Cie in Paris, to be placed underneath an ordinary grand piano.

Pedaliter. A quasi-Latin term derived from *pedalis* (a part 'for the feet') to indicate that a piece of organ music so labelled is played by both hands and feet. The word appears to have arisen as an antithesis to MANUALITER and was so used by Schlick (1511). Although it does not indicate a piece played by pedals alone, it does in practice imply one with a developed pedal part. Sometimes composers used it to suggest a large-scale work in several 'voices' (e.g. Scheidt's '*Benedicamus* à 6 voc. pleno organo pedaliter', 1624). However, in the third section of his *Clavier-Übung* Bach seems to have contrasted *manualiter* with a phrase such as 'canto fermo in basso'; but *pedaliter* itself also appeared in music from his circle, chiefly outside the context of organ chorales and pedal melodies, as for example in the autograph manuscript of BWV535a, and in Buxtehude's C major Praeludium in the 'Johann Andreas Bach Buch'.

PETER WILLIAMS

Pedalklavichord (Ger.). *See* PEDAL CLAVICHORD

Pedalklavier (Ger.). *See* PEDAL PIANOFORTE.

Pedalling. The art of using the tone-modifying devices operated on the modern piano by pedals. In the earlier history of the instrument similar, and other, devices were operated by hand stops, knee levers or pedals. The mechanisms of these devices are described in PIANOFORTE, §I, and in articles on individual stops and pedals.

1. To *c*1790. 2. *c*1790 to 1830. 3. From *c*1830.

1. TO *c*1790.   The number and type of tone-modifying devices on 18th-century pianos varied substantially. Cristofori, the maker of the earliest pianos, used only the UNA CORDA, which is found on two of his three surviving instruments. The *una corda* also appears on an early piano from the Iberian peninsula. The earliest extant pianos from Germany, made in the 1740s by Gottfried Silbermann, were the first to have a sustaining (damper-raising) stop. The effect produced by this stop imitates the sound of the Pantaleon, a type of large dulcimer also made by Silbermann, and was popular in mid-18th-century Germany. The term PANTALON STOP was used for a stop found in some unfretted clavichords (Adlung, 568) and the name 'Pantalon' was given to pianos with wooden hammers and no dampers. Silbermann also used an ivory mutation stop, which imitates the sound of the harpsichord by means of small pieces of ivory brought into contact with the strings just above the hammer's striking point.

A sustaining device was usual on later 18th-century German and Austrian grand pianos, and during the last quarter of the century the mechanism was normally operated by knee levers. The MODERATOR also became common at this time. At first the moderator mechanism was operated by a hand stop, but by the 1790s a knee lever was used for this too. A BASSOON STOP operated by a knee lever is found on some later 18th-century German and Austrian pianos. From Backers (1772) onwards, the standard disposition of English grands was two pedals: sustaining and *una corda*.

It is difficult to generalize about the stops, levers and pedals available on 18th-century square pianos. Whereas many earlier English squares had three levers inside the piano (two to raise the ends of the damper rail and one to operate the BUFF STOP), some later instruments had no levers or pedals. A proliferation of tone-modifying devices, including lid swells (*see* SWELL, §2), was fashionable with some on the Continent, but the trend was much criticized by others. Hand stops were later replaced by pedals in

England, but both knee levers and pedals were used on continental squares towards the end of the century, with a preference for the former.

No pedal markings exist in music before the 1790s and other sources are generally reticent on the subject, although a few authors mention the use of the sustaining lever. C.P.E. Bach commented that 'the undamped register of the fortepiano is the most pleasing and, once the performer learns to observe the necessary precautions in the face of its reverberations, the most delightful for improvisation'. Charles Burney was less enthusiastic about a performance without dampers given in 1770 by Anne Brillon de Jouy in Paris:

She was so obliging as to play several of her own pieces both on the harpsichord and piano forte [Burney]. . . I could not persuade Madame B to play the piano forte with the stops on – *c'est sec*, she said – but with them off unless in arpeggios, nothing is distinct – 'tis like the sound of bells, continual and confluent.

Evidently some use was made of the undamped register and presumably of other registers too, but tone-modifying devices do not appear to have been widely accepted throughout most of the 18th century. Their use cannot have been very subtle, since they were often operated by hand stops. Descriptions suggest that they were generally thought of in the same way as organ or harpsichord registers.

2. c1790 TO 1830.   Daniel Steibelt published the first music with pedalling indications in his *6me Pot Pourri* and his *Mélange* op.10, both of which appeared in Paris in 1793. The pedalling in these pieces is of a somewhat rudimentary nature, with the sustaining pedal apparently held down for several bars at a time. It is possible that these indications simply define the outer parameters of passages in which the performer raises and depresses the dampers at will. However, pedalling indications in a slightly later concerto by Boieldieu suggest that pianists were still accustomed to raising the dampers for several bars at a time, or even whole sections of a movement: the indications 'Grande Pédalle toute la Variation' and 'Sourdine aux accords seulement' mean 'sustaining pedal for the whole variation' and 'lute for the chords only'. In Steibelt's two works, new, distinctively pianistic writing begins to appear, notably the *tremolando* for which he was to become (in)famous and the accompanying texture in which the sustaining pedal allows a bass note to be sustained below other notes or chords which complete the harmony.

While some regarded Steibelt's innovations as mere gimmickry, others began to use similar techniques to develop a new style. Chief among the latter were members of the London Pianoforte School. Cramer seems to have introduced printed pedalling in London, in his second concerto of 1797. However, later commentators singled out Dussek as the most significant pioneer of pedalling in his generation. His first pedal markings appeared in the *Military Concerto* op.40 of 1798, but the technique in this work suggests that he had been using the pedals for some time previously. Clementi, the oldest member of the School, included pedal markings in some works of the late 1790s, but they represent a much less developed approach than that of his younger contemporaries.

Some German and Austrian musicians were very conservative in their use of the pedals (or levers). For example, while Beethoven's approach shared many similarities with that of members of the London Pianoforte

School, Hummel was cautious: 'Hummel's partisans accused Beethoven of mistreating the piano, of lacking all clearness and clarity, of creating nothing but confused noise the way he used the pedals' (Czerny, 1842). Hummel later wrote that 'though a truly great artist has no occasion for the pedals to work upon his audience by expression and power, yet the use of the damper pedal, combined occasionally with the piano pedal (as it is termed), has an agreeable effect in many passages'. At around the same time, Kalkbrenner observed that 'in Germany the use of the pedals is scarcely known'. Pedal markings appeared in music by German and Austrian composers a little later than in England and France.

The terminology of early pedal markings has caused some confusion. In England, the term for the sustaining pedal was 'Open Pedal' while in Vienna it was 'Senza Sordini' ('S.S.').

Shortly after 1800 Viennese-style grands acquired something of a 'standard' disposition of tone-modifying devices. The knee levers were replaced by four pedals: *una corda*, moderator, bassoon and sustaining. To these were sometimes added a second moderator and 'Turkish music' ('Janissary stop'), a stop with bells, drum and triangle or cymbal. A similar four-pedal disposition existed in France, although a LUTE STOP often replaced the bassoon. Pedals other than the sustaining, moderator and *una corda* were never highly regarded by professionals and largely died out in the 1830s. In England, the only pedals generally used were the *una corda* and sustaining. The latter was sometimes divided (as was the damper rail itself) to allow selective sustaining.

Refinements in pedalling technique developed quickly at the beginning of the 19th century. Accounts of Dussek's playing suggest that he gave the effect of continuous pedalling while retaining clarity in his playing. This effect requires syncopated pedalling, in which the pedal is raised on the beat and depressed again shortly afterwards. Dussek's notation is too imprecise to show this, but syncopated pedalling is suggested by the markings in Clementi's Fantaisie op.48 (1821).

3. FROM c1830.   As 19th-century pianos became more resonant, increasingly sophisticated pedalling was called for; it is clear that Chopin, Liszt and some of their contemporaries exhibited all the essentials of a modern technique. These pianists had individual pedalling styles distinguished, for example, by the clarity of their playing and the extent to which they used the *una corda*. Some, including Beethoven, Kalkbrenner and Thalberg, made extensive use of the *una corda*, but others objected to the changes of timbre that its use caused in the middle of phrases, and reserved it for special effects in discrete sections. Extensive use of the pedals was condemned by a few writers: Friedrich Wieck lamented what he perceived as the excesses of pianists he associated particularly with Paris.

After the middle of the 19th century, the only significant development in pedalling was the invention of the selective tone-sustaining pedal. J.L. Boisselot exhibited such a device at the Paris exposition of 1844 and other mechanisms designed to achieve the same, or similar, effect followed. However, the principle of selective tone-sustaining became established only after Steinway patented the SOSTENUTO PEDAL in 1874. A few composers indicated this pedal in scores, but many others were reluctant to use it, especially in Europe, and its adoption by leading makers was a gradual process.

Pedalling has been acknowledged as an extremely important element of performance. Following the emergence of pedalling in piano music of the 1790s, some tutors devoted significant space to it (Milchmeyer, Adam, Steibelt), but it was not, however, until the pioneering work of Schmitt (1875) and Lavignac (1889) that the subject received detailed treatment.

BIBLIOGRAPHY

ClinkscaleMP

C.P.E. Bach: *Versuch über die wahre Art das Clavier zu spielen* (Berlin, 1753/R, 2/1787; Eng. trans., 1974), 431

J. Adlung: *Anleitung zu der musikalischen Gelahrtheit* (Erfurt, 1758/R, 2/1783)

J.P. Milchmeyer: *Die wahre Art das Pianoforte zu spielen* (Dresden, 1797)

L. Adam: *Méthode de piano du Conservatoire* (Paris, 1804)

D. Steibelt: *Méthode de piano* (Paris and Leipzig, 1809)

J.N. Hummel: *Ausführliche, theoretisch-practische Anweisung zum Piano-forte Spiel* (Vienna, 1828, 2/1838; Eng. trans., 1829), iii, 62

F. Kalkbrenner: *Méthode pour apprendre le pianoforte* (Paris, 1830; Eng. trans., 1862), 10

C. Czerny: *Vollständige theoretisch-practische Pianoforteschule* (Vienna, 1838–9; Eng. trans., 1839)

C. Czerny: *Erinnerungen aus meinem Leben* (MS, 1842, A-Wgm; ed. W. Kolneder, 1968; Eng. trans., MQ, xlii (1956), 302–17

F. Wieck: *Clavier und Gesang* (Leipzig, 1853; Eng. trans., 1988)

H. Schmitt: *Das Pedal des Clavieres* (Vienna, 1875; Eng. trans., 1893)

A. Lavignac: *L'école de la pédale* (Paris, 1889)

R.E.H. Harding: *The Piano-forte: its History Traced to the Great Exhibition of 1851* (Cambridge,1933/R, 2/1978)

F.J. Hirt: *Meisterwerke des Klavierbaus* (Berlin, 1955; Eng. trans., 1968)

C. Burney: *Music, Men and Manners in France and Italy*, ed. H.E. Poole (London, 1969, 2/1974), 19–20 [based on Journal, 1771, and *The Present State of Music in France and Italy*, 2/1773]

J. Banowetz: *The Pianist's Guide to Pedaling* (Bloomington, IN, 1985)

W. Cole: 'Americus Backers; Original Forte Piano Maker', *The Harpsichord and Pianoforte Magazine*, iv (1987), 79–85

D. Rowland: *A History of Pianoforte Pedalling* (Cambridge, 1993)

S. Pollens: *The Early Pianoforte* (Cambridge, 1995)

DAVID ROWLAND

Pedal note. The lowest of the series of notes that can be sounded on a brass instrument with a given setting of any slide or valves. The term derives from the association of deep sounds with the pedals of an organ. The lowest octave of the serpent and the ophicleide consists of pedal notes (*C–c* for the most common size). Pedal notes have been used on the trombone from Berlioz onwards: on the B♭ trombone, the pedals are B♭' down to E'. French horns with shorter tube lengths (such as the B♭ side of the double horn) can sound pedal notes easily; they are difficult on instruments with longer lengths such as the horn in 12' F. Pedal notes are used frequently on tubas and euphoniums, but rarely on trumpets and cornets, and then only in showy solos. For instruments with a high proportion of cylindrical tubing, such as trombones, the air column does not have a mode of vibration at the correct frequency to support the fundamental (first harmonic) of the pedal note, which can only be sounded because of a 'co-operative regime' in which its higher harmonics are supported by higher modes of resonance of the tube. As a result, these pedal notes have a bright but hollow tone quality.

See ACOUSTICS, §IV.

ARNOLD MYERS

Pedal organ. Strictly the chest, towers, chamber, etc., given to the pipes of the pedal department, as distinct from the pedal-keys or PEDAL-BOARD which play them or which, in instruments without a Pedal organ, play the stops of the manual(s). Since the late 14th century the largest organs had some kind of Pedal organ, though this may not have included the largest pipes or have been more than an extension of the manual, itself playing a BLOCKWERK. By 1600 in central Germany, the Pedal organ often contained three distinct chests, themselves often divided, and including as well as the biggest bass pipes some of the highest flute and reed solo stops. In other regions (e.g. France) the Pedal might be in a separate enclosure behind the main case and have no registers below 8' pitch. The preponderance and eventual monopoly of bass stops in the 18th- and 19th-century Pedal organ meant that the department became less versatile than it had traditionally been.

PETER WILLIAMS/NICHOLAS THISTLETHWAITE

Pedal pianoforte (Fr. *piano à pédalier, clavier de pédales*; Ger. *Pedalflügel, Pedalklavier*; It. *pianoforte organistico*). A piano equipped with a pedal-board like that of an organ. Four types are known: those in which the pedals operate separate hammers to strike the same strings as the keys; those in which a separate set of strings with its own soundboard is installed below the main soundboard; those with a separate box containing pedals, action and strings, on which the piano itself is set; and uprights, where wire pull-downs on the keys are activated by the pedals. The pedal notes usually sound at the 16' pitch over a two-octave range. Some 18th-century instruments have a SHORT OCTAVE arrangement, such as the Johann Schmidt piano of the first type, now in the Metropolitan Museum of Art, New York. The third type was also known in the 18th century; Mozart had such an instrument, made probably by Anton Walter, and his father reported to Nannerl that the box was extremely heavy.

Some pedal pianos may have been used, like the PEDAL CLAVICHORD and PEDAL HARPSICHORD, as practice instruments for organists. Mozart, however, improvised on his instrument in public, and perhaps performed the Piano Concerto in D minor K466 on it. A large number of pedal pianos, mostly of the third type, were made in the 19th and early 20th centuries; a few American examples exist, as well as European makes. In Paris, an instrument of the third type was invented by Pleyel, Wolff & Cie; the Viennese maker Joseph Brodmann also built instruments of this type (see illustration).

Schumann persuaded Mendelssohn to institute classes in pedal piano playing at the Leipzig Conservatory and wrote two works for the instrument: the *Studien* op.56 and *Skizzen* op.58. Other 19th-century composers who wrote music specially for the instrument include Alkan (*Benedictus* op.54, *11 grands préludes et une transcription* op.66, *Impromptu sur le choral de Luther* op.69 and some études and fugues) and Gounod (*Fantaisie sur l'hymne national russe* and *Suite concertante*, both with orchestra).

BIBLIOGRAPHY

J. Handschin: 'Das Pedalklavier', *ZMw*, xvii (1935), 418–19

E. and P. Badura-Skoda: *Mozart-Interpretation* (Vienna, 1957; Eng. trans., 1962/R, as *Interpreting Mozart on the Keyboard*)

EDWIN M. RIPIN/EDWIN M. GOOD

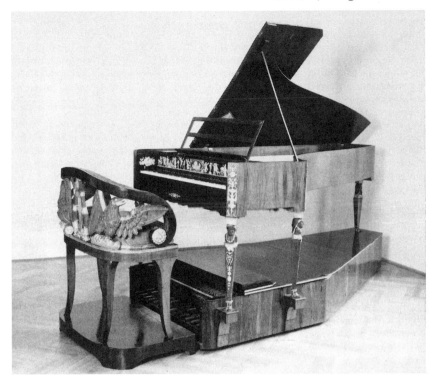

Pedal pianoforte by Joseph Brodmann, Vienna, c1815 (Kunsthistorisches Museum, Vienna)

Pedal point. A long, sustained note held through many bars while movement continues in other parts of the piece. The expression is derived from organ playing, where the technique exploits the organist's ability to hold down a low pedal note indefinitely while playing above it with the hands. 'Pedal point' generally refers to a low bass note, but it may also be applied to a long-held note elsewhere in the texture. The note most commonly note chosen for pedal point is the dominant, but the tonic is also sometimes used. As is to be expected, examples abound in organ music. One of the most celebrated outside that idiom is the low D held throughout the fugue 'Die Gerechten Seelen sind in Gottes Hand', which concludes the third movement of Brahms's *German Requiem*. Pedal point is a required element in the FUGUE D'ÉCOLE, where it is placed just before the stretto (*see* STRETTO (i)), but it is otherwise no more characteristic of fugue than of any other genre of composition.

PAUL M. WALKER

Pedal steel guitar. A development of the lap steel guitar (*see* HAWAIIAN GUITAR) in which the application of pedals enables the player to change instantaneously from one tuning to another. As performing technique developed, players of the Hawaiian guitar came to depend on using a variety of open tunings. In order to be able to move between these tunings at will, players began to use instruments with more than one neck. However, this meant that instruments became increasingly unwieldy as more necks were added. In the 1940s makers such as Bigsby in California and Epiphone in New York started to offer a solution by limiting the number of necks to two but adding pedals which, attached to a system of 'changers' and 'fingers' on the instrument, would enable the player to alter tunings as desired. At first players were happy to operate the systems as designed, using the pedals to move to new tunings as if they had changed necks. But gradually guitarists adapted the system to provide some novel musical effects, and used the pedals to change the pitch of one string while another was sounding. One of the first recorded examples of this 'slurring' effect, which is now considered to be the pedal steel guitar's most characteristic sound, is featured in a solo played by Bud Isaacs on Webb Pierce's 1954 song *Slowly*. From about that time the pedal steel guitar almost completely replaced the lap steel guitar, especially in country music where the pedal steel guitar became a virtually compulsory component.

The standard number of pedals for a twin-necked instrument is eight. Pitch-changing knee-levers (usually four in number) were added later, giving the instrument even greater versatility. Most pedal steel guitars are fitted with ten strings on each of two necks, although some have eight, 12 or 14. Twin-neck guitars usually have one set of strings tuned to a chord of E^9, and the other to C^6. Until the 1970s many of the large guitar manufacturers such as Fender and Gibson made pedal steel guitars, but as manufacturing costs increased and demand subsided, the market was largely left to small, independent makers such as Sho-Bud and Emmons, joined in the 1990s by newer makers, such as Matses and Morrell, all in the USA.

BIBLIOGRAPHY
T. Wheeler: *American Guitars: an Illustrated History* (New York, 1982)
T. Bacon: *The Ultimate Guitar Book* (London, 1991)
G. Gruhn and W. Carter: *Electric Guitars and Basses: a Photographic History* (San Francisco, 1994)

TONY BACON

Pedardo [Pedart], Antonio. *See* PATART, ANTONIO.

Pedersøn [Pedersen], Mogens [Petreo, Magno] (*b* c1583; *d* ?Copenhagen, ?Jan/Feb 1623). Danish composer and instrumentalist. He was one of the four musicians led by Melchior Borchgrevinck who were sent by King Christian IV to study with Giovanni Gabrieli in Venice in 1599. On their return in 1600 he continued his apprenticeship to Borchgrevinck until, in August 1603, he was appointed an instrumentalist in the royal chapel. He must have shown exceptional promise since in the spring of 1605 he was given leave to travel 'wherever he can advance himself in his art and learning', and, provided with a handsome personal recommendation in Italian from Christian IV to Gabrieli, he returned to Venice. This time he remained for four years; before returning home he published there his first book of madrigals, dedicating it to Christian IV in gratitude for the privilege of studying with Gabrieli and as a demonstration of what he had learnt. He rejoined the royal chapel in September 1609, but in 1611 the king sent him to England in company with Hans Brachrogge, Jacob Ørn and Martinus Otto to serve his sister Anne, James I's queen, since he was involved in a war with Sweden and would thus for a time have no use for them. There is no record of the activities of the four musicians in England, but they seem to have been in contact with Francis Tregian, since some of their music is found in manuscripts that he copied while imprisoned for recusancy between 1609 and 1619. One of the manuscripts (GB-Lbl Eg.3665) contains ten five-part madrigals identified as from 'Magno Petreo Dano Libro secundo 1611'. This second book of madrigals by Pedersøn is otherwise unknown; it is not known where it was published (if indeed it ever was) or whether Tregian made his copies from the composer's manuscript. No doubt also dating from his stay in England are two five-part pavans for viols (his only known instrumental music) of which only three parts survive (in GB-Lbl Add.30826–8). In July 1614 Christian IV made a brief, unofficial visit to England and took three of his musicians home with him; Pedersøn remained behind for another month. In 1618 he was appointed assistant director of the royal chapel under Borchgrevinck and given charge of six choirboys, the first native musician to achieve such a high position in the musical establishment of the Danish court. He was granted a vicariate at Roskilde in 1621. His name occurs in the official records for the last time in January 1623; his wife received payment for the maintenance of the six boys in February, and his post was taken over by Hans Nielsen in April, so it is reasonable to suppose that he died in January or February of that year.

Pedersøn is the most important Danish composer before Buxtehude and the only one of the Danish musicians educated by Christian IV who seems to have persevered with composition – or at least by whom enough music remains to allow a reasonably balanced impression of his abilities as a composer to be formed. His madrigals (31 for five voices, and two three-part madrigalettos) are generally of a very high standard and can bear comparison with their Italian models. Their style may be described as post-Marenzio, i.e. they are up to date and expressive without departing from the polyphonic tradition. There are parallels in them with Italian pieces. That Pedersøn was familiar with Monteverdi's latest music, for example, is apparent from his setting of Guarini's *T'amo mia vita* (1608), in which he unmistakably borrowed material from Monteverdi's setting of the same text (book 5, 1605), though he did not follow him in his addition of a continuo part.

Pratum spirituale (1620) reveals quite a different side of Pedersøn. It is a collection of church music – the earliest surviving substantial example of settings of Danish words by a Danish composer – which provides five-part polyphonic versions of some of the liturgical melodies set out for use in the post-Reformation church in Denmark in Hans Thomissøn's *Salmebog* (1569) and Niels Jespersen's *Graduale* (1573). In his dedication to Crown Prince Christian, whom he said he taught, Pedersøn expressed the hope that his collection would not only be of use to the nation but would also be performed in schools, by which he no doubt meant the cathedral schools and larger grammar schools, which provided choirs to lead the singing in the larger churches. This practical intention is apparent in the essentially homophonic style of the settings of the Danish psalms, the melodies of which would also be sung by the congregation. Of the 37 pieces in the collection, 31 are settings of either Gregorian melodies or Lutheran chorales. These are systematically arranged, with the pieces proper to Christmas, Easter and Whitsun first, followed by a number of psalms not restricted to any particular feast. The last six pieces, also for five voices, are freely composed and comprise two sets of responses, one to Danish, the other to Latin words, an abbreviated Latin mass for Lutheran use, and three fine Latin motets. They are in a masterly early Baroque polyphonic style which reveals Pedersøn as a composer of character who was not obviously dependent on Venetian models. He represents the highpoint of Christian IV's achievements for Danish music.

WORKS

Madrigali, libro primo, 5vv (Venice, 1608); ed. in Dania sonans, i (Copenhagen, 1933); 3 ed. in Cw, xxxv (1935)
[Madrigali, libro secondo], 5vv (?printed, 1611); lost except for 10 madrigals, 5vv, GB-Lbl Eg.3665; ed. in Dania sonans, iii (Egtved, 1967)
2 madrigaletti, 3vv, 1619¹³; ed. in Dania sonans, ii (Egtved, 1966)
Pratum spirituale, 5vv (Copenhagen, 1620); ed. K. Jeppesen in Dania sonans, i (Copenhagen, 1933); mass and 3 Latin motets ed. H. Glahn in Music in Denmark at the Time of Christian IV, iv (Copenhagen, 1988)
2 pavans, 5 viols, Lbl Add.30826–8 [3 parts only]

BIBLIOGRAPHY

DBL (K. Jeppesen)
A. Hammerich: Musiken ved Christian den Fjerdes hof (Copenhagen, 1892)
T. Dart and B. Schofield: 'Tregian's Anthology', ML, xxxii (1951), 205–16
J.P. Jacobsen: 'Mogens Pedersøn', Dansk kirkesangs årsskrift 1961–62, 106–17
D. Arnold: 'Gli allievi di Giovanni Gabrieli', NRMI, v (1971), 943–72
J. Bergsagel: 'Danish Musicians in England 1611–14: Newly-Discovered Instrumental Music', DAM, vii (1973–6), 9–20
Heinrich Schütz und die Musik in Dänemark: Copenhagen 1985
N. Krabbe: Træk af musiklivet i Danmark på Christian IVs tid (Copenhagen, 1988)
O. Kongsted: 'Christian IV und seine europäische Musikerschaft', Europa in Scandinavia: kulturelle und soziale Dialoge in der frühen Neuzeit: Kiel 1992, 115–26
H.W. Schwab: 'Italianità in Danimarca: Zur Rezeption des Madrigals am Hofe Christians IV', ibid., 127–53

JOHN BERGSAGEL

Pederzuoli [Pederzoli, Pedezzuoli], **Giovanni Battista** (*d* after 1691). Italian composer and organist, partly active in Austria. He was *maestro di cappella* of S Maria Maggiore, Bergamo, from 12 February 1664 until 26 January 1665. In 1677 he was appointed organist at the court of the Dowager Empress Eleanora in Vienna and in

1682 succeeded Antonio Draghi as her Kapellmeister, a position he retained until her death in 1686. He may have remained in Vienna as a member of the emperor's Kapelle, but only one work attributed to him, the oratorio *L'anima in transito* (1692), bears a date later than 1686. During his service in Vienna, music at the Habsburg court was almost entirely dominated by Draghi, but he composed more sacred dramatic works than any other late 17th-century Habsburg musician except Draghi. He provided Eleonora's Kapelle with a new *sepolcro* (a type of oratorio performed at Vienna during Holy Week) every year from 1683 to 1686. Like the works of Draghi his operas and oratorios are in the rather conservative middle Baroque style favoured by the Emperor Leopold I. His sinfonias show both French and Venetian influence. In his arias he occasionally called for some unusual instrumental colour, such as three viols in two arias of the oratorio *Sant'Elena* (1683), but in general he scored for voice and continuo only. In *Sant'Elena* he achieved another unusual effect by writing the chorus of demons for a quartet of basses. His ensemble numbers are usually simpler than Draghi's, as are his recitatives, which contain no florid arioso patterns. His melodies include occasional expressive chromatic writing reminiscent of the early 17th century. Among his smaller works are ten *accademie* or philosophical cantatas, which are the earliest examples of this genre written for Vienna. They were probably performed at sessions of the Italian academy founded at Vienna in 1657, of which Pederzuoli's patron Eleanora and his chief librettist, Minato, were members. All begin with four-part sinfonias in dance forms.

WORKS

in A-Wn unless otherwise stated

DRAMATIC

I presagi della sorte (festa musicale) Vienna, 6 Jan 1677, music lost
Vienna festeggiante (serenata) Vienna, 1679
Ragguaglio della fama ('servizio di camera') Vienna, 18 Nov 1680
Il giudice di villa (intermedio), Vienna, 1681, perf. with A. Scarlatti: Amor non vuole inganni [= Gli equivoci nel sembiante]
Il monte Chimera (trattenimento musicale, N. Minato), Vienna, Augarten, 9 July 1682
Le fonti della Boezia (festa musicale, Minato), music lost (prepared for Vienna, 1682, but unperf.)
Introduzione d'una festa e ballo di zingare (Minato), Vienna, carn. 1684
Didone costante, Vienna, Hofburg, carn. 1685, music lost
Le ricchezze della madre dei Gracchi ('introduzione a un balletto') Vienna, 6 Jan 1685, *A-Wgm* (lib only)
Scherzo musicale in modo di scenica rappresentazione (Minato), Vienna, carn. 1685
Musica, pittura e poesia (trattenimento musicale, Minato), Vienna, Bellaria, 24 July 1685
Musica per una festa di carnevale (Minato), Vienna, carn. 1686
L'ossequio della bizzarria ('introduzione a un balletto') Vienna, carn.
L'ozio ingannato ('musica di camera', Minato)

ORATORIOS

La sete di Cristo in croce (Minato), Vienna, 15 April 1683
Sant'Elena (Minato), Vienna, 1683
Le lagrime più giuste di tutte le lagrime (Minato), Linz, 30 March 1684
La bevanda di fiele (Minato), Vienna, 20 April 1685
La sorte sopra la veste di Cristo (Minato), Vienna, 11 April 1686, music lost
L'anima in transito (Pezuoli), Vienna, 1692
San Pietro piangente

OTHER VOCAL

[6] Accademie (Minato), perf. 1685
[4] Cantate per l'accademia per sua maesta cesarea, dell' imp. Eleonora, *A-Wn*; facs. in ICSC, xvi (1985)
Trialogo nel natale del Signore, Wn

Sonetto per le felicissime nozze, Vienna, 1685, *Wn* [for the marriage of Maria Antonia, Archduchess of Austria, and Maximilian Emanuel, Elector of Bavaria]
Madrigal, 5vv, *I-Nf*

BIBLIOGRAPHY

EitnerQ; La MusicaD; SartoriL; SchmidlDS
E. Wellesz: 'Die Opern und Oratorien in Wien von 1660–1708', *SMw*, vi (1919), 5–138
P. Nettl: 'Zur Geschichte der kaiserlichen Hofmusikkapelle von 1636–1680', *SMw*, xvi (1929), 70–85; xvii (1930), 95–104; xviii (1931), 23–35; xix (1932), 33–40
A. Bauer: *Opern und Operetten in Wien* (Vienna, 1955)
H. Knaus: 'Wiener Hofquartierbücher als biographische Quelle für Musiker des 17. Jahrhunderts', *Anzeiger der Österreichischen Akademie der Wissenschaften, philosophisch-historische Klasse*, cii (1965), 178–206
O.E. Deutsch: 'Das Repertoire der höfischen Oper, der Hof- und der Staatsoper in Wien', *ÖMz*, xxiv (1969), 369–70, 379–421
H. Knaus: 'Die Musiker in den geheimen kaiserlichen Kammerzahlamtsrechnungsbüchern (1669, 1705–1711)', *Anzeiger der Österreichischen Akademie der Wissenschaften, philosophisch-historische Klasse*, cvi (1969), 14–38
R. Klein: 'Musik im Augarten', *ÖMz*, xxviii (1973), 239–49
L. Bennett: *The Italian Cantata in Vienna, c.1700–c.1711* (diss., New York U., 1980)
R. Flotzinger, ed.: *Geschichte der Musik in Oesterreich*, ii (Vienna, 1995)

LAWRENCE E. BENNETT

Pedrazzini, Giuseppe (*b* Pizzighettone, nr Cremona, 13 Jan 1879; *d* 19 Oct 1957). Italian violin maker. He was a pupil of Romeo Antoniazzi in Milan, then began to work on his own there. He quickly gained recognition and won awards at various exhibitions, including those in Rome in 1920 and in Cremona in 1937. He modelled his instruments after various patterns, especially those of Stradivari, G.B. Guadagnini and Amati, all of which he interpreted freely. Tonally his work is among the best of the early 20th-century Italian makers. He was a meticulous and elegant craftsman; the scrolls of his instruments are always deeply carved, and the symmetrically rounded curves of the bouts and flanks provide a distinctive touch. Besides new instruments, he made a number of skilful antiqued copies. He used a variety of different labels and, depending on the period, one of three different brands. A good part of his output was exported, and he had particularly close ties with Hawkes & Son (later Boosey & Hawkes) in London. Among his pupils and associates were Ferdinando Garimberti, P. Parravicini and his nephew N. Novelli.

BIBLIOGRAPHY

VannesE
W. Henley: *Universal Dictionary of Violin and Bow Makers*, i–v (Brighton, 1959–60); vi, ed. C. Woodcock as *Dictionary of Contemporary Violin and Bow Makers* (Brighton, 1965)
U. Azzolina: *Liuteria italiana dell'Ottocento e del Novecento* (Milan, 1964)

ERIC BLOT/JAAK LIIVOJA-LORIUS

Pedreira, José Enrique (*b* San Juan, Puerto Rico, 2 Feb 1904; *d* San Juan, 6 Jan 1959). Puerto Rican music educator and composer. He took piano lessons in San Juan with Ana and Rosa Sicardó before studying piano and composition in New York with Zygmunt Stojowski for five years. In 1928 he returned to Puerto Rico, where he established himself as a teacher of piano, founding his own academy in Santurce in 1931. Among his pupils were Alba Rosa Castro, Irma Isern and José Raul Ramírez. Although he was primarily a teacher, Pedreira is acknowledged as the most significant Puerto Rican composer of his generation. His stylistic evolution was gradual, from

Romanticism through an identifiably Puerto Rican Impressionism to a more personal idiom that is especially evident in his eloquent *danzas*. He represents the transition between Quintón (1881–1925) and the nationalist composers of the 1950s.

WORKS
(*selective list*)

Inst: Pf Conc., d, 1936; vn, pf duos, incl. Elegía India; numerous pf works, incl. mazurkas, waltzes, danzas, op fantasias, nocturnes, études, caprices, and 1 sonata
Vocal: 3 diálogos con el silencio, song cycle, 1956; many songs, 1934–54
El jardín de piedra (ballet), 1957
Principal publisher: E.B. Marks

BIBLIOGRAPHY

R. Sacarello: 'José Enrique Pedreira y la escuela de Stojowsky', *Puerto Rico ilustrado* (15 June 1940)
H. Campos-Parsi: 'El fin del Modernismo: Pedreira', *Le gran enciclopedia de Puerto Rico*, ed. V. Báez, vii (Madrid, 1976), 266–8

GUSTAVO BATISTA

Pedrell, Felipe [Felip] (*b* Tortosa, 9 Feb 1841; *d* Barcelona, 9 Aug 1922). Catalan composer, musicologist and teacher. He began his musical studies at the age of seven while a chorister at Tortosa Cathedral, receiving instruction in solfège, harmony and the transcription of popular song from Juan Antonio Nin y Serra. He was otherwise self-taught in music. During his early career he wrote a great deal of vocal music, mostly sacred, but devoted himself increasingly to opera and zarzuela after moving to Barcelona as deputy director of the Light Opera Company of the Teatro Circo in 1873. His operas *L'ultimo Abenzeraggio* (1874) and *Quasimodo* (1875) had their premières at the Gran Teatro del Liceo in that city. A year in Italy (1876–7) aroused his interest in musicology, and in Roman libraries he researched music history, aesthetics, folklore and early music. Subsequently he spent two years in Paris, where he composed opera and came under the influence of Wagner. After returning to Spain he settled in Barcelona and concentrated on musicology. He began publishing two journals in 1882: *Salterio sacro-hispano*, in which he published many works by earlier Spanish composers, and *Notas musicales y literarias*. In 1888 he intoduced the periodical *La ilustración musical hispano-americana*, which contained some of his most important research, and also contributed numerous articles to other periodicals, especially *La España musical*. His operatic activities resumed with *Eda* (1887), *Little Carmen* (1888), and *Mara* (1889), all commissioned by a friend in New York. In 1890 he began work on his monumental *Els Pirineus* (*Los Pirineos*), an operatic trilogy with prologue, which blended the quotation of medieval and Renaissance music with modern harmony and Wagnerian leitmotif. In conjunction with its completion a year later he published the book *Por nuestra música*, in which he set forth his views regarding Spanish national opera.

Pedrell moved to Madrid in 1894 and was appointed professor of choral singing at the conservatory, professor of higher studies at the Ateneo, and was elected to the Real Academia de Bellas Artes. He spent ten productive years in the capital composing, promoting the performance of sacred music, founding the Isidorian Choir, organizing concerts, editing music, and giving lectures. He also composed the opera *La Celestina*, intended as the second opera after *Els Pirineus* in a triptych dedicated to *Patria*, *Amor*, and *Fides*, the motto of the Catalan Jocs Florals ('Floral games'). The third opera was never written. Although he completed a final dramatic work *El Comte Arnau* upon his return to Barcelona in 1904, he gradually abandoned composition and spent his remaining years arranging the large amount of material he had collected, publishing it in several major works, and rearranging or re-editing existing work.

Pedrell was the founder of modern Spanish musicology and contributed greatly to the revival of church music in Spain. He wrote extensively on Spanish liturgical music and made substantial collections and editions of both early and contemporary Spanish sacred music. His most important editions include the complete works of Victoria and the series Hispaniae Schola Musica Sacra. His biographical writings include a series in *Revista musical catalana* (1904–10) entitled 'Musichs vells de la terra', biographies of Victoria and Eximeno, and a bio-bibliographical dictionary of Spanish, Portuguese, and Latin American musicians. His critical writings include a study of Spanish popular song. One of his major works was the *Catàlech de la Biblioteca musical de la Diputació de Barcelona*, in which he collated much of what he had already published in books and articles. His endeavours inspired the succeeding generation of scholars, and he encouraged the early career of Anglès. The Festschrift *Escritos heortásticos*, published in his honour in 1911, contains a complete list of all his publications and compositions up to that date; subsequent lists based on this are not always representative, for although he was at first ambitious to become a Spanish equivalent of Wagner, in his later years he destroyed many of his scores, recognizing that his major talents lay elsewhere. His lack of success as a composer was a source of frustration to him, and it is difficult today to assess his stature because much of his music remains in manuscript, with few modern editions or recordings. He strove to make a major contribution to national music in Spain, especially Catalonia, and was prolific: his output includes not only songs, choral works, and operas but many chamber and orchestral compositions as well. His works for the piano consist mostly of salon-style dances as well as arrangements, fantasias, rhapsodies, and variations based on popular operatic themes. None of this music, however, has found its way into the standard repertory. Perhaps his most important achievement in composition was to inspire other composers through his writings, lectures and private instruction. Albéniz, Granados and Falla all benefited from his tutelage and held him in high esteem.

WORKS
(*selective list; complete list in Bonastre*)

STAGE

El último Abencerraje (op, 4, J.B. Altés), 1868, unpubd; rev. as L'ultimo Abenzeraggio (F. Fors de Casamayor), 1870, unpubd; rev., with new nos., Barcelona, Liceo, 14 April 1874, excerpts (Barcelona, 1874); rev., Barcelona, Liceo, 8 Oct 1889
Les aventures de Cocardy, 1873 (ob, Gelée–Bertal), unperf.
Quasimodo (op, 4, J. Barret, after V. Hugo), Barcelona, Liceo, 20 April 1875
Le roi Lear (op, 5, A. Baralle), 1877, unperf.
Mazeppa (poema lírico, 9 nos., A. de Lauzières de Thémines), 1878
Tasso à Ferrara (poema lírico, 1, Lauzière de Thémines), Madrid, Apollo, 1881
Cleopâtre (op, 4, Lauzières de Thémines), 1878, unperf.
Eda (ópera cómica), 1887, unperf.
Little Carmen (ópera, 3), 1888
Mara (ópera cómica, 4), 1889, unperf., unpubd
Els Pirineus [Los Pirineos] (op, prol., 3, V. Balaguer), 1891, Barcelona, Liceo, 4 Jan 1902, vs (Barcelona, 1893) [pt 1 of trilogy]

La Celestina: tragi-comedia lírica de Calisto y Melibea (op, 4, Pedrell, after F. de Rojas), 1902, excerpts, concert perf., Barcelona, 1921, vs (Barcelona, 1903) [part 2 of trilogy]
El Comte Arnau ('festival lirich-popular', 2 pts, J. Margall), vs (Leipzig, 1911)
Zarzs: Ells i Elles (1, J. Riera i Bertrán), 1873; La guardiola (3, E. Vidal i Valenciano), 1873; Lluch-Llach (2, A. Ferrer i Codina), 1873 [orig. El diplomático (ob)]; Lo rei tranquil (Riera), 1873; La veritat i la mentida (3, C. Colomer), 1873; Los secuestradores (zarzuelita, 3 nos.), 1889

INSTRUMENTAL

Orch: Marche-hymne and Fête (march), 1871; Sym., D, 1872; Scherzo fantastique, 1872; Elegía a Romea, 1875; Meditación fúnebre, 1875; Mila, 1876; La veu de las montanyas, 1877; March triomphale, 1878; Gavotte, c, 1879; Gavotte, a, 1880; I trionfi, suite, 1880; Marxa fúnebre, 1885
Chbr: Elegía a Foruny, vl, vc, pf, hmn, 1875; Himne a Venus, sop.fl, gui, hp, hmn, pf, 1880; Jesús als pecadors, T, str qt, pf, 1880; Llevant Déu, escena religiosa, 1, str qt, pf, 1880; Preghiera dell'orfanello, vc, str quintet, 1880; serenata, str, hmn, pf, 1881
Pf: Los cantares, Horas tristes (melodías características), 1862; Sonata, 1864, Scènes, 1866; Estudios melódicos, 2 books (1866, 1867); Hojas de álbum, 1867; Escenas infantiles, 4 hands, 1880; 26 pièces pour le piano, 1881; La veu de las montayas, 1892; many waltzes, nocturnes, impromptus, mazurkas and romances, as well as transcrs., arrs., fantasies and rhapsodies based on operatic themes
Sacred: Stabat mater, 3vv, 1856; Mass, 2vv, org, 1857; Mass, 3vv, org, 1858; Stabat mater, 2vv, orch, 1858; Salve regina, 3vv, org, 1860; 2 Masses, 3vv, org, 1861; Mass, 3 solo vv, vv, org, 1864; Alleluia (small orat), 4 solo vv, vv, org, 1865; Mass, 3vv, org, 1865; Dixit dominus y Magnificat, 4vv, org, 1862; Dixit dominus y Magnificat, 4vv, org, 1866; Mass, 3vv, org, 1866; Stabat mater, vv, orch, 1866; Requiem, 3vv, orch, 1868; 3 Lamentations, 4vv, hmn, 1869; 2 Masses, 4vv, org, 1869; Missa brevis, 1875; Salve regina-Filiae Jerusalem, S, vv, st qt, hmn, 1875; Missa solemnis, 3 solo vv, vv, orch, hp, org, 1876; Requiem, 4 solo vv, vv, 1876; Te Deum, 4 solo vv, vv, orch, hp, org, 1876; Salterio sacro Hispano, 2–4vv, org, 1882; In captivitatem comploratio, 4vv, orch, 1906; many other small works, incl. 6 settings of the Ave Maria, 2 of the Benedictus, 4 Hymns, Bone pastor (motet), Christus factus est, Miserere and Gozos
Other choral: Cant de la montanya, 1877; Cançó llatina, 1878; Serenata, 4vv, 1879; La festa de Tibulus, vv, vla, vc, pf, 1879; Don Ramon i Don Joan, SATB, 1902; La Matinada, solo vv, vv, offstage orch, 1905; Visió de Randa, solo vv, vv, orch, 1905; Glossa, vv, orch, 1906

VOCAL

Songs for 1v, pf: Despedida, 1858; La serenata-La ermita, 1862; La pescadorcita, 1863; 7 melodías, 1863; Ecos de Italia, 1864; 6 Lieder, 1864; Melodías, 1864; Cantos de la infancia, 1866; Embriaguez, 1867; Noches de España, 1871; 3 Lieder, 1871, Balada, 1875; Lágrimas, 1875; Consolations, 1876; 14 Lais, 1879; 16 Lieder, 1879; Balada y preghiera, 1880; Cant dels mariners Catalans, 1880; Sirventés, 1880; 14 melodías, 1881, Amarosa, 1884; Avuy farà un any, 1884; Mai més, 1884; Mignon, 1884; Aires andaluces, 1889; Aires de la tierra, 1889; Canciones arabescas, 1906; Vita nuova, 1921

WRITINGS

Apuntes y observaciones sobre estética musical (Barcelona, 1866)
Gramática musical o manual expositivo de la teoría del solfeo, en forma de diálogo (Barcelona, 1872, 3/1883)
Las sonatas de Beethoven (Barcelona, 1873)
Los músicos españoles en sus libros (Barcelona, 1888)
Por nuestra música (Barcelona, 1891/R; Fr. trans., 1891)
Diccionario técnico de la música (Barcelona, 1894, 2/1899/R)
Diccionario biográfico y bibliográfico de músicos y escritores de música españoles, portugueses y hispano-americanos antiguos y modernos (Barcelona, 1894–7) [A–Gaz only]
'Folk-Lore musical castillan du XVIe siècle', *SIMG*, i (1899–1900), 372–82
Emporio científico e histórico de organografía musical española antigua (Barcelona, 1901)
Prácticas preparatorias de instrumentación (Barcelona, 1902)
'La musique indigène dans le théâtre espagnol du XVIIe siècle', *SIMG*, v (1903–4), 46–69
La cançó popular catalana (Barcelona, 1906)

Documents pour servir à l'histoire du théâtre musical: la festa d'Elche ou le drame lyrique liturgique espagnol (Paris, 1906)
Musicalerías (Valencia, 1906) [selection of critical articles]
Antología de organistas clásicos españoles (Madrid, 1908/R1968 as *Classical Spanish Organists*)
Càtalech de la Biblioteca musical de la Diputació de Barcelona (Barcelona, 1908–9)
'Jean I d'Aragon, compositeur de musique', *Riemann-Festschrift* (Leipzig, 1909), 229–240
'L'églogue "La forêt sans amour" de Lope de Vega, et la musique et les musiciens du théâtre de Calderon', *SIMG*, xi (1909–10), 55–104
'Jacopone da Todi, los *Stabat mater* y la *Música*', *Revista de estudios franciscanos* (April–May, 1910), 129–147
Músicos contemporáneos y de otros tiempos (Paris, 1910)
Jornadas de arte (Paris, 1911) [memoirs and articles, 1841–91]
Orientaciones (Paris, 1911) [memoirs and articles, 1892–1902]
La lírica nacionalizada (Paris, 1913)
Tomás Luis de Victoria Abulense (Valencia, 1918) [based on *T.L. de Victoria: Opera omnia*, viii, 1913]
P. Antonio Eximeno (Madrid, 1920)

EDITIONS

Many edns of early Spanish music in *Salterio sacro-hispano* (1882–)
Hispaniae schola musica sacra (Barcelona, 1894–8/R)
Teatro lírico español anterior al siglo XIX (La Coruña, 1897–8)
T.L. de Victoria: Opera omnia (Leipzig, 1902–13)
El organista litúrgico español (Barcelona, 1905)
Antología de organistas clásicos españoles (Madrid, 1908)
Cancionero musical popular español (Valls, 1918–22, 3/1958)
with H. Anglès: *Els madrigals i la missa de difunts d'En Brudieu*, PBC, i (1921)

BIBLIOGRAPHY

R. Mitjana: *Felipe Pedrell* (Málaga, 1901)
N. Otaño, ed.: *Al Maestro Pedrell: escritos heortásticos* (Tortosa, 1911) [with list of works by A. Reiff; this list repr. in *AMw*, iii (1921), 86–97]
F. Pedrell: *Musiquerías* (Paris, c1911) [autobiography]
H. Anglès: *Catàleg dels manuscrits musicals de la Collecció Pedrell* (Barcelona, 1921)
F. Pedrell: *Jornadas postreras* (Valls, 1922) [autobiography]
L. Villalba Muñoz: *Felipe Pedrell, semblanza y biografía* (Madrid, 1922)
'Al ilustre compositor y musicólogo insigne Felipe Pedrell, fundador del nacionalismo musical español y padre de la musicología española, en el quincuagésimo aniversario de su muerte', *AnM*, xxvii (1972) [whole issue]
E. Istel: 'Felipe Pedrell', *MQ*, xi (1925), 164–91
M. Jover: *Felipe Pedrell (1841–1922): vida y obra* (Tortosa, 1972)
F. Bonastre: *Felipe Pedrell: acotaciones a una idea* (Tarragona, 1977) [incl. complete list of works]
T. Snow: '"La Celestina" of Felipe Pedrell', *Celestinesca*, i/3 (1979), 19–32
M.C. Gómez-Elegido Ruizolalla: 'La correspondencia entre Felipe Pedrell y Francisco Asenjo Barbieri', *Recerca musicològica*, iv (1984), 77–242
J. Casanova: 'Presència poética en la música de la Renaixença', *Revista musical catalana*, no.43 (1988), 27–31
A. Gallego: 'Nuevas obras de Falla en América: El Canto a la Estrella, de "Los Pireneos" de Pedrell', *Inter-American Music Review*, xi/2 (1991), 85–102
F. Cortès i Mir: *El nacionalismo musical de Felip Pedrell a través de sus óperas: Els Pirineus, La Celestina y El Comte Arnau* (diss., U. Autònoma of Barcelona, 1996)

WALTER AARON CLARK

Pedrini, Teodorico (*b* Fermo, 30 June 1671; *d* Beijing, 10 Dec 1746). Italian composer, theorist and instrument maker. He was the first Lazarist missionary to settle in China, and contributed to the cultural exchange between China and the West during the late Ming and early Qing dynasties. He was educated in Rome and arrived in China in 1711 after an arduous nine-year journey. There he succeeded the Portuguese Jesuit Tomás Pereira as court musician to Emperor Kangxi. Pedrini remained in China until his death, working closely with the emperor and simultaneously fulfilling his religious life and missionary goals. Life in the Chinese court was politically complex, and Pedrini was deeply involved in intrigues between the emperor, the Jesuits and Rome during the Rites controversy. Despite earning Kangxi's esteem, he was twice imprisoned by the emperor.

There were many harpsichords at the Chinese court, gifts from foreign visitors, and there is evidence that Pedrini himself built instruments in China. His musical abilities were highly regarded by the emperor, who declared Pedrini's lack of the Chinese language to be unimportant, since 'harpsichords are tuned with the hands, and not with the tongue'. Pedrini's op.3 sonatas (MS, Beijing National Library; the title-page bears the anagrammatic name 'Nepridi') are his only known extant compositions; they are strongly influenced by (and include several quotations from) Corelli's op.5 set, to which they pay homage in the style, number, structure and types of movements. Pedrini also completed the fifth volume of *Lulu Zhengyi* ('A True Doctrine of Music'; Beijing, 1713), on Western music theory, begun by Tomás Pereira.

BIBLIOGRAPHY

A.B. Duvigneau: 'Théodoric Pedrini, prêtre de la mission, protonotaire apostolique, musicien à la cour impériale de Pékin', *Bulletin catholique de Pékin* (1937), 312–23

G. Gild-Bohne, ed.: *Das Lü Lü Zheng Yi Xubian: ein Jesuitentraktat über die europäische Notation in China von 1713* (Göttingen, 1991)

J. Lindorff: 'The Harpsichord and Clavichord in China During the Ming and Qing Dynasties', *Early Keyboard Studies Newsletter*, viii/2 (1994), 1–8

Y.B. Tao: *Zhongxi Yinyue Jiaoliu Shi Gao* [The history of musical exchange between China and the Western world before 1919] (Beijing, 1994)

JOYCE LINDORFF

Pedro del Puerto. *See* ESCOBAR, PEDRO DE.

Pedrollo, Arrigo (*b* Montebello Vicentino, 5 Dec 1878; *d* Vicenza, 23 Dec 1964). Italian composer. He studied first with his father Luigi, an organist and band conductor, and later at the Milan Conservatory with Gaetano Coronaro, Amintore Galli and Luigi Mapelli, earning a diploma in composition in 1897; his graduation composition, a symphony, was first conducted by Toscanini (June 1900). After a short career as a pianist, he began a successful career as an opera composer: between 1908 and 1936 he had eight operas performed, some several times, in Italy and abroad. In 1912 his *Juana* won the Sonzogno competition. He was also active as a conductor and founded the Milan and Turin radio symphony orchestras (1928–34). In 1920 he was appointed director of the Istituto Musicale in Vicenza (where he also held conducting appointments 1922–9). He later taught composition at the Milan Conservatory (1930–41). From 1941 to 1959 he was director of the Liceo Musicale Cesare Pollini, Padua. His pupils included Galliera, Maderna, Scimone and Santi.

The dramatic conception and musical language of Pedrollo's operas are strongly reminiscent of 19th-century ideals, and his debt to the Italian tradition, as well as to Wagner and Strauss, and to Berlioz and Debussy, is equally evident. The originality of his work lies mainly in the subtleties of his harmonic language and especially in the wonderful palette of his orchestration, but the dramatic tension of Pedrollo's his operas is not consistently sustained.

WORKS

OPERAS

Terra promessa (quadro lirico, C. Zangarini), Cremona, Ponchielli, 18 Feb 1908; rev. (poema drammatico, 3 pts), after 1913 [pt 2 'La morte di Mosè' corresponds, with variants, to version of 1908]

Juana (3, C. De Carli), Vicenza, Eretenio, 3 Feb 1914

La veglia (1, C. Linati, after J.M. Synge: *The Shadow of the Glen*), Milan, Filodrammatici, 2 Jan 1920; rev. 1921

L'uomo che ride (3, A. Lega, after V. Hugo: *L'homme qui rit*), Rome, Costanzi, 6 March 1920

Rosmunda (4, L. Siciliani), *c*1920, unperf.

Maria di Magdala (3, A. Rossato), Milan, Dal Verme, 11 Sept 1924

Delitto e castigo (3, G. Forzano, after F.M. Dostoyevsky: *Crime and Punishment*), Milan, Scala, 16 Nov 1926

Primavera fiorentina (1, M. Ghisalberti, after G. Boccaccio), Milan, Scala, 28 Feb 1932

La fattoria Polker (Rossato), 1935, unperf.

L'amante in trappola (1, G. Franceschini), Vicenza, Verdi, 22 Sept 1936

La regina di Cirta [Sofonisba] (3, Lega), 1943–4, unperf.

Il giglio di Alì (3, E. Romagnoli), 1948, unperf.

OTHER WORKS

Ballets: Oriente; Giuditta, Bologna, 1916; Aziadée, Florence, Pergola, 1935

Orch: Sym., d, 1900; Preludio sinfonico, F, 1912; Conc., d, pf, chbr orch, 1933–53; Icaro, sym. poem, 1951; Suite su temi armeni, 1951; Castelli di Giulietta e Romeo, sym. poem, 1952; Concertino, ob, str, 1960; Mascherata

Vocal: 2 poemetti, chorus, orch, 1918; Dialogo della Divina Providenza di S Caterina da Siena (cant., A. Barolini), solo vv, chorus, orch, 1948; songs

Other inst: Sonata, vn, pf, 1908; Qt, vn, va, vc, pf, 1910; Elegia, str qnt, 1935; Pf Qt, 1941; Trio, f♯, 1941; Qt, A, inc., 1944; Canzone del Don, vc, pf, 1948; Pf Trio, 1962

BIBLIOGRAPHY

P. Petrobelli: 'Arrigo Pedrollo: una figura d'artista', *Musica d'oggi*, viii (1965), 82–3

F. Grassi, ed.: *Arrigo Pedrollo nel centenario della nascita (1878–1978)* (Padua, 1979)

PIERLUIGI PETROBELLI

Pedroso, Manuel de Moraes (*b* Miranda do Douro; *fl* 1750–70). Portuguese theorist and composer. After several years' residence at Oporto he published there a 47-page *Compendio musico, ou Arte abbreviada* (1751, 2/1769) divided into three parts: rudiments, accompanying and counterpoint. The last part gives rules for composing arias, recitatives, duets, minuets, concertante pieces and symphonies. An autograph Lamentations for soprano and organ dated 1751 survives at the Biblioteca Nacional in Lisbon. An imposing *Te Deum* for four voices with strings and organ (1762; published in A. von Gavel: *Investigaciones musicales de los archivos coloniales*, Lima, 1974) and a brilliant soprano aria, *Dichoso seras*, with violins, flute and continuo, are now in the Archivo Arzobispal, Lima. (*DBP*; *StevensonRB*)

ROBERT STEVENSON

Pedrotti, Carlo (*b* Verona, 12 Nov 1817; *d* Verona, 16 Oct 1893). Italian composer and conductor. He was intended for a business career, but showed exceptional musical talent at an early age, composing orchestral pieces and organizing a group of fellow students to perform them under his direction. After a period of study with the Veronese teacher Domenico Foroni he turned his attention to opera; his first two attempts were not performed, but the third, *Lina*, was successfully given at the Teatro Filarmonico in Verona in 1840. Its successor, *Clara di Mailand*, may not have been performed, but his reputation was growing and won him the appointment of conductor at the Italian opera in Amsterdam, where he stayed for four seasons, gaining valuable experience and producing at least one more opera of his own, *La figlia dell'arciere*.

In 1845 he returned to Verona, where he remained until 1868, at first supporting himself by teaching but later doubling the posts of opera coach and conductor at the Teatro Filarmonico and the Teatro Nuovo. This was the time of Pedrotti's main work as a composer: the ten operas he produced during this period, especially those in the *buffa* or *semiseria* style, established his reputation throughout Italy; his first major success, *Fiorina* (1851), carried his name outside Italy as well, and in 1856 his best work, *Tutti in maschera*, was quickly recognized as a minor masterpiece of *opera buffa*, reaching Vienna in 1865 and Paris in 1869. Another important success came with *Guerra in quattro* in Milan in 1861.

In 1868 Pedrotti was appointed director of the Liceo Musicale and director and conductor of the Teatro Regio in Turin. He threw himself into the musical life of the city, making radical improvements in the style and quality of the performances at the opera, and founding in 1872 a weekly series of Concerti Popolari at the Teatro Vittorio Emanuele, using the orchestra and chorus of the Teatro Regio. These concerts, which introduced many of the works of Beethoven, Wagner and other foreign composers to Italian audiences, were the first of their kind in Italy and constitute a landmark in the late 19th-century revival of Italian interest in instrumental music. In both these undertakings Pedrotti was sustained by the appointment, in 1876, of Giovanni Depanis as impresario of the Teatro Regio (whose son, Giuseppe, had already been deeply involved in the foundation of the Concerti Popolari and was later to write their history). Depanis was an admirer of Wagner, and his first season included an important performance of *Lohengrin*, preceding which Pedrotti went to Munich for a personal meeting with the composer. Following its successful Italian première, conducted by Angelo Mariani (1871, Bologna), the opera had proved a spectacular failure in Milan in 1873, but the Turin production was a success and gave a new impetus to Wagner performances in Italy. Pedrotti was also responsible for a number of Italian premières at the Teatro Regio, as well as the third Italian production of *Carmen* – which had to be cancelled after two disastrous performances, only to return in triumph at the end of the same season.

Pedrotti's 14 seasons put the Teatro Regio on a level that rivalled La Scala, and placed Turin beside Milan as one of the chief musical centres of Italy. But in the process the composer Pedrotti was extinguished: in 1870 he produced *Il favorito*, the only one of his own operas given in Turin during his entire directorship, and shortly afterwards wrote his last opera, *Olema la schiava* (Modena, 1872), for the singer Isabella Galletti-Gianola.

In 1882 Pedrotti left Turin for Pesaro, where he had been appointed the first director of the Liceo Musicale established by the *comune* of Pesaro in accordance with the terms of Rossini's will. He spent ten years administering and inspiring the new institution and in 1892 organized the celebrations for the centenary of Rossini's birth; but early in the following year ill-health forced him to tender his unwillingly received resignation. He returned to his family home at Verona, where he suffered from acute nervous depression and after only a few months of retirement committed suicide by throwing himself into the river Adige.

As a composer, Pedrotti was highly regarded in his day. Technically accomplished and a brilliant orchestrator (he was selected in 1869 to write the 'Tuba mirum' for Verdi's projected Rossini requiem), he was at his best in *opera buffa*, where his cultured eclecticism, rhythmic vitality and lightness of touch made an immediate appeal. His masterpiece, *Tutti in maschera*, is full of happy invention and tuneful ensemble writing, and has deservedly been revived well into the 20th century. But even here (and more so in his serious operas) he was the representative of a dying style. He was perfectly aware of Verdi, and by the 1880s regarded his own works as 'roba da vecchi' ('old men's stuff') and strenuously opposed their performance. His influence as an orchestra director was more significant: he was probably the first Italian conductor in the modern sense of the word, the eldest of an important group of late 19th-century composer-conductors that included Bottesini, Mariani, Faccio, Mancinelli and Mascheroni. It was he who prepared the orchestra and public that gave Toscanini his first sustained success at Turin in 1895–8.

WORKS

OPERAS

Antigone (os, M.M. Marcello), unperf.
La sposa del villaggio (op semiseria, Marcello), unperf.
Lina (op semiseria, 2, Marcello), Verona, Filarmonico, 2 May 1840, excerpts (Milan, 1840)
Clara di Mailand (os, 3), Verona, Filarmonico, 1840, but ?unperf.
Matilde (os, 3), Amsterdam, Italiano, spr. 1841, but ?unperf.
La figlia dell'arciere (op semiseria, 2, F. Romani), Amsterdam, Italiano, 29 Feb 1844
Romea di Montfort (os, 3, G. Rossi), Verona, Filarmonico, 19 Feb 1846, I-Mr*, vs (Milan, 1846)
Fiorina, o La fanciulla di Glaris (op semiseria, 2, L. Serenelli Honorati), Verona, Nuovo, 22 Nov 1851, Mr*, vs (Milan, 1852)
Il parrucchiere della reggenza (op comica, 3, Rossi), Verona, Nuovo, 5 May 1852, Mr*, vs (Milan, 1852)
Gelmina, o Col fuoco non si scherza (op semiseria, 3, G. Peruzzini), Milan, Scala, 3 Nov 1853
Genoveffa del Brabante (os, 3, Rossi), Milan, Scala, 20 March 1854, excerpts (Milan, 1854)
Tutti in maschera (commedia lirica, 3, Marcello, after C. Goldoni: L'impresario delle Smirne), Verona, Nuovo, 4 Nov 1856, Mr*, vs (Milan, 1857); in Fr. as Les masques (C.-L.-E. Nuitter and Beaumont [A. Beaume]), Paris, 1869
Isabella d'Aragona (os, prol, 2, Marcello), Turin, Vittorio Emanuele, 7 Feb 1859, Mr*, vs (Milan, n.d.)
Guerra in quattro (ob, 3, Marcello), Milan, Cannobiana, 25 May 1861; rev. Trieste, 22 Feb 1862, Mr*, vs (Milan, 1862)
Mazeppa (tragica, 4, A. de Lauzières de Thémines), Bologna, Comunale, 3 Dec 1861, Mr*, vs (Milan, 1861)
Marion de Lorme (os, 3, Marcello, after V. Hugo), Trieste, Comunale, 16 Nov 1865
La vergine di Kermo (os, 3, F. Guidi), Cremona, Concordia, 16 Feb 1870 [incl. music by Cagnoni, Ricci, Ponchielli, Pacini and others]
Il favorito (tragedia lirica, 3, G. Bercanovich), Turin, Regio, 15 March 1870, excerpts (Milan, n.d.)
Olema la schiava (os, 4, F.M. Piave), Modena, Municipale, 4 May 1872, Mr*, vs (Milan, n.d.)

OTHER WORKS

Salve regina, 4vv, unacc. (Milan, n.d.); other sacred works
Ov., D, orch (Milan, n.d.)
Songs, incl. In morte di Bellini (Milan, 1835)

BIBLIOGRAPHY

E. Hanslick: 'Opern und Theater in Italien', *Musikalische Stationen* (Berlin, 1880/R)
I. Valetta: Obituary, *Nuova antologia*, cxxxi (1893), 251–68
T. Mantovani: *Carlo Pedrotti* (Pesaro, 1894)
L. Torchi: 'Carlo Pedrotti', *RMI*, i (1894), 137–41
G. Depanis: *I concerti popolari ed il Teatro regio di Torino* (Turin, 1914–15)

C. Bianchi: 'Carlo Pedrotti a Torino', *Musicalbrandé*, no.16 (1962), 10–11

V. Mazzonis, ed.: *Il Teatro regio di Torino* (Turin, 1970)

T.G. Kaufman: *Verdi and his Major Contemporaries* (New York, 1990), 155–68

C.A. Traupman: *I dimenticati: Italian Comic Opera in the Mid-Nineteenth Century* (diss., Cornell., 1995)

MICHAEL ROSE

Peebles, David (*fl* 1530–76; *d* ?1579). Scottish composer. A canon of the Augustinian Priory of St Andrews, he is described as 'ane of the cheiff musitians into this land' by Thomas Wood (i), whose contemporary partbooks (*IRL-Dtc, GB-Eu, Lbl, US-Wgu*) contain all his surviving music. According to Wood, Peebles composed the motet *Si quis diligit me* in about 1530 and presented it to James V 'being a musitian, he did lyke it verray weill'. The motet is a cantus firmus composition in post-Josquin style, incorporating some structural imitation and revealing a striking melodic gift. Other music of this period by Peebles must be lost. The anonymous Mass '*Felix namque*' for six voices (MB, xv, no.4) is stylistically similar and may be his work.

In 1550 'David Pablis, canonicus' signed a matriculation roll of students at St Leonard's College in the University of St Andrews. In the 1560s, at the time of the Reformation, Lord James Stewart, half-brother of Mary Queen of Scots and Prior of St Andrews, turned Protestant. When Earl of Moray and regent, he commissioned Peebles to set the psalm tunes for four voices. There are 106 of these settings with the tune in the tenor, according to contemporary practice. All are written in a simple chordal style; but as might be expected from an able polyphonist, individual parts are always interesting and harmonic propriety is strictly observed.

After the Reformation canons often lived on at their priory or convent – with the ground divided among them – and many of them married. A charter of land rent was granted in 1571 to David Peebles and his wife Katherine Kinnear by the commendator of the priory, the Catholic Robert Stewart, 7th Earl of Lennox (another half-brother of Mary's). Peebles seems to have remained a Catholic: Robert Stewart commissioned from him a Latin motet, *Quam multi, Domine*, in 1576, a setting for four voices of Psalm iii, which shows a knowledge of contemporary European developments in dramatic and madrigal-inspired sacred music. Peebles died in December 1579, according to Laing (see Johnson, 3/1853), who cited the 'Register of Confirmed Testaments' kept at the Scottish Record Office, Edinburgh. Unfortunately, the volume for 1579 is now missing. He had certainly died by 1592: his wife is described as 'relict of David Peablis' in her will of that year.

BIBLIOGRAPHY
J. Johnson, ed.: *The Scots Musical Museum*, i (Edinburgh, 1787, enlarged D. Laing 3/1853)

D.H. Fleming, ed.: *St Andrews Kirk Session Register 1559–1600*, i: *1559–82* (Edinburgh, 1889)

F. Grant, ed.: *The Commissariot Record of St Andrews, Register of Testaments, 1549–1800*, Scottish Record Society Commissariot Records, pt.15 (Edinburgh, 1901)

D.H. Fleming: *The Reformation in Scotland* (London, 1910)

J.M. Anderson, ed.: *Early Records of the University of St Andrews, 1413–1579*, Scottish History Society Publications, ser.3, viii (Edinburgh, 1926)

KENNETH ELLIOTT

Peeling-horn. *See* WHITHORN.

Peellaert [Pellaert], **Auguste** [Augustin] (**-Philippe-Marie-Ghislain**), Baron de (*b* Bruges, 12 March 1793; *d* Saint Josse-ten-Noode, Brussels, 10 April 1876). Belgian composer. The son of one of Napoleon's chamberlains, he spent his youth in Paris and studied the piano and harmony with J.-J. de Momigny. In 1813 his family returned to Bruges, where he intended to pursue an artistic career, but in 1815, when his father became bankrupt, he decided to join the army, eventually reaching the rank of lieutenant-colonel. Peellaert was a prolific composer who devoted himself chiefly to vocal music. Claiming musical kinship with Rossini, whose friend he became in 1860, he concentrated on *opéra comique*, often writing his own librettos. His sense of local colour and dramatic expression also induced him to try his hand at *grand opéra*. Although several of his works were well received at La Monnaie, the simplicity of their melodies ensuring them a certain success, they were never staged in Paris. Some fragments of his operatic works were published in Brussels. He also wrote many songs, church music and orchestral and chamber works. After 1850 he confined himself to unpretentious operettas, and at the end of his life he wrote, in disillusionment: 'I have done a little of everything without succeeding at anything' (*Cinquante ans de souvenirs recueillis en 1866*, Brussels, 1867).

WORKS
(*selective list*)

operas first performed at Brussels, Théâtre de la Monnaie, unless otherwise stated

Stage: L'heure du rendez-vous (oc, 1, Peellaert), Ghent, 16 March 1819, *B-Bc**; Le sorcier par hasard [Le souper magique] (oc, 1, Peellaert), Courtrai, 16 May 1820, *Bc**; Agnès Sorel (oc, 3, J.N. Bouilly and E. Dupaty), 3 Aug 1824, *Bc**; Le barmécide, ou Les ruines de Babylon (opéra, 3, G. de Pixérécourt), 5 July 1825, *Bc**; Teniers, ou La noce flamande (oc, 1, Bouilly and M.J. Pain), 9 March 1826, *Bc**; L'exilé (oc, 2, T. Anne, A. Dartois and A. Tully, after W. Scott: *Old Mortality*), 25 Sept 1827, *Bc**; Faust (drame lyrique, 3, E. Théaulon), 19 Feb 1834, *Bc**; Le coup de pistolet (oc, 1, Léon), 22 March 1836; Louis de Male (grand opéra, 4, J. Vanderbelen), 14 Nov 1838, *Bc**; Le Barigel (oc, 1, G. Oppelt), 3 Nov 1842, *Bc**; Monsieur et Madame Putiphar (opérette comique, 1, Peellaert), Brussels, Château des Fleurs, 19 Aug 1857, *Bc**

Other: masses; 2 pf trios; duo, 2 hp; songs

HENRI VANHULST

Peerce, Jan [Perelmuth, Jacob Pincus] (*b* New York, 3 June 1904; *d* New York, 15 Dec 1984). American tenor. He studied with Giuseppe Borgatti and from the mid-1940s was chosen by Toscanini to sing in his broadcasts and recordings of *La bohème*, *La traviata*, *Fidelio*, *Un ballo in maschera* and the last act of *Rigoletto*. He made his stage début in Philadelphia in 1938 as the Duke of Mantua and joined the Metropolitan in 1941, making his first appearance as Alfredo; he stayed with that company until 1968. He toured abroad with many ensembles, specializing in the Italian and French *spinto* repertories, and in 1956 he became the first American to sing with the Bol'shoy since the war. In 1971 he made his Broadway début as Tevye in *Fiddler on the Roof*. He also appeared in films, and recorded popular songs in addition to Jewish liturgical music. In his prime Peerce was most admired for a remarkably even scale, a strong technique, and a voice with a dark vibrancy in the middle register and a metallic ring at the top, points confirmed by his recordings under Toscanini. Though his diminutive size precluded an ideal romantic illusion, he was an actor of restraint and dignity.

BIBLIOGRAPHY

GV (G. Gualerzi; S. Smolian)

A. Levy: *The Bluebird of Happiness: the Memoirs of Jan Peerce* (New York, 1976)

J. Hines: 'Jan Peerce', *Great Singers on Great Singing* (Garden City, NY, 1982), 224–30

Obituary, *New York Times* (17 Dec 1984)

MARTIN BERNHEIMER/R

Peers, Edward. *See* PEARCE, EDWARD.

Peerson [Pearson], Martin (*b* probably at March, Cambs., between 1571 and 1573; *d* London, bur. 15 Jan 1651). English composer, virginalist and organist. He was probably the son of Thomas and Margaret Peerson of March: evidence of his parentage can be derived from his will and the March marriage registers. This couple married in 1570, but it seems likely that Thomas died during the next few years and that Martin's mother was the 'Margaret Peersonn' who married in 1573: hence the suggested date of birth for the composer. Probably at a comparatively early stage in his career he came under the patronage of the poet Fulke Greville. On May Day 1604 his setting of *See, O see, who is heere come a maying* was performed as part of Ben Jonson's *Private Entertainment of the King and Queene* at the house of Sir William Cornwallis at Highgate (now in London). In 1606, on the same occasion as Jonson, he was convicted of recusancy and thus most probably had Catholic sympathies at that time. A letter of 7 December 1609 states that he was then living at Newington (Stoke Newington, London) and had composed several lessons for the virginals, his principal instrument. Peerson took the BMus degree at Oxford in 1613 and for this would have had to subscribe to the Thirty-nine Articles and thus to Protestantism. From 1623 to 1630 a 'Martin Pearson' was sacrist at Westminster Abbey: this was probably the composer. Between June 1624 and June 1625 Peerson took office as almoner and Master of the Choristers at St Paul's Cathedral; there is evidence to suggest that he was later made a petty canon. Although all cathedral services ceased at the end of 1642 following the outbreak of the Civil War, he retained the title 'almoner' and along with the other petty canons and the vicars-choral had special financial provision made for him. He was buried in St Faith's Chapel under St Paul's.

The first 14 pieces in Peerson's *Private Musicke* are ayres for solo voice with accompaniment of three viols, nos.15–23 are duets or dialogues, and *See, O see, who is heere come a maying* (for mixed forces a 6) completes the set. All are secular, and all except the last have short choruses at the ends of the verses which, even when contrapuntal and imitative, could as a rule be easily memorized, thus allowing any onlookers to participate in the music-making. The volume contains some attractive songs and is notable for using and combining elements from a number of different genres, e.g. the ayre, madrigal, consort song (especially of the type in Thomas Ravenscroft's publications) and verse anthem. Although it presented no novelties of style in 1620, it was up to date in including fragments of declamatory rhythm in some of the voice parts, and the specific suggestion of extemporized accompaniment on virginals or lute over the bass line was an original feature.

The 'organ part' of Peerson's *Mottects or grave chamber musique* of 1630 consists of a two-part score (a *basso seguente* and usually the uppermost vocal or instrumental part) with some figures added to the bass – the first instance of a figured bass in an English published collection; in none of the numbers is the organ part essential (although it might substitute for other parts) and it could in many cases have been a later addition. Nor does one find in this music any of the melodic clichés of the *stile nuovo* or rhythms or textures basically dissimilar from those already established in the English madrigal, verse anthem or secular song. Thus the collection differs markedly from Walter Porter's *Madrigales and Ayres* of 1632 and in general derives from the past. It is worth noting too that Peerson's weakest pieces are to be found here: some of these might in fact be of much earlier date. However, certain pieces show interesting, individual traits. Although there are a few lively songs, an impressive feature is the intense, introspective gloom of a good deal of this music, created by minor keys, low-lying parts, chromaticism and especially by the frequent use of augmented chords.

A sombre mood characterizes a number of Peerson's anthems, which in the main belong to the second decade of the 17th century. Here he stands out as one of the most modern composers of that decade in employing dramatic solo melodies, madrigalian harmonies and sometimes quite elaborate word-painting. Many of his anthems, verse and full, contain individual and expressive music, and a work such as *Fly ravisht soule* bears comparison with the anthems of Gibbons. The motets to Latin texts probably date from about the turn of the century. Their quality is hard to assess because of the loss of the cantus part, but they, too, probably contain some of Peerson's finest music. Like the verse anthems, however, they do not always sustain the interest of their initial ideas.

The four surviving keyboard pieces show a range of style and genre that may reflect the range of Peerson's total output for keyboard. *The Fall of the Leafe* and *The Primerose* are attractive genre pieces that have found enough favour in modern times to be performed and even recorded fairly often: like the *Alman*, they are reminiscent of his older contemporary Giles Farnaby's miniatures. *Piper's paven* is however a fine large-scale reworking of Dowland's piece, and suggests that the lost keyboard music could have included substantial works of considerable interest. Peerson's skill in instrumental construction is seen, too, in the works for string consort, which have a freshness of design, and a textural and melodic beauty, that make them well worth playing and hearing. In general they are polyphonically uncomplicated but far from superficial. While Peerson makes use of such devices as 'chain-canon' imitation, in passages which are harmonically static or increasing in tension (see bars 14–44 of Fantasia no.4, entitled *Delicate*), these are only a part of his technical repertory. He is capable of springing surprises, as in the bass-viol flurry of quavers in *Delicate*: and in this regard the five-part fantasia *Attendite* is especially notable, with a wealth of invention and a beautiful passage in Db followed by a perfectly convincing return to the home key of D minor in only 28 beats.

Two idiosyncrasies of Peerson's music are the use now and again of unprepared 4ths, rare at the time, and a strange, mannered kind of degree inflection (ex.1). While

Ex.1 *O Love thou mortall speare*

counterpoint of any complexity was beyond his technique and probably alien to his temperament, his experiments with form and unusual harmonic procedures are interesting. It seems likely that keyboard playing and extemporization had considerable influence on his musical style and were the source of much of his unconventional treatment of dissonance.

WORKS

Editions: *English Ayres: Elizabethan and Jacobean*, ed. P. Warlock and P. Wilson (London, 1927–31) [W]
M. *Peerson: Opera omnia*, ed. R. Rastall (in preparation)

ANTHEMS
verse unless otherwise stated

All laude and praise, a 5, *GB-Lbl* (also attrib. T. Ravenscroft)
Blow out [up] the trumpet, a 5, *Cp*, *DRc*, *Lbl*, *Ob*, *Y*
Bow down thyne eare O Lord (2p. Preserve thou my soule; 3p. Be mercifull unto mee O Lord), a 5, *Cp* (inc.)
By Euphrates flowrie side, full, 5vv, *Lbl* (inc.)
Fly ravisht soule (2p. Rest thee [there] awhile; 3p. Muse still thereon [Nayle prints]; 4p. Raine eyes), a 5, *Lbl*, *Ob*
I am brought into so great trouble (2p. My heart panteth), a 5, *Lbl*
I am small (2p. Thy word is tride; 3p. Trouble and heaviness), a 5, *Ob*
I called upon the Lord (2p. All nations compassed mee; 3p. They kept mee in on every side; 4p. They came about mee like bees), a 5, *Ob*
I will magnifie thee O Lord (2p. O Lord my God; 3p. Which sitteth in the heavens), a 6, *DRc*, *Lbl*, *Och*
Lord ever bridle my desires, full, 5vv, 1614⁷; ed. in EECM, xi (1970), 150–54
O God that no time doest despise, full, 4vv, 1614⁷; ed. in EECM, xi (1970), 69–71
O God when thou wentest before the people (2p. It is well seene O God), a 5, *Lbl*, *Ob*
O goe not from me (2p. Many oxen; 3p. They gape upon me), a 5, *Lbl* (also attrib. H. Palmer), *Ob*
O Lord in thee is all my truste (2p. No, no, not so thy will is bent; 3p. Haste thee O Lord), a 5, *Och* (inc.)
O let me at thy footstoole fall, full, 5vv, 1614⁷; ed. in EECM, xi (1970), 124–29
O Lord thou hast searched me out (2p. Thou art about my path; 3p. Thou hast fashioned me; 4p. Whether shall I goe then), a 5, *Lbl*
O that my wayes (2p. I will thanke thee), a 5, *Lbl*
O that my wayes (2p. I will thanke thee), a 6, *Lbl*
Pleade thou my cause, a 5, *Lbl*
Praise the Lord (2p. Yea as long; 3p. O put not your trust), a 5, *Ob*
Who will rise up (2p. But when I said), full, 5vv, *Lbl*

MOTETS ETC
all motets, 5 voices, in Ob, lacking cantus part

Deus omnipotens; Hora nona dominus Jesus (2p. Latus eius lancea miles perforavit); Laboravi in gemitu meo; Levavi oculos meos in montes (2p. Ecce non dormitabit); Mulieres sedentes (2p. Christus factus est); Nolite fieri sicut equus et mulus (2p. Multa flagella peccatoris); O Domine Jesu Christe; O Rex gloriae; Pater Fili paraclete; Quid vobis videtur de Christo; Redemptor mundi
1 psalm-tune harmonization, 1621¹¹ [setting used for Pss l, lxx, cxxxiv]

SECULAR VOCAL

Private Musicke or The First Booke of Ayres and Dialogues … being Verse and Chorus, 4, 5, 6vv/viols, acc. virginals/lute/b viol (London, 1620) all ed. in Heydon:
   Ah were she pittifull, W iv, 26; At her faire hands (W. Davison), W vi, 34; Can a mayd?; Come pretty wagge and sing (2p. Then with reports); Disdaine that so doth fill mee; Gaze not on youth (2p. I onely seeke to please mine eye); Hey the horne the horna; Is not that my fancies queene?; Locke up faire lids (P. Sidney); Love her no more

   Now Robin laugh and sing, W iv, 21; O I doe love; O pretious time, W iv, 13; Open the dore; Pretty wantons sweetly sing; Resolv'd to love (H. Constable); See, O see, who is heere come a maying (B. Jonson); Since just disdayne; Sing love is blinde; The spring of joy is dry; Upon my lap my soveraigne sits (R. Verstegan); What neede the morning rise

Mottects or Grave Chamber Musique … some Ful, and some Verse and Chorus, 5, 6vv/viols, org/virginals/b lute/bandora/Irish harp (London, 1630) [all texts, except Where shall a sorrow, from F. Greville: *Caelica Sonnets*]; all ed. in Baxter and Foote:
   Cupid my prettie boye; Farewell sweet boy; Love is the peace; Love the delight (2p. Beautie her cover is; 3p. Time fayne would stay); Man dreame no more (2p. The floud that did); Man dreame no more; More then most faire (2p. Thou window of the skie)

   O false and treacherous probabilitie; O love thou mortall speare (2p. If I by nature); Selfe pitties teares; Under a throne; Was ever man so matcht with boye; Where shall a sorrow (2p. Dead noble Brooke); Where shall a sorrow (2p. Dead noble Brooke); Who trusts for trust (2p. Who thinkes that sorrows felt); You little starres (2p. And thou O love)

Wake sorrow (2p. Arbella), a 5, *GB-Lbl* Add.29372–6 [mourning song for Arabella Stuart]

CONSORT MUSIC

6 fantasia-almain sets and a seventh almain, a 6, *IRL-Dm* Z.3.4.1–6 [no. 5 only], *GB-Lbl* Add. 17786–91, *Och* 423–8 [only fantasias nos.1–4, entitled 'Acquaintance', 'Beauty', 'Chowse' and 'Delicate'], no.4 ed. in MB, ix (1955, 2/1962), 165–70; the anonymous fantasia a 6 preceding Peerson's work in *IRL-Dm* Z.3.4.1–6 is probably also by him
1 fantasia, a 5, inc., *GB-Lbl* Add. 37402–6 [entitled 'Attendite'], *Och* 716–20

KEYBOARD

Alman, Pipers paven [after J. Dowland], The Fall of the Leafe, The Primerose: *Cfm* 32.G.29; ed. J.A. Fuller Maitland and W.B. Squire, *The Fitzwilliam Virginal Book* (London and Leipzig, 1894–9/R), i, 359–60; ii, 238–41, 422, 423

BIBLIOGRAPHY

*Le Huray*MR (chap.9)
C. van den Borren: *Les origines de la musique de clavier en Angleterre* (Brussels, 1912; Eng. trans., 1914 as *The Sources of Keyboard Music in England*)
C.S. Emden: 'Lives of Elizabethan Song Composers: Some New Facts', *Review of English Studies*, ii (1926), 416–22, esp. 421
M. Eccles: 'Jonson and the Spies', *Review of English Studies*, xiii (1937), 385–97, esp. 392
M. Wailes: 'Martin Peerson', *PRMA*, lxxx (1953–4), 59–71
A. Jones: *The Life and Works of Martin Peerson* (diss., U. of Cambridge, 1957)
I. Spink: 'English Seventeenth-Century Dialogues', *ML*, xxxviii (1957), 155–63
M. Eccles: 'Martin Peerson and the Blackfriars', *Shakespeare Survey*, xi (1958), 100–06
McD. Emslie: 'Nicholas Lanier's Innovations in English Song', *ML*, xli (1960), 13–27
R.M. Baxter: *Martin Peerson's 'Mottects or Grave Chamber Music' (1630)* (diss., Catholic U., Washington DC, 1970)
M.H. Foote: *Martin Peerson's 'Mottects or Grave Chamber Mvsique': Fulke Greville's 'Treatie of Humane Love'* (diss., U. of California, Santa Barbara, 1977)
R. Charteris: 'Consort Music Manuscripts in Archbishop Marsh's Library, Dublin', *RMARC*, xiii (1977), 27–63
R. Charteris: 'Another Six-Part Fantasia by Martin Peerson?', *Chelys*, ix (1980), 4–9
R. Charteris: *A Catalogue of the Printed Books on Music, Printed Music and Music Manuscripts in Archbishop Marsh's Library, Dublin* (Kilkenny, 1982)
J. Heydon: *Martin Peerson's 'Private Musicke': A Transcription, Edition, and Study of an Early 17th-Century Collection of English Consort Songs* (diss., U. of Oregon, 1990)
P. Phillips: *English Sacred Music 1549–1649* (Oxford, 1991)

AUDREY JONES/RICHARD RASTALL

Peer-Southern. American firm of music publishers. It was founded in New York in 1928 by Ralph Peer as the Southern Music Publishing Co. in cooperation with the Victor Talking Machine Co. Peer had spent several years in the southern USA collecting ethnic music and jazz, and the company became a major publisher and distributor of this music. In 1932 when Victor withdrew, Peer, who was president of Southern, became its sole owner (he remained at the head of the firm until his death in 1960). In 1940 he established the Peer International Corporation. This, together with Southern, became known as the Peer-Southern Organization, which from 1940 included the American Performing Rights Society, from 1941 Melody Lane Publications and La Salle Music Publishing Company, and from 1943 the Charles K. Harris Music Publishing Company.

Peer-Southern is the principal publisher of Ives and the sole publisher of David Diamond, Fuleihan, Rudolf Maros, Orrego-Salas, Manuel Ponce, Revueltas, Saygun, Serebrier and Shapero. Peer also represents the catalogues of Ediciones Mexicanas de Música, Pan American Union of Washington and Wagner & Levien of Mexico City; Southern Music Publishing Co. is the exclusive representative of A. Cranz of Brussels, Editorial Argentina de Música of Buenos Aires, Editorial Cooperative Interamericana de Compositores of Montevideo, Enoch & Cie of Paris (partial catalogue), C. Gehrman of Stockholm (partial catalogue), Israeli Music Publications, Liber-Southern of London and R.E. Westerlund AB of Helsinki.

W. THOMAS MARROCCO, MARK JACOBS

Peeters, Flor [Florent] (*b* Tielen, province of Antwerp, 4 July 1903; *d* Antwerp, 4 July 1986). Belgian composer, organist and teacher. At the Lemmens Institute, Mechelen, he studied Gregorian chant with van Nuffel, the organ with Depuydt and composition with Mortelmans. He won the highest distinction, the Lemmens-Tinel Prize, was appointed professor at the institute in 1923 and succeeded Depuydt as professor of organ in 1925. Also in 1923 he was made assistant at St Rombouts Cathedral, Mechelen, where he later became organist in succession to Depuydt. He was professor of organ at the Ghent Conservatory (1931–48) and professor of organ and composition at the Tilburg Conservatory in the Netherlands (1935–48). From 1948 to 1968 he was organ professor at the Antwerp Conservatory, which he directed between 1952 and 1968. He received many honours: in 1958 he was made a Commander of the Order of St Gregory the Great and he was awarded honorary doctorates by the Catholic universities of America (1962) and of Leuven (1971). In 1971 he was elevated to the peerage by King Baudouin with the personal title of baron; he was the third Belgian musician since 1830 to receive this honour.

Peeters won renown as a teacher both in Europe and the USA, where he often gave masterclasses at Boys Town, Nebraska. In 1968 the Belgian Ministry of Flemish Cultural Affairs commissioned him to give an annual masterclass at Mechelen Cathedral, providing 20 scholarships for students from countries having cultural links with Belgium. Peeters's didactic publications include a practical edition of old Flemish music, *Oudnederlandsche meesters voor het orgel*, and a summary of his teaching methods, *Ars organi*, published with text in Flemish, French, German and English. He also wrote a *Practische methode voor gregoriaansche begeleiding* based on the Vatican edition of plainchant, which was simultaneously published in French and English. As a performer he made numerous commercial recordings and gave over 1200 recitals throughout Europe, the Philippines, South Africa and the USA, where he completed ten transcontinental tours during the period 1946–71. His programmes featured Bach, the Flemish masters and contemporary

works including his own compositions, and invariably contained a work by Franck.

Although Peeters composed chamber music, piano works, songs and much sacred choral music, the development of his technique and his highly individual style may best be studied in the organ works. Certain influences early in his career were quickly absorbed into his own idiom: as a student at the Lemmens Institute he followed a tradition of highly disciplined training for Roman Catholic church musicians. His fluent melodic line is influenced by Gregorian chant, Flemish Renaissance polyphony and often by Flemish folk themes. Of contemporaries, an admiration for Dupré is reflected in the dedication and design of the *Variationen und Finale über ein altflämisches Lied* op.20, the *Toccata, fuga en hymn op 'Ave maris stella'* op.28 is dedicated to Peeters's greatest friend, Tournemire, and has some resemblance to the improvisatory techniques characteristic of Tournemire's style, as do other works of the same period. The friendship between the two organist-composers was long and close. Tournemire began an intensive correspondence with him in 1930, but their only meeting was in 1936, when Tournemire invited Peeters to give his début recital at Ste Clotilde, Paris, where he was *organiste titulaire*. In 1939 Tournemire bequeathed to Peeters the organ console that Franck had used at Ste Clotilde.

Peeters's works are characterized by a preference for classical forms. From the start he explored many possibilities of variation technique and his vast output of chorale preludes shows great skill in handling miniature form. He frequently experimented with polyrhythm, polytonality and complex contrapuntal devices, as in the *Passacaglia e Fuga* op.42. The Sinfonia op.48, dedicated to Peeters's wife, was composed in August 1940, directly after the German invasion. Its severe, dissonant harmonic language expressed his rebellion against the occupation. Peeters's refusal to play for the Germans during the war resulted in the confiscation of his passport, but he continued to travel to the Netherlands for masterclasses and to act as a courier between Belgian and Dutch cathedral authorities. Peeters worked on his Organ Concerto op.52 throughout 1944. The family had to flee their home at the height of the Allied bombing, but returned in the summer, and this joyful, optimistic work was completed during the liberation of the city by British troops. The Concerto is the emotional antithesis of the Sinfonia. It is gay and spontaneous, with strong melodic and contrapuntal interest and a suave, lyrical middle movement. In this work the chief departure from conventional form is the placing of the cadenza at the beginning of the last movement. This cadenza gives a fine exposition of the themes in clear, bright textures featuring virtuoso pedal passages; with some modifications it was later published as the Concert Piece op.52a.

Typical of the longer works is the contrast of vigorous, contrapuntal, rhythmic outer sections with subdued, contemplative material for the second subject where the influence of plainchant and folksong is discernible in the melodic shape. (A good example is the *Vlaamsche Rhapsodie* op.37). After the period of the *Lied Symphony* op.66 Peeters's style changed, gradually becoming more introspective and restrained in the chorale preludes and other pieces of the early 1950s, reaching a culmination in the Six Lyrical Pieces op.116. Peeters was much in demand as a consultant and by the early 1970s a further stylistic development reflected his increasing interest in modern tracker-action instruments; notable examples are the Concertino op.122 and the *Paraphrase on 'Salve regina'* op.123, where open textures, thematic economy and an emphasis on linear interest particularly suit the clear-cut timbres of these organs. Perhaps the most important example is the *Sonata quasi una fantasia* op.129 where all the thematic material derives from the major 7th and minor 2nd at the opening.

After 1978 a fracture in the spinal column and increasing osteoporosis terminated further extensive touring, although he was able to give occasional concerts and continued composing. His last public recital was in Mechelen Cathedral during the 1982 Flanders Festival. Two weeks later, his wife Marieke died. He reworked an earlier piece, *Adagio* (the name of their last family home), into the Ricercare op.134, and dedicated it to her memory. During the last years, his contribution to music brought further international awards and a new Prix Flor Peeters was created by the Société Belge des Auteurs, Compositeurs et Editeurs (SABAM) in Belgium.

WORKS

(selective list)

published works only

for list of unpublished works, see G. Peeters (1996)

SACRED CHORAL

Ave verum, Exurgens Joseph, op.7, SA, org, 1923; 4 Motets, op.9, 4vv, org, 1924; O Maria die daar staat, op.12/32, 2/4vv, pf/org, 1928; Missa in honorem Sancti Josephi, op.21, SATB, org, 1929; Missa in honorem reginae pacis, op.30, 2vv, org, 1933; Naar Bethlehem, op.32, Bar, 2vv, org, 1934; Sing to God with gladness (Ps xcix), op.40/2, SATB, org, 1936; TeD, op.57, SATB/TTB/SSA, org, 1945; Missa festiva, op.62, 5vv, org, 1947; 4 Motets, op.63, 4vv, 1947

4 Motets, op.64, 4vv, 1947; Tu es sacerdos, op.78, TTB, org, congregation, 1954; Missa laudis in honorem sancti Joannis Baptistae, op.84, SATB, org, 1956; Prayer on Christmas Eve, SATB, op.85/4; In excelsis gloria, SATB, org, op.85/5, 1956; Evening Prayer, op.87/2, 2vv/SATB, org, 1958; Flos carmeli, op.89a, 1/2vv, org, 1958; Inviolata, op.89b, 4vv, org, 1958; Missa choralis, op.91, SATB, org, congregation ad lib, 1958; Jubilee Mass, op.92, 4vv, org, 1958

Entrata festiva, op.93, unison, 2 tpt, 2 trbn, org, timp ad lib, 1959; 2 Anthems, op.94, SATB, 1959; The Lord's Prayer, op.102, 2vv/SATB/solo v, org, 1960; Wedding Song, op.103, solo v, SATB, org, 1960; Mihi autem nimis (Ps cxxxviii), op.105, SATB, org, 1961; 2 Anthems, op.107, SATB, org, 1961; Mag, op.108, SATB, org, 1961; In silent night, op.110, SATB, org, 1963; In convertendo (Ps cxxv), op.111, SATBB, 1963; Missa simplex, or Confraternity Mass, op.112, unison vv, org, 1963; 4 Old Flemish Christmas Carols, op.115, SATB, 9 wind, org, 1964; Canticum gaudii, op.118, SATB, 2 tpt, 2 trbn, org, 1971–2; Ps cxxviii, op.120, solo vv, chorus, org, 1972; Pss xxiii/xxii, op.124, solo vv, chorus, org, 1973; Gebed voor de kerk, op.137, 1v, SATB, pf, org, 1983

ORGAN

4 Improvisaties, op.6, 1923; 10 Pedal Studies, op.11, 1925; Symfonische Fantasie, op.13, 1925; Variationen und Finale über ein altflämisches Lied, op.20, 1929; Toccata, fuga en hymn op 'Ave maris stella', op.28, 1933; Vlaamsche Rhapsodie, op.37, 1935; Elégie, op.38, 1935; 10 Orgelchoräle, op.39, 1936; Passacaglia e fuga, op.42, 1938; Suite modale, op.43, 1938; Sinfonia, op.48, 1940; Aria, op.51a, 1945; Concert Piece, op.52a, 1952; 35 Miniatures, op.55, 1945

Variations on an Original Theme, op.58, 1945; 4 Pieces, op.59, 1945; Lied Sym., op.66, 1948; Chorale Preludes, opp.68–70, 3 sets of 10, 1948; 4 Pieces, op.71, 1949; 3 Preludes and Fugues, op.72, 1950; Alma redemptoris mater, op.73/1, 1951; Chorale Preludes on Gregorian Hymns, opp.75–7, 3 sets of 10, 1953–4; 2 Chorale Preludes, op.81, 1955; Prelude, Canzona e Ciacona, op.83, 1955; Solemn Prelude, op.86/3, 1956

Festival Voluntary, op.87/1, 1957; Praeludien und Hymnen, op.90, 1958; 30 Short Chorale Preludes on Well-Known Hymns, op.95, 1959; Domenica XI post pentecosten, op.99, 1960; Hymn Preludes for the Liturgical Year, op.100, 24 vols., 1959–64; Partita on 'Almighty God of Majesty', op.109, 1962; Praeludiale, op.113, 1964; 6 Lyrical Pieces, op.116, 1966; 10 Inventionen zum liturgischen Gebrauch, op.117, 1969; 10 Preludes on Old Flemish Carols, op.119, 1972; Paraphrase on 'Salve regina', op.123, 1973; Introduzione, fugato con corale supra 'Pro civitate', op.126, 1976; Little Choral Suite, op.130, 1977; Partita on 'Puer nobis nascitur', op.127, 1977; Sonata quasi una fantasia, op.129, 1977; Ricercare, op.134, 1981; Partita op 'Lieve Vrouwe van de Kempen', op.135, 1983; Prière pour une paix, op.139, 1985

OTHER WORKS

Vocal: De wiedsters, op.2/3, chorus 2/4vv, pf/org, 1926; 6 Alice-Nahon liederen, op.3, S, pf, 1923; Speculum vitae, op.36, 1v, org, 1935; De Morgen in 't Bosch, op.44 no.2, chorus 2vv, pf, 1940; Ivory Tower, op.47, 1v, pf, 1940; 6 Love Songs, op.50; 6/ Zuid-Afrikaanse liederen, op.65, chorus 4vv, 1947

With org: Org Conc., op.52, 1944; Conc., op.74, org, pf, 1951; Choral Fantasy on 'Christ the Lord has Risen', op.101, org, brass, 1960; Concertino, op.122, positive org, hpd, 1973; Ubi caritas et amor (cant.), op.128, T, org, 1977

Other inst: Pf Suite, op.18, 1928; 10 Schetsen uit het Kinderleven, op.27, pf, 1934; 2 pf sonatines, opp.45–6, 1940; Aria, op.51b/c, vn/vc, pf, 1945; Sonata, op.51, tpt, pf, 1945; Toccata, op.51d, pf, 1945; Steenhof Suite, op.53/1, pf, 1944; Trio, op.80a, fl, cl, bn, 1955; Suite, op.82, 4 trbn, 1955; 10 Bagatelles, op.88, pf, 1958; Larghetto, op.106, pf trio, 1961; 12 Chorale Preludes, op.114, pf, 1964; Aria, op.51b, tpt, brass band, 1977; Invention op de naam Johan Fleerackers, op.133, pf, 1981; Preambulum op de naam Jan de Smedt, op.138b, pf, 1984

Principal publishers: Augsburg, Dessain, Elkan-Vogel, Gray, Herder, Heuwekemeyer, Lemoine, Metropolis, Novello, Oxford University Press, C.F. Peters, Schott, Schwann, Summy-Birchard

EDITIONS AND PEDAGOGICAL WORKS

Oudnederlandsche meesters voor het orgel/Les maîtres anciens néerlandais pour grand orgue, 3 vols. (Paris, 1938–46)
Practische methode voor gregoriaansche begeleiding/Méthode pratique pour l'accompagnement du chant grégorien (Mechelen, 1943)
with C. Tournemire: *Opera selecta pro organo Johannis Cabanilles*, 3 vols. (Brussels, 1948)
Anthologia pro organo, 4 vols. (Brussels, 1949–59)
Ars organi, 3 vols. (Brussels, 1952–4)
Little Organ Book (Boston, 1957)
Alte Orgelmusik aus England und Frankreich (Mainz, 1958)
Altniederländische Meister für Orgel oder Harmonium (Mainz, 1958)
with M.A. Vente: *De orgelkunst in de Nederlanden van de 16de tot de 18de eeuw* (Antwerp, 1971)

BIBLIOGRAPHY

P. Visser: *Flor Peeters, Organist* (Turnhout, 1950)
E. Donnell Blackham: *An Analytical Study of the Formal Treatment of the Cantus Firmus in 30 Chorale Preludes by Flor Peeters* (diss., Brigham Young U., 1962)
G. Beechey: 'The Organ Music of Flor Peeters', *Quarterly Record*, lii (1967), no.207, pp.72–86
W. Giles: 'The Organ Music of Flor Peeters: Opus 100', *Journal of Church Music*, ix (1967), 8–10, 43
J. Lade: 'The Organ Music of Flor Peeters', *MT*, cix (1968), 667–9
M.-Th. Buyssens: *Bibliografie Meester Flor Peeters* (Antwerp, 1971)
J. Hofmann: *A Study of Pedagogical Values found in Selected Organ Works of Flor Peeters* (diss., U. of Rochester, 1973)
J. Bate: 'Flor Peeters at 70', *MT*, cxiv (1973), 185–6
G. Peeters: 'Flor Peeters on his 70th Birthday', *Music: the AGO and RCCO Magazine*, vii/12 (1973), 28–9
R. Schuneman: 'To Flor Peeters: a 70th Birthday Tribute', *The Diapason*, lxiv/8 (1973), 2 only
J. Hofmann: *Flor Peeters: his Life and his Organ Works* (Fredonia, 1978)
G. Peeters and R. Schroyens: *Flor Peeters, 1903–1986: Allegro energico* (Mechelen, 1991)
G. Peeters: *Flor Peeters: chronologische catalogus van 3ij oeuvre* (Brussels, 1996)

JENNIFER BATE

Peetrinus [Peetrino, Peeters], **Jacobus** [Giaches] (*b* Mechelen, *c*1553; *d c*1591). Dutch composer, active in Italy. Doorslaer suggested that he was the same person as Jacobus Pieters who is recorded as a boy chorister at St Rombout, Mechelen, on 28 August 1561. A singer known as Petrinus is mentioned in the *Liber punctorum* of the Cappella Sistina, Rome, in 1572. Peetrinus dedicated his first compositions, *Il primo libro de madrigali*, from Milan in 1583, which suggests that he was probably living there at that time. His two books of spiritual canzonettas were published in Rome, and, according to the dedication of the *Liber primus motectorum*, he spent the latter part of his career there under the patronage of the Count of Montfort, a relative of the Fugger family. The canzonettas proved to be Peetrinus's most popular works, not only in Italy, but also in northern Europe where several of them were reprinted in collections published in Antwerp, Dillingen and Frankfurt. The five-voice motet *Surge illuminare* from the 1591 volume was also copied, within a few years of its publication, into the choirbooks of the Egidienkirche, Nuremberg (now in *D-Nla*).

WORKS

SACRED VOCAL

Il primo libro delle melodie spirituali, 3, 4vv (Rome, 1586); 1 ed. in vander Straeten
Il primo libro del Iubilo di S Bernardo con alcune canzonette spirituali, 3, 4vv (Rome, 1588, enlarged 2/1589 with 6 new works)
Liber primus motectorum, 5vv (Venice, 1591)

Spiritual canzonetta, 1586², canonic motet, 1591²⁶ (doubtful, attrib. 'Paul: Peet')

SECULAR VOCAL

Il primo libro de madrigali, 4vv (Venice, 1583), inc. [incl. inst work] 2 works, 3vv, 1589¹¹

BIBLIOGRAPHY

Vander StraetenMPB, vi
G. van Doorslaer: 'J. Peetrinus compositeur Malinois', *Bulletin du Cercle archéologique, littéraire et artistique de Malines*, xxvii (1922), 23–38
W.H. Rubsamen: 'The International "Catholic" Repertoire of a Lutheran Church in Nürnberg (1574–1597)', *AnnM*, v (1957), 229–327
                                                    IAIN FENLON

Pegbox (Fr. *cheviller*; Ger. *Wirbelkasten*; It. *cassa dei bischeri*). In violins and bowed string instruments generally, the wooden box-like structure, generally open on top (sometimes partly or wholly open at the back as well), into which are fitted the tuning-pegs that hold the strings and regulate their tension (*see* VIOLIN, fig.2). In most bowed string instruments, the wooden pegs are inserted laterally into the pegbox; that is, the holes for the pegs are bored in the sides of the pegbox, and the tapered pegs run from one side through the other side of the pegbox, the shank of the peg being at right angles to the string.

In some bowed strings, as in the *lira da braccio*, the pegs are not lateral but frontal, the pegs being inserted not at the side but from the front (top) downwards, the pegbox being open below (*see* LIRA DA BRACCIO, figs.1 and 2). This type of pegbox is often leaf- or heart-shaped. In the case of frontal pegs whose pegheads are on top, the strings are strung either directly to the peg-shanks on top, or the strings run through holes, bored just above the nut, down to the peg-ends below.

Plucked string instruments often use pegboxes with lateral pegs, but sometimes a 'pegboard' is employed instead. The latter generally consists of a surface or 'board', approximately rectangular, into which pegs are inserted so that for the most part the peg-heads are regulated from the back, and the peg-ends protrude from the front surface of the pegboard, the strings running directly from the pegs to and over the nut (*see* GUITAR, fig.9). The pegboard or pegbox is often thrown back at an angle to the fingerboard in many guitars; in some lutes this angle is as much as 90 degrees.

Conventional pegs are maintained in place by friction from the pegholes. Modern instruments, however, often rely on worm-gear mechanisms to achieve more accurate tuning and to secure holding by mechanical means (*see* GUITAR, fig.1). On earlier instruments the functions of pegs and pegbox were occasionally performed by comparable mechanical means of tightening the strings, such as the 'watch-key' tuner of the ENGLISH GUITAR.

                                              DAVID D. BOYDEN

Pegg, Bob (*b* Long Eaton, Derbyshire, 5 Dec 1944). English songwriter, singer and musician. He was much influenced by British traditional music. After performing, while still at school, in the eclectic world of the early English folk revival, Pegg went to Leeds University (1963–9) where he did fieldwork on the musical traditions of the Yorkshire Dales and edited a pioneering journal on traditional and folk club music called *Abe's Folk Music* (1966–9). His conclusion that 'folk' or 'traditional' music could not be defined usefully outside its social context was not universally accepted in Britain at the time, and caused a stir even in 1976, when it was propounded in his book *Folk*. The instrumental composition of the Dales dance bands and chapel orchestras influenced the line-up of the folk-rock band MR FOX, which Bob and CAROLE PEGG formed in 1970. At this point Pegg began to work seriously as a songwriter, producing material that was characteristically narrative and melody-based. He became best known for extended pieces of storytelling like *The Gipsy* and *Bones*. The formation of Mr Fox was also the beginning of 20 years as a touring musician. In 1975, Pegg moved to the West Yorkshire Pennines, an area that became the subject of his Calderdale Songs, commissioned by the Hebden Bridge Festival in 1978 and released on the CD *The Last Wolf* (1996). During this period he also produced music for radio, television, theatre and film. He moved in 1990 to the Highlands of Scotland, where he is now an arts worker in Ross and Cromarty. Recent projects have included: scores for the community dramas Macbeth and Storm; the introduction of American Sacred Harp singing to the Highlands; investigations into Pictish music with harpist Bill Taylor; research and performance of music of the Great Glen with E. Mairi MacArthur; and creation of soundposts for Pictavia visitor centre in Brechin.

WRITINGS

B. Pegg: *Folk: A Portrait of English Traditional Music, Musicians and Customs* (London, 1976)

RECORDINGS

He Came from the Mountains, perf. B. Pegg, C. Pegg, Trailer LER 3016 (1971)
And Now It Is So Early: Songs of Sidney Carter, perf. B. Pegg, C. Pegg, S. Carter, Galliard GAL 4017 (1972)
Bob Pegg and Nick Strutt, perf. B. Pegg, N. Strutt, Transatlantic TRA 265 (1973)
The Shipbuilder, perf. B. Pegg, Transatlantic TRA 280 (1974)
Ancient Maps, perf. B. Pegg, Transatlantic TRA 299 (1975)
The Last Wolf, perf. B. Pegg, Rhiannon RHYD 5009 (1996)
Breaking the Silence: Music inspired by the Picts, perf. B. Pegg, B. Taylor, The Highland Council PICT 001 (1997)
                                                    DAVE ARTHUR

Pegg, Carole (Anne) [Carolanne] (*b* Nottingham, 19 Sept 1944). English folk-rock and neo-traditional singer, fiddle player, songwriter and ethnomusicologist. In the early 1960s she was a resident singer at the Nottingham folk club. From 1964 to 1969, she and her husband BOB PEGG ran the traditional club the Sovereign in Leeds, and performed together on the national folk circuit. She introduced to the folk scene the English fiddle style (comprising short choppy bow strokes, double-stopping, drones and no vibrato), learnt from traditional fiddlers, including Jinky Wells, Peter Beresford and Harry Cox.

The Peggs recorded their interpretations of Sydney Carter's songs on *And Now it is So Early* (Galliard), and their own songs on *He Came from the Mountains* (Transatlantic, 1971), by which time they had launched the experimental and controversial folk-rock band MR FOX. Carole Pegg's singer-songwriter album *Carolanne* (1973) mixed traditional English influences with rock and country music, and featured the guitarist Albert Lee. She went on to form Magus with Graham Bond while continuing to perform solo.

From the mid-1970s Pegg studied anthropology at the University of Cambridge. After completing a PhD on music and society in Suffolk, she has continued to lecture on the anthropology of music and performance in the University's Department of Social Anthropology. During the late 1980s and throughout the 1990s, she undertook field research in Mongolia and Inner Mongolia. She was chairperson to the UK chapter of the International Council for Traditional Music (1989–94) (now the British Forum for Ethnomusicology), a founding co-editor of the *British Journal of Ethnomusicology* and is currently its reviews editor.

WRITINGS

Music and Society in East Suffolk (diss., U. of Cambridge, 1986)
'Tradition, Change and Symbolism of Mongol Music in Ordos and Xilingol, Inner Mongolia', *Journal of the Anglo-Mongolian Society*, xii (1989), 67–72
'Mongolian Conceptualisations of Overtone Singing (xöömii)', *BJE*, i (1992), 31–54
'Ritual, Religion and Magic in West Mongolian (Oirad) Heroic Epic Performance', *BJE*, iv (1995), 77–98
Mongolian Music, Dance and Oral Narrative: Performing Diverse Identities (Washington DC, 2000)

BIBLIOGRAPHY

F. Woods: 'A Sapphire for Carole Pegg', *Folk Review*, ii/2 (1972), 8–9
K. Dallas: 'Rockin' Pegg', *Let it Rock: the New Music Review* (1973)
J. Fairley: *Folk Roots* [forthcoming]

ROBIN DENSELOW

Pegolotti, Tomaso (*fl* Scandiano, nr Modena, *c*1698). Italian composer. The title-page of his only extant work, *Trattenimenti armonici da camera a' violino solo, e violoncello* (Modena, 1698), dedicated to Foresto d'Este, Marchese di Scandiano, indicates that he was from Scandiano. He designated himself 'Vicesegretario, e Cancelliere della medema A.S.', implying that he was a skilled amateur or dilettante. The 12 works in the collection, the first a *sonata da chiesa* and the others *sonate da camera*, are in four movements. The opening movements are slow, the second fast (alternately Capriccio and Balletto), and, except in the first sonatas, these are followed by two dance movements. Neither instrument is required to play beyond third position, but the passage-work and string crossings are demanding and indicate a familiarity with current string styles and technique. As the cello part has no figures and participates on almost equal melodic terms with the violin, it seems that the works were intended as true duos; the etching of a cellist and violinist on the title-page strengthens this conjecture.

NONA PYRON

Peguilhan, Aimeric de. *See* AIMERIC DE PEGUILHAN.

Pehr, Joseph. *See* BEER, JOSEPH.

Peinemann, Edith (*b* Mainz, 3 March 1937). German violinist. At four she began lessons with her father Robert Peinemann, leader of the Mainz Stadtorchester. From 1951 she studied with Heinz Stanske in Heidelberg and from 1953 to 1956 with Max Rostal at the GSM in London. In 1956 she won the Munich International Competition and began to tour Europe, quickly becoming recognized as one of the best German soloists. In 1960 she formed a duo with the Austrian pianist Jörg Demus, specializing in the Beethoven and Brahms sonatas, and in 1962 she started her regular visits to the USA which have taken her to many of the major festivals there. Her New York orchestral début was made in 1965 with the Beethoven Violin Concerto accompanied by the Cleveland Orchestra under George Szell; and soon after that she played Bartók's Second Concerto with the New York PO under William Steinberg. She has also toured South America, Japan and South Africa. In 1964 she became professor of violin at the Musikhochschule in Frankfurt. A sensitive player with an ample, well focussed but occasionally slightly hard tone, she excels in Bach and the Classical and Romantic repertory, although she is also a fine interpreter of the Berg and Stravinsky concertos. In 1990 she made an outstanding recording of the Reger Concerto. Her other recordings include the Dvořák Concerto with the Czech PO under Peter Maag.

TULLY POTTER

Peire Cardenal (*b* Le Puy-en-Velay, ?1180; *d* ?Montpellier, ?1278). Troubadour. His place of birth, in the modern département of Haute-Loire, is known through his *vida*; a number of members of his family are also traceable there. The estimated date of his birth is based on a document which mentions a certain 'Petrus Cardinalis' who was employed as a clerk in 1204 by Raimon VI, Count of Toulouse. The *vida* tells us that Peire lived to be nearly 100 years old, and that he probably died in Montpellier, the principal residence of Jaime I, King of Aragon (1213–76). As a small boy, Peire attended a clerical school in order to learn reading and singing. It is doubtful whether he ever became a priest, but he did write a large number of Marian poems.

Over 90 poems have been attributed to him, of which three only have survived with melodies. It is evident from the *vida* that at least some of the others were intended to be sung: we are told that he kept a *jongleur* to sing his sirventes. Topical references and bitter attacks on both the nobility and the clergy are often the dominant themes of his poems, many of them inspired by the Albigensian crusade. Two of the three extant melodies are contrafacta of songs by troubadours of an earlier generation.

WORKS

Editions: *Poésies complètes du troubadour Peire Cardenal*, ed. R. Lavaud (Toulouse, 1957) [complete text edn]
Der musikalische Nachlass der Troubadours, ed. F. Gennrich, SMM, iii (1958) [complete music edn]
Las cançons dels trobadors, ed. I. Fernandez de la Cuesta and R. Lafont (Toulouse, 1979) [complete music edn]

The Extant Troubadour Melodies, ed. H. van der Werf and G. Bond (Rochester, NY, 1984) [complete music edn]

Ar mi posc eu lauzar d'amor, PC 335.7 [contrafactum of: Guiraut de Bornelh, 'Non posc sofrir qu'a la dolor', PC 242.51] (composed 1204–8, according to Lavaud)

Rics hom que greu ditz vertat a leu men, PC 335.49 [contrafactum of: Raimon Jordan, 'Vas vos soplei, domna Premeiramen', PC 404.11]

Un sirventes novel voill comensar, PC 335.67 (composed 1232–3, according to Lavaud)

BIBLIOGRAPHY

K. Vossler: *Peire Cardinal, ein Satiriker aus dem Zeitalter der Albigenserkriege* (Munich, 1916)

S. Vatteroni: 'Le poesie di Peire Cardenal', *Studi mediolatini e volgari*, xxxvi (1990), 73–259; xxxix (1993), 105–218; xl (1994), 119–202; xli (1995), 165–212; xlii (1996), 169–251

For further bibliography see TROUBADOURS, TROUVÈRES.

ROBERT FALCK

Peire d'Alvernhe (*fl* 1149–70). Troubadour. He was possibly the son of a burgher in Alvergne, and may have sought the patronage of the counts of Barcelona, Provence and Toulouse. His famous sirventes, *Chantarai d'aquest trobadors* (whose melody does not survive), satirizes several contemporaries, including Raimbaut d'Aurenga, Giraut de Bornelh and Bernart de Ventadorn. The song was once thought to have been composed in conjunction with the procession from Bordeaux to Tarazona in 1170 of Aliénor, daughter of Henry II of England and Eleanor of Aquitaine, to marry Alfonso VIII of Castile, but that has been shown to be improbable. Peire composed about 24 poems, but only two survive with melodies (ed. in van der Werf): a *tenso* with Bernart de Ventadorn (PC 323.4; *F-Pn* fr. 844) and a *canso*, *Dejosta·ls breus jorns e·ls loncs sers* (PC 323.15; *F-Pn* fr.20050 and 22543). The latter is through-composed, and in its conservative texture and range it resembles the melodies of Bernart. The *tenso* is one of the most melismatic of troubadour melodies, and differences between the two extant versions suggest that the melismas are ornamental.

BIBLIOGRAPHY

A. Del Monte, ed.: *Peire d'Alvernhe* (Turin, 1955) [complete edn]

M. de Riquer: *Los trovadores: historia, literari y textos* (Barcelona, 1975), i, 311–41

H. van der Werf: *The Extant Troubadour Melodies* (Rochester, NY, 1984), 230*–32* [incl. music edns]

E. Aubrey: *The Music of the Troubadours* (Bloomington, IN, 1996)

For further bibliography see TROUBADOURS, TROUVÈRES.

ELIZABETH AUBREY

Peiró, José [Joseph]. See PEYRÓ, JOSÉ.

Peirol (*b* Peirol, Auvergne, ?1160; *d* after 1221). Troubadour. He was born in Peirol Castle, and is described in his *vida* (*I-Rvat* 5232, f.147) as 'a poor knight of Auvergne' ('paubres cavalliers d'Alverge'). Information in the *vida* and his own works indicates that he may have been in the service of the Dauphin of Auvergne at Clermont until about 1202. The earliest firm date that can be established is 1188 – the probable date of composition of *Quant amors trobet partit* and the period of preparation for the third crusade. This 'crusading *tenso*' (see Aston) is Peirol's best-known work, and takes the form of a debate with Love as to whether it would be better to take the cross or serve his lady. The only other work containing biographical allusion which may be dated with any certainty is *Pus flum Jordan ai vist e·l monimen* (PC 366.28), written in Jerusalem at the conclusion of the fifth crusade in 1221 or 1222. It seems likely that he did not live much beyond

1221. One version of his *vida* states that he died in Montpellier, but this cannot be documented.

Ex.1 *I-Ma* R71, f.48

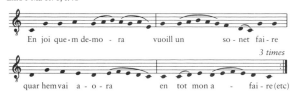

Although there are references in his poems to Vienne (PC 366.1 and 20), Blacatz (PC 366.5 and 25) and possibly Marseilles (PC 366.5, and in one version of his *vida* in *F-Pn* fr.1749, f.208), these are not definite indications of his whereabouts or service. A 'Marqueza' is mentioned in one poem (PC 366.4) but not identified further; the 'Seign En Heralh' in another (PC 366.27a) is Heraclius of Polignac, to whom the poem is addressed. The joint authorship of some poems with Gaucelm Faidit (PC 366.17) and Dalfi d'Alvernha (PC 366.10 and 30) gives an indication of the literary circle within which Peirol worked. (It is doubtful that this was the Peirol of the poem jointly composed with Bernart de Ventadorn, PC 366.23.)

Of the 34 poems attributed to Peirol, 17 survive with music. Of these, only *Per dan que d'amor m'aveigna* inspired later imitations. In the opening stanza of *M'entension ai tot' en un vers meza*, Peirol stated his intention to compose a *vers*; he next considered that a *chansoneta* would be more readily learnt, but that such songs are too frivolous; he finally concluded that it would be better to compose a *vers* in order to demonstrate his skill (*saber*). A number of the songs call themselves *vers* (e.g. *D'un bon vers*), but more are termed *sonet*. Both *D'un sonet* and *En joi que·m demora* are designated *sonet* in the first stanza, and *chansoneta* in the last, suggesting that the two terms may be related. Musically it appears possible to distinguish the two genres: the *vers*, although it may have a repeated *AB* structure at the beginning, is more often through-composed and richly melismatic (see

Ex.2 *I-Ma* R71, f.48v

Be dei chantar, *D'un bon vers* and *M'entension*); the *sonet* is slightly less melismatic and employs repeating melodic schemes – it is in essence more concise and tonally clear than the rather diffuse style of the *vers*. The *sonets D'un sonet vau pensan* and *En joi que·m demora* both begin with the leap of a 5th, and the latter employs only four melodic phrases for 12 lines of text (ex.1). *Be dei chantar* is not entirely through-composed, but even the incipient repeated *AB* form at the beginning is largely disguised. The final line is likewise a varied and even more richly melismatic version of the first line (ex.2). In addition, the cadential plan seems less clear than that of ex.1 and the final cadence appears to be completely unmotivated by what has gone before.

WORKS

Editions: *Peirol: Troubadour of Auvergne*, ed. S.C. Aston (Cambridge, 1953) [complete text edn]
　Der musikalische Nachlass der Troubadours: I, ed. F. Gennrich, SMM, iii (1958) [complete text edn]
　Las cançons dels trobadors, ed. I. Fernandez de la Cuesta and R. Lafont (Toulouse, 1979) [complete edn]
　The Extant Troubadour Melodies, ed. H. van der Werf and G. Bond (Rochester, NY, 1984) [complete edn]

Atressi co·l cignes fai, PC 366.2
Be dei chantar pos amors m'o enseigna, PC 366.3
Camjat m'a mon consirier, PC 366.6
Cora qu·m fezes doler, PC 366.9
D'eissa la razo qu'en soill, PC 366.11
Del seu tort farai esmenda, PC 366.12
D'un bon vers vau pensan com lo fezes, PC 366.13
D'un sonet vau pensan, PC 366.14
En joi que·m demora, PC 366.15
Mainta gens me malrazona, PC 366.19
M'entension ai tot' en un vers meza, PC 366.20
Mout m'entremis de chantar volentiers, PC 366.21
Nuls hom no s'auci tan gen, PC 366.22
Per dan que d'amor m'aveigna, PC 366.26 [contrafacta: 'A l'entrant del tens salvage', R.41; 'Vite perdite me legi', 2vv (Notre Dame conductus)]
Quant amors trobet partit, PC 366.29 (written in 1188 during the preparations for the third crusade)
Si be·m sui loing et entre gent estraigna, PC 366.31
Tot mon engeing e mon saber, PC 366.33

BIBLIOGRAPHY

MGG1 (F. Gennrich)
U. Sesini: *Le melodie trobadoriche nel Canzoniere provenzale della Biblioteca Ambrosiana* (Turin, 1942), 204
M. Switten: 'Metrical and Musical Structure in the Songs of Peirol', *Romantic Review*, li (1960), 241–55
J. Boutière and A.-H. Schutz: *Biographies des troubadours* (Paris,1950, rev. 2/1964 by J. Boutière), 303ff
For further bibliography see TROUBADOURS, TROUVÈRES.

ROBERT FALCK

Peitsche (Ger.). *See* WHIP.

Peixinho, Jorge (Manuel Rosado Marques) (*b* Montijo, 20 Jan 1940; *d* Lisbon, 30 June 1995). Portuguese composer. After completing his studies in piano and composition at the Lisbon Conservatory with Artur Santos and Jorge Croner de Vasconcelos (1951–8), he studied with Boris Parena and with Petrassi at the Accademia di S Cecilia in Rome, where he obtained the diploma in composition in 1961. In 1960 he also worked with Nono in Venice and with Boulez and Stockhausen at the Musik-Akademie in Basle. He took part in the Darmstadt summer courses (1960–70) and from 1962 directed contemporary music courses in Portugal and South America. In 1970 he founded the Grupo de Música Contemporânea de Lisboa (GMCL), with whom he played an important part in promoting the works of contemporary Portuguese and foreign composers. He performed with GMCL in many European countries. At the same time he gained a reputation as a teacher, pianist and lecturer. As a composer he received various prizes and took part in various festivals in Europe and South America. He was professor of composition at the Lisbon Conservatory (1985–95).

Peixinho was an outstanding figure in Portuguese music during the second half of the 20th century and in the 1960s played a pioneering role in opening up the country to the musical language of the avant garde. His solid formal training was complemented by a great creativity, resulting in a large and varied, politically relevant output. According to Luis de Pablo, one detects in his music 'an enormous effort to discipline a volcanic temperament within a set of rules, self-imposed with great lucidity'.

WORKS
(selective list)

GMCL denotes the Grupo de Música Contemporânea de Lisboa, an ensemble with a variable instrumental combination

Orch. Políptico, chbr orch, 1960; Sobreposições, 1960; Conc. sax, orch, 1961; Diafonia, chbr orch, 1963; Políptico II, 1964; Kinetofonias, 1965–8; Nomos, 1967; Sucessões simétricas II, 1971; Sucessões simétricas III, 1974; Mémoires ... miroirs ... , clvd, str, 1980; Retrato de Helena, chbr orch, 1982; Concerto de outono, ob, orch, 1983; Alis, chbr orch, 1990; Hp Conc., 1995

Vocal: Fascinação (textless), S, fl, cl, 1959; Tríptico (C. de Barcelos, F. Pessoa, S. V. do Céu) 1: Bar, male chorus, brass, perc; 2: S, Mez, female chorus, 11 insts; 3: S, str trio, small orch, 1959–60; A cabeça do grifo (Pessoa), S, mand, pf, 1960, rev. S, va, hp, pf, 1980; Estrela (E.A. Blásquez), S/Bar, pf, 1962; Coracão habitado (E. de Andrade), Mez, fl, vc, pf, 1965; Eurídice reamada (H. Helder), 5 solo vv, chorus, orch, 1968; Recitativo II (R. Brandão, Helder), S, Mez, hp, 1970; Vocaliso (textless), Mez, pf, 1970–82; A lira destemperada (L. de Camões), S, trbn, perc, 1972; Voix (C. Rasson), Mez, chbr orch, 1972; Voix-en-jeux, Mez, chbr orch, 1972–6; Madrigal I, chorus, 1975; Leves véus velam, S, fl, hp, va, perc, 1980; Ah! A angústia, a raiva vil, o desespero (de Barcelos), S, fl, hp, 2 perc, 1980; Canto para Anna Livia, S, Mez, A, chbr ens, 1981; À flor das águas verdes, chorus, 1982; Ulivi aspri e forti (R. Cresti), Mez, fl, vc, 1984; Ciclo-valsa II, T, pf, db, perc, velophone, musical boxes, 1984, rev. S, pf, perc, GMCL, velophone, musical boxes, 1985; Greetings, Mez, fl, bn, vc, perc, 1985; Llanto por Mariana (F. García Lorca), S, fl, cl, pf, 2 vn, va, vc, 1986; Credo, T, chbr ens, 1988; A capela de Janas, S, chbr ens, 1989; Cantos de Sophia, S, gui, 1990; Memória de Marília, S, Bar, chbr ens, 1990; Viagem da natural invenção, 2 solo vv, ens, 1991–4; Ja a roxa manhã clara, chorus

Chbr: 4 Evocação, chbr ens, 1960; Episódios, str qt, 1960; Dominó, fl, perc, 1963–4; Estrutura, fl, perc, 1963–4; Sequência, fl, perc, cel, 1963–4; Morfocromia, chbr ens, 1963–8; Situações 66, fl, cl, tpt, va, hn, 1966; Recitativo III, hp, fl, perc, tape, 1969; CDE, cl, vn, vc, pf, 1970; Lov I, pf, fl, perc, tape, 1971; Nocturnal, chbr ens, 1971; As quatro estações, chbr ens, tape, 1972; Ma fin est mon commencement (Homenagem a Machaut), chbr ens, tape, 1972; 4 peças para Setembro vermelho, chbr ens, 1972; A idade do ouro, chbr ens, tape, 1973; Morrer em Santiago, 6 perc, 1973; Recitativo IV, chbr ens, tape, 1974; Coral, GMCL, 1974; A aurora do socialismo (Madrigale capriccioso), chbr ens, tape, 1975; ... e isto é só o início, hein?, GMCL, 1975; Canto da Sibila, cl, perc, pf, 1976; Elegia, va, trbn, pf, perc, 1976; Música em água e mármore, fl, tpt, hp, gui, vn, vc, synth, 1977; Madrigal II, cl qnt, 1977; Lov II, vc, pf, fl, perc, tape, 1978, rev. 1983; O jardim das delícias, GMCL, 1979; Faites vos jeux, mesdames, messieurs!, hn, vc, hp, pf, 1979, rev. fl, pic, vc, hp, pf, 1981; Ciclo-valsa, GMCL, velophone, musical boxes, 1980; Warsaw Workshop Waltz, cl, trbn, vc, pf, 1980; Novo canto da Sibila, cl, pf, perc, 1981; Madame Borbolet(r)a, children's insts, musical toys, 1981; Serenata per A., fl, b fl, pic, gui, pf, perc, 1981; O jardim de Belisa, chbr ens, 1984; Canzone da suonare I, fl, cl, tpt, va, hp, vib, 1984; Canzone da suonare II, fl, cl, vc, hp, vib, 1984; Metaformoses, chbr ens, 1984; Remake, fl, vc, hp, pf, 1985; Qt, 4 sax, 1985; Ouçam a soma dos sons que soam, chbr ens, 1986; Sine nomine, GMCL, 1987; O quadrado azul, ob, va, db, pf, 1987; Deux pièces meublées, chbr ens, 1988; Passage intérieur, sax, elec gui, b gui, synth, elec perc, 1989; Mediterrânea, chbr ens, 1991; Floreal, chbr ens, 1992; ... silenciosa rosa/rio do tempo ... fl, vn, va, vc, hp, 1994

1–2 Insts: 2 espressioni, tpt, hpd, 1959; 2 pequenos estudos para Aldo Hans, 2 vn, 1961; Imagens sonoras, 2 hp, 1961; Recitativo I, hp, 1971; Recit, vc, 1971; Welkom, vn, va, 1972; Solo, db, 1976; L'oiseau-lyre, gui, 1982; Sax-blue, a sax, sopranino sax, elecs, 1982–4; The Missing Miss, vn, 1985; Glosa II, fl, 1990–4; Fantasia-impromptu, a sax, pf, 1991

Pf: 5 pequenas peças, 1959; Sucessões simétricas I, 1961; Estudo I, 1969; Lov, pf, tape, 1971–7; Estudo II, 1972; Estudo III, 1976; Music Box, pf, tape, 1983–5; Red Sweet Tango, 1984; Estudo IV, amp pf, 1984; Miss Papillon, pf, tape, 1985; Villalbarosa, 1987; Aquela tarde ..., 1988; 3 Pieces, 1989–92; Nocturno no cabo do mundo, 3 pf, 1993; Janeira, 1995

Dramatic: A pousada das Chagas (film score), 1970; Brandos costumes (film score), 1972; O prisioneiro (film score), 1978; other scores incl. incid music

El ac: Sincronia-objecto, 1967, Elegia a Amílcar Cabral, 1973; Luis Vaz 73, 1973–4, rev. 1974–5; Electronicolirica, 1979; Canto germinal, 1989

Principal publishers: Salabert, Musicoteca

Principal recording companies: Tecla, Sassetti, Portugalsom, Poly-Arte International, Jorsom

BIBLIOGRAPHY

R.V. Nery and P.F. de Castro: *Sínteses da cultura portuguesa: História da música* (Lisbon, 1991)

E. Vaz Palma: 'Entrevista com o compositor Jorge Peixinho', *Arte musical*, 4th ser., no.1 (1995), 4–17

J. de Lemos, J. Machado and T. Castanheira: *Homenagem a Jorge Peixinho* (Lisbon, 1996)

J. Machado and J. Machado: *Catálogo da obra completa de Jorge Peixinho* (Lisbon, forthcoming)

ADRIANA LATINO

Pejačević [Pejacsevich], Dora (*b* Budapest, 10 Sept 1885; *d* Munich, 5 March 1923). Croatian composer. She studied at the Croatian Music Institute in Zagreb then briefly in Dresden with Sherwood and in Munich with Courvoisier. For the most part, however, she was self-taught and developed her musical talents through contact with other artists and intellectuals, such as Karl Kraus. Her ancestral home was at Našice (near Osijek), but she also travelled extensively to Budapest, Munich, Prague and Vienna. After 1921 she lived mainly in Munich.

Her works were performed most frequently outside Croatia; part of her Symphony, for example, was first given in Vienna (25 January 1918) and the complete work was performed later in Dresden. Her late Romantic idiom, enriched with Impressionist harmonies and lush orchestral colours, evolved as she strove to break free from drawing-room mannerisms and conventions. She introduced the orchestral song into Croatian music, though among her vocal works her greatest achievement is the *Drei Gesänge* op.53 for voice and piano. Her late piano miniatures are lyrical and meditative evocations, such as the two nocturnes op.50, or else robust dance movements containing grotesque elements, as in the *Humoreske und Caprice* op.54. The Piano Quintet op.40, String Quartet op.58, the Symphony and the Piano Concerto display both an accomplished technique and a striving towards integration of motivic and thematic material. In the *Phantasie concertante* op.48 for piano and orchestra and in the Piano Sonata in Ab, op.57, she followed the Lisztian concept of the single movement sonata-fantasy.

In Croatia her work concurred with the modernist movement in literature and the secession in the visual arts: without breaking new ground she helped to bring a new range of expression into the traditional musical language. Almost all of her 57 known compositions

survive as a single collection, in the Croatian Music Institute in Zagreb.

WORKS
(*selective list*)

Orch: Pf Conc., g, op.33, 1913; Sym., f♯, op.41, 1916–18; Phantasie concertante, d, op.48, pf, orch, 1919; Ov., d, op.49, 1919

Vocal: 7 Lieder (W. Wickenburg-Almásy), op.23, 1v, pf, 1907; Verwandlung (K. Kraus), op.37b, 1v, orch, 1915; Liebeslied (R.M. Rilke), op.39, 1v, orch, 1915; Mädchengestalten (Rilke), op.42, 1v, pf, 1916; 2 Schmetterlingslieder (K. Henckell), op.52, 1v, orch, 1920; 3 Gesänge (F. Nietzsche), op.53, 1v, pf, 1920

Chbr: Pf trio, D, op.15, 1902; Pf Qt, d, op.25, 1908; Sonata, D, op.26, vn, pf, 1909; Pf Trio, C, op.29, 1910; Elégie, op.34, vn, pf, 1913; Sonata, e, op.35, vc, pf, 1913; Pf Qnt, b, op.40, 1915–18; Slawische Sonate, bb, op.43, vn, pf, 1917; Méditation, op.51, vn, pf, 1919; Str Qt, C, op.58, 1922

Pf: 6 Phantasiestücke, op.17, 1903; Blumeleben, op.19, 1904–5; 4 Klavierstücke, op.32a, 1912; Sonata: bb, op.36, 1914; 2 nocturnes, op.50, 1919, 1920; Humoreske und Caprice, op.54, 1920; Sonata, Ab, op.57, 1921

BIBLIOGRAPHY

K. Kos: *Dora Pejačević* (Zagreb, 1982)

Dora Pejačević, 1885–1923: Našice 1985 ed. Z. Veber [In Croatian with Eng. summaries]

KORALJKA KOS

Pejović, Roksanda (*b* Belgrade, 11 Dec 1929). Serbian musicologist. She studied at the Belgrade Academy of Music (MA 1964) and the University's department of art history. She gained the doctorate from the University of Ljubljana in 1975 with a dissertation on musical instruments on medieval monuments in Serbia and Macedonia. She taught at the Stanković School of Music in Belgrade (1957–75) and at the Faculty of Music (1975–95). Her chief musicological interests are medieval musical instruments as represented in Byzantine and Serbian medieval art, Serbian Romantic music and the study of musical life in Serbia in the 19th and 20th centuries.

WRITINGS

'Musique serbe contemporaine', *Zvuk*, nos.77–8 (1967), 78–87

'Hrvatski muzički umetnici i kompozitori u Beogradu između dva rata' [Croatian musicians and composers in Belgrade between the two World Wars], *Arti musices*, iii (1972), 119–45

Glasbeni instrumenti na srednjeveškim spomenikih v Srbiji in Makedoniji [Musical instruments on Medieval monuments in Serbia and Macedonia] (diss., U. of Ljubljana, 1975)

Barokni koncert [The Baroque concerto] (Belgrade, 1982)

Istorija muzike jugoslovenskih naroda [The history of Yugoslav music], i (Belgrade, 1983)

Predstave muzičkih instrumenata u srednjovekovnoj Srbiji [Musical instruments in Medieval Serbia], ed. S. Rajičić (Belgrade, 1984)

'Musical Instruments Depicted or Sculptured on Antique Monuments in the Northern Part of the Balkan Peninsula', *ICTM Study Group on Music Archaeology: Conference II: Stockholm 1984*, i, 145–56

'Šta se u beogradskoj sredini smatralo muzički savremenim, modernim i avangardnim u periodu između dva svetska rata' [What was considered contemporary, modern and avant-garde in Belgrade between the two World Wars], *Medjimurje*, nos.13–14 (1988), 172–85

Srpsko muzičko izvođaštvo romantičarskog doba [Performing musicians in the Romantic period] (Belgrade, 1991)

Muzikolog Stana Đurić-Klajn: istoriografska, esejistička i kritičarska delatnost (Belgrade, 1994)

Opera i balet Narodnog pozorišta u Beogradu (1882–1941) [Opera and ballet in the National Theatre, Belgrade] (Belgrade, 1996)

'Češki muzičari u srpskom muzičkom životu (1844–1918)' [Czech Musicians in Serbian Musical Life (1844–1918)], *Novi zvuk*, no.8 (1996), 51–58; no.9 (1997), 65–74; Eng. trans. in *New Sound*, viii (1996), 57–64; ix (1997), 65–75

MELITA MILIN

Pękalski, Jozef Tadeusz Benedykt (*d* ?Kraków, *c*1761). Polish musician. He was probably ordained a priest in Warsaw, for it is known that he studied theology there in

1726–7. In 1739 he was appointed director of the vocal chapel of the Rorantists at Wawel Cathedral, with which he may have been connected before (perhaps as a member of this chapel). As the director of the Rorantist chapel, he must be given credit for the survival of the music of that group. A considerable part of this music (several hundred works, some dating back to the 16th century) has survived, copied or with additions in his own hand. The authorship of a manuscript treatise on music, *Discordia concors, sive de magna arte musica tractatus IV* (destroyed in World War II), is also attributed to him.

BIBLIOGRAPHY

A. Chybiński: 'Nowe materiały do dziejów królewskiej kapeli rorantystów w Kaplicy Zygmuntowskiej na Wawelu' [New materials from the Sigismund chapel on Wawel Hill concerning the history of the Royal Rorantist Collegium], *Księga pamiątkowa ku czci Oswalda Balcera* (Lwów, 1925), 133–51

ZYGMUNT M. SZWEYKOWSKI

Pekelis, Mikhail Samoylovich (*b* Kiev, 29 July/10 Aug 1899; *d* Moscow, 20 March 1979). Russian musicologist. He graduated from the Kiev Conservatory in 1922 and two years later became a member of staff of the Moscow Conservatory. He was appointed senior lecturer in 1925 and professor in 1930; he held the chair of Russian music history (1934–5), and the chair of history of the music of the Soviet peoples (1937–41). After teaching at the Sverdlovsk, Kiev and Gor'ky Conservatories (1943–55) Pekelis returned to Moscow, where from 1955 he was professor and chairman of the faculty of music history at the Gnesin Musico-Pedagogical Institute. Pekelis's research was concerned with the history of Russian music. He devoted three books to his main interest, the life and work of Dargomïzhsky, and wrote articles and papers on Glinka, Musorgsky, Borodin and Mikhail Gnesin. He was general editor of and contributor to the two-volume *Istoriya russkoy muzïki* (1940) and edited and wrote articles for the journal *Muzïkal'noye nasledstvo*. Although he was a scholar of impressive erudition and wide experience, he was severely criticized by the Soviet authorities in 1948.

WRITINGS

Aleksander Sergeyevich Dargomïzhskiy: biograficheskiye svedeniya i analiz tvorchestva [Biographical information and an analysis of his works] (Moscow, 1932)
ed.: *Istoriya russkoy muzïki* [History of Russian music] (Moscow, 1940)
Dargomïzhskiy i narodnaya pesnya: k probleme narodnosti v russkoy klassicheskoy muzïke [Dargomïzhsky and folksong: the problem of nationalism in Russian classical music] (Moscow, 1951)
ed.: *A.S. Dargomïzhskiy: izbrannïye pis'ma* [Collected letters], i (Moscow, 1952)
ed.: *M.P. Musorgskiy: izbrannïye pis'ma* (Moscow, 1953)
'Neizvestnaya partitura Glinki' [An unknown score of Glinka], *SovM* (1954), no.9, pp.67–9
'Ëzopova rech' v tvorchestve Musorgskogo' [Aesopian language in Musorgsky's works], *SovM* (1956), no.7, pp.75–80
'Ob avtobiografii Dargomïzhskogo', *SovM* (1957), no.7, pp.89–97
ed.: *A.S. Rabinovich: izbrannïye stat'i i materialï* [Collected articles and materials] (Moscow, 1959)
'Muzïkal'no-ésteticheskiye vozzreniya i literaturnïye trudï M.F. Gnesina' [The view of musical aesthetics and the literary works of Gnesin], *M.F. Gnesin: stat'i, vospominaniya, materialï*, ed. R.V. Glezer (Moscow, 1961) pp.64–79
ed.: 'M.P. Musorgsky: pis'ma k V.V. Stasovu' [Musorgsky: letters to Stasov], *Muzïkal'noye nasledstvo* (1962), 350–56
Aleksandr Sergeyevich Dargomïzhskiy i yego okruzheniye [Dargomïzhsky and his circle] (Moscow, 1966–73)
'Musorgskiy: pisatel', dramaturg' [Musorgsky: writer and dramatist], *SovM* (1967), no.6, pp.92–103
'Dargomïzhskiy i Shchepkin', *SovM* (1969), no.2, pp.88–93
'Dva avtografa' [Two autographs], *SovM* (1969), no.9, pp.67–74 [the librettos for Musorgsky's *Boris Godunov* and *Khovanshchina*]
ed., with A.A. Orlova: *M.P. Musorgskiy: literaturnoye naslediye* [Literary legacy] (Moscow, 1971)
'Russkaya pevitsa L.I. Karmalina' [The Russian singer L.I. Karmalina], *SovM* (1972), no.11, pp.84–91

EDITIONS

Aleksandr Sergeyevich Dargomïzhskiy: Polnoye sobraniye sochineniy [Complete collection of works] (Moscow, 1947–67)

JOACHIM BRAUN

Pękiel [Pechel, Peckel, Pekel, Pekell, Pekiel, Penckel], **Bartłomiej** (*d* ?Kraków, *c*1670). Polish composer and organist. Mattheson claimed that he was of German origin. The contents of a charter given to him in 1641 show that he entered the service of the Warsaw court during the reign of Władysław IV (i.e. not before 1633). On 27 March 1637, when he appeared as a godfather in the records of the collegiate church of St Jan, Warsaw, he was described as 'organarius S[acrae] R[egiae] M[aiestatis]'. At the court he was associated with Marco Scacchi, director of music from 1628 to 1649, and he became deputy director from 1641 or 1644: Feicht maintained that from 1633 Scacchi was occupied only with opera and secular music in general at the court and entrusted the sacred music to Pękiel. The task of educating the choirboys had long been entrusted to him, and after Scacchi's departure from Warsaw in 1649 Pękiel took sole charge of the administration of the royal chapel, although the title of director was not assigned to him until 1653. Later that year, because of the war with the Cossacks, he was appointed to serve and protect the queen, and after the capture of Warsaw by the Swedes in 1655 and the dissolution of the court he left Warsaw. He moved to Kraków, where in 1658, after the death of Franciszek Lilius, he became director of music in the Wawel cathedral chapel. He was also in close touch with the Rorantist chapel, in particular with its director, M.A. Miśkiewicz. The last archival reference to him as director of music dates from 1664, but as a new director (Daniel Fierszewicz) did not take up his post until 1670 or 1671 it may be assumed that he died at or shortly before this time. Evidence connected with the lost *Missa super 'Veni sponsa'* and *Missa Wąchocianna* seems to indicate that during his stay at Kraków he had contacts with Cistercian abbeys and monasteries in southern Poland.

Pękiel was the leading Polish composer of the middle Baroque period. One can distinguish in his work a Warsaw period and a Kraków period. In the former he composed dramatic concertato works (e.g. the dialogue *Audite mortales*), polychoral masses accompanied by numerous instruments (mainly wind) and with independent instrumental passages (*Missa 'La Lombardesca'*, and the 14-part mass), and purely instrumental pieces such as the canon, in the style of a variation ricercare, in *Xenia Apollinea*. The organ fugue discovered by Gołos also probably dates from this period, as do the arrangements of dances for lute attributed to Pękiel in a manuscript at Gdańsk but more likely to be by a number of different composers. During his Kraków period he composed only sacred works for the cathedral chapel and also – indeed primarily – for the male Rorantist chapel. They embrace masses (for four to eight voices) and *a cappella* motets (which, however, were doubtless performed with organ accompaniment). From both melodic and rhythmic points of view Pękiel's polyphony is decidedly Baroque in character, even in works written in a traditional *a cappella* style, and even though he did not renounce the religious modes it is emphatically tonal. A particularly significant work is the four-part mass that Miskiewicz named *Missa pulcherrima ad instar Praenestini* (the reason for this use of Palestrina's name has not been established). It is recognized as the outstanding Polish work of its type of the entire 17th century. Pękiel derived the themes from his own works (mainly of the Warsaw period), from Gregorian chant and particularly from Polish sacred songs, especially carols. Pękiel's music was known in Germany as well as in Poland, as manuscripts in Berlin and Lüneburg testify.

WORKS

Edition. *Pękiel, B.: opera omnia*, I–II, ed. Z. Dobrzańska-Fabiańska, MMP, ser. A, i (1994), 6–106

MASSES

Missa brevis, 4vv, 1661; ed. in WDMP, lxii (1966)
Missa 'De resurrectione Domini', a 6, formerly *PL-GD*, now *Kp* (inc.)
Missa in defectu unius contraltus, 4vv, ?1661–9, *Kk*
Missa 'La Lombardesca', 8vv, 2 vn, 3 trbn, bc (org); ed. in WDMP, lxxiv (1976)
Missa paschalis, 4vv, bc (org), 1662; ed. in WDMP, lviii (1965, 2/1978)
Missa pulcherrima ad instar Praenestini, 4vv, 30 Jan 1669; ed. in WDMP, xvii (1938, 4/1972)
Missa secunda, 4vv, 18 March 1661, *Kk*
Missa senza cerimonie (i), 8vv, bc (org), ?1661–9, *Kk*
Missa senza cerimonie (ii), 8vv, bc (org), ?1661–9, *Kk*; ed. in Opieński
Missa super 'Veni sponsa', 8vv, *PL-Wu* (inc., frag. only) (see Perz, 1970)
Missa Wąchocianna, a 13, lost (see Perz, 1974)
Missa, 4vv, 1664, *Kk*; ed. M. Pielech (Warsaw, 1993)
Missa, 5vv, 5 insts, lost (see Perz, 1974)
Missa 'a 14', 8vv, 2 vn, 3 va (ad lib), 2 cornettinos, 3 trbn, bombard, bn, db, bc (org) [Ky and Gl only]; ed. in WDMP, lxix (1971, 2/1980)
2 masses, a 12–13, lost, (see Maciejewski)

OTHER SACRED VOCAL

Assumpta est Maria, 4vv, ?1661–9; ed. H. Feicht, *Muzyka staropolska* (Kraków, 1966)
Audite mortales, dialogue, 6vv, 2 va da gamba, db, bc (org), before 1649; ed. in WDMP, iv (1929, 2/1968)
Ave Maria, 4vv, ?1661–9; ed. H. Feicht, *Muzyka staropolska* (Kraków, 1966)
Canite bene, sumite, 3vv, 2 va, bn, bc (org), lost, formerly *D-Lm*
Domine, ne in furore tuo, 4vv, ?1661–9, *PL-Kk* (inc.)
Dulcis amor Jesu, 5vv, bc (org); ed. Z.M. Szweykowski, *Muzyka w dawnym Krakowie* (Kraków, 1964)
Magnum nomen Domini, 4vv, ?1661–9; ed. in WDMP, xix (1948, 3/1971)
Nativitas [conceptio] tua, 4vv, ?1661–9; ed. H. Feicht, *Muzyka staropolska* (Kraków, 1966)
O adoranda Trinitas, 4vv, ?1661–9, *Kk*
O salutaris hostia, 4vv, ?1661–9, *Kk* (inc.)
Patrem rotulatum (i), 4vv, 1661; ed. in WDMP, lii (1963, 2/1969)
Patrem rotulatum (ii), 4vv, 1664; ed.in WDMP, lii (1963, 2/1969)
Quae est ista, 4vv, ?1661–9, *Kk* (inc.)
Resonet in laudibus, 4vv, ?1661–9; ed. in WDMP, xix (1948, 2/1964)
Salvator orbis, 4vv, ?1661–9, *Kk*
Sub tuum praesidium, 4vv, ?1661–9; ed. H. Feicht, *Muzyka staropolska* (Kraków, 1966)
5 lits., a 5–11, 2 motets: all lost (see Maciejewski)

INSTRUMENTAL

40 dances, lute, ?1649–55, *PL-GD* (authenticity doubtful); ed. in WDMP, xxx (1955, 4/1965)
Canon in tres partes, a 6, in Xenia Apollinea (Venice, 1643); ed. in Kmicic-Mieleszyński (1958)

Fugue, org; ed. in Gołos (1973); facs. in Gołos (1972)
1 sonata, a 2, lost (see Maciejewski)

BIBLIOGRAPHY

DEUMM (W. Sandelewski); *EitnerQ*; *GerberNL*; *MatthesonGEP*
J. Surzyński: *Matka Boska w muzyce polskiej* [The Mother of God in Polish music] (Kraków, 1905)
A. Poliński: *Dzieje muzyki polskiej w zarysie* [A history of Polish music in outline] (Lwów, 1907), 127, 129, 131, 133–4
Z. Jachimecki: *Wpływy włoskie w muzyce polskiej* [Italian influences in Polish music] (Kraków, 1911), 300ff
H. Opieński and G. Koeckert: *La musique polonaise* (Paris, 1918, 2/1929)
H. Feicht: 'Bartłomiej Pękiel', *Przegląd muzyczny*, i/10–12 (1925)
H. Feicht: *Kompozycje religijne Bartłomieja Pękiela* [Pękiel's sacred compositions] (diss., U. of Lwów, 1925); repr. in H. Feicht, *Studia nad muzyką polskiego renesansu i baroku* (Kraków, 1980)
H. Feicht: '"Audite mortales" Bartłomieja Pękiela', *KM*, no.4 (1929), 166–96
Z. Jachimecki: *Muzyka polska w rozwoju historycznym* [Polish music in its historical development], i/1 (Kraków, 1948), 202ff
A. Chybiński: *Słownik muzyków dawnej Polski do roku 1800* [Dictionary of early Polish musicians to 1800] (Kraków, 1949)
W. Kmicic-Mieleszyński: 'Geneza "Cribrum musicum"' [The genesis of 'Cribrum musicum'], *Muzyka*, ii/3 (1957), 3–17
W. Kmicic-Mieleszyński: 'Kanony Bartłomieja Pękiela' [Pękiel's canons], *Muzyka*, iii/1–2 (1958), 72–89
H. Feicht: 'Muzyka w okresie polskiego baroku' [Music in the Baroque period in Poland], *Z dziejów polskiej kultury muzycznej*, i: *Kultura staropolska* [From the history of Polish musical culture, i: Early Polish culture], ed. Z.M. Szweykowski (Kraków, 1958), 157–229, esp. 187ff, 210ff; repr. in H. Feicht, *Studia nad muzyką polskiego renesansu i baroku* (Kraków, 1980), 87–182
Z. Stęszewska: 'Z zagadnień staropolskiej muzyki tanecznej' [Some problems of early Polish dance music], ibid., 252, 254, 256, 258
K. Swaryczewska: 'Kanoniczny ricercar wariacyjny Pękiela' [Pękiel's canonic variation ricercare], *Muzyka*, iii/4 (1958), 44–8
Z. Stęszewska: 'Konkordancje "polskich" melodii tanecznych w źródłach od XVI do XVIII wieku' [Concordances of 'Polish' dance melodies in sources from the 16th century to the 18th], *Muzyka*, xi/2 (1966), 94–105
Z.M. Szweykowski: 'Some Problems of Baroque Music in Poland', *Musica antiqua Europae orientalis: Bydgoszcz and Toruń 1966*, 294–309
A. Szweykowska: 'Kapela królewska Jana Kazimierza w latach 1649–1652' [The royal chapel of Jan Kazimierz, 1649–52], *Muzyka*, xiii/4 (1968), 40–48
H. Feicht: 'An Outline of the History of Polish Religious Music', *Poland's Millennium of Catholicism*, ed. M. Rechowicz (Lublin, 1969), 449–533, esp. 526–7
M. Perz: 'Strzępki nieznanej mszy Bartłomieja Pękiela' [Fragments of an unknown mass by Bartłomiej Pękiel], *Muzyka*, xv/1 (1970), 81–5
A. Szweykowska: 'Notatki dotyczące kapeli królewskiej w XVII wieku' [Notes about the royal chapel in the 17th century], *Muzyka*, xvi/3 (1971), 91–8
K. Mrowiec: *Pasje wielogłosowe w muzyce polskiej XVIII wieku* [Polyphonic Passions in Polish music of the 18th century] (Kraków,1972), 31, 182, 186
J. Gołos: *Polskie organy i muzyka organowa* (Warsaw, 1972; Eng. trans., 1992, as *The Polish Organ, i: The Instrument and its History*)
Z. Surowiak: *Zbiory muzyczne proweniencji pod-krakowskiej* [Collections of music from the Kraków area], Musicalia vetera: katalog tematyczny rękopiśmiennych zabytków dawnej muzyki w Polsce [Musicalia vetera: thematic catalogue of manuscript treasures of early Polish music], ed. Z.M. Szweykowski, ii/1 (Kraków, 1972)
J. Gołos: 'Nieznana kompozycja Bartłomieja Pękiela' [An unknown composition by Pękiel], *RM*, xvii/4 (1973), 5 only
M. Perz: 'Inwentarz przemyski (1677)' [A Przemyśl catalogue of 1677], *Muzyka*, xix/4 (1974), 44–69
T. Maciejewski: 'Inwentarz muzykaliów kapeli karmelickiej w Krakowie na Piasku z lat 1665–1685' [The Inventory of Musical Materials of the Carmelite Monastery at Kraków from the years 1665–1685], *Muzyka*, xxi/2 (1976), 77–99
I. Poniatowska: 'De l'expression dramatique dans L'Audite Mortales de B. Pekiel', *Quadrivium*, xviii/2 (1977), 175–91

E. Zwolińska: 'Pękiel, Bartłomiej', *Polski Słownik Biograficzny*, xxv (Wrocław, 1980), 736–7

Z. Dobrzańska: 'Uwagi na temat pisowni nazwiska Bartłomieja Pękiela' [Notes on the Spelling of Bartłomiej Pękiel's Surname], *Muzyka*, xxxiv/1 (1989), 37–48

B. Przybyszewska-Jarmińska: 'The Sacred Dramatic Dialogue in Seventeenth-Century Poland', *Musica Jagellonica*, i (1995), 7–22

MIROSŁAW PERZ

Pekinel. Turkish piano duo. The twin sisters Güher and Süher Pekinel (*b* Istanbul, 29 March 1953) began their studies in Ankara with their mother, gave their first duet concert at the age of six and subsequently studied at the Paris Conservatoire, the Frankfurt Hochschule für Musik, the Curtis Institute, Philadelphia (with Rudolf Serkin), and the Juillard School. They won prizes as a duo in several international competitions, and in 1984 were engaged by Karajan for the Salzburg Easter Festival. Since then they have given numerous recitals throughout the world and performed with leading conductors and orchestras. While technically a match for any of their fellow duettists, their playing is marked by a meticulous and probing musicianship, and their chosen repertory, much of which they have recorded, reflects their essential seriousness. Their Mozart is full of subtle inflections, but kept within a relatively narrow dynamic range, while their Schubert is emotionally rich and impressively moulded. Their playing in general is characterized by breadth of vision and a pervasive lyrical impulse, but they can suspend their natural cantabile where appropriate in favour of a more angular and percussive approach, as can be heard in their pioneering recording of the two-piano version of Stravinsky's *The Rite of Spring*.

JEREMY SIEPMANN

Peking. See BEIJING.

Peking opera. See BEIJING OPERA.

Pēktis. One of the more common and earlier terms for the Greek angular harp (see MAGADIS, and TRIGŌNON). The word appears a number of times in the Eastern Greek author Anacreon (*fl* 6th century BCE). Although the term itself is Greek (from *pēgnuein*, 'to fasten'), the instrument is associated with the territory of Lydia by authors such as Pindar, Herodotus and Sophocles, and there is no reason to doubt that it came from that area.

See also GREECE, §I, 5(iii)(b).

BIBLIOGRAPHY

M. Maas and J.M. Snyder: *Stringed Instruments of Ancient Greece* (New Haven, CT, 1989), 147–9

M.L. West: *Ancient Greek Music* (Oxford, 1992), 71–2

T.J. Mathiesen: *Apollo's Lyre: Greek Music and Music Theory in Antiquity and the Middle Ages* (Lincoln, NE, 1999), 272–5

JAMES W. McKINNON

Pelé, Robert le. See ROBINET.

Pelemans, Willem (*b* Antwerp, 6 April 1901; *d* Berchem-Sainte-Agathe, Brussels, 28 Oct 1991). Belgian critic and composer. He began studying harmony and counterpoint at the age of 18 with Paul Lagye, but as a composer he is mostly self-taught. After World War I he participated in the experiments of the avant-garde theatre group 'Rataillon', conducted by Albert Lepage. His early experimental compositions were performed there. Meanwhile he was very active in cultural circles in Brussels, promoting Flemish musical life. For a few years he taught musical history at the conservatory of Malines. From 1944 until

his death he was the influential music critic of the liberal newspaper *Het laatste nieuws*. As president of the Union of Belgian Composers he successfully promoted Belgian music. His output was prolific and varied. He held his place among Flemish composers because of his autodidactic and empirical approach to music. Simplicity and clear expression are the main characteristics of his music.

WORKS
(*selective list*)

Op: La rose de Bakawali (chbr op, A. Lepage, from Hindustani), 1938; Le combat de la vierge et du diable (chbr op, J. Weterings), 1949; De mannen van Smeerop (M. Kröjer, after C. de Coster), 1952, Antwerp, 1963; De nozem en de nimf (chbr op, L. Bruylants), 1960, Radio Brussels, 1961

Other dramatic: De geschiedenis van het tinnen soldaatje (radio play, after H.C. Andersen), 1945; Miles gloriosus, ballet, 1945; Herfstgoud [Autumn Gold], ballet; Pas de quatre, ballet, 1969

Choral: De wandelende Jood (orat, A. Vermeylen), spkr, mixed vv, orch, 1929; Floris en Blancefloer (episch zangspel, H. Opdebeeck), spkr, S, A, T, Bar, 2B, mixed vv, orch, 1947–8; Een vogel van sneeuw (concertante cant., W.M. Roggeman), Mez, T, fl, ob, str, 1964

6 syms., 1936–9

Other orch: Vn Conc., 1954; Cello Conc., 1961; Org Conc., 1964; Conc. no.5, 1966; Concertino no.5, chbr orch, 1966; Pf Conc. no.3, 1967; Conc., 2 pf, 1973; Sax Conc., 1976

Other works: Choral music, many chbr and inst works, pf pieces, songs

Principal publishers: CeBeDeM, Maurer

WRITINGS

Architectonische muziek (Brussels, 1927)
Muziek beluisteren (Brussels, 1932)
Geest en klank (Brussels, 1941)
De vlaamse muziek en Peter Benoit (Brussels, 1971)

BIBLIOGRAPHY

CeBeDeM directory

C Mertens: *Hedendaagse muziek in België* (Brussels, 1967)

CORNEEL MERTENS/DIANA VON VOLBORTH-DANYS

Pelesier, Victor. See PELISSIER, VICTOR.

Pelham, Peter (*b* London, 9 Dec 1721; *d* Richmond, VA, 28 April 1805). American organist, harpsichordist, teacher and composer of English birth. He was the son of Peter Pelham, a mezzotint portrait engraver who settled in Boston in 1726. The earliest recorded public concert of secular music in the New World was held at the family's house on 30 December 1731, and the family also supported other musical activities in the city. Pelham studied with Charles Theodore Pachelbel for nine years from the age of 12, first in Newport, Rhode Island and later in Charleston, South Carolina. There Pelham taught the spinet and the harpsichord, his students describing him as 'a Genteel Clever young man' and 'verey chomical and entertaining'. He was the first organist at Trinity Church, Boston (1744–9), and was organist of Bruton Parish Church in Williamsburg, Virginia, from 1755 to 1802; his evening performances (1769) at Bruton Church included works by Handel, Vivaldi and William Felton. He conducted the Virginia Company of Comedians' production of *The Beggar's Opera* in 1768 and performed a dirge (now lost) at a Masonic funeral at Bruton Church in 1773. Pelham also held non-musical posts in Williamsburg: he was supervisor for the printing of money (1758–75) and town gaol-keeper (1770–80). He became blind in 1802, after which his daughter Elizabeth briefly succeeded him as organist of Bruton Church.

The only surviving piece definitely by Pelham is a minuet melody (ed. J.S. Darling, *A Little Keyboard Book*,

Williamsburg, VA, 1972). His 1744 manuscript copybook of harpsichord lessons (M. Myers private collection, Bloomington, IL) contains two further minuets that may also be by Pelham. These simple, didactic works are well crafted and appealing. The book also includes works by Handel, Arne, Pepusch, Maurice Greene, Davidson Russel, Marchant, Robert Valentine, Jean Baptiste Loeillet (i) and Charles Pachelbel.

BIBLIOGRAPHY

N.A. Benson: *The Itinerant Dancing and Music Masters of Eighteenth Century America* (diss., U. of Minnesota, 1963)
R. Stevenson: 'The Music that George Washington Knew: Neglected Phrases', *Inter-American Music Review*, v (1982–3), 19–77
H. Joseph Butler: 'Harpsichord Lessons in the New World: Peter Pelham and the Manuscript of 1744', *Early Keyboard Journal*, xii (1994), 39–70

H. JOSEPH BUTLER

Peli [Pelli], **Francesco** (*b* ?Modena, *c*1680; *d* ?Munich, 1740/45). Italian composer and teacher. Nothing is known of his early years. From 1708 to 1731 he was chamber composer to Rinaldo d'Este, Duke of Modena, and in 1720 he was described as a citizen of Modena, where he is thought to have directed a highly regarded singing school from 1715. In 1731 he may have been in Brno, where his oratorio *L'ultima persecuzione di Saule contro Davidde* was performed for Cardinal Wolfgang Hannibal von Schrattenbach, Bishop of Olmütz. On 6 November 1734 Peli arrived at the court of Elector Karl Albrecht of Bavaria in Munich with three Italian-trained female singers, including his own pupil Christina Monchicca. In the same year he was appointed music teacher to Crown Prince Maximilian Joseph, who succeeded as elector in 1745. Peli composed operas for the Munich court for the carnivals of 1736 and 1737. French influences are apparent in his musical style.

WORKS
SECULAR DRAMATIC

Giove pronubo (componimento per musica, I. Zanelli), Modena, 1728
Temide (componimento per musica, Zanelli), Modena, 1729
La clemenza di Tito (os, 3, P. Metastasio), Munich, carn. 29 Jan 1736, *D-Mbs*
La constanza in trionfo o vero L'Irene (os, C.M. Perozzo di Perozzi), Munich, carn. 1737

Doubtful: Ipermestra (os, 3), Munich, 22 Oct 1736

SACRED

L'ultima persecuzione di Saule contro Davidde (orat, G. Tagliazucchi), Modena, 1708
Il battesimo di Constantine imperatore (orat), Bologna and Brno, Lent 1720

Laudate Dominum, 4vv, str, org, 1719, *I-Baf**

ROBERT MÜNSTER

Pelinski, Ramón (Adolfo) (*b* Corpus, 31 Aug 1932). Argentine musicologist and pianist. After studying piano and composition at the Conservatory of Córdoba he moved to Paris (1959) and studied musicology with Chailley and analysis with Messiaen. He later studied philosophy in Kraków with Roman Ingarden and musicology in Munich, where he wrote an essay on Spanish vocal music at the beginning of the 17th century (1971). He settled in Canada (1973) where he first taught musicology until 1977 at the University of Ottawa before moving to the University of Montreal. He then specialized in, wrote on, and recorded traditional Inuit music. Pelinski also founded tango ensembles: 'Tango X 4', the first group dedicated to tango in Canada; 'Tango X 3',

specializing in traditional tango, and 'Métatango', devoted to contemporary tango in the style of Astor Piazzolla. Pelinski has also worked for the restoration of the Ermita de S Cristóbal in Spain where he has organized festivals of traditional music since the early 1990s. In 1995 he retired from teaching and settled in San Cristóbal, Spain.

WRITINGS

with R.M. Casamiquela: *Músicas de canciones totémicas y populares y de danzas araucanas* (La Plata, 1966)
Die weltliche Vokalmusik Spaniens am Anfang des 17. Jahrhunderts (Tutzing, 1971)
with L. Suluk and L. Amarook: *Inuit Songs from Eskimo Point* (Ottawa, 1979)
La musique des Inuit du Caribou: 5 perspectives méthodologiques (Montreal, 1981)
ed.: *Tango nomade: etudes sur le tango transculturel* (Montreal, 1995)

JEAN-PASCAL VACHON

Pelio, Giovanni. *See* PELLIO, GIOVANNI.

Pelison [Peliçon, Peliso, Pellisson, Pellissonus; Johannes de Bosco (*fl* 1399). French composer, possibly identifiable with BOSQUET.

Pélissier [Pellissier], **Marie** (*b* 1706/7; *d* Paris, 21 March 1749). French singer. She married the impresario Pélissier soon after her début at the Paris Opéra in 1722, and sang at his theatre in Rouen. After her husband's bankruptcy, she returned to Paris and appeared at the Opéra in a revival of Collasse's *Thétis et Pélée* on 16 May 1726 to considerable acclaim. Later that year she attracted even greater applause for her creation of Thisbe in Rebel and Francoeur's *Pyrame et Thisbé*. Sensing danger, Cathérine-Nicole Le Maure returned in December from one of her 'retirements', and a fierce rivalry developed between the two singers and between their respective supporters, the 'mauriens' and 'pélissiens'. On 15 February 1734 Pélissier was dismissed after a scandal involving her lover Dulis. She fled to London, but returned to sing at the Opéra on 19 April 1735, remaining there until her retirement in October 1741. Among the many roles she created were five in operas of Rameau: Aricia in *Hippolyte et Aricie*, Emilie in *Les Indes galantes*, Telaira in *Castor et Pollux*, and Iphise in both *Les fêtes d'Hébé* and *Dardanus*.

Pélissier's voice was small and, initially at least, somewhat forced. She was nevertheless regarded as an heir to the famous Marthe Le Rochois in the emotional power of her declamation and the eloquence of her gestures and facial expressions, though she never equalled Le Rochois' stature.

BIBLIOGRAPHY

F. Parfaict and C. Parfaict: *Histoire de l'Académie royale de musique depuis son établissement jusqu'à présent* (MS, 1741, F-Pn)
C.-E. Aïssé: *Lettres de Mlle Aïssé à Madame C*** (1725–33)* (Paris, 1787)
E.J.F. Barbier: *Chronique de la régence et du règne de Louis XV* (Paris, 1857)
M. Marais: *Journal et mémoires … sur la régence et le règne de Louis XV (1715–1737)* (Paris, 1863–8)
A. Jullien: *Amours d'opéra au XVIIIe siècle* (Paris, 1907), 59–88
G. Sadler: 'Rameau's Singers and Players at the Paris Opéra: a Little-Known Inventory of 1738', *EMc*, xi (1983), 453–67

GRAHAM SADLER

Pelissier [Pelesier, Pelliser, Pellesier], **Victor** (*b* ?Paris, *c*1740–50; *d* ?New Jersey, *c*1820). French composer, arranger and horn virtuoso, active in the USA. He was first mentioned in the USA as a horn player in a concert advertisement in Philadelphia (1792). In 1793 he went to New York to play in the orchestra of the Old American Company, becoming one of its principal composers and arrangers. He returned to Philadelphia (1811–14) where he published *Pelissier's Columbian Melodies* (1811–12), consisting of 12 volumes of songs, dances and instrumental pieces arranged for the piano, many of which were written for New York and Philadelphia theatres. The manuscript score and parts of his incidental music to William Dunlap's play, *Voice of Nature*, demonstrate details of early theatre orchestration. He was a prolific composer who displayed 'variety of thought and readiness of invention, with the full knowledge of the power of the orchestra' (Parker). Pelissier, perhaps the first significant French composer active in the USA, introduced there the practice of having an independent accompaniment part in his songs with a separate staff for the voice, and frequently placed the melody in the accompaniment while the voice held a note. His *Ariadne* was one of the earliest and most influential melodramas in the country. Although Eitner has attributed the *Amusements variés avec accompagnement de musette* to Pelissier, the authorship is doubtful.

WORKS

Collection: *Pelissier's Columbian Melodies*, i–xii (Philadelphia, 1811–12) [PCM]; ed. K. Kroeger, RRAM, xiii-xiv (1984)

STAGE

Edwin and Angelina, or the Banditti (op, 3, E.H. Smith, after O. Goldsmith), New York, 19 Dec 1796, 2 songs in PCM, I, vi
Ariadne Abandoned by Theseus in the Isle of Naxos (melodrama), New York, 1797
Sterne's Maria, or The Vintage (op, 2, W. Dunlap), New York, 14 Jan 1799, 3 songs in PCM, xi
The Fourth of July, or Temple of American Independence (spoken pantomime), New York, 4 July 1799, lost
A Tale of Mystery (melodrama, 3, T. Holcroft), New York, 16 March 1803, collab. J. Hewitt, 2 dances in PCM, I
Voice of Nature (incid music, Dunlap), New York, 1803, *US-NYp*
Valentine and Orson (melodrama), New York, 1805, song in PCM, xii
The Lady of the Lake (melodrama), Philadelphia, 1 Jan 1812, songs in PCM, iii, iv
The Bridal Ring (melodrama), Philadelphia, 10 Feb 1812, ov., dances, 2 marches in PCM, iii–vii
The Wandering Melodist, 2 songs, Philadelphia, 1810, *Cn*, *CA*; 16 works, selections arr. (1v, pf)/pf solo, PCM, i–xii; others, some performed Philadelphia, lost

OTHER WORKS

Vocal: Ode on the Passions, spkr, pf, PCM, v; songs, mostly lost
Inst: Sym., G, *c*1780, *CH-BEsu*; A Grand Ov., arr. pf, PCM, i; March, variations, 1812, arr. pf, PCM, x; March to Canada, pf (Philadelphia, 1813)

BIBLIOGRAPHY

GroveO (A.D. Shapiro)
J.R. Parker: 'Musical Reminiscences: Pelliser', *The Euterpeiad*, iii/3 (1822–3), 18
W. Dunlap: *A History of the American Theatre* (New York, 1832, 2/1963)
C. Durang: *History of the Philadelphia Stage, 1749–1855* (MS, *c*1855, *US-PHhs*)
J. Mates: *The American Musical Stage before 1800* (New Brunswick, NJ, 1962)
R.J. Wolfe: *Secular Music in America, 1801–1825: a Bibliography* (New York, 1964) [with list of works]
K. Kroeger, ed.: *Pelissier's Columbian Melodies: Music for the New York and Philadelphia Theaters* (Madison, WI, 1984)
K. Kroeger: 'Victor Pelissier's Masonic March', *The Sonneck Society for American Music*, xiii/3 (1987), 96–8

ANNE DHU McLUCAS

Pelitti. Italian family of instrument makers. Luigi Pelitti (*b* 1736, *d* after 1780) founded a workshop in Varese in the mid-18th century, and his sons Paolo Aquilino (*b* 1765, *d* after 1800) and Giovanni (*b* 1775, *d* after 1818) continued it. It initially made harpsichords and church organs but soon turned to brass instruments. Both keyboard and brass instruments by Paolo Aquilino possibly survive: a natural horn signed 'P. Pelitti' and dated 1795 (Museo degli Strumenti musicali, Rome), and a square piano signed 'Pater Aquilinus, Varisiensis' (Castello Sforzesco, Milan). Three of Giovanni's children also made brass instruments: Paolo (1802–44), who founded the family's workshop in Milan, Giuseppe (1811–65) and Carlo (1818–64). When Paolo moved to Genoa in 1828, setting up a new workshop there, Giuseppe took over the Milan firm, soon entrusting management of the workshop to the young Carlo. Giovanni's daughter Maria Theresa was the mother of the Milanese wind instrument maker Alessandro Maldura (*b* 1830).

Giuseppe Pelitti led the firm to notable success. Among his many inventions were the euphonium-like *bombardino* (1835), its name still used in Italy for such instruments; the *pelittone* (1845), a contrabass tuba in C of lasting success; the *genis* (1847), a flugelhorn in E♭; and several *duplex* or double instruments, also called *gemelli*, whose invention was later claimed by Adolphe Sax. In 1860 Giuseppe's son Giuseppe Clemente (1837–1905) established his own firm in Milan, making woodwinds and brass instruments marked 'Clemente Pelitti' (e.g. a clarinet in Nuremberg, MIR 460). On his father's death the two firms were merged under the younger Giuseppe's leadership. He too devised numerous instruments, among them the *trombone basso Verdi* (1881) – a contrabass trombone – which provided the low brass in Italian orchestras until the adoption of the tuba in the 1920s. After Giuseppe's death his widow Antonietta Corso (*b* 1834; *d* 1912) directed the firm until her death in 1912; it was sold to the Milanese firm Bottali in 1915. Further details of the firm's history are given in R. Meucci: 'The Pelitti Firm' (*HBSJ*, vi, 1994, pp.304–33).

RENATO MEUCCI

Pellaert, Auguste de. *See* PEELLAERT, AUGUSTE DE.

Pelleg [Pollak], Frank (*b* Prague, 24 Sept 1910; *d* Haifa, 20 Dec 1968). Israeli harpsichordist, pianist, composer and educationist of Czech birth. He made his public début as a pianist at the age of 12. He studied first at the Prague Academy of Music and later at Prague University (1929–31). In 1936, at the invitation of Bronisław Huberman, he settled in Israel. After gaining a distinction in the 1939 Geneva International Competition he became sought after as a performer; following an engagement at the 1947 Prague Festival he made lengthy annual tours abroad, appearing under, among other conductors, Klemperer, Paray, Dorati, Celibidache, Solti, Fricsay and Bertini. In 1939 Pelleg was among the founders of the Institute for Jewish Music Research, and in 1949 he became director of the music department of the Ministry of Education and Culture in the new state of Israel. In 1951 he moved to Haifa, where he was among the founders of the Haifa SO and its music director until his death; he was also music director of the Municipal Theatre from its establishment in 1961. The 1954 ISCM Festival took place in Haifa through his initiative. He instigated premières of music by Dallapiccola, Petrassi and Gerhard, and took part in the first performances of Israeli music including Tal's Concerto for harpsichord and electronic music, Natra's Variations for piano and orchestra and Partos's *Agada*. Though Pelleg's repertory ranged widely, he specialized in Bach and other Baroque music (he recorded a good deal) and was noted for his insistence that the harpsichord should be treated as a modern instrument and its tonal possibilities fully exploited, even in 18th-century music. His lectures in Israel and abroad, full of vitality and humour, were highly popular; he also composed and wrote books on music appreciation, and in sum made an outstanding contribution to the development of music in Israel. His pupils included the pianists Alexis Weissenberg, Israela Margalit and Yahli Wagman. After his death a prize for musicological research and a harpsichord prize were set up in his memory.

WILLIAM Y. ELIAS

Pellegrin, Claude Mathieu (*b* Aix-en-Provence, 25 Oct 1682; *d* Aix-en-Provence, 10 Oct 1763). French composer. The son of a pharmacist in Aix, he joined the cathedral choir school of St Sauveur on 5 November 1696 (while Cabassol was *maître de chapelle*). He became Poitevin's pupil, probably when the latter again became *maître de chapelle* on 5 May 1698. Pellegrin was appointed organist of Aix Cathedral but was dismissed in May 1705 because he had written secular music. He was restored to his position on 2 May 1706 and was described as 'serviteur du Chapitre'. On 20 June in that year he was appointed *maître de chapelle* in succession to Poitevin. He was ordained priest on 3 November 1717 and appointed 'bénéficier' on 29 June 1719. On 15 January 1724 he was granted a year's leave of absence: five days later he was admitted to the Ste Chapelle in Paris as a *chapelain ordinaire*. In March 1730 the Aix chapter instituted proceedings against him before the Grand Council, and on 4 May 1731 Pellegrin resumed his duties at Aix Cathedral, fulfilling his obligations there until May 1748. He continued to compose, enjoying successes as far afield as Lyons, and supervised the early musical studies of E.J. Floquet and others.

The secular pieces that lost him his post in 1705 are no longer extant. His surviving sacred works are in the music collection of the former school of St Sauveur (in *F-AIXm*), often in several versions showing considerable and complex differences, something quite usual in the practice of the time. Some marches and fanfares – probably an introduction to the *Te Deum* – survive (in *B-Bc*).

The indications in the separate parts show that Pellegrin had large forces of singers and instrumentalists available, ranging from 42 musicians in *De profundis* to 50 for the *Benedictus* in A. Instrumental colour is a feature of his style; the bassoon or bassoons often replace the serpent, while flutes, oboes, trumpets and sometimes even the flageolet, fife, *tambours militaires* and kettledrums (in the *Te Deum*) enhance the colours of the string instruments and allow the composer to produce original combinations. He even used rattles to imitate musketry.

Unlike many composers of the Provençal school (for instance Jean Audiffren), Pellegrin wrote for the traditional five-part French chorus, and devised some unusual combinations. In particular, he used treble voices in unison on their own (in the *Benedictus*, *Te Deum* and *Venite*) and played on variations of voices in a figural manner. The orchestra is usually in three real parts (*dessus de violon*, *hautes-contre de violon* and bass instruments),

but there are some passages in four or five parts (in the Requiem), and in those cases the desks were divided to achieve the requisite effect.

Pellegrin took little interest in the contrapuntal complexities found at the same period in the composers of the Ile de France, but his directions bear witness to his care for detail in the interpretation of his works and the resulting sound: he indicates nuances in the Requiem ('doux', 'moins doux', 'fort'), while directions such as 'ardy', 'gracieux un peu gay', 'brusqué', 'un peu hardiment' indicate the tempo and effect he wanted. His works, widely performed in France in the 18th century, are evidence of the vitality of the Provençal school. A *Dissertation sur la musique française et italienne* (in *F-Pn*) can also be attributed to him.

WORKS
principal sources: B-Bc, F-AIXm, AR

Motet, Dominus regnavit, 1v, str, bc, 1745

Motets, 5vv, fl, ob, bn, str, tpt, bc: De profundis, 1708; 2 Mag; TeD and Marches et fanfares, 1745; Messe pour les morts and De profundis, 1763; Beatus vir; 2 Benedictus; Dixit Dominus; In convertendo; Jub; Veni de Libano; Venite exultemus Domino

BIBLIOGRAPHY

BrenetM

C.F. Bouche: *Essai sur l'histoire de la Provence* (Marseilles, 1785), ii

E. Marbot: *Les maîtres de chapelle de St Sauveur au XVIIIe siècle* (Aix, 1905)

J.-R. Mongrédien: *Catalogue thématique des sources du grand motet français, 1663–1792* (Munich, 1984)

M. Signorile: *Musique et société: le modèle d'Arles à l'époque de l'absolutisme (1600–1789)* (Geneva, 1994)

J. Duron: 'Le grand motet à l'époque de Rameau: le cas de Claude Mathieu Pellegrin (1682–1763), maître de chapelle à la cathédrale Saint-Sauveur d'Aix-en-Provence', *La musique dans le midi de la France*, i: *XVII–XVIII siècle* (Paris, 1996), 133–78

MARCEL FRÉMIOT/MARC SIGNORILE

Pellegrin, Abbé **Simon-Joseph** [La Roque; La Serre; Pellegrin-Barbier; Chevalier Pellegrin] (*b* Marseilles, 1663; *d* Paris, 5 Sept 1745). French librettist, poet and playwright. Son of a magistrate, he entered a Servite monastery and later became a naval chaplain. He arrived in Paris in 1703 to consolidate a literary career already begun with his *Cantiques spirituels* (1701) and other sacred verse. In 1704 he gained some notoriety by submitting two poems for an Académie Française literary prize, both of which won. Thanks to the support of Mme de Maintenon, he was allowed to leave the Servites and join the Cluniac order, which freed him from monastic obligations but provided no financial support. He subsequently eked out a living by producing religious verse to be sung to popular melodies (this comprising in all an estimated 500,000 lines) and numerous plays, of which the best known is the tragedy *Pélopée* (read at Versailles in 1710; revised and staged in 1733). By 1705 he had turned to opera. According to the *Mercure de France*, C.-H. Gervais's setting of his libretto *Renaud* was rehearsed in that year but not performed; Desmarets's opera of the same name (1722) probably reuses this poem. Pellegrin went on to collaborate with composers of the stature of A.C. Destouches, Montéclair and Rameau. *Jephté* (1732), the earliest French libretto based on a biblical subject and the first to win him real acclaim, brought him into conflict with the church. He had earlier sought to avoid such opprobrium by adopting pseudonyms (which makes identification of some of his work problematic), to no avail: he was eventually debarred from saying Mass.

Though almost universally reviled in literary circles, Pellegrin was one of the most talented librettists of his generation. His tendency to rework themes that had already been treated in spoken tragedies (including his own) led him to give less prominence to the amorous entanglements prevalent in the *tragédie en musique*; as in the first version of his play *Pélopée*, incest provides a motivating force in *Théonoé* and *Hippolyte et Aricie*, innocence betrayed in *Jephté*. These last two librettos in particular demonstrate a considerable flair for dramatic construction, psychologically convincing characters and colourful divertissements, and include some felicitous if uneven verse. His preface to *Hippolyte*, a work deriving material from Euripides, Seneca, and Racine's *Phèdre*, shows the care with which he sought to improve on aspects of Racine's masterpiece, and his concern for dramatic verisimilitude and the proper treatment of the supernatural.

WRITINGS
(only those relating to music)

THEATRICAL WORKS
(each work is followed by its composer and year of performance; published in Paris and performed at the Opéra unless otherwise stated)

Tragédies en musique, each with prol and 5 acts: *Renaud, ou La suite d'Armide*, C.-H. Gervais, rehearsed 1705; Desmarets, 1722; *Médée et Jason* [as La Roque], J.-F. Salomon, 1713; *Télémaque et Calypso*, Destouches, 1714; *Théonoé* [as La Rocque], Salomon, 1715; *Polydor* [as La Serre; attrib. Pellegrin in Girdlestone (1972)], Stuck, 1720; *Télégone*, Lacoste, 1725; *Orion* [with J. de Lafont], Lacoste, 1728; *Jephté*, Montéclair, 1732; *Hippolyte et Aricie* [as Chevalier Pellegrin, his brother], Rameau, 1733; *Antigone*, Arianne, 1722, unperformed; *Loth*, n.d., unperformed
Opéras-ballets, each with prol and 3 entrées: *Les fêtes de l'été* [with Mlle M.-A. Barbier], Montéclair, 1716; *Les plaisirs de la campagne* [with Barbier], Bertin de la Doué, 1719; *Les caractères de l'Amour* (labelled 'ballet héroïque'; later 4th entrée by Bonneval), Collin de Blamont, 1736 (concert performance, Tuileries), 1738; ?addns to Montdorge, *Les fêtes d'Hébé*, Rameau, 1739
Other operas: *Le jugement de Paris* [with Barbier] (pastorale héroïque, prol, 3), Bertin de la Doué, 1718; *La princesse d'Elide* (ballet héroïque, prol, 3), A. de Villeneuve, 1728; *Alphée et Aréthuse* (new prol for Campra's *Aréthuse*), Montéclair, 1752
Opéras comiques with vaudevilles: *Arlequin à la guinguette* (3), 1711, Foire St Laurent; *Le pied de nez* (3), 1718, Foire St Laurent; *La fiancée du roi Garbe* (prol, 3), 1719, Foire St Laurent; *Arlequin, rival de Bacchus* (3), 1727, Comédie-Italienne
Plays with music (Comédie-Française): *Le nouveau monde* (comédie, prol, 3), J.-B.M. Quinault, 1722; *Le divorce de l'amour et de la raison* (comédie), Quinault, 1723; *Le Pastor-Fido* (pastorale héroïque), Collin de Blamont (according to Fétis), 1726
Divertissements *Les présents des dieux* (idylle héroïque including 3 entrées), Collin de Blamont, Versailles, 1725; *Le Parnasse* (pastiche), Collin de Blamont, Lully, Campra, Destouches, Mouret, 1729

SACRED TEXTS
(all published in Paris)

Cantiques spirituels . . . accompagnés d'hymnes . . . sur des airs d'opéra, vaudevilles choisis, et sur les chants de l'église (1701)
Histoire de l'Ancien et du Nouveau Testament . . . mis en musique sur des airs de vaudeville (1702, 2/1713)
Noëls nouveaux . . . et chansons spirituels . . . sur des chants anciens, 7 vols. (1702–28, 2/1729)
Airs notés des cantiques . . . noëls nouveaux et chansons spirituelles (1705, 2/1728)
Les psaumes de David et les cantiques de l'Ancien et du Nouveau Testament, sur les plus beaux motifs de MM. Lambert, Lully et Campra (1705)
Nouveaux recueils de noëls (1715, 1722, 1725)
Les proverbes et parabôles de Salomon, mis en musique sur des airs et des vaudeules (1725)

Noëls nouveaux (1725–35)
Concert spirituel . . . sur une version du psaume 'Dominus regnavit; exultet terra' (1727), music by Villeneuve
L'Imitation de Jésus-Christ, mise en cantiques spirituels sur les plus beaux airs des meilleurs auteurs (1727)

BIBLIOGRAPHY

E. de Bricqueville: *Deux abbés d'opéra au siècle dernier: Joseph Pellegrin, François Arnaud* (Amiens, 1889)
C.M. Girdlestone: *Jean-Philippe Rameau: his life and work* (London, 1957, 2/1969)
C.M. Girdlestone: *La tragédie en musique (1673–1750) considérée comme genre littéraire* (Geneva, 1972)
G. Sadler: 'Rameau, Pellegrin and the Opéra: the Revisions of "Hippolyte et Aricie" during its First Season', *MT*, cxxiv (1983), 533–7
R. Fajon: *L'Opéra à Paris du Roi Soleil à Louis le Bien-Aimé* (Geneva, 1984)
C. Kintzler: *Poétique de l'opéra français de Corneille à Rousseau* (Paris, 1991)
G. Burgess: '"Le théâtre ne change qu'à la troisième scène": the Hand of the Author and Unity of Place in Act V of *Hippolyte et Aricie*', *COJ*, x (1998), 275–87
C. Dill: 'Pellegrin, Opera and Tragedy', *COJ*, x (1998), 247–57
B. Norman: 'Remaking a Cultural Icon: *Phèdre* and the Operatic Stage', *COJ*, x (1998), 225–45
L. Rosow: 'Structure and Expression in the *scènes* of Rameau's *Hippolyte et Aricie*', *COJ*, x (1998), 259–73

GRAHAM SADLER

Pellegrini, Domenico (*b* Bologna, early 17th century; *d* after 1682). Italian guitarist and composer. He was a member of the Accademia dei Filomusi, a performer in the Concerto Palatino (both in Bologna) and one of several guitarists whose works were published by Giacomo Monti. His *Armoniosi concerti* contains guitar pieces combining the *battute* and *pizzicato* styles, in the manner of Foscarini, Corbetta and Granata; many of them are dedicated to fellow members of the Accademia.

Pellegrini's style is conservative by mid-17th century standards, with almost no use of *campanelas* passages or the upper octaves of the bass strings; some of the pieces do not even include strummed chords, like Foscarini's early lute-style pieces. The preface contains important pedagogical information on arpeggiation, dynamics, slurs and ornaments. Three of the five surviving copies also contain an engraved frontispiece of the composer, clearly showing long fingernails on his right hand. The pieces include a *battaglia francese*, using motifs from French lute tablature, and a series of *passacaglias* 'per tutte le lettere, e per diversi altri tuoni cromatici', which modulate through all 24 major and minor keys before returning to the original tonality.

WORKS

2 secular cants.: Amor tiranno (Bologna, 1649; words only), Vuol l'ultima risoluzione della sua donna, 1v, bc, 1662, *I-MOe*
Armoniosi concerti sopra la chitarra spagnuola (Bologna, 1650/*R*), 8 ed. in Hudson
Several pieces, in Libros de diferentes cifras de guitarra escogida de los mejores autores, Madrid, 1709, anon., *E-Mn*
Sacred cant.: Dicite mortales, 1v, bc, *GB-Lbl*

BIBLIOGRAPHY

R. Strizich: 'Ornamentation in Spanish Baroque Guitar Music', *JLSA*, v (1972), 37–8
R. Hudson: *The Folia, the Saraband, the Passacaglia, and the Chaconne* (Stuttgart, 1982)
O. Gambassi: *Il concerto palatino della signoria di Bologna* (Florence, 1989), 234
G.R. Boye: *Giovanni Battista Granata and the Development of Printed Guitar Music in Seventeenth-Century Italy* (diss., Duke U., 1995), 92–8, 113–14
G.R. Boye: 'Performing Seventeenth-Century Italian Guitar Music: the Question of an Appropriate Stringing', *Performance on Lute,*

Guitar, and Vihuela: Historical Practice and Modern Interpretation, ed. V. Coelho (Cambridge, 1997), 180–94

GARY R. BOYE

Pellegrini [Pellegrino], Ferdinando (*b* ?Naples, *c*1715; *d* ?Paris, *c*1766). Italian composer, harpsichordist and organist. His career took him to Rome, Lyons, Paris and probably London (*c*1763–5). In Paris (1762) he served La Pouplinière, whose brother-in-law the Abbé de Mondran described Pellegrini as a 'true demon at the keyboard'. A series of works, largely for harpsichord, was issued from about 1753 to 1770 in Paris and London. The keyboard style is somewhat shallow, making much use of conventional *galant* string and keyboard mannerisms. The sonatas with violin are noteworthy in that most follow Giardini's model, maintaining a concertante equality between violin and harpsichord parts. Torrefranca claimed that several movements from opp.2 and 10 were actually by Galuppi, Rutini and Platti. The latter opus, however, was published as 'opera X et ultima', indicating Pellegrini's death before publication. The music may have been left incomplete, causing the Paris publisher (Bureau d'Abonnement de Musique) to flesh out the full six sonatas, promised to subscribers the previous year, by borrowing.

WORKS

op.

1	6 trietti, 2 vn, bc (Paris and Lyons, *c*1753)
1	6 sonates, hpd, avec une lettre sur les pièces de clavecin en rondeau (Paris, *c*1754; as op.2, London, 1765)
—	4 concerts, hpd, 2 vn, vc (Paris, 1758; London, 1763)
4	6 sonates, hpd, vn acc. (Paris, 1759; London, 1763)
5	6 sonates, hpd (Paris, 1760); as 6 Lessons (London, 1764)
6	6 sonates, hpd (Paris, 1763)
7	6 sonates, hpd, vn acc. (Paris, *c*1765); nos.2, 6, 3 (London, *c*1765)
—	16 nouveaux préludes, hpd (Paris, *c*1766)
9	6 concerts, hpd, 2 vn, va, vc (Paris, 1766); as op.6 (London, 1766)
10	6 sonate, hpd, vn (Paris, 1766)
—	3 sonatas in 6 sonates, hpd (Paris, *c*1760) [incl. works by other Italians]
—	6 duets 2vv, bc, in 12 duo italiens (Paris, *c*1760) [incl. works by other Italians]
—	[8] chansons italiennes, 1v, bc (harp/gui/hpd) (Paris, *c*1760)

BIBLIOGRAPHY

EitnerQ; FétisB; GerberL; NewmanSCE

G. Cucuel: *La Pouplinière et la musique de chambre au XVIIIe siècle* (Paris, 1913/R), 254

F. Torrefranca: 'Intermezzo di date e documenti', *RMI*, xxvi (1919), 291–331

F. Torrefranca: 'Influenza di alcuni musicisti italiani vissuti a Londra su W.A. Mozart (1764–65)', *Musikwissenschaftlicher Kongress: Basle 1924*, 336–62

F. Torrefranca: *Le origini italiane del romanticismo musicale: i primitivi della sonata moderna* (Turin, 1930/R), 488, 716

R.R. Kidd: *The Sonata for Keyboard with Violin Accompaniment in England (1750–1790)* (diss., Yale U., 1967), 136

R.R. Kidd: 'The Emergence of Chamber Music with Obbligato Keyboard in England', *AcM*, xliv (1972), 122–44, esp. 138

RONALD R. KIDD

Pellegrini, Giulio. Singer, husband of Clementine Moralt (*see* MORALT family, (5)).

Pellegrini, Valeriano (*b* Verona, ?*c*1663; *d* Rome, 18 Jan 1746). Italian soprano castrato and composer. He sang in the Chiesa Nuova and the Cappella Sistina choir in Rome, at Cardinal Ottoboni's private concerts and in Bononcini's *La fede publica* in Vienna (1699). From 1705 to 1716 he was in the service of the Elector Palatine at Düsseldorf, where he created the difficult role of Gheroldo (requiring a range of *c'* to *b"*) in Steffani's *Tassilone* (1709) and was knighted. During this period he also appeared at Venice (as Nero in Handel's *Agrippina*, 26 December 1709) and London. Pellegrini served the elector in other capacities; he acquired for him a large collection of medals at Verona in 1708, but in 1715 the painter Sebastiano Ricci shamelessly fobbed him off with a bogus Correggio. Pellegrini made his London début on 9 April 1712 at a concert in the Old Spring Garden, but did not appear on the stage until the following November. Handel composed for him Mirtillo in *Il pastor fido*, the title role in *Teseo* and probably Lepidus in *Silla*. He seems to have been a technically proficient rather than a glamorous singer. By 1728 he had lost his voice and become a priest. In his last years in Rome he was dependent on charity. There is a soprano cantata by him in *D-Dl* (*EitnerQ*). A caricature of Pellegrini by Pierleone Ghezzi survives (*I-Rvat* Cod. Ottob. Lat.3116 c.162).

WINTON DEAN, JOHN ROSSELLI

Pellegrini, Vincenzo (*b* Pesaro, *c*1562; *d* Milan, 23 Aug 1630). Italian composer. He studied at the seminary in Pesaro, and from 1594 was a canon in the city's cathedral. It has been suggested that he was also *maestro di cappella* and organist of the cathedral, but while the first theory might be confirmed by two payments to a 'ms Vincenzo m.ro di capella' in 1582, there is no documentation to support the second. His 1599 collection of *Canzoni* is dedicated to Livia della Rovere, wife of the Duke of Urbino, in whose service Pellegrini worked before moving to Milan (see Radiciotti, 1891). On 23 April 1603 he travelled to Rome with the delegation representing the Pesaro curia. In the same year he was elected vicar-capitular, holding the post until 25 February 1604. During his time in Pesaro he had a number of pupils, including Galeazzo Sabbatini, later organist of the cathedral. On the recommendation of Cardinal Federico Borromeo, Pellegrini was appointed *maestro di cappella* of Milan Cathedral on 19 October 1611. On 3 February 1612 he asked the Pesaro chapter for three months' leave to visit Milan, but he settled permanently in the city, while maintaining the title of canon of the Pesaro curia. His connections with the Rovere family continued: autograph letters to the duke's secretary, Abbot Giulio Brunetti, survive; the motets of the *Sacri concentus* (1619) are dedicated to Francesco Maria II della Rovere; and Pellegrini was present at the wedding celebrations between Federico Ubaldo della Rovere and Claudia de' Medici in May 1621.

Pellegrini took up his post at Milan Cathedral on 26 February 1612; with a quarterly stipend of 375 lire, the same as his predecessor G.C. Gabussi. However, under his direction the quality of the choir suffered and Pellegrini was held responsible. Some of the singers were dismissed and in 1625 Pellegrini was under the threat of being replaced (the correspondence relating to this process involved Monteverdi). Pellegrini held on to his post, and in November 1628 asked for an increase in his stipend to enable him to publish some of his works for use in religious services. On 17 June 1630 he made his will, leaving a third of his music to a *maestro di cappella* in Milan, another third to Pesaro Cathedral, and the final third to the convent of S Agostino, Pesaro. Some of his money was left to Pesaro Cathedral so that a chapel could be built and a patronage established, the obligation being that three masses be said weekly, and the feast of S Vincenzo be celebrated. There is no further reference to him in the cathedral records after 2 August 1630, and it is probable that he died of the plague.

Pellegrini's sacred music, described as austere and conservative, has often been linked to late 16th-century style, respecting the dictates of the Council of Trent. While the bulk of his sacred music is in the *a cappella* style, in his more modern compositions, such as the solo motets, the use of ornaments, rhythm and dissonances for expressive purposes, suggest the influence of the new *stile rappresentativo*. Pellegrini's most successful works are his instrumental canzonas. They reveal a lively imagination, clarity and serenity. Most follow a tripartite scheme with sections in duple then triple then duple time with a different theme. Themes return superimposed or juxtaposed with entries following quickly on one another, in a sort of concluding stretto that is particularly effective. Often the initial idea, fragmented, transformed and elaborated, is the source of the entire piece: this characteristic makes him a unique figure in the context of music in Milan.

WORKS
published in Venice, unless otherwise stated

Canzoni de intavolatura d'organo fatte alle francese, libro primo (1599); ed. in CEKM, xxxv (1972); facs. (Bologna, 1976)
Missae octo, 4–5vv (1603)
Missarum liber primus (1604)
Magnificat decem (1613)
Sacri concentus, 1–6vv, org (1619)
5 motets (1615[13]); 4 other works, 3–4vv (1617[2])
8 lucernar, 5vv, 5 hymns, 4vv, 19 posthymns, 5, 8vv, 5 ants, 4–5vv, symphonia, 4 insts, in Pontificalia ambrosiana ecclesiae ad vesperas musicali concentui accomodata (Milan, 1619[3])
10 lucernar, 5vv, 4 hymns, 4vv, 29 posthymns, 5, 8–9vv, 3 ants, 4–5vv, in Pontificalia ambrosiana ecclesiae ad vesperas musicali concentui accomodata (Milan, 1619[4])
3 works (Milan, 1623[3]); 2 works (Milan, 1626[5])
Mass, 6vv, bc, D-MÜs; requiem, 5vv, MÜs; 8 masses, 4–5vv, I-Md; mass, 4vv, Ad; mass, 5vv, Rc [may be the same as the mass printed in 1603]
2 Mag, 5–6vv, bc, D-MÜs
2 ants; 7 intonazioni per il Miserere; 2 ints, 5–6vv; lit all'ambrosiana: I-Ma
50 motets, 3–6vv, bc, D-MÜs [17 also in Sacri concentus (1619)]
2 Pater noster, 5, 9vv; Versetto asperges me: I-Md
1 work in L. Zacconi, Canoni musicali proprii e di diversi autori, PESo

BIBLIOGRAPHY
EitnerQ; SchmidlD
MS documents, I-PESo
A. Banchieri: *Lettere armoniche* (Bologna, 1628/R), 144–5 [incl. a letter to D. Vincenzo Pellegrini]
G. Radiciotti: 'Brevissimi cenni su lo stato dell'arte musicale nelle Marche durante il secolo XVI', *Strenna marchigiana*, ii (1891), 142–56
G. Radiciotti: *I musicisti marchigiani dal sec. XVI al XIX* (Rome, 1909), 126
M. Donà: *La stampa musicale a Milano fino all'anno 1700* (Florence, 1961)
G. de Florentiis and G.N. Vessia, eds.: *Sei secoli di musica nel duomo di Milano* (Milan, 1986)
M. Toffetti: *La canzone strumentale a Milano (1572–1647)* (diss., U. of Milan, 1991)
P. Giorgini: *La cappella musicale del duomo di Pesaro* (diss., U. of Urbino, 1996–7)
PIER PAOLO SCATTOLIN/AUSILIA MAGAUDDA and DANILO COSTANTINI

Pellegrino, Ferdinando. *See* PELLEGRINI, FERDINANDO.

Pellegrino, Il. Nickname of DELLA VALLE, PIETRO.

Pellegrino, Ron(ald Anthony) (*b* Kenosha, WI, 11 May 1940). American composer and performer. After early

training as a clarinettist, he studied theory, composition and philosophy at Lawrence University (BM 1962) and later studied with Kolisch, Leibowitz and Crane at the University of Wisconsin (MM 1965, PhD 1968). He began working in electronic music in 1967 and in 1969 published *An Electronic Music Studio Manual*, which became the standard text on the Moog synthesizer. He directed the electronic music studios at Ohio State University (1968–70) and the Oberlin Conservatory (1970–73) and was associate professor at Texas Tech University, Lubbock (1978–81). He established the Leading Edge music series (a forum for contemporary music performance and scholarship) and published his book, *The Electronic Arts of Sound and Light* (1983). Pellegrino's works reflect his interest in psychoacoustics and psycho-optics, creating works whose sonic and visual aspects are either integrated through, or derived from, common electronic sources. He founded two electronic music performance ensembles, the Real Electric Symphony (R*ES) and the Sonoma Electro-Acoustic Music Society (SEAMS), and has developed a theory of music based on the structure and behavior of waves and vibrations, which he calls 'cymatic music'. He has written articles on various topics including synthesizers and laser composition.

WORKS
Elec and mixed media: Figured, film, perc, tape, 1972; Metabiosis IV, mixed media, 1972; S & H Explorations, cl, elec, 1972; Cries, film, perc, tape, 1973; Kaleidoscopic Electric Rags, 1974; Video Slices, film, perc, tape, 1975; Ephemeral Forms, mixed media, 1976; Metabiosis VI, mixed media, 1977; Setting Suns and Spinning Daughters, mixed media, 1978; Words and Phrases, 1v, perc, elec, 1980; Siberian News Release, perc, elec, 1981; Laser Seraphim and Cymatic Music, mixed media, 1982; Spring Suite, elec, 1982; a few other works
Tape, inst and vocal: Dance Drama, S, timp, 1967; The End of an Affair, perc, tape, 1967; Passage, tape, 1968; Markings, S, timp, tape, 1969; ETT/Y, tape, 1970; Leda and the Swan, S, synth, 1970; Phil's Float, cl, tape, 1974; Wavesong, pf, tape, 1975; Issue of the Silver Hatch, perc, 1979

Principal publishers: American Society of University Composers, Electronic Arts

STEPHEN RUPPENTHAL/DAVID PATTERSON

Pellegrino di Zanetto (Micheli). Italian violin maker, son of ZANETTO DA MONTICHIARO.

Pellesier, Victor. *See* PELISSIER, VICTOR.

Pelletier, (Louis) Wilfrid (*b* Montreal, 20 June 1896; *d* New York, 9 April 1982). Canadian conductor and music educationist. After studying with François Héraly (1904–14) and subsequently working with Alexis Contant and Alfred Laliberté, in 1915 Pelletier won the Prix d'Europe and moved to Paris with his first wife, Berthe Jeannotte. There he studied with Isidore Philipp (piano), Marcel Samuel-Rousseau (harmony), Charles Bellaigue (opera repertory) and Charles-Marie Widor (composition). After moving to New York in 1917 he was engaged, on the recommendation of Monteux, as a répétiteur at the Metropolitan Opera. In 1921 he was made assistant conductor. In 1928 he became director of the company's French repertory, and in 1932 conductor of the Sunday Night Opera Concerts. He served as house conductor until 1950, during which time he initiated the Metropolitan Auditions of the Air (1936), regularly conducted the New York PO's children's concerts and was guest conductor, under Toscanini, of the NBC SO.

In April 1935 he gave his first concert as founding conductor of the reorganized Montreal SO, and in November instigated a series of children's concerts. In June 1936 he led the inaugural programme of the Montreal Festival. In 1940 he left the Montreal SO and in 1942, together with Claude Champagne, persuaded the provincial government to establish the Conservatoire de Musique de Québec à Montréal. Pelletier was director until 1961, and made it the pre-eminent musical institution in French Canada. From 1951 to 1966 he was artistic director of the Quebec SO, and from 1961 to 1970 music director in the Ministry of Cultural Affairs of the Quebec government. His honours included CMG (1946), Chevalier of the Légion d'Honneur (1947) and Companion of the Order of Canada (1968). In 1966 the largest concert hall at the new Place des Arts in Montreal was named Salle Wilfrid-Pelletier. Pelletier married the American singer Queena (Tillotson) Mario in 1925, and the soprano Rose Bampton in 1937.

BIBLIOGRAPHY

W. Pelletier: *Une symphonie inachevée* (Montreal, 1972) [autobiography]

C. Huot: *Wilfrid Pelletier: un grand homme, une grande oeuvre* (Montreal, 1996)

CHARLES BARBER, JOSÉ BOWEN

Pelli, Francesco. *See* PELI, FRANCESCO.

Pellicani, Giovanni Battista Sanuti. *See* SANUTI PELLICANI, GIOVANNI BATTISTA.

Pelliccia, Arrigo (*b* Viareggio, 20/21 Feb 1912; *d* Rome, 20 July 1987). Italian violinist and viola player. He studied first with his father, then at the conservatory in Bologna and later took postgraduate courses with Arrigo Serato at the Accademia di S Cecilia and with Carl Flesch in Berlin. Inaugurating a brilliant concert career in 1931, he specialized, as a soloist, in contemporary music. After World War II he divided his time between leading the orchestra of the Pomeriggi Musicali at Milan, playing the viola with the Santoliquido-Pelliccia-Amfiteatrov Trio, the Rome Quartet and the Boccherini Quintet, and the violin as a soloist with the Virtuosi di Roma, and performing as a soloist on both the violin and the viola, making many appearances abroad. He recorded Mozart's duos for violin and viola with Grumiaux, to great acclaim. From 1939 to 1959 he taught at the Naples Conservatory, and then at the Rome Conservatory. (J. Creighton: *Discopaedia of the Violin*, Toronto, 1974, 2/1994)

PIERO RATTALINO/R

Pellio [Pelio, Pello], Giovanni (*fl* 1578–97). Flemish composer, active in Italy. He was a priest. He was in the service of Don Serafino Fontana in Venice at least between 1578 and 1584, and his *Primo libro delle canzoni spirituali a cinque voci* (Venice, 1578, incomplete) is dedicated to Fontana by Giovanni Bassiano, who probably supervised the printing of the work. Pellio described himself as 'Fiamengo' in the dedication of his *Primo libro delle canzoni spirituali a sei voci* (Venice, 1584). A second book for six voices appeared in 1597. He contributed one madrigal to G.B. Moscaglia's *Secondo libro de madrigali a quattro voci con alcuni di diversi eccellenti musici di Roma* (RISM 1585²⁹).

PIER PAOLO SCATTOLIN

Pelliser, Victor. *See* PELISSIER, VICTOR.

Pellisson [Pellissonus] (*fl* 1399). French composer, possibly identifiable with BOSQUET.

Peloponnesios, Petros. *See* PETROS PELOPONNESIOS.

Peloubet, (Louis Michel François) Chabrier (de) (*b* Philadelphia, 22 Feb 1806; *d* Bloomfield, NJ, 30 Oct 1885). American maker of woodwind instruments and reed organs. His father, Louis Alexander de Peloubet, was a French royalist who fled during the Revolution to Germany, where he learnt to make flutes, fifes and clarinets. In October 1803 he emigrated to New York, where he married in 1805; he advertised in the *Albany Argus* as 'musical instrument maker' from 26 November 1810 to 28 May 1811. Chabrier Peloubet, who undoubtedly learnt the woodwind maker's trade from his father, was in business in New York from 1829 until 1836, when he transferred his family to Bloomfield, New Jersey. His first factory was in 'Pierson's Mill', 3 Myrtle Court; in 1842 he moved to 86 Orange Street. After these premises were destroyed by fire in 1869, he built two new factory buildings on Orange Street.

In 1849 the Peloubet firm began production of melodeons (the first in the USA) and reed organs; advertisements for them appeared in newspapers in Newark, New Jersey, during the 1850s and 60s and instruments were sold by H. Warren and Chickering in New York, and through J.C. Bates in Boston. The firm grew appreciably during the 1850s. Peloubet's son Jarvis (1833–1902) joined him in the family business and in 1860 they produced 90 melodeons to the value of $8000, most of them apparently small instruments for home use.

Although Peloubet manufactured melodeons and reed organs for 31 years, only three of these survive: two in the museum of the Bloomfield Historical Society and one in a private collection. The Bloomfield instruments display evidence of careful workmanship and good intonation and tone. Four of Peloubet's clarinets and 20 flutes survive. The latter range in complexity from the boxwood, one-key instrument in E♭ with brass and ivory fittings (Library of Congress, Washington DC, Dayton C. Miller collection no.79) to the eight-key cocuswood instrument in C with silver fittings and an ivory head (Miller no.1556).

It is difficult to date Peloubet's flutes and clarinets. None of the clarinets is dated; of the flutes, 12 have Peloubet's numbers, which may be serial, but none is dated. All are stamped (usually on the foot-joint) 'C. Peloubet New York (City)', and all but five say 'Factory Bloomfield NJ'.

CHARLES H. KAUFMAN

Pelplin Keyboard Tablatures (*PL-PE* 304–8, 308a). *See* SOURCES OF KEYBOARD MUSIC TO 1660, §2(iii).

Peña, Paco (*b* Córdoba, 1 June 1942). Spanish guitarist. At the age of six he heard Ramón Montoya playing in Córdoba football stadium. Peña made his first professional appearance aged 12. In his early 20s, he decided to pursue his career abroad, making his London début in 1963. He settled in Britain in 1966. Since then, his reputation as a refined interpreter of traditional flamenco-guitar forms has remained unequalled. He has made many recordings, including a 'flamenco mass' composed for the 1988 Wrocław Festival. He founded the Paco Peña

Flamenco Centre in Córdoba in 1981, and was made professor of flamenco at Rotterdam University in 1985.

JAMES WOODALL

Pena Costa, Joaquín (*b* Barcelona, 1 March 1873; *d* Barcelona, 25 June 1944). Spanish musicologist and music critic. He qualified in law at Barcelona University, but began his career writing criticism for various Barcelona newspapers. Although he never gave up criticism, his greatest work was as a musicologist and music organizer. He was strongly influenced by Pedrell and centred his efforts on making Wagner's music known: to this end he founded the Asociación Wagneriana (1901), translated Wagner's operas and writings and wrote several studies of his music. Later he extended his field to other composers and to other forms, including lieder. In 1940 he started to translate Riemann's *Musik Lexikon* into Spanish, but was persuaded by Higini Anglès to change the project into the writing of a new dictionary that would better answer the needs of the Spanish public. After his death it was continued by Anglès and published as the *Diccionario de la música Labor* (Barcelona, 1954). (*LaborD* [incl. introduction])

JOSÉ LÓPEZ-CALO

Peñalosa [Penyalosa], Francisco de (*b* Talavera de la Reina, *c*1470; *d* Seville, 1 April 1528). Spanish composer. More works by him survive than by any of his Spanish contemporaries, even though it is also clear that quite a considerable number of his compositions have been lost. Six complete masses, six *Magnificat* settings, five hymns, three Lamentation settings, over 20 motets and 11 songs are attributed to him in Iberian or New World sources; surprisingly, it appears that none of his music has been preserved elsewhere.

Relatively little is known about his life before his appointment to the Aragonese royal chapel on 11 May 1498; the document recording his appointment gives only his place of birth. He served there until the death of King Ferdinand in 1516, his salary having been increased in May 1501 to 30,000 maravedís, the maximum paid to a singer-chaplain in that household. Although Cristóbal de Villalón described him as *maestro de capilla* (*Ingeniosa comparación entre lo antigua y lo presente*, Valladolid, 1539), he is not referred to elsewhere under this title. He was, however, 'maestro de música' (music teacher) to the king's grandson, Ferdinand, who was brought up and educated in Burgos; Peñalosa held this position from 1511. In December 1505 he had been presented, at royal request, to a canonry at Seville Cathedral, but the position was contested and it was several years before the case was decided in his favour. He visited Seville from time to time while continuing to serve at court, but he took up residence there following the king's death. In the autumn of 1517 he received an invitation to go to Rome, and he served as a member of the papal choir until the death of Leo X (December 1521). Even the high esteem of the pope was insufficient to convince the chapter of Seville Cathedral to allow Peñalosa to receive the income from the canonry *in absentia*, and in the summer of 1518 he renounced it for the position of Archdeacon of Carmona. After the pope's death he returned to Seville, resumed his canonry and in March 1525 was granted the rights to the post of treasurer. He died in Seville on 1 April 1528 and was buried in the cathedral.

Villalón's homage to 'the celebrated Francisco de Peñalosa … whose skill in composing and singing surpassed even that of music's inventor, Apollo' reflects the composer's fame in his own country, and he was also renowned in Rome, primarily, it would appear, as a singer. No works are attributed to him in manuscripts associated with the Cappella Sistina or in other Italian sources, but it is clear that he was composing motets for King Ferdinand's chapel before he travelled to Rome. The late 16th-century inventories preserved at Tarazona Cathedral list a number of works that are now lost, including a book of his masses. In addition, an inventory of the library of the Duke of Calabria lists a further 'libro de Peñalosa' which is probably no longer extant. The works that do survive reveal a composer of great skill, whose musical idiom is rooted in the lingua franca of the Franco-Flemish school. Peñalosa would have met composers such as Pierre de La Rue and Alexander Agricola during their visits to Spain in the early 16th century, and it is probably not by chance that both Peñalosa and La Rue composed masses based on Urrede's well-known canción *Nunca fue pena mayor*. Indeed, it has been suggested that these masses were composed for the wedding in 1497 of Philip the Fair and Juana, second daughter of Ferdinand and Isabella, although this was a year before Peñalosa entered the king's service. It is not yet possible to date any of the other masses, but it is likely that his *Missa 'L'homme armé'* and perhaps the *Missa 'Por la mar'* (which cites the *L'homme armé* melody in the Sanctus) were composed for specific occasions.

All Peñalosa's masses are for four voices and are built round a cantus firmus in the tenor; in general the cantus firmus also pervades the entire texture through imitation. Almost all his borrowed melodies are secular, and most are of French origin; even in his *Missa 'Ave Maria peregrina'*, the one mass based on plainchant, he cites Hayne van Ghizeghem's *De tous biens plaine* in the final Agnus Dei. The *Missa 'El ojo'*, the meaning of whose title remains unclear, is the simplest and most concise of his mass settings, with the melody confined, apparently unadorned and mostly in long note values, to the tenor. It may be the earliest of his masses: all the others that survive display a much greater integration of the borrowed melody and a more experimental approach to structure. The latter is achieved through contrasts of texture and scoring (duos and trios are sometimes used in contrast to the full texture, which is at times expanded to five or six voices), metre (ternary and binary) and declamation (contrapuntal sections alternating with passages of homophony). Canonic writing is characteristic of Peñalosa's masses, particularly in the final Agnus Dei: the most outstanding example is found in the *Missa 'Ave Maria'*, where the *Salve regina* melody is sung in canon simultaneously with the tenor of Hayne's chanson in retrograde. Such technical feats are worthy of any of his Franco-Flemish contemporaries.

His *Magnificat* and Lamentation settings, hymns and some of the motets are based on plainchant, and are generally imitative in texture. Of the motets, his setting of *Ave regina celorum* is closest to the cantus-firmus style of his masses. Although some of his motets have specific liturgical functions, the majority set non-liturgical texts and are often penitential in tone – the predominant themes are the Passion and redemption – and may well have served in devotional contexts. With no predetermined plainchant melody, these motets are freely composed, their structure being articulated by contrasts of texture and scoring. In particular, the rhetorical use of sections of homophony to highlight key words or phrases, very often set in a quasi-recitational manner, conveys the textual message to the listener in an enhanced and compelling manner.

If Peñalosa's motets are highly original and experimental, his songs are more conventional, with the notable exception of *Por las sierras de Madrid*: this is a compositional tour de force that combines several melodies simultaneously, including four refrains underlined, in the bass, by the phrase 'Loquebantur variis linguis magnalia Dei' ('they spoke in different tongues of the wonderful works of God'). The incomplete *Tú que vienes de camino* is also unusual: in the table of contents of the Cancionero Musical de Palacio it is listed as an *ensalada*, but it is impossible to tell from the surviving material whether it conforms to the structure of the *ensalada* as it developed later in the 16th century. Most of Peñalosa's songs were added to the Cancionero after its original compilation in about 1500; all are villancicos and all set verse that develops the conventional courtly love themes. The musical style follows that cultivated by Juan del Encina in the 1490s, but generally with an increased use of imitation. A single *romance*, *Los braços traygo*, is attributed to Peñalosa in another source (*E-Bbc* 454).

Peñalosa's versatility and skill as a composer undoubtedly mark him out as the leading composer of his generation. Through his connections with Seville Cathedral he may well have directly influenced Morales; he certainly made a major contribution to the flowering of polyphony in the Iberian peninsula during the 16th century.

WORKS

for 4 voices unless otherwise stated

Editions: *Francisco de Peñalosa: Collected Works*, ed. J.M. Hardie (Ottawa, 1994–) [H]
Francisco de Peñalosa opera omnia, ed. D. Preciado (Madrid, 1986–91) [P]

MASSES, MASS MOVEMENTS AND MAGNIFICAT SETTINGS

Adieu mes amours, *E-TZ* 2–3
Ave Maria peregrina, ed. in MME, i (1941, 2/1960/R)
El ojo, *TZ* 2–3, *P-Cug* M.12
L'homme armé, *E-TZ* 2–3
Nunca fue pena mayor, ed. in MME, i
Por la mar, *TZ* 2–3
Kyrie, 3vv, *Boc* 5
Kyrie, *TZ* 5
Kyrie, Sanctus, Agnus Dei 'feriales' (inc.), *TZ* 5
Gloria, Credo (BVM), *TZ* 2–3
Magnificat, 1st tone, 3rd tone, 4th tone, 6th tone, 8th tone (2 settings); all in P ii

MOTETS

Adoro te, Domine, 3vv, H, P i; Ave regina celorum, H, P i; Ave vera caro Christe, H, P i; Ave vere sanguis domini, H, P i; Ave verum corpus, H, P i; Deus qui manus tuas, H, P i; Domine Jesu Christe, qui neminem, H, P i; Domine, secundum actum meum, H, P i; Emendemus in melius, H, P i; In passione positus, H, P i; Inter vestibulum ac altare, H, P i; Ne reminiscaris, 3vv, H, P i; Nigra sum sed formosa, 3vv, H, P i
O decus virgineum, *TZ* 2–3; O domina sanctissima, 3vv, H, P i; Pater noster, H, P i; Precor te, Domine, H, P i; Sancta Maria, sucurre miseris, 3vv, H, P i; Sancta mater istud agas (wrongly attrib. 'Iusquin' in *Bbc* 454), H, P i, also ed. in MRM, ix (1996); Transeunte Domino, 5vv, H, P i; Tribularer si nescirem, H, P i; Unica est columba mea, 3vv, H, P i; Versa est in luctum, H, P i
Lamentation settings: Aleph: Quomodo obscuratum est, *TZ* 2–3; Aleph: quomodo obtexit caligine, *TZ* 2–3; Et factum est postquam, *TZ* 2–3

HYMNS

Gloria, laus, *TZ* 5; Jesu nostra redemptio, *TZ* 2–3, ed. in Cw, lx (1957); O lux beata Trinitas, *TZ* 2–3, ed. in Cw, lx; Sacris solemnis, *TZ* 2–3, ed. in Cw, lx; Sanctorum meritis, *TZ* 2–3, cd. in Cw, lx

SECULAR

Alegraos, males esquivos, 3vv, ed. in MME, x; A tierras agenas, 3vv, ed. in MME, x (1951); De mi dicha no se spera, 3vv, ed. in MME, x; El triste que nunca os vio, 3vv, ed. in MME, v (1947); Lo que mucho se desea, 2vv, ed. in MME, x; Los braços traygo, 3vv, ed. in Ros-Fàbregas; Niña, erguideme los ojos, 3vv, ed. in MME, v; Por las sierras de Madrid, 6vv, ed. in MME, x; Pues vivo en perder la vida, 3vv, ed. in MME, v, and in Ros-Fàbregas; Que dolor mas me doliera, 3vv, ed. in MME, x; Tú que vienes de camino (inc.), 3vv, ed. in MME, x

DOUBTFUL AND MISATTRIBUTED WORKS

Kyrie 'in feriis', *E TZ* 5 (attrib. Montes and Peñalosa)
Sicut cervus, 2vv (tr, Requiem Mass, attrib. Peñalosa in *TZ* 5; by Ockeghem)
Domine Jesu Christe qui hora diei, *SE* (Anchieta), *Sc* 5-5-20 (Anchieta), *TZ* 5 (Peñalosa), *E-Vp* 5, *P-Cug* M.12, *Cug* M.32, II
Memorare piissima, *E-Bbc* 454, *Sc* 1 (Escobar), *Sc* 5-5-20 (Escobar), *Tc* 21 (Peñalosa), *TZ* 2–3 (Escobar), *P-Cug* M.12, *Cug* M.32, H, P i
O bone Jesu, *E-Bbc* 454 ('Penyalosa'), *Boc* 5, *SE* (Anchieta), *TZ* 2–3 (Antonio de Ribera), *P-Cug* M.12, *Cug* M.32, *Cug* M.48, *Cug* M.53, 1519² (Compère), P i
Qui expansis – Qui prophetice – Christus Dominus factus est, *E-TZ* 5, H

LOST WORKS

numbered according to Calahorra Martinez

Credo, *E-TZ* 5 (321)
Magnificat (127)
Ave Maria (377); Vide Domine (28)

BIBLIOGRAPHY

StevensonSM
F.A. Barbieri, ed.: *Cancionero musical de los siglos XV y XVI* (Madrid, 1890/R)
C. Lynn: *A College Professor of the Renaissance: Lucio Marineo Siculo among the Spanish Humanists* (Chicago, 1937)
R. Stevenson: *La música en la Catedral de Sevilla, 1478–1606: documentos para su estudio* (Los Angeles, 1954, enlarged 2/1985)
R. Stevenson: 'The Toledo Manuscript Polyphonic Choirbooks and some other Lost or Little Known Flemish Sources', *FAM*, xx (1973), 87–107, esp. 100, 102
J.M. Hardie: *The Motets of Francisco de Peñalosa and their Manuscript Sources* (diss., U. of Michigan, 1983)
T.W. Knighton: *Music and Musicians at the Court of Fernando of Aragon, 1474–1516* (diss., U. of Cambridge, 1984), i, 288
P. Calahorra Martinez: 'Los fondos musicales en el siglo XVI de la Catedral de Tarazona, i: Inventarios', *Nassarre*, viii/2 (1992), 9–56
T. Knighton: 'A Day in the Life of Francisco de Peñalosa', *Companion to Medieval and Renaissance Music*, ed. T. Knighton and D. Fallows (London, 1992), 79–84
E. Ros-Fàbregas: *The Manuscript Barcelona, Biblioteca de Catalunya, M.454: Study and Edition in the Context of the Iberian and Continental Manuscript Traditions* (diss., CUNY, 1992)
T. Knighton: 'Francisco de Peñalosa: New Works Lost and Found', *Encomium musicae: a Festschrift in Honor of Robert J. Snow*, ed. D. Crawford (forthcoming)

TESS KNIGHTON

Peñalosa, Juan de (*b* c1515; *d* ?Toledo, 1579). Spanish organist of Jewish descent. He served as assistant to the blind Francisco Sacedo, who was principal organist of Toledo Cathedral from 22 January 1541 until his death shortly before 7 August 1547. Peñalosa, who had by then become a priest in the Toledo diocese, was elected his successor on 31 December 1549. From 30 June 1552 he had to divide his stipend with another organist Francisco López. Peñalosa applied 11 years later for the post of organist of Palencia Cathedral, which had become vacant on the death of Francisco de Soto in summer 1563. On 5 January 1564 the Palencia chapter dismissed him, since he seemed to be attempting to seek double employment with the Toledo and Palencia chapters. Apparently he remained at Toledo until 1579. No relationship to Francisco de Peñalosa has yet been discovered, nor do any of his compositions survive.

BIBLIOGRAPHY

F. Rubio Piqueras: *Música y músicos toledanos* (Toledo, 1923)
M.S. Kastner: 'Palencia, encrucijada de los organistas españoles del siglo XVI', *AnM*, xiv (1959), 115–64, esp. 140
J. López-Calo: *La música en la catedral de Palencia*, i: *Catalogo musical. Actas capitulares (1413–1684)* (Palencia, 1980), esp. 474
D. Preciado: 'El organista Juan de Peñalosa, "primera víctima" quizá del estatuto de limpieza de sangre toledano', *El órgano español II: Madrid 1986*, 147–8

ROBERT STEVENSON

Peña y Goñi, Antonio (*b* San Sebastián, 2 Nov 1846; *d* Madrid, 13 Nov 1896). Spanish music critic and composer. His early musical training was with José Juan Santesteban, organist and *maestro de capilla* at San Sebastián. He spent his youth in France, as a student at Paris and Bordeaux, and later studied harmony at the Madrid Conservatory. He composed numerous works for the piano, a symphonic poem, *Vasconia*, and fantasy, *Pan y Toros*, for orchestra, and a 'patriotic Basque song' *¡Viva Hernani!* for solo voice, chorus and orchestra (Madrid, Teatro Real, 21 Dec 1875), which enjoyed great success. But he is best known as a critic; he began on *El imparcial* and then, with Manuel de la Revilla, founded the periodical *La crítica*. He also contributed to the *Revista contemporánea*, *El globo*, *El tiempo*, *La Europa*, *La Ilustración española y americana*, *La Correspondencia musical* and *La epoca*. He was named professor of music history and criticism at the Escuela Nacional de Música y Declamación in Madrid in 1879 and in 1892 was elected to the Real Academia de S Fernando, an honour he had declined in 1873 through excessive modesty.

Peña y Goñi was an opponent of Italianism and a supporter of Wagner, whose work he helped make known in Spain. He enthusiastically defended the zarzuela, and his chief work, *La ópera española y la música dramática*, is of the greatest importance in tracing its origins and documenting its history. He was the founder of modern music criticism in Spain.

WRITINGS

only those on music

La obra maestra de Verdi: Aida, ensayo crítico musical (Madrid, 1875)
Nuestros músicos: Barbieri (Madrid, 1875)
Rienzi (Madrid, 1875)
Impresiones musicales: colección de artículos de crítica y literatura musical (Madrid, 1878)
Impresiones y recuerdos: Carlos Gounod (Madrid, 1879)
'Miguel Marqués y la sinfonía en España', *Revista contemporánea*, no.26 (1880), 455
La ópera española y la música dramática en España en el siglo XIX (Madrid, 1881)
Cristina Nilsson: discurso biográfico leído en el gran salón teatro de la Escuela nacional de música y declamación en la función celebrada el 26 de diciembre de 1881 para solemnizar la adjudicación del primer premio Nilsson (Madrid, 1882)
'Luis Mancinelli y la Sociedad de conciertos de Madrid', *Revista contemporánea*, no.81 (1891), 597; no.82 (1891), 32
La ópera cómica española: desde 1838 hasta nuestros días (Madrid, 1892)
Los maestros cantores de Nuremberg de Richard Wagner (Madrid, 1893)
Cajón de sastre (Madrid, 1894)

BIBLIOGRAPHY

FétisB
A. Peña y Goñi: 'Mi retrato', *La Ilustración musical hispano-americana* (1892) [autobiography]
L. Carmena y Millán: 'Antonio Peña y Goñi', *Cosas del pasado: música, literatura y tauromaquia* (Madrid, 1904), 35
'Peña y Goñi (Antonio)', *Enciclopedia universal ilustrada europeo-americana* (Madrid, 1905–30), xliii, 429–30
J. Subirá: *La música en la Academia: historia de una sección* (Madrid, 1980), 102–3, 113–14, 232

GUY BOURLIGUEUX

Penberthy, James (*b* Melbourne, 3 May 1917; *d* 29 March 1999). Australian composer. He received his early musical tuition from his father. After active naval service during World War II he studied at the Melbourne University Conservatorium, graduating in composition in 1950. He undertook further study from 1950 to 1952 in London, Manchester, Paris and Florence. From 1953 to 1973 he lived in Perth, dividing his time mainly between composition and journalism. From 1947 to 1950 he was musical director of the National Opera and Ballet in Melbourne: later he was instrumental in the foundation, in Perth, of the Western Australian Ballet (1953) and Opera (1967) companies. He taught at the NSW Conservatorium and the Northern Rivers College of Advanced Education from 1974 to 1982. His interest in music-theatre has been reflected in the composition of many operas and ballets, the most notable success perhaps being the opera *Dalgerie* based on an Australian aboriginal subject. His musical style, essentially Romantic and, like Antill, Douglas and Sculthorpe, consciously nationalist, has drawn largely upon early 20th-century sources; from 1965 to 1975, however, he also occasionally explored serial, aleatory and computer methods.

WORKS

(selective list)

11 operas incl. Ophelia of the Nine Mile Beach (comic op, 1, Penberthy), 1955, Hobart, Theatre Royal, July 1965; The Earth Mother (tragic op, 3, D.R. Stuart, Penberthy), 1957–8, unperf.; Dalgerie (tragic op, 1, M. Durack, after her novel: *Keep Him My Country*), Perth, Somerville Auditorium, 22 Jan 1959); Stations (space op, 3, Harwood), 1975, unperf.; Henry Lawson (3, Penberthy, after stories and poems by H. Lawson), 1988–9, unperf.

27 ballets incl. Beach Inspector and the Mermaid (Penberthy), Perth, 1958; Kooree and the Mists, Perth, 1960; Fire at Ross's Farm (after Lawson), Perth, 1961

9 syms. incl. no.6 'The Earth Mother', 1962; 2 film scores; 4 pf concs.; concs. for vn, va, vc, fl, ob, cl, bn, hn, sax, tpt; other music for orch/str orch; band pieces

Many choral works incl. Cant. on Hiroshima Panels (J.J. Jones), S, T, Bar, chorus, orch, 1959; Commentaries on Living (G. Harwood), nar, chorus, orch, 1972; Southland (Harwood, Penberthy), Bar, 2 SATB, orch, 1991; song cycles, other vocal music

Chbr music incl. 3 str qts; kbd works incl. sets of preludes and studies, pf; 2 org pieces

MSS in *AUS-Smc*

Microfilms in *Pml*

BIBLIOGRAPHY

A.D. McCredie: *Catalogue of 46 Australian Composers and Selected Works* (Canberra, 1969), 16
J. Murdoch: *Australia's Contemporary Composers* (Melbourne, 1972), 157–62
J.A. Meyer: 'James Penberthy', *Australian Composition in the Twentieth Century*, ed. F. Callaway and D. Tunley (Melbourne, 1978), 81–7

DAVID SYMONS

Pencerdd. One of two bardic classes distinguished in medieval Welsh legal theory. *See* BARD, §2, and WALES, §II, 1.

Pencerdd Gwalia. *See* THOMAS, JOHN.

Pencerdd Gwynedd. *See* ROBERTS, JOHN HENRY.

Penckel, Bartłomiej. *See* PĘKIEL, BARTŁOMIEJ.

Penco, Rosina (*b* Naples, April 1823; *d* Porretta, nr Bologna, 2 Nov 1894). Italian soprano. After an unrecorded début she sang in Dresden and Berlin in 1850, and Constantinople in 1850–51, chiefly the lyric coloratura parts of Rossini, Bellini and Donizetti, and was renowned for her trill. Before Verdi wrote Leonora in *Il trovatore* for her (1853, Rome) he heard that she had 'many virtues' though 'imperfect'; she was also described as 'very pretty' and 'a devil' to her fellow singers. Verdi prized her combination of agility with passionate dramatic temperament; he later suggested her for *La traviata* and for the heavier part of Amelia in *Un ballo in maschera* (which she eventually sang in 1861 at Covent Garden and the Théâtre Italien, Paris). He complained in 1858 that she had retreated into the bel canto style 'of thirty years ago' – her range included Norma, Elvira in *I puritani* and Paolina in Donizetti's *Poliuto* – instead of moving forward into 'the style of thirty years hence'. She sang frequently in Madrid (to 1857), London (1859–62), Paris (most years from 1855 to 1872) and St Petersburg (to 1874).

BIBLIOGRAPHY
ES (R. Celletti)
J. Budden: *The Operas of Verdi* (London, 1973–81)
M. Conati: *La bottega della musica: Verdi e la Fenice* (Milan, 1983)
JOHN ROSSELLI

Penderecki, Krzysztof (*b* Dębica, 23 Nov 1933). Polish composer and conductor. He first came to prominence as an explorer of novel string textures and for many years his name was popularly synonymous with avant-garde Polish music. His subsequent allusions to 18th- and 19th-century idioms and genres, in his choral and operatic works as well as in his purely instrumental pieces, has produced a substantial body of work which challenges many assumptions about the nature and purpose of contemporary music.

1. Life. 2. Music up to 1974. 3. Music after 1975.

1. LIFE.   Penderecki studied composition privately with Franciszek Skołyszewski and then (1954–8) with Malawski and Wiechowicz at the State Higher School of Music (now the Academy) in Kraków. On graduating, he joined the staff of the school as a teacher of composition. His first major success came in 1959 when *Strofy* ('Strophes'), *Emanacje* ('Emanations') and *Psalmy Dawida* ('Psalms of David') were awarded the top three prizes at a competition organized by the Union of Polish Composers. Subsequently he came to the attention of two influential figures who were to prove crucial in bringing his music to audiences outside Poland: the publisher Hermann Moeck (who had heard *Strophes* at the 1959 Warsaw Autumn Festival) and Heinrich Strobel, director of the music division at SWF. In his capacity as director of the Donaueschingen Music Days, Strobel commissioned several of Penderecki's works, the first being *Anaklasis*, composed in 1959–60. In a short period Penderecki earned a reputation as one of the most innovative composers of his generation, especially for his experiments in notation, the perception of time, and extended instrumental techniques. He received an award at UNESCO (1961, for *Tren*, 'Threnody') and the

Westphalia and Italia Prizes (1966 and 1967 respectively, for the *St Luke Passion*), the Sibelius Gold Medal (1967) and the Polish State Prize, first class (1968); and later the Herder, Honegger and Grawemeyer awards, the latter for Symphony no.4.

From 1966 Penderecki accepted many composition residencies abroad, including appointments at the Volkwäng Hochschule für Musik, Essen (1966–8), in Berlin under the aegis of the Deutscher Akademischer Austauschdienst (1968–70), and at Yale University (1973–8). In 1972 he was appointed rector of the Kraków Academy, a post he held for 15 years, during which time martial law was imposed in Poland. There have been festivals of his music both in Kraków and, periodically since 1980, at his restored manor house in nearby Lusławice, where he has cultivated a fine garden, including a labyrinth and arboretum.

Penderecki's career as a conductor began in earnest in 1972, when he recorded seven of his own works for EMI. He has since conducted mainly in the USA and throughout Europe, becoming associated with the music of Shostakovich as well as his own works. From 1987 to 1990 he was artistic director of the Kraków PO, and in 1988 he became principal guest conductor with the NDR SO, Hamburg.

Penderecki has received honorary doctorates from several European and American institutions and is an honorary member of many learned academies. In 1990 he was made a Chevalier de Saint Georges and in addition received the Grosses Verdienstkreuz der Bundesrepublik Deutschland. Other honours include the Österreichisches

Krzysztof Penderecki in 1993

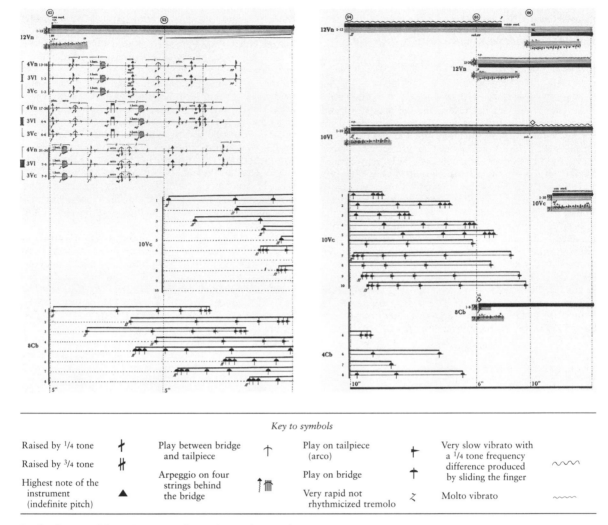

Key to symbols

Raised by 1/4 tone	♯	Play between bridge and tailpiece	↑	Play on tailpiece (arco)	⊤
Raised by 3/4 tone	♯♯				
Highest note of the instrument (indefinite pitch)	▲	Arpeggio on four strings behind the bridge	↑ ⫙	Play on bridge	⊤
				Very rapid not rhythmicized tremolo	⌇

Very slow vibrato with a 1/4 tone frequency difference produced by sliding the finger	∿
Molto vibrato	∿

Penderecki: 'Tren. Ofiarom Hiroszimy', figures 62–66 inclusive (pub.

Ehrenzeichen für Wissenschaft un Kunst (1992) and the Monacan Ordre du Mérite Culturel (1993).

2. MUSIC UP TO 1974.   Penderecki's juvenilia show characteristically vigorous rhythmic and lyrical melodic traits, in the vein of enriched neo-classicism prevalent in Poland in the postwar decade. The prizewinning works of 1958–9, however, advance rapidly from a mix of Stravinskian and Webernian choralism (*Psalms of David*) to Boulezian gestures (*Strophes*). Penderecki never fully engaged with orthodox serial techniques, preferring to absorb certain permutational procedures and to explore textural writing and effects which were to lead to the full-blown sonorisms of subsequent scores. *Emanations*, with its two string orchestras tuned a semitone apart, thus paved the way for *Anaklasis*, *Fonogrammi* and *Tren* ['Threnody'], works which use novel graphic notation and what was to become a characteristically broad-brush approach to musical materials and their development. Scored mostly for strings, these later works create a highly Expressionistic soundworld by means of quarter-tone clusters, wedges and group glissandos; a range of vibratos, tremolos and percussive effects, and by exploiting the flexibility of time–space notation. Alongside comparable

pieces by Xenakis and Ligeti, *Threnody* remains a classic avant-garde statement of the period, not least because it represented directness of expression at a time of advanced post-serial complexity. Originally entitled *8′ 37″*, the work was subsequently given an emotive title which was symptomatic of Penderecki's burgeoning fascination with historical events and storylines, especially those of a traumatic nature.

Graphic notation and extended instrumental techniques featured in many Polish orchestral works of the 1960s. However, unlike most of his contemporaries, Penderecki proved an instinctive dramatist; this quality is apparent from earlier choral pieces as well as his magnum opus of the 1960s, the *St Luke Passion*, the work which brought him genuine popular acclaim. Like Benjamin Britten's *War Requiem*, composed in 1961, the Passion touched on a contemporary spirit of reconciliation, which was all the more remarkable for it being composed in communist Poland and first performed in the Federal German Republic (in Münster Cathedral). It was also the cause of disquiet among the more purist avant-garde critics for its eclecticism, which may now be seen as a portent of the polystylism which soon surfaced elsewhere. But Penderecki had already rocked the boat with the concluding major triads in the *Stabat mater* (incorporated in the *Passion*) and *Polymorphia*, and in this gritty reworking of the Baroque genre he confidently incorporated chant, recitative and chorales. The choral writing, as adventurous as his instrumental textures, sometimes emulates electronic sounds, and the serial pitch organization (two 12-note rows are used) includes the B–A–C–H motif as a bridge to the more traditional elements in the score. It retains a clear narrative structure, and contains cyclic devices and set pieces, of which the 'Stabat mater' is the most substantial. The raw and austere expression of the *Passion* conveys an apocalyptic vision held in check, to be unleashed in more visceral form in later works.

A penchant for themes on the human condition lies behind many of the choral commissions. *Dies irae* commemorates the dead of Auschwitz, while *Kosmogonia* was written for the 25th anniversary of the United Nations. And yet by integrating vocal lines into the instrumental textures or by translating texts into Latin, as in *Dies irae*, or assembling them in a number of languages, as in *Kosmogonia*, he frequently places the listener at a remove. There is, however, a less sombre combination of reflection and ecstasy in *Utrenia*, the sequel to the *St Luke Passion* and his most symphonic choral work of the 1960s and 70s. Its assimilation of Eastern Orthodox rites is especially vivid, and the open exuberance of the 'Resurrection' is uncommon in Penderecki's work of the period. While retaining many serial practices of the 1960s, his musical language now integrates diatonic triads and emphasizes certain interval classes, most notably the minor 3rd. The *Magnificat* (1974), with its triple fugue (in 'Quia respexit'), polyrhythmic textures and extreme juxtapositions, may be regarded as the summation of his early oratorio style.

3. MUSIC AFTER 1975.   Like a number of his contemporaries and compatriots, Penderecki relaxed his compositional language in the mid-1970s to give lyrical melody the central role in both his vocal and instrumental music. Turning-points were the orchestral *Przebudzenie Jakuba* ('The Awakening of Jacob'), scored additionally for 12 ocarinas, and, more particularly, the First Violin Concerto, written for Isaac Stern. While retaining some earlier methods, the concerto marks out future territory in its discursive, narrative structure and in its focus on two intervals, the semitone and tritone. The semitone has been the unmistakable cornerstone of Penderecki's vocabulary throughout his career, and unresolved chains of semitones, commonly separated by a tritone, have been the most conspicuous aspect of his melodic style since the mid-1970s. This *idée fixe* was crucial to Penderecki's development of his own brand of neo-romanticism. He had, to many observers, however, created a neo-Brucknerian idiom that seemed even more retrogressive than the eclecticism of the *St Luke Passion*. In truth, this later style owes less to late 19th- and early 20th-century German traditions than is commonly supposed; rather it recalls the motivic and symphonic procedures of Liszt and Paderewski and in its dark expressivity echoes the work of his compatriot, Mieczysław Karłowicz. Where Penderecki differs is in his modernistic fixation on deliberately restricted technical means: intervallic repetition, doggedly persistent rhythms, sombre orchestral colours and a tendency to deploy his ideas rhetorically.

In contrast to the voyeurism of his first opera, *The Devils of Loudun* (1969), where the profane is dominant,

Penderecki's second stage work is styled a *sacra rappresentazione*. While both works are opera–oratorio hybrids, *Paradise Lost* (1975–8) draws on a variety of early genres, such as Renaissance Florentine entertainments, with their extravagant scenic tableaux and dances. Given its Christian message of innocence, degradation and purification, with Adam and Eve as unwitting victims, it is curious that Penderecki created only superficial differences between the musical material assigned respectively to God and Satan. His intervallic *idée fixe*, containing the medieval 'diabolus in musica', is appropriate for fallen angels, but it also in effect depicts heaven, giving Milton's account a fatalistic gloss and sapping any vestiges of dramatic momentum. That said, there are impressive set pieces, notably towards the end of Act 2, where visions of death, pestilence, war and flood are contained within a favoured formal device, the passacaglia.

Penderecki's third and fourth operas, *Die schwarze Maske* and *Ubu Rex*, allowed him to indulge his musical and dramatic neuroses. The former is his finest *danse macabre*, a hysterical Grand Guignol whose absurdity is matched by music of manic intensity and drive (as in much of his work, there is an almost cinematic quality to the emotional directness of the music). The central female role, Benigna, dominates the second half of the opera in music of unusual melodic breadth, lessening its overwhelming gloom. The use of pastiche and quotation, apparent in both *Paradise Lost* and *Die schwarze Maske*, comes into its own in *Ubu Rex*. Penderecki's adaptation of Jarry's grotesque, scatalogical tale is replete with affable references to operatic styles as varied as Rossini, Musorgsky and Shostakovich. Not attaining the innovative synthesis of either Stravinsky or Weill, *Ubu Rex* remains something of an aberration in Penderecki's output, but one whose melodic and harmonic language is refreshingly light-spirited.

More central to Penderecki's output after 1975 are the oratorios, among them the *Polish Requiem*, *Seven Gates of Jerusalem* and *Credo*, all large-scale works. Whereas the Polishness of *Die schwarze Maske* and *Ubu Rex* lies in their storylines, the *Te Deum* and *Requiem* rely on musical quotation: the hymn *Boże coś Polskę* ('God, who hast protected Poland') is the centrepiece of the former work, while a second Old Polish hymn, *Święty Boże* ('Holy God'), occurs in the 'Recordare' of the *Requiem*. To the outside observer, such iconography may seem excessively sentimental, but in the context of events in Poland during the years 1979–81 it was timely and appropriate: Cardinal Wojtyła of Kraków, to whom the *Te Deum* is dedicated, had been elected to the papacy in October 1978; the trade union Solidarity was established in 1980; and in December 1981 martial law was imposed on the country by the then communist authorities. Penderecki's music came to represent much of the struggle between church and state (although, unlike Lutosławski and Górecki, he maintained some links with the Polish political establishment during the harsh years after 1981), hence the commission by Solidarity to compose a piece for the unveiling of the Gdańsk memorial to those killed in anti-government riots at the shipyard in 1970. The *Lacrimosa*, scored for soprano and chorus, was later to become part of the *Polish Requiem*.

This quasi-political, patriotic role seems to have spurred Penderecki to develop his neo-romantic language to a point where conventions from the Renaissance and the

18th and 19th centuries are openly acknowledged. Diminished and dominant harmonies, cadential formulae and melodic phrases (most noticeably those beginning with a rising minor 6th), are now part of his vocabulary. Elsewhere, in the *Requiem*, where many of the sections are dedicated to individuals or mass martyrs in Polish history, Penderecki also employs choral and instrumental textures derived from his own music of the 1960s, achieving a hitherto unmatched stylistic and technical synthesis. Terror-driven it may be, like much of his music, but it does touch common ground with many audiences, especially within a political-religious context.

Later choral works, especially the *Credo*, show an increasingly softer, 19th-century harmonic bias. Some, again, incorporate Polish hymns (e.g. in the 'Crucifixus' of the *Credo*), and the influence of Bach is much more obvious than before. When deprived of a religious text or commemorative occasion, as in the chamber and orchestral music, Penderecki's compositional rationale can seem vulnerable to accusations of indulgent rhapsodizing. Nevertheless, works like the String Trio and Clarinet Quartet are permeated by a relaxed, conversational tone.

Orchestral monumentalism remains however, and in many cases relies on extended sonata forms to provide cohesion, showing a preference for multi-sectioned, single-movement works, e.g. the second, fourth and fifth symphonies, whose structures are articulated primarily by alternating fast and slow material. Among the most persuasive of the concertante works are the Second Cello Concerto (written for Rostropovitch) and the Second Violin Concerto. The former, like the *Requiem*, brings bite to his neo-romantic idiom by assimilating textural elements from his music of the 1960s, although the overall gestural language remains resolutely 19th-century. The latter concerto is essentially an expanded sonata allegro, with many refined sonorities. Its subtitle, 'Metamorphoses', is indicative of the cyclical elements and procedures which have formed the basis of Penderecki's music for over two decades.

The Third Symphony, unusually, has five distinct movements, with a passacaglia reminiscent of that in the *Magnificat*. For all its reliance on Mahler, it is the sustained central adagio, completed in 1995, after the fourth and fifth symphonies, which makes the strongest case for Penderecki's new communicable language. In 1998 he wrote in a foreword to a catalogue of his sketches that he felt he was getting close to the essence of music. By implication, these views are somewhat dismissive of his music of the 1960s, arguably his most distinctive contribution to 20th-century culture. Penderecki is a composer who has consistently engaged with the issues of the outside world, sometimes with piety, often with apparent anger and never without passion. Nevertheless, his stylistic shifts have often raised more questions than answers.

WORKS

DRAMATIC

Najdzielniejszy z rycerzy [The Most Valiant of Knights] (children's op, 3, Penderecki, after E. Szelburg-Zarembina), 1965, collab. M. Stachowski; Poznan, Teatr Lalki i Aktora 'Marcinek', 15 March 1965

The Devils of Loudun (op, 3, Penderecki, after A. Huxley), 1968, Hamburg, Staatsoper, 20 June 1969

Paradise Lost (sacra rappresentazione, 2, C. Fry, after J. Milton), 1975–8, Chicago, Lyric Opera, 29 Nov 1978

Die schwarze Maske (op, 1, H. Kupfer and Penderecki, after G. Hauptmann), 1984–6, Salzburger Festspiele, 15 Aug 1986

Ubu rex (op, 2, Penderecki and J. Jarocki, after A. Jarry), 1990–91, Munich, Bayerische Staatsoper, 6 July 1991

Incid music, incl. music for puppet theatre, 1957–67

Film scores, incl. Rękopis znaleziony w Saragossie [The Saragossa Manuscript] (dir. W. Has), 1963

VOCAL

Psalmy Dawida (trans. J. Kochanowski), chorus, perc, cel, hp, 2 pf, 4 db, 1958

Strofy [Strophes] (Menander, Sophocles, Isaiah, Jeremiah, Omar Khayyám), S, reciter, 10 insts, 1959

Wymiary czasu i ciszy [Dimensions of Time and Silence], 40vv, perc, str, 1959–60

Stabat mater, 3 choruses, 1962

Passio et mors domini nostri Jesu Christi secundum Lucam, S, Bar, reciter, children's chorus, 3 choruses, orch, 1963–6

Cantata in honorem Almae Matris Universitatis Iagellonicae sescentos abhinc annos fundatae, 2 choruses, dbn, brass, perc, pf, org, 1964

Pieśń żałobna ku czci B. Rutkowskiego [Funeral Song in memory of Rutkowski], chorus, 1964

Dies irae [Bible, Aeschylus and others], S, T, B, chorus, orch, 1967

Utrenia (Jutrznia) (Old Slavonic, New Testament), S, Mez, T, B, B profundo, 2 choruses, orch

Złożenie Chrystusa do grobu [The Entombment of Christ], 1969–70

Kosmogonia (Old Testament, Sophocles and others), S, T, B, chorus, orch, 1970

Zmartwychwstanie Pańskie [The Lord's Resurrection], 1970–71

Canticum canticorum Salomonis, 16vv, orch, 1970–73

Ecloga VIII (Virgil), 6 male vv, 1972

Magnificat, B, 7 male vv, boys' chorus, 2 choruses, orch, 1974

Te Deum, S, Mez, T, B, chorus, orch, 1979–80

Lacrimosa, S, chorus, 1980

Polskie requiem, S, A, T, B, chorus, orch, 1980–84, rev. 1993

Agnus Dei, chorus, 1981, arr. str, 1984

Pieśń Cherubinów [Song of Cherubim] (Old Slavonic), SSAATTBB, 1986

Veni creator, SSAATTBB, 1987

Benedicamus Domino, TTTBB, 1992

Benedictus, SATB, 1993

Agnus Dei, S, A, T, B, chorus, orch, 1995 [movt 10 of Requiem der Versöhnung, collab. Berio, Cerha, Dittrich and others]

7 Gates of Jerusalem (Pss, Old Testament), 2S, A, T, B, reciter, 3 choruses, orch, 1996

Hymne an den heiligen Daniel, SATB, wind insts, 1997

Hymne an den heiligen Adalbert, SATB, orch, 1997

Credo, S, 2 Mez, T, B, children's chorus, chorus, orch, 1998

ORCHESTRAL

Epitafium Artur Malawski in memoriam, str, timp, 1958

Emanacje [Emanations], 2 str orch, 1958

Anaklasis, str, perc, 1959–60

Tren [Threnody 'To the Victims of Hiroshima'], 52 str, 1960

Fonogrammi, fl, chbr orch, 1961

Polymorphia, 48 str, 1961

Fluorescencje, 1961–2

Kanon, 52 str, tape delay, 1962

3 utwory w dawnym stylu [3 Pieces in Old Style], str, 1963 [from film score Rękopis znaleziony w Saragossie]

Violin Concerto, 1963, withdrawn

Sonata, vc, orch, 1964

Capriccio, ob, 11 str, 1965

De natura sonoris I, 1966

Capriccio, vn, orch, 1967

Uwertura pittsburska [Pittsburgh Overture], ww, perc, pf, 1967

Concerto per violino grande, 1967, rev. as Cello Concerto no.1, 1972

De natura sonoris II, 1970–71

Partita, hpd, elec gui, b gui, hp, db, chbr orch, 1971, rev. 1991

Prélude, ww, perc, dbs, cel, pf, 1971

Symphony no.1, 1972–3

Intermezzo, 24 str, 1973

Przebudzenie Jakuba [The Awakening of Jacob], 1974

Violin Concerto no.1, 1976–7

Adagietto from Paradise Lost, 1979

Symphony no.2 'Wigilijna' [Christmas Symphony], 1979–80

Cello Concerto no.2, 1982

Concerto per viola (vc/cl), orch, 1983
Symphony no.3, 1988–95
Adagio (Symphony no.4), 1989
Sinfonietta, str, 1990–91 [orch of Str Trio, 1990–91]
Flute Concerto, 1992, rev. cl, orch, 1995
Symphony no.5, 1992
Violin Concerto no.2, 1992–5
Sinfonietta no.2, cl, str, 1994 [orch of Cl Qt, 1993]
Entrata, brass, timp, 1994
Passacaglia, str, 1996

OTHER WORKS

Chbr: Sonata, vn, pf, 1953; 3 miniatury, cl, pf, 1956; 3 miniatury,
   after J. Harasymowicz, vn, pf, 1959; Str Qt no.1, 1960; Mensura
   sortis, 2 pf, 1963; Str Qt no.2, 1968; Actions, jazz ens, 1971; Der
   unterbrochene Gedanke, str qt, 1988; Str Trio, 1990–91; Qt, cl,
   vn, va, vc, 1993
Solo inst: Capriccio per Siegfried Palm, vc, 1968; Capriccio, tuba,
   1980; Cadenza, va/vn, 1984; Per slava, vc, 1985–86; Preludium,
   cl, 1987; Divertimento, vc, 1994
Tape: Psalmus, 1961; Brygada śmierci [Brigade of Death] (incid
   music, J. Smoter, after L. Weliczker), 1963; Ekechejria (Pindar),
   1972; seeORCHESTRAL [Kanon, 1962]

Principal publishers: Moeck, PWM, Schott

WRITINGS

'Możliwość regeneracji sztuki jest dla mnie pewnikiem' [For me, the
   possibility of art's regeneration is a certainty], RM, xxxix/1–2
   (1995), 2–3
Labirint czasu: pięć wykładów na koniec wieku (Warsaw, 1997);
   expanded Eng. trans.: Labyrinth of Time: Five Addresses for the
   End of the Millennium (Chapel Hill, 1998)

BIBLIOGRAPHY

H. Schiller: 'Z warsztatu młodych' [From the workshop of the
   young], RM, iii/13 (1959), 16–20
T.A. Zieliński: 'Der einsame Weg der K. Penderecki', Melos, xxix
   (1962), 318–23
B. Pociej: 'Krzysztof Penderecki: en traditionell kompositör', Nutida
   musik, ix/1–2 (1965–6), 15–18
Z. Mycielski: 'Passio et mors Domini nostri Jesu Christi secundum
   Lucam Krzysztofa Pendereckiego', RM, x/10 (1966), 3–7
T. Nordwall: 'Krzysztof Penderecki: studium notacji i
   instrumentacji', Forum musicum, no.2 (1968), 79–112
T.A. Zieliński: 'Technika operowania instrumentami smyczkowymi
   w utworach Krzysztofa Pendereckiego' [The technique of the use
   of string instruments in Penderecki's works], Muzyka, xiii/1
   (1968), 74–92
K. Lisicki: Szkice o Krzysztofie Pendereckim [Sketches on Penderecki]
   (Warsaw, 1973)
K. Bilica: '"Ofiarom Hiroshimy: Tren" Krzysztofa Pendereckiego',
   Muzyka, xix/2 (1974), 45–71
A. Chłopecki: 'Penderecki i film', Kino, ix/12 (1974), 25–30
L. Erhardt: Spotkania z Krzysztofem Pendereckim [Meetings with
   Penderecki] (Kraków, 1975)
B. Kaack: 'Pendereckis Zwölftonreihe: Versuch einer Interpretation
   des Eröffnungschores der Lukaspassion', Musica, xxix/1 (1975),
   9–15
Koncepcja, notacja, realizacja w twórczości Krzysztofa
   Pendereckiego (Kraków, 1975)
Muzyka, xxi/2 (1976) [Penderecki issue]
M. Schuler: 'Tonale Phänomene in Pendereckis Lukaspassion',
   Melos, ii/6 (1976), 457–60
T. Świercz: Technika chóralna w dziełach wokalno-intrumentalnych
   Krzysztofa Pendereckiego [Choral technique in Penderecki's vocal-
   instrumental works] (Gdańsk, 1976)
M. Komorowska: 'Penderecki w teatrze', Dialog, xxvi/11 (1979),
   131–41
B. Murray: 'Paradise Lost: a New Opera of Krzysztof Penderecki',
   Polish Music, no.1 (1979), 37–43
W. Schwinger: Krzysztof Penderecki: Begegnungen, Lebensdaten,
   Werkkommentare (Stuttgart, 1979, 2/1994); expanded Eng. trans.
   Krzysztof Penderecki: his Life and Work (London, 1989)
R. Chłopicka: 'Tradycja gatunkowa w Pasji wg św. Łukasza
   Krzysztofa Pendereckiego' [Generic tradition in Penderecki's St
   Luke Passion], Muzyka w muzyce, ed. L. Polony (Kraków, 1980),
   182–213
R. Chłopicka and K. Szwajgier, eds.: Współczesność i tradycja w
   muzyce Krzysztofa Pendereckiego [Modernity and tradition in
   Penderecki's music] (Kraków, 1983)
A. Ivashkin: Kristof Penderetski: monograficheskiy ocherk
   [Monograph] (Moscow, 1983)
R. Robinson and A. Winold: A Study of the Penderecki St Luke
   Passion (Celle, NJ, 1983)
J. Chomiński and K. Wilkowska-Chomińska: 'Synteza
   nowoczesności i tradycji' [Synthesis of modernity and tradition],
   Wielkie formy wokalne (Kraków, 1984), 458–86 [on the St Luke
   Passion]
J. Wnuk-Nazarowa: 'O Koncercie skrzypcowym Pendereckiego' [On
   Penderecki's Violin Concerto], Mieczysławowi Tomaszewskiemu
   w 60–lecie urodzin, ed. T. Malecka (Kraków, 1984), 76–99
I. Nikolska: 'O ewolucji twórczości instrumentalnej Krzysztofa
   Pendereckiego' [The evolution of Krzysztof Penderecki's
   intrumental writing], Muzyka, xxxii/1 (1987), 31–53
W. Schwinger: 'Dämonen, Engel und Gespenster: der
   Opernkomponist Krzysztof Penderecki', Oper Heute, x (1987),
   175–204
T. Meyer: 'Man kann nur einmal Avantgardist sein: Gespräche mit
   Krzysztof Penderecki', NZM, cl (1989), 17–22
R. Chłopicka: 'Czarna maska Krzysztofa Pendereckiego:
   ekspresjonistyczna wizja tańca śmierci [Penderecki's "Die
   schwarze Maske": an expressionistic vision of the dance of death],
   Krakowska szkoła kompozytorska 1888–1988, ed. T. Malecka
   (Kraków, 1992), 227–64
K. Szwajgier: '"De natura sonoris" no.1 i no.2 Krzysztofa
   Pendereckiego: studium porównawcze' [Penderecki's "De natura
   sonoris" nos.1 and 2: a comparative study], ibid., 215–26
M. Tomaszewski: 'Słowo i dźwięk u Krzysztofa Pendereckiego'
   [Word and sound in Penderecki] (Kraków, 1992), 305–33
P. Ćwikliński and J. Ziarno: Pasja o Krzysztofie Pendereckim
   (Warsaw, 1993)
R. Chłopicka: 'Problem dobra i zła w twórczości scenicznej
   Krzysztofa Pendereckiego' [The problem of good and evil in
   Penderecki's stage works], Muzyka, słowo, sens, ed. A. Oberc
   (Kraków,1994), 113–34
M. Tomaszewski: Krzysztof Penderecki i jego muzyka: cztery eseje
   [Penderecki and his music: four essays] (Kraków, 1994)
M. Tomaszewski, ed.: The Music of Krzysztof Penderecki: Poetics
   and Reception (Kraków, 1995)
B. Jacobson: A Polish Renaissance (London, 1996)
A. Behrendt: 'Der unterbrochene Gedanke? Krzysztof Pendereckis
   Klarinettquartett und seine Kammermusik nach 1980', Jeder nach
   seiner Fasson, ed. U. Liedtke (Saarbrücken, 1997)
D. Mirka: The Sonoristic Structuralism of Krzysztof Penderecki
   (Katowice, 1997)
Z. Baran, ed.: Krzysztof Penderecki Itinerarium: wystawa szkiców
   muzycznych [Exhibition of musical sketches] (Kraków, 1998)
R. Chłopicka: 'Styl i jego przemiany w muzyce Krzysztofa
   Pendereckiego' [Style and its transformations in Penderecki's
   music], Dysonanse, no.3 (1998), 12–19
R. Robinson and R. Chłopicka, eds.: Studies in Penderecki, i
   (Princeton, 1998)

ADRIAN THOMAS

Penet, Hilaire [Hylaire] (b diocese of Poitiers, ?1501).
French composer. A document of 1515 places him 'in his
15th year of age or thereabouts'. He appears in a rollbook
of the papal court from May 1514 as one of three
choirboys – all apparently sent to Rome by Louis XII of
France the previous year – in the charge of Carpentras.
He became a regular member of the papal chapel by 1516
and joined Leo X's private musicians in 1519. The
following year he left Rome on a paid leave of absence
from which he seems not to have returned. Manuscripts
and printed collections invariably refer to Penet by his full
name, no doubt to distinguish him from the older
composer who is identified simply as 'HILAIRE'.
   Penet's motet Descendit angelus Domini circulated
widely and served as a model for masses by Palestrina
and Costanzo Porta. Its lucid polyphony, moulded with a
judicious balance of full textures and voice pairing, makes
its popularity readily understandable. Clarity and smooth

craftsmanship also mark Penet's chansons – all settings of popular melodies – and his other sacred works.

WORKS

Magnificat, 4vv, 1534[7], 1543[19] (Esurientes); ed. A.T. Merritt, *Treize livres de motets parus chez Pierre Attaingnant en 1534 et 1535*, v (Monaco, 1960)
Magnificat, 4vv, *I-MOd* IV
Descendit angelus Domini, 4vv, 1532[10], and many other sources (see Crawford); ed. L. Pruett, *The Masses and Hymns of Costanzo Porta* (diss., U. of North Carolina, 1960); Virgo prudentissima, 5vv, 1534[5], 1543[3], Bc Q27/I; ed. A. Smijers, *Treize livres de motets parus chez Pierre Attaingnant en 1534 et 1535*, iii (Paris, 1936)
Au joly boys, 3vv, 1553[22], 1578[14]; Il fait bon aimer l'oysillon, 3vv, 1553[22], 1578[14]; Vray dieu d'amours, 4vv, 1557[15], 1559[9], 1575[5]

BIBLIOGRAPHY

F.X. Haberl: 'Die römische "Schola cantorum" und die päpstlichen Kapellsänger bis zur Mitte des 16. Jahrhunderts', *VMw*, iii (1887), 189–296; repr. as *Bausteine für Musikgeschichte*, iii (Leipzig, 1888/R)
H.-W. Frey: 'Michelagniolo und die Komponisten seiner Madrigale', *AcM*, xxiv (1952), 147–97
H.-W. Frey: 'Regesten zur päpstlichen Kapelle unter Leo X. und zu seiner Privatkapelle', *Mf*, viii (1955), 58, 178, 412; ix (1956), 46, 139
S.R. Charles: 'Hillary-Hyllayre: How Many Composers?', *ML*, lv (1974), 61–9
D. Crawford: *Sixteenth-Century Choirbooks in the Archivio Capitolare at Casale Monferrato*, RMS, ii (1975)

JOSHUA RIFKIN/R

Penherski, Zbigniew (*b* Warsaw, 26 Jan 1935). Polish composer. He studied composition with Stefan Poradowski in Poznań (1955–6) and with Szeligowski at the Warsaw Academy (1956–9). He has received a number of Polish composition prizes, and in 1969 was awarded a Dutch government scholarship.

Though he developed in the 1960s many of the compositional and notational techniques then prevalent in Polish music, he has maintained a certain distance from their associated expressiveness. In much of his music there is a deft economy of means and an emotional reticence (even when dealing with subject matter as visceral and lurid as that contained in his opera *Zmierzch Peryna*, 'The Twilight of Peryn') which serves to objectify the musical experience. Much of this comes from his adherence to counterpoint, numerical patterning and closed musical forms. His music may be delicate as well as intense, as in *Musica humana* (1963), a tribute to his father, who was shot dead in 1939. Many of his later works possess a meditative quality owing to their harmonic continuums and driving percussion, though *Sygnały II* ('Signals II') is more openly expressive.

WORKS
(selective list)

Op: Dziewczęta zza muru [Girls from Behind the Wall] (1, L.E. Stefański), 1961, withdrawn; Mały książę [The Little Prince] (1, Penherski, after A. de Saint-Exupéry], 1962, withdrawn; Sąd nad Samsonem [The Judgement of Samson] (radio op, J. Prutkowski and Penherski), 1968, Warsaw, 23 Sep 1969; Zmierzch Peryna [The Twilight of Peryn] (3, K. Meissner after J.I. Kraszewski), 1971–2, Poznań, 6 Oct 1974; Edgar, syn Walpora [Edgar, Son of Walpor] (3, Penherski, after S.I. Witkiewicz], 1982; Wyspa róż [Rose Island] (Meissner, after S. Mrożek), 1989
Vocal: Ostinata (old Arabic), chorus, orch, 1960; Obrazki chóralne [Choral Pictures] (K. Iłłakowicz), chorus, 1960; 3 pieśni cygańskie [3 Gypsy Songs] (J. Ficowski), female chorus, 1961; 3 pieśni [3 Songs] (old Pol. texts), chorus, 1961; Kontrasty, vv, orch, 1962; 3 recitativi (R. Tagore), S, pf, perc, 1963; Musica humana (Bible), Bar, chorus, orch, 1963; Missa abstracta, T, spkr, chorus, orch (Bible, T. Różewicz), 1966; Cantatina, chorus, children's orch, 1969, withdrawn; Hymnus laudans (medieval hymn), chorus, chbr

orch, 1970; 3 impresje (Tagore), S, pf, perc, 1985; Cantus, chorus, 1992
Orch: Kroniki mazurskie I [Mazurian Chronicles I], orch, tape, 1965; Kroniki mazurskie II, orch, tape, 1973; Anamnesis, 1975; String Play, str, 1980; Kroniki szkockie [Scottish Chronicles], 1987; Sygnały I [Signals I], 1992; Sygnały II, 1995
Other: Muzyka uliczna [Street Music], cl, tpt, perc, accdn, 2 pf 8 hands, 1966; 3M-H1, tape piece, 1969; Kwartet instrumentalny, 4 opt. insts, 4 metronomes, tape, 1970; Incantationi I, 6 perc, 1972; Symfonia radiowa, tape piece 2 pfmrs, 1975; Incantationi II, 7 pfmrs, 1976; Jeux partis, sax, perc, 1984; Introdukcja, cl, trbn, vc, pf, 1994; Genesis, B, vv, ens, tape
Music for children, film and radio scores, incid music
Principal publisher: PWM, Agencja Autorska

BIBLIOGRAPHY

GroveO (A. Thomas)
T. Marek: 'A New Polish Opera: The First Day of History', *Polish Music*, no.2 (1973), 28–31
Z. Penherski: 'Radio Symphony for Two Performers', *Polish Music*, no.3 (1978), 27–31

ADRIAN THOMAS

Penigk [Pönick, Poenicke], **Johann Peter** (bap. Untermassfeld, nr Meiningen, 6 July 1666; *d* after 1719). German organ builder. Together with Johann Gottlieb Döltzsche, Johann Ernst Hähnel, David Haussdörffer and Christoph Thielemann, Penigk belongs to a significant group of central German organ builders of the 18th century of whom a careful historical assessment has yet to be made. He was working in Hof around 1691. On 20 December 1700 he obtained the citizenship of Zwickau, where he married in 1701 and later purchased his father-in-law's house. The construction of the Glauchau organ (St Georg, 1701–3; burnt in 1712) was negotiated by the Kantor, Johann Christian Friedel, and by the organist, Johann Gottlob Meischner, also noted as a lawyer and composer. In 1714 Penigk tested the new Gruber organ in Schwarzenbach. He built at least ten organs in Saxony, Thuringia and Bavaria with characterful dispositions. The organ at Kürbitz (1720) possessed a colourful specification; its very beautiful façade survives.

BIBLIOGRAPHY

F. Oehme: *Handbuch über ältere und neuere Orgelwerke im Königreiche Sachsen*, iii (Dresden, 1897)
W. Hüttel: *Musikgeschichte von Glauchau und Umgebung* (Glauchau, 1995), 105, 227, 230 only

WALTER HÜTTEL

Penillion. A Welsh form of improvised song with harp accompaniment, also known as 'canu penillion'. *See* WALES, §II, 3(i).

Penn, William (Albert) (*b* Long Branch, NJ, 11 Jan 1943). American composer. He studied with Pousseur and Kagel at SUNY, Buffalo (BFA 1964, MA 1967), and received the PhD from Michigan State University, East Lansing (1971). At the Eastman School, where he was a faculty member from 1971 to 1978, he pursued further studies in composition with Wayne Barlow. He was staff composer for the New York Shakespeare Festival (1974–6) and from 1975 was associated with the Folger Shakespeare Theatre and Sounds Reasonable Records in Washington DC. He went on to serve as visiting professor at various institutions including the universities of Texas, Connecticut, Arizona and South Carolina. He has received awards from ASCAP and the NEA (1974–6), and has been nominated for a Grammy Award. His output covers a wide range of genres including jazz and mixed media. Penn's intensely dramatic music draws on a general poetic inspiration to which melody, harmony, texture and instrumentation all correspond. His style connects lyric, theatrical, experimental and popular musical ideas. He has also explored experimental sound sources. His compositional interests include music for the theatre, film, television and radio.

WORKS

Dramatic: At Last Olympus! (musical), 1969; The Boy who Cried 'Wolf' is Dead (musical), 1971; The Pied Piper of Hamelin (musical), 1971; The Canticle (musical), 1972; Confessions of a Serial Killer (film score), 1987; incid music, mixed media works

Inst: Str Qt, 1968; Spectrums, Confusions and Sometime: Moments beyond the Order of Destiny, orch, 1969; Chbr Music no.1, vn, pf, 1971; Sym., 1971; Ultra mensuram, 3 brass qnts, 1971; And Among the Leaves we were Passing, synth, 1972; Chbr Music no.2, vc, pf, 1972; Designs, wind, jazz qnt, perc, 1972; Inner Loop, band, 1973; Niagara 1678, band, 1973; Night Music, fl choir, 1973; Mr Toad's Wild Adventure, orch, 1993; Sax Conc., 1994; The Revelations of St John the Divine, wind ens, 1995; other inst works

Vocal: Miroirs sur le Rubaiyat, pf, nar, 1974; A Cornfield in July and The River, medium v, 25 pfmrs, 1990; songs

Principal publishers: C.F. Peters, Theodore Presser, Seesaw

DAVID COPE

Penna, Lorenzo (*b* Bologna, 1613; *d* Bologna, 31 Oct 1693). Italian composer and theorist. There have in the past been doubts about Penna's date of birth, but it is confirmed by secondary sources. Nothing is known of his life before he entered the Carmelite monastery of S Martino in Bologna on 18 March 1630. After a year's novitiate he took vows, and until 1642 devoted himself almost exclusively to the religious life in S Martino, where he was a master of novices from 1639. He was probably permitted to pursue his musical studies in Bologna or elsewhere from 1642 to 1656. In 1656 he took up the post of *maestro di cappella* at S Ilario, Casale Monferrato. He must have begun theological studies at Ferrara University about 1660, since he was awarded his doctorate of theology on 23 June 1665. Some two years later he became *maestro di cappella* at the cathedral of S Cassiano at Imola, whose chapter archives reveal that he served a probationary year before being confirmed in the appointment. He resigned in 1669, by which time he was a member of the Accademia dei Risoluti and the Accademia dei Filaschisi in Bologna.

After leaving Imola Penna entered the Carmelite monastery at Mantua, where he remained until 1672, possibly performing duties of a musical nature. In 1672 and 1673 he was *maestro di cappella* at the church of the Carmine at Parma. He then probably returned to Bologna, where in 1676 he became a member of the Accademia Filarmonica. The events of his remaining years can again only be conjectured. Since most of his published works appeared in Bologna from 1677 onwards it may be assumed that he remained there until his death, the date of which can again be deduced only from secondary sources, of which the *Liber religiosorum mortuorum* of S Martino is the most reliable.

Penna's musical output consists almost entirely of church music in a style that is basically that of Palestrina as modified by his successors. The single exception is the volume of *Correnti francesi*, which in texture is similar to contemporary chamber sonatas. His *Primi albori musicali*, a theoretical work of some importance, was used very widely; its three volumes deal respectively with the rudiments of music, counterpoint and continuo playing.

WORKS

Messe e salmi concertati, 5vv, 2 vn ad lib, bc, op.1 (Milan, 1656)
Psalmorum totius anni modulatio, una cum missa, et falsis bordon, 4/5vv, op.3 (Milan, 1669)
Correnti francesi 2 vn, violetta, vle, bc (hpd) (Bologna, 1673)
Il sacro parnaso delli salmi, 4, 8vv, op.8 (Bologna, 1677)
Reggia del sacro parnaso ... ordinate in messe piene e brevi, 4, 8vv, op.9 (Bologna, 1677)
Galeria del sacro parnaso ornata con adornamenti di messe piene, e brevi, 4, 8vv, insts, op.10 (Bologna, 1678)
Messa ... a capella, 4–5vv (Bologna, 1679), lost

WRITINGS

Li primi albori musicali per li principianti della musica figurata (Bologna, 1672, 4/1684/R, 5/1696)
Direttorio del canto fermo (Modena, 1689)
Les éléments du contrepoint (MS, 1690, F-Pc) [excerpt from vol.ii of *Li primi albori musicali*]

BIBLIOGRAPHY

G. Schünemann: *Geschichte des Dirigierens* (Leipzig, 1913/R), 131ff
F.T. Arnold: *The Art of Accompaniment from a Thorough-Bass* (London, 1931/R), 133
K.H. Holler: *Giovanni Maria Bononcini's Musico prattico in seiner Bedeutung für die musikalische Satzlehre des 17. Jahrhunderts* (Strasbourg, 1963), 36–7, 76, 85, 87ff, 101
J.-H. Lederer: *Lorenzo Penna und seine Kontrapunkttheorie* (diss., U. of Graz, 1970)
J.-H. Lederer: 'Zur Lebensgeschichte Lorenzo Pennas: eine biographische bibliographische Studie', *KJb*, lv (1971), 25–31
J.-H. Lederer: 'Zur Kontrapunkttheorie Lorenzo Pennas', *SMw*, xxviii (1977), 105–14
E. Apfel: *Geschichte der Kompositionslehre*, i (Wilhelmshaven, 1981)

JOSEF-HORST LEDERER

Pennard (*fl c*1400). English composer. His only known work is a four-part setting of the Credo, ascribed to him in the Old Hall Manuscript (ed. in CMM, xlvi, 1969–73; no.89) and recurring anonymously elsewhere. The tenor (*Te iure laudant*, a Trinity antiphon) is disposed in 20 loosely isorhythmic sections. The text alternates between the upper parts for each section, the residual melismatic portions themselves forming a roughly isorhythmic pattern. A solus tenor part is provided. Bukofzer suggested a pairing with the first Gloria in *GB-Lbl* Add.40011B, and put forward Pennard as its possible composer. It is based on another Trinity antiphon, *Tibi laus*, and the alternating melismas of the top part create a similar isorhythmic pattern, though the tenor isorhythm is unlike the Credo, having a second statement in diminution. (M.F. Bukofzer: *Studies in Medieval and Renaissance Musik*, New York, 1950, p.107)

For bibliography see OLD HALL MANUSCRIPT.

MARGARET BENT

Pennario, Leonard (*b* Buffalo, NY, 9 July 1924). American pianist. His earliest teachers included the pianists Isabelle Vengerova and Olga Steeb, and the composer Ernst Toch. At the age of 12 he made his début, playing Grieg's Concerto with the Dallas SO. His New York début came seven years later, in Liszt's E♭ Concerto with the New York PO under Rodzinski in Carnegie Hall. In 1952 he gave his first European performances, including his London début, and then toured extensively, winning praise for the power and brilliance of his playing. As a chamber musician he has worked and recorded with Heifetz and Piatigorsky, among others. He gave the first performance of Miklós Rózsa's Piano Concerto (1966), composed for him, with the Los Angeles PO under Mehta. In the 1970s he expanded his repertory to include popular works, notably music by Gottschalk and Gershwin.

BIBLIOGRAPHY
'It is the Ultimate Reward', *Piano Quarterly*, no.82 (1973), 3–7
[interview]

GEORGE GELLES/BETH E. LEVY

Pennauer, Anton (*b c*1784; *d* Vienna, 20 Oct 1837). Austrian music publisher. His father Kaspar, a musician, advertised his services as a copyist in the *Wiener Zeitung* between 1786 and 1799. In 1821 Anton Pennauer made an application ('as a music teacher') to open a music shop which was at first refused several times; on 20 February he was granted permission to open 'a music shop in a suburban community', but nevertheless began his activities as a music publisher in the Viennese suburb of Leopoldstadt on 20 May 1822. A long struggle with the authorities resulted finally, on 1 March 1825, in permission for an art and music shop, which Pennauer opened in the city on 5 July 1825. The publishing house was already in difficulty at the end of 1830; in 1834 it was declared bankrupt and its stock was transferred to Anton Diabelli. Pennauer died completely impoverished. As a publisher he was extremely ambitious: he brought out works by Georg Hellmesberger (i), Henri Herz, Franz and Ignaz Lachner, Mayseder, Randhartinger and Voříšek, as well as 17 compositions by Schubert, including important piano works and lieder. His publications were notable for their excellent graphical production.

BIBLIOGRAPHY
DeutschMPN
A. Weinmann: *Verzeichnis der Musikalien des Verlages Anton Pennauer* (Vienna, 1981)

ALEXANDER WEINMANN

Penne, Antoine de (*b* nr Valenciennes, end of 16th century; *d* after 1616). Flemish composer. He began his career as a boy singer at Cambrai Cathedral, later rising to the position of *maître de chapelle* there. Only sacred works by him remain, and in these he is said to have been influenced by Eustache du Caurroy. Penne could certainly have known Du Caurroy, as the latter was a prizewinner in 1576 and 1583 in the composition contests held during the Cecilian festival at Évreux. Most of his few known works, written for two and three choruses, are incomplete; only parts for the first chorus remain. All Penne's surviving works are in the Médiathèque Municipale at Cambrai. One manuscript (*F-CA* 15) contains the first (four-part) chorus of a 12-part mass dated 1612 and the first four-part chorus of another; two other manuscripts contain the first (five-part) chorus of a Credo dated 1615 (*F-CA* 16) and a six-part motet, *Anima*, dated 1615 (*F-CA* 7939). Coussemaker attributed to Penne two further masses, one for two voices and one for four; these are now lost.

BIBLIOGRAPHY
C.-E.-H. de Coussemaker: *Notice sur les collections musicales de la Bibliothèque de Cambrai* (Paris, 1843/R)
D. Launay: 'Les motets à double chœur en France dans la première moitié du XVIIe siècle', *RdM*, xxxix–xl (1957), 173–95

LAVERN J. WAGNER

Pennequin, Jean (*fl* Arras, *c*1577–85). French composer. In 1577, when his five-voice chanson *Dieu vous gard messagers fidelles du printemps* (published in his 1583 volume) won the silver lyre prize in the St Cecilia competition at Evreux, 'Jehan Pennequin' was described as 'maître des enfants de chœur' at Arras Cathedral. Six years later the title-page of his *Chansons nouvelles à quatre et cincq parties et une à huict* (Douai, 1583)

referred to him as canon in the same church. The collection contains 31 settings of texts of a serious, moral, philosophical and religious character. A six-voice motet by Pennequin, *Quem vidistis, pastores*, published at Nuremberg (RISM 1585[1]), illustrates his command of the imitative genre.

BIBLIOGRAPHY
T. Bonnin and A.Chassant: *Puy de musique érigé à Evreux, en l'honneur de Madame Sainte Cécile* (Evreux, 1837)
W. Rubsamen: 'The International "Catholic" Repertoire of a Lutheran Church in Nürnberg (1574–1597)', *AnnM*, v (1957), 229–327

FRANK DOBBINS

Pennetier, Jean-Claude (*b* Châtellerault, 16 May 1942). French pianist. He studied at the Paris Conservatoire, where he received *premiers prix* in piano (in the class of Lucette Descaves), chamber music and analysis. He won second prize in the 1961 Marguerite Long-Jacques Thibaud Competition, first prize in the 1965 Montreal Competition and second prize in the 1968 Geneva Competition. He is an active champion of new French music and has given the first performances of works by Philippe Hersant, Michel Merlet and Maurice Ohana; he has also performed with leading contemporary music ensembles, including Domaine Musical and Ars Nova. Among his recordings are sensitive, poised accounts of Schumann's Fantasy op.17 and several of Schubert's sonatas, as well as music for piano and strings by Chausson, Brahms and Schubert (with Régis and Bruno Pasquier and Roland Pidoux). Pennetier taught chamber music at the Paris Conservatoire from 1985 to 1992, in which year he was appointed to the piano faculty at the Conservatoire National de Région de Paris.

CHARLES TIMBRELL

Pennisi, Francesco (*b* Acireale, 11 Feb 1934). Italian composer. He was born into a cultured Sicilian family, whose independent resources permitted him to develop his singular gifts in both the visual arts and music without the constraints imposed by a search for early recognition. In 1953 he moved to Rome, to study within the university faculty of arts (1954–5), and to pursue private composition lessons with Robert W. Mann (1954–9). Thereafter he taught himself, maintaining an oblique but canny view over the wilder reaches of the avant garde. In 1960 he became one of the founder-members (along with Evangelisti, Clementi and others) of the Roman new music association Nuova Consonanza. Another major source of new discoveries was the annual Palermo International New Music Week, founded in 1960, the third edition of which included the first public performance of his music (*L'anima e i prestigi* of 1962).

For much of the 1960s, Pennisi lived out – if more as an ironic onlooker than as an intensely committed practitioner – the compositional dilemmas of the day. In particular, he found himself uncomfortably fascinated by the interplay between compositional determinism and chance, and by the question of how to sustain productivity when the avant garde's most exciting aesthetic achievements seemed to have come and gone. While not following Evangelisti into a studied silence, he registered the 'posthumous' nature that seemed to afflict new music at the time by such titles as *Fossile* (1966) and *Mould* (1968) – a minimal play with the crumbs left after the feast (an image from Leonardo da Vinci that Pennisi used to preface another work of 1968, *Choralis cum figuris*). One mode of rescue from such self-imposed frugality was offered by his other major talent – penmanship. His first piece of musical theatre, *Silvia simplex (Ornitoscopia)* (1971–2), offered a profusely illustrated lecture on birds, alive with colour and intricate detail, while soprano and chamber ensemble provided a calculatedly modest background.

In retrospect, Pennisi cheerfully acknowledged that he was evading, however stylishly, the problem of composition. His way out of the *impasse* was one shared by several contemporaries (notably Donatoni): that of reaffirming the pleasure of musical play. His characteristically elegant chamber works of the mid-1970s, a number of them gathered together to form the cycle *Carteggio*, show a crisp concision, and a delight in ornament much seized on – somewhat to the composer's dismay – in discussions of his music. In effect, he is more interested in a form of melodic elaboration in which it is impossible to determine what is 'ornament', and what 'ground'. *Carteggio* also confirmed Pennisi's enduring delight in plucked, evanescent sound, as manifested by his frequent use of the harpsichord, and later guitar and harp.

But more crucially, this relish for the delicacies of timbre came to the fore in the series of works for orchestra with or without soloist, that were a distinctive component of Pennisi's output from the late 1970s on. His exploration of unexpected instrumental affinities, and of the endless variety of chamber groupings that could momentarily emerge, was often set in perspective by an unmoving, intricate magma from the orchestral tutti (an implicit homage, this last, to the work of his friend and fellow Sicilian, Clementi). Those works that set one or more soloists against the orchestra characteristically feature solo instruments – flute and harp are favoured choices – the fragility of which might seem to risk engulfment by their more massive sound environment, but which survive undaunted.

Pennisi's idiosyncratic musical theatre found further outlet in his *Descrizone dell'Isola Fernandea* (1982), based on a contemporary account of one of the stranger episodes in Sicilian history. In 1831 a volcanic island emerged in a much-used shipping lane off the southern coast of Sicily. While powers and principalities debated ownership of this 'new territory', eventually named after the King of the Two Sicilies in a pre-emptive strike, the island disobligingly resubmerged. On stage, the Neapolitan bureaucrat Signor Marzolla reads his account. Signor Wright, an English explorer who had contributed some pleasing sketches to the original publication, instead sings an aria of amazement, while the tutor to the royal household seizes the chance to draw out a symbol of worldly vanity. A fortune-teller reads the cards, and the 'allegory of the island' evokes wider and more phantastic interpretations of the singular event. Needless to say, it is not Signor Wright's sketches that form the backdrop, but those, splendidly evocative, by Pennisi himself.

In the decade that followed, Pennisi's instrumental output continued unabated – testimony to the resiliently inventive energy unleashed by resolving the 'dark night' of the late 1960s and 70s. But he also permitted himself a more exuberant and lyrical use of the voice, notably in his radio opera *Aci il fiume* (1986) and in a number of subsequent works such as the cantata *O lux beatissima* (1994). His inventive forays into musical theatre expanded to admit collaboration. Where previously he had put together words, music and design in a creative equipoise,

in *L'esequie della luna* (1991) the dramaturgical structure was provided by Roberto Andò, working from a brief prose work by the Sicilian poet Lucio Piccolo, and the stage was articulated by the scenic sculptures of Enzo Cucchi. Perhaps it was this freedom from multiple responsibility that allowed Pennisi to produce his richest theatrical score yet. All proliferates from the startling conceit of the moon falling from the sky. Around it, amidst popular mourning and official indifference, there starts up a nocturnal echo-chamber in which the intricate, multi-layered history of Sicilian culture resists time's invitation to lie quiet.

WORKS

DRAMATIC

Sylvia simplex [Ornitoscopia] (Pennisi), 1971–2, Venice Festival, 10 Sept 1972

Descrizione dell'Isola Ferdinandea (1, chbr op, Pennisi), 1982, Rome, Olimpico, 19 Oct 1983

Aci il fiume (radio op, Ovid, de Góngora), 1986

L'esequie della luna (music theatre, R. Ando, after L. Piccolo), 1991, Gibellina, Case di Lorenzo, 23 July 1991

Tristan (E. Pound), 1995, Venice, Goldoni, 1995

ORCHESTRAL

Alternazione, 1960–61; La lune offensée, 1971–2; Fantasia, vc, orch, 1977; Andante sostenutu, 1977; Gläserner Tag, 1978; La partenza di Tisias, va, orch, 1979; Memorie e varianti, 1980; Arioso mobile, fl, orch, 1981; Per Agamennone, 1983; L'arrivo dell'unicorno, hp, orch, 1984–5; Postilla per Aldo Clementi, hp, orch, 1985; Eclisse a Fleri, a fl, + b fl, orch, 1985; Duetto e orizzonte, fl, gui, orch, 1987 [from music theatre work L'esequie della luna, 1991]; Intonazione per foresta ariostea, tpt, orch, 1989; Angelica in bosco, hp, orch, 1990; Una cartolina da Selim (omaggio a Mozart), 1991; Scena, fl, orch, 1997

VOCAL

Vocal-orch: A Cant. on Melancholy (R. Burton), S, orch, 1967; La vigne di Samaria (Bible: *Prophets*), chorus, orch, 1974; Era la notte (T. Tasso), S, hpd, orch, 1982; O lux beatissima, cant., S, S, chbr orch, 1994

Solo vocal: L'anima e i prestigi (L. Piccolo), Mez, 3 trbn, vib, perc, 1962; Invenzione seconda (E. Montale), S, fl, sax, trbn, hp, 3 perc, db, 1963; Fossile (after T.S. Eliot), Bar, fl, cl, b cl, hn, hpd, cel, va, 2 perc, 1966; Serena (N. d'Agostino), S, fl, prep pf, db, 1973; Chanson de blois (C. d'Orléans, F. Villon), S, gui, pf, 1977 [incl. in Trittico di blois]; The Garden (A. Marvell), S, hpd/pf, 1983; I mandolini e le chitarre (L. Piccolo), S, a fl, hp, pf, 1986; L'inganno della rete (Piccolo), S, fl, gui, hp, 1988; Petite chanson de blois (C. d'Orléans, F. Villon), S, gui, pf, 1988 [incl. in Trittico di blois]; Al precario sentiero (Pennisi), S, gui, 1990; Purpureas rosas (de Góngora), 2 S, Bar, cl qt, 1990; 6 versi del Foscolo da Saffo, S, str qt, 1991; Silva resonat (Virgil), B, cl, pf, 1991; 2 notturni (U. Foscolo da Saffo), S, gui, str, 1992; The Wild Swans (W.B. Yeats), S, cl, hn, bn, pf, str trio, 1992; Medea dixit (Ovid), S, fl, b cl, hn, pf, str trio, 1993; Altro effetto di luna (Montale), S, fl, vc, hp, pf, 1996

CHAMBER

3 or more insts: Invenzione, 3 cl, cel, cymbals, 1961; Invenzione, 3 cl, cel, 1963, unpubd; Qnt in 4 parts, fl, tpt, trbn, pf + hmn, perc, 1965; Palermo, aprile, 18 insts, 1965–6; Trio, fl, hn, db, 1966; Choralis cum figuris, fl, ob, cl, bn, perc, vn, db, 1968; Mould, hpd, pf, cel, hmn, 3 perc, 1968; A tempo comodo, metronome, insts (2–4 players), 1970; Carteggio, fl, vc, hpd (in various combinations), 1974–6 [cycle]; Lipsia, fl, vc, hpd, 1975 [incl. in Carteggio]; Scritto in margine, 2 vn, va, 1975; Hortus fragilis, 2 pf, fl, ob, cl, bn, hn, gui, 1976; Nuit sans étoiles, 2 vn, va, hpd, 1977–8; Notturnino, 3 gui, 1978; Movimento, wind qnt, 1980; 2 canzoni natalizie etnee, fl, cl, b cl, hn, hp, perc, vn, va, vc, db, 1982–3; Per Elettra, fl, ob, cl, bn, hn, perc, 1984; Alba, 4 gui, 1987; 3 pezzi, cl, va, pf, 1987–90; Méliès, fl, va, pf, 1987–90; Icaro a Capodimonte, gui, str qt, 1995; Se appare il dubbio, fl, cl, vc, pf, perc, 1996; Etude-rhapsodie, fl, cl, pf, 1997

2 insts: Note e paragrafi sull'op.15, (hp, hpd)/2 hpd, 1971; Lettera a Charles Ives, fl, hpd, 1974 [incl. in Carteggio]; Sopra la lontananza, vc, hpd, 1976 [incl. in Carteggio]; Acanthis, fl, pf,

1981; Sesto trio, a fl, pf, 1981; Introduzione al Grecale, fl, hp, 1984; La muse endormie, va, prep pf, 1981, version for vc, 1985; Dal manoscritto Sloan, hpd, hp, 1988, version for pf, gui [incl. in Trittico di blois]; Piccolo campionariod'echi della Valrameau, 2 hpd, 1991; Duettino augurale nel segno della Bilancia, fl, vn, 1992; Duettino augurale nel segno della Bilancia, fl, vn, 1993; Preludietto e coda sul nome Goffredo, fl, pf, 1994; Echi per Aldo, 2 pf, 1995

Solo inst: Musica, pf, 1960; Afterthoughts, pf, 1962; 2 studi, hpd, 1963, unpubd; Commento a Euro, fl + a fl, 1975 [incl. in Carteggio]; Bien loin d'ici, db, 1976; Paysage avec la lune, hpd, 1976 [incl. in Carteggio]; Voce, vc, 1977 [incl. in Carteggio]; Madame Récamier, hp, 1978; Intermezzo, gui, 1979; Promenade, prep pf, 1980; Oh Lilibeo!, a fl, 1982; 2 piccole rapsodie, hp, 1982–3; In un foglio, pf, 1983; Piccolo labirinto, gui, 1989

Principal publishers: BMG Ariola, Edipan, Ricordi, Suvini Zerboni

WRITINGS

'Wagner ad Acireale', La Sicilia (1966), Sept, 28
'Pianoforte contemporaneo a Brescia e Bergamo', Spettatore musicale, iv/May (Bologna, 1969), 5 only
'Su Questo di Franco Donatoni', Spettatore musicale, v/Dec (1970), 16 only
'Frammento di conversazione fra XY e Francesco Pennisi', Autobiografia della musica contemporanea, ed. M. Mollia (Rome, 1979)
Deragliamento (Rome, 1984)
'Trans, neo, proto, post ... ', La Musica, no.1 (1985)
'Divagazioni sull'inchiostro di china', La Musica, no.3 (1985)
'Una questione di iconologia', La Musica, no.19 (1988)
'Su alcune composizioni con la voce', La vocalità nella musica italiana contemporanea: Rome 1988
'Minima memoralia', Nuova Consonanza: trent'anni di musica contemporanea in Italia, ed. D. Tortora (Lucca, 1990)
'Postfazione a tre partiture', Labirinti, no.3 (1990)
Programme notes: Francesco Pennisi, ed. G. Seminara (Palermo, 1992), 84–98

BIBLIOGRAPHY

Grove6 (C. Annibaldi); GroveO (D. Osmond-Smith)
P.E. Carapezza: 'Letture: Francesco Pennisi, Hymn (per orchestra), Roma 1963', Collage, no.5 (1965), 99 only
N. d'Agostino and F. Pennisi: 'Per Sylvia (stralcio di conversazione)', Spettatore musicale, vii/5 (1972), 18; corrigenda in vii/6 (1972), 32
S.E. Failla: 'Pennisi', Cronache musicali, no.25 (1982)
S.E. Failla: 'Miniature e labirinti', Aquario, iii/5 (1984)
S.E. Failla: 'Siciliani antichi e moderni', Cronache musicali, no.32 (1984)
T. Geraci: 'Rapsodie e tarocchi', Cronache musicali, no.33 (1985)
R. Zanetti: La musica italiana del Novecento (Busto Arsizio, 1985)
S. Ragni: 'La "Descrizione dell'Isola Ferdinandea" di Francesco Pennisi: un frammento musicale di storia siciliana', Annali dell'Università per Stranieri di Perugia (1990)
D. Tortora: Nuova Consonanza: trent'anni di musica contemporanea (Lucca, 1990)
R. Andò: 'Il poetà barocco e gli dei della città', Orestiadi di Gibellina: musica (Milan, 1991) [festival booklet]
P. Petazzi: '"Orestiadi" di Gibellina', Sonus, iii/2 (1991), 20–23
G. Seminara, ed.: Francesco Pennisi (Palermo, 1992)
G. Seminara, ed.: Omaggio a Francesco Pennisi (Milan, 1994)

DAVID OSMOND-SMITH

Pennsylvania, University of. University in Philadelphia. It appointed its first professor of music in 1875; its music department awards graduate and postgraduate music degrees. See PHILADELPHIA, §6.

Pennywhistle [tin whistle] (Fr. flageolet, flûteau d'un sou, flûte en fers blanc; Ger. Blechflöte; Sp. flauta metálica; Flem. blikken fluit, fluitje van een cent). A popular form of DUCT FLUTE. It was invented by Robert Clarke (1816–82), a farm labourer who lived in Coney Weston, Suffolk. He was a talented performer on a small wooden six-holed duct flute, possibly a FLAGEOLET. He copied this instrument with help from the local blacksmith using the newly available tinplate. After a dispute with the farmer over his wages, he started to make tin whistles for sale in 1843; he later moved to Manchester, walking there with his materials in a barrow. He started manufacture in a hut but when he became successful he purchased a larger property in nearby New Moston. Shortly thereafter he was exporting all over the world, particularly to Ireland where his tin whistles became the most popular and easily available instrument for traditional music.

Clarke's first tin whistle was called the 'Meg' ('meg' being the Lancashire name for a halfpenny, the price for which he sold them). The Meg had six finger-holes in front and a wooden block crimped into the mouthpiece. Later he produced, by the same method, a larger instrument in the key of C, which became universally known as the Pennywhistle. The origin of the name is uncertain. Clarke's price was threepence a dozen wholesale. It is said that they were so called because street musicians played them for pennies. Clarke tin whistles were made in other keys but these were only available until just after the turn of the century. The business remained in the family until 1986, when it was purchased by Jim Weedon. He later produced a pennywhistle in the key of D, together with a new version named the 'Sweetone', which has a plastic mouthpiece.

See also TIN WHISTLE.

BIBLIOGRAPHY

D. Thompson and L. Thompson: 'Folk Musical Instruments at the Kutztown Folk Festival', Pennsylvania Folklife, xxxi (1982), 158–61
Na Feadánaigh: the Whistle Players (Glyndon, MN, 1984–5) [pubn of the Penny Whistle Society]
P. Varlet: 'Le flageolet ou tin whistle', Tradition vivante, xi (1987), 223–30
N. Dannatt: The Pennywhistle: the Story of Robert Clarke and his Famous Tinwhistle 1843–1993 (Tonbridge, 1993)

NORMAN DANNATT

Penorcon. The name given by Praetorius (2/1619) to a nine-course bass ORPHARION tuned $G'–A'–C–D–G–c–e–a–d'$. His illustration (see BANDORA, fig.2) confirms his description:

The Penorcon is an instrument of almost the same kind, only its body is a little broader than that of the Bandora, and its neck or fingerboard is quite wide, so that nine courses of strings can pass over it. In length it is somewhat less than the Bandora and greater than an Orpharion.

Praetorius is the only source for the name 'penorcon', but there is some incomplete music 'for 3 Orph' and 'for iii Wiers' [i.e three viols] in the Cambridge consort books (GB-Cu Dd.3.18 f.55–6 [orpharion parts], Dd.5.20 f.10^v and Dd.5.21 f.11 [viol parts]) that seem to require a bass orpharion, possibly a Penorcon, pitched $B\flat'–C–F–B\flat–d–g–c'$.

BIBLIOGRAPHY

PraetoriusSM, ii
D. Gill: 'An Orpharion by John Rose', LSJ, ii (1960), 33–40
D. Gill: 'The Orpharion and Bandora', GSJ, xiii (1960), 14–25
L. Nordstrom: 'The Cambridge Consort Books', JLSA, v (1976), 70–103

IAN HARWOOD/LYLE NORDSTROM

Penson, Robertson & Co. [Penson & Robertson; later Alexander Robertson & Co.]. Scottish music publishers, founded in Edinburgh about 1807 by William Penson and Alexander Robertson. Penson (b c1776; d Edinburgh, after 1828) was a music teacher in Edinburgh in 1809, and from 1810 to 1816 leader of the orchestra at the Theatre Royal; in 1819 he became the first secretary of the Professional Society of Musicians. Robertson (d Edinburgh, 22 Sept 1819) was a music engraver at the

Luckenbooths, Edinburgh, in 1800 and a music teacher in Libberton's Wynd in 1808.

By 1811 Penson, Robertson & Co., having started in business as music sellers, had a publishing house in Princes Street. From 1818 they also ran a music academy at Robertson's house. After Robertson's death the firm was reorganized. Penson left it to concentrate on private teaching, which he continued until his death or retirement in 1829. In 1822 Robertson's two sons, Alexander and John, took over the business, which became Alexander Robertson & Co. In 1837 John Steuart Grubb (1811–67) acquired the firm.

Among quantities of ephemeral sheet music (much of which they themselves arranged), the firm published William Marshall's outstanding *Scottish Airs* in 1822 and his posthumous second collection in 1845; jointly with ROBERT PURDIE, they reissued the publications of Nathaniel GOW after the latter's bankruptcy in 1827. (*KidsonBMP*, 190–93)

H.G. FARMER/DAVID JOHNSON

Pentagramma (It.). Five-line STAFF.

Pentangle, the. British folk fusion band. BERT JANSCH and JOHN RENBOURNE, two of Britain's leading acoustic guitarists with established solo careers, led the band, which also included singer Jacqui McShee, bass player Danny Thompson and drummer Terry Cox. *Pentangle* (Transatlantic, 1968), their first album, was a light, sophisticated blend of folk, blues, classical and jazz musics. It was followed later the same year by the double-album *Sweet Child* (Transatlantic) and then by a subtle folk crossover album, *Basket of Light* (Transatlantic, 1969), which remained in the British top 10 chart for four weeks. Its success was helped by the track 'Light Flight', a technically complicated song with a time signature that switched from 5/8 and 7/8 to 6/4, used as the theme music to a BBC television drama series.

The Pentangle took folk-blues and traditional songs out of the folk club scene and on to the international concert circuit but were criticized for being easy-on-the-ear. They attempted to enliven their style in 1970 by introducing electric guitars on the *Cruel Sister* album (Transatlantic), while *Solomon's Seal* (Rep., 1972) featured fuzz guitar on the folk club standard 'Sally Free and Easy'. They had, however, lost their momentum and split up soon after its release. The band re-formed briefly in the early 1980s, and McShee was re-united with Jansch in 1989 for the Pentangle album *So Early in the Spring* (Plane), although they were the only members of the original band involved.

ROBIN DENSELOW

Pentatonic. A term applied to a scale, or, by implication, a musical style or system that is characterized by the use of five pitches or pitch-classes. The term is used more strictly to describe the so-called ANHEMITONIC pentatonic collection, which is typified by the set C–D–E–G–A; of the five modes arising from the collection, the major (i.e. with tonic C) is generally regarded as 'the (common) pentatonic scale', although the Aeolian mode is also important.

The strict sense of the term Pentatonic is justified, given the rarity of hemitonic pentatonic scales (e.g. the Japanese *in* or the Korean *kyemyŏnjo*) and the aptness of the term 'pentachord' to describe conjunct diatonic collections (for instance, Beethoven's 'Ode to Joy' theme). It was in this sense, moreover, that Carl Engel coined the term

in 1864, and as far back as Burney writers referred to 'gapped' or 'incomplete' scales of this sort. (Scrupulous musicologists have rightly cautioned against these adjectives, but the scales do indeed afford the cultivated Western ear interpretative ambiguities between pentatonic and heptatonic hearings). One may further refine the notion of the pentatonic by recognizing the distinctiveness of the scale's minor third 'steps'; hence the motif G–A–C is more characteristically pentatonic than C–D–E, even though both belong to the same pentatonic scale.

Once described variously as the 'Chinese scale' or the 'Scotch scale', the pentatonic scale has impressed commentators since at least the mid-19th century for its astonishing ubiquity. A significant feature of such diverse musical traditions as those of the British Isles, West Africa and Amerindian America (among countless others), pentatonicism may well be a musical universal (Chailley, pp.111–28; Nettl, p.42), and many have taken for granted its historical primitivism (Helmholtz, p.257; Suchoff, 1976, p.371; Trân). The ethnocentric problems involved in generalizing about scales, however, remind us that defending such grand claims would require the most careful methodology, as pentatonic usage varies widely from one tradition to another. For instance, the Chinese system – for which the very propriety of the term 'pentatonic' has been questioned (Shen, p.3) – is based on a universe of 12 perfect 5ths, featuring a pentatonic 'core' plus two 'exchange tones' (*bianyin*), embellishments that in both theory and practice fill in the minor 3rds (ex.1a);

Ex.1
(a) Chinese *gong* scale   (b) Japanese *yo* scale

whereas the Japanese *gagaku* tradition, while ostensibly founded on this same system, differs in its use of the exchange tones, which assume the nature of METABOLE rather than passing notes (ex.1b). The *sléndro* tuning of Javanese gamelans is pentatonic, though in this case the intervals are more nearly equidistant.

Ex.2 Weber: *Turandot*, end of theme

Still, such modal and tuning issues notwithstanding, the universalist hypothesis seems compelling, and although the question of primordial scales is far from resolved, a general consensus does exist concerning at least the importance of the pentatonic in the history of music. Whether it is explained in terms of mono- or

Ex.3 Chopin: *Krakowiak* op.14

polygenesis, this 'king' of scales (Trân) warrants further research.

The rise of diatonic tonality seems to have temporarily extinguished pentatonicism from music (other than folk and traditional musics) in the West. The Romantics, however, in their quest for originality, undertook notable (if isolated) experiments using pentatonic materials in the 19th century. These innovations can be understood ideologically in two ways: as part of a rejection of the conventional musical language, with a new emphasis on sonorous colour; and as an embodiment of the Romantic fascination with the 'Oriental' (exoticism), with folk art (primitivism, nationalism) and with medieval Christianity archaism (exx.2, 3 and 4 respectively). Carl Maria von

Ex.4 Liszt: Kyrie from *Missa Choralis*, theme

Weber, apparently the first of the 19th-century pentatonicists, used an 'Air chinois', copied note for note from Rousseau's *Dictionnaire de musique*, as the theme for his incidental music to Schiller's *Turandot* (see ex.2). Chopin's famous Etude in G♭ owes something of its peculiar pentatonic sound to a technical issue – the right hand playing on black keys – but the earlier *Krakowiak*, op.14 (see ex.3), confirms his familiarity with the scale. Liszt employed pentatonicism to a striking degree, especially in his solo piano and sacred music (see ex.4). Other composers who used the pentatonic scale include Mendelssohn, Berlioz, Wagner, 'the Five', Mahler, Dvořák, Puccini, and above all the Impressionists. Though modest in comparison with later practice, 19th-century pentatonicism represents both a subtle change in melodic sensibility away from common-practice diatonicism and also a reaction against what must have seemed the cloying tendencies of chromaticism.

In the 20th century, thanks in large part to Debussy and Bartók (exx.5, 6), the pentatonic scale earned its

Ex.5 Debussy: *Nuages*

Ex.6 Bartók: *Bluebeard's Castle*, Bluebeard's glory

place among the materials of Western art-music and, consequently, became somewhat less 'marked' despite its enduring association with various folk and traditional musics. For Debussy and Ravel, the scale's inherent tonal ambiguities were surely as attractive as its exotic implications. Debussy's direct acquaintance with the pentatonic – through exposure to the gamelan at the 1889 Paris Exhibition – represents a significant change from Weber's armchair anthropology earlier in the century. A further

step was taken by Bartók and Kodály, who, in search of their Hungarian musical roots, amassed thousands of vernacular melodies, a portion of which were pentatonic. As composer, Bartók spoke of 'the tyrannical rule of the major and minor keys' and described his own pentatonicism as 'the most suitable antidote for the hyperchromatism of Wagner and his followers'. This decidedly un-Schoenbergian 'antidote' proved useful to other composers as well, including Stravinsky (ex.7), Hindemith

Ex.7 Stravinsky: *The Rite of Spring*, 'Spring Rounds'

and Vaughan Williams. The partitioning of the chromatic aggregate into 'white-' and 'black-note' sets accounts for some less overt pentatonic usage, for instance, in Villa Lobos and Ligeti.

Certain genres of American popular music exhibit pentatonic elements, especially those genres most directly related to African American traditions: from the spiritual (ex.8) to jazz, Motown and rock.

Theorists, generating the pentatonic scale from a cycle of perfect 5ths, have observed a host of scalar properties that may be acoustically or psychologically desirable. For instance, the set enjoys unique multiplicity of interval classes (<032140>) and so-called 'optimum consonance' (Huron). It is both 'well-formed' (Carey) and 'coherent' (Agmon), and exhibits the 'f to f♯ property' (Zweifel), all assurances of scalar and modulatory integrity. The extent to which these features account for the apparent universality of pentatonicism, however, remains speculative.

BIBLIOGRAPHY

H. von Helmholtz: *Die Lehre von den Tonempfindungen als physiologische Grundlage für die Theorie der Musik* (Brunswick, 1863, 5/1896; Eng. trans., 1875, 2/1885/R)

C. Engel: *The Music of the Most Ancient Nations* (London, 1864/R)

Z. Kodály: 'Ötfokú hangsor a magyar népzenében' [Pentatonicism in Hungarian folk music], *Zenei szemle*, i (1917); Eng. trans., *EthM*, xiv (1970), 228–42

B. Szabolcsi: *A melódia története: vázlatok a zenei stílus múltjából* (Budapest, 1950, 2/1957; Eng. trans., 1965, as *A History of Melody*, Ger. trans., 1959, as *Bausteine zu einer Geschichte der Melodie*)

J. Chailley: *Formation et transformation du langage musical* (Paris, 1955)

C. Brăiloiu: 'Pentatony in Debussy's Music', *Studia memoriae Belae Bartók sacra*, ed. B. Rajeczky and L. Vargyas (Budapest, 1956, 3/1959)

C. Brăiloiu: *Problèmes d'ethnomusicologie*, ed. G. Rouget (Geneva, 1973; Eng. trans., 1984)

A. Labussière: 'Rhythme enfantin, pentatonismes et giusto syllabique dans les créations mélodiques des enfants', *RdM*, lxii (1976), 25–85

B. Suchoff, ed.: *Béla Bartók Essays* (London, 1976)

H. Avenary: 'The Northern and Southern Idioms of Early European Music: a New Approach to an Old Problem', *AcM*, xlix (1977), 27–49

D. Beveridge: 'Sophisticated Primitivism: the Significance of Pentatonicism in Dvořák's American Quartet', *CMc*, no.24 (1977), 25–36

Ex.8 African American spiritual

Yes ev'ry time I feel the Spi-rit   mo-vin' in my heart,   I will pray!

V.K. Trân: 'Is the Pentatonic Universal? A Few Reflections on Pentatonicism', *World of Music*, xix/1–2 (1977), 76–84

S. Gut: 'Liszt et Debussy: comparaison stylistique', *Liszt-Studien II: Eisenstadt 1978*, 63–77

M. Kolinski: 'The Structure of Music: Diversification Versus Constraint', *EthM*, xxii (1978), 229–44

R. Gauldin: 'The Cycle-7 Complex: Relations of Diatonic Set Theory to the Evolution of Ancient Tonal Systems', *Music Theory Spectrum*, v (1983), 39–55

B. Nettl: *The Study of Ethnomusicology: Twenty-Nine Issues and Concepts* (Urbana, IL, 1983)

J. Oliveira: 'Black Key versus White Key: a Villa-Lobos Device', *LAMR*, v (1984), 33–47

J.R. Wheaton: *The Diatonic Potential of the Strange Sets: Theoretical Tenets and Structural Meaning in Gustav Mahler's 'Der Abschied'* (diss., Yale U.,1988)

N. Carey and D.Clampitt: 'Aspects of Well-Formed Scales', *Music Theory Spectrum*, xi (1989), 187–206

S.-Y. Shen: *Chinese Music and Orchestration* (Chicago, 1991)

G. Hajdu: 'Low Energy and Equal Spacing: the Multifactorial Evolution of Tuning Systems', *Interface* [Amsterdam], xxii (1993), 319–33

D. Huron: 'Interval-Class Content in Equally Tempered Pitch-Class Sets: Common Scales Exhibit Optimal Tonal Consonance', *Music Perception*, xi (1994), 289–305

E. Agmon: 'Coherent Tone-Systems: a Study in the Theory of Diatonicism', *JMT*, xl (1996), 39–59

M. Beckerman: 'Dvořák's Pentatonic Landscape: the Suite in A Major', *Rethinking Dvořák: Views from Five Countries*, ed. D. Beveridge (Oxford, 1996), 245–54

P. Zweifel: 'Generalized Diatonic and Pentatonic Scales: a Group-Theoretic Approach', *PNM*, xxxiv/1 (1996), 140–61

J. Day-O'Connell: *Pentatonicism in Nineteenth-Century Music* (diss., Cornell U., in preparation)

JEREMY DAY-O'CONNELL

Pentecontachordon. A name given by lexicographers to the Sambuca lincea, an enharmonic harpsichord or ARCICEMBALO, invented by FABIO COLONNA, and described by him in 1618.

Pentecostal and Renewal church music. The music and worship of (1) that group of Christian sects whose defining characteristic is the belief that the occurrence on the day of Pentecost recounted in the second chapter of the *Acts of the Apostles* not only signalled the birth of the Church but described an experience available to believers in all ages, namely, baptism in the Holy Spirit; and (2) those churches, either belonging to or outside the mainstream denominations, that were touched by the Charismatic Renewal movement of the latter half of the 20th century. Associated with these traditions is a distinctive repertory of songs and choruses expressing, often in a vivid and personal manner, individual and collective experience of the Christian faith.

1. The Pentecostal tradition. 2. The Charismatic tradition.

1. THE PENTECOSTAL TRADITION.   The Pentecostal Movement in America, strongly influenced by Methodism and the Holiness Movement (out of which it grew), is considered to have emerged at the turn of the 19th and 20th centuries, with outpourings of the Holy Spirit manifested in North Carolina (1896), Kansas (1901) and California (1906). At the beginning all leaders preached the Wesleyan doctrine of sanctification as a 'second work of grace', and the 'third blessing' as baptism in the Holy Spirit, with speaking in tongues as evidence. So strong was the teaching on baptism in the Holy Spirit that at a very early stage at least six hymnals with the title *Pentecostal Hymns* were used within the movement. From its meagre beginnings Pentecostalism has grown into a

global force within Christendom, crossing denominational barriers in a way that few other movements have managed. Missionary activity on the part of several of the long-established Pentecostal Churches, international crusades by leading evangelists such as Oral Roberts, religious broadcasting and the proliferation of Christian television networks have all contributed to its worldwide spread. Today, there are three broad groups of Pentecostal believers: (1) classical Pentecostals, belonging to Churches whose origins date back to the beginning of the 20th century, for example, the Assemblies of God, the Church of God (Cleveland, TN), the Pentecostal Holiness Church, and the International Church of the Foursquare Gospel; (2) neo-Pentecostals, who accept baptism in the Holy Spirit but choose to stay within the mainstream denominations; and (3) charismatics, whose affiliation and doctrinal beliefs lie outside the classical Pentecostal or main denominational frameworks, but whose faith is centred on the distinctively Pentecostal blessings and phenomena, namely, baptism in the Holy Spirit with the spiritual gifts, such as divine healing, of *1 Corinthians* xii.8–10. In 1992 it was estimated that about a quarter of all Christians belonged to Pentecostal or charismatic denominations.

Music, often highly spiritual and improvisatory, has always been a significant feature of Pentecostal worship. The Movement's immediate musical roots lay in the traditional congregational songs common to many other denominations, particularly the hymns of Isaac Watts and Charles Wesley. But even more widespread and characteristic were the Holiness Movement songs, which focussed on purity of heart, eradication of sin and a deeper walk with God (e.g. *The Cleansing Wave*), camp-meeting songs, concerned with man's earthly trials, conversion to the Christian life, and the experience of joy on the path to heaven (e.g. *Our Lord's Return to Earth*), and gospel songs, which were songs of personal testimony and heartfelt belief in Jesus Christ, especially during times of trial (e.g. *Blessed Assurance*). The more distant origins of Pentecostal music, however, may be found in biblical traditions of music and worship. In the Old Testament music clearly had both a 'functional' and a 'spiritual' aspect: in everday life it was used, for example, in social contexts, as a martial accompaniment to physical work, for didactic purposes, and as an element in liturgy; but sacred song could also be a vehicle for expressing the deeper dimensions of human thought and experience. The functional aspect is of primary importance to Pentecostals, for whom music must be easily accessible, capable of reflecting the 'everyday life' of the believer and allowing the worshipping community to convey its needs to God (as, for example, in Reuben Morgan's *Your Unfailing Love*: 'When my burden keeps me doubting, when my memories take the place of you, Jesus come'). But it is also necessary for sacred music to reinforce theological belief and impart spiritual truths, thus helping people to grow closer to their Creator (as in songs concerned with healing, the second coming of Christ, spiritual baptism and the workings of the Holy Spirit). The use of various musical instruments, the importance of singing psalms and scriptural songs, and the rebirth, within the Charismatic Movement, of dance in worship, may be directly attributed to Old Testament example (see Alford, 688).

2. THE CHARISMATIC TRADITION.   During the early decades of the 20th century, as the Pentecostal Movement

developed, a freer, more demonstrative kind of worship evolved whose influence would eventually leave no branch of the Western Church untouched. In the 1950s and 1960s a 'neo-Pentecostal' style of worship began to appear, particularly in the USA and Great Britain, among small groups of Christians belonging to the mainstream denominations. At first these 'charismatic fellowships' would mainly gather in homes or in smaller rooms of churches for prayer-meeting type services. But as the Charismatic Renewal movement gathered worldwide momentum, it was only a matter of time before its characteristic style of worship, known as 'Praise and Worship', whose hallmark was an intensely personal form of group singing called 'praise singing', began to be be incorporated into the normal services of individual churches. Many Christians of hitherto traditional persuasion – Methodists, Presbyterians, Baptists, Mennonites, Anglicans/Episcopalians, Lutherans, Roman Catholics – came to realize that their worship, though outwardly proper and beautiful, seemed inwardly void and unimaginative, lacking freshness and life-giving spirituality. By contrast, Charismatic Renewal brought a fresh 'wind of the Spirit', imparting a new vitality and meaning by restoring an emphasis on dynamic worship, in both a personal and corporate way. Worship could be an experience of joy and celebration, often manifested in enthusiastic, winsome singing, the raising of hands, exclamations of verbal praise, and, at times, spontaneous spiritual dance. The study of scripture (aided by new versions of the Bible) also plays a vital part in this type of worship, and in many churches there has been a renewed interest in the Eucharist, but praise and praise singing remain central.

Although a casual observer might easily interpret congregational praise singing as primarily emotional, its authenticity is supported by biblical practice. Some theologians see the 20th-century Charismatic Renewal movement as the spiritual restoration of Davidic worship around the Ark of the Covenant, especially through praise singing. A number of elements in Praise and Worship are based on Old Testament models and represent a liberating trend by allowing expression of the whole body and person. The joyous intensity and robust, exuberant style of praise singing is a response to Psalm lxvi.1–2, 'Make a joyful noise unto God all ye lands: sing forth the honour of his name: make his praise glorious', as well as other exhortations such as 'cry aloud' (Psalm lv.17) and 'shout for joy' (Psalm v.11); even 'laughter' is not excluded (Psalm cxxvi.2) from worship. Such singing is often accompanied by bowing and kneeling (Psalm xcv.6: 'Come, let us worship and bow down; let us kneel before the Lord our maker'), clapping of hands and shouting (Psalm xlvii.1: 'O clap your hands all peoples; shout to God with a voice of triumph'), lifting up of hands (Psalm cxxxiv.2: 'Lift up your hands in the sanctuary, and bless the Lord'), and – perhaps the most surprising of all – dancing (Psalm cl.4: 'Praise him with the timbrel and dance'; and *2 Samuel* vi.14: 'David danced before the Lord with all his might').

The charismatic service allows for a type of freedom and spontaneity whereby pastor and 'worship leader', who form a dual team, do not feel the need to be in complete control of the progress of the meeting. It is assumed that unexpected changes of direction will occur, as motivated by the Holy Spirit, although this does not

mean that an eclectic, free-for-all pattern emerges but rather that a type of 'guided spontaneity' prevails in which events in the service are anticipated but not prescribed or predicted. The worship leader – a kind of master of ceremonies responsible for guiding the direction of the service – chooses and leads the songs, leads prayer, quotes scripture and provides commentary. The ability of the congregation to 'flow with the Spirit' as directed through the worship leader is essential. A common freedom and excitement of praise is often shared by worship leader and congregation alike, resulting in improvised and creative worship that emanates from the very hearts of the participants, who may express themselves in prayer, testimonies, word of knowledge, prophecy, and expressions of praise in singing, shouting and dancing.

The key to praise singing lies in the participation of the congregation, for praise music is not primarily to be listened to but rather to be sung (choir items and organ playing, therefore, are usually of lesser importance). The music generally consists of short, often repetitive choruses and other scripture songs, whose antecedents may be found in the Pentecostal camp-meeting and gospel songs (see §1 above). The voice of the worship leader, amplified by an efficient sound system, is of primary importance in leading the singing, although gestures (not necessarily the conventional directing patterns) are often used to indicate the beginning and ending of phrases. The singing is usually reinforced by a back-up group of 'praise singers' (or an individual co-singer) and instrumentalists, but rather than functioning as a choir the singers encourage participation through their visual exuberance and their leadership in physical movements.

The musical characteristics of praise singing are very much bound up with popular music styles and performing practice, for example, the use of pop-derived harmonies, rhythms and instrumentation (drums, piano, synthesizers, guitars and, in large churches, wind instruments). Some of the most prominent charismatic churches engage arrangers and copyists on a weekly basis to provide new instrumental charts for praise singing. The result is a type of 'sacra-pop' that has become the dominant musical style in such worship. The development of electronic technology has been an important factor in the growth of the genre, for sound reinforcement systems and electronic and amplified instruments permit an enormous array of sounds and dynamic levels not previously available. Nevertheless, a wide range of practice exists, and in many churches the style of singing remains simple, with minimal use of instruments and electronic support.

The kind of praise singing described above has somewhat displaced traditional congregational song and the use of the hymnal, not least because holding a hymnbook inhibits the worshippers from raising or clapping their hands. The most widespread practice is to sing from memory, with some use of the overhead projector to provide the words. However, 'liturgical' churches of charismatic persuasion tend to blend their use of memorized choruses and scripture songs with use of the hymnal and the servicebook. In the early stages, Praise and Worship music was mostly passed on by oral tradition, for example, the chorus 'Seek ye first' (1972) and the simple repetitive 'Alleluia' (1972). Other typical and universally known charismatic songs, many of them in a direct, folklike idiom, include 'This is the day' (1967), 'I exalt Thee' (1976), 'I will enter his gates with thanksgiving' (1976), 'Praise the name of Jesus' (1976), 'Give thanks' (1978), 'I love you Lord' (1978) and 'We bring the sacrifice of praise' (1984). What is considered to be the first published collection of Praise and Worship music, *Scripture in Song* by David and Dale Garratt, appeared in New Zealand in 1968. Today most collections are published in the USA, by companies such as Maranatha Music, Vineyard Music and Integrity Music, including, respectively, *Maranatha! Music, Praise, Hymns and Choruses* (1987, 4/1997), *Songs of the Vineyard* (1980s–) and *Hosanna Music Songbooks* (1987–). Another significant source, devoted primarily to Praise and Worship music but in hymnal format, is *Songs and Praise for Worship* (1992). Praise and Worship choruses also appear side by side with more traditional hymns in various denominational hymnals, for example, *The United Methodist Hymnal* (1989), *The [Southern] Baptist Hymnal* (1991) and the Church of the Nazarene's *Sing to the Lord* (1993), and also in such non-denominational books as *The Hymnal* (1986) and *Celebration Hymnal* (1997). Further resources include *Hillsongs Australia* (1993, originating in Australia but produced in the USA by Integrity Music) and *Renew: Songs and Hymns for Blended Worship* (1995).

The Praise and Worship phenomenon, with its central activity of praise singing, is regarded by some commentators as a peripheral movement. But this is to fail to recognize its extraordinary growth and impact during the 20th century. Praise singing is not bound by denominational barriers but rather fosters a natural ecumenicity: persons of all ages, from varying theological, ethnic and cultural traditions, can share in it together, bringing with them the distinctiveness of their backgrounds. It would not be unreasonable to predict that the new spirit of praise singing will exert an increasing influence on Christian worship during the 21st century.

BIBLIOGRAPHY
GENERAL
P. Fleisch: *Zur Geschichte der Heiligungsbewegung* (Leipzig, 1910)
D. Gee: *The Pentecostal Movement* (London, 1949)
C. Conn: *Like a Mighty Army* (Cleveland, 1955)
K. Kendrick: *The Promise Fulfilled: a History of the Modern Pentecostal Movement* (Springfield, MO, 1961)
E. Bucke: *The History of Methodism* (Nashville, TN, 1964)
F. Bruser: *A Theology of the Holy Spirit: the Pentecostal Experience and the New Testament Witness* (Grand Rapids, MI, 1970)
W. Menzies: *Anointed to Serve: the Story of the Assemblies of God* (Springfield, MO, 1971)
V. Synan: *The Holiness Pentecostal Movement in the United States* (Grand Rapids, MI, 1971)
M. Dieter: 'Wesleyan-Holiness Aspects of Pentecostal Origins: as Mediated through the Nineteenth Century Holiness Revival', *Aspects of Pentecostal Charismatic-Origins*, ed. V. Synan (Plainfield, NJ, 1975), 59
D. Dayton: *Theological Roots of Pentecostalism* (Grand Rapids, MI, 1987)
L. Duncan: 'Music Among Early Pentecostals', *The Hymn*, xxxviii (1987), 11
D. Hustad: 'The Historical Roots of the Pentecostal and Neo-Pentecostal Movements', *The Hymn*, xxxviii (1987), 10
D. Alford: 'Pentecostal and Charismatic Music', *Dictionary of Pentecostal and Charismatic Movements*, ed. S.M. Burgess, G.B. McGee and P.H. Alexander (Grand Rapids, MI, 1988), 688
R. Webber: *Signs of Wonder: the Phenomenon of Convergence in Modern Liturgical and Charismatic Churches* (Nashville, TN, 1992)
D. Hustad: *Jubilate II: Church Music in Worship and Renewal* (Carol Stream, IL, 1993)
B. Liesch: *The New Worship* (Grand Rapids, MI, 1996)
R. Webber: *Ancient–Future Worship: a Model for the 21st Century* (Wheaton, IL, 1999)

PRAISE AND WORSHIP
G. Truscott: *The Power of his Presence* (San Diego, CA, 1969)
B. Mumford: *Entering and Enjoying Worship* (Greensburg, PA, 1975)
C. Baker: *On Eagles' Wings* (Seattle, 1979)
R. Allen: *Praise: a Matter of Life and Breath* (Nashville, TN, 1980)
R. Allen and G. Borror: *Worship: Rediscovering the Missing Jewel* (Portland, OR, 1982)
A. Ortland: *Up with Worship: how to Quit Playing Church* (Ventura, CA, 1982)
J. Cornwall: *Let us Praise* (South Plainfield, NJ, 1983)
J. Cornwall: *Let us Worship* (South Plainfield, NJ, 1983)
C. Johansson: *Music and Ministry* (Peabody, MA, 1984)
P. Baker: *Contemporary Christian Music: Where it Came from – What it is – Where it's Going* (Westchester, IL, 1985)
J. Cornwall: *Elements of Worship* (South Plainfield, NJ, 1985)
T. Law: *The Power of Praise and Worship* (Tulsa, 1985)
R. Webber: *Worship is a Verb* (Waco, TX, 1985)
L. Boschman: *The Prophetic Song* (Shippensburg, PA, 1986)
J. Hayford: *Worship his Majesty* (Waco, TX, 1987)
K. Osbeck: *The Endless Song: Music and Worship in the Church* (Grand Rapids, MI, 1987)
B. Sorge: *Exploring Worship: a Practical Guide to Praise and Worship* (Buffalo, NY, 1987)
D. Bloomgren, D. Smith and D. Christoffel: *Restoring Praise and Worship* (Shippensburg, PA, 1989)
L. Boschman: *The Rebirth of Music* (Shippensburg, PA, 1990)
J. Cornwall: *Worship as David Lived it* (Shippensburg, PA, 1990)

J. RANDALL GUTHRIE

Pentland, Barbara (Lally) (*b* Winnipeg, 2 Jan 1912; *d* Vancouver, 5 Feb 2000). Canadian composer. She began composing at the age of nine, shortly after her first piano lessons, persisting in her pursuit of music despite poor health and parental opposition. Winnipeg provided a flourishing, if limited, musical environment in the 1920s, and it was the piano sonata writing of Beethoven that Pentland emulated during this period. While attending a private boarding school in Montreal (1927–9) she studied the piano and theory with an English organist, Frederick H. Blair, who encouraged her to continue music studies. She proceeded to Paris in 1929 and became a composition pupil of Cécile Gauthiez. Gauthiez's teaching was in the Franckian tradition, and the characteristic thick textures and chromatic harmonies remained in Pentland's music until the late 1930s, as is evident in the Five Piano Preludes (1938), the Rhapsody for piano (1939) and the Piano Quartet (1939).

After returning to Winnipeg in 1930, Pentland continued her studies with Gauthiez by correspondence for 18 months. During the next six years she composed a great deal, winning several local competitions; at the same time she studied the piano and organ and frequently performed her piano music in public. She then won a fellowship in composition to the Juilliard School, where she studied with Frederick Jacobi (1936–8) and Bernard Wagenaar (1938–9). Exposure to new music in New York had a decisive effect: she was particularly impressed by the work of Paul Hindemith, which provided a model for her increasing interest in counterpoint. She returned again to Winnipeg in 1939 and was appointed to the music advisory committee and an examiner in theory at the University of Manitoba. In the summers of 1941 and 1942 she studied at Tanglewood with Aaron Copland, whose influence, which encouraged her to a more lucid style, is shown most strikingly in the similarity between her Piano Variations (1942) and Copland's own (1930). Also contributing to the leaner textures of her music was a neo-classical tendency, a primary feature from the early 1940s to the late 1950s.

Persuaded that her works would have more chance of performance in a larger centre, Pentland moved to Toronto in 1942, and in the following year she was appointed to teach theory and composition at the conservatory. During the 1940s she gained a reputation as a headstrong member of the avant garde. Her developing contrapuntal leanings are seen in the Sonata Fantasy (1947), in which the opening few bars present the material for the entire work. This direction was stimulated by her first significant exposure to serial music, in the summers of 1947 and 1948 at the MacDowell Colony, where Dika Newlin introduced her to many of Arnold Schoenberg's compositions; the Wind Octet (1948) was her first consciously serial work. In 1949 she joined the music department of the University of British Columbia, Vancouver, where she taught until 1963, when she resigned to give her attention to composition.

The main influence on Pentland's mature style was the music of Anton Webern, which impressed her during a European visit in 1955. She attended the Darmstadt summer courses and the ISCM Festival, and in the following year returned to hear her Second Quartet played at the ISCM Festival in Stockholm. The *Symphony for Ten Parts* (1957), in its compactness and clarity, displays Webern's influence: three tightly-knit movements are built from melodic and rhythmic shapes established in the short introduction. A new interest in timbre, also Webernian, is expressed in such instrumental combinations as that of xylophone with double bass, as well as in the alternation of dry, percussive sections with passages of greater lyricism.

Pentland's later works are economical, the textures swept clean of the scales and arpeggios of her music of the 1940s. 12-note serialism, used freely, is a means of control. A distinctive feature is the touch of humour in the syncopated rhythms, light melodies or brisk staccatos. Retrograde is also a frequently encountered technique: a work or section often concludes with a reversal of the initial serial statement, sometimes providing material for a coda or recapitulation.

In the late 1960s Pentland began to use aleatory techniques and quarter-tones. There are short aleatory passages in the *Trio con alea* (1966), the Third String Quartet (1969), *News* (1970) and *Mutations* (1972), permitting the performer freedom in rhythmically varying, repeating and articulating given pitches; the last aleatory section in a work may function as a cadenza. The use of quarter-tones is principally decorative and confined to string parts, though there are some in the vocal line of *News*. Also during this period Pentland wrote numerous short piano pieces for children, strictly miniatures of her mature style. She maintained an active career until the early 1990s, when ill health curtailed her ability to compose. She was made a Member of the Order of Canada in 1989.

WORKS
(selective list)

Stage: Beauty and the Beast (ballet-pantomime), 2 pf, 1940; The Lake (chbr op, 1, D. Livesay), SATB, small orch, 1952

Orch and vocal orch: Lament, 1939; Arioso and Rondo, 1941; Holiday Suite, 1941; Conc., vn, small orch, 1942, arr. vn, pf, 1945; Colony Music, pf, str, 1945; Sym. no.1, 1945–8; Variations on a Boccherini Tune, 1948; Conc., org, str, 1949; Sym. no.2, 1950; Ave atque vale, 1951; Ricercar, str, 1955; Conc., pf, str orch, 1956; Sym. for 10 Parts (Sym. no.3), 1957; Sym. no.4, 1959; Strata, 1964; Cinéscene, chbr orch, 1968; News, Mez, orch, tape,

1970; Variations concertantes, pf, orch, 1970, also arr. 2 pf; Five-Plus (Simple Pieces for Str), 1971; Res musica, str orch, 1975

Vocal: Ruins: Ypres, 1917 (G.H. Clarke), 1v, pf, 1932; Ballad of Trees and the Master (S. Lanier), chorus, 1937; Dirge for a Violet (D.C. Scott), chorus, 1939; Song Cycle (A. Marriott), 1v, pf, 1942–5; At Early Dawn (Hsiang Hao), T, fl, pf, 1945; Epigrams and Epitaphs, rounds, chorus 2–4vv, 1952; Salutation of the Dawn (Sanskrit text), SATB, 1954; What is Man? (Apocrypha: *Ecclesiasticus* xviii), SATB, 1954; 3 Sung Songs (Chin. text, trans. C.M. Candlin), SATB, 1964, also arr. medium v, pf, 1964; Sung Songs nos.4–5 (J'Sin Ch'I-Chi, trans. Candlin), Mez, pf, 1971; Disasters of the Sun (D. Livesay), Mez, inst ens, tape, 1976; Ice Age (Livesay), S, pf, 1986

Chbr and solo inst: Pf Qt, 1939; Sonata, vc, pf, 1943; Str Qt no.1, 1945; Vista, vn, pf, 1945; Sonata, vn, pf, 1946; Wind Octet, 1948; Weekend Ov. for Resort Combo, cl, tpt, pf, perc, 1949; Sonata, vn, 1950; Str Qt no.2, 1953; Duo, va, pf, 1960; Canzona, fl, ob, hpd, 1961; Pf Trio, 1963; Variations, va, 1965; Trio con alea, str trio, 1966; Septet, hn, tpt, trbn, vn, va, vc, org, 1967; Str Qt no.3, 1969; Reflections, accdn, 1971; Interplay, accdn, str qt, 1972; Mutations, vc, pf, 1972; Occasions, brass qnt, 1974; Phases, cl, 1977; Eventa, fl, cl, trbn, vn, vc, hp, 2 perc, 1978; Trance, fl, pf/hp, 1978; Variable Winds, solo ww (4 versions), 1979; Elegy, hn, pf, 1980; Str Qt no.4, 1980; Commenta, hp, 1981; Tellus, fl, vc, pf, perc, cel, 1981–2; Septet, hn, tpt, trbn, vn, va, vc, org, 1982; Qnt, pf, str, 1983; Tides, vn, mar, hp, 1984; Str Qt no.5, 1985; Intrada and Canzona, rec qt, 1988; Adagio, vc, pf, 1991

Pf: 5 Preludes, 1938; Rhapsody, 1939; Studies in Line, 1941; Variations, 1942; Sonata, 1945; Sonata Fantasy, 1947; Dirge, 1948; 2 Sonatinas, 1951; Sonata, 2 pf, 1953; Interlude, 1955; 3 Duets after Pictures by Paul Klee, pf 4 hands, 1958; Toccata, 1958; Fantasy, 1962; Echoes no.1 and no.2, 1964; Maze, Casse-Tête (Labyrinthe, Puzzle), 1964; Puppet Show, pf 4 hands, 1964; Shadows (Ombres), 1964; 3 Pairs, 1964; Hands Across the C, 1965; Space Studies, 1966; Suite Borealis, 1966; Music of Now, bks 1–3, 1969–70; Vita brevis, 1973; Ephemera, 1974–8; Tenebrae, 1976; Vincula, 1983; Horizons, 1985; Canticum, Burlesca and Finale, 1987; Small Pieces for a Shrinking Planet, 1990

Also incid music for radio plays and film scores, incl. The Living Gallery, 1947

MSS in *CDN-Tcm*; other material in *On*

Principal publishers: Avondale, BMI Canada, Berandol, Waterloo

BIBLIOGRAPHY

EMC2 (K. Winters and J. Beckwith); *GroveW* (S. Eastman Loosley, G.G. Jones) [incl. further bibliography]

R. Turner: 'Barbara Pentland', *Canadian Music Journal*, ii/4 (1958), 15–26

'Barbara Pentland: a Portrait', *Musicanada*, no.21 (1969), no.21, pp.8–9

S. Eastman and T.J. McGee: *Barbara Pentland* (Toronto, 1983)

T.J. McGee: 'Barbara Pentland in the 1950s: String Quartet No.2 and Symphony for Ten Parts', *SMC*, ix (1984), 133–52

G. Dixon: 'The String Quartets of Barbara Pentland', *Canadian University Music Review*, xi/2 (1991), 94–121

D.G. Duke: 'Notes Towards a Portrait of Barbara Pentland: Issues of Gender, Class and Colonialism in Canadian Music', *Musicworks*, lxx (1998), 16–20

SHEILA EASTMAN LOOSLEY/ROBIN ELLIOTT (work-list, bibliography with GAYNOR G. JONES)

Penzel, Christian Friedrich (*b* Oelsnitz, 25 Nov 1737; *d* Merseburg, 14 March 1801). German Kantor and composer. He studied music first under the Oelsnitz Kantor J.G. Nacke, and then at the Thomasschule, Leipzig (1749–56). Penzel studied law at Leipzig from 1756 until 1761. After an unsuccessful attempt in 1762 to obtain his father's position as sexton at Oelsnitz, in 1765 he succeeded A.F. Graun as Kantor at Merseburg.

Penzel is chiefly remembered for his numerous copies of Bach's works, some of which are important sources for modern editors. These copies (from sources at the Thomasschule and in the possession of W.F. Bach) comprise mainly cantatas, but also instrumental music. His manuscript collection was inherited by his nephew

Johann Gottlob Schuster who sold most of it to Franz Hauser in 1833 (now in *D-Bsb*), while the remainder was acquired by the Leipzig publisher C.F. Peters (now in *LEm*). Of his own compositions all that survive are four four-part arias (Leipzig, 1780) and the motet, *Wenn Christus seine Kirche schützt* (Leipzig, 1777), modelled on the chorale chorus 'Und wenn die Welt voll Teufel wär' from Bach's cantata *Ein feste Burg*.

BIBLIOGRAPHY
Y. Kobayashi: *Franz Hauser und seine Bach-Handschriftensammlung* (diss., U. of Göttingen, 1973)
W. Wiemer, ed.: *Johann Sebastian Bach und seine Schule: Neu entdeckte Choral- und Liedsätze aus der Bach-Choral-Sammlung (1780) von C.F. Penzel* (Kassel, 1985)
K. Lehmann: ' Neues zur Vorgeschichte der Bach-Sammlung Franz Hausers', *Beiträge zur Bachforschung*, vi (1988), 65 81
K. Lehmann: ' Bachiana unter "Tabak & Cigaretten": die Bach-Sammlung des Leipziger Verlages C.F. Peters in der ersten Hälfte des 19. Jahrhunderts', *BJb 1996*, 49–76
RICHARD JONES/PETER WOLLNY

Peperara, Laura. See PEVERARA, LAURA.

Pepi, Jorge (*b* Cordoba, Argentina, 28 March 1962). Argentine pianist and composer. He studied music in Argentina until 1980 when an Argentine government bursary enabled him to pursue his studies in Europe. He gained a diploma as a pupil of Edith Fischer and also attended the Académie Menuhin at Gstaad. He studied composition with Eric Gaudibert at Geneva. He began writing music for the Théâtre de l'Ephémère in Lausanne in 1985. In 1991 his *Metamorfosis I* for piano was awarded a prize by Edition musicale suisse and it was also chosen to represent Argentina at the International Composers Forum. His chamber opera *La caccia al tesoro* ('The Treasure Hunt') was awarded a prize by the Société Suisse des Auteurs in 1993 and performed at the Geneva Archipel and Wien Modern festivals in 1995. *Extravagario* won first prize at the Gerona international competition and *Amalgama* the Gilson prize in 1995.

Thanks to his extrovert temperament, Jorge Pepi has an acute sense of theatricality in his music. In recent years he has turned increasingly towards forms of pure music. Each work being the continuation of its predecessor (as in the *Metamorfosis* series), his output gives the impression of a long quest, a kind of 'treasure hunt' in itself.

WORKS
(*selective list*)
Septet, fl, cl, str qt, hpd, 1983; Escalera, vn/fl/cl, str trio, 1984; Lieder ohne Worte, 2vv, str trio, 1984; Block, pf 4 hands, 1986; Bagatelles, hp, cl, vc, 1987; Metamorfosis I, pf, 1989; La caccia al tesoro (chbr op, D. Buzzati), 1990–92; Metamorfosis II, 12 str, 1991; Extravagario (P. Neruda), 1v, fl, vc, pf, 1993–4; Amalgama, 10 insts, 1995; Metamorfosis III, pf, ob, perc, 1995; Metamorfosis IV, 9 insts, 1995; Metamorfosis V, chbr orch, 1996; Puna, fl, 1996; Cadenza, fl, ob, cl, bn, tpt, hn, trbn, 2 perc, 1997; Nacht Stücke, 7 pieces, vn, vc, pf; Metamorfosis VI, vn, vc, accdn

BIBLIOGRAPHY
'A propos de Metamorfosis I de Jorge Pepi', *Dissonanz/Dissonance*, no.31 (1992)
J.-P. Amann: ' Musique pour une fin de siècle', *Revue musicale de Suisse romande*, xlvii (1994), 114–20
JEAN-PIERRE AMANN

Pépin, (Jean-Josephat) Clermont (*b* St Georges-de-Beauce, PQ, 15 May 1926). Canadian composer, pianist and teacher. As a boy he studied the piano and harmony with Georgette Dionne. In 1937 he was awarded a composition prize from the Canadian Performing Rights Society (later the Composers, Authors and Publishers Association of Canada) and went to Montreal to study harmony and counterpoint with Claude Champagne and the piano with Arthur Letondal. In 1941 he received a scholarship from the Curtis Institute in Philadelphia, where he studied composition with Rosario Scalero and the piano with Jeanne Behrend. Upon his graduation in 1944, he returned to Montreal and spent two years at the conservatoire studying with Jean Dansereau (piano), Champagne (composition) and Barzin (conducting). Three further CAPAC awards enabled him to continue his studies at the Toronto Conservatory with Arnold Walter (composition) and Lubka Kolessa (piano).

In 1949 Pépin won the Prix d'Europe, a yearly scholarship granted by the Académie de Musique de Québec that enabled him to make a six-year sojourn in Paris, where he studied the piano with Yves Nat and Lazare Lévy, and composition with Jolivet and Honegger. In analysis courses with Messiaen he became acquainted with the music of Berg and Schoenberg as well as with Messiaen's *Turangalîla-symphonie*. These discoveries deeply modified his own style, which up to this time had relied heavily on Franck and Rachmaninoff. In his symphonic poems *Guernica* (1952) and *Le rite du soleil noir* (1955) he made partial use of serialism, extending this technique in works such as the String Quartet no.2 (1955–6), the Symphony no.2 (1957), *Hyperboles* (1960) and *Nombres* (1962). These are marked by a keen sense of rhythm and an attention to textural contrast.

From 1955 to 1964 and again from 1977 to 1987 Pépin held the post of professor at the Montreal Conservatoire. In 1960 he became director of studies. On a 1964 Canada Council grant he was able to visit 35 conservatories and schools of music in major European cities and become acquainted with their teaching methods, courses and administrative structures. Soon after his return he was appointed director of the Montreal Conservatoire, a position he held from 1967 to 1973. From 1969 to 1972 he was also national president of the Jeunesses Musicales du Canada. He served as the president of CAPAC from 1981 to 1983.

As an educator he addressed the complex problem which he refers to as the 'decolonization of the ear'. Consolidating his concern, in 1965 he co-founded, with musical colleagues, sociologists and artists, the Centre d'Etudes Prospectives du Québec. Modelled on a similar institute in Paris which he visited a few months earlier, the centre studied the technical, economic, social and cultural causes of modern evolution. An initial study, devoted to the effects of noise pollution, appeared in 1970.

It is perhaps through his association with scientists that Pépin has been able to view his music in relation to significant physical phenomena in the universe. Each of the *Monades* (1964–86) (taking their name from Leibnitz) focusses on a 'single active and indivisible substance'. *Quasars* (1967) was inspired by the discovery of quasars in 1963 and *La messe sur le monde* (1975, rev. 1990) reveals Pépin's profound admiration for Theilhard de Chardin and his quest for spirituality through scientific research.

Pépin was awarded the 'Prix de musique Calixa-Lavallée' in 1970 and was made officer of the Order of Canada in 1981. In 1984 he received a Master's degree in Public Administration. The following year he established the 'Clermont-Pépin' prize to encourage young artists from his native region (Beauce). His book *Le décideur et la prospective* (Editions Clermont-Pépin) appeared in 1987.

WORKS
(selective list)

STAGE

Ballets: Les portes de l'enfer, 2 pf, 1953; L'oiseau-phénix, orch, 1956; Porte-rêve, orch, 1957–8

Incid music: Athalie (Racine), 1956; Le malade imaginaire (Molière), 1956; La nuit des rois (W. Shakespeare), 1957; L'heure éblouissante, 1961; Le marchand de Venise (Shakespeare), 1964

ORCHESTRAL

Variations, str, 1944; Pf Conc. no.1, c♯, 1946; Adagio, str, 1947–56; Variations symphoniques, 1947; Sym. no.1, b, 1948; Pf Conc. no.2, 1949; Nocturne, pf, str, 1950–57; Guernica, sym. poem, 1952; Le rite du soleil noir, sym. poem, 1955; Fantaisie, str, 1957; Sym. no.2, 1957; Monologue, 1961; Nombres, 2 pf, orch, 1962; 3 Miniatures, str, 1963; Monade I, str, 1964; Sym. no.3 'Quasars', 1967; Monade III, vn, orch, 1972; Chroma, 1973; Prismes et cristaux, str, 1974; Sym. no.4 'La messe sur le monde', nar, chorus, orch, 1975, rev. 1990; Sym. no.5 'Implosion', 1983; Mar Conc., 1988

VOCAL

With orch: Cantique des cantiques (Bible), SATB, str, 1950; Fantaisie (Fr.-Can. folksongs), T, SATB, orch, 1957; Mouvement (Fr.-Can. folksongs), chorus, orch, 1958; Hymne au vent du nord (A. des Rochers), T, orch, 1960; Pièces de circonstance (J. Tetreau), children's vv, school band, 1967; 4 miniatures beauceronnes, children's chorus, orch, 1987

Songs: La feuille d'un saule (Chin.), S, pf, 1940; Chanson d'automne (P. Verlaine), T, pf, 1946; Les ports (Chadourne), Bar, pf, 1948; Cycle Eluard (P. Eluard), S, pf, 1949; 3 incantations d'une galaxie lointaine (C. Pepin), S, pf, 1987; Paysage, S, cl, vc, pf, 1987

CHAMBER AND INSTRUMENTAL

Chbr: 3 menuets, str qt, 1944; Str Qt no.1, 1948; Str Qt no.2 'Variations', 1955–6; Ronde villageoise, str orch, 1956; Suite, pf trio, 1958; Str Qt no.3 'Adagio et fugue', 1959; Str Qt no.4 'Hyperboles', 1960; Séquences, fl, ob, vn, va, vc, 1972; Monade IV 'Réseaux', vn, pf, 1974; Str Qt no.5, 1976; Interaction, 7 perc, 2 pf, 1977; Trio no.2, vn, vc, pf, 1982; Monade VII, vn, va, 1986

Solo inst: Passacaglia, org, 1950; 4 monodies, fl, 1955; 3 pièces pour la légende dorée, hpd, 1956; Monades VI 'Réseaux', vn, 1974–

Pf: Andante, 1939; Short Etudes no.1, 1940; Thème et variations, 1940; Pièce, 1943; Toccate, op.3, 1946; Short Etudes nos.2–3, 1946, 1947; Sonata, 1947; Thème et variations, 1947; Etude atlantique, 1950; Short Etude no.4, 1950; Suite, 1951, rev. 1955; 2 préludes, 1954; Short Etude no.5, 1954; Ronde villageoise, 2 pf, 1961, rev. 1986; Toccate no.3, 1961

Principal publishers: Clermont-Pépin, MCA, Western

BIBLIOGRAPHY

EMC2 (G. Potvin)

G. Potvin: 'Musique: l'année de Clermont Pépin', *Le Devoir* [Montreal] (6 April 1974)

K. MacMillan and J. Beckwith, eds.: *Contemporary Canadian Composers* (Toronto, 1975)

J.W. Schuster-Craig: *Compositional Procedures in Selected Works of Clermont Pépin* (diss., U. of Kentucky, 1987)

A. Freedman: *An Analysis of Clermont Pépin's Implosion* (MA thesis, San Diego State U., 1988)

DORITH R. COOPER/MARIE-THÉRÈSE LEFEBVRE

Pepper, Art(hur Edward jr) (*b* Gardena, CA, 1 Sept 1925; *d* Panorama City, CA, 15 June 1982). American jazz alto and tenor saxophonist. In 1943 he played in the big bands of Benny Carter and Stan Kenton. After serving in the US Army he toured with Kenton as the band's outstanding soloist (1946–51) and also performed freelance in Los Angeles. Thereafter his career was hampered by a series of prison terms for drug abuse, though he attempted several times to resume playing and issued several acclaimed recordings for the Contemporary label between 1957 and 1960, including *Intensity* (1960). In 1964 he

adopted the tenor saxophone and began to play free jazz, then in 1968 returned to mainstream jazz by joining Buddy Rich's band; serious ailments forced his departure in the following year, however. From 1977 until his sudden death he gave a series of sensational bop performances in Japan and New York. He was the subject of a documentary, *Art Pepper: Notes from a Jazz Survivor* (1982).

Pepper was a leading figure in West Coast jazz, a movement with which he was associated not only because of his choice of location and musical colleagues but also because of his light, clear, precise sound on the alto saxophone. However, he was a stronger, more fiery improviser than his fellow West Coast musicians, as is amply demonstrated by his recordings in 1957 and 1960 with Miles Davis's rhythm section. In the mid-1960s, under the overwhelming influence of John Coltrane, he took up the tenor saxophone, on which his playing stressed intense and expressive noise elements. Eventually, having returned to the alto instrument, he combined the two approaches in performances such as *Cherokee* (on the album *Saturday Night at the Village Vanguard*, 1977, Cont.), in which traditional bop lines erupt at explosive moments into squeals, growls and flurries of notes.

BIBLIOGRAPHY

J. Tynan: 'The Return of Art Pepper', *Down Beat*, xxvii/8 (1960), 17–18

J. Tynan: 'Art Pepper's Not the Same', *Down Beat*, xxxi/22 (1964), 18–19, 40

C. Marra: 'Art Pepper: "I'm Here to Stay!"', *Down Beat*, xl/4 (1973), 16–17

L. Underwood: 'Pepper's Painful Road to Pure Art', *Down Beat*, xlii/11 (1975), 16–17, 34

A. and L. Pepper: *Straight Life: the Story of Art Pepper* (New York, 1979, 2/1994) [incl. discography by T. Selbert]

P. Welding: 'Art Pepper: Rewards of the Straight Life', *Down Beat*, xlvi/18 (1979), 16–19 [incl. discography]

Oral history material in *US-NEij*

BARRY KERNFELD

Pepper, J(ames) W(elsh) (*b* Philadelphia, 1853; *d* Philadelphia, 28 July 1919). American music publisher and band instrument maker. He worked as an engraver in his father's printing business, gave music lessons and in 1876 founded a publishing house at 9th and Filbert streets in Philadelphia. From copper plates and a manually operated press he issued instrumental tutors, quicksteps and from 1877 to 1912 a monthly periodical entitled *J.W. Pepper's Musical Times and Band Journal* (later the *Musical Times*). Around 1887 he acquired a structure at 8th and Locust streets which came to be known as the J.W. Pepper Building, accommodating a large salesroom, an instrument factory and a printing plant, equipped with steam-powered presses to produce sheet music on a large scale. During the next four decades the firm published nearly 200 new titles a year; except for a small group of sacred songs issued by Pepper Publishing Co. in 1901–4, these were all orchestral and band works intended for civic, commercial and school ensembles. Many compositions and arrangements appeared in journals – *Quickstep*, *Brass and Reed Band*, *Ballroom*, *Theatre and Dance* and *Opera House*. The *J.W. Pepper Piano Music Magazine* was begun in 1900, and a separate 20th-century series was also established. Among the composers whose works were published by Pepper were Sousa, Pryor, Grafulla, Southwell, William Paris Chambers, Nick Brown, Thomas H. Rollinson, William Henry Dana and Fred Luscomb. Publication of new works ceased in 1924.

Pepper sold more than 70,000 brass instruments and a similar number of drums, woodwind and string instruments. His instruments were moderately priced and, like his sheet music, intended for a mass audience. Controversy concerning the invention of the SOUSAPHONE culminated in a claim by C.G. Conn to have invented it in 1898, although Pepper had introduced a prototype as early as 1893. The manufacture of Pepper instruments continued until J.W. Pepper & Son was formed in 1910, after which most instruments sold by the firm were imported. On Pepper's death the direction of J.W. Pepper & Son was assumed by Howard E. Pepper (1882–1930), in turn succeeded by his widow, Maude E. Pepper. The firm was sold in 1942 and moved to Valley Forge, Pennsylvania, in 1973. Guided by Harold K. Burtch and his son Dean C. Burtch, who became president on his father's death in 1963, the firm grew by the mid-1980s to be the largest retailer of sheet music for instrumental ensembles in the USA.

BIBLIOGRAPHY

J.W. Pepper's Musical Times and Band Journal (Philadelphia and Chicago, 1877–1912)

W.H. Dana: *J.W. Pepper's Guide ... Arranging Band Music* (Philadelphia, 1878)

W.H. Dana: *J.W. Pepper's Guide ... Orchestra Music* (Philadelphia, 1879)

LLOYD P. FARRAR

Pepping, Ernst (*b* Duisburg, 12 Sept 1901; *d* Berlin, 1 Feb 1981). German composer. On leaving school he went, in 1922, to study at the Berlin Hochschule für Musik, where his composition teacher was Gmeindl. His early music was immediately well received: he was awarded the Mendelssohn Prize in 1926, and works of his were performed at the 1927 Donaueschingen Festival and the 1928 Baden-Baden Festival. After a temporary job as an arranger of film scores, he worked as a freelance musician in Mülheim from 1930, and in 1934 he moved to a post at the Kirchenmusikschule in Berlin-Spandau, where he remained for the rest of his career. In addition, he taught at the Berlin Hochschule für Musik from 1953 to 1968. Pepping was a member of the Berlin Academy of Arts and of the Munich Academy of Fine Arts. His numerous awards included the Berlin Kunstpreis für Musik (1948), the Lübeck Buxtehude Prize (1951), the Düsseldorf Robert Schumann Prize (1956), prizes given by the Bremen Philharmonic Society (1962) and the Bavarian Academy of Fine Arts (1964), and an honorary doctorate of the Free University of Berlin.

Pepping's earliest instrumental compositions show his search for new means of expression within an essentially constructivist and strict contrapuntal style. The continuing influence of 16th- and 17th-century music is already evident, particularly in the use of cantus firmus technique, a tendency to linearity, Baroque concerto forms and a broadening of tonality on the basis of the church modes. The theoretical foundation of these features is expounded in Pepping's books, *Stilwende der Musik* and *Der polyphone Satz*. After turning his back on the experiments of his first pieces, he concentrated on choral music, where he employed two distinct manners: one rigorously polyphonic and the other freer and more readily influenced by the text. In his later choral works (from about 1948) these two approaches were increasingly intermingled, enabling Pepping to construct effective large-scale forms. The contents of his *Spandauer Chorbuch* are particularly representative of these austere works intended principally

for use in the Protestant Church. In his *a cappella* pieces, such as the *Missa 'Dona nobis pacem'* and the *Passionsbericht des Matthäus*, Pepping's 'essential gift in the sphere of polyphony' (see Poos, p.51) is combined with a madrigal style rich in imagery; whereas such works as the *Te Deum* transcend their liturgical purpose with magnificent passages for brass reminiscent of Hindemith. Pepping's secular vocal music includes a number of choruses which make great demands on the singers, and four song cycles comprising together around 70 songs which were all written during the period 1945–6. These songs, which Moser described as 'lovingly chiselled', unite simple melodic lines with motivic development in the piano.

As with the choral music, most of Pepping's organ pieces are for church use, and their construction is largely governed by cantus firmi. On the other hand, his piano music has a gay insouciance and often employs Classical or Baroque forms. Of the three symphonies, the first bears the mark of Haydn, while the second encompasses severe polyphony and lyrical expansiveness, closing with a passacaglia. This neo-Baroque tendency, found at all periods in Pepping's work, is indicative of the constancy of his musical evolution. While he has maintained links with the major currents in German Protestant church music, his archaism represents a highly personal return to the past.

WORKS
SACRED VOCAL
unacc. chorus unless otherwise stated

Choralsuite, small chorus, large chorus, 1928; Kanonische Suite in 3 Chorälen, male chorus 3vv, 1928; Deutsche Choralmesse, 6vv, 1928; Hymnen, 4vv, 1929; Kleine Messe, 3vv, 1929; Choralbuch, 30 pieces, 4–6vv, 1931; Ps xc, 6vv, 1934; Spandauer Chorbuch, 20 vols., 2–6vv, 1934–8, rev. G. Grote, 4 vols., 1962; Uns ist ein Kind geboren, 4vv, 1936; 6 kleine Motetten, 4vv, 1937; Ein jegliches hat seine Zeit, 4vv, 1937; 3 Evangelien-Motetten, 1937–8; Deutsche Messe 'Kyrie Gott Vater in Ewigkeit', 4–6vv, 1938

25 Weihnachtslieder, 2–3vv, 1938; Missa 'Dona nobis pacem', 4–8vv, 1948; O Haupt voll Blut und Wunden, A/Bar, orch, 1949; Missa brevis, 1950; Passionsbericht des Matthäus, 4–10vv, 1950; Liedmotetten nach Weisen der Böhmischen Brüder, 1951–3; Bicinien, 1954–5; TeD, solo vv, chorus, orch, 1956; Das Weltgericht, 4vv, 1958; Die Weihnachtsgeschichte des Lukas, 4–7vv, 1959; Neues Choralbuch, 3–4vv, 1959; Johannes der Täufer, Vesper für Chor, 1961; Ps viii, 1962; Ps xxiii, 1962; Gesänge der Böhmischen Brüder in Variationen, 1963; Aus hartem Weh die Menschheit klagt, 3–4vv, 1964; Ps cxxxix, A, chorus 4vv, orch, 1964; Deines Lichtes Glanz, 4–6vv, 1967

SECULAR VOCAL

Choral: Sprüche und Lieder (J.W. von Goethe, R.M. Rilke, J. von Eichendorff), 3–5vv, 1930; Das gute Leben, 3 pieces, 4vv, 1936; Lob der Träne, 4vv, 1940; Das Jahr (J. Weinheber), 4vv, 1940; Der Wagen (Weinheber), 4–5vv, 1940–41; Der Morgen, 4 solo vv, 6 solo vv, 1942; 33 Volkslieder, female/children's chorus 2–3vv, 1943; Heut und ewig (Goethe), 1948–9; Die wandelnde Glocke (Goethe), 1952

Song cycles: Liederbuch nach Gedichten von Paul Gerhard, 1945–6; As ik hier dit Jaar weer (K. Groth), 1946; Haus- und Trostbuch (C. Brentano, Goethe, W. Bergengruen, F.G. Jünger, etc), 1946; Vaterland (Jünger), 1946

ORGAN

Chorale Partita 'Wer nur den lieben Gott lässt walten', 1932; Chorale Partita 'Wie schön leuchtet der Morgenstern', 1933; Grosses Orgelbuch, 3 vols., 1939; Kleines Orgelbuch, 1940; Toccata and Fugue 'Mitten wir im Leben sind', 1941; Conc no.1, 1941; Conc no.2, 1941; 4 Fugues, D, c, E♭, f, 1942; 2 Fugues, c♯, 1943; 3 Fugues on B–A–C–H, 1943 [also for pf]

Partita no.1 'Ach wie flüchtig', 1953; Partita no.2 'Wer weiss, wie nahe mir mein Ende', 1953; Partita no.3 'Mit Fried und Freud', 1953; Böhmisches Orgelbuch, 1953; Hymnen, 1954; 12 Chorale Preludes, 1958; Sonata, 1958; 25 Orgelchoräle nach Sätzen des

Spandauer Chorbuches, 1960; Preludes/Postludes to 18 Chorales, 1969

OTHER WORKS

Orch: Prelude, 1929; Invention, 1930; Partita, 1934; Lust hab ich g'habt zur Musika, Variationen zu einem Liedsatz von Senfl, 1937; Syms: no.1, 1939, no.2, 1942, no.3 'Die Tageszeiten', 1944; Serenade, 1944–5; Variations, 1949; Pf Conc, 1950; 2 Orchesterstücke über eine Chanson des Binchois, 1958

Chbr: Variations and Suite, 2 vn, 1932; Str Qt, 1943; Sonata, fl, pf, 1958

Pf: Sonatine, 1931; 2 Romanzen, 1935; 3 Sonatas, 1937; Tanzweisen und Rundgesang, 1938; 3 Fugues on B–A–C–H, 1943 [also for org]; Sonata no.4, 1945; Phantasien, 1945; Variations, 2 sets, 1948; Zuhause, 1950

Principal publishers: Bärenreiter, Schott

WRITINGS

Stilwende der Musik (Mainz, 1934)
Der polyphone Satz, i: Der cantus-firmus-Satz (Berlin, 1943, 2/1950); ii: Übungen im doppelten Kontrapunkt und im Kanon (Berlin, 1957)

BIBLIOGRAPHY

K. Laux: Musik und Musiker der Gegenwart (Essen, 1949), chap. 'Ernst Pepping'
H.J. Moser: Die evangelische Kirchenmusik in Deutschland (Berlin, 1954)
K.H. Wörner: Neue Musik in der Entscheidung (Mainz, 1954)
W. Hamm: Studien über Ernst Peppings drei Klaviersonaten (diss., U. of Würzburg,1955)
A. Dürr: ' Gedanken zum Kirchenmusik-Schaffen Ernst Peppings', Musik und Kirche, xxxi (1961), 145–72
D. Manicke: ' Gruss an Ernst Pepping zum 70. Geburtstag', Musica, xxv (1971), 501–5
W.B. Weeks: The Use of the Chorale in the Organ Works of Ernst Pepping (DMA diss., U. of Arizona, 1971)
H. Poos, ed.: Festschrift Ernst Pepping (Berlin, 1972) [incl. bibliography and list of works]
A. Adrio: 'Die Weisen der Böhmischen Brüder im Werk Ernst Peppings', Musicae scientiae collectanea: Festschrift Karl Gustav Fellerer, ed. H. Hüschen (Cologne, 1973), 23–34
F.M. Beyer: ' Ernst Pepping zum Gedenken', Musica, xxxv (1981), 1995–7
D.L. Brown: An Analysis of the Free Organ Compositions of Ernst Pepping (diss., Michigan State U., 1981)
K.D. Hüschen: Studien zum Motettenschaffen Ernst Peppings (Regensburg, 1987)

KLAUS KIRCHBERG

Pepusch, Johann Christoph (b Berlin, 1667; d London, 20 July 1752). German composer and theorist. He was the son of a Protestant minister and studied music theory under one Klingenberg (probably not the son of the Stettin organist Friedrich Gottlieb Klingenberg as Hawkins stated, but perhaps an elder relation), and practice under Grosse, a Saxon organist. From the age of 14 he was employed at the Prussian court, where he remained until about the end of the 17th century. According to Hawkins he resolved to leave Germany after witnessing the execution without trial of a Prussian officer accused of insubordination 'and put himself under the protection of a government founded on better principles'. After travelling through Holland, some time after September 1697 he settled in London, where he remained for the rest of his life; from 1707 he lived at Hooker's (later Boswell) Court near Lincoln's Inn Fields. He is known to have frequented the concerts of Thomas Britton at Clerkenwell, and it was probably there that he became acquainted with the poet and dramatist John Hughes, with whom he later collaborated in a number of works. His first permanent employment in London was as a viola player, and later harpsichordist at Drury Lane Theatre in 1704. His only stage work from this period was the pasticcio Thomyris, Queen of Scythia, but he was well known as a composer

of instrumental music, much of it published in both Amsterdam and London, and as a performer in and organizer of public and private concerts.

In January 1708 he joined the opera company operating from Vanburgh's Queen's Theatre in the Haymarket. There he served as violinist, harpsichordist, and agent for the soprano Margherita de l'Epine. The German traveller Zacharias Conrad von Uffenbach described a concert he attended in June 1710 at which l'Epine sang, accompanied by members of the opera house band directed by Pepusch from the harpsichord. Pepusch and l'Epine were married some time between 1718 (the traditional date, but now impossible to establish) and 1723; their only son, who died in July 1739 after showing considerable talent and promise, was baptized on 9 January 1724.

In July 1713 Pepusch, along with William Croft, was awarded the degree of DMus at Oxford; the music he submitted for this occasion, including the ode Hail, queen of islands! Hail, illustrious fair, has not survived. In 1714 Pepusch moved to Drury Lane as musical director and over the next two seasons contributed four essays in the genre of the English masque: Venus and Adonis, Myrtillo and Laura, Apollo and Daphne and The Death of Dido. These were intended as independent afterpieces, with plots that are completely self-contained, interpolate no real element of comedy, and have a tragic dénouement. In autumn 1716 he transferred to Lincoln's Inn Fields, where he served as musical director for much of the next 15 years but he composed little of importance for the stage.

Sometime after this date Pepusch became involved with the musical establishment of James Brydges, Earl of Carnarvon, and he was replaced by John Ernest Galliard as musical director at Lincoln's Inn Fields for the 1717–18 season. His presence at Cannons, Brydges's estate near Edgware in Middlesex, can be documented from as early as December 1717, and he and George Frideric Handel were both there in April 1718. Although he was again active at Lincoln's Inn Fields for the 1718–19 season, Pepusch seems to have been appointed musical director at Cannons in mid-1719 with a salary of £25 per quarter, perhaps as a consequence of Brydges' reorganization of his household on his elevation to the title of first Duke of Chandos in April of that year. Pepusch was responsible for providing music for the duke's chapel and chamber on a regular basis until mid-1721, presumably dividing his time between Cannons and his London house. After this date the duke cut back his musical establishment in response to financial losses, but Pepusch continued to provide occasional musicians from London until 1725, when organized musical activity at Cannons seems to have ceased.

Pepusch provided two new works for the 1723–4 season at Lincoln's Inn Fields, The Union of the Three Sister Arts and a revision of Betterton's The Prophetess, or The History of Dioclesian, and presumably conducted the band for the famous series of pantomimes between 1723 and 1730 featuring the theatre owner John Rich as Harlequin and music by Galliard. He was almost certainly in charge for the opening night of John Gay's famous satire The Beggar's Opera on 29 January 1728, for which he probably composed the overture and may have arranged the airs (although the printed bass lines do not reflect his elegance and technical skill). A sequel, Polly, was published in 1729, but censorship prevented its performance on stage until after Pepusch's death. Pepusch

1. Johann Christoph Pepusch: portrait by Thomas Hudson, c1735 (National Portrait Gallery, London, on deposit Beningbrough Hall)

an overture that uses one of the opera's popular tunes, has tended to overshadow his own music. His earliest surviving works are mostly instrumental and include well over 100 violin sonatas and several recorder and flute sonatas. These are mostly modelled on the four-movement plan of Corelli, whose sonatas and concertos Pepusch later edited for publication in London. Particularly interesting are the manuscript sets of sonatas composed for various English violinists, each containing 16 works in as many different keys, thus anticipating (and going beyond) the similar arrangement of Bach's two- and three-part Inventions. (Pepusch included B major in addition to the keys that Bach used.)

Most, if not all, of Pepusch's church music was written for the Duke of Chandos. It consists mainly of verse anthems in which soloists and chorus alternate, often with quite elaborate instrumental accompaniment. The *Magnificat* is similarly composed, though on a larger scale, and may well have been written to celebrate the opening of the chapel at Cannons in August 1720. Some anthems exist in versions for male voices and continuo, which may reflect the economies forced upon the duke in the 1720s, or possibly performances at the Academy of Ancient Music after the boys of St Paul's and the Chapel Royal had been withdrawn in 1731. Some of Pepusch's most attractive vocal writing is found in the secular cantatas, written, according to Hughes's preface to the

probably retired from the theatre at the end of the 1732–3 season and subsequently concentrated primarily on his antiquarian interests.

In 1735, when he moved to Fetter Lane, Pepusch reorganized the Academy of Ancient Music (of which he had been a founder-member in 1726) as a seminary for the musical instruction of young boys. In December 1737 he was made organist of the Charterhouse, and in 1745 (the year before his wife died) he was elected a Fellow of the Royal Society, to whom he delivered a paper 'Of the Various Genera and Species of Music Among the Ancients'. Throughout his career he was much sought after as a teacher, his pupils including Boyce, Benjamin Cooke, J.H. Roman, John Travers, George Berg, James Nares and Ephraim Kellner. After his death Travers and Kellner shared with the Academy of Ancient Music their master's extensive and important library of books and music, among which was the collection of virginal music now known as the Fitzwilliam Virginal Book.

Largely as a result of Burney's estimate of him, posterity has tended to look upon Pepusch as an academic pedant who opposed Handel's cause in England. He was certainly the most learned musical antiquarian of his day, but to regard him only in this way is to ignore the lively theatre music and the elegant English cantatas, which are mostly carefully composed, but by no means dry. And though the success of *The Beggar's Opera* contributed to Handel's difficulties in promoting Italian opera for the Royal Academy, there is no indication of any personal or professional enmity between the two men. Even after 1728 Pepusch subscribed to publications of Handel's operas, and he also arranged performances of his music by the Academy of Ancient Music.

The unprecedented popularity of *The Beggar's Opera*, for which Pepusch may have supplied only the basses and

2. Title-page of Pepusch's 'Six English Cantatas', bk 2 (London: Walsh & Hare, 1720)

first printed collection, 'as an Experiment of introducing a sort of Composition which had never been naturaliz'd in our Language'. Pepusch's cantatas are italianate in their structure of two arias separated (and usually preceded) by recitative and in the almost invariable use of the da capo form, but the music itself often tends towards the kind of English tunefulness that kept his most famous cantata, *Alexis*, popular for over a century. *Alexis* is for voice and continuo only, but most of the other cantatas include an obbligato instrument, which Pepusch combined in skilful counterpoints with the voice and bass. Many cantatas were sung as interludes in the theatre, but some at least were designed for more intimate performance. Four out of the six cantatas in the second printed volume (dedicated to the Duke of Chandos) include a part for solo recorder (fig.2) and were probably performed at Cannons.

Pepusch's writing in his masques is intentionally italianate, with da capo arias, secco recitatives and typical Italian instrumentation using strings and woodwind; there is hardly any use of chorus or dances. These masques, in particular the longest and most successful, *Venus and Adonis*, are virtually operatic presentations in miniature.

Pepusch seems to have retired from composition after about 1729 and devoted himself mainly to the study and performance of ancient music. His most important theoretical work, *A Treatise on Harmony*, was published anonymously in 1730, possibly at the instigation of his pupil, Viscount Paisley, and revised the following year. It represents a last-ditch attempt to restore solmization as a basis for the instruction of harmonic theory.

Pepusch's brother Heinrich Gottfried (*d* 1750), an oboist employed by the Elector of Brandenburg, visited London in 1704; no compositions by him are known.

WORKS
thematic catalogue in Cook (1982)

DRAMATIC
all performed in London; all printed works published in London

Thomyris, Queen of Scythia (pasticcio, P.A. Motteux), Drury Lane, 1 April 1707; recits ? arr. Pepusch; songs (*c*1719)

Venus and Adonis (masque, C. Cibber, after Ovid: *Metamorphoses*), Drury Lane, 12 March 1715; score and parts *GB-Lcm*, songs (1716)

Myrtillo and Laura (pastoral masque, Cibber), Drury Lane, 5 Nov 1715; score *Lam*, frags. *Bu, Cfm, Ob*

Apollo and Daphne (masque, J. Hughes), Drury Lane, 12 Jan 1716; score *Lcm*, frags. *Lam, Ob, US-Wc*

The Death of Dido (masque, B. Booth, after Virgil: *Aeneid*), Drury Lane, 17 April 1716; *GB-Lam*

The Prophetess, or The History of Dioclesian (op with spoken dialogue, T. Betterton and J. Dryden, after J. Fletcher and P. Massinger), Lincoln's Inn Fields, 28 Nov 1724, music lost

Alexis and Dorinda (afterpiece), Lincoln's Inn Fields, 15 April 1725, music lost, ?by Pepusch

The Beggar's Opera (ballad op, J. Gay), Lincoln's Inn Fields, 29 Jan 1728; ? airs arr. Pepusch, ? ov. by Pepusch (1728/R)

The Wedding (ballad op, E. Hawker), Lincoln's Inn Fields, 6 May 1729; ov. by Pepusch (1729)

Polly (ballad opera, 3, Gay), Little Theatre, Haymarket, 19 June 1777; ? by Pepusch (1729); 1777 score arr. S. Arnold, *US-CAh*

Songs and other music for various stage works in *GB-Lam, Och* and pubd singly and in 18th-century anthologies

Doubtful: music in Marsaniello, or A Fisherman Prince, Lincoln's Inn Fields, 29 March 1729; prelude, songs *Lam* [revival of T. D'Urfey: *The History of the Rise and Fall of Marsaniello*]

ODES

Ye gen'rous arts and muses join [Britannia and Augusta] (J. Hughes), in honour of the Duke of Devonshire, 1707, 2 S, 2 rec, 2 ob, 2 vn, va, bn, bc, *B-Bc, GB-Lbl*

Hail, queen of islands! Hail, illustrious fair [Peace, Apollo and Britain], for Peace of Utrecht, 1713, music lost, text in *Gu*

Fame and Isis joined in one [Ocean's Glory, or A Parley of Rivers], coronation of George I, 1714, ?unperf., music lost, text in D'Urfey: *Wit and Mirth, or Pills to Purge Melancholy*, i (London, 1719)

To joy, to triumphs [Fame and Cambria] (Hughes), for birthday of Princess of Wales, 1716, 2 S, tpt, rec, ob, hp, 2 vn, va, vc, bc, *Lam, Lcm*

Great Phoebus, who in thy unwearied race, for St Cecilia's Day, S, A, 2 T, B, SSATB, ob, tpt, 2 vn, va, bc, *Lam*, ?by Pepusch

OTHER SECULAR VOCAL
cantatas unless otherwise stated; some of those in collections also published separately

6 English Cantatas, bk 1 (London, 1710/R), texts by Hughes: Airy Cloe, proud and young [Cloe], S, 2 ob, 2 vn, va, bc; As beauty's goddess [The Island of Beauty], S, bc; Fragrant Flora, hast, appear! [The Spring], S, vn, bc; Miranda's tunefull voice and fame [Miranda], S, vn, bc; See! from the silent groves [Alexis], S/T, bc [vc, kbd]; While Corydon the lovely shepherd [Corydon], S, rec; bc

6 English Cantatas, bk 2 (London, 1720/R):   Cleora sat beneath a shade (J. Slaughter), S, rec, bc; Kindly fate at length release me (L. Theobald), S, tpt, 2 vn, va, bc; Love frowns in beauteous Myra's eyes (Myra, Hughes), S, rec, bc; Menalcas once the gayest swain (Gee), S, rec, bc; When loves soft passion (J. Blackley), S, rec, bc; While pale Britannia pensive sate [Britannia] (Cibber), S, tpt, 2 vn, va, bc

2 cants. in 12 Cantatas in English … by Several Authors (London, *c*1720):   On fam'd Arcadia's flow'ry plains (pastoral, Hughes), S, ob, bc;
The god of love had lost his bow, S, bc

The Union of the Three Sister Arts (musical entertainment, ?Walsh), S, T, B, SATB, 2 ob, 2 vn, va, bc, 1723, frag. *GB-Ckc*, songs (1723)
An hapless shepherd, S, 2 vn, bc, *GB-Bu*;

Crudel, ingrata, S, hpd, vc, *Lbl*; Fonte adorato, A, bc, *Lbl*; Hymen, source of human bliss, S, A, T, B, SATB, ob, 2 vn, va, bc, *Lam* ?by Pepusch; No, no, vain world [The Meditation], 2 S, 2 rec, 2 ob, vn solo, 2 vn, va, bc, perf. in *The Lady Jane Gray* (play, N. Rowe), 1715; *Lam, Lcm*; S'io peno e gemo, S, ob, bc, *Lcm*; Twas on the eve, S, bc, *Lcm*; Victorious Caelia charming fair, S, A, SATB, 2 vn ,va, bc, *Lam* ?by Pepusch; Vorrei scoprir, S, vn, bc, *Lcm*; Wake th' harmonious voice and string (serenata, Hughes), for the marriage of Lord Cobham to Mrs Anne Halsey, 2 S, ob, rec, 2 vn, va, bc, *Lam, Lcm*

Lost, cited in Chandos library inventory of Aug 1720, see Baker: A severa battaglia; Mirar il caro ogetto; Non ti bastava, oh Clori; Strephon, young uncautious boy, 1v, insts; Sur les flots inquiets de la mer, 1v, bc; The muses once to Phoebus came, 1v, insts

Lost, texts in J. Hughes, *Poems on Several Occasions With Some Select Essays in Prose* (London, 1735):   Foolish love! I scorn thy darts; On silver Tyber's vocal shore [Cupid and Scarlatti]; Why too amorous heroe [The Soldier in Love]; Young Strephon by his folded sheep

Other lost cants., cited in *LS*
Doubtful: As Silvia in a forest lay [Sylvia's Moan], madrigal, SATB, *Lam, Lms*

SACRED VOCAL

Mag, S, A, T, B, SATB, ob, bn, tpt, 2 vn, va, vc/db, org, before Oct 1721, ?autograph *GB-Lbl*

Motets: Beatus vir, SATB, *Lbl, Lcm*; Laetatus sum, SATB, *Lcm*; Te aeternum Patrem, SAT, *US-Wc*

Anthems: Blessed is the man, S, S, A, T, B/SATTB, 2 vn solo, 2 vn, va, vc/db, bc, *GB-Lam*; I will magnifie thee O Lord, T/TTB, bc, *Lam*; Lord Thou art become gracious, S, A, T, B/SAATB, ob, tpt, 2 vn, va, vc/db, bc, before Aug 1720, *Lam*; O be joyfull in God, A/SATB, ob, 2 vn, db, vc, *Lbl*, rev. for S, S, A, T, B/SATB, ob, 2 vn, va, vc, org, before Aug 1720, *Lam*; O give thanks, S, A, B/SATB, ob, 3 vn, b, before Aug 1720, *Ob*; O praise the Lord, S, bc, in J. Weldon, *Divine Harmony: 6 Select Anthems* (London, 1716–17); O praise the Lord, A, A, B/SATB, 2 bn/vc, bc, *Lcm, LF, Ob*; O praise the Lord, T, B/TTTB, bc, *Lam*; O sing unto the Lord,

S, S, B, 2 vn, org, *Lbl*, rev. for SSATB, 2 vn, va, b, before Aug 1720, *Lwa*, *Ob*; Rejoyce in the Lord, S, A, T, T, B/SATB, fl, ob, tpt, 2 vn, va, bc, before Aug 1720, *Lam*

I will magnifie thee O God, S, unison vv, 2 vn, bc, arr. of Bassani's motet Alligeri amores, *Cfm*, *Lbl*, *Och*, *WO*

Lost anthems, cited in Chandos library inventory of Aug 1720, see Baker and Beeks (1993): O come let us sing, SSB, insts; The Lord is King, SATB, insts

Lost anthems, cited in Chapel Royal workbook of 1749: I will give thanks unto thee; O God, thou art my God

INSTRUMENTAL

op.

[1]   VI sonates, rec, bc [kbd/bn] (Amsterdam, 1705–6); as Six Sonatas or Solos (London, 1707); ed. F.J. Giesbert (Mainz, 1939), ed. in Moecks Kammersmusik, xi, xxi–xxiii (Celle, 1939)

?   [16] Sonates, vn, bc, pts 1–2 (Amsterdam, 1707), incl. in XXIV Solos (London, 1708)

—   A Second Set of [6] Solos, rec, bc [bn/b rec/hpd/org] (London, 1709); ed. H. Ruf (Mainz, 1963), ed. W. Hess (Winterthur, 1982)

—   Airs, 2 vn (London, 1709), for 2 rec (London, 1709)

3   XII sonates, 2 vn/ob/fl, bc [org/vc] (Amsterdam, before Oct 1711), 11 in Twelve Sonatas in Parts ... Corrected by Mr Wm Corbett (London, 1710); 6 ed. in Mitteldeutsches Musikarchiv, 2/i–ii (1955–7)

4   XII sonates, vn, vc/bc (Amsterdam, before Oct 1711), lost, advertised in *Post-Man*, 16 October 1711

5   X sonates, vn, bc (Amsterdam, *c*1711–12) [pt 3 of op.2], 8 in XXIV Solos (London, 1708)

6   X sonates, vn, bc (Amsterdam, *c*1711–12) [pt 4 of op.2]

7   X sonates, nos.1–8 for fl/ob, vn, bc, no.9 for fl, va da gamba, bc, no.10 for rec, fl, bc (Amsterdam, *c*1717–18), lost, listed in Le Cene catalogue, 1737

8   VI concerts, 2 rec, 2 fl/ob/vn, bc (Amsterdam, *c*1717–18) [not all playable with this scoring]; ed. D. Lasocki (London, 1974)

Concerto grosso, D, tpt, str, *D-ROu*, ed. G. Blechert (Leipzig, 1980); Sinfonia à 5, G, 2 fl, 2 vn, bc, *ROu*; concerto 'Partie Englitair', C, vn, 3 ob, bc, *SWl*; concerto grosso, a, 4 vn, va, b, *GB-Ob*; 5 concerto grossi, G, D, F, F, e, 1/2 vn, str, *D-Dl*; concerto grosso, D, 2 vn, str, *POTh*; 2 concertos, a, d, 2 vn, va, b, *US-Wc*; concerto grosso, G, vn, str, bc, *S-Uu*; concerto grosso, str, B♭, *GB-Lbl*; Concerto grosso, A, vn, 2 vn, va, b, *Lam*

Lost concs.: 5 for tpt, ob, 4 vn, va, b; 4 in six pts; 1 for ob, insts; 3 for unspecified insts; all cited in Chandos library inventory of Aug 1720, see Baker; 1 for flageolet, insts, 1717, and others perf. in London theatres and concert halls, see *LS*

43 Trio sonatas, 20 for 2 vn, bc, 20 for other combinations, 3 for 2 tr insts, b, *D-Dl*, *ROu*, *GB-Lam*, *Lbl*, *Lcm*, *Och*, *US-R*, *Wc*

6 sets of 16 solos or sonatas, vn, b viol/hpd, *B-Bc*, *D-Bsb* according to Eitner, *GB-CDp*, *Lbl*, *S-Uu*, *US-R* [12 from set 2 pubd in opps.5 and 6]; 8 solos or sonatas, vn, b viol/hpd, *J-Tn*; 16 solos or sonatas, vn, b viol/hpd, *B-Bc*; 5 Select Sonatas, ?vn, bc, *US-R*; other sonatas, vn, bc, *GB-Ckc*, *Lbl*, *Lcm*, *Mp*; sonatas or solos, fl, bc [some also for vn], *D-ROu*, *GB-Lcm*, BENcoke; sonata, ob/vn, bc, *D-ROu*; other sonatas pubd singly or in 18th-century anthologies

Miscellaneous pieces, kbd, *B-Bc*, *GB-BENcoke*, *Cu*, *Lam*, *Lbl*, *Lco*, *Ldc*, *Mp*, *Ob*, *US-NYp*

THEORETICAL WORKS

Rules, or A Short and Compleate Method for Attaining to Play a Thorough Bass upon the Harpsichord or Organ, by an Eminent Master [?J.C. Pepusch] (London, *c*1730)

A Treatise on Harmony: Containing the Chief Rules for Composing in Two, Three and Four Parts (London, 1730, 2/1731/R)

'Of the Various Genera and Species of Music Among the Ancients', *Philosophical Transactions of the Royal Society*, xliv (1746), 266–75

A Short Account of the Twelve Modes of Composition and their Progression in Every Octave (MS, 1751), lost

EDITIONS

The Score of the 4 Setts of Sonatas ... Compos'd by A. Corelli ... the Whole Carefully Corrected by Several Most Eminent Masters, and Revis'd by Dr Pepusch (London, 1732)

The Score of the 12 Concertos ... compos'd by Arcangelo Corelli ... the Whole Carefully Corrected by Several Most Eminent Masters, and Revis'd by Dr Pepusch (London, 1732)

BIBLIOGRAPHY

BurneyH; EitnerQ; FiskeETM; GroveO (D.F. Cook); *HawkinsH; LS*

J. Downes: *Roscius anglicanus* (London, 1708/R); ed. J. Milhous and R.O. Hume (London, 1987)

'Pepusch's Will', *MT*, xliv (1903), 312 only

C.W. Hughes: 'Johann Christopher Pepusch', *MQ*, xxxi (1945), 54–70

C.H.C. and M.I. Baker: *The Life and Circumstances of James Brydges, First Duke of Chandos* (Oxford, 1949)

A.J.E. Lello: 'Dr Pepusch', *MT*, xciii (1952), 209–10

J. Wilson, ed.: *Roger North on Music* (London, 1959)

H.W. Fred: *The Instrumental Music of Johann Christopher Pepusch* (diss., U. of North Carolina, 1961)

H.D. Johnstone: 'An Unknown Book of Organ Voluntaries', *MT*, cviii (1967), 1003–7

J.G. Williams: *The Life, Work and Influence of J.C. Pepusch* (diss., U. of York, 1976)

D.F. Cook: '*Venus and Adonis*: an English Masque "After the Italian Manner"', *MT*, cxii (1980), 553–7

D.F. Cook: *The Life and Works of Johann Christopher Pepusch, 1667–1752* (diss., U. of London, 1982)

G. Beeks: '"A Club of Composers": Handel, Pepusch and Arbuthnot at Cannons', in A. Hicks and S. Sadie, ed., *Handel Tercentenary Collection* (London, 1987), 209–21

G. Beeks: 'The Chandos Anthems of Haym, Handel and Pepusch', *Göttinger Händel-Beiträge*, v (1993), 161–93

For further bibliography see BALLAD OPERA.

MALCOLM BOYD/GRAYDON BEEKS (with D.F. COOK)

Pepys, Samuel (*b* 23 Feb 1633; *d* London, 26 May 1703). English naval administrator, diarist (1660–69) and gentleman-amateur composer and performer on the viol, theorbo, flageolet, recorder and guitar. He had a good ear, sang at sight, received singing lessons and practised the *trillo* (a vocal ornament that John Playford's *Introduction* of 1654 had made available in England); and in 1662 he attempted composition under John Birchensha's instruction. He usually employed friends to provide or help him with accompaniments to the vocal parts that he wrote (e.g. *Beauty retire* and *It is decreed*); there is no evidence that he could write in tablature himself. He tried to study musical theory in 1667–8 from Morley's *Plaine and Easie Introduction* (1597), Playford's *Introduction* and other works, learnt the gamut and bought a spinet. He came to possess Kircher's *Musurgia*, Mersenne's *Harmonie universelle*, Birchensha's *Templum musicum* and Descartes' *Compendium* (in the original and in Lord Brouncker's translation of 1653). Ten years after the diary period he employed a domestic musician, Cesare Morelli, to set songs and write out, with guitar tablature, a collection of his favourite pieces. A few of his songs survive (*GB-Cmc*).

Pepys's diary affords a detailed knowledge of Restoration domestic music, including the level of amateur musical ability and the taste for declamatory song. He favoured Henry Lawes's recitatives, composed his own recitative vocal part for a soliloquy by Ben Jonson and had Morelli set 'To be or not to be' (a speech Pepys learnt by heart in 1664) as a recitative. His friendship with an actress, Mrs Knepp, brought him into contact with Nicholas Lanier, a copy of whose *Hero and Leander* (*c*1628) he might have obtained during winter 1665–6 and which Morelli transcribed between 1679 and 1681. Pepys appreciated the nature of recitative. In 1667, hearing Giovanni Battista Draghi sing part of an Italian opera he had composed, he commented (12 February):

My great wonder is how this man doth do to keep in memory so perfectly the music of the whole Act, both for the voice and for the instrument too … But in Recitativo the sense much helps him, for there is but one proper way of discoursing and giving the accent.

And hearing groups of Italian singers later that year, he remarked (16 February) 'In singing, the words are to be considered and how they are fitted with notes, and then the common accent of the country is to be known', and on 7 April, 'The better the words are set, the more they take in of the ordinary tone of the country whose language the song speaks'. Unconsciously following arguments appropriate to the Florentine Camerata, he disliked partsongs and wished the words to be always intelligible in performance; yet he enjoyed tuneful Italian songs with words of diluted meaning, such as *La cruda, la bella* and *S'io muoio*.

While the diary shows that there was a certain amount of circulation of songs and instrumental music in manuscript, especially by professional teachers, one may reasonably assume that for the most part Pepys got his songs from printed sources, that the majority of the songs mentioned in his diary can be related to available publications and that the latter can be identified. In addition to books mentioned above, he possessed and used the three volumes of Henry Lawes's *Ayres and Dialogues* (1653, 1655, 1658), at least five of John Playford's vocal and instrumental publications, Richard Dering's *Cantica sacra* (1662), William King's *Poems of Mr Cowley and Others* (1668) and Pietro Reggio's *Songs* (1680).

WRITINGS

The Letters of Samuel Pepys and his Family Circle, ed. H.T. Heath (Oxford, 1955)
Diary, ed. R. Latham and W. Matthews (London, 1970–83) [see vol.x for commentary on the diary's musical references]

BIBLIOGRAPHY

McD. Emslie: 'Pepys' Shakespeare Song', *Shakespeare Quarterly*, vi (1955), 159
McD. Emslie: 'Pepys' Songs and Song-Books in the Diary Period', *The Library*, 5th ser., xii (1957), 240–55
McD. Emslie: 'Milton on Lawes', *Music in English Renaissance Drama*, ed. J.H. Long (Lexington, KY, 1968), 96
J.E. Hearsey: *Young Mr. Pepys* (New York, 1974)
S. Race: 'Samuel Pepys, Music Lover', *The Consort*, no.39 (1983), 498–501

McDONALD EMSLIE

Pepys Choirbook (*GB-Cmc* Pepys 1236). *See* SOURCES, MS, §IX, 3.

Pepys Manuscript (*GB-Cmc* Pepys 1760). *See* SOURCES, MS, §IX, 8.

Pequeno, Mercedes (de Moura) Reis (*b* Rio de Janeiro, 8 Feb 1921). Brazilian music librarian and musicologist. She graduated from the National School of Music of the University of Brazil (now the Federal University of Rio de Janeiro) in 1973, and then pursued library science studies in the Administrative Department of Public Service, graduating in 1943. In 1951 she was appointed chief of the music division of the National Library in Rio de Janeiro, founding and organizing the music and sound recording collection and archives. She retired from that position in 1990, having built up the most comprehensive public music library in Brazil. From the 1960s to the 1990s she organized numerous exhibits (18 of them with printed catalogues that she compiled) on the life and works of European and Brazilian composers. She has participated in numerous national and international conferences of music research and music libraries and belonged to several international editorial boards. She first collaborated in the early 1940s on the *Revista brasileira de música*, then co-authored *Bibliografia musical brasileira (1820–1950)* with Luiz Heitor Corrêa de Azevedo and Cleofe Person de Mattos (Rio de Janeiro, 1952), and published *A música militar no Brasil no século XIX* (Rio de Janeiro, 1952). In 1994 she became a member of the Brazilian Academy of Music, for which she has coordinated the computerized Brazilian Music Bibliography project.

GERARD BÉHAGUE

Per, Il. *See* RUGERI.

Perabo, (Johann) Ernst (*b* Wiesbaden, 14 Nov 1845; *d* Boston, 29 Oct 1920). German-American pianist, teacher and composer. He began piano lessons with his father at the age of five, and was able to play all of Bach's '48' from memory by the age of 12. His family moved to New York in 1852, but he went back to Germany to complete his musical education. Between 1858 and 1865 he studied with Johann Andersen in Eimsbüttel, near Hamburg, then attended the Leipzig Conservatory, where his teachers included Moscheles, Alfred Richter, Moritz Hauptmann and Reinecke. He returned to the USA in 1865, and gave a number of concerts in the West before settling in Boston, where he made his first appearance with the Harvard Musical Association on 19 April 1866. He became well known as a pianist and as a composer and arranger of piano music. He gave a notable series of concerts where he performed the complete solo piano works of Schubert. Perabo was also renowned as a teacher: among his many pupils was Amy Beach. His works for the piano include *Moment musical* op.1, Scherzo op.2, Prelude op.3, Waltz op.4, Three Studies op.9, Pensées op.11, *Circumstance, or Fate of a Human Life* op.13 (after Tennyson) and Prelude, Romance and Toccatina op.19. His arrangements include ten transcriptions from Sullivan's *Iolanthe* op.14, concert fantasies on themes from Beethoven's *Fidelio* opp.16 and 17, and transcriptions of Schubert's 'Unfinished' and Anton Rubinstein's 'Ocean' Symphony.

JOSEPH REZITS

Perabovi [Parabovi, Perabuoni], **Filippo** [Francesco]**Maria** (*b* Bologna; *fl* 1577–1601). Italian composer and singer. He is recorded as a salaried musician at the Gonzaga court in Mantua in 1577 and 1578, and is later noted as a substitute *maestro di canto*, replacing Giulio Guarnieri, for two and a half months at the beginning of 1580 in the ducal chapel of S Barbara there. According to Bertolotti he was paid as a singer at the court in 1582, but by 1584 was *maestro di cappella* at Carpi. He evidently spent much of his early career at Mantua: in his only known work, *Il primo libro de madrigali a cinque et a sei* (Venice, 1588), the dedication to the new Duke of Mantua, Vincenzo Gonzaga, speaks of his wish to continue 'nella servitù ch'io haveva molti anni sono col Sereniss. Sig. suo Padre'. He was *maestro della musica* of the Confraternità dell'Annunziata in Viadana when his book was published, but he returned to Mantua and is recorded as a singer there at S Barbara between December 1592 and August 1601. The book includes two madrigal cycles each of seven stanzas and concludes with a setting of Guarini's *Tirsi morir volea*.

BIBLIOGRAPHY

BertolottiM; FenlonMM

P. Canal: *Della musica in Mantova* (Venice, 1881/R), 655–774

A. de Maddalena: *Le finanze del ducato di Mantova all'epoca di Guglielmo Gonzaga* (Milan, 1961), 231

P.M. Tagmann: 'La cappella dei maestri cantori della basilica palatina di Santa Barbara a Mantova (1565–1630): nuovo materiale scoperto negli archivi mantovani', *Civiltà mantovana*, iv (1970), 376–400

IAIN FENLON

Peragallo, Mario (*b* Rome, 25 March 1910; *d* Rome, 23 Nov 1996). Italian composer. He studied composition with Vincenzo di Donato and Casella. Between 1950 and 1954 he was artistic director of the Accademia Filarmonica Romana, and he was involved in the Società Italiana di Musica Contemporanea for many years (secretary, 1950–56; president, 1956–60 and 1963–85).

From the beginning of his career Peragallo was attracted to opera, at first following a lyrical, realistic manner halfway between Zandonai and late Puccini; the librettist Forzano also played a large part in shaping both *Ginevra degli Almieri* and *Lo stendardo di San Giorgio*. His postwar works did not abandon expansive lyricism, but the dramatic aspect became progressively more modern (e.g. *La collina*, with its seven solo episodes, with choral and orchestral introductions), as did the musical language; 12-note techniques were first used in *La gita in campagna*. His instrumental music of the period reveals similar characteristics (e.g. the Violin Concerto and *In memoriam*), and subsequently Peragallo moved cautiously in the direction of an avant-garde idiom (e.g. *Forme sovrapposte*), also experimenting with the interaction between traditional instruments and new sources of sound: *Vibrazioni* uses the 'tiptofono', a percussion ensemble of his own invention, while *Emircal* is for voices, orchestra and tape.

WORKS
(*selective list*)

Ops: Ginevra degli Almieri (melodrama, 3, G. Forzano), Rome, Opera, 12 Feb 1937; Lo stendardo di San Giorgio (melodrama, 3, Forzano), Genoa, Carlo Felice, 9 March 1941; La collina (madrigale scenico, after E.L Masters: *Spoon River*), Venice, Fenice, 27 Sept 1947; La gita in campagna (1, A. Moravia after *Andare verso il popolo*), Milan, Scala, 25 March 1954; La parrucca dell'imperatore (rondò scenico, G. Maselli), Spoleto, Festival, 12 June 1959

Orch: Conc. for Orch, 1939; Pf Conc. no.1, 1949; Fantasia, 1950; Pf Conc. no.2, 1951; Vn Conc., 1954; Forme sovrapposte, 1959

Choral and solo vocal: Sinfonia lirica, 1v, orch, 1929; De profundis, chorus, 1952; In memoriam, corale e aria, chorus, orch, 1955; Emircal (St Augustine), vv, orch, tape, 1980; songs

Chbr: Balletto, pf, 1927; Str Qt, 1933; Str Qt, 1934; Concertino, pf qt, 1935; Str Qt, 1937; Musica, 2 str qts, 1948; Fantasia, pf, 1953; Vibrazioni, fl, tiptophone, pf, 1960; other pf and org pieces

Principal publishers: Ricordi, Suvini Zevboni, Universal

BIBLIOGRAPHY

DEUMM (E. Restagno); *GroveO* (R. Pozzi); *MGG1* (M. Mila)

H. Fleischer: 'La collina di Mario Peragallo', *Il diapason* (1951), nos.3–4

L. Pestalozza: 'Peragallo, scrivere per l'opera', *Il verri*, ii/4 (1958), 153–60

M. Mila: *Cronache musicali 1955–1959* (Turin, 1959), 217–18

F. d'Amico: *I casi della musica* (Milan, 1962), 18–20

R. Zanetti: *Musica italiana del Novecento* (Busto Arsizio, 1985), 1236–50

V. Fellegara: 'L'ultimo Peragallo', *Gli anniversari musicali del 1997*, ed. P. Pederra and P. Santi (Milan, 1997), 577–8

R. Zanetti: 'Mario Peragallo: musicista moderno "con judico"', ibid., 579–607

VIRGILIO BERNARDONI

Perahia, Murray (*b* New York, 19 April 1947). American pianist. He began piano lessons at an early age with Jeanette Haien and later graduated from Mannes College in conducting and composition while continuing his piano studies with Artur Balsam. Before embarking on a solo career, he completed an unusually full musical formation by spending summers at Marlboro, Vermont, where he was encouraged by Rudolf Serkin and collaborated in chamber music with such outstanding musicians as Casals and members of the Budapest Quartet; he also studied at this time with the veteran pianist Mieczysław Horszowski. In March 1972 he made his début with the New York PO

Murray Perahia

and later that year won first prize at the Leeds International Piano Competition. That led the following year to his first London recital, at the Queen Elizabeth Hall, and his first concert at the Aldeburgh Festival, where he became a regular visitor, often accompanying Peter Pears; from 1981 to 1989 he was one of the artistic directors of the festival.

Perahia's sensibility and the naturalness and lyrical impulse of his phrasing, together with the finish of his playing, were always recognized as exceptional. After his first prize at the Leeds competition it was predictable that he would become a distinguished pianist, but the direction and extent of his development as a solo player might not have been foreseen. He acknowledges that he owes much to the advice, inspiration and friendship of Vladimir Horowitz. During the 1980s and 90s his playing acquired a more sharply defined declamation and the command of a larger scale than hitherto, and one sensed within the frame of each performance a bolder rhetoric and more space for the music to breathe. Earlier, he was not usually thought of as a virtuoso or a 'big' player; by 2000 (although this is not his most frequented territory) he could be as thrilling as anyone in the *Rhapsodie espagnole* of Liszt.

Perahia is a consummate Bach player who has recorded the six English Suites, and he has also made a successful case for re-establishing the Handel suites and many of the Scarlatti sonatas as rewarding repertory for pianists. In the late 1970s he began to record all the Mozart concertos with the English Chamber Orchestra, directing them from the piano, and achieved a set of consistent excellence which has not been surpassed as a version on modern instruments. His discography also includes fine recordings of Mendelssohn (a composer he has consistently championed), together with Beethoven sonatas and all the concertos (with the Concertgebouw Orchestra conducted by Haitink). More recently, his recordings of Schumann's *Kreisleriana* and Piano Concerto and Chopin's Ballades and two concertos have been acclaimed; his Chopin discography is substantial and has been particularly admired. His repertory in the 20th century has hardly extended beyond Bartók, although it has included Tippett's First Sonata; but to everything he touches, whether as concerto soloist, solo recitalist, chamber musician or accompanist – or indeed conductor – he has brought distinction and a musical ease that has seemed effortless. It is given to few artists to develop as Perahia has done and to be able to renew so vividly our experience of a wide range of great music, while appearing to impose themselves on it so lightly.

BIBLIOGRAPHY

A. Blyth: 'Branching Out', *Gramophone*, lxix/Oct (1991), 60–61

STEPHEN PLAISTOW

Peralta, Angela (*b* Puebla, 6 July 1845; *d* Mazatlán, 30 Aug 1883). Mexican soprano. When she sang a cavatina from Donizetti's *Belisario* for Henriette Sontag during the latter's visit to Mexico, Sontag prophesied an international future for her. At the age of 15 she made her début at the Gran Teatro Nacional, singing in *Il trovatore*. She made her Milan début at the age of 17 in *Lucia di Lammermoor* and followed it with an equally successful Turin début in *La sonnambula*. Hailed everywhere in Europe as 'the Mexican nightingale', she toured the Continent during 1862–5 and sang as far afield as Egypt. Because of her European successes, which she repeated in

a series of later tours, she was on her return to Mexico in 1866 guaranteed 20% of the receipts of every opera in which she was to sing; but she preferred to organize her own company. She travelled over the whole of Mexico, singing in *Lucia* 166 times, *La sonnambula* 122 times, and *La traviata*, *Dinorah*, *I puritani*, *Norma* and others a lesser number of times.

Peralta organized the Mexican première of Verdi's Requiem, which was given on 12 October 1877, 'in memory of three noble liberators, Juárez, Lincoln and Thiers'. She sang in the productions of Melesio Morales's *Ildegonda* and *Gino Corsini* and in Aniceto Ortega's Aztec opera, *Guatimotzin* (13 September 1871). An album of 19 of her original piano pieces was published (Mexico City, 1875). She died of yellow fever in the Pacific port of Mazatlán, at the age of 38, while on tour with her own company.

BIBLIOGRAPHY

E. Olavarría y Ferrari: *Reseña histórica del teatro en México* (Mexico City, 1895), ii, 337, 373, 380; iii, 106–14
A. de María y Campos: *Angela Peralta, el ruiseñor mexicano* (Mexico City, 1944)
R. Stevenson: *Music in Mexico: a Historical Survey* (New York, 1952/R), 201–3, 206, 210
G. Carmona: *La música de México: período de la independencia a la Revolución (1810–1910)* (Mexico City, 1984), 102–10, 124–37

ROBERT STEVENSON

Peralta Escudero, Bernardo de (*b* Falces, Navarra; *d* Burgos, 4 Nov 1617). Spanish composer. In 1605 he was *maestro de capilla* at Alfaro and in 1607 he applied for a similar post at El Burgo de Osma; he was rejected and afterwards became *maestro de capilla* at Santo Domingo de la Calzada Cathedral. In 1609 he was summoned to Burgos where he became *maestro de capilla*, a post he held until his death; he was also made a canon but without the right to vote. He was evidently held in high esteem by his contemporaries since on 9 December 1611 he was elected to replace Francisco de Silos as *maestro de capilla* of Zaragoza Cathedral, and on 3 May 1616 he was invited to serve the royal chapel at Madrid in the same capacity; he declined both appointments, declaring, characteristically, that he would 'prefer the galleys to Madrid'.

Peralta's works are up-to-date polychoral compositions of the lively, bustling type preferred by Philip III. His *Magnificat primi toni* for three choirs (judged 'bom' by João IV of Portugal; one copy reached Puebla in Mexico) is freely composed; he exploited the vocal groups fully in dynamic, textural and spatial contrasts, and set expressively individual words such as 'esurientes'. He was one of the first Spanish composers to attempt this sort of word-painting.

WORKS

Missa pro defunctis, 8vv; Magnificat primi toni, 12vv (3 choirs); 6 villancicos, 4, 6, 8, 12vv; romance, 3vv, *E-Mn*, *V*, *Zs*, Puebla Cathedral, Mexico; Magnificat, ed. S. Barwick: *Sacred Vocal Polyphony in Early Colonial Mexico* (diss., Harvard U., 1949)
Salve regina, 7vv; 12 villancicos, 3–8vv, lost, cited in *JoãoIL*

BIBLIOGRAPHY

JoãoIL
L. Siemens Hernández: 'La Seo de Zaragoza, destacada escuela de órgano en el siglo XVII', *AnM*, xxi (1966), 153–4, 158
D. Preciado: 'Alonso de Tejeda (†1628): pequeña biografía', *TSM*, liii (1970), 81–5
D. Preciado: 'Vidal de Arce, maestro de capilla de la catedral de Palencia', *TSM*, lvi (1973), 108–17, esp. 112

ROBERT STEVENSON

Peranda [Perandi, Perande], **Marco Gioseppe** (*b* Rome or Macerata, *c*1625; *d* Dresden, 12 Jan 1675). Italian composer and singer. He may have been a pupil of Carissimi in Rome, as was Christoph Bernhard, who took him to Dresden between 1651 and 1656. He was first employed as an alto singer in the chapel of Johann Georg II, heir to the electorate; in 1656 this chapel was combined with the court chapel, in which he continued to sing. By 1661 he was vice-Kapellmeister, and in 1663 he succeeded Vincenzo Albrici as Kapellmeister. From the death of Schütz in 1672 until his own death he was first Hofkapellmeister. Though the electoral court continued to be Lutheran until 1697, Peranda remained a Catholic. Court journals show that he visited Italy in 1667.

Peranda's importance as a composer undoubtedly lies primarily in the field of the sacred concerto. His many such works, together with his other sacred music and his stage and instrumental works, as well as similar works by Albrici, were far more representative of the repertory of the Dresden court in the period from about 1660 to 1680 than the music of Schütz, which was seldom performed in the court chapel after 1656. There are indeed very few features common to the older German school represented by Schütz and the newer Italian school, whose chief members were Bontempi, Albrici and Peranda. The attack on the new theatrical church music in the funeral oration for Schütz by the chief court preacher Geier was mainly directed against Peranda as a papist and as the exponent of a style described as 'broken'. The most notable characteristics of this style are the free combination of tutti concertato- and solo arioso-style passages with solo aria strophes. Peranda sets these sections off from one another by using changes in meter, and by contrasting few and many voices, vocal and instrumental sections, syllabic and linear writing, and block harmony and brilliant decorative writing. His works are indebted to the Roman motet style of Graziani and others, but also exhibit the influence of contemporary German sacred music, particularly in the use of instruments. Together with Albrici he contributed to the early history of the so-called 'concerto-aria cantata' in Dresden. Like some other composers Peranda set new devotional Latin texts more often than biblical and liturgical ones. Only in his handling of German words – for example in *Herr, wenn ich nur dich habe, Verleih uns Frieden* and the recently identified *St Mark Passion* (once attributed to Schütz) – did he approach the style of comparable works by Schütz, such as the second set of *Symphoniae sacrae* and the Passions. He often used consciously beautiful sounds for purely musical ends and not simply to illustrate the words. He appears to have laid the foundations of the 18th-century motet style (Bach's apart) in central Germany, and he exerted considerable influence on his central and north German contemporaries.

WORKS

OPERAS

Dafne (5, G.A. Bontempi), Dresden, 3 Sept 1671, collab. Bontempi, *B-Bc* (score, 1863), *D-Mbs* (score, *c*1870)
Jupiter und Io (Bontempi or C.C. Dedekind), Dresden, 16 Jan 1673, collab. Bontempi, only lib extant

ORATORIOS

Historia von der Geburt des Herrn Jesu Christi, Dresden, 25 Dec 1668, lost
Historia des Leidens und Sterbens unsers Herrn ... Jesu Christi nach dem Evangelisten St. Marcum, Dresden, 20 March 1668, *D-LEm*

(attrib. H. Schütz); ed. in *H. Schütz: Sämmtliche Werke*, i (Leipzig, 1885)
Il sacrifico di Jefte, Bologna, 1675, only text extant

MASSES

Missa, 6vv, 5 insts, bc, *D-Bsb*
Missa 4/8vv, 5 insts, bc, *Bsb* Bokemeyer
Missa B. Agnetis, 6/11vv, 10 insts, bc, copied 1671, *CZ-KRa*
Missa, 5/10vv, 12 insts, bc, copied 1672, *KRa*
Missa brevis, 4vv, 4 insts, bc, *D-Bsb*
Missa brevis, 6vv, 6 insts, bc, *Bsb*
Kyrie, 5vv, 7 insts, bc, *Bsb* Bokemeyer

CONCERTOS, MOTETS

Principal sources: *CZ-KRa*, *D-Bsb* Bokemeyer, *Dl* Grimma and 19th-century copies of Bokemeyer sources, *S-Uu* Düben
Abite dolores, 2vv, 2 insts, bc; Accurrite gentes, 3vv, 3 insts, bc; Ad cantus ad sonos, 3vv, 3 insts bc; Ad dulces amores, 2vv, bc; Audite peccatores, 2vv, 2 insts, bc; Cantemus Domino, 3vv, bc; Cor mundum crea in me, 1v, 3 insts, bc; Credidi propter quod locutus sum, 3 solo vv, 4vv, 5 insts, bc; Da pacem Domine, 3vv, 3 insts, bc; Dedit abyssus vocem suam, 4vv, bc; Dic nobis Maria, 3vv, 3 insts, bc; Dies sanctificatus illuxit, 1v, 3 insts, bc; Diligam te Domine, 3vv, 3 insts, bc; Dum proeliaretur, 2vv, 3 insts, bc; Ecce ego mittam piscatores, 3vv, 3 insts, bc; Factum est proelium, 6/11vv, 7 insts, bc; Fasciculus myrrhae, 5/10vv, 10 insts, bc; Florete fragrantibus, 3vv, 3 insts, bc
Gaudete, cantate, 3vv, 2 insts, bc; Hac luce cunctos, 3vv, 5 insts, bc; Herr, wenn ich nur dich habe, 3vv, 3 insts, bc; Jesu dulcis, Jesu pie, 3vv, 3 insts, bc; Laetentur coeli, 5/10vv, 7 insts, bc; Languet cor meum, 3vv, 3 insts, bc; Laudate Dominum omnes gentes, 5vv, 5 insts, bc; Laudate pueri, 4vv, bc; Miserere, 6/12vv, 12 insts, bc; Missus est angelus, 3 solo vv, 5vv, 5 insts, bc; O ardor, o flamma, 2vv, 2 insts, bc; O bone Jesu, 1v, 2 insts, bc; O fideles modicum, 4vv, 3 insts, bc; O Jesu mi dulcissime, 3vv, 5 insts, bc; Peccavi o Domine, 3vv, 2 insts, bc; Per rigidos montes, 1v, 3 insts, bc; Plange anima suspira, 3vv, bc; Propitiare, 5/10vv, 5 insts, bc
Quis dabit capiti meo, 3vv, 3 insts, bc; Quo tendimus mortales, 3vv, bc; Repleti sunt omnes, 2vv, 6 insts, bc; Rorate cherubim, 3vv, 2 insts, bc; Si Dominus mecum, 4vv, 2 insts, bc; Si vivo mi Jesu, 1v, 2 insts, bc; Si vivo mi Jesu, 3vv, 3 insts, bc; Spirate suaves, 2vv, 3 insts, bc; Sursum deorsum, 3vv, 3 insts, bc; Te solum aestuat, 3vv, 3 insts, bc; Timor et tremor, 4vv, 2 insts, bc; Valete risus, 2vv, bc; Veni Sancte Spiritus, 4/8vv, 5/10 insts, bc; Verleih uns Frieden, 3vv, 2 insts, bc; Vocibus resonent, 3vv, 3 insts, bc

SECULAR

Seguace d'amore, 3vv, 2 insts, bc, *S-Uu*

BIBLIOGRAPHY

EitnerQ; FürstenauG; GaspariC
R. Engländer: 'Zur Frage der "Dafne" (1671) von G.A. Bontempi und M.G. Peranda', *AcM*, xiii (1941), 59–77
W. Steude: 'Die *Markuspassion* in der Leipziger Passionen-Handschrift des Johann Zacharias Grundig', *DJbM*, xiv (1969), 96–116
G. Spagnoli: *Letters & Documents of Heinrich Schütz, 1656–1672: an Annotated Translation* (Ann Arbor, 1990)
W. Steude: 'Zur Musik am sächsischen Hof in Dresden während der Regierung Kurfürst Johann Georgs II', *Dresdner Hefte*, no.33 (1993), 69–79
M. Frandsen: *The Sacred Concerto in Dresden, ca. 1660–1680* (diss., U. of Rochester, 1996) [incl. work-list, inventory of lost works and transcrs. of 23 works by Peranda]
M. Frandsen: 'Albinci, Peranda und die Ursprünge der Concerto-Aria-Kantate in Dresden', *Schütz-Jb*, xviii (1996), 123–39

WOLFRAM STEUDE (with MARY E. FRANDSEN)

Perandreu, José (*fl* ?mid-17th century). Spanish composer. From the occurrence of his works in *E-E* Plut.56 67-ñ along with pieces by José Ximénez and Pablo Bruna, and the stylistic affinities between them, it seems likely that he was active in the middle of the 17th century. He is represented by nine pieces – four settings of the Spanish *Pange lingua* and five works of the tiento type. The *Pange lingua* pieces apparently form a group, each containing the cantus firmus in a different voice; the accompanying parts form interesting and at times rhythmically complex counterpoint. The tientos (one ed. H. Anglés, *Antología de organistas españoles del siglo XVII*, i, Barcelona, 1965) all adopt the Spanish tradition of divided keyboard (*medio registro*) with either one or two solo parts given to the right hand in continuously spun-out figuration that develops from successive points of imitation. Though they have fared badly with music historians because of their excessive length and monotony, they do reveal a certain melodic lilt, a variety of rhythmically interesting figuration and ingenious transformations of the initial motifs.

BIBLIOGRAPHY

ApelG

F. Pedrell: 'Music Vells de la terra', *Revista musical catalana*, v (1908), 177

W. Apel: 'Die spanische Orgelmusik vor Cabanilles', *AnM*, xvii (1962), 15–29

ALMONTE HOWELL

Per arsin et thesin. *See* ARSIS, THESIS.

Peraza. Spanish family of instrumentalists and organists. Many of them were namesakes whose exact relationship is unclear.

(1) **Jerónimo de Peraza (de Sotomayor) (i)**   (*b* ?Seville, *c*1550; *d* Toledo, 26 June 1617). He was the son of Juan Peraza, the most famous shawm player of his day, who was employed at Salamanca, Valencia, Seville and Toledo. Jerónimo's teacher was probably Pedro de Villada (*d* 15 Oct 1572), organist at Seville Cathedral; Peraza succeeded him on 1 September 1573. Installation of a new large organ, begun in 1567 by the Flemish 'Mestre Jox', had recently been completed. On 8 April 1575 Peraza was asked to draw up in cooperation with the builder two books describing the stops, one to be placed in the cathedral archive. Two months later he had not complied and, moreover, was absent without leave. Despite the chapter's efforts to please him by appointing his brother Juan as instrumentalist at a high salary, he continued to give trouble. The chapter considered that Jerónimo had deceived them when he accepted from Toledo a better offer which included a chaplaincy. He was elected organist at Toledo on 27 November 1579 and installed on 21 March 1580; he served that cathedral for 36 years. On at least one occasion the Seville Cathedral authorities tried to tempt him back, but Toledo responded on 8 March 1602 by raising his salary still further and by allowing him even more liberal leaves of absence to attend to his business interests.

Francisco Correa de Arauxo, in *Facultad orgánica* (Alcalá de Henares, 1626), mentioned Peraza as the first at Seville to have intabulated verses in the 8th tone ending on D instead of the usual G. The Jerónimo de Peraza appointed suborganist at Seville on 19 October 1594 was a namesake, possibly (3) Jerónimo Peraza (ii). A monothematic tiento of excellent quality in the 8th tone, notable for its use of accidentals, survives, as an addition to a copy of *Facultad orgánica* (in *P-La*), and is described there as 'Obra de Peraza'.

(2) **Francisco de Peraza (i)**   (*b* Salamanca, 1564; *d* Seville, 23 June 1598). Youngest brother of (1) Jerónimo de Peraza (i) and an exceptionally precocious player. He spent his childhood at Seville and Toledo, where his father was principal shawm player in the cathedral establishments. At the competition held on 16 May 1584 at Seville to decide on a successor to Diego del Castillo, Peraza so impressed Cardinal Rodrigo de Castro, Archbishop of

Seville, that he asked the cathedral chapter to award him the organist's prebend, at an annual salary of 200 ducats. Francisco Pacheco described the occasion in *Libro de descripcion* (Seville, 1599): 'Finding that Guerrero [the *maestro de capilla*] was confronting the competitors with some of the hardest tests of skill known to musicians, but that scarcely had he announced a task before Francisco Peraza had accomplished it to perfection, even adding his solution of variants to the problem, the cardinal was overwhelmed with admiration of such skill found only in the rarest prodigies'. Within two years Peraza's salary had been increased substantially; on 6 June he was awarded another 1000 reales annually, which gave him a stipend closely in line with Guerrero's. The *maestro de capilla* generously 'embraced him and exclaimed that he had an angel in every finger'. Philippe Rogier, *maestro de capilla* to Philip II, also held him in high esteem. Because he was widely in demand, Peraza often overstayed his leaves. The chapter dismissed him on 27 June 1590 for a long and unauthorized absence, but reinstated him later that year.

He was the only Spanish organist of the time whose portrait has survived. The many compositions – keyboard works, villancicos, *chanzonetas*, motets and *sainetes* (theatre music) – mentioned by Pacheco, his first biographer, are no longer extant. The identity of the Pedraza or Peraza who composed a single surviving organ piece superscribed 'Medio registro alto, Tono I' (divided keyboard, 1st mode), printed from a 17th-century Escorial manuscript in L. Villalba Muñoz's *Antología de organistas clásicos* (Madrid, 1914, rev. 2/1971 by S. Rubio), has been disputed. The many sequential passages in the right hand give the work a Baroque flavour, placing Francisco de Peraza ahead of his time if it is truly his.

(3) **Jerónimo de Peraza (ii)**   (*b* Toledo, 1574; *d* Palencia, 21 July 1604). Nephew of (1) Jerónimo de Peraza (i). On 20 December 1594 he defeated Sebastián Martínez Verdugo in a competition for the post of organist of Palencia Cathedral, left vacant by Pedro de Pradillo. He was ordained in 1600. On 14 July he played in Valladolid for the entry of King Philip III, and on 26 June 1603 played for the king's visit to Palencia. He remained as organist at Palencia until his death from tertian fever, a form of malaria.

(4) **Francisco de Peraza (ii)**   (*b* Seville, 1595/6; *d* ?Madrid, after 1635). Son of (2) Francisco de Peraza (i). His uncle (1) Jerónimo de Peraza (i), organist of Toledo Cathedral, brought Francisco up to be his successor. At a public trial of skill on 6 and 7 March 1618 Peraza was considered superior to Francisco Correa de Arauxo, his only competitor for the Toledo post, and was confirmed on 30 June 1618. During the following years he fell into disfavour with the Toledo chapter. He returned twice after long absences without leave (22 May 1619 and 1 April 1621); after fleeing for a third time from his creditors in Toledo he tendered his resignation, which was accepted on 9 September 1621.

The Cuenca Cathedral chapter engaged him for two years beginning 12 October 1624, with an excessive annual salary, and on 29 July 1626 voted him a canon's salary provided that he took orders; however, he failed to keep the agreement and on 9 October was dismissed for unauthorized absence. After this he was organist of the Convento Real de la Encarnación in Madrid. From 7 June

1628 to 17 August 1629 he was organist and prebendary of Segovia Cathedral. In 1636 the future João IV of Portugal gave him 400 silver réis for a book of tientos brought by him to the ducal residence at Vila Viçosa.

BIBLIOGRAPHY

JoãoIL

M.S. Kastner: Introduction to *Francisco Correa de Arauxo: Libro de tientos y discursos*, MME, xii (1952), 14–17, 268–76

M.S. Kastner: 'Palencia, encrucijada de los organistas españoles del siglo XVI', *AnM*, xiv (1959), 115–64, esp. 157

D. Preciado: 'Francisco de Peraza II, vencedor de Francisco Correa de Araujo', *TSM*, liii (1970), 6–15, esp. 7

D. Preciado: 'Francisco de Peraza II, organista de la Catedral de Segovia', *TSM*, lvi (1973), 3–9

D. Preciado: 'El pulgar izquierdo del organista Francisco de Peraza I', *TSM*, lvi (1973), 35–8

D. Preciado: 'Jerónimo de Peraza II, organista de la Catedral de Palencia', *TSM*, lvi (1973), 69–80

J.E. Ayarra Jarne: 'Un documento de excepcional interés', *RdMc*, ii (1979), 300–06, esp. 300

J. López-Calo: *La música en la Catedral de Palencia* (Palencia, 1980), 544–71 passim [Jerónimo de Peraza (ii)]

K.H. Müller-Lancé: 'Arten der Tonalität des 16. und 17. Jahrhunderts', *AnM*, xxxviii (1983), 187–92 [harmonic analysis of 'Medio registro alto, tono I', *Antología de organistas clásicos*, i (1914), ed. Luis Villalba Muñoz]

J. López-Calo: *La música en la Catedral de Segovia* (Segovia, 1988), i, 20–21

M. Martínez Millán: *Historia musical de la Catedral de Cuenca* (Cuenca, 1988), 117–18

J. López-Calo: *Documentario musical de la Catedral de Segovia*, i (Santiago de Compostela, 1990), 93–4

R. Stevenson: 'Francisco Guerrero (1528–1599): Seville's Sixteenth-Century Cynosure', *Inter-American Music Review*, xiii/1 (1992–3), 21–98, esp. 46–9, 51–2 [portrait of Francisco de Peraza (i), 47]

L. Jambou: 'Reflexiones y documentos sobre dinastías de maestros de capilla y organistas de los siglos XVI–XVIII', *Nassarre: Revista aragonesa de musicología*, xii/2 (1996), 161–84, esp. 168–79

ROBERT STEVENSON

Perches Enríquez, José (*b* Chihuahua, 1882; *d* Los Angeles, 1939). Mexican pianist and composer. His first teachers were his father, José Perches Porras, a pianist, organist and conductor, and his mother, Antonia Enríquez y Terrazas, a concert pianist. A child prodigy, by the age of 10 he had already given many recitals. At 16 he made a triumphal appearance at the casino in Chihuahua, which won him a scholarship from the governor for studies at the National Conservatory in Mexico City, where he studied with Julio Ituarte. After graduation he began to teach and give concerts throughout Mexico as well as Central and South America. He was a professor of piano at the National Conservatory from 1906 to 1931. In 1934, for reasons of health, he moved to Los Angeles, where he later died. He composed a large quantity of salon music for piano, and his *Secreto eterno* (*Danza orientale*) achieved international popularity, along with *Alicia* (*Vals*) and *Toño* (*Danza*). All these works were published by A. Wagner y Levien.

BIBLIOGRAPHY

F.R. Almada: *Diccionario de historia-geografía y biografía chihuahuense* (Chihuahua,1975)

WALTER AARON CLARK

Perchival, Charles Theodore. See PACHELBEL family, (3).

Percussion (Fr. *instruments à percussion*; Ger. *Perkussion, Schlagzeug*; It. *percussione*). A term used to describe instruments, in particular Western orchestral and band instruments, that are played by shaking, or by striking either a membrane (e.g. drums and tambourines; *see* MEMBRANOPHONE) or a plate or bar of wood, metal or other hard material (e.g. cymbals, triangles, xylophone; *see* IDIOPHONE). They can also be divided into instruments that produce a sound of definite pitch (e.g. kettledrums, celesta) and those that do not (e.g. snare drum, gong). The term is also used to designate the section of the Western orchestra containing these instruments (Fr. *batterie*; Ger. *Schlagzeug*; It. *batteria*); the percussionist may also be called upon to produce a variety of sound effects.

The rise of percussion within the orchestra is primarily a development of the 20th century (but *see also* JANISSARY MUSIC). An interest in orchestral colour and texture led composers such as Debussy (*La mer*, 1903–5) and Richard Strauss (*Don Quixote*, 1896–7 and *Eine Alpensinfonie*, 1911–15) to expand the percussion section; Satie in *Parade* (1913) made use of a variety of sound effects, including sirens, starting pistols, bouteillophone and typewriter. Such composers as Stravinsky, Bartók and Varèse gave the element of rhythm, and percussion instruments, a new importance within the orchestra and chamber ensemble. The rise of Latin American dance bands in the 1930s brought with it a new group of percussion instruments, of Afro-Cuban origin; these instruments and others of non-European cultures, such as the Asian and other non-Western instruments studied and used by Henry Cowell, made their way into the orchestra. Composers who have used percussion with special originality and effectiveness include Messiaen, Britten and Stockhausen. In jazz, dance bands, rock and pop music the percussion is most commonly handled by a single player using a DRUM KIT.

The development of music in the 20th century has brought about a situation where any strange sound or sound effect not produced by conventional orchestral instruments ends up in the percussion section. The single percussionist in Ligeti's *Aventures* (1962) and *Nouvelle aventures* (1962–5) requires the following:

a rack with carpet and carpet beater; an open wooden box with four rubber bands (the box to act as a resonating chamber when the rubber bands are plucked); sandpaper taped to the floor (to be scraped by the player's feet); paper bags (to pop); newspaper, brown grease-proof paper and tissue paper (to tear); toy frog (to squeak); balloons (to squeak); cloth (to tear); book (to flick pages); tin foil (to rustle); empty suitcase (to hit); metal dustbin and tray of crockery (crockery to be thrown into dustbin); tin can and hammer; sandpaper blocks; bass drum, snare drum, xylophone, glockenspiel, suspended cymbal and güiro.

Many other late 20th-century works have unusual requirements, some calling for instruments invented by the composer. In Richard Rodney Bennett's Waltz from *Murder on the Orient Express* (film score, 1973) a steam effect is created with a cylinder of carbon dioxide. Birtwistle's *The Mask of Orpheus* (1973–84) calls for a 'Noh Harp', the effect being achieved by suspending five metal bars over a timpani, the player striking the bars and moving the timpani pedal to create an eerie sound. Henze's *Voices* (1973) requires three thunder sheets, a starting pistol, wine glasses, a jew's harp, three penny whistles and a referee's whistle. In George Benjamin's *At First Light* (1982) a ping pong ball is dropped into a glass (a suitable glass should maximize the number of times the ball bounces); the player also tears newspaper. Benedict Mason's *!* (1992) calls for a waterphone (invented by Dick Waters; water is activated in a special vessel by striking or bowing rods welded to the rim), a *binzasara* (a

Japanese rattle consisting of wooden slabs strung together), a gourd in water, a rainmaker (rain machine), an *udu* pot (an Igbo instrument, a vessel played by striking one of the openings with the hand, a beater or against the body), theatre lighting, a cuckoo (whistle), hosepipe whistles, devil chaser (bamboo stick), trihorn (three-bulb car horn), *Schwirrbogen* (a bow mounted on a stick with elastic stretched across the bow, which emits a whining sound when whirled around the player's head) and patum pipes (a length of plastic tubing containing beads). Unusual instruments and sound effects have appeared in all types of music, and virtually anything may be expected of the percussionist in the late 20th century.

The Javanese gamelan may have provided a model for the Western percussion ensemble, a group of performers playing a wide variety of percussion and sound-effects instruments. One of the earliest public performances by such an ensemble took place in 1933; the work was Varèse's *Ionisation* (1931), for 13 performers playing 39 instruments, including some borrowed from Latin American music and jazz. Other early works for percussion ensemble included Cowell's *Ostinato pianissimo* (1934), which uses Latin American instruments, Western percussion and Asian instruments such as gongs and Indian 'rice bowls' (*jalatarang*), and John Cage's *First Construction in Metal* (1939), which calls for five differently pitched thunder sheets, four brake drums, four gongs resting on pads and a water gong. Lou Harrison and Carlos Chávez also made significant contributions to the medium. In such works, which employ many instruments apart from those developed within the concepts of Western harmony and melody, the elements of colour, texture and rhythm are developed to a high degree of complexity. Since the 1950s many composers have written for the percussion ensemble, which by the end of the century had become a part of many university music programmes. The ensembles Nexus, Les Percussions de Strasbourg and Ensemble Bash have commissioned many new works. Solo percussionists have included Evelyn Glennie, James Wood and Keiko Abe; all have also composed for the medium. Wood's *Stoichea* (1988) calls for more that 600 instruments, played by 16 percussionists. The percussionist and scholar James Blades has, through his writings, helped to define a history and scholarship for percussion instruments. *See* INSTRUMENTS, CLASSIFICATION OF; see also entries on individual instruments.

BIBLIOGRAPHY

BeckEP; BladesPI

The Percussionist (1963–4) [from 1980–81 as *Percusssive Notes: Research Edition*; from 1985–6 with *Percussive Notes*]

D. Bajzek: *Percussion: an Annotated Bibliography with Special Emphasis on Contemporary Notation and Performance* (Metuchen, NJ, 1988)

T. Siwe: *Percussion Ensemble and Solo Literature* (Champaign, IL, 1993)

T. Siwe: *Percussion Solo Literature* (Champaign, IL, 1995)

JAMES HOLLAND, JANET K. PAGE

Percussions de Strasbourg, Les. French percussion ensemble. It was formed in 1961 by six young percussionists, all of whom were members of Strasbourg symphony orchestras. Although the repertory for such a group was virtually non-existent at the time, the ensemble was sponsored by Pierre Boulez, who was fascinated by the possibilities it offered. Other composers were immediately attracted to the idea of writing for the ensemble, and in 1965 it gave a concert devoted entirely to percussion.

Although the players have changed over the years, the group remains true to the original concept of presenting percussion instruments – Western, Oriental and African – in the language of contemporary avant-garde music. Over 170 compositions have been dedicated to the group (including Xenakis's *Persephassa* (1969) and *Pleïades* (1978)); and the players are constantly adding new instruments and sonorities to the hundreds already in use. Messiaen called the ensemble 'pioneers in the evolution of percussion in contemporary music', and wrote for it the percussion parts in *Sept haïkaï* (1962), *Couleurs de la cité céleste* (1963) and *Et exspecto resurrectionem mortuorum* (1964). Les Percussions de Strasbourg have also been very active in education, with 'Percustra', an introduction to music through body, voice and percussion instruments. They tour regularly throughout the world and have made numerous recordings.

JAMES HOLLAND

Perdeholtz, Lucas. *See* BERGHOLZ, LUCAS.

Perdendosi (It.: 'losing itself', 'dying away'; reflexive gerund of *perdere*, 'to lose'). A term equivalent to *diminuendo* and *descrescendo* but implying the ultimate arrival at complete silence. A famous example appears just before the end of Beethoven's Violin Concerto.

$\square$

Perdigo (*b* Lespéron, Ardèche; *fl* 1195–1220). Troubadour. Several conflicting versions of his *vida* exist, all presenting highly contestable facts; it seems likely, however, that he was born the son of a poor fisherman in a small village called Lespéron in the bishopric of Gévaudon (Ardèche). According to one source, he retired to the monastery of Silvabela; this has not been identified but it may be the monastery at Silvacana (Aix), founded by Raimon I of Baux in 1144. According to the *vida* all his songs were written during this period. His surviving work includes eight love-songs (three with melodies, all in *I-Ma* R.71 sup.: *Los mals d'amor ai eu be totz apres*, PC 370.9; *Tot l'an mi ten amors d'aital faisso*, PC 370.13; *Trop ai estat mon Bon Esper no vi*, PC 370.14), a religious verse, a *cobla* and a sirventes. He was also a partner in three partimens with Dalfi d'Alverne, Gaucelm Faidit, and Raimbaut de Vaqeiras with Ademar de Poitiers. His style seems to have been highly influential particularly on Italian poets, many of whom translated and imitated his works. The wide distribution of his poems among the sources also attests his popularity. The construction of his melodies is quite unsophisticated: they are all fairly elaborate in style and through-composed to the extent of lacking even melodic rhymes between the individual phrases.

BIBLIOGRAPHY

K. Lewent: 'Zu den Liedern des Perdigon', *Zeitschrift für romanische Philologie*, xxxiii (1909), 670–87

H.J. Chaytor, ed.: *Les chansons de Perdigo* (Paris, 1926)

E. Hoepffner: *Les troubadours dans leur vie et dans leurs oeuvres* (Paris, 1955)

M. de Riquer: *Los trovadores: historia literaria y textos* (Barcelona, 1975), ii

E. Aubrey: *The Music of the Troubadours* (Bloomington, IN, 1996)

For further bibliography *see* TROUBADOURS, TROUVÈRES.

IAN R. PARKER

Perdomo Escobar, José Ignacio (*b* Bogotá, 5 June 1917; *d* 1980). Colombian musicologist. Concurrently with law, he studied music theory, composition and music history at the Bogotá National Conservatory under Guillermo Uribe Holguín and Antonio María Valencia. After working as a cataloguer at the National Library, he was appointed secretary of the National Conservatory (1935–40). He then became a priest, and was later a canon at Bogotá Cathedral. Besides law he worked mainly in Colombian music history, particularly the colonial period, and Colombian folklore. His *Historia de la música en Colombia* (Bogotá, 1938, 5/1980) was the first to appear and is still useful, as is his *El Archivo musical de la Catedral de Bogotá* (Bogotá, 1976); his valuable instrument collection is now housed at the Biblioteca Luis Angel Arango, Bogotà.

BIBLIOGRAPHY

E. Bermudez: 'Historia de la musica vs. historias de los músicos: la obra de J.I. Perdomo Escobar', *Revista de la universidad nacional* [Bogota], i/3 (1984), 5 17 [incl. list of writings]

E. Bermudez: *Colección de instrumentos musicales … José Ignacio Perdomo Escobar* (Bogotà, 1986)

GERARD BÉHAGUE

Peregrine tone. *See* TONUS PEREGRINUS.

Peregrino di Zanetto (Micheli). Italian violin maker, son of ZANETTO DA MONTICHIARO.

Pereira, Domingos Nunes (*d* nr Lisbon, 29 March 1729). Portuguese composer. He was a priest, who after serving as *mestre de capela* of the Casa da Misericórdia, Lisbon, held a similar position at Lisbon Cathedral from about 1690 until 1719. His works, which were all sacred, are apparently all lost. They included eight-part responsories for Holy Week and the Office of the Dead, vesper psalms (including *Laudate pueri Dominum* and *Confitebor*, both for eight voices), Lessons for the Dead and a four-part *Laudate Dominum, omnes gentes*, as well as vilhancicos for four to eight voices. (D. Barbosa Machado: *Bibliotheca lusitana*, i, Lisbon, 1741/*R*, pp.713–14; music entries ed. R.V. Nery as *A música no ciclo da Bibliotheca lusitana*, Lisbon, 1984, 64, 189–90)

ROBERT STEVENSON

Pereira, Marcos Soares (*b* Caminha, *c*1595; *d* Lisbon, 7 Jan 1655). Portuguese composer, elder brother of João Soares Rebelo. He was a priest. He succeeded Roberto Tornar as *mestre de capela* at Vila Viçosa about 1629, and when the Duke of Bragança became King João IV in 1640 he accompanied him to Lisbon, where he was royal choirmaster until his death. All his music is lost, but the royal library included the following sacred works by him: for triple choir (12 voices) a mass, five vesper psalms, two motets and a *Te Deum*; for double choir (eight voices) two vesper and two compline psalms, a responsory for 8 December, an invitatory and lessons for the Office of the Dead, and calendas for 24 June, 12 August and 4 October. There were also ten vilhancicos, one for 12 voices, the others for smaller groups.

BIBLIOGRAPHY

DBP; JoãoIL

D. Barbosa Machado: *Bibliotheca lusitana*, iii (Lisbon, 1752/*R*), 410–11; music entries ed. R.V. Nery as *A música no ciclo da Bibliotheca lusitana* (Lisbon, 1984)

J. Mazza: 'Dicionário biográfico de músicos portugueses', *Ocidente*, xxv (1945), suppl., 86, 96

ROBERT STEVENSON

Pereira, Tomás [Sancho] (*b* São Martinho do Vale, Barcelos, 1 Nov 1645; *d* Beijing, 24 Dec 1708). Portuguese organist, theorist and organ builder. He was a Jesuit missionary; his 36-year stay in China produced far-reaching cultural exchange. His accomplishment in music, mathematics and diplomacy led to his being invited to Beijing by Emperor Kangxi. He astounded the emperor with a demonstration of musical notation, repeating Chinese melodies flawlessly after one hearing. Kangxi's subsequent creation of an academy to study ancient Chinese music culminated in the four-volume *Lulu Zhengyi* ('A True Doctrine of Music'). A fifth volume, on Western music theory, was begun by Pereira and completed by Teodorico Pedrini, his successor as court musician; the whole was published in Beijing in 1713.

Pereira built several organs in Beijing for the Catholic church and for the emperor, including one which played Chinese songs mechanically. He also wrote Chinese hymns, his only known compositions. At Kangxi's behest Pereira was instrumental in negotiating the 1689 Treaty of Nerchinsk between Russia and China, the first such treaty between Asia and Europe.

BIBLIOGRAPHY

L. Pfister: *Notices biographiques et bibliographiques sur les Jésuites de l'ancienne mission de Chine, 1552–1773* (Shanghai, 1932–4/*R*).

J. Canhão: 'Um músico português do século XVII na corte de Pequim: o padre Tomás Pereira', *Boletím da Associação portuguesa de educação musical*, lv (1987), 9–15; Eng. trans., *Review of Culture*, no.4 (1988), 21–33

G. Gild-Bohne, ed.: *Das Lü Lü Zheng Yi Xubian: ein Jesuitentraktat über die europäische Notation in China von 1713* (Göttingen, 1991)

J. Lindorff: 'The Harpsichord and Clavichord in China During the Ming and Qing Dynasties', *Early Keyboard Studies Newsletter*, viii/2 (1994), 1–8

JOYCE LINDORFF

Pereira Salas, Eugenio (*b* Santiago, 19 May 1904; *d* Santiago, 17 Nov 1979). Chilean musicologist. He studied at the University of Chile, chiefly under Domingo Santa Cruz (licentiate 1928), and at the universities of Paris (1926–8) and California (1933–4). At the University of Chile he served as dean of the faculty of philosophy and education (1953–7), as a member of the university council (1958–64) and as chairman of the department of history (1952–70); he was elected president of the Chilean Academy of History. His thorough study of Chile's music history provides a comprehensive account from the beginnings of the colony to the end of the 19th century; his publications also contain valuable bibliographical information.

WRITINGS

Cantos y danzas de la patria vieja (Santiago, 1940)

Los origenes del arte musical en Chile (Santiago, 1941)

Notas para la historia del intercambio musical entre las Américas antes del año 1940 (Washington DC, 1942; Eng. trans., 1943)

'Los estudios folklóricos y el folklore musical en Chile', *RMC*, no.1 (1945), 4–23

Le música de la isla de Pascua (Santiago, 1947)

Guía bibliográfica para el estudio del folklore chileno (Santiago, 1952)

with M. Abascal Brunet: *Pepe Vila: la zarzela chica en Chile* (Santiago, 1952)

Historia de la música en Chile, 1850–1900 (Santiago, 1957)

'Algúnos cantos infantiles de Chile', *Folklore americano*, nos.15–16 (1967–8), 25–39

Art and Music in Contemporary Latin America (London, 1968) [lecture delivered 16 May 1967 at Canning House, Belgrave Square, London]

Biobibliografia musical de Chile desde los origenes a 1886 (Santiago, 1978)

'La vida musical en Chile en el siglo XIX', *Die Musikkulturen Lateinamerikas im 19. Jahrhundert*, ed. R. Günther (Regensburg, 1982), 237–59

BIBLIOGRAPHY
L. Merino: 'Don Eugenio Pereira Salas (1904–1979), fundador de la historiografía musical en Chile', *RMC*, no.33 (1979), 66–87

GERARD BÉHAGUE

Perelmuth, Jacob Pincus. *See* PEERCE, JAN.

Perényi, Miklós (*b* Budapest, 5 Jan 1948). Hungarian cellist. He began his studies at the age of five with Miklós Zsámboki and Ede Banda at the Franz Liszt Academy in Budapest, and gave his first concert when he was nine. He was a pupil of Mainardi at the Accademia di S Cecilia, Rome, where he obtained his diploma in 1962, and with Casals in Zermatt, Puerto Rico and Marlboro between 1965 and 1972. In 1974 he was appointed a professor at the Franz Liszt Academy. Perényi has performed throughout Europe and the USA, and has appeared frequently, often in partnership with András Schiff, at the Mondsee International Chamber Music Festival. In 1990 he took part in the première of Kurtág's Double Concerto. His recordings include concertos by Haydn, Dvořák, Hindemith, Ligeti and Lutosławski, and many chamber works. Renowned for his noble, lyrical line and warmth of tone, he plays a Gagliano cello dated 1730.

PÉTER P. VÁRNAI/R

Perera, Ronald (Christopher) (*b* Boston, 25 Dec 1941). American composer. He studied with Leon Kirchner at Harvard (BA 1963, MA 1967), then with Gottfried Michael Koenig at the Studio voor Elektronische Muziek, University of Utrecht (1968). An extended study of electronic and computer music culminated in his *The Development and Practice of Electronic Music* (Englewood Cliffs, 1975), a major text which he edited with Jon Appleton. He has been a MacDowell Colony Fellow four times (1974, 1978, 1981, 1988) and in 1976 and 1988 received fellowship awards from the NEA. The Paderewski Fund (1972), the Goethe Institute (1974) and the Massachusetts Arts Council (1983) have commissioned works from him. From 1968 to 1970 he taught at Syracuse University and, in 1970, at Dartmouth College; in 1971 he joined the faculty of Smith College, Northampton, Massachusetts, where he was appointed to the Elsie Irwin Sweeney Chair in music. In *Alternate Routes* (1971), a score for the Dartmouth Dance Company, Perera conceived of all sounds as having kinetic properties: either wild runs and spins or delicate, subtle departures from complete stillness. In contrast to this physical orientation, his settings of three poems by Günter Grass (1974) use quotations of jazz, march music and a Johann Strauss waltz to evoke the nostalgic or even bizarre inner experiences of the personae. Many of Perera's works are available from Opus One, Albany, and CRI Records.

WORKS
Ops: The Yellow Wallpaper (C. Perkins Gilman), 1989; S. (J. Updike), 1995
Orch: Chanteys, 1976; The Saints: 3 Pieces for Orch with Audience Participation, 1990
Chbr and solo inst: Suite, pf, 1966; Improvisation for Loudspeakers, tape, 1969; Reverberations, org, tape, 1970; Alternate Routes, dance score, elec, 1971; Reflex, va, tape, 1973; Fantasy Variations, pf, elec, 1976; Bright Angels, org, perc, tape, 1977; Tolling, 2 pf, tape, 1979
Choral: Mass, solo vv, chorus, orch, 1967; Did You Hear the Angels Sing? (S. Miller), S, SATB, org, 1968; 3 Night Pieces, S, A, SSAA, vc, perc, pf, 1974; Everything That Has Breath (Bible: *Pss* cxlviii, cl), male/female/mixed 2vv, tape, 1976; other works
Songs: Dove sta amore (L. Ferlinghetti), S, tape, 1969; 5 Summer Songs (E. Dickinson), S, pf, 1972; Apollo Circling (J. Dickey), S,

pf, 1972; 3 Poems of Günter Grass, Mez, chbr ens, tape, 1974; Children of the Sun (R.L. Stevenson), S, hn, pf, 1979; The White Whale (H. Melville), Bar, orch, 1981; Crossing the Meridian (various poets), T, chbr ens, 1982; The Outermost House (H. Boston), nar, S, ens, 1991
Principal publishers: E.C. Schirmer, Boosey & Hawkes, Music Associates of New York

DAVID COPE

Peretola, Decimo Corinella da. *See* MEI, GIROLAMO.

Pereira da Costa, António. *See* COSTA (i), (10).

Pereyra-Lizaso, Nydia (*b* Rocha, 12 May 1916). Uruguayan composer. She began her musical studies at the Conservatorio Teresiano in Rocha with Dolores Bell and Carmen Barrera; later she moved to Montevideo for advanced studies with Wilhelm Kolischer (piano), Tomás Mujica (counterpoint and fugue) and Enrique Casal-Chapí (composition). Her *Cuatro miniaturas* for violin and viola won a chamber music award at the GEDOK competition in Mannheim in 1966 (with Ernst Krenek, Werner Egk and Nadia Boulanger as the jurors); she also won several times (1959, 1964, 1966, 1967, 1978) the Casa de Teatro stage music award with incidental music for plays performed by the Comedia Nacional de Montevideo. Her chamber and vocal music reveals styles varying from contrapuntal techniques to a medieval troubadour-like character as well as 20th-century influences, mainly Hindemith. She has also written pedagogical works for children. She taught for many years at the Kolischer conservatory and at the Instituto de Enseñanza Musical.

WORKS
(*selective list*)
Chbr music: Divertimento, str; Christmas Cant.; Str Qt; Adagio y allegro, cl, pf, 1958; Allegro y andante, Bb-cl, pf, 1965; Cuatro miniaturas, vn, va/cl, 1966
Vocal: Canción sobre Juan Ramón Gimenez, 1v, pf, 1954; 2 canciones (C. Gómez Martínez), 1v, pf, 1956; 3 canciones (E. de Cáceres), vocal qt or choir, 1956; 6 canciones (R.M. Rilke), Mez, pf, 1959; 3 canciones (E. de Cáceres), S, pf, 1967
Pf: Sonata no.1, 1955; Sonata no.2, 1958; Sonatina, 1967; 3 piezas para niños, 1967; Sonatina, G, 1963; 2 miniaturas, 1968
Incid music

BIBLIOGRAPHY
Uruguayos contemporáneos, iii (Montevideo, 1965)
S. Salgado: *Breve historia de la música culta en el Uruguay* (Montevideo, 1971, 2/1980)

SUSANA SALGADO

Perez, David [Davide] (*b* Naples, 1711; *d* Lisbon, 30 Oct 1778). Italian composer. He was the son of Giovanni Perez and Rosalina Serrari, both Neapolitans (the surname Perez, of Spanish origin, was fairly common in the former Kingdom of the Two Sicilies). At the age of 11 he became a student at the Conservatorio di S Maria di Loreto in Naples, where he remained until 1733, studying counterpoint with Francesco Mancini, singing and keyboard playing with Giovanni Veneziano, and the violin with Francesco Barbella. On completion of his studies, Perez immediately entered the service of the Sicilian Prince of Aragona, Diego Naselli. His first known pieces, the Latin cantatas *Ilium palladio astu subducto expugnatum* and *Palladium*, performed in Palermo's Collegio della Società di Gesù for the laurelling festivities, date from 1734. For the next few years he was active in Palermo and Naples, his patron having become chamberlain to King Carlo I. His first opera, *La nemica amante*, was composed for the king's birthday in 1735 and performed in the gardens of the Neapolitan royal palace and later in the Teatro S

Perez's 'Alessandro nell'Indie', Act 1 scene xi, Opera do Tejo, Lisbon, 31 March 1755; engraving by Michel Le Bouteux after design by Giovanni Carlo Galli-Bibiena

Bartolomeo. In the libretto's dedication the impresario of the theatre, Angelo Carasale, referred to Perez and Pergolesi as 'dei buoni virtuosi di questa città'. In 1738 he was appointed *vicemaestro di cappella* of Palermo's Cappella Palatina, the church dedicated to S Pietro in the royal palace, and became *maestro* the following year, succeeding Pietro Puzzuolo.

In the early 1740s Perez firmly established himself as a mature master. The opera he composed for the Teatro Alibert, Rome, for the carnival of 1740 was not performed due to the sudden death of Pope Clement XII, but on his return to Naples he staged an *opera buffa* (*I travestimenti amorosi*) and a serenata (*L'amor pittore*) at court, and an *opera seria* (*Il Siroe*) at the Teatro S Carlo, the latter performed by Caffarelli and Manzuoli. Opera was not an easy enterprise in Palermo and, until 1744, most of Perez's compositions as *maestro di cappella* there were serenatas and church music. He also composed church music for Naples, and two operas for the carnival of 1744 in Genoa. After March 1748 he was granted leave of absence and never returned to Palermo, although he continued to receive half his Palermo salary until his death. He proceeded to stage his operas in rapid succession in Naples, Rome, Florence, Venice, Milan, Turin and Vienna. In February 1749 he competed with Niccolò Jommelli in a public examination for the position of *maestro di cappella* at the Vatican. Cardinals Albani and Passionei helped grant Jommelli the appointment, although Perez was popular with the musicians (Girolamo

Chiti, *maestro di cappella* of S Giovanni in Laterano, commented that Perez 'composes, sings and plays as an angel' and 'is very much superior to Jommelli in groundwork, singing and playing. He is, however, an imaginary hypochondriac').

In 1752 the King of Portugal invited Perez to become *mestre de capela* and music master to the royal princesses, a position he occupied until his death. The substantial annual stipend, coupled with the excellent musical and theatrical resources of the Portuguese court, undoubtedly influenced his decision to remain in Lisbon. The ambition of the new king was to depart from his father's music policy, which favoured church music, and give Italian opera a central position at court. Sumptuous scenic treatment was the rule, and Perez's operas were mounted by such famous designers as Berardi, Dorneau, Bouteux and Galli-Bibiena (see illustration). Equally important were the great singers who appeared at the Portuguese court, including Raaf, Elisi, Manzuoli, Gizziello and Caffarelli.

The nature of Perez's output changed in the aftermath of the Lisbon earthquake of 1 November 1755. The court withdrew from the theatres, and no operas were produced for seven years (and thereafter only in a less spectacular fashion). In the last 23 years of his life, Perez wrote only a few new operas; however, he wrote a huge amount of church music, covering almost all the rituals and practices of the two main musical chapels of Lisbon, the royal chapel and the Seminário da Patriarcal. Because he never left Portugal, his international acclaim slowly declined. Nevertheless, Gerber noted that by 1766 Perez's compositions were known and in demand in Germany and that in 1790 he was 'one of the most celebrated and beloved composers among the Italian masters . . . one of the latest composers who maintained the rigour of counterpoint'. In 1774 Perez became by acclamation a member of the Academy of Ancient Music in London, where the only full-scale piece printed in his lifetime, the *Mattutino de' morti*, was published by Bremner. His music, particularly that for the church, was widely copied in Italy. During the last four years of his life he suffered from a chronic disease, eventually losing his sight, but continuing to compose. In 1778 Maria I (one of his pupils) made him a Knight of the Order of Christ; and when he died she ordered his funeral to be conducted with pomp at court expense.

Perez composed more than 45 dramatic works between 1733 and 1777, about half of which were operas written between 1744 and 1755, the period during which he concentrated almost exclusively on the genre. Excerpts from *Arminio*, *La Didone abbandonata*, *Ezio*, *Il Farnace*, *Solimano* and *Vologeso* were published in London by John Walsh, and many works exist in manuscript. In the *opere serie* written before 1752 he was often bound by the forms of Metastasian opera. *Il Siroe*, *Andromaca* and *Alessandro nell'Indie* (1744 version) are prime examples: 20 or more full da capo arias (more than half accompanied by strings alone) are consistently used, with between one

and four accompanied recitatives, usually a single duet, a perfunctory three-movement sinfonia and a simple choral finale for the principals. The arias are usually written in the Baroque concerto idiom, with extravagant word-painting in the orchestra and extensive vocal bravura passages. Adhering to Metastasio's prescription of character definition as the sum of a pattern of dramatic reversals, each aria usually depicts a single affect, with few exceptions. These latter include *Artaserse* and *Alessandro*, which each contain a scene complex of related arias and accompanied recitatives.

With *Il Demofoonte* in 1752, as Perez began his lengthy residence in Lisbon, the monumental idiom declined and a sentimental style gained increasing prominence, with a resultant clarity of texture, greater symmetry of phrase, frequent rhythmic motifs and an emphasis on the pathetic. Formal modifications include the frequent absence of ritornellos, truncated da capo arias, between five and nine accompanied recitatives and several small ensembles. Perez's operas of the 1750s frequently display an orchestral mastery superior to that of the contemporary Italian opera school, incorporating features that appeared in his church music of the 1740s. The strings are in three to five parts, the wind are often used for solo passages, and there is less doubling of the vocal part and an increase in concertante passages. Among the better examples of this later manner are *Olimpiade*, *Il Demofoonte*, *L'Ipermestra* and *Alessandro nell'Indie* (1755 version). Several works written after 1757 reflect French influence. *Creusa in Delfo*, for example, contains extensive finales, prominent chorus and ballet scenes, and accompanied recitative for two to five characters.

Demetrio (1766 version) represents a transitional aesthetic, in which Perez combined a modified Baroque dramaturgy with a more up-to-date musical style: he eliminated 14 Metastasio aria texts, used eight accompanied recitatives and two duets for moments of personal reflection, and gave the da capo aria more musical and dramatic coherence. *Solimano* (1757) is his acknowledged masterpiece. It contains 14 *dal segno* arias, one cavatina and six accompanied recitatives, the scope and procedures of which are exceptional; several times the individual numbers are integrated into large-scale scene complexes. The flexibility of form, dramatic contrasts and musical vitality of the work are due in large part to the juxtaposition of *buffo* and *seria* idioms and to an interchange of compositional technique between aria and accompanied recitative. Kretzschmar (1919) claimed that *Solimano* 'belongs under the heading of masterworks . . . richness of invention and of feeling, originality of means and of form, everything is therein, which makes an art great' and 'if all opera composers of the Neapolitan school had been of his stamp, there would have been no need of a Gluck'.

Perez's two long periods of employment offered ample opportunities to write for the church. In the early part of his career he is reported by Florimo to have 'enriched with his compositions' Palermo's Cappella Palatina, but there are also many pieces that were written for Naples. In Lisbon, his deep religiosity and that of his pupil, the Princess Maria, combined with the musical policy of the court, led him to concentrate on church music for the last 23 years of his life. His first mass is dated February 1736. In most of his early works he made good use of orchestral and choral resources, taking great care over their treat-

Ex.1 *Stabat Mater*, 1774, beginning (organ part not shown)

ment. The Mass in E♭ (1740), for example, is scored for two choirs (the final 'Cum Sancto Spiritu' is a ten-voice fugue), full strings divided, in some sections, into two orchestras, and woodwind (no clarinets), horns and trumpets in pairs. The orchestral writing includes muted strings, 'seconda corda' passages for the violins, an abundance of crescendos and diminuendos, and solo parts for the woodwind and the viola. He treated solo vocal passages like operatic arias; most fugues or fugato sections have symmetrical thematic entries, and the pieces in the *stile antico* are conservative in harmony and notation.

The later church music written at Lisbon is quite different from the earlier works. The orchestral writing is as detailed, but instruments such as recorders and lutes are no longer employed. There are fewer separate sections for solo voices, and in most pieces one or more soloists emerge from the choir for short passages, thus creating numerous distinct vocal textures. A striking difference is that the counterpoint, although remaining strict, is more eloquent and sentimental, and rarely are the modern and archaic styles distinctly juxtaposed. The beginning of the 1772 *Stabat mater* (ex.1) serves as an example of his later style, in which the musical presentation of the words acquires pietist overtones. The sections alternate freely between polyphonic and chordal writing, and the harmony is elaborate, with much use of chromaticism. On the whole the style is strongly in favour of variety over coherence, and therefore thematic recurrence is not a regular feature.

18th-century critics often ranked Perez with Hasse and Jommelli; Burney found 'an original spirit and elegance in all his production'. 19th-and 20th-century commentary, based for the most part on a few earlier operas, has generally downgraded this judgment. A more complete examination of his works affirms the stature his contemporaries assigned to him. While he was essentially a transitional figure in 18th-century opera, he was nevertheless one of the great composers of *opera seria*, and as a church composer, he wrote some of the finest Roman Catholic music of the 18th century.

WORKS
SACRED
for 4 voices and organ or basso continuo unless otherwise stated

masses, etc.
In A (Ky, Gl), S, A, SATB, vns, bc, 1736, *I-Nc*; in A, *P-EVc, La*; in B♭ (Ky, Gl), SSATB, orch, 1766, *La**; in B♭ (Ky, Gl), SSATB, orch, *D-Mbs, GB-Lcm, I-Fc, P-La*; in b, SATB, orch, *D-Hs*; in C, S, S, B, org/bc, *Mbs*; in c, S, A, SATB, vn, obs, hns, org/bc, *I-Baf**; in D♭, SSATB, org/bc, *P-Lf*; in D, SSAATTBBB, orch, 1736, *I-Nc*; in E♭ (Ky, Gl), S, S, A, T, T, B, SSAATTBBB, 2 orchs, 1740, *Nc**; in E♭ (Ky, Gl), baptism of José, son of Maria I, S, S, SSAATTBB, orch, 1761, *D-Mbs, GB-Lcm, I-Mc, Nc, Nf, P-La**; in e (Ky, Gl), *Lf*; in F (Ky, Gl), SATB, orch, *GB-Lcm, P-EVc*; in G, SSATB, orch, *D-Hs*; in G, SSAATTBBB, orch, *I-Nc, Nf*; in g (Ky, Gl), *P-Ln, VV*; Requiem in c, SATB, bn obbl, org/bc, 1763, *Lf, Ln, VV*; Cr in A, S, S, A, T, B, SSATB, orch, *La*; Cr in C, SATB, vns ad lib, 1742, *I-Nc**, *PLcon*; Cr pastorale in C, SATB, orch, *PLcon*; Cr in D, SSATB, orch, *D-Mbs, GB-Lcm, I-Nf, P-La*; Cr in D, SATB, orch, *Ln*; Cr in D, S, S, A, A, T, T, B, SSAATTBBB, orch, *D-Mbs, I-BGc, I-Mc, Nc, Nf*; Cr in F, SSAATTBBB, orch, *Nc*; Cr in G, SATB, orch, *P-Lf*

antiphons
Alma Redemptoris mater, D, *P-Lf*; Ascendente Jesu, B♭, 1756, *La, Lf**; Ave regina coelorum, D, SSATB, *Lf*; Beatus Laurentius, F, *Ln*; Cum turba multa, D, 1757, *Lf**; Missus est Gabriel angelus, D, *I-Af, P-Ln*; Nativitas tua, c, *I-Rf, P-Lf, Ln*; O quam suavis, c, *Lf, Ln, VV*; O quam suavis, D, SSATB, org/bc, 1772, *Lf*, Ln, VV*; O sacrum convivium, D, 1772, *La*, Lf, Ln*; Quae est ista, E, *Lf*; Regina coeli laetare, A, SSATB, org/bc; Salutate Mariam, B♭, S, S,

SSATB, org/bc, 1774, *Ln**; Salve regina, B♭, SATB, org/bc, *D-Bsb*; Salve regina, B♭, A, vns, va ad lib, org/bc, *A-Ed*; Salve regina, c, S, SATB, org/bc, 1765, *P-Lf**; Salve regina, E♭, 1760, *Lf**; Salve regina, E, *Ln*; Salve regina, f, SAAT, org/bc, 1739, *A-W, D-Bsb, Dl, Rp, P-Lf**; Sancta Maria succurre, B♭, *EVc*; Sancta Maria succurre, c, *Lf, Ln, VV*; Te gloriosus apostolorum, B♭, *Lf, Ln*

psalms
Confitebor tibi, D, B, SSAATTBBB, org/bc, *P-Ln*; Confitebor tibi, F, S, SATB, org/bc, *Lf*; Dixit Dominus, B♭, SATB, orch, *I-Nc*; Dixit Dominus, D, S, S, A, T, B, B, SATB, *P-Lf*; Dixit Dominus, F, *EVc, Lf*; Domine probasti me, C, SSAATTBB, org/bc, *Lf*; In exitu Israel, D, SSAATTBBB, org/bc, *I-Mc, PAc, Rvat*, 2nd version: *D-Bsb, Mbs, GB-Lbl, P-Lf, Ln, VV*; Laetatus sum, C, S, A, T, B, org/bc, *Lf*; Lauda Jerusalem, B♭, SATB, org/bc, 1759, *Lf**; Laudate pueri, A, S, S, A, SATB, org/bc, *A-Wn, D-Mbs, I-Mc, Nc, Rf, Rvat*; Laudate pueri, A, S, S, A, SATB, org/bc, *D-Bsb, Rp, I-Nc, P-Ln, VV*; Laudate pueri, C, *Ev*; Laudate pueri, D, S, orch, *I-Gi(l)*; Laudate pueri, F, SSATB, orch, *Nc*, Memento Domine David, D, SSAATTBBB, org/bc, *D-Bsb, Rp, GB-Lbl, I-BGc, Mc, Nc, Rvat, P-Lf, Ln, VV*, ed. in *Corps complet de musique d'église* (Paris, 1829); Miserere, c, SATB, 1749, *D-Mbs, E-ZAc* (with added str), *I-Rvat**, exam piece for Vatican appointment; Miserere, c, 1757, *P-EVc, La, Lf*, Ln*; Miserere, c, S, S, A, T, B, SATB, org/bc, *Lf, Ln*; Miserere, c, S, A, T, B, B, SATB, org/bc, *GB-Lbl, Lcm, I-Nc*; Miserere, f, SSATB, bn obbl, org/bc, 1764, *A-Wn, D-Rp, Mbs, I-Mc, Nc, P-Lf**; Nisi Dominus, A, S, SATB, org/bc, *Lf, Ln, VV*; Nisi Dominus, B♭, S, SSATB, org/bc, *Lf*; Nisi Dominus, C, S, orch, *I-Nc*; Vespers, A, 1766, *P-Lf**; Vespers, D, *Lf, Ln*; Vespers, D, 1768, *Lf**; Vespers, G, SATB, vn, org/bc, *I-NT, PLcon*

responsories
Credo quod redemptor meus vivit, c, death of King of Spain, SATB, org/bc, 1747, *P-Lf**; Credo quod redemptor meus vivit, d, S, S, A, T, B, SATB, orch, 1772, as *Mattutino de'morti* (London, 1774); Credo quod redemptor meus vivit, g, S, A, T, B, SATB, org/bc, *I-Fc, Mc, P-La, Ln, VV*; Hodie concepta est, A, *BRs, EVc, Lf, Ln*; Hodie nobis coelorum rex, D, for Christmas, 1756, *Ln*; Hodie in Jordane, B♭, for Epiphany, *BRs, Lf, Ln, VV*; Hodie nobis coelorum rex, D, *D-Bsb, GB-Lbl, I-Af, P-BRs, EVc, Lf, Ln*; In columbae specie, F, S, SATB, vn, org/bc, *EVc*; In monte Oliveti, a, for Maundy Thursday, *EVc*; In monte Oliveti, g, *EVc*; In monte Oliveti, c, 1758, *I-Nc, P-Lf*, Ln, VV*; In monte Oliveti, f, *Lf*; Omnes amici mei, d, for Good Friday, 1758, *D-Rp, I-Nc, P-EVc, Lf*, Ln, VV*; Omnes amici mei, d, S, T, B, org/bc, *EVc, Ln*; Omnes de Saba venient, F, for Epiphany, S, S, S, S, vn, org/bc, *EVc*; Regis Tharsis, F, for Epiphany, S, SSAT, vn, org/bc, *EVc*; Regnum mundi, A, *Ln*; Regnum mundi, C, S, S, A, T (female soloists), org/bc, 1772, *Ln**; Sicut ovis, a, for Easter Saturday, 1758, *D-Rp, I-Nc, P-EVc, Lf, Ln*

lamentations
Aleph. Ego vir videns, F, for Good Friday, ?1749, A, fl, hn, vn, va, b, *A-Wn, I-BGc*; De lamentatione Jeremiae prophetae, g, for Good Friday, 1761, *Nc, P-Lf*, Ln, VV*; De lamentatione Jeremiae prophetae, for Good Friday, ?1749, (oboe lunghi), rec, hn, vn, va, b, *A-Wn, I-BGc*; Incipit lamentatio Jeremiae Prophetae, c, for Maundy Thursday, 1763, *Nc, P-BRs* (pts, with added hns and bn), *Lf*, Ln, VV*; Lamed. Matribus suis dixerunt, G, for Good Friday, ?1749, S, A, fl, hn, vn, va, b, *A-Wn, I-BGc*

sequences
Lauda Sion, B♭, 1757, *D-Bsb, Mbs, P-La, Lf**; Lauda Sion, B♭, *Lf*; Lauda Sion, d, SATB, vn, org/bc, *I-PLcon*; Stabat mater, c, 1772, *GB-Lbl*; Stabat mater, f, *P-Ln, VV*; Stabat mater, f, *Lf*; Veni Sancte Spiritus, C, SATB, vns, org/bc, *I-PLcon*; Victimae paschali laudes, C, SATB, orch, *Mc*

hymns
Mag, D, SSATB, orch, *I-Nc*; O salutaris hostia, E♭, SATB, orch, *P-Ln*; TeD, A, *Lf, Ln*; TeD, C, SSAATTBBB, org/bc, 1774, *Lf**; TeD, D, SSAATTBBB, org/bc, *Lf, Ln*; TeD, D, acclamation of Queen Maria I, 1777, SSAATTBBB, hn, tpt, 2 vc obbl, db, org/bc, *Lf*; TeD, D, SSAATTBBB, org/bc, 1776, *Lf**; TeD, D, SSAATTBBB, org/bc, *Lf*; TeD, D, 1760, *La, Lf**; TeD, D, SATB, orch, *CH-E*; TeD, D, S, S, A, T, SATB, orch, *P-Cug*; Tibi Christe splendor patris, A, S, str, *CH-E*

Haec dies quam fecit Dominus (grad), D, SSAATTBBB, org/bc, *D-Mbs, GB-Lbl, I-Af, Mc, Nc, Rf, Rsc, Rvat, P-BRs, Lf, Ln, VV*; Rorate coeli de super (int), E♭, 3vv, *A-Wn*

motets

Amore Jesu gaudeo, B♭, SSATB, orch, 1772, *P-La**; Amore Jesu gaudeo, G, SSATB, orch, 1776, *P-La**; Beatissimae Virginis Mariae, A, *Lf*; Defuncto Herode, E♭, *I-Af, P-Ln,Vs,VV*; Factum est silentium in coelo, B♭, *EVc* (with added vns and hn) *Lf, Ln, VV*; Jesus junxit se discipulus suis, A, *Lf, Ln*; Magister dic nobis, C, *Ln*; Media nocte, D, *I-Af, P-Lf, Ln, VV*; O Margarita poenitens, c, *GB-Lcm,P-Lf*; Regnum et civitatem istam, b, 1756, *Lf*, Ln*; Repleta est, G, *Lf*; Sacram beati Vicentis martyris, D, 1756, *Lf**; Sancte Paule apostole, F, 1756, *Lf**; Te excelsis fons sapientiae, F, *Ln*; Virtute magna, C, 1756, *I-Af, P-Lf**, Ln*

litanies and novenas

Litany of the BVM, C, *P-BR, Ln*; Litany of the BVM, G, SATB, org/bc, *La, Ln*, alternatim lit, with short verses in Port. marked 'povo'; Litany of the BVM, G, *Ln*; Novena of St Margarita of Cortona, D, 1777, *La*; Novena of the Most Sacred Heart of Jesus, D, *Ln, VV*; Novena of the Most Sacred Heart of Jesus, G, 1763, *La*

concert motets

Care Jesu o sponse amate, G, S, vns, org, *CH-Af*; Jesu dilecte amabo te, G, S, vns, b, *D-DO*; Jesum amare desidero, E♭, S, orch, *CH-BM*; Jesu o bone salvator, f, S, vn, va, b, org/bc, *SAf*; Ne timeas Maria, D, S, orch, *BM*; O anima quid amas, A, S, S, str, org/bc, *SAf*; O flos amice, G, S, orch, *H-PH*; Sanctus Deus in aula, A, S, S, str, *CH-E*; Tornat coelum ruinas minatur, G, S, orch, 1749, *D-Rp** (under pseud. of Perez's patron 'Egidio Lasnel' (Diego Naselli)); Tota pulchra es amica mea, G, S, str, *DO*; Unica est columba mea, D, A, orch, *CZ-OP*

ORATORIOS

La passione di Gesù Cristo nostro Signore (P. Metastasio), 1742, ?*DK-Kk* (under pseud. of Perez's patron 'Egidio Lasnel' (Diego Naselli)), lib *GB-Lbl*

Il martirio di S Bartolomeo, 1749, *I-Pca, Ras*

Giefte, 1750, music lost, lib *Rsc, Vgc*

Il ritorno di Tobia, 1753, music lost, lib *PLcom*

OPERAS
drammi per musica in three acts unless otherwise stated

La nemica amante, Naples, Palazzo Reale, 4 Nov 1735, music lost, lib *I-Bc, Fm, Mb*

I travestimenti amorosi (ob, 2, A. Palomba), Naples, Palazzo Reale, 10 July 1740, *Mc, US-Wc*

Il Siroe, re di Persia (P. Metastasio), Naples, S Carlo, 4 Nov 1740, *I-Nc* (Act 1); rev. Lisbon, Corte, 12 Sept 1752, *D-Hs, I-Vnm, P-La**, S-Skma*

Demetrio [1st version] (Metastasio), Palermo, 13 June 1741, *B-Bc,F-Pn, P-La**; revived Naples, 18 Dec 1748, under pseud. of Perez's patron 'Egidio Lasnel' (Diego Naselli)

Alessandro nell'Indie [1st version] (Metastasio), Genoa, Falcone, carn. 1744, *A-Wn, GB-Lbl, I-Vnm, P-La, S-Skma, US-BEm*

Merope (A. Zeno), Genoa, Falcone, carn. 1744, *F-Pn, I-Vlevi, P-La*

Leucippo (favola pastorale, G.C. Pasquini), Palermo, S Cecilia, 1744, *F-Pn*

L'errore amoroso (commedia), Palermo, S Lucia, carn. 1745, music lost, lib *I-PLcon*

L'amor fra congionti (commedia), Palermo, S Lucia, carn. 1746, music lost, lib *I-PLcon, Rli*

Artaserse (Metastasio), Florence, Pergola, aut. 1748, *D-Hs, GB-Lcm, I-Nc, Vnm, P-La, Ln, S-Skma, US-BEm*

La Semiramide riconosciuta (Metastasio), Rome, Alibert, 3 Feb 1749, *GB-Lbl, P-La*, arias in *I-Fc, Gl* and *MOe*

La clemenza di Tito (Metastasio), Naples, S Carlo, 1749

Andromaca, Vienna, Hof, 1750, *A-Wn, US-Wc*, as Andromeda,*GB-Lbl, I-Nc*

Vologeso (Zeno), Vienna, Hof, 1750, *A-Wn*, Favourite Songs (London, 1759); rev. as Lucio Vero, Verona, 1754, as La Berenice, Verona, carn. 1762, arias in *I-Nc, MOe* and *P-La*

Ezio (Metastasio), Milan, Regio Ducal, 26 Dec 1750, *F-Pn*, Favourite Songs (London, 1755)

Il Farnace (Zeno, rev. ?A.M. Lucchini), Turin, Real, carn. 1751, *F-Pn** (Act 1), *P-La**, Favourite Songs (London, 1759)

La Didone abbandonata (Metastasio), Genoa, 1751, *GB-Lbl, I-Vnm, P-La**, S-Skma, US-Wc*, Favourite Songs (London, 1761)

La Zenobia (Metastasio), Milan, Regio Ducal, aut. 1751, *P-La*, arias in *I-MAav, Nc* and *PLcon*

Il Demofoonte (Metastasio), Lisbon, Corte, aut. 1752, *D-Hs, GB-Ob, I-Vn, P-La**, Ln, S-Skma*

Olimpiade (Metastasio), Lisbon, Corte, spr. 1753, *B-Bc, D-Hs, GB-Lbl, Lcm, I-Vnm, P-La**, S-Skma,US-Wc*; also perf. as serenata in the queen's chambers, 31 March 1753

L'eroe cinese (Metastasio), Lisbon, Corte, 6 June 1753, *P-La**, arias in *GB-Lbl, Lcm, I-Vnm* and *US-Wc*

Adriano in Siria (Metastasio), Lisbon, Salvaterra, carn. 1754, *D-Hs, GB-Lbl, Lcm, I-Vnm, P-La, Ln, S-Skma,US-BEm*

L'Ipermestra (Metastasio), Lisbon, Real Corte, 31 March 1754, music lost, lib *D-Hs, GB-Lbl, Lcm, I-Vnm, P-La, S-Skma, US-Wc*

Alessandro nell'Indie [2nd version] (Metastasio), Lisbon, Opera do Tejo, 31 March 1755, *GB-Lbl, P-La, Ln*

Re Pastore, Cremona, spr. 1756, music lost, lib *I-Lurago, sormani, Rsc*

Solimano (G. Migliavacca), Lisbon, Ajuda, carn. 1757; rev. (?B. Martelli), Lisbon, Salvaterra, 31 March 1768, *F-Pn, GB-Lbl* (facs. in IOB, xlv, 1978), *Lcm, I-Nc, P-LA, US-Wc*; Favourite Songs (London, n.d.)

Arminio (pasticcio, Salvi), London, King's, 1760, Favourite Songs (London, 1760)

Demetrio [2nd version] (Metastasio), Lisbon, Salvaterra, carn. 1766, *D-Hs, F-Pn, GB-Lcm, I-Nc, P-VV**, La, US-Wc*

Creusa in Delfo (dramma per musica misto di cori e danze, 2, G. Martinelli), Lisbon, Salvaterra, carn. 1774, *P-La*

Doubtful: Astarto, Palermo, 1743; Medea, Palermo, 1744; L'isola incantata, Palermo, 1746

OTHER DRAMATIC

Ilium Palladio astu subducto expugnatum (cant.), Palermo, Collegio della Società di Gesù, 1734, *I-PLcom*

Palladium (cant.), Palermo, Collegio della Società di Gesù, 1734, *PLcom*

Il trionfo di Venere (serenata), king's marriage, Palermo, 1738

L'atalanta (serenata), queen's birthday, Palermo, 1739

L'amor pittore (componimento drammatico, N. Giovo), Naples, Palazzo Reale, 24 July 1740, music lost, lib *Nc*

Iason aureo vellere potitus (cant.), Palermo, Pelicella, 1740, *PLcom*

La reggia del Sole (serenata), queen's birthday, Palermo, Real Palazzo, 1741, music lost, lib *GB-Lbl*

L'eroismo di Scipione, Palermo, 1741, lost, mentioned in *FétisB*

La stirpe di Achille (serenata, N. Marini), queen's nameday, Palermo, Real Palazzo, 10 July 1742, music lost, lib *Lbl*

Il natale di Giunone (serenata, Marini), queen's birthday, Palermo, Real Palazzo, 1742, music lost, lib *Lbl*

Il regno della Sirene (serenata, Marini), Palermo, Real Palazzo, 10 July 1743, music lost, lib *Lbl*

L'isola disabitata [1st version] (componimento drammatico, 1, P. Metastasio), Palermo, 1748, *I-Nc*

Posson ben le stagion (cant. pastorale, 2 pts) Rome, Cesare Capranica's chamber, 1749, *Tf*

La vera felicità (componimento drammatico, 3, M.B. Martelli), Lisbon, Queluz, 5 July 1761, music lost, lib *P-Cug, Cul, Ln, Lt*

L'isola disabitata [2nd version] (componimento drammatico, 1, Metastasio), Lisbon, Queluz, 19 March 1767, *La*

Le cinesi (componimento drammatico che introduce a un ballo, 1, Metastasio), Lisbon, Queluz, 1769, music lost, lib *Cug, Lac, Lt*

Il ritorno di Ulisse in Itaca (componimento drammatico, 1, Martelli), birth of the infanta, Lisbon, Queluz, 9 June 1774, music lost, lib *BR-Rn, I-Rsc*

L'eroe coronato (serenata, G. Martinelli), unveiling of statue of José I, Lisbon, Casa da Alfândega, 7 June 1775, music lost, lib *F-Pa, I-Bc, Rsc, Vgc, P-Cug, Cul, Lac, Ln, US-Cn, Wc*

La pace fra la virtù, e la bellezza (componimento drammatico, 1, Metastasio), Lisbon, Ajuda, 17 Dec 1777, *P-La*

INSTRUMENTAL AND DIDACTIC

6 sonate, 2 vn, b, op.1 (Paris, n.d.)

Trio, d, 2 vn, vc, *S-SK*

Trio, D, 2 vn, vc, *P-Ln*

Concerto, G, fl, 2 vn, b, *B-Bc*

Andantino, Allegro, C, hpd, *P-Pn*

Sonata, D, hpd, *Ln*

12 solfeggi, S, S, b, *D-Hs, I-BGc, Rrostirolla*

Chief sources in *A-Wn; D-Bsb; GB-Lbl,Lcm; I-Bc, La, Mc, Nc, Pn, Vsm; US-BEm, Wc* (see also *EitnerQ*)

BIBLIOGRAPHY

BurneyH; EitnerQ; FlorimoN; MGG1 (P. Giurleo)

S.M. Vercelli: *Nelle funebre pompe del Signor Arcimaestro in Musica David Peres* (Lisbon, 1779)

S. Bertini: *Dizionario storico-critico degli scrittori di musica e de' più celebri artisti di tutte le nazioni si' antiche che moderne*, iii (Palermo, 1815)

H. Kretzschmar: 'Aus Deutschlands italienischer Zeit', *JbMP*, viii (1901), 45–61

H. Abert: *Niccolò Jommelli als Opernkomponist* (Halle, 1908)

H. Kretzschmar: *Geschichte der Oper* (Leipzig, 1919)

U. Prota-Giurleo: *Musicisti napoletani alla corte di Portogallo* (Naples, 1923)

W. Vetter: 'Gluck und seine italienischen Zeitgenossen', *ZMw*, vii (1924–5), 609–46

E. Soares: *David Perez, Subsidios para a biografa' do celébre mestre de musica de camera de D. Josè* (Lisbon, 1935)

L. Russo: *Metastasio* (Bari, 1945)

E.O.D. Downes: *The Operas of Johann Christian Bach as a Reflection of the Dominant Trends in Opera Seria 1750–1780* (diss., Harvard U., 1958)

P.J. Jackson: *The Operas of David Perez* (diss., Stanford U., 1967)

G. Allroggen: 'Piccinnis Origille', *ANMg*, no.15 (1975), 258–97

A. McCredie: 'La riforma operistica prima di Gluck e il teatro musicale eroico tedesco dello Sturm und Drang', *Ricerche musicali*, v (1981), 86–108

M.C. de Brito: *Opera in Portugal in the Eighteenth Century* (Cambridge, 1989)

W.C. Holmes: *Opera Observed: Views of a Florentine Impresario in the Early Eighteenth Century* (Chicago, 1993)

M. Dottori: *The Church Music of Davide Perez and Niccolo Jommelli, with Especial Emphasis on their Funeral Music* (diss., U. of Wales, 1997)

MAURICIO DOTTORI, PAUL J. JACKSON

Pérez (Roldán), Juan (bap. Calahorra, 26 Dec 1604; *d* ?Zaragoza, after 1672). Spanish composer. López-Calo identifies him with the Juan Pérez, nephew of the chaplain and musician Pedro Pereda, who became a choirboy at Calahorra Cathedral in 1617 and left for Sigüenza in December that year. In 1634 he was in Toledo seeking to become *cantor* (tenor) at the cathedral. In 1636 he was working as *maestro de capilla* and canon at the collegiate church of Berlanga, but in November he moved to Toledo Cathedral as *claustrero* and choirmaster, obtaining the tenor's prebend in June 1638. In 1639 he was offered the post of *maestro de capilla* at Calahorra. By December 1641 he was at Málaga Cathedral, hoping to become *maestro de capilla* there; however, the competition was not officially called until March 1642. He won the post, but had left by 30 October 1645, possibly owing to disagreements with musicians of the chapel. From at least 15 March 1648, the day his mother died, he was *maestro de capilla* at the Madrid Convent of the Incarnation. A letter to King João IV of Portugal, dated 22 June 1654, tells of Pérez Roldán's fame and at the same time describes him as lazy and prone to attributing others' work to himself. In February 1655 he received an invitation to return to his old post in Málaga, which he rejected because his travel costs had not been paid in advance. In 1661 he was presbyter and the king's chaplain, as well as *maestro de capilla* at the Convento de la Encarnación; he still held all these posts in 1664, when he was a judge in the competition for the mastership of Segovia Cathedral. By 18 June 1667 he was no longer working at the Madrid convent, and on 22 July he was appointed *maestro de capilla* of Segovia Cathedral; however, by 26 October 1670 he had disappeared, taking everything with him, including his scores, and breaking all his commitments. In 1671 he took up the post of *maestro de capilla* at León Cathedral, but was pensioned in October. His debts were forgiven and he was granted 300 ducats for his retirement in exchange for turning certain musical scores over to the church. However, in December 1671 he became *maestro de capilla* at the cathedral of Nuestra Señora del Pilar,

Zaragoza, and at once had to take charge of the music for Christmas and Epiphany. Immediately after these festivities, on 9 January 1672, the chapter decided that, due to Pérez Roldán's age, the care of the children should pass to the organist, Joseph Muniesa, who must not have been much younger. The last news of Pérez Roldán is in a letter, dated 13 February 1672, from Joaquín Falqués, the king's chaplain and musician of the royal chapel, addressed to him in Madrid. Also, Andrés Lorente listed him among the good modern masters in *El porqué de la música* (Alcalá de Henares, 1672; p.560). In November 1673 there was a new *maestro de capilla* at El Pilar. Most of Pérez Roldán's works are preserved in the cathedrals of Zaragoza, which, considering his reluctance to give his compositions to any church, would suggest that he died in that city. In August 1673 one of his works (a *Misa de la Batalla*) was handed over by a *cantor* of Segovia Cathedral, Pedro de la Puebla, to settle a debt he had contracted with the chapter.

During his life Pérez Roldán was considered a great composer, and a century later Iriarte, in his poem *La música*, placed him among the great Spanish composers. He comes across as having had a solid training in counterpoint, as demonstrated by both his old-style compositions and his villancicos, which are elaborate and of great melodic and harmonic interest. His use of dissonance and modulation confers upon his works a clearly recognizable personal style. His madrigal *Ah del sol* is one of the few known 18th-century Spanish works for instrumental ensemble. The music for *Tetis y Peleo* can almost certainly be attributed to him. It was composed to celebrate the Peace of the Pyrenees and the marriage of María Teresa, daughter of Phillip IV, to Louis XIV. Pérez Roldán re-used fragments from *Tetis* to create villancicos to the Resurrection and to the Virgin, with new text by Vicente Sánchez, incumbent of El Pilar and habitual collaborator with its *maestros de capilla*.

WORKS

SACRED VOCAL

14 masses, *E-E*(2), *Lc*(2), *SE*(9), *Zac*(1): 5 for 4vv; 3 for 8vv, acc.; 2 for 4vv, org; 1 for 8vv, org, other acc.; 1 for 10vv, hp, 2 other insts; 1 for 12vv; 1 for 12vv, acc.

2 Requiem settings: 1 for 4vv, *Ac*; 1 for 8vv, acc., *Zac*

4 Offices of the Dead: Liberame Domine, 8vv, hp, acc., Parce mihi Domine, 8vv, b, hp, Regem cui omnia vivunt, 8vv, org, other acc., all *E*; Taedet animam meam, 12vv, hp, *SE*

2 ants, 4vv, *SE*: Asperges me, Vidi aquam

4 Mag settings: 3 for 10–12vv, acc., *SE*; 1 for 12vv, hp, 2 org, other acc., *E*

2 lits: 1 for 6vv, acc., *SE*; 1 for 8vv, hp, org, *E*

1 hymn: Ave maris stella, 8vv, org, other acc., *SE*

4 Lamentations, *SE*: 2 Cogitavit Dominus, 10vv, acc., 2 Misericordiae Domini, 9vv, 2 bajoncillos, bn, other acc.

4 motets: Crux fidelis, 8vv, hp, org, *Zac*; Dulcissima Maria, 5vv, *Zac*; Introduxit me rex, 12vv, *E*; Sepulto Domino, 4vv, ed. in Lira sacro-hispana, ser.1, i (Madrid, 1869)

12 pss: Beatus vir, 8vv, 2 insts, *J*; Cum invocarem, 8vv, acc., *SE*; Cum invocarem, 12vv, hp, 2 org, other acc., *E*; Dixit Dominus, 8vv, hp, *SE*; Dixit Dominus, 8vv, hp, org, other acc., *E*; Laetatus sum, 10vv, b, hp, *SE*; Laetatus sum, 12vv, vn, other acc., *SE*;. Lauda Jerusalem, 5vv, acc., *E*; Laudate Dominum, 6vv, hp, *Zac*; Miserere, 8vv, acc., *SE*; Miserere, 8vv, org, other acc., *E*; Qui habitat, 8vv, hp, 2 org, other acc., *E*

1 reservation: Tantum ergo, 8vv, org, other acc., *Zac*

52 villancicos, 2–12vv, mostly with acc., 17 dated 1658–72, mainly in *Zac* (4 inc.), others in *D-Mbs*, *E-Bc*, *E*, *SE*

SECULAR VOCAL

Music for Tetis y Peleo (comedy, J. de Bolea), Zaragoza, Casa de Comedias, Feb 1672, *E-Zac*

No recates favores (tono humano), 4vv, acc., *E*

INSTRUMENTAL

Ah del sol (madrigal), 4 insts, acc., 1672, *E-Zac*
Untitled piece, 12 pts, hp, *Zac* (inc.), may be for voices, but no text
    survives

LOST WORKS

2 masses, 1 for 12vv, 1 dated 1692; pss, 2 choirs; 2 sets of
    Complines, 8vv, 2 hp, org; motets, 6–8vv; Salve, 8vv; hymns, 8vv:
    E-MO according to *LaborD*
Bk of masses, *Mp*, according to Alvarez Pérez
Motete a la Asunción, 8vv, listed in 18th-century MS inventory of
    works by composers at El Pilar, *Zac*
Motete a la Ascensión, 7vv, listed in a MS inventory of *c*1715, *Zac*
Crux fidelis, 8vv, hp, org; ps, 6vv: *Bc* according to *LaborD*
Que llegan ya ciudadanos (Christmas villancico), 1v, 4 choirs, Ay
    traydor a la niña no tires (villancico for the Conception), 1v, 6vv,
    listed in *JoãoIL*
Villancicos in score, formerly in *Pac, SE, V*

BIBLIOGRAPHY

J.M. Alvarez Pérez: 'La polifonía sagrada y sus maestros en la
    catedral de León durante el siglo XVII', *AnM*, xv (1960), 141–63,
    esp. 152, 163
J. López-Calo: 'Corresponsales de Miguel de Irizar (II)', *AnM*, xx
    (1965), 209–33
A. Llordén: 'Notas históricas de los maestros de capilla en la catedral
    de Málaga (1641–1799)', *AnM*, xx (1965), 105–60
M. Agulló y Cobo: 'Documentos para las biografías de músicos de
    los siglos XVI y XVII', *AnM*, xv (1970), 105–24
L. Jambou: ' Documentos relativos a los músicos de la segunda mitad
    del siglo XVII de las Capillas Reales y Villa y Corte de Madrid,
    sacados de su Archivo de Protocolos', *RdMc*, xii (1989), 469–514
J. López-Calo: *Documentario musical de la catedral de Segovia*
    (Santiago de Compostela,1990)
C. Cabellero Fernández-Rufete: 'Miguel Gómez Carmago:
    correspondencia inédita', *AnM*, xlv (1990), 67–102
L.A. González Marín: *Música para los ministriles de El Pilar de
    Zaragoza (1671–1672)* (Zaragoza, 1991)
L.A. González Marín: 'Tetis y Peleo o la restauración del teatro
    musical barroco aragonés', *Rolde*, lxiii–lxiv (1993), 47–58
L.A. González Marín: 'Pérez Roldán, Juan', *Gran Enciclopedia
    Aragonesa* (Zaragoza, 1998)
L.A. González Marín: 'Pérez Roldán, Juan', *Diccionario de la música
    española e hispanoamericana*, ed. E. Casares Rodicio (Madrid,
    2000)

LUIS ANTONIO GONZÁLEZ MARÍN

Perez de Alba, Alonso. *See* ALBA, ALONSO DE.

Pérez de Albéniz, Mateo. *See* ALBÉNIZ, MATEO PÉREZ DE.

Pérez de la Parra, Ginés (*b* Orihuela, Alicante, bap. 7 Oct
1548; *d* Orihuela, 15 Nov 1600). Spanish composer. His
name is sometimes given erroneously as Juan Ginés Pérez.
On 15 October 1562, just after his 14th birthday, he was
chosen to direct the music in the collegiate church (from
1564 the cathedral) at Orihuela. From 23 February 1581
he was choirmaster of Valencia Cathedral, where one of
his pupils was Juan Bautista Comes. After frequent
unauthorized absences he left early in 1595 at the chapter's
request and settled again at Orihuela, where from May
1595 he was a canon of the cathedral, although he did
not act as choirmaster. On 14 November 1600 he made
his will, which was executed on 25 November by his
brother Juan. He was highly regarded by his contemporaries. His collected works, 'ready for the press', were to
be found at Orihuela Cathedral in 1636 but had
disappeared by 1727. Some 50 works by him do, however,
survive elsewhere in 20th-century copies (some incomplete). They show that he had a preference for homophonic
textures, which are seen at their best in glowing chordal
passages that resemble Victoria. There is much expressive
chromatic alteration, and in the motets in Catalan
composed for the sacred drama *El misterio de Elche*,

unrelated chords, such as E and B♭ major, boldly appear
in quick succession.

WORKS

Sacred vocal: Benedictus, 4vv; Magnificat, 5vv; 6 vesper psalms, 4vv;
    Advent responsory, 3vv; 3 motets, 5vv; Latin hymn, 5vv, ed. in
    Hispania schola musica sacra, v (Barcelona, 1896/*R*)
Catalan motets, 3, 4vv, ed. J. Pomares Perlasia, *La 'Festa' o misterio
    de Elche*
Other sacred vocal: music for the Office of the Dead; vesper psalms;
    canticles; other liturgical compositions; motets: *E-MA, SEG, VAc,
    VAcp, Zac*

BIBLIOGRAPHY

J. Blasco: 'Un célebre hijo do Orihuela: introduction to *Hispaniae
    schola musica sacra*, ed. F. Pedrell, v (Barcelona, 1896/*R*)
S. Rubio: 'La música del "Misterio" de Elche', *TSM*, xlviii (1965),
    61–71; music suppl., 1–24
J. Climent: 'La música en Valencia durante el siglo XVII', *AnM*, xxi
    (1966), 211–41, esp. 218, 221
J. Climent: *Historia de la música valenciana* (Valencia, 1989)
R. Stevenson: 'Spanish Polyphonists in the Age of the Armada', *Inter-
    American Music Review*, xii/2 (1991), 17–114, esp. 47

ROBERT STEVENSON

Pérez Gutiérrez, Mariano (*b* Pisón de Castrejón, Palencia,
11 Sept 1932; *d* Madrid, 9 Feb 1994). Spanish musicologist, choral conductor and music pedagogue. He studied
music during his theological training at the Seminario
Conciliar, Palencia (1948–55), and after winning a
scholarship in 1956 he attended the Real Conservatorio
Superior de Música in Madrid. In 1967 he obtained a
degree in canonical law from the Universidad Pontificia
de Comillas, Cantabria, and he served as choral director
at the cathedral in Santiago de Compostela, 1964–9. He
joined the faculty of the Conservatorio Superior de
Música, Seville, in 1969, and was professor of aesthetics
and music history (1969–74), then assistant director
(1974–8) and director (1978–85). He earned the title
magister chori in 1983 from the Gregorian Institute at the
Catholic University of Paris, and in 1984 took the
doctorate in philosophy at the University of Seville. He
also studied privately with Chailley in Paris. From 1985
until his death he was professor at the Real Conservatorio
de la Música in Madrid. He also served as president of
the ISME, Spain, vice-president of the Sociedad Española
de Musicología (1984–7) and founder (1988) and editor
of the journal *Música y Educación*. In addition to his
activities as a scholar, teacher and conductor, he also
composed more than 70 works, including masses and
works for orchestra, some of which were published.

WRITINGS

Música sagrada y lenguas modernas (Madrid, 1967) [trans. of
    Musique sacrée et langues modernes, Paris, 1964; incl. 'Música
    sagrada y lenguas vernáculas en España', 137–55]
Oficio de Difuntos con música (Madrid, 1968)
'Origen y naturaleza del jubilus aleluyático', *TSM*, lv (1972), 107
    only; 117–8; lvi (1973), 17–23, 45–52, 81–4, 104–7; lvii (1974),
    40–43
'La estética clasicista de Ravel', *Revista de ideas estéticas*, no.132
    (1975), 289–308
'El binomio Falla-Ravel o la confluencia enigmática de dos genios
    paralelos e independientes', *TSM*, lix (1976), 107–19
'El París que vivió Manuel de Falla y sus concomitancias estéticas',
    Revista de ideas estéticas, no.138 (1977), 115–35
'La concepción armónica de Ravel', *AnM*, xxx (1977), 2–33
Comprende y ama la música (Madrid, 1979)
El universo de la música (Madrid, 1980, 2/1995)
'La música culta andaluza a través de la historia', *Los andaluces*
    (Madrid, 1980), 381–418
Falla y Turina a la luz de su espistolario (Madrid, 1982)
'Falla y Turina hermanados e el París de sus sueños', *AnM*, xxxviii
    (1982), 129–48

Orígenes y antecedentes de la polifonía (diss., U. of Seville, 1984) [3 vols.]

'El iberismo en la música europea; el hispanismo de Ravel', *España en la música de occidente: Salamanca 1985*, ii, 341–8

Diccionario de la música y de los músicos (Madrid, 1985) [3 vols.]

La estética musical de Ravel (Madrid, 1987)

'Los conservatorios españoles: historia, reglamentación, planes de estudio, centros, profesorado y alumnando', *Música y educación*, vi/3 (1993), 17–48

'Breve reseña histórica sobre la educación musical en España y comparación con otros países', *Música y educación*, vii/1 (1994), 19–28

BIBLIOGRAPHY

J.M. de Mena: *Historia del Conservatorio Superior de Música de Sevilla* (Seville, 1984), 135–84

E. Rey García: 'Mariano Pérez Gutiérrez (1932–1994)', *RdM*, xviii (1995), 361–2

ISRAEL J. KATZ

Pérez Martínez, Vicente (*b* Cifuentes, nr Madrid; *d* Madrid, 2 Jan 1800). Spanish liturgist and singer. He may have been the Vicente Andrés Pérez from Cifuentes (*b* 4 Feb 1746) who was admitted as a choirboy to the *seises* of Toledo Cathedral in 1756. In 1770 he entered the royal chapel in Madrid as a tenor and remained there until his death. During his career, he was especially noted for his excellence as a singer, teacher and interpreter of plainsong, and for his activity in chapel affairs. He collected and annotated many documents concerning the chapel (now in *E-Mn*) along with autographed theoretical works from his library. His major work is the *Prontuario del cantollano gregoriano … según práctica de la muy santa primada iglesia de Toledo*, a three-volume anthology of plainsong submitted to the Imprenta Real in 1786 but not published until 1799–1800 after years of delays and a personal appeal to the prime minister Godoy. An enlarged second edition appeared in 1828–9, edited by A. Hernández. It is the most extensive plainsong collection printed in Spain, containing nearly 1000 pages of music. Based on the practices of Toledo, carefully prepared and collated with numerous manuscripts, it is an invaluable source of the chants used in Spain over several centuries, including those for vespers, compline and the proper and ordinary of the mass.

BIBLIOGRAPHY

SubiráHME

M. Soriano Fuertes: *Historia de la música española* (Madrid, 1855–9)

B. Saldoni: *Diccionario biográfico-bibliográfico de efemérides de músicos españoles* (Madrid, 1868–81/R)

N. Álvarez Solar-Quintes: 'La imprenta musical en Madrid en el siglo XVIII', *AnM*, xviii (1963), 161–95

F.J. León Tello: *La teoría española de la música en los siglos XVII y XVIII* (Madrid, 1974)

ALMONTE HOWELL

Pérez Maseda, Eduardo (*b* Madrid, 12 Aug 1953). Spanish composer. He studied music at the Madrid Conservatory (1969–81) and took a degree in sociology at the University of Madrid (1972–7). He has worked as a consultant in the department of musical activities for the municipality of Madrid. He won prizes for . . . *Y ved cómo la Creación se ensancha ante nuestros ojos* (1981), the Cello Concerto (1981) and the Sonata I (1983, for piano). His Sonata II (1985, for violin) won the New York Musician's Accord prize and received its first performance in that city. His *Me recuerdas tanto y nada* was chosen for the 1989 ISCM Festival in Amsterdam. He has given many courses and seminars on music, sociology and aesthetics, and has published two books and several essays and articles.

His most important orchestral work is *La cruz, el ciprés y la estrella* (1989). Immediately afterwards he began composing his first opera, on St John of the Cross. Entitled *Luz de oscura llama* (1991), it was given its first performance in Madrid and was an outstanding success.

WORKS
(*selective list*)

Op: Luz de oscura llama (prologue, 3, C. Janés), 1989–91, Madrid, Sala Olimpia, 1991

Vocal: . . . Y ved cómo la Creación se ensancha ante nuestros ojos (Virgil, H.D. Thoreau, Blanco White, F. López Serrano), chorus, children's chorus, 2 fl, 2 tpt, trbn, 4 perc, 1981; Me recuerdas tanto y nada (Música nocturna), S, fl, perc, gui, vn, vc, 1987; Swan (El peso de la sombra) (J. Villiers de l'Isle-Adam), nar, Ct, perc, pf, vc, tape, 1989; La cruz, el ciprés y la estrella (St John of the Cross, Lao-Tse, F. de la Torre and others), spkr, S, Bar, chorus, orch, 1989

Orch: Conc., vc, chbr orch, 1981; La cruz, el ciprés y la estrella, suite, 1991 [based on choral work]; Retorno a la luz, 1993

Chbr and solo inst: Sonata I, pf, 1983; El hierro y la luz, fl, ob, cl, bn, hn, perc, 2 vn, va, vc, 1984; Traspasa el aire todo . . ., 2 fl, ob + eng hn, cl, b cl, bn, tpt, pf/cel, perc, 2 vn, va, vc, db, 1984; Sonata II, vn, pf, 1985

Other works, incl. pf pieces, chbr pieces, el-ac works

WRITINGS

El Wagner de las ideologías: Nietzsche-Wagner (Madrid, 1983; rev. as *Música como idea, música como destino: Wagner-Nietzsche*, 1993)

Alban berg (Madrid, 1985)

BIBLIOGRAPHY

E.M. Mihura: 'Il tribuna de jóvenes compositores', *Ritmo*, no.534 (June 1983)

E. Franco: 'La cruz, el ciprés y la estrella', *El país* (4 April 1990)

J.A. Vela del Campo: 'Una ópera sobre Sam Juan de la Cruz', *El país* (5 April 1991)

E. Franco: 'La luz en Pérez Maseda', *El país* (29 Jan 1994)

JOSÉ LUIS TEMES

Pérez Prado, (Dámaso) [Prado, Pérez] (*b* Matanzas, 11 Dec 1916; *d* Mexico City, 14 Sept 1989). Cuban pianist, bandleader, composer and arranger. After a formal musical training in Matanzas he moved to Havana in the early 1940s, where he played the piano and arranged for the orchestra of Paulina Alvarez (1942) and the well-known Orquesta Casino de la Playa (1943–6). His growing incorporation of big band jazz influences was not well received, and he left Cuba in 1947, settling in Mexico City the following year. Establishing a mambo big band, he made several recordings through the next decade, including his famous *Mambo No.5* and *Qué rico el mambo*. While often criticized for falsely claiming to have invented the mambo, his popularization of this genre in mainstream North America is undisputable, and his recordings of *Cherry Pink and Apple Blossom White* (1955) and *Patricia* (1958) made it to the top of the US charts for several weeks.

Remembered more for his goatee and vocal exclamations than for his musical talents, the self-titled 'Mambo King' was a brilliant pianist and an accomplished arranger. His appeal for non-Latino audiences lay in his use of dramatic horn lines and simple, less rhythmically complex arrangements than those of authentic Cuban bands. Among the most commercially successful of all Latin musicians, he was also popular in South and Central America through his appearances in dozens of Mexican film musicals. In addition to his dance hits, he wrote more ambitious, serious works for mambo orchestra, such as *Voodoo Suite* (1954), *Mosaico Cubano* (1956) and *La suite de las Américas* (1958–9), and also arranged classical favourites by Rachmaninoff and Grieg in mambo style.

LISE WAXER

Pérez Puentes, José Angel (*b* Havana, 20 Sept 1951). Cuban composer and guitarist. He studied guitar with Isaac Nicola and Jesús Ortega, later taking lessons with Brouwer, Ichiro Suzuki and Antonio Lauro, and studying composition with Bernaola. Since 1976 he has toured nationally and internationally as a concert guitarist. An award winner in various national composition competitions, he won the national composition prize (1979) in the symphonic, popular and children's categories and was commissioned to write the compulsory test piece (1985) for the International Guitar Competition in Puerto Rico. In the 1980s he formed a duo with Teresa Madiedo and founded the Ensemble de Guitarras de La Habana. Since 1992 he has lived in Ecuador, where he has given recitals, conducted the Banda Municipal de Quito and taught the guitar and composition.

Perez Puentes's compositions make ample use of contemporary techniques such as improvisational devices, polychords and polystylistic writing. However, in recent years he has turned towards neo-romanticism, quoting from the works of the great classical composers, jazz and traditional Cuban music. Most notable among his works are three instructive children's concertos, the guitar pieces that exploit the technical and expressive possibilities of the instrument, the *Divertimento para varios y algunos* for two guitars, based on traditional peasant themes, in which the guitarists also act as percussionists, and the *Variaciones sin tema* for wind quintet. These are variations on variations, using a range of musical language to create a neo-romantic mood.

WORKS
(selective list)

Choral: Y solo ha de verse la luz, S, Bar, spkr, mixed vv, orch, 1983; Carrusel I, children's chorus, 1985; Carrusel II, children's chorus, 1985; Senza parole, mixed vv, 1985

Orch: Concierto para niños no.3, 1980; Para un hada con hilos de oro, gui, orch, 1981; De donde crece la palma, 1987

Chbr: Concierto para niños no.1, gui, fl, ob, cl, perc, kbd, 1976; Sonata no.1, trp, pf, 1976; Para dos amigos, 2 gui, 1977; Concierto para niños no.2, pic, fl, ob, cl, bn, perc, kbd, 1978; Ireme, 2 gui, 1979; Oda al sol, 3 insts, 1980; Divertimento para varios y algunos, 2 gui+perc, 1981; Toccata, vc, pf, 1981; Polipuntos y contrafonías, 3 perc, 1982; Gamas II, str qt, 1983; Etc., etc. . . . 2 gui, 1984; Variaciones sin tema, wind qnt, 1985; Estimulaciones no.2, gui ens, 1986; La vieja ciudad y el poeta, 2 gui, 1987; Insomnio para un día invierno, fl, gui ens, 1988

Solo inst: Fantasía del amor, gui 4 hands, 1981; Gamas I, 1v, 1982; Mixtificaciones, pf, 1982; 2 piezas, gui 1986; Preludios, gui, 1986; Ostinato, gui, 1987; Con si con la, gui, 1989

ALBERTO ALÉN

Perezzani, Paolo (*b* Suzzara, 7 Sept 1955). Italian composer. He graduated in philosophy at Bologna University and studied composition with Sciarrino, teaching under him at Città di Castello from 1985 to 1988. He was appointed in 1989 to teach harmony and counterpoint at the Mantua Conservatory, and between 1994 and 2000 was artistic director of the Reggio nell'Emilia 'Di Nuovo' Festival. Since *Diario* at the Venice Opera Prima in 1982, his works have been performed regularly at major international contemporary musical events. In 1992 he won the Vienna International Competition with his orchestral *Primavera dell'anima*.

Perezzani regards composition as essentially a speculation upon the nature of sound. His technique owes much to the refined experimentation with timbres which Sciarrino has pursued, sometimes at the borders of silence. He is concerned less with internal relationships than with trying to formulate the most subtle of sonorities – from the harmonic and timbral richness of instrumental gesture to the imaginary world of a dying woman's final rambling thoughts in *Donna dei dolori*.

WORKS
(selective list)

Stage: Gli Uccelli (incid music), 3 fl, 3 vn, cl, hp, perc, tape, 1981

Orch: Primavera dell'anima, 1990; Machina symphoniaca, 1995

Vocal: Imagine si ceci, male v, bn, vc, 1993

Chbr and solo inst: Diario, 2 fl, pf, 1980; Episodio sul vuoto, pf 4 hands, 1980, rev. 1986; Notturno, va, pf, 1981; Passo a due, cl, pf, 1981; Aspera, 2 vn, va, 1982; Le superfici del tempo, fl, cl, str qt, 1984; Studio per le superfici del tempo, cl, 1984; In quella vibrazione, va, cl, pf, 1984, rev. 1989 for vc, cl, pf; Con slancio, fl, cl, vn, vc, pf, 1985; L'ombra dell'angelo, fl/a fl, 1985; Tlön, 3 gui, 1985; Intimi voli, db, 1986; Hrön, 2 gui, 1987; Il tempo, fl, cl, vc, pf, 1987; Il volto della notte, fl, b cl, pf, 1987; Amore e addio, 11 str, 1988; Arouette, fl, vn, 1988; Vocativo, bcl, db, 1989; Radura con flauto (e roveto), fl, insts, 1991; D'incenso, catrame e lillà, b cl, 1992; Vento di rosa, b fl, 1992; Pim sta per parlare, sax qt, 1993; Sonata, 2 hpd, 1993; 3 piccoli pezzi, insts, 1994; Str Qt no.1, with live elecs, 1996

Tape: Donna dei dolori (P. Valduga), 1994

Principal publishers: Ricordi, Edipan

GIORDANO FERRARI

Perfall, Karl Freiherr von (*b* Munich, 29 Jan 1824; *d* Munich, 14 Jan 1907). German administrator and composer. After studying law, he was briefly a civil servant before becoming a pupil of Moritz Hauptmann in Leipzig (1848–9). Moving back to Munich, he directed the Liedertafel from 1850 and founded and conducted the Oratorienverein in 1854; he was appointed court intendant by Ludwig II in 1864, provisional intendant of the Nationaltheater in 1867, intendant in 1869 and general intendant in 1872. An energetic and practical administrator, he greatly improved the theatre itself (renovating the building in 1869 and installing electric lighting as early as 1882) and the scope and standard of the performances. He took up Wagner's cause with what seems to have been genuine and independent enthusiasm, and in the face of dictatorial hostility from the composer, who even tried to enforce his suspension upon the king. *Die Meistersinger* (1868), *Das Rheingold* (1869) and *Die Walküre* (1870) were all first performed during his intendancy, and over 700 Wagner performances were given in 25 years. In 1878 he proposed to the king that the Munich Opera, having benefited so greatly from Wagner's music, should pay the composer a 10% royalty until the discharge of the deficit that had accumulated after the Bayreuth Festival of 1876; this was a crucial step in saving Bayreuth. Wagner and his early champions give a prejudiced view of Perfall, but Bülow found him both artistically and administratively very competent. The Munich Opera Festival, which began in the summer of 1875, was founded by him. He retired in 1893 and published two books on theatre history. His own operas, *Sakuntala* (1853), *Das Konterfei* (1863), *Raimondin* (1881; revised as *Melusine*, 1885) and *Junker Heinz* (1886; revised as *Jung Heinrich*, 1901), were performed in Munich with moderate success.

WRITINGS

Ein Beitrag zur Geschichte der königlichen Theaters in München (Munich, 1894)

Die Entwicklung des modernen Theaters (Munich, 1899)

BIBLIOGRAPHY

S. Röckl: *Ludwig II. und Richard Wagner*, 2 vols.: i: *1864–1865* (Munich, 1903/*R*, 2/1913); ii: *1866–1883* (Munich, 1920)

A. von Mensi-Klarbach: *Alt-Münchner Theater-Erinnerungen* (Munich, 1923, enlarged 2/1924)

E. Stemplinger: *Richard Wagner in München (1864–1870): Legende und Wirklichkeit* (Munich, 1933)

E. Newman: *The Life of Richard Wagner*, iv (London, 1947/*R*)

A. Ott: 'Die Münchner Oper von den Anfangen der Festspiele bis zur Zerstörung des Nationaltheaters', *Musik in Bayern*, i (Tutzing, 1974), 313–26

JOHN WARRACK

Perfect cadence [authentic cadence; final cadence; full cadence; full close] (Fr. *cadence parfaite, cadence authentique*; Ger. *Ganzschluss, vollkommene Kadenz*; It. *cadenza perfetta, cadenza intera*). A CADENCE consisting of a dominant chord followed by a tonic chord (V–I), normally both in root position. In some theoretical writings the term is extended to cover any cadence ending on the tonic, thus including the plagal form (IV–I) as well as the 'authentic' form; particularly in American writings, it is sometimes specified that a cadence is not 'perfect' unless the uppermost voice sounds the tonic note in the final chord.

JULIAN RUSHTON

Perfect consonance. The INTERVAL of a unison, 5th, octave or any of their compounds (12th, 15th, etc.), when neither augmented nor diminished. The term is contrasted in much medieval polyphonic theory with 'imperfect consonance', a simple or compound 3rd or 6th (*see* COUNTERPOINT, §2). The diatonic FOURTH, although usually defined as a dissonance in that context, has since been considered a CONSONANCE when understood as the inversion of the perfect fifth; as a result, the term 'perfect interval' is generally taken to include the 'perfect 4th', and its compounds in addition to the medieval perfect consonances.

JULIAN RUSHTON

Perfect interval. A PERFECT CONSONANCE, or a simple or compound perfect 4th.

Perfectio (Lat.: 'perfection'). A term used in theoretical writings on mensural music from the mid-13th century onwards. It refers to a quality of ligatures that depended on the value of the final note of the ligature. The final note was normally assumed to be a long unless its normal shape was modified. If the last note was of normal shape (for an ascending ligature this meant with a stem descending to the right, for a descending ligature this

TABLE 1

Quality	Shape		Value
cum proprietate et perfectione			breve-long
sine proprietate et cum perfectione			long-long
cum proprietate et sine perfectione			breve-breve
sine proprietate et sine perfectione			long-breve
cum opposita proprietate			semibreve-semibreve

meant without stem) then the ligature had perfection and the last note was a long. If the ascending ligature ended in a note with no descending stem, or if the descending ligature ended in two notes in an oblique form, then the ligature had no perfection and the last note was a breve. A quality of ligatures that depended on the value of the initial note of the ligature, PROPRIETAS ('propriety'), was governed by similar rules, which for a two-note ligature *cum opposita proprietate* (which had an ascending stem to the left) overruled the above conventions governing perfection and resulted in a pair of semibreves. The usual shapes for two-note ligatures are shown in Table 1. Ligatures of three, four and more notes were governed by the same rules, with all but the first and last notes understood to be breves (except in the case of opposite propriety, when the second note was always a semibreve, or where a note is graphically distinguished as a long or a maxima).

See also RHYTHMIC MODES and NOTATION, §III, 2(viii) and 3.

BIBLIOGRAPHY

F. Reckow: 'Proprietas und Perfectio: zur Geschichte des Rhythmus, seiner Aufzeichnung und Terminologie im 13. Jahrhundert', *AcM*, xxxix (1967), 115–43

W. Frobenius: 'Perfectio' (1973), *HMT*

PETER WRIGHT

Perfect pitch. *See* ABSOLUTE PITCH.

Perfidia (It.). A term used mainly during the 17th and 18th centuries to designate the persistent repetition of a figure or motif. Its use as a technical term in music would have been suggested by a meaning that was current in the 17th and 18th centuries but is now obsolete: 'obstinacy' or 'persistence'. Berardi, in his *Documenti armonici* (1687, pp.17–20), defined the perfidia as the continuation of a figure according to one's whim ('continuare un passo à capriccio'). His eight music examples clarify his meaning: against a cantus firmus a second voice (higher or lower) develops a contrapuntal line in which the same rhythmic figure is repeated in each bar except the last. Berardi's first example, headed 'Della semiminima col punto sincopata, e perfidiata con trè Crome', is given in ex.1. Brossard, who knew Berardi's treatise, offered a similar but broader definition in his *Dictionaire* (1701): 'an affectation to do always the same thing, to follow always the same pattern'. Brossard's understanding of the term includes the 'fuga perfidiata' as well as ostinato basses. His wider definition permitted him to equate the perfidia with Zarlino's 'pertinacia' (*Le istitutioni harmoniche*, 1558, iii): in Zarlino's examples it is the melodic pattern of the counterpoint to a cantus firmus that remains constant, while the note lengths are changed – the opposite of Berardi's examples, in which rhythm is the constant factor and pitches change. Walther (*Musikalisches Lexicon*, 1732) and Rousseau (*Dictionnaire de musique*, 1768) both followed Brossard's definition closely. Three short passages of music attributed to Torelli (in manuscripts in *I-Bsp*) are given the label 'perfidia' (nos.65–7 in Giegling's catalogue, 1949); the first may be spurious, and the second and third are part of the same work. They are 29, 28 and 13 bars in length, are scored for two violins and bass, and feature brilliant figuration for the violins over a sustained bass pedal. It is reasonable to assume that they originally formed part of longer works. A similar passage, but without the heading 'perfidia', occurs at the end of the second movement of Corelli's sonata op.5 no.3 (*see* CADENZA, ex.6). There is a loose connection between

Ex.1 A. Berardi: *Documenti armonici* (Bologna, 1687)

Berardi's and Torelli's terminology: in both cases passages of figuration are heard either against a slow-moving cantus firmus or above a static bass. The perfidia is discussed by P. Whitmore in *Unpremeditated Art: the Cadenza in the Classical Keyboard Concerto* (Oxford, 1991), 38–41.

ANDREW V. JONES

Performance. Music-making is a virtually universal human activity. At its most fundamental, it is a form of private biological necessity (in that, for example, individual survival is assisted by being sung to as a baby by a birth mother). At its most elevated, musical performance is public property; it played a pivotal role in some of the earliest traces of elaborate Western art, with the story of Orpheus, a pre-Homeric hero (thus now of at least some 3000 years' standing), possessing the legendary ability to tame wild animals and resist the Sirens by singing and by playing the lyre. Across the ages and throughout world civilizations it is the actual, direct, live experience of music that seems to have been integral to the human culture carried forward from its apparent European origins some 40,000 years ago to the modern world (Mithen, 1996, pp.159–63).

1. General considerations. 2. Role of the performer. 3. Basic elements. 4. Learning to perform.

1. GENERAL CONSIDERATIONS. It can be argued that, in this modern world, music performed is perhaps the most widely disseminated kind of public property. In the 1980s and 90s – and for all that the following may prove to be forgotten names from mass entertainment – Queen, Madonna and, later, the Spice Girls were truly global cultural phenomena, and what they were all doing was performing music for other people. In the field of classical or art music, a similar effect has been known for centuries, from Blondel in the 12th to Paganini in the 19th and, we might conjecture, Casals and Segovia in the 20th. Musical performance, then, seems to have a double aspect in human culture, in that it is both endemic, more or less evenly spread throughout the species and its history since prehistoric times, yet also value-bearing. Just as 'fixed' works of art are held to range from the ephemeral (lost in history and never intended to be kept) to the preservable (deliberately saved artefacts, curiosities, social objects) to the canonical (enduring works of 'genius'), so musical performance can range from something ordinary to a level that becomes a gold standard – although we shall encounter, with the example of Inuit throat games (which in early ethnomusicology would have been called 'primi-tive' music) the challenge of what may well amount to ephemeral genius.

In the Western art tradition, musical performance is commonly understood, and not surprisingly, in something like the way that are the works of music that performance brings to life, so that a familiar list of musicological categories is available: the historical, analytical and psychological dimensions. In performance studies, however, each of these dimensions must take on a special flavour. The history of performance was essentially mute until the 20th century with its invention of non-human storage of music (see §2 below). Time and again, therefore, earlier epochs characterize performance as something valid only for the present, or for veiled, mediated recollection; and though performance may have been reflected, represented and even to some extent 'recorded' in literary or visual art, music in performance was not essentially open to scientific or even philosophical inspection: 'the composer works slowly and intermittently . . . the performer in impetuous flight; the composer for posterity, and the performer for the moment of fulfilment. The musical artwork is formed; the performance we experience' (Hanslick, 1854; 1986, p.49). Analytically too – to address the second dimension mentioned above – the 'work' of music has typically taken precedence over any of its 'realizations'. Technical commentary on music since the Middle Ages has largely been restricted to commentary on general musical practices (see the comment in §4 on musical treatises) and on notated pieces or repertories. Only in the late 20th century did momentum begin to gather for the study of 'music in performance . . . where analysis, cultural studies, hermeneutics, and performance practice meet' (Bowen, 1999, p.451). Thirdly, music psychology may also be considered inchoate in respect of (as it were) real-time music, for all the strides that have been taken in building models of contemplative musical understanding. We are hardly in a better position than was Lucretius in *De rerum natura* some 2000 years ago to ask interesting questions about the essence of ongoing human experience, although it will be possible to codify modern thinking on the fundamental specifics of contemplating musical performance (see §3). Finally, in these introductory comments, the dimensions of interpretation and notation must also be mentioned, since these concomitants of mainstream musicology are evidently central to the phenomenon and to the study of musical performance; issues entailing them are threaded through the following discussion, which addresses the role of the performer, including the somewhat altered status of performance in the 20th century, the basic elements of musical performance that have nevertheless endured and, more briefly, the musical training and learning of the performer.

For the psychology of performance, *see* PSYCHOLOGY OF MUSIC, §IV.

2. ROLE OF THE PERFORMER. The role of the performer in Western music is nowadays typically characterized in two ways. First, the performer is seen as the composer's ambassador, with decisive powers, a perception that is at least as old as the mid-18th-century: 'What comprises good performance? The ability through singing or playing to make the ear conscious of the true content and affect of a composition. Any passage can be so radically changed by modifying its performance that it will be barely recognizable' (Bach, 1753; 1949, p.148). That is an enduring truth, and in some senses it must be the case that

the great composer-performers, such as Boulez and Britten in recent times, are likely to be offering the 'truest' content and affect of at least their own music (but Rachmaninoff is a cautionary case of a maestro who gave up performing his concertos because he felt that the younger generation of concert pianists included some who could offer better interpretations).

Secondly, however, there has been an emphasis fuelled by social science to examine the relativities and interdependencies of music-making and posit a more democratic picture in which those for whom performances are performed have a supposedly equal significance:

... as cognitive psychology has taught us, the temporal materialization of a musical artwork emanates not from the composer alone or from the performer alone but from a triarchical interrelationship among composer, performer, and listener ... for performers to discharge faithfully their aesthetic responsibilities, they must give considerable attention not only to their understanding of the composer's demands and desires but also to the sensibilities of the audience (Narmour, 1988, p.318).

Certainly, through the commercialization of classical music, performing has become strikingly market-led, and since at least as early as the rise of the public concert in the 18th century (Raynor, 1972, pp.314–30) market forces have been significant in the careers of professional performers. Historically, the sensibilities performers have most needed to flatter in approximately the last three centuries have been those of music critics, who were diagnosed by Hans Keller (1987) as constituting an entirely phoney profession but who have been and remain potent arbiters of public taste all the same. Whether we choose to see the performer as a creative vessel of transmission from composer to audience, or as cog in a three-cog mechanism that can never work with only two cogs – and this may come down to the question of whether the art of music conveys a message or is pure activity – there is no known ramified art of music that is performer-less (a notion with which composers using electronic sound generation have indeed toyed, working interestingly against the grain of existing musical constraints).

The place of performance in the history of music changed in the 20th century with the onset of mechanical and acoustic, and afterwards electronic, recording (see RECORDED SOUND).

We may be witnesses, the only direct witnesses there will ever be, to the beginning of the music of the future. Is it not easy to imagine that two thousand years or five thousand from now people will say that Western music really only got going properly during the twentieth century from which distant time there date the earliest proper sonic and visual records, following that strange 'mute' early period of music history that spanned the Greeks (of which we know essentially nothing), via medieval polyphony (of which we know a certain amount), to, say, Mahler, the last great pre-technological composer (of whose work and times we know much more but not, really, enough: none of his performances survive recorded, and there are just memories mythically handed on to indicate that he was one of the greatest-ever conductors)? (Dunsby, 1995, pp.15–16).

Musical performance no longer has a lost, silent history but impinges on current practice: we have precious little idea of how Blondel actually performed his songs and of the impression they made, but we have a very good idea of how Schoenberg performed his *Pierrot lunaire* since he conducted a sound recording of it in 1940, 28 years after its composition (now issued on CD) – a continuity that spans nearly the whole century. It is no surprise, then, that in the modern musical world, where we are becoming used to access to sonic history and its visual context,

performance is being interrogated continually by the concept of 'authenticity' (Kivy, 1995), or by what it has been suggested should be called 'authenticism' (Taruskin, 1988), the consensus seeming to be that 'historical authenticity alone will never lead us to a true revival without an admixture of a degree of our own artistic beliefs and instincts' (Lang, 1997, p.179): we shall see how inherent in musical performance is the human agent to whom Lang refers.

3. BASIC ELEMENTS. What has endured through the electronic revolution is what might be called the basic elements of musical performance: understanding, actuality and the ineffable – performance being an activity of sentient human beings, an activity that draws on the past and unfolds into the future (satisfying our eagerness to perceive what happens next), but one that exists in that inevitably mobile time called the present.

Understanding follows from sentience and is not restricted to 'high' art. Compare what a conductor is doing in London at a symphony concert with what a female Inuit is doing in northern Canada performing a largely unobserved but locally, socially significant throat game. The conductor is probably highly educated, having learnt a great deal about organology, music history, music theory and so on, and earning large sums of money. Without having achieved a wide cultural assimilation, the conductor would be useless. The Inuit, on the other hand, knows very many more concepts of snow than the Londoner's, and has no concern about the history and theory of Western music. Yet the Inuit performer may actually be singing 'better' than the celebrated conductor is conducting. It is worth bearing this in mind when reading of how sophisticated the musical understanding of some performers needs to be: 'the interpreter, in order to produce more than just an idiosyncratic response, must rely on a combination of sound technical analysis and relevant musicological scholarship' (Cone, 1995, p.242); similarly, of conductors, 'however extensive the scope of his imaginative powers, his comprehension will remain limited unless he is adequately equipped with knowledge' (Scherchen, 1929; 1933, p.18). This may be true in our culture, but analysis and scholarship are of no direct 'emic' (or one might say 'native') concern to the Inuit performer. What 'understanding' really means, then, in musical performance in general, with an eye to other cultures, and to other forms of judged public exposure (see Green and Gallway, 1987, for an application of sport-training methods to musical performance), is informed intensity. The importance of this may be easiest to grasp by contemplating its opposite: where, in all the musics of the world, is there found communal music-making that is fundamentally uninformed and careless? Probably as near to nowhere as makes no difference.

Actuality is the reason that people flock to live performances, and again this is a transcultural fact. The technological revolution mentioned above has not altered this. There have been cases where live performance has been challenged, notoriously by the Canadian pianist Glenn Gould who in 1964, in his 30s, gave up public performance in favour of the recording studio ('no famous musician had ever done anything like it', Page, 1987, p.xii). However, the excitement of actually witnessing performance seems to be at the sharp end of musical practice, the authentic medium for informed intensity, and unlikely to disappear. This excitement surely lies to some extent in the stimulus to be found in any communal activity, there being something that touches our primeval sensibility in the 'buzz' of a crowd of people. Yet the excitement depends too on a feature proper to music, which is the nature of sound, for it remains true that any electronic reproduction of non-electronic Western music (and probably any non-electronic human music at all) is not in fact a reproduction but a mere simulacrum, an approximation. It is only in live performance, offering 'real' sound and a balance of the expected with the unexpected, that the capacity for plenitude in human musical experience can be fully satisfied (see Clynes, 1982, and Wallin, 1991). That is from the listening side, and it almost goes without saying that performers themselves, *pace* Gould and the unquestionable integrity and depth of his arguments about his own artistic personality, perform differently in public from how they do in private; and this difference between the public and the private is a common human experience in everyday life.

What is called above the 'ineffable' can be discussed under many different rubrics – artistry, charisma, inspiration, magic, star quality – none of which can ever quite capture a quality to which performers would nevertheless not aspire if they did not believe that audiences were acutely sensitive to it. This ineffable quality of musical performance at its highest is bound up with our tendency to believe that something may be 'perfect', and that this is the ideal of artistic experience (see Kant, 1790; 1987, pp.79–84, although noting that unfortunately Kant believed music to be of only secondary importance), an ideal in delicate balance with the fact that real-time musical performance is inevitably contingent, always involving an element of risk (Dunsby, 1995, pp.12–14). Musical performance is held to have a special social power equal, according to Lévi-Strauss, to that of myth, both music and myth being 'instruments for the obliteration of time'; Lévi-Strauss goes so far as to ascribe truly magical powers to the results of musical performance during which he claims 'we enter into a kind of immortality' (Lévi-Strauss, 1964; 1970, p.16; see also Nattiez, 1993, pp.15–19).

4. LEARNING TO PERFORM. The requirements of musical performance in Western culture are stringent. As with the learning of different languages, training is most likely to succeed when begun in childhood, usually between the ages of five and eight. One measure of what is required is provided by the Associated Board of the Royal Schools of Music, by far the world's largest assessment body for educational music-making of many different varieties, administering in the UK alone more than 300,000 individual examinations annually. It indicates some eight or nine years of almost daily practising as a prerequisite for reaching a level on one instrument or in singing that might qualify the student for tertiary-level study. Only after a further three or four years of intensive, full-time study combined with performing experience might a student be ready to (for example) take an audition for a semi-professional orchestra. The proportion of trained performers who go on to be able to work professionally is small, and the proportion who can become soloists is minute. As one source of professional advice to young performers puts it: 'On the realities of the music business . . . unlike the business world, the amount of effort and time put in to master your craft in the arts does not pay off with predictable success. It is difficult to separate

reality and fantasy when trying to be good enough to "make it"' (Dunkel, 1990, p.51). Thus professional performers are somewhat rare among the population. They also tend to be specialized; a case such as Mozart, considered by his father Leopold to have the potential to become as great a violinist as he was a pianist, is wholly exceptional. Amateur musical performance, on the other hand, is a huge human phenomenon, from Caribbean steel bands to Welsh choirs, from the Inuit throat games of the western north Atlantic coast and the northern Pacific Rim to the didgeridoo players of native Australia.

Learning musical performance to any significant level has always been arduous but also immensely satisfying, as might be expected of an activity that has demonstrably health-improving clinical effects (*see* MUSIC THERAPY). Musicians throughout the centuries have written about performing, and it is from treatises on performance that our views on the interpretation of pre-20th-century music back to the Middle Ages are principally founded. However, it has always been agreed that one cannot effectively learn to perform, be it singing or playing, from a book, or from musical notation, given that 'the text carries no more than the minimal necessary information for a new performance. It is not the composition itself' (Boorman, 1999, p.406), and given that Lang's 'beliefs and instincts' are always in play, making each interpretation unique. Rather, the history of performance shows multi-generational chains of apprenticeship and pedagogy, for instance in religious orders, or in traditions linked to repertory and instrument (one fascinating case being the genealogy of the modern style of piano playing, which can be traced back largely to Beethoven through Czerny, Liszt and succeeding generations in both Europe and the USA). It would be pure speculation to suppose that no-one is likely to learn to perform from a computer, yet it can be asserted that technology has so far had little specific impact on becoming a performer, but for the profound effects mentioned above of musical recording.

BIBLIOGRAPHY

C.P.E. Bach: *Versuch über die wahre Art das Clavier zu spielen* (Berlin, 1753/R, 2/1787 Eng. trans., 1949/R as *Essay on the True Art of Playing Keyboard Instruments*)

I. Kant: *Kritik der Urteilskraft* (1790; Eng. trans., 1987, as *Critique of Judgment*)

E. Hanslick: *Vom Musikalisch-Schönen: ein Beitrag zur Revision der Ästhetik der Tonkunst* (Leipzig, 1854/R, 16/1966; Eng. trans., 1891/R 1986, as *On the Musically Beautiful: a Contribution towards the Revision of the Aesthetics of Music*)

H. Scherchen: *Lehrbuch des Dirigierens* (Leipzig, 1929; Eng. trans., 1933, *Handbook of Conducting*)

C. Lévi-Strauss: *Le cru et le cuit* (Paris, 1964; Eng. trans., 1970, as *The Raw and the Cooked: Introduction to the Science of Mythology*)

H. Raynor: *A Social History of Music from the Middle Ages to Beethoven* (London, 1972)

M. Clynes, ed.: *Music, Mind, and Brain: the Neurophysiology of Music* (New York, 1982)

B. Green and W.Gallway: *The Inner Game of Music* (London, 1987)

H. Keller: *Criticism* (London, 1987)

T. Page, ed.: *The Glenn Gould Reader* (London, 1987)

E. Narmour: ' On the Relationship of Analytical Theory to Performance and Interpretation', *Explorations in Music, the Arts, and Ideas*, ed. E. Narmour and R. Solie (Stuyvesant, NY, 1988), 317–40

R. Taruskin: ' The Pastness of the Present', *Authenticity and Early Music*, ed. N. Kenyon (Oxford, 1988), 137–207

S. Dunkel: *The Audition Process* (New York, 1990) [Juilliard Performance Guides no.3]

N. Wallin: *Biomusicology: Neurophysiological, Neuropsychological and Evolutionary Perspectives on the Origins and Purposes of Music* (Stuyvesant, NY, 1991)

J.-J. Nattiez: *Le combat de Chronos et d'Orphée* (Paris, 1993)

E. Cone: 'The Pianist as Critic', *The Practice of Performance: Studies in Musical Interpretation*, ed. J. Rink (Cambridge, 1995), 241–53

J. Dunsby: *Performing Music: Shared Concerns* (Oxford, 1995)

P. Kivy: *Authenticities: Philosophical Reflections on Musical Performance* (Ithaca, NY, 1995)

S. Mithen: *The Prehistory of the Mind: a Search for the Origins of Art, Religion and Science* (London, 1996)

P. Lang: *Musicology and Performance* (New Haven, CT, 1997)

B. Nettl and M.Russell, eds.: *In the Course of Performance: Studies in the World of Improvisation* (Chicago, 1998)

S. Boorman: 'The Musical Text', *Rethinking Music*, ed. N. Cook and M. Everist (Oxford, 1999), 403–23

J. Bowen: 'Finding the Music in Musicology', *Rethinking Music*, ed. N. Cook and M. Everist (Oxford, 1999), 424–51

JONATHAN DUNSBY

Performing practice. A term adapted from the German *Aufführungspraxis* (in America the usage 'performance practice' is generally preferred).

I. Western. II. Non-Western and traditional music.

I. *Western*

As applied to Western music, the subject involves all aspects of the way in which music is and has been performed, and its study is of particular importance to the modern performer concerned with historically informed performance. Topics that may be considered aspects of performing practice include notational ones (i.e. the relationship between written notes and the sounds they symbolize, especially such matters as rhythm, tempo and articulation); improvisation and ornaments; instruments, their history and physical structure and the ways in which they are played; voice production; matters of tuning, pitch and temperament; and ensembles, their size, disposition, and the modes in which they are directed. Performing practice is generally approached through the study of treatises and instruction books, critical writings and iconographical material, as well as actual instruments and music. The present article summarizes the issues involved in different periods; particular topics relevant to instruments and their use are treated in separate entries.

1. General. 2. Medieval monophony: (i) Sacred (ii) Secular. 3. Polyphony to 1400. 4. 15th- and 16th-century music. 5. 1600–1750. 6. 1750–1800: (i) Continuity and change (ii) Performer and composer (iii) Instruments (iv) Performances. 7. The 19th century: (i) Sources (ii) The orchestra (iii) The piano (iv) Performance and interpretation. 8. The 20th century.

1. GENERAL. Musical notation can be understood as a set of instructions indicating to the performer how the composer wished the music to sound. From the accent signs of the ancient Greeks and the staffless neumes of some medieval manuscripts (which reminded singers of the general shape of melodies they already knew, but did not indicate exact pitches or intervals) to the carefully marked scores of most 20th-century composers, methods of notation have changed radically over the centuries, along with the attitudes of composers to the degree of detail and precision they wished to offer the interpreter. Not all the elements of a performance can be fixed in writing. Even in the 20th century, when composers took more care than ever before to state exactly the quality and duration of each sound, different performances of a piece (including sometimes those by the same musician) varied in tempo, phrasing, articulation, timbre and so on. The amount and kind of deviation from a precisely determined ideal tolerated (or even encouraged) by composers have depended partly on convention – habit and training – and partly on the temperaments of the individuals involved and the practical requirements of particular situations – the size of the ensemble, the acoustics of the performing area, the nature of the occasion, and so on. Throughout history musicians in the Western world have cherished those ambiguities of notation that have allowed performers some freedom and given musicians and listeners alike the impression that a piece of music is created anew each time it is heard. The principle that the performers should be allowed some scope to 'interpret' the notation subjectively was challenged successfully for the first time in the 20th century, with the advent of recordings and electronic means of fixing a composition in its definitive form once and for all.

In considering the kinds of information written music of the past supplies to performers, the student of performing practice must make a distinction between those elements of the original notation that may be misleading or confusing to a modern performer unless translated into symbols with which he is familiar, and those that originally had a fixed meaning which is now lost or ambiguous. The problems created by the first category are generally faced by editors, and are thus dealt with under EDITING. Consideration of the second category is complicated by the fact that some signs permitted but did not demand particular styles of performance, while others changed their meanings over the years. Thus it is not entirely clear how the rhythms of plainchant and medieval secular monophony were interpreted, or even whether the notation demanded a particular solution; scholars disagree in their transcriptions of the time values of some early polyphony; the hypothesis that the Renaissance mensural system indicated precise tempos and tempo relationships is being questioned; the application to German and Italian music of the French 17th- and 18th-century rules of rhythmic alteration – the convention that allows or demands quavers to be played unequally even though they are notated in equal values – has been sharply challenged; and performers are beginning to learn that some signs for particular bowings and articulations in use today meant quite different things to late 18th- and 19th-century musicians. In short, the student of performing practice must investigate carefully the precise meanings of musical symbols in each period of music history and attempt to discover how they have changed over the years.

Perhaps even more important, scholars must try to establish the amount of freedom allowed the performer, by determining which aspects of performance were not fixed on paper during a particular period. Unwritten conventions make up the most difficult but also the richest category of problems of performing practice. In fact, all players and singers must ask themselves certain basic questions about the compositions they perform, most of which have not been precisely answered by composers: the exact tempo, whether alterations of the written rhythms are allowed or expected, which sonorities are best suited to the piece being played, how each note should be articulated, whether or not melodic embellishments are permitted or forbidden within the convention in question, whether the players are expected to improvise (or prepare for themselves before the performance) sections of the composition, and so on. The 'correct' tempo of a piece, for example, depends on a number of variable features, among them the size of the ensemble and of the concert hall and the mood of the performers on the day of the concert. Even since the invention and widespread adoption of the metronome, musicians and listeners have tolerated widely divergent tempos for the same piece (and, indeed, arguments continue about the accuracy and appropriateness of many composers' metronome markings). Singers must learn how, when, and whether to embellish their melodic lines, and how to sing florid ornamentation, before they can perform late Renaissance solo songs or late Baroque operatic arias in the way audiences first heard them. Some music calls for the addition of improvised or semi-improvised parts. Many modern performers of medieval music, for example, add drones and heterophony to the unadorned melodies of the troubadours and trouvères; harpsichordists and organists must learn how to invent their own part above a figured bass when they accompany 17th- and 18th-century music; and soloists must prepare cadenzas not supplied by the composers when they perform 18th- and 19th-century concertos and arias. Instrument makers and players have acquired a great deal of collective experience in reproducing the timbres of Baroque music by building replicas of old instruments and relearning the techniques required to play them, and this area of 'practical research' is gradually widening to encompass the timbres of medieval and Renaissance music on the one hand, and late 18th- and 19th-century music on the other. Concurrently with their attempts to clarify the nature of old instruments by learning to play them again, students of performing practice have sharpened their perceptions of the sonorities of the past by studying matters of pitch level, tuning and temperament, research that often yields surprisingly practical results.

The further back one goes in music history, the fewer aspects of performance there are that composers established precisely in writing. The 20th century was something of an exception to that general rule, and offers examples of both extremes: on the one hand the meticulous, almost obsessively careful, markings of Schoenberg, Berg and Webern and the well-known aversion of Stravinsky to 'wilful' interpreters of his music, and on the other the controlled, and sometimes uncontrolled, improvisations introduced into their scores by John Cage and other members of the avant garde since 1945. Composers of the 19th century, beginning with Beethoven, greatly increased the number and precision of their directions for performance by indicating tempos (by means of the metronome as well as by the use of conventional terms), phrasings, bowings, dynamics and so on. In the 17th and 18th centuries tempos were indicated only approximately by means of a fairly well understood convention using descriptive terms; some but not all bowings were marked, and performers were expected to realize keyboard accompaniments above a bass, and in many instances to embellish their own parts. In music before 1600 many aspects of compositions that later became a part of their very conception were left to the performers to determine (and presumably to change from occasion to occasion), such as the choice of voices and instruments, the accidentals required by the rules of *musica ficta*, and the way the syllables of vocal music were made to fit the notes.

Answers to many questions about performing practice – even for music of the not very distant past – can be found only by examining indirect evidence, such as the musical institutions of a period. Thus the subdiscipline of performing practice involves the study of social history, as well as the history of musical instruments (organology), of musical subject matter in works of art (iconography), of theoretical treatises, and of the music itself. Archival documents are often the only way to discover the number of performers engaged for a given occasion, what sorts of events were accompanied by music, and so on. And investigations of the organization and rules of various institutions – the minstrel guilds of the Middle Ages, the courts, cathedrals and academies of the Renaissance and the Baroque era, and the concert societies of the 19th century, for example – are often necessary prerequisites for discovering various details about the way music was performed in past times.

Some, and perhaps many, basic questions about past performing practice can never be answered completely. One can never know, for example, the quality of voice most cultivated by the virtuoso singers of the Italian Renaissance, or the exact specifications of most medieval instruments. Moreover, one might reject on aesthetic grounds some of the qualities most prized by past musicians (early recordings convincingly demonstrate how much taste changed even during the 20th century). Reproducing as closely as one can the techniques and timbres known to be appropriate to a given period can never replace performances that are musically convincing to the audience; and yet the means and style of performance imagined by a composer are so indissolubly bound up with the whole musical fabric that he or she has set down, that the communication and impact of the composition are seriously impaired if the sounds imagined are not at least kept in mind when preparing modern performances.

The study of performing practice as a subdiscipline of musicology has been fostered by an implicit distinction between that which standard notation may indicate precisely – namely an exact pitch (within a given tuning) and duration for each note – and that which requires a knowledge of the style for its proper interpretation. While this approach may be extended to music in non-European notations, it is obvious that for societies without a written tradition distinctions cannot be made between the way the music looks on the page – its style considered in the abstract – and the way it sounds. Thus performing practice is an inseparable part of the central concerns of ethnomusicologists who work with orally transmitted repertories, and of those scholars who work with the music of ancient civilizations, such as those of Egypt, Greece and Rome.

2. MEDIEVAL MONOPHONY.

(i) Sacred. The principal sources of information about the performance of Western medieval sacred monophony are the chant manuscripts themselves and the writings of theorists. Owing to the widespread preservation of such sources a great deal is known about plainchant performance in the Middle Ages (for a fuller account see Hiley, B(i)1989). However, as is frequently the case in the discussion of performing practice, problems such as contradictory accounts or missing details create obstacles that prevent the confident reconstruction of such performances. Any modern performance, therefore, must depend

considerably on subjective interpretation. Furthermore, unlike more complex music, monophonic chant can support a very wide range of interpretation and still remain ostensibly true to the notes preserved in the sources.

The case of the Eastern (Orthodox) Churches is different, for in some traditions the melodies have been transmitted orally for more than a millennium. Questions naturally arise, therefore, as to the constancy of the transmission, especially since in the best-documented tradition – BYZANTINE CHANT – very grave changes may be seen to have occurred.

For the reconstruction of chant performance, several aspects have to be considered. The first is liturgical context: the function of the chant in the ceremony, the forces needed to sing it, and other practical considerations such as the position of the singers in the building. Such matters were clearly of great importance through the ages, but only gradually were they set out in written documents. The earliest surviving sources in which liturgical ceremonies are described in any detail are the *Ordines romani*, dating from the 7th–9th centuries, regarding Roman liturgical practice; somewhat over two dozen are extant (ed. M. Andrieu, *Les Ordines romani du haut Moyen-Age*, Leuven, 1931–61), many of them copied in the Carolingian period by Frankish churchmen concerned to follow Roman usage. The most widespread monastic Rule, that of St Benedict (*c*530), also sets out broad guidelines about how the canonical Hours are to be performed. During the following centuries such documents became more detailed and were available for a greater number of churches, particularly monastic ones. The Rules of religious orders such as the Cistercians (in the 12th century) and the Dominicans (in the 13th) are full of specific information about liturgical usage. From the 13th century onwards ordinals survive from a number of important churches (Chartres, Paris, Salisbury etc.), providing enough detail to make possible the reconstruction of these aspects of liturgical performance. Knowledge of performance conditions can also help in the reconstruction of the content of liturgical services: for example, if the performance conditions obtaining in a 9th-century service also applied in a 7th-century service of the same kind, there is a strong possibility that the same melody was sung in the 7th century as in the 9th, even though no notated sources for the earlier period exist.

A second aspect, concerning the way the chant sounded, is much more problematic. Little is known about the sort of voice production favoured over the centuries, or about dynamic level or tempo: vocal colour, loudness and speed affect the way chant is sung and heard, but the musical sources are silent on such matters. It is not even clear if all genres of chant were performed in the same way. There are, however, indications that tempo varied according to the solemnity of the day: the more important the occasion, the slower the tempo. One of the earliest such recommendations is a passage in a *Regula canonicorum* of Chrodegang of Metz (*c*755; *PL*, lxxxix, 1069), which states that the number of singers and the rank of the feast day were the determining factors. The Cistercian *Instituta patrum de modo psallendi* (13th century) refers on numerous occasions to faster and slower singing (*GerbertS*, i, 5–8; see also Van Dijk, B(i)1950). Information of a more specific nature is given in a passage in the *Commemoratio brevis de tonis et psalmis modulandis* of

about 900, which says that in the antiphons for Office psalms, antiphon and psalm were delivered in the same tempo, but the final repeat of the antiphon was sung at half the speed ('duplo dumtaxatur longius'). Canticle antiphons, however, were sung slowly from the start.

The most detailed account of chant singing almost until modern times is Conrad von Zabern's *De modo bene cantandi* of 1474 (discussion and partial translation in Dyer, B(i)1978). It warns against such faults as aspirating notes within a syllable, over-nasal tone, distorted vowel colours, forced high notes (but trumpet-like low notes are recommended), and lazy delivery and inappropriate posture. The vast majority of texts relating to performance matters simply recommend moderation in choice of tempo and pitch, together with sweetness of voice production. (Many texts are discussed in Müller-Heuser, B(i)1963).

Johannes de Grocheio, writing at the end of the 13th century, is something of a special case. He compared chant genres to those of secular music, whose characteristics he described in more detail in an earlier passage. Thus, for example, he stated that the gradual and alleluia were sung 'in the manner of a *stantipes* or of a *cantus coronatus*, so that they may bring devotion and humility to the hearts of their hearers'; the *stantipes* was previously described as difficult, both textually and musically, which 'makes the minds of young men and girls dwell on it', and the *cantus coronatus* is 'composed entirely from longs, perfect longs', also implying some ceremoniousness. The sequence that follows is, on the other hand, 'sung in the manner of a *ductia*, so that it may make [the hearers] joyful', the *ductia* having been described as 'light and rapid in its ascents and descents'. Yet just when a distinction between grave and lively seems to be emerging, Grocheio states that the offertory 'is sung in the manner of a *ductia* or of a *cantus coronatus*'.

Very rarely, there are hints of what may be called an aesthetic appreciation of tempo. In the *Scolica enchiriadis* (9th century) it is stated: 'Whereas one melody is better sung more quickly, another is sweeter when sung more slowly. For one can know by the very formation of a melody whether it is composed of fast or slow phrases' (Schmid, B(i)1981, p.89; Erickson, in Palisca, B(i)1995, p.53).

Another clear sign that chant was not always sung in a flat and featureless manner is the existence of a small number of 10th-century chant books in which the neumes are supplemented with small letters, most of which have significance for pitch and rhythm, a few for delivery (*see also* NOTATION, §III, 1). The meaning of these letters is explained in a letter reputedly written by Notker of St Gallen at the end of the 9th century (see J. Froger, *EG*, v, 1962, pp.23–72). Among those concerning delivery are 'f' (*cum fragore seu frendore feriatur*: 'to be performed with harsh or percussive attack'), 'k' (*clange*: 'with a ringing tone'), 'p' (*pressionem*: 'driving forward'; *prensionem*: 'with urgency') and 'r' (*rectitudinem vel rasuram … crispationis*: 'with straight or forthright vibratoless [tone]').

Many more such significative letters refer to rhythmic detail, for example 'c' (*cito* or *celeriter*: 'to be performed rapidly and quickly') and 't' (*trahere*: 'drag out'; or *tenete*: 'hold'). The same manuscripts that are rich in significative letters contain many details of notation that are rare or unknown elsewhere; they include *episemata* and the deliberate modifying or distorting of the normal neume shape to suggest a different significance. These and many other features have occasioned extensive discussion, the chief issue being whether they can be interpreted in mensural rhythmic terms, and, if so, which rhythmic values are appropriate. On the one side, many have argued that the rhythmic indications are no more than nuances, agogic modifications of the basic flow. This is more or less the position adopted in the early years of this century by the monks of Solesmes; it became known as 'equalist' because all notes are basically of equal length. On the opposite side, the 'mensuralists' have been of varying opinions, some proposing two basic mensural units in the ratio 2:1, while others prefer three or more units (in the ratio 3:2:1 or 4:2:1, etc.). Further scope for varied note values is provided when they are grouped in bars, with the necessary flexibility to accommodate shorter, longer or dotted notes. While such meanings can be read into the notation, there is almost no firm contemporary evidence – in theoretical writings, for example – that these were envisaged. It is true that several authors speak of long notes, but with reference only to the closing notes of phrases. Only the *Commemoratio brevis* (*c*900, therefore contemporary with the manuscripts richest in notation detail) attaches proportional value to long and short notes: 'The longer values consist of the shorter, and the shorter subsist in the longer, and in such a fashion that one has always twice the duration of the other, neither more nor less' (see Bailey, B(i)1979, p.103). Yet the necessary link between such statements and the notational signs is lacking.

It is not surprising, therefore, that a wide range of interpretations have been proposed, ever since Lambillotte made mensural transcriptions from the early St Gallen manuscript *CH-SGs* 359. Pothier believed that the notational signs were a limited and chronological phenomenon and ignored them for the purposes of making the Vatican editions of chant, the *Graduale romanum* (1908) and the *Antiphonale romanum* (1912). This was the cause of the famous break with Solesmes, whose own chant editions, produced under the leadership of Mocquereau, add supplementary bars and dots indicating agogic nuances. For a group of scholars, including Houdard and Riemann, the text-syllable had to maintain a constant length, the notes being shorter or longer depending on how many were allotted to the syllable in question. Wagner transcribed with minim, crotchet and quaver, later with dotted crotchet, crotchet and quaver (in *AdlerHM*). Jeannin used only crotchet and quaver. (For other mensuralist transcriptions see Jammers, B(i)1937 and Vollaerts, B(i)1958.) Dechevrens had the interesting idea that many notes of Gregorian chant were of ornamental rather than structural significance, and he transcribed accordingly. His transcriptions, though barred, have melodic ornamental flourishes: the music thus resembles, at least on the rhythmic surface, the melodies of Coptic chant taken down from oral tradition. The adoption of one of the other mensuralist interpretations, on the other hand, may result in a performance closer to that of Greek Orthodox chant today. Furthermore, the guttural, forceful and vibrant delivery of Orthodox singers need not be ruled out as an impossibility for Western chant. There is, however, no evidence that Latin singers ever used the *ison* or drone note of late Byzantine chant, which in any case does not seem to be documented in the East before the 15th century (Jammers,

B(i)1962, p.185; refuted by Nowacki, B(i)1985–6, p.260). The term 'paraphonista' used in a few early *Ordines romani*, sometimes adduced in this context, simply means 'cantor' (Van Dijk, B(i)1963, pp.346–7).

No matter how much scholars read into chant notation and into theoretical writings, these sources cannot be expected to provide a full understanding of performing practice. One of the few hints as to how much remains unexplained may be found in the treatise of Hieronymus de Moravia, who not only gave rules about which notes should be longer than others, but also wrote about 'special effects' in singing chant (see Cserba, B(ii)1935, pp.lxii ff, 181ff). He stated that most notes in chant are equal in length, but with five exceptions: the first note of a chant if it is the same as the final, the *plica longa* (a liquescent neume), the penultimate and final notes of a phrase, and the second note of a phrase. The 'special effects' include various types of vibrato on the long notes; some, including various grace notes (*reverberatio*, *nota mediata*), were peculiar to French singers.

These last remarks are a reminder that chant is a changing, living tradition, and was (and still is) subject to regional variation as well as to changes that happen over time. Later additions to the chant repertory from the 14th century onwards include melodies sometimes found with mensural or semi-mensural notation; these are mostly new melodies, and do not necessarily suggest that the same rhythmic style of performance was applied to the older parts of the repertory. The wholesale revisions of the 17th and 18th centuries (for example NEO-GALLICAN CHANT) meant that the restoration movements of the 19th century (most particularly that of Solesmes) had to reconstruct a long-dead tradition. That chant is part of a living liturgical tradition, therefore, means that for practical purposes decisions have to be made for which hard evidence is, strictly speaking, lacking.

(ii) Secular. It was presumably in the realm of secular monophonic music that the concept of performance was principally fostered in the 12th and 13th centuries. The question of how medieval concepts of performance arose, and of how they were related not only to issues of social status but also to questions of domestic space and court decorum, may yet prove to be one of the most challenging areas of research in medieval performing practice. It is uncertain at present whether performers expected 'audiences' to keep silent, or whether listeners were generally accustomed to sit or stand. If there were discussions after the performance, we know little of the critical language employed. The consideration of such issues requires close attention to the nature of court experience, very remote from the modern scholar's own. A Franco-Italian manuscript of the mid-14th century (fig.2), shows a knight performing before the court of King Arthur. The 'performer' stands before his 'audience' and is separated from them by a space that the modern eye instantly recognizes from the concert hall. The courtiers stand in deference to their monarch's state, but it remains uncertain whether such attendants in the Middle Ages (or long after) would have drawn a sharp distinction between listening and simply waiting in attendance. The call to stand while a musician sang was simply another call upon their obligation of service that they could not deny. Nor it is clear where the performance shown in the picture is taking place. The presence of a throne suggests the great hall, a

large and impersonal space used for council and ceremonial meals, and in no sense a specialized place for music.

The secular music of the Middle Ages survives in a more imperfect state than plainchant. A large corpus of secular monophony exists – Latin songs by clerics, other non-liturgical melodies setting Latin words (e.g. conductus), Spanish *Cantigas de Santa María*, English songs, Italian *laude*, German Minnelieder, and chansons in old French by trouvères and in Old Occitan (Provençal) by troubadours – but there is little information about music intended chiefly for instruments and about the songs of the lower classes. Moreover, most of the courtly songs that survive were written down in staff notation (as opposed to staffless neumes, which served merely as reminders of melodies already known) only from the 13th century onwards. And the manuscript sources often record widely divergent or even completely different versions of the music intended for particular poems – a probable indication that the repertory was transmitted chiefly by oral tradition. For several reasons, then, it should be assumed that only a fragment, and perhaps a small fragment, of the music that must once have been performed outside the patronage of the church has survived.

Most of the important details about the performance of this repertory can never be known. Most past debate on the performance of medieval secular monophony has centred on two questions of fundamental importance: the nature of rhythm in medieval song, and the extent to which instruments took part in its performance.

Secular monophonic melodies are notated mostly in neumes which unambiguously indicate the pitches but not precise time values. However, some trouvère melodies – for example, a number of those in the 13th-century Chansonnier Cangé (*F-Pn* fr.846) – appear in a semi-mensural notation in which the scribe seems to have distinguished between some but not all longs and breves in a rather inconsistent way (or in a manner designed to make the notation look like that of a polyphonic source). Moreover, some trouvère melodies (but very few) were interpolated into 13th-century motets where their rhythms as well as their pitches are unambiguous. These questionable indications that secular songs were sometimes sung in strictly measured time have led some 20th-century

(a)

(b)

(c)

(d)

1. Miniature from the 'Cantigas de Santa María', Spain, late 13th century (E-E b.I.2, ff.39v, 268r, 179v, 260r): (a) fiddle and citole (b) trumpet (c) cymbals (d) psaltery

2. King Arthur and his courtiers listening to a knight singing to the gittern: miniature from the 'Roman du Roi Meliadus di Leonnoys' written (1352–62) for Louis II, titular King of Naples (GB-Lbl Add.12228, f.223r)

scholars, beginning with Beck (B(ii)1910) and Aubry (B(ii)1909), to conclude that all trouvère melodies were regulated by RHYTHMIC MODES – repeating patterns in triple metre. Indeed, virtually the entire corpus of secular song has been subjected by scholars to interpretation in modal rhythms, even though the particular pattern to be applied in individual cases is by no means always clear, and scholars have not agreed in their transcriptions.

Other scholars have used both duple and triple metres in their transcriptions, deciding between them apparently on aesthetic grounds. Still others, notably Van der Werf (B(ii)1972), have favoured more or less unmeasured rhythms, suggesting that most medieval song was declaimed freely, while not ruling out metrical and even modal transcriptions of dance-songs and some other chansons. This hypothesis has the virtue of claiming (at least by implication) that the notation indicates in the most efficient way possible the solutions to the musical problems at hand.

Similar controversy surrounds the question of instrumental participation. Some scholars find no justification for the addition of instruments; others add them freely, and still others take some middle position. Their arguments centre on a consideration of three points: the instruments commonly played during the Middle Ages and the musicians who played them; the information derived from musical sources, miniatures, literary works and archival documents; and the way musicians in other cultures with monophonic song repertories perform their music. Professional singers and instrumentalists of the Middle Ages were called *jongleurs*, minstrels, or, in German, *Spielmänner*. The terms describe musicians of widely differing sorts. There were poor vagabonds and wayfarers who sang songs, played popular tunes, juggled, did acrobatic tricks, or entertained townspeople and villagers with trained bears and monkeys; and there were *jongleurs*, associated with noblemen or aristocratic society, who were chiefly responsible for the performance of courtly songs. *Jongleurs* attended schools from time to

time to renew their repertories and they were expected to play a number of instruments.

Few instruments from the Middle Ages have survived, so knowledge of the medieval instrumentarium is based almost entirely on secondary evidence. This includes lists of instruments in literary works of the 12th, 13th and 14th centuries (such as Machaut's enumerations in his poems *Remède de Fortune* and *La prise d'Alexandrie*, and the lists in the anonymous 14th-century *Echecs amoureux*), which were apparently intended to be encyclopedic. Paintings and other art works depict large numbers of instruments; the well-known illuminations in the late 13th-century *Cantigas de Santa María* (E-E b.I.2) show Christian, Jewish and Moorish musicians playing instruments at the court of Alfonso X ('el Sabio'), King of Castile and León (1252–84) (fig.1). Among the instruments in the various lists are fiddles in several different shapes, rebecs, hurdy-gurdies, lutes, diverse sorts of guitars and psalteries, citoles, harps, rottes, transverse flutes, a variety of flageolets and recorders (some of them with two or more tubes), shawms, cornetts, *douçaines* (probably soft straight-capped shawms), bagpipes of one sort or another, and trumpets and percussion instruments.

It is by no means clear what music each of these instruments played. If they did take part in performances of medieval secular song, they may have accompanied singers by doubling them literally or heterophonically or by adding drones, preludes, interludes and postludes to the written melodic lines; or they may on occasion have performed the songs completely instrumentally, replacing the singers. (The selfconscious, middle-class Meistersinger of the 15th and 16th centuries, who modelled themselves to an extent on the earlier Minnesinger, forbade instrumental participation, but this should scarcely affect interpretation of medieval practices).

The case for instrumental participation in the performance of medieval secular song rests partly on literary and pictorial evidence (fig.2). The pictorial evidence is often of questionable value. The scene shown in fig.2 is separated in time from the text it illustrates by more than a century, and the text calls for a harp, not the gittern that is shown. The Arthurian setting of the text, placing the narrative in a time remote from the original readers, and surely securing certain freedoms for the painter, does little to strengthen the authority of the picture. The case for instrumentation also rests partly on the nature of the instruments involved, and partly on the non-historical claim that monophonic repertories are apt to be treated in similar ways in different cultures.

A passage from Huon de Mery's *Le tournoiement de l'Antechrist* suggests that instrumentalists at least on occasion accompanied singing: 'The *jongleurs* stood up, took fiddles and harps, and sang us songs, *lais*, tunes, verses, and refrains, and *chansons de geste*' (translation from *NOHM*, ii, 228–9). The principal reason for supposing that these songs might sometimes have been accompanied by drones derives from the nature of the instruments themselves, some of which – notably the hurdy-gurdy, the bagpipe, and various double pipes and recorders – could not be played without drones. (It is perhaps suggestive that the hurdy-gurdy lost its social standing as a courtly instrument in the 14th and 15th centuries just at the time when monophonic music was going out of fashion.) And the fiddle, perhaps the most versatile and hence most important of the medieval courtly *bas* (that is, soft, as opposed to *haut*, or loud) instruments, was often supplied with drone strings or else tuned in a way to facilitate playing with drones, as Hieronymus de Moravia pointed out in the 13th century.

The highly ornamented character of the 13th- and 14th-century monophonic dances and some medieval songs has given rise to the speculation that instrumentalists played heterophonically – that is, by sounding simultaneously slightly varying versions of the same melody. While the evidence is far from conclusive, the theory is attractive, and it receives some support from the non-historical but nevertheless persuasive fact that heterophony, along with drones and improvised preludes, interludes and postludes, regularly occurs in west European local traditions and in many non-Western cultures (for example, in those Islamic countries that are thought to have influenced so deeply the character of the medieval instrumentarium).

3. POLYPHONY TO 1400. Craig Wright (B(i)1989) has neatly summarized the essential circumstances of medieval performance: 'Medieval music manuscripts carried no presumption of absolute pitch, nor any indication of tempo, dynamics, instrumentation [or] vocal ornamentation . . . All these the performer was expected to supply himself, drawing on a fund of musical experience and using his skill to extend and refine the accepted practices of his day'. The 'accepted practices' of medieval polyphony extended from the performance of elaborate counterpoint to impromptu treatments of plainchant. Many kinds of evidence illuminate them, but the writings of the theorists are the most consistently valuable because the musical manuscripts have not been systematically examined for the information they may provide. Pictorial sources, literary texts and archives also make a contribution, but when all the available information is assembled the result is only a collage drawn from different repertories, procedures and levels of musical literacy.

The composed polyphony of the Middle Ages is generally regarded as music for soloists, but the evidence suggests a more flexible practice which was much the same whether the polyphony was composed or extemporized. Elias Salomo, a French priest from Périgord, but writing *in curia romana*, stipulated one singer to a part in extemporized parallel organum, conceding that the lowest voice might be reinforced if necessary. In 13th-century Paris the tally of singers deputed to sing organum at Notre Dame was usually the same as the number assigned to the unadorned plainchant, so as many as six might be involved in the performance of two-part polyphony. Wright proposed that a soloist sang all parts save the tenor, but this cannot be confirmed. Among the pictorial sources, the 'Notre Dame' manuscript W_2 shows three (or possibly four) singers in the initial to Perotinus's *Salvatoris hodie* in three parts (f.31r), while a two-part version of *Presul nostri* has four singers (f.92r). These images draw deeply on the iconography of Psalm xcvii, *Cantate Domino* (ii), and their value in this context is open to question.

Two illustrations from the same tradition, but perhaps with a greater claim to authority, have been discovered in English psalters of 1310–20. The work of the same artist, they show three tonsured singers performing the three-voice motet *Zelo tui langueo/Reor nescia/ [Omnes de Saba]*. The tenor of the motet is derived from the Gradual for Epiphany and the pictures show a singer wearing the starred vestment prescribed for Epiphany by a Sarum ordinal of the 14th century. This is an unusual concatenation of evidence and might serve for a clear ruling about the performance of this motet. However, the artist's contemporary Jacobus of Liège declared that nothing prevented a two-part piece having more than one singer on either tenor or discantus. In view of this evidence it would be difficult to maintain that the aesthetic of medieval polyphony positively demanded a single voice to a part, even if such performances were common.

Some refinements of performing practice are recoverable. The theorists reveal that standards of intonation among the best singers were very high, as might be expected in repertories so consistently based on the octave and 5th rather than the 3rd and 6th (where the ear accepts a greater latitude). Jacobus of Liège disdained any singer who deviated from perfection by as little as a Pythagorean comma, less than a quarter of a semitone, and he associated loss of accuracy in this regard with 'tremulous voices'. This may be a reference to a 'straight' tone allowing the ear to savour the intervals. Many other refinements, however, are beyond recall. Elias Salomo's instruction that a singer 'should lift his voice from note to note in the manner of the French' will probably always remain a mystery, and it is far from clear what Pseudo-Garlandia meant by *nobilitatio*, 'an augmentation or diminution of the same sound'. This is conceivably a reference to dynamics. Hieronymus de Moravia gave some richly metaphorical descriptions of vocal ornamentation and Roesner has used them to reconstruct the nuances of Parisian *organum duplum*. They include the 'harmonic flower', the 'stormy note' ('nota procellaris'), the 'open flower', the 'sudden flower' and 'reverberation', defined by Hieronymus in gratifyingly precise terms. To lay his account beside *organum duplum* as it appears in the sources, blocked out in the ligatures of square notation, is to appreciate the distance that could separate symbol from sound in medieval polyphony.

Hieronymus de Moravia's principal subject when he described these ornaments was the embellishment of

3. Nakers, two shawms, bagpipe, two trumpets, fiddle and portative organ accompanying a wedding procession: miniature showing the marriage of Polynices and Tydeus to Argia and Deipyle from the 'Thebiad of Statius', Padua, c1380–90 (IRL-Dcb W.76A, f.13v)

chant. Performing practice was strongly influenced by plainchant and therefore by 'the organs which generate the human voice' (Engelbert of Admont). By modern standards, the performer of polyphony before 1400 was often a musician with an exceptional experience of consort singing acquired in the choral performance of plainchant. Elias Salomo, though concerned with extemporized organum, may reveal the broader priorities that were instilled into such singers by their rulers or precentors in rehearsal, marking the pauses on the book to ensure good ensemble and seeking a good blend of *voces concordes*. The outstanding concern seems to be unanimity of every kind. The terminology of 'head' voices and 'chest' voices was well established by 1300, and Hieronymus de Moravia emphasized that the different types should not be mixed. Jacobus of Liège confirmed that singing chant in unison required the singers to be 'equal in everything' ('omnino equales'). It is possible to imagine how organum and conductus counted as an especially exacting form of being 'equal in everything' during performance, for in these two genres the participating voices sang the same text and respired together, demanding careful adjustment of phrasing and, in pursuit of precise tuning, the colour of vowels.

The gradual dissolution of this vocal predominance, with all its technical and aesthetic values, owed much to a sweeping social and musical change between 1300 and 1500; by the end of this period composed polyphony touched many more human lives than at the beginning. At present, the balance of the evidence favours belief in a vocal predominance until at least 1400, but the material is not definitive nor is it too abundant for rapid review. Johannes de Grocheio discussed instruments with monophonic secular music, not composed polyphony. English polyphony of the 14th century was composed for vocal ensembles of stable constitution making little or no use of the organ; a survey of the French and Italian sacred repertories might reveal something similar. The two-part madrigals and ballatas of the Italian Trecento appear in most of the sources as vocal duets, while the sources of Landini's music show considerably more full and partial texting in the lower parts than the published edition suggests. A picture in the Squarcialupi Codex (*I-Fl* Med.Pal.87) famously shows Landini playing the portative organ surrounded by other instruments, but the only known description of his music in performance reveals the three-part ballata *Orsù gentili spiriti* sung by two girls and a man (a perfectly plausible scoring). In French chansons of the Machaut tradition the prevailing texture comprises a texted cantus accompanied by up to three textless parts. Eustache Deschamps (probably Machaut's nephew) mentioned a 'triplicité des voix' for the best performance of chansons with tenor and contratenor; if musicians ever regarded the more angular contratenors of this repertory as artistic vocal music it was perhaps precisely because they were not 'faciles ad pronuntiandum', in the words of Jacobus of Liège. The possibility that these underparts were generally texted seems remote; perhaps they were vocalized wordlessly. Machaut himself invited 'orgues, cornemuses ou autres instruments' for his three-part ballade 33 *Nes que on porroit*, a piece he regarded as 'very novel' and 'very foreign'; whatever he intended by this call for instruments (Leech-Wilkinson, B(ii)1993, is the first to have offered a convincing explanation), theorists throughout the period portrayed instrumentalists as musicians working more by *usus* than by *ars*. Only Arnulf of St Ghislain, whose dates are unknown, evoked a situation with the potential for far-reaching change. The instrumentalists that he described were clerics capable of composing and performing pieces that no singer would attempt to rival, and who remedied their own want of musical knowledge by consorting (perhaps in more senses than one) with trained musicians.

Medieval concepts of musical beauty, as they are understood today, have often been contrasted with those attributed to the Renaissance. J.I. Wimsatt, for example (*Chaucer and his French Contemporaries*, Toronto and London, 1993), argued that 'Machaut and his contemporaries ... make no attempt to imitate or stir the passions', and it is impossible to imagine such a remark being made about a Renaissance madrigalist. However, there is no single line of development to be discerned. Some of the language used by 16th-century musicians to describe the ideals of the Italian madrigal, surely the most intensely 'Renaissance' musical form, is foreshadowed by chant theorists half a millennium earlier. About 1100 John 'of Afflighem' (Johannes Cotto) ruled that a musical setting should express the meaning of the words ('quod verba sonant cantus exprimere videantur'), and it remains unproved that a Latin song known to him would have been performed with fewer nuances of phrasing, tone-colour or pace than a polyphonic madrigal four centuries later, whatever other contrasts the difference of musical texture might impose. The rise of measured polyphony, however, probably shifted the aesthetic ground of medieval music, at least in the polyphonic sphere. Before 1300, the dialectic between precisely measured and not so precisely measured performance was an important intellectual and aesthetic issue for musicians; that is why some of the most suggestive information about performing practice relates to music without precise measure (*organum duplum* is the clearest example) or music which had newly acquired it (Hieronymus de Moravia's ornamented plainchant). By the 1320s this situation had changed. The Ars Nova treatises suggest an aesthetic based upon the scrupulous calibration of duration and pitch, neither broaching the question of how different polyphonic textures might express 'quod verba sonant' nor hinting at the wealth of nuance in performance noted by their Ars Antiqua forebears. A language about the affective union of music and poetry, known to the plainchant theorists, lost pertinence when composed polyphony, exulting in scrupulous measurement and perhaps a certain objectivity, became the medium of high art. The gradual recuperation of that language for polyphony is a significant chapter in the history of performing practice and deserves a study to itself.

4. 15TH- AND 16TH-CENTURY MUSIC. Occasions for informal music-making are seldom recorded systematically. Passing remarks in literary and historical writings and the evidence of works of art depicting commonplace reality or traditional themes in contemporary guises are our chief source of information about such areas of Renaissance activity as aristocratic music-making (with or without professional assistance), the character of

4. *Singers performing from a note roll (rotulus): miniature from Machaut's 'Livre du voir dit', c1390 (F-Pn fr.9221, f.16r)*

informal music in middle-class homes, and the extent to which peasants and the poorer urban dwellers played and sang in taverns, at fairs, at home and at work. But formal musical activity is easier to document, for records of payments to musicians often survive, as well as traces of the institutional framework within which the music was performed. Accordingly, much research into the performing practices of the 15th and 16th centuries has focussed on these formal occasions and the churches, courts and civic institutions that supported them.

By the 16th century the most important churches and cathedrals in western Europe had polyphonic choirs, and

5. *Secular song accompanied by a portative organ: detail from a 15th-century French tapestry in the Musée des Beaux-Arts, Angers*

in many cases separate singing groups for performing plainchant. These ensembles were responsible for providing music for the daily liturgical ceremonies, the celebration of Mass as well as Office hours, and for more elaborate performances on feast days and other extraordinary celebrations. Church and cathedral choirs counted among their members the best-trained musicians and almost all the greatest composers except those who performed similar duties at princely courts. They regularly performed the finest and most complex masterpieces of the age. On average, leading 16th-century choirs seem to have consisted of between 20 and 30 singers, although the number varied a great deal; by mid-century the cathedral in Antwerp employed as many as 69 singers, while small provincial centres must have been content with but a handful. Many churches seem to have reorganized and consolidated their musical establishments during the 15th century, and the size of vocal ensembles tended to increase as the century progressed. Nonetheless, even some of the largest and most distinguished ensembles (e.g. the papal chapel) frequently performed polyphony with one singer to a part, especially in polychoral music and mass sections with reduced scoring.

Except in convents (whose musical practices remain largely mysterious), women were excluded from participation in liturgical services, so the polyphony of church and cathedral was sung by all-male choirs. Lower lines were taken by tenors and basses, and the highest parts were typically given to falsettists. (Castrato singers were unknown before 1550 and relatively rare for the rest of the century.) Many churches also maintained a half-dozen or more choirboys, providing for their liberal-arts education and musical training (liturgy, notation, counterpoint, improvisation, and often one or more instruments). In

6. Unaccompanied church choir: woodcut from 'Practica musice' (1496) by Gaffurius

some musical establishments choirboys were a regular feature, taking the top lines of polyphonic compositions; in others, the boys more often formed a separate ensemble by themselves and with their teachers. A number of polyphonic choirs in the 15th and early 16th centuries were proportioned in ways that may seem top-heavy by modern standards: in 1469, for example, Charles the Bold directed that the Burgundian court chapel choir should comprise at least six falsettists, three tenors, two contratenors (men with tenor-range voices but specializing in contratenor parts) and three basses when singing polyphony. Virtually every 15th-century choir whose voice distribution can be determined follows some variant of this pattern, whether the top be boys or adult falsettists; by the late 16th century, however, more equal distributions seem to have become the norm.

By the mid-16th century some churches employed a group of instrumentalists, normally playing loud instruments such as shawm, cornett, trombone and dulcian. Their precise role varied from place to place and should probably not be overestimated: in many churches they played only for wordless portions of the service, and in others their participation with the singers was carefully circumscribed. By the end of the century, however, musicians had begun to cultivate the sonorous possibilities of mixing voices and instruments in the concerted polychoral compositions of the Gabrielis and other Venetian musicians, for example, and in the music of the German italophile Michael Praetorius, whose *Syntagma musicum* (1614–18) offers comprehensive instructions for scoring *concerti* in the early Baroque 'colossal' style. Unambiguous documentation for the use of wind instruments in church during the 15th and early 16th centuries is difficult to find, but the reluctance of church authorities to permit instrumental participation evidently did not extend to the organ. Organs, sometimes of substantial size, were commonplace in European churches well back into the Middle Ages, and throughout the Renaissance organists either doubled singers or alternated regularly with them. An extensive repertory of plainchant settings, toccatas and preludes, and examples of improvisatory technique, suggest the style in which they performed.

Because of the nature of much secular documentation, together with the traditional professional secrecy of the guilds, relatively little is known about the way instrumentalists were educated, or even about their repertory. The rigid medieval distinction between *haut* (loud) and *bas* (soft) bands relaxed but by no means disappeared over the course of the Renaissance. *Haut* ensembles followed an evolving but stereotyped pattern, beginning in the 15th century with typically a few shawms and a slide trumpet (later a trombone), growing by about 1500 to four or five players (sometimes with various sizes of shawm), and with cornetts and dulcians supplementing and later supplanting the shawms in the 16th century. *Bas* ensembles were much more various, admitting a vast array of plucked and bowed strings, recorders, flutes, organs and other instruments. These bands, loud and soft alike, probably learnt to improvise dance music, typically in the 15th century by adding one or two contrapuntal lines around a tenor cantus firmus (e.g. a basse danse), and in the 16th century by harmonizing a melody played in the top voice and by embellishing the melody when it was repeated. But instruments also played all sorts of composed music, not only chansons, madrigals and other secular music (with or without singers) but motets and even mass movements as well. By the middle of the 16th century such publishers as Attaingnant in Paris and Susato in Antwerp were producing little books of textless music, usually dances with unspecified and presumably very flexible instrumentation, for use by amateur and professional bands of all types; and, by the last decades of the century, independent instrumental ensemble music (e.g. the canzonas of such composers as Florentio Maschera and Giovanni Gabrieli, or the well-known English viol fantasias) had become very sophisticated indeed.

The musical establishment at the court of a king or prince was a microcosm of the outside world. A choir with its organist supplied music for the ordinary services in the prince's chapel, and the chapel singers may also normally have taken part as soloists in secular entertainments sponsored by the court. Most princes also employed one or more bands of *haut* instrumentalists – cornett players, trombonists, shawm players and the like – who played for dancing and outdoor entertainments, and a corps of trumpeters and drummers who served to announce the prince ceremonially during peacetime as well as in battles. And some princes also engaged a few virtuoso *bas* instrumentalists – lutenists, recorder players, viol players and the like – to play chamber music.

Many courts may have enjoyed music at daily meals. Certainly, varied programmes by vocal, instrumental and mixed ensembles enlivened banquets and special meals when the prince entertained important guests. In his cookery book, *Banchetti, composizioni di vivande e apparecchio generale* (Ferrara, 1549), Cristoforo Messisbugo, steward to the Este family, described several typical occasions in the late 1520s when members of the court in Ferrara played host to visitors, and music was supplied by virtually all of the musical establishment; not only singers from the chapel choir took part, but also individual virtuosos, groups of shawms, cornetts and trombones, viols and flutes, and mixed *concerti* consisting of a group of singers, a group of viol players, and one or more groups of wind and string players. Similarly, Massimo Troiano, an Italian at the court of Munich in the 1560s, wrote a detailed account of the music performed at banquets and other celebrations when Duke Wilhelm of Bavaria married Renée of Lorraine in 1568 (fig.9); and Ercole Bottrigari, in *Il desiderio* (1594), explained how many of the townspeople of Ferrara joined the courtly musicians to prepare imposing *concerti* for performance at special events at the Este court late in the century. Doubtless the wind bands of princes played regularly for dancing, and chamber musicians were frequently called upon to entertain the prince and his courtiers with chansons, madrigals and the like.

In sum, a great deal of scholarship concerning the performing practices of the Renaissance has concentrated

7. Civic procession accompanied by a wind band of three shawms and a folded trumpet: miniature from a French translation (1455–60) of Boccaccio's 'Teseide' (A-Wn 2.617, f.39r)

8. *Trombone, shawm, cornett and bass viol accompanying dance: detail of engraving, 'The Aulterer's Bridge' (c1570), by Jost Amman*

of the 15th and 16th centuries it is now useful and possible, at least in broad terms, to imagine an 'ideal' instrumentation within the habits of the time and place. The ideals were often violated, of course; but over the years, again broadly speaking, they show a surprising consistency. For almost any piece of Renaissance Latin sacred polyphony, *a cappella* choral performance with falsettists on the top line represents a plausible ideal; for most vernacular songs, throughout the period, voices without accompaniment seem also to have been the preferred medium, but with one singer on a part and with boys, women, or girls on the top line or lines. The notion that textless lines in the sources, most famously in the 15th-century chansons, were meant for instruments has not survived close scrutiny: instruments (especially lute and harp) may have been at least a possibility, but singers, either supplying words or vocalizing on a neutral vowel sound, seem better to represent the usual ideal of the time.

The music sung by church and chapel choirs was prepared in large choirbooks set on a lectern around which the musicians gathered. In the 16th century much music was printed in partbooks. Scores were not in general use but were reserved for keyboard players and, in the second half of the 16th century, for students of counterpoint. Players of chordal instruments other than keyboards, particularly plucked string instruments such as the lute and the guitar, might prepare special parts in tablatures which incorporated all or most of the melodic lines of the polyphonic music they wished to play. Before they performed a composition, Renaissance musicians (and indeed those of later times) had to agree about a number of things besides instrumentation: the tempo, which might not be implied by the mensuration sign; how the text was to be added to the notes in vocal music; which accidentals were to be added to the written notes

on basic questions of instrumentation: how many singers to put on a part, and what kind, and what instruments, if any. Apart from tablatures and other tell-tale notations, almost no Renaissance source gives a reliable clue to the composer's preference, and thus instrumentations must be reconstructed as probabilities based on surviving circumstantial evidence. For most mainstream repertories

9. *The Bavarian court chapel under Lassus performing at a banquet in celebration of the marriage of Duke Wilhelm of Bavaria to Renée of Lorraine in Munich, 1568: engraving by Nikolaus Solis*

10. Church service with a choir accompanied by cornetts and trombones: engraving from 'Encomium musices' (Antwerp: Philip Galle, c1590)

following the rules of *musica ficta*; whether or not to embellish the written notes; and, if so, where and how.

The theory of one *tactus* of invariable speed can probably not be sustained for the 15th and 16th centuries, and therefore mensuration signs do not indicate absolute tempos. Various 16th-century writers commented that tempo was variable, dependent at least partly on the character of the words (or the choreography, in the case of dance music). Nevertheless, in extended compositions with changes of mensuration, the relationships between the various tempos seem often to have involved simple arithmetical relationships indicated by proportions. In principle, music in so-called duple proportion, indicated by a slash (and in ₵) moved twice as fast as music in *integer valor* (C); the *brevis* (and every other note value) sounded half as long under the proportional sign. Similarly, music in triple proportion, indicated by C3 or some other sign, moved three times as fast, three semibreves under the proportional sign sounding in the time of one *brevis* of *integer valor*; and in *proportio sesquialtera*, indicated by 3, 3/2 or some other sign, the music moved one and a half times as fast as in *integer valor*, three semibreves under the proportional sign taking the same time as two in *integer valor*. The four basic mensuration signs of the 14th and 15th centuries were C (*tempus imperfectum cum prolatione imperfecta*), O (*tempus perfectum cum prolatione imperfecta*), ₵ (*tempus imperfectum cum prolatione perfecta*) and ☉ (*tempus perfectum cum prolatione perfecta*). It is difficult to understand how these were interrelated when they

followed directly one after another, with the changes occurring simultaneously in all voices. Mendel's rule of thumb that semibreves (and not breves) remain the same when the mensuration changes from O to C and vice versa is helpful and in most cases produces good musical results. Except for special instances, however, complex mensuration ceased to be a concern of composers from the late 15th century onwards. As ₵ became by far the most common mensuration sign, appearing regularly at the beginning of a piece, it obviously lost its proportional significance and became essentially the new *integer valor*; the chief difficulties facing the performer of 16th-century music thus involve fairly elementary features of the mensural system: for example how ₵ should be interpreted when juxtaposed with the old C or O. How C, O, ₵ and ₵ relate to one another when all voices change mensuration signs simultaneously is probably explained by saying that the *semibrevis* stayed the same in *integer valor* and was halved in value under the proportional signs. As to the question of when the composer intended *proportio tripla* and when *proportio sesquialtera*, it can be said that most shifts in tempo in the 16th century seem to involve *proportio sesquialtera* regardless of the sign used to indicate the change, although there are fairly frequent exceptions to this rule of thumb.

Like mensural practice, the principles of text underlay are more difficult to discover for 15th- than for 16th-century music. About 1500 Josquin des Prez and his contemporaries took more pains than any previous composers to write melodic lines that closely fitted the texts they set, and the following generation of composers (from about 1530 on), led by Adrian Willaert, perfected the union of notes and syllables. During the 15th century, however, most music was highly melismatic, and composers seem often not to have conceived their melodic lines so that text syllables fitted them in only one way. In short, text underlay in the 15th century was left to the performers. Principles of 15th-century text underlay may yet be formulated from the evidence supplied by some manuscripts of the time. But most manuscripts do not indicate precisely where the text syllables are to be sung, and no scholar has succeeded in demonstrating that scribes intended to supply that kind of information. Modern musicians, therefore, are forced to base their decisions on the theoretical evidence of the following century, and especially on the advice given by G.M. Lanfranco (*Scintille di musica*, 1533), Gioseffo Zarlino (*Le istitutioni harmoniche*, 1558) and Gaspar Stoquerus (*De musica verbali libri duo*, c1570). Harrán (C1973) has shown that Zarlino's rules for text underlay derive from Lanfranco's, and Lowinsky (*Festschrift Heinrich Besseler*, 1961) explained that Stoquerus's importance lies in his awareness of changes in style between the period of Josquin and his own day. Zarlino's ten rules for text underlay may be summarized as follows: long and short syllables should be combined with notes or figures of corresponding value; only one syllable should be sung to a ligature; a dot augmenting a note should not be assigned a new syllable; a change of syllable should not normally be made on or immediately after a crotchet or shorter note; notes immediately following a dotted semibreve or minim and of smaller value than the dots are not usually assigned a syllable; if a syllable must be sung to a crotchet, another syllable may be given to the note following; a syllable should be sung to the first note of a piece (regardless of its value) and to the first note after a rest; individual words or syllables should not be repeated, although in very melismatic music it is acceptable to repeat a whole clause whose meaning is complete by itself; if the penultimate syllable of a composition is long it may be sung to a melisma; and the last syllable should coincide with the last note. Commonsense application of these rules gives a satisfactory text underlay, at least for most songs, motets and wordier movements of the mass; more serious difficulties, at least for the modern editor and performer, attend mass movements for which the sources give no hint of intended underlay (for example, a Kyrie whose scribe has written 'Kyrie' under the first notes, 'leison' under the last, and 'e' somewhere in the middle). These apparently caused no trouble to singers of the time (any such problem would have been very easy for composers and scribes to solve), and indeed text underlay for such movements is not hard to improvise today, at least when singing one to a part; whether it was thought important for sections to underlay text together, and, if so, how this was accomplished in practice, are not known.

Besides expecting performers to fit the syllables to the notes, 15th- and 16th-century composers also intended that they add sharps and flats to the written notes, following the rules of *musica ficta*. These rules, as summarized by Lowinsky, Berger and others from theoretical evidence, give two reasons for adding accidentals, *causa necessitatis* and *causa pulchritudinis*. Reasons of necessity govern perfect consonances: tritones, diminished 5ths and augmented octaves should normally be made

perfect. Aesthetic reasons dictate the rules governing imperfect consonances: perfect consonances should be approached by the nearest imperfect consonances; major 6ths expand to an octave, for example, and minor 6ths contract to a 5th. Related to this regulation, leading notes should be raised in all cadential formulae (except in Phrygian cadences, where the second degree descends to the *finalis* by a semitone). And, in the 16th century, the 3rd in final chords should be made major. While the rules themselves are quite simple, their application often creates difficulties. The largest body of evidence showing the way 16th-century musicians added unspecified accidentals, the intabulations for lute and other plucked string instruments of vocal music of every sort, reveals that instrumentalists disagreed in their solutions to particular passages, even though they generally followed the precepts of *musica ficta*, and, indeed, often added many more accidentals than a modern editor would think seemly.

Several instruction books on instrumental technique, notably those by Ganassi dal Fontego (*Fontegara*, 1535) and Diego Ortiz (*Trattado de glosas*, 1553), reveal that instrumentalists during the first two-thirds of the 16th century considered improvised or quasi-improvised ornamentation a necessary part of their technical equipment; and such works as Coclico's *Compendium musices* (1552) suggest that singers needed some of the same skills. Certainly virtually every lutenist who arranged sacred and secular music for his instrument included runs, turns and trills in his intabulations. Musicians performing in an ensemble probably did little more than decorate cadences and perhaps add divisions or *passaggi* to one or two passages within a composition. Ortiz supplied performers with numerous formulae which they could use for those purposes. Whenever a madrigal or motet was performed by a solo singer with lute accompaniment, and whenever instrumental arrangements (and dance music) allowed a single player to dominate the texture, embellishment probably became a more prominent feature of the performance. Ganassi's tables of ornaments seem to have been designed to transform a relatively simple solo melodic line into an elaborate vehicle for the virtuoso performer, and Ortiz included versions of several compositions for solo viol and keyboard in which the viol player imposes on the music a florid line which is more than merely an embellishment of the original. During the last quarter of the 16th century a series of instruction books, by Girolamo Dalla Casa, G.B. Bovicelli, Giovanni Bassano, Riccardo Rognoni and various others, described and explained the extremes to which virtuoso singers and players went in displaying their agility and inventiveness, even at the expense of the composer's intentions. Indeed, the excesses of the late 16th-century virtuosos probably led composers such as Caccini and Monteverdi to incorporate bravura elements into their music in an effort to reduce the extent to which the performer strayed from the written notes.

The 15th and 16th centuries were times of great change in the nature of instruments and the way they were played. Harpsichords and other similar keyboard instruments came into general use early in the 15th century. The trombone evolved from the slide trumpet in the middle of the century. Late in the 15th century lutenists developed a technique of playing polyphonic music with their fingers to replace the outmoded method of playing single lines with a plectrum. The crumhorn was probably invented later in the century and the viol evolved at the same time (relatively few years before the violin family came into existence, presumably during the first quarter of the 16th century). About 1500, too, many instruments came to be built in families tuned either in 4ths or 5ths (flutes, recorders, viols, crumhorns and various others) or less regularly, like lutes.

Consorts of like instruments, the instrumental equivalent of the *a cappella* choir, were particularly favoured during the early 16th century. Usually three sizes of instruments took part in a four-part ensemble, the smallest (e.g. a treble recorder in G) playing the top line, two middle-sized instruments (e.g. tenor recorders in C) playing the two middle lines, alto and tenor, and the largest instrument (e.g. a bass recorder in F) playing the bottom line. Because of inherent weaknesses in some sizes of some instruments these pure consorts were sometimes modified. Alto trombones were musically less satisfactory than the standard tenor trombones, for example, and so the top parts in wind bands were often taken by either cornetts or shawms (depending on the quality of sound desired). Trombones, viols or some other bass instrument often played beneath three recorders. However, mixed consorts of unlike instruments were also common, and during the 16th century ensembles tended to become more elaborate and more varied. Often a chordal instrument, a lute or a keyboard, doubled all the voices in a polyphonic composition, and from the custom of supporting an ensemble in this way grew the Baroque technique of basso continuo. Similarly, 'terraced dynamics', traditionally associated with Baroque music, probably originated before 1600, when so many of the instruments in general use the possibilities of controlling dynamic nuances were relatively limited. Crescendos and diminuendos are impossible, or nearly so, on many 16th-century instruments, such as flutes, recorders, crumhorns, harpsichords and organs.

Keyboard instruments in the 16th century were tuned by preference in mean-tone temperament, a practical method for dividing the Pythagorean comma so that 3rds and 5ths more closely approach just intonation than they do with equal temperament. But equal temperament was also widely adopted during the Renaissance – on all fretted string instruments, for example. Bottrigari (*Il

11. *Consort of recorders: woodcut from the title-page of 'S'ensuyvent plusieurs basses dances tant communes que incommunes' (Lyons: Moderne, c1530–38)*

desiderio*, 1594) and others discussed the problem of combining instruments of different temperaments.

Attempts to determine the pitch level at which Renaissance music was performed have met with varying success. A number of surviving 16th-century recorders and cornetts (two of the few contemporary instruments whose pitch can be tested more or less accurately) are tuned about a semitone above modern pitch, but this was by no means a universal standard: pitch clearly varied from place to place (and some places recognized more than one standard simultaneously), and in vocal ensembles pitch levels may have been set without reference to any outside source and may thus have been in effect flexible. Various theories of systematic pitch shiftings have been developed – for example, that English sacred music of the 16th century should be sung a minor 3rd higher than its apparent notated pitch, or that late 16th-century sacred music written in *chiavette* or high clefs (treble clef on the top line rather than soprano) should be transposed down a 3rd or 4th – but none has yet found universal favour or wide application.

Ganassi, Ortiz and other writers on string and wind instruments imply that single notes were generally played in a more or less detached manner during the 16th century. Ortiz's description of slurred notes suggests that they are something of an exception in his time, and both Ganassi and Dalla Casa (*Il vero modo di diminuir*, 1584) recommended varied and sophisticated double tonguings for even the fastest passage-work. Scattered references suggest that vibrato was available to 16th-century instrumentalists as a special effect (and thus presumably not as a constant presence), but most issues of style and interpretation are either ignored by the contemporary writers on music, or referred to so fleetingly or cryptically that they cannot be interpreted without doubt. Modern performers of Renaissance music are still, in many important respects, on their own.

5. 1600–1750. Baroque performers enjoyed many of the same freedoms as earlier musicians. They were expected to make many of the same kinds of decisions about a wide range of problems as their counterparts in the Middle Ages and the Renaissance, although gradually the conventions changed. There was no sharp break with earlier traditions, merely a slow evolution. For example, early 17th-century performers still had to add a few unspecified accidentals to their parts, but composers came increasingly to write down all the sharps and flats they expected to hear, albeit following a slightly different practice from the modern one. Similarly, the older practice of expecting changes of tempo to follow simple arithmetical proportions, indicated by mensuration signs, did not die out completely until the 18th century, even though complex combinations of mensuration signs or time signatures seldom appeared in music of the Baroque era. Moreover, performers in the 17th and 18th centuries could still play much music on whatever instruments suited the parts. Scoring was not entirely fixed, in spite of the fact that composers began more and more to indicate precisely which instruments they intended, and to write parts idiomatically conceived for those instruments.

Direct musical instruction is plentiful for the Baroque period where many publications dealt with specific instruments and with the voice. These range from treatises and prefaces addressing the needs of accomplished musicians to countless rather primitive manuals aimed at

12. *Mixed consort of trombone, organ, cornett, violin, lute and bass viol accompanying two singers: painting from the 'Album amicorum' of Hieremias Buroner, Augsburg, 1592–9 (GB-Lbl Eg.1554, f.2r)*

amateurs. Two encyclopedic works – Praetorius's *Syntagma musicum* (1614–18) and Mersenne's *Harmonie universelle* (1636–7) – provide a wealth of information about instruments and performing practice at the beginning of the era, while at its close four great treatises provide something of a summation: Quantz's *Versuch einer Anweisung die Flöte traversiere zu spielen* (1752), on flute playing; C.P.E. Bach's *Versuch über die wahre Art das Clavier zu spielen*, i (1753), on keyboard playing; Leopold Mozart's *Versuch einer gründlichen Violinschule* (1756), on violin playing; and J.F. Agricola's *Anleitung zur Singekunst* (1757), on singing. Scholars continue to debate the precise character of these works. As composers, these four authors are orientated towards the new world of pre-Classical, Rococo and *galant* styles, but for all that their treatises must, to some extent, reflect their early training in the older techniques of the Baroque era. Agricola's volume is, in fact, an extensively glossed translation of P.F. Tosi's *Opinioni de' cantori antichi e moderni* (1723) and so enshrines the practices of the earlier period. How far these can be used to elucidate Baroque practice is a question to which a simple and definitive answer is unlikely to be forthcoming. So, too, is the question of whether they set down general principles valid for all 18th-century music, or whether their remarks merely clarified local usages and customs. These four

volumes nevertheless supply the most comprehensive picture of the way music of the period was performed.

Treatises are usefully supplemented by other kinds of documentary evidence from the period: letters (by such eminent musicians and intellectuals as Monteverdi, Mersenne and Constantijn Huygens), the diaries and memoirs of a musically alert élite (Pepys, Evelyn, Ludovic Huygens, Charles Burney) and the accounts of musical performances which appeared in newspapers and periodicals (themselves a new development). Archival records relating to the musical establishments of courts and churches throw much light on such matters as the emergence of the orchestra in the 17th century. They can also sharpen our sense of the skills and versatility expected of musicians in this period.

Paintings and engravings contribute greatly to our knowledge of performing practice in the era. It is still true, though to a much lesser extent than for earlier periods, that our knowledge of certain kinds of musical instrument (violin bows before the late 17th century, for instance) is heavily dependent on iconographical evidence. Pictures can throw light on such questions as the number of musicians involved and their disposition in certain kinds of ensemble.

The value of individual pictures as evidence is first and foremost determined by their accuracy (often a reflection

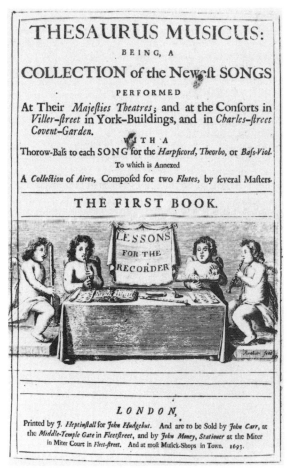

THESAURUS MUSICUS:

BEING, A

COLLECTION of the Newest SONGS

PERFORMED

At Their *Majesties Theatres*; and at the Conforts in *Viller-street* in York-Buildings, and in *Charles-street Covent-Garden*.

WITH A

Thorow-Bafs to each SONG for the *Harpficord*, *Theorbo*, or *Bafs-Viol*.

To which is Annexed

A *Collection* of Aires, Compofed for two *Flutes*, by feveral Mafters.

THE FIRST BOOK.

LESSONS FOR THE RECORDER

LONDON,

Printed by *J. Heptinftall* for *John Hudgebut*. And are to be Sold by *John Carr*, at the *Middle-Temple Gate* in *Fleetftreet*, and by *John Money*, Stationer at the Miter in Miter Court in *Fleet-ftreet*. And at moft Mufick-Shops in Town. 1693.

13. *Title-page of John Hudgebut's 'Thesaurus musicus' (1693)*

of the artist's own interest in music). On the one hand, the interiors of Jan Vermeer (1632–75) and his contemporaries give beautiful and quasi-photographic depictions of people holding or playing instruments. There is, for example, typical Dutch realism in Pieter de Hooch's *The Music Party*, dating from the early 1660s, which gives informative illustrations of a violin, recorder, cittern and bass viol – though what repertory this rather irregular mixed consort might be playing remains a mystery (fig.14). On the other hand, the caricatures of Pietro Longhi (1702–85) or William Hogarth (1697–1764) may give distorted images which nevertheless convey useful information about such matters as performing contexts. Caution is always needed in assessing the musical content of iconographical sources; we need to ask why it has been included (*see* ICONOGRAPHY).

Most of the really new performing practices of the Baroque period arose from three causes: an increased consciousness of national styles, and especially of the difference between French and Italian music and ways of playing it; the rise and development of the technique of improvising a chordal accompaniment over a basso continuo (a technique rooted in 16th-century conventions); and a new desire on the part of composers and performers to be brilliant and expressive in playing or singing melodies. This last is signalled by the rise of the violin family, the decline of the viol family (except for the bass viol), and the virtual disappearance of instruments, such as the crumhorn, which were incapable of dynamic nuance.

Many of the most important innovations of the 17th century – the invention of opera, the rise of an autonomous instrumental music, the development of the violin, the incredibly rapid increase in the amount of music requiring a thoroughbass accompaniment, and so on – are identified with Italian composers. The rhetorical style of the new and expressive recitative in opera (soon transferred to instruments in the early 17th-century canzona and sonata) and the 'singing' melodies in the arias of early and mid-Baroque operas, cantatas and oratorios, made different demands on performers from the balanced, classical, polyphonically intricate music of the 16th century. And the Italian manner soon dominated music in many parts of western Europe, especially in the Germanic countries. France, on the other hand, resisted Italian influence

14. *'The Music Party': oil painting by Pieter de Hooch (1663); the instruments are (left–right) bass viol, recorder, cittern and violin (Cleveland Museum of Art)*

(except, paradoxically, for the most influential of all 17th-century French composers, the Italian Lully). The reticent declamation of classical theatre set to music in the *tragédies lyriques* of the second half of the 17th century differed significantly from the more flamboyant Italian operatic style. And French music was shaped by the predilection of musicians and audiences for dance music, with its emphasis on rhythmic detail; for lute music, with its need to elaborate single chords in order to keep the fragile sound alive; and for music that expressed some literary or at least non-musical idea (character-pieces, *hommages* and the like) and which thus placed great importance on subtle changes of sonority and on a rich, decorative surface. Before the Restoration, Britain remained largely untouched by the competing claims of French and Italian musical styles. Even after 1660 – and in the face of royal support for French and Italian music – composers continued to produce works which in their contrapuntal textures and mannered use of expressive dissonance demonstrate continuity with a quite specifically English tradition. This sense of a separate musical identity is less strong in the 18th century, when the latest musical novelties imported from the Continent were much appreciated and foreign virtuosos often enjoyed remarkable successes in London (by far the largest and most cosmopolitan centre in Europe).

Each of the two main styles of the Baroque period presupposed a different technique of playing and singing, a fact that should always be kept in mind when considering particular aspects of performing practice during the period. French music was very different from Italian in its ornamentation, for example, and the principles for applying it. The extent to which the two competing national styles interpenetrated, particularly in 'peripheral' countries like Germany, remains debatable. Few other aspects of performing practice will elicit such diverse or

such heated scholarly opinion as, for example, the question of the propriety of applying French ornaments or French rhythmic alterations to the music of J.S. Bach (*see* NOTES INÉGALES, §3). Paradoxically, the very fact of Germany's being outside these two main performing traditions helps explain why we owe to German musicians (Muffat, Quantz) the most thorough instructions on how to perform in the French and Italian styles: the conventions could not be taken for granted.

The technique of composing an independent bass line, which guided performers of keyboards and plucked string instruments in devising their chordal accompaniment, was something quite new in the early 17th century. The operas, secular monodies and sacred *concerti* by Peri, Caccini, Cavalieri and Viadana, published in the first decade of the 17th century, were the earliest volumes to include a figured or unfigured basso continuo. But the practice has its roots deep in the 16th century, when it was common for harpsichordists, organists and lutenists to double the singers of both secular and sacred music. Performers gradually realized that it was easier to invent a chordal part than to prepare a special score in order to follow the vocal lines exactly. Short scores and so-called 'organ basses' – with a *basso seguente* (a part made up of the lowest sounding line) and some sketchy indication of one or more upper parts – began to appear about 1575, and after 1600 more and more music was published with an obligatory thoroughbass.

A number of writers in the 17th and 18th centuries set down rules for playing from figured bass, among them Banchieri (1605), Agazzari (1607), Werckmeister (1698), Gasparini (1708), Heinichen (1728), Mattheson (1731) and C.P.E. Bach (1753–62). F.T. Arnold and Peter Williams have conveniently summarized the information about continuo playing to be found in these and other treatises of the period, which change slightly from generation to generation and from country to country. Most Baroque writers on thoroughbass stressed grammatical correctness – how to play the right harmony, which notes to double, how best to space chords, and so on – rather than instructing their readers as to how to make an accompaniment stylish and elegant. While it is impossible to formulate general principles that would be valid for the entire Baroque period about the most appropriate sort of accompaniment, it would not be unrealistic to attempt to describe ideal continuo realizations for a particular repertory (e.g. mid-17th-century French opera recitative, or mid-18th-century German solo song) by combing the theorists carefully for passing remarks about what constitutes good style, and by examining the relatively rare examples of written-out realizations. Nevertheless, the answers to questions about how full the accompaniment should be, the extent to which the accompanist might double the solo line (or lines), how imitative or contrapuntal the texture should be, how widely spaced the chords and so on depend not just on the style of a particular repertory, but on circumstances that may change with each performance – such as the instruments available and the skill of the performers.

The instruments used for accompaniments during the Baroque period similarly changed with the generations, the country and the genre. Early 17th-century Italian operas and grand concerted vocal music were inclined to include a wide variety of chordal accompanying

15. 'The Concert': painting by Pietro Longhi (1741)

instruments among the members of the 'orchestra', not only harpsichords and organs, but also lutes, chitarroni, theorbos, harps, lironi and guitars, as well as one or more melodic instruments (bass viol or violone) to strengthen the written bass line; on the other hand, the chitarrone alone (without viol) was a favourite accompanying instrument for solo songs during the same period. Agazzari, in his treatise *Del sonare sopra il basso* (1607), distinguished between foundation and ornamenting instruments, that is, between chordal instruments such as organ and harpsichord, and melody instruments 'which disport themselves and play counterpoints' such as lutes, harps and violins. Thus he seemed to envisage the possibility that melody instruments, too, could play a more or less contrapuntal 'realization' of the harmonies over the written bass. In the 17th and early 18th centuries chamber music continuo practice seems to have been quite varied. There is little reason for assuming an obligatory partnership between a keyboard and a melodic bass-line instrument, and it is likely that Corelli and others who specified 'violone ò cembalo' for the bass parts of their sonatas really did regard either instrument as sufficient (although, for marketing reasons, title-pages tend to emphasize minimum requirements rather than ideal resources). By the mid-18th century, however, C.P.E. Bach was recommending a keyboard instrument and cello as 'the most complete accompaniment', one which could not be criticized.

In the orchestras of the Opéra in Paris in the late 17th and early 18th centuries, keyboard continuo was regarded as essential in vocal numbers and three-part *ritournelles* but took no part in dance music or *symphonies*. It seems likely that this practice was followed by the orchestras for the late 17th-century semi-operas in England. In larger orchestras of the 18th century it was not unusual to find two harpsichords, one (playing with cello and sometimes double bass) to support singers or instrumental soloists, and the other (playing with cello, bassoon and double bass) to support the principal string section of the orchestra; in a smaller orchestra one harpsichord usually sufficed. Even though the keyboard instrument is not always clearly heard while playing continuo, its presence is crucial, for it gives the orchestral sound brightness and a slight cutting edge.

The differences between French and Italian musical styles are apparent from the surviving music, and the differences in manner of performance were described in detail by a number of writers. The techniques and styles of realizing figured basses can be deduced from treatises, surviving realizations, and the nature of the composition to be performed (*see* CONTINUO). The third new aspect of Baroque performing practice – the expressiveness and brilliance in singing or playing melodic lines – is not so easy to reconstruct, since it is impossible to describe objectively qualities of sound and manners of perform-ance. It is unclear, for example, how much dynamic contrast was cultivated in the 16th century, or to what extent Renaissance performers made use of crescendos and diminuendos in shaping the phrases of motets and madrigals. Baroque writers on the voice and vocal technique, such as Caccini in *Le nuove musiche* (1601/2), Christoph Bernhard in *Von der Singe-Kunst oder Maniera* (*c*1649) and Tosi in *Opinioni de' cantori antichi e moderni* (1723), all discussed dynamic nuance in detail, and encouraged singers to practise *messa di voce*, the

gradual swelling and diminishing of a single pitch. Moreover, those instruments incapable of making cres-cendos and diminuendos because of their construction, such as the crumhorn and the wind-capped shawms in general, disappeared from common use in the 17th century, while instruments with only a limited capacity for dynamic nuance, such as the transverse flutes and recorders of the Renaissance, went into a decline. At the same time the brilliant and expressive violin and those instruments that could imitate its effects, such as the cornett, came into a new prominence. Put another way, the instruments which flourished were those that could have a solo (rather than a predominantly consort) role. The less flexible, consort-orientated woodwind (which constituted the *haut* (loud) music so frequently referred to in early 17th-century sources) were displaced by more refined instruments with a solo potential developed (principally by the Hotteterre family) in France and the second half of the 17th century.

An inventory of instruments owned by the Württemberg court in 1718 (including such items as 15 'good Munich violins', seven French basses, oboes at different pitches and a couple of French bassoons) has a separate section listing disused items where we find sets of flutes, rackets, crumhorns and cornetts. All told, it gives a fascinating picture of a radical shift in taste which had rendered whole classes of instruments obsolete. Indeed, one of the principal differences between Renaissance and Baroque performing practice may well have been the greater reliance of earlier musicians on 'terraced dynamics' (abrupt changes of dynamic level from section to section). This practice is often incorrectly described as a new characteristic of Baroque music, though the technique better fits the nature of Renaissance instruments and instrumentation, and especially the habit of scoring festive motets and madrigals for several different self-contained groups – for example, an ensemble of singers, joined by a consort of wind instruments, one of plucked strings, another of bowed instruments and so on. The concept has continuing relevance in the Baroque period through, for example, the concertino–ripieno contrasts fundamental to the concerto grosso style; but it is important to recognize that this is structural – a matter of instrumen-tation rather than performing practice.

The relatively great power and brilliance of the violin, and the bel canto singer (particularly the virtuoso castrato, whose voice combined force with agility), could achieve the new rhetorical affects demanded by composers of the 17th and 18th centuries in a way that earlier instruments could not. The emphasis on dynamic nuance went hand in hand with the attitude to vibrato, which was treated as an ornament rather than as a constituent of good tone production. The amount of vibrato favoured seems to have varied greatly in the course of the 17th and 18th centuries. Mersenne (who praised the violinist Bochan's use of 'certains tremblemens qui ravissent l'esprit') noted that vibrato was less used in 1636 than it had been in the past. At the end of the 17th century, Roger North thought it was a 'late invention' (and eloquently described the ways in which it could be varied for different expressive effects). Some writers (Muffat, Bremner) insisted that vibrato should be suppressed in orchestral music, where it simply interferes with good tuning. But the character of performances in the Baroque period was determined also

16. Chamber music ensemble with harpsichord, cello, two violins, viola and a singer: engraving (1769) by Daniel Nikolaus Chodowiecki

by new techniques of ornamentation and by new attitudes towards notated rhythm.

In their rather careful stipulation of the vocal ornaments required, composers of the early 17th century, including Monteverdi and Caccini, seem to have been reacting against the excesses of late 16th-century virtuosos, whose elaborate *passaggi* sometimes destroyed almost completely the composer's intended effects. Caccini, stressing that the function of ornamentation was to underline the emotional content of what was being sung, allowed some additional embellishment, and even encouraged the development of rubato and dynamic effects. Except perhaps for an occasional decoration at important cadences, complex division can have had no place in recitative (especially in view of its status as heightened speech). While simple strophic arias might well have been embellished profusely by some singers, Monteverdi and his contemporaries often made ornamental figures an integral part of their compositional style, so that additional embellishment can hardly have been tolerated. In *Orfeo* (1607) Monteverdi provided an elaborately decorated version above the basic vocal line for the aria 'Possente spirto' (which also has virtuoso instrumental ritornellos). Here – the point at which Orpheus must summon all his rhetorical skills to persuade Charon to allow him across the Styx – the expressive function of such ornamentation is clear (although, ironically, Charon is lulled to sleep rather than moved by Orpheus's

eloquence). As the ratio of arias to recitative scenes in Italian operas increased, so the conventions of embellishment changed. By the 18th century, with the firm establishment of the da capo aria as the chief musical 'number' in *opera seria*, singers were clearly expected to ornament the repetition of the initial section of each composition, and they were allowed, as well, to add brief cadenzas to the final cadences of each section, and possibly even to embellish modestly the initial statement of the first section as well as the second. Tosi described the practice, and several arias survive with embellishments written in by 18th-century musicians.

The practice of embellishing Italian instrumental music in the Baroque period involved a gradual evolution from a flexible convention rooted in earlier practice to a more rigidly defined set of options, where in some cases ornamentation was required and in others it was possible but not necessary. Performers were more or less free to add a variety of graces (short, clearly defined ornaments that apply to single notes) in both fast and slow movements, whether or not the composer had indicated them. Thus trills can always be added to cadences, and the music permits the addition of appoggiaturas, mordents, slides, turns and other changing or passing notes (*see* ORNAMENTS and IMPROVISATION). In some instances, notably in slow movements notated only with a structural outline of the melody, it was obligatory for the performer to add more elaborate ornamental figuration. Here one can see that, over the course of the 17th century, division or diminution techniques rooted in Renaissance practice (but still fostered, particularly in England) gave way to a more sweeping improvisatory style of florid embellishment. The most celebrated written-out exemplar in this style is the 1710 Roger edition of Corelli's op.5 violin sonatas, which has graces for the adagios of part 1 supposedly supplied by the composer. Other examples of florid embellishment for Corelli sonatas survive, most of them in manuscript. Telemann's *Sonate metodiche* (1728, 1732) were advertised as being 'very useful to those who wish to apply themselves to cantabile ornamentation', but the most systematic treatment of the subject comes in Quantz's *Versuch* (1752), where several chapters are devoted to the decoration of simple intervals and then to the manner of treating Adagio movements.

French musicians used a greater number of signs than Italians to indicate a more varied repertory of graces; moreover, they put much less emphasis on the performer's ability to add melodic figuration. Since they normally wrote out instrumental slow movements more completely than Italians, and did not make use of da capo forms in their operas, the principal opportunities for *passaggi* were lacking in French music. Composers such as François Couperin (ii), who prepared a detailed table of graces for his important treatise, *L'art de toucher le clavecin* (1716), advised the performer to pay close attention to the signs indicated in the printed music and to follow the composer's instructions closely – remarks symptomatic of the greater control French composers wished to exercise over the circumstances of performance, and, indeed, of the greater importance of surface detail and refinement of sonority in French musical style in general. Quantz made the point that whereas performers wishing to embellish pieces in the Italian style needed to understand harmony and the principles of composition, no such knowledge was needed for the ornamentation of French music.

Moreover, French musicians were more precise in their application of the principles of rhythmic freedom than musicians in other countries. Performers everywhere and in various historical periods have modified the rhythms notated by composers, and flexibility of rhythm is certainly desirable in Baroque music. The Italian Girolamo Frescobaldi, for example, wrote a series of enlightening prefaces to his volumes of keyboard music in the early 17th century which make clear, among other things, the importance of *tempo rubato* in the performance of his compositions (significantly, he commented that the tempo should be as free in his toccatas as in the madrigals of his day). But 17th- and 18th-century French writers on music (Bacilly, Loulié, J.-M. Hotteterre, François Couperin (ii) and many others) described certain rhythmic modifications that came to be closely associated with the music of their countrymen and which were applied to the written notes in particular situations. Thus, some notes written in equal values were intended to be played unequally. Moderately fast quavers moving stepwise, for example, might be grouped in pairs and each pair played unequally, normally with the first note lengthened (either a lot or a little), but sometimes with the first note shortened and the second lengthened.

When and how to apply the conventions governing rhythmic alteration – especially for notated DOTTED RHYTHMS – in the Baroque era has been one of the most fiercely debated issues in recent years. In some compositions (for example, many French overtures) it may be that a dotted quaver followed by a semiquaver, or even a dotted crotchet followed by a quaver, ought to be performed with the short notes sounding even shorter than written. In some compositions the dotted figures are smoothed out and turned into triplets; and in others equal quavers are dotted, or quaver upbeats are played as semiquavers in order to maintain the pattern of rhythms evidently intended by a composer in a particular movement. Much French music (and indeed much Baroque music of all countries) was derived from dance forms and rhythms, and in performance the underlying rhythmic patterns of the dance must be brought out. All of these slight modifications of the written rhythms – NOTES INÉGALES, over-dotting, under-dotting and dance rhythms – give some of the music of the 17th and 18th centuries, especially that composed in France, its lilting, easy grace and its sophisticated refinement of surface detail.

Composers in the Baroque period, unlike those in earlier times, often used a word or phrase to indicate the approximate tempo at which they wished their compositions to be played: *lento, adagio pesante, allegro ma non tanto*, and the like. These are inevitably vague, and they often suggest the mood as much as the speed of a composition. Moreover, they were often used inconsistently by composers or defined in contradictory ways by different writers on music from the period. Georg Muffat (*Ausserlesener Instrumental-Music*, 1701) warned that the Italians played movements marked Adagio, Grave and Largo much more slowly than his compatriots, whereas they took those marked Allegro, Vivace and Presto 'incomparably faster'. Yet these terms offer the most precise surviving information about the tempo of Baroque music. Various writers, such as Brossard and Grassineau in their dictionaries of musical terms and Leopold Mozart in his treatise on violin playing, defined these descriptive terms in prose. In addition, Quantz in his treatise on flute playing included a systematic table of groups of tempos, with an approximation of absolute speeds measured against the human pulse (Table 1), and he gave even more precise descriptions of the tempos proper to various dances.

Modern performers have concerned themselves not only with styles of playing Baroque music but also with the revival of precise sonorities. More often than not,

TABLE 1: Tempos indicated by Quantz

(after Donington, *Interpretation of Early Music*, 1974 edn., p.391)
   The approximate speeds are given for music in common time; the metronome readings should be doubled for music in *alla breve* time.

1. Allegro assai (including allegro molto, presto, etc)   crotchet = 160

2. Allegro (including poco allegro, vivace, etc)   crotchet = 120

3. Allegretto (including allegro ma non tanto, non troppo, non presto, moderato, etc)   crotchet = 80

4. Adagio cantabile (including cantabile, arioso, pomposo, maestoso, larghetto, soave, dolce, poco andante, affettuoso, alla siciliana, adagio spiritoso, etc)   crotchet = 40

5. Adagio assai (including adagio pesante, lento, largo assai mesto, grave, etc)   crotchet = 20

increased knowledge about the details of Baroque instruments and performing practices has brought with it an increased sensitivity to the sound of older music and a heightened awareness of the connection between musical style and the history of technology. Thus 20th-century instrument makers copied ever more closely the details of surviving instruments of the 17th and 18th centuries in the realization that the so-called 'improvements' of modern technology (often intended to eliminate mechanical disadvantages) may destroy some essential quality of sound. Moreover, modern builders (especially of keyboard instruments) have come to appreciate the vast differences between, say, a 16th-century Italian harpsichord and its 18th-century French counterpart, and have passed on to players and listeners their conviction that the best instrument for a particular piece is the sort for which it was originally intended. The concept of a 'period instrument' is rather different for the violin family from what it is for keyboard and wind instruments where, by and large, the Baroque versions differ so much from their modern equivalents that they are essentially distinct instruments. (No amount of alteration could make an 18th-century flute or trumpet function as a modern instrument.) Violinists, however, still prize 17th- and 18th-century instruments above all others – and many internationally famous violinists perform Romantic and 20th-century repertory on instruments made in the Baroque era but extensively modified since (through resetting the neck, strengthening the bass-bar and substituting a thicker soundpost). One of the paradoxes of the modern world is that while Stradivari is acknowledged as the greatest violin maker of all time, every surviving Stradivari instrument has been altered ('improved') to conform to 19th-century notations of how a violin should sound. Those ('period-instrument') players who feel that Baroque and Classical repertory is best served by instruments set up as they were when the music was composed use either newly made replicas or older instruments restored to their pre-19th-century condition. And, of course, they use bows which, as far as possible, match those in use at the time the music they are playing was composed. Related to this concern to reproduce as exactly as possible the original timbre of older music is the persuasive case scholars have made that older conventions of performance should be observed even when they run counter to modern tastes. Thus, writers such as Winton Dean have argued that castrato roles in Baroque opera should be sung by women (a common 18th-century solution when no castratos were available) rather than by tenors or baritones in transposed versions which destroy the sonorities conceived by the composer. (Assigning castrato roles to countertenors is the most common modern solution to the problem, though it is virtually without historical precedent.)

The increasing use of old instruments or of accurate modern reproductions has in many cases required performers to relearn techniques by studying instruction books published during the 17th and 18th centuries. Thus keyboard players have studied and adopted the fingerings included in such sources as English virginal books or François Couperin's *L'art de toucher le clavecin* (1716; *see* FINGERING, §I, 1). For wind players, the study of Baroque tonguing conventions provides similar insights into articulation and phrasing. Musicians who play on violins (that is to say, violins set up as they would have

been in the 17th or 18th century: *see* VIOLIN, §I, 4) have had to learn an entirely new technique, particularly in the use of pre-Tourte bows. While some useful information can be gleaned from the instrumental tutors published before 1750, it is not until the end of the Baroque era that we find treatises written by truly accomplished violinists (Geminiani, Herrando, Leopold Mozart, L'abbé le fils and Tartini) addressed to players of more than amateur aspirations. Moreover, violinists must take into account the differences between the more rhythmic, dance-orientated playing technique of the French (described in detail by Georg Muffat in the preface to *Florilegium secundum*, 1698) and the freer singing tone and more varied bowings of the Italian musicians of the period.

Once they have acquired the proper instruments and learnt to play them, modern performers of Baroque music must then decide at what pitch they should play and in which temperament. An international standard pitch was not established until the 20th century. Pitch seems to have varied fairly widely from place to place; and even within one city various pitches were used for different ensembles. Praetorius who (confusingly) reversed what even in 1619 appears to have been the usual application of the terms 'Chor Thon' and 'Cammer Thon', noted the use of other regional variations on these two basic pitch standards. In 18th-century Germany, chamber pitch (Cammerton) was a tone lower than that to which church organs were tuned (Chorton); but a low chamber pitch a minor 3rd beneath Chorton was also used (*see* PITCH, §I, 2). Some modern performers of Baroque chamber music have adopted a lower pitch standard, normalized for convenience a semitone below the modern level (i.e. at $a' = 415$). It is, however, fast becoming recognized that such factors as vocal ranges or the kind of sound quality wanted from string instruments make it appropriate to regard pitch – like so many other aspects of performance – as something which needs to be considered in relation to particular repertories. Similarly, investigation of the way instruments were tuned in earlier times (in various kinds of mean-tone temperament or in other more elastic tunings for keyboard instruments, for example) has shown that old techniques were not only practical but also capable of adding nuances unknown in performance of more recent music. Mean-tone tuning, favoured in the early Baroque period, produces a spectrum in which the most-used chords (broadly speaking, the pivotal chords in keys with fewest accidentals) have beautifully pure 3rds while those in more remote tonalities vibrate with dissonance (or, in the case of the 'wolf' chord, are unusable). The 'circulating' temperaments which became standard in the 18th century (and which are implied by the term 'well tempered') retain something of this chiaroscuro, while allowing modulation through any tonal area.

The modern orchestra had its origins in the lavish ensembles assembled for late 16th- and early 17th-century court festivities, such as the Florentine *intermedi*, the French *ballet de cour* and the English masque (Monteverdi's *Orfeo* orchestra is essentially like this – a spectacularly varied ensemble assembled for a specific court festivity). It became regularized as a relatively fixed ensemble of instruments with strings as its core in the mid-17th century, with Lully's Petits Violons du Roi and the opera orchestras of Venice. The size and disposition of 17th-century orchestras varied enormously. On the one hand, there are reports of Corelli directing ensembles which would be very large even by modern standards, while on the other we know that he performed concerti grossi in the 1690s with an ensemble of just nine players.

The practice of regularly including a 16'-pitch string instrument on the bass line seems to have originated in Italy in the late 17th century; such an instrument had no place in 17th-century French or English orchestras. A number of these organizations achieved great fame. Lully's orchestral discipline set new standards everywhere in western Europe, and his elaborate instrumentation encouraged wind players to develop new and mechanically improved instruments; the oboe, and the Baroque flute and recorder, probably developed as a direct result of the need for more brilliant and more reliable wind timbres which could combine well with strings in French orchestras. And the orchestra at the court of Mannheim in the 18th century astounded listeners with its refined playing and its control of a variety of effects: diminuendo, crescendo and so on. But these organizations differed in many particulars from the modern orchestra, not only in the types of instruments used and their playing styles, but also in the number of musicians employed, the way they were arranged, and the kinds of balance between strings, wind and continuo instruments they aimed to achieve. The wind parts, for example, were often doubled in 18th-century orchestras, producing a substantial counter-force to the relatively few string players.

As with orchestral music, much choral repertory was likely to have been performed with quite small forces. In the early 1980s Joshua Rifkin initiated a debate (which still continues) when he suggested that Bach may have used very small instrumental and vocal ensembles with, typically, a single voice to each part for performances of his cantatas and Passion settings in Leipzig. Rifkin argued his case on the basis of surviving performing parts and on Bach's own 'Entwurff einer wohlbestallten Kirchen Music' of 1730 in which he described the numbers of musicians he needed to fulful his obligations to the various Leipzig churches. There is evidence that the situation in Leipzig may have been paralleled in many other German centres.

6. 1750–1800.

(i) Continuity and change. Performing practices of the late 18th century followed on with little change from those of the earlier part of the century; however, changes in musical style, experimentation in the construction of musical instruments, and new performing situations and aesthetics all brought changes in performance. It is clear that performing styles continued to undergo gradual change during the course of the 19th and 20th centuries: by the end of the 19th century musicians were playing on instruments vastly different from those of Mozart's time and designed to be part of a new musical aesthetic; the advent of recordings has allowed us to hear the changes that took place during the 20th century, a period in which many performers believed that they continued to follow traditions reaching back to the late 18th. Most performers and audiences from the late 18th century onwards (at least until the mid-20th) were accustomed to performing and hearing most music, whether new or old, in a common style – that suited to the instruments and aesthetic of their own time. What is more, instruments, and in some cases musical perceptions, were considered to have improved with each generation. Thus Mozart reorchestrated Handel's *Messiah*; Beethoven and Brahms wrote cadenzas in their own styles for Mozart's Piano Concerto in D minor

K466 (Beethoven's cadenza is much longer and has far wider-ranging modulations than any of Mozart's, and Brahms's has chains of orchestrally conceived tremolo accompaniments unlike anything used by Mozart); Wagner and others 'corrected' Beethoven's symphonies; and late 19th-century singers sang music by Mozart and Verdi very much alike.

Although there had been some interest from the 1950s and even earlier in how the music of Mozart might have been performed, a more general awareness that the study of performing practice could be relevant to music of the late 18th century came about only in the 1970s, as an extension of work on music of the Baroque and earlier periods. The corresponding entry in *The New Grove Dictionary of Music and Musicians* (1980) devoted little space to music after 1750, invoking the idea of continuity of tradition from the mid-18th century to the present, but *The New Grove Dictionary of Musical Instruments* (1984) added an extended discussion on this period. By the end of the 20th century much detailed work had been carried out on performing practices of music after 1750.

(ii) Performer and composer. The relationship between performer and composer remained in the late 18th century much the same as that of the age that preceded it. In a concerto performance the performer was often also the composer, and the work was tailored to his or her talents. A manuscript might be written in a way that only the composer-performer could readily interpret. Leaving aside the cadenzas and *Eingänge* to be added (*see* CADENZA, EINGANG and IMPROVISATION, §II, 4(i)), Mozart, for example, did not fully write out every detail in the solo part of some of his piano concertos but left some passages of figuration in shorthand (e.g. the third movement of K482 and the last movement of K491, in which long notes provide an outline to be realized as passage-work; and K537, where the left-hand part is missing in a number of bars), notated few dynamic nuances, provided figures to indicate that the soloist was to realize a continuo accompaniment in tutti passages, and occasionally left a passage sparely ornamented (as in the Andante of K451, for which Mozart composed an ornamented version at the request of his sister). Composers expected that other professional performers would ornament soloistic works such as concertos or arias as appropriate and in their own individual style: Dittersdorf could comment that as a boy he had once ornamented a piece 'quite in the Huber style' (that is, in a style recognizable as that of Karl Huber, principal violinist of the church orchestra in which Dittersdorf also played). Individualistic interpretation, yet within the bounds of accepted style, was also appreciated, certainly by the end of the century: the pianist Marie Bigot was praised at the beginning of the 19th century by both Haydn and Beethoven, Beethoven remarking 'That is not exactly the character which I wanted to give this piece, but go right on. If it is not wholly mine, it is something better'.

But performers (and audiences) otherwise expected a composer to write with someone particular in mind, providing music that showed off his or her strengths and downplayed weaknesses. Thus Mozart wrote stately old-fashioned arias in *Idomeneo* for the elderly Anton Raaff and remarked of the composition of *Die Entführung aus dem Serail* that he 'had sacrificed something to the flexible throat of Mlle Cavallieri'. Composers were likewise acutely aware of the capabilities of the instruments for which they wrote: Haydn lamented that Marianne von Genzinger, for whom he was composing some sonatas, did not own a piano by Schantz, his favourite maker, 'because everything can be better expressed' on such an instrument; he further wrote, 'I know I ought to have composed this sonata for the capabilities of your instrument, but I find this difficult because I am no longer used to writing this way' (1790).

In published works, intended for sale to performers not necessarily in direct contact with the composer, notation had to be complete enough to explain the composer's intentions. Thus it tended to become more detailed towards the end of the century, but still left up to the player many details of articulation, dynamic and rhythmic nuance, etc. Burney, for example, commented on hearing the Besozzi brothers (oboe and bassoon) play:

[Their compositions] are in a peculiar manner adapted to display the powers of the performers; but it is difficult to describe their style of playing. Their compositions when printed, give but an imperfect idea of it. So much expression! Such delicacy! Such a perfect acquiescence and agreement together, that many of the passages seem heart-felt sighs, breathed through the same reed. No brilliancy of execution is aimed at, all are notes of meaning. . . . each *forte*, *piano*, *crescendo*, *diminuendo*, and *appoggiatura*, is observed with a minute exactness, which could be attained only by such a long residence and study together (*BurneyFI*, 2/1773).

(iii) Instruments. During the second half of the 18th century the piano replaced the harpsichord, although not everywhere at once. The key-bed of the late 18th-century piano was shallower, the string tension less and the action lighter than those of a modern instrument, all combining to produce a delicate sound and to enable the pianist to play quickly and lightly. Two distinct types of action were in use: the *Prellmechanik* or 'Viennese', with an extremely light touch, favoured in Germany and Austria, and the English, favoured in England and France (*see* PIANOFORTE, §I, 5). Mozart's works from the 1770s were written for a five-octave, wooden-framed piano with small, hard, leather-covered hammers and Viennese action. His own concert instrument (Anton Walter, *c*1780, now in the Mozart Geburthaus, Salzburg) originally had hand stops to raise the dampers; the knee levers were added later. Detailed study of this instrument has revealed that it may have been altered considerably after Mozart's death to conform to the style in vogue around 1800 (Latcham, E1997): thus this instrument, long held as a standard for the performance of Mozart's music, may not provide us with the information we would like to have concerning Mozart's style of playing. But the changes in timbre produced with either hand stops or knee levers were expressive options rather than an integral part of the sound as on a modern piano. The light action is fundamental to the concept of a piece such as the *perpetuum mobile* Presto of the finale of Mozart's concerto K271 (1777); this action also supports the flexibility of dynamics and delicate touch called for by Mozart's many small-scale articulation marks. Beethoven, in the Sonata op.13 (*Pathétique*; 1797–8), used the limitations of the instrument to create a tension that is an essential part of the rhetoric of that work: the gradual crescendo from *p* to *ff* combined with an outward expansion to almost the highest and lowest notes of the instrument seems to push the limits of the instrument and of its musical expression, an effect entirely absent on a modern grand piano with its larger range, sturdier frame

and even sound (ex.1). He continued to use instruments of the Viennese type throughout his life. By the mid-1790s Haydn was composing for an instrument with English action; the instrument had a range of five and a half octaves and was heavier than the Viennese piano, with a more sonorous sound and damping that was purposely less effective (Sonata in C, HXVI:50). It was the legato sound concept of the English instruments that came to dominate in the 19th and 20th centuries. According to Czerny, Beethoven described Mozart as having a 'fine but choppy [*zerhacktes*] way of playing, no *ligato*'; this comment must be understood in the context of the instrument in use and of changes in taste.

Woodwind instruments were constructed throughout most of this period, as in the Baroque era, with the idea that each individual note and thus also each scale had a characteristic sound. The oboe of the period, while it tended to have a narrower bore and smaller tone holes than earlier types, still had only two keys; chromatic notes were still produced by cross-fingerings, which had a more veiled sound. It was a softer instrument than the Baroque oboe and played more easily in the high register; the note *f'''* is used in Mozart's Quartet for oboe and strings K370/368*b* (1777) and began to appear in fingering charts in the 1790s. The variety of wind colourings was increased in the late 18th century with the rise of the clarinet and associated instruments such as the basset-horn. Many clarinettists played with the reed against the upper lip rather than the modern position: the reed-above position allowed the player to make rapid leaps and play especially high, while the reed-below position gave the softest tone. The flute began to acquire additional keys late in the century. Tromlitz, writing in 1791, still advocated the use of an instrument with two keys, for E♭ and D♯ (just as Quantz had done), a register (tuning device in the foot joint) and a graduated screw-cork; additional keys could be used to make the first octave more even and trills better in tune, suggesting that players and makers were beginning to move towards a more even sound by the last decade of the century, if not earlier. The added keys, according to Tromlitz, were useful in slow movements but not in fast ones; their use for improved facility was a later development. Both flutes and oboes could be provided with

Ex.1 Beethoven: Sonata op.13, 1st movt, bars 299–310

several middle joints of varying lengths to accommodate variations in pitch standards in different regions (*see* PITCH).

Tromlitz makes it clear that singing remained the model for instrumental playing, and indicated that players were to use varied patterns of articulation based on tonguing syllables. He favoured finger vibrato (*flattement*), although others were using breath vibrato (*see* VIBRATO). For brass instruments the ability to play the complete scale, so that the instrument could be used melodically, was gaining importance. The art of hand-stopping on the horn, developed around 1750, reached a high level, and by the end of the century various experimental trumpets, for example the keyed trumpet for which Haydn wrote, had appeared.

The late 18th century was a period of transition for string instruments. Greater volume and brilliance began to be required of these instruments in order to fill the larger halls now needed for new audiences. This was achieved in a variety of ways: greater tension was produced through use of higher pitch, the neck began to be tilted back, the strings became longer for more resonance, the bass-bar and soundpost were made more substantial. Gut strings remained the most common, but metal-wound strings were increasingly used on the lower strings of violin, viola and cello towards the end of the century. Treatises of the period recommend a variety of ways of holding the violin, varying from at the breast to the chin-braced grip that would be later universally adopted (L'abbé *le fils*); the latter allowed greater freedom of movement in the left hand for easier shifting, and freer vibrato. The cello was placed between the knees with the weight supported on the calves or supported on a footstool or small peg. Leopold Mozart's influential treatise (*Versuch einer gründlichen Violinschule*, 1756) recommended avoiding unnecessary finger activity, although Galeazzi (*Elementi teorico pratici di musica*, 1791–6) advocated the use of higher positions for expressive purposes, providing violin G-string fingerings up to the 8th position. Open strings were generally avoided when stopped notes were possible, and sequences were played with matching fingerings. Vibrato was generally used sparingly, as an expressive ornament, although Geminiani (*The Art of Playing on the Violin*, 1751) appears to have recommended a continuous vibrato in the modern fashion.

The construction of bows was the subject of much experimentation, with various versions of straight and concave bows being developed. The use of a greater amount of hair and of a ferrule to hold it flat also helped the player achieve greater volume and brilliance. Such bows produced greater volume and a larger dynamic range, and led to the development of new styles of articulation. Convex bows such as that employed by Leopold Mozart commonly produced an articulated, non-legato stroke, with dynamic nuances on long notes for variety of expression. Transitional and Tourte-style bows had a larger repertory of bow strokes, a more immediate attack, and a more sonorous cantabile style. But all these kinds of bow, of old and new design, were used together in the same orchestras, and uniformity of bowing was rare. The variety of instruments and bows in use makes the establishment of a suitable combination for a particular work a difficult matter, and in cases where the composer's preference is not known, the particular relationship that may have existed between the instrument used and the music itself remains unknown. (For further discussion of bows and bowing techniques *see* BOW).

(iv) Performances. All kinds of performances took place, and performers and ensembles were praised for their nuanced dynamics, their ensemble and their good taste. Extensive rehearsal, insisted on by Haydn, and also employed by Mozart to reach his musical ends, (see, for example, his account of the preparations for *Idomeneo*), seems to have been uncommon. Performance traditions varied from place to place: it is clear that we must be careful about general comments. Sources of such information include: documentary material (see, for example, Edge and Eisen, both in 'Performing Mozart's Music', E1991–2); manuscript music (Edge, in Zaslaw, E1996); newspaper reports (McVeigh, E1993); letters (Mozart, Haydn); diaries (Burney, Rosenbaum, Zinzendorf) and autobiographies (Dittersdorf, Dülon, Grétry) of musicians and audience members; works of literature (Fanny Burney); iconography; dictionaries (Rousseau, Koch); and the commentaries of travellers (Burney, Schubart). Burney, for example, provided many accounts of performances heard in the various places he visited in the 1770s, with comments on the performance of church music in various places (noting, for example, that the serpent was an especially favoured accompaniment in France); descriptions of opera houses he visited, with accounts of the sort of music performed, the behaviour of the audience and the technique and talents of the singers; and accounts of private academies and public concerts, noting the size and disposition of the performing forces, and commenting on the use of unusual instruments and on performing techniques, all from the perspective of an educated Englishman. Burney also noted that the French continued to maintain a pronounced independent style of performance and taste in spite of the encroachment of the Italian style.

A keyboard instrument continued to be used in the orchestra in many places to play the continuo line. The instrument was often a piano rather than a harpsichord by the 1780s, and the keyboard player played unobtrusively, doubling the principal parts in the right hand or, in louder passages, playing chords. Mozart played continuo in the tuttis of his piano concertos and according to one report was known to have conducted a symphony from the keyboard. Nannerl Mozart accompanied symphonies on the harpsichord in Salzburg in 1778. By the end of the century, however, as direction of the orchestra passed from the keyboard player to the principal violinist, the keyboard instrument disappeared or else the seat at the keyboard became a position of honour. Haydn 'presided at the keyboard' during performances of his London symphonies in that city, and the honorary function of the instrument was well enough established for Haydn to make it the subject of wit, bringing the instrument forward suddenly as a soloist in the coda of the finale of Symphony no.98.

Orchestra size varied from place to place and according to the performance venue, but there were two general styles of orchestration: the French, followed also in some Austrian and German cities, and the Italian. In the French tradition there was a stronger middle part, and thus more violas; in the Italian, a strong treble and a treble–bass polarity. In many Italian orchestras, and also in Salzburg (see table of orchestra sizes in Zaslaw, E1989, pp.458–9), there were more basses than cellos (*see* ORCHESTRA).

A subject of much discussion has been the use of articulation marks by composers, especially Mozart. In his case it seems most likely that whether the symbol appeared as a dot or a stroke or something in between was in most cases a result of the speed with which he wrote down the music (Riggs, E1997). Clear dots appear under slurs as an indication of *portato*, but otherwise there seems to be no attempt to distinguish between dots and strokes, and indeed it seems clear from examining copies of Mozart's music that his contemporaries did not recognize a distinction. Many theorists from the second half of the 18th century recognized only a single type of articulation marking, which was, according to C.P.E. Bach, to be executed 'according to the length of the note . . . whether the tempo is fast or slow, whether the dynamic is *forte* or *piano*'. Others recognized two signs, but there was no agreement as to their intended articulation. No specific style of performance is implied by either dots or strokes in Mozart's music, except in the case of long strokes in certain works with organ (for example, the church sonata K144) where they appear to indicate that the organ line is to be played unison rather than realized (Eisen, E1991). Rather, interpretation is to be determined by context, according to an understanding of the meaning of the passage. Theorists recognized that different styles of articulation were needed also for notes not provided with articulation marks. Thus according to J.F. Reichardt (*Ueber die Pflichten des Ripien-Violinisten*, 1776): 'the bowstroke in an Adagio is very different from that in an Allegro, and contrasts mainly in that the former remains more on the string than in the Allegro'.

See also ARTICULATION AND PHRASING; ARTICULATION MARKS; IMPROVISATION, §II, 4 and INSTRUMENTATION AND ORCHESTRATION, §3.

7. THE 19TH CENTURY.   It had become increasingly apparent by the end of the 20th century that the idea of continuity of tradition even from the 19th century into the 20th was problematic. In a period of such experimentation and change as the 19th century, exactly whose traditions were continued? And how are they related to what a composer might have heard or envisaged? What especially distinguishes this period is the vast amount of source material: owing to advances in technology and the rise of literacy, there are literally thousands of eyewitness accounts of performers and performances. In part because of this sometimes bewildering variety of material, but also because tradition was long considered eminently satisfactory as a guide, many of even the central works of the modern repertory have not yet appeared in scholarly editions.

(i) Sources.   As in any other period of music history, the materials used by musicians themselves are primary evidence of their practices. Manuscript parts and conducting scores from the 19th century exist in abundance, although many were lost in fires or wars or just thrown away to make room for the new. A complete set of manuscript material associated with the origin of a work is usually as good a record of its early performance history as of its compositional genesis. Players liked to sign and date their parts; alterations to the musical text bespeak the decisions made while preparing the work for its première, the compromises reached between composers and performers, and the lessons learnt by composers from the players. The number of parts alone tells a great deal about the size of the performing forces. Original manuscript parts often resolve dilemmas resulting from printer's errors or other interruptions in the transmission of the composer's intention to the printed page. Assessment of such materials – without which there would be neither a Paris *Don Carlos* nor a viable *Benvenuto Cellini* – is one of the most intriguing tasks of modern musicology. Standards in such musicological investigation have been set by new complete editions of the works of Rossini, Verdi and Wagner.

Published music too needs careful study. Chopin, for example, published works simultaneously in France, Germany and England, resulting in as many as half a dozen authentic sources for a single work. Editors must separate the intentional discrepancies from the unintentional, and determine which variants are so substantial as to merit publication of separate versions, considering at the same time that some elements may have been considered variable by the composer: there may be no one 'correct' version.

Other useful material includes opera production books, the manuscript notebooks in which singers kept track of their cadenzas (e.g. those of Laure Cinti-Damoreau) and the corrected or amplified published editions of composers' works prepared for their pupils, as in the case of Jane Stirling's copies of Chopin. Iconographical sources, including lithographs and photographs, depict costumes, sets, and the disposition of the singers at an opera, the number and disposition of orchestral players, methods of holding instruments, and performance spaces and situations. Method books, many intended for the training of professional performers, offer information on instruments, sound production, performing techniques and interpretation (a useful bibliography of these appears in Brown and Sadie, A1989). Treatises on orchestration (Kastner, 1837; Berlioz, F1843; Gevaert, 1863 and 1885; Prout, 1876, 1897–9) discuss instruments, their tone qualities and their use, orchestral placement and what the writer felt could be improved; those on conducting (Berlioz, 1856; Wagner, F1869) discuss techniques and philosophies of performance. Berlioz insisted on the conductor's responsibility to follow the composer's intent, while later treatises, such as that of Wagner, favour schemes for modernizing works to suit the large symphony orchestra.

The writings of composers (Berlioz, Spohr, Wagner), performers (William Thomas Parke, Gustave-Hippolyte Roger) and bystanders (Chorley) provide much important material. Berlioz in his *Mémoires*, for example, described musical conditions in Paris, and also recounted in vivid style the problems encountered in the course of his tours: the logistics of raising orchestras and hiring halls, playing standards, rehearsal practices, and practices of substitution when instruments such as the english horn were unavailable. Accounts in periodicals provide information about dates of performance, the progress of tours and performance repertory. The reports of critics are often revealing. Composer-critics (E.T.A. Hoffmann, Weber, Schumann, Berlioz, Liszt, Wagner) in particular were sensitive to details of performance, sometimes even discussing a particular artist's style of ornamentation. In any event, newspaper journalism is more accurate as to who actually played than the printed programmes, and it is our chief source for understanding how performances were received by the public. The RIPM project (Répertoire International de la Presse Musicale) indexes 19th-century periodicals, providing scholars with access to much useful material.

Edison's tinfoil phonograph (1877) inaugurated the era of sound reproduction, offering an important new type of source for the study of performing practice. The early technology worked most successfully with solo instrumentalists, who could get close to the recording apparatus: Joachim and Sarasate both left revealing recorded performances. Joachim, for example, played in a style using little vibrato. Singers too were successfully recorded, and many of their earliest recordings document 19th-century styles. Maurel and Tamagno, the first Othello and Iago (Verdi, *Otello*), made recordings in the early years of the 20th century, as did Adelina Patti, a singer well known to Verdi, who praised her 'purest style of singing'. The last castrato of the Cappella Sistina, Alessandro Moreschi, also left recordings, our only aural documents of this voice quality of such importance to Roman Catholic church music and to 18th-century opera. Although he was the last of a dying tradition, his voice is like nothing else, reaching into the high range with great power and clarity. But even more astonishing to modern ears is his singing style, which is truly that of his age, making heavy use of portamento and dramatic sobbing effects. The seriousness of intent of the modern discipline of performing practice still finds such obvious emotion a little embarrassing.

(ii) The orchestra. Central to the musical life of the 19th century was the rise of the philharmonic society and the symphony orchestras. The Paris Société des Concerts du Conservatoire was founded in 1828, inspired by curiosity about Beethoven's music; the Philharmonic Symphony Society of New York and the Vienna Philharmonic both trace their origin to 1842. The Leipzig Gewandhaus Orchestra flourished under Mendelssohn from 1835. Concerts sponsored by the Philharmonic Society of London can be traced to 1813, as can those of the Vienna Gesellschaft der Musikfreunde. Characteristic of these orchestras was a clear breach with continuo practice, public concert series supported by subscription and leadership by a true conductor. The orchestra of the 19th century was a youthful institution, not yet constrained by precedents. Spohr experimented in the 1810s with his *Taktirstäbchen* ('directing baton'), which replaced the violin bow, and along with Weber gave rise to modern conducting and to discussions of the proper role of the composer-conductor. By contrast, Spontini and others conducted with a baton held in the centre, and all manner of stamping of the floor and tapping on candle racks was considered by many to be the only successful way to coordinate a performance (although these practices, it must be added, were deplored by many).

Orchestral seating arrangements were varied. The members of the Gewandhaus Orchestra stood to perform, but other orchestras were seated. Proper balance between chorus and orchestra was achieved by Berlioz and others by placing the orchestra behind the chorus on raised tiers. For the popular monster concert the conductor was to be found in the centre of his forces, surrounded by assistant conductors and mirrors. From the 1860s Verdi devoted considerable attention to the seating arrangement of his orchestras, insisting that the double basses be placed together to improve ensemble and that the strings surround the wind instruments to create a homogeneous sound (*see* ORCHESTRA).

Four bassoons had been common in many orchestras since the 18th century, but the practice of doubling the wind section gained momentum as the century progressed. The addition of piccolo, english horn, contrabassoon and other instruments vastly enhanced the symphonic palette. An equally sweeping change in the sound of orchestras resulted from new mechanisms for the traditional instruments. These allowed instrumentalists to master the vivid melodic figurations and the new spectrum of keys that progressive composers required. But the increase in the number of keys on woodwind instruments was only part of the story of the performing practice of those instruments: there were many experiments in key configuration, in bore proportions and sound-producing mechanisms: some clarinettists (especially in England and Italy) were still playing with the reed against the upper lip in the 1830s, and for all the woodwinds there were several competing concepts of sound, which led to different styles of instrument in different places and sometimes even to the use of radically different instruments within the same orchestra (*see* FLUTE §4(iii)(d)). This lack of uniformity kept orchestras individual and colourful in sound.

From the same period come piston and rotary valves for brass instruments (*see* VALVE (i)). By the end of the 1820s piston-valves were common in Paris, and by mid-century rotary valves of increasing technical perfection were widely used. But, as with woodwinds, local tastes varied. There was considerable resistance to the valve horn, as the characteristic inequalities of tone of the natural horn were considered essential to the nature of the instrument. Although a valve horn class was established under Meifred at the Paris Conservatoire in 1833, it was discontinued on his retirement in 1864 and not reformed until 1896. Brahms's Trio op.40 (1865) was conceived with the natural horn in mind. Schumann, on the other hand, worked to develop an idiomatic technique for the valve horn. The bass of the brass section was particularly variable as early valves were not effective with the wide bore of the large instruments: the serpent was employed by Berlioz and Mendelssohn, and the ophicleide remained in use at the Paris Opéra until 1874 and in English orchestras until the end of the century. Different styles of instrument developed in different places: Wieprecht's Bass-Tuba in F (1835) in Germany; the tuba in 8′ C, with its large four-octave range, in France (works written with this instrument in mind pose difficulties for players using other instruments); the bombardon in Italy; and Červený's large-bore instrument in eastern Europe and Russia (from the early 1880s).

The conversion of string instruments into the high-powered models now almost universally in use resulted in a dramatic change in string sonority. It is thought that fewer than 30 or so good violins escaped remodelling for volume, a process that lengthened necks and fingerboards, heightened bridges and permitted the increased tension of metal strings. The widespread adoption of the Tourte bow almost completed the modernization of the violin: gut E and A strings remained in use into the 20th century.

The philharmonic societies were adventurous in their choice of repertory, at least in the first half of the century (music by Beethoven held a special fascination for many) but by the 1850s works by popular favourites such as Weber and Mendelssohn were programmed season after season. Old masters began to dominate concert programmes just as they do today. Enthusiasm for novelty slackened as the decades passed, and responsibility for promotion of new music largely shifted to more progressive organizations.

(iii) The piano.   Like other instruments, the piano developed along somewhat different lines in different places. The simple and light action of the enlarged Viennese piano of Graf and Stein was favoured in parts of Europe for most of the century, though the London instruments of Broadwood and Clementi had their admirers. By the 1820s metal framing had been added to the piano to allow it to support the greater string tension required for greater volume, at the expense, it was held, of some degree of nuance. The repetition action patented by Sébastien Erard in 1821 made the heavier-tensioned instruments workable. Combined with the greater mass of felt-covered hammers (from the 1840s) and carefully devised striking points (in which Erard was also a pioneer), the resultant tone was more sustained, richer in overtones and more uniform throughout the compass of the instrument. But the widespread assumption that by the 1860s the piano, with its one-piece cast-iron frame, had reached a final plateau of development is demonstrably false. The tone of the 1892 Steinway concert grand in the Smithsonian Institution, used by Paderewski for an American tour, projects a velvety mellowness quite unlike the steely, more brilliant tone of comparable instruments of the late 20th century.

(iv) Performance and interpretation.   During the 19th century, advances in technology allowed music, and musicians, to travel further afield. Travelling virtuosos required modern instruments and skilled instrumentalists when they arrived to perform, and often stimulated progress in cities and towns formerly content with indifferent standards. As early as the 1830s a successful opera at La Scala would be required within a season or two in London, Paris, Vienna and St Petersburg (the commercial ramifications of this were quickly recognized, by the house of Ricordi in particular). Wagner's music reached Boston within a few months. Musical compositions, in short, strayed further and further from home, and the increasingly complex annotations in published music reflect these developments (*see also* ORNAMENTS, §9).

Even so, individual markings were not always interpreted in the same way. Spohr, for example, used vertical strokes over notes to indicate, in different contexts, legato bowing and short, sharp *martelé* strokes. Many composers employed both dots and strokes, but the notation did not always have the same meaning. The French generally followed J.L. Adam (*Méthode du piano du Conservatoire*, 1802) in using the marks to indicate the length of notes: he gave the strokes as the shortest, the dots as longer and dots under slurs as the longest. But Germans emphasized the degree of accent: Fröhlich (*Kontrabass-Schule*, 1829) considered that strokes indicated the more powerful staccato, the dots a more gentle style. Baillot (*L'art du violon: nouvelle méthode*, F1834) used the dot for *martelé*, where the bow stays in contact with the string, and the wedge for light bouncing strokes, whereas Ferdinand David (*Violinschule*, 1863) used the marks in the opposite way (Brown, E1993). (For further discussion of bowing in this period, *see* BOW, §II, 3).

The existence of different pitch standards in different places as well as a general rising trend brought demands for an international standard (*see* PITCH, §I). A standard of $a' = 435$ (the *diapason normal*) was established in Paris in 1859. It was soon adopted in Britain, and more generally at an international conference in Vienna in 1885. But although some Italian opera houses adopted the new standard in the late 1860s, Verdi found it necessary to inquire in 1871 whether the wind in the orchestra and the stage band at La Scala would play at a uniform pitch level, and when on tour in the final decade of the century the clarinettist Richard Mühlfeld sent a tuning-fork ahead so that the piano might be tuned to his preferred pitch; his instruments suggest that this was about $a' = 440$, lower than was usual in many places by that time.

The rise of the modern conservatory considerably elevated standards of performance. Important conservatories existed in Paris (1794, reorganized 1816), Prague (1811), Vienna (1817), Leipzig (1843) and St Petersburg (1862). Graduates had a systematic training and attained a new technical security, prompting them to extend the technical possibilities of their instruments. The Paris Conservatoire was especially influential through the many method books produced by its instructors. As the century progressed, conservatory teachers seem to have done much to establish what has become the standard repertory.

Amateur music-making was similar to that in the preceding century. Properly bred young ladies studied the piano and harp; aristocratic dilettantes still played the flute. As mechanization made the piano cheaper to produce, it found its way into the parlour of every tasteful family. Music was more popular than ever, and a proper view of the performance history of, say, Meyerbeer's *Robert le diable* will not exclude the piano fantasies and the promenade quadrilles based on it, just as the study of performing practice in general must also deal with such durable traditions as the performance of Handel's *Messiah* by a large massed chorus, with soloists producing a sound capable of filling the large halls in which the performances took place.

The musical text was often treated with greater freedom in the 19th century than was acceptable in the 20th. Liszt, for example, noted after his retirement from concert-giving that

I then frequently performed . . . the works of Beethoven, Weber and Hummel, and I confess to my shame that in order to compel the bravos of an audience . . . I had no scruples against changing their tempos and intentions; I even went so far as insolently to add to them a host of passages and cadenzas.

One can therefore understand Berlioz's surprise on the occasion when Liszt performed Beethoven's Hammerklavier Sonata with 'not a note . . . left out, not one added'. In spite of his penitence, the 'tradition' passed on by Liszt in his later years to numerous pupils like the young Rosenthal was one in which editorial licence was taken for granted. In private and public performances solo works and sometimes even concertos were preceded by improvised (or prepared) preludes designed to set the mood. Sometimes works were joined together with similar interludes.

The invention of the metronome gave composers another means of documenting their wishes. Beethoven, in his initial enthusiasm, wrote down metronome marks for all the symphonies and quartets to op.95 (as well as for the Piano Sonata op.106 and a few slighter works). He placed great faith in the metronome, yet new markings devised as substitutes for those he had lost were often significantly different: Beethoven's marks represent how he imagined the work in his head at the time. Whether these marks are performable or not has been the subject of much discussion. Schumann provided metronome markings in most major genres except the songs (those for the piano music were revised after his death by his wife and may indicate her tempos rather than his). The belief that Robert Schumann's metronome was faulty was not shared by the composer. But how is a marking such as the 'Nicht schnell ♩ = 100', given in the first edition (1850) of the third of his *Romanzen* op.94 for oboe and piano, to be used? This work, like many others, progresses through a detailed series of tempo modifications: *ritard*, *in tempo*, *zurückhaltend*, and so on, and the metronome marking can indicate only a starting- point. Later in the century Brahms and Wagner registered their strong reservations about metronome markings, Brahms noting that 'As far at least as my experience goes, everybody has, sooner or later, withdrawn his metronome marks'. Brahms seems to have considered his painstaking written designations as the best indications of tempo, and contemporary timings and his own metronome markings provide clues about what the speed might have been. He considered tempo to be fluid, and that *accelerando* and *ritardando* were essential in achieving the desired expression. (For further discussion of the implications of metronome markings for performing practice *see* METRONOME (i).)

It is not clear how much freedom to vary the pulse was sanctioned by 19th-century performers. Czerny considered rubato to be an important means of expression, recognizing 11 types of subtle rhythmic deviation (all determined by the emotion of the passage) within the framework of constant tempo. As used by Chopin in his early works, 'rubato' probably referred to the practice of allowing the melody to fall behind the regular pulse provided by the bass. According to Liszt, rubato was a matter of taste: 'a metronomical performance is certainly tiresome and nonsensical: time and rhythm must be adapted to and identified with the melody, the harmony, the accent and poetry'.

Practices of ornamentation were varied. Italian opera was embellished well into the century and a number of examples of the practice are preserved, including those for arias by Rossini, Donizetti, Bellini and others prepared by the soprano Laure Cinti-Damoreau (*Méthode*, 1849). Both Rossini and Verdi, however, disapproved of the excessive interpolation of embellishments into their music. At the end of the 20th century the question of adding embellishment to Schubert's music was the subject of discussion. Johann Michael Vogl, who often sang with Schubert, left ornamented versions of many songs. Yet the musical style with which Schubert can be more generally associated seems to have used little added embellishment, even though contemporaries such as Hummel allowed some. With composers such as Hummel, whose *Anweisung* (1828) advocates principal-note starts for trills, the trill became less an intensifier of harmony and more an element of texture. Beginning with the generation of Mendelssohn and Schumann, most trills are to be played starting on the main note and unterminated unless specified otherwise. However, Fétis and Moscheles (*Méthode des méthodes*, 1840) continued to advocate an upper-note start.

Attempts in the final decades of the 20th century to produce performances of 19th-century music in historically informed styles revealed excellent reasons for doing so and for continuing to investigate and experiment with the repertories and performance styles of the century: a metronome marking close to Beethoven's own points up, for example, the multi-level metric complexity of a movement such as the Scherzo of the Third Symphony (Orchestre Révolutionnaire et Romantique, cond. John Eliot Gardiner, DG 445 944–2, 1994); the characteristic sound of the ophicleide creates a colourful bass, admirably suited to Mendelssohn's luminous orchestration (*Midsummer Night's Dream* overture, Orchestra of the Age of Enlightenment, cond. Charles Mackerras, Virgin VC 90725–2, 1988); the four Erard harps in the *Valse* of Berlioz's *Symphonie fantastique*, placed in Roger Norrington's recording (London Classical Players, EMI CDC 7 49541 2, 1989) at the front of the orchestra as Berlioz had recommended, stunningly dominate the texture. Many such popular works had been, by the end of the 20th century, recorded in several different historically informed interpretations.

8. THE 20TH CENTURY. Music historians are able to study the performing practice of the 20th century quite differently from that of earlier centuries because of the development of sound recording. For the first time in history, the performances themselves were preserved, rather than just documentary evidence about them. This had a profound effect on performance during the 20th century. The dissemination of recordings meant that musicians could hear themselves, and could influence each other more directly than in earlier periods. The performing practice of one generation was also preserved for study by later generations, giving them unprecedented insight into the development of their own performing practice.

A survey of recordings over the 20th century reveals a number of clear trends: the growing use of continuous vibrato, the decreasing use of portamento, a trend towards a narrower range of tempos within movements, a trend towards more accurate and literal interpretation of note values, a growing insistence on rhythmic clarity, a trend towards greater homogeneity of ensemble (in tone quality, phrasing and rhythm) and a general rise in standards of accuracy and discipline. There was also a tendency towards increasing volume, and greater force and intensity of expression, which was associated with changes in instruments during the century.

The brilliant-toned metal flute, first adopted by the French, largely replaced the softer-toned wooden flute (except in period performance) by the second half of the century; the fuller-toned German bassoon largely replaced the quieter, more subtle French bassoon; violinists increasingly adopted the metal E string from the 1930s onwards, and more powerful bow-holds came to predominate over the traditional 19th-century grips used by Joachim's generation. Brass instruments tended during the century to become wider in bore, producing a broader, more massive tone. The powerful concert Steinway piano came to predominate in the second half of the century; earlier pianists had used a variety of makes of piano, many of them lighter in touch and more delicate in tone.

The increasing power of instruments was associated with a general increase in the use of vibrato to intensify tone. In the early years of the century, vibrato was used only to a very limited extent by wind players, and most did not use it at all. Many string players adhered to Joachim's advice: 'A violinist whose taste is refined and healthy will always recognize the steady tone as the ruling one'. Ysaÿe encouraged a trend towards a more liberal (though delicate) use of vibrato, but it was Kreisler, closely followed by Heifetz, who initiated the continuous use of vibrato on the violin, which was echoed in viola and cello playing. The use of vibrato by woodwind players similarly increased during the century. It was led by the French, particularly pupils of the flautist Paul Taffanel, and it had spread, on both the flute and the oboe, to most of Europe and the USA by the 1940s. The spread of vibrato was less general on the bassoon, and only sporadic among clarinettists.

Singing followed the general trend towards greater power, together with wider, more continuous vibrato. Though vocal styles in the early years of the century varied greatly, much of the singing of the period was more delicate, and more restrained in its vibrato, than later in the century.

While power and the use of vibrato generally increased, the use of portamento decreased. Until the 1930s, the habitual use of emphatic portamento was common among string players. The trend towards more sparing and subtle portamento was encouraged by a number of prominent players and teachers, including Flesch on the violin and Casals on the cello. This involved not only changes in shifting technique and choice of fingerings, but also a fundamental change in attitude to portamento as an ornament in a melodic line. Portamento which occurred simply as a convenient way of moving from one position to another gradually became unacceptable. Among singers there was a similar trend from frequent and prominent portamento towards a preference for lines in which portamento was reserved for points of particular emphasis or softening.

There were major changes during the century in approaches to rhythm, with a general tendency towards the more literal interpretation of note values. In the early part of the century, musicians often 'over-dotted' dotted rhythms (see above, §5) and lightened and hurried groups of short notes. This freedom on the small scale was paralleled by freedom on the larger scale: tempo was often flexible within movements, tending to accelerate in loud and vigorous passages, and to slow down in quieter and more gentle ones, so that a second subject in a movement of a sonata or symphony would often be given a quite different tempo from the first subject. Such freedom, both in detail and on the large scale, gradually lessened. The hurrying of short notes and the over-dotting of dotted rhythms came to be regarded as undisciplined and unclear, and acceleration came to denote lack of control. That is not to say that all freedom was lost, only that it was more restrained than earlier in the century.

This development was associated with a trend towards greater clarity and rhythmic precision, which was linked in turn with discipline and rehearsal. Most early 20th-century orchestras were rhythmically imprecise by later standards, partly because many of them were under-rehearsed and irregular in their membership (the sending of deputies to rehearsals in Paris and London, for example, was deplored by Stravinsky and Henry Wood). But the trend towards modern precision was not simply a matter of more rehearsal time. Session musicians in the late 20th century routinely achieved rhythmic precision with little

rehearsal, whereas regular and thoroughly rehearsed ensembles of the early 20th century, such as Stokowski's Philadelphia Orchestra, and the Léner and Bohemian quartets, played with a looser approach to rhythmic detail. The difference was a matter not just of competence but also of expectation and style. Even solo pianists of the early 20th century were, compared to later pianists, informal in their approach to rhythm. The arpeggiating of chords, and styles of rubato which often led to lack of synchronization between melody and accompaniment, were practised, to a varying extent, by pianists of many different schools and nationalities.

Such freedom was not restricted to pianists. Solo instrumentalists and singers in the early 20th century were often freer in relation to accompanists than musicians of later generations. This kind of freedom, between solo and accompaniment, and between the two hands of a pianist, was clearly linked to earlier styles of *tempo rubato* described in the 18th and 19th centuries. The trend later in the 20th century was towards a stricter approach to rhythmic coordination.

Alongside these general trends, various forces were at work during the century, including the development of recording and its industry. At the beginning of the century, all musicians played either to themselves or to an audience which heard the performance only once. By the end of the century the principal means of hearing classical music was by recordings, which could be repeated many times. This development had a subtle but profound influence on performing practice. At the beginning of the century there were substantial contrasts between performers in different countries and of different schools, but as the century wore on a growing uniformity of style and approach could be discerned, as the availability of recordings (and the general development of international communication and transport) enabled musicians to be influenced by each other. At the beginning of the century, minor inaccuracies during a performance were of little importance; the overriding aim was to convey the thrust of the piece of music to an audience which might rarely hear it again. By the end of the century, recordings had accustomed both musicians and audiences to expect a very high standard of competence and accuracy, an expectation enhanced by the development of sophisticated editing techniques. Recordings also enabled musicians to listen to themselves and to learn exactly what they sounded like. The late 20th-century musician was therefore selfconscious to a degree which had been impossible before the invention of recording. This too contributed to the general increase in accuracy, and to the gradual refinement of the habits associated with a less selfconscious age, such as the routine use of portamento and the rhythmic looseness of traditional rubato. The abandonment of old habits, however, was largely restricted to performers of 'classical' music. Rubato independent of the beat continued to be an essential component of the new jazz and popular performing styles. As the split between classical and popular music widened, classical performance became more strictly controlled and more concerned with precision of detail and faithfulness to the text, leaving some of the traditional freedoms to the popular genres. It is as if classical performers felt obliged to demonstrate that they were serious by distancing their styles from those of popular performers.

A new influence on performance in the second half of the century was the growth of interest in the reconstruction of historical performing practice. A few musicians (notably the Dolmetsch family) had pioneered the use of period instruments since the late 19th century, and the performance of 'old music' had always been carried on by small numbers of specialists. But from the 1960s onwards there was an enormous growth in the performance of Renaissance and medieval music by groups performing on period instruments (originals or reproductions) and attempting period vocal styles. The use of period instruments not only extended the performed repertory back to earlier and earlier music, but also provided a new approach to the familiar repertory of the 18th and 19th centuries. For further discussion see EARLY MUSIC.

The end of the century saw contrasted approaches to performance co-existing side by side. In new music, late 20th century composers ranged from those who wished to exert strict control over every detail of performance to those who wished to control almost nothing (see ALEATORY), or for whom conventional concepts of performance had ceased to be meaningful. As the period movement reached early 20th-century repertory, such as the music of Elgar, a new contrast became apparent: between period-style Elgar as performed in the late 20th century, and Elgar's own recorded performances from the 1920s. Knowledge of historical recordings began to reveal, for the first time, the extent to which attempts to reconstruct earlier performing styles take place within the conventions of the performer's own time.

BIBLIOGRAPHY

A General. B Medieval (i) Sacred (ii) Secular. C Renaissance. D Baroque. E Classical. F Romantic. G 20th century.

A: GENERAL

A. Beyschlag: *Die Ornamentik der Musik* (Leipzig, 1908/R)
A. Schering: 'Vom musikalischen Vortrage', *JbMP 1930*, 9–23
R. Haas: *Aufführungspraxis der Musik* (Potsdam, 1931/R)
A. Schering: *Aufführungspraxis alter Musik* (Leipzig, 1931)
E.T. Ferand: *Die Improvisation in der Musik* (Zürich, 1938)
W. Apel: *The Notation of Polyphonic Music 900–1600* (Cambridge, MA, 1942, 5/1961)
F. Dorian: *The History of Music in Performance: the Art of Musical Interpretation from the Renaissance to our Day* (New York, 1942/R)
M.F. Bukofzer: 'The Beginnings of Choral Polyphony', *Studies in Medieval & Renaissance Music* (New York, 1950), 176–86
H.-P. Schmitz: *Prinzipien der Aufführungspraxis alter Musik* (Berlin, 1950)
J.M. Barbour: *Tuning and Temperament: a Historical Study* (East Lansing, MI, 1951/R, 2/1953)
C. Sachs: *Rhythm and Tempo* (New York, 1953)
T. Dart: *The Interpretation of Music* (London, 1954, 4/1967/R)
H. Keller: *Phrasierung und Artikulation: ein Beitrag zu einer Sprachlehre der Musik* (Kassel, 1955; Eng. trans., 1965)
D.J. Grout: 'On Historical Authenticity in the Performance of Old Music', *Essays on Music in Honor of Archibald Thompson Davison* (Cambridge, MA, 1957), 341–7
S. Corbin: *L'église à la conquête de sa musique* (Paris, 1960), 150–89
R. Donington: *The Interpretation of Early Music* (London, 1963, 4/1989)
G. Frotscher: *Aufführungspraxis alter Musik* (Wilhelmshaven, 1963, 8/1997; Eng. trans., 1981)
A.J. Ellis and A. Mendel: *Studies in the History of Musical Pitch* (Amsterdam, 1969/R)
M. Vinquist and N. Zaslaw: 'Bibliography of Performance Practice', *CMc*, no.8 (1969) [whole issue]; no.10 (1970), 144–72; pubd separately as *Performance Practice: a Bibliography* (New York, 1971); suppl., *CMc*, no.12 (1971), 129–49; no.15 (1973), 126–40
J. Westrup: *Musical Interpretation* (London, 1971)
J.A. Bank: *Tactus, Tempo and Notation in Mensural Music from the 13th to the 17th Century* (Amsterdam, 1972)

D. Barnett: *The Performance of Music: a Study in Terms of the Pianoforte* (New York, 1972)
C. MacClintock, ed.: *Readings in the History of Music in Performance* (Bloomington, IN, 1979)
L. Dreyfus: 'Early Music Defended against its Devotees: A Theory of Historical Performance in the Twentieth Century', *MQ* xlix (1983) 297–322
N. Harmoncount: *Der musikalische Dialog* (Munchen and Kassell, 1984); trans. as *The Musical Dialogue* (London, 1989)
D. Leech-Wilkinson, R. Taruskin, N. Temperley: 'The Limits of Authenticity: a Discussion', *EMMc* xii (York, 1984), 3–25
H. Haskell: *The Early Music Revival: a History* (London and New York, 1988)
R. Jackson: *Performance Practice, Medieval to Contemporary: a Bibliographical Guide* (New York, 1988)
N. Kenyon: ; ed.*Authenticity and Early Music* (Oxford and New York, 1988)
H.M. Brown and S. Sadie, eds.. *Performance Practice: Music after 1600* (London, 1989)
P. Kivy: *Authenticities: Philosophical Reflections on Musical Performance* (Ithaca and London, 1985)
C. Lawson and R. Stowell: *The Historical Performance of Music: an Introduction* (Cambridge, 1999)

B: MEDIEVAL

(i) Sacred

L. Lambillotte: *Antiphonaire de saint Grégoire: fac-similé du manuscrit 359 de Saint-Gall* (Brussels, 1851, 2/1867)
L. Lambillotte: *Esthétique, théorie et pratique du chant grégorien* (Paris, 1855)
A. Dechevrens: *Du rythme dans l'hymnographie latine* (Paris, 1895)
G.L. Houdard: *Le rythme du chant dit grégorien d'après la notation neumatique* (Paris, 1898)
P. Wagner: *Einführung in die gregorianischen Melodien*, ii (Fribourg, 1905, 2/1912/R)
J. Jeannin: *Etudes sur le rythme grégorien* (Lyons, 1926)
E. Jammers: *Der gregorianische Rhythmus: antiphonale Studien* (Strasbourg, 1937, 2/1981)
S.J.P. Van Dijk: 'St Bernard and the *Instituta patrum* of St Gall', *MD*, iv (1950), 99–109
E.A. Bowles: 'Were Musical Instruments Used in the Liturgical Service during the Middle Ages?', *GSJ*, x (1957), 40–56
H. Hucke: 'Zum Problem des Rhythmus im gregorianischen Gesang', *IMSCR VII: Cologne 1958*, 141–2
W. Krüger: *Die authentische Klangform des primitiven Organum* (Kassel, 1958)
J.W.A. Vollaerts: *Rhythmic Proportions in Early Medieval Ecclesiastical Chant* (Leiden, 1958, 2/1960)
H. Anglès: 'Die Mehrstimmigkeit des Calixtinus von Compostela und seine Rhythmik', *Festschrift Heinrich Besseler*, ed. E. Klemm (Leipzig, 1961), 91–100
E.A. Bowles: 'The Organ in the Late Medieval Liturgical Service', *RBM*, xvi (1962), 13–29
E. Jammers: *Musik in Byzanz, im päpstlichen Rom und im Frankenreich: der Choral als Musik der Textaussprache* (Heidelberg, 1962)
F. Müller-Heuser: *Vox Humana: ein Beitrag zur Untersuchung der Stimmästhetik des Mittelalters* (Regensburg, 1963, rev. 2/1997 by D. Gutknecht and K.W. Niemöller)
S.J.P. Van Dijk: 'Gregory the Great, Founder of the Urban "Schola cantorum"', *Ephemerides liturgicae*, lxxvii (1963), 335–56
R.G. Weakland: 'The Performance of Ambrosian Chant in the 12th Century', *Aspects of Medieval and Renaissance Music: a Birthday Offering to Gustave Reese*, ed. J. LaRue and others (New York, 1966/R), 856–66
H. Tischler: 'How were Notre Dame Clausulae Performed?', *ML*, l (1969), 273–7
E. Rohloff: *De Quellenhandschriften zum Musiktraktat des Johannes de Grocheio* (Leipzig, 1972)
J. Dyer: 'Singing with Proper Refinement from *De modo bene cantandi* (1474) by Conrad von Zabern', *EMc*, vi (1978), 207–27
J. McKinnon: 'Representations of the Mass in Medieval and Renaissance Art', *JAMS*, xxxi (1978), 21–52
T. Bailey, ed.: *Commemoratio brevis de tonis et psalmis modulandis: Introduction, Critical Edition, Translation* (Ottawa, 1979)
E. Roesner: 'The Performance of Parisian Organum', *EMc*, vii (1979), 174–89
J. Dyer: 'A Thirteenth-Century Choirmaster: the *Scientia artis musicae* of Elias Salomon', *MQ*, lxvi (1980), 83–111

H. Schmid, ed.: *Musica et Scolica enchiriadis: una cum aliquibus tractatulis adiunctis* (Munich, 1981)

E. Nowacki: 'The Gregorian Office Antiphons and the Comparative Method', *JM*, iv (1985–6), 243–75

C. Page: 'The Performance of Ars Antiqua Motets', *EMc*, xvi (1988), 147–64

D. Hiley: 'Chant', *Performance Practice: Music before 1600*, ed. H.M. Brown and S. Sadie (London, 1989), 37–54

C. Wright: *Music and Ceremony at Notre Dame of Paris, 500–1550* (Cambridge, 1989)

A.W. Robertson: 'The Mass of Guillaume de Machaut in the Cathedral of Reims', *Plainsong in the Age of Polyphony*, ed. T.F. Kelly (Cambridge, 1992), 100–39

C. Page: 'Johannes de Grocheio on Secular Music: a Corrected Text and a New Translation', *PMM*, ii (1993), 17–41

R. Bowers: 'To Chorus from Quartet: the Performing Resource for English Church Polyphony, c.1390–1559', *English Choral Practice c.1400–c.1650: a Memorial Volume to Peter le Huray*, ed. J. Morehen (Cambridge, 1995), 1–47

J.W. McKinnon: 'Lector Chant versus Schola Chant: a Question of Historical Plausibility', *Laborare fratres in unum: Festschrift Lászó Dobszay*, ed. J. Szendrei and D. Hiley (Hildesheim, 1995), 201–11

C.V. Palisca, ed.: *Musica enchiriadis and Scolica enchiriadis* (New Haven, CT, 1995) [Eng. trans. by R. Erickson, incl. introduction and notes]

C. Page: 'An English Motet of the 14th Century in Performance: Two Contemporary Images', *EMc*, xxv (1997), 7–32

(ii) Secular

P. Aubry: *Trouvères et troubadours* (Paris, 1909, 2/1910; Eng. trans., 1914)

J.B. Beck: *La musique des troubadours* (Paris, 1910/R)

S.M. Cserba, ed.: *Hieronymus de Moravia O.P.: Tractatus de musica* (Regensburg, 1935)

L. Hibberd: 'On "Instrumental Style" in Early Melody', *MQ*, xxxii (1946), 107–30

G. Reaney: 'Voices and Instruments in the Music of Guillaume de Machaut', *RBM*, x (1956), 3–17, 93–104

E.E. Lowinsky: 'Early Scores in Manuscript', *JAMS*, xiii (1960), 126–73

F.Ll. Harrison: 'Tradition and Innovation in Instrumental Usage 1100–1450', *Aspects of Medieval and Renaissance Music: a Birthday Offering to Gustave Reese*, ed. J. LaRue and others (New York, 1966/R), 319–35

G. Reaney: 'The Performance of Medieval Music', ibid., 704–22

J. Smits van Waesberghe: 'Singen und Dirigieren der mehrstimmigen Musik im Mittelalter: was Miniaturen uns hierüber lehren', *Mélanges offerts à René Crozet*, ed. P. Gallais and Y.-J. Riou (Poitiers, 1966), 1345–54

I. Bent: 'A 12th-Century Extemporizing Technique', *MT*, cxi (1970), 33–7

H. Van der Werf: *The Chansons of the Troubadours and Trouvèrs* (Utrecht, 1972)

L. Gushee: 'Two Central Places: Paris and the French Court in the Early Fourteenth Century', *GfMKB: Berlin 1974*, 135–51

K. Polk: 'Ensemble Performance in Dufay's Time', *Dufay Conference: Brooklyn, NY, 1974*, 61–75

G. Foster: *The Iconology of Musical Instruments and Musical Performance in Thirteenth-Century French Manuscript Illumination* (diss., CUNY, 1977)

C. Page: 'Machaut's "Pupil" Deschamps on the Performance of Music', *EMc*, v (1977), 84–91

D. Hoffmann-Axthelm: 'Instrumentensymbolik und Aufführungspraxis: zum Verhältnis von Symbolik und Realität in der mittelalterlichen Musikanschauung', *Basler Jb für historische Musikpraxis*, iv (1980), 9–90

A. von Ramm: 'Style in Early Music Singing', *EMc*, viii (1980), 17–20

B. Thornton: 'Vokale und Gesangtechnik: das Stimmideal der aquitanischen Polyphonie', *Basler Jb für historische Musikpraxis*, iv (1980), 133–50

Studies in the Performance of Late Mediaeval Music: New York 1981 [incl. H.M. Brown: 'The Trecento Harp', 35–73; W. Arlt: 'The "Reconstruction" of Instrumental Music: the Interpretation of the Earliest Practical Sources', 75–100; D. Fallows: 'Specific Information on the Ensembles for Composed Polyphony, 1400–1474', 161–92]

J. McKinnon: 'Iconography', *Musicology in the 1980s: Boston 1981*, 79–93

J. Nadas: 'The Structure of the MS Panciatichi 26 and the Transmission of Trecento Polyphony', *JAMS*, xxxiv (1981), 393–427

K.-J. Sachs: 'Arten improvisierter Mehrstimmigkeit nach Lehrtexten des 14. bis 16. Jahrhunderts', *Basler Jb für historische Musikpraxis*, vii (1983), 166–83

C. Page: *Voices and Instruments of the Middle Ages: Instrumental Practice and Songs in France, 1100–1300* (Berkeley, 1986)

J. Stevens: *Words and Music in the Middle Ages: Song, Narrative, Dance and Drama, 1050–1350* (Cambridge, 1986)

N. Kenyon, ed.: *Authenticity and Early Music* (Oxford, 1988)

S. Huot: 'Voices and Instruments in Medieval French Secular Music: on the Use of Literary Texts as Evidence for Performance Practice', *MD*, xliii (1989), 63–113

C. Page: 'Polyphony before 1400', *Performance Practice: Music before 1600*, ed. H.M. Brown and S. Sadie (London, 1989), 79–106

L. Welker: 'Some Aspects of the Notation and Performance of German Song around 1400', *EMc*, xviii (1990), 235–46

J. Caldwell: 'Plainsong and Polyphony 1250–1550', *Plainsong in the Age of Polyphony*, ed. T.F. Kelly (Cambridge, 1992), 6–31

T. Knighton and D. Fallows, eds.: *Companion to Medieval and Renaissance Music* (London, 1992)

D. Leech-Wilkinson: '*Le voir dit* and *La Messe de Nostre Dame*: Aspects of Genre and Style in the Late Works of Machaut', *PMM*, ii (1993), 43–73

T.J. McGee: 'Singing without Text', *Performance Practice Review*, vi (1993), 1–32

M.L. Switten: *Music and Poetry in the Middle Ages: a Guide to Research on French Occitan Song, 1100–1400* (New York, 1995)

C. Page: 'Listening to the Trouvères', *EMc*, xxv (1997), 638–59

T.J. McGee: *The Sound of Medieval Song: Ornamentation and Vocal Style according to the Treatises* (Oxford, 1998)

C: RENAISSANCE

R. Molitor: *Die nachtridentinische Choral-Reform zu Rom* (Leipzig, 1901–2/R)

M. Kuhn: *Die Verzierungs-Kunst in der Gesangs-Musik des 16.–17. Jahrhunderts (1535–1650)* (Leipzig, 1902/R)

H. Besseler: *Die Musik des Mittelalters und der Renaissance* (Potsdam, 1931/R)

M. Bukofzer: 'On the Performance of Renaissance Music', *Music Teachers National Association: Proceedings*, xxxvi (1941), 225–35

A. Mendel: 'Pitch in the 16th and Early 17th Centuries', *MQ*, xxxiv (1948), 28–45, 199–221, 336–57, 575–93

I. Horsley: 'Improvised Embellishment in the Performance of Renaissance Polyphonic Music', *JAMS*, iv (1951), 3–19

E.T. Ferand: 'Improvised Vocal Counterpoint in the Late Renaissance and Early Baroque', *AnnM*, iv (1956), 129–74

C. Jacobs: *La interpretación de la música española del siglo XVI para instrumentos de teclado* (Madrid, 1958)

C. Dahlhaus: 'Zur Theorie des Tactus im 16. Jahrhundert', *AMw*, xvii (1960), 22–39

H.K. Andrews: 'Transposition of Byrd's Vocal Polyphony', *ML*, xliii (1962), 25–37

M.B. Collins: 'The Performance of Sesquialtera and Hemiolia in the 16th Century', *JAMS*, xvii (1964), 5–28

Mother Thomas More [M. Berry]: 'The Performance of Plainsong in the Later Middle Ages and the 16th Century', *PRMA*, xcii (1965–6), 121–34

E.T. Ferand: 'Didactic Embellishment Literature in the Late Renaissance: a Survey of Sources', *Aspects of Medieval and Renaissance Music: a Birthday Offering to Gustave Reese*, ed. J. LaRue and others (New York, 1966/R), 154–72

D. Wulstan: 'The Problem of Pitch in Sixteenth-Century English Vocal Polyphony', *PRMA*, xciii (1966–7), 97–112

C. Jacobs: 'Spanish Renaissance Discussion of Musica ficta', *Proceedings of the American Philosophical Society*, cxii (1968), 277–98

H.M. Brown: 'Accidentals and Ornamentation in Sixteenth-Century Intabulations of Josquin's Motets', *Josquin des Prez: New York 1971*, 475–522

H.M. Brown: 'On the Performance of Fifteenth-Century Chansons', *EMc*, i (1973), 3–10

H.M. Brown: *Sixteenth-Century Instrumentation: the Music for the Florentine Intermedii*, MSD, xxx (1973)

D. Harrán: 'New Light on the Question of Text Underlay Prior to Zarlino', *AcM*, xlv (1973), 24–56

R.B. Lynn: *Renaissance Organ Music for the Proper of the Mass in Continental Sources* (diss., Indiana U., 1973)

H.M. Brown: 'Embellishment in Early Sixteenth-Century Italian Intabulations', *PRMA*, c (1973–4), 49–83

P. Gossett: 'The Mensural System and the "Choralis Constantinus"', *Studies in Renaissance and Baroque Music in Honor of Arthur Mendel*, ed. R.L. Marshall (Kassel and Hackensack, NJ, 1974), 71–107

M. Lindley: 'Early 16th-Century Keyboard Temperaments', *MD*, xxviii (1974), 129–51

W.F. Prizer: 'Performance Practices in the Frottola', *EMc*, iii (1975), 227–35

H.M. Brown: *Embellishing Sixteenth-Century Music* (London, 1976)

H.M. Brown: 'The Performance of Fifteenth-Century Chansons: Problems of Instrumentation and Ornamentation', *Current Thought in Musicology*, ed. J.W. Grubbs and L. Perkins (Austin, 1976)

B. Dickey: 'Untersuchungen zur historischen Auffassung des Vibratos auf Blasinstrumenten', *Basler Jb für historische Musikpraxis*, ii (1978), 77–142

L. Litterick: 'Performing Franco Netherlandish Secular Music of the Late Fifteenth Century: Texted and Untexted Parts in the Sources', *EMc*, viii (1980), 474–85

D. Bonge: 'Gaffurius on Pulse and Tempo: a Reinterpretation', *MD*, xxxvi (1982), 167–74

E. Schroeder: 'The Stroke Comes Full Circle: Φ and ₵ in Writings on Music, ca. 1450–1540', *MD*, xxxvi (1982), 119–48

A.M.B. Berger: 'The Relationship of Perfect and Imperfect Time in Italian Theory of the Renaissance', *EMH*, v (1985), 1–28

R. Stewart: 'Voice Types in Josquin's Music', *TVNM*, xxxv (1985), 97–189

H.M. Brown: 'Notes (and Transposing Notes) on the Transverse Flute in the Early Sixteenth Century', *JAMIS*, xii (1986), 5–39

D. Harrán: *Word-Tone Relations in Musical Thought from Antiquity to the Seventeenth Century* (Neuhausen-Stuttgart, 1986)

T.J. McGee: 'Instruments and the Faenza Codex', *EMc*, xiv (1986), 480–90

R. Greenlee: '*Dispositione di voce*: Passage to Florid Singing', *EMc*, xv (1987), 47–55

R. Sherr: 'Performance Practice in the Papal Chapel during the 16th Century', *EMc*, xv (1987), 453–62

J. Rosselli: 'The Castrati as a Professional Group and a Social Phenomenon, 1550–1850', *AcM*, lx (1988), 143–79

H.M. Brown: 'Bossinensis, Willaert and Verdelot: Pitch and the Conventions of Transcribing Music for Lute and Voice in Italy in the Early Sixteenth Century', *RdM*, lxxv (1989), 25–46

W. Elders: 'The Performance of Cantus firmi in Josquin's Masses based on Secular Monophonic Song', *EMc*, xvii (1989), 330–41

R.C. Wegman: 'Concerning Tempo in the English Polyphonic Mass, c.1420–70', *AcM*, lxi (1989), 40–65

S. Bonta: 'The Use of Instruments in Sacred Music in Italy 1560–1700', *EMc*, xviii (1990), 519–535

G. Houle: '*Doulce memoire*: a Study of Performance Practices* (Bloomington, IN, 1990)

L. Korrick: 'Instrumental Music in the Early 16th-Century Mass: New Evidence', *EMc*, xviii (1990), 359–70

G. Towne: 'A Systematic Formulation of Sixteenth-Century Text Underlay Rules', *MD*, xliv (1990), 255–87; xlv (1991), 143–68

Le concert des voix et des instruments à la Renaissance: Tours 1991

L. Earp: 'Texting in 15th-Century French Chansons: a Look Ahead from the 14th Century', *EMc*, xix (1991), 195–210

D. Slavin: 'In Support of "Heresy": Manuscript Evidence for the *a cappella* Performance of Early 15th-Century Songs', *EMc*, xix (1991), 179–90

S. Bonta: 'The Use of Instruments in the Ensemble Canzona and Sonata in Italy, 1580–1650', *Recercare*, iv (1992), 23–43

S. Keyl: '*Tenorlied*, *Discantlied*, Polyphonic Lied: Voices and Instruments in German Secular Polyphony of the Renaissance', *EMc*, xx (1992), 434–45

T. Knighton and D. Fallows, eds.: *Companion to Medieval and Renaissance Music* (London, 1992)

T. Knighton: 'The *a cappella* Heresy in Spain: an Inquisition into the Performance of the Cancionero Repertory', *EMc*, xx (1992), 560–81

K. Kreitner: 'Minstrels in Spanish Churches, 1400–1600', *EMc*, xx (1992), 532–46

K. Polk: *German Instrumental Music of the Late Middle Ages: Players, Patrons, and Performance Practice* (Cambridge, 1992)

A.M.B. Berger: *Mensuration and Proportion Signs: Origins and Evolution* (Oxford, 1993)

G. Dixon: 'The Performance of Palestrina: Some Questions, but Fewer Answers', *EMc*, xxii (1994), 666–75

J.G. Kurtzman: 'Tones, Modes, Clefs and Pitch in Roman Cyclic Magnificats of the 16th Century', *EMc*, xxii (1994), 641–65

R. Sherr: 'Competence and Incompetence in the Papal Choir in the Age of Palestrina', *EMc*, xxii (1994), 606–29

N. Mitchell: 'Choral and Instrumental Pitch in Church Music, 1570–1620', *GSJ*, xlviii (1995), 13–32

J. Morehen, ed.: *English Choral Practice c.1400–c.1650: a Memorial Volume to Peter le Huray* (Cambridge, 1995)

M.A. Roig-Francolí: 'Playing Consonances: a Spanish Renaissance Technique of Chordal Improvisation', *EMc*, xxiii (1995), 461–71

B. Turner: 'Spanish Liturgical Hymns: a Matter of Time', *EMc*, xxiii (1995), 477–82

D. Fallows: *Songs and Musicians in the Fifteenth Century* (Aldershot, 1996)

N. O'Regan: 'The Performance of Palestrina: Some Further Observations', *EMc*, xxiv (1996), 145–54

D: BAROQUE

BoydenII

H. Goldschmidt: *Die italienische Gesangsmethode des XVII. Jahrhunderts und ihre Bedeutung für die Gegenwart* (Breslau, 1890, 2/1892/R)

M. Kuhn: *Die Verzierungs-Kunst in der Gesangs-Musik des 16.–17. Jahrhunderts (1535–1650)* (Leipzig, 1902/R)

A. Schering: 'Zur instrumentalen Verzierungskunst im 18. Jahrhundert', *SIMG*, vii (1905–6), 365–85

H. Goldschmidt: *Die Lehre von der vokalen Ornamentik* (Charlottenburg, 1907/R)

A. Dolmetsch: *The Interpretation of the Music of the XVIIth and XVIIIth Centuries Revealed by Contemporary Evidence* (London, 1915, 2/1946/R)

P. Brunold: *Traité des signes et agréments employés par les clavecinistes français des XVIIe et XVIIIe siècles* (Lyons, 1925/R)

H. Keller: *Die musikalische Artikulation, insbesondere bei Joh. Seb. Bach* (Stuttgart, 1925)

F.T. Arnold: *The Art of Accompaniment from a Thorough-Bass as Practised in the XVIIth and XVIIIth Centuries* (London, 1931/R)

C.S. Terry: *Bach's Orchestra* (London, 1932/R)

E. Borrel: *L'interprétation de la musique française (de Lully à la Révolution)* (Paris, 1934/R)

A. Carse: *The Orchestra in the XVIIIth Century* (Cambridge, 1940/R)

J.A. Westrup: 'Monteverdi and the Orchestra', *ML*, xxi (1940), 230–45

J.M. Barbour: 'Bach and "The Art of Temperament"', *MQ*, xxxiii (1947), 64–89

M.F. Bukofzer: 'Checklist of Baroque Books on Music', *Music in the Baroque Era* (New York, 1947), 417–31

P. Aldrich: 'Bach's Technique of Transcription and Improvised Ornamentation', *MQ*, xxxv (1949), 26–35

P. Aldrich: *Ornamentation in J.S. Bach's Organ Works* (New York, 1950/R)

D.D. Boyden: 'The Violin and its Technique in the 18th Century', *MQ*, xxxvi (1950), 9–38

W. Emery: *Bach's Ornaments* (London, 1953/R)

F. Rothschild: *The Lost Tradition in Music*, i: *Rhythm and Tempo in J.S. Bach's Time* (London, 1953/R)

W. Kolneder: *Aufführungspraxis bei Vivaldi* (Leipzig, 1955, 2/1973)

A. Mendel: 'On the Pitches in Use in Bach's Time', *MQ*, xli (1955), 332–54, 466–80

H.-P. Schmitz: *Die Kunst der Verzierung im 18. Jahrhundert* (Kassel, 1955, 4/1983)

E.T. Ferand: *Die Improvisation in Beispielen aus neun Jahrhunderten abendländischer Musik*, Mw, xii (1956, 2/1961; Eng. trans., 1961)

E.T. Ferand: 'Improvised Vocal Counterpoint in the Late Renaissance and Early Baroque', *AnnM*, iv (1956), 129–74

P. Aldrich: 'The "Authentic" Performance of Baroque Music', *Essays on Music in Honor of Archibald Thompson Davison* (Cambridge, MA, 1957), 161–71

D.D. Boyden: 'Dynamics in Seventeenth- and Eighteenth-Century Music', ibid., 185–93

V. Duckles: 'Florid Embellishment in English Song of the Late 16th and Early 17th Centuries', *AnnM*, v (1957), 329–45

D.D. Boyden: 'Monteverdi's *violini piccoli alla francese* and *viole da brazzo*', *AnnM*, vi (1958–63), 387–402

E.T. Ferand: 'Embellished "Parody Cantatas" in the Early 18th Century', *MQ*, xliv (1958), 40–64

D.D. Boyden: 'Geminiani and the First Violin Tutor,' *AcM*, xxxi (1959), 161–70 [postscript in xxxii (1960), 40–47]

E. Bodky: *The Interpretation of Bach's Keyboard Works* (Cambridge, MA, 1960/R)

D.D. Boyden: 'The Missing Italian Manuscript of Tartini's *Traité des agrémens*', *MQ*, xlvi (1960), 315–28

N. Broder: 'The Beginnings of the Orchestra', *JAMS*, xiii (1960), 174–80

R. Donington: *Tempo and Rhythm in Bach's Organ Music* (London, 1960)

J. Eppelsheim: *Das Orchester in den Werken Jean-Baptiste Lullys* (Tutzing, 1961)

S. Babitz: 'On Using J.S. Bach's Keyboard Fingerings', *ML*, xliii (1962), 123–8

A. Geoffroy-Dechaume: *Les 'secrets' de la musique ancienne* (Paris, 1964/R)

F. Neumann: 'La note pointée et la soi-disant "manière française"', *RdM*, li (1965), 66–92; Eng. trans. in *EMc*, v (1977), 310–24

G.J. Buelow: *Thorough-Bass Accompaniment according to Johann David Heinichen* (Berkeley, 1966, 2/1986)

S. Babitz: 'Concerning the Length of Time that Every Note must be Held', *MR*, xxviii (1967), 21–37

R. Donington: 'A Problem of Inequality', *MQ*, liii (1967), 503–17

F. Neumann: 'The Use of Baroque Treatises on Musical Performance', *ML*, xlviii (1967), 315–24

M. Collins: 'A Reconsideration of French Overdotting', *ML*, i (1969), 111–23

A. Schnoebelen: 'Performance Practices at San Petronio in the Baroque', *AcM*, xli (1969), 37–55

P. Williams: *Figured Bass Accompaniment* (Edinburgh, 1970)

R. Donington: *A Performer's Guide to Baroque Music* (London, 1973)

M. Seares: 'Aspects of Performance Practice in the Recitatives of Jean-Baptiste Lully', *SMA*, viii (1974), 8–16

I. Smit Duyzentkunst and K. Vellekoop, eds.: *Bachboekt* (Utrecht, 1975) [incl. bibliography]

S. Babitz: *Note-Separation in Musical Performance and Other Matters*, Early Music Laboratory Bulletin, xiii (1976)

G.J. Buelow: 'A Lesson in Operatic Performance Practice by Madame Faustina Bordoni', *A Musical Offering: Essays in Honor of Martin Bernstein*, ed. E.H. Clinkscale and C. Brook (New York, 1977), 79–96

R. Donington: 'What is Rhythmic Alteration?', *EMc*, v (1977), 543–4

D. Fuller: 'Dotting, the "French Style" and Frederick Neumann's Counter-Reformation', *EMc*, v (1977), 517–43

F. Neumann: 'Facts and Fiction about Overdotting', *MQ*, lxiii (1977), 155–85

E. Harris: 'Baroque Vocal Performance Practice', *Alte Musik als ästhetische Gegenwart: Bach, Händel, Schütz: Stuttgart 1985*, i, 263–4

A. Newman: *Bach and the Baroque: a Performing Guide to Baroque Music with Special Emphasis on the Music of J.S. Bach* (New York, 1985)

G. Moens-Haenen: *Das Vibrato in der Musik des Barock* (Graz, 1998)

J. Butt: 'Improvised Vocal Ornamentation and German Baroque Compositional Theory: an Approach to "Historical" Performance Practice', *JRMA*, cxvi (1991), 41–62

M. Cyr: *Performing Baroque Music* (Portland, OR, 1992)

M.A. Parker, ed.: *Eighteenth-Century Music in Theory and Practice: Essays in Honor of Alfred Mann* (Stuyvesant, NY, 1994)

P.F. Broman: 'The Emperor's New Clothes: Performance Practice in the 1990s', *STMf*, lxxvi–lxxvii (1994–5), 31–56

R.W. Duffin: 'Performance Practice: Que me veux-tu? What do you Want from me?', *Early Music America*, i (1995), 26–36

P. Downey: 'Performing Purcell's "Exotick" Trumpet Notes', *Performing the Music of Henry Purcell*, ed. M. Burden (Oxford, 1996), 49–60

M. Vanscheeuwijck: 'The Baroque Cello and its Performance', *Performance Practice Review*, ix (1996), 78–96

A. Parrott: *The Essential Bach Choir* (Woodbridge, 2000)

E: CLASSICAL

GroveI (§6; R. Winter)

A. Dolmetsch: *The Interpretation of the Music of the XVIIth and XVIIIth Centuries Revealed by Contemporary Evidence* (London, 1915, 2/1946/R)

O. Schreiber: *Orchester und Orchesterpraxis in Deutschland zwischen 1780 und 1850* (Berlin, 1938/R)

E. and P. Badura-Skoda: *Mozart-Interpretation* (Vienna, 1957; Eng. trans., 1962/R, as *Interpreting Mozart on the Keyboard*)

P. Mies: 'Die Artikulationszeichen Strich und Punkt bei Wolfgang Amadeus Mozart', *Mf*, xi (1958), 428–55

A. Gottron: 'Wie spielte Mozart die Adagios seiner Klavierkonzerte?', *Mf*, xiii (1960), 334 only

F. Rothschild: *The Lost Tradition of Music*, ii: *Musical Performance in the Times of Mozart and Beethoven* (London and New York, 1961)

Der junge Haydn: Graz 1970

O. Biba: 'Die Wiener Kirchenmusik um 1738', *Jb für österreichische Kulturgeschichte*, i/2 (1971), 7–79

J. Webster: 'Violoncello and Double Bass in the Chamber Music of Haydn and his Viennese Contemporaries', *JAMS*, xxix (1976), 413–38

T.E. Warner: 'Tromlitz's Flute Treatise: a Neglected Source of Eighteenth-Century Performance Practice', *A Musical Offering: Essays in Honor of Martin Bernstein*, ed. E.H. Clinkscale and C. Brook (New York, 1977), 45–62

J. Webster: 'The Bass Part in Haydn's Early String Quartets', *MQ*, lxiii (1977), 390–424

L.F. Ferguson: *Col basso and Generalbass in Mozart's Keyboard Concertos: Notation, Performance, Theory, and Practice* (diss., Princeton U., 1983)

L.F. Ferguson: 'The Classical Keyboard Concerto: Some Thoughts on Authentic Performance', *EMc*, xii (1984), 437–45

L.F. Ferguson: 'Mozart's Keyboard Concertos: Tutti Notations and Performance Models', *MJb 1984–5*, 32–9

H. Macdonald: 'To Repeat or Not to Repeat?', *PRMA*, cxi (1984–5), 121–37

A.P. Brown: *Performing Haydn's 'The Creation': Reconstructing the Earliest Renditions* (Bloomington, IN, 1986)

F. Neumann: *Ornamentation and Improvisation in Mozart* (Princeton, NJ, 1986)

J. Spitzer and N. Zaslaw: 'Improvised Ornamentation in Eighteenth-Century Orchestras', *JAMS*, xxxix (1986), 524–77

S.P. Rosenblum: *Performance Practices in Classic Piano Music: their Principles and Applications* (Bloomington, IN, 1988)

N. Zaslaw: 'When is an Orchestra Not an Orchestra?', *EMc*, xvi (1988), 483–95

M.S. Morrow: *Concert Life in Haydn's Vienna: Aspects of a Developing Musical and Social Institution* (Stuyvesant, NY, 1989); see also review by D. Edge, *Haydn Yearbook* 1992, 108–67

N. Zaslaw: *Mozart's Symphonies: Context, Performance Practice, Reception* (Oxford, 1989)

J. Webster: 'On the Absence of Keyboard Continuo in Haydn's Symphonies', *EMc*, xviii (1990), 599–608

C. Eisen: 'The Mozarts' Salzburg Copyists: Aspects of Attribution, Chronology, Text, Style, and Performance Practice', *Mozart Studies*, i, ed. C. Eisen (Oxford, 1991), 253–99

P. Whitmore: *Unpremeditated Art: the Cadenza in the Classical Keyboard Concerto* (Oxford, 1991)

'Performing Mozart's Music', *EMc*, xix/4 (1991 [incl. C. Eisen: 'The Old and New Mozart Editions', 513–32]); xx/1 (1992 [incl. D. Edge: 'Mozart's Viennese Orchestras', 64–88; C. Eisen: 'Mozart's Salzburg Orchestras', 83–103]); xx/2 (1992)

C. Brown: 'Dots and Strokes in Late 18th- and 19th-Century Music', *EMc*, xxi (1993), 593–610

D. Charlton: '"A *maître d'orchestre* … Conducts": New and Old Evidence on French Practice', *EMc*, xxi (1993), 340–53

S. McVeigh: *Concert Life in London from Mozart to Haydn* (Cambridge, 1993)

J. Spitzer: 'Players and Parts in the 18th-Century Orchestra', *Basler Jb für historische Musikpraxis*, xvii (1993), 65–88

L.E. Miller: 'C.P.E. Bach and Friedrich Ludwig Dülon: Composition and Improvisation in Late 18th-Century Germany', *EMc*, xxiii (1995), 65–80

V.W. Goertzen: 'By Way of Introduction: Preluding by 18th- and Early 19th-Century Pianists', *JM*, xiv (1996), 299–337

N. Zaslaw, ed.: *Mozart's Piano Concertos: Text, Context, Interpretation* (Ann Arbor, 1996) [incl. D. Edge: 'Manuscript Parts

as Evidence of Orchestral Size in the Eighteenth-Century Viennese Concerto', 427–60]
B. Harrison: *Haydn's Keyboard Music: Studies in Performance Practice* (Oxford, 1997)
R. Riggs: 'Mozart's Notation of Staccato Articulation: a New Appraisal', *JM*, xv (1997) 230–77
M. Latcham: 'Mozart and the Pianos of Gabriel Anton Walter', *EMc*, xxv (1997), 382–400
C. Brown: *Classical and Romantic Performing Practice 1750–1900* (Oxford, 1999)

F: ROMANTIC

BerliozM
W.T. Parke: *Musical Memoirs* (London, 1830/R)
P. Baillot: *L'art du violon: nouvelle méthode* (Paris, 1834)
M. Garcia: *Traité complet de l'art du chant* (Paris, 1840–47/R; Eng. trans., 1893, as *Hints on Singing*; new Eng. trans., 1975–84)
H.F. Chorley: *Music and Manners in France and Germany* (London, 1841/R)
H. Berlioz: *Grand traité d'instrumentation et d'orchestration modernes* (Paris, 1843, 2/1855/R; Eng. trans., 1856, rev. 2/1882/R by J. Bennett)
H. Berlioz: *Les soirées de l'orchestre* (Paris, 1852/R, 5/1895; Eng. trans., 1956/R); ed. L. Guichard (Paris, 1968)
A. Elwart: *Histoire de la Société des concerts du Conservatoire impérial de musique* (Paris, 1860, enlarged 2/1864)
L. Spohr: *Selbstbiographie* (Kassel, 1860–61; Eng. trans., 1865/R, 2/1878/R); ed. E. Schmitz (Kassel, 1954–5)
H.F. Chorley: *Thirty Years' Musical Recollections* (London, 1862/R, abridged 2/1926/R by E. Newman)
R. Wagner: *Über das Dirigieren* (Leipzig, 1869; Eng. trans., 1887, 4/1940/R)
E. Hanslick: *Geschichte des Concertwesens in Wien* (Vienna, 1869–70/R)
R. Wagner: *Mein Leben* (pubd privately, 1870–81); ed. M. Gregor-Dellin (Munich, 1963; Eng. trans., 1983)
F. Weingartner: *Ueber das Dirigieren* (Leipzig, 1896, 5/1920); Eng. trans., 1906, 2/1925; repr. in *Weingartner on Music & Conducting* (New York, 1969)
A. Dandelot: *La Société des concerts du Conservatoire de 1828 à 1897* (Paris, 1898, many later edns, enlarged 1923 as *La Société des concerts du Conservatoire (1828–1923)*)
H. Knödt: 'Zur Entwicklungsgeschichte der Kadenzen im Instrumentalkonzert', *SIMG*, xv (1913–14), 375–419
A. Carse: *The Orchestra from Beethoven to Berlioz* (Cambridge, 1948/R)
A.G. Huber: *Ludwig van Beethoven: seine Schüler und Interpreten* (Vienna, 1953)
P. Badura-Skoda, ed.: *Carl Czerny: Über den richtigen Vortrag der sämtlichen Beethoven'schen Klavierwerke* (Vienna, 1963; Eng. trans., 1970)
D. Shawe-Taylor and others: 'Schubert as Written and as Performed', *MT*, civ (1963), 626–8
H. Grundmann and P. Mies: *Studien zum Klavierspiel Beethovens und seiner Zeitgenossen* (Bonn, 1966, 2/1970)
P. Stadlen: 'Beethoven and the Metronome: I', *ML*, xlviii (1967), 330–49
N. Temperley: 'Berlioz and the Slur', *ML*, l (1969), 388–92
F. Weingartner: *Weingartner on Music & Conducting* (New York, 1969)
W.S. Newman: 'Beethoven's Pianos versus his Piano Ideals', *JAMS*, xxiii (1970), 484–504
W.S. Newman: 'On the Rhythmic Significance of Beethoven's Annotations in Cramer's Etudes', *GfMKB: Bonn 1970*, 43–7
W.S. Newman: *Performance Practices in Beethoven's Piano Sonatas* (New York, 1971)
G. Beechey: 'Rhythmic Interpretation', *MR*, xxxiii (1972), 233–48
K. Drake: *The Sonatas of Beethoven as he Played and Taught them*, ed. F.S. Stillings (Cincinnati, 1972)
A. Caswell: 'Mme Cinti-Damoreau and the Embellishment of Italian Opera in Paris: 1820–1845', *JAMS*, xxviii (1975), 459–92
W.S. Newman: 'Freedom of Tempo in Schubert's Instrumental Music', *MQ*, lxi (1975), 528–45
W. Weber: *Music and the Middle Class: Social Structures of Concert Life in London, Paris, and Vienna* (London, 1975)
W.S. Newman: 'The Performance of Beethoven's Trills', *JAMS*, xxix (1976), 439–62
R. Winter: 'Second Thoughts on the Performance of Beethoven's Trills', *MQ*, lxiii (1977), 483–504

R. Winter: 'Performing Nineteenth-Century Music on Nineteenth-Century Instruments', *19CM*, i (1977–8), 163–75
D. Coe: 'The Original Production Book for *Otello*: an Introduction', *19CM*, ii (1978–9), 148–58
R.W. Oldani: '*Boris Godunov* and the Censor', *19CM*, ii (1978–9), 245–53
L. Wright: 'A New Source for *Carmen*', *19CM*, ii (1978–9), 61–71
E.M. Frederick: 'The "Romantic" Sound in Four Pianos of Chopin's Era', *19CM*, iii (1979–80), 150–53
O. Biba: 'Concert Life in Beethoven's Vienna', *Beethoven, Performers, and Critics: Detroit 1980*, 77–93
T. Higgens: 'Whose Chopin?', *19CM*, v (1981–2), 67–75
D.K. Holoman: 'The Emergence of the Orchestral Conductor in Paris in the 1830s', *Music in Paris in the Eighteen-Thirties: Northampton, MA, 1982*, 374–430
W. Schenkman: 'Beyond the Limits of Urtext Authority: a Contemporary Record of Early Nineteenth-Century Performance Practice', *College Music Symposium*, xxiii/2 (1983), 145–63
W. Crutchfield: 'Vocal Ornamentation in Verdi: the Phonographic Evidence', *19CM*, vii (1983–4), 3–54
R. Winter: 'The Emperor's New Clothes: Nineteenth-Century Instruments Revisited', *19CM*, vii (1983–4), 251–65
W.A. Bebbington: *The Orchestral Conducting Practice of Richard Wagner* (diss., CUNY, 1984)
R. Stowell: *Violin Technique and Performance Practice in the Late Eighteenth and Early Nineteenth Centuries* (Cambridge, 1985)
D.J. Koury: *Orchestral Performance Practices in the Nineteenth Century: Size, Proportions, and Seating* (Ann Arbor, 1986)
G. Harwood: 'Verdi's Reform of the Italian Opera Orchestra', *19CM*, x (1986–7), 108–34
C. Brown: 'Bowing Styles, Vibrato and Portamento in Nineteenth-Century Violin Playing', *JRMA*, cxiii (1988), 97–128
E. Galkin: *A History of Orchestral Conducting* (New York, 1988)
W.S. Newman: *Beethoven on Beethoven: Playing his Piano Music his Way* (New York, 1988)
R. Taruskin: 'Resisting the Ninth', *19CM*, xii (1988–9), 241–56
A.B. Caswell, ed.: *Embellished Opera Arias* (Madison, WI, 1989)
C. Brown: 'Historical Performance, Metronome Marks and Tempo in Beethoven's Symphonies', *EMc*, xix (1991), 247–58
H.J. Macdonald: 'Berlioz and the Metronome', *Berlioz Studies*, ed. P. Bloom (Cambridge, 1992), 17–36
D. Rowland: *A History of Pianoforte Pedalling* (Cambridge, 1993)
R. Stowell, ed.: *Performing Beethoven* (Cambridge, 1994)
D. Montgomery: 'Modern Schubert Interpretation in the Light of the Pedagogical Sources of his Day', *EMc*, xxv (1997), 101–18
B.D. Sherman: 'Tempos and Proportions in Brahms: Period Evidence', *EMc*, xxv (1997), 462–77
D.M. Di Grazia: 'Rejected Traditions: Ensemble Placement in Nineteenth-Century Paris', *19CM*, xxii (1998–9), 190–209

G: 20TH CENTURY

CampbellGC
F. Weingartner: *Ueber das Dirigieren* (Leipzig, 1896, 5/1920); Eng. trans., 1906, 2/1925; repr. in *Weingartner on Music & Conducting* (New York, 1969)
L. Auer: *Violin Playing as I Teach it* (New York, 1921/R)
D. Alexanian and P. Casals: *L'enseignement du violoncelle: traité théorique et pratique du violoncelle* (Paris, 1922)
C. Flesch: *Die Kunst des Violinspiels*, i (Berlin, 1923, 2/1929; Eng. trans., 1924, 2/1939); ii (Berlin, 1928; Eng. trans., 1930)
P. Taffanel and P. Gaubert: *Méthode complète de flûte* (Paris, 1923, 2/1958)
H. Becker and D. Rynar: *Mechanik und Ästhetik des Violoncellspiels* (Vienna, 1929/R)
I. Yampol'sky: *Osnovï skripichnoy applikaturï* [The principles of violin fingering] (Moscow, 1933, enlarged 3/1955; Eng. trans., 1967)
C. Flesch: *Memoirs* (London, 1957/R, 2/1958; Ger. orig., Freiburg, 1960, 2/1961)
I. Galamian: *Principles of Violin Playing and Teaching* (Englewood Cliffs, NJ, 1962, 2/1985)
H.C. Schonberg: *The Great Pianists* (New York, 1963, 2/1987)
B. Schwarz, ed.: *Carl Flesch: Violin Fingering, its Theory and Practice* (London, 1966/R)
B. Bartolozzi: *New Sounds for Woodwind* (London, 1967, 2/1982; It. orig., Milan, 1974)
H.C. Schonberg: *The Great Conductors* (New York, 1967)
D. Wooldridge: *Conductor's World* (London, 1970)

J.B. Steane: *The Grand Tradition: Seventy Years of Singing on Record* (London, 1974)

R.M. Philip: *Some Changes in Style of Orchestral Playing, 1920–1950, as Shown by Gramophone Recordings* (diss., U. of Cambridge, 1975)

B. Boretz and E.T. Cone, eds.: *Perspectives on Notation and Performance* (New York, 1976)

E. Brody: 'Viñes in Paris: New Light on Twentieth-Century Performance Practice', *A Musical Offering: Essays in Honor of Martin Bernstein*, ed. E.H. Clinkscale and C. Brook (New York, 1977), 45–62

E.W. Galkin: *A History of Orchestral Conducting: in Theory and Practice* (New York, 1988)

R. Philip: *Early Recordings and Musical Style: Changing Tastes in Instrumental Performance, 1900–1950* (New York, 1992)

R. Hudson: *Stolen Time: the History of Tempo rubato* (Oxford, 1994)

R. Taruskin: *Text and Act: Essays on Music and Performance* (Oxford, 1995)

For further bibliography, *see* IMPROVISATION; MUSICA FICTA; ORNAMENTS, and THOROUGHBASS.

II. Non-Western and traditional music

1. Introduction. 2. Definition. 3. Sources. 4. Scholarly approaches and issues.

1. INTRODUCTION.   This section will focus on studies of performing practices worldwide conducted primarily by ethnomusicologists. An outline of the range of meanings denoted by performing practice is followed by a survey of sources for the study of performing practice and their approaches, the central issues that have arisen and some applications of knowledge about performing practice.

Not all ethnomusicologists use the term performing practice, but most have studied it. The term, or its more common variant 'performance practice', figures relatively rarely in titles of books or articles and is missing from the index of definitive works on ethnomusicology, but this does not indicate a lack of interest. Rather, performing practice is so central to knowledge of the world's musics that it has usually been integrated into studies rather than set aside as an independent field of study. Performing practice has, in fact, been one of the prime areas of ethnomusicological investigation, particularly in the third quarter of the 20th century, when many studies of non-Western and other traditional musics were devoted to defining normative performance.

While some ethnomusicologists have studied questions of performing practice as a direct outgrowth of Western musicology and have brought to this study the issues raised by historical musicologists, others have been impelled by their involvement in performance and a consequent need to make sense of musical practice. Still others are motivated by anthropologically or sociologically informed interests in human behaviour. The influence of practice theory and the work of Pierre Bourdieu, in particular, is extensive and growing.

The issues that occupy scholars and performers of Western art music, specifically those concerning authenticity and the feasibility and desirability of re-creating earlier European performing practices, have no direct analogies in ethnomusicology. There is widespread and largely tacit agreement, however, that performing practice can and should be studied. Conflicts may arise between champions of contemporary practice and scholars of older ones, but these are relatively infrequent. A notable instance is the mixed reception in Japan of revisionist histories of Japanese court music by Laurence Picken and associates (see Picken, 1982–90). Considerable efforts have been made in various parts of the world to document older practices that appear to be changing or vanishing altogether, but this is rarely done for the sake of historically accurate reconstruction. The vast majority of performer-scholars do not attempt to reinstate earlier practices, by choice or for lack of evidence. Rather, fidelity to teachers' models and observed practice are the rule. This is due in part to the predominance of non-native scholarship and the resultant deference towards experts born into the tradition. As scholars (and some performers) have developed more sophisticated understanding of longstanding processes of cultural exchange and change in virtually every part of the world, notions of purity and authenticity have become irrelevant except as tropes in local discourses on music that may themselves become the subject of study. Similarly, musics which were once presumed to be 'hybrid' or 'impure' and therefore unworthy of study are now the focus of considerable scholarly attention as are processes of change.

2. DEFINITION.   Performing practice is generally understood by ethnomusicologists to refer to the conventions that govern music-making and accompanying activities, such as dance, theatre and ritual in a socially, culturally and historically defined context. These conventions delimit a range of appropriate choices in performance and, increasingly, are understood to be situated, negotiable and often gendered. In other words, despite their apparent stability they are subject to change and highly dependent on context and power relations between performers and others who influence performances, such as patrons, scholars and audiences. For the most part, the conventions of performing practice are unwritten and, in some cases, unarticulated, but they are nonetheless observable in performance. They extend beyond a single composition, being linked to or defined for a particular time period, group of musicians, set of pieces – a single genre, an entire repertory – and types of performance.

Ethnomusicologists have been mostly concerned with that which is traditional and typical and with variations thereon. Ethnomusicological research stresses the synchronic over the historical; most publications concern contemporary performing practice, not because of a lack of interest in earlier practices or an assumption that current practice is essentially the same as earlier practice, but because of the difficulty of pursuing historical research in musical traditions that are primarily or exclusively transmitted orally/aurally.

In ethnomusicological writing there is overlap between the concepts of 'performing practice' and 'style' since both terms refer to ways of doing. Yet the two concepts are usually distinguishable; 'style' often refers to the way a piece is composed regardless of the way it is performed (performing practice), or about certain ways of performing those pieces. Style does not cover such aspects as piece selection, a piece's transformation within performance, or instrumentation and orchestration (role assignment), which define the constitution of ensemble. These issues belong to the domain of performing practice.

Performing practice is thus related to but at least partly separable from the pieces performed. But what is the piece? Transferring performing practice as it is used in Western musicology requires that ethnomusicologists distinguish between an item (song, composition or piece) and its normative realizations. Studies of performing practice for notated musics may deal with aspects of interpretation similar to those considered by scholars of European art music. But the concept of performing practice is also viable in traditions where notation either does not exist or plays a less central role, such as when it is used for archival or pedagogical reasons, but not in performance. Thus, it is more useful to think of performing practice as a range of possibilities for realizing some sort of representation of a piece; this representation may be written in great detail, sketched in mnemonics or a completely mental phenomenon.

Almost every kind of music-making is less reifiable as text than most European art music, partly because much of it is not notated. Even for Japanese, Chinese, Arab and Javanese traditions of musical notation, where this distinction between 'text' and 'act' (Taruskin, 1995, p.356) might seem clear, there may be problems due to the necessity of aurally transmitted knowledge for interpretation. When no notation is used, defining realization in performance can be complicated. For instance, solo improvisations such as the Middle Eastern *taqasim* are open to such variations that one can only describe a performance, not prescribe a specific *taqsim*. Yet much can be said about the performing practice associated with *taqasim*, as Scott Marcus does in his study of common patterns of modulation in Middle Eastern improvisation (1992). Even when a piece is notated, one must ask whether the notation represents the most important aspects of the piece or simply the ones that are easiest to write down or are most likely to be needed by less experienced performers. In Javanese gamelan music, for example, the commonly notated *balungan* is only one melodic strand and may not be the most important. Some performers and scholars maintain that an unplayed melody abstracted from the live sound and heard only in the musicians' heads is the best representation of the piece. This has generated substantial discussion of the nature of this essence and its realizations (Sutton, 1979; Sumarsam, 1984; Perlman, 1994).

Even in the most integrated cases, such as improvised performances where the abstract concept of a constant composition hardly applies, distinguishing between the structure that is created in performance and the performing practice with which that structure is created provides two complementary perspectives on the performance. The problem of filtering performing practice can be reformulated by defining performing practice not with respect to the details of a particular piece, but as the things musicians must know in order to perform a certain group of pieces or even an entire repertory suitable for ceremonies, nightclub shows or formal concerts. The questions that could be asked concern appropriateness: which sort of piece, performed by whom, when and how.

3. SOURCES. Sources for the study of performing practice, and hence the methods of study, vary greatly among different musics. Ethnomusicologists undertake ethnographic studies of current practice, elicitation of oral histories and analysis of notation that draw on written and iconographic materials. They also rely on older recordings and archaeological evidence where available.

(i) Ethnographic data and performance study. Since the early 1960s ethnomusicologists have favoured working in the present, conducting interviews, observing performances, recording and, perhaps more important than anything else, pursuing practical study from a variety of musicians. Ethnographic work contrasts with the methods of historical musicologists owing to the availability of living sources. Often a substantial portion of performing practice is implicit, deducible from the actions of experienced performers in particular circumstances. The scope of the unsaid varies greatly, requiring a variety of approaches to eliciting that which has not yet been articulated in words. Often the most fruitful approach is practical study which enables the scholar to participate in performance, experiencing the working of conventions from within and gauging responses to his or her musical choices (Kippen, 1992; Brinner, 1995).

(ii) Oral history. In order to study both performing practice of earlier times and change over time, observation of and participation in contemporary practice are clearly insufficient. Eliciting oral histories is an approach used worldwide. Interviewers seek to document changes within living memory and hope for echoes of still earlier practices. For completely non-literate societies this is the primary and often sole resource of historical study.

(iii) Notation. Many musical traditions rely on some form of notation, but the 'notes themselves' often lack crucial information as to how they are to be performed. Tablature for the Chinese *qin*, for example, includes precise indications for playing techniques, but durations are left to the player's interpretation, which is informed though not fully determined by performing practice handed down from teacher to pupil. In this case, as in many others, the notation serves largely as a set of mnemonics for a repertory that has been transmitted and memorized in a fundamentally aural manner. Practice can change substantially under these conditions, as demonstrated by Picken and other researchers who examined early notation of music exported to medieval Japan from Tang dynasty China; evidence demonstrates that crucial aspects of performing practice, particularly tempo and ornamentation, must have changed significantly over the past 1000 years, even as the same pieces continued to be played by *gagaku* musicians (Marett, 1986). Based on this material, as well as evidence from medieval Europe and Central Asia, Picken has proposed a far-reaching continuum of performing practice in dance music (1982–90, ii). The introduction of notation is likely to alter performing practice substantially in a formerly aural tradition, as shown in Ruth Davis's study of Tunisian performing practice (1992).

(iv) Textual evidence. Written sources that document earlier performing practice include comments attached to notation, descriptions of performances and lists of performers or ensembles. Comments on notation may convey information about variations in performing practice, with possible repetitions or substitutions indicated, for example. Texts concerning performances and performers may indicate what was played in particular circumstances, including the constitution of an ensemble, the sequence of pieces or genres and the interaction between performers and audience. For instance, George Sawa has shown continuities between medieval and modern Arab performing practice in his interpretation of 10th-century Arab treatises (1989) and Carol Meyers has speculated on the type of music performed by Jewish women in biblical times, based on passages in the Bible (Marshall, 1993). There are also examples of recent music traditions. The recovery of African retentions in early African-American musical practice based on accounts of slaves

written by whites is a particularly large and varied project of this sort.

(v) Archaeological and iconographic evidence. Meyers's speculation on questions of gender and performing practice in biblical Israel also relied on terracotta figurines to support the interpretation of textual evidence. Lise Manniche's marshalling of a panoply of iconographic, textual and other archaeological evidence from ancient Egypt is a particularly comprehensive undertaking (1991). Working with manuscript illustrations from Mughal India, Bonnie Wade has recovered aspects of performing practice at a crucial juncture in Indian music history, namely the mixing of Indian and foreign instruments and practices occasioned by the Mughal conquest (1998).

(vi) Recordings.   Recordings are an important source for studying performing practice from the late 19th and early 20th centuries onwards. Jihad Racy (1988) and, more recently, Henry Spiller (1996) and Amy Stillman (1996) have used early recordings of Arab, Sundanese and Hawaiian musics to ascertain changes in performing practice. In the Middle East, for example, this wealth of early recordings bears witness to a period of great change, a shift from smaller ensembles with one performer to a part and substantial improvisation, divergent interpretations and ornamentations to larger orchestras with unified sound ideals, string sections, greater stress on composition and more unified conceptions of the piece, greatly aided in many cases by notation (see Davis, 1992). Of course, the severe time limitations of early recordings, the decontextualization of performance and the difficulty of recording large ensembles limit the types of questions one can approach. Nevertheless, performers involved in the revivals of musics as disparate as Jewish klezmer and Amerindian songs have made use of early recordings not only for repertory but to learn earlier ways of performing that repertory (Witmer, 1991). Recordings, especially those made in the field by the researcher, are also particularly helpful for tackling the difficult problem of distinguishing between ornamentation and the simpler, more basic, or more essential aspects of a piece. Ethnomusicologists sometimes compare differing performances of a piece or repetitions within a piece in order to separate the varying details, the so-called surface of the music, from what is presumed to be the more permanent or stable core.

4. SCHOLARLY APPROACHES AND ISSUES.   Studies of performing practice vary in scope, focus, theoretical assumptions, methodology and emphasis. The scope of generalization in studies of performing practice may be as limited as a short time period, a single community, or a lineage of performers, and it may be as broad as a continent or other large cultural area, such as the Indian subcontinent (Wade, in Béhague, 1984), Jewish musical traditions (Shiloah, 1992) or the African diaspora (Brown, 1992). The focus of a study may be the piece as independent entity, the scholar then asking what is the range of ways that it can be performed (Nettl and Foltin, 1972; Vetter, 1981) or the way in which components are assembled into larger performance sequences (Picken, 1982–90; Racy, 1983; Schuyler, in Béhague, 1984; al-Faruqi, 1985). Others address a more generalized, systemic level as Robert Garfias has done for Japanese *gagaku* (1975), David Morton for Thai music (1976), Anderson Sutton for Javanese gamelan (1993) and

Lawrence Witzleben for Chinese instrumental music (1995). The phenomena studied under the rubric of performing practice range from aspects of intonation, ornamentation and playing techniques (Garfias, 1975; Wade, in Béhague, 1984) to the constitution of ensembles (Berliner, 1978, p.112), from the realizations of individual pieces to the considerations that govern the choice of repertory for an entire occasion (Nettl and Foltin, 1972; Vetter, 1977 and 1981; Schuyler, 1984; Sugarman, in Béhague, 1988).

The theoretical assumptions methodologies and emphases that shape studies of performing practice have changed rapidly over time. Though early reports from missionaries, explorers and other travellers during the age of exploration can hardly be considered ethnomusicological studies, such sources convey more information about aspects of performing practice, however tersely and subjectively, than about other aspects of foreign musics (Harrison, 1973). These accounts constitute the bulk of early textual evidence for ethnomusicologists working in many parts of the world (Bohlman, 1988; Bor, 1988). Comparative musicologists working from the late 19th century to the mid-20th focussed on scales, instruments and items of repertories rather than on practice though contextual information is often scattered in field reports. The dominance of so-called armchair analysis, removed from sites of performance, precluded the analysis of processes of musical performance.

It was with the rise of ethnomusicology in the mid-20th century that aspects of performing practice began to receive considerable attention. This body of work exhibits a tendency to normative generalizations, often based on an individual or a small sample. This is taken to an extreme in the work of Alan Lomax, whose cantometrics project sought correlations between social structure and song style. For Lomax, cantometrics is a term that means style of performance, i.e. performing practice, including aspects such as the type of ensemble, the musical relationships between the singer and instrumentalist, and the degree of ornamentation (Lomax, 1968; see critique in Henry, 1976). At the same time a large body of ethnomusicological work has filtered out performing practice by looking for essential features of compositions or pieces to find points of connection between them, just as comparative musicologists had done earlier.

The new emphasis on performance advocated in the 1970s by folklorists such as Richard Bauman urged ethnomusicologists to pay more attention to events and the processes played out in them as opposed to the more systemic accounts of earlier work. This led to the development of new field methodologies and to collections of articles devoted to performing practice (McLeod and Herndon, 1980; Béhague, 1984). The authors in Gerard Béhague's collection, in particular, showed how performing practice is contingent on context.

In the 1990s, alongside a continued interest in process and event, attention has shifted to individual agency, to the multiplicity of viewpoints within a community or tradition and to the constructedness of norms in which performers, critics and scholars are implicated. The relationship between practice and theory, both oral and written, has been one such direction (Zemp, 1979; Schuyler, 1990; Marcus, 1992; Weintraub, 1993; Barz and Cooley, 1997). Much of this change in orientation is due to recent sociological and anthropological concerns such as the growing influence of Bourdieu's concept of 'habitus' in ethnomusicological work (Waterman, 1991, pp.50–54). Concurrently, many scholars have given closer attention to the intersection of gender and performing practice, demonstrating that one can study which pieces are appropriate for a given occasion, for example, or how an ensemble for a particular performance context should be constituted with regard not only to instrumentation but also, for example, to gender and social status (Meyer, Teeter and Weiss, in Marshall, 1993; Sugarman, 1997; Walton, 1997). Scholars have also broadened the scope of musical investigation to include popular musics (Booth, 1991–2) and the performance of traditional musics in new contexts (Rasmussen, 1989).

Perhaps the most important contribution of ethnomusicology to the study of performing practice is that performing practice itself becomes the subject of interpretation. Going beyond analyses of source materials for the purpose of determining what performing practice is for a given music, ethnomusicologists attempt to analyse why those particular conventions have formed in order to determine what relationship this formation may have with other cultural and social aspects. Interpretation may focus on aesthetics, sociological concerns, world-view or other cultural issues. Lomax's ambitious and methodologically flawed global mapping of song style and social structure is one example (1968). In a far more focussed and successful study, Anthony Seeger not only describes how men of the Suya people in Brazil perform *Akia* songs, but he also interprets the social significance of this practice (Mcleod and Herndon, 1980). Studying the performing practice associated with Balinese *gender wayang*, Lisa Gold has shown the narrative and ritual links that join shadow play and life-cycle ceremonies (1992, 1998). Benjamin Brinner has analysed the interaction that takes place in the performance of Javanese gamelan, explaining it in terms of the intertwining of musical and social forces and issues (1995).

Writings on performing practice in the world's musics are not usually as concerned with prescriptive agendas as many writings on historical practice in European art music are, yet some research on performing practice is practically motivated and more prescriptive than descriptive; such research is conducted with the goal not only of documenting current, or somewhat older, practice but of seeking out the 'best' or the most representative practice as a basis for standardized teaching. Such work is generally associated with and often instigated by national institutions for education in performing arts, and the standardization or codification of performing practice may serve a political agenda. Nationalist works are further differentiated from most other works on performing practice in that they are conducted by local researchers rather than foreign scholars. In the case of Central Java the displacement of the royal courts by national conservatories as training-grounds and extravagant patrons of the arts led to a similar shift in the custodianship of court-based performing practices, although these did not remain unmodified (Brinner, 1995, pp.158–9). Certain performing practices also became emblematic of regional identity and thus politically charged (Sutton, 1991). Similar processes have been played out elsewhere as post-colonial governments created national arts institutes with far-reaching pedagogical and curatorial mandates (Davis, 1997, p.2). Even when creation of a unified standard is not the goal, standardization may take place at a lower level as examples of regional practices are simplified to fill curricular needs at conservatories (Witzleben, 1995, p.132).

Study of performing practice has been a standard part of the training of many ethnomusicologists, due in part to Ki Mantle Hood's championship of the ideal of bi-musicality. Bi-musicality is primarily a pedagogical tool rather than a field of intellectual inquiry; the student absorbs the conventions of the music to be studied rather than researching them. As instruction in a broad variety of musical traditions has become more widespread and readily available through much of the Western world, many musicians in addition to ethnomusicologists have developed an eclectic musicianship based not only on acquisition of playing techniques and specific items of repertory, but also on absorption of some aspects of performing practices from highly diverse sources.

BIBLIOGRAPHY

A. Lomax: *Folk Style and Culture* (Washington DC, 1968)

B. Nettl and B. Foltin jr: *Daramad of Chahargah: a Study in the Performance Practice of Persian Music* (Detroit, 1972)

F.Ll. Harrison: *Time, Place and Music: an Anthology of Ethnomusicological Observation c.1550 to c.1800* (Amsterdam, 1973)

R. Garfias: *Music of One Thousand Autumns: the Tôgaku Style of Japanese Court Music* (Berkeley, 1975)

E.O. Henry: 'The Variety of Music in a North Indian Village: Reassessing Cantometrics', *EthM*, xx (1976), 49–66

D. Morton: *The Traditional Music of Thailand* (Berkeley, 1976)

R. Vetter: *Formal Aspects of Performance Practice in Central Javanese Gamelan Music* (thesis, U. of Hawaii, 1977)

P. Berliner: *The Soul of Mbira: Music and Traditions of the Shona People of Zimbabwe* (Berkeley, 1978)

R.A. Sutton: 'Concept and Treatment in Javanese Gamelan Music, with Reference to the Gambang', *AsM*, xi/1 (1979), 59–79

H. Zemp: 'Aspects of 'Aré'aré Musical Theory', *EthM*, xxiii (1979), 5–48

N. McLeod and M.Herndon, eds.: *The Ethnography of Musical Performance* (Norwood, PA, 1980) [incl. A. Seeger: 'Sing for your Sister: the Structure and Performance of Suya *Akia*', 7–42]

R. Vetter: 'Flexibility in the Performance Practice of Central Javanese Music', *EthM*, xxv (1981), 199–214

L. Picken, ed.: *Music from the Tang Court* (Oxford, 1982–90), esp. 'Aspects of the Suite-Form in East Asia', ii, 100–08 [vol.ii co-edited by R.F. Wolpert]

A.J. Racy: 'The Waslah: a Compound-Form Principle in Egyptian Music', *Arab Studies Quarterly*, v (1983), 396–403

G. Béhague, ed.: *Performance Practice: Ethnomusicological Perspectives* (Westport, CT, 1984) [incl. B.C. Wade: 'Performance Practice in Indian Classical Music', 13–52; R. Knight: 'The Manding Contexts', 53–90; P. Schuyler: 'Berber Professional Musicians in Performance', 91–148]

Sumarsam: 'Inner Melody in Javanese Gamelan', *Karawitan: Source Readings in Javenese Gamelan and Vocal Music*, i, ed. J. Becker and A. Feinstein (Ann Arbor, 1984), 245–304

R.A. Sutton: 'Who is the Pesindhèn? Notes on the Female Singing Tradition in Java', *Indonesia*, xxxvii (1984), 118–31

L.I. al-Faruqi: 'The Suite in Islamic History and Culture', *World of Music*, xxvii/3 (1985), 46–64

A. Marett: 'In Search of the Lost Melodies of Tang China: an Account of Recent Research and its Implications for the History and Analysis of Tôgaku', *Musicology Australia*, ix (1986), 29–38

J. Baily: *Music of Afghanistan: Professional Musicians in the City of Herat* (Cambridge, 1988)

P.V. Bohlman: 'Missionaries, Magical Muses, and Magnificent Menageries: Image and Imagination in the Early History of Ethnomusicology', *World of Music*, xxx/3 (1988), 5–26

J. Bor: 'The Rise of Ethnomusicology: Sources on Indian Music c.1780–1890', *YTM*, xx (1988), 51–73

A.J. Racy: 'Sound and Society: the Takht Music of Early Twentieth-Century Cairo', *Selected Reports in Ethnomusicology*, vii (1988), 139–70

J. Sugarman: 'Making Muabet', ibid. 1–42

A. Rasmussen: 'The Music of Arab Americans: Performance Contexts and Musical Transformations', *Pacific Review of Ethnomusicology*, v (1989), 15–33

G. Sawa: *Music Performance Practice in the Early Abbasid Era, 132–320 AH/750–932 AD* (Toronto, 1989)

P. Schuyler: 'Hearts and Minds: Three Attitudes towards Performance Practice and Music Theory in the Yemen Arab Republic', *EthM*, xxxiv (1990), 1–18

L. Manniche: *Music and Musicians in Ancient Egypt* (London, 1991)

R.A. Sutton: *Traditions of Gamelan Music in Java: Musical Pluralism and Regional Identity* (Cambridge, 1991)

C.A. Waterman: '*Juju* History: toward a Theory of Sociomusical Practice', *Ethnomusicology and Modern Music History*, ed. S. Blum, P.V. Bohlman and D.M. Neuman (Urbana, IL, 1991), 49–67

R. Witmer: 'Stability in Blackfoot Songs, 1909–1968', ibid., 242–53

G. Booth: 'Disco *Laggi*: Modern Repertoire and Traditional Performance Practice in North Indian Popular Music', *AsM*, xxiii/1 (1991–2), 61–83

E. Brown: 'The African/African American Idiom in Music: Family Resemblances in Black Music', *African Musicology: Current Trends*, ii, ed. J.C. Djedje (Los Angeles, 1992), 115–34

R. Davis: 'The Effects of Notation on Performance Practice in Tunisian Art Music', *World of Music*, xxxiv/1 (1992), 85–114

L. Gold: 'Musical Expression in the Wayang Repertoire: a Bridge between Narrative and Ritual', *Balinese Music in Context*, ed. H. Oesch and D. Schaareman (Winterthur, 1992), 245–75

J. Kippen: 'Tabla Drumming and the Human-Computer Interaction', *World of Music*, xxxiv/3 (1992), 72–98

S.L. Marcus: 'Modulation in Arab Music: Documenting Oral Concepts, Performance Rules and Strategies', *EthM*, xxxvi (1992), 171–95

J.M. Schechter: *The Indispensable Harp: Historical Development, Modern Roles, Configurations, and Performance Practices in Ecuador and Latin America* (Kent, OH, 1992)

A. Shiloah: *Jewish Musical Traditions* (Detroit, 1992)

K. Marshall, ed.: *Rediscovering the Muses: Woman's Musical Traditions* (Boston, 1993) [incl. S. Weiss: 'Gender and *Gender*: Gender Ideology and the Female *Gender* Player in Central Java', 21–48; C. Meyers: 'Drum-Dance-Song Ensemble: Women's Performance in Biblical Israel', 49–67; E. Teeter: 'Female Musicians in Pharaonic Egypt', 68–91]

A. Miner: *Sitar and Sarod in the 18th and 19th Centuries* (Wilhelmshaven, 1993)

R.A. Sutton: *Variation in Central Javanese Gamelan Music: Dynamics of a Steady State* (DeKalb, IL, 1993)

A.N. Weintraub: 'Theory in Institutional Pedagogy and "Theory in Practice" for Sundanese Gamelan Music', *EthM*, xxxvii (1993), 29–39

C. Perlman: *Unplayed Melodies: Music Theory in Postcolonial Java* (diss., Wesleyan U., 1994)

B. Brinner: *Knowing Music, Making Music: Javanese Gamelan and the Theory of Musical Competence and Interaction* (Chicago, 1995)

R. Taruskin: *Text and Act: Essays on Music and Performance* (Oxford, 1995)

J.L. Witzleben: '*Silk and Bamboo*' Music in Shanghai: the Jiangnan Sizhu Instrumental Ensemble Tradition* (Kent, OH, 1995)

M. Perlman: 'Conflicting Interpretations: Indigenous Analysis and Historical Change in Central Javanese Music', *AsM*, xxviii/i (1996–7), 115–40

H. Spiller: 'Continuity in Sundanese Dance Drumming: Clues from the 1893 Chicago Exposition', *World of Music*, xxxviii/2 (1996), 23–40

A.K. Stillman: 'Sound Evidence: Conceptual Stability, Social Maintenance and Changing Performance Practices in Modern Hawaiian Hula Songs', *World of Music*, xxxviii/2 (1996), 5–22

G.F. Barz and T.J.Cooley, eds.: *Shadows in the Field: New Perspectives for Fieldwork in Ethnomusicology* (New York, 1997)

R. Davis: 'Cultural Policy and the Tunisian *Ma'lûf*: Redefining a Tradition', *EthM*, xli (1997), 1–21

J.C. Sugarman: *Engendering Song: Singing and Subjectivity at Prespa Albanian Weddings* (Chicago, 1997)

S.P. Walton: *Heavenly Nymphs and Earthly Delights: Javanese Female Singers, their Music, and their Lives* (diss., U. of Michigan, 1997)

L. Gold: *The Gender Wayang Repertoire in Theater and Ritual: a Study of Balinese Musical Meaning* (diss., U. of California, Berkeley, 1998)

B. Wade: *Imaging Sound* (Chicago, 1998)

HOWARD MAYER BROWN (I, 1), DAVID HILEY (I, 2 (i)), HOWARD MAYER BROWN/CHRISTOPHER PAGE (I, 2 (ii)), CHRISTOPHER PAGE (I, 3), HOWARD MAYER BROWN/KENNETH KREITNER (I, 4), HOWARD MAYER BROWN/PETER WALLS (I, 5), JANET K. PAGE (I, 6), D. KERN HOLOMAN, ROBERT WINTER/JANET K. PAGE (I, 7), ROBERT PHILIP (I, 8), BENJAMIN BRINNER (II)

Performing Right Society [PRS]. *See* COPYRIGHT, §III, 16(i).

Pergament, Moses (*b* Helsinki, 21 Sept 1893; *d* Gustavsberg, nr Stockholm, 5 March 1977). Swedish composer and music critic of Finnish birth. Compared with his Swedish colleagues (he became a Swedish citizen in 1918) Pergament had a cosmopolitan background and training: he was born into a Jewish family; he studied in St Petersburg as a violinist (and served as such for four years in the Helsinki Philharmonic Society) and in Berlin at the Stern Conservatory; he also trained as an opera conductor; and he spent much of the interwar period in Berlin and Paris before settling permanently in Stockholm. There he worked steadily as a composer and as one of the city's most influential and trenchant music critics, with some part-time choral and orchestral conducting.

The varied experiences of Pergament's formative years gave him a breadth of perspective which is obvious in his vast output and which sets him apart from his compatriots. His interest in Russian music (particularly Musorgsky) and German Expressionism is balanced with Impressionist touches and later French traits, notably from Les Six. Besides this, some of his most important works treat Jewish themes and are partly influenced by Hebrew cantillation. *Den judiska sången* (1944) is a central work, and the orchestral *Rapsodia ebraica*, written in protest at the massacres under the Nazis and parodying *Deutschland über alles*, is another Jewish-inspired piece. Pergament's major works also include the ballet *Krelantems och Eldeling*, composed for the Ballets Suédois, the chamber opera *Himlens hemlighet*, choral works, songs, various orchestral pieces and chamber compositions of many kinds.

WORKS
(selective list)

Stage: Krelantems och Eldeling (ballet), 1920–21; Vision (ballet), 1923, Helsinki, 1925; Himlens hemlighet [The Secret of Heaven] (chbr op, after P.F. Lagerkvist), Stockholm, 1953; Eli (mystical play, N. Sachs), Stockholm, 1959

Choral orch: Hosiannah, 1928; Nedanförmänskliga visor [Subhuman Songs] (G. Fröding), 1936; Den judiska sången [The Jewish Song] (R. Josephson), choral sym., 1944; De sju dödssynderna [The Seven Deadly Sins] (K. Boye), 1963; Al nahrat bavel (Bible), cant., 1974

Songs with orch: 4 kinesiska sånger, 1946; Ångest [Anguish], 1963; 4 dikter av Edith Södergran, 1966; Drömmen om mullen och vindarne [The Dream of the Earth and the Winds], 1969

Orch: Dibbuk, vn, orch, 1935; Rapsodia ebraica, 1935; Swedish Rhapsody, 1940; Kol nidre, vc, orch, 1949; Vn Conc., 1950; Pf Conc., 1952; Vc Conc., 1954; Violino Grande Conc., 1965; Fantasia differente, vc, str, 1970; Intermezzo, fl, str, 1973

Chbr: Suite, vn, vc, 1919; Sonata, vn, pf, 1918–20; Str Qt no.1, 1918–22; Pf Trio, 1924; Str Qt no.2, 1952; Str Qt no.3, 1967; Pezzo, 4 fl (1 player), 1972

Other works: over 100 songs, *c*60 choral pieces

Principal publisher: Nordiska Musikförlaget

WRITINGS

Svenska tonsättare (Stockholm, 1943)
Vandring med fru musica (Stockholm, 1943)
Ny vandring med fru musica (Stockholm, 1944)
Jenny Lind (Stockholm, 1945)
'Franz Berwald', *MMR*, lxxvi (1946), 176–82
'Gösta Nystroem: Swedish Composer',*ML*, xxvii (1946), 66–70
'Hilding Rosenberg: a Journey in Modern Swedish Music', *ML*, xxviii (1947), 249–57

BIBLIOGRAPHY

L. Rosenblüth: 'Arvet från två Kulturer', *Nutida musik*, vii/3 (1963–4), 7–10 [incl. list of works]
G. Larsson: 'Moses Pergament and "The Jewish Song"', *Kungl. musikaliska akademien årsskrift* (Stockholm, 1979), 28–40

HANS ÅSTRAND

Pergament, Ruvim Samuilovich (*b* Petrozavodsk, 30 Aug/9 Sept 1906; *d* Petrozavodsk, 6 March 1965). Karelian composer, violinist and conductor. He was one of the founders of the school of composers and the first chairman of the Union of Composers in the Karelian republic. His studies in the violin class at the Petrograd Conservatory (1914–17, 1920–26) were interrupted by the war and he began to compose music independently in consultation with R.I. Mervol'f at the conservatory. In 1926 he began working as a violinist in Petrozavodsk, directing the music departments at the theatres of Working Youth and Young Viewers. His acquaintance with the ethnographer, poet and musician V.P. Gudkov, drew to his attention the local northern Russian, Pomor, Karelian-Lyudik, Finnish and Vepsian traditions. He became aware of the diverse forms of folk music (runic and pastoral), as well as the work being done to revive the *kantele* (both the natural and harmonic types of the instrument) and to expand the repertory for the ensembles made up of its various types. Continuing Russian nationalist practices, he doggedly practised harmonizing folk melodies.

His first large-scale composition – the symphonic poem *Ayno* for soprano and orchestra – commemorated the centenary of the first published edition of the Kalevala. The work was successful with audiences both in concert and on radio; Sollertinsky commented that '*Ayno* is a fine and serious piece'. The thematic material is generated by using variation technique to develop the Karelian wedding song *Priletal oryol* ('An Eagle Came Flying'). The work is imbued with symphonic intensity in the spirit of Rimsky-Korsakov and in part of Sibelius; along with the *Karelian Suite* (1938) it opened up a path for the composition of large-scale orchestral genres in Karelia.

During the 1940s Pergament concentrated on operatic works. His comic opera *Kumokha*, based on Karelian folk tales about a wooden clown, was given a concert performance in 1948 but, following the party resolution about Muradeli's opera *The Great Friendship*, the opera was declared formalist. In 1959 *Kumokha* was revised and the music (especially the dance numbers and games) became very popular. The one-act opera *Tri brata* ('Three Brothers'; 1949), after Karelian songs about Vyaynemeynen, Illmoyllin and Yogamoyn, was conceived in epic terms and might have become a milestone in the establishment of Karelian music for the stage, but for the same ideological reasons it suffered a hapless fate; it was performed only in 1985 by students of the Petrozavodsk Conservatory. The opera employs leitmotifs that come close to standard runic melodies. Pergament gave clear proof of his lyrical gifts with psychological expressiveness bound up with the rivalry between the brothers over the capricious but beautiful Katerina.

During the 1950s and 60s Pergament continued the vein of folkloric symphonism; *Iz severnogo al'boma* ('From a Northern Album') is a lyrical orchestral suite that reinterprets the traditions of Russian and European romanticism as embodied by Tchaikovsky and Grieg, but nonetheless contains original harmonic turns. Many of his major works have remained in manuscript.

WORKS
(selective list)

Ops: Kumokha (V. Chekhov and N. Ruban), 1944–6, rev. 1959, Petrozavodsk, 1959; Tri brata [Three Brothers] (1, V. Gudkov, after Kalevala), 1948–9, concert perf., Petrozavodsk, 1985
Inst: Karel'skaya syuita [Karelian Suite], orch, 1938; Ov., kantele orch, 1944; Liricheskiye stranitsï [Lyrical Pages], kantele orch, 1949; Vn Conc., 1949, unfinished; Pesni Zaonezh'ya [Song of the Trans-Onega Region], fantasy, pf qnt, 1950, Vepsskaya rapsodiya [Vepsian Rhapsody], orch, 1952; Iz severnogo al'boma [From a Northern Album], lyrical suite, orch, 1955; 6 p'yes, kantele, wind qt, 1956; 10 fortepiannïkh p'yes dlya detey [10 Piano Pieces for Children], 1958; 4 p'yesï, vn, pf, 1960
Vocal: Ayno (after Kalevala, trans. V. Bel'sky), S, orch, 1936; Poèma o devushkakh partizankakh [Poem about the Partisan Girls] (B. Shmidt), female chorus, orch, 1947; Pionyorskaya syuita [Pioneer Suite] (Yu. Nikonova), children's chorus, orch, 1954; Chudesnaya devushka [The Wonderful Girl], chorus, bayan (1959); Lesnaya nasha storona [Our Land of Forests] (A.I. Titov), chorus (1959); Nad rekoy luna svetila [The Moon was Shining over the River] (V. Voynovich), chorus (1959); Pesni dlya detey shko l'nogo vozrasta [Songs for Children of School Age], chorus (1959)
Incid music for theatre and puppet theatre, wind band music and folksong arrs., incl. Finskiye pesni [Finnish Folksongs], S, pf (1948)

Principal publishers: Muzgiz, Sovetskiy kompozitor

BIBLIOGRAPHY

G.I. Lapchinsky: *Zhizneutvyorzhdayushcheye tvorchestvo* [Life-affirming creative work] (Petrozavodsk, 1961)
A.I. Gladïsheva: 'O pretvorenii vepsskogo fol'klora karel'skikh kompozitorov' [Interpreting the Vepsian folklore of Karelian composers], *Vzaimoobogashcheniye natsional'nïkh muzïkal'nïkh kul'tur* (Kazan, 1981)
V.K. Koshelyov: 'K izucheniyu tvorchestva R.S. Pergamenta: opït orkestrovki operï "Tri brata"' [A contribution towards studying the creative work of Pergament: an attempt at orchestrating the opera 'Three Brothers'], *Sovremennoye kompozitorskoye tvorchestvo, fol'klor Karelii, khudozhestvennoye naslediye* (Petrozavodsk, 1986)
L.M. Butir: 'Simfonichesakaya muzïka Karelii' [The symphonic music of Karelia], *Professional'naya muzïka Karelii: ocherki*, ed. Yu.G. Kon and N.Yu. Grodnitskaya (Petrozavodsk, 1995), 12–16

OL'GA ALEKSANDROVNA BOCHKARYOVA

Pergolesi, Giovanni Battista (*b* Iesi, Marche, 4 Jan 1710; *d* Pozzuoli, nr Naples, 16 March 1736). Italian composer. He was a leading figure in the rise of Italian comic opera in the 18th century.

1. Life. 2. Posthumous fame. 3. Works.

1. LIFE.   His grandfather, Cruciano Draghi, was a shoemaker, a son of Maestro Francesco from Pergola; he married a woman from Iesi in that town on 1 January 1663. The family was known as 'Pergolesi' from the town of their origin (although the composer's elder brother and sister were entered in the baptismal register under the name 'Draghi'). In the files of the conservatory where he studied, Giovanni Battista is entered under the name 'Jesi', although he called himself 'Pergolesi'; in contemporary records the form 'Pergolese' is also used.

The composer's father, Francesco Andrea Draghi-Pergolesi, was a surveyor, and in that capacity formed links with the nobility of Iesi. One such nobleman was the godfather of Giovanni Battista, the third child; another defended his interests in a dispute over the will after his father's death on 27 May 1732 (his mother had died in 1727). The composer's two brothers and one sister died in infancy, and even as a child Giovanni Battista seems to have been sickly: it is significant that he was confirmed as early as 27 May 1711. The caricaturist Pier Leone Ghezzi met the composer in Rome in 1734 and sketched his profile that May. After Pergolesi's death Ghezzi expanded the sketch to a full-length caricature with a note that he suffered greatly from a deformed leg and limped (fig.1). This is the only likeness of Pergolesi linked with any certainty to the composer. He died from tuberculosis.

According to later tradition, Pergolesi received his elementary musical training from the *maestro di cappella* at Iesi, Francesco Santi, and was instructed on the violin by Francesco Mondini, the public music master. Through the Marquis Cardolo Maria Pianetti, of Iesi, he was sent to study at the Conservatorio dei Poveri di Gesù Cristo in Naples at some time between 1720 and 1725. Gaetano Greco, *maestro di cappella* of the conservatory until his death in 1728, was Pergolesi's instructor in composition; Greco was succeeded for a few months by Leonardo Vinci and then, from October 1728, by Francesco Durante. Pergolesi did not have to pay maintenance or tuition expenses at the conservatory because he took part in musical performances, first as a choirboy, later as a violinist and as *capoparanza* (the leading violinist of one of the groups of instrumentalists made available by the conservatory for performances in Naples and the surrounding area). Villarosa, whose account is based on a manuscript by Giuseppe Sigismondo, wrote in superlatives of his skill and improvisations as a violinist.

1. *Giovanni Battista Pergolesi: caricature by Pier Leone Ghezzi, pen and ink, 1734 (I-Rvat Cod. Ottob. lat.3116,.f.139v)*

A *dramma sacro* by Pergolesi, *Li prodigi della divina grazia nella conversione di S Guglielmo Duca d'Aquitania*, was performed by the conservatory in summer 1731 at the monastery of S Agnello Maggiore. Such performances were part of a tradition whereby the Naples conservatories gave their advanced students the opportunity to make their public débuts as composers; they were commissioned to compose *drammi sacri*, three-act religious operas with *buffo* scenes. After Pergolesi's death *S Guglielmo* was twice revised, once as a two-part opera (in Rome, 1742).

Pergolesi must have left the conservatory in the late summer of 1731. A Mass in D probably dates from this era and he received his first opera commission in 1731, which reflects his growing and influential patronage. The libretto chosen was *Alessandro Severo*, written by Zeno for Venice in 1716 and now revised as *Salustia*. It would seem, from the fact that the author of the text for the intermezzo (possibly Domenico Caracajus) himself set the recitatives of the second part to music, that Pergolesi had to compose the music in haste. The most famous member of the cast for *Salustia*, Nicolini, died on 1 January 1732; Gioacchino Conti was brought from Rome, two roles changed hands, and Pergolesi had to make last-minute alterations. Accordingly, the opera was not staged until the second half of January 1732, and apparently it had little success; the second opera of the season, *Alessandro nell-Indie* by the court *maestro di cappella* Francesco Mancini, followed as early as 2 February.

In 1732 Pergolesi became *maestro di cappella* to Prince Ferdinando Colonna Stigliano, equerry to the Viceroy of Naples. *Lo frate 'nnamorato*, his first *commedia musicale*, was performed at the Teatro dei Fiorentini in Naples on 27 September 1732; the libretto was by G.A. Federico, a lawyer and the leading Neapolitan comedy writer of the time. *Lo frate 'nnamorato* met with unusual success. The performances may have continued into 1733, and for Carnival 1734 Pergolesi had to revise the work for a new cast. When there was a new production of the opera in 1748, at the Teatro Nuovo, the work was said to have been recited and sung in the city streets for the previous 20 years.

There were earthquakes in 1731 and again in November 1732; the archbishop summoned the people to services of atonement and the municipality elected St Emidius, protector against earthquakes, as the city's special patron saint. A vow was taken to celebrate his festival annually with a solemn mass and double vespers, and the decree was formally proclaimed on 31 December 1732 in the church of S Maria della Stella. Villarosa reported that Pergolesi composed for the occasion a mass for double chorus, a *Domine ad adjuvandum me* and the psalms *Dixit Dominus*, *Laudate* and *Confitebor*. It is probable that the Mass in F and perhaps the vesper introit *Deus in adjutorium* ('Domine ad adjuvandum me'), as well as other vesper psalms, were performed on this occasion; the extant psalm *Laudate pueri*, however, belongs among Pergolesi's last works. The brief interval (19 days) between the election of St Emidius and the celebration suggests that the mass (the autograph of which is dedicated to the saint) may have been written earlier, or for a later celebration of the event.

During Carnival 1733 the theatres in Naples remained closed as a sign of atonement. For the empress's birthday (28 August 1733) Pergolesi was commissioned to write an opera, *Il prigioniero superbo* (after Silvani's libretto

La fede tradita e vendicata). The impresario had engaged an unusual and small cast: there was no primo uomo and the prima donna was an alto. The text of the intermezzo, *La serva padrona*, was written by Federico. For some reason the first performance did not take place until 5 September 1733; there were further performances continuing into October. On 23 February 1734, presumably because of his services during the festivities in honour of St Emidius, Pergolesi was appointed deputy to the *maestro di cappella* of the city, Domenico Sarro, with the right to succeed him.

In March 1734 the claimant to the Neapolitan throne, Charles Bourbon, approached the city with Spanish troops. The Austrians, who had ruled Naples since 1707 through a viceroy, retreated into the citadel and remained there until the beginning of May; on 10 May Charles celebrated his solemn entry into the city and reinstated the Kingdom of Naples. Pergolesi's patron, the Prince of Stigliano, had withdrawn to Rome. Another Neapolitan nobleman, Marzio Domenico IV Carafa, Duke of Maddaloni, ordered a performance of a mass by Pergolesi in the church of S Lorenzo in Lucina, Rome, on the festival of St John Nepomuk (16 May 1734); this was the Mass in F (probably performed earlier in Naples), which aroused great interest, if only because the Neapolitan 'number' mass was unusual in Rome. In his diary Ghezzi reported mockingly that it was an extraordinary event and a 'musica spaventosa' performed by all the singers and violinists of Rome. In Valesio's chronicle it is stated that the *maestro di cappella* had been specially brought from Naples at the expense of the duke's mother (an aunt of the Prince of Stigliano). Because of the congestion in the church, it was noted, the floor and the corner of the choir rostrum subsided.

It may have been in connection with the performance that Pergolesi entered the Duke of Maddaloni's service as *maestro di cappella*. He probably returned to Naples in the duke's entourage in June 1734. The duke was interested in literature and was an amateur cellist; Pergolesi's cello sinfonia was no doubt composed for him. The duke's uncle and guardian, Lelio Carafa, Marquis d'Arienzo, was among the closest friends of King Charles, and in September 1734 was entrusted with the supervision of the opera house. Pergolesi was commissioned to write an opera for the birthday of the king's mother on 25 October 1734. The libretto chosen was Metastasio's *Adriano in Siria*; the text of the intermezzo (now known as *Livietta e Tracollo*) was supplied by Tommaso Mariani. One of the most famous singers of the 18th century, Caffarelli, who had been admitted into King Charles's musical establishment, was engaged as primo uomo. In setting the libretto Pergolesi had to take note of Caffarelli's wishes, and Metastasio's text was considerably rewritten. This was Pergolesi's last serious opera for Naples. In a statement by the impresario of the Teatro S Bartolomeo to the Marquis d'Arienzo in 1735, Pergolesi is no longer mentioned among the composers who could be called on, and in a second document it is stated that he was esteemed as a musician but that his last opera had failed to please.

It must accordingly have come as some compensation to Pergolesi that his mass in S Lorenzo in Lucina had aroused the interest of the Roman public; he was commissioned to set Metastasio's *L'olimpiade* for the Teatro Tordinona in Rome for Carnival 1735. Metastasio, who had reports sent to him in Vienna about the preparations for the première, became indignant: the chorus which he required had been omitted, and the cast was mediocre. Nevertheless, Pergolesi (who apparently wrote most of the opera in Naples) had to make further alterations for the singers; he composed one new aria, and in four others drew on *Adriano in Siria*. The performances began in January. After a few days they were interrupted when the Rome theatres were closed because of the death of Maria Clementina Stuart-Sobieski, wife of the pretender to the English throne. Performances were resumed on 23 January, but the theatres were again closed on 1 and 2 February for the Candlemas festival; by 5 February the next opera, Ciampi's *Demofoonte*, was in production. Grétry's report, which depends on Duni for its evidence, states that *L'olimpiade* was a failure and that a member of the audience threw an orange which struck Pergolesi on the head (one of the many traditional stories about him). It must be admitted that initially *L'olimpiade* did not apparently enjoy any special success; but it lived on in multiple restagings, and some passages in the opera, such as the aria 'Se cerca, se dice', were later considered unrivalled for dramatic effect; Galuppi, Hasse, Jommelli and others based their own settings of the text on Pergolesi's model. It was also heard in numerous pasticcio versions throughout Europe, including the one given on 20 April 1742 at the King's Theatre, London, as *Meraspe*. An extensive manuscript tradition attests the fact that *L'olimpiade* was still highly esteemed by connoisseurs and operagoers in the second half of the century.

Pergolesi's health seems to have deteriorated in summer 1735. He had his last theatrical success with *Il Flaminio*, a comedy on a text by Federico produced in the Teatro Nuovo in Naples in autumn 1735; the libretto refers to Pergolesi as organist of the royal chapel. The comedy was performed again in winter 1737 at the Teatro dei Fiorentini, and for Carnival 1743 it was given in Siena as a *divertimento giocoso*; it was also staged with a new production of *Lo frate 'nnamorato* in the Teatro Nuovo in Naples in 1748 and 1749. Pergolesi was commissioned to write a serenata (*Il tempo felice*) for the wedding of Raimondo di Sangro, Prince of Sansevero, at Torremaggiore in December 1735. According to the libretto, dated 9 November 1735, the second part was set by Nicola Sabatino because Pergolesi was in poor health.

Early in 1736 Pergolesi moved into the Franciscan monastery in Pozzuoli founded by the ancestors of his patron, the Duke of Maddaloni. His aunt, Cecilia Giorgi, from Iesi, who had been his housekeeper, remained in Naples; he is said to have handed his possessions over to her, which suggests that he did not expect to recover. According to Boyer, during his final illness Pergolesi composed the cantata *Orfeo*, the *Stabat mater* and (his last work) the *Salve regina* in C minor for soprano and strings (the cantata was in fact written before *Il Flaminio*). Villarosa, however, said that Pergolesi's last work was the *Stabat mater*, written for the noble fraternity in the church of S Maria dei Sette Dolori in Naples as a replacement for Alessandro Scarlatti's *Stabat mater*. Pergolesi, aged 26, died in Pozzuoli and was buried in the common pit next to the cathedral. The Marquis Domenico Corigliano di Rignano, who then owned the *Stabat mater* manuscript and was a friend of the first Pergolesi biographer, Villarosa, had a memorial tablet for him set up in the cathedral at Pozzuoli; the inscription on it was by Villarosa. In September 1890 a side-chapel of the

2. Scene from part 2 of an early Paris production of Pergolesi's intermezzo 'La serva padrona': engraving, after 1752

cathedral was prepared as Pergolesi's burial chapel and the memorial tablet was transferred there.

2. POSTHUMOUS FAME.   Highly romanticized accounts of Pergolesi's life written in the late 18th and the 19th centuries distorted his career and influence, but he was clearly among the most successful and respected composers of his generation. He wrote regularly for the Teatro S Bartolomeo from the moment he left school, his comic works in minor theatres were enormously popular, he was appointed *vicemaestro* to the royal chapel at the age of 22, and was offered the protection and commissions of Naples's most important royal families. The almost universal fame he attained posthumously represented a new phenomenon in music history. Shortly after his death a collection of four of his cantatas was published: this was the first time that cantatas had been printed in Naples, and as early as 1738 a second edition appeared. Queen Maria Amalia of Naples ordered in 1738 that *La serva padrona* and *Livietta e Tracollo* be performed, and added: 'Questo autore è difonto, ma fu uomo grande'. President De Brosses called Pergolesi 'mon auteur d'affection' as early as 1739. Pergolesi's fame was spread by performances of *Lo frate 'nnamorato, Il Flaminio, L'olimpiade* and his church music, but above all by travelling troupes of players who took his comedies, particularly *La serva padrona*, into their repertory. The work received at least 24 new productions in its first ten years at places that included Rome, Spoleto, Parma, Milan, Fermo, Graz, Lucca, Venice, Munich, Dresden, Modena, Siena and Hamburg. Remarkably, and uncharacteristically for its day (and in contrast to *Livietta*), *La serva padrona* remained largely unaltered in its text throughout its 18th-century performance history. It was given on 1 August 1752 in Paris, where it had first been

heard in 1746. This second series of performances met with a tremendous response (fig.2) and was the cause of the Querelle des Bouffons, the pamphlet war between the supporters of traditional French opera and the proponents of Italian *opera buffa*; Pergolesi's name came to symbolize the aesthetics of J.-J. Rousseau and the 'progressive' party. Two printings of *La serva padrona* appeared in Paris in 1752; these were followed by two editions of a French adaptation under the title *La servante maîtresse* by Baurans, and in 1759 by the appearance of *The Favourite Songs in the Burletta La serva padrona* in London.

Livietta e Tracollo, the *Salve regina* and above all the *Stabat mater* achieved equally widespread fame. The *Stabat mater*, first published in London in 1749, became the most frequently printed single work in the 18th century. It was also circulated in many adaptations, including one by Bach (as *Tilge, Höchster, meine Sünden*). The vogue for Pergolesi caused many works to be wrongly attributed to him, creating a confusion that has long persisted and is reflected in the early *Opera omnia* (1939–42), and corrected in the new *Complete Works*. Among the most important misattributions are an intermezzo, *Il maestro di musica* (based largely on a work by Auletta), the song *Tre giorni son che Nina*, sets of trio sonatas and harpsichord lessons, two flute concertos and six *Concerti armonici* (details of these misattributed works are given in the work-list below).

3. WORKS.   Pergolesi's music is among the earliest consistently to reflect the new principles of an evolving 'natural' or 'galant' style in the 18th century. Writers such as Mattei and Manfredini a generation later praised him for his regular and well-developed motifs, and for his expressive text-setting, although much of this can be traced to Vinci and other earlier composers. Above all,

3. *Autograph MS of part of the Kyrie from Pergolesi's Mass in F (3rd version) (I-Nc)*

his music seems spontaneous and fresh, often with a distinctive Neapolitan character tinged by a popular style, Spanish motifs and alternately comic, sentimental and heroic gestures. His operas reflect the social and intellectual upheaval of early 18th-century Naples, the comic ones (such as *Il Flaminio*) in particular exploring a new rising and ambitious middle class.

A collection of Pergolesi's *solfeggi* (two- and three-part exercises in melody) is extant; traces of modality and elements of the doctrine of proportion can be seen in them. If they represent student work at the conservatory, they are a unique document of the methods of instruction used there, but they give little indication of any special talent for composition. Otherwise the earliest extant work by Pergolesi is the cantata *Questo è il piano* (*Ritorno*), dated 24 April 1731. It bears the marks of an exercise in composition: its two arias, constructed from musical 'blocks' of one and a half to several bars, are exemplary models of the da capo form. *S Guglielmo*, his *dramma sacro*, also gives the impression of being a student work; one can sense the didactic purpose behind it as well as the instructor's correcting hand. The most remarkable parts are the *buffo* scenes; Pergolesi already used with great skill and accuracy the gesture-like style of *buffo* melody which had been developed by Neapolitan intermezzo composers during the preceding decade.

Pergolesi had the good fortune to be able to apply himself at an unusually early age to what was then the most important musical genre, the *opera seria*. All his *opere serie* were written under unfavourable circumstances. *Salustia* has conservative features not to be found in his later works; this may be connected with the choice of libretto and with the fact that the intended primo uomo, Nicolini, was at the end of his career (and died before it was performed). No other of Pergolesi's operatic characters has the grandeur and pathos of Marziano, intended for Nicolini: it is like an echo of the music of the high Baroque era. The notable influence of the *buffo* melody in some of the arias is a new and significant departure for Pergolesi. The style, so disjointed in *Salustia*, is more polished in *Il prigioniero superbo*. Pathos is replaced by sentimentality and gallantry, and formal accompanying figures become more prominent in the orchestral writing. Because of the unusual cast there are none of the splendid soprano arias that normally highlight an *opera seria*. This makes the opera a strangely colourless work, for Pergolesi was not yet able to turn the performers' lack of virtuosity to account so as to increase the dramatic intensity.

Adriano in Siria is an excellent example of the extent to which the composition of an *opera seria* could be influenced by the demands of a single singer. The alterations to Metastasio's libretto affected not only the part of Pharnaspes (composed for Caffarelli) but also the relationship of his arias to those of the other performers, which in turn affected their number, position and character. Of Metastasio's 27 aria texts, only ten were retained: eight were omitted, nine replaced by different texts; one additional new aria was inserted, making ten new arias altogether. Caffarelli's three arias are extended beyond anything else in Pergolesi's music up to that date; they are the focal points of the opera. Each of these expresses a different 'affection', but the expression is subordinated to the need for allowing Caffarelli the opportunity to shine vocally; this is done differently each time and with new effects. The unusual care and precision which Pergolesi lavished on the arias of the supporting cast is still more remarkable. In *L'olimpiade*, composed for Rome, the special requirements which Pergolesi had to fulfil were comparatively modest. The fact that in *L'olimpiade* he used arias from no opera older than *Adriano in Siria* might be taken to suggest that he was conscious of his recent development as an artist. *L'olimpiade* is characterized by idyllic and delicate tone-colours, smooth, expressive melodies with reserved virtuosity, free treatment of the text (for example with verbal repetitions of the kind used in *opera buffa*) and a greater intensity of feeling. Pergolesi excelled as a dramatic composer in his variety of mood, figure and expression.

Of Pergolesi's two *commedie musicali* the earlier, *Lo frate 'nnamorato*, is his first completely independent work and also the most important extant example of the genre. It is in Neapolitan dialect, and a local note is prominent in its music. Folksong-like pieces, *seria* arias, *seria* parodies and *buffo* numbers are juxtaposed with great assurance. Federico's text for *Il Flaminio* is particularly dependent on the contemporary upheaval in social status under the Spanish regime; Flaminio, a bourgeois without noble title, aspires to express himself in aristocratic Italian, though he cannot leave his Neapolitan roots, as his opening aria 'Mentre l'erbetta' (borrowed by Stravinsky for *Pulcinella*) illustrates. The roles were performed by *commedia dell'arte* actors, and the spontaneity, juxtaposition and stratification of styles in the music surely flows from that influence. Pergolesi's music seems to be full of allusions and quotations, only a few of which can be deciphered. In *Il Flaminio*, unlike *Lo frate 'nnamorato*, the *parti serie* and *parti buffe* are clearly differentiated, and what were later to be known as *parti caricate* are introduced; using a wide stylistic repertory, Pergolesi endowed these roles with unusually personal and individual traits.

La serva padrona, the intermezzo to *Il prigioniero superbo*, is a work of true genius. Pergolesi's basic method of portrayal is the gesture-like *buffo* style, which he developed to an unsurpassed vitality and effectiveness. Federico's libretto, exuding in a particularly inventive way the rhythms and inflections of Neapolitan dialect, provided him not only with effective *buffo* scenes but also with a plot which develops logically between credibly drawn characters. It was possible both for the characters to express themselves naturally within the idiom of the music and for the music to make clear the characters' motivation. Mariani's libretto for *Livietta e Tracollo*, the intermezzo to *Adriano in Siria*, is less unified, but still consistently implies the dialect of its origin. Pergolesi's *buffo* style is still more concentrated and cryptic than in *La serva padrona*, but the individual numbers are not part of a plot which develops in a credible way; instead they appear as single pieces (including some of a characteristically melancholy and tender tone for Livietta).

In his masses Pergolesi used a style that had recently been developed in Naples, in which only the Kyrie and the Gloria were set to music on a large scale (fig.3). The Kyrie is made up of a long 'Christe' fugue with concertante elements, framed by a slow introduction and a broad cadence on the words 'Kyrie eleison'. The Gloria is divided into choral, ensemble and solo movements. Pergolesi produced different versions of his masses in D and F, for one, two and four choruses (there was still a demand for polychoral music on festive occasions). These are not, however, genuinely polychoral, for the music, designed for one chorus in five parts (with double soprano), is merely assigned to several choruses so as to achieve antiphonal and tutti effects. There is no early evidence for the authenticity of the Mass in F published under Pergolesi's name in Vienna in 1805, but it is similar in style to his known masses. This may be explained by Guglielmo della Valle's statement (*Memorie storiche del p.m. Giambattista Martini*, Naples, 1785) that the dukes of Maddaloni held performances of church music each year on the third Sunday in September in the Neapolitan parish church of S Maria dei Sette Dolori (where their family had its burial vault), and that Pergolesi composed music for this occasion which the Maddaloni family had jealously guarded.

Pergolesi's psalm settings are intended for vespers. They too are on a large scale and are divided into choral and solo sections, with concertante movements for soloists and chorus. The solo sections in Pergolesi's church music are two-section, aria-like pieces, different from the typical opera and oratorio arias and apparently derived from the vocal and instrumental concerto movement. Many of the choral movements, too, betray the same influence, and some of them show signs of being reduced polychoral settings. Within its stylistic bounds, Pergolesi's church music is distinguished by the lively declamation of the text and the melodic charm of the solo sections, and by the rich contrasts of the choral ones. It may have influenced the later work of his teacher, Francesco Durante, and of Leonardo Leo, both of whom survived Pergolesi. The *Stabat mater* for two solo voices and strings, his most famous work, was evidently written in competition with Alessandro Scarlatti's *Stabat mater* for the same voices and instruments. A comparison between the works shows Pergolesi's new approach to the concertante vocal movement and his development of the 'church aria', as well as the earliest application to sacred music of the style of expressive sensibility. The work stirred considerable controversy at home and abroad for its religious propriety and musical style. Padre Martini's traditional views towards counterpoint incited some to criticize Pergolesi's setting, while others found it 'galant', expressive and new. The same bittersweet tone is present in the *Salve regina* in C minor for solo soprano and strings, composed (like the *Stabat mater*) at the very end of Pergolesi's life.

Most of the instrumental music under Pergolesi's name is wrongly attributed; his few authentic pieces are insignificant by comparison with his vocal music. The apparently authentic double harpsichord concerto is among the earliest examples of the keyboard concerto and demonstrates (along with other early Italian examples) a parallel development of the genre outside Germany.

WORKS

Editions: *G.B. Pergolesi: Opera omnia*, ed. F. Caffarelli (Rome, 1939–42/R) [C]

[Of the 148 works in this edition, 69 are misattributed, 49 are questionable and only 30 may be considered genuine. A large number of works attributed to Pergolesi, some of which may be authentic, were omitted. For further information see Paymer: *Giovanni Battista Pergolesi:* (1977)]

G.B. Pergolesi: The Complete Works, ed. B.S. Brook and others (New York and Milan, 1986–) [B]

Title	Genre, acts	Libretto	First performance	Sources, edn; remarks
Salustia	os, 3	?S. Morelli, after A. Zeno: *Alessandro Severo*	Naples, S Bartolomeo, Jan 1732	*I-Mc, Nc*; C ix; B i
[Nibbio e Nerina]	int, 2	?D. Caracajus	Naples, S Bartolomeo, Jan 1732	perf. with Salustia; music lost; recit in pt 2 set by Caracajus
Lo frate 'nnamorato	commedia musicale, 3	G.A. Federico	Naples, Fiorentini, 27 Sept 1732; rev. Naples, carn. 1734	*B-Bc, GB-Lbl, I-Mc, Nc*; C ii; B vii
[Capetà Cola, Spaviento e Giulietta]	introduction, balli		Naples, Fiorentini, 27 Sept 1732	perf. with Lo frate 'nn-amorato; music lost
Il prigioniero superbo	os, 3	after F. Silvani: *La fede tradita e vendicata*	Naples, S Bartolomeo, 5 Sept 1733	*Nc*; C xx; B ii
La serva padrona [characters: Serpina, Umberto]	int, 2	Federico	Naples, S Bartolomeo, 5 Sept 1733	perf. with Il prigioniero su-perbo; *A-Wgm, Wn, B-Bc, Br, D-Dl, W, F-Pn, I-Bc, BGc, Fc, Gl, Mc, Nc, PAc, PESc, Rsc, Tf, Vc*; C xi/1, sinfonia spu-rious, probably Viennese; B v
Adriano in Siria	os, 3	P. Metastasio	Naples, S Bartolomeo, 25 Oct 1734	*GB-Lbl, I-Nc*; C xiv; B iii
[Livietta e Tracollo/La contadina astuta]	int, 2	T. Mariani	Naples, S Bartolomeo, 25 Oct 1734	perf. with Adriano in Siria; *B-Bc, Br, GB-Lbl, I-Bc, Fc, Mc, Nc, PESc, Rsc, Tf*; C xi/3; B vi
L'olimpiade	os, 3	Metastasio	Rome, Tordinona, ? 2 Jan 1735	*A-Wn, B-Bc, Br, D-Dl, F-Pn, I-BGc, Mc, MOe, Nc, Rsc*, C xxiv; B iv
Il Flaminio	commedia musicale, 3	Federico	Naples, Nuovo, aut. 1735	*B-Bc, I-Nc* [Act 3*]; C xii; B viii

Works based on or related to Livietta e Tracollo: Il ladro finto pazzo, Milan, Regio, 1739; Il finto pazzo (addns C. Goldoni), Venice, S Samuele, May 1741, addl arias by P. Chiarini, rev. Goldoni and Chiarini as Amor fa l'uomo cieco, Venice, 1742; Il Tracollo, Venice, S Moisè, aut. 1744; Livietta, Venice, S Moisè, carn. 1746; La finta polacca, Rome, 2 Feb 1748; Il ladro convertito per amore, Venice, 1750; Tracollo, medico ignorante, Paris, 1753; Le charlatan

Spurious works: Ricimero, 1732 [probably an alternative title for Il prigioniero superbo]; Il geloso schernito, C iii [probably pasticcio by P. Chiarini, sinfonia by B. Galuppi]; La contadina astuta [characters: Tabarano, Scintilla], C xi/2 [pasticcio (B. Saddumene) based on 2 ints by J.A. Hasse: La contadina and Il tutore, and 1 duet from Pergolesi's Il Flaminio; also known as Il Tabarano]; Il maestro di musica, Paris, Opéra, 19 Sept 1752, C xxv [pasticcio based largely on P. Auletta: Orazio, but incl. 2 authentic arias – 'Son timida fanciulla', C xxv, 67, and 'Non vo' più dargli ascotto', C xxv, 45, and 1 authentic duet – 'Venite, deh siate gentile', C xxv, 51; also perf. as Le maître de musique, Paris, Comédie-Italienne (Bourgogne), 31 May 1755]

SACRED DRAMAS AND ORATORIOS

Li prodigi della divina grazia nella conversione di S Guglielmo Duca d'Aquitania (dramma sacro, 3, I. Mancini), Naples, monastery of S Agnello Maggiore, sum. 1731, C iv, B ix

La fenice sul rogo, ovvero La morte di S Giuseppe (orat, 2), ? Naples, Oratorio dei Filippini, 1731, C i, B iv

Spurious: Septem verba a Christo in cruce moriente prolatae (orat), *CH-Zz*, vs ed. H. Scherchen as *Die sieben Worte des Erlösers* (Vienna, 1952); Planctus animo poenitentis ad matrem dolorosam (orat), *GB-Lbl*; Oratorio della Passione; La morte d'Abel (orat), *CH-Zz*; Il pentimento, *GB-Lbl, Lcm*; La nascita del Redentore (orat), lost, said by Villarosa, probably mistakenly, to be in *I-Nf*

LITURGICAL

Mass [Ky–Gl] (D): version 1, S, A, SSATB, orch, ? sum. 1731, C xv/2, B xi; version 2, SSATB, SSATB, 2 orch; version 3, S, A, SSATB, orch, incl. Qui tollis, Quoniam, from Mass in F of 1734 and arr. of Cum Sancto spiritu from Sicut erat; other arrs. not authentic

Mass [Ky–Gl] (F): version 1, S, A, SSATB, orch, ? perf. Naples, S Maria della Stella, 31 Dec 1732, ? perf. Rome, S Lorenzo in Lucina, 16 May 1734, C xviii, B xii; version 2, SSATB, SSATB, 2 orch, C vi; version 3, solo vv, SSATB, SSATB, SSATB, SSATB, 2 orch; version 4, new version of Ky

Confitebor, ps, SSATB, orch, ? perf. Naples, S Maria della Stella, 31 Dec 1732, C viii, B xiii

Deus in adjutorium (Domine ad adjuvandum me), int, S, SSATB, orch, ? perf. Naples, S Maria della Stella, 31 Dec 1732, C xvii/1, B xiii

Dixit Dominus, ps (D), S, A, SSATB, SSATB, orch, ? perf. Naples, S Maria della Stella, 31 Dec 1732, C viii, B xiii

In coelestibus regnis, ant, A, str, org, C xvii/1, B xiii

In hac quam decora, motet, S, A, T, B, SSA, TTB, 2 orch, C xvii/1 (inc.), B xv

Laudate pueri, ps, S, SSATB, orch, late work, C viii, B xiii; authentic except for alternative version of Quis sicut Dominus, C xiii, 252

Salve regina, ant (a), S, str, org, C xv/1, B xv

Salve regina, ant (c), S, str, org; composed at Pozzuoli, 1736, C xv/1, B xv

Stabat mater, seq (f), S, A, str, org; composed at Pozzuoli, 1736, C xxvi, B xiv

Doubtful: Aura sacratis amoris, S, orch, *B-Bg*; Conturbat mentem, S, orch, *D-Bsb,W*; De placido torrente, *B-Bg*; Deus misereator nostri; Dixit Dominus, ps (B♭), SATB, orch, *D-MÜs*; Dixit Dominus, ps (D), C viii; Ecce pietatis signa, S, orch, *I-Mc*; Ecce superbos hostes, S, orch, *B-Bg*; In campo armato pugno, S, orch, *D-Bsb*; Laetatus sum, C viii; La Maddalena al sepolcro, S, *I-Ac*; Miserere mei (a), *D-SWl*; Miserere mei (B♭), formerly Königsberg; Miserere mei (C); Miserere mei (d), *GB-Lbl*; Miserere mei (F), *F-Pn*; Miserere mei (g), *B-Bc, F-Pn, GB-Lbl*; O salutaris hostia, T, B, bc, *Lbl*; Peccator crudelis, *I-Vnm*; Salve regina (f), C xv/1; Sequentia olim tempore missae septem dolorum, *D-LÜh*; Sol resplendet, *GB-Ob*; Te ergo quaesimus, S, T, hpd, *I-Rsc*; Tuba et timpano, S, orch, *B-Bg*; Utique resonando, *I-Nf*

Spurious: Mass [Ky–Gl] (F) (Vienna, 1805); Missa Pergolesiana [Messa estense] (D), C xxiii; Missa solemnis [Messa solenne] (C), C xxiii; Requiem, C xvi; Credo (C), Incarnatus (G), Sanctus (a), Sanctus (d), Agnus Dei (G), Agnus Dei (b), inc.: all C xxiii; Credo

(D), SATB, str, org, C xix suppl.; Agnus Dei (b), ed. R.F. Goldman (New York, 1949); Adoro te devote, C xvii/1; Ave verum, C xvii/1; Beatus vir, C viii; Dies irae, parody of Stabat mater, C xxvi; Dixit Dominus (C), by L. Leo, C viii; Dorme, benigne Jesu, by F. Durante, C xvii/1; Mag, by Durante, C xvii/1; Miserere (c), 2 settings, C xiii; O sacrum convivium, C xvii/1; Pro Jesu dum vivo, C xvii/1; Quis sicut Dominus, C viii; Salve regina (c), C xv/1; Sanctum et terribile, C viii; Siste superba fragor, C xvii/1; Super flumina, C xvii/2; Vexilla regis, C xvii/1

CHAMBER CANTATAS AND DUETS

4 cantate da camera … di G.B. Pergolesi, raccolte di Gioacchino Bruno, op.2 (Naples, after 1736): Chi non ode e chi non vede (Segreto tormento), S, str, bc; Dalsigre, ahi mia Dalsigre (Lontananza), S, bc, in *GB-Lbl* as Nigella, ahi mia Nigella; Luce degli occhi miei (L'addio), S, str, bc; Nel chiuso centro (Orfeo), S, str, bc, before aut. 1735; all ed. in C x, B xvi

Cants.: Della città vicino, S, str, bc, *D-MÜs*; Questo è il piano, questo è il rio (Ritorno), A, str, bc, 24 April 1731, C xxii, B xvi

Cants. (doubtful): A te torna il tuo Fileno, S, str; Berenice che fai; Che farò, che; Clori se mai rivolgi (Il canto del pastore), C x; Contrasti crudeli; Ecco, Tirsi, quel mirto (Proposta) – Or responderti debbo (Risposta), C x; In queste spiagge amene (Amor fedele), C x; L'aura, il ruscello, il fonte; Ove tu, ben mio, non sei, S, str; Quest'è amor, quest'è fede, *MÜs*

Cant. (spurious): Cor prigioniero, C xxii

Duets (spurious): Deh t'accheta, C xix, by G. Sellitto; Io mi rido; Mo che te stregno, C xix, suppl.; Se mi lasci, o mio contento, C xix, by G.M. Orlandini; Tu non rispondi, C xix, by G.A. Giai; Tu resterai mia cara, C xix; Tu vuoi ch'io viva, C xix, by D. Terradellas; Una povera fanciulla, C xix, by ?Orlandini

ARIAS
spurious unless otherwise stated

Ah, che sento in mezzo al core, C xxii; Ahi, che soffersi o Dio, C xxii; Ah mi dividon l'anima, C xix, also attrib. G. Chinzer; Amerò finché il mio core, C xxii; Basta così t'intendo, C xix, by R. di Capua; Ben che s'ascondono, doubtful, *B-Bc*; Bendato pargoletto, C xxii; Cara tu ridi, C xxii; Chi non crede, C xxii, by B. Galuppi; Chi tento, doubtful, *GB-Lcm*; Confusa, smarrita, C xix, by L. Vinci; Con quel volto sì vezzoso, doubtful, *Lbl*; Dio s'offende, e l'uom ne giace, doubtful; È pur ver, C xxii, by A.M. Bononcini; Empio amor, amor tiranno, C xxii, doubtful; Il mio cor innamorato, doubtful, *B-Bc*; Immagini dolenti, C xix, by G. Scarlatti; Ingrata non sarò, C xxii, by L. Leo

L'amato mio sposo, ed. in Il teatro illustrato, no.126 (Milan); La ragion, gli affetti, doubtful, *GB-Lbl*; Le luci vezzose del caro mio bene, doubtful, *Lbl*; Le souhaît, doubtful; Madre, e tu, inquista sposa, doubtful; Misero me, qual gelido tormento, acc. recit, C xix; Nacqui agli affanni in seno, doubtful; Non mi negar, ed. A. Parisotti, Arie antiche (Milan, 1930); Non mi tradir mai più, C xxii, by A. Scarlatti; Non so d'onde, C xix; Non ti minaccio sdegno, C xix; Non ti son padre, doubtful, *Lbl*; Partò, qual pastorello, doubtful, *B-Bc*; Pellegrino ch'infolto orror, doubtful; Pensa bene, mi dicesti, C xxii; Pensa, se avrò, mia cara, C xxii; Per esser più vezzose, C xxii; Per fuggirti io peno avrò, doubtful; Piangerò tanto, C xxii; Qual dolente pastorello, C xxii, by G. Lampugnani; Quant'inganni insegna amore, C xxii

Saggio nocchiero, doubtful, *Bc*; Se al labro mio non credi, ed. in Aus dem goldenen Zeitalter des Belcanto, ii (Mainz); Se amor ti compose, C xxii, by F. Arresti; Sentir d'un vago oggetto, C xxii; Sentirsi il petto accendere, C xxii, by Lampugnani; Se per te viva io sono, C xxii, by A.M. Bononcini; Se tu m'ami, C xxii, by A. Parisotti; Serbi l'intatta fede, C xix; Si cangia in un momento, C xxii; So ch'è fanciullo amore, C xix; Talor se il vento freme, C xix, by Terradellas; Tergi quel pianto, o cara, doubtful, *Bc*; Tra fronda e fronda, doubtful; Tre giorni son che Nina, C xxii, ? by V.L. Ciampi; Tremende oscure atroci, doubtful, *Bc*; Un caro e dolce sguardo, doubtful; Un ciglio che sa piangere, C xxii; Vado a morir ben mio, doubtful; Vanne a seguire (Ingrato core), C xxii, by A.M. Bononcini; Va tra le selve ircane, C xix; Vorrei poter almeno, C xxii

OTHER VOCAL

42 solfeggi, 2vv; 64 solfeggi, 3vv; solfeggio, hpd acc.: all in B xviii
Venerabilis barba cappucinorum, Scherzo fatto ai Cappuccini di Possuoli, T, B, 1735, B xviii
Doubtful: Per voi mi struggo in pianto, canon, 3vv, C xxii

INSTRUMENTAL

Conc. (Bb), solo vn, 2 vn, va, bc, C xxi; Conc. (C), 2 hpd, 2 vn, va, b; Sonata (F), org, C xxi; Sinfonia (F), vc, bc, C xxi; Sonata (G), vn, bc, movt 2 as Sonata (A), hpd, C xxi: all in B xvii

Doubtful: Piccola sinfonia (Eb), 2 vn, va, b, *I-Rsc*; Simphonia (Bb), 2 vn, va, vc, *US-R*; Simphonia (F), 2 vn, va, vc, *R*; Sinfonia [di apertura] (G), 2 vn, va, bc, hns, C xix; Symphonia (D), 2 vn, va, b, *CZ-Pnm*; Trio (Bb), 2 vn, bc, *I-Nc*, attrib. 'Pergola'

Extremely doubtful: 2 concs. (D, G), fl, 2 vn, bc, C xxi; Conc. a 5 (F), 3 vn, va, b, hns, org, C xxi; Simphonia (C), 2 vn, va, tpts, timp, *US-CA*; Sinfonia (D), 2 vn, va, b, hns, *S-SK, L*; Sinfonia [d'apertura] (D), 2 vn, va, b, fls, obs, tpts, timp, C xix; Sonatas nos.2 (C), 4 (G), 5 (C), 6 (Bb), hpd, C xxi; Sonata a 3 nos.13 (g), 14 (C), 2 vn, bc, C v

Spurious: 6 concerti armonici, concertinos, 4 vn, va, bc (The Hague, 1740), by U.W. van Wassenaer, C vii; 8 Lessons, hpd (London, 1771), no.2 in C xxi, nos.1, 5 by G.B. Martini; A Second Set of 8 Lessons, hpd (London, 1778), nos.2, 7 in C xxi; Propter magnam (G), org (London, 1831); Sinfonia (Bb), 2 vn, va, b, *L*, by J.G. Graun; Sonata (G), hpd, C xxi, ? by D. Alberti; 12 Sonatas a 3, 2 vn, b (London, 1771), by D. Gallo, C v; Trio (Bb), 2 vn, b, *Skma*, by F. Ruge; Trio (F), 2 vn, b, *Skma, Uu*

BIBLIOGRAPHY
SOURCE STUDIES, CATALOGUES, RESEARCH

F. Walker: 'Two Centuries of Pergolesi Forgeries and Misattributions', *ML*, xxx (1949), 297–320

F. Degrada: 'Alcuni falsi autografi pergolesiani', *RIM*, i (1966), 32–48

M.E. Paymer: *Giovanni Battista Pergolesi: a Thematic Catalogue of the Opera Omnia with an Appendix Listing Omitted Compositions* (New York, 1977)

H. Hucke: 'Pergolesi: Probleme eines Werkverzeichnisses', *AcM*, lii (1980), 195–224

B. Brook and M.E.Paymer: 'The Pergolesi Hand: a Calligraphic Study', *Notes*, xxxviii (1981–2), 550–78

Studi pergolesiani I: Iesi 1983

Pergolesi (Naples, 1986)

Studi pergolesiani II: New York 1986

B.S. Brook: 'Stravinsky's "Pulcinella": the "Pergolesi" Sources', *Musiques, signes, images: liber amicorum François Lesure*, ed. J.-M. Fauquet (Geneva, 1988), 41–66

M.E. Paymer and H.W.Williams: *Giovanni Battista Pergolesi: a Guide to Research* (New York,1989)

F. Degrada: 'False attribuzioni e falsificazioni nel catalogo delle opere di Giovanni Battista Pergolesi: genesi, storica e problemi critici', *L'attribuzione, teoria e pratica: Ascona 1992*

BIOGRAPHY AND CRITICISM

BurneyH; FlorimoN

P. Boyer: 'Notice sur la vie et les ouvrages de Pergolèse', *Mercure de France* (July 1772)

C. de Rosa, Marquis di Villarosa: *Lettera biografica intorno alla patria ed alla vita di Gio. Battista Pergolese, celebre compositore di musica* (Naples, 1831, enlarged 2/1843)

G. Annibaldi: *Alcune delle notizie più importanti intorno al Pergolesi recentemente scoperte: il Pergolesi in Pozzuoli: vita intima* (Iesi, 1890)

G. Radiciotti: *G.B. Pergolesi: vita, opere ed influenza su l'arte* (Rome,1910, 2/1935)

A. della Corte: *Pergolesi* (Turin, 1936)

S.A. Luciani, ed.: *G.B. Pergolesi (1710–1736): note e documenti*, Chigiana, iv (1942)

F. Walker: 'Pergolesiana', *ML*, xxxii (1951), 295–6

F. Walker: 'Pergolesi Legends', *MMR*, lxxxii (1952), 144–8, 180–83

F. Degrada: 'Falsi pergolesiani: dagli apocrifi ai ritratti', *Convegno musicale*, i (1964), 133–42

F. Degrada: 'Linee d'una storia della critica pergolesiana',*Convegno musicale*, ii (1965), 13–43

P. Petrobelli: 'Pergolesi and Ghezzi Revisited', *Music in the Classic Period: Essays in Honor of Barry S. Brook*, ed. A.W. Atlas (New York, 1985), 213–20

J. Blume: 'Sempre in contrasti: Heiterkeit und Empfindsamkeit bei Pergolesi', *NZM*, Jg.147 (1986), no.2, pp.4–7

G. Rotondella: 'Giovanni Battista Pergolesi: fra leggenda e realtà', *Rassegna musicale Curci*, xxxix/2 (1986), 17–19

OPERAS AND CANTATAS

J.-J. Rousseau: *Lettre de MM. du coin du roi à MM. du coin de la reine sur la nouvelle pièce intitulée La servante maîtresse* (Paris,1754)

F. Walker: 'Orazio: the History of a Pasticcio', *MQ*, xxxviii (1952), 369–83

D.E. Monson: *Recitativo semplice in the opere serie of G.B. Pergolesi and his Contemporaries* (diss., Columbia U., 1982)

H.E. Beckwith: *Giovanni Battista Pergolesi and the Chamber Cantata* (diss., U. of Maryland, 1983)

H. Weber: 'Der Serva-padrona-Topos in der Oper: Komik als Spiel mit musikalischen und sozialen Normen', *AMw*, xlv (1988), 87–110

F. Degrada: '"Lo frate 'nnamorato" e l'estetica della commedia musicale napoletana', *Napoli e il teatro musicale in Europa tra Sette e Ottocento: Studi in onore di Friedrich Lippmann*, ed. B.M. Antolini and W. Witzenmann (Florence, 1993), 21–35

SACRED AND INSTRUMENTAL MUSIC

F. Degrada: 'Le messe di Giovanni Battista Pergolesi: problemi di cronologia e d'attribuzione', *AnMc*, no.3 (1966), 65–79

M.E. Paymer: *The Instrumental Music Attributed to Giovanni Battista Pergolesi: a Study in Authenticity* (diss., City U. of New York, 1977)

H. Hucke: 'Pergolesi's "Missa S Emidio"', *Music in the Classic Period: Essays in Honor of Barry S. Brook*, ed. A.W. Atlas (New York, 1985), 99–115

M. Marx-Weber: 'Die G.B. Pergolesi falslich zugeschriebenen Miserere-Vertonungen', *Florilegium musicologicum: Hellmut Federhofer zum 75. Geburtstag*, ed. C.-H. Mahling (Tutzing, 1988), 209–18

J. De Ruiter: 'Wahre Kirchenmusik oder Heuchelei?: zur Rezeption des Stabat mater von Pergolesi in Deutschland bis 1820', *Mf*, xliii (1990), 1–15

HELMUT HUCKE, DALE E. MONSON

Peri, Achille (*b* Reggio, nell'Emilia, 20 Dec 1812; *d* Reggio, nell'Emilia, 28 March 1880). Italian composer. He studied in his native city with two local teachers, Gregori (piano) and Rabitti (harmony and composition), and then spent several years in Paris studying with Carafa. He assembled an opera company in Paris and toured the provinces, putting on his first stage work, *Una visita a Bedlam*, in Marseilles in 1839. Economic difficulties forced him to return to Italy where the first of his serious operas, *Il solitario*, was performed in 1841. Several of those that followed had considerable success, particularly *Dirce* (1843), *Tancreda* (1847) and his best work, the biblical drama *Giuditta*, which, after a disastrous première at La Scala in 1860, was revived there two years later with great success. His last two operas, also performed at La Scala in 1861 and 1863, were complete failures, causing him to give up writing for the stage. Peri was also *maestro di cappella* of Reggio Cathedral, for which he composed a large amount of church music of slight value, and conductor at the opera there. As an opera composer he was an imitator of Donizetti and Mercadante.

WORKS

OPERAS

Una visita a Bedlam (operetta), Marseilles, 1839, 1 duet, vs (Paris, n.d.)

Il solitario (os, 2, G. Bassi), Reggio nell'Emilia, Comunale, 29 May 1841

Ester d'Engaddi (dramma tragico, 3, S. Cammarano), Parma, Reggio, 19 Feb 1843, *I-Mr**, vs (Milan, n.d.)

Dirce (tragedia lirica, 3, P. Martini), Reggio nell'Emilia, Comunale, May 1843

Tancreda (dramma lirico, 3, F. Guidi), Genoa, Carlo Felice, 26 Dec 1847, excerpts, vs (Milan, n.d.)

Orfano e diavolo (melodramma comico, 3), Reggio nell'Emilia, Comunale, 26 Dec 1854

I fidanzati (melodramma, 3, F.M. Piave), Genoa, Carlo Felice, 7 Feb 1856, *Mr**, vs (Milan, 1856)

Vittore Pisani (melodramma, 3, Piave), Reggio nell'Emilia, Comunitativo, 21 April 1857, *Mr**, vs (Milan, n.d.)

Giuditta (melodramma biblico, 3, M.M. Marcello), Milan, Scala, 26 March 1860, *Mr**, vs (Milan, 1861)

L'espiazione (os, 3, T. Solera), Milan, Scala, 7 Feb 1861, *Mr**, vs (1861)

Rienzi (os, 3, Piave), Milan, Scala, 26 Dec 1862, *Mr**, excerpts, vs (Milan, ?1863)

VOCAL
all published in Milan

Choral: De profundis, 4vv, org; Salve regina

Songs, pubd before 1855: Il pianto, arietta; Sotto il salice piangente, romanza; Te pur mia vita, romanza

Songs, after 1855; Torquato Tasso alla tomba di Eleonora, romanza: L'addio della giovine nizzarda, scena, aria

INSTRUMENTAL
all published in Milan

Chbr: Str Qt (before 1855); Qnt, 2 vn, va, 2 vc

Pf: Armonie originali; Buon augurio, valzer; Farfalla, capriccio; Gran valzer fantastico; Mazzetto di fiori, notturno; Mie veglie, sonata; Rimembranze di Milano, mazurka di concerto; Un saluto a Napoli, tarantella; Ricreamento moderno ed utile: nuove suonatine precedute da esercizi, 4 hands

BIBLIOGRAPHY

FétisB; SchmidlD; StiegerO

G. Masutto: *Maestri di musica italiani del XIX secolo: notizie biografiche* (Venice, 1884), 136–7

T. Kaufman: *Verdi and his Major Contemporaries* (New York, 1990)

GIOVANNI CARLI BALLOLA

Peri, Jacopo ['Zazzerino'] (*b* Rome or Florence, 20 Aug 1561; *d* Florence, 12 Aug 1633). Italian composer, singer and instrumentalist. His most significant contribution was his development of the dramatic recitative for musical theatre. His most characteristic examples of this style are found in *Euridice* (1600), the earliest opera for which complete music has survived.

1. LIFE. Although Peri may have been born in Rome, he claimed descent from Florentine nobles with a long record of public service. He settled in Florence at an early age, and on 1 September 1573 he was taken into the convent of SS Annunziata 'to sing laude to the organ'. His musical education came under Cristofano Malvezzi, who included a four-part ricercare by him in his print of 1577 and the madrigal *Caro dolce ben mio* in his first book of five-part madrigals (1583). On 1 February 1579 Peri began service as organist at the Badia at a yearly salary of 15 scudi. He held the post until April 1605, and by 1586 he was also employed as a singer at S Giovanni Battista. The young Peri was praised by A.F. Grazzini for his instrumental and vocal performances, knowledge and grace, but Grazzini was annoyed that Peri's talents as a musician appeared to be insufficiently recognized. In 1584 the Duke and Duchess of Mantua spoke of Peri's endearing qualities. Although there is no known documentation it is likely that he participated during the 1580s in the discussions of the so-called Camerata which met in the house of Giovanni de' Bardi. When later recalling his father's acquaintances in a letter to G.B. Doni, Pietro de' Bardi praised Peri's performances on the organ and other keyboard instruments, his compositions and his singing, in which, he said, he intelligently imitated speech in sound.

In 1588, shortly after the accession of Grand Duke Ferdinando I, Peri's name first appeared as an official employee of the Medici court with a monthly salary of six scudi, which was increased to nine scudi in September 1590. His earliest recorded connection with a dramatic production had been in February 1583, when he had collaborated with Malvezzi, Alessandro Striggio (i) and others in composing music (which is lost) for the *intermedi* to Giovanni Fedini's comedy *Le due Persilie*. In 1589 he took part in the festivities celebrating Ferdinando's marriage to Christine of Lorraine. He performed the role of Arion in the fifth *intermedio* for Girolamo Bargagli's comedy *La pellegrina*, singing his own aria *Dunque fra torbid'onde* in which he illustrated the miraculous powers of music. According to the descriptive commentary published with the music in 1591 he captivated the audience, accompanying himself with amazing skill on the chitarrone. Peri's costume for this role is depicted in a sketch by Bernardo Buontalenti (see illustration).

Peri apparently met with musicians, poets and philosophers at the home of Jacopo Corsi during the 1590s. With the encouragement and collaboration of Corsi and Ottavio Rinuccini he wrote music for the latter's short pastoral *Dafne*. Although *Dafne* was reportedly planned as early as 1594, the earliest recorded performance was during Carnival 1597–8. Pietro de' Bardi described the event as including a few numbers in short scenes, which were recited and sung privately in a small room. The first version was subsequently improved for later Florentine performances in 1599, 1600 and 1604. Although details of the casting are unknown Peri sang the role of Apollo in some of them.

Peri's next and most significant collaboration with Rinuccini was in their opera *Euridice*, first produced for the Florentine celebrations of the wedding of Maria de' Medici and Henri IV, King of France. The première took place before a small audience in the Palazzo Pitti on 6 October 1600, although the libretto contains the dedicatory date of 4 October. Peri's musical rivals, Giulio Caccini and Emilio de' Cavalieri, each had a part in this

Jacopo Peri's costume for the role of Arion in the fifth intermedio for Girolamo Bargagli's comedy 'La pellegrina': sketch by Bernardo Buontalenti, pen and ink, 1589 (I-Fn)

initial performance: Caccini rewrote music for the parts sung by his musicians (the role of Eurydice, three choral numbers, and solos for some nymphs and shepherds), while Cavalieri appears to have directed the production. The set and costume designers are unknown (Ludovico Cigoli may have been one), but the décor was quite simple in comparison with Caccini's spectacular *Il rapimento di Cefalo* presented three nights later (and in which Peri sang). In the preface to the publication of *Euridice*, Peri identified prominent members of the original cast: Francesco Rasi (Aminta), Antonio Brandi (Arcetro), Melchior Palantrotti (Pluto) and a boy soprano, Jacopo Giusti, from Lucca (Daphne, the messenger). Handwritten annotations on a copy of the original libretto name additional singers, including Peri himself in the role of Orpheus (see Palisca, 1964). Peri also listed in the preface four instrumentalists, who played from behind the scenes. *Euridice* received high praise, particularly from Marco da Gagliano, who was impressed not only by the work but also by Peri's own expressive singing. The composer's rivals, however, found the recitatives tedious and the stage designs inadequate. In 1616 Peri and Rinuccini supervised a revival in Bologna.

After 1600 Peri continued to serve the Medici court. His later professional activities were primarily in composition, although he sang the role of Neptune in an unnamed ballo on 14 February 1611, and again in a new version of the ballo, now named *Mascherate di ninfe di Senna*, on 5 May 1613. He wrote at least some of the music for the celebrations of the wedding of Prince Cosimo in 1608, and his setting of one of the choruses of the younger Michelangelo Buonarroti's *Il giudizio di Paride* (*Poichè la notte con l'oscure piume*), performed during the festivities, reappeared with a new text (*Se tu parti da me, Fillide amata*) in his 1609 volume of songs. Few other compositions from this period survive, but contemporary reports and librettos indicate that at least in the 1610s he wrote much for dramatic productions. Among these *intermedi*, ballets and equestrian shows were some of the most spectacular court *feste* that had ever been seen in Florence. Peri generally collaborated with other Florentine composers, particularly Marco da Gagliano and Francesca Caccini. He may have specialized in writing recitatives for these productions, but there is no evidence that this was his exclusive concern.

Peri's close relationship with the Mantuan court during the early years of the 17th century is documented by numerous letters, mostly sent to Ferdinando Gonzaga, and by his active membership in the Accademia degli Elevati. The composer planned two large-scale projects for Mantua: *Le nozze di Peleo e Tetide* (libretto by Francesco Cini), intended for the Gonzaga wedding festivities of 1608 but rejected in favour of Rinuccini and Monteverdi's *Arianna*, and *Adone* (libretto by Jacopo Cicognini), projected for a performance in 1620. He composed songs, now lost, on texts by various members of the Mantuan court. The Gonzagas frequently praised his talents. In 1618 the duke and duchess recommended him for an appointment in Florence as 'Camarlingo dell'Arte della Lana', a position that he held initially with a monthly salary of ten scudi. In Florence too his talents did not go unrecognized, and in 1616, with Francesca Caccini and her husband, G.B. Signorini, he accompanied Cardinal Carlo de' Medici to Rome, while in 1619 the publisher Zanobi Pignoni was moved by the 'continual requests' for his music to reissue his 1609 volume of songs, to which he now added several more recent works.

In his later years Peri collaborated with G.B. da Gagliano on three *sacre rappresentazioni*, performed before the Compagnia dell'Arcangelo Raffaello, and with Marco da Gagliano on two operas, both to texts by Andrea Salvadori. The first of these operas, *Lo sposalizio di Medoro ed Angelica*, based on an episode from Ariosto's *Orlando furioso*, was staged at the Palazzo Pitti on 25 September 1619 in honour of the election of the Emperor Ferdinand II, brother-in-law of Grand Duke Cosimo II. An extant libretto of 1623 reports numerous revisions, probably for a proposed but unrealized performance in Mantua in 1622. The second opera with Marco da Gagliano, *La Flora*, was in honour of the wedding in 1628 of Duke Odoardo Farnese of Parma and Margherita de' Medici. Peri composed only the role of Clori. For these festivities Peri had originally planned a different opera, *Iole ed Ercole*, also on a libretto by Salvadori. Although there is no evidence that this work was fully composed, a lament of Iole, *Uccidimi, dolore*, is attributed to Peri (in *CZ-Pnm* II La 2 and in *I-Bc* Q49). In 1630 Peri suffered a serious illness and on 15 March 1630 prepared his will. He died three years later and was buried in the church of S Maria Novella.

Composition for Peri was often a slow and apparently difficult task, a circumstance that may explain the number of works he left incomplete. His most natural musical activity seems to have been performance. Severo Bonini said that he could move the hardest heart to tears through his singing, and he also praised his superb instrumental accompaniments. Marco da Gagliano claimed that no one could fully appreciate Peri's music until he had heard dramatic interpretations by the composer himself. In the preface to *Euridice* Peri suggested that the secret of his expressive singing lay not only in his written embellishments but much more in the subtle nuances and graces which can never be completely indicated in notation. His success brought praise from many other contemporaries but also created inevitable jealousies. The most famous attack came in the form of a satirical sonnet by Francesco Ruspoli, presenting otherwise unfounded slurs on his professional reputation and family. Stefano Rosselli, in a commentary on the sonnet, explained the implications of the poem and also added valuable information on the composer's character and appearance. Peri was very slender and of medium height, and had long, blond hair, this last feature being reflected in his well-known nickname, 'Zazzerino'.

2. WORKS. Peri's earliest published compositions are in various styles. The sectional ricercare in four parts (1577) combines a number of themes through standard contrapuntal devices. The madrigal for five voices (1583), basically homophonic but occasionally enlivened by imitations, is a syllabic setting of an ottava. In the more expansive aria for the *intermedio* of 1589 the tenor soloist has elaborate embellishments, which are at times echoed by two other voices. The publication of 1591 provides a simple four-part instrumental accompaniment despite the reference in the commentary to the composer's own performance on the chitarrone.

Peri's first complete drama in music, *Dafne*, follows the literary genre of the tragicomic pastoral. Rinuccini's libretto tells of the slaying of the Pythian dragon, Apollo's boasts to Cupid, Cupid's revenge by afflicting Apollo with love for Daphne, Daphne's transformation into a laurel tree and Apollo's final grief. Printed librettos for Peri's setting survive from the 1600 and 1604 performances, but only fragments of the music are preserved in two manuscripts of Florentine origin (now in *I-Fn* and *B-Bc* respectively). Two of the six excerpts are ascribed to Corsi in the latter source. The four pieces presumably by Peri consist of the Prologue sung by Ovid, a choral monody *Almo Dio, ch'il carr'ardente*, Venus's ottava *Chi da' lacci d'amor* and the messenger's narrative *Qual' nova meraviglia!* The last-named setting is the only surviving excerpt with a non-strophic text and a consistent recitative style. Since the words deviate somewhat from the librettos of 1600 and 1604 this piece may represent the recitative writing in the earliest version of the pastoral. The vocal line has no written embellishments, and few dissonances with the slow-moving bass. Two of the strophic numbers in *Dafne* closely resemble later pieces by Peri with similar poetic structure. The music for the Prologue was adapted for the Prologue to *Euridice*, while the music for *Chi da' lacci d'amor* reappears in modified form in *Torna, deh torna, pargoletto mio*, published in Pietro Benedetti's *Musiche* of 1611. Similar relationships to other contemporary songs suggest that Peri may have at times employed stock formulae for standard types of poetry.

Peri and Rinuccini's second collaboration, *Euridice*, is a significant advance on the experimental *Dafne*. The longer libretto has a more intricate design, and the music a wider range of expressive techniques. Tragedy, who sings the Prologue, dismisses fear, bloodshed and sorrow and then calls for sweeter emotions to be evoked through the forces of music. In the classical tale which follows, Rinuccini's Orpheus only temporarily loses his beloved Eurydice. Once successful in the underworld he makes an unconditional return with his wife to the joyous land of shepherds and nymphs. Although the text provides poignant expressions of intense grief by Orpheus and the chorus, lighter emotions and simple narration are just as prominent. Following the Prologue of seven stanzas, the libretto may be divided into five scenes, each concluded by a strophic number which reflects on the preceding events. In these interludes Peri mixed choral writing, usually in four or five parts, with stanzas for solo voices. The texts have simple rhyme and metrical patterns, mostly with lines of seven or eight syllables, which sharply contrast with the freer rhyming of the 7- and 11-syllable lines elsewhere in the libretto. Outside the interludes the only comparable texts occur in two short songs for Tirsi and Orpheus. In setting the strophic poetry Peri imposed musical organization in three ways: through the re-use of material from one stanza to another, either in exact repetition or in strophic variations; through recurring rhythmic and melodic patterns within single stanzas; and through frequent use of refrains.

The continuous recitatives in the scenes between the set choral numbers contain Peri's most innovatory writing in *Euridice*. He described this style as 'an intermediate course, lying between the slow and suspended movements of song and the swift and rapid movements of speech'. The pacing of the voice and accompaniment is carefully coordinated with the rising and falling tensions in the text, thereby achieving a broad scale of emotional expression. In the narrative sections of the libretto the singer imitates the rhythmic and melodic inflections of a normal speaking voice. Peri's slower accompaniment moves according to the principal words of the text, showing no apparent regard for large-scale tonal design. More intense sections are created by unprepared dissonances, suspensions and frequent rests for the voice; by unexpected harmonic progressions; and at times by altering the normal motion of the bass. These devices are well illustrated in Orpheus's impassioned monologues *Non piango e non sospiro*, which is sung after he hears of Eurydice's death, and *Funeste piaggie, ombrosi, orridi campi*, which is delivered at the gates of the underworld.

Peri's extant opera with Gagliano, *La Flora*, treats the origin of flowers, symbolic of Florence and Parma, the two cities honoured in the wedding festivities of 1628. Blossoms are transformed from the tears of joy shed by Zephyr upon finally winning his beloved Clori. Peri's contribution, the role of Clori, consists of the virtuoso aria *O campagne d'Anfitrite* in Act 2 and numerous recitatives. The aria, in the form of strophic variations, contains far more embellished phrases for the voice than does Peri's earlier surviving dramatic music. The accompaniment is more active and supplies a short ritornello between each stanza. As in *Euridice*, the recitatives range from a normal narrative to a highly emotional style; the latter is used particularly in Act 4 when Clori jealously believes that Zephyr has turned his affections to another nymph.

Only a few fragments remain from Peri's other dramatic works. The above-mentioned *Torna, deh torna, pargoletto mio*, patterned after Venus's song in *Dafne*, is an aria of Venus from the Rinuccini ballo of 1611 later named *Mascherate di ninfe di Senna* (1613). In his setting of the ottava text Peri used a modification of the first four lines of music for the second half of the song. The triple metre with hemiolas is retained from the earlier version in *Dafne*. One other fragment from the *Mascherate di ninfe di Senna* survives in manuscript but is unattributed and consists only of four lines of recitative.

Peri's song collection, *Le varie musiche* (1609), contains four settings of Petrarch sonnets, each divided into four parts; nine madrigals with non-strophic texts; four arias with extra stanzas printed after the music; and one strophic aria with minor variations written out for each stanza. The sonnets and six of the solo madrigals mix Peri's recitative style with phrases of more lyrical character. Embellishments are confined to occasional turns and trills or to short cadential roulades. The remaining three madrigals, for two and three voices, contain passages of imitation, of note-against-note writing and of a single voice emphasized against an accompaniment. The four arias with extra stanzas of text are in triple metre throughout and frequently repeat melodic and rhythmic patterns. The aria in strophic-variation form, *Se tu parti da me, Fillide amata*, is unique in this collection, since each stanza presents a sharp distinction between recitative and aria styles. The second edition of *Le varie musiche* (1619) omitted this song and one madrigal but contains seven additional strophic arias, including simple dance-songs, one recitative setting and several pieces in mixed styles. The few further songs by Peri that have survived in other prints or manuscripts from the period include *O dell'alto appenin figlio sovrano*, with four sections partly using strophic-variation technique, and three solos in a style similar to the expressive monologues in *Euridice*: *Se da l'aspro martire*, *Tu dormi e 'l dolce sonno* and *Uccidimi, dolore*; as was mentioned above, this last piece may be a survival from Peri's incomplete *Iole ed Ercole* of 1628.

For the opening of *Euridice*, see OPERA, §II, 1, fig.1.

WORKS

DRAMATIC

first performed in Florence unless otherwise stated

title	librettist	first performance	remarks; sources
Dafne	O. Rinuccini	Palazzo Corsi, carn. 1597–8	collab. J. Corsi; rev. 1598–1600; frags. *B-Bc*, *I-Fn*, see Porter (1965) and Carter (1989)
Euridice	Rinuccini	Palazzo Pitti, 6 Oct 1600	5 scenes; collab. G. Caccini; (Florence, 1600/R, repr. 1607), ed. in RRMBE, xxxvi–vii (1981)
Le nozze di Peleo e Tetide	F. Cini	unperf.	planned for Mantua, 1608
Adone	J. Cicognini	unperf.	comp. 1611, planned for Mantua, 1620
Lo sposalizio di Medoro et Angelica	A. Salvadori, after L. Ariosto	Palazzo Pitti, 25 Sept 1619	collab. M. da Gagliano; rev. c1622
Iole ed Ercole	Salvadori	unperf.	planned for Florence, 1628; ?frag. 'Uccidimi, dolore' in *CZ-Pnm* and *I-Bc*, ed. in RRMBE, l (1985)
La Flora, o vero Il natal de' fiori	Salvadori	Palazzo Pitti, 14 Oct 1628	collab. M. da Gagliano, only Clori's music by Peri (Florence, 1628)

Sacre rappresentationi (all collab. G.B. da Gagliano): La benedittione di Jacob (G.M. Cecchi, rev. Cicognini), 1622; Il gran natale di Christo salvator nostro (Cicognini), 1622; La celeste guida, o vero L'arcangelo Raffaello (Cicognini), 1624

Other: Intermedio I in G. Fedini: Le due Persilie, 1583; Intermedio V in G. Bargagli: La pellegrina (Rinuccini), 1589, RISM 1591[7]; [Torneo] (M. Buonarroti), Pisa, 1605; Chorus in Il giudizio di Paride (Buonarroti), 1608, ed. in RRMBE, l (1985) [Ballo], 1611, rev. as Mascherate di ninfe di Senna (Rinuccini), 1613, collab. M. da Gagliano and others, ed. in RRMBE, l (1985); [?Torneo] (G.C. Villifranchi), 1613, collab. M. da Gagliano and others, ed. in

RRMBE, l (1985); [Marte e Amore] (F. Saracinelli), 1614; Intermedi to Veglia delle grazie (G. Chiabrera), 1615; Guerra d'Amore (festa a cavallo, Salvadori), 1616, collab. P. Grazi and G.B. Signorini; [Ballo] (Saracinelli), collab. L. Allegri; Guerra di bellezza (festa a cavallo, Salvadori), 1616, collab. Grazi; [Ballo] (? A. Striggio (ii)), Mantua, 1620; La precedenza delle dame (Salvadori), 1625

Doubtful: Ballo della cortesia (Buonarroti), 1614 [collab. A. Brunelli or by F. Caccini]; La liberazione di Tirreno ed Arnea (Salvadori), 1617 [? by M. da Gagliano]

SONGS

for 1v, bc, unless otherwise stated, all ed. in RRMBE, l (1985)

Le varie musiche … 1–3vv, con alcune spirituali in ultimo, per cantare, hpd, chit, ancora la maggior parte di esse per sonare semplicemente, org (Florence, 1609, enlarged 2/1619) [1609, 2/1619]

Al fonte, al prato (Cini), 2vv, bc (bc also has text), 1609, 2/1619

Anima, ohimè, che pensi, che fai (Rinuccini), 1609, 2/1619

Bellissima regina (Rinuccini or Chiabrera), 1609, 2/1619, *I-Fc* Barbera

Care stelle, 2/1619

Caro dolce ben mio, perchè fuggire (L. Celiano), 5vv, 1583[16]

Caro e soave legno (Rinuccini or B. Barbarino), 3vv, bc (bc also has text), 1609, 2/1619

Che veggio, ohimè, che sento, 2/1619 *Fn* Magl.XIX.114

Con sorrisi cortesi (Chiabrera), 2vv, bc (bc also has text), 1609

Freddo core che in amore, 2/1619

Hor che gli augelli, 2/1619, 1620[13]

Ho visto al mio dolore (A. Striggio (ii)), in G. Montesardo: L'allegre notti di Fiorenza (Venice, 1608), 1609, 2/1619

In qual parte del ciel, in qual idea (F. Petrarch), 1609, 2/1619, *B-Bc* 704

Intenerite voi, lacrime mie (Rinuccini), 2vv, bc, *Bc* 704, *I-Fn* Magl.XIX.66

Lasso ch'io ardo et altri non me 'l crede (Petrarch), 1609, 2/1619

Lungi dal vostro lume, 1609, 2/1619

O core infiammato, 2vv, bc (bc also has text), 2/1619, *Fn* Magl.XIX.114

O dell'alto appenin figlio sovrano (Saracinelli), in Brunelli: Scherzi … libro secondo (Venice, 1614)

O dolce anima mia, dunque è pur vero (G.B. Guarini), 3vv, bc (bc also has text), 1609, 2/1619

O durezza di ferro e di diamante, 1609, 2/1619

O miei giorni fugaci, o breve vita (Rinuccini), 1609, 2/1619, *Fn* Magl.XIX.115 (arr. kbd)

Qual cadavero spirante, 2/1619

Quest' humil fera un cor di tigre o d'orsa (Petrarch), 1609, 2/1619

Se da l'aspro martire, *CZ-Pnm* II La 2

Se tu parti da me, Fillide amata (Buonarroti), 1609, *I-Fc* Barbera (with text Poichè la notte con l'oscure piume (Buonarroti))

Solitario augellino, 1609, 2/1619

Torna, deh torna, pargoletto mio (Rinuccini), in P. Benedetti: Musiche (Florence, 1611), *Vm* Ms 10318 (codex 742)

Tra le donne onde s'onora (?Rinuccini), 1609, 2/1619, *Fc* Barbera (with text Fra le donne ond'il bel Arno (Rinuccini))

Tra le lagrime e i sospiri, 2/1619

Tu dormi e 'l dolce sonno, *CZ-Pnm* II La 2, *GB-Lbl* Add.30491, *I-Fc* Barbera

Tutto 'l dì piango e poi la notte quando (Petrarch), 1609, 2/1619

Uccidimi, dolore (Salvadori), *CZ-Pnm* II La 2, *I-Bc* Q49 (possibly from op Iole ed Ercole)

Un dì soletto (Chiabrera), 1609, 2/1619

INSTRUMENTAL

Ricercare, a 4, in C. Malvezzi: Il primo libro de ricercari (Perugia, 1577, inc.), *Fn* Magl.XIX.107; ed. in RRMR, xxvii (1978)

BIBLIOGRAPHY

FortuneISS; PirrottaDO; SolertiMBD

F. Ruspoli: sonnets, with commentary by S. Rosselli, *I-Fn* Magl.VII.572; ed. A. de La Fage, *Essais de diphthérographie musicale* (Paris, 1864/R)

E. Vogel: 'Marco da Gagliano: zur Geschichte des florentiner Musiklebens von 1570–1650', *VMw*, v (1889), 396–442, 509–68

G.O. Corazzini: *Jacopo Peri e la sua famiglia* (Florence, 1895)

A. Solerti: *Le origini del melodramma* (Turin, 1903/R)

A. Solerti: *Gli albori del melodramma* (Milan, 1904–5/R)

O.G. Sonneck: '"Dafne", the First Opera: a Chronological Study', *SIMG*, xv (1913–14), 102–10

M. Mila: 'Jacopo Peri (Firenze 1561–1633)', *RaM*, vi (1933), 219–27

F. Boyer: 'Les Orsini et les musiciens d'Italie au début du XVIIe siècle', *Mélanges de philologie, d'histoire et de littérature offerts à Henri Hauvette* (Paris, 1934), 301–10

F. Ghisi: *Alle fonti della monodia: due nuovi brani della 'Dafne'* (Milan, 1940/R)

F. Ghisi: 'An Early Seventeenth Century MS, with Unpublished Italian Monodic Music by Peri, Giulio Romano and Marco da Gagliano', *AcM*, xx (1948), 46–60

F. Ghisi: 'Ballet Entertainments in Pitti Palace, Florence, 1608–1625', *MQ*, xxxv (1949), 421–36

N. Fortune: 'A Florentine Manuscript and its Place in Italian Song', *AcM*, xxiii (1951), 124–36

N. Pirrotta: 'Temperamenti e tendenze nella Camerata fiorentina', *Le manifestazioni culturali dell'Accademia nazionale di Santa Cecilia* (Rome, 1953); Eng. trans. in MQ, xl (1954), 169–89, and in N. Pirrotta: *Music and Culture in Italy from the Middle Ages to the Baroque* (Cambridge, MA, 1984), 235–53

A.M. Nagler: *Theatre Festivals of the Medici, 1539–1637* (New Haven, CT, 1964/R)

C.V. Palisca: 'The First Performance of "Euridice"', *The Department of Music, Queens College of the City University of New York: Twenty-Fifth Anniversary Festschrift*, ed. A. Mell (Flushing, NY, 1964), 1–23; repr. in C.V. Palisca: *Studies in the History of Italian Music and Music Theory* (Oxford, 1994), 432–51

W.V. Porter: 'Peri and Corsi's *Dafne*: Some New Discoveries and Observations', *JAMS*, xviii (1965), 170–96

F.A. D'Accone: 'The *Intavolatura di M. Alamanno Aiolli*: a Newly Discovered Source of Florentine Renaissance Keyboard Music', *MD*, xx (1966), 151–74, esp. 154

A.M. Monterosso Vacchelli: 'Elementi stilistici nell'"Euridice" di Jacopo Peri in rapporto all'"Orfeo" di Monteverdi', *Claudio Monteverdi e il suo tempo: Venice, Mantua and Cremona 1968*, 117–27

N. Pirrotta: *Li due Orfei: da Poliziano a Monteverdi* (Turin, 1969, enlarged 2/1975)

H.M. Brown: 'How Opera Began: an Introduction to Jacopo Peri's *Euridice* (1600)', *The Late Italian Renaissance, 1525–1630*, ed. E. Cochrane (New York and London, 1970), 401–43

S. Reiner: 'La vag'Angioletta (and others), i', *AnMc*, no.14 (1974), 26–88

E. Strainchamps: 'New Light on the Accademia degli Elevati of Florence', *MQ*, lxii (1976), 507–35

F.W. Sternfeld: 'The First Printed Opera Libretto', *ML*, lix (1978), 121–38

T. Carter: 'Jacopo Peri (1561–1633): Aspects of his Life and Works', *PRMA*, cvi (1978–9), 50–62

B.R. Hanning: 'Glorious Apollo: Poetic and Political Themes in the First Opera', *Renaissance Quarterly*, xxxii (1979), 485–513

J.W. Hill: 'Oratory Music in Florence, i: *Recitar cantando*, 1583–1655', *AcM*, li (1979), 108–36, esp. 121

G.A. Tomlinson: *Rinuccini, Peri, Monteverdi, and the Humanist Heritage of Opera* (diss., U. of California, Berkeley, 1979)

T. Carter: 'Jacopo Peri', *ML*, lxi (1980), 121–35

B.R. Hanning: *Of Poetry and Music: Power, Humanism, and the Creation of Opera* (Ann Arbor, 1980)

T. Carter: 'Jacopo Peri's *Euridice* (1600): a Contextual Study', *MR*, xliii (1982), 83–103

C.V. Palisca: 'Peri and the Theory of Recitative', *Studi musicali*, xv (1982), 51–61; repr. in idem: *Studies in the History of Italian Music and Music Theory* (Oxford, 1994), 452–66

T. Carter: 'A Florentine Wedding of 1608', *AcM*, lv (1983), 89–107

T. Carter: '*Serate musicali* in Early Seventeenth-Century Florence: Girolamo Montesardo's *L'allegre notti di Fiorenza* (1608)', *Renaissance Studies in Honor of Craig Hugh Smyth*, ed. A. Morrogh and others (Florence, 1985), i, 555–68

T. Carter: *Jacopi Peri (1561–1633): his Life and Works* (New York and London, 1989)

W. Kirkendale: *The Court Musicians in Florence during the Principate of the Medici* (Florence, 1993), 189–243

WILLIAM V. PORTER (with TIM CARTER)

Periáñez, Pedro (*b* Babilafuente, *c*1540; *d* Santiago de Compostela, before 3 May 1613). Spanish composer. He may have been the singer Periáñez who was a member of the viceroyal *capilla* at Naples in February 1558. After working in Almería as *maestro de capilla* Periáñez took up a similar post as successor to Juan Cepa at Málaga. The competition for the position in late September 1577 included composing overnight a motet on *John* xvii.11*b* and a villancico, adding two voices to a given cantus firmus and improvising other counterpoints, and adding a third voice to the duo that had been used 26 years earlier at the competition won by Cristóbal de Morales. A chapter vote was taken on 16 October, and Periáñez was declared the winner. In the meantime he had been offered the post of *maestro de capilla* of Córdoba Cathedral, but he accepted the offer from Málaga. On 1 August 1583 he took up a more attractive position at the cathedral in Santiago de Compostela, which he held for the rest of his life. His duties included not only direction of the music but also the organization of dances and playlets by the choirboys for Corpus Christi. Málaga attempted to win him back with the offer of a canonry on 7 June 1595, when he was visiting the city. In 1612 he retired from the post at Santiago, and on 3 April offered to give half his salary to Bernardo de Peralta of Burgos; but a competition was held of which 'Antonio Carrera' (his uncle; *see* CARREIRA family, (3)), *mestre de capela* at Braga, was named the winner on 2 July 1612. A five-voice motet, *Ave domina Maria*, which survives in manuscript (at *E-E*), is printed in Eslava y Elizondo's *Lira sacrohispana*.

BIBLIOGRAPHY

StevensonSCM

S. Tafall Abad: 'La capilla de música de la catedral de Santiago: notas históricas', *Boletín de la Real academia gallega*, xxvi (1931), 73–82, 109–12, 129–37

A. Llordén: 'Notas históricas de los maestros de capilla y organistas, mozos de coro y seises de la catedral de Málaga', *AnM*, xvi (1961), 99–148, esp. 141; xix (1964), 71–93, esp. 73

R. Stevenson: 'Spanish Polyphonists in the Age of the Armada', *Inter-American Music Review*, xii/2 (1991–2), 17–114, esp. 47–8

ROBERT STEVENSON

Peričić, Vlastimir (*b* Vršac, 7 Dec 1927). Yugoslav composer and writer on music. He studied composition with Rajičić at the Belgrade Academy until 1951, and with Uhl in Vienna (1955–6). He was a professor at the Marinković Music School, Belgrade (1948–51), and the Slavenski Music School (1951–5), and then joined the Belgrade Academy of Music as an assistant (1955–61), lecturer (1961–5) and from 1965 as professor; from 1988 to 1993 he was professor ordinarius. Peričić's music is characterized by its sound construction and polished craftsmanship. Generally neo-classical in style, his works frequently exhibit lively rhythms and a marked contrapuntal variety. His principal works, written mostly during the 1950s, show a fondness for strong thematic links between the various parts. Outstanding among these is the *Simfonijeta* (1957) with its excellent handling of contrapuntal devices. Peričić has latterly concentrated on writing, his principal works being a comprehensive reference book on Serbian composers and a large multi-lingual dictionary of musical terms. He has contributed extensively to lexicographical works on music.

WORKS
(selective list)

Orch: Sym. Movt, 1951; Simfonijeta, str, 1957

Choral, unacc.: Rukovet I – pesme iz Vranja, 1948; Rukovet II – pesme iz Makedonije, 1948; Veče na školju [Evening on the Island], 1948; Grm [The Bush], 1948; Rukovet III – pesme iz Dalmacije, 1949

Chbr: Str Qt, 1950; Sonatina, vn, pf, 1951; Fantasia quasi una sonata, g, va, pf, 1954, arr. d, vn, pf, 1954; Suite, 3 vn, 1955

Songs, 1v, pf: Šumske idile [Forest Idylls] (V. Nazor), 1950; Bila jednom ruža jedna, 1953; 3 pesme Rabindranata Tagore, 1957; Noć bez jutra [Night without a Dawn] (V. Popa), 1959; Gradinar [The Gardener] (Tagore), 1964

Pf: Tema sa varijacijama, 1948; Sonata, 1949; Sonatina, 1951

Principal publishers: Prosveta, Srpska akademija nauka i umetnosti, Univerzitet umetnosti, Udruženje kompozitora Srbije

WRITINGS

with D. Skovran: *Nauka o muzičkim oblicima* [On musical forms] (Belgrade, 1961, 7/1991)

with M. Radenković: *Pregled nauke o harmoniji* [Survey of harmony] (Belgrade, 1962)

'Stvaralački lik Vojislav Vučkovića' [The creative figure of Vučkovič], *Zvuk*, no.57 (1963), 161–84

'Druga simfonija Vasilija Mokranjca' [The second symphony by Mokranjac], *Zvuk*, no.69 (1966), 505–12

Josif Marinković: Život i dela (Belgrade, 1967)

Razvoj tonalnog sistema [The evolution of the tonal system] (Belgrade, 1968)

'Stanojlo Rajičić', *Pro musica* (1968), no.34

'Vasilije Mokranjac', *Pro musica* (1968), nos.30–31

ed.: *Vojislav Vučković umetnik i borac* [Vučkovič artist and combatant] (Belgrade, 1968)

Muzički stvaraoci u Srbiji [Musical composition in Serbia] (Belgrade, 1969)

Stvaralački put Stanojla Rajičića [The creative path of Stanojlo Rajičić] (Belgrade, 1971)

'Četvrta simfonija Vasilija Mokranjca' [The fourth symphony by Mokranjac], *Pro musica* [Belgrade], no.65 (1973), 16–19

'Beleške o formalnoj strukturi Mokranjčevih Rukoveti' [Notes on the formal structure of the *Rukoveti* by Stevan Mokranjac], *Pro musica* [Belgrade], extra no. (1981)

Višejezični rečnik muzičkih termina [Multilingual dictionary of musical terms] (Belgrade, 1985, 2/1997)

'Kompozicije na tekstove iz Vukove zbirke/Vertonungen von Texten aus Vuks Liedersammlung', in V. Bojić: *Vukovo nasledje u evropskoj muzici/Vuks musikalische Erben* (Belgrade and Munich, 1987)

'Josip Slavenski und seine Astroakustik', *Musiktheorie* (1988), 1

'Dejan Despić: Kontrast tonaliteta', *Zvuk* (1989), no.3, pp.86–7

Instrumentalni i vokalno-instrumentalni kontrapunkt (Belgrade, 1987)

Vokalni kontrapunkt (Belgrade, 1991, 2/1997)

ed.: *Folklor i njegova umetnička transpozicija III: Belgrade 1991* (Belgrade, 1991)

BIBLIOGRAPHY

D. Skovran: 'Peričić Vlastimir', in V. Peričić: *Muzički stvaraoci u Srbiji* [Composers in Serbia] (Belgrade, 1969), 378–82

D. Despić: 'Vlastimir Peričić – portret umetnika' [Vlastimir Peričić – portrait of the artist], *Pro musica* [Belgrade], no.140 (1989), 5–6

'Vlastimir Peričić', *Godišnjak Srpske akademije nauka i umetnosti* [Annual of the Serbian Academy of Sciences and Arts for 1988] (Belgrade, 1989) [bio-bibliography]

D. Despić: 'Razgovor sa Vlastimirom Peričićem' [A conversation with Vlastimir Peričić], *Novi zvuk*, no.2 (1993), 5–10; Eng. trans. in *New Sound*, no.2 (1993), 5–10

NIALL O'LOUGHLIN

Pericope (Gk. *perikopē*: 'passage', from *perikoptein*: 'cut off'). In Christian liturgies an extract from the Bible or other ecclesiastical source intended for public recitation or chanting, for example, Old Testament lesson, EPISTLE or GOSPEL.

Périer, Jean (Alexis) (*b* Paris, 2 Feb 1869; *d* Paris, ?3 Nov 1954). French baritone. He studied with Taskin and Bussine at the Paris Conservatoire and made his début in 1892 as Monostatos (*Die Zauberflöte*) at the Opéra-Comique, where he remained (except from 1894 to 1900) until 1920. His repertory lay chiefly in operetta (he sang leading roles in the first performances of Messager's *Véronique* in 1898 and *Fortunio* in 1907) but he also sang Don Giovanni, Lescaut, Sharpless and was the first Pelléas (Opéra-Comique, 30 April 1902) and the first Ramiro (*L'heure espagnole*). He sang Pelléas at the Manhattan Opera in 1908 and appeared at Monte Carlo, but remained firmly a part of the Parisian musical and theatrical scene. He acted in several films between 1900 and 1938. His was essentially a declamatory art, and even with limited gifts as a singer he created convincing characters with the help of his clear diction and his ability as an actor. Seven published recordings of his voice (on cylinders, later issued as discs) were made about 1905.

HAROLD BARNES

Perigourdine [perijourdine]. A French folkdance, usually in 3/8 or 6/8, from the region of Périgord in south-west France, similar to the PASSEPIED. The best-known example in art music is in Verdi's *Rigoletto* (Act 1 scene iii).

Perile, Joseph. See RIEPEL, JOSEPH.

Perinet. See PERRINET [Perinetus] and FONTAINE, PIERRE.

Perinet, Joachim (*b* Vienna, 20 Oct 1763; *d* Vienna, 4 Feb 1816). Austrian dramatist, pamphleteer and actor. He swiftly squandered a sizeable inheritance, thereafter living penuriously by his wits. His stage career swung between the Leopoldstadt and Wieden/Wien theatres, for both of which he supplied a string of mainly ephemeral farces, dramatic caricatures, travesties and parodies. The most popular were a series of Singspiel adaptations of comedies by Philipp Hafner, including *Die Schwestern von Prag* (1794), which remained in the repertory of the Theater in der Leopoldstadt (later Carltheater) until 1859 and may have influenced *Die Meistersinger von Nürnberg* through its interrupted serenade scene and street riot. *Kaspar der Fagottist, oder Die Zauberzither*, long (but wrongly) held to have influenced the story line of *Die Zauberflöte*, is an entertaining rescue opera with some social satire; it and a few of Perinet's other stage works have been successfully revived in recent years. Perinet's pamphlets include *Mozart und Schikaneder: ein theatralisches Gespräch* (Vienna, 1801), written, like so many of his works, in doggerel verse. Though seldom rising above the level of competence, he played an important part in the development of the repertory of Vienna's suburban theatres.

BIBLIOGRAPHY
GroveO (T. Bauman) [incl. list of librettos]
G. Gugitz: 'Joachim Perinet: ein Beitrag zur Wiener Theatergeschichte', *Jb der Grillparzer-Gesellschaft*, xiv (1904), 170–223
G. Gugitz: 'Joachim Perinets Broschüren und Gedichte: nebst dem Versuche einer ersten vollständigen Bibliographie und Chronologie seiner sämtlichen Werke', *Zeitschrift für Bücherfreunde*, ix (1905–6), 154–69
PETER BRANSCOMBE

Perini, Annibale (*b* north Italy, *c*1560; *d* Graz, late 1596). Italian composer and organist. Following the tradition begun by Annibale Padovano, who was probably his uncle, he and Simone Gatto continued to import Venetian musical style to Graz. He arrived there from Venice about 1575, and in 1579 was appointed organist of the court chapel of Archduke Karl II, who provided for his further training. On the archduke's death in 1590 he went as organist to the Protestant collegiate church at Graz. When he introduced the Venetian style there it pleased the Protestant nobility but displeased the church authorities, who remained obstinately loyal to music in the traditional German style. In 1594 he returned to the court at Graz, which had remained Catholic, and in 1595 was confirmed in his post as court organist under Archduke Ferdinand. A collection of 40 of his motets for four to 12 voices, along with similar pieces by Gatto, was edited posthumously by Orazio Sardena (Venice, 1604, inc., 1 in MAM, xlvii, 1979). An eight-part *Missa super Benedicite omnia opera Domini* (*SI-Lng* 340) and a few motets also survive. The seven-part *Cantate Domino* is one of his finest works: it is found in six sources (including the *Promptuarii musici*, RISM 1612³), and Christoph Demantius used it as a model for a mass.

BIBLIOGRAPHY
H. Federhofer: 'Annibale Perini', *Mf*, vii (1954), 402–14
H. Federhofer: *Musikpflege und Musiker am Grazer Habsburgerhof der Erzherzöge Karl und Ferdinand von Innerösterreich (1564–1619)* (Mainz, 1967)
HELLMUT FEDERHOFER

Perino Fiorentino [Perino degli Organi] (*b* ?Florence, 1523; *d* 1552). Italian lutenist and composer. As a child he was a pupil of Francesco da Milano; his position as Francesco's protégé apparently placed him in high regard at the court of Pope Paul III, for he is mentioned in the papal account books as recipient of a cash gift at the age of 13 (in January 1537) and again in the following year. His name appears twice more after Francesco's death in 1543–4.

Five of Perino's compositions were published in *Intabolatura de lauto di M. Francesco Milanese et M. Perino Fiorentino, suo discipulo* (RISM 1547²¹), a collection made up principally of Francesco's pieces. The volume was reprinted three times up to 1566, and some of its pieces probably appeared in Phalèse's now lost fifth book, *Des chansons, gaillardes, paduanes et motetz reduitz en tabulature de luc* (Leuven, 1547, see *BrownI*). Three of the pieces are fantasias. Two of them show a grasp of composition in an imitative style; the third is chordal, with diatonic melodies and ornamented cadences. Two other pieces are intabulations of four-part madrigals by Arcadelt: *O felici occhi miei* and *Quanti travagli*. The Siena Lutebook (*NL-DHgm* 20.860) contains Perino's parody on Francesco's *Fantasia de mon triste* (which is based on Richafort's chanson *De mon triste desplaisir*).

BIBLIOGRAPHY
BrownI
E.A. Wienandt: 'Perino Fiorentino and his Lute Pieces', *JAMS*, viii (1955), 2–13
H.C. Slim: 'Francesco da Milano (1497–1543/44)', *MD*, xviii (1964), 63–84; xix (1965), 109–28
R.K. Falkenstein: *The Late Sixteenth-Century Repertory of Florentine Lute Song* (diss., SUNY, 1997)
ELWYN A. WIENANDT/IAIN FENLON

Period. The interval of time between successive events, such as rhythmic pulses or peaks in a vibration pattern; commonly, a musical statement terminated by a cadence or built of complementary members, each generally two to eight bars long and respectively called 'antecedent' and 'consequent'. A musical period has been compared with a sentence, or period, in rhetoric. Zarlino, in *Le istitutioni harmoniche* (1558), associated the two concepts when he described the cadence as a *punto di cantilena*, which could not appear until the sense of the underlying text had been completed (p.221); in this sense a period, however short or long, extends until its harmonic action has come to a close. It is this view of structure that governed musical form for much of the 18th century, extending below and above the period itself, from two-and four-bar phrases to entire movements. With the technique of *Fortspinnung* a composer such as Bach could build long periods out of short figures and motifs; the harpsichord cadenza to the first movement of Brandenburg Concerto no.5, for instance, constitutes a harmonic period 43 bars long (another example, in which a four-note motif in semiquavers is extended to a 12-bar period, is quoted in FORTSPINNUNG, ex.1). Wagner extended this concept of period to apply to large-scale musico-dramatic units, although he often used an interrupted cadence, instead of a conclusive one, to terminate a 'period' in his music dramas.

Symmetry provides another defining element in period structure. Complementary figures and phrases establish a regular pattern of movement that allows the listener to anticipate the final point of arrival in a self-contained unit, for example the last bar of the theme or a variation in a theme and variations movement. When a period, such as that formed by the theme of the slow movement of Haydn's 'Surprise' Symphony, is built of two 'equal' members – the first of which is punctuated by an imperfect cadence, the second by a perfect cadence, and both of which are themselves further divisible into two equal parts – it is said to be 'regular' or 'normal'.

Regular period-like structures can be found in music from as early as the 13th century; the two strains of an *estampie* were designated *primus punctus* and *secundus punctus*, and their respective endings 'ouvert' and 'clos'. This symmetrical pattern, which is fitted to music for dancing and to settings of poetry built in quatrains, has been pervasive in music to the present day. However, it was primarily in the 18th century that the manipulation of period structure became the most important feature of musical form, because of the interplay of symmetry and cadential harmony that characterizes the musical language of the time. Classical composers were specially resourceful in building long periods by extending one or both of a pair of complementary phrases beyond their regular length by internal repetitions, interrupted cadences and harmonic digressions. A striking example of extended phrase lengths is provided by the first movement of Mozart's String Quintet in C K515, whose 368 bars (making it the longest first movement of all his quartets and quintets) can be divided into 11 periods.

Period structure in music was discussed extensively by 18th-century theorists. Koch's *Versuch einer Anleitung zur Composition* (1782–93) provides the most comprehensive treatment, beginning with short symmetrical patterns, discussing the compression and extension of phrases and periods and eventually arriving at what he called *Hauptperioden*, namely the principal sections in a large-scale form (exposition, development, recapitulation). There has been considerable disagreement on the terms used to discuss period structure, and even on the exact nature of the period itself; and the 19th-century view, which has sought to narrow it to two phrases each usually consisting of two, four or eight bars, has limited the period to the regular construction.

In the terminology of Hugo Riemann, 'period' expresses a purely rhythmic, hierarchical concept (*see* RHYTHM).

See also ANALYSIS, §II, 2, and OUVERT.

BIBLIOGRAPHY

L.G. Ratner: 'Eighteenth-Century Theories of Musical Period Structure', *MQ*, xlii (1956), 439–54, repr. in *Classical Music*, ed. E. Rosand (New York, 1985), 85–100

P. Benary: 'Zum periodischen Prinzip bei J.S. Bach', *BJb 1958*, 84–93

G. Massenkeil: *Untersuchungen zum Problem der Symmetrie in der Instrumentalmusik W.A. Mozarts* (Wiesbaden, 1962)

C. Dahlhaus: 'Wagners Begriff der "dichterisch-musikalischen Periode"', *Beiträge zur Geschichte der Musikanschauung im 19. Jahrhundert*, ed. W. Salmen (Regensburg, 1965), 179

C. Dahlhaus: 'Phrase et période: contribution à une théorie de la syntaxe musicale', *Analyse musicale*, xiii (1988), 37–44

G. Fisher: 'System and Impulse: Three Theories of Periodic Structure from the Early Nineteenth Century', *CM*, xlix (1992), 29–47

L.G. Ratner: *Romantic Music: Sound and Syntax* (New York, 1992)

C. Rosen: 'Ritmi di tre battuti in Schubert's Sonata in C minor, D958', *Convention in Eighteenth- and Nineteenth-Century Music: Essays in Honor of Leonard G. Ratner*, ed. W.J. Allenbrook, J.M. Levy and W.P. Mahrt (Stuyvesant, NY, 1992), 113–21

LEONARD G. RATNER

Periodicals. The present article provides a general account of musical periodicals and their history; it is supplemented by a comprehensive list of musical periodicals, arranged by continent and country, with an alphabetical index. Periodical editions of music are presented in a separate section.

In this article, dates given normally represent first and last volumes or, in certain special cases, issues; dates given with an oblique stroke (e.g. 1971/2) refer to a volume beginning in one year and ending in another. Fuller information on title changes and on breaks in a periodical's run will be found in the lists.

For a comprehensive list and index of musical PERIODICALS see volume 28.

I. General. II. Continental and national surveys.

I. General

1. Definitions, nomenclature. 2. Origins. 3. History.

1. DEFINITIONS, NOMENCLATURE. Periodicals are publications appearing at regular (or sometimes irregular) intervals and, normally, furnished with serial numbers indicating annual volumes. They primarily contain such material as essays, reports, critiques and news items. In addition to their periodical mode of publication they have in common with newspapers an intention of continuance, an approach determined by publisher or editor, an objective of variety of content and to some extent contemporary relevance. In music, the concept of the periodical also includes yearbooks, annual reports and the proceedings of institutions, almanacs on music and similarly orientated publications; works published in fascicles (part-works, serials etc.) are to be distinguished from periodicals proper.

The essential criterion is that of periodical appearance, be it regular (daily, weekly, fortnightly, monthly, bi-monthly, quarterly, half-yearly or annually) or occasional. The term 'journal' came into English with the connotation of 'daily' as a translation of the French 'journal'. The expression 'journal' generally had this French sense at the end of the 17th century (i.e. diary, newspaper, periodical). J.P. Kohl, editor of the *Hamburgische Berichte von neuen gelehrten Sachen*, defined the term in the preface to the first annual volume in 1732, alluding to the change of meaning:

A *journal* … is to the French what the Greeks called *ephemerides*, the Romans *diarium*, the Italians a *giornale*, and the Germans a *Tag-Buch*. In all these languages however it also means, by extension of its original significance, a paper or a publication which appears not monthly but daily, or at least weekly. Similarly the word 'journal' has undergone the same change or alteration, so that it means today not so much a weekly paper with the latest learned news but any publication that appears either monthly, quarterly or yearly.

In musical publications the term 'journal' first appeared in the titles of French and Belgian periodicals, for example in the periodical edition of music *L'écho, ou Journal de musique françoise, italienne* (Liège, 1758–66). In Germany, where H.C. Koch's *Journal der Tonkunst* (Brunswick and Erfurt, 1795) may be noted, it was gradually replaced by the perfectly adequate German word 'Zeitschrift', which was also considered by contemporary dictionaries a substitute for 'journal and periodical writings' (as in the supplement of 1813 to J.H. Campe's dictionary). In England the word 'journal' first appeared in a main title in the periodical edition of music *The Monthly Musical Journal*, edited by Thomas Busby in London in 1801. 'Journal' was often used along with expressions relating to periodicity, e.g. 'Monthly Journal' (or simply 'Monthly'); similarly in French 'journal mensuel' and in German compounds such as 'Monatsschrift'. Other virtually synonymous titles used in English were 'Magazine', 'Review', 'Register', 'Gazette', 'Record', 'Circular', 'Guide', 'Herald', 'Times', 'Reporter', 'News' etc.; in French 'Echo', 'Chronique', 'Revue', 'Gazette', 'Album', 'Courrier', 'Moniteur', 'Presse' etc.; and in German 'Beiträge', 'Nachrichten', 'Briefe', 'Magazin', 'Blatt', 'Archiv', 'Rundschau', 'Zeitung' etc. Some of these terms also occur in the titles of daily papers. From the beginning various such names were used equally for musical periodicals and for periodical editions of music.

2. ORIGINS. Periodical publications consisting solely of pieces of music preceded music periodicals (in the sense used in this article) in almost all countries except Germany and Austria. The first such editions appeared in England and France in the 1690s. Such periodicals exercised an enduring influence. The practice of furnishing each number or year of a musical journal or almanac with musical appendixes or supplements is no doubt attributable to them. So is the two-part format, with one part devoted to practice and the other to theory: that arrangement appears in the late 18th century and in the 19th, as in the *Musikalische Realzeitung* (1788–90) published by Bossler with its 'practical part', *Musikalische Anthologie für Kenner und Liebhaber*, William Ayrton's *The Harmonicon* (1823–33) and *The Flutist's Magazine; and Musical Miscellany* (1827–?1830), or the publications by Schott (Mainz) of *Der Minnesänger* (1834–8) and *Der Gesellschafter* (1837–8). In the second half of the 18th century and the first of the 19th periodical editions of music also included supplements with articles on theory and critiques of new books and works. Musical periodicals in the narrower sense seem to have developed from these literary supplements in England, Russia and Bohemia. *The Literary Part of the Musical Magazine* of *The New Musical and Universal Magazine* (1774–5) can be considered a prototype.

Other factors too played an important part in the rise of musical periodicals. Occasional musical items in newspapers and musical reports in general journals may be seen as forerunners. For example the literary and political journal *Mercure galant* (*Mercure de France* from 1724), founded in 1672 by the writer Donneau de Visé and published until 1832, carried important notices on musical events, and is specially relevant to French opera. In Germany the *Monathliche Unterredungen* of E.W. Tentzel (1680–1707) offered an essay with comments on musical compositions and an article about the use of musical instruments in church services (September 1692). German scholarly journals of the time contain essays on 'Musik und Oper der Italiener' (*Historische Remarques der neuesten Sachen in Europa des 1699ten Jahrs*, Hamburg, 1699–1700) and contributions on the 'Missbrauch der Kirchenmusik' and on the 'Verwerffung der musicalischen Harmonie' in the church (*Nova literaria Germaniae*, Hamburg, April 1704), with announcements

and discussions of books on music. In England Peter Motteux's *The Gentleman's Journal, or The Monthly Miscellany, by Way of Letters to a Gentleman in the Country, consisting of News, History, Philosophy, Poetry, Musick* (1691/2–4) offers commentary on Purcell's music with reports on musical events and announcements of books. Moral weeklies, which were primarily journals of instruction, occasionally contained references to opera. In 1710 Joseph Addison published in the *Spectator* three satirical and critical articles about Italian opera in England. One issue of *Der Vernünfftler* (Hamburg, 1713/14), the first publication of the kind in Germany, edited by Johann Mattheson, contained his article 'Theatralische Remarques' on J.P. Förtsch's *Thalestris* and Reinhard Keiser's *Julius Cäsar* and *Iphigenie*. *Der Patriot* (Hamburg, 1724–8), as the organ of the Teutsch-Übende Gesellschaft, a society devoted to the promotion of the German language and to works, written in it, at first contained articles or conduct during opera performances but later included essays on stage sets and machinery, performers and dance; no.25 of the first volume was devoted exclusively to opera in Hamburg and took a rationalist attitude towards illusionism in Baroque opera. In his moral weekly *Vernünfftige Tadlerinnen* (Leipzig, 1725), too, Gottsched tried to influence his readers with opinions and verdicts on various opera-related topics.

As this conspectus shows, music had assumed a place, even if peripheral, in magazines and journals of the 17th and early 18th centuries long before the establishment of true musical periodicals. Their emergence had the deeper purpose of providing the musical endeavour of the time with its own platform. The ground for the earliest musical periodicals, which began in 1722 with Mattheson's *Critica musica*, was thus prepared by scholarly journals of an encyclopedic nature and moral weekly magazines devoted to learning and improvement.

3. HISTORY. The intellectual history of an epoch is strikingly reflected in its periodicals. This applies not only to general journals but also to musical ones, the articles and reports of which offer a variety of material for study as regards the outlook of the era. The first musical periodicals of the 18th century represent the publications of individual personalities, whom F.W. Marpurg called 'periodical writers' (*Der critische Musicus an der Spree*, i, 1749). They saw their task as consisting essentially in assisting the development of musical knowledge and ensuring its recognition by the critical exegesis of literature. These early musical periodicals are partly in the tradition of the encyclopedic scholarly journals and partly in the tradition of weeklies designed to serve education and moral improvement.

If these periodicals were mainly for musical connoisseurs, succeeding ones were increasingly concerned with the music of their own time, musical life and institutions. This was connected with the emergence of musical life into the public domain instead of its confinement within a more exclusive social group. Not only connoisseurs ('Kenner') but also musical amateurs ('Liebhaber') were drawn into the journals' circle of interest. The didactic and critical tendencies of the age of rationalism, at first prominent, retreated during the later 18th century, with the growing middle-class musical public, before a striving for the 'general' and a more marked tendency towards immediacy. While all the musical periodicals of the first half of the 18th century were published in Germany, in the second half France and the Netherlands, and then Austria and England, produced their first musical journals.

1798, the year the *Allgemeine musikalische Zeitung* was founded in Leipzig, saw a new phase of development in the history of musical periodicals which continued until the end of World War I, characterized by its orientation towards the universal rather than the specialist journal. The development towards comprehensive journals on the one hand and to ever narrower specialist fields on the other reached its apogee at different times during the 19th century in different European countries and the USA.

In addition to the journals of wide scope, of the standing of the *Allgemeine musikalische Zeitung* (Leipzig, 1798/9–1848), *Le ménestrel* (Paris, 1833/4–1914, 1919–1940) or *The Musical Times* (London, 1844/5–), which covered all the musical activities of their time, there were many others, some of them important, that concentrated on particular musical centres, especially the chief cities of Europe – in Germany, Berlin and (especially) Leipzig, and in the USA (mainly Boston). With the increasing development of musical life the large general periodicals and the more locally orientated journals were joined by those catering for special interests. This trend began in the 1840s and gained momentum in the second half of the century. For example, the foundation of choral societies and the organization of music festivals gave rise to publications largely devoted to choral singing and vocal music. Developments in instrument manufacture demanded the appearance of specialist periodicals. Reforms in music education led to numerous periodicals dealing with general educational matters or more specific ones such as piano or singing pedagogy, or eurhythmics on the Jaques-Dalcroze system, or notation (e.g. John Curwen's Tonic Sol-fa method). Liturgical reforms, the revival of hymns and sung services and the founding of church music organizations encouraged the appearance of many more. The increasing cultivation of instrumental and vocal music also gave rise to periodicals dealing with particular genres, including chamber music, popular music (for such instruments as the guitar, mandolin and zither), and even light music, including that of the music halls and smoking concerts.

The widespread commercialization of musical life after 1870 led to an increase in journals serving groups of like interest, whose task was mainly to further professional interests. Continuing specialization led to the provision of periodicals and yearbooks devoted to individual composers, for example Wagner. The consolidation of musicology as a discipline and the formation of musicological societies initiated the publication of musicological journals in the later 19th century. During this development the general journals came to devote significantly more attention to practical matters of music and musical life, while research articles and studies appeared in specialist ones. In the 19th century the development of national schools, mainly in north-east and south-east Europe, led to the founding of periodicals stressing the national element, in Scandinavia as well as in the Slavonic countries, Hungary and Greece. Outside Europe and North America, the first music periodicals appeared in the later 19th century and the early 20th; these were mainly devoted to national music and musical life, such as that of Australia, Japan, Mexico and New Zealand.

Towards the end of the 19th century came recognition of a need, in music as in other cultural areas, to proceed

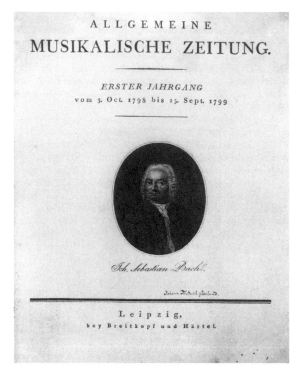

1. Title-page of the first issue of the 'Allgemeine musikalische Zeitung' (Leipzig, 1798)

outwards from national groups into international ones. As opposed to the national element so dominant in the 19th century, international cooperation was seen as an urgent task in order to constrain further national fragmentation and compartmentalization, in music as well as musicology. The International Musical Society, founded in 1899, the first of its kind, published two important periodicals to further such aims; both lasted until the beginning of World War I (1914).

As in all branches of cultural life, the end of World War I occasioned a turning-point in the development of musical periodicals. The fundamental change of the years after 1918 is reflected in the titles of certain new periodicals. Together with general periodicals (some revived, others newly established), which were mainly concerned with the musical life of the time, there were many concerned solely with modern musical developments, for example impressionism or expressionism, or the structural and tonal problems of modern music. The range of specialized journals was widened by the development and spread of gramophone records and by the new directions of research taken by teachers and theorists such as Heinrich Schenker.

In particular, the musicological specialist journals underwent notable expansion in many countries between the wars, partly because of the founding of more musicological societies (e.g. in France, Germany, Sweden, Great Britain, Switzerland and Belgium). In some countries outside Europe, for example in parts of Latin America, musical periodicals came into existence only after 1940. In several countries, activity in musical periodicals was halted or even destroyed by World War II. Only a few were able to reappear after the end of the war in 1945. At the end of the 1940s and still more in the 1950s and 60s the number of musical periodicals in the advanced countries of the world increased considerably and, by the 1970s, presented an uncommonly varied total picture. The new journals are for the most part general ones dealing with the musical life of their own time and country, e.g. in Austria, Germany and Great Britain, as well as several concerned with traditional specialist areas such as music education, church music, instrument making, vocal and choral music or folk music. New topics such as copyright, sound reproduction (records, tape, electronic instruments, stereophony) and jazz, as well as beat, country music and (increasingly) pop and rock music, are all covered by periodicals. Periodicals concerned with records in particular can be seen as a mirror of various repertories, famous virtuosos, singers and conductors; the importance of technical and commercial aspects should also be emphasized. The progress of musicology after World War II, in Europe and especially in the USA, found expression in the establishment of musicological periodicals and yearbooks. Some sought to cover all areas of the discipline; others were (and are) confined to particular periods, composers, genres or instruments.

Since the early 19th century, and particularly since 1850, many music periodicals have been issued by music publishing firms with the propagation of their own music publications as an important objective; when such factors have been permitted to influence editorial policy, such periodicals may give a highly partial view of the musical scene. Many others, for example the official organs of institutions or learned societies, or independently owned periodicals, are unaffected by such factors. Commercial considerations over the years have increasingly dictated the necessity for periodicals to include advertising material; the nature of such advertising may often provide clues as to a periodical's readership.

Sound reproduction, electro-acoustical experimentation and electronic technology have increasingly been topics for consideration in music periodicals. This development began in the mid-1950s. Journals devoted to musical instruments came to discuss new electronic technology and its application to keyboards, guitars, drums, woodwind and other instruments. There are specialized journals dealing with the promotion of experimental and improvised music. From the later 1970s computer music came to be considered. Some periodicals deal with the role of science and technology, or with methods and issues arising from the use of contemporary technology in such fields as multimedia art-forms, sound sculpture as generated by computer and electro-acoustic composition; in the USA, the application of computers and technology to the study of music and musicology is a favoured topic.

II. Continental and national surveys

1. Africa. 2. America: (i) Canada (ii) United States of America (iii) Latin America. 3. Asia: (i) India (ii) Israel (iii) Japan. 4. Australasia. 5. Europe: (i) Austria (ii) Belgium (iii) France (iv) Germany (v) Great Britain (vi) Italy (vii) The Netherlands (viii) Russia (ix) Central eastern European countries (x) Scandinavia (xi) Spain and Portugal (xii) Switzerland.

1. AFRICA.   Music journals on the African continent reflect a musical culture either European or European-influenced. The first African journals with a regular musical component came from the French-ruled Algeria and Tunisia; these were devoted to the theatre and the fine arts generally as well as music, e.g. *Lorgnette bônoise*

(Bône [now Annaba], 1897/8), *Alger artistique* (Algiers, 1898) and *La revue noire* (Tunis, 1898). The first exclusively musical journals were *Le bulletin musical* (Mustapha [now Algiers], 1904–6) and *L'avenir musical de Tanger* (Algiers, 1904–14), organ of the Algiers Conservatory. Similarly most African music periodicals continue to represent institutions or organizations. Among the more important were the *Newsletter* published 1948–53 by the African Music Society founded in 1947 in Roodeport near Johannesburg (continued 1954–1975/6 as *African Music*), which was concerned with investigations into folk music, popular music, dance and poetry in Africa, and the journal of the All-Africa Church Music Association (Salisbury, Zimbabwe, 1963–). Further attempts towards a more systematic view of African music are seen in *Notes on Education and Research in African Music*, published by the Institute of African Studies of the University of Ghana since 1967, and in *The Nigerian Music Review* (1977–), published by the Department of Music, University of Ife. In South Africa, the musicological journal *Ars nova* was founded in 1969 at the Department of Musicology, University of South Africa; it was joined by the *South African Journal of Musicology* (Pretoria, 1981–) of the Musicological Society of Southern Africa. Two specialized journals are the *South African Journal of Music Therapy* (Cape Town, 1982–) and the *Nuusbrief*, later *Cantando Gaudeamus* (Bloemfontein, ?1989–), published by the South African Choral Society.

2. CANADA.

(i) Canada.   Musical supplements were published in Canadian literary journals from 1839, but musical journals as such appeared in Canada only from the mid-1840s, at first in French-speaking areas, where the earliest Canadian musical centres had been established: *Le ménestrel* (Quebec, 1844–5) which presumably derived its title from the Paris journal, and *L'artiste* (1860). Probably one of the first Canadian music journals in English was *The Musical Journal* (1887–?1890). Besides numerous short-lived publications there have been three significant longer-lasting periodicals: *Le passe-temps* (1895–1935, 1945–9), *Canadian Music Trades Journal* (1900/01–1932/3) and *The Violin* (1906/7, called *Musical Canada* from 1907 to 1933). In more recent times Canadian music journals have generally concentrated on the various facets of musical life, as did the *Canadian Review of Music and Art* (1942–1947/8), devoted to musical life, to conductors, composers and performers and more widely to musical education. The first journal, published by the Canadian Music Council was *The Canadian Music Journal* (Sackville, NB, later Toronto, 1956/7–1961/2), followed by *Les cahiers canadiens de musique/The Canada Music Book* (1970–76). Mention should also be made of Canada's leading opera journal *Opera in Canada* (from July 1963 *Opera Canada*; 1960–), published by the Canadian Opera Guild. Other music journals are devoted to music education, for example the journal of the Canadian Association of University Schools of Music (1971–9), continued as *Canadian University Music Review* (1980–), or on Canadian composers, folk music and the music industry. A first step towards a Canadian musicological periodical is represented by *Studies in Music* (1976–87, 1991–), with contributions exclusively by members of the music faculty of the University of Western Ontario. Journals specializing in early music appeared, such as *Le tic-toc-choc*, later

Journal de musique ancienne (1979–89) and *Musick* (1979–), published by the Vancouver Society of Early Music. In 1983 the yearly newsletter *Periodica Musica* was founded as organ of RIPM, which is involved in the cataloguing and indexing of musical periodicals, published by the Centre for Studies in 19th-Century Music at the University of British Columbia, from 1986 at the University of Maryland, USA. There are several periodicals devoted to contemporary music, among them *Array Newsletter* (1972/3–1978), intended to improve communication between composers and performers. *Musicworks* (1978–) deals with new music from Stockhausen to John Cage, microtonal music and experimental developments in visual art and dance. *SoundNotes* (1991–), a single-handed effort by the composer and author Colin Eatock, reports on the new music scene across Canada. *Circuit* (1991–) deals with postmodernism and is orientated towards continental Europe.

(ii) United States of America.   In the USA, the forerunners of true musical periodicals were periodical music publications, obviously English-influenced. The first, edited by Amos Doolittle and Daniel Read, was *The American Musical Magazine* (1786–7), which consisted of compositions by American and English composers. But a successor, *The Musical Magazine*, edited by Andrew Law (1792–1801), offered in addition to 'Psalm and Hymn Tunes' an essay – an exception to the general trend in early USA musical periodicals, which however cannot be seen as a first step, historically, towards a true musical journal. The *Ladies' Literary Museum, or Weekly Repository* (1817–20) was a literary journal which included musical supplements from 1818, and from 1819 turned occasionally to musical topics.

The Euterpeiad, or Musical Intelligencer (1820/21–1823), edited by J.R. Parker, may be seen as the first true musical periodical in the USA. In addition to a serial conspectus of musical history it offered mainly news and reviews of Boston musical life, which was becoming increasingly lively in the 1820s. Among other early, short-lived periodicals are *The Euterpeiad* (1830/31–1831), containing essays on musical and stylistic questions, biographical sketches and anecdotes about well-known musicians as well as discussion of printed music and concert reviews, and *The Musical Magazine, or Repository of Musical Science, Literature and Intelligence* (1839–1841/2), which strove to familiarize its readers with the European musical scene. The first really ambitious musical journal was *Dwight's Journal of Music* (1852–81). In a circular of 1852 its editor John Sullivan Dwight (1813–93) stressed the independence of his publication: 'The tone to be impartial, independent, catholic, conciliatory, aloof from musical clique and controversy, cordial to all good things, but not eager to chime in with any powerful private interest of publisher, professor, concert-giver, manager, society or party'. The journal offered essays on such composers as Handel, Haydn, Mozart and Beethoven, and on music history, theory, education and style, together with critical reports on the musical scene and announcements of new compositions. Another more comprehensive musical periodical of extra-regional significance was the New York publication *Musical America* (1898–9, 1905–64, 1987–92), while other general musical periodicals focussed on individual centres, for example *The Musical Leader and Concert-Goer* (Chicago, 1895–

1967) and the *Pacific Coast Musician* (Los Angeles, 1911–48), the oldest important Californian musical periodical.

As musical culture spread in the 1870s, numerous publications appeared dealing with particular interests. The movement, European in origin, towards the revival of church music and sung services led in the USA to the publication of several church music magazines, such as *Caecilia* (Regensburg, 1874–6; New York, 1877–), the journal of the American Cecilia Society, *The Catholic Choirmaster* (1915–64), the journal of the Society of St Gregory of America, incorporated in 1965 into *Caecilia*, and *The Church Music Review* (1901/2–1934/5) of the American Guild of Organists. With the growing commercialization of musical life these were joined by periodicals devoted to the music trade, such as *The Music Trades* (1890–), or to the sale of musical instruments, e.g. *Music Industry* (?1906–). Other publications were concerned with light music, e.g. *Metronome* (1885–1961), and the various branches of music entertainment, e.g. *The Billboard* (1894/5–). Interest in music education reform led to the foundation of journals dealing generally with the subject, e.g. *The Etude* (1883–1957), which circulated widely, and *The Musician* (1896–1948), or with new methods of notation, e.g. *Tonic Sol-fa Advocate* (1881/2–1885/6), the organ of the Tonic Sol-fa movement in the USA and Canada.

Many special interests were incorporated into the framework of musical publications of the 20th century. In a deliberate campaign for progressive European music and for the compositions of the incipient American avant garde the magazine *Modern Music* (at first *The League of Composers' Review*) was founded (1924–46). On the other hand, *Chord and Discord* (1932–1963, 1969), as

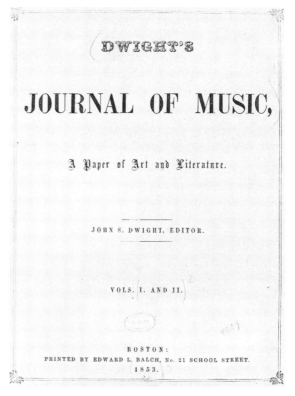

2. Title-page of the first issue of 'Dwight's Journal of Music' (Boston, 1852)

the magazine of the Bruckner Socity of America, was devoted to the works of Bruckner and Mahler. Next to appear were journals representing the interests of operatic societies, such as *Opera, Concert and Symphony*, from 1952 *Counterpoint* (1934–53) of the San Francisco Opera Association, and *Opera News* of the Metropolitan Opera Guild (1936/7–), which contains news of the Metropolitan Opera and the Guild and is a leading organ of both the Metropolitan and the international operatic scene. Sheets dealing with records, jazz and film music followed at the beginning of the 1940s. The following decades saw an upsurge of musicology in the USA. The first comprehensive musicological periodical *The Musical Quarterly* (1915–) was founded by the pioneer of American musicology O.G.T. Sonneck; successive editors have followed his declared policy of securing contributions from the best scholars regardless of nationality. As well as essays on various aspects of musicology, there later followed selective book, music and record reviews and 'Current Chronicle' (reports on performances of new music) as well as quarterly book and record lists. Among more recent musicological journals are the *Journal of Renaissance and Baroque Music* (from 1948, *Musica disciplina*; 1946/7–) and the *Journal of the American Musicological Society* (1948–). Mention should also be made of *Notes*, the organ of the American Music Library Association (1943/4–), with its comprehensive bibliographical contributions and useful conspectuses of new music, books and records. *The Music Index* (1949–), published in monthly parts and collected in annual volumes, offers a continuous guide, in the form of an author and contents index, to over 100 musical periodicals mainly in English. In 1967 the periodical *RILM Abstracts* was founded by the International Association of Music Libraries Archives and Documentation Centres with the International Musicological Society and the American Council of Learned Societies, designed to provide a conspectus of all significant musicological writing. The *RIdIM/RCMI Newsletter* (1975/6–), the organ of the Répertoire International d'Iconographie Musicale, published by the Research Center for Music Iconography of the City University of New York, provides a coverage of research in music iconography, addressing issues relevant to the music of both Western and non-European cultures.

In addition to these important publications devoted to documentation and research, attention has been given to the cataloguing and classifying of sources and documents to increase their accessibility and usefulness to scholarship, for example in the *Music Cataloging Bulletin* (founded 1970) of the Music Library Association. Mention should also be made of some library journals, such as *Cum notis variorum* (1976–89), the newsletter of the Music Library at the University of California, Berkeley, reporting on acquisitions and meetings, *Impromptu* (1982–?5), which notified librarians, scholars and musicians about the activities of the Music Division of the Library of Congress, and *The Full Score* (1985–), the newsletter of the Music Library at UCLA, which is concerned with research based on the library's materials. Other specialist preoccupations reflected in periodicals of the 1970s were concentrated more than before on particular countries, in respect either of historical studies or of the contemporary situation. Thus *Bach* (1970–), the periodical of the Riemenschneider Bach Institute, offers analyses and essays on the forms, styles and performances of the music of Bach and other Baroque composers, with translations of significant theoretical and musicological works, as well as *Bach Perspectives* (1995–), published by the University of Nebraska. *Ethnomusicology Newsletter*, later *Ethnomusicology*, was founded in 1953 by the Society for Ethno-Musicology and soon became a leading organ in this field, joined since 1983 by *Ethnomusicology at UCLA* and since 1995 by *Ethnomusicology Online*. Specific ethnic groups are considered in *Asian Music* (1968/9–), focussing on performing arts traditions, and in the *Chinese Music General Newsletter*, from 1979 *Chinese Music* (1978–), the organ of the Chinese Music Society of North America, as well as in *Music from China News* (1991–) and *Music in China* (1998–). The twice-yearly *The Black Perspective in Music* (New York, 1973–90) is devoted to the historical study of the African and black American musical tradition and its revival. It was joined by the *Black Music Research Newsletter* (from 1988 *Bulletin*) (1977/8–1990) and the *Black Music Research Journal* (1980–), published by the Institute for Research in Black American Music of Fisk University, mainly devoted to theoretical, sociological and aesthetic problems of the living musical traditions and their historical past, more recently followed by *Lenox Avenue* (1995–) of the Center for Black Music Research at Columbia College, Chicago.

Emphasis has recently been laid on research in American music. *The Sonneck Society Newletter* (1975–) provides information; more substantial is *American Music* (1983–), edited by the same society, covering not only art music but also jazz, folk, country and gospel. The *Newsletter* of the Institute for Studies in American Music (1971/2–) deals with folk and urban music in both North and South America. Most important are the *Inter-American Music Review* (1978/9–), edited by Robert Stevenson, relevant for the history of Latin and North American music, and the *Latin American Music Review* (1980–), edited by Gerard Béhague, which continues the tradition of Chase's *Yearbook for Inter-American Musical Research* (1965–77), with articles based on original Latin American material. International folk music research was considered in the *Yearbook for Traditional Music* (1969–86) of the International Council for Traditional Music. Besides *The Journal of Musicology* (1982–), which covers a wide variety of branches of the discipline, there are several scholarly journals devoted to particular areas. Music education periodicals include *Update* (1982–), for teachers on a national level, the *Philosophy of Music Education Review* (1993–) and *Teaching Music* (1993/4–) of the Music Educators National Conference, and music psychology, such as *Psychomusicology* (1981–) and *Music Perception* (1983/4–). Some journals are concerned with particular periods such as *19th Century Music* (1977/8–) and *Divisions* (1978–80), which dealt with the Baroque, including translations of theoretical works. Music theory occupies an important place in the realm of periodicals, with *In Theory Only* (1975–) of the Michigan Music Theory Society, *Music Theory Spectrum* (1979–) of the Society for Music Theory and *Music Theory Online* (1993–). Several periodicals deal with particular genres, such as chamber music or choral music; religious traditions are considered in *Folk Mass and Modern Liturgy Magazine* (1973/4–), *Musica judaica* (1975/6–) of the American Society for Jewish Music and *Hymnology Annual* (1991–), which is on an international basis. The

Journal of Research in Singing (1977/8–), *Voice*, later renamed *The Voice of Chorus America* (1978–) and *Ars Lyrica* (1981–) are concerned with vocal music; some journals are devoted to opera, such as *The World of Opera* (1978/9) and especially *The Opera Quarterly* (1983/4–), while the *AIVS Newsletter* (1976–), published by the American Institute for Verdi Studies and renamed *Verdi Newsletter* in 1977, includes a bibliography of publications on the composer since 1974. Periodicals devoted to composers more generally include *The Composer* (1969/70–1981), while *Women of Note Quarterly* (1993–) is concerned with women composers; others, published by societies, are dedicated to individual composers such as the *Bulletin* of the Arnold Schoenberg Institute (1975–6) and the *Journal of the Arnold Schoenberg Institute* (1976/7–1995/6), the *Journal of the American Liszt Society* (1977–), *The American Brahms Society Newsletter* (1983–) and *Beethoven Forum* (1992–). Several journals are devoted to special instruments or groups, among them *The Winds Quarterly* (1980–81), the *Flute Journal* (1981–) and *ClariNetwork* (1982–8). Periodicals in the field of sound reproduction are numerous and include the *Antique Phonograph Monthly* (1973–93) and the *ARSC Newsletter* (1977–), while record reviewing is the concern of *Fanfare: the Magazine for Serious Record Collectors* (1977/8–), *Record Review* (1977–84) and *New Review of Records* (1994–) as well as *Resound* (1982–), from the Archives of Traditional Music, which deals with archival materials (tapes, disc and cylinder recordings). Other technical developments, especially computer applications for musical purposes, are covered by the *Computer Music Journal* (1977–), *Computing and Musicology* (1985–) and *Computers in Music Research* (1989–). There are also increasing numbers of journals devoted to popular music and jazz.

(iii) Latin America. The first authenticated music periodical of Mexico and Central America is *El violín* (Mexico City, 1862). That in South America is *L'Union musicale* (Rio de Janeiro, 1852–?; traceable only bibliographically), followed by the Venezuelan opera journal *Dulcamara* (1873/4), the *Boletín musical* (Buenos Aires, 1878–?) and in Venezuela *El arte musical* (1878–?), the *Revista musical e de bellas artes* (Rio de Janeiro, 1879–80) and the *Montevideo musical* (1885–?1939), published for half a century by the Instituto Verdi and exercising a significant influence in Latin America. At first its only successors were isolated and short-lived music publications, but this situation changed radically at the beginning of the 1940s. From then on many musical periodicals were published, concerned with day to day happenings of musical life (for example *Polifonía*, Buenos Aires, 1944–?82, *Buenos Aires musical*, 1946–?78, or the important *Nuestra música*, Mexico City, 1946–53), music education (*Armonía*, Panama City, founded in 1943), church music (*Música sacra*, Petrópolis, 1941–59), modern music (*Música viva*, Rio de Janeiro, 1940–41) or folk music (*Anuario de la Sociedad folklórica de México*, Mexico City, 1938/40–1959); *Folclore* (São Paulo, 1953–; *Revista brasileira de folclore*, Rio de Janeiro, 1961–76, or *Revista colombiana de folclor* (1947–) and light music (*La canción*, Buenos Aires, founded in 1942). Another important publication is the *Revista musical (chilena)* (Santiago, 1945–), brought into being by the Instituto de Extensión Musical, the governing body of Chilean musical life since 1940; at first based on North American and

European models, it later developed a certain independence as a review of Chilean and Latin American art and indigenous and folk music from the colonial epoch to the present. Mention should be made of the more recent *Heterofonía* (Mexico City, 1968–), which became the official journal of the Conservatorio Nacional de Música, and the monthly *Revista do músico* (Rio de Janeiro, 1974–), both of which deal with the current musical life of their countries. The first periodicals devoted to musicology were the *Boletín latino-americano de música* (Montevideo, 1935–46), published from 1941 by the Instituto Interamericano de Musicología, and *Música viva* (Montevideo, 1942), which contained important contributions on the history of South American music. The establishment in 1965 of a musicological society in Argentina gave rise to a specialized journal, the *Argentine Review of Musicology* (Buenos Aires, 1973–), which places its main emphasis on ethnomusicology and folklore as well as covering historical, sociological and aesthetic questions. The 1980s saw the establishment of musicological journals in other South American countries, such as the *Revista musical de Venezuela* (Caracas, 1980/81–), since 1982 the official organ of the Sociedad Latinoamericano de Investigaciones Musicales, founded in September 1982 under F.C. Lange, or the *Boletim da Sociedade brasileira de musicologia* (São Paulo, 1983–). Other musicological periodicals emphasize the special traditions of the country concerned, such as the *Revista colombiana de investigación musical* (Bogotá, 1985–). The *Boletín andino de música* (Cochabamba, 1988–) deals with research and bibliography of traditional Bolivian music. Further specialized music journals are concerned with opera (for example *Ayer y hoy de la opera*, Buenos Aires, 1977–92), new music and contemporary composition (*Pauta*, Mexico City, 1982–) and folk and popular music (*A Contratiempo*, Bogotá, 1987–) as well as current musical life, such as *Boletín de música* (Havana, 1970–), which lists new works by Cuban composers, the *Boletim de documentação musical* (São Paulo, 1977–81), since 1982 forming a section of *Caderna de música* (São Paulo, 1980–), which lists Brazilian works in supplementary catalogues, or *Música brasileira* (Rio de Janeiro, 1996–).

3. ASIA.

(i) India. The earliest Indian music periodical was the *Annual Report of the Bengal Music School* (1871–?). This was followed by *Oriental Music* (1892–3), devoted to indigenous music. Two important periodicals founded by Indian institutions appeared in the 1930s: *The Journal of the Music Academy Madras* (1930–), which contains contributions on Western as well as Indian music (mainly on Hindu music), and *Music of India* (1937–8), the organ of the Calcutta Music Association. The 1960s saw the establishment of the *Indian Music Journal* (1964–) and at the beginning of the 1970s the foundation of the Indian Musicological Society; an English supplement to the periodical *Sangit Kala Vihar* served from November 1970 as its official organ, from 1971 as *Journal of the Indian Musicological Society, incorporating Sangeet Kala Vihar*, from 1973 *Journal of the Indian Musicological Society*. It deals mainly with Indian music and related arts.

(ii) Israel. The first music periodical of Palestine, as it then was, was the journal *Hallel* (1930), published by the Institute for New Music. After the founding of Israel various musical periodicals appeared. *Bat-kol* (1956,

1960–61) and *Tatzlil* (1960–70) represent local journals in which Israeli scholars published their research, while material from the congresses of the Israel Institute for Religious Music were printed in the yearbook *Dukhan* (1960–66). The *Bulletin of the Israel Musicological Society* (1968–) provides reports on that society. Since 1971 Israel has produced *Orbis musicae*, a specialized musicological journal, and since 1978 *Israel Studies in Musicology*, containing contributions on various topics, including music theory and ethnomusicology; the first volume has served as a Festschrift for Edith Gerson-Kiwi and Hanoch Avenary. In 1983/4 the scholarly yearbook *Music in Time* appeared, from the Rubin Academy of Music and Dance, with articles by well-known musicians and music educators.

(iii) Japan.   Japan's first musical periodical, *Ongaku zasshi* (1890–98), appeared at the end of the 19th century. This and its successors were manifestly influenced by the Western tradition, for example *Ongaku-shinpō* (1904–7), whose title reflects that of Schumann's journal *Neue Zeitschrift für Musik*. It contains essays, theoretical studies and reports on European musical life. Among the periodicals of the following years those mainly devoted to European music are the journals *Ongaku* (1910–22), and *Philharmony* (1927–), the organ of the NHK SO. Those devoted to traditional Japanese music in general began to appear towards the end of the 1920s: outstanding is *Tōyō ongaku kenkyū* (1936–42, 1951–) published by the Society for Research in Asiatic Music. But periodicals concerned with specific types of Japanese music hardly appeared before the 1940s; an example is *Engeki sekai* (1942–), which consists of studies of the *kabuki* and its music. There are however numerous magazines on records and jazz, e.g. *Chikuonki to kyōiku* (1931–) and *Swing Journal* (1947–), known by its Japanese name of *Suingu jānaru* until 1987. The establishment of the Musicological Society of Japan in the 1950s led to the publication of the country's first specialized journal of musicology, *Ongak-ugaku* (1954–), mainly based on European models but also containing articles on Japanese music. Similarly, the *Bulletin of Musashino academia musicae* (1962–) is a yearbook in which historical questions and current problems of musicology, especially of the Western world, are discussed by both native and foreign authors.

4. AUSTRALASIA.   The oldest music periodical of Australia is *Williams's Musical Annual and Australian Sketch Book* (1858). Apart from music supplements, which were clearly appropriated from the *Illustrated Journal of Australasia* (1855), it contains only ephemera about musical life in Melbourne. It was followed by the *Adelaide Musical Herald and Journal of Literature* (1862/3). Like these, later periodicals mainly devoted to the musical life of individual centres such as Melbourne, Adelaide and Sydney were generally short-lived. Of particular importance was the periodical *Music and Dance* (founded as *The Australian Musical News*, 1911–63/4), which provided graphic reports on events and circumstances in various parts of Australia. Among later publications two are of special interest: *The Canon* (1947/8–1966) and *Con brio* (1973), the journal of the NSW State Conservatorium of Music. More specialized magazines were or are concerned with jazz, e.g. *Jazz Notes (and Blue Rhythm)* (1941–62), which for a time relied heavily on the English journal *Jazz Music*; or with records, e.g. *Record Guide* (1953–8); or with copyright, e.g. the *APRA*

3. *Title-page of the fortieth issue of the 'Bulletin of Musashino academia musicae', iii (Tokyo, 1969)*

Journal (1969–92) and *Music and Copyright* (1989–), published by the Australian Copyright Council. The establishment of musicological studies in the 1960s in Australia led to the publication of several periodicals, such as *Studies in Music* (1967–92) and *Miscellanea musicologica* (1966–90), published by the music departments at the universities of Western Australia and Adelaide respectively, as well as *Musicology* (from 1985 *Musicology Australia*) (1964–), the organ of the Musicological Society of Australia, with articles on the music of various continents, the Indian and Pacific Oceans, Australian Aborigines and Australian composition, and the society's *Newsletter* (1977–). Periodicals devoted to music education include the *International Journal of Music Education* (1983–), published by the University of Western Australia and later by the University of Reading, Great Britain, and *Australian Music Teacher* (1990–). Emphasis is laid on Australian music in *Australian Record and Music Review* (1989–), in the *Newsletter* (1995–) of the Centre for Studies in Australian Music and in *Music Forum* (1996–), the journal of the Music Council of Australia.

The New Zealand Muse: a Musical Paper (1880) is the first authenticated New Zealand musical periodical; it was followed by the *The New Zealand Musical Monthly* (1888–90), whose coverage included Australia. The journal *The Triad* (1893/4–1927) was of particular importance; in its early years it was mainly devoted to music, offering essays, news and music supplements, though it later turned more to literature and art. Day to day musical life was dealt with in *Music in New Zealand* (1931–7). Important articles on New Zealand composers, musicians, publications and criticism appeared in *Music Ho* (1941–8). *Third Stream* (1968) was founded on an attempt to establish an important New Zealand music periodical, but it ceased publication after four numbers for financial reasons. In 1979 *Canzona*, the organ of the Composers' Association of New Zealand, started publication and after some years widened its scope to general musical topics. The leading journal of today is *Music in New Zealand* (1988–), from the music publisher W. Dart, which covers all fields from rock and pop to classical music.

5. EUROPE.

(i) Austria.   Austria's first music periodical, *Der musikalische Dilettante* (1770–73), founded by J.F. Daube, can in a sense be considered a scholarly journal in Mattheson's tradition: it is essentially a primer of composition and theory, with pieces by Daube and others. An important source for information about opera at the beginning of the 19th century is the *Wiener Hof-Theater-Almanach* (1804–16), called from 1805 the *Wiener Hof-Theater-Taschenbuch*, edited by H.J. Collin and I.F. Castelli. The *Wiener Theater-Zeitung* (1806–60), edited by Adolf Bäuerle (1786–1859), sought to fulfil the function of a Viennese music periodical; *Thalia* (1810–11), edited by I.F. Castelli, played an analogous role for opera – Castelli was sharply critical of Italian productions. The *Wiener allgemeine musikalische Zeitung* (1813), edited by Ignaz von Schönholz, did not long withstand the competition of the *Wiener Theater-Zeitung*; it was followed by the comprehensively conceived *Allgemeine musikalische Zeitung, mit besonderer Rücksicht auf den österreichischen Kaiserstaat* (1817–24) which, especially under the editorship of F.A. Kanne (1778–1833), successfully espoused Beethoven's cause and is an important source-book for the musical life of those years. The short-lived *Wiener Journal für Theater, Musik und Mode* (1806) was initially popular in Vienna. Ten years later there appeared the *Wiener Moden-Zeitung*, from 1817 *Wiener Zeitschrift für Kunst, Literatur, Theater und Mode* (1816–48); alongside Bäuerle's *Wiener Theater-Zeitung* it owned special weight at a time when no true music periodical existed; in 1816 and 1825–8 it published reviews of operatic productions in Vienna (including works by Auber, Bellini, Boieldieu, Donizetti, Meyerbeer, Mozart, Rossini and Weber).

The *Allgemeiner musikalischer Anzeiger* (1829–40), edited by Castelli, contained mainly reviews of new music; it was joined by the important *Allgemeine Wiener Musik-Zeitung* (1841–8) edited by August Schmidt (Aloys Fuchs also collaborated on it). The *Neue Wiener Musik-Zeitung* (1852–60) of Franz Glöggl jr had such notable contributors as Simon Sechter and Gustav Schilling; it offered substantial articles on music history as well as regular weekly reports on the Hofoper and news of musical events. On its demise, Selmar Bagge (1823–96) founded the *Deutsche Musik-Zeitung* (1860–62); he understood the importance of securing as contributors such important figures as Eduard Hanslick, Gustav Nottebohm, W.J. von Wasielewski and Arrey von Dommer, and thus of setting high standards. It was continued by the new series of the *Allgemeine musikalische Zeitung* (Leipzig, 1863–5), which Bagge edited from 1863, but many facets of Viennese musical life could be covered only in reports from correspondents.

In the second half of the 19th century and the first decades of the 20th new specialist periodicals were founded, for example those dealing with choral music, such as *Die Liedgenossen* (1861–5), which arose as choral societies and glee clubs developed. The organization of professional musicians into associations for the furtherance of their interests led to the publication of corresponding journals such as the *Österreichische Musiker-Zeitung* (1875–8; new series 1893–1934). The Austrian contribution to Wagner was *Parsifal* (1884–8). The resurgence of Catholic church music led to the founding of such publications as the *Gregorianische Rundschau* (1902–13), edited by Johann Weiss, which included material on the plainchant research at Solesmes, and its sequel *Musica divina* (1913–38) under the aegis of the Schola Austriaca. Attempts at the reform of music education led to such periodicals as the *Musikpädagogische Zeitschrift* (1911/12–1927). In 1904 the noted Viennese critic and composer Richard Heuberger founded the yearbook *Musikbuch aus Österreich* (1904–13), which contains valuable critical and musicological essays.

The first musicological yearbook, *Studien zur Musikwissenschaft* (1913–), was founded by Guido Adler as *Beihefte* of the Denkmäler der Tonkunst in Österreich (published in Germany). The music and theatre periodical *Der Merker* (1909/10–1922) offered, together with substantial articles on Vienna's musical past, the first reports on the new Viennese School of Arnold Schoenberg; but it was not until the advent of the *Musikblätter des Anbruch* (1919–37) that a clear new forum became available, after

4. Title-page of the first issue of the 'Musikbuch aus Österreich' (Vienna and Leipzig, 1904)

World War I, for the discussion of a new direction for music. Similar aims were pursued by *23: Dreiundzwanzig: eine Wiener Musikzeitschrift* (1932–7) edited by Willi Reich. New theories of music were also diffused by periodicals, e.g. the teaching of Schenker in his journal *Der Tonwille* (1921–4) and his yearbook *Das Meisterwerk in der Musik* (Munich, Vienna and Berlin, 1925–30), while *Der Dreiklang* (1937/8) was concerned with promulgating these doctrines after Schenker's death. Further music journals were devoted to particular composers, such as *Bruckner Blätter* (Klosterneuburg, later Vienna, 1929–42). From 1946 the *Österreichische Musikzeitschrift* fulfilled the role of a general music periodical in the broadest sense, concerned with current Austrian musical life as well as the country's past. Specialist journals include *Der Opernfreund* (1956–64), dealing primarily with contemporary issues in music drama in Vienna. Among periodicals devoted to particular composers are the *Chopin-Jahrbuch* (1956, 1963, 1970) and the *Nachrichtenblatt* of the Österreichische Richard-Wagner-Gesellschaft, Landesstelle Steiermark (1959–1988) and its sucessor *Richard Wagner Nachrichten* (1989/90–), as well as the *Richard Strauss Blätter* (1971/2–1978; new ser., 1979–), each number of which is devoted to one of the composer's principal works. Musicological organs are, since 1956, *Kommission für Musikforschung: Mitteilungen* of the Österreichische Akademie der Wissenschaften, since 1967 the *Beiträge* of the Österreichische Gesellschaft für Musik, and since 1977 *Musicologica austriaca* (the last two published in Germany). *Komponist und Musikerzieher* (originally called *Der Komponist*) has appeared since 1971 as the organ of the Österreichischer Komponistenbund.

The following decades show a wide variety of more than 50 current music periodicals, most of them being supported by the Austrian state. The traditional special topics have been pursued, such as church music (*Praxis der Kirchenmusik*, 1981–, of the Protestant Church) and the concern for new religious music (*Musik und Leben*, 1987–), folk music (*Musikanten-Express*, 1982–7, and *Briefe des Steirischen Volksliedwerkes*, from 1985 *Der Vierzeiler*, 1980–) and music instruments (*Okey*, 1994–, dealing with organs and keyboards). Other journals are devoted to Viennese music life – to opera and concert (*Der neue Merker*, 1989/90–) and from jazz (*Jazz live*, 1983–?94) to the musical (*Musical-Cocktail*, 1994–). There are important scholarly yearbooks and the like, which are devoted to individual Viennese composers such as *Nachrichten zur Mahler-Forschung* (1976–) of the Internationale Gustav Mahler-Gesellschaft, the *Bruckner-Jahrbuch* (1980–) of the Bruckner-Institut Linz, *A propos Haydn* (1983) of the Haydn-Gesellschaft Wien, *Mitteilungen* (1986/7–1993/4) of the Internationale Schönberg-Gesellschaft, *Mitteilungen: Schubert durch die Brille* (1988–) of the Internationales Schubert-Institut Wien (published in Germany) and *Die Fledermaus* (1990–) of the Wiener Institut für Strauss-Forschung. Newer areas are music therapy (*ÖBM*, from 1993 *Musiktherapeutisches Forum*, 1985–), contemporary music (*KompAkt 23*, 1987, published by the Austrian Section of the Internationale Gesellschaft für Neue Musik), electronic keyboards (*Manual*, 1986/7–) and new developments in electro-acoustic techniques (*Elektroakustik, Akusmatik & Raum*, 1992–, published by the Austrian section of the Internationale Gesellschaft für Neue Musik).

(ii) Belgium.   The earliest periodical publications in the southern Netherlands (present-day Belgium) included music ones: beginning with *Récréations harmoniques, ou recueil de chansons françaises* (1756–7), they appeared in some profusion. But the earliest musical periodical in the strict sense was the *Gazette musicale de la Belgique* (1833/4), founded by F.-J. Fétis in the year after his return to Belgium. The *Annuaire dramatique de la Belgique* (1839–47), edited by Félix Delhasse, contains critiques of musicians and composers and of concerts in Brussels; *La Belgique musicale, beaux-arts, belles-lettres* (1839) and its continuation *La revue musicale belge* (1840–59) are also locally orientated. A more broadly based music periodical was Delhasse's *Le guide musical* (1855–1917/18), which contained substantial contributions on current musical life, and which under Maurice Kufferath (1852–1919) became a forum for the discussion of Wagner's work; after World War I *La revue musicale belge* (1925–39), organ of the Sociétés Musicales et Dramatiques, continued the tradition of that journal but with a more objective approach. *Muziekwarande* (1922–31) focussed mainly on Flemish music and its composers. An important periodical, *La revue internationale de musique* (Paris and Brussels, 1938/9–1952), extended its coverage to France. There also appeared periodicals devoted to special topics, such as Catholic church music, for example *Musica sacra* (1881/2–1964) or the *Courrier de Saint-Grégoire* (1889–1914), and some dealing with liturgical issues such as *Ad te levavi* (1959–67) or *Gewijde dienst* (1961–5); others dealt with modern music, such as *Musica viva* (1936), edited by Hermann Scherchen or *La Sirène*, from 1938 *Syrinx* (1937–46). With the founding in 1931 of the Vereniging voor Muziekgeschiedenis te Antwerpen, Belgium achieved its first musicological journal, *Vlaamsch jaarboek voor muziekgeschiedenis* (1939–42, 1959, 1977). The *Revue belge de musicologie* was founded in 1946 by the Société Belge de Musicologie, particularly for the study of the musical history of the Low Countries. It has been joined by the *Brussels Museum of Musical Instruments Bulletin* (1971–), concerned with the investigation of historical and folk instruments, and later by the *Mededelingen van het Ruckers-Genootschap* (1982–91). Several periodicals are devoted to particular instruments, mainly to the organ, such as *De schalmei* (1946–50), continued as *De Praestant* (1952–72), followed by *Orgelkunst* (1978–) and *Organum novum* (1994–). Some are published by societies, such as *L'organiste* (1969–), from the Union Wallonne des Organistes, and *Orgel positief* (1985), from the Vlaamse Orgel Vereniging. The restoration of historical organs is covered by *La renaissance de l'orgue* (1968–94) and the manufacturing of music instruments in general by *Celesta* (1987–). Other periodicals are published by opera houses, for example *De Munt/La Monnaie* (1986/7–), or concert societies, such as *Filharmonia* (1989/90–1995). Journals devoted to particular composers include *Feuilles wagnériennes* (1960–66), published by the Association Wagnérienne de Belgique, *Cahiers Albert Roussel* (1978–9, 1981) by Les Amis Belges d'Albert Roussel and *Le paon* (1981–), published by the Association Kodály-Belgique. Musicological periodicals underwent further specialization, such as music education, for example *Orphée apprenti* (1987–94), music of the past, as in *Musica 'antiqua'* (1983/4–) and the *Jaarboek van het Vlaams centrum voor*

oude muziek (1985–7), while new directions in musical philosophy are explored in *Musicae scientiae* (1997–).

(iii) France. The appearance of music journals in the strict sense in France was preceded by numerous periodical publications of music, e.g. in the *Meslanges de musique latine, françoise et italienne* (1725–32), issued by Ballard. Musical reports and news were granted a measure of space in general cultural journals, e.g. *Mercure de France* (at first *Mercure galant*) from 1672. At the beginning of the development of French music periodicals mention should be made of the long-running almanac, the *Calendrier historique des théâtres de l'opéra, et des comédies françoise et italienne et des foires* (1752–1793/4, 1800–01, 1815). The first purely musical French periodical, *Sentiment d'un harmoniphile sur différens ouvrages de musique* (1756), consisted of two issues, in the first of which Abbé de Morambert offered learned essays in Mattheson's style; this was followed by the *Journal de musique historique, théorique et pratique* (1770–71); continued as *Journal de musique par une Société d'amateurs* (1773–7) in which N.E. Framery (editor until April 1771) wrote about new trends in music and discussed theory. In 1775–83 appeared the *Almanach musical*, which offered a conspectus of the Parisian musical scene in its numerous lists of composers, performers, publishers and printers, concerts and opera. Equally significant for Paris was the *Annuaire dramatique* (1805–1821/2), giving names and addresses of the directors, actors, musicians and other employees of all the Parisian theatres. Information about Parisian musical events, though no regular critiques, was also provided by *Correspondance des amateurs musiciens* (1802/3–1805), edited by Cocatrix.

The *Revue musicale* (1827–35), founded by F.-J. Fétis, was the first significant French music periodical of the 19th century: in addition to historical essays and biographies of contemporary composers it contained detailed notices of performances in Paris. Its amalgamation with the *Gazette musicale de Paris*, founded in 1834, resulted in the *Revue et gazette musicale de Paris* (1835–80), which enjoyed particular success. It had the services of notable writers, including Liszt and Berlioz as well as Fétis; Berlioz published his articles on Rameau and on Beethoven's symphonies in this journal, and Meyerbeer's operas were prominently featured. Of equal stature were *Le ménestrel* (1833/4–1940) and *La France musicale* (1837/8–1870). The former developed into a journal of considerable renown, concerned both with historical matters and with contemporary events and offering valuable reports on Paris and other European musical centres. It also published for the first time, before they appeared separately, important works such as Lussy's *Traité de l'expression musicale* which defended Rossini and the Italian school.

Along with these, specialized publications developed in the later 19th century. The formation of choral unions brought into being journals on choral singing, e.g. *L'orphéon: moniteur des orphéons et sociétés chorales de France, d'Algérie et de Belgique* (1855–1939). The revival of liturgical traditions gave rise to periodicals on church music generally and on the current reforms, e.g. *Musica sacra: revue du chant liturgique et de la musique religieuse* (1874/5–1901) or the monthly publication of the Paris Schola Cantorum, *La tribune de Saint-Gervais* (1895–1929). Discussions of Wagner's music led to the founding of the *Revue wagnérienne* (1885/6–1887/8). The system of notation developed by the Galin-Paris-Chevé school resulted in publications designed to propagate the method, e.g. *La réforme musicale* (1856–70) and its sequels. Other specialist publications owed their origin to the increasing spread from the 1860s of light music and its ancillary commercialization in cabaret and music hall, e.g. *La lyre phocéenne: echo des théâtres et des cafés concerts* (1866/7) or *L'art lyrique et le music-hall* (1896–1901). The cultivation of the 'chanson' played a salient part, engendering such journals as *La chanson française* (1874, 1876/7) and *La chanson* (1902–?1922), which covered research into the chanson and its poetry. The increasing expansion from the 1870s had the further consequence of the inception of periodicals with bibliographical digests of French music, old and new, e.g. *Le bibliographe musical* (1872–6) continued as the *Catalogue des nouvelles oeuvres musicales françaises* (called the *Bibliographie musicale française* for most of its run; 1875–1920).

The rise of French musicology at the turn of the century and the establishment of a French section of the International Musical Society led to the founding of various musicological publications. The *Revue d'histoire et de critique musicales* (1901–12), founded by Jules Combarieu, was the first of the kind; in 1912 it was amalgamated with the *S.I.M. Revue musicale mensuelle* (originally entitled *Le Mercure musical*; 1905–14), published by the French section of the International Musical Society. *L'année musicale* (1911–13), edited by leading French musicologists, contained important historical and critical articles; to its final issue Michel Brenet contributed her important 'Bibliographie des bibliographies musicales'. The *Revue de musicologie* (originally the *Bulletin de la Société française de musicologie*; 1917/19–) began publication before the end of World War I and has remained the main organ of French musical scholarship. The 1920s saw the inception of the important general periodical *La revue musicale* (1920–91), founded by Henry Prunières, which soon developed into a forum for the French avant garde and also followed modern music in other countries; the *Revue Pleyel* (1923/4–1926/7) also covered general musical life. The interest in organ music and organ playing gave rise to various specialized periodicals, e.g. the *Bulletin trimestriel des Amis de l'orgue* (*L'orgue* from 1939; 1929–). Mention should also be made of *L'opéra-Comique*, published by the Association des Amis de l'Opéra-Comique (1929–32). There were also journals devoted to records, such as *Disques* (1934–47) and its successor of the same name (1948–62) and, from the 1930s, to jazz, e.g. *Jazz hot* (1935–9, 1945).

Several lapsed journals resumed publication at the end of World War II. Among the new journals, special mention should be made of *Contrepoints* (1946–?1951), which was concerned not only with the general musical scene but also dealt vigorously with new musical developments. As regards opera, the Académie Nationale de Musique et de Danse began publication of *L'Opéra de Paris* (1950–67), the official organ of the Théâtres Lyriques. A publication of note is *Opéra international* (1977–), which had begun publication in 1961 as the *Opéra 61* (later with title changes to reflect the year). *L'avant-scène opéra* (1976–) contains excellent articles on operas, devoting each issue to a single work. The decades from the 1950s were notable mainly for musicological publications, dealing either with documentation

JOURNAL
DE MUSIQUE
HISTORIQUE, THÉORIQUE
ET PRATIQUE,

Sur la Muſique ancienne & moderne, les Muſiciens & les Inſtrumens de tous les temps & de tous les Peuples.

PREMIER VOLUME.

JANVIER 1770.

A PARIS,

Chez VALLAT-LA-CHAPELLE, Libraire, ſur le Perron de la Sainte-Chapelle, au Palais.

Et au *Bureau du Journal de Muſique*, rue Montmartre, près la rue Tiquetonne.

M. DCC. LXX.

Avec Approbation & Privilége du Roi.

and research, such as *Bulletin du Centre de documentation de musique internationale* (1951–4), or with particular periods, such as *Annales musicologiques*, issued from 1953 by the Société de Musique d'Autrefois and containing studies of medieval and Renaissance music, or with developments in musicology, such as the quarterly *Musique en jeu* (1970–78), devoted mainly to the semiology of music.

From the 1970s a considerable number of French music journals were devoted to national music life, such as *Le monde de la musique* (1978/9–) and *La lettre du musicien* (1984–), but there were also local journals such as the *Annuaire musical et chorégraphique de la Haute-Ga-*ronne, later *Annuaire musique et danse* (1987/8–) or on an international level, including opera, *Music & Opera around the World* (1997/8–). *Les cahiers de l'animation musicale*, from 1986 *Les cahiers du CENAM* (1976–93), each number of which was devoted to a particular aspect of French music life (festivals, music in school, instrument manufacture), should be noted. During the late 1980s and early 90s new journals dealing with instruments appeared, including the yearbook *Piano* (1987–), *Keyboards magazine* (1987–), *Guitarist magazine* (1989–), *Les cahiers de la guitare* (1982–) and *Guitar & Bass* (1993–), as well as *Clarinette magazine* (1984–93) and *Traversières* (1991) of the Association de la Flûte, and also, for collectors of instruments, *Larigot* (1988–), of the Association des Collectionneurs d'Instruments de Musique à Vent. There have also been a number of journals issued by various centres and societies devoted to specialist topics, such as *Les cahiers de la Société Jean-Philippe Rameau* (1980); *Analyse musicale*, from 1994 *Musurgia* (1985/6–), issued by the Société Française d'Analyse Musicale; and *Les Cahiers de CIREM* (1986–), published by the Centre International de Recherches en Esthétique Musicale of Rouen University.

(iv) Germany. The first periodicals – in fact the earliest of all such musical publications – arose in Germany in the first half of the 18th century. Their starting-point was provided by the two main types of general publication at that time, the scholarly periodicals and the moral weeklies; these were their immediate models. The earliest music periodicals appeared as a succession of fascicles contributed by individual musicians and theorists aiming to instruct and, particularly, to foster the development of a scientific approach to music in reviews of publications from both older and more recent musical literature. The very first such periodical, edited by Johann Mattheson in 1722, already exhibits all the characteristics, as its title shows: *Critica musica, d.i. Grundrichtige Untersuch- und Beurtheilung vieler theils vorgefassten, theils einfältigen Meinungen, Argumenten und Einwürffe, so in alten und neuen, gedruckten und ungedruckten musicalischen Schrifften zu finden, zur möglichsten Ausrottung aller groben Irrthümer und zur Beförderung eines besseren Wachsthums der reinen harmonischen Wissenschaft, in verschiedene Theile abgefasset, und stück-weise heraus gegeben* ('Critica musica, that is, searching critiques and assessments of the many opinions, arguments and objections, whether preconceived or spontaneous, that are to be found in old and new, printed or handwritten, papers on music. Designed to eradicate so far as possible all vulgar error and to promote a freer growth in the pure science of harmony. Arranged in several parts and issued separately'). As a model Mattheson cited the German scholarly publication *Acta eruditorum* (1682–1782) and at the same time offered a justification of the choice of this medium for his argument: 'Since I can discern that the matter is too weighty to be advanced suddenly or with one single work, I have determined to undertake this enterprise at intervals'. In a section 'Neues von musicalischen Sachen und Personen', he published commentaries on the music and performance of operas currently being mounted in various European cities. By contrast with *Critica musica*, which typifies the scholarly journal, Mattheson's anonymously published *Der musicalische Patriot* (1728) typifies the moral weekly. It consists of 43 'discourses' and appeared in weekly sheets; its title was derived from the organ of the 'German-speaking community' in Hamburg, the *Patriot* (1724). Mattheson included a list of all the operas produced in Hamburg since 1678, but he was mainly concerned with protecting music against decadence and outmoded techniques; his moralizing tone is unmistakable.

A parallel to *Critica musica* is offered by Lorenz Mizler's *Neu eröffnete musikalische Bibliothek, oder Gründliche Nachricht nebst unpartheyischem Urtheil von musikalischen Schriften und Büchern* (1736/8–1754), which embodies the scholarly type of publication in an even more significant way. In his periodical, which in 1738 became the organ of his Correspondirende Societät

6. Title-page of the first issue of 'Critica musica' (Hamburg, 1722)

der Musicalischen Wissenschaften, he sought to investigate music in its acoustical and physiological as well as its practical and theoretical aspects, with the aim of extending the knowledge of music as a natural science. It also contains essays on the merits and significance of opera, such as Gottsched's 'Gedanken vor den Tragödien und Comödien' and Uffenbach's 'Von der Würde der Singgedichte oder Vertheidigung der Oper'. At the same time he brought out the periodical *Musikalischer Staarstecher* ('Musical Eye-opener'; 1739/40) as a practical supplement. In a sense J.A. Scheibe's *Critischer Musicus* (1737/8–1739/40) was the spiritual successor to Mattheson's *Der musikalische Patriot*. Scheibe too sought to exercise an educational influence and thereby to affect the formation of taste. In this he followed both the title and the content of the *Critische Dichtkunst* (1730) of his teacher J.C. Gottsched, whose rules for poetics Scheibe applied to music.

F.W. Marpurg published anonymous didactic essays in letter form in *Der critische Musicus an der Spree* (1749/50); this weekly also contained perceptive comments on musical misconceptions and debate with J.F. Agricola on French and Italian music. Marpurg's *Kritische Briefe über die Tonkunst* (1759/60–1764) included critiques of musical works and, for the first time, anecdotes as well as essays in letter form; above all, it was the vehicle for Marpurg's polemic against G.A. Sorge. These may be considered the last musical representatives of the typical moralizing weekly. Marpurg's most significant achievement among the periodicals he edited were the *Historisch-kritische Beyträge zur Aufnahme der Musik* (1754/5–1778) in which he sought to continue Mizler's tradition but laid more stress on the practical. The contributions included short essays, reviews of historical, critical and didactic writings, biographical information on musicians, and news of court orchestras, theatres and music societies; there is discussion of the state of opera in Berlin and Paris and catalogues of operas performed in Paris, 1645–1752, and in Venice. Classifiable as a scholarly journal it was of fundamental importance in the development of musical periodicals.

Such periodicals were aimed at the musical connoisseur. J.A. Hiller, who in his *Wöchentliche Nachrichten und Anmerkungen die Musik betreffend* (1766/7–1770) set out to cover the interests of the amateur, opened up a new line of development. His was the first such periodical to appear weekly. It included discussions of performance, announcements of publications and essays on musical topics. Hiller gave special prominence to musical events and commentaries on opera productions in Dresden, Vienna and other cities. Among the essays, his own 'Kritischer Entwurf einer musikalischen Bibliothek' (1768), in which he discussed critically the writing on music available to him, deserves special mention. In the periodicals of the ensuing years an increasing part was played by discussions of contemporary music. Thus J.N. Forkel, in his *Musikalisch-kritische Bibliothek* (1778–9), dealt with musical life and institutions, and the scientific background and general state of music; he detected, and strove to combat, a deterioration. In addition the musical almanacs he edited in 1782–4 and 1789, with their numerous catalogues, as well as essays, reviews, condensed biographies and news items, afford valuable and varied insights into contemporary musical life. Similarly J.F. Reichardt, in his *Musikalisches Kunstmagazin* (1782–91), sought to arrest the 'decay of art'. He supplied analyses and commentaries on compositions (such as Gluck arias) and extracts from the writings of Herder, Goethe and Kant. In his *Musikalisches Wochenblatt* (1791/2) he tried to influence the formation of taste among connoisseurs and amateurs with critiques of important compositions and writings whether of German, Italian, French or English origin. The *Berlinische musikalische Zeitung historischen und kritischen Inhalts* (1793/4) followed the same general pattern.

In contrast to the critical periodical of the age of the Enlightenment, there emerged in the later 18th century a trend towards the general or universal, with emphasis on a greater immediacy, like Nicolai's *Allgemeine deutsche Bibliothek* (1765–1802) and the *Allgemeine Litteratur-Zeitung* (1785). Hiller's *Wöchentliche Nachrichten und Anmerkungen die Musik betreffend* and the journals of Forkel and Reichardt had shown this tendency, but the first to do so comprehensively was the *Allgemeine musikalische Zeitung* (Leipzig, 1798–1848; see fig.1). It represents the highest period of development in the 18th century and at the same time ushered in a new era in the history of musical periodicals. Its division – into (*a*) essays, (*b*) biographical information, (*c*) reviews, first of theoretical works and second of music, (*d*) descriptions of instruments, (*e*) news items, in and from letters, and (*f*) miscellaneous – became a model for future magazines. Friedrich Rochlitz, editor from 1798 to 1818, realized this plan in exemplary fashion: he raised the journal to a high intellectual level and founded its international reputation as the leading musical periodical. It was the first such journal to use an extensive panel of collaborators; no fewer than 130 can be identified in its first decade. The editor from 1818 to 1827 was Gottfried Härtel. He was succeeded by G.W. Fink, who was unable to maintain its intellectual level or to sustain the competition of the *Neue Zeitschrift für Musik*. His successors were C.F. Becker, Moritz Hauptmann and J.C. Lobe. In 1848 Breitkopf & Härtel discontinued publication on the grounds of a changed situation in which there was 'no further place for a general musical journal'.

The next most important and comprehensive music periodical in Germany was the *Neue Zeitschrift für Musik*, founded by Robert Schumann (with Friedrich Wieck, Ludwig Schunke and Julius Knorr) in 1834. Its contents were organized on the same lines as those of the *Allgemeine musikalische Zeitung*, but its intellectual outlook, dominated by Schumann until 1844, was entirely different from the earlier journal's rationalism. Schumann's aim was to use his periodical – which he saw as the standard-bearer of the Romantic movement in music – to improve the musical resources of Germany, depleted after the deaths of Weber, Beethoven and Schubert, and affected by increasing superficiality and the domination of the virtuoso, and to restore the 'poetry of art' to its rightful position. To this end he used the journal as a forum for the creative artist, excluding the dilettante. Schumann edited the journal with true independence and with the highest artistic motivation; but under his successor Franz Brendel, editor from 1845 to his death in 1868, it became increasingly the organ of the 'new German' school of Liszt and others, and not all the composers of the time agreed with its views (see for example the *Erklärung* against Brendel's journal of 1860, initiated by Brahms and also signed by Joachim, Grimm and Scholz). Brendel also defended Wagner's operas in particular; Schumann's own essay on a production of *Tannhäuser* appeared in 1852. In 1887 it became the organ of the Allgemeiner Musikverein and went through a variety of phases, under different management, up to 1974. From 1975, when it amalgamated with *Melos*, it appeared as *Melos/NZ Neue Zeitschrift für Musik*; from 1979 it was again separately published as *NZ Neue Zeitschrift für Musik*.

The only comparable universal journal was the new series of the *Allgemeine musikalische Zeitung* (1863–5), which, however, did not regain its former high level. It was a continuation not only of the journal of the same name (1798–1848) but also of the *Deutsche Musik-Zeitung* edited by Selmar Bagge (see §5(i) 'Austria' above). Despite its vaunted independence it could not always remain above factional dispute. In 1866 it was continued as the *Leipziger allgemeine musikalische Zeitung* and then (1869–82) reappeared under its original title. Under Bagge's editorship (1866–8) the emphasis was on contemporary music-making, while under Friedrich Chrysander (1868–71, 1874–82), who considered it a continuation of his *Jahrbücher für musikalische Wissenschaft* (1863–7), it increasingly covered music history and scholarship.

From the beginning of the 19th century there were numerous journals dealing with individual musical centres. J.F. Reichardt brought out the *Berlinische musikalische Zeitung* (1805–6) concerned with local musical life and containing reviews of published music in which Reichardt aimed to provide 'justice for the artist and instruction for the art-lover'. Nor did the later Berlin music journals have any lasting life. In 1821–3 came the *Zeitung für Theater und Musik*, edited by August Kuhn, and in 1824–30 the more important *Berliner allgemeine musikalische Zeitung* edited by A.B. Marx, who aimed 'to serve not only artists and connoisseurs but also the general public of cultivated music-lovers' – he justified the music of his own time in accordance with this dictum, especially that of Beethoven and Spontini. *Iris im Gebiete der Tonkunst* (1830–41), edited by Ludwig Rellstab, provided essentially a conspectus of musical events and publications. The first to attempt a more comprehensive policy, with special regard to historical perspective, was the *Berliner musikalische Zeitung* (1844–7), which was replaced by the influential *Neue Berliner Musikzeitung* (1847–96) published by Bote & Bock. The *Signale für die musikalische Welt* (1843–1941), brought out by Bartholf Senff in Leipzig, earned a wider distribution by the broad scope of its news coverage and became an important source not only for Leipzig musical life but for wider developments. It also contains news and detailed accounts of major operatic productions at home and abroad. In the Rhineland two important music journals were inaugurated by the Cologne critic Ludwig Bischoff (1794–1867), the *Rheinische Musik-Zeitung für Kunstfreunde und Künstler* (1850/51–1859) and the *Niederrheinische Musik-Zeitung für Kunstfreunde und Künstler* (1853–67); their tradition was pursued by the *Rheinische Musik-Zeitung* (1900–37), edited by Gerhard Tischer.

Along with those of a general nature and those concerned with local centres, more and more periodicals came into being, from the 1840s, devoted to special areas of music. The establishment of choral societies and glee clubs led to the founding of periodicals devoted to choral singing, e.g. *Die Sängerhalle* (1861–1908), continued as *Deutsche Sängerbundeszeitung* (since 1958 entitled *Lied und Chor*; 1909–). Advances in instruments favoured the appearance of new periodicals, general or particular, e.g. the *Zeitschrift für Instrumentenbau* (1880/81–1942/3) founded by Paul de Wit in Leipzig. Reformist ideas in music education brought into being such periodicals as *Der Klavierlehrer* (1878–1931) and *Die Stimme: Centralblatt für Stimm- und Tonbildung* (1906/7–1934/5). The reawakening of interest in Gregorian chant, the renovation of the Catholic liturgy and the establishment of church music (or Cecilian) associations led to the foundation of journals such as the two edited by Franz Witt, *Fliegende Blätter für katholische Kirchenmusik* (1866–) and *Musica sacra* (1868–1937). Efforts to reactivate the Lutheran hymn and the Protestant liturgy lay behind the foundation of journals for evangelical church music such as *Siona: Monatsschrift für Liturgie und Kirchenmusik zur Hebung des gottesdienstlichen Lebens* (1876–1920) and the *Korrespondenzblatt des Evangelischen Kirchengesangvereins für Deutschland* (1887–1933). The extension of musical life led to the creation of journals dealing with individual genres, such as chamber music, e.g. *Die Kammermusik* (1897/8–1901), popular music, e.g. *Echo vom Gebirge* (1883–1934) and military music, e.g. *Deutsche Militär-Musiker-Zeitung* (1879–1944), and also journals concerned with musicians' professional interests, e.g. *Deutsche Musiker-Zeitung* (1870–1933), the organ of the Allgemeiner Deutscher Musiker-Verband. Other periodicals aimed to publicize the work of a particular composer, for example Wagner, in the *Anregungen für Kunst, Leben und Wissenschaft* (1856–61), which concentrated on Wagner and the 'Kunstwerk der Zukunft', the *Bayreuther Blätter* (1878–1938) and the Wagner yearbooks (1886 and 1906–8, 1912–13).

In the second half of the 19th century the development of musicology gave rise to a new kind of periodical. *Cäcilia* (1824–48), edited by Gottfried Weber in Mainz, was a hybrid of the scholarly periodical of the 18th century and the new specialized musicological publication. It inclined to the former in its rationalistic outlook, to the latter in its choice of topics and its large number of important contributors. It was *Cäcilia* that Chrysander took as his model in his *Jahrbücher für musikalische Wissenschaft* – the first attempt at an independent musicological journal. From 1868 Chrysander continued his efforts on behalf of musicology in the *Allgemeine musikalische Zeitung* (Leipzig), but that collapsed in 1882 for lack of competent correspondents and no doubt also because of increasing competition from the daily press. While the *Musikalisches Wochenblatt* (1870–1910), published by E.W. Fritzsch, emphasized contemporary music-making, the musicological efforts of Chrysander, Philipp Spitta and Adler found an outlet in the *Vierteljahrsschrift für Musikwissenschaft* until 1894 (the year of Spitta's death). The founding of this publication completed the separation of the general music periodical and the musicological one foreshadowed by Chrysander's *Jahrbücher* and Eitner's *Monatshefte für Musikgeschichte* (1869–1905), which contain valuable studies of source material from the 15th century to the 17th. Musicological aims were also pursued by the *Bach-Jahrbuch* (1904–), the *Beethovenjahrbuch* (1908–9) and the *Gluck-Jahrbuch* (1913–18), as well as the *Jahrbuch der Musikbibliothek Peters* (1894–1940), which published seminal musicological studies and valuable classified bibliography of music literature. From 1899 the newly founded International Musical Society published two important musicological periodicals. While one of them, the *Zeitschrift der Internationalen Musik-Gesellschaft*, was primarily concerned with the actualities of musical life, with essays, critiques, announcements and reports as well as advertisements and reviews, the *Sammelbände der Internationalen Musik-Gesellschaft* dealt with research designed to deepen the understanding of music, by exploring new areas of musical history besides covering music theory and the relation of music to the other arts and the sciences. Both publications, which attained high reputations, lasted until the beginning of World War I (1914).

There developed from the 1870s, in succession to the universally orientated music periodical (of which the Leipzig *Allgemeine musikalische Zeitung* was the last true representative in Germany), a newer type of general musical journal, entirely factual in content and largely concerned with practical music and musical life: for example the *Musikalisches Wochenblatt* (1870–1910), the *Allgemeine (deutsche) Musik-Zeitung* (1874–1943), the *Neue Musik-Zeitung* (1880–1928) and *Die Musik* (1901/2–1942/3).

World War I caused a hiatus in the development of German musical periodicals. A few of the great mass-circulation journals maintained publication; these were then joined by numerous new ones with modern ideas. The preoccupation with modern music was crystallized in periodicals partly or wholly devoted to new directions in music. At the focal point was *Melos*, founded in Berlin in 1920 by Hermann Scherchen, which adopted a decidedly cosmopolitan stance: it dealt mainly with structure, tonality and atonality, and the relationship between words and music. The realm of specialized music publications was further extended by the youth music movement, as in *Die Musikantengilde: Blätter der Erneuerung aus dem Geiste der Jugend* (1922/3–1930), and through popular cultural aspirations, as in *Musik im Leben: eine Zeitschrift der Volkserneuerung* (1924–30).

Several journals devoted to opera began to appear; various opera houses started to publish annuals, beginning with the Jahrbuch of the Deutsches Opernhaus in Charlottenburg (1919/20–1922/3) and *Die Oper* of the Königsberger Opernhaus (1930/31–1933/4). On the musicological front, two pioneer journals were founded in 1918, the *Zeitschrift für Musikwissenschaft* (1918/19–1935) and the *Archiv für Musikwissenschaft* (1918/19–1926). The successor of the both music periodicals, published by the International Musical Society, as the organ of the International Musicological Society, was *Acta musicologica* (initially *Mitteilungen*; 1928–), which survived World War II. Since about 1967 musicological studies have been supplemented by reports on research in particular countries, periods, genres or composers. Special mention should also be made of the *Zeitschrift für vergleichende Musikwissenschaft* (1933–5), edited by Robert Lachmann in association with E.M. von Hornbostel and Johannes Wolf, which was concerned exclusively with ethnomusicological matters and was the first journal of its kind to deal with non-European music. In succession to the *Zeitschrift für Musikwissenschaft* there appeared the *Archiv für Musikforschung* (1936–43), while *Deutsche Musikkultur* (1936/7–1944) was devoted as much to musical life as to musicology.

In the years 1933 to 1945 the few existing periodicals, whether old or new, became increasingly imbued with the political theology of the National Socialist regime and were either subordinated to or invigilated by state institutions. In World War II German music periodicals almost came to a standstill; many journals ceased publication or appeared in a much reduced form. But from 1945 there was a rapid revival, and by about 1950 there were already many periodicals to meet particular interests. The immediate development was in the general music periodical, now concentrated even more closely on practical matters in public musical life, such as *Musica* (1947–96) and *Musik und Gesellschaft* (1951–90), continued by *Motiv: Musik in Gesellschaft anderer Künste* (1991), of which only one issue appeared.

An important part was played by specialist publications: some represented successors of earlier journals, as in evangelical and Catholic church music, e.g. *Musik und Kirche* (refounded 1947; 1929–) and *Zeitschrift für Kirchenmusik* (refounded 1949; 1866–) and of music education, e.g. *Musik im Unterricht* (refounded 1949; 1903–68), amalgamated with *Kontakte* (1958–68) to form *Musik & Bildung* (1969–) and covering the whole of music education, and the *International Music Educator* (1960–72), and its sequel *International Music Education* (1973–92), organs of the ISME. Another specialized area was opera, such as *Oper und Tanz* (1961–), a kind of union journal, *Opernwelt* (1960/61–) and its annual *Oper* (1966–); the *Jahrbuch der Komischen Oper Berlin* (1960/61–1971/2) and its successor *Musikbühne* (1974–7), devoted to an exploration of Walter Felsenstein's idea of realistic music drama in the GDR, succeeded by *Oper heute* (1978–90); *Oper und Konzert* (1963–97) and the informative arts bulletin *Orpheus* (1973–). *Das Opernglas* (1980–) focusses on Hamburg, but contains reports from Berlin, Bonn, Cologne, New York and Salzburg. More recently, the *Jahrbuch für Opernforschung* (1985–90) can be viewed as a forum for studies in the literary and social history of operatic production with essays particularly on librettos. *Musik & Theater*

(1986–7) is a comprehensive international artistic journal concerned with opera, ballet, dance and music drama. Such specialized areas, including also folk music and light music, were augmented by new ones such as copyright, e.g. *Musik und Dichtung* (1954/5), modern techniques of sound reproduction, e.g. *Fono Forum* (1956–), electroacoustic experimentation, e.g. the *Gravesaner Blätter* (1955/6–1966) and jazz, e.g. *(Das internationale) Jazz-Podium* (Vienna, 1952–4; Munich etc., 1955–). In the field of musicology, *Die Musikforschung* has been published since 1948 as the journal of the Gesellschaft für Musikforschung, the resurrected *Archiv für Musikwissenschaft* since 1952, the *Deutsches Jahrbuch der Musikwissenschaft* (Leipzig, 1956–77), continued as *Jahrbuch Peters* (1978–87) and the *Beiträge zur Musikwissenschaft* (East Berlin, 1959–92). There are also specialist journals of individual institutions, e.g. the *Jahrbuch des Staatlichen Instituts für Musikforschung Preussischer Kulturbesitz* (1968–), with contributions on historical and systematic musicology, and the *Hamburger Jahrbuch für Musikwissenschaft* (1974–) of the musicological institute of Hamburg University. Other periodicals of a musicological nature are devoted to more specialized topics, such as *Ars organi* (1952/3–), *Zfmth, Zeitschrift für Musiktheorie* (1970–78) and the *Beethoven-Jahrbuch* (1953/4–1981), the *Händel Jahrbuch*, second series (1955–), *Acta sagittariana* (1963/4–), relating to Schütz, and the *Schütz-Jahrbuch* (1979–), the *Haydn-Studien* (1965/7–) and the *Hindemith-Jahrbuch* (1971–), as well as the *Göttinger Händel-Beiträge* (1984–). Regarding documentation and bibliography, *Fontes artis musicae* (1954–), the organ of the International Association of Music Libraries, Archives and Documentation Centres (IAML) has to be mentioned. In 1984 *Imago Musicae*, yearbook of Répertoire International d'Iconographie Musicale (RIdIM), was founded.

Among further specialized musicological journals are *Beiträge zur Gregorianik* (1985–), with research reports on the interpretation of plainchant, and several dedicated to individual instruments, such as the yearbook of the International Viola Research Society, *Die Viola* (1979–), which reports on the instrument's literature, repertory, history and technique, and the periodicals *Flöte aktuell* (1986–), *Die Klarinette*, since 1989 *Oboe, Klarinette, Fagott* (1986–), and the *Piano-Jahrbuch* (1980–83). There are also periodicals devoted to organ building, such as *ISO-Information* (1969–90), issued by the International Society of Organbuilders, and *Organ: Journal für die Orgel* (1998–), concerned with interpretation and performing practice as regards new instruments. Other journals concerned exclusively with music of the past include *Concerto: das Magazin für alte Musik* (1983/4–), which carries reports of early music and opera performances, and *Alte Musik aktuell* (1986–), published by Pro Musica Antiqua. At the opposite end of the spectrum stand periodicals devoted to new music, such as the series on composers, *Musik-Konzepte* (1977/8–), less a journal than a series of regularly issued, single thematic volumes, with new information mostly on 20th-century composers. There is also *Musiktexte: Zeitschrift für neue Musik* (1983–), concerned with compositional and aesthetic issues.

The Leipzig journal *Positionen* (1988–), founded as *Beiträge zur neuen Musik*, appeared from no.8 as *Forum für experimentelle und grenzüberschreitende Musik*; this drastic change reflects political developments surrounding the reunification of Germany in 1990 and the different situation that ensued: the new orientation of the periodical that it represented was highly significant for the former GDR. Matters of music pedagogy always receive increasing attention: *Musik in der Schule* (East Berlin, 1949/50–), strongly linked to practical issues, now serves under new democratic circumstances and deals with the training of music teachers and the improvement of musical education. Alongside this is *Üben & Musizieren* (1983–), the newsletter of the Akademie für Musikpädogogik Mainz and other groups. *Musik und Unterricht* (1990–) is regarded as a basic and comprehensive journal, a successor to *Zeitschrift für Musikpädagogik* (1976–89). Lastly, *MusE: Zeitschrift für Musik und Eltern* (1991–2–) should be mentioned for its concern with arts and cultural educational issues in Germany. The area of music pedagogy was affected by the marked interest during the 1908s in interdisciplinary studies, and the yearbook *Musikpädagogische Forschung* (1980–) provided a forum for interdisciplinary research, with material not only on theory, method and practice but also basic work on music psychology and didactics. There have been similar trends in the fields of music theory, with the journal *Musiktheorie* (1986–) tending towards an art-theoretical outlook, and music psychology, where the *Jahrbuch Musikpsychologie* (1984–92), published by the Deutsche Gesellschaft für Musikpsychologie, moves between psychology and musicology and deals with the problems of access to music, and also since the 1970s has noted the development of music therapy: considered in journals from *Musiktherapie* (1973–4) through *Musik + Medezin* (1975–82) to *Musiktherapeutische Umschau* (1980–) and such specialist publications as *Musik und Kommunikation, MUK: Hamburger Jahrbuch zur Musiktherapie und intermodalen Medientherapie* (1987/8–) and *Musik-, Tanz- und Kunsttherapie* (1990–).

(v) Great Britain. Surviving music periodicals from the end of the 17th century and the early 18th offer series of vocal compositions; but general cultural and historical journals from the end of the 17th century onwards allocated space to reports on individual composers and musical events. The first tentative step towards a true musical periodical was arguably taken by *The Literary Part of the Musical Magazine* of *The New Musical and Universal Magazine* (1774–5); this was followed by the first independent musical publication, T. Williams's *The Review of New Musical Publications* (1784), which contains useful bibliographical information. Besides two short-lived music periodicals in the early 19th century, the *Quarterly Musical Register* (1812) and Arding and Merritt's *The English Musical Gazette, or Monthly Intelligencer* (1819), *The Quarterly Musical Magazine and Review* (1818–28) and *The Harmonicon* (1823–33) contain significant articles on London musical life. *The Musical World* (1836–91) was England's first comprehensive music periodical; in some aspects it was modelled on its German and French predecessors. It contained not only historical articles but also detailed reports from the main European musical centres, together with critiques of publications and performances. An even more widespread significance was to be attained by the monthly *The Musical Times and Singing Class Circular*, founded by J.A. Novello in 1844 as a continuation of *Mainzer's Musical Times and Singing Circular* (1842–4): now called *The Musical Times*, it is the oldest of all

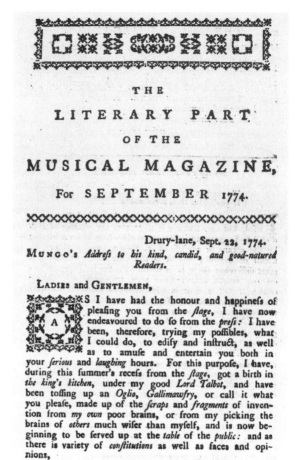

7. Title-page of the first issue of 'The Literary Part of the Musical Magazine' (London, 1774)

musical journals with a continuous record of publication. At first its main task was envisaged as the furtherance of the popular resurgence of singing brought about by Joseph Mainzer, John Hullah and others, in line with the policies of the Novello publishing house. Thus J.A. Novello wrote in the prospectus of his journal, contained in the last issue of *Mainzer's Musical Times*:

The music of the chorus will, in future, occupy at least three pages; and the greatest care will be exercised in its selection. The literary department will be superintended with an assiduous desire to combine interesting intelligence of the current month; reports of important musical performances, and a brief chronicle of minor events as they transpire; especially with a view to what may be interesting to Choral Societies and Singing Classes, including the announcement of all publications expressly adapted to their use.

But *The Musical Times* soon developed into a music periodical covering all aspects of music and musical life, and commanded general respect. From the 1870s it also covered opera, with articles on operatic organizations, English opera houses, individual operas from all over Europe (with perhaps less attention to those of Wagner), ballet and melodrama. From the 1920s to the 90s it had a special association with the Royal College of Organists, which contributed to a renewal of interest in church music. The current policy is to strive for a broad view that maintains a careful balance between historical articles and contributions on present-day music and musical life, and thus to continue the two basic types of periodical, the general and the scholarly. In the late 1990s, after several changes in ownership, it became a quarterly. Among the music periodicals of broad scope Augener's *The Monthly Musical Record* (1871–1960) should be mentioned, with its wide-ranging contributions on a variety of topics and detailed reports on music centres in and outside Britain.

Many journals were established to cover special topics from the middle of the 19th century onwards. With John Curwen's development of the Tonic Sol-Fa method, *The Tonic Sol-Fa Reporter* (1851, 1853–1920) was founded as the main organ for its propagation and published in association with *The Tonic Sol-Fa Record* (1904–6) of the Tonic Sol-fa College. The cultivation of choral music led to the establishment of periodicals specially concerned with choral singing, often in association with church music, such as *The Choir and Musical Record* (1863–78), aimed at clergymen, organists, choirmasters and choristers, whose tastes it sought to influence, *The Organist and Choirmaster* (1893–1920) and *The Choir (and Musical Journal)* (1910–64). Other periodicals were devoted to church music of various denominations, such as *The Musical Standard* (1862–71, continued in three other series until 1933), which also covered musical events in general, the Scottish *The Presbyterian Psalmodist* (1871–3) and *The Nonconformist Musical Journal* (1888–1910).

The increasing spread of musical life and its commercialization led in the 1870s to the foundation of periodicals concerned with the music trade, such as the *London and*

8. Title-page of the first issue of 'The Musical Times and Singing Class Circular' (London, 1844)

Provincial Music Trades Review (1877–1971) and *Musical Opinion (and Music Trade Review)* (1877/8–). Several periodicals dealt with individual instruments or groups of instruments; among the most important was *The Strad* (1890/91–), which is concerned with the whole range of bowed string instruments and is addressed equally to professional musicians and to amateurs. The controversy about Wagner in the 1880s, and the formation of a London branch of the Wagner Society under the chairmanship of his biographer and translator W.A. Ellis, led to the founding of *The Meister* (1888–95), which acted as an extension of the *Bayreuther Blätter*. Musicological activities first crystallized in periodical form with the *Proceedings of the (Royal) Musical Association* (1874/5–), which published papers read to the association and thus catered for research and discussion of the scientific, aesthetic and historical aspects of music. The first periodical devoted solely to such topics was *The Musical Antiquary* (1909/10–1912/13), edited by G.E.P. Arkwright, which also contained valuable studies of source material. *Music & Letters*, founded by A.H. Fox Strangways in 1920, was recognized within its first year of publication as the leading journal of English musicology; it covers a broad range of topics and includes a sizable critical section. Its title stressed the relation between music and literature and between word and note – as in song, opera and oratorio – and it also stood for the journal's emphasis on a high literary level. Among the progressively orientated periodicals Granville Bantock's *New Quarterly Musical Review* (1893/4–1895/6), mainly concerned with contemporary music, should be mentioned. But the main representative of progressive trends was *The Chesterian* (1915–19; new series 1919–61), edited by G. Jean-Aubry from 1919, which concentrated on modern Russian and French music. *Tempo* (1939–), published by Boosey & Hawkes, is devoted almost exclusively to modern music. A significant area of interest was opened up in the 1920s with the advent of gramophone records, which gave rise to numerous publications, notably *The Gramophone* (1923–), which offers detailed record reviews and contains useful discographies. Further specialization led to the production of journals dealing with the manufacture or reconstruction of historic instruments, such as *The Organ* (1921/2–), which contains articles with descriptions of important organs, while *The Consort* (1929–), founded in the course of the revival of early music associated with Arnold Dolmetsch, is mainly concerned with the use and manufacture of instruments modelled on historical ones and the music apt to them.

The period after World War II ushered in a series of significant general musical periodicals. Among them was *Con brio: a Scots Magazine for the Modern Music Lover* (1946–51), important for musical life in Scotland. Mention should be made of the *Music-Journal* (from 1948 *Music-Survey*; 1947–52), with reports on concerts and accounts of new books, compositions, periodicals and records, and *The Score* (1949–61) which, among essays on history, theory and performing practice, emphasized contemporary composers, notably Messiaen, Schoenberg, Stravinsky and Britten. *Music and Musicians* (1952–) aims to keep the music lover in touch with current musical events. Since the 1950s, specialist opera journals have appeared in increasing number. In 1950 the Earl of Harewood founded the journal *Opera* (1950–), which he edited for its first three years, his intention being to include items on all subjects of interest to the intelligent operagoer. With Harold Rosenthal as editor, *Opera* continued to develop into the highly regarded journal it is today, covering opera in Britain and elsewhere, including festivals; it devotes much space to new works. *Opera Annual* (1954/5–1961/2), also edited by Rosenthal, contained accounts of the previous season's productions in various opera houses, with details of singers, conductors and repertories. By contrast there are periodicals with more scholarly aims. With *The Music Review*, founded by Geoffrey Sharp in 1940 and edited by him single-handed until 1974, England had a second musicological periodical, comparable to *Music and Letters*; it soon achieved international recognition. It contains scholarly studies and critical essays, biographical material on composers and detailed analyses (especially of works of the Classical and Romantic periods, as well as the 20th century), often by leading British and continental scholars. Later musicological journals turned to more specialized areas, especially instruments: *The Galpin Society Journal* (1948–) is devoted to the history, construction and function of early instruments, while the *Bulletin* of the Viola da Gamba Society (1948–68), continued as *Chelys* (1969–), contain scholarly articles on the viol's technique and repertory and *The (English) Harpsichord Magazine*, from 1987 *The Harpsichord and Fortepiano Magazine* (1973/7–), which also deals with other keyboard instruments. Finally, *Early Music* (1973–) deals with instruments of the Middle Ages, Renaissance and Baroque, and with repertory and performing practice. In a similar way *Early Music History* (1981–) is devoted to manuscript studies, analyses, iconography and criticism as well as social issues before 1700, as is the *Journal* of the National Early Music Association, from 1991 *Leading Notes* (1984–), whereas *Early Music Today* (1993–) is more a news journal for the promotion, performance, study and enjoyment of early music, as too is *Early Music Review* (1994–). There are journals dealing with special areas of church music, e.g. hymnology in *News of Hymnody* (1982–) and plainchant in *Plainsong & Medieval Music* (1992–). Besides several music educational journals, there are several in the field of music psychology, such as *Psychology of Music* (1973–) of the Society for Research in Psychology of Music and Music Education, and for music therapy, the *British Journal of Music Therapy* (1968–87), the *Journal of British Music Therapy* (1987–), and the *Bulletin* of the British Society for Music Therapy (1987–). The *IAMS Newsletter* (1993–), as organ of the Institute of Advanced Musical Studies at King's College, London, serves the interaction of teaching and research and the dialogue between the disciplines.

Journals concerned with particular composers include *The Haydn Society of Great Britain Newsletter*, from 1993 *Haydn Society Journal* (1979–), containing scholarly studies and reviews, *Wagner* (1980–) and *Wagner News* (1980–), both continued from *The Wagner Society Newsletter*, from 1971 *Wagner* (1965–80), consisting of contributions of a scholarly nature, and *The Bruckner Journal* (1997–), organ of an informal Bruckner Society. In ethnomusicology, the *British Journal of Ethnomusicology* (1992–) is a continuation of the *Bulletin* of the International Council for Traditional Music (UK Chapter) (1983–90), publishing scholarly essays on traditional music. Besides many general pop music journals, *Popular Music* (1981–) is an interdisciplinary periodical, dealing

from a scholarly point of view with the musicological, literary, sociological and economic issues. An interdisciplinary tendancy can be also seen in opera research as regards the *Cambridge Opera Journal* (1989–), devoted to the study of various musicological, literary and dramatic aspects as well as from anthropological, historical and philosophical viewpoints. Electronic technology has become an increasingly important, with *Electronics & Music Maker* (1981/2–1985/6), continued as *Music Technology* (1986/7–1994), considering modern technology of keyboards, guitars, drums, woodwind and other types, including articles on sound recording and reproduction, and *Rhythm for the Contemporary Drummer, Percussionist and Programmer* (1987–), dealing with new electronic drum technology. Other periodicals are devoted to promoting experimental musics, such as *Rubberneck* (1985–), dealing with improvised music, or cover all aspects of computer music, such as *Future Music* (1992–), which also contains news, reviews of music equipment and profiles of musicians, and *Organised Sound* (1996–), dealing with methods and issues of contemporary technology in multimedia performance, sound sculpture and electro-acoustic composition.

(vi) Italy. The earliest Italian musical periodicals, which go back to the last decades of the 18th century, were mostly devoted to the theatre in general and to the opera stages of Italy or the whole of Europe, such as the *Foglio periodico e ragguaglio de' spettacoli musicali* (1808–9), the *Indice, o sia Catalogo dei teatrali spettacoli italiani di tutta l'Europa* (1764–1823), which covers Italian theatres and Italian opera on foreign stages and contains a list of singers, composers and librettists of operas performed in Italy, or *Il censore universale dei teatri* (from 1838, *Il corriere dei teatri*; 1829–40); they sometimes included dance, as in *I teatri: giornale drammatico, musicale e coreografico* (1827–31) and the *Rivista teatrale: giornale drammatico, musicale e coreografico* (1831–5). There were also yearbooks, either concerned with the country's musical past, e.g. *I fasti musicali* (1818) and *La Polinnia europea, o sia Biblioteca universale di musica* (1823), or, on a higher intellectual plane, dealing with general artistic as well as purely musical subject matter, as in the weekly *Notizie teatrali, bibliografiche e urbane* (1825). There were also musical almanacs with biographical notes on composers and general musical news, e.g. *Rossini e la musica* (1827) or *La virtù e la musica* (1831).

The first significant general music periodical in Italy was the *Gazzetta musicale di Milano* (1842–8, 1850–62, 1866–1912; from 1903 *Musica e musicisti*, from 1906 *Ars et labor*, and revived later as *Musica d'oggi*) which gave special attention to Italian opera, in Italy and abroad, and deserves special mention for its chronological lists of productions at La Scala and La Fenice. It also provided biographical, historical and bibliographical contributions and reports on Italian and other main musical centres. Besides smaller-scale journals, some of which were locally orientated and ephemeral such as the *Gazzetta musicale di Firenze* (1853–9), founded by E. Picchi, which espoused Meyerbeer's cause, and the *Gazzetta musicale di Napoli* (1852–68) or *L'Italia musicale* (1847/8–59), which offered detailed critiques of recent operas, there were others such as *L'arpa* (1853/4–1902) or *Il trovatore* (1854–1913), which enjoyed a wide circulation by covering the arts in general while according music a leading place. Another important publication was *La cronaca musicale*

(1896–1917), edited by T. Mantovani, with its articles on historical subjects. But the comprehensive general music periodical of high quality was the *Rivista musicale italiana* (1894–1955), which offered important articles by well-known contributors, news of musical events at home and abroad, and catalogues and critiques of recent publications; it was continued in 1967 as the *Nuova rivista musicale italiana*.

There were periodicals serving individual interests from the 1860s onwards. The increasing cultivation of chamber music brought into being specific publications such as *Boccherini* (1862–82), the organ of the Società del Quartetto in Florence, and the *Giornale della Società del quartetto di Milano* (1864/5). Endeavours to restore church music and the well-known controversy about the liturgy led to the publication of numerous periodicals, among which *Musica sacra* (1877–1942; continued 1956–), the journal of the Cecilian Society in Milan, and the *Rassegna gregoriana* (1902–14), the journal of the Scuola Superiore di Musica Sacra di Roma, were specially influential. There were also important yearbooks and proceedings of music academies, e.g. the *Atti dell' Accademia del R. istituto musicale di Firenze* (1863–1941). Controversies over Wagner's music and the foundation in Bologna of a branch of the Wagner Society engendered the *Cronaca wagneriana* (1893–5), followed in 1909 by the *Rassegna wagneriana*.

Other fields of interest covered by periodicals included new musical publications (e.g. the *Bollettino bibliografico musicale*, 1899/1900–1933), the music trade (e.g. *870 ottocentosettanta*, 1906–9), popular instruments such as the guitar and the mandolin (e.g. *Il plettro*, 1911–43) and light music (e.g. *Ba-ta-clan*, 1897–1902). *Ars nova* (1916/17–1918/19), the journal of the Società Italiana di Musica Moderna, dealt exclusively with the music of the neoclassical school typified by Casella. *Musica d'oggi* (1919–42) covered current musical life in general. The important general periodical *La rassegna musicale* (1928–62), edited by G.M. Gatti, contained important essays by well-known authors, musical news from home and abroad, and lists and reviews of new publications, while *Note d'archivio per la storia musicale* (1924–43), sponsored by Raffaele Casimiri, provided a variety of information and documentation on Italian musical history. The political influence of the Fascist regime made itself felt in journals such as *Rivista nazionale di musica* (1920–43) and *Bollettino dei musicisti* (from 1934, *Il musicista*; 1933/4–43), the organ of the Sindacato Nazionale Fascista dei Musicisti.

After World War II several substantial music periodicals were founded, some with novel features. Among general ones, *La rassegna musicale* was continued as the *Quaderni della Rassegna musicale* (1964–72); it devoted each volume to a single topic. Specialized ones, besides those devoted to jazz or recordings, e.g. *Musica jazz* (1945–) and *Musica e dischi* (1945–), include music education journals *Educazione musicale* (1964–75) and *Musica domani* (1971–), the quarterly publication of the Società Italiana per l'Educazione Musicale. The resurgence of Italian musicology since around 1950 gave rise to several substantial periodicals which together offer a general conspectus of the discipline: notable are the *Rivista italiana di musicologia* (1966–), the journal of the Società Italiana di Musicologia, *Quaderni della Rivista italiana di musicologia* (1966), and *Chigiana: rassegna di studi musicologici* (1964–), of the Accademia Musicale Chigiana, which

contains essays either commemorating a composer's anniversary or specially written for the annual Settimana Musicale in Siena. Of strictly scholarly character is *Studi musicali* (1972–), with important articles by Italian and foreign authors. Others are concerned with the life and works of individual composers, e.g. the two series of the *Bollettino del Centro rossiniano di studi* (1955/6–1959/60, 1967–), *Verdiana* (1950/1) and the *Bollettino quadrimestrale dell'Istituto di studi verdiani* (1958–). Some specialize in the medieval period, e.g. *Quadrivium: rivista di filologia e musicologia medievale* (1956–89), or discuss new scientific methods, e.g. *Music and Communication* (1970–).

The following decades show a wide variety of Italian music periodicals. General music periodicals have had an important place in present-day Italian musical life, among them *Musica/Realtà* (1980–), dealing with music, culture and society, past and present, the *Annuario musicale italiano* (1981–), published by the Centro Italiano de Iniziativa Musicale (CIDIM), and *Il giornale della musica* (1985–), containing information about musical events, new recordings, music publications and musicological activities at Italian universities. There are several periodicals devoted to church music, notably *Rivista internazionale di musica sacra/International Church Music Review* (1980–), which contains articles by leading authors on liturgical music of all periods. The *Istituto di Musica Vincenzo Amato: Quaderni* (1985–) discusses theological, philosophical and aesthetic aspects of sacred music, including that of the Byzantine church, and *Cantus planus* (1992–?1996) is devoted to Gregorian chant. Other special fields are music therapy (*Bollettino d'informazione A.I.S.Mt.*, 1975–, of the Associazione Italiana Studi di Musicoterapia) and music theory and education (e.g. *Analisi: rivista di teoria e pedagogia musicale*, 1990–). The numerous journals dealing with instruments include both the particular (*Liuteria*, 1981–, *Piano Time*, 1983–) and the general (*Strumenti musicali*, 1979–, is devoted to acoustic and electronic instruments). Others are concerned with contemporary music, e.g. *La musica* (1985–8), *Konsequenz* (1994–) and *Notizie dell'Archivio sonoro di musica contemporanea* (1987–). New technical developments are discussed in *Quaderni LIMB* (1981–) of the Laboratorio Permanente per l'Informatica Musicale, while *Quaderni di informatica musicale* (1982–) of the Studio di Sonologia Computazionale E. Varèse deals with the technology of electronic music and composition and *Sonus* (1989–) with analysis, computer music and new instrumental techniques.

(vii) The Netherlands. The *Samenspraaken over Muzikaale beginselen*, published in eight numbers in Amsterdam in 1756 by J.W. Lustig, was a scholarly periodical in the tradition of Mattheson, whose pupil Lustig was and on whose writings Lustig's were to some extent based. The first 19th-century periodical was the Groningen monthly *Amphion* (1818–22), which was organized on the lines of the Leipzig *Allgemeine musikalische Zeitung*; it contained critiques, news and biographical anecdotes as well as articles. The Viennese type of theatre, music and fashion periodical is to be found with *Omnibus: journal mensuel de la littérature, des anecdotes, des faits politiques, des théâtres, de la musique et des modes* (1835–6). In 1836 the *Muzijkaal tijdschrift*, the first official organ of the Maatschappij tot Bevordering der Toonkunst, appeared; it offered short articles on musical

questions, announcements and criticisms of music by Dutch and other composers, biographical notes on well-known musicians and news items. Among the more comprehensive general musical periodicals was *Caecilia: algemeen muzikaal tijdschrift van Nederland* (1844–1944), founded by F.C. Kist, which included historical studies, for example on the origins of opera, the musical life of Utrecht from 1400, church music and folksinging, together with detailed discussions of musical works, especially by contemporary composers. Other general musical journals include the *Weekblad voor muziek* (1894–1909), the organ of the musicians' union in Amsterdam.

There were also numerous periodicals devoted to particular areas of music, a few of them dating from the first half of the century. The revival of Catholic church music and Gregorian chant led to the publication of such journals as *De Gregoriaan, of Bijdragen ter bevordering van het Gregoriaansch gezang* (1834–7) and the *Sint Gregorius-blad* (1876–?1995), from 1911 the organ of the Nederlandsche Sint Gregorius Vereeniging. The spread of choral activity in the Netherlands, with the foundation of choirs associated with particular denominations, led to the establishment of periodicals either dealing with vocal activity in general, such as *Zangersalmanak* (1881–2), which contains a complete list of choral societies in the Netherlands, and *Euphonia* (1919–71), or concentrating on folksong, e.g. *De varende zanger* (1911–22), or acting as the journals of particular societies, e.g. *Ons maandblad* (1908/9–1916/17), organ of the Christelijke Oratoriumvereeniging, or *De stem des volks* (1927–), organ of the Bond van Arbeiders-Zangvereenigingen in Nederland. Among other such publications of those decades, special importance attaches to the yearbook *Bouwsteenen* (1869/72–1874/81), published by the Vereeniging voor Nederlandsche Muziekgeschiedenis and devoted to the country's musical past. With the *Tijdschrift der Vereeniging voor Noord-Nederlands muziekgeschiedenis* (1882/5–) Dutch musicology gained its main specialist journal, of which the central function was the study of early Flemish composers. The *Maandblad voor muziek* (1888/9–1893/4), the organ of the Wagner-Vereeniging te Amsterdam, should also be mentioned. These were joined in the 1920s by two leading general music periodicals, *Symphonia* (1923–60), partly the journal of the Federatie van Amateur Symphonie Orkesten, and *De muziek* (1926/7–1932/3), the organ of the Federatie van Nederlandsche Toonkunstenaars-Vereenigingen, which was incorporated into *Caecilia* in 1933. After World War II, *Mensch* (*Mens* since 1948) *en melodie: algemeen maandblad voor muziek* was founded (1946) as a factual, generally orientated music periodical providing reports on events in the Netherlands and abroad, with articles on a wide range of topics including modern music, historical questions and non-European music. By contrast, *Sonorum speculum* (1958–74), the organ of Donemus, was concerned exclusively with current Dutch musical life and new Dutch music. This journal of information was continued as a twice-yearly publication, *Key Notes* (1975–97), which covers Dutch musical life more widely, dealing with the cultivation of chamber music, orchestral activities, teaching and concert life. In the musicological world, besides *Mededelingenblad* (1961–8), published by the Vereniging voor Nederlands Muziekgeschiedenis, several specialist publications have appeared: *The Organ Year-book* (1970–) deals mainly with historic organs and other keyboard instruments, while *Electronic Music Reports* (1969–71), prepared by the Institute of Sonology at Utrecht, reported on new scientific methods in the electro-acoustic field; it was continued as *Interface* (1972–93), which dealt mainly with questions on the borders of music, science and technology. It has been continued by the *Journal of New Music Research* (1994–), which is mainly devoted to computer music. Besides these important Dutch periodicals, some of them still alive, there are few music journals coming into existence. They are devoted to ethnomusicological aspects, such as *CHIME* (1990–), the newsletter of the European Foundation for Chinese Music Research; to music of the past, such as *Tijdschrift voor oude muziek* (1986–), containing articles on music history and performances and listings of concerts; to contemporary music, *Opscene* (1987–), dealing with avant garde and independent music; to music instruments, e.g. *Piano Bulletin* (1984–), published by the European Piano Teachers Association, with information about repertory, technique, interpretation and new recordings; or to opera, for example *Opera jaarboek* (1980–85) of the Nederlandse Operastichting and *Odeon* (1990–) of the Nederlandse Opera, with news and synopsis of operas performed there. There are journals dealing with country music, such as *Country gazette* (1973–), or with all kinds of pop music, such as *Nashville Tennessee* (1984–), covering country and rock and roll, or with jazz, such as *Jazz-press*, from 1978 *Jazz nu* (1976–), notable for the high quality of its articles.

(viii) Russia. The general press in Russia carried material on music in the 18th century, for example items and articles about the history and aesthetics of music and early examples of criticism. Cultural journals contained reports on musical events. The first periodical publications of music were compositions issued in series such as *Muzïkal'nïye uvesel'nïya* (1774–5), a collection of pastimes and entertainments with songs and instrumental dances, and *Journal de musique pour le clavecin ou piano forte* (1785–94) which consisted mainly of opera extracts.

The first attempt in the direction of a true musical periodical was *Literaturnoye pribavleniye k 'Nuvellistu'* (1844–74), the literary supplement to the periodical music publication *Le nouvelliste* (1840–1906); this consisted mainly of biographical sketches of such composers as Schubert, Chopin, Mendelssohn and Cherubini and studies of the music of various European and other countries. It was followed by *Le monde musical/Muzïkal'nïy svet* (1847–78), which adopted a conservative stance and published reports in chronicle form and lighter essays as well as music supplements with works by leading Classical and Romantic composers, or salon pieces. Among subsequent periodicals are the ultra-conservative *Muzïkal'nïy sezon* (1869/70–1870/71); *Muzïkal'nïy vestnik* (1870–72), consisting of a musical part with pieces by undistinguished Russian and German composers and a literary part with biographical sketches of western European composers and reports on musical life abroad; and *Muzïkal'nïy listok* (1872/3–1876/7), noted for the contributions of the outstanding critic G.A. Laroš. A comprehensive and influential music periodical was the *Russkaya muzïkal'naya gazeta* (1894–1917), founded by the important scholar N.F. Findeyzen (1868–1928) in St Petersburg: it represented a more progressive outlook and offered contributions on significant sources of Russian musical history and articles on musical history, theory, interpretation, education and ethnology, as well as providing a forum for important correspondence later collected in book form (notably between Musorgsky and V.V. Stasov). Also of significance was *Muzïka* (1910/11–1915/16), which was concerned mainly with contemporary music, especially that of Skryabin; it was here that B.V. Asaf'yev, later to attain fame as a musicologist, began his career as a critic. *Muzïkal'nïy sovremennik* (1915/16–1916/17), edited by A.N. Rimsky-Korsakov, the composer's son, contains useful material towards a history of Russian music, for example the correspondence between Balakirev and Rimsky-Korsakov, 1862–98, as well as informative special issues on Skryabin (1915), Taneyev (1916) and Musorgsky (1917).

Besides these there appeared, from the 1840s, periodicals devoted to theatre and music, e.g. *Repertuar russkogo i Panteon vsekh yevropeyskikh teatrov* (1842–53) which from 1847 offered mainly careful and detailed reports on music, and *Teatral'nïy i muzïkal'nïy vestnik* (1856–60), an art periodical through which A.N. Serov exerted an important influence. *Muzïka i teatr* (1867/8), edited by Serov and his wife, adopted a deliberately provocative stance to induce polemics, and so acted as a forum for the current controversies. *Yezhegodnik imperatorskikh teatrov* (1892–1915) contains important factual data on Russian musical life and articles on the history of Russian music; *Teatr i iskusstvo* (1897–1918) and *Rampa i zhizn'* (1909–12) should also be mentioned for their relevance to the musical situation in the early 20th century. Other music periodicals founded in the early 20th century covered specialized interests. Thus *Muzïkal'nïy truzhenik* (1906–10), devoted to the interests of professional musicians and teachers, sought to extend their musical horizons with articles about composers, correspondence and news items. By contrast, the aims of *Muzïka i zhizn'* (1908–12) were national and cultural, including the aim of bringing music to the people as a whole.

All periodicals were brought to an end by the October Revolution of 1917. In the new era that dawned, music and musical life took new paths, as the titles of new periodicals reflected: *K novïm beregam* ('Towards new shores') (1923) or *Muzïkal'naya nov'* ('New territory in music') (1923–4). There was an increase in the number of periodicals on contemporary music-making whose contributors were mostly themselves composers, such as *Sovremennaya muzïka* (1924–9), the journal of the Assotsiatsiya Sovremennoy Muzïki of the State Academy of the History of the Arts in Moscow. Ideas for the reform of musical life were expressed in, for example, *Muzïkal'naya kul'tura* (1924), while the reform of music education, of musicological research and socio-musical questions were dealt with in *Muzïkal'noye obrazovaniye* (1926–30). The special nature and tasks of Soviet music were discussed in such journals as *Muzïka i revolyutsiya* (1926–9). The interests of amateur musicians were catered for by, for example, *Proletarskiy muzïkant* (1929–32). With the foundation (1932) of the Union of Soviet Composers the leading general music journal of the USSR, *Sovetskaya muzïka* (1933–), made its first appearance: it reflects not only the development of Soviet music and its main genres (song for the people, folk art, programmatic orchestral music, opera, ballet, oratorio and cantata) but also provides a conspectus of Soviet musicology from the 1930s, partly in the form of popularized scholarly

contributions. Another comprehensive periodical, *Muzïkal'naya zhizn'*, appeared first in 1957/8; it offers entertainingly written articles on modern compositions or on works that have been unfairly neglected or misjudged. In 1972 Ukraine achieved its own general music periodical *Muzyka*, in its own language, dealing almost exclusively with Ukrainian music and musical life. The preoccupation with Russian folk music and its relation to Soviet music led to the establishment of *Muzïkal'naya fol'kloristika* (1973–). After *perestroika*, two more general music periodicals came into existence in 1989, the *Rossiyskaya muzïkal'naya gazeta* and the *Muzïkal'naya gazeta*, later under the title *Muzïkal'noye obozreniye*. After the break-up of the USSR in 1992 the chief general music periodical *Sovetskaya muzïka* (1933–) changed its title to *Muzïkal'naya akademiya*; it now includes material on the music on the Russian Orthodox church and has also published material on the history of Russian Soviet music.

(ix) Central eastern European countries.

(a) Bulgaria. Only when Bulgaria was liberated from the Turks in 1878 did its independent musical development begin. The first periodical was *Gusla* (1891), soon followed by *Kaval* (1894/5–1901/2). Succeeding periodicals, like these, were general musical journals, some of which also dealt with the theatre, while *Muzikalen vestnik* (1904–28) was mainly devoted to music education. The country's most important music periodical is *Balgarska muzika* (originally *Muzika*), founded in 1948 as the organ of the Union of Bulgarian Composers and of the Culture and Arts Committee, containing articles, reports and news about Bulgarian music, musical life and education. The *Informatsionni muzikalni byuletin*, published since 1969 by the Union of Bulgarian Composers, has the prime purpose of informing the rest of the world about Bulgarian musical life and its organizations. The beginning of the 1970s saw the establishment of the first musicological periodical *Balgarsko muzikoznaniye* (1971–) and later of *Muzikoznanie* (1977–), published by the Institute of Musicology at the Bulgarian Academy of Sciences.

(b) Croatia. The earliest musical periodical in Croatia was *Sv. Cecilija* (1877–), which, concerned with both sacred and secular music, represents a substantial source for Croatian musical life. The existing journals were joined by newcomers that gave composers and scholars the opportunity to publish their music or research, whether in general periodicals such as *Glazbeni vjesnik* (1927–31) or in specialist journals such as *Ćirilometodski vjesnik* (1933–40), devoted to church music. After World War II a number of general music periodicals were founded, such as *Muzičke novine* (1946–8). In 1969 Josip Andreis and others, founded the yearbook *Arti musices* at the musicological department of Zagreb Music Academy. Specializing in aesthetics and sociology, Ivan Supičić founded the *International Review of the Aesthetics and Sociology of Music*, originally *The International Review of Music Aesthetics and Sociology* (1970–), which has gained a high reputation. Other periodicals are devoted to music education, such as *Tonovi* (1986–) and ethnomusicology, *Bašćinski glasi* (1992–).

(c) Czech Republic. The founding of independent musical periodicals in the Czech lands was preceded by news items on music in daily papers of the 18th and 19th centuries, such as the *Pražské poštovské noviny* (1719–86), the

Prager Intelligenzblatt (1774–1811) and the *Prager Zeitung* (1825–48), as well as in cultural and socio-historical journals, e.g. *Časopis Českého musea* (1832–1908) and *Česka včela* (1834–56). J.F. von Schönfeld's *Jahrbuch der Tonkunst von Wien und Prag* (1796) printed accounts of opera orchestras in the national theatres of Vienna and Prague and articles on operas. But the *Allgemeine musikalische Zeitung* (Leipzig, 1798–1848) offers the main source for reports on the work of Czech composers. The earliest attempt at a Czech music periodical was the literary supplement to the song collection *Věnec* (1843). The first independent music periodical was *Caecilie* (1848–9), devoted mainly to the interests of organists and teachers. More important for Czechs were its successors *Dalibor* (1858–69) and *Slavoj* (1862–5). The earliest Moravian periodical was *Hlasy hudební* (1873). Special importance attaches to the controversies between the journal *Dalibor* (1878/9–1927) and *Hudební listy* (1884/5–1887/8) about the national character of Czech music and about Wagnerianism. A significant general musical journal is *Česká hudba* (1895–1939), which originally consisted solely of musical compositions, but from 1904 had a regular literary supplement which then developed into a reputable periodical. As a counterblast to more conservative journals such as *Hudební revue* (1908–20) the periodical *Smetana* (1910/11–1926/7) espoused the cause of progressive Czech music. Among specialist music periodicals are *Cecilie* (later *Cyrill*; 1874–1948), devoted to Catholic church music in Bohemia, Moravia and Silesia, and *Hudební sborník* (1913–14) in musicology. The creation of Czechoslovakia in 1918 fostered an expansion of musical life, leading to the publication of new periodicals. Several were concerned with contemporary music, e.g. *Der Auftakt* (1920/21–1938), *Klíč* (1930/31–1933/4) and *Rytmus* (1935–48); there was also the specialist *Musikologie* (1938–58). After World War II *Hudební rozhledy* (1948/9–) was made into a general music periodical by the Union of Czechoslovak Composers. The Czech Academy of Sciences began publication of *Hudební věda*, a specialist musicological journal, in 1961. In Moravia the general periodical *Opus musicum* was founded in 1969, while musicological articles and reports have been published annually since 1966 in the *Series musicologica* of the *Sborník prací Filosofické fakulty* of the University of Brno.

(d) Estonia.   The first Estonian music magazine, *Laulu ja mängu leht* (1895/6–1898), played a leading role in the country's cultural life, with material on education and writings about music history, musicians and cultural events. The periodicals of the 1920s and 30s, apart from *Eesti lauljate liidu muusikaleht* (1924–40) were short-lived. In the 1980s and the early to mid-90s the periodical *Teater, muusika, kino* functioned as the only musical journal, containing articles and reviews on the performing arts, until 1997, when *Music in Estonia*, the organ of the recently founded Estonian Music Council, was established. The weekly newspaper *Sirp* usually contains two pages devoted to music.

(e) Greece.   The first music periodical of Greece was *Armonia* (1900–02); the annual of the *Odion Athinon* had appeared since 1871. Further music journals followed at short intervals, devoted to music and musical life, mainly of Athens; but material on Byzantine music was published in non-musical periodicals. Since the 1970s, specialized journals have come into existence, devoted to high fidelity and stereophony. The first periodical in the field of musicology, *Mousikología*, was founded in 1985 by a group of Greek musicologists and is focussed on research into Greek music; musicology is presented here for the first time in Greece as a modern science in its historic and systematic outlines following the central European tradition.

(f) Hungary.   General cultural periodicals, published in the first half of the 19th century in Hungary, deal mainly with literature, art and the theatre but contained only brief items on music. The first true Hungarian music periodical, Kornél Ábrányi's *Zenészeti lapok* (1860–76), espoused the cause of a national style while also accepting the western European tradition; it includes essays and substantial discussions of performances (mainly in Budapest theatres and concert halls), including little-known material on Brahms's appearances as a pianist in 1867 and 1869. The foundation of the Philharmonic Society (1867), the Academy of Music (1875) and an independent opera house (1884) led to an increase in the number of music periodicals, but most were short-lived. There followed other general music periodicals, some of considerable duration, such as *Zenélő Magyarország* (1894–1913), *Magyar zenészek lapja* (1897–1904), *A zene* (1909–44) and *Zenei szemle* (1917–29, new series 1947–9). There were also periodicals for Gypsy music (e.g. *Magyar cigányzenészek lapja*, 1908–31), concert guides (*Harmonia*, 1893–6), music trade journals (*Zenekereskedelmi közlöny*, 1911–14), and journals of music societies (*Magyar zenészek lapja*, 1917–38) and choral unions (*Magyar dal- és zeneközlöny*, 1895–1944). A wider field was covered by the church music periodicals of various denominations such as *Katolikus egyházzenei közlöny* (1894–1918), *Protestáns zeneközlöny* (1902–14) and *Református zeneközlöny* (1905–6). Most notable of recent publications are the journals *Muzsika* (1958–), *Magyar zene* (1960–) and the news sheet *Hungarian Music News* (1969–). Since 1961 Hungary has possessed, in the *Studia musicologica Academiae scientiarium Hungaricae*, a musicological publication which, though mainly concerned with Hungarian music history, also deals with general musicological problems and takes a particular interest in the autograph material in the nation's libraries. It was joined by a few general music journals of a more informative character, such as *Hungarian Music News* (from 1989 *Quarterly*) (1969–), published by the Budapest Office of Music Competitions, and briefly by *Hungarian Dance News* (1985–6).

(g) Poland.   In the early 19th century Polish composers sent reports on Polish music to foreign journals, e.g. J. Elsner in the Leipzig *Allgemeine musikalische Zeitung*. The Warsaw composer Karol Kurpiński founded Poland's own first music periodical, the *Tygodnik muzyczny* (1820–21), which dealt mainly with the life and work of Polish Composers, especially in song and opera. The next really significant development was the appearance of *Ruch muzyczny* (1857–62) published in Warsaw by the leading Polish music critic Józef Sikorski. Among other general music periodicals mention should be made of *Echo muzyczne i teatralne*, from 1885 *Echo muzyczne, teatralne i artystyczne* (1883/4–1907), which made an important contribution to Polish musical life. In addition to general publications specialist ones arose in the 1880s, for example on church music and hymnology (*Muzyka*

kościelna, 1881–1902), Polish folksongs and national songs (the supplement to the song collection *Lutnia polska*, 1885, connected with the earliest Polish choral society) and to answer the needs of organists (*Muzyka i śpiew*, 1912–31). The development of musicology in Poland and the creation of professorial chairs led to the publication of the first Polish musicological journal, *Kwartalnik muzyczny* (1911/13–1913/14, continued 1928/9–1933 and 1948–1950), devoted to the history of Polish music, aesthetics and theory of music; in 1928 it became the organ of the musicological school of Lwów and from 1948 of the musicological section of the Union of Polish Composers. The most important periodicals between the wars were the monthly *Muzyka* (1924–38) edited by Mateusz Gliński and the quarterly *Muzyka polska* (1934–9) brought out by a group of young Polish composers. Just after World War II Polish musical life experienced a resurgence which eventually gave rise to a multiplicity of journals. In addition to general periodicals such as *Ruch muzyczny* (1945–9, continued 1957–) and *Muzyka* (1950–56), in which current controversies were aired, specialist publications appeared concerned for example with national folk music (*Poradnik muzyczny*, 1947–91), with music in schools (*Śpiew w szkole*, 1957–), with national opera (*Opera viva*, 1961–3) and with jazz. Mention should also be made of the significant musicological periodicals *Studia muzykologiczne* (1953–6) and *Muzyka* (1956–96), dealing with the history and theory of music as well as criticism, and *Annales Chopin* (1956–). *Res facta* (1967–) is devoted to contemporary music in Poland and abroad. *Polish Musicological Studies* (1977–1986) contains scholarly articles already published, representing Polish musicological thinking, to give foreign readers insight into the methods and areas of research of Polish musicology. Regarding the music holdings of the libraries of Poland, the *Biuletyn muzyczny* (1974–8), continued by *Biblioteka muzyczna* (1979–1983/4), represent the Polish section of IAML. As regards Chopin Societies and similar organizations, from all over the world, a *Bulletin of the Council of Agreement* (1984–5), continued by *Chopin in the World* (1986), published by the International Federation of Chopin Societies, was published. Modern sound reproduction (recording, phonography, audio equipment) is covered in *Studio* (1992–).

(h) Romania. The earliest Romanian music journal, *Eco musicale* (1869–71), was followed by the periodical of the Romanian Music Society in Sibiu, *Raportul general al Comitetului reuniunei române de musică din Sibiiu* (1878/9–1905/6), which provided a significant stimulus to Romanian musical life. Numerous short-lived music periodicals appeared in the following years dealing partly with the other arts as well as music, such as *Lyra românâ* (1879–80). Of far-reaching significance for national musical life towards the end of the 19th century was *România musicală* (1890–1904); in the first half of the 20th, *Muzica* (1916–25) also played an important role, encouraging the independence of Romanian composers by fostering the national heritage of folk music. In 1951 *Muzica*, the organ of the Composers' Union, was founded; it contains articles and discussions, mainly on new works, and reports on musical life. Scholarship on recent musical history and contemporary Romanian music are to be found in *Studii şi cercetări de istoria artei* (1954–) published by the Romanian Academy of Sciences, which

has also appeared in French since 1964. Since 1965 there have been published *Studii de muzicologie*, issued by the Composers' Union, and *Lucrări de muzicologie*, issued by the Conservatorul de Muzică G. Dima in Cluj, both dedicated primarily to research in Romanian music, past and present, as well as general problems of musical scholarship, teaching, style analysis and interpretation.

(i) Slovakia. The first Slovak periodical containing studies and miscellanies on music was *Hudba – spev – tanec* (1949/50–1950/51), serving amateur musical life. It was followed by the important organ of the Union of Slovak Composers, *Slovesnká hudba* (1957–71), which commented on musical life. The function of musicology as a university discipline initiated *Musicologica slovaca* (from 1990 *et europaea*), founded in 1969 by the Slovak Academy of Sciences. The importance should also be stressed of *Hudobný život* (1969–) and *Slowakische Musik* (1969–90). The 1990s gave rise to a intensifying of musicology in certain specific fields, including ethnomusicology, with *EthnoMusicologicum* (1993–), systematic musicology, with *Systematische Musikwissenschaft/Systematic Musicology* (1993–) and the musicology of today, in *Musicologica actualia* (1997–).

(j) Slovenia. The first Slovenian music periodical, *Cäcilia/Cecilija* (1958–9), devoted mainly to music in the rural areas and aimed at country organists and teachers, was published in Ljubljana; it appeared in both German and Slovenian, in monthly parts. It was followed by the monthly *Cerkveni glasbenik* (1878–1945, 1976–) of the Cecilian Society of Ljubljana, devoted to church music and musical culture. More specialist music periodicals followed during the 1920s, such as *Nova muzika* (1928–9), dealing with new music. After World War II the situation of Slovenian periodicals improved still further, especially as regards general periodicals concerned with the musical life of their regions, such as *Slovenska glasbena revija* (1951–60). A specialist musicological review, founded and edited by Dragotin Cvetko, was published at Ljubljana University from 1965, the *Muzikološki zbornik/Musicological Annual*; its main emphasis is on the connection between Slovenia and the European music of the past. The *Bilten* (1993–) of the Slovenian Musicological Society provides news about musicological events in the country, reports on research projects and news of conferences. Mention should be also made of the *Jahresbibliographie der Volksballadenforschung/Annual Bibliography of Folk Ballad Research* (1971–90) of the Institute for Slovenian Folklore at the Slovenian Academy of Sciences and Arts. There are also periodicals dealing with music education, such as *Glasbeno-pedagoški zbornik Akademije za glasbo v Ljubljani* (1995–) and *Glazba v šoli* (1995–).

(k) Ukraine. Ukrainian cultural periodicals contained reports on musical events, for example the *Journal d'Odessa* (1821–9), published in French and from 1827 also in Russian, on opera productions. In the field of musicology the first autochthone yearbook *Ukraïns'ke muzykoznavstvo* (1964–) was founded in Russian, from 1967 with a Ukrainian title. In 1970 Ukraine achieved also its own general music periodical, *Muzyka*, in its own language, dealing almost exclusively with Ukrainian music and musical life.

(l) Yugoslavia. The first music periodical in Yugoslavia, *Glasnik Pevačke družine 'Kornelije'* (1883), of which

only one issue appeared, was mainly devoted to the founder of Serbian national music, the composer Kornelije Stanković (1831–65). *Srpski muzički list* (1903), produced in Novi Sad, contained news of local musical life for Serbian readers in the south-eastern Austro-Hungarian empire. After World War I, numerous general musical periodicals appeared, such as *Muzika* (1928–9), the organ of the Union of Yugoslav Musicians, *Muzički glasnik* (1931–4, 1938–41) and the most important journal, *Zvuk* (1932–6), which contained scholarly articles on all aspects of music history and folk music, analyses of new works, concert critiques and book reviews of Yugoslav authors. After World War II, the short-lived but important journals *Muzika* (1948–51) and *Savremeni akordi* (1954–61) should be mentioned. Other periodicals were published by societies, such as the contiuation of *Zvuk* (1955–66, 1967–86) by the Union of Yugoslav Composers and *Pro musica* (1964–) by the Society of Music Artists of Serbia. Since 1987, Matica Srpska in Novi Sad has published two specialized scholarly periodicals, in the area of folkloristic research (*Folklor u Voivodini*) and on theatre and music (*Zbornik Matice srpske za scenske umetnosti in muziku*). Newly founded periodicals include a further continuation of *Zvuk* on an international basis, *Novi zvuk* (1993–), and *MT/Muzički talas* (1994–).

(x) Scandinavia.

(a) Denmark. The first music periodical in Denmark was C.F. Cramer's *Musik* (1788/9), the Copenhagen continuation of his *Magazin der Musik* (1783–1784/6) published in Hamburg. It contained mainly news about orchestras and concert institutions at home and abroad and material about musicians and their works, as well as a history of the Berlin Opera, with a commentary on Salieri's *Les Danaïdes*, and the libretto of Kunzen's opera *Holger Danske*, performed in 1789 in Copenhagen. The first music periodicals to be published by Danes followed in the 1830s, for example the 20 issues of the *Musikalsk tidende* (1836), edited by A.P. Berggreen, and the entertaining journal *Figaro vom Auslande* (1838). Of higher value as regards music history was the *Tidsskrift for music* (1857–9), edited by Immanuel Rée. In the later 19th century other general musical periodicals were founded, some including sections on theatre or literature and art, e.g. in *Nordisk tidsskrift for musik (og theater)* (1871/2–1872/3), *Musikbladet: ugerevue for musik og theater* (1884–1893/5) and *Mignon: ugeblad for musik, literatur og kunst* (1897–8). There were also journals of singing or choral societies, such as *Heimdal* (1845), edited by Berggreen, the organ of the Nordisk Sanger-Forening; some were on a denominational basis. In the 19th century and the early 20th musical societies played a decisive part in national musical life, and this was reflected in the periodicals and news sheets of institutions, such as societies of organists (like the *Medlemsblad for Dansk organistforening*, 1904–; from 1920 *Dansk kirkemusiker-tidende*), orchestral associations (like the *Orkesterforeningens medlemsblad*, of the Københavns Orkester-forening, 1902/3–1911) or music clubs (like the *Dansk musiker-tidende*, from 1991 *Musikeren*, the organ of the Danske Musikeres Lands-Forbund (Dansk Musiker Forbund), 1911–, and the *Dansk musik tidsskrift*, the organ of Unge Tonekunstnerselskab, 1925/6–1971). The last is the most important Danish general music periodical, containing seminal musicological and bibliographical material, but it was also the organ for new musical

directions with composers as authors, including Berg, Bartók and Zemlinsky. Its continuation *DMT* (1972/3–) is devoted to contemporary music, mainly by Danish and other Scandinavian composers, and to music aesthetics. In the years 1942–6 there was *Levende musik*, a news sheet for the Musikpaedagogisk Forening; as a general periodical it mainly covered topical events, with a national tendency, but it also published scholarly work. The first purely scholarly music periodical was the *Aarbog for musik* (1922–4), published by the Musikologisk Samfund which also brought out the *Musikhistorisk arkiv* (1931–9). With the *Dansk aarbog for musikforskning* (1961–) of the Dansk Selskab for Musikforskning (founded in 1954), Denmark achieved a specialist musicological journal; it contained essays on Danish music and also embraced a wide variety of research topics, from Greek antiquity to Webern. In 1967–72 it was joined by *Information om nordisk musikforskning* and in 1975 by the yearbook *Musik & forskning*, both published by the musicological institute of the University of Copenhagen, the latter containing articles primarily by members of that institute. Similar periodicals followed in 1991, the yearbook *Caecilia* and the working papers *Da capo*, both published by the musicological institute of the University of Århus. In a more specific area, the Danish Organ Society (founded in 1970) has published since 1971 the journal *Orglet*, devoted to organ building, past and present, the *Dansk orgelårbog* (1981/2–) and since 1984 *Orglet: B*.

A wide range of topics are covered by specialist periodicals: ethnomusicology, in *Acta ethnomusicologica* (1969–); new methods in electro-acoustics, in *Electronic Music and Musical Acoustics* (1975–7), of the Department of Musical Acoustics of the University of Århus; music education, in *Opus* (1981–92) and *Modus* (1987–), the organ of the Dansk Musik paedagogisk Forening; in traditional music, such as *Folkemusikhusringen*, from 1990 *Dansk Folkemusik*, from 1995 *Folkemusik i Danmark* (1980–1, 1989–), and *Folkemusik scenen* (1995–); and in music of the past, such as the newsletter of the Centre of Historical Music (1977–80) and the *Båndjournalen* (1983/4–1984/5) of that institution, which consists of cassettes with texts and music. There are also periodicals that concentrate on particular composers, such as *Vivaldi informations* (1971/2–1973), published by the International Antonio Vivaldi Society, and *Espansiva* (1994–), the journal of the Carl Nielsen Society.

(b) Finland. Regular reviews of music appeared in Finalnd in Helsinki newspapers from the end of the 1820s. The country's first music periodical was *Säveleitä* (1887–90), consisting for two years of two separate parts, one with articles on the history of Finnish music, the other with music. The first Finnish journal in Swedish, carrying articles on music as well as on other arts, was *Euterpe* (1901–5) (like others, of short duration) that appeared in the first two decades of the 20th century. The 1920s and 30s saw the establishment of longer-lasting periodicals, such as *Suomen musiikkilehti* (1923–46) and *Musiikkitieto* (1933–46); these were amalgamated as *Musiikki* (1947–51). This was followed by the admirably edited *Uusi musiikkilehti* (1954–7). Since 1958 the Suomen Säveltaiteilijain Liito and the Suomen Musiikkitieteellinen Seura have produced a joint yearbook, *Suomen musiikin vuosikirja*, with essays, discussions of cultural questions and reports, critiques of books and records and statistical

information, while the results of scholarly research are published in *Musiikki* (1971–), the organ of Suomen Musiikkitieteellinen Seura. It was joined by the yearbook *Musiikkitiede* (1989–94), of the Musicological Institute of the University of Helsinki. Further tendencies to specialization gave rise to new music periodicals: in ethnomusicology, *Musiikin suunta* (1983–) and *Etnomusikologian vuosikirja* (1986–); in composition and music theory, *Sävellys ja musiikinteoria* (1991–), published by the Sibelius Academy; in folk music, *Kansanmusiikki* (1973–90); and in music education, *Musiikkikasvatus-/Finnish Journal of Music Education* (1996–). The *Finnish Music Quarterly* (1985–) is a representative journal of the country's musical culture, mainly for foreign readers.

(c) Norway.   The first Norwegian periodicals, in the 1820s, were serial publications of music, consisting solely of songs or piano pieces, for example *Norske lyra* (1825). The first steps towards a music periodical were taken in *Cecilia* (1838/9), the literary part of the periodical music edition *Musikjournal*, which contained rudimentary theory and essays. The first true Norwegian music periodical was *Musikalsk søndagsblad* (1839/40), which consisted primarily of translations of articles from central European journals such as the *Neue Zeitschrift für Musik* (1834–), soon followed by other music periodicals, notably the monthly *Nordisk musik-tidende* (1880–92), an invaluable source of information about Norwegian music and musicians in the 1880s and 90s. Many of the following music journals were short-lived. The first periodical published by an institution was *Musikbladet* (1908–21), the organ of the Music Conservatory of Oslo, then combined with *Sangerposten* (1910–21), which represented a group of choral associations, and continued in 1927 as *Tonekunst*, supported by five organizations, among them the Society of Norwegian Composers and the Norwegian Organists' Association. With the *Norsk musikerblad* (1914–) Norway achieved its first general music periodical, devoted mainly to the nation's music and musical life. The importance of the choral movement in Norway led to a series of periodicals related to singing, the first of which was *Sanger-tidende* (1864/5), which appeared as a supplement to the third year of the *Norsk skytter- og jagt-tidende* (the shooting and male choral societies were important in the national independence movement that led to the divorce from Sweden in 1905). Mention should also be made, as important periodicals in this context, of *Sangertidende* (1884–95), *Tonens makt* (1909–), the news sheet for members of the Norsk Arbeidersangerforbund, and *Norsk sang* (1946–84), published by the Norges Landssangerforbund established in 1921. As a musicological forum Norway had *Norsk musikkgranskning* (1937–1962/71), a yearbook published by the Norsk Samfund for Musikkgranskning, and since 1968 *Studia musicologica norvegica*, of the musicological society Norsk Musikkforskerlag (founded in 1964).

The jazz movement started during World War II with *Rytme* (1941–61). In 1966 the Norwegian Jazz Association published its journal, *Jazznytt*. Exclusively devoted to folk music are *Spelemannsbladet* (1941–) and *Årbok for norsk folkemusikk* (1991–). Besides the musicological yearbook mentioned above, the most important Norwegian music periodicals of today are *Norsk kirkemusikk* (1947/8–), devoted to church music, *Musikk i skolen*, 1956–, and *Norsk musikktidsskrift*, 1964–, dealing with

pedagogical aspects of music teaching as well as *Ballade*, 1977, which is devoted to contemporary music.

(d) Sweden.   In Sweden the earliest periodical publication of music was *Musikaliskt tidsfördrif* (1789–1834), edited by the composer Olof Åhlström, containing music by Swedish and other composers; its 46-year run constitutes one of the longest to be found in this genre. The first true Swedish music periodical was *Euterpe* (1823), which was followed by a series of other general music periodicals, such as *Läsning uti musikaliska ämnen* (1827–9), *Stockholms musik-tidning* (1843–4) and its successor *Ny tidning för musik* (1853–7), both published by Abraham Hirsch, the latter giving a most colourful picture of Stockholm musical life in the 1850s in its reviews. The most important and comprehensive music periodical of the 19th century was *Svensk musik-tidning* (1881–1913), rich in material, mainly in the field of biography and to some extent scholarly essays. There were also numerous periodicals dealing with theatre and music, e.g. *Tidning för teater och musik* (1835–6) and above all the *Svenska scenen* (from 1919 *Scenen*; 1914/15–1941) of the Svenska Teaterförbundet. With the increasingly developing musical life of Sweden in the late 19th century and especially the early 20th, there emerged many specialized journals, beginning with those devoted to church music and musicians, which also took account of the interest of teachers, e.g. *Musikalisk kyrkotidning* (1847–50). In addition choral societies brought out their own journals, such as *Svenska sångarförbundet* (from 1922 *Sångartidningen*; 1915–95); these were sometimes denominational, e.g. *Sången* (1921–69), the organ of the Svenska Baptisternas Sångarförbund. Periodicals published by professional musical organizations also affected the development of music in Sweden, e.g. *Musikern* (1908–9), continued as *Svenska musikerförbundets tidning* (from 1920 *Musikern*; 1910–) and the *Auktorn* (1928–30), the organ of the performing rights society, Svenska Tonsättares Internationella Musikbyrå, which later issued *Ord och ton*, from 1986 *STIM-nytt* (1970–) and as *Svensk musik* (1986–). Musicological research is catered for by the Svenska Samfundet för Musikforskning and its organ the *Svensk tidskrift för musikforskning* (1919–), which contains musicological studies and is central in the development of Swedish musical scholarship; the society also published the monthly *Ur nutidens musikliv* (1920–25), dealing with contemporary music. More recently the cause of modern music in Sweden has been advanced by *Nutida musik* (1957/8–), published by Swedish radio; this periodical has contributed significant links between Swedish music and international musical life, especially as regards recent compositional techniques.

In more recent times, periodicals devoted to church music have played an important role, such as the *Svensk kyrkomusik* (1967–83), published by Kyrkomusikernas Riksförbund, then incorporated into *Kyrkomusikernas tidning* (1936), and *Kyrkokör-journalen* (1990–) of Sveriges Kyrkosångsförbund. Several journals deal with musical instruments, including conservation and technology, as in the *News* (1977–) and *Journal* (1978–) of the Musikhistoriska Museet Stockholm, particular instruments, such as *Gitarr och luta* (1968–) and *Orgelforum* (1979–), and folk music instruments, as the *Newsletter* of the Study Group of Folk Musical Instruments (1977–) of the International Folk Music Council. Other special areas are opera and ballet, as in *På operan* (1978/9–1995/6), published by the royal theatres, and *Musikdramatik* (1978–); particular composers, as in *ILC Quarterly* (1971–), from 1979 *Liszt Saeculum* of the International Liszt Centre, with research on original material; and traditional music – research in the yearbook *Sumlen* (1976–), traditional music festivals in the ethnic journal *Lira* (1994–) and combined with jazz in *Musik* (1994–8).

(xi) Spain and Portugal. The first Spanish music periodicals appeared in the 1840s. *La Iberia musical y literaria* (1842–5), founded by M. Soriano Fuertes and edited by J. Espín y Guillén, was the first significant one; it contained articles on various topics – instrumentation, the activities of performers, and Spanish and foreign music. Most of the periodicals that followed lasted only a short time, but among them the locally orientated *Gaceta musical de Madrid* (1855–6), issued by H. Eslava, strove to elevate the level of Spanish musical life. Among the periodicals of the 1860s, *La España musical* (1866–74) contains essays on Wagner's operas and Liszt's symphonic poems, and the *Almanaque musical* (1868) includes articles by Felipe Pedrell, the founder of Spanish musicology, on Wagner. Later in the century there appeared Pedrell's weekly *Notas musicales y literarias* (1882–3) and two periodicals concerned with Latin American music: *Ilustración musical hispana-americana* (1888–96) and *La música ilustrada hispano-americana* (1898–1902). Church music periodicals are specially significant for Spain: the monthly *La música religiosa en España* (1896–9), edited by Pedrell, and the quarterly *Tesoro sacro musical* (1917–78), which included music and dealt with both past and present. At the beginning of the 20th century was founded the fundamental periodical devoted to research on Catalan music, issued by the important choral association Orféo Catalá, *Revista musical catalana* (1904–36). All music periodicals ceased publication in July 1936 because of the beginning of the Spanish Civil War; only a few resumed afterwards. Other notable 20th-century periodicals include *Ritmo* (1929–90). Since 1946 the Instituto Español de Musicología has issued the *Anuario musical*, which gives extensive treatment to Spanish musical history and to archival studies, more recently also on ethnomusicological topics; several volumes have served as Festschriften, either dealing with composers of the past (Morales, 1953; Cabezón, 1966), or dedicated to eminent Spanish musicologists (Subirá, 1963; Pedrell, 1972). The Sociedad Española de Musicología, in Madrid, founded the semi-annual *Revista de musicología* in 1978 with contributions, partly by well-known Spanish musicologists, mainly dealing with early Spanish music history, in the Middle Ages, the Renaissance and Baroque, emphasizing church music and liturgical questions; some articles are also devoted to music instruments, primarily organs, and ethnomusicological topics. The volume of 1982 functioned as a Festschrift for Samuel Rubio, the society's founder and first president and first editor of its organ. It was joined in 1979 by *Butlletí de la Societat catalana de musicología* and in 1981 by *Recerca musicológica*, published by the Universidad Autónoma de Barcelona. The *Revista musical catalana*, from 1990 *Catalunya música* (1984–), is not a revival of the earlier periodical of the same title but is more devoted to Catalan music life. Among other specialized journals, *Apromur*, from 1985 *Musicae* (1984–), of the Asociación para la Promoción de la Música Religiosa, sacred music in general and *Nassarre:*

revista aragonesa de musicología (1985–) published by the Institución Fernando el Católico, Sección de Música Antigua, with early religious music; *Nueva música* (1990–) is concerned with contemporary music, *Música y educación* (1988–) with music pedagogical research, and, *Música y tecnología*, from 1989 *Keyboard* (1986–) deals with the technology of musical instruments. Bibliographical studies are covered by the *Anuario de la prensa musical española* (1980/81–) of the Instituto de Bibliografía Musical in Madrid, and musical documentation by *AEDOM* (1994–), the newletter of the Asociación Española de Documentación Musical.

In 18th-century Portugal, articles on music appeared occasionally in general cultural periodicals, like the critical descriptions of operatic practice in the *Gazeta literária* (1762). The *Jornal do Conservatório* (1839/40), founded by the composer J.D. Bomtempo (1775–1842), may be considered the earliest Portuguese music periodical; it was issued weekly and consisted mainly of critical writings and accounts of the activities of the Lisbon Royal Conservatory. In the later 19th century there followed locally orientated publications such as the *Gazeta musical de Lisboa* (1872/3–1874/6) and the *Gazeta musical* (1884–6), and periodicals dealing with music and the other arts, such as *Amphion* (1884–98). Another important periodical of high repute was M.A. Lambertini's *A arte musical* (1899–1915). *A arte musical: revista de doutrina, noticiário e crítica* (1930/31–73), the country's general musical periodical, contains short articles, accounts of Portuguese and foreign music and critical notices; it was published from 1945 by the Juventude Musical Portuguesa. The quarterly *Canto gregoriano* (1956/7–1984), published by the Centro de Estudos Gregorianos (Lisbon) dealt with the promotion of Gregorian chant in highly specialized articles, some by musicologists from Paris and Solesmes. It was joined by the *Nova revista de música sacra* (1971–), planned along the lines of its forerunner *Música sacra* (1927–8) with articles on religious music and liturgy. Guided by the principles of Vatican Council II, priority is given to Gregorian chant. Music and liturgy are also dealt with in the *Boletím de música liturgica* (1973–86) and specially on Gregorian chant in *Modus* (1987–92). Other periodicals are devoted to music education, such as *APEM: boletim informativo* (1972–), published by the Associação Portuguesa de Educação Musical, the national branch of ISME, to new ideas on music aesthetics, in *Informação musical* (1981–3), founded by the Sector de Animação, and to the history of performances of opera and ballet in Lisbon in the opera house organ *S. Carlos revista* (1986–).

(xii) Switzerland. The growth of Swiss musical life at the beginning of the 19th century led to the widespread foundation of music societies; the first annual periodical was the *Protokoll der Schweizerischen Musik-Gesellschaft*, which from 1808 to 1856 testifies to the society's activities. But the Swiss periodical with the oldest tradition is the *Neujahrsgeschenk an die Zürcherische Jugend von der Allgemeinen Musikgesellschaft in Zürich* (1813–), which evolved from the New Year bulletins of the music society Ab dem Musiksaal (1685–1812) and of the Musikgesellschaft zur Deutschen Schule in Zürich (1713–1812), and contained quotations from the Bible and from poetry with vocal and instrumental compositions. Since 1830 the bulletins have consisted of musical biographies with material on the activities of composers (such as

Wagner and Busoni in Zürich) and essays on Swiss musicians; they offer a rich source for Zürich music history, and bear witness to a gradual change of attitude among the authors, from the serious amateur to the cultured and also the professional music historian. The first true Swiss musical periodical, the highly respected *Schweizerische Musikzeitung/Revue musicale suisse*, was founded by J.R. Weber in 1861 as the *Sängerblatt* of the Bernischer Kantonalgesangverein. By its second year, when it was called the *Schweizerisches Sängerblatt*, it began to expand its subject matter, and by 1879, now the *Schweizerische Musikzeitung und Sängerblatt*, it had developed into a general periodical. In 1901 it became the organ of the Schweizerischer Tonkünstlerverein and thus a forum for Swiss music, exerting much influence, even beyond the country. It ceased publication in 1983.

The importance attached to choral singing and above all the male-voice choir in 19th-century Switzerland, in the tradition of H.G. Nägeli, led to the establishment of journals of individual choirs such as *Der Konkordianer* (1883–?1952/3) of the Männerchor Konkordia Bern, as well as bulletins of cantonal choral societies, e.g. *L'écho musical* (1865–81) of the Société Cantonale des Chanteurs Vaudois. Some such periodicals were partly directed towards national cultural aims, e.g. *Der Volksgesang* (in 1897/8 *Schweizerische Zeitschrift für Gesang und Musik*; 1893/4–1904/5). There later appeared the *Schweizer Musikerblatt* (1915–97) of the Schweizerischer Musikerverband, specially concerned with the professional interests of Swiss musicians, as well as publications of a more popular kind, e.g. *Musikzeitung: Zeitschrift für Harmonie- und Blechmusik* (1908–11), the official organ of the Nordwestschweizerische Musikverbände, and others on a denominational basis, e.g. *Der Organist* (1923–47), the journal of the Schweizerische Reformierte Organisten-Verbände. Among other music periodicals were several dealing with the restoration of Protestant congregational and choir singing, such as *Der evangelische Kirchenchor* (1895/6–1974), from 1897 the journal of the Schweizerischer Kirchengesangsbund, and others devoted to the revival of Gregorian chant and associated with the new Cecilian associations, whether on a broad basis, such as *Der Chorwächter* (from 1960 *Katholische Kirchenmusik*; 1876–), the journal of the Schweizerische Cäcilien-Vereine, and *Caecilia* (1879–97), from 1887 the journal of the Sociétés de Sainte-Cécile de la Suisse Romande, or more specific. Music education journals include the annual reports of conservatories, e.g. that of Zürich (1876–), and periodicals designed to propagate Jaques-Dalcroze's eurhythmic methods, such as *Le rythme* (1916–74). The leading education organ was the *Schweizerische musikpädagogische Blätter* (1912–59) of the Schweizerischer Musikpädagogischer Verband, which was absorbed into the *Schweizerische Musikzeitung* in 1960.

The new directions of music in the 1920s led to the appearance of *Dissonances* (1923/4–1946), which mainly contained essays on modern music. The development of musicology and the founding of the Schweizerische Musikforschende Gesellschaft gave rise to the publication of the *Schweizerisches Jahrbuch für Musikwissenschaft* (1924–38), which published contributions on Swiss and other music history. The *Mitteilungen* (from 1937 *Mitteilungsblatt*; 1934–80) of the society, on the other hand, contain miscellaneous material mainly on Swiss musical history with, since 1948, a bibliography of newly published Swiss musical literature. From 1981 it was continued by the *Schweizer Jahrbuch für Musikwissenschaft*, including the *Schweizer musikbibliographie*, as the leading musicological periodical of the country. The *Schweizerische Musikzeitung* (1861–1983) was continued after 1984 by *Dissonanz*, published by the Schweizerischer Tonkünstlerverein, including a list of new Swiss compositions by members. The Schweizerischer Musikpädagogischer Verband resumed independent publication of its organ in 1984, as *Schweizer musikpädagogische Blätter/Cahiers suisses de pédagogie musicale*. Regarding contemporary music, the important *Mitteilungen der Paul Sacher Stiftung* (1988–) should be mentioned. There is a wide variety of musical periodicals, reflecting a picture of growing specialization, with a large number of choir and brass band association papers or organs of folkloric music as well as journals devoted to various branches of popular music (rock, pop, country etc.) and jazz.

BIBLIOGRAPHY

A Commentaries: (i) Periodicals of the written word: non-musical (ii) Periodicals of the written word: musical (iii) Periodicals of the written word: specific (iv) Editors. B Bibliographies: (i) Musical periodicals (ii) General music literature. C Article indexes: (i) Musical periodicals (ii) Non-musical periodicals.

A: COMMENTARIES
(i) Periodicals of the written word: non-musical
(PM – Periodica musica)

J.O. Opel: *Die Anfänge der deutschen Zeitungspresse 1609–1650* (Leipzig, 1879), 179ff

L. Salomon: *Die Anfänge des deutschen Zeitschriftenwesens*, i (Leipzig, 1900)

G. Calmus: 'Drei satirisch-kritische Aufsätze von Addison über die italienische Oper in England (London, 1710)', *SIMG*, ix (1907–8), 131–45

J. Bobeth: *Die Zeitschriften der Romantik* (Leipzig, 1911/R)

G. Menz: *Die Zeitschrift: ihre Entwicklung und ihre Lebensbedingungen* (Stuttgart, 1928)

L.N. Richardson: *A History of Early American Magazines, 1741–1789* (New York, 1931/R)

E.H. Lehmann: *Die Anfänge der Kunstzeitschrift in Deutschland* (Leipzig, 1932)

E. Brümmer: *Beethoven im Spiegel der zeitgenössischen rheinischen Presse* (Würzburg, 1933)

A. Goldschmidt: *Die Musik in deutschen Almanachen* (diss., U. of Leipzig, 1935)

F.L. Mott: *A History of American Magazines* (Cambridge, MA, 1938–68)

E. Merbeck: *Die Münchner Theaterzeitschriften im 18. Jahrhundert* (Bottrop, 1941)

J. Kirchner: *Das deutsche Zeitschriftenwesen*, i: *Von den Anfängen des Zeitschriftenwesens bis zum Ausbruch der Französischen Revolution* (Leipzig, 1942), 103–4, 145–7, 259–63

H. Jahrsetz: 'Titelworte in Zeitschriften und Zeitungen', *Der Jungbuchhandel*, vii (1953), 164ff

Heinz Becker: 'Die frühe hamburgische Tagespresse als musikgeschichtliche Quelle', *Beiträge zur hamburgischen Musikgeschichte*, ed. H. Husmann (Hamburg, 1956), 22–45

W. Drop: 'Het Nederlandse muziekleven tussen 1815 en 1840 in tijdschriften weerspiegeld', *TVNM*, xviii/4 (1959), 181–202

W. Matthäus: 'Beiträge zur Musikgeschichte Bonns in den Jahren 1772–1791: Quellen und Berichte aus zeitgenössischen Tageszeitungen', *Bonner Geschichtsblätter*, xxi (1967), 136–52

J.F. Schoof: *A Study of Didactic Attitudes on the Fine Arts in America as expressed in Popular Magazines during the Period 1786–1800* (diss., Ohio State U., 1967)

A. Weinmann: *Der Alt-Wiener Musikverlag im Spiegel der 'Wiener Zeitung'* (Tutzing, 1976)

C.-H. Mahling: 'Bemerkungen zur "Illustrirten Zeitung" als Quelle zur Musikgeschichte des 19. Jahrhunderts', *FAM*, xxix (1982), 158–60

H.R. Cohen, S. L'Ecuyer Lacroix and J. Léveillé: *Les gravures musicales dans 'L'illustration' 1843–1899* (Quebec and New York, 1983)

R. Verti: 'La presenza della musica nei periodici bolognesi dal 1800 al 1830', *PM*, i (1983), 6–9

H.R. Cohen and S. L'Ecuyer Lacroix: 'Indexation de l'iconographie musicale dans la presse illustrée du dix-neuvième siècle: présentation d'une méthode', *FAM*, xxxi (1984), 96–107

D. Legány: 'Hungarian Periodicals, 1800–1840', *PM*, ii (1984), 17 only

W. Reid Cipolla: 'Present Activities regarding Union Catalogues of Periodicals in the United States of America', *FAM*, xxxi (1984), 51–4

M.G. Brindisino: 'Notizie musicali sui periodici politico-letterari salenti (Puglia) dalla seconda metà del sec. XIX sino al 1911', *PM*, iii (1985), 19–25

A.F. Ivaldi: 'Théâtre et musique dans la Gazetta di Genova de 1800 à 1814', ibid., 8–18

B.H. Miller: 'A Research Report on "Magazine Music" published in Non-Musical Periodicals', *PM*, iv (1986), 18–20

P. Bloom: '"Politics" and the Musical Press in 1830', *PM*, v (1987), 9–16

L. Langley: 'Italian Opera and the English Press, 1836–1856', *PM*, vi (1988), 3–10

Z. Roman: 'Italian Opera Premières and Revivals in the Hungarian Press, 1864–1894', ibid., 16–20

G. Seaman: 'Nineteenth-Century Italian Opera as seen in the Contemporary Russian Press', ibid., 21–4

H.R. Cohen: 'Verdi in Paris: Reflections in "L'illustration"', *PM*, vii (1989), 5–12

M. Conati: 'Il giornalismo teatrale lombardo degli anni 1830 e la "Strenna teatrale europea"', *PM*, viii (1990), 19–20

B.H. Miller: 'Magazine Music of the Jugendstil and Expressionist Movements', *PM*, ix (1991), 1–13

I. Susaeta Llombart: *La música en las fuentes hemerográficas del siglo XVIII español: referencias musicales en la 'Gaceta de Madrid', y artículos de música en los papeles periódicos madrileños* (diss., U. Complutense de Madrid, 1993)

B.H. Miller: 'Household Periodicals: an Unstudied Source of American Music', *FAM*, xlii (1995), 311–19

(ii) Periodicals of the written word: musical

E. von Lannoy: 'Was ist die Aufgabe einer musikalischen Zeitung?', *Neue Wiener Musik-Zeitung*, i (1852), 1–2

H. Riemann: 'Unsere Musikzeitungen', *Präludien und Studien* (Leipzig, 1895/R), 13–21

F. Krome: *Die Anfänge des musikalischen Journalismus in Deutschland* (Leipzig, 1897)

O.G. Sonneck: 'Die musikalische Zeitschriften-Literatur', *ZIMG*, i (1899–1900), 388–90

J.-G. Prod'homme: 'Essai de bibliographie des périodiques musicaux de langue française', *RdM*, i (1917–19), 76–90

T. Haas: 'Die Wiener Musikzeitschriften', *Der Merker*, x (1919), 671–6, 699–702, 733–6

H. Koch: *Die deutschen musikalischen Fachzeitschriften des 18. Jahrhunderts* (diss., U. of Halle, 1923)

A. Schering: 'Aus der Geschichte der musikalischen Kritik in Deutschland', *JbMP 1928*, 9–23

A. Pougin: 'Notes sur la presse musicale en France', *EMDC*, II/vi (1931), 3841–59

K. Dolinski: *Die Anfänge der musikalischen Fachpresse in Deutschland* (Berlin, 1940)

H.E. Johnson: 'Early New England Periodicals Devoted to Music', *MQ*, xxvi (1940), 153–61

Å. Davidsson: 'Svensk musiktidskrifter', *STMf*, xxvii (1945), 95–126; Eng. trans., *FAM*, xxxiii (1986), 194–210 [19th-century periodicals]

F.C. Campbell: 'Some Current Foreign Periodicals', *Notes*, v (1947–8), 189–98

B.S. Yagolim: 'Russkaya muzikal'naya periodika po 1917 goda' [The Russian music periodical before 1917], *Kniga: issledovaniya i materiali*, iii (Moscow, 1960), 335–59

E. Rohlfs: *Die deutschsprachigen Musikperiodica 1945–1957: Versuch einer strukturellen Gesamtdarstellung als Beitrag zur Geschichte der musikalischen Fachpresse* (Regensburg, 1961)

C.E. Wunderlich: *A History and Bibliography of Early American Musical Periodicals, 1782–1852* (diss., U. of Michigan, 1962/R)

I. Fellinger: *Verzeichnis der Musikzeitschriften des 19. Jahrhunderts*, i: *Historischer Überblick* (Regensburg, 1968)

P. Berri: 'I periodici musicali genovesi: da La musica a Musicalia', *Liguria*, xxxvii (1970), 21–4

N. Zaslaw: 'Free Music Periodicals', *CMc*, no.10 (1970), 140–43

C.B. Grimes: *American Musical Periodicals, 1819–1852: Music Theory and Musical Thought in the United States* (diss., U. of Iowa, 1974/R)

K. McMorrow: 'Canadian Music Periodicals', *Notes*, xxxvi (1979–80), 904–13

I. Fellinger: 'Union Catalogues of Music Periodicals', *FAM*, xxvii (1980), 13–17

I. Fellinger: 'Aspekte der Mozart-Auffassung in deutschsprachigen Musikzeitschriften des 19. Jahrhunderts', *MJb 1980–83*, 269–77

I. Fellinger: 'Report of the Working (Project) Group on Music Periodicals', *FAM*, xxviii (1981), 97–8; xxix (1982), 36–8; xxx (1983), 46–7; xxxi (1984), 48–50; xxxii (1985), 35–7; xxxiii (1986), 37–8; xxxiv (1987), 21–2; xxxv (1988), 35–6; xxxvi (1989), 17–18; xxxvii (1990), 21–2; xxxviii (1991), 20–21; xxxix (1992), 31–3; xl (1993), 151 only; xli (1994) 129–30, 207 only; xlii (1995), 184 only; xliii (1996), 208 only; xliv (1997), 188–9; xlv (1998), 166–7; xlvi (1999), 152–3; xlvii (2000), forthcoming

Periodica musica [*PM*], ed. RIPM under auspices of the IMS and IAML (Vancouver, later Collegepark, MD, 1983–91)

G. Brosche: 'Zur Situation der Österreichischen Musikzeitschriften', *FAM*, xxx (1983), 47–9

I. Fellinger: 'Reflections on Nineteenth-Century Periodicals and Musicological Research', *PM*, i (1983), 5–6

L. Langley: 'The Use of Private Papers, Correspondence and Archives of the Publishing Trade in British Music Periodicals Research', ibid., 12–13

V. Vavrinecz and M. Gráf-Forrai: 'The Project of a Union Catalogue of Hungarian Periodicals of Music and Related Arts', *FAM*, xxx (1983), 51–2

S. Wallon: 'Les périodiques musicaux en France dans les bibliothèques municipales de Province', ibid., 49–51

G.B. Anderson: 'Unpublished Periodical Indexes at the Library of Congress and Elsewhere in the United States of America', *FAM*, xxxi (1984), 54–60

H. Garceau: 'Notes sur la presse musicale religieuse en France de 1827 à 1861', *PM*, ii (1984), 6–13

C. Lindahl: 'Past Efforts regarding Union Catalogues of Periodicals in the United States of America', *FAM*, xxxi (1984), 50–51

M. Donà: 'The Present State of Music Periodicals in Italy', *FAM*, xxxii (1985), 37–9

D. van den Hul: 'Present-Day Music Periodicals in the Netherlands', ibid., 40–41

A. Zecca-Laterza: 'Cataloghi collettivi per i periodici musicali in Italia', ibid., 39 only

Z. Blažeković: 'The First Music Journals in Croatia', *PM*, iv (1986), 12–13

J.A. Deaville: 'The Earliest Known Inventories of European Journals', ibid., 14–17

P. Krause: 'Zum gegenwärtigen Stand der Musikzeitschriften in der Deutschen Demokratischen Republik', *FAM*, xxxiii (1986), 39–44

K. Michałowski: 'Musikbibliographie der Zeitschriften in Polen', ibid., 45–51

M.A. Ester-Sala: 'Revistes de musicología: un fet aïllat' [Musicology journals: an isolated phenomenon], *Revista Musical Catalana*, 2nd ser., no.32 (1987), 49–50

E.-B. Fanger: 'Catalogues of Music Periodicals in Denmark: from Traditional Card Files to Electronic Data Processing', *FAM*, xxxiv (1987), 124–6

K. McMorrow: 'Music Periodicals in Canada', ibid., 250–54

Ø. Norheim: 'Norwegian Music Periodicals in Past and Present', ibid., 121–4

M. Suhonen: 'Music Periodicals in Finland', ibid., 127–32

I. Freire de Andrade: 'Portuguese Music Periodicals', *FAM*, xxxv (1988), 174–9

D. van den Hul: 'Early Music Periodicals in the Netherlands', ibid., 171–4

B. Huys: 'Belgian Music Periodicals: their National and International Interest', ibid., 179–84

C.-H. Mahling: 'Zur Beurteilung der italienischen Oper in der deutschsprachigen Presse zwischen 1815 und 1825', *PM*, vi (1988), 11–15

J. Torres Mulas: 'Polirritmia: un apunte sobre hemerografía musical', *Ritmo*, suppl. to no.593 (1988), 161–3

M. Conati: 'I periodici teatrali e musicali italiani a metà Ottocento', *PM*, vii (1989), 13–28

I. Fellinger: 'Periodica', *Modern Music Librarianship: Essays in Honor of Ruth Watanabe*, ed. A. Mann (Stuyvesant, NY, and Kassel, 1989), 193–214

T.F. Heck and R. Yoshimura: 'Japanese Musical Term Retrieval in "RILM" On-Line: a Status Report and Comparison to "The Music Index" and "Zeitschriftendienst Musik"', *FAM*, xxxvi (1989), 31–7

S. Mori: 'A Historical Survey of Music Periodicals in Japan: 1881–1920', ibid., 44–50

J. Torres: 'La prensa periódica musical española en el siglo XIX: bases para su estudio', *PM*, viii (1990), 1–11

C. Clark: 'POMPI: Popular Music Periodicals Index', *FAM*, xxxviii (1991), 32–7

S. Friedmann: 'The Special Situation Regarding Music Periodicals in Colombia', ibid., 110–17

R. Kitson: 'English and American Periodicals Treated by RIPM: a Report', *PM*, ix (1991), 23–7

J. Torres Mulas: *Las publicaciones periódicas musicales en España (1812–1990): estudio crítico-bibliográfico* (Madrid, enlarged 2/1991)

H. Vanhulst: 'Les revues musicales et la critique en Wallonie et à Bruxelles au XIXème siècle', *PM*, ix (1991), 14–22

I. Antonio: 'Impression of Music – Periodicals Press and Documentation in Brazil', *FAM*, xxxix (1992), 235–45

V. Čižik: 'Slowakische Musikzeitschriften', ibid., 39–43

I. Fellinger: 'Die Auseinandersetzung mit dem Oratorium als Kunstgattung in deutschen Musikzeitschriften der zweiten Hälfte des 19. Jahrhunderts', *IMSCR XV: Madrid 1992* [*RdMc*, xvi (1993)], 1636–42

I. Fellinger: 'Die gegenwärtige Situation der Musikzeitschriften in Deutschland', *FAM*, xxxix (1992), 169–75

W. Pigła: 'Die Warschauer Musikzeitschriften (1850–1914)', ibid., 50–56 [orig. pubd in Pol.]

G.R. Seaman: 'New Zealand Periodicals with Musical Content', ibid., 211–19

J. Wilgocki: 'Polnische musikwissenschaftliche Zeitschriften aus der Perspektive von 80 Jahren (1911–1991)', ibid., 43–50

E.-B. Fanger: 'Überblick über die historische Entwicklung dänischer Musikzeitschriften', *FAM*, xl (1993), 323–31

M. Capra: 'Alla ricerca dei periodici musicali: in margine alla pubblicazione dei periodici musicali delle biblioteche della Campania', *RIM*, xxxii (1997), 367–82

C. Giglio: 'La musica nei periodici dell'Ottocento e del primo Novecento pubblicati a Palermo', *Fonti musicali italiane*, ii (1997), 95–153

T. Grande: 'Neapolitan Music Periodicals in the Second Half of the 19th Century', *FAM*, xliv (1997), 151–68

T.F. Heck: 'The Illustration of Music Periodicals, c.1880–1914: a Question of Halftones and 'Whole'-Tones', ibid., 307–30

J. Ludvová: *Německé hudební časopisy v Čechách 1860–1945* [German music periodicals in Bohemia], *HV*, xxxiv (1997), 205–23

J. Torres Mulas: 'Music Periodicals in Spain: Beginnings and Historical Development', *FAM*, xliv (1997), 331–42

M.W. Davidson: 'Mid-Nineteenth-Century American Periodicals: a Case Study', *Notes*, liv (1997/8), 371–87

M. Geering: 'Schweizer Musikzeitschriften: Gestern und Heute', *FAM*, xlv (1998), 273–81

C. Giglio: 'Music Periodicals in Palermo: the Nineteenth and Early Twentieth Centuries', ibid., 250–72

(iii) Periodicals of the written word: specific

A.B. Marx: 'Ueber den Anforderungen unserer Zeit an musikalische Kritik: in besonderm Bezuge auf diese Zeitung', *Berliner allgemeine musikalische Zeitung*, i (1824), 3–5, 9–11, 17–19

A.B. Marx: 'Andeutung des Standpunktes der [Berliner allgemeinen musikalischen] Zeitung', ibid., 444–8; v (1828), 493–4

H. Dorn: 'Berliner allgemeine musikalische Zeitung', *Caecilia* [Mainz], viii (1828), 179–86

L. Stierlin: *Die 'Neujahrstücke' der frühern Musikgesellschaften bis 1812* (Zürich, 1857)

S. Bagge: 'Rückblick und Abschied von den Lesern der deutschen Musikzeitung', *Deutsche Musik-Zeitung*, iii (1862), 409 only

J.H. Scheltema: 'Caecilia, algemeen muzikaal tijdschrift van Nederland', 1844–1893 (The Hague, 1893) [also incl. *Nederlandsch muzikaal tijdschrift*]

G. Wustmann: 'Zur Entstehungsgeschichte der Schumannischen "Zeitschrift für Musik"', *ZIMG*, viii (1906–7), 396–403

H. Otto: 'Was bietet uns das "Musik-Instrument"?', *Das Musik-Instrument*, v (1916), 66–7

O. von Hase: 'Allgemeine musikalische Zeitung', *Breitkopf & Härtel: Gedenkschrift und Arbeitsbericht* (Leipzig, 4/1917–19/R), i, 149–51; ii, 31–7

G. Kinsky: 'Zur Geschichte der Gründung der "Neuen Zeitschrift für Musik"', *ZfM*, Jg.87 (1920), 1–5

H. Mersmann: 'Zehn Jahre "Melos"', *Melos*, ix (1930), 58–63

H. Ehinger: 'Die Rolle der Schweiz in der "Allgemeinen musikalischen Zeitung" 1798–1848', *Festschrift Karl Nef* (Zürich and Leipzig, 1933), 19–47

A. Heuss: 'Augenblicksaufnahmen der ZFM aus ihren drei letzten Jahrzehnten', *ZfM*, Jg.100 (1933), 30–33

A. Schering, W. Niemann and M. Unger: 'Ein Wort zum Jubiläumsjahrgang der "Zeitschrift für Musik" aus den Reihen ihrer früheren Schriftleiter', ibid., 27–30

I. Wyzewska: *La revue wagnérienne: essai sur l'interprétation esthétique de Wagner en France* (Paris, 1934)

R.R. : 'Jedan dački glazbeni list' [A student's music periodical], *Hrvatska tamburica*, i/7–8 (1936), 51 only [describes the Serbian pubn *Đačka lira*]

M. [Bruckner-]Bigenwald: *Die Anfänge der Leipziger 'Allgemeinen musikalischen Zeitung'* (Hermanstadt [Sibiu], 1938/R)

L. Kretzer: *Die 'Wiener allgemeine Theaterzeitung' Adolf Bäuerles 1806–1860* (diss., U. of Berlin, 1941)

P.A. Scholes: *The Mirror of Music 1844–1944: a Century of Musical Life in Britain as Reflected in the Pages of the 'Musical Times'* (London, 1947/R)

J.M. Barbour: '"Allgemeine musikalische Zeitung": Prototype of Contemporary Musical Journalism', *Notes*, v (1947–8), 325–37

A. vander Linden: 'La place de la Hollande dans l'"Allgemeine musikalische Zeitung" (1798–1848)', *IMSCR V: Utrecht 1952*, 293–5

A. Fleury: *Die Musikzeitschrift 'Caecilia' 1824–48* (diss., U. of Frankfurt, 1953)

G. Pietzsch: 'Die erste pfälzische Musikzeitschrift', *Pfälzische Heimatblätter*, ii (Neustadt, 1954), 30ff [discusses the *Musikalische Real-Zeitung*, 1788–90]

H. Husmann: '"Annales musicologiques": ein neues internationales musikwissenschaftliches Jahrbuch', *Mf*, ix (1956), 202–6

Hugo Becker: 'Die Geschichte der "Schweizerischen Musikzeitung": ein Rückblick zu Beginn des 101. Jahrgangs', *SMz*, ci (1961), 2–15

D.W. Krummel: 'Twenty Years of *Notes* – a Retrospect', *Notes*, xxi (1963–4), 56–82

P.L. Miller: 'Twenty Years After', ibid., 55–6 [discusses *Notes*]

I. Fellinger: 'Das Brahms-Bild der "Allgemeinen musikalischen Zeitung" (1863–1882)', *Beiträge zur Geschichte der Musikkritik*, ed. Heinz Becker (Regensburg, 1965), 27–54

G.A. Marco: 'And Radiate its Own Vitality': "The Music Review" over Twenty-Five Years', *MR*, xxvi (1965), 236–46

E. Salzman: '"Modern Music" in Retrospect', *Composer*, no.17 (1965), 2–5

M. Vogel: 'Nietzsche und die "Bayreuther Blätter"', *Beiträge zur Geschichte der Musikkritik*, ed. Heinz Becker (Regensburg, 1965), 55–68

A. Briner: *Musikgeschichte aus der Perspektive Zürichs: die 'Neujahrsblätter' der Allgemeinen Musikgesellschaft Zürich 1813–1965* (Zürich, 1966)

L. Ager: 'Fanfare', *MT*, cviii (1967), 1001–2

J.R. Holmes: *'The Musical Quarterly': its History and Influence on the Development of American Musicology* (diss., , U. of North Carolina, 1967)

L. Ager: 'Sounding Brass', *MO*, xci (1967–8), 317 only, 319 only, 321 only [discusses *The Sackbut*]

C.C. von Gleich: *Die Bedeutung der 'Allgemeinen musikalischen Zeitung' 1798–1848 und 1863–1882* (Amsterdam, 1969) [incl. repr. of *Beiblatt*, April 1850]

Z. Pilková: 'Listy Hudební matice–Tempo', *HRo*, xii (1969), 362–7

R. Schmitt-Thomas: *Die Entwicklung der deutschen Konzertkritik im Spiegel der Leipziger 'Allgemeinen musikalischen Zeitung' (1798–1848)* (Frankfurt, 1969)

N. Temperley: 'MT and Musical Journalism, 1844', *MT*, cx (1969), 583–6

A. Briner: 'The Early Zürich *Neujahrsblätter*', *Studies in Eighteenth-Century Music: a Tribute to Karl Geiringer*, ed. H.C.R. Landon and R.E. Chapman (New York and London, 1970/R), 86–91

H. Strobel: '50 Jahre "Melos"', *Melos*, xxxvii (1970), 221–3

B. Dânsorean: 'Revista muzica" (1916–1925), etapă importantă a culturii muzicale Româneşti', *LM*, vii (1971), 61–9

G. Diezel: *Funktion der Zeitschrift: 'Musik in der Schule' bei der Verwirklichung der Bildungs- und Erziehungsziele der*

Sozialistischen Schule in der Deutschen Demokratischen Republik (diss., Humboldt U., Berlin, 1971)

H.G. Otto: 'Wissenschaft und Theater: einige Anmerkungen zu den "Jahrbüchern der Komischen Oper"', *MG*, xxi (1971), 319–23

W. Siegmund-Schultze: 'Rückblick auf die "Händel-Jahrbücher" (1955–1970)', *HJb 1971*, 129–35

A. Briner: '"Dreiundzwanzig": eine Zeitschrift der Neuen Wiener Schule', *SMz*, cxii (1972), 205–10

M. Jankowska: '"Tygodnik muzyczny" Karola Kurpińskiego – pierwsze polskie czasopismo muzyczne' [Kurpiński's 'Tygodnik muzyczny': the first Polish music journal], *Kultura i społeczeństwo*, xvi (1972), 189–200

R. Ceely: 'Communications', *PNM*, xi/1 (1972–3), 258–61

E. Senior: 'In the Beginning: Twenty Years of "Music and Musicians"', *Music and Musicians*, xxi/1 (1972–3), 18 only

H.E. Karjala: *A Critical Analysis of 'School Music Magazine' 1900–1936* (diss., U. of Minnesota, 1973)

H. Oesch: 'Das "Melos" und die Neue Musik', *Festschrift für einen Verleger: Ludwig Strecker zum 90. Geburtstag*, ed. C. Dahlhaus (Mainz, 1973), 287–94

R. Vogler: *Die Musikzeitschrift 'Signale für die musikalische Welt' 1843–1900* (Regensburg, 1975)

P. Schnaus: *E.T.A. Hoffmann als Beethoven-Rezensent der Allgemeinen musikalischen Zeitung* (Munich, 1977)

J.H. Alexander: 'Brainard's (Western) Musical World', *Notes*, xxxvi (1979–80), 601–14

M. Lederman: *The Life and Death of a Small Magazine (Modern Music 1924–1946)* (Brooklyn, NY, 1983)

Z. Roman: 'Periodica musica', *FAM*, xxx (1983), 70–72

J.A. Deaville: 'Anregungen für Kunst, Leben und Wissenschaft: an Introduction and Index', *PM*, ii (1984), 1–5

R. Pejović: '*Savremeni akordi*', *Zvuk*, i (1985), 107–8

R. Verti: 'The *Indice de' teatrali spettacoli*, Milan, Venice, Rome 1764–1823: Preliminary Research on a Source for the History of Italian Opera', *PM*, iii (1985), 1–7

K. Szerző: 'The Most Important Hungarian Music Periodical of the 19th Century: *Zenészeti lapok* (Musical Papers) (1860–1876)', *PM*, iv (1986), 1–5

G.B. Anderson: *Music in New York during the American Revolution: an Inventory of Musical References in 'Rivington's New York Gazette'* (Boston, 1987)

T. Grande: 'The *Gazzetta musicale di Napoli* 1852–1868', *PM*, v (1987), 17–23

K. Szerző: '"Il celebre maestro . . .": Reports on Liszt in the *Gazzetta musicale di Milano* in the Years 1870–1886', ibid., 24–31

M. Lazić: 'Sto pedeset godina horskog pevastva u Vojvodini' [150 years of choral singing in Vojvodina], *Sveske matice srpske*, ser.: *Umetnosti*, iii (1988), 5–42 [incl. sections on *Gudalo* and *Gusle*]

D. Snigurowicz: '*L'art musical: musique, théâtre, beaux-arts*: a Music Publisher's *organe de maison*', *PM*, viii (1990), 13–18

R. Pejović: 'Four Editions of the Yugoslav Magazine *Zvuk*', *New Sound*, i (1993), 29–52

J.A Robles-Cahero: '*Revista musical de Mexico* (1919–20): la primera revista musical moderna', *Pauta*, xii/45 (1993), 20–26

C. Heyter-Rauland: 'Neues zur "Cäcilia: eine Zeitschrift für die Musikalische Welt"', *FAM*, xli (1994), 340–57

K. Ellis: *Music Criticism in Nineteenth-Century France: La revue et gazette musicale de Paris, 1834–80* (Cambridge, 1995)

K. Laitinen: '*Suomen musiikkilehti* 1923–46: the Story of a Finnish Periodical', *FAM*, xlii (1995), 320–24

L. Merino: 'Situación actual de la investigación musical en Chile a la luz de la "Revista musical chilena"', *Situación de la musica clásica en Chile* (Santiago de Chile, 1995), 49–58

P. Elliot: *Pro-musica: Patronage, Performance and a Periodical: an Index to the Quarterlies* (Canton, MA, 1997)

(iv) Editors

G.W. Cooke: *John Sullivan Dwight, Brook-Farmer, Editor and Critic of Music* (Boston, 1898)

E. Reichel: 'Gottsched und Johann Adolph Scheibe', *SIMG*, ii (1900–01), 654–68

A. Storch: *J.A. Scheibes Anschauungen von der publizistischen musikalischen Historie, Wissenschaft und Kunst* (diss., U. of Leipzig, 1923)

H. Ehinger: *Friedrich Rochlitz als Musikschriftsteller* (Leipzig, 1929/R)

M. Faller: *Johann Friedrich Reichardt und die Anfänge der musikalischen Journalistik* (Kassel, 1929)

E. Rosenkaimer: *Adolph Scheibe als Verfasser seines Critischen Musicus* (Bonn, 1929)

R. Pessenlehner: *Hermann Hirschbach: der Kritiker und Künstler* (Regensburg, 1932)

R. Pessenlehner: 'Robert Schumann und die "Neue Zeitschrift für Musik"', *ZfM*, Jg.100 (1933), 18–27

H. Edelhoff: *Johann Nikolaus Forkel: ein Beitrag zur Geschichte der Musikwissenschaft* (Göttingen, 1935)

E.N. Waters: 'John Sullivan Dwight, First American Critic of Music', *MQ*, xxi (1935), 69–88

E. Böhm: *Hans Paul Freiherr von Wolzogen als Herausgeber der 'Bayreuther Blätter'* (diss., U. of Munich, 1943)

P. Kehm: *Die 'Neue Zeitschrift für Musik' unter Robert Schumanns Redaktion 1834–1844* (diss., U. of Munich, 1943)

B.C. Cannon: *Johann Mattheson: Spectator in Music* (New Haven, 1947/R)

J.C. Haskins: 'John Rowe Parker and the Euterpeiad', *Notes*, viii (1950–51), 447–56

W. Franke: *Der Theaterkritiker Ludwig Rellstab* (Berlin, 1964)

H. Kirchmeyer: 'Ein Kapitel Adolf Bernhard Marx: über Sendungsbewusstsein und Bildungsstand der Berliner Musikkritik zwischen 1824 und 1830', *Beiträge zur Geschichte der Musikanschauung im 19. Jahrhundert: Kassel 1964*, 73–101

J.H. Davies: 'Entente-cordiale: G. Jean-Aubry and a Generation of Anglo French Musical Journalism in The Chesterian', *FAM*, xiii (1966), 31–3

L.B. Plantinga: *Schumann as Critic* (New Haven, CT, 1967/R)

H.J. Serwer: *Friedrich Wilhelm Marpurg (1718–1795): Music Critic in a Galant Age* (diss., Yale U., 1969/R)

I. Fellinger: 'Friedrich August Kanne als Kritiker Beethovens', *GfMKB: Bonn 1970*, 383–6

P.A. Bloom: *François-Joseph Fétis and the 'Revue musicale'* (diss., U. of Pennsylvania, 1972/R)

I. Fellinger: 'Mattheson als Begründer der ersten Musikzeitschrift (*Critica musica*)', *New Mattheson Studies*, ed. G.J. Buelow and H.J. Marx (Cambridge, 1983), 179–97

C. Lickleder: *Choral und figurierte Kirchenmusik in der Sicht Franz Xaver Witts anhand der 'Fliegenden Blätter' und der 'Musica sacra'* (Regensburg, 1988)

A. Randier-Glenisson: 'Maurice Schlesinger, éditeur de musique et fondateur de la "Gazette musicale de Paris", 1834–1846', *FAM*, xxxviii (1991), 37–48

E.D. Bomberger: 'Alfred Michaelis and the Leipziger *Musikzeitung*', *FAM*, xliv (1997), 234–47

B: BIBLIOGRAPHIES

(in addition to the specialist bibliographies below, music periodicals are listed in national and regional union catalogues of general literature and general periodicals, as well as in the general catalogues of individual libraries and collections)

(i) Musical periodicals

MCL, xi ('Zeitschriften')

F.J. Fétis: 'Revue des journaux de musique publiés dans les divers pays de l'Europe', *Revue musicale*, ii (1827), 313–20

E.G.J. Grégoir: *Recherches historiques concernant les journaux de musique depuis les temps les plus reculés jusqu'à nos jours* (Antwerp, 1872)

W. Freystätter: *Die musikalischen Zeitschriften seit ihrer Entstehung bis zur Gegenwart: chronologisches Verzeichniss der periodischen Schriften über Musik* (Munich, 1884/R)

E. Vander Straeten: *Nos périodiques musicaux* (Ghent, 1893) [Belg. periodical edns of the 18th and 19th centuries, music periodicals of the 19th]

'Periodische Schriften', *JbMP 1894–1938*

F. Krome: *Die Anfänge des musikalischen Journalismus in Deutschland* (Leipzig, 1897), 68–71

J.-G. Prod'homme: 'Essai de bibliographie des périodiques musicaux de langue française', *RdM*, i (1917–19), 76–90

T. Haas: 'Die Wiener Musikzeitschriften', *Der Merker*, x (1919), 671–6, 699–702, 733–6

A. Shteynberg: 'Muzikal'niy periodiki za 15 let (1917–1932)', *SovM* (1933), no.6, pp.147–51

M. [Bruckner-]Bigenwald: *Die Anfänge der Leipziger 'Allgemeinen musikalischen Zeitung'* (Hermannstadt [Sibiu], 1938/R), 90–92

L. Fairley: 'A Check-List of Recent Latin-American Music Periodicals', *Notes*, ii (1944–5), 120–23

F.C. Campbell: 'Some Current Foreign Periodicals', *Notes*, v (1947–8), 189–98

R.S. Hill: 'German Wartime Music Periodicals', ibid., 199–206

F. Campbell, G. Eppink and J. Fredericks: 'Music Magazines of Britain and the United States', *Notes*, vi (1948–9), 239–62; vii (1949–50), 372–6

R. Schaal: 'Europäische Musikzeitschriften 1945–1948', *Jb der Musikwelt*, ed. H. Barth (Bayreuth, 1949/50), 111–23

A. Riedel: *Répertoire des périodiques musicaux belges* (Brussels, 1954)

D. Lindner: 'Musikzeitschriften in Österreich: Versuch einer Bibliographie', *ÖMz*, x (1955), 39–46

J.B. Coover: 'A Bibliography of East European Music Periodicals', *FAM*, iii (1956), 219–26; iv (1957), 97–102; v (1958), 44–5, 93–9; vi (1959), 27–8; vii (1960), 16–21, 69–70; viii (1961), 75–90; ix (1962), 78–80; x (1963), 60–71

J.-A. Thoumin: *Bibliographie rétrospective des périodiques français de littérature musicale 1870–1954* (Paris, 1957)

K.-H. Köhler, ed.: *Musik: Verzeichnis der in der Musikabteilung der Deutschen Staatsbibliothek nach 1945 laufend gehaltenen Zeitschriften* (Berlin, 1958)

W.P. Malm: 'A Bibliography of Japanese Magazines and Music', *EthM*, iii (1959), 76–80 [25 music and dance periodicals]

E. Rohlfs: *Die deutschsprachigen Musikperiodica 1945–1957* (Regensburg, 1961)

F. Blum: 'East German Music Journals: a Checklist', *Notes*, xix (1961–2), 399–410

A Union List of Music Periodicals in the Libraries of Northern California, ed. Northern California Chapter of the MLA (Berkeley, CA, 6/1979)

Union List of Music Periodicals in Canadian Libraries, ed. Can. Library Association (Ottawa, 1964, rev. 2/1981 by L.C. Lewis)

V. Telec: *Soupis hudebních periodik v Universitní knihovně v Brně* (Brno, 1964)

A. Töröková and V. Dvořák: *Súpis hudobných periodík v Univerzitnej knižnici v Bratislave* (Bratislava, 1966)

F. Blum: 'Music Serials in Microform and Reprint Editions', *Notes*, xxiv (1967–8), 670–79

I. Fellinger: *Verzeichnis der Musikzeitschriften des 19. Jahrhunderts* (Regensburg, 1968); suppls in *FAM*, xvii (1970), 7–8; xviii (1971), 59–62; xix (1972), 41–4; xx (1973), 108–11; xxi (1974), 36–8; xxiii (1976), 62–6

M.A. Baird: *Union List of Periodicals in Music in the Libraries of the University of London and Some Other London Libraries* (London, 1969)

N. Benzoor, ed.: *Bibliography of the Jewish Music Periodicals in Hebrew, Yiddish and Other Languages* (Haifa, 1970)

W.J. Weichlein: *A Checklist of American Music Periodicals, 1850–1900* (Detroit, 1970)

M. Svobodová: *Hudební periodika v českých zemích 1796–1970 a na Slovensku 1871–1970* (Olomouc, 1971)

Chikuji kankōbutsu sōgō mokuroku (Tokyo, 1972; enlarged 1979 as *Ongaku kankei chikuji kankōbutsu shozai mokuroku/Union List of Periodicals in Music*, rev. 1993)

K. Musioł: 'Bibliografia śląskich czasopism muzycznych' [Bibliography of Silesian musical periodicals], *Slaskie studie historyczno-teologiczne*, xxii (1972), 335–62 [summaries in Eng., Ger., Russ.]

M. Svobodová: 'Music Journals in Bohemia and Moravia 1796–1970', *FAM*, xix (1972), 22–41

P. Krause: *Musikperiodika: Zeitschriften, Jahrbücher, Almanache: Bestandsverzeichnis* (Leipzig, 1974)

M. Svobodová and J. Potúček: 'Music Journals in Slovakia 1871–1970', *FAM*, xxi (1974), 32–6

T.G. Everett: 'An Annotated List of English-Language Jazz Periodicals', *JJS*, iii/2 (1975–6), 47–57; v/2 (1978–9), 99–103; contd in *Annual Review of Jazz Studies*, iv (1988), 214–16

C.E. Lindahl: 'Music Periodicals: Early (and Later) Musical Instrument Journals', *Notes*, xxxiii (1976–7), 86–102; 'Music Periodicals', ibid., 308–16, 851–64; further lists in xxxiv (1977–8), 883–93; xxxv (1978–9), 323–35, 895–902; xxxvi (1979–80), 662–72; xxxix (1982–3), 106–16

E. Bartlitz and W. Reich, eds.: *Zeitschriftenverzeichnis Musik: Nach weis der von der Bibliotheken der DDR seit 1945 gehaltenen Musikperiodika* (Dresden, 1977)

C. Lawrence Mekkawi: 'Music Periodicals: Popular and Classical Record Reviews and Indexes', *Notes*, xxxiv (1977–8), 92–107

Union List of Music Periodicals, ed. Texas Chapter of the MLA (n.p., 1978)

J.M. Meggett: *Music Periodical Literature: an Annotated Bibliography of Indexes and Bibliographies* (Metuchen, NJ, 1978)

B. Huys: 'Lijst van orgeltijdschriften bewaard in enkele Belgische bibliotheken', *Orgelkunst*, ii (1979), 28–32

A. Zecca Laterza: *Catalogo dei periodici musicali delle biblioteche lombarde* (Milan, 1979)

S. Milligan: 'Music and Other Performing Arts Serials available in Microform and Reprint Editions', *Notes*, xxxvii (1980–81), 239–307

W. Pigła, ed.: *Katalog zagranicznych czasopism muzycznych w bibliotekach polskich* (Kraków, 1980; rev. 2/1993 by J. Wilgocki as *Zagraniczne czasopisma muzyczne w bibliotekach polskich*)

L. Schwenger and J. Strömgren, eds.: *Faelleskatalog over udenlandske musiktidsskrifter i danske biblioteker* (Copenhagen, 1980)

C.E. Lindahl: 'Music Periodicals in U.S. Research Libraries in 1931: a Retrospective Survey', *Notes*, xxxvii (1980–81), 864–70 [Europe]; xxxviii (1981–2), 73–9 [Europe, pt 2], 320–26 [US]

I. Fellinger: 'List of Union Catalogues of (Music) Periodicals', *FAM*, xxviii (1981), 323–7

Union Catalogue of Music Serials in Queensland Libraries, ed. Queensland Division of the Australian Branch of IAML (Brisbane, 1982–3)

S.M. Fry: 'New Periodicals', *Notes*, xxxix (1982–3), 833–6; contd as 'New Music Periodicals', xl (1983–4), 275–8, 761–5; xli (1984–5), 259–63, 699–703; xlii (1985–6), 268–73, 763–6; xliii (1986–7), 292–6; xliv (1987–8), 293–6; contd by D. Coclanis: 'New Periodicals', 736–9; xlv (1988–9), 306–9, 769–72; xlvi (1989–90), 411–14, 966–7; xlvii (1990–91), 429–32, 1196–8; xlviii (1991–2), 564–7, 1332–6; xlix (1992–3), 666–8; contd by S. Eggleston, xlix (1992–3), 1554–6; l (1993–4), 663–7, 1483–90; li (1994–5), 657–63, 1377–9; lii (1995–6), 537–42, 1230–34; liii (1996–7), 534–40, 1231–4; liv (1997–8), 748–52; contd by K. Little, lv (1998–9), 170–72, 724–5

L.I. Solow: 'Index to "Music Periodicals" Reviewed in *Notes* (1976–1982)', *Notes*, xxxix (1982–3), 585–90

G. Seaman: 'Nineteenth-Century Russian Music Periodicals: an Annotated Checklist' pt 1, *PM*, ii (1984), 14–16; pts 2–3, iv (1986), 6–11

K.P. Glennan: 'Music periodicals published in Los Angeles County, 1900–1985: a Bibliography', *California's Musical Wealth: Glendale, CA, 1985*, 107–22

A. Hodges and R. McGill, eds.: *The British Union Catalogue of Music Periodicals* (London, 1985; rev. and enlarged 2/1998 by J. Wagstaff to include the holdings of 6 Irish libraries)

I. Pechotsch-Feichtinger: 'Verzeichnis österreichischer Musikzeitschriften, 1945–1980', *FAM*, xxxii (1985), 160–71

J. Bourne: *Union Catalogue of Music Serials in Victorian Libraries 1985* (Clayton, Victoria, 1986)

A. Claes: *Catalogues der Belgische muziektijdschriften tot 1985 uitgegeven en bewaard in de Koninklijke bibliotheek Albert I (1833–1985)* (Brussels, 1987 [for 1833–1985]); contd by B. Huys (1993 [1986–92], 1996 [1986–95]) [mimeograph]

J. Mota and M. Infiesta: 'Revistas wagnerianas', *Monsalvat*, no.163 (Sept 1988), 52–5

G. Vachia, P. Krümm and J.-C. Klein: 'Recensement des périodiques musicaux', *Vibrations*, no.5 (1988), 275–88

T.E. Warner: *Periodical Literature on American Music, 1620–1920: a Classified Bibliography with Annotations* (Warren, MI, 1988)

I.M. Freire de Andrade: 'Ediçoes periódicas de música e periódicos musicais em Portugal', *Boletim da Associação portuguesa de educação musical*, no.62 (1989), 47–50

S.J. Lin: 'Music Periodicals in Japan – a Comprehensive List', *FAM*, xxxv (1988), 116–28; contd and indexed by H. Kishimoto in xxxvi (1989), 38–43

D. Robinson: *Music and Dance Periodicals: an International Directory & Guidebook* (Voorheesville, NY, 1989)

Katalog der Musikzeitschriften/Catalogue of Music Periodicals, ed. Bavarian State Library (Munich, 1990–) [CD-ROM as *Katalog der Notendrucke, Musikbücher und Musikzeitschriften*, 1998]

L.M. Fidler and R.S. James, eds.: *International Music Journals* (New York, 1990)

V.H. Pelote: 'An Annotated Bibliography of British Periodicals (1930–40)', *Annual Review of Jazz Studies*, v (1991), 91–107

W. Pigła, ed.: *Centralny katalog polskich czasopism muzycznych i wydawnictw ciągłych o tematyce muzycznej: zbiory polskie* [The union catalogue of Pol. musical periodicals and serial pubns on the subject of music] (Warsaw, 1991)

J. Torres Mulas: *Las publicaciones periódicas musicales en España (1812–1990)* (Madrid, 2/1991)

M. O'Mara, ed.: *Union Catalogue of Music Serials in Australian Libraries* (Brisbane, 1992)

M. Svobodová and B. Geist: *Soupis cizojazyčných hudebních periodik* [List of foreign-language music periodicals] (Prague, 1992)

M. Suhonen: *Suomalaiset Musiikkilehdet* [Finnish music periodicals] (Helsinki, 1993)

J. Torres Mulas: *Periódicos musicales en bibliotecas españolas: primer repertorio* (Madrid, 1993)

E.-B. Fanger: *Katalog over musiktidsskrifter i danske forskningsbiblioteker* (Copenhagen, 1997)

T. Grande: *Catalogo dei periodici musicali delle biblioteche della Campania* (Naples, 1997)

Nihon no ongaku zasshi: kaidai-shu [Musical journals in Japan: explanatory notes], ed. Nihon Kindai Ongakukan (Tokyo, 1999)

(ii) General music literature

J.N. Forkel: *Allgemeine Litteratur der Musik, oder Anleitung zur Kenntnis musikalischer Bücher* (Leipzig, 1792/R)

C.F. Whistling: *Handbuch der musikalischen Literatur* (Leipzig, 1817, suppls.1–10 [for 1818–27]; rev. 2/1828/R by A. Hofmeister; suppls.1–3, 1829–39/R); contd for 6 vols. as *C.F. Whistlings Handbuch der musikalischen Literatur* (1844–67; vols.vii-xix, 1868–1943 as *Hofmeisters Handbuch der Musikliteratur: Verzeichnis sämtlicher Musikalien, Musikbücher, Zeitschriften, Abbildungen und plastischen Darstellungen* and from 1943 as *Deutsche Musikbibliographie*)

C.F. Becker: *Systematisch-chronologische Darstellung der musikalischen Literatur von der frühesten bis auf die neueste Zeit* (Leipzig, 1836/R; suppl. 1839/R)

H. Hirschbach: *Musikalisch-kritisches Repertorium aller neuen Erscheinungen im Gebiete der Tonkunst* (Leipzig, 1844; vol.ii 1845 as *Repertorium für Musik*)

A. Gebhart: *Repertorium der musikalischen Journalistik und Literatur* (Dillingen, 1850)

A. Büchting: *Bibliotheca musica oder Verzeichniss aller in Bezug auf die Musik . . . im deutschen Buchhandel erschienenen Bücher und Zeitschriften* (Nordhausen, 1867 [for 1847–66], 1872 [1867–71])

R. Eitner: *Bücherverzeichnis der Musik-Literatur aus den Jahren 1839 bis 1846 im Anschluss an Becker und Büchting* (Leipzig, 1885)

A. Aber: *Handbuch der Musikliteratur in systematisch-chronologischer Anordnung* (Leipzig, 1922/R), §E [52 music periodicals, 1754–1920]

E. Blom: *A General Index to Modern Musical Literature in the English Language* (London, 1927/R) [incl. periodicals, 1915–26]

B.D. Rocha da Silva Guimarães: *Primeiro esboço duma bibliografia musical portuguesa, com uma breve noticia histórica da música no nosso país* (Oporto, 1947)

Á. Davidsson: *Bibliografi över svensk musiklitteratur 1800–1945* (Uppsala, 1948, enlarged 2/1980)

W. Kahl and W.M. Luther: *Repertorium der Musikwissenschaft: Musikschrifttum, Denkmäler und Gesamtausgaben in Auswahl (1800–1950)* (Kassel, 1953), §E

K. Michałowski: *Bibliografia polskiego piśmiennictwa muzycznego* [Bibliography of Pol. music literature] (Kraków, 1955; suppl. 1964)

F. Lesure, ed.: *Ecrits imprimés concernant la musique*, RISM, B/VI/1–2 (1971)

C: ARTICLE INDEXES

(i) musical periodicals

Bibliographie des Musikschrifttums, ed. Institut für Musikforschung (Leipzig, 1936–9 [for 1936–8], 1941 [for 1939]; Frankfurt, 1954–64 [for 1950–59] ed. W. Schmieder; Hofheim am Taunus, from 1969 Mainz, 1968–98 [for 1960–87])

D.H. Daugherty, L. Ellinwood and R.S. Hill: *A Bibliography of Periodical Literature in Musicology and Allied Fields October 1938 – September 1940 with a Record of Graduate Theses* (Washington DC, 1940–43/R)

The Music Index: the Key of Current Music Periodical Literature, ed. Information Service (Detroit, 1949–/R) [reprinted as microfiche version]

C. Wallbaum: 'Index of Articles Published in Selected Musical Periodicals', *Brio*, i–x (1964–73)

Music Article Guide (Philadelphia, 1965/6–1995/6)

P. Suárez Urtubey: *La música en revistas argentinas* (Buenos Aires, 1970)

P. Copenhaver and P. Craig: 'Annotated Bibliography of Articles appearing in the National Association of College Wind and Percussion Instructors Journal, Fall 1968 thru Spring 1973', *NACWPI Journal, USA*, xxii/2 (1973–4), 15–21

Anuario de la prensa musical española, Instituto de Bibliografia Musical (Madrid, 1982– [for 1980/81–])

H.R. Cohen: 'An Introduction to the Fourth 'R': le répertoire international de la presse musicale du dix-neuvième siècle (RIPMxix)', *PM*, i (1983), 1–2

D.C.S. Snigurowicz: *L'art musical: 1860–70, 1872–94: Prototype RIPM Catalogue and Keyword-Author Index: an Assay of RIPM Methodology and Introductory Study of the Journal* (thesis, U. of British Columbia, 1983)

C. Clark and A. Linehan, eds.: *POMPI: Popular Music Periodicals Index* (1984/6–) [yearly cumulations]

E.W. Marasinghe: *Periodicals Index to Oriental Music* (Peradeniya, 1987/R)

F.C. Lange: 'Bibliografia: Revista musical de Venezuela', *Revista musical de Venezuela*, xiv (1993), 307–27

International Index to Music Periodicals (Alexandria, VA, 1996–) [CD-ROM and on-line index]

(ii) Non-musical periodicals

E. Refardt: *Verzeichnis der Aufsätze zur Musik in den nichtmusikalischen Zeitschriften der Universitätsbibliothek Basel* (Leipzig, 1925/R)

A.S. Wolff, ed.: *Speculum: Journal of Medieval Studies 1926–1961: a Check-List of Articles, Notes and Book Reviews pertaining to Music* (Denton, TX, 1961–)

S. Papierz: *Muzyka w polskich czasopismach niemuzycznach w latach 1800–1830* [Music in Pol. non-musical periodicals in the period 1800–1830], vol.2 (Kraków, 1962)

P. Kast: 'Bibliographie der Aufsätze zur Musik in aussermusikalischen [italienischen] Zeitschriften I', *AnMc*, no.1 (1963), 90–112; contd by other compilers in no.2 (1965), 144–228; no.3 (1966), 122–32; no.4 (1967), 207–367; no.5 (1968), 338–56; no.7 (1969), 248–70; no.9 (1970), 363–77; no.14 (1974), 506–26

T. Livanova: *Muzikal'naya bibliografiya russkoy periodicheskoy pechati XIX veka* [Music bibliography of Russ. 19th-century periodicals], ii (Moscow, 1963 [for 1826–50]); v/1, with O. Vinogradova (1971 [1861–70])

E. Szczawińska: *Muzyka w polskich czasopismach literackich i społecznych 1864–1900* [Music in Pol. literary and social periodicals in the period 1864–1900] (Kraków, 1964; ed. S. Dziki, 1973 [for 1831–63])

E. Szczawińska: *Muzyka w polskich czasopismach literackich i artystycznych 1901–1918* [Music in Pol. literary and art periodicals] (Kraków, 1971)

J. Szwedowska: *Muzyka w czasopismach polskich XVIII wieku* [Music in Pol. periodicals of the 18th century] (Kraków, 1975 [for 1730–64]; 1984 [1764–1800])

C. Höslinger: *Musik-Index zur 'Wiener Zeitschrift für Kunst, Literatur, Theater und Mode', 1816–1848* (Munich, 1980)

M.C. Peñas: 'Bibliografia de los articulos de interés musicológico en revistas navarras de estudios locales, entre 1941 y 1985', *RdMc*, ix (1986), 263–5

IMOGEN FELLINGER

Perissone, Francesco Bonardo. *See* BONARDO PERISSONE, FRANCESCO.

Perissone [Pierreson, Pyrison] **Cambio** (*b* ?*c*1520; *d c*1562). Singer and composer of South Netherlandish origin, active in Italy. In Doni's *Dialogo della musica* (Venice, 1544), he is described as a 'valente giovane' and as the possessor of a fine voice and a perfect technique. 'Perissone fiamengo' was granted a privilege by the Venetian senate (2 June 1545) to print a volume of madrigal settings of Petrarch's sonnets. On 14 July 1548 he was named a provisional, unsalaried member of the chapel at S Marco. Shortly after this, through a personal intervention by the doge, he became a regular member; he remained in the ducal chapel for at least ten years after that.

Perissone belonged to a circle of well-known Venetian musicians, including Parabosco and Donato, all pupils of Willaert. Two sonnets by Girolamo Fenaruolo (printed in 1546) mention Perissone next to Parabosco and Rore, as composers and friends of the printer Antonio Gardane. A connection with Rore is suggested by the presence of his pieces (including the first appearance of *Anchor che col partire*, a text also set by Perissone) in the *Primo libro a quattro voci* (1547[14]), and of works by Perissone in Rore's second and third books of five-voice madrigals. Perissone also wrote the dedicatory letter for Gardane's first edition of Rore's *Vergine bella* (1548) (present in the alto partbook only).

During the years 1545 to 1550 Perissone published four volumes of secular music. If he also wrote sacred music most of it must be lost; a single motet survives in print, and although a 'Pyrison', resident in Venice, is said in a letter of 25 November 1549 to have written a mass at the behest of a German merchant, the work is not known to survive. (Eitner's identification of a mass in *D-Bsb* 40091 as this work is mistaken.)

In 1552 Ortensio Lando (*Sette libri di cataloghi*) described him as living, singing and playing in Venice. During the 1550s Perissone was a member of the Compagnia di S Marco, a group of ducal singers who performed elsewhere in Venice, especially in the *scuole grandi*. He became a brother in the Scuola di S Marco in 1557.

When Perissone died, sometime in the 1560s, he was still considered a young man: Domenico Veniero in a sonnet lamented the musician as one who had been granted to his friends for but a brief time. The composer's names are here the subject of word-play: 'Ben *perì suon*, quel suona il nome stesso'; 'Quand egual *Cambio* in *Cambio* a noi fia dato/Di sì gran *Cambio*?'. To this sonnet Veniero's friend Fenaruolo answered in a similar vein: 'In un punto *perì suon* sì pregiato/E 'n sua vece mandò tristi lamenti/(*Duro Cambio*) il mar d'Adria in ogni lato.'

Perissone was indebted to Rore and Willaert, modelling his four-voice madrigals on those of Rore, and his villanellas and five-voice madrigals on those of Willaert. Particularly striking is Perissone's choice of four dialogue texts (published in *Il secondo libro*, 1550) and of two Petrarch sonnets (*Cantai hor piango* and *I piansi hor canto*, published in *Madrigali a cinque voci*, 1545) also set by Willaert in the *Musica nova* (1559). There are some explicit musical relationships between the sonnet settings by the two men. Since Willaert is unlikely to have modelled his pieces on the work of a young singer, Perissone probably had access to his teacher's madrigals in the *Musica nova* before its publication.

WORKS

Canzoni villanesche alla napolitana, 4vv (Venice, 1545); 1 piece in *BurneyH*, iii, 215; 1 ed. in Cw, viii (n.d.), 20; 2 ed. in *EinsteinIM*
Madrigali, 5vv (Venice, 1545); ed. in SCMad, ii (1987)
Primo libro di madrigali, 4vv (Venice, 1547[14]); ed. in SCMad, iii (1989)
Il segondo libro di madregali, 5vv (Venice, 1550)
Ad te Domine, 5vv, 1549[7]
Secular pieces in 1544[6], 1544[16], 1548[11], 1549[31], *c*1550[19], 1554[28], 1557[25], 1560[22], 1561[15], 1562[8], 1569[20]

BIBLIOGRAPHY

CaffiS; *EinsteinIM*
R. Eitner: 'Zwei Briefe von Georg Wytzel', *MMg*, viii (1876), 157–9
R.B. Lenaerts: 'La chapelle de Saint-Marc à Venise sous Adriaen Willaert (1527–1562)', *Bulletin de l'Institut historique belge de Rome*, xix (1938), 205–55
R. Giazotto: *Harmonici concenti in aere veneto* (Rome, 1954)
H. Meier: 'Zur Chronologie der Musica Nova Adrian Willaerts', *AnMc*, xii (1973), 71–96
J. Glixon: 'A Musicians' Union in Sixteenth-Century Venice', *JAMS*, xxxvi (1983), 392–421
G. Ongaro: *The Chapel of St. Mark's at the Time of Adrian Willaert* (diss., U. of North Carolina, Chapel Hill, 1986)
M. Feldman: *City Culture and the Madrigal in Venice* (Berkeley, 1995)

JAMES HAAR

Perkholtz, Lucas. *See* BERGHOLZ, LUCAS.

Perkins, Carl (*b* Tiptonville, TN, 9 April 1932; *d* Nashville, TN, 19 Jan 1998). American rock and roll singer, guitarist and songwriter. A rural upbringing exposed him to the blues music of his negro sharecropper neighbours which profoundly marked his later, highly influential, guitar style. In the mid-1950s Perkins became one of the principal recording artists for Sam Phillips's Sun label in Memphis. Through compositions such as *Blue Suede Shoes*, *Put your Cat Clothes On* and *Boppin the Blues*, he made a major contribution to the foundation of rock and roll and rockabilly music.

Like Chuck Berry, Perkins had an ear attuned to the argot and fashions of young Americans in the 1950s and the ability to distil these in a pithy lyric. Another Sun artist, Elvis Presley, made *Blue Suede Shoes* into a global rock and roll anthem in 1956. Perkins's own version of the song was a big hit in the United States but other recordings met with less commercial success. During the 1960s Perkins alternated between rock and country music, and for several years he toured with Johnny Cash for whom he wrote the hit song *Daddy Sang Bass*. His final recordings were issued posthumously on the album *Go Cat Go!* (Dinosaur, 1996) and featured duets with such admirers as George Harrison and Paul McCartney, Paul Simon and Willie Nelson. See also D. McGee: *Go, Cat, Go* (New York, 1995).

DAVE LAING

Perkins, Leeman L(loyd) (*b* Salina, UT, 27 March 1932). American musicologist. He took the BFA at the University of Utah in 1954 and the PhD at Yale in 1965 and began teaching at Boston University during summer 1964. In autumn 1964 he joined the music department of Yale University, where he taught until moving to the University of Texas at Austin in 1971. In autumn 1975 he was visiting associate professor at Columbia University, where he was appointed professor of music history in 1976; he chaired the department from 1985 to 1990. His principal area of research has been the music and theoretical writings of the late 15th and early 16th centuries. His investigations of manuscripts of sacred and secular vocal polyphony have led to several scholarly editions and show a concern for the editorial practices involved in presenting this music in modern transcriptions.

WRITINGS

The Motets of Jean Lhéritier (diss., Yale U., 1965)
'Notes bibliographiques au sujet de l'ancien fond musical de l'Eglise de Saint Louis des Français à Rome', *FAM*, xvi (1969), 57–71
'Mode and Structure in the Masses of Josquin', *JAMS*, xxvi (1973), 189–239
'Toward a Rational Approach to Text Placement in the Secular Music of Dufay's Time', *Dufay Conference: Brooklyn, NY, 1974*, 102–14
'Antoine Busnois and the d'Hacqueville Connection', *Musique naturelle et musique artificielle*, ed. M.B. Winn (Montreal, 1979), 49–64
'The Mellon Chansonnier as a Central European Source', *Musica antiqua VI: Bydgoszcz 1982*, 651–67

'The L'homme armé Masses of Busnoys and Okeghem: a Comparison', *JM*, iii (1984), 363–96

'Musical Patronage at the Royal Court of France under Charles VII and Louis XI', *JAMS*, xxxvii (1984), 507–66

'Modern Methods, Received Opinion and the Chansonnier', *ML*, lxix (1988), 356–64

'Toward a Typology of the "Renaissance" Chanson', *JM*, vi (1988), 421–47

'Ockeghem's *Prenez sur moi*: Reflections on Canons, Catholica, and Solmization', *MD*, xliv (1990), 119–83

ed., with P. Lefferts: *CMc*, nos.45–7 (1990) [Sanders Festschrift issue]

'At the Intersection of Social History and Musical Style: the Rondeaux and Virelais of the Manuscript Torino J.II.9', *The Cypriot-French Repertory of the Manuscript Torino J.II.9: Paphos 1992*, 433–62

'Text and Music in the Chansons of Busnoys: the Editorial Dilemma', *L'edizione critica tra testo musicale e testo letterario: Cremona 1992*, 165–79

'Modal Strategies in Okeghem's *Missa Cuiusvis toni*', *Music Theory and the Exploration of the Past*, ed. C. Hatch and D.W. Bernstein (Chicago, 1993), 59–71

'Modal Species and Mixtures in a Fifteenth-Century Chanson Repertory', *Modality in the Music of the Fourteenth and Fifteenth Centuries/Modalität in der Musik des 14. und 15. Jahrhunderts*, ed. U. Günther, L. Finscher and J. Dean (Neuhausen-Stuttgart, 1996), 177–201

Music in the Age of the Renaissance (New York, 1999)

EDITIONS

Jean Lhéritier: Opera omnia, CMM, xlviii (1969)
with H. Garey: *The Mellon Chansonnier* (New Haven, CT, 1979)
Masters and Monuments of the Renaissance (New York, 1980–)

PAULA MORGAN

Perkowski, Piotr (*b* Oweczacze, 17 March 1901; *d* Otwock, nr Warsaw, 12 Aug 1990). Polish composer and teacher. He studied composition with Statkowski at the Warsaw Conservatory and privately with Szymanowski in Warsaw and Roussel in Paris (1926–8), where he also attended the Ecole des Sciences Politiques. Between the wars he organized the Association of Young Polish Musicians in Paris. He was director of the Toruń Conservatory (1938–9), president of the Polish Composers' Union (1945–9) and a professor at the conservatories of Warsaw (1946–51, 1954–73) and Wrocław (1951–4); his pupils included Baird, Kotoński and Rudziński. Among the awards he received are the Kraków Music Award and a prize from the Polish Ministry of Culture (1966).

The main influences present in Perkowski's work are Szymanowski and post-Impressionist French music; his style is traditional, faithful to the primacy of melody. In earlier works there are qualities of emotional restraint and subtle, poetic atmosphere; his later music is often modelled on the rhythms and melodies of Polish folk music. Such pieces as the orchestral *Nokturn* and the Violin Concerto no.2 blend a specifically Polish emotional depth with programmatic intentions. Several of his compositions were lost during World War II.

WORKS
(*selective list*)

Ballets: Swantewit (3, Perkowski and J. Kapliński, after old Slavonic legend), 1930, rev. 1945–7, Poznań, 1948; Balladyna (2, after J. Słowacki), 1960–64, Warsaw, 1965; Klementyna (3, O. Obarska), 1963, Bytom, 1969

Orch: Pf Conc., lost; Fantasia, pf, orch, lost; Szkice toruńskie [Toruń Sketches], 1938 [only 2nd of 3 movts survives]; Vn Conc. no.1, 1938, lost, reconstructed 1947–8; Fantasia, 1939; Taniec rosyjski [Russian Dance], 1949; Sym. no.2, 1952–5; Uwertura warszawska, 1954; Nokturn, 1955; 3 tańce lubelskie [3 Lublin Dances], 1956; Vn Conc. no.2, 1959–60; Sinfonia drammatica, 1963; Vc Conc., 1973, rev. 1978; W stronę Atmy [In the Direction of Atma], str, pf, perc, 1978

Vocal-orch, choral: Sym. no.1, solo vv, chorus, org, orch, 1925, lost; Epitafium na śmierć Nikosa Belojanisa (cant., J. Hordyński), Bar, chorus, orch, 1952; Suita weselna [Wedding Suite], S, T, chorus, orch, 1952 [after Mazurian folk music]; Poematy Aben-Azama, Bar, small orch, 1975; choral songs and cants. on folk themes

Chbr: Krakowiak, vn, pf, 1926; Fantasia, fl, va, pf, 1926, lost; Sextet, cl, hn, tpt, pf trio, 1926, lost; Str Qt, 1930; Elegia, vc, org/pf, 1945; Karolowi Szymanowskiemu [To Szymanowski], vn, pf, 1952; Poemat, fl, pf, 1954; Sonatina, tpt, pf, 1954; Sonata, ob, pf, 1955; Str Qt no.2, 1978

Songs (1v, pf): 2 pieśni japońskie [2 Japanese Songs] (R. Kwiatkowski), 1924; 3 pieśni japońskie (Kwiatkowski), 1924; 2 pieśni (M. Pawlikowska, L. Staff), 1928–30; W imionniku [In the Album] (A. Mickiewicz), 1955; Ptaszek [A Little Bird] (A. Pushkin), 1959; Niebo w ogniu [Sky on Fire] (E. Szemplinska), 1969; others

Pf: Preludia, lost; Bagatelle, 1926; Etude, 1926; Sonata, 1926, lost, reconstructed 1949; 4 krakowiaki, 1927; 2 preludia, 1928; Łatwe utwory [Easy Pieces], 2 books, 1947, 1949; 4 łatwe utwory, 1953; 5 łatwych utworow, 1953

Principal publishers: Eschig, PWM

BIBLIOGRAPHY

Z. Mycielski: '"Swantewit" Perkowskiego', *Odrodzenie* (1948), 36 only

J. Cegiella, ed.: *Szkice do autoportretu polskiej muzyki współczesnej* [Sketches for a self-portrait of Polish contemporary music] (Kraków, 1976)

T. Kaczyński: 'Stowarzyszenie Młodych Muzyków Polaków w Paryzu' [The Association of Young Polish Musicians in Paris], *Muzyka*, xxiii/3 (1978), 5–15

BOGUSŁAW SCHÄFFER/R

Perle, George (*b* Bayonne, NJ, 6 May 1915). American composer and theorist. He studied composition with Wesley La Violette (1934–8) and Krenek (early 1940s), and was awarded the BA at DePaul University (1938) and the PhD at New York University (1956). A member of the faculty at the University of Louisville (1949–57), the University of California, Davis (1957–61), and Queens College, CUNY (1961–84), he has also held visiting professorships at Yale University (1965–6), the University of Southern California (summer 1965), SUNY, Buffalo (1971–2), the University of Pennsylvania (1976, 1980), Columbia University (1979, 1983), the University of California, Berkeley (Ernest Bloch Professor, 1989) and New York University (1994). He was elected to the American Academy of Arts and Letters (1978) and the National Academy of Arts and Sciences (1985); awards include the Pulitzer Prize (1986) in music (for Wind Quintet no.4), the MacArthur Fellowship (1986) and two Guggenheim Fellowships (1966, 1974). His book *The Operas of Alban Berg* (1980) won the Otto Kinkeldey Award of the American Musicological Society and the ASCAP Deems Taylor Award (1981). The articles 'Webern's 12-Tone Sketches' and 'The Secret Program of the *Lyric Suite*' also won the ASCAP Deems Taylor Award in, respectively, 1975 and 1978. He has been composer-in-residence at Tanglewood Music Center (1967, 1980, 1987), at the Marlboro Music Festival (1993) and with the San Francisco SO (1989–91). He was elected to the Institute of the American Academy and Institute of Arts and Letters in 1978.

In the 1930s Perle was among the first American composers to be attracted by the music and thought of Schoenberg, Berg and Webern. His interest, however, was not so much in the 12-note system itself as in the idea of a generalized systematic approach to dodecaphonic composition. Using some of the fundamental concepts of the 12-note system, such as set and inversion, he developed an approach to composition which attempts to incorporate

such 12-note ideas with some of the basic kinds of hierarchical distinction found in tonal practice, such as the concept of a 'key' as a primary point of reference. His system of '12-note tonality' (originally referred to as 'the 12-tone modal system'), developed continuously from 1939 (and in collaboration with Paul Lansky from 1969–73), is in simplest terms an attempt to create useful distinctions and differentiations in a 12-tone context by defining functional characteristics of pitch-class collections, in terms of the intervals formed by component pairs of notes, on the one hand, and the properties of these same pairs with respect to axes of symmetry, points about which they are symmetrically disposed, on the other. (In an abstract sense these two concepts are roughly analogous to familiar notions of 'mode' and 'key' in tonal music.)

The harmonic vocabulary of 12-note tonality is exclusively derived from 'cycle sets', ordered 12-note statements of complete collections of symmetrically related dyads (*see* TWELVE-NOTE COMPOSITION). The cyclic set differs from the general 12-note series not only in its structure but also in its use: akin to a scale in diatonic tonality, its function is referential, not literally determining note-to-note motion on the compositional surface. Paired forms of the cyclic sets generate arrays of chords which are related to one another by different types of symmetry. This approach was anticipated in some works by Berg (the first movement of the *Lyric Suite* and Act 2 scene i of *Lulu*) and Bartók (the fourth and fifth quartets) in their use of symmetrical relations as a basis for their harmonic language. Perle's approach does not define explicit procedures for composition but rather outlines a large and highly structured network of pitch-class and formal relations which can then serve as points of reference for compositional development. (In this sense, too, it is like tonal composition in that the composer's 'system' is a general guide to a musical language and a given composition constructs a unique interpretation of that language.)

Though most of Perle's compositions to 1967 and all since then are based on this approach, Perle has also written works that he described as

'freely' or 'intuitively' conceived, combining various serial procedures with melodically generated tone centers, intervallic cells, symmetrical formations, etc. A rhythmic concept, or rather ideal, toward which I progressed in these and other works was that of a beat, variable in duration but at the same time as tangible and coherent as the beat in classical music, and of an integration between the larger rhythmic dimensions and the minimal metric units.

These works include the Quintet for Strings (1958), three wind quintets (1959, 1960, 1967), and a series of monophonic works for solo instruments (1942–65). A consistent thread which runs through these pieces, as well as later works, is the construction of rhythmic relations through inter-tempo equivalences: e.g. triplet quavers in one tempo might equal crotchets in another. While this is a widely used technique, Perle uses it in a highly personal way, which has the effect of creating a general feeling of continuous rubato, adding a subtle flexibility to the underlying rhythmic sense. Interrelations of metre, rhythm, tempo, phrase structure and formal design are basic to his compositional thinking.

In comparison with much music of the time, the 'sound' of Perle's music and the manner in which he unfolds his musical ideas are usually straightforward and relatively uncomplicated. His music eschews the veneer of the avant garde and what he considers the wrong-headed association of musical complexity with perceptual difficulty. The complexities that concern him are those arising from the many levels on which his pitch, pitch-class and motivic relations interact and interrelate, and for him difficulties are only in making these relations as interesting and understandable as possible. In many of his compositions a few relatively simple musical ideas will appear in different ways and contexts so that the character and quality of these ideas become richer in the process.

Perle's writings on 20th-century music, particularly that of Schoenberg, Berg and Webern, Bartók and

Skryabin, have contributed much to a wider and deeper understanding of it. His work on Skryabin has made an important contribution in showing how analytical insights may be derived from idiosyncratic features of a composer's notation, while his book *Serial Composition and Atonality* has become a standard text. His most extensive work has been on the music of Berg and has revealed in great depth and detail the richness and subtlety of Berg's work, dispelling popular notions that Berg's music, in contrast with that of Schoenberg and Webern, is arbitrary in its use of 12-note and serial procedures; the two-volume *The Operas of Alban Berg* is also a detailed study of his life and complete works. After studying the materials for the incomplete third act of *Lulu*, in 1963, he published a series of articles which conclusively demonstrated that the opera could be accurately completed, and prepared the way for the publication of the complete opera in 1985. In January 1977 Perle discovered a score of Berg's *Lyric Suite*, annotated by the composer. The annotations unfold a secret programme inspired by Berg's love for Hanna Fuchs-Robettin, the wife of a Prague industrialist and sister of Franz Werfel. Her initials combine with Berg's to give the basic cell of the work, B–F–A–B♭ (in German, H–F–A–B). This discovery, together with Berg's letters to Hanna Fuchs-Robettin, uncovered by Perle at the same time and spanning the period from 1925 to Berg's death in 1935, refuted the description of Berg's life and character that had been authorized by his widow and accepted by every biographer of the composer.

Perle's work is deeply conservative in that his main effort has been to build a musical world whose logic and power is as consistent as that of traditional tonal practice. While this was also Schoenberg's aim in constructing the 12-note system, for Perle there was an intolerable contradiction in Schoenberg's concept of the 12-note series as 'invented to substitute for some of the unifying and formative advantages of scale and tonality' at the same time as it 'functions in the manner of a motive'. Perle's cyclic sets act solely as the basis of the harmonic and contrapuntal syntax of his music: they do not function as motifs. Though initially inspired by the Vienna school, his later writings (*The Listening Composer*) reveal a close connection with Skryabin, Bartók, and Stravinsky as well. He argues that the seemingly disparate aspects of post-tonal music share structural elements that derive from a common source – inversional and cyclic symmetry inherent in the 12-note scale – and that this implies a system of relations as coherent as that of diatonic tonality.

WORKS
(*selective list*)

ORCHESTRAL
Solemn Procession, band, 1947; 3 Movts for Orch, 1960; Serenade no.1, va, chbr orch, 1962; 6 Bagatelles, 1965; Vc Conc., 1966; Serenade no.2, 11 insts, 1968; Concertino, pf, wind, timp, 1979; A Short Sym., 1980; Serenade no.3, pf, chbr orch, 1983; Dance Fantasy, 1986; New Fanfares, brass ens, 1987; Lyric Intermezzo, 15 players, 1987; Sinfonietta I, 1987; Pf Conc., no.1, 1990; Sinfonietta II, 1990; Adagio, 1992; Pf Conc. no.2, 1992; Transcendental Modulations, 1993

CHAMBER
For 6 insts: For Pf and Wind, fl, eng hn, cl, hn, bn, pf, 1988; Critical Moments, fl + pic, B♭ cl + E♭ cl + b cl, vn, vc, pf, perc, 1996
5 insts: Qnt for Str, 2 vn, 2 va, vc, 1958; 4 Wind Qnts no.1, 1959; no.2, 1960; no.3, 1967; no.4, 1984; Sonata a cinque, b trbn, A cl + E♭ cl + b cl, vn, vc, pf, 1986; Nightsong, fl, cl, vn, vc, pf, 1988; Duos, hn, str qt, 1995

4 insts: Str Qt no.2, 1942, unpubd; Str Qt no.5, 1960, rev. 1967; Str Qt no.7, 1973; Sonata a quattro, fl, cl, vn, vc, 1982; Windows of Order (Str Qt no.8), 1988; Brief Encounters (Str Qt no.9), 1998
2 insts: Lyric Piece, vc, pf, 1946; Sonata quasi una fantasia, cl, pf, 1972; Sonata, vc, pf, 1985

SOLO INSTRUMENT
Str: Sonata, va, 1942; Hebrew Melodies, vc, 1945; Sonata, vc, 1947; Sonata no.1, vn, 1959; Monody II, db, 1962; Sonata no.2, vn, 1963; Solo Partita, vn, va, 1965
Winds: 3 Sonatas, cl, 1943; Monody I, fl, 1960; 3 Inventions, bn, 1962
Pf: Pantomime, Interlude, and Fugue, 1937; Little Suite, 1939, unpubd; Modal Suite, 1940; 6 Preludes, 1946; Sonata, 1950; Short Sonata, 1964; Toccata, 1969; Suite in C, 1970; Fantasy-Variations, 1971; 6 Etudes, 1976; Ballade, 1981; 6 New Etudes, 1984; Sonatina, 1986; Lyric Intermezzo, 1987; Phantasyplay, 1995; 6 Celebratory Inventions, 1995; Chansons cachées, 1997; Musical Offerings, left hand, 1998; 9 Bagatelles, 1999

VOCAL
2 Rilke Songs, Mez, pf, 1941; 'And so the Swans …', a cappella chorus, 1961; Sonnets to Orpheus, a cappella chorus, 1974; Songs of Praise and Lamentation, chorus, orch, 1974; 13 Dickinson Songs, S, pf, 1977–8

INCIDENTAL MUSIC
The Birds (Aristophanes, trans. W. Arrowsmith), solo vv, chorus, fl + pic, E♭ cl + bar sax, tpt, trbn, va, cel + hpd + hmn + pf, perc, 1961

Principal publishers: Presser, Boelke-Bomart, Gunmar, ECS Publishing

WRITINGS
(*selective list*)

'Evolution of the Tone-Row: the Twelve-Tone Modal System', *MR*, ii (1941), 273–87; It. trans. in *Boletín latíno-americano de música*, v (1941), 421–34
'Twelve-Tone Tonality', *MMR*, lxxiii (1943), 175–9
'Integrative Devices in the Music of Machaut', *MQ*, xxxiv (1948), 169–76
'The Chansons of Antoine Busnois', *MR*, xi (1950), 89–97
'Schoenberg's Late Style', *MR*, xiii (1952), 274–82
'The Harmonic Problem in Twelve-Tone Music', *MR*, xv (1954), 257–67
'The Possible Chords in Twelve-Tone Music', *The Score*, no.9 (1954), 54–63
'Symmetrical Formations in the String Quartets of Béla Bartók', *MR*, xvi (1955), 300–12
'The Music of Miriam Gideon', *Bulletin of American Composers Alliance*, vii/4 (1958), 2–6
'The Music of Lulu: a New Analysis', *JAMS*, xxi (1959), 185–200
'Theory and Practice in Twelve-Tone Music (Stadlen Reconsidered)', *The Score*, no.25 (1959), 58–64
'Atonality and the Twelve-Note System in the United States', *The Score*, no.27 (1960), 51–9; Sp. trans. in *Buenos Aires musical*, xiv (1959), 40–51
Serial Composition and Atonality: an Introduction to the Music of Schoenberg, Berg, Webern (Berkeley, 1962, 6/1991)
'An Approach to Simultaneity in Twelve-Tone Music', *PNM*, iii/1 (1964–5), 91–101
'The Character of Lulu: a Sequel', *MR*, xxv (1964), 311–19
'*Lulu*: the Formal Design', *JAMS*, xvii (1964), 179–92
'A Note on Act III of *Lulu*', *PNM*, ii/2 (1963–4), 8
'*Lulu*: Thematic Material and Pitch Organization', *MR*, xxvi (1965), 269–302
'Pierrot Lunaire', *The Commonwealth of Music, in Honor of Curt Sachs*, ed. G. Reese and R. Brandel (New York, 1965), 307–12
'The Score of *Lulu*', *PNM*, iii/2 (1964–5), 127–32
'Erwiderung auf Willi Reichs Aufsatz "Drei Notizblätter zu Alban Bergs *Lulu*"', *SMz*, cvii (1967), 163–5
'The Musical Language of *Wozzeck*', *Music Forum*, i (1967), 204–59
'Die Personen in Bergs *Lulu*', *AMw*, xxiv (1967), 283–90
'Die Reihe als Symbol in Bergs "*Lulu*"', *ÖMz*, xxii (1967), 589–93; Eng. trans. in *Essays on the Music of J.S. Bach and Other Divers Subjects: a Tribute to Gerhard Herz*, ed. R.L. Weaver (Louisville, KY, 1981), 304–8
'*Woyzeck* and *Wozzeck*', *MQ*, liii (1967), 206–19
'*Wozzeck*: ein zweiter Blick auf das Libretto', *NZM*, Jg.129 (1968), 218–21

'Representation and Symbol in the Music of *Wozzeck*', *MR*, xxxii (1971), 281–308

'Webern's Twelve-Tone Sketches', *MQ*, lvii (1971), 1–25

Review of A. Schoenberg: *Style and Idea*, ed. L. Stein (London, 1975), *MQ*, lxii (1976), 435–41

'Berg's Master Array of Interval Cycles', *MQ*, lxiii (1977), 1–30

Review of J. Maegaard: *Studien zur Entwicklung des dodekaphonen Satzes bei Arnold Schönberg* (Copenhagen, 1972), *MQ*, lxiii (1977), 273–83

'The Secret Programme of the *Lyric Suite*', *MT*, cxviii (1977), 629–32, 709–13, 809–13

'The String Quartets of Béla Bartók', *A Musical Offering: Essays in Honor of Martin Bernstein*, ed. E.H. Clinkscale and C. Brook (New York, 1977), 193–210

Twelve-Tone Tonality (Berkeley, 1977, enlarged 2/1996)

'The Cerha Edition', *International Alban Berg Society Newsletter*, no.8 (1979), 5–7; repr. in *PNM*, xvii/2 (1979), 251–9

'The Complete "Lulu"', *MT*, cxx (1979), 115–20

'Berg, Alban', *Grove6*

with P. Lansky: 'Atonality', 'Twelve-Note Composition', *Grove6*

'"Mein geliebtes Almschi": Briefe von Alban und Helene Berg an Alma Mahler Werfel', *ÖMz*, xxxv (1980), 2–15

The Operas of Alban Berg, i: *Wozzeck* (Berkeley, 1980)

'Das Film-Zwischenspiel in Bergs Oper *Lulu*', *ÖMz*, xxxvi (1981), 631–8; Eng. orig. in *International Alban Berg Society Newsletter*, no.11 (1982), 3–8

'Friedrich's *Lulu*', *Tempo*, no.137 (1981), 2–7

'Der Tod der Geschwitz', *ÖMz*, xxxvi (1981), 19–28

'The "Sketched-In" Vocal Quartet of *Lulu*, Act III', *International Alban Berg Society Newsletter*, no.12 (1982), 12–13

'Scriabin's Self-Analyses', *MAn*, iii (1984), 101–22

'An Introduction to *Lulu*', *OQ*, iii/3 (1985), 87–111

'Berg: Martyr to His Profession', *ON*, xlix/9 (1984–5), 10–13

The Operas of Alban Berg, ii: *Lulu* (Berkeley, 1985)

Review of the 1985 edition of *Lulu*, *Notes*, xliii (1987), 915–18

'Some Thoughts on an Ideal Production of *Lulu*', *JM*, vii (1989), 244–53

'The First Four Notes of *Lulu*', *The Berg Companion*, ed. D. Jarman (London, 1989), 269–89

The Listening Composer (Berkeley, 1990)

'Pitch-Class Set Analysis: an Evaluation', *JM*, vii (1990), 151–72

'Programme Notes, Chronology and Bibliography', *An Affair With Numbers: the Music of Alban Berg*, ed. G. Hall (BBC, 17–19 Jan 1992), 4–72, 81

'Symmetry, the Twelve-Tone Scale, and Tonality', *Contemporary Music Review*, vi/2 (1992), 81–96

'Krenek', *MQ*, lxxvii (1993), 145–53

'Standortbestimmung', *ÖMz*, lxxvii (1993), 152–60

The Right Notes: Twenty-Three Selected Essays by George Perle on Twentieth-Century Music (Stuyvesant, NY, 1995)

Style and Idea in the Lyric Suite of Alban Berg (Stuyvesant, NY, 1995)

'Berg's Style of Freedom', *MT*, cxxxix (1998), 12–31 ed.: *Alban Berg: Lyric Suite/Lyrische Suite. The Secret Vocal Part/Die geheime Gesangsstimme* (Vienna, 1999)

BIBLIOGRAPHY

H. Weinberg: 'The Music of George Perle', *American Composers Alliance Bulletin*, x/3 (1962), 6–11

L. Kraft: 'The Music of George Perle', *MQ*, lvii (1971), 444–65

P. Lansky: *Affine Music* (diss., Princeton U., 1973)

B. Saylor: 'A New Work by George Perle', *MQ*, lxi (1975), 471–5

O. Knussen: 'George Perle, Composer', *Tempo*, no.137 (1981), 38–40

R. Swift: 'A Tonal Analog: the Tone-Centered Music of George Perle', *PNM*, xxi1–2 (1982–3), 257–84

M. Boriskin: 'Six New Etudes: a Strand of Perle's', *Clavier*, xxvi/4 (1987), 11–15

D. Miller: 'Perle on Perle', *George Perle* (n.p., 1987), 5–22 [interview]

J. Carson: 'A Talk with George Perle on Music History, Tonality, and Composing', *Strings*, iv (1989), 40–43

P. Lansky: 'The Listening Composer', *George Perle: a Catalog of Works* (Boston, 1991), 6–7

E. Antokoletz: 'Twelve-Tone Tonality', *Twentieth-Century Music* (Englewood Cliffs, NJ, 1992), 426–7

P. Carrabré: *Twelve-Tone Tonality and the Music of George Perle* (diss., CUNY, 1993)

International Journal of Musicology, iv (1995) [Perle 80th birthday Festschrift issue; incl. E. Antokoletz: 'George Perle's *The Listening Composer*', 13–23; J. Smith: 'George and the Dragon: Reflections from a Chopin Etude', 25–43; J. Carr: 'George Perle and the Computer: an Uneasy Alliance', 207–15; C. Porter: 'Five to Four Complexities in George Perle's *Nocturne*', 217–29; P. Carrabré: 'Music as Linguistic Analog', 231–9; P. Lansky: 'Being and Going', 241–52; J. Leleu: 'La notion de "Background Structure" chez George Perle: de l'étude du langage musical au déchiffrement des oeuvres', 253–90; Eng. trans. in *International Journal of Musicology*, v (1996), 287–322; D. Pitt: 'What is Tonality?', 291–300; D. Headlam: 'Tonality and Twelve-Tone Tonality: the Recent Music of George Perle', 301–33]

D. Headlam: Introduction to G. Perle: *The Right Notes: Twenty-Three Selected Essays by George Perle on Twentieth-Century Music* (Stuyvesant, NY, 1995), x–xiii

S. Rosenhaus: *Harmonic Motion in George Perle's Wind Quintet no.4* (diss., New York U., 1995)

A. Whittall: 'Double Dealer', *MT*, cxxxvii (1996), 25–7

M. Graubart: 'The Writings of George Perle', *Tempo*, no.196 (1996), 37–41

M. Steinberg: *The Concerto* (New York and Oxford, 1998), 337–42

PAUL LANSKY

Perlea, Jonel (*b* Ograda, Romania, 13 Dec 1900; *d* New York, 29 July 1970). Romanian conductor and composer, active also in the USA. He studied in Munich and Leipzig and, except for a year at Rostock (1924–5), conducted mostly in Bucharest, becoming musical director at the Romanian Opera in 1934. He spent the last year of the war in a German internment camp. Afterwards, he conducted opera in Italy, and went to the Metropolitan, New York, in 1949, making his début with *Tristan und Isolde*. The urgency, clarity and beautiful orchestral sonority of that performance were remarkable, and he made an equally strong impression that season in *Carmen*, *La traviata* and *Rigoletto*. He became the victim of internal intrigues and stayed at the Metropolitan for only one season (the new general manager in 1950 offered him only *Die Fledermaus*).

Perlea continued to conduct opera in Italy (giving the première of Nino Rota's *Il capello di paglio di Firenze* in Palermo in 1955), but his American career was unsuccessful. Weakened by a heart attack in 1957, then crippled by a stroke, he learnt to conduct with his left arm alone. In his later years, having become a naturalized American, he taught and conducted at the Manhattan School of Music, was musical director of the Connecticut SO (from 1955) and once more made a stirring impression with his performances of *Tosca* for Sarah Caldwell's American National Opera Company in 1967. His compositions, somewhat in the style of Hindemith, include works for orchestra, a string quartet, a piano quintet and songs.

MICHAEL STEINBERG

Perlemuter, Vlado [Vladislas] (*b* Kowno [now Kaunas], 26 May 1904). French pianist of Polish birth. He moved to Paris at an early age and studied privately with Moszkowski, from whom he received his grounding as a virtuoso. He then studied with Cortot at the Paris Conservatoire, where he won a *premier prix* in 1919, the *prix d'honneur* in 1920 and the Prix Diémer in 1921. He also worked with Robert Lortat and privately with Ravel, whose complete works he was among the first to perform in public. Numerous concerts and recordings established his international reputation after 1945. His recordings of Ravel's works reveal a wide range of sonorities and, in such works as *Gaspard de la nuit*, strong evocations of orchestral instruments. His Chopin playing is also outstanding: in the Etudes, the Ballades and the Mazurkas in particular he achieves a wonderful range of tone-colour, a rhythmic subtlety, and a balance between line and detail that would be difficult to surpass. That he is less renowned than others whose readings of Chopin cannot compare with his own is perhaps due, on the one hand, to an occasional lapse of memory, and on the other to a temperament that is self-effacing – and no doubt to a conception of the music that is very grand and simple, and neither fastidious nor showy. From 1951 to 1976 he was a leading professor at the Paris Conservatoire, where his students included Michel Dalberto, Jean-François Heisser and Jacques Rouvier. He has also given master-classes in Canada, Japan and Great Britain. Perlemuter described his work with Ravel in a book written with Hélène Jourdan-Morhange, *Ravel d'après Ravel* (Lausanne, 1953; Eng. trans., 1988).

BIBLIOGRAPHY

J. Methuen-Campbell: 'A Master of Nuance', *Records and Recordings*, xxii/7 (1978–9), 16–18
J. Methuen-Campbell: *Chopin Playing* (London, 1981)
J. Roy: 'Vlado Perlemuter: les leçons du maître', *Le monde de la musique*, no.123 (1989), 36–41
C. Timbrell: *French Pianism* (White Plains, NY, and London, 1992, enlarged 3/1999)

WILLIAM GLOCK/CHARLES TIMBRELL

Perli, Lisa. *See* LABBETTE, DORA.

Perlis, Vivian (*b* Brooklyn, NY, 26 April 1928). American musicologist. She was educated at the University of Michigan (BM 1949, MM 1952), where she studied the history of music and also the piano and harp. A graduate student in musicology at Columbia University (1962–4), she taught the history of music at several colleges in New England before becoming a reference librarian at Yale University in 1967. In 1972 Perlis founded Oral History, American Music, also based at Yale, and has continued as its director. The project is an extensive repository on tape and videotape of source material on composers and other major figures in American music. Her other activities have included lecturing and teaching for the American Studies programme and the School of Music at Yale. She has collaborated on several recordings and television documentaries, the latter including *Memories of Eubie* (1980), on the jazz pianist Eubie Blake. Her work represents an imaginative and timely contribution to the investigation of the recent history of American music.

WRITINGS

'Ives and Oral History', *Notes*, xxviii (1971–2), 629–42
Charles Ives Remembered: an Oral History (New Haven, CT, 1974)
ed., with H.W. Hitchcock: *An Ives Celebration: Brooklyn, NY and New Haven, CT, 1974*
'The Futurist Music of Leo Ornstein', *Notes*, xxxi (1974–5), 735–50
Two Men for Modern Music: E. Robert Schmitz and Herman Langinger (Brooklyn, NY, 1978)
'Charles Ives: Victorian Gentleman or American Folk Hero?', *Folk Music and Modern Sound*, ed. W. Ferris and M.L. Hart (Jackson, MS, 1982), 141–50
ed.: *Charles Ives Papers* (New Haven, CT, 1983)
with A. Copland: *Copland* (New York, 1984–9) [Copland's autobiography]
'Monumenta Americana Revisited', *A Celebration of American Music: Words and Music in Honor of H. Wiley Hitchcock*, ed. R.A. Crawford, R.A. Lott and C.J. Oja (Ann Arbor, 1990), 439–48

PAULA MORGAN

Perlman, Itzhak (*b* Tel-Aviv, 31 Aug 1945). Israeli violinist. He initially taught himself to play, first on a toy fiddle and then on a child's violin. At four he was stricken with poliomyelitis which left him permanently disabled. During a year's convalescence he continued to practise and he then entered the Tel-Aviv Academy of Music to study with Rivka Goldgart. By the time he gave his first solo recital, at ten, he had already made a number of appearances with the Ramat-Gan and Broadcasting Orchestras. In 1958 he played twice on the 'Ed Sullivan Show' on television in New York and decided to remain there, making a nationwide US tour and entering the Juilliard School of Music to study with Dorothy Delay and Ivan Galamian. He made his Carnegie Hall début in 1963 and the following year won the Leventritt Memorial Award. In 1965 he toured his native country and in the 1965–6 and 1966–7 seasons he visited most of the major North American cities. In the 1967–8 season he made major débuts in Europe, including London and Paris, and since then he has been recognized not just as the finest violinist of his generation but as one of the greatest musical talents to emerge since World War II.

Although he has to play sitting down, Perlman is an immensely strong violinist with no discernible flaws in his technique, producing a big tone of great beauty and phrasing with immense breadth when the music demands it. An outgoing, genial character, he is able to call on deep reserves of emotion and humanity; and he has dominated the last quarter of the 20th century with performances ranging from the scintillating to the Olympian. When he is on his best form he can match any player of the past in the major concertos, from Bach onwards, although his approach to Baroque and Classical works is unashamedly Romantic. His numerous recordings include the Bach solo sonatas and partitas, the Paganini *Caprices* and much of the virtuoso repertory, as well as profound interpretations of Bach's Double Concerto and Mozart's Sinfonia concertante with Zukerman; the Mozart sonatas with Barenboim; the Beethoven and Brahms concertos with Barenboim conducting; the Beethoven sonatas with Ashkenazy; and the Berg and Stravinsky concertos with Ozawa. In chamber music he has often been heard, in the concert hall or on recordings, with such colleagues as Barenboim, Zukerman, Ashkenazy, Martha Argerich, Bruno Canino and Lynn Harrell. For many years Perlman has been associated with the Aspen Music Festival in Colorado, and he teaches at Brooklyn College, New York. In 1996 he was awarded the Royal Philharmonic Society's gold medal. Although he has generally made light of his disability, he has on occasion been a trenchant spokesman for the disabled. Works have been written for him by Robert Mann, Earl Kim and Robert Starer. He plays the 1714 'Soil' Stradivari.

BIBLIOGRAPHY

B. Schwarz: *Great Masters of the Violin* (London, 1983), 601–6
D. Rooney: 'Courage and Ability', *The Strad*, c (1989), 300–03
R.D. Lawrence: 'Pearls of Wisdom', *The Strad*, c (1989), 304–8
H. Roth: *Violin Virtuosos from Paganini to the 21st Century* (Los Angeles, 1997), 220–27
B.L. Sand: 'Introducing Professor Perlman', *The Strad*, cvi (1995), 1146–51

TULLY POTTER

Perm'. Russian city, on the western slopes of the Urals. From 1940 to 1957 it was known as Molotov. The musical life of the city has traditionally centred on the opera house built in 1878. Perm''s first opera season took place the following year, when *A Life for the Tsar*, *Ruslan and Lyudmila*, *Faust* and *Aida* were performed. Amateur music-making existed at a high level in the late 19th century, and the city's amateur orchestra performed symphonies and piano concertos by such composers as Beethoven and Liszt. The works of Mozart, Schubert, Glinka and Tchaikovsky were heard at chamber and orchestral concerts under the aegis of the Philharmonic Society (1908–12). Concerts of sacred music were organized by church choirs, and featured works by Arkhangel'sky, Grechaninov, Haydn and others. Between 1890 to 1917 there was a remarkable growth in the number of folk choirs in Perm'. Village and factory choirs (in 1913 there were a total of 290) performed folksongs and works by major Russian composers; between 1911 and 1913 scenes from *A Life for the Tsar*, in a production by A.D. Gorodtsov, were performed by peasants in numerous locations in and around the city.

After the upheavals of the Revolution the city's musical life was resumed in the 1920s. Much of the opera house's repertory consisted of now forgotten works with an ideological slant. A powerful impulse was given to the opera house's development by the evacuation to Perm' during World War II of the troupe of the Leningrad Opera and Ballet Theatre and of a number of leading Russian musicians. All the operas and ballets of Tchaikovsky have been performed in Perm''s opera house, which was renamed after that composer in 1965. In 1969 it became the Permskiy Gosudarstvennïy Akademicheskiy Teatr Operï i Baleta imeni P.I. Chaikovskogo (Tchaikovsky State Academic Theatre of Opera and Ballet). In the 1980s a Tchaikovsky festival and a Prokofiev festival were held in the city. For several decades after World War II there was a tradition of Monday symphony concerts in Perm'. The Urals State Chamber Choir, founded in 1975, tours frequently and has established a reputation as one of the best choirs in Russia; its repertory consists mainly of Russian sacred music.

Political changes in the late 1980s brought increased artistic freedom, and led to the creation of a number of new musical organizations: chamber, vocal and folk ensembles, and secular and church choirs. A composers' union was formed in Perm' by ten local composers. Under its auspices major operatic, orchestral, choral and chamber works have been composed and performed. In 1991 a children's school of composition, the only such institution in Russia, was founded in the city. The annual Perm' Festival, inaugurated in 1992, features well-known Russian performers; artists to have appeared at the festival include the pianist Nikolay Petrov, the violinist Sergey Stadler and the conductors Vladimir Fedoseyev, Vladimir Spivakov, Pavel Kogan and Mikhail Pletnev.

Musical education in Perm' is provided by 15 children's music schools, a music college (founded in 1924) and the Institute for Culture and the Arts (1975). The development of recording is a recent feature of musical life in the city, and the two leading studios have released CDs and cassettes of both classical and variety music.

BIBLIOGRAPHY

V.S. Verkholantsev: *Gorod Perm': yego proshloye i nastoyashcheye* [The city of Perm': its past and present] (Perm', 1913)
Yu. Keldïsh, ed.: *Muzïkal'naya èntsiklopediya* (Moscow, 1973–)
B.V. Asaf'yev: *Narodnopevcheskoye delo v Permskoy gubernii* [Folksong activity in the Perm' province] (Leningrad, 1980)

IGOR' VLADIMIROVICH ANUFRIYEV

Permont, Haim (*b* Vilnius, 1950). Israeli composer of Lithuanian birth. He studied at the Rubin Academy in Jerusalem with Kopytman among others and at the University of Pennsylvania (PhD 1985), where his teachers included George Crumb, Richard Wernick and Jay Reese. After accepting a lectureship at the Rubin Academy in 1985, he became dean of theory and composition (from 1995). In 1996 he was appointed composer-in-residence of the Haifa SO. His honours include prizes from CBS and ASCAP, Israeli ACUM prizes (1993–4) and the Israeli Prime Minister's Prize (1995).

Believing that music emanates from realignments with tradition, Permont has endorsed a pluralistic compositional attitude. *Elegy*, a meditative work for piano and orchestra, exemplifies this view: bitonal harmonies produce a rich modality, while octatonic patterns and structures derived from major 3rds and tritones are also characteristic. His vocal settings project a romantic aesthetic. *Like the Leaden Sky Before It Rains*, written in commemoration of the victims of Terezín, illustrates his imaginative use of a range of compositional idioms, from traditional tonality to dense atonal counterpoint. (R. Fleisher: *Twenty Israeli Composers*, Detroit, 1997).

WORKS
(*selective list*)

In memoriam, orch, 1982, rev. 1996; Suite, pf (1986); For Oboe, ob, str trio, 1988; Hazar La-Darom [A Return to the South] (A. Kovner), A, orch (1989); Pf Qnt, 1989; Like the Leaden Sky Before It Rains (Terezín boy, trans. L. Goldberg), A, SATB, orch, 1990; Niggun 1, fl, orch, 1990; Symphonette, orch, 1992; Haben yakir li [Dear Son of Mine] (op, T. Al-Yagon), 1995; Niggun 2, hp, orch, 1996

JEHOASH HIRSHBERG

Permutation fugue. A type of composition that brings together certain characteristics of fugue and of canon, namely: (1) The voices enter successively, as in fugue, each waiting until the preceding voice has stated the opening theme. (2) Entries alternate between tonic and dominant. (3) Each voice, once it has completed its statement of the opening theme, continues by stating two or three additional themes of the same length, all voices stating these themes in the same order. (4) There is almost no non-thematic material; that is, when a voice has completely stated all themes, it begins the series over again, either immediately or after a rest, and restates all themes, again in the same order. A classic example of a permutation fugue is the opening chorus of Bach's cantata *Himmelskönig, sei willkommen* BWV182. The German term *Permutationsfuge* was coined in 1938 by Werner Neumann to describe the most common way in which Bach's vocal fugues, especially those in his early works such as BWV182, were constructed. The word reflects the manner in which the themes appear in myriad vertical permutations, for which reason the composer must be sure that the themes function properly in INVERTIBLE COUNTERPOINT. Permutation fugue grew out of an interest in combining fugue with invertible counterpoint manifested among a circle of German composers working in Hamburg and Lübeck in the 1660s and 70s that included Reincken, Weckmann, Bernhard, Buxtehude and Theile. Although the sonatas of Reincken's *Hortus musicus* include several fugues with most of the above characteristics, Theile wrote what is probably the first true permutation fugue for his *Musicalisches Kunst-Buch*, and it was probably from this treatise, which circulated widely in central Germany, that Bach acquired the idea. Because certain elements of the 'classic' fugue are not present, such as the use of episodes or thematic statements in related keys, there is some disagreement among present-day scholars on whether permutation fugues should be thought of in the same category as fugue. There is no questioning, however, that musicians of Bach's time would have so classified them. (P. Walker: 'The Origin of the Permutation Fugue', *The Creative Process*, Studies in the History of Music, iii (New York, 1992), 51–91)

PAUL WALKER

Pernambuco. State in north-east Brazil. It had one of the earliest musical establishments in the Portuguese colony. The city of Olinda, founded in the mid-16th century, became during that century the seat of a bishopric, and remained the seat of the diocese until 1833. The first known *mestre de capela* at Olinda was Gomes Correia, appointed in 1564 and succeeded by the end of the century by Paulo Serrão. Several names of 17th-century *mestres de capela* survive in church documents, but not a single composition has been discovered. In the city of Recife (the capital of Pernambuco) musical institutions developed, especially during the 17th and 18th centuries. A large number of documents reveal some 600 musicians (instrumentalists, singers, composers and organ builders) working in the area at that period. A frequently praised musician of the 17th century is João de Lima, whose works were considered worthy of publication even 50 years after his death 'for the instruction of music professors'. Another musician of excellent reputation as a composer and performer was Inácio Ribeiro Noya, born in Recife in 1688; however none of his works is extant. The mulatto Manoel de Almeida Botelho (*b* 1721) was described in a contemporary account as 'one of the most famous composers of the present age'. His works (e.g. a four-part mass with two violins, a *Lauda Jerusalem*, three *Tantum ergo* settings and various sonatas and toccatas for keyboard and for guitar) were eagerly sought in Lisbon by professional musicians. The composer to have gained most attention, however, is Luiz Álvares Pinto (1719–?1789), who was *mestre de capela* at S Pedro dos Clérigos in Recife (1782–9) and who founded the Irmandade de Cecília dos Músicos in the same city in about 1787. A setting of the *Te Deum* by him was discovered by Jaime Diniz in 1967. The main organ builder of 18th-century Brazil, Agostinho Rodrigues Leite (1722–86), was also a native of Recife; he built organs for Recife and Olinda and also for Salvador (Bahia) and Rio de Janeiro. Other musicians or *mestres de capela* of colonial Pernambuco to have been studied are Manoel da Cunha, Jerônimo de Souza Pereira, Máximo Pereira Garros, Jerônimo Coelho de Carvalho and Salvador Francisco Leite (son of the organ builder). Secular musical activities during the colonial period in Pernambuco were apparently limited.

During the 19th century performances of art music were concentrated in Recife and focussed principally on sacred music and opera and, later, amateur salon music, from which much of the local piano repertory developed. A number of European musicians, such as the Italian Joseph Fachinetti (*c*1810–*c*1870), settled in the city, greatly contributing to operatic and concert life and to music education. Several concert organizations were founded during the century, including the Sociedade Teatral, the Sociedade Filarmônica and the Ateneu Musical do Recife, as well as several theatres, such as the Teatro de Apolo, Casa da Ópera, Teatro da Rua da Praia and Teatro S Isabel. In the latter part of the century several native composers emerged, notably Euclides Aquino da Fonseca (1854–1929) and Marcelino Cleto (1842–1922).

Although 20th-century musical life in Recife developed steadily, it did not offer the same opportunities as the other major Brazilian cities of Rio de Janeiro, São Paulo and Salvador. Thus renowned native Pernambucan composers, such as Marlos Nobre, made their careers elsewhere in Brazil. However, Recife contains a number of organizations that have helped to sustain musical life in the city; these include a symphony orchestra and the music departments of the Federal University of Pernambuco and of several private schools. In addition, the city has been a major centre of regional popular music, with famous Carnival parades, *maracatus*, and some of the most celebrated figures in contemporary Brazilian popular music, notably Chico Science.

BIBLIOGRAPHY

F.A. Pereira da Costa: *Anais pernambucanos* (Recife, 1951–66; 2/1983–7)
J.C. Diniz: *Músicos pernambucanos do passado* (Recife, 1969–71)
J.C. Diniz: *Notas sobre o piano e seus compositores em Pernambuco* (Recife, 1980)
T. de Oliveira Pinto: 'Musical Difference, Competition, and Conflict: the Maracatu Groups in the Pernambuco Carnival, Brazil', *Latin American Music Review*, xvii/2 (1996), 97–119

GERARD BÉHAGUE

Perne, François-Louis (*b* Paris, 4 Oct 1772; *d* Laon, 26 May 1832). French music historian, composer, singer and double bass player. He sang in the parish church choir of St Jacques-de-la-Boucherie in Paris, taking music lessons from the choirmaster, the Abbé d'Haudimont. He sang in the chorus of the Opéra from 1792 until 1799, then played the double bass in the Opéra orchestra until 1816. He was appointed professor of harmony at the Conservatoire in 1813, having worked as Catel's assistant from 1811. In 1815 he was entrusted with the administration of the Conservatoire, serving as inspector general from 1816 to 1822 and succeeding the Abbé Roze as librarian in 1819. He also played the double bass in the orchestra of the Tuileries chapel from its reopening in 1802. He retired in 1822 to the département of Aisne, where he continued private studies until his death.

Perne is best known for his writings on the history of music. He took an early interest in both Greek and medieval music and, as a tireless researcher, brought together an impressive number of documents. In an age in which composers and theorists alike tackled their problems uncritically and were indiscriminate in repeating or commenting on the opinions of others, Perne insisted on going back to the ancient and medieval texts and studying them in their original languages. He lacked the time – and perhaps the talent – needed to put them into proper form and to construct informed theories from them. He took a particular interest in the problems of the notation of Greek music and read a paper on this subject at the Institut de France in 1815.

Most of his historical writings were not published; a few extracts appeared in the early volumes of Fétis's *Revue musicale* (1828–30). Fétis, who acquired Perne's library after his death, catalogued 23 writings on music left in manuscript, some of which had been completed, others of which had only been sketched. A collaborative project of 1815 focussing upon Machaut's poetic and musical works was never completed. His most important edition of early music, the only one to be published, is his transcription of the works of the Chastelain de Couci, with piano accompaniment, in Francisque Michel's *Chansons du Châtelain de Coucy* (Paris, 1830). There is as yet no comprehensive study of his scholarly work.

He wrote few compositions, of which none has enjoyed a high reputation. Besides two masses and a few smaller sacred choral works, he composed incidental music for Racine's *Esther*, an Andante for oboe and orchestra and some piano music, of which the *Six sonates faciles* are noteworthy. A number of Perne's musical manuscripts and letters are in the Bibliothèque Nationale in Paris; his library, which was given to Fétis and eventually acquired by the Bibliothèque Royale in Brussels, includes manuscript transcriptions of polyphonic music and theoretical treatises.

WRITINGS

'Notice sur les manuscrits relatifs à la musique [de l'Eglise grecque]', *Revue musicale*, i (1827), 231–7

'Quelques notions sur Josquin Després', *Revue musicale*, ii (1827), 265–75

'Notice sur un manuscrit du XIIIe siècle', *Revue musicale*, ii (1827), 457–67, 481–90

'Recherches sur la musique ancienne: découverte dans les manuscrits d'Aristide-Quintilien . . . d'une notation musicale grecque', *Revue musicale*, iii (1828), 433–41, 481–91; iv (1828), 25–34, 219–28, 402–5

'Recherches sur la musique ancienne: nouvelle exposition de la séméiographie musicale grecque', *Revue musicale*, v (1829), 241–50, 553–60; viii (1830), 98–107; ix (1830), 129–36

'Polémique', *Revue musicale*, vi (1829), 25–31 [on a passage from a Mozart quartet]

'Curiosités historiques de la musique: description d'un tableau de l'église Saint-Rémy à Reims', *Revue musicale*, xiv (1834), 91–3 [posth.]

BIBLIOGRAPHY

FétisB

L.-J. Francoeur: 'Notice des travaux de M. Perne', *Dictionnaire des découvertes, inventions* (Paris, n.d.)

Obituary, *Revue musicale*, xii (1832), 141–3 [incl. Deglaire: Funeral speech, orig. pubd in *Journal de l'Aisne*, 29 May 1832]

F.J. Fétis: 'Notice sur M. Perne, ancien inspecteur général du Conservatoire et membre correspondant de l'Institut', *Revue musicale*, xii (1832), 145–8 [obituary]

Catalogue de la bibliothèque de F.J. Fétis acquise par l'Etat belge (Brussels, 1877) [pubn of the Bibliothèque royale de Belgique]

P. Lefèvre: *Un savant musicologue: François-Louis Perne (1772–1832)* (?Laon, 1980) [offprint, source unknown, *F-Pn*]

JEAN MONGRÉDIEN/KATHARINE ELLIS

Pernet, André (*b* Rambervillers, Vosges, 6 Jan 1894; *d* Paris, 23 June 1966). French bass. He studied at the Paris Conservatoire with André Gresse and made his début at Nice in 1921. After seven years in the French provinces he was engaged in 1928 by the Paris Opéra and became their leading bass; from 1931 he also appeared at the Opéra-Comique. At the Opéra he was much admired as Boris Godunov, Don Quichotte, Méphistophélès and Don Giovanni. He created, among other parts, the title roles in Milhaud's *Maximilien* (1932) and Enescu's *Oedipe* (1936) and Shylock in Hahn's *Le marchand de Venise* (1935). He made guest appearances throughout Europe and appeared in the film version of Charpentier's *Louise*. His many recordings reveal a firm, supple voice of ample range and a notable feeling for words.

HAROLD ROSENTHAL/R

Perneth. *See* PERRINET.

Pernye, András (*b* Újpest, 19 Nov 1928; *d* Budapest, 4 April 1980). Hungarian musicologist and music critic. He studied the clarinet and recorder and was a pupil of Kodály, Szabolcsi, Bartha, Bárdos and Kókai at the Budapest Academy of Music (diploma in musicology 1958). Subsequently he was music critic of the newspaper *Magyar nemzet* (1959–75) and the periodicals *New Hungarian Quarterly*, *Muzsika* and *Kritika*, and from 1964 a lecturer in music theory and history at the Budapest Academy of Music. He also gave 250 lectures on jazz on Hungarian Radio (1962–9). In 1975 he was awarded the Erkel Prize. His writings include studies of Berg and Puccini and the scenario of István Láng's ballet based on Thomas Mann's *Mario und der Zauberer*. He has edited Dunstaple's *Magnificat secundi toni* (1974), one of Byrd's *Salve regina* settings (1975) and, in a series of 16th- and 17th-century keyboard pieces, Daniel Croner's *Tabulature* (1987).

WRITINGS

Puccini (Budapest, 1959)

A jazz (Budapest, 1964, 2/1966)

A német zene története 1750-ig [History of German music up to 1750] (Budapest, 1964)

Szabó Ferenc (Budapest, 1965)

Alban Berg (Budapest, 1967)

'Alban Berg und die Zahlen', *SMH*, ix (1967), 141–54

Hét tanulmány a zenéről [Seven essays on music] (Budapest, 1973)

Előadóművészet és zenei köznyelv [Performing art and the musical vernacular] (Budapest, 1974)

A nyilvánosság: zenei írások [Publicity: musical writings], ed. J. Breuer (Budapest, 1981) [collected writings of Pernye]

Fél évezred fényében: írások a zenéről [In the light of half a millenary: writings on music], ed. J. Breuer (Budapest, 1988) [collected writings of Pernye]

MÁRIA ECKHARDT

Peroni, Giovanni. *See* PERRONI, GIOVANNI.

Perosi, Lorenzo (*b* Tortona, 20 Dec 1872; *d* Rome, 12 Dec 1956). Italian composer and church musician. After attending the conservatories of Rome and Milan, he went to Regensburg in 1893 to study church music with Haberl. He was made choirmaster of S Marco, Venice (1894), ordained priest (1895) and appointed music director of the Cappella Sistina (1898); meanwhile he was becoming widely known as a conductor of his own oratorios. But an acute spiritual crisis, the culmination of eight years of growing psychological disturbance, forced him to abandon his Rome post in 1915, and in 1922 he entered a mental hospital. In 1923 he was sufficiently cured to resume his position, which officially he held until his death. His recovery, however, was incomplete, his relapses frequent: later intermittent musical activities were a mere appendix to his career. In 1930 he was honoured with membership of the Reale Accademia d'Italia.

Around the turn of the century Perosi's oratorios had an extraordinary international success: Rolland wrote enthusiastically in the composer's praise. Though his reputation waned quickly, the embers of his early fame persist, and it is not only Vatican interest that keeps his music in the Italian repertory. For, naive and eclectic though it was, Perosi's talent was genuine, and his best pieces retain an appealing freshness and gentle spirituality. These qualities found their most durable expression not in the oratorios but in the best of the many smaller religious works, often strongly influenced by Gregorian chant and 16th-century polyphony. (Perosi was the first modern Italian composer to be significantly influenced by pre-Classical music.) The once famous oratorios have lasted less well, and their eclecticism – drawing, for example, on plainsong, Renaissance polyphony, Bach, the Wagner of *Lohengrin*, and even Mascagni – has often been ridiculed. Yet they contain passages which are persuasive in their lyrical sincerity and their sense of the numinous, and others which graphically illustrate the drama, whether the pursuit of the Israelites by the Egyptians in *Mosè* or the sufferings of the soul on the threshold of death in *Transitus animae*. Such moments do much to compensate for passages where the music seems facile and improvised.

WORKS
(selective list)

ORATORIOS

La passione di Cristo secondo San Marco, 1897; La trasfigurazione di Cristo (Bible, etc.), 1898; La risurrezione di Lazzaro (Bible: *John*), 1898; La risurrezione di Cristo (Bible: *Matthew*), 1898; Il natale del Redentore (*Matthew*, *Luke*), 1899; L'entrata di Cristo in Gerusalemme (*Matthew*, *Luke*), 1900; La strage degli innocenti (mainly *Matthew*), 1900; Mosè (A. Cameroni, P. Croce, after Exodus), 1900; Stabat mater, 1904; Il giudizio universale (G. Salvadori, P. Miscatelli, Perosi), 1904; Dies iste, 1904

Transitus animae (Liturgy, etc.), 1907; In patris memoriam (Requiem Mass, Bible: *Job*), 1909; Vespertina oratio (frags. from Ps xxx, Vexilla regis, etc.), 1912, perf. 1928; In transitu Sancti Patris Nostri Francisci (Ps cxli, 2 antiphons), 1936; Natalitia (Breviary), 1937; Il nazareno (sacra rappresentazione, T. Onofri, Perosi), 1942–4, perf. 1950; 5 others, 1913–30, unpubd

OTHER WORKS

Church music: 33 masses surviving complete, incl. 4 messe di requiem, 2 missae pro defunctis; c350 other works, incl. 13 settings of the Magnificat, 10 of the Tantum ergo

Orch (mainly unpubd): Conc., small orch, 1901; Tema con variazione, 1902; Scherzo, pic, orch, 1902; 2 vn concs., 1903, 1916; Pf Conc., 1916; Cl Conc., 1928; Conc., large orch; 10 suites named after Italian cities, 1899–1918, 1 inc.; 10 other pieces

Other inst (mainly unpubd): 200 little pieces, cl, pf, 1928; 18 str qts, 1928–9, 1 pubd; 5 pf qnts, 1930–31; Sonata, va, pf; Sonata, vn, pf, org music

MSS in *I-Rvat*

Principal publishers: Bertarelli, De Santis, Musica Sacra, Pustet, Ricordi

BIBLIOGRAPHY

A. Cameroni: *Lorenzo Perosi e i suoi primi quattro oratori* (Bergamo, 1899)

R. Rolland: 'Don Lorenzo Perosi', *Musiciens d'aujourd'hui* (Paris, 1908, many later edns; Eng. trans., 1915/R), 168–74

A. Damerini: *Lorenzo Perosi* (Rome, 1924)

A. Paglialunga: *Lorenzo Perosi* (Rome, 1952)

M. Glinsky: *Lorenzo Perosi* (Milan, 1953)

A. Damerini: *Lorenzo Perosi* (Milan, 1953)

Musica sacra, 2nd ser., ii (1957), 65–96 [Perosi number, incl. articles by G. Biella, E. dalla Libera, L. Migliavacca, A. Paglialunga, L. Perosi]

M. Rinaldi: *Lorenzo Perosi* (Rome, 1967) [incl. list of works, 545ff, and bibliography, 589ff]

V. Zaccaria: 'Catalogo dei manoscritti musicali di Lorenzo Perosi esistenti nella Biblioteca Vaticana', *NRMI*, vi (1972), 235

M. Bruni: *Lorenzo Perosi, il cantore evangelico* (Turin, 1972)

T. Onofri: *Lorenzo Perosi nei giorni imolesi* (Imola, 1977)

T. Onofri: 'Contributi per un carteggio perosiano', *Rivista internazionale di musica sacra*, iii (1982), 395–405; iv (1983), 90–108, 190–202, 316–35; v (1984), 76–91

T. Onofri: 'Lorenzo Perosi "conferenziere"', *Rivista internazionale di musica sacra*, viii (1987), 208–28

JOHN C.G. WATERHOUSE

Perotinus [Perrotinus, Perotinus Magnus, Magister Perotinus, Pérotin] (*fl* Paris, *c*1200). Composer of organa, conductus and, probably, motets. He was almost certainly active at the cathedral of Notre Dame, Paris, and was the most important of the musicians involved in the revision and updating of the *Magnus liber organi* attributed to Leoninus. His achievements are mentioned in two documents from the late 13th century, the treatises of Johannes de Garlandia (Hieromymus de Moravia's compilation)

and Anonymus 4. No works are ascribed to Perotinus in musical sources, but Anonymus 4 mentions seven of his compositions, all of which can be identified in manuscripts of the 13th and 14th centuries with reasonable certainty. Other compositions have been attributed to him on stylistic grounds by modern scholars.

1. Biography. 2. Works.

1. BIOGRAPHY.   The identity of Perotinus is largely a matter of speculation. Circumstantial evidence points to his being at Notre Dame at the end of the 12th century and beginning of the 13th. Edicts reforming the celebration of the Circumcision Office (1 January) and the Feast of St Stephen (26 December) issued in 1199 by the Bishop of Paris, Eudes de Sully, mention performance of the Vespers responsory, the third and sixth Matins responsories, the gradual and alleluia of the Mass and the Benedicamus Domino 'in triplo vel quadruplo vel organo'. Perotinus's four-voice settings of the graduals *Viderunt omnes* (for Christmas and Circumcision) and *Sederunt principes* (for St Stephen) are often dated on the basis of these edicts, although it is not improbable that they were in the repertory before Eudes' reforms, or even that one or both were composed in response to the edicts (if so, they would probably date from 1201 or later, owing to the papal interdict of 1200). *Triplum* and *organum* (*duplum*) versions of the other items on Eudes' list also appear in the *Magnus liber*, but these cannot be ascribed to Perotinus. However, one of Perotinus's conductus, *Salvatoris hodie*, is assigned to Mass on the Feast of the Circumcision in *GB-Lbl* Egerton 2615, and it is possible that this work stems from Eudes' reform. Perotinus appears to have worked with the poet Philip the Chancellor (*d c*1237); his conductus *Beata viscera* is a setting of Philip's poem, and some of his organa are found with motet texts that are also attributed to Philip.

The title 'magister', employed by both Johannes de Garlandia and Anonymus 4, indicates that Perotinus, like Leoninus, earned the *magister artium*, undoubtedly in Paris, and that he was licensed to teach. The diminutive form of his name, 'Perotinus' (for 'Petrus', a Latinization of the French 'Pérotin'), was probably a mark of respect bestowed by his colleagues; the appellation 'magnus', used by Anonymus 4, testifies to the esteem in which he was held, even long after his death. If Perotinus's career was similar to those of other Parisian ecclesiastics involved with music, such as Adam of St Victor, Albertus Cantor, Leoninus and Philip the Chancellor, he could have held a prominent position within the cathedral hierarchy. In fact, Perotinus has been identified with two important members of the Notre Dame administration, the theologian Petrus Cantor (*d* 1197) and Petrus, Succentor of Notre Dame from 1207 or earlier until *c*1238. The first of these identifications is improbable from a chronological standpoint, but Petrus Succentor is a possible candidate, not least because of the role played by the succentor in overseeing the celebration of the liturgy in the cathedral. Husmann's hypothesis that Perotinus was associated with the parish church of St Germain-l'Auxerrois and that he was something of a court composer to the French king Philippe-Auguste is no longer accepted.

2. WORKS.   Virtually everything known about Perotinus's musical activity is extrapolated from a passage in the treatise of Anonymus 4 (ed. Reckow, 1967, i, 46). Noting that Leoninus, the *optimus organista* ('best man

with organum'), 'made' the *Magnus liber* to embellish the liturgy, he remarks:

[This *liber*] was in use up to the time of the great Perotinus, who made a redaction of it ['abbreviavit eundem'] and made many better clausulas, that is, *puncta*, he being the best *discantor*, and better [at discant] than Leoninus was. . . . This Magister Perotinus made the best *quadrupla*, such as *Viderunt* and *Sederunt*, with an abundance of striking musical embellishments [colores armonicae artis]; likewise, the noblest *tripla*, such as *Alleluia, Posui adiutorium* and [*Alleluia*], *Nativitas* etc. He also made three-voice conductus, such as *Salvatoris hodie*, and two-voice conductus, such as *Dum sigillum summi Patris*, and also, among many others, monophonic conductus, such as *Beata viscera* etc. The book, that is, the books of Magister Perotinus, were in use in the choir of the Paris cathedral of the Blessed Virgin up to the time of Magister Robertus de Sabilone, and from his time up to the present day.

Crucial to an understanding of Perotinus's work is the meaning of the verb 'abbreviare' as used in the above passage. It could mean 'to shorten', and Anonymus 4's remark is often taken in that sense, as indicating that Perotinus shortened Leoninus's *liber* by curtailing the size of individual organa, replacing *organum purum* with discant clausulas and substituting one clausula for another. A group of 154 clausulas in *I-Fl* plut.29.1 (ff.178–83v, clausulas 289–442; ed. R.A. Baltzer, Le magnus liber organi de Notre-Dame de Paris, v, Monaco, 1995) could have been used to achieve this result; these clausulas have been ascribed to Perotinus by some modern scholars (see Ludwig, 1910; Waite, 1961; Sanders, 1967). However, most of the other clausulas in this manuscript (ff.147–84 v) are ambitious compositions, and their use in the organa would, if anything, expand the size of the original settings. A number of these clausulas bear a stylistic resemblance to the known works of Perotinus, which are also conceived on a large scale in comparison with the organa generally supposed to belong to the Leoninian corpus, and do not suggest a 'reduction' in any sense. 'Abbreviare' is probably better understood as meaning 'to write down' or 'to make a redaction'; this reading is consistent with Anonymus 4's use of the word elsewhere in his treatise. If Perotinus 'made a redaction of [Leoninus's *liber*]', in effect he prepared a new 'edition' of it, a process that could have involved both 'abbreviation' and the introduction of 'many better clausulas, that is, *puncta*', as well as the addition of wholly new compositions. The idea of a redaction, or edition, accords with Anonymus 4's suggestion that Perotinus used a more developed system of rhythmic notation than Leoninus had, one in which the full system of rhythmic modes was operative, and in which some elements of mensural notation were present ('These principles [of notation] are used in many books of the *antiqui*, and this from the time of the great Perotinus, and during his time, . . . and similarly from the time of Leo, to some extent [*pro parte*!]'; ed. Reckow, 1967, i, 46). It also fits with his allusion to 'the book, that is, the books of Magister Perotinus', following immediately upon what is in effect a description of the *Magnus liber* as we know it from such manuscripts as *D-W* 628 and *I-Fl* plut.29.1. Ludwig (1910) suggested that the former manuscript transmitted the two-voice organa more or less as Leoninus had created them, and that (for the most part) its two clausula cycles date from the time of Perotinus, while the latter manuscript preserved the *organa dupla* in Perotinus's revision, in addition to much else by him. This formulation is undoubtedly too simple; the collections in both sources

Ex.1 *Alleluia, Nativitas*

A -   [- brahe]

were certainly culled from several layers of the Notre Dame repertory, so that they reflect less the input of one specific composer or 'editor' than what was available to the scribe at the time of copying. But the Parisian origins of *I-Fl* plut.29.1, its close ties to Notre Dame and the fact that it was copied only a decade or two after Perotinus is likely to have been active, all suggest that this manuscript may indeed by the prime witness to his work.

We know from Anonymus 4 that Perotinus wrote organa for three and four voices, as well as conductus for one to three voices, and that he 'made' numerous 'better' clausulas, most of them presumably in two voices, for use in Leoninus's *Magnus liber*. Although Anonymus 4 refers to him as 'optimus discantor', implying that he was known in particular for his work in the various genres of discant, there is no reason to suppose that he did not compose *organa dupla* with passages in *organum purum* as well; indeed *organum purum* is a striking feature of his two four-voice organa. In any event, it is not possible to identify any *organa dupla* (or any sustained-note passages in such pieces) as his work. Perotinus probably also played a role in the early development of the motet. If, as seems likely, he was active through much of the first quarter of the 13th century or beyond, it is unlikely that he did not have direct contact with the new genre. Although Anonymus 4 does not ascribe any motets as such to Perotinus, this may be insignificant since although the theorist evidently knew the genre, he seems not to

Ex.2 *Viderunt omnes*

Vi -

[- derunt]

Ex.3 *Sederunt principes*

[Se-]

[- derunt]

Ex.4 *Alleluia, Nativitas*

[Allelu-]   - ya.

Ex.5 *Viderunt omnes*

[Vide-]

- runt

have taken it much into account in his treatise. Motet versions of Perotinus's two four-voice organa were included in *E-Mn* 20486 (and in reduced form in two other manuscripts, including the Parisian *Magnus liber* source *D-W* 1099); these texts are attributed elsewhere to Perotinus's collaborator and likely colleague at Notre Dame, Philip the Chancellor. In addition, several other organa and clausulas ascribed to Perotinus by modern scholars are also transmitted with motet texts written by Philip. Many early motets, including those that may be by Perotinus and Philip, were probably understood to be clausulas of sorts, and thus they may number among Perotinus's 'many better clausulas, that is, *puncta*' mentioned by Anonymus 4.

Perotinus's compositions for three and four voices are milestones in the history of Western music. With the possible exception of the three-voice conductus *Congaudeant catholici* ascribed to the Notre Dame cantor Albertus Parisiensis in the Codex Calixtinus, these are the first known pieces conceived for more than two independent parts. The upper voices often lie in a similar range and move in a similar style, frequently in phrases of identical length. This suggests that the polyphonic fabric may initially have been conceived in two parts, with additional voices being written in imitation of the second part or contrived from it. As ex.1 from *Alleluia, Nativitas* shows, each upper voice is written as a separate 'duet' with the tenor line, without much regard for the harmonic effect that these upper voices produce when combined. The polyphonic fabric is rooted in stable blocks of consonance, here based on *f* and, later, *g*, ordinarily built out of perfect

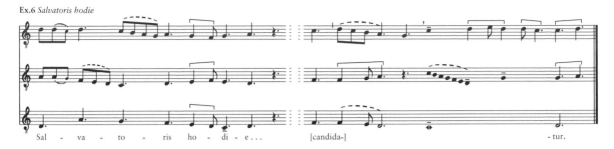

Ex.6 *Salvatoris hodie*

Sal - va - to - ris ho - di - e...   [candida-]   - tur.

concords, within which the upper voices intertwine to produce relatively frequent dissonant clashes. The use of dissonance within a consonant framework is cultivated with striking effect in the opening of *Viderunt omnes* (ex.2), where, after an intonation establishes the underlying consonant sonority, each phrase begins with a major 7th against the tenor in two or all three of the upper voices and then projects this discord forward in rhythmically energized polyphony before resolving it to a form of the initial concord. The tension generated by the prolongation of this dissonance significantly enhances the strength and formative power of the underlying consonance, allowing Perotinus to extend it over a very large span. Through the use of this and other stylistic elements Perotinus was able to create works on an unprecedented scale. This is doubtless one of the devices Anonymus 4 had in mind when he mentioned the *quadrupla*'s 'abundance of striking musical embellishments'. Another of the colores employed by Perotinus to enhance and extend his work was rondellus, or voice exchange; elements of this can be seen in exx.1 and 2, but in ex.3, from *Sederunt principes*, rondelli dominate the texture, yielding an extended variation design as the melodic ideas are passed from voice to voice. Still other colores are deployed to articulate the end of a clausula or larger work: in *Alleluia, Nativitas* a commonly used *copula non ligata* formula is inserted as a brief cadenza-like flourish to bring its setting of 'alleluia' to a close (ex.4).

All of these devices reveal a composer keenly interested in clearly articulated structure and balanced design. The voice exchange in ex.3 shows a sensitivity to the possibilities inherent in the manipulation of multi-voice texture that belies the somewhat mechanical process that might seem to have been at work in creating the polyphonic fabric of ex.1. Perotinus often achieved formal shaping by balancing passages with differing textures. Above a sustained-note tenor, he sometimes deployed the upper voices in note-against-note fashion, but other times he differentiated them with individual rhythmic patterns in overlapping phrases, which generated a discant of sorts above the tenor in which one voice might move in the 5th rhythmic mode while another moves in 1st (ex.5, from *Viderunt omnes*). The systematic overlapping of rhythmic *ordines* in combination with the use of different rhythmic modes seen here is typical of many of the more 'advanced' two-voice clausulas. The developing sense of tonal balance which these examples display can be seen also on a much larger level in the formal design of entire settings (see Reckow, 1973; Flotzinger, 1984).

Unlike the *organum purum* in the two-voice settings in the *Magnus liber*, which usually flow in rhapsodic, wide-ranging, rhythmically 'free' melismas, the melodic idiom used by Perotinus in his sustained-note writing is highly

disciplined, moving in balanced phrases with clearly defined, patterned rhythms of the sort codified in the system of rhythmic modes. Some works (e.g. the two four voice organa) limit their rhythmic designs to the 1st, 5th and 6th modes, and to variations of them such as the so-called alternative form of the 3rd mode. Others, such as *Alleluia, Nativitas* and *Alleluia, Posui adiutorium*, however, draw upon the full range of temporal relationships inherent in the six modal patterns. Since the three 'trochaic' modes (1, 5 and 6) are probably earlier than the others, it is sometimes thought that these distinctions in rhythm usage reflect different stages in the evolution of Perotinus's style. But in fact all of his organa were conceived against the background of the fully developed modal system. Thus *Viderunt omnes* and *Sederunt principes* include hocketing passages in the 'imperfect' 1st mode, while the most 'advanced' of his organa (with the greatest degree of rhythmic variety), *Alleluia, Posui adiutorium*, is cited by Anonymus 4 for a passage in the 1st 'irregular' mode (ed. Reckow, 1967, i, 84). In their rhythmic clarity and precision these *organum purum* lines are similar to Perotinus's discant writing, and may be one of the factors prompting Anonymus 4's characterization of him as 'optimus discantor'. The rhythmic patterning reduces the stylistic disparity between *organum purum* and discant clausulas within a larger setting, and thereby heightens the unity of the work as a whole. Nonetheless, something of the florid quality of Leoninus's lines can be detected in the cadential gesture in ex.5, and, using a slightly different vocabulary, in the melodic embellishments applied to individual syllables in Perotinus's conductus and the flourishes that conclude the melismatic *caudae* placed at important structural points in the text (ex.6, the beginning and end of the first strophe of *Salvatoris hodie*).

As the opening of *Beata viscera* shows (x.7), the strong sense of tonal order and the balanced melodic phrases to

Ex.7 *Beata viscera*

Be - a - ta   vi - sce-ra Ma-ri - e vir-gi - nis

which it contributes, manifest throughout Perotinus's works for two or more voices, also inform his monophony, despite the absence of the formative constraints of a polyphonic texture and clearly perceptible modal rhythm. This tendency towards lucidity, order and balance, equally evident in the melodic profile, the phrase structure, the rhythmic planning or the harmonic idiom of the music, would become an important feature not only of much later French music, but also of 13th-century English polyphony, most strikingly in the Summer Canon and the repertory in the Worcester Fragments.

See also MAGNUS LIBER; RHYTHMIC MODES; SOURCES, MS, §IV, 4.

ATTRIBUTED WORKS

† – *compositions cited by Anonymus 4 as by Perotinus; all other works are attributed by Husmann on stylistic grounds*

Editions: *Polyphonies du XIIIe siècle: le manuscrit H 196 de la Faculté de médecine de Montpellier*, ed. Y. Rokseth (Paris, 1935–9) [R]

Die drei- und vierstimmigen Notre-Dame-Organa: Kritische Gesamtausgabe, ed. H. Husmann, Publikationen älterer Musik, xi (Leipzig, 1940/R) [complete except for conductus]

Thirty-five Conductus for Two and Three Voices, ed. J. Knapp, Collegium musicum, vi (New Haven, CT, 1965) [K]

The Works of Perotin, ed. E. Thurston (New York, 1970) [T]

The Montpellier Codex, ed. H. Tischler, RRMMA, ii–viii (1978–85) [M]

Notre-Dame and Related Conductus: Opera omnia, ed. G.A. Anderson (Henryville, PA, 1979–) [A]

The Conductus Collections of MS Wolfenbüttel 1099, ed. E. Thurston, RRMMA, xi–xiii (1980) [C]

The Earliest Motets (to circa 1270): a Complete Comparative Edition, ed. H. Tischler (New Haven, CT, 1982) [E]

Les quadrupla et tripla de Paris, ed. E.H. Roesner, Le magnus liber organi de Notre-Dame de Paris, i (Monaco, 1993) [complete except for conductus]

FOUR-VOICE ORGANA

†Viderunt omnes ℣. Notum fecit dominus, T, E (gradual for Christmas and Circumcision; motet versions: Vide prophecie and Homo cum mandato dato; texts have medieval attrib. Philip the Chancellor)

†Sederunt principes ℣. Adiuva, T, E (gradual for St Stephen; motet versions: De Stephani roseo sanguine and Adesse festina; texts have medieval attrib. Philip the Chancellor)

THREE-VOICE ORGANA

Sancte Germane ℣. O sancte Germane, R (resp for St Germanus and other confessor bishops; motet version: Associa tecum in patria; text has medieval attrib. Philip the Chancellor)

Terribilis ℣. Cumque (resp for Dedication of a Church)

Virgo ℣. Sponsus, R (resp for St Catherine)

Exiit sermo ℣. Sed siceum (gradual for St John the Evangelist)

Alleluia, Pascha nostrum (Easter)

†Alleluia, Nativitas, R, T, E (Nativity of BVM motet version of the clausula on Ex semine: Ex semine rosa prodit spina/Ex semine Abrahe divino; text attrib. Philip the Chancellor by modern scholars)

Alleluia, Dilexit Andream (St Andrew)

†Alleluia, Posui adiutorium, R, T (*commune sanctorum* for Confessor-Bishops)

Benedicamus Domino (i)

Benedicamus Domino (ii)

Benedicamus Domino (iii)

CLAUSULAS

Mors, 4vv, E (for Alleluia, Christus resurgens; motet version: Mors que stimulo/Mors morsu nata venenato/Mors a primi patris; text attrib. Philip the Chancellor by modern scholars)

In odorem, 3vv, E (for Alleluia, Dilexit Andream; motet version: Mens fidem seminat/In odorem; text attrib. Philip the Chancellor by modern scholars)

Et illuminare, 3vv, E (for gradual Omnes de Saba ℣. Surge; motet versions)

Et gaudebit, 3vv, E (for Alleluia, Non vos relinquam; motet version: Homo qui vigeas/Et gaudebit; text attrib. Philip the Chancellor by modern scholars)

Et exaltavi, 3vv, E (for Alleluia, Posui adiutorium; motet version: Et exaltavi plebis humilem/Et exaltavi; text attrib. Philip the Chancellor by modern scholars)

Numerous 2-voice clausulas (attrib. by Ludwig, 1910; Waite, 1961; Sanders, 1967)

CONDUCTUS

†Salvatoris hodie, 2vv and 3vv, K, T, A, C

†Dum sigillum summi Patris, 2vv, K, T, A

†Beata viscera, 1v, T, A, C (text has medieval attrib. Philip the Chancellor)

BIBLIOGRAPHY

MGG1 (H. Husmann; also 'Ars Antiqua', H. Besseler; 'Notre-Dame-Epoche', H. Husmann)

F. Ludwig: ' Die liturgischen Organa Leonins und Perotins', *Riemann-Festschrift* (Leipzig, 1909/R), 200–13

F. Ludwig: *Repertorium organorum recentioris et motetorum vetustissimi stili*, i/1 (Halle, 1910/R), 15–16, 23ff, 60

F. Ludwig: ' Perotinus Magnus', *AMw*, iii (1921), 361–70

A. Gastoué: *Les primitifs de la musique français* (Paris, 1922)

R. von Ficker, ed.: *Perotinus: Organum quadruplum Sederunt principes* (Vienna and Leipzig, 1930)

J. Handschin: ' Zur Leonin-Perotin-Frage', *ZMw*, xiv (1931–2), 319–32

J. Handschin: ' Zur Geschichte von Notre Dame', *AcM*, iv (1932), 5–17, 49–55, 104–5

H. Schmidt: *Die drei- und vierstimmigen Organa* (Kassel, 1933); part previously pubd as 'Zur Melodiebildung Leonins und Perotins', *ZMw*, xiv (1931–2), 129–34

Y. Rokseth, ed.: *Polyphonies du XIIIe siècle: le manuscrit H 196 de la Faculté de médecine de Montepellier*, iv (Paris, 1939), 48–62

H. Husmann: Introduction to *Die drei- und vierstimmigen Notre-Dame-Organa*, Publikationen älterer Musik, xi (Leipzig, 1940/R)

Y. Rokseth: ' La polyphonie parisienne du treizième siècle: étude critique à propos d'une publication récente', *Les cahiers techniques de l'art*, i/2 (1947), 33–47

F. Gennrich: 'Perotins Beata viscera Mariae virginis und die "Modaltheorie"', *Mf*, i (1948), 225–41

H. Tischler: ' New Historical Aspects of the Parisian Organa', *Speculum*, xxv (1950), 21–35

F. Gennrich, ed.: Perotinus Magnus: *Das Organum Alleluja Nativitas gloriose virginis Marie und seine Sippe*, Musikwissenschaftliche Studien-Bibliothek, xii (Darmstadt, 1955)

A. Machabey: ' A propos des quadruples pérotiniens', *MD*, xii (1958), 3–25

W.G. Waite: ' The Abbreviation of the *Magnus liber*', *JAMS*, xiv (1961), 147–58

G. Birkner: ' Notre Dame-Cantoren und -Succentoren vom Ende des 10. bis zum Beginn des 14. Jahrhunderts', *In memoriam Jacques Handschin*, ed. H. Anglès and others (Strasbourg, 1962), 107–26

H. Husmann: ' St. Germain und Notre-Dame', *Natalicia musicologica Knud Jeppesen septuagenario collegis oblata*, ed. B. Hjelmborg and S. Sørenson (Copenhagen, 1962), 31–6

H. Husmann: ' The Enlargement of the *Magnus liber organi* and the Parish Churches St. Germain l'Auxerrois and Ste. Geneviève-du-Mont', *JAMS*, xvi (1963), 176–203

H. Husmann: ' The Origin and Destination of the *Magnus liber organi*', *MQ*, xlix (1963), 311–30

H. Tischler: ' The Dates of Perotin', *JAMS*, xvi (1963), 240–41 [response to E.H. Sanders' article, *JAMS*, xv, 1962, pp.249–91, esp. 280]

H. Tischler: ' Perotinus Revisited', *Aspects of Medieval and Renaissance Music: a Birthday Offering to Gustave Reese*, ed. J. LaRue and others (New York, 1966/R), 803–17

H. Tischler: ' The Early Cantors of Notre Dame', *JAMS*, xix (1966), 85–7

F. Reckow, ed.: *Der Musiktraktat des Anonymus 4* (Wiesbaden, 1967), esp. i, 45–6, 99–102

E.H. Sanders: ' The Question of Perotin's Oeuvre and Dates', *Festschrift für Walter Wiora*, ed. L. Finscher and C.-H. Mahling (Kassel, 1967), 241–9

J. Chailley: *Histoire musicale du moyen age* (Paris, 2/1969), 158–61

R. Flotzinger: *Der Discantussatz im Magnus liber und seiner Nachfolge* (Vienna, 1969)

F. Reckow: ' Das Organum', *Gattungen der Musik in Einzeldarstellungen: Gedenkschrift Leo Schrade*, ed. W. Arlt and others (Berne and Munich, 1973), 434–96, esp. 478–81

E.H. Sanders: ' The Medieval Motet', ibid., 497–573

R.A. Baltzer: *Notation, Rhythm, and Style in the Two-Voice Notre-Dame Clausula* (diss., Boston U., 1974)

S. Brunner: *Die Notre-Dame-Organa der Handschrift W2* (Tutzing, 1982)

H. Tischler: ' Pérotin and the Creation of the Motet', *MR*, xliv (1983), 1–7

P. van Poucke: *Magister Perotinus magnus: Organa quadrupla generaliter, inleidende reconstructieve Studie* (diss., Rijksuniversitett Gent, 1983)

R. Flotzinger: 'Zu Perotin und seinem "Sederunt"', *Analysen: Beiträge zu einer Problemgeschichte des Komponierens: Festschrift* fur Hans Heinrich Eggebrecht zum 65. Geburtstag, ed. W. Breig, R. Brinkmann and E. Budde (Wiesbaden, 1984), 14–28

R. Flotzinger: '"De Stephani roseo sanguine": vom Quadruplum zur einstimmigen Motette', Mf, xxxvii (1984), 177–90

T.B. Payne: 'Associa tecum in patria: a Newly Identified Organum Trope by Philip the Chancellor', JAMS, xxxix (1986), 233–54 [incl. edn]

R. Stelzle: Der musikalische Satz der Notre Dame-Conductus (Tutzing, 1988)

C. Wright: Music and Ceremony at Notre Dame of Paris, 500–1500 (Cambridge, MA, 1989), esp. 288–94

T.B. Payne: Poetry, Politics and Polyphony: Philip the Chancellor's Contribution to the Music of the Notre Dame School (diss., U. of Chicago, 1991)

Perotinus Magnus, Musik-Konzepte, no.107 (2000)

S. Pinegar: ' Between Pope and Monarch: The Edicts of Eudes de Sully Concerning Liturgical Polyphony at the Cathedral of Notre Dame, Paris' (forthcoming)

EDWARD H. ROESNER

Perotti, Giovanni Agostino [Giannagostino] (b Vercelli, 12 April 1769/70; d Venice, 28 June 1855). Italian composer, teacher and writer on music. He received his first musical training from his older brother Giovanni Domenico Perotti. About 1790 he went to Bologna to study under Mattei. His setting of Metastasio's oratorio Abele was performed in Bologna in 1794 and a one-act comic opera, La contadina nobile, in Pisa in 1795. That year he went to Vienna as a keyboard player at court and from 1798 was in London. About 1801 he returned to Italy and settled in Venice. Here he was associated with the neo-classical academies such as the Corpo Accademico dei Sofronimi, the Accademia Veneta Latteraria, the Accademia Veneta della Bella Lettere and, in 1812, the Ateneo Veneto, which the leading figures in the city's artistic and cultural life were involved in during the Napoleonic period. In 1811 he won a prize in Livorno for his Dissertazione ... [sullo] stato attuale della musica in Italia, which was translated into French in its entirety and in part into German and English, and widely discussed. This Dissertazione, Perotti's most important theoretical work, is a treatise on musical aesthetics, uniting the tradition of Padre Martini and the Bologna school with 18th-century rationalist opera criticism (Algarotti and Arteaga) and Venetian neo-classical ideals (Cicognara and Diedo). In 1811 Perotti was appointed maestro primo at S Marco in Venice, but it was only in 1817, on the death of Bonaventura Furlanetto, that he could properly assume the post, which he held until 1855. As the maestro di cappella of S Marco, Perotti promoted several reforms concerning the re-ordering and expansion of the chapel's music archive, the use of women's voices in performances of old sacred music, the singing school for young choristers and the re-creation of the Società di S Cecilia (1832).

Perotti was essentially a composer of sacred music. In the context of music written for S Marco his work constitutes a period of transition between the old Venetian practice of the 18th century and the more modern one of the 19th, represented by his successor Antonio Buzzolla. His masses are still dominated by the concertante structure of soloists and tutti, the survival of the traditional a cappella style and of mixed style. Sometimes in his psalm settings and requiem masses Perotti seems consciously to be imitating the style of Marcello and Lotti. His theoretical and musical works became increasingly traditional and dogmatic – as can be seen from his criticism of Rossini's Stabat mater (1842). Nevertheless, they made a lasting impact on cultural and musical life in 19th-century Venice.

An understanding of Perotti as an intellectual and musician can be gained from the correspondence he had with important figures and artists of his time, such as Emanuele Cicogna, Stanislao Mattei, Marco Santucci (all I-Vmc), Simon Mayr (Vmc, BGc), Gaetano Gaspari (MOe), Saverio Mercadante (Nc), Giovanni P. Schulthesius and his friend Donizetti, who dedicated his opera Belisario to him.

WORKS

Abele (orat, P. Metastasio), Bologna, 1794, D-Dl, I-Bc (inc.)

La contadina nobile (comic op), Pisa, 1795, lost

Exultate Deo, 4vv, org (Venice, n.d.); 125 sacred works for soloists, chorus and orch, incl. masses, mass sections, canticles, hymns, Lamentations, motets, ps settings, vespers, I-Vsm, Vlevi, for details see Passadore and Rossi (1994–6); other sacred works and fugues, D-Dl; Mass, collab. Pacini, I-Li; 16 fugues, Bc

Pf: Sonata, 6 hands, D-Dl; Concerto, 4 hands, I-TVco; 6 sonate, 4 hands, Adria, Conservatorio Antonio Buzzolla; Sonata, 4 hands, TV-co; Theme and Variations, 2, 4 hands, Vnm, CHf, R VI; 3 sonate, A-Wn; Sonata, I-Tn; Variations on Diletta immagine, OS, Vnm; other pieces, Mc

WRITINGS

Il buon gusto della musica (Venice, 1808) [poem]

Dissertazione ... determinare in tutta la sua estensione e con gli opportuni confronti il gusto, e lo stato attuale della musica in Italia (Venice, 1811; Fr. trans., 1812; partial Ger. trans. as 'Preisschrift über den Zustand der Musik in Italien', AMZ, xv (1813), 3–10, 17–25, 41–3; partial Eng. trans in The Harmonicon, i (1823), 137–9, 164–6, 183–5); review in Il Polografo, ii (1812), 387–9; Perotti's reply in F. Aglietti: 'Relazione accademica (1812)', Alteneo veneto (1814), 47–9

'Cenni critici sullo Stabat mater di Rossini', GMM, i (1842), 41–2, 47–9

'Sugli studii e sulle opere di Benedetto Marcello', GMM, ii (1843), 125–6, 132–4

Guida per lo studio del canto figurato (Milan, 1846)

Metodo chiaro e facile per il Piano Forte (MS, D-Dl)

'Biografia de Giovanni Agostino Perotti de Vercelli', 1851, in G. Gaspari: Zibaldone (MS, I-Bc, UU.12), ii, 401–5 [autobiography]

BIBLIOGRAPHY

CaffiS; EitnerQ

C. Gervasoni: Nuova teoria di musica (Parma, 1812/R), 228–30

P. Zannini: 'Relazione accademica', Ateneo veneto (1817), 113 [Perotti's Discorso sulla vita di Giuseppe Haydn]

C. Dionisotti: Notizie biografiche dei vercellesi illustri (Biella, 1862/R), 228–9

G. Masutto: Della musica sacra in Italia (Venice, 1889), i, 75–6

A. Luzio, ed.: Carteggi verdiani, iv (Rome, 1947), 138–51 [Donizetti's letters to Perotti]

A. Ziino: 'La Dissertazione sullo stato attuale della musica italiana (Venezia 1811) di Giovanni Agostino Perotti e una lettera inedita di G. Paisiello', Quadrivium, xxii/1 (1981), 201–13

G. Fornari: '"Determinare in tutta la sua estensione ... lo stato attuale della musica in Italia": Giannagostino Perotti e la ricerca di un primato perduto', Chigiana, xliii, new ser. xxiii (1993), 9–26

F. Passadore and F. Rossi: San Marco: vitalità di una tradizione: il fondo musicale e la cappella dal Settecento a oggi (Venice, 1994–6), i, 108–27; iii, 832–902

L. Sirch: '"L'emerito Giannagostino Perotti, riputatissimo e nelle pratiche e nelle teoriche della scienza": note su Percotti maestro di Cappella a San Marco (1811–1855)', La cappella musicale di San Marco nell'età moderna: Venice 1994, 527–67

F. Passadore: 'Hausmusik e sonatismo classico nella musica pianistica di Giovanni Agostino Perotti', La musica strumentale nel Veneto fra '700 e '800: Padua 1996

HOWARD BROFSKY/LICIA SIRCH

Perotti, Giovanni Domenico (b Vercelli, 20 Jan 1761; d Vercelli, 24 March 1825). Italian composer. He studied with Fioroni in Milan before 1779 and with Martini and Mattei in Bologna in late 1780 and early 1781. In March 1781 he was admitted to the Accademia Filarmonica there and from sometime later that year until his death was maestro di cappella at Vercelli Cathedral. Despite this rather insular career he had several operas performed, two at important theatres: *Agesilao re di Sparta* at the Teatro Argentina, Rome (1789), and *La vittima della propria vendetta* at La Fenice, Venice (1808). Two other opera scores are in the Dresden Landesbibliothek: *Zemira e Gandarte* (Alessandria, 1787) and *Bianca di Melfi*. 15 sacred works, an aria and sketches are also in Dresden; 22 sacred works, sketches and letters in the Bologna Conservatory library; and a symphony and two quartets in that of Genoa (other works in *I-Mc, Rc, Td, Tn*). Perotti was the first teacher of his more famous younger brother, Giovanni Agostino Perotti.

BIBLIOGRAPHY

EitnerQ

C. Gervasoni: *Nuova teoria di musica* (Parma, 1812/R), 227–8

C. Dionisotti: *Notizie biografiche dei vercellesi illustri* (Biella, 1862/R)

HOWARD BROFSKY

Perpessas, Harilaos (*b* Leipzig, 10 May 1907; *d* Sharon, MA, 19 Oct 1995). Greek composer. He was a pupil of Schoenberg for a year in Berlin, where he met Skalkottas, but he remained opposed to Schoenberg's compositional methods. He went to Greece for the first time in January 1934, attracting notice there as a composer. In 1948 he moved to New York, where he lived in virtual seclusion, reportedly declining commissions for film scores from Spyros Skouras, the president of Twentieth Century-Fox. In 1992 he moved to a residential home in Sharon, Massachusetts.

Together with Mitropoulos, who admired and conducted his music, and Skalkottas, he is generally considered one of the first Greek composers to have turned aside from musical nationalism. His orchestral frescoes, influenced by Strauss and Mahler, Debussy and Ravel, abound in rich, chromatic polyphony driven to powerful and dramatic climaxes, with wide-leaping melodies. In the mid-1970s he wrote a large mystical treatise, *The Opening of the Seventh Seal*, which remained in manuscript. An ever-revising perfectionist, he kept his scores from publication.

WORKS

Orch: Dionysos Dithyramben, pf, orch, before 1934; 3-movt orch piece (?Sym. no.1), 1934; Prelude and Fugue, c, orch, 1935, rev. ?1970s; Sym. no.2, ?1936–7, completed as Sym. 'Christus', 1948–50; Sym. Variations on Beethoven's Eighth Sym., 1953–60; orch of J.S. Bach: Die Kunst der Fugue, 1953–6; orch of L. van Beethoven: Str Qt no.12, E♭, op.127

Other works: Pf Sonata, ?1928–32, ?destroyed; Str Qt, ?1928–32, ?destroyed; Restoration, tetralogy, 1963–73: The Song of the Concentration Camp [= Prelude and Fugue, 1935], The Opening of the Seventh Seal (Liberation) (Hippolytus: *Philosophumena*), solo vv, SATB, orch, Conjunction, orch, The Infinite Bliss, orch

BIBLIOGRAPHY

G. Leotsakos: 'Perpessas, Herilaos', *Pangosimo viografiko lexico* [Universal biographical dictionary], viii (Athens, 1988)

P.E. Gradenwitz: 'Requiem to a Forgotten Composer', *The Athenian*, no.272 (1996), 16–18

S.D. Heliadelis: 'Harilaos Perpessas, o agnostos Siatistinos klassikos synthétis ke philosophos' [Harilaos Perpessas, the unknown classical composer and philosopher from Siatista], *Elymiaka* [Salonica], no.43 (1999), 93–110

GEORGE LEOTSAKOS

Perpetuum mobile (Lat.). *See* MOTO PERPETUO.

Perra [Perras], **Margarita** [Margherita] (*b* Monastir [now Bitola, Macedonia] or Salonica, 15 Jan 1908; *d* Zürich, 2 Feb 1984). Greek soprano. She studied at the Salonica State Conservatory and then at the Berlin Hochschule für Musik; there, in 1927 as Norina, she caught the attention of Bruno Walter, who engaged her for the Städtische Oper. She appeared as Nuri in d'Albert's *Tiefland* and as Cupid in Gluck's *Orfeo ed Euridice* (1927) and sang the title role in the Berlin première of Paul Graener's *Hanneles Himmelfahrt* (1928). She later moved to the Berlin Staatsoper, having toured in Spain, Argentina and Brazil. In 1935 she was engaged by the Vienna Staatsoper and was highly praised as Mozart's Konstanze under Felix Weingartner. She repeated the role in Salzburg (1935) and at Glyndebourne (1937), and had further successes as the Queen of Night, Susanna, Pamina and other Mozart roles. In 1936 she sang Gilda at Covent Garden. Having married in 1937, she settled in Zürich and until 1944 appeared only in recitals, but returned to the operatic stage for a season in Vienna (1946–7). Her firm, well-schooled voice possessed a gently glowing tone colour.

BIBLIOGRAPHY

Obituary, *Opera*, xxxv (1984), 376–7

G. Leotsakos: disc notes, *Ellinikó Lyrikó Théatro, 100 chronia, 1888–1988*, YP 4–6, A/A 14564–6 (1988), 148–51

GEORGE LEOTSAKOS

Perrachio, Luigi (*b* Turin, 28 May 1883; *d* Turin, 6 Sept 1966). Italian composer, pianist and writer on music. He studied the piano in his native city and later in Vienna, and also read law at Turin University. As a composer he was largely self-taught, though eventually (1913) he gained a diploma in composition as well as piano at the Liceo Musicale, Bologna. He taught the piano at the Turin Liceo Musicale (1925–40), and then composition in the same institution until 1955. A keen propagandist for contemporary music through his activities as conductor, pianist and writer, he also fought ardently for the reform of Italian musical education. Extreme modesty kept him from publishing more than a very little of his music: only a few piano works, songs and harp pieces were ever printed. Most of these derive in some way from the Debussy-Ravel tradition, sometimes with notable sensitivity. The *Nove poemetti*, for example, show an excellent command of a wide variety of Debussian techniques, ranging from the intricate, evanescent arabesques of no.4 ('Libellule') to the brooding, shadowy chord progressions of no.3 ('La notte dei morti', perhaps the finest of the set). The striking 25 Preludes (Perrachio's best-known work) are more architectonic in conception, and sometimes show a truly modern toughness; yet here too Debussy and Ravel are rarely lost sight of for long. Perrachio's unpublished large-scale compositions are sometimes even bolder harmonically: the opening of the Piano Concerto, marked *aspro e rabbioso*, is violent to the point of uncouthness. Neither in this nor in other unpublished works, however, do the manuscripts quite bear out the high claims made for Perrachio by some Italian writers.

WORKS
(*selective list*)

Stage: Mirtilla (op, N. Costa), 1937–40, unperf.; La calunnia, ballet, 1952

Orch: 3 notturni a G. Verdi, 1929; Piccola suite, 1930; Taccuino, 1930; Pf Conc., 1931–2; Vn Conc., 1932; other works

Vocal: Sii benedetto creato, chorus, orch, 1956; Il creato, cant., Bar, orch, 1961; songs, several to Piedmontese dialect texts; folksong arrs. etc.

Chbr: Str Qt no.1, 1910; Pf Qnt, 1919; Str Qt no.2, 1930; Sonata popolaresca no.2, vn, pf, 1936; many other works

Pf: 9 poemetti, 1917–20; Il re guardiano delle oche, duet (1922); In nomine Hyeronimi, 3 pieces, 1925; La luna, duet (1925); 25 preludi, 1927; Valses (1953); other pieces

Hp: Sonata popolaresca no.1, before 1926; 3 pezzi (1926)

Principal publishers: Amprino (Turin), Carisch, Curci (Naples and Milan), Pizzi (Bologna), Ricordi

MSS in *I-Tco*

WRITINGS

L'opera pianistica di Claude Debussy (Milan, 1924)
Il 'clavicembalo ben temperato' di J.S. Bach (Milan, 1926)
Treatises on harmony and composition, many articles

BIBLIOGRAPHY

G.M. Gatti: 'Luigi Perrachio', *Critica musicale*, i (Florence, 1918), 229–35 [repr. in G.M. Gatti: *Musicisti moderni d'Italia e di fuori* (Bologna, 1920, 2/1925), 87–98]
M. Castelnuovo-Tedesco: 'Luigi Perrachio: Nove poemetti', *Il pianoforte*, ii (1921), 253 4
A. Casella: 'Jeunes et indépendants', *ReM*, viii/3 (1926–7), 62–70
M. Saint-Cyr: 'Luigi Perrachio', *Rassegna dorica*, iii (1931–2), 191–4
E. Desderi, G.M. Gatti and P. Rattalino: 'Ricordo di Luigi Perrachio', *Musicalbrandé* [Turin], viii/32 (1966), 2–6
G. Pestelli: 'Luigi Perrachio scrittore di musica', *Ghedinie l'attività musicale a Torino fra le due guerre: Turin 1986*, 156–64
A. Piovano: 'Principali connotazioni stilistiche nell'opera di Luigi Perrachio', ibid., 117–55

JOHN C.G. WATERHOUSE

Perrault, Charles (*b* Paris, 12 Jan 1628: *d* Paris, 15/16 May 1703). French author and lawyer, younger brother of CLAUDE PERRAULT. After studying for several years at the Collège de Beauvais in Paris and then at the Sorbonne he undertook private study and in collaboration with his brothers Nicolas and Claude made a burlesque verse translation of the sixth book of Virgil's *Aeneid*. In 1651 he became a lawyer, but his literary activities gradually took up more of his time. In 1654 he wrote his first light verses and got to know a number of Parisian writers, in particular Philippe Quinault, whom he welcomed to his house at Viry-sur-Orge. In 1663 he became secretary to Colbert. He was a member of the Conseil des Bâtiments and the Petite Académie, and in 1671 he was elected to the Académie Française, where he attracted attention through his innovations. In 1673 Colbert appointed him *contrôleur général des bâtiments, jardins, arts et manufactures du roi*, a post that he resigned in 1682. In 1683 he was excluded from the Petite Académie. From 1696 he devoted much of his time to writing his *Mémoires*.

In 1659 Perrault had attended the first performance of the *Pastorale d'Issy* (words by Perrin and music by Cambert), after which he was concerned with Lully's manoeuvres to obtain his monopoly of opera production, which finally succeeded in 1669. It was then that Perrault obtained from Louis XIV the use of the theatre in the royal palace for the performance of Lully's works. Although librettos were submitted to the Petite Académie for approval, the production of Lully's *Alceste* in 1674 was the occasion for violent attacks by Racine and Boileau. Charles Perrault, with the aid of his brother Pierre, defended Quinault by publishing a *Critique de l'opéra, ou Examen de la tragédie intitulée 'Alceste, ou Le triomphe d'Alcide'* (1674) and *Lettre à monsieur Charpentier … sur la préface de l'Iphigénie' de monsieur Racine* (?1680). These pamphlets emphasized the specific nature of *tragédie en musique* and put forward the foundations of a poetics for this new French operatic genre. The *Alceste* controversy also foreshadowed the quarrel that broke out in 1687 when Perrault read his poem *Le siècle de Louis le grand* to the Académie Française. This text started the quarrel between the

supporters of the old and the new in French art in which he was in conflict with Boileau and Racine. Thoroughly modern in outlook, he defended the age of Louis XIV and expressed his preference for the new genre of opera, compared with Greek music with its lack of harmony: he shared these views with his brother Claude. In his *Parallèle … des anciens et des modernes* (1688–97) and in his appreciations of Quinault's librettos he praised Quinault for writing 'simple verse, well suited to musical setting' and in *Les hommes illustres qui ont paru en France pendant le XVIIème siècle* (1696–1700) defended Lully as 'a French and Italian genius'.

In 1682 Perrault wrote *Le banquet des dieux pour la naissance de Monseigneur le Duc de Bourgogne*, a libretto that shows that he fully understood the nature of Lullian opera; he provided a *galant* theme, simple verses for the recitatives, *airs* and choruses, and detailed instructions for the instrumental movements. The music was composed by Claude Oudot, but it is lost, as also is *Titon et l'Aurore* (1677), an earlier operatic collaboration between Perrault and Oudot. The works that principally made Perrault's reputation, however, and by which he is best remembered are the dozen or so *Contes*, which he wrote over a period of several years and collected for publication in Paris in 1697. The *Histoires, ou Contes du temps passé* include such familiar tales as *La belle au bois dormant*, *Cendrillon* and *La barbe bleue*, which, like most of the others, have inspired a wide range of music up to the 20th century, notably operas and ballets by, among others, Rossini, Tchaikovsky, Offenbach, Massenet, Dukas, Ravel and Bartók.

BIBLIOGRAPHY

P. Bonnefon: 'Charles Perrault: essai sur sa vie et ses ouvrages', *Revue d'histoire littéraire de la France*, xi (1904), 365–420
P. Bonnefon: 'Charles Perrault, littérateur et académicien', ibid., xii (1905), 549–610
P. Bonnefon: 'Les dernières années de Charles Perrault', ibid., xiii (1906), 606–57
A. Hallays: *Les Perrault* (Paris, 1926)
M. Soriano: *Le dossier Perrault* (Paris, 1972)
J. Barchilon and P. Flinders: *Charles Perrault* (Boston, 1981)
M. Couvreur: *Jean-Baptiste Lully: musique et dramaturgie au service du prince* (Brussels, 1992)
W. Brooks, B. Norman and J.M. Zarucchi: 'La querelle d'*Alceste*: anciens et modernes avant 1680'; introduction to *Philippe Quinault: Alceste*, ed. W. Brooks (Geneva, 1994), pp.ix–lxi

LAURENCE DE LAUBADÈRE/MANUEL COUVREUR

Perrault, Claude (*b* Paris, 25 Sept 1613; *d* Paris, 9 Oct 1688). French polymath, elder brother of CHARLES PERRAULT. He studied medicine and qualified as a doctor in Paris in 1641. Boileau was one of his patients before becoming one of his detractors. His medical practice was soon confined to his immediate circle of acquaintances; but he had many other interests. He concerned himself with physics and anatomy and in 1666, on its foundation, was admitted to the Académie des Sciences, where he directed studies in natural history, a field in which he also published new and penetrating observations. His abilities extended to music and architecture as well. When it was decided that the Louvre should be given a façade befitting its monumental grandeur, Perrault entered the competition. He probably benefited from the influential position of his brother Charles, who gave him steadfast support throughout his life. The result was the colonnade of the Louvre built under the supervision of François d'Orbay between 1666 and 1670. If this work cannot be attributed to him with absolute certainty, it is said that as an architect he was responsible for many technical innovations adopted on the building site. His most notable architectural achievements include the Paris Observatory and the Arc de Triomphe of the Porte Saint-Antoine (demolished in 1716). In 1673 Colbert entrusted him with the task of translating Vitruvius's ten volumes on architecture: he was thus the first man of his time to make a study of this remarkable work.

Perrault's work relative to music appears in his *Essais de physique, ou Recueil de plusieurs traités touchant les choses naturelles* (Paris, 1680–88, 2/1721). He formulated a remarkable theory about the ear and studied the phenomenon of sound vibration. He learnt about Aristoxenus's theories and was familiar with the acoustics of the theatres of antiquity and of the buildings of his own day, just as he also knew about the qualities of ancient instruments as well as of 17th-century ones. He was a committed 'moderne', as witness his *Mythologie des murs de Troye* (1653), intended to lend support to the epic *Les murs de Troye, ou L'origine du burlesque*, written in collaboration with his younger brothers Nicolas and Charles. Like Mersenne, he considered modern polyphonic music superior to the purely monodic music of classical antiquity. These views find polemical expression in the unpublished dialogue *Savoir si la musique à plusieurs parties a été connue et mise en usage par les anciens*, which was intended as preface to the treatise *De la musique des anciens*, published in the second volume of the *Essais de physique*. In it he defended continuo and the French opera, which he had seen taking its first steps in 1672 with Gilbert and Cambert's *Les peines et les plaisirs de l'amour*. When the *Alceste* quarrel broke out in 1674 he wrote to Colbert in support of Lully, who like Chambonnières and Hotteterre was a friend of his. He died of an infection which he caught while dissecting a camel's body in the royal gardens.

BIBLIOGRAPHY

H. Gillot: *La querelle des anciens et des modernes en France* (Paris, 1914)
A. Hallays: *Les Perrault* (Paris, 1926)
J. Barchilon: 'Les frères Perrault à travers la correspondance et les oeuvres de Christian Huygens', *XVIIème siècle*, lvi (1962), 19–36
A. Picon: *Claude Perrault (1613–1688), ou La curiosité d'un classique* (Paris, 1988)
P. Vendrix: *Aux origines d'une discipline historique: la musique et son histoire en France aux XVIIe et XVIIIe siècles* (Liège, 1993)

LAURENCE DE LAUBADÈRE/MANUEL COUVREUR

Perrichon, Julien [Jean] (*b* Paris, 6 Nov 1566; *d* ?Paris, *c*1600). French lutenist and composer. He was the son of Jehan Perrichon, court viol and shawm player. His early lute studies were probably with the famous Vaumesnil, *valet de chambre* and lutenist to the king from 1560 to 1574. Perrichon may have continued his training with Vaumesnil's successors, Jean de La Fontaine and Samuel de La Roche; the 'young Perrichon' is mentioned in court records from 1576 to 1578 as a student of the lute. By 1595 he was *valet de chambre* and lute player to King Henri IV. Apparently he died a few years later: Antoine Francisque, in his *Trésor d'Orphée* of 1600, spoke of him in the past tense.

Perrichon was accorded unusual recognition in his own day. Praetorius described him as an excellent master. Mary Burwell also mentioned him in her lutebook (1652, *GB-BEcr*), and in 1636 Mersenne listed Perrichon among half a dozen great masters of the previous generation. His works were widely reprinted in a variety of important collections, including those of Francisque, Besard, Dowland, Praetorius and Fuhrmann. Here and there, notably in the collections of Besard, Dowland and Fuhrmann, works by Julien Perrichon are incorrectly ascribed to his father Jehan.

WORKS
all for lute

Galliard in A. Francisque: *Trésor d'Orphée* (Paris, 1600); ed. H. Quittard (Paris, 1906)
4 galliards, 3 courantes, volta, 1603[15]; ed. J.B. Besard, A. Nachtsheim and M. Esch, *Praeludien, Fantasien und Tänze aus Thesaurus Harmonicus* (Köln 1603), i (Bad Ems, 1989)
Courante, 1610[25]
3 courantes, 4–5 insts, 1612.[16]
La nonette, 1615[24]
5 preludes, 3 courantes, volta: *GB-Cfm*, Lord Herbert of Cherbury's Lutebook

BIBLIOGRAPHY

EitnerQ; MersenneHU
F. Lesure: 'Recherches sur les luthistes parisiens à l'époque de Louis XIII', *Le luth et sa musique: Neuilly-sur-Seine 1957*, 209–23

RUTH K. INGLEFIELD

Perrin, Jean (*b* Lausanne, 17 Sept 1920; *d* Lausanne, 24 Sept 1989). Swiss composer and pianist. After studying in Lausanne, he continued his piano studies with Franz-Joseph Hirt in Berne, Edwin Fischer in Lucerne and Yves Nat in Paris, where he also had the opportunity to study composition with Nadia Boulanger and Darius Milhaud (1947–8).

During his active career, Perrin taught piano at the conservatories in Lausanne and Sion; he also wrote about music and for more than 20 years he edited programme notes for the Lausanne Chamber Orchestra. The list of his compositions includes over 50 works. Perrin was a man of erudition but also of great modesty which did not always serve the promotion of his works. On the eve of the live broadcast of the première of his string quartet on French speaking radio stations worldwide, he died unexpectedly in his sleep.

His music, always fundamentally tonal, was the fruit of long and rigorous work. He explored various means of achieving a language of extreme harmonic complexity, which came close to a kind of polytonality, whereby the composer could give free rein to his sense of mystery and wonder.

WORKS
(selective list)

Conc. grosso, pf, orch, op.6b, 1952; Sonatas, 1953–6: op.7, hn, pf; op/8, vn, pf; op.10b, pf; op.11, vc, pf; op.12b, fl, pf; Sym. no.2, op.15, orch, 1959; Mass, 4 solo vv, chorus, orch, op.19, unfinished; Pf Qt, op.23, 1965; Sym. no.3, op.24, orch, 1966; Drei deutsche Lieder (B. Brecht, A. Goes, G. Politzer), A, orch, 1967–8; De profundis, op.26, 4 solo vv, chorus, orch, 1968–70; Vc Conc., op.27, 1972; Canticum laudis, op.32, 4vv, fl, ob, cl, 2 bn, tpt, trbn, db, 1974; Marche funèbre, op.38, orch, 1978; Pf Conc., op.41, 1978; 6 préludes, op.45, pf, 1980–81; Vn Conc., 1986; Str Qt, 1988

BIBLIOGRAPHY

J. Matter: 'Entretien avec Jean Perrin à l'occasion de son soixantième anniversaire', *Revue musicale de Suisse romande*, xxxiv (1981), 116–18
'Hommage à Jean Perrin', *Revue Repères*, no.1 (1981)
J.L. Matthey: *Catalogue de l'oeuvre de Jean Perrin* (Lausanne, 1982)

JEAN-PIERRE AMANN

Perrin, Pierre ['L'abbé'] (*b* Lyons, *c*1620; *d* Paris, bur. 26 April 1675). French poet, librettist and co-creator, with ROBERT CAMBERT, of French opera. He was active in Paris from about 1645. In 1653 he married Mme La

Barroire, a 61-year-old widow who borrowed heavily to help him buy the post of *Introducteur des ambassadeurs* at the court of Gaston d'Orléans. The marriage was annulled and she died shortly afterwards, leaving Perrin to face debts during much of his remaining life.

Perrin's earliest lyric poetry dates from the mid-1650s, when he began supplying court composers with texts for songs, dialogues, motets and other works. In 1659 he collaborated with Cambert on the *Pastorale*, a simple, five-act stage work, first given at Issy and subsequently performed before the king, queen and Cardinal Mazarin. Perrin, in gaol at the time, recounted the events and essayed his theories on vernacular opera in a letter to Cardinal della Rovere (1659; published in *Les oeuvres de poésie*, Paris, 1661; Eng. trans in Auld), whom he had met at Gaston's court. At Mazarin's suggestion, a second *pastorale* followed: *Ariane, ou Le mariage de Bacchus*, the libretto for which Perrin fashioned to the wedding of Louis XIV and the Infanta of Spain. The work was rehearsed in public (c1660–61), but was overshadowed by the imported Italian operas and never formally performed. A third libretto (*La mort d'Adonis*), set to music by J.-B. Boësset, also remained unstaged, though excerpts were sung before the king. After the deaths of Gaston (1660) and Mazarin (1661), Perrin turned away from lyric drama and began writing motets and Elevations for the royal chapel. Several of his Latin texts were set by *sous-maîtres de la chapelle*, in particular Du Mont, Expilly and Gobert, and four volumes of his sacred verse were published. He also provided Boësset with secular texts for the queen's *concert de chambre*.

Perrin, however, still harboured aspirations to establish a national opera, and in about 1666 he sent Jean Baptiste Colbert, the king's minister, a large manuscript collection of his lyric works, the *Recueil de paroles de musique* (F-Pn, transcr. in Auld), in the preface of which he exposed his operatic theories and, cleverly exploiting national vanities, suggested that the king should foster a French form of opera. He was rewarded on 28 June 1669, when Louis XIV accorded him a 12-year privilege to establish 'Académies d'Opéra' in France. Perrin and Cambert renewed their association, and took on the machinist the Marquis de Sourdéac and the rich financier the Sieur de Champeron as their business managers. The company's inaugural production, *Pomone*, opened on 3 March 1671. Later considered the first true French opera, it involved much ballet, spectacle and machinery; it ran for 146 performances and would have made a healthy profit for Perrin and Cambert but for the unscrupulous actions of Sourdéac and Champeron, who pocketed most of the takings. In June 1671 Perrin again found himself in prison for insolvency and soon afterwards started to sell off rights to his privilege. By early 1672 most rights had passed to the composer Sablières and his librettist Guichard; even so, a second opera by Cambert was in production at the Académies and plans were afoot for a third work, most probably a revised version of *Ariane*. Lully visited Perrin in gaol on 13 March 1672 and persuaded him to surrender the entire privilege; in return, Perrin was assured a pension and enough money to repay his outstanding debts. Squabbling broke out over the ownership of the privilege, but Lully, backed by Louis XIV, eventually gained control of the monopoly. Although Perrin was freed from financial problems, his theatrical career was over.

Perrin's conception of opera was strongly linked to the pastoral play and, in contrast to Italian opera, relied on a simple plot, being more concerned with communicating emotions through the union of words and music than with developing dramatic intrigues. In true French theatrical tradition his librettos incorporated ballets, spectacle and elaborate machine effects; he also provided panegyrical prologues in honour of Louis XIV. Nevertheless his poetry was harshly criticized, even ridiculed, causing him to defend his theatrical style in a preface to the libretto of *Pomone* (Paris, 1671/R) and his sacred style in the foreword to the *Cantica pro Capella Regis* (Paris, 1665; foreword repr. in Auld). Passages in *Pomone*, in particular, attracted adverse comment; his un-classical use of comic episodes, facile rhymes, earthy language and workaday visual imagery seem to have offended many listeners and may have led to the criticism relayed by Saint-Evremond that 'people listened to the music with delight, the words with disgust'. Such opinions, along with Perrin's poor judgment of character and lack of business acumen, have tended to overshadow both the importance of his contribution to the development of French opera and the scholarly value of his theoretical writings.

BIBLIOGRAPHY

C. de Saint-Evremond: 'Les opera: comedie', *Oeuvres meslées*, xi (Paris, 1684; Eng. trans., 1728)

A. de Boislisle: *Les débuts de l'opéra français* (Paris, 1875)

A. Pougin: *Les vrais créateurs de l'opéra français: Perrin et Cambert* (Paris, 1881)

C. Nuitter and E. Thoinan: *Les origines de l'opéra français* (Paris, 1886)

H. Prunières: 'Lully and the Académie de musique et de danse', *MQ*, xi (1925), 528–46

R. Isherwood: *Music in the Service of the King: France in the Seventeenth Century* (Ithaca, NY, 1973)

S. Pitou: *The Paris Opéra: an Encyclopedia of Operas, Ballets, Composers, and Performers*, i: *Genesis and Glory, 1671–1715* (Westport, CT, 1983)

P. Danchin: 'The Foundation of the Royal Academy of Music in 1674 and Pierre Perrin's Ariane', *Theatre Survey*, xxv/1 (1984), 53–67

L.E. Auld: *The Lyric Art of Pierre Perrin, Founder of French Opera* (Henryville, PA, 1986)

C. Kintzler: 'De la pastorale à la tragédie lyrique: quelques éléments d'un système poétique', *RdM*, lxxii (1986), 67–96

L. Sawkins: 'Chronology and Evolution of the *grand motet* at the Court of Louis XIV: Evidence from the *livres du roi* and the Works of Perrin, the *sous-maîtres* and Lully', *Jean-Baptiste Lully and the Music of the French Baroque: Essays in Honor of James R. Anthony*, ed. J.H. Heyer (Cambridge, 1989), 41–79

C. Bashford: 'Perrin and Cambert's "Ariane, ou Le mariage de Bacchus" Re-examined', *ML*, lxxii (1991), 1–26

J. de la Gorce: *L'opéra à Paris au temps de Louis XIV: histoire d'un théâtre* (Paris, 1992)

CHRISTINA BASHFORD

Perrin d'Angicourt (*fl* 1245–70). French trouvère. The fact that his name appears twice as a partner of Jehan Bretel in the jeux-partis *Perrin d'Angicourt, respondés* and *Prince del pui*, and (probably as judge) in other jeux-partis involving Bretel, Gaidifer d'Avion, Lambert Ferri, Jehan de Grieviler and Audefroi (?Louchart) – R.295, 546, 664, 978, 1121, 1838 and 1925 – indicates a close association with Arras. Moreover, *J'ai un joli souvenir*, *Quant partis sui* and perhaps *Quant li cincenis s'escrie* are designated as *chansons couronnées*, presumably by the Arras *puy*. Among the nine towns that might be considered as Perrin's possible birthplace, the most likely is Achicourt, less than 5 km to the south of Arras. Gillebert de Berneville sent a song (R.138) to Perrin, while the latter dedicated *Quant voi en la fin* to Henri III, Duke of Brabant, and *Lors quant je voi* to Gui de Dampierre, Count of Flanders. Of greater importance is the dedication of *Quant li biaus estés repaire* to Charles of France, the youngest brother of Louis IX (St Louis). Charles, who became Count of Anjou in 1246 and King of Sicily in 1266, is known as the patron of Adam de la Halle and Rutebeuf. He was a partner of Perrin in the jeu-parti *Quens d'Anjou*, a judge with Perrin in *Encor sui cil* (R.644), and in *Perrin d'Angicourt, respondés*, in which Perrin appears as respondent. The Petrus de Angicuria who appears as *rector capellae* in the service of Charles in a Naples document of 1269 may be identifiable with the trouvère.

Perrin was one of the more prolific trouvères, and some of his 35 songs survive in as many as 11 sources. Strophes employing different line lengths are in the majority, a peak of complexity being reached with *Quant partis sui* (five different line lengths), *Quant voi en la fin* and *Helas, or ai je trop duré* (four each). There are five isometric decasyllabic strophes, and decasyllables appear in two heterometric strophes, but Perrin clearly preferred shorter verses, particularly those of seven syllables. Six poems employ fixed refrains and another six have variable refrains. Five, or possibly six, served as models for later contrafacta.

The *chansons couronnées J'ai un joli souvenir* and *Quant partis sui* are in an authentic C mode, with a clear sense of tonal direction. The former leaps vigorously from the final to the 5th at the opening, while the latter begins at the octave and descends gradually over the first two phrases. Perrin clearly had a preference for modes with a major 3rd above the final. (In eight of his works, the modal structures vary among different manuscript readings.) All of the original melodies are in bar form except that for *Il convient qu'en la chandele*, which ends an otherwise non-repetitive structure with variants of the first and third phrases. *J'ai un joli souvenir* and *Quant partis sui* show the composer's ability at employing techniques of development in the cauda; both also display heightened rhythmic activity at cadential areas, a trait to be found in several other chansons by Perrin. Only three works (*Onques por esloignement*, *Quant li biaus estés repaire* and the doubtful *Je ne sui pas esbahis*) survive in mensural notation (in *F-Pn* fr.846), all three being in the 2nd mode. The very regular disposition of ligatures in *Haute esperance* also seems to hint at the 2nd mode, but in most chansons ligature patterns are more irregular. *Au tens novel* and *Il ne me chaut* are among the plainer of the melodies, while *Il convient qu'en la chandele, J'ai un joli souvenir, Lors quant je voi* and *On voit souvent* are among the more florid.

WORKS

Edition: *Trouvère Lyrics with Melodies: Complete Comparative Edition*, ed. H. Tischler, CMM, cvii (1997)

(V) etc. indicates a MS (using Schwan sigla: *see* SOURCES, MS) containing a late setting of a poem

Amours dont sens et courtoisie, R.1118 (V)
Au tens novel, R.573 (V)
Biau m'est du tens de gäin qui verdoie, R.1767 = 1755 [?model for anon. 'Quant Amours vit que je l'aloignoie', R.1684 (no music)]
Bone Amour, conseilliez moi, R.1665 (V)
Chancon veul faire de moi, R.1669
Haute esperance garnie, R.1162 (V)
Honeur et bone aventure, R.2088 [model for anon. 'J'ai bon espoir d'avoir joie', R.1725]
Il convient qu'en la chandele, R.591

Il feroit trop bon morir, R.1428
Il ne me chaut d'esté ne de rosee, R.552
J'ai un joli souvenir, R.1470
Jamès ne cuidai avoir, R.1786 [model for anon. 'Quant voi blanchoier la flour', R.1980]
Je ne chant pas pour verdour, R.2017 (R, V)
Li jolis mais ne la flour qui blanchoie, R.1692 [model for anon. 'Mere au dous roi, de cui vient toute joie', R.1743; ? Phelipe de Remi, 'Bone Amours veut tous jours c'on demaint joie', R.1731 (late, different melody)]
Lors quant je voi le buisson en verdure, R.2118
Onques a faire chanson, R.1858
Onques ne fui sans amour, R.1964
Onques por esloignement, R.672 (V)
On voit souvent en chantant amenrir, R.1391 = 1409 (R, V)
Quant je voi l'erbe amatir, R.1390 (V)
Quant li biaus estés repaire, R.172 (V)
Quant li biaus estés revient, R.1243
Quant li cincenis s'escrie, R.1148 [model for anon. 'Quant li nouviaus tens define', R.1382]
Quant partis sui de Provence, R.615 (R, V)
Quant voi en la fin d'esté, R.438 (V)
Quant voi le felon tens finé, R.460 [model for anon. 'J'ai maintes fois d'Amours chanté', R.411] (R, V)

WORKS OF PROBABLE JOINT AUTHORSHIP

Perrin d'Angicourt, respondés, R.940 (with Jehan Bretel)
Perrins amis, mout volentiers saroie, R.1759 (no music)
Prince del pui, vous avés, R.918 (with Jehan Bretel)
Quens d'Anjou, prenés, R.938 (with Charles d'Anjou)

DOUBTFUL WORKS

Contre la froidour, R.1987 (M)
Helas, or ai je trop duré, R.429 (V)
Je ne sui pas esbahis, R.1538
Mais ne avris ne prins tans, R.288 (no music)
Tres haute Amors qui tant s'est abessie, R.1098

BIBLIOGRAPHY

F.-J. Fétis: *Histoire générale de la musique*, v (Paris, 1876/R), 41 [edn of *Au tens novel*]
G. Steffens: *Die Lieder des Troveors Perrin von Angicourt* (Halle, 1905)
A. Långfors, A. Jeanroy and L. Brandin, eds.: *Recueil général des jeux-partis français* (Paris, 1926)
R. Dragonetti: *La technique poétique des trouvères dans la chanson courtoise: contribution à l'étude de la rhétorique médiévale* (Bruges, 1960/R)

For further bibliography *see* TROUBADOURS, TROUVÈRES.

THEODORE KARP

Perrine (*d* probably Paris, after 1698). French theorist and lute teacher. His surname alone is known. His two publications were designed to revive the declining fashion for the lute by abandoning the traditional tablature for staff notation. The *Livre* deals with continuo playing, where the tablature was an obstacle to playing in ensembles. The *Table* (the second part of the *Livre*) has useful realizations of cadence formulas in *style brisé*. The *Pieces* has an important *Advertissement* on the operation of *brisure*. It also contains 31 lute pieces by Ennemond and Denis Gaultier transcribed into staff notation. Although Perrine's transcriptions are ingenious, and shed light on many aspects of performance, they are complicated in comparison with tablature and must have been expensive to print.

WRITINGS

Livre de musique pour le lut, contenant une metode nouvelle et facile pour aprendre à toucher le lut sur les notes de la musique (Paris, 1679/R)
Et une table pour aprendre à toucher le lut sur la basse continüe pour accompagner la voix (Paris, 1682, 2/1698)
Pieces de luth en musique avec des regles pour les toucher parfaitement sur le luth et sur le clavessin (Paris, 1680)

BIBLIOGRAPHY

A. Bailes: 'An Introduction to French Lute Style of the XVIIth Century', *Le luth et sa musique II* [Tours 1980], ed. J.-M. Vaccaro (Paris, 1984), 213–28

D.J. Buch: '*Style brisé, Style luthée*, and the *Choses luthées*', *MQ*, lxxi (1985), 52–67

D. Ledbetter: 'What the Lute Sources Tell us about the Performance of French Harpsichord Music', *The Harpsichord and its Repertoire*, ed. P. Dirksen (Utrecht, 1992), 59–85

Y. de Brossard: *La collection de Sébastien de Brossard* (Paris, 1994)

DAVID LEDBETTER

Perrinet [Perinetus, Perneth, Prunet] (*fl* late 14th or early 15th century). French composer. He has been tentatively identified with Perrinet Rino, an instrumentalist active in the court of King Alfonso the Magnanimous in Barcelona in 1417, although Pierre Fontaine was also known as Perrinet and was at Rouen in the late 14th century before moving to the Burgundian court. A certain Perrinet d'Acx is also known to have been in the service of the King of Navarre from 1374 to 1386. Perrinet's compositions comprise a three-part Kyrie and a four-part Credo (ed. in CMM, xxix, 1962 and in PMFC, xxiii, 1989–91). In the Apt Manuscript (*F-APT*), the Credo is attributed to 'Bonbarde'; the composer may thus have been a shawm player. Two otherwise unknown works, a Gloria and a Credo (unless the latter is the above Credo), were mentioned by the Anonymus 5 of Coussemaker (*CoussemakerS*, iii, 379–98 esp. 396a).

BIBLIOGRAPHY

H. Anglès: 'Gacian Reyneau am Königshof zu Barcelona in der Zeit von 139 … bis 1429', *Studien zur Musikgeschichte: Festschrift für Guido Adler* (Vienna, 1930/*R*), 64–70

H. Stäblein-Harder: *Fourteenth-Century Mass Music in France*, MSD, vii (1962), 28, 47, 66–7, 95

U. Günther: 'Quelques remarques sur des feuillets récemments découverts à Grottaferrata', *L'Ars Nova italiana del Trecento: Convegno II: Certaldo and Florence 1969* [*L'Ars Nova italiana del Trecento*, iii (Certaldo, 1970)], 315–97

M. del C. Gómez: *La música en la casa real Catalano-Aragonesa 1336–1442*, i (Barcelona, 1977)

M. del C. Gómez: 'Neue Quellen mit mehrstimmiger geistlicher Musik der 14. Jahrhunderts in Spanien', *AcM*, l (1978), 208–16, esp. 211–14

GILBERT REANEY

Perron [Pergamenter], **Karl** (*b* Frankenthal, Pfalz, 3 June 1858; *d* Dresden, 15 July 1928). German bass-baritone. He studied with Julius Hey in Berlin and Julius von Stockhausen in Frankfurt, making his début in 1884 at Leipzig as Wolfram. In 1892 he moved to Dresden, where he was engaged at the Hofoper until 1913. There he created John the Baptist in *Salome* (1905), Orestes in *Elektra* (1909) and Ochs in *Der Rosenkavalier* (1911). In addition to his Strauss roles he sang Don Giovanni, Count Almaviva (*Le nozze di Figaro*), Hans Heiling, Nélusko (*L'Africaine*), Thomas' Hamlet, Escamillo and Yevgeny Onegin. At Bayreuth between 1889 and 1904 he sang Amfortas, Wotan, King Mark and Daland. A powerful actor, he sang with great authority.

ELIZABETH FORBES

Perroni, Anna. Italian singer, sister of Rosa Borosini. *See* BOROSINI family, (3).

Perroni [Peroni], **Giovanni** (*b* Oleggio, Novara, 1688; *d* Vienna, 10 March 1748). Italian cellist and composer. He probably received his training in his native city or at the provincial capital, Novara, an active musical centre, where in 1711 he took part in celebrations connected with the translation of the relics of S Gaudenzio. His first

position was at the ducal court of Parma, where he served between 1704 and 1714. In 1718 he was *maestro di cappella* of S Maria delle Grazie, Milan, and a member of the court orchestra there. He left in 1720 to seek employment at the imperial court in Vienna, where he was appointed a cellist on 1 April 1721. Payment records at the imperial court indicate a quick rise to fame, for by the end of the decade he was the highest paid cellist, with an annual salary of 1800 florins. He served in this capacity until his death, having been retained by the Empress Maria Theresa in spite of the substantial reduction of musical forces at court during the early years of her reign. In 1726 Perroni married Anna d'Ambreville, an Italian singer of French descent, who sang major roles in northern Italy before 1721 and was thereafter employed at the imperial court in Vienna.

Except for a cello concerto, Perroni's extant compositions are all dramatic music. His early works were composed in collaboration with his brother Giuseppe Maria, a violinist active in Novara, Milan and Vienna. His later, independent compositions consist of stereotyped alternations of short recitatives with extended da capo arias and lack either dramatic or musical interest. His cello concerto, however, is of some significance, showing his talent and knowledge of the capabilities of his instrument.

WORKS
lost unless otherwise stated

ORATORIOS

La costanza della pietà trionfante nel glorioso S Gaudenzio, Novara, 1711, collab. G.M. Perroni
Le delizie notturne della santità, Oleggio, 1712, collab. G.M. Perroni
La santità coronata o Il trionfo de' tre fiori, Milan, 1714, collab. G.M. Perroni
L'impegno delle virtù, Milan, 1718
Dialogo pastorale, Milan, 1720
Il sagrificio di Noè (S. Stampiglia), Vienna, 5 March 1722, *A-Wn*
Giobbe (L. Villati di Villatburg), Vienna, 22 Feb 1725, *Wn*
La gara delle virtù per esaltare l'anima grande di S Carlo (Arrighini), Vienna, 1727, *Wn*

OTHER WORKS

Nicodemo (cant.), Milan, 1716
Gesù nell'orto, Gesù flagellato, Gesù coperto di spine, Gesù crocifisso (cant. cycle), Milan, 1718
Cant. (J.B. Pusterla), Vienna, 4 Nov 1729
Elisabetta (cant., F. Brunamotti), Vienna, 19 Nov 1730

Conc., vc, 2 vn, violetta, bc, *Wn*

BIBLIOGRAPHY

KöchelKHM

A. Bauer: *Opern und Operetten in Wien: Verzeichnis ihrer Erstaufführungen in der Zeit von 1629 bis zur Gegenwart* (Graz, 1955)

G. Barblan: 'La musica strumentale a Milano dalla seconda metà del Cinquecento a tutto il Seicento', *Storia di Milano*, xvi (Milan, 1962), 589–618 [pubn of the Fondazione Treccani degli Alfieri per la storia di Milano]

G. Barblan: 'La musica strumentale e cameristica a Milano nel '700', ibid., 619–60

RUDOLF SCHNITZLER

Perroquette. A type of bird organ. *See* BIRD INSTRUMENTS.

Perrot, Jules (Joseph) (*b* Lyons, 18 Aug 1810; *d* Paramé, 24 Aug 1892). French dancer and choreographer. *See* BALLET, §2(ii).

Perrot [Peron, Peros, Pierrot] **de Neele** (*fl* Arras, mid- to late 13th century). French trouvère. His period of activity may be deduced from the works attributed to him: the partner for the jeux-partis was Jehan Bretel, a prominent and prolific trouvère of Arras who flourished in the mid-13th century, and who died in 1272; furthermore, Perrot identified himself at the end of the 'Sommaires en vers de poèmes' that introduces a collection of narrative verse (characterized by Jordan as a collection of 'classic literary works') contained in a source dated 1288. The ascription reads: 'Ce fist Peros de Neele, qui en trover tos s'escrevele' ('Peros de Neele made this, who nearly broke down in tears while writing'). The one song by Perrot that is not a jeu-parti is a Marian song in bar form.

WORKS

Editions: *Recueil général des jeux-partis français*, ed. A. Långfors, A. Jeanroy and L. Brandin (Paris, 1926) [J]
Trouvère Lyrics with Melodies: Complete Comparative Edition, ed. H. Tischler, CMM, cvii (1997) [T]

Amis Peron de Neele, R.596, J, T iv, no.345 (jeu-parti with Jehan Bretel)
Douce vierge, röine nete et pure, R.2113, T xiii, no.1208
Jehan Bretel, respondés, R.942, J, T vii, no.558 (jeu-parti)
Pierrot de Neele, amis, R.1518, J (jeu-parti with Jehan Bretel)
Pierrot, li ques vaut pis a fin amant, R.297, J, T iii, no.177 (jeu-parti with Jehan Bretel)

BIBLIOGRAPHY

L. Jordan: 'Peroc de Neeles gereimte Inhaltsangabe', *Romanische Forschungen*, xvi (1903), 735
M. Stewart: 'The Melodic Structure in Thirteenth-Century "Jeux-Partis"', *AcM*, li (1979), 86–107

ROBERT FALCK

Perry, George Frederick (*b* Norwich, 1793; *d* London, 4 March 1862). English composer. He was a member of Norwich Cathedral choir under Beckwith. After leaving the choir he studied the piano, the violin, harmony and composition, all with local musicians, and in about 1818 he succeeded Binfield as leader of the orchestra at the Theatre Royal, Norwich. While still resident in Norwich he composed two oratorios, both performed there, and the overture to *The Persian Hunters* (of which the rest of the music was by C.E. Horn) for the Lyceum Theatre, London.

In 1822 he moved to London, where he was appointed musical director of the Haymarket Theatre; there he provided music in whole or in part for several dramatic pieces. A few years later he became organist of the Quebec Chapel, St Marylebone. When the Sacred Harmonic Society was formed in 1832, Perry was chosen to be leader of the orchestra, and at its first concert on 15 January 1833 extracts from two of his oratorios were performed. Perry was an assiduous supporter of this society, never missing a concert for 16 years. When Joseph Surman was dismissed as conductor in 1848, Perry acted as conductor for a time, but when he was not appointed permanent conductor he resigned from the society. During his membership his oratorio *The Death of Abel* was performed several times, despite the fact that it generally resulted in a loss to the society. In 1846 he resigned his post at Quebec Chapel and became organist of Trinity Church, Gray's Inn Road.

Perry is notable chiefly for his persistence in composing oratorios, and his relative success in having them performed, at a time when the works of English composers were little regarded in oratorio circles. The music of these works lacks originality, being based mainly on the style of Haydn's *Creation*, with occasional reminiscences of Handel and Mozart. He also wrote additional accompaniments to a number of Handel's oratorios for use by the Sacred Harmonic Society, and several anthems, including *The queen shall rejoice* in honour of the birth of the Princess Royal (1840), which was performed by the Sacred Harmonic Society with a choir of 500.

WORKS
all printed works published in London

Ov. to The Persian Hunters, London, Lyceum, 13 Aug 1817, pf score (*c*1817)
Family Jars (operatic farce, J. Lunn), London, Haymarket, 26 Aug 1822
Morning, Noon and Night (comic op, T.J. Dibdin), London, Haymarket, 9 Sept 1822
The Death of Abel (orat, G. Bennett), Norwich, *c*1816, *US-NYp*, vs (1846)
Elijah and the Priests of Baal (orat, J. Plumptre), Norwich, 12 March 1819 (*c*1830)
The Fall of Jerusalem (orat, E. Taylor, after H.H. Milman), Hanover Square Rooms, 20 Feb 1832, vs (1834)
Belshazzar's Feast (orat), Sacred Harmonic Society, 10 Feb 1836
Hezekiah (orat), 1847, excerpts in vs (1847)
3 anthems: Blessed be the Lord God of Israel, 1838; The queen shall rejoice, 1840; I will arise
Songs, pf pieces

BIBLIOGRAPHY

DNB (R.H. Legge)
A.H. Mann: *Norwich Musical Events* and *Norwich Musicians* (MS, GB-NWr, 434–9)
'Mr Perry's New Oratorio', *The Harmonicon*, x (1832), i, 57 only

NICHOLAS TEMPERLEY

Perry, Julia (Amanda) (*b* Lexington, KY, 25 March 1924; *d* Akron, OH, 24 April 1979). American composer. She studied at Akron University and Westminster Choir College (BM 1947, MM 1948), and took a conducting course at the Juilliard School of Music (1950–51). She spent two summers at the Berkshire Music Center, studying choral singing with Hugh Ross (1949) and composition with Luigi Dallapiccola (1951). She went on to study with Dallapiccola in Florence and briefly with Boulanger in France (1952), winning the Boulanger Grand Prize for her Viola Sonata. Other honours included Guggenheim fellowships (1954, 1956) and a National Institute of Arts and Letters Award (1964). *Stabat mater* (1951), which launched her career, was performed in both the USA and Europe; her *Study for Orchestra* was performed by the New York PO in 1965. Her career was curtailed because of physical health problems in the early 1970s.

Perry's early works, mostly songs and choral music, show a strong influence of spirituals. *Prelude for Piano* (1946, rev. 1962) draws on the blues, using an extended harmonic vocabulary of major 7ths, 9ths and 11ths, blue notes, chord substitutions and the common blues poetic form *AAB*. While living in Europe, her music became increasingly instrumental and abstract, focussing on the concise treatment of small motivic cells. Overt references to her native black culture are absent in these restrained, neo-classical works. Pitch centres are established through reiteration, the melodic-harmonic language is often dissonant, and rhythmic complexity emerges in shifting subdivisions and syncopation. *Homunculus C.F.*, written shortly after her return to the USA, is among her most innovative works, gradually unfolding pitches in a chord of the 15th. With the civil rights struggles of the 1960s, she renewed her use of black American musical idioms, but shifted her references to contemporary, urban genres. *A Suite Symphony* draws on rock and roll and rhythm and blues. *Bicentennial Reflections* offers a cautionary tale of American race relations, developing a racial dynamic with the aid of visual and textual elements.

WORKS

OPERAS

The Cask of Amontillado (The Bottle) (1, Perry and V. Card, after E.A. Poe), 1953; New York, 1954; The Selfish Giant (3, Perry, after O. Wilde), 1964; Mary Easty (?The Symplegades), 1964–74, unfinished

VOCAL

Choral: Carillon Heigh-ho (Perry), SATB (1947); Is There Anybody Here?, women's vv, 1947; The Lord is Risen, men's vv, 1947; Chicago (C. Sandburg), nar, chorus, orch, 1948; Ruth (sacred cant.), SATB, org, 1950; Our Thanks to Thee (Perry), A, SATB, org (1951); Stabat mater (J. da Todi, trans. Perry), A/Mez, str qt/str orch, 1951; Ye Who Seek the Truth (Perry), T, SATB, org (1952); Be Merciful Unto Me, O God (Ps lvii.1–2), S, B, SATB, org (1953); Song of Our Savior (Perry), S, SATB (1953); Frammenti dalle lettere di Santa Caterina, S, SATB, chbr orch, rev. 1957; Hymn to Pan (J. Fletcher), SATB, org/pf, 1963; Sym. no.7 'USA', SATB, orch, 1967 or ?1969; Missa brevis, SATB, org

Other vocal: Deep Sworn Vow, 1v, pf, ?1947; King Jesus Lives, 1v, pf, 1947; To Elektra, 1v, pf, 1947; Lord, What Shall I Do?, spiritual, 1v, pf (1949); By the Sea (Perry), high v, pf (1950); Free at Last, spiritual, high v, pf (1951); I'm a Poor Li'l Orphan in This Worl', spiritual, medium v, pf (1952); Alleluja (Bible: Matthew xxviii.1, 2, 5, 6), medium v, org, 1954; A Short Service from The Mystic Trumpeter (W. Whitman), T, tpt, 1954; How Beautiful are the Feet (Bible: Isaiah lii.7), medium v, pf/org (1954); Parody (P. Sides), Bar, pf, 1954; Quinary Quixotic Songs (Triptych) (Perry), B-Bar, fl, cl, va, bar bn, pf, 1976; Bicentennial Reflections (Perry), T, 2 cl, 3 perc, elec b gui, 1977; 5 Songs, Mez, str qt, by 1977; 7 Contrasts (?7 Songs), Bar, chbr orch

INSTRUMENTAL

Orch: A Short Piece, 1952 [reorchd 1955 as A Short Piece for Large Orchestra, reorchd 1965 as Study for Orchestra]; Homage to Vivaldi (Requiem for Orch, Vivaldiana), 1959, rev. 1964; 3 Spirituals; 4 Spirituals, ?1960s; Sym. in 1 Movt (Sym. no.1), vas, dbs, 1961; Sym. no.2, 1962; Sym. no.3, 1962, rev. 1970; Contretemps, 1963; Vn Conc., 1963–5, rev. 1968; Sym. no.4, 1964, ?rev. 1968; Sym. no.5 'Integration', 1966–7; Sym. no.8, 1968–9; Module, 1969 or 1975; Pf Conc. 'In 2 Uninterrupted Speeds', 1969, rev. as Pf Conc. no.2, 1969; Sym. no.9, 1970; Sym. no.10 'Soul Sym.', Bar, orch, 1972; Sym. no.12 'Simple Sym.' (Children's Sym.), 1973; Solstice, str, by 1976; A Suite Sym., 1976; Ballet (Dance), chbr orch

Band: Sym. Band sym. (?Sym. no.6), 1966; Venus Moon, 1971 or 1972; Fireworks on Mars, by 1972; Football Game Salute, 1972; Marching Band Salute, by 1972; Panorama, by 1972; Space Adventure Sym. (Space Sym.), 1972–5; Sym. no.11, 1972 [uncertain forces]; Theme Song 'Gimme that Ol' Time Religion', 1973; Suite, brass, perc, 1978

Chbr and solo inst: Sonata, va, pf, ?1952; Pastoral (Septet), fl, str sextet, 1959; Homunculus C.F., hp, cel + pf, 8 perc, 1960; The Beacon, 2 eng hn, 2 t sax, 2 bn, 2 tpt, 1963; Quartette (Sym. no.13), fl, ob, cl, a sax, bn, 1963; Composition, ob, opt. pf, 1960s, arr. as Serenity, cl, 1972; Soundouts, 3 tpt, 2 trbn, 1970–71; Tom Thumb Series, perc ens, 1972; Divertimento, fl, ob, a sax, t sax, bn, 1974–6

Pf: Prelude (?Lament), 1946, rev. 1962; Pearls on Silk, 1947; Suite of Shoes, 1947; 2 Easy Pieces, 1972; Miniature (1973); 3 Pieces for Children

MSS in US-NA; Jackson State University, Jackson MS; American Music Research Center, University of Colorado, Boulder; US-NYamc; Peer-Southern

Principal publishers: Carl Fischer, Galaxy, Peer-Southern

Principal recording comapnies: CRI, Koch, Leonarda

BIBLIOGRAPHY

O. Smith: 'Julia Perry Acclaimed in Europe for Music', Akron [OH] Beacon Journal (6 July 1952)
W. Brinkey: 'They All Say: "Look at the American Signora!"', Life (23 Dec 1957)
Obituary, BPM, vii (1979), 282; viii (1980), 264 [correction]
M.D. Green: Black Women Composers: a Genesis (Boston, 1983)
J.M. Edwards: 'Julia Amanda Perry', International Dictionary of Black Composers, ii, ed. S. Floyd (Chicago, 1999), 914–22

J. MICHELE EDWARDS

Perry, Lee [Perry, Rainford Hugh; 'Scratch'] (b Kendal, Hanover Parish, 20 March 1936). Jamaican reggae producer. He moved to Kingston in the mid-1950s and began to work with the producer Clement 'Sir Coxone' Dodd on his mobile sound system. Moving into studio production and working as Coxone's talent scout, in 1965 Perry helped to produce some of the early recordings made by Bob Marley's vocal group, the Wailers. That same year he began recording under his own name; his first hit record Chicken Scratch earned him the nickname Scratch, by which he became popularly known. In 1967 he formed a band, the Upsetters, around the brothers Carlton (drums) and Aston 'Family Man' Barrett (bass guitar). The following year, as the rock steady beat slowed into a new rhythmic format, Perry's innovatory hit record People Funny Boy helped to create what became known as reggae. In 1969 Perry teamed the Upsetters' instrumentalists with the Wailers' vocal trio and began to make the group recordings that launched Bob Marley's international career, including Small Axe, My Cup, Mr Brown and Duppy Conqueror. Perry effectively co-wrote some of Marley's mid-period songs, and their close collaboration continued sporadically until Marley's death in 1981.

Perry opened his Kingston recording studio, the Black Ark, in 1974, where for Island Records he produced some of the most important works of the reggae movement: Max Romeo's War Inna Babylon (1976), Junior Murvin's Police and Thieves (1977), the Upsetters' Super Ape dub album and the Congos' Heart of the Congos (1978). During this time he also worked with several European rock musicians. Since 1980 he has continued to record and distribute his work in Europe.

Perry's eccentric and avante-garde productions, conceived and recorded under notoriously primitive conditions, are best known for their odd effects including heavy repeating echo, spacey tape rewind, distortion, sudden noises, animal sounds and disorientating instrumental absences. He pioneered the technique of scratching records which was later an important part of the hip hop sound.

BIBLIOGRAPHY

S. Davis: Reggae International (London, 1983)
C. Wilson: disc notes, Lee 'Scratch' Perry: Chicken Scratch, Heartbeat CD HB 53 (1989)
S. Davis: Bob Marley (London, 1994)
B. Mack: 'Return of the Super Ape: the Lives and Times of Lee "Scratch" Perry', Grand Royal, no.2 (1995)
S. Heilig: 'Showtime with Scratch', The Beat, xvi/5–6 (1997)

STEPHEN DAVIS

Perse, Edward. See PEARCE, EDWARD.

Persen, John (b Porsanger, 9 Nov 1941). Norwegian composer. He was educated from 1968 at the Oslo Conservatory, studying with Finn Mortensen. In addition to his work as a composer, he has been active in different organizations – as chairman of Ny Musikk, the Norwegian branch of the ISCM (1974–6) and as director of the Ultima-Oslo Contemporary Music Festival.

His musical style is neo-Expressionist, and he has characterized his Orkesterverk II, written for a television ballet, as 'naked and brutal'. He also uses electronic means in his music, in which sound planes and structures are predominant; he sometimes exploits limited musical material to the utmost, and on occasion the influence of jazz is detectable. He has mainly written chamber music and orchestral works, in addition to an opera Under kors og krone ('Beneath Cross and Crown', M. Mikkelsen,

1985). His chamber work *Et cetera* was named Work of the Year in Norway in 1988, and the orchestral *ČSV* (the title is Sami, and means 'dare to show that you are Sami') won a competition in connection with the opening of the new Oslo concert hall in 1976.

BIBLIOGRAPHY

N. Grinde: *Norsk musikkhistorie* (Oslo, 4/1993)

RUNE J. ANDERSEN

Persia. See IRAN.

Persian Gulf [Arabian Gulf]. For a discussion of the music of this area *see* ARABIAN GULF and ARAB MUSIC; for a discussion of the music of the Iranian south coast *see* IRAN, §I, 1.

Persiani, Fanny. *See* TACCHINARDI-PERSIANI, FANNY.

Persiani, Giuseppe (*b* Recanati, *c*1799–1805; *d* Paris, 13 Aug 1869). Italian composer. He was taught the violin by his father, but was left an orphan in 1814. He played in the Teatro Valle orchestra in Rome and from 1820 at the S Carlo in Naples, where he also studied at the conservatory under Zingarelli and Tritto. He was *maestro di cappella* in Cerignola, but by late 1824 he had settled in Rome, where he composed oratorios. The first of his 11 operas, *Piglia il mondo come viene* (1825, Florence), was an instant success; his subsequent stage works, in the Bellinian mould, were sought by impresarios at home and abroad. All but three were produced between 1825 and 1829. He owed much of his subsequent fame to the soprano Fanny Tacchinardi, whom he married in 1830. She sang in many of his operas, but Persiani's most famous opera, *Ines de Castro* (1835, Naples), was a vehicle for Malibran. His last opera, *L'orfana savoiarda* (1846, Madrid), was a fiasco. In 1847 he was named impresario of the Royal Italian Opera in Covent Garden, London, but because of competition with Verdi's *I masnadieri* at the Haymarket, his season was a failure. The couple moved to Paris; he ended his career as a singing teacher.

The music of *Ines de Castro* is structured in the Donizetti style, with four-part arias ending in virtuoso cabalettas. The vocal style is very difficult; the role of Ines has a range of over two octaves. Like many of its contemporaries, the opera ends with a mad scene and death.

WORKS
operas unless otherwise stated

Piglia il mondo come viene (ob, 2, A. Anelli), Florence, Pergola, 26 Dec 1825

L'inimico generoso (2), Florence, Pergola, 17 Oct 1826

Attila in Aquileja (A. Sografi), Parma, Ducale, 31 Jan 1827

Danao re d'Argo (2, F. Romani), Florence, Pergola, 16 June 1827

Gastone di Foix (Romani), Venice, Fenice, 26 Dec 1827, *I-Vt*

Il solitario (C. Bassi), Milan, Scala, 20 April 1829

Eufemio di Messina, ossia La distruzione di Catania (Romani), Lucca, del Giglio, 20 Sept 1829; as I saraceni in Catania, Padua, 29 July 1832; as Il rinnegato, Naples, 1837

Costantino in Arles (3, P. Pola), Venice, Fenice, 26 Dec 1829, *Vt*

Ines de Castro (tragedia lirica, 3, S. Cammarano), Naples, S Carlo, 28 Jan 1835, *Mc, US-Bp*

Il fantasma (3, Romani), Paris, Italien, 14 Dec 1843

L'orfana savoiarda (3), Madrid, Circo, 25 July 1846

BIBLIOGRAPHY

G. Radiciotti: *Teatro, musica e musicisti in Recanati* (Recanati, 1905), 109–60

G. Tebaldini: 'Giuseppe Persiani e Fanny Tacchinardi', *RMI*, xii (1905), 579–91

H. Bushnell: *Maria Malibran: a Biography of the Singer* (University Park, PA, 1979), 181–4

P. Ciarlantini: *Giuseppe Persiani e Fanny Tacchinardi: due protagonisti del melodramma romantico* (Ancona, 1988)

T.G. Kaufman: 'Giuseppe and Fanny Persiani', *Donizetti Society Journal*, vi (1988), 123–51

MARVIN TARTAK

Persichetti, Vincent (*b* Philadelphia, 6 June 1915; *d* Philadelphia, 14 Aug 1987). American composer, educator and pianist. At the age of five he enrolled in the Combs Conservatory (Philadelphia), where he studied the piano, organ and double bass; he also studied theory and composition with Russell King Miller, his most influential teacher. While in high school, he acquired professional experience performing on the radio, in churches and in recital. After graduating from Combs (BMus 1935), he served as head of its theory and composition departments while studying the piano with Samaroff and composition with Nordoff at the Philadelphia Conservatory (MMus 1941, DMus 1945), and conducting with Fritz Reiner at the Curtis Institute. In 1941 he was appointed head of the theory and composition departments at the Philadelphia Conservatory. He joined the faculty of the Juilliard School in 1947, where he became chairman of the composition department (1963) and of the literature and materials department (1970). From 1952 he also served as director of publications for Elkan-Vogel.

Persichetti's prodigious musical output exemplifies a principle that was also fundamental to his teaching and theoretical writing: the integration into a fluent working vocabulary of the wealth of materials placed at a composer's disposal by the expansion of musical language over the course of the 20th century. Drawing on a wide range of expressive possibilities, from simple diatonicism to complex atonal polyphony, Persichetti produced an array of works whose varied moods, styles and levels of difficulty bewildered those who sought an easily identifiable musical personality or a conventional chronological pattern of development.

Despite Persichetti's precocious attainment of compositional fluency, his early works show the influence of Stravinsky, Bartók, Hindemith and Copland; not until the 1950s did he truly achieve his own distinctive voice. Within that decade alone, however, he produced nearly 50 compositions, among them some of his finest and most frequently performed works. During this period he also developed a formal design particularly well suited to his creative temperament. This formal concept, in which a series of short sections, usually based on a single theme, is integrated into a large formal structure, underlies the Concerto for Piano–Four Hands, the Symphony no.5, the Piano Quintet, the Piano Sonata no.10 and the String Quartet no.3, all of which are among Persichetti's most important compositions.

Persichetti himself identified two main currents within his creative disposition: one 'graceful' and the other 'gritty'. Beyond this, his music is characterized by lucid textures, sparse gestures, epigrammatic forms, a fondness for pandiatonic and polytonal harmony, a playful rhythmic vitality and a pervasive geniality of spirit. Like that of Mozart and Ravel, Persichetti's music often suggests the innocence and childlike joy of pure musical creativity. Hence many works for beginners stand, with neither condescension nor apology, alongside more difficult compositions. The importance with which he regarded his pieces for children is indicated by the fact that one of his most ambitious works, the opera *The Sibyl*, a harsh allegory based on the folktale *Chicken Little*, draws most of its thematic material from the *Little Piano Book*. *The Sibyl* was the 20th work in a series Persichetti called 'Parables', which he defined as 'non-programmatic musical essays about a single germinal idea'. He began the series in 1965, completing the 25th addition in 1986. Many of the 'Parables' are written for monophonic instruments and are based on motifs from other compositions.

Persichetti often 'cross-referenced' his own works explicitly, regarding his output as a sort of bibliography from which he could draw at any time. Perhaps the most important of his 'bibliographical' works is the collection *Hymns and Responses for the Church Year*, a contemporary hymnal with texts drawn from a variety of poetic sources, both traditional and modern. He returned to this collection frequently to borrow thematic material for compositions of many types and dimensions. His last complete work is a second volume of such hymns. Another quasi-religious work, which Persichetti often described as his most significant opus, is *The Creation*, a large oratorio on his own text, drawn from mythological, scientific, poetic and biblical sources.

Although Persichetti made substantial contributions to many musical genres, his piano works are worthy of particular mention. Comprising a sizable portion of his output, these provide a microcosmic representation of his work as a whole, while offering a comprehensive survey of contemporary piano techniques. Also important are his works for wind band, which reveal a natural affinity for the medium. The Symphony no.6 has become a staple of the band repertoire.

Persichetti's many works of intermediate difficulty, his ecumenical attitude regarding contemporary compositional techniques and his warm, engaging and witty personal manner made him a favourite on American college campuses, where he was frequently invited as a guest lecturer. Among his many honours and awards are three Guggenheim Fellowships, two grants from the National Foundation on the Arts and Humanities and a grant from the National Institute of Arts and Letters, of which he was a member from 1965. Many of his works were commissioned by the country's leading orchestras and institutions. His writings include the monograph *William Schuman* (with F.R. Schreiber, New York, 1954) and *Twentieth Century Harmony* (New York, 1961).

WORKS
all published unless otherwise stated

OPERA

The Sibyl (Parable XX) (1, Persichetti, after fable: *Chicken Little*), op.135, 1976; Philadelphia, Pennsylvania Op Theatre, 13 April 1985

LARGE INSTRUMENTAL ENSEMBLE

Orch: Concertino, op.16, pf, orch, 1941; Dance Ov., op.20, 1942; Sym. no.1, op.18, 1942, unpubd; Sym. no.2, op.19, 1942, unpubd; Fables, op.23, nar, orch, 1943; The Hollow Men, op.25, tpt, str, 1944; Sym. no.3, op.30, 1946; Fairy Tale, op.48, 1950; Serenade no.5, op.43, 1950; Sym. no.4, op.51, 1951; Sym. for Str (Sym. no.5), op.61, 1953; Sym. no.7 'Liturgical', op.80, 1958; Pf Conc., op.90, 1962; Introit, op.96, str, 1964; Sym. no.8, op.106, 1967; Night Dances, op.114, 1970; Sym. no.9 'Sinfonica janiculum', op.113, 1970; A Lincoln Address, op.124, nar, orch, 1972; Conc., op.137, eng hn, str, 1977
Band: Divertimento, op.42, 1950; Psalm, op.53, 1952; Pageant, op.59, 1953; Sym. for Band (Sym. no.6), op.69, 1956; Serenade no.11, op.85, 1960; Bagatelles, op.87, 1961; So Pure the Star, chorale prelude, op.91, 1962; Masquerade, op.102, 1965; Turn not thy Face, chorale prelude, op.105, 1966; O Cool is the Valley (Poem for Band), op.118, 1971; Parable IX, op.121, 1972; A Lincoln Address, op.124a, nar, band, 1973; O God Unseen, chorale prelude, op.160, 1984

VOCAL

Choral: Mag and Nunc, op.8, SATB, pf, 1940; Canons, op.31, SSAA/TTBB/SATB, 1947; 2 Cummings Choruses (e.e. cummings), op.33, 2vv, pf, 1948; Proverb, op.34, SATB, 1948; 2 Cummings Choruses, op.46, SSAA, 1950; Hymns and Responses for the Church Year (W.H. Auden and others), op.68, 1955; Seek the Highest (F. Adler), op.78, SAB, pf, 1957; Song of Peace (anon.), op.82, TTBB/SATB, pf, 1959; Mass, op.84, SATB, 1960; Spring Cantata (Cummings), op.94, SSAA, pf, 1963; Stabat mater, op.92, SATB, orch, 1963; Te Deum, op.93, SATB, orch, 1963; 4 Cummings Choruses, op.98, 2vv, pf, 1964; Winter Cantata (11 Haiku), op.97, SSAA, fl, mar, 1964; Celebrations (cant., W. Whitman), op.103, SATB, wind ens, 1966; The Pleiades (cant., Whitman), op.107, SATB, tpt, str, 1967; The Creation (Persichetti), op.111, S, A, T, Bar, SATB, orch, 1969; Love (Bible: Corinthians), op.116, SSAA, 1971; Glad and Very (Cummings), op.129, 2vv, 1974; Flower Songs (Cant. no.6) (Cummings), op.157, SATB, str, 1983; Hymns and Responses for the Church Year, vol. 2, op.166, 1987
Solo: 2 Chinese Songs, op.29, 1945; E.E. Cummings Songs, op.26, 1945, unpubd; 3 English Songs (17th century), op.49, 1951, unpubd; Harmonium (W. Stevens), song cycle, op.50, S, pf, 1951; Carl Sandburg Songs, op.73, 1957, unpubd; Emily Dickinson Songs, op.77, 1957; Hilaire Belloc Songs, op.75, 1957; James Joyce Songs, op.74, 1957; Robert Frost Songs, op.76, 1957, unpubd; Sara Teasdale Songs, op.72, 1957, unpubd; A Net of Fireflies (Jap., trans. H. Steward), song cycle, op.115, 1970

CHAMBER AND SOLO INSTRUMENTAL

3 or more insts: Serenade no.1, op.1, 10 wind, 1929; Str Qt no.1, op.7, 1939; Concertato, op.12, pf qnt, 1940; Serenade no.3, op.17, vn, vc, pf, 1941; Pastoral, op.21, ww qnt, 1943; Str Qt no.2, op.24, 1944; King Lear, op.35, ww qnt, timp, pf, 1948; Serenade no.6, op.44, trbn, va, vc, 1950; Pf Qnt, op.66, 1954; Str Qt no.3, op.81, 1959; Parable II, op.108, brass qnt, 1968; Str Qt no.4 (Parable X), op.122, 1972; Parable XXIII, op.150, vn, vc, pf, 1981
1–2 insts: Sonata, op.10, vn, 1940; Suite, op.9, vn, vc, 1940, unpubd; Fantasy, op.15, vn, pf, 1941, unpubd; Serenade no.4, op.28, vn, pf, 1945; Vocalise, op.27, vc, pf, 1945; Sonata, op.54, vc, 1952; Little Rec Book, op.70, 1956; Serenade no.9, op.71, 2 rec, 1956; Serenade no.10, op.79, fl, hp, 1957; Infanta marina, op.83, va, pf, 1960; Serenade no.12, op.88, tuba, 1961; Serenade no.13, op.95, 2 cl, 1963; Masques, op.99, vn, pf, 1965; Parable [I], op.100, fl, 1965; Parable III, op.109, ob, 1968; Parable IV, op.110, bn, 1969; Parable VII, op.119, hp, 1971; Parable VIII, op.120, hn, 1972; Parable XI, op.123, a sax, 1972; Parable XII, op.125, pic, 1973; Parable XIII, op.126, cl, 1973; Parable XIV, op.127, tpt, 1973; Parable XV, op.128, eng hn, 1973; Parable XVI, op.130, va, 1974; Parable XVII, op.131, db, 1974; Parable XVIII, op.133, trbn, 1975; Parable XXI, op.140, gui, 1978; Parable XXII, op.147, tuba, 1981; Serenade no.14, op.159, ob, 1984; Parable XXV, op.164, 2 tpt, 1986

KEYBOARD

Pf: Serenade no.2, op.2, 1929; Poems, vols.1–2, opp.4–5, 1939; Sonata no.1, op.3, 1939; Sonata no.2, op.6, 1939; Sonata, op.13, 2 pf, 1940; Poems, vol. 3, op.14, 1941; Sonata no.3, op.22, 1943; Variations for an Album, op.32, 1947; Sonata no.4, op.36, 1949; Sonata no.5, op.37, 1949; Sonata no.6, op.39, 1950; Sonata no.7, op.40, 1950; Sonata no.8, op.41, 1950; Sonatina no.1, op.38, 1950; Sonatina no.2, op.45, 1950; Sonatina no.3, op.47, 1950; Conc., op.56, 4 hands, 1952; Parades, op.57, 1952; Serenade no.7, op.55, 1952; Sonata no.9, op.58, 1952; Little Pf Book, op.60, 1953; Serenade no.8, op.62, 4 hands, 1954; Sonatina no.4, op.63, 1954; Sonatina no.5, op.64, 1954; Sonatina no.6, op.65, 1954; Sonata no.10, op.67, 1955; Sonata no.11, op.101, 1965; Parable XIX, op.134, 1975; 4 Arabesques, op.141, 1978; Little Mirror Book, op.139, 1978; Reflective Studies, op.138, 1978; Mirror Etudes, op.143, 1979; 3 Toccatinas, op.142, 1979; Sonata no.12, op.145, 1980; Winter Solstice, op.165, 1986
Other: Sonatine, op.11, org pedals, 1940; Hpd Sonata no.1, op.52, 1951; Org Sonata, op.86, 1960; Shimah b'koli, op.89, org, 1962;

Drop, Drop Slow Tears, chorale prelude, op.104, org, 1966; Parable V, op.112, carillon, 1969; Parable VI, op.117, org, 1971; Do Not Go Gentle, op.132, org pedals, 1974; Auden Variations, op.136, org, 1977; Dryden Liturgical Suite, op.144, org, 1980; Hpd Sonata no.2, op.146, 1981; Hpd Sonata no.3, op.149, 1981; Song of David, op.148, org, 1981; Hpd Sonata no.4, op.151, 1982; Hpd Sonata no.5, op.152, 1982; Hpd Sonata no.6, op.154, 1982; Parable XXIV, op.153, hpd, 1982; Hpd Sonata no.7, op.156, 1983; Little Hpd Book, op.155, 1983; Hpd Sonata no.8, op.158, 1984; Serenade no.15, op.161, hpd, 1984; Give Peace, O God, chorale prelude, op.162, org, 1985; Hpd Sonata no.9, op.163, 1985

Principal publisher: Elkan-Vogel

BIBLIOGRAPHY

EwenD

R. Evett: 'The Music of Vincent Persichetti', Juilliard Review, ii/2 (1955), 15–30

W. Schuman: 'The Compleat Musician', MQ, xlvii (1961), 379

D.M. Rubin: 'Vincent Persichetti', ASCAP in Action (1980), spr., 8

R. Schackelford: 'Conversation with Vincent Persichetti', PNM, xx/1–2 (1981–2), 104–34

J. Hilfiger: Comparison of Some Aspects of Style in the Band and Orchestral Music of Vincent Persichetti (diss., U. of Iowa, 1985)

J.B. Smith: Golden Proportion in the Published Solo Piano Music of Vincent Persichetti (diss., U. of Missouri, Kansas City, 1987)

D.L. and J.L. Patterson: Vincent Persichetti: a Bio-Bibliography (Westport, CT, 1988)

D.A. Morris: Life of Vincent Persichetti, with Emphasis on Works for Band (diss., Florida State U., 1991)

WALTER G. SIMMONS

Persile, Giuseppe. See PORSILE, GIUSEPPE.

Persimfans [Pervïy Simfonicheskiy Ansambl' bez Dirizhyora] (Russ.: 'First Conductorless Symphony Ensemble'). Moscow orchestra active from 1922 to 1932. See MOSCOW, §3.

Persinger, Louis (b Rochester, IL, 11 Feb 1887; d New York, 31 Dec 1966). American violinist, pianist and teacher. He had early lessons in Colorado, appearing in public at the age of 12. His main studies were at the Leipzig Conservatory (1900–04) under Hans Becker (violin), Carl Beving (piano) and Nikisch (conducting), who described him as 'one of the most talented pupils the Leipzig Conservatory ever had'. He then settled in Brussels for three years, combining studies under Ysaÿe with concerts in Belgium and Germany and two summers' coaching from Thibaud. Returning to the USA, he made his début on 1 November 1912 with the Philadelphia Orchestra under Stokowski, followed by many engagements with orchestras. In 1914 Nikisch invited him to become leader of the Berlin PO and in 1915 he became leader of the San Francisco SO. Two years later he resigned to form his own string quartet and to direct the Chamber Music Society of San Francisco (1916–28), where he began his teaching career. One of his earliest pupils was Yehudi Menuhin, whose family followed Persinger to New York in 1925. An accomplished pianist, he was the accompanist for Menuhin's first New York recital in 1926 and on his American tour in 1928–9. On his 75th birthday Persinger gave a recital at the Juilliard School, playing half the programme on the piano and half on the violin.

Persinger taught at the Cleveland Institute of Music (1929–30), and in 1930 succeeded Auer at the Juilliard School, where he taught the violin and chamber music until his death. Among his pupils were Isaac Stern, Ruggiero Ricci, Guila Bustabo and Camilla Wicks. He said that his unorthodox teaching method was 'based on keeping a child's interest, in sensing what might be amusing or arresting to him, and in using as few pedantic words as possible. I teach through the sound of the instrument'. Menuhin wrote that Persinger 'has done perhaps more than anyone else to establish a genuine American school of violin playing'. He served as a member of the jury in the Queen Elisabeth and Wieniawski competitions, and published transcriptions and editions of violin music.

BIBLIOGRAPHY

CampbellGV; SchwarzGM

R. Magidoff: Yehudi Menuhin: the Story of the Man and the Musician (Garden City, NY, 1955/R, 2/1973)

M.C. Hart: 'Louis Persinger: a Tribute on his 75th', Juilliard Review, ix/1 (1961–2), 4

Y. Menuhin: 'Louis Persinger', Juilliard Review Annual, v (1966–7), 15

Obituaries, Juilliard News Bulletin, v/3 (1966–7), 1; New York Times (1 Jan 1967)

J. Creighton: Discopaedia of the Violin, 1889–1971 (Toronto, 1974)

Y. Menuhin: Unfinished Journey (London, 1977, 2/1996)

BORIS SCHWARZ

Persoens [Persones], Josquino (fl 1563–8). Flemish composer, active in Austria and Italy. He entered the service in Brussels of Margaret of Austria, Regent of the Low Countries and wife of Ottavio Farnese, Duke of Piacenza and Parma, on 5 August 1563 at a monthly salary of 3 scudi. He was summoned to Italy to the court of Ottavio at Parma and was a member of the musical establishment there from 23 September 1563 until the end of March 1568. During this time he studied with Cipriano de Rore whose influence is reflected in stylistic and expressive aspects of Persoens's madrigals. It is worth noting that Rore was also at the court of Margaret at Brussels before going to Parma. Persoens's Libro primo de' madrigali a quattro voci (Parma, 1570²⁸) consists of 23 pieces, including two ascribed to Jean d'Arras, another Fleming in the service of the Parma court from 1566. The dedication to the Duke of Parma states that the compositions are 'the first fruits of a plant which has grown with the nourishment of the sweet dew of the immortal Cipriano Rore'. A manuscript copy of a mass for six voices has been attributed to him by Vander Straeten and Eitner.

BIBLIOGRAPHY

EitnerQ; Vander StraetenMPB, vi

N. Pelicelli: 'Musicisti in Parma nei secoli XV–XVI', NA, ix (1932), 112–29, esp. 114–5

FRANCESCO BUSSI/ LAVERN J. WAGNER

Persoit [Persois], Jean Pierre Marie (b ?Mirecourt, 1782–3; d after 1854). French bowmaker. He was one of the first bowmakers (if not the first) to be hired by the young J.B. Vuillaume; he seems to have worked in this studio for at least 15 years (1823–41 according to Millant; 1828–43 according to Vatelot). It nevertheless remains difficult to recognize his work under the Vuillaume stamp. His best bows, especially those with octagonal sticks, are remarkably close to the Tourte style, though there are small but telling differences: the octagonals are not so sharply planed; the heads are rather more squared; the frogs are more solid and with shallower throats; and the distinctive buttons have unequally wide bands which cover most of the ebony. Persoit's round-shafted bows are more personal and generally bulkier than the Tourte ideal. Most are also slightly short. His work is only rarely seen today but much appreciated. His brand PRS is stamped on the stick under the frog and under the lapping, occasionally as many as three times, although sometimes not at all. It is possible that Persoit left Paris after 1854 either to retire or to be cared for.

BIBLIOGRAPHY

J. Roda: *Bows for Musical Instruments of the Violin Family* (Chicago, 1959)

W.C. Retford: *Bows and Bow Makers* (London, 1964)

R. Millant: *J.B. Vuillaume: sa vie et son oeuvre* (London, 1972)

E. Vatelot: *Les archets français* (Nancy, 1976)

J. Liivoja-Lorius: 'The Bows of Persois', *The Strad*, xci (1980–81), 254–6

P. Childs: *Jean Pierre Marie Persoit: his Life and Work* (Montrose, NY, 1993)

JAAK LIIVOJA-LORIUS

Person, Gobelinus [Persona] (*b* Paderborn, 1358; *d* monastery of Böddeken, nr Paderborn, 17 Nov 1421). German historian, theorist, cleric and reformer. He was first educated at Paderborn. In 1384 he travelled to Italy, where he studied theology and canon law and held several posts at the papal court under Urban VI. In 1386 he was ordained priest at Genoa and in 1389 he returned to Paderborn. In 1405 he was pastor in Warburg, and in 1410 court chaplain to Bishop Wilhelm von Berg of Paderborn; he was made canon in 1411, and in 1416 he became deacon of St Marien, Bielefeld. In 1418, because of poor health, he retired to the Augustinian monastery of Böddeken and attempted to reform its greatly declining discipline.

Person is known principally as a historian. His *Cosmodromius*, a history of the world, is valuable as a chronicle of Paderborn, particularly for the years 1347–1418; his life of St Meinolf, canon of Paderborn Cathedral and founder of the Böddeken monastery in the first half of the 9th century, is also valuable as a historical document. Person is said to have prepared in March 1417 a book 'for the Ordinary of the Divine Office and Ceremonials', now lost. In his treatise *Tractatus musicae scientiae* (formerly *D-Hs* Realkat. ND VI 4582, lost in World War II), completed in 1417, he presented in nine chapters a conventional treatment of the terminology and the use of modes in plainchant (he also complained about irregularities in the church's musical tradition). He defined music as 'an art that proportionally judges the intervals and consonances of voices' (Müller, 180; see also Yudkin, 66) and, following Isidore of Seville (*Etymologiae* iii.19), divided music into three parts: harmonic, organic and rhythmic. Person also discussed tone-syllables, solmization and mutation, and compositional techniques within the modes (tones). The treatise does not contain musical examples, but in the source it was followed by a tonary in a different hand illustrating part of its contents.

BIBLIOGRAPHY

MGG1 ('Gobelinus Person'; H. Hüschen);*RiemannL 12*

M. Gerbert: *De cantu et musica sacra* (St Blasien, 1774/*R*), ii, 111

U. Chevalier: 'Persona (Gobelin)', *Répertoire des sources historiques du Moyen Age: bio-bibliographie* (Paris, 2/1905–7/*R*), 3584–5

H. Müller: 'Der *Tractatus musicae scientiae* des Gobelinus Person (1358–1421)', *KJb*, xx (1907), 177–96

J.P. Kirsch: 'Gobelinus, Person', *The Catholic Encyclopedia*, vi (New York, 1909)

P. Eickhoff: 'Mitteilungen', *ZMw*, vii (1924–5), 253 only

D. Berg: 'Gobelin Person', *Lexikon des Mittelalters*, iv (Munich, 1989), 1528

M. Bernhard: 'Das musikalische Fachschrifttum im lateinischen Mittelalter',*Rezeption des antiken Fachs im Mittelalter*, Geschichte der Musiktheorie, ed. F. Zaminer, v (Darmstadt, 1990), 37–104

J. Yudkin, ed.: *De musica mensurata: the Anonymous of St. Emmeram* (Bloomington, IN, 1990)

GORDON A. ANDERSON/C. MATTHEW BALENSUELA

Persones, Josquino. *See* PERSOENS, JOSQUINO.

Persuis, Louis-Luc Loiseau de (*b* Metz, 4 July 1769; *d* Paris, 20 Dec 1819). French composer and conductor. He spent his early childhood in the provinces, where he was educated by his father, himself a composer and choirmaster at the cathedrals of Angers and Metz. As a young man Louis-Luc was a violinist in the Metz orchestra and then tried his luck in Paris, arriving there in 1787 on the eve of the Revolution. He played in theatre orchestras, first at the Montansier and then at the Opéra. In 1805 he became chorus master, stage director and, in 1810, conductor of the Opéra; at the same time he was principal assistant conductor in the emperor's orchestra. He had also been appointed professor of singing at the Conservatoire when it was founded in 1795, but he left in 1802 when reform measures involved the abolition of a number of posts. In 1818, while acting as administrator at the Opéra, he also helped to build up the company at the Théâtre Italien, under the direction of Paer.

Persuis's works were mainly for the stage and included operas, *opéras comiques*, ballets and occasional dramatic works. He often wrote in collaboration with other composers; with Jean-François Le Sueur he composed *L'inauguration du temple de la Victoire* and *Le triomphe de Trajan* (both 1807). The latter, a propagandist piece written to glorify Napoleon, was well attuned to the neoclassical tastes of contemporary audiences and was a huge success. Two of his other music dramas are notable examples of their time: *Fanny Morna, ou L'écossaise*, with its setting of landscaped gardens and weeping willows, marks a unique point in the history of the pre-Romantic sensibility; and *La Jérusalem délivrée* exemplifies the tendency of contemporary French opera to look back to medieval subjects. The work is weak in itself but opens with a remarkable overture which was to feature prominently in anthologies of French symphonic music under the Empire; it displays a force and originality for which the rest of Persuis's compositions does not prepare us. He was also prominent in the 19th-century revival of religious music, and from 1802 was a member of the Chapelle Royale, first as a director, then as *compositeur de la musique*. When the Bourbons returned to power Persuis was replaced by Plantade.

WORKS

STAGE

first performed in Paris unless otherwise stated

La nuit espagnole (oc, J. Fiévée), Feydeau, 14 June 1791

Estelle (oc, 3, Villebrune), National, 17 Dec 1793

Phanor et Angéla (oc, 3, Faur), Feydeau, July 1798

Léonidas, ou Les Spartiates (opéra, R.C.G. de Pixérécourt), Opéra, 15 Aug 1799, *F-Po*, collab. A.-F. Gresnick

Fanny Morna, ou L'écossaise (drame lyrique, 3, E. Favières), OC (Favart), 22 Aug 1799

Le fruit défendu (opéra, 1, E. Gosse), OC (Favart), 7 March 1800

Marcel, ou L'héritier supposé (oc, 1, Pixérécourt), OC (Favart), 12 Feb 1801

L'inauguration du Temple de la victoire (tragédie lyrique, 1, Baour-Lormain), Opéra, 2 Jan 1807, collab. J.-F. Le Sueur

Le retour d'Ulysse (ballet, 3, Milon), Opéra, 24 Feb 1807

Le triomphe de Trajan (tragédie lyrique, 3, J. Esménard), Opéra, 23 Oct 1807, *Po*, collab. J.-F. Le Sueur

La Jérusalem délivrée (tragédie lyrique, 5, P.-M. Baour-Lormian, after T. Tasso: *Gerusalemme liberata*), Opéra, 15 Sept 1812

Nina, ou La folle par amour (ballet, 2, Milon), Opéra, 23 Nov 1813

L'épreuve villageoise, ou André et Denise (ballet, Milon), Opéra, 4 April 1815

L'heureux retour (opéra-ballet, 1, Milon), Opéra, 25 July 1815, collab. H.-M. Berton and R. Kreutzer

Le carnaval de Venise, ou La constance à l'épreuve (ballet, 2, Milon), Opéra, 22 Feb 1816, collab. Kreutzer

Les dieux rivaux, ou Les fêtes de Cythere (opéra-ballet, 1, M. Dieulafoy and C. Briffaut), Opéra, 21 June 1816, *Po*, collab. Berton, Kreutzer and G. Spontini

Der Zauberschlaf (ballet, 2), Vienna, 16 Jan 1818, collab. A. Gyrowetz

OTHER WORKS
MSS in F-Pn

Sacred: Leçon de Jérémie pour la Chapelle impériale, 19 April 1810; Pange lingua et tantum ergo, Motet pour la Chapelle du roi; Prière pour Louis XVI; Veni, Creator, alla breve, after 1800

Secular: Chant français, 'Vive le roi, vive la France' (de Bouillé), chorus, orch, 1814; Chant guerrier, 'De Lutèce enfans généreux', 1815; 6 romances, 1v, pf: 1 Le vieux Robin Gray, 'Quand les moutons sont dans la bergerie' (C. Florian), 2 Romance marotique, 'Faire voudrais belle Marie', 3 'Je suis à peine à mon aurore' (C. Dupin), 4 Romance savoyarde, 'Pauvre Jeannette' (Florian), 5 'Avant d'aimer le beau Lisis' (Dupin), 6 'Eglé rêveuse et languissante' (C. Lefébure)

BIBLIOGRAPHY

Choron-FayolleD; EitnerQ; FétisB; MGG1 (B. Bardet)

C. Poisot: *Histoire de la musique en France depuis les temps les plus reculés jusqu'à nos jours* (Paris, 1860)

G. Chouquet: *Histoire de la musique dramatique en France* (Paris, 1873/R)

M. Brenet: *Les concerts en France sous l'ancien régime* (Paris, 1900/R)

A. Soubiès: *Le théâtre italien de 1801 à 1913* (Paris, 1913)

D.H. Foster: 'The Oratorio in Paris in the 18th Century', *AcM*, xlvii (1975), 67–133

P. Constant: *Histoire du Concert spirituel 1725–1790* (Paris, 1975)

D. Pistone: *La musique en France de la Révultion à 1900* (Paris, 1979)

J. Mongrédien: *J.F. Lesueur: contribution à l'étude d'un demi-siècle de musique française, 1780–1830* (Berne, 1980)

J. Mongrédien: *La musique en France des Lumières au Romantisme, 1780–1830* (Paris, 1986)

N. Wild: *Dictionnaire des théâtres parisiens au XIXe siècle* (Paris, 1989)

JEAN MONGRÉDIEN/LAURINE QUETIN

Perth. City in Australia. Situated on the western seaboard, Perth, the capital of Western Australia, is one of the most isolated cities of its size in the world (its population was over one million in the late 1990s). Before the days of rapid communications its isolation hindered the development of a flourishing musical life. During the middle years of the 19th century, vocal music was the staple diet of what was then a British colony, there being little in the way of instrumental music because of the dearth of competent musicians.

In 1887 the colony's first orchestra, the Fremantle Orchestral Society, was established. It was not, however, until 1936 that the first firm foundations for the future development of professional orchestral music in Perth were laid when the Perth SO became the Australian Broadcasting Commission SO, later the West Australian SO. This has now grown to an 89-player orchestra which presents the state's principal orchestral series in the Perth Concert Hall, the leading music auditorium in Western Australia. The orchestra also plays in the pit of His Majesty's Theatre for the seasons of the Western Australian Opera Company (founded 1967) and the West Australian Ballet Company (founded 1952). The West Australian SO is funded by both the federal government and the West Australian state government.

Concerts in Perth range from large orchestral and choral concerts presented by the West Australian SO, usually with visiting international conductors and artists, through chamber music seasons promoted by Musica Viva, to numerous smaller events ranging from perform-ances of Baroque music on original instruments to avant-garde or multi-arts productions of music written by Western Australian composers. The University of Western Australia figures strongly in the performances of 18th- and 20th-century music, while the Western Australian Conservatorium of Music has a national reputation for the quality of its jazz and music theatre productions. Since 1953 the University of Western Australia, together with the state government of Western Australia, has organized the annual Festival of Perth, in which music plays an important role. It is the longest established festival of its kind in Australia and balances the presentation of Western Australian musicians and ensembles with that of eminent international visitors.

Of growing significance in the musical life of Perth are performances by musicians who have recently migrated to Australia and who still practise the musical arts of their home country. In 1982 the Ethnic Music Centre (now the Kulcha) was established to support and promote the work of these musicians. More recently the organization Ab Music was established to provide support for the training of Australian aboriginal musicians and the dissemination of their work.

Music education in Perth during the 19th and early 20th centuries remained largely in the hands of private teachers. During the 1950s music as a class subject came to be accepted into the school system, and it is currently one of the listed subjects for the annual tertiary entrance examinations. Tertiary-level studies are available at the University of Western Australia, where students can elect to specialize in performance, musicology, composition or music education, or at Edith Cowan University, which offers performance and music education.

BIBLIOGRAPHY

A.H. Kornweibel: *Apollo and the Pioneers* (Perth, 1973)

C. Buttrose: *Playing for Australia: a Story about ABC Orchestras and Music in Australia* (Sydney, 1982)

J.E. Farrant: *Music in Western Australia 1900–1950* (diss., U. of Western Australia, forthcoming)

MARGARET SEARES

Perti, Giacomo Antonio (*b* Bologna, 6 June 1661; *d* Bologna, 10 April 1756). Italian composer. During his 60 years as *maestro di cappella* of S Petronio, Bologna, he achieved fame both as a composer of sacred music, opera and oratorio and as a teacher: such illustrious musicians as Giuseppe Torelli and G.B. Martini were among his pupils.

1. LIFE. At the age of nine he began to study music in Bologna with his uncle Lorenzo Perti and with Rocco Laurenti, from whom he learnt the rudiments of organ playing. He started to study singing in 1670 and the year after he took up humanistic studies with the Jesuits at S Lucia. In 1675 he began the study of counterpoint with his uncle and he later studied with Petronio Franceschini. In 1678 his first music to be performed, a mass, was given in S Tomaso al Mercato; two other works, a motet and a *Magnificat* (both for eight voices), date from that year. In 1679 he wrote his first operatic music – the third act of *Atide* – and the oratorio *S Serafia*. In 1680 he wrote a Mass in D with two trumpets (claimed by Martini to be the first of its kind), which was performed in S Sigismondo. In 1681 he was admitted as composer to the Accademia Filarmonica, where he was *principe* in 1687, 1693, 1697, 1705 and 1719, when he was made 'diffinitore perpetuo'. Several months later he went to Parma for further

contrapuntal studies with Giuseppe Corso (called Celano). Here, as is clear from a six-year correspondence with Celano, he decisively formed his church music style, especially that of the concerted masses and psalms of the 1680s and 90s. In 1688 he published his first opus, *Cantate morali e spirituali*, dedicating it to the Emperor Leopold I, who eventually rewarded him with a precious chain of gold. In the following year he was in Venice, probably for the production of his opera *La Rosaura*, and from there he applied for the vacant position of *vicemaestro di cappella* of S Petronio. He was unsuccessful, possibly because of the influence of G.P. Colonna, the *maestro di cappella* (during the famous dispute over the consecutive 5ths of Corelli, Perti had sided with Corelli against Colonna).

Perti was chosen to succeed his uncle Lorenzo as *maestro di cappella* of the cathedral of S Pietro in 1690. In 1696 he was called from there to be *maestro di cappella* of S Petronio, where he spent the rest of his life, except for a few short journeys to Florence, Rome (1703 and 1747) and Naples (1703). Simultaneously he held similar posts at S Domenico (1704–55, G.M. Alberti deputizing for him from 1734) and the Madonna di Galliera (1706–50). According to Martini he was offered a position at the court of the Emperor Leopold I in 1697 in succession to Antonio Draghi, but there is no other record of this. Because of financial difficulties at S Petronio, Perti began his career there without a fixed group of musicians. Until February 1701 musicians were hired only for the required festive occasions. With the restoration of the *cappella musicale*, however, the group was re-established with 24 regular musicians. It was enlarged for festive occasions (especially the patronal feast on 4 October) to as many as 153 in 1718 and 1719. In 1723 the regular group numbered 36, the highest number during Perti's term.

Perti enjoyed considerable fame and favour with several important personages, including Ferdinando III de' Medici, for whom he wrote church music and operas, which were staged at Pratolino, and the Emperor Charles VI, to whom he dedicated his op.2. In 1740 the emperor made him a royal councillor. His correspondence reveals a longstanding rapport with the Duchess Aurora Sanseverino of Piedimonte d'Alife, who was a member of a Bolognese family; he regularly sent compositions to her for use at her court. His correspondence also indicates that he was held in high regard by Fux, Caldara, Pasquini, Corelli and other influential musicians. Padre Martini held him in the highest esteem and included six examples of his contrapuntal music in his *Esemplare ossia Saggio fondamentale pratico di contrappunto* (1774–5). Among Perti's students were Torelli, Gabrielli, Pistocchi, Aldrovandini, P.P. Laurenti, G.B. Martini and F.O. Manfredini.

2. WORKS.   For the musicians at S Petronio (discussed above) Perti wrote masses (consisting of Kyrie and Gloria only, with a few separate Credo settings), motets, psalms, hymns, antiphons and *Magnificat* settings, as well as instrumental music intended for the liturgy. Most of these are festive works in Bolognese-style counterpoint calling for strings and occasionally trumpets and other obbligato instruments, in addition to solo voices and choruses. There are also works in strict *a cappella* style or with simple basso continuo accompaniment. According to Gaspari, Martini divided Perti's sacred works into two halves: one was left to S Petronio, most of which is still extant, and one to S Lucia, most of which is lost. Many of the extant works are in Perti's own hand or in manuscripts that he carefully corrected. In many cases there survive not only scores but also parts, which reveal interesting continuo practices and revisions by Perti himself and others. A large group of separate *versetti* intended as substitutes for sections of the masses show the adaptability of the masses to occasions of varying degrees of splendour. They and especially the motets and psalms reveal Perti as a vocal composer of considerable skill, in complete command of his craft. He himself acknowledged that Luigi Rossi, Carissimi and Cesti inspired his melodic style. Similar qualities are obvious in his operas, oratorios and solo cantatas, which are characterized by melodic inventiveness, variety of form, the use of concerted solo instruments (especially trumpet and cello) and dialogues between voices and instruments with independent melodic material. He projected a treatise on counterpoint as his op.3, but it was never completed. His purpose as stated in the preface was 'to demonstrate with the greatest brevity and clarity possible the manner of applying all the principles of music to the modern style': this statement indicates his characteristic ability to adapt his well-founded musical skills to the changes of style that occurred during his long creative life.

WORKS

OPERAS

lost unless otherwise stated

dm – *dramma per musica*

Atide [Act 3] (dm, 3, T. Stanzani), Bologna, Formagliari, 23 June 1679, lib (Bologna, 1679) [Act 1 by G.F. Tosi, Act 2 by P. degli Antoni]

Marzio Coriolano (dm, 3, F. Silvani), Venice, SS Giovanni e Paolo, 20 Jan 1683

Oreste in Argo (drama [per musica], 3, G.A. Bergamori), Modena, Spelta, carn. 1685, *I-MOe*

L'incoronazione di Dario (dm, A. Morselli, rev. G.M. Rapparini), Bologna, Malvezzi, 13 Jan 1686

La Flavia (dm, 3, Rapparini), Bologna, Malvezzi, 16 Feb 1686, *MOe*

La Rosaura (dm, 3, A. Arcoleo), Venice, S Angelo, carn. 1689, *D-SWl, I-MOe*

Dionisio Siracusano (dm, A. Salvi), Parma, Ducale, carn. 1689

Brenno in Efeso (dm, 3, Arcoleo), Venice, S Salvatore, 1690

Il Pompeo (dm, N. Minato), Genoa, Falcone, carn. 1691

L'inganno scoperto per vendetta (dm, Silvani), Genoa, Falcone, 1691, *MOe*

Furio Camillo (dm, 3, M. Noris), Venice, S Salvatore, carn. 1692, *D-Bsb*

Nerone fatto cesare [Nerone infante] (dm, 3, Noris), Venice, S Salvatore, 1693, *SWl, I-Rsc* (inc.); sinfonia by Giuseppe Torelli

La forza della virtù (dm, 3, D. David, with alterations), Bologna, Malvezzi, 25 May 1694

Laodicea e Berenice (dm, Noris), Venice, S Salvatore, 26 Dec 1694; rev. as L'inganno trionfante in amore

Penelope la casta (dm, Noris), Rome, Tordinona, 25 Jan 1696

Fausta restituita all'impero (dm, 3, N. Bonis), Rome, Tordinona, 19 Jan 1697

?Perseo (P.J. Martello), Bologna, 1697, collab. others

Apollo geloso (Martello), Bologna, Formagliari, 16 Aug 1698

La prosperità di Elio Sejano (drama musicale, Minato), Milan, Ducale, carn. 1699, collab. A.F. Martinenghi and A. Vanelli

Ariovisto [Act 1] (drama musicale, 3, P. d'Averara), Milan, Ducale, Sept 1699, collab. F. Ballarotti and P. Magni

Lucio vero [Acts 2 and 3] (dm, 3, A. Zeno), Bologna, 1700

Astianatte (dm, Salvi, after J. Racine: *Andromaque*), Florence, Pratolino, 1701; sinfonia by Giuseppe Torelli

Dionisio rè di Portogallo (dm, Salvi), Florence, Pratolino, Sept 1707

Il Venceslao, ossia Il fratricida innocente (dm, Zeno), Bologna, Malvezzi, 19 May 1708

Ginevra principessa di Scozia (dm, Salvi, after L. Ariosto: *Orlando furioso*), Florence, Pratolino, aut. 1708

Berenice regina d'Egitto (dm, Salvi), Florence, Pratolino, Sept 1709

Demetrio (Salvi), Florence, Pratolino, 1709 [according to G.B. Martini]

Il riso nato tra il pianto (drama da rappresentarsi, ?A. Aureli), Bologna, 11 Feb 1710, collab. others

Rodelinda regina de' Longobardi (dm, Salvi, after P. Corneille: *Pertharite, roi des Lombards*), Florence, Pratolino, aut. 1710

Faramondo (Zeno), Bologna, 1710

Il più fedele tra i vassalli (dm, Silvani), Bologna, 1710, collab. others

Il Cortegiano (A. Basili), Palestrina, 1739, prol only

Foca, Munich

Rosinda ed Emireno (Arcoleo), *A-Wn*, never perf.

revs. of ops by others: L'eroe innocente, ovvero gli equivoci del sembiante by A. Scarlatti, Bologna, 1679; Pompeo Magno by D. Freschi, Bologna, 1687; Teodora Augusta by D. Gabrielli, Bologna, 1687; Il re infante by C. Pallavicino, Bologna, 1694

ORATORIOS
music in I-Bsp; librettos, where extant, Bc

S Serafia [I due gigli porporati nel martirio de S Serafia e S Sabina] (L. Lotti), Bologna, 23 Feb 1679

Abramo [Abramo vincitore; Agar; Agare scacciata; Sara] (G. Malisardi), Bologna, 10 Dec 1683, score also in *I-MOe* (facs. in IO, iv, 1986)

Mosè (G.B. Giardini), Modena, 1685, score also in *MOe*

Oratorio della Passione [Gesù al Sepolcro] (G.A. Bergamori), Bologna, 1685, score also in *Ac* (facs. in BMB, section 4, 85, 1977), *Bc*

La Beata Imelde Lambertini, Bologna, late March 1686, score also in *Bc*

La passione di Cristo [Oratorio sopra la passione del Redentore; Affetti di compassione alla morte del Redentore], Bologna, 1694

S Galgano (Bergamori), Bologna, 1694

Cristo al limbo, Bologna, 28 March 1696

La morte del giusto overo Il transito di S Giuseppe (B. Sandrinelli), Venice, c1700, lost

La sepoltura di Cristo, Bologna, 21 March 1704

S Petronio (G.B. Rampognani), Bologna, 17 March 1720, score also in *Bc*

La passione del Redentore, Bologna, 11 April 1721

L'amor divino [I conforti di Maria Vergine] (C.I. Frugoni), Bologna, 26 March 1723

La nascita del Signore

Il figlio prodigo

Pasticcio orats: La morte delusa, Milan, 1703, lost; I trionfi di Giosuè [Giosuè in Gabaon], Florence, 1704

?8 other orats

Profetia à 8, score also in *Bc*, *D-MÜs*; Profetia di Nabucodonosor, score also in *I-Bc*

SACRED VOCAL

Messa e salmi concertati, 4vv, insts, chorus, op.2 (Bologna, 1735)

7 canzonette in aria marmoresca sopra le 7 principali feste di Nostra Signora (Bologna, 1780)

28 masses, 1v, chorus, bc, insts [Ky, Gl only]; 11 Cr, 1v, chorus, bc, insts

c120 pss, cantica, hymns, solo vv, chorus, bc, insts

54 motets, solo vv, chorus, bc, insts

83 versetti; miscellaneous sacred works, *I-Bsp*

1 motet, B, 2 vn, bc, 1695¹

Principal sources: *A-Wn*, *I-Ac*, *Bc*, *Bsp*, *Fc*, *Vc*, incl. many autographs

SECULAR VOCAL

Cantate morali e spirituali, 1–2vv, vn, op.1 (Bologna, 1688; 4 /R1969 in BMB, lxxxv–lxxxvi)

93 cants. (dialogues, serenades, accademie), solo vv, bc; 49 cants., solo vv, bc, insts; 30 arias: *I-Ac*, *Bsp*

INSTRUMENTAL
manuscripts in I-Bsp

Sonata, d, in Sonate per camera a violino e violoncello di vari autori (Bologna, c?1700)

15 sinfonie avanti la messa; 2 sinfonie avanti il prologo; 2 sinfonie avanti l'oratorio; 3 sinfonie

1 sonata à 4

3 adaptations of concs. or sonatas by G. Torelli

BIBLIOGRAPHY

ES (L.F. Tagliavini); *GaspariC*; *RicciTB*

G.A. Perti: Letters (MSS, *I-Bc* K.44, P.143–6)

F. Parisini: *Carteggio inedito del P. Giambattista Martini coi più celebri musicisti del suo tempo* (Bologna, 1888/R)

F. Vatielli: *Arte e vita musicale a Bologna* (Bologna, 1927/R)

N. Morini: *La R. Accademia filarmonica di Bologna* (Bologna, 1930/R)

F. Vatielli: 'L'oratorio a Bologna negli ultimi decenni del Seicento', *NA*, xv (1938), 26–35, 77–87

J. Berger: 'Notes on Some 17th-Century Compositions for Trumpets and Strings in Bologna', *MQ*, xxxvii (1951), 354–67

F. Giegling: 'Giacomo Antonio Perti (1661–1756)', *Mf*, viii (1955), 445–52

G. Vecchi: 'Giacomo Antonio Perti a duecento anni della morte (1661–1756)', *Atti e Memorie della Deputazione di Storia Patria per le provincie di Romagna*, new ser., vii (1955–6), 255–71

M. Fabbri: 'Giacomo Antonio Perti', *Musicisti lombardi ed emiliani*, Chigiana, xv (1958), 133–40

G. Vecchi, ed.: *La musica barocca a Bologna … Giacomo Antonio Perti (1661–1756)* (Bologna, 1961)

J. Berger: 'The Sacred Works of Giacomo Antonio Perti', *JAMS*, xvii (1964), 370–77

M. Fabbri: 'Nuova luce sull'attività fiorentina di Giacomo Antonio Perti, Bartolomeo Cristofori e Giorgio F. Haendel', *Chigiana*, new ser., i (1964), 143–90

M.L. Orlandi: *La musica strumentale di G.A. Perti* (thesis, U. of Bologna, 1965–6)

M.N. Schnoebelen: *The Concerted Mass at San Petronio in Bologna, ca. 1660–1730* (diss., U. of Illinois, 1966)

R. Schnitzler: *The Passion-Oratorios of Giacomo Antonio Perti* (thesis, Ohio, U., 1967)

A. Schnoebelen: 'Performance Practices at San Petronio in the Baroque', *AcM*, xli (1969), 37–55

G. Vecchi: 'Il "Nerone fatto Cesare" di Giacomo Antonio Perti a Venezia', *Venezia e il melodramma nel Seicento*, ed. M.T. Muraro (Florence, 1976), 299–318

A. Schnoebelen: *Padre Martini's Collection of Letters in the Civico museo bibliografico musicale in Bologna* (New York, 1979)

M. De Angelis: 'Il teatro di Pratolino tra Scarlatti e Perti: il carteggio di Giacomo Antonio Perti con il principe Ferdinando de' Medici (1705–1719)', *NRMI*, xxi (1987), 606–40

O. Gambassi: *La cappella musicale di S. Petronio: maestri, organisti, cantori e strumentisti dal 1436 al 1920* (Florence, 1987), 30–33, 156–89, 332, 488

J. Riepe: 'Gli oratorii Giacomo Antonio Perti: cronologia e ricognizione delle fonti', *Studi musicali*, xxii (1993), 115–232

M. Vanscheeuwijck: 'La cappella musicale di San Petonio ai tempi di Giovanni Paolo Colonna (1674–1695): organizzazione esemplare di una istituzione musicale', *La cappella musicale nell'Italia della Controriforma*, ed. O. Mischiati and P. Russo (Florence, 1993), 303–24

M. Vanscheeuwijck: *De religieuze muziekproduktie in de San Petronio-Kerk te Bologna ten tijde van Giovanni Paolo Colonna (1674–1695)* (diss., U. of Ghent, 1995)

ANNE SCHNOEBELEN (with MARC VANSCHEEUWIJCK)

Pertile, Aureliano (*b* Montagnana, nr Padua, 9 Nov 1885; *d* Milan, 11 Jan 1952). Italian tenor. He studied with Orefice in Padua and made his début at Vicenza in *Martha* in 1911. After further studies in Milan with Manlio Bavagnoli he began to attract notice in 1913–14 at the S Carlo, Naples, singing in *Madama Butterfly* and *Carmen*, and then at the Costanzi, Rome (1915–16), La Scala (1916) and at the Colón, Buenos Aires (1918). He achieved fame in 1922 for his performance in *Mefistofele* at La Scala under Toscanini, whose favourite tenor he then became. Still at La Scala, where he appeared every year until 1937, he scored notable successes as Lohengrin, Puccini's Des Grieux, Edgardo, Andrea Chénier, Canio, Radames, Riccardo, Don Alvaro and Manrico, and took the title roles in the premières of Boito's *Nerone* (1924) and Mascagni's *Nerone* (1935). He sang until 1946, in the later years appearing frequently as Otello. From 1945 he taught at the Milan Conservatory. His voice was not particularly powerful and the tone, rather thick in the middle register, took on nasal and guttural inflections. It became smooth and mellifluous, however, in lyrical moments as well as vibrant and incisive in dramatic ones.

Pertile stood out because of his fine enunciation, variety of expression and unusual interpretative gifts, as can be heard in recordings from his best years (1922–32), including solos from *Andrea Chénier* and *Adriana Lecouvreur*, and Radames in a complete *Aida* from La Scala. At his peak Pertile was widely held, in Italy and Argentina, the equal of the most famous tenors of the period. Less fortunate in the USA (he sang at the Metropolitan only during the 1921–2 season), he was very popular at Covent Garden (1927–31), especially as Manrico, Radames and Canio.

BIBLIOGRAPHY

ES (E. Gara); *GV* (E. Gara, R. Celletti; R. Vegeto)
D. Silvestrini: *I tenori celebri: Aureliano Pertile e il suo metodo di canto* (Bologna, 1932)
P. Morby: 'Aureliano Pertile', *Record Collector*, vii (1952), 244–60, 267–83 [with discography by H.M. Barnes and V. Girard]
J.B. Steane: *The Grand Tradition* (London, 1974/R), 156–8
B. Tosi: *Pertile: una voce, un mito* (Venice, 1985)
W.R. Moran, ed.: *Herman Klein and the Gramophone* (Portland, OR, 1990)

RODOLFO CELLETTI/VALERIA PREGLIASCO GUALERZI

Pertinaro, Francesco. *See* PORTINARO, FRANCESCO.

Peru, Republic of (Sp. *República del Perú*). Country in South America. It is situated on the Pacific western seaboard and covers an area of 1,285,216 km², bordered by Ecuador, Colombia, Brazil, Bolivia and Chile. The country declared independence from Spain in 1821 and achieved full independence in 1824. The legal existence of Amerindian communities was recognized in the constitution after 1920. The population of 25·66 million (2000 estimate) is predominantly Amerindian and mestizo, and the original Inca language of Quechua is spoken by *c*16·5% as the second official language, Spanish being the first. Aymara is spoken by some 3%, mainly in the Southern Andes.

I. Art music. II. Traditional and popular music.

I. Art music

1. Colonial period. 2. After independence.

1. COLONIAL PERIOD.   Peru, the administrative centre of practically all Spanish South America from the Spanish conquest (1526) until the 18th century, occupied with Mexico the most important place in the Spanish colonial empire. During the colonial period Lima (the 'City of Kings') and Cuzco, the city of the Incas, developed an active cultural life. At Cuzco music was cultivated at the cathedral and the Seminario de S Antonio Abad (founded 1598), where polyphonic music and instrument playing were taught. The music archive of the seminary contains a rich collection of post-1600 colonial manuscripts of Spanish and Peruvian works, including a large number of polyphonic *villancicos*, *tonadas*, *jácaras*, liturgical works with and without ascription, and dramatic works such as *loas*, *comedias* and *sainetes*. There is evidence that as early as 1553 the first and second books of Morales's masses (Rome, 1544) were in use at Cuzco, with other volumes of motets and *Magnificat* settings. Gutierre Fernández Hidalgo (*c*1547–1623), the most substantial composer in 16th-century South America, held the post of *maestro de capilla* at Cuzco for a few years before moving permanently to Sucre in Bolivia.

Missionary work was keenly pursued in Peru, as in the other Spanish colonies. The Franciscan Juan Pérez Bocanegra included in his *Ritual formulario e institución de curas* (Lima, 1631) a four-part polyphonic piece titled *Hanacpachap cussicuinin*, to a text in the Quechua language, to be sung 'in processions when entering the church'; it is the earliest example of polyphony printed in the New World. Fray Gregorio Dezuola (de Zuola) (*d* 1709), active at the convent of S Francisco in Cuzco, left a book known as the Dezuola Manuscript, which contains 17 songs, mostly polyphonic, with Spanish texts (with the exception of a 'Credo romano'). Only two items of the collection have been ascribed; one to Francisco Correa de Arauxo, the other to Tomás de Herrera, who was appointed organist of Cuzco Cathedral in 1611. Herrera's piece is a short song, *Hijos de Eva tributarios*, for two altos and tenor, and is the earliest known example of vernacular polyphony in Peru.

Lima, the capital of the viceroyalty of Peru, developed a musical life unequalled by any other South American city. The cathedral (consecrated 1572) employed many well-paid singers and instrumentalists and attracted several famous *maestros de capilla*. The post was created in 1612 and its responsibilities included conducting the orchestra and the choir, the composition of works for all occasions, the teaching of polyphony, financial administration and acting as intermediary between the archbishop, the chapter and the musicians. Tomás de Torrejón y Velasco was *maestro de capilla* from 1676 to 1728, and his works (extant at Lima and Cuzco) were performed throughout Spanish America. His fame also rests on his opera *La púrpura de la rosa* (1701, libretto by Calderón de la Barca), the first produced in the New World, which indicates the extent of the *maestro de capilla*'s involvement in the whole musical life of the city. His successor, the Italian-born Roque Ceruti, who went to Peru primarily as the director and conductor of the viceroy's private chapel and orchestra, exerted a decisive influence by introducing the bel canto style. Another Italian musician associated with Lima Cathedral, Andrés Bolognesi, active at the turn of the 19th century, was responsible for organizing and developing local opera.

The first native Peruvian composer of church music was José de Orejón y Aparicio, considered the most talented Peruvian musician of his time. He was appointed organist of the cathedral in 1742, and in 1760 he succeeded Ceruti as the acting choirmaster. Among his many works his *Passion for Good Friday* for double chorus and orchestra and a solo cantata *Mariposa de sus rayos* reveal his inventive treatment of melody and harmony. Extant works of Juan Beltrán, Melchor Tapia and Bonifacio Llaque, all cathedral musicians, indicate that church music declined at Lima during the early 19th century.

2. AFTER INDEPENDENCE.   The splendour of colonial musical life had no counterpart in the years of the struggle for independence (1820–80), during which operas and salon music predominated. Church music continued to be written in a secularized Romantic style, as can be seen in some works by José Bernardo Alcedo (1788–1878), composer of the Peruvian national anthem.

At the end of the 19th century Peruvian composers, who had become more technically competent, began to turn to Peruvian folklore for inspiration. Immigrant musicians were the first to treat Peruvian subjects in works written within the Romantic tradition, such as the successful opera *Atahualpa* (1875) by the Italian Carlo Enrico Pasta (1817–98) and the *Rapsodia peruana* by

Claudio Rebagliati (1843–1909). This Romantic nationalism was adopted by José María Valle Riestra (1859–1925), educated in London, Paris and Berlin, in his opera *Ollanta* (1900), and by Luis Duncker Lavalle (1874–1922), who wrote piano pieces in a semi-popular style inspired by the most characteristic mestizo folk-music genres. The various generations of early 20th-century composers developed musical nationalism within concurrent European styles. Music of the Quechua-speaking Indians, which is pentatonic and displays distinctive rhythmic features, became a source of national identity. The Amerindian style is found in varying degrees in the works of Daniel Alomía Robles (1871–1942), Manuel Aguirre (1863–1951), Luis Pacheco de Céspedes (*b* 1895), Carlos Sánchez Málaga (1904–95) and many others. Theodoro Valcárcel (1900–42), the most prolific and imaginative Peruvian composer of his generation, at first adopted an impressionistic style and later evolved a refined form of nationalism.

With the arrival in Peru in the 1920s and 30s of the European composers and musicologists Andrés Sas (1900–67) and Rudolf Holzmann (1910–92), Peruvian art music was revitalized. Sas and Holzmann taught practically all the Peruvian musicians of that generation, and made available in Peru a much-needed solid academic training. Holzmann promoted the study of contemporary composition techniques and aesthetic attitudes, particularly the music of the Second Viennese School and of Hindemith. As the head of the musicological service of the National School of Folk Music and Dance in Lima, Holzmann encouraged research into colonial music and was active in the study of Peruvian folk and traditional music. Sas concentrated his studies on the indigenous music of his adopted country and specialized in Peruvian pre-Columbian and colonial music.

An awareness of contemporary international currents appears in the works of younger composers such as Enrique Iturriaga (*b* 1918), Celso Garrido-Lecca (*b* 1926), Francisco Bernado Pulgar Vidal (*b* 1929), Enrique Pinilla (1927–89) and Alejandro Núñez Allauca (*b* 1931) in their use of atonal expressionism, neo-classicism or serialism. Iturriaga has become a leading figure in modern Peruvian composition; he has gradually turned from large nationalist works to dodecaphony. The outstanding figures of the Peruvian avant garde include César Bolaños (*b* 1931), Edgar Valcárcel (*b* 1932), José Malsio (*b* 1924), Leopoldo La Rosa (*b* 1931) and Pozzi Escot (*b* 1931). Most of those named have had links with foreign music institutions: Bolaños and Valcárcel have been Fellows of the Di Tella Institute of Buenos Aires; Garrido-Lecca spent two years at the Columbia–Princeton Electronic Music Center, USA; Pozzi Escot has taught for several years at the New England Conservatory of Music and at Wheaton College, USA; Pinilla studied at the Hochschule für Musik in Berlin, and Iturriaga received lessons in Paris from Arthur Honegger. In the late 1970s and 80s a number of younger composers emerged on the Peruvian scene revealing a dynamic, eclectic production. The most notable figures at that time were Walter Casas Napán (*b* 1939), Pedro Seiji Asato (*b* 1940), Teófilo Alvarez (*b* 1944), Douglas Tarnawiecki (*b* 1948), Luis David Aguilar (*b* 1950) and José Carols Campos (*b* 1957).

See also LIMA.

BIBLIOGRAPHY

StevensonRB

C. Raygada: 'Panorama musical del Perú', *Boletín latino-americano de música*, ii (1936), 169–214

C. Sanchez Málaga: 'La música en el Perú', *Nuestra música*, ii (1947), 72–7

C. Arróspide de la Flor and R. Holzmann: 'Catálogo de los manuscritos de música existentes en el Archivo Arzobispal de Lima', *Cuaderno de estudio*, iii/7 (1949), 36–49; enlarged in *StevensonRB*, 114–30

R. Barbacci: 'Apuntes para un diccionario biográfico musical peruano', *Fénix*, no.6 (1949), 414–510

R. Vargas Ugarte: 'Un archivo de música colonial en la ciudad del Cuzco', *Mar del Sur*, v/26 (1953), 1–10

C. Raygada: 'Guía musical del Perú', *Fénix*, no.12 (1956–7), 3–77; no.13 (1963), 1–82; no.14 (1964), 3–95

R. Stevenson: 'Opera Beginnings in the New World', *MQ*, xlv (1959), 8–25

R. Stevenson: *The Music of Peru: Aboriginal and Viceroyal Epochs* (Washington DC, 1960)

C. Vega: 'Un códice peruano colonial del siglo XVII', *RMC*, nos.79–82 (1962), 54–93

E. Pinilla: 'Informe sobre la música en el Perú', *Historia del Perú*, ix, ed. J. Mejía Baca (Lima, 1980), 363–77

E. Iturriaga and J.C. Estenssoro: 'Emancipación y República: siglo XIX', *La música en el Perú* (Lima, 1985), 103–24

E. Pinilla: 'La música en el siglo XX', *La música en el Perú* (Lima, 1985), 125–213

J. Quezada: 'La música en el virreinato', *La música en el Perú* (Lima, 1985), 65–102

J.C. Estenssoro: *Música y sociedad coloniales: Lima 1680–1830* (Lima, 1989)

II. Traditional and popular music

The varieties of traditional and popular music in Peru correlate with different social groups and regions. The musics of indigenous communities and of mestizos of the Andean highlands represent the two most prominent style complexes. *Criollos* (creoles, i.e. American-born of Spanish descent, generally of European heritage), Afro-Peruvians on the Pacific coast and lowland indigenous groups in the Amazonian rain forest perform different styles. The audiences for recent urban-popular genres tend to cross regional boundaries but are still often delineated by ethnicity and class.

1. Documentation and collections. 2. Pre-Columbian music. 3. Highland indigenous music. 4. Lowland indigenous music. 5. Highland mestizo music. 6. Coastal *criollo* and Afro-Peruvian music. 7. Music of highland migrants in cities.

1. DOCUMENTATION AND COLLECTIONS.   Information about pre-Columbian Peruvian music comes from 16th- and 17th-century chronicles, church documents and archaeological instruments and iconography (*see* INCA MUSIC). The archaeological record is strongest for pre-Columbian coastal cultures. Museum collections in Lima (e.g. Museo Nacional de la Cultura Peruana), North America and Europe house instruments and ceramics that depict instruments or musical activities. The most important sources for highland music and dance in the preconquest and early colonial periods include the chronicles of Felipe Guaman Poma de Ayala who discusses indigenous music, dances and festivals and provides illustrations and song texts; Guaman Poma also makes mention of, or illustrates, early colonial musical practices and instruments.

Don Baltasar Jaime Martínez Campañón y Bujanda documented and provided illustrations of costumed dances, harp and violin in Trujillo on the north coast for the second half of the 18th century. There are a few scattered references to highland and coastal music in travellers' accounts during the 18th and 19th centuries, but indigenous and mestizo music is poorly documented for this period. Victor Guzmán Cáceres and Daniel Alomía Robles collected *criollo*, mestizo and indigenous music in the early 20th century but their material remains largely unpublished. The Harcourts worked in Peru, Ecuador and Bolivia between 1912 and 1924 and produced the first major study of Andean music and instruments (1925). In more recent years a number of substantial general studies and printed collections of pre-Columbian, indigenous, mestizo, and *criollo* music and song texts have been published (e.g. *see* STEVENSON, ROBERT MURRELL).

The Harcourts made early cylinder recordings, 168 of which were published in transcription (1925). 190 field recordings made by Isabel Aretz in 1942 are housed in the Instituto Interamericano de Etnomusicología y Folklore (Caracas). There is a collection of Andean music in the Archives of Traditional Music at Indiana University. Sound, photo and video documentation of traditional Peruvian music and dance is now centred at the Archivo de Música Tradicional Andina at the Pontificia Universidad Católica del Perú in Lima (catalogue, 1995); archive recordings are being reissued on the US based Smithsonian Folkways label.

2. PRE-COLUMBIAN MUSIC. Wind, drums, and ideophones were the only instruments used in the Peruvian highlands and on the coast before the arrival of the Spanish in 1532 (fig.1); there is little information about pre-Columbian music of the Peruvian Amazon. Many of the prominent types of pre-Columbian instruments were still used in performance in the late 20th century, although terminology, tunings and materials of construction have sometimes changed.

There is archaeological evidence for vertical notched flutes for the coast and highlands (fig.1*b*). Now known as KENA, as well as by other local names, end-blown notched flutes were known in the highlands as *pinkullu* (also *pincollo*, *pingollo*) in the pre-Columbian period. Archaeological ceramic whistles, ocarinas and whistle jars indicate that the technology for duct flutes existed before the Spanish conquest, yet there is no early evidence for pre-Columbian vertical duct flutes. One of the most common indigenous instruments, end-blown duct flutes (often called *pinkullu* or *pinkillu*) may have been modelled on the European recorder during the colonial period. An extant example of a transverse flute with two finger-holes from coastal Moche culture has been found.

Archaeological panpipes from the coast, especially from Nasca culture (see fig.1*a*), have been studied by a number of scholars. Findings indicate that high-pitched tunings were favoured, that single-row instruments were predominant, that intervals both smaller and larger than European semitones were included, and that panpipes were sometimes played in consort with two sizes tuned in octaves. The 16th-century chronicler Garcilaso describes panpipe performance in the southern Peruvian-Bolivian highlands involving double-row interlocking practice, with different parts (*tiple*, tenor, contralto, *contrabajo*) suggesting that different sized panpipes may have been played in consort to create parallel polyphony as in the late 20th century. PANPIPES were called *antara*, and *siku* (or *sico*).

Trumpets were the other main pre-Columbian wind instruments. Curved and straight trumpets without stops were made of ceramic, metal and conch shells, while conch-shell trumpets are depicted as important in Inca culture by Guaman Poma. Ceramic single-headed drums have been found on the coast. Drawings by Guaman

Poma show a variety of different sized double-headed drums. Interestingly, he shows women playing both large and small double-headed drums. In the late 1990s the small double-headed *tinya* is the only instrument played by indigenous women in the Peruvian Andes. Leg rattles are also depicted by Guaman Poma.

From chroniclers' and early missionaries' accounts it is clear that in Inca society music was associated with monthly festivals, and was closely bound to indigenous religion and agriculture. Garcilaso suggests that masked dances were indigenous to Cuzco.

3. HIGHLAND INDIGENOUS MUSIC. Quechua, the language of the Inca empire and a lingua franca favoured by early colonial missionaries, is spoken throughout most of the Peruvian sierra and among highland migrants in coastal cities. In Peru, Aymara (the second most prominent Andean Amerindian language) is largely restricted to the *departamento* of Puno: in the province of Huancané on the northwest side of Lake Titicaca and in Chucuito province on the south side, with both Quechua- and Amyara-speaking communities in the province of Puno located between Huancané and Chucuito. Academics and state institutions have used 'Quechua' and 'Aymara' as cultural categories for convenience; indigenous groups have sometimes strategically used these concepts as the basis of political ethnic groupings. Notions of a Quechua or Aymara culture or 'nation', however, tend to be alien to the discourse of rural villagers who more frequently define their identities in specific community and regional terms. The main generalizable musical difference between Quechua- and Aymara-speaking communities is that vocal music is usually central in the former and relatively unimportant in the latter. Otherwise, indigenous Andean music is best understood in regional terms.

Spanning regional and ethnolinguistic differences, certain aesthetic preferences, musical practices and stylistic features are common to indigenous Andean music. The music tends to involve short sections of between two and four phrases which are repeated in various ways: *AABB*, *AABBCC*, *ABAB*. There is often a good deal of motivic repetition between sections and a single, short piece will often be repeated for a long time during festivals. Scales vary from three to seven notes according to region, and to genre within the same region, but often include an initial minor 3rd. Melodic shape tends to be either undulating or descending, or both. There is a preference for dense timbres involving complex overtone structures and for relatively wide intonational variation for any given pitch. There is also a preference for dense, overlapping textures within the overall approaches of wide unison, heterophony and parallel polyphony for group performance. High tessitura in vocal, wind and string music is favoured, with all flutes except panpipes being overblown and young women being the preferred singers. Most indigenous music is in duple metre and involves syncopated rhythms. A prototypical Andean rhythmic feel, basic to genres such as the HUAYNO, *carnavale*, *hyalas*, *kh'ajelo* and others, subtly fluctuates between a quaver and two semi-quavers figure and a quaver triplet. With the exception of the small double-headed *tinya* drum, indigenous instrumental performance is restricted to males.

In the Lake Titicaca region of Puno, various panpipe styles are heard during the dry season (April to October). The double-row *sikuri* style is prominently performed by

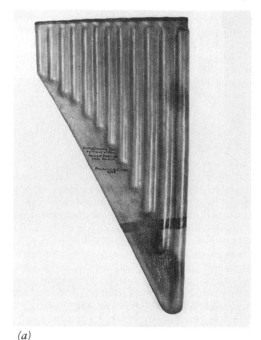

(b)

(a)

(c)

(d)

1. Pre-Columbian instruments: (a) clay panpipes (Nazca period, 400–1000 CE), Pitt Rivers Museum, Oxford; (b) notched flute of clay (Chancay period, 1300–1438 CE), Museum für Völkerkunde, Leipzig; (c) copper bells surmounted by dancing figures (Mochica period, 400–1000 CE), private collection; (d) whistling pot in the form of a dead man beating a drum above a group of dancing figures accompanied by panpipes (Mochica period), Linden-Museum, Stuttgart

community ensembles ranging from 12 to over 50 players for public festival dancing and weddings. As with most panpipe traditions in this region, *sikuri* performances involve paired musicians performing their individual panpipe rows in interlocking fashion. Communities and micro-regions in the Lake Titicaca area use specific types of consorts with panpipes cut to different sizes to render parallel polyphony. A common style diffused from the Aymara district of Conima after the 1920s involves nine panpipe sizes (three groups of three) tuned in parallel 3rds, 5ths and octaves. Other consort styles render parallel 4ths, 5ths, and octaves or simply parallel octaves.

A variable number of panpipe players accompany the group with large double-headed drums (*bombos* or *wankara*); the rhythms played are modelled on the rhythms of a given melody. As common for much of the music in the southern area, *sikuri* music is standardly in AABBCC form in duple metre and involves a good deal of syncopation. Several scales are used; six- and seven-note series with a minor 3rd and flattened 7th are common. Among Aymara communities on the north shore of Lake Titicaca, several single-row panpipe styles are still occasionally performed, as are the huge double-row *chiriguano* panpipes in three parallel octaves without

2. (a) Baile de la Honda dancers accompanied by pinkullo (fipple flute) players, Mariangani, Cuzco; (b) close-up of a pinkullo player

drums during May in Huancané. In the province of Lampa, Quechua communities perform double-row *ayarachis* panpipes in parallel octaves accompanied by thin *caja* drums. Both Aymara and Quechua communities south of the lake in Puno, Monquegua and Tacna perform the *sikumoreno* style. The double-row *sikumoreno* panpipes are cut to produce two or three parallel octaves. With their faster tempos, Western snare and base drum accompaniment, and more staccato blowing technique, *sikumoreno* ensembles have a more sprightly quality than most other panpipe styles. In the same region, notched end-blown flutes are also played to accompany specific festival dances during the dry season. Known by a variety of dance-specific names such as *chokela* or *pulipuli*, these cane flutes are approximately 55 cm in length and have six top finger-holes and a thumb-hole. They are played in unison in large ensembles with or without drum accompaniment, with the flutes typically overblown to produce the high ranges preferred by indigenous Andeans.

The *pinkillu* (or *pinkullu*) and *tarka*, two end-blown duct flutes, are the primary indigenous instruments played during rainy season festivals in the Titicaca region. Performed in unison to accompany circle dances, *pinkillu* music is in AABBCC form with a six- or seven-note scale. Some six to 20 *pinkullu* players are accompanied by almost an equal number of large, deep sounding, indigenous snare drums (*cajas*). *Tarkas* are carved wooden duct flutes with six finger-holes and a mouthpiece fashioned to split the octave partially and produce a reedy sound. Performed in consorts of between two and four different sizes in parallel 4ths, 5ths, and octaves, they are accompanied by Western snare and bass drums which play syncopated patterns mirroring the given melody. *Tarka* music in AABBCC form is typically pentatonic.

The other instrumental ensembles of the southern region include 10 to 15 transverse cane or wooden flutes cut for parallel 4ths, 5ths and octaves. The transverse flutes are supported by snare and bass drums to accompany specific costumed dances at any time of year. Valveless animal horn or metal trumpets (*pututus*) are played during the Carnival season in Puno, usually as drones within a flute ensemble or as noise makers during celebration. CHARANGO, a small guitar variant with five duple or triple courses, are used by young indigenous men to perform the *kh'ajelo* genre for courting in the Titicaca area. A number of *charangos* will be performed in unison

for dancing, the young men forming half a circle facing the young women who sing in responsorial fashion to the men. Beginning in the 19th century, brass bands have become increasingly important in indigenous communities throughout Peru.

The non-specialized, communal-participatory character of music-making in the Titicaca region has influenced musical form. Music is primarily learnt by playing within public festival performance. There may be a 'rehearsal' the night before a festival but this is usually a session for composing new pieces and is attended only by the most dedicated community musicians. Many community members only join the group during the festival. Motivic repetition, long repetition of any given piece (a piece lasting a minute is typically repeated 20 to 30 times), and stock genre formulae help people to rapidly learn the new compositions during performance. An ensemble's new compositions are stressed in Aymara communities in Puno as well as in Quechua communites in other regions such as Ayacucho. Elsewhere, the same music may be used annually as an index of a particular event.

Indigenous music in northern Puno and the departments of Cuzco, Apurimac, north-eastern Arequipa, Ayacucho, Huancavelica and parts of Junín form another musical area. Here panpipe performance is rare. Several large end-blown notched or duct flutes are played solo or in unison for agricultural ceremonies with or without drum accompaniment during the rainy season. A long wooden *pinkullu* (a duct flute approximately 1·5 metres long) is played for agricultural and livestock rituals in Arequipa with *tinya* (small drum) and in southern Cuzco without drum accompaniment. In southern Cuzco this same large *pinkullu* is played during the ritual battles that take place between communities during the rainy season. Smaller *pinkullo* and *tinya* are played in pipe-and-tabor fashion to accompany communal agriculture work in Junín (fig.2). Informal, solo performance of the smaller *kena* (notched flute, approximately 36 cm long) is common in this region and in northern Peru, and *kenas* have been incorporated into festival dance ensembles comprising violins or mandolins, harp, accordion and drums for performance at any time of year. Ensembles comprising one to three transverse wooden or cane flutes playing six- or seven-note descending melodies in unison with snare and bass drums are common for festival dancing throughout the year in Cuzco and Apurimac. In Cuzco village headmen play conch-shell trumpets to herald their presence to district authorities during festivals. Long valveless, side-blown wooden or cane trumpets (1·5 to 3 metres in length or more, e.g. *clarín*, *llungur*) are played for agricultural ceremonies in Junín and Huancavelica as well as in locations in northern Peru such as Cajamarca. In Apurimac, Ayacucho, Huancavelica and Junín, circular cow-horn trumpets (*wakrapuku*) are performed during village bullfights. In Junín, one or two *wakrapuku* are used in combination with *tinya*, violin and female singing in tritones for the marking of cattle during the feast of St James (25 July).

Music for strings is highly developed and more widespread than music for indigenous wind instruments in this musical area. Diffused to Andean peoples early in the colonial period by missionaries, the diatonic harp and violin are primary instruments performed solo, used together in duos, or as parts of larger ensembles to accompany singing and dance (fig.3). In keeping with indigenous aesthetics, the violin is heavily bowed, creating a dense sound, and often played in its higher ranges with slides and other ornaments. In Ayacucho and Huancavelica harp-violin duos are used to accompany the famous scissors dance (*danzaq*), a highly-specialized, esoteric tradition. Solo and group *charango* performance, primarily by young indigenous men for courting, is found in pockets throughout this musical area. Indigenous *charango* performance involves the strumming of single-line melodies, sometimes punctuated by two-finger chords, against the backdrop of open thin metal strings, producing the dense buzzy sound favoured by indigenous Andeans.

From the departments of Ancash and Huanuco to the north, string and brass bands are prominent. Pipe-and-tabor performance with *pinkullu* or a single-row panpipe

3. Quena (notched flute) and harp players in procession at an Inca sun-worshipping festival, Cuzco

(e.g. *antara*) is more common than in southern Peru. In Cajamarca, the *antara* is a single-row panpipe tuned to pentatonic scale for the solo performance of mestizo genres like the *huayno* and *triste* in informal contexts. Several *kenas* performed with snare drum and cymbals are a typical festival dance ensemble in the northern department of Lambayeque. *Pinkullus* or side-blown flutes performed with drums or other instruments are also used for dancing in the north, and various types of indigenous trumpets are played in festivals and work-related rituals and parties. In general, however, mestizo ensembles and genres, or urban-popular styles like salsa and *chicha*, are the mainstay in northern Peru.

Quechua songs are sung within, and in reference to, a wide variety of occasions including agricultural labour and rituals for livestock, the building of homes and roof-raising parties, for life-cycle events including 'first hair-cutting' for children, courting, child-rearing, weddings, funerals and wakes and for the whole gamut of festival religious and dance occasions. Like the music itself, Quechua song texts tend to involve relatively short lines and a high degree of repetition within and across strophes, often with only subtle paradigmatic substitutions made from one line to another. Depending on context, the length of strophes can be quite flexible within a single song performance. The texts are often highly metaphoric using nature imagery, or will include concrete mention of specific activities and social roles for the given context. While both men and women sing, women, and especially young women, are the favoured vocalists because of the preference for high vocal ranges. Singing style typically involves forceful nasal-throat singing, although in private contexts women also sing in a soft, high, delicate style. Women often use ornamental falsetto glides, especially to punctuate the end of lines and sections. Unison and heterophonic singing among groups of women or men is typical; responsorial singing between men and women also commonly takes place in courting and on festival occasions such as Carnival where sexual relations are paramount. In such contexts male-female song duels, including playful taunts and insults, emerge.

4. LOWLAND INDIGENOUS MUSIC.   There are several small indigenous societies in the Amazon region of Peru who speak languages related to the Tupi-Carib, Panoan, Arawakan and Jívaro families: to date relatively little detailed ethnomusicological research has been done among these groups. Extant information suggests that, like Amazonian societies elsewhere, communal singing and dancing represent central musical activities with instrumental accompaniment varying between specific societies, and purely instrumental music being less common. Drums, panpipes, vertical flutes, trumpets and rattles have been reported for a number of groups. Within the same small-scale society there is often a wide variety of vocal genres and styles ranging from the soft, non-metred, melismatic singing of laments to forceful group chanting with regular, repetitive rhythms. Among the societies studied, unison and heterophonic singing are most common. Scales tend to vary widely. In contrast to highland peoples, songs often play an important role in curing procedures among indigenous Amazonian groups. Songs are vehicles for the telling of myths and history as well as being related to life-cycle events and subsistence activities. Music is also commonly used by shamans in

combination with hallucinogens to transcend mundane experience.

5. HIGHLAND MESTIZO MUSIC. The music is associated with Peruvians who are identified or self-identify as mestizo may be characterized as incorporating more Iberian elements relative to highland indigenous performers. This situation is obscured by the facts that indigenous music, dance and ceremony also variously incorporate European elements, and that ethnic identities in Peru are highly context-sensitive and fluid. A few mestizo musical traits may be generalized for highland Peru. These include strophic song forms, the use of parallel 3rds and 6ths, an emphasis on European string and wind instruments and in certain genres the use of hemiola moving between 3/4 and 6/8 metres. While intensive and extensive repetition is favoured by indigenous musicians, mestizos tend to favour a higher level of musical contrast, e.g. juxtaposing pieces in different metres within a medley. As compared with indigenous performers, mestizos also typically prefer more moderate pitch ranges and greater textural-timbral clarity. As in indigenous communities, mestizo song texts may be in the indigenous language or Spanish, or both, although there will be a higher percentage of Spanish texts among mestizos relative to the indigenous population. Whereas indigenous genres are highly context-specific, major mestizo genres such as the *huayno* (*wayno*, *wayño*), the *marinera*, the *yaraví*, marches and hymns are widely diffused and musically identifiable across regions.

The *huayno* is the most important highland mestizo song-dance genre. *Huaynos* are in a moderate-to-quick simple duple metre, often with an extra beat at major cadences. The rhythmic underpinning, a subtle yet constant shifting between a quaver and two semiquaver movement and a quaver triplet, is a hallmark feature. Musical forms such as *AABB* and *ABAB* are common. Within sections, antecedent phrases typically end on a cadence in the relative major and the final section on a cadence in the relative minor chord with rather static harmonies, involving III, VI, V and i chords, accompanying four-, six-, seven-, or most commonly five-note melodies. *Huaynos* often end with a musically distinct and more animated *fuga* section. According to mestizo composers such as Julio Benavente Díaz from Cuzco, the *huayno* is the genre of choice for expressing deeply-felt sentiments and important ideas. The strophic texts cover an extremely wide range of topics including humorous or joking themes, topical and overtly political songs, happy and sad love songs, songs about work, songs of leave-taking or celebrating specific locations, songs about death or the loss of one's parents. Text lines frequently do not rhyme.

The *huayno* is a couple or group dance which, depending on the region, involves fast rhythmic footwork (e.g. Cuzco to Junín) or a softer forward shuffle step (Puno). The upper body position is relatively erect and static; couples and groups in line or circle formations may hold hands or dance independently holding handkerchiefs or yarn cords with pompoms. The dancing typically becomes more animated in the *fuga* section. The genre is performed in the full range of mestizo musical contexts from family celebrations and drinking parties to public Catholic festivals and stage presentations. Indigenous people in southern Peru often use the term *huayno* generically for song; indigenous people also perform the specific *huayno* genre described here. Within specific

regions other terms such as *carnavales*, *kh'ajelo* (Puno), *huayllachas* (Arequipa), *huaylas* (Junín), and *kashua* (Cajamarca) are used both by mestizo and indigenous musicians to refer to what are closely allied musical variants of the *huayno*.

The MARINERA is the second most prominent mestizo song-dance genre in Peru. It is related stylistically to the *cueca* of Chile and Bolivia, and the *zamba* of Argentina; it was known in Lima as the *zamacueca* in the early 19th century. While some historians have suggested Hispanic roots for the dance, others suggest Afro-Peruvian derivation; 19th-century commentators often associated it with Afro-Peruvians. Performed in moderate tempo, *marineras* are in 6/8 metre and feature hemiola rhythms. The entire form (e.g. *AABBCCBB*) is usually repeated twice (called *la primera* (the first) and *la segunda* (the second)) with a quick break in between. Like the *huayno*, the *marinera* typically juxtaposes phrases in the relative major and minor keys with the final cadence on the minor. The texts are typically restricted to light romantic themes. The *marinera* is a graceful couple dance in which the dancers wave a *pañuelo* (handkerchief) in one hand. Three regional choreographic variants, from the highlands, Lima and the north coast, are distinguished by Peruvians. As with the *huayno*, the *marinera* is danced in the full range of public festivals and private social gatherings in the north and in the southern sierra. In northern regions such as Lambayeque, the *marinera* is a particularly prominent genre.

During the 18th century the *yaraví* was a widespread popular genre with a relatively broad thematic-emotional scope and lyrics occasionally in Quechua. In the contemporary period, *yaraví* refers to a slow, lyrical, romantic song genre with strophic Spanish texts treating sad or sombre topics such as unrequited love, and separation from home and family. The term *yaraví* was perhaps derived from a pre-Columbian generic designation for song and poetry, *harawi*, but by 1754 it had already come to signify *cancion triste* (sad song). Typically written in 3/4 metre, the music alternates between 3/4 and 6/8 rhythms (*sesquialtera*) but sometimes also includes dramatic *retardandos* at cadences such that the sense of pulse and metre become obscured. Like other mestizo genres the *yaraví* juxtaposes the relative major and minor keys. *Yaravís* are performed at serious moments on social occasions, and may be performed instrumentally in religious contexts (e.g. in religious processions).

Unlike these widespread genres and the ubiquitous brass bands, mestizo ensemble types are often region-specific, as are solo instrumental styles. Large string ensembles, known as *estudiantinas*, are closely associated with Puno but historically have had a presence in urban Cuzco, Ayacucho and elsewhere. They comprise a guitar section (between two and five) that supplies a prominent bass line as well as harmonic accompaniment; one or two *charangos* providing strummed chordal accompaniment; and several mandolins, violins and often *kenas* as the principal melody instruments. In addition to performing the generalized mestizo song types, in Puno *estudiantinas* also play arranged versions of local indigenous panpipe and flute music. Popularized within the romantic-nationalist *indigenista* movement in the early 20th century, *estudiantinas* typically perform in theatre and other stage settings. In Cuzco, a local style of *orquesta* providing music for public festival dancing comprises harp, accordion, between one and three violins, two *kenas* and bass drum. In the Apurimac, Ayacucho, Huancavelica area, ensembles comprising guitars and mandolins, or harps and violins, are common as are other string combinations and the inclusion of *kenas*. The festival dance *orquesta* of Junín combines numerous saxophones and clarinets with the ensemble core of harp and violin. A 'typical' festival dance orchestra of Lanbayeque comprises several *kenas*, snare and bass drums and cymbals. In Cajamarca, ensembles combining violins, snare and bass drums, or guitars, violins, *kenas* and percussion are frequently heard. A plethora of ad hoc instrumental combinations is found throughout Peru.

In Cuzco, Apurimac, Ayacucho and to the north, regionalized solo harp traditions are important: in northern Peru, as in Ecuador, a second musician will sometimes beat percussion parts on the harp. Prominent solo mestizo *charango* styles, which juxtapose strummed-chordal and plucked-melodic sections, are regionally centred on Ayacucho, Cuzco, Arequipa and Puno. A solo guitar style combining classical guitar technique with local musical elements is associated with Ayacucho. Important practitioners of this style, such as Raúl García Zarate, play bass lines derived from Ayacuchan harp performance, the melody in parallel 3rds on the higher strings with prominent vibrato and extended bass runs between musical phrases and sections.

Large public festivals to celebrate the feast day of a town's patron saint are the single most important type of occasion for mestizo music and dance throughout most of highland Peru. Locally specific as well as widely diffused dance-drama traditions are a central component of most patronal fiestas. Derived from colonial *autos sacramentales* (religious conversion plays), European Carnival dances and perhaps pre-existing indigenous dances, dance–dramas involve a troupe of masked and often costumed performers whose festival presentation enacts or alludes to historical, topical or mythical characters and happenings. Widespread dance–dramas often parody or characterize 'outsiders' such as jungle Indians, Spaniards, blacks or supernatural beings such as devils. Central and southern Peru remain a stronghold for spirited dance drama performance.

6. COASTAL 'CRIOLLO' AND AFRO-PERUVIAN MUSIC. In Peru, the term *criollo* implies Iberian–Peruvian cultural orientation and heritage; *criollo* culture is most strongly associated with Lima and the coast, as well as sometimes with élites in provincial cities. From the colonial period through to the late 20th century, the music associated with *criollo* culture was largely derived from cosmopolitan and European sources, including European classical and urban-popular styles and military band music. Theatre music, especially the *zarzuela* (music drama), was important for diffusing European styles. The *marinera Limeña* was an early distinctive *criollo* popular form and at the end of the 19th century this genre, along with the waltz and the polka, was the mainstay of popular *criollo* music. Among these, the *vals criollo* (waltz) emerged as the most important in the early 20th century, and came to be almost synonymous with *música criolla* after the mid-20th century.

The *vals criollo* was influenced by the jota and the mazurka, the three genres becoming popular in Lima in the mid-19th century. Largely rejected by the upper classes, during the first three decades of the 20th century the *vals criollo* was the primary genre among the *criollo*

working class and poor. Used for dancing, waltzes were common to drinking parties and family celebrations. They were performed variably with guitar, *laúd* or *bandúrria* (fig.4) to support the singing of texts which commented on working-class life and personal experience, often involving themes of conflict, suffering, loneliness and unrequited love. According to Stein (1982), they projected the world view of pessimism and fatalism of their proletariat composers. The grass roots performance of the *vals* declined in the mid-1920s due to the new influence of the mass media and foreign styles such as the tango, Mexican *rancheras* and North American forms such as the fox-trot. After the 1950s the *vals criollo* shed its working-class associations and was nostalgically adopted as the musical emblem for Limeña *criollo* culture in general. An important style change was the addition of the Afro-Peruvian *cajón* (wooden-box drum played with the hands) (Romero, 1985). Although of particular significance in the Lima context, the *vals criollo* is also performed throughout Peru.

While *música criolla* has incorporated Afro-Peruvian elements such as the *cajón* and certain rhythmic features, Romero (1985) suggests that the small Afro-Peruvian minority was basically assimilated into *criollo* culture. Afro-Peruvian and white *criollo* musicians had been mutually influencing each other for some time; the black performance of the coastal *marinera* in the 19th century is one example. After the turn of the 20th century, Afro-Peruvian communities ceased to perform distinct black genres such as the *alcatraz*, the *penalivio*, the *ingá* and the *agua'e nieve*, among others. Beginning in the 1950s, however, an Afro-Peruvian revivalist movement inspired the formation of folkloric troupes that performed styles presented as black traditions.

7. MUSIC OF HIGHLAND MIGRANTS IN CITIES. Once considered the bastion of *criollo* culture, Lima underwent a major transformation in the decades following World War II, due to highland migration. Waves of highlanders from different states created a market for commercial recordings and shows featuring various regional styles;

4. Harp and bandurria (guitar) players in the courtyard of a colonial home, Lima, early 20th century

the *huayno* was the primary genre within this phenomenon. Live performances were held on weekends in *coliseos* (stadiums or large tents), and radio programmes dedicated to regional *huayno* music emerged in the 1950s. A star system of highland performers was created with the emphasis on specific styles mirroring the size of the migrant population from that region at given points in time. Music from Junín, Ancash, Huancavelica, Cuzco and Ayacucho was the first to be recorded. Stars such as El Picaflor de los Andes from Junín and La Pastorita Huaracina from Ancash dressed in stylized regional costumes, sang songs from and about home and were backed by 'typical orchestras' of their area to appeal to these specific migrant populations. Their performances blended indices of regional identity with elements of 'urban sophistication' such as singing with wide vocal vibrato and tight instrumental arrangements.

The commercial sphere of Andean music was paralleled and supported by regional migrant clubs in the capital. Regional clubs existed in Lima from the early 20th century but increased tremendously in number after the 1950s. They organized patronal fiestas in the city, often including the dance groups and ensemble types that performed in their home towns. The clubs also held smaller parties and dances, engaging recording artists from their regions or playing commercial recordings of *huaynos* as well as other popular international styles such as Colombian *cumbia*. The clubs from certain regions became the basis for organizing highland-style ensembles: e.g. Puno regional clubs formed panpipe groups in the city. By the early 1980s the last of the commercial *coliseos* had disappeared and the clubs had effectively taken over the organization of highland musical events in Lima. These trends were reproduced in other Peruvian cities.

In the 1960s a new form of pan-highland migrant music known as *chicha* or *cumbia Andina* began to emerge in Lima. At first appealing to the teenage and young adult children of highland migrants, *chicha* is a fusion of the melodic structure of *huaynos* with the rhythm of Colombian *cumbia* performed with electric instruments (guitars, bass and keyboards), trap set, and Caribbean percussion (*timbales*, *guiro*, cow-bell). Actual *huaynos* are sometimes set to *cumbia* rhythm; more often *chicha* songs are new compositions. The majority of texts are about romantic love, often unrequited, but *chicha* songs also speak to the struggles and aspirations of the working- and lower-class children of highland migrants in cities. Major national *chicha* stars such as Los Shapis and Grupo Alegría had great mass appeal in the 1980s. The style remained vital in the 1990s as the emblem for a new Peruvian identity fusing images of Andean roots, modernity and urbanity.

BIBLIOGRAPHY
AND OTHER RESOURCES

D. Gonzáles Holguin: *Vocabulario de la lengua general de todos el Perú llamada lengua Quichua o del Inca* (Lima, 1608)

R. and M. Harcourt: *La musique des Incas et ses survivances* (Paris, 1925, rev. 2/1957 by S.L. Moreno as *La música de los Incas*)

C. Vega: *La música de un códice colonial del siglo XVII* (Buenos Aires, 1931)

B.J. Martínez Compañón y Bujanda: *Trujillo del Perú a fines del siglo XVIII* (Madrid, 1936/R)

F. Guaman Poma de Ayala: *Nueva corónica y buen gobierno* (Paris, 1936/R)

I. Garcilaso de la Vega: *Comentarios reales de los Incas* (Buenos Aires, 1945)

P. Verger: *Fiestas y danzas en el Cuzco y en los Andes* (Buenos Aires, 1945)

L. Bertonio: *Vocabulario de la lengua aymara* (La Paz, 1956)

J.R. Pineda: 'El wayno del Cuzco', *Folklore americano*, nos.6–7 (1958–9), 129–245

C. Pagaza Galdo: 'El yaraví', *Folklore americano*, nos.8–9 (1960–61), 75–141

R. Holzmann, ed: *Panorama de la música tradicional del Perú* (Lima, 1966)

C. Pagaza Galdo: *Cancionero andinio sur* (Lima, 1967)

R. Stevenson: *Music in Aztec and Inca Territory* (Berkeley and London, 1968/R)

T.D. Lucas: 'Songs of the Shipibo of the Upper Amazon', *Yearbook for Inter-American Musical Research*, vii (1971), 59–67

R.J. Smith: *The Art of Festival as Exemplified by the Fiesta to the Patroness of Otuzco: la Virgen de la Puerta* (Lawrence, KS, 1975)

J.M. Arguedas: *Señores e indios* (Buenos Aires, 1976)

A. Rossel: *Arqueología sur del Perú* (Lima, 1977)

C. Santa Cruz: *El waltz y el valse criollo* (Lima, 1977)

R.C. Smith: 'Deliverance from Chaos for a Song, a Social and Religious Interpretation of the Ritual Performance of Amuesha Music' (diss., Cornell U., 1977)

Mapa de los instrumentos musicales de uso popular en el Peru, ed. Instituto Nacional de Cultura (Lima, 1978)

D.R. Bernal: *La múliza* (Lima, 1978)

J. Haeberli: 'Twelve Nasca Panpipes: a Study', *EthM*, xxiii (1979), 57–73

J. Schechter: 'The Inca *Cantar Histórico*: a Lexico-Historical Elaboration on Two Cultural Themes', *EthM*, xxiii (1979), 191–204

S. Stein: 'El vals criollo y los valores de la clase trabajadora en la Lima de comienzos del siglo XX', *Socialismo y participación*, xvii (1982), 43–50

R.E. Vásquez: *La práctica musical de la población negra en Perú* (Havana, 1982)

J.A. Llorens: *Música popular en Lima: criollos y andinos* (Lima, 1983)

A. Valencia: *El siku bipolar altiplanico*, i: *Los sikuris y sikumorenos* (Lima, 1983)

J.G. Carpio Muñoz: *Arequipa: música y pueblo* (Arequipa, 1984)

R.C. Smith: 'The Language of Power: Music, Order and Redemption', *LAMR*, v/2 (1984), 129–60

T. Turino: 'The Urban-Mestizo Charango Tradition in Southern Peru: a Statement of Shifting Identity', *EthM*, xxviii/2 (1984), 253–69

C. Bolaños: 'Música y danzas en el antiguo Perú', *La música en el Perú*, ed. Patronato Popular y Porvenir Pro Música Clásica (Lima, 1985), 11–64

E. den Otter: *Music and Dance of Indians and Mestizos in an Andean Valley of Peru* (Delft, 1985)

R. Romero: 'La música tradicional y popular', *La música en el Perú*, ed. Patronato Popular y Porvenir Pro-Musica Clásica (Lima, 1985), 217–83

R., E. and L. Montoya: *La sangre de los cerros: antología de la poesia quechua que se canta en el Perú* (Lima, 1987)

C. Bolaños: *Les antaras Nasca: historia y análisis* (Lima, 1988)

T.R. Turino: 'The Music of Andean Migrants in Lima, Peru: Demographics, Social Power, and Style', *LAMR*, ix/2 (1988), 127–50

C. Vasquez Rodríguez and A. Vergara Figueroa: ¡*Chayraq! Carnival ayacuchano* (Lima, 1988)

R. Romero: 'Musical Change and Cultural Resistance in the Central Andes of Peru', *LAMR*, xi.1 (1990), 1–35

T.R. Turino: 'Somos el Perú: Cumbia Andina and the Children of the Andean Migrants in Lima', *Studies in Latin American Popular Culture*, ix (1990), 15–37

T.R. Turino: 'The State and Andean Musical Production in Peru', *Nation-State and Indian in Latin America*, ed. J. Sherzer and G. Urban (Austin, 1991), 259–85

D.A. Olsen: 'Implications of Music Technologies in the Pre-Columbian Andes', *Musical Repercussions of 1492: Encounters in Text and Performance*, ed. C.E. Robertson (Washington, 1992), 65–88

R. Romero, ed.: *Música, danzas y mascaras en los Andes* (Lima, 1993)

T.R. Turino: *Moving Away from Silence: the Music of the Peruvian Altiplano and the Experience of Urban Migration* (Chicago, 1993)

Catalogo 1985–1993, ed. Archivo de Música Tradicional Andina (Lima, 1995)

Cosmología y música en los Andes: Berlin 1992, ed. M.P. Baumann (Frankfurt, 1996)

RECORDINGS WITH INFORMATIVE DISC NOTES

Indian Music of the Upper Amazon (Peru and Bolivia), FE 4458 (1954) [incl. notes by H. Tschopik]

Huayno Music of Peru, i, Arhoolie CD 320 (1989) [incl. notes by J. Cohen]

Mountain Music of Peru, i, SF 40020 (1991) [incl. notes by J. Cohen]

Mountain Music of Peru, ii, SF 40406 (1994) [incl. notes by J. Cohen and T. Turino]

Traditional Music of Peru, i: *Festivals of Cusco*, SF 40466 (1995) [incl. notes by G. Cánepa-Koch and others]

Traditional Music of Peru, ii: *The Mantaro Valley*, SF 40467 (1995) [incl. notes by R. Romero]

From the Mountains to the Sea: Music of Peru – the 1960s, Arhoolie CD 400 (1996) [incl. notes by J. Cohen]

Traditional Music of Peru, iii: *Cajamarca and the Colca Valley*, SF 40469 (1996) [incl. notes by R. Romero and others]

Traditional Music of Peru, iv: *Lambayeque*, SF 40469 (1996) [incl. notes by R. Romero and others]

Traditional Music of Peru, v: *Andean Music of Peru*, SF 40470 (1997) [incl. notes by R. Romero]

GERARD BÉHAGUE (I), THOMAS TURINO (II).

Perugia. City in the Umbria region of Italy. In the 13th century Perugia was the leading centre of the devotional societies that practised the singing of *laude*. The first such confraternity, the Compagnia dei Disciplinati or Flagellanti, was founded in 1260 by Raniero Fasani. From the 14th century until about the mid-16th the city's government engaged several minstrels (*canterini*), who provided musical and poetic entertainment twice daily for the magistrates, and at least twice monthly for the populace, at concerts held in public squares. In the last quarter of the 14th century the *canterino* Ercolano di Gilio (Gigli) da Perugia won wide recognition for his abilities as an improviser.

The earliest documentation of the practice of sacred polyphony in the cathedral of S Lorenzo is provided by three manuscript versions of the versicle *Benedicamus Domino* dating from the end of the 14th century (*I-PEd* Cod.15). From 1433 musical activity is regularly documented in the *Libri contabili* and in 1521 the chapel was officially established with a papal brief from Leo X. The *maestri di cappella* include the papal singer Ivo Barry (1535–6), Giorgio Mirreo di Cambrai (1551–75), Vincenzo Cossa (1591–1620), Francesco Marcorelli (1635–41), Francesco Bagaglia (1694–1740), Baldassarre Angelini (1740–62), Francesco Zannetti (1762–88), Luigi Caruso (1788–1823), Giuseppe Rossi Bonaccorsi (1823–33), Ulisse Corticelli (1845–80), Agostino Mercuri (1880–92), Giuseppe Scudellari (1892–1901) and Raffaele Casimiri (1905–8). Among the most representative of the second generation of trecento composers was Niccolò da Perugia, author of madrigals, and cacce on texts by Sacchetti and Soldanieri, among others. An important Perugian figure, responsible for the diffusion in Italy of French musical style in the early 15th century, was Matteo da Perugia, first *maestro di cappella* at Milan Cathedral.

The construction of organs in the city's various churches began in the mid-15th century. Perugia's principal organ builders were Bevenate di Francesco (S Agostino, 1494, S Simone del Carmine, 1504), Luca Biagi (S Maria Nuova, 1584), Pietro Fedeli (S Lorenzo, 1785) and Angelo Morettini (19th century). Several makers of string instruments settled in Perugia in the 16th and 17th centuries, including Martino and Lorenzo di Pietro, Lutio di Lorenzo Mucetti, who introduced lyre making into the city, and Pietro Pavolo di Gerolamo.

After the founding of a university in 1275 humanistic studies and activities gained ground in Perugia. A collection of frottola texts, *Il libro de amore chiamato Ardelia* by Baldassaro Olympo delli Alexandri, was printed in 1520, and was important for the dissemination of humanism. In 1561 Raffaele Sozi instituted the Accademia degli Unisoni, whose principal aim was the theory and practice of music. Following the will of Bishop Napoleone Comitoli a public school of plainchant was instituted in 1621 at the church of S Bartolomeo, and was first directed by Nicolò Magnanini. In the late 16th century and early 17th the printer Pietroiacomo Petrucci was active in Perugia; in 1577 he published Malvezzi's *Ricercari a quattro* and in 1603 Arcadelt's first book of four-part madrigals. Other music publishers working in the city in the 16th and 17th centuries included Eredi del Bartoli, Angelo Laurenzi and Girolamo Costanti.

The reorganization of the Accademia degli Unisoni under the protection of S Cecilia in 1604 prompted the construction of an oratory next to the church of S Maria Nuova. The building was used exclusively by the *accademici* throughout the 17th century for performances of sacred musical dramas; similar performances took place in the church of S Filippo Neri, built in 1649. From 1690 to 1705 the singer, composer and historiographer G.A. Bontempi lived in Perugia, publishing his *Historia musica* there in 1695.

The first opera known to have been performed in Perugia was Cavalli's *Giasone* (1663). In March 1717 a group of 60 noblemen arranged to give the city its first public theatre, the Teatro del Pavone. Constructed under the direction of Costantino Ranieri and Alessandro Baglioni, it was completed in 1723, and in 1726 the promoters of the enterprise formally constituted the Nobile Accademia del Casino to supervise it. In 1765 the original wooden theatre, known as the Teatro della Nobile Accademia del Casino, or Teatro del Pavone (after the peacock depicted on the curtain), was rebuilt in stone to a design by Pietro Carattoli, who used the Teatro Argentina in Rome as a model; it was in a horseshoe shape, with four tiers comprising 82 boxes. A group of affluent citizens, in competition with the Accademia del Casino, which was patronized exclusively by the nobility, subsidized the construction of a new theatre, the Nuovo Teatro Civico del Verzaro, inaugurated in 1781 with Francesco Zannetti's *La Didone abbandonata* and Giacomo Rust's *Artaserse*. The Italian première of Rossini's *Moïse et Pharaon* was given at the Verzaro in 1829. In 1874 it was renamed Teatro Francesco Morlacchi; in 1942, having been donated to the city's administration, it became the Teatro Comunale Morlacchi. Another theatre, the Teatro Turreno, was erected mainly to present spectacles for the less affluent social classes; it was inaugurated in 1891 with Pedrotti's *Tutti in maschera*.

The Congregazione dell'Oratorio di S Filippo Neri, established in 1615, was the centre of oratorio performance in Perugia. From 1689 the Accademia degli Unisoni celebrated the feast of St Cecilia in the oratory of the same name adjoining the Chiesa Nuova. Many oratorios, particularly cantatas for Christmas Eve, were sponsored by the Compagnia dei Nobili del Gesù. In the late 17th century and the early 18th there was a flourishing local school of oratorio, with composers such as Pietro Giacomo Bacci, Francesco Bagaglia and Giovanni Bernardino

Serafini, and subsequently Baldassarre Angelini, Francesco Zannetti and Luigi Caruso.

A musical institute was founded in 1790 by Luigi Caruso; in 1873 it was named after Francesco Morlacchi, and in 1967 it became a state conservatory. The history of music has been taught at the university since 1957. The annual Sagra Musicale Umbra, founded in 1937, is a festival devoted mainly to choral and symphonic religious works. The Associazione Amici della Musica, founded in 1946 and presided over by A.B. Gatteschi, sponsors concerts throughout the year, presenting renowned virtuosos and many contemporary works. In 1983 the Centro di Studi Musicali in Umbria was founded with the aim of promoting research into the region's musical heritage.

BIBLIOGRAPHY

R. Strohm: 'Neue Quellen zur liturgischen Mehrstimmigkeit des Mittelalters in Italien', *RIM*, i (1966), 77–87
A.W. Atlas: 'The Accademia degli Unisoni: a Music Academy in Renaissance Perugia', *A Musical Offering: Essays in Honor of Martin Bernstein*, ed. E.H. Clinkscale and C. Brook (New York, 1977), 5–24
B. Brumana: 'Luigi Caruso e la cappella musicale del duomo di Perugia dal 1788 al 1823', *NRMI*, xi (1977), 380–405
B. Brumana: 'Per una storia dell'oratorio musicale a Perugia nei secoli XVII e XVIII', *Esercizi: arte, musica, spettacolo*, iii (1980), 97–167
B. Brumana and M.Pascale: 'Il teatro musicale a Perugia nel Settecento: una cronologia dai libretti', *Esercizi: arte, musica, spettacolo*, vi (1983), 71–134
M.M.R. Ventura, ed.: *Teatro Francesco Morlacchi: archivio storico* (Perugia, 1983)
B. Brumana: *Il fondo musicale dell'archivio di San Pietro a Perugia: catalogo* (Perugia, 1986)
G. Ciliberti: 'Repertorio delle fonti musicali umbre dal XIII al XV secolo e dei musicisti arsnovistici di provenienza umbra', *Bollettino della Deputazione di storia patria per l'Umbria*, lxxxv (1988), 219–70
N. Guidobaldi: 'Music Publishing in Sixteenth- and Seventeenth-Century Umbria', *EMH*, viii (1988), 1–36
B. Brumana and G.Ciliberti: 'Umanesimo e tradizione orale: nuovi documenti sui canterini a Perugia nel XV secolo', *NRMI*, xxiii (1989), 579–91
B. Brumana and G.Ciliberti: *Musica e musicisti nella cattedrale di S. Lorenzo a Perugia (XIV–XVII secolo)* (Florence, 1991)
B. Brumana: *L'archivio musicale della cattedrale di S. Lorenzo a Perugia: catalogo* (Perugia, 1993)
B. Brumana: *Teatro musicale e accademie a Perugia tra dominazione francese e restaurazione (1801–1830)* (Florence, 1996)
G. Ciliberti: *Musica e società in Umbria tra Medioevo e Rinascimento* (Turnhout, 1998)

ELVIDIO SURIAN/BIANCAMARIA BRUMANA

Perugia, Matteo da [Perusiis, Perusio, Perusinus, Matheus de]. *See* MATTEO DA PERUGIA.

Perusso, Mario (*b* Buenos Aires, 16 Sept 1936). Argentine conductor and composer. He studied at the Di Tella Institute of Buenos Aires and began his musical career as a singer in the opera chorus of the Teatro Colón. He was appointed opera conductor at the Teatro Argentino in La Plata (1967) and was appointed to several conducting posts throughout Argentina. He became deputy conductor and (since 1998) artistic director of the Teatro Colón in Buenos Aires.

Between 1966 and 1968 he wrote a one-act opera in Spanish, *La voz del silencio*, based on an idea of his own with a libretto by Leónidas Barrera Oro. Without being set at any particular time or place, the work deals with human conflict in the aftermath of a devastating catastrophe, such as a nuclear explosion. It was first performed at the Colón on 27 November 1969 and was recorded in 1971. Musically it belongs to the avant garde of the 1960s, with free atonality and no adherence to conventional forms. The orchestra plays the most important part and generates considerable dramatic tension.

Perusso's second opera is the one-act *Escorial*, completed in 1987 (though the first sketches date back to 1973). He wrote his own libretto (in Spanish), an adaptation of the play of the same name by Michel de Ghelderode set in the Escorial palace in Spain and dealing with a role-change between the king and his clown. Also atonal, it includes some elements drawn from Renaissance music. Its first performance was at the Colón in December 1989, conducted by Perusso himself.

In 1992 he wrote *Guayaquil*, a lyric drama in seven scenes, on a libretto by Agustín Pérez Pardella. This atonal work deals with an interview between José de San Martín and Simón Bolívar. The composer conducted the première in the Teatro Colón on 8 June 1993. In 1991 he began work on an opera based on the play by Octavio Paz, *Sor Juana Inés de la Cruz*.

Perusso's orchestral works include the *Tres movimientos sinfónicos* (1956), the *Elegía* (1964) and *La eternidad y el viento*. He has also written the *Cantos de guerra* for soprano and orchestra (1965), the *Partita* (1967) for solo cello and the *Invenzioni* (1967) for string quartet.

JUAN MARÍA VENIARD

Perwer, Şivan (*b* Sori, Urfa province, Turkey, 23 Dec 1955). Kurdish singer and composer. He was born into a poor peasant family and struggled to attend school in a nearby village; he began singing while in primary school. While Kurdish music was banned in Turkey, he learnt many songs by listening to Kurdish radio broadcasts from Armenia, Iraq and Iran, and his music contributed to the upsurge of nationalist and leftist cultural and political movements in the 1970s. Facing persecution for his singing, he took refuge in Germany in 1976 and resettled in Sweden, continuing to perform and compose songs in the steadily growing Kurdish diaspora. He is well known for his political songs, which emphasize the struggle of workers and peasants and the national liberation movements of the Kurds. His recordings included four tapes and two records before his exile and 25 cassettes by 1991, totalling about 500 pieces by the late 1990s. He usually accompanies his songs on the *tanbūr* and often sings duets with his wife Gulistan. Since 1995 his performances have been broadcast by the Kurdish satellite channel Med-TV, based in Europe.

BIBLIOGRAPHY
AND OTHER RESOURCES

M. Baksi: *The Kurdish Voice: Shivan Perwer* (1986)
Siwan Perwer: chants du Kurdistan, Auvidis A 5145 (1989)
S. Blum and A. Hassanpour: '"The Morning of Freedom Rose Up": Kurdish Popular Song and the Exigencies of Cultural Survival', *Popular Music*, xv (1996), 325–43

AMIR HASSANPOUR, STEPHEN BLUM

Perz, Mirosław (*b* Zielonagóra, nr Szamotuły, 25 Jan 1933). Polish musicologist. He studied musicology with Chybiński at Poznań University (1951–4) and with Feicht at Warsaw University (1954–6); he also studied the organ at the Poznań Music School (1952–4). He continued his musical training in Warsaw, where he studied the organ (1954–9), conducting with Bohdan Wodiczko (1960–64) and composition with Tadeusz Szeligowski (1959–63). From 1956 to 1959 he was conductor of the Chamber Choir of the National PO in Warsaw. In 1957 he began working in the musicology institute at Warsaw University, where in 1966 he obtained the doctorate with a dissertation on Mikołaj Gomółka. In 1971 he was appointed reader and head of the department of Polish music history in the musicology institute at Warsaw University; from 1977–93 he was reader at the University of Poznań. He was visiting professor at the universities of Calgary (1986) and Kansas (1986–7).

Perz has concentrated mainly on the music of the Middle Ages and the Renaissance; working from both Polish and foreign sources, he is responsible for the discovery of many important early Polish works and other archival material. Notable achievements include his reconstruction of the Stary Sącz fragments, his monograph on Gomółka and editions of sources of polyphony in Poland.

WRITINGS

'Handschrift Nr.1361 der Öffentlichen Städtischen Raczyński-Bibliothek in Poznań, als neue Quelle zur Geschichte der polnischen Musik in der II. Hälfte des XV. Jahrhunderts', *The Works of Frederick Chopin: Warsaw 1960*, 588–92

'Die Vor- und Frühgeschichte der Partitur in Polen', *Festschrift aus Anlass der Erhebung des Steirmärkischen Landeskonservatoriums zur Akademie für Musik und darstellende Kunst in Graz* (Graz, 1963), 129–38

'Kapela Zamoyskich i kolegiacka w Pilicy' [The Zamoyski chapel and the collegiate church chapel in Pilica], *Z dziejów muzyki polskiej*, vii (Bydgoszcz, 1964), 41–54

'Opracowanie muzyczne Pieśni-legendy o św. Stanisławie' [Musical settings of the legend of St Stanislaw], *Średniowiecze: studia o kulturze*, ed. J. Lewański (Warsaw, 1965), 322–36

Mikołaj Gomółka: monografia (diss., U. of Warsaw, 1966; Warsaw, 1969, 2/1981)

'Motety Marcina Leopolity' [The motets of Marcin Leopolita], *Studia Hieronymo Feicht septuagenario dedicata*, ed. Z. Lissa (Kraków, 1967), 155–89

'Nieznany polski traktat chorałowy Marka z Płocka (1518)' [The unknown Polish hymn treatise by Mark of Płock (1518)], *Muzyka*, xiii/4 (1968), 75–80

'Szesnastowieczne księgi głosowe z Olkusza i Sandomierza' [16th-century partbooks from Olkusz and Sandomierz], *Muzyka*, xiii/4 (1968), 11–27

'Cechy socjologiczne polskiej kultury muzycznej XVI stulecia' [Sociological features of 16th-century Polish musical culture], *Musica antiqua II: Bydgoszcz 1969*, 197–207 [with Fr. summary]

'Rękopiśmienne partesy olkuskie' [Manuscript partbooks from Olkusz], *Muzyka*, xiv/2 (1969), 18–44

'Die Einflüsse der ausgehenden italienischen Ars Nova in Polen', *L'Ars Nova italiana del Trecento: Convegno II: Certaldo and Florence 1969* [*L'Ars Nova italiana del Trecento*, iii (Certaldo, 1970)], 465–83

'Organalne Sanctus Agnus z zaginionego rękopisu Lat.Q.I 201' [An organum Sanctus Agnus from the lost MS Lat.Q.I 201], *Muzyka*, xv/3 (1970), 20–34

'Trasformazioni dello stile e della pratica dell'organo dei secoli XVI e XVII in Polonia', *Musica strumentale e vocale strumentale dal Rinascimento al Barocco: Bologna 1970*, 33–45

'Quattro esempi sconosciuti del "cantus planus binatim" in Polonia', *Quadrivium*, xii/1 (1971), 93–117

'Starosądecki urywek motetów średniowiecznych w Bibliotece Uniwersyteckiej w Poznaniu' [The Stary Sącz fragment of medieval motets in the Poznań University Library], *Muzyka*, xvi/1 (1971), 77–82; Eng. trans. as 'The Oldest Source of Polyphonic Music in Poland: Fragments from Stary Sącz', in *Polish Musicological Studies*, i (1977), 9–57

'Organum, Conductus und mittelalterliche Motette in Polen: Quellen und Probleme', *IMSCR XI: Copenhagen 1972*, 593–6; Pol. orig., 'Organum, conductus i średniowieczny motet w Polsce: źródła i problemy', *Muzyka*, xviii/4 (1973), 3–11

'Inwentarz przemyski (1677)' [A Przemyśl catalogue of 1677], *Muzyka*, xix/4 (1974), 44–69

'Wyznaczniki początków renesansu muzycznego w Polsce' [Factors determining the beginnings of Renaissance music in Poland], 'Missarum quattuor vocibus liber primus Marci Scacchii Romani', 'Kilka uwag o źródłach i repertuarze polifonii retrospektywnej we

Włoszech i Polsce' [Some thoughts on the origins and repertory of backward-looking polyphony in Italy and Poland], *Polsko-włoskie materiały muzyczne/Argomenti musicali polacco-italiani: Warsaw 1971 and Bardolino 1972* [*Pagine*, ii (1974)], 57–70; 217–37; 277–90

'Poglądy na muzykę w Polsce XVI stulecia' [Opinions about 16th-century Polish music], *Renesans: sztuka i ideologia: Kraków 1972*, ed. T.S. Jaroszewski (Warsaw, 1976), 59–80

'Die Publikationen älterer Musik in Polen', *Musica slavica*, i (1977), 38–55

'Koncepcja historii muzyki polskiej jako dyscypliny naukowej' [The conception of Polish music history as a scholarly discipline], *Z zagadnień muzykologii współczesnej*, ed. A. Neuer (Warsaw, 1978), 35–50

'Staropolskie opracowania polifoniczne tekstów o św. Stanisławie Biskupie' [Old Polish polyphonic settings of texts by Bishop (St) Stanisław], *Summarium*, vii (1978), 103–18

'Znajomość i recepcja laudy włoskiej w Polsce XV i XVI wieku' [Knowledge and reception of the Italian lauds in 15th- and 16th-century Poland], *Pagine*, iii (1979), 59–80

'Czterysta lat gomółkowych *Melodii* 1580–1980; czyli o początkach polskiej deklamacji muzycznej' [400 years of Gomółka's *Melodie*, 1580–1980: the beginnings of Polish musical recitation], *Muzyka*, xxv/3 (1980), 3–22

'Zur Textunterlegungspraxis in der Mehrstimmigkeit des 14. und 15. Jahrhunderts und über einige in Polen neu- und wiedergefundene Quellen dieser Zeit', *Musik und Text in der Mehrstimmigkeit des 14. und 15. Jahrhunderts: Wolfenbüttel 1980*, 327–49

'La chiesa e la musica in Polonia e nei paesi limitrofi (966–1600)', *Common Christian Roots of the European Nations: Rome 1981*, 649–56

'The Lvov Fragments: a Source for Works by Dufay, Josquin, Petrus de Domarto and Petrus de Grudencz in 15th-Century Poland', *TVNM*, xxxvi/1 (1986), 26–51; Pol. orig., 'Fragmenty lwowskie: źródło dzieł Dufaya, Josquina, Piotra z Domarto i Piotra z Grudziąda w Polsce XV wieku', *Muzyka*, xxxiii/3 (1989), 3–46

'Il carattere internazionale delle opere di Mikołaj Radomski', *MD*, xli (1987), 153–9

'Polish Contributions to the Problem of Polyphonic Repertories in the 14th and 15th Centuries', *IMSCR XIV: Bologna 1987*, 175–81

Melodie na Psałterz polski Mikołaja Gomółki: interpretacje i komentarze [The *Melodie na Psałterz polski* by Mikółaj Gomółka: interpretations and commentaries] (Kraków, 1988)

'Sztuka sekretnej chromatyki w "Melodiach" Mikołaja Gomółki' [The secret chromatic art of the *Melodie* by Mikołaj Gomółka], *Muzyka*, xxxiii/4 (1988), 3–28

'Le canzone di Cesare Borgo', *Seicento inesplorato: Lenno, nr Como 1989*, 55–64

'Interpretacje muzycznego sacrum w kontekście polskiej tradycji' [Interpretation of the sacrum in the context of the Polish tradition], *Współczesna polska religijna kultura muzyczna jako przedmiot badań muzykologii: Lublin 1989*, 21–35

'Na tropie śpiewnika krakowskiego c.1470: rzecz o fragmencie Biblioteki Jagiellońskiej nr 8a' [On the trail of a Kraków songbook of c1470: about fragment no.8a from the Jagiellonian Library], *Muzyka*, xxxiv/1 (1989), 3–35; It. trans. in *Studi in onore di Giuseppe Vecchi*, ed. I. Cavallini (Modena, 1989), 235–46

'Wawelska przeszłość muzyczna: mity i domniemana rzeczywistość' [Music of the Wawel's past: myths and alleged realities], *Muzyka*, xxxv/4 (1990), 3–15

'Kontrafaktury ballad w rękopisie Krasińskich (*PL-Wn* 8054)' [A ballad from the Kraśiński manuscript *PL-Wn* 8054], *Muzyka*, xxxvii/4 (1992), 89–111

'The Structure of the Lost Manuscript from the National Library in Warsaw, no.378 (*WarN* 378)', *From Ciconia to Sweenlink: donum natalicium Willem Elders*, ed. A. Clement and E. Jas (Amsterdam, 1994), 1–11

'Śladem Adama z Wągrowca (zm. 1629)' [In the footsteps of Adam of Wągrowiec (d 1629)], *Muzyka*, xli/3 (1996), 3–18

EDITIONS

M. Gomółka: *Melodie na Psalterz Polski I–III*, WDMP, xlvii–xlix (1963–6, 2/1981–3)

Sources of Polyphony up to c.1500, AMP, xiii–xiv (1973–6)

Mikołaj Radomski: Magnificat i inne utwory [Magnificat and other works] (Kraków, 1987)

ZOFIA HELMAN

Pes (i) (Lat.: 'foot', 'fundament', 'ground'). In some English sources of polyphony dating from the second half of the 13th century (mostly the so-called Worcester Fragments, now in the Bodleian Library and Worcester Cathedral: *see* WORCESTER POLYPHONY) *pes* is the usual designation for the untexted non-Gregorian tenor of certain motets; it was freely invented or, more rarely, borrowed from a song or a dance-tune. The term generally denotes a strict or varied melodic ostinato, in contrast to the purely rhythmic ostinatos into which continental motet composers fashioned their cantus firmi. While the cantus firmus motets written in England follow continental precepts, the *pes* motets are an English speciality.

Ex.1 L. A. Dittmer, ed.: *The Worcester Fragments* (1957), no.17

At first *pes* seems to have designated the supporting voice of motets whose upper two voices engage in voice-exchange (the commonly accepted term for a 13th-century technique that more precisely would be called phrase-exchange). In such motets the phrase elements of the *pes* are fairly short (ex.1), typically producing the polyphonic design:

> CBED
> BCDE
> AAA'A'

(The same compositional procedure, but without the designation of the tenor as *pes*, occurs in some passages of English CONDUCTUS, both *cum littera* and *sine littera*.) SUMER IS ICUMEN IN (see also for facsimile) can appropriately be included in this group of compositions, especially in view of its alternative Latin text. Some of the motets

Ex.2 E. H. Sanders, ed.: *English Music* (1979), no.44

without voice-exchange have *pedes* with rather long repeated elements, which are, however, generally subdivisible into variant segments (ex.2).

In addition to the Summer Canon, there are two cases in which the *pes*, not so designated in the manuscript, carries an ostinato text (*English Music*, no.45, and *US-PRu* Garrett 119, no.B1). A few compositions in which only one upper voice, supported by two *pedes* (e.g. *primus pes* and *secundus pes*), has text constitute a special kind of accompanied solo song. (A similar, though much later specimen – early 15th-century – of probable English origin is a Latin song, supported by a slow italianate tenor which is designated as a rondellus (*I-TRmp* 87, ff.252v–253); cf also Cornysh's *A robyn, gentyl robyn*.) The term *pes* evidently became common enough in the 'Worcester school' to be applied to the lowest voice of three motets actually based on plainchant cantus firmi (*English Music*, nos.67, 73, 80). The following compositions have a bottom voice specifically and properly labelled *pes*: *English Music*, nos.47–51, 53–4; the Summer Canon; the Worcester Fragments, nos.7, 17, 30, 74, 75. No medieval writer on music reported the use or meaning of the term in the English polyphony of the time.

BIBLIOGRAPHY

HarrisonMMB

K.J. Levy: 'New Material on the Early Motet in England: a Report on the Princeton MS Garrett 119', *JAMS*, iv (1951), 220–39

L.A. Dittmer: 'Beiträge zum Studium der Worcester-Fragmente', *Mf*, x (1957), 29–39

L.A. Dittmer: *The Worcester Fragments: a Catalogue Raisonné and Transcription*, MSD, ii (1957)

E. Apfel: *Studien zur Satztechnik der mittelalterlichen englischen Musik* (Heidelberg, 1959), chap.1

E.H. Sanders: 'Tonal Aspects of 13th-Century English Polyphony', *AcM*, xxxvii (1965), 19–34

H. Tischler: 'A Three-Part Rondellus in Trent MS 87', *JAMS*, xxiv (1971), 449–57

E.H. Sanders, ed.: *English Music of the Thirteenth and Early Fourteenth Centuries*, PMFC, xiv (1979)

P.M. Lefferts: *The Motet in England in the Fourteenth Century* (Ann Arbor, 1986)

ERNEST H. SANDERS

Pes (ii) [podatus] (Lat.: 'foot'). In Western chant notations a neume signifying two notes, the second higher than the first. It is so called because its shape often resembles that of a foot. (For illustration *see* NOTATION, Table 1; see also M. Huglo: 'Les noms des neumes et leur origine', *EG*, i, 1954, pp.53–67.)

Pesamment (Fr.: 'heavily'). *See* PESANTE.

Pesante (It.: 'heavy', 'weighty'). A direction usually applying to a whole passage or a whole piece rather than to individual notes or phrases. It was used frequently by Schoenberg but can be found as far back as the early 18th century, also in the French adverbial form *pesamment*.

Pesanterin. Instrument mentioned in *Daniel*. *See* BIBLICAL INSTRUMENTS, §3(xiii).

Pesarino, Il. Nickname of BARTOLOMEO BARBARINO.

Pesaro. City in Italy, in the Marches region. At the peak of the Malatesta family's splendour in the early 15th century, Du Fay, on his first visit to Italy, probably stayed in Pesaro and Rimini (1420–26), writing the motets *Vasilissa* *ergo gaude* (1420) for Cleofe Malatesta, *Apostolo glorioso* (1426) for Pandolfo Malatesta and the chanson *Resveilles vous* for the wedding of Carlo Malatesta and Vittoria Colonna (July 1423). During the same period Hugo de Lantins was also probably in the service of the Malatestas. Later in the century an anonymous contemporary chronicler reported spectacular musical events in Pesaro for the wedding of Costanzo Sforza and Camilla of Aragon, referring to polychoral singing heard during the ceremony in the cathedral (28 May 1475). The Mass was celebrated with the concurrence 'of numerous organs, pipes and trumpets, and drums, accompanying two separate groups of many singers, the one alternating with the other, and there were about 16 singers in each' (De Marinis, 1946, p.11).

From the time of Duke Francesco Maria I the Urbino court began to gravitate towards Pesaro. Under Guidobaldo II (duke from 1538) the court's musical activity received a boost with the presence of Paolo Animuccia, Leonardo Meldert, Dominique Phinot and the singer and instrumentalist Virginia Vagnoli. Phinot's five-voice *Mottetti* were the first music book published by Bartolomeo Cesano (active in Pesaro 1554–9), who also published one of Vincenzo Ruffo's books of *Madrigali* (1555) and G.B. Corvo's *Divina et sacra hebdomadae sancte* (1556).

In the 16th century a family of harpsichord makers maintained a workshop in Pesaro; 14 of their instruments built between 1533 and 1600 have survived. Zarlino, in his *Istitutioni harmoniche* (Venice, 1558, p.164), remarked that in 1548 he commissioned 'Maestro Dominico Pesarese raro et eccellente fabricattore di simili instrumenti' to construct a harpsichord that could give the temperament and modulation of the three genera, the diatonic, chromatic and enharmonic. The instrument, which has not yet been located, provided 19 divisions to the octave, with extra keys for all the sharps as well as between E and F and B and C. Other instrument makers were Tibaldo Fattorini (16th century) for lutes, Carlo Cortesi (*fl* 1612), Carlo Brandini, Antonio Mariani (*d* 1680), Sabatino Sacchini (*fl* 1686) for bowed instruments, and Antonio Pace (17th century) and Vincenzo and Francesco Polinori (18th century) for organs.

In the second half of the 16th century the Augustinian monk Paolo Lucchini (*c*1535–1598) was a music teacher in Pesaro, as his treatise *Della musica* shows. This work, of which a contemporary manuscript copy exists (*I-PESo* 2004), covers many aspects of 16th-century music theory and practice and is subdivided into three main sections: 'Della theorica', 'Del valore delle note e delle proporzioni', and 'Della pratica del contrapunto e del comporre'. The theorist Ludovico Zacconi (1555–1627), a native of Pesaro, began his musical studies in 1575 with Lucchini before settling in Venice about 1577. He returned to Pesaro in 1596 to be prior of the Augustinian monastery until his retirement in 1612; he remained in Pesaro until his death, writing the second part of his *Prattica di musica* (Venice, 1622).

Vincenzo Pellegrini (1594) and Pietro Pace (1597) are mentioned in cathedral documents. In the 17th century numerous musical performances took place at the homes of the nobility, and in the premises of academies such as the Accademia dei Disinvolti (founded 1645).

The event that helped to link musical life in Pesaro with that of other Italian centres was the establishment of the Teatro del Sole, designed and decorated by Niccolò Sabbatini (1574–1654), a native of Pesaro. It was inaugurated during Carnival 1637 with Hondedei's

Asmondo, and throughout the century staged works that had already appeared mainly in Rome and Venice. It was semicircular and the stage was relatively small (about 8 metres square), but it had elaborate scenery and machinery. The first part of Sabbatini's *Pratica di fabricar scene e machine ne' teatri* (Pesaro, 1637–8) is a description of the new theatre. Major improvements in its structure were made by the construction of one box for dignitaries in 1678 and the erection of three tiers of boxes between 1682 and 1694, when performances were suspended. In the 18th century works that appeared in Naples, Venice and Rome were performed there as well as works by local composers, including the premières of G.M. Ruggeri's *Armida abbandonata* (1715) and G. De Sanctis's *La serva scaltra* (1762). In 1723 and 1790 additional improvements were made in the boxes and ceiling of the theatre.

On 6 March 1816 the city council decided to build a new theatre on the same site, to provide employment for needy workmen. It was designed by the architect Pietro Ghinelli, completed on 30 January 1817 and named Teatro Nuovo. During the period of construction the Teatrino della Pallacorda was used for opera performances, and continued to be until the end of the century. Rossini was the city's most illustrious native composer, and the Teatro Nuovo opened on 10 June 1818 with his opera *La gazza ladra*, under his direction: throughout the century Rossini's works were the most often performed. In 1854 the theatre was closed for a year for renovations; it reopened as the Teatro Rossini. After Rossini's death a series of performances, which included *Semiramide*, *Otello* and the *Stabat mater* (with Teresa Stolz), were organized in August 1869 and called 'Pompe Funebri Rossiniane'. At the end of the 19th century and the beginning of the 20th works by Leoncavallo, Puccini and Mascagni (with a première of his *Zanetto* on 2 March 1896) dominated the seasons.

The Biblioteca Oliveriana, founded in 1756, holds musical sources, librettos and stage-setting documents. In accordance with Rossini's will, a Liceo Musicale was founded in 1882 (a conservatory from 1940); it has been directed by renowned figures including Pedrotti, Mascagni, Zanella, Zandonai, Alfano and Liviabella. A workshop for electronic music was established in 1971. The library contains manuscript and printed sources (*c*20,000 volumes) and a collection of portraits of musicians. The conservatory has published *Cronaca musicale* (1896–1917) and an *Annuario*. It houses the Tempietto Rossiniano, which has an extensive collection of the composer's autographs, including some operas, the *Petite messe solennelle* and the chamber compositions of his Paris period.

In 1955 the Fondazione Rossini (established 1940) set up the Centro Rossiniano di Studi; it publishes a *Bollettino*, has edited chamber compositions in the series Quaderni Rossiniani and in 1979 began the critical edition of Rossini's complete works. Since 1980 the Rossini Opera Festival has been held annually during August. The house where Rossini was born is now a small museum.

BIBLIOGRAPHY

DEUMM (F. Piperno); *GroveO* (P. Fabbri)

C. Cinelli: *Memorie cronistoriche del Teatro di Pesaro dall'anno 1637 al 1897* (Pesaro, 1898)

G. Radiciotti: 'La musica in Pesaro', *Cronaca musicale*, x (1906), 21–8, 46–9

G. Radiciotti: 'La cappella musicale del duomo di Pesaro (sec.
XVII–XIX)', *Cronaca musicale*, xviii (1914), 41–8, 65–75

E. Paolone: 'Codici musicali della Biblioteca Oliveriana e della
Biblioteca del R. Conservatorio di musica di Pesaro', *RMI*, xlvi
(1942), 186–200

T. De Marinis, ed.: 'Le nozze di Costanzo Sforza e Camilla
d'Aragona celebrate a Pesaro nel maggio 1475: narrazione
anonima, accompagnata da trentadue miniature di artista
contemporaneo', *Nozze Ricasoli–Firidolfi Ruffo di
Guardialombarda* (Florence, 1946)

A. Melica: 'Catalogo ragionato della Raccolta Rossini del
Conservatorio di Pesaro', *Bollettino del Centro rossiniano di studi*,
v (1960), 31–4, 53–7, 90–92

B. Cagli and M.Bucarelli, eds.: *La casa di Rossini* (Modena, 1989)
[exhibition catalogue]

D. Fornaciari: *L'ombra sacra della Quercia d'Oro: musica e
spettacolo alla corte dei Della Rovere di Pesaro e Urbino nel 500*
(diss., U. of Florence, 1990–91)

A. Brancati, ed.: *I centodieci anni del Liceo musicale Rossini
(1882–1992) oggi Conservatorio in Pesaro* (Pesaro, 1992)

E. Gamba and V. Montebelli, eds.: *Macchine da teatro e teatri di
macchine: Branca, Sabbatini, Torelli scenotecnici e meccanici del
Seicento – Catalogo della mostra* (Urbino, 1995)

ELVIDIO SURIAN/MARCO SALVARANI

Pescetti, Giovanni Battista (*b* Venice, *c*1704; *d* Venice, 20
March 1766). Italian composer. He studied with Antonio
Lotti, organist at S Marco, Venice, and opera composer.
He became friendly with his fellow student Baldassare
Galuppi with whom he collaborated in writing and
revising operas. An early mass by Pescetti impressed J.A.
Hasse. From 1725 to 1732 he supplied operas to various
Venetian theatres. In April 1736 he appeared as a
harpsichordist in London where, the following autumn,
he replaced Porpora as director of the Opera of the
Nobility, the rival company to Handel's. After its collapse
Pescetti remained in London, contributing operas or arias
in pasticcios; he also published (1739) a set of keyboard
sonatas, which include arrangements of the overture and
arias in his opera *La conquista del velo d'oro*. It is likely
that Pescetti left London around 1745, when the rebellion
of Prince Charles and the Highland clans made the city
inhospitable to Catholic Italians. In 1747 he returned to
providing operas in Venice. On 27 August 1752 he applied
for the position of second organist at S Marco, and finally
obtained the appointment on 16 May 1762.

Pescetti's opera arias are notable for their easily singable
lines, simple accompaniments, short, clearly articulated
phrases and restricted harmonic vocabulary. He was
nevertheless capable of fugal writing, as in his overture to
La conquista del velo d'oro, in several of his sonatas and
in his church music. Burney faulted him for a lack of fire
and of fertility of invention.

WORKS

OPERAS AND OTHER DRAMATIC
music lost unless otherwise stated

LKH - *London, King's Theatre in the Haymarket* VS - *Venice, Teatro
S Samuele*

Nerone detronato (G. Pimbaloni), Venice, S Salvatore, carn. 1725,
arias *GB-Lbl*, Favourite Songs (London, 1740)

Il prototipo (D. Lalli), VS, aut. 1726

La cantatrice (Lalli), VS, Ascension 1727

Gli odii delusi dal sangue (A.M. Lucchini), Venice, S Angelo, 1728,
acts 1 and 3 by B. Galuppi

Dorinda (pastorale, Lalli), VS, Ascension 1729, collab. Galuppi

I tre difensori della patria (A. Morselli), Venice, S Angelo, aut. 1729;
as Tullio Ostilio, wint. 1740

Costantino Pio, Rome, palace of Cardinal Ottoboni, 1730, for the
birth of the Dauphin, *F-Pn*

Siroe re di Persia (P. Metastasio), Venice, 1731, collab. Galuppi [rev.
of Vinci]

Alessandro nelle Indie (Metastasio), Venice, S Angelo, carn. 1732,
arias *I-Bas*

Demetrio (Metastasio), Florence, Pergola, carn. 1732; rev., LKH, 12
Feb 1737, Favourite Songs (London, 1737)

La conquista del velo d'oro (A.M. Cori), LKH, 28 Jan 1738, *GB-Lbl*,
arias in Le delizie dell'opere, ii (London, 1740)

L'asilo d'amore (int, Metastasio), LKH, spr. 1738

Diana e Endimione (serenata, Metastasio), London, New, 1 Dec
1739, arias in Le delizie dell'opere, ii (London, 1740), Favourite
Songs (London, *c*1740)

Olimpia in Ebuda (P.A. Rolli, after L. Ariosto: *Orlando furioso*),
LKH, 15 March 1740, doubtful, formerly attrib. J.A. Hasse

Busiri, ovvero Il trionfo d'amore (Rolli), London, New, 10 May 1740

Ezio (Metastasio), Venice, Grimani, carn. 1747

Farnace (Lucchini), Florence, Pergola, carn. 1749

Fra i due litiganti il terzo gode (ob, G. Lorenzi), Venice, S Cassiano,
spr. 1749, aria *I-Vc*

Arianna e Teseo (P. Pariati), Florence, Pergola, carn. 1750

Il Farnace (Metastasio), Siena, Rinnovati, 1750; as Adriano in Siria,
Reggio nell'Emilia, Moderno, 1750

Artaserse (Metastasio), Milan, Regio, 26 Dec 1751, *Fc*

Tamerlano (A. Piovene), VS, carn. 1754, collab. G. Cocchi

Solimano (G.A. Migliavacca), Reggio nell'Emilia, Moderno, 1756,
Favourite Songs (London, 1765)

Zenobia (Metastasio), Padua, Nuovo, June 1/61, *P-La*

Andimione, *D-Hs*

Contribs. to the following pasticcios: Sabrina (Rolli), LKH, 26 April
1737, Favourite Songs (London, 1737); Arsaces (A. Salvi, Rolli),
LKH, 29 Oct 1737; Angelica e Medoro (C. Vedova), London,
Covent Garden, 10 March 1739, Favourite Songs (London, 1739);
Merode e Olympia, 1740, Favourite Songs (London, 1740);
Alessandro in Persia (F. Vanneschi), LKH, 31 Oct 1741, Favourite
Songs (London, 1741); Aristodemo, tiranno di Cuma (Rolli),
LKH, 3 April 1744; Ezio (Metastasio), LKH, 24 November 1764;
Lionel and Clarissa (London, n.d.)

SACRED

Gionata (orat), Padua, ?before 1769, *I-Pca*

Cr, Gl, *GB-Ob*, Ky, Gl, *D-Dkh*

INSTRUMENTAL

[10] Sonate, hpd (London, 1739); hpd sonata and 4 org works, *I-Vc*;
Sonata, hpd, *Gl*; Lesson no.11 in kbd collection, *GB-Ob*

BIBLIOGRAPHY

CaffiS, ii

F. Torrefranca: *Le origini italiane del romanticismo musicale: i
primitivi della sonata moderna* (Turin, 1930/*R*)

S. dalla Libera: 'Cronologia musicale della basilica di San Marco in
Venezia', *Musica sacra* [Milan], 2nd ser., vi (1961), 133–5

F. Degrada: 'Le sonate per cembalo e per organo di Giovanni Battista
Pescetti', *Chigiana*, new ser. iii (1966), 89–108

M. Fabbri: 'Giovanni Battista Pescetti e un concorso per maestro di
cappella a Firenze', *RIM*, i (1966), 120–26

C.M. Taylor: 'From Losses to Lawsuit: Patronage of the Italian
Opera in London by Lord Middlesex, 1739–45', *ML*, lxviii
(1987), 1–25

JOHN WALTER HILL

Pesch, Gregor. *See* PESCHIN, GREGOR.

Pescheur [Lepescheur]. French family of organ builders.
They worked in Paris during the 17th century. Nicolas
Pescheur (*b* Paris, 1555; *d* Paris, 1616) was the son of a
merchant from the quarter of St Germain-des-Prés. He
probably trained at first with the organ builder Raoul
Bourdet, and then with Jan Langhedul during their stay
in Paris (1585–90). In partnership with Claude Danyon,
he worked at Chaource in Burgundy. After returning to
Paris, he pursued a modest career combining organ
building with the post of organist at St Sulpice. From
1610, enriched by the teaching of Carlier, he entrusted
this work to his sons. Of his four sons from his marriage
to Catherine Henry, a musician's daughter, two became
organ builders. Pierre Pescheur (*b* Paris *c*1590; *d* Paris,
1637) was taught by his father Nicolas and then by Paul
Maillard. He learnt organ building in the Titelouze style

with Valéran De Héman in 1610–12, and built organs to commissions his father had obtained, eventually succeeding him. After some smaller projects, he built the organ in Amiens Cathedral (1620–24), and in Paris at St Paul (1623) and St Gervais (1628), where pipework survives. The organs at Aubervilliers (c1630; pipework survives) and St Etienne-du-Mont, Paris (1631–6), were his greatest instruments. He married a mason's daughter, and they had one son, Charles, who became a painter. With his master, De Héman, he founded the classical Parisian school of organ building. His most prominent pupil was Pierre Desenclos. Aubin Pescheur (b c1595; d after 1630), another son of Nicolas Pescheur, is only known as an employee of Maillard (Rennes, 1628).

BIBLIOGRAPHY

F. Raugel: *Les grandes orgues des églises de Paris* (Paris, 1927)
N. Dufourcq: *Documents pour servir à l'histoire de l'orgue* (Paris, 1934)
P. Hardouin: 'La composition des orgues que pouvaient toucher les musiciens parisiens aux alentours de 1600', *La musique instrumentale de la renaissance* [Paris, 1954], 259–68
P. Hardouin: 'Jeux d'orgues du XVIe siècle', *RdM*, lii (1966), 163–84
P. Hardouin: 'Facteurs parisiens du XVIIe siècle: les Pescheurs', *Connaissance de l'orgue*, xix–xx (1976), 26–32; xxi (1977), 18–25

PIERRE HARDOUIN

Peschin [Pechin, Pečin, Pesch, Pesthin, Pitschner, Posthinus], **Gregor** (b ?Prague, c1500; d ?Heidelberg, after 1547). Bohemian composer. He received his musical training in the court chapel of Lajos II in Budapest, serving there until 1526. From 1527 to 1539 he was a member of the court chapel of Matthäus Lang, Prince-Bishop of Salzburg, where he and Paul Hofhaimer were colleagues as organists. His skill in playing the organ won him the high opinion of his musical patron. In 1539 he went to Neuburg an der Donau in the service of Count Palatine Ottheinrich, subsequently Elector of Heidelberg (1556–9); this move was probably connected with the building of a large organ for the castle in Neuburg by Hans Schachinger of Munich (the work was commissioned on 26 June 1537). When Count Palatine Ottheinrich had to leave the duchy of Pfalz-Neuburg in 1544 after his bankruptcy, Peschin followed him and his retinue into exile, going first to Heidelberg. He is mentioned, along with the lutenist Sebastian Ochsenkun, in Elector Friedrich II's accounts books for 1546. The last extant document concerning Peschin is a letter he wrote to his friend, the composer and printer Hans Kilian of Neuburg, on 18 November 1547, attached to the so-called 'Heidelberg chapel inventory' of 1544 (D-HEu Cod.Pal.Germ.318). Peschin probably wrote part of the inventory as well. Drawn up before Ottheinrich went into exile, it lists 105 compositions by Peschin (including five masses, four epitaphs on members of the ducal family, about 30 motets and over 50 German songs), mentioning some of them several times. 12 of his song settings are included in Sebastian Ochsenkun's lute tablature, compiled in 1558 at the request of the elector of the time, Ottheinrich of the Palatinate (RISM 1558[20]). Those few of Peschin's songs that survive owe much to the compositional tradition of Hofhaimer, and the classical perfection to which Hofhaimer brought the Tenorlied is continued in his work.

WORKS

Edition: *Das Deutsche Gesellschaftslied in Österreich von 1480–1550*, ed. L. Nowak, DTÖ, lxxii, Jg.xxxvii/2 (1930/R) [N]

Missa dominicalis (Missa super dominicale minus), 4vv (alternative Ag, 6vv), *D-Mbs* Mus.ms.69
Motets: Beati omnes qui timent/Ecce sic benedicitur, 4vv, *Rp* B220–222; Cum ascendisset aurora, 6vv, *Rp* B211–15; Dominus dixit ad me, 4vv, *Rs* 2⁰, Liturg. 18; Dulces exuviae dum fata, 4vv, *Rp* B220–222; Deus qui sedes super thronum/Quia tu solus laborem, 4vv, *Rp* B220–222; Praeceptum novum de vobis, 4vv, *Rp* B220–222; Si bona suscepimus, 4vv, *Rp* B211–215; Sic enim Deus dilexit mundum, 4vv, *Rp* B211–215; Vocem iocunditatis/Ecce ducem nostrum . . . Franciscus Sforcia Dux Mediolaniensis, 8vv, *Mbs* Mus.ms.1536, 1564[1] (anon.)
Ode: Collis o heliconii, 4vv, 1539[26]
Sacred songs: Es wöll uns Gott genedig sein, 4vv, 1558[20]; Herr das du mich so gestürtzet, 4vv, 1558[20]; Herr durch Barmhertzigkeyt, 4vv, 1558[20]; Im friede dein, o Herre mein, 4vv, 1558[20]; Invocabat autem Samson, 4vv, 1558[20]; Mein seel erhebt den Herren, 4vv, 1558[20]; O Herr, nit ferr, sey dein, 4vv, 1558[20]; Wol dem die ubertrettung gross, 4vv, 1558[20]
Secular songs: All ding auff erdt, 6vv, *Rp* B282 (T only); Die aller holdseligst, 4vv, 1558[20], N; Ein stund vermag, 5vv, *Rp* B282, (T only); Es mag wol noch geraten, 5vv, *Rp* B282 (T only); Dort niden an dem Rheyne, 4vv, 1558[20], N; Fraw ich bin euch von hertzen hold, 4vv, 1539[27], N (also attrib. Senfl); Freud und muet het mich, 4vv, 1558[20]; Glueck hoffnung gib, 4vv, 1556[28], N; Herrlich und schön, 5vv, *Rp* B282 (T only); Ich hab ein hertz, glaub mir, 5vv, *Rp* B282 (T only); Mag ich Zuflucht in eer und zucht, 4vv, 1539[27], N; Mein hertz fert hin, 5vv, 1556[29], N; Mich fretzt unglück so vast hart, 4vv, 1540[7], N; Oft wünsch ich jr, 1539[27], N; Und wer der winter noch so kalt, 4vv, 1558[20], N; Wer das elendt Bauer wil, 5vv, *Rp* B282 (T only)
About 100 other works (masses, motets, songs, epitaphs), lost, listed in *HEu* Pal.Germ.318 (see Lambrecht)

BIBLIOGRAPHY

L. Nowak: 'Das deutsche Gesellschaftslied in Österreich von 1480 bis 1550', *SMw*, xvii (1930), 21–52
H. Spies: 'Beiträge zur Musikgeschichte Salzburgs im Spätmittelalter und zu Anfang der Renaissancezeit', *Mitteilungen der Gesellschaft für Salzburger Landeskunde*, lxxxi (1941), 80–84, 89–91
S. Hermelink: 'Ein Musikalienverzeichnis der Heidelberger Hofkapelle aus dem Jahre 1544', *Ottheinrich: Gedenkschrift zur 400jährigen Wiederkehr seiner Kurfürstenzeit in der Pfalz*, ed. G. Poesgen (Heidelberg, 1956), 247–60
A. Layer: 'Pfalzgraf Ottheinrich und die Musik', *AMw*, xv (1958), 258–75
G. Pietzsch: 'Quellen und Forschungen zur Geschichte der Musik am kurpfälzischen Hof zu Heidelberg bis 1622', *Abhandlungen der geistes- und sozialwissenschaftlichen Klasse der Mainzer Akademie der Wissenschaften und der Literatur*, 6th ser., vi (Wiesbaden, 1963)
J. Lambrecht: *Das 'Heidelberger Kapellinventar' von 1544 (Codex Pal.Germ.318): Edition und Kommentar* (Heidelberg, 1987)

JUTTA LAMBRECHT

Pesciolini, Biagio (b Prato; d after 1609). Italian composer. When he published his first volume of music, in 1563, he was *maestro di cappella* of Volterra Cathedral. He was canon and *maestro di cappella* to the provostry of Prato at least for the period 1571–81 and is again recorded at Prato in 1599, but only as a canon. Brunelli implied that he was still alive in 1610. The influence of the directives of the Council of Trent concerning the composition of church music is evident in his works, especially in the masses of 1599. Brunelli praised him highly for his skill in double counterpoint, especially when improvising.

WORKS
all printed works published in Venice

SECULAR VOCAL

Il primo libro de madrigali, 5, 6vv (1563), inc.
Il secondo libro de madrigali, 6vv (1571), inc.
Il terzo libro de madrigali, 6vv (1581)

SACRED VOCAL

Missae, motecta ut dicunt, juxta formam Concilij Tridentini, 8, 10, 12vv (1599)
Mottetti, messe e Magnificat, libro primo, 5, 6, 8, 10vv (1605)

MS works, *D-Bsb*

BIBLIOGRAPHY

EitnerQ; SchmidlD; PitoniN

A. Brunelli: *Regole et dichiarationi di alcuni contrapunti doppii* (Florence, 1610)

PIER PAOLO SCATTOLIN

Pešek, Libor (*b* Prague, 22 June 1933). Czech conductor. He studied with Karel Ančerl, Václav Neumann and Václav Smetáček at the Prague Academy and worked as a répétiteur, first at the Plzeň Opera and then at the Prague National Theatre. He gained his early conducting reputation with the Prague Chamber Harmony, a wind band he founded and directed (1958–64), and the Sebastian Orchestra, Prague. He was chief conductor of the Czech Chamber Orchestra, 1970–77, and the Slovak PO, 1980–81, and in 1982 was appointed conductor in residence of the Czech PO. During the 1970s he worked frequently in the Netherlands, and in 1987 he became music director of the Royal Liverpool PO, which he brought to greater international prominence with a USA tour in 1992 and through an impressive series of recordings; in 1993 the Liverpool orchestra also became the first non-Czech orchestra to open the Prague Spring Festival. Pešek appears frequently with other major orchestras in Europe and North America, and is principal guest conductor of the Prague SO. He has conducted a number of stage works for films and television, including Dvořák's *Rusalka*, Benda's *Medea* and Stravinsky's *Pulcinella* and *The Soldier's Tale*. He is a fervent advocate of Suk, whose *Asrael* and other works he has recorded; his discography also includes a fresh, idiomatic cycle of Dvořák symphonies, Smetana's *Má vlast*, and works by Britten, Janáček, Skryabin, Linek, Krommer and Ryba. In 1996 in Britain he was appointed an honorary KBE.

NOËL GOODWIN

Pesenti, Benedetto (*b* Venice, *c*1545; *d* after 1591). Italian composer. He was a priest. According to his nephew Giovanni Battista, who wrote the dedication, dated 15 October 1591, to his *Primo libro de madrigali a cinque voci* (Venice, 1591), the compositions published in it, as well as some others, had been left with him while Benedetto, here referred to as an abbot, was away from Venice on ecclesiastical business some months earlier. His madrigals, according to his nephew, are 'composed according to the science of the most excellent musicians Adrian Willaert and Cipriano de Rore, teachers of the above mentioned [Pesenti]'. If indeed he studied with Willaert (*d* 1562), then he must have been born no later than about 1545. However, his madrigals, which include a setting of a canzone in nine parts and several *madrigali spirituali*, show none of the mastery of either of his alleged teachers, and he is best considered a competent amateur. One motet for five voices was published by Phalèse (in RISM 1609¹).

DAVID NUTTER

Pesenti, Martino (*b* Venice, *c*1600; *d* Venice, *c*1648). Italian harpsichordist and composer. He appears to have spent all his life in Venice, where he was a pupil of G.B. Grillo. He was blind from birth, so he was unable to participate in the large-scale productions cultivated in Venetian churches and theatres. Devoting himself instead almost entirely to chamber music, he had a large following in the private sector of society; his patrons included local noblemen, the Habsburg Archduke Leopold and successive Viennese ambassadors to Venice.

Pesenti's published works include at least seven volumes of madrigals and canzonettas, three of arias and five of dances, but only one of church music. His style is simple, almost austere, and is thus similar to that of much of the sacred music of Venetian and provincial parish churches in the 1610s and 20s, when several decrees prohibiting florid writing and elaborate accompaniment were issued. The duet textures of most of his works are uncluttered and usually homophonic; apart from canon at the unison he admits little counterpoint, there are few melismas in his vocal works, and his solo arias are very short. He is best remembered for his instrumental music, but it is remarkably similar in idiom to his vocal works: indeed the suites (ballettos) and passamezzos in some of his volumes are dance-songs, and the correntes of his op.10 can be performed vocally or instrumentally.

In Pesenti's madrigals the bass becomes progressively more important. Notably stationary basses characterize several works in op.11, while another, *Cieco viato*, is built on a strophic bass. He used a variety of chaconne, passacaglia and simple ostinato basses in op.16. The bulk of his dances are short and simple correntes and galliards. They are conceived essentially for harpsichord, which may be supplemented by string instruments (lutes and *viole* are mentioned in the preface to op.15). The dances of op.15 have attracted special attention because Pesenti intended them for performance on a keyboard instrument with separate keys for enharmonic notes (e.g. $a\sharp$ and $b\flat$). Most are presented in two versions – 'diatonic' and 'chromatic' or 'enharmonic'; the latter two amount only to transpositions, but often to keys with numerous sharps or flats. The intrinsic musical value of these works is far below that of the op.15 passamezzos in which the bass is emphasized by long, flowing divisions. Pesenti acknowledged his use of tritones, sevenths, ninths and other dissonances in a note to performers in his first book of correntes, and recommended them for their beauty (*vaghezza*) provided that the tempo was taken presto. Typically these dissonances occur as passing notes in the quaver figurations in the treble of the first half and the bass of the second half of each work. Conversely, Pesenti recommends a very long beat (*battuta longhissima*) in his ballettos. The three-voice example in the first book of correntes contains several strophes in duple metre but concludes with a fast movement in triple metre.

WORKS

MADRIGALS

Il primo libro de madrigali, 2–4vv, bc (Venice, *c*1619, 2/1628)

Il secondo libro de madrigali, lost

Il terzo libro de madrigali, 2–5vv, bc (hpd/other insts) (Venice, 1628, 2/1639)

Il quarto libro de madrigali, 2–6vv, alcuni concertati con violini, con alcune canzonette et un ballo sopra la gagliarda di 5 passi con bc, op.9 (Venice, 1638); Ardo ma non ardisco in Whenham, ii, 311–21

Madrigali concertati, 2–3vv, bc, libro quinto, op.11 (Venice, 1641)

Capricci stravaganti e musicali pensieri, passi e mezi da cantar, canzoni, et alcuni madrigali, 2–3vv, bc, [libro sesto], op.16 (Venice, 1647)

Ultime musicali e canore fatiche, 2–3vv (Venice, 1648)

ARIAS ETC.

Arie, libro primo, lost

Arie, 1v … gui, libro secondo (Venice, 1633); Così Nilio cantò, ed. K. Jeppesen, *La flora*, ii (Copenhagen, 1949), 16

Arie, 1v, hpd/chit/other inst, con una cantata in fine … libro terzo (Venice, 1636); O biondetta lascivetta ed. in *La flora*, ii, 18

Correnti alla francese, gagliarde, e balletti da cantarsi, 1v, hpd/other inst, con un brando … libro primo, op.10 (Venice, 1639)

INSTRUMENTAL MUSIC

Il primo libro delle correnti alla francese, hpd, other insts (Venice, c1619, 2/1635/R, 'con una aggionta di alcune correnti et un balletto a 3')

Il secondo libro delle correnti alla francese ... con alcune correnti spezzate a tre, hpd, other insts (Venice, 1630)

Correnti alla francese, balletti, gagliarde, pass' e mezi ... libro terzo, hpd, other insts, op.12 (Venice, 1641)

Correnti, gagliarde, e balletti diatonici, trasportati parte cromatici, e parte henarmonici, con un balletto a 3, passi e mezi a 2 & a 3 ... libro quarto, hpd, other insts, op.15 (Venice, 1645/6); 4 correntes, 5 galliards, 5 ballettos and the 2-part passamezzo in DM, xxxvi (1964); selections in AMI, vii (1897) [including a balletto and passamezzo (no.20) incorrectly attrib. G.B. Fontana]

14 correntes in *I-Tn* Foà vi; 1 galliard in Foà vii

Suites and dances in *PL-Kj*

SACRED MUSIC

Missae ... con sacris cantionibus, 1–3vv, bc (Venice, 1643)

1 motet, 2vv, bc, in 1642[4]

BIBLIOGRAPHY

Mischiati1

C. Morey: 'The Diatonic, Chromatic, and Enharmonic Dances by Martino Pesenti', *AcM*, xxxviii (1966), 185–9

E. Selfridge-Field: *Venetian Instrumental Music from Gabrieli to Vivaldi* (Oxford, 1975, 3/1994)

J. Whenham: *Duet and Dialogue in the Age of Monteverdi* (Ann Arbor, 1982)

L.F. Tagliavini: 'The Art of "not leaving the instrument empty": Comments on Early Italian Harpsichord Playing', *EMc*, xi (1983), 299–308

P. Barbieri: 'I temperamenti ciclici da Vicentino (1555) a Buliowski (1699): teoria e pratica "archicembalistica"', *L'organo*, xxi (1983), 129–208

C. Stembridge: 'The cimbalo cromatico and Other Italian Keyboard Instruments with Nineteen or More Divisions to the Octave (Surviving Specimens and Documentary Evidence)', *Performance Practice Review*, vi (1993), 33–59

J. Whenham: 'Martino Pesenti's "Madrigali guerrieri, et amorosi"', *Claudio Monteverdi und die Folgen: Detmold 1993*, 267–89

ELEANOR SELFRIDGE-FIELD

Pesenti [Vicentino], **Michele** (*b* Verona, *c*1470; *d* May, 1528). Italian priest, composer, singer and lutenist. With Tromboncino and Cara, he was one of the most important frottola composers. He was born in Verona in about 1470, the son of Alberto and Umilia Pesenti. Since he was a priest, he must have studied at the Scuola degli Accoliti in his native city, an institution founded by Pope Eugene IV that produced other cleric-composers, among them Marchetto Cara. Pesenti's first known position was in Ferrara, where he served Cardinal Ippolito I d'Este, acting as a procurer of music and instruments as well as a lutenist, singer and composer. Already in 1504 he wrote to the cardinal from Venice promising to come to Ferrara as soon as an unnamed gentleman returned his lute. From 1506 his name appears in Ippolito's payment registers, and it remains there, except for a probably illusory break in 1510, up to 1514. In this capacity he was resident with Ippolito in Rome in 1513 and 1514, where he thrice petitioned Pope Leo X for benefices. He apparently left Rome in 1515, when Ippolito wrote to his brother Alfonso in Ferrara asking him to put the musician in prison.

At some point after this Pesenti entered the services of Leo himself: on 30 August 1521 the pope, calling him 'musicus, cubicularius et familiaris continuus comensalis noster', granted him a benefice in the church of SS Fermo e Rustico in his native Verona. By late 1522 he was in Mantua as a member of the staff of Marchese Federico Gonzaga. He was still in Mantua on 13 July 1524, when Federico gave 'Pre Michele da Verona, nostro musico' 25 lire for one of the musician's servants, but he left the city

by early 1525, going first to Rome, where Clement VII granted him minor Veronese benefices on 21 February. He had returned to his native city by May of the same year, when he became rector of SS Fermo e Rustico. Here he apparently had extensive restoration done to the church, since there remains a stone tablet with the following words: 'SANCTORUM / FIRMI ET / RUSITICI ECCLESIAM / DOMUMQ. MICHAEL / MUSICUS / RESTAURAVIT / MDXXV'. Pesenti died, probably after a long illness, in May 1528; he was replaced as rector of the church on 5 June of this year.

As a frottolist, Pesenti ranks with Lurano and just after Tromboncino and Cara in historical importance. His works are characterized by a remarkable freedom and variety of formal solutions, ingenious twists of melody, and a light, popular flavour. Pesenti often wrote his own poetry: in Petrucci's editions, eight pieces are marked 'C[antus] et V[erba]', signifying that he also wrote the text as well as the music. He is important for the early period of the frottola rather than for the later, more subtle period. Nearly all his 36 surviving frottolas (16 *barzellete*, 7 *ode*, 5 *villotta*-like settings, 2 *strambotti*, 2 *canzonette*, 1 *capitolo*, 1 *madrigal*, and 2 Latin odes) were in print by 1514. Only one, *Alma gentil, sein voi fusse* (1521[6]), appeared after Petrucci's last book of frottolas. This is also his only setting of a madrigal text, although it still has the typical non-imitative contrapuntal style of the frottola. *So ben che lei non sa* (1513[1]) stands at the border between madrigal and villotta. Unlike the other leading frottolists, Pesenti wrote no *laude*.

Pesenti is particularly significant for his early adoption of popular tunes into his works. Two frottolas, *Spenta m'hai del pecto amore* (1507[3]) and *Io voria esser cholu* (1509[2]), incorporate the text and tunes of 'Bel alboro, ch'è nato nella via' and 'Turluru, la capra è mozza' respectively. Even more notable are several early villotta-like compositions, which adopt the popular tune throughout the piece. *Dal lecto me levava* (1504[4]), which imitates the sounds of the stork, resembles the later villotta in its textures, its all-vocal scoring, and the bawdy undercurrent to its text. Indeed, Pesenti was one of the earliest Italian Renaissance composers to write secular compositions in which all parts were intended to be sung. In Petrucci's first book of frottolas (1504[4]) two of his pieces have texts in all voices throughout and two others have texts in all voices in the refrain. Pesenti also seems to have delighted in musical and textual repartee with his contemporaries: his *Io son de gabbia* forms a part of a complex of 'birdsong' *strambotti*; his *Io son l'ocel che con le debil ali* includes as its fully texted tenor the cantus of Cara's *Io son l'ocel che sopra i rami d'oro*, and is also a part of the complex; and his *L'acqua vale al mio gran focho* is a *risposta* to Tromboncino's *Non val acqua al mio gran foco*, adopting Tromboncino's cantus as its bassus. Pesenti's *S'io son stato a ritornare* is answered by Antico's *Questo tuo lento tornare*, which bears the rubric 'Risposta de "S'io son stato a ritornare"' in Petrucci's seventh book of frottolas. Pesenti is included among other frottolists, including Tromboncino and Cara, in Filippo Oriolo's poem *Monte Parnassus* of about 1520.

Pesenti's name appears in many different forms. Two pieces in the 1520 reprint of Antico's *Frottole, libro tertio* (1517[1]) are ascribed to Michele Vicentino. Once thought to be another composer, this is now thought to be Pesenti (see Rubsamen, 1961). In the first two editions of Antico's collection (1513 and 1518) two works are ascribed to 'D. Michael V.', but Petrucci, in his *Frottole, libro undecimo* (1514[2]), attributed one of them to 'D[on] M[ichael]'. Petrucci ascribed several of Pesenti's pieces in this way, and it seems almost certain that the editor of the 1520 reprint erred in the resolution of the earlier abbreviation and that the correct attribution should be to "D[on] Michael V[eronensis]", that is, Pesenti, who was both a priest and a native of Verona.

Pesenti also composed two secular compositions with Latin texts: *Inhospitas per Alpes* and *Integer vitae*, the latter a treatment of a Sapphic ode by Horace. Both are carefully set so that the melody mirrors the natural accents of the words. The latter was also set by Tromboncino, perhaps while he was in Ferrara, since the two works show marked similarities. Two four-voice motets survive, both in printed collections. One of these, *Tulerunt dominum meum*, is also included in Glarean's *Dodecachordon* (1547). Glarean writes glowingly of the motet, commenting on the music's 'great emotion and innate sweetness and tremendous power' in its depiction of Mary Madgalene weeping at the tomb of Christ. It is a large motet in three parts that demonstrates fully Pesenti's ability to compose in the formal Franco-Flemish style. Glarean, in fact, originally thought that the motet was by Josquin and writes that some people attribute it to Isaac, though in the copy of the treatise he sent to his pupil Johannes Aal he added a handwritten note assigning the piece correctly to 'Pre Michel de Verona'.

Pesenti's music seems to have been widely known, even after his death. Marguerite of Navarre translated into French his *Che faralla, che diralla* (1513[1]), which deals with a lover exacting his revenge on his beloved by becoming a friar; she described the music as 'rather pedestrian'. Verdelot set the cantus of his *O dio, che la brunetta mia* (1504[4]) for six voices (1541[16]), and Pesenti's work itself appeared, without the altus and ascribed to Costanzo Festa, in *Il vero libro di madrigali a tre voci di Costanzo Festa* (1539).

WORKS

Editions O. Chilesotti: *Saggio sulla melodia popolare del Cinquecento* (Milan, 1889) [Chiles]
Ottaviano Petrucci, Frottole, Buch I und IV, ed. R. Schwartz, Publikationen älterer Musik, viii (Leipzig, 1935/R) [S]
F. Torrefranca: *Il segreto del Quattrocento* (Milan, 1939) [T]
Le frottole nell'edizione principe di Ottaviano Petrucci, ed. G. Cesari and others, Ima, 1st ser., i (1954) [C]
Le frottole per canto e liuto intabulate da Franciscus Bossinensis, ed. B. Disertori, IMa, 2nd ser., iii (1964) [D]

Secular: Adio, signora, adio, 1504[4], S, C; Ahimé, ch'io moro, 1504[4], S, C, D; Ahimé, lasso, ahimé dolente, 1505[6], D; Alma gentil, sein voi fusse, 1521[6], ed. in Rubsamen (1961); Amor, poi che non poi, 1505[6], Chiles; Ardo e bruscio, 1504[4], S, C; Ben mille volte al dì, 1504[4], S, C, ed. in Rubsamen (1961); Che faralla, che diralla, 1513[1], ed. in SCMA, iv (1941), K. Jeppesen, *Italia sacra musica*, ii (Copenhagen, 1962); Dal lecto me levava, 1504[4], S, C, T; Deh, chi me sa dir novella, 1507[4], D; Dime un pocho che vol dire, 1504[4], S, C
Fuggir volio el tuo bel volto, 1504[4] (attrib. 'Micha C. & V.'), S, C; Inhospitas per Alpes, 1504[4], S, C, D; Integer vitae, 1504[4] (Horace) (*I-Fn* 27 with text 'Io son de gabbia'), S, C, D; Io son l'ocel che con le debil ali, 1507[4]; Io voria esser cholu, 1509[2], D; L'aqua vale al mio gran foco, 1504[4], S, C; Non è pensier che'l mio secreto, 1507[4], D; Non mi doglio già d'amore, 1504[4] (G. Visconti), S, C; O bon, egli è bon, 1505[6] (doubtful, attrib. 'D. M.' in tavola, but 'M. C.' over music), 1511 (attrib. 'M. C.'), D, ed. in Rubsamen (1961); O dio, che la brunetta mia, 1504[4] (attrib. 'Micha. C. & V.'), S, C; Passando per una rezolla, 1504[4], S, C; Poi che'l ciel e la fortuna, 1504[4] (attrib. 'Micha. C. & V.'), S, C, D

Quando lo pomo vien, *I-Fc* 2440 (doubtful, attrib. 'Pr. Michael'), 1514[2] (attrib. 'B. T.'), 1516[2] (attrib. 'Marchetto Cara'), ed. F. Luisi, *Il secondo libro di frottole di Andrea Antico* (Rome, 1975–6), T; Questa è mia, l'ho fatta mì, 1504[4] (attrib. 'Michaelis C. & V.'), S, C; Se in tutto hai destinato, 1504[4], S, C; Sempre l'è come esser, 1504[4] (attrib. 'Michaelis Cantus & Verba'), S, C; Sia felice la tua vita, 1505[4], C; Sì, me piace, 1504[4] (attrib. 'Micha. C & V. a voce mutate'), S, C; S'io son stato a ritornare, 1504[4] (attrib. 'Micha. C. & V.'), S, C, D; So ben che lei non sa, 1513[1], ed. SCMA, iv (1941); Spenta m'hai del pecto amore, 1507[3], D; Trista e noiosa, 1504[4], S, C; Tute lamenti a torto, 1504[4] (A. Tebaldeo), S, C; Una legiadra donna, 1504[4], S, C; Vieni hormai, non più tardare, 1505[5], S, C
Sacred: Manus Domini, 1521[6], ed. K. Jeppesen, *Italia sacra musica*, ii (Copenhagen, 1962); Tulerunt Dominum meum, 1519[2], ed. C. Miller, *Henricus Glarean: Dodecachordon*, MSD, vi, 1965

BIBLIOGRAPHY

EinsteinIM; *PirrottaDO*
D. Heartz: 'Les goûts réunis, or the Worlds of the Madrigal and the Chanson Confronted', *Chanson & Madrigal 1480–1530: Cambridge, MA, 1961*, ed J. Haar (Cambridge, MA, 1964), 88–138
W. Rubsamen: 'From Frottola to Madrigal: the Changing Pattern of Secular Italian Vocal Music', ibid., 51–87
K. Jeppesen: 'Über italienische Kirchenmusik in der ersten Hälfte des 16. Jahrhundert', *SM*, iii (1962), 149–60
K. Jeppesen: *La frottola* (Århus and Copenhagen, 1968–70)
H. Glarean: *Dodecachordon* (Basle, 1547/R; Eng. trans., MSD, vi, 1965)
H.C. Slim: 'Musicians on Parnassus', *Studies in the Renaissance*, xii (1965), 134–63
F. Luisi: 'Il secondo libro di frottole di Andrea Antico', *NRMI*, viii (1974), 491–535
E. Paganuzzi: 'Michael Musicus e la lapide di S. Fermo e Rustico in Cortalta', *Atti e memorie dell'Accademia di Agricoltura, Scienze e Lettere di Verona*, ser. vi, xxvii (1975–6), 91–101
E. Paganuzzi: 'Notizie veronesi su Marchetto Cara e Michele Pesenti', *RIM*, xi (1976), 7–24
E. Paganuzzi and others: *La musica a Verona* (Verona, 1976)
F. Luisi: *La musica vocale nel Rinascimento* (Turin, 1977)
W. Prizer: 'Lutenists at the Court of Mantua', *JLSA*, xiii (1980), 4–34
L. Lockwood: 'Adrian Willaert and Cardinal Ippolito I d'Este: New Light on Willaert's Early Career in Italy, 1515–1521', *EMH*, 5v (1985), 85–112
W. Prizer: 'Isabella d'Este and Lucrezia Borgia: the Frottola at Mantua and Ferrara', *JAMS*, xxxiii (1985), 1–33
W. Prizer: 'Games of Venus: Secular Vocal Music in the Late Quattrocento and Early Cinquecento', *JM*, ix (1991), 3–56
W. Prizer: 'Local Repertories and the Printed Book: Antico's Third Book of Frottole (1513)', *Music in Renaissance Cities and Courts: Studies in Honor of Lewis Lockwood*, ed. J.A. Owens and A.M. Cummings (Warren, MI, 1997), 347–71
C. Gallico: *Rimeria musicale popolare italiana nel Rinascimento* (Lucca, 1996)

WILLIAM F. PRIZER

Pes flexus. *See* TORCULUS.

Pesindhèn [pasindhèn, pesinden]. Female singer in Central Javanese gamelan. Commonly several *pesindhèn* participate in a performance, singing in alternation or in unison depending on context. They are prominent in shadow plays (*wayang kulit*), interacting with the puppeteer (*dhalang*). They sing *sindhènan*, as a featured solo or as one of many melodic strands in the gamelan texture (*sindhènan* also refers to mixed-gender choral song for court dances).

Sindhènan is fixed for some pieces, but for most pieces the *pesindhèn* draws on stock texts and melodic phrases, parsing *wangsalan*, richly allusive couplets of 12-syllable lines, into eight- and four-syllable units, sung (with various interjections) to melodic formulae that lead to principal pitches in the composition according to modal constraints, incorporating substantial individual variation. Usually *sindhènan* is rhythmically free, unlike male choral melodies (*gérongan*), and is closely related to the *rebab* melody.

Recently the voice of the *pesindhèn* has been heavily amplified. She is often visually prominent in performance and on cassette covers, while other performers are anonymous. Paid more than male singers and instrumentalists, *pesindhèn* confer status on their patrons: the more famous and numerous the singers hired, the richer the patron appears. Despite this star status, allegations of immorality, based on singers' close associations with men, have led some singers to prefer the euphemistic label *waranggana* ('nymph').

In West Java the *pasindén* is a recent addition (mid-20th century onwards) to the *gamelan saléndro* ensemble. The *pasindén* plays a prominent role in *wayang golék* (rod puppet theatre, accompanied by *gamelan saléndro*), where the increasing focus on her melody has resulted in changes to the musical texture of the ensemble.

See also INDONESIA, §§III and V, i; and MARDUSARI, NYAI TUMENGGUNG.

BIBLIOGRAPHY

S. Gitosaprodjo: *Ichtisar teori sindenan* [Summary of the theory of *sindhènan*] (Malang, 1971)
R.A. Sutton: 'Who is the Pesindhèn? Notes on the Female Singing Tradition in Java', *Indonesia*, no.37 (1984), 118–31
T.S. Suparno: *Laporan penelitian sindenan andegan Nyi Bei Mardusari* (Surakarta, 1985)
R.A. Sutton: 'Identity and Individuality in an Ensemble Tradition: the Female Vocalist in Java', *Women and Music in Cross-Cultural Perspective*, ed. E. Koskoff (Norwood, CT, 1987), 111–30
S.P. Walton: *Mode in Javanese Music* (Athens, OH, 1987)
Supadmi: *Cengkok-cengkok srambahan dan abon-abon* [Basic patterns and filler phrases] (Oakland, CA, 1989)
I. Kurniatun: *Garap sindenan ayak-ayak laras slendro cengkok Nyi Supadmi* [Nyi Supadmi's patterns of vocal treatment for *ayak-ayak laras slendro*] (Surakarta, 1992)
N.I. Cooper: *The Sirens of Java: Gender Ideologies, Mythologies and Practice in Central Java* (diss., U. of Hawaii, 1994)
S.P. Walton: *Heavenly Nymphs and Earthy Delights: Javanese Female Singers, their Music, and their Lives* (diss., U. of Michigan, 1997)
BENJAMIN BRINNER

Peskó. Hungarian family of musicians.

(1) Zoltán Peskó (i) (*b* Zsolna, 24 Aug 1903; *d* Budapest, 12 April 1967). Organist. He studied with Dezső Antalffy-Zsiross and Aladár Zalánfy at the National Hungarian Royal Academy of Music, obtaining his diploma in 1927, and in Berlin with Heitmann and Jöde (1928–9). For many years he was organist and choirmaster of the Lutheran church in Budapest, and was involved in many Hungarian church music reforms. He was one of the most eminent Hungarian organists of the 1930s and 1940s. His interests included school music, and he was responsible for the introduction of recorders into Hungarian schools.

(2) György Peskó (*b* Budapest, 16 April 1933). Organist and pianist, son of (1) Zoltán Peskó (i). He studied at the Liszt Academy under Sebestyén Pécsi (organ) and Zoltán Horusitzky (piano), obtaining his diplomas in 1959 and 1961 respectively. He became organist of the Lutheran church in Buda Castle, and in 1969 joined the teaching staff of the Budapest Conservatory. He has given concerts in Germany, Austria, Switzerland, Yugoslavia, Finland, Poland and elsewhere and is the first Hungarian organist to have performed the complete cycle of Bach's organ works. An excellent Bach

interpreter, he keeps his virtuoso technique rigorously within the appropriate stylistic framework. His robust temperament makes his performances colourful and dramatic, in a repertory ranging from Bach to Liszt and Reger.

(3) Zoltán Peskó (ii) (*b* Budapest, 15 Feb 1937). Conductor and composer, son of (1) Zoltán Peskó (i). He graduated from the Liszt Academy in 1962, having made his début conducting the Hungarian Radio and Television SO in 1960; between 1963 and 1966 he studied composition under Petrassi and Ferrara in Italy, and conducting under Boulez in Switzerland. He was assistant conductor (to Maazel) of the Deutsche Oper and Berlin Radio SO (1966–9), and conductor at the Deutsche Oper (1969–73), also teaching at the Berlin Hochschule für Musik (1969–72). He made his début at La Scala in 1970, and four years later was appointed principal conductor at the Teatro Comunale, Bologna, where he presented a repertory ranging from *Carmen* and *Le nozze di Figaro* to *Billy Budd* and *The Fiery Angel*. He was principal conductor at the Teatro La Fenice, Venice, 1976–7, and of the RAI SO, Milan, 1978–82. He is a notable interpreter of contemporary music, and has given the premières of several of Dallapiccola's works and works by Xenakis, Bussotti, Donatoni, Jolivet, Kurtág and Rihm. He gave the first performance of the German version of Liebermann's *La forêt* at Schwetzingen in 1988, and the première of Azio Corghi's *Blimunda* in Milan in 1990. His orchestration of Musorgsky's *Salammbô* was first performed and recorded in Milan in 1980. Peskó's own compositions are in an avant-garde idiom, and include a string quartet *Tensions*, *Trasformazione* for orchestra, *Bildnis einer Heiligen* for soprano, children's choir and chamber ensemble, and *Jelek* for keyboard instruments.

PÉTER P. VÁRNAI/NOËL GOODWIN

Pesori, Stefano (*b* Mantua; *fl* 1648–75). Italian guitarist, guitar teacher and composer. He served various members of the Italian nobility including the marquises M.A. Sagramosi, B. Gherardini and G. Pozzo. He published five books for the guitar, with pieces in the *battute*, pizzicato and combination *battute*-pizzicato styles, and including songs. The books contain lengthy prose passages and letters, often up to half of the book's length, which are unfortunately of little pedagogical value. Several contain lists of his students, arranged according to social status. The style is tailored to amateurs, rarely exceeding the lower positions, avoiding complex textures and rhythms, as well as *campanelas*, and rather archaic by post-1650 standards, especially when compared to the works of contemporary guitarists such as Corbetta, Bartolotti and Granata.

WORKS

Galeria musicale ... compartita in diversi scherzi di chitarrigia (Verona, 1648), 1 saraband ed. in Hudson
Lo scrigno armonico ... per suonare in concerto con basso, violino, manacordo, & altri instrumenti ... con l'intavolatura della chitarra spagnola, op.2 (?Mantua, n.d./R)
Toccate di chitarriglia, parte terza (Verona, n.d.)
I concerti di chitarriglia (Verona, n.d.)
Ricreationi armoniche, overo toccate di chittariglia (?Verona, c1675) [printed prefatory material and MS music]

BIBLIOGRAPHY

W. Kirkendale: *L'Aria di Fiorenza, id est Il ballo del Gran Duca* (Florence, 1972), 25, 42, 65f, 79
R. Hudson: *The Folia, the Saraband, the Passacaglia, and the Chaconne* (Stuttgart, 1982)

G.R. Boye: *Giovanni Battista Granata and the Development of Printed Guitar Music in Seventeenth-Century Italy* (diss., Duke U., 1995), 151–7

G.R. Boye: 'Performing Seventeenth-Century Italian Guitar Music: the Question of an Appropriate Stringing', *Performance on Lute, Guitar, and Vihuela: Historical Practice and Modern Interpretation*, ed. V. Coelho (Cambridge, 1997), 180–94

GARY R. BOYE

Pessard, Emile (Louis-Fortuné) (*b* Paris, 29 May 1843; *d* Paris, 10 Feb 1917). French composer and teacher. His father was a flautist, his mother a pianist, and his brother became a distinguished political journalist. At the age of 13 he composed a miniature comic opera for three characters, *La lettre de faire-part*, to words by his brother, which played 23 times in the puppet theatre in the passage Jouffroy in 1857. He then studied at the Ecole Niedermeyer for 3 months before enrolling at the Conservatoire to learn piano (with Laurent), organ (with Benoist), harmony (with Bazin) and composition (with Carafa). He won a *premier prix* in harmony there in 1862 and the Prix de Rome in 1866 with his cantata *Dalila*, which was performed at the Opéra Comique on 21 Feb 1868. After leaving the Conservatoire, he played the flute, double bass and timpani in various Parisian orchestras, and then in 1878 was appointed inspector of vocal teaching in the Paris municipal schools. The following year he was admitted to the Légion d'Honneur, and in 1890 he became director of vocal teaching at that institution's establishment in St Denis. From 1881 until his death he was a professor of harmony at the Conservatoire, where his pupils included Ravel, and from 1891 to 1899 he wrote music criticism for *L'événement*.

Pessard's operas, of which contemporary biographers list quite a few more than seem to have been published or even performed, were genially received, and *Les folies amoureuses* in particular was quite successful. His songs, too, attracted praise: Debussy, for example, copied out 'Chanson d'un fou', and the resulting manuscript was published as Debussy's composition in 1932.

WORKS
all printed works published in Paris

STAGE
all first performed in Paris

La lettre de faire-part (miniature oc, H. Pessard), Marionettes, passage Jouffroy, 1857

La cruche cassée (oc, 1, H. Lucas and E. Abraham), OC (Favart), Feb 1870, vs (1872)

Don Quichotte (opérette-bouffe, 1, A. Deschamps, after M. de Cervantes), Salle Erard, 13 Feb 1874 (1873)

Le char (oc, 1, P. Arène and A. Daudet), OC (Favart), 18 Jan 1878, vs (1878)

Le capitaine Fracasse (oc, 3, C. Mendès, after T. Gautier), Lyrique, 2 July 1878, vs (1878)

Tabarin (opéra, 2, P. Ferrier), Opéra, 12 Jan 1885, vs (1885)

Tartarin sur les Alpes (?incid music, 4, C. de Courcy and P. Bocage, after Daudet), Gaîté, 17 Nov 1888

Les folies amoureuses (oc, 3, A. Lénéka and E. Matrat, after J.-F. Regnard), OC (Lyrique), 15 April 1891, vs (1891)

Une nuit de Noël (M. Lefèvre and Roddaz), Ambigu, 1893

Mam'zelle Carabin (opérette, 3, F. Carré), Bouffes-Parisiens, 3 Nov 1893

La dame de trèfle (oc, 3, C. Clairville and M. Froyez), Bouffes-Parisiens, 13 May 1898

L'armée de vierges (opérette, 3, E. Depré and L. Héral), Bouffes-Parisiens, 15 Oct 1902

L'épave (opérette, 1, Depré), Bouffes-Parisiens, 17 Feb 1903

Castor et Pollux (fantaisie-bouffonne, Deschamps), 2vv, orch/pf (1880)

La fiancée du trombone à coulisse (symphonologue en vers, P. Bilhaud)

La grande batelière (oc, 3, M. Boucheron and Xanrof)

Jeanne Hachette (drame lyrique, 3 acts and 6 tableaux, E. Dubreuil)

Le muet (opérettomime, Galipaux)

Les plaideurs (oc, 3, Adenis and Harthmann, after Racine)

3 one-act ocs: Gifles et baisers (P. Barbier), Huguette (G. Prévost), Laridon (Morel-Retz)

Excerpts from Pessard's operas pubd in *Fleurs mélodiques*, ed. H. Cramer (1878–85)

Arrs. by Pessard and others of opera excerpts for chbr groups and pf

OTHER WORKS

Choral: at least 17 pieces, incl. Dalila (cant., E. Vierne), 1866; Ave Maria, chorus, org, vn/vc, pf/hp (1873); Petite messe solennelle, 2vv, org (1878); some sacred works pubd in *Lyra sacra*, no.1 (1875); many secular works pubd in *L'orphéon des écoles* (1880–89)

Songs: over 50 pubd separately, many repr. in 20 mélodies, i (n.d.), 20 mélodies, ii (?1895), Joyeusetés de bonne compagnie (1873); at least 6 duets

Orch. 2 suites, 1 march, other works

Chbr: at least 9 pieces, incl. Wind Qnt, op.6 (1882); Pf Trio, op.19 (1877); 3 pièces, fl, pf, op.28 (1886)

Pf: *c*20 publications, incl. 4 mazurkas; 4 romances sans paroles; 3 sonatines; 2 nocturnes; 25 pièces, op.20 (1878); 10 pièces, pf 4 hands, op.22 (1878); 20 pièces nouvelles, op.26 (1885); arrs. of orch works of Pessard

Harmonization and arrs. of La marseillaise for orch; band; 1v, pf; 2vv; 3vv; male chorus

BIBLIOGRAPHY

FétisB

C.E. Curinier: *Dictionnaire national des contemporains* (Paris, 1889–1906)

E.M. di Rienzi: *Panthéon des lettres, des sciences et des arts: profils contemporains* (Paris, 1893)

M. Sansone: 'The *verismo* of Ruggero Leoncavallo: a Source Study of *Pagliacci*', *ML*, lxx (1989), 342–62

CORMAC NEWARK

Pessozi. *See* BESOZZI family.

Pes stratus (Lat.). A neume characteristic of chants composed in Francia. *See* GALLICAN CHANT, §6; *see also* NOTATION, §III, 1.

Pest. Hungarian town, united in 1873 with Buda and Óbuda to form BUDAPEST.

Pestelli, Giorgio (*b* Turin, 26 May 1938). Italian musicologist. He was first taught music by his great-uncle, the composer Luigi Perrachio, and then studied the piano with Lodovico Lessona at the Turin Conservatory (diploma 1961), and took an arts degree at the University of Turin under Mila in 1964. In the same year he became an assistant lecturer in music at Turin, where he later became lecturer (1969) and professor (1976). Pestelli's main interests lie in the relationship between music and literature, the history of criticism, and 18th- and 19th-century music. His first work, a study of the sonatas of Domenico Scarlatti, proposed a new chronological ordering of the sonatas based on stylistic evidence; and he has edited two volumes of sonatas by Platti (1978, 1986). He was a member of the editorial board of the *Rivista italiana di musicologia* (1977–85), artistic director of the orchestra and chorus of the Turin RAI (1982–5) and joint editor of *Storia dell'opera italiana* (Turin, 1987). He is on the editorial boards of the complete critical edition of Verdi's works (by the University of Chicago Press and Ricordi) and the journals *Nuova rivista musicale italiana* (from 1990) and *Il saggiatore musicale*. He is a music critic for the Turin newspaper *La stampa*.

WRITINGS

Le sonate di Domenico Scarlatti: proposta di un ordinamento cronologico (Turin, 1967)

'Contributi alla storia della forma-sonata: sei sonate per cembalo di Girolamo Sertori', *RIM*, ii (1967), 131–9

'Giuseppe Carpani e il neoclassicismo musicale della vecchia Italia', *Quaderni della RaM*, no.4 (1968), 105–21

'La coscienza contemporanea nel giovane Debussy', *Chigiana*, xxv, new ser. v (1968), 215–27

'Le poesie per la musica monteverdiana: il gusto poetico di Monteverdi', *Claudio Monteverdi e il suo tempo: Venice, Mantua and Cremona 1968*, 349–60

'Beethoven a Torino e in Piedmonte nell'Ottocento', *NRMI*, iv (1970), 1013–86

'Le riduzioni del tardo stile verdiano', *NRMI*, vi (1972), 372–90

'"Claudine ou Le petit commissionaire" di Antonio Bartolomeo Bruni (1794)', *Quadrivium*, xiv (1973), 217–34

'Le toccate per strumento a tastiera di Alessandro Scarlatti nei manoscritti napoletani', *AnMc*, no.12 (1973), 169–92 [incl. incipits]

'Corelli e il suo influsso sulla musica per cembalo della suo tempo', *Nuovi studi corelliani: Fusignano 1974*, 37–51

'Il repertorio italiano all'estero: trionfo barocco e illuminismo alle corti europee', *Storia dell'opera*, ed. A. Basso and G. Barblan (Turin, 1976), i/2, 3–98

ed.: *Il melodramma italiano dell'Ottocento: studi e ricerche per Massimo Mila* (Turin, 1977) [incl. 'I *Cento anni* di Rovani e l'opera italiana', 605–30]

'Mozart e Rutini', *AnMc*, xviii (1978), 290–307

L'età di Mozart e di Beethoven (Turin, 1979, 2/1991; Eng. trans. 1984)

'Musica, linguaggio, declamazione: il contributo di Condillac alla definizione del problema', *Musica e spettacolo a Parma nel Settecento: Parma 1979*, 227–35

'La "generazione dell' 80" e la resistibile ascesa della musicologia italiana', *Musica italiana del primo Novecento: Florence 1980*, 31–44

'Osservazioni sul primo tema del Quarto Concerto op.58 di Beethoven', *AnMc*, xxii (1984), 437–55

'Bach, Handel, D. Scarlatti and the Toccata of the late Baroque', *Bach, Handel, Scarlatti Tercentenary Essays*, ed. P. Williams (Cambridge, 1985), 277–91

Di tanti pàlpiti: cronache musicali 1972–86 (Pordenone, 1986)

ed.: *Beethoven* (Bologna, 1988)

'Una nuova fonte manoscritta per Alessandro e Domenico Scarlatti', *RIM*, xxv (1990), 100–18

'"Gewiss nicht aber. . .", sulle Waldszenen di Robert Schumann', *Livro de Homenagem a Macario Santiago Kastner*, ed. M.F.C. Rodrigues, M. Morais and R.V. Nery (Lisbon, 1992), 287–306

'Musica', *La cultura italiana del Novecento*, ed. C. Stajano (Rome, 1996), 459–79

CAROLYN GIANTURCO/TERESA M. GIALDRONI

Pesthin, Gregor. *See* PESCHIN, GREGOR.

Pestrino, Giulio dal. *See* ABONDANTE, GIULIO.

Peter [Petraeus], Christoph (*b* Weida, Vogtland, 1626; *d* Guben, 4 Dec 1669). German composer and music editor. His first appointment was as schoolmaster and Kantor at Grossenhain, Saxony. He moved in 1655 to Guben, where he was Kantor until his death. He worked closely there with the poet and civic official Johann Franck. 40 melodies in the latter's *Geistliches Sion* (1672), the first part of his *Teutsche Gedichte*, are by Peter, and he referred to Peter's skills in the second part, *Irdischer Helicon* (1674). Peter's *Andachts-Zymbeln* is an anthology of chorales by various composers which also contains preliminary instructional matter, a letter of 1524 from Luther to Spalatin, and testimonials to Peter from Franck and others. It may well be significant that he inscribed it to the mayor and corporation of Guben in the year in which he arrived at Guben and that he received rights of citizenship there early the following year. *Precationis thuribulum* (RISM 1669¹) consists of masses by Saxon composers based on familiar chorales and set for various combinations of voices and instruments with continuo. The *Geistliche*

Arien includes settings of poems by, among others, Franck, Johann Rist and Paul Gerhardt, and Peter explained that they are for solo voice (with instruments) 'so that the words can be better understood'.

WORKS

Andachts-Zymbeln oder andächtige … Lider und … Arien, 4, 5vv (Freiburg, 1655); 19 ed. in *ZahnM*

Letzte Segens-Wort … durch Johann Francken auffgesetzet, 5vv (Frankfurt an der Oder, 1655)

Brautlied aus dem 1. Capitel des hohen Liedes Salomonis, 8vv (Frankfurt an der Oder, 1661)

Geistliche Arien … auf die hohen Jahres Feste und Psalmen Davids, 1v, 5 viols/other insts, bc (Guben, 1667); 2 ed. in *WinterfeldEK*; 4 ed. in *ZahnM*

40 lieder in J. Franck: Geistliches Sion (Guben, 1672); 1 ed. in *WinterfeldEK*; 13 ed. in *ZahnM*

BIBLIOGRAPHY

WaltherML; *WinterfeldEK*; *ZahnM*

K. Ameln, C. Mahrenholzand W. Thomas, eds.: *Handbuch der deutschen evangelischen Kirchenmusik*, iii/1 (Göttingen, 1936)

J. Grimm: 'Die Andachts-Zymbeln des Christoph Peter (1655)', *Jb für Liturgik und Hymnologie*, xiv (1970), 152–79

PERCY M. YOUNG

Peter, Henry. *See* PETYR, HENRY.

Peter, Johann Friedrich [John Frederik] (*b* Heerendijk, the Netherlands, 19 May 1746; *d* Bethlehem, PA, 13 July 1813). German composer, organist and minister. He was educated at the Moravian schools in the Netherlands and Germany, finally entering the theological seminary of the church at Barby, Saxony. After his graduation in 1769, he was sent to America in 1770. From 1770 to 1780 he served the northern Moravian communities of Nazareth, Bethlehem and Lititz, Pennsylvania. In 1780 he was transferred to the southern community of Salem, North Carolina, where he spent the next ten years in various church positions, including that of musical director to the Salem congregation. In 1790 he was again transferred to the north, serving successively at Graceham (Maryland), Hope (New Jersey) and Bethlehem again. Although his official position was often that of schoolteacher, clerical assistant or diarist, unofficially he was always concerned with music. While a student at the seminary he copied much of the music that came his way. When he went to America he took with him an extensive library of instrumental works in manuscript, including several works by J.C.F. Bach which survive only in Peter's copies. Although he must have studied with such Moravian composers as Johann Daniel Grimm (1719–60) and C.F. Gregor, it is thought that he gained more from his studies of the works he copied than from formal instruction.

Peter composed six quintets for two violins, two violas and cello, and about 105 concerted anthems and solo songs. The musical style of the quintets is close to that of the early Classical masters, such as Stamitz, Vanhal and early Haydn. They were completed in Salem in 1789 and are the earliest known chamber music composed in America. Peter's anthems and solo songs feature graceful vocal writing and a considerable depth of musical expression. The orchestral accompaniment of these works, for strings and organ with occasional woodwind and brass, is always well worked out and often elaborate. His sacred vocal music is the finest body of concerted church music written in America at the time and compares well with that of European Moravian composers of his era. Manuscripts of his music are in *US-BETm* and WS.

See also MORAVIAN CHURCH MUSIC, §II.

BIBLIOGRAPHY
D.M. McCorkle: *Moravian Music in Salem* (diss., Indiana U., 1958)
W.E. Schnell: *The Choral Music of Johann Friedrich Peter (1746–1813)* (diss., U. of Illinois, 1973)
T.J. Anderson: *The Collegium Musicum Salem, 1780–1790: Origins and Repertoire* (diss., Florida State U., 1976)
M. Gombosi: *A Day of Solemn Thanksgiving: Moravian Music for the Fourth of July 1783, in Salem, North Carolina* (Chapel Hill, NC, 1977)
C.D. Crews: *Johann Friedrich Peter and his Times* (Winston-Salem, NC, 1990)

KARL KROEGER

Peter, Simon (*b* 1743; *d* 1819). American Moravian composer, brother of JOHANN FRIEDRICH PETER. *See also* MORAVIANS, MUSIC OF THE, §3.

Peterborough. American town in New Hampshire. It is the location of the MACDOWELL COLONY.

Peterlein, Johann. *See* PETREIUS, JOHANN.

Peter of Blois (*b* Blois, *c*1135; *d* ?France or ?London, 1211/12). French writer of Latin lyric poetry. He studied at Tours, Bologna and Paris, tutored William II of Sicily in Palermo 1166–8 and served the archbishops of Rouen (*c*1172–4), Canterbury (*c*1174–*c*1209) and York (1201–2) as well as King Henry II of England (*c*1184–9). He was chaplain and secretary to Eleanor of Aquitaine (1191–5) and gained among other posts a canonry at Chartres (between 1176–9) and archdeaconries at Bath (1182) and London (*c*1200). Though known primarily from and for his voluminous collection of about 300 letters (assembled 1184–1202), Peter also wrote rhetorical and religious treatises, and was renowned as a poet, earning the praise of his contemporary Walter of Châtillon. As many as 53 songs have been ascribed to him (see Dronke, 1984), several of which (given below) have musical settings in the Notre Dame conductus repertory, only nine (one with a surviving melody) are supported by contemporaneous evidence. Two different Peters have been proposed (see Southern, 1992), both poets with similar careers, which complicates the questions of authorship and attribution of the songs.

WORKS

Editions: *Notre Dame and Related Conductus: Opera omnia*, vi, ed. G.A. Anderson (Henryville, PA, 1981) [ND]
Secular Medieval Latin Song: an Anthology, ed. B. Gillingham (Ottawa, 1993) [SM]

A.[no.] – *number in Anderson (1972)*
F.[no.] – *number in Falck (1981)*
monophonic conductus unless otherwise stated; for fuller information see Dronke, 1984

A globo veteri, A.K74, F.2; ND, SM (sequence, lai-like repetitions of phrases)
Dum iuventus floruit, D-Mbs Clm 4660, f.4r, A.L75; SM (melody only in unheighted neumes)
Ex ungue primo teneram, F-Pn 3719, f.23r, f.37v; SM (through-composed, 3 pairs of strophes, ending melisma)
Olim sudor Herculis, A.K4, F.250; ND, SM (sequence with refrain)
Vacillantis trutine, GB-Cu Ff.i.17, f.1r, A.L48; SM (sequence with refrain)
Veneris prosperis, 2vv, A.J28, F.359; ND, SM (strophic)
Vitam duxi iocundam sub amore, A.K36, F.386; ND, SM (strophic)

DOUBTFUL WORKS

Fons (or Flos) preclusus sub torpore, A.K72, A.L145 (different melody), F.172; ND (attrib. Philip the Chancellor); contrafactum of A.L145, 'Povre viellece m'assaut', R.390 (strophic)
In nova fert animus via gressus, A.K29, F.176; ND (attrib. Philip the Chancellor; single surviving strophe, melismatic)

Non te lusisse pudeat, A.K47, F.223; ND, SM (15th-century attrib. Peter in GB-Lbl Harl.3672; medieval attrib. Stephen Langton (*d* 1228) in GB-Ob Laud.Misc.650; modern attrib. Philip the Chancellor; strophic)
Qui seminat in loculis, A.K22, F.284; ND (strophic, ending melisma)
Quo me vertam nescio, A.K28, F.292; ND, SM (medieval attrib. Philip the Chancellor in D-DS 2777; sequence, melismatic)
Vite perdite, 2vv, A.J35, F.387; ND, SM (modern attrib. Walter of Châtillon; contrafacta: Hue de Saint Quentin, *fl* 1221, 'A l'entrant du tens sauvage', R.41; Peirol, 'Per dan que d'amor m'aveigna', PC 366.26; strophic, cantio (AAB) form; ABABCDCD)

BIBLIOGRAPHY

PL, ccvii
J.A. Robinson: 'Peter of Blois', *Somerset Historical Essays* (London, 1921), 100–40
E. Braunholtz: 'Die Streitgedichte Peters von Blois und Roberts von Beaufeu über den Wert des Weines und des Bieres', *Zeitschrift für romanische Philologie*, xlvii (1927), 30–38
R.R. Bezzola: *Les origines et la formation de la littérature courtoise en occident, 500–1200*, i (Paris, 1963), 31–46
R. Southern: 'Peter of Blois: a Twelfth-Century Humanist?', *Medieval Humanism and Other Studies* (Oxford, 1970), 104–32
G.A. Anderson: 'Notre Dame and Related Conductus: a Catalogue Raisonné', *MMA*, vi (1972), 152–229; vii (1973), 1–81
J. Gildea, ed.: *L'Hystore Job: an Old French Verse Adaptation of Compendium in Job by Peter of Blois* (Liège and Villanova, PA, 1974–9)
P. Dronke: 'Peter of Blois and Poetry at the Court of Henry II', *Medieval Studies*, xxxviii (1976), 185–235; rev. in *The Medieval Poet and his World* (Rome, 1984), 281–339
R. Falck: *The Notre Dame Conductus: a Study of the Repertory* (Henryville, PA, 1981)
P. Dronke: 'Profane Elements in Twelfth-Century Literature', *Renaissance and Renewal in the Twelfth Century*, ed. G. Constable and R.L. Benson (Cambridge, MA, 1982), 569–92
C.J. McDonough, ed.: *The Oxford Poems of Hugh Primas and the Arundel Lyrics* (Toronto, 1984)
R. Southern: 'The Necessity for Two Peter of Blois', *Intellectual Life in the Middle Ages: Essays Presented to Margaret Gibson*, ed. L. Smith and B. Ward (London, 1992), 103–18
E. Revell, ed.: *Later Letters of Peter of Blois* (Oxford, 1993)
L. Wahlgren: *The Letter Collections of Peter of Blois: Studies in the Manuscript Tradition* (Göteborg, 1993)

THOMAS B. PAYNE

Peter of Cambrai [Petrus Cameracensis] (*fl* mid-13th century). French composer. He was an Augustinian canon of the abbey of St Aubert in Cambrai; a catalogue of ecclesiastical authors names him as a composer of conductus and of neumas to an office of St Elizabeth of Hungary with texts by Gerard of Saint-Quentin-en-Isle. The office is most likely that in *F-CA* 38, beginning 'Gaudeat Hungaria'; the neuma to its fifth Matins responsory is the tenor of the anonymous motet *Un chant renvoisie* (*F-Pa* 3517–18, f.14r). An undated life of St Dympna, probably dating from the mid-13th century, is ascribed to a certain Petrus Cameracensis, who may be the same individual.

BIBLIOGRAPHY

F. Heuckenkamp: *Die heilige Dimphna* (diss., U. of Halle, 1887)
B. Haggh: *Two Offices for St Elizabeth of Hungary* (Henryville, PA, 1995)

BARBARA H. HAGGH

Peters. German firm of music publishers. Originally founded in Leipzig, it is now an international group of independent companies in Germany, Great Britain and the USA. On 1 December 1800 the Viennese composer and Kapellmeister FRANZ ANTON HOFFMEISTER (1754–1812) and the Leipzig organist Ambrosius Kühnel (1770–1813) opened a 'Bureau de Musique' in Leipzig. Attached to this publishing house were an engraving works, a printing works and a shop selling printed music and instruments. The first publications included chamber music by Haydn and Mozart, as well as almost forgotten keyboard works by J.S. Bach, of which the firm published a complete edition in 14 volumes. J.N. Forkel entrusted his monograph on Bach to the publishers in 1802, and they also acquired several compositions by Beethoven (opp.19–22, 39–42). Hoffmeister moved back to Vienna in 1805, while Kühnel, continuing alone, increased the collaboration with Forkel, and promoted the publication of Ernst Ludwig Gerber's *Neues historisch-biographisches Lexikon der Tonkünstler* (1812–14). By 1813 the firm had published works by J.F. Reichardt, Dotzauer, Johann Andreas Streicher, Türk, Lauska, Tomášek and Vincenc Mašek; the first works by Louis Spohr were published, and Spohr collaborated with Kühnel's successors for decades.

In 1814 the publishing business was bought by Carl Friedrich Peters (*b* Leipzig, 30 March 1779; *d* Sonnenstein, Bavaria, 20 Nov 1827), a bookseller of Leipzig, and it became known as 'Bureau de Musique C.F. Peters'. The Battle of Leipzig (1813) had a deleterious effect on the sale of printed music, and Peters's business difficulties were aggravated by the fact that he suffered from bouts of severe depression; he was subsequently committed to an asylum. Besides Spohr and Weber, Peters published works by Hummel, Field, Grosheim, Klengel, Ries and other lesser-known composers.

The manufacturer Carl Gotthelf Siegmund Böhme (1785–1855) bought the firm in 1828 and played an active role in the formation of the first confederation of music publishers for the purpose of securing legal copyright protection. In collaboration with Czerny, Siegfried Dehn, F.C. Griepenkerl and Moritz Hauptmann he brought out many works by J.S. Bach. After Böhme's death the firm became a charity foundation under the supervision of the town council of Leipzig. On 21 April 1860 it was bought by Julius Friedländer, a book- and music seller of Berlin, who invented a speed printing press for producing sheet music. In 1863 Max Abraham (1831–1900), a doctor at law, became a partner in the business and in 1880 sole owner. Under Abraham's purposeful direction C.F. Peters won a worldwide reputation. Together with Carl Gottlieb Röder, Abraham recognized the importance of the mechanical press for printing music, and used it to advantage with the Edition Peters series, begun in 1867. It was produced well and cheaply, with light green jackets (for earlier composers' works not affected by copyright restrictions), or pink (for original works acquired by the publisher). Abraham acquired the complete works of Grieg and from the business relationship grew a life-long friendship. First editions of Wagner, Brahms, Bruch, Köhler, Moszkowski and Sinding appeared, edited by noted musicologists and interpreters. In 1894 the Musikbibliothek Peters, founded by Abraham, was donated to the city of Leipzig and made available free of charge to the general public. Since 1953 this comprehensive collection has been in the Leipziger Städtische Bibliotheken, which has made it accessible by producing bibliographies. In 1895 the *Jahrbuch der Musikbibliothek Peters* appeared, which in 1956 became the *Deutsches Jahrbuch der Musikwissenschaft*.

After Abraham's death in 1900 the business was inherited and managed by his nephew Henri Hinrichsen (*b* Hamburg, 5 Feb 1868; *d* Auschwitz [Oświęcim], 1942), who had been head clerk from 1891 and a partner from 1894. Hinrichsen developed into a far-sighted and circumspect businessman, who was also a patron of the arts. He acquired songs by Wolf, as well as works by Mahler, Reger, Pfitzner and Schoenberg, and seven symphonic poems by Richard Strauss (acquired from Aibl, 1932). In 1907 the *Volksliederbuch für Männerchor* first appeared. In 1917 Hinrichsen bought the Swiss firm of Rieter-Biedermann, and in 1926 he made possible the purchase of the Heyer collection of musical instruments in Cologne, which formed the basis for the museum of musical instruments in the University of Leipzig. The honorary degree of doctor of philosophy was conferred on Hinrichsen by Leipzig University in 1929. In 1931, the year of the death of his assistant Paul Ollendorff, Henri Hinrichsen's eldest son Max (*b* Leipzig, 6 July 1901; *d* London, 17 Dec 1965) joined the firm as a partner. His second son, Walter (*b* Leipzig, 23 Sept 1907; *d* New York, 21 July 1969), also joined the firm that year, followed in 1933 by the third son, Hans-Joachim (1909–40). The composer Wilhelm Weismann (1900–80), who had worked for the firm from 1929, had considerable influence upon its development and output until his retirement in 1966.

Walter Hinrichsen left Germany in 1936, and in 1948 founded the C.F. Peters Corporation in New York. Max Hinrichsen left the parent firm in 1937, and in 1938 created Hinrichsen Edition in London. In 1939 Henri and Hans-Joachim Hinrichsen, who had become co-partner with his father in 1937, were forced to yield to sanctions of the Nazi regime and Johannes Petschull (*b* 1901) took over the management of the firm. In 1940 he acquired the firm of Litolff, founded in Brunswick in 1828.

After World War II the original Leipzig firm was restored to the Hinrichsen family and received a licence to continue publishing in March 1947. In 1949–50 it was again confiscated, this time by the East German government, and became a state-owned business (VEB). As such it was subject to new cultural, political and editorial development. In addition to its attention to the humanist musical heritage and the support of important national and international traditions it was soon concerned with the promotion of the work of contemporary composers in eastern Europe (Eisler, E.H. Meyer, Butting, Dessau, Ottmar Gerster, Geissler, Khachaturian, Schnittke, Shostakovich). The firm produced revised editions as well as comprehensive new editions (Skryabin, Chopin, Debussy, Fauré, Satie, Mahler and Vivaldi). From 1949 to 1969 the firm was under the direction of the book- and music seller Georg Hillner. In 1969 the musicologist Bernd Pachnicke took over its direction; he was succeeded by Norbert Molkenbur in 1983.

In 1950 Walter and Max Hinrichsen took Petschull to West Germany and formed a partnership with him, creating the new firm of C.F. Peters Musikverlag in Frankfurt with Petschull as managing partner. After the reunification of Germany in 1989, C.F. Peters Frankfurt took over the former communist-supervised Leipzig firm and transferred most of its publishing activities to Frankfurt. In 1993, after having twice been confiscated, the publishing house was finally restored to its rightful owners.

Each of the three Western companies has published a substantial share of the original Peters catalogue as well as developing its own independent publishing programme. The Frankfurt firm, whose managers in 1999 were Johannes Petschull and Karl Rarichs, acquired the music publishing firm of M.P. Belaieff in 1971 and in 1974 Edition Schwann. The C.F. Kahnt catalogue was purchased in 1989. In addition to the original Peters, Belaieff, Schwann and Kahnt catalogues, the Frankfurt firm publishes much contemporary music, including works by Genzmer, Globokar, Goldmann, Heider, Kagel, Ligeti, Sheriff and Tüür. Another main area of activity is the publication of Urtext editions based on the latest research into sources, especially of large-scale choral repertory of the 18th and 19th centuries.

Hinrichsen Edition Ltd in London (renamed Peters Edition Ltd in 1975) initially focussed on English music, notably choral and organ repertory, together with pedagogic works and music for amateur performers (including brass bands); it published the periodical *Music Book* (formerly *Hinrichsen's Musical Year Book*) until 1961. Following Max Hinrichsen's death, his widow Carla took over the direction of the firm until 1976 when Jonson Dyer was appointed managing director. He was succeeded in 1995 by Nicholas Riddle. As Peters Edition, the firm has prioritized Urtext editions, including the piano works of Debussy and Ravel, and contemporary music (by James Dillon, Ferneyhough, Rebecca Saunders and Jonathan Dove).

One of the first priorities of the New York branch of the firm was to reissue the Edition Peters publications. It also publishes the American Music Awards sponsored by Sigma Alpha Iota, the American Wind Symphony Editions, the New York Public Library Music Publications, and the Walter Hinrichsen Award (under the auspices of the American Academy of Arts and Letters). Another major commitment is to the publication of contemporary music; since 1948 close to 3000 works (of which 90% are contemporary) have been introduced. The Peters catalogue lists among its composers Babbitt, Cage, Cowell, Crumb, Davidovsky, Morton Feldman, Lou Harrison, Hovhaness, Ives, Schoenberg, Christian Wolff and Wuorinen. The firm has also become the American agent for a number of European publishers. After Walter Hinrichsen's death, his widow Evelyn continued to maintain the high standards of the firm as well as expanding the catalogue. His son Henry Hans Hinrichsen became president of the firm in 1978, and was succeeded by Stephen Fisher (a staff member since 1964) in 1983. On 19 December 1983 Evelyn Hinrichsen and C.F. Peters were awarded the American Music Center's Letter of Distinction for their continued commitment to the advancement of new music. At the beginning of 1998 Nicholas Riddle was appointed president and chief executive officer, combining these roles with management of the London company.

BIBLIOGRAPHY

H. Lindlar: *C.F. Peters Musikverlag: Zeittafeln zur Verlagsgeschichte 1800–1867–1967* (Frankfurt, 1967)
H.M. Plesske: 'Bibliographie des Schrifttums zur Geschichte deutscher und österreichischer Musikverlage', *Beiträge zur Geschichte des Buchwesens*, iii (1968), 135–222
W. Lichtenwanger: 'Walter Hinrichsen', *Notes*, xxvi (1969–70), 491–3
H.-M. Plesske: *Der Bestand Musikverlag C.F. Peters im Staatsarchiv Leipzig: Geschäftsbriefe aus den Jahren 1800 bis 1926* (Leipzig, 1970)
H. Lindlar: 'Zur Geschichte der Musikbibliothek Peters', *Quellenstudien der Musik: Wolfgang Schmieder zum 70. Geburtstag*, ed. K. Dorfmüller and G. von Dadelsen (Frankfurt, 1972), 115–23
'The C.F. Peters Company', *Music Journal Annual* (1973), 56, 96–7
P. Gülke: 'Edition Peters: 175 Jahre Musikverlag in Leipzig', *Musik und Gesellschaft*, xxv (1975), 749–52
B. Pachnicke, ed.: *Edition Peters, 1800–1975* (Leipzig, 1975)
H.W. Hitchcock: 'C.F. Peters Corporation and Twentieth-century American Music', *Introduction to Music Publishing*, ed. C. Sachs (New York, 1981), 15
D. Fog: *Zur Datierung der Edition Peters: auf Grundlage der Greig-Ausbagen* (Copenhagen, 1990)
I. Lawford-Hinrichsen and N. Molkenbur: 'C.F. Peters – ein deutscher Musikverlag im Leipziger Kulturleben: zum Wirken von Max Abraham und Henri Hinrichsen', *Judaica Lipsiensia: zur Geschichte der Juden in Leipzig* (Leipzig, 1994), 92–109
S. Popp and S. Shigihara, eds.: *Max Reger: Briefwechsel mit dem Verlag C.F. Peters* (Bonn, 1995)
F. Benestad and H. Brock, eds.: *Edvard Grieg: Briefwechsel mit dem Musikverlag C.F. Peters 1863–1907* (Frankfurt, 1997)
I. Lawford: *Grieg and his Publishers* (London, 1997)
I. Lawford-Hinrichsen: *Music Publishing and Patronage: CF Peters: 1800 to the Holocaust* (Kenton, Middx, 2000)

HANS-MARTIN PLESSKE, FRANCES BARULICH

Peters [Lazzaro], Bernadette (*b* Queens, NY, 28 Feb 1948). American actress and singer. One of the most distinctive of Broadway performers, she made her stage début at the age of 10 in a revival of *The Most Happy Fella* in 1958. She played a supporting role in *George M!* (1968) and scored her first major success with the off-Broadway *Dames at Sea* (1968). She played Mabel in *Mack and Mabel* (1974), Dot in *Sunday in the Park with George* (1983), Emma in *Song and Dance* (1985), the Witch in *Into the Woods* (1987), Marsha in *The Goodbye Girl* (1993) and Annie Oakley in the revival of *Annie Get Your Gun* (1999). She has won two Tony awards, the first for *Song and Dance* and the second for *Annie Get Your Gun*. Her musical film credits include *Pennies from Heaven* (1981), for which she won a Golden Globe Award, and *Annie* (1982). She has also appeared in numerous non-singing films, including Mel Brook's *Silent Movie* (1976) and *Impromptu* (1991). She provided singing voices for the animated *Beauty and the Beast 2: the Enchanted Christmas* (1997) and *Anastasia* (1997).

Her voice is as distinctive as her classical beauty. She does not have the typical Broadway belt voice, but rather adapts her versatile instrument to the particular needs of each character. The voice can be either as beautiful or as grotesque as she decides it should be, depending on the role. Her tremendous talent, vocal ability and professional attitude have earned her the well-deserved reputation as one of the finest musical theatre performers of her time.

WILLIAM A. EVERETT, LEE SNOOK

Peters, Reinhard (*b* Magdeburg, 2 April 1926). German conductor. He was a pupil of Thibaud and Cortot, and on one occasion performed as the soloist in a violin concerto and a piano concerto in the same concert. In 1952, after he had received first prize in conducting at the Besançon Festival, he began his career at the Städtische Oper in Berlin. He was principal Kapellmeister in Düsseldorf from 1957 to 1960 and Generalmusikdirektor in Münster from 1961 to 1970, and in 1970 became permanent guest conductor of the Deutsche Oper, Berlin. From 1975 to 1979 he was music director of the Philharmonic Hungaria, with whom he made several recordings. He often conducts without a baton, and commands a wide repertory; his guest appearances have been in Japan, and North and South America. In 1966 he conducted the première of Blacher's *Zwischenfälle bei einer Notlandung* at the Hamburg Staatsoper, and in 1970 he conducted *Die Zauberflöte* at Glyndebourne.

Other premières he has conducted include Reimann's *Melusine* (1971), Sutermeister's *Madame Bovary* (1967) and the first symphonies of Yun (1984) and Detlev Glanert (1985).

HANS CHRISTOPH WORBS/R

Peters, Roberta (*b* New York, 4 May 1930). American soprano. She studied with William Hermann and was engaged by the Metropolitan at 19, without previous stage experience. She made her début in 1950 as Zerlina, a last-minute replacement for Nadine Conner; her official début was to have been as the Queen of Night, two months later. By her 25th anniversary with the company she had given 303 performances of 20 roles in 19 operas, notably Gilda, Despina, Norma, Rosina, Oscar, Zerbinetta and Lucia. Later she attempted to broaden her repertory in lyric soprano roles, playing Violetta, Mimì and Massenet's Manon outside New York and performing in musical comedy. She performed at Covent Garden (*The Bohemian Girl* under Beecham, 1951), in Salzburg (*Die Zauberflöte*, 1963), Vienna (1963), Munich (1964) and Berlin (1971), and with the Kirov and Bol'shoy companies (1972). A singer of considerable charm and flute-like accuracy, Peters maintained the Pons and Galli-Curci tradition of coloratura singing at a time when the more dramatic attitudes of Callas and, later, Sutherland were in vogue. She recorded several of her most successful roles, including Zerbinetta and Rosina with Leinsdorf and the Queen of Night with Böhm.

BIBLIOGRAPHY

R. Peters and L.Biancolli: *A Debut at the Met* (New York, 1967)
J. Hines: 'Roberta Peters', *Great Singers on Great Singing* (Garden City, NY, 1982), 231–9

MARTIN BERNHEIMER/R

Peters, W(illiam) C(umming) (*b* Woodbury, Devon, 10 March 1805; *d* Cincinnati, OH, 20 April 1866). American music publisher. He emigrated to the USA from England in about 1820. In 1827 he was active in Pittsburgh as a clarinettist, music teacher and proprietor of one of the city's first music shops. Between 1828 and 1831 he composed a Symphony in D in two movements, numerous marches and dances, and arranged opera overtures for the Harmonist orchestra. He was also organist at Trinity Episcopal Church in Pittsburgh. In 1830 Peters's Musical Repository was located at 19 Market Street; in 1831 he was in partnership with W.C. Smith and J.H. Mellor at 9 Fifth Avenue. He sold his business interests to his partners in 1832 and moved to Louisville, establishing himself as a teacher and dealer in pianos and operating a school and circulating music library.

In the three decades before the Civil War about 200 of Peters's arrangements and compositions were published. Between 1838 and 1866 W.C. Peters owned or had an interest in no fewer than ten publishing companies in Louisville, Baltimore, Cincinnati, New York and St Louis. His earliest publications were his own songs and keyboard pieces that were first published by Hewitt & Jaques.

Peters, Browning & Co., Louisville, was formed in about 1840 by W.C. Peters, his brother-in-law Samuel Browning (*d* Texas, 1844) and probably his brother Henry J. Peters (*d* Texas, 1877). This was followed around 1841 by Peters & Co., Louisville, and Peters & Co., Cincinnati (W.C. Peters and Henry J. Peters). Peters & Webster, Louisville, was formed in 1845 at about the same time as Peters & Field, Cincinnati, and Peters & Field, St Louis, with Joel Field. Popular composers in their

catalogue were Stephen Collins Foster, Henry Russell, E.W. Gunter and William Striby. The inventory was increased with sheets acquired from John F. Nunns and Kretchmar & Nunns, Philadelphia.

In 1849 W.C. Peters established the firm W.C. Peters, Baltimore. Some sheets have the imprint W.C. Peters & Co., Baltimore, but no source has been found to identify a partner or partners. While in Baltimore, W.C. Peters stated that he 'still had an interest' in the Louisville and Cincinnati companies, and for a time tried to unite them with interlocking plate numbers.

W.C. Peters's sons, William M. Peters, Alfred C. Peters and John L. Peters, became active in the companies in the late 1840s and early 1850s. In 1848 William M. Peters joined Peters & Field which then became Peters, Field & Co. A new plate number series was begun by this company. One or more of the sons may have been part of W.C. Peters & Co., Baltimore, which published the *Baltimore Olio and Musical Gazette* (12 Numbers). This contained music, excerpts from pedagogical works, biographical sketches, reviews and notices of concerts and other topics of current musical interest, some of the latter written by pianist-composer Charles Grobe.

In 1851 W.C. Peters moved to Cincinnati and with his sons William and Alfred formed W.C. Peters & Sons, 'successors to Peters, Field & Co.'. W.C. Peters & Sons issued piano methods and exercises by Hünten, Burgmüller, Czerny and Henri Herz, and teaching manuals for other instruments. They also published masses, motets, antiphons, hymns and responses for the Roman Catholic Church, most of which were adapted and arranged or composed by W.C. Peters. Among the European composers represented are Giuseppe Baini, Diabelli, Pietro Terziani, Gaspare Spontini, Louis Lambillotte, Michael Haydn, J.N. Hummel and Vincent Novello. The Americans include Raynor Taylor, Benjamin Carr, Benjamin Carr Cross, H.D. Sofge, Henry Bollmann and W.C. Peters.

In 1857 William M. Peters was replaced by his brother John L. Peters, and William appears to have established his own business. John L. Peters also opened stores in New York and St Louis. Under the names W.C. Peters & Sons, A.C. Peters & Brother and J.L. Peters & Brother they continued to publish popular songs, many with texts about the Civil War, and by 1862 the plate numbers on new sheets issued were above the number 4000. Popular composers in their inventory were Henri Herz, Vincent Wallace, William Iucho, Stephen Glover and Charles Grobe.

In March 1866 the company premises were destroyed by fire and the Peters company lost its entire stock of music and all the plates acquired by W.C. Peters over a period of more than forty years. On 20 April 1866, one month after the fire, W.C. Peters died of heart failure. John L. Peters then began to expand his New York and St Louis businesses, buying the stock of H.M. Higgins, Chicago (1867), A.E. Blackmar, New York, J.J. Dobmeyer & Co., St Louis and DeMotte Brothers, Chicago (all 1869). J.L. Peters sold the Cincinnati firm to J.J. Dobmeyer & Co. in 1868 and the New York firm to C.H. Ditson & Co. in 1877. J.L. Peters, St Louis, published until 1885 and was an active music store until 1892. Meanwhile, in Louisville Henry Peters and his partners had bought back the business from D.P. Faulds in 1855 (sold to them in 1851) and resumed business as Peters, Webb & Co. until

1861, when the company was named Webb, Peters & Co. Henry J. Peters dissolved his Louisville partnership in 1877 and moved to Texas where he died soon afterwards.

BIBLIOGRAPHY

H. Dichter and E. Shapiro: *Early American Sheet Music: its Lure and its Lore, 1768–1889* (New York, 1941, repr. with corrections as *Handbook of Early American Sheet Music, 1768–1889*)

E.G. Baynham: *The Early Development of Music in Pittsburgh* (diss., U. of Pittsburgh, 1944)

S.V. Connor: *The Peters Colony of Texas* (Austin, 1959)

E.C. Krohn: *Music Publishing in the Middle Western States before the Civil War* (Detroit, 1972)

R.D. Wetzel: *Frontier Musicians on the Connoquenessing, Wabash and Ohio* (Athens, OH, 1976)

G.R. Keck: *Pre-1875 American Imprint Sheet Music in the Ernst C. Krohn Special Collections, Gaylord Music Library, Washington University, St Louis, Missouri: a Catalog and Descriptive Study* (diss., U. of Iowa, 1982)

R.D. Wetzel: 'The Search for William Cumming Peters', *American Music*, i/4 (1983), 27–41

F.C. Krohn: *Music Publishing in St. Louis* (Warren, MI, 1988), 51

R.C. Vitz: *The Queen City and the Arts: Cultural Life in Nineteenth-Century Cincinnati* (Kent, OH, 1989)

S. Saunders and D.L. Root, eds.: *The Music of Stephen C. Foster* (Washington DC, 1990)

M. Korda: *Louisville Music Publications of the 19th Century* (Louisville, 1991)

R.D. Wetzel: 'Catholic Church Music in the Midwest before the Civil War: The Firm of W.C. Peters & Sons', *American Music Life in Context and Practice to 1865*, ed. J.R. Heintze (New York, 1994), 203–30

RICHARD D. WETZEL

Petersen [Pietersen], David (*b* Lübeck, *c*1650; *d* before 5 May 1737). Dutch composer and violinist of German extraction. He went to Lund (Sweden) with Gregor Zuber (*fl* 1633–73), possibly his tutor and almost certainly his mentor; both were employed as university musicians there during the early 1670s. From shortly before 1680 onwards Petersen was in Amsterdam; it is not clear whether he worked as a professional musician. Considering his *Speelstukken* of 1683 (a set of violin sonatas modelled after J.J. Walther's *Scherzi* of 1676) and a possible connection between Walther and Amsterdam (as expressed in Walther's *Hortulus chelicus*), it is possible that Walther taught Petersen. Petersen dedicated the *Speelstukken* to an Amsterdam burgomaster and subsequently received a few small city appointments, which he held until his death. He died somewhere outside Amsterdam.

The *Speelstukken* are by far his most important compositions; they are in a virtuoso style with many polyphonic passages, rapid scales and other figures, and the use of high positions. He also wrote numerous continuo songs to Dutch poems mostly by Abraham Alewijn, a close friend. Alewijn dedicated his play *Amarillis* (1693) to Petersen with the suggestion that he set it to music, but the extent to which Petersen fulfilled this wish is not known; some of his songs are on texts derived from the play.

Petersen belongs to the generation of Dutch composers that includes Johannes Schenk, Carolus Hacquart, Servaas de Konink and Hendrik Anders, all of whom were influenced by German, French and Italian music. Their work, however, was superseded by the Italian-orientated music that dominated the Dutch Republic from about 1710 onwards.

WORKS

Speelstukken (12 sonatas), vn, bc (Amsterdam, 1683/R)

Zede- en harpgezangen (24 songs) (A. Alewijn), 1v, bc (Amsterdam, 1694)

8 Cont songs, Boertige en ernstige minnezangen, 1v, bc (Amsterdam, 3/1705, 4/1705, 5/1709)

Incid music in Andromeda (play, F. Rijk, after P. Corneille), Amsterdam, 1730, lost

BIBLIOGRAPHY

J. Schröder: 'David Petersen: ein Geiger im Amsterdam des 17. Jahrhunderts', *Alte Musik: Praxis und Reflexion*, ed. P. Reidemeister and V. Gutmann (Winterthur, 1983), 267–71

R. Rasch: Introduction to *Speelstukken* (Utrecht, 1989) [facs.]

G. Andersson: 'Stadsmusikanter, i stifts- och universitetsstaden Lund under 1600- och 1700-talet', *STNf*, lxxiii (1991), 33–68

RUDOLPH A. RASCH

Petersen, Lauritz Peter Corneliys. *See* CORNELIUS, PETER (ii).

Petersen Quartet. German string quartet. It was founded in 1979 at the Hanns Eisler Hochschule für Musik, Berlin, by Ulrike Petersen, Uta Fiedler, Friedemann Weigle and Hans-Jakob Eschenburg. Its mentor was Wolf Dieter Batzdorf of the Berlin Quartet and its members took part in masterclasses by Thomas Brandis, Rudolf Koeckert, Siegmund Nissel and Sándor Végh. In 1983 Fiedler was replaced by Gernot Süssmuth. The ensemble won prizes at a number of competitions – Prague in 1984, Evian in 1985, Florence in 1986 and Munich in 1987 – and from 1988 to 1992 it was quartet-in-residence at East German Radio, although it also began to tour widely. At first its members played in East German orchestras but in 1989 it became a full-time ensemble. In 1992 Petersen was replaced as leader by Conrad Muck, a pupil of Rudolf Ulbrich and Wolfgang Marschner. During the 1990s the quartet established a position among the top German ensembles, notable for its technical polish and its intellectual grasp of a repertory ranging from Haydn and Boccherini to contemporary music. Its recordings, including on the one hand penetrating accounts of late Beethoven quartets and the Schubert C major Quintet and on the other hand works by Ervín Schulhoff, Pavel Haas and Boris Blacher, have won praise from the critics. In 1997 the group gave the first performance of Siegfried Matthus's *Das Mädchen und der Tod*. In 2000 Daniel Bell became second violinist and Eschenburg was replaced as cellist by Jonáš Krejčí, formerly of the Škampa Quartet.

BIBLIOGRAPHY

C.M. Solare: 'Aiming for Perfection', *The Strad*, cx (1999), 463–7

TULLY POTTER

Peterson, John Willard (*b* Lindsburg, KS, 1 Nov 1921). American composer of gospel hymns and cantatas. *See* GOSPEL MUSIC, §I, 1(v).

Peterson, Oscar (Emmanuel) (*b* Montreal, 15 Aug 1925). Canadian jazz pianist. He studied classical piano from the age of eight, and when he was 14 won a local talent contest. During his late teens he played on a weekly Montreal radio show and throughout the mid-1940s was heard with Canada's Johnny Holmes Orchestra, playing in a style that blended elements from the styles of Teddy Wilson, Art Tatum, Nat 'King' Cole, Erroll Garner and others. Norman Granz invited him to appear at Carnegie Hall in 1949 in a Jazz at the Philharmonic concert and from that time onwards managed his career. Peterson toured regularly with Jazz at the Philharmonic during the early 1950s and formed his own trio using the combination, popularized by Cole, of piano, guitar and double bass. His most popular trio, the other members of which were fellow black musicians Herb Ellis (guitar) and Ray

Brown (double bass), remained together from 1953 until 1958, when the guitarist was replaced by a drummer, Ed Thigpen. In this form the group, considered by many to have been the ideal vehicle for Peterson's unique talents, remained intact from 1959 until 1965, when Sam Jones (double bass) and Louis Hayes (drums) replaced Brown and Thigpen. In 1964 they recorded *The Oscar Peterson Trio Plus One* (Mer.) with Clark Terry.

In the early 1970s Peterson began concentrating on unaccompanied performances, proving incontestably that he was one of the greatest solo pianists in the history of jazz – though he had already recorded as an unaccompanied soloist (*My Favorite Instrument*, 1967, Saba). From the mid-1970s he played with symphony orchestras throughout North America and joined established jazz musicians such as Dizzy Gillespie, Clark Terry, Joe Pass and Niels-Henning Ørsted Pedersen for a number of memorable performances. Ill-health, including a severe stroke, kept him inactive for much of the early 1990s, though he gave a concert in Carnegie Hall in June 1995.

Because of his extraordinary technique and his comprehensive grasp of jazz piano history, Peterson is often compared with Art Tatum, with whom he shares an exceptional gift for inspiring awe from musicians, critics and listeners alike. Unlike Tatum, however, who often played in an arhythmic or rhythmically irregular manner, Peterson is devoted to maintaining a sense of hard-driving swing.

BIBLIOGRAPHY

EMC2 (M. Miller)

R. Palmer: 'Oscar Peterson', *Jazz Journal*, xxi/3 (1968), 4–6

L. Feather: 'Oscar', *From Satchmo to Miles* (New York, 1972/R), 187–96

L. Lyons: *The Great Jazz Pianists: Speaking of their Lives and Music* (New York, 1983), 130–43

R. Palmer: *Oscar Peterson* (Tunbridge Wells, 1984) [incl. discography]

G. Lees: *Oscar Peterson: the Will to Swing* (Toronto, 1988/R)

BILL DOBBINS

Peterson, Wayne T. (*b* Albert Lea, MN, 8 March 1927). American composer. He studied at the University of Minnesota (BA 1951, MA 1953, PhD 1960) where his teachers included Paul Fetler, Earl George and James Aliferis. A Fulbright Scholarship (1953–4) enabled him to spend a year at the RAM where he studied with Lennox Berkeley and Howard Ferguson. He has held teaching appointments at San Francisco State University (from 1960), Indiana University (1992) and Stanford University (1992–4), and fulfilled commissions for the San Francisco SO, Louisville Orchestra and Freiberg SO, the American Composer's Orchestra and the Fromm and Koussevitzky foundations. He has received awards from the Minnesota Centennial Composition Contest (1958), the American Society of Harpists (1985) and the American Academy and Institute of Arts and Letters (1986). In 1990 he was a visiting artist at the American Academy in Rome and in 1992 won a Pulitzer Prize for *The Face of the Night, The Heart of the Dark*.

Peterson is an open-minded enthusiastic listener and a self-confessed eclectic. His music is characterized by strikingly intricate and intensely active rhythms, profuse and inventive melodic and contrapuntal lines and secure, if at times elusive, formal structures. His works range in mood from driving and devilishly playful to sensuous. Later compositions employ an increasingly tonal idiom. Originally a jazz pianist, he began composing under the influence of Copland and Stravinsky before becoming absorbed by the music of Schoenberg and Sessions. He has also acknowledged Boulez, Carter and Wuorinen as important influences.

WORKS

INSTRUMENTAL

Orch: Free Variations, 1958; Introduction and Allegro, 1959; Exaltation, Dithyramb and Caprice, 1961; Clusters and Fragments, str, 1968; Transformations, chbr orch, 1986; Triology, chbr orch, 1988; The Widening Gyre, 1990; The Face of the Night, The Heart of the Dark, 1991; And the Winds Shall Blow, sax qt, orch, 1994; Theseus Ov., 1995

Chbr: Metamorphosis, wind qnt, 1967; Phantasmagoria, pic + fl + a fl, E♭ cl + cl + b cl, cb, 1969; Capriccio, fl, pf, 1973; Diatribe, vn, pf, 1975; Encounters, pic + fl, cl + b cl, hn, tpt, vn, vc, perc, pf, 1976; Rhapsody, vc, pf, 1976; An Interrupted Serenade, fl, vc, hp, 1978; Doubles, 2 fl, cl, b cl, 1982; Sextet, pic + fl + a fl, cl + b cl, vn, vc, perc, hp, 1982; Str Qt no.1 (1983); Ariadne's Thread, pic + fl + a fl, ob, cl + b cl, hn, vn, perc, hp, 1985; Duodecaphony, va, vc, 1987; Labyrinth, fl, cl, vn, pf, 1987; Mallets Aforethought, perc qt, 1990; Str Qt no.2 'Apparitions, Jazz Play', 1991; Diptych: Aubade, Odyssey, pic + fl + a fl, cl + b cl, vn, vc, perc, pf, 1992; Duo, vn, pf, 1993; Janus, fl, ob, cl, hn, tpt, vn, va, vc, perc, pf, 1993; Vicissitudes, pic + fl + a fl, cl + b cl, vn, vc, perc, pf, 1995; Windup, sax qt, 1997; arrs. incl. works by Ravel (Sonatine), De Falla (4 Spanish Songs)

VOCAL

Choral: Can Death Be Sleep (J. Keats), 1955; Earth, Sweet Earth (G.M. Hopkins), 1956; Ps lvi, 1959; An E.E. Cummings Triptych, 1962; An E.E. Cummings Cant., SATB, pf/sextet, 1964; Spring (T. Nash), 1970; A Robert Herrick Motley, 1997

Solo: 3 Songs (L. Tennyson, T.S. Eliot, Hopkins), S, pf, 1957; Ceremony After a Fire Raid (D. Thomas), S, pf, 1969; Dark Reflections (J. Joyce, E. St Vincent Millay, T. Campbell), S, vn, pf, 1980; arr. Debussy (Song Cycle)

Principal publishers: Peters, Trillenium, Seesaw, Lawson-Gould, Boosey & Hawkes

BIBLIOGRAPHY

R. Commanday: 'Composer Wayne Peterson', *San Francisco Chronicle* (13 Oct 1991)

ROBERT P. COMMANDAY

Peterson-Berger, Wilhelm (*b* Ullånger, Ångermanland, 27 Feb 1867; *d* Östersund, 3 Dec 1942). Swedish composer and writer. After matriculating in Umeå he studied the organ and composition at the Stockholm Conservatory (1886–9); he then went to Dresden (1889–90), where his teachers included Kretzschmar (orchestration). He returned to Umeå to teach music and languages (1890–92), and went again to Dresden as a music educationist (1892–4). In 1895 he settled in Stockholm, where he was music critic of the *Dagens nyheter* from 1896 to 1930, except for a period when he was stage manager at the Stockholm Opera (1908–10) and for an Italian visit in 1920–21. From 1930 he lived at his villa on Fröson in Jämtland, northern Sweden.

Peterson-Berger's criticism immediately aroused great interest, and in 1896 he became well known as the composer of the piano pieces *Frösöblomster* and the song collection *Svensk lyrik*. In both fields he made a major contribution to the Swedish national-Romantic movement. His Wagnerian aesthetic standpoint was expressed in a series of music dramas, for which he wrote the texts, creating a Swedish Gesamtkunstwerk. *Arnljot*, based on the story of the warrior Arnljot Gelline from Sturlasson's *Saga of St Olav*, has often been viewed as the Swedish national opera. Each summer from 1936 it has been performed, as a spoken drama with incidental music, at Fröson. The comedy *Domedagsprofeterna*, concerning a wager as to the date of the Last Judgment, presents a charming blend of lyrical freshness with textual and musical 17th-century pastiche. *Adils och Elisiv* combines the restraint of a saga with a yearning for peace and reconciliation determined by the period at which it was composed (after World War I); there are melodic features of Italian opera.

The most successful of Peterson-Berger's symphonies is the third, a work permeated by Scandinavian nature mysticism and drawing on the Sami *jojkar* music notated by Karl Tirén. The other symphonies are also more or less programmatic, and the Violin Concerto is a work of nature lyricism. Peterson-Berger's lyrical gift appears to greatest advantage in the piano miniatures and songs, among which the Karlfeldt songs, highly varied in mood, hold a special position. While still at school he had directed and sung in choirs, and his early compositions include some notable choruses, often suggested by nature and outdoor life. His material progress was hindered by the many enemies he made through his criticism; he attacked showy virtuosity and dry academicism with satire, but also with profound conscientiousness. Although his attitudes became increasingly negative, particularly with regard to new music, his writing was marked by idealism and, by reason of its breadth and colour, it had an enormous influence on Swedish cultural life. A Peterson-Berger Society has been founded within the Royal Musical Academy, Stockholm.

WORKS

MUSIC DRAMAS
all texts by Peterson-Berger

Ran, 1899–1900; Stockholm, 20 May 1903 [text pubd Stockholm, 1898]

Lyckan [The Happiness], 1903; Stockholm, 27 March 1903 [text pubd Stockholm, 1903]

Arnljot, 1907–9; Stockholm, 13 April 1910 [text pubd Stockholm, 1906, rev. 2/1910, 3/1956; Ger. trans. 2/1914]

Domedagsprofeterna, 1912–17; Stockholm, 21 Feb 1919 [text pubd Stockholm, 1912]

Adils och Elisiv, 1921–4; Stockholm, 27 Feb 1927 [text pubd Stockholm, 1919]

ORCHESTRAL

Orientalisk dans, 1890; Majkarneval i Stockholm, ov., 1892–3; Förspel till Sveagaldrar, ov., 1897; Sym. no.1 'Baneret' [The Banner], B♭, sketched 1889–90, composed 1903, rev. 1932–3; I somras [Last Summer], suite, pf/orch, 1903; Sym. no.2 'Sunnanfärd' [The Journey to the South], E♭, 1910; Sym. no.3 'Same-Ätnam' [Lappland], f, 1913–15; Romans, d, vn, pf/orch, 1915; Koral och fuga ur Domedagsprofeterna, concert arr., 1915; Earina [Spring], suite, 1917; Italiana, suite, 1922; Conc., f♯, vn, pf/orch, 1928; Sym. no.4 'Holmia' [Stockholm], A, 1929

Sym. no.5 'Solitudo', b, 1932–3; Törnrosasagan [The Tale of the Sleeping Beauty], suite, 1934 [based on Lyckan]; Ur Frösöblomster, suite, small orch, 1934

Orchestration of E. Grieg: *Norwegian Dances*, op.35, 1931

Arrs. by other hands of 47 pieces for orch, 65 for military band, 9 for 1v, military band

CHORAL

Österländsk dansscen (Peterson-Berger), S, T, chorus, 2 pf, 1892; 5 dikter ur Arne (B. Björnson, trans. Peterson-Berger), 1891–3; Hvile i skogen [At Rest in the Forest] (J.S.C. Welhaven), 1894; 6 sånger (E.J. Stagnelius, C. Snoilsky, Peterson-Berger, Swed. trad., M.Y. Lermontov, trans. Peterson-Berger), 1891–4; Album (J.P. Jacobsen, H. Nyblom, Welhaven, Björnson), 8 songs, op.11, 1890–94; 10 sånger (Peterson-Berger, P.D.A. Atterbom, J. Moe, Welhaven, E. van der Recke, Björnson, Nor. and Russ. trad., trans. Peterson-Berger), 1892–5; Vårsång III [Spring Song III] (Peterson-Berger), 1895

Sveagaldrar (cant., Peterson-Berger), solo vv, chorus, pf/orch, 1897; Dalmarsch (E.A. Karlfeldt), unison, pf and vn ad lib, 1902, arr. pf, 1906; I Mora (Karlfeldt), unison chorus, pf, 1903; Finsk idyll (J.L. Runeberg), 3 songs, Bar, 4 solo vv, male chorus, 1903;

Norrlandsminnen [Norrland Memories] (Peterson-Berger), unison/partsong, 1906; Fjällvandrarsång [Mountain Wanderers' Song] (G.W. Bratt), 1907; Bröllopssång [Wedding Song] (K.E. Forsslund), T, Bar, chorus, org, 1909

Svensk frihetssång (after Bishop Thomas), unison, pf, 1910; Sorgehymn vid August Strindbergs bår [Funeral Hymn at Strindberg's Bier] (E.W. Hülphers), T, male vv, 1912; Riddargossarnas sång [Song of the Knight Boys] (K.G. Ossiannilsson), unison, 1912; De tysta sångerna [The Silent Songs] (Karlfeldt), T, male vv, 1914; Aubade ur Domedagsprofeterna (Peterson-Berger), Bar, SSAATTBB, orch, 1916; Norrbotten (cant., A. Carlgren), solo vv, chorus, pf/orch, 1921

Kantat vid Umeå stads 300-årsjubileum (Peterson-Berger), solo vv, chorus, vn, org, pf, military band/pf, 1922; Kantat vid Kungliga Teaterns i Stockholm 150-årsjubileum (Peterson-Berger), solo vv, chorus, orch/pf, 1922, rev. 1935–6; Irmelin (Jacobsen, trans. Peterson-Berger), mixed vv, 1927, arr. T, male vv (1934); Aspåkerspolska (Karlfeldt), 1927; När jag för mig själv i mörka skogen går [When I walk alone in the dark forest], 1927; Som stjärnorna på himmelen [Like the Stars in the Firmament], 1927

Jungfrun under lind (Recke, trans. Peterson-Berger), 1927; Brudsviten hälsar Elisiv [The Bridal Suite Greets Elisiv] [from opera] (Peterson-Berger) (1927); Soluppgång [Sunrise] (cant., Peterson-Berger), S, B, 4 solo vv, boys' chorus, chorus, orch/pf, 1929; Jämtlandssången [Song of Jämtland] (Peterson-Berger), unison, pf, 1931; Danslek ur Ran [Dance Game from Ran] (Peterson-Berger), chorus/(chorus, pf) (1931), arr. male chorus (1941); Svensk medborgarsång [Swed. Civic Song] (Peterson-Berger, after Bishop Thomas), unison, orch, 1934; En Stockholmssång (J. Bergman), unison, 1935

Fansång [Banner Song] (Peterson-Berger), 1936; Idrottssång (Peterson-Berger) (1937); Kör ur Arnljot (Peterson-Berger), male vv (1944); Anne Knutsdatter (C.P. Riis, after Nor. trad.) (1950); Kan det tröste [May it console] (C. Winther) (1950); Les compagnons de la Marjolaine (trad.) (1950); Skogssång [Song in the Wood] (A.T. Gellerstedt) (1950); Solefallssång [Sunset Song] (N. Rolfsen) (1950); Stämning [Mood] (S. Elmblad) (1950); Jämtlands sångarförbunds hembygdshälsning [The Jämtland Union of Singers' Greeting from their Native Place], male vv (1953)

MALE-VOICE QUARTETS

En fjällfärd [A Mountain Journey] (Peterson-Berger), 1893; Husarvisa [Hussar Song], 1894; 5 sånger (G. Fröding, A.V. Rydberg, Runeberg, Swed. trad.), 1895–6; Guldfågel [Golden Bird] (Snoilsky), 1903; Juninatt (Lermontov, trans. Peterson-Berger), 1903; Killebukken [The Lamb] (Björnson), 1903; I furuskogen [In the Pine Forest] (Nyblom, trans. Peterson-Berger), 1903; Stämning [Mood] (Jacobsen, trans. Peterson-Berger), 1903; Hyllning till Jämtland [Homage to Jämtland] (Peterson-Berger), 1910

Hembygdshälsning (Peterson-Berger), 1911, arr. unison chorus; 4 dikter (Karlfeldt), 1911–12; Sommarkväll [Summer Evening] (Prince Wilhelm), 1912, arr. chorus; Asra (H. Heine, trans. Peterson-Berger), 1912; Gillets skål [A Toast to the Guild] (J.W. Dumky), 1913; Dalslands hembygdssång (T. Arne), 1916, arr. unison/partsong; Jutta kommer till Folkungarna [Jutta Comes to Folkungarna] (V. von Heidenstam), 1922; Kompankörer (Karlfeldt), 1924

VOCAL ORCHESTRAL

Florez och Blanzeflor (O. Levertin), 1v, orch, 1898; Älven till flickan [The River to the Girl] (Rydberg), 1v, orch, 1899; Skogsrået [The Wood Spirit] (Rydberg), B-Bar, orch, 1899; Gullebarns vaggsånger [The Cradle Songs of Darling Children] (V. von Heidenstam), Mez, orch, 1913; Til Majdag (Jacobsen), 1v, orch, 1926; Serenata (Nyblom), Mez/Bar, orch, 1932; Det lysned i skoven [It dawned in the forest] (Moe), Mez/Bar, orch, 1934; Höstsång [Autumn Song] (Heidenstam), 1v, orch, 1936

Orchestration of P. Heyse: *Dyvekes sange* (Drachmann), 1923

SONGS
all for 1v, pf

3 sånger (Jacobsen, Recke), 1887; Aftonstämning [Evening Mood] (D. Fallström), 1888; Och riddaren drog uti österland [And the knight went to the east] (A. Strindberg), 1892; 4 visor i folkton [4 Folk Ballads], op.5, 1892; Jämtlandsminnen [Jämtland Memories] (Peterson-Berger), op.4, 1893; Ur minnesångarna i Sverige (Atterbom), op.7, 1895; 2 orientalske sange (H. Drachmann), op.8, 1895; 3 sånger (Recke, trans. Peterson-Berger), op.10, 1895;

Ur en kärlekssaga [From a Love Story] (Peterson-Berger, after G. Walling), op.14, 1896

2 dikter (B. Mörner), 1896; 2 sånger (Moe, trans. Peterson-Berger, Nyblom), op.9, 1895–6; Marits visor [Marit's Songs] (Björnson), op.12, 1896; Mor Britta [Old Britta] (F.A. Dahlgren), 1898; 5 Dichtungen (F. Nietzsche), 1901; 3 sånger ur Arnljot (Peterson-Berger), Bar, pf, 1909; Vainos sånger ur Arnljot (Peterson-Berger), 1909; 4 Gedichte (Huch), 1910; Svensk lyrik, serie I (Heidenstam, Levertin, Fröding, Rydberg), 6 vols., 1896–1913; Frukttid (A. Österling), 1915; 2 orientaliska fantasier (H. Heine), 1923

Svensk lyrik, serie II (Karlfeldt), 7 vols., 1900–28; Svensk lyrik, serie III (Strindberg, Österling, B. Bergman, Fröding), 6 vols., 1911–24; 3 andliga sånger av G***** [3 Sacred Songs of G*****], 1924; 2 romantiska visor (J.W. von Goethe, B. Bergman), 1932

CHAMBER

Sonata no.1, e, op.1, vn, pf, 1887; Bolero, Cantilena, vn, pf, 1888; Melodi, F, vn, pf, 1889; Preludium, 2 vn, 1889; Berceuse, vc, pf, 1891; Lyrisk sång, vn, pf, 1895; Suite, op.15, vn, pf, 1896; 3 melodier ur Frösöblomster, vn, pf (1904); Irmelin Rose, vn, pf (1909); Serenad ur 4 danspoem, vn, pf (1909); Sonata no.2, G, vn, pf, 1910; Melodi, d, vn, pf, 1916; En visa utan ord [A Song without Words], vn, pf, 1916; 5 sånger, vn, pf (1917) [from songs]; Danslek ur Ran [Dance Game from Ran], org/hmn (1922); Vid Frösö kyrka, org/hmn (1923); Gratulation ur Frösöblomster, vn, pf (1923); Canzone, Melodia, vn, pf (1952); Preludium, Intermezzo, 2 vn (1952)

Arrs.: O. Bull: Saeterjentens söndag, vn, pf, 1891; 20 jämtpolskor [collected by S. Sahlin], 2 vn, 1902; Jämtlandssången [trad. bridal melody], 2 vn (1932)

PIANO

En herrskapstrall [A Genteel Tune], 1883; Valse burlesque, 1886; Canzonetta, 1888, arr. vn, pf (1925); Valzerino, 1892; Vikingabalk [Viking Code], pf/pf duet, 1893; Brudmarsch [Bridal March], 1895; Damernas album [Ladies' Album], op.6, 1895; Tonmålningar [Tone Pictures], op.13, 1896; Frösöblomster, op.16, 1896; 6 låtar [6 Melodies], 1897; Invention a 2 voci, 1897; Glidande skyar [Gliding Skies], 1897; Inledning till skådespelet Sveagaldrar (1897); Stjärngossarna [The Star Boys], 1897; Norrländsk rapsodi, 1898; 4 danspoem, 1900, Serenad arr. vn, pf (1909); Frösöblomster: ny samling [Frösö-Flowers: New Collection], 1900

I somras [Last Summer], 1903; Ur sagospelet Lyckan (1903); Scener och motiv ur Ran (1904); Danslek ur Ran [Dance Game from Ran] (1906); Dalmarsch (1906); Kung Junis intåg, 1907; Sånger [from songs], 2 vols. (1907, 1913); Färdminnen [Travel Memories], 1908; Ur Arnljot (1909); Böljebyvals (1909); Frösöblomster III: I Sommarhagen, 1914; 3 albumblad i dansform, 1917; Earina [Spring], 1917; Vallåt [Herding Melody], 1917; Ur Domedagsprofeterna (1919); September, 1920; Italiana, 1922; Ingrid och Ulf Tufvessons bröllop (1922) [from Ran]; 3 nya danspoem, 1914–23

Anakreontika I, 1922–3; 3 tondikter, 1924–6; Solitudo, 1932; På fjället i sol [On the Mountain in the Sunshine], 1932; Anakreontika II, 1935; Mirres menuett (1952)

Arrs.: E. Sjögren: 10 romanser, 1896; Svensk folkmusik, 2 vols., 1906

Principal publishers: Elkan & Schildknecht, Gehrmans, Hansen, Lundquist

WRITINGS

Essays on music in Dagens nyheter (1896–1936)

Svensk musikkultur (Stockholm, 1911)

Richard Wagner som kulturföreteelse (Stockholm, 1913; Ger. trans., 1917)

'The Life Problem in Wagner's Dramas', MQ, ii (1916), 658–68

'The Wagnerian Culture Synthesis', MQ, vii (1921), 45–56

P. B.-recensioner (Stockholm, 1923) [selected criticism]

'Beethoven aus Römischen Horizont', Die Musik, xvii (1924–5), 416–23

Melodins mysterium (Stockholm, 1937)

Om musik, ed. T. Fredbärj (Stockholm, 1942)

Minnen, ed. T. Fredbärj (Uppsala, 1943)

Från utsiktstornet, ed. T. Fredbärj (Östersund, 1951)

TRANSLATIONS

Richard Wagners skrifter i urval (Stockholm, 1901)

P. Quinault: Armida, 1907–8, unpubd

R. Wagner: Tristan och Isolde (Stockholm, 1908)

G. Keller: Romeo och Julia från byn (Stockholm, 1919)

Also trans. of works by Nietzsche

BIBLIOGRAPHY

Wilhelm Peterson-Berger: festskrift den 27 februari 1937, ed. E. Arbman and others (Stockholm, 1937) [incl. list of works and writings]

B. Carlberg: Wilhelm Peterson-Berger (Stockholm, 1950)

B. Wallner: 'Till den himmelske fadern: en vuolleh som symfoniskt tema', STMf, xxxviii (1956), 87–110

S. Beite: Wilhelm Peterson-Berger: en känd och ökänd tondiktare [Wilhelm Peterson-Berger: a known and notorious composer] (Östersund, 1965) [incl. bibliography and discography]

L. Hedwall: 'Anteckningar kring Wilhelm Peterson-Bergers pianosviter', STMf, xlix (1967), 41–117

L. Hedwall: 'Wilhelm Peterson-Berger', Schwedische Musik einst und heute (1970), 88 [special Ger. issue of Musikrevy]

G. Percy: 'Five Swedish National Romantics', Tradition and Progress in Swedish Music, ed. B. Pleijel (Stockholm, 1973), 92–100 [Musikrevy, special issue]

A.V. Sundkvist: Wilhelm Peterson-Berger, Sven Kjellström och Västerbotten (Umeå, 1975)

Musikrevy, xxxiv/1 (1979) [Peterson-Berger issue, incl. articles by S. Stolpe, A. Aulin, M. Tegen, G. Percy, F. Abenius and L. Hedwall]

L. Hedwall: Wilhelm Peterson-Berger: Life and Works (Stockholm, 1984) [pubn of the Swedish Music Information Centre]

G. Norell: Wilhelm Peterson-Berger och dikten (Arboga, 1991)

F. Bohlin: 'Om jojkarna i Peterson-Bergers samiska symfoni' [On jojkar music in Peterson-Berger's Samish symphony], Thule: årsbok Kungl. skytteanska samfundet 1993, 101–13

ROLF HAGLUND

Peterszoon, Dirk. Dutch musician, son of PETER JANSZOON DE SWART.

Pétillement (Fr.: 'crackling'). A kind of staccato bowing. See BOW, §II, 2(iv).

Petipa, (Victor) Marius (Alphonse) [Marius Ivanovich] (b Marseilles, 11 March 1818; d Gurzuf, Crimea, 2/15 July 1910). French ballet-master and choreographer. See BALLET, §2(iv).

Petit [first name unknown] (b early 18th century; d ?Paris, after 1752). French violinist and composer. Although various 18th-century writers attested Petit's reputation, his career is obscure. He was one of Tartini's four French pupils, along with Pagin, La Houssaye and de Tremais, whose violin playing pleased the Parisian public during the middle of the century. When Petit made his début at the Concert Spirituel on Christmas Day 1738, playing a concerto of his own, he was in the service of the Polish King Stanislaus at the latter's court-in-exile at Lunéville. At subsequent appearances in 1741 and 1742 Petit played a sonata by Leclair and concertos by Leclair and Tartini. He was living in Paris in 1753.

According to Marpurg and Gerber, Petit's compositions are in the style of Tartini, but little can be judged from the few small pieces published in anthologies, which are all that have survived. Titon du Tillet considered Petit the equal of the best Italian violinists of the day, while to d'Aquin Tartini's stature could be discerned merely from his having produced students of the calibre of Pagin and Petit. According to Pincherle, Petit also studied with Leclair l'aîné. Pincherle incorrectly assigned Petit the initials J.C.; in fact J.C. Petit was music director to the Duke of Saxe-Eisenach and the Margrave of Baden-Durlach before 1730, and published Apologie de l'exellence de la musique (London, c1740). The books of violin duets (Paris, 1788–9) attributed by Gerber and Vidal to Tartini's pupil Petit are the work of a younger Petit who in 1788 and 1789 was a violin teacher and member of the orchestra of the Théâtre Italien in Paris and was subsequently a violinist at the Opéra-Comique for 30 years. According to Fétis, this man had among his children a horn player Charles (b Paris, 1783) and a pianist-composer Camille (b Paris, 27 April 1800). It is not known whether the two violinists named Petit were related, or whether they were related to various other French musicians of that name active in the 17th and 18th centuries.

BIBLIOGRAPHY
FétisB; GerberL; GerberNL
E. Titon du Tillet: Le Parnasse françois, suppl.i (Paris, 1743/R)
P.-L. d'Aquin: Lettres sur les hommes célèbres … sous le règne de Louis XV (Paris, 1752)
F.W. Marpurg: 'Nachricht von verschiedenen berühmten Violinisten und Flötenisten itziger Zeit zu Paris', Historisch-kritische Beyträge zur Aufnahme der Musik, i (Berlin, 1754–5/R), 166 /5
A. Vidal: Les instruments à archet (Paris, 1876–8/R)
L. de La Laurencie: L'école française de violon de Lully à Viotti (Paris, 1922–4/R1971)
M. Pincherle: Jean-Marie Leclair l'aîné (Paris, 1952/R)
NEAL ZASLAW

Petite reprise (Fr.). See REPRISE.

Petit Jehan [Petitjean], **Claude** ['L'Abbé'] (d ?Metz, before 1604). French composer and singer. Documents in the archives of Meurthe-et-Moselle indicate that in August 1562 a 'Petit Jehan' received a payment from the chapter of the collegiate church of St George in Nancy for the education of a young choirboy; 'Claude Petit Jan' was mentioned as 'maistre des enffans de choeur' of the same church in February 1565 and in September of that year as 'maistre des chantres'. In June 1571 his name appeared as choirmaster of Metz Cathedral, but by April 1575 he was master of the choristers at Verdun Cathedral. In the same year he directed a group of singers brought from Verdun and Toul to Nancy for the funeral service of Claude de France, Duchess of Lorraine. They may have performed a Requiem Mass that he is reported to have written: a document of 1603 orders the binding of a book 'composed by the late M Petitjean'. In 1567 the choirmaster of Verdun won a prize at the annual music competition at Evreux with his four-voice setting of Ronsard's sonnet Ce riz plus doux. He seems likely to be the composer of the four-voice chanson Je suis devenu amoureux published in RISM 1569⁹ with an attribution to 'Petit Jan' and reissued in RISM 1578¹³ with the more specific ascription to 'Cl. Petit Jehan' (this chanson is ed. in SCC, xix, 1991). In April 1592 'Claude Petit Jehan de Metz' was paid by the chapter of Toul Cathedral for composing 'quelques pièces de musicque'. A number of singers at Metz had the name 'Petitjean', among them Henry (d 1550), his nephew Jean (d 1552), and Jacques Petitjean, who like Claude was sometimes called 'L'Abbé'. The earlier confusion with PETIT JEAN DE LATRE was resolved by Lesure.

BIBLIOGRAPHY
J.-B. Pelt: Etudes sur la cathédrale de Metz (Metz, 1930)
P. Marot: Recherches sur les pompes funèbres des ducs de Lorraine (Nancy, 1935)
F. Lesure: 'Petit Jehan de Lattre (†1569) et Claude Petit Jehan (†1589)', Renaissance-muziek 1400–1600: donum natalicium René Bernard Lenaerts, ed. J. Robijns and others (Leuven, 1969), 155–6
FRANK DOBBINS, PASCAL DESAUX

Petit jeu. An organ registration on the Positif department of the Classical French organ, analogous to the GRAND JEU, with which it was often played in alternation. See also REGISTRATION, §I, 5.

Petkov, Dimitar (b Raykovo, 4 May 1919). Bulgarian composer. He studied chemistry in Sofia (1938–42) and subsequently graduated from the State Academy of Music. From 1946 to 1952 he directed the folksong and dance ensemble of the Ministry of the Interior; during the period 1958–60 he taught theory at the Sofia Music Academy, studying at the Moscow Conservatory between these periods. He was director of the Sofia National Opera (1954–62, 1975–8) and adviser in the Bulgarian Embassy, Prague (1962–7). Between 1969 and 1972 he was one of the vice-presidents of the committee for arts and culture in Sofia. From 1972 he was president of the Bulgarian Composers' Union. Most of his works are songs, often serving as examples of Bulgarian socialist realism.

WORKS
(selective list)
5 cantatas, incl. Septemvriyska legenda, 1954, Komunisti, 1966; Rekviyem za matrosa [Requiem for a Sailor], 1968; 3 polifonichni piesi, fl, cl, bn, 1954; Krivata pateka [The Crooked Path] (children's operetta), 1956; Rozhen sliza ot Rodopa [Rozhen Descends from Rhodope] (orat), 1967; Nespokoyni sartsa [Restless Hearts] (operetta), 1976; Zamlaknalite kambani [Silenced Bells] (op), 1988; Zlatna esen [Golden Autumn] (songs and arias), 1900–92; 2 suites, solo vv, children's chorus, orch; 25 solo songs, 50 choral songs, c300 children's/mass songs, film scores

Principal publisher: Nauka i izkustvo

BIBLIOGRAPHY
Entsiklopedya na balgarskata muyikalna kultura (Sofia, 1967)
V. Krastev: Ocherki po istoriya na balgarskata muzikalna kultura [Sketches on the history of Bulgarian musical culture] (Sofia, 1977)
E. Pavlov: Dimitar Petkov: monografiya (Sofia, 1987)
LADA BRASHOVANOVA

Petra-Basacopol, Carmen (b Sibiu, 5 Sept 1926). Romanian composer. After attending the philosophy faculty at Bucharest University (1945–9), she studied composition with Jora and Leon Klepper and orchestration with Rogalski at the Bucharest Academy (1949–56), where in 1962 she became a lecturer. Petra-Basacopol took the doctorate at the Sorbonne under the supervision of Chailley with a thesis entitled L'originalité de la musique roumaine à travers les oeuvres d'Enescu, Jora et Constantinescu (Bucharest, 1968). In 1968 she attended the summer courses in Darmstadt. Her essentially neoromantic music remains within the framework of the Romanian national style, though she has experimented with harmonic and textural elements including clusters and new instrumental techniques. Petra-Basacopol has composed prolifically for the harp. In her theatrical works she has gained inspiration particularly from Romanian subject matter. Her many awards include the 1980 Enescu Prize.

WORKS
(selective list)
Stage: Miorița (ballet, 1, choreog. O. Danovski), 1980, Constanța, Fantasio, 15 May 1981; Coeur d'enfant (children's op, 2, E. D'Amicis), 1983, Bucharest, Română, 18 Aug 1985; Ciuleandra (ballet, 2, L. Rebreanu), 1985–6, Cluj-Napoca, Română, 28 June 1987; Apostol Bologa (op, prol, 2, epilogue, after Rebreanu), 1990; Les sept corbeaux (ballet, 2, after J.L.C. and W.C. Grimm), 1996
Vocal: Crengile [The Branches] (M. Dumitrescu), chorus, orch, 1966
Orch: Sym. no.1, 1955; Țara de piatră [The Country of Stone] 1959; Pf Conc., 1961; Triptic simfonic, 1962; Vn Conc. no.1, 1963; Vn Conc. no.2, 1965; Conc., hp, str, timp, 1975; Conc., str, 1981; Vc Conc., 1982; Fl Conc., 1994
Chbr and solo inst: Studii, hp, 1958; Pf Trio, 1959; 6 preludii, hp, 1960; Impresiuni din Muzeul Satului [Impressions from the Village Museum], pf, 1960; Sonata, fl, hp, 1961; Octet, ww, db, xyl,

1969; Trio, fl, cl, bn, 1974; Qt, fl, pf trio, 1978; Trio, fl, cl, hp, 1980; The Jungle Book, hp, 1990; Wind Qnt, 1992

BIBLIOGRAPHY

W.G. Berger: *Ghid pentru muzica instrumentală de cameră* [Guide to instrumental chamber music] (Bucharest, 1965)

V. Cosma: *Muzicieni români* (Bucharest, 1970)

OCTAVIAN COSMA

Petracchi, Francesco [Franco] (*b* Pistoia, 22 Sept 1937). Italian double bass player. He studied the double bass, conducting and composition at the Accademia di S Cecilia in Rome and made his solo début in 1961 at La Fenice in Venice. He has appeared extensively throughout Europe as a soloist and has also worked as a conductor. Several works have been dedicated to him, including Mortari's *Concerto per Franco Petracchi* (1966), Bucchi's *Concerto grottesco* (1967) and Rota's *Divertimento concertante* (1968–9). An influential teacher, he has been a professor at conservatories in Bari, Rome and Geneva, and his masterclasses at the Accademia Musicale Chigiana in Siena have attracted students from around the world. Among his recordings is an acclaimed account of Bottesini's Gran Duo with Ruggiero Ricci and the RPO. He plays a double bass by Gaetano Rossi, an unusually large instrument for a soloist.

RODNEY SLATFORD

Petraeus, Christoph. *See* PETER, CHRISTOPH.

Petrarch [Petrarca, Francesco] (*b* Arezzo, 20 July 1304; *d* Arquà, 18 July 1374). Italian poet and humanist man of letters. The son and grandson of notaries active in Florence, Petrarch himself never lived in Florence and only rarely visited it; his family had been exiled from the city and their confiscated property was not returned. In 1312 Petrarch's family moved to Avignon, where the papal court had recently settled. Francesco was educated in nearby Carpentras, then (1316) sent to study law at Montpellier. In 1320 he went to Bologna to continue his studies, beginning a pattern of alternate periods of residence in Italy and Provence that was to last until 1353, when he moved to Italy for good.

Petrarch returned to Avignon at the time of his father's death in 1326. He and his brother lived for a short time on their patrimony, but in 1330 Petrarch entered the service of two ecclesiastical members of the Roman Colonna family. About this time he received the tonsure; he may or may not have taken minor orders, and he never married. Over his life he accumulated canonries and other ecclesiastical benefits from the income on which he lived; but he rarely assumed canonical duties, and lived as far as possible the life of an independent man of letters.

The famous Laura was first seen by the poet in Avignon in 1327; the sonnets celebrating his love for her were written over a long period, the first redaction of the *Canzoniere* being undertaken in 1342. More poems were written after Laura's death in 1348, and the final text and arrangement of the *Canzoniere* occupied Petrarch intermittently throughout his life. The sonnets and canzoni of the *Canzoniere*, the *Trionfi* and scattered lighter poems in Italian represented for Petrarch, who was not sanguine about the state of vernacular literature, only a small part of his literary activity, most of which was devoted to biographies of classical figures, reflective essays and dialogues, epic poetry, and above all letter-writing, all in Latin.

During the 1330s Petrarch travelled in northern Europe; in 1336, the year of his celebrated climb of Mt Ventoux, he visited Rome for the first time. He settled in the country in Vaucluse in 1337, near to, but not in, crowded Avignon, which he detested. In 1340 he accepted the sponsorship of King Roberto of Naples as a candidate for poetic 'coronation'; the ceremony took place on the Capitol in Rome in April 1341. Petrarch's view of Rome as the proper residence for both pope and emperor, and his later support of Cola di Rienzo, were part of his humanistic reverence for Latin antiquity, as was his lifelong thirst for literary fame.

Parma and Vaucluse were Petrarch's 'Cisalpine' and 'Transalpine' homes in the next decade. He was now a great celebrity, sought after as an ambassador and orator on state occasions in Italy, France and imperial domains. The rulers of Milan, Verona, Ferrara and Mantua all paid court to him. His circle of friends, among whom the most celebrated was Boccaccio, was large and was carefully cultivated through visits and correspondence. After 1353 his residence for eight years was Milan, where he was close to the Visconti; in 1361 he moved to Padua, then to Venice, and again in 1368 to Padua. The gift of a piece of land in the Euganean hills enabled him to build his final country retreat at Arquà.

Petrarch was fond of music. Among his friends were the singer Ludovicus da Beeringhen (called 'Socrates'), a Ferrarese musician named Tommaso Bambasio to whom the poet left his lute, and a certain Confortino. Although only one poem, the madrigal *Non al suo amante*, survives in a contemporary polyphonic setting (by Jacopo da Bologna), other occasional verse may have been given by the poet to performers for their own use. Very little of Petrarch's verse belongs to the category of *poesia per musica* (ballatas and madrigals); it is not surprising that Trecento composers did not set his sonnets and canzoni, any more than they did the serious poetry of Dante.

Although Petrarchan echoes may be found in the poetry of Boiardo and Lorenzo de' Medici, the revival of Petrarchism important in the history of music begins with the work of Benedetto Gareth ('il Chariteo'), in whose verse, made for musical performance, Petrarchan metaphors were relentlessly exploited and given 'existential reality' (Wilkins). The poetry of Tebaldeo and Sasso, and above all the enormously popular *strambotti* of Serafino de' Ciminelli dall'Aquila, belong to this late 15th-century phase.

Pietro Bembo's thorough study of Petrarch resulted in an edition of the *Canzoniere* (1501) that was a model for the more than 160 editions printed in the 16th century; Bembo's theories on Tuscan Italian as a literary language depended heavily on examples provided by Petrarch; and his own poetry in Petrarchistic vein gave inspiration to at least two generations of Italian poets, including Alamanni, Ariosto, Caro, Cassola, Colonna, Della Casa, Gambara, Guidiccioni, Molza, Navagero, Sannazaro and Bernardo Tasso – all of whom provided texts for madrigalists. Petrarch's verse itself was set, at first occasionally in the later period of the frottola and among the early madrigalists, then more regularly. Whole collections, such as Matteo Rampollini's *Musica … sopra di alcuni canzoni del divin poeta M Francesco Petrarca* (*c*1545) were devoted to Petrarch, whose poetry was set with special seriousness and grandeur by Willaert and the Venetian circle around him. Settings of Petrarch became less frequent in the later 16th-century madrigal, but they never entirely disappeared. The number of madrigals to Petrarchan texts is enormous; but it is not quite so large as lists of titles (*VogelB*) would lead one to believe. Many poems found in madrigal collections begin with a few words borrowed from Petrarch, then go their own way.

Petrarchism spread over Europe in the 16th century. In France Marot and St Gelais cultivated a poetic style influenced by the Petrarchism of Serafino; Du Bellay and Baïf began a more serious adaptation of Petrarchan themes and language to French poetry, much of which received musical setting. In England translators and imitators of Petrarch began with Wyatt, Surrey and other poets printed in Tottel's *Miscellany* (1557), which includes an anonymous sonnet beginning 'O Petrarke hed and prince of poets all'. Sidney and other Elizabethan sonneteers continued English Petrarchism in richer form, but with little influence on the madrigal of the period.

Among more recent settings of Petrarchan verse might be cited songs by James Hook (*c*1792), several Schubert songs, the celebrated Liszt songs and piano pieces, choral works by Moniuszko (1855) and Tommasini (1918), and Schoenberg's Serenade op.24.

BIBLIOGRAPHY
MODERN EDITIONS
only those important for music

A. Solerti, ed.: *Rime disperse di Francesco Petrarca o a lui attribuite* (Florence, 1909)
G. Contini, ed.: *Canzoniere* (Turin, 5/1974)

STUDIES

EinsteinIM; VogelB
A. Graf: 'Petrarchismo ed antipetrarchismo', *Attraverso il Cinquecento* (Turin, 1888, 2/1926), 3–86
C. Culcasi: *Il Petrarca e la musica* (Florence, 1911)
W.H. Rubsamen: *Literary Sources of Secular Music in Italy (ca. 1500)* (Berkeley, 1943/R)
E.H. Wilkins: *The Making of the 'Canzoniere' and Other Petrarchan Studies* (Rome, 1951)
E.H. Wilkins: *Studies in the Life and Works of Petrarch* (Cambridge, MA, 1955)
L. Baldacci: *Il petrarchismo italiano nel Cinquecento* (Milan, 1957, 2/1974)
N. Pirrotta: 'Due sonetti musicali del secolo XIV', *Miscelánea en homenaje a Monseñor Higinio Anglés* (Barcelona, 1958–61), 651–62
E.H. Wilkins: *Life of Petrarch* (Chicago, 1961)
D.T. Mace: 'Pietro Bembo and the Literary Origins of the Italian Madrigal', *MQ*, lv (1969), 65–86
C. Rawski: 'Petrarch's Dialogue on Music', *Speculum*, xlvi (1971), 303–18
D. Stevens: 'Petrarch's Greeting to Italy', *MT*, cxv (1974), 834–6
P. Petrobelli: '*Un leggiadretto velo* ed altre cose petrarchesche', *RIM*, x (1975), 32–45
T. Greene: *The Light in Troy: Imitation and Discovery in Renaissance Poetry* (New Haven, CT, 1982)
F. Ersparmer: 'Petrarchismo e manierismo nella lirica del secondo Cinquecento', *Storia della cultura veneta*, iv/1: *Il Seicento*, ed. G. Arnaldi and M.P. Stocchi (Vicenza, 1983), 189–222
N. Pirrotta: *Music and Culture in Italy from the Middle Ages to the Baroque: a Collection of Essays* (Cambridge, MA, 1984)
M. Feldman: 'The Composer as Exegete: Interpretations of Petrarchan Syntax in the Venetian Madrigal', *Studi musicali*, xviii (1989), 203–38
M. Feldman: *City Culture and the Madrigal at Venice* (Berkeley, 1995)
JAMES HAAR

Petrassi, Goffredo (*b* Zagarolo, nr Palestrina, 16 July 1904). Italian composer. Along with Dallapiccola, he is the most significant Italian composer of the mid-20th century.

1. Education and earlier works. 2. The concertos for orchestra and later works.

1. EDUCATION AND EARLIER WORKS. Petrassi's birthplace, Zagarolo, is a village in the Roman countryside with no lack of musical connections: on top of a nearby hill stands the fortress of Palestrina, and in the centre of the village is the Palazzo Rospigliosi named after the family of Cardinal Giulio Rospigliosi, who was known first as an opera librettist and then as Pope Clement IX. Young Goffredo's family moved to Rome in 1911 and it was as a result of this that the seven-year-old had his first contact with music. He was sent to school in Via dei Coronari, and as the Scuola Cantorum of S Salvatore in Lauro was situated next to the school, it seemed natural to send the boy, who had shown that he had a good voice, to study at this choir school. The music which Goffredo Petrassi encountered as a chorister – that of Palestrina, Josquin, Animuccia and Anerio – demonstrates the similarity between the Scuola Cantorum and the schools which centuries before had cultivated the Roman polyphonic tradition. At the Scuola Cantorum the young Petrassi received the same sort of musical education as Palestrina and many other musicians had centuries before. Practical concerns, however, forced Petrassi at the age of 15 to find a job in a music shop. In quiet moments he played a piano in the back of the shop, and attracted the attention of Alessandro Bustini, the distinguished teacher of piano and composition at the Conservatorio di S Cecilia. He decided to teach him and thus get him into the conservatory, where he could have a first-rate musical education. In the space of a few years the young Petrassi moved from 16th century world of Palestrina to a contemporary world dominated by the figures of Bustini, Casella, Respighi and Bernardino Molinari, together with all those musicians who, in the early years of the century, were attempting to pull Italian musical life out of the operatic furrow it had ploughed almost exclusively for centuries. Petrassi experienced no conflict in the juxtaposition of these two areas of his education: according to his own words, the experience of Renaissance polyphony retreated into a sort of limbo, ready to spring forth as an adult composer tackling demanding themes. The plural nature of Petrassi's education, its all-inclusive quality a reflection of his environment, is the key to understanding his music; as will be seen, Petrassi was able not only to pursue different impulses but also to bring them together in a wide-ranging musical outlook.

The beginning of Petrassi's career is customarily marked by the success of his *Partita* for orchestra, written in 1932; his winning two competitions with it, together with receiving performances at ISMC festivals, put him on to the international stage. Although Casella and Edward J. Dent are regarded as being responsible for drawing wider attention to Petrassi, Casella had already noticed the composer some months before when he heard the *Tre cori*, Petrassi's graduation piece from the conservatory. The *Tre cori* remained unpublished, but they at once revealed Petrassi's considerable ability in dealing with the orchestral and choral material. The brilliant Partita was soon followed by other orchestral works, such as the *Ouverture da concerto* of 1931 and the first Concerto for Orchestra of 1933–4. It is not difficult to see in them the influence of the rhythmic vigour and contrapuntal complexity of Hindemith, the polytonal conflicts of Stravinsky and the rhythmic geometry of Casella, but over and above those influences one finds an assured, virtuosic mastery of the orchestra, practically an unknown skill in Italian orchestral music of that period. His experience as a chorister was to come to the surface in *Salmo IX*, composed between 1934 and 1936. To judge from the vast forces employed and the often angular quality of the music, the work seems to convey more the impressions he may have had of the great Roman basilicas rather than of Palestrina's style. The memory of those spaces, volumes and echoes passes, however, through the filter of Stravinsky's *Symphony of Psalms* and *Oedipus rex* which were both heard in Rome in that same period. Yet Petrassi's experience of polyphony is easily recognized in the treatment of the choral part which is structured in sections that follow each other seamlessly. At this time, works for orchestral and vocal forces dominated Petrassi's output: in 1940 his *Magnificat* for soprano, chorus and orchestra showed a more lyrical and subtle approach to the re-examination of the sacred style which had given rise to *Salmo IX*. The following year produced the *Coro dei morti*, described as a 'dramatic madrigal for male voices, brass, three pianos, double-basses and percussion', a setting of a passage from Leopardi's *Operette morali* and a move, therefore, from the sacred to the philosophical. This work quickly became famous, and shows the beginnings of Petrassi's tendency to treat his relationship with musical language as a source of dramatic inspiration. Disinclined to express emotions directly, Petrassi found himself in the peculiar position of presenting his own intellectual struggle as an abstract drama: a unison, an interval, a pause, a pulsating rhythm and sometimes the vaguest of melodic reminiscences are the outward signs of this abstract drama. The *Coro dei morti* is characterized by clear-cut opposition of melodic tonal sections with highly contrapuntal and far less tonal ones. The dilemma at the heart of the work is one which Petrassi was to explore in his compositions over the following decade, and it was almost in order to make his inner struggle more explicit that at this time Petrassi moved towards theatrical music.

Petrassi's work in the theatre produced two ballets, *La follia di Orlando* and *Ritratto di Don Chisciotte*, and two operas, *Il cordovano* and *Morte dell'aria*. Through these he focussed on one of the basic tools of his style, irony, which he saw as the perfect means to disguise (with abstraction and ambiguity) his responses to events. Petrassi was not concerned as to whether he should be a tonal, neo-classical or 12-tone composer: he had no belief in the certainty of any definitive approach, but only in the certainty of the struggle and torment of life, and his musical language is the diary of these uncertainties. One of the greatest works in his whole output, *Noche oscura* (1951), a cantata for mixed chorus and orchestra, provides a lesson in the way these stylistic directions pile up, interweave and erode one another. It is a setting of the poem by St John of the Cross on the theme of the solitary path of a mystic who renounces all links with humanity to approach the Beloved, namely Christ. The desolate solitude of this interior journey is symbolized by a cell of four notes (two ascending minor seconds linked by a descending major third). For Petrassi this four-note pattern acquires the character of a mystic formula, and it reappears in later compositions – such as *Beatudines* (1968–9) and *Orationes Christi* (1974–5) – in which he developed the ideas of human responsibility and solitude. Entire compositions develop from the intervallic elaboration and transformation of this formula, moving gradually from mostly contrapuntal textures and dark timbres towards less astringent harmonies and brighter timbres. Many commentators have seen Petrassi's studied management of such material as a move towards serial procedures. But it should be realized that the composer's relationship with 12-tone technique was never one of complete conformity. Petrassi saw 12-tone technique as a way of manipulating the musical material in the most rational and economically controlled manner; although he made occasional horizontal use of the method, he was never committed to it with the fervour of many composers in the 1950s. The real objective of Petrassi's technical grapplings was the arrival at a linguistic concentration and abstraction which would act as a shield against any manner of rhetoric.

2. THE CONCERTOS FOR ORCHESTRA AND LATER WORKS. Nothing reflects better Petrassi's creative exploration of questions of technique and style than his series of concertos for orchestra. 17 years separate the first, written in 1934 in the wake of the success of the *Partita*, and the second, composed in 1951 to a commission from the Basle Chamber Orchestra. Although the difference between these two works lies in a more concentrated and adroit use of the material, in both Petrassi treats it according to the rules of classical thematicism. There is an increase in rhythmic vigour and the models of Hindemith and Stravinsky are now joined by Bartók whose sublime silences and freely germinating counterpoint particularly attracted Petrassi. The prestige of the organizations which now commissioned Petrassi's works is an indication of his international reputation. After the Basle Chamber Orchestra came the Südwestfunk of Baden-Baden for whom Petrassi wrote his Third Concerto for Orchestra, subtitled 'Récréation concertante', in 1952–3. From the very beginning, the exposition of a long series with various notes repeated several times demonstrates the freedom of Petrassi's use of 12-tone technique and, given the ironic, light and elegant character of the score, it is evident that for him the series is only a device with which to escape the thematic tradition. Yet Petrassi had no hesitation in turning back to this tradition as soon as a suitably dramatic opportunity arose. In the

Goffredo Petrassi

fourth and last movement, marked *adagio moderato*, the four-note pattern of *Noche oscura* reappears to initiate an episode of a lyrical intensity probably unequalled in Petrassi's entire output. To lend a 12-tone series a strong melodic inflection in the manner of Berg, who was unsurprisingly Petrassi's favourite of the Second Viennese School composers, seems to be his aim in the Fourth Concerto for Orchestra in which the light, agile style of writing for the string orchestra gives way in the third movement, marked *lentissimo*, to a melodic series of rare lyrical intensity. His approaches towards serial technique continued in 1955 with his Fifth Concerto for Orchestra, and in 1957 with the sixth, which were written in response to commissions from the Boston SO and the BBC. To describe these concertos for orchestra solely in terms of their greater or lesser adherence to serial techniques would be to overlook the complexity of Petrassi's struggles with his material which would be at their most productive at the end of the 1950s. It has been noted how in the Third Concerto for Orchestra one of the high points comes about through the reappearance of the four-note theme from *Noche oscura*; other concertos are also characterized by the insistent use of certain key intervals and other quotations – for example, one of three notes taken from the *Coro dei morti* appears in the Fifth Concerto for Orchestra. Although these intervals and brief thematic figures become increasingly important in the writing of the concertos, various chamber works dating from the end of the 1950s onwards demonstrate their full significance and mark the most important method used by Petrassi during his career. A string quartet composed in 1958 shows clearly how certain intervals (major third, minor sixth and tritone) have become the protagonists of the composition. The result is an abstract and athematic style in which the interval takes on a fully dramatic character. This laconic mode of expression, with its wealth of allusive possibilities, provided Petrassi with the language which best suited him, a language of gestures sculpted from the musical material with a graphic precision and simplicity. With this string quartet Petrassi showed that he was absolutely sure in his approach; other, strongly characterized elements were added, with a new focus on timbre.

The *Serenata*, also composed in 1958, is scored for flute, harpsichord, percussion, viola and double-bass, a bright array of instrumental timbres whose clear, vibrant colours are an essential element in each intervallic gesture and which are juxtaposed in a series of solo cadenzas. The precise exploration of timbre continued in 1962 with the *Seconda Serenata-Trio*, which explores only different plucked sounds (harp, guitar and mandolin). By this stage each new work marked the conquest of new territory, as in 1964 did *Tre per sette* (the title refers to the three performers, on flute, oboe and clarinet, playing seven different instruments in all) which explores varieties of intervals and timbres in the woodwind family. Petrassi explores new terrain in these scores but the music has none of the acerbity which often marks experimental works: one can hear that the composer is working in a highly congenial context, and within the supremely concise writing allusions and poetic extracts multiply as if the musical material had at last suddenly become malleable and able to reveal hidden treasures. In subsequent years there was an upsurge in the number of solo works aimed at exploiting this miraculous richness of

timbre: *Souffle* for solo flute, from 1969, *Elogio per un'ombra* for violin and *Nunc* for guitar of 1971, *Ala* in 1972 for flute and harpsichord and *Alias* in 1977 for guitar and harpsichord. This was Petrassi's preferred terrain, and on it he created some of his masterpieces; his attention to it did not mean that other areas were neglected, if anything the achievements in one field were transplanted into another.

In 1964 Petrassi wrote his Seventh Concerto for Orchestra, a rather troubled score which sprang from a previous work, *Prologo e cinque invenzioni*, written in 1962 to a commission from the Portland Junior Symphony Orchestra. Unhappy with the original work, Petrassi recast it entirely as the Seventh Concerto, but its didactic origins explain why the various sections are given over to different instruments of the orchestra, with brilliant solo episodes which reflect the solo cadenzas in the chamber works. The superb cadenza for xylorimba in the third section is a perfect example of how Petrassi's chamber style had successfully been absorbed into his orchestral writing. That Petrassi's chamber writing with its virtuosity of timbres and intervals took his orchestral writing towards this point can be seen in two different but equally important examples, the Flute Concerto of 1960 and the Eighth Concerto for Orchestra of 1970–2. The structure of the Flute Concerto – determined by the numerous, extended cadenzas for the solo instrument which direct the orchestral flow like magnetic poles – reflects the spirit of his chamber music, with its alternation of cadenzas and intervallic schemes. In the Eighth Concerto for Orchestra, extreme intervallic economy and brilliant rhythmic variety across the overall orchestral framework generate a new type of musical material: instead of the nervy, precise calligraphies of the works for a few instruments, the frothing material produces music like fine swirling dust. As the signs multiply, they generate a message, a total greater than the sum of all the parts: it is the sort of experience which has become familiar over the years from abstract painting, and Petrassi is, unsurprisingly, passionate and knowledgeable about modern art. Attention to abstract forms of writing did not draw Petrassi away from the moral themes which had illuminated the choral-orchestral works of his youth. The *Beatudines* (subtitled 'A Witness to Martin Luther King') for baritone and five instruments (1969), the *Orationes Christi* for mixed choir, brass, violas and cellos (1975) and the *Poema per archi e trombe* (1977–80) continued to develop more or less explicitly the themes of solitude and human suffering, which were now explored with more unusual combinations of voices and instruments.

The chamber works which at the end of the 1960s signalled such a fertile development in Petrassi's music were also those on which he expended the greatest care. In 1967, his *Estri* for 15 players seemed in its title alone to make an utterly characteristic artistic declaration: the term *estro*, meaning both caprice and talent, has a long history in Italian instrumental music; it is difficult to translate, but should not be understood merely as the glorification of imagination. Unpredictable and possibly wayward in character, *estro* also implies the revelation of one's mystery to an observer. Undoubtedly the *estro musicale* was destined to find its perfect form in a style of composition dependent on the balancing of intervals and timbres, in the technique of which Petrassi acquired a rare mastery, and his final works are like the coming together of various *estri* of reminiscence and different emotions. The nostalgia for a certain sort of salon virtuosity implied by the title of the *Grand septuor avec clarinette concertante* of 1977–8 is belied by the sense of irony produced by the alienating sounds of guitar and percussion. Petrassi's last great chamber work is entitled *Sestina d'autunno*, and bears the explanatory subtitle *Veni, creator Igor*. It was composed in 1981 on the tenth anniversary of the death of Stravinsky, the composer who had made such a profound mark on Petrassi's early years and the subsequent development of his music. It is written for six players: viola, cello, double-bass, guitar, mandolin and percussion instruments. The variety of colour which, as is often the case with Petrassi, tends towards darker shades, the frail and somewhat alienating sound of the plucked strings and the percussion, the graceful linearity of phrases whose simplicity is more charged with meaning than ever, and the clarity of the form, borrowed from the old Italian strophic form of six lines (a *sestina*), display to the utmost that synthesis of sobriety and intensity which Petrassi pursued tirelessly for so many years.

WORKS

DRAMATIC

La follia di Orlando (ballet, with narrative recitatives from L. Ariosto, choreog. A.M. Milloss), 1942–3, Milan, Scala, 12 April 1947

Il cordovano (op, 1, E. Montale, after M. de Cervantes: *Entremes del viejo celoso*), 1944–8, Milan, Scala, 12 May 1949; rev. 1958, Milan, Piccola Scala, 18 Feb 1959

Ritratto di Don Chisciotte (ballet, 1, Milloss), 1945, Paris, Champs-Elysées, 21 Nov 1947

Morte dell'aria (op, 1. T. Scialoja), 1949–50, Rome, Eliseo, 24 Oct 1950

4 incid scores, 1930–54, unpubd; 9 film scores, 1948–65, unpubd

ORCHESTRAL

Preludio e fuga, str, 1929, unpubd; Divertimento, C, 1930, unpubd; Conc. for Orch, 1931: Ouverture da concerto, 1931, rev. 1933, Passacaglia, unpubd; Partita, 1932; Conc. for Orch no.1, 1933–4; Pf Conc., 1936–9; La follia di Orlando, suite, 1942–3 [from ballet]; Ritratto di Don Chisciotte, suite, 1945 [from ballet]; Conc. for Orch no.2, 1951; Conc. for Orch no.3 (Récréation concertante), 1952–3; Conc. for Orch no.4, str, 1954; Conc. for Orch no.5, 1955; Conc. for Orch no.6 (Invenzione concertata), brass, perc, str, 1956–7; Saluto augurale, 1958, unpubd; Fl Conc., 1960; Prologo e 5 invenzioni, 1961–2; Conc. for Orch no.7, 1964 [incl. material from Prologo e 5 invenzioni and chbr work Musica di ottoni]; Conc. for Orch no.8, 1970–72; Poema, tpt, str, 1977–80; Frammento, 1983

CHORAL

Acc.: 3 cori, chorus, orch, 1932, unpubd; Ps ix, chorus, brass, perc, 2 pf, str, 1934–6; Magnificat, S, chorus, orch, 1939–40; Coro dei morti (madrigale drammatico, G. Leopardi), male vv, brass, 3 pf, perc, 5 db, 1940–41; Noche oscura (cant., St John of the Cross), chorus, orch, 1950–51, Orationes Christi, chorus, brass, vas, vcs, 1974–5; Kyrie, chorus, str, 1986

Unacc.: Nonsense (Lear, trans. C. Izzo), 1952; Sesto non-senso (Lear, trans. Izzo), 1964; Motetti per la Passione (liturgical texts), 1965; 3 cori sacri, 1980–83

OTHER VOCAL

Salvezza (G. Gozzano), 1v, pf, 1926; Canti della campagna romana, folksong arrs., 1v, pf, 1927, collab. N. Nataletti; La morte del cardellino (Gozzano), 1v, pf, 1927, unpubd; 2 liriche su temi della campagna romana, 1v, pf, 1927, unpubd; Per organo di Barberia (S. Corazzini), 1v, pf, 1927, unpubd; Campane (V. Breccia), 1v, pf, 1929, unpubd; 3 liriche antiche italiane (G. Cavalcanti, 13th century), 1v, pf, 1929, no.2 pubd; Pioggia dai peschi (M. Saint-Cyr), 1v, pf, 1929, unpubd; Colori del tempo (V. Cardarelli), 1v, pf, 1931; Benedizione (Bible: *Genesis*), 1v, pf, 1934; O sonni, sonni, folk lullaby, 1v, pf, 1934; Vocalizzo per addormentare una bambina, 1v, pf, 1934, arr. 1v (1938); Lamento d'Arianna (L. de Libero), 1v, pf, 1936, arr. 1v, wind qnt, tpt, hp, str qt (1938); 2 liriche di Saffo Rome (trans. S. Quasimodo), 1v, pf, 1941, arr. 1v,

wind qnt, tpt, hp, str qt, 1945; 4 inni sacri (latin texts), T, Bar, org, 1942, arr. T, Bar, orch, 1950; 3 liriche (Leopardi, U. Foscolo, E. Montale), Bar, pf, 1944; Miracolo (F. de Pisis), Bar, pf, 1944

Gloria in excelsis Deo, S, fl, org, 1952, unpubd; Propos d'Alain (E.A. Chartier), Bar, 12 insts, 1960; Beatitudines 'Testimonianza per Martin Luther King' (Bible: *Matthew*), B/Bar, E♭-cl, tpt, timp, va, db, 1968–9

CHAMBER AND SOLO INSTRUMENTAL

5 or more insts: Sonata da camera, hpd, 10 insts 1948; Serenata, fl, hpd, perc, va, db, 1958; Musica di ottoni, 4 hn, 4 tpt, 3 trbn, tuba, timp, 1961–3 [incl. material from Prologo e 5 invenzioni, orch, 1961–2 and forms basis of Conc. for Orch no.7]; Estri, 15 pfmrs, 1966–7, Ottetto di ottoni, 4 tpt, 4 trbn, 1968; Grand septuor avec clarinette concertante, cl, tpt, trbn, vn, vc, gui, perc, 1977–8; Sestina d'autunno 'Veni, creator Igor', va, vc, db, gui, mand, perc, 1981–2; Laudes creaturarum 3 cl, 2 trbn, vc, 1982; Inno, 12 brass, 1984

3–4 insts: Sinfonia, siciliana e fuga, str qt, 1929, unpubd; Fanfare, 3 tpt, 1944, rev. 1976; Str Qt, 1958; Str Trio, 1959; Seconda serenata-trio, hp, gui, mand, 1962; Tre per sette, pic+fl+a fl, ob+eng hn, E♭-cl+cl, 1964; Odi, str qt, 1973–5

2 insts: Sonata in tre brevi movimenti continui, vc, pf, 1927, unpubd; Sonata in tre brevi movimenti continui, vc, pf, 1927, unpubd; Sarabanda, fl, pf, 1930, unpubd; Introduzione e allegro, vn, pf, 1933, arr. vn, 11 insts (1934); Preludio, aria e finale, vc, pf, 1933, arr. vc, chbr orch, 1939, destroyed; Invenzione, 2 fl, 1944, rev. as Dialogo angelico, 1948; 5 duetti, 2 vc, 1952, unpubd; Ala, pic + fl, hpd, 1972; Alias, gui, hpd, 1977; Duetto, vn, va, 1985

Solo: Egloga, pf, 1926, unpubd; Partita, pf, 1926; Siciliana e marcetta, pf 4 hands, 1930; Toccata, pf, 1933; Piccola invenzione, pf, 1941, unpubd; Divertimento scarlattiano, pf, 1942, unpubd; Invenzioni, pf, 1944; Petite pièce, pf, 1950, rev. 1976; Suoni notturni, gui, 1959; Souffle, pic + fl + a fl, 1969; Elogio per un'ombra, vn, 1971; Nunc, gui, 1971; Oh les beaux jours!, pf, 1976 [incl. material from Piccola invenzione, 1941 and Divertimento scarlattiano, 1942]; Violasola, 1978; Flou hp, 1980; Romanzetta, fl, pf, 1980

MSS in *CH-Bps*

Principal publishers: Ricordi, Suvini Zerboni, Universal

WRITINGS

'Perché i giovani musicisti non scrivono per il teatro', *Scenario*, iv (1935), 459

'Il festival internazionale di musica', *Scenario*, v (1936), 482

Taccuino di musica (Rome, 1944) [incl. reproductions of unpubd works]

'Scuola di composizione', *Il mondo* [Rome] (16 June 1945), no.6, p.12

'Le mie avventure con la danza', *Musica* [Rome], i (1946), 135

'Sulla musica religiosa', *Il campo*, i (1946), 153

'Seminario di composizione', *Chigiana*, xxxiii, new ser., xiii (1976), 307–29

ed. C. Vasio: *Autoritratto* (Laterza, 1992)

Many contributions to *Cosmopolita* [Rome], ii–iii (1945–6) [on Stravinsky, Walton, Bloch and others]

For fuller list see *KdG* (J. Noller)

BIBLIOGRAPHY

KdG (J. Noller)

M. Mila: 'Ultime tendenze della musica italiana: un giovane, Goffredo Petrassi', *Domus*, vii/74 (1934), 54

G. Gavazzeni: 'Musicisti nuovi: Goffredo Petrassi', *Bollettino mensile di vita e cultura musicale*, ix (1935), 115–19

G.M. Gatti: 'Modern Italian Composers: I Goffredo Petrassi', *MMR*, lxvii (1937), 1–3

L.[F.] D'Amico: *Goffredo Petrassi* (Rome, 1942) [incl. reproductions of unpubd works; extract, 'I lavori giovanili di Petrassi', *RaM*, xv (1942), 1–10]

M. Maglia: 'Le dernier Petrassi', *Il diapason*, i/3 (1950), 19

G. Gavazzeni: 'Due balletti di Petrassi', *La musica e il teatro* (Pisa, 1954), 241–57

R. Vlad: 'Petrassi', 'La noche oscura', *Modernità e tradizione nella musica contemporanea* (Turin, 1955), 217–35

K. Gaburo: 'Goffredo Petrassi: the Man and his Music', *Musical Courier*, cliv/3 (1956), 6, 30

J.S. Weissmann: *Goffredo Petrassi* (Milan, 1957, 2/1980) [in Eng.]

R. Vlad: 'La dodecafonia in Italia', *Storia della dodecafonia* (Milan, 1958), 204–19

F. D'Amico: 'Astrattismo puro del secondo Petrassi', *L'Italia domani*, ii/10 (1959), 14

J.S. Weissmann: 'Petrassi's Early Choral Music', *Ricordiana*, iv/2 (1959), 4; It. trans. in *Musica d'oggi*, new ser., ii (1959), 342

J.S. Weissmann: 'Goffredo Petrassi and his Music', *MR*, xxii (1961), 198–211

G.M. Gatti, ed.: 'L'opera di Goffredo Petrassi', *Quaderni della RaM*, no.1 (1964) [Petrassi issue]

G. Turchi: 'Profilo di Goffredo Petrassi', *Terzo programma* (1964), no.3, p.266

A. Gentilucci: 'Goffredo Petrassi: Quartetto per archi – Trio per archi', *Musica università*, iv/3 (1966), 32

C. Marinelli: 'La musica strumentale de camera di Goffredo Petrassi', *Chigiana*, xxiv, new ser., iv (1967), 245–84

B. Porena: 'I concerti di Petrassi e la crisi della musica come linguaggio', *NRMI*, i (1967), 101–91

R. Vlad: *Musica moderna* (1967–9), v, 129–60 [2 Petrassi issues]

L. Pinzauti: 'A colloquio con Goffredo Petrassi', *NRMI*, ii (1968), 482–93

J.C.G. Waterhouse: *The Emergence of Modern Italian Music (up to 1940)* (diss., U. of Oxford,1968), 741ff

C. Annibaldi: *Goffredo Petrassi: catalogo delle opere e bibliografia* (Milan, 1971, rev. 2/1980 with M. Monna)

A.E. Bonelli: *Serial Tecniques in the Music of Goffredo Petrassi* (diss., U. of Rochester, 1971)

C. Annibaldi: 'Alfredo Casella a Goffredo Petrassi: 23 lettere inedite', *NRMI*, vi (1972), 553–71

L. Maggini: *L'opera di Goffredo Petrassi* (diss., U. of Florence, 1973)

O. Stone: 'Goffredo Petrassi's Concerto for Pianoforte and Orchestra: a study of Twentieth-Century Neo-Classic Style', *MR*, xxxix (1978), 240–57

G. Zosi: *Ricerca e sintesi nell'opera di Goffredo Petrassi* (Rome, 1978)

L. Lombardi: *Conversazioni con Petrassi* (Milan, 1980)

R. Piacentini: *I concerti per orchestra fi Goffredo Petrassi* (thesis, U. of Turin, 1983–4)

F. Amico: 'Goffredo Petrassi', *Komponisten des 20. Jahrhunderts in der Paul Sacher Stiftung*, ed. F. Meyer, J.M. Jans and I. Westen (Basle, 1986), 237–46

L. Lombardi: 'Spannung vertritt die Form: ein Gespräch mit Goffredo Petrassi', *NZM*, cxlvii/3 (1986), 21–5

E. Restagno, ed.: *Petrassi* (Turin, 1986)

L.G. Barrow: 'The Rebirth of Choral Music in Italy', *American Choral Review*, xxxii/1–2 (1990), 17–22

L. Di Fronzo: 'Teatralità e madrigalismo nei Nonsense di Goffredo Petrassi', *Analisi*, ii/5 (1991), 7–22

L. Galliano: 'Incontro con Goffredo Petrassi di Luciana Galliano: la germinazione della musica nella musica stessa', *Sonus* [Potenza], iii/4 (1991), 19–22 [interview]

D. Spini: 'Petrassi e il tempo', *NRMI*, xxviii (1994), 354–62

ENZO RESTAGNO

Petratti, Francesco (*b* Cremona; *fl c*1620). Italian composer and string player. He was in the service of Paolo Giordano II, Duke of Bracciano, before 1620 and of Marquis Ludovico Barbone in the early 1620s. He published *Il primo libro d'arie a una et due voci con un dialogo in fine* (Venice, 1620; one piece for 2vv transcr. in Stevens, 291); Monteverdi, a fellow Cremonese, saw it through the press at the request of the Duke of Bracciano.

BIBLIOGRAPHY

G. Pontiroli: 'Notizie di musicisti cremonesi dei secoli XVI e XVII', *Bollettino storico cremonese*, xxii (1961–4), 149–92

D. Stevens: 'Monteverdi, Petratti, and the Duke of Bracciano', *MQ*, lxiv (1978), 275–94

Petre, Henry. See PETYR, HENRY.

Petreius [Petrejus, Petri, Peterlein], **Johann** (*b* Langendorf, nr Würzburg, 1497; *d* Nuremberg, 18 March 1550). German printer. He began his studies at the University of Basle in 1512, receiving the baccalaureate there in 1515 and the MA two years later. In 1519 he was employed as proofreader by his relative, Adam Petri, in Basle. He became a citizen of Nuremberg in 1523. Although Petreius was not officially entered as printer in the city records until 1526, publications survive from as early as 1524 and he appears to have established his own type foundry by 1525. After his death the business was taken over by his son-in-law, Gabriel Hayn, who continued printing until 1561.

An extremely prolific printer (about 800 publications are known) and a well-educated man, Petreius devoted his professional efforts to a variety of subjects, notably theology, science, law and the classics. Although music forms but a small part of his output, he was known for the superior quality of his work in this field, using the single-impression technique developed by Attaingnant. In addition to printing the first of Forster's collections, Petreius apparently functioned as his own editor in selecting the works for other collections. Unfortunately this tradition was not continued by Hayn, whose music publications are limited to a handful of religious books.

MUSIC EDITIONS

(selective list)

all published in Nuremberg

H. Neusidler: Ein newge ordnet künstlich Lautenbuch, I (1536[12])

Der ander Theil des Lautenbuchs (1536[13])

S. Heyden: Musicae, id est artis canendi, libri duo (1537)

Tomus primus psalmorum selectorum, 4–5vv (1538[6])

Modulationes … quas vulgo motetas vocant, 4vv (1538[7])

Liber quindecim missarum (1539[1])

Tomus secundus psalmorum selectorum, 4–5vv (1539[9]/R in *MGG1*)

Harmoniae poeticae Pauli Hofheimeri et Ludovici Senflii (1539[26])

G. Forster, ed.: Ein Ausszug … teutscher Liedlein (1539[27])

S. Heyden: De arte canendi … libri duo (1540)

G. Forster, ed.: Selectissimarum mutetarum … tomus primus, 4–5vv (1540[6])

G. Forster, ed.: Der ander Theil … teutscher Liedlein (1540[21])

N. Listenius: Musica (1541)

Cantiones centum, 3vv (1541[2])

G. Forster, ed.: Tomus tertius psalmorum selectorum, 4–5vv (1542[6])

Guter, seltzamer … teutscher Gesang, 4–5vv (1544[19])

M. Luther: Geistlicher Geseng und Psalmen (1545)

Responsoria quae annuatim in Veteri Ecclesia … cantari solent (1550)

GABRIEL HAYN

L. Lossius: Psalmodia (1553)

Geystliche Lieder (1557)

BIBLIOGRAPHY

Brown1; *MGG1* (T. Wohnhaas)

J.H.G. Ernesti: *Die Woleingerichtete Buchdruckerey* (Nuremberg, 1721/R), fol. f 1*v*

A. Schmid: *Ottaviano dei Petrucci … und seine Nachfolger im sechzehnten Jahrhunderte* (Vienna, 1845/R)

P. Cohen: *Musikdruck und -drucker zu Nürnberg im sechzehnten Jahrhundert* (Nuremberg, 1927)

J. Benzing: *Die Buchdrucker des 16. und 17. Jahrhunderts im deutschen Sprachgebiet* (Wiesbaden, 1963, 2/1982)

K. Gudewill: 'Bemerkungen zur Herausgebertätigkeit Georg Forsters',*Musik und Verlag: Karl Vötterle zum 65. Geburtstag*, ed. R. Baum and W. Rehm (Kassel, 1968), 299–305

R.L. Wynn: *The French and German Works in 'Trium vocum cantiones centum':a Performing Edition and Commentary* (diss., U. of Colorado, 1969)

E. Soltesz: 'Bisher unbestimmte Petreius-Druckschriften', *Gutenberg-Jb 1980*, 105–112

M. Teramoto: *Die Psalmmotettendrucke des Johannes Petrejus in Nürnberg (gedruckt 1538–1542)* (Tutzing, 1983)

H.M. Brown: Foreword to *Trium vocum cantiones centum*, Renaissance Music in Facsimile, xxvi (New York, 1986)

J.E. Lindberg: *Origins and Development of the Sixteenth-Century Tricinium* (diss., U. of Cincinnati, 1988)

M. Teramoto and A.Brinzing: *Katalog der Musikdrucke des Johannes Petreius in Nürnberg* (Kassel, 1993) [Review by J. Kmetz in *Notes*, li (1994–5), 1291–4]

MARIE LOUISE GÖLLNER

Petrella, Errico (*b* Palermo, 10 Dec 1813; *d* Genoa, 7 April 1877). Italian composer. His father was a Neapolitan naval officer stationed in Palermo, so his Sicilian birth was accidental. In 1815 the family returned to Naples, where Petrella began his musical studies at the age of eight with the violinist Del Giudice. Soon afterwards he started attending classes at the Naples Conservatory, where in 1825 he won a free place as a boarder. Among his first instructors there was the young Bellini, though he studied mainly with Furno and Francesco Ruggi and later with the director Zingarelli. When only 14 years old, he was invited by the impresario Sangiovanni to write an *opera buffa* for the local Teatro La Fenice. It is said that up to this time he had never attended a public opera performance; yet, in spite of opposition from his teachers, he accepted, and in August 1829 produced *Il diavolo color di rosa* with great success. For this audacity he was expelled from the conservatory before he had finished the full course, though he continued to study privately with Ruggi. Four more works in the Neapolitan tradition (with spoken dialogue and local dialect for the *buffo*) followed at the more important Teatro Nuovo over the next thirteen years, though his first attempt at a serious subject was turned down by the Teatro S Carlo in 1835, on the grounds that the composer was too young and not sufficiently well known. In 1843 as the result of a quarrel over fees he stopped composing and supported himself by giving singing lessons and was later appointed (at least temporarily) music director at the Teatro Nuovo. In 1851 he made a brilliant return to composition with *Le precauzioni*, which received 40 performances, and in the following year *Elena di Tolosa* met with such enthusiasm at the Teatro del Fondo that it was transferred after nine days to the S Carlo. It was at this time that Petrella was taken up by the Milanese publisher Lucca. In 1854 he produced his first serious opera at the S Carlo, *Marco Visconti*, with such success that from this moment on he concentrated almost entirely on serious works.

Marco Visconti made Petrella known throughout Italy, where he became the most performed composer of his generation after Verdi. A commission followed from La Scala, Milan (*L'assedio di Leida*, 1856), and in 1858 he produced there the best-known of all his serious operas, *Jone*. The next operas had little success, but with *La contessa d'Amalfi* (Turin, 1864) Petrella produced another work that was to remain in the repertory for many years, later providing the background for a novel by Gabriele D'Annunzio.

The operas from *Celinda* (Naples, 1865) onwards show a strong influence of French *grand opéra*, which had become very popular in Italy at that time. In 1869 Petrella embarked on a setting of Manzoni's famous novel *I promessi sposi* with Ghislanzoni (the librettist of *Aida*), a project that prevented him from accepting the invitation to contribute to the *Messa per Rossini*, a composite setting designed to mark the anniversary of that composer's death the previous year. The opera was performed amid much publicity at Lecco, where the action of the novel begins, but Manzoni himself did not attend the première, as was widely believed. The great success of *I promessi sposi* stimulated Ponchielli to revise his older setting of the same subject, which later eclipsed Petrella's opera.

Petrella was one of the last composers of the old Neapolitan tradition. His first works earned him comparisons with Paisiello and Cimarosa – to the indignation of

Verdi, who wrote in 1871: 'Let's have the honest truth. … Petrella is a poor musician; his masterpiece, *Le precauzioni*, may please the amateurs with a few attractive violin tunes, but as a work of art it can't stand up, not only to the great works, but even to operas like [the Riccis'] *Crispino*, *Follia in Roma*, etc.' (Abbiati, 1959). This view was not shared by other contemporary musicians, who saw in *Le precauzioni* a spirited and full-blooded (if not very refined) example of late *opera buffa*.

Petrella was vigorous but unequal in his work: the vitality and exuberance that stood him in good stead in the comic vein were not sufficient for his serious operas, in which the melodic inspiration (central to his conception of opera) does not sustain the passion which his subjects demand; in face of the formal problems of dramatic music he was too easily content with commonplace solutions. Nevertheless, there is a real advance in dramatic consistency from *Marco Visconti* to *Jone* (particularly in the last act) and, side by side with curious ineptitudes, there are genuine beauties in the operas. The works of his last few years show a new refinement of style: in *I promessi sposi* there is more imagination in the accompaniments, and the theme of simple life is treated with a sensitivity unusual amid the thunder of contemporary Italian opera, recalling Bellini's lyrical approach.

Though sometimes despised by the critics, Petrella's most successful operas remained in the repertory of smaller Italian opera houses up to the time of World War I. As one of the most performed composers of the generation between Donizetti and Puccini, Petrella has a distinctive place in the history of Italian opera.

WORKS

OPERAS

mels – *melodramma serio*
melss – *melodramma semiserio*
melt – *melodramma tragico*

Il diavolo color di rosa (ob, 2, A.L. Tottola), Naples, Fenice, Aug 1829, *I-Nc**

Il giorno delle nozze, ovvero Pulcinella marito e non marito (commedia, 2, Tottola), Naples, Nuovo, 28 Jan 1830, *Nc**

Lo scroccone (commedia, 2, ? G. Peruzzini), Naples, Nuovo, 8 Feb 1834

La Cimodocea (melss), composed for Naples, S Carlo, *c*1835, inc.

I pirati spagnuoli (mels, 2, G.E. Bidera), Naples, Nuovo, 13 May 1838; rev. Nuovo, 16 July 1856; *Nc*, vs, excerpts (Milan, n.d.)

Le miniere di Freinbergh (melss, 2, Bidera), Naples, Nuovo, 16 Feb 1843; rev. Nuovo, 29 May 1853; *Nc*, vs, excerpts (Milan, n.d.)

Il carnevale di Venezia, ossia Le precauzioni (ob, 3, M. d'Arienzo), Naples, Nuovo, 11 May 1851; rev. Genoa, 30 Nov 1853; rev. Milan, 15 Feb 1858; *Mc**, *Nc*, vs (Naples, ?1853; Milan, n.d.)

Elena di Tolosa (melss, 3, D. Bolognese), Naples, Fondo, 12 Aug 1852, *Nc*, vs (Rome, ?1852; Milan, n.d.)

Marco Visconti (melt, 3, Bolognese, after T. Grossi), Naples, S Carlo, 9 Feb 1854, *Mr**, *Nc*, vs (Milan, 1855)

L'assedio di Leida, o Elnava (melt, prol, 3, Bolognese, after M. Cuciniello: *Elnava*), Milan, Scala, 4 March 1856 *Mr**, *Nc*, vs (Milan, 1856; Naples, ?1856)

Jone, o L'ultimo giorno di Pompei (dramma lirico, 4, Peruzzini, after E. Bulwer-Lytton), Milan, Scala, 26 Jan 1858 *Mr**, *Nc*, vs (Milan, ?1863; Naples, n.d.)

Il duca di Scilla (mels, 4, Peruzzini and L. Fortis, after V. Séjour), Milan, Scala, 24 March 1859, *Mr**, *Nc*, vs (Milan, ?1859; Naples, ?1859)

Morosina, ovvero L'ultimo de' Falieri (melt, 3, Bolognese, after Séjour), Naples, S Carlo, 6 Jan 1860, *Mr**, *Nc*, vs (Milan, ?1859; Naples, ?1859)

Il folletto di Gresy (commedia lirica, 3, Bolognese, after E. Scribe: *La part du diable*), Naples, Fondo, 28 Aug 1860, *Mr**, *Nc*, vs (Milan, ?1860)

Virginia (melt, 3, Bolognese, after V. Alfieri), Naples, S Carlo, 23 July 1861, *Mr*, *Nc*, vs, excerpts (Milan, n.d.)

La contessa d'Amalfi (mels, 4, Peruzzini, after O. Feuillet: *Dalila*), Turin, Regio, 8 March 1864, frag. *Trt**, *Nc*, vs (Turin, 1864)

Celinda (melt, 3, Bolognese), Naples, S Carlo, 11 March 1865, *Nc*, vs (Turin, 1865)

Caterina Howard (melt, 4, G. Cencetti, after A. Dumas *père*), Rome, Apollo, 7 Feb 1866, *Rsc**, vs (Milan, 1866; Turin, n.d.)

Giovanna [II] di Napoli (dramma lirico, prol, 3, A. Ghislanzoni), Naples, S Carlo, 27 Feb 1869, *Mr**, *Nc*, vs (Milan, 1869)

I promessi sposi (melss, 4, Ghislanzoni, after A. Manzoni), Lecco, Sociale, 2 Oct 1869, *Mr**, vs (Milan, 1870)

Manfredo (dramma lirico, prol, 3, G.T. Cimino, not after Byron), Naples, S Carlo, 24 March 1872, *Mr**, vs (Milan, 1872)

Bianca Orsini (mels, 4, Cimino), Naples, S Carlo, 4 April 1874, *Mr**, vs (Milan, 1874)

Diana, o La fata di Pozzuoli (ob, R. d'Ambra), c1876, not perf., *Mr**, vs (Milan, 1878)

Salambò, ossia Solima (opera-ballo, Ghislanzoni), inc., *Mr**

OTHER WORKS

Inno a Vittorio Emanuele II (D. Bolognese), Naples, S Carlo, 7 Nov 1860, *I-Nc*

Gran marcia cavalleresca … in occasione del gran torneo in Firenze, 1868

Messa funebre per la morte di Angelo Mariani, June 1873

Sacred works, albums of songs, vocal exercises, etc.

BIBLIOGRAPHY

FétisB; *FlorimoN*

G. Carotti: *Cenni biografici e ritratto di Errico Petrella* (Turin, 1877)

F. Guardione: *Di Errico Petrella e della traslazione della salma da Genova a Palermo* (Palermo, 1908)

G. Cosenza: *La vita e le opere di Errico Petrella* (Rome, 1909)

G. Siciliano: *Di Errico Petrella musicista palermitano* (Palermo, 1913)

G. Pannain: 'Saggio su la musica a Napoli nel sec. XIX, da Mercadante a Martucci', *RMI*, xxxvi (1929), 203–10; xxxvii (1930), 231–42; rev., abridged in *Ottocento musicale italiano: saggi e note* (Milan, 1952), 134–9

F. Schlitzer: 'Opere e operisti in un carteggio di Giovannina Lucca', *Mondo teatrale dell'Ottocento* (Naples, 1954), 183–212

F. Abbiati: *Giuseppe Verdi*, iii (Milan, 1959), 425

A. Camurri: 'I "promessi sposi" di Petrella', *La Scala*, nos.117–18 (1959), 32–5

M. Morini: 'Antonio Ghislanzoni, librettista di Verdi', *Musica d'oggi*, new ser., iv (1961), 56–64, 98–103

F. Fano: 'Musica e teatro a Napoli negli ultimi due secoli', *Storia di Napoli*, x (1971), 677–755

G. De Santis: *Antonio Ghislanzoni e il Teatro di Lecco* (Lecco, 1977)

J. Budden: *The Operas of Verdi*, ii (Oxford, 1978, 2/1992), 20–30

A. Pavarani Bello: 'Ghislanzoni-Manzoni e il melodramma', *Il 'Vegliardo' e gli 'Anticristi': studi su Manzoni e la Scapigliatura*, ed. R. Negri (Milan, 1978), 166–92

F. Portinari: *Pari siamo! Io la Lingua, Egli ha il Pugnale: storia del melodramma ottocentesco attraverso i suoi libretti* (Turin, 1981)

B. Baratelli: 'I Promessi sposi di Antonio Ghislanzoni', *Experienze letterarie*, ix (1986), 4, 41–80

T. Kaufmann: *Verdi and his Major Contemporaries: a Selected Chronology of Performances with Casts* (New York, 1990), 179–220

S. Werr: *Die Opern von Errico Petrella: Rezeptionsgeschichte, Interpretationen und Dokumente* (Vienna, 1999)

MICHAEL ROSE/JULIAN BUDDEN, SEBASTIAN WERR

Petreo, Magno. *See* PEDERSØN, MOGENS.

Petrescu, Ioan D(umitru) (*b* Podu-Bărbierului, Dîmboviţa district, 28 Nov 1884; *d* Bucharest, 9 May 1970). Romanian musicologist. He studied music at the Nifon Seminary, Bucharest (1895–1902), the Bucharest Conservatory (1924–8) and the Schola Cantorum in Paris under Amédée Gastoué (1928–31). He studied theology at Bucharest University (1902–7), and served as a priest in Bucharest and Paris before being appointed to teach Byzantine musical palaeography and Gregorian chant at the Bucharest Academy of Religious Music (1934–40) and the Bucharest Royal Academy of Music (1941–8). He was noted for his studies in Byzantine music, for his transcriptions and choral arrangements of early Romanian church music and for his authoritative research into medieval manuscripts from Paris, Grottaferrata and Bucharest. He established the study in Romania of comparative Byzantine musical palaeography and of the theories of psalm music transcription, making notable contributions to the study of the Byzantine modes, repertory (Christmas carols, antiphons, imperial masses) and representative composers of liturgical music.

WRITINGS

Les idiomèles et le canon de l'office de Noël (Paris, 1932)

'Les principes du chant d'église byzantin', *Actes du 4e congrès des études byzantines: Sofia 1934* [*Bulletin de l'Institut archéologique bulgare*, ix–x (1935–6)], i, 242–9

Transcrierea muzicii psaltice (Bucharest, 1937)

Condacul Naşterii Domnului [Nativity plainsongs] (Bucharest, 1940)

Laudele ingropării Domnului …(Bucharest, 1940)

Etudes de paléographie musicale byzantine, 2 vols. (Bucharest, 1967–84)

BIBLIOGRAPHY

G. Panţiru: 'O valoroasă contribuţie românească la studiul muzicii bizantine', *Muzica*, xviii (1968), no.1, pp.36–41; no.3, pp.29–33; no.7, pp.48–52

V. Cosma: *Muzicieni români: lexicon* (Bucharest, 1970), 354–5

T. Moisescu: *Prolegomene bizantine* (Bucharest, 1985)

VIOREL COSMA

Petri. German family of church musicians and composers.

(1) Balthasar Abraham Petri (*b* Sorau [now Żary, Poland], 3 Dec 1704; *d* Behnau [now Bieniów], 8 July 1793). Kantor. He was Kantor in Sorau and later a pastor in Behnau. He is said to have composed the motets *Musica laeta sonet* and *Decantabat populus* (both for 12 voices) and *Unser Herr Jesus Christus in der Nacht* (eight voices).

(2) Georg Gottfried Petri (*b* Sorau, 9 Dec 1715; *d* Görlitz, 6 July 1795). Kantor and composer, brother of (1) Balthasar Abraham Petri. After studying law for four years in Halle he practised that profession for a short time in several places; he was appointed lecturer in law in Halle in 1740, and then served as a private tutor for government officials. From 1748 he was the music director in Guben, and was assistant headmaster there from 1763 (in 1755 he had applied unsuccessfully for the post of Thomaskantor in Leipzig). When he became Kantor in Görlitz in 1764 his well-known teaching abilities as well as his knowledge of music and foreign languages were cited. He continued in that office, also directing the music at the church of St Peter und St Paul, until his death.

Petri was a prolific composer, especially of church music, but his only proven extant work is the second part of the two-volume *Musikalische Gemüths-Belustigungen* (Pförten [Brody], 1761–2), consisting of songs, keyboard pieces and violin pieces. He composed at least three yearly cycles of church cantatas and other occasional sacred works (some of the texts were published in the *Lausitzisches Magazin* from 1768); for the 200th anniversary of the Gymnasium at Görlitz in 1765 he composed *Gesang der drei Männer im Feuerofen*, a *drama musicum*, and published the essay *Oratio saecularis, qua confirmatur coniunctionem studii musici cum reliquis litterarum studiis erudito non tantum utilem esse, sed et necessariam videri* (Görlitz, 1765). According to an advertisement in the *Oberlausitzer Monatsschrift* of 1796, Petri's library at his death contained about 1000 musical works. He himself had written more than any other composer, but there were 102 works by Telemann and others by

Agricola, Bach, Doles, Graun, Hasse and Homilius. The two masses marked 'Petri' in the Luckau church archives may be by him (Biehle attributed them to (3) Johann Samuel Petri).

(3) **Johann Samuel Petri** (*b* Sorau, 1 Nov 1738; *d* Bautzen, 12 April 1808). Kantor, teacher and writer on music, son of (1) Balthasar Abraham Petri. Although at first kept away from musical activities by his father, he taught himself to play keyboard instruments and ultimately secured permission to have regular instruction from an organist (according to an autobiographical sketch in his *Anleitung*). He also taught himself to play the violin, flute, cello and harp. In 1762 he became a music teacher at the Pädagogium in Halle; there he met W.F. Bach and there was a fruitful exchange of musical ideas. From 1763 to 1770 he was Kantor and school teacher in Lauban (now Lubań), and from 1770 he held a similar post at Bautzen.

Petri's most important work was his pedagogical treatise *Anleitung zur practischen Musik, vor neuangehende Sänger und Instrumentspieler* (Lauban, 1767, enlarged 2/1782/*R*); the second edition had nearly three times as many pages as the first and included a new essay on music history. As he hoped to produce a book that could serve as a complete musical library for poor musicians, he included a wide variety of subjects: thoroughbass, playing keyboard instruments, strings and the flute, and organ building and playing (all with practical examples), as well as hints for the performance of church music. The work breaks the traditional mould for 18th-century music manuals (C.P.E. Bach, Quantz and Leopold Mozart) which, apart from providing a comprehensive introduction to music pedagogy and aesthetics, deal with only a single instrument. Petri's *Anleitung zur practischen Musik* is of historical importance as it provides thorough instructions on the playing of several musical instruments, as well as on singing. Gerber, who greatly respected Petri, praised the work as a good general text for amateurs, and it was closely studied by Jean Paul (see Schünemann). Petri's known compositions include 68 sacred works for chorus and orchestra (four have parts for solo voices) in the parish church at Żary, several Passion cantatas cited by Biehle (one published in vocal score, Leipzig, 1790) and a work for Easter in the library of his uncle (2) Georg Gottfried Petri; the two masses at Luckau may be by him or by his uncle.

(4) **Christopher Petri** (*b* Sorau, 1758). Kantor and composer, son of (1) Balthasar Abraham Petri. He studied in Leipzig and was Kantor in Lauban from 1782. He published a cantata, *Rinaldo und Armide* (vocal score, Leipzig, 1782), *Lieder und Rundgesänge* (Leipzig, 1784) and *Sechs kleine Klavier-Sonaten* (Leipzig and Sorau, 1786).

BIBLIOGRAPHY

GerberL

'Verzeichnis einer Sammlung von Kirchenmusiken', *Oberlausitzer Monatsschrift* (1796) [catalogue of the library of Georg Gottfried Petri]

M. Friedlaender: *Das deutsche Lied im 18. Jahrhundert*, i (Stuttgart and Berlin, 1902/*R*)

G. Tischer and K. Burckard, eds.: 'Musikalienkatalog der Hauptkirche zu Sorau N./L.', *MMg*, xxxiv (1902), suppl.

M. Gondolatsch: 'Georg Gottfried Petri, Kantor in Görlitz 1764–95, und sein musikalischer Nachlass', *ZMw*, iii (1920–21), 180–88

H. Biehle: *Musikgeschichte von Bautzen bis zum Anfang des 19. Jahrhunderts* (Leipzig, 1924)

G. Schünemann: 'Jean Pauls Gedanken zur Musik', *ZMw*, xvi (1934), 385–404, 459

V. Schwarz: 'Johann Samuel Petris Anweisungen zum Beziehen, Bekielen und Stimmen besaiteter Tasteninstrumente', *Der klangliche Aspekt beim Restaurieren von Saitenklavieren: Graz 1971*, 87–99

G. Weinberger: 'Zu Problemen des Finger- und Pedalsatzes in den Orgelwerken Bachs', *Musica sacra*, cv (1985), 277–88, 372–8

E. Kooiman: 'La technique de pédale: Kittel, Tuerk, Petri et Bach', *Bulletin de l'Association François-Henri Cliquot de Poitiers*, xiii (1986), 22–33

L.J. Hizer: *Performance Practice According to Johann Samuel Petri's 'Anleitung zur praktischen Musik': an Annotated Translation* (diss., Washington U., 1991)

LOTHAR HOFFMANN-ERBRECHT

Petri, Egon (*b* Hanover, 23 March 1881; *d* Berkeley, CA, 27 May 1962). German pianist and teacher of Dutch descent, later active in the USA. At the age of five he had violin lessons with his father, Henri Petri, then leader of the Leipzig Gewandhaus Orchestra. Following the family's move to Berlin in 1889 he became a pupil of the pianist Teresa Carreño. He also learnt the organ and the horn, and as a teenager studied composition and theory with Kretschmar and Draeseke. From 1901, when he joined Busoni's masterclass at Weimar, the piano became his chosen instrument. Busoni took a deep interest in his development and later described him as being his 'most genuine pupil'. Petri corrected the manuscripts of Busoni's operas and piano works, and also collaborated with him in editing Bach's keyboard works.

He made his début in Holland in 1902, although initially failed to establish a successful career. In 1905 he became a professor at the Royal Manchester College of Music and remained there until 1911, after which he returned to Berlin as Busoni's assistant. From 1921 to 1925 Petri taught at the Hochschule für Musik and pursued a busy concert schedule, with an intensive tour of Russia in 1923. He lived at Zakopane in Poland from 1925, and this remained his base until the outbreak of the Second World War. The 1930s was the busiest decade in his career. A notable American début in January 1932 opened a new chapter in both his concert and teaching activity, and he subsequently became a naturalized American. From 1940 to 1946 he was visiting professor at Cornell University, but following a serious illness he decided to move to the West Coast, and settled in California as a teacher and lecturer at Mills College, Oakland, where he remained for a further decade. He also taught at the San Francisco Conservatory. His pupils included Carl Szreter, Franz Joseph Hirt, Gunnar Johansen, Vitya Vronsky, Earl Wild, Grant Johannsen and Ernst Lévy, as well as John Ogdon, who attended his masterclasses in Basle.

Although a large-scale player in the Busoni mould, Petri's playing differed in many respects to that of his teacher. He was considerably more dutiful in regard to both correct style and adherence to the printed text. In contrast to the tonal richness of Busoni's playing, Petri's piano sound frequently had a rough edge to it. His playing was noted for a massiveness of conception and for its dedicated interpretative insight. Particularly admired in Bach, Beethoven and Liszt, Petri was also a staunch advocate of his mentor's compositions, a number of which he recorded.

JAMES METHUEN-CAMPBELL

Petri, Johann. *See* PETREIUS, JOHANN.

Petri, Michala (*b* Copenhagen, 7 July 1958). Danish recorder player. She began recorder lessons at five and left school at 11 to be tutored privately, concentrating on music from the age of 14. In 1969 she was awarded the Jacob Gade prize, which enabled her to have regular recorder lessons with Ferdinand Conrad at the Staatliche Hochschule für Musik und Theater in Hanover while also studying the flute in Copenhagen. Until 1981 she performed mostly with her mother Hanne (harpsichord) and brother David (cello), in the Petri Trio; she then performed with Hanne alone until 1992, when she formed a duo with her husband, the Danish guitarist and lutenist Lars Hannibal. Recognized as a consummate technician, she is also known for her distinctive tone, fluidity of line and expressive phrasing. Using recorders at modern pitch, she has taken the recorder beyond the early music movement to mainstream audiences, performing with James Galway, Heinz Hollinger, Pinchas Zukerman, the Academy of St Martin-in-the-Fields, the Berlin PO and others. A recording partnership with the jazz keyboard player Keith Jarrett (1990–92) inspired greater flexibility in her playing. As a soloist Petri has expanded the recorder repertory with (mainly Romantic) virtuoso transcriptions and by commissioning new works. She has published the Michala Petri Recorder Series and editions of csakan music.

BIBLIOGRAPHY
K. Wollitz and M. Bixler: 'An Interview with Michala Petri', *American Recorder*, xxvii/1 (1986), 4–8
R. Quandt: 'Michala Petri', *Tibia*, xiv/1 (1989), 341–5
G. Schliess: 'Das Instrument als Poet und Schmerzenskind: die Blockflötistin Michala Petri', *Fono forum* (1997), no.5, 50–55

DAVID LASOCKI

Petrić, Ivo (*b* Ljubljana, 16 June 1931). Slovene composer and conductor. He studied composition at the Ljubljana Academy of Music (1950–58) with Škerjanc and conducting with Švara. In 1962 he founded the Slavko Osterc Ensemble, a flexible group of about 20 players. He has directed this ensemble in outstanding recordings and performances of much adventurous contemporary music, including his own, in Slovenia and across Europe. The group ceased to operate regularly after the early 1980s. Petrić was editor-in-chief of Edicije Društva slovenskih skladateljev, the publishing section of the Association of Slovenian Composers, from 1972 to 1979. From 1979 to 1995 he was the artisitic director of the Slovenian PO. During this period he also produced a large number of recordings with the orchestra with numerous guest conductors from Slovenia and abroad. The music chosen included, as well as the standard repertory, many modern Slovenian works.

Under the influences of his teacher Škerjanc and of the music of Slavko Osterc, Petrić's music developed a refined and economical style of great melodic appeal. His early works were neo-classical, somewhat indebted to Hindemith, with a lively rhythmic subtlety and restrained melodic lines; the Clarinet Concerto (1958) is an excellent example. A change of style followed at about the time when the Slavko Osterc Ensemble was founded, and Petrić discovered the potentiality of freer expression and more advanced instrumental techniques, particularly for the harp. *Elégie* and, above all, the prizewinning *Croquis sonores* mark this change decisively. The latter work shows Petrić's propensity for clean textures and beautifully scaled forms within its short duration. Further pieces written for the ensemble – *Sept mouvements* (Radio-Televizija Belgrade Award 1963), *Mozaïki, Nuances en couleurs* and the Divertimento of 1970 – show complete mastery of new techniques; *Mozaïki* is outstanding for its lucid thinking and imaginative solo clarinet writing. Although Petrić had written three moderately conventional symphonies, he rarely wrote large orchestral works in the early 1960s, with *Symphonic Mutations* standing on its own as a boldly conceived piece in the new style. *Epitaph* and *Integrali v barvi* ('Integrals in Colours'), on the other hand, are clearly an extension of his chamber miniatures, with their fastidious attention to detail and their refined textures. *Epitaph* integrates a small concertante chamber group with orchestra, while the second work, sub-titled 'Sonorous reflections on Kosovel's poetry', neatly summarizes the composer's approach. Petrić has a feeling for the sensuous and telling, but always restrains it by a natural instinct for the right scale and manner; the greatest strength of his music is in its lack of pretence and artifice.

Petrić's music during the 1970s included many outstanding orchestral works which used freely coordinated lines with a system of conductors' cues. Notable is the violin concerto *Trois Images*, a large-scale lyrical work of 25 minutes' duration. The concentration on melodic lines and orchestral colours is particularly clear in this work and *Nocturnes et jeux*. There was also a complementary development in a series of well-crafted chamber pieces, written often for his friends. During the early 1980s Petrić began to feel the need to return to barred notation, partly for the practical reason of simplifying performance, but also to enhance the corporate rhythmic characteristics that he felt needed strengthening. Nevertheless, there was no return, except in the occasional recreational piece, to any form of traditional tonality.

WORKS
(selective list)

ORCHESTRAL

Sym. no.1 'Goga', 1954; Conc. grosso, str, 1956; Divertimento, wind, perc, 1956; Sym. no.2, 1957; Fl Conc., 1957; Cl Conc., 1958; Conc., hp, str, 1959; Koncertantna suita, bn, str, 1959; Histoire de Ferdinand, musical tale, nar, orch, 1959; Sym. no.3, 1960; Concert Ov., 1960; 3 skladba, hn, orch, 1960; Koncertantna glasba, wind qnt, str, timp, 1962; Sym. Mutations, 1964; Epitaph, cl, vn, vc, str, hp, perc, 1966; Integrali v barvi [Integrals in Colours], 1968; Intarzije [Intarsia], fl, cl, bn, chbr orch, 1968; Burlesque pour les temps passés, tpt, str, 1969; Musique concertante, pf, orch, 1971; Dialogues concertantes, vc, orch, 1972; 3 images, vn, orch, 1973; Fresque symphonique, 1973; Nocturnes et jeux, 1973; Episodes lyriques, ob, chbr orch, 1974; Gemini Conc., vn, vc, orch, 1975; Tako je godel Kurent [This is the Way to do the Kurent], va, orch, 1976; Hommage à Johannes, 1978; Jeux concertants, fl, orch, 1978; Toccata concertante, perc, orch, 1979; Groharjeve impresije [Impressions of Grohar's Paintings], 1980; Conc. for orch, 1982; Slika Doriana Graya [Picture of Dorian Gray], 1984; Adagio, 1985; Tpt Conc., 1986; Dresdener Konzert, 15 solo str, 1987; Moods and Temperaments, 1987; After so Many Years, 1989; Toccata, 1989; Gallus Metamorphoses, 1992; Fantasy, str, hp, 1993; Jubilee Conc. for Celea, str, 1994; Scottish Impressions, 1994; Štiri letni časi po Groharjev platnih [Four Seasons after Grohar's Canvases], 1995

CHAMBER AND SOLO INSTRUMENTAL

Wind Qnt no.1, 1953; Sonata, bn, pf, 1954; Prélude et scherzino, hp, 1955; Sonata, fl, pf, 1955; Sonatina, ob, pf, 1955; Variacije na temo Bele Bartóka [Variations on a theme of Bartók], vn, pf, 1955; Str Qt, 1956; Štiri skladbe [4 Pieces], pf, 1956; Mala suita [Little Suite], wind, 1956; Sonata, cl, pf, 1957; Wind Qnt no.2, 1959; Sonata, hn, pf, 1960; Sonatina, hn, pf, 1961; 3 esquisses, fl, str qt, 1961; Šest skladb [6 Pieces], fl, pf, 1961; Trije kontrasti [3

Contrasts], vn, pf, 1961; Elégie sur le nom de Carlos Salzedo, hp, 1962; Croquis sonores, b cl, hn, perc, hp, pf, db, 1963
7 mouvements, ob, cl, hn, tpt, hp, vn, vc, 1963; De profundis, tuba, tam-tam, b drum, 1963; Mozaïki, cl, trbn, hp, vc, perc, 1964; Jeux à 3 – jeux à 4, fl, cl, vc, hp, perc, 1965; Nuances en couleurs, fl, bn, pf, hp, vc, 1966; Petit conc. de chambre, ob, eng hn, b cl, hn, hp, str trio, db, 1966; Lirizmi, hn, pf, 1969; Quatuor 1969, str qt; Divertimento for Slavko Osterc, ens, 1970; Gravures, ww trio, 1971; Meditacije [Meditations], pf trio, 1971; Gemini Music, vc, pf, 1971; Les paysages, pf, 1972; Capriccio, vc, 8 insts, 1973; Summer Music, fl, pf, 1973; Autumn Music, vn, pf, 1974; Concert Improvisations, ob, vn, va, vc, 1974; Wind Qnt no.3, 1974; Dialogi, 2 vn, 1975; Gemini Concertino, vn, hn, ens, 1975; Cadenza, trbn, 1976; Capriccio Wannenhorn, fl, 1976; Sonata, vn, 1976; Winter Music, cl, pf, 1977; Fanfare in nokturni, brass qnt, 1977; Trio Labacensis, str trio, 1977; Capriccio parentium, tpt, 1978; Koncert, 5 perc, 1978; Nocturne d'été, vn, gui, 1978; Contacts, cl, perc, 1979; Esquisses poetiques, ob, 9 insts, 1979; Marcifabialom, cimb, 1979; Quatuor 1979, str qt, 1979; American Impressions, vn, vc, pf, 1980; Brass Minimusic, 2 tpt, 2 trbn, 1980; Gemini Cimbalon, 2 cimb, 1980; Introduction k kontaktom, b cl, perc, 1981; Music for 5, hn, 4 perc, 1981; Duo concertante, rec, vc, 1982; 3 kratke skladbe, bn, pf, 1982; Leipziger Kammermusik, ob, tpt, va, perc, pf, 1983; Brass Minimusic no.2, 2 tpt, 2 trbn, 1984; Winter Elegy, ob, pf, 1984; Quatuor 1985, str qt; Fantazije in nokturni, cl, vc, pf, 1986; Rondeau, str trio, pf, 1987; Battere à 3, perc, 1988; Hornspiele, hn, 1989; Chbr Sonata no.1, ob, va, b cl, hp, 1991; Chbr Sonata no.2, fl, eng hn, vn, vc, hpd, 1991; Sonata no.2, hn, pf, 1991; Toccata, pf, 1991; Portrait d'automne, str qt, 1992; Sonata, sax, pf, 1992; 2 portraits, 2 vn, pf, 1993; Pf Sonata no.1, 1993; Burlesque, 4 sax, 1994; Elegy, eng hn, str qt, 1994; Hommage à Sergej Prokofjev, ob, cl, vn, va, db, 1994; Pf Sonata no.2, 1994; Pejsaži [Landscapes], ob, va, 1995; Summer Games, cl, vc, pf, 1995; Ww Trio 95; Štiri preludiji [4 Preludes], sax, 1996; Diptich, 12 sax, 1996; Pomladna simfonija [Spring Sym.] wind qnt, str trio, db, perc, 1996

OTHER WORKS

Vocal: Je sais pour le printemps (cant), 1961; Pierrot de la mort (chbr cant), 1962; Aus den Sonetten an Orpheus (R. Rilke), T, chbr orch, 1965; Igre, 1v, hp, 1965; Igre II, 1v, hp, chbr ens, 1966; 3 satire po Krilovu, chorus, hn, tpt, trbn, perc, pf, 1970; Pesem življenja [Song of Life], Mez, orch, 1981
Odisej 67 (ballet), 1967

Principal publishers: Breitkopf & Härtel, Deutsche Verlag für Musik, Društvo slovenskih skladateljev (Ljubljana), Peters, Pizzicato (Udine)

WRITINGS

'Razvoj glasbene misli 20. stoletja' [Review of 20th-century thinking on music], Sodobnost, x (1962), 385–96, 509–17, 612–21, 767–80
'Slavko Osterc: Mouvement symphonique', Zvuk, no.53 (1962), 297–302
'Glasbena grafika: glasbeni jezik bodočnosti?' [Musical graphics: the musical language of the future?], Sodobnost, xi (1963), 151–8
'Alojz Srebotnjak: monologi', Sodobnost, xi (1963), 4, 370–73
'Jubilej ansambla Slavko Osterc', Zvuk, nos.83–4 (1973), 1, 39–42

BIBLIOGRAPHY

T. Reich: Susreti sa suvremenim kompozitorima Jugoslavije [Meetings with contemporary Yugoslav composers] (Zabreb, 1972), 238–41
A. Rijavec: 'Problem forme v delih Iva Petrića' [The problem of form in the work of Ivo Petrić], MZ, xi (1975), 101–8
N. O'Loughlin: Slovenian Composition since the First World War (diss., U. of Leicester, 1978)
A. Rijavec: Slovenska glasbena dela [Slovenian musical works] (Ljubljana, 1979), 223–32
A. Rijavec: 'Skladateljska skupina okrog ansambla "Slavko Osterc"/Komponistengruppe um das Ensemble "Slavko Osterc"', Slovenska glasba v preteklosti in sedanjosti, ed. P. Kuret (Ljubljana, 1992), 260–69
N. O'Loughlin: 'Melodic Workings in the Music of Ivo Petrić', MZ, xxix (1993), 107–19

NIALL O'LOUGHLIN

Petridis, Petros (John) (b Nigde, Turkey, 23 July 1892; d Athens, 20 Aug 1977). Greek composer. During his education in Istanbul at the Zografeion High School (c1902–6) and at the American Robert College (until 1911) he studied the piano with Hegey, reputedly a pupil of Liszt, and harmony with Italo Selvelli. From 1911 to 1914 he read law at the Sorbonne and political science at the Ecole Libre des Sciences Politiques. In Paris he met Riadis, Varvoglis and Theodoros Spathis and abandoned his planned career for music. He took Greek nationality in 1913. For brief periods he was a pupil of Albert Wolff (1914) and of Roussel (1919) but considered himself self-taught. He contributed music reviews to the Musical Times (1915–31) and to the Christian Science Monitor; for more than 50 years he was a music critic for such prominent Greek newspapers as Vima and Kathimerini. In this capacity he replaced the superficial style current in Greece by assessments based on technical study. During 1918–19 he directed the information office of the Greek Embassy in London, at the same time lecturing on Greek folklore and music at King's College. He taught modern Greek at the Sorbonne (1919–21) and after 1922 divided his time between Athens and Paris. In 1959 he was elected a member of the Athens Academy and also a corresponding member of the French Academy in succession to Sibelius.

Petridis has slowly gained recognition as a highly significant figure in Greek musical history, although his compositions are rarely perofrmed. His early works, from Kléftikoi horoi ('Cleftic Dances', 1922) to Dighenis Akritas (1933–9), a gigantic, programmatic fresco dedicated to a 10th-century Byzantine hero, include some of the finest achievements of Greek orchestral literature: based on Greek folk music, they demonastrate sound construction, solid counterpoint and a certain harmonic daring. Around the 1930s, as Petridis gravitated increasingly towards the Orthodox Church, his harmony became more conventional. More than any other composer of his generation he orientated himself towards Byzantine chant, writing in a modal or polymodal contrapuntal style that became increasingly ascetic. His melodies tend to move stepwise within a narrow compass, shunning bold modulations, while his orchestration and polyphony are sober, avoiding superficial effect and adhering to traditional forms (fugue, variations, symphony, etc.). The tension in his creativity between East and West, asceticism and sensuality, authority and individual freedom, are clearly depicted in his unperformed opera Zefyra or Zemfyra.

WORKS

STAGE

Kyra phrossyni, ballet; Theseus, ballet; Zefyra (Zemfyra) (op, 3 Petridis, after G. Drossinis), 1923–5, rev. 1958–64, concert perf., Athens, National State Opera, 30 April 1991; Iphigenia in Tauris (incid music, Euripides), 1941, Athens, Greek National, 15 Oct 1941; O prameteftis [The Pedlar] (ballet, 2, Petridis, after Y. Gryparis), 1941–3, Athens, National State Opera, 6 May 1944

INSTRUMENTAL

Orch: Paneghyri [The Village Fair], 1920–24, ?destroyed; Kléftikoi horoi [Cleftic Dances], 1922, rev.; Eisagogi se tria ellinika thémata [Ov. on Gk. themes], before, 1926, ?destroyed; Sym. no.1 'Greek', g, 1928–9; Conc. grosso, wind, timp, 1929; Gk. Suite, 1929–30; Va Conc., before ?1932, ?lost, ?destroyed; Dighenis Akritas, sym., after Byzantine epic, ?1933–9; Studies, small orch, perf. 1934; Pf Conc. no.1, c, 1934, ?rev. 1948; Vyzantini thyssia [Byzantine Offering], 1935; Ionian Suite, 1936; Vc Conc., 1936, lost; Pf Conc. no.2, d, 1937; Conc. no.1, str, 1939; Chorale and Variations no.2 on 'Christos anesti', str, 1939; Chorale and Variations no.1 on 'Kyrie ton dynameon', str, 1940; Uvertura se dhyo ellinika thémata [Ov. on 2 Gk. Themes], destroyed, transcr. military band, 1940; Sym. no.2 'Lyric', d and a, 1941; Sym. no.4 'Doric'

('Pindos'), c, 1942; Largo, str, 1944; Issagoghi penthimi ke heroiki [Funeral and Heroic Ov.], 1944; Sym. no.3 'Parisian', D, 1944–6; Sym. no.5 'Pastoral', F, 1949–51, rev. 1972–3, lost; Conc., orch, 1951; Vn Conc., 1972; Conc., 2 pf, 1972; Emvatirion poreias [Marching March], military band; Pénthimon emvatirion [Funeral March], military band; Heroikon emvatirion [Heroic March], military band

Chbr: Sonata, fl, pf, before 1932, ?destroyed, ?lost; Sonata, vc, pf, before 1932, ?destroyed, ?lost; Kammersymphonie, ww qt, str qt, before 1932, ?destroyed, ?lost; Pf Qt, before 1932, ?destroyed, ?lost; The Modal and Bimodal kbd, pf, after 1932; Pf Trio, 1933/1934; Str Qt, 1951, inc.

OTHER WORKS

Choral: Hayos Pavlos [St Paul] (orat, Petridis, from Bible), nar, S, Mez, T, B, 8 subsidiary solo vv, chorus, orch, 1950–51

Requiem ya ton aftokratora [Requiem for the Emperor] (Petridis, after Orthodox funeral mass), S, Mez, T, B, chorus, orch, 1952–64

Solo vocal: 4 mélodies grecques (A. Valaoritis, trad.), S, pf, 1917–22; Ti ypermacho stratigo, Byzantine church monody, S, A, T, B, pf/org, 1920; 5 mélodies grecques (K. Krystallis, K. Palamas, L. Mavilis, Y. Gryparis), S, pf, 1924; Thrylos agapis [The Legend of Love] (L. Porphyras), Mez, pf/orch, 1925; 13 Songs (T. Dekker and others), S, pf, 1945, lost; 40 mélodies populaires grecques harmonisées, S, pf; Arrs. of songs by E. Riadis

2 scores for son et lumière, Akropolis, Athens

Principal publisher: Schott, Greek Ministry of Culture and Sciences

WRITINGS

ed. V. Fidetzis: 'Ta prota keimena' [The early texts], Moussikologhia, nos.7–8 (1989), 130–67 [collection of articles orig. pubd in Esperia, Greek-speaking London newspaper, 22 May–16 Sept 1916]

Folklore and Greek Music (London, 1919) [lecture at King's College, London, 21 March 1919]

BIBLIOGRAPHY

MGG1 (M.E. Dounias)

G. Sklavos: 'Petridis, Petros', Megali elliniki engyklopaedia [Great Greek Encyclopedia], xx (Athens, 1932), 122 only

S.K. Spanoudi: 'I exelixis tis hellenikis moussikis apo tou 1821 mehri ton imeron mas' [The development of Greek music from 1821 to the present], Helios, vii (Athens, c1950), 1035 only

S.K. Spanoudi: 'Petridis, Petros', Helios, xv (Athens, c1950), 844 only

F. Anoyanakis: 'I mousiki stin neoteri Ellada' [Music in modern Greece], in K. Nef: Istoria tis moussikis [Gk. edn of Einführung in die Musikgeschichte] (Athens, 1958), 593–4

G. Leotsakos: 'Petridis opos ton ézisa' [My personal recollections from Petridis], To vims tis kyriakis (4 Sept 1977) [obituary]

G. Leotsakos: 'Petridis, Petros', Pangosmio viografiko lexico [Univeral biographical dictionary], viii (Athens, 1988), 244–5

For further bibliography and list of works see Moussikologhia, nos.7–8 (1989), 119–29

GEORGE LEOTSAKOS

Petrie, George (b Dublin, 1 Jan 1790; d Dublin, 17 Jan 1866). Irish artist, antiquary, violinist and folksong collector. His father, a portrait painter and miniaturist of Scottish descent, wished him to be trained as a surgeon, but Petrie showed a much greater inclination towards landscape painting, developing a particular skill in the area of draughtsmanship. In 1828 he was elected to the Royal Irish Academy and to the Royal Hibernian Academy, becoming librarian of the latter in 1830 and president in 1857.

In his introduction to The Ancient Music of Ireland (1855), Petrie notes that 'from my very boy-days, whenever I heard an air which in any degree touched my feelings, or appeared to me to be either an unpublished one, or a better version of an air than what had already been printed, I never neglected to note it down'. Several of these tunes found their way to Thomas Moore (ii) and appeared in his Selection of Irish Melodies, which were serially published from 1808; Petrie was also a substantial

contributor to a collection by his friend Francis Smollet Holden the younger. He met Edward Bunting soon after the latter published the second volume of A General Collection of the Ancient Irish Music in 1809, and remained his lifelong friend. Although he offered Bunting his complete collection, only 17 of the 'airs' were included in the 1840 volume, Bunting being unhappy with Petrie's requirement that his involvement be acknowledged. The founding of the Society for the Preservation and Publication of the Melodies of Ireland, with Petrie as president, and the devastating effects of the famine of 1846–7 on the musical life of the peasantry, stimulated the publication in 1855 of a small portion of the melodies as The Ancient Music of Ireland, with piano accompaniments written in the main by his daughter. A brief posthumous second volume was published in 1882. The complete manuscript of 2148 melodies was passed to C.V. Stanford, who removed a number of duplicates and published the remaining 1582 items in three volumes between 1902 and 1905, without song texts or piano accompaniment, with the assistance of the Irish Literary Society of London.

Petrie's importance is in the isolation of what have now come to be known as 'tune families'. He disputed Bunting's assertion that 'a strain of music, once impressed on the popular ear, never varies', and noted as many as 50 variants of a single melody. Although perhaps less of a practical musician than Bunting, he was probably the finer scholar, and The Complete Collection must be regarded as one of the most important 19th-century resources of Irish traditional music.

WRITINGS

The Petrie Collection of The Ancient Music of Ireland (Dublin, 1855)
Ancient Music of Ireland (Dublin, 1882)

BIBLIOGRAPHY

C. Graves: 'Address on the loss sustained by Archaeological Science in the death of George Petrie, LL.D.', Proceedings of the Royal Irish Academy, ix (1867), 325–36

W. Stokes: The Life and Labours in Art and Archaeology of George Petrie (London, 1868)

C.V. Stanford, ed.: The Complete Collection of Irish Music as Noted by George Petrie (London, 1902–5)

G.J. Calder: George Petrie and the Ancient Music of Ireland (Dublin, 1968)

DAVID COOPER

Petrini. German family of harpists and composers, of Italian descent.

(1) Petrini [first name unknown] (b Germany, after 1660; d Berlin, 1750). Harpist. He was a chamber musician at the court of Frederick the Great and the Berlin opera house for many years. In 1736 he was one of 17 musicians who moved with the court of Frederick the Great from Ruppin to Rheinsberg. In 1740 C.P.E. Bach composed a harp sonata for him. Marpurg wrote that Petrini was one of the greatest virtuosos of his time, and that he played in all 24 keys with equal dexterity.

(2) (Marie) Therese Petrini (b Berlin, 1736; d Berlin, after 1800). Singer and harpist, daughter of (1) Petrini. She received both singing and harp lessons from her father, and after his death followed him as harpist at the court of Frederick the Great, where J.F. Agricola taught her to sing with thoroughbass. She was said to have 'the soul of her father'. In 1754 she was a singer and harpist at the chapel of Margrave Karl Albrecht of Brandenburg-Schwedt in Berlin. She often sang publicly in Berlin, including the second soprano part at the première of C.H.

Graun's *Der Tod Jesu* (1755) at Berlin Cathedral. Later she was a chamber musician in Strelitz.

(3) **Francesco** [François, Franz] **Petrini** (*b* Berlin, 1744; *d* Paris, 1819). Harpist, teacher and composer, son of (1) Petrini. He studied the harp with his father, whom he soon surpassed in virtuosity. In 1765 he became harpist and chamber musician at the court of Mecklenburg-Schwerin, where he also studied composition. In 1769 he went to Paris, and in 1770 gave his début at the Concert Spirituel and published his op.1, a set of six sonatas for harp with optional violin accompaniment, dedicated to Prince Louis of Rohan. By 1787 he had published numerous works for the harp, including sonatas with violin accompaniment, concertos, duets, collections of airs and variations and symphonies with harp. When other harpists were leaving Paris during the Revolution, Petrini remained; several of his works written after 1800 have titles inspired by contemporary political events, among them *Bataille du Wagram* (1809), commemorating the Empire's victory over the Austrians. He began the monthly journal *Glaneur lyrique* in about 1795, and published a harp method (reprinted up to the 20th century) and several books on harmony. The Fourth Concerto op.29 is remarkable for its romantic cadenza in the first movement (see Vernillat). According to Gerber, he was still active in Paris in 1813.

His son Henri Petrini (*b* Paris, 1775; *d* Paris, *c*1800), to whom he taught the harp, revealed a marked talent as a harpist. He composed two sets of sonatas as well as some other pieces for the harp; he died young.

WORKS
extant works only; published in Paris, undated unless otherwise stated

Orch: 5 concs., hp, orch, 2 as op.18 (arr. for hp of works by 'Mr Bach' and 'Mr J.-B. Davaux', *c*1782), no.1 as op.25 (1786), no.3 as op.27, no.4, B♭, as op.29 (1793, see *GerberL*); 4 syms., hp, fl, 2 hn, str, op.36
Duos: 2 hp/(hp, pf)/2 pf, op.7 (?1773); 2 hp (vn, bc, ad lib), op.31
Sonatas (hp, vn ad lib): 6 as op.1 (1769); 6 as op.3; 2 as op.4; 3me livre, op.9; 2 as 4me livre, op.10 (*c*1780); 1 as op.39; 4 as op.40 (1801)
Airs with variations (hp): 3 petits airs, op.2 (1774); 2me recueil, op.8 (1774); 3me recueil, with vn, ob (1774); 4me–5me recueil, with vn, ob, op.12–13 (*c*1778); 6me recueil, with bn, vc, op.14 (1778); 7me recueil, op.15; op.16 (1779); op.17 (*c*1780–*c*1785); 3me recueil, ii, with fl, 2 vn, op.19 (1783); airs, ouvertures, sonata movements, pubd in *Delamanière at Delaplanque*, i/11 (*c*1790), in *GB-Lbl*; variations on Le réveil du peuple de Gaveaux, Vive Henri IV, Bataille du Wagram; several others pubd separately
Other works: 6 divertimentos, hp, fl, vn, bc (1772); 3 preludes, hp, bc

WRITINGS

Méthode de harpe (Paris, n.d. [?lost], rev. 1796 as *Abrégé de la méthode de harpe avec la manière de l'accorder*)
Nouveau système de l'harmonie en 60 accords (Paris, 1793)
Règles de l'harmonie, rendues plus faciles par une suite de leçons en forme de préludes, op.51 (Paris, n.d.)
Etude préliminaire de la composition, selon le nouveau système de l'harmonie en 60 accords (Paris, 1810)

BIBLIOGRAPHY
Choron-FayolleD; *FétisB*; *GerberL*; *GerberNL*; *MCL*
F. Marpurg: *Historisch-kritische Beyträge zur Aufnahme der Musik* (Berlin, 1754–78/*R*), 158
C. von Ledebur: *Tonkünstler-Lexicon Berlin's* (Berlin, 1861/*R*), 414–15
E.B. Schnapper, ed.: *British Union Catalogue of Early Music Printed before 1801* (London, 1957)
F. Vernillat: 'La littérature de la harpe en France au XVIIIe siècle', *RMFC*, ix (1969), 162–85
H.J. Zingel: *Die Entwicklung des Harfenspiels*, iv (Leipzig, 1969), 170, 172, 174

ALICE LAWSON ABER-COUNT

Petri Nylandensis, Theodoricus. *See* THEODORICUS PETRI NYLANDENSIS.

Petrobelli [Pietrobelli], **Francesco** (*b* Vicenza; *d* Padua, 31 March 1695). Italian composer and organist. He described the contents of his first published work (1643) as the 'products … of my earliest youth'. He was a member of the clergy. On 9 June 1647 he competed unsuccessfully for the organist's position at Vicenza Cathedral, but on 22 August he was appointed *maestro di cappella* of Padua Cathedral at an annual salary that in 1659 reached 150 ducats. In November 1652 he was at the court of Innsbruck with several companions. Although pensioned on 8 November 1684, he may have played one of the organs at S Antonio in Padua after this date; he continued to publish to the end of his life. He was chiefly a composer of concerted church music; his one surviving opera, *Il Teseo in Creta*, is old-fashioned by Venetian standards, and its melodic writing is often rambling and dull.

WORKS
SACRED
published in Venice unless otherwise stated

Motetti, 1v (1643)
Motetti, 2–5vv, op.2 (1651)
Motetti, 2, 3vv, e Letanie della B.V., lib.2, op.5 (Antwerp, 1660, but perhaps originally pubd Venice, 1657; see Walther)
Psalmi, 2–4vv, 2 vn, org [?op.6] (1662)
Musiche sacre concertate con istromenti, 3vv, 2 vn, va, bn/str, bc, op.8 (Bologna, 1670); 1 psalm in *Seventeenth-Century Italian Sacred Music*, xi (New York, 1995)
Sacri concentus, 2 or more vv, 2 vn, va, bc (Bologna, 1670) [? = Musiche sacre]
Ave beata virgo, 1670[1]
Motetti, antifone, e letanie della B. Vergine, 2vv, org, op.11 (Bologna, 1677)
Psalmi breves, 8vv, op.16 (1684)
Salmi dominicali, 8vv, op.19 (1686), ?lost
Psalmi, 8vv, op.25 (1694) [also as op.17]

OPERAS

Angelica in India (P.P. Bissari), Vicenza, 1656; authorship doubtful, lib of Teseo in Creta attributes an 'Angelica' to Petrobelli, music lost
Il Teseo in Creta ('A.P.D.'), Padua, 1672, *I-Vnm*

OTHER SECULAR
printed works published in Venice unless otherwise stated

Scherzi amorosi, 2–3vv, op.4 (1652)
Scherzi amorosi, 2–3vv, vns ad lib, op.7 (1668)
Musiche da camera, 2–4vv, vns, op.9 (Bologna, 1673)
Cantate, 1, 2vv, bc, op.10 (Bologna, 1676)
Musiche da camera, op.15 (1682), according to Fétis
Scherzi musicali per fuggir l'ozio, 2–3vv, insts, op.24 (1693), ?lost
Cantata, 2vv, 2 ob, bc, *D-Bsb*; perhaps identical with a cantata from op.9
Aria, *I-Fn*

BIBLIOGRAPHY
EitnerQ; *FétisB*; *GaspariC*; *GerberL*; *GerberNL*; *MGG1* (O. Mischiati); *RicordiE*; *SennMT*; *VogelB*; *WaltherML*
G. Mantese: *Storia musicale vicentina* (Vicenza, 1956)
A. Sartori: *Documenti per la storia della musica al Santo e nel Veneto* (Verona, 1977)
F. Passadore: 'I musicisti del Santo e della Cattedrale di Padova in antologie sacre dei secoli xvi e xvii', *Contributi per la storia della musica sacra a Padova* (Padua, 1993), 191–212

THOMAS WALKER/R

Petrobelli, Pierluigi (*b* Padua, 18 Oct 1932). Italian musicologist. He studied composition with Pedrollo at the Liceo Musicale of Padua and took an arts degree (1957) at the University of Rome, having completed a dissertation on Tartini under Luigi Ronga. After teaching liberal arts subjects in secondary schools for two years, he continued his music studies at Princeton University under Lockwood, Mendel and Strunk with the aid of a Fulbright Grant (MFA 1961). He also spent some time at Harvard University and the University of California, Berkeley, where in 1963 he collaborated on a thematic catalogue of the university library holdings of 18th-century instrumental music. On his return to Italy he resumed secondary school teaching (1963–4) and was appointed librarian-archivist at the Istituto Nazionale di Studi Verdiani, Parma (1964–9), becoming director in 1980. From 1968 to 1972 he was lecturer and later reader in music history at the University of Parma; in 1970 he also assumed direction of the library of the Pesaro Conservatory. He took the *libera docenza* in 1972 and was appointed lecturer in music at King's College, London (1973–6), and reader in musicology there (1977–80). He was professor of music history at the universities of Perugia (1981–3) and Rome 'La Sapienza' (1983), and Visiting Professor of Italian culture and civilization at the universities of California, Berkeley (1988) and Harvard (1996). He was on the editorial board of *Rivista Italiana di Musicologia* (1968–72), and has been a member of the Advisory Board (1973–90) and the Commission Mixte (from 1990) of the Répertoire International des Sources Musicales (RISM). He is the editor of *Studi verdiani*, which he founded in 1982, and he has been a member of the Accademia Filarmonica Romana since 1994.

Petrobelli is one of the best trained of the postwar generation of Italian musicologists, and has played an active part in international musicological circles (he was a member of the Programme Committee of the 1972 IMS conference in Copenhagen). One of his main interests has been the life and works of Tartini: his earliest research, in his university dissertation *Contributi alla conoscenza della personalità e dell'opera di Giuseppe Tartini* (1957), was followed by a book and several articles. Other interests include Verdi (particularly his creative processes), Venetian opera of the early 17th century, the Italian Ars Nova and 20th-century music, particularly Dallapiccola.

WRITINGS

'L'"Ermiona" di Pio Enea degli Obizzi e i primis spettacoli d'opera veneziani', *Quaderni della RaM*, no.3 (1965), 125–41
'Due mottetti francesi in una sconosciuta fonte udinese', *CHM*, iv (1966), 201–14
'Francesco Manelli: documenti e osservazioni', *Chigiana*, xxiv, new ser. iv (1967), 43–66
'"Ahi, dolente partita": Marenzio, Wert, Monteverdi', *Claudio Monteverdi et il suo tempo: Venice, Mantua and Cremona 1968*, 361–76
Giuseppe Tartini: le fonti biografiche (Vienna, London and Milan, 1968)
'Some Dates for Bartolino da Padova', *Studies in Music History: Essays for Oliver Strunk*, ed. H. Powers (Princeton, NJ, 1968), 94–112
'L'Alceste di Calzabigi e Gluck e l'illuminismo e l'opera', *Quadrivium*, xii/2 (1971), 279–94
'Balzac, Stendhal e il "Mosè" di Rossini', *Annuario 1965–1970 del Conservatorio G.B. Martini di Bologna* (1971), 203–19
with H. Weinberg: 'Roger Sessions e la musica americana', *NRMI*, v (1971), 249–63
'The Italian Years of Anton Raaff', *MJb 1973–4*, 233–73
'"Un leggiadretto velo" ed altre cose petrarchesche', *RIM*, x (1975), 32–45
'La partitura del "Massimo Puppieno" di Carlo Pallavicino', *Venezia e il melodramma nel Seicento*, ed. M.T. Muraro (Florence, 1976), 273–97
'"Don Giovanni" in Italia: la fortuna dell'opera e la sua influenza', *AnMc*, no.18 (1978), 30–51
'Haydn e lo "Sturm und Drang"', *Chigiana*, xxxvi, new ser. xvi (1979), 65–72

'John Dowland e la musica a Firenze alla fine del '500', *Firenze e la Toscana dei Medici nell'Europa del Cinquecento: Florence 1980*, ii, 539–48
'Il musicista di teatro settecentesco nelle caricature di Pierleone Ghezzi', *Antonio Vivaldi: Venice 1981*, 415–26
'Goldoni at Esterhaza: the Story of his Librettos set by Haydn', *Joseph Haydn: Vienna 1982*, 314–18
'Violin Technique in Rome during the First Half of the 18th Century', *Jakob Stainer und seine Zeit* (Innsbruck, 1984), 175–85
'"Il Re pastore": una serenata', *MJb 1984–5*, 109–14
'Il mondo del teatro in musica nelle caricature di Pierleone Ghezzi', *Le muse galanti: la musica a Roma nel Settecento* (Rome, 1985), 109–17
'On "Reading" Musical Caricatures: some Italian Examples', *Imago musicae*, ii (Lucca, 1985), 135–42
'Pergolesi and Ghezzi Revisited', *Music in the Classic Period: Essays in Honor of Barry S. Brook*, ed. A.W. Atlas (New York, 1985), 213–20
'"Il re pastore" von Johann Adolph Hasse (Dresden, 1755)', *Dresdner Operntraditionen* (Dresden, 1986), 174–85
'Poesia e musica', *Letteratura italiana*, ed. A. Asor Rosa, vi (Turin, 1986), 229–44
'Un caso di trasmissione e recezione delle forme di cultura musicale: la musica di Verdi', *IMSCR XIV: Bologna 1987*, 285–7
'On Dante and Italian Music: Three Moments', *COJ*, ii (1990), 219–49
'"Il re pastore" di Guglielmi e di Mozart', *Mozart e i musicisti italiani del suo tempo: Rome 1991*, 43–53
'Mozart e la lingua italiana', *Convegno mozartiano: Rome 1991*, 37–46
'Problemi di ecdotica nel repertorio operistico: a proposito di "Così fan tutte"', *L'edizione critica tra testo musicale e testo letterario: Cremona 1992*, 319–25
Tartini, le sue idee e il suo tempo (Lucca, 1992)
'Boito e Verdi', *Arrigo Boito: Venice 1993*, 261–73
'Rossini nell'opera e nella vita di Verdi', *La recezione di Rossini ieri e oggi: Rome 1993*, 15–25
'Tre poemi', *Studi su Luigi Dallapiccola*, ed. A. Quattrocchi (Lucca, 1993), 5–13
Music in the Theater: Essays on Verdi and other Composers (Princeton, 1994)
'Dallapiccola e Busoni', *Dallapiccola: letture e prospettive: Empoli 1995*, 25–33
'Le sonate per organo di Gaetano Valeri', *Le fonti della ricerca musicale: studi per Claudio Sartori*, ed. M. Donà and F. Lesure (Lucca, 1997)

EDITIONS

with W. Rehm: W.A. Mozart: *Il re pastore*, Neue Ausgabe sämtlicher Werke, ii/5–9 (Kassel, 1985)
with M. Girardi: *Messa par Rossini* (Milan, 1988)
G. Rossini: *Petite messe solennelle*, Fondazione Rossini (forthcoming)

CAROLYN GIANTURCO

Petrograd. *See* ST PETERSBURG.

Petros Bereketes. *See* BEREKETES, PETROS.

Petros Byzantios (*b* Neochorios, Bosphorus, mid-18th century; *d* Iaşi, 1808). Romaic (Greek) composer and scribe. First mentioned in the records of the Ecumenical Patriarchate as second *domestikos* (1771), he rose over the next three decades through the hierarchy of patriarchal cantors, serving as first *domestikos*, *lampadarios* (1789–1800) and, in succession to Jakobos Peloponnesios, *prōtopsaltēs* (1800–05). Dismissed from this last position by Patriarch Kallinikos IV for entering into a second marriage, he left Constantinople for Kherson in the Crimea (thereby acquiring the sobriquet *ho fugas*, 'the fugitive') and later travelled to Iaşi, Moldavia, where he died.

In 1791, together with JAKOBOS PELOPONNESIOS, Petros founded the Third Patriarchal School of Music. Wheareas the conservative Jakobos would teach only chants in traditional styles to be sung with considerable rhythmic freedom, Petros, according to his student Chrysanthos of Madytos, supplemented the older repertories with the works of his own teacher PETROS PELOPONNESIOS and favoured a steady pulse. Numerous autograph manuscripts of the period 1773–1806 show how he significantly advanced Petros Peloponnesios's work, composing many chants to fill out the latter's hymnodic and psalmodic collections (including supplementary *katabasiai* for his Heirmologion). He also continued to produce florid realizations (*exēgēseis*) of older chants, not only by Petros Peloponnesios but also by composers such as Balasios, Daniel the Protopsaltes, Manuel Gazes, Joannes Kladas and Joannes Koukouzeles, by writing out orally transmitted melismas.

Although Petros Byzantios was fluent in the melismatic and neumatic papadikē and stichērarion styles, his syllabic setting of the entire Heirmologion for the Divine Office, which forms the basis of modern performances of Byzantine kanons, is probably his most influential work; it was edited and transcribed by CHOURMOUZIOS THE ARCHIVIST and published in 1825. His other chants for the Divine Office include several Great Doxologies, settings, in the 'new sticheraric style', of the opening verses of Lauds ('Hoi ainoi') at Orthros and the 'lamplighting' psalms at Hesperinos, and an *amomos* (Psalm cxviii). For the eucharistic liturgies he wrote communion verses for Sundays and feasts of the liturgical year and a modally ordered series of eight Cherubic hymns. A number of his major original and exegetical works were first published in Chrysanthine editions (see bibliography). Petros is also said to have written secular songs (see Romanou) and to have been an accomplished performer of Arabo-Persian music on the ney and tanbur (Papadopolous). (For a fuller list of works, including manuscripts featuring Petros's original notation, see Chatzēgiakoumēs, 1975, pp.364–7.)

BIBLIOGRAPHY

CHRYSANTHINE MUSIC EDITIONS

P. Ephesios, ed.: *Neon anastasimatarion metaphrasthen kata tēn neophanē methodon tēs mousikēs hypo tōn en Kōnstantinoupolei mousikologiōtatōn didaskalōn kai epheuretōn tou neou mousikou systēmatos* [New anastasimatarion transcribed according to the newly appeared method of the musical teachers and inventors of the new musical system] (Bucharest, 1820)

T. Phōkaeus, ed.: *Tameion anthologias* [Treasury of an anthology] (Constantinople, 1824) [transcr. Chourmouzios the Archivist]

Chourmouzios the Archivist, transcr. and ed.: *Heirmologion tōn katabasiōn Petrou tou Peloponnēsiou meta tou Syntomou heirmologiou Petrou Prōtopsaltou tou Byzantiou* [Heirmologion of the *katabasiai* of Petros Peloponnesios with the *Short Heirmologion* of Petros Byzantios the Protopsaltes] (Constantinople, 1825/R)

T. Phōkaeus, ed.: *Tameion anthologias* [Treasury of an anthology] (Constantinople, 1834) [transcr. Gregorios the Protopsaltes]

I. Lampadarios and Stephanos the First Domestikos, eds.: *Pandektē* (Constantinople, 1850–51) [transcr. Gregorios the Protopsaltes]

STUDIES

Chrysanthos of Madytos: *Theōrētikon mega tēs mousikēs* [Great theoretical treatise on music] (Trieste, 1832/R)

G.I. Papadopoulos: *Historikē episkopēsis tēs byzantinēs ekklēsiastikēs mousikēs apo tōn apostolikōn chronōn mechri tōn kath' hēmas (1–1900 m. Ch.)* [An historical survey of Byzantine ecclesiastical music from apostolic times to our own (1–1900 CE)] (Athens, 1904/R)

G.T. Stathēs: 'Hē synchysē tōn triōn Petrōn (dēl. Bereketē, Peloponnēsiou kai Byzantiou' [The confusion of the three Peters (i.e. Bereketes, Peloponnesios and Byzantios], *Byzantina*, iii (1971), 213–51

C.G. Patrinelis: 'Protopsaltae, Lampadarioi and Domestikoi of the Great Church during the Post-Byzantine Period (1453–1821)',

Studies in Eastern Chant, iii, ed. M. Velimirović (London, 1973), 141–70

G.T. Stathēs: *Ta cheirographa byzantinēs mousikēs: Hagion Oros* [The MSS of Byzantine Music: Holy Mountain] (Athens, 1975–93)

M. Chatzēgiakoumēs: *Cheirographa ekklēsiastikēs mousikēs (1453–1820)* [MSS of ecclesiastical music] (Athens, 1980)

A. Şirli: *The Anastasimatarion: the Thematic Repertory of Byzantine and Post-Byzantine Musical Manuscripts (the 14th-19th centuries)*, i (Bucharest, 1986)

K. Romanou: *Ethnikēs mousikēs periēgēsis 1901–1912: hellēnika mousika periodika hōs pēgē ereunas tēs historias tus neoellēnikēs mousikēs* [A journey in national music, 1901–12: Greek music periodicals as a research source for the history of modern Greek music] (Athens, 1996)

ALEXANDER LINGAS

Petros Peloponnesios (*b* c1730; *d* Constantinople, 1778). Greek chanter, composer and teacher of Byzantine music. He received his first music lessons in monastic communities in Smyrna (Papadopoulos). In 1764 he travelled to Constantinople, where he became associated with the well-known *prōtopsaltēs* of Hagia Sophia, Joannes Trapezountios, with whom he chanted as second *domestikos* in the right choir. He held this office until his promotion to *lampadarios* (leader of the left choir) between 1769 and 1773. He was made an instructor in the second patriarchal school of music, founded in 1776, and from this time his reputation as an important teacher and composer was established. It is reported that he was also a specialist in Armenian and Turkish music and that he composed melodies based on the oriental *maqāmāt*.

Petros contributed a number of original compositions to the Offices and liturgies of the Greek Church, including complete sets of Cheroubic Hymns and communion chants in all eight modes, as well as music for funerals, ordinations, baptisms, weddings etc. In addition, he composed exercises and lessons for students of chant. Although his life as a composer was short (he died prematurely when a plague swept Constantinople in 1778), he proved to be the most prolific writer of the post-Byzantine period and his works are available in many musical anthologies from the 18th and 19th centuries.

Apart from original compositions, Petros produced many 'interpretations' of older chant melodies, writing a full realization (*exēgēsis*) of the ornamental signs in the neumatic line of the earlier manuscripts. This system was further developed by PETROS BYZANTIOS, his pupil, and subsequently employed by the three reformers of Byzantine notation, CHRYSANTHOS OF MADYTOS, GREGORIOS THE PROTOPSALTES and CHOURMOUZIOS THE ARCHIVIST. One manuscript in particular, *GR-AOk* ε 103 (late 18th-century), contains Petros's interpretations of works by the 14th-century musicians JOANNES GLYKYS and JOANNES KOUKOUZELES.

Petros Peloponnesios was the first to introduce the *syntomon* ('quick') melodies into the liturgical anthologies. These were designed for ordinary services requiring simple, unembellished chants. The revisions he made between 1765 and 1775 of virtually all the earlier music books (anastasimatarion, heirmologion and doxastarion) quickly gained a wide reputation; they gradually replaced the older editions and settings of PANAGIOTES THE NEW CHRYSAPHES, BALASIOS and GERMANOS OF NEW PATRAS, and are still predominant within the Greek chant repertory. Continuing the work of Joannes Trapezountios, Petros developed a simpler, more analytical system of musical writing which contributed to the formulation that took place in the early 19th century.

BIBLIOGRAPHY

FétisB

G.I. Papadopoulos: *Symbolai eis tēn historian tēs par' hēmin ekklēsiastikēs mousikēs* [Contribution to the history of our ecclesiastical music] (Athens, 1890/R), 318–24

K.A. Psachos: *Hē parasēmantikē tēs byzantinēs mousikēs* [The notation of Byzantine music] (Athens, 1917, 2/1978)

S. Karas: *Hē byzantinē mousikē sēmeiographeia* [Byzantine musical semiography] (Athens, 1933)

H.J.W. Tillyard: 'Byzantine Music at the End of the Middle Ages', *Laudate*, xi (1933), 141–51

D. Stefanović and M. Velimirović: 'Peter Lampadarios and Metropolitan Serafim of Bosnia', *Studies in Eastern Chant*, i, ed. M. Velimirović (London, 1966), 67–88

P. Georgiou: 'Petros ho Peloponnēsios', *Thrēskeutikē kai ēthikē enkyklopaideia* [Encyclopedia of religion and ethics], x (Athens, 1967), 318–24

G. Stathēs: 'I synchysē tōn triōn Petrōn' [The confusion of the three Peters], *Byzantina*, iii (1971), 213–51

C.G. Patrinelis: 'Protopsaltai, Lampadarii and Domestikoi of the Great Church during the Post-Byzantine Period (1453–1821)', *Studies in Eastern Chant*, iii, ed. M. Velimirović (London, 1973), 141–70

D.E. Conomos: 'Sacred Music in the post-Byzantine Era', *The Byzantine Legacy in Eastern Europe*, ed. L. Clucas (New York, 1988), 83–105

For further bibliography *see* BYZANTINE CHANT.

DIMITRI CONOMOS

Petrov, Andrey Pavlovich (*b* Leningrad, 2 Sept 1930). Russian composer. He studied composition first at the Rimsky-Korsakov Music College (1945–9), then at the Leningrad Conservatory (1949–54) in Yevlakhov's composition class. He served as chairman of the Leningrad Composers' Union from 1964, and in 1992 was appointed president of the St Petersburg Philharmonic Society. He was awarded the title of People's Artist of the USSR in 1990. He has also received two State Prizes of the USSR (1967, 1976) and the State Prize of Russia (1996), as well as awards for his film scores.

Petrov's first endeavours were in the fields of orchestral music (the symphonic poem *Radda i Loyko*) and ballet (*Bereg nadezhdi*, 'Shore of Hope'). Petrov continued to write for the theatre throughout the 1970s and early 80s. The subjects of these works, such as the operas *Pyotr Pervïy* ('Peter I') and *Mayakovsky nachinayetsya* ('Mayakovsky Begins'), and the ballet *Pushkin*, frequently have their roots in the cultural history of Russia and, in particular, St Petersburg. Petrov acknowledges history, literature and painting as the chief source of his creative impulses. In the 1980s he produced a series of concertos and the *Romanticheskiye variatsii* ('Romantic Variations'), which are notable for their orchestral resourcefulness; the 1990s saw the appearance of a series of symphonies based on Christian themes. His film music and songs have nonetheless been the mainstay of his output. In both genres he has successfully transformed both the familiar and occasionally banal idiom of old Russian romance and the styles of contemporary popular song, with results that are memorable in their melodic invention and, in the film scores, consistently suited to the dramatic context at hand. Though his style is usually diatonic and consonant, he has been resourceful in his exploitation of a wide range of stylistic influences, from Bach to jazz and from Russian traditional music to avant-garde sonoristic techniques. Petrov's aim to discover a unifying harmony between different spheres of creativity is epitomized by his opposition to the division between 'high' art and popular culture; in terms of his artistic ideals he remains essentially a Romantic. Performers who have championed his music include the baritone Sergey Leiferkus and the conductors Yevgeny Svetlanov and Yury Temirkanov.

WORKS
(selective list)

Stage: Bereg nadezhdï [Shore of Hope] (ballet, 3, Yu. Slonimsky), 1959; V ritme serdtsa: mï khotim tantsevat' [In the Rhythm of the Heart: We Want to Dance] (musical, 2, after V. Konstantinov and B. Ratser), 1967; Sotvoreniye mira [The Creation of the World] (ballet, 3, N. Kasatkina, V. Vasilyov), 1971; Pyotr Pervïy [Peter I] (op, 3, Kasatkina, Vasilyov), 1975; Pushkin: razmïshleniya o poète [Pushkin: Reflections on the Poet] (ballet, 2, Kasatkina, Vasilyov after A.S. Pushkin), spkr, Mez, chorus, orch, 1978; Mayakovsky nachinayetsya [Mayakovsky Begins] (op, 2, M. Rozovsky), 1985; Master i Margarita [The Master and Margarita] (ballet, 1, B. Èyfman, after M. Bulgakov), 1987

Orch and vocal orch: Radda i Loyko [Radda and Loyko], sym. poem, after M. Gor'ky: *Makar Chudra*, 1954; Prazdnichnaya uvertyura [Festive Ov.], 1955; Pesni nashïkh dney [Songs of our Time], 1964; Pamyati pogibshïkh v godï blokadï Leningrada [To the Memory of those who Perished in the Blockade of Leningrad], poem, org, str, 4 tpt, 2 pf, perc, 1966; Sotvoreniye mira [Creation of the World], 3 suites from the ballet, 1968, 1969, 1975; Pyotr Pervïy [Peter I] (vocal-sym. frescoes, Kasalkina, Vasilyov) 1972; Puskin, sym., spkr, Mez, 2 pf, orch, 1977; Vn Conc., 1983; Master i Margarita: po prochtenii Bulgakova [The Master and Margarita: on Reading Bulgakov], fantastic sym., 1985; Concertino-buffo, chbr orch, 1987; Memoria, vn, chbr orch, 1987; Romanticheskiye variatsii [Romantic Variations], 1988; Pf Conc., 1989; Rus' kolokol'naya [The Bells of Old Russia], variations on a theme by Musorgsky, 1990; Sym. no.1 'na temï khristianskikh gimnov' [On Christian Anthems], 1992; Sym. no.2 'na temï khristianskikh gimnov', 1992; Vremya Khrista [The Time of Christ], choral sym., 1995

Vocal: Prostïye pesni [Simple Songs] (G. Rodari), S, B, pf, 1956; 5 vesyolïkh pesen [5 Cheerful Songs] (S. Marshak, S. Mikhalkov, Rodari, Ye. Serova), 1960; Pateticheskaya poèma [A Passionate Poem] (N. Aseyev, V. Bryusov, L. Martïnov, V. Mayakovsky, B. Pasternak, I. Sel'vinsky, A. Voznesensky), B/Bar, 2 pf, perc, 1969

Chbr: Str Qt, 1993

Film scores: Chelovek-Amfibiya [The Amphibious Man] (V. Chebotaryov, K. Kazanksy), 1961; Put' k prichalu [The Road to the Mooring Place] (G. Daneliya), 1962; Ya shagayu po Moskve [I Stroll through Moscow] (Daneliya), 1963–4; Beregis' avtomobilya [Beware of the Car] (E. Ryazanov), 1965–6; Stariki–razboyniki [The Old Brigands] (Ryazanov), 1971–2; Sluzhebnïy roman [An Office Affair] (Ryazanov), 1977–8; Garazh [The Garage] (Ryazanov), 1979; Osenniy marafon [An Autumn Marathon] (Daneliya), 1979; O bednom gusare zamolvite slovo [Put in a Word for the poor Hussar] (Ryazanov), 1980–2; Vokzal dlya dvoikh [A Railway Station for Two] (Ryazanov), 1982; Zhestokiy romans [A Cruel Romance] (Ryazanov), 1984; Nebesa obetovannïye [The Promised Heaven] (Ryazanov), 1991; Peterburgskiye taynï [St Petersburg Secrets] (V. Orlov, D. Pchyolkin, V. Zobin), TV serial, 1994–6

BIBLIOGRAPHY

A. Koenigsberg: *Andrey Petrov* (Moscow, 1959)

A. Chernov: 'Romanticheskaya ustremlyonnost'' [A Romantic orientation], *SovM* (1966), no.6, pp.37–40

M. Byalik: 'Garmoniya kontrastnïkh nachal' [The harmony of contrasting principles], *SovM* (1970), no.11, pp.18–25

L. Markhasyov: *Andrey Petrov znakomïy i neznakomïy* [Petrov familiar and unfamiliar] (Leningrad, 1973, 2/1995)

Andrey Petrov: sbornik statey [Andrey Petrov: a collection of articles], ed. M. Druskin (Leningrad, 1981)

A. Petrov, N. Kolesnikova: *Dialog o kinomuzike* [A dialogue about film music] (Moscow, 1982)

B. Kats: *Prostïye istinï kinomuzïki* [The simple truths of film music] (Leningrad, 1988)

OL'GA MANUL'KINA

Petrov, Nikolay (Arnol'dovich) (*b* Moscow, 14 April 1943). Russian pianist. He entered the Central School of Music in Moscow as a child and remained there for ten years, studying with the renowned pedagogue Tat'yana Kestner. In 1961 he became a pupil of Zak at the Moscow

Conservatory and the following year won second prize at the inaugural Van Cliburn Competition at Fort Worth, Texas. He was awarded the silver medal at the 1964 Queen Elisabeth Competition in Brussels. During the Cold War years Petrov held a virtually unique status among younger Soviet pianists, as he was permitted to tour widely and to display, at least superficially, some of the liberal Western attitudes of the 1960s. A pianist of seemingly limitless technical resource, Petrov commands a repertory encompassing the gamut of the piano literature. Besides acting as an ambassador for the music of such Soviet composers as Khachaturian, Khrennikov, Shchedrin and Eshpay earlier in his career, he has made a speciality of presenting larger-scale works from the 19th-century virtuoso piano literature. Notable is his dazzling recording of the 1838 version of Liszt's six *Etudes d'exécution transcendante d'après Paganini*, previously deemed to be unplayable. Although Petrov is not an interpreter of great originality, the authority and musical thoroughness of his readings are always impressive.

BIBLIOGRAPHY

M. Zilberquit: *Russia's Great Modern Pianists* (Neptune, NJ, 1983)

JAMES METHUEN-CAMPBELL

Petrov, Osip (**Afanas'yevich**) (*b* Yelizavetgrad [now Kirovograd], 3/15 Nov 1806; *d* St Petersburg, 28 Feb/12 March 1878). Russian bass. His date of death is often given incorrectly as 27 February/11 March or 2/14 March, the latter being the date of his burial. He first sang in a church choir, at the same time teaching himself the guitar; he was also taught the clarinet by a friend. In 1826 he was taken into Zhurakhovsky's travelling company, making his début in Yelizavetgrad in Cavos's *The Cossack Poet*, and shortly after joining the troupe of Ivan Fyodorovich Stein: here he was much influenced by working with the great actor Mikhail Shchepkin. Continuing his self-education, with help from Cavos in singing and Hunke for piano and theory, he made rapid progress, singing in various different operatic genres and acting in plays. In 1830 Petrov made his St Petersburg début, soon winning wide recognition for his talents. At the première of *A Life for the Tsar* (1836) he set a tradition for the interpretation of Ivan Susanin with a performance of overwhelming dramatic power (see illustration): Glinka himself recounted how the chorus of Poles set upon Petrov so violently that he had genuinely to defend himself. Other roles written for Petrov and created by him include Glinka's Ruslan (1842), the Miller in Dargomïzhsky's *Rusalka* (1856), Oziya in Serov's *Judith* (1863), Vladimir in Serov's *Rogneda* (1865), Leporello in Dargomïzhsky's *The Stone Guest* (1872), Ivan the Terrible in Rimsky-Korsakov's *The Maid of Pskov* (1873), Varlaam in Musorgsky's *Boris Godunov* (1874), Prince Gudal in Rubinstein's *The Demon* (1875) and the Mayor in Tchaikovsky's *Vakula the Smith* (1876). In April 1876 the Mariinsky Theatre held a celebration to mark his 50th anniversary on the stage: he was presented with a gold medal by the tsar and a diamond-studded gold wreath, on each leaf of which was engraved the name of one of the 100 operas in which he had sung. For Petrov's jubilee Tchaikovsky wrote his Nekrasov cantata *To Touch the Hearts of Men*.

Petrov's voice, which ranged from B′ to f♯′, from a rich, profound bass to a flexible baritone in the high register, was greatly admired for its warmth, depth and evenness of delivery; and his vivid personality and generous

Osip Petrov as Ivan Susanin in Glinka's 'A Life for the Tsar', Act 4 scene iii, St Petersburg, 1870s

perception made him especially successful as a character actor. His non-Russian roles included Rossini's Figaro, Bellini's Oroveso, Meyerbeer's Bertram, Herold's Zampa and Weber's Kaspar. But his embodiment of essential Russian types in a bass voice of peculiarly Russian character provided many different composers with an example and an inspiration: Stasov was not exaggerating when at the jubilee he declared that 'Petrov may be considered one of the founders of Russian opera as we know it'. Petrov married the contralto Anna Yakovlevna Vorob'yova, who sang thereafter under her married name.

BIBLIOGRAPHY

V.V. Stasov: *Sobraniye sochineniy* [Collected works] (St Petersburg, 1894–1906)

E. Lastochkina: *Osip Petrov* (Moscow and Leningrad, 1950)

V. Bogdanov-Berezovsky, ed.: *M. Glinka: Zapiski* [Memoirs] (Leningrad, 1953; Eng. trans., 1963)

P.A. Markov, ed.: *Teatral'naya entsiklopediya*, iv (Moscow, 1965)

D. Brown: *Mikhail Glinka: a Biographical and Critical Study* (London, 1974/R)

JOHN WARRACK/R

Petrov, Stoyan (*b* Sofia, 19 Aug 1916; *d* Sofia, 18 Feb 1996). Bulgarian musicologist. After graduating in theory (1943) and performing (1944) at the Bulgarian State Music Academy in Sofia, he studied music history at the Moscow Conservatory under R.I. Gruber, V.M. Belyayev and Klyment Kvitka (1944–53). He held posts as music editor at Radio Sofia (1945–9), head of the art schools department at the Committee of Science, Art and Culture (1953–4), deputy rector of the Bulgarian State Conservatory (1954–6), and secretary of the musicologists' section of the Union of Bulgarian Composers (1958–62). In 1955 he became reader in the history of Bulgarian music at the Bulgarian State Conservatory; in 1971 he was appointed head of the music history department there. Petrov made a special study of medieval Bulgarian music, Byzantine chant and ancient Bulgarian folk music.

WRITINGS

ed., with S. Stoyanov: *15 godini balgarska muzikalna kultura* [15 years of Bulgarian musical culture] (Sofia, 1959)

Ocherki po istoriyata na balgarskata muzika [Sketches on the history of Bulgarian musical culture] (Sofia, 1959)

Balgarskata narodna pesen prez vekovete [Bulgarian folksong through the ages] (Sofia, 1961)

'Béla Bartók and Bulgarian Musical Culture', *SM*, v (1963), 491–506; Ger. versions in *Studia musicologica aesthetica, theoretica, historica: Zofia Lissa w 70. roko urodzin*, ed. E. Dziębowska (Kraków, 1979), 367–77

'Pesni za Kiril i Metodiy' [Songs about Cyril and Methodius], *1100 godini slavyanska pismenost* (Sofia, 1963), 489

'Pevcheskata kultura na Banatskite Balgari' [The song culture of the Banat Bulgarians], *IIM*, xi (1965), 79–147 [incl. Russ. and Fr. summaries]

'Tvortsi, pametnitsi i traditsii na starobalgarskata muzikalna kultura' [Creators, monuments and traditions of old Bulgarian musical culture], *Kliment Okhridski: sbornik ot statii po sluchay 1050 godini ot smartta mu* [St Clement of Ohrid: a collection of essays commemorating the 1050th anniversary of his death], ed. B.S. Angelov and others (Sofia, 1966), 393–403

'Sur quelques nouveaux procédés méthodologiques de recherche sur le folklore musical en Bulgarie et les autres pays balkaniques', *Etudes balkaniques et sud-est européennes I: Sofia 1966*, ii, 1041–53

'Rolyata na vazrozhdenskite i revolyutsionni pesni po vreme na aprilskoto vastanie, 1876' [The role of the Revival and revolutionary songs during the April Insurrection, 1876], *Godishnik na balgarskata darzhavna konservatoriya*, iv (1968), 1

with H. Kodov: *Old Bulgarian Musical Documents/Staroulgarski muzikalni pametnici* (Sofia, 1973)

EDITIONS

Pesni na rusko-balgarskata boyna druzhba [Songs of Russo-Bulgarian war comradeship] (Sofia, 1969)

LADA BRASHOVANOVA

Petrova, Anna Yakovlevna (Vorob'yova) (*b* St Petersburg, 2/14 Feb 1817; *d* St Petersburg, 13/26 April 1901). Russian contralto. Her mother, Avdot'ya Vorob'yova (*d* 1836), and her mother's former husband, Yakov Stepanovich Vorob'yov (1766–1809), were leading singers of their day. Trained originally for ballet, she studied singing with Glinka, among others, and identified closely with that composer's musical outlook. After her début as Pippo in Rossini's *La gazza ladra* in 1833, she created the part of Vanya in *A Life for the Tsar* (1836) and later Ratmir in *Ruslan and Lyudmila* (1842). She and her husband Osip Petrov were recognized as pioneers of the Russian nationalist school of music, notably by the critic and musicologist Stasov, who described her voice as 'one of the most exceptional and astonishing in all Europe: size, beauty, strength, gentleness'. Petrova also excelled in the bel canto operas of Rossini and Bellini, in which her singing was compared to that of Albani and Viardot. Her reminiscences were published in *Russkaya starina*, xxvii (1880), 611–17.

BORIS SEMEONOFF

Petrová, Elena (*b* Modrý Kameň, 9 Nov 1929). Czech composer. She studied the piano with Karel Hoffmeister, musicology at Charles University, Prague, and composition with Jan Kapr at the Janáček Academy of Musical Art, Brno. She has spent her whole career teaching music theory at Charles University. Her main creative interest is in vocal and dramatic music, for which she writes her own texts and scenarios. Her opera *Kdyby se slunce nevrátilo* ('Suppose the Sun did not Return') demonstrates her concise approach to musical utterance and a tendency towards modality in her harmonic language. Petrová's works have won several prizes, in her own country and abroad (Philadelphia, 1968; Czech National Competition, 1971 and 1972; Denver, 1975; Mannheim, 1976 and 1978).

WORKS
(selective list)

Opera: Kdyby se slunce nevrátilo [Suppose the Sun did not Return] (Petrová, after F.C. Ramuz), 1982–3

Ballets: Slavík a růže [The Nightingale and the Rose] (after O. Wilde), 1969; Podivuhodná raketa [The Remarkable Rocket] (after Wilde), 1970; Šťastný princ [The Happy Prince] (after Wilde), 1971; Slunečnice [Sunflower] (after Ovid), 1972

Orch: Sym., 1968; Slavnostní předehra [Festive Ov.], 1975; Sym., 1976; Smuteční hudba [Mourning Music], 1981; Passacaglia, 1982; Sym. Interludes, 1983

Vocal: Písně o čase [Songs about Time], Bar, pf, 1958, arr. pf, 1960; Žluté balady [Yellow Ballades] (F. García Lorca), Bar, pf, 1964; Písně starého měsíce [Songs of the Old Moon] (Chin. poetry), S, chbr orch, 1965; Azalea, melodrama, spkr, chbr orch, 1966; Madrigaly, chbr chorus, 1966; Noci [To the Night] (cant., V. Nezval), T, chorus, orch, 1969; Klytie, melodrama, spkr, nonet, 1969; Pět slovenských písní [5 Slovak Songs], men's vv, 1969; Tanbakzan, spkr, chbr orch, 1981; Nářek královny Ningal [Mourners of Queen Ningal], S, chbr chorus, 1992; Sluneční sonáta [Sunny Sonata] (Petrová), S, pf, 1992, arr. pf; Caprices (Petrová), female vv, 1993

Inst: Pf Sonata, 1960; Eclogues, b cl, 1965; 2 str qts, 1965, 1968; Prelude and Passacaglia, org, 1969; Invocations, b cl, 1972; Inspirace [Inspirations], pf 4 hands, 1973; Pantomime, b viol, 1974; Impromptus, pf, 1979, 1989; Str Qt, 1991; Pf Sonata, 1992; Capricci, b cl, perc, 1993; Str Qt, 1994; Commedy dell arte, hps, 1995; Etudes, pf 4 hands, 1996

Principal publishers: ČHF (Czech Music Fund), Panton

BIBLIOGRAPHY

ČSHS

A.I. Cohen: *International Encyclopedia of Women Composers* (New York, 1981, 2/1987)

A. Šerých: 'Konfese Eleny Petrové' [Confession of Elena Petrová], *Opus musicum*, xviii/8 (1986), 239–41

F. Mihaly: *Osobnosti novohradu* [Nový Hrad personalities] (Lučenec, 1995)

ANNA ŠERÝCH

Petrova, Mara (*b* Sliven, 15 May 1921; *d* 1997). Bulgarian composer. One of the earliest Bulgarian woman composers to be well documented, she graduated in 1945 from the Sofia Academy of Music, where her teachers were Stoyanov (composition), Vladigerov (piano) and Goleminov (orchestral conducting). Her talent revealed itself at an early age through her children's songs, instrumental pieces and a short operetta. She was an editor, a teacher at the Institute for Music and Choreography in Sofia (1972–83) and a critic. Her large output, embracing many genres, includes over 260 children's songs, as well as orchestral and chamber works. Her music, based on Bulgarian classical and folk traditions, exhibits clear formal structures and rich melodic invention; it has been performed and recorded in Bulgaria, Poland, Germany, the former Czechoslovakia, Switzerland and the former USSR.

WORKS
(selective list)

Orch: Mladezhka syuita [Youth Suite], 1953; Moyata rodina [My Homeland], ov., 1965; Yunosheska syuita [Youth Suite], str, timp, 1970; Sym. 'April 1876', 1981

Vocal: Blue-Eyed (song), 1v, orch, 1947; Lullaby (song), 1v, orch, 1953; Triptych, 1v, orch, 1972

Chbr and solo inst: Pf Variations, 1945; Small Sonata, pf, 1946; Prelude, pf, 1948; Bulgarian Dance, 1951; Dance, 3 bn, 1957; Prelude, 3 bn, 1960; Scherzo, fl, pf, 1964; Sofiyska syuita [Sofia Suite], 1969; Skitsi [Sketches], fl, ob, bn, 1977
Children's songs
Principal publishers: Muzika, Nauka i Izkustvo

BIBLIOGRAPHY
S. Lazarov: 'Mara Petrova', *Balgarska muzika*, xxiii/5 (1972), 15–17
N. Kaufman: 'Za muzikata na Mara Petrova', *Balgarska muzika*, xxxii/5 (1981), 30–33

MAGDALENA MANOLOVA

Petrović, Ankica (*b* Sarajevo, 5 May 1943). Bosnian-Hercegovinan musicologist. She studied music theory (BA 1968) and musicology and ethnomusicology (BA 1974) at the University of Sarajevo and took the PhD at Queen's University, Belfast in 1977 with a dissertation on *ganga*, a form of Bosnian traditional rural singing. She was a music producer at Radio Sarajevo (1967–79) and assistant professor (1979–86) and associate professor (1986–92) at the Sarajevo Academy of Music. Her research is focussed on Eastern-European traditional music, the aesthetics of rural Bosnian and Balkan music, Sephardi music traditions in Bosnia and the Balkans, and various styles of religious chant. She is the author and producer of numerous radio broadcasts on traditional music for the BBC, Kol Israel Jerusalem and Radio Brussels, and has been involved with the recordings *Traditional Music on the Soil of Bosnia and Hercegovina* (Diskoton, 1986) and *Bosnia: Echoes from an Endangered World* (Smithsonian Folkways, SF 40407, 1993).

WRITINGS
'Staroslavensko obredno pjevanje u Škaljarima u Boki Kotorskoj' [Old Slavonic ritual chant in Škaljari, Boka Kotorska], *Zvuk* (1975), no.1, pp.51–7
Ganga, a Form of Traditional Rural Singing in Yugoslavia (diss., Queen's U. of Belfast, 1977)
'Kulturološka i muzička analiza pasionskog napjeva Gospin plač na otoku Hvaru' [Cultural and musicological analysis of the Passion song *Gospin plač* from the island of Hvar], *Yugoslav Folklore Association: Congress XXIX: Hvar 1982*, 61–7
'Sacred Sephardi Chants in Bosnia', *World of Music*, xxiv/3 (1982), 35–51
'Kulturološki prikaz obrednih sefarskih napjeva iz Bosne' [Cultural issues in ritual Sephardi melodies in Bosnia], *Sveske Instituta za proučavanje nacionalnih odnosa*, vii–viii (1984), 11–115
'Lokalni idiomi u obrednim napjevima sefarskih Jevreja u Bosni' [Local idioms in the religious melodies of Sephardi Jews in Bosnia], *Međuakademijskog koordinacionog odbora za ispitivanje tradicionalne narodne religiozne obredne muzike u Jugoslaviji: Sarajevo 1984*, 57–85
'Primjena Ellisovih konstatacija o skalama na neke oblike tradicionalne muzike u Jugoslaviji' [An application of Ellis's conclusions about scales to some forms of traditional music in Yugoslavia], *Yugoslav Folklore Association: Congress XXXII: Sombor 1985*, 489–93
'Tradition and Compromises in the Musical Expressions of the Sephardic Jews in Bosnia', *Traditional Music of Ethnic Groups (Minorities): Zagreb 1985*, 213–21
'Narodni elementi u pjevanju latinske mise među Malisorima u Tuzi, Crna Gora' [Folk elements in Latin Mass chants among Malisors in Tuzi, Montenegro], *Makedonski folklor*, xix/37 (1986), 201–11
'Oriental-Islamic Cultural Reflections on Musical Folk Muslim Expressions in Bosnia and Herzegovina, Yugoslavia', *Al Mathurat al Sha'biyyah*, ii/2 (1987), 10–19
'Vidovi manifestovanja kulturnog tradicionalizma u obredno-religijskoj muzici jermenske zajednice u starom Jerusalemu' [Manifestations of cultural traditionalism in the ritual religious music of the Armenian community in the old city of Jerusalem], *Folklor i njegova umetnička transpozicija [I]: Belgrade 1987* [, ii, 59–62 [summaries in Eng., Fr., Ger., Russ.]
'Paradoxes of Muslim Music in Bosnia and Herzegovina', *Asian Music*, xx/1 (1988), 128–47

'Generalne kulturne odrednice muzike sefardskih Jevreja u Jugoslaviji' [General cultural determinations in the music of Sephardi Jews in Yugoslavia], *Zbornik radova Muzičke akademije u Sarajevu*, i (1989), 53–72
'Tradicionalna muzika sefardskih Jevreja na našem području' [Traditional music of Sephardi Jews in the Yugoslav region], *Bilten Jevrejske opštine u Sarajevu*, iii (1989), 29–39
'Correlation between the Musical Content of Jewish Sephardic Songs and Traditional Muslim Lyrics *Sevdalinka* in Bosnia', *Proceedings of the Tenth World Congress of Jewish Studies: Jerusalem 1989*, ed. D. Asaf (Jerusalem, 1990), D, ii, 165–71
'Women in the Music Creation Process in the Dinaric Cultural Zone of Yugoslavia', *Music, Gender, and Culture*, ed. M. Herndon and S. Ziegler (Wilhelmshaven, 1990), 71–84
'Les techniques du chant villageois dans les Alpes Dinariques (Yougoslavie)', *Cahiers de musiques traditionelles*, iv (1991), 103–15
'Cultural Factors affecting Changes in the Musical Expression of the Sephardic Jews in Yugoslavia', *History and Creativity in the Sephardi and Oriental Jewish Communities: Jerusalem 1988*, ed. T. Aleksander and others (Jerusalem, 1994), 273–84
'The Eastern Roots of Ancient Yugoslav Music', *Music-Cultures in Contact: Convergences and Collisions*, ed. M.J. Kartomi and S. Blum (Sydney and New York, 1994), 13–20
'The Status of Traditional Music in Eastern Europe', *Folklore and Traditional Music in the Former Soviet Union and Eastern Europe*, ed. J. Porter (Los Angeles, 1997), 49–59

ZDRAVKO BLAŽEKOVIĆ

Petrović, Danica S. (*b* Belgrade, 2 Dec 1945). Serbian musicologist. She graduated from the Belgrade Academy of Music in 1970 and became an assistant at the Institute of Musicology at the Serbian Academy of Sciences and Arts in Belgrade. She studied in Oxford with Egon Wellesz and gained the doctorate from the University of Ljubljana in 1980, with a dissertation on Oktōēchos in the musical tradition of southern Slavs. She was made professor of music history at the University of Arts, Novi Sad, in 1993.

Petrović's musicological interests include Slavonic music manuscripts of the 15th to the 19th centuries, Greek-Slavonic and Russian-Serbian cultural links in the 18th century, and links between Serbian music and European musical traditions of the 19th century. Her research has demonstrated the continuity of Serbian music from late medieval times to the present. She has contributed to the complete edition of Stevan Mokranjac's works and prepared facsimile editions of *Orthodox Church Singing of the Serbian People* by Kornelije Stanković (Belgrade, 1994).

WRITINGS
'A Liturgical Anthology Manuscript with the Russian "Hammer-Headed" Notation from A.D.1674', *Musica antiqua III: Bydgoszcz and Toruń 1972*, 293–321
'One Aspect of the Slavonic Oktoechos in Four Chilandari Music Manuscripts', *IMSCR XI: Copenhagen 1972*, 766–74
'Le chant populaire sacré et ses investigateurs', *Srpska muzika kroz vekove/La musique serbe à travers les siècles*, ed. S. Đurić-Klajn (Belgrade, 1973), 275–92
'Church Elements in Serbian Ritual Songs', *Beiträge zur Musikkultur des Balkans*, i, ed. R. Flotzinger (Graz, 1974), 109–25
'Byzantine and Slavonic Octoechos until the 15th Century', *Musica antiqua IV: Bydgoszcz 1975*, 175–90
'Music for some Serbian Saints in Manuscripts Preserved in Roumania in Comparison with Different Melodic Versions Found in Other Manuscripts', *International Congress of Byzantine Studies XIV: Bucharest 1971*, ed. M. Berza and E. Stanescu, iii (Bucharest, 1976), 557–64
'Hymns in Honour of Serbian Saints in Music Manuscripts of the Monastery of Chilandar and in Printed Editions', *Studies in Eastern Chant*, iv (1978), 134–9
'Ukrainian Melodies in the Serbian Monastery of Krka (Dalmacia)', *MZ*, xiv (1978), 35–49

Osmoglasnik u muzičkoj tradiciji Južnih Slovena [Oktōēchos in the musical tradition of Southern Slavs] (diss., U. of Ljubljana, 1980; Belgrade, 1982) [with Eng. summary]
'The Importance of the Chilandari Music Manuscripts for the History of Serbian Church Music', *Musica antiqua VI: Bydgoszcz 1982*, 223–36
'A Russian Musical Manuscript in the Belgrade Patriarchal Library: a Contribution to the Study of Russo-Serbian Cultural Links in the 18th Century', *Musica antiqua VII: Bydgoszcz 1985*, 273–88
'Different Stages of Written and Oral Tradition in the Serbian Church Singing using the Example of the Trisagion Hymn', *Cantus Planus IV: Pécs 1990*, 293–302
'Baroque and Serbian Chant in the 17th and 18th Centuries', *Zapadnoevropski barok i vizantijski svet: Belgrade 1989*, ed. D. Medaković (Belgrade, 1991), 95–102
'The Eleven Morning Hymns Eothina in Byzantine and Slavonic Traditions', *Cantus Planus V: Éger 1993*, 435–48
'A South Slavonic Sticherarion in a 17th Century Neumatic Manuscript in the Monastery of the Great Lavra',*Laborare fratres in unum: Festschrift Laszlo Dobszay zum 60. Geburtstag*, ed. J. Szendrei and D. Hiley (Hildesheim, 1995), 249–60

EDITIONS

Stevan St. Mokranjac: Serbian Chant: Osmoglasnik, Sabrana djela, vii (Belgrade, 1996)
Stevan St. Mokranjac: Serbian Chant: Ordinary, Special and Festal Chant, Sabrana djela, viii (Belgrade, 1997)

DIMITRIJE STEFANOVIĆ

Petrovics, Emil (*b* Nagybecskerek [now Zrenjanin, Serbia], 9 Feb 1930). Hungarian composer. He studied with Farkas at the Liszt Academy of Music (1952–7). His first international success came when a string quartet won a prize in the 1959 Liège competition. From 1960 to 1964 he was musical director of the Petőfi Theatre, Budapest, and in 1964 he was appointed professor at the academy of dramatic art. He became professor at the Liszt Academy of Music in 1969, heading its composition department from 1978 to 1995, and president of the Hungarian Association for Copyright Protection in 1983. He was general director of the Hungarian State Opera (1986–90). His awards include the Erkel Prize (1960, 1963), the Kossuth Prize (1969) and the Bartók-Pásztory Prize (1993).

Petrovics's first instrumental pieces, notably the Flute Concerto and the String Quartet, show an absorption of influences from Falla, Prokofiev and Ravel as well as the Hungarian tradition. Although these pieces gained some attention, it was the one-act opera *C'est la guerre* that quickly established his reputation. Broadcast in 1961, the work was staged at the Hungarian State Opera in the following year and enthusiastically received; further productions were put on in Oberhausen, Nice and Sarajevo. The opera is Puccinian in its dramaturgy, but the declamatory style looks back to *Wozzeck*, and its free 12-note technique is a further link with Berg. Nonetheless the work has an individual musical character and a striking dramatic power. It was followed by a comic opera, *Lysistrate*, written in 1962 for concert performance but staged in Budapest (1971) and East Berlin (1972).

After developing his style in a series of instrumental works, Petrovics produced the large-scale oratorio *Jónás könyve* ('The Book of Jonah'), a work which displays his lyrical vein. He returned to composition for the stage with a full-length opera based on Dostoyevsky's *Crime and Punishment*, produced in Helsinki in 1970 and Wuppertal in 1971. Although much of the novel had to be abandoned, the opera is distinguished by Petrovics's gift for underlining dramatic situations and, above all, by his handling of Hungarian prose. Here again the music is freely atonal with more or less serial episodes; the polyphonic textures

owe much to the Second Viennese School, but the vocal style is fully in accord with the Magyar language. Dramatic moments and sections of closed musical form are masterfully balanced. The weight of his later output lies in his cantatas on Hungarian texts and world literature. A confrontation with loneliness, the loss of values and death underlies these works, which are given distinction by different combinations of vocal forces. Petrovics has gradually returned to tonality, retaining a characteristic atmosphere through the use of elemental musical gestures and expressive lyricism.

WORKS
(selective list)

Ops: C'est la guerre (1, M. Hubay), 1960–61; Lysistrate (after Aristophanes), 1962, rev. for stage 1971; Bűn és bűnhődés [Crime and Punishment] (3, G. Maar, after F. Dostoyevsky), 1969
Cants.: no.1 'Egyedül az erdőben' [Alone in the Forest] (M. Eminescu), S, chbr orch, 1956; no.2 'Ott essem el én' [Dying in Action] (S. Petőfi), male chorus, orch, 1972; no.3 'Fanni hagyományai' [Fanny's Heritage] (G. Czigány, after J. Kármán), S, chbr orch, 1978; no.4 'Mind elmegyünk' [We shall All be Gone] (S. Weöres), female chorus, chbr orch, 1980; no.5 'Törökországi levelek' [Letters from Turkey] (Czigány, after K. Mikes), B, chbr orch, 1981; no.6, 'Szonya monológja' [Sonya's Monologue] (after A.P. Chekhov: Dyadya Vanya [Uncle Vanya]), S, chorus, orch, 1986; no.7 'Pygmalion' (after Lucretius, Ovid), nar, chorus, orch, 1994–5; no.8 'Panasz és vigasz' [Complaint and Consolation] (L. Szabó), T, pf, 1996; no.9 'A Dunánál' [The Danube] (A. József), Tr, S, Bar, chorus, orch, 1998
Other vocal works: Serbian Songs, 1v, ens, 1955; Jónás könyve [The Book of Jonah] (orat, M. Babits), 1966; choral pieces, songs, folksong arrs.
Inst: Cassazione, brass qnt, 1953; Fl Conc., 1957; 4 Self-Portraits in Masks, hpd, 1958; Str Qt no.1, 1958; Passacaglia in Blues, bn, pf, 1964; Sym., str, 1964; Wind Qnt, 1964; Magyar gyermekdalok [Hungarian Childrens' Songs], fl, pf, 1974; 2 mouvements: no.1, cimb, no.2, 2 cimb, 1977; Salome (ballet, after O. Wilde), fl, tpt, hp, perc, 1978; Rhapsody no.1, vn, 1982; Rhapsody no.2, va/vc, 1984; Concertino, tpt, orch, 1990; Str Qt no.2, 1991; Vörösmarty, ov., orch, 1993; Piangendo e meditando, str, 1997
Incid music for theatre, cinema, radio and TV

Principal publisher: Editio Musica Budapest

BIBLIOGRAPHY

I. Fábián: 'Two Opera Composers', *Tempo*, no.88 (1969), 10–19
I. Földes, ed.: *Harmincasok: Beszélgetések magyar zeneszerzőkkel* [Those in their thirties: conversations with Hungarian composers] (Budapest, 1969), 125–45, 213–6
G. Kroó: *Ungarische Musikgeschichte – gestern und heute* (Budapest, 1980), 208–14
B.A. Varga, ed.: *Contemporary Hungarian Composers* (Budapest, 5/1989), 280–4

JÁNOS KÁRPÁTI/PÉTER HALÁSZ

Petrovsky Theatre. Moscow theatre built in 1780. *See* MOSCOW, §3.

Petrucci, Brizio (*b* Massalombarda, nr Ferrara, 12 Jan 1737; *d* Ferrara, 15 June 1828). Italian composer. He studied at the seminary in Imola and, from 1750, law at the University of Ferrara, receiving his doctorate in 1758. He also studied music with Pietro Berretta (1703–59), *maestro di cappella* at the cathedral in Ferrara. Turning to music as a profession, he became coadjutor to Pietro Marzola, *maestro di cappella* at the cathedral, and his successor in 1784. He held this post until the first decade of the 19th century.

Petrucci's early career reflects an interest in dramatic music, his first known work being choruses for a tragedy, *Giovanni di Giscala* (1760, Ferrara). In 1762 he helped found the Accademia dei Dilettanti di Musica, where in 1763 his oratorio *La madre de' Maccabei* was performed. Two *opere serie* were staged at Ferrara in 1765; in the second, *Demofoonte*, his pupil, the celebrated Lucrezia Aguiari, made one of her early appearances. He also served as *maestro al cembalo* at the Bonacossi and Scroffa theatres and produced a comic opera in 1770. Later he concentrated on sacred music; according to Fétis, his psalms with large orchestra were famous throughout Italy. A Requiem of 1822 was also well known, perhaps partly because of the age at which he wrote it.

WORKS

STAGE

Choruses for Giovanni di Giscala (tragedia), Ferrara, 1760
Ciro riconosciuto (os, P. Metastasio), Ferrara, Bonacossi, carn. 1765, *I-FEd*
Demofoonte (os, Metastasio), Ferrara, Bonacossi, 26 Dec 1765, arias *Gl* (Lucca, 1765), *PAc*
Nitteti (dramma per musica Metastasio), Mantua, Vecchio, carn. 1766
I pazzi improvvisati (ob), Ferrara, Bonacossi, carn. 1770, *FEd*
Teseo in Creta (azione teatrale, G.F. Fattiboni), Cesena, for election of Cardinal Opizio Pallavicini as Protector of Cesena, 1771

OTHER VOCAL

La madre de' Maccabei (orat), Ferrara, 1763
Davide eletto al trono (orat), Imola, 1769
La Virtù condottiera della Gloria (cant.), Imola, 1775
La pace italica (cant., G. Muzzarelli), Ferrara, 1815
Sacred: many works, mostly 4vv, orch, some 3–4vv, org, *I-FEd*, *MAav*, incl.: masses; Requiem, 1822; Te Deum; Stabat mater; psalms; hymns; litanies; Mass (Ky–Gl), 4vv, orch, E♭, *D-MÜs*; Tui sunt coeli, solo v, insts, *?Bsb*

□

Petrucci, Ottaviano (dei) (*b* Fossombrone, 18 June 1466; *d* ?Venice, 7 May 1539). Italian publisher. He was the first significant publisher of polyphonic music.

1. LIFE.   Apart from the evidence of his birth and his family's residence in Fossombrone for some generations, nothing certain is known of Petrucci's life before 1498. He is thought to have been among the young men whom Guidobaldo I, Duke of Urbino, allowed to be educated at court. On 25 May 1498 Petrucci was granted a Venetian privilege for 20 years. His petition stated that he had discovered what many had sought, a way to publish 'canto figurado'. He added that it would make the printing of chant much easier also; but this was probably no more

than self-advertisement, given that he did not seek to include chant in his privilege, nor, probably, did he print any. His request was for the exclusive right to print both 'canto figurado' and 'intaboladure dorgano et de liuto'. The privilege also included a ban on the importation or sale of these repertories in the Venetian states by anyone else.

Petrucci's first book, the *Harmonice musices odhecaton A*, was backed by Amadio Scotto and Niccolo di Raffaele, both experienced in the publishing trade. It does not survive intact and lacks a publication date, but the dedication (to Girolamo Donato, a leading Venetian nobleman, diplomat and humanist) is dated 15 May 1501. The music of this volume, a collection of chansons and other secular pieces, was edited by the Dominican friar Petrus Castellanus. The success of the venture must have been quickly evident: several reprintings of parts of it were needed within two years, and two new editions appeared, in 1503 and 1504. The intervening years were devoted to books of masses by the most highly regarded composers, starting with Josquin Des Prez and Brumel, as well as two motet volumes (see illustration) and the two books, *Canti B* and *Canti C*, which continued the *Odhecaton* series.

In 1504, with his first volume of frottolas, Petrucci launched into a new and popular repertory. This was intended from the beginning to be part of a series, and both it and many of the subsequent ten volumes went through more than one edition. From 1504 until 1509 Petrucci seems to have been consistently successful: he published at least 27 new titles, reissuing a number of these and earlier volumes, often without changing the date in the colophon. Among them are volumes of music for lute, perhaps published in reaction to the privilege accorded to Marco Dall'Aquila in 1505.

Petrucci's last publication at Venice appeared on 27 March 1509. His next volume was published in Fossombrone on 10 May 1511. Petrucci had not lost contact with his home town during his Venetian years: in 1504 he had been a councillor representing Fossombrone in Urbino, and in 1505 and 1507 a city official. In 1508 he had revisited Fossombrone, and resettled there at some time

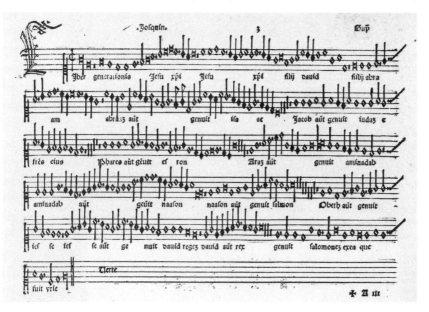

Opening of Josquin's motet 'Liber generationis Jesu Christi' from the superius partbook of 'Motetti C' (Venice: Petrucci, 1504)

in 1509 or 1510. The decision to leave Venice probably reflects his (and others') growing concern about the effects of the League of Cambrai war on Venetian business, a papal interdict on trade with the city and the spread of the plague.

Petrucci's output at Fossombrone began slowly. He acquired the patronage of the distinguished theologian and Bishop of Fossombrone, Paulus de Middelburgh, for whom he printed two non-musical works. One of these, Paulus's *Paulina de recta Paschae* of 1513 (a plea for reform of the liturgical calendar), was Petrucci's largest and most sumptuous volume. His only two musical volumes during these years, one each in 1511 and 1512, continued series begun earlier in Venice: in 1514 he printed a third volume of Josquin's masses.

This last was Petrucci's first volume printed under a new privilege, obtained from the pope in October 1513, protecting his books of polyphony and organ tablature in the papal states for 15 years. It was paralleled by a privilege granted to Andrea Antico, an ambitious wood-cutter who appears deliberately to have set out to compete with Petrucci. In the same year, on 26 September, Jacomo Ungaro received a Venetian privilege, issued without prejudice to any earlier grant. Scotto and Raffaele petitioned on Petrucci's behalf in June 1514, pointing out that he was the inventor of music printing and that his partners had not yet recouped their investment. The second claim seems unlikely, given the continuous production for more than ten years; but the further point that Raffaele was too infirm to support his family without the benefit of Petrucci's privilege may well have been true. Their petition was no doubt a defence against not only Ungaro (who, as a type founder, may have been protecting technical modifications), but also Luc'Antonio Giunta (who had recently printed *Cantorinus*, a popular musical treatise) and perhaps also Antico. However, the renewal of Petrucci's privilege, coupled with the Roman one for the papal states, encouraged him to print a volume of motets in 1514 and two of masses, besides new editions of Josquin's first two books. He also continued to be a leading member of the ruling councils of Fossombrone.

The suspension of his activities between 1516 and 1519 is more apparent than real. Pope Leo X had ousted the ducal family of della Rovere from Urbino and placed Lorenzo de' Medici on the throne. Petrucci, as a leading citizen of a town loyal to the exiled rulers, played a significant role in the tension between the new duke and his cities. His printing output included a few concealed editions of earlier volumes and a small text by his bishop. He also planned to publish M. Fabio Calvo's translation of Hippocrates. An extant manuscript (in *I-Rvat*) suggests that it appeared on 1 January 1519, but the volume itself, which caused Petrucci some contractual problems and another visit to Rome, does not appear to have been printed.

After Lorenzo de' Medici's death in 1519, Petrucci began to print again. He produced three motet volumes in 1519, and apparently Pisano's *Musica* and a volume of which only fragments survive [*Musica XII*], both in 1520, as well as a number of reprintings of these and earlier volumes. In 1520 he opened a paper mill at Acqua Santa near Fossombrone, which seems to have been his principal source of income, for he ceased printing. (There is no evidence that Petrucci printed the *Prognosticon* of Paulus de Middelburgh dated 1523.) Some of his typographical material appears to surface in the volume of Eustachio Romano's duos printed by Dorico in Rome in 1523. Petrucci continued to be active in local politics for another decade. According to Schmid, he was recalled to Venice in 1536 to help print Latin and Italian classical texts. Neither his place of death nor site of burial is known.

2. PUBLICATIONS.   Throughout his career Petrucci used multiple-impression type methods. The secret he averred he had discovered was that of printing both staves and music by setting and printing the two layers separately. In fact this was not new, for it had already been used by printers of liturgical music; but Petrucci did make the technique feasible for polyphony by developing much finer type material. His method produced work of an elegance hardly equalled since.

At first, Petrucci seems to have sent the sheet of paper through the press three times – once for the notes and other musical signs, once for the staves and once for the text. This permitted great freedom in arranging the material of each layer, while also requiring precise alignment. During 1503 he seems to have realized that staves and text could be printed together, reducing the number of passes through the press to two. From then onwards, the physical appearance of his book and the technical processes remained unchanged (until his last two books), although the quality of both materials and workmanship gradually declined.

At first, Petrucci seems to have acquired much of his music from the friar Petrus Castellanus. The two produced an international repertory, appealing and accessible to professional musicians. The first frottola volumes in 1504 mark a shift in Petrucci's intended market. These books (and the volumes of lute tablature and lute songs which began to appear in 1507) offer a simpler repertory and seem to be addressed as much to dilettantes as to professionals. At the same time, Petrucci must have acquired new suppliers of music: there is evidence suggesting contacts with the Ferrarese court and other sources.

When Petrucci moved back to Fossombrone, he seems to have intended merely to complete projects already begun in Venice. The hiatus caused by the political situation, or by his loss of contact with his purchasers, was partly filled by the three non-musical books, of which the *de recta Paschae* is outstanding, and is proof that Petrucci had not yet, in 1513, abandoned his artistic standards. A small collection of new titles in 1514–15 suggests a fresh start in music printing, drawing on new sources. However, with the change of power in the duchy of Urbino, the situation deteriorated, and subsequent publications consisted mostly of reprintings of earlier titles. Even the three new books of 1519 appear to be a political response rather than a continuation of earlier work, as they might at first seem.

In 1520 Petrucci undertook two volumes of a new Roman or Florentine repertory. Neither survives complete, though both show significant changes in his printing-house practice. Apart from these two volumes, the year 1520 (and perhaps 1521) was devoted to the last reissues of earlier volumes.

Petrucci's production represents a major portion of the surviving music in each of the genres he covered. His three volumes devoted primarily to chansons appeared at the beginning of his career, and, as a group, show the changing styles of around 1500. The many books of frottolas, on the other hand, survey the field very thoroughly, and show the various forms in their different guises and changing popularity. Petrucci's books of masses, mass sections and motets, perhaps inherently more conservative, cover the transition from works of Josquin's generation to those of his immediate successors, and even their followers, including Willaert and Festa, who formed the Italian style of the next decades. Finally, the last two books are of particular interest for their early evidence of the transition from frottola to the new madrigalian forms. Petrucci, or his editor, seems always to have been sensitive to prevailing taste: among the few volumes that were not reprinted are those for lute, or voice and lute, perhaps because they seem to be aimed specifically at amateurs.

The readings preserved in Petrucci's editions have recently been criticized for being inaccurate and arbitrary. While there is no evidence that he regarded his editorial role differently from that of a manuscript scribe, there is much evidence of the care with which he transmitted the readings. This evidence includes stop-press and manuscript corrections, as well as cancel leaves.

Petrucci's legacy was seen as a major one by his contemporaries: the music he printed was widely disseminated and frequently copied into manuscripts. Various volumes (Josquin's masses and the *Motetti de la corona*) were reprinted by Pasoti and Dorico in 1526, and others were the basis of books published by Schoeffer and probably also by Giunta. To these men, scribes as well as printers, Petrucci's editions represented reliable usable copies of much of the most important music of the time, as trustworthy as any manuscript copy. They also presented music with an elegance which encouraged Antico, Dorico and Schoeffer (and through them many others) to continue to print music.

For another illustration *see* PRINTING AND PUBLISHING OF MUSIC, fig.5.

PUBLICATIONS
VENICE

Harmonice musices odhecaton A (after 15 May 1501, 14 Jan 1503, 25 May 1504/R), ed. H. Hewitt (Cambridge, MA, 1942); Canti B (5 Feb 1502/R, 4 Aug 1503), ed. in MRM, ii (1967); Motetti A (9 May 1502, 13 Feb 1505), some ed. in SC Mot, i (1991); Josquin Desprez: Misse [I] (27 Sept 1502, [c1505]); J. Obrecht: Misse (24 March 1503); Motetti de passione ... B (10 May 1503, Sept 1504); A. Brumel: Misse (17 June 1503); J. Ghiselin: Misse (15 July 1503/R); P. de La Rue: Misse (31 Oct 1503/R); Canti C (10 Feb 1504/R); A. Agricola: Misse (23 March 1504/R); Motetti C (15 Sept 1504), some ed. in SC Mot, ii (1991); Frottole I (28 Nov 1504), ed. R. Schwartz (Leipzig, 1935); Frottole II (5 Jan 1505, 29 Jan 1508); Frottole III (6 Feb 1505, 26 Nov 1507); M. de Orto: Misse (22 March 1505); Motetti IV (4 June 1505), some ed. in SC Mot, iii (1991); Josquin Desprez: Misse II (30 June 1505/R); Fragmenta missarum (31 Oct 1505); Motetti a cinque I (28 Nov 1505; 1508, lost); Frottole IV ([1505], 31 Aug 1507); Frottole V (23 Dec 1505, 21 May 1507), ed. R. Schwartz (Leipzig, 1935); Frottole VI (5 Feb 1506); Lamentationes Jeremie I (8 April 1506); Lamentationum Jeremie II (29 May 1506); H. Isaac: Misse (20 Oct 1506); G. van Weerbecke: Misse (7 Jan 1507); F. Spinacino: Intabolatura de lauto I (before 27 March 1507/R); F. Spinacino: Intabolatura de lauto II (31 March 1507/R); Frottole VII (6 June 1507); Magnificats I (14 Oct 1507; lost); J. Martini: Hymnorum I (1507; lost); Laude II (11 Jan 1508); Missarum diversorum autorum I (29 Jan 1508); G.M. Alemanni: Intabolatura de lauto III (20 June 1508; lost); Dammonis: Laude I (7 July 1508); J. Dalza: Intabolatura de lauto IV (31 Dec 1508/R); Frottole IX (22 Jan 1509); F. Bossinensis: Tenori e contrabassi I (27 March 1509/R)

FOSSOMBRONE

F. Bossinensis: Tenori e contrabassi II (10 May 1511/R); Frottole X (1512; lost); Paulus de Middelburgh: Paulina de recta Paschae (8

July 1513); B. Castiglione: Epistola de vita (29 July 1513); Messa corale [1513], unlikely to be Petrucci; Josquin Desprez: Misse III (1 March 1514/R, [1516]); Motetti de la corona [I] (17 Aug 1514, [1516], [1519]), some ed. in SC Mot, iv (1991); Frottole XI (24 Oct 1514); Josquin Desprez: Misse II (11 April 1515/R, [1517]); J. Mouton: Misse I (11 Aug 1515, [1520]); A. de Févin: Misse (22 Nov 1515, [1520]); Missarum decem libri duo (1515; lost); Josquin Desprez: Misse III (29 May 1516/R, [1517–18], [1520]); Paulus de Middelburgh: Parabola Christi (20 Nov 1516); Hippocrates, trans. Calvo (1 Jan 1519), ?not printed; Motetti de la corona II (17 June 1519, [1520]), some ed. in SC Mot, v (1992); Motetti de la corona III (7 Sept 1519), some ed. in SC Mot, v (1992); Motetti de la corona IV (31 Oct 1519), some ed. in SCMot v (1992); B. Pisano: Musica (23 May 1520); [Musica XII] [1520]

BIBLIOGRAPHY

A. Schmid: *Ottaviano dei Petrucci da Fossombrone ... und seine Nachfolger im sechzehnten Jahrhunderte* (Vienna, 1845/R)
F.X. Haberl: 'Drucke von Ottaviano Petrucci auf der Bibliothek des Liceo filarmonico in Bologna', MMg, v (1873), 49–57, 92–9
A. Vernarecci: *Ottaviano de' Petrucci da Fossombrone* (Fossombrone, 1881, 2/1882/R)
E. Vogel: 'Der erste mit beweglichen Metalltypen hergestellte Notendruck', JbMP 1895, 47–60
A. Einstein: 'Das elfte Buch der Frottole', ZMw, x (1927–8), 613–24
M. Cauchie: 'A propos des trois recueils instrumentaux de la série de l'odhecaton', RdM, ix (1928), 64–7
K. Jeppesen: 'Die neuentdeckten Bücher der Lauden des Ottaviano dei Petrucci', ZMw, xii (1929–30), 73–89
G. Reese: 'The First Printed Collection of Part-Music (the Odhecaton)', MQ, xx (1934), 39–76
J. Marix: 'Harmonice musices odhécaton A: quelques précisions chronologiques', RdM, xvi (1935), 236–41
C.L.W. Boer: *Chansonvormen op het einde van de XVde eeuw: een studie naar aanleiding van Petrucci's 'Harmonice musices odhecaton'* (Amsterdam, 1938)
E.T. Ferand: 'Two Unknown Frottole', MQ, xxvii (1941), 319–28
C. Sartori: *Bibliografia delle opere musicali stampate da Ottaviano Petrucci* (Florence, 1948)
C. Sartori: 'A Little-Known Petrucci Publication: the Second Book of Lute Tablatures by Francesco Bossinensis', MQ, xxxiv (1948), 234–45
A. Einstein: *The Italian Madrigal* (Princeton, NJ, 1949/R)
C. Sartori: 'Nuove conclusive aggiunte alla "Bibliografia del Petrucci"', CHM, i (1953), 175–220
A.-M. Bautier-Régnier: 'L'édition musicale italienne et les musiciens d'Outremonts au XVIe siècle (1501–1563)', La Renaissance dans les provinces du nord: Arras 1954, 27–49
F.J. Norton: *Italian Printers, 1501–1520* (London, 1958)
D. Plamenac: 'Excerpta Colombiniana: Items of Musical Interest in Fernando Colón's Regestrum', Miscelánea en homenaje a Monseñor Higinio Anglés (Barcelona, 1958–61), ii, 663–87
G. Ceccarelli: *Notizie biografiche di Ottaviano De' Petrucci* (Fossombrone, 1966)
Commemorazione di Ottaviano de' Petrucci: Fossombrone 1966 (Fossombrone, 1968)
C.W. Chapman: 'Printed Collections of Polyphonic Music Owned by Ferdinand Columbus', JAMS, xxi (1968), 34–84
K. Jeppesen: *La frottola, i: Bemerkungen zur Bibliographie der ältesten weltlichen Notendrucke in Italien* (Copenhagen, 1968)
S. Boorman: 'Petrucci at Fossombrone: the 'Motetti de la Corona', IMSCR XI: Copenhagen 1972, 295–301
G. Drake: *The First Printed Books of Motets: Petrucci's Motetti A numero trentatre (Venice, 1502) and Motetti de Passione, de Cruce, de Sacramento, de Beata Virgine et huius modi (Venice, 1503)* (diss., U. of Illinois, 1972)
S. Boorman: *Petrucci at Fossombrone: a Study of Early Music Printing, with Special Reference to the 'Motetti de la Corona', 1514–1519* (diss., U. of London, 1976)
S. Boorman: 'Petrucci's Type-Setters and the Process of Stemmatics', Formen und Probleme der Überlieferung mehrstimmiger Musik im Zeitalter Josquins Desprez: Wolfenbüttel 1976, 245–80
G. Ceccarelli and M. Spaccazocchi: *Tre carte musicali a stampa inedite di Ottaviano Petrucci* (Fossombrone, 1976)
T. Noblitt: 'Textual Criticism of Selected Works Published by Petrucci', Formen und Probleme der Überlieferung mehrstimmiger Musik in Zeitalter Josquins Desprez: Wolfenbüttel 1976, 201–44
M. Picker: 'The Motet Anthologies of Petrucci and Antico Published between 1514 and 1521: a Comparative Study', ibid., 181–99

S. Boorman: 'The "First" Edition of the Odhecaton A', *JAMS*, xxx (1977), 183–207

J. Noble: 'Ottaviano Petrucci: his Josquin Edition and some Others', *Essays Presented to Myron P. Gilmore*, ed. S. Bertellii and G. Ramakus, ii (Florence, 1978), 433–45

S. Boorman: 'Petrucci at Fossombrone: some New Editions and Cancels', *Source Materials and the Interpretation of Music: a Memorial Volume to Thurston Dart*, ed. I. Bent (London, 1981), 129–53

C. Gallico: 'Dal laboratorio di Ottaviano Petrucci: immagine, trasmissione e cultura della musica', *RIM*, xvii (1982), 187–206

R. Agee: 'The Venetian Privilege and Music Printing in the Sixteenth Century', *EMH*, iii (1983), 1–42

S. Boorman: 'A Case of Work and Turn: Half-Sheet Imposition in the Early Sixteenth Century', *The Library*, 6th ser., viii (1986), 301–21

W. Elders: 'Le problème de l'authenticité chez Josquin et les éditions de Petrucci: une investigation préliminaire', *FAM*, xxxvi (1989), 108–15

H.M. Brown: 'The Mirror of Men's Salvation: Music in Devotional Life about 1500', *Renaissance Quarterly*, xliii (1990), 744–73

M.K. Duggan: *Italian Music Incunabula: Printers and Type* (Berkeley, 1992)

S. Boorman: 'Printed Books of the Italian Renaissance from the Point of View of Manuscript Study', *RdMc*, xvi (1993), 2587–602

B.J. Blackburn: 'Lorenzo de' Medici, a Lost Isaac Manuscript, and the Venetian Ambassador', *Musica Franca: Essays in Honor of Frank A. D'Accone*, ed. I. Alm, A. McLamore and C. Reardon (New York, 1996), 19–44

STANLEY BOORMAN

Petrus Bonus de Burzellis. *See* PIETROBONO DE BURZELLIS.

Petrus Cameracensis. *See* PETER OF CAMBRAI.

Petrus Capuanus. *See* PETRUS DE AMALFIA.

Petrus de Abano [Petrus Aponensis] (*b* ?Abano, nr Padua, 1257; *d* Padua, ?1315). Italian philosopher and doctor. He studied at Padua and spent some time at Paris; later he became a professor at Padua University. Music is discussed in two of his works, the *Conciliator differentiarum philosophorum et precipue medicorum* (Venice, 1476) and the *Expositio Problematum Aristotelis* (Mantua, 1475). They contain the traditional notion of music as a discipline of the Quadrivium, but also interesting references to musical practice. Rhythm is related to pulse beats, and mention is made of the instruments *rubeba* and *viella*, the forms of the *muteti* and *rote*, and the practice of 'bordonizare'.

BIBLIOGRAPHY

L. Thorndike: *A History of Magic and Experimental Science*, ii (New York, 1923), 917ff

F. Alessio: 'Filosofia e scienza: Pietro da Abano', ed. G. Folena *Storia della cultura veneta*, ii (Vicenza, 1976), 171–206

F.A. Gallo: 'La trattatistica musicale', ibid., 469–76

F. ALBERTO GALLO

Petrus de Amalfia [Petrus Capuanus] (*b* ?Amalfi; *fl* 2nd half of the 14th century). Italian theorist. He was probably a member of the Amalfi nobility: in the 13th century a Petrus Capuanus de Amalfia was a cardinal, and an Andreas Capuanus was a canon in the choir of Amalfi Cathedral. Petrus's treatise, entitled *Compendium artis motectorum Marchecti* (ed. F.A. Gallo, Ant MI, *Scriptores*, i/1, 1966, pp.41–8), purports to be a summary of the mensural theory of Marchetto da Padova. In fact, however, it describes an Italian notation quite different from that of the early 14th century in that it is strongly influenced by the notation of 14th-century France. Petrus described a system containing three measures: *tempus perfectum* or *duodenarium* with each *brevis* divided into 12 *minime*, *tempus imperfectum* or *octonarium* with eight

minime, and *tempus imperfectissimum* or *quaternarium* with four *minime*.

BIBLIOGRAPHY

F.A. Gallo: *La teoria della notazione in Italia dalla fine del XIII all'inizio del XV secolo* (Bologna, 1966), 71ff

F.A. Gallo: 'Die Notationslehre im 14. und 15. Jahrhundert', *Die mittelalterliche Lehre von der Mehrstimmigkeit*, ed. H.H. Eggebrecht and others (Darmstadt, 1984), 259–356, esp. 319ff

F. ALBERTO GALLO/ANDREAS BÜCKER

Petrus de Cruce [Pierre de la Croix] (*fl c*1290). Composer and theorist. One of the most important French musicians of the later 13th century, he won the praise of such commentators as Jacobus of Liège, for whom he was 'that worthy practical musician, who composed so many beautiful and good pieces of mensural polyphony and followed Franco's precepts' (CSM, iii, vol.7, 1973, p.36), and Guy de Saint-Denis, for whom he was 'Master Petrus de Cruce, who was the finest practical musician and particularly observed the custom of the church of Amiens' (*GB-Lbl* Harl.281, ff.92r–v).

Apparently a native and resident of Amiens, and a member of a family prominent in that city from the 12th century to the early 14th, Petrus is likely to have studied at the University of Paris as a member of the Picard nation, earning there the title Magister (see Johnson). His student years would have been between 1260 and 1290, as he was evidently a younger contemporary of Franco (see Franco's *Ars cantus mensurabilis* of *c*1280), and Franco experimented with his mensural innovations, as Jacobus of Liège reported (CSM, iii, vol.7, 1973, p.38). Two of Petrus's motets occupy a place of honour at the beginning of the seventh fascicle of the Montpellier Codex (*F-MOf* H196) and thus date from before *c*1290. In 1298 Petrus sojourned in the king's castle in Paris and participated in the composition of a monophonic rhymed office for St Louis, perhaps the well-known *Ludovicus decus regnancium*. In 1301–2 he resided in the palace of Bishop Guillaume de Maçon of Amiens, where he was probably a senior cleric and a participant in the liturgy of the episcopal chapel. If still alive, he was no longer at the cutting edge of innovation in the 1320s, when Robert de Handlo and Jacobus of Liège placed him among their older figures as opposed to the *moderni*. Petrus bequeathed a book of polyphony to Amiens Cathedral, a gift first recorded in the inventory of the cathedral treasury in 1347.

Petrus is cited several times by Guy de Saint-Denis for his expertise in the details of the liturgy and chant of Amiens. No major work on plainchant survives under his name, but he is the author of a brief tonary reflecting Amiens usage, the *Tractatus de tonis* (CSM, xxix, 1976). He may also have turned his hand to an essay on the notation of mensural music, but again no major work survives. Two treatises, the *Ars motettorum* of Petrus de Picardia (CSM, xv, 1971, pp.16–24) and an anonymous *Ars musicae mensurabilis secundum Franconem* (CSM, xv, 1971, pp.31–57), have been attributed to him by modern scholars, but neither contains the innovations for which he was famed.

Petrus's major achievement in the development of mensural music was to progress beyond Franco's subdivision of the breve, such that not only the traditional two (unequal, i.e. minor and major) or three (equal, i.e. minor), but up to seven semibreves could occupy the value of a breve. He therefore stipulated that any two successive groups of semibreves (equivalent to two breves) must be separated by a *punctus*; this contrasts with the tradition codified by Franco, for whom such separation was necessary only for more than four successive semibreves, since four were inevitably recognized as two groups of two. Petrus de Cruce also seems to have been the first to introduce the dot as a symbol of *divisio*, or separation; Franco still used the *tractulus*, or small stroke, which he also referred to in the conventional manner as *divisio modi*. Jacobus of Liège well conveyed the sense of adventure that marked the experimentation Petrus carried on in his motets, describing how he 'sometimes put more than three semibreves for a perfect breve. At first he began to put four semibreves for a perfect *tempus*. . . . Thereafter he went further and put for one perfect *tempus* now five semibreves, now six, and now seven . . .' (CSM, iii, vol.7, 1973, pp.36–7).

The proliferation of semibreves naturally brought with it a corresponding deceleration in the speed of the breve. Petrus Le Viser, who knew no subdivision of the breve beyond that of Petrus de Cruce, held that this style required the slowest beat available (the *mos longus* in Le Viser's system). In contrast, for Jacobus of Liège the motets of Petrus de Cruce, though too advanced for the traditional fast beat (*cita mensuratio*), merely required a relatively moderate adjustment (*media mensuratio*) in the speed of the *tempus*. Jacobus further reported on the next step, when 'someone else, however, put for a perfect *tempus* not only five, six, or seven semibreves, but also eight and sometimes nine . . .' (CSM, iii, vol.7, 1973, p.38). According to Handlo this other musician was evidently Johannes de Garlandia (the Younger), who must have been active during the earliest years of the 14th century. In contrast to his comments on Petrus de Cruce, Jacobus expressed no approval here, presumably because the three *gradus* of Johannes de Muris's ternary mensural system (cf the *Notitia artis musice*), of which he disapproved, would in effect seem to have been brought about as soon as the figure nine was reached. To this most advanced style of notation Jacobus assigned his slowest beat (*morosa mensuratio*), in which the duration of the semibreve equalled that of the Franconian breve (CSM, iii, vol.7, 1973, p.36).

Petronian semibreves were generally restricted to tripla, whose increasing subdivision of the breves was more often syllabic than melismatic. Their performance was necessarily too rapid for each semibreve to be measured precisely. An analogous situation had existed in the decades around 1200 when a long (i.e. a *longa duorum temporum*) was divisible not only by two, but also by three or four breves, which were *ultra mensuram* (because of their speed they were not subject to precise measurement; cf the *Discantus positio vulgaris*). Similarly, around 1290 the semibreves in any group of four or more were simply shorter than short; and their delivery, as Jacobus of Liège testified (CSM, iii, vol.7, 1973, pp.38–9, 85–6), was equal, not yet requiring the conception of *semibrevis minorata* and *semibrevis minima*. (A variety of post-Petronian attempts at differentiations of value led eventually to the codifications of the French Ars Nova; for an early attempt *see* PETRUS LE VISER). The motetus generally continued to exhibit steady and perceptible modal rhythm – usually mode 1. It is these circumstances that must have caused Jacobus of Liège to approve of Petrus's motets as being still in accordance with Franconian tradition.

The two motets whose tripla Jacobus cited as examples are in *I-Tr* Vari 42 (nos.24 and 14), and in *F-MOf* H196, where they open the seventh fascicle (nos.236 and 237): *S'amours eust point de poer/Au renouveler du joli tans/Ecce* and *Aucun ont trouvé chant/Lonc tans me sui tenu/Annuntiantes*. The triplum of the latter is also cited in association with Petrus de Cruce by Robert de Handlo and the Faenza Anonymus (CSM, xv, 1971, 66–72), and it is quoted without attribution in two further anonymous late Ars Antiqua treatises, the *De cantu organico* (Anglès 1958, p.21) and the *Ars musicae mensurabilis secundum Franconem* (CSM, xv, 1971, p.42). In addition, Handlo and the *Ars musicae mensurabilis secundum Franconem* refer to an unattributed and otherwise unknown Latin triplum, *Novum melos promere*, in contexts suggesting Petrus de Cruce as author. Six other motets containing French tripla with Petronian characteristics and therefore possibly composed by Petrus are *Aucuns vont souvent-/Amor qui cor/Kyrie eleison* (*I-Tr* 42, no.13, *F-MOf* H196, no.247), *Amours qui se me maistrie/Solem iustitie/Solem* (*MOf*, nos.272, 321), *Lonc tans ai atendu/Tant ai souffert/Surrexit* (*MOf*, no.281), *Pour chou que j'aim/Li jolis tans/Kirieleison* (*MOf*, no.282), *Aucun qui ne sevent/Iure tuis/Maria* (*MOf*, no.300) and *Je cuidoie bien metre/Se j'ai folement/Solem* (*MOf*, no.315).

In Petronian motets the tenors as a rule move in longs, which are often unpatterned. In view of the retardation of the speed of the lower voices by the parlando in the triplum, the musical construction of the motetus often seems closer to the tenor than to the triplum (ex.1). The latter, by far the most rapid of the three voices, never hockets with the motetus, and its register is somewhat higher than that of the other two parts. Hence, Petronian

Ex.1
from *Aucun ont trouvé chant/Lonc tans me sui tenu/Annuntiantes*, F-MOf H196 no.237

motets tend to give the impression of a triplum supported by two lower and slower voices, one of which (motetus) has a text of its own. The highly irregular structure of the French verses with their precipitous rhythms and declamation seems quite capricious and often approaches rhymed prose. In a rather romantic way the music is primarily oriented toward the virtuoso of declamation. Generally, these motets with their shapeless tenors resist all analytical search for rational phrase structures; the same tendency is already in evidence in many motets of the Franconian period.

The post-Petronian evolution in France produced the system of four prolations with minim equivalence, a considerable departure from Petrus's notational practice. 14th-century English and Italian notations, however, were based on the Petronian principle of subdivision of the breve, accommodating varying numbers of semibreves between two puncti (or between ligatures, larger note values, rests, or any combination of these).

See also MOTET, §I, 1 and NOTATION, §III, 3.

BIBLIOGRAPHY

H. Anglès: 'De cantu organico: tratado de un autor catalán del siglo xiv', *AnM*, xiii (1958), 3–24

E.H. Sanders: 'The Medieval Motet', *Gattungen der Musik in Einzeldarstellungen: Gedenkschrift Leo Schrade*, ed. W. Arlt and others (Berne, 1973), 497–573

M. Huglo: 'De Francon de Cologne à Jacques de Liège', *RBM*, xxxiv–xxxv (1980–81), 44–60

F.A. Gallo: 'Die Notationslehre im 14. and 15. Jahrhundert', *Die mittelalterliche Lehre von der Mehrstimmigkeit, Geschichte der Musiktheorie*, ed. F. Zaminer, v (Darmstadt, 1984), 257–356

H. Ristory: *Post-franconische Theorie und Früh-Trecento: die Petrus de Cruce Neuerungen und ihre Bedeutung für die italienische Mensuralnotenschrift zu Beginn des 14. Jahrhunderts* (Frankfurt, 1988)

E.H. Roesner, F. Avril and N.F. Regalado: *Le Roman de Fauvel in the Edition of Mesire Chaillou de Pesstain* (New York, 1990), 30–38

P.M. Lefferts, ed. and trans.: *Robertus de Handlo: Regule/The Rules, and Johannes Hanboys: Summa/The Summa* (Lincoln, NE, 1991), 17–20

G.P. Johnson: *Aspects of Late Medieval Music at the Cathedral of Amiens* (diss., Yale U., 1991)

ERNEST H. SANDERS/PETER M. LEFFERTS

Petrus de Domarto. *See* DOMARTO, PETRUS DE.

Petrus de Picardia (*fl* 1250). French theorist. Hieronymus de Moravia included a short treatise by him in a compendium of treatises on various aspects of the music of his time. The work, the *Ars motettorum compilata breviter*, appears in two other sources as well, but is anonymous in both. The Parisian source, *F-Pn* lat.16663, has been printed twice in modern editions (*CoussemakerS*, i, 136*b*–139*b*; S.M. Cserba, ed.: *Hieronymus de Moravia O.P.: Tractatus de musica*, 259–63); an incomplete Swedish source, *S-Uu* C 453, is discussed by C.A. Moberg (*STMf*, x, 1928, pp.62–7). These two, together with *I-Nn* XVI A 15, were used for a critical edition by F.A. Gallo (CSM, xv 1971, pp.9–30).

Petrus based his treatise on Franco of Cologne and Johannes de Burgundia, a follower of Franco. It is an exposition of Franconian principles, illustrated by reference to various motet tenors, most of them mentioned or quoted in other contemporary sources. The work is in four short sections, discussing notation in simple figures, ligatures, rests and the rhythmic modes. It is designed as a condensation of its authorities addressed, as Petrus stated in the introduction, to 'novi auditores' who wish to be instructed briefly. Its importance lies in the large number of motet tenors mentioned, thus giving an idea of the distribution of certain pieces. Although it has been suggested that Petrus de Picardia is actually the composer PETRUS DE CRUCE, Hüschen's theory that they are two separate individuals is more plausible. Petrus de Cruce is cited by other theorists for his division of the breve into as many as seven semibreves – a practice adopted in his motets. In Petrus de Picardia's *Ars motettorum compilata breviter* the breve is divided into only two or three semibreves, following more closely the tradition of Franco of Cologne.

BIBLIOGRAPHY

MGG1 (H. Hüschen)

H. Riemann: *Geschichte der Musiktheorie im IX.–XIX. Jahrhundert* (Berlin, 2/1921/R; Eng. trans., 1962/R)

F. Ludwig: 'Die Quellen der Motetten ältesten Stils', *AMw*, v (1923), 185–222, 273–315, esp. 291; repr. in *SMM*, vii (1961)

R. Stephan: 'Theoretikerzitate', *Mf*, viii (1955), 85–8

M. Huglo: 'De Francon de Cologne à Jacques de Liège', *RBM*, xxxiv–xxxv (1980–81), 51–4

F.A. Gallo: 'Die Notationslehre im 14. und 15. Jahrhundert', *Die mittelalterliche Lehre von der Mehrstimmigkeit, Geschichte der Musiktheorie*, ed. F. Zaminer, v (Darmstadt, 1984), 259–356, esp. 268–9

H. Ristory: *Post-franconische Theorie und Früh-Trecento* (Frankfurt, 1988)

ALBERT SEAY/C. MATTHEW BALENSUELA

Petrus de Sancto Dionysio (*fl* 14th century). French theorist. He was from the abbey of St Denis on the outskirts of Paris and is known only as the compiler of the *Tractatus de musica*, which probably dates from shortly after 1321. The treatise is in two parts: the first, 'Musica theoretica', is largely derived from the *Notitia artis musice* of Jehan des Murs; the second, 'Musica practica', is a collection of rules on mensural notation drawn from at least two sources. Part of the *Tractatus* was published as Coussemaker's Anonymus 6 (*CoussemakerS*, iii, 398–403).

BIBLIOGRAPHY

K. von Fischer: 'Eine wiederaufgefundene Theoretikerhandschrift des späten 14. Jahrhunderts (Chicago, Newberry Library, MS 54.1...)', *Schweizer Beiträge zur Musikwissenschaft*, i (1972), 23–33

U. Michels, ed.: *Johannes de Muris Notitia artis musicae*, CSM, xvii (1972), 38–41; appx, 147–66 [edn of *Tractatus de musica*]

A. Gallo: 'Die Notationslehre im 14. und 15. Jahrhundert', *Die mittelalterliche Lehre von der Mehrstimmigkeit, Geschichte der Musiktheorie*, ed. F. Zaminer, v (Darmstadt, 1984), 259–356, esp. 277–8

GORDON A. ANDERSON/C. MATTHEW BALENSUELA

Petrus frater dictus Palma ociosa (*b* Bernaville, Ponthieu; *fl* 1336). French theorist. According to his *Compendium de discantu mensurabili* (ed. Wolf) he was a Cistercian monk at Cercamp Abbey, near Frévent in the Pas-de-Calais. His name may indicate a deformed hand which, as the *Summa musice* implies (lines 692–6; ed. Page), would have interfered with his learning and teaching of the Guidonian scale, particularly if it was his left hand.

Petrus's treatise survives along with standard works by Guido and Johannes Cotto and a series of anonymous tracts in *D-EF* Ampl.8°94, ff.59*v*–68. Its three chapters treat *discantus simplex* (intervals and note-against-note counterpoint), *falsa musica* (*musica ficta*) and *flores musice mensurabilis* (decorated counterpoint). The first of these is treated conventionally. The second is mainly concerned with making 3rds and 6ths major when they resolve outwards; sharps and flats are to be understood as raising and lowering pitches; certain motets and rondelli chromatically alter plainchant tenors, though Petrus avoids that in his examples; B♭ and D may be solmized as *ut*. The numerous examples suggest a striking tolerance of consecutive semitones, though it would seem in the light of the third chapter that these should be understood as underlying progressions which in practice would be elaborated.

The third chapter is remarkable for providing, at a very early date, an analytically conceived description of Ars Nova motet style. The 'flowers of measured music' (Petrus's equivalent of other theorists' *contrapunctus diminutus*) decorate note-against-note counterpoint; they are to be recognized by their being reducible to a single pitch; their character is determined by the mensuration in use, and since the potential decorations of possible progressions are innumerable, Petrus provides examples covering all combinations of modus, tempus and prolation. The 12 examples serve as models for composing over a chant: the composer may set out the decorated discantus line 'in whatever way seems most appropriate according to each group of notes', as shown in examples 'selected just as one might compose'.

The purpose of Petrus's treatise is indicated by its contents. The examples are strikingly similar to surviving Ars Nova motets in their melodic and rhythmic style. Nine of the 12 are based on Sanctus chants; they are all in two voices and could perhaps have been improvised. Cistercian houses did not normally favour decorated polyphony; Petrus therefore seems to have been providing a practical manual on polyphonic mass composition in a simple but up-to-date style for use outside his own order. His sophisticated understanding of Ars Nova music can only have been acquired from study of recent motets by Vitry and his immediate followers.

BIBLIOGRAPHY

J. Wolf: 'Ein Beitrag zur Diskantlehre des 14. Jahrhunderts', *SIMG*, xv (1913–14), 504–34

K.-J. Sachs: *Der Contrapunctus im 14. und 15. Jahrhundert* (Wiesbaden, 1974)

C. Page: *The 'Summa musice': a Thirteenth-Century Manual for Singers* (Cambridge, 1991), 72, 158

D. Leech-Wilkinson: 'Written and Improvised Polyphony', *Polyphonies de tradition orale*, ed. C. Meyer (Royaumont, 1993), 170–82

DANIEL LEECH-WILKINSON

Petrus Le Viser (*fl c*1290–1300). Theorist. He is known only through certain rules regarding mensural polyphony attributed to him in the *Regule* of Robert de Handlo (ed. Lefferts). Petrus Le Viser was the first to acknowledge the existence of different stylistic categories requiring different tempos for the beat. He posited three speeds at which the beat (*tempus* – i.e. the breve) could be taken: *mos* (i.e. manner) *longus*, *mos mediocris* and *mos lascivus*. The last of these, applying principally to the Franconian tradition, was equivalent to the modern 'allegro', in both senses of the word. It was now conceived as sufficiently fast for the characteristic unequal rhythm of the 3rd and 4th modes (*brevis recta* – *brevis altera*) to be equalized (two *breves recte*): 'But in the *mos lascivus* we reject any altered breve and any inequality of breves and affirm their equality; hence, two breves between two longs are equal in the *mos lascivus*, and both longs are imperfect'.

Whereas 12 to 15 years earlier Lambertus had still regarded this as a conceptual impossibility, Petrus Le Viser gave recognition to what came to be known as *modus imperfectus*. He added that the latter could not of course apply if three breves consistently intervened

between two longs. The speed of the *tempus* was fast enough to accommodate no more than the conventional two or three semibreves per breve; these were performed in the Franconian manner. ('It was these semibreves in the *mos lascivus* that gave rise to a good many *hoketi lascivi* [merry hockets] …') Examples of the *mos lascivus* with binary mensuration of the long occur in the Bamberg manuscript (*D-BAsp* Ed IV 6, no.86) and Montpellier manuscript (*F-MOf* H196, nos.153, 260, 261, 311), and also in a few English compositions, notably several in *US-Cum* 654 app.

The *mos mediocris* accommodates three, four or five semibreves in a *brevis recta* (e.g.: *F-MOf* no.281; *I-Tr* Vari 42, nos.4, 7, 12, 23; *GB-Onc* 362, no.9). 'But in this *mos* two semibreves are equal, three unequal, four equal and five unequal.' This passage doubtless reflects the evolutionary process that had apparently been set in motion, somewhat earlier, by Petrus de Cruce when he began to enlarge to four the number of semibreves set for a breve. These were necessarily performed too fast to be rhythmically differentiated. (In fact, Petrus Le Viser still stipulated that if four or five semibreves took the place of a breve, they could only be melismatic, i.e. turns or similar ornaments in which the first of five notes could hardly be more than an acciaccatura; see ex.1.) Four equal semibreves in one voice set against two semibreves in another (e.g. *I-Tr* no.7) could easily cause the latter to become equal, in effect producing *tempus imperfectum*. The contrapuntal evidence in applicable motets (three semibreves in one voice set against four or two in another) indicates that in a group of three semibreves the last was equivalent to the first two (the *via nature* of the early 14th century).

Petrus was thus the first to recognize at least special categories of imperfect mensuration on the two levels of *modus* and *tempus*. At the same time he unwittingly introduced what later came to be known as *prolatio minor*, since each of a group of four semibreves (in effect, minims) in *mos mediocris* has half the value of each of a group of two.

Petrus Le Viser's attempt at precise mensural definition of fractional semibreves was apparently not accepted by other musicians, among them Petrus de Cruce, whose more advanced motets, in which the breve could be

Ex.1 *GB-Onc* 362, no.9 (read in *mos mediocris*)

divided by up to seven semibreves, were performed in the *mos longus*. Here the customary reading of groups of two or three semibreves continued to obtain, probably because the large number of allowable semibreves per beat was conducive to the retention of the Franconian tradition.

The *mensurationes* of JACOBUS OF LIÈGE are similar to the *mores* of Petrus Le Viser, except that the conservative Jacques explained them as largely representing historical layers: (1) *citissima* for compositions written in longs and breves only, such as older hockets, in which 'the perfect breve has no more value than the present-day minim', e.g. Pérotin; (2) *cita* for Franconian motets; (3) *media* for Petronian motets; and (4) *morosa* for the 'moderns', e.g. Philippe de Vitry (*CoussemakerS*, ii, 400*b*–401). He reported no imperfect mensuration for either (2) or (3).

BIBLIOGRAPHY

H. Besseler: 'Studien zur Musik des Mittelalters, ii: Die Motette von Franko von Köln bis Philipp von Vitry', *AMw*, viii (1926), 137–258, esp. 159

E.H. Sanders: 'Duple Rhythm and Alternate Third Mode in the 13th Century', *JAMS*, xv (1962), 249–91, esp. 250–57 [the interpretation of *mos longus* and *mos mediocris* is partly in error]

S. Gullo: *Das Tempo in der Musik des XIII. und XIV. Jahrhunderts* (Berne, 1964), 22–5, 30–32

P.M. Lefferts, ed. and trans.: *Robertus de Handlo: Regule/The Rules, and Johannes Hanboys: Summa/The Summa* (Lincoln, NE, 1991), 22–4, 104–9

ERNEST H. SANDERS

Petrus optimus notator, Magister (*fl* mid-13th century). Musical scribe active in Paris. In the period following the generations of Perotinus and Robertus de Sabilone, he was involved, along with Johannes 'Primarius' and others, in copying the *Magnus liber* of Notre Dame, work that resulted in the transcription of the repertory from a modal to a mensural system of notation. He is mentioned only by the theorist Anonymus 4 (ed. Reckow, 1967, i, 46, 50). Anonymus 4's text implies that Petrus's activity preceded that of Franco of Cologne; it is possible, however, that Petrus 'the best notator' was actually a somewhat younger figure, PETRUS DE PICARDIA, on whose compendium *Ars motetorum compilata breviter* (ed. F.A. Gallo, CSM, xv, 1971) Anonymus 4 appears to have drawn. Identification with Petrus de Cruce (Coussemaker and others) is unlikely.

EDWARD H. ROESNER

Petrus Palma Ociosa. *See* PETRUS FRATER DICTUS PALMA OCIOSA.

Petrus Trothun Aurelianis, Magister (*fl* early or mid-13th century). Singer. He was active in Paris, about the time of Robertus de Sabilone, probably at Notre Dame. His singing of plainchant was praised by the theorist Anonymus 4 (ed. Reckow, 1967, i, 50), who also remarked that he knew little or nothing about the rhythm of measured music.

IAN D. BENT

Petrželka, Vilém (*b* Brno, 10 Sept 1889; *d* Brno, 10 Jan 1967). Czech composer and teacher. He studied at the Brno Organ School with Janáček (1905–8) and privately in Prague with Novák (1913–14). He lectured in composition and theory at the Brno Conservatory (1919–52) and at the academy (1947–60), where he became professor in 1957. From his Novák-like beginnings, he developed remarkably as a composer: his use of new methods of composition, daring for its time, aroused admiration, but later he inclined more towards the traditional school. Apart from the monumental cantata *Námořník Mikuláš*

('Mikuláš the Sailor'), the most valuable of his works are the chamber compositions. In them he made striking use of harmony, metre and rhythm and showed a refined technique in a style that was basically homophonic, though with frequent use of imitation. His works show no direct relation to folk music. Petrželka completed and orchestrated Janáček's Mass in E♭. He taught a number of composers, among them Zdeněk Blažek, Sokola, Kaprálová, Jan Novák, Josef Berg and Křivinka. He was also a critic for newspapers in Ostrava and Brno.

WORKS
(*selective list*)

Orch: Suite, chbr orch, 1925; Dramatická předehra [Dramatic Prelude], 1932; Partita, str, 1935; Sinfonietta, 1941; Vn Conc., 1943; Pastoral Sinfonietta, 1951; Sym., 1956

Vocal: Samoty duše [Solitudes of the Soul], song cycle, 1919; Štafeta [Relay], song cycle, 1v, str qt, 1927; Námořník Mikuláš [Mikuláš the Sailor] (cant., J. Wolker), 1929; Horník Pavel [Pavel the Miner] (op), 1938; Písně milostné [Love Songs], 1939; To je má zem [This is my Country], male chorus, 1940

Chbr and solo inst: Písně poezie a prózy [Songs of poetry and prose], pf, 1917; Z intimních chvil [From Intimate Moments], vn, pf, 1918; Fantasy, str qt, 1927; Suite, pf, 1930; Sonata, vc, 1930; Sonata, vn, pf, 1933; 4 Impromptus, vn, pf, 1940; Divertimento, wind qnt, 1941; Serenade, 9 insts, 1945; Str Qt no.5, 1947; Divertimento, vc, pf, 1947; 2 Pieces, vc, pf, 1947; Miniatures, wind qnt, 1953

Principal publishers: Hudební Matice, Panton, Supraphon

MSS in CZ-*Bm*

BIBLIOGRAPHY

J. Racek: *Leoš Janáček a současní moravští skladatelé* (Brno, 1940)

L. Firkušný: *Vilém Petrželka* (Prague, 1946)

I. Petrželka: *Vilém Petrželka* (Prague, 1988)

JAN TROJAN

Pets. *See* PAEZ.

Pet Shop Boys, the. English pop group. It was formed in 1981 by a pop music journalist, Neil Tennant (*b* North Shields, Northumberland, 10 July 1954), and Chris Lowe (*b* Blackpool, 4 Oct 1959). They had their first success with the song *West End Girls*, a number one hit in Britain and the USA in early 1986 which heralded a string of chart singles including four UK number one singles. Their sometimes excellent material is mostly original, although *Always on my Mind* (1987) was a cover version of the Elvis Presley standard. *Where the streets have no name/Can't keep my eyes off you* (1991) was a 'hi-energy' version of a U2 number and a Frankie Valli song segued together, while *Go West* (1993) was a remake of the Village People's 1979 gay anthem. They were probably at their peak in the late 1980s with their duet with Dusty Springfield, *What have I done to deserve this?* (1987), and *Heart* (1988), although their melodic touch never really left them. In 1999 they returned to the charts with their album *Nightlife*.

With Erasure, the Pet Shop Boys are the last in a long line of arty, camp synthesizer duos which stretches back to Sparks in the 1970s and continued into the 1980s with Yazoo, Blancmange and Soft Cell. However, the Pet Shop Boys' style is instantly recognizable: Tennant's dead-pan recitatives are combined with Lowe's disco and Balearic beats. The band have also shown a predilection for grandly operatic ballad styles, as on their 1991 hit *Jealousy*. Their work carries with it obvious camp overtones with songs such as *Shopping* (1987) and *Can you forgive her?* (1993), and a quintessentially English wry sense of humour and understatement, suggested in the titles of some of their albums: *Please* (1986), *Actually*

(1987) and *Very* (1993). Their melodramatic and highly theatrical performances on stage are reminiscent of a bygone pop age, when show and spectacle were applauded, not ridiculed.

BIBLIOGRAPHY

C. Heath: *The Pet Shop Boys: Literally* (London, 1991)
C. Heath: *The Pet Shop Boys versus America* (London, 1993)

DAVID BUCKLEY

Pettersson, (Gustaf) Allan (*b* Västra Ryd, Uppland, 19 Sept 1911; *d* Stockholm, 20 June 1980). Swedish composer. He was brought up, together with three older siblings, in crowded and basic conditions in a poor working-class area of southern Stockholm. His irascible blacksmith father and pious mother – who had an appealing singing voice and played the guitar – had bitter conflicts and eventually divorced. Pettersson played the violin in his youth at political meetings, funerals and silent films, though he received no formal training until his mid-teens. He applied to the Swedish Royal Academy of Music in Stockholm in 1926 but gained admission only later, studying the violin with Ruthström, the viola with Runnquist, harmony with Nordqvist and counterpoint with Melchers (1930–38). He played chamber works, theatre music and jazz, and was the viola player in the first Swedish performance of Schoenberg's *Pierrot lunaire* (1937). Although he won a position in 1939 as a section violist in the Concert Society (now the Royal Stockholm PO), a scholarship to study with Vieux in Paris postponed the start for a year. He kept the position until 1953 but stopped playing in the orchestra in 1950. He gained a reputation as a fine, sensitive musician and an irritable, difficult person.

Pettersson had intermittently written music since 1934. To further his goals as a composer, in the second half of the 1940s he studied privately: harmony with Herbert Rosenberg, counterpoint with Olsson, orchestration with Mann and composition with Blomdahl. He went back to Paris between 1951 and 1953, where his principal teacher was Leibowitz. On his return to Stockholm, he concentrated on composition; but worsening rheumatoid arthritis was eventually to turn him into an invalid, unable after 1968 even to attend concerts. Nevertheless in that year he finally achieved a public breakthrough with the première of his Seventh Symphony by the Royal Stockholm PO under Dorati.

In the 1970s Pettersson won various important Swedish prizes and awards. Frequent articles in the Swedish press centred on his chronic illness, colourful character and identification with the weak, poor and disadvantaged of society. In 1975, when the Stockholm PO decided not to take his music on tour, he became notorious by banning the orchestra from playing his music; the ban lasted a year, during which, unusually, Pettersson wrote little or no music. After his death, interest in his music increased internationally, especially in Germany. There an Allan Pettersson Gesellschaft issued six yearbooks, CPO began recording his complete works, and a series of concerts (in 1994–5) programmed almost all of them.

Pettersson's early compositions consist of chamber music and songs. The crucial work among these is the 24 *Barfotasånger* ('Barefoot Songs'), which he wrote in the 1940s to his own poetry. Some of the songs recall ballads or romances, folk tunes or church hymns; while others recall Schubert's *Winterreise*. They are mostly diatonic with simple accompaniments in structures of some

sophistication. Poetic themes include loneliness and longing, poverty, sorrow and death, suffused with religious implication. His orchestral music, all of which came afterwards, may be an attempt to deal with the losses these songs project and to realize on a large scale the struggles which lie behind them. Melodies from the *Barfotasånger* reappear later, sometimes as fragments (e.g. in Symphony no.2), sometimes in longer quoted sections (e.g. in the Second Violin Concerto and Symphony no.14). They may supply intervallic material for the larger works or blossom as calmer areas in very turbulent music.

Around 1950 Pettersson wrote his last two chamber works, which technically were the most advanced music he ever composed. In the Concerto for violin and string quartet, hysterical repetition, cold vibratoless chorales, arco and pizzicato beyond the bridge, deliberate mistuning via quarter-tones, and a very wide variety of articulations for all the instruments advance an impression of irony and provocation, sometimes wild, sometimes harrowingly distant. Just as alarming technically and emotionally are the Seven Sonatas for two violins. Like the concerto, they use Hindemith and Bartók as models to create a different sound world. Pettersson asks for strict observance of 'the prescribed string designations, which are given for *timbral* reasons, and the bowing indications, which all aim for a particular expression'. Characteristically that expression is harsh, distorted and agitated; occasionally there is grim humour. Both concerto and sonatas reveal comprehensive mastery of composition for strings. So do Pettersson's three concertos for string orchestra, all completed in the 1950s. The first owes something to Bartók's *Divertimento*; better known is the Third, whose long *mesto* middle movement became Pettersson's first recorded work. All three concertos demand considerable virtuosity; they also reveal the extreme contrasts and musical fragmentation which mark his symphonies of the 1950s.

Pettersson wrote 17 symphonies, from about 1950 to 1980. No.1 exists in two substantial incomplete (but orchestrated) manuscripts. No.17 is also incomplete. Most are on a very large scale: only three last fewer than 30 minutes (nos.10, 11 and 16), and only two have more than one movement (nos.3 and 8). The single-movement 9th and 13th symphonies last over an hour. The completed symphonies may be grouped into nos.2–4, 5–9 and 10–16. The first group emphasizes struggle and conflict, typically through irregular, rapidly changing chromatic lines in complex textures sometimes approaching atonality, and the opposition of these lines to smoother, slower, diatonic melodies. Such serenity as occasionally emerges is either insecure or final, suggesting either unattainable peace, or resignation and death. The next group exhibits more expansive writing and more diatonic harmony, often paring down thematic and harmonic material to a minimum and proceeding by ostinato and other repetition. The ethereal coda to the 7th Symphony has a harmonic support almost exclusively of a repeated B minor triad which continues for about six minutes.

No.10 is the fiercest and most concentrated of the symphonies. All of them in the third group contain highly charged music. Many simultaneous ideas and their doublings, typically at high speed and loud volume, and in heavy orchestration and syncopated melodic planes, compete in extreme musical struggle. Adding to the tension may be lines at very high tessitura, especially in the high strings and high brass. For all these reasons, these symphonies are the hardest to perform, although the last (no.16), together with the viola concerto, is more relaxed and transparent.

Thematic shapes and their individual developments, especially in the first and third groups of symphonies and the concertos (from the 1950s and 1970s), share procedures traceable to Pettersson's studies of serialism under Leibowitz. Although never genuinely serial, some of Pettersson's works have chromatic or 12-note themes which are developed in whole or in part in inversion, retrograde, or both. The music always retains tonality on a large scale, although achieved goals of diatonic triads are scarce in his purely orchestral music from the 1970s. Such goals are more common in his only orchestral music to include voices: Symphony no.12 and *Vox humana*. The former sets texts from Neruda's *Canto general*. It deals with oppression and strife, in a personal rather than political commentary. Both works identify with the oppressed and struggling outsider in grim, frequently tragic circumstances.

Although he completed 15 symphonies and several concertos, these works owe little to traditional formal patterns. Pettersson once observed that his symphonic form actually broke up symphonic structures. Although occasionally like the orchestral music of Mahler, Berg, Sibelius or Bartók, his is more extreme. The vigorous heterophony suggests struggle and defiance, while the more lyrical, often hauntingly beautiful passages could, in his words, 'calm a child's weeping'. He considered his own sufferings and blessings, especially from childhood, the source of his creativity. Through his music he felt himself 'a voice crying out . . . which is threatened with drowning in the noise of the times'.

WORKS

INSTRUMENTAL

Syms.: no.1, 1950–51, inc.; no.2, 1952–3; no.3, 1954–5; no.4, 1958–9; no.5, 1960–62; no.7, 1966–7; no.8, 1968–9; no.9, 1970; no.10, 1971–2; no.11, 1971–3; no.12, 'De döda på torget' [The Dead on the Square] (P. Neruda), chorus, orch, 1973–4; no.13, 1976; no.14, 1978; no.15, 1978; no.16, a sax, orch, 1979; no.17, 1980, inc.

Other orch: 3 concs., str, 1949–50, 1956, 1956–7; Sym. Movt, 1973; Vn Conc. no.2, 1977–8; Va Conc., 1979

Chbr and solo inst: 2 elegier, vn, pf, 1934; Fantasistycke, va, 1936; 4 improvisationer, str trio, 1936; Sketch for str qt, 1936, inc.; Andante espressivo, vn, pf, 1938; Romanza, vn, pf, 1942; Lamento, pf, 1945; Fugue, E, ob, cl, bn, 1948; Vn Conc. no.1, vn, str qt, 1949; 7 sonatas, 2 vn, 1951

VOCAL

Choral: Vox humana (Neruda and other S. American poetry), 4 solo vv, chorus, str, 1974

Solo vocal: 6 songs (G. Björling and others), medium v, pf, 1935; 24 Barfotasånger [Barefoot Songs] (Pettersson), medium v, pf, 1943–c1949, 6 songs arr. E. Hemberg, chorus, 1969, 8 songs arr. A. Dorati, medium v, orch, 1970

Principal publisher: Nordiska Musikförlaget

WRITINGS

'Att fiska toner' [Fishing for music], *Röster i radio* (6–12 April 1952)
'Dissonance – douleur', *Musique contemporaine – revue internationale*, nos.4–6 (1952), 235–6
'Den konstnärliga lögnen' [The artistic lie], *Musiklivet*, xxviii/2 (1955), 26–7
'Symfoni nr 2', Stockholm Konserthuset, 29 April 1955, pp.2–4 [programme notes]
'Allan Pettersson: Konsert nr 3 för stråkorkester', *Nutida musik*, i/5 (1957–8), 14–16
'Symfoni nr 3', Stockholm, 14 Oct 1959, pp.3, 5–7 [programme notes]
'Anteckningar' [Notes], *Nutida musik*, iv/4 (1960–61), 19 only

Barfotasånger och andra dikter [Barefoot songs and other poems] (Stockholm, 1976)

BIBLIOGRAPHY
AND OTHER RESOURCES

U. Stenström: 'Allan Pettersson: komponerande och grubblande son av Söder' [Allan Pettersson: composing and brooding son of the South Side], *Nutida musik*, i/5 (1957–8), 6–11
G. Fant: 'Den sista symfonikern' [The last symphonist], *Nutida musik*, vii/2 (1963–4), 11–13
R. Davidson: 'Allan Petterssons sextiotalssymfonier' [Allan Pettersson's symphonies of the 1960s], *Nutida musik*, xvii/2 (1973–4), 30–36
'Allan Pettersson – vem är det?' [Allan Pettersson – who is he?], TV documentary, dir. S. Hammar, Swedish Radio TV2 (Sweden, 1974)
B. Hedman and B. Berg: *Allan Petterssons 24 Barfotasånger: notationer kring en skivinspelning* [Allan Pettersson's 24 Barefoot songs: notations around a recording] (Stockholm, 1975)
'Poem: en resa i själens och naturens landskap' [Poem: a voyage in the landscape of the soul and of nature], TV Film, dir. B. Engström, Swedish Radio TV1 (Sweden, 1976)
L. Aare: *Allan Pettersson* (Stockholm, 1978)
P. Rapoport: 'Allan Pettersson and his Symphony no.2', *Opus est: Six Composers from Northern Europe* (London, 1978), 108–32, 199–200
'Människans röst (Vox humana)' [Voice of Humanity], TV documentary, dir. P. Berggren, Swedish Radio TV2 (Sweden, 1979)
P. Rapoport: *Allan Pettersson* (Stockholm, 1981)
L. Hedwall: *Den svenska symfonin* [The Swedish symphony] (Stockholm, 1983), 370–79
M.T. Vogt, ed.: *Allan Pettersson Jb* (Wuppertal, 1986–92) [6 vols]
'Sången om livet. Det förbannade! Det välsignade!' [The song of life. The damned! The blessed!], TV documentary, dir. P. Berggren, Swedish Radio TV2 (Sweden, 1987)
R. Davidson: 'Allan Pettersson', *Musiken i Sverige* [Music in Sweden], ed. L. Jonsson and H. Åstrand, iv (Stockholm, 1994), 463–75
M. Kube, ed.: *Allan Pettersson (1911–1980): Texte, Materialien, Analysen* (Hamburg, 1994)
M. Nicolin, ed.: *Musik von Allan Pettersson: Konzerte 1994/95 und ein Symposion* (Wuppertal, 1994)
L. Barkefors: *Gallret och stjärnan: Allan Petterssons väg genom Barfotasånger till symfoni* [The grate and the star: Allan Pettersson's path through the Barefoot songs to the symphony] (Göteborg, 1995)

PAUL RAPOPORT

Petti, Paolo (*b* Rome; *d* Rome, 1678). Italian composer and musician. He appears to have spent his whole life in Rome, where he was a pupil of Silvestro Durante and then *maestro di cappella* of S Maria Maggiore and a musician at the Castel S Angelo. According to Pitoni he died young. In his handling of both textures and learned contrapuntal techniques he was a skilful exponent of the polychoral style much cultivated in Rome.

WORKS

Motet, 3vv, bc, 1675[3]

4 masses, 16–17vv, 1670–78, *I-Rli**, *Rsg**; 1 ed. L. Feininger (Rome, 1956)
Mag, 3vv, bc; 4 ps, 9–10, 16vv, one dated 1665: *D-Bsb**
2 orats: Assalone, 5vv, insts; Bersabea, 5vv: lost
Cant., 1v, *I-Rvat*; 4 arias, 1v, *A-Wn*; madrigal, 5vv, *GB-Cfm*, *Lbl* (contrafactum)

BIBLIOGRAPHY

MGG1 (O. Mischiati); *PitoniN*
L. Feininger: 'La scuola policorale romana del Sei e Settecento', *CHM*, ii (1956–7), 193–7

Petty, Tom [Thomas] (*b* Gainesville, FL, 20 Oct 1952). American rock singer and songwriter. As a teenager he formed Mudcrutch, influenced by the 'British invasion', with Benmont Tench (keyboards) and Mike Campbell (guitar). The trio moved from Florida to California

(1976), renaming the group Tom Petty and The Heart-breakers and adding Ron Blair (bass guitar) and Stan Lynch (drums) to the line-up. Between 1976 and 1999 they recorded ten albums of Petty's songs. Among his most commercially successful compositions were 'American Girl' from the début album, 'Don't do me like that' (*Damn the Torpedoes*, 1979), 'Don't come around here no more' (*Southern Accents*, 1985) and 'Into the Great Wide Open' (*Into the Great Wide Open*, 1991). Petty also made two solo albums. Through his well-crafted songs and his work with such performers as Bob Dylan (with whom the group toured in the 1980s and 90s) and George Harrison, he has been one of the leading figures of mainstream rock for more than two decades. With Dylan and Harrison, Petty was also a member of the 'supergroup' the Traveling Wilburys.

DAVE LAING

Petyr [Petre, Peter], Henry (*b c*1470; *d* after 1516). English composer. He graduated BMus at Oxford in 1516, having spent 30 years in the study and practice of music. Only one of his works, a 'Playn Song' Mass in *GB-Lbl* Add.5665 (without Kyrie), has survived. The title refers to the fact that the notation is adapted from plainchant symbols. In fact only two note values are used: breve and semibreve, though other instances of the same convention also use the minim. This interpretation of the notational symbols is confirmed by their appearance from time to time in the cantus firmus voice only of ritual polyphonic items in the early 16th century. (Taverner's 'Plainsong' mass also uses a restricted range of values but does not employ plainchant symbols.) Petyr's mass has little merit besides its ingenuity.

JOHN CALDWELL

Petyrek, Felix (*b* Brno, 14 May 1892; *d* Vienna, 1 Dec 1951). Austrian pianist, composer and teacher. In Vienna he studied the piano with Godowsky and Sauer, musicology with Adler and composition with Schreker (1912–15, 1917–19). Several of Schreker's pupils at this time, such as Grosz, Hába, Krenek, Rathaus and Rosenstock became close friends: Petyrek was to be responsible for many first performances of their piano and chamber works. He used his first appointment to a teaching post in piano, at the Salzburg Mozarteum, as the opportunity to place his many talents, as solo pianist, teacher, composer and performer, at the service of contemporary music, and this he continued to do in Berlin (Musikhochschule, 1921–3), Abbazia, Slovenia (1923–6), Athens (Odeon, 1926–30), Stuttgart (Musikhochschule, succeeding Wilhelm Kempff, 1930–39), Leipzig (Musikhochschule and University, 1939–45). In 1949 he returned to Vienna, where he taught in several faculties at the Musikakademie, as it then was, and set up an archive of folksong.

While the core of his oeuvre is the vocal and piano music, his melodrama *Die arme Mutter und der Tod* (1922, operatic version 1929) (which employs Sprechgesang), the sextet and the Sinfonietta (both monothematic in conception) helped equally to establish his reputation as an original artist. The *Sechs groteske Klavierstücke* (1914–19), with their pregnant rhythms, staccato-martellato effects, disruptive changes of tempo, and bitonal tendencies, were much praised in progressive circles and frequently performed. He composed piano duos and duets in the 1930s, after marrying the pianist Renate Helene Lang, his second wife. Hindemith, among others, took an interest in Petyrek, and he was invited to Donaueschingen in 1923 and 1925, making him spiritually a co-founder of the ISCM. The Swiss poet and anthroposophist Hans Reinhart had a great influence on his stage works, including the three subtle settings of Reinhart's versions of Andersen. Mahler's influence has been overstated: at the start of his career Petyrek was very receptive to Schreker's sphere of expression but later became more critical of his musical language. As an acknowledged interpreter of contemporary music he was closer to Hindemith, Stravinsky (critics at one time often called him the 'Viennese Stravinsky') and Bartók, without renouncing the colourful melodic style and instumentation of his former teacher. He shared Bartók's interest in collecting the folksongs of eastern and central-southern Europe, and adapting them in his own compositions. Petyrek favoured formal originality, strong rhythms and inventive melodic language. But his particular strength probably lay in his independent efforts to secure emancipation from major–minor tonality without following Schoenberg and his circle into the 12-note technique. His path involved freely atonal structures, bitonal or polytonal combinations, extreme chromaticism, and then a return once more to tonal allegiances.

WORKS
(*selective list*)

Stage: Komödie (pantomime, Festenberg), Vienna, 1922; Tahi (pantomime, J. Algo), Hanover, 1928; Die arme Mutter und der Tod (op, Reinhart), Winterthur, 1933; Der Schatten (Nachtstück, H. Reinhart), Basle, 1937; Der Garten des Paradieses (dramatische Rhapsodie, Reinhart), Leipzig, 1942

Orch: Arabische Suite, 1918; Scherzo, b, 1919; Sinfonietta, 1921; Conc., F, 2 pf, orch, 1931; Conc., 2 pf, orch, 1949; 2 Concs. for orch

Chbr: Sonata, e, vn, pf, 1913; Qnt, 1914; 2 Kammermusiklieder, 1919; Pf Trio, 1921; Sextet, cl, pf, str qt, perf. 1922; Divertimento, wind, 1922; Fischmarkt in Athen, str trio

Pf: Sonata, D; Variationen und Tripelfuge über ein eigenes Thema, 1915; 24 ukrainische Volkweisen, 1919–20; Passacaglia und Fuge, d, 1922; 6 groteske Klavierstücke, 1923; Choral, Variationen und Sonatine, 1924; 6 griechische Rhapsodien, 1927; 11 kleine Kinderstücke, 1927; 3 sonatas, 1928; Toccata, 1931; 6 Konzertetüden, 2 pf, 1934; Toccata und Fuge, 2 pf, 1934; Burleske, 1941; Variation über ein Thema von Verdi, 2 pf, 1941; Sonatina, C, 1947; 5 sonatas, 1956

Vocal: Lukians Gesänge griechischer Hetären, S, pf; 2 japanische Haikos, S, cl, pf; 10 slawische Volkslieder, v, str trio; 2 jüdische Hochzeitslieder, 3vv, ob, str qt; Lieder aus dem West-östlichen Diwan (J.W. von Goethe), chorus; Beduinischer Diwan, chorus 8vv; 5 heitere Lieder (J.W. von Goethe), male chorus; Steirische Bauernhochzeit, chorus; Jugendland (E.C. Kolbenheyer), chorus 6vv, 1936; Wir tragen ein Licht (F. Höller), chorus 5vv, 1936; Gotischer St Georg (A. Pichler), chorus 8vv, 1939

Principal publishers: Doblinger, Österreichischer Bundesverlag, Tonger, Ullmann, Universal

BIBLIOGRAPHY
MGG1 (K. Komma)

H. Weiskopf: 'Die Gestalt Felix Petyrek', *Neue Musik-Zeitung*, xlix (1928), 497

F. Schwebsch: 'Felix Petyrek', *ZfM*, Jg.105 (1938), 588–93

R.F. Brauner: 'Felix Petyrek', *Österreichische Zeitschrift für Musik*, iii (1951), 94–6

K. Komma: 'Schicksal und Schaffen sudetendeutscher Komponisten', *Stifter-Jb*, iii (1953), 83, 88, 111

C. Ottner: 'Moderner Musikbolschewist - wie der Herr, so der Knecht: Felix Petyrek, ein vergessener Schüler Franz Schrekers', *Österreichische Musik, Musik in Österreich: Beiträge zur Musikgeschichte Mitteleuropas: Theophil Antonicek zum 60. Geburtstag*, ed. E.T. Hilscher (Tutzing, 1998), 605–31

L. Mahn: *Felix Petyrek* (Tutzing, 1998)

C. Ottner: 'Was damals als unglaubliche Kühnheit erschine': Franz Schrekers Wiener Kompositionsklasse: Studien zu Wilhelm Grosz, Felix Petyrek und Karol Rathaus (Frankfurt, 2000)

CARMEN OTTNER

Petz. See PAEZ.

Petz, Johann Christoph. See PEZ, JOHANN CHRISTOPH.

Petzold, Christian. See PEZOLD, CHRISTIAN.

Petzold, Rudolf (*b* Liverpool, 17 July 1908; *d* Michaelshoven, Cologne, 17 Nov 1991). German composer and teacher of music. His interest in music was first aroused as a ten-year-old in Liverpool by the English conductor and Handel expert John Tobin. From 1930 to 1933 he studied at the Cologne Musikhochschule (composition with Jarnach, piano with Peter Dahm). He worked as a freelance composer (1933–41) and taught music theory at the Cologne Musikhochschule (1937–8). From 1941 to 1942 he again lectured on music theory, this time at the Frankfurt Musikhochschule. He returned to Cologne in 1946 to teach composition and stayed there until 1970, becoming successor to Jarnach in 1955 and later holding the appointment of deputy director (1960–69). After his retirement in 1970 Petzold devoted himself entirely to composing. He received the Robert Schumann Prize in 1958 and the Silver Medallion of the Cologne Musikhochschule in 1968.

His work falls into three periods. In the first, ending in about 1949 (opp.1–26), Petzold wrote mostly chamber music in a late Romantic style of broadened tonality. The middle period, up to about 1961 (Violin Concerto op.38), is characterized by increasingly free atonality. Of his work after 1962 the 'imaginary ballet' Incarnatus est homo is particularly important. In these later works tonality is suspended, making way, in many cases, for the application of serial techniques.

WORKS
(selective list)

Chbr and solo inst: Str Qt no.1, op.14, 1934; Sonata, op.19, vn, pf, 1936; Str Qt no.2, op.24, 1944; Str Qt no.3, op.34, 1954; Sonata, op.46, vn, pf, 1968–9; Str Qt no.4, op.48, 1972; Str Sextet, op.50, 1976; pf works opp.5, 20, 26, 27, 45

Vocal: Mass, op.30, chorus, 1949; Te Deum, op.32, double chorus, org, 1950; Komm heiliger Geist (F. Werfel), op.36, chorus, orch, 1957; Die Lerche, op.40, S, chorus, orch, 1962; Incarnatus est homo, op.43, chorus, orch, 1966; Contemplatio, op.49, chorus, orch, 1973–4; Voces humanae, op.47, chorus, 1975; songs opp.10, 23, 25, 29

Orch: Sinfonietta, op.21, str, 1940; Sym. no.2, op.33, 1952; Chbr Sym., op.35, 1955; Conc., op.38, vn, str, 1960

Principal publisher: Gerig

BIBLIOGRAPHY

H. Lemacher: 'Rudolf Petzold', ZfM, Jg. 112 (1951), 227–31
J. Schwermer: 'Das Chorschaffen Rudolf Petzolds', Lied und Chor, lxiii (1971), 52–3
R. Lück, ed.: Das Komponistenportrait (Cologne, 1971)
Obituary, Das Orchester, xl (1992), 204 only

RUDOLF LÜCK/R

Peudargent [von Huy], Martin (*b* Huy, *c*1525–30; *d* after 1587). Flemish composer. He was for much of his career in the service of the Duke of Kleve as Kapellmeister. In his first work, published in 1555, he referred to himself as 'musicus' in the court of Duke Wilhelm V of Jülich-Kleve-Berg in Düsseldorf. Oridryus, in his treatise *Practicae musicae* (Düsseldorf, 1557), referred to him in friendly terms and described him as *praefectum* in the duke's chapel. Peudargent is known to have been present at Jülich in 1585 for the marriage of Duke Johann-Wilhelm and the Margravine Jakobe von Baden, and he was named by Graminäus as the principal musician there. It is clear that he remained for more than 30 years in the service of the Duke of Kleve; by 1587, when he petitioned his master for assistance, he had become blind and was no longer able to support his family.

Peudargent's style conforms to that current in the Low Countries and the Rhineland at the time. His motets are predominantly imitative and the texts are handled with a sure sense of balance. The underlay is notably syllabic and the harmonic idiom is markedly 'tonal' in feeling.

WORKS

Liber primus sacrarum cantionum, 5vv (Düsseldorf, 1555), ed. H. Kümmerling (Frankfurt, 1979)
Liber secundus sacrarum cantionum, 5, 6vv (Düsseldorf, 1555)
8 motets, 19 chansons, Novi prorsus et elegantis libri musici (Düsseldorf, 1561), bassus only extant
Motets, 1553⁹, 1556³
1 chanson, 6vv, 1553²⁵, its superius, ornamented, in G. dalla Casa: *Il vero modo di diminuir* (Venice, 1584)

BIBLIOGRAPHY

R. Federhofer-Königs: Johannes Oridryus und sein Musiktraktat (Düsseldorf 1557) (Cologne, 1957)
G. Pietzsch: 'Die Jülich'sche Hochzeit 1585', Studien zur Musikgeschichte des Rheinlandes, ii: Karl Gustav Fellerer zum 60. Geburtstag, ed. H. Drux, K.W. Niemöller and W. Thoene (Cologne, 1962), 166–89

JOSÉ QUITIN/HENRI VANHULST

Peuerl [Bäuerl, Peyerl], Paul (*b* ?Stuttgart, bap. 13 June 1570; *d* after 1624). German composer, organist and organ builder. From 1602 onwards he was an organist at Horn, Lower Austria, and, from 1 November 1609 at the latest, at the church of the Protestant school at Steyr, Upper Austria, though he was not definitely appointed there until mid-February 1614. He built or renovated, among others, organs for churches at Steyr (1613), Enns (1615) and Horn (1606 and 1615) and a two-manual instrument for the church of the Cistercian Wilhering Abbey, Upper Austria (1619). None of these instruments has survived, though from our knowledge of the specification of the last-named we can conclude that his organs were of the *werkprinzip* type. In 1625 he had to flee from Steyr as a religious refugee, after which nothing more is heard of him.

Peuerl published four collections of his own compositions while he was at Steyr. His name is linked above all with the creation of the variation suite. There is still research to be done on the antecedents of this form, which possibly include early 16th-century Italian lute music and the variations of the English virginalists; the form was soon taken up by Schein, Posch and others. Peuerl's suites consist of four dances: paduana, intrada, 'dance' and galliard. The 'dance' ('Däntz') is the basic theme; the other three are variations of it, the paduana being the closest to it and the intrada and galliard more distant. Peuerl, like H.L. Hassler, Aichinger, Schein and others, was one of the few German composers of the early Baroque period to compose italianate instrumental canzonas. He was also the first German composer to write (in his 1625 volume) for the Italian texture of two melody instruments and continuo. To some extent his songs (1613) follow traditional German adaptations of Italian forms such as madrigal and balletto, but they also hark back to the court songs and *Bergreihen* of 16th-century Germany.

WORKS

Edition: *P. Peuerl und I. Posch: Instrumental- und Vokalwerke*, ed.
K. Geiringer, DTÖ, lxx, Jg.xxxvi/2 (1929/R)

Newe Padouan, Intrada, Däntz unnd Galliarda, a 4 (Nuremberg,
1611); 3 in Amoenitatum musicalium hortulus (Leipzig, 1622),
lost; 9 intabulated for kbd, *A-LIm*

Weltspiegel, das ist neue teutsche Gesänger … sampt zweyen
Canzonen, 5vv (Nuremberg, 1613)

Ettliche lustige Padovanen, Intraden, Galliarden, Couranten und
Däntz, a 3 (Nuremberg, 1620), inc.

Gantz neue Padouanen, Auffzüg, Balletten, Couranten, Intraden und
Däntz, a 3 (Nuremberg, 1625), ?lost, *D-Bgk* according to Eitner

BIBLIOGRAPHY

EitnerQ
P. Frankl: *Paul Peuerl, ein österreichischer Vokal- und
Instrumentalkomponist um 1600* (diss., U. of Vienna, 1915)
K. Geiringer: 'Paul Peuerl', *SMw*, xvi (1929), 32–69
R. Flotzinger: 'Einige neue Daten zu Paul Peuerl', *Mitteilungen der
Österreichischen Gesellschaft für Musikwissenschaft*, no.5 (1975),
16
W. Tuschner: 'Paul Peuerl als Orgelbauer in der Welser
Stadtpfarrkirche', *Oberösterreichische Heimatblätter*,
Sonderdruck, xxxii (1978), 63–72
K.A. de Mol: *Tonal Practices in Early Seventeenth Century German
Dances* (diss., Northwestern U., 1990)
OTHMAR WESSELY/DOROTHEA SCHRÖDER

Peutinger, Conrad (*b* Augsburg, 14 Oct 1465; *d* Augsburg,
28 Dec 1547). German diplomat, humanist and patron of
music. After studies in Basle and several Italian cities he
returned to Augsburg in 1497 as secretary of the town
council. He became a trusted adviser of Emperor Maximilian I (*d* 1519) and an important link between the
artistic activities of Augsburg and the imperial court. In
1521, during the reign of Charles V, he met Luther and
tried unsuccessfully to get the reformer to recant. Peutinger
was bound to musicians by both friendship and correspondence. He aided the work of the music printer Erhard
Oeglin and Petrus Tritonius, the composer of Horatian
ode settings. He was closely associated with Veit Bild, the
Benedictine theorist and composer, and Othmar Lusci-
nius, the theorist and humanist. His correspondence with
Nicolaus Ellenbog reveals their mutual interest in literature and music. He wrote the postscript to *Liber
selectarum cantionum* (RISM, 1520⁴), a collection of
motets by Josquin, Obrecht, Senfl, and others, that Senfl
published in Augsburg in honour of Maximilian I.

BIBLIOGRAPHY

MGG1 (A. Layer)
E. König, ed.: *Konrad Peutingers Briefwechsel* (Munich, 1923)
CLEMENT A. MILLER

Peverara [Peperara], Laura (*b* Mantua, *c*1550; *d* Ferrara, 4
Jan 1601). Italian virtuosa singer. She was brought up in
Mantuan courtly circles, the daughter of a respected
Mantuan intellectual who was tutor to the princes of that
city. She was clearly a singer of great excellence and
charm, as well as a dancer and harpist of considerable
skill. She appears to have been present as a singer in
Verona in the late 1570s. She was the first and the
dominant member of the famous Ferrarese group of
singers (*concerto delle donne*, which also included Anna
Guarini, Livia d'Arco and, in some role and for some
period at least, Tarquinia Molza) from its foundation in
1580 until its dissolution in 1598. Peverara's singing was
the subject of numerous laudatory poems by various
authors including Tasso, who became acquainted with
her in Mantua in 1563 or 1564 (Tasso's poems for her
are listed in Maier; for others see Durante and Martellotti).
Peverara's marriage, to the Ferrarese Count Annibale

Turco on 22 February 1583, was an occasion for elaborate
festivities, including the preparation under Tasso's supervision of the madrigal anthology, *Il Lauro verde* (Ferrara,
1583¹⁰). Two other anthologies were compiled in her
honour: *Il Lauro secco* (Ferrara, 1582⁵) and a manuscript
collection (*I-VEaf* 220), probably from very early in 1580.

BIBLIOGRAPHY

NewcombMF
B. Maier, ed.: *Torquato Tasso: Opere*, i (Milan, 1963), index of
names
A. Newcomb: 'The Three Anthologies for Laura Peverara,
1580–1583', *RIM*, x (1975), 329–45
E. Durante and A. Martellotti: *Cronistoria del concerto delle dame
principalissime di Margherita Gonzaga d'Este* (Florence, 1979,
2/1989)
ANTHONY NEWCOMB

Pevernage [Bevernage, Beveringen], Andreas [André, An-
dries] (*b* Harelbeke, nr Kortrijk, 1542/3; *d* Antwerp, 30
July 1591). Flemish composer. On 21 January 1563 he
was appointed choirmaster of St Salvator, Bruges, and on
22 September of the same year he was named to a similar
post at Onze Lieve Vrouwkerk, Kortrijk. He remained in
Kortrijk until 1577 although he held a prebend at St
Willibrordus in Hulst in 1564. In 1578 Kortrijk fell briefly
to Calvinist rule. By the following year Pevernage had
secured the position of choirmaster at St Jacob, Bruges.
This city too fell to the Calvinists and Catholic services
were suppressed there from May 1581 until 1584. On 1
October 1584 he was reappointed to his former position
at Kortrijk and less than a year later became choirmaster
at Antwerp Cathedral where he remained until his death.
He was buried by the cathedral's altar of St Anne.
Antwerp archives confirm that Pevernage rebuilt the
music library destroyed by the Calvinist rebellion and
that he was active in humanist circles surrounding the
Plantin press.

Pevernage's sacred output includes *Laudes vespertinae*
(Antwerp, 1604), a posthumous collection of 14 Marian
antiphons and sacrament hymns intended for Antwerp
confraternity services, and six masses, also published
posthumously. The *Cantiones sacrae* (1578), a collection
of sacred and secular motets, includes 25 occasional
works written in honour of such notable contemporaries
as Margaret of Parma, Louis de Berlaimont (Archbishop
of Cambrai), and seven princes of Kortrijk's St Cecilia
guild. A seven-voice hymn to the patroness of music, *O
virgo generosa*, was reportedly sung at concerts held at
the composer's home.

Pevernage's four books of chansons include over 100
works that appear to be planned according to the type of
text set (whether spiritual or profane), voicing and mode.
They are mostly for five voices and set texts by poets such
as Clément Marot and Philippe Desportes. The first book
(1589) includes an epitaph for Plantin, *Pleurez muses,
attristez vos chansons*, while book 3 includes more
madrigalistic chansons characterized by picturesque and
dramatic text expression. Pevernage was awarded a
stipend of £50 by the city of Antwerp for the publication
of book 4 and the volume opens with a musical tribute to
the city, *Clio, chantons*. In addition to his work as a
composer, Pevernage also edited the popular and influential anthology *Harmonia celeste* (1583). The volume
includes seven of his own madrigals. Four additional
madrigals appear in other Italian music anthologies issued
in Antwerp by Phalèse and Bellère.

ENCOMIVM MVSICES

Devotional print showing the six-voice motet 'Nata et grata polo' by Pevernage, supported by the figures of Harmonia, Musica and Mensura: engraving by A. and C. Collaert, after Joannes Stradanus, from 'Encomium musices' (Antwerp: Philip Galle, c1590)

WORKS

[6] Missae, 5–7vv (Antwerp, 1602); inc.
[39] Cantiones aliquot sacrae, 6–8vv, quibus addita sunt [25] elogia nonnula (Douai, 1578, 2/1602 omits elegies and incl. 1 new motet); 1 ed. F. Commer, Collectio operum musicorum batavorum, viii (Berlin, n.d.)
4 motets, 1564[3-5]
5 motets: Dignus es Domine, 4vv; Gloria in excelsis Deo, 9vv; Laude pia Dominum, 5vv; Nata et grata polo, 6vv; Osculetur me, 5vv: engraved in devotional prints by J. Sadeler and A. Collaert (for P. Galle) (n.p., 1587–90); ed. I. Bossuyt and J. van Deun, *Andreas Pevernage (1542/43–1591): Beeldmotetten* (Bruges, 1985)
14 motets, Laudes vespertinae B. Mariae Virginis (Antwerp, 1604, 2/1629[2], 3/1648)
3 motets, *A-Ws*
Chansons … livre premier, contenant chansons spirituelles, 5vv (Antwerp, 1589); Chansons … livre second, 5vv (Antwerp, 1590); Chansons … livre troisième, 5vv (Antwerp, 1590); Chansons … livre quatrième, 6–8vv (Antwerp, 1591): all ed. in RRMR, lx–lxiv (1983)
Chansons … tant spirituelles que prophanes, 5vv (Antwerp, 1606)
Chansons … a six, sept, et huict parties (Antwerp, 1607)
5 works in 1583[14]; 1 in 1583[15]; 2 in 1589[9]; 2 in 1591[10]; 3 in 1597[10]
2 bicinia, 1590[19]

BIBLIOGRAPHY

G. Caullet: *Musiciens de la collégiale Notre-Dame à Courtrai d'après leurs testaments* (Kortrijk and Bruges, 1911)
L. Willems: 'A. Pevernage's Cantiones sacrae, 1578', *Tijdschrift van het boek - en bibliotheekswezen*, ix (1911), 3–18
J.A. Stellfeld: *Andries Pevernage: zijne leven, zijne werken* (Leuven, 1943)
G.R. Hoekstra: *The Chansons of André Pevernage (1542/43–1591)* (diss., Ohio State U., 1975)
R. de Man: 'André Pevernage en Kortrijk (1543–1591)', *Handelingen van de Geschied en Oudheidkundige Kring Kortrijk*, xliv (1977), 3–42
G.R. Hoekstra: 'An Eight-Voice Parody of Lassus: André Pevernage's "Bon jour mon coeur"', *EMc*, vii (1979), 367–77
R. Rasch: *De cantiones natalitiae en het kerkelijke muziekleven in de zuidelijke Nederlanden gedurende de zeventiende eeuw* (Utrecht, 1985)
B. Bouckaert and others: 'Andreas Pevernage (1542/3–1591) en het muziekleven in zijn tijd', *Musica antiqua*, x/4 (1993), 161–75
G.R. Hoekstra: 'The Reception and Cultivation of the Madrigal in Antwerp and the Low Countries, 1555–1620', *MD*, xlviii (1994), 125–87

KRISTINE FORNEY

Peyer, Andreas. *See* BAYER, ANDREAS.

Peyer, Gervase de. *See* DE PEYER, GERVASE.

Peyer [Bayer, Beyer], Johann Baptist (*b c*1680; *d* Vienna, 10 April 1733). Austrian organist and composer. He may have received his education at Heiligenkreuz monastery, where another Johann Baptist Peyer (1651–1726) worked as *camerarius major* from 1693 to 1698; the younger (and possibly related) J.B. Peyer was active as organist and musical instructor there from 1698. He worked for the Empress Eleonora, widow of Leopold I, from about 1712 until her death in 1720, and thereafter at the central court chapel under the direction of J.J. Fux. The major extant source of keyboard works by Peyer (*D-Bsb* 1220, copied in Vienna, *c*1780) gives rise to considerable confusion over attributions. Riedel accepted the copyist's ascription of the prelude and fugues in the first fascicle to Andreas Bayer (1710–49), court organist at Würzburg, and of those in fascicles 2–3 to J.B. Peyer. Fascicle 4 contains a two-movement sonata in the newer Italian manner, ascribed simply to 'Sig^e Beÿer'.

The 100 pieces in fascicles 2–3 show signs of liturgical intentions (selections ed. R. Walter, Süddeutsche Orgel-meister des Barock xiii–xiv, Altötting, 1980–81); all but the last few are grouped according to the eight church tones, and titles such as 'Capriccio pro Elevatione' and 'Fuga post Dona nobis' occur. But in style they do not conform to the conventional Austro-German verset. Some pieces are in an old-fashioned ricercare style, like the fugue on the Easter Alleluia; more significant are those pieces written in a lively, modern instrumental manner, and showing strikingly progressive tendencies in texture, melodic style, rhythmic patterns and key structure. These create a simplified *galant* effect closer to the new keyboard sonata than to Baroque liturgical fugue.

If Andreas Bayer were the author of the whole manuscript, fascicles 2–3 would fit into a logical chain encompassing the sonata in fascicle 4. Andreas belonged to the generation of Alberti and Paradies; the sonata composer Platti, whose *Sonates pour le clavessin* op.1 appeared in Andreas's lifetime, was active at the Würzburg court. The alternative is to regard J.B. Peyer as a remarkably forward-looking individualist among his Viennese contemporaries. The Viennese origin of the manuscript can be explained by the close association between the courts of Vienna and Würzburg, while the ascription in fascicles 2–3 could be a copyist's error. But no firm conclusions can be drawn in the absence of corroborative evidence.

BIBLIOGRAPHY

KöchelKHM; MGG1 (F.W. Riedel)

A. Fuchs: *Thematisches Verzeichniss einer Sammlung Orgel-Compositionen von Beyer* (MS, *D-Bsb* 516)

L. von Köchel: *J.J. Fux* (Vienna, 1872/*R*)

O. Biba: 'The Unknown Organ Music of Austria', *The Diapason*, lxii/2 (1970–71), 10–11, 18, 27

S. Wollenberg: 'The Jupiter Theme: New Light on its Creation', *MT*, cxvi (1975), 781–3

S. Wollenberg: *Viennese Keyboard Music in the Reign of Karl VI (1712–40)* (diss., U. of Oxford, 1975)

R. Walter: 'Der Kaiserliche Hoforganist Johann Baptist Peyer (Bayer) und seine Preambuli e Fughe', *Die süddeutsch-österreichische Orgelmusik im 17. und 18. Jahrhundert: Innsbruck 1979*, 201–25

SUSAN WOLLENBERG

Peyerl, Paul. *See* PEUERL, PAUL.

Peyko, Nikolay Ivanovich (*b* Moscow, 12/25 March 1916; *d* Moscow, 1 July 1995). Russian composer. He studied at the Moscow Conservatory Music Academy (1933–7) with G.I. Litinsky (composition) and I.V. Sposobin (harmony), and at the conservatory itself (1937–40) with Myaskovsky (composition), Zukkerman (analysis) and Rakov (orchestration). In 1943 he joined the conservatory staff, becoming Shostakovich's assistant in 1944 and later taking his own composition class. He was also professor and head of the composition department at the Gnesin Institute. In 1964 he received the title Honoured Art Worker of the RSFSR. His music has deep links with the Russian tradition, and in particular with the epic Russian symphony; in this he was at first a close follower of Myaskovsky. Subsequently, however, he was influenced by Stravinsky, Prokofiev and Shostakovich, and in the 1960s he began working with 12-note methods, though still within a tonal framework. His orchestration is masterly, and his vocal works show a particular delicacy and poetic understanding.

WORKS
(selective list)

8 syms.: 1945, 1946, 1957, 1965, 1968, 1972, 1980, 1986
Other orch: Pf Conc., 1943–7; Iz russkoy starinï [From Old Russia], sym. suite, 1948; Moldavskaya syuita [Moldavian Suite], 1949–50; Sem' p'yes na temï narodov SSSR [7 Pieces on Themes of the Peoples of the USSR], sym. suite, 1950; Zhanna d'Ark [Joan of Arc] (ballet, V. Burmeister), 1953–5, rev. 1981; 2 concert suites, vn, orch, 1953, 1968; Simfonicheskaya ballada [Symphonic Ballad], 1956; Iz yakutskikh legend [From Yakutsk Legend], sym. suite, 1940–57; Conc.-Sym., 1974; Abakadaya (ballet), 1983; Ob conc., ob, chbr orch, 1983; 12 aforizmov i postlyudiya [12 Aphorisms and Postlude], 1993
Choral orch: Ivan Groznïy [Ivan the Terrible], 1967; Dneydavnikh boy [The Battle of Distant Days], 1981
Chbr: Pf Qnt, 1961; 2 str qts, 1962, 1965
Song cycles (G. Apollinaire, A. Blok, S. Esenin, N. Zabalotsky, Amer. poets, old Chin. poets etc.)

Principal publishers: Muzïka, Sovetskiy kompozitor

WRITINGS

'27 simfoniya N.Ya. Myaskovsky', 'Vospominaniya ob uchitele' [Reminiscences about a teacher], *Myaskovsky: stat'i, pis'ma, vospominaniya* [Myaskovsky: articles, letters, reminiscences] (Moscow, 1959), 78–95

'Dve instrumental'nïye minaturï (kompozitsionnïy analiz p'yes O. Messiana i V. Lyutoslavskogo)' [Two instrumental miniatures (compositional analysis of pieces by Messiaen and Lutosławski)], *Muzïka i sovremennost'*, ix (Moscow, 1979), 262–310

BIBLIOGRAPHY

V. Zukkerman: 'Moldavskaya syuita N. Peyko', *SovM* (1951), no.11, pp.28–41

G. Grigor'yeva: *N.I. Peyko* (Moscow, 1965)

G. Grigor'yeva: 'Vokal'naya lirika N. Peyko i yego tsikl na stikhi N. Zabolotskogo' [The vocal writing of N. Peyko and his cycle on verses by N. Zabolotsky], *Muzïka i sovremennost'*, viii (Moscow, 1974), 90–108

Ye. Ribakina: *N.I. Peyko: ocherk zhizni i tvorchestva* [Peyko: life and works] (Moscow, 1980)

GALINA GRIGOR'YEVA

Peyró [Peiró], José [Joseph] (*b* Aragon, ?*c*1670; *d* 1720). Spanish composer. He began his career as second musician (most likely harpist or guitarist) in the troupe of Joseph Andrés in 1701, and in 1703 he was performing in Mallorca. Peyró was the 'músico de Valencia' who arrived in Madrid between August 1710 and September 1711 to join the highly successful company of Joseph Garcés. He probably performed again in Madrid between March 1714 and April 1715, for at some time during this period he donated 60 reales de vellón in honour of the Virgin Mary to the actors' guild, the Congregación de Nuestra Señora de la Novena. In 1719 the officials organizing the performance of *autos sacramentales* for the Corpus Christi celebrations in Madrid made an urgent request that Peyró travel to Madrid as quickly as possible in order to participate in the *autos* that year. Peyró explained that he was unable to work because he was suffering the aches and pains of an illness 'of Gallic origin'. The harpist and composer Juan de Lima Sequeiros took Peyró's place for the *autos* of 1719, while Peyró performed with the company of Joseph Garcés in Valencia and Granada for the 1719–20 season.

Peyró composed solos, *recitados* and ensemble songs for plays and *auto sacramentales*. His music attests to the co-existence of different styles in theatrical music of the early 18th century. In particular, his music for 18th-century revivals of Calderón's *autos El lírio y la azucena* and *Primer refugio del hombre* demonstrate Peyró's expertise with the italianate, pan-European style (with its da capo arias, greater vocal coloratura and busy obligato violin and oboe parts) fashionable in the first and second decades of the 18th century. The largest collection of Peyró's works is in the 'Manuscrito Novena', a large anthology compiled in the early years of the 18th century with music for some of the most often performed plays in the Spanish repertory of the late 17th and early 18th centuries. Housed for many years in the archive of the actors' guild in Madrid (in the parish church of S Sebastián), this extremely important manuscript is now on display in the Museo de Teatro in Almagro. In it Peyró is credited with the music for eight plays and two *autos sacramentales*, a total of 53 separate pieces. Another important manuscript compiled in the early years of the 18th century (*E-Mn* 13622) contains music by Peyró for a *comedia* by Lanhini y Sagredo and for *El jardín de Falerina* by Calderón. Peyró's music cannot be associated with 17th-century productions of *El jardín de Falerina*, but it may well have been used for revivals in 1715–20 in Madrid and elsewhere. Other theatrical songs by Peyró survive in manuscripts in Barcelona Cathedral and the Biblioteka Jagiellónska, Kraków (the latter originally compiled in Valencia).

BIBLIOGRAPHY

SubiráHME

Genealogía, origen y noticias de los comediantes de España (MS, *E-Mn* 12918; ed. N.D. Shergold and J.E. Varey, *Fuentes para la historia del teatro en España*, ii, London, 1985)

R. Eitner: 'Ein spanisches handschriftliches Sammelwerk von 1704', *MMg*, xv (1883), 32–7, esp. 33

F. Pedrell: *Teatro lirico español anterior al siglo XIX* (La Coruña, 1897–8)

J. Subirá: 'Un manuscrito musical de principios del siglo XVIII', *AnM*, iv (1949), 181–91

L.K. Stein: 'El "Manuscrito Novena", sus textos, su contexto histórico-musical y el músico Joseph Peyró', *RdMc*, iii (1980), 197–234

L.K. Stein: 'Música existente para comedias de Calderón de la Barca', *Calderón y el teatro español del siglo de oro: Madrid 1981*, 1161–72

L.K. Stein: *Songs of Mortals, Dialogues of the Gods: Music and Theatre in Seventeenth-Century Spain* (Oxford, 1993)

L.K. Stein: 'Las convenciones del teatro musical y la herencia de Juan Hidalgo', *Bances Candamo y el teatro musical de su tiempo (1662–1704)*, ed. J.A. Gómez (Oviedo, 1995)

LOUISE K. STEIN

Peyser [née Gilbert], **Joan** (*b* New York, 12 June 1931). American editor and writer on music. She studied at Smith College (1947–9), Barnard College (BA 1951), and with P.H. Lang at Columbia University (MA 1956, further study until 1958). She has written numerous articles for such periodicals as *Commentary*, *Vogue*, *Hi-Fi/Stereo Review* and *Opera News*, and is the author of many pieces for the Sunday *New York Times* which were based on interviews with European and American musicians. From 1977 to 1984 she was editor of the *Musical Quarterly*. Her books, *The New Music* (1971) and *Boulez*

(1976), are intended as a history of music from 1880 to the present; the first discusses Schoenberg, Stravinsky, Webern and Varèse, and the second, Stockhausen, Cage, and Babbitt in addition to Boulez.

WRITINGS

The New Music: the Sense behind the Sound (New York, 1971, 2/1980 as *Twentieth-Century Music: the Sense behind the Sound*)

Boulez: Composer, Conductor, Enigma (London, 1976)

ed: *The Orchestra: Origins and Transformations* (New York, 1986)

Bernstein: a Biography (New York, 1987, 2/1998)

The Memory of all That: the Life of George Gershwin (New York, 1993)

The Music of My Time (White Plains, NY, 1995)

PAULA MORGAN

Pez [Petz], Johann Christoph (*b* Munich, 9 Sept 1664; *d* Stuttgart, 25 Sept 1716). German composer, instrumentalist and singer. His family had long been connected with music at the Peterskirche, Munich, whose choir school he attended, receiving a firm grounding in plainsong and polyphony. About 1675 he went to the Jesuit school at Munich, where he was an important member of the choir and orchestra (his main instruments were viol and lute) and took an important part in the annual school plays. He sang tenor at the Peterskirche for some time and in 1687 became choirmaster there. However, since he was forbidden to introduce a more modern style of church music there (the authorities wanted nothing but plainsong and polyphony), he moved in 1688 to the Munich court as a chamber musician. The Elector Max Emanuel believed in sending promising composers abroad to study, so Pez spent the years 1689–92 in Rome, absorbing the styles of Corelli and of Carissimi and his followers.

Musical life at the Munich court was at a low ebb in the early 1690s (Max Emanuel lived mainly in Brussels), and in 1694 Pez left for Bonn to reorganize the musical establishment of Joseph Clemens, Archbishop-Elector of Cologne, who was also Bishop of Liège. He was given the title of Kapellmeister in 1696. In 1701 the outbreak of the War of the Spanish Succession caused him to return to Munich, where, however, music was almost non-existent. For the next five years he kept church music going but in 1706 moved to Stuttgart as Kapellmeister at the Württemberg court. He remained there until his death.

Pez's music shows strong Italian influence, the result not only of his visit to Italy but also of his contacts with other Italian-trained musicians in Munich, especially Kerll, who was one of the first composers to bring the Italian concertato style of church music there. His published masses and psalms are very compact, with little repetition of words or division of long movements into self-contained sections. Unlike Kerll he made little use of counterpoint – his choral writing is largely homophonic but with great variety of texture and rhythmic liveliness – but Kerll's influence shows in the relationship between solo and tutti voices. There is much close interplay between the two groups: extended solo passages are rare except in Benedictus sections. His instrumental parts are simple – the strings usually double the voices or accompany a bass solo in a trio texture – and on the whole he rarely used recurrent themes for voices or instruments. Neither masses nor psalms contain much ornamental solo writing, which is, however, found in the solo cantatas of the *Corona stellarum*; these 12 works also display Pez's melodic gift and ability to write convincing accompanied recitative and arioso. The trio-sonata movements which precede each cantata suggest that his instrumental style was strongly influenced by Corelli.

WORKS

Edition: *J.C. Pez: Ausgewählte Werke*, ed. B.A. Wallner, DTB, xxxv, Jg.xxvii, xxviii (1928) [incl. important introduction] [W]

SACRED
all published in Augsburg

Prodromus optatae pacis, sive Psalmi de Dominicus e Beata Virgini in officio vespertino, 8vv, 2 vn, va, bc (org), op.2 (1703)
Jubilum missale sextuplex, 8vv, 2 vn, va, bc (org) (1706); 1 in W
Corona stellarum, 1v, 2 vn, bc, op.4 (1710); 3 cants. in W

DRAMATIC WORKS, CANTATAS
lost unless otherwise stated

Il giudizio di Marforio (festa da camera), 1695
Trajano, imperator romano, 1696 (Bonn, 1699); W
Il riso d'Apolline (serenata teatrale), 1701
Fileno e Silvia (cant), ?D-Bsb

Speculum vanitatis, sive Bononius; Abdolonymus christianus: in P.F. Lang, Theatrum solitudinis asceticae (Munich, 1717)

School ops: In solo Deo unica quies, 1684; Viriles constantia, 1686; Jonathus Machabaeus, 1686; Matthias e captivo rex, 1702; Guilelmus e Duce, 1703; Aquitaniae Eremita, 1703; Tamerlanes, 1706: all lost

INSTRUMENTAL

Duplex genius ... 12 constans symphoniis, 2 vn, archiviola, bc (Augsburg, 1696; also pubd as op.1, 1701); W
Sonate da camera ... Several Suites of Overtures and Airs, parte I, 1/2 fl, bc, (London, ?1710)
1 sonata, 2 vn, bc, in Harmonia mundi (London, 1707); 1 work, 2 fl, in Choice Italian and English Music (London, 1709); 1 sonata, fl, bc, in 10 Sonates (Amsterdam, c1710)
Conc. pastorale, 2 fl, 2 vn, 2 va, bc, W; 3 suites, kbd, A-Wn; other MSS of inst music in ?D-Bsb, Dl, ROu

BIBLIOGRAPHY

J. Sittard: *Zur Geschichte der Musik und des Theaters am württembergischen Hofe*, i (Stuttgart, 1890/R), 84ff
A. Scharnagl: 'Die katholische Kirchenmusik von der tridentinischen Reform bis zum Abschluss der Regensburger Restauration', *Music in Bayern*, ed. R. Münster and H. Schmidt (Tutzing, 1972), 261–72
M. Rosenblum and others: 'A Concert of Baroque Music for Viola d'Amore', *JVdGSA*, vi/2 (1981), 46–9

ELIZABETH ROCHE

Pezel [Pecelius, Petzel, Petzoldt, Bezel(d), Bezelius], **Johann Christoph** (*b* Glatz, Silesia, 1639; *d* Bautzen, 13 Oct 1694). German town bandsman and composer. He probably attended the Gymnasium in Bautzen, near Glatz, and possibly travelled widely before taking up a musical appointment. He spent his whole career as a member of various town bands. He was a *Ratsmusiker*, one of a humble yet privileged class of musicians that derived from the old tower watchmen-trumpeters and became increasingly important as musicians for civic functions during the 17th century. The *Ratsmusiken* corps had both brass and string instruments and it is as a string player that Pezel was first mentioned. In 1664 the Leipzig town council agreed to increase their town band from seven members to eight and Pezel was appointed fourth *Kunstgeiger*. In 1670 he was promoted to *Stadtpfeifer*, the equivalent to being named 'Master' of his particular craft. This was a life appointment. His first important musical publication, *Hora decima musicorum*, dates from that year. The confusion over his name also began at this time: the title-page carries the name Johanne Pezelio but the dedication is signed Johann Bezeld and other variants appeared later. One result is the confusion of the identities of Johann Pezel, town bandsman, with Johann or Jan Pecelius (some of whose works are in *CZ-KRa*; *ČSHS*

mentions records, now lost, which show the Czech Pecelius to have been a member of the Augustinian order, and his surviving compositions are all for the church). It seems unlikely that the matter will ever be resolved.

Pezel was apparently dissatisfied with his musical position and made attempts to improve it, applying at one stage for the post of Kantor at the Thomaskirche, Leipzig, a position his experience as a *Stadtpfeifer* in no way qualified him to fill. He applied also to be a member of the Dresden *Ratsmusiken* corps. In 1681 plague broke out at Leipzig and he moved to Bautzen, where he remained until his death. Contemporary commentators, notably Printz in his *Phrynides Mytilenaei* of 1696, indicated that he was better educated than his musical position required. His ability to understand Italian was particularly unusual, and he seems to have written several literary commentaries during his years in Leipzig, although none has survived.

The works for which Pezel is remembered are contained in his two important collections for the five-part cornett and trombone ensembles that were characteristic of the *Ratsmusiken*. During his time at Leipzig, music for such a combination was performed twice daily from the *Rathaus* tower, a practice that was apparently widespread in Germany. The two collections are *Hora decima musicorum* (Leipzig, 1670) and *Fünff-stimmigte blasende Music* (Frankfurt, 1685). The first book contains 40 one-movement sonatas separately numbered. Although strings are given as an alternative to wind, the dedication and the musical figuration show clearly which was the intended instrumentation. The most interesting question concerning this book is the grouping of the pieces. The order of the sonatas falls into groupings of tonality, so Riemann (*SIMG*, v, 1904–5, p.501) proposed that the book was actually a set of 11 suites each of two to nine movements. This rather arbitrary and impracticable notion lacks historical proof and reason.

Downs put forward another possibility, noting that, apart from six sonatas (nos.1–5 and 40), the pieces alternate between duple and triple metre and fit together in key to make two-movement sonata pairs (e.g. no.6, duple, and no.7, triple, both in A minor). Sonatas nos.1 and 2 each have three sections instead of two, the first two sections in duple metre and the third in triple. They make a satisfactory sonata entity on their own. Sonatas nos.3, 4 and 5 have the sequence C, C, 3/2 all in F, which suggests their performance together as a three-movement work. There are no striking thematic relationships between the pairs but such pairing practice is mentioned in Praetorius and it is certainly a viable theory.

Fünff-stimmigte blasende Music is a collection of 76 pieces, mostly intradas but with examples of various dance forms such as saraband, courante, allemand and bal (balleta). There are some obvious pairings of dance movements denoted by recurring melodic motifs, but these are surprisingly few, and there appears to be no recognizable formal pattern in which to arrange the contents.

This music for tower musicians is most characteristic of Pezel. It was also an old, hardy and fairly stereotyped tradition. This is hardly progressive music; the musical opportunities are not great, the colour range is limited and the musical development in each piece rudimentary. The main variety in Pezel's music comes from his cunning exploitation of texture to utilize his limited palette to the full. He wrote smoothly, with the outer voices predominating and the bass line moving more slowly and strongly to set up simple triadic harmony. There are seldom more than four real parts, since the tendency is to pair instruments – the second cornett moving parallel with the first, for instance. Climaxes are often achieved by increasing the complexity of the texture rather than by dynamic means, and all the works consist of rapidly alternating imitative and homophonic sections. Yet within this stereotyped style Pezel managed to produce music that is often lively and interesting, thereby proving his superiority over the many other contemporary *Ratsmusiker* composers.

WORKS

Edition: *J.C. Pezel: Turmmusiken und Suiten*, ed. A. Schering, DDT, lxiii (1928/R) [S]

INSTRUMENTAL

Musica vespertina Lipsica, oder Leipzigische Abend-Music (12 suites containing 101 pieces), 2 vn, 2 va, bn/vle, bc (Leipzig, 1669); 36 in S

Hora decima musicorum Lipsiensium, oder Musicalische Arbeit zum Ab-blasen (40 sonatas), (2 cornetts, 3 trbn)/(2 vn, 2 va, vle) (Leipzig, 1670; repr., Dresden, 1674, as Supellex sonatarum selectarum); 12 in S; sonatas 12–40, ed. A. Müller (Dresden, 1930); some ed. E.H. Meyer, *Turmmusik* (Leipzig, 1960); ed. A.F. Lumsden (London, 1967); 12 ed. K. Brown (New York, 1982)

Musicalische Gemüths-Ergetzung (10 suites containing 90 pieces), 2 vn, va, bc/vle (Leipzig, 1672)

[110] Bicinia variorum instrumentorum, 2 clarini, 2 vn, bn, bc (Leipzig, 1675); nos.61–75, ed. R.P. Block (London, 1970–72)

Delitiae musicales, oder Lust-Music (7 suites containing 63 pieces), 2 vn, 2 va, bn/vle, bc (Frankfurt, 1678); 27 in S

Fünff-stimmigte blasende Music (76 works), 2 cornetts, 3 trbn (Frankfurt, 1685); 16 in S; ed. K. Schlegel (Berlin, 1960); ed. A.F. Lumsden (London and Leipzig, 1960–66); some ed. E.H. Meyer, *Turmmusik* (Leipzig, 1960)

Opus musicum [25] sonatarum, 2 vn, 3 va, bn/vle, bc (Frankfurt, 1686)

Gigue seu canon perpet., a 4, entered in J.V. Meder's album, Leipzig, 1670/1671

VOCAL

Des Menschen-Lebens Eitelkeit (Es schallt die gantze Welt von lauter Eitelkeit), funeral ode, canon a 4, 1672 (n.p., n.d.)

Lobwürdiger Namens-Irrthum (Das trifft ja garnicht ein), funeral ode, canon a 4 (Leipzig, 1673)

Sacred songs, 1v, bc, in J. Feller: Devotus studiosus, oder Der andächtige Student (Leipzig, 1682) [also contains melodies by J. Schelle; the melodies are not individually attrib. either composer]

Des Abends, Morgens und Mittags, cant., A, T, B, 2 va d'amore, 2 va, bc (MS, 1690, D-F Ms. Mus.449)

2 masses, Lat. and Ger. sacred works, 1–5vv, insts, D-AN, Bsb, F, FBa, HAf, LEt, Nla

1 Ger., 1 Lat. sacred works (doubtful), Bsb

LOST WORKS

[24] Schöne lustige und anmuthige neue Arien (C. Weise), 1v, 2 vn, 2 va, bn/vle, bc (Leipzig, 1672)

Musica curiosa Lipsiaca (Leipzig, 1685 or 1686, probably new edn of Musica vespertina Lipsiaca, see Eller)

30 sacred works, cited by J.G. Schwartze, Kantor of Bautzen, in inventory dated 3 Dec 1700

Ger. sacred work, 4vv, 6 insts, formerly D-GMl (attrib. G. Pezold)

OTHER
announced but possibly never published

Braut-messen, 4–12vv (1669)

Concerten … über David Eliä Heydenreichs geistliche Oden, 6–12vv (1669)

Decas sonatarum, 2 cornetts, 4 trbn (1669)

Fasciculus sacrarum cantionum, 3–12vv (1669)

Magnificat X, 6–12vv (1669)

Missae, 6–12vv (1669)

Kurze lustige Balletten, 2 vn, va, vle/4 va (Leipzig, 1669–71)

Jocosa, 3–5 va (1671)

Musicae vespertinae … ander Theil, a 1–5 (1671)

Seria, 3–5 va (1671)

Musicalische Seelenerquickungen (Leipzig, 1675)

Jahrgang über die Evangelia, 3–5vv, 2–5 insts (1676) [1678 according to *GerberNL*]

Intraden, cornett, 3 trbn (?1676) [announced in preface to Musica vespertina, 1669, pts II and III announced 1670 and 1676; probably only 1 or 2 pts pubd, 1676, see *GerberNL*]

WRITINGS
announced 1678, possibly never published

Observationes musicae (?1683)

Infelix musicus

Musica politico-practica

BIBLIOGRAPHY

MeyerMS; MGG1 (R. Eller)

A. Schering: 'Die Leipziger Ratsmusik von 1650 bis 1775', *AMw*, iii (1921), 17–53

J.A. Wattenbarger: *The Turmmusik of Johann Pezel* (diss., Northwestern U., 1957)

A.L. Murphy: *The Bicinia variorum instrumentorum of Johann Christoph Pezel* (diss., Florida State U., 1959)

A. Downs: 'The Tower Music of a Seventeenth Century Stadtpfeifer: Johann Pezel's *Hora decima* and *Fünffstimmigte blasende Music*', *Brass Quarterly*, vii (1963–4), 3–33

E.A. Wienandt: *Johann Pezel (1639–1694): a Thematic Catalogue of his Instrumental Works* (New York, 1983)

E. Frebiger: *Johann Christoph Pezel: Stadtpfeifer zu Budissin* (Bautzen, 1994)

E. Fiebig: 'Ein tüchtiger Musiker und angesehener Bürger: Johann Christoph Pezel, Stadtpfeifer in Bautzen von 1681 bis 1694', *Das Orchester*, xliii/5 (1995), 10–16

ADRIENNE SIMPSON

Pezold [Petzold], Christian (*b* Königstein, 1677; *d* Dresden, ? by 2 June 1733). German organist and composer. Records describe him as organist at the Dresden court in 1697. From 1703 he was organist at the Sophienkirche in Dresden, and in 1720 he wrote a cantata for the consecration of the Silbermann organ recently built there; it was first performed by the Dresden Kreuzkirche choir. In 1709 he was appointed court chamber composer and organist. Concert journeys took him to Paris in 1714, and to Venice in 1716. He also wrote a piece for the consecration of the Silbermann organ in Rötha, near Leipzig. His death date is usually given as 2 July 1733, but Schaffrath's letter of application for his post is dated 2 June and the competition for the vacancy was held on 22 June.

Mattheson (*Der vollkommene Capellmeister*, 1739) described Pezold as one of the most famous organists, and Gerber reckoned him 'one of the most pleasant church composers of the time'. C.H. Graun was among his pupils. His few surviving instrumental works include three trios, two partitas for viola d'amore, 11 fugues for organ or harpsichord, a suite and single pieces for harpsichord, an *Orgeltabulatur* (two- and four-part chorales, 1704) and a *Recueil de 25 concerts pour le clavecin*, dating from 1729 (all in manuscript, D-Dl).

The works for harpsichord and organ have a distinctive virtuoso brilliance, with much use of scale and arpeggio figuration. A cantata, *Meine Seufzer, meine Klagen (Bsb)*, contains free forms, independent of the da capo scheme.

BIBLIOGRAPHY

EitnerQ; FürstenauG; GerberL

G. Hempel: 'Johann Sebastian Bach und der Dresdner Hoforganist Christian Petzold', *BJb* 1956, 156–61

H.-J. Schulze: 'Ein "Dresdner Menuett" im zweiten Klavierbüchlein der Anna Magdalena Bach', *BJb* 1979, 45–64

P. Damm: 'Bemerkungen zu zwei Kammermusikwerken mit Corno da caccia von J.J. Fux und Chr. Petzold', *Zur Entwicklung der*

instrumentaler Kammermusik in der ersten Hälfte des 18.
Jahrhunderts: Blankenburg, Harz, 1983, 67–76
M. Willer: '"Sonderfälle", "Modeerscheinungen" und das
"Normale": Konzertsatzkonzeptionen in begleiteten und
unbegleiteten Klavierkonzerten vor 1750', Beiträge zur Geschichte
des Konzerts: Festschrift Siegfried Kross, ed. R. Emans and M.
Wendt (Bonn, 1990), 95–113

DIETER HÄRTWIG

Pezzo (It.). *See* PIECE.

Pfaefferli, Christoph. *See* PIPERINUS, CHRISTOPH.

Pfannhauser, Karl (Robert) (*b* Vienna, 2 Feb 1911; *d* Vienna, 5 Oct 1984). Austrian musicologist. After taking the doctorate in classics and history, he established a reputation as an authority on Austrian church music. In 1945 he founded the series Österreichische Kirchenmusik: Publikationen für den praktischen und wissenschaftlichen Gebrauch (nine volumes to 1949), containing music from Haydn to Bruckner, with his own introductions and notes. He also wrote carefully researched programme notes for performances by the Vienna Hofmusikkapelle and other concerts, including many for the works of the Austrian composer Raimund Weissensteiner.

His most important writings are on Mozart: he proved that six works (KAnh.A 1–4, 22, 23), hitherto believed to be authentic, were copies of works by C.G. Reutter and J.E. Eberlin; he showed K139/47a to be the *Waisenhausmesse*; he found Mozart's copy of Michael Haydn's *Tres sunt*; he established the date of the first performance of the Mass K427/417a; and he showed that the 'Coronation' Mass K317 had nothing to do with the shrine at Maria Plain near Salzburg.

WRITINGS

'Die Anfänge des christlichen Wechselgesanges', *Opuscula philologica*, vi (Baden, 1934), 40–42
'Mozart hat kopiert', *Acta mozartiana*, i (1954), 21–5, 38–41
'Zu Mozarts Kirchenwerken von 1768', *MJb* 1954, 150–68
'Auf den Spuren der Mozart-Überlieferung in Oberösterreich', *Festschrift des Linzer Landestheaters* (Linz, 1956), 15–27
'Wer war Mozarts Amtsnachfolger?', *Acta mozartiana*, iii/3 (1956), 6–16
'Mozarts kirchenmusikalische Studien im Spiegel seiner Zeit und Nachwelt', *KJb*, xliv (1959), 155–98
'Nannerl Mozarts Tagebuchblätter: eine Forschungsstudie zur gleichnamigen Publikation von Walter Hummel', *Mitteilungen der Internationalen Stiftung Mozarteum*, viii/1–2 (1959), 11–17
'Eine menschlich-künstlerische Strauss-Memoire', *Festschrift Alfred Orel zum 70. Geburtstag*, ed. H. Federhofer (Vienna and Wiesbaden, 1960), 139–50
'Mozarts "Krönungsmesse"', *Mitteilungen der Internationalen Stiftung Mozarteum*, xi/3–4 (1963), 3–11
'Kleine Köcheliana', *Mitteilungen der Internationalen Stiftung Mozarteum*, xii/3–4 (1964), 24–38
'Epilegomena Mozartiana', *MJb* 1971–72, 268–312

RUDOLF KLEIN

Pfannmüller [Phanmüller, Phanmulner], **Friedrich** (*b* Hirschau, Upper Palatinate, *c*1490; *d* Prague, before Whitsuntide 1562). German organ builder. He was based in Amberg in the Upper Palatinate (a district of eastern Bavaria), where he is mentioned as a citizen in 1547. He restored the organ of St Johann, Regensburg, in 1538, and that of St Martin, Amberg, in 1549. The so-called 'Yellow Organ' he built for St Mikuláš, Cheb, in 1549–52 (three manuals, 30 or 35 stops) led to the commission to build a large organ in the Renaissance gallery of Prague Cathedral (simultaneously the palatine church and the chapel of the Habsburg court). This work occupied him from 1553 until his death; it was completed after 1566 by Joachim and Albrecht Rudner (the organ was later played

on by Carl Luython). Although the transition from double chests to slider-chests was happening in Pfannmüller's area during his career, he continued frequently to place more comprehensive mixtures on a separate chest controlled by a spring-valve. Besides his richly articulated Principal choruses (e.g. 16', 8', 4', 2⅔', 2', Zimbel, or 8', 4', 2⅔', 2', 1⅓', 1', Zimbel), he built stopped diapasons, flutes and regals; his organs also show a tendency towards wide-scale ranks of the Low Countries type, perhaps instigated by Flemish members of the royal chapel. His son Friedrich became organist of St Mikuláš, Cheb, where he played his father's instrument; he was succeeded there in 1562 by his brother Wolfgang Pfannmüller, who died in 1611.

BIBLIOGRAPHY

MGG1 (R. Quoika)
D. Mettenleiter: *Musikgeschichte der Oberpfalz* (Amberg, 1867)
E. Trolda: 'Varhany v dómu svatovítském' [Organs in St Vít Cathedral (Prague)], *Cyrill*, liii (1927), 57–60
K. Riess: *Musikgeschichte der Stadt Eger im 16. Jahrhundert* (Brno, 1935)
R. Quoika: 'Die Prager Kaiserorgel', *KJb*, xxxvi (1952), 35–46
R. Quoika: *Die altösterreichische Orgel der späten Gotik, der Renaissance und des Barock* (Kassel, 1953)
L. Tomší: 'Varhanářství v západních Čechách v době renesanční' [Organ Building in Western Bohemia in the Renaissance], *Minulostí Západočeského kraje*, xv (1979), 251–3

HANS KLOTZ/JIŘÍ SEHNAL

Pfeffinger, Philippe-Jacques (*b* Strasbourg, 15 Dec 1765; *d* Paris, *c*1821). French composer and teacher. In 1790 he became *maître de musique* for the city of Strasbourg and for the Temple Neuf. He studied composition with Ignace Pleyel and composed several patriotic songs and cantatas. After obtaining a law degree from the University of Strasbourg in 1791 he accompanied Pleyel to London, where he met Haydn and developed a liking for Handel's oratorios. From 1794 he was active in Paris as a composer and teacher. His compositions include *romances*, light piano works and chamber music; Choron and Fayolle considered them conservative but showing a good knowledge of harmony.

WORKS
many published in Paris

Stage: Zaire (op, 2, Voltaire), unperf., lost
Vocal: cants.; many romances; patriotic works, incl. Hymne à la vertu
Inst: Sonate concertante, pf 4 hands, op.16; Trio, pf, hn/vn, vc, op.18; Vive Henri IV, variations, pf, vn, vc, lost; caprices, fantasias, variations, potpourris, pf; variations, hpd

BIBLIOGRAPHY

Choron-FayolleD; EitnerQ; FétisB
J.F. Lobstein: *Beiträge zur Geschichte der Musik im Elsass und besonders in Strassburg* (Strasbourg, 1840), 49
M. Vogeleis: *Quellen und Bausteine zu einer Geschichte der Musik und des Theaters im Elsass 500–1800* (Strasbourg, 1911/R)

FRÉDÉRIC ROBERT

Pfeife (i) (Ger.). *See* PIPE (i).

Pfeiffe (ii). For pipes in organs, *see under* ORGAN STOP.

Pfeiffe (iii). *See* WHISTLE.

Pfeiffer, Carl August (*b* Karlsruhe, before 1753; *d* after 1768). German composer. He was a choirboy at Karlsruhe in 1753 and studied the violin and composition at Mannheim in 1762 before entering the Karlsruhe court orchestra as a violinist in 1763; he became Konzertmeister in 1765 but apparently left Karlsruhe before 1768. His music is typical of the third quarter of the 18th century, with relatively concise movements and stylistic features resembling those of the second generation of Mannheim composers. His fast movements are dominated by motivic and rhythmic material but also include passages of italianate lyricism; an interesting feature of the Clarinet Concerto is the operatic 'Recitativo – Andante' that precedes the slow movement proper. The Symphony in D has all three movements joined together without a break (and with no internal repeated sections), a format more typical of C.P.E. Bach; this, together with the location of this manuscript, suggests that Pfeiffer visited Berlin. His flute quartets, except for the three-movement one in E minor, each consist of a moderately paced first movement and a minuet. The Bassoon Concerto in B♭ attributed to Franz Anton Pfeiffer at Weimar (*D-WRl*) may also be by Carl August Pfeifer. He is not to be confused with a Carl Pfeifer who composed six Austro-Styrian ländler for fortepiano. (*EitnerQ*)

WORKS

Bn Conc., C; Cl Conc., E♭, *US Wc* ed. D.J. Rhodes (London, 1999); Menuetto, orch; 5 quartetti, fl, vn, va, vc; Sonata à tre, G, fl, vn, vc, all *D-KA*; Sinfonia, D, orch, *Bsb*

D.J. RHODES

Pfeiffer, Franz Anton (*b* Windischbuch, nr Boxberg, 16 June 1752; *d* Ludwigslust, 22 Oct 1787). German composer and bassoonist. He studied the double bass at Mannheim, where he later claimed to have played in the court orchestra. He also studied the bassoon, and in about 1772 he left for Munich to continue his studies of the instrument with Felix Rheiner. After playing in travelling theatre orchestras in the Frankfurt area, he was appointed bassoonist in the Mainz court orchestra in 1778. It was probably here that Pfeiffer began to compose for the bassoon, performing this music at court and on concert tours. In 1783 he entered the court orchestra of the Duke of Mecklenburg-Schwerin at Ludwigslust. His six Bassoon Quartets op.1 are dedicated to Prince Friedrich Wilhelm of Prussia, before whom he played and who offered him a position in Berlin. He married the contralto Maria Johanna Clara Lanius (1765–1856) in 1787. He was widely praised for his superb technique and musicality. The impression of his seal on his will depicts a bassoon in minute detail, including an octave key and a hand rest, the earliest evidence of the former in Germany.

As a composer, Pfeiffer was apparently influenced by Carl Stamitz. His collection of bassoon music was sold to the Mannheim court by his widow and may have included works by Stamitz and others in addition to unattributed music, arrangements and transcriptions, some possibly by Pfeiffer. His music shows a fine understanding of the bassoon's nature and idiom as a solo instrument and explores its range to the full. It is composed in an attractive, *galant* style, with rhythmic and motivic first subjects and lyrical, italianate second subjects. His finest music undoubtedly lies in the concertos and especially in the bassoon quartets. His *Engloise* and bassoon sonatas and trio are probably early works; several bassoon quartets exist in earlier manuscript versions, which Pfeiffer later revised, presumably for publication by J.J. Hummel.

Franz Anton Pfeiffer has frequently been confused with other (unrelated) bearers of the same surname, particularly JOHANN PFEIFFER, but also with the Austrian composer and bass Franz Pfeiffer (*b* ?1750s; *d* ?Vienna, ?1830s), who sang at the Theater in der Leopoldstadt,

Vienna, and had a number of pieces, mainly for piano, published in Vienna. There was also a Viennese flautist named Anton Pfeiffer.

WORKS

MSS in D-SWl unless otherwise stated

Concs. (for bn, orch, unless otherwise stated): 2 in C; 3 in B♭, 1 ed. A. Hennige (Munich, 1986); 2 in F, 1 inc.; B♭, op.7, C, op.8, both (Berlin and Amsterdam, by 1803), ?lost, ? identical with MS concs.; 1 for ob, bn, orch, F, ed. W. Spiess (Prague, 1979); B♭, Weimar, Thüringisches Hauptstaatsarchiv, doubtful, ? by C.A. Pfeiffer; 2 in C, doubtful

Other orch: Engloise, 2 ob, 2 hn, 2 vn, b, D

Chbr: 8 qts, bn, vn, va, vc, nos.1–6 pubd as op.1 (Berlin and Amsterdam, 1784–5), nos.1–8 ed. D.J. Rhodes (New York, 1998); Trio-Divertimento, F, bn, vn, vc, ed. D.J. Rhodes (New York, 1998); 2 sonatas (B♭, B♭), bn, vc, ed. D.J. Rhodes (Barrhill, Ayrshire, 1994); 2 qts, bn, vn, va, vc, ed. D.J. Rhodes (New York, 1998), 2 sonatas, bn, vc, ed. D.J. Rhodes (Barrhill, Ayrshire, 1995), 2 duettos, bn/vc, vn, ed. D.J. Rhodes (Barrhill, Ayrshire, 1998), all doubtful

BIBLIOGRAPHY

EitnerQ; FétisB; GerberL; GerberNL; JohanssonH; SchillingE
J.N. Forkel: *Musikalischer Almanach für Deutschland . . . 1783* (Leipzig, 1782/*R*)
C.F. Cramer, ed.: *Magazin der Musik* (Hamburg, 1783/*R*)
AMZ, vi (1803–4), 686 only
D.J. Rhodes: 'Franz Anton Pfeiffer and the Bassoon', *GSJ*, xxxvi (1983), 97–103
D.J. Rhodes: *The Life and Works of Franz Anton Pfeiffer (1752–1787) with an Edition of his Music* (diss., Queen's U. of Belfast, 1983) [incl. edn of works, except doubtful]
D.J. Rhodes: 'Franz Anton Pfeiffer (1752–1787) – Bassoonist and Composer', *Journal of the International Double Reed Society*, xxii (1994), 7–29

D.J. RHODES

Pfeiffer, Georges Jean (*b* Versailles, 12 Dec 1835; *d* Paris, 14 Feb 1908). French pianist and composer. His great-uncle, J. Pfeiffer, was a leading piano maker in Paris, and his father, Emile Pfeiffer, whom he later succeeded, was a partner in the piano firm of Pleyel, Wolff & Cie. He studied piano with his mother, Clara Pfeiffer, a former pupil of Kalkbrenner, and composition with Maleden and Damcke. A programme of his works, including the operetta *Le capitaine Roche* and the Piano Trio op.14, was well-received at the Salle Pleyel-Wolff in 1862. He made his London debut at St James's Hall, playing his Second Piano Concerto. His early compositions were praised by Pougin for their melodic variety and polished form. The Piano Quintet op.41 won the Chartier Prize and in 1877 his sonata for two pianos won the prize of the Société des Compositeurs de Musique. In later years he performed infrequently, devoting himself mainly to composition. *Le légataire universel* (1901), after the comedy by J.F. Regnard (1708), is considered his finest stage work. He was a music critic for *Voltaire*, a frequent judge of the piano *concours* at the Conservatoire, and president of the Société des Compositeurs de Musique.

WORKS

(selective list)

all printed works published in Paris

Stage: Le capitaine Roche (operetta), op.19, perf. 1862; Agar (lyric scena), March 1875; L'enclume (oc, 1, P. Barbier) (1884); Le légataire universel (ob, 3, J. Adenis and L. Bonnemère, after Regnard), Paris, OC (Favart), 6 July 1901 (1897)

Orch: Pf Conc. no.1, op.11 (1859); Pf Conc. no.2, op.21 (1864); Sym., op.31; Jeanne d'Arc, sym. poem, 1872; Pf Conc. no.3, op.86 (1883); Marine, sym. study, op.131 (1893)

Chbr: Pf Qnt, op.41; Pf Trio, op.14; Vc Sonata, op.28; Vn Sonata, op.66; Sonata, 2pf

Songs, pf solos, studies

WRITINGS

'De l'interprétation des signes d'ornements chez les maîtres anciens', *RHCM*, iii (1903), 513

BIBLIOGRAPHY

FétisB; FétisBS

L. Auge de Lassus: 'G.-F. Pfeiffer et son oeuvre', *Revue musicale* (1 April 1908)

A. Pougin: Obituary, *Le ménestrel* (22 Feb 1908)

A.J. HIPKINS/DAVID CHARLTON/CHARLES TIMBRELL

Pfeiffer, Johann (*b* Nuremberg, 1 Jan 1697; *d* Bayreuth, 7 Oct 1761). German composer and violinist. He learnt the violin with various teachers and later studied jurisprudence at the universities of Leipzig (from 1717) and Halle-Wittenberg (from 1719). He spent six months as director of music for Count Heinrich XI von Reuss at Schleiz before entering the Weimar court orchestra as a violinist in 1720. In 1726 he was made Konzertmeister, a post apparently left vacant since J.S. Bach's departure in 1717. Pfeiffer's *Trauermusik* for Duke Ernst August's late wife, Eleonore Wilhelmine, was performed later that year, and between August 1728 (or 1729) and January 1730 he accompanied the duke on a tour of the Low Countries and France.

In or about May 1732 Pfeiffer was in Berlin, and in December 1733 he was offered a post at Bayreuth as a court violinist and music tutor to the margrave's daughter-in-law, Friederike Wilhelmine (sister of the future King Frederick the Great). On 8 November 1734 he was appointed Kapellmeister at Bayreuth with a salary of 300 gulden (increased to 480 gulden by 1737). Friederike's husband succeeded as margrave in May 1735, and together they set about expanding the musical life at court, and thereby increasing Pfeiffer's opportunities as a composer. On 20 September 1752 he married the widowed Dorothea Hagin, by whom he had two sons, Friederich (1754–1816), a lawyer by profession and an able violinist, and Johann Heinrich, who died in infancy. In 1752 or 1753 Pfeiffer was awarded the honorary title of 'Hofrat' (privy councillor), and his salary was increased; by the time of his death it stood at 1375 Reichsthaler.

Much of Pfeiffer's music is lost, or remains unidentified or misattributed (he usually signed his manuscripts simply 'del Sign. Pfeiffer'). According to Schrickel, he distinguished himself at Weimar by composing charming Singspiels, but except for the Bayreuth serenata *Das unterthänigste Freudenopfer*, no such works by him are known, and only two vocal pieces (possibly from stage works) remain. Despite claims advanced by Gerber and Fétis, no sacred music by him has been found. Instrumental music forms the bulk of his output, most of it undoubtedly composed at Bayreuth. In style it is perhaps most closely comparable with that of Bach. Both Gerber and Schilling comment on the high regard in which his ouvertures (orchestral suites) were held. Five of these recall Bach's first suite in their scoring for two oboes, bassoon and strings; they consist typically of a French overture, a *forlana*-like Cantabile, a fugal Alla breve, a bourrée-like Allegro (or Presto) and a Menuet with a trio for the wind instruments alone. The scoring and structure of the other suites vary considerably. The surviving concertos show both three- and four-movement schemes; the layout slow–fast–slow–fast is one commonly found in the chamber works too. Some of the symphonies attributed to him may be by Johann Michael Pfeiffer.

WORKS

VOCAL

Trauermusik, 1726, lost

Das unterthänigste Freudenopfer, serenata, 1739, lost

Cant. (Ps xlvi), 1758, lost

Arias: L'agnello in tanto senza timore, lv, 2 fl, 2 hn, str, bc, D-F; Penche [?=Benche] sempre crudel meco, B, str, lost, listed in Breitkopf catalogues; Se il sol non feconda/Vox prima di more, lv, 2fl, 2hn, str, org, F

Perdon in grazia, S, S, B, bn, str, lost, listed in Breitkopf catalogues

CONCERTOS

all with strings and basso continuo

Conc., B♭, bn, D-MÜu

4 concs., fl: G, SWl, ed. D.J. Rhodes (Barrhill, Ayrshire, forthcoming); G, S-Skma, ed. D.J. Rhodes (Barrhill, Ayrshire, 1993); G, D-Bsb; b, Bsb

Conc., B♭, lute, As

Conc., E♭, ob, ROu; ed. D.J. Rhodes (Barrhill, Ayrshire, 1995)

Conc., ob d'amore, lost, listed in Breitkopf catalogue, 1764

Conc., A, va da gamba, Bsb; GB-Lbl

4 concs., vn: C, S-L (inc.); D, D-Dl, f, 1726, Dl, B♭, Dl, 15 others lost, listed in Breitkopf catalogues

Conc., vn piccolo: F, MÜu; 9 others lost, listed in Breitkopf catalogues

OTHER ORCHESTRAL

8 overtures (orch suites): D, D-DS; D, SWl, ed. D.J. Rhodes (Barrhill, Ayrshire, forthcoming); e, Bsb, ed. D.J. Rhodes (Barrhill, Ayrshire, forthcoming); G, DS; G, Dl, SWl, ed. D.J. Rhodes (Barrhill, Ayrshire, forthcoming); g, SWl, ed. D.J. Rhodes (Barrhill, Ayrshire, forthcoming); B♭, Dl, c, SWl, ed. D.J. Rhodes (Barrhill, Ayrshire, forthcoming); 3 others lost, formerly D-DS; 14 others lost, listed in Breitkopf catalogues

6 partitas, lost, listed in Breitkopf catalogues

2 syms.: D, S-Uu; Sinfonie a piu stromenti (Paris and Lyons, 1764); 4 others lost (1 formerly D-DS, 1 formerly SI, 2 listed in Breitkopf catalogues), some by ?J.M. Pfeiffer

CHAMBER

4 arias a 5 (B♭, g, F, F), ob, 2 vn, va, bc, D-HRD

Conc. a 4 (g), ob, bn, vn, vc, Bsb

3 sonatas (C, D, f♯), vn, bc, Bsb (inc.); sonata (G), vn, bc, Rtt

Sonata a 4 (G), fl, ob, hn, b, DS, ed. R. Lauschmann (Leipzig, 1939/R); Sonata (D), hpd, va da gamba, HRD, ed. L. Schäffler (Hanover, 1938/R); Sonata a 3 (B♭), ob, vn, b, Rtt; Sonata a 5 (A), 2 ob d'amore, 2 va, b, Bsb; Sonata a 3 (B♭), va d'amore, vn, b, CZ-Pnm, D-DS, GB-Lbl, ed. C. Kint (Leipzig, 1935), ed. I. White (Chipperfield, Herts., 1977)

Trio (c), vn, ob, b, D-Dl

Verstelle dich, o Freundin, in der Liebe, arr. lute, As

Lost: Sonata (G), fl, hpd, formerly DS; 2 sonatas (c, F), hpd, vn/ob, listed in Breitkopf catalogues; Sonata (g), hpd, vn, listed in Breitkopf catalogues; Sonata a 3 (D), va, vn, b, listed in Breitkopf catalogues

BIBLIOGRAPHY

BrookB; FétisB; EitnerQ; GerberNL; LipowskyBL; MCL, iv; MGG1 (H. Unverricht); *RiemannL12; SainsburyD; SchillingE*

L. Schrickel: *Die Geschichte des Weimarer Theaters von seinen Anfängen bis heute* (Weimar, 1928)

E. Schenk, ed.: *Johann Wilhelm Hertel: Autobiographie* (Graz, 1957), 41, 74, 90 [with editorial note]

I. Sander: 'J. Pfeiffer', *Archiv für Geschichte von Oberfranken*, xlvi (1966), 129–81

R. Brockpähler: *Handbuch zur Geschichte der Barockoper in Deutschland* (Emsdetten, 1964)

A. Baumgartner: *Musik der Klassik* (Salzburg, 1982)

DAVID J. RHODES

Pfeiffer, Johann Michael [Jean Michel] (*b* Franconia, *c*1750–60; *d* ?London, after 1800). German composer. The earliest record of him concerns the performance of his *Amore in puntiglio* in Venice in 1773; he undoubtedly lived in Venice for a time, since much of his music was published there under his own imprint. According to Fétis he lived in Mannheim around 1780 and later in London, and Eitner repeats Thayer's statement that he spent his last years in London. Pfeiffer composed in a variety of genres, notably keyboard duets, and some of his works appeared under several different publishers' imprints; this fact, together with the large number of extant copies, reflects their popularity during his lifetime. The keyboard sonata *Il maestro e scolare* was especially successful, as was the children's keyboard tutor *La bambina al cembalo*, which includes a divertimento with accompanying solo voice in the first two movements and violin in the finale. Pfeiffer may have been the composer of a number of symphonies attributed to JOHANN PFEIFFER, while some of his works have been misattributed to the later composer Michael Traugott Pfeiffer.

WORKS

Vocal: Amore in puntiglio (farsa in prosa con arie di musica), Venice, 1773, ?lost, mentioned by Eitner; A Collection of 6 Italian and 6 English Songs, 2–3vv, pedal hp/pf/hpd (London, 1789)

Orch: Conc., G, hpd, 2 vn, b (Venice, n.d.), ed. R. Steglich (Hanover, 1932/R), arr. per 2 hpd, D-Dl; Sinfonia, D (Venice, 1779); Sinfonia no.2, D (Venice, n.d.)

Chbr: 6 sonate . . . per esercizio a contratempi, 2 vn (Venice, 1785), as duetti for vn, va, D-Bsb, for va, vc, I-BRc; 2 sonatas, hpd, vn, b, D-Bsb; 3 pieces and 1 conc., hpd/pf, fl, vc (London, 1789), ?lost, listed in *GerberNL* and *FétisB*

Kbd (for hpd/pf unless otherwise stated): 12 petites pièces caractérisées, et 1 sonate, 4 hands (Venice, 1784); La bambino al cembalo (Venice, 1785); 2 sonates, hpd 4 hands (Venice, n.d.); Duett, 4 hands, op.1 (London, ?1795); Il maestro e scolare, sonata, 4 hands (Munich, ?1805/R); Il y a de la malice dedans, sonata, 4 hands (Mannheim and Munich, n.d.), ? = Sonata, 4 hands (Mannheim, n.d.) ?lost, listed *FétisB*; 2 sonatas, pf 4 hands (Hamburg and Altona, n.d.); Sonata, hpd 4 hands, Fughetta, 2 hpd, both D-Bsb

BIBLIOGRAPHY
Choron-FayolleD; EitnerQ; FétisB; GerberL; GerberNL; SainsburyD
E. Forbes, ed.: *Thayer's Life of Beethoven* (Princeton, NJ, 1964), i, 69

D.J. RHODES

Pfeiffer, (Johann) Michael Traugott (*b* Wilfershauzen, Bavaria, 5 Nov 1771; *d* Wettingen, Switzerland, 20 May 1849). Bavarian teacher. He was the first to apply Pestalozzian principles to school music teaching. Son of a Bavarian Kantor, he studied the violin and then went to Switzerland in 1792 to study languages and philosophy at Solothurn. Eight years later he had risen to the rank of secretary to the cantonal government of Aargau. Inspired by Pestalozzi's writings and a brief acquaintance with his experimental teaching at Burgdorf, Pfeiffer abruptly left the civil service to set up private schools at Solothurn in 1804 and Lenzburg in the following year. It was during his work in those schools, not (as Fétis claimed) as a member of Pestalozzi's staff, that Pfeiffer evolved the method of teaching music which was to secure approval from Pestalozzi himself.

The application of Pestalozzi's educational principles to separate subjects was often undertaken by specialist teachers, the master subsequently approving his disciples' work in appropriate cases. Following that pattern, Pfeiffer devised a 'Pestalozzian' syllabus which ensured that children were made familiar with particular phenomena before encountering the symbols which represented them, and that the complexities of notation were broken down into their simplest elements before children were required to study them. He thus divided the study of musical rudiments into separate parts: the rhythmic element was studied first, the melodic next and the dynamic third.

Only after separate study were those sections reconciled, allowing the full significance of musical notation to be considered.

With Pestalozzi's approval, the results of Pfeiffer's work were published by H.G. Nägeli, the Zurich music publisher who was also an active educational reformer, under the following titles: *Die Pestalozzische Gesangbildungslehre nach Pfeiffers Erfindung* (1809), *Gesangbildungslehre nach Pestalozzischen Grundsätzen paedagogisch begrundet von Michael Traugott Pfeiffer, methodisch bearbeitet von Hans Georg Nägeli* (1810) and *Auszug der Gesangbildungslehre . . .* (1812). Pfeiffer later published jointly with Nägeli *Gesangbildungslehre für den Männerchor* (1817) and *Chorgesangschule* (1821).

BIBLIOGRAPHY
J. Keller: *Michael Traugott Pfeiffer, der Musiker, Dichter und Erzieher* (Frauenfeld, 1894)
H. Lobmann: *Die Gesang-Bildungslehre nach Pestalozzischen Grundsätzen* (diss., U. of Leipzig, 1908)
B. Rainbow: *The Land without Music: Musical Education in England, 1800–1860, and its Continental Antecedents* (London, 1967)
R. Lorenz: *Musikpädagogik in der ersten 30 Jahren des 19. Jahrhunderts am Beispiel Carl Gottlieb Herings* (Mainz, 1988)

BERNARR RAINBOW

Pfeiffer, Tobias Friedrich (*b* in or nr Weimar, ?1751; *d* ?Düsseldorf, ?1805). German tenor, pianist and composer. He worked as an actor-singer in Weimar and then in Gotha (1778). From 1779 to 1780 he performed at the Elector of Cologne's theatre in Bonn, where he became acquainted with Johann van Beethoven, a tenor in the elector's service. He lodged with the Beethoven family until his departure, and in return gave Johann's son, the young Ludwig, piano lessons. During the next ten years he continued to travel; in 1789 he became a member of Joseph Seconda's Leipzig theatrical company, which performed his musical interlude (or prelude) *Die Freuden der Redlichen* (to words by Schocher) with great success. He settled in Düsseldorf in 1794 or 1795, and worked as a music teacher, receiving regular payments from Beethoven through Nicolaus Simrock. His compositions, which also included a cantata, *Der Friede* (*c*1801), and possibly piano variations (perhaps composed by Franz Pfeiffer; *see* PFEIFFER, FRANZ ANTON), appear to be lost.

BIBLIOGRAPHY
EitnerQ; FétisB; GerberNL; SainsburyD
M. Solomon: *Beethoven* (London, 1977)

D.J. RHODES

Pfendner, Heinrich (*b* Hollfeld, Upper Franconia, *c*1590; *d* Würzburg, *c*1631). German composer and organist. He studied with Aichinger and Erbach at Augsburg and with Cifra in Italy. His first publication, in 1614, describes him as organist to the Bishop of Gurk, Austria; the dedication (which is dated 1611 – possibly a misprint) states that its contents had been performed in private at the bishop's house for some time before this, so one may assume that he had also been employed there for some time. In 1615 he moved to Graz as court organist to Archduke Ferdinand II, and from 1618 until his death he was organist and Kapellmeister to the Bishop of Würzburg.

Pfendner, a prolific composer of Latin church music, was one of an important group of south German and Austrian composers who in the early 17th century developed the form of the concertato motet for few voices originating with Viadana; in doing so he was no doubt inspired by his training in Italy and with Aichinger. His

1614 volume is important in that, apart from those of Aichinger himself, it was one of the earliest motet collections with continuo to be published by a German composer. Of the motets in this collection and in three further books (1623–30) a few include independent instrumental parts, and there is also a 'sonata a cappriccio' for three instruments and continuo which is clearly based on the canzona pattern much used by Italian composers, including Cifra. Pfendner's vocal writing shows other italianate influences, such as the use of dialogue and refrain or rondo form, where the refrain is usually in triple time and the intervening passages are in a typical duet style, with progressions in parallel 3rds. He set the texts imaginatively. He preferred a basically syllabic approach which he enhanced by a certain amount of ornate writing, rhythmic and textural variety, short contrasting phrases and a growing conception of the function of the continuo as a separate, important element of the whole. The two organ canzonas are sectional and employ frequent changes of metre; both display typical early 17th-century keyboard figuration and contain colourful harmonies.

WORKS
printed works except anthologies published in Würzburg unless otherwise stated

Delli motetti, 2–8vv, bc (org) (Graz, 1614, enlarged 2/1625 as Motectorum liber primus)
Motectorum liber secundus, 2–8vv, bc (org) (1623)
Motectorum liber tertius, 2–8vv, bc (org) (1625)
Motectorum liber quartus, 2–8vv, bc (org) (1630)
Psalm 1, 8vv (1645)
Motets, incl. some repr. from above vols., 1623², 1626², 1626⁴, 1627¹, 1627², 1629¹, 1645⁵
2 canzonas, org, *c*1620, *D-Mbs*; ed. in CEKM, xl/iii (1976)

LOST WORKS
Mariale in omnes festivitates BVM (1645)
Missae, 4–8vv (1645)
Liber quintus missae (1648)

BIBLIOGRAPHY
EitnerQ; EitnerS; GerberNL
A. Adrio: *Die Anfänge des geistlichen Konzerts* (Berlin, 1935)
M. Sack: *Leben und Werk Heinrich Pfendners* (diss., Free U. of Berlin, 1954)

A. LINDSEY KIRWAN/ERICH SCHWANDT

Pfeyl, Johann. German printer who succeeded to the firm of JOHANN SENSENSCHMIDT.

Pfister, Hugo (*b* Zürich, 7 Sept 1914; *d* Küsnacht, nr Zürich, 31 Oct 1969). Swiss composer and teacher. He trained as a schoolteacher, then studied the piano and music theory with Czeslaw Marek. He taught music in the Teachers' Training College in Küsnacht for most of his life. He composed in a light French manner until 1956–7 when he went to study in Paris with Nadia Boulanger; he then quickly developed an individual style integrating linear thinking, a widely enlarged tonality with polytonal characteristics, and polyrhythmic textures stemming from the music of Bartók, Schoenberg and Berg. In many of his works the main formal force is a rhythmic impulse, combined with astute melodic and timbral invention. Pfister wrote much incidental music for stage and radio plays performed primarily in Germany and Switzerland.

WORKS
(selective list)

4 esquisses, fl, 1956; Sonatine bitonale, pf, 1957; Preambolo, aria e ballo, cl, gui, db, 1958; Orchester-Ballade, 1959; Fantaisie concertante, fl, hn, hp, str, 1959–60; Augsburger Serenade, fl, gui,
str trio, 1961; Sonata, 2 tpt, timp, str, 1962; Aegäisches Tagebuch, ob, str, perc, 1963; Partita, orch, 1964; Mobili a 3, fl, cl, pf, 1965; Duo concertante, va, vc, str, 1965–6; Ottobeuren-Quintett, wind qnt, 1966; Ikebana, 3 hp, 1968; 5 Sketches, 2 perc, orch, 1967, rev. 1969

Principal publishers: Eulenburg (Zürich), Heinrichshofen

BIBLIOGRAPHY
A. Briner: 'Zur Musik von Hugo Pfister', *SMz*, cv (1965), 322–6
G. Fierz: 'Gedenkblatt für Hugo Pfister', *Spektrum* [Zürich], no.49 (1970), suppl.
R. Tschupp: *Hugo Pfister* (Zürich, 1973)

ANDRES BRINER/CHRIS WALTON

Pfitzner, Hans (Erich) (*b* Moscow, 5 May 1869; *d* Salzburg, 22 May 1949). German composer, conductor and musical polemicist.

1. LIFE.   His father, an orchestral violinist who in 1872 moved from Moscow back to his native Germany, was leader of the Stadttheater orchestra in Frankfurt. Pfitzner claimed that he had some of his earliest musical experiences as a youthful spectator in the orchestra pit during opera performances in which his father was playing. He received his formal musical education at the Hoch Conservatory, Frankfurt, between 1886 and 1890, studying the piano with James Kwast and composition with Iwan Knorr. While he explored a wide range of contemporary musical, literary and philosophical preoccupations with his friends James Grun and Paul Cossmann (son of conservatory cello teacher Bernhard Cossmann), the Hoch Conservatory was closely associated with the outspoken hostility of its Brahmsian director, Bernhard Scholz, towards Wagner, Liszt and the New German school. A student cello concerto by Pfitzner was condemned by Scholz for harmonic irregularities and the inclusion of three trombones; these Scholz considered lamentable signs of Wagnerian influence. Pfitzner's music was henceforth to occupy an idiosyncratic stylistic position between New German Modernism and a more regressive allegiance to Schumann, Weber and the world of German Romantic opera.

Pfitzner's career as a teacher and conductor began in Mainz, where his Wagnerian, specifically *Tannhäuser*- and *Lohengrin*-orientated opera *Der arme Heinrich* was first performed in 1895. In the same year Ibsen's play *Gildet på Solhaug* was produced as *Das Fest auf Solhaug* with incidental music by Pfitzner. While those works began to shape his subsequent reputation as a theatre composer, he had already produced a considerable body of non-theatrical music, including some 30 songs, chamber music and the choral ballad *Der Blumen Rache*. It was the two early stage works, however, whose success carried him forward to a teaching post at the Stern Conservatory in Berlin (1897-1907). His ten years there saw the consolidation of his reputation, his elopement with Kwast's daughter Maria ('Mimi') to England in 1899 (they were married in Canterbury) and the first performance of his second opera *Die Rose vom Liebesgarten* (1901). This was an elaborate pageant, based on a painting by Hans Thoma, in which elements of *Parsifal* were reinterpreted in a spirit of Rosicrucian mysticism, its allegorical characters including ethereal Germanic nobles, woodland folk, fairies, the Star Maiden and Sun Child, a primitive bog-dweller, dwarfs and giants. The opera was given an important production in Vienna by Gustav Mahler and Alfred Roller in 1905, the year in which Kleist's *Das Kätchen von Heilbronn* was produced in

1. Hans Pfitzner: portrait by Willi Geiger, 1932 (Städtische Galerie im Lenbachhaus, Munich)

Berlin with music by Pfitzner. More incidental music followed in 1906, composed for the fairy tale play *Das Christ-Elflein* by his friend Ilse von Stach; he later (1917) turned this into a *Spieloper* with spoken dialogue, revising the text but retaining the original title. Here the complex fin-de-siècle symbolism of *Die Rose vom Liebesgarten* was replaced with the homespun sentimentality of a German Christmas morality play for children; it anticipated some of the preoccupations of the *Blut und Boden* school of the National Socialist period and occasioned a significant stylistic retreat into diatonic tunefulness.

In 1907 Pfitzner moved to Strassburg (now Strasbourg), where he was to run the conservatory, act as chief conductor of the city's symphony orchestra and, from 1910, direct the opera during a period when its short-term junior conductors included the young Furtwängler, Klemperer and Szell. Regarding his conservatory duties primarily as facilitating his conducting activities, Pfitzner was now able to indulge his enthusiasm for German Romantic opera, publishing E.T.A. Hoffmann's *Undine* for the first time in vocal score (1908), reviving Heinrich August Marschner's *Der Templar und die Jüdin* in a version of his own in 1912 and devising a new edition of Marschner's *Der Vampyr* (staged in Stuttgart in 1922). His central creative preoccupation during this period, however, was his opera *Palestrina* (designated 'a musical legend'), whose libretto he completed in 1911, using historical sources to elaborate the essentially fictitious story of Palestrina's 'rescue' of polyphonic music (by composing the *Missa Papae Marcelli*) from the reforming zeal of the Council of Trent. The completed opera was first performed in Munich in 1917, at the height of World War I (fig.2), and rapidly established itself as the most moving and coherent of all Pfitzner's expressions of idealistic, 'inspiration'-orientated musical conservatism. The work brought him into contact with the novelist Thomas Mann, who was fascinated by Pfitzner's characterization of the opera as marked by a valedictory 'sympathy with death' (by comparison with the lively optimism of *Die Meistersinger von Nürnberg*). Mann nevertheless found Pfitzner rather difficult ('not born to feel at ease') and the two men's later creative and intellectual divergence was symbolically marked by the inclusion of Pfitzner's signature on the public letter of April 1933 in the *Münchener Neuester Nachrichten* condemning Mann's supposedly un-German lecture on the 50th anniversary of Wagner's death ('Leiden und Grösse Richard Wagners').

By that time Pfitzner's creative idealism had been irrevocably scarred by his deep personal identification with Germany's defeat in 1918 and the country's ensuing humiliation. The return of Alsace-Lorraine to France had occasioned his removal from Strassburg to Munich in 1918. In his increasingly polemical expressions of anti-Modernist adherence to traditional German artistic values, as manifested in Classical and Romantic music, he created a public persona that seemed rather crudely to

2. Angels' scene from Act 1 of Pfitzner's 'Palestrina', Prinzregententheater, Munich, 1917, with Karl Erb as Palestrina; set design by Adolf Linnebach

underline his identification with the world-weary Palestrina in his 'Musical Legend'. His pamphlet *Futuristengefahr*, published in the year of *Palestrina*'s first performance (1917) was followed in 1920 by *Die neue Aesthetik der musikalischen Impotenz*, an extended diatribe against Paul Bekker's book on Beethoven, in which the critic developed the notion that a 'poetic idea' underlay the specifically musical structures and processes of Beethoven's major works. Pfitzner's attack stressed the uncontingent and self-sufficient nature of musical 'inspiration' ('*Einfall*') in a manner that occasioned heated debate in the German and Austrian musical press. Non-operatic works like the Eichendorff cantata *Von deutscher Seele* (1921) were increasingly interpreted as musical manifestos supporting his ostensibly proto-fascist rejection of foreign, Jewish and 'international bolshevik' influences on German culture. Regarding the wider intellectual life of Europe as decadent, Pfitzner became increasingly isolated from all but conservative sympathizers within the Weimar Republic.

His world-weary exasperation with jazz from America, as much as with the 'New Music' of Schoenberg and his school, led Pfitzner almost inevitably to entertain high hopes for a 'renewed' Germany under National Socialism; Hitler's 1923 visit to his hospital bedside, bizarrely engineered by his old Jewish friend Paul Cossmann (who supported and published Pfitzner in his *Süddeutsche Monatshefte*), marked the composer in a way that his subsequently confused and occasionally antagonistic relationship with the Nazis did not altogether warrant. The full complexity of his theoretically 'apolitical' artistic relations with the world of power and political reality were explored in his last opera, *Das Herz*, first performed simultaneously in Berlin and Munich in 1931. The prevailing darkness of the work owed much to the personal tragedy of his wife's death in 1926, but the concluding, dream-like escape by the early 18th-century black magician Dr Daniel Athanasius from the horror of public execution poignantly revealed artistic transcendence coinciding with political evasion: the doctor dies in his cell and his spirit is seen walking into Elysian fields to greet the wife for whose earlier death he had been responsible. In the first act of this often surprisingly dissonant and even experimental-sounding work, Athanasius's Faustian pact with temporal and daemonic powers (he uses the black arts to bring the Duke's son back to life) is nevertheless central to the dramatic action.

From 1933 Pfitzner's public life was marked by alternating phases of grudging public prominence and bitter and angry withdrawal. An unfolding sequence of personal tragedies included his ultimate failure to prevent Cossmann from perishing in Theresienstadt in 1942 (although he had successfully interceded on his behalf in 1933), the death of his eldest son Paul in 1936, his subsequent estrangement from two of his other children (Peter and Agnes) and the suicide of his daughter Agnes in the year of both his 70th birthday and his marriage to Mali Stoll (1939). Pfitzner suffered further disasters with the destruction of his Munich house in a 1943 air-raid and the loss of his son Peter in Russia in 1944; in 1945 he found himself interned opposite Richard Strauss's villa in Garmisch-Partenkirchen. He was already installed in an old-people's home when he began to undergo de-Nazification in 1947. The toll of these experiences on his health was ultimately fatal; he died in May 1949 in Salzburg, some two weeks after attending an 80th-birthday concert.

2. WORKS. In the light of Pfitzner's investment in the ideology of Romantic idealism, brought to a sharply coherent music-theoretical focus by Heinrich Schenker during the same period, it is striking that his most interesting works are characterized by disjunct and fractured surface features. Individual compositions, like his output as a whole, seem intent on avoiding conventional signs of structural and stylistic 'organic unity' that the aesthetic philosophy of 'inspiration', linked to a belief in 'purely musical' values and processes, entailed for thinkers as diverse as Schenker and Schoenberg. In stylistic terms Pfitzner's output embraced advanced post-Wagnerian chromatic harmony (occasionally tending towards atonality), an almost Impressionistic sound palette (whole-tone scales are used in the *fin-de-siècle* nature-music of his op.18 setting of Goethe's *An den Mond*), diatonic melodic writing that harks back to the Romantic operas of Weber and Lortzing, grandiose late-Romantic effects in the manner of Richard Strauss, a predilection for bony linear counterpoint and an occasional recourse to pastiche effects of deliberate archaism (as in *Palestrina*).

Pfitzner wrote in all the major genres available to him, apart from the large-scale orchestral symphony (his only works to bear the designation 'symphony' are the op.36a arrangement for orchestra of his second string quartet, the op.44 *Kleine Symphonie* and the one-movement Symphony in C, op.46). His four large-scale operas, excluding *Das Christ-Elflein*, represent major contributions to post-Wagnerian German musical theatre, their internal anomalies being eloquently summarized and even thematized in *Palestrina*. That work's epigraph from Schopenhauer ('… alongside the history of the world there goes, guiltless and unstained by blood, the history of philosophy, of science and the arts') is ostentatiously contradicted by the second act, in which a meeting of the Council of Trent fails to achieve democratic consensus and concludes with a street brawl that the German nobleman, Cardinal Madruscht, quells with a murderously cathartic volley of gunfire.

A comparable masterpiece to *Palestrina* is the similarly fractured cantata *Von deutscher Seele*, which represented a quintessence of Pfitzner's style in its marriage of the Romantic poetry of Eichendorff (he wrote numerous *Lieder* to Eichendorff texts) with patriotic German nationalism and nostalgia. The work was deemed appropriate to feature prominently in the first *Reichsmusiktage* festival in Düsseldorf in 1938, the year that saw the publication in Berlin of a collection of extracts from Pfitzner's writings ominously titled *Hört auf Hans Pfitzner!*. The first section of the cantata ('Mensch und Natur') is distinguished by a typically eclectic stylistic range, stage-managed in such a way as to lead from the advanced *Stimmungsmusik* of the orchestral 'Abend-Nacht' interlude into the highly original Protestant-sounding chorale which crowns it. The subsequent sections are less well-integrated. German Romantic soulfulness is finally turned into a nationalistic peroration of crudely rhetorical character in the setting of *Der Friedensbote*; the work became a fitting monument to the unresolved contradictions which made Pfitzner's conservatism so rich and revealing a contribution to German music in the first half of the 20th-century.

WORKS

STAGE

op.

— Das Fest auf Solhaug (incid music, H. Ibsen), 1889–90; Mainz, 28 Nov 1895

— Der arme Heinrich (Musikdrama, 3, J. Grun and Pfitzner, after H. von Aue), 1891–3, Mainz, 2 April 1895

— Die Rose vom Liebesgarten (romantische Oper, prol., 2, epilogue, Grun), 1897–1900, Elbergeld, 9 Nov 1901

17   Das Käthchen von Heilbronn (incid music, H. von Kleist), 1905, Berlin, 19 Oct 1905

20   Das Christ-Elflein (incid music, I. von Stach), Munich, 11 Dec 1906, rev. (Spieloper, 2, Pfitzner, after Stach), Dresden, 11 Dec 1917

— Gesang der Barden für 'Die Hermannsschlacht' (incid music, Kleist), 1906

— Palestrina (musikalische Legende, 3, Pfitzner), 1911–15, Munich, 12 June 1917

39   Das Herz (Drama für Musik, 3, H. Mahner-Mons), op.39, 1930–31, Berlin and Munich, 12 Nov 1931

CHORAL

— Der Blumen Rache (Ballade, F. Freiligrath), A, female vv, orch, 1888

— Rundgesang zum Neujahrsfest 1901 (E. von Wolzogen), B, mixed/male vv, pf, 1900

16   Columbus (F. von Schiller), chorus 8vv, 1905

25   2 deutsche Gesänge (A. Kopisch, J.F. von Eichendorff), Bar, male vv ad lib, 1915–16

28   Von deutscher Seele (cant., Eichendorff), 4 solo vv, chorus, orch, org, 1921

38   Das dunkle Reich (Chorphantasie, Michelangelo, J.W. von Goethe, C.F. Meyer, R. Dehmel), solo vv, orch, org, 1929

48   Fons salutifer (E.G. Kolbenheyer), chorus, orch, org, 1941

49   2 Male Choruses, 1941

53   3 Songs, male chorus, small orch, 1944

57   Kantate (Goethe: Urworte orphisch), 4 solo vv, chorus, orch, org, 1948–9, completed R. Rehan

OTHER VOCAL

With orch: Herr Oluf (ballad, J.G. von Herder), op.12, Bar, orch, 1891; Die Heinzelmännchen (A. Kopisch), op.14, B, orch, 1902–3; Lethe (C.F. Meyer), op.37, Bar, orch, 1926

Lieder, 1v, pf: 6 Jugendlied, 1884–7; 7 Lieder, op.2, 1888–9; 3 Lieder, op.3, 1888–9; 4 Lieder, op.4, 1888–9; 3 Lieder, op.5, 1888–9; 6 Lieder, op.6, 1888–9; 5 Lieder, op.7, 1888–9; 5 Lieder, op.9 (J.F. von Eichendorff), 1888–9; 3 Lieder, op.10, 1901; 5 Lieder, op.11, 1901; Untreu und Trost, 1903; 4 Lieder, op.15, 1904; An den Mond, op.18 (J.W. von Goethe), 1906; 2 Lieder, op.19, 1905; 2 Lieder, op.21, 1907; 5 Lieder, op.22, 1907; 4 Lieder, op.24, 1909; 5 Lieder, op.26, 1916; 4 Lieder, op.29, 1922; 4 Lieder, op.30, 1922; 4 Lieder, op.32 (Meyer), 1923; Alte Weisen, op.33 (G. Keller), 1923; 6 Liebeslieder, op.35 (R. Huch), 1924; 6 Lieder, op.40, 1931; 3 Sonette, op.41, 1931; Die schlanke Wasserlilie (1949)

INSTRUMENTAL

Orch: Scherzo, c, 1887; Pf Conc., E♭, op.31, 1922; Vn Conc., b, op.34, 1923; Sym., c♯, op.36a, 1932 [after Str Qt no.2]; Vc Conc., G, op.42, 1935; Duo, op.43, vn, vc, pf/small orch, 1937; Kleine Sym., G, op.44, 1939; Elegie und Reigen, op.45, 1940; Sym., C, op.46, 1940; Vc Conc., a, op.52, 1944; Fantasie, op.56, 1947

Chbr and solo inst: Sonata, f♯, op.1, vc, pf, 1890; Pf Trio, F, op.8, 1896; Str Qt no.1, D, op.13, 1902–3; Pf Qnt, C, op.23, 1908; Sonata, e, op.27, vn, pf, 1918; Str Qt no.2, c♯, op.36, 1925; 5 Klavierstücke, op.47, 1941; Str Qt no.3, c♯, op.50, 1942; 6 Studien, op.51, pf, 1943; Sextet, g, op.55, cl, vn, va, vc, db, pf, 1945

WRITINGS

Gesammelte Schriften (Augsburg, 1926–9)
Über musikalische Inspiration (Berlin, 1940)
ed. W. Abendroth: Reden–Schriften–Briefe (Berlin, 1955)

BIBLIOGRAPHY

Grove6 (H. Wirth) [incl. further bibliography]
P.N. Cossmann: Hans Pfitzner (Munich, 1904)
W. Riezler: Hans Pfitzner und die deutsche Bühne (Munich, 1917)
T. Mann: 'Hans Pfitzner', Betrachtungen eines Unpolitischen (Berlin, 1919)
A. Morgenroth: Hört auf Hans Pfitzner! Kernsätze aus Pfitzners Schriften (Berlin, 1938)
E. Valentin: Hans Pfitzner: Werk und Gestalt eines Deutschen (Regensburg, 1939)
H. Rutz: Hans Pfitzner: Musik zwischen den Zeiten (Vienna, 1949)
K.F. Müller: In memoriam Hans Pfitzner (Vienna, 1950) [incl. complete work-list]
Mitteilungen der Hans Pfitzner-Gesellschaft (Munich, 1954–)
L. Schrott: Die Persönlichkeit Hans Pfitzners (Freiburg and Zürich, 1959)
H. Rectanus: Leitmotivik und Form in den musikdramatischen Werken Hans Pfitzners (Würzburg,1967)
W. Diez: Hans Pfitzners Lieder: Versuch einer Stilbetrachtung (Regensburg, 1968)
H. Rectanus: 'Pfitzner als Dramatiker', Beiträge der Geschichte der Oper, ed. H. Becker (Regensburg, 1969), 139–45
J. Newsom: 'Hans Pfitzner, Thomas Mann and "The Magic Mountain"', ML, lv (1974), 136–50
F. Wamlek-Junk: Hans Pfitzner und Wien. Sein Briefwechsel mit Victor Junk und andere Dokumente (Tutzing, 1986)
Hans Pfitzner und die musikalische Lyrik seiner Zeit: Hamburg 1989
J.P. Vogel: Hans Pfitzner, mit Selbstzeugnissen und Bilddokumente (Reinbek bei Hamburg, 1989)
G. Busch-Salmen and G.Weiss, eds.: Hans Pfitzner: Münchener Dokumente, Bilder und Bildnisse (Regensburg, 1990)
J. Williamson: The Music of Hans Pfitzner (Oxford, 1992)
O. Toller: Pfitzner's Palestrina: the 'Musical Legend' and its Background (London, 1997)
M.H. Kater: Composers of the Nazi Era: Eight Portraits (New York, 2000)

PETER FRANKLIN

Pfleger, Augustin (b Schlackenwerth, nr Carlsbad [now Karlovy Vary], c1635; d ?Schlackenwerth, after 23 July 1686). German composer of Bohemian birth. Schlackenwerth was the Bohemian residence of the dukes of Saxe-Lauenburg, and Pfleger had found employment there as Kapellmeister to Duke Julius Heinrich by the time he published his op.1 in 1661. In 1662 he went to Güstrow as vice-Kapellmeister to Duke Gustav Adolph of Mecklenburg. He was kept very busy as a composer there and wrote 89 sacred concertos in 1664 alone. In 1665 he was appointed Kapellmeister to the Schleswig-Holstein court at Gottorf and was commissioned to compose the ceremonial music for the opening of the University of Kiel. He left there on 16 May 1673, but his destination is unknown; his successor was Johann Theile. By 23 July 1686 he had returned to Schlackenwerth and was once again Kapellmeister to the court of Saxe-Lauenburg.

Pfleger's op.1 is a collection of 18 small sacred concertos to Latin texts, primarily biblical. They are scored for a small ensemble of singers with little instrumental participation other than continuo and are based on Italian models, in both the choice and the treatment of the texts. The four Latin odes for the inauguration of Kiel University are in a stiff, ceremonial style, while the two with German texts are more forward-looking and show similarities to some of Buxtehude's aria cantatas. The individual works surviving in manuscript were most likely composed at Gottorf. Latin still predominates, but there are more non-biblical, devotional and mixed texts than in op.1. These works are moreover more richly scored, have much more prominent instrumental parts and include more contrapuntal writing. Pfleger dedicated his cycle of 72 cantatas for the church year to the Flensburg city council, so they too may date from his Gottorf years. Many are dramatic dialogues, with both allegorical and biblical characters. Their German texts, based on the appointed gospel for the day, skilfully combine biblical passages, strophic poetry and an occasional chorale, which are set in contrasting arioso, concerto or aria styles.

The French lexicographer Sébastien de Brossard owned a copy of Pfleger's op.1 and characterized it as 'one of the best of its time'. In their settings of composite texts, his later works figure significantly in the development of the German sacred cantata.

WORKS

Editions: *A. Pfleger: Geistliche Konzerte*, ed. F. Stein, EDM, 1st ser., l, lxiv (1961, 1964) [S i–ii]
for full details see Nausch; all MSS in S–Uu

[18] Psalmi, dialogi et motettae, 2–5vv, bc, op.1 (Hamburg, 1661)
Odae concertantes … in Actu Inaugurationis lusit musicorum chorus et compositione … Augustini Pflegeri, 1, 5vv, insts, in J. Torquato: Inaugurationis panegyrica descriptio (Kiel, 1666)

German

all except *O barmherziger Vater* constitute a cycle of cantatas for the church year

Ach, dass ich Wassers genug hätte, 5vv, 2 va, ed. in Cw, lii (1938); Ach, die Menschen sind umgeben mit viel Krankheit, 5vv, 3 va; Ach Herr, du Sohn Davids, 4vv, 2 va, S i; Ach, wenn Christus sich liess finden, 5vv, 3 va, S i; Christen haben gleiche Freud, 5vv, 2 vn, S i; Der Herr ist ein Heiland, 4vv, 3 va da braccio; Der Herr ist gross von Wundertat, 5vv, 2 vn, S ii

Der Mensch ist nicht geschaffen zum Müssiggang, 4vv, 2 vn, 2 va da braccio; Die Ernte ist gross, 5vv, 2 vn, va da gamba, S ii; Erbarm dich mein, O Herre Gott, 5vv, 2 vn, 2 va da braccio; Es wird das Szepter von Juda nicht entwendet werden, 5vv, 2 vn, 2 va, S i; Friede sei mit euch, 4vv, vn, 2 va da gamba; Fürchtet den Herrn, 5vv, 2 vn; Gestern ist mir zugesaget, 4vv, 2 vn, S i; Gott bauet selbst sein Himmelreich, 3vv, 2 vn, S ii

Gottes Geist bemüht sich sehr, 4vv, 2 vn, 2 va da braccio; Gott ist einem König gleich, 4vv, 2 va; Herr, haben wir nicht, 4vv, 3 va; Herr, wann willst du mich bekehren, 3vv, 3 va; Herr, wer wird wohnen in deiner Hütten, 4vv, 3 va; Herr, wir können uns nicht nähren, 5vv, 2 va; Heute kann man recht verstehen, 4vv, 2 vn, 2 va da braccio; Heut freue dich, Christenheit … der Heiland, 4vv, 2 vn, 2 va da braccio, S i

Heut freue dich, Christenheit … vom Himmel, 4vv, 2 vn, 2 va da braccio, S i; Heut ist Gottes Himmelreich, 5vv, 2 vn, 2 va da braccio, S i; Hilf, Herr Jesu, lass gelingen, 4vv, 3 va, S i; Ich bin das Licht der Welt, 5vv, 3 va; Ich bin ein guter Hirte, 3vv, 2 vn, 2 va da gamba/da braccio; Ich bin wie ein verirret' und verloren Schaf, 4vv, 2 vn; Ich danke dir, Gott, 5vv, 3 va

Ich gehe hin zu dem, 5vv, 2 vn, 2 va da gamba; Ich sage euch, 4vv, 2 vn, 2 va da braccio; Ich suchte des Nachts in meinem Bette, 4vv, 2 vn, 2 va; Ich will meinen Mund auftun, 4vv, 2 vn, S ii; Im Anfang war das Wort, 4vv, 3 va, S i; Jesu, lieber Meister, 4vv, 3 va; Jesus trieb ein' Teufel aus, 5vv, 2 va, S ii; Jetzt gehet an die neue Zeit, 5vv, 2 va

Kommt, denn es ist alles bereit, 4vv, 3 va da braccio; Kommt her, ihr Christenleut, 5vv, 2 va, S i; Lernet von mir, 4vv, 3 va; Mache dich auf, 4vv, 2 vn, S i; Meine Tränen sind meine Speise, 4vv, 2 vn, 2 va da braccio; Mein Sohn, woll't Gott, 3vv, 3 va; Meister, was soll ich tun, 5vv, 3 va; Meister, welches ist das fürnehmste; Gebot, 5vv, 3 va; Meister, wir wissen, 5vv, 3 va

Mensch, lebe fromm, 3vv, 2 vn; Merket, wie der Herr uns liebet, 4vv, 3 va; Mich jammert des Volkes, 5vv, 2 vn; Nun gehe ich hin, 5vv, 2 vn; O barmherziger Vater, lv, 4 va; O Freude, und dennoch Leid, 4vv, 2 vn, 2 va da braccio; O, Tod, wie bitter bist du, 4vv, 2 va da braccio; Preiset ihr Christen mit Hertzen und Munde, 5vv, 2 vn, 2 va da braccio; Saget der Tochter Sion, 4vv, 2 vn, 2 va; Schauet an den Liebes Geist, 4vv, 2 vn

Siehe dein Vater, 5vv, 3 va, S ii; Sollt nicht das liebe Jesulein, 4vv, 2 va, S i; So spricht der Herr, 4vv, 3 va, S ii; Triumph! Jubilieret, 6vv, 2 vn, 2 va; Und er trat in das Schiff, 5vv, 3 va, S ii; Und es war eine Hochzeit zu Cana, 4vv, 2 va, S ii; Und Jesus ward verkläret vor seinen Jüngern, 6vv, 2 vn, 2 va, S ii; Wahrlich, ich sage dir, 4vv, 2 vn, 2 va da braccio; Wahrlich, ich sage euch, 4vv, 3 va

Weg mit aller Lust und Lachen, 3vv, 2 va, S ii; Wenn aber der Tröster kommen wird, 5vv, 2 vn, 2 va da braccio; Wenn die Christen sind vermessen, 4vv, 3 va; Wenn du es wüsstest, 4vv, 2 va; Wer ist wie der Herr unser Gott, 4vv, 3 va; Wir müssen alle offenbar werden, 5vv, 3 va; Zwar bin ich des Herren Statt, 4vv, 3 va

Latin

Ad te clamat cor meum, 1v, 4 insts; Confitebor tibi, 4vv, 2 vn, va; Cum complerentur dies, 5vv, 2 va, 2 va da gamba; Diligam te Domine, 5vv; Dominus virtutum nobiscum, 5vv, 2 vn, va, va da gamba; Eheu mortalis, 4vv, 3 va; Fratres, ego enim accepi a Domino, 3vv, 3 va; Inclina Domine, 4vv, 4 va; In tribulatione, 4vv, 3 va da braccio; Justorum animae in manu Dei sunt, 1v, 4 va; Laetabundus et jucundus, 4vv, 2 vn; Laetatus sum in his, 4vv, 2 vn, 2 va

Lauda Jerusalem, 4vv, 2 vn, 2 va; Laudate Dominum, omnes gentes, 4vv, 4 insts (2 versions); Laudate pueri, 3vv, 3 va da gamba; Missus est angelus, 3vv, 2 va; Nisi Dominus aedificavit, 2vv, 2 vn; O altitudo divitiarum, 5vv, 4 va; O divini amor, 1v, 4 va; O jucunda dies, 2vv, 2 vn, 2 va da gamba; Si quis est cupiens, 1v, 2 vn, 2 va da gamba; Veni Sancte Spiritus, 8vv, 10 insts; Veni Sancte Spiritus, 4vv, 2 vn, 2 va

LOST WORKS

89 Lat. sacred concs., 2–5vv, 1664, cited in Güstrow catalogue, Mecklenburgisches Geheimes und Hauptarchiv, Schwerin
9 Ger. cants., 1–5vv, insts; 4 Lat. cants., 1, 3vv, insts: formerly St Michaelis Chorbibliothek, Lüneburg, or *D-LEt*, or the court at Ansbach

BIBLIOGRAPHY

F. Stein: 'Ein unbekannter Evangelienjahrgang von Augustin Pfleger', *Festschrift Max Schneider zum 60. Geburtstag*, ed. H.J. Zingel (Halle, 1935), 126–36
F. Blume: 'Augustin Pflegers Kieler Universitäts-Oden', *AMf*, viii (1943), 5–26; repr. in F. Blume: *Syntagma musicologicum: gesammelte Reden und Schriften*, i, ed. M. Ruhnke (Kassel, 1963)
A. Nausch: *Augustin Pfleger, Leben und Werke: ein Beitrag zur Entwicklungsgeschichte der Cantate im 17. Jahrhundert* (Kassel, 1954)
F. Stein: Introduction to EDM, I (1961)
B. Grusnick: 'Die Dübensammlung: ein Versuch ihrer chronologischen Ordnung', *STMf*, xlvi (1964), 27–82; xlviii (1966), 63–186
F. Krummacher: *Die Überlieferung der Choralbearbeitungen in der frühen evangelischen Kantate* (Berlin, 1965)
E. Hehr: 'An Anonymous Motet Manuscript in Brossard's Library Partially Identified', *MR*, xlvii (1986–7), 77–88
M. Märker: *Die protestantische Dialogkomposition in Deutschland zwischen Heinrich Schütz und Johann Sebastian Bach* (Cologne, 1995)
G. Webber: *North German Church Music in the Age of Buxtehude* (Oxford, 1996)

KERALA J. SNYDER

Pflock (Ger.). *See* ENDPIN.

Phagotum. A kind of bagpipe invented about 1515 by Afranio degli Albonesi of Pavia, in an unsuccessful attempt to improve the popular bagpipe of Pannonia (where he was living, now in Serbia) with its double chanter and no drones. Later, in Italy, Afranio perfected the phagotum with the help of Giovanni Battista Ravilio of Ferrara, playing a solo on it at a feast given in Mantua by the Duke of Ferrara in 1532. In 1539 Afranio's nephew Teseo Ambrosio, professor of Syriac at the University of Bologna, described and illustrated the instrument in his book *Introductio in Chaldaicam linguam, Syriacam atque Armenaicam at decem alias linguas.* In 1565 Teseo gave a sheet of instructions for playing the instrument to a friend, to whom he had presented 'uno de suoi fagoti'. Apparently a number of examples of the phagotum were made. Mersenne briefly discussed the instrument in *Harmonicorum libri*, xii (1636) and *Harmonie universelle* (1636–7), but it is not mentioned by Agricola, Zacconi, Praetorius or other Renaissance writers.

As the illustration shows, the phagotum consisted of two connected pillars, about 45 to 55 cm in height, with a purely ornamental pillar on the front and a shorter pillar at the back through which the air from the bellows was conveyed to the instrument. The two main pillars

Rear view of Afranio's phagotum from Teseo Ambrosio's 'Introductio in Chaldaicam linguam…' (1539)

were each divided into an upper and a lower part: the upper part was bored with two parallel cylindrical tubes united at the top, forming one continuous doubled-back bore pierced with holes for the fingers and keys; the lower part contained a single metal reed. The left-hand pillar, with a reed of silver, provided a diatonic scale of ten notes from *c* upwards, while the right-hand pillar was fitted with a reed of brass and had a compass of ten notes from G to *b*. By cross-fingering, chromatic notes could be obtained, and either pillar could be silenced or sounded at will by a special key. From the back of the instrument, which was rested on the knees during performance, a flexible pipe passed to a bag held under the left arm; this formed an air reservoir, supplied with wind from bellows fastened under and actuated by the right arm, as in the Irish ('uilleann') and Northumbrian bagpipes.

The phagotum was used by Afranio not for 'vain and amatory melodies' but for 'divine songs and hymns'. The music could be played either in one or two parts, and Teseo in his instructions said that he had seen a phagotum with three large pillars or sets of tubes.

The name 'phagotum', like the Italian form '*fagoto*' in the description of the 1532 feast and the manuscript instructions, probably arose because the instrument resembled 'a bundle of sticks' (a faggot). However, although the name '*fagotto*' was subsequently applied to the bassoon (because its bore, like that of the phagotum,

was doubled back within the instrument), the two instruments were not otherwise related. While essentially a curiosity of limited distribution, Afranio's phagotum is historically significant as the earliest known use of the doubled-back bore, and in its use of an elaborate key mechanism.

BIBLIOGRAPHY

F.W. Galpin: 'The Romance of the Phagotum', *PMA*, lxvii (1940–41), 57–72

W.A. Cocks: 'The Phagotum: an Attempt at Reconstruction', *GSJ*, xii (1959), 57–9

H.M. Brown: 'A Cook's Tour of Ferrara in 1529', *RIM*, x (1975), 216–41

FRANCIS W. GALPIN/GUY OLDHAM/BARRA R. BOYDELL

Phairau, Luang Pradit (*b* Samut Songkhram, Thailand, 1881; *d* 1954). One of the two most highly-regarded central Thai musicians during the reigns of Rama V, VI and VII (*see also* PHATAYAKOSOL, CANGWANG THUA). Born as Sorn, the young musician was discovered by Prince Woradet (a member of the Thai royal family) during a music competition and was taken to the capital and made a royal page; he eventually attained the title 'Cangwang' (one of the highest ranks for the royal pages). He quickly became the best *ranāt ēk* (xylophone) player in the palace, which effectively made him the leader of the palace *pī phāt* ensemble. He served the prince for several decades, living in Burapha Palace and making the prince's household famous for its music. He accompanied the prince to Java in 1915 and King Rama VII to Cambodia in 1929–30, bringing back instruments as well Javanese and Khmer musical repertory that he adapted to Thai music. In 1925 King Rama VI recognized Sorn's talents and contributions by conferring on him the honorific name Luang (an aristocratic title) Pradit ('invent', 'make' or 'devise') Phairau ('beautiful sound') and giving his family the hereditary surname Silapabanleng ('the art of musical performance'). He is considered the originator of many musical techniques and concepts now central to the practice of central Thai court music, including the technique of sustaining pitches on the xylophone by trilling or rolling the mallets (*krǭ*) and developing the compositional practice known as *thao* that involves expanding or contracting pre-existing melodies. He is also considered the first composer to write in a programmatic fashion, imitating the sounds of nature, and he extended the most expansive metrical framework, three *chan*, to six *chan* (*see* THAILAND, §I, 2(ii)). Two of his children, Prasidh Silapabanleng (*b* 1915) and Chin Silapabanleng (1906–88), became famous in their own rights as musicians; Prasidh is a composer in the Western art music tradition and Chin was involved in bringing Thai classical music into the public school curriculum. The Luang Pradit Phairau Foundation, a school for traditional Thai music and dance, was established by his children and is now overseen by his grandchildren.

DEBORAH WONG

Phalèse. Flemish family of music publishers. They were active in Leuven and Antwerp from 1545 to 1674.

(1) **Pierre Phalèse (i)** (*b* Leuven, *c*1505–10; *d* Leuven, 1573–6). He was the son of Augustin vander Phaliesen, a brewer, and Marguerite van Poddeghem. He may have been related to Arnold vander Phaliesen, a painter in Leuven from 1499, and the organist Antoine vander Phalisen (*d* 17 March 1487). In 1541 Phalèse became a bookseller to the University of Leuven, where from 1545

to 1552 he published a number of scholarly books, some of them jointly with another Leuven publisher and printer, Martin de Raymaker (Rotarius). During these years Phalèse also published five books of chansons arranged for lute; they were printed for him by JACOB BAETHEN, S. Sassen and R. Velpen, as Phalèse was at that time only a bookseller, not a printer. The five books are, however, all printed with the same type that Phalèse used from 1553, for the second volume of *Hortus musarum* and his other lute books.

Phalèse applied for and on 29 January 1552 received a privilege to print music from movable type. After his early lute publications Phalèse published a number of chanson and motet books featuring composers of the Low Countries, especially Clemens non Papa and Crécquillon. Beginning in 1560, however, he showed a bolder and more international approach. In 1561 he published *Cantuale . . . usum . . . ecclesiae Amstelredamensis*, for use by the combined choirs of the Amsterdam churches, printed by single-impression type in Gothic neume notation, which he used again in 1563 for *Psalmi . . . cum hymnis*. In 1563 Phalèse began to issue a new series of lute books entitled *Theatrum musicum*. The same year he published Francisco Guerrero's eight-part settings of the *Magnificat* using a large type (see illustration) similar to that used by Attaingnant and Du Chemin in Paris for their folio publications. Phalèse also published a number of books by Lassus and Rore, often reprints of volumes issued by Le Roy & Ballard.

In 1570 Phalèse began the association with the Antwerp printer JEAN BELLÈRE, a partnership continued by (2) Pierre Phalèse the younger until Bellère's death in 1595. Bellère was a bookseller with important international connections; he probably helped finance publications and ensured their better distribution, even in Antwerp. It was, however, still Phalèse who printed them. Bellère came from Liège and it may have been through this connection that the Liège musician Jean de Castro acted in 1574 and 1575 as musical adviser, supplying Phalèse with the latest French and Italian compositions for publication.

Apart from the Gothic and large choirbook types, Phalèse also owned a smaller, ordinary music type, used for chanson and motet publications, and lute tablature types. The smaller music type was also used by Jean Bogard in Douai. All the types are clear and well defined,

although the tablature is not as elegant as those used by French publishers. Nevertheless, Phalèse's printing is of a high standard, with texts carefully underlaid, and he was the first printer in the Low Countries to print lute books in a format with the two parts so arranged that players seated around a table could perform from one copy. When Phalèse visited Antwerp in 1570 to be examined by King Philip's proto-typographer, Plantin declared that Phalèse was 'expert in the art of printing music, which he did exclusively, and well versed in Latin, French and Flemish'.

The date of Phalèse's death is unrecorded: various books were published 'chez Pierre Phalèse' from 1574 to 1576. However, in 1574 his eldest son Corneille also published a volume by Lassus, the first part of his *Patrocinium musices* (a reprint of the Munich edition of 1573) but he did not continue as a printer. Corneille's younger brother, (2) Pierre Phalèse (ii), published three further parts of the *Patrocinium musices* in 1577 and 1578, signing himself on the title-page 'apud Petrum Phalesium juniorem'. As the title-pages of the volumes published by the firm between 1574 and 1576 do not carry this signature, it is most likely that these were published by Pierre Phalèse the elder. He probably died, therefore, in about 1576.

(2) Pierre Phalèse (ii) [the younger]   (*b* Leuven, *c*1545; *d* Antwerp, 13 March 1629). Son of (1) Pierre Phalèse (i). His name appears in 1563 in the matriculation register of the University of Leuven, but he does not seem to have completed his studies. He took over the firm after his father's death and three parts of *Patrocinium musices* (1577–8) were his first publications. He moved to Antwerp and registered in the Guild of St Luke in 1581, married Elisabeth Wisschavens in 1582 and in the same year set up his press in the Kammerstraat, at the sign of 'De rode leeuw'. He stayed there until 1608 when he moved to 'Den Coperen Pot' and shortly afterwards changed the name of the house to 'Koning David'. Phalèse continued the association with Jean Bellère until the latter's death in 1595. He used the same typographical material as his father, and continued to print chansons, motets and other religious music, as well as music for lute. Phalèse also published many volumes of Italian madrigals, including four celebrated collections: *Harmonia celeste* (1583, edited by Pevernage, reprinted five times between 1589 and 1628); *Musica divina* (1583, edited by Phalèse himself, reprinted seven times between 1588 and 1634), *Symphonia angelica* (1585, edited by Waelrant, reprinted four times between 1590 and 1629), and *Melodia olympica* (1591, edited by Philips, reprinted three times between 1594 and 1630). These and other collections reflect the popularity of Italian music in the Low Countries at this time. He also published a large number of madrigal books devoted to single Italian composers, including Agazzari, Anerio, Croce, Frescobaldi, Marenzio, Monteverdi, Mosto, Pallavicino, Rossi and Vecchi. Gastoldi's *Balletti a cinque voci* (1596), was reprinted seven times between 1601 and 1631, and sacred and secular music by the English composers living in Antwerp, Dering and Philips, was also published. Among Phalèse's lute publications, *Pratum musicum* by the Antwerp lutenist Emanuel Adriaenssen (1584), containing arrangements of madrigals and chansons as well as a few Flemish songs, holds an important place.

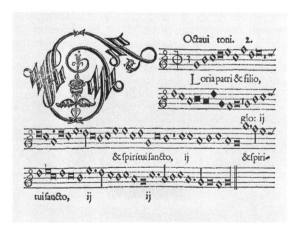

Opening of the superius voice of the 'Gloria Patri' from Francisco Guerrero's 'Canticum beatae Mariae, quod Magnificat nuncupatur' (Leuven: Phalèse, 1563), printed in large type

(3) Madeleine Phalèse (*b* Antwerp, bap. 25 July 1586; *d* Antwerp, 30 May 1652). Daughter of (2) Pierre Phalèse (ii). She and her sister, Marie (*b* Antwerp, bap. 10 Dec 1589; *d* Antwerp, *c*1674), enrolled in the Guild of St Luke as 'Filles Phalèse' in 1629 after their father's death, and for the next 45 years continued to run the family business, publishing some 180 volumes of madrigals, masses and motets. The proportion of madrigals to sacred music is not as high as in their father's time, but the composers are mostly Italians, and many volumes are reprints of collections originally issued by the Venetian firms of Gardano, Vincenti and Magni. After Madeleine Phalèse's death in 1652, a detailed list of the assets of the business was drawn up which gives some indication of its importance. The firm owned over 375 kg of music type and had a stock of music valued at over 3000 florins. Wages to journeymen printers and other expenses from June 1652 to July 1653 were more than 1000 florins. The document also lists the firm's outstanding debts, some of which were declared irrecoverable, and mentions its commercial ties with Italian music publishers. Although Marie Phalèse continued to manage the firm for another 20 years after her sister's death, the house of Phalèse did not recover its former stature. With the decline of Antwerp at the end of the 16th century, and the rise of Amsterdam during the 17th, music printing, like other aspects of trade and culture, became important in the northern Netherlands as it declined in the southern provinces.

PUBLICATIONS
(*selective list*)

P. PHALÈSE (i)
all published in Leuven

Des chansons reduictz en tablature de lut. . . livre premier [–V] (1545²¹/*R*, 1546²¹, 1546²⁸, 1547²⁰/*R*, 1547²³/*R*); Hortus musarum (1552²⁹, 1553³³/*R*); Premier [–VII] livre des chansons, 4vv (1552¹², 1552¹³, 1552¹⁴, 1552¹⁵, 1554²², 1560⁶) [livre I by De Latre]; Premier [–II] livre des chansons, 5–6vv (1553²⁴, 1553²⁵); Liber I [–IX] cantionum sacrarum, 5–8vv (1554¹, 1554², 1554³, 1554⁴, 1555⁴, 1555⁵) [liber V by Manchicourt, liber IX lost]; Clemens non Papa: Missae . . . tomus I [–X] (1556–60) ed. Bernet Kempers, CMM iv; Liber I [–VII] cantionum sacrarum, 4vv (1559) [books I–VI by Clemens non Papa, ed. Bernet Kempers, CMM iv, book VII by T. Crécquillon, ed. H.L. Marshall, *Musicological Studies*, xxi]; O. de Lassus: Tiers [–IV] livre des chansons (1560–64); Premier [–III] livre du recueil des fleurs de la divine musique (1560⁷, 1569¹⁰, 1569¹¹); A. Willaert: Moteta, 4–6vv, liber primus [–II] (1561), ed. H. Zenck, CMM iii; Cantuale usum ecclesiae Amstelredamensis (1561); F. Guerrero: Canticum Beatae Mariae quod Magnificat (1563); Psalmi, 1v (1563)

Theatrum musicum (1563); F. Viaera: Nova et elegantissima . . . carmina (1564); G. Pacoloni: Longe elegantissima tribus testudinibus ludenda carmina (1564/*R*); O. de Lassus: Sacrae lectiones, 4vv (1566); G. de Turnhout: Cantiones, 4–5vv (1568) [lost]; S. Vredeman: Nova . . . carmina, liber I [–II] (1568–9); Luculentum theatrum musicum (1568²³); Selectissimarum sacrarum cantionum . . . liber I [–III] (1569⁴, 1569⁵, 1569⁶); O. de Lassus and C. de Rore: Liber primus [–II] sacrarum cantionum (1569⁷, 1569⁸); G. de Turnhout: Sacrarum . . . cantionum . . . liber unus, 3vv (1569), ed. L. Wagner, RRMR ix–x; J. de Castro: Chansons & madrigales, 4vv (1570); O. de Lassus and C. de Rore: Premier [–IV] livre des chansons, 4–6vv (1570⁵, 1570⁶); Clemens non Papa: Missa defunctorum, 4vv (?1570) [lost]

P. PHALÈSE (i) with J. bellère
all published in Leuven and Antwerp

Praestantissimorum divinae musices, 4–6vv (1570¹); Hortulus cytharae (1570³⁴); Selectissima . . . carmina (1570³⁵); J. de Castro: Sacrarum cantionum . . . liber unus, 5–8vv (1571); O. de Lassus: Livre cinquiesme de chansons nouvelles, 5–8vv (1571), ed. H. Hümmerling (Düsseldorf, 1974); *Denkmäler Rheinischer Musik*, xvii; O. de Lassus: Primus (–III) liber modulorum 5vv (1571–3) [liber III lost]; O. de Lassus: Moduli, 5vv (1571); Liber primus

leviorum carminum, 4vv (1571¹⁴/*R*); Livre de musique, 2vv (1571¹³); Theatrum musicum (1571¹⁶), ed. G. Vellekoop (Rotterdam, 1958); Een duytsch musyck boeck (1572¹¹), ed. in UVNM, xxvi (1903); C. de Rore: Sacrae cantiones (1573); Petit trésor des danses (1573) [lost]; J. Flori: Modulorum . . . liber unus, 3vv (1573)

Thesaurus musicus (1574¹²); J. de Castro: Triciniorum sacrorum . . . liber unus (1574), ed. I. Bossuyt (Leuven, 1997); J. de Castro: La fleur des chansons, 3vv (1574³); J. de Castro: Livre de mélanges, 4vv (1575); O. de Lassus: Liber motettarum, 3vv (1575); P. de Monte: Sonetz, 5–7vv (1575); R. Viola: Carminum pro testudine liber (1575) [lost]; J. de Castro: Chansons, odes . . . de Pierre Ronsard, 4–8vv (1576); T. Crécquillon: Opus sacrarum cantionum, 4–8vv (1576); O. de Lassus: Cantiones, 2vv (1577) [lost]

C. PHALÈSE

O. de Lassus: Patrocinium musices, liber I (Leuven, 1574)

P. PHALÈSE (ii) with J. bellère
all published in Antwerp

J. de Castro: Chansons, madrigaux, 3vv (1582); J. de Castro: Livre de chansons, 3vv (1582); O. de Lassus: Libro de villanelle moresche, 4–8vv (1582); Hortulus citharae vulgaris (1582¹⁶); Chorearum molliorum collectanea, 4vv (1583²¹/*R*); Harmonia celeste, 4–8vv (1583¹⁴/*R*); Musica divina, 4–7vv (1583¹⁵/*R*); Symphonia angelica, 4–6vv (1585¹⁹/*R*); J. de Castro: Chansons, 5vv (1586); R. del Mel: Madrigali, 6vv (1588); R. del Mel: Sacrae cantiones, 5–12vv (1588); J. de Castro: Madrigali, 3vv (1588); G.B. Mosto: Madrigali, 5vv (1588); J. van Turnhout: Madrigali, 6vv, libro I (1589); Bicinia sive cantiones suavissimae (1590¹⁹)

J. de Castro: Recueil des chansons, 3vv (1591); Il lauro verde, 6vv (1591⁸); Melodia olympica, 4–8vv (1591¹⁰/*R*); E. Adriaenssen, arr.: Novum pratum musicum (1592²²/*R*); J. de Castro: Chansons, stances, 2vv (1592); J. de Castro: Sonets avec une chanson, 2vv (1592), ed. I. Bossuyt (Leuven, 1997); J. de Castro: Triciniorum sacrorum liber unus (1592); O. de Lassus: La fleur des chansons, 4–8vv (1592⁹); O. de Lassus: Cantiones italicae (1593) [lost]; G.P. da Palestrina: Cantiones sacrae, 4vv (1593); L. Marenzio: Madrigali, 5vv, libro I–V (1593); M. Thalman: Missae, 4–6vv (1593) [lost]; J. Desquesnes: Madrigali, 5vv . . . libro I (1594); G.B. Galeno: Madrigali, 5vv . . . libro I (1594); L. Marenzio: Madrigali, 6vv (1594¹⁴); J.P. Sweelinck and C. Verdonck: Chansons, 5vv (1594⁵)

P. PHALÈSE (ii) alone
published in Antwerp unless otherwise stated

O. de Lassus: Cantiones, 2vv (Leuven, 1577); O. de Lassus: Patrocinium musices . . . secunda (–4) pars (Leuven, 1577–8); E. Adriaenssen, arr.: Pratum musicum (1584¹²/*R*); J. de Castro: Harmonie joyeuse, 4vv (1595); Il trionfo di Dori (1595²); G.G. Gastoldi: Balletti, 5vv (1596); P. Philips: Il primo libro de madrigali, 6vv (1596⁸); Madrigali, 8vv (1596⁸); Paradiso musicale (1596¹⁰); Il vago alboreto (1597¹⁵); Le rossignol musical (1597¹⁰); P. Philips: Madrigali, 8vv (1598); Orazio Vecchi: Convito musicale (1598); Litaniae septem deiparae virgini, 4–5vv (1598)

F. Anerio: Madrigali, 6vv (1599); M. Pottier: Selectissimarum missarum flores, 4–8vv (1599¹); C. Verdonck: Poésies françoises, 5–10vv (1599); A. Agazzari: Madrigali harmoniosi, 6vv (1600); De floridi virtuosi d'Italia, 5vv (1600⁸); G. de Macque: Madrigaletti, 6vv (1600); G.B. Mosto: Madrigali, 6vv (1600); E. Adriaenssen, arr: Pratum musicum (1600¹⁸) Ghirlanda di madrigali, 6vv (1601⁵); A. Agazzari: Madrigali, 5vv (1602); G. Eremita: Madrigali, 6vv, libro I (1602); G.G. Gastoldi: Balletti, 3vv (1602); A. Pevernage: Missae, 5–7vv (1602)

L. Marenzio: Cantiones sacrae (1603); P. Maulgred: Cantiones sacrae, 4–8vv (1603); G.P. da Palestrina: Cantiones sacrae, 5vv (1603); P. Philips: Madrigali, 6vv . . . libro II (1603); Orfeo Vecchi: Cantiones sacrae, 6vv (1603); C. Verdonck: Madrigali, 6vv (1603); P. Rimonte: Missae, 4–6vv (1604), ed. P. Calahorra (Zaragoza, 1982); B. Pallavicino: Madrigali, 5vv (1604); A. Pevernage: Laudes vespertinae (1604); Fiori musicali, 3vv (1604¹³); Madrigali pastorali, 6vv (1604¹⁰); G.P. da Palestrina: Cantiones sacrae, 5vv (1605); A. Pevernage: Chansons, 5vv (1606); R. Giovannelli: Madrigali, 5vv (1606); B. Pallavicino: Madrigali, 6vv . . . libro I (1606); A. Pevernage: Chansons . . . tant spirituelles, 5vv (1606);

J. de Castro: Madrigali, 3vv (1607); O. de Lassus: Cantiones sacrae, 5–8vv (1607) [lost]; O. de Lassus: Magnificat 8 tonorum (1607) [lost]; L. Marenzio: Madrigali, 4vv (1607); A. Pevernage:

Chansons, 6–8vv (1607); P. Rimonte: Cantiones sacrae, 4–7vv (1607); Canzonette alla romana (1607[14]); G. Frescobaldi: Madrigali, 5vv, libro I (1608), ed. C. Jacobs (London, 1983); M. Serra: Missae, 4vv (1608[1]); Orfeo Vecchi: Cantiones sacrae, 5vv (1608); L. Marenzio: Madrigali, 5vv . . . libro VI–IX (1609); Bicinia sive cantiones (1609[18]/R); Florilegium sacrarum cantionum, 5vv (1609[1])

F. Anerio: Canzonette, 4vv (1610); G.G. Gastoldi: Concenti musicali, 8vv (1610[15]); L. Marenzio: Villanelle, 3vv, libro I–V (1610); L. Marenzio: Madrigali, 6vv, libro I–VI (1610 and 1610[16]); L. Marenzio: Madrigali spirituali, 5vv (1610); Novi frutti musicali: madrigali, 5vv (1610[14]); D. Poncet: Douze pseaumes de David (1611); Orazio Vecchi: Canzonette, 4vv (1611); M. Pottier: Missae, 8vv (1611); G. Guami: Canzonette francese, 4–8vv (1612); B. Pallavicino: Madrigali, 5vv, libro VI (1612); P. Philips: Cantiones sacrae, 5vv (1612); Orazio Vecchi: Missae, 6–8vv (1612[1]); G. Moro: Concerti ecclesiastici (1613); P. Philips: Cantiones sacrae, 8vv (1613), ed. J. Steele; P. Philips: Gemmulae sacrae, 2–3vv (1613); B. Pallavicino: Madrigali, 5vv, libro VII (1613); Il Parnasso: Madrigali, 6vv (1613[10])

O. de Lassus: Cantiones sacrae, 3–4vv (1613); P. Rimonte: Missae, 4–6vv (1614); P. Rimonte: El Parnaso español, 4–6vv (1614); G. Croce: Madrigali, 5vv (1615); Jean Deschamps: Novae missae novem, 5–8vv (1615); C. Monteverdi: Madrigali, 5vv, libro III [–V] (1615); A. Terzachus: Psalmi vesperarum, 4vv (1615); P. Bonhomme: Missae, 6–12vv (1616); P. Philips: Deliciae sacrae, 2–3vv (1616[6]); Il helicone (1616[10]); R. Dering: Cantiones sacrae, 5vv (1617); J. Rijspoort: Moraele spreekwoorden, 4–5vv (?1617)

G. Croce: Madrigali, 6vv (1618); R. Dering: Cantica sacra, 6vv (1618), ed. P. Platt (London, 1974); L. Nervius: Missae decem, 4–7vv (1618); S. Rossi: Madrigali, 5vv, libro I (1618); S. Bernardi: Missae, 4–5vv (1619[1]); W. Brade: Melodieuses paduanes (1619) [lost]; L. Leoni: Sacri flores, 2–4vv (1619): poera omnia; J.P. Sweelinck: Cantiones sacrae, 5vv (1619); R. Dering: Canzonette, 3vv (1620); R. Dering: Canzonette, 4vv (1620[16]) ed. P.Platt (Musica Britannica xxv); F. Costantini: Sacrae cantiones, 8vv (1621[1]); G. Finetti: Concerti ecclesiastici, 2–4vv (1621); H. Liberti: Cantiones sacrae, 4–5vv (1621) [lost]; G. Croce: Cantiones sacrae, 8vv (1622); H. Praetorius: Cantiones sacrae, 8vv (1622); P. Lappi: Sacrae melodiae, 1–6vv (1622); G. Belli: Concerti ecclesiastici, 2–3vv (1622)

P. Philips: Litaniae Beatae Mariae Virginis, 4–9vv (1623); L. Nervius: Cantiones sacrae, 8vv (1623); L. Nervius: Magnificat (1624); L. Nervius: Missae sacrae, 8vv (1624); L. Barberio: Cantiones sacrae, 5–8vv (1624); F.M. Guaitoli: Missa et motetta, 8vv (1624); T. Pecci: Canzonette, 3vv . . . libro I (1624[12]); C. Rondino: Cantiones sacrae, 2–3vv (1624[7]); L. de Hodemont: Armonica recreationi, 3vv (1625); H. Praetorius: Missae, 5–8vv (1625); G.B. Cocciola: Concentus harmonici ecclesiastici, 2–5vv (1625); L.G. da Viadana: Missarum, 4vv . . . liber I (1625[1a]); A. Bianchi: Motetta, 1–4vv (1626); Corona sacra (1626[4]); P. Bonhomme: Harmonia sacra, 5–12vv (1627); L. Nervius: Fasciculus cantionum sacrarum, 4–6vv (1628); P. Philips: Paradisus sacris cantionibus, 1–3 vv, 1a pars (1628); Laudes vespertinae, 4–6vv (1629[2])

HEIRS OF P. PHALÈSE
all published in Antwerp

C. Burgh: Hortus marianus, 4vv (1630); P. Philips and N. Pisanio: Litaniae Beatae Virginis Mariae, 4–8vv (1630[2]); H. Hollander: Parnassus ecclesiasticus, 1–4vv (1631); B. Richard: Litaniae Beatae Virginis Mariae (1631) [lost]; G.B. Ala: Luscinia sacra, 2–4vv (1633); G. Messaus: Missae, 5–12vv (1633); P. Philips: Paradisus sacris . . . secunda [–tertia] pars, 1–3vv (1633); G.B. Ala: Pratum musicum (1634[2]); H. Hollander: Jubilus filiorum Dei, 1–4vv (1634); G. Messaus: Cantiones sacrae, 8vv (1635) [lost]; Gratulationes marianae, 4–12vv (1636); A. Marino: Psalmi vesperarum, 4vv (1637); F. Colombini: Mel musicum, 2–5vv (1638); F. Colombini: Nectar caelicum, liber II, 2–4vv (1639); F. Colombini: Cantiones sacrae, 2–7vv, liber III (1639)

A. Grandi (i): Cantiones sacrae, liber I, 2–8vv (1639); A. Grandi (i): Cantiones sacrae, liber III, 1–5vv (1639); C. Monteverdi: Madrigali, 5vv, libro VI (1639); J. Willems: Primitiae Marianae, 6–8vv (1639); S. Todeschi: Sacrae cantiones, 2vv (1639); A. Grandi (i): Motetorum, 2–4vv, liber VI (1640); G. Hayne: Moteta sacra, 2–4vv . . . liber I (1640); G.B. Rovetta: Motetti concertati . . . op.5 (1640); G. Sabbatini: Madrigali . . . concertati, 2–4vv (1640); F. Colombini: Madrigali concertati, 5vv (1640); J. Dromal: Sertum musicum, 4–6vv (1640); J. Dromal: Convivium musicum, 2–6vv (1641); G. Sabbatini: Sacrarum laudum, liber II . . . op.7

(1641); J. Dromal: Corona sanctorum, 2vv (1641); Paradisus sacris cantionibus (1641[1]); J. Dromal: Missae sex, litaniae . . . , 4–7vv op.4 (1642); G. Sabbatini: Sacrae Laudes, 2–5vv, liber I, op.3 (1642) N. a Kempis: Symphoniae, op.4 (1642); Quadriga musicalis, 5–12vv (1642); J. Stadlmayr: Missae novem (1643); O. Tarditi: Motectorum, 2–4vv, liber IV, op.13 (1643); G. Hayne: Motetti overo madrigali, 5vv, op.2 (1643); O. Tarditi: Litaneae concertatae, 3+5vv (1644)

Gasparo Casati: Sacri concentus, 2vv (1644); G. Casati: Sacri concentus, 3–5vv (1644); N. a Kempis: Symphoniae 1–3 instrumentorum (1644); B. Marini: Corona melodica . . . op.15 (1644); D. Philetaero: Dei, deiparae . . . laudes, 5vv (1645); F. Colombini: Ambrosia sacra . . . liber III (1646); G. Hayne: Motetti sacri, 3–5vv (1646); J. Loisel: Surculus olivae . . . op.2 (1646) [lost]; Gasparo Casati: Operis primis pars . . . moteta (1647[4]); Gasparo Casati and P. Cornetti: Primi partus foetus . . . suavissimis modulis (1647[3]); N. a Kempis: Symphoniae 1–5 instrumentorum, op.2 (1647); L. Pietkin: Sacri concentus, liber I . . . op.1 (1648)

G.B. Rovetta: Bicinia sacra . . . liber III (1648); G.B. Rovetta: Manipulus et messe musicus, 2–3vv (1648); J. Loisel: Modulationes, 3–4vv, op.4 (1648); G.B. Rovetta: Motetta concertata, 2–4vv (1648); Tiburtius van Brussel: De gheestelycke tortel-duyve (1648); Gasparo Casati: Amoenum rosarium . . . op.5 (1649); G. Hayne: Moteta sacra, 2–4vv (1649); N. a Kempis: Symphoniae 1–5 instrumentorum, op.3 (1649); G.B. Rovetta: Gemma musicalis, liber IV (1649); J. Loisel: Motetta sacra, 2–3vv (1649); J.B. Verrijt: Flammae divinae, 2–3vv, liber I, op.5 (1649); Gasparo Casati: Sacri concentus, 2vv (1650); F. della Porta: Cantionum . . . liber I [–II], op.3 (1650); M. Cazzati: Corenti & balletti (1651[7]); G.B. Chinelli: Missarum, 3–5vv, liber II (1651); G.P. Finatti: Missae, motetta . . . op.2 (1652); Godefridus: Fasciculus musicus (1652); B. Graziani: Motetta, 2–6vv (1652); A. Poggioli: Delectus sacrarum cantionum, 2–5vv (1652)

G.B. Rovetta: Novi concentus sacrae, 2–4vv (1653); G. Casati: Motetta, 1–2vv, op.1 pars 1 (1654) F. della Porta: Cantionum . . . liber III, op.4 (1654); P. Hurtado: Cantiones natalitiae, 1–5vv (1655); G. Sabbatini: Sacrae laudes . . . liber I, op.3 (1656); S. Vesi: Motetti, 1v . . . op.3 (1656); Ph. van Steelant: Missa et motetta, 5–6vv, op.1 (1656); M. Cazzati: Motetti e hymni, 1v (1656) M. Cazzati: Suonate, op.18 (1657); J.-F. a Kempis: Cantiones natalitiae (1657); D. Castello: Sonate concertate . . . libro I [–II] (1656 and 1658); F. Foggia: Concentus ecclesiastici, 2–6vv (1658); B. Marcesso: Sacra corona (1659[2])

G. Borremans: Cantiones natalitiae, 5vv (1660); F. Petrobelli: Motetti, 2–3vv, liber II, op.5 (1660); N. Monferrato: Motetti concertati, 2–3vv, libro I, op.3 (1660); A. Vermeeren: Missae et motetta, 1–4vv (1660); Florida verba (1661[1]); G. Verlit: Missae et motetta, 4–6vv (1661); M. Cazzati: Motetti, 2–4vv . . . op.12 (1662); G.B. Halbos: Vermaeckelijcke duytsche liedekens, 3–5vv (1663); M. Cazzati: Tributo di sagri concerti, op.23 (1663); M. Uccellini: Sonate correnti . . . op.4 (1663); Tyrocinium musicum (1664); G. Bussé: Het gheestelyck Blomhofken (1664); M. Cazzati: Motetti, 2vv, op.10 (1665); G. Legrenzi: Sentimenti devote, op.6 (1665); J. Vander Wielen: Cantiones natalitiae, 4–5vv (1665); A. Vermeeren: Missae et motetta, liber III (1665); M. Cazzati: Motetti, 2vv, op.10 (1665); G. Legrenzi: Sentimenti devoti, 2–3vv, op.6 (1665); Compositioni sacri, 1–4vv (1665[2]); Benedictus a Sancto Josepho: Missae, litaniae . . . op.1 (1666); J. Berckelaers: Cantiones natalitiae, 4vv (1667); A. Grossi: Orfeo Pellegrino, op.4 (1667); Cantiones natalitae (1667[3])

M. Uccellini: Compositioni armoniche . . . libro VII (1668); M. Uccellini: Sonate sopra il violino, libro VII (1668); G. de Verlit: Missae et motetta . . . 3–4vv (1668); G.B. Vitali: Recueil des dances . . . livre V (1668[10]); M. Uccellini: Sinfonie boscarecie . . . op.8 (1669); J. Berckelaers: Cantiones natalitiae, 2–5vv (1670); G. Bart: Philomela sacra, 1–3vv (1671); C. Dumont: Missae et motetta, op.1 (1671); L. Royet: Missa, litania, 2–5vv (1671); P.F. Munninckx: Balletti, allemande, 3vv (1672); D. Becker: Musicalische lendt-vruchten, 3–5vv (1673); Benedictus a Sancto Josepho: Corona stellarum, 1–4vv (1673); J. Cocx: Ferculum musicum (1673); G. Doré: Motetta et psalmi, 3–4vv (1673); G. Bart: Missae et motetta, 3–5vv (1674); M. Cazzati: Suonate a 2 violini . . . op.18 (1674)

BIBLIOGRAPHY

BNB (E. van Even)*; BrownI; GoovaertsH*

A. Goovaerts: *De muziekdrukkers Phalesius en Bellerus te Leuven en te Antwerp 1546–1674* (Antwerp, 1882)

S. Clercx-Lejeune: 'Les éditions musicales anversoises du XVIe siècle', *Gedenkboek der Plantin Dagen, 1555–1955* (Antwerp, 1956), 264–375

H.D.L. Vervliet: *Sixteenth Century Printing Types of the Low Countries* (Amsterdam, 1968)

S. Bain: *Music Printing in the Low Countries in the Sixteenth Century* (diss., U. of Cambridge, 1974)

H. Vanhulst: 'Un succès de l'édition musicale: le *Septiesme livre des chansons a quatre parties* (1560–1661/63)', *RBM*, xxxii–xxxiii (1978–9), 97–120

H. Vanhulst: 'Édition comparative des instructions pour le luth, le cistre et la guitare publiées à Louvain par Pierre Phalèse (1545–1570)', *RBM*, xxxiv–xxxv (1980–81), 81–105

H. Vanhulst: 'L'instruction pour le cistre parue dans la version anversoise de l'*Hortulus citharae* (1582)', *RBM*, xxxvi–xxxviii (1982–4), 65–87

H. Vanhulst: *Les Phalèse éditeurs et imprimeurs de musique à Louvain* (diss., Free U. Brussels, 1984)

H. Vanhulst: 'Tassus et ses éditeurs: Remarques à propos de deux lettres peu connues', *RBM*, xxxix–xl (1985–6), 80–100

R. Rasch: 'The *Livre septième*', *IMSCR XIV: Bologna 1987*, i, 306–18

H. Vanhulst: *Catalogue des éditions de musique publiées à Louvain par Pierre Phalèse et ses fils 1545–1578* (Brussels, 1990)

H. Vanhulst: 'A Fragment of a Lost Lutebook Printed by Phalèse (Leuven, c1575)', *TVNM*, xl (1990), 57–80

A.T. Gross: 'A Musicological Puzzle: Scrambled Editions of the Phalèse *Livre Septième* in Two London Libraries', *FAM*, xl (1993), 283–313

H. Vanhulst: 'Le contrat d'apprentissage conclu en 1562 entre Pierre Phalèse et Jean Laet', *From Ciconia to Sweelinck: donum natalicium Willem Elders*, ed. A. Clement and E. Jas (Amsterdam, 1994), 155–9

L. Guillo: 'Les caractères de musique utilisés des origines à environ 1650 dans les anciens Pays-Bas', *Yearbook of the Alamire Foundation*, ii (1997), 183–235

A.T. Gross: 'The Firm of Phalèse: a Modest Venture', *Yearbook of the Alamire Foundation*, ii (1997), 269–78

H. Vanhulst: 'Les mises en tablature originales dans le *Theatrum musicum* de Pierre Phalèse (Leuven, 1563)', *'La musique, de tous les passetemps le plus beau': hommage à Jean-Michel Vaccaro*, ed. F. Lesure and H. Vanhulst (Paris, 1998), 343–68

SUSAN BAIN/HENRI VANHULST

Phanmüller [Phanmulner], Friedrich. *See* PFANNMÜLLER, FRIEDRICH.

Phantasie (Fr., Ger.). *See* FANTASIA.

Phantasiestück. *See* FANTASIESTÜCK.

Phantasy. An old English spelling of FANTASIA, adopted in competitions established in 1905 by WALTER WILSON COBBETT and the Worshipful Company of Musicians as the name for a new type of chamber music piece. Cobbett saw phantasies as a 'modern analogue' to the viol fantasias of Tudor and Stuart times: his aim was to elicit works for specified ensembles, of modest length, and without breaks between the contrasting sections, in which the composer's imagination would be given free play. The first competition (1905) was for a phantasy for string quartet, the second (1907) was for one for piano trio. Entrants had to be British, and prizewinners included William Hurlstone (1905), Frank Bridge (1905, 1907), Joseph Holbrooke (1905) and John Ireland (1907). Awards for a string quartet phantasy based on British folk songs (1916) and dance phantasy for piano and strings (1919) were won respectively by Herbert Howells and Armstrong Gibbs. Cobbett also commissioned phantasies from Bridge (piano quartet, 1910), Benjamin Dale (viola and piano, 1911), John McEwen (string quintet, 1911), Thomas Dunhill (piano, violin and viola, 1911), Vaughan Williams (string quintet, 1912) and others. Britten's Phantasy for oboe and strings (1932), though not written for a Cobbett competition, belongs in the same tradition.

BIBLIOGRAPHY

'British Chamber Music', *MT*, lii (1911), 242–3 [report of a lecture by W.W. Cobbett]

E. Walker: 'The Modern British Phantasy', *Music Student*, viii (1915), suppl.17, pp.17–27; W.W. Cobbett: 'Obiter dicta', ibid., 27–31

'Cobbett Competitions and Commissions', 'Phantasy', *Cobbett's Cyclopedic Survey of Chamber Music* (London, 1929–30; enlarged 2/1963/R by C. Mason), iii

CHRISTOPHER D.S. FIELD

Phasing. The effect of a type of signal processing unit on electronically produced sound. The unit is often operated by means of a foot-pedal. *See* ELECTRIC GUITAR, §2.

Phatayakosol, Cangwang Thua (*b* Thonburi, Thailand, 1881; *d* 1938). One of the two most highly-regarded central Thai musicians during the reigns of Rama V, VI and VII (*see also* PHAIRAU, LUANG PRADIT). His parents and grandparents were musicians; their home near the bank of the Chao Phraya River in Thonburi was famous as a house of music. He directed the *pī phāt* ensemble at the Bang Khun Phrom Palace, home of Prince Boriphat, half-brother to King Rama V; this ensemble, known for its virtuosity, made some ten recordings (on 78 r.p.m. records). The title 'Cangwang' was conferred on him by Prince Boriphat. He was considered equally good on virtually all instruments and composed a large number of musical works; at least 15 are still played today. His performance style, as passed on to his students, is known as the Thonburi style; his descendants still live in his house and his grandchildren direct a *pī phāt* ensemble regarded as carrying on his style.

DEBORAH WONG

Phelippon. *See* BASIRON, PHILIPPE.

Pheloung, Barrington (*b* Sydney, 10 May 1954). Australian composer. He went to England in 1972 in order to study at the RCM, and received his first ballet score commission while still a student. He has subsequently composed for the concert platform, dance, theatre, film, television, radio and CD ROM. In 1979 he was appointed musical adviser to the London Contemporary Dance Theatre and has since toured with them in the UK and abroad as their principal conductor. Pheloung is best known for his music to the British television series *Inspector Morse*, recordings of which were awarded platinum, gold and silver discs in 1994. He was appointed visiting professor of film composition at the RCM in 1995.

Pheloung's film scores include the simple yet effective chamber music for *Truly, Madly, Deeply*, and the larger-scale work *Nostradamus*, notable for its references to early 16th-century music and the inclusion of period instruments within atmospheric orchestral and choral textures. In addition to his work for the media, he has composed a large number of chamber and orchestral pieces.

WORKS
(*selective list*)

Film scores: Friendship's Death (dir. P. Wollen), 1987; Truly, Madly, Deeply (dir. A. Minghella), 1991; Nostradamus (dir. R. Christian), 1993; The Mangler (dir. T. Hooper), 1994; Twin Dragons (dir. P. Janssens), 1996; Jackie (dir. A. Tucker), 1997

TV music: Boon, 1985; Inspector Morse, 1988–92; Portrait of a Marriage, 1990; Red Empire, 1990; Events at Drimaghleen, 1991; Briefest Encounter, 1992; The Secret Agent, 1992; Dancing

Queen, 1993; The Killing of Kennedy, 1993; 7 Wonders of the World, 1994; Dalziel and Pascoe, 1995–7; Cinder Path, 1996; Inside Out, 1996; The Gift, 1997

Radio music: 2 Planks and a Passion (A. Minghella), 1986; La bête humaine (E. Zola), 1993; Double Indemnity (J.M. Cain), 1993; Dead Perfect, 1994; Kind Hearts and Coronets (R. Hamer), 1995; The Merchant of Venice (W. Shakespeare), 1996; The Playboy of the Western World (J.M. Synge), 1997

Incid music (theatre): 2 Planks and a Passion (Minghella, dir. D. Boyle), 1985; Made in Bangkok (Minghella, dir M. Blakemore), 1986; The Foreigner (dir. J. Broadhurst), 1987; Bite of the Night (H. Barker, dir. D. Boyle), 1988; Epicoene (B. Jonson, dir. Boyle), 1989; After the Fall (A. Miller, dir. Blakemore), 1990; The Ride down Mount Morgan (Miller, dir. Blakemore), 1991

Ballets: Stone Figures, 1977; Fugue, 1979; Study, 1981; Run Like Thunder, 1983; Rite Electric (choreog. T. Jobe), 1985; The Phantasmagoria, 1987; Ace of Spades, 1989; A Midsummer Night's Dream (choreog. R. Cohan), 1993

Other: Mir-ah-Chashafti-Lehachsir, 2 pf, London, 1992; Gui Conc., Nottingham, 1994; Gui Qt, London, 1994; Str Qt no.6, London, 1994; Vc Conc., Glasgow, 1994; Double Gui Conc., Bath, 1995; Sinfonietta, Norwich, 1995; Double Bass Conc., Glasgow, 1996

Music for CD ROM games

Principal publisher: Polygram

DAVID BURNAND

Phelps, Lawrence Irving (*b* Somerville, MA, 10 May 1923; *d* Boston, 22 Feb 1999). American organ builder. He studied conducting, the organ and several orchestral instruments at the New England Conservatory of Music, Boston. He sought to design an organ which would restore the fundamental principles of the so-called 'classic organ', typified by the 17th century Schnitger school, yet which in its approach to technical problems and its greater versatility would be a genuinely modern instrument. He worked first with G. Donald Harrison at the Aeolian-Skinner Organ Co., Boston and from 1949 as an independent consultant. His most important design project of the period was the 235-rank (Aeolian-Skinner) organ for the First Church of Christ, Scientist, Boston. This was noted for tonal and technical innovations such as dissonant mutations and refinements to electrical and winding systems. Appointed tonal director in 1958 (and later President) of Casavant Frères, Quebec, then one of the world's largest organ companies, he was the first major builder in North America to return to the making of mechanical action (tracker) organs. Tonally, he successfully reconciled in these organs two of the main schools of organ building and composition (German Baroque and French Classical); technically, he introduced sophisticated improvements in the action, special low-pressure reeds, advanced playing aids, etc. During his 14 years at Casavant he produced some 650 organs, ranging from traditionally-based classic models to the technical challenge of a four-manual circular organ suspended from the roof (Lewis and Clark College, Portland, Oregon), its sound working entirely by reflection. From 1972 to 1981 he headed his own company in Erie, Pennsylvania, and in 1974 built England's first American-made organ, for the 1300th anniversary of Hexham Abbey, Northumberland. From 1981 Phelps directed the development of custom organs at the Allen Organ Co., Pennsylvania, returning to Boston in 1995 to oversee the major restoration of his instrument in the First Church of Christ, Scientist.

Phelps's organs are noted for their musically functional qualities; their tonal design is based firmly on the musical requirements of all periods while eschewing antiquarianism, and their exceptionally subtle key action further assists the musician. This rethinking of each principle of organ design was as a result of his perfect distillation of two art forms: the art of organ building and the art of musical performance, as the technical innovations he developed. Phelps was a Board Member of the International Society of Organ Builders and American Editor of its journal until 1980 and a visiting lecturer at Westminster Choir College, Princeton, from 1969–71. He wrote many articles on the organ's history, design and acoustical problems, and his influence as pioneer and reformer has been widespread.

BIBLIOGRAPHY

O. Ochse: *The History of the Organ in the United States* (Bloomington, IN, 1975)

J. Norman: *The Organs of Britain: an Appreciation and Gazetteer* (Newton Abbot, 1984)

M. Forsyth-Grant: *Twenty-one Years of Organ-Building* (Oxford, 1987)

J. D'Aigle: *L'Histoire de Casavant Frères, facteurs d'orgues, 1880–1980* (Sainte Hyacinthe, 1988)

DAVID TITTERINGTON

Phelyppis [Phillips, Phillipps], **Thomas** (*b c*1450). English composer. He wrote a carol for three voices, *I love, I love, and whom love ye* in the Fayrfax manuscript (*GB-Lbl* Add.5465; ed. in MB, xxxvi, 1975), an important collection of early Tudor partsongs. In the manuscript he is styled 'Syr', but at that time this term was frequently applied to priests as well as to knights and baronets. A Thomas Philips is recorded as a chorister and boy-bishop at Salisbury Cathedral in 1465 and vicar-choral there in 1473; he was also a vicar-choral at St George's Chapel, Windsor, from 1477 to 1490.

BIBLIOGRAPHY

HarrisonMMB

R.L. Greene, ed.: *The Early English Carols* (Oxford, 1935, 2/1977), 264, 479–80

J. Stevens: *Music & Poetry in the Early Tudor Court* (London, 1961, 2/1979), 364, 441

DAVID GREER

Pherecrates (*fl* 440–*c*420 BCE). Greek comic poet. He won victories at the City Dionysia and the Lenaea between 440 and 430 BCE. 19 titles and 250 fragments of his work are known. In a fragment of the *Cheiron* (preserved in Pseudo-Plutarch, *On Music*, 1141d–1142a = Edmonds, frag.144b), he presents Music (*mousikē*), personified as a woman, describing the various outrages she has endured at the hands of modern composers, all of whom were active in the 5th century. As the fragment begins, Justice asks how this came to pass, and Music replies:

MUSIC: My woes began with Melanippides. He was the first who took and lowered me, making me looser [*chalarōteran*] with his dozen strings [*chordais dōdeka*]. Yet after all I found him passable compared with the woes I suffer now. But Cinesias, cursed Athenian, producing exharmonious twists in every strophe has so undone me that in the poesy of his dithyrambs, like reflections in a shield, his dexterity appears to be left-handed. Yet still and all I could put up with him. But Phrynis inserted his own spinning-top [*strobilon*], bending and twisting me to total corruption, having twelve harmoniai [*dōdech' harmonias*] in his five strings [*pentachordois*]. Yet him too in the end I could accept, for if he slipped he got back on again. But Oh, my dear! Timotheus buried and crushed me most shamefully!

JUSTICE: And who is this Timotheus?

MUSIC: A redhead from Miletus. I say he's caused me more woes than all the others put together, doing those perverted ant-crawlings [*ektrapelous murmēkias*]. And when he finds me on a walk alone, he undoes me and pays me off with his twelve strings.

The precise meaning of each of Pherecrates' plays on words is not certain, but the irony of 'left-handed dexterity'; the deprecating epithet 'redhead', a slave's name; the general imagery of modern musicians raping

Music with various tools or implements; the expansion of the kithara to as many as 12 strings; and the winding chromaticism commonly associated with Timotheus are unmistakable. This lament of Music is a most valuable supplement to knowledge of the 'new music' at Athens.

A second, very short fragment appears just a few lines later in Pseudo-Plutarch's *On Music* (1142a). It may be an additional passage from the *Cheiron*; if so, it probably still refers to the style of Timotheus in describing 'exharmonious high-pitched whistlings; he filled me up with turns like a cabbage'.

See also GREECE, §I; PHRYNIS OF MYTILENE; MELANIPPIDES; and TIMOTHEUS.

BIBLIOGRAPHY

A. Körte: 'Pherekrates', *Paulys Real-Encyclopädie der classischen Altertumswissenschaft*, xix/2 (1938), 1989–90

I. Düring: 'Studies in Musical Terminology in 5th-Century Literature', *Eranos*, xliii (1945), 176–97

J.M. Edmonds, ed. and trans.: *The Fragments of Attic Comedy* (Leiden, 1957–61), i, 206–85

G. Pianko: 'Un comico contributo alla storia della musica greca: Chirone di Ferecrate', *Eos*, liii (1963), 56–63

W.D. Anderson: *Ethos and Education in Greek Music* (Cambridge, MA, 1966), 50–55

W. Süss: 'Über den Chiron des Pherecrates', *Rheinisches Museum*, cx (1967), 26–31

E.K. Borthwick: 'Notes on the Plutarch *De Musica* and the *Cheiron* of Pherecrates', *Hermes*, xcvi (1968), 60–73

D. Restani: 'Il *Chirone* di Ferecrate e la "nuova" musica greca', *RIM*, xviii (1983), 139–92

A. Barker, ed.: *Greek Musical Writings*, i: *The Musician and his Art* (Cambridge, 1984), 236–8

D. Restani: 'In margine al *Chirone* di Ferecrate', *RIM*, xix (1984), 203–5

M.L. West: 'Analecta musica', *Zeitschrift für Papyrologie und Epigraphik*, xcii (1992), 28–9

W.D. Anderson: *Music and Musicians in Ancient Greece* (Ithaca, NY, 1994), 127–34

THOMAS J. MATHIESEN

Phidil. *See* FIDDLE.

Philadelphia. City in Pennsylvania, USA. It is one of the country's principal musical centres; the Philadelphia Orchestra and Curtis Institute of Music are known throughout the world. The city is also recognized for the excellence of its other educational institutions and for the Fleisher Collection of Orchestral Music, housed at the Free Library of Philadelphia and the largest and most comprehensive collection of its type.

Philadelphia was founded in 1682 by William Penn of England on land granted to him by Charles II as a place of refuge for victims of religious persecution. The city prospered and soon became the largest in the colonies; it was the capital of the new nation (1776–1800) and its commercial and cultural centre until it yielded that position to New York about 1820. The original settlers were English Quakers who had little interest in music, but Penn's hospitality to other religious groups ensured the growth of musical activities. German immigrants who began arriving about 1700 brought musical instruments with them, built organs, composed hymns and published more than 20 editions of German hymnbooks. Philadelphia was a leading centre for music printing; of the colonial hymnbooks in English, the largest and most significant was *Urania, or A Choice Collection of Psalm-Tunes, Anthems, and Hymns*, compiled by James Lyon (Philadelphia, 1761).

1. Concerts. 2. Opera. 3. Choral singing. 4. The Musical Fund Society. 5. Popular music and jazz. 6. Educational institutions. 7. Music publishing. 8. Instrument makers.

1. CONCERTS. During the colonial period, music-making took place mainly in the church, the home and the social club. The earliest known private concert was given in 1734, the first known public concert in 1757. Subscription concerts featuring a chamber orchestra were initiated in that year, including music by contemporary English, Italian, German and Bohemian composers, largely through the efforts of Governor John Penn and Francis Hopkinson, a distinguished statesman and amateur composer and performer.

After the Revolutionary War, a substantial number of professional musicians from Europe arrived in Philadelphia. Rayner Taylor, Alexander Reinagle and Benjamin Carr were the leading figures in the city's musical life around the turn of the century. They had emigrated from England and were active as performers, composers, conductors, teachers and concert managers. About 1809, Frank Johnson settled in Philadelphia and soon gained recognition, despite prejudice against black American musicians, for the high quality and originality of his band's performance of military and dance music. After his band's visit to England in 1837, Johnson toured widely and introduced the 'promenade concert' to American audiences. With the inauguration of the Musical Fund Society in 1820 (see §4 below), musical activity in the city greatly increased. It was not until the second half of the 19th century, however, that the city had a resident orchestra of importance. Taking its name from an earlier group that had come from Germany in 1848, the Germania Orchestra, under the direction of Carl Lenschow, gave annual series of concerts from 1856 to 1895. The conductor and impresario Theodore Thomas also presented one or two concert series each season between 1864 and 1891. During the centennial celebration of American independence in 1876 the Thomas Orchestra gave concerts throughout the summer but, as the programmes were too weighty and the hall too far from the centre of the city to attract a large audience, Thomas suffered a great financial loss.

Concerts were given by visiting orchestras, including the Boston SO, the New York PO and the New York SO, from the 1890s to about 1926. The city's own orchestra had its beginnings in spring 1900 when two concerts, under the direction of Fritz Scheel, were held for the benefit of the families of soldiers killed in the war with Spain in the Philippines. A guarantee fund was raised so that the Philadelphia Orchestra, with 85 musicians, could be formed, and its first concert was given, under Scheel, on 16 November 1900. Scheel quickly strengthened the orchestra by engaging players trained in Europe; he gave American premières of works by major European composers and introduced concerts for children in 1902. After his death in 1907 he was succeeded by Karl Pohlig, who returned to Germany in 1912.

The appointment of Leopold Stokowski as conductor in 1912 helped seal the orchestra's eventual reputation as one of the world's finest ensembles. His dynamic direction was constantly in evidence in his introduction of contemporary works to a conservative audience; he presented American premières of works by Busoni, Mahler, Skryabin, Stravinsky, Schoenberg and Varèse. He also experimented with the seating of the players and with orchestral sonorities. The orchestra gained national attention in 1916 with the first American performance of Mahler's Eighth Symphony; 1068 musicians participated in nine performances. Under Stokowski the orchestra's size was increased to 104 and it became widely known through its many recordings, beginning in 1917; through radio broadcasts, dating from 1929; and through three films, starting with *The Big Broadcast of 1937*. In 1933, with the assistance of telephone engineers, Stokowski pioneered stereophonic recording. In 1936 the Philadelphia Orchestra made the first of its many transcontinental tours, giving 36 concerts in 27 cities. Stokowski retained the title of conductor until he retired in 1941.

Eugene Ormandy was appointed music director in 1938, a post he held for an unparallelled 42 years, retiring in 1980 as conductor laureate. He was particularly admired for his development of the rich sonority for which the orchestra was celebrated. Beginning in 1949, he introduced the orchestra to audiences in South America, Europe and Asia; in 1973 the Philadelphia Orchestra became the first American orchestra to perform in mainland China. Riccardo Muti was music director from 1980 to 1992. His tenure was notable for its emphasis on contemporary music and for concert performances of complete operas. Wolfgang Sawallisch, music director from 1993, increased dwindling attendance by focussing on well-known composers. Many of the world's great conductors and performing artists have appeared with the orchestra, beginning with the pianist Ossip Gabrilovich, who was soloist at the opening concert, and including Richard Strauss in 1904 and Weingartner in 1905. Rachmaninoff, who lived in Philadelphia for a period, performed and recorded there and dedicated several of his works to the orchestra.

The orchestra performs regularly at the Academy of Music, but the hall's acoustics are inadequate for orchestral performances and unsuitable for recording; a new performing arts centre is scheduled to open in 2001. During the summer the orchestra plays for six weeks at the Mann Center for the Performing Arts, an outdoor auditorium built in 1976 in Fairmount Park as the Mann Music Center, and renamed in 1999. Charles Dutoit was appointed artistic director and principal conductor of the summer season in 1990. Between 1930 and 1975 the orchestra gave outdoor concerts at the Robin Hood Dell, also in Fairmount Park.

Outdoor concerts have long been popular with Philadelphia audiences; between 1896 and 1920, for example, a concert series given at the suburban Willow Grove amusement park attracted thousands of listeners. During a three-month season, Frederick Stock with the Theodore Thomas Orchestra, Walter Damrosch with the New York SO and Victor Herbert with his own group gave two concerts a day over two to five weeks. Band concerts were also given under the direction of John Philip Sousa, Arthur Pryor and Giuseppe Creatore. A summer festival with indoor concerts was held at the suburban Ambler campus of Temple University between 1967 and 1980, and the Pittsburgh SO was in residence for about ten years.

Chamber orchestras and small ensembles were established in Philadelphia as early as the 1750s, and since that time countless amateur and professional organizations have been formed. Among the most prominent of the professional groups was the Curtis String Quartet (1932–81). The members were graduates of the Curtis Institute, and the quartet travelled widely and made many recordings. The Philadelphia String Quartet, made up of members of the Philadelphia Orchestra, was formed in 1959 and in 1967 became the quartet-in-residence at the University of Washington. Members of the Philadelphia Orchestra frequently give chamber music concerts. The Philadelphia Chamber Music Society, established in 1986, brings prominent chamber groups and soloists to the city.

The Concerto Soloists, founded in 1965 by Marc Mostovoy, is the city's principal professional chamber orchestra. In addition to its own subscription series, it performs at music festivals and accompanies various vocal groups. The Bach Festival, the Amerita Chamber Players, 1807 and Friends and the Mozart Orchestra are among the more than 60 non-profit musical organizations that are active in the region. Several ensembles specialize in the performance of early music on period instruments: the American Society of Ancient Instruments, founded by Ben Stad (1925); Philomel, the area's foremost baroque ensemble (1976); Piffaro (formerly the Philadelphia Renaissance Wind Band, 1985); and the Philadelphia Classical Symphony, founded by Karl Middleman (1994). Groups specializing in contemporary music include Relâche (1977) and Orchestra 2001 (1988). The Network for New Music (1984) and the Composer's Forum sponsor performances of music by living composers. The Hildegard Players, founded by Sylvia Glickman (1991), specializes in the music of women composers, past and present.

2. OPERA. The earliest known performance of a musical drama in Philadelphia was *Flora, or Hob in the Well*, a ballad opera given by an English company in 1754. In 1757 Francis Hopkinson mounted an elaborate production of Thomas Arne's masque *Alfred*. Both the Society Hall Theatre, built by David Douglass in 1759, and the Southwark Theatre, which opened in 1766 with Arne's *Thomas and Sally*, staged productions of plays and operas given by the American Company. Although the Quakers and other religious groups expressed their moral opposition to theatrical performances, comic operas by leading British composers were frequently performed, often soon after their premières in London. In 1767 the first American ballad opera was announced: *The Disappointment*, attributed to Andrew Barton. The performance was cancelled because of the highly satirical plot and the work was not performed until 1976, although two editions of the libretto were published in the 18th century. During the revolutionary period expensive theatrical entertainments were prohibited, except during the time of the British occupation, and the ban remained in effect until 1789.

After the ban was lifted, Philadelphia became one of the nation's main theatrical centres. The New Company, founded in 1792 by Reinagle and Thomas Wignell, recruited a large number of singers and composers from England. Although the principal repertory was from London, several composers who lived in Philadelphia wrote original operas; among the most successful were *The Archers* (1796) by Carr, *The Volunteers* (1795) by Reinagle and *The Aethiop* (1814) by Taylor. Of prime importance to the success of opera was the construction in 1793 of the New Theatre (later known as the Chestnut or Chesnut Street Theatre), the most splendid theatre in the USA; it seated nearly 2000 people, and its design was based on the Theatre Royal at Bath in England.

1. Interior of the New (Chestnut Street) Theatre, Philadelphia, opened 1793: engraving from the 'New York Magazine' (1794)

Exceptions to the English character of the repertory were the performances by a troupe of French refugees from Santo Domingo in 1796–7 and by John Davis's French Opera Company of New Orleans in 1827; the latter troupe enjoyed such success that it returned eight times over a 16-year period. Lorenzo da Ponte, a familiar figure in Philadelphia during his later years, was instrumental in bringing the first Italian companies to the city and in igniting an enthusiasm for Italian opera that has been maintained ever since. Rossini and Bellini were the most frequently performed composers by both the Montressor (1832–3) and the Rivafinoli (1834) opera companies. The immense popularity of Bellini's La sonnambula (1836, with 61 performances over the next three years) almost dealt a death-blow to English opera. One of the few exceptions was The Enchantress by Michael Balfe, which was given 32 times within a ten-week period in 1846. Philadelphia saw the première in 1845 of the first American grand opera, Leonora by William Henry Fry, which was written in the Italian style and admired so much that it was performed 16 times that season. The Havana Opera Company introduced the operas of Verdi to the city in 1847.

With the erection of the Academy of Music in 1857, the city acquired the finest opera house in the country. Built by the Philadelphia firm of Napoleon Le Brun and modelled after La Scala, the house has three balconies, an impressive interior and nearly 3000 seats. It is the oldest existing opera house in the USA and was declared a National Historic Landmark in 1963; it remains the principal opera and concert hall in the city. Many first American performances were given there, including Faust (in German, 1863), Der fliegende Holländer (in Italian, 1876) and Boito's Mefistofele (1880). In the second half of the 19th century, two additional opera houses were opened: the Chestnut Street Opera House (1885) and the Grand Opera House (1888). With three houses available, the city was able to attract touring companies that featured the finest European stars. A number of American premières were directed by Gustav Hinrichs at the Grand: Cavalleria rusticana (1891), L'amico Fritz (1892), Les pêcheurs de perles (1893), Manon Lescaut (1894) and Hinrich's own opera, Onti-Ora (1890).

The Metropolitan Opera of New York first appeared in Philadelphia in 1885, and in 1889 gave the first complete performance in the city of the Ring cycle, under Anton Seidl. From that time until 1968, when production costs became prohibitive, the company presented an annual season in Philadelphia, ranging from six to 25 performances a year. Oscar Hammerstein, challenging the supremacy of the Metropolitan, built an opulent 4000-seat theatre called the Philadelphia Opera House (1908). It was sold to the Metropolitan in 1910 and was renamed the Metropolitan Opera House. After 1931 it was seldom used and it was destroyed by fire in 1948.

Since the end of World War I many local opera companies have been formed; the Philadelphia Civic Opera Company (1924–30) gave the American premières of Strauss's Ariadne auf Naxos and Feuersnot, and the Philadelphia Grand Opera Company (1926–43) that of Berg's Wozzeck (1931) with the Philadelphia Orchestra conducted by Stokowski. The Pennsylvania Grand Opera Company (1927) was later re-formed as the Philadelphia-La Scala Company. After several mergers and name changes, the Civic Grand and the Lyric Grand emerged as the major opera companies in the city, performing primarily the popular Italian repertory. In 1976 they merged to form the Opera Company of Philadelphia, the only professional opera company in Philadelphia today. The local music schools regularly produce operas, and the American Music Theater Festival, founded in 1984 under Marjorie Samoff, occasionally presents contemporary operas.

3. CHORAL SINGING. Choral singing has flourished in Philadelphia since the end of the 18th century. In 1784 Andrew Adgate organized the Institution for the Encouragement of Church Music, renamed the Uranian Academy (1787–1800). The city's large German population supported several singing societies. The Männerchor (1835–1962), the Junger Männerchor (from 1850) and Arion (1854–1969) have been disbanded, but Harmonie (1855) and eight other German choral groups remain active. Other important early choruses were the Abt Male Chorus, led successively by Michael Cross and Hugh Archibald Clarke; the Philadelphia Choral Society, conducted by Henry Gordon Thunder from 1897 to 1946; the Treble Clef Club (1884–1934) and the Eurydice Chorus (1886–1918), both for women; the Fortnightly Club (1893); the Palestrina Choir (1915–48); and the Accademia dei Dilettanti di Musica (1928–60). Still

flourishing are the male-voice Orpheus Club (1872); the Mendelssohn Club (1874); Singing City (1947); the Philadelphia Singers (1971), the city's principal professional choir; the Pennsylvania Pro Musica (1972); and the Choral Arts Society (1982).

4. THE MUSICAL FUND SOCIETY.   What is probably the oldest music society in the USA in continuous existence was founded in February 1820 by a group of professional and amateur musicians who had been playing quartets for their own enjoyment for several years. Among the founders were the musicians Benjamin Carr, Rayner Taylor, J. George Schetky and Benjamin Cross, and the painter Thomas Sully, who made portraits of his fellow members. Inspired by the Royal Society of Musicians of Great Britain, the society was dedicated to 'the relief of decayed musicians and the cultivation of skill and diffusion of taste in music'. Its initial public concert was presented on 22 April 1821 and featured Beethoven's Symphony no.2; in 1822 Haydn's *Creation* was given by more than 100 performers to an audience of nearly 2000. The society maintained its own orchestra and around 1900 was actively involved in the establishment of the Philadelphia Orchestra.

William Strickland, a distinguished architect and member of the society, designed the Musical Fund Hall (1824), which was used for the society's many concerts and for other musical and non-musical events. Noted for its fine acoustics, the hall attracted renowned artists such as Maria Malibran, Jenny Lind, Henriette Sontag, Adelina Patti, Henri Vieuxtemps and Louis Moreau Gottschalk. *Die Zauberflöte* had its first American performance there (1841, in English). The building fell into disrepair in the 20th century and was demolished in 1982 after repeated efforts to preserve it had failed; the façade remains but the hall itself has been replaced by a residential development. The society's large music and document collection, which includes early editions and manuscripts of European music as well as music by Pennsylvania composers, went to the library of the University of Pennsylvania.

In the late 20th century the society focussed its attention on fostering the careers of emerging young artists and ensembles through the awarding of grants, scholarships and a Musical Fund Society Award for career advancement. The society also supports musicians and music education in the Philadelphia area, offers free public concerts and sponsors occasional competitions for new music. Most notable was the world-wide competition in 1928 in which the first prize was shared by Bartók, for his String Quartet no.3, and Casella, for the original version of his Serenata. The international competition is now sponsored by the society's Edward Garett McCollin Fund; the 1994 prize was awarded to Judith Lang Zaimont for her Symphony no.1, performed by the Philadelphia Orchestra in January 1996.

5. POPULAR MUSIC AND JAZZ.   In the 19th century Philadelphia was an important centre for the composition, publication and performance of popular music, and by the second half of the century more than 100 composers were writing songs and dances for the theatre and salon. Minstrel shows were enthusiastically received, and in 1855 the first black minstrel theatre was opened. The local minstrel performer James Bland composed songs that attained phenomenal success, especially *Carry me back to old Virginny* (1878) and *Oh, dem golden slippers*

(1879). The latter became the 'theme song' of the Mummers, who established clubs and formally inaugurated the annual tradition in 1901 of dressing in extravagant costumes and parading on New Year's Day while performing on banjos, guitars, saxophones and glockenspiels. In the first half of the 20th century, more conventional bands played for dancing at the Woodside and Willow Grove amusement parks and in large hotels and ballrooms. Visiting big bands such as those of Tommy Dorsey and Glenn Miller and vocal soloists such as Frank Sinatra performed to standing-room-only crowds at the Earle Theatre.

Gospel singing, which was encouraged in the many black American churches, strongly influenced the development of popular music, and gospel groups such as the Clara Ward Singers performed internationally. At the height of their fame their recordings sold in the millions. Starting in the 1940s, Philadelphia became a significant centre for jazz performance with such noted groups as the Miles Davis Quintet, Art Blakey's Jazz Messengers and the John Coltrane Quartet in residence. Coltrane's home is now a museum. A wealth of influential jazz musicians have had connections with Philadelphia, including the saxophonists Stan Getz, Gerry Mulligan, Odean Pope and Grover Washington jr; the trumpeters Dizzy Gillespie and Lee Morgan; the cornettist Rex Stewart; the guitarist Eddie Lang; the singers Ethel Waters, Eddie Jefferson and Pearl Bailey; and members of the Barron, Bryant, Heath and Massey families.

Dick Clark's 'American Bandstand' (fig.2), which began as a local television programme, was broadcast nationally from 1957 to 1964 and brought fame to many Philadelphia popular musicians including Frankie Avalon, Fabian and James Darren. Bill Haley and the Comets (from nearby Chester) were early pioneers of rock and roll in the 1950s, and Chubby Checker introduced the 'Twist' in the 1960s. By 1960 the city had become known for a distinctive brand of black American popular music often referred to as Philadelphia Soul. Among the best-known exponents of the style in the 1970s and 80s were Patti LaBelle and Teddy Pendergrass. Philadelphia Soul also influenced two local rock musicians who gained national fame, Daryl Hall and John Oates.

The city was an important recording centre. Philadelphia International Records, founded by Kenneth Gamble and Leon Huff in 1971, was responsible for many musicians who made hit recordings in the 1970s, and the expertise of Sigma Sound Studios led such well-known performers as Stevie Wonder to record in Philadelphia. In the early 1990s Boyz II Men, who formed their group at the Philadelphia High School for the Creative and Performing Arts, became successful recording artists.

Jazz clubs flourished in the city during the 1950s and 60s. Of particular importance was the Philadelphia Clef Club of Jazz and Performing Arts, initiated in 1966 by the Black Musicians' Union. It was a thriving organization with 700 members, but along with many other jazz clubs it fell into decline during the 1970s and 80s. In the 1990s, with a renewal of interest, a large number of city and suburban jazz clubs opened. The Clef Club received funding for a new building (1995) with a 200-seat auditorium and classrooms for students. Mellon PSFS Bank sponsors an annual jazz festival and popular music events are held regularly at the Spectrum (a sports stadium), the Keswick Theatre, the Electric Factory, the

2. Dancers on 'American Bandstand', Philadelphia, late 1950s, with Dick Clark (rear, on the podium)

waterfront and elsewhere. In the summer months, outdoor concerts are given at the Robin Hood Dell East and the Mann Center for the Performing Arts. The Philadelphia Folk Festival, held annually in a nearby suburb since 1962, continues to attract well-known performers.

6. EDUCATIONAL INSTITUTIONS.   The first institution for general musical instruction was the American Conservatorio (1822–54), founded by Filippo Trajetta. The Musical Fund Society established an academy of music (1825–32) but it was financially unprofitable. The two most significant music conservatories at the end of the 19th century were the Philadelphia Musical Academy and the Philadelphia Conservatory of Music (both 1870); they merged in 1963 and the institution, with an expanded curriculum, was renamed the Philadelphia College of the Performing Arts (1976). After its merger with the Philadelphia College of Art in 1985, the school was called the University of the Arts; it awards both undergraduate and graduate degrees. The Settlement Music School opened in 1908; from a student body of 40 in its first year it grew to approximately 7000 students at its five branches. It is the largest community arts school in the country and provides high quality music instruction for its students regardless of age, background or ability to pay.

The Curtis Institute of Music is one of the foremost conservatories in the USA. Founded in 1924 by Mary Louise Curtis Bok (fig.3), president of the school until her death in 1970, it offers scholarships in performance and composition and attracts world-renowned musicians as

3. Mary Louise Curtis Bok, founder and president of the Curtis Institute of Music

teachers. Well-known alumni include Samuel Barber, Leonard Bernstein, Lukas Foss, Gary Graffman (director of the Institute in the 1990s), Eugene Istomin, Jaime Laredo, Gian Carlo Menotti, Anna Moffo, Ned Rorem and Peter Serkin. It offers both BM and MM degrees and a professional diploma. The Academy of Vocal Arts (1935) is another highly regarded institution that awards scholarships to most of its students.

Two large universities offer undergraduate and graduate degrees in music. In 1875 the University of Pennsylvania (founded in 1740) appointed Hugh Archibald Clarke professor of the science of music; this, one of the earliest chairs of music in an American university, was held by Clarke for 50 years. He concerned himself only with theory and composition; music history was later added to the curriculum but not performance, although the university maintains both choral and instrumental performing groups. In the 1960s the music department gained an international reputation in composition, musicology and music theory under the chairmanship of George Rochberg. The department continues to maintain a distinguished faculty and awards the BA, MA and PhD degrees in these fields as well as the PhD in ethnomusicology. The university's music library, named after the musicologist Otto E. Albrecht, is recognized as one of the finest on the eastern seaboard.

The Temple University school of music dates from 1913, although honorary degrees in music were granted as early as 1897. A department of music education was initiated in 1923 and a separate college of music was established in 1962. In 1986 the New School of Music, founded in 1943 by the members of the Curtis String Quartet, merged with Temple to form the New School Institute, and in the same year the college was renamed the Esther Boyer College of Music in recognition of its benefactor. Temple University awards BM, MM and MMT degrees, the DMA in composition and performance and the PhD in music education. It offers performing experience in some three dozen ensembles, and it sponsors a Music Preparatory Division, a Community Music Program and a Center for Gifted Young Musicians.

In the nearby suburbs, undergraduate and graduate music degrees are awarded at Immaculata College and West Chester University. Other colleges, such as Haverford and Swarthmore, offer music courses and support choral and orchestral ensembles.

7. MUSIC PUBLISHING.   Philadelphia was the pre-eminent music publishing centre in the USA until about 1850, when it was superseded by New York. The earliest music published was in a hymnbook printed by Christopher Sauer in 1752, and the first publication to contain full pages of music using movable type was *The Youth's Entertaining Amusement*, compiled in 1754 by William Dawson. Early music publishers were John Aitken (1787–1811), Thomas Dobson (1787–98), John Christopher Moller and Henri Capron (1793–4) and Filippo Trisobio (1796–8). Benjamin Carr, with his family and his associate J. George Schetky, published great quantities of music intermittently from 1793 until 1830. The firm of George Willig, established in 1794, was the leading publishing house in the first half of the 19th century; it was sold to Lee & Walker in 1856 and to Oliver Ditson in 1875. Other significant firms include George E. Blake (1803–c1850), Allyn Bacon, under various firm names (1816–80), John G. Klemm (1823–83), Fiot, Meignen & Co.

(1835–63), G. André & Co. (1850–79) and W.H. Boner (1865–1900). J.W. Pepper (1876) moved to the suburb of Valley Forge in 1973 and within a few years became the largest retailer of instrumental ensemble sheet music in the USA. Theodore Presser's firm moved to Philadelphia in 1884 and to the suburb of Bryn Mawr in 1949, acquired Oliver Ditson (1931) and Elkan-Vogel (1970), and became one of the foremost music publishing firms in the country. Presser is also known for its publication of the monthly musical magazine *Etude* (1883–1957) and for its charitable work. In 1906 the firm established the Presser Home for Retired Music Teachers, operated by the Presser Foundation. The foundation also provides music scholarships and grants to colleges for the construction of music buildings.

8. INSTRUMENT MAKERS.   From its earliest history, the city has had capable instrument makers. The Swedish organ builder Gustavus Hesselius constructed harpsichords as early as 1742, and John Behrent produced the first piano made in the colonies in 1775. James Juhan advertised himself in 1783 as the manufacturer of a mysterious 'great North American fortepiano'. Charles Albrecht began manufacturing pianos in 1789, and Charles Taws shortly thereafter; his sons continued the business until the 1830s. John I. Hawkins took out the first patent for an upright piano ('portable grand') in 1800. Thomas Loud jr began to manufacture pianos in 1816, and the business was continued by members of his family until 1854. From 1828 until 1878 Conrad Meyer was one of the country's leading piano makers. The Prussian piano maker Johann Heinrich Schomacker settled in Philadelphia in 1837; his firm continued under later generations until about 1935.

Violin makers also have a long history in Philadelphia. John Albert, like many other Germans, came to the USA in 1848; his shop was continued by family members until about 1921. Other important violin makers include the shops of Carmen Primavera, established in 1888 and continued by the House of Primavera, and of William Moennig, established in 1909 and still active.

BIBLIOGRAPHY

GroveA ('Centennial Exhibition', M.F. Schleifer)

C. Durang: 'The Philadelphia Stage', *Philadelphia Sunday Despatch* (1854, 1856,1860) [series of articles; compiled by T. Westcott as *History of the Philadelphia Stage, between the Years 1749 and 1855*, 1868, *US-PHu*; similar compilations as *The Philadelphia Stage* in PHlc, and *History of the Philadelphia Stage* in PHhs]

W.G. Armstrong: *A Record of the Opera in Philadelphia* (Philadelphia, 1884/R)

L.C. Madeira: *Annals of Music in Philadelphia and History of the Musical Fund Society from its Organization in 1820 to the Year 1858* (Philadelphia, 1896/R)

O.G.T. Sonneck: *Early Concert-Life in America (1731–1800)* (Leipzig, 1907/R), 65–157

R.R. Drummond: *Early German Music in Philadelphia* (New York, 1910/R)

H.M. Lippincott: *Early Philadelphia: its People, Life and Progress* (Philadelphia, 1917)

J. Curtis: *One Hundred Years of Grand Opera in Philadelphia* (MS 1920, PHf, PHhs)

Pennsylvania Composers and their Compositions, ed. Pennsylvania Federation of Music Clubs (Philadelphia, 1923)

F.A. Wister: *25 Years of the Philadelphia Orchestra, 1900–1925* (Philadelphia, 1925/R)

A. Aston and J. Kelpius: *Church Music and Musical Life in Pennsylvania in the Eighteenth Century*, ed. Pennsylvania Society of the Colonial Dames of America (Philadelphia, 1926–47)

A.A. Parker: *Music and Musical Life in Pennsylvania in the Eighteenth Century* (Philadelphia,1926–7)

R.D. James: *Old Drury of Philadelphia: a History of the Philadelphia Stage, 1800–1835* (Philadelphia, 1932)

T.C. Pollock: *The Philadelphia Theater in the Eighteenth Century* (Philadelphia, 1933/R)

A.H. Wilson: *A History of the Philadelphia Theatre 1835 to 1855* (Philadelphia, 1935/R)

R.A. Gerson: *Music in Philadelphia: a History of Philadelphia Music, a Summary of its Current State and a Comprehensive Index Dictionary* (Philadelphia, 1940/R)

G.M. Rohrer: *Music and Musicians of Pennsylvania* (Philadelphia, 1940/R)

W.J. Perlman and S. Spaeth: *Music and Dance in Pennsylvania, New Jersey, and Delaware* (New York, 1954)

D.W. Krummel: *Philadelphia Music Engraving and Publishing, 1800–1820: a Study in Bibliographical and Cultural History* (diss., U. of Michigan, 1958)

H. Kupferberg: *Those Fabulous Philadelphians: the Life and Times of a Great Orchestra* (New York,1969)

The Musical Fund Society of Philadelphia (Philadelphia, 1970)

E.C. Wolf: 'Music in Old Zion, Philadelphia, 1750–1850', *MQ*, lviii (1972), 622–52

P. Hart: *Orpheus in the New World: the Symphony Orchestra as an American Cultural Institution* (New York, 1973), 139–68

J.J. Kelley: *Life and Times in Colonial Philadelphia* (Harrisburg, PA, 1973)

T. Cummings: *The Sound of Philadelphia* (London, 1975)

E. Southern: 'The Philadelphia Afro-American School', *BPM*, iv (1976), 238–56

E.J. Southern: 'Musical Practices in Black Churches of Philadelphia and New York, ca.1800–1844', *JAMS*, xxx (1977), 296–312

O.E. Albrecht: 'Opera in Philadelphia, 1800–1830', *JAMS*, xxxii (1979), 499–515

J.A. Taricani: 'Music in Colonial Philadelphia: Some New Documents', *MQ*, lxv (1979), 185–99

D. Webster: 'The Curtis Institute: a Decade of Change', *High Fidelity/Musical America*, xxx/3 (1980), MA20–22, 39 only

R.F. Weigley: *Philadelphia: a 300-Year History* (New York, 1982)

A.B. Ballard: *One More Day's Journey: the Story of a Family and a People* (New York,1984)

J.F. Marion: *Within These Walls: a History of the Academy of Music in Philadelphia* (Philadelphia, 1984)

S.L. Porter: *With an Air Debonair: Musical Theatre in America 1785–1815* (Washington DC, 1991)

K. Smith: *Catalog of the Music of Pennsylvania Composers* (Wynnewood, PA, 1992)

K.K. Preston: *Opera on the Road: Traveling Opera Troupes in the United States, 1825–60* (Urbana, IL, 1993)

S.E. Murray: 'Music and Dance in Philadelphia's City Tavern 1773–1790', *American Musical Life in Context and Practice to 1865*, ed. J.R. Heintze (New York,1994), 3–47

J. Ardoin, ed.: *The Philadelphia Orchestra: A Century of Music* (Philadelphia, 1999)

OTTO E. ALBRECHT (1–4, 6–8; 6 with NINA DAVIS-MILLIS), TOM DI NARDO (5)/EVE R. MEYER

Philbert [Rebillé, Philbert; Rebillé, Philibert] (*b* Thouars, 1639; *d* after March 1717). French flautist, singer, musette player and oboist. According to Michel de la Barre and Johann Joachim Quantz, Philbert was the first to distinguish himself on the one-keyed transverse flute in France. His name first appears in the accounts of the *Menus Plaisirs* in 1667, in which he was designated a 'joueur de flutte ordinaire' in the royal *cabinet*. On 18 August 1670 he was appointed to the Hautbois et Musettes de Poitou. Excelling in singing and comic mimicry as well as in playing the flute, musette and oboe, Philbert was celebrated in a poem by Alexandre Lainez and as Dracon in *Les caractères* by La Bruyère. He is reputed to have married the widow of Jean Brunet, at whose home he frequently played, after an unsavoury affair in which she had her husband poisoned so that she could marry Philbert. The flautist supposedly went to prison on account of this, but was later acquitted. Although he resigned his position in the royal chamber music at the end of 1689, he continued to appear in private performances at court,

often with the flautist René Pignon Descoteaux and the guitarist and theorbo player Robert de Visée. There are no records of him after he left the Hautbois et Musettes de Poitou at the end of March 1717. His only existing works are two unaccompanied melodies, an *air* and a minuet, in two French manuscripts – *Airs propre pour le timpanon* (*F-Pc* Rés.F845, p.21) and André Danican Philidor's *Suite des dances pour les violons, et hautbois* of 1712 (*Pn* Vm⁷ 3555, p.112).

BIBLIOGRAPHY

J. Ecorcheville: 'Quelques documents sur la musique de la Grande Ecurie du Roi', *SIMG*, ii (1900–01), 608–42, esp. 633–8

J.-G. Prod'homme, ed.: 'Mémoire de M. de la Barre: sur les musettes et hautbois', *Ecrits de musiciens (XVe–XVIIIe siècles)* (Paris, 1912/R), 244–5

M. Benoit: *Versailles et les musiciens du roi, 1661–1733* (Paris, 1971)

J.M. Bowers: '"Flauste traversenne" and "Flûte d'Allemagne": the Flute in France from the Late Middle Ages up through 1702', *Recherches sur la musique française classique*, xix (1979), 33–42

M. Benoit: *Dictionnaire de la musique en France aux XVIIe et XVIIIe siècles* (Paris, 1992)

JANE M. BOWERS

Philharmonia Baroque Orchestra. American period-instrument orchestra. Based in Berkeley, it was founded by Nicholas McGegan in 1985 and is now acknowledged to be one of the leading Baroque ensembles in the USA. Its lively, well-turned playing can be heard in many recordings, including several Handel oratorios. Performances and recordings by its smaller offshoot ensemble, the Arcadian Academy, directed by McGegan at the keyboard, have attracted consistent critical approbation, especially in little-known Italian music of the 17th century.

JONATHAN FREEMAN-ATTWOOD

Philharmonic. A term widely used, along with such cognates as Philharmonia or Philarmonia, for musical organizations. Discussion of such organizations will be found under the name of the city or country where they are located. *See* especially LONDON, §VI, 2, §VIII, 3, and NEW YORK, §5. For Philharmonia miniature scores *see* WIENER PHILHARMONISCHER VERLAG.

Philibert. *See* PHILBERT.

Philidor [Filidor]. French family of musicians. The family name was originally Danican (possibly a corruption of 'Duncan'), and according to La Borde the name 'Philidor' derives from the family's earliest known musician, Michel Danican, whose oboe playing supposedly inspired in Louis XIII a comparison with the Italian oboist Filidori. It seems likely that the musician who pleased Louis XIII was the father of another Michel Danican (*b* Dauphiné, *c*1610; *d* ?Bordeaux, Aug 1659) and of Jean Danican (*b* ?Dauphiné, *c*1610; *d* Paris, 8 Sept 1679), the first member of the family whose name appears in documents as 'Danican dit Filidor'. By 1645 Jean was in the royal service as oboist in the musketeers, and both he and Michel (ii) were employed in the Grande Ecurie, the branch of the royal musical establishment that supported military and other outdoor performances, Michel by 1651 as a member of the Cromornes et Trompettes Marines, and Jean around 1654 in the same ensemble and by 1659, if not before, among the Fifres et Tambours. Jean may also have composed (it is unclear whether the designation 'Philidor *le père*' in the lost volume 25 of the Philidor Collection refers to him or to his son André). Two of Jean's many children became musicians, and were also known increasingly by the name Philidor: (1) André

Danican Philidor *l'aîné*; and (2) Jacques Danican Philidor (i) *le cadet*. The rest of the family stems directly from them (fig.1).

BIBLIOGRAPHY

BenoitMC; *EitnerQ*; *FétisBS*; *LaBordeE*

E. Thoinan: 'Les Philidor, généalogie biographique des musiciens de ce nom', *France musicale* (22 and 29 Dec 1867; 5, 12 and 19 Jan; 2, 9 and 16 Feb 1868)

M. Benoit: *Versailles et les musiciens du roi, 1661–1733* (Paris, 1971)

D. Herlin: *Catalogue du fonds musical de la Bibliothèque de Versailles* (Paris, 1995)

J.-F. and N. Dupont-Danican Philidor: *Les Philidor: une dynastie de musiciens* (Paris, 1995)

N. Dupont-Danican Philidor: *Les Philidor: répertoire des oeuvres, généalogie, bibliographie* (Paris, 1997)

(1) André Danican Philidor [*l'aîné*; *le père* after 1709] (*b* ?Paris, *c*1652; *d* Dreux, 11 Aug 1730). Music librarian, composer and instrumentalist, son of Jean Danican. The date of his birth is unknown, but his death certificate gave his age as 'approximately 78'. In 1659 he was named to the position formerly held by Michel Danican in the Cromornes et Trompettes Marines and from 1667 to 1677 he served as *hautbois* in the royal musketeers. From 1670 his name appears in librettos of Lully's ballets and operas as a performer on a number of woodwind and percussion instruments (as of 1714 he owned 33 instruments including oboes, flutes, recorders, bassoons, musette and drums). In 1678 he was named a drummer in the Fifres et Tambours and he was appointed to the prestigious 12 Grands Hautbois du Roi in 1681; from 1682 he served as *ordinaire de la musique de la chapelle* and in 1690 he and three other wind players officially joined the Petits Violons. As a member of these ensembles Philidor played for military ceremonies, balls, theatrical works and services in the royal chapel, and also took part in military campaigns.

Although Philidor *l'aîné* probably composed occasional pieces (marches, signal airs, dances etc.) throughout his career, he did not begin to compose for the stage until after Lully's death in 1687. A flurry of compositional activity in 1687–8 suggests that he may have been trying to position himself as a candidate for Lully's post of *surintendant* of the king's music, but in 1689 the position went to Michel-Richard de Lalande. During the carnival season of 1700, Philidor, his nephew Pierre and his son Anne composed a number of divertissements for perform-

2. André Danican Philidor: portrait, c1710 (private collection); the music is his 'Marche royalle à 3 dessus de hautbois pour la marche françoise', 1678

ance at Marly, largely for the entertainment of the Duchess of Burgundy, wife of the king's eldest grandson.

Philidor *l'aîné* married twice; by his first marriage in 1672 to Marguerite Mouginot he had 17 children, among whom were Alexandre Danican Philidor (*b* Paris, July 1676; *d* Versailles, 6 Jan 1684), who despite his tender age held a post among the Cromornes et Trompettes Marines from 1679–83; (3) Anne Danican Philidor; Michel Danican Philidor (*b* Versailles, 12 Sept 1683; *d* Paris, 19 May 1723), a timpanist to the king and godson of Michel-Richard de Lalande; and François Danican Philidor (i) (*b* Versailles, 17 March 1689; *d* Paris, 13 March 1717), a flautist who composed two volumes of

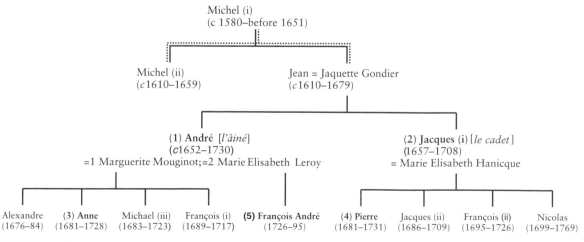

1. Philidor family tree

Michel (i)
(c 1580–before 1651)

Michel (ii)   Jean = Jaquette Gondier
(c1610–1659)   (c1610–1679)

(1) André [*l'aîné*]   **(2) Jacques** (i) [*le cadet*]
(c1652–1730)   (1657–1708)
=1 Marguerite Mouginot; =2 Marie Elisabeth Leroy   = Marie Elisabeth Hanicque

Alexandre   **(3) Anne**   Michael (iii)   François (i)   **(5) François André**   **(4) Pierre**   Jacques (ii)   François (ii)   Nicolas
(1676–84)   (1681–1728)   (1683–1723)   (1689–1717)   (1726–95)   (1681–1731)   (1686–1709)   (1695–1726)   (1699–1769)

Pièces pour la flûte traversière (Paris, 1716 and 1718) and who is often confused with his cousin of the same name. By his second marriage in 1719 to Elisabeth Leroy he had six children, including (5) François-André Danican Philidor.

Philidor *l'aîné* is best remembered for his work as the king's music librarian, in which capacity he presided over an enormous effort to collect and preserve music not only from Louis XIV's reign, but as far back as that of Henri IV. 1684 is often cited (without documentation) as the year of his appointment, but in 1694 Philidor himself claimed that he had been working as music librarian for 30 years. (The earliest known score he copied for the royal library is dated 1681.) Philidor shared the post with the violinist François Fossard until the latter's death in 1702 and thereafter occupied it alone. Although Philidor had a number of assistants, he himself copied dozens of volumes. The dedications to the king in the series of Lully ballets he prepared reveal his consciousness of the historical value of his work. In addition to his work for the king, Philidor copied music for other aristocratic and royal patrons. In 1694 he and Fossard were granted a privilege to print some of the music from the king's collection, but they published only a single anthology of *Airs italiens* (Paris, 1695). Philidor had intended that his son Anne succeed him as music librarian, but it was his son-in-law Jean-Louis Schwartzenberg, known as Le Noble, who took up the post.

Manuscripts emanating from Philidor's workshop are found in many libraries and private collections. The so-called Philidor Collection, formerly in the Bibliothèque du Conservatoire, included 59 volumes when it was inventoried by Nicolas Roze in the early 19th century; almost half have since disappeared. (Some of the lost volumes contained music by members of the Philidor family.) This collection is now housed in the Bibliothèque Nationale, which also holds a significant number of other volumes copied by Philidor's workshop. Another substantial collection is located in the Bibliothèque Municipale, Versailles, and a large body of manuscripts that Philidor prepared for the Count of Toulouse (the illegitimate son of Louis XIV) belonged to St Michael's College, Tenbury, until 1978, when the collection was sold; at that time a number of volumes returned to Paris and Versailles.

WORKS

for further details see Harris-Warrick and Marsh, pp.18–21 and Dupont-Danican Philidor, pp.91–7; all printed works published in Paris

Stage (music in MS, many libs pubd): Midas (mascarade), before 1685, lost except 1 march, *F-Pn* Rés.F.921; Le canal de Versailles (ballet), Versailles, 16 July 1687, *Pn* Collection Philidor, vol.xxxviii; La princesse de Crète (comédie-héroïque mêlée d'entrées de ballet), Marly, Jan 1688, *Pn* Collection Philidor, vol.lii, lost, excerpts in *V* Ms.Mus.139–43; Le mariage de la grosse Cathos (mascarade), Versailles, 1688, *Pn* Collection Philidor, vol.liv (facs. (Cambridge, 1994); see Harris-Warrick and Marsh); Le roi de la Chine (mascarade), Marly, 7 and 8 Jan 1700, *US-BEm*; Les Savoyards (mascarade), Marly, 21 and 22 Jan 1700, *BEm*; La noce de village (mascarade), Marly, 4 Feb 1700, *BEm*; Le vaisseau marchand (mascarade), Marly, 18 Feb 1700, *BEm*; La fête d'Arcueil, Arcueil, 1 July 1700, *BEm*; Le cercle d'Anet (divertissement), 1717, *F-V* Mus.139–43

Inst: Pièces de trompettes et timballes, 1er livre (1685); Suite de danses . . . qui se jouent ordinairement aux bals chez le roi, vn, ob (1699) [incl. works by other composers]; Pièces à deux basse de viole, basse de violon et basson (1700/*R*); Partition de plusieurs marches et batteries de tambour tant françaises qu'étrangères, *F-V*

Ms.Mus.168 [incl. works by other composers]; dances, marches, occasional pieces in MS anthologies in *B-Bc*, *F-Pn*, *Po*, *V*, *US-Wc*
Doubtful: La mascarade du jeu d'échecs, Marly, 19 Feb 1700, *BEm* [attrib. Philidor *l'aîné* in lib, to Pierre Philidor in score copied by Philidor *l'aîné*]

BIBLIOGRAPHY

F.-J. Fétis: *Revue musicale* (9 Aug 1827)
E.H. Fellowes: 'The Philidor Manuscripts', *ML*, xii (1931), 116–29
A. Tessier: 'Un fonds musical de la bibliothèque de Louis XIV: la collection Philidor', *ReM*, nos.111–15 (1931), 295–302
F. Waquet: 'Philidor l'aîné', *RdM*, lxvi (1980), 203–16
C. Massip: 'La collection musicale Toulouse-Philidor à la Bibliothèque nationale', *FAM*, xxx (1983), 184–207
R. Harris-Warrick and C.G. Marsh: *Musical Theatre at the Court of Louis XIV: 'Le mariage de la grosse Cathos'* (Cambridge, 1994)

(2) Jacques Danican Philidor (i) *[le cadet]* (*b* Paris, 5 May 1657; *d* Versailles, 29 May 1708). Instrumentalist and composer, son of Jean Danican and younger brother of (1) André Danican Philidor *l'aîné*. In 1667 he joined his father in the Fifres et Tambours, a position which took him on several military campaigns. When his father died in 1679 he took over his post among the Cromornes et Trompettes Marines and in 1682 he joined the Grands Hautbois. In 1690 he became an official member of the Petits Violons as a bassoonist and he also performed in the royal chapel. He appears also to have been an instrument maker; when he died he owned 'tools serving to make musical instruments' in addition to 44 instruments, most of them woodwinds. Only a few of his marches and dances survive in manuscript anthologies; the volumes of the Philidor Collection containing more of his works have been lost.

Philidor *le cadet* had 12 children, among whom four were musicians: (4) Pierre Danican Philidor; Jacques Danican Philidor (ii) (*b* Paris, 7 Sept 1686; *d* Pamplona, 25 June 1709), who was to have inherited his father's position in the Fifres et Tambours but was killed in Spain while serving as a drummer in the guards of the Duke of Orléans; François Danican Philidor (ii) (*b* Versailles, 12 Jan 1695; *d* Paris, 27 Oct 1726), who joined the Grands Hautbois in 1716 after also having served as a drummer to the Duke of Orléans, and who at the time of his death had the title of timpanist to the Queen of Spain; and Nicolas Danican Philidor (*b* Versailles, 1 Nov 1699; *d* Versailles, 8 Sept 1769), who succeeded his brother Pierre as a *grand hautbois* (1726) and as a viol player in the king's chamber (1731) and later played serpent in the royal chapel.

(3) Anne Danican Philidor (*b* Paris, 11 April 1681; *d* Paris, 8 Oct 1728). Composer, instrumentalist and entrepreneur, son of (1) André Danican Philidor *l'aîné*. He was named after his godfather, the Duke of Noailles. He was granted the *survivance* of his father's post in the Grands Hautbois in 1698 and joined the royal chapel in 1704 and the Petits Violons by 1712. He composed sacred and instrumental music, and by the age of 20 had at least five stage works produced. He also collaborated with his father in his duties as a royal music librarian. He was apparently well regarded at court: the king and two other members of the royal family signed his wedding contract in 1706. In 1725 he founded the Concert Spirituel to provide musical entertainment on days when, for religious considerations, the Académie Royale de Musique (the Opéra) was closed. The first concert was on 18 March in the Salle des Suisses of the Tuileries palace, and the series, which lasted until 1790, promoted instrumental and sacred vocal music. In December 1727 Philidor expanded his enterprise by initiating the Concerts Français, a series primarily of secular concerts featuring French cantatas. He resigned from the directorship of both series a few months before his death in 1728 and was replaced by J.-J. Mouret. The Concerts Français lasted only until 1730 on a regular basis, though annual concerts were given during the next three years. Philidor also directed concerts for the Duchess of Maine and was superintendent of music for the Prince of Conti.

WORKS

Stage: L'amour vainqueur (pastorale), Marly, 9 Aug 1697 (Amsterdam, 1698), *F-Pn* (olim *Pc*) Collection Philidor, vol.xlv, lost; Diane et Endymion (pastorale-héroïque), Marly, 1698, *Pa*, *Pn* (olim *Pc*); Les amazones (mascarade), Marly, 21 Jan 1700, *US-BEm*; Le lendemain de la noce de village (mascarade), Marly, 5 Feb 1700, *BEm*; Danaé (op, 5, E. Le Noble), Marly, 16 Dec 1701, *F-Pn*; Le jugement de Pâris, before 1712, lost, except ov. in *V* Ms. Mus.139–43
Sacred: motets, lost; TeD, 4vv, *Pn*
Inst: Premier livre de pièces, fl/rec/vn/ob, bc (1712/*R*); Second livre de pièces, fl/rec/vn/ob, bc (1714/*R*); marches, dances, *Pn*, *V* Mus.139–43

BIBLIOGRAPHY
PierreH
S. Blondel: 'Origine du Concert spirituel', *Chronique musicale*, iv (1874), 5–11
D. Tunley: 'Philidor's "Concerts Français"', *ML*, xlvii (1966), 130–34
M. Barthélemy: 'Une oeuvre inconnue d'Anne Danican Philidor au Conservatoire royal de musique de Liège', *RMFC*, xv (1975), 91–5

(4) Pierre Danican Philidor (*b* Paris, 22 Aug 1681; *d* Versailles, 30 Aug 1731). Composer and instrumentalist, son of (2) Jacques Danican Philidor (i) *le cadet*. He began composing at an early age; a pastorale of his composition was performed at court in 1697. He was granted the inheritance of his father's post among the Grands Hautbois the same year and by 1708 when his father died was also playing for the royal chapel and among the Petits Violons. In 1716 he became a member of the *chambre du roi* as a viol player, where his colleagues included François Couperin and Marin Marais. In 1717 and 1718 he published three books of suites, half of them intended for two unaccompanied flutes, the others for two treble instruments and continuo. In 1726 he resigned his post in the Grands Hautbois in favour of his younger brother Nicolas, but remained as a viol player until shortly before his death, when he gave that post as well to Nicolas.

WORKS

Stage: Pastorale, Marly, 3 Aug 1697 and Versailles, 3 Sept 1697, *F-V*; La mascarade du jeu d'échecs, Marly, 19 Feb 1700, *US-BEm* [attrib. Philidor *l'aîné* in lib, to Pierre Philidor in score copied by Philidor *l'aîné*]; L'églogue de Marly (divertissement), Marly, 4 Jan 1702 and Versailles, 8 Jan 1702, lib pubd, music lost; Apollon et Daphné (pastorale-héroïque), Marly, 1703, lib pubd, music lost
Inst: 6 suites, 2 fl, and 6 suites, ob/fl/vn, bc (Paris, 1717 and 1718; 2/1718); 6 suites, 3 fl/ob/vn and La marche du régiment de la Calotte (Paris, *c*1722/*R*); marches, dances, *F-V*

(5) François-André Danican Philidor (*b* Dreux, 7 Sept 1726; *d* London, 31 Aug 1795). Composer, youngest son of (1) André Danican Philidor *l'aîné*, and half-brother of (3) Anne Danican Philidor. Although he was best known to his contemporaries as a chess player, his stage works show him to be one of the most gifted French composers of his generation.

1. LIFE. As a page-boy in the royal chapel at Versailles, he received a good musical education with André Campra, the *maître de chapelle*; he also learnt the favourite pastime

of the musicians, chess. In 1738 he had a motet performed and favourably received in the chapel, and though he left Versailles for Paris in 1740, his works continued to be performed there. Another motet was heard at the Concert Spirituel in 1743. Philidor's early music is lost, but was presumably modelled on that of his master.

From 1740 Philidor lived in Paris, performing, teaching and, in the family tradition, copying music. He also assisted Rousseau, in an unknown manner, with *Les muses galantes*. His skill at chess marked him out earlier than his musical gifts. At the Café de la Régence he came into contact with many of the brightest minds of the time, including Diderot who was to call him, in *Le neveu de Rameau*, 'Philidor le subtil'. He met, studied with and defeated France's leading player, Légal. In 1745 he left Paris on a concert tour of the Netherlands with Geminiani and Lanza; when Lanza's daughter died, however, the tour was cancelled and Philidor, stranded, supported himself by chess. Some British officers helped him to travel to London, thus beginning his lifelong connection with England. He established himself as the strongest player of central and northern Europe (though he never played the leading Italian masters), and particularly impressed by simultaneous blindfold play. In 1748, at Aachen, he wrote his *L'analyze des échecs* (later revised as *Analyse du jeu des échecs*). With the help of the Duke of Cumberland, whom he met at Eindhoven, the book was published in London (1749); it was later translated into several languages and had numerous editions into the 20th century. Philidor remained in England until 1754, returning in 1771 and 1773, then annually for a season from 1775 until 1792, giving lectures and demonstrations subscribed by the St James Club and moving in the same circles as Dr Johnson and Dr Burney.

Philidor's return to Paris in 1754 was encouraged by friends such as Diderot, but his efforts to establish himself as a composer met with mixed fortunes. A trial motet, *Lauda Jerusalem*, for a post at Versailles was deemed too Italian (unfortunately none of Philidor's sacred music survives). During his travels he had encountered the newest Italian music, including the Neapolitan style which had made such an impression in France during his absence abroad. Appearing in the aftermath of the Querelle des Bouffons, Philidor's early operas show the unmistakable imprint of Pergolesi.

After writing his one instrumental work, a set of quartets inappositely named *L'art de la modulation*, he began his successful career as a theatre composer in 1756. His italianate style, rejected by Rebel (the director of the Opéra) as unsuitable for that institution, was no obstacle in *opéra comique*, and from 1759 to 1765 Philidor produced 11 *opéras comiques* of which eight were decidedly successful; after *Le sorcier* (1764) he became the first composer to be called on the stage at the Comédie-Italienne. *Tom Jones* (1765) was at first a failure, and, as later with *Ernelinde*, Sedaine was called in to revise the libretto. *Ernelinde* (1767) was performed 18 times at the Opéra (fig.3), briefly revived in 1769 under the title *Sandomir, prince de Dannemarck* and presented in Brussels in 1772. The version played at Versailles in 1773 and the Opéra in 1777 was completely revised, in five acts; with public taste modified by Gluck, real success replaced the earlier *succès d'estime* and it was paid the compliment of parody.

3. Costume design by Louis-René Boquet for Nicolas Gélin as Rodoald in 'Ernelinde, princesse de Norvège', 1767 (Bibliothèque et Musée de l'Opéra, Paris)

Philidor's later musical production was more sporadic. He produced his major choral work, the *Carmen saeculare* (1779), in London at the suggestion of Giuseppe Baretti, who adapted the libretto from several odes of Horace including the one which gives the work its title. Masonic symbolism graces the title-page of the finely engraved score. *Carmen saeculare* was admired, published and performed in London and Paris. Philidor's career was now divided between the two capitals, but he continued to teach music and to write for the French theatre and the Concert Spirituel. His later tragedies, *Persée* and *Thémistocle*, had scant success; he was accepted neither by the Gluckists nor by the Italian devotees, while in comedy he suffered from the competition of Grétry.

At the outbreak of war between England and France, Philidor was in London, and was unjustly put on the list of émigrés. He died, separated from his family, at 10 Little Ryder Street, and was buried from St James's, Piccadilly; the exact location of his grave is not known. There is a bust of Philidor by Augustin Pajou and a portrait by Cochin, engraved by Saint-Aubin in 1772 (fig.4).

2. WORKS.   Educated in both French and Italian styles, and undoubtedly acquainted with contemporary German music, Philidor is usually acknowledged to have possessed the greatest technical ability of the early composers of *opéra comique*. He probably intended no affront to ingrained French traditions, but he was undoubtedly of use to those who did, such as the *philosophes* and his librettist A.A.H. Poinsinet. As a composer he was not lacking in self-criticism, as the four versions of *Ernelinde* testify; but he allowed free rein to a natural fluency supported by too good a memory, of obvious value in chess but dangerous for a composer. The problem of what Burney called Philidor's 'Italian plunder', which led to charges of deliberate plagiarism, is especially acute in *Ernelinde*. The likeliest explanation is that he read, heard and subconsciously assimilated to such effect that he was unaware of the extended near-quotations that appear in some of his scores.

Besides occasional collaboration with such leading authors as Favart and Sedaine, Philidor worked with Louis Anseaume in *Le soldat magicien*, and with A.F. Quétant in the brilliantly successful *Le maréchal ferrant*. But Philidor's literary sense was relatively undeveloped. His chief collaborator was Poinsinet, whom the memoirs of Jean Monnet and Grimm's *Correspondance littéraire* present as possessed of little poetic ability, but of a monumental conceit and gullibility which made him the butt of innumerable practical jokes. Nevertheless, after *Sancho Pança* Poinsinet wrote the three works with which Philidor's career reached its apogee, *Le sorcier*, *Tom Jones* and *Ernelinde*.

Philidor was the first French composer successfully to use a modern Italian style in the major theatres. He was

4. François-André Danican Philidor: engraving by Augustin de Saint-Aubin after Charles-Nicolas Cochin II, 1772

preceded by Duni in *opéra comique*, but *Ernelinde* was a pioneering attempt to modernize the dramatic and musical character of the Paris Opéra. He soon developed a more ornate melodic style than was usual in *comédie mêlée d'ariettes*, and applied the Italian style to French forms at the Opéra well before Gluck. As noted by Garcin (*Traité du mélo-drame*, 1772), he was superior to his early rivals in his instrumentation, which though seldom elaborate is always telling. His work benefits from the solid but undeniable virtues of his harmony, and from melodic invention which, if not strikingly individual, is effectively used in characterization.

Philidor's early comedies subject the mixture of social classes and human foibles, like gullibility and greed, to scrutiny under the guise of farce. *Blaise le savetier* deals with such mundane matters as evading the rent by compromising the landlord. Simple domestic farce (*Blaise* and *Le soldat magicien*) developed into sophisticated comedy (*Tom Jones* and *Les femmes vengées*); rustic dramas in which the dialogue is spiced with *patois* (*Le maréchal ferrant* and *Le bûcheron*) culminate in *Le sorcier*.

Parody of serious genres appears in the simile aria 'Je suis comme une pauvre boule', which marks the height of Sancho Panza's difficulties in governing his 'island'. In *Le bûcheron* the aria for the woodcutter, its chopping motif already heard in the overture, breaks off for the draught of wine that gives him enough strength for a roulade. Mercury then offers him three wishes, singing accompanied recitative ('sostenuto' in the score). The reference to *tragédie lyrique* was doubtless appreciated at Versailles, where it was given two weeks after its première. Another such parody is Julien's conjuration in *Le sorcier*.

Philidor's inventive use of onomatopoeia often marks an *air* dealing with a *métier*: the woodcutter, blacksmith and coachman (*Le maréchal ferrant*); Blaise the wine-maker (*Le sorcier*); and hunters (*Tom Jones*). It is part of an affection for making the commonplace musical; the first number in *Le soldat magicien* is a game of backgammon. *Le bûcheron* and *Le sorcier* demand male singers capable of grotesque falsetto to *d″*. Another favourite comic genre is the sung invoice, in *Le soldat magicien*, *Le bûcheron* and *Le maréchal ferrant*.

In ensemble writing Philidor pioneered the simultaneous use of compound and simple metres in *Le maréchal ferrant*, *Tom Jones* and the battle music of *Ernelinde*. In the quartets and quintets of *Blaise le savetier* and *Le soldat magicien* Philidor manages to convey the utmost confusion while remaining musically transparent; among the best of these ensembles is the septet in *Le bûcheron*. Poinsinet did not take full advantage of Philidor's abilities in *Sancho Pança* and *Le sorcier*, but another masterly septet ends the second act of *Tom Jones*.

Philidor's occasional and possibly unintended plagiarism damaged his reputation and contributed to a controversy, dwarfed by the subsequent Gluck–Piccinni quarrel, over *Ernelinde*. Even the clear echo of Gluck's *Orfeo ed Euridice* in *Le sorcier* ('Nous étions dans cet âge') is inexact, and forms part of a well-constructed opera in which the music is otherwise all new; it dispenses with the traditional timbres.

The success of Monsigny and Grétry in *opéra comique* ended Philidor's supremacy, which he never regained, although several of his works continued in the repertory of the Comédie-Italienne (which by then had merged with the Opéra-Comique). Given a good libretto like *Les femmes vengées* (1775), he could still write a successful comedy. *Carmen saeculare* (1779), an extended cantata in four parts and over 20 separate movements, sets texts from several of Horace's *Odes*; only the fourth part is based on *Carmen saeculare* itself. With solo (recitative and aria) and choral sections including an ingenious double fugue, it is a remarkable compendium of late 18th-century affects.

Neither of the serious operas that followed achieved a *succès d'estime* comparable to that of *Ernelinde*, and neither is as dramatically effective. *Persée* was one of the few *tragédies lyriques* of this period not to be published; but there is distinguished solo and choral music in this resetting of Quinault, especially when Philidor evokes an older French style (as in the opening chorus and the sleep scene). The reconciliation scene in *Thémistocle*, using a melody from the overture, is touching, its surroundings comparatively uninspired.

Philidor pursued two careers for much of his working life, yet his operatic output is considerable, with a high proportion of effective works, and even his failures include fine numbers. But his musical productivity declined with his popularity, and he did little to maintain the impetus he gave to stylistic change in comic and serious genres.

WORKS
all printed works published in Paris

STAGE
opéras comiques and first performed in Paris, unless otherwise stated

OC – Opéra-Comique
PCI – Comédie-Italienne
PSL – Théâtre de la Foire St Laurent

Le diable à quatre, ou La double métamorphose (3, M.-J. Sedaine), OC (PSL), 19 Aug 1756; pastiche with some new music by Baurans, J.-L. Laruette and Philidor (1757)
Blaise le savetier (1, Sedaine, after La Fontaine), OC (Foire St Germain), 9 March 1759 (1759), excerpts pubd separately
L'huître et les plaideurs, ou Le tribunal de la chicane (1, Sedaine), OC (PSL), 17 Sept 1759
Le quiproquo, ou Le volage fixé (1, Moustou), PCI (Bourgogne), 6 March 1760, excerpts (n.d.)
Le soldat magicien (1, L. Anseaume), OC (PSL), 14 Aug 1760 (?1760)
Le jardinier et son seigneur (1, Sedaine), OC (Foire St Germain), 18 Feb 1761 (1761)
Le maréchal ferrant (2, A.F. Quétant), OC (PSL), 22 Aug 1761 (1761), excerpts pubd separately
Sancho Pança dans son isle (1, A.A.H. Poinsinet, after M. de Cervantes: *Don Quixote*), PCI (Bourgogne), 8 July 1762 (?1762), excerpts pubd separately
Le bûcheron, ou Les trois souhaits (1, Guichard and N. Castet), PCI (Bourgogne), 28 Feb 1763 (?1763), excerpts pubd separately
Les fêtes de la paix (1, C.-S. Favart), PCI (Bourgogne), 4 July 1763, excerpts pubd with lib
Le sorcier (2, Poinsinet), PCI (Bourgogne), 2 Jan 1764 (?1764)
Tom Jones (3, Poinsinet, after H. Fielding), PCI (Bourgogne), 27 Feb 1765; rev. (3, Sedaine), 30 Jan 1766 (1766); vs ed. N. McGegan (London, 1978)
Le tonnelier (oc, 1, N.-M. Audinot and A.-F. Quétant, after La Fontaine: *Le cuvier*), PCI (Bourgogne), 16 March 1765 (c1765); collab. Alexandre, Ciapalanti, Gossec, Kohaut, J. Schobert and J.-C. Trial
Ernelinde, princesse de Norvège (tragédie lyrique, 3, Poinsinet, after F. Silvani: *La fede tradita, e vendicata*), Opéra, 24 Nov 1767; rev. as Sandomir, prince de Dannemarck, Opéra, 24 Jan 1769 (1769/R1992 in FO, lvi); rev. as Ernelinde (5, Sedaine), Versailles, 11 Dec 1773; rev., Opéra, 8 July 1777; vs (5 acts) ed. A. Pougin and C. Franck (1883), excerpts pubd separately
Le jardinier de Sidon (2, R.T.R. de Pleinchesne, after P. Metastasio: *Il re pastore*), PCI (Bourgogne), 18 July 1768 (?1768), excerpts pubd separately

L'amant déguisé, ou Le jardinier supposé (1, Favart and C.-H. de Voisenen), PCI (Bourgogne), 2 Sept 1769 (1770)

La rosière de Salency (3, Favart), Fontainebleau, 25 Oct 1769, excerpts with lib (1769), collab. Blaise, Duni, Monsigny, van Swieten

La nouvelle école des femmes (3, A. Mouslier de Moissy), PCI (Bourgogne), 22 Jan 1770, F-Pn

Le bon fils (1, F.A. Devaux [G.A. Lemonnier]), PCI (Bourgogne), 11 Jan 1773, excerpts (n.d.)

Zémire et Mélide (Mélide, ou Le navigateur) (2, C.G. Fenouillet de Falbaire), Fontainebleau, 30 Oct 1773 (1774), MS in 3 acts, intended for Opéra, Po

Berthe (3, Pleinchesne), Brussels, Monnaie, 18 Jan 1775, collab. H. Botson, Gossec, I. Vitzthumb

Les femmes vengées, ou Les feintes infidélités (1, Sedaine), PCI (Bourgogne), 20 March 1775 (1775)

Persée (tragédie lyrique, 3, J.F. Marmontel, after P. Quinault), Opéra, 27 Oct 1780, Po, excerpts pubd separately

Thémistocle (tragédie lyrique, 3, E. Morel de Chédeville), Fontainebleau, 13 Oct 1785 (1786)

L'amitié au village (3, Desforges [P.-J.-B. Choudard]), Fontainebleau, 18 Oct 1785, excerpts Pn

La belle esclave, ou Valcour et Zéïla (1, A.J. Dumaniant), Théâtre du Comte de Beaujolais, 18 Sept 1787 (?1787)

Le mari comme il les faudrait tous, ou La nouvelle école des maris (1, de Senne), Théâtre du Comte de Beaujolais, 12 Nov 1788

Bélisaire [Acts 1 and 2] (3, A.-L. Bertin d'Antilly, after Marmontel), OC (Favart), 3 Oct 1796 [Act 3 by H.-M. Berton]

Contribs. to: M.A. Charpentier: Le retour du printemps, perf. privately, Dec 1756; J.C. Gillier: Les pèlerins de la Mecque, PSL, 1758; J.-B.-M. Quinault: Le triomphe du temps, Versailles, 10 Dec 1761; Au Dieu qui vous enchaine, ariette in 1763 edn of J.-J. Rousseau: Le devin du village

Inc.: Protogène (Sedaine), 1779

Spurious: Le rendez-vous (P. Légier), 1763; La bagarre (P. van Maldere), 1763; Les puits d'amour, ou Les amours de Pierre de Long et de Blanche Bazu (Landrin), 1779; Le dormeur éveillé (Marmontel), 1783 [music by N. Piccinni]

OTHER WORKS

Sacred vocal (all lost): Motets, perf. 1738, 1743, 1770; Latin music, motet, perf. 1752/3; Lauda Jerusalem, Ps cxlvii, motet, perf. 1754; Requiem, perf. 1764 [in memory of Rameau]; TeD, perf. 1786

Secular vocal: A Hymn to Harmony (W. Congreve), perf. 1754, lost; 6 ariettes for L.E. Billardon de Sauvigny: Histoire amoureuse de Pierre de Long et … Blanche Bazu, pubd with the novel (1765); 12 ariettes périodiques (Paris, ?1766, with 12 ariettes by J.-C. Trial); L'été, cantatille, S, orch (n.d.); Carmen saeculare (Horace), London, Freemasons' Hall, 26 Feb 1779 (1788); An Ode on His Majesty's Recovery (Ode anglaise), London, Hanover Square Rooms, 8 June 1789, lost; songs

Inst: L'art de la modulation, 6 qts, ob/fl/vn, 2 vns, bc (1755)
Numerous pieces in contemporary collections

BIBLIOGRAPHY

Choron-FayolleD; DNB (T. Seccombe); EitnerQ; PierreH
Prospectus [for the pubn of Ernelinde] (Paris, 1768)
Lettre à M. le Chevalier de *** à l'occasion du nouvel opéra [Ernelinde] (Paris, 1768)
Réflexions sur un prospectus où l'on propose par souscription la partition complète d'Ernelinde … par M. T*** (Paris, 1768)
L. Petit de Bachaumont and others: Mémoires secrets pour servir à l'histoire de la république (London, 1777–89)
G. Baretti: The Introduction to the Carmen Saeculare (London, 1779)
R. Twiss: Chess (London, 1787–9)
A.E.M. Grétry: Mémoires, ou Essais sur la musique (Paris, 1789, enlarged 2/1797/R)
P.L. Ginguené: 'France', Encyclopédie méthodique: musique, i (Paris, 1791/R)
R. Twiss: Miscellanies (London, 1805)
F.M. von Grimm: Correspondance littéraire (Paris, 1812–14); ed. M. Tourneaux (Paris, 1877–82/R)
'Das Carmen Seculare des Horatius, von Philidor in Musik gesetzt', Caecilia [Mainz], v (1826), 45–8
J. Lardin: Philidor peint par lui-même (Paris, 1847); extract in Le Palamède, 2nd ser., vii (1847), 2–3
G. Allen: The Life of Philidor, Musician and Chessplayer (New York, 1858, enlarged 2/1863/R, 3/1865)
A. Pougin: 'Philidor', GMP, xxvi (1859), 303–5, 318–20, 327–9
A. Pougin: 'André Philidor', Chronique musicale, iv (1874), 241–8; v (1874), 74–82, 203–8; vi (1874), 22–32, 105–12, 200–07; vii (1875), 10–16, 111–19, 215–23; viii (1875), 20–26, 118–25, 264–75
C. Piot: 'Particularités inédites concernant les oeuvres musicales de Gossec et de Philidor', Bulletin de l'Académie royale des sciences, des lettres et des beaux-arts de Belgique, 2nd ser., xl (1875), 624–54
A. Pougin: Introduction to vocal score of F.-A. Philidor: Ernelinde (Paris, 1883/R)
P. Fromageot: Les compositeurs de musique versaillais (Versailles, 1906)
H. Quittard: 'Le bûcheron, opéra-comique de Philidor', RHCM, vii (1907), 421–4
H. Quittard: 'Ernelinde de Philidor', RHCM, vii (1907), 469–74
H. Quittard: 'Le sorcier, opéra-comique de Philidor', RHCM, vii (1907) 537–41
G. Cucuel: Les créateurs de l'opéra-comique français (Paris, 1914)
G. E. Bonnet: 'La naissance de l'opéra-comique en France', ReM, ii/6–8 (1921), 231–43
G.-E. Bonnet: 'L'oeuvre de Philidor', ReM, ii/9–11 (1921), 223–50
G.-E. Bonnet: Philidor et l'évolution de la musique française au XVIIIe siècle (Paris, 1921)
M. Pincherle: 'Ernelinde et Jomelli', ReM, iv/7–9 (1922–3), 67–72
E. Blom: '"Tom Jones" on the French Stage', Stepchildren of Music (London, 1925/R)
B. Harley: 'Music and Chess', ML, xii (1931), 276–83
C.M. Carroll: François-André Danican Philidor: his Life and Dramatic Art (diss., Florida State U., 1960)
C.M. Carroll: 'The History of "Berthe" – a Comedy of Errors', ML, xliv (1963), 228–39
J.G. Rushton: Music and Drama at the Académie Royale de Musique, Paris, 1774–1789 (diss., U. of Oxford, 1970)
J.F. Magee: A.D. Philidor: his Life in Pictures and Stories: a Scrapbook of Portraits, Letters, Clippings (MS, US-NYp)
J.G. Rushton: 'Philidor and the Tragédie Lyrique', MT, cxvii (1976), 734–7
C.M. Carroll: 'A Classical Setting for a Classical Poem: Philidor's Carmen Saeculare', Studies in Eighteenth-Century Culture, vi (1977), 97–111
E.A. Cook: The Operatic Ensemble in France, 1673–1775 (diss., U. of East Anglia, 1989)
M. Couvreur: 'Diderot et Philidor: le philosophe au chevet d'Ernelinde', Recherches sur Diderot et l'Encyclopédie, xi (1991), 83–107
J.G. Rushton: Introduction to F.-A. Philidor: Ernelinde, FO, lvi (1992)
P. Vendrix, ed.: L'opéra-comique en France au XVIIIe siècle (Liège, 1992)
RMFC, xxviii (1993–5) [Philidor issue]
D. Charlton: 'The romance and its Cognates: Narrative, Irony and vraisemblance in Early Opéra Comique', Die Opéra comique und ihr Einfluss auf das europäische Musiktheater im 19. Jahrhundert: Frankfurt 1994, 43–92
C. Rollin: Philidor: il musicista che giocava a scacchi (Brescia, 1994)
D. Charlton: 'The Overture to Philidor's Le bûcheron (1763)', D'un opéra l'autre: hommage à Jean Mongrédien, ed. J. Gribenski, M.-C. Mussat and H. Schneider (Paris, 1996), 231–42

REBECCA HARRIS-WARRICK (1, 4), JULIAN RUSHTON/
REBECCA HARRIS-WARRICK (Introduction, 2, 3),
JULIAN RUSHTON (5)

Philip II, King of Spain. Spanish ruler and patron of music. See under HABSBURG family.

Philipoctus de Caserta. See CASERTA, PHILIPPUS DE.

Philipp, Adolf (b Hamburg, 29 Jan 1864; d New York, 30 July 1936). German composer, librettist, singer, actor and theatre manager, active in the United States. He began a career as a tenor with operetta companies in Germany and Austria. In 1890 Gustav Amberg brought him to New York to sing operetta roles, though he also sang in opera, most notably in the role of Turridu in Cavalleria rusticana (November 1891). In 1893 Philipp opened the Germania Theater (formerly Aberle's Theatre), where he produced musical comedies modelled after Harrigan's stage works, until 1902. He composed, wrote the librettos for, and appeared in such portrayals of German-American immigrant life on New York's East Side as *Der Corner Grocer aus der Avenue A* (1893), *Arme Maedchen* (1893), *Ein New Yorker Brauer* (1894) and *New York bei Nacht* (1897). *Ein New Yorker Brauer* was performed more than 700 times in New York up to 1909. Revised as *Über'n grossen Teich*, it received more than 1300 performances in Germany, and was given on Broadway as *From Across the Pond* (1907). Others of Philipp's German works were also adapted for the Broadway stage, the most successful being *Alma, wo wohnst du?* (*Alma, Where do you Live?*, 1909). *Adele* (1913), *Two Is Company* (1915) and *The Girl who Smiles* (1915) are apparently the only original English-language operettas that he composed, written under his pseudonyms Jean Briquet and Paul Hervé. Philipp's activities were greatly reduced because of World War I, though he wrote and appeared in an anti-German play, *Tell That to the Marines* (1918). He also produced and appeared in films, his Adolf Philipp Film Corporation issuing *The Midnight Girl*, *Oh! Louise*, and *My Girl Suzanne* in 1919. His last musical comedy was *Mimi* (1920). Philipp's compositions exhibit an assimilation of many musical styles, from Viennese waltz operettas and French comic opera to the American musical theatre of Harrigan and David Braham. (*GänzlEMT*; *GroveA*)

JOHN KOEGEL

Philipp, Franz (*b* Freiburg, 24 Aug 1890; *d* Freiburg, 2 June 1972). German organist and composer. He studied the organ with Adolf Hamm in Basle and read literature and philosophy at Freiburg University. In spite of partial deafness incurred during World War I, he took the post of organist and choirmaster at St Martin, Freiburg (1914), where he developed a reputation as an improviser and prolific church composer in the Brucknerian style. In 1924 he became director of the Karlsruhe Conservatory, which he quickly raised to the status of Musikhochschule. After attempting to conform with the National Socialist ideology by composing 'Volkskantaten', works he later sought to withdraw, and facing political difficulties because of his dedication to Catholic church music, he resigned from his post in 1941, citing reasons of poor health. He retired to Freiburg where he continued to compose songs and choral music in a retrospective, often contrapuntal style. The Franz-Philipp-Gesellschaft published the periodical *Vox* from 1960 to 1972.

WORKS
(selective list)

Choral-orch: Friedensmesse, op.12, 1920; Sancta Elisabeth, op.24, 1932; Hymne zum Lob der Arbeit (H. Lersch), op.33, 1934; Zwischen Zeit und Ewigkeit (H. Thoma), op.65, 1950; De profundis, op.83, 1956; Missa symphonica: Credo in unum Deum, op.85, 1960

Choral: Missa laudate Dominum, op.28, 1932; Heiliges Vaterland (G. Stammler), op.32, 1935; Ewiges Volk (G. Schumann), op.45, 1939; Freiburger Psalter, op.57, 1951; Mater Dei (Ein Marienleben), op.60, 1954; numerous sacred and secular works

Other: Sym. 'Eine Gedächtnisfeier für meinen lieben Sohn Johannes', d, op.97, orch, 1960; chbr music; songs

BIBLIOGRAPHY

Franz Philipp 70 Jahre (Freiburg, 1960) [pubn of the Franz-Philipp-Gesellschaft]

F. Ruh: 'Franz Philipp: Porträt des alemannischen Komponisten', *Ekkhart-Jb* (Freiburg, 1971), 108–14

C. Schmieder: '"Cantate Domino": Franz Philipp zum 100. Geburtstag', *Kirchenmusikalische Mitteilungen für die Erzdiözese Freiburg*, xxviii (Freiburg, 1991), 21–31

FRIEDRICH BASER/WOLFGANG RUF

Philipp, Isidore [Isidor] (*b* Pest [now Budapest], 2 Sept 1863; *d* Paris, 20 Feb 1958). French pianist and teacher of Hungarian birth. At the Paris Conservatoire he received a *premier prix* in 1883 in the class of Georges Mathias, one of Chopin's former students. He also studied with Saint-Saëns and Théodore Ritter. In the 1880s he met Liszt, made his Paris début with Chopin's Concerto in E minor and played for Rubinstein and Tchaikovsky. In 1890 he performed Widor's Fantasy for piano and orchestra in London, receiving praise for his beautiful touch and perfect technique. He was an ardent champion of the music of Saint-Saëns, Widor and Fauré, performing often as a chamber musician.

Philipp was a renowned teacher, at the Paris Conservatoire (1903–34), the American Conservatory at Fontainebleau (1921–33) and privately in Paris (until 1940) and New York (1941–56); among his students were Jeanne-Marie Darré, Nikita Magaloff, Guiomar Novaës and Phyllis Sellick. He published more than 100 volumes of technical exercises, including *Exercices pratiques* (Paris, 1897), *Exercises for the Independence of the Fingers* (New York, 1898), *Etudes techniques* (Paris, 1904) and *Complete School of Technique* (Bryn Mawr, 1908), edited many works of the standard piano literature and composed a number of short piano pieces. His recordings include elegant accounts of two works of Saint-Saëns, the Violin Sonata in D minor, with André Pascal, and the Cello Sonata in C minor, with Paul Bazelaire.

WRITINGS

Quelques considérations sur l'enseignement du piano (Paris, 1927)
Le piano et la virtuosité (Paris, 1931)
'Souvenirs sur Anton Rubinstein, Camille Saint-Saëns et Busoni', *Revue internationale de musique*, nos.5–6 (1939), 907–12

BIBLIOGRAPHY

H. Bellamann: 'Isidore Philipp', *MQ*, xxix (1943), 417–25

J. Methuen-Campbell: *Catalogue of Recordings by Classical Pianists*, i (Chipping Norton, 1984)

C. Timbrell: *French Pianism* (White Plains, NY, and London, 1992, enlarged 2/forthcoming)

D. LeBlanc: 'The Teaching Philosophy of Isidor Philipp', *Clavier*, xxxv/2 (1996), 14–17

C. Timbrell: 'Isidore Philipp: his Life and Legacy', *Journal of the American Liszt Society*, no.40 (1996), 48–83

CHARLES TIMBRELL

Philippe, Pierre [Philippi, Pietro]. *See* PHILIPS, PETER.

Philippe de Bourbon (*b* St Cloud, 2 Aug 1674; *d* Versailles, 2 Dec 1723). French patron and musician. He was Duke of Chartres and (after the death of his father in 1701) Duke of Orléans, and from 1715 Regent of France. A nephew of Louis XIV, he grew up in Paris and played the flute, guitar, harpsichord and viol. He studied music with Etienne Loulié and composition with Marc-Antoine Charpentier, Nicolas Bernier and Charles-Hubert Gervais, his lifelong valet whom he appointed *intendant* of his music in 1700. He was keenly interested in Italian music and employed both French and Italian musicians. His earliest known work was an opera, *Philomèle*, written in collaboration with Charpentier in 1694 and played three times in his residence, the Palais Royal. The duke forbade its publication and it is lost. Helped by Gervais, he composed *Penthée*, an opera which was probably rehearsed on 21 October 1703 at Fontainebleau and performed on 16 July 1705 and 15 March 1709 at the Palais Royal; the libretto was by Marquis de la Fare, his captain of the guard, and was published in the marquis's *Poésies* (1755). The *Suite d'Armide, ou Jerusalem délivrée*, also written in collaboration with Gervais, was rehearsed on 2 October 1704 at Fontainebleau, sung at the Palais Royal in February 1705, and perhaps again at Fontainebleau on 17 October 1712. The libretto, based on Tasso's epic, was by the duke's former tutor Bernard Requeleyne, Baron de Longepierre; it was printed, without the prologue, in 1812 by Nicolas Morceau. The duke again forbade publication of these two operas, but they survive in manuscript (in *F-Pa*). Philippe is said to have assisted also in the composition of Gervais's *Hypermnestre* (1716): the two *tambourins* of Act 2 are indeed heard in *Penthée* (Act 2). He also composed motets (lost), two *airs* (*Je suis né pour le plaisir* and *Insensés, nous ne voyons pas*), four cantatas (lost; texts in J. Bachelier, *Recueil de cantates*, The Hague, 1728) and two instrumental pieces (in *F-Pn*, *V*). Philippe's operatic music is italianate in style, brilliantly orchestrated and includes some fine *airs*.

BIBLIOGRAPHY

GroveO (J.A. Sadie) [with further bibliography]

M. Barthélemy: 'Un foyer musical en France au début du XVIIIe siècle: le Palais-Royal', *Cahiers musicaux*, no.14 (1957), 27–35

C.M. Girdlestone: *La tragédie en musique (1673–1750) considérée comme genre littéraire* (Geneva, 1972), 164–9, 182–5

J.H. Shennan: *Philippe, Duke of Orléans: Regent of France 1715–1723* (London, 1979)

J.A. Sadie: 'Paris and Versailles', *Man and Music: the Late Baroque Era*, ed. G.J. Buelow (Englewood Cliffs, 1993), 129–89

J.-P. Montagnier: *Un mécène-musicien: Philippe d'Orléans, Régent* (Bourg-la-Seine, 1996)

CUTHBERT GIRDLESTONE/JEAN-PAUL MONTAGNIER

Philippe de Vitry. *See* VITRY, PHILIPPE DE.

Philippines (Republika ng Pilipinas). Country in South-east Asia comprising a complex archipelago on the western rim of the Pacific Ocean to the north-east of Indonesia.

I. General. II. Indigenous and Muslim-influenced traditions. III. Western art music. IV. Popular music. V. Dance.

I. General

The Philippine islands have become isolated from centres of cultural change in insular and continental South-east Asia. A strong Hindu influence in Java and Bali and a Buddhist mission in Thailand made scarcely any impression on the Philippines: there are no temples like those of Borobudur or Angkor Wat, stories of the *Mahābhārata* and the *Rāmāyaṇa* (popular in South-east Asian countries) are not represented in shadow plays, and Hindu gods are much less known than in Indonesia. Islam was the only great Asian tradition that left a significant mark among powerful groups in southern Mindanao and the Sulu islands, while Spanish and American institutions changed the cultural patterns of about 90% of the population, now totalling about 70 million. This vast majority, living in most parts of the islands, speak only eight languages, whereas the remaining 10% speak more than 100. The major 38 cultural-linguistic groups are represented in fig.1. The contrast illustrates how 10% of the population has preserved a culture related to their languages, while 90% of the population brought about new literary forms.

Three principal minority groups (including those influenced by Islam) live in two separate areas, the north and the south. Altogether, these three cultural groups comprise about 8% of the Philippine population, divided more or less evenly between those settled in the Cordillera mountain range in northern Luzon, the inland peoples of Mindanao, Palawan and Mindoro, and the Muslim groups in southern Mindanao and the Sulu islands. A fourth group may be added: the Negrito, a very small group living in scattered areas of Luzon and in remote southern mountain areas.

The traditions of these minorites are related to those of other cultural groups in continental and insular Southeast Asia. There are common elements in their settlements, house structure, tattooing, basket weaving, cultivation of rice and root crops, habit of chewing betel-nuts, kinship systems, communication with spirits, practice of divination and shamanism. Some aspects of indigenous culture, such as the cultivation of rice and use of pottery and bamboo, may have ancient origins. Former land bridges with continental Asia relate flora, fauna and early man in the Philippines to those of the mainland.

In spite of the above similarities, cultural differences do exist, in particular between the northern Luzon peoples and the Mindanao groups in the south. In the north, the Negrito, a Spanish term for a culture with the local names Aeta, Ita, Abyan, Agta and Dumagat, are the oldest inhabitants of the Philippines. They were formerly an itinerant group and are now partly settled in widely scattered areas in different parts of Luzon, in the provinces of Camarines Norte, Albay, Quezon, Bataan, Zambales, Isabela and Cagayan. The Negrito are similarly widely dispersed in the southern Philippines, living in communities in the island of Negros, as well as in Palawan, Panay and eastern Mindanao. These groups have persisted with their cultural ways, perhaps for thousands of years, although they are now influenced by their neighbours. Several anthropologists and linguists have studied their culture through the years.

The Kalingga, Ifuago, Bontok, Tingguian, Ibaloi, Isneg, Karao and Kankanay, referred to here as the Cordillera groups, are a completely different culture with a complex agricultural system; they formerly practised headhunting. They appoint 'priests' or specialists to lead prayers in complex rituals related to the cultivation of rice and use flat gongs without bosses and derivatives of the bamboo plant as their principal musical instruments. The Ilonggot in eastern Luzon are a people apart from the Cordillera with a similar culture.

In the south, mountain peoples in the islands of Mindanao, Palawan and Mindoro practise a slash-and-burn or swidden agriculture. The languages they speak (Ata, Bagobo, Bukid, Bilaan, Mandaya, Manobo, Mansaka, Palawan, Subanen, Tagakaolo, Tagbanwa, Tiboli and Tiruray) belong to those of a different group from the north. These mountain peoples grow a large species of bamboo, which accounts for the increased size of their tube zithers and other instruments. Their most important musical instruments are heavy, suspended gongs (*agung*), used as dowry and inheritance and played in all sorts of community activities.

In the 14th century, seafarers and trade with Indonesia introduced Islam into southern Mindanao among peoples living near the Mindanao river and the Sulu islands (the Magindanao, Maranao, Tausug, Sama-Samal, Badjao, Yakan and Jama Mapun). This brought about changes in political systems, education, dress and food taboos and

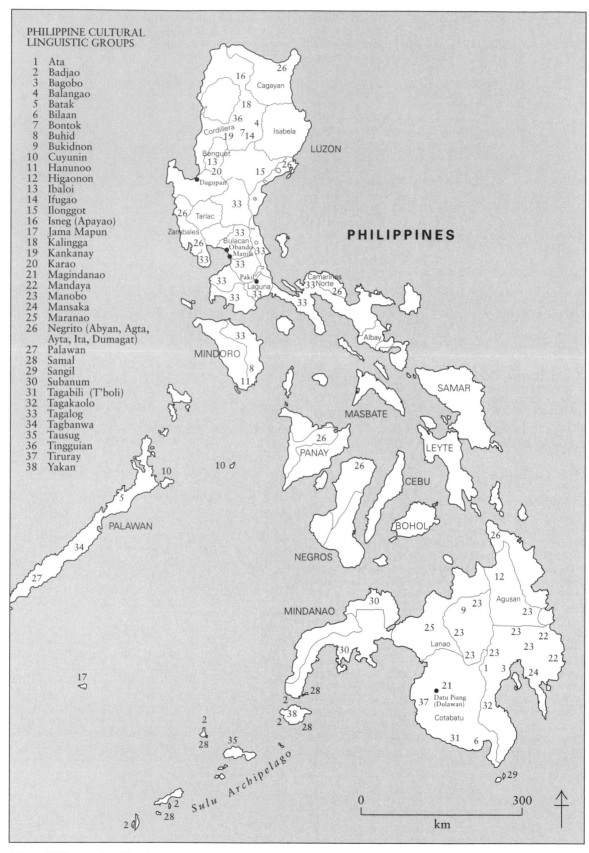

PHILIPPINE CULTURAL
LINGUISTIC GROUPS

 1 Ata
 2 Badjao
 3 Bagobo
 4 Balangao
 5 Batak
 6 Bilaan
 7 Bontok
 8 Buhid
 9 Bukidnon
10 Cuyunin
11 Hanunoo
12 Higaonon
13 Ibaloi
14 Ifugao
15 Ilonggot
16 Isneg (Apayao)
17 Jama Mapun
18 Kalingga
19 Kankanay
20 Karao
21 Magindanao
22 Mandaya
23 Manobo
24 Mansaka
25 Maranao
26 Negrito (Abyan, Agta,
      Ayta, Ita, Dumagat)
27 Palawan
28 Samal
29 Sangil
30 Subanum
31 Tagabili (T'boli)
32 Tagakaolo
33 Tagalog
34 Tagbanwa
35 Tausug
36 Tingguian
37 Tiruray
38 Yakan

1. Map of Philippine cultural-linguistic groups

introduced the practice of polygamy. These peoples became skilled in woodwork, brassware and especially in the performance of the gong-chime (*kulintang*), which was added to the existing ensembles of suspended gongs (*agung*).

Two centuries later, the Spanish introduced Christianity, Spanish law and feudal land tenure; in 1898, the United States brought an American way of life, leaving a democratic political system that distinguishes the Philippines from its neighbours. The 'Westernized' peoples of the Philippines may be divided geographically north to south according to the eight languages they speak: Ilokano, Pangasinan, Kapangpangan, Tagalog, Bikol, Waray, Sebuano and Hiligaynon. Stone churches, which exist in almost every town in the Philippines, in a courtyard surrounded by the houses of the landed gentry, symbolize the foundation of a Westernized culture that has produced folksongs (*kundiman*) and, since the early 20th century, renowned performers and composers of European classical music.

Under the influence of technology and mass media, musical interest has come to centre on popular music, transmitted mostly through radio, television and recordings. Popular songs are sung in the vernacular by local celebrities with large followings and played by groups in indigenous styles.

BIBLIOGRAPHY

GEWM, iv ('The Lowland Christian Philippines', C. Canave-Dioquino; 'Upland Peoples of the Philippines', J. Maceda; 'Art Music of the Philippines in the 20th Century', R. Santos; 'Islamic Communities of the Southern Philippines', R. Santos; 'Popular music in the Philippines', R. Santos)

J. Maceda: 'Music in the Philippines', in M. Hood and J. Maceda: *Music*, Handbuch der Orientalistik, Abt. iii, Bd.vi (Leiden, 1972), 28–39

W.G. Solheim: 'An Earlier Agricultural Revolution', *Scientific American*, ccxxvi/4 (1972), 34–41

J. Maceda: 'Music in the Philippines in the Nineteenth Century', *Musikkulturen Asiens, Afrikas und Ozeaniens im 19. Jahrhundert*, ed. R. Günther (Regensburg, 1973), 215–31

J. Maceda: 'Music in Southeast Asia: Tradition, Nationalism, Innovation', *Cultures*, i/3 (1974), 75–94

J. Maceda: 'Southeast Asian Arts: Music', *Encyclopaedia Britannica: Macropaedia*, ed. W.E. Preece (Chicago, 15/1974), 873–8

J. Maceda: 'A Search for an Old and a New Music in Southeast Asia', *AcM*, li (1979), 160–69

J. Maceda: *A Manual of a Field Music Research with Special Reference to Southeast Asia* (Quezon City, 1981)

J. Maceda: 'Contemporary Music in the Philippines and Southeast Asia', *National Centre for the Performing Arts Journal* [Bombay], xii/4 (1983), 31–5

J. Maceda: 'A Concept of Time in a Music of Southeast Asia', *EthM*, xxx (1986), 11–53

II. Indigenous and Muslim-influenced traditions

In the northern Philippines, indigenous music is represented by the Negrito, a very small minority mostly from Luzon, and the people of the Cordillera mountain range, a larger population. In the south, the indigenous and Muslim-influenced peoples live separately. There, the influence of Islam is discernible in many singing styles and in some flute and reedpipe music, but there is no apparent Muslim influence in the music of the gong ensemble *kulintang* or in terms of other musical instruments.

1. Northern Philippines: (i) Negrito music in Luzon (ii) Cordillera music in Luzon (iii) Vocal music. 2. Southern Philippines: (i) General (ii) Gongs and gong ensembles (iii) Solo instruments and other ensembles (iv) Vocal music.

1. NORTHERN PHILIPPINES.

(i) Negrito music in Luzon. Among the Negrito in Bataan, marriage rituals and those for honouring the dead or curing the sick still exist. In a marriage ceremony (*ambahan*), ritual singing, dancing and jumping around a fire are essential elements. The singing style consists of a few lines of melismatic melodies sung by a leader and repeated responsorially by the crowd of men and women. The Negrito often speak of a need for gongs, but when provided with one they do not seem to have a traditional musical structure for its performance. The *bansi* (flute) is used as a courting instrument; the *kuryapi* (two-string lute) is still remembered, though it has long since disappeared from this region. The Negrito in Zambales have instruments similar to the *kimbal* (conical drum) used by the Ibaloi. They make a bamboo zither with two parallel strings connected by a bridge, as well as a flute with a chip on its ledge similar to that of Mindanao (see fig.14a below). In Zambales, the Negrito's five-string guitar resembles that of their Westernized neighbours.

In the northern part of Quezon province, among the Dumagat of eastern Luzon, the musical bow, a rare instrument in the Philippines, is most probably an original Negrito musical instrument and is the single instrument that is found only among the Dumagat, being unknown to other indigenous groups. It is made from the midrib of a palm, with two strings of thin vine connecting the two ends of the midrib. To increase the strings' resonance the performer places the convex side of the palm midrib in his open mouth, between his teeth. A simple, three-note melody is repeated many times (two notes a 3rd apart, played on two strings, and one note at the interval of a 4th). Other possible resonators include a tin can, on which the palm midrib is placed, and the performer's own chest, on which the tin can in turn may be set. The other musical instruments played by the Dumagat have been borrowed from adjacent cultures, just as song texts contain words from their neighbours.

(ii) Cordillera music in Luzon.

(a) Gongs and gong ensembles. *Gangsa*, flat gongs of bronze or brass (*see* GANGSA (i)), are found only in the north, principally in the Cordillera mountain range of Luzon (fig.2). There are some similarities between Luzon gongs and gongs found among the mountain peoples in central Vietnam (similarities in name, performance context and playing technique), which may indicate musical and even prehistoric relationships between the two mountain peoples. The gongs have a diameter of approximately 30 cm, and their perpendicular rims are about 5 cm high, producing diffused sounds of an unfocussed pitch. The Bontok play gongs with sticks in an ensemble of six or more players as they dance in circular patterns. On occasion, one or a pair of dancers improvise beats with several dance postures while resting in place. The Kalingga play gongs with sticks as well as the hands. The Ibaloi use only two gongs together with two conical drums, while the Karao play with several gongs as they dance in rows.

Gangsa are played in such ceremonies as peace pacts between two communities, the inauguration of a new house or rice field, life-cycle celebrations given by the rich, or weddings. Gongs are stored by families inside their houses; they are lent only for special occasions, with the borrower taking full responsibility for their care and

2. Kalingga gangsa (flat gong) ensemble, early 1900s

safe return: if a gong was dropped and broken it would be the duty of the borrower to replace it, which might mean crossing mountains to obtain a gong of similar tonal quality from a neighbouring tribe.

The value of a gong is measured in different ways: it may be offered as a dowry, sold or exchanged for animals, land and property. During ceremonies, a succession of community leaders perform on the *gangsa* or dance to its music. *Gangsa* music itself enjoys a certain preference among the Kalingga: during recreation and other secular occasions when *gangsa* playing is not allowed, young boys and girls continue to play its music using other instruments (zithers, tubes, buzzers, xylophones, pan-pipes). Whether plucked, struck or blown, the *gangsa* rhythm is accompanied by recognizable *gangsa* sounds; there is such an interest in *gangsa* music that the original solo music for bamboo instruments has been neglected and almost forgotten.

Gong ensembles of the north vary in their instrumentation: some consist entirely of gongs, others are combined with drums. The *topayya* ensemble, found among the Kalingga and Tingguian, consists of six flat gongs played with the palms of both hands as if the gongs were drums. Each performer carries his own gong suspended from his belt. He sits on his heels, laying the instrument on his lap with the open side facing down. Four performers with the biggest gongs of diminishing size use hand techniques consisting of a two-part repetition of movements, each part lasting about a quaver (at crotchet = *c*116). The first part is a stroke of the left palm on the centre of the gong, which makes a ringing sound. The second part consists of the same stroke, staccato, followed by a strong slap and a

slide of the right hand from the centre to the outer edge of the gong away from the performer, the effect being an abrupt sound, followed by a swishing noise. The two parts are repeated continually. The four gongs have staggered entrances: the first gong, called *balbal*, begins the rhythm with the movements just described; the second, *salbat*, plays the same rhythm, but its first beat starts on the second beat of the *balbal*; the first beat of the third gong, *katlo*, will coincide with the second beat of the *salbat*, and similarly, the first beat of the fourth, *kapat*, will coincide with the second beat of the *katlo*. The overall effect is a mixture of faintly rising melody and harmony produced by the first left-hand beat of each gong and the combination of tapping and sliding sounds in the second beat of all four gongs. On top of this vibrating medley, the fifth gong, *pokpok* or *opop*, sounds a two-tone ostinato. The sixth gong, *anungos*, has a freer pattern, which may also turn into an ostinato (ex.1).

The *itundak* or *tinebtebak*, an ensemble of seven gongs with different rhythms used by the Karao, accompanies dances with music played by beating sticks on the centres of the gongs instead of playing them with the hands. Here, the *gangsa* has a V-shaped wooden handle from which the gong is suspended by a string. The left hand holds the handle while the right strikes the gong with a cloth-headed stick. Among the Karao, the inner (ventral) side of the gong is struck, while among the Kalingga the dorsal side is struck. The Karao's ensemble has seven performers, each playing a rhythm on his own gong, each of which has a distinct timbre.

The rhythms of five principal gongs in the *itundak* ensemble are shown in ex.2. Gongs are played during big

Ex.1 Kalingga *topayya gangsa* ensemble; rec. and transcr. J. Maceda

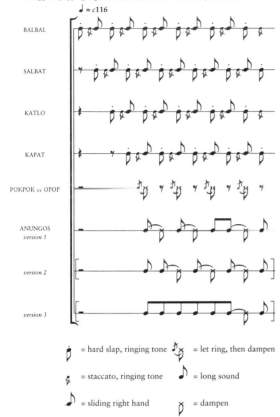

feasts, especially in the *babeng*, traditionally given by rich men of the community. While men play the gongs, women dance in rows, either advancing and retreating in slow dance steps with discreetly lifted legs, or making clockwise and anticlockwise formations. The right leg is raised and swings sideways from the knee in time with the music; then the woman hops forward on her left foot, with her arms raised straight in front of her. The *tinebtebak* dance has a different rhythm and dance position: as the left foot steps forward, the body's full weight is put on it; after this the body leans backwards, transferring its weight to the heel of the right foot.

In the *palook*, an ensemble of gongs struck with sticks, played by the Kalingga and Bontok, the back sides of seven gongs are beaten in one or two rhythms by seven men who assume various body movements and dancing postures (fig.3). In single file they advance sideways in short steps, first led by one end of the line then by the other; occasionally they move forward making a serpentine line. Sometimes they scarcely lift their feet and at other times they raise them high. The gongs are held in different positions: swinging, rocking raised above the shoulder or lowered to the ground. Body positions include crouching, standing upright, stooping or swaying. The women enter later: they appear suddenly, encircle the men and thus end the dance.

The *kulimbet* ensemble of the Ibaloi, consisting of two long, narrow barrel drums (one high-pitched and one low) and one gong, plays in a curing ceremony in which a couple dance anticlockwise around a sacrificial pig. The woman, as celebrant and principal dancer, wields a knife in her right hand; suddenly, the knife drips blood. The sick person revives and the knife is handed to the owner of the house for safe-keeping.

In the *inila-ud*, an ensemble of three gongs and one cylindrical drum found among the northern Kalingga and Tingguian, the first gong is called *patpat*, the second *kebang*, the third *sapul* and the drum *tambul*. Each gong is laid (dorsal side up) on the lap of a performer, who strikes it with the left hand using a stick, while tapping it with the palm of the right hand. In the *pinala-iyan* ensemble (four gongs and one drum) of the same two groups, the first and third gongs (*talagutok* and *saliksik*) are laid on the ground with the rims down and are each struck with two sticks. The second gong, *pawwok*, is held upright, in a slanting position with its base touching the ground. The fourth gong, *pattong*, is laid with its open side up, the stick beats on this ventral side of the gong. The *tambul* is played with two sticks. In a third ensemble, the *pinalandok* (six gongs), the *gangsa* are suspended from the belts of the six players, who slap them with both hands. The musical form used is the same as that of the *topayya*.

In the Ifugao *gangha* (three gongs), one gong (*tobop*), higher-pitched with more brilliant overtones, is played with the hands: the left hand taps while the right fist slides on the instrument. The other two gongs (*hibat*, *ahot*) are played with sticks beating on their inner (ventral) side. The *gangha* are played during harvest ceremonies or the inauguration of a new house, and accompany line dances (*tayao*) by men in semi-crouching positions with their arms stretched forward, and with open palms turned up. In another position the left hand stretches forward with the right arm bent at the elbow.

The Isneg have an ensemble consisting of *hansa* (two gongs) and *ludag* (one conical drum). The gongs are played by women while the long drum, which needs more force to produce loud sounds, is played by men. The ensemble accompanies two kinds of dances: *tabok* and *talip*. In the Ibaloi *sulibao* ensemble (two gongs, two conical drums and a pair of iron clappers), one deep-toned drum (*kimbal*) starts a rhythmic ostinato, immediately followed by the higher-pitched drum (*sulibao*) in another rhythm (fig.4). One gong (*pinsak*) is held in the

Ex.2 Karao *itundak gangsa* ensemble; rec. and transcr. J. Maceda

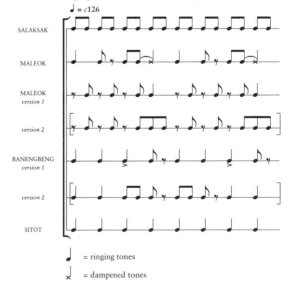

3. Palook ensemble of struck gongs played by the Bontok-Sagada people

left hand by its V-shaped handle, its dorsal side touching the forearm; the ventral side of the gong is struck with a soft stick held in the right hand. The second gong (*kalsa*) is played similarly, but has a freer part. The clappers (*palas*) provide another rhythmic improvisational part of the *kalsa* (ex.3). A Negrito ensemble composed of *talibeng* (bamboo drum) and *palayi* (gong) is played in an *anito* (spirit) ceremony to cure the sick. Among the Negrito of Zambales a cooking-pan is used instead of a gong, as the proper gong is no longer available.

(b) Solo instruments and other ensembles. Instruments made from bamboo, wood and other tropical materials do not enjoy the same prestige as gongs. However, they have important uses in rituals and secular activities. Timbres vary with the materials used (bamboo predominates), the shapes of the instruments and the manner in which they are played; often these timbral qualities are more important than rhythm and melody.

Idiophones. Most of the idiophones in the north are made of bamboo. Bamboo percussion tubes (Kalingga *tongatong*; Isneg *tungtung*; Negrito *talibengan*) are played by holding the body of the tube, open end up, in the right hand. The tube's closed lower end is then struck against a hard block of stone or wood while its open end is covered and uncovered by the palm of the left hand. Among Kalingga boys and girls, seven tubes are played during hours of recreation to imitate *topayya* (gong) music. Originally the tubes were used to accompany dances done by a *dawak* (medium) to drive away bad spirits from a person's body. The Isneg play these percussion tubes as solo instruments. The Negrito percussion tube, comprising three bamboo segments, is longer than the Kalingga variety. A second type of bamboo percussion tube, the quill-shaped *patang-ug* (Kalingga) or *patanggo* (Isneg), is held near its base by the right hand and is struck against a hard object (e.g. another tube, a stone or the handle of a large knife). A second tone is produced by stopping a hole at the tube's base with the third finger. Among the Kalingga, this instrument is played on the way to a peace pact or an important celebration; it is believed to prevent ill-omens from befalling the celebration. An ensemble of six such tubes may also be played to imitate *topayya* music.

The *patatag* (Kalingga), an instrument comprised of six separate bamboo xylophone staves, is played with one segment laid on the lap of each performer. The ensemble uses the techniques of *topayya* music: the left hand, which strikes the blade with a stick, corresponds to the left hand's motions on the *topayya*, while strokes and slides by the right-hand stick correspond to the right hand's motions in *topayya* playing.

The bamboo buzzer (Kalingga *balingbing*, fig.5; Isneg *pahinghing*, *paginggeng*; Ibaloi *pakkung*) has a slit

Ex.3 Ibaloi *sulibao* ensemble; rec. and transcr. J. Maceda

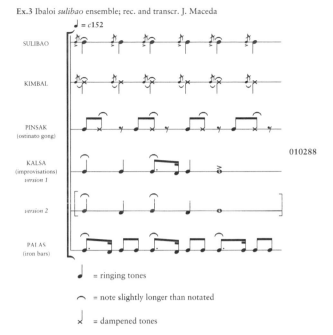

010288

♩ = ringing tones

⌒ = note slightly longer than notated

✗ = dampened tones

4. Instruments of the Ibaloi sulibao ensemble: (a), (b), Kalsa and pinsak (gongs), (c) palas (iron clappers), (d), (e) sulibao and kimbal (conical drums)

dividing the bamboo tube in half, allowing the halves to vibrate and buzz when one half is struck against the heel of the left hand. The instrument is played by young girls in the evening for recreation, or along paths to drive away evil spirits lurking there. The Kalingga use six of the instruments together as in *topayya* music.

For the bamboo clapper *hangar* (Ifugao), two halves of a bamboo tube are shaped and narrowed towards the middle of the tube, making them flexible enough to flap against each other. In one ritual, men singers rhythmically strike the carcass of a sacrificed pig with this instrument to produce the clapping sounds.

The jew's harp (Kalingga *ulibao*, *giwong*, *onnat*; Ibaloi *ko-ding*; Bontok *alibaw*, *abafiw*, *afiw*, *olat*, *ulibaw*; Isneg *oribao*; Negrito *kulibao*; Ifugao *biqqung*, *guyud*) in the north may be of brass, bronze or bamboo, with or without a string. Most jew's harps in the Cordillera are made of a copper alloy but have the same names as those of bamboo. Among the Ifugao, the jew's harp with a string to pull and make the blade vibrate is called *guyud*, while that without a string is the *biqqung*. There are various rhythms associated with the jew's harp, but none is characteristic of any one region. Among the Kalingga the *giwong* is used to imitate gong sounds and vocal music.

Two wooden instruments are the percussion yoke-bar (Ifugao *bangibang*, *pattung*; fig.6) and percussion beams (Ilonggot *pamagekan*). The first is a yoke-shaped bar with a small handle at its middle, which is held by the left hand as the right hand strikes one side of the bar, producing a ringing tone. A set consists of three such bars each played with a different rhythm. Hundreds of sets of *bangibang* may be played together by men from several villages when a violent death has occurred, or as part of other ceremonies. The percussion beams are played in pairs, one long and one short. The long beam is laid on the ground, and rhythms are played on it by five people, each with two sticks. At the same time, a drone is played on the shorter beam by one person. The music is used in an *anito* (spirit) ceremony to drive away malevolent spirits

5. *Kalingga balingbing (bamboo buzzer)*

from the sick. Percussion beams of another type are used by the Tiruray. They are played, suspended, by two men; one beats an ostinato on a single beam, while the other plays the melody on two or three beams.

Chordophones. Zithers form an important class of chordophone in the north. The bamboo polychordal tube zither (Kalingga *kolitong, kulibit*; Ilonggot *kolesing*; Isneg

kuritao, uritang) has from 5 to 11 strings, which are plucked by fingers of both hands (thumb plus the two or three fingers next to it). The tones are distributed between the right- and left-hand fingers to form a melodic ostinato through the alternate use of left and right hands. The parallel-string tube zither (Kalingga *dungadung*; Isneg *pasing*; Negrito *tabengbeng*) has two strings joined in the middle by a bridge or platform that is beaten with a stick, producing deep sounds (fig.7). The board zither (Ifugao *taddeng*; Ibaloi *kaltsang*) among the Ifugao has three strings of bamboo or wire, or three iron strands, which are tapped to imitate gong sounds, while among the Ibaloi it has four wire strings that are plucked.

The musical bow of the Agta Negrito of eastern Luzon can have as its resonator the performer's mouth. Alternate plucking on the two strings by fingers of the right and left hands produces a simple rhythmic pattern of three tones. Other types of musical bow use different resonators: a tin can pressed against the chest or a pig's bladder resting on the two bow-strings.

The Ilonggot have a three-string fiddle (called *kulibao, gisada* or *litlit*) that is similar to but larger than the three-string fiddle (*gitgit*) of a southern Philippines group, the Hanunoo.

In addition to the above chordophones, some northern groups have adopted European-type instruments. The violin (Kalingga *biyolin*) is used to play song melodies; the guitar (Negrito *gitara*) is used to play one or two chords in a fast rhythm to accompany dances that imitate animal movements.

Aerophones. In addition to various types of flute, northern aerophones include panpipes, a stopped-flute ensemble and reedpipes. In the lip-valley or deep-notched flute (Kalingga *tongali, paldong*), the shape of the rim and the number (three plus one), size and placement of stops correspond exactly with those of lip-valley Mindanao flutes; the northern flute is shorter, however. The duct flute with an internal plug is found among the Ifugao (*ongiyong*), Ibaloi (*kulasing*), Kalingga (*olimong*) and Balangao (*kaleleng*). The *kulasing* and *olimong* have three plus one stops. The 'chip on tube' flute with external duct (Ilonggot *tolali*; Negrito *bulungudyung*) is arranged so

6. *Set of three bangibang (percussion yoke-bars) of the Ifugao*

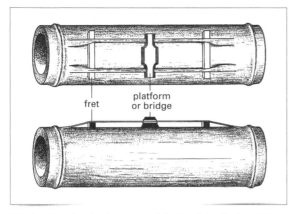

7. Tube zither showing the two parallel strings joined in the middle by a bridge or platform

that between the chip and the tube a small passage allows the flow of air against the edge of a hole into the tube chamber (see fig.15b below). The *tolali* and *bulungudyung* have three plus one stops.

The main characteristic of the bamboo nose flute (Bontok *kaleleng*; Isneg *bali-ing*; Kalingga *tongali, enongol*) is that its blowing-hole is bored through a bamboo node (fig.8). It has three plus one stops, and melodies played on it usually have a descending pattern. This type of flute is found almost nowhere else in the Philippines (though one has been seen in Palawan), a limited distribution that invites comparison with nose flutes elsewhere in South-east Asia.

The panpipes (Bontok *diwdiw-as, diwas*), a raft of five tubes, are no longer played in the Cordillera. The stopped-pipe ensemble (Kalingga *saggeypo*), comprising a set of five pipes, one for each player, may occasionally be played; its music simulates that of the *topayya* gong ensemble. The *hupep* of the Ifugao is an idioglot single-reed pipe about 7 mm in diameter and 24 cm long.

(iii) Vocal music. Among peoples of the Cordillera in Luzon there are no generic terms for song, only names for particular song forms. Among the Ibaloi, the *badiw* (leader-chorus singing) is the principal vocal form. It is used in ceremonies for the dead (*du-udyeng, ta-tamiya*) as well as on such occasions as weddings, *peshit* (anniversary feasts celebrated by rich couples) and thanksgiving rituals. In a *du-udyeng*, which may last for several nights, the *badiw* singers may speak in riddles,

invite spirit-relatives to drink rice wine with the living or talk of properties left by the deceased, of humorous conversations between a song character and the evening's host and of plants and animals related to the deceased's entourage. At a *peshit*, the lines of verse in the *badiw* extol the virtues of the man being honoured. Leading members of each village take turns in these praise songs. The leader's verses are extemporized, but his melody follows a traditional pattern. The chorus repeats the last syllables of his lines in slower rhythm, and as it finishes its own melody, the leader must be ready with his next line (ex.4). This continuous opposition between leader and chorus lasts a long time, testing the soloist's creative ability and imagination.

Among the Bontok, one of the most important feasts is the *chuno*, the last of three ceremonies to commemorate the wedding of rich citizens. Another is the *ap-apoy*, held after the planting season to prevent calamities befalling the community. The *kay-aya* celebrates a war victory, and the *siyenga* is a curing ritual. The leader-chorus song form is used for all these occasions; specific songs include the Bontok *churwassay*, a funeral song for an older person who has just died, which uses a characteristic singing technique in which meaningless vowels are repeated many times before a word is formed (ex.5).

With the Kalingga, the *dango* and *ading* song forms are traditional in important ceremonies such as peace pacts, weddings and discussions, and are used to express a declaration, greeting or statement related to the occasion. The restrained manner of singing, the economy in the use of notes and the formality of the event indicate these songs' importance in the society. In the *ading* (ex. 6) slides, uncertain pitches, trills, stops and speech-like sounds are particularly characteristic. After the initial

Ex.4 Ibaloi *badiw*, song for ceremonies; rec. and transcr. J. Maceda

8. Tongali (bamboo nose flute) of the Kalingga people

Ex.5 Bontok *churwassay*, funeral song; rec. and transcr. J. Maceda

Ex.6 Kalinga *ading*, song for formal occasions; rec. and transcr. J. Maceda

song declarations and discussions, other types of song follow, including the *ullalim* (epic), *ogayam* (ballad), *balaguyos* and *salidomay* (popular songs). Other occasions for singing occur in curing ceremonies (*dawak*), laments for dead relatives (*ibil*, *alba-ab*), lullabies (*owawi*) and others.

2. SOUTHERN PHILIPPINES.

(i) General. Pre-Western traditions in the southern Philippines exist in the large island Mindanao, the Sulu archipelago and two smaller western islands, Palawan and Mindoro. In addition, in the islands of Panay and Negros, there are isolated minority groups who have retained their pre-Hispanic musical heritage though surrounded for four centuries by peoples who have become musically Westernized. Indigenous peoples are more widely scattered in these islands, while Muslims are centralized in western Mindanao and the Sulu archipelago.

Instruments found only among Islamic groups are principally the *kulintang* (gong-chime), *gabbang* (xylophone), *saunay* (single-reed aerophone), *biola* (violin) and *gandang* (two-headed drum). Not all these instruments may have been brought to the islands by a Muslim culture; their presence may be the result of trade relations that the coastal people of Mindanao and island dwellers of Sulu had with several islands in Indonesia and Malaysia. The most common instrument among the Muslim groups is

the *kulintang*, generally played in a group with other instruments. The *saunay* is a solo instrument, and the *gabbang*, though sometimes treated as a solo instrument, generally accompanies the *suling* (ring flute), the *biola* (violin) or a secular song (fig.9).

Instruments found among both indigenous peoples and Muslim groups are the *agung* (suspended bossed gong with wide rim), *palendag* (lip-valley flute), *suling* (ring flute), duct flute with a chip on its ledge, *kudyapi* (two-string lute), *kubing* (jew's harp), *kagul* (percussion beams) and the tube zither with parallel strings. The AGUNG with a wide, turned-in rim and high boss has the widest distribution among bronze instruments, found among practically all groups in Mindanao, Sulu and Palawan (fig.10). The indigenous groups do not generally use the *kulintang* except as an instrument borrowed from the Muslims. The most developed *agung* ensembles are those of the Tiruray, Tiboli and Bagobo; they are also played in pairs or in simple ensembles among the Manobo, Mansaka, Bukidnon, Mandaya, Subanen, Palawan and Tagbanwa. An interesting *agung* ensemble without a melody is found among groups in Palawan and Mindoro; its musical interest lies in timbral qualities and rhythmic counterpoint.

The polychordal tube zither is played only by the indigenous groups of Mindanao, while the parallel-string tube zither is used by the Maranao and Magindanao. Among the Tiruray, the polychordal tube zither is played by two women: one, holding one end of the tube, plays a melody on three strings, while the other, grasping the other end of the tube, plays a drone on two strings. Among the Tiboli and the Palawan the zither may also be played in unison with a *kudyapi*. Other instruments that appear only among indigenous groups are the single-string spike fiddle, stamping-tube, stamping-stick, log drums and board drums. A single-string spike fiddle is found among the Bilaan, Higaonon, Bukidnon and the Manobo. The stamping-tube was reported among the Manobo of Agusan; the stamping-stick among the Bukidnon is used agriculturally, to bore holes in which to drop seeds. The log drum of the Tagakaolo is similar to the board drum with jar resonators of the Yakan, which is suspended from a frame with the board lying a few centimetres above the ground. Two inverted jars, one big and one small, are suspended from the frame, their mouths barely touching the board. Two performers beat a steady rhythm in unison on one end of the board, while a third

9. *Gabbang (bamboo-keyed xylophone) and biola (violin) of the Samal people, Zamboanga*

10. Agung (bossed gong) ensemble of the Tagakaolo people, Mindanao Island

performer improvises another rhythm with changing patterns at the other end of the board.

(ii) Gongs and gong ensembles. As in the north, bronze or brass gongs are the most important instruments, but in the south they are all bossed (with a protrusion in the centre). The presence of the boss and the structure of the gongs themselves both account for a difference in musical aesthetics between the north and the south: gongs in the south make round, full sounds in contrast to the diffused, unfocussed tone qualities of gongs in the north. Suspended bossed gongs are older instruments than the smaller gongs laid in a row (KULINTANG) that were introduced in Sulu and in a limited area in southern Mindanao, probably through trade and commerce with the outside world. The arrival of *kulintang* in the Philippines, after hanging gongs, means that the musical concepts of 'melody-producing' gongs-in-a-row and 'punctuating' suspended gongs were initially separate entities, becoming fused over time. The music of the *kulintang* in the south is built on scales with identifiable pitches in contrast to the indefinite pitches of the northern flat gongs. Sound on bossed gongs (*agung*) may be cut off quickly by damping the boss with the left hand to produce short, drum-like effects. The lighter gongs of the Tiruray, with high-pitched sounds, are allowed to vibrate freely, while the heavy, suspended gongs of the Magindanao (*gandingan*) vibrate in long, low sounds.

While men are assigned to play the heavy gongs, adolescent or young boys and girls play the melody on the *kulintang*. In the town of Dulawan, boys practise it as a sport, competing with each other in virtuosity and musical skill; they make rhythmic permutations on three or four suspended gongs as a test of speed and endurance. In other towns adept women display their individual improvisational styles. Some *kulintang* are made in Lanao and Cotabato, but the older hanging gongs (*agung*) may have come from Kalimantan, Sarawak or Sabah, while the *Kulintang* gongs in a row probably came from the Moluccas, with whose chiefs the Magindanao Sultanates were associated politically. The *agung* (with a high boss

and a wide rim) are the most valuable gongs; different types are widely distributed among Islamic and other groups in Mindanao, Sulu and Palawan.

Gong-chime ensembles, known as *kulintang* among the Badjao, Magindanao, Maranao, Samal, Tausug and Yakan, vary from group to group in their exact composition, the common element being the presence of the gong-chime, *kulintang*, itself (fig.11). The five instruments in the Magindanao *kulintang* ensemble are the *kulintang* (a gong-chime of eight gongs), *babendil* (gong with turned-in rim), *agung* (one or a pair of larger gongs with wide turned-in rims), *gandingan* (two pairs of gongs with narrow rims) and the *debakan* (cylindrical drum). The *babendil* is played with one or a pair of sticks striking its rim to produce thin, metallic sounds. The *agung* gives off short, dampened sounds, in contrast to the *gandingan*, which produces long, low vibrations. The *debakan* adds the sharp sounds of a struck membrane. (For melody of the *kulintang* and ostinatos of the other four instruments, see ex.7). In the Maranao *kulintang* ensemble the *gandingan* is absent. With the Yakan, not only is the *gandingan* absent, but the *babendil* is replaced by a lone bamboo pole laid on the ground and struck with two sticks as a percussion instrument. Among the Tausug and Samal the *kulintang* is accompanied by a double-headed drum (*gandang*) and suspended gongs *tunggalan* and *duahan*. The *duahan* consists of two gongs, one of which (*huhugan* or *buahan*) has a narrow rim similar to that of the Magindanao *gandingan*; the other is a wide-rimmed *pulakan* similar to that of the Magindanao and Maranao *agung*. The Badjao *kulintang* is accompanied by two *agung* and a cylindrical drum.

In all these ensembles it is the *kulintang* that carries the melody. Compositions for the *kulintang* are based on rhythmic modes. Three modes (*duyug*, *sinulug*, *tidtu*) used by the Magindanao are sometimes similar to those used by other groups in name, structure or both. The Magindanao mode name *sinulug* is similar to *sinug*, a term used by the Tausug, but the rhythms of the two are not identical. The Magindanao *tidtu*, an iambic rhythm

11. Kulintang ensemble of the Magindanao people, Mindanao Island, with (from left to right) gandingan and babendil (gongs), debakan (cylindrical drum), agung (bossed gong) and kulintang (gong-chime, front)

with beats in the ratio 2:3, appears not only in the Sulu and Mindanao areas, but also in other areas among non-Muslims as a rhythm without a particular name. Among the Magindanao, melodic development on the *kulintang* is based on nuclear tones; permutations and variations on two or three tones are the performer's main concern. Yakan *kulintang* music includes the continuous, extremely fast repetition of a simple melodic pattern. In Tausug *kulintang* compositions the *kuriri* pattern is used; it consists of descending melodic passages and fast repeating rhythms, while among the Maranao, loudness, virtuosity in handling of the mallets and a kind of dialogue between instrumental parts are important characteristics of *kulintang* pieces.

Gong ensembles with only suspended gongs consist of *agung*-type gongs with wide turned-in rims. Among the Tiruray the *agung* ensemble is made up of five small light gongs with delicate sounds, played by five men or women. The smallest, *segarun*, leads the group with a steady beat, and the others follow with their respective rhythms (ex.8). This ensemble is played at weddings, big gatherings and meetings to entertain visitors. The Bagobo and Tagakaolo *agung* ensemble usually consists of eight wide-rimmed gongs suspended from a beam in vertical rows and played by two people. A standing man plays the melody, while another man or woman, kneeling, taps an ostinato on the lowest-hung, lowest-sounding gong. After a certain time, the melody performer stops playing, but the ostinato player continues. The melody performer starts to dance in small steps away from the gongs, following the ostinato rhythm of the remaining gong player. Eventually the dancer returns to his original position and again plays his gongs, this time in a faster tempo. Among the Palawan and Tagbanwa the *agung* ensemble includes two small

Ex.7 *Duyug* mode, *kulintang* ensemble, Magindanao; rec. and transcr. J. Maceda (Maceda, 1964)

⌒ = slightly longer than notated
‿ = slightly shorter than notated

suspended gongs (*sagung* among the Tagbanwa), one, two or three big suspended gongs (*agung*) and one small cylindrical drum. In the Palawan ensemble there is another pair of smaller gongs (*sanang*), each played by a performer with two sticks. There is an alternation of emphasis between the two performers: while one plays his rhythmic permutations loudly, the other plays his beats softly and without permutations. Together with the other instruments in the ensemble they create complex cross-rhythms. The Tagbanwa *agung* ensemble is similar to that of the Palawan, except that the music of the smaller pair of gongs (*babendil*) is not so developed. Among the Subanun an *agung* 'ensemble' is one gong (with wide turned-in rim) played by two performers: one player beats the boss with a padded stick and damps it with his knee; the other taps the rim of the gong with two sticks, producing a thin, contrasting sound.

The Hanunoo *agung* ensemble consists of two light gongs played by two men squatting on the floor: one man beats with a lightly padded stick on the bosses of the two gongs, the other strikes with a stick on the rim of one of the gongs. Both performers play in simple duple rhythms. The Magindanao *agung* ensemble consists of one *agung* (gong with turned-in rim) and a *tambul* (cylindrical drum). The *tambul* maintains a fast, steady, rhythmic pattern while the *agung* provides a counterpoint with its mixture of slow and fast patterns.

(iii) Solo instruments and other ensembles. Most instruments in the south are made of bamboo and are blown, plucked or struck; with bamboo flutes, the shape of the mouthpiece, number of holes and size of the bamboo may be clues to their distribution in South-east Asia generally (Maceda, 1990). Instruments whose sounds are produced by other materials (e.g. wood, skin, vine, bean pod, wire, seashell) extend the range of sound qualities. Ensembles without gongs comprise a combination of two instruments (e.g. tube zither and two-string lute), or two persons sharing different parts of the same instrument (e.g. bamboo zither), or a song with instrumental accompaniment (e.g. xylophone and voice), or two instruments of the same type (e.g. a pair of two-headed drums) or a variety of instruments.

(a) Idiophones. The jew's harp, *kubing*, is widespread among groups in the southern Philippines and is known by this name among the Bagobo, Bilaan, Bukidnon, Magindanao, Mansaka, Palawan, Subanun, Tiruray and Yakan (fig.12). Its bamboo filament is vibrated by plucking. It is made from various kinds of bamboo in

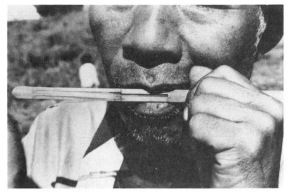

12. Kubing (jew's harp) of southern Mindanao

many sizes and shapes, producing various sounds and dynamics. Some jew's harps are barely audible, with quick sound-decay; others twang loudly and vibrate for a long time, like a reed. Colour and timbre can also vary according to the tongue placements of the performer. Plucking the jew's harp with the tongue placed near the alveolar ridge produces vibrations similar to the vowel 'i'; other vowels can be suggested as well, using other tongue placements. The jew's harp can thus simulate words, phrases, simple conversations and speeches. Using this instrument young boys and girls 'converse' in front of their elders without being understood by them.

The Bukidnon *talupak* or stamping-stick is a chordophone used as an idiophone. It is a bamboo tube zither having many parallel strings with a common fret attached at the upper end of the tube. A slit that almost divides the bamboo in half allows one side of the tube to flap against the other each time the instrument is struck on the ground to bore holes in which to plant rice seeds. Another instrument connected with rice growing is the *tagutok*, used by the Maranao. It is a bamboo scraper consisting of two sticks rubbed back and forth across a serrated bamboo tube to drive away animals from a field where rice is almost ready for harvest.

Other bamboo instruments of the south are the bamboo slit-drum (Maranao *agong a bentong*) and the trough xylophone (Tausug *gabbang*). The Maranao play two *agong a bentong* like *agung* in an ensemble with bamboo xylophone and cylindrical drum. The Tausug *gabbang* has about 16 to 19 bamboo keys tuned to a heptatonic scale with equal intervals. The melody is divided between the leading line (*ina*, 'mother') and a following line in the

Ex.8 Drone and melody, Tiruray *agung* ensemble; rec. and transcr. J. Maceda

lower register (*anak*, 'child'). As a solo instrument it is used for preludes to songs; it is also an important accompanying instrument for all secular songs and for the *biola*.

Two additional idiophones are the Hanunoo *buray dipay*, a bean-pod rattle used for merrymaking in ensemble with other kinds of instrument, and the *kalutang*, also found among the Hanunoo, percussion sticks played in pairs to produce harmonies of 2nds, 3rds or 4ths.

(b) Chordophones. The types of chordophone used in the south include lutes, zithers and fiddles. On the two-string lute, known as the *kudyapiq, kusyapiq* or *kutyapiq* among the Bukidnon, Magindanao, Maranao and Tag-banwa, one string provides a rhythmic drone (fig.13); the other has movable frets allowing melodies to be played in two different pentatonic scales, one containing semitones, the other anhemitonic (ex.9). Excellent soloists among the Magindanao of Cotabato play melodic patterns resembling those of *kulintang* melodies. Among these groups a *kudyapiq* may also be played with a *saluray* (bamboo tube zither), *kutet* (one-string fiddle) or *tumpung* (duct flute). A four-part ensemble consists of the *kudyapiq*, jew's harp, fiddle and flute.

Zithers include the polychordal tube zither (Tiruray *togo*; Bukidnon *tangkol*; Bilaan *sluday, sloray*; Mansaka *takol*; Ata *saluray*; Mangguangan *tangko*), which has an anhemitonic pentatonic tuning and on which melodic patterns are repeated over long periods (fig.14), and the parallel-string bamboo tube zither (Maranao *seronga-gandi*; Hanunoo *kudlung*; Mandaya *takumbo*; Subanun *tabobok*; Tagakaolo *katimbok*), which, like the northern Philippines *dungadung*, is also played by striking the bridge that connects the two strings. Among the Tiruray, two pairs of parallel strings are played with one stick. The Maranao instrument has a half-open lid on one end of the tube, struck to provide a sound quality contrasting with that of the resonating tube chamber.

The one-string fiddle (Mandaya and Manobo *duwagey, kogut*; Bukidnon *dayuray, dayuday*) is used to play melodies with quick triplet patterns. Some groups, such as the Tausug, have adopted a European-type violin, which they call *biola* or *biyula*.

13. *Kudyapiq (two-string lute) of the Maranao people, Mindanao, with (left to right) kubing (jew's harp), tumpung (duct flute) and saluray (tube zither)*

Ex.9 *Kudyapiq* music, southern Philippines; rec. and transcr. J. Maceda

(c) Aerophones. Flutes are the most important class of aerophone in the south. The transverse flute (Hanunoo *lantuy*; Buhid *palawta*; Cuyunin, Batak and Tagbanwa *tipanu*) has six stops (five among the Hanunoo) and is tuned diatonically. End-blown flutes include notched flutes and various types of duct flute. The most widespread notched flute is the lip-valley or deep-notched type (Magindanao and Bagobo *palendag*; Tiruray *falendag*; Mansaka *parundag*), which generally has three plus one stops. The lips control and affect the air flow through minute changes and create a degree of tonal control and sensitivity not possible in flutes with differently shaped blowing-holes (e.g. the ring flute, *suling*). In addition, the Tagbanwa have a short notched flute with no stops (an example is held by the National Museum of the Philippines), whose native name has not been recorded.

The ring flute (Magindanao, Tiruray, Manobo, Bukidnon and Tausug *suling*; Maranao *inse*) is a type of duct flute whose sound is produced by adjusting the ring on the mouthpiece in relation to the blowing-hole. Among the Tausug the *suling* may be played in ensemble with the *biola*. With the Maranao, an ensemble consists of the *suling, kudyapiq*, jew's harp, bamboo zither and metal dish.

The duct flute (Hanunoo *pituh*) is diatonically tuned and has finger-holes but no thumb-hole. Transverse flutes among the Tagbanwa and Hanunoo (*palawta*) are diatonically tuned and have five or six holes. The other duct flutes in the south are defined by the position of the attached plug or chip which forms the duct. In the external-duct flute with a chip tied on to its rim ledge (Bukidnon *pulala*; Manobo *lantoy*), a narrow passage between the chip and the ledge allows air to be blown into the tube itself, producing a sound much like that of a whistle (fig.15*a*). A third type is the external-duct flute with a chip tied on to the tube of the flute (Hanunoo *bangsiq*; Magindanao *tumpung*; fig.15*b*). The *tumpung* here has three plus one stops.

Other types of aerophone in the south include trumpets and a single-reed instrument. The *budyung* is a bamboo trumpet found among the Hanunoo and Mandaya; among the Bukidnon the same word denotes a shell trumpet that is used as a signalling or call device. The single-reed pipe (Tausug *saunay, sahunay*) has six finger-holes and no thumb-hole. Its melody line is a continuous flow of changing pitches produced by circular breathing interspersed with mordents.

(d) Membranophones. Cylindrical drums with one or two heads are known in the southern Philippines. The *gimbal* of the Mandaya, Tagbanwa and Palawan is a

single-headed cylindrical drum played with two sticks, used as part of a gong ensemble or with other instruments.

(iv) Vocal music. Indigenous and Muslim-influenced cultures in the south differ in the types of songs they sing and in the singing styles they use. The latter use both a tense, high-pitched style with complex melismas, as well as a relaxed style in the natural speaking range with less melisma. Indigenous groups prefer the relaxed style, and have in addition other techniques such as responsorial singing and songs imitating the sounds of musical instruments.

The Islamic musical tradition is represented by various song types. Among the Tausug, the melismatic style is exemplified in the *lugu*, highly melismatic solo songs sung in Arabic, mostly by women, for Islamic ceremonies (e.g. Ramadan and the birthday of Muhammad) and local rituals such as weddings and funerals. Five songs of the *lugu* tradition are the *jikil, sail, tarasul, baat* and *langan bataq-bataq*. The *jikil* serves as a vehicle for virtuoso singing in competitions and entertainments; *sail* is used sometimes to mean the *lugu* song style used at weddings and wakes; *tarasul* are commentaries on verses from the Qur'an; *baat* are highly refined allusions to love; and *langan bataq-bataq* are lullabies with texts about love, nature and life. *Lugu* songs are sung in free tempo with weak or no metric beats; the melodic phrases seem slow because of the long held notes separating melismas from each other. Although few of the people understand Arabic, they value highly the refinements of *lugu* singing: women who study this tradition undergo personal training with a leading guru of the community. The Tausug use the second, more relaxed style for secular affairs such as entertainment at weddings and social gatherings. A male or female singer is generally accompanied by a *gabbang* and a *biola*. Texts are in Tausug rather than Arabic, and melodies are metrical. The *liyangkit* (ballad) is a metrical song sung in the lower register using two or three notes.

Among the Magindanao in Cotabato, a Muslim group, four characteristic types of song are the *tutol* (epic), *bang* (call to prayer), *sindil* (song of insinuation) and *bayok* (love-song). The *tutol* tells of the exploits of heroes like Rajah Indara Patra, a man of noble birth who makes fantastic flights to the palace of the clouds and fights with legendary monsters to save his people from destruction (see ex.10, the beginning of the epic in which a greeting to Allah is expressed in melisma, showing the use of long notes, trills, mordents, fast notes and a long descending melodic line). The *bang* is sung on Fridays and has the same function as bellringing in Christian communities of

the Philippines (see ex.11, in which another form of melisma with a long vocalise on a vowel is sung in a

Ex.11 *Bang*, Muslim call to prayer, southern Philippines, rec. and transcr.
J. Maceda

Ex.12 *Sarankunay*, Muslim song of insinuation, southern Philippines; rec. and transcr. J. Maceda

relaxed voice). The *bang* contrasts greatly with the strained technique used for the *sindil* (ex.12), in which vowel changes, microtonal variation and the bell-like quality of the voice give a sensual effect to the performance. In a performance recorded in 1954, one singer who had been trained by a visiting musician from the Near East sang the *bang* in a relaxed low voice, while another, trained in the local style, sang it in the same melismatic, high-pitched, strained manner used for secular songs such as the *sindil*. The *bayok* (ex.13), usually sung in the more

Ex.13 *Isaden*, Muslim *bayok*, love-song; rec. and transcr. J. Maceda

relaxed style by the women of the village, has a simple melodic line and more use of repeated tones, with a syllabically set text. Among the Maranao, however, *bayok* are more complex songs. Along with the *darangan* (a type of epic), they are the most popular song for weddings and festivities in Lanao; the singers are specialists who become centres of attraction at social gatherings where, as protagonists, they vie with each other in extemporizing allusions and double meanings, much to the delight of their audience.

Indigenous peoples make less use of the melismatic style; their songs are in a more syllabic style, centring on a few notes as in Western psalm singing (see ex.14, a Tiruray courting-song from western Mindanao). Among the Manobo, songs are metrical and imitate the plucking sounds of a bamboo zither. Leader-chorus singing prevails among the Tagbanwa: in one ceremony a woman leader sings and dances around jars of rice wine prepared for the

Ex.10 Magindanao epic *Raja Indara Patra*; rec. and transcr. J. Maceda

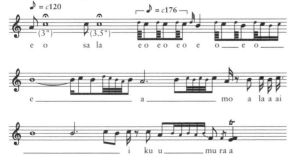

14. *Saluray (polychordal tube zither) and kudlung (two-string lute) played by the Ata, eastern Mindanao*

occasion and placed at the centre of the house; she tries to communicate with deities and invites them to join the festivity. As she dances a group of young girls follow her, and as she sings the chorus repeats the last syllables of her lines (ex.15). The Tagbanwa believe that when she falls into a trance spirits enter her body and through her suck the first wine from the bamboo tubes placed in the jars.

In a wine-drinking festivity, participants sing verses whose lines must rhyme and have certain numbers of syllables. Other songs use traditional prose texts. In both the verse and prose forms there are many metaphors and allusions; archaic words often provoke long discussions, even among older speakers, regarding the real meaning of certain words.

There are two types of courting-song among the Hanunoo: the *urukay* in eight-syllable verses accompanied by the *kudyapi*, a six-string guitar, and the *ambahan* in seven-syllable verses accompanied by the *gitgit*, a three-string fiddle.

Epic songs may be sung at a wedding, in gatherings to entertain guests or simply as evening entertainment for the villagers themselves. Epics are common in Mindanao, and Palawan, among the Manobo, Agusan and Bukidnon, and among the Mandaya, Mansaka and Bagobo groups whose tales describe the lives of the heroes Agyu, Tuwaang and Ulahingan. Epics may last one or more nights and are attended with keen interest. The singer performs either sitting or lying down. In the *manggob*, an epic among the Mansaka, the singing style requires extra vowels and syllables to be added to the words. These additions obscure the words themselves so that even a native speaker of the language who is unfamiliar with the epic will not

be able to follow the story. Among the Palawan, epic melodies are long lines with the text sung syllabically and enunciated clearly; changes of tonal structure and pitch identify the various characters in the epic.

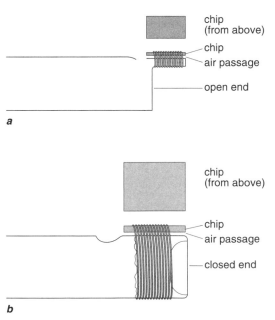

15. *External duct flutes with (a) chip tied to the rim ledge, and (b) chip tied to the tube*

Ex.14 *Lingung rasak*, Tiruray courting song; rec. and transcr. J. Maceda

Among indigenous peoples in Mindanao, some songs are accompanied by instruments such as the *kudlung* (two-string lute), *saluray* (tube zither; see fig.15 above) or *palendag* (lip-valley or deep-notched flute). Other song forms include debates, narrative solo songs, dance-songs and speech-like songs. Among the Magindanao some skilful whistlers using only tongue and lips can simulate difficult passages of flute melodies.

Ex.15 Tagbanwa medium's song; rec. and transcr. J. Maceda

III. Western art music

1. Spanish period, 1521–1896. 2. American period, 1898–1946. 3. Independence, after 1946.

1. SPANISH PERIOD, 1521–1896.   With close to four centuries of rule over the Philippine archipelago, Spain left an indelible musical imprint and caused an almost complete obliteration of Asian musical traditions in some areas. The first Spanish soldiers brought priests, who taught Filipinos how to sing plainchant for Mass and other Christian services and how to play various instruments. These priests received musical training in Spain before coming to the Philippines; a few were composers of religious music. One of the first teachers known was the Franciscan Geronimo Aguilar, an excellent musician who started teaching in 1586. He was succeeded in 1606 by Juan de Santa Marta (formerly a tenor at Zaragoza Cathedral), who gathered 400 boys from different provinces and trained them in singing, playing and instrument-making at Lumbang (near Manila). After their training, these boys were sent back to their respective home towns, where they taught others.

In 1742 the Archbishop of Manila, Juan Rodriguez Angel, founded a singing school at Manila Cathedral. In the 19th century the school was known as Colegio de Niños Tiples (School of Boy Sopranos); it admitted boys of over six who could pass the entrance requirements. The curriculum was patterned after that of the Madrid Conservatory; singing teachers used the solfège book by Hilarion Eslava, and courses in harmony, composition, piano, organ and strings were given by a staff of clergy and laymen. Two other churches in Manila that taught music to young boys were the convents of S Agustin and S Domingo.

These and similar institutions elsewhere in the Philippines provided a large base of amateur and professional musicians who evolved a syncretic style using Philippine and Western elements. Musicians trained at these schools included the pianists Antonio Garcia (1865–1919), Hipolito Rivera (1866–1900) and Ramon Valdes (d 1902); the violinists Andres Dancel (1870–98), Cayetano Jacobe (fl 1893), Bibiano Morales (b 1872) and Manuel Luna y Novicio (1858–83); and the composers José Canseco jr (1843–1912), Simplicio Solis (1864–1903), Fulgencio Tolentino (fl 1887), Julio Nakpil (1867–1960) and Julian Felipe (fl 1898).

The church schools taught mainly religious music. The most famous composer of church music was Marcelo Adonay (1848–1928), whose works show the variety of common musical forms used by friar musicians at that time. Besides liturgical settings, Adonay's works include a descriptive fantasy, *The Tarumba of Pakil*, for chorus and brass band, using a native Philippine setting to honour the Virgin Mary, and *Rizal Glorified*, a hymn with orchestral accompaniment in praise of a national hero.

In Philippine provinces new musical forms developed around the new religious and secular activities. The *pasyon* is a chanted story of the Passion, sung in the vernacular during Lent; the *santa-cruzan* and *flores de mayo* are annual celebrations with special songs for the Blessed Virgin Mary, and the *dalit* is a mournful plaint in her honour. Secular songs include the *tagulaylay*, a recitative lament; the *awit*, a chanted story based on the crusades; and the *kumintang*, a war song, now known as a love song. Stage plays that developed are the *moro-moro*, with a stereotyped theme depicting encounters between Muslims and Christians; the *duplo*, a form usually performed during the ninth day of a series of prayers; the *cenaculo*, a drama on the Passion and death of Christ; and the *carillo*, a shadow play with suspended cardboard figures.

In Manila and nearby provinces, literary musical organizations that appeared in the late 19th century presented a wide range of light musical programmes, concerts, operas, literary and brass band contests. Operas found special favour among a cosmopolitan audience; Italian opera companies that toured the orient made long visits to Manila and exerted such a strong influence that airs from *La traviata*, *Rigoletto*, *William Tell* and *Poet and Peasant* became popular household tunes.

As Spain ruled the islands through Mexico, there were some Mexican as well as Spanish and European influences on Philippine folk music. The *cariñosa*, *pandango*, *polka*, *dansa*, *rigodon* and other dance forms of the Philippines show traces of the Spanish habanera, jota, tango and fandango, and even of the French *valse* and rigaudon. The *kundiman* (love song) and the *balitao* (serenade or dance) are native Philippine versions of 19th-century European musical genres. The instruments used in the *rondalla* (plucked string orchestra) – the *banduria*, *laud*, *octavina*, *guitara* and *bajo* – are adaptations of European and Mexican string instruments. One of the few bamboo organs constructed in the 19th century exists in Las Piñas (near Manila), built in 1818 by the Augustinian Diego Cera.

The Revolution of 1896 against Spain incited a sense of nationalism among composers, who collaborated with Tagalog playwrights to write zarzuelas depicting Philippine life and culture. The libretto for the first operetta, *Sandugong panaginip* ('The Dream Pact'), was written by Pedro A. Paterno (1858–1911) with music by Ladislao Bonus (1854–1908). Other zarzuela composers included Francisco Buencamino (1883–1972), Juan de S. Hernandez (1881–1945) and José A. Estella (1870–1943), who wrote music for *El diablo mundo* to a libretto by Rafael del Val. Another well-known play, *Walang sugat* ('Unhurt'), was written by Severino Reyes (1861–1942), with music by Fulgencio Tolentino.

2. AMERICAN PERIOD, 1898–1946.   The public co-educational system introduced by the Americans facilitated the teaching not only of Philippine but also of foreign folksongs, which quickly spread throughout the whole country. American jazz and film music gained favour among the younger generation of the upper middle class. As regards European classical music, new methods of piano teaching were introduced by Baptista Battig, a German Benedictine missionary who had studied with Ludwig Deppe. She taught the piano at the music school (founded 1908) of St Scholastica's College for women, where her influence was lasting. The Conservatory of Music (founded 1916) at the University of the Philippines helped to raise standards of performance and to increase public appreciation for European classical music. The first two directors of the school, Wallace W. George and Robert L. Schofield, were succeeded in 1926 by Alexander Lippay, a Viennese conductor and composer who introduced changes in the curricula and appointed European artists as members of staff. He resigned in 1931 to found

a new school, the Manila Academy of Music. He also helped to organize and develop the Manila SO, which became disciplined and highly proficient under his direction. The conservatory continued under Francisco Santiago (1889–1947), its first Filipino director, who together with Nicanor Abelardo (1893–1934) and Antonio Jesus Molina (1894–1980) formed a triumvirate of composers well known for their nationalism, teaching and creative work. The works of other composers, Bonifacio Abdon (1876–1944), Buencamino, Estella and Hernandez, showed the prevailing musical taste of that time.

In 1903 the Philippine Constabulary Band, which continued a long tradition of brass bands, was founded under the direction of Walter H. Loving (*fl* 1903–15; *d* during the Japanese Occupation, 1942–5). It won an international band contest at the St Louis Exposition (1904), participated at the inauguration of President William H. Taft (1909), the first governor-general of the Philippines and, in 1915, performed at the Panama Canal Exposition, under the baton of Pedro B. Navarro (1879–1951).

The first Filipino artists to gain recognition abroad were the singers Jovita Fuentes (1905–78), Isang Tapales, Mercedes Matias and José Mossegeld Santiago-Font, and the violinists Ramón Tapales (1906–95), Ernesto Vallejo (*d* 1945) and Luis Valencia (1912–82). A new interest in native Philippine music was encouraged by Jorge Bocobo, president of the University of the Philippines, who in 1924 created a research committee consisting of Francisca Reyes-Tolentino (1899–1933), Francisco Santiago and Molina and Antonino Buenaventura (*b* 1904), which travelled over the main islands and collected folksongs and dances.

The occupying Japanese discouraged jazz and the music of the allied nations, favouring the performance of Philippine and other Eastern musical forms. Prizes were given for compositions using native themes; Filipino soloists were encouraged to give concerts. Alfredo Lozano (*b* 1912) organized the New Philippine SO, composed entirely of Filipino musicians. Various Filipino conductors gave concerts, including Francisco Santiago, who presented an all-Philippine programme. One of the few music schools that remained open during the war was the Philippine Conservatory of Music (affiliated with the Philippine Women's University), which was directed by the singing teacher Felicing Tirona (*d* 1952).

Although Japanese music was played almost daily on the radio, and the works of the Japanese composer Koszak Yamada were performed in a special concert, Japanese music had no effect on the style and content of Philippine music.

3. INDEPENDENCE, AFTER 1946.   Philippine music showed a growth of cultural consciousness and nationalism after independence. The number of music schools increased greatly, offering BMus courses in the piano and organ, string and wind instruments, singing, theory, composition and music education; some offer an MMus.

Several organizations were founded to foster the development of music. The National Music Council, an agency of the UNESCO National Commission of the Philippines, organized the Regional Music Conference of South-east Asia in 1955. This meeting was followed in 1966 by a symposium on the musics of Asia, in which musicians from India, Indonesia, Ceylon, China, Japan,

Vietnam, Thailand and the Philippines, as well as from the West, participated. Founded by Jovita Fuentes, the Music Promotion Foundation of the Philippines was created in 1956 to promote the development of music and musicians in the country through grants, commission awards and scholarships. Its functions were taken over by the Cultural Center of the Philippines in 1986. The Manila Symphony Society continued to support its orchestra, which amplified its concert activities under the direction of Herbert Zipper; subsequent music directors were Oscar Yatco (from 1970) and Sergio Esmilla (until the mid-1980s, when the orchestra disbanded owing to financial difficulties). Among many other active performing groups are the National PO, the Filipino PO, the Philippine Choral Society, the Philippine Madrigal Singers, the Opera Guild of the Philippines and the Pangkat Kawayan (bamboo orchestra). The Philippine PO, established in 1982 and subsidized by the Cultural Center of the Philippines and the Philippine Philharmonic Society, originated as the CCP PO, founded in 1973 out of the Filipino Youth SO, which was formed in 1946. The Philippine Youth Orchestra was created by the University of the Philippines in 1974, and is subsidized by the Cultural Center.

The League of Filipino Composers was established in 1955, with 11 charter members: Antonino Buenaventura (b 1904), Rodolfo Cornejo (1909–91), Bernardino Custodio (b 1911), Felipe de Leon (1912–92), Lucrecia Kasilag (b 1918), Antonio Molina, Eliseo Pajaro (1915–84), Hilarion Rubio (1902–85), Lucino Sacramento (1908–84), Lucio San Pedro (b 1913) and Ramón Tapales (1906–95). The league holds annual music festivals that feature new works. A younger generation of composers includes Laverne dela Peña (b 1959), Jonas Baes (b 1961), Conrad del Rosario (b 1958), Kristina Benitez (b 1945), Arlene Chongson (b 1959) and Virgina Laico-Villanueva (b 1952). Popular composers and film music arrangers include Francisco Buencamino jr (b 1916), Miguel Velarde jr (b 1913), Ariston Avelino (b 1911), Restituto Umali (b 1916) and Tito Arevalo (b 1911). The ethnomusicologist José Maceda (b 1917) has collected and studied the musics of many ethnic groups throughout the Philippines and in parts of south-east Asia; he has also composed a number of avant-garde compositions using native materials.

The Philippine Women's University sponsored the Bayanihan Folk Arts Centre's extensive collection (founded 1957) of indigenous instruments and tape recordings of various ethnic musics of the Philippines for use by the faculty in lecture recitals. From 1958 the Bayanihan Dance Company, through its many international tours, has made Philippine culture known abroad.

The Cultural Center of the Philippines (inaugurated 1969) was designed to serve as a showcase for works by Philippine artists. Music, dance, drama and visual art of various styles have been presented in the centre's national and international festivals. The National Music Competition for Young Artists was established in 1973 to develop and promote Philippine music and discover young musical talent through regional and national competitions and festivals. The Filipino Society of Composers, Authors and Publishers was founded in 1965. For music teachers there are the Philippine Society for Music Education (1971) and the Piano Teachers Guild of the Philippines (1973).

The music colleges of the University of the Philippines, the Philippine Women's University, the Silliman University and the Asian Institute for Liturgy and Music all have staff trained in Western techniques and native music, and conduct courses in Philippine and Asian music. The Philippine Music Ensemble was established in 1983 by teachers and students of the PWU College of Music, to preserve and disseminate Filipino music of all kinds. Its four sections consist of a Muslim gamelan, a chorale, an *angklung* ensemble and a guitar quartet.

IV. Popular music

1. Early sources. 2. The emergence of Filipino pop. 3. The contemporary situation.

1. EARLY SOURCES. Filipino popular music may be traced to songs sung in the course of everyday living: work, war and drinking songs, lullabies and ballads. Western contact in 1521 brought Spanish colonization and Christianization to the islands; this produced musicians trained in the performance of Western music and resulted in new forms of music adapting Western idioms (e.g. jota, habanera and valse), which became the accompaniment to indigenous dances at town fiestas and celebrations.

After three centuries, Spanish occupation gave way to the American period (1898–1946), the influence of which is still strongly felt. Early in American colonial rule the *kundiman* or Filipino love song reigned supreme. Also prevailing were songs from the *sarswela*, an adaptation of the Spanish zarzuela. These musical plays, depicting love of country in time of revolution or espousing traditional values over encroaching foreign customs, waned with the establishment of dance-hall cabarets, musical reviews and vaudeville.

Radio, cinema and the American recording industry all aggressively promoted American popular music; by the 1920s Filipino bands were playing foxtrots, charlestons and tangos. Nicanor Abelardo, revered as one of the composers who raised the *kundiman* to the level of art song, led one such group, playing at the cabaret at night and teaching at the University of the Philippines College of Music by day. Traditional folksongs arranged in dance rhythms were in the repertory, as were movie themes popularized through radio and variety shows. At this same time, recording companies such as Victor and Columbia recorded *kundiman* and *sarswela* songs by Francisco Santiago, Constancio de Guzman and Abelardo.

American music was banned during the Japanese occupation, but when the Americans returned in 1945 the euphoria of liberation reinforced further the Filipino fascination with Americana. In the 1950s and 60s American popular culture was so strong that performers were often gauged on how well they could copy US singers, with contests for the Filipino counterparts of US pop stars. Philippine pop music by then meant Western pop, and it eventually incorporated the whole range of Western styles.

2. THE EMERGENCE OF FILIPINO POP. Despite the seemingly absolute reign of Western pop music, small pockets resisted the trend. Villar Records, founded in the early 1950s, recorded over 500 albums and 300 singles of *kundimans*, folksongs and local pop songs, including the well-known *Dahil sa iyo* ('Because of you'), written by Mike Velarde, the composer Antonio Maiquez's *Sapagkat kami ay tao lamang* ('For we are only human')

and Manuel Villar's *Diyos lamang ang nakakaalam* ('Only God knows').

In the 1960s pop idols who had begun by singing foreign songs (exemplified by Nora Aunor and Eddie Peregrina) began recording original compositions with English lyrics and forms. Foreign songs were also translated into Pilipino: Celeste Legaspi's highly acclaimed 1975 concert at the Cultural Centre of the Philippines, for example, featured Cole Porter, Burt Bacharach and Jim Webb songs translated by the poet Rolando Tinio.

By the 1970s the desire of composers to produce truly Filipino music that would find acceptance among the young found expression in *Ang himig natin* ('Our music') by Joey Smith and the Juan de la Cruz Band. Considered the first *Pinoy* (slang for Filipino) rock piece, it spoke of the lonely struggle of Filipino musicians for acceptance by an audience addicted to foreign music, arguing that Filipinos would only achieve true unity when they could appreciate and sing their own songs.

In 1974 the band Hotdog achieved success with *Ikaw ang Miss Universe ng buhay ko* ('You are the Miss Universe of my life') and *Pers lab* ('First love'), the first songs in the style that later became known as the Manila Sound, characterized by sentimental subjects and lyrics in Taglish, the urban student argot that combines English and Tagalog.

This new movement was facilitated by a Broadcast Media Council memorandum requiring all radio stations to play at least one Filipino composition per hour (this later became two and, in 1977, three per hour). The first Metro Manila Popular Music Festival was also organized in 1974; Ryan Cayabyab's *Kay ganda ng ating musika* ('How beautiful is our music') won the top prize, but the most record sales were generated by *Anak* ('Child') by Freddie Aguilar, and Heber Bartolome's *Tayo'y mga Pinoy* ('We are Filipinos'). *Anak*, based on the familiar Filipino theme of children risking pitfalls by not heeding their parents' advice, enjoyed unprecedented success and was translated into several foreign languages. The humorous *Tayo'y mga Pinoy* criticized Filipinos aping American ways; also decrying American influence on Philippine culture was a song contributed by one of the country's most enduring singing groups, the Apo Hiking Society, graphically called *American Junk*.

3. THE CONTEMPORARY SITUATION.   Though Philippine popular musical forms are predominantly derived from or inspired by the West, in language and spirit they are now Filipino. Traditional views on undying love and a resignation to heartbreak, carry-overs from the *kundiman*, still prevail in local ballads as sung by figures such as Celeste Legaspi, Basil Valdes and Sharon Cuneta. Protest songs, born in time of revolt (against Spain, the US and the Marcos regime) have begotten what is now called 'alternative music', which focusses on social conditions, environmental issues and human rights. Prominent exponents are Susan Fernandez Magno, Jess Santiago, Gary Granada and the duo Inang Laya.

Francis Magalona pioneered rap with his famous *Mga kababayan ko* ('My countrymen'), a call for patriotism. Rock and folk music exhibits the influence of the musical patterns, rhythms and instruments of indigenous musics. Joey Ayala and his group Bagong Lumad ('New natives') were the front-runners of this trend, using a *hegalong* (two-string lute) and *kubing* (jew's harp) together with electric guitar, bass and drums. Such combinations of instruments have blurred the distinctions between rock, folk and alternative music, evolving what could be best described as ethnic rock (or pop). Among its exponents are the groups Ang Grupong Pendong, Waling-Waling, Pinikpikan, and singers Grace Nono and Bayang Barrios. Full-length musicals and rock operas are also being written in increasing numbers, by composers such as Ryan Cayabyab.

At the end of the 20th century all-Filipino recordings stood at 60% of the industry's total output against 40% for foreign artists, reversing the conditions of the 1980s. The bestselling artists are rock bands that play mostly original music, and the major label is OPM (Original Pilipino Music); the same acronym is consciously used for the association of pop singers called Organisasyon ng Pilipinong Mangaawit. After years of imitating Western pop, indigenization has taken over, with a strong consciousness of Filipino identity that has inspired creators and performers of popular music to look back to their roots.

BIBLIOGRAPHY

AND OTHER RESOURCES

INDIGENOUS AND MUSLIM-INFLUENCED TRADITIONS

J.M. Garvan: *Ethnography of the Manobo Peoples of Eastern Mindanao* (Manila, 1912)

L.W. Benedict: *A Study of Bagobo Ceremonial, Magic and Myth* (New York, 1916)

E.A. Manuel: *The Maiden of the Buhong Sky* (Quezon City, 1958) [from the *Tuwaang* epic]

I. Leaño: *The Ibaloi Sings for the Dead* (diss., Philippine Women's University, Manila, 1960)

L.A. Reid: 'Ritual and Ceremony in Mountain Province: Dancing and Music', *Philippine Sociological Review*, ix/3–4 (1961), 55–82

J. Maceda: *The Music of the Magindanao* (diss., UCLA, 1963)

M. Maquiso: *An English Edition and a Critical Study of a Manobo Epic, Ulahingan*, i (diss., Silliman University, 1968)

E.A. Manuel: *Agyu: the Ilianon Epic of Mindanao* (Manila, 1969)

W.R. Pfeiffer: *Manobo Music Traditions and Some Other Ethnic Music Traditions of Mindanao* (Honolulu, 1969)

T.M. Kiefer: disc notes, *Music from the Tausug of Sulu: Moslems of the Southern Philippines*, Ethnosound EST 8000–1 (1970)

N.R. Macdonald: 'Oral Literature among the Palawan of the Makagwaq Valley', *Dialogue for Development: Cagayan de Oro 1972*, ed. F.R. Demetrio (Cagayan de Oro, 1975), 441–53

R.D. Trimillos: 'The Setting of Vocal Music among the Tausug', *Sulu Studies*, i (1972), 65–80

R.D. Trimillos: *Tradition and Repertoire in the Cultivated Music of the Tausug of Sulu, Philippines* (diss., UCLA, 1972)

N. Madale: *The Radia Indarapatra: a Study of a Maranao Tutol* (diss., U. of the Philippines, 1973)

U. Cadar and R. Garfias: 'Some Principles of Formal Variation in the Kolintang Music of the Maranao', *EthM*, xviii (1974), 43–55

J. Maceda: 'Drone and Melody in Philippine Musical Instruments', *Traditional Drama and Music of Southeast Asia*, ed. M.R. Osman (Kuala Lumpur, 1974), 246–73

J. Maceda: disc notes, *Ang Mga Kulintang sa Mindanao at Sulu*, U. of the Philippines (1977)

J. Maceda: 'Philippinen', *Musikgeschichte in Bildern*, i/3 (Leipzig, 1979), 144–63

M.T. Yraola: 'Ang musika ng mga Bontok Igorot sa Sadanga, lalawigang bulubundukin', *Musika Jornal* [Quezon City], iii (1979), 41–112

A. Martenot and J. Maceda: disc notes, *Sama di Sitangkai: Philippines – Archipel de Sulu*, Orstom-Selaf Ceto 793 (1980)

M.T. Yraola: 'The Music of the Bontok in Luzon', *Filipiny*, Polyjazz (1981) [disc notes]

J. Maceda: 'A Cure of a Sick *bgapipat* in Dulawan, Cotobato, Philippines', *AcM*, lvi (1984), 92–104

F. Prudente: *Musical Process in the Gasumbi Epic of the Buwaya Kalinga People of Northern Luzon* (diss., U. of Michigan, 1986)

R. Georsua: *Traditional Practices among the Subanen in Lapuyan, Zamboanga del Sur, with Special Reference to Music* (thesis, U. of the Philippines, 1987)

M. Mora: 'The Sounding Pantheon of Nature', *AcM*, lix (1987), 187–212

A. Nicolas: *Ritual Transformations and Music Parameters: a Study of Selected Headhunting Rites in Southern Cordillera, Northern Luzon* (thesis, U. of the Philippines, 1987)

J. Maceda: disc notes, *Kulintang and Kudyapiq: Gong Ensemble and Two-Stringed Lute among the Magindanaon in Mindanao, Philippines*, U. of the Philippines UPCM-LP (1989)

E. Rivera Mirano: *Subli, isang sawau sa apat na tinig* [*Subli*, one dance in four voices] (Manila, 1989)

J. Maceda: 'In Search of Sources of Hemitonic and Anhemitonic Scales in Southeast Asia', *AcM*, lxii/2–3 (1990), 192–223

N. Revel-MacDonald and J. Maceda: disc notes, *Philippines: musique des hautes terres Palawan*, Chant du Monde LDX 274865 (1992)

M. Mora: 'The Last Kiss and the Return after Murder: a Case Study of Meaning and Context in Instrumental Performance among the T'boli (Philippines)', *Anthropological Forum*, vi/3 (1992), 385–94

Asian Music, xxvii/2 (1996), 1–148 [Kulintang/Kolingtang issue, ed. M. Hatch]

J. Maceda: 'Aspects of Research on Gongs and Gong-Related Instruments in Asia', *Themes and Variations. Writings on Music in Honour of Rulan Chao Pian*, ed. B. Yung and J.S.C. Lau (Cambridge, MA, 1994), 278–89

E. Rivera Mirano: *Ang mga Tradisyonal na Musikang Pantinig sa Lumang Bauan, Batangas* (Manila, 1997)

J. Maceda: *Bamboo and Gongs: a Panorama of Philippine Musical Instruments* (Quezon City, forthcoming)

J. Maceda: 'Upland Peoples of the Philippines', *Garland Encyclopaedia of Music* (forthcoming) (iv)

WESTERN ART MUSIC

F.R. Hernandez: *Our Outstanding Filipino Composers* (Manila, n.d.)

F.A. Ylagan: *Tagalog Popular and Folk Songs as a Reflection of Tagalog Life and Culture* (diss., U. of the Philippines, 1934)

E.M. Pajaro: *Philippine Symphony* (diss., U. of Rochester, NY, 1953)

E.A. Manuel: *Dictionary of Philippine Biography* (Quezon City, 1955–70)

C.J. Astraquillo: *A Study and Evaluation of Vocal Art Music in the Philippines during the First Half of the 20th Century* (diss., Indiana U., 1963)

A. Faurot: *Culture Currents of the World: an Introduction to Art and Music for Filipino Students* (Dumaguete City, 1967)

A.J. Molina: *Music of the Philippines* (Manila, 1967)

R. Bañas y Castillo: *Filipino Music and Theater* (Quezon City, 1969/R)

M.B. Bautista and others: *Beautiful Philippines in Panoramic Music* (Manila, 1969)

P. Brooks: 'Manila's New Cultural Center', *Art in America*, lvii (1969), 140–42

F.P. de Leon: 'Poetry, Music and Social Consciousness', *Philippine Studies*, xvii (1969), 266–82

H.F. Samson: *Contemporary Filipino Composers: Biographical Interviews* (Quezon City, 1976)

A. Roces, ed.: *Filipino Heritage: the Making of a Nation* (Manila, 1977–8)

L.R. Kasilag, ed.: *The League of Filipino Composers: 1989 Directory and Catalogue of Selected Works* (Manila, 1989)

N.G. Tiongson, ed.: *Tuklas Sining: Essays on Philippine Arts* (Manila, 1991)

R.P. Santos and C.C. Dioquino, eds.: *CCP Encyclopedia of Art*, vi: Philippine Music (Manila, 1994)

POPULAR MUSIC

Philippine Panorama (4 Dec 1977) [Manila Sound issue]

T.G. Maceda: 'Pinoy Pop', *Cultural Center of the Philippines Encyclopedia of Philippine Art*, vi, ed. N.G. Tiongson (Manila, 1994), 107–13

R.P. Santos: 'The American Colonial and Contemporary Traditions', *Cultural Center of the Philippines Encyclopedia of Philippine Art*, vi, ed. N.G. Tiongson (Manila, 1994), 46–69

D.G. Besa: *A Summary Report on the Cultural Situation in the Philippines: Music* (Manila, 1997) [The Japan Foundation Manila Office]

J. and A. Baes: 'East–West Synthesis or Cultural Hegemony in Philippine Popular Music' *Perfect Beat*, iv/1 (1998), 47–55

V. Dance

1. Cultural and historical background. 2. Indigenous traditions. 3. Muslim traditions. 4. Christian and lowland Filipino traditions.

1. CULTURAL AND HISTORICAL BACKGROUND.   The many indigenous dances of the Philippine archipelago have varied origins. Dances derived from South-east Asia are related to social life and/or religious rites, wine-drinking festivities, fighting, celebrations of pacts, victories, weddings, births, deaths and funerals. Certain dances are performed to conciliate gods or spirits, or to beg them to drive away human illness or crop disease, increase the rice harvest or mark certain occasions (e.g. tilling the soil or harvesting sugar cane and rice). Philippine dances are remarkable for their wide diversity: they include dances during rain-calling ceremonies (among the Bontok), fish dances (Badjao and Tausug), a ritual dance for a good fish catch (Badjao), princess and slave dances (Maranao), dances for royalty, nobility and commoners (Davao), a torture dance, a comic honey-gathering dance and a potato-thief dance (Negrito), a spider-game dance (Tagbanwa), various animal and bird dances, dances associated with weddings, funerals and sacrifices, as well as hunting, mock duel and mock fight dances.

Early Spanish writers on Philippine dances include Antonio Pigafetta (1491–c1535) and the Jesuits Pedro Chirino (1557–1635) and Francisco Colin (d 1660). Chirino related that the people in Mindanao made offerings to idols in their homes; the Tagalog-speakers called their priests or priestesses *katalonan*, and the Visayans, *babailan*. These priests danced to the sound of a bell in sacrificial offerings in private houses, especially where there was sickness. Colin described dances he saw:

The banquet was interrupted with local music, in which one or two persons sing and the rest respond. Their dances generally go with the beating of the bells, which seem of hollow metal sound. The beating is shrill and rapid in a war dance, but with measured variations which verily elevates one or puts him in suspense. The hands generally hold a towel or a spear or shield, and with the one or the other make their rhythmic movements, which are full of meaning. At other times, with empty hands, movements are made corresponding with those of the feet – now slow, now fast, now forward, now backwards, now together, now separately, but always with such grace and vivacity that they have not been judged as undignified to add solemnity to our Christian festivities. The children dance and sing with no less ability than the grown-ups.

2. INDIGENOUS TRADITIONS.   Dances of isolated groups, having been least subject to change, are among the most interesting in the Philippines. The vigorous and mimetic dances of groups such as the Negrito and the Batak require agility and endurance. Negrito dances are accompanied by the drum or guitar, Batak dances by gongs and drums, or by rhythms beaten out on a long percussion log. In trance dances, performed mostly by women among the Tagbanwa and other groups, the shaman claims communication with spirits and possession by one or more of them.

The colourful dances of the Bontok, Ifugao, Benguet, Apayao and Kalingga tribes of the mountain province of Luzon are performed during large celebrations called *peshit* and *kañao*. A leader and several other men dancing in rhythmic unison form twisting lines, spirals, circles and serpentine patterns, each man beating a gong. Dance steps are usually earth-bound and include shuffling feet, flexing toes, light skips, mincing, cutting steps and low hops and jumps. Hands are held either with closed fists, or with the thumb out and fingers held together, or loosely. Some dances are accompanied by song and speech. The tempo usually gets faster and faster as the dance proceeds.

Dances of the Ifugao include the *dinnyya* (festival dance), wedding dance and the *bangibang* (war or funeral dance); of the Bontok, the *takik* (flirtation or wedding dance) and the *pattong* (war dance); of the Kalingga, the pot dance, where women pile seven pots on their heads, and a wedding dance; of the Benguet region, the *tayaw*, the offering of sacrificial pigs by a priestess to the god Kabuniyan, and the *tchungas*, a victory dance over ghosts of slain enemies. With the advance of westernization, some of these dances, especially the trance dances of the shamans, are increasingly difficult to view.

Instruments of the various tribes include gongs of varying timbres, drums, metal sticks beaten together, and the *takik*, a piece of iron hit with stone.

3. MUSLIM TRADITIONS.   Muslim Filipinos, possessed of legendary courage, withstood repeated Spanish attempts at conquest and subjugation, and the arts of attack and self-defence (*silat*, *bersilat*) are celebrated in some of their men's dances. Although their culture has been receptive to Arab influence as well as Chinese, Hindu and Javanese, it has retained its individuality. The women's dances are characterized by inner intensity and absorption, mysticism, a languid grace, much use of the upper torso, nuance of facial expression, flowing arm movements (the fingers sometimes held close and stiff, sometimes circling), the flexed elbow, the shifting of body weight from one bent and turned-out knee to the other, the use of *singuel* (metal anklets/bells) and the expert manipulation of fans. In Moroland dances improvisation is allowed, and the dancers perform according to their mood. Contrapuntal movements are sometimes used; the feet may follow a vigorous rhythm while head, arm and hand movements are languid, leisurely and smooth.

Among Muslim Filipinos the better-known dances are the Tausug *pangalay* (wedding dance), the *sua–sua* ('orange tree', a courtship dance) and the *kandiñgan* (a wedding dance whose name may derive from *gandangan*, the two-headed cylindrical drum used to accompany it), the fish dances of the Yakan and the *sagayan* (war dance) and *kazaduratan* (women's dance) of the Maranao. The *ka-singkil* (royal fan dance) of the Maranao is performed between four or more criss-crossed bamboo poles.

Instruments for such dances include *agung* (gongs), *kulintangan* (gong-chimes), bamboo xylophones and drums.

4. CHRISTIAN AND LOWLAND FILIPINO TRADITIONS.   In their zeal to promote Christianity the Spaniards destroyed indigenous and Hindu images and forbade native ceremonies and rituals. Dances such as the jota and habanera were introduced and adapted; gradually a new style evolved, which was softer, more rounded and gracious in the new Castilian manner. The costumes took on elements of Spanish dress, and the fan was used to attract attention subtly, or to hide a modest blush. Percussion no longer dominated the music, and the native *kudyapiq* (two-string lute) gave way to the Spanish guitar. Sentimentality was introduced in sad interludes between lively moments, as in the *jota moncadeña* and the *purpuri* (potpourri). Modified versions of balancing dances of Asian origin and of indigenous wine-offering dances appeared in the *pandango sa ilaw* ('dance with oil lamps' from Mindoro),

binasuan and *abaruray*. Such 'bird dances' as the *sinalampati* (dove), *pabo* (turkey) and *itik* (duck) evolved. Waltz, polka, mazurka, *paso doble* and other ballroom steps were paraphrased and sometimes used at random, as in *bailes de ayer* ('dances of yesteryear', a quadrille from Tarlac Province), *polkabal* (polka-waltz), *polka sala* (ballroom polka) and *jotabal* (jota-waltz).

The bamboo-pole dance (also found in Thailand, Laos and India) came to be danced in slow triple time. Mock war dances (*maglalatik*, *magbabao*) and mock duel dances (*palo-palo*) between Moors and Christians developed. Coconut shells were held instead of shields and swords, clicked together and against shells held by strings close to the body.

Dances arising among the Catholic Filipinos included the *subli*, or dance in honour of the Holy Cross, in which men danced in a bent-over position; the *bulaklakan*, a garland dance, performed in May; and the *putong*, in which an honoured person, sitting between two girls dressed as angels, was crowned. Childless women danced and sang at midnight in the Maytime procession of the *turumba* (in Pakil, Laguna) and at the fiesta of St Pascual Bailon (in Obando, Bulacan). The *salubong* involved the re-enactment of the meeting of the risen Christ and his mother. Dances of drunkenness (*binadyong*), quarrelling (*bakya*, *pukol*) and embarrassed bridegrooms (*pandang-pandang*) emerged.

In 1924 Jorge Bocobo, president of the University of the Philippines, created the University Committee on Philippine Folk Songs and Dances. A member of the committee, Francisca Reyes-Tolentino, wrote several books describing dances found during their fieldwork and initiated the teaching of these folkdances in Philippine schools. Further research into and recording of traditional dances has been continued by scholars and organizations, including the Philippine Folk Dance Society.

The pioneer Filipino choreographer Leonor Orosa (*b* 1917) produced the first Philippine folkloric ballet in 1941, *Trend: Return to Native*, followed by others such as *Vinta!* and *Filipinescas: Philippine Life, Legend and Lore in Dance*. Traditional dances are performed by travelling groups such as the Bayanihan Dance Company; they also continue to serve as a resource and inspiration for contemporary Philippine dance-theatre.

BIBLIOGRAPHY

P. Chirino: *Relación de las Yslas Filipinas y de lo que en ellas hàn travajado los Padres de la Compañia de Jesus* (Rome, 1604); ed. as *Relación de las Islas Filipinas/The Philippines in 1600* (Manila, 1969); Eng. trans. in Blair and Robertson, xii (1903–9)

F. Colin: *Labor evangelica, ministerios apostolicos de los obreros de la compania de Jesus, fundacion y progressos de su provincia en las Islas Filipinas* (Madrid, 1663)

A. Pigafetta: *Primo viaggio intorno al globo terracqueo ossia ragguaglio della navigazione alle Indie Orientali per la via d'occidente, fatta dal Cavaliere Antonio Pigafetta* (Milan, 1800); Eng. trans. in Blair and Robertson, xxxiii (1903–9)

E.H. Blair and J.A. Robertson, eds.: *The Philippine Islands 1493–1898*, xii, xxxiii (Cleveland, 1903–9)

S.Y. Orosa: *The Sulu Archipelago and its People* (Yonkers-on-Hudson, NY, 1923, enlarged 2/1970)

F.R. Tolentino: *Philippine National Dances* (New York, 1946)

H.O. Beyer and J.C. de Veyra: *Philippine Saga: a Pictorial History of the Archipelago since Time Began* (Manila, 1947)

L.A. Reid: 'A Guinaang Wedding Ceremony', *Philippine Sociological Review*, ix/3–4 (1961), 1–54

L.A. Reid: 'Ritual and Ceremony in Mountain Province: Dancing and Music', *Philippine Sociological Review*, ix/3–4 (1961), 55–82

H. de la Costa, ed.: *Readings in Philippine History* (Manila, 1965)

W.H. Scott: *Pre-Hispanic Source Materials for the Study of Philippine History* (Manila, 1968)

L.O. Goquingco: *The Dances of the Emerald Isles: a Great Philippine Heritage* (Quezon City, 1980)

N.G. Tiongson: *Tuklas Sining: Essays on the Philippine Arts* (Manila, 1991)

M.Y. Orosa: *Philippines 2000: a Vision for the Nation* (Manila, 1995)

JOSÉ MACEDA (I, II), LUCRECIA R. KASILAG (III), DELLA G. BESA (IV), LEONOR OROSA GOQUINGCO (V)

Philippon. *See* BASIRON, PHILIPPE.

Philippot, Michel Paul (*b* Verzy, 2 Feb 1925; *d* Vincennes, 28 July 1996). French composer. Attracted at first to the study of science, he enrolled in Dandelot's harmony class at the Paris Conservatoire (1945–8) and discovered the composers of the Second Viennese School as a student of Leibowitz (1946–50). He joined ORTF in 1949, where he was successively a music producer (to 1959), assistant to Pierre Schaeffer in the Groupe de Recherches Musicales, then to Henri Barraud at France-Culture. Soon in charge of music programmes (1964–72), he became technical adviser to Radio France 1972–5, and later the Institut National de l'Audiovisual (1983–9). He taught musicology and aesthetics at the Universities of Paris I and Paris IV (1969–76), and composition at the Paris Conservatoire (1970–90). His pupils included Philippe Manoury, François Nicolas, Denis Cohen, Yves-Marie Pasquet and Nicolas Bacri. In 1976 he set up the music department at the Brazilian State University of São Paolo, which he directed until 1982.

Philippot's music was born of a controlling passion for rigour. Marked from the first by the discipline of dodecaphony (his First Piano Sonata is indebted to Schoenberg's Suite op.25), renouncing literary titles and even the resources of the human voice, Philippot's music is nonetheless not ungrateful to the ear. The austerity of his work in the 1950s yielded steadily to a fluidity which harks back to Debussy and to Schoenberg's Variations op.31. The limpidity of his orchestration is always at the service of an essentially contrapuntal way of thinking. His scores resemble a subtle play with mirrors, where the elements reflect one another, neglecting the notion of theme and development in favour of the principle of continuous variation and a balance of musical planes, lines and colours.

WORKS
(*selective list*)

Orch: Ov., chbr orch, 1949; Composition no.1, str, 1959; Composition no.2, str, pf, hp, 1974; Composition no.4, 1980; Carrés magiques, 1983; Conc., vn + va, orch, 1984

Chbr and solo inst: Variations, 10 insts, 1957; Transformations triangulaires, 12 insts, 1963; Composition no.1, vn, 1965; Org Sonata, 1971; Passacaille, 12 insts, 1973; Composition no.2, vn, 1975; Octet, cl, hn, bn, str qt, db, 1975; Composition no.3, vn, 1976; Str Qt no.1, 1976; Septet, 1977; Str Qt no.2, 1982; Quintet, fl, cl, vn, vc, pf, 1984; Str Qt no.3, 1985; Pf Qnt, 1986; Composition no.4, vn, 1988; Str Qt no.4, 1988; Ludus sonoritatis, 8 insts, 1989; Contrapunctus X, 10 insts, 1994; Méditation, 12 insts, 1994

Tape: Etude no.1, 1951; Etude no.2, 1957; Etude no.3, 1962

Pf: Sonata no.1, 1947; Sonata no.2, 1973; Composition no.4, 1975; Composition no.5, 1976; Composition no.6, 1977

Vocal: 4 mélodies (G. Apollinaire), S, pf, 1948

Incid music, film scores

Principal publishers: Boelke & Bomart, Billaudot, Salabert

WRITINGS

Liberté sous condition (Paris, 1954)
Igor Stravinsky (Paris, 1965)
La lucidité de René Leibowitz (Paris, 1973)
Diabelli diabolico (São Paulo, 1979)
Défense et illustration du langage musical (Paris, 1982)

GÉRARD CONDÉ

Philippus, Petrus. *See* PHILIPS, PETER.

Philippus de Caserta. *See* CASERTA, PHILIPPUS DE.

Philips (i). Dutch recording company. Taking advantage of the invention of the LP and of technological developments pioneered by its parent company Philips Gloeilampenfabrieken (especially the invention of the Musicassette and the CD), the Philips label gained a reputation for the high technical quality of its recordings of classical Western music. Its espousal of hitherto little-known repertories and commitment to ambitious multi-volume series and cycles had a profound impact on the tastes and listening habits of a broad public.

Philips Gloeilampenfabrieken, the electrical company based in Eindhoven, entered the record industry in 1929, when it started producing hardware for shellac (78 r.p.m.) discs. In 1946 Philips took over the Dutch arm of Decca and signed an agreement allowing it to distribute Decca material in Europe. It was not until 1950 that Philips entered the record business in its own right, when mainly at the instigation of the president, Frits Philips, Philips Phonographische Industrie (PPI) was established in Baarn, a village about 50 km from Amsterdam. This move was well-timed to take advantage of the recent invention of the LP. The pressing of LPs, which had started in a test factory at Doetinchem, continued in a newly built factory in Baarn, and before long the technical superiority of the pressings attracted a world-wide clientèle. In 1964 Philips consolidated its technical leadership by introducing the Musicassette, which replaced the open-reel tape for domestic use. The convenience and low price of the new format contributed to a massive growth in the recording industry which lasted until the recession of the late 1970s.

The first Philips recording – Tchaikovsky's Symphony no.4 and Grieg's *Peer Gynt*, with Willem van Otterloo conducting the Hague Residentie Orchestra – was made in 1950. Recording activities followed in other European countries and distribution deals were signed with companies in Europe and the USA: between 1951 and 1960, Philips issued recordings from the US-based CBS under licence in Europe, and from 1955 to 1968 Columbia Records distributed Philips material in the USA on the Epic label. Philips then found a new US partner in Mercury (ii), whose 'Living Presence' recording technology was introduced into Philips recordings.

Despite being in the technical vanguard and its advances in distribution, Philips had to establish its own identity by acquiring its own artists and repertory. An important step was taken in 1953, when a contract was signed with the Amsterdam Concertgebouw Orchestra, then conducted by Eduard van Beinum. The relationship with this orchestra continued after van Beinum's death in 1959 with Eugen Jochum and Bernard Haitink. Also important was the decision to engage Vittorio Negri to conduct series of neglected works by Vivaldi and Albinoni. The phenomenal success of I Musici's Vivaldi recordings, especially of *The Four Seasons*, not only boosted the company's prestige and commercial fortunes but also helped launch the Baroque revival. Another composer whose fortunes Philips helped to restore was Paganini, with the first recordings of the violin concertos nos.4 (Arthur Grumiaux, 1954) and 3 (Henryk Szeryng, 1969).

Throughout the late 1950s and the 60s Philips continued to build its classical music catalogue. Recordings were made with pianists Clara Haskil, Claudio Arrau and Ingrid Haebler, the singer Elly Ameling, the Quartetto Italiano and the Beaux Arts Trio, Raymond Leppard (with the English Chamber Orchestra) and the Concertgebouw (the complete symphonies of Bruckner and Mahler conducted by Haitink). A relationship with the Bayreuth Festival was established leading to Karl Böhm's live recording of the *Ring* (released 1966–7) and bearing its finest fruit in Pierre Boulez's recording of the same work (released on CD audio and video).

The expansion of the Philips label depended on light and popular as well as classical repertory, including film music. The first LP to sell over one million copies was the original cast recording of Lerner and Loewe's *My Fair Lady* (1956). In the 1960s the label established itself in the teenage market by signing contracts with several acts, including Pretty Things, Merseybeats, Walker Brothers, the Four Seasons, Wayne Fontana and the Mindbenders and (through a production agreement with the Island label) the Spencer Davis Group and Millie. In France, the Philips roster included the Swingle Singers, Jacques Brel, Nana Mouskouri and Johnny Hallyday, in the Netherlands, the Dutch Swing College Band, and in Germany, Caterina Valente and Esther and Abi Ofarim. In the UK, Philips also issued popular recordings on the Fontana and Phonogram labels from Winifred Attwell, Dusty Springfield, Shirley Bassey and others. In addition, Philips entered into marketing or distribution deals with labels such as Immediate, Planet, Page One, and established the label Vertigo as an outlet for progressive groups such as Black Sabbath and Status Quo. Although Philips ceased to issue popular music in the late 1980s, film was an important and continued source of revenue from 1959, when the soundtrack of the film of *Porgy and Bess* was released. Other successes have included *Saturday Night Fever* (1977), *Grease* (1978) and *Shine* (1997).

Alongside its classical and popular activities, Philips took account of the commercial potential of the broader international market. In Nigeria in the mid-1950s, for example, Philips issued modern dance music, including *Highlife* (later Afrobeat), *jújú* and other Muslim styles for the local market, while the Spanish offices issued much flamenco, such as the 1966 recordings of Manitas de Plata. The company's work in ethnographic recordings, if overshadowed by its other activities, provided an important resource for the study and enjoyment of folk and traditional musics from around the world. One significant contribution was its participation in the UNESCO Collection of Traditional Music, devoted to documenting the musics of the world. Begun by Alain Daniélou and Paul Collaer in 1961 in collaboration with the International Music Council, this scholarly collection was published in several series through the 1970s and 80s by Bärenreiter Musicaphon, Odeon-EMI and Phonogram on the Philips label. Of a less scholarly nature was the series 'Song and Sound the World Around', issued in the 1960s and 70s.

In 1972 Polygram was formed as a holding company for Philips (PPI) and Deutsche Grammophon; in 1962 Philips Gloeilampenfabrieken had acquired a 50% stake in Deutsche Grammophon and Siemens a 50% stake in Philips (PPI). At the same time, PPI changed its name to Phonogram International but continued to trade under the Philips label. The new Polygram company acquired the American labels Mercury and Casablanca and later purchased A&M, Island and Motown. In 1979 Polygram acquired Decca, so becoming the most powerful music group in the world. Within the Polygram umbrella the three classical-music labels, Decca, Deutsche Grammophon and Philips, retained their independence with regard to artists and repertory.

In the 1970s, after Erik Smith took over as head of A&R, the Philips label embarked on an ambitious programme to record operas, a repertory that until then it had neglected. In 1971 Jessye Norman made her recording début as the Countess in *Le nozze di Figaro*, the start of a long association with the label. Apart from Mozart, operas by Verdi (early operas), Rossini, Haydn (with Antal Dorati conducting) and Tippett were recorded; Tippett was championed by Colin Davis, who also recorded a series of operas and large-scale works by Berlioz. Other artists recruited in the 1970s included Neville Marriner (with the Academy of St Martin-in-the-Fields), Alfred Brendel and José Carreras.

In 1979 the economic slow-down caught up with the Philips label and sales dropped. However, the invention by Philips Gloeilampenfabrieken of the CD, developed in collaboration with Sony and launched in 1982–3, revived the company's fortunes. On the crest of the CD boom of the 1980s, the Philips label (from 1983 under a new name, Philips Classics Productions) continued to recruit artists, including Mitsuko Uchida, Viktoria Mullova, Gidon Kremer, Riccardo Muti, Frans Brüggen and John Eliot Gardiner. The relationship with Gardiner and Brüggen signalled a new interest in early music and the use of period instruments, confirmed when Philips engaged Philip Pickett to make recordings of English stage music and acquired (in 1996) the Gimmell label, the vehicle for Peter Phillips's recordings of Renaissance choral music with the Tallis Scholars. Further, Valery Gergiev was contracted to conduct the Kirov company in Russian opera. There was a move towards 20th-century music, possibly motivated by falling sales of the standard 18th- and 19th-century favourites. The early 1990s also saw an interest in 'crossover' (fusing classical with jazz, pop or light music), represented most clearly by the joint venture with Philip Glass's label Point Music and by several recordings of 'cult', new age and world music. This diversification was increasingly adopted as a survival strategy at a time, in the mid-1990s, when sales of CDs continued to fall. CD Video had not proved commercially viable and attempts to develop a Digital Compact Cassette (DCC) came to nothing.

The Philips label attempted to adapt to these new realities, but in 1998 it sold its majority share in Polygram to Seagram, breaking the link with Philips Gloeilampenfabrieken. A new company, Universal Classics, was formed from Philips, Decca and Deutsche Grammophon. In 1999 Philips and Decca merged their operations, bringing Philips's location in the Netherlands to an end.

Along with other CD companies, Philips benefited commercially from reissues of earlier analogue recordings in digital form. What distinguished the Philips label was the scale and ambition of these reissues, many of them multi-volume box sets. These include the Wagner Edition, an edition of recordings of the pianist Sviatoslav Richter and, most importantly, the Complete Mozart Edition (master-minded by Erik Smith), issued in 1990–91 to commemorate Mozart's bicentenary. In 1998 an even larger project, Great Pianists of the 20th Century, was begun, involving an unprecedented collaboration with recording companies both within and outside the Polygram group.

BIBLIOGRAPHY

Grove6 ([Gramophone], B. Bicknell and R. Philip; also Sound Recording Transmission and Reproduction', D.E.L. Shorter and J. Berwick)

M. Ruppli: The Mercury Labels: a Discography (Westport, CT, and London, 1993)

JAMES CHATER (with DAVE LAING and JANET TOPP FARGION)

Philips [Philippes, Phillips], **Mr (ii).** Name under which PHILIP VAN WILDER is often found in English manuscripts.

Philips [Phillipps, Phillips], **Peter** [Philippe, Pierre; Philippi, Pietro; Philippus, Petrus] (b ?London, 1560–61; d Brussels, 1628). English composer and organist. He spent his maturity in the Spanish Netherlands, and for this reason has often been regarded as a member of the Flemish school; yet on the title-pages of all his publications he was at pains to describe himself as 'Inglese' or 'Anglo'. Apart from Byrd he was the most published English composer of his time.

1. LIFE.   His date of birth is inferred solely from his certificate of residence in Brussels, dated 4 August 1597, which gives his age as 36. The first known reference to him is as a choirboy at St Paul's Cathedral, London, in 1574. There is evidence that he was later a pupil of Byrd. His earliest known composition, a keyboard pavan in the Fitzwilliam Virginal Book (GB-Cfm Mus.32.G.29), is dated 1580, with the superscription 'The first [that] ever Phi[lips] mad[e]'. The piece was later extremely popular and was arranged and transformed by other musicians. In 1582 Philips was mentioned in the will of Sebastian Westcote, almoner of St Paul's. Westcote had been in charge of the music and choirboys, being appointed during the reign of Queen Mary. A stubborn adherent to Roman Catholicism and frequently in trouble with the authorities, Westcote seems to have enjoyed a measure of royal protection. He left in his will £5 each to four boys 'now remayninge in my howse' and 'to Peter Phillipps likewise remayninge withe me five poundes thirtene shillings fower pence'. Early in August 1582, shortly after his master's death, Philips fled England 'pour la foy Catholique' as the Brussels certificate attests. He stopped on 18 August for a few days at the English College in Douai. On 20 October he arrived in Rome and was received at the English College there. The entry in the Pilgrims' Book at the college reads: 'Petrus Philippus Anglus diocesis [blank space] receptus fuit hospitio 20 Octob: 1582.ad.12.dies'.

   The college at this time received many such refugees and was in hard straits financially. But it had a powerful protector in Cardinal Alessandro Farnese, who became Philips's patron for the next three years. Philips continued at the same time to act as organist for the college, and in 1585 the appointment of Felice Anerio as maestro di cappella seems to have confirmed the direction of the young man's studies. He later included music by Anerio and Palestrina in his own publications, and his style always remained deeply indebted to the conservative Roman tradition.

   On 22 February 1585 Lord Thomas Paget, a prominent English Roman Catholic refugee, arrived at the college accompanied by two servants. Philips entered his service and departed with him on 19 March. They travelled together for the next five years, visiting Genoa (September 1585), Madrid (October 1585) and France (September 1586). 1587 and the first half of 1588 were spent in Paris, except for a brief journey to Brussels in March 1588. In June they went to Antwerp shortly before the sailing of the Spanish Armada, and in February 1589 settled in Brussels. Early in 1590 Paget died, and Philips may have written the Pavan and Galliard Pagget in his memory, though this pair is undated in the Fitzwilliam Virginal Book; a much later and peripheral source (S-Uu Mus.408), however, suggests that the dedication may have been to Lord Thomas's younger brother Charles, a notorious double agent.

   Philips settled in Antwerp in 1591 and 'maintcyncd him self by teaching of children of the virginals, being very cunning thereon'. On 26 May of the same year he married Cornelia de Mompere in the cathedral. His wife died in July 1592, two months after the birth of their daughter, Leonora, who was baptized on 7 June of that year. Leonora's godfather was Cornelis Pruym, a notable patron of music who had links with Hubert Waelrant, Emanuel Adriaensen and Cornelis Verdonck, whom he employed for 20 years. Through such connections Philips was assured of an entrée into the musical and artistic life of Antwerp, witnessed by the selection of the Flemish composers represented in his first publication, Melodia olympica, issued by Phalèse in 1591. It is a large anthology of Italian madrigals edited by Philips, and including four of his own madrigals. The selection is conservative, suitable for cultivated amateurs, and reflects the styles that most influenced Philips: Marenzio is represented by five madrigals, G.M. Nanino by four and Palestrina and Verdonck by three each. Philips dedicated the work to Giulio Balbani, a prominent Italian banker.

   In 1593 Philips visited Amsterdam 'to sie and heare an excellent man of his faculties'. This was no doubt Sweelinck, who composed a complimentary set of variations on Philips's pavan of 1580 and was held in high regard by Philips. On his return journey in September, Philips fell ill, and stayed for three weeks at Middelburg 'conversant with such as delighted in musicq'. An Englishman, Roger Walton, denounced him to the Dutch authorities as having been involved in a plot against the life of Queen Elizabeth. Philips, Walton and another accused, Robert Pooley, were all arrested and taken to The Hague for interrogation and to await reports from London. Inquiries were made with the help of the acting English ambassador, George Gilpin. While in prison Philips composed the Pavan and Galliard Dolorosa (the manuscript, D-Bsb, Mus.40316, bears the inscription 'composta in prigione'). The version in the Fitzwilliam Virginal Book is dedicated to 'Treg.', i.e. a member of the Tregian family: Francis Tregian the younger was the compiler of this collection and copied much of Philips's other music (e.g. in GB-Lbl Eg.3665). The inquiries exonerated Philips; he was released and able to return to Antwerp before Christmas.

   Philips's first book of six-part madrigals was published in 1596. The dedication, dated 8 January, was to Alessandro di Giunta, a member of the Florentine family of printers and booksellers, resident in Antwerp. The texts he chose, like those for his other two collections, are almost all of the most frivolously amorous type of poesia *per musica*. The most notable poet represented is Guarini, and the anonymous verse *Amor di propria man*, a scarcely concealed description of love-making, is one of the many imitations of Guarini's *Tirsi morir volea*. Marenzio's setting of *Tirsi* had become famous; Philips made a keyboard version of it and followed its general design in his own madrigal. By now Philips was becoming increasingly well known, and single works of his appeared in many printed collections over the next 40 years or so.

In 1597 the Archduke Albert admitted Philips as a member of his household, as attested in the certificate of residence in Brussels, dated 4 August. Philips's signature, 'Pier Philippe', on this document is the only surviving authentic one (see facsimile in MB, xxix, p.xxii). In 1598 Phalèse published Philips's sole collection of eight-part madrigals. The title-page designates him as 'Organista del Serenissimo Alberto'; he retained his position as one of the three organists of the vice-regal chapel until his death. The dedicatee of the madrigals was the English Roman Catholic freebooter, Colonel William Stanley, and they had an immediate success, being reprinted in the following year.

According to his marriage contract, after the death of his wife and then his only child (Leonora died in December 1599) Philips had agreed to share his wife's inheritance with her brothers and sisters. The contract itself does not survive, but an orphan-master's document (*weesmeesters-document*) of 1601 describes its administration (see Spiessens). Philips was obliged to account for all receipts and expenditures from the date of his wife's death until the reading of the will, and to prepare an inventory and valuation of his house and its contents, including his music books. In the event, the debts owing proved to be greater than the value of the property, so the inheritance was refused. Philips still owed money to Anthony Chambers, an English cornett player at the Brussels court, to 'Sr. Junta' (probably Alessandro di Giunta) and to 'Sr. Orsuch' (probably Jean Orsucchi Bernardszoon, a merchant from Lucca who lived in Antwerp from 1597 to 1610).

Archduke Albert married Isabella of Spain on 18 April 1599 and thereafter they ruled as joint regents. The poor economic state of the Spanish Netherlands was exacerbated by the archduke's extravagance and the salaries of minor court employees, often in arrears, were constantly augmented by the practice of simony. Philips, however, was ordained a priest on 24 March 1609, and the entry in the Archief Aartsbisdom Mechelen (reg. 60, f. 142*v*) describing him as 'Petrus Philippi, beneficiatus nostrae diocesis' suggests that he had taken minor orders at some time beforehand. His subsequent series of prebendaries at Soignies, Tirlemont and Béthune were thus technically legitimate, though there is no evidence that he was ever resident at any of these places, nor that he even functioned as a priest.

Philips's first printed sacred compositions were three motets in the second and third parts of Herrer's anthology *Hortus musicalis* (RISM 1609[14-15]). One of these, *Vulnera manuum*, is a contrafactum of his madrigal, *Ditemi, O diva mia*, first published in *Melodia olympica*. In the following year Phalèse printed Philips's first major collection of sacred music, the 69 *Cantiones sacrae* for five voices, 'for the principal feasts of the whole year and the common of the saints'. The dedication was to the Virgin Mary, 'for the consolation and salvation of

Christian people, the confirmation and amplification of the Catholic, Apostolic and Roman faith, and the extirpation and confusion of Heresy and Heretics'. The motets are organized according to the liturgical calendar, unlike those of the later sets. In all his sacred collections Philips showed a marked propensity for strictly liturgical texts (particularly antiphons, Marian antiphons and responds). Most of these appear to be drawn from the breviary rather than direct from scripture, and he seldom set freely chosen texts such as psalm verses as earlier Renaissance composers did. Nothing could make his post-Tridentine, Counter-Reformation attitude more plain.

In 1613 two further sets were published, the 30 *Cantiones sacrae* for eight voices and a set of 31 two- and three-part motets with organ continuo, the *Gemmulae sacrae*. He dedicated the eight-voice motets to St Peter, and the *Gemmulae* to Pierre de Campis, a chaplain and singer of the Brussels royal chapel. Another set of two- and three-voice motets with continuo followed in 1616, the *Deliciae sacrae*, dedicated to Albert and Isabella. In the meantime his services as an organ player had been in demand. He had travelled to Malines in 1611 with others of the royal chapel to inspect the new organ there and to perform at the Easter services; he later personally approved Langhedul's restoration of the royal chapel organ in Brussels (30 December 1624). Philips's salary for four months in 1613, including travelling and living expenses, was about 305 florins. His fame was at its height in this second decade of the 17th century. His madrigal sets went through reprintings, the hydraulic engineer Salomon de Caus included some of his instrumental music in two treatises, and in 1615 the Valenciennes publisher Jean Vervliet (or perhaps the Jesuit, Guillaume Marci) invited him to contribute to a book called *Les rossignols spirituels* (RISM 1616[7]). This was a collection of adaptations of popular tunes with simple bass parts added by Philips, set to verses in French for the religious instruction of children. A counterblast to similar Protestant compilations, it also contains three four-part Latin pieces, one of which is an otherwise unknown *Hodie Maria virgo caelos ascendit* for three sopranos and tenor by Palestrina; perhaps Philips obtained it personally from the composer in his Roman days. *Les rossignols* went through four editions, the last appearing in 1647 without Philips's name.

During this period Philips enjoyed the presence of some illustrious colleagues in the royal chapel. In 1611, for instance, the chapel director was Géry Ghersem; other notables included Jan van Turnhout, and Philips's fellow organists Joachim Zacharias and Peeter Cornet. In 1613 an even more famous figure arrived – John Bull, who had fled England to avoid prosecution for adultery. Philips may possibly have met him on an earlier visit in 1601. The meeting of the two most internationally renowned English keyboard players of the day, both of the same generation, gives rise to fascinating speculation, but nothing is known of their mutual reactions.

Economic conditions at the court continued to be hard. Salaries were still often in arrears, and employees were sustained by irregular *ex gratia* payments; in August 1617, for instance, Philips received a gift of 250 florins, and on 13 October 1620 another of 300. On 25 January 1621 Philips exchanged his prebend of St Vincent for a perpetual chaplaincy in St Germain, Tirlemont. According to the title-page of his next publication, the *Litaniae*

Beatae Mariae Virginis (Antwerp, 1623), he also became canon of Béthune.

The Archduke Albert died in 1621, and on 12 March Philips headed the procession of chaplains of the royal chapel in the funeral cortège. An engraving of the procession by Corneille Galle appears in Jacques Francart's *Pompa funebris … Albertii Pii* (Brussels, 1623). Allegedly drawn from life, Philips appears as a tall, straight-backed figure with a lean face and a pointed beard, but so unfortunately do at least two of the other chaplains. This is his only known portrait (see illustration). His last publication came out in the year of his death, a monumental collection which includes his first published monodies, *Paradisus sacris cantionibus* (Antwerp, 1628). This comprises 106 motets for one, two and three voices, all with continuo. Like the *Gemmulae and Deliciae* they were among his most successful compositions, since each set was reprinted no fewer than three times.

The only record of Philips's death is in the contemporary diary of Dr John Southcote. Under a list of 'Dead Friends and Acquaintance' for the year 1628, Southcote entered: 'Peeter Philips Pr. Bruxelles'. No further information has come to light, and doubts regarding Southcote's testimony have been based solely on a misunderstanding of the publication dates of the *Paradisus*.

The *Paradisus* was printed for the third time in 1641, the last time any of Philips's music was printed until Hawkins's *General History* (London, 1776). He had been famous enough in his lifetime and his music spread as far afield as Lisbon and Stockholm. But it never penetrated south of the Alps, despite Henry Peacham's encomium in *The Compleat Gentleman* (London, 1622): 'Nor must I here forget our rare countryman, Peter Philips, organist to their *altezzas* at Brussels and now one of the greatest masters of music in Europe. He hath sent us over many excellent songs, as well motets as madrigals. He affecteth altogether the Italian vein'. Not until the late 19th century

Peter Philips leading the procession of chaplains at the funeral of Archduke Albert: engraving by Corneille Galle from Jacques Francart's 'Pompa funebris … Albertii Pii' (Brussels, 1623)

was there a real awakening of interest in his music. The publication of the Fitzwilliam Virginal Book established him as a major figure in the English keyboard school, and one of its editors, W.B. Squire, also published a few of the madrigals and motets. The work of R.R. Terry, who performed many of the motets at Westminster Cathedral in the early part of this century and published several of them, was also crucial in the re-establishment of Philips's music; since then a handful of his motets have remained in both Roman Catholic and Anglican repertories.

2. WORKS.   Like Byrd, Philips distinguished himself at whatever branch of music he tried his hand. No northern continental composer could compete in terms of versatility in keyboard, instrumental ensemble, secular and sacred vocal music, and in this Philips held to the English tradition. As Peacham said, however, his vocal music 'affecteth altogether the Italian vein', and few English traits are to be found in it.

His keyboard music is another matter. Much of it is fairly early, most of it was copied by Francis Tregian into the Fitzwilliam Virginal Book (1609–19) and many of the pieces have precise dates. The first piece, the pavan of 1580, has already been mentioned in view of its extraordinary popularity. Its cantus firmus-like last strain was imitated by many other composers, including Morley and Dowland, and a Dutch composer, Willem Swart, even turned it into a carol, *Wy engelen gret* (in *Den lusthof der nieuwe mysycke*, Amsterdam, 1603). The next dated piece, a 'fantasia' of 1582, is clearly an ornamented intabulation of an unidentified polyphonic vocal composition. The genre is rather un-English (only Farnaby appears to have cultivated it to any degree) so the piece may date from after Philips's arrival in Rome. It is the first of a series of such compositions in which he wove fantastic keyboard figuration around madrigals and chansons by Marenzio, Lassus and Striggio, one of his own madrigals (*Fece da voi*) and even (in 1603) Giulio Caccini's famous monody, *Amarilli*. His latest example seems to be the setting of Lassus's *Margott laborez* (dated 1605) where, typically, the original all but disappears in a welter of ornamentation, and the vivacious rhythm of the chanson is completely destroyed. Such pieces, immensely popular with continental keyboard players and lutenists, hold little appeal for modern musicians no longer familiar with the originals from which they stem. Much more immediately attractive are the idealized dance pieces in the English tradition, of which there are unfortunately only seven by Philips. Four of them, the Pavan and Galliard Dolorosa and the Pavan and Galliard Pagget, are masterpieces. In both pairs pavan and galliard use the same musical material and the Dolorosa is Philips's only extended essay in chromaticism; it was later recast as a lute piece (but not by Philips, who was no lutenist; see D. Lumsden: *Anthology of English Lute Music*, London, 1954, nos.9–10). So fine is the polyphonic balance within these two sets that they also exist in arrangements as splendid five-part ensemble pieces, probably by Philips himself.

Considering Philips's 30 years as a professional organist, his legacy in this genre is disappointing. Only one liturgical organ piece survives, a setting of the Pentecost sequence, *Veni Sancte Spiritus* (in *GB-Och* 89, where it is wrongly titled *Veni creator Spiritus*). The chant, in a strong triple rhythm, is in the bass, with Philips's usual virtuoso figuration above, but with a cadence and a pause at the end of every line. Curiously, Philips set all the verses; there is no provision for *alternatim* performance. One important 'abstract' fantasia has been preserved: that in the Fitzwilliam Virginal Book (no.84; no.88 in the same collection is evidently an intabulation of an as yet unidentified vocal model) is notable for its 39 numbered entries of a single subject (also used by Byrd and Cornet).

Of the ensemble music, a few pieces were published, but most remains in scattered manuscript sources, some of doubtful authenticity. The most important group is probably that in the Tregian anthologies (*GB-Lbl* Egerton 3665 and *US-NYp* Drexel 4302). The repertory divides into two main types: 'idealized' and 'practical' dance music. Especially fine in their polyphonic balance are the five-part arrangements of the Dolorosa and Pagget pavan and galliard pairs; indeed it is hard to say whether the ensemble or keyboard version came first. The rich six-part Passamezzo Pavan, on the other hand, is independent of Philips's 1592 setting for keyboard (Fitzwilliam Virginal Book no.76). Some of both types of dance pieces are arrangements of other composers' music, principally Cavalieri (*Aria del Gran Duca*), Augustine Bassano, Morley and Tregian himself. Peter Holman has plausibly suggested that most of this repertory was for violin rather than viol consort.

The heart of Philips's music undoubtedly lies in his madrigals and motets. The madrigals demonstrate his adherence to the Roman tradition. They show his complete mastery of this chosen style within its characteristic limits: an easy command of contrapuntal technique, a liking for suave harmonic progressions and a restrained attitude towards word-painting. *Nero manto vi cinge*, with its black notation, is an isolated instance of eye music. None of his later music suggests that he showed much interest in or understanding of the harmonic and declamatory experiments taking place in Ferrara, Mantua, Venice and Florence.

In the motets, Philips achieved a surprisingly wide range within the restrictions of his language. Some of the five-voice *Cantiones sacrae* may apparently date back to before 1591, since *Gaude Maria Virgo* is found in a slightly different version, ascribed to Thomas Morley, in an English manuscript of that date (see Pike, *ML*, 1969). So it is natural that some seem more old-fashioned than others. Some, like *Pater noster*, are set in a severe, archaic polyphonic style complete with a plainchant cantus firmus; *Viae Syon lugent* maintains a strict canon. Others are madrigalian in style, with vivid word-painting (sometimes more vivid than in the actual madrigals) and much use of purely chordal harmony (e.g. *O beatum et sacrosanctum*, *Tibi laus*). Philips seems particularly to have favoured respond texts, perhaps because they aided him in constructing a satisfactory musical design with the return of earlier material. Variation, in these circumstances, is usually restricted to the exchange of the two upper voice parts.

The eight-voice *Cantiones sacrae* of 1613 are nearly all for two choirs of equal voices. Again the Roman rather than the Venetian tradition asserts itself. More homophonically conceived than the five-part motets, they occasionally reach the heights of brilliant figuration (*Hodie nobis de caelo*) and sometimes even polyphonic intricacy (*Caecilia virgo*). The *Litaniae* of 1623, however, as far as one can tell from the incomplete state of the

surviving partbooks, are of an austere, one-note-per-syllable character.

Composition of the huge collection of 'few-voice' motets printed as the *Gemmulae*, *Deliciae* and *Paradisus* may possibly have been influenced by the diminishing number of capable singers available in the archducal chapel, or may be simply following an Italian fashion. The first two contain duets and trios, the third solos as well, all with basso continuo. Pike argued convincingly that some may be adaptations of fully choral works for four, or even as many as eight, voices. The continuo part consists of a left- and right-hand staff, which, while it is not in itself harmonically complete, often suggests imitative entries not in the voice parts. The style varies from writing that could have been taken straight out of a 16th-century motet (*O bone Jesu*, from the *Gemmulae*) to extravagantly florid passages (e.g. *Veni sponsa Christi* from *Deliciae* and *O fons vitae* from the *Paradisus*). Such *fioriture*, however, sometimes seem stiff and contrived by comparison with the better Italian composers and do not integrate well with the essentially simple harmonic idiom. Only once did Philips revert to the chromaticism of his youthful Pavan Dolorosa, and that was at the words 'tu humilitasti' in *Dominus Deus virtutum* (1616).

WORKS

Editions: *The Fitzwilliam Virginal Book*, ed. J.A. Fuller Maitland and W.B. Squire (Leipzig, 1894–9/*R*1963) [F]

P. Philips: Select Italian Madrigals, ed. J. Steele, MB, xxix (1970) [M]

Peter Philips: Fifteen Motets for Solo Voice and Continuo, ed. L. Pike (Newton Abbot, 1991) [P]

P. Philips: *Cantiones Sacrae Octonis Vocibus (1613)*, ed. J. Steele, MB, lxi (1992) [C]

P. Philips: *Cantiones Sacrae Quinis Vocibus (1612)*, ed. J. Steele (Dunedin, 1992) [S]

MOTETS

Cantiones sacrae, pro praecipuis festis totius anni et communi sanctorum, 5vv (Antwerp, 1612; 1617 with bc (org)) [1612]

Cantiones sacrae, 8vv (Antwerp, 1613; 2/1625 with bc (org)) [1613a]

Gemmulae sacrae, 2–3vv, bc (org) (Antwerp, 1613) [1613b]

Deliciae sacrae, 2–3vv, bc (org) (Antwerp, 1616⁶) [1616]

Paradisus sacris cantionibus consitus, 1–3vv, bc (org) (Antwerp, 1628) [1628]

Works in 1609¹⁴, 1609¹⁵, 1622², 1629²

Absterget Deus, 1v, 1628, P; Adjuva nos Deus, 5vv, 1612, S; Alma redemptoris mater, 5vv, 1612, S; Alma redemptoris mater, 8vv, 1613a, C; Anima Christi, 2vv (CC), 1628; Anima Christi, 2vv (CT), 1628; Apparuerunt apostolis, 2vv, 1628; Ascendit Deus, 2vv, 1613b; Ascendit Deus, 5vv, 1612; Assumpsit Jesu, 3vv, 1628, ed. in Zercher; Assumpta est Maria, 5vv, 1612, S; Ave Domina, 2vv, 1628; Ave gratia plena, 5vv, 1612, S; Ave Jesu Christe, 8vv, 1613a, C; Ave Maria gratia plena, 5vv, 1612, S; Ave regina caelorum, 5vv, 1612, S; Ave regina caelorum, 8vv, 1613a, C; Ave serenissima virgo Maria, 2vv, 1613b; Ave verum corpus Christi, 5vv, 1612, S; Ave verum corpus, natum de Maria virgine, 2vv, 1613b; Ave verum corpus, natum de Maria virgine, 3vv, 1628, ed. in Zercher; Ave virgo gloriosa, 2vv, 1628

Beata Agnes, 5vv, 1612, S; Beata Caecilia, 2vv, 1628; Beata Dei genitrix, 2vv (CT), 1628; Beata Dei genitrix, 2vv (CB), 1613b; Beata Dei genitrix, 8vv, 1613a, C; Beata es virgo Maria, 2vv, 1628; Beati estis, 8vv, 1613a, C; Beatus Laurentius, 5vv, 1612, S; Beatus vir qui inventus est, 3vv, 1628, ed. in Zercher; Beatus vir qui inventus est, 5vv, 1612, S; Beatus vir qui timet Dominum, 2vv, 1616; Benedic Domine, 3vv, 1613b; Benedicta sit Sancta Trinitas, 8vv, 1613a, C; Benedictus Deus noster, 8vv, 1613a, C; Benedictus Dominus, 8vv, 1613a, C

Caecilia virgo, 8vv, 1613a, C; Cantabant sancti canticum novum, 5vv, 1612, S; Cantantibus organis, 2vv, 1628; Cantantibus organis, 5vv, 1612, S; Cantate Domino, 2vv, 1613b; Cantemus Domino, 2vv, 1628; Caro mea vere est cibus, 2vv, 1616; Christus resurgens, 2vv, 1628; Christus resurgens, 5vv, 1612, S; Cibabit nos pane, 3vv, 1613b; Clamaverunt justi, 2vv, 1613b; Conceptio tua,

5vv, 1612, S; Confirma hoc Deus, 2vv, 1613b; Confirma hoc
Deus, 3vv (CCT), 1622²; Confirma hoc Deus, 3vv (CCB), 1613b;
Confitebor tibi, Domine, 1v, 1628, P; Confitebor tibi, Domine, 2vv
(CT), 1628; Confitebor tibi, Domine, 2vv (CB), 1616;
Congratulamini mihi omnes, 3vv, 1616; Corona aurea, 2vv (CT),
1628; Corona aurea, 2vv (CB), 1616; Corona aurea, 5vv, 1612, S;
Crux fidelis, 3vv, 1628, ed. in Zercher; Cum audisset, 2vv, 1613b;
Cum jucunditate, 5vv, 1612, S; Cum jucunditate, 8vv, 1613a, C
Descendit angelus Domini, 2vv, 1613b; Desiderium anima ejus, 1v,
1628, P; Deus canticum novum, 2vv, 1628; Deus in nomine, 2vv,
1628; Deus qui beatae scholasticae, 5vv, 1612, S; Deus qui beatam
Mariam, 5vv, 1612, S [simpler version in GB-Lbl Add.18936–9];
Disciplinam et scientiam, 5vv, 1612, S; Domine Deus meus, 5vv,
1612, S; Domine inclina caelos, 3vv, 1613b; Domine Jesu Christe,
2vv, 1613b; Domine ostende nobis, 2vv, 1628; Domine probasti
me, 1v, 1628, P; Domine quinque talenta, 2vv, 1616; Dominus
Deus virtutem, 2vv, 1616; Domus mea, 2vv, 1628
Ecce iste venit, 2vv, 1613b; Ecce panis angelorum, 3vv, 1616; Ecce
panis angelorum, 8vv, 1613a, C; Ecce sacerdos, 2vv, 1628; Ecce tu
pulchra es, 3vv, 1628, ed. in Zercher; Ecce tu pulchra, 8vv, 1613a,
C; Ecce vicit Leo, 5vv, 1613a, C; Ego sum panis vivus, 2vv, 1613b;
Ego sum panis vivus (2p. Et panis), 5vv, 1612, S; Elegerunt
apostoli, 5vv, 1612, S; Elegi abjectus esse, 5vv, 1612, S;
Emendemus in melius, 2vv, 1616; Exaltabo te Domine, 3vv,
1613b; Exultate justi in Domino, 3vv, 1628; Exurge Ignati, 3vv,
1628, ed. in Zercher; Exsurgens Maria, 8vv, 1613a, C
Factum est silentium, 3vv, 1628, ed. in Zercher; Factum est
silentium, 5vv, 1612, S; Factus est repente, 2vv, 1628; Felix
namque, 2vv, 1616; Fuit homo missus a Deo, 3vv, 1616; Gabriel
angelus, 2vv, 1628; Gabriel angelus, 3vv, 1616; Gabriel angelus,
5vv, 1612, S; Gaudeamus omnes in Domino, 2vv, 1628;
Gaudeamus omnes in Domino, 5vv, 1612, S; Gaudeamus omnes in
Domino, 8vv, 1613a, C; Gaude Maria virgo (2p. Virgo
prudentissima), 5vv, 1612, S (attrib. Morley in GB-Lbl
R.M.24.D.2; see Pike, ML, 1969); Gaudens gaudebo, 8vv, 1613a,
C; Gaudent in caelis, 3vv (CCB), 1616; Gaudent in caelis, 3vv
(CAT), 1628, ed. in Zercher; Gaudent in caelis, 5vv, 1612, S;
Gentes Philippus ducit, 3vv, 1628, ed. in Zercher; Gentes Philippus
ducit, 5vv, 1612, S; Gentes Philippus ducit, 8vv, 1613a, C;
Gloriosae virginis, 2vv, 1628
Haec est praeclarum, 2vv, 1628; Haec est virga, 2vv, 1628; Haec est
virgo sapiens, 2vv (CT), 1628; Haec est virgo sapiens, 2vv (CB),
1616; Hic est beatissimus, 2vv, 1628; Hic est praecursor dilectus,
3vv, 1616; Hic est vere martyr, 3vv, 1616; Hodie Beata Virgo
Maria, 5vv, 1612, S; Hodie concepta est, 8vv, 1613a, C; Hodie in
monte, 8vv, 1613a, C; Hodie nata est Beata Virgo Maria, 2vv,
1616; Hodie nobis, 2vv, 1628; Hodie nobis caelorum Rex, 2vv,
1616; Hodie nobis de caelo, 8vv, 1613a, C; Hodie Sanctus
Benedictus, 5vv, 1612, S; Hodie Symon Petrus, 3vv, 1616; Hodie
Symon Petrus, 5vv, 1612, S; Homo quidam, 2vv, 1613b
In illo tempore, 3vv (CCB) (i), 1613b; In illo tempore, 3vv (CCB) (ii),
1616; In mediis indicae, 3vv, 1628, ed. in Zercher; In splendenti
nube, 5vv, 1612, S; Inter vestibulum et altare, 2vv, 1616; Intuens
in caelum, 2vv, 1628; Inviolata intacta, 2vv, 1628; Iste cognovit
justitiam, 2vv (CT), 1628 (i); Iste cognovit justitiam, 2vv (CT),
1628 (ii); Iste est Joannes, 5vv, 1612, S; Iste est qui ante Deum,
5vv, 1612, S; Iste homo, 3vv, 1628, ed. in Zercher; Iste sanctus,
2vv, 1628; Iste sanctus pro lege Dei, 1v, 1628, P; Isti sunt qui
viventes, 2vv, 1628; Isti sunt qui viventes, 5vv, 1612, S; Isti sunt
triumphatores, 2vv, 1616; Isti sunt viri sancti, 2vv, 1628; Jubilate
Deo omnis terra, 8vv, 1613a, C
Laetamini cum Maria, 2vv, 1628; Laetatus sum, 2vv (CT), 1628;
Laetatus sum, 2vv (CB), 1616; Laudate pueri Dominum, 1v, 1628,
P; Loquebantur variis linguis, 5vv, 1612, S; Magi ab oriente, 6vv,
1609¹⁴; Maria Magdalena, 5vv, 1612, S; Maria virgo assumpta
est, 3vv, 1628, ed. in Zercher; Media vita in morte sumus, 5vv,
1612, S; Misericordias Domini, 2vv, 1628; Misi digitum meum,
5vv, 1612, S; Modo veniet dominator, 5vv, 1612, S; Mulieres
sedentes, 5vv, 1612, S; Nativitas tua, 2vv, 1613b; Nativitatem
beatae Mariae, 3vv, 1628, ed. in Zercher; Ne reminiscaris
Domine, 5vv, 1612, S; Ne timeas Maria, 2vv, 1628; Ne timeas
Maria, 5vv, 1612, S; Nisi quia Dominus erat in nobis, 2vv, 1613b
O admiranda, 2vv (CC), 1628; O admiranda, 2vv (CT), 1628; O
beata Maria, 2vv, 1628; O beatum et sacrosanctum diem, 5vv,
1612, S; O beatum Martinum, 5vv, 1612, S; O bone Jesu, 2vv
(CT) (i), 1613b; O bone Jesu, 2vv (CT) (ii), 1628; O crux ave, 2vv
(CB), 1628; O crux ave, 2vv, 1628; O crux splendidior, 5vv,
1612, S; O dilecte, 1v, 1628, P; O divini amoris immensitas, 1v,
1628, P; O doctor optime, 2vv, 1628; O Domine Jesu Christe, 2vv

(CB) (i), 1613b; O Domine Jesu Christe, 2vv (CB) (ii), 1613b; O
Domine Jesu Christe, 2vv (CB) (iii), 1616
O fons vitae, 2vv, 1628; O ignis qui semper luces, 2vv, 1628; O lux
beata Trinitas, 3vv, 1616; O Maria domina nostra, 1v, 1628, P; O
Maria mater et Joannes, 5vv, 1612, S; O Maria virgo dulcissima,
2vv, 1628; O memoriale, 2vv, 1628; O nomen Jesu, 5vv, 1612, S;
O panis candidissime, 2vv, 1628; O pastor aeternae, 8vv, 1613a,
C; O piissime Jesu, 3vv, 1628, ed. in Zercher; O pretiosum, 2vv,
1628
O quam bonus, 2vv, 1628; O quam mira sunt hac omnia, 1v, 1628,
P; O quam suavis, 2vv (CT) (i), 1613b; O quam suavis, 2vv (CT)
(ii), 1628; O quam suavis, 8vv, 1613a (i), C; O quam suavis, 8vv,
1613a (ii), C; O rex gloriae, 2vv, 1628; O sacrum convivium, 2vv
(CC), 1628; O sacrum convivium, 2vv (CT), 1613b; O sacrum
convivium, 3vv, 1613b; O salutaris hostia, 1v, 1628, P; O salutaris
hostia, 2vv (CC), 1628; O salutaris hostia, 2vv (CT), 1628; O
salutaris hostia, 2vv (CB), 1613 b; O salutaris hostia, 3vv, 1616; O
si quando videbo gaudium, 1v, 1628, P; O virum mirabilem, 2vv,
1613b; O virum mirabilem, 5vv, 1612, S
Panis angelicus, 3vv, 1616; Panis dulcissime, 2vv, 1613b; Panis
sancte, 2vv, 1613b; Panis sancte, panis vive, 8vv, 1613a, C;
Paratum cor meum, 3vv, 1628, ed. in Zercher; Pater noster, 5vv,
1612, S; Pauper sum ego, 8vv, 1613a, C; Puer qui natus est nobis,
3vv, 1616; Quae est ista quae ascendit, 8vv, 1613a, C; Quae est
ista quae processit, 1v, 1628, P; Quae est ista quae processit, 2vv
(CB) (i), 1616; Quae est ista quae processit, 2vv (CB) (ii), 1628;
Quae est ista quae processit, 5vv, 1612, S; Quanti mercenarii, 2vv,
1628 (after Palestrina); Qui manducat meam carnem, 2vv, 1616
(after F. Anerio); Quo progrederis, 2vv, 1628
Recordare Domine, 2vv, 1613b; Redemptor orbis, 4vv, 1629²;
Regina caeli laetare, 5vv, 1612, S; Regina caeli laetare, 8vv, 1613a,
C; Regnum mundi, 2vv, 1628; Rogo te dulcissime Jesu Christe,
5vv, 1612, S
Salvator mundi, 2vv, 1613b; Salve regina, 6vv, GB-Och 21 (score);
Salve regina, mater misericordiae, 5vv, 1612, S; Salve regina, vita
dulcedo, 8vv, 1613a, C; Salve salutaris victima, 2vv, 1613b; Salve
salutaris victima, 5vv, 1612, S; Salve sancte Pater, 3vv, 1616; Salve
virgo florens, 2vv, 1628; Sancta et immaculata, 2vv, 1628; Sancta
Maria, 2vv, 1628; Sancta Maria, 3vv, 1628, ed. in Zercher; Sancte
Paule apostole, 2vv, 1616; Sancti mei qui in carne, 5vv, 1612, S;
Sicut misit me vivens Pater, 3vv, 1616; Si quis vult venire, 2vv,
1628
Spem in alium, 2vv, 1616; Spiritus Sanctus, 2vv, 1628; Spiritus
Sanctus, 3vv, 1616; Stella caeli, 2vv, 1628; Stella quam viderunt
magi, 5vv, 1612, S; Sub altare Dei, 2vv, 1628; Sub tuum
praesidium, 1v, 1628, P; Sub tuum praesidium, 3vv, 1628, ed. in
Zercher; Surgens Jesus, 2vv, 1628; Surgens Jesus, 5vv, 1612, S;
Surge Petre, 5vv, 1612, S; Surge propera amica mea, 3vv, 1616;
Surrexit pastor bonus, 2vv, 1613b; Symon Petre antequam de
navi, 5vv, 1612, S
Tibi laus, tibi gloria, 2vv, 1613b; Tibi laus, tibi gloria, 5vv, 1612, S;
Tota pulchra es, 2vv, 1628; Tradent enim vos, 2vv, 1628; Tristitia
vestra, 5vv, 1612, S; Tu es pastor, 3vv, 1616; Tu es Petrus, 8vv,
1613a, C; Tu es vas electionis, 5vv, 1612, S
Veni dilecte mi, 2vv, 1616; Veni electa mea, 2vv, 1613b; Veni electa
mea, 3vv, 1616; Veni in hortum meum, 6vv, 1609¹⁴; Veni sponsa
Christi, 2vv, 1628; Veni sponsa Christi, 3vv, 1616; Veni sponsa
Christi, 5vv, 1612, S; Venite et videte, 2vv, 1628; Viae Syon
lugent, 5vv, 1612, S; Videntes stellam, 2vv, 1613b; Videntes
stellam, 3vv, 1622²; Virgo prudentissima, 2vv, 1628; Virgo
prudentissima [2p. of Gaude Maria virgo]; Vita dulcedo, 1v, 1628;
Vive Jesus, 5vv, 1629² (attrib. L. Caullier in 2/1648); Voce mea ad
Dominum, 2vv, 1616; Vulnera manuum (contrafactum of Ditemi,
O diva mia), 8vv, 1609¹⁵, 1613a, C

Litaniae Beatae Mariae Virginis, in ecclesia Loretana canisolitae, [1]
4vv, [4] 5vv, [3] 6vv, [1] 9vv, bc (org) (Antwerp, 1623)

Masses (? litanies) and psalms, some inc., now lost, listed in EitnerQ

ed.: Les rossignols spirituels (Valenciennes, 1616⁷)

MADRIGALS

Il primo libro de madrigali, 6vv (Antwerp, 1596) [1596]
Madrigali, 8vv (Antwerp, 1598) [1598]
Il secondo libro de madrigali, 6vv (Antwerp, 1603) [1603]

Works in 1591¹⁰, 1596⁸, 1596¹⁰, 1598¹⁵, 1601⁵

Amor che vuoi, 6vv, 1591¹⁰; Amor di propria man, 6vv, 1596, M;
Amor sei bei rubini, 4vv, 1591¹⁰; Apra la porta d'oro, 6vv, 1596;
Baciai ma che mi, 6vv, 1596; Baciai per haver vita, 6vv, 1596, M;

Cantai mentre dispiacqu'al mio bel sole, 6vv, 1596, M; Chi vuol vedere un bosco, 6vv, 1603, Chiesi un guardo, 6vv, 1603; Chi vi mira, 6vv, 1596, M; Come potrò, 8vv, 1598, M; Correa vezzosamente, 6vv, 1603, M; Deh ferma, 6vv, 1603, M; Di perle lagrimose, 6vv, 1596; Dispiegate, guancie amate, 8vv, 1598, M; Ditemi, O diva mia, 8vv, 1591¹⁰; Donna mi fugg'ogn'hora, 8vv, 1598

Echo figlia, 8vv, 1598; Era in acquario il sole, 6vv, 1603, M; Fece da voi partita, 6vv, 1596, M [see also KEYBOARD]; Filli leggiadra e bella, 8vv, 1598, Hor che dal sonno vinta, 8vv, 1598, M; Il dolce mormorio, 6vv, 1596, M; Io son ferito, 6vv, 1596; Lascian le fresche linfe, 6vv, 1596; Lasso, non è morir, 6vv, 1603, M; Madonna udite, 6vv, 1603; Mentre hor humile, 6vv, 1596, M; Nero manto vi cinge, 6vv, 1603; Non è ferro, 6vv, 1603 124; Non è, non è più cor, 6vv, 1603, M; Non più guerra, pietate, 8vv, 1598, M; Nov'herbe e vaghe fiori, 5vv, 1596¹⁰, M; O che dolce morire, 6vv, 1601⁵

Passando con pensier, 8vv, 1598, M; Perchè con tanto ardore, 6vv, 1603, M; Perchè non debbo, 8vv, 1596⁸; Piangea Fillide mia, 6vv, 1603; Poi che voi non volete, 6vv, 1596, M; Porta nel viso Aprile, 6vv, 1603; Questa che co' begl'occhi, 8vv, 1598, M; Questa mercè ch'amore, 6vv, 1603, M; Questa vinta mortale, 6vv, 1603, M; Qui sott'ombrosi mirti, 6vv, 1603, M; Scherza madonna e dice, 6vv, 1603, M; Se per gridar, 8vv, 1598; Si, me diceste, 6vv, 1596; Tanta ne' capei biondi, 6vv, 1603; Tocca la vista mia, 6vv, 1603, M; The nightingale, 5vv, 1598¹⁵; Ut re mi fa sol la, 6vv, 1596, M; Voi volete ch'io muoia, 4vv, 1591¹⁰, M

KEYBOARD
in GB-Cfm Mus.32.G.29 unless otherwise stated

Amarilli, 1603 (after G. Caccini); F i, 329
Benedicam Dominum, GB-Och 1113
Bon jour mon cueur, 1602 (after Lassus); F i, 317
Chi fara fede al cielo (after A. Striggio (i)), also in S. de Caus: *Les raisons des forces mouvantes*, i (Frankfurt, 1615/R), f.38v; F i, 312
Fantasia (Chi fara fede; after Striggio, another setting), *B-Lu* Mus.888; ed. in Archives des Maîtres de l'Orgue, x (Paris, 1910), 153
Fece da voi (after the madrigal in Il primo libro); F i, 288
Le rossignuol, 1595 (after Lassus); F i, 346
Margott laborez, 1605 (after Lassus); F i, 332
Tirsi [morir volea], Freno [Tirsi il desio], Cosi morirò (after Marenzio); F i, 280
Veni creator Spiritus, GB-Och 89 (actually Veni Sancte Spiritus)
Almande, Och 1003, 1113
Fantasia, 1582; F i, 354
Fantasia; F i, 335
Passamezzo Pavan and Galliard, 1592; F i, 299
Pavan and Galliard Dolorosa, 1593; F i, 321
Pavan and Galliard Pagget; F i, 291
Pavan, 1580; F i, 343
Galliard; F i, 351

OTHER INSTRUMENTAL

3 trios, in S. de Caus: *Institution harmonique*, ii (Frankfurt, 1615); ed. in Archives des Maîtres de l'Orgue, x (Paris, 1910), 169
Aria a 4, 1621¹⁹
Fuga a 4, pavan, *I-Tn* Giordano 7, Foà
Pavan and galliard, 1607²⁸
Pavan and Galliard Dolorosa, Pavan and Galliard Pa[get], pavan and galliard, 5 dances, 6 settings of dances by A. Bassano, Holborne, Morley, Galilei: *GB-Lbl* Eg.3665
Fantasia, pavan a 6, *Ob* Mus.Sch.E.437–42
Pavan Passamezzo, *Ob* Mus.Sch.E.437–42, *Och* 423–8 [called Deo gratias], *US-NYp* Drexel 4302; ed. in MB, ix (1955, 2/1962), 155
Pavan [1580] and galliard, in T. Morley: *The First Booke of Consort Lessons* (London, 1599); ed. S. Beck (New York, 1959)

BIBLIOGRAPHY

P. Bergmans: *L'organiste des archiducs Albert et Isabelle: Peter Philips* (Ghent, 1903)
A.G. Petti: 'New Light on Peter Philips', MMR, lxxxvii (1957), 58–64
L. Pike: '"Gaude Maria virgo": Morley or Philips?', ML, l (1969), 127–35
J. Steele: 'Calendar of the Life of Peter Philips': introduction to *Peter Philips: Select Italian Madrigals*, MB, xxix (1970), pp.xvi–xxi
L. Pike: 'Peter Philips' Les rossignols spirituels', The Consort, no.27 (1971), 50–63
L. Pike: 'The Performance of Triple Rhythms in Peter Philips' Vocal Music', The Consort, no.28 (1972), 88–105
L. Pike: 'The First English "Basso continuo" Publication' [*Gemmulae sacrae*], ML, liv (1973), 326–34
J.R. Zercher: *The Three-Voiced Motets of Paradisus Sacris Cantionibus by Peter Philips: an Edition with Commentary* (diss., U. of Missouri, Kansas City, 1983)
G. Spiessens: 'De Antwerpse Periode van Peter Philips ca 1561–1628', *Musica Antiqua*, vii (1990), 108–13
D. Charlier: 'Attribution d'une fantaisie du "Liber fratrum cruciferorum leodiensium"', RBM, xlvi (1992), 247–8
D.J. Smith: *The Instrumental Music of Peter Philips: its Sources, Dissemination and Style* (diss., U. of Oxford, 1994)
D.J. Smith: 'Further Light on Peter Philips', Annual Byrd Newsletter, iii (1997), 8–9

JOHN STEELE

Philips, Thomas. *See* PHELYPPIS, THOMAS.

Philip the Chancellor (*b* Paris, *c*1160–70; *d* Paris, ?26 Dec 1236). French theologian and Latin lyric poet. He was the illegitimate son of Philippe, Archdeacon of Paris (*d* 1184–5), and part of an aristocratic family from Nemours whose members included chamberlains to Louis VII and Philippe II Auguste, and bishops of Paris, Meaux, Noyon and Châlons. He studied theology and possibly canon law in Paris, became Archdeacon of Noyon between 1202 and 1211 and was made chancellor of Notre Dame in the early months of 1217, retaining both posts until his death. As chief overseer of education in Paris, Philip was active during a time of crisis and evolution within the city's schools, and his authority dwindled steadily as a result of conflicts with the university. He vigorously protested the election of William of Auvergne as Bishop of Paris, and defied him on the accumulation of ecclesiastical benefices in 1235. Although Philip is often portrayed as an enemy of the newly established mendicant orders, such claims have been exaggerated; he was even buried in a Franciscan house, and possibly donned the habit just before his death. He was afterwards vilified by the Dominican chronicler Thomas of Cantimpré in his *Bonum universale de apibus*, and lauded by the poet Henri d'Andeli, whose *Dit du Chancelier Philippe* fantastically recounts his last moments.

In addition to his influential *Summa de Bono* (1230s) and an unedited corpus of over 700 sermons (catalogued by Schneyer), Philip remains one of the most prolific of medieval lyric poets, with 83 texts ascribed to him in medieval sources and dozens of others suggested by modern scholars. His poetic style has been described as vitriolic in its rhetoric, virtuosic in its rhyming, word play and use of images, learned in its classical and biblical references, and prophetic in its appropriation of the voices of Christ, the Church, and other allegorical personae to admonish and condemn (see Dronke). Philip particularly favoured apostrophes to mankind (*Homo*), and the *altercatio*, or debate poem, where two or more personified contenders argue theological, moral or ethical controversies in the manner of the jeu parti and the *disputationes* of the Paris schools.

Although no conclusive evidence proves he was a composer, and though many of his songs are contrafacta or prosulas of pre-existent works, Philip was nonetheless closely attuned to the music of his day. Nearly all his poems include musical settings and these exploit the entire gamut of genres and styles available to Notre Dame composers. His conductus range from simple strophic songs to melismatic through-composed works which use the latest rhythmic and constructive devices. Several poems reveal contact with the composer Perotinus; indeed Philip texted his organa, conductus and discant clausula, thus furnishing some of the earliest examples of the medieval MOTET. The organum prosulas survive with single voices which can be recognized as parts of Perotinian organa; it is unclear whether they were intended to be performed monophonically, with all the voices of the organum, or with the tenor alone. Philip deserves consideration as one of the principal forces behind Notre Dame music. He is often confused with Philippe de Grève, a dean of Sens (*d* 1220), who left no known writings.

WORKS

Editions: *Notre Dame and Related Conductus: Opera omnia*, ed. G.A. Anderson (Henryville, PA, 1979–) [ND]
The Montpellier Codex, i–viii, ed. H. Tischler, RRMMA, ii–vii (1978–85) [MC]
The Earliest Motets (to circa 1270): a Complete Comparative Edition, ed. H. Tischler (New Haven, CT, 1982) [EM]
Secular Medieval Latin Song: an Anthology, ed. B. Gillingham (Ottawa, 1993) [SM]

A.[no.] – *number in Anderson, MMA, vi–vii (1972–3)*
F.[no.] – *number in Falck (1981)*
G.[no.] – *number in Gennrich (1957)*

MONOPHONIC CONDUCTUS
including sequences, hymns, French chansons and pieces without music

medieval attributions

Ad cor tuum revertere, A.K10, F.6; ND
Aristippe quamvis sero, A.K3, F.19; ND
Ave gloriosa virginum regina, A.K75, F.28; ND (sequence; French contrafacta)
Beata nobis gaudia reduxit, A.K44, F.41; ND (for the coronation of Louis VIII, 1223)
Beata viscera Marie virginis cuius, A.K14, F.42; ND (music by Perotinus; unlikely medieval attrib. Walter of Châtillon; French contrafacta)
Bonum est confidere in dominorum, A.K37, F.50; ND
Ceciderunt in preclaris (sequence)
Christus assistens pontiphex, A.K48, F.61 (for the installation of Philip's uncle Peter of Nemours as Bishop of Paris, 1208)
Crux de te volo conquere, A.K59, F.71; ND (unlikely medieval attribs. Jacopone da Todi and Bernard of Clairvaux)
Cum sit omnis caro fenum, A.L3, F.76; SM
Excutere de pulvere, A.K26, F.113; ND
Ex[s]urge dormis domine, A.K24, F.118; ND
Festa dies agitur, A.N16, F.121; ND (Latin rondeau)
Fontis in rivulum, A.K6, F.130; ND
Homo considera, A.K56, F.156; ND (French contrafacta)
Homo natus ad laborem et avis, A.L7, F.159; SM
Homo natus ad laborem tui status, A.K1, F.160; ND (possible confusion with 'Homo natus ad laborem et avis')
Homo qui semper moreris, A.K32, F.162; ND
Homo vide que pro te patior, A.K53, F.164; ND (unlikely medieval attrib. Bernard of Clairvaux)
In hoc ortus accidente, A.K5, F.174; ND
Inter membra singula, A.L2, F.186; SM
Li cuers se vait de l'oil, L.32.1, R.349 (Latin contrafactum of 'Quisquis cordis'; other French and Provençal contrafacta)
Luto carens et latere, A.F1, M6; F.200; ND (also 3vv version; Latin rondeau)
Nitimur in vetitum, A.K54, F.219; ND (French contrafacta)
O labilis sortis humane status, A.K30, F.234; ND
O mens cogita, A.K57, F.240; ND
Pater sancte dictus Lotarius, A.K61, F.267; ND (for the installation of Pope Innocent III, 1198)
Phebus per dyametrum (*PL-WRu* I.Q.102; text only, goliardic stanzas)
Que est ista que ascendit transiens (*US-BAw* 88; sequence)
Quid ultra tibi facere, A.K17, F.288; ND
Quisquis (or Si quis) cordis et oculi, A.K52, F.291; ND (French and Provençal contrafacta, including 'Li cuers se vait')
Quo vadis quo progrederis, A.K31, F.293; ND
Quomodo cantabimus, A.K25, F.296; ND
Rex et sacerdos prefuit, A.K49, F.308; ND (on a dispute between Pope Innocent III and Emperor Otto IV, 1209–10)

Si vis vera frui luce, A.K40, F.329; ND (sequence)
Sol est in meridie, A.N17, F.332; ND (Latin rondeau)
Sol oritur in sidere, A.K13, F.333; ND
Suspirat spiritus, A.L6, F.344; ND (French and Latin contrafacta, both monophonic and polyphonic)
Tempus adest gratie, A.M51, F.345; ND (Latin rondeau)
Thronus tuus Christe Jhesu (*US-BAw* 88; text only; sequence)
Vanitas vanitatum, A.K18, F.355; ND
Ve mundo a scandalis, A.K27, F.356; ND
Veni sancte spiritus spes, A.N19, F.363; ND (French contrafacta also employed as refrains in motets; Latin rondeau)
Venit Jhesus in propria, A.K42, F.365; ND (on the fall of Jerusalem, 1187)
Veritas equitas largitas, A.K62, F.375; ND (Latin lai; French and Provençal contrafacta; possible references to the reign of Louis IX under the regency of Blanche of Castile, 1226–36)
Veritas veritatum, A.K19, F.376; ND
Vide quo fastu rumperis, A.K11, F.381; ND
Vitia virtutibus, A.L4, F.388; SM

modern attributions

Adulari nesciens, A.K35, F.10; ND
Aque vive dat fluenta, A.K65, F.18; ND (part of a group with 'Terit Bernardus' and 'In paupertatis predio' in *I-Fl* Plut.29.1, fasc.10, after the central collection of Philip's works)
Aurelianis civitas, A.K60, F.25; ND (on the massacre of students in Orléans, 1236; found within a series of Philip's works in *Fl* Plut.29.1, fasc.10; textual correspondences with a sermon of his from 1230)
Clavus clavo retunditur, A.K51, F.64; ND (on the loss of the holy nail of St Denis, 1233)
Cum omne quod componitur, A.K59, F.74; ND
Dic homo cur abuteris (text only; also attrib. Bernard of Clairvaux)
Dogmatum falsas species, A.K55, F.97; ND
Homo cur degeneras, A.K68, F.157; ND
Homo cur properas, A.K69, F.158; ND
In paupertatis predio, A.K64, F.179; ND (part of a group with 'Terit Bernardus' and 'Aque vive dat fluenta' in *Fl* Plut.29.1, fasc.10, after the central collection of Philip's works)
In superna civitate (sequence; associated with 'Ceciderunt in preclaris')
Lignum vite querimus (sequence; text only)
O Christi longanimitas, A.Q99 (text only; also attrib. Bernard of Clairvaux; also found with incipit 'O mira Christi pietas')
O curas hominum, A.K21, F.231; ND
Post peccatum hominis (text only; goliardic stanzas)
Quod Iude murmuracio, A.L22, F.294; ND (*F-Pn* lat.15139, with Philip's 'Inter membra' and 'Agmina milicie')
Quomodo sunt oculi (text only)
Tuum Syon exilium (text only)
Terit Bernardus, A.K63, F.347; ND (part of a group with 'Aque vive dat fluenta' and 'In paupertatis predio' in *I-Fl* Plut.29.1, fasc.10, after the central collection of Philip's works)

POLYPHONIC CONDUCTUS
medieval attributions

Ave virgo virginum verbi, 3vv, A.F16, A.P44; F.39; ND
Centrum capit circulus, 2vv, A.J38, F.57; ND
Dic Christi veritas, 3vv, A.C3, F.94; ND (used for Philip's conductus prosulas 'Bulla fulminante' and 'Vesti nuptiali'; on the conflict between Innocent III and King Philippe II Auguste over Ingeborg of Denmark, 1198)
Gedeonis area, 3vv, A.15, F.143; ND
Luto carens et latere, 3vv, A.F1, A.M6; F.200; ND (also 1v version; Latin rondeau)
Mundus a mundicia, 3vv, A.F17, F.212; ND (possible Provençal contrafactum)
O Maria virginei flos, 3vv, A.E14, F.239; ND
Regis decus et regine, 2vv, A.J47, F.301; ND

modern attributions

Caput in caudam vertitur, 2vv, A.J3, F.54; ND (immediately before 2 works by Philip in *I-Fl* Plut.29.1, fasc.7)
Clavus pungens acumine, 2vv, A.J39, F.65; ND (on the loss of the holy nail of St Denis, 1233)
Consequens antecedente, 2vv, A.H2, F.68; ND
Deduc Syon uberrimas, 2vv, A.68, F.85; ND
Heu quo pregreditur, 2vv, A.J26, F.155; ND
Inflexu causuali verbum, A.P18; ND
Luget Rachel iterum, 2vv, A.J40, F.199; ND

Non livoris ex rancore, 3vv, A.F14, F.222; ND (between works by Philip in *Fl* Plut.29.1, fasc.6)

Quod promisit ab eterno, 2vv, A.G6, F.295; ND (cauda is texted)

Regnum dei vim patitur, 2vv, A.H33, F.302; ND

Relegentur ab area, 3vv, A.C6, F.304; ND (music possibly by Perotinus; cauda is texted)

ORGANUM PROSULAS
medieval attributions

Adesse festina/Adiuva me domine, 1v, A.A12, G.58; ND (music from the verse of Perotinus's organum Sederunt principes, 4vv; paired with 'De Stephani')

Associa tecum in patria/Sancte [Eligi], 1v, A.K80, F.22; ND (music from the organum Sancte Germane, 3vv, which has modern attrib. Perotinus; text indicates the prosula was intended for St Eligius, not Germanus; on the transfer of a relic of Eligius from Noyon to Paris, 1212)

De Stephani roseo sanguine/Sederunt, 1v, A.A11, G.57; ND (music from Perotinus's organum Sederunt principes, 4vv; paired with 'Adesse festina')

Homo cum mandato dato/Omnes, 1v, A.A10, G.3; ND (music from Perotinus's organum Viderunt omnes, 4vv; paired with 'Vide prophecie')

Vide prophecie/Viderunt, 1v, A.A9, G.2; ND (music from Perotinus's organum Viderunt omnes, 4vv; paired with 'Homo cum mandato')

CONDUCTUS PROSULAS
medieval attributions

Bulla fulminante, 1v, A.L5, F.53; SM (from Philip's conductus: 'Dic Christi veritas', music possibly by Perotinus; Latin contrafactum, 'Veste nuptiali')

Minor natu filius, 1v, A.K82, F.208; ND

Veste nuptiali, 1v, A.K81, F.377; ND (see 'Bulla fulminante')

modern attributions

Anima iuge lacrimas, 1v, A.K45, F.15; ND (strophes successively notated; can be combined to form 3-voice piece)

Crucifigat omnes, 3vv, A.D3, F.70; ND (call to the fifth Crusade, 1219–20; Latin contrafacta)

MOTETS
medieval attributions

Agmina milicie/Agmina, 3vv, G.532; EM (conductus motet; music possibly by Perotinus; French and Provençal contrafacta)

Homo quam sit pura/Latus, 3vv, G.231; EM (strophic conductus motet; Latin contrafactum 'Stupeat natura')

In omni fratre tuo/In seculum, 2vv, G.197; MC

In veritate comperi/Veritatem, 3vv, G.451; EM (conductus motet; questionable lost medieval attrib. Bishop William of Auvergne)

Lacqueus conteritur/Lacqueus contritus, 2vv, G.95; MC

Venditores labiorum/Eius [or Domino], 2vv, G.760; EM (double motet, combined with triplum 'O quam necessarium', G.759, probably by a different author)

modern attributions

Doce nos hodie/Docebit, 3vv, G.345; EM (conductus motet; possibly the work intended for *CZ-Pak* N.VIII, instead of the probably spurious 'Doce nos optime')

Et exaltavi plebis humilem/Et exaltavi, 3vv, G.517; EM (conductus motet; found before 'Agmina milicie' in *I-Fl* Plut.29.1, fasc.8; music has modern attrib. Perotinus)

Ex semine rose prodit spina/Ex semine Abrahe divino/Ex semine, 3vv, G.483/484; EM (double motet, both texts by Philip; music by Perotinus; French contrafacta)

Flos de spina rumpitur/Regnat, 3vv, G.437; EM (conductus motet; music has modern attrib. Perotinus)

Homo qui vigeas/Et gaudebit, 3vv, G.313; EM (conductus motet; music has modern attrib. Perotinus; French contrafacta)

Latex silice/Latus, 4vv, A.A2, F.190, G.228; EM (strophic conductus motet)

Manere vivere/Manere, 2vv, G.70; EM (Latin contrafactum; music has modern attrib. Perotinus)

Mens fidem seminat/In odorem, 2vv, G.495; EM (music has modern attrib. Perotinus; textual correspondences with Philip's *Summa de Bono*; French contrafacta)

Mors que stimulo/Mors morsu nata venenato/Mors, 3vv, G.255/254, MC (double motet; see 'Mors a primi'; Latin contrafactum)

Non orphanum te deseram/Et gaudebit, 2vv, G.322; EM (music has modern attrib. Perotinus; French contrafactum)

Nostrum est impletum/Nostrum, 3vv, G.216; EM (conductus motet; music has modern attrib. Perotinus; French contrafactum)

Velut stelle firmamenti/Et gaudebit, 3vv, G.315; EM (double motet with 'Ypocrite pseudopontifices'; the music has modern attrib. Perotinus; French and Latin contrafacta)

Ypocrite pseudopontifices (1v), G.316; EM (triplum of double motet, 3vv; surviving moteti include the modern attrib. 'Velut stelle'; music of the source clausula has modern attrib. Perotinus; French contrafactum)

DOUBTFUL, SPURIOUS OR TENTATIVE ATTRIBUTIONS
monophonic conductus: medieval attributions

Angelus ad virginum, A.O15 (later polyphonic versions; English contrafacta)

Ave dei genetrix et immaculata (text only; conflicting attrib. Robert Grosseteste)

Dum medium silentium tenerent, A.K15, F.99; ND (medieval ascription to Walter of Châtillon more probable since part of a sermon Walter gave at the University of Bologna, *c*1174)

Inter natos mulierum ut testatur (sequence)

J'ai un cuer mout lait ma ioie m'annour, L.253.1, R.202b ('Thibaut', perhaps Thibaut d'Amiens, identifies himself as poet in text)

Missus Gabriel de celis (*I-Fl* Plut.25.3; sequence; also attrib. 'prior Montis Acuti')

O amor deus deitas, A.L56 (*CH-Bu* B XI 8)

Pange lingua (or Collaudemus) Magdalene (hymn; often associated with 'Aestimavit hortulanum' and 'O Maria noli'; modern attrib. Alexander Neckham, 1157–1217, more likely)

Quo me vertam nescio, A.K28, F.292; ND (modern attrib. Peter of Blois)

Venite exultemus regnante, A.Q1 (*CH-Bu* B XI 8; text only)

Virgo templum trinitatis (*I-Fl* Plut.25.3; text only; gloss on 'Ave Maria')

monophonic conductus: modern attributions

Aestimavit hortulanum (hymn; associated with 'Pange lingua Magdalene' and 'O Maria noli'; see 'Pange lingua' for discussion)

Alabaustrum frangitur, A.K50, F.12; ND (found prior to central collection of Philip's works in *I-Fl* Plut.29.1, fasc.10)

Dum medium silentium componit, A.K16, F.98; ND (apparently confused with Walter of Châtillon's 'Dum medium silentium tenerent' in *D-DS* 2777: latter poem was entered, but former intended)

Fons (or Flos) preclusus, A.L145, A.K72, F.129; ND (modern attrib. to Peter of Blois; French and Provençal contrafacta)

In nova fert animus via gressus, A.K29, F.176 (modern attrib. Peter of Blois)

Nec mare flumini (text only; attrib. Peter of Blois and Bernard of Clairvaux)

Non te lusisse pudeat, A.K47, F.223; ND (also attrib. Peter of Blois and Stephen Langton)

O Maria noli flere (hymn: often associated with 'Pange lingua Magdalene' and 'Aestimavit hortulanum'; see 'Pange lingua' for discussion)

O Maria O felix puerpura, A.K58, F.237; ND (found in a group of Philip's works in *I-Fl* Plut.29.1, fasc.10; French contrafactum)

Post dubiam post nugatorium (text only; modern attrib. Peter of Blois)

Regis et pontificis (sequence)

Veri solis radius lucerna, A.K66, F.371; ND

polyphonic conductus: modern attributions

Austro terris influente, 2vv, A.G1, F.26; ND (cauda is texted)

Dum sigillum summi patris, 2vv, A.J24, F.100; ND (music by Perotinus)

Gratuletur populus, 2vv, A.H6, F.147; ND

O levis aurula, 2vv, A.J34, F.235; ND

Veni creator spiritus recreator, 3vv, A.E13, F.361; ND

motets: medieval attributions

Doce nos optime/Docebit, 3vv, G.346; EM (conductus motet; possibly confused with 'Doce nos hodie')

In salvatoris nomine, 1v, G.452; MC (triplum of double motet; probably included among Philip's works only because of connection with 'In veritate comperi')

motets: modern attributions

Memor tui creatoris/Et gaudebit, 2vv, G.320; EM (contrafactum of 'Velut stelle firmamenti'; music has modern attrib. Perotinus)

Mors a primi patris (1v), G.256; MC (quadruplum to be combined with 'Mors morsu' and 'Mors que stimulo' to form triple motet, 3vv; music has modern attrib. Perotinus; this text probably not by Philip on stylistic grounds)

Mors vite vivificatio/Mors, 2vv, G.257; EM (contrafactum of 'Mors morsu'; music has modern attrib. Perotinus)

O quam necessarium (1v), G.759; EM (triplum of double motet, 3vv; motetus 'Venditores labiorum' attrib. Philip)

Serena virginum/Manere, 4vv, A.A1, F.323, G.69; EM (strophic conductus motet; music has modern attrib. Perotinus; contrafactum of 'Manere vivere')

Stupeat natura/Latus, 2vv, G.232; EM (strophic; contrafactum of 'Homo quam sit pura')

BIBLIOGRAPHY

P. Meyer: 'Henri d'Andeli et le Chancelier Philippe', *Romania*, i (1872), 190–215

P. Aubry: 'Un chant historique latin du XIIIe siècle: Le saint Clou de Saint-Denys (1233)', *Mercure musical*, i (1905), 423–34

N. Fickermann: 'Ein neues Bischofslied Philipps de Grève', *Studien zur lateinischen Dichtung des Mittelalters: Ehrengabe für Karl Strecker*, ed. W. Stach and H. Walther (Dresden, 1931), 37–44

F. Gennrich: *Bibliographie der ältesten französischen und lateinischen Motetten*, SMM, ii (1957)

R. Steiner: 'Some Monophonic Latin Songs composed around 1200', *MQ*, lii (1966), 56–70

H. Husmann: 'Ein Faszikel Notre-Dame-Kompositionen auf Texte des Pariser Kanzlers Philipp in einer Dominikanerhandschrift', *AMw*, xxiv (1967), 1–23 [incl. edns of *Homo considera, Homo quam sit, Ve mundo*]

J.B. Schneyer: *Repertorium der lateinischen Sermones des Mittelalters für die Zeit von 1150–1350*(Münster, 1969–90), 818–68 [incl. catalogue of Philip's sermons]

G.A. Anderson: 'Notre Dame and Related Conductus: a Catalogue Raisonné', *MMA*, vi (1972), 152–229; vii (1973), 1–81

G.A. Anderson: 'Thirteenth-Century Conductus: Obiter Dicta', *MQ*, lviii (1972), 349–64

R. Falck: *The Notre Dame Conductus: a Study of the Repertory* (Henryville, PA, 1981), 110–19 [incl. catalogue, 138–256]

C. Page: 'Angelus ad virginem: a New Work by Philippe the Chancellor?', *EMc*, xi (1983), 69–70

T.B. Payne: 'Associa tecum in patria: a Newly Identified Organum Trope by Philip the Chancellor', *JAMS*, xxxix (1986), 233–54

P. Dronke: 'The Lyrical Compositions of Philip the Chancellor', *Studi medievali*, 3rd ser., xxviii (1987), 563–92

C.M. Wright: *Music and Ceremony at Notre Dame of Paris* (Cambridge, 1989), 294–300

T.B. Payne: *Poetry, Politics and Polyphony: Philip the Chancellor's Contribution to the Music of the Notre Dame School* (diss., U. of Chicago, 1991)

For further bibliography see CONDUCTUS; MOTET.

THOMAS B. PAYNE

Philipus Francis (*fl* mid-15th century). ?Bohemian composer. An identification has been suggested with PHILIPPE BASIRON but the style of his music is clearly Germanic.

WORKS
all in CZ-Ps D.G.IV.47

Missa 'Hilf und gib Rat' (Gl, Cr, San, Ag), 4vv; ed. in Snow, 330–72

O gloriosa mater/Salve regina/Gaude rosa, 4vv, also in *I-TRmp* 1376 (89); ed. in Snow, 373–84 (probably orig. Ky of Missa 'Hilf und gib Rat'; see Strohm)

Sanctus–Agnus Dei, 3vv

Regina celi, 3vv

BIBLIOGRAPHY

StrohmR

R.J. Snow: *The Manuscript Strahov D.G.IV.47* (diss., U. of Illinois, 1968)

JEFFREY DEAN

Philistines, music of the. See JEWISH MUSIC, §II, 3.

Phillipps, Peter. See PHILIPS, PETER.

Phillips, Anna Maria. See CROUCH, ANNA MARIA.

Phillips, Arthur (*b* Winchester, 1605; *d* Harting, Sussex, 27 March 1695). English organist and composer. He became a clerk of New College, Oxford, in 1622, and organist of Bristol Cathedral in 1638. In 1639 he succeeded Richard Nicholson as organist of Magdalen College, Oxford, and as professor of music in that university; he graduated BMus on 9 July 1640. He left England for France as organist to Queen Henrietta Maria and returned after the Restoration, when he 'was entertained in the family of [John] Caryl, a gentleman of the Romish persuasion in Sussex' (Hawkins).

An imaginative set of variations for keyboard on a four-bar ground (in *GB-Lbl*) is in Thomas Tomkins's hand and is assigned to Tomkins in the index of the manuscript (which is in the hand of Nathaniel Tomkins). Although it is known, from a note in the manuscript *F-Pc* Rés.1122, that Tomkins did write a set of variations on this same ground, the music itself bears an ascription to Phillips (in Thomas Tomkins's hand) and in style the ground resembles the other keyboard variations attributed to Phillips. The consort pieces are notable for their active bass parts.

WORKS

Hear O thou shepherd, anthem, *GB-WO* (inc.)

10 airs, tr, b, *Ob*

2 pavans, 2 [airs], corant, 2 tr, b, *Ob*

Almaine, corrante, serrabrand, *Och* (inc.) [b only]

Ground, kbd, *Lbl* [24 vars.]; ed. in MB, v (2/1964)

Ground, kbd, *US-NYp* [22 vars.]

The Requiem, or the Liberty of an imprisoned Royalist, 1641, The Resurrection, 1649 and other settings of verse by T. Pierce, lost

BIBLIOGRAPHY

DNB (L.M. Middleton); *HawkinsH*

J.A. Caldwell: *British Museum Additional Manuscript 29996: Transcription and Commentary* (diss., U. of Oxford, 1965)

J.A. Irving: *The Instrumental Music of Thomas Tomkins (1572–1656)* (diss., U. of Sheffield, 1984)

JOHN CALDWELL/ALAN BROWN

Phillips, Burrill (*b* Omaha, NE, 9 Nov 1907; *d* Berkeley, 22 June 1988). American composer and pianist. His theory and composition teachers were Edwin Stringham at the Denver College of Music (1928–31) and Howard Hanson and Bernard Rogers at the Eastman School (BM 1932, MM 1933). He has been a faculty member at Eastman (1933–49, 1965–6), the University of Illinois (professor, 1949–64), the Juilliard School (1968–9) and Cornell University (1972–3), as well as visiting composer at the universities of Texas, Kansas, Southern California and Hawaii. Among his awards are two Guggenheim Fellowships (1942–3, 1961–2) and an award from the American Academy of Arts and Letters (1944). He was a Fulbright Lecturer at the University of Barcelona (1960–61). He received commissions from the League of Composers (Scherzo for orchestra, 1944), the Koussevitzky Foundation (*Tom Paine*, overture for orchestra, 1946), the Fromm Foundation (*The Return of Odysseus*, 1956) and the Elizabeth Sprague Coolidge Foundation (String Quartet no.2, 1958).

Phillips's first important orchestral work, *Selections from McGuffey's Reader* (1933), was an immediate success and established his reputation as a composer with a consciously American style – a reputation that has tended to overshadow the subsequent development of his musical language. The elements of his early style – an emphasis on melodic line, a rich harmonic texture, and rhythmic associations with jazz – had evolved by the late

1930s and early 1940s into a drier, more acerbic idiom, with asymmetrical rhythms and broadened expressiveness. Many of the works written in the 1940s and 1950s reveal a new intensity and compression; imitative counterpoint is characteristic of the piano writing. In the early 1960s Phillips began to work with free serial techniques, less sharply accented rhythms, and an increasing sense of fantasy. Although he can in no sense be considered an imitator of earlier models, his works show a clarity of line and texture that reflects his great admiration for the music of Domenico Scarlatti and Purcell.

WORKS

STAGE

Katmanusha (ballet), 1932–3; Play Ball (ballet), 1937; Step into my Parlor (ballet), 1942; Don't We All (op buffa, 1, A. Phillips), 1947; Dr. Faustus (incid music, C. Marlowe), org, brass qt, timp, 1957; Nine from Little Rock (film score), 1964; La piñata (ballet, choreog. J. Limón), chbr orch, 1969; The Unforgiven (op, 3, A. Phillips), 1981; other incid music

ORCHESTRAL

Selections from McGuffey's Reader, 1933; Sym. concertante, chbr orch, 1935; Courthouse Square, 1935; Concert Piece, bn, str, 1942, arr. bn, sym. band/pf, 1953; Pf Conc., 1942; Scherzo, 1944; Tom Paine, ov., 1946; Scena, chbr orch, 1946; Conc. grosso, str qt, chbr orch, 1949; Triple Conc., cl, va, pf, orch, 1952; Perspectives in a Labyrinth, 3 str orchs, 1962; Soleriana concertante, 1965; Theater Dances, 1967; Fantasia, sym. band, 1968; Yellowstone, Yates, and Yosemite, t sax, sym. band, 1972

VOCAL

Declaratives (T. Boggs, e.e. cummings, B. Phillips), SSAA, chbr orch, 1943; What will Love do and The Hag (R. Herrick), SSAA, 1949; A Bucket of Water (A. Phillips), SATB, pf, 1952; The Age of Song (W. Raleigh, T. Campion, J. Donne, W. Shakespeare), SATB, 1954; The Return of Odysseus (A. Phillips), Bar, nar, chorus, orch, 1956; The First Day of the World (A. Phillips), TTBB, pf, 1958; 4 Latin Motets, SATB, 1959; Canzona III (A. Phillips), S, fl, pf, perc, 1964; Canzona IV (A. Phillips), S, fl, perc, 1967
That Time may Cease (Marlowe), TTBB, pf, 1967; Canzona V (A. Phillips), SATB, pf, 1971; Eve Learns a Little (A. Phillips), S, 4 ww, pf, 1974; The Recesses of my House (A. Phillips), S, cl, pf, perc, 1977; Hernán y Marina (A. Hurtado), S, pf, 1981; Song in a Winter Night (B. Noll), S, pf, 1981; Letters from Italy Hill (A. Phillips), S, fl, cl, str qt, pf, 1984

CHAMBER AND SOLO INSTRUMENTAL

Pf works incl. 4 sonatas, 1942–60; Toccata, 1944; Music, 1949–50; Serenade, pf duet, 1956; Commentaries, 1983
Qts incl. 2 str qts, 1939–40, 1958; Partita, pf qt, 1947; Conversations and Colloquies, 2 vn, 2 va, 1950; Ob Qt, 1967
Sonatas: vn, pf, 1941; vc, pf, 1948; org, 1964; vn, hpd, 1965
Other: Trio, 3 tpt, 1937; Piece, 6 trbn, 1940; 4 Figures in Time, fl, pf, 1952; A Rondo of Rondeaux, va, pf, 1954; Music for this Time of Year, wind qnt, 1954; Sinfonia brevis, org, 1959; 3 Nostalgic Songs, fl, pf, 1962; Intrada, wind ens, perc, pf, vn, vc, 1975; Huntingdon Twos and Threes, fl, ob, vc, 1975; Scena da camera, vn, vc, 1978; Canzona VI, wind qnt, 1985

MSS in US-R, Wc

Principal publishers: Elkan-Vogel, Fallen Leaf, C. Fischer, Hargail, Presser, Southern

BIBLIOGRAPHY

J.T. Howard: *Our American Music* (New York, 1931, enlarged 4/1965)
C.R. Reis: *Composers in America* (New York, 1938, 2/1947/R)
J.T. Howard and A. Mendel: *Our Contemporary Composers* (New York, 1941/R)
B. Phillips: 'Saluting the American Composer: Burrill Phillips', *Music Clubs Magazine*, 1 (1970–71), 6, 8–9, 19 [incl. autobiographical statement]

ANN P. BASART

Phillips, Harvey (Gene) (*b* Aurora, MO, 2 Dec 1929). American tuba player and teacher. After studying at the Juilliard School (1950–54) and the Manhattan School (1956–8), he played with numerous ensembles and orchestras, and was a founder member of the New York Brass Quintet. From 1971 to 1994 he was professor at the Indiana University School of Music where in 1973 he financed the First International Tuba Symposium-Workshop and sponsored his first 'Octubafest' of student recitals. Phillips also co-founded several organizations, including the Tubists Universal Brotherhood Association (1972) and the International Brass Society (1975). In 1975 he gave a series of five recitals at Carnegie Hall in which he played 39 pieces, including many composed for him. Phillips's technique was prodigious and flexible, his tone smooth and perfectly focussed, even in the lowest register. He commissioned works from such composers as David Baker, Morton Gould, Wilder, Heiden and Schuller, many of which he recorded.

DENNIS K. McINTIRE

Phillips, Henry (*b* Bristol, 13 Aug 1801; *d* London, 8 Nov 1876). English baritone. Born to theatrical parents, he made his first appearance as a boy soprano at the Harrowgate theatre about 1807; he afterwards went to London. As a student and young professional Phillips worked with musicians who traced their artistic lineage from Handel, whose works, together with those of Purcell, supplied much of his repertory. In 1824 he sang the role of Caspar in the first performance in English of Weber's *Der Freischütz* (much adapted for the English Opera House); from 1825 he performed regularly at the Concert of Ancient Music; and in 1826 he sang under Weber. This rapid advance owed much to the guidance of Sir George Smart. In the 1830s he created roles in operas by Loder, Barnett and Balfe. Phillips insisted on having a ballad in his operatic roles, whether or not written by the original composer, for such songs could be highly lucrative. In addition to performing in London, he regularly toured provincial centres.

In the 1840s Phillips's career suffered from changes in theatre managements and from his own actions. In 1841 he was publicly criticized by Balfe for undermining the latter's managerial aspirations. His musical lectures, to which he frequently had recourse, were financially unsuccessful, as was a trip to the USA in 1844–5; nonetheless the songs that resulted from his American experiences are his best. On return to London he was unable to regain his former position. After appearing in Wallace's *Maritana* (1845) his operatic career was virtually at an end. He sang in the première of *Elijah* (1846, Birmingham), but Mendelssohn, who directed the performance, entrusted the major role to Staudigl. *On Lena's Gloomy Heath*, a scena Mendelssohn wrote for Phillips the same year, proved disappointing. In 1847 he sang in *Elijah* under the composer's direction in London; thereafter his vocal powers seem to have waned, and increasingly he turned to glee-singing and then to teaching. His farewell concert took place in 1863.

Phillips composed several songs, and his writings include *The True Enjoyment of Angling* (1843), an angler's manual that extols the charms of countryside in florid prose and mediocre song, *Hints on Musical Declamation* (1848) and *Musical and Personal Recollections during Half a Century* (1864).

BIBLIOGRAPHY

DNB (J.C. Hadden)
English Opera House. Statement and Correspondence between Mr. Balfe, and Mr. H. Phillips, Relative to the Affairs of the Above

Theatre (London, 1841) [and correspondence in *The Times* (16 April 1841)]

J.E. Cox: *Musical Recollections of the Last Half-Century* (London, 1872), i, 187–91, 341–2

C.L. Kenney: *A Memoir of Michael William Balfe* (London, 1875/R), 155

Obituary, *MT*, xvii (1875–6), 694–5

G. Biddlecombe: *English Opera from 1834 to 1864 with Particular Reference to the Works of Michael Balfe* (New York, 1994), 38, 79

GEORGE BIDDLECOMBE

Phillips, John (*d* London, *c*1765). Welsh music engraver, active in England. He and his wife Sarah kept a music shop in London from about 1740 to about 1765, and engraved many works for composers who published their own compositions. Among these were Geminiani (*The Art of Playing on the Violin*, 1751), Arne (*Thomas and Sally*, 1761) and E.T. Warren (*A Collection of Catches, Canons and Glees*, 1763). They also worked for other publishers, including JOHN JOHNSON (ii) and James Oswald. The quality of their engraving was excellent; Hawkins stated that John Phillips adopted and improved upon the ideas of Fortier, and devised his own set of punches after many experiments. On Phillips's death in about 1765, his widow continued the business until 1775. (*HawkinsH*; *Humphries-SmithMP*; *KidsonBMP*)

FRANK KIDSON/PETER WARD JONES

Phillips, Montague F(awcett) (*b* London, 13 Nov 1885; *d* Esher, 4 Jan 1969). English composer. He was educated at the RAM, where he won the Henry Smart and Macfarren scholarships and other awards. He first made a name with popular ballads composed for his wife, the soprano Clara Butterworth (1888–1997), who also starred in the work to which his fame was due above all, the light opera *The Rebel Maid* (1921). For the centenary of the RAM in 1922 he composed *The Song of Rosamund* and he was for many years professor of harmony and composition there. He composed many works for orchestra, but only the lighter pieces, which showed off his talents to greater advantage, made any real mark.

WORKS
(selective list)

Stage: The Rebel Maid (light op, 3, A.M. Thompson, G. Dodson), London, Empire, 12 March 1921 [incl. Fishermen of England]; The Golden Triangle (light op), unperf., unpubd.

Orch: Boadicea, ov., 1907; 2 pf concs., 1907, 1919; Sym., c, 1911; Phantasy, vn, orch, 1912; Heroic Ov., 1914; In Maytime, 1923; A Hillside Melody, 1924, rev. 1946; Dance Revels, 1927; A Forest Melody, 1929; 3 Country Pictures, 1930; Village Sketches, 1932; The World in the Open Air, 1933; A Surrey Suite, 1936; A Moorland Idyll, 1936; Revelry, ov., 1937; Empire March, 1941; Sinfonietta, C, 1943; Festival Ov., 1944; Hampton Court, ov., 1954

Many pieces for pf, incl. Berceuse (1910); Nocturne (1910); Violetta, air de ballet, op.43 no.1 (1926); Arabesque, op.43 no.2 (1927); Jacotte (1928); arrs. of orch works

Voice and orch: The Death of Admiral Blake, Bar, chorus, orch (1913); The Song of Rosamund, scena, S, orch (1922)

Song cycles: Dream Songs (E. Teschmacher) (1912); Sea echoes (N.B. Marsland) (1912); Calendar of Song (H. Simpson) (1913); The Fairy Garden (H. Simpson), op.21 (1914); Flowering Trees (N.B. Marsland), op.31 (1919); From a Lattice Window (E. Lockton), op.33 (1920); Old-World Dance Songs (K.M. Luck) (1923)

Many other songs for 1v, pf; partsongs; many arrs. of own songs and songs of others

Principal publishers: Ascherberg, Hopwood & Crew, Chappell, Novello & Co

ANDREW LAMB

Phillips, Peter (i). *See* PHILIPS, PETER.

Phillips, Peter (ii) (*b* Southampton, 15 Oct 1953). English choral director. He was awarded an organ scholarship at St John's College, Oxford, in 1972 and read music under David Wulstan. During this time he gained experience in directing vocal ensembles, and founded the Tallis Scholars in 1973. Besides giving concerts and making recordings with the Scholars (including the complete English anthems of Tallis), he is a frequent guest conductor with other vocal ensembles. Phillips' research has focussed on sacred music of the Tudor and early Stuart periods (published as *English Sacred Music 1549–1649*, London, 1991), and he is also active as a journalist, writing a weekly column for *The Spectator*. In 1995 he became publisher of the *Musical Times*. In addition to his activities in the field of Renaissance music, he has maintained a long-standing association with John Tavener, conducting the Tallis Scholars in first performances of several of his works.

FABRICE FITCH

Phillips, Sid [Simon] (*b* London, 14 June 1907; *d* Chertsey, 23 May 1973). English jazz clarinettist, bandleader and arranger. He studied the violin and piano as a child and taught himself theory and harmony. In his late teens he began playing the saxophone and the clarinet and performed with his brothers' band in Europe. He worked as a staff arranger for a music publisher and as a music director for the Edison-Bell Gramophone Co. From 1930 he wrote arrangements for Bert Ambrose and led his own quintet. Later he joined Ambrose's band (1933), with which he recorded on clarinet and alto and baritone saxophones (1933–7). In 1937 Phillips visited the USA, where he broadcast and recorded with American musicians. After serving in the RAF he formed another quintet (1946) and composed several symphonic works for the BBC SO (as Simon Phillips). From 1949 until his death he led his own dixieland band; among his sidemen were George Shearing, Colin Bailey, Tommy Whittle and Kenny Ball. Phillips made several recordings as a leader from 1928 into the 1970s.

BIBLIOGRAPHY

J. Godbolt: *A History of Jazz in Britain, 1919–50* (London, 1984)

D. Fairweather: 'Phillips, Sid', in I. Carr, D. Fairweather and B. Priestley: *Jazz: the Essential Companion* (London, 1987)

E.S. Walker: 'Sid Phillips: the Early Years', *Storyville*, no.130 (1987), 143

J. Chilton: *Who's Who of British Jazz* (London, 1997)

NEVIL SKRIMSHIRE/ALYN SHIPTON

Phillips, Theophilus K. Ekundayo (*b* Nigeria, 1884; *d* 1969). Nigerian composer. After a time as organist at the church of St Paul, Breadfruit, Lagos, he studied the piano, organ and violin at Trinity College of Music (1911–14). On his return he was appointed organist at Christ Church, Lagos, remaining in this post until 1962. Most of his compositions are sacred choral works. As an exponent of the cultural and musical importance of Yoruba music and language, his works, many of which set Yoruba texts, show a predilection for speech rhythm, pentatonic scales and simple harmonic progressions. A major contributor to the growth and popularity of church and art music in Nigeria, Phillips provided compositional inspiration for such prominent Nigerian composers as Fela Sowande and Ayo Bankole. He was awarded the honorary doctorate by the University of Nsukka in 1964. His book *Yoruba Music* (Johannesburg, 1953) is an early study of theoretical aspects of indigenous African musical practices.

WORKS
(*selective list*)

Org: Prelude

Choral with acc.: Choral Suite, solo vv, chorus, pf; Yoruba Cant., SATB, org; Emi ogbe oju mi soke wonni (I will lift up mine eyes), S, org

Unacc. choral: Nigerian National Anthem; Magnificat in Yoruba, C

DANIEL AVORGBEDOR

Phillips [Phillipps], Thomas. *See* PHELYPPIS, THOMAS.

Philodemus (*b* Gadara, 110–100 BCE; *d* ?Herculaneum, 40–35 BCE). Epicurean philosopher, poet and critic of music. Philodemus went to Italy in about 65 BCEand remained there until his death. He was the author of a treatise *On Music*, extensive parts of which have survived in a series of fragments discovered in the Herculaneum papyri, buried by the eruption of Mount Vesuvius in 79 CE. Excavations beginning in the mid-18th century brought the first of the papyri to light, and attempts at a reconstruction of the treatise have been published since the end of the 18th century. In 1884 Johann Kemke established a text including additional material that had been discovered; he proposed that Philodemus's treatise was comprised of four books, the first of which was a doxography of the music theory of the Academy, the Peripatetics and the Stoics (including Diogenes of Babylon); the second (essentially lost) and third provided a fuller explanation of the theory of the Academy and the Peripatetics; and the fourth presented Philodemus's polemic against Diogenes and other Stoics. Until the 1980s Kemke's text was the basis for most modern scholarship, despite objections to his arrangement that were periodically raised on various grounds. With the later work of Rispoli, Neubecker and Delattre, however, Kemke's interpretation (and much of his text) has been largely supplanted. Delattre has proposed on papyrological and contextual grounds that all the fragments belong to the fourth book of Philodemus's *On Music* and that the treatise was not necessarily restricted to four books. In Delattre's reconstruction, the first 47 columns provide a summary of the theory of Diogenes of Babylon and the balance of the treatise is devoted to Philodemus's refutation of the arguments of the Stoics.

For Philodemus, music was irrational and so could not influence the soul in any choice or avoidance of action. When it accompanied a text, it added nothing but listening pleasure. In Philodemus's view, reports of the powerful effects of music are simple nonsense: music has never in itself manifested ethos, and it cannot be considered among things of serious worth.

Despite the dogmatism and excessive vehemence with which Philodemus sometimes pursues such arguments, his treatise has value, especially as a reflection of late stages in the development of ethos theory. Several passages add significantly to the ancient evidence regarding Damon. Existing scholarship evaluating the treatise, its arguments and the place of Philodemus will certainly be reviewed and most probably revised in light of Delattre's new complete critical edition (forthcoming).

WRITINGS

J. Kemke, ed.: *Philodemi de musica librorum quae exstant* (Leipzig, 1884)

D.A. van Krevelen: *Philodemus: De Muziek, met vertaling en commentar* (Hilversum, 1939)

G.M. Rispoli, ed. and trans.: *Il primo libro del Peri mousikēs de Filodemo* (Naples, 1969)

G.M. Rispoli: 'Filodemo sulla musica', *Cronache ercolanesi*, iv (1974), 57–84

A.J. Neubecker, ed. and trans.: *Philodemus: Über die Musik IV. Buch* (Naples, 1986)

D. Delattre: 'Philodème, de la musique: livre IV', *Cronache ercolanesi*, xix (1989), 49–143

BIBLIOGRAPHY

T. Gomperz: *Zu Philodem's Büchern von der Musik: ein kritischer Beitrag* (Vienna, 1885)

E. Holzer: 'Zu Philodemos Peri mousikēs', *Philologus*, lxvi (1907), 498–502

L.P. Wilkinson: 'Philodemus on Ethos in Music', *Classical Quarterly*, xxxii (1938), 174–81

O. Luschnat: *Zum Text von Philodems Schrift De musica* (Berlin, 1953)

A.J. Neubecker: *Die Bewertung der Musik bei Stoikern und Epikureern: eine Analyse von Philodems Schrift De musica* (Berlin, 1956)

A. Plebe: *Filodemo e la musica* (Turin, 1957)

W.D. Anderson: *Ethos and Education in Greek Music* (Cambridge, MA, 1966), 153–76, 189–91

H. Schueller: *The Idea of Music* (Kalamazoo, MI, 1988), 92–4

G.M. Rispoli: 'Elementi di fisica e di etica epicurea nella teoria musicale di Filodemo di Gadara', *Harmonia mundi: musica e filosofia nell'antichità: Rome 1989*, 69–103

THOMAS J. MATHIESEN

Philolaus [Philolaos] (*fl c*450–400 BCE). Pythagorean philosopher. A contemporary of Socrates and teacher of Democritus, he came from Croton (southern Italy), famous for its religious community associated with Pythagoras. After the destruction of the community in about 450 BCE, he escaped to Thebes, a leading musical centre, where he taught some of the Pythagoreans whom Plato knew. He was the first to commit the precepts of Pythagoras to writing. Fragments from two of his works survive: the *Bacchae* (Diels, 44b17–19), and *On Nature* (*Peri physios*; Diels, 44b1–16), originally a multi-volume work, according to Nicomachus of Gerasa who quoted from it (Diels, 44b6). The authenticity of these fragments (written in the Doric dialect) has been disputed, but most scholars now regard them as genuine.

The fragments, together with the accounts of Aëtius (Diels, 44a9–13, 15–21) and Boethius (44a26), embrace a variety of subjects. In the fragment on music (44b6), Philolaus begins as a traditional Pythagorean philosopher with an explanation of *harmonia*, whose function is to bring into accord all the principles of opposition of which the cosmos is composed; but his own concluding analysis of the structural components of *harmonia* suggests a stronger link with musical practice (Philolaus himself was active as an aulos player; Diels, 44a7) than with Pythagorean doctrine.

Philolaus's nomenclature in effect adumbrates the tuning techniques of musicians: thus, *harmonia*, his term for octave (*diapasōn*: the concord running 'through all the notes'), denotes the harmonic framework or 'fitting together' of the octave's components; the 5th (*diapente*: the concord running 'through five notes'), he called *dioxeian* – 'through the high-pitched notes'); and the 4th (*diatesserōn*: 'through four notes') is *syllaba* – the first 'grab' of the fingers on the strings of the tilted lyre. What the Pythagoreans and Plato called *leimma* (limma) – the semitone 'left over' after the subtraction of two whole tones from the 4th – Philolaus named *diesis* ('passing through'), a term reserved by later theorists for the quarter-tone.

In his analysis of intervals smaller than a whole tone, Philolaus departed radically from Pythagorean doctrine, the hallmark of which is the treatment of musical intervals as numerical ratios. Using the numbers constituting these ratios as addable, not correlated, entities, Philolaus (as reported by Boethius) posited an array of micro-intervals, computed in units of 14 – *apotomē* (large semitone), 13 – *diesis* (small semitone), 1 – *komma* (comma; the difference between the large and small semitones) and $\frac{1}{2}$ – *schisma* (half of a comma). This process of bisecting musical intervals is so mathematically unsound (the proper method being the multiplication and division of ratios) that scholars have judged Philolaus's analysis unworthy of a Pythagorean thinker. It is possible, however, that he was treating musical intervals not as mathematically expressible proportions but, after the practice of musicians, as units in a tonal continuum governed solely by the capacities of the human voice and ear.

WRITINGS

H. Diels, ed.: *Die Fragmente der Vorsokratiker* (Berlin, 1903, rev. 6/1951–2/R by W. Kranz; Eng. trans., 1948, 2/1959)
A. Barker, ed.: *Greek Musical Writings*, ii: *Harmonic and Acoustic Theory* (Cambridge,1989), 36–9, 261–2

BIBLIOGRAPHY

J. Burnet: *Early Greek Philosophy* (London, 1892, 4/1945), 277ff
E. Frank: *Plato und die sogennanten Pythagoreer* (Halle, 1923/R), 263ff
W. Burkert: *Weisheit und Wissenschaft: Studien zu Pythagoras, Philolaos und Platon* (Nuremberg, 1962; Eng. trans., rev., 1962, as *Lore and Science in Ancient Pythagoreanism*)
C.J. de Vogel: *Pythagoras and Early Pythagoreanism* (Assen, 1966)
K. von Fritz: 'Philolaos', *Paulys Real-Encyclopädie der klassischen Altertumswissenschaft*, suppl.xiii (Munich, 1973), 453–83
C.A. Huffman: *Philolaus of Croton: Pythagorean and Presocratic* (Cambridge, 1993) [incl. commentary on the fragments]

FLORA R. LEVIN

Philomathes [Philomates], **Venceslaus** [Václav] (*b* Neuhaus [now Jindřichův Hradec], *c*1480; *d* after 1532). Bohemian theorist. His textbook *Musicorum libri quatuor, compendiose carmine elucubrati* (Vienna, 1512) arose out of his studies and lecturing at the University of Vienna in the years immediately preceding its publication. The whole of music theory is set forth in elegant Latin hexameters, showing a humanistic influence that is also demonstrated by the dedicatory verses, for instance the one by Joachim Vadian. The mnemonic value of writing in verse had been invoked by Guido of Arezzo, but was almost unique in the Renaissance. The structure of the book was also original: the first two sections are on the conventional *cantus planus* and *cantus figuratus* (pitch and rhythm respectively), but before turning to counterpoint and composition in the last section Philomathes inserted a section on 'direction' (*regimen*) and voice-production. The textbook had a wide resonance. It was reprinted not only in Vienna in 1523, but twice by Georg Rhau (Leipzig, 1518, as *Liber musicorum quatuor*; Wittenberg, 1534) and also (with alterations) in Strasbourg in 1543; Fétis referred to another Vienna edition of 1548. Rhau quoted many of Philomathes's verses as mnemonics in his own *Enchiridion utriusque musicae* (1517), as did (through Rhau's influence) Johannes Galliculus in his *Isagoge de compositione cantus* (1520) and Martin Agricola throughout his writings (1528–39). Agricola went so far as to publish a commentary, *Scholia in Musicam planam Venceslai Philomatis* (1538), for the use of his schoolboys in Magdeburg. Through these and other writers Philomathes exercised an indirect influence on 16th-century central-European music pedagogy second only to that of Gaffurius.

Several of Philomathes's statements have received particular attention. He was the first to point out the octave relationship between the ranges of the discantus and tenor parts and between those of the altus and bassus. He considered that the copious use of imitative passages, in parallel with the versification of the words, would result in a 'subtile poema'. He emphasized beating time regularly with the hand or with a staff. After publishing his textbook Philomathes seems to have returned as a priest to southern Moravia. He wrote a Latin *Institutio grammatica* (Kraków, 1525), and in the early 1530s he collaborated with Beneš Optát and Petr Gzel: he advised them on their Czech translation of the New Testament (1533), and his section 'Etymologia' was combined with their 'Orthographia' to form the oldest Czech grammar, *Grammatyka czeská* (Náměšt' nad Oslavou, 1533). This is the last that is known of him.

BIBLIOGRAPHY

ČSHS; EitnerQ; FétisB; MGG1 (J. Bužga)
G. Schünemann: *Geschichte des Dirigierens* (Leipzig, 1913/R), 41–5
V. Helfert: 'Musika Blahoslavova a Philomatova', *Sborník Blahoslavův, 1523–1923*, ed. V. Novotný and R. Urbánek (Přerov, 1923), 121–51
H. Funck: *Martin Agricola* (Wolfenbüttel, 1933), 65–8
J. Trojan: *Muzika Václava Philomatha z Jindřichova Hradce (1512)* (diss., U. of Brno, 1950)
O. Wessely: 'Alte Musiklehrbücher aus Österreich', *Musikerziehung*, vii (1953–4), 128–32, 205–9, esp. 205–6
A. Truhlář and others: *Rukovět' humanistického básnictví v Čechách a na Moravě od konce 15. do začatku 17. stoleti* (Prague, 1973)
G. Friedhof: Introduction to Beneš Optát, Petr Gzel, Václav Philomates: *Grammatyka czeská: die Ausgaben von 1533 und 1588* (Frankfurt and Munich, 1974)
B. Meier: *Die Tonarten der klassischen Vokalpolyphonie nach den Quellen dargestellt* (Utrecht, 1974; Eng. trans., 1988), 41–2
W. Werbeck: *Studien zur deutschen Tonartenlehre in der ersten Hälfte des 16. Jahrhunderts* (Kassel, 1989), 87–9, 112–18, 189–91

KLAUS WOLFGANG NIEMÖLLER, JEFFREY DEAN

Philomela. *See under* ORGAN STOP.

Philosophy of music.

I. Introduction. II. Historical survey, antiquity–1750. III. Aesthetics, 1750–2000. IV. Anglo-American philosophy of music, 1960–2000. V. Contemporary challenges.

I. Introduction

1. A sceptical beginning. 2. Entries in *Grove's Dictionary*.

1. A SCEPTICAL BEGINNING.   Short and long discussions of music saturate the history of Western philosophy. Similar discussions of philosophy saturate the history of Western music. Yet referring to 'the philosophy of music' often surprises academics and laypersons alike. Some declare they did not know there was such a subject; perhaps that is because there have been few devoted philosophers of music. If one were to list known philosophers solely devoted to music, or known musicians devoted to philosophy (a devotion that in much earlier times would still have kept them in the class of musicians), one might not come up with a single name. However, were one to name philosophers and musicians who have contributed to the subject, one could produce a seemingly unending list and a list of the greatest names: Pythagoras, Plato, Aristotle, Boethius and so on through to the present. Most philosophical engagement with music has taken place in the context of (*a*) philosophers developing cosmological and metaphysical systems in which each subject and type of phenomenon, including music, is assigned its proper place; (*b*) philosophers treating music

as one of the arts within their different philosophical systems of aesthetics; and (c) musicians – composers, performers, theorists, and critics – drawing on, and thus contributing to, philosophy to explain the foundations, rationale and more esoteric aspects of their theories, practices and products. Even so, scepticism about the subject remains.

Typically, the Western philosophy of music has been treated as a history of competing philosophical theories about the music most approved of at any given time – sacred music, serious music, classical music – hence generating a canonic discipline of the best that has been said about the best music produced. Yet even on this canonic level fluctuation in theory type, methodological commitment and chosen phenomena has been broad. Sometimes the fluctuation has produced scepticism as to whether there is a distinct field that is the philosophy of music and a belief that any such field is a hotchpotch of more or less connected theories produced by philosophers and musicians of the Western tradition. Others have admired this same tradition, seeing the connections between the different philosophical explorations of music as interestingly sustaining and interacting with the explorations that constitute Western philosophy as a whole. Between the extremes of scepticism and admiration have laboured the theorists, troubled in their different periods by all that has been left out of, or included in, the canon: types of argument, types of philosopher, types of music, types of musician. Sometimes their resulting theories have been absorbed into the canon, sometimes as central, sometimes as marginal. Often they have helped generate new fields – musicology (and 'new musicology'), music theory and analysis, ethnomusicology and anthropology, the physics of sound (acoustics), the sociology of, psychology of and social history of music – fields that have contributed to, or competed with what, at any given time, has constituted the canonic line of the philosophy of music. If, now, one still wants to grant that there is something approaching a sustained discipline of the philosophy of music, probably it is best understood, like the history and practice of music itself, as a family (or families) of theories, objects and practices happily and unhappily connected in relations of continuity and rupture, benevolent and malevolent debate, competition, influence, admiration and affection.

From another methodological point of view, whether one should speak of the philosophy of music on a particular species level, as one does, say, of the philosophy of biology or of law, or, as many have, only on the genus level, as part of a general aesthetics or philosophy of art, depends on how particularistic or unique one takes music (and each of the other arts) to be. 'The aesthetics of one art is that of the others; only the material is different', declared Robert Schumann. But just as one may argue that philosophical questions raised by biological phenomena are sufficiently particular for questions appropriate to 'the philosophy of science' as a genus discipline to fail to cover them, or that questions raised about law are inadequately covered by the general questions of ethics, so one may argue that music is too particular to be exhausted by the general questions of aesthetics. Certainly, from a historical point of view, music deserves to be treated as a particular if only by virtue of the extraordinary and distinctive breadth of use and significance it has sustained. For music has been treated not

only as one of the major arts but also as a significant science and, for an extraordinarily long time, as a mainstay of a liberal arts education. In its different roles, music has been treated as theoretical speculation and idea, as practice, production and performance, as expression and craft, as natural phenomenon and cosmological force.

Nevertheless, for all this breadth, does the same assertion of particularity hold true when music is made the subject of philosophy? The difficulty inherent in that question has most interestingly lain in the 'of' in 'the philosophy of music'. It has not lain in the obvious and pervasive truth that philosophers have used music, often with great depth, in their thinking, or that musicians have used philosophy with similar depth in theirs; it has lain in the less obvious thought that the practice and theory of music has historically represented a deep resistance to its being made the object of a systematic philosophical theory. There is a problem in making any particular subject the object of a general philosophical theory, but the claim here is more specific to music's peculiar historical engagement with philosophy. Allied repeatedly with human emotion, with purely sensuous expression, with cosmology, mystery and mathematical abstraction, with useless and unnatural (artificial) function, with purely transient or temporal existence, with non-conceptual communication and, finally, with the often underestimated channel of the human ear (the ear is merely 'the channel of the heart', the eye 'the channel of the mind'), theorists and practitioners have been remarkably successful in making the 'art of tone' resist the philosophical bid to provide for music an exhaustive rational, logical or conceptual account.

The long history of music's being described negatively, in terms of what it is not, does not have, or cannot and should not do, has often been used to prove either music's impoverishment because music fails of philosophical account or philosophy's impoverishment because philosophy fails to control music. In the ruling dualistic terms of Western thought, some theorists have suggested that music's history is just the history of human passion, and that since philosophy's demand for reason has so often opposed itself to what passion offers, music has symbolized philosophy's antidote. One way to counter the resistance has been to make music's 'art of tone' subservient to poetry's 'art of word', or to render music rational, conceptual or logical in conformity with philosophical law. In the 19th century, Nietzsche spoke of the resistance and of the related struggle between music and philosophy when, in *The Birth of Tragedy*, he suggested that 'perhaps music represents a realm of wisdom from which the logician is exiled. Perhaps art is . . . a necessary correlative of, and supplement for, science?' He had the long history of Western philosophy and music explicitly in mind. It was a history going back to ancient, Athenian quarrels between reason and feeling, mind and body, truth and illusion, desire and obligation, freedom and constraint, and to at least one of music's origins, namely, in *mousikē*: the desired contribution of the passionate muses to the project of educating the soul and to the distrust of some philosophers that the muse of music could in fact educate the soul. Regarding contemporary debate, a comparable struggle is articulated as a conflict between authoritarian and non-authoritarian social and cultural forms, or in gendered terms, between patriarchal and matriarchal discourses (see §V below). In order to accommodate music's endless resistance or philosophy's endless self-reflection, perhaps the headword 'philosophy of music' should be rejected, since it tends to embody an assumption that music can be, or historically has been, captured by and controlled within the constraints of philosophical method. 'Philosophy and/or music' may better capture their suggestive history of interactive equality and tension and leave dialectically open the issue of their relation. The headword may not only indicate what the entry will contain but also how the subject will be approached, as a necessary excursus into one specific history of music's complex relations with philosophy will now demonstrate.

2. ENTRIES IN 'GROVE'S DICTIONARY'. We now examine changing attitudes in the English-speaking musical world by a consideration of the treatment of the topic in the *Grove* dictionaries from the earliest discussion (in 1927) to the present day (2000). *Grove's Dictionary*, historically, has epitomized a mainstream if not always subtle position of extreme scepticism towards the existence of, and interest in, the philosophy of music, perhaps typifying attitudes prevalent among musicians in Great Britain. In its third edition (1927) – the earliest to have an entry even approaching a direct discussion of philosophy and music – the author, Sir Percy Buck, introduced readers to the subject under the headword 'Aesthetics'. This choice of rubric justified Buck's beginning his account 'about the year 1750' when the term 'aesthetics' first came explicitly into use for the 'science which investigates the Beautiful'. Though he provided no more historical information, and concerned as he was to expound his favoured aesthetic theory, he still explained something about a tradition of the philosophers' engagement with music whose temporal and conceptual scale extended far beyond that mid-18th-century year. Yet what he wrote was quite disparaging:

'Aesthetics' has come to mean two different things to two different groups of thinkers. To the pure metaphysician it still stands for the investigation of Beauty as a thing in itself – a speculation which attracted even the earliest Egyptian and Greek thinkers – and to him Beauty is an absolute, outside of us, independent of its effect on mind and of human reaction to it. To the psychologist, however, Aesthetics has, by common consent, been narrowed down to the consideration of the Fine Arts: *i.e.* the arts concerned with sight and hearing (Architecture, Sculpture, Poetry, Painting and Music).

The connection between aesthetics and the modern classification of the fine arts has been sustained by more than the psychologists' common consent. It was, and remains, the standard starting account among many metaphysicians and historians of the arts (Kristeller, 1951). Yet Buck, preferring the psychologists' method, was determined to get metaphysics out of the way:

The single metaphysical problem 'What is Beauty?' thus resolves itself into a number of practical questions which may be stated in some such form as this: 'How and why do we as human beings become affected by, and pass judgement on the quality of, works of art?'.

He had already loaded his argument by assuming that metaphysics should be resolvable into practical, as opposed to theoretical, questions. He explained:

It would serve no purpose to attempt to summarise here even the chief theories of the metaphysicians. From Socrates, Plato and Aristotle to Plotinus and the Neoplatonists in Greece, from Leibniz to Lessing, Baumgarten, Kant, Hegel and Schopenhauer in Germany; from Descartes and Diderot to modern time in France; from Bacon to Bosanquet in England, we are met with an endless stream of conflicting dogmatism. Few people pretend to understand (and most people doubt the ability of anyone to understand) what the majority of the above writers really want to say, and to those to whom metaphysics is

not an end in itself the whole output of human thought in this field seems to be distressingly dreary and sterile. For the metaphysicians write – and possibly it is proper that metaphysicians should write – as if they had never once allowed themselves to be thrilled by any manifestation of Beauty. It is therefore permissible to say that no student of music will love his art one whit the less for giving a wide berth to all that the metaphysicians have written.

Buck turned to the 'psychologist [who] approaches the subject from an entirely different standpoint', and who deals with an experience that is 'always two-sided, being a reaction to a stimulus'. He did not particularly mention music again, finding his points applicable to the fine arts in general. Yet he did hint at fairly standard answers to what are still the predominant questions of a musical aesthetics with a predilection for psychology: What is Beauty? is it objective? law-like? does beauty reside in the object, the work of art, or in the hearer's response? what is the nature of an emotional response? what is the relation between the work of art (the stimulus) and the response? how, more generally, should one describe the relation between music and human nature, between music's 'psychic energy' or formal movement and the movement of our 'inner lives', or between how music moves and why we feel moved when we listen to music? What is surprising about Buck's answers was the implication that they were free of metaphysical assumption and carried solely by mere commonsense. At best, they were carried by that 18th-century British tradition of philosophical psychology that devised a theoretical ideal of commonsense – a shared faculty of sense – to guide its inquiries.

According to Buck, beauty resides in the response to a particular stimulus, in our feelings stirred by this particular object; yet not every feeling so stirred results in an aesthetic judgment. We judge aesthetically only when we take an interest in how artists have objectified their feelings, because art is the presentation of an idea through a medium; we find a work of art beautiful when our response is akin to the feeling in the artist that originated it. Much 'barren [i.e. philosophical] discussion', he wrote, could be avoided if we understood that a work's appeal lies not in the immediacy of our feeling-response but in how that response is mediated through the intellect, because the intellect contributes the knowledge of how the work is arranged. The intellect gives credence and shape to the emotion, the feeling of pleasure or displeasure, approbation or disapprobation, on the basis of which we judge. However, our judgment is not merely a reflection of our personal tastes; if it were, we could not guarantee objectivity in our practice of criticism. Criticism, rather, is the application of aesthetic principles derived on the basis of an acquired expertise about the technical and stylistic properties of art. Buck did not name these principles; he remarked only that they were conventional, not law-like; he then simply grounded their purported objectivity in 'sincerity'. One 'ultimate and eternal question', he wrote, governs the entire enterprise of aesthetic judgment and criticism: 'Is the artwork genuine? Was it born because the catharsis of its author compelled him to create?'. If critics who ask this question are sincere, their answers and judgments will be, and in their sincerity, he concluded, they will have engaged with the problems of aesthetics.

Music's expression, its embodiment of the emotions and its capacity to prompt catharsis (purification of feeling) in listeners are incontrovertible topics of musical aesthetics, although some would argue the topics, prompting as they do the central issue of the source and objectivity of expression, taste, judgment, criticism. Do musical works express or embody the composers' feelings, ideas or intentions? Do works express or mean something through their own form and content as linguistic sentences or utterances mean something independently of the particular persons who utter them? Are expressive or emotive predicates attributable to works themselves: may we say of the music itself that it is sad? Are the judgments and evaluations of musical works based on listeners' responses; if so, under what conditions of feeling and intellect? or are such judgments based on the emotive content we find in the form and content of the works themselves?

These classic questions of objectivity and subjectivity lie behind Robert Donington's entry, still under the rubric 'Aesthetics', in *Grove5* (1954). Noting first the Greek origin of the term *aisthanesthai* ('to perceive'), Donington observed that the term had come more broadly to refer to the 'theory of artistic experience'. He did not say more but remarked on how rewarding aesthetics was for those with speculative talent, although he warned against untrained dabbling. He noticed how much 'unrivalled confusion' the subject has promoted, even among 'the trained', and then stated that the philosophical aspect was beyond the scope of the dictionary.

In the earlier editions of *Grove's Dictionary*, a discussion of aesthetics was included without any presumption that the dictionary was offering philosophical coverage. In the first (1877–89), when the editors specifically excluded certain topics and modes of inquiry from their concerns, philosophy was not mentioned among them. Its absence is further confirmed by the noticeable omission of entries on philosophers who contributed to music in that capacity. Although Rousseau was entered in the first edition, he was not recognized for his philosophical views on music (though they were mentioned) but for his compositions and music theory (specifically his debate with Rameau). Schopenhauer, now widely regarded as 'the musician's philosopher', entered *Grove* only in the fifth edition, as briefly did Nietzsche (the entry mostly concerned his relationship to Wagner). Further, when it was considered, aesthetics was not specifically connected to philosophy; it was not even treated with special reference to music, as Donington confirmed when, in referring his readers to an aesthetician he admired, he mentioned Benedetto Croce (1902), not usually known for his remarks on music despite his influential work on language and expression.

Unlike Buck, Donington did not promote a preferred method. Though he granted that psychology has much to contribute to aesthetics, he remarked that it had not yet been very successful in its contributions. He granted that critics had written much that was useful, but again warned against an attempt at philosophical explanation. He praised Wagner for his inspired and voluminous intuitions and developments of opera and myth, but chided him for attempting philosophical explanation. Although he regarded philosophy as beyond his scope, he showed an awareness of when his themes called for philosophical account: 'The question of the principles on which a work of art can be judged good of its kind is one on which both psychologists and critics can throw much light', he wrote, 'but only a philosopher can (with their assistance) frame a really accurate answer'. Without claiming any such accuracy, he offered guidelines as to how the question might be approached.

Donington first observed that music may be described according to its emotional or physical aspects, noting that its physical aspects were treated elsewhere (under 'Acoustics'). We need only to know for aesthetics that certain vibrations and combinations of sounds give rise to certain reactions, perhaps of monotony or distress. The emotional aspects are then dealt with by psychology, by theories that show how auditory experiences vary conventionally and habitually in all sorts of ways against the background of shared human faculties. He continued more speculatively: although aesthetic pleasures include natural beauties, 'works of art are unique in putting us in touch with another mind'. A basic feature of artistic experience is communication by artists through works of art. Artists communicate their intentions to give pleasurable or satisfying feelings to listeners through the medium of music. To achieve this, composers tend to use contrasts: harshness raises a desire for sweetness, and resolution is felt when sweetness is offered. Discord finds resolution in concordance: when it does not, we speak of composers as 'ahead of their time', although this does not necessarily mark progress. He finally suggested that the impact of music might depend upon primordial associations that are worked out unconsciously, but offered no more detail. He concluded that, even had his thoughts not been accurate, he hoped he had been asking the right questions.

That Donington was approaching some of the right questions is not in doubt; that his answers were not entirely convincing is beside the point. What matters is this: in how many more editions would *Grove* assign the writing of an entry on aesthetics to theorists who felt the need, either because of disinclination, modesty or inadequacy, to disavow the contribution of philosophy in an encyclopedic coverage of 'music and musicians'?

The position changed in *Grove6* (1980). The entry's headword was now 'Aesthetics of music', and subtitled as 'the philosophy of the meaning and value of music'. It was extended considerably and was written by the Canadian philosopher Francis Sparshott. Aware of the difficulties of adequate representation of so large a topic, he began by delimiting its scope:

The term 'aesthetics of music' normally designates attempts to explain what music means: the difference between what is and what is not music, the place of music in human life and its relevance to an understanding of human nature and history, the fundamental principles of the interpretation and appreciation of music, the nature and ground of excellence and greatness in music, the relation of music to the rest of the fine arts and to other related practices, and the place or places of music in the system of reality.

Here are captured most of the central questions pertinent to the philosophical discussion of music in its history and in the present day: the ontological questions of being and classification, the epistemological questions of experience, knowing and meaning and the normative questions of criticism, appreciation, judgment and value, and the functional questions of music's role in education and entertainment, culture and society. Sparshott went on to delimit the scope of the enterprise in terms of the modern disciplines from which it is differentiated:

aesthetics is to be distinguished from the psychology and sociology of musical composition, performance and listening; from the history of musical practice; from the physics of sound and the physiology of the ear; from the analysis and description of all particular works and traditions in music; and from all other kinds of empirical inquiry, even though fruitful discussions in aesthetics may in practice be inseparable from some such inquiries.

While acknowledging that 'aesthetics' had sometimes been used to include some or all of the modes of inquiry he had just put aside, Sparshott then added, against this, that aesthetics had also maintained a much narrower use, to refer only to those attempts to establish a rational basis for enjoyment and evaluation. He did not favour either side: the first was too broad, the second too narrow. Instead, he stated his intention simply to record 'what has been thought and said' by philosophers and philosopher-musicians 'about music in the tradition of Western Civilisation', although suggestions were added about how this tradition 'might be enriched by contributions from elsewhere', specifically from the long traditions of aesthetics, philosophy and the arts in China and India. He mentioned the concept of 'rasa' in Indian poetics, a sort of 'relish', that might have served Western aesthetics better than that of expression, and China's great system of equipoises, a cosmological system (social and aesthetic) that allows 'the theory of music and ceremonies', as Yueh Chih wrote, to embrace 'the whole nature of man'.

Sparshott's reasons for some of the inadequacies he saw in the aesthetics of music provide a new perspective on the scepticism that still concerns us. The field, he suggested, has received a noticeable lack of attention because (a) not all writers who would like to philosophize about music have the requisite knowledge of the technical complexities of music's production and notation; (b) there has been a strong prejudice that musical value does not extend past its notes or forms into extra-musical areas of human experience and value; and (c) that the humanities have long assigned music a low place, as merely an emotional or ornamental art of entertainment, of insignificant use in serious matters of culture. 'At least the first of these reasons remains operative', he noted, concluding that 'modern theorizing about music rises above the arcane and the nugatory less often than does comparable writing about the visual arts'.

His own discussion tried to alleviate that impression to the extent that he offered a chronology of what had best been said and by whom in Western philosophy about Western music, from antiquity until the late 20th century (see §2 below for his account from antiquity to 1750). His account highlighted precisely the kinds of judgment, choice and prejudice that have historically been at stake in the topic. Unlike Buck and Donington, Sparshott showed how far music itself has been an essentially contested concept and the Western philosophy of music an essentially contested field. His account suggested that, if scepticism is to be retained, it should be of the constructive kind that allows essentially contested fields and concepts to be admitted to the contest. Denying that a given mode of inquiry is genuine or worthwhile might at times be a valuable, even a necessary, position to take within a field, but it should not be taken, as one might read the early *Grove* entries, as externally representing the field as a whole.

Sparshott's entry was published under the headword 'Aesthetics of music', although he knew that the title referred to a discipline and set of concerns that came into their own only in the mid-18th century. That was the time when music achieved (or so it is argued) its emancipated status as a fine art, when it acquired sufficient autonomy for its focus to move away from its external functional and occasional extra-musical functions in church and court to the secular and bourgeois concert-hall aesthetic of works, performances and reception (see §3). Sparshott associated the paradigm change of this period, as many theorists do, with the beginnings of modern theorizing about music, a type of theorizing that gave modern meanings to the theoretical terms of the previous sentence. It was also a type of theorizing that helped sustain the three kinds of concerns Sparshott identified as sometimes detrimental to the modern aesthetics of music: the new analytical focus on technical matters of composition and form; the formalist separation of specifically or purely musical value from extra-musical association, and the 'bourgeois' relegation of music to the sphere of leisure or mere, albeit fine, entertainment. These tendencies, however, constitute only a small part of the modern aesthetics of music, an aesthetics often reckoned as marking the period in which the relations between philosophy and music received more explicit attention in theory and practice than ever before.

The modern period saw musicians engaging in philosophy and philosophers engaging in music. It heard that music, under its condition of freedom and emancipation, was infinite expression, absolutely philosophical, the last true religion, the pure expression of the world's Will, the supreme carrier of the Dionysian spirit of tragedy in the modern age. It saw the plastic arts aspiring to the non-discursive, abstract and supremely expressive Romantic condition of absolute or purely instrumental music. It witnessed music, in the form of the symphony, opera or song, disclosing utopian and revolutionary dreams or prophesies for the future of humanity. It saw music, operatic and instrumental, being so feared for its power over the public that it was sometimes strictly censored.

Yet it was also a period of radical distrust of music's metaphysical and political imports, a period in which evolutionary science, psychology, history and sociology gave independent, empirical credence to, and justification for, the development of new musical genres. It was a period in which the discipline of music developed internally motivated forms of analysis and criticism that attended to the specifically musical, technical and expressive aspects of musical composition, notation, form and performance.

All these tendencies – the Romantic, the formalist, the speculative, analytical, positivistic and empirical, the psychological, political and sociological – are part of the modern aesthetics of music. They are also the tendencies of modern philosophy *per se*. Some may reasonably find the 'arcane and nugatory' in the most extreme manifestations of any of these tendencies, in the worst excesses of metaphysical speculation, in the worst excesses of formalism and positivism, and so on. More pertinent is the treatment here of the period before the establishment of the modern aesthetics of music: the views and approaches just mentioned can be found in more or less similar forms before 1750 (as, more or less, Sparshott's chronology shows). Yet this approach also shows a tendency to treat this history before the modern aesthetics of music as a pre-history, as if all the issues and concerns of philosophers writing about music, and musicians engaging in philosophy, were leading up to and resulting in these modern concerns (especially with the autonomy of music). Perhaps this tendency encourages the acceptance of the title 'aesthetics of music' as appropriate to the entire field.

It is common among modern aestheticians and modern philosophers to read the history of Western philosophy and music in terms of standardized periods, such as Antiquity, the Middle Ages, Renaissance, Enlightenment, Romanticism, Modernism; it is usual, furthermore, to suggest the development of themes from one period to another, a development that need not follow a straight, progressivist or unified line. Many theorists show how, in each of these periods, contemporary writers often justified their particular claims by showing their origin and authority in antiquity (or another early period) as a way to assert a difference from, and rejection of, their immediate predecessors' claims. Such is the repeated pattern in the arts behind the quarrels between 'the old and new', 'the conservative and progressive' and 'the ancients and moderns'. Although, as a general point, this way of writing history has some justification, its sometimes severe limitations need to be acknowledged.

One alternative is to confine 'the aesthetics of music' to the modern Western period, to acknowledge the paradigm shift of the mid-18th century without underestimating the obvious continuities that also transcend the shift: this is the approach of the present entry. It offers (in §3) a discrete discussion of the aesthetics of music, surveying the dominant concerns of the modern field. This discussion tracks the concerns predominantly associated with what is normally called 'continental' philosophy, a literature mostly written in German. It puts aside the Anglo-American contribution (discussed in §4) as well as certain other distinct issues, thereby reflecting contemporary disciplinary divisions and allegiances which, despite some recent erosion, institutionally at least still hold sway. In the entire entry the influence of non-Western thought shows itself noticeably underdeveloped in the contemporary philosophical field.

This separation of the Anglo-American contribution is especially pertinent because it reflects a tendency among modern philosophers to distinguish musical aesthetics from the philosophy of music, or aesthetics from the philosophy of the arts (a distinction originally made by Hegel). Many want to avoid the assumption that philosophical (for example ontological) problems prompted by the world of the arts are automatically to be associated with the traditional concerns of aesthetics (about judgment, beauty, nature etc.), or that the concerns of aesthetics are exhaustively treated by reference to the arts (for example judgments of natural beauty). Now, as before, the naming of our enterprise carries assumption and significance and, at best, encourages lively contest. Such contest becomes evident within and between the ensuing surveys, in which judgments, qualifications, prejudices and preferences are left more or less explicit. It is appropriate and timely that this entry should be self-reflectively concerned not only about its topic but also about its status as a dictionary entry: for usually such entries presuppose solutions to the problems about objectivity and representation that occupy philosophers as precisely the problems still in need of solution.

II. Historical survey, antiquity–1750

1. Hellenic and Hellenistic thought. 2. Early Christian thought. 3. Medieval thought. 4. Renaissance thought. 5. Baroque thought. 6 Rationalism. 7. Enlightenment.

1. HELLENIC AND HELLENISTIC THOUGHT. The commonest positions in the aesthetics of music are borrowed and developed from classical antiquity. Greek musical practice being inaccessible, the theories related to it have been freely adapted to the practice of whatever day it might be – a licence less available to those who similarly exploited classical writings on less fugitive arts. The language of musical aesthetics has thus often suggested a certain remoteness from what was actually going on.

Although 'music' (mousikē) is a Greek word, classical Greece did not use it to mean what we call music. It had no word for that. Etymologically, the word means 'the business of the Muses', who were goddesses of poetic inspiration. As a body of practice, the 'music' of classical Greece extended to cover all imaginative uses of language and dance, and as an object of theoretical study 'music' was largely the study of scale-construction and tuning systems. But this divergence between Greek conceptualization and our own dwindled in Hellenistic times.

Among the debris of ancient thought we may distinguish at least six views about the nature and significance of music. The first view is assigned to the thinkers, mostly anonymous, associated with the name of Pythagoras (6th century BCE), traditionally the first to take note of the relevance of certain small-number ratios to the intervals recognized as consonant and invariant in the music of the day. By the 5th century BCE the Pythagoreans were speculating that similar ratios should be discoverable everywhere in the world. That music embodies numerical principles and somehow answers to the laws of nature seems already to have been accepted everywhere, from China to Babylon; the Pythagorean contribution was to make this hitherto mysterious relationship amenable to rational inquiry. The ratios found in musical intervals were sought in the distances of planets, in the compositions of stuffs, in the souls of good men and in everything that contributed to cosmic order. Musical structures should thus have analogues in the human mind and in the world at large, and their felt but ineffable meaningfulness should be explicable by those analogies. Music was important as the only field in which these ratios had been discovered rather than merely postulated. But the mathematicians of the 4th century BCE borrowed the name 'music' for the branch of their study devoted to the theory of proportions, and the specifically audible varieties and manifestations of such proportions became theoretically accidental. The doctrine that music was or ought to be an 'abstract' system of relationships stateable in a set of equations has haunted musical aesthetics ever since, although the habit of linking music to astronomy by a supposed 'music of the spheres' died with Kepler (1619).

The second Greek view of music adapted the Pythagorean ideas to fit the notion, popular then as now, that national music expressed national character or *ethos*. Damon of Athens seems to have done the adapting in the middle of the 5th century BCE (see Lasserre, 1954). National styles or 'modes' were construed as essentially scale systems, whose intervals are generated by ratios characteristic of the personality types and behaviour patterns of their users, Dorians, Phrygians and the like. Damon thought of music as primarily a means of moral indoctrination. Plato, from whom these ideas descend to modern times, cut them loose from their mathematical underpinnings: his *Republic* (c380 BCE) merely postulates a series of causal connections, as follows. The specific mental characteristics that assign a person to a given sort find expression in corresponding patterns of thinking; these patterns achieve utterance in characteristic forms of poetical speech, and such formal speech evokes a fitting melodic and rhythmical accompaniment. To hear, and especially to perform, the resulting music will tend to re-create the originating mental characteristics, so that the student performer becomes the same sort of person as his composer-teacher. The charms of music are thus the same as those exerted by an attractive personality, except that music is expressive through and through whereas the excellence of a man may require him to be inexpressively reticent. In this Platonic version of the *ethos* theory, the expressiveness of music reflects that of an actual or possible poetic text. This answers to the Greek practice of teaching gentlemen to accompany themselves on plucked strings, leaving wind instruments and bravura generally to low-born professionals. The verbalizing version of *ethos* theory has the advantage over the mathematicizing version that it calls for no cosmological commitments; on the other hand, this modesty leaves it with no hidden resources to counter empirical rebuttals.

A third view of music, which has also proved perennial, is implicit in the histories of music that survive from the first centuries of our era. Like the analogous histories of other arts, these sources take a technical view of music: its history is the progressive mastery of more and more elaborate instruments, performing techniques and sound patterns. Music is seen as exploring the possibilities of a self-contained world of sound. However, this view of cultural history is modified by an assumption derived from Aristotle's cosmology and reinforced by cultural nostalgia for the classical age of Greece. The world of sound, like the world at large, is not infinite; the possibilities to be explored are not endless; and the fruitful development of the art of music was completed long ago at a period defined by that completion as classical. This complication of the progressivist view of music has also been revived from time to time, with the idealized classical age suitably updated; but its revivers are mostly musical revolutionaries who modify the theory by claiming that new worlds of music can be substituted for the old, so that new explorations can proceed – even if, as conserva-tives will protest, the new worlds cannot sustain human life. In its extreme form, this last modification becomes the claim that every serious musical work is or should be a self-contained musical universe.

The ancient progressivist theories of music history, whether or not they held that progress must end somewhere, ran counter to a deep-seated belief in social degeneration, which assigned the 'golden age' to a technically primitive past. When these tendencies collide, we have a view of music history in which musicians continually press for innovations which statesmen and moralists untiringly resist. Plato, writing as a moralist, reinterpreted the conflict between reactionary and pro-gressive musicians as one between two kinds of music: one, the true music, rationally based and logically developed, exemplifies the structural principles of all reality, including the human mind; the other music, impressionistic and fantasticated, merely imitates the sounds of nature and the passing show of temporary feelings. Variants of this contrast, which despite its incoherence is deeply rooted in Plato's general metaphysic, keep reappearing in the history of aesthetics, most recently in Adorno's pitting of the severities of dodecaphony against the confectionery of the culture industry. The contrast has been strikingly reflected in recent decades in

debates over the proprieties of interpretation: a music whose vocation is subtly to mould the perceptible surface of sound is a performer's art for which composers merely provide the material, but if music is to unfold profound tonal structures it must be elaborated in the study and its performer must reveal only such treasures as the composer has buried for him.

The reason why the underlying view of music history whose vicissitudes we have traced gives rise to such continued controversy is that it starts by equating the progress of music with the elaboration of its means rather than with the exploration of deep structures. Even the intonational researches whereby the Greek theorists finally excogitated a unified system, within which the originally incommensurable tribal modes could each appear as a possible variant, were represented as a mere development of new possibilities of modulation rather than as an investigation of the nature of modality as such.

A less tendentious account of the division within music that the ancient histories of music sought to explicate is adumbrated in Aristotle's *Politics* (*c*330 BCE): there are two musics because there are two uses for music. Rituals and festivals call for an exciting and ecstatic music, demanding virtuosity of its performers and moving its audience to a salubrious frenzy. A gentleman needs a different sort of music to play for his recreation, as one of the amenities of everyday life. 'What passion cannot Music raise and quell?', Dryden was to ask. But not all music has the raising and quelling of passion as its function.

A fourth view of music was sketched by Aristoxenus (*c*300 BCE), a student of Aristotle. He refuted the Pythagorean numerology and the *ethos* theory that was built on it by pointing out that the ratios generating harmonies are inaudible, and music is concerned with the audible. What can be heard is sounds in relation. The ear certainly needs the aid of memory and mind, but the contribution of memory is to make protracted structures perceptible, and the intellect is called on, not to intuit any underlying reality, whether cosmic or psychic, but to grasp the mutual relations of notes within the system of a scale. Music is thus a self-contained phenomenological system, and the significant form of any work is not derived from its relation to any other reality but is identical with the principle of its own organization. Why men should make such things and delight in them Aristoxenus does not say, but no Aristotelian need ask: any refined exercise of mind and senses is inherently delightful, for man is by nature hungry for information. Aristoxenus concedes that such audible constructions may acquire by association an ethical significance, but that is adventitious.

Aristoxenus's embryonic formalism strikes a responsive chord today, but was little noted in antiquity. To Ptolemy in the 2nd century CE, he was only the bellwether of one of the two extremist schools of musical theory, the latter-day Pythagoreans being the other. Ear and reason are judges of harmony, says Ptolemy, the ear establishing the facts and the reason divining their explanation. Musical theorists, like astronomers, must lay bare the design that unifies the phenomena, thus showing that the real is not irrational. He complained that the Aristoxenians trust the ear alone and forgo theoretical explanation, while the Pythagoreans trust reason at the cost of observational accuracy. The philosophy of music is thus shown to involve difficulties of principle that are still central in 20th-century philosophy of science.

A fifth view of music was current among the followers of Epicurus, represented by Lucretius in the 1st century BCE, for whom music was nothing but a source of innocent pleasure, natural in the sense that it represents a complex use of man's natural endowments: 'Every creature has a sense of the purposes for which he can use his own powers'. Such elaborations, discovered by accident and developed by experience, afford relaxation, distraction in distress and an outlet for excess energy. No further explanation of musical delight is possible or necessary, and the pretensions of highfalutin theories are merely absurd. The Epicurean tradition did not survive the triumph of Christianity, but such Philistine mutterings remain a permanent possibility for aesthetics, one that is congenial to most of us some of the time and to some of us most of the time.

A sixth, sceptical view goes beyond the Epicureans by agreeing that music is a diversion but denying that it is natural. Musical practice is conventional through and through: it may have effects on the character, but only because it is believed to have them. In fact, the Sceptics denied that music could be an object of knowledge, since it is constituted by the relations between notes, which themselves have no reality; and what is unreal cannot be known. This ontological scepticism, known to us from the work of Sextus Empiricus (3rd century CE), was to find, when less crudely stated, a permanent place in musical aesthetics.

The last four of these ancient traditions, the ones that flourished after the Greek cities lost their independence, allow music no social or civic significance. When an art claims autonomy, it may be a sign that it accepts a peripheral place in the culture of its day.

2. EARLY CHRISTIAN THOUGHT.   The Stoics had slighted music as irrelevant to the life of reason, and the Church Fathers followed them in finding it irrelevant to salvation. Yet music played an important part in the liturgy. This generated some tension. In fact, we find St Augustine (4th century) torn between three attitudes to music: exaltation of musical principles as embodying principles of cosmic order; ascetic aversion from music-making as carnal; and a recognition of jubilation and congregational song as respectively expressing inexpressible ecstasy and promoting congregational brotherhood. Being a rhetorician and not a musician by training, he thought of the numerical side of music as embodied in poetic metres rather than in music proper, but the other two attitudes left him agonizing: it is as if a man were seduced by worship.

Medieval musical aesthetics, while preserving the Augustinian attitudes, resembles medieval philosophy of culture generally in basing itself on the attempt by Boethius (6th century) to consolidate the consensus of classical philosophy, whose three-tiered metaphysical and epistemic structures readily adapted themselves to the notion of a triune God. Boethius thought of music as a branch of mathematics, unlike other branches in that its proper manifestations are perceptible and affective as well as intelligible. There are three musics: *musica mundana*, cosmic music, the 'harmony' or order of the universe; *musica humana*, human music, the order of the virtuous and healthy soul and body; and *musica instrumentalis*, music in use, the audible music men make. This framework haunted musical thought for a millennium. Its significance lies in its Neoplatonic and Christian implications. Man, according to Neoplatonism, can and should associate himself with the higher, intelligible level of reality, but turns in his weakness to the lower, sensuous level. Now, the human voice is not an artefact, but a direct embodiment of intelligence: in a sense, it belongs to *musica humana*. Stoics such as Epictetus had taught that man attunes himself with the eternal Mind by an intellectual 'song' of praise: that is, by philosophy. Christian writers – using, like St John Chrysostom (c400), the homely analogy of work songs that ease men's necessary toil – had adapted this rhetoric to a literal advocacy of psalmody, audible praise facilitating mental praise of a personal God. This complex of thought now gives rise to a new version of the old dichotomy between two musics: a low, sensual, instrumental, secular music is contrasted with an exalted, intellectual, vocal, sacred music. This dichotomy is reinforced by another Boethian doctrine, that the artist, in this case the music theorist who understands practice, is better than the mere practitioner, in this case the player or singer who uncomprehendingly follows the guidance of his training or his instrument: 'it is the definition of a beast, that he does what he does not understand', as Guido of Arezzo (c1030) unkindly remarked of singers.

3. MEDIEVAL THOUGHT.   Boethius, by treating music as a mathematical science, gave it a high place in the life of the mind (higher than rhetoric, for instance), but cut it off from secular song and dance. This sealed the fate of musical aesthetics in the early Middle Ages. The art of music became a rational mystery underlying practice, and medieval theorists tended to be preoccupied with ways of calculating and representing musical ratios. Since these ratios are exemplified everywhere in the cosmic economy, allegorical interpretations of all sorts abound, without any one of them being much developed or emphasized. However, in the 9th century the philosopher Eriugena used the fact that the cosmic order is one of simultaneous complexity to explain the peculiar value of polyphony. For the first time, musical harmony was equated with the internal relationships of an audible object.

The drive towards polyphony and polyrhythm was one of the factors that led to the development of a graphic, mensural notation, without which such complex music could scarcely be learnt and certainly could not be transmitted throughout the newly cosmopolitan and bookish culture of the 11th century and after. The introduction of such a notation, as systematized by Franco of Cologne around 1216, was not itself a contribution to aesthetics but transformed aesthetics by radically changing the nature of the art. It facilitated complexities of a wholly new order; it liberated musical time immediately from the tyranny of the syllable, and ultimately from any expressiveness based on words; it enabled the composer to be an intellectual working at his desk, rather than a performing musician; and finally, as Nelson Goodman and Thurston Dart have stressed in different ways, it lent emphasis and authority to those aspects of music that it recorded, so that a composition came to be defined by its score. Thus the abandonment of conventional notation by the advanced composers of our day left some musicians feeling as if the solid ground of their art had vanished from under their feet.

The notation that evolved for the sacred music of the Middle Ages had not only to record musical facts but also to disclose them as rational. Hence abstruse controversies arose about the nature of perfect and imperfect numbers, and the metaphysical superiority of triple (trinitarian) over duple (manichean) relations. But by the early 14th century a more sophisticated and subtle logic led in aesthetics, as in philosophy at large, to a rejection of the equation between rationality and structural simplicity. The new mood appeared in a passing remark of Johannes de Muris (1319): 'What can be sung can be written down'. The reactionary Jacques de Liège (c1330) attacked the 'new art' as lascivious, incoherent and above all irrational: if three is admittedly the perfect number, why admit imperfections? But he was too late.

Medieval aesthetics in general rests on the ancient theory of beauty, as that which gives immediate pleasure when perceived, rather than on any theory of art. Allegorical explanations are introduced only when the literal level is exhausted: it may be true that polyphony mirrors the universe, but beauty must be experienced before it is explained, and the fundamental fact is that counterpoint sounds well. This position allows of little theoretical development; but Roger Bacon, among others, drew the conclusion that the most beautiful work would be one that pleased all the senses at once, and in which music formed only one component (De Bruyne, 1947).

4. RENAISSANCE THOUGHT.   A versatile mathematical intelligence does not demand simple forms but adapts itself to the complexities of the real. The advances of late medieval logic thus prepare the way for the conclusion that mathematical considerations have no essential bearing on music. In the later 15th century, the view of music as the branch of mathematics that pertains to sounds tends to give way to a humanist view of music as a sonorous art, to which mathematics is relevant only as calculating or explaining means to musical ends otherwise determined. Johannes de Grocheo had already made the essential point around 1300, urging that the mathematical *science* of music was not the same as the *art* of music, which was the application of such theory to singing. This art was not a branch of mathematics, and neither *musica mundana* nor *musica humana* had any place in it. His cool Aristotelian pragmatism made little headway in that age of numerological hermeticism. But Tinctoris in the late 15th century, and yet more clearly Glarean in 1547, remodelled the theory of music on the basis of its actual history, practice and effects. They thought of music primarily as a form of human activity rather than as a closed science or a model of the cosmos; and the conventional ethical associations of old and new modes received less attention than the actual effects that genius and discipline may achieve. Tinctoris (c1473–4), enumerating and classifying the effects claimed for music, was content to cite authorities; but a century later writers such as John Case (1586) put flesh on his bones. Such humanism comes the more readily because no myth claims divine origin for polyphony. God may have taught Adam to sing his praise, and Jubal to play upon instruments, as J.A. Scheibe still maintained in 1754; but counterpoint was invented by men in historical times.

Glarean already sensed a crisis in music, a tension between polyphonic skill and melodic feeling, between art and nature. Zarlino, in 1558, attempted a synthesis involving a subtle humanization of the ancient *ethos* theory. Of all musical effects, he says, the ear is judge. But

the ear finds a fundamental contrast between the feeling-tone of joyful major and mournful minor triads. Instead of finding metaphysical reasons why each mode should reflect a different type of character or feeling, he appeals to experience to testify to a correlation of harmonies with feeling within a single harmonic scheme. Then, instead of saying (with Plato) that the harmony and rhythm of a piece should be determined by those actually inherent in the accompanied words and their meanings, he demands that harmony and rhythm be those perceived as suiting the general feeling-tone of the subject matter of the words.

While thus adapting ancient proprieties to a modernized and humanized form in which they have remained so familiar as to seem obvious, Zarlino introduced another fateful concept of a quite different tendency. Just as a poem may have a subject, such as the fall of Troy, so does a musical composition have a subject but this is a musical subject, a theme, a series of sounds. Music is about music. It is thus at once autonomous, through its melodic organization, and heteronomous, through its harmonic and rhythmic affectivity.

Zarlino's professional Venetian compromise between ancient theory and modern practice was soon challenged by the mainly amateur circle formed at Florence around Giovanni de' Bardi, whose chief theorist was Zarlino's pupil Vincenzo Galilei (1581). They pointed out that Greek humanism, now the acknowledged ideal, had rested on the practice of a monodic and heteronomous music in which a singing line traced and induced a flow of emotion: the gentleman troubadour, long ignored or disparaged by theorists, came into his own now that gentlemen were writing the books. Polyphonic music cannot raise and quell passions, because the effects of simultaneous melodies must cancel out. To emulate the fabled effects of Greek music at Alexandrian feasts, arcane and autonomous pattern-making must be replaced by the expressive voice of a natural man. And what is expressed is merely sentiment and speech, not (as in Plato's fantasy) character and thought. Significantly, this polemic is launched in the name of Boethius's second level against his third; the revival of Neoplatonism might have encouraged the opposition to take the yet higher ground of Boethius's first level, but the unfashionableness of logic and mathematics seems to have discouraged them from doing so.

Zarlino (1588) found the obvious reply to the Florentine arguments: music is music, it is not rhetoric. But that was the point at issue: rhetoric was the cornerstone of a courtly education, musicians' music was work for monks and lackeys. The debate continued and, *sotto voce*, continues yet; but, as the 17th century saw, it was rather unnecessary, since the Venetians had in mind a public and ceremonious music, and the Florentines envisaged a music for a more private use.

5. BAROQUE THOUGHT.   Towards 1700, the controversies between old and new musics settled down to a squabble of gentlemen over their amusements. The favoured contrast was that between stiff French correctness and supple Italian invention. The divergent styles found different rationales. Le Cerf de la Viéville (1704–6) claimed for the French party that the accepted rules formulated the established requirements of good taste and stood for reason and method as against the vagaries of fancy and passion. Raguenet (1702) maintained that the Italians, trained to music from the cradle, could dispense with rules because their underlying principles

had become second nature. If they took risks, it was because they had developed a sense for when something risky would come off. The arguments on both sides are closely analogous to those used at the time in controversies over painting and literature. Both parties occupy the lowest ground of sentimental humanism: hedonism and a courtly ambience are assumed, and the rules appealed to turn out to be no more than recipes for a rational enjoyment.

If humanistic thought can find for music a deeper significance than that of mere amusement, it must be through its working on human passion. Here an issue had been left unsettled between Venice and Florence: how does music most fitly express feeling? Through the 17th century and after, three modes were mooted. Music may follow the inflections of a voice speaking in passion – a device practically abandoned at Florence soon after it was first tried, but still theoretically entertained by Grétry 200 years later; it may echo the sense of a text word by word, as a man who gestures while he speaks – Rosseter (1601) thought it vulgar to do so, Morley (1597) thought it absurd to do otherwise; or it may convey the general tone of its text. All three modes were defended around 1600, and confused (as by Richard Hooker in 1617) with the very different doctrine of *ethos* according to which music mirrors not passion but character. But what if there is no text to accompany? The rise of a purely instrumental music that is more than an accompaniment for dancing seems to call for compositional principles that are purely structural, but how can these be used without sacrificing humanistic meaning? 'Sonata, what do you want of me?', asked Fontenelle (Rousseau, 1753).

Answers to this newly pressing problem were sought from the art of rhetoric. There were three good reasons for this. First, it afforded the only actual model for the articulation of temporally extended forms on a large scale; secondly, it formed the basis of genteel education; and thirdly, of most direct relevance, the ancient treatises on rhetoric had as their avowed aim the systematic analysis of the passions and the means of working on them – so that J.J. Quantz (1752) could say that 'The orator and the musician have, at bottom, the same aim'.

Rhetoric was actually used in two ways. First, theorists of the Baroque age tried to describe musical forms and figures by making various figurative uses of terminology derived from the articulations and ornamentations of discourse. These systems, never stabilized, died out as our special vocabulary for describing musical forms gradually made its way. And second, musical theorists tried to adapt directly to music the programme for a scientific rhetoric first enunciated in Plato's *Phaedrus* (*c*375 BCE): an analysis of human passions and the ways to arouse them. These attempts leaned heavily on Descartes' treatise on the passions (1649), which argued that the most complex emotions could be shown to result from the mechanical combination of a few simple psychological components by a strict causal necessity. Such writers as Mattheson (1739) offer elaborate analyses of the emotions along these lines, with detailed specifications of the corresponding musical devices. The resulting emotive packages are mediated by dance forms, since in a dance a complete musical complex, often with ethnic and hence ethical connotations, is already wedded to gesture and thus as it were integrated into a way of life. On examination, the mediation proves somewhat programmatic: the musical

specifications could be at best sketchily correlated with the analyses of the passions, since only a few simple musical variables had an emotive significance that could be specified. In theory, that would not detract from a Cartesian analysis, which actually called for the reduction of complexities to combinations of a few simple forms; but in practice the Cartesian programme has rather limited application, and the more elaborate versions of the 'theory of affections' were eventually abandoned (*see* AFFECT, THEORY OF THE).

Such theories of emotive meaning admit an important ambiguity: are the feelings in question to be worked on or only to be symbolized? The more sophisticated authors write as if the primary function of the emotive meaning were to make the music intelligible. A work of art has to be unified as well as articulated, and Mattheson's requirement that each piece confine itself to a single emotion suggests that at least part of what is at stake is the use of a consistent manner as a unifying principle. But the question was not clearly posed, and evocation of the represented passion was not ruled out. What was excluded was the demand that the composer be imbued with the feeling he expresses or imparts. This exclusion showed that music was being assimilated to rhetoric and not to poetry: traditionally, the poet is inspired by the feeling he arouses, while the orator must keep cool to control his audience.

To the extent that the doctrine of affections pertains to the meaning rather than to the effects of music, its intellectual affinities are not with the Cartesian 'hydraulics of the animal spirits' already alluded to, but with the later contention of such Enlightenment sages as Holbach and Hume that it is the function of reason to articulate and thus to civilize the passions.

We have noted the demand that each piece be dominated by a single mood. Such a demand envisages the composer as master of various styles. The notion of style is imported into musical theory in the 17th century from its original home in rhetoric, which required of the orator the ability to speak in diverse literary manners and to suit diverse occasions. The Baroque age found this notion useful when coping with the survival of contrapuntal church music alongside a basically monodic secular music. No longer are there rival musics: the accomplished musician knows how to write church music, theatre music or chamber music, in a diversity of national manners.

6. RATIONALISM.   It was not only through the doctrine of affections that Descartes left his mark on the aesthetics of music. He (1649) and his friend Mersenne (1636–7) both attempted once more the impossible task of rationalizing the mathematical basis of harmony. More important was Rameau's (1722) successful interpretation of harmony itself as a system on the Cartesian plan, reducing the bewildering variety of possible chords to the simple system of triads and their inversions. The modern notion of harmony, already implicit in Zarlino, thus suddenly acquires an intelligible basis and occupies the centre of musical thought. As the notion of the 'position' of a chord suggests, music comes to be envisaged as occupying a 'space' with vertical (chordal) and horizontal (cadential) dimensions. The Baroque vocabulary borrowed from rhetoric does not fit this way of thinking about music, and it becomes easier to think of it in formal, even in architectural, terms.

Rameau himself pointed out the more immediate significance of his theories. The squabbles of italophile and francophile cliques and cabals over operatic styles and persons, which through most of the 18th century retained the interest of the lay public, mostly concerned the style of vocal writing. They were therefore trivial in comparison with the issue of principle between the theories and practices that put melody first and those that put harmony first. Melody tends to be interpreted heteronomously, in terms of what it expresses; in giving harmony priority over melody Rameau laid new foundations for the autonomy of music, at the same time making it easier for instrumental music to take up a central position that it had never before occupied and from which it has yet to be evicted.

Rameau's revolutionary move coincided with, and purported to incorporate, a more fundamental discovery. This was Joseph Sauveur's almost single-handed development of the science of acoustics, making sounds into objects susceptible of systematic investigation and description. The scepticism of Sextus Empiricus was finally refuted, and from then on music could be slowly, subtly and profoundly transformed into an art of sound (see PHYSICS OF MUSIC). Meanwhile, Rameau fastened on the overtone series, already identified by Mersenne but now explicated by Sauveur, as affording a natural basis for the harmonic relations he was expounding. Musical structures were thus founded on nature – not the nature of the heavens, or of the soul, or of the eternal objects of mathematics, but the nature of sound itself.

In seeking a basis in nature for the structures he explored, Rameau was typical of his age. The reference to 'nature', which might be most variously conceived, is one aspect of a convergence between the criticism of music and that of the other arts that continued throughout the 18th century. The notion of the 'fine arts' had been conceived when palaces became museums in the 16th century; its gradual emergence reflects the dominance of monarchic courts, making symbolic use of acquisition and display. Like other cultural movements of the epoch, this conceptual unification of the fine arts had to be validated by an appeal to classical antiquity, and the only rationalization to be found there was the concept of 'arts of imitation' implicit in Plato's *Republic* and explicit in his *Epinomis* (*c*350 BCE).

Music, then, like other arts, must imitate what is not art; and what is not art is nature. But the nature of what? The growing separation of composer and performer from their public meant that the honorific answer of the ancient *ethos* theory, that music directly shows and moulds character, would no longer do; and the difficulty of finding any other laudatory answer threatened to relegate music to the last place in the pecking order of the arts. Among the early systematizers of the arts, Dubos (1719) held that music imitated the voice, and gave pleasure through the style of that imitation. Batteux (1746), arguing that all the arts exist to portray an idealized nature, seems to have been the first to think of music as a language of the heart that is natural because it precedes all conventions.

Rameau's breathtaking proposal of a Cartesian science of music did not fit into these systematizations of the arts, and seemed politically objectionable at a time when progressive thinkers were exalting the natural voice of the natural man (see Diderot, 1823). Its impact, though in the long run decisive, was therefore delayed.

7. ENLIGHTENMENT. Batteux's description of music as the language of the heart, itself a sentimental blurring of the contemporary doctrine of affections, was developed by Rousseau (1781) into a popular and durable theory about the origin and nature of language. The first human speech must have been a chant that expressed thought and feeling together; developed languages confine themselves to communicating thought, leaving to music, in its original form of song, the task of expressing feeling. Such expression was indeed the true function of all art. And since Rousseau equated nature with human nature, and this with the naively passionate side of man as opposed to the artificial 'rationality' his schooling imposed on him, music 'imitated nature' more than any other art did. But only melody is thus vindicated. Harmony and counterpoint, gothic and barbarous inventions designed merely to produce a volume of agreeable sound, fall altogether below the level of art.

The compilers of the *Encyclopédie*, the foundation of progressive thought in the later 18th century, followed Rousseau in deriving beauty from 'nature' interpreted as simplicity and truth but did not agree on the consequences for music. D'Alembert (1751) disparaged music in a way that had become traditional, for the poverty of its representational resources. Diderot (1751), however, set music highest among the arts; not for Rousseau's reasons, but because musical relationships are perceived directly and not mediated through interpretation of content, so that music gives imagination more freedom.

Diderot's appeal to imagination invokes an alternative tradition in aesthetics, according to which the fine arts were not exercises in imitation that call for rationalized skill but sources of 'pleasures of the imagination' open to the free play of creative genius. To this school, dominant in British aesthetics throughout the 18th century, not the poem but the landscape garden, in which artifice merges with the infinite, was the paradigm of art. It is this view of art and music that Romanticism was to develop. Meanwhile Kant (1790), systematizer of the Enlightenment and synthesizer of British and German aesthetics, acknowledged both conflicting evaluations of music: of all arts it is the least rational and the most delightful, a language of feeling that contrives to be universal in scope only by forswearing all cognitive meaning, so that it can never be integrated into the truly human life of reason.

Such odious comparisons between the arts were not universal. G.E. Lessing (1766) pointed out that different arts used such heterogeneous means that it was pointless to compare them. Music, deployed through time, must relate to other realms of experience than do those arts whose works are extended in space and presented all at once; how can they be thought to compete? And J.G. Herder (1800) denounced all attempts to set up hierarchies of the arts, especially that of Kant.

III. Aesthetics, 1750–2000

1. THE RISE OF AESTHETICS.   The theoretical reflections on the status of music as an art and as a form of

meaningful articulation, which constitute what is now termed the 'aesthetics of music', are often seen as merely a continuation of philosophical reflection upon music of the kind that began with the Greeks. However, the aesthetics of music cannot be said to have existed before the second half of the 18th century in Europe. The word 'aesthetics' derives from the Greek *aisthanesthai*, 'perceive sensuously', but perception became a decisive issue for philosophy only in the empiricism of Locke and Hume.

Given the increasing success of the natural sciences, rationalist philosophers of the 17th century had argued that the mathematical intelligibility of the world was proof that its true structure can be explained independently of the vagaries of sensuous perception. Leibniz summed up the implications of the rationalist view for music in the dictum that music was 'the unconscious counting of a mind which is unaware of its own numeracy'. Against the rationalist view, the empiricists maintained that our access to the world's intelligibility lies in the impressions made by the world on the senses, which constitute the prior basis of scientific knowledge. In his *Aesthetica* (1750), Alexander Baumgarten, himself schooled in the Leibnizian tradition, prepared the ground for the new subject of 'aesthetics' by focussing attention on the value of what appears as sensuously true in everyday life even if it has no claims to scientific status, such as a successful painting of a particular object. J.G. Hamann, in his *Aesthetica in nuce* (1762) and in other work, linked insistence on the senses as the prior means of access to the truth to the claim that this access also requires natural languages that cannot be reduced to a 'general philosophical language'. He saw languages primarily as celebratory expressions of the divine harmony of creation, rather than as the means of representing an objective world. This led him to the claim that the oldest language was music and to his giving a prominent philosophical role to literature.

Hamann's understanding of language is echoed by Herder, Rousseau and others during the second half of the 18th century, but they dispute the divine origin of language, seeing language instead as connected to the natural expressivity that is the basis of music. Herder, for example, claims that all natural sound is music, and that music is the language of emotion. Language thus ceases to be thought of as descending from divine naming and gains a new freedom from theology. This freedom is crucial to the emergence of music aesthetics, because it also changes the status of music, by questioning the idea that music, as itself a kind of language, could be seen in Pythagorean terms as part of a divinely ordered nature. The aesthetics of music emerges, therefore, at the moment when it is no longer self-evident what either language or music really is.

2. SUBJECTIVITY, LANGUAGE AND MUSIC.   The new conceptions of language in the 18th century come to be linked to the 'world-making' capacity of the post-feudal individual subject. When language is no longer understood as just re-presenting a 'ready-made' world, it can become a means of revealing what otherwise remains inarticulate. In the same way, aesthetics becomes a distinct philosophical topic when reflection on art becomes concerned with what art can articulate that theology, philosophy and science cannot. The new aesthetic approach to the arts is accompanied and influenced by changes in the status of instrumental music in the second half of the 18th century.

These changes are linked to the move of the most important theories of art away from the idea of art as 'mimesis': instead of art imitating or representing an extra-aesthetic order of truth, it becomes significant for its own sake. It is therefore not fortuitous that the least representational form of art, wordless instrumental music, should come to be seen by many as the highest form of art.

The emergence of 'absolute music' corresponds to changes in the conception of the human subject which begin in the 17th century and dominate philosophy in early modernity. The first theorist to think of music primarily in terms of the listener was Descartes, whose grounding of knowledge in the thinking subject's certainty of its own existence became the most significant moment in the origin of modern philosophy. In 1618, Descartes claimed that music requires imaginative activity on the part of the listener if the differing bars of a piece are to be made into a discernable unity. This theoretical claim is accompanied by a related change in music praxis: from the 17th century onwards, European music increasingly becomes more a spectacle, rather than just a ritual or a collective participatory activity. The listener's role therefore becomes more individualized, and more attention is paid to music's subjective effects. However, a prophetic tension already becomes apparent with regard to the subject who listens to music. Rationalists like Descartes think musical effects are calculable in terms of a scientific theory, but the suspicion that music might resist such a theory will later lead to specifically aesthetic views, for which music is a manifestation of the freedom of the subject and therefore immune to scientific explanation.

The interrelated social and conceptual changes of this period are accompanied by moves away from polyphonic music, which is understood as reflecting a fixed divine order, towards a harmonically based music, in which the composer's melody plays a new, 'expressive' role. Especially in Italy, this new conception of the role of music goes hand in hand with the rise of opera and with accompanying theoretical debates about the relative status of music and language. The move away from the dominance of polyphony is also regarded as a rejection of the idea that the essence of music is mathematics: Mattheson maintained, for example, that 'the art of notes draws its water from the well of nature and not from the puddles of arithmetic' (1739, p.16).

However, the nature in question is still a nature conceived of in rationalist terms, which composers depict with the intention of arousing moral sentiments in their listeners; they do not attempt to make the listeners undergo the emotions depicted in the music. The move from music being understood as expressing something to a *listener* who is its 'object', to C.F.D. Schubart's idea in the 1780s of expressing oneself as a subject in *music* as one's object, is another of the essential changes that lead to the founding of aesthetics proper. A vital factor here is the increased importance of the notion of the musical work as an autonomous, rather than a functional, entity. These changes also highlight tensions that result between positions that consider music from the point of view of the composer, of the listener, of the performer or of the music itself.

The aesthetics of music results, then, from debates about the relative importance of language and music in the 17th and 18th centuries, from the rise of modern individualism and from the importance of art in a culture increasingly secularized by the scientific and social achievements of the Enlightenment. From Saint-Evremond's declaration in 1678 that 'The Musick must be made for the Words, rather than the Words for the Musick' (1705; Eng. trans., 1930, p.210), one moves by the end of the 18th century to Wilhelm Heinse's remark in 1776–7 that 'Instrumental music . . . expresses such a particular spiritual life in man that it is untranslatable for every other language' (1795–6, iii, 83), to W.H. Wackenroder's claim in 1797 that music 'speaks a language which we do not recognize in our everyday life' (1910, edn, p.167), and to J.N. Forkel's assertion in 1778 that music 'begins . . . where other languages can no longer reach' (p.66). When the Enlightenment assumption that truth can be represented only in semantically determinate language is questioned, the role of music in philosophical thinking becomes vital. Before this time theorists regarded the feelings aroused by music as wholly able to be articulated via the objective ways of naming them, a conception captured in Fontenelle's famous question: 'Sonata, what do you want of me?'. This question was soon to become very outmoded.

3. KANT: JUDGMENT, IMAGINATION AND MUSIC. The most influential philosophical moves away from Enlightenment assumptions about music are indirectly occasioned in the 1780s and 90s by Immanuel Kant. Kant himself had no great knowledge of music, and maintained that, as merely a beautiful play of sensations, music was the lowest form of art. His initial importance for the aesthetics of music actually derives from his theory of knowledge (1781). His revolutionary claim is that objective knowledge can be understood only as a product of the cognitive acts of a subject. If the intelligibility of objects in the world can be brought about only via synthesizing acts of the mind, the mind can no longer be just the imitator of pre-existing objects. Descartes' idea that the activity of the imagination is necessary for the constitution of music is extended by Kant into the idea that all knowledge of the world depends on the workings of the imagination.

If the imagination could be said to function in terms of fixed, ultimately mathematical rules like the rest of nature, rationalist assumptions about music's harmonious links to the rest of nature, of the kind shared by Descartes and composers such as Rameau, would still hold. However, while accepting that the imagination does partly function in terms of rules, Kant rejects claims about nature's inherent structure, arguing that we ourselves 'give the law' to nature as it appears to us, so that we cannot know nature as it is 'in itself'. The essence of nature 'in itself' for his contemporaries Diderot, Rousseau, Herder and the *Sturm und Drang* movement is manifest in dynamic conflicts of the kind also present in human passions and in living organisms, which cannot be explained solely by scientific laws. The relationship of the imagination – which is itself in some way part of nature – to truth and language therefore becomes a central issue in this period. Rousseau did not think of music as a reflection of a universal form of intelligibility accessible to all rational beings; instead, he links musical melodies to particular natural languages which 'grow' in specific cultures. His idea of nature as the source of art helps open the way for Kant's later notion of the 'genius'. In his *Critique of Judgment* (*Kritik der Urteilskraft*, 1790), Kant regards the nature-derived imaginative ability of the genius to *produce* new formal rules as the basis of art. Those aspects of art that cannot be wholly derived from existing rules, and which therefore depend on the spontaneity of the subject, play a vital role in Kantian and post-Kantian music aesthetics.

Kant also sought ways of resolving key problems that emerge from his epistemology via reflection on art. In order to suggest how the passive reception of data from the world can become the active rendering of that data into forms of knowledge, he had introduced (1781) the idea of 'schematism', the ability of the subject to apprehend something *as* something, rather than receive a mass of sensory data. The relationship of this ability to the freedom of the subject, which Kant regards as the condition for art to be possible at all, becomes crucial in his later work. A piece of music can be described in terms of laws of physics, that is, it can be categorized as sounds of different pitches and durations. If it is to be apprehended as music, however, the listener must be able to hear the sounds as notes, thus as significant in relation to other not immediately contiguous sounds. This ability cannot be rule-bound, because it is required every time a new series of sensory data is heard as music. Furthermore, the listener can relate the elements of music to each other in any number of different ways in aesthetic 'play'. Kant insists that the ability to apprehend something as a work of art is not wholly conceptual, even though it depends on the same activity of the subject that is the condition of possibility of conceptual knowledge.

Two questions arise here. The first concerns the status of a conceptual description of music in relation to what the music itself makes intelligible to the listener. The second concerns the boundary between musical and verbal articulation: if language cannot say all that is to be said about music, this boundary cannot be drawn by verbal language alone. Kant helps open up these questions in his notion of the 'aesthetic idea' – 'the representation of the imagination which gives much to think about, but without any . . . *concept* being able to be adequate to it, which consequently no language can completely attain and make comprehensible' (1790; 1974 edn, p.193). Post-Kantian Romantic music aesthetics explores in depth the idea of languages that would be adequate to the imagination's ability to make the world intelligible in ways that scientific laws cannot explain.

4. ROMANTICISM: PHILOSOPHY, MUSIC AND LITERATURE. Music's dependence on mathematically expressible proportions and connection to the imagination and feelings are linked in Romantic thought to the Kantian problem of the relationship between the deterministic world of the natural sciences and the ethical and aesthetic world of human freedom. Attempts to reconcile the conflict between these two aspects of existence form the basis of German Idealist and Romantic philosophy. These attempts are associated with the exploration at the end of the 18th century of the new possibilities inherent in the dynamic form of the sonata. The sonata offers a formal framework of implicit and explicit rules, and freedom for the imagination to develop this framework by the exploitation of contrast and contradiction. At the same time, it demands that the framework resolve in its conclusion the apparent contradictions it contains. In his *System des Transcendentalen Idealismus* (1800), F.W.J. Schelling gives a culminating role to art as that which

manifests a reconciliation of the contradictions between necessity and freedom, arguing that the freedom of the subject must itself actually be part of nature, and that nature therefore cannot be conceived of solely in deterministic terms. Beethoven seems to have been an admirer of Schelling, and Hegel's Schelling-influenced philosophical system has often been regarded as analogous to Beethoven's sonata movements.

The interplay between the musical and the philosophical is characteristic of early Romantic thought, for which there is no absolute difference between the forms in which the arts and the sciences are articulated and thus no final boundary between language and music. Friedrich Schlegel maintained in 1798 that music is 'the highest of all arts. It is the most general [art]. Every art has musical principles and when it is completed it becomes itself music. This is true even of philosophy' (*Literarische Notizen*, 1980 edn, p.151), and he asked whether, in instrumental music, 'the theme . . . is not as developed, confirmed, varied and contrasted as the object of meditation in a sequence of philosophical ideas?' (1988, p.155).

Schlegel exemplifies the Romantic idea that what is revealed in all forms of artistic and cognitive articulation, be it verbal language, painting or music, is understanding of both the inner and outer world. The Romantics attached no inherent priority to referential language, because we may come to understand an aspect of the world, such as temporality or emotions or even a landscape, more appropriately via music. There is also a musical aspect, most obviously manifest in poetry, to any use of language, and music itself can involve a 'referential' aspect, of the kind present in such works as Haydn's *The Seasons*. Schlegel also links music's resistance to determinate semantic meaning to his conception of Romantic 'irony', which puts in doubt the truth of what one says even as one says it. In 1798 his friend Novalis claimed that the world is an endless series of changing relationships, which was best understood through music because music was not directed towards referentially fixing objects in the world. Novalis's loosening of the boundary between language and music is echoed in Herder's view in *Kalligone* (1800) that music is a temporalized 'energetic' art, not a finished product or work, and is valuable for precisely that reason.

The change in the status of wordless music also gives rise in Romanticism to the first methodologically elaborated conception of 'literature'. Schlegel and Novalis see musical forms as providing the model for the rhythmic and other attributes of verbal texts, which take them beyond both their pragmatic and referential functions and the limitations of rule-bound language, giving the texts a value for their own sake. Schlegel asserts that: 'the method of the novel is that of instrumental music' (1980, p.146), and he even talks of the 'musical' aspects of Kant's philosophy. The Enlightenment contrast between music's supposed failure to say anything important and the primacy of verbal language is therefore turned on its head in Romantic thought; this inversion is later epitomized by Walter Pater's assertion in 1877 that 'All art constantly aspires to the condition of music' (1961, p.129). Novalis also points the way both to the non-representational art characteristic of 20th-century Modernism and to the recent musical avant garde's use of elements of language as non-semantic elements of musical composition, when, linking them to music, he imagines 'Poems, just pleasant sounding and full of beautiful words, but also without any meaning or context . . . like fragments of the most diverse things' (1978, p.769). The Romantics initiate far-seeing reflections on the historical interplay between language and music, content and form, and these reflections do not give the one an inherent superiority over the other.

In his *Philosophie der Kunst* (1802–3), Schelling characterizes music in the terms he uses to reconcile the Kantian division between the world in itself and the world as appearance, between the 'real' and the 'ideal' aspects of the world and ourselves. Art works make the 'ideal' manifest in 'real' objects, revealing how productive freedom combines with the necessities dictated by the material of the work. Language is itself 'the complete work of art' (1859, i/5, p.358), and the other arts are seen as analogous to language. Schelling maintains that music is an inferior form of articulation, because its physical manifestation as sound (*Klang*) means that it is merely transitory. Music's dependence on temporal succession relates it to human self-consciousness, which also links together moments of time in meaningful succession, transcending temporality even as it depends upon it. Rhythm is therefore the principle both of music and of the self for Schelling: without a unification of differing moments, which both makes a succession into a rhythm and makes differing experiences into my experiences, there could be neither music nor a self. Rhythm, the 'music in music' (ibid., 322), is consequently the very condition of possibility of an intelligible world, in which successions of phenomena become meaningful by being unified into identifiable entities. Not only is rhythm therefore also the basis of melody and harmony, but music, as the interplay of difference and identity, can be said to be 'nothing but the heard rhythm and the harmony of the visible universe' (ibid., 329). Everything in the universe gains its identity from its endless relationships to other things, in the same way as each moment of a rhythmic sequence becomes determinate only by being apprehended as part of a whole.

In Romantic philosophy 'the Absolute', the whole that is necessary for finite things to have an identity, is revealed to us only via our sense of the limitations of what we know. This sense of limitation is manifested in concern with music's attempt to say the 'unsayable'. The Romantic philosopher K.W.F. Solger's dialogue *Erwin* (1815) makes some of the most emphatic claims concerning music's relationship to the Absolute: 'the effect of music consists in the fact that in the sensation of every present moment a whole eternity emerges in our mind. Music . . . therefore really achieves what is not achievable for the usual activity of the understanding. But it also does not achieve it for real objects, but only in the universal empty form of time' (Dahlhaus and Zimmermann, 1984, pp.146–7). In order to achieve the real unification of the finite and the infinite, music, Solger asserts, must link itself to other forms of art, a conception that Wagner would soon try to realize in his idea of the *Gesamtkunstwerk*, but which Solger saw as realized in the 'complete musical church service, in the singing of holy hymns before paintings of divine actions' in inspiring architectural surroundings.

5. SCHOPENHAUER, HEGEL AND SCHLEIERMACHER. Schelling suggested in 1811 that 'because sound and note seem to arise only in [the] battle between spirituality and corporeality, music alone can be an image of . . . primeval

nature and its movement' (*Die Weltalter*, 1946 edn, p.43), and he relates music to Dionysus in a manner later echoed by Nietzsche. Much of Schelling's conception of this period was appropriated by Schopenhauer in *Die Welt als Wille und Vorstellung* (1819). However, unlike Schopenhauer and many who follow him, Schelling still thinks of music as linked to rationality, because music tries to come to terms with rationality's origins in what discursive rationality itself can never finally explain. For Schopenhauer, the world of the transient appearances ordered by science is the product of a single self-contradicting power, the 'Will', which is 'an endless striving' (1966, p.240). Any manifestation of the Will must sustain itself against other manifestations that will eventually destroy it. Awareness of the Will comes about through the constant imperative to appropriate other parts of the world in order to subdue the lack generated by our ever-present bodily and emotional needs. If we remain subjected to these needs there can be no possibility of contentment. Music is most closely analogous to the Will and is the most important form of art, because it least represents the world of appearance. Even though the Will cannot be represented as appearance, music is supposed to be an 'image/representation' (*Abbild*) of the Will, so that 'One could . . . just as well call the world embodied music as embodied Will' (ibid., 366). The tensions and resolutions in a melody and the temporality of music echo the self-consuming nature of the Will at the same time as offering an aesthetic escape from dependence on it. The point is not that we experience the emotions that music articulates – that would merely be a further form of subjection to the Will – but that music should turn them into aesthetically significant forms. Schopenhauer regards these forms as analogous to Platonic 'Ideas', and this is supposed to explain the connection of music to mathematical forms. The inconsistencies in Schopenhauer's position have often been pointed out, but he had a remarkable impact on the history of music, the aesthetics of music and the other arts: Wagner regarded reading Schopenhauer as a decisive moment in his intellectual and musical development.

In his *Ästhetik* (1835), Hegel, like Herder and Schelling, defines the arts through their mutual relationships in a historical and philosophical hierarchy, but claims that the 'science of art . . . is in our time much more necessary than in times when art for itself as art provided complete satisfaction' (1965, i, 21). Art, the 'sensuous appearing of the Idea' (p.117), is understood via an historical account of the developing relationships of thought to the object world. The final phase of art is 'Romantic' art, which moves away from 'classical' (Greek) art's concern with the sensuous beauty of the object towards the Christian realization that the highest truth lies in the mind's ability to transcend the (dis)appearing sensuous world. Music is therefore the 'key note' of Romanticism, because it does not represent external objects. Its 'principle' is 'subjective inwardness' (ii, 320), and it is the culmination of the aesthetic liberation of mind by the transformation of the merely sensuous (*sinnlich*) into 'meaning' (*Sinn*). However, instrumental music has no capacity for revealing anything about the external world of science, history and society. This leads Hegel to a version of musical formalism. The philosopher's ability to assert in conceptual language that music is a one-sided form of articulation is evidence for Hegel of why, in modernity, art is transcended by

philosophy, whose task is to explicate the relationships between the principles of the sciences.

For Hegel, instrumental music's lack of semantic content is merely a deficiency on the part of music, which conceptual thought can overcome. Schopenhauer, on the other hand, gives all music the same 'meaning', because it is the means of temporarily escaping finitude via its *lack* of worldly meaning. A true description of music would be the 'true philosophy' for Schopenhauer: whereas Schopenhauer thinks that description is impossible, Hegel claims to provide it. This version of the paradigmatic opposition between music as a higher and a lower form of language reappears in many subsequent theorists: Kierkegaard (*Enten-eller*, 1843), for example, suspects music for its merely transient, if highly seductive effects, which contrast with the ethical seriousness of real communication. The question underlying the future of music aesthetics now becomes a hermeneutic question: should music be interpreted in its own terms, or in terms of something else, like philosophy, psychology or physics? The answers to this question will link music aesthetics to major philosophical and ideological battles in the modern world.

F.D.E. Schleiermacher's too often neglected aesthetics is based on his theory of hermeneutics, the 'art of interpretation'. Interpretation is an 'art', because there can be no prior rules for dealing with texts or utterances that make new sense even though they violate existing rules. Instead of isolating music in the manner of formalism, which thinks that music must be understood solely via its own criteria, Schleiermacher regards those criteria as themselves inextricably linked to other forms of articulation. He relates music to gesture and mime, because both are non-verbal, and maintains that 'the mobility of self-consciousness' – which he regards as vital to all art – is evident in both. The idea of the mobility of self-consciousness leads him to develop Kant's notion of schematism in relation to music. Sounds in nature are not music, and music is possible only through new syntheses of sounds, which depend on the subject, as composer, performer or listener, to constitute them as music. Verbal language can have either a closer or a more distant relationship to music: the specifically aesthetic issue is the 'transition to music' from the pre-musical. This transition depends upon 'free productivity', which forms sounds into new significant configurations. Free productivity must play a role, in differing degrees, not just in the composer or the performer but also in the listener.

The essential aspect is therefore the acknowledgement, through interpretative activity, of the other person's freedom to articulate and thereby give pleasure and new insight. Because the relevant aspects of the context of any interpretation must be chosen from an indefinite number of possibilities, there can be no definitive rules for this choice. Most crucially, verbal language is itself never completely semantically determinate: it always depends upon shifting contexts for its meaning. As such, 'even in the most strict kind of utterance the musical influence will not be absent' (1977, p.160), and the musical influence can play a role in how the utterance should be understood. Art, as in Kant, is 'free production of the same functions that also occur in the bound activity of mankind' (1974, p.375). Verbal languages differ from music because the referential and pragmatic 'bound' aspect tends to dominate. However, in metaphor this aspect is relativized: a metaphor can make us notice new aspects of the world, even if we cannot say what the metaphor means beyond its literal meanings. This brings verbal language closer to the ways in which music brings to our attention what we may not be able to state in words. Music is therefore closest to poetry, in which the concern is not with the general referential aspect of language but with the articulation of a particular aspect of life in a particular form. The paraphrase of a metaphor or a poem, or the verbal description of music, cannot exhaust what is paraphrased or described. After Schleiermacher, theories that take in all dimensions of the understanding of music become increasingly rare.

6. FORMALISM.   The enormous and continuing impact of Eduard Hanslick's *Vom Musikalisch-Schönen* (1854) should be understood in relation, first, to its intended refutation of the 'unscientific aesthetics of sentiment/feeling' (1990, p.21), and, secondly, to the music of Hanslick's time against which it was directed – the 'programme music' of Berlioz, Liszt, Wagner and others, which used literary and other verbal models to extend the range of musical expression. Hanslick argued that Schumann's claim that 'the aesthetics of one art is that of the others, only the material is different' (p.23) ignored the fact that the beauty of an art is inseparable from its specific techniques. He therefore maintained that 'in aesthetic investigations the beautiful object and not the feeling subject should first be investigated' (p.22), and that aesthetics should strive for the rigour of a natural science.

Hanslick successfully highlighted ways of looking at music as an 'autonomous' art: instead of describing the feelings evoked by hearing the music, the music critic analyses the specific harmonic, melodic and rhythmic characteristics of the music itself. The reasons for the shortcomings of Hanslick's approach had, though, already been suggested by the Romantics: the boundaries between the musical and the non-musical are not as absolute as he (sometimes) wished to make them. The incorporation into music of the previously non-musical is almost definitive of music history, and any attempt to interpret music solely in its own terms is inherently unrealizable. E.T.A. Hoffmann had already shown in his account of Beethoven's Fifth Symphony that it was possible to combine technical analysis of music with an – admittedly extravagant – metaphorical description of that music. Although technical analysis can generate 'verifiable' results, there is no reason to think that metaphorical interpretation cannot reveal just as much of the piece *qua* music. Hanslick fails to reflect sufficiently on the contested criteria that can be used to decide between the many ways of discussing a piece of music. There are no 'scientific' criteria for such hermeneutic decisions, and the criteria cannot be established merely from the side of the work itself.

Hanslick's core idea is that music's 'content and object' are 'sounding moved forms' (1990, p.75), and he takes instrumental music as his model. The musical material – harmony, rhythm and melody – expresses 'musical ideas', which are determinate in a way that subjective feelings can never be, and are 'their own purpose'. 'Music just wants to be grasped as music' (p.77), but music is also 'a language which we speak and understand but cannot *translate*' (p.78): 'in language the note is only the *means* to the expression of something which is completely alien to this means, while in music the note appears as its *own purpose*' (p.99). Hanslick relies, then, on an untenable conception of language, which makes the existence of literature incomprehensible, because it denies that language itself has a 'musical', non-pragmatic aspect. In order to stress music's distance from representation, Hanslick actually presupposes an aesthetics of representation for the other arts, thereby ignoring Romantic insights, themselves based on the understanding of music, which show that *any* form of art could not validly be said to be art if it were understood merely in terms of representation. Hanslick attempts to overcome the opposition between form and content by claiming that the content of music is in fact its forms, rather than what it might represent or make us feel. The claim that music's form is its content is not *a priori* implausible, but to assess its plausibility one needs to employ the resources of a contextual approach, in which the forms are located both aesthetically and historically. Hanslick's desire for a formalist understanding of music meant that he was not sufficiently prepared to historicize his conception. In this he will be followed by many subsequent approaches to music, particularly those that regard musical analysis as the only methodologically tenable approach to music.

7. DISINTEGRATION.   Hanslick's account of the scope of aesthetics of music rules out neither the importance of music for emotional life nor the possible philosophical import of music. However, Hanslick does exemplify a new tendency for aesthetics to aim at the same kind of rigour as is assumed to be present in the natural sciences. This leads to the exclusion of many approaches as merely 'subjective' and unworthy of academic consideration. The discipline of aesthetics now also tends more and more towards schematic attempts – often, like that of Friedrich Theodor Vischer, modelled on Hegel – at thoroughgoing systematization. Such works lack the sense of philosophical discovery that characterizes early Romantic approaches to aesthetics, and the desire to complete the system too often results in a Procrustean treatment of the particular arts.

The writings of the composers of the era, such as Berlioz, Wagner and Liszt, on the other hand, contribute little to sustained philosophical insight into music, even though they are essential documents of the aesthetically crucial interplay – and frequent incongruity – between verbally formulated conceptions of music and actual musical production. The composers also testify to an interest in combining music with the other arts, as suggested by Solger, in the name of the achievement of a higher kind of art, an interest that culminates in Wagner's music dramas. Although many of the ideas the composers embrace derive from Romantic thought, the subtle differentiations of that thought are sometimes neglected, for instance in Wagner's unqualified declaration in *Oper und Drama* (1852) that 'the linguistic capability of the orchestra can clearly be described as the capacity to announce the *unsayable*', namely the 'feeling' that rational verbal language is incapable of expressing. Instead of proposing a complex interplay between language and music, Wagner – who elsewhere sometimes sustains a more differentiated view – here makes a rigid division between the two.

Unlike the best of Romantic music aesthetics and hermeneutics, which regards both the separation of subject and object and other absolute distinctions in aesthetic theory as mistaken, the authors of the music aesthetics of the second half of the 19th century often concentrate exclusively either on music as an expression of subjective feeling or on the objectifiable aspects of music. The falling apart of the two sides is not just an issue for aesthetic theory: it also relates to a more general intellectual division between the arts and the sciences, which affects all later theorists. A symptomatic text of the era in this respect is Hermann von Helmholtz's *Die Lehre von den Tonempfindungen als physiologische Grundlage für die Theorie der Musik*, first published in 1863, a truly masterly account, based on the physics of sound, of the constitution of the harmonic relationships between notes and of their effect on human physiology. Helmholtz ends with a chapter on 'Relations to Aesthetics' in which he insists that the tonal systems he has examined are not an object of science as such, but 'a work of artistic invention' (1913 edn, p.587). The task of aesthetics, though, is to find the 'laws and rules' (p.588) of beauty, even though these are consciously present neither to the producer nor to the recipient of music. This leads Helmholtz, as many subsequent theorists will also be led, back to the issues that concerned Kant and the Romantics. He suggests, for example, that 'we understand pleasure in the beautiful . . . as a law-bound correspondence with the nature of our mind' (p.589), but this is only because, like Kant, he thinks we must assume a *sensus communis* in matters of taste. Once Helmholtz leaves the passive aspects of the realm of perception, where his account is exemplary, he is forced into what is really hermeneutic territory, which, as Schleiermacher had already shown, and as Hugo Riemann argued against Helmholtz, involves the active rather than just the receptive capacities of the subject. Helmholtz also underestimates the need for an awareness – of the kind his contemporary Willhelm Dilthey tried to reintroduce into academic discourse – of the inescapability of attention to context in all forms of understanding.

A further characteristic tendency of music aesthetics in the second half of the 19th century is the attempt to graft music on to a theory of human nature. Charles Darwin asserts in 1871 that 'musical tones and rhythm were used by our half-human ancestors, during the season of courtship', and that it would therefore be 'opposed to the principle of evolution' to think that 'articulate speech', as the 'latest . . . [and] highest, of the arts acquired by man' (1972, p.284), was the source of humanity's musical capacities. Music is in fact the source of language, whose fundamental aspect is rhetorical, because it is based on the need to charm a sexual partner. Darwin thus adopts a familiar Romantic topos, as well as something akin to Schopenhauer's metaphysics of the Will, but he does not give any serious reasons why music should come to be an autonomous form of *art*.

Edmund Gurney (1880) attempts to add on a theory of musical autonomy to Darwin's theory that music is dependent upon emotional excitation (although he later moves away from Darwin's view). Gurney is left with a paradigmatic problem: if it is the case that musical works are, *qua* music, independent of any emotion from outside music (even though they also gave other forms of pleasure), all music would seem, as it did for Schopenhauer, to have essentially the same significance. The source of Gurney's problem is his rigid separation between a referential conception of verbal language and music: he assumes, mistakenly, that non-musical emotions are all

namable and that musical feelings must be purely musical. Gurney's position exemplifies a central problem for any aesthetics that wishes to hold on to the autonomy of music at the same time as connecting music to the social and historical world.

Friedrich Nietzsche's account of music in *Die Geburt der Tragödie* (1872) mixes Schelling's link of music to Dionysus with Schopenhauer's metaphysics of music and the Will, while connecting Wagner's music dramas to Greek tragedy. Tragedy, as music was for Schopenhauer, is closest to the Will (Dionysus), because it transforms the destructive and chaotic aspects of human existence into the form of art. By 1878, though, Nietzsche already asserts, in the light of his engagement, after writing *Die Geburt der Tragödie*, with materialist conceptions of science of his day, that 'In itself no music is deep and significant, it does not speak of the "Will"' (*Sämtliche Werke*, 1980, ii, 175), and that 'Music is precisely not a general, supra-temporal language' (p.450). The twists and turns in his conception of music and in his relationship to Wagner are underpinned by his antipathy to any art or any conception of art that echoes Christian redemptive metaphysics, which he regards as an obstacle to confronting the realities of human finitude. He also comes to attack Wagner, in the name of a formalist musical autonomy, for giving up 'all style in music, in order to make of it what he needed, a theatre-rhetoric, a means of expression . . . he increased the linguistic capacity of music into the unmeasurable' (vi, 30). At times, though, Nietzsche sees aesthetics as 'nothing but an applied physiology' (p.418), and, like Darwin, as 'bound to . . . biological preconditions' (p.50). At other times – like the early Romantics, and in a manner that will eventually influence deconstructive approaches to interpretation – he claims that music is the reminder that the world 'has once again become "infinite" for us: to the extent that we cannot reject the possibility that it contains infinite interpretations in itself' (iii, 627).

This conception, however, is often reduced to another version of Schopenhauer's metaphysics, when he claims that the 'will to power' 'interprets', by repressing one aspect of itself in favour of another. Nietzsche's influential rejection of the notion of truth as adequate representation of a ready-made world leads him to regard all forms of articulation as potentially deceptive, and thus as all ultimately 'aesthetic'. His assessments of music vary so much because he constantly undercuts the differing bases, from biology, to psychology, to metaphysics, upon which those assessments are built. Nietzsche points to a disintegration that takes place in aesthetics when hopes for the capacity of art to replace theological meaning by establishing harmonious new relationships between the human and the natural are undermined both by the advances of the natural sciences and by the failure of these advances to be accompanied by equivalent moral and aesthetic progress. The crisis of forms in post-Wagnerian music at the end of the 19th century clearly relates to these developments: once the harmonic tonal system comes to be seen as optional, the relationship of music to a meaningful natural order seems increasingly to be a 'merely human' projection. The problem for 20th-century music aesthetics lies in finding a response to this crisis that could both sustain a critical perspective and do justice to new forms of musical production.

8. The 20th century: artists.   In 20th century 'classical' music the tension between the post-traditional sense of liberation from established forms, and the fear that a 'merely human' order might turn out to be no meaningful order at all, was brought to a head by what Schoenberg terms the 'emancipation of dissonance', the renunciation of a tonal centre around which composition is organized.

An intriguing speculative interpretation of the emancipation of dissonance is to be found in Thomas Mann's novel *Doktor Faustus* (1947), which follows the life of the fictional German composer Adrian Leverkühn whose 'compositions' involve elements derived from descriptions of the work of Mahler, Schoenberg and others. Mann connects the fate of the avant-garde composer, who insists that 'even a silly order is better than none at all', to the fate of Germany as it descends into the barbarism of the Nazi period. *Doktor Faustus* is questionable in a variety of respects because establishing relationships between music, ethics, society and politics in the 20th century is fraught with difficulties. However, the most significant composers were themselves clearly convinced of the existence of such relationships, and the continuing rejection of much of their music by large parts of the listening public suggests the importance of that conviction. The vital aesthetic question here is how the move of the most innovative music away from the tastes of the majority of its audience is to be interpreted. Carl Dahlhaus suggests that, while the music aesthetics of the 19th century aimed to explicate the musical experience of the educated lay person, the music aesthetics of the 20th century becomes an aesthetics for experts which reflects on the legitimacy of the new compositional techniques (Dahlhaus, Zimmermann, 1984).

Writing in 1957, Pierre Boulez sees advances in the technology of sound production as making possible 'a category of works free at last from all constraint outside what is specific to themselves'. He regards this possibility as 'quite an abrupt transformation, when one considers that previously music was a collection of codified possibilities applicable to any work indifferently' (Thévenin, 1991, p.179). Boulez seems untroubled by the fact that the notional lack of any 'codified possibilities' must give rise to difficulties for those listening to the music in question: if there is nothing 'codified' about the music, what grounds does one have for terming it music at all? It is therefore no coincidence when, the following year, Milton Babbitt argues that advanced composition is increasingly becoming like research in physics and will become inaccessible to the general public.

John Cage is also among those composers who regard liberation from the forms of the past as an unquestioned improvement, but he does so from a perspective that aims beyond a supposedly restrictive conception of 'music'. He offers an alternative between the position common to Boulez and Babbitt – 'if [the composer] does not wish to give up his attempts to control sound, he may complicate his musical technique towards an approximation of the new possibilities and awareness' – and his own position: 'one may give up the desire to control sound, clear his mind of music, and set about discovering means to let sounds be themselves rather than vehicles for man-made theories or expressions of human sentiments' (1973, p.10). Cage proposes a series of not necessarily compatible conceptions: he concurs with Herder, in the idea that

music is not limited to intentional human creations, and with Kant's view of art, in the idea that it is a 'purposeful purposelessness' (p.12); at the same time, he endorses a very radical version of what was adumbrated by the advocates of music's autonomy from extra-musical meaning. Cage does claim that 'the coming into being of something new does not by that fact deprive what was of its former place', but his anarchic optimism contrasts sharply with the worries of the composers who did the most to create the situation to which he responds so positively.

Stravinsky's writings on music aesthetics contain a number of observations on the interpretation and performance of music which prefigure the 'authenticity' movement, but the writings would not receive the attention they do if they were not by Stravinsky (it is not even clear to what extent they were all by him anyway). The lectures entitled *La poétique musicale* (1942) espouse a neo-classicism which, as it did for the later Nietzsche before him, involves favouring minor French talents – for Nietzsche it was Bizet, for Stravinsky, Gounod – over the 'bad musicians of modern Germany: the Liszts, the Wagners, the Schumanns'. The 'essential aim' of music should be 'to promote a communion, a union of man with his fellow-man and with the Supreme Being'. This union is being destroyed because 'Modern man is progressively losing his understanding of values and his sense of proportions', and this 'leads us infallibly to the violation of the fundamental laws of human equilibrium'. Like later conservative thinkers, such as Scruton (1997), Stravinsky interprets effects as causes, failing to see how the musical and other cultural symptoms which understandably disturb him have deep social and economic roots and cannot just be attributed to the misuse of freedom on the part of those he blames for the symptoms. His repeated appeals to the need for a 'foundation' that would reveal the hollowness of 'unrestricted freedom', and for an 'established order' to which one should submit as an artist and human being, are based in the last analysis on a dogmatic theology which completely fails to come to terms with the complex realities of the secularized modern world.

Schoenberg is profoundly aware of the problems created by his farewell to many of the established foundations of musical composition. His writings testify to a constant tension between the drive for authentic innovation and the desire to legitimate that innovation in terms of existing traditions. His account of his role in the 'emancipation of dissonance' raises important points with regard to his music's relationship to verbal language, describing how he only became able to use the new non-harmonically based style 'to construct larger forms by following a text or poem' (1975, p.217), the lack of recognizable chordal patterns having ruled out other ways of structuring a larger compostion. In his longer compositions before the development of his new method of 'composition with 12 tones', the 'differences in size and shape of [the text or poem's] parts and the change in character and mood were mirrored in the shape and size of the composition, in its dynamics and tempo, figuration and accentuation, instrumentation and orchestration. Thus the parts were differentiated as clearly as they had formerly been by the tonal and structural functions of harmony' (pp.217–8). However, in that case, the hard-won musical autonomy established in music at the end of the 18th century is now renounced in favour of a renewed subordination to the text. Schoenberg's essential concern is that his music should embody an order of the kind possessed by harmonically based music. He suggests that the artist 'will wish to know consciously the laws and rules that he has conceived "as in a dream"' and that 'he must find, if not laws and rules, at least ways to justify the dissonant character of these harmonies and their successions' (p.218). In the search for specifically musical forms of order, Schoenberg arrives at a method which he claims to have 'esthetic and technical . . . support which advances it from a mere technical device to the rank and importance of a scientific theory' (p.220). He accordingly presents the method of 'composition with 12 tones', which he developed in the early 1920s, as the 'foundations for a new procedure in musical construction which seemed fitted to replace those structural differentiations provided formerly by tonal harmonics' (p.218).

Arguments over the significance of Schoenberg's new method continue to this day. Do listeners actually listen to such music with tonal ears, and is the method therefore, as Hindemith and others have claimed, still in fact reliant on a natural order of harmony based on the intervals between notes with less complex mathematical ratios? Or is the perception suggested by Hindemith's argument merely a habit that has developed in the West over the centuries? The more significant issue here, as Mann realized, lies in the consequences that could be drawn from adopting either of these assumptions. The tendency has been for many on the authoritarian and conservative side to insist that there is a natural order upon which music relies, which the avant garde senselessly transgresses, and for many on the left to insist that one cannot naturalize something that is inextricably connected to other developments in culture and society. Given the growing openness of the public to music from the most diverse cultures, this issue seems likely to be settled in favour of the relativity of music to historically based norms, but the underlying tension persists between the desire to naturalize and the desire to historicize because music has become ever more clearly linked to an awareness of the essentially contested nature of cultural norms.

9. THE 20TH CENTURY: THEORISTS.   The most significant theoretical development in the music aesthetics of the 20th century is the emergence of sophisticated theories of music's connections to society and history, which extend the exploration of music's relationship to subjectivity to the ways in which individual subjectivity is at least in part consituted by socially generated structures and practices, including language, economics and music itself. Many of the other major theories of music, on the other hand, either are questionable elaborations of positions from previous music aesthetics, or fail to deal with the real aesthetic questions.

Large parts of the philosophical work on music in Britain and the USA from the 1920s onwards reflect the impact of the new 'analytical' philosophy of language of Frege, Russell and Carnap, which assumes that the philosophical explanation of thought can be achieved by the logical analysis of language. Until the later Wittgenstein – who will maintain, in line with Romantic hermeneutics, that 'Understanding a sentence in language is much more related to understanding a theme in music than one thinks' – such philosophy often stifles thinking about those aspects of language the Romantics regarded

as inseparable from music, though it does offer invaluable insights into the logic of our understanding of the object-world. Analytical approaches to philosophy draw on powerful support from the natural sciences, which study the rule-bound subjective aspect of music in new forms of physiology and psychology, and study the objective aspect of music, in acoustics, information theory and other physically based disciplines. The aesthetics of music, though, is inherently at odds with philosophy which, like 'logical positivism', relegates statements about music as an art to 'meaninglessness', on the assumption that the meaning of a statement lies only in the ways in which it can be scientifically verified. Controversies over the relationship between verbal language and music now take on a new significance, which comes to be reflected in the divide between analytical and 'phenomenological', and hermeneutic approaches that still dominate contemporary philosophy. In certain respects this divide echoes the divide between positions that see music as a timeless category and positions that think it impossible to separate the understanding of music from its history.

Until recently much of analytical philosophy worked mainly on the objectifying assumption that meanings are phenomena to be explained in terms of the rules for the use of language. It also considers music in mainly objectifying terms, looking, for example, at notional laws governing the hearing of the musical object, or at whether the object has 'representational properties'. The advocates of phenomenology closest to its founder, Edmund Husserl, such as Roman Ingarden (1973; Eng. trans., 1986), are concerned to give exhaustive descriptions of the structures via which the world is 'given to us', and they often deal with ontological issues similar to those that concern analytical philosophers, such as the status of the musical work *qua* score and *qua* performance. Ingarden argues, for example, that the musical work is a 'purely intentional object', reducible neither to the score nor to a specific performance (or set of performances).

Susanne K. Langer (1942) incorporates music into a view, derived from Ernst Cassirer, of humankind as distinguished from the animal world by its ability to produce symbols. Langer's often exhilarating position remains, though, unhappily suspended between analytical assumptions about the 'fixed meanings' which refer to objects in the world in verbal language, and a Romantic awareness, based on Kant's notion of schematism, of the need to explore ways of making sense beyond discursive language. For Langer, music becomes the 'logical expression' of feelings, and has no 'literal meaning'. It has 'all the earmarks of a true symbolism, except one: the existence of an *assigned connotation*' (1942, p.240), and is an 'unconsummated symbol' of the form of feelings, rather than of feelings themselves, or of objects in the world. However, it is clear that living metaphors also have no 'assigned connotation', and that music cannot be limited to expressing just the *form* of feelings. The strict division Langer requires between music and language therefore not only fails to theorize language adequately but also fails to do justice to key aspects of music.

Hermeneutic and phenomenological approaches to language and art associated with the work of Martin Heidegger assume that humankind is inherently characterized by the need to understand its own facticity. This 'always already' present *existential* need is the inescapable basis of any subsequent *theoretical* attempt to understand ourselves and the world. A hermeneutic aesthetics of music therefore does not see it as necessary to make definitive methodological divisions between the differing dimensions of language, or between language and music, because these divisions are constituted in continually changing practices of understanding. In his essay 'Grundfragen der Musikästhetik' (1926), Heidegger's pupil Heinrich Besseler announces that 'the real goal of all music theory and music history today should be termed hermeneutics' (p.78). Like Heidegger, Besseler wishes to get away from the idea that the truth about phenomena like music is a purely theoretical or scientific matter: 'Music originally becomes accessible to us as a manner/melody of human being'('Weise menschlichen Daseins', p.45). Music is part of human 'being in the world'. The task of aesthetics, as it was in the Romantic tradition, is to make us understand better what we are in relation to music and what music is in relation to us: these questions cannot be divorced. The questions are historical because there can, as the history both of music and of music aesthetics shows, be no final answer to them. Besseler confirms the significance of his approach in the notion of *Gebrauchsmusik* ('functional music' or 'music for use'), which reflects the new musical production of the early Hindemith, Eisler and others. He also challenges notions of musical autonomy, arguing that 'The everydayness away from which high art wishes to lead is the life-element of *Gebrauchsmusik*' (p.43), and asks 'What role does music play in the context of the particular existence and its everydayness?' (p.42). This position is itself a historical reaction to the failure of so much music theory at that time to come to terms with the new roles of music in a society which was in ideological, social, economic and political crisis.

The exploration of music's relationship to society exemplified by Besseler is unthinkable without the emergence of the sociological tradition of Marx, Dilthey and Max Weber. However, many Marxist sociological approaches to music aesthetics, such as those of Georg Lukács and Zofia Lissa, remain, despite the importance of their attempts to show how musical and socio-historical transformations are inextricably linked, trapped within a model of art as primarily a representation of historical reality and as merely a 'reflex' of its historical circumstances. Because it does not offer an adequate account of musical autonomy, let alone of the revolutionary utopian promise of reconciliation that music seems to offer its listeners suggested by Ernst Bloch (1918), this model often makes it incomprehensible that the same music can be highly valued, for differing reasons, in the most diverse modern societies. The challenge facing a sociologically orientated aesthetics of music is therefore to do justice to seemingly incommensurable realms. Analysis of historically specific social, economic and political constellations has to be combined with analysis of music which becomes aesthetically significant only because it transcends such constellations.

The strength of the work in music aesthetics of the philosopher, critic and composer T.W. Adorno, on whose theories Mann relied for parts of *Doktor Faustus*, lies in his combination of the refusal to ignore the continuing importance of the Western classical tradition of autonomous music with a critical stance which accepts that art may have become inadequate as a means of responding to the extremes of modern history. Adorno directs his

aesthetics against the 'culture industry'. In capitalist societies where virtually anything can become a commodity to be bought and sold, art with an immediate popular appeal will tend to function as a compensation for existing injustices, and will therefore encourage uncritical acceptance of the *status quo*. The freedom of the subject is threatened when subjects become the passive objects of cultural products made to fit the artificially created demands of the market. The music of the heroic bourgeois period, particularly that of Beethoven, had seemed at times to offer symbolic indications of a reconciliation between the new freedom of the individual and the need to create new forms of collective social justice. It did so, Adorno argues, by being true to the specific, collectively generated, technical demands and possibilities of the art form itself, rather than by aiming to please its recipients or to be immediately comprehensible. The task of music aesthetics is to bring out the more general truth of the most significant music, at the same time as doing justice to the particularity of the musical work, which is, as it was for Kant, a value in itself. The problem is that music no longer can be regarded as true if it is beautiful in the manner of the tradition of Western classical music: that tradition's means of extending the ability of the modern subject to express itself have, particularly since Wagner, become clichéd and 'ideological'. The difficulties of composing modern music are thus incorporated into a wider theory of how music relates to the individual and of how the individual is subjected to the pressures of modern rationalized societies.

Despite his pessimistic assessment of modernity, Adorno tries to sustain both the autonomy of music and the notion that music still has a potential to keep alive the idea of a fulfilled human existence. This leads him to revise Romantic notions of the relationship between music and language: 'As language, music moves towards . . . the absolute unity of thing and sign, which is lost in its immediacy to all human knowledge' (1970; Eng. trans., 1984, p.154). Music 'makes a fool of the spectator by continually promising meanings – and even intermittently granting meanings – which are for it in fact only, in the truest sense of the word, means towards the death of meaning, and in which [meanings] it for that reason never exhausts itself' (pp.154–5). Like the Romantics, Adorno sustains an interplay between what can be stated in verbal language and what music may communicate through its unique historical configuration of material. Within Adorno's own context new music can only keep alive possibilities of meaning by refusing to be assimilated into the dominant ways of making sense of the modern world. The musical avant garde of Schoenberg, Berg and Webern, which resists interpretation in terms of straightforward enjoyment, is seen as the music that is true to the demands of philosophically serious music aesthetics. Adorno's position, particularly in *Philosophie der neuen Musik* (1949), where he stylizes the difference between Schoenberg and Stravinsky into a paradigm of the conflicts in modern music, is often unnecessarily dogmatic, and his moves from immanent analysis of works to their wider social meanings are sometimes questionable. However, his requirement that art, the sphere in which the most developed possibilities of human freedom can be explored, be subject to rigorous aesthetic and historical criticism rings increasingly true at a time when the culture industry and those who administer it threaten to obliterate differentiated aesthetic judgment in so many areas of the contemporary world.

Adorno may well represent the end of a tradition of aesthetic theory which was certain of its ability to make substantial connections of Western music to a wider story about history and philosophy. Now, in an era of incommensurability between philosophical traditions and of 'decentred' artistic production, such enterprises are often seen as underestimating the complexity of the task of establishing large-scale links between the theorization of art and the writing of history. What, then, are the future tasks of music aesthetics if it renounces a 'grand narrative' (Lyotard) of Western art and if the very category 'work of art' is now threatened? Since its inception, aesthetics has always been a hybrid discipline. Its decline from the speculative heights of the early 19th century was in part a result of many of its concerns becoming the object of more specific disciplines, particularly in the natural sciences. However, the power of the early conceptions, beginning with Baumgarten, lay in their disturbing the boundaries between scientific and other conceptions of the world by showing that art poses questions that cannot be definitively answered from within any of these particular conceptions. When aesthetics competes with disciplines with their own rigorous methodological criteria it must in one sense fail: the aesthetics of music will not, for example, give us testable results of the kind offered by musical analysis. However, the inextricable links between aesthetics and hermeneutics are today again becoming important both for the study and the praxis of music, and for philosophy.

The notorious problems concerning the appropriate ways to carry out musical analysis relate to problems that have also bedevilled the analytical philosophy of language. The underlying dilemma is a circularity, in which the results of any investigation must depend on the initial decision as to what it is that is being analysed. This dilemma was already recognized by Kant when he introduced the notion of schematism in his theory of judgment, was developed by Schleiermacher and was made central to 20th-century philosophy by Heidegger and Wittgenstein. Criteria for judgment, be it in semantics or music analysis, cannot legitimate themselves, so there can be no definitive way of establishing a universally valid starting-point for any kind of analysis. The choice that music aesthetics now faces lies between the analytical development of Hanslick's formalism, and hermeneutic attempts, represented in recent years by Carl Dahlhaus, Hans Heinrich Eggebrecht, Roger Scruton and others, to keep alive interactions of music with other ways of understanding and experiencing the world and ourselves. Such interactions ensue of necessity from the fact that all understanding, be it of referential language or Beethoven's 'Eroica' Symphony, is possible only via the contexts in which what is to be understood is already pre-theoretically disclosed to us. When we understand, we do not understand sentences via the rules of language: instead we understand the world of which we are a part. If we did not have prior ways of understanding the world we would never even be able to learn rules for understanding utterances, because we could not get to the point of understanding what it is to learn a rule at all. In a phrase of the philosopher of language Donald Davidson, the hermeneutic conception erases 'the boundary between knowing a language and knowing our way around in the world generally'. Music can contribute to our knowing our way around the world, even as it reminds us in its own ways that the understanding of anything always also involves aspects that remain hidden to us. Recent developments in musicology and music aesthetics suggest that a hermeneutically orientated approach can assimilate the analytical insistence on the autonomy of music at the same time as showing how the idea that music is mere abstract form fails to explain why so many kinds of music matter so much, in so many different contexts, to so many people.

IV. Anglo-American philosophy of music, 1960–2000

1. Ontology. 2. Performance. 3. Expressiveness. 4. Understanding. 5. Evaluation. 6. Future directions.

1. ONTOLOGY.   Ontology is the study of the manner, matter and form in which things exist; so the ontologist might ask: what kind of thing is a musical sound or a musical work? Few philosophers have recently addressed the first question (an exception being Scruton, 1997), but several discuss the second.

Although Goodman (1968) characterized the work as the set of its accurate performances, in fact he regarded it as a set of 'descriptions' encoded in and relative to a notational system. Anything that satisfied these descriptions was an instance of the given work. As a nominalist, Goodman avoided talk of abstract entities, but a person more inclined to realism might regard the work not as a set of descriptions but as an abstract object, in particular as a sound-structure. This Platonist view has a long history. Its entailments include the following: that musical works exist eternally and are discovered by their composers; that a single work could be discovered by different people; that composers, working independently and at a temporal and social distance from each other, would write the same work if they specified the same sound-structure.

The main alternative to Platonism is a contextualist ontology, which ties the work's identity to features that depend for their character on the socio-historical setting within which it is made. Accordingly, works are created, not discovered, and identical sound-structures specified in very different socio-musical contexts are likely to result in distinct works. Contextualism was developed mainly by Levinson (1990). Because he took the composer's identity to generate relational features of the work that are crucial to its identity, he thought that different composers spelling out the same sound-structure inevitably composed different works. Also, he regarded a work's instrumentation and the appropriate manner of sound production to be essential to its identity. On all these points he has been criticized from a Platonist perspective by Kivy (1993). Levinson focussed on works dating from the early 19th century. His proposals are less plausible for earlier times, because far less detail then was specified by the composer, both as regards what is to be sounded and the instruments to be used. One might respond to this (as Goehr, 1992, did) by concluding that the concept of the musical work, with its regulative function, did not emerge until 1800. Alternatively, one could hold that a thinner but still legitimate conception prevailed before 1800. Works can be thin or thick in constitutive properties; over the past six centuries they have tended to become thicker, with more detail specified and less freedom granted to the performer. A number of factors lie behind this trend, such as the development of an increasingly complex notational system and the progressive standardization of instruments and orchestras.

On this last view, musical works are not of a uniform ontological type. A similar conclusion emerges when one considers differences across musical types at a given time. For instance, jazz pieces are ontologically much thinner, and purely electronic works are much thicker, than most classical ones. Works conveyed by notations addressed to performers are always ontologically thinner than the performances that instance them, because notations are silent on many matters that must be decided by the player. But the notations or model instances that are the basis of jazz improvisations are more skeletal than those specifying classical works, so the jazz musician has more freedom than his or her classical counterpart. Meanwhile, purely electronic compositions are for playback under standard conditions, not for performance. (The person who controls the settings of a hi-fi in playing a CD does not perform the works on it, whether these are Beethoven's or are purely electronic.) Accordingly, in the case of purely electronic pieces all the acoustic details that are reproduced under appropriate conditions characterize the work itself.

2. PERFORMANCE.   In the case of classical music, philosophers typically have focussed more on works and the listener's experience of them than on performances (exceptions include Mark, 1981; Thom, 1993; and Godlovitch, 1998). Some who write on jazz (Alperson, 1984; Brown, 1996) and on rock (Gracyk, 1996) have discussed improvisation and the manner in which live performances differ from those generated in the recording studio, but the philosophical literature on these musical kinds is as yet under-developed. Meanwhile, the performer's interpretative contribution is little discussed (but see Krausz, 1993).

However, one performance issue, that of authenticity, has been widely debated by philosophers in the last decade. An authentic performance is one that instances the work, which is done by faithfully executing those of the composer's instructions that are work-constitutive, whether or not it also duplicates some original performance (Davies, 1987). Because a work's specification always under-determines many details of its performance, many different performances can be equally faithful to it. There are huge practical difficulties in finding authoritative scores, in mastering the instruments and performing practices of former times and in interpreting the composer's prescriptions in light of the notational conventions and musical practices they presuppose. Moreover, there is some philosophical uncertainty, especially as regards works historically removed from the present, about which of the properties publicly indicated by the composer are to be counted as work-determinative. Yet authenticity would appear to be attainable in many cases, since performers often can comply with all the instructions and indications conveyed by the composer, thereby delivering a faithful instance of his work.

There are many kinds of authenticity in which music figures (Kivy, 1995), including that associated with the performer's personal autonomy. But if we are interested in musical works as the creations of their composers, the faithfulness with which the composer's work-determinative instructions are met must be central to the enterprise of performance. This is not to deny that a performance is evaluated also in terms of other qualities, but it is to say that authenticity normally should not be traded for the sake of heightening other performance values. If this last assertion does not appear to be a commonsense platitude, as it should, perhaps this is because of the inflated claims sometimes made on behalf of authentic performances. Of more philosophical relevance is the understandable doubt that modern listeners can experience the work as its composer's contemporaries did, in which case it can seem that authenticity must be pointless. Yet this need not be so, as long as we value performances for successfully instancing the works they are of, thereby acknowledging our musical heritage and all the subsequent works built on that foundation. Besides, such painstaking care is taken with the details of most works by their composers that it is reasonable to predict that authentic performances usually will be more revealing and rewarding than the alternatives for audiences who are receptive to works of the kind being performed.

3. EXPRESSIVENESS.   The traditional view, that emotions are purely inner sensations distinguished by their phenomenal structures, has been rejected in favour of one that recognizes as no less essential to an emotion's identity certain desires, attitudes, suppositions and beliefs about its object, along with appropriate behavioural expressions and causal conditions. In the 19th century, Hanslick anticipated the modern view and concluded that purely instrumental music could not express human emotions. In effect, he argued that music was incapable of conveying propositional attitudes or of picking out intentional objects (and neither was it sentient, of course). Although a few current authors have not regarded works as expressive of emotions – for instance, Raffman (1993) has suggested that expressiveness attaches to performances, not works – most reject Hanslick's conclusion. Indeed, accounting for music's expressiveness has been the major preoccupation of Anglo-American philosophers of music in recent decades.

Although Susanne Langer's theory (1942) remains touted by music educationists, it presupposes the crude, traditional view of emotions. Moreover, its account of music's expressive power – as depending on an opaque and indescribable connection between the form of emotions and of music – lacks explanatory power. (But for a recent defence of Langer, see Addis, 1999.) Similarly unsatisfactory is Goodman's analysis (1968) of art's expressiveness as involving metaphorical exemplification, for it is clear neither how music illustrates the literary device of metaphor nor how the notion of exemplification, by which the music provides a sample of an emotion in expressing that emotion, applies to it (see Beardsley, 1981). Meanwhile, the claim that we experience an irreducible analogy between music's movement and human expressive behaviour (Scruton, 1974, 1997) identifies without accounting for the phenomenon that is so puzzling.

One prominent analysis, sometimes known as the 'contour' theory, notes that expressive character is sometimes ascribable to a face or body without reference to felt-emotions or the intentional contexts they suppose (Kivy, 1989; Davies, 1994); for instance, the face of a St Bernard dog looks sad, without regard to the way the dog happens to be feeling. The expressiveness of instrumental music is similar, arising from a resemblance experienced between human appearances with an expressive character and the dynamic contour and pattern of the music. In his version of the theory, Kivy denied both that music was about, and that it often moved listeners to echo, the emotions expressed in it. Neither of these positions is entailed by the contour theory and, without them, it is better placed to explain why we would attach importance to music's expressive character.

The contour theory cannot explain how music could express 'higher', more cognitive emotions, such as pride, hope, envy and patriotism, which lack distinctive outward appearances. Those who think that music is capable of expressing such emotions have argued that music is able to invoke or otherwise 'hook into' the cognitive aspects and attitudes that are distinctive to them (Levinson, 1990). Complementarily, some philosophers (see Robinson, 1994, and Levinson, 1996) and musicologists (cited in Robinson, 1997) have suggested that instrumental works should be heard as developing a narrative about a persona hypothesized by the auditor. This narrative provides both a human subject to whom emotions can be attributed and a context allowing for the expression of subtle, cognitively complex feelings. Whether this kind of imaginative engagement is required for the recognition and appreciation of the expressive properties of instrumental music, or, instead, if it leads to responses that are merely occasioned by the music, are topics that will continue to be debated.

A longstanding but frequently criticized theory holds that music's expressiveness can be analysed reductively as its power to awaken a response in a suitably prepared listener. The listener does not respond to the music's expressiveness; that is, the music's expressiveness does not precede the listener's response, either as its object or as its cause. Rather, the music is expressive in virtue of arousing the listener as it does. New and more refined versions of 'arousalism' continue to be advanced (see Ridley, 1995, and Matravers, 1998). The appeal of this theory no doubt stems from the recognition that we could not easily explain the interest of music were it not for its capacity to stimulate the listener's emotions.

4. UNDERSTANDING.   It is frequently acknowledged that comprehending listeners must have a grasp of a work's style and type, so that they can distinguish the expected from the surprising and can synthesize the perceptual manifold in a fashion that reflects the music's telos or organizational principles. In this regard, Meyer's theory (1956) of the listening process is widely accepted (although his account of music's expressiveness as depending primarily on delays in the fulfilment of such expectations seems unduly narrow). According to Meyer, educated auditors bring to their listening expectations internalized from experiences of similar pieces and earlier parts of the current one, and these reflect the likelihood of various continuations from any moment in the work. More generally, the cognitive character of listeners' understandings, which must be informed by knowledge of the relevant idioms and conventions, is emphasized over alternative accounts that characterize the appeal of music as purely visceral.

However, this is not to accept the tradition according to which the appreciation of instrumental music depends on recognition of its formal structure and is fundamentally opposed to emotional responses other than those that delight in the work's formal unity and ingenuity. The intellectual and emotional are not exclusive and opposed;

neither is the one always self conscious while the other is mindless. Appreciation may be revealed in the emotional response music calls from a person as much as in his or her verbal reports, and we might reasonably doubt that listeners comprehend music if they are never moved emotionally by it; but neither of these observations counts against the claim that music's comprehension is ineradicably cognitive. Many recent philosophers hold that a work's formal structure will usually be of interest to listeners who grasp it, but these philosophers are not narrow formalists. Listeners should be able to recognize prominent musical ideas (such as themes), to identify their repetitions, variants and recapitulations as such, and to describe the music's unfolding, but this need involve neither an internal commentary in terms of textbook models nor a knowledge of musical technicalities and the musicologist's vocabulary (Kivy, 1990; Davies, 1994). Moreover, so intimate often is the connection between a piece's formal structure and its expressive pattern that listeners' accounts of, or responses to, the latter are no less indicative of their appreciation than would be their descriptions of the former.

Though the above position is far from strict formalism, it is rejected by Levinson (1997), who follows the 19th-century author, Edmund Gurney, in arguing that almost all musical understanding and appreciation comes from tracking the music's progress moment by moment. Not only is it unnecessary for listeners to attend to overarching form, it is impossible for them to hear musical units that extend over more than about one minute. What is heard earlier can affect how later passages sound, but listeners need be aware only of the outcome, not of the connections that underlie it. The art of listening involves practical rather than intellectual knowledge – know-how rather than propositional awareness – and the understanding achieved may not be capable of articulation.

Levinson intends his account to defend the person who responds to the passing surface of music without reflecting on what he or she hears. If his claims are controversial, it is because he presents them as appropriate for the listener whose aim is to understand an extended classical work. The kind of listening he recommends might be thought to be more appropriate for other musical kinds or for the listener whose primary focus is not the work as such, and who yields to the music's subliminal effects without attending to what is actually heard.

5. EVALUATION.   Music plays so central a role in the lives of many people that there can be no doubting how highly it is valued. As a primarily abstract art form, it cannot be important for the informational significance of its content. This has been seen as posing a problem for analyses of its profundity (Kivy, 1990), but it could be that the distinctness or separation of the musical realm from the actual world is crucial to music's value, not only for providing an enjoyable alternative to reality but also for intensifying the appeal of the formal and expressive relations that it explores (Sparshott, in Alperson, 2/1994; Goldman, 1995; Budd, 1996).

Although it is sometimes maintained that music is valuable mainly as a source of knowledge (through direct acquaintance with the emotions it expresses and arouses, say), or because of its humanizing and moralizing power, a more plausible view recognizes that musical works are valued for the pleasure that attends their appreciation. An interest in a sufficient number of works might, indeed, yield the desirable side-effects mentioned, but individual works interest us for themselves and are valued according to the pleasurable experiences they provide. Not all works are enjoyable: some are revealed as trite and dull, and then are to be avoided, while others, though worthwhile, are harrowing and depressing. But, in general, musical works reward those who take the trouble to understand them, and this includes works in which the expression of negative emotions contributes to the creation of a whole the worth of which can be seen to depend on the part they play.

The pleasure provided by the listening experience is taken not only in purely sensuous elements but also in the complex relation between a work's content and the manner in which it unfolds (Levinson, 1996). Sometimes formal relations are important; at other times expressiveness is prominent; and most often it is the complex interdependence of these two, as well as other features salient to an experience of the music's progress, that is the object of appreciation. In order to hear the interplay between the music's content and form, the listener's perceptions must be informed (if only implicitly, as a result of repeated hearings of appropriately similar works) by a sense of the musical conventions, constraints and possibilities within and against which the composer operates.

Further kinds of musical value include a work's originality and its influence on later works. These values are derivative: unless the work in question provides an enjoyable experience, or leads to subsequent works that do so, its originality and impact are of no moment.

It should be apparent from the earlier discussion of performance that we esteem, as well as works, the performer's efforts, both as these succeed in delivering a faithful version of the work and also as they are creative in going beyond that which is supplied by the composer, so that what is sounded forth presents an interesting and satisfying interpretation. In addition, we admire the sheer skill of the virtuoso player (Mark, 1980; just as we admire the technical brilliance of the composer of complicated fugues), but, in general, we expect virtuosity to be at the service of the work rather than an end in itself (just as we expect composers to produce music that sounds interesting, whatever structural complexities are hidden within it). Good performance is valued for its own sake. This is apparent from the fact that improvised music is of interest, as are those kinds in which works are so ontologically minimal that the focus falls mainly on the player; and we do not condemn a performance if it reveals a poor work to be just that.

6. FUTURE DIRECTIONS.   Our understanding of music and its relation to those who make and listen to it might be broadened by a fuller consideration by Western philosophers of the many musics of non-Western cultures and non-classical types of Western music. This should provide a new perspective on familiar issues as well as raising others hitherto undiscussed. Even in the discussion of Western classical music, the range of issues canvassed has been restricted or slanted: the focus has fallen more on works than on performances, on purely instrumental music than on other kinds, on expressiveness than on ontology, on what is common to listeners' responses than on what differs, and on music considered in isolation rather than on its connection to morality, personal identity and social relations more generally (for an exception see

Higgins, 1991). Moreover, philosophers ignore the general implications of modern technology for our experience of music and, more particularly, differences between recordings and live performances.

V. Contemporary challenges

1. The ideological. 2. Cognitive science. 3. Technology and the experimental. 4. Popular music. 5. The present.

1. THE IDEOLOGICAL.   Many challenges arise out of the remarkable surge of recent interest in the interactions of both music and philosophy with social and cultural theory, feminist criticism and theory, post-structuralism and postmodernism. These interactions tend to stress the connections between music and the world – with the ordinary conditions and experiences of men's and women's lives – to counter the more positivistic, alienated and abstracted discourse of formalism they take to have long dominated academia. These challenges often consist in replacing the dominant theoretical discourse with a preferred one. Theorists tend to articulate their positions by urging us to move away from the establishment discourse towards a preferred alternative:

(i) from the high, élite, fine tradition of classical or serious art towards the practices and rituals of popular, non-Western (non-European) music;

(ii) from the division between composer and performer, the commodified work-concept, the masterpiece, the fixed score (text) and the differentiated and fixed genres (sonata, symphony, concerto) towards performer-composer continuity, improvised performances, forms and contents, spontaneous music-making and interactive genres;

(iii) from the mentalistic, voyeuristic, intellectual, concert-hall form of passive or unbodily listening and watching towards active, participatory, dynamic, bodily and erotic acts of musical engagement;

(iv) from the élite and institutionalized concert hall towards public and open performance spaces;

(v) from the separation or remove of music from life towards its social context (say, its involvement in and contribution to social action);

(vi) from principles and ideals of unity, sameness and singularity towards plurality, difference and diversity, from the ideal of correct (*Werktreue*) or authentic interpretation towards that of multiple and diverse interpretations; and

(vii) from the pure music itself towards those who, in multiple and diverse ways, engage impurely (i.e. as real people) with music.

Some contemporary theorists seek to undermine the traditional (Western) discourse of bi-polarities (body/mind; sense/reason; feeling/thought; fact/norm), a discourse that has allowed theorists to disregard or exclude one side in favour of the other. They suspect this discourse because they take it to be the 'ideological machinery' for the sustained oppression of women (perhaps women composers and musicians, or women's music conceived in anti-essentialist terms), and of minority groups (composers, performers, musicians and their musics) (Kramer, 1990; McClary, 1990). Yet it often looks as if the dichotomous discourse is perpetuated when the challenge is articulated in terms of replacing the terms of one discourse with those of another. Mostly, that is a false impression. Some theorists assert their difference from, and rejection of, the concepts and claims of the traditional discourse as a necessary act of political separatism. Some see their function to be essentially negative or critical, that is, to expose the dominant historical discourse for the prejudices it tries to conceal behind the mask, typically, of 'reason', 'purity' and 'humanity'. In either case, the point is to stress that the preferred discourse does not fall prey to the same hegemonic or ideological forms as the rejected one. In other words, a rejected discourse that claims, for example, to speak for all but obviously does not, would be replaced by one that explicitly stresses (say) diversity, range, locality and particularity precisely as a way to expose the former's pretence while trying to avoid the pretence itself.

As so described, these contemporary aims suggest an interesting paradox when applied to the history of Western music and philosophy. Recall the idea that, from the earliest times, established academicians sometimes liked to conceive of music as antithetical to philosophy. They attributed to music properties of the 'irrational', 'uncontrollable', 'emotional' and 'insignificant', properties they also often assigned to woman or the 'feminine'. Paradoxically, when they chose to value music, they stressed qualities (say) of form, reason and meaning that rendered music least, one might say, like music – least affective, least musical. That way, the academy could control what it most feared. Contrarily, when they chose not to value music, and saw it threatening society's established forms, they assigned to it all the 'negative' values that enabled music to remain most musical. Symbolic of the discarded feminine, so the counter-argument goes, music secretly carried all the values (of feeling, passion, of the body etc.) that the academy of oppressive society tried to conceal, by relegating them to the non-serious, the secular and the popular. Music thus named what the established society refused to name; it served as society's principle of resistance, of non-identity and, potentially, of the establishment's undoing (Leppert, 1993).

A relevant conclusion for the present discussion follows from this argument. Assuming that Western philosophy, or the philosophy 'of the academy', has reflected or, in its worst condition has tended to reflect society's oppressive tendencies, if it now stands any chance of producing a successful philosophy of music, it will do so the more it adopts values for itself that it has historically assigned to music. It is more likely to do this when it positively embraces music as music and no longer relegates it to a position of the incomprehensible 'other'. The problem is whether, under this condition, it will still be able to produce a 'philosophy of', if, that is to assume, thinking about philosophy as a 'philosophy of' inherently assumes a position of dominance and control.

2. COGNITIVE SCIENCE. From the most contrary perspective, the engagement of philosophy with music has been challenged and reshaped by the increasing interest philosophers and theorists have taken in cognitive psychology and cognitive science. This engagement has tended music towards its being empirically well-grounded. Being so grounded – so that music may receive accurate and objective analysis – is a longstanding aspiration of the philosophical enterprise and, in many quarters, remains so.

Early developments in structural linguistics since the 1930s led to attempts to describe music as a 'language' or 'code', whose fundamental principles of organization were analogous to those of verbal language and other semiotic systems (see SEMIOTICS). The central principle

motivating this analogy was the Saussurean dualism of 'speech' (*parole*) and 'language' (*langue*). Speech consists of concrete verbal or musical utterances; language represents underlying rules and structural relations. Knowledge of the latter is necessary for receiving and producing the former. The rules (at the level of *langue*) that relate the sounds of speech to one another are conventional: they form a code shared by the speakers of a particular language. The stress on conventional codes or on the cultural relativity of musical languages recalls Langer's application to music of Cassirer's philosophy of language. It also recalls the work by the pioneers of structural linguistics (notably Jakobson, 1932). In the 1950s–70s theorists as diverse as Cooke (1959), Pagnini (1974) and Gasparov (1976) all explored the parameters of musical structure – acoustics, rhythm, harmony, form, scale – against the theoretical background of structural linguistics. Structural linguistics has also been significantly developed, and sometimes usurped, by semiotic or semiological theory. Taking music as a sign, the task has been either to show, formalistically, the way in which music refers to itself (here its meaning is specifically musical) or, anti-formalistically, how the sign refers to or mediates the 'extra-musical' cultural or ideological world (Nattiez, 1975). The challenge of semiotics has been to show simultaneously the extent to which music acts like a language, but achieves its meaning in a way other languages do not (Lévi-Strauss, 1964; Ruwet, 1972 and Faltin, 1978).

At the same time, theorists have been showing a renewed interest in universal structure, and in this regard may be distinguished from those who have focussed on convention or, by long extension, on cultural ideology. The shift towards universality has followed the advances of the theory of generative grammar whose proponents focus on the universal 'deep structure' that is purportedly common to all languages and supersedes each language's conventional 'surface structure'. Attempts to apply this sort of generative grammar to music can be found in Asch's theory of musical analysis (1974), Blacking's theory of innate musical comprehension (1973) and Arkad'yev's theory of a universal concept of rhythm (1992).

However, by far the most influential application of the generative approach to music is found in the collaborative work of Fred Lerdahl and Ray Jackendoff (1983). They offer a rule-based model that attempts to account for the musical intuitions of listeners acculturated to classical tonal music. The theory has two rhythmic components: grouping structure, which parses the musical surface into motifs, phrases and sections; and metrical structure, which assigns a grid of strong and weak beats. The theory also has two pitch-hierarchical components: time-span reduction, which assigns degrees of structural importance to events in relation to the rhythmic structure; and prolongational reduction, which assigns a hierarchy of tension and relaxation to events. The reductions are represented by tree diagrams which are different from syntactic trees in linguistic theory. The rules that assign these structures are of two types: well-formed rules, which characterize hierarchical structures within each component; and preference rules, which rank well-formed structures according to perceptual plausibility. Some of these rules, such as those based on Gestalt principles, are hypothesized to be psychological universals, while others are taken to be style-specific.

Their work has given rise to many empirical predictions and experiments. It has also helped establish a strong connection between music theory and cognitive science. From a philosophical perspective, their model falls within the framework of modular theories of mental representation. Thus, Anglo-American philosophers engaged with cognitive theory, science or psychology have tended, when thinking about music, to focus on the mental act of listening. Their general concern (confirmed by Raffman, 1993) has been with mental representation, with the idea that perception, broadly defined, is an operation in which the mind represents the world to itself. This representation may be more or less abstract, ranging as it does from the most basic sensorial responses or sensations to the most complex, conscious thoughts. Theorists, Raffman writes, disagree on what governs the process of mental representation in the case of listening, but Lerdahl and Jackendoff have argued that it is governed by a musical grammar, by analytical and innate rules stored in the unconscious mind that allow us to represent what is given to us in hearing as a coherent or intelligible structure.

Though some contemporary cognitivists have gone on to use (more or less directly) Lerdahl and Jackendoff's model to stress music's non-conceptual or ineffable meaning (Raffman), others have used it to stress the strong cognitive and conceptual dimension of listening (DeBellis, 1995). Both uses have depended on establishing a connection between music's physical or formal features and the perceptual features of listening. These connections are established when listeners enter into intentional contexts, such that what we hear is more than the merely physical features of music. We hear pitch rather than mere acoustical frequency (Raffman), patterns of closure, say, rather than merely sequences of sounds (DeBellis). (Compare also Scruton's theory of metaphorical listening, 1997.) The theories generally differ given the extent to which they take the intentional contexts to be cognitively or theoretically laden. Some stress the unconscious operations governing mental operations; others, the impact on listening of, say, consciously knowing a music theory. DeBellis, for example, investigates the logical relationships between hearing and musical analysis, arguing that for some listeners and contexts, music perception is non-conceptual, for others, laden with music-theoretic concepts: 'Music-theoretical terms (closure, etc.) have a certain kind of explanatory status, and . . . the value of hearing music in those terms sometimes derives from that status'. His intent is to bring explanation and interpretation into rapprochement. This intent has two advantages: first, it brings the philosophy of music in touch with music theory (thus perhaps countering Sparshott's objection that philosophers are insufficiently literate about music); secondly, it gives to the philosophy of music, with its interest in listening, interpretation and meaning, a scientific, empirical or theoretically sound foundation without reducing music to mere science.

3. TECHNOLOGY AND THE EXPERIMENTAL.   Many theorists have used the pervasive presence of recording, computers and other new forms of technology to challenge traditional ontological views about music, the musical work and performance. What, they have asked, is the status of a recording? How is it related ontologically to its performance, or to the work itself? Is the status of the recording or work altered if the composer dispenses with the medium of live performance, or if the composer composes directly into the technology, thereby dispensing with notation, traditional instruments and performance, and, hence, with the ontological differentiation between work and reproduction? Answers to these questions have partly depended on the type of the ontological theory supported (more or less Platonist, nominalist, contextual: see §IV, above) and partly on how much theorists have taken into account the diverse revolutions and experiments in compositional, notational and performing techniques of the 20th century. Up to now, the practice and theory of both John Cage and Glenn Gould seem to have proved the two most common reference points for Anglo-American philosophers.

More broadly, developments in electronic, acoustic, aleatory, spatial and minimalist musics have all forced transformations in music's traditional conceptual and ontological packaging. Often in line with 'alternative' discourses of the postmodern, some of these developments have symbolized the move away from fixed to open specification of musical features, especially when the compositional process has stressed indeterminacy, chance and randomness. In other cases, the shift has been in the opposite direction, making the determinate but interpretatively flexible qualities of traditional notation absolutely precise and absolutely fixed through computer techniques.

Musical packaging has also been affected, modified or utterly transformed as practitioners and theorists have moved away from tonal to sound organization, from sound to noise organization, from noise to temporal organization, from temporal to spatial organization. Part of what has conceptually, ontologically and politically been at stake here has been the upholding or breaking down of barriers, (a) between the different art forms (to what extent do we see or hear spatial music?), (b) between the different functions of 'classical' musicians (composers, performers, listeners), (c) between the so-called élite and popular forms of music-making, and (d) between the aesthetic domain and the ordinary and between art and nature. Some theorists have claimed that music (and they have produced music accordingly) can lead listeners (back) into nature, (back) into the ordinary world of sound. Some have rejected the idea that music represents in any sense at all: music is found in the world, and does not exist at an aesthetic or representational distance from it. Some have claimed that contemporary experiments of music reveal new and radical forms of expression, thus subverting with more or less success the increasingly heard, conservative, or at least backward-looking, assertion that tonal music (however broadly or narrowly defined) is the one true or natural musical language.

Other writers have suggested of the new musics (some or all) that they are experiments for the sake of such, that they have no ontological or aesthetic interest, and, if anything symbolizes the end of music (in Hegelian terms) at the end of the 20th century, it is the fact that the conceptual or philosophical interest of contemporary musical forms has so often surpassed their aesthetic or musical interest. The claim that these experiments have no musical interest tends to beg the question as to what music is, what it can be, and what it is for. And the claim that aesthetic interest remains the most, if not the only, relevant standard needs more support, especially if one holds that interests, including aesthetic ones, change as languages, techniques and social forms change. The purportedly special preserves of both music and the aesthetic domain remain under negotiation. Two more sophisticated, though very different, critiques by philosophers of radical experiment have been offered (Adorno, 1958 and Cavell, 1969).

4. POPULAR MUSIC.   Ontological, aesthetic and social claims have been challenged by theorists who have taken their primary examples from jazz, rock, rap and fusion (Brown, 1996). They have contributed to the philosophical debate by stressing, first, the many 'trans-' or 'intertextual' relations that hold between different instances of music, given current techniques of quotation, sampling and allusion, and secondly, the deep dependence and interaction of ontological models on and with social and cultural forms of production (Frith, 1981; Leppert and McClary, 1987; Middleton, 1990). When, and to the extent that, their theories have been read back into the 'élite' production of classical music, part of the intent has been to show that classical music is just one of many forms of music production in the world, and that, if philosophers are to address music, they should not automatically assume that the music should be classical music (and typically late 18th- and early 19th-century music). In other words, the stress on 'just one of the many' has been a political act of theory intended to undermine classical music's longstanding hegemony largely by revealing the contingency of classical music's underlying conceptual and aesthetic paradigms. The recent noticeable rise of interest in opera, a genre that offers all kinds of interactions between the classical, élite, popular, social and aesthetic, has also reflected the methodological shifts associated with these interactions (Abbate, 1991; McClary, 1992; Goehr, 1998).

Theorists of the popular have also wanted to show the value of different kinds of music or their broad and pervasive impact on all sorts (and classes) of persons in society. Here they have sustained a most provocative suggestion that, because those who listen to popular forms of music far outnumber (and the gap is growing) those who listen to classical forms, then if philosophers really want to understand how music moves, what it means and how it is social, they should look at the musics that do still move, do still mean and do still interact with the social at the end of the 20th century.

Conservative theorists of the classical have tended to respond more or less explicitly with an ardently-felt evaluative argument: the purpose of a philosophical theory is not merely to describe the musics that do move and mean, but the musics that (they believe) should move and mean. If society is benefited by its musics, then it matters to which musics it gives value, and popular music is not for the most part the music, they argue, that we should value (Scruton, 1997). Many of these theorists have sought psychologically, naturalistically, or tradition-based arguments to explain the value they find in their preferred exemplars of classical music.

Not all philosophers engaged with classical music believe their choice of examples is so ideologically or evaluatively loaded. Some merely write about what they know most about and most like. Some engage in traditional forms of speculation about music's being and meaning without any apparent regard for the political, social or historical: they believe they stand in a position of philosophical detachment. Yet other theorists continue to engage philosophically with classical music, fully realizing that their choice does not exclude others making alternative choices and contrary evaluations and, further, that fruitful and critical interactions can be achieved between different modes of philosophical inquiry, modes that might focus on different areas of musical production. One consequence at least of this more expansive or open approach has been to caution philosophers about the limitations of a monological or unilinear approach towards even the classical domain. When philosophers speak about music, what kinds of instances, and which instances, of music are they speaking specifically about? Why, for example, the usually overriding emphasis on purely instrumental music among certain groups of philosophers? Should we not be as concerned about the reference of 'music' as much as we are about the reference of 'philosophy'?

5. THE PRESENT.   Perhaps the most significant challenge to the philosopher's engagement with classical music has come from the mere fact of the present. For most of the history of the discipline, philosophers who have thought about music have thought about the music of their own time. Of course, they have compared it with a more or less idealized past that sometimes they chose to favour but, on the whole, they were concerned with the contemporary and present. To a large extent, and most especially among the Anglo-Americans interested in classical music, the focus on the contemporary has become increasingly opaque or, in some cases, has disappeared altogether. Over a century ago, Dilthey (1985) called the modern age the 'age of historical consciousness', and what he noticed in that age was the extent to which 'we feel surrounded by our entire past'. Over a century later, the question is whether this feeling has become too great a burden. Despite the abundance of forms of modern or contemporary music, many philosophers seem much more comfortable focussing on examples produced in the past, usually in the 18th and 19th centuries. However, engaging philosophically with past examples produces a very distinctive kind of philosophy: sometimes a philosophy of ideal types, sometimes a philosophy of too fixed or rigidified a past. The question remains whether the idealization or fixity is justified and under what terms. What kind of philosophy is produced when it treats its subject or examples as ahistorical products that conform to static and general principles of classification? Under hermeneutical influence, some theorists suspect that the attitude we take towards our past, whether we idealize or reject it, always reveals more about the present than it does about the past. This suspicion also pervades much of contemporary musicology, especially the recent debate over authenticity (Kenyon, 1988).

Some theorists have suggested that our philosophical thinking about music always seems to trail behind our thinking about other artistic and cultural forms. Some think that this trailing positively symbolizes music's ability to resist the appropriative trends of competing, contemporary theories. Others see the trailing negatively to reflect the establishment's reluctance to subject music's purported mystery to commonplace or worldly account. Others think very little about any of these issues and continue to hold fast to the long established tradition of asking certain sorts of philosophical questions about music: What is it? Does it express? How does it mean? Is it like language or any other of the arts? Is its meaning tied to our emotional lives? Is it connected to emotion? What is the relation between music and sound, music and tone? What is musicality and musicianship? Can music teach or instruct? What is its role in education? Can it tell the truth? What is listening? What kind of performance is musical performance? Is it mental, is it bodily? What human or social interests does music serve? Does it serve any interests uniquely? What is the role of technique and craft? What are the proper preserves of philosophy and its philosophy of music? What is the relation between music and language, symbolic form, and myth? What is music's relationship to dance?

To a great extent, philosophers continue to develop models of investigation – analytic, formal, hermeneutical, phenomenological, semiotic, post-structuralist, sociological, cultural – to treat the seemingly perpetual questions of their discipline. The choice of method often reflects the particular traditions of philosophy developed in different languages and countries (Russia, Hungary, Bulgaria, France, Italy, Japan, China, India and Scandinavia, to mention some of the countries not specifically considered above). To an equally great extent, philosophers have recently been noticeably preoccupied by the assumptions of the enterprise in which they engage. The most neutral conclusion to draw is that the struggle between the two enterprises – the positive offering of methods and claims and the sceptical self-reflection – continues to keep philosophy's engagement with music most animated, and the philosophy most philosophical.

BIBLIOGRAPHY

A General. B Historical survey: (i) Hellenic and Hellenistic (ii) Early Christian and medieval (iii) Renaissance and Baroque (iv) Rationalism and Enlightenment (v) 18th century (vi) 19th century (vii) 20th century. C Anglo-American philosophy of music since 1960. D Contemporary challenges.

A: GENERAL

StrunkSR1
F. Nietzsche: *Die Geburt der Tragödie aus dem Geiste der Musik* (Leipzig, 1872/R; Eng. trans., 1993)
H. Ehrlich: *Die Musik-ästhetik in ihrer Entwickelung von Kant bis auf die Gegenwart* (Leipzig, 1882)
J. Legge, trans.: 'Yo Kî or Record of Music', *The Sacred Books of China: the Texts of Confucianism*, iv: *The Lî Kî*, The Sacred Books of the East, xxviii (Oxford, 1885/R), 92–131
W. Wiora: *Die vier Weltalter der Musik* (Stuttgart, 1901/R; Eng. trans., 1965)
B. Croce: *Estetica come scienza dell' espressione e linguistica generale* (Milan, 1902, 11/1965; Eng. trans., 1909, 2/1922/R)
P. Moos: *Die Philosophie der Musik von Kant bis Eduard von Hartmann* (Stuttgart, 1922/R)
F. Gatz, ed.: *Die Musik-Ästhetik grosser Komponisten* (Stuttgart, 1929)
F. Gatz, ed.: *Musik-Ästhetik in ihren Hauptrichtungen* (Stuttgart, 1929)
R. Schäfke: *Geschichte der Musikästhetik in Umrissen* (Berlin, 1934, 3/1982)
W.D. Allen: *Philosophies of Music History* (New York, 1939/R)
P.H. Lang: *Music in Western Civilization* (New York, 1941/R, 2/1997)
P.O. Kristeller: 'The Modern System of the Arts', *Journal of the History of Ideas*, xii (1951), 496–527; xiii (1952), 17–46
H.J. Moser: *Musikästhetik* (Berlin, 1953)
J. Portnoy: *The Philosopher and Music* (New York, 1954/R)
E. Fubini: *L'estetica musicale dal Settecento a oggi* (Turin, 1964, 3/1987; Eng. trans., 1990)
H. Pleasants, ed. and trans.: *Schumann on Music: a Selection from the Writings* (New York, 1965)
D. Zoltai: *A zeneesztétika, i: Ethosz és affektus* [A history of the aesthetics of music, i: Ethos and affect] (Budapest, 1966, 2/1969; Ger. trans., 1970 as *Ethos und Affekt*)
C. Dahlhaus: *Musikästhetik* (Cologne, 1967; Eng. trans., 1982)

W. Kaufmann, ed.: *The Basic Writings of Nietzsche* (New York, 1968)
J.M. Masson and M.V. Patwardhan: *Aesthetic Rapture* (Poona, 1970)
S. Bimberg and others, eds.: *Handbuch der Musikästhetik* (Leipzig, 1979)
P. le Huray and J. Day, eds.: *Music and Aesthetics in the Eighteenth and Early-Nineteenth Centuries* (Cambridge, 1981, 2/1988)
E. Lippman, ed.: *Musical Aesthetics: a Historical Reader* (New York, 1986–90)
C. Dahlhaus and R. Katz, eds.: *Contemplating Music: Source Readings in the Aesthetics of Music* (New York, 1987–93)
B. Bujic, ed.: *Music in European Thought, 1851–1912* (Cambridge, 1988)
A. Bowie: *Aesthetics and Subjectivity from Kant to Nietzsche* (Manchester, 1990)
L. Goehr: *The Imaginary Museum of Musical Works* (Oxford, 1992)
E. Lippman: *A History of Western Musical Aesthetics* (Lincoln, NE, 1992)
P. Alperson, ed.: *What is Music?: an Introduction to the Philosophy of Music* (University Park, PA, 1994)
W. Bowman: *Philosophical Perspectives on Music* (Oxford, 1998)

B: HISTORICAL SURVEY
(i) Hellenic and Hellenistic

StrunkSR1
H.S. Macran, ed. and trans.: *The Harmonics of Aristoxenus* (Oxford, 1902/R)
I. Düring: *Ptolemaios und Porphyrios über die Musik* (Göteborg, 1934/R)
E. Barker, ed. and trans.: *The Politics of Aristotle* (Oxford, 1946, 2/1948/R)
R.G. Bury, trans.: 'Against the Musicians', *Sextus Empiricus*, iv (London and Cambridge, MA, 1949/R)
C. Bailey, ed. and trans.: *Titi Lucreti Cari De rerum natura libri sex* (Oxford, 1950)
F. Lasserre, ed.: *Plutarque: de la musique* (Olten, 1954)
A.J. Neubecker: *Die Bewertung der Musik bei Stoikern und Epikureern* (Berlin, 1956)
E. Hamilton and H. Cairns, eds.: *Collected Dialogues of Plato* (New York, 1961/R)
E.A. Lippman: *Musical Thought in Ancient Greece* (New York, 1964/R)
W.D. Anderson: *Ethos and Education in Greek Music* (Cambridge, MA, 1966)
K. Meyer-Baer: *Music of the Spheres and the Dance of Death* (Princeton, NJ, 1970/R)

(ii) Early Christian and Medieval

ReeseMMA; RiemannG; StrunkSR1
PG, lv, 3552-7 [St John Chrysostom, commentary on the psalms]
Augustine: 'De musica', *Writings of Saint Augustine*, ed. R.C. Tagliaferro, Fathers of the Church, ii (New York, 1947)
Boethius: *De institutione musica*; ed. and Eng. trans. in C.M. Bower, *Fundaments of Music* (New Haven, CT, 1989); extracts in *StrunkSR1*
Guido of Arezzo: *Regulae rhythmicae*, in *GerbertS*, ii, 25–42; ed. J. Smits van Waesberghe (Buren, 1985)
Franco of Cologne: *Ars cantus mensurabilis*, in *CoussemakerS*, i, 117–36; ed. F. Gennrich (Darmstadt, 1957); extracts in *StrunkSR1*
Johannes de Grocheio: *De musica* (c1300); ed. and Eng. trans., A. Seay in *Johannes de Grocheo: Concerning Music* (Colorado Springs, 1967)
Jacques de Liège: *Speculum musicae*; ed. R. Bragard, CSM, iii (1955–73)
Jehan des Murs: *Notitia artis musicae* (1321), in *GerbertS*, iii, 256–7, 292–301, 312, 313–15
J. Tinctoris: *Complexus effectuum musices* (c1472–5), in *CoussemakerS*, iv, 191; ed. in CSM, xxii (1975–8); ed. and Eng. trans. in R. Strohm and J.D. Cullington, *Egidius Carlerius, Johannes Tinctoris: On the Dignity and the Effects of Music* (London, 1996)
J. Tinctoris: *Liber de arte contrapuncti* (1477), in *CoussemakerS*, iv, 76–153; ed. in MSD, v (1961)
H. Abert: *Die Musikanschauung des Mittelalters und ihre Grundlagen* (Halle, 1905/R)
E. de Bruyne: *L'esthétique du Moyen Age* (Leuven, 1947; Eng. trans., 1969)
T. Dart: *The Interpretation of Music* (London, 1954, 4/1967/R)

N. Goodman: *Languages of Art: an Approach to a Theory of Symbols* (Indianapolis, 1968, 2/1976)
C.V. Palisca and W. Babb, eds. and trans.: *Hucbald, Guido and John on Music: Three Medieval Treatises* (New Haven, CT, 1978)

(iii) Renaissance and Baroque

ReeseMR; StrunkSR1
H. Glarean: *Dodecachordon* (Basle, 1547/R); Eng. trans., MSD, vi (1965)
G. Zarlino: *Le istitutioni harmoniche* (Venice, 1558, 4/1589/R; Eng. trans. of pt iii, 1968)
V. Galilei: *Dialogo della musica antica et della moderna* (Florence, 1581/R)
J. Case: *The Praise of Musicke* (London, 1586)
G. Zarlino: *Sopplimenti musicali* (Venice, 1588/R)
T. Morley: *A Plaine and Easie Introduction to Practicall Musicke* (London, 1597/R); ed. R.A. Harman (London, 1952/R, 2/1963/R)
P. Rosseter: *A Booke of Ayres* (London, 1601/R)
R. Hooker: *Of the Lawes of Ecclesiasticall Politie* (London, 1617/R, 7/1639)
J. Kepler: *Harmonices mundi libri V* (Linz, 1619; Eng. trans., 1997)
R. Descartes: *Les passions de l'âme* (Amsterdam, 1649/R; Eng. trans., 1911–12)
A. Kircher: *Musurgia universalis* (Rome, 1650/R)
F. Raguenet: *Parallèle des italiens et des français en ce qui regarde la musique et les opéras* (Paris, 1702/R; Eng. trans., 1709/R)
J.L. Le Cerf de la Viéville: *Comparaison de la musique italienne et de la musique françoise* (Brussels, 1704–6/R)
J. Mattheson: *Das neu-eröffnete Orchestre* (Hamburg, 1713/R)
J. Mattheson: *Der vollkommene Capellmeister* (Hamburg, 1739/R; Eng. trans., 1981)
J.J. Quantz: *Versuch einer Anweisung die Flöte traversiere zu spielen* (Berlin, 1752/R, 3/1789/R; Eng. trans., 1966 as *On Playing the Flute*, 2/1985)
C.P.E. Bach: *Versuch über die wahre Art das Clavier zu spielen* (Berlin, 1753–62/R, 5/1925; Eng. trans., 1949)
J.A. Scheibe: *Abhandlung vom Ursprunge und Alter der Musik* (Altona, 1754/R)
M.C. Boyd: *Elizabethan Music and Musical Criticism* (Philadelphia, 1940, 2/1962/R)
M.F. Bukofzer: *Music in the Baroque Era* (New York, 1947)
P. Nettl: *Luther and Music* (Philadelphia, 1948/R)
M.F. Bukofzer: *Studies in Medieval and Renaissance Music* (New York, 1950/R)
H. Lenneberg: 'Johann Mattheson on Affect and Rhetoric in Music', *JMT*, ii (1958), 47–84, 193–236
E. Bodky: *The Interpretation of Bach's Keyboard Works* (Cambridge, MA, 1960/R)
F. Blume, ed.: *Renaissance and Baroque Music* (New York, 1968) [trans. of *MGG* articles]
C.V. Palisca: *The Florentine Camerata: Documentary Studies and Translations* (New Haven, CT, 1989)

(iv) Rationalism and Enlightenment

MersenneHU; StrunkSR1
R. Descartes: *Musicae compendium* (Utrecht, 1650/R, 2/1656; Eng. trans., 1653)
J.B. Dubos: *Réflexions critiques sur la poésie et sur la peinture* (Paris, 1719, 7/1770/R; Eng. trans., 1978)
J.-P. Rameau: *Traité de l'harmonie réduite à ses principes naturels* (Paris, 1722/R; Eng. trans., 1971)
C. Batteux: *Les beaux-arts réduits à un même principe* (Paris, 1746/R, 2/1773/R)
D. Diderot: *Lettre sur les sourds et les muets* (Paris, 1751)
J. le Rond d'Alembert: 'Discours préliminaire des éditeurs', *Encyclopédie ou Dictionnaire raisonné des sciences, des arts et des métiers*, ed. D. Diderot and others, i (Paris, 1751; Eng. trans., 1965)
C. Avison: *An Essay on Musical Expression* (London, 1752, enlarged 2/1753/R, 3/1775)
J.-J. Rousseau: *Lettre sur la musique française* (Paris, 1753)
G.E. Lessing: *Laoköon* (Berlin, 1766/R; Eng. trans., 1957)
J. Beattie: *Essays: on Poetry and Music, as they Affect the Mind* (Edinburgh, 1776, 3/1779)
J.-J. Rousseau: 'Essai sur l'origine des langues', *Traités sur la musique* (Geneva, 1781), ed. C. Kintzler (Paris, 1993); Eng. trans. (New York, 1966)
A.E.M. Grétry: *Mémoires, ou Essais sur la musique* (Paris, 1789, enlarged 2/1797/R)
I. Kant: *Kritik der Urteilskraft* (Berlin, 1790/R; Eng. trans., 1952/R)
J.G. Herder: *Kalligone* (Leipzig, 1800/R)
D. Diderot: *Le neveu de Rameau* (Paris, 1823; Eng. trans., 1964)
H. Scherchen: *Vom Wesen der Musik* (Winterthur, 1946; Eng. trans., 1950)

(v) 18th Century

C. de. Saint-Evremond: *Oeuvres meslées* (London, 1705); Eng. trans. (London, 1728; selection repr. in *The Letters of Saint-Evremond*, ed. J. Hayward, London, 1930)
A. Baumgarten: *Aesthetica* (Frankfurt, 1750/R)
J.-P. Rameau: *Démonstration du principe de l'harmonie* (Paris, 1750)
J.G. Hamann: *Aesthetica in nuce* (1762); ed. J. Nadler, *Johann Georg Hamann: Sämtliche Werke*, ii (Vienna, 1950), 195–217
J.N. Forkel: *Musikalisch-kritische Bibliothek* (Gotha, 1778–9/R)
I. Kant: *Kritik der reinen Vernunft* (Riga, 1781 and many other edns)
I. Kant: *Kritik der Urteilskraft* (Berlin, 1790/R; Eng. trans., 1952/R); ed. W. Weischedel, *Werkausgabe*, x (Frankfurt, 1974)
W. Heinse: *Hildegard von Hohenthal* (Berlin, 1795–6)
L. Schubart, ed.: *C.F.D. Schubart: Gesammelte Schriften und Schicksale* (Stuttgart, 1839–40/R)
F. von der Leyen, ed.: *W.H. Wackenroder: Werke und Briefe* (Jena, 1910)
L. Schneider, ed.: *W.H. Wackenroder: Werke und Briefe* (Heidelberg, 1967)
H.J. Mähl, ed.: *Novalis: Werke, Tagebücher und Briefe*, ii: *Das Philosophisch-theoretische Werk* (Munich, 1978)
F. Schlegel: *Literarische Notizen, 1797–1801*, ed. H. Eichner (Frankfurt, 1980)
P. le Huray and J. Day, eds.: *Music and Aesthetics in the Eighteenth and Early-Nineteenth Centuries* (Cambridge, 1981, 2/1988)
F. Schlegel: *Kritische Schriften und Fragmente 1–6*, ed. E. Behler and H. Eichner (Paderborn, 1988)
R. Otto, ed.: *J.G. Herder: Kritische Wälder* (Berlin, 1990)

(vi) 19th Century

A. Schopenhauer: *Die Welt als Wille und Vorstellung* (Leipzig, 1819, enlarged 3/1859/R; Eng. trans., 1958, 2/1966/R)
G.W.F. Hegel: *Ästhetik* (Berlin, 1835, 2/1842/R; Eng. trans., 1965, 1975/R, as *Aesthetics: Lectures on Fine Art*)
F. Schleiermacher: *Hermeneutik und Kritik* (Berlin, 1838; Eng. trans., 1977)
F.T. Vischer: *Ästhetik oder Wissenschaft des Schönen* (Reutlingen, 1840–57/R)
F. Schleiermacher: *Vorlesungen über die Ästhetik*, ed. C. Lommatzsch (Berlin, 1842/R)
R. Wagner: *Oper und Drama* (Leipzig, 1852/R; Eng. trans., 1913)
E. Hanslick: *Vom Musikalisch-Schönen* (Leipzig, 1854, 17/1971; Eng. trans., 1891/R); ed. D. Strauss (Mainz, 1990)
A.W. Ambros: *Die Grenzen der Musik und Poesie* (Leipzig, 1855/R, 2/1872; Eng. trans., 1893)
F.W.J. Schelling: *Philosophie der Kunst* (1802–3) (Stuttgart, 1859; Eng. trans., 1989)
C. Darwin: *The Descent of Man and Selection in Relation to Sex* (London, 1871; repr. 1972)
C. Darwin: *The Expression of Emotions in Man and Animals* (London, 1872)
W. Pater: *Studies in the History of the Renaissance* (London, 1877, 6/1901 as *The Renaissance*); ed. K. Clark (Cleveland, 1961)
F. Nietzsche: *Menschliches, Allzumenschliches* (Leipzig, 1878; Eng. trans., 1986)
E. Gurney: *The Power of Sound* (London, 1880/R)
F. Nietzsche: *Die fröhliche Wissenschaft* (Leipzig, 1882; Eng. trans., 1974)
G. Engel: *Ästhetik der Tonkunst* (Berlin, 1884)
E. von Hartmann: *Die deutsche Ästhetik seit Kant* (Berlin, 1886)
F. Nietzsche: *Der Fall Wagner* (Leipzig, 1888; Eng. trans., 1899)
C.G. von Maasen, ed.: *E.T.A. Hoffmanns Sämtliche Werke* (Munich, 1908, 2/1912)
M. Schröter, ed.: *F.W.J. Schelling: Die Weltalter* (Munich, 1946/R; Eng. trans., 1942/R)
A. Schopenhauer: *Sämtliche Werke* (Frankfurt, 1966)
G. Colli and M. Montinari, eds.: *F. Nietzsche: Sämtliche Werke* (Berlin, 1967–82) [critical edn]

(vii) 20th Century

H. Riemann: *Die Elemente der musikalischen Ästhetik* (Berlin, 1900)
H. Kretzschmar: *Musikalische Zeitfragen* (Leipzig, 1903)
H. Schenker: *Neue musikalische Theorien und Phantasien* (Vienna, 1906–35/R; Eng. trans., 1979)
W. Hilbert: *Die Musikästhetik der Frühromantik* (Remscheid, 1911)

A. Halm: *Von zwei Kulturen der Musik* (Stuttgart, 1913, 3/1947)

E. Bloch: *Der Geist der Utopie* (Munich, 1918/R, 2/1923)

P. Moos: *Die Philosophie der Musik* (Stuttgart, 1922/R) [enlarged edn of *Moderne Musikästhetik in Deutschland* (Berlin, 1902)]

H. Besseler: 'Grundfragen des musikalischen Hörens', *JbMP 1925*, 35–52; repr. in *Musikhören*, ed. B. Dolpheide (Darmstadt, 1975), 48–73

H. Besseler: 'Grundfragen der Musikästhetik', *JbMP 1926*, 68–80

B.V. Asaf'yev: *Muzïkal'naya forma kak protsess* [Musical form as process] (Moscow, 1930–47, 3/1971; Eng. trans., 1977)

I. Stravinsky: *Poétique musicale* (Cambridge, MA, 1942; Eng. trans., 1970)

Z. Lissa: *O specyfice muzyki* [On the specific qualities of music] (Warsaw, 1953; Ger. trans., 1957)

Z. Lissa: *Podstawy estetyki muzycznej* [Questions of music aesthetics] (Warsaw, 1953; Ger. trans., 1954)

L. Wittgenstein: *Philosophical Investigations* (Oxford, 1953, 3/1968/R)

T. Georgiades: *Musik und Sprache* (Berlin, 1954, 2/1974; Eng. trans., 1982)

K. Huber: *Musikästhetik*, ed. O. Ursprung (Ettal, 1954)

T.W. Adorno: *Musikalische Schriften* (Berlin, 1959)

T.W. Adorno: *Ästhetische Theorie* (Frankfurt, 1970/R, 6/1996; Eng. trans., 1984)

J. Cage: *M: Writings '67–'92* (Middletown, CT, 1973)

R. Ingarden: *Utwor muzyczny i sprawa jego tozsamosci* (Kraków, 1973; Eng. trans., 1986 as *The Work of Music and the Problem of its Identity*)

R. Scruton: *Art and Imagination* (London, 1974/R)

J.J. Nattiez: *Fondements d'une sémiologie de la musique* (Paris, 1975)

A. Schoenberg: *Style and Idea*, ed. L. Stein (London, 1975)

H.H. Eggebrecht: *Musikalisches Denken* (Wilhelmshaven, 1977)

H. Besseler: *Aufsätze zur Musikästhetik und Musikgeschichte* (Leipzig, 1978)

C. Dahlhaus: *Die Idee der absoluten Musik* (Kassel, 1978, 2/1987; Eng. trans., 1984, 2/1989)

A. Halm: *Von Form und Sinn in der Musik* (Wiesbaden, 1978)

P. Kivy: *The Corded Shell: Reflections on Musical Expression* (Princeton, NJ, 1980)

R. Scruton: *The Aesthetic Understanding* (London, 1983)

C. Dahlhaus and M. Zimmermann, eds.: *Musik zur Sprache gebracht: musikästhetische Texte aus drei Jahrhunderten* (Munich, 1984)

M. Budd: *Music and the Emotions* (London, 1985/R)

A. Bowie: 'Music, Language and Modernity', *The Problems of Modernity: Adorno and Benjamin*, ed. A. Benjamin (London, 1989), 67–85

M. Frank: *Einführung in die frühromantische Ästhetik* (Frankfurt, 1989)

T.W. Adorno: *Beethoven: Philosophie der Musik* (Frankfurt, 1993, 2/1994; Eng. trans., 1998)

A. Bowie: *From Romanticism to Critical Theory* (London, 1997)

C: ANGLO-AMERICAN PHILOSOPHY OF MUSIC SINCE 1960

S.K. Langer: *Philosophy in a New Key* (Cambridge, MA, 1942/R, 3/1957/R)

L.B. Meyer: *Emotion and Meaning in Music* (Chicago, 1956/R)

N. Goodman: *Languages of Art* (Indianapolis, IN, 1968, 2/1976)

R. Scruton: *Art and Imagination* (London, 1974/R)

T.C. Mark: 'On Works of Virtuosity', *Journal of Philosophy*, lxxvii (1980), 28–45

M.C. Beardsley: 'On Understanding Music', *On Criticizing Music: Five Philosophical Perspectives*, ed. K. Price (Baltimore, 1981), 55–73

T.C. Mark: 'Philosophy of Piano Playing: Reflections on the Concept of Performance', *Philosophy and Phenomenological Research*, xli (1981), 299–324

P. Alperson: 'On Musical Improvisation', *Journal of Aesthetics and Art Criticism*, xliii (1984), 17–29

P. Alperson, ed.: *What is Music?: an Introduction to the Philosophy of Music* (New York, 1987, 2/1994)

S. Davies: 'Authenticity in Musical Performance', *British Journal of Aesthetics*, xxvii (1987), 39–50

P. Kivy: *Sound Sentiment* (Philadelphia, 1989)

P. Kivy: *Music Alone: Philosophical Reflections on the Purely Musical Experience* (Ithaca, NY, 1990)

J. Levinson: *Music, Art, and Metaphysics* (Ithaca, NY, 1990)

K. Higgins: *The Music of our Lives* (Philadelphia, 1991)

L. Goehr: *The Imaginary Museum of Musical Works: an Essay in the Philosophy of Music* (Oxford, 1992)

P. Kivy: *The Fine Art of Repetition: Essays in the Philosophy of Music* (Cambridge, 1993)

M. Krausz, ed.: *The Interpretation of Music* (Oxford, 1993)

D. Raffman: *Language, Music, and Mind* (Cambridge, MA, 1993)

P. Thom: *For an Audience: a Philosophy of the Performing Arts* (Philadelphia, 1993)

S. Davies: *Musical Meaning and Expression* (Ithaca, NY, 1994)

J. Robinson: 'The Expression and Arousal of Emotion in Music', *Journal of Aesthetics and Art Criticism*, lii (1994), 13–22

A.H. Goldman: *Aesthetic Value* (Boulder, CO, 1995)

P. Kivy: *Authenticities: Philosophical Reflections on Musical Performance* (Ithaca, NY, 1995)

A. Ridley: *Music, Value and the Passions* (Ithaca, NY, 1995)

L.B. Brown: 'Musical Works, Improvisation, and the Principle of Continuity', *Journal of Aesthetics and Art Criticism*, liv (1996), 353–69

M. Budd: *The Values of Art: Pictures, Poetry, and Music* (London, 1996)

T.A. Gracyk: *Rhythm and Noise: an Aesthetics of Rock* (Durham, NC, 1996)

J. Levinson: *The Pleasures of Aesthetics* (Ithaca, NY, 1996)

J. Levinson: *Music in the Moment* (Ithaca, NY, 1997)

J. Robinson, ed.: *Music & Meaning* (Ithaca, NY, 1997)

R. Scruton: *The Aesthetics of Music* (Oxford, 1997)

S. Godlovitch: *Musical Performance: a Philosophical Study* (London, 1998)

D. Matravers: *Art and Emotion* (Oxford, 1998)

L. Addis: *Of Mind and Music* (Ithaca, NY, 1999)

D: CONTEMPORARY CHALLENGES

F. de Saussure: *Cours de linguistique générale* (Paris, 1916/R, 5/1955; Eng. trans., 1959)

T.W. Adorno: *Dissonanzen: Musik in der verwalteten Welt* (Göttingen, 1958, 6/1982)

D. Cooke: *The Language of Music* (Oxford, 1959/R)

R. Jakobson: 'Musikwissenschaft und Linguistik' (1932), *Selected Writings*, i (Monton, 1962, 2/1971)

C. Lévi-Strauss: *Le cru et les cuit* (Paris, 1964; Eng. trans., 1969/R)

S. Cavell: *Must we Mean what we Say?* (New York, 1969/R)

N. Ruwet: *Langage, musique, poésie* (Paris, 1972)

J. Blacking: *How Musical is Man?* (Seattle, 1973)

M. Asch: *Analyse générative de la mélodie des chorals de Bach* (Rome, 1974)

M. Pagnini: *Lingua e musica* (Bologna, 1974)

J.J. Nattiez: *Fondements d'une sémiologie de la musique* (Paris, 1975)

B. Gasparov: 'Le fonctionnement sémantique des musiques vocales et instrumentales', *Versus: Quaderni studi semiotici*, xiii/1 (1976), 11–18

P. Faltin: 'Musikalische Bedeutung: Grenzen und Möglichkeiten einer semiotischen Ästhetik', *International Review of the Aesthetics and the Sociology of Music*, ix (1978), 5–33 [incl. Eng. summary]

S. Frith: *Sound Effects: Youth, Leisure, and the Politics of Rock 'n Roll* (New York, 1981)

F. Lerdahl and R. Jackendoff: *A Generative Theory of Tonal Music* (Cambridge, MA, 1983)

W. Dilthey: *Poetry and Experience*, v: *Selected Works*, ed. R.A. Mackreel and F. Rodi (Princeton, 1985)

R. Leppert and S. McClary, eds.: *Music and Society: the Politics of Composition, Performance, and Reception* (Cambridge, 1987)

N. Kenyon, ed.: *Authenticity and Early Music: a Symposium* (Oxford, 1988)

L. Kramer: *Music as Cultural Practice, 1800–1900* (Berkeley, 1990)

S. McClary: 'Towards a Feminist Criticism of Music', *Canadian University Music Review*, x/2 (1990), 9–18

R. Middleton: *Studying Popular Music* (Philadelphia, 1990)

C. Abbate: *Unsung Voices: Opera and Musical Narrative in the Nineteenth Century* (Princeton, NJ, 1991)

S. McClary: *Feminine Endings: Music, Gender, and Sexuality* (Minneapolis, 1991)

M. Arkad'yev: *Vremennïye strukturï novo-yevropeyskoy muzïki* [Temporal structures of new European music] (Moscow, 1992)

S. McClary: *Georges Bizet: Carmen* (Cambridge, 1992)

R. Leppert: *The Sight of Sound: Music, Representation, and the History of the Body* (Berkeley, 1993)

D. Raffman: *Language, Music, and Mind* (Cambridge, MA, 1993)

M. DeBellis: *Music and Conceptualization* (Cambridge, 1995)

L.B. Brown: 'Musical Works, Improvisation, and the Principle of Continuity', *Journal of Aesthetics and Art Criticism*, liv (1996), 353–69

R. Scruton: *The Aesthetics of Music* (Oxford, 1997)

L. Goehr: *The Quest for Voice: Music, Politics, and the Limits of Philosophy* (Oxford and Berkeley, 1998)

LYDIA GOEHR (I, V), F.E. SPARSHOTT/LYDIA GOEHR (II), LYDIA GOEHR, ANDREW BOWIE (III), STEPHEN DAVIES (IV)

Philovalensis, Hieronim. *See* WIETOR, HIERONIM.

Philpot, Lucy. *See* ANDERSON, LUCY.

Phinot [Finot, Finotto], **Dominique** [Dominico] (*b* c1510; *d* c1556). Franco-Flemish composer. He was described by Girolamo Cardano as 'Gallus'. He appears to have spent at least part of his career in Italy: in a document of May 1544, Duke Guidobaldo II of Urbino proposed that he be appointed *cantor* in the cathedral, while a further two documents, dated 26 March 1545 and 20 November 1555, indicate that 'Finotto musico' was employed in the court of Urbino. Though he is not known to have resided in Lyons, evidence of his close associations with the city are contained in four volumes of motets and chansons published there by Godefroy and Marcellin Beringen in 1547 and 1548. The dedicatees had Lyonese connections (for example, César Gros was a prominent citizen and patron), some of the chanson texts are by the local poets Maurice Scève and Charles Fontaine, and other texts deal with subjects of local interest. A passage in Cardano's *Theonoston* implies that Phinot was executed for homosexual practices.

The outstanding works in the Beringen volumes are the eight-voice double-choir sacred pieces *Iam non dicam*, *O sacrum convivium*, *Sancta trinitas*, *Tanto tempore* and *Incipit oratio Hieremiae*, which, as Carver observed, are the first mature examples of polychoral writing based on constant thematic interaction between alternating ensembles. These compositions were highly esteemed, especially in Germany, during the late 16th and early 17th centuries, and appear to have been known by Palestrina and Lassus.

Phinot was celebrated in his day for finely crafted five-voice motets such as *Non turbetur cor vestrum*, in which typically Netherlandish imitative counterpoint predominates. His chansons cover a variety of musical styles suited to topics ranging from mordant anti-clerical anecdotes to courtly poems and imitations of Ovid and Catullus. The animated homophony of *Si vous voulez* and supple polyphony of *Puisque mon coeur* are rooted in established styles of chanson composition. Among the more innovative pieces are *Vivons, m'amye*, *Qu'est-ce qu'amour?* and *Par un trait d'or*, in which polychoral dialogue and secular poetry are imaginatively aligned. Potent expressive devices, too, such as the triple suspensions underscoring 'meschamment' in *Je l'hay perdu* and Eb harmony on the word 'mort' in *Mort et amour* and elsewhere recall similar musical metaphors in the early Italian madrigal, while the music of *Quand je pense au martire* is sensitively keyed both to Jean Martin's skilful translation of Bembo's *Quand'io penso al martire* and to Arcadelt's madrigal setting of the latter.

Writers such as Luis Venegas de Henestrosa, Cornelius Blockland and Pietro Pontio (*Ragionamento*, Parma, 1588) cited Phinot's work as being worthy of emulation. Hermann Finck (*Pratica musica*, 1556) ranked him with Gombert, Crecquillon and Clemens non Papa, while Pietro Cerone (*El melopeo y maestro*, Naples, 1613/R) claimed that Palestrina composed in Phinot's style.

WORKS

Edition: *Dominici Phinot opera omnia*, ed. J. Höfler and R. Jacob, CMM, lix (1972–) [H]

MASSES AND MAGNIFICAT SETTINGS

Missa 'Quam pulchra es', 4vv, 1544[5] (on Lupi's motet)
Missa 'Si bona suscepimus', 4vv, 1544[1] (on Sermisy's motet)
Pleni sunt coeli, 2vv, 1543[19]
Magnificat [1st tone], 4vv (Venice, 1554)
Magnificat [4th tone], 4vv (Venice, 1555)
Magnificat [8th tone], 4vv (Venice, 1555)

MOTETS
for 5 voices unless otherwise stated

Liber primus mutetarum quinque vocum (Lyons, 1547) [=H i]
Liber secundus mutetarum sex, septem et octo vocum (Lyons, 1548) [=H iv]
Liber secundus mutetarum quinque vocum (Pesaro, 1554) [=H ii]

Ad Dominum cum tribularer, H i; Angustiae mihi sunt undique, 4vv, 1549[9]; Apparens christus, H i; Ascendo ad patrem meum, H i; Aspice Domini, 1543[3]; Auribus percipe Domine, H i; Ave Maria gratia plena, H ii; Ave virgo gloriosa, 1543[3]; Beata es virgo Maria, H i; Beati omnes qui timent Dominum, H ii

Caecus sedebat secus viam, 1543[3]; Cerne meos ergo gemitus, 6vv, H iv; Cives apostolorum et domestici Dei, H ii; Clare sanctorum senatus apostolorum, H ii; Concede nobis Domine, H i; Congregatae sunt gentes, 1543[3]; Descendit angelus Domini, H ii; Descendit de caelis, H ii; Deus in nomine tuo, 1543[3]; Dixit Jesus discipulis suis, H ii; Domine nonne bonum semen seminasti, H i; Domine non secundum peccata nostra, H ii

Ecce ego mitto vos, 6vv, H iv; Ecce sacerdos magnus, 10vv, H ii; Ecce tu pulcher es, H ii; Ego sum panis vitae, 1549[6]; Ego sum qui sum, H i; Emitte Domine sapientiam, H i; Exaudiat te Dominus, 6vv, H iv; Exaudi Domine deprecationem meam, 6vv, H iv; Exsurge, quare obdormis, 1538[4]; Fundata est domus Domini, H i; Gabriel angelus locutus est, H i

Hic est dies praeclarus, H ii; Hoc est praeceptum meum, H i; Homo quidam fecit cenam, H ii; Homo quidam fecit cenam, 5vv, 1541[3]; Iam non dicam vos servos, 8vv, H iv; Illuminare Hierusalem, 1549[6]; Illuxit nobis dies, 1543[3]; Incipit oratio Hieremiae, 8vv, H iv; Inclina Domine aurem tuam, H ii; In craticula te Deum, 6vv, H iv; In illo tempore dixit Jesus, H ii; Iste sanctus pro lege Dei sui, H ii; Istorum est enim regnum caelorum, H i

Laetatus sum, H ii; Martinus Abrahae sinu laetus, H ii; Memor fui nocte nominis tui, 3vv, 1549[14]; Missus est Gabriel angelus, H i; Ne derelinquas me, Domine, 1538[4]; Non turbetur cor vestrum, 1543[3]; Non turbetur cor vestrum, H i; O altitudo divitiarum, 4vv, 1538[5]; O martyr egregie doctor veritatis, H i; O quam gloriosum est regnum, H i; O sacrum convivium, 8vv, H iv; Osculetur me osculo oris sui, 4vv, 1538[5]; Osculetur me osculo oris sui, H i

Pacem meam do vobis, H i; Panis quem ego dabo, 1553[16]; Pater manifestavi nomen tuum, H i; Pater noster, H ii; Pater peccavi in caelum, 1538[4]; Prolongati sunt dies mei, H i; Quae est ista, 6vv, H iv; Quam pulchri sunt gressus tui, H i; Regina caeli laetare, H i; Repleti sunt omnes spiritu sancto, H i

Salve regina misericordiae, H i; Sancta trinitas unus deus, 7vv, H ii; Sancta trinitas unus deus, 8vv, H iv; Sanctorum omnium gaudia inclyta, 7vv, H iv; Si bona suscepimus, H i; Sit nomen Domini benedictum, 6vv, H iv; Spiritus meus attenuabitur, 1538[4]; Stella ista sicut flamma, 6vv, H iv; Stetit angelus ad sepulchrum Domini, H ii; Surge propera amica mea, 6vv, H iv; Sustinuimus pacem, 6vv, H iv

Tanto tempore vobiscum sum, 4vv, 1549[9]; Tanto tempore vobiscum sum, H i; Tanto tempore vobiscum sum, 8vv, H iv; Te gloriosus apostolorum chorus, H i; Tua est potentia, H i; Usque modo non petistis quicquam, H i; Usque quo Domine oblivisceris me, H i; Valde honorandus est, 4vv, 1549[9]; Veni sponsa Christi, H ii; Videns dominus flentes, 1543[3]; Vidi speciosam, 4vv, 1549[9]; Vidi turbam magnam, H ii; Virga Jesse floruit, 4vv, 1539[13]; Virgo parens, 7vv, H iv; Zachee festinans descende, H ii

PSALMS

I sacri et santi salmi de David profeta, 4vv (Venice, 1554) [1554]

Beatus vir [2nd tone], 1554; Beatus vir [3rd tone], 1554; Confitebor tibi Domine [2nd tone], 1554; Confitebor tibi Domine [3rd tone], 1554; Dixit Dominus [1st tone], 1554; Dixit Dominus [1st tone], 1554; Donec ponam inimicos tuos [1st tone], 4vv, 1550[1]
Labores manuum tuarum [4th tone], 4vv, 1550[1]; Laetatus sum [1st tone], 1554; Lauda, Hierusalem, Dominum [3rd tone], 1554;

Laudate Dominum omnes gentes [2nd tone], 1554; Laudate Dominum omnes gentes [5th tone], 1554; Laudate pueri Dominum [4th tone], 1554; Laudate pueri Dominum [8th tone], 1554; Nisi Dominus aedificaverit [8th tone], 1554

CHANSONS

for 4 voices unless otherwise stated: all ed. in H iii

Premier livre contenant trente et sept chansons (Lyons, 1548)

Second livre contenant vingt et six chansons (Lyons, 1548)

Adieu, Loyse, 8vv; Amour et mort ont faict leur assemblée; Belle ne suis (response to Plus doulcement); Bouche de satin cramoysi (Forcadel); Catin, ma gentille brunette (C. Fontaine); Catin veult que souvent la voye (Fontaine); Ce corps tant droit; Comme en beauté

Dame Margot; D'estre amoureux n'ay plus intention (C. Marot); De ton amour; Doy-je espérer; En chascun lieu (M. d'Amboise); En feu ardant (Bembo/J. Martin); Frèrot un jour; Ha mes amys (Amboise); Hault le boys, m'amye Margot, 12vv (canonic); Ingrate suis (response to Quand je te voy); Je l'hay perdu bien meschamment (Fontaine)

Laissez cela, disoit une nonette; Las, pourquoy donc (Marot); L'eau qui distille (Bembo/Martin); Le coeur et l'oeil; Le concours discordant (canonic); L'esprit vouloit (M. Scève); Lynote (Marot); Madame ayant l'arc d'Amour (Scève); Maugré Saint-Gelais; Moins dure ou plus (M. de Saint-Gelais) (response to Si vous voulez); Mort et amour un soir se racontrèrent

Navré m'avez (Fontaine); On dira ce que l'on vouldra (Marot); 'Ostez la main, ma mère nous regarde'; Paovre de joye (Scève); Par ce propos; Par toy je vis (Fontaine); Par un trait d'or (Forcadel), 8vv; Petite fleur; Plorez, mes yeulx, plorez à chauldes larmes; Plus doulcement; Possible n'est d'estre amoureux (Forcadel); Pour bien aymer; Pour ton amour j'ay souffert tant d'ennuis (Marot); Puisque mon coeur est vers toy malvenu; Puisqu'il vous plaist (J. Peletier Du Mans); Pyrrhus, le Roy d'Epire

Quand je pense au martire (Bembo/Martin); Quand je te voy; Qu'est-ce qu'amour (G. de la Perrière), 8vv; Quinconques soit qui en vertu travaille (Forcadel) (canonic); Si je la tien; Si je mourois; Si j'en dy bien (Saint-Gelais); Si la beauté, qui vous rend si aymable (Saint-Gelais); Si le mien coeur, 5vv (canonic, response to Trop loing de moy); Si le regard (?Saint-Gelais); Si par aymer et souffrir (Marot); Si vous voulez moins dure devenir (Saint-Gelais)

Ta beauté me donne espérance (Fontaine); Taisez-vous donq (response to Laissez cela); Tous les malheurs (Peletier Du Mans); Trop loing de moy, 5vv (canonic); Un gros prieur (Marot); Une nonain de l'abbesse; Une fillette à son vicaire alla; Vivons, m'amye, 8vv

MADRIGALS

S'in veder voi madonna, 6vv, 1541[16]

Simili a questi smisurati monti (Sannazaro), 8vv, 1561[10]

BIBLIOGRAPHY

MGG1 (F. Lesure); *ReeseMR*

A. Saviotti: 'La musica alla corte dei Duchi di Urbino', *La Cronica Musicale* [Pesaro], xxx (January 1909), 119

R. Casimiri: 'Un accenno poetico a Giosquino e Finoto di F. Spinola', *NA*, viii (1931), 143–5

L. Werner: 'Una rarità musicale della biblioteca vescovile di Szombathely', *NA*, viii (1931), 89–105, esp. 91

P. Hansen: *Liber Secundus Mutetarum by Domenico Phinot: a Modern Transcription with an Introduction* (diss., Eastman School of Music, Rochester, NY, 1935)

P. Hansen: *The Life and Works of Dominico Phinot* (diss., U. of North Carolina, 1939)

P. Hansen: 'The Double-Chorus Motets of Dominico Phinot', *RN*, iii (1950), 35–7

V.L. Saulnier: 'Dominique Phinot et Didier Lupi, musiciens de Clément Marot et des marotiques', *RdM*, xliii (1959), 61–80

J. Höfler: 'Dominique Phinot i počeci renesansnog višehorskog pevanja' [Dominique Phinot and the beginnings of Renaissance polyphoral music], *ZVUK*, no.100 (1969), 497–515 [with Eng. summary]

J. Höfler: 'Nekaj zgodnejših primerov italijanskega dialoga: prispevek k vprašanju renesančnega večzborja' [Some early examples of the Italian *dialogo*: a contribution to the problems of Renaissance polychoral music], *MZ*, viii (1972), 40–56 [with Eng. summary]

C.A. Miller: 'Jerome Cardan on Gombert, Phinot, and Carpentras', *MQ*, lviii (1972), 412–19

R. Jacob: 'Dominique Phinot', *Cultural Aspects of the Italian Renaissance: Essays in Honour of Paul Oskar Kristeller*, ed. C.H. Clough (Manchester, 1976), 425–39

N. O'Regan: 'The Early Polychoral Music of Orlando di Lasso: New Light from Roman Sources', *AcM*, lvi (1984), 234–51

A.F. Carver: *Cori spezzati: the Development of Sacred Polychoral Music to the Time of Schütz* (Cambridge, 1988)

L. Guillo: *Les éditions musicales de la Renaissance lyonnaise* (Paris, 1991)

F. Dobbins: *Music in Renaissance Lyons* (Oxford, 1992)

F. Piperno: 'Guidubaldo II della Rovere, la musica e il mondo', *Saggiatore musicale*, iv (1997)

R. Jacob: *The chansons and madrigals of Dominique Phinot (fl c1510–c1556)* (diss., U. of Aberdeen, forthcoming)

ROGER JACOB

Phoenicians, music of the. *See* JEWISH MUSIC, §II, 3.

Phon. A unit of LOUDNESS. *See also* SOUND, §4.

Phonikon. A baritone brass instrument invented by VÁCLAV FRANTIŠEK ČERVENÝ.

Phonofiddle. A one-string variant of the STROH VIOLIN.

Phonographic Performance Ltd [PPL]. *See* COPYRIGHT, §III, 16(iv).

Phonotype. Italian record company. It was founded in Naples in 1901 by Raffaele Esposito (1865–1945). The catalogue consisted of recordings by local popular artists and a few minor opera singers. In 1917 Fernando De Lucia (1860–1925) began a series of about 300 records for Phonotype, made over a period of four years. He recorded a wide range of opera and song, including *Il barbiere di Siviglia* and *Rigoletto*, with highly developed embellishment. During World War II the matrices were hidden; they have since been rediscovered and pressings made from them. Other Phonotype artists included Angeles Ottein and Benvenuto Franci.

ELIOT B. LEVIN

Phorbeia (Gk., also *phorbea*, *phorbaia*; Lat. *capistrum*). A mouthband shown in many illustrations of auletes playing the double aulos. The term also refers to a horse's halter, which bears a remarkable resemblance to the device shown in a particularly detailed view of an aulos player on a red-figure amphora (*c*480 BCE) attributed to the Kleophrades Painter and preserved in the British Museum (E 270; *see* AULOS, fig.2).

The *phorbeia* is mentioned by Plutarch (*On the Control of Anger*, 456b–c) and described by scholiasts and some of the lexicographers. The comments tend to be brief, and the function of the *phorbeia* remains unclear in the literary and iconographic sources. Plutarch observes that MARSYAS employed special devices – a *phorbeia* and *peristomios* – when he played the aulos. He explains these terms by quoting two lines now commonly attributed to Simonides: 'Marsyas, it seems, suppressed the violence of his breath with a *phorbeia* and *peristomios*, composed his countenance and concealed the distortion: "He fitted his forehead locks with gleaming gold and his blustering mouth with leather straps and bound behind"'. A *peristomios* is something that goes around a mouth. Plutarch is probably using the terms as synonyms, and the two of them together convey a reasonably clear sense of the appearance of the *phorbeia*. Moreover, the reference to Marsyas's 'blustering mouth' evokes the hissing and spitting sounds that emerge from a poorly sealed embouchure, especially as the pressure of the performer's breath increases.

Hesychius's *Lexicon* defines the *phorbeia* as a skin placed around the mouth of the aulete to prevent his lips from parting. Experiment with reconstructions demonstrates the aptness of this definition. With two mouthpieces, the difficulty of maintaining a tight seal is considerable, especially over a long period. The *phorbeia* allows the performer to maintain a relaxed embouchure: by sealing the mouth and holding the lips together against the pressure of the breath, it prevents the reed from being choked by a tight embouchure – or stopped from beating altogether – and allows the lips to exercise sensitive adjustments in pressure on the reed. In addition, with the *phorbeia*, the mouthpiece itself can easily be withdrawn by increments from the mouth in order to shorten the reed; without the *phorbeia*, it is difficult to maintain a tight seal around the mouthpieces while moving them in and out of the mouth to adjust pitch and timbre. Contrary to common conjecture, the *phorbeia* does not provide special support for cheeks, enabling them to act like a bellows, except in the sense that it allows the facial muscles to relax because they do not need to maintain a sealed embouchure. There is no easy explanation for the fact that aulos players are often shown without the *phorbeia*, but experiment does indicate that short and simple phrases can be played on the auloi without greatly taxing the embouchure. Thus, it may be conjectured that the *phorbeia* was introduced to allow auletes to play the longer, more difficult compositions characteristic of the innovatory style of the auletic competitions. Players of the salpinx, too, often wore the *phorbeia*, which must have served the same purpose as it did for the aulos. In the illustration of Epiktetos (*c*520–490) for an eye kylix, a satyr wears the *phorbeia* while sounding the salpinx over his shoulder (London, British Museum, E 3).

The *phorbeia* is rarely shown without the aulos – or some other instrument – in the aulete's mouth, but one kylix (New York, Metropolitan Museum of Art, kylix 96.9.18) does show an aulete adjusting the *phorbeia* while holding both auloi in his left hand at his waist; the illustration clearly indicates that the *phorbeia* has a slit or hole for each mouthpiece (confirmed by a volute krater in Tarento, Museo Nazionale, IG 8263). As the aulete prepares to play, the mouthpieces must then be inserted through the holes into the mouth.

BIBLIOGRAPHY

A.A. Howard: 'The *Aulos* or Tibia', *Harvard Studies in Classical Philology*, iv (1893), 29–30

C. Sachs: *The History of Musical Instruments* (New York, 1940), 138–9

H. Becker: *Zur Entwicklungsgeschichte der antiken und mittelalterlichen Rohrblattinstrumente* (Hamburg, 1966), 120–29

D. Paquette: *L'instrument de musique dans la céramique de la Grèce antique: études d'organologie* (Paris, 1984)

A. Bélis: 'La phorbéia', *Bulletin de correspondance hellénique*, cx (1986), 205–18

T.J. Mathiesen: *Apollo's Lyre: Greek Music and Music Theory in Antiquity and the Middle Ages* (Lincoln, NE, 1999), 218–22

THOMAS J. MATHIESEN

Phorminx. The term most commonly used for a string instrument in the *Iliad* and *Odyssey* (written between 850 and 750 BCE but preserving stories from oral tradition about events from the Mycenaean period, over 400 years earlier). The word is also found in Archaic period texts such as the Homeric hymns. It is still seen in early 5th-century literature, but in works from the end of that century it is seldom found.

The phorminx of the Mycenaean Greeks, as works of art attest, was a lyre (CHORDOPHONE) with a shallow wooden soundbox with a rounded base, similar in most details to the earlier lyre of Minoan Crete and, like it, having two arms that often curved in and out in an ornamental fashion, supporting a crossbar to which seven strings were fixed with leather strips (*kollopes*) for friction. The instrument was held upright, and played in the same manner as the later KITHARA.

The same shape and mode of playing are seen in the art of the Geometric period (*c*1100–800 BCE), although the arms are sometimes straight, and only a few strings are shown (for artistic reasons; the actual number probably did not change). Although other types of lyre begin to be found in works of art from about 800 BCE, the phorminx (with straight arms, its seven strings again visible) is still seen more often and in more locations than other lyres until the end of the 7th century.

Representations of the phorminx made between 600 and 525 BCE are much less common than those of the kithara or chelys lyra, and are from areas as distant as Greek Asia Minor, Rhodes, Egypt and Etruscan Italy as well as from Athens. But the phorminx appears in over 40 representations from the late 6th century and throughout the 5th, mostly on Athenian vase paintings.

From the 7th century, pairs of bosses or circles were often painted on the soundbox, and after 475 BCE these were sometimes turned into eyes; no other lyre has this apotropaic feature. The arms, early and late, were often decorated, though in ways that changed markedly.

Homer and the writers of the Archaic era described the phorminx as the instrument of Apollo, who sometimes played it to the singing of the Muses; in the early 5th century PINDAR spoke of it as owned by Apollo and the Muses. In fact the kithara had long since replaced the phorminx as Apollo's instrument, but the Muses inherited it: they play it in some half-dozen 5th-century vase paintings. Other female figures, mythological and mortal, also play the phorminx. Both Homer and the Archaic period writers mentioned it in connection with dancing; in the 5th century Bacchylides and Pindar also placed it in the context of dancing, as do scenes on a substantial group of vase paintings.

BIBLIOGRAPHY

B. Aign: *Die Geschichte der Musikinstrumente des Ägäischen Raumes bis um 700 vor Christus* (Frankfurt, 1963)

M. Wegner: *Griechenland*, Musikgeschichte in Bildern, ii/4 (Leipzig, 1963, 2/1970)

M. Wegner: 'Musik und Tanz', *Archaeologia Homerica*, iii (1968), 3–18

M. Maas: 'The Phorminx in Classical Greece', *JAMS*, ii (1976), 34–55

M. Maas and J.M. Snyder: *Stringed Instruments of Ancient Greece* (New Haven, CT, 1989)

MARTHA MAAS

Phrase. A term adopted from linguistic syntax and used for short musical units of various lengths; a phrase is generally regarded as longer than a MOTIF but shorter than a PERIOD. It carries a melodic connotation, insofar as the term 'phrasing' is usually applied to the subdivision of a melodic line. As a formal unit, however, it must be considered in its polyphonic entirety, like 'period', 'sentence' and even 'theme'.

See also ANALYSIS; ARTICULATION AND PHRASING; RHYTHM, §§I, 4; II, 13.

Phrygian. The common name for the third of the eight church modes, the authentic mode on E. In the Middle Ages and Renaissance the Phrygian mode was described in two ways: as the diatonic octave species from *e* to *e'*, divided at *b* and composed of a second species of 5th (semitone–tone–tone–tone) plus a second species of 4th (semitone–tone–tone), thus *e–f–g–a–b* + *b–c'–d'–e'*; and as a mode whose FINAL was *e* and whose AMBITUS was *d–e'*. Most theorists pointed out that the division of the Phrygian octave species at the 5th, *b*, did not correspond with musical practice in 3rd-mode Gregorian chants, nor for that matter later in Renaissance polyphonic works whose principal and final degree was E. They observed that the sixth degree, *c'*, which is the tenor of the corresponding third psalm tone, was a much more prominent scale degree than *b* in compositions in the Phrygian mode. Tinctoris, however, in chapter 19 of *Liber de natura … tonorum* (1476), which discusses appropriate beginning pitches for polyphonic compositions in each of the modes, implied that the fourth degree, *a*, could be regarded as the most important note in the Phrygian mode after the final *e* and its octave *e'*.

The expression 'Phrygian mode' is often used as a covering term for Renaissance and Baroque polyphonic compositions whose final sonority is an E major triad established by a Phrygian cadence and whose parts range more or less within the Phrygian or HYPOPHRYGIAN ambitus; their principal cadence degrees, other than the final, are A, C, G and occasionally D. This polyphonic application of the Phrygian mode is sometimes found transposed up a 4th in the *cantus mollis* (i.e. with a one-flat signature), so that the final becomes *a* and all other modal functions and relations are also a 4th higher in terms of their notated degrees.

'Phrygian mode', or 'Phrygian scale', is frequently used with reference to European folksongs and diatonic non-Western melodies whose final or apparent tonic is related to the scale type in a manner similar to that of the Phrygian church mode. The most characteristic feature of such melodies is the presence of a scale degree a semitone above the final or apparent tonic; this is sometimes called an 'upper leading note'.

For the early history of Greek-derived modal names *see* DORIAN. *See also* MODE.

HAROLD S. POWERS

Phrygian cadence. A CADENCE in which the lowest part descends to the final or tonic by a semitone.

Phrygian music. *See* ANATOLIA.

Phrynis of Mytilene [Mitylene] (*fl* Athens, *c*450–420 BCE). Greek kitharode and composer of *nomoi*. None of his works has survived. He went to Athens from Lesbos (*c*450 BCE) and had already become well known by 423; in that year Aristophanes (*Clouds*, 969–70 and scholium) deplored the difficult vocal writing that contemporary composers had learnt from him. About half a dozen years later, Timotheus boasted of a victory over Phrynis and called him *ton Iōnokamptan*, 'the Ionian [decadent] bender' (Edmonds, frag.20). As in Aristophanes' *dysko-lokamptous*, there is a reference to *kampai* (literally 'bends') in the melodic line; at times writers applied the term to metrical structure as well. After a century, however, Aristotle's pupil Phaenias of Eresus named

Phrynis and Timotheus alike as examples of classical excellence (Athenaeus, xiv, 638b); and Aristotle himself, or a member of his school, said of the two poets that the one would not have been possible without the other (*Metaphysics*, i.1, 993b16; of disputed authorship).

According to Pseudo-Plutarch's *On Music* (1133b), Phrynis complicated kitharoedic techniques by varying the mode and metre. He was contemporary with the renowned Theban aulete PRONOMUS, supposedly the first to play all the modes on one and the same double aulos. The tradition that he had been a singer to the aulos before he learnt the kithara (scholiast on Aristophanes, above) may merit serious consideration. Proclus (*Useful Knowledge*, in Photius, *Bibliotheca*, 320a33), writing about 450 CE, stated that Phrynis had revolutionized the *nomos* by combining the hexameter with a free metre and using more than seven strings (*chordai*). According to Plutarch (*On Progress in Virtue*, 83e–84b; *Sayings of the Spartans*, 220c), Phrynis added two strings, but when he attempted to introduce his innovations to Sparta, Ekprepes the Ephor removed two of them, admonishing him not to 'murder music'. A similar story is told of Timotheus (*Ancient Customs of the Spartans*, 238c–d; Boethius, *De institutione musica*, i.1).

The strongest evidence comes from the *Cheiron*, a fragment of the Old Comedy of the later 5th century BCE; preserved in Pseudo-Plutarch's *On Music* (1141d–1142a), it is the lament of Music (*mousikē*), personified as a woman, who has suffered various outrages at the hands of modern composers (*see* PHERECRATES, MELANIPPIDES). Phrynis, she declares, inserted his own spinning-top (*strobilon*), bending and twisting her to total corruption with 12 *harmoniai* (*dōdech' harmonias*) in his five strings (*pentachordois*). The sexual imagery of the entire fragment is reasonably clear; *strobilos* must therefore have been a term both of sexual slang and of technical musical meaning. In the former context, it may refer to the *olisbos*, a leather phallus (see Anderson, p.132); no convincing hypothesis has yet been presented for its musical meaning. It is nevertheless evident that in the history of kitharoedic composition the Greeks ranked Phrynis second only to Timotheus as a revolutionary.

BIBLIOGRAPHY

J.M. Edmonds, ed. and trans.: *Lyra graeca*, iii (London and Cambridge, MA, 1927, 2/1928/R), 267–8

W. Riemschneider: 'Phrynis', *Paulys Real-Encyclopädie der classischen Altertumswissenschaft*, xx/1 (Stuttgart, 1941), 925–30

G. Pianko: 'Un comico contributo alla storia della musica greca: Chirone di Ferecrate', *Eos*, liii (1963), 56–63

E.K. Borthwick: 'Notes on the Plutarch *De musica* and the *Cheiron* of Pherecrates', *Hermes*, xcvi (1968), 60–73

M.L West: 'Analecta musica', *Zeitschrift für Papyrologie und Epigraphik*, xcii (1992), 28–9

D.A. Campbell, ed. and trans.: *Greek Lyric*, v (Cambridge, MA, and London, 1993), 62–9

W.D. Anderson: *Music and Musicians in Ancient Greece* (Ithaca, NY, 1994), 127–34

WARREN ANDERSON/THOMAS J. MATHIESEN

Phthora (Gk.). A sign in Byzantine music referring to a transition from one *ēchos* (mode) to the next (*see* ĒCHOS, §2). Each of the eight *ēchoi* has its own *phthora*, but in effect only six are used. There is an explanation of their functions in a treatise by MANUEL CHRYSAPHES.

Phylypps. Clerk at Winchester College, 1523–6, possibly identifiable with THOMAS PHELYPPIS.

Physharmonika. (1) The name given by Anton Haeckl of Vienna to a small REED ORGAN first made in 1821.

(2) An ORGAN STOP.

Physics of music. This article is concerned with the history of vibration theory as it relates to music. For further information *see* ACOUSTICS and SOUND.

1. To Mersenne. 2. From Huygens to Sauveur and Newton. 3. The age of Euler. 4. From Chladni to Ohm. 5. The age of Helmholtz. 6. 20th century.

1. TO MERSENNE. The basic ideas of the physics of music were first obtained in the 17th century. Acoustic science then consisted mainly in the study of musical sounds; in fact, music provided both questions and techniques for the study of vibration. Music gave experience in comparing the pitch and timbre of tones, and so the means for careful experiment on sound; musical instruments offered empirical information on the nature of vibration; and, rather remarkably, the Pythagorean ratios of traditional music theory provided frequency ratios.

Early in the 17th century it was realized that the sensation of pitch is appropriately quantified by vibrational frequency – that is, pitch 'corresponds' to frequency. This realization came as part of a preliminary understanding of consonance and dissonance. Once the correspondence had been made, it was possible to determine the relative vibrational frequencies of tones from the musical intervals they produced. When relative frequencies were known, there was the challenge of determining frequencies absolutely; and the first measurements were made during the century. The idea that pitch corresponds to frequency motivated efforts to understand overtones, since, during most of the 17th century, it seemed paradoxical that a single object could vibrate simultaneously at different frequencies. This paradox was resolved by the end of the century through an initial understanding of the 'principle of superposition'. Also by this time the connection between overtones and timbre was noticed, and beats were explained quantitatively. During most of the century, sound was described as a succession of pulses, its wave nature being understood qualitatively. But late in the century the first mathematical analysis of the propagation of sound waves was made.

At least since the time of the Pythagoreans, musical intervals had been characterized by the length ratios of similar and equally tense strings – 2:1 for the octave, and so on. In music theory these ratios, although based on string lengths, were usually understood in purely arithmetical terms. As Palisca (1961) has shown, scepticism about arithmetical dogmatism in music led to an interest in the physical determinants of pitch. Around 1590 Vincenzo Galilei showed that various ratios could be associated with an interval. For example, if the strings' tensions rather than their lengths were considered, the ratio for the octave would be 1:4 rather than 2:1. Also, Francis Bacon (1627) was dissatisfied with arithmetical analysis of musical sound and recommended that empirical information be obtained from instrument makers. Even Kepler (1619), who was inspired by the Pythagorean idea of a celestial harmony, criticized the Pythagoreans for overemphasizing arithmetical considerations when judging the consonance of musical intervals. But the validity of the traditional ratios remained apparent, so the emphasis shifted and there was interest in finding physical (rather than numerological) reasons for using them. Descartes (1650; written in 1618) suggested that the octave was the first consonance because it was the interval obtained most easily by overblowing flutes.

The ambiguity originally demonstrated by Vincenzo Galilei was resolved most clearly by his son Galileo (1564–1642). By considering the sound that reaches the ear rather than the vibrating object that produces it, Galileo came to realize that pitch corresponds to frequency and showed that musical intervals could be uniquely characterized by frequency ratios. To explain why some intervals are more consonant than others, one of the 'musical problems' that he proposed to solve, Galileo wrote, in 1638, that 'the length of strings is not the direct and immediate reason behind the forms [ratios] of musical intervals, nor is their tension, nor their thickness, but rather, the ratios of the numbers of vibrations and impacts of air waves that go to strike our eardrum' (see Drake, 1974). He asserted that the degree of consonance produced by a pair of tones is determined by the proportion of impacts from the higher tone that coincide with impacts from the lower. (Benedetti had realized by 1563 that pitch corresponded to frequency, but his idea had not become known. In the early 17th century Beeckman, Descartes and Mersenne made statements about this correspondence, but Galileo's presentation was the clearest.)

Mersenne, who specialized in the physics of music, experimented extensively to relate vibrational frequencies to other properties of sources of sound. According to Mersenne's Law, the (fundamental) frequency of a string of given material is proportional to $\sqrt{T}/l\sqrt{m}$, where l is the length, T the tension and m the mass per unit length. In his experiments to establish this, which he described (1636–7), Mersenne tuned pairs of strings that differed in one or two properties. The musical interval indicated the strings' relative frequencies, and the dependence of frequency on each variable was found separately. To a certain extent the law was known by others; for example, the explicit statement that the frequency is inversely proportional to the square root of the density is due to Galileo. Mersenne tried to find for the vibrating air column a relation similar to the one he had found for the string. Although there is no simple precise relation between the frequency of a pipe and its dimensions, Mersenne did observe various effects of length, width and blowing pressure on the pitches of organ pipes, and he noted the octave difference between open and closed pipes.

Assuming that Mersenne's Law holds even for a string so long that its vibrations can be counted visually, Mersenne estimated the frequency of a note, that is, he found experimentally the constant of proportionality in the law. Some decades later Robert Hooke may have made a direct measurement of frequency; in 1665 he wrote about estimating the frequency of a fly's wings' vibration from its buzz. In 1681 he demonstrated before the Royal Society a way of making musical sounds 'by the striking of the teeth of several Brass Wheels, proportionally cut as to their numbers, and turned very fast round, in which it was observable that the equal or proportional stroaks of the Teeth, that is 2 to 1, 4 to 3, etc., made the musical [intervals]'. Hooke's wheel (usually known as Savart's wheel), which demonstrates explicitly that pitch corresponds to frequency, could have been used to make a rough measurement of frequencies.

Mersenne realized the importance of overtones, and urged his numerous correspondents to seek an explanation of them. In the case of an open string he identified at least four harmonic overtones, typically finding it paradoxical that a string should vibrate at different frequencies simultaneously. He also raised the problem of understanding instruments, such as the trumpet marine and the wind instruments, in which harmonics are produced separately.

2. FROM HUYGENS TO SAUVEUR AND NEWTON.   Like Galileo, Christiaan Huygens was the son of a musician, played a number of instruments and was interested in consonance and dissonance. Around 1673, influenced by Mersenne, he gave a derivation (under simplifying assumptions) of Mersenne's Law for the vibrating string. Like Mersenne, he was interested in overtones. He estimated absolute frequency, and understood the relationship between wavelength and pipe length.

In 1677 the mathematician John Wallis published a report on experiments showing that the overtones of a vibrating string, which are harmonic, are associated with the existence of nodal points on the string; according to him the phenomenon had been known to the Oxford musicians for a number of years. In his experiments a string was made to vibrate in a higher mode by resonance with a string tuned so that either its fundamental or one of its harmonics was at the pitch of the mode. Paper riders showed the nodal points. Wallis suggested that a similar situation must exist for wind instruments. He observed that the tone of a string was 'rough' if the string was excited at a potential node. In 1692 Francis Robartes published a similar description of nodes and harmonics in connection with his study of the scales of the trumpet and the trumpet marine.

At the beginning of the 18th century Joseph Sauveur proposed the development of a science of sound, which would be called 'acoustique'. His own studies, which grew out of an interest in music and a background in mathematics, dealt with the physics of musical sound. He seems to have been the first to recognize that the frequency of the beats produced by a pair of notes is equal to their frequency difference, and was able to determine frequencies absolutely, probably to within a few per cent, by counting the beat frequency for two low-pitched organ pipes tuned a small semitone apart in just intonation (frequency ratio 25:24). Like Wallis and Robartes, but independently of them, he explained that nodes are present when a string vibrates in a higher mode. He introduced the terms 'son harmonique', 'noeud' and 'ventre'.

Sauveur noted that organ builders had intuitively discovered the harmonic pitches, which they mixed by means of stops to obtain various timbres. As Fontenelle, *secrétaire perpétuel* of the Paris Académie, reported: 'Nature [had] the strength to make musicians fall into the system of harmonic sounds, but they fell into it without knowing it, led only by their ear and their experience. Sauveur has given a very remarkable example of this'. Sauveur remarked that the organist mixes the stops 'almost the way the painters mix colours', and that 'by the mixture of its stops, the organ is only imitating the harmony that nature observes in sonorous objects'. Fontenelle referred essentially to the principle of superposition in his explanation of harmonics: 'each half, each

third, each quarter of the string of an instrument makes its partial vibrations while the total vibration of the entire string continues'. In 1713 Sauveur ingeniously derived Mersenne's Law with a constant of proportionality for the ideal string that was correct but for a factor of $\sqrt{10}/\pi$. He did this by considering a horizontal string, hanging in a curve because of the gravitational field, which he treated as a compound pendulum. (In the same year Brook Taylor also gave a derivation. His style of analysis belongs to the 18th century, Sauveur's to the 17th.) The most important of Sauveur's ideas for later developments was the implicit theme of superposition, which appeared in his studies of beats, harmonics and timbre.

Newton first commented on musical sound in some of his early papers on optics. In a major achievement of the *Principia* (1687–1726) he analysed the propagation of sound mathematically. (His analysis was correct except for his use of Boyle's Law for the relation between pressure and volume rather than the adiabatic law, which was not known until the beginning of the 19th century.) Recognizing that the velocity of sound equals the product of wavelength and frequency, and using Mersenne's and Sauveur's determinations of the frequencies of organ pipes, Newton was able to conjecture 'that the wavelengths, in the sounds of all open pipes, are equal to twice the lengths of the pipes'.

3. THE AGE OF EULER.   The audible overtones of taut strings and of other bodies used to make music are harmonious to the ear. In the 18th century it was popularly believed that the overtones of all natural bodies were harmonious (see for example *BurneyH*, i, 164), and some readers claimed that Rameau had founded his system of harmony upon this idea; in fact Rameau's extensive passages on acoustics are confused and often misrepresented the knowledge in his time.

The dominant acoustic problem of the 18th century was to calculate the fundamental and the overtones of a given sonorous body. In 1713 Taylor attempted to determine the motion of the monochord on the basis of Newton's rational mechanics. His pioneer approach was fruitful for later work, but he himself could not carry it through without restricting the shape of the string to be a single sine wave. He confirmed Mersenne's Law and showed that its constant of proportionality is $\frac{1}{2}$. In 1727 Johann Bernoulli proposed a model of the string as a set of n little balls connected by massless cords and calculated the fundamental frequency for a few small values of n. Both Taylor and Bernoulli had equations from which they could have calculated the frequencies and nodes of the overtones, but neither of them did so. Bernoulli's discrete model, which had been proposed in the previous century, was to be studied in increasing detail, but it contributed nothing to acoustics.

In 1727, too, Euler published his *Dissertatio physica de sono*, a clear, short pamphlet that at once became a classic and guided acoustical research for about 75 years. Euler divided sounds into three kinds: the tremblings of solid bodies, such as the reeds of wind instruments, strings, chimes and drumskins; the sudden release of compressed or rarefied air, as by clapping the hands; and the oscillations of air, either free or confined by a chamber, such as the tube of a flute, an organ pipe or a trumpet. The first two kinds refer to the production of sound, the third also to its transmission to the ear.

Euler recalled Newton's determination of the speed of sound in air. Although the ideas upon which that determination rested seemed to be correct, the numerical result was far too small to agree with measured values. The problem of correcting Newton's analysis was to dog theorists for the whole century and to remain unsolved until 1868; however, the early theorists gradually came to see that mechanical principles could give correct ratios of frequencies, even if the pitch of the fundamental was incorrect, and they often reported their results in terms of such ratios. Fortunately for the earlier theories of music, it is the ratios that determine musical intervals. Similarly, pitches of all instruments were only uniformly incorrect; two instruments predicted to be consonant would be so indeed. Thus musical acoustics could make spectacular advances in the 18th century despite the standstill on what would seem to be the basic and central problem of physical acoustics.

In his next significant work on acoustics, *Tentamen novae theoriae musicae* (1739), Euler presented a developed theory of consonance, based upon an explicit, mathematical rule for determining the 'simplicity' of a set of frequencies such as those making up a chord. He derived his rule from ideas of the ancients, Ptolemy in particular. It could not take account of difference tones and summation tones, for they had not yet been reported, but it permitted Euler to determine by routine calculations the most complete systems of scales or modes ever published. The last chapter sketches a theory of modulation. Euler thus began to construct a mathematical theory of the consonance of a progression of chords.

The 7th and the combination of the 6th and the 5th have high measures of dissonance yet were often used by musicians of the 18th century. To explain this fact, Euler many years later suggested that 'we must distinguish carefully the ratios that our ears really perceive from those that the sounds expressed as numbers include' ('Conjecture', 1764). In the equally tempered scale there are no exact consonances, yet the ear seems to hear the ratio 2:3 when its irrational, equal-tempered substitute $1:2^{0.583}$ is sounded. The ear tends to simplify the ratio perceived, especially if the dissonant tones follow after a harmonious progression; for example, 36–45–54–64 is indistinguishable from 36–45–54–63, which is the same set of ratios as 4–5–6–7. The paper closes with the suggestion that the music of the day had already replaced Leibniz's basic numbers 2, 3 and 5, beyond which 'music had not yet learned to count', by 2, 3, 5 and 7. Apparently Euler was not familiar with Tartini's beats, though by the time he wrote this work they had been demonstrated. In the succeeding paper on the 'true character of modern music' (1764), Euler reasserted the position he took in his treatise: consonances and dissonances are not essentially different but just sounds that are more 'simple' or less so, according to the value of his numerical measure. The ancients admitted a smaller range of consonances than do the moderns; both the ancient and the modern practices perfectly obey the principles of harmony, but the modern composers have achieved 'a very considerable extension of the limits of ancient music'. Euler recommended that the musical scale of 12 notes based on the numbers 2, 3 and 5 be augmented by 12 more, based on the numbers 2, 3, 5 and 7; all of these 'foreign notes' are obtained by multiplying one of the usual notes by 7. A harpsichord with 24 keys per octave should be constructed so as to try

out this extended scale. Presumably Euler did not know of Vito Trasuntino's celebrated *arcicembalo* of 1606 (now in the Civico Museo of Bologna), which has 31 keys per octave. These works on the theory of harmony are exceptional in Euler's research on acoustics, the rest of which concern strictly physical problems.

It is now known that a body in undergoing a free vibration at a single frequency must assume a shape proportional to some particular one. The amplitude of vibration is arbitrary, but both the proper frequency of the vibration and the generating shape, which is the normal mode that corresponds to it, are determined uniquely. The several normal modes correspond to the several pure tones that a free sonorous body may emit simultaneously; the sound of such a body is thus a mixture of its normal mode frequencies. What this mixture is depends upon the amplitudes given to the several normal modes, and therefore on the way in which the body is set into vibration. This idea, of central and indispensable importance in acoustics, is due to Daniel Bernoulli. One of the few scientists of the 18th century who produced important experiments as well as important theory, he formed it gradually upon the basis of accumulated musical experience, simple theoretical assumptions and calculations, and experimental checks. He was not only the first to conceive of vibratory motions in this way but also the first to calculate the complete set of proper frequencies and normal modes for a particular vibrating body. He chose to consider first a heavy cord hung up from one end, but he saw and stated that his ideas were general and would apply to musical bodies (see his papers of 1732–3 and 1734–5). His results showed that the partials of the hanging cord were incommensurable and not harmonious; he showed also that a normal mode of higher frequency had a greater number of nodes than did one of lower frequency.

Euler and Bernoulli in friendly competition poured out a torrent of research on the small vibrations of bodies. Of course the long-awaited explanation of the tones and frequencies of the monochord fell into their hands at once. All the modal shapes were found to be sine waves, as Taylor could have shown but did not; and their frequencies follow the series 1–2–3–4 .... The transverse vibrations of elastic bars or chimes, variously supported at their ends, confirmed abundantly the facts suggested by Bernoulli's work on heavy cords (see Bernoulli, 1741–3, and Euler, 1734–5, 1744 and 1772). Only for exceptional bodies or conditions are the modal shapes sinusoidal; most of the partials are strikingly dissonant. The theory showed Bernoulli where to expect the nodes; by supporting a chime 'with the tips of two fingers' at the predicted nodes and then striking it he could easily induce a vibration in the corresponding pure mode. He recorded the tones 'by observing, as best as I was able, the consonant sound on my harpsichord'. The idea that harmony could be founded upon the 'naturalness' of the progression of partials was destroyed. Rather, as it appeared, bodies fit for making music are most unusual ones, having been selected precisely because their series of partials are harmonious to the ear. Of course the traditional idea that 'simplicity' made a chord harmonious, which had been rendered precise by Euler, was not affected. Nature had been shown not to be simple in this regard. The idea, then commonly attributed to Rameau, that simplicity was harmonious because favoured by nature, was thereby destroyed. Euler (1739) also explained the long-known phenomenon of resonance by showing that if an (undamped) harmonic oscillator is driven at its natural frequency the amplitude of its vibration increases without limit.

The methods used to calculate the modal forms and frequencies of bodies were special; the motions considered, likewise, were special. Daniel Bernoulli had claimed that any free vibration of a sounding body could be regarded as a superposition of its simple modes with various amplitudes, but there were no general principles upon which proof of such a statement could be attempted. At the mid-century, the Newtonian framework of mechanics was vastly expanded by Euler and Jean Lerond d'Alembert to make possible a concise mathematical description, in principle, of all motions of a body. These statements came later to be called 'differential equations of motion'; for bodies having infinitely many degrees of freedom, such as a bar or drumhead or chamber full of air, they are 'field equations', for they govern the local motion at each place in the body. On the basis of these equations, supplemented by suitable additional conditions on the boundary of the body, it is possible to ask whether Bernoulli's principle of superposed simple oscillations is valid. The mathematical tools developed in the 18th century were insufficient to answer the question, but in the 19th century mathematicians were to justify application of Bernoulli's idea to a multitude of vibrating bodies, and it forms an indispensable part of acoustics today.

A great controversy on this and related matters began in 1749, when d'Alembert published his discovery of the field equation for a taut cord; the other disputants were Euler, Bernoulli and, later, Joseph Louis Lagrange. From the very beginning the solutions of d'Alembert's equation indicated that every possible form of string could be generated by suitable waves travelling both to the right and to the left with the same speed, namely, $\sqrt{T/m}$. Euler based all of his discussion of the matter on this fact alone; d'Alembert contended that only particular 'equations' were amenable to mathematics; Bernoulli claimed that use of a sufficient number of simple modes would explain everything with any accuracy desired. The dispute was of a technical nature, unresolvable with the mathematics then known, and in the 18th century it bore no direct fruit for acoustics. However, both Bernoulli and Euler pursued the subject in the constructive spirit that characterized all their work; each showed that his approach could produce new and valuable information about sounding bodies.

Bernoulli (1753 and 1762), proceeding by analogy to his concept of transverse vibrations in strings and bars, formed a special theory of longitudinal vibrations of air in wind instruments. He found that the partials of a closed pipe followed the progression 1–3–5–7 .... He analysed the tones of an organ pipe à cheminée and concluded that his results were in accord with his formula for determining the length of a consonant uniform pipe. He also calculated the series of partials of a conical horn.

The year 1759 is decisive for acoustics, for in that year Euler derived the general field equations for vibrations of air in one, two or three dimensions. The modern theory of aerial acoustics rests upon these 'partial differential' equations or upon modifications of them so as to take account of internal friction and the conduction of heat. Euler's own research on them (1759) entered into only the simplest cases. He introduced the method of 'separation of variables', which is still the starting-point for solving many problems of aerial acoustics. He also determined the laws of propagation of cylindrical and spherical waves, calculating the diminution of their amplitudes as they spread out from a source. Euler had communicated some of his results to Lagrange during the weeks in which he discovered them. Lagrange applied them at once (1760–61) and extended the analysis in various directions. He obtained the field equations for longitudinal vibration of air in a tube of general cross-section; this equation was rediscovered over a century later, called the 'Webster horn equation', and put to extensive use in the design of loudspeakers.

One simple phenomenon remained ill-comprehended. If, as the theory asserts, sonic motion consists of waves running both ways continually, how can part of a string remain long at rest, and how can an echo be heard successively? In 1765 Euler easily showed how the opposing waves may simply annul each other for periods of time. He did so by explaining the general solution of the one-dimensional equation in terms of pulses which obey definite rules of reflection upon reaching a terminus such as the end of a wire, the vent or stopper of a pipe, or the face of a cliff. For example, he exhibited (1772) the complete solution for motion of a monochord plucked to triangular form and then released, thus settling the old problem of Beeckman, Mersenne and Taylor.

On the basis of this formulation of the transverse vibrations of a straight elastic bar in terms of a single partial differential equation, Euler in 1772 and 1774 calculated the frequencies and nodal forms of the modes corresponding to all six possible kinds of support. In 1782 Riccati published still more accurate calculations concerning the first six modes of a bar free at both ends, along with a detailed verification by experiments on chimes of brass and steel. The theory has been universally accepted ever since and is usually called 'the Bernoulli-Euler theory'.

In the second half of the 18th century theories for vibrating bodies of more complicated kinds were proposed, but the only success lay in Euler's field equations ('De motu vibratorio tympanorum', 1764) for a perfectly flexible drumhead, discovered in 1759. Euler obtained some particular solutions, but mathematical analysis was too primitive then to do much more. An epoch of acoustics closed with Euler's death in 1783. That the great achievements of the 18th century were only imperfectly recognized and in some cases had to be rediscovered in the 19th may be due partly to the lack of a textbook or even a treatise for specialists. The nearest to the latter is Euler's 'Sectio quarta de motu aëris in tubis' (1771), which is the last section of his treatise on fluid mechanics; the final chapters are devoted to the hyperbolic horn and the conical flute.

4. From Chladni to Ohm.   The research of the 18th century produced mainly theory such as to consolidate and extend understanding already formed by musical experience and by known experiments. It was nearly always presumed tacitly that music was first produced and then transmitted to the ear, which registered exactly the sound that fell upon it. There were occasional remarks about the nature of the ear, but little more than that. Rameau (1737) wrote: 'What has been said of sonorous bodies should be applied equally to the fibres which carpet

1. *Ernst Chladni demonstrating his experiment for determining nodal patterns; drawing (1800) by an unknown artist in the Deutsches Museum, Munich*

the bottom of the ear; these fibres are so many sonorous bodies, to which the air transmits its vibration, and from which the perception of sounds and harmony is carried to the soul'. Riccati suggested (1767) that the auditory nerve was 'a bundle of nerves which by the smallest degrees pass from the lowest tone to the highest, and the one of these that corresponds to unison with a sounding body is set a-trembling'. Such an ear, if its fibres were tuned at intervals of one tenth of a comma, would smooth over small differences of frequency but otherwise would be a perfect receiver.

In 1787 appeared a pamphlet by Ernst Chladni, *Entdeckungen über die Theorie des Klanges*, which opened a new period in physical acoustics. Mathematics had dominated the subject for a century; now, for the first time, a master experimentist who understood and knew how to use existing theory broke new ground with experiments which at once suggested and demanded a

theory of a new kind. To Chladni the idea of partials with their nodes corresponding to various kinds of support was second nature. He chose to determine them by experiment for thin, springy plates, and did so by scattering fine sand over the surface, supporting the plate at points conjectured to be nodal, and stroking the free edge with a violin bow (fig.1). He used this technique first to confirm the Bernoulli-Euler theory of straight rods; then he turned his attention to thin elastic surfaces, mainly circular discs but also square plates.

The enormous variety of nodal patterns Chladni obtained may be illustrated by the samples in fig.2. He recorded the frequencies in terms of musical pitches. His results reveal the intricacy of response that must be expected in the most idealized sounding-board of a musical instrument. To explain his figures by a theory that would correlate the nodal patterns with the frequencies has remained a major open problem of acoustic

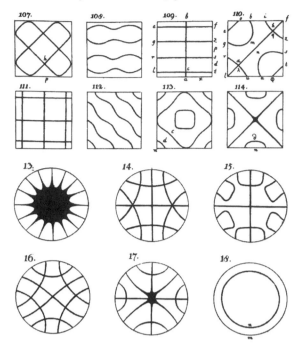

2. Examples of some nodal patterns obtained by Chladni, from his 'Die Akustik' (1802)

theory; it has been a continuing stimulus to search of principle, and cannot be regarded as solved.

The publication of Chladni's classic work *Die Akustik* (1802) gave a clear indication of change. In the new century the physics of music was to emphasize observation. By the end of that century, observation was to reveal that some of the problems of musical acoustics were more complex than they had seemed. The timbre and acoustical nuances of interest to the performing artist sometimes arose from effects too complicated to be included in the developing physical theories. For example, while the wolf note of the cello may be readily understood as an unavoidable problem of a resonant chamber of specified dimensions, the degree and type of orthotropy or directionally orientated elasticity in the cane of an oboe reed – possibly related in some way to the silicon content which makes cane from one particular region preferable to that from another – is a complicated problem far beyond the mathematical simplifications necessary to describe the physics of music.

To explain Chladni's sand figures in the vibrating plate challenged several generations of experimentists and theorists. After a few initial mistaken steps, a theory of the vibrating plate with appropriate boundary conditions evolved in the 19th century, but further experiments by Savart, Faraday, Lord Rayleigh (J.W. Strutt) and many others revealed phenomena beyond its range. The dilemma remained until 1931, when Andrade and Smith showed that the sand did not rest along the stationary nodal curves but rather moved on the surface until it reached lines at which the maximum acceleration of the plate equalled the gravitational constant g. For oscillations of large amplitude such lines approach the nodal lines on either side, but in moderate motion they may be far from them (fig.3). Thus Chladni and others after him were not right in interpreting the lines of sand as nodal lines;

perhaps the lines of sand as interpreted by Andrade could be determined by the theory, but so far they have not been. The status of the now standard theory of elastic plates remains neither supported nor controverted by Chladni's famous results. Andrade and Smith found, as had Rayleigh, that better consistency was obtained if the violin bow used by Chladni and those who followed him was replaced at a fixed location by a mechanical driver of constant frequency.

Experiments on the physics of music require precise determination of the absolute frequency of a sustained tone. Without such a determination it is not possible to analyse the frequencies of the various components of a musical note. Cagniard de Latour (1819) made a contribution to the measurement of absolute pitch (fig.4). He developed the siren in a form, later improved by Seebeck (1841) and Helmholtz (1863), and perfected by Koenig (1867, published 1881), which made absolute measurement possible. To a bellows chamber Cagniard affixed one plate with a series of holes; he rotated a second plate with identical holes so as to open and close the matching holes alternately. He therefore produced a tone of the desired loudness at a frequency determined by the speed of rotation. In the early 19th century it was difficult to maintain that speed constant, and many people throughout the rest of the century described their efforts to do so.

The most important tool for investigators in the 19th century was provided by Scheibler, a silk merchant who lived near Düsseldorf. In a pamphlet of 1834, in which he humbly acknowledged his limitations as a writer on science, he described his 'tonometer', which for the first time made it possible to determine absolute pitch precisely. His instrument was copied, improved and widely used for fundamental studies during the rest of the century. In fact, one of Scheibler's original instruments was still being used by Alexander J. Ellis, 50 years after its construction, to determine the pitches of 16th- to 19th-century organs and the tuning-forks of historically prominent musicians.

In his long summary of these measurements Ellis observed, for a', frequencies ranging from 374 to 567 Hz

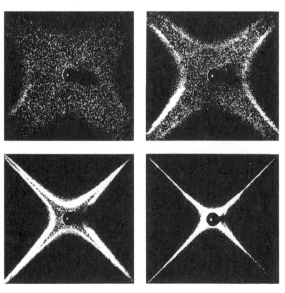

3. Sand figures for increasing amplitude (from Andrade and Smith, 1931)

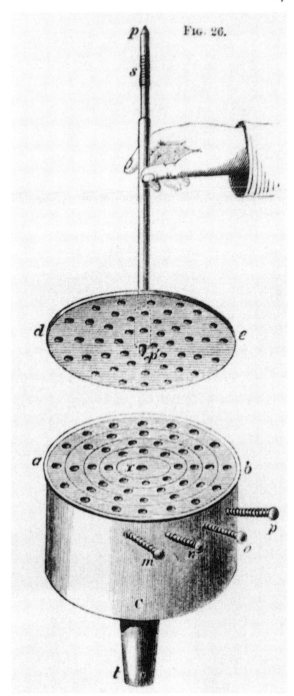

FIG. 26.

4. *Cagniard de Latour's siren (1819) for measuring absolute pitch (from Tyndall, 'Sound', 1898)*

the total average pitch was $a' = 440$ Hz, there were national differences. More important, there were variations of pitch during individual performances, depending upon the dominance of the various sections of the orchestra or upon the soloist.

The tonometer Scheibler described in 1834 was an array of 56 tuning-forks. One fork was tuned to $a' = 440$ Hz, the second to a, one octave below, and the rest at 4-Hz intervals in the octave. Through the careful counting of beats, the absolute frequency of an unknown tone in any 4-Hz interval could be established. At a congress of physicists in Stuttgart in the year he described his invention Scheibler introduced $a' = 440$ Hz and pressed for its selection; that value became known as the 'Stuttgart pitch'. Scheibler had made this choice not for some fundamental reason relating to scales, consonance or intonation, but because he had observed that 440 Hz was the mean of the frequencies of the a' on pianos in Vienna as they varied with temperature.

Scheibler's equally tempered scale, which he calculated to four decimal places, was a consequence of his choice of $a' = 440$ Hz rather than a preconceived notion. Among the many attempts to provide an absolute standard this 'Stuttgart pitch' was unique in that for the first time the proposed value had meaning; it could be measured with precision. Scheibler's tonometer, developed at the same time, provided the necessary tool.

One type of experiment in the 19th century was designed less as a part of the developing new ideas than as a confirmation of the conjecture of an earlier century. In the 18th century it had been relatively easy to perceive the nodes of transverse vibration of a string or a bar, but it was not until 1820 that Jean-Baptiste Biot, using polarized light through a transparent doubly refracting solid, demonstrated the existence of nodal patterns in the interior of a solid in longitudinal oscillation. This technique of photoelasticity had been discovered in a different context by Brewster (1816).

Kundt (1866), with a variation on Chladni's original experiment with the sand figures on plates, demonstrated the existence of nodal patterns in a column of air in a transparent glass tube by means of his 'dust figures' (fig.5). He observed the distribution into nodal patterns of a fine powder which he had sprinkled in the tube. His famous dust figures became the main method in the 19th century for determining the velocity of sound in various gases and, by means of an ingenious adaptation, the velocity of sound in solids.

Knowledge of the physics of music in the early 19th century had advanced sufficiently to provide an essential background for Helmholtz's experiments between 1854 and 1862. His work culminated in the penetrating study described in his great classic of 1863 *Die Lehre von den Tonempfindungen als physiologische Grundlage für die Theorie der Musik*.

The theorists of the 18th century had tried again and again to repair Newton's failure to calculate a value for the speed of aerial sound that squared with experiment. They had eliminated all sources of possible error but one: Newton's having taken the pressure in sonic motion to be proportional to the density, just as it is in air at rest. The mechanical theories had yielded correct ratios of frequencies and hence correct musical intervals, but they could account for the diminution of sound only through its spreading outwards as it progressed. According to them,

(cycles per second). Although the frequency generally increased from the 16th century to the 19th, there were wide fluctuations at any given time (*see* PITCH). In this context the study by van der Pol and Addink (1939) is interesting; their electronic arrangement permitted them to measure continuously, to an accuracy of 0·2 Hz, the pitch of an orchestra during a performance. In comparing 450 radio broadcasts of orchestras in England, France, Germany and the Netherlands, they found that, although

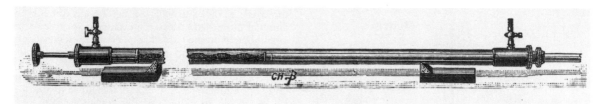

5. Kundt's glass tube from 'Catalogue des appareils d'acoustique construits par Rudolph Koenig' (1889)

air once set in motion to and fro between the plane walls of an elastic box would go on sounding for ever. Real sounds die out in time. Otherwise there could be no music. It is equally necessary that all audible sounds travel at sensibly the same speed. A complete theory of propagation must account for all these facts.

Pierre-Simon de Laplace suggested by degrees in the years 1816–22 that the sonic motion was too rapid to allow differences of temperature in the neighbouring parts of the air to equalize through conduction of heat. He showed that in a 'sudden compression', later called an 'adiabatic motion', the pressure of a gas was proportional not simply to the density, but to the density raised to the power of the ratio of specific heats. Substituting this relation into Euler's formula for the speed of sound in general, Laplace at once replaced Newton's numerical value by one that agreed well with measurements. It was still not clear just why the motion should be adiabatic. The matter was settled in a masterly research by Gustav Kirchhoff (1868). He began from the general field equations of motion which James Clerk Maxwell had obtained from his kinetic theory of gases just the year before; these, in turn, reflected the idea of internal friction due to George Gabriel Stokes, the conduction of heat as described by Fourier, the theory of interconvertibility of heat and work as elaborated by James Prescott Joule and Rudolf Julius Emmanuel Clausius, and the framework of continuum mechanics established by Augustin-Louis Cauchy. All the centuries of experience in rational mechanics were brought to bear on the problem of determining the behaviour of plane sound waves in a gas. Kirchhoff proved that for waves of low frequency the speed was given approximately by Laplace's formula, and that all such waves travelled at the same speed. However, for waves in the audible range the motion is not quite adiabatic, although it is more nearly so the slower (not the faster) is the oscillation. All sound waves are damped through the combined effects of viscosity and the conduction of heat, and sounds of higher pitch are damped out more quickly than are graver tones. 'Ultrasonic' waves, whose frequencies are very high, exhibit 'dispersion': the speed of propagation increases with frequency.

The velocity of sound in a solid had been measured first by Biot in 1808 in his experiments on waves propagating through nearly a kilometre of the newly constructed iron water pipes in Paris. Ingredients for Helmholtz's analysis were provided by the rapid, phenomenal development of the linear theory of elasticity in the 1820s by Claude-Louis Navier, Siméon-Denis Poisson and Cauchy.

Meanwhile, in his work on the conduction of heat in the first decades of the 19th century Fourier had shown how to represent any curve by superposing sine waves corresponding to the frequencies 1, 2, 3 …. This theorem and generalizations or analogues of it not only substantiated Daniel Bernoulli's viewpoint on acoustics but also became the basis for countless analyses of the tones, overtones and dissonant beats of musical instruments as well as unmusical ones.

Finally, as a prelude to the contributions of Helmholtz, there was the statement of Georg Ohm, better known for his law in electricity, who in 1843 proposed what became known as Ohm's Law of Acoustics. Ohm suggested that musical sounds depended only on the distribution of energies among the harmonics and had no dependence on differences of phase. The physical demonstration of Ohm's Law of Acoustics was the major accomplishment of Helmholtz, and the theory remained without effective challenge until the middle of the 20th century.

5. THE AGE OF HELMHOLTZ. Helmholtz provided a classic analysis of the role of overtones. To do so he needed an instrument sufficient to identify the existence and determine the strength of a suspected overtone. Furthermore, he was the first to understand fully that analysis of consonance and dissonance, let alone the existence of combination tones and the timbre of musical instruments, required more than the physics of the vibrating structure; analysis had to include the interaction of the sound from that source of vibration impinging upon another vibrating structure, the human ear. Helmholtz met the need for an instrument by developing his resonator. In its early crude form it was a spherical glass chamber with a hole at either end (fig.6), of size such that when exposed to a specific frequency the resonant cavity enabled him to identify that frequency when one aperture of the sphere was placed in the ear by means of a melted wax earpiece.

To achieve a proper analysis, Helmholtz applied to the detailed study of the human ear his great talents as one of the outstanding physiologists of the 19th century. Helmholtz, who is said to have been a competent pianist in addition to having exceptional talents as a universalist in physics and physiology, developed a two-manual harmonium to produce the overtones, difference tones and summation tones he wished to study. He systematically tested the applicability of Ohm's Law of Acoustics by using his metallic reeded harmonium, improved versions of the Cagniard de Latour siren and the Scheibler tonometer, and a greatly improved model of his own resonator, which Rudolph Koenig had perfected.

It is not possible here to give much detail of Helmholtz's discoveries beyond his demonstration of the general principles enunciated in Ohm's Law. He observed that the range of 30–40 Hz in the beating of high overtones produced the most unpleasant sensation. Some may contest this on aesthetic grounds, but Helmholtz's research shed light on the centuries of debate on the subject of consonance.

Of the many particulars of his work beyond the consideration of Ohm's Law, one must be mentioned

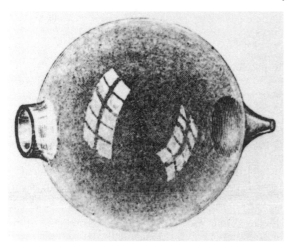

6. *Helmholtz resonator from 'Die Lehre von den Tonempfindungen'* (1863; Eng. trans., 1875/R1954)

because it set straight a previous misconception concerning the mystery of 'Tartini's beats': if two pure tones are sounded, and if the ear hears a tone the frequency of which is the difference of the two, the tone heard is called a 'difference tone'. Their discovery generally is credited to Tartini, who wrote of them in 1754. If date of publication is the criterion, however, the discovery must be credited to the German organist Georg Andreas Sorge, who published a description of the same phenomenon in

7. *Hermann von Helmholtz*

1745. Before Helmholtz the usual explanation for the difference tones is that stated by Thomas Young, among others. Such a tone, according to Young, was the beating of upper partials at a frequency high enough to provide a sound an octave below the lower of the two sounded notes. That this was a conjecture which led to absurdity was demonstrated by Helmholtz's discovery of higher combination tones, which he called 'summation tones'. The measured difference tone had a frequency which was the difference between two sounded notes, whereas the summation tone lay above the highest tone, with a frequency equivalent to the sum of the two sounding frequencies. Unlike the difference tone, which requires no special aural acuity to perceive, the summation tone is extremely difficult to hear. The discovery of its existence not only eliminated the conjectures of Young and others but also provided evidence for Helmholtz's theory of the non-linearity of the ear.

A receptor such as the ear, as would be expected from a knowledge of the mechanical behaviour of other portions of the human body, performs in a manner which is best represented by recourse to non-linear mechanics. The expected behaviour is entirely different from that in the world of linearized physics, with its focus restricted to the inaudible whisper and the invisible vibration, that is, to infinitesimal phenomena. In the linearly interpreted world, the sums of different solutions are still solutions, superposition prevails, and elementary harmonic analysis is possible. This corresponds to the general behaviour of the sources of sound in musical instruments. If non-linearity prevails, the sums of solutions are not generally solutions, superposition does not apply, and the resulting response contains elements produced by the non-linear receptor itself. Thus the human ear, first described in mathematically acceptable terms by Helmholtz, is capable of providing sounds not actually present in the musical instruments which supply the stimuli. The purely aural harmonics are in the form of sums and differences of the frequencies of the fundamental and the overtones of a given note, and in the amazing matrix of possible combinations of sums and differences when an interval or a chord is sounded. Hence the rudimentary physics of the vibration of musical instruments provides an indication of general behaviour but cannot explain the timbre.

Like many solemn pronouncements in science, Ohm's Law of Acoustics was more a summation of the accumulated wisdom of a preceding century than the sudden declaration of a newly conceived discovery. However, Helmholtz's years of experimentation in musical acoustics gave far more than mere substance to those conjectures; he provided in enormous detail and breadth the foundations for a century of further research.

The research of Helmholtz and Koenig, like that of other scholars of similar calibre, was not at once universally accepted. Mercadier (1872) criticized Helmholtz for having concentrated on the study of sustained tones rather than upon the melodious flow of the music. Koenig, too, was attacked. A sequence of correspondence in *Nature* indicates that although many of his contemporaries revered Koenig, as is affirmed by Thompson (1890–91) when describing Koenig's research and his visit to Koenig's remarkable workshop at the Quai d'Anjou on the Seine, he had some detractors, Ellis being one of them. It is difficult to see how Ellis, on the basis of what turned out to be his own flimsy measurements on a single,

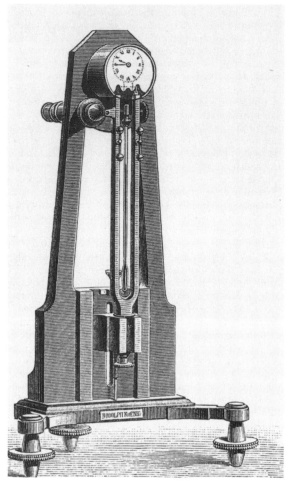

8. Koenig's clock tuning-fork from 'Catalogue des appareils d'acoustique' (1889)

questionable instrument, could claim that the tuning-forks of all Koenig's tonometers were seriously in error, particularly in view of the accuracy which Koenig had achieved with his 'clock tuning-fork', among other instruments (fig.8).

In Koenig's clock tuning-fork, the clock mechanism was driven by a 64-Hz tuning-fork which, with added weights, was adjustable between 62 and 68 Hz. It was possible to observe the motion of the opposite prong of the tuning-fork under the microscope in order to examine the Lissajous figures. Matching the clock tuning-fork to an unknown frequency, and observing the loss or gain of time of the fork-driven clock compared with a standard clock, provided the most precise measurement of frequency in the 19th century. Koenig had also developed the Scheibler tonometer to a remarkable instrument which would permit the determination of frequency over the entire audible range with what may be called 20th-century precision.

The accuracy of Koenig's tuning-forks (fig.9) became legendary. Each one was stamped with his own initials, to attest to his personal inspection of the validity of the stated frequency. Ellis, in his translator's notes accompanying Helmholtz's tome, described in detail the range of the tuning-forks and their prices in 1885 when they still were available from Koenig's own workshop. Nevertheless, Ellis was adversely critical of them. He used Appunn's reed tonometer, borrowed from the South Kensington Museum, and too rapidly concluded that Koenig's tuning-forks erred by 2 to 12 Hz from their stated frequencies. Koenig, questioning the accuracy of the instrument Ellis had used, stoutly defended the accuracy of his own tuning-forks and of his correction of the earlier measurements of Lissajous, who had been appointed by the Académie to set the standard for the French 'diapason normal' of $a' = 435$ Hz. (Lissajous had used a siren and had introduced the famous Lissajous figures in carrying out the commission.)

That was not the end of the discussion. Rayleigh entered the argument. He described a series of experiments which revealed that, when two reeds were vibrating in the

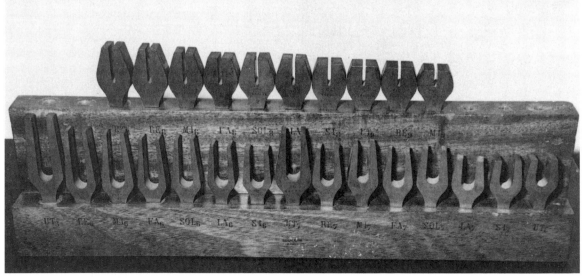

9. Koenig's tuning-forks (US Military Academy at West Point, New York)

immediate vicinity of one another, as in the instrument Ellis had used, the observed beats would be in error, for stated reasons, if they were compared with those for the same unknown frequency ascertained by means of separated tuning-forks, as in Koenig's instrument. Rayleigh's analysis and experiment supported Koenig's claim of precision. One could wish that in the final letter in this series Ellis had been as gracious to the craftsmanship of Koenig as he was to the ingenuity of Rayleigh.

6. 20TH CENTURY.   The 18th century saw the laying of a firm theoretical foundation for the physics of music, and the mechanical ingenuity of the great 19th-century experimentalists succeeded in providing empirical support for many of the theoretical predictions concerning the nature of sound and the operation of musical instruments. 20th-century acoustics has been dominated by the electronic revolution, which placed in the hands of scientists an immensely improved set of tools for measurement and computation. The resulting increase in the precision of both experiment and calculation has revealed that classical linear acoustics is incapable of describing many important aspects of the physics of music. In the last decades of the 20th century it increasingly became recognized that non-linear dynamics must be used to describe the behaviour of continuously excited instruments such as woodwinds and bowed strings (see Hirschberg, Kergomard and Weinreich, eds., 1995).

One of the most important practical problems in acoustics which was solved by electronic techniques was that of obtaining an accurate graphical record of the waveform of a sound. In the 17th century Galileo had described the possibilities of interpreting displacement against time, using traces of scratches from a vibrating stylus drawn across a metallic surface. In 1849 Guillaume Wertheim, a notable experimental physicist in 19th-century solid mechanics, while studying the 'deep tone' longitudinal vibration of rods (see Bell, 1973), had recorded the detail of vibration by a method he attributed to Duhamel. A tiny needle attached to a vibrating rod produced a trace on a transversely moving glass plate coated with carbon. Such mechanical methods of determining waveforms, with their limitations of frequency and other problems, were improved throughout the second half of the 19th century. Before the development of the vacuum tube revolutionized such experiments, the 'phonodeik', devised by Dayton C. Miller (1909), gained much attention. The sensitive receiver of Miller's device was a diaphragm of thin glass at the end of a resonator. A tiny steel spindle mounted in jewel bearings attached to the diaphragm by a thin thread made possible the photographing of the trace of the sound produced by the many different musical instruments which Miller investigated (fig.10). The device still had limitations of frequency response which had characterized the previous methods of mechanical measurement in this area. Miller's photographs filled the literature and influenced attitudes on musical acoustics until the mid-20th century.

The essential problem of all mechanical devices for recording sound vibrations lay in the difficulty of achieving an adequately rapid response from the mechanically moving parts. In 1897, J.J. Thomson demonstrated that a beam of electrons (which he described as a 'cathode ray') could be accelerated across an evacuated glass tube to create a visible spot on a fluorescent screen. A deflection of the beam by an electronic voltage could be observed as

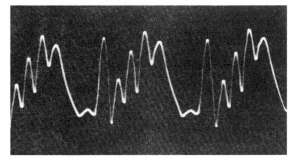

10. *Phonodeik trace for the tone of an oboe (from Miller, 1916)*

a movement of the visible spot. Since the electron beam, the only moving part of this system, is almost without mass, it is in principle capable of extremely rapid response. By the middle of the 20th century the cathode ray oscilloscope had become the standard method of observing the waveforms of the electrical signals generated by microphones or other vibration transducers (*see* SOUND, §3).

Access to electronic amplification and filtering techniques made it much easier to determine the frequency and spectral content of sound. Frequency measurement systems based on tuning forks were replaced by electro-mechanical meters like the Stroboconn, and later by meters which used the piezoelectric effect in a quartz crystal to provide a highly stable frequency standard. In the last 30 years of the century the phenomenal development of computers and other microprocessor-based devices led to another revolution, in which analogue electrical techniques have largely been supplanted by digital techniques. The first stage in the investigation of a sound signal consists of a digital sampling, with the signal being stored in the computer memory as a set of numbers. Subsequently a variety of sophisticated signal processing techniques can be applied, and any portion of the recorded signal can be readily reconstructed for detailed study, modification or reproduction (*see* RECORDED SOUND, §II, and SIGNAL (ii)).

The impact of the age of electronics has been so great in terms of the variety and magnitude of measurement in musical acoustics, as well as in some other areas, that it would be impossible in a short history to do more than emphasize a few important points. In one sense, the successes of Helmholtz and of Koenig had led to a hiatus in which few advances were made until well into the 20th century, despite the continued interest in acoustics and musical acoustics of one of the great late 19th-century scientists, Rayleigh, who continued to experiment and write on the subject until his death in 1919. The most influential book ever published on acoustics is Rayleigh's *The Theory of Sound* (1877), which gives a fairly reliable account of the accepted theory and experiment of its period.

By the end of the 19th century a fair understanding of impulsively excited instruments, such as plucked strings or struck bars, had been reached. If the energy imparted to the instrument by the excitation was not too great, the problem could be treated as the free decay of the normal modes of the system; the nature of the excitation determined the initial mode amplitudes. The situation was less satsifactory for continuously excited instruments, such as wind and bowed string instruments. In the 1850s

Helmholtz, among others, had performed experiments to study the phenomenon of bowing, and had identified the idealised string behaviour now known as 'Helmholtz motion'. Further studies of this motion were reported by C.V. Raman in 1918. Helmholtz had also investigated the excitation mechanisms of reed woodwind and brass instruments. Several researchers, including Rayleigh and especially Strouhal (1878), had developed an understanding of the principle of edge tones, which were believed to be related to sound production in the flute. However, although theoretical models based on these researches appeared to encompass the basic physics of the instruments, such musically important issues as the variation of timbre with change of playing parameters were not explained.

The pioneering work of Helmholtz and Rayleigh did not take into account an aspect of the physics of continuously excited musical instruments which is now recognised to be of crucial importance. This is the strongly non-linear relationship which is usually at the heart of the excitation mechanism. In the case of a reed woodwind instrument, for example, the relationship between the pressure difference across the reed and the rate of air flow through it is much more complicated than a simple linear proportionality. Because of this non-linearity, a sinusoidal driving pressure in the air column of the instrument can generate an air flow into the air column with a rich mixture of frequency components. Henri Bouasse (1929–30) was the first to recognize the significance of the non-linear excitation mechanism in wind instruments; his work in this field was later taken up and greatly extended by Arthur Benade (1976). A non-linear dynamical treatment of the bowed string has also been presented by McIntyre, Schumacher and Woodhouse (1983).

The classical theory of sound wave propagation rests on an approximation proposed by Euler, which is appropriate to waves of small amplitude. The original, non-linear partial differential equations of acoustics are replaced by linear 'wave equations'. However, non-linear waves of air do occur in nature: they are an everyday occurrence in the flight of aeroplanes and also are easy to produce in the laboratory. A non-linear wave of condensation concentrates energy. If heard as a sound, such a wave seems to be louder after a short time. The linear acoustics, culminating in the work of Kirchhoff, cannot account for this 'reinforcement', for according to it, all parts of a wave travel at the same speed. Important research by Riemann (1858–9) and Hugoniot (1887, 1889) showed that Euler's original, non-linear partial differential equations of gas dynamics, if not simplified by assuming the motion to be small from the outset, did predict reinforcement. Unfortunately, however, Euler's theory predicts also that all plane waves will reinforce: every small condensation, not only those deliberately produced as music, would become audible. That is not surprising in a theory that allows sounds to continue unabated for ever because it neglects all internal causes of damping. Thus in the late 19th century two different theories, partly contradictory, were needed in order to explain the propagation of one and the same sound. This awkward artificiality persisted for a century. Finally Coleman and Gurtin (1965), working within a conceptual framework due in part to Walter Noll, succeeded in subsuming the two older theories as approximations to a master theory which displays the behaviour of plane waves of arbitrary amplitude in a body of dissipative material. They calculated a 'critical amplitude' determined by the conditions of the medium. Sounds feebler than that amplitude are damped from the start; sounds stronger than that are reinforced and hence are perceived as louder at first; of course they, too, are finally damped out by internal friction and the conduction of heat, according to Kirchhoff's theory.

The human ear is an extremely sensitive organ, and the pressure variation caused by even a painfully loud sound is typically less than 0·1% of the mean atmospheric pressure. The small-amplitude approximation proposed by Euler is thus more than adequate for the description of almost all audible sound waves. Inside the mouthpiece of a trombone, on the other hand, the pressure can vary by around 10% when a very loud note is being played. It has been shown by Hirschberg and others (1996) that in these circumstances non-linear wave propagation in the trombone air column is musically important. Shock waves reminiscent of those generated by the 'sonic boom' of a supersonic aircraft are generated in the air column, giving rise to the rasping blare which characterizes the timbre of a loudly blown brass instrument.

There was one part of musical acoustics in which dramatic advances were made in the early 20th century, namely room acoustics, of obvious importance not only for the audience but also for the performing musician (see ACOUSTICS, §I). Wertheim (1851), in a memoir on the vibration of sounds in air, had emphasized that although we spend our daily lives responding to sounds produced in rooms, cupboards, glasses, bottles and other receptacles of air, physicists in the mid-19th century were concerned solely with behaviour in infinite space and in cylindrical tubes with open ends. With his characteristic thoroughness in experiment, Wertheim proceeded to provide measurements to broaden this focus. His basic criticism of the experiments of his contemporaries, however, remained essentially valid until the contributions, between 1898 and 1917, of Wallace Clement Sabine.

Sabine's collected papers on room acoustics present the results of a nearly single-handed achievement of importance in the physics of music. He brought the problems of reverberations, reflections, resonance and absorption in an auditorium to such a state of understanding that for the first time it became possible to design such a structure successfully on rational grounds, in advance of its construction. An outstanding example of his work was the design of the Boston Music Hall, which from its formal opening on 15 October 1900 was acclaimed for its fine acoustics. Directly from Sabine's original ideas and experiments enormous development took place in the engineering and the physics of room acoustics, during the 20th century; by its close, sophisticated computer modelling techniques had made it possible for the acoustical consequences of architectural design choices to be explored and understood before the commencement of building.

Another important area which developed greatly in the 20th century was the study of the human response to particular types of sound. This field, in which physics, psychology and physiology overlap, is often described as psychophysics or psychoacoustics. Many of the findings of 19th-century acousticians were reports of their own perceptions, and were criticized by Mercadier and others for lack of objectivity. In the 20th century a careful methodology was developed, involving suitably designed tests on large numbers of subjects. To a large extent these tests answered the criticisms by providing data on average perceptions which were in principle subject to verification.

Great care is necessary in designing the protocols and techniques used in psychoacoustic testing. In 1924 Wegel and Lane reported on tests carried out using a faint probe tone to investigate the generation of aural harmonics. These are distortion products introduced by the ear when presented with a purely sinusoidal sound wave. The finding of Wegel and Lane that many such aural harmonics were clearly audible was later shown to be due to a fault in the experimental technique (see Clack, Edreich and Knighton, 1972). It is now accepted that although such distortion products are generated by the inner ear, they are normally at such a low level as to be musically insignificant.

The ability to record, manipulate and synthesize musical sounds has made it possible to design and carry out systematic and reproducible psychoacoustic tests which have helped to answer some of the questions which intrigued the acousticians of previous centuries. Ohm's Law, stating that the human ear is insensitive to the relative phases of the partials in a complex sound, was conclusively disproved (see Plomp, 1976). In 1980 Carl Stumpf had suggested that the initial transient in the sound of a musical instrument was a crucial clue in identifying the instrument; this was verified by psychoacoustical studies carried out by Berger (1964) and by Grey and Moorer (1977).

At the end of the 20th century, the speed and memory capacity of computers continued to grow at a remarkable rate. As a consequence, it became possible to program into even a modest desktop computer a set of equations representing the theoretical behaviour of an instrument, and to obtain rapid predictions of the behaviour of the model. This proved to be of great value in testing theoretical predictions, since the equations are usually too complicated to be solved analytically. On the experimental side, laser-based vibration measuring equipment of very high accuracy has been added to the already impressive array of techniques being used to study both the detailed motion of musical instruments and the physiological responses of human and animal hearing systems.

Looking back over more than three centuries of sustained work on the physics of music, an acoustician at the end of the 20th century could not but marvel at the achievements of the past. Nevertheless, we are still a long way from being able to explain many of the features of musical sound and musical instruments which are of fundamental importance to musicians. To develop theoretical and experimental techniques to a level of accuracy that matches the sophistication of the musician's perception is the great challenge facing musical acoustics at the dawn of the 21st century.

BIBLIOGRAPHY

MersenneHU
J. Kepler: *Harmonice mundi libri V* (Linz, 1619; Eng. trans., 1997)
F. Bacon: *Sylva sylvarum* (London, 1627, 10/1676)
R. Descartes: *Musicae compendium* (Utrecht, 1650/R, 4/1695; Eng. trans., MSD, viii, 1961)
R. Hooke: *Micrographia* (London, 1665/R)
J. Wallis: 'On the Trembling of Consonant Strings: Dr Wallis's Letter to the Publisher concerning a New Musical Discovery', *Philosophical Transactions of the Royal Society*, xii (1677), 839–42

I. Newton: *Philosophiae naturalis principia mathematica* (London, 1687/R, 3/1726; Eng. trans., 1729/R), ii/2, propositions xlvii–l; ed. A. Koyré and I.B. Cohen (Cambridge, 1972)
F. Robartes: 'A Discourse concerning the Musical Notes of the Trumpet, and the Trumpet Marine, and of Defects of the Same', *Philosophical Transactions of the Royal Society*, xvii (1692), 559–63
[B. Le B. de Fontenelle]: 'Sur un nouveau système de musique', *Histoire de l'Académie royale des sciences* [1701] (Paris, 1704), 123–39
J. Sauveur: 'Système general des intervalles des sons', ibid. [1701] (Paris, 1704), *Mémoires*, 297–364
[B. Le B. de Fontenelle]: 'Sur l'application des sons harmoniques aux jeux d'orgues', ibid. [1702] (Paris, 1704), 90–92
J Sauveur: 'Application des sons harmoniques a la composition des jeux d'orgues', ibid. [1702] (Paris, 1704), *Mémoires*, 308–28
B. Taylor: 'De motu nervi tensi', *Philosophical Transactions of the Royal Society*, xxviii [1713] (1714), 26–32
[B. Le B. de Fontenelle]: 'Sur les cordes sonores, et sur une nouvelle détermination du son fixe', *Histoire de l'Académie royale des sciences* [1713] (Paris, 1716), 68–75
J. Sauveur: 'Rapport des sons des cordes d'instruments de musique aux fleches des cordes; et nouvelle détermination des sons fixes', ibid. [1713] (Paris, 1716), *Mémoires*, 324–48
J.P. Rameau: *Nouveau système & musique théorique* (Paris, 1726/R; Eng. trans., 1975, ed. B.G. Chandler); ed. J.-F. Kremer (Bourg-la-Reine, 1996)
J. Bernoulli: Theoremata selecta, pro conservatione virium vivarum demonstranda', *Commentarii Academiae scientiarum imperialis petropolitanae*, ii (1727), 200–07; repr. in *Opera omnia* (Lausanne, 1942/R), iii, 124–30
L. Euler: *Dissertatio physica de sono* (Basle, 1727); repr. in *Opera omnia*, III/i (Leipzig, 1926), 182–96
D. Bernoulli: 'Theoremata de oscillationibus corporum filo flexibili connexorum et catenae verticaliter suspensae', *Commentarii Academiae scientiarum imperialis petropolitanae*, vi (1732–3), 108–22
D. Bernoulli: 'Demonstrationes theorematum suorum de oscillationibus corporum filo flexibili connexorum et catenae verticaliter suspensae', ibid., vii (1734–5), 162–73
L. Euler: 'De minimis oscillationibus corporum tam rigidorum quam flexibilium methodus nova et facilis', ibid., vii (1734–5), 99–122; repr. in *Opera omnia*, II/x, ed. F. Stüssi (Leipzig, 1947), 17–34
J.P. Rameau: *Génération harmonique, ou Traité de musique théorique et pratique* (Paris, 1737), proposition xii; ed. and trans. in D. Hayes: *Rameau's Theory of Harmonic Generation* (diss., Stanford U., 1968)
L. Euler: 'De novo genere oscillationum', *Commentarii Academiae scientiarum imperialis petropolitanae*, xi (1739), 128–49; repr. in *Opera omnia*, II/x, ed. F. Stüssi (Leipzig, 1947), 78–97
L. Euler: *Tentamen novae theoriae musicae, ex certissimis harmoniae principiis dilucide expositae* (St Petersburg, 1739); repr. in *Opera omnia*, III/i (Leipzig, 1926), 197–427
D. Bernoulli: 'Excerpta ex litteris a Daniele Bernoulli ad Leonhardum Eulerum', *Commentarii Academiae scientiarum imperialis petropolitanae*, xiii (1741–3), 1–15
D. Bernoulli: 'De vibrationibus et sono laminarum elasticarum commentationes physico-mathematicae', ibid., xiii (1741–3), 105–20
L. Euler: 'Additamentum I de curvis elasticis', *Methodus inveniendi lineas curvas maximi minimive proprietate gaudentes* (Lausanne and Geneva, 1744), 63–97; repr. in *Opera omnia*, I/xxiv (Leipzig, 1952)
J. Lerond d'Alembert: 'Recherches sur la courbe que forme une corde tendue mise en vibration', *Histoire de l'Académie royale des sciences et des belles lettres de Berlin*, iii [1747] (1749), 214–19
J.P. Rameau: *Démonstration du principe de l'harmonie servant de base à tout l'art musical théorique et pratique* (Paris, 1750/R)
D. Bernoulli: 'Réflexions et éclaircissements sur les nouvelles vibrations des cordes exposées dans les Mémoires de l'Académie de 1747 & 1748', *Mémoires de l'Académie royale des sciences et des belles lettres de Berlin*, ix (1753), 147–95
L. Euler: 'De la propagation du son', ibid., xv (1759), 185–264; repr. in *Opera omnia*, III/i (Leipzig, 1926), 428–507
J.-L. Lagrange: 'Nouvelles recherches sur la nature et la propagation du son', *Mélanges de philosophie et de mathématique de la Société royale de Turin*, ii (1760–61), 11–172; repr. in *Oeuvres de Lagrange*, i, ed. J.-A. Serret (Paris, 1867), 151–316

D. Bernoulli: 'Recherches physiques, mécaniques et analytiques, sur le son et sur les tons des tuyaux d'orgues différemment construits', *Histoire de l'Académie des sciences de Paris* (1762), 431–85

L. Euler: 'Conjecture sur la raison de quelques dissonances généralement reçues dans la musique', *Mémoires de l'Académie royale des sciences et des belles lettres de Berlin*, xx (1764), 165–73; repr. in *Opera omnia*, III/i (Leipzig, 1926), 508–15

L. Euler: 'De motu vibratorio tympanorum, *Novi commentarii Academiae scientiarum imperialis petropolitanae*, x (1764), 243–60; repr. in *Opera omnia*, II/x, ed. F. Stüssi (Leipzig, 1947), 344–59

L. Euler: 'Du véritable caractère de la musique moderne', *Mémoires de l Académie royale des sciences et des belles lettres de Berlin*, xx (1764), 174–99; repr. in *Opera omnia*, III/i (Leipzig, 1926), 516–39

L. Euler: Eclaircissements plus détaillés sur la génération et la propagation du son, et sur la formation de l'écho, ibid., xxi (1765), 335–63; repr. in *Opera omnia*, III/i (Leipzig, 1926), 540–67

L. Euler: Sur le mouvement d'une corde qui au commencement n'a été ébranlée, que dans une partie', ibid., xxi (1765), 307–23; repr. in *Opera omnia*, II/x, ed. F. Stüssi (Leipzig, 1947), 426–50

G. Riccati: 'Delle vibrazioni delle corde sonore', *Delle corde ovvero fibre elastiche schediasmifisico-matematici* (Bologna, 1767), 65–104

L. Euler: 'Sectio quarta de motu aëris in tubis', *Novi commentarii Academiae scientiarum imperialis petropolitanae*, xvi (1771), 281–425; repr. in *Opera omnia*, II/xiii, ed. C.A. Truesdell (Leipzig, 1955), 262–369

L. Euler: 'De chordis vibrantibus disquisitio ulterior', ibid., xvii (1772), 381–409

L. Euler: 'De motu vibratorio laminarum elasticarum ubi plures novae vibrationum species hactenus non pertractatae evolvuntur', ibid., xvii (1772), 449–87; repr. in *Opera omnia*, II/xi/1, ed. F. Stüssi (Leipzig, 1957), 112–41

G. Riccati: 'Delle vibrazioni sonore dei cilindri', *Memorie di matematica e fisica della Società italiana delle scienze*, i (Verona, 1782), 444–525

E.F.F. Chladni: *Entdeckungen über die Theorie des Klanges* (Leipzig, 1787/R)

E.F.F. Chladni: *Die Austik* (Leipzig, 1802)

J.B. Biot: 'Expériences sur la propagation du son à travers les corps solides et à travers l'air, dans des tuyaux très-allongés', *Mémoires de physique et de chimie de la Société d'Arcueil*, ii (1809/R), 405–23

D. Brewster: 'On the Communication of the Structure of Doubly Refracting Crystals to Glass, Muriate of Soda, Fluorspar, and Other Substances, by Mechanical Compression and Dilatation', *Philosophical Transactions of the Royal Society*, cvi (1816), 156–78

C. Cagniard de Latour: 'Sur la sirène, nouvelle machine d'acoustique destinée à mesurer les vibrations de l'air qui constituent le son', *Annales de chimie et de physique*, 2nd ser., xii (1819), 167–71

J.-B. Biot: 'Sur une nouvelle propriété physique qu'acquièrent les lames de verre quand elles exécutent des vibrations longitudinales', ibid., 2nd ser., xiii (1820), 151–5

F. Savart: 'Mémoire sur la communication des mouvements entre les corps solides', ibid., 2nd ser., xiv (1820), 113–72

P.S. Laplace: *Traité de mécanique céleste*, xii (Paris, 1825); repr. as *Oeuvres de Laplace*, v (Paris, 1843–7)

M. Faraday: 'On a Peculiar Class of Acoustical Figures; and on Certain Forms Assumed by Groups of Particles upon Vibrating Elastic Surfaces', *Philosophical Transactions of the Royal Society*, cxxi (1831), 299–318

J.H. Scheibler: *Der physikalische und musikalische Tonmesser* (Essen, 1834)

A. Seebeck: 'I. Beobachtungen über einige Bedingungen der Entstehung von Tönen', *Annalen der Physik und Chemie*, liii (1841), 417–36

G.S. Ohm: 'Ueber die Definition des Tones, nebst daran geknüpfter Theorie der Sirene und ähnlicher tonbildender Vorrichtungen', ibid., lxi (1843), 497–565

G.S. Ohm: 'I. Noch ein paar Worte über die Definition des Tones', ibid., lxii (1844), 1–18

G. Wertheim: 'Mémoire sur la propagation du mouvement dans les corps solides et dans les liquides', ibid., 3rd ser., xxxi (1851), 19–36

G. Wertheim: 'Mémoire sur les vibrations sonores de l'air', ibid., 3rd ser., xxxi (1851), 385–432

J. Lissajous: 'Mémoire sur l'étude optique des mouvements vibratoires', ibid., 3rd ser., li (1857), 147–231

G.B. Riemann: 'Ueber die Fortpflanzung ebener Luftwellen von endlicher Schwingungsweite', *Abhandlungen der Königlichen Gesellschaft der Wissenschaften zu Göttingen, mathematischen Classe*, viii (1858–9), 43–65; repr. in *Bernard Riemann's Gesammelte mathematische Werke*, ed. R. Dedekind and H. Weber (Leipzig, 1876), 145–64; ed. R. Narasimhan (Berlin, 1990)

H. von Helmholtz: *Die Lehre von den Tonempfindungen als physiologische Grundlage für die Theorie der Musik* (Brunswick, 1863, 4/1877; Eng. trans. 1875, 2/1885/R, 6/1948, as *On the Sensations of Tone*)

A.A. Kundt: 'I. Ueber eine neue Art akustischer Staubfiguren und über die Anwendung derselben zur Bestimmung der Schallgeschwindigkeit in festen Körpern und Gasen', *Annalen der Physik und Chemie*, cxxvii (1866), 497–523

J. Tyndall: *Sound* (London, 1867, 3/1875/R, 5/1893)

G. Kirchhoff: 'Über den Einfluss der Wärmeleitung in einem Gase auf die Schallbewegung', ibid., cxxxiv (1868), 177–93; repr. in *Gesammelte Abhandlungen* (Leipzig, 1882, suppl. 1891 ed. L. Boltzmann), 540–56

E. Mercadier: 'Sur l'histoire de l'acoustique musicale', *Journal de physique théorique et appliquée*, i (1872), 109–12

A.J. Ellis: 'Koenig's Tuning-Forks and the French "Diapason Normal"', *Nature*, xvi (1877), 85 only

R. Koenig: Note, *Proceedings of the American Philosophical Society*, xvii (1877), 80–83

A.J. Ellis: 'The Radiometer and its Lessons', *Nature*, xvii (1877–8), 26–7

R. Koenig: Letter, *Nature*, xvii (1877–8), 162 only

Lord Rayleigh [J.W. Strutt]: 'Absolute Pitch', *Nature*, xvii (1877–8), 12–14

Lord Rayleigh [J.W. Strutt]: *The Theory of Sound* (London, 1877–8, 2/1894–6)

C. Strouhal: 'Über eine besondere Art der Tonerregung', *Annalen der Physik und Chemie*, new ser., v (1878), 216–51

A.J. Ellis: 'The History of Musical Pitch', *Nature*, xxi (1879–80), 550–54

R. Koenig: 'Bemerkungen über die Klangfarbe', *Annalen der Physik und Chemie*, new ser., xiv (1881), 369–93

A.J. Ellis: 'Translator's Notice', in H. von Helmholtz: *On the Sensations of Tone* (London, 2/1885/R)

P.H. Hugoniot: 'Mémoire sur la propagation du mouvement dans les corps et spécialement dans les gaz parfaits', *Journal de l'école polytechnique*, lvii (1887), 3–97; lviii (1889), 1–125

S.P. Thompson: 'The Researches of Dr. R. Koenig on the Physical Basis of Musical Sounds', *Nature*, xliii (1890–91), 199–203, 224–7, 249–53

D.C. Miller: 'The Phonodeik', *Physical Review*, xxviii (1909), 151 only

D.C. Miller: *The Science of Musical Sounds* (New York, 1916/R)

W.C. Sabine: *Collected Papers on Acoustics* (Cambridge, MA, 1922/R)

R.L. Wegel and C.E. Lane: 'The Auditory Masking of One Pure Tone by Another', *Physical Review*, 2nd ser., xxiii (1924), 266–85

H. Bouasse: *Instruments à vent* (Paris, 1929–30/R)

E.N. da C. Andrade and D.H. Smith: 'The Method of Formation of Sand Figures on a Vibrating Plate', *Proceedings of the Physical Society of London*, xliii (1931), 405–11

C. Huygens: *Oeuvres complètes*, ed. Société Hollandaise des Sciences, xviii (The Hague, 1934), 483–95; xix (1937), 359–77; xx (1940), 1–173

D.C. Miller: *Anecdotal History of the Science of Sound to the Beginning of the 20th Century* (New York, 1935)

B. van der Pol and C.C.J. Addink: 'The Pitch of Musical Instruments and Orchestras', *Philips Technical Review*, iv (1939), 205–10

C. Truesdell: 'The Theory of Aerial Sound, 1687–1788', *Leonhardi Euleri opera omnia*, II/xiii (Leipzig, 1955), pp.xix–lxxvi

I.B. Cohen, ed.: *Isaac Newton's Papers & Letters on Natural Philosophy* (Cambridge, MA, 1958, 2/1978), 177–99

C. Truesdell: 'The Rational Mechanics of Flexible or Elastic Bodies, 1638–1788', *Leonhardi Euleri opera omnia*, II/ii/2 (Leipzig, 1960), 15–141

C.V. Palisca: 'Scientific Empiricism in Musical Thought', *Seventeenth Century Science and the Arts*, ed. H.H. Rhys (Princeton, NJ, 1961), 91–137; repr. in C. Palisca: *Studies in the History of Italian Music and Music Theory* (New York, 1994), 146–67

K.W. Berger: 'Some Factors in the Recognition of Timbre', *JASA*, xxxvi (1964), 1888–91

B.D. Coleman and M.E. Gurtin: 'Waves in Materials with Memory, II: On the Growth and Decay of One-Dimensional Acceleration Waves; III: Thermodynamic Influences on the Growth and Decay of Acceleration Waves', *Archive for Rational Mechanics and Analysis*, xix (1965), 239–98; repr. in B.D. Coleman and others: *Wave Propagation in Dissipative Materials* (New York, 1965)

D.P. Walker: 'Kepler's Celestial Music', *Journal of the Warburg and Courtauld Institutes*, xxx (1967), 228–50

T.D. Clack, J. Edreich and R.W. Knighton: 'Aural Harmonics', *JASA*, lii (1972), 536–41

J.F. Bell: 'The Experimental Foundations of Solid Mechanics', *Handbuch der Physik*, ed. S. Flügge, vi/A/1 (Berlin, 1973), 1–813, esp. 254–7

S. Drake, ed. and trans.: G. Galilei: *Two New Sciences* (Madison, WI, 1974, 2/1989), 96–108

S. Dostrovsky: 'Early Vibration Theory: Physics and Music in the Seventeenth Century', *Archive for History of Exact Sciences*, xiv (1975), 169–218

A.H. Benade: *Fundamentals of Musical Acoustics* (New York, 1976, 2/1990)

R. Plomp: *Aspects of Tone Sensations* (New York, 1976)

C.A. Taylor: *Sounds of Music* (London, 1976)

C. Truesdell: 'History of Classical Mechanics', *Die Naturwissenschaften*, lxiii (1976), 53–62, 119–30

J.M. Grey and J.A. Moorer: 'Perceptual Evaluation of Synthesised Musical Instrument Tones', *JASA*, lxi (1977), 454–62

M.E. McIntyre, R.T. Schumacher and J. Woodhouse: 'On the Oscillations of Musical Instruments', *JASA*, lxxiv (1983), 1325–45

M. Campbell and C. Greated: *The Musician's Guide to Acoustics* (London, 1987/R)

A. Hirschberg, J. Kergomard and G. Weinreich, eds.: *Mechanics of Musical Instruments* (Vienna, 1995)

J.G. Roederer: *The Physics and Psychophysics of Music* (New York, 3/1995)

A. Hirschberg and others: 'Shock Waves in Trombones', *JASA*, xcix (1996), 1754–8

N.H. Fletcher and T.D. Rossing: *The Physics of Musical Instruments* (New York, 2/1998)

SIGALIA DOSTROVSKY/MURRAY CAMPBELL (1–2), JAMES F. BELL, C. TRUESDELL/MURRAY CAMPBELL (3–6)

Piacenza. City in northern Italy. There is evidence of a local liturgy dating from the 4th century in a letter from St Jerome to the deacon of Piacenza, Presidius (384). A bull issued by Pope Innocent IV (6 February 1248) confirming the city's privilege of a *studium generale* (i.e. a university), with faculties of canon and civil law, philosophy, literature, the sciences and the liberal arts, recognizes the existence of schools of music attached to chapters and monasteries of the Benedictine, Cistercian, Dominican, Servite and Franciscan orders. This early liturgical and musical activity in Piacenza is also shown by the neumatic manuscripts in the two major archives. S Antonino, the first cathedral (begun in the 4th century), contains the famous Antiphoner Gradual (12th century) which still shows some traces of Ambrosian influence in Piacenza's long tradition of plainchant. The present cathedral (1122) has 22 music manuscripts from before the 11th century to the 16th, a fine collection of printed music (particularly rich in single extant copies) and precious 16th-century manuscript anthologies. A 12th-century codex, the *Liber Magistri* (I-PCd 65), contains rich illuminations of instruments (*tensibilia*, *inflatilia*, *percussionales*), an antiphoner, a gradual, a psalter, a sequentiary, a tonary, a compendium of musical theory and a troper with one of the rare examples of *Quem quaeritis*. Raimbaut de Vaqeiras, Jacopo da Bologna and Giovanni da Cascia were all probably active in or near Piacenza. Duke Galeazzo Maria Sforza, who was assassinated in 1476, intended but failed to establish *cappelle* in the principal cathedrals of the duchy, from Milan to Piacenza. Francesco Sforza employed the dancing-master Domenico da Piacenza (*c*1450), who taught another Piacentine, Antonio Cornazano. The links between the Sforza and Josquin Des Prez are reflected in the cathedral archive and in the marquetry-work in the choir of S Sisto, which represents music and musical instruments.

The *cappelle* of the major churches flourished during the 16th century: S Pietro, S Agostino, S Antonino, S Maria di Campagna (housing an imposing organ by Carlo Serassi, 1822), S Francesco, S Giovanni in Canale (1557–1732, the last *maestro di cappella* being Geminiano Giacomelli) and the cathedral. There music was encouraged by Bishop Claudio Rangoni (1596–1619); the most important *maestri di cappella* between about 1570 and about 1780 were the 'Frenchman' Luigi Roinci, G.C. Quintiani, Tiburtio Massaino, Michelangelo Serra, G.A. Grossi, Giuseppe Allevi, F.M. Bazzani, G.B. Benzoni and Giuseppe and Giacomo Carcani.

Academies flourished in the 16th century, including those of Guido della Porta, Alessandro Colombo and especially Annibale Malvicino. The latter was attended by Antonfrancesco Doni, also a member of the Accademia Ortolana. He dedicated to some influential men of Piacenza three parts of his *Dialogo della musica* (1544), in which appear such local musicians as P.J. Palazzo, Tommaso Bargonio, Claudio Veggio and Gerolamo Parabosco. The Farnese, dukes of Parma and Piacenza from 1545, provided patronage and employment. Under Ottavio Farnese (1556–86) and his wife Margaret of Austria, governor of the Low Countries, Flemish composers and singers flocked to the duchy. In spite of the harsh character of Ranuccio I (1586–1622) life at his court could be festive (Fabritio Caroso dedicated to him his *Il ballarino*, 1581). Odoardo (1625–46) was a patron of Monteverdi, whose ballet *La vittoria d'amore* was performed in the Cittadella (1641) for the birth of Ottavio, Odoardo's seventh son. Ranuccio II (1646–94) encouraged musical drama; his three marriages provided opportunities for musical festivities. Through Elisabetta Farnese, the consort of Philip V of Spain, the Farnese were succeeded by Bourbons; under them Piacenza lost importance relative to Parma. Notable musicians during the Farnese period included Giuseppe Villani and his sons Gasparo and Gabriele and, under the patronage of the Bourbons, Giuseppe and Giacomo Carcani. Other natives of Piacenza included Sebastiano Nasolini, Giuseppe Nicolini, Giuseppe Ferranti (1888–1937), highly regarded by Debussy and Toscanini, and Amilcare Zanella.

From 1644 to about 1720 operas were given sporadically in the Teatro di Palazzo Gotico (also called Teatro Nuovo), built by Cristoforo Rangoni (called Ficcarelli) with four rows of boxes; it was inaugurated with a performance of Francesco Sacrati's *La finta pazza* given by the Febiarmonici. Other first performances there included Olivo's *Ratto d'Elena* (1646) and Cavalli's *Coriolano* (1669), probably in the absence of the composer. More active, especially in the 18th century, were the Teatro delle Saline (1593–1804) and the Regio Ducal Teatro della Cittadella (first half of the 17th century to 1797). The former specialized in *opera buffa*; the latter gave performances of both *opera seria* (A. Ziani, Chelleri, T. Albinoni, Carcani, Jommelli, Sacchini) and later *opera buffa* (Galuppi, Gazzaniga, V. Fioravanti, Tritto, G. Nicolini, Paisiello, Cimarosa). The Cittadella theatre won esteem in the late 17th century with a team consisting of the composer Bernardo Sabadini, the impresario Giuseppe

Calvi and the designers Ferdinando and Francesco Galli-Bibiena. On 10 September 1804 the Teatro Comunitativo (now Teatro Municipale) opened with a performance of *Zamori, ossia L'eroe dell'Indie* by Simon Mayr. It is still one of the major provincial Italian opera houses (*teatri di tradizione*); it has five rows of boxes and seats about 1500. It was built by Lotario Tomba and important improvements were made between 1826 and 1830 by the designer Alessandro Sanquirico. Among the artists who performed there were Paganini (1812, 1818 in a contest with K.J. Lipiński, 1834) and Toscanini (1900, 1920). The 19th-century repertory in Piacenza was dominated by Rossini (15 operas performed between 1814 and 1838) and Verdi (almost all the major operas starting with *Nabucco* in 1843) and included works by Bellini, Donizetti, Puccini, Mascagni, Meyerbeer and Massenet. Wagner was introduced into the repertory with a performance of *Lohengrin* in 1889, and Mozart with *Così fan tutte* in 1961.

The Accademia dei Filarmonici, the Filarmonici di Trebbia and the Università di Filarmonici were founded in the mid-18th century. The Casino de' Virtuosi di Musica was associated with the Teatro della Cittadella, and the Società Filarmonica was active from the beginning of the 19th century. From 3 August 1822 the Accademia di Studio Musicale held regular weekly meetings throughout the 19th century to spread knowledge of both old and contemporary Italian vocal and instrumental music. The Scuola Musicale was founded in 1839 with the purpose of supplying members of the chorus and orchestra to the Teatro Municipale; it was named after Nicolini in 1914, recognized by the state in 1933 and became a conservatory in 1970. It has a fine concert hall; its library holds an interesting music collection. Directors of the Scuola Musicale have included Giuseppe Jona, Primo Bandini, Giovanni Spezzaferri, Marcello Abbado and Giuseppe Zanaboni. In 1953 Zanaboni founded the Gruppo Ciampi to promote Piacenza's musical heritage; Francesco Bussi's 1987 foundation of the Monumenti Musicali Piacentini e Farnesiani has a similar aim.

The province of Piacenza includes the monastery at Bobbio, founded by the Irish St Columba in 599, which is famous for its collection of manuscripts in the notation of St Gallen (it is likely that the *Planctus de obitu Caroli* was written at Bobbio); Monticelli d'Ongina, the residence of Franchinus Gaffurius between 1480 and 1483; and Castell'Arquato, where the archives of the Collegiata contain the only extant copy of Monteverdi's *Sacrae cantiunculae*.

BIBLIOGRAPHY

DEUMM (F. Bussi); *MGG2* (F. Bussi); *RicordiE* (F. Bussi)
E. Nasalli Rocca: 'Dalla Scuola vescovile allo Studio generale di Piacenza', *Bollettino storico piacentino*, xxxix (1944), 19–28
A. Rapetti: 'Il teatro ducale della Cittadella'; 'Il teatro ducale di Palazzo gotico', *Bollettino storico piacentino*, xlvi (1951), 1–10, 45–51
C. Censi: *Il Liceo musicale 'G. Nicolini' di Piacenza* (Florence, 1952)
F. Bussi: *Alcuni maestri di cappella e organisti della cattedrale di Piacenza (sec. XVI–XIX)* (Piacenza, 1956)
F. Bussi: *L'Antifonario-Graduale della Basilica di S Antonino in Piacenza (sec. XII)* (Piacenza, 1956/R)
M. Picker: 'Josquiniana in some Manuscripts at Piacenza', *Josquin des Prez: New York 1971*, 247–60
F. Bussi: *Due importanti fondi musicali piacentini: la biblioteca-archivio capitolare del duomo e la biblioteca del Conservatorio 'Giuseppe Nicolini'* (Piacenza, 1972)
F. van Benthem: 'Einige Musikintarsien des frühen 16. Jahrhunderts in Piacenza und Josquins Proportionskanon "Agnus Dei"', *TVNM*, xxiv (1974), 99–111
O. Mischiati: *L'organo di Santa Maria di Campagna a Piacenza* (Piacenza, 1980)
D. Rabitti: 'Orchestre e istituzioni musicali piacentine', *Orchestre in Emilia-Romagna nell '800 e '900* (Parma, 1982), 37–59
M.G. Forlani: *Il Teatro Municipale di Piacenza (1804–1984)* (Piacenza, 1985)
F. Bussi: 'Frivolezza mondana e fasto austero: dicotomìa della musica alla corte di Ranuccio I', *I Farnese nella storia d'Italia* (Florence, 1988), 365–79
M. Genesi: 'Il coro ligneo di S. Sisto a Piacenza: uno specimen di strumentario italiano rinascimentale', *Strenna piacentina*, x (1988), 101–14
F. Bussi: 'I teatri d'opera a Piacenza prima della costruzione del Teatro Municipale', *NRMI*, xxiv (1990), 456–64
M.L. Bussi: *Musica e musicisti presso i Ser.mi Duchi Farnese in Piacenza (1545–1731)* (Piacenza, 1991)
F. Bussi: 'La musica a Piacenza dai Visconti (1313) e gli Sforza fino all'avvento dei Farnese (1545)', *Storia di Piacenza*, iii (Piacenza, 1997), 909–45

FRANCESCO BUSSI

Piacenza, Domenico da. *See* DOMENICO DA PIACENZA.

Piacenza, Giuseppe Allevi. *See* ALLEVI, GIUSEPPE.

Piacere, a. *See* A PIACERE.

Piacevole (It.: 'agreeable', 'pleasant'). A word that appears as a qualification to tempo designations. The finale of Beethoven's Violin Sonata in A op.12 no.2 and the opening of Elgar's Serenade op.20 are marked *allegro piacevole*.

Piaf [Gassion], Edith (Giovanna) (*b* Paris, 19 Dec 1915; *d* Plascassier, nr Grasse, 10 Oct 1963). French singer and actress. Her mother Anita Maillard was a singer and her father Louis-Alphonse Gassion was a fairground acrobat. Her early childhood was fraught with illness, she became temporarily blind through infection, and was passed from one lodging to another, eventually staying with her grandmother who worked in a bordello. At the age of nine she joined her father on tour and began to sing while he performed his routine. It was as a street singer that she was discovered in Paris by the proprietor of the nightclub Le Gerny's, Louis Leplée, who launched her as 'La môme Piaf' ('the little sparrow') in October 1935. She was an immediate success and was engaged to record and to sing on radio. At first her repertory drew on popular songs of the day, but very soon songwriters began to write material specially for her and she found in Marguerite Monnot, Michel Emer and Raymond Asso authors and composers who understood her style perfectly.

A film career began almost as soon as she had achieved her early fame, and during World War II she remained in France and continued to record and make films, as well as appearing in the play *Le bel indifférent* which Cocteau wrote for her. In 1945 she recorded the first of her worldwide successes, *Les trois cloches*, with the group Les Compagnons de la Chanson and the following year recorded *La vie en rose*, her most famous song. With these songs she had a huge success in New York in 1947 and for the next few years became a transatlantic star. Illness, drug addiction and alcoholism dogged her later years, and her reputation was increased with several well-publicized affairs and marriages. Her love affair with the champion boxer Marcel Cerdan, who was killed in an air crash, caught the public's imagination and seemed to be the subject of some of her love songs such as *L'orgue des amoureux* (1949), *Hymne à l'amour* (1950) and *La belle histoire d'amour* (1960).

Piaf was the inheritor of a great tradition of Parisian chanson, the logical successor to such *chanteuses réalistes* of the 1920s as Yvonne George, Damia and Frehel. At the same time she was one of the singers who began to create a new, more international style of Parisian song, more readily exportable. Her early songs such as Monnot's *Mon légionnaire* (1937) and Emer's *L'accordeoniste* (1940) belong unmistakably to the old music-hall tradition. Although her voice was strong she soon developed a microphone technique and her later performances seem to belong to the world of international pop music rather than the Paris *café-concert*. Her later recordings, using larger orchestras, choirs and echo-chambers have none of the charm of her earlier performances and melodramatic effects detract from the simplicity of her singing. Her ability to invest the lyrics with pathos and, too seldom, humour, continued to be impressive. Among her later songs the most celebrated are *Milord* (1959) by Monnot and Georges Moustaki and *Non, je ne regrette rien* (1961) by Michel Vaucaire and Charles Dumont. Her last appearances were in Paris at the Bobino music hall in March 1963, her very final performance at the Opera house in Lille at the end of the same month. Despite, or perhaps because of, the sad personal life which she seemed to bring to her songs, Piaf's fame and popularity have remained in the decades since her death. All her recordings remain in print, and several plays and films about her have introduced her songs to later generations.

BIBLIOGRAPHY

E. Piaf: *Au bal de la chance* (Paris, 1958; Eng. trans. as *The Wheel of Fortune*, 1965)
E. Piaf: *Ma vie* (Paris, 1964; Eng. trans., 1990)
S. Berteaut: *Piaf* (Paris, 1969; Eng. trans., 1970)
J. Montserrat: *Edith Piaf et la chanson* (Paris, 1983)
P. Ribert: *Témoignages sur Edith et Chansons de Piaf* (Paris, 1984)
M. Crosland: *Piaf* (London, 1985)
B. Marchois: *Piaf: Emportée par la foule* (Paris, 1995)

PATRICK O'CONNOR

Piaggio, Celestino (*b* Concordia, Entre Ríos, 20 Dec 1886; *d* Buenos Aires, 28 Oct 1931). Argentine composer and conductor. He studied in Buenos Aires with Aguirre, Andrés Gaos, Carlos Marchal and Alberto Williams. In 1908 he won the European Prize which took him to the Schola Cantorum in Paris, where he studied composition with D'Indy. He was in Romania when World War I began, and was forced to stay. Back in Paris in 1919, he took conducting lessons with Nikisch. He was later offered the directorship of the Bucharest Conservatory, but he turned it down in favour of returning to Argentina in 1921 where some of his compositions were already known. He became the conductor of the Colon Theatre orchestra and he was also a member of the Symphonic Association of Buenos Aires, an organization set up to promote Argentine music. Piaggio's music is indebted to French models, in particular *mélodie*. Though his output is small, its quality has assured its continued performance in Argentina.

WORKS

Inst (composed before 1910 unless otherwise stated): Andantino, str orch; 2 arabescos, pf; Gavota y danza, str orch; Hoja de álbum, vn, orch; Humorística, pf; Los días, pf; Miniature, str orch; Minuetto, pf; Página gris, pf; Tonada, pf; Ov., orch, 1914; Sonata en do sostenido menor, pf, 1916; Homenaje a Julián Aguirre, pf, 1925

Songs: 3 romanzas, *c*1903; 3 mélodies; Stella matutina; Ici-bas; Chanson du canard

JUAN MARÍA VENIARD

Piamor, John. *See* PYAMOUR, JOHN.

Pian, Rulan Chao (*b* Cambridge, MA, 20 April 1922). American ethnomusicologist. She was educated at Radcliffe College, Cambridge, MA, in Western music history and theory with A.T. Merritt (BA 1944, MA 1946), and gained the PhD at Harvard University (1960) with a dissertation on the Song dynasty, influenced by Yang Lien-sheng and in particular by John M. Ward. Her father, Yuen Ren Chao, a composer and linguist, has also had a significant influence upon her musical interests. She began teaching Chinese at Harvard University in 1947 while a part-time graduate student. In 1961 she also joined the music department, teaching Chinese music. She was made professor of east Asian languages and civilizations and professor of music in 1974, until her retirement, when she was made professor emeritus (1992). She was appointed fellow of the Academica Sinaica in Taiwan in 1994.

Her publications on Song dynasty (960–1279) musical sources, Peking opera, Peking drum songs and other historical and contemporary genres provide not only a wealth of musical data and analytical insights, but also illustrate diverse methods and issues in music studies. Her teaching at Harvard University, public lectures in China (Mainland China, Hong Kong and Taiwan) and informal discussions in her home in Cambridge, MA, a place where scholars often gathered, inspired generations of students of Chinese music. Since the late 1970s, Pian travelled to China regularly, bringing the latest Western ideas and publications there, and returning to America with a wealth of fieldwork data and audio-visual recordings, materials that preserve and illustrate Chinese music to American audiences. As a teacher of Chinese language she was also able to examine narrative singing and other oral and performing literature of China as expressions that are both verbal and musical.

WRITINGS

Song Dynasty Musical Sources and their Interpretation (diss., Harvard, 1960; Cambridge, MA, 1967)
'The Function of Rhythm in the Peking Opera', *The Musics of Asia*, ed. J. Maceda (Manila, 1971), 114–31
'Text Setting with the *Shipyi* Animated Aria', *Words and Music: the Scholar's View*, ed. L Berman (Cambridge, MA, 1972), 237–70
'Aria Structural Patterns in the Peking Opera', *Chinese and Japanese Music Drama*, ed. J.I. Crump and W.P. Malm (Ann Arbor, MI, 1975), 65–86
'Modes, Transposed Scales, Melody Types and Tune Types', *IMSCR XII: Berkeley 1977*, 536–44
'A Complete Translation and Transcription of the Medley Song *The Courtesan's Jewel Box*', *Chinoperl Papers*, viii (1978), 161–206
'A Study of the Use of Music as a Narrative Device in the Medley Song *The Courtesan's Jewel Box*', *Chinoperl Papers*, xi (1980), 9–31
'Musical Elements in the Peking Opera, *The King's Farewell*', *Chinoperl Papers*, xii (1983), 61–83
'The Twirling Duet: a Dance Narrative from Northeast China', *Music and Context: a Festschrift for John M. Ward*, ed. A.D. Shapiro (Cambridge, MA, 1985), 210–41
ed.: *Zhao Yuanren yinyue zuopin quanji* [The complete musical works of Yuen Ren Chao] (Shanghai, 1987)
'Higashi ajia no ongaku no tayosei to no kankei' [Diversity and interrelationships of the musics of East Asia], *Nippon on ongaku, Ajia no ongaku*, iii (1988), 145–58
'The Flower Songs of Lotus Mountain: a Study of Performance Content', *New Perspectives on Music: Essays in Honor of Eileen Southern*, ed. J. Wright and S. Floyd (Waren, MI, 1992), 341–54
'Return of the Native Ethnomusicologist', *YTM*, xxiv (1992), 1–7

'Text Setting and the Use of Tune Types in Chinese Dramatic and Narrative Music', *Text, Tone, and Tune: Parameters of Music in Multicultural Perspective*, ed. B.C. Wade (New Delhi, 1993), 201–33

'Music and the Confucian Sacrificial Ceremony', *Enchanting Powers: Music in the World's Religions*, ed. L.E. Sullivan (Cambridge, MA, 1997), 237–62

J.S.C. LAM

Piana, Giovanni Antonio. *See* PIANI, GIOVANNI ANTONIO.

Pianelaio de Firençe, Jachopo (*fl* 1386–90). Italian composer, from Florence. He is documented as an artisan (a slipper manufacturer) from about 1386 to 1390 (see Di Bacco), and probably belonged to the Compagnia dei Laudesi di S Zenobi in Florence. Only one simple two-voice ballata by him survives, in *GB-Lbl* 29987 (f.47; ed. in CMM, viii/5, 1964, p.41, and in PMFC, x, 1977, p.91): *Come tradir pensasti*, the first lines of text of which are cited in documents from Bologna (1382) and Udine (1331) (see Fiori). The music of this ballata was also employed for a lauda, *Come se' da laudar*.

BIBLIOGRAPHY

G. Corsi, ed.: *Poesie musicali del Trecento* (Bologna, 1970), 234–5
K. von Fischer: 'Quelques remarques sur les relations entre les laudesi et les compositeurs florentins du Trecento', *L'Ars Nova italiana del Trecento: Convegno II: Certaldo and Florence 1969* [*L'Ars Nova italiana del Trecento*, iii (Certaldo, 1970)], 247–52
G. Di Bacco: 'Alcune nuove osservazioni sul codice di Londra' (British Library, MS Additional 29987), *Studi musicali*, xx (1991), 181–234
A. Fiori: 'Ruolo del notariato nella diffusione del repertorio poetico-musicale nel medioevo', *Studi musicali*, xxi (1992), 211–35, esp. 234–5
G. D'Agostino: 'La tradizione letteraria dei testi poetico-musicali del Trecento', *'Col dolce suon che da te piove': studi su Francesco Landini e la musica del suo tempo in memoria di Nino Pirrotta*, ed. M.T.R. Barezzani and A. Delfino (Florence, 1999), 389–428

GIANLUCA D'AGOSTINO

Piani [Piana, Piano], **Giovanni Antonio** [Desplanes, Jean-Antoine] (*b* Naples, 1678; *d* ?Vienna, after 1759). Italian violinist and composer. One of the five sons of the Bolognese–Neapolitan trumpet player Pietro Giacomo Piana who became professional musicians, he was trained at the Conservatorio della Pietà dei Turchini under Vinciprova and Cailò. He arrived in Paris in 1704, and by 1712 he was leading violinist to Louis Alexandre de Bourbon, Count of Toulouse and Admiral of the French Fleet.

In 1721 he became a musician at the imperial court in Vienna, where he was the highest-paid instrumentalist. An article in the *Mercure de France* (June 1738) recounted that Piani was 'an excellent violinist, highly esteemed in Paris at the beginning of this century, to whom a really fatal catastrophe happened in Venice where he was accused of having forged several signatures and condemned to have his hand cut off'. This anecdote was repeated by Fétis and others, who failed to notice that the story was retracted by the editor as false in the August issue of the same periodical. Piani in fact remained at the imperial court at least until 1757, rising to the position of director of instrumental music; he served with Carlo Tomaso Piani, perhaps a relative. A violinist Piani or Piana, who worked at the court of Count Carl at Cassel from 1710 to 1725, was apparently no relation.

In 1712 in Paris he published his op.1, a collection of 12 sonatas, six for violin and continuo and six for flute or violin and continuo (ed. by Jackson). This work is of considerable historical importance: by means of an extended preface and unusually thorough markings in the music itself, Piani offered detailed information about dynamics, fingering, bowing, ornamentation and indications of tempo and character. The *privilège général* awarded Piani on 29 May 1712 mentions the publication of vocal works, but none are extant; an 'op.2', of six sonatas for flute and continuo, often cited in reference works, stems from an erroneous citation by Walther of six of the sonatas of op.1.

BIBLIOGRAPHY

FétisB; KöchelKHM; La LaurencieEF; La MusicaD; WaltherML
B.G. Jackson: Preface to *G.A. Piani: Sonatas for Violin Solo and Violoncello with Cembalo … Opera Prima*, RRBME, xx (1975)
E. Selfridge-Field: 'The Viennese Court Orchestra in the Time of Caldara', *Antonio Caldara: Essays on his Life and Times*, ed. B.W. Pritchard (Aldershot, 1987), 115–51

NEAL ZASLAW

Pianino (It.: 'small piano'). (1) A common term in a number of European languages for a small upright piano. It is said to have been introduced by PLEYEL (ii) of Paris in 1815 to distinguish that firm's small upright instruments (designed by JEAN HENRI PAPE, based on a model of 1811 by Robert WORNUM (ii)) from the larger type of upright, or *piano droit*. By 1840 German and Austrian firms had begun to produce similar small uprights under the name pianino. The term 'cottage piano', introduced by Wornum, has also gained currency for small uprights (*see* PIANOFORTE, fig.25). Collard & Collard's smallest upright models were known as 'microchordons'.

(2) The name applied by CHAPPELL to a type of small GLASSCHORD produced during the first quarter of the 19th century with a keyboard of piano dimensions and a simple downstriking hammer action. The compass was 37 notes, c to c'''. An example of 1815 is in the Victoria and Albert Museum, London.

BIBLIOGRAPHY

T. Norlind, ed.: *Systematik der Saiteninstrumente*, ii: *Geschichte des Klaviers* (Stockholm, 1939), 219–34
D.S. Grover: *The Piano: its Story from Zither to Grand* (London, 1976), 137–40
H. Schott: *Victoria and Albert Museum: Catalogue of Musical Instruments*, i: *Keyboard Instruments* (London, 1985, 2/1998), 108
R. Palmieri, ed.: *Encyclopedia of Keyboard Instruments*, i: *The Piano* (New York, 1994), 259–60

HOWARD SCHOTT

Pianissimo. *See* PIANO (i).

Piano (i) (It.: 'flat', 'low'). The standard dynamic mark for soft playing, abbreviated *Pia.*, *Pian.* and *P* in the 18th century, today customarily expressed by *p*. In the early 17th century the word 'echo' often served instead: both Domenico Mazzocchi (1638) and W.C. Printz (1668) equated the two. In the anonymous *A Short Explication* (London, 1724) *ecco* and *echus* were described as being signified by *dim* and *piano*. The superlative form *pianissimo*, abbreviated in the 18th century *pian^mo*, *pmo*, *pssmo*, is today normally abbreviated *pp*, but Brossard (*Dictionaire*, 1703) gave *pp* as meaning only *più piano* whereas *pianissimo* was represented by *ppp*, and several other 18th-century theorists agreed with him: Vivaldi often progressed from *p* to *pp* and then to *pian^mo*, so it is likely that he followed the same convention. The instruction *tocca pian piano* is found in the Capirola Lutebook of 1517 (*US-Cn*), and *tocchi pian piano* appears in Monteverdi's *Orfeo* (1607). Verdi used *ppppp* in his Requiem

and Tchaikovsky *pppppp* in his Sixth Symphony, but in a context where the results are inevitably more like *mp*.
See also TEMPO AND EXPRESSION MARKS.

DAVID FALLOWS

Piano (ii). Abbreviation of PIANOFORTE.

Piano, Giovanni Antonio. *See* PIANI, GIOVANNI ANTONIO.

Piano a coda (It.). *See* GRAND PIANOFORTE.

Piano à prolongement (Fr.). *See* SOSTENENTE PIANO, §5.

Piano à queue (Fr.). *See* GRAND PIANOFORTE.

Piano armonico (It.). *See* SOUNDBOARD (i).

Piano à sons soutenus (Fr.: 'sustained-sound piano'). *See* SOSTENENTE PIANO, §5.

Piano carré (Fr.). *See* SQUARE PIANOFORTE.

Piano droit (Fr.). *See* UPRIGHT PIANOFORTE.

Piano duet. Piano duets are of two kinds: those for two players at one instrument, and those in which each of the two pianists has an instrument to him- or herself. Although the one-piano duet has the larger repertory, it has come to be regarded as a modest, essentially domestic branch of music compared with the more glamorous two-piano duet. The reason probably lies in the fact that the comparatively cramped position of two players at one keyboard inhibits an element of virtuoso display possible to pianists with the complete range of the keyboard at their disposal. Schubert was the one great composer to write extensively for the medium, although many composers, from Mozart to Ligeti, have added important works and a wide range of entertaining pieces.

Both types of duet began a more or less continuous history in the mid-18th century, but each had some isolated precursors. The earliest duets at one keyboard instrument are English and date from the early 17th century. A three-hand piece, *A Battle, and No Battle* (MB, xix, no.108), has been ascribed to John Bull; there are pieces by Nicholas Carleton and Thomas Tomkins in a manuscript that once belonged to Tomkins (*GB-Lbl* Add.29996). The two composers were close friends and neighbours in Worcestershire and the pieces may well have been composed for them to play together. Tomkins's duet (MB, v, no.32) is a fancy, that by Carleton an extended and finely constructed In Nomine. The superscription to this piece, 'A Verse for two to play on one Virginal or Organ', suggests a domestic as well as a quasi-liturgical use.

The domestic character of the one-piano duet is also brought out in the famous Mozart family portrait of about 1780 by Johann Nepomuk de la Croce. It was obviously posed for in the Mozart home, for a portrait of their mother looks down from the wall on Wolfgang and Nannerl, who are playing a duet (and exhibiting a hand-crossing technique), and Leopold, who holds a violin. Mozart and his sister played duets in London in 1764–5 and the sonata K19*d* dates from that time. Leopold is alleged (by Nissen, *Biographie W.A. Mozarts*, 1828) to have claimed in a letter of 9 July 1765 that 'in London, little Wolfgang wrote his first piece for four hands. No-one has ever written a four-hand sonata before'. Einstein, however (*Mozart: his Character, his Work*, 1945), regarded the quotation as at least suspect.

The first duets to be printed were Charles Burney's four sonatas of 1777; he also wrote a *Sonate à trois mains* (1780). He had a six-octave piano made by Merlin expressly for duets, 'ladies at that time wearing hoops which kept them at too great a distance from each other' (Burney's article 'Ravalement' in *Rees's Cyclopaedia*). Burney also wrote of awkwardness and embarrassment likely to be caused initially by 'the near approach of the hands of the different persons'. Between 1778 and 1780 Johann Christian Bach published some duets among his op.15 and op.18 sets of sonatas which, with other and probably earlier sonatas that remained in manuscript, became prototypes for those of Clementi, three each in op.3 (1779) and op.14 (1786), and Mozart, K381/123*a* (1772), 358/186*c* (1774), 357/497*a* (unfinished), 497 (1786) and 521 (1787). A notable feature of the duet sonatas of Clementi and Mozart is their frequent recourse to quasi-orchestral textures (ex.1); this is not uncommon in solo music, but composers naturally took advantage of the fuller sonority available from four hands. Mozart's early K358 and 381 have affinities with his divertimentos, but his later works have all the richness of texture of his mature instrumental style. The expansive K497 has two symphonic movements and one concerto-like one and

Ex.1 Clementi: op.3 no.1

begins with a portentous slow introduction, and K521 is clearly in a concertante style.

The ability of four hands to cope with rich textures probably accounted for a spate of arrangements of symphonies and other orchestral works for piano duet. About 1798–1800 the London publisher Birchall brought out all Haydn's London symphonies in this form, and duet arrangements of these and of symphonies by Mozart, Beethoven and later composers remained the chief means whereby amateur musicians became familiar with the standard orchestral repertory until the arrival of the gramophone record in the 20th century. Anything and everything was so arranged. Liszt arranged his orchestral rhapsodies, all his symphonic poems and even *Via crucis*; and such intractable or seemingly intractable works as Bach's *St Matthew Passion*, Haydn's *The Creation*, Verdi's *Requiem*, all Strauss's tone poems and symphonies, as well as complete operas (e.g. Wagner's entire *Ring* cycle and *Tristan*, Gounod's *Faust*), appeared in duet form. It was at one time possible to buy almost the complete works of Saint-Saëns as duets.

Mozart composed a variation set and a fugue, and Clementi some rondos, for piano duet. Beethoven composed a lightweight sonata (op.6) and a few other works, but it was left to Schubert to exploit the medium to the full. His works, which range from the tiniest of waltzes to the vast Grand Duo (op.140, D812), and which occur throughout his output from his earliest surviving composition, the G major Fantasy (D1) written in 1810 when he was 13, to several duets composed in the last year of his life, constitute a body of duet music unparalleled by any other composer. Most important are the B♭ sonata (op.30, D617), the Grand Duo, which was once thought to be a reduction of a lost 'Gastein' symphony, the *Divertissement à la hongroise* (op.54, D818), the F minor Fantasy (op.103, D940) and the *Lebensstürme* duo (op.144, D947). Schubert also composed rondos, variations, sets of marches and groups of dances, including ländler and polonaises.

19th-century composers found sets of national or pseudo-national dances eminently suited to the duet medium. Schumann composed polonaises in imitation of Schubert, some of which he incorporated with his *Papillons* op.2. Brahms's Waltzes and Hungarian Dances are justly famous, as are the splendid Slavonic Dances of Dvořák and the Norwegian Dances of Grieg. Reger composed German dances and Moszkowski, with less native instinct, Spanish and Polish dances. Folk music lay at the root of Tchaikovsky's and Balakirev's arrangements of Russian folksongs, Busoni's more expansive *Finnländische Volksweisen* (op.27) and Arnold van Wyk's Improvisations on Dutch Folk Songs (1942).

Meanwhile, substantial works appeared from time to time. In the Classical era, sonatas were composed by Pleyel, Dussek, Türk, Hummel, Diabelli, Kuhlau and others, and works in sonata form were later composed by Mendelssohn (*Allegro brillante* op.92), Grieg (whose Symphonic Pieces op.14 were rescued from an abortive symphony), Moscheles, Rubinstein, Hindemith, Toch, Arnell, Poulenc, Berkeley, Persichetti and others. Other substantial works for piano duet include Chopin's early *Variations sur un air national de Moore* (cleverly reconstructed from a damaged manuscript by Jan Ekier), Brahms's Variations on a Theme by Schumann op.23, Nicodé's *Eine Ballscene* op.26, which owes a little to Weber and more to Schumann's *Papillons*, Koechlin's Suite op.19, Carse's Variations in A minor, Ladmirault's *Rhapsodie gaélique*, Starer's *Fantasia concertante* and Richard Rodney Bennett's *Capriccio*. Stravinsky's *The Rite of Spring* exists independently as a duet (but for ease of execution is sometimes played on two pianos as performed by Stravinsky and Debussy together).

Weber set a new fashion with his *Six petites pièces faciles* op.3 in 1801, which he followed with two further sets of short and highly engaging pieces in 1809 (op.10) and 1819 (op.60). His lead was followed by innumerable composers in the 19th and 20th centuries and sets of short pieces proliferated. Among the most significant are Schumann's *Bilder aus Osten* op.66, Alkan's *Trois marches*, Rubinstein's *Bal costumé* (possibly the longest single work for piano duet), Dvořák's *Legends* op.59, Satie's *Trois morceaux en forme de poire*, Debussy's two suites (one from each end of his career), the early *Petite suite* (1889) and the more representative *Six épigraphes antiques* (1914), Milhaud's *Suite provençale*, Rawsthorne's *The Creel* (tiny but characteristic pieces inspired by Izaak Walton), and duets by Wallingford Riegger. Several French suites are delightfully evocative of childhood, notably Bizet's *Jeux d'enfants* op.38, Fauré's *Dolly* op.56, Ravel's *Ma mère l'oye* and Inghelbrecht's *La nursery*.

Duets have long been recognized as educationally valuable. Haydn's little variation set *Il maestro e lo scolare* is, as its title implies, one of many pieces for teacher and pupil. Others have been composed for young people with parts of equal difficulty. Czerny composed a *Practical Method for Playing in Correct Time* op.824, which was also the aim behind the *Pianoforte Method* of Annie Curwen, much used in England. Apart from specialists in the field, composers who have successfully simplified their styles in the service of education include Bruckner, Godowsky, Arensky, Rachmaninoff, Stravinsky, Milhaud, Dello Joio, Seiber, Walton and Thea Musgrave.

If we except an arrangement of a Crecquillon chanson for two keyboards (MME, ii, 158), duets for two instruments (as opposed to two players at one instrument) also began in England, with a small piece by Farnaby in the Fitzwilliam Virginal Book, and there are pre-Classical compositions for the medium by Couperin and by Bernardo Pasquini (whose 14 sonatas for two figured basses require simultaneous improvisation from the duettists). The modern history of the repertory may be said to begin with the two-keyboard works of the three Bach brothers, Wilhelm Friedemann, Carl Philipp Emanuel and Johann Christian. Clementi composed two sonatas and Mozart one (K448/375a) as well as a fugue (K426), and there are some works by Dussek. In the time of Beethoven and Schubert few were written, and it was not until the Romantic era that there was an enthusiastic resumption of two-piano writing. Liszt arranged Beethoven's Ninth Symphony as well as his own Faust and Dante symphonies, symphonic poems and both concertos. Piano concertos are normally published in two-piano form to facilitate practice. They are outside the scope of this article, though they outnumber original large-scale works for two pianos, many of which exist in more than one form. Schumann's Andante and Variations op.46 originally had parts for two cellos and horn; Brahms's Variations on a Theme of Haydn op.56*b* has its orchestral counterpart, and his F minor sonata op.34*b* exists as a piano quintet. Reger's Variations and Fugue on a Theme of Mozart op.132*a* also appeared in orchestral form and as a one-piano duet, and Busoni's *Fantasia contrappuntistica* as a piano solo. These, together with two other big sets of variations by Reger, Saint-Saëns's Variations on a Theme of Beethoven op.35, Debussy's *En blanc et noir*, with its disturbing undertones of war, Stravinsky's Sonata, Bartók's Sonata for two pianos and percussion, Rachmaninoff's two suites, Hindemith's Sonata, Messiaen's *Visions de l'amen* and Henri Martelli's sonata are among the biggest works for the medium. Debussy's *Lindaraja* of 1901 is significant as being the first of his great Spanish pieces. Among popular repertory pieces are Chopin's posthumous Rondo op.72, Arensky's suites, Milhaud's *Scaramouche* and short pieces by Bax, Infante and others. Curiosities are Grieg's second piano parts to Mozart solo sonatas and Ives's Three Quarter-Tone Pieces for pianos tuned a quarter-tone apart. Notable modern works include sonatas by Genzmer and Cooke, variations by Mervyn Roberts and Geoffrey Bush, Louis Aubert's Suite op.6, Vaughan Williams's Introduction and Fugue and works by Martin, Hessenberg, Tailleferre, Britten, Berkeley and Jürg Wyttenbach. The avant garde is represented by works by Cage and Cardew. In this highly professional field there is little educational music (unless Bartók's arrangements of pieces from *Mikrokosmos* be considered such), though Gurlitt and others composed easy pieces. On a lighter level there was a vogue for brilliant arrangements of Johann Strauss waltzes and other light classics in the mid-20th century, dispensed with skill and urbanity by the Austrian pianists Rawicz and Landauer and other specialist teams.

Some modifications and multiplications of the duet medium have occurred, many of humorous intent. Close liaison is desirable for the gentleman and two ladies required for a proper performance of W.F.E. Bach's *Das Dreyblatt* for three players at one keyboard; it is inevitable in Chaminade's *Les noces d'argent* op.13, which squeezes four players together at one piano. Czerny composed works for three players at one piano and for four at four, Smetana for four at two, and there was an arrangement of Wagner's *Meistersinger* overture for six players at three pianos. Willem Coenen composed a *Caprice concertante* for 16 pianists at eight pianos. The English pianist Cyril Smith, after an illness which left him partly incapacitated, played with Phyllis Sellick arrangements for three hands at two pianos; several original works have been composed for this combination. 31 pianists at 16 pianos were assembled on one platform at the first of Gottschalk's 'monster concerts' in Rio de Janeiro on 5 October 1869.

BIBLIOGRAPHY

H. Wetzel: 'Schubert's Werke für Klavier zu vier Hände', *Die Musik*, vi (1906–7), 36–44
K. Ganzer and L. Kusche: *Vierhändig* (Munich, 1937, 2/1954)
A. Rowley: *Four Hands – One Piano* (London, 1940)
W. Georgii: *Klaviermusik* (Zürich, 1941, 5/1976)
W. Altmann: *Verzeichnis von Werken für Klavier vier- und sechshändig sowie für zwei und mehr Klaviere* (Leipzig, 1943)
H.M. Miller: 'The Earliest Keyboard Duets', *MQ*, xxix (1943), 438–57
M. Carner: 'Piano Duets', *Making Music*, no.13 (1950), 4–6
H. Moldenhauer: *Duo-Pianism* (Chicago, 1950)
F. Dawes: 'Nicholas Carlton and the Earliest Keyboard Duet', *MT*, xcii (1951), 542–6
D.I. Sonnedecker: *Cultivation and Concepts of Duets for Four Hands, One Keyboard, in the Eighteenth Century* (diss., Indiana U., 1953)
H. Schmitt: *Studien zur Genese und Stilistik des Satzes für zwei Klaviere zu vier Händen* (Saarbrücken, 1965)
D. Townsend: 'The Piano Duet', *Piano Quarterly*, no.61 (1967), 14–18
D.A. Weekley: *The One-Piano, Four-Hand Compositions of Franz Schubert* (diss., Indiana U.,1968)
E. Lubin: *The Piano Duet* (New York, 1970)
C. McGraw: *Piano Duet Repertoire* (Bloomington, IN, 1981)
M. Hinson: *Music for More than One Piano* (Bloomington, IN, 1983)
M. Hinson: *The Pianist's Guide to Transcriptions, Arrangements, and Paraphrases* (Bloomington, IN,1990)
S.J. Sloane: *Music for Two or More Players at Clavichord, Harpsichord, Organ* (New York, 1991)
G.L. Maxwell: *Music for Three or More Pianists* (Metuchen, NJ, 1993)
H. Ferguson: *Keyboard Duets from the 16th to the 20th Century* (Oxford, 1995)

FRANK DAWES

Piano éolien (Fr.: 'aeolian piano'). A keyboard instrument in which the strings were activated by jets of compressed air. *See* SOSTENENTE PIANO, §2.

Pianoforte [piano]. A keyboard instrument distinguished by the fact that its strings are struck by rebounding hammers rather than plucked (as in the harpsichord) or struck by tangents that remain in contact with the strings (as in the clavichord).

The present article treats the history and technique of the instrument; for discussion of the repertory *see* KEYBOARD MUSIC, §III. Additional information on the contributions of particular makers is given in their individual articles.

In the Hornbostel-Sachs classification of instruments the piano is reckoned as a box zither.

I. History of the instrument. II. Piano playing.

I. History of the instrument

1. Introduction. 2. Origins to 1750. 3. Germany and Austria, 1750–1800. 4. England and France to 1800. 5. The Viennese piano from 1800. 6. England and France, 1800–60. 7. Spain 1745–1850. 8. North America to 1860. 9. 1860–1915. 10. From 1915.

1. INTRODUCTION. The piano has occupied a central place in professional and domestic music-making since the third quarter of the 18th century. In addition to the great capacities inherent in the keyboard itself – the ability to sound simultaneously at least as many notes as one has fingers and therefore to be able to produce an approximation of any work in the entire literature of Western music – the piano's capability of playing notes at widely varying degrees of loudness in response to changes in the force with which the keys are struck, permitting crescendos and decrescendos and a natural dynamic shaping of a musical phrase, gave the instrument an enormous advantage over its predecessors, the clavichord and the harpsichord. (Although the clavichord was also capable of dynamic expression in response to changes in touch, its tone was too small to permit it to be used in ensemble music; the harpsichord, on the other hand, had a louder sound but was incapable of producing significant changes in loudness in response to changes in touch.) The capabilities later acquired of sustaining notes at will after the fingers had left the keys (by means of pedals) and of playing far more loudly than was possible on the harpsichord made this advantage even greater.

The instrument's modern name is a shortened form of that given in the first published description of it (1711) by Scipione Maffei where it is called 'gravecembalo col piano, e forte' ('harpsichord with soft and loud'). 18th-century English sources used the terms 'pianaforte' and 'fortepiano' interchangeably with 'pianoforte'; some scholars reserve 'fortepiano' for the 18th- and early 19th-century instrument, but the cognate is used in Slavonic countries to refer to the modern piano as well. The German word 'Hammerklavier' might refer to the piano in general, or alternatively to the square piano as distinct from the grand piano ('Flügel').

There is no continuity between the remote 15th-century precursors of the piano described by Henri Arnaut de Zwolle around 1440 (see DULCE MELOS) and the origins of the instrument as discussed in §2 below, though references made in letters dated 1598 from Hippolito Cricca of Ferrara to Duke Cesare d'Este in Modena suggest that an instrument with dynamic flexibility (perhaps equipped with a striking mechanism) was used in the d'Este court in Ferrara during the late 16th century. These letters make repeated reference to a special *instromento pian et forte, istromento piane e' forte, instromento pian e' forte* and *instromento piano et forte*. An octave spinet (now in the Metropolitan Museum of Art, New York) made in 1585 by Francesco Bonafinis may have been converted to a tangent piano in the 17th century, providing further evidence that there were isolated attempts to construct string keyboard instruments with striking mechanisms prior to Bartolomeo Cristofori's invention made around 1700 (see §2 below).

The modern piano consists of six major elements: the strings, the metal frames, the soundboard and bridges, the action, the wooden case and the pedals. There are three strings for each note in the treble, two for each note in the tenor, and one for each note in the bass. The massive metal frame supports the enormous tension that the strings impose (approximately 18 tons or 16,400 kg). The bridges communicate the vibrations of the strings to the soundboard which enables these vibrations to be efficiently converted into sound waves, thereby making the sound of the instrument audible. The action consists of the keys, the hammers, and the mechanism that impels the hammers towards the strings when the keys are depressed. The wooden case encloses all of the foregoing. The right pedal (the 'loud' or 'sustaining' pedal) acts to undamp all the strings enabling them to vibrate freely regardless of what keys are depressed. The left pedal (the 'soft pedal' or 'una corda') acts to reduce the volume of tone, either by moving the hammers sideways so that they strike only two of the three strings provided for each note in the treble and one of the two strings provided for each note in the tenor, or by bringing the hammers closer to the strings, thus shortening their stroke, or – on some upright pianos – by interposing a strip of cloth between the hammers and the strings to produce a muffled tone. The middle pedal, when present, acts to keep the dampers raised on only those notes being played at the moment the pedal is depressed.

Logically, the ideal form of the piano is the 'grand', the wing-shape of which is determined by the fact that the strings gradually lengthen from the treble at the right to the bass at the left. Theoretically, the length of the strings might be doubled for each octave of the instrument's range, but this would be impractical for an instrument having a range of over seven octaves, as the modern piano does, and even the earliest pianos with a range of only four octaves employed some shortening of the strings in the extreme bass. The rectangular 'square' piano, which like the grand has its strings in a horizontal plane, and which was popular in the 18th and 19th centuries, has been entirely superseded by various types of 'vertical' or 'upright' piano, which have their strings in a vertical plane; the fact that uprights take up less room outweighs the disadvantage imposed by the more complex action they must use.

2. ORIGINS TO 1750.   The musical advantages initially possessed by the piano were not generally recognized at the time of its invention even though the instrument made its first appearance in a highly developed form, the work of a single individual, BARTOLOMEO CRISTOFORI, keeper of instruments at the Medici court in Florence. Despite warmly argued claims on the part of such other men as Christoph Gottlieb Schröter and Jean Marius, there now seems to be no doubt that Cristofori had actually constructed a working piano before any other maker was even experimenting in this field. The detailed description of an 'arpicimbalo di nuova inventione' in an inventory of the Medici instruments for 1700 establishes that he had by that year already completed at least one instrument of this kind. A precise date is found in an inscription made by Federigo Meccoli (a court musician in Florence) in a copy of Gioseffo Zarlino's *Le istitutioni harmoniche*, which states that the 'arpi cimbalo del piano e' forte' was invented by Cristofori in 1700. Cristofori's accomplishment as seen in the three surviving pianos made by him, all of which date from the 1720s, would be difficult to exaggerate. His grasp of the essential problems involved in creating a keyboard instrument that sounded by means of strings struck by hammers was so complete that his action included features meeting every challenge that would be posed to designers of pianos for well over a century. Unfortunately, the very completeness of his design resulted in a complicated mechanism, which builders were apparently unwilling to duplicate if they could possibly devise anything that would work and at the same time be simpler to make. As a result, much of the history of the 18th-century piano is the history of the gradual reinvention or readoption of things that were an integral part of Cristofori's original conception; and it was only with the introduction in the 19th century of increasingly massive hammers that the principles discovered by Cristofori could no longer provide the basis for a completely satisfactory piano action, requiring the still more complicated mechanism known today.

The essential difficulty in creating a workable instrument in which the strings are to be struck by hammers is to provide a means whereby the hammers will strike the strings at high speed and immediately rebound, so that the hammers will not damp out the vibrations they initiate. In order to provide for immediate rebounding, the strings must not be lifted by the impact of the hammer and must therefore be thicker and at higher tension than those of a harpsichord, and the hammers must be tossed towards the strings and be allowed to fly freely for at least some small part of their travel. The smaller this distance of free flight is, the more control the pianist has over the speed with which the hammer will strike the string and accordingly over the loudness of the sound that it will produce. Unfortunately, the smaller this distance is, the more likely the hammer is to jam against the strings or bounce back and forth between the strings and whatever device impelled it upwards when the key was struck;

hence when the distance of free flight is made small to permit control of loudness, the hammer is likely to jam or bounce and damp out the tone. Cristofori solved this problem with a mechanism that enabled the hammer to be brought quite close to the string but caused it to fall quite far away from it even if the key was still held down. Devices of this kind are called escapements and they lie at the heart of all advanced piano actions. In addition, Cristofori provided a lever system that caused the hammers to move at a high speed, and a 'check' (or 'back check') which would catch the hammer after it fell so as to eliminate all chance of its bouncing back up to restrike the strings. Finally, his action provided for silencing the strings when the keys were not held down, using slips of wood resembling harpsichord jacks which carried dampers and rested on the ends of the keys.

These features are all visible in fig.1, which shows the action of the piano of 1726 (fig.2) in the Musikinstrumenten-Museum of Leipzig University. When the key is depressed, the pivoted jack mortised through it pushes upwards on a triangular block attached to the underside of the intermediate lever, which in turn bears on the hammer shank near its point of attachment, providing for a great velocity advantage. (Although the jack rises only about as fast as the front of the key is depressed, the free end of the intermediate lever rises approximately twice as fast and the hammer rises four times more rapidly still.) The escapement is provided by the pivoted jack, which tilts forward just before the hammer reaches the string so that, when the hammer rebounds, the block on the underside of the intermediate lever contacts the padded step at the back of the jack rather than the tip of the jack. As a result, even if the key is held down, the hammer falls to a point at least 1 cm below the strings. Adjustment of the point at which the jack tilts forward is achieved by bending the wire that supports the pad against which the jack is held by the spring. The further forward this pad is, the earlier the jack slips away from the block and the sooner escapement takes place.

The construction of Cristofori's pianos is similar to that of an 18th-century Italian harpsichord of the thick-cased type, except that it employs a novel inner bentside that supports the soundboard. The inner bentside and

soundboard are structurally isolated from the stress-bearing sections of the case, rendering the soundboard more resonant. Cristofori obviously recognized the necessity of using thicker strings at higher tension. Thus, the gap between the pinblock or wrest plank and the belly rail (the stout transverse brace that supports the front edge of the soundboard) through which the hammers rise to strike the strings is bridged by a series of wooden braces ('gap spacers') not found in Italian harpsichords. These braces contribute to preventing the wrest plank from twisting or bending into the gap at its centre and are therefore of vital importance in keeping the entire structure from twisting out of shape or collapsing. (The means of ensuring the straightness and integrity of the wrest plank and case structure continued to be one of the principal concerns of piano makers throughout the 18th century.)

Two of Cristofori's three surviving pianos have an inverted wrest plank in which the tuning-pins are driven completely through, with the strings attached to their lower ends after passing across a nut attached to the underside of the wrest plank. According to Maffei, this plan was adopted to provide more space for the action, but it provides at least two other advantages: since the strings bear upwards against the nut, the blow of the hammer, instead of tending to dislodge them, upsetting the tuning and adversely affecting the tone, seats them even more firmly; second, the inverted wrest plank permits placement of the strings close to the top of the action, so that the hammers need not be tall to reach the strings. They can therefore be quite light, an important factor, since Cristofori's lever system, providing for an acceleration of the hammer to eight times the velocity with which the key is depressed, automatically causes the player to feel (at the key) the weight of the hammer multiplied eightfold.

The sound of the surviving Cristofori pianos is very reminiscent of that of the harpsichord owing to the thinness of the strings compared with later instruments and the hardness of the hammers; but it is less brilliant and rather less loud than that of a firmly quilled Italian harpsichord of the time. These points are mentioned in Maffei's account as reasons for the lack of universal

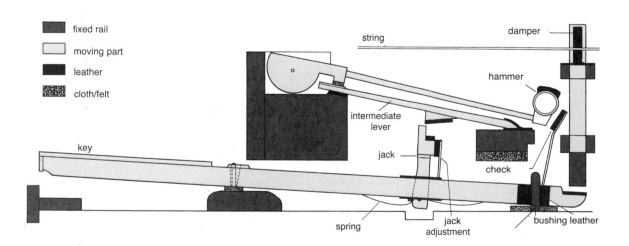

1. *Action of a piano by Bartolomeo Cristofori, 1726 (shown in fig.2)*

2. Piano by Bartolomeo Cristofori, Florence, 1726 (Musikinstrumenten-Museum, University of Leipzig)

praise for the instrument, as is the fact that contemporary keyboard players found the touch difficult to master (in Germany, where the clavichord was used as both a teaching and a practice instrument, no such objection seems to have been raised when the piano became known). On two of the surviving Cristofori pianos it is possible to slide the keyboard sideways so that the hammers strike only one of the two strings provided for each note. Possibly it was the desire to include such a device that caused Cristofori to space his strings widely rather than placing the unisons struck by each hammer close to one another with a wider space between. Apart from this *una corda* capability, Cristofori's pianos make no provision for alteration of the tone by stops or other such devices; however, one would not expect to find such a provision in view of the lack of any multiplicity of stops in Italian harpsichords.

There seems to have been little direct result in Italy of Cristofori's monumental achievement. Maffei, in his account, clearly recognized the important differences between Cristofori's pianos and the harpsichord (even if he had no better name for the new instrument than 'harpsichord with soft and loud'), and an interesting collection of 12 sonatas for the instrument that includes dynamic markings implying crescendos and decrescendos was published in 1732 (Lodovico Giustini's *Sonate da cimbalo di piano e forte*). But only a handful of other Italian instrument makers seem to have followed in

Cristofori's footsteps, notably Giovanni Ferrini and Domenico del Mela. It was left primarily to German, Spanish and Portuguese builders and musicians to exploit his work in the years after his death in 1732.

A German translation of Maffei's account was published in Johann Mattheson's *Critica musica*, ii (1725) where it was presumably seen by Gottfried Silbermann, who is reported to have begun experimenting on pianos of his own in the 1730s. He is said to have offered one for Bach's inspection, and at the composer's adverse reaction to its heavy touch and weak treble to have gone on to further experiments resulting in improved instruments, a number of which were bought by Frederick the Great. These are reported to have met with Bach's complete approval when he visited Potsdam in 1747. The two Silbermann pianos owned by Frederick that have survived have actions identical with those in the surviving Cristofori instruments; it seems more than likely that by the time Silbermann made them he had seen an example, whereas his earlier attempts had failed as a result of having been based on the diagram accompanying Maffei's description – which Maffei admitted had been drawn from memory without the instrument before him. Silbermann retained Cristofori's inverted wrest plank and the equidistant spacing of the strings (fig.3) and he used the hollow hammers made of rolled paper found in the 1726 instrument which, together with the check replacing silk strands, evidently replaced the small blocks shown in

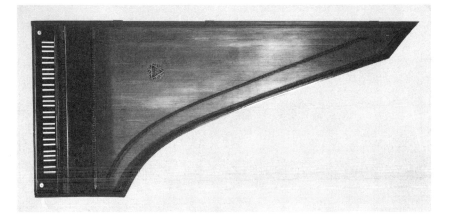

3. Piano by Johann Heinrich Silbermann, Strasbourg, 1775 (Staatliches Institut für Musikforschung [Preussischer Kulturbesitz], Berlin)

Maffei's diagram. As might be expected from a representative of the north European keyboard instrument building tradition, Silbermann included hand stops for raising the treble and bass dampers in addition to devices for sliding the keyboard sideways so that the hammers would strike only one of the two strings provided for each note. Thus, these two most characteristic means of modifying the piano's tone, integral to all modern pianos, were found together as early as the 1740s.

Although Gottfried Silbermann and his nephew Johann Heinrich Silbermann seem to have made direct copies of Cristofori's hammer action, virtually unchanged except for the addition of damper-lifting mechanisms, other German makers, some of whom may perhaps not even have been explicitly informed of Cristofori's work to the extent of knowing of the existence of 'hammer harpsichords', devised a host of less complicated actions, many adapted to the rectangular clavichord-shaped square pianos. In an early example, a hammer hinged to the back

of the case is thrust upwards by a block at the end of the key, reducing Cristofori's mechanism to an absolute minimum. This type of action became known as the *Stossmechanik* and is the principle upon which the later English builders and their followers built their pianos (see §4 below). The great period of piano building in the German-speaking world is not, however, represented by these developments or even by Silbermann's work, which with the death of his son seems to have led to no direct line of Cristofori-inspired instrument building. Rather, a different approach evolved – using a type of action known as the *Prellmechanik* – which dominated German piano building for the next 75 years.

3. GERMANY AND AUSTRIA, 1750–1800. Whereas Cristofori, the Silbermanns and the later piano makers of other schools sought to create a harpsichord capable of dynamic expression, the main thrust of German and Austrian piano building in the later part of the century

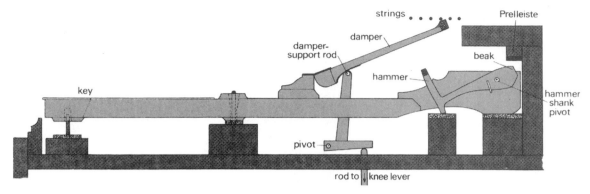

4. *Prellmechanik action without escapement mechanism from an anonymous south German square piano, c1770 (Royal College of Music, London); to allow space for the hammer, the rear of the key is narrower than the front; the dampers are beneath the strings and disengage when the hinged end rises with the key; the knee lever lowers the damper-support rod to disengage all the dampers simultaneously*

seems to have been towards creating an instrument that would be like a louder clavichord (Austria, Germany and Scandinavia being virtually the only countries in which the clavichord was still esteemed at this period). These German and Austrian pianos have a relatively clear singing tone and an extremely light touch (12–20 grams). The simplest of the so-called square models with the *Prellmechanik* show clearly the inspiration of their origin: all that separates them from the clavichord is the addition of a nut at the rear to determine the speaking length of the strings, and the replacement of the tangent by a hammer hinged to the back of the key. In the simple *Prellmechanik* most commonly (and apparently exclusively) used in square models, each of the hammer shanks is attached to its own key – either directly to the top or side (fig.4), or by a wooden or metal fork or block (the *Kapsel*) – with the hammer head towards the player. A point (the 'beak') on the opposite end of the hammer shank extends beyond the end of the key. This beak is stopped vertically either by the underside of the hitch-pin apron or by a fixed rail called the *Prelleiste*: as the back of the key rises, the hammer is thereby flipped upwards towards the string. As the distance from the tip of the beak to the hammer shank pivot is far shorter than the distance from the pivot to the hammer, the hammer ascends much more rapidly than does the back of the key. An adequate free-flight distance had to be left as there was no escapement mechanism to prevent the hammers from restriking the string or blocking and interrupting the tone. A significant number of these pianos had uncovered hammer heads, giving a harpsichord-like sound. Others had only a meagre covering of leather on the hammers.

The development of an individual escapement for the *Prellmechanik* is credited to Johann Andreas Stein (1728–92), a keyboard instrument maker in Augsburg. In some of Stein's instruments the labels are missing, altered or falsified, so there has been confusion in the dating of his earliest pianos. But some of the questionable instruments are also signed and dated with silver pencil on the underside of the soundboard (Latcham, D1998). The claviorgan, a combination of organ and piano made by Stein in 1781 (now in the Historiska Museum, Göteborg), is the oldest known dated piano with the *Prellmechanik* escapement. By 1777 a type of action with an escapement mechanism must have evolved sufficiently to satisfy Mozart when he visited Stein in Augsburg (Mozart

complained of hammers jamming on other instruments). The harpsichord-piano of the same year, located now in the Museo Civico di Castelvecchio, Verona, has stationary mounted hammers while the individual escapement hoppers are hinged to the keys (*Zuggetriebe*; see Pfeiffer, C1948). The hammer heads are still uncovered.

In the developed *Prellmechanik* there is an individual hinged escapement hopper for each key instead of a stationary rail serving all keys. Each hopper has a notch into which the beak of the hammer shank fits, and each hopper has its own return spring (fig.5). As the key is depressed, the beak is caught by the top of the notch in the escapement hopper, lifting the hammer. The combined arcs traversed by the key and the hammer shank cause the beak to withdraw from the escapement hopper and slip free just before the hammer meets the string, after which it is free to fall back to its rest position. When the key is released, the beak slides down the face of the escapement hopper back into the notch.

An important feature in such pianos is the extremely small and light hammers (see fig.19 below); their thin leather covering (instead of felt) is vital to these instruments' clavichord-like delicacy of articulation and nuance. Typically, the Stein action has either round hollow hammers similar to those of the Silbermanns but made of barberrywood (see Koster and others, C1994), or short solid hammers usually made of pearwood (the *Kapseln* are also of felt-covered pearwood). Surviving Stein instruments from 1781 to 1783 all have the round hollow hammers, as do the instruments of J.D. Schiedmayer, who worked for Stein from 1778 to 1781. In Stein's instruments each key has a post supporting the hammer in a rest position above the level of the keys; this rest post is provided with a soft cloth which helps absorb the shock of the returning hammers thus preventing them from

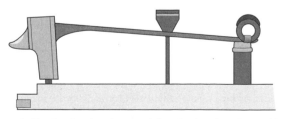

5. *Prellmechanik with escapement, believed to have been first used by Stein, from a Heilman piano of c1785 (private collection)*

6. Piano by Johann Andreas Stein, Augsburg, 1788 (Germanisches Nationalmuseum, Nuremberg); see also fig.7

rebounding, a useful function in the absence of a true back check. To place the action in its proper position (behind the wrest plank in a grand) a 'sled' or drawer about 5 cm high is slipped under the action. The keyboard itself is generally of spruce or lime with ebony key slips for the naturals and with sharps of dyed pearwood topped with bone or ivory.

The individual dampers are fitted into a rack above the strings, which the player can raise by means of two joined knee levers under the keyboard; the claviorganum of 1781 has hand stops for this purpose. Some of Stein's instruments have hand levers for other stops, but these are probably not original. On the outside the Stein case (figs.6 and 7) has a double curved bentside. Inside, the liners for the soundboard are made of solid wood and reach down to the baseboard. The frame is braced by two or three members perpendicular to the spine (the straight side of the instrument) and two or three diagonal supports. The case is closed at the bottom by a thick baseboard with the grain running parallel to the straight part of the bentside, and is usually veneered in plain walnut or cherry with a band of moulding around the lower edge. The soundboards of Stein's instruments are of quarter-sawn spruce, graduated in thickness and with a system of ribbing glued to the underside. Typical of Stein's ribbing systems is the position of the long diagonal rib, glued very close to the bridge. The compass of all Stein's pianos is

five octaves, F' to f'''. Some variations of detail and design in Stein's late instruments, e.g. the shape of the action parts and the use of gap spacers, wire-guided dampers, and slides to raise the action, were continued by his children until 1805.

It has not yet been discovered how knowledge of Cristofori's hammer action reached Vienna. The Viennese court account books of 1763 record a fee to Johann Baptist Schmidt 'for a concert on the fortipiano', the first documented usage of this term (this may have been a square piano): Quite a number of the oldest extant Viennese pianos have the *Stossmechanik* rather than Stein's *Prellmechanik* (Huber, D1991); Stein was probably not using his new mechanisms before 1780 (Latcham, D1993, D1998). A number of piano makers came to Austria from South Germany and Bohemia in the later 18th century, most notable among them Anton Walter (1752–1826). In about 1782 W.A. Mozart bought a piano from Walter (Rampe, D1995). Certain alterations to the action suggest that this piano and two other instruments of Walter's earliest creative period could originally have had a *Stossmechanik* action.

In the mid-1780s Walter developed the *Prellmechanik* further, departing significantly from Stein's model (Luithlein, F1954; Rück, D1955). The escapement hoppers are tilted forward with the effect that the hammers, which are longer and larger and rest close to the level of the key

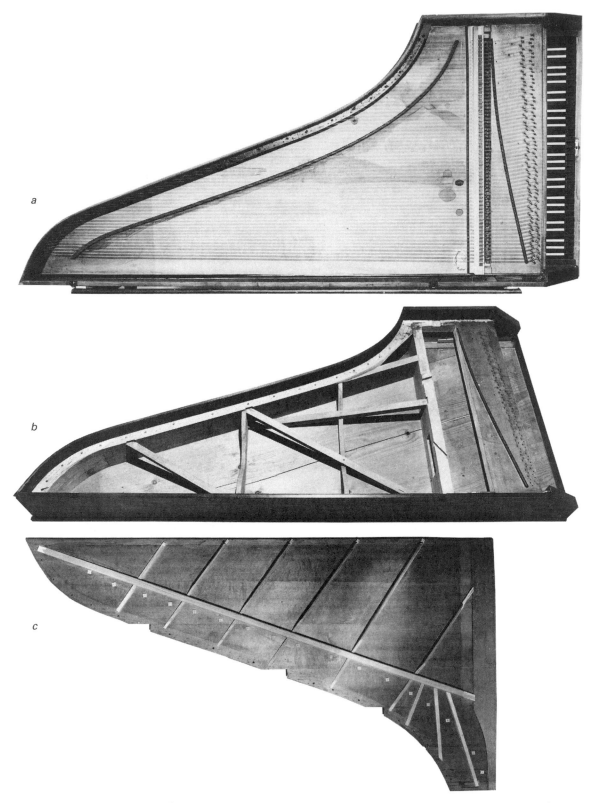

7. *Piano by Johann Andreas Stein, Augsburg, 1788 (Germanisches Nationalmuseum, Nuremberg): (a) plan view; (b) internal structure from above, with soundboard removed; (c) underside of soundboard*

(there are no rest posts as such), decelerate as they rise, and their beaks gradually slip out from the notches in the hoppers. A movable rail adjusts the point at which the beak finally leaves the notch. There is a sprung back-check rail to prevent the hammers from rebounding. After about 1785 brass *Kapseln* were used in Vienna as well as the wooden felt-covered *Kapseln* of the Stein action (the two types continued in parallel use for some 20 years). The double-pointed iron axle of the hammer fits into two shallow sockets in a springy, U-shaped fork of brass. This invention, attributed to the Viennese piano maker Johann Jakob Seidel [Seydel] (1759–1806), allowed more precise and relatively frictionless movement of the hammer shank and greater efficiency of manufacture (for illustration of a later version of this action, see fig.18 below). Both Stein's and Walter's actions are capable of great expressivity and dynamic variation, but Walter's, with its check rail, could produce greater volume, suiting the fashion for virtuoso performance. In expressive power, subtlety and the production of swiftly repeated notes, if not in volume, the *Prellmechanik* with back check (described in the 19th century as the 'Viennese action'; see §5 below) was undoubtedly superior to the various *Stossmechanik* actions then being built.

The cases of these pianos at first resembled those of south German and Austrian harpsichords. The body was usually plain, made of native woods (walnut, cherry, oak, yew), sometimes solid wood and sometimes veneered. The naturals usually had ebony key slips and the sharps were dyed black, with slips of bone or ivory. From the mid-1790s some keyboards had ivory or bone slips on the naturals as well; the cases of these instruments were usually of mahogany, and in more expensive instruments were decorated with brass appliqué work, partly gilded. In some instruments (e.g. by Ignatz Kober, Johann Jakob Könnicke, L. Gress) the soundboard has a rose. The compass was usually F' to f''' or g'''; the treble register was extended only towards the turn of the century. Most pianos were double-strung in the bass and middle registers, with the treble triple-strung from about a' to c'', while most square pianos were double-strung throughout. Strings were usually of soft low-carbon phosphorous steel ('iron strings') with brass in the lowest octave. Many makers used 'copper' (red brass) for the lowest notes. The low notes of square pianos usually had overspun strings made of silvered, tinned or zinc-covered copper wire on a brass or iron core. Contemporary sources and significant differences in scaling, as well as several preserved claviorgans, provide evidence that pianos were built (or played) in different pitches: low chamber pitch (a' = $c405$–25), high chamber pitch (a' = $c430$–40), and choir pitch (a' = $c450$–65).

Both grand and square pianos usually had one or more devices to change tone colour, known as mutations or stops. Sometimes, especially in earlier instruments, they were divided into bass and treble areas. The *forte* stop raises all the dampers. The *piano* or mute stop (or *sourdine*) inserts a strip of cloth between strings and hammers, producing a slightly muted colour. The lute or harp stop (rarer) presses a leather or fabric-covered strip against the strings close to the bridge, the effect being a lute-like sound that quickly dies away. The stops could be operated by hand, as on an organ, or by knee levers (square pianos usually used hand levers). At the end of the 1790s the so-called bassoon stop (probably originating

in Prague) became fashionable. It was a strip of wood supporting a roll of paper, silk or extremely thin parchment, pressed against the bass strings to give them a buzzing sound. The kind of sound expected by instrument makers, musicians and audiences was clearly not firmly established at first, and tone colours of different instruments might resemble those of the clavichord, harpsichord, dulcimer, harp or pantaleon. Many instruments of the period had hammer heads without leather covers, the result being a very bright, harpsichord-like sound. Until the end of the 18th century the central concern of piano makers was clearly to build an action which would be easy to operate, subtle and capable of swift repetition of notes, with a reliable damping system, and to balance a rounded bass with good tone colour against an expressive, not too weak treble. Volume and carrying power do not seem to have been a priority. Besides iconographical evidence, this is indicated by the fact that a great majority of preserved 18th-century south German and Austrian pianos originally had no sticks to hold their lids open. Grand pianos were usually played with the lid closed; or when performances were given on a larger scale the entire lid was removed (Huber, G1987). The distributed and importance of square pianos should not be underestimated; for average musicians and amateurs they were easier to acquire than the far more expensive grand pianos, which must have been largely reserved for the aristocracy until the last quarter of the 18th century.

At the end of the 18th century some 60 piano makers and organ builders were active in Vienna. Instruments made in the tradition of J.A. Stein should be regarded as the typical pianos of the early Viennese Classical period, in particular those made by his two children, Nannette Stein (later Streicher) and Matthäus Andreas Stein (known as André Stein), who moved their workshop from Augsburg to Vienna in 1794 (Frère & Soeur Stein à Vienne). German makers of note include Stein's pupil J.D. Schiedmayer in Erlangen; J.L. Dulcken (ii) in Munich; the brothers Johann Gottfried (1736–1808) and Johann Wilhelm Gräbner (1737–98) in Dresden; and C.F.W. Lemme (1747–1808) and J.J. Könnicke (1756–1811) in Brunswick (Könnicke moved to Vienna in 1790). J.E. Schmidt (1757–1804), who was appointed court organ builder in Salzburg in 1785 on the recommendation of Leopold Mozart, and Ferdinand Hofmann (1756–1829) also worked in the Stein tradition in Vienna. Notable among the followers of Anton Walter were his pupil Kaspar Katholnik (1763–1829) and Michael Rosenberger (1766–1832). There was a third Viennese tradition of piano making, its most important maker being Ignatz Kober ($c1755$–1813). Features of his instruments include very precisely made *Stossmechanik* actions and a rose on the soundboard. The oldest preserved signed and dated Viennese piano was made in 1787 (Kunsthistorisches Museum, Vienna) by Gottfried Mallek (1731–98).

4. ENGLAND AND FRANCE TO 1800.   Before 1765 the pianoforte did not occupy a prominent position in France or Britain. Nevertheless, scattered documentary sources indicate that, as in northern Germany, some early examples were heard and admired during the 1730s and 40s. Writing to his brother James from London on 17 May 1740, Thomas Harris (1712–85) reported that

Handel had 'played finely on the Piano-forte' the day before (Dunhill, G1995). As he did not explain what this instrument was, we may conclude that both men had seen it previously. Charles Jennens, Handel's librettist for *Messiah*, owned a 'Piano-forte Harpsichord', sent from Florence as early as 1732, together with 'a book of Sonatas compos'd purposely for the Piano forte', presumably Giustini's. In about 1740 Samuel Crisp (1706–83) returned from Italy with a pianoforte made in Rome by an Englishman named Wood. In 1747 Charles Burney played it at the country home of his new patron Fulke Greville. Listeners were delighted by its tone, and its 'magnificent and new effect' of light and shade produced simply 'by the finger'. It was, however, severely limited by poor repetition. 'Nothing quick could be executed upon it', wrote Burney, but he perfected the performance of slow and solemn pieces, and some 'pathetic strains [from] Italian operas', exciting 'wonder and delight in the hearers'. Greville liked it so much that he prevailed on Crisp to sell it to him for 100 guineas – about double the price of a new harpsichord. Roger Plenius, a London harpsichord maker, made an improved version about 1750 but met with little encouragement; he was declared bankrupt in 1756. On 27 June 1755 the Rev. William Mason wrote from Hanover to the poet Thomas Gray: 'I bought at Hamburg such a Pianoforte, and so cheap! It is a Harpsichord too, of 2 Unisons, and the Jacks serve as Mutes when the Pianoforte is played by the cleverest Mechanism imaginable'. The maker's name is not known, but Friedrich Neubauer was advertising such combination instruments in Hamburg in 1754, as well as clavichords and harpsichords, and hammer-action instruments called *Pantelong*, evidently inspired by Hebenstreit's giant dulcimer (known as pantaleon). By 1758 Neubauer had moved to London where he advertised the same instruments, dropping the name 'Pantelong' in favour of 'Piano forte'. Thus hammer instruments of both German and Italian designs were seen in London before 1760. Nevertheless, in an environment dominated by the harpsichord, pianos were comparatively scarce and undeveloped, and had little influence on repertory or performance.

In Paris there was a similarly slow response. In 1716 Jean Marius presented plans to the Académie des Sciences for a *clavecin à maillets*. But the originality of his invention was successfully challenged in the courts and no such instrument is known to have been completed by Marius. In 1759 the academy saw another novel harpsichord, made by 'Weltman' (possibly the Dutch maker Andries Veltman), containing both conventional jacks and a hammer action; again there was no discernible response. After Gottfried Silbermann's death (Dresden, 1753) his pianoforte design was perpetuated by his nephew Johann Heinrich Silbermann in Strasbourg. The latter's instruments, described in Paris in *L'avant coureur* of 6 April 1761, were bichord grands of five octaves, with hand-operated stops to raise the dampers. The prodigious asking price – 1500 livres – would have deterred all but the wealthiest patrons; reportedly there were only four of these *piano e forte clavecins* in Paris. Schobert and Eckard probably played on such instruments when the opportunity arose. The preface of Eckard's Sonatas op.1 (1763) explains that dynamic markings appear so as to make the music 'equally useful to performers on the harpsichord, clavichord or pianoforte'.

The tardy acceptance of the piano was soon to be rapidly accelerated by events in London. In September 1761 Princess Charlotte of Mecklenburg-Strelitz became queen of England, aged 17. Her enthusiastic harpsichord playing and penchant for modern music led to the selection of J.C. Bach as her music master by 1763. Burney reported that after J.C. Bach's arrival in London to prepare works for the opera season of 1762–3, 'all the harpsichord makers tried their mechanical powers at piano-fortes, but their first attempts were always on the large size till Zumpé … constructed small piano-fortes of the shape and size of the virginal'. Johannes Zumpe (1726–90) emigrated to London around 1750 and studied instrument making with Burkat Shudi. He set up his own workshop in 1761, at first supplying metal-strung English guitars, but then turned to pianos. His earliest surviving square pianos date from 1766.

In the same year, on the title page of J.C. Bach's six keyboard sonatas op.5, Bach first nominated the piano-forte as an alternative to the harpsichord. Zumpe's instruments were enthusiastically endorsed by Bach, Burney, Mason and, by association, the queen herself. For several decades this type of square piano was much the most popular form of pianoforte throughout Europe and North America. Burney attributed this to its sweet tone, good repetition, compact size and low price: the instruments sold at 16 to 18 guineas, about a third of the cost of a harpsichord.

Zumpe's standard keyboard (fig.8) has 58 playing notes (G', A'–f''') and a distinctive dummy sharp attached to the lowest note. The action, commonly called English single action, is shown in fig.9. Instead of the jack and intermediate lever of Cristofori's action, Zumpe used a wire (the pilot) mounted on a key with a leather-covered button at its upper extremity which acted directly on the hammer. There is no escapement or back check. A sprung damper-lever is hinged to the back of the piano case above the strings. The damper is raised by a thin wooden or whalebone rod (the sticker); the whalebone damper spring expedites its return once the key is released. Though the lack of escapement hinders subtlety of expression, it makes the mechanism almost indestructible and repetition very prompt. Zumpe's hammers are attached by flexible leather hinges (eliminating rattling sounds), and their tiny limewood heads are covered with one or two thin layers of smooth goatskin. An important innovation is that, compared with a clavichord, the strings are much thicker and at higher tensions. This combination of hammers and strings produces a remarkably pleasant tone. Initially, one hand stop was provided to raise the dampers, but, to counter objections that the lingering harmonies were too intrusive Zumpe changed to separate hand stops for bass and treble in 1767, enabling the player to damp the bass while employing the singing, undamped tone in the treble. From 1769 the buff stop was added; this pressed soft leather against the end of the strings so that, with the full damper lift, the sound resembled the gut-strung tones of Hebenstreit's dulcimer (though in Britain it was likened to the harp). Alternatively, with the buff stop on and the dampers engaged the sound resembled the pizzicato of violins.

Zumpe's design was never patented and, since demand far outstripped his ability to supply, a host of other makers soon began producing imitations. Between 1768 and 1775 these included, in London, Johannes Pohlman,

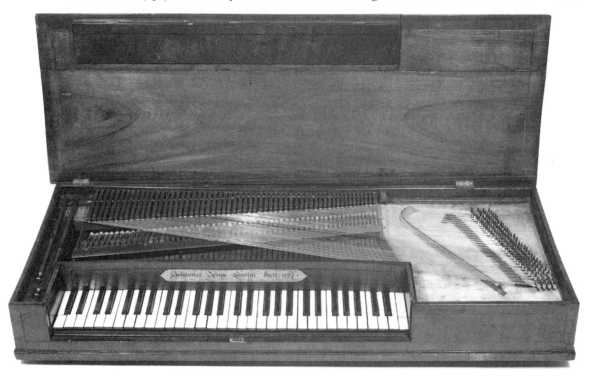

8. *Square piano by Johannes Zumpe, London, 1767 (Victoria and Albert Museum, London)*

Adam Beyer, Frederick Beck, George Fröschle, Christopher Ganer and Thomas Garbutt; in York, Thomas Haxby; and in Paris, Baltazar Péronard and Johann Kilian Mercken. In Paris some makers tried an alternative system using unleathered hammer heads and *Prellmechanik* (i.e. with hammers attached to keys), among them Adrien l'Epine in 1772, but tonally such designs were inferior to the 'English pianoforte', as Zumpe's invention was known. By 1784 pianos of the Zumpe type (fig.10) were widely used in France, North America, the Low Countries, Spain, Portugal, Italy, Germany and Austria. Makers included Krogmann (Hamburg), Steinbrück (Gotha), Hubert (Ansbach), Juan del Mármol (Seville), the Meyer brothers (Amsterdam), Henri van Casteel (Brussels), Sébastien Erard (Paris) and Wilhelm Zimmermann (Paris). Beyer and Ganer improved Zumpe's design, enlarging the soundboard, adding a swell that worked by raising part of the lid, and sometimes fitting pedals to work the stops. In 1774 Fröschle introduced a brass under-damper; other

makers ignored this improvement until John Broadwood, who had manufactured square pianos from 1780, included it in his patent of 1783. A still better damper was invented by William Southwell of Dublin who also managed to extend the compass to *c''''* without encroaching on the soundboard or increasing the size of the instrument.

In 1786 John Geib patented an escapement with an intermediate lever ('double action'), based on the Cristofori-Silbermann action (fig.11). Longman & Broderip, who bought rights to Geib's and Southwell's patents, sold square pianos that were delightful in their touch and tone, and deservedly popular. The Schoene brothers, who took over Zumpe's business in about 1783, appear to have introduced a variant form of Zumpe's action in 1786, using an intermediate lever without escapement; Erard and other French makers adopted it for square pianos until about 1820. Zumpe's single action continued in use until at least 1815 in pianos of inferior quality.

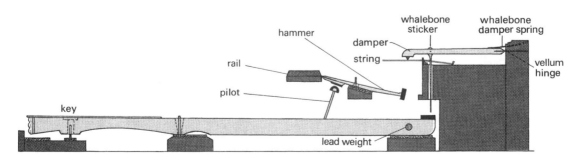

9. *Zumpe-style single action from a 1775 square piano inscribed as by Jacob and Abraham Kirkman*

In February 1771 Americus Backers announced an exhibition in London of his 'new-invented original Forte Piano' – the direct ancestor of the modern grand. An example dated 1772 with serial number 21 (at St Cecilia's Hall, Edinburgh) resembles a Kirkman harpsichord in appearance, but its many advanced design features suggest years of development. Backers's action dispenses with Cristofori's intermediate lever: the jack works directly on the hammer butt, having a forced escapement regulated by a set-off screw under the hammer rail. Its great advantage was that it could be easily adjusted by the owner with an ordinary tuning hammer. It has a true check as invented by Cristofori, so repetition is excellent. Two pedals attached to the front legs established the pattern for modern pianos: the left works an *una corda* and the right is the earliest known sustaining pedal, which allows a general raising of the dampers without taking a hand from the keys.

Backers pianos were used by J.C. Bach and his protégé Johann Samuel Schroeter for concerto performances in London and would certainly have been known by Clementi. After Backers's death his pioneering work was continued by Stodart and John Broadwood, who made the most significant advances in tone. An action from a Broadwood grand piano of 1799 is shown in fig.12. Backers and Stodart had placed the striking point at about one-twelfth of the sounding length but Broadwood moved it to between one-ninth and one-tenth. He also gave the bridge a rectangular cross-section, carved in a sawtooth pattern to give all three unison strings an equal sounding length and tension. Then, about 1790, he divided the bridge into two lengths (fig.13), separating the brass strings in the bass from the steel ones of the treble and tenor; by stretching the different metals to their optimum tensions he achieved a purer tone. It was allegedly to please Dussek that Broadwood made his first five-and-a-half octave grand, its compass extended to c'''', in about 1791. Haydn took a Longman & Broderip grand with this range to Vienna after his London visits. The first six-octave Broadwood ($C'–c''''$) is reported to have been made in 1794. Broadwood's innovations were swiftly copied by other English makers and then by Erard, but were not generally adopted in Vienna until about 1820 (see §5 below). By 1790 French makers were constructing grand pianos to various designs. Having established a good reputation for square pianos, the Erard firm began manufacturing concert pianos in the late 1790s after the return in 1794 of Sébastien Erard from a period in London. They used the English grand action and case construction, but added extra mutation pedals including a moderator and a harp or buff stop. Erard grand pianos quickly achieved international renown (see §6 below).

5. THE VIENNESE PIANO FROM 1800. Of the 200 or so Viennese instrument makers listed in Haupt's study (D1960) for the period 1791–1815, at least 135 were keyboard instrument builders. Most prominent were: Anton Walter, who from about 1817 to 1824 was in partnership with his stepson Joseph Schöffstoss (1767–1824); Johann Schantz, who had taken over the workshop of his deceased brother Wenzl in 1791, and whose business was continued from 1831 by Joseph Angst (c1786–1842); and Nannette Streicher and her brother Matthäus Andreas Stein, who had their own separate firms after 1802. After 1823 Nannette Streicher was in partnership with her son Johann Baptist, who continued the business after her death in 1833; from the late 1850s he was in partnership with his son Emil Streicher, who took over in 1871 and dissolved the firm in 1896. Other noteworthy makers included Matthias Müller (1770–1844), the number and ingenuity of whose inventions rival those of J.A. Stein in the 18th century; Joseph Brodmann (c1771–1848), whose workshop was taken over by his pupil Ignaz Bösendorfer in 1828 and continued by his son Ludwig Bösendorfer from 1859; and Conrad Graf, who in 1804 married the widow of the piano builder Jacob Schelkle, and in 1811 moved his workshop to Vienna.

Several trends of the first half of the 19th century were already discernible by 1800. The five-octave range of the German and Viennese pianos was expanded, and the keyboards were changed from black naturals and white-topped sharps to white naturals and black sharps as on the modern keyboard. The number of tone-altering devices increased. The case structure was made heavier to accommodate the increasing size of the instruments and their heavier stringing.

Few Viennese pianos from the first years of the 19th century appear to have survived, but several extant instruments by Anton Walter with a range of F' to g''' may be from this period. An early instrument by Nannette Streicher (Germanisches Nationalmuseum, Nuremberg) with a range of five and a half octaves, F' to c'''', has most of the characteristics of a late J.A. Stein piano (see §3 above) including wooden *Kapseln*, but the naturals of the keyboard are ivory, and the grain of the bottom is parallel to the spine. Later surviving instruments by Nannette Streicher indicate that about 1805 she adopted the Walter action type with metal *Kapseln* and back checks.

The earliest known signed and dated Viennese action pianos with damper pedals instead of knee levers are by Nannette Streicher (1811; Germanisches Nationalmuseum, Nuremberg) and Joseph Brodmann (1812; Musikinstrumenten-Museum, Staatliches Institut für Musikforschung, Berlin). With one (early) exception the extant pianos by Conrad Graf all have pedals.

By the 1820s a typical Viennese grand piano was nearly 2·3 metres long and 1·25 metres wide, with a range of six or six and a half octaves and usually with two to six pedals. Certain types of space-saving and decorative upright instruments, such as the 'giraffe' (fig.15) and 'pyramid' pianos, were popular (see UPRIGHT PIANO-FORTE), as well as smaller versions of the square such as the *Nähtisch* ('sewing table'), the *Orphica* (a tiny portable harp-shaped piano; for illustration see ORPHICA) and the *Querflügel* ('cocked hat'). An invention of 1800 by Mathias Müller had special significance: his *Ditanaclasis*, made at first with two keyboards opposite each other and from 1803 with a single keyboard, is an ancestor of the modern pianino or cottage piano (Haupt, D1960), its strings running from near the level of the floor rather than from keyboard level. In the second quarter of the century larger squares with the Viennese action were also made.

The 1820s and 30s were also a time of many inventions and improvements in the piano in Vienna. Soundboard structure, *Kapseln*, the keyboard and down-bearing devices for the nut and bridge seem to have received the most attention. In 1823 J.B. Streicher patented his down-striking action (Pfeiffer's *Zuggetriebe*; see §3 above), of which there are several surviving examples, and in 1831 he invented an 'Anglo-German' action in which the layout

10. Zumpe-style square piano, and a cello: painting, 'The Cowper and Gore Families' (1775) by Johann Zoffany (Yale Center for British Art, New Haven, CT)

of the traditional Viennese action is combined with the action principle of the English piano (fig.16; this type of action had also appeared in some English and German-Austrian pianos in the late 18th century, but was never widely adopted). Streicher used a system of iron bars in 1835, and Friedrich Hoxa is reputed to have been the first Austrian to use a full iron frame, in 1839; Friedrich Ehrbar (1827–1905) was one of the first in Vienna to use the iron frame (see §6 below). But these developments were behind their English counterparts by 15 or 20 years, and fortunately the basic design of the Viennese wooden instrument with its interlocking structure was more capable than that of the English of sustaining increased string tension. Graf, the most eminent Viennese builder from the early 1820s until his retirement in 1841, remained faithful to wooden framing (fig.17). The relative virtues of English- and Viennese-style pianos – their touch and timbre – were keenly debated on many occasions. Research indicates that German composers from Beethoven to Schumann and Brahms never wavered in their allegiance to the Viennese piano. But as the century progressed, the demands of musical taste elsewhere and

the predominant playing technique of the period accentuated the disadvantages of the Viennese action, rendering it unable to compete in the international market. Joseph Fischhof, a juror at the Great Exhibition of 1851, complained bitterly in his *Versuch einer Geschichte des Clavierbaues* (1853) about the other judges' emphasis on volume alone, which discriminated against the already sparsely represented Viennese pianos built to satisfy the Austrian taste for fine nuances and expressive playing.

Just as the demand for more volume with a stronger fundamental tone and fewer overtones meant heavier stringing and consequently a thicker and stronger case structure, the hammers and dampers of the Viennese piano also became heavier (figs.18 and 19, below), although the simplicity of the action did not change and some Viennese makers retained until late in the century the thin layer of leather over the felt hammer-covering that had become common by the middle of the century. Inevitably, however, the heavier action destroyed that delicacy of touch and crispness of tone which had distinguished the earlier instruments. Pfeiffer suggested that pianists used to the English action were disturbed by

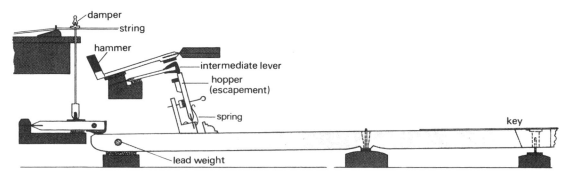

11. Geib-type double action from a piano of c1800 by Broderip & Wilkinson

the feeling of the hammer falling back to the rest position, which is not noticeable in an action where the hammers are not attached to the key. He also explained that the key-attached hammer had another disadvantage: the striking-point varies according to the depth of the key dip when the hammer hits the string; therefore, when the total key dip was increased as the Viennese action got heavier, this inconsistency was accentuated. However, Pfeiffer (C1948) considered that the allegedly poor capacity for repetition of the Viennese action was much exaggerated. On the same subject, Joseph Fischhof (C1853) had already commented that repetition was to be performed by the pianist, not the piano maker. Viennese pianos were still produced in the second half of the 19th century but were discontinued as a standard model by Bösendorfer in 1909; some were made to order by Bösendorfer during the next decade and a few makers of less expensive instruments in Vienna continued to use the developed *Prellmechanik* even later. In the end the decline of the Viennese action was due to changing aesthetic paradigms in playing as well as building pianos. Viennese pianos required both a sensitive, sympathetic pianist of the old school, and a piano maker who was a skilful technician and worked with intuitive feeling, since the action was much harder to adjust with precision than a modern action with its many adjusting screws.

The modern instrument, which has become more of a machine, is also better suited to modern piano playing, which calls for great volume and precision. In this connection it is worth noting that Viennese piano makers were particularly reluctant to expand their firms (Bösendorfer, F1898), so that there was hardly any industrial manufacturing of instruments on a large scale in Austria. Viennese piano-building stands for a traditional craftsmanlike approach, and 19th-century industrialization was foreign to it. However, several Viennese piano makers in the second half of the 19th century did endeavour to comply with the west European standard. The most important firms of this period were J.B. Streicher & Sohn, Ludwig Bösendorfer, J.M. Schweighofer's Söhne and Friedrich Ehrbar. As well as making the usual Viennese instruments, all these firms also built pianos with the

English action, and even with a double repeating action. Innovations such as the cross-strung solid-cast frame, and the double scale deriving from the research of the physicist Helmholtz, were already being introduced in Vienna about 1875 (Schelle, B1873; *Die Pianoforte von Schweighofer*, 1892).

In the wake of the harpsichord revival of the 20th century there was from World War II a new interest in the early models of piano with *Prellmechanik* as proper instruments for the stylistic investigation and historically accurate performance of the Classical masters such as Haydn, Mozart and Beethoven. Replicas of pianos by Stein and his contemporaries have been produced by Hugh Gough and Adlam-Burnett (England), Philip Belt (USA), Martin Scholz (Switzerland), Rück and Neupert (Germany) and others, and these have promoted a widespread recognition of the virtues of the 18th-century Viennese piano for its own repertory. By the late 1970s progress in reconstructing contemporaneous orchestral instruments and their playing techniques made it feasible to perform a Mozart concerto with instruments resembling the originals.

In the early 1980s makers such as Robert Smith and Margaret Hood (USA) and Neupert began producing replicas of the larger Viennese pianos of Graf, Streicher and Dulcken. Since the early 1990s Christopher Clark (Cluny, France) and Paul McNully (Divišor, Czech Republic) have also become famous for the high standard of their instruments. Many such builders concentrate on using the same materials and techniques as the original makers. These instruments, as well as the restorations of E.M. Frederick, Edward Swenson (both USA), Gert Hecher and Albrecht Czernin (Austria) and others, provide an opportunity to extend keyboard performing practice to include the piano repertory of the 19th century.

6. ENGLAND AND FRANCE, 1800–60. During the first half of the 19th century English and French instrument makers transformed their low-tensioned, light-action fortepianos of five or five and a half octaves into massively powerful, seven-octave instruments closely resembling the modern piano. Prominent London manufacturers of the period included the firms of Broadwood, Clementi (later Collard & Collard), Kirkman and Stodart; in Paris, the

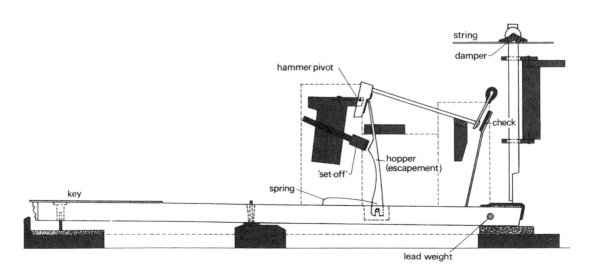

12. *English grand piano action from a Broadwood piano of 1799 (Royal College of Music, London)*

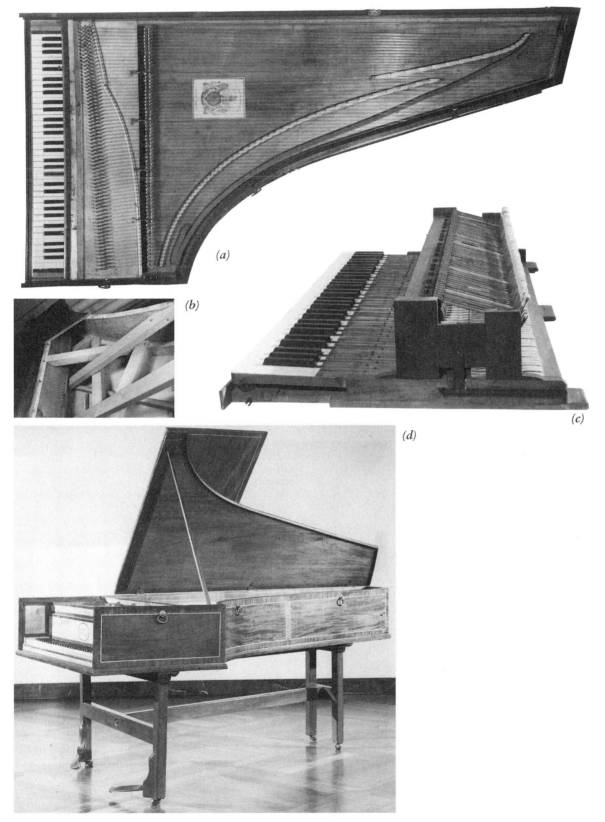

13. Grand piano by John Broadwood & Son, London, 1794 (Smithsonian Institution, Washington, DC); (a) plan view; (b) detail of internal bracing showing a rather heavier structure than that in fig.7; (c) action; (d) general view

Erard and Pleyel firms were dominant. Erard, which also ran a successful London branch, was perhaps the single most important source of innovation among these makers.

In the quest for greater power and dynamic range, which was the driving force behind these changes, string diameters and tensions were progressively increased. On the grand pianos of John Broadwood about 1801, the iron wire used for the note c'' is under a tension of about 10 kg per string – virtually the same as that used in Zumpe's square pianos 30 years earlier. But by 1815, thicker wire was used in both grands and squares, with a tension of about 15 kg per string for c''. Thereafter the increase was inexorable: 24 kg by 1825, 42 kg by 1850. Such high tensions were made possible only by using harder steel wire and ever-stronger forms of bracing in the case construction, progressing towards the full iron frame.

To match these heavier strings the weight of the hammers was more than doubled (fig.19). The more powerful, richer sonorities of the later pianos are directly related to energy input, which cannot be manufactured inside the instrument, but must come ultimately from the player's fingers. This has a profound effect on the touch, illustrated by comparing the minimum weight required to sound a note on instruments made 60 years apart. Typically, an English grand of around 1800 requires only 34 grams to sound c'', but on a piano of 1860 the same note requires 80 grams. To ease the burden on the player, piano makers were compelled to reduce the gearing ratio between the finger and the hammer head. Until about

1810 English piano keys had a touch depth of about 7.5 mm, but by 1845 this had increased to 9 mm and by 1860 to 10 mm. This depth of movement required taller sharps, while the natural key heads were lengthened from 40 mm to 50 mm, encouraging a more vigorous attack with extended fingers rather than the quiet hand and curved finger techniques of the 18th century.

The extra tensile strength obtained from hardened steel strings, together with the physical properties of much tauter wire, demanded softer and thicker hammer coverings to suppress the undesirable inharmonicities produced by prominent upper partials. Many materials were tried, including woven cloth or matted fur applied over the traditional layers of leather, but compressed felt gave the best results. This led to the production of specialist hammer felts and new arts of voicing (or 'toning') the hammers. The *fortissimo* became much more powerful than before, and the *pianissimo* quieter by contrast, but there was some loss in articulation, especially noticeable in the lower notes where the tone develops more slowly.

Sébastien ERARD and his nephew Pierre introduced many successful solutions to the problems created by the heavier and deeper touch, and their numerous patents of this period also chronicle the ways in which piano construction was modified so as to bear hugely augmented loads. As early as 1808 Sébastien Erard's patent drawings show a downward-sloping wrest plank with agraffes (metal staples, one for each note, secured to the wrest plank to provide a bearing for the strings which pass underneath and at the same time defining one end of the

14. Typical mid-19th-century south German square piano accompanying a violin and flute; painting, 'Family Concert in Basle' (1849), by Sebastian Gutzwiller in the Kunstmuseum, Basle

15. Giraffe piano by Ernst Rosenkranz, Dresden, c1815 (Neupert Collection, Germanisches Nationalmuseum, Nuremberg); the right-hand view shows the instrument with the fronts removed to reveal a layout resembling that of a grand piano (here a vertical adaptation of the Viennese action); the pedals (from left to right) are: sustaining pedal, bassoon stop (up to e♭'), full moderator (celeste), half-moderator, una corda, janissary stop

speaking-length of each string). In this arrangement the wrest plank is stronger and the hammer blow hits the strings against their bearing, which prevents their displacement and, together with the equalized unison string lengths introduced by Broadwood, helps to preserve the tuning. But the main focus of the 1808 patent was an entirely new action: Erard's *mécanisme à étrier*. In this the intermediate lever (omitted in English grand actions)

was reintroduced, but adapted to operate a downward-pulling action on a rear extension of the hammer butt. After escapement the 'stirrup mechanism' quickly re-engages the hammer so that notes may be repeated with small motions of the key. This ability to repeat notes when the key was only partially returned became increasingly important as more massive hammers produced a heavier touch. English makers paid insufficient

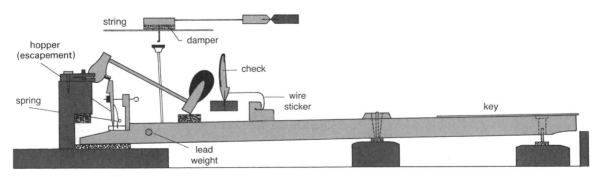

16. Anglo-German action from a piano of c1845 by Johann Streicher of Vienna (private collection)

17. Grand piano (once owned by Robert and Clara Schumann) by Conrad Graf, Vienna, 1839 (Gesellschaft der Musikfreunde, Vienna, on loan to the Sammlung alter Musikinstrumente, Kunsthistorisches Museum, Vienna)

attention to these developments, most preferring the simplicity and reliability of the action invented by Backers. In December 1821, just months before the 1808 patent expired, Pierre Erard filed a patent for another repetition action (fig.20; the patent was approved the following year). This one, with only minor modifications, provides the basis of all modern grand piano actions. After escapement, the hammer falls away by only a short distance, about 10 mm below the strings, where it rests on a sprung repetition lever. As the finger releases the key the intervention of this lever allows the hopper to re-engage the hammer quickly; so that for repeated notes it is not necessary that the key return to its original position. One of the secondary results of higher string tensions can be seen in Erard's change to under-dampers which, aided by a spring, press firmly against the strings to quell their energetic vibrations.

The construction of an entirely wooden case that would resist the enormous aggregate forces of the string tension demanded ever more drastic buttressing. For this reason there was much interest in down-striking actions because these allowed the case to have bulky wooden struts passing right through the instrument behind the sound-board. However, the better reliability of up-striking actions was ultimately persuasive. Early six-octave English grands used five steel arches to bridge the gap between wrest plank and belly rail – as in Beethoven's Broadwood

of 1817. That instrument may be seen as the end of the line for piano development without metal framing. In 1820 James Thom and William Allen jointly patented a 'compensation frame', in which brass and steel tubes were placed above the strings to connect the wrest plank to a metal hitch-pin plate along the bentside. Part of their idea was to allow for slight movements of the hitch-pin plate, and to use the expansion and contraction of the tubes under changing temperatures to push or pull the frame, so maintaining the original string tension. Their system was very effective in practice. Grands made under this patent by William Stodart were vastly more stable at high tension than any previous piano. Other makers responded with more modest schemes using three to five steel struts (fig.21). In most English square pianos after 1825 a metal hitch-pin plate on the right was braced against the wrest plank by a single strut. In Erard's 1825 patent the grand's wrest plank is reinforced with a steel plate fastened underneath, and struts bear against a metal plate at the bentside through adjustable screws.

Facility of repetition was of paramount importance to French makers, yet many of their square pianos from the early part of the 19th century feature a simple two-lever action without escapement. With this mechanism rapid reiteration was possible with practice, but as hammers increased in weight it became more difficult to prevent rebounds and double strikes. London makers, using the

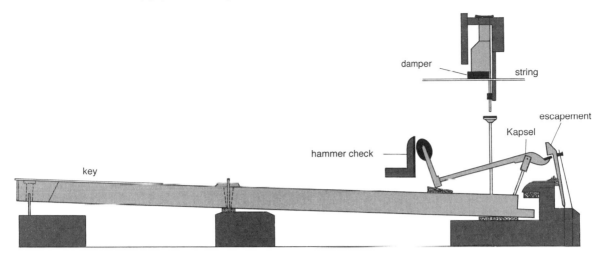

18. Prellmechanik (Viennese action) from a piano of 1826 by Conrad Graf (private collection)

more subtle escapement action of fig.11, countered this problem by adding a wire-mounted check – before 1830 on expensive models. Erard likewise added a check; the firm designed and patented a succession of innovatory actions for square pianos between 1820 and 1840, but few of these found their way into regular production. Many French square pianos employed triple stringing rather than augmenting the tone with heavier bichords as favoured in England.

Once again, as the 14-year term for the grand repetition action expired, Erard applied for another, dated December 1835, effectively preventing British rivals from using a wide selection of useful innovations. In all this time Broadwood had taken out only three quite trivial patents. It was not until the Great Exhibition of 1851 in London, when the jury awarded its most prestigious medal to Erard, that Broadwood's complacency was exposed. As the world's largest and most commercially successful manufacturers they were aggrieved at the decision, though many friends rallied to defend them, claiming that Broadwood's tone was superior – a notoriously subjective matter. (A grand piano of 1855 by Erard is shown in fig.22.)

Among British manufacturers the square piano declined rapidly after 1840 as improved uprights won approval for domestic use. In 1810 more than 80% of pianos produced in London had been squares, but by 1850 this had dwindled to less than 7%. Part of the reason for the square's demise was its increasing size: as the compass increased from five-octaves to seven such instruments inevitably grew not only longer but proportionally wider and deeper, becoming massively cumbersome pieces of furniture. The upright instrument provided an alternative. Most uprights of the period had the soundboard and strings raised above the keys – chiefly for acoustical reasons. 'Upright grands' up to 8·5 feet (2·66 m) tall incorporated the structure and action of the horizontal grand with minimal modification, the hammers striking from the back. More compact forms were basically square pianos raised vertically, using diagonal stringing; for these William Southwell designed the 'sticker action'. The first cabinet uprights, in which the strings descend to within a small distance of the floor, were five-octave instruments patented in 1800 by JOHN ISAAC HAWKINS, an Englishman

living in Philadelphia (*see also* UPRIGHT PIANOFORTE). Just over four feet high, his absurdly named 'Portable Grand Piano-forte' was in some technical respects far ahead of its time. But Hawkins was primarily an engineer, not a musical instrument maker; he paid little attention to the touch and the pianos were not a success. Southwell's sticker action (fig.23) proved useful in tall cabinet uprights (1820–50) which, like Hawkins's piano, had the wrest plank at the top. Even with an escapement such actions were not equal to *prestissimo* playing, but the structural stability of the cabinet form, in which the action could be placed entirely in front of the strings, was so superior that other forms were soon obsolete. The shortcomings of the upright action were addressed most successfully by Robert Wornum, who developed the 'tape-check' mechanism (fig.24). A light brass spring, connected to the hammer butt by a linen tape, acquires tension as the hammer approaches the strings and tweaks it away from the strings promptly, preventing rebounds or dwelling on the string. With minor modifications to improve reliability in the escapement, and with relocation of the dampers, Wornum's invention became the prototype for modern upright actions.

To reduce the height of these front-striking uprights to the absolute minimum a simple diagonal disposition of the strings was adopted, as advocated by Thomas Loud (1802) and seen in Wornum's early instruments. But in 1828 Jean Henri Pape in Paris devised the prophetic concept of overstringing, placing the bass strings on a separate bridge in the otherwise unused area of the soundboard at the bottom right beyond the tenor bridge. The bass strings passed over the tenor in a system that has since worked well in grands. In Pape's fashionable console pianos of around 1840 the top of the case was only slightly higher than the keys, an arrangement made possible by having the rear of the keys cranked downwards. However, the compactness of such designs was achieved at the cost of some loss in sonority and in the reliability of the action. From 1835 to 1860 the most popular form of domestic instrument was the dependable 'cottage piano', a cabinet piano of modest height (one of *c*1825 is shown in fig.25).

Changing perceptions on the use of the sustaining tone and mutation stops were partly conditioned by the

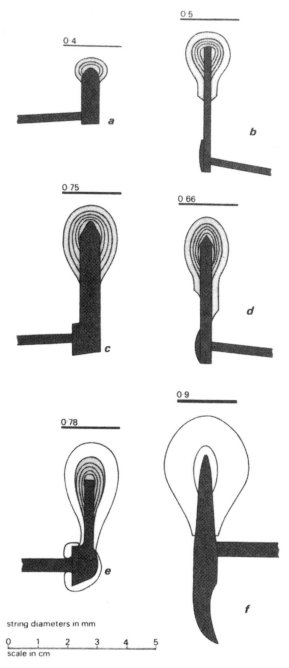

19. Comparison between six piano hammers and strings (all sounding the note f'), showing the gradual increase in mass of both as the instrument developed: a) South German Heilmann, c1785–c1790; b) English (Broadwood), c1806; c) Viennese (Graf), 1826; d) English (Broadwood), c1823; e) French (Erard), c1825; f) American (Steinway), c1970

increasing power of the piano throughout this period. Beethoven's Erard grand, presented to him by the maker in 1803, had four pedals typical of French instruments up to 1825. The harp pedal produced a pizzicato sound that could be used with or without sustaining effects. (When not sustained, the tone was usually called 'lute'.) The moderator produced a muffled tone by interposing cloth tabs between the hammers and strings. The *una corda*, which Louis Adam (1804) recommended in conjuction with the fourth, sustaining pedal as the *jeu céleste*, was commended by Beethoven to Viennese makers. Parisian square pianos often had a BASSOON STOP, operating only from middle C downwards, whose buzzing sound added rhythmic impulse to dance music. Pianos from London were usually equipped simply with two pedals, as found on modern instruments. On early 19th-century grands and uprights the left pedal provided a genuine *una corda* or *due corde* throughout the compass, but this was often compromised after 1830 when the tenor and bass were not always tricords. The right pedal lifted the dampers. The changing use of this pedal, in consequence of the stronger reverberation of more tautly strung pianos, caused many makers to seek ways of providing selective sustaining mechanisms. The simplest was Broadwoods' split pedal, which could lift the bass and treble dampers separately, while the most complicated and least copied was the SOSTENUTO PEDAL pioneered by Boisselot and exhibited in Paris in 1844. In spite of the plethora of other mechanical aids, when felt-covered hammers became the norm after 1830, most pianos were provided only with the keyboard-shifting 'soft' pedal and the damper-lifting SUSTAINING PEDAL.

7. SPAIN, 1745–1850.   The earliest extant Spanish piano, dating from about 1745, was made in Seville by Francisco Pérez Mirabal. Whilst the action resembles Cristofori's 1720 model with a non-inverted wrest plank, the case has a double-curve bentside and other features of construction more typical of Sevillian harpsichord-making. Its compass 9is *G'–d'''*. Unusually, it possesses trichord stringing where one set of strings could be silenced with a hand-operated stop of leather pads. Two other, unsigned, Spanish pianos with a Florentine-style action are known: a *G'–g'''* instrument from the Pérez Mirabal workshop, and a *C–d'''* instrument with bichord stringing whose case suggests a different school of construction. The early presence of pianos in Seville may be related in some way to the marriage of the Portuguese infanta Maria Bárbara and the Spanish crown prince Fernando in 1729 and to the Spanish court's residence in Andalusia during the following four and a half years. Maria Bárbara brought her music teacher, Domenico Scarlatti, with her to Spain. It appears probable that both were familiar with the piano and during the early years of her marriage the princess may already have owned a Florentine instrument that could have inspired Pérez Mirabel to develop similar instruments. None of the grand pianos built by Mirabal's successor in Seville, Juan del Mármol, is known to have survived; however a number of his square pianos, made from the 1780s onwards in the English style, are extant. Some of his instruments were exported to Latin America and a Juan de Mármol (father or son) emigrated to Mexico at the end of the century, as did Adam Miller, a German who moved to Mexico after working in Madrid. Information on piano building in Madrid prior to 1780 is not available. As far as the royal harpsichord maker Diego Fernández is concerned, it is not clear whether he made such instruments himself or whether a few of his harpsichords were later converted into pianos.

Grand pianos (Sp. *pianos de cola*) were usually known as *clavicordios* (or *claves*) *de piano* or *de martillos* (i.e.

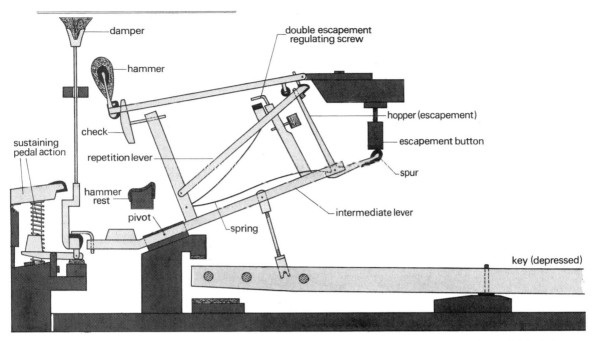

20. *Erard repetition action after the English patent drawing of 1821; the intermediate lever, pivoted to its flange, simultaneously lifts the hopper and pulls down the damper; the action is shown with the key depressed, the hammer having fallen back to its check*

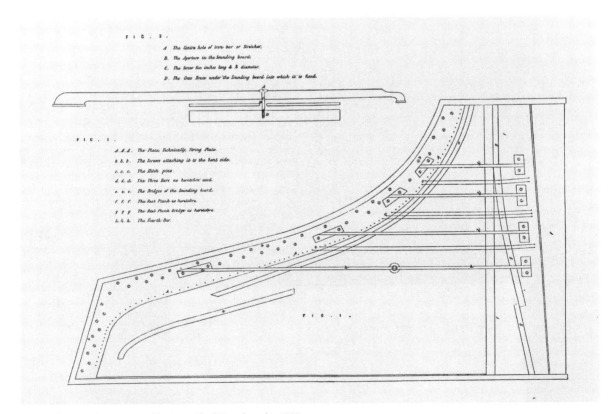

21. *Iron bracing scheme patented by James Shudi Broadwood in 1827*

'piano- or hammer-harpsichords') during the 18th century. Square pianos were called *fortepianos* or *pianos fortes* (later known as *pianos cuadrilongos* and most recently as *pianos de mesa*). The term *fortepiano* seems to have been introduced together with the first such instruments from England during the 1770s. In the following decades the most up-to-date models were imported from England and Madrid makers advertised themselves as exponents of the English style. Foremost of these was FRANCISCO FLÓREZ, a court piano maker who became familiar with the work of English makers, including that of J.J. Merlin, during a year-long stay in England. His younger rival and successor in the royal favour, FRANCISCO FERNÁNDEZ, at first followed the English style but later tried to found a Spanish school of construction using native woods, while at the same time following developments abroad, particularly in France. Other Madrid piano makers in the first half of the 19th century showed little originality. An exception was the immigrant Jan Hosseschrueders, a Dutch carpenter who founded a firm in Madrid in 1814, later known as HAZEN and still in operation today. Hosseschrueders patented a transposing piano in about 1824.

Little research has been carried out on the piano in other regions of Spain. It appears, however, that at the beginning of the 19th century German influence was uppermost in Catalonia. Many Catalan square pianos are

to be found incorporating knee levers and a *Prellmechanik* (see §§3 and 5) comprising a *Prelleiste*, hammers held in brass *Kapseln*, but no back checks. In 1848 the French firm of Boisselot opened a branch in Barcelona (later owned by the Spanish firm of Bernareggi). This was a symptom of the increasing popularity of French instruments in Spain. As the 19th century progressed few Spanish firms could compete directly with the large factories in other countries and many smaller Spanish firms came to rely on cheaper parts from abroad for assembly in Spain.

8. NORTH AMERICA TO 1860. Pianos were used and made in North America by the 1770s. The earliest known reference to a piano there is a notice in the *New-York Gazette and Weekly Mercury* of 17 September 1770 listing a 'fortepiano' for sale by the Englishman David Propert; in Boston, Propert advertised that he taught the piano and in 1771 performed 'some select pieces on the forte piano', at the Concert Hall. In the same year in Virginia Thomas Jefferson and Robert Carter bought pianos from London. In 1772 John Scheiuble [Sheybli] announced in New York that he made and repaired pianos, and in 1774 he advertised for sale 'one hammer spinnet', which he may have made himself. Another German craftsman, John [Johann] Behrent, usually credited with making the first piano manufactured in North

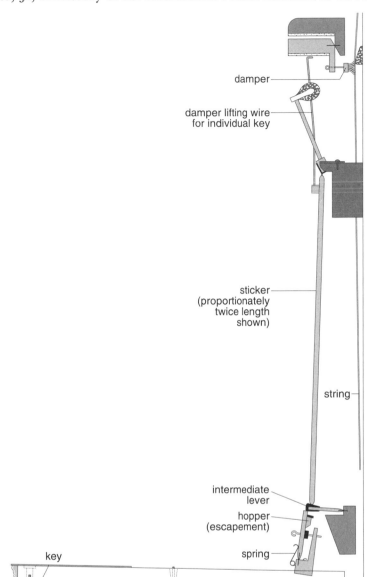

damper

damper lifting wire
for individual key

sticker
(proportionately
twice length
shown)

string

intermediate
lever

hopper
(escapement)

key

spring

America, advertised in Philadelphia in 1775 that he had made an instrument 'by the name of Piano Forte, of Mahogany, in the manner of an harpsichord, with hammers and several changes'. Although both manufacture and emigration diminished during the Revolutionary War, from the mid-1780s many builders emigrated from Europe to the USA, among them Thomas Dodds (active in New York from 1785), Charles Albrecht (Philadelphia, c1785), Charles Taws (New York, 1786; Philadelphia, 1787) and John Geib (New York, 1797), who claimed by 1800 to have built 4910 pianofortes. In Milton, Massachusetts, the American-born Benjamin Crehore was building pianos by the 1790s. The type most often played and owned by Americans was the square piano, which remained in favour until the 1880s. The typical early square had wooden framing, a range of five to five and a half octaves (*F′–c″″*), English action (although Albrecht made some with German action), and changes in registration activated by hand stops.

As early as 1792 Dodds & Claus noted the need to prepare their wood 'to stand the effect of our climate', a prime concern of American builders throughout most of the 19th century. JOHN ISAAC HAWKINS, an English civil engineer working in Philadelphia, included an iron frame and iron bracing rods in his ingenious 1800 patent for a small upright piano. Although his invention did not succeed musically, it represents one of the earliest attempts to use iron to withstand climatic changes. In 1825 Alpheus Babcock, a Boston maker who had worked with Crehore, was the first to be issued a patent (17 December 1825) for a one-piece metal frame, which he claimed would be 'stronger and more durable than a wooden frame or case' and, because the strings and metal frame would expand or contract equally, would prevent the instrument being 'put out of tune by any alteration in the temperature of the air'. He fitted this frame in a piano typical of the late 1820s, a mahogany square with decorative stencilling, two pedals and a compass of six octaves (*F′–f″″*); only

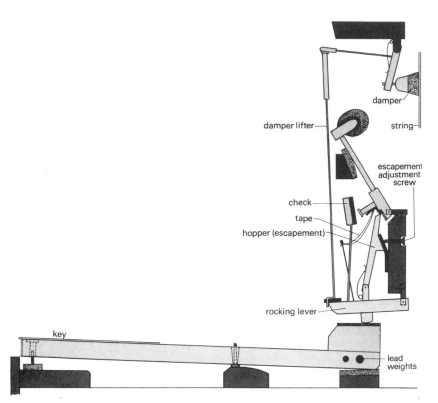

24. Wornum's tape-check action for upright pianos, patented in 1842; the tape assists the return of the hammer to check

two Babcock squares with an iron frame are extant (fig.26). Many builders, especially in New York and Baltimore, opposed the iron frame, claiming that it resulted in a thin and nasal tone quality. Instead, many used the heavy wooden bracing and a solid five-inch (12·7 cm) wooden bottom for stability in tuning. But by the 1840s, wooden framing alone was not strong enough to withstand the enormous tension required by the piano's expanded compass (seven octaves, A″–a″″) and the rigours of American climatic extremes.

By the 1830s American makers of square pianos were using the Erard repetition action. In 1840 the Boston piano maker Jonas Chickering, with whom Babcock worked from 1837 to 1842, patented a metal frame with a cast-iron bridge for a square piano, and in 1843 he patented a one-piece metal frame for grands. He was the first to devise a successful method of manufacturing and selling pianos with metal frames and was the first major American builder to make grand pianos, for which he won special notice at the Great Exhibition in London (1851). Metal frames and felt-covered hammers made American squares characteristically heavy and sonorous instruments. The Chickering factory, with about 300 workers, made over 10% of the 9000 pianos produced in the USA in 1851. After a fire destroyed the factory in late 1852 the firm built a vast new factory (fig.27) and by the 1860s it employed over 500 workers. The Chickering firm set the standard for the American piano industry: production of high-quality pianos with metal frames, an extensive steam-powered factory operation whose workers developed highly specialized skills, an energetic sales programme, and support for musical events and performers.

In 1853, the year of Jonas Chickering's death, the Steinway firm was established in New York; within a decade it had equalled the Chickering firm in production and prestige. Like Chickering, the firm designed pianos

25. Cottage piano by Clementi & Co., London, c1825 (private collection)

26. *Square piano with a one-piece metal frame made by Alpheus Babcock in Philadelphia, c1835 (Smithsonian Institution, Washington, DC)*

with metal frames, patenting in 1859 a new overstringing arrangement for the grand piano which transformed the sound of the instrument and was eventually adopted by manufacturers throughout the world (see also §9 below). The demand for pianos grew throughout the century. According to statistics gathered by Loesser, Ehrlich and Dolge, one in every 4800 Americans bought a new piano in 1829; by 1851 the figure had risen to one in 2777, and by 1870 to one in 1540.

9. 1860–1915.   The great change in the period from 1860 to World War I was the shift in piano manufacture from the craft shop to a factory system. Manufacturers

before this time, such as Broadwood, the largest in the world with more than 300 employees, used no machinery and achieved virtually no economies of large-scale production. The typical small craft shop used labour-intensive methods to make a few instruments each year. The spread of factories brought a tremendous growth in piano production, making much less expensive instruments available to more modest households. The greatest change of this type took place in the USA, where production, as shown in Table 1, increased by 15 times between 1870 and 1910. Germany's output increased eight times and Britain's three times, while France's production rose only

27. *View of the Action Room in the Chickering Pianoforte Manufactory, Tremont Street, Boston USA in 1887*

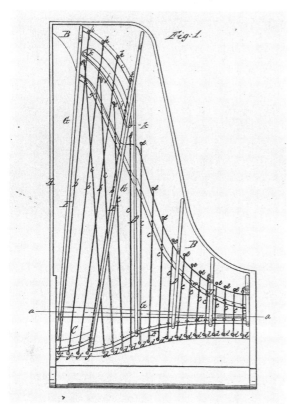

28. Detail from Henry Steinway's patent for an overstrung piano, dated 20 December 1859

about 20%. It has been estimated that, based on comparative income levels, the cost of pianos approximately halved from 1850 to the end of the century. Such growth suggests that the second half of the century saw the actualization of aspirations often expressed in the first half: that even the most modest cottage might have a piano on which the greatest music would be played, that the piano would become the household's altar, the drawing-room's orchestra, the centre and focus of the concert hall. Pianists continued to be leading stars of the musical world. International tours by Rubinstein, Bülow, Paderewski and others continued the tradition begun by such pianists as Liszt, Thalberg and Clara Schumann, bringing the highest realms of pianism to ever-greater numbers of people.

TABLE 1: Estimates of piano production, 1870–1980 (in thousands)

Year	Britain	France	Germany		USA	Japan	USSR	Korea
c1870	25	21	15		24			
c1890	50	20	70		72			
c1910	75	25	120		370		10	
c1930	50	20	20		120	2		
c1935	55	20	4		61	4		
			W	E				
c1960	19	2	16	10	160	48	88	
c1970	17	1	24	21	220	273	200	6
c1980	16	3	31	28	248	392	166	81

Note: estimates for 1960, 1970 and 1980 are taken from United Nations 'Growth of World Industry' and 'Yearbook of Industrial Statistics'; for earlier years see Ehrlich, 1976

This period also saw the beginnings of the standardization of what may justly be called the modern piano. Innovations of earlier years, such as overstringing, metal frames, felt hammer-coverings, refinements in actions, and the extension of the range from five octaves to seven or seven and a third, were combined and improved. Types and shapes of instruments were somewhat simplified as the century wore on. Large vertical pianos, such as cabinet pianos and 'giraffes', disappeared to be replaced by smaller uprights, standing only 4 to 5 feet (c1·2 to 1·5 m) in height. Such instruments were rapidly becoming the pianos of choice in middle-class European homes by the 1860s, and Broadwood made its last square in 1866. The Americans and Canadians retained their affection for the square for some decades longer. When, after 1865, Theodore Steinway began to concentrate production on the upright at the expense of the square, even workers in the factory objected, and American makers produced larger and larger squares as the century went along. But Steinway, which had made its first uprights in 1862, produced its last square in 1888, and in 1904 the association of American piano manufacturers gathered together all the squares they could find at their meeting in Atlantic City, New Jersey, and burnt them in a bonfire. Many squares survive as relics, but as the symbolism showed, their manufacture had essentially ceased.

Steinway's 1859 patent for overstringing grand pianos (fig.28) produced what was essentially the modern grand (fig.29). It combined elements of earlier designs: the one-piece iron frame, patented for squares by Babcock, and for grands by Chickering (see §8 above); overstringing, which was pioneered by Jean Henri Pape for small uprights in the 1820s and was widely in use in squares; and the divided bridge, used by John Broadwood in the 18th century and refined in shape by Henry Steinway so that in combination with overstringing the bridge was brought closer to the centre of the soundboard, where vibrating efficiency was greater. Other design innovations came especially from the imagination of Theodore Steinway: the metal action frame, which prevented the warping of the action; the 'duplex scale', which proportioned the lengths of non-speaking parts of strings to the speaking parts in order to enhance the partials and the tone; and the laminated case, which was stiffer and more durable and, by some accounts, improved the tone with more efficient reflection of vibrations across the soundboard. His brother Albert Steinway patented the sostenuto pedal, the middle pedal in most modern grands, which allowed the sustaining of notes whose dampers were already up when the pedal was depressed. Many of these elements were copied by other makers, though Europeans on the whole did not use the sostenuto pedal until after World War II. Some experiments in redesigning keyboards were carried out, notably Józef Wieniawski's double-keyboard instrument with the treble on the right in one and on the left in the other (1876), Ferdinand Clutsam's concave keyboard (1907), and Paul von Janko's six-row, paired whole-tone keyboard (1882). These had only temporary success, Janko's more than the others. (*See* KEYBOARD.)

The Erard action became the most common, though other types were in use. Bösendorfer continued to provide Viennese as well as Erard actions until about 1910. Such makers as Broadwood, Chickering, Pleyel and Blüthner used actions of their own design for quite a time, but by

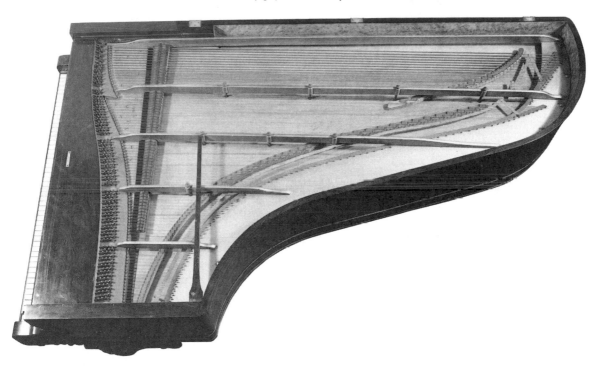

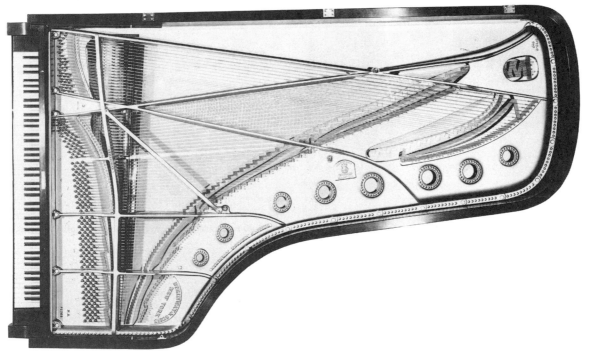

29. Plan views of grand pianos by Steinway, New York: a) straight-strung, 1857 (Smithsonian Institution, Washington, DC); b) overstrung 'model D', developed c1900

the early 20th century most of these had fallen out of use. Some makers, especially the English and French companies, held back from adopting the one-piece iron frame with overstringing, Broadwood making its first overstrung grand only in 1897 and Erard in 1901. Both continued to make straight-strung pianos after that. Blüthner used (throughout the 20th century) aliquot stringing in the top

three octaves, with a fourth string above the others which vibrates sympathetically.

The die was cast in 1867, when at the Paris Exposition the piano competition was decisively won by the Americans. Steinway and Chickering argued inconclusively about which had taken the more important prize. Both were winners, and the outcome was dramatic. They were

30. Full grand piano (Style II) by Bechstein (reproduction after a photograph from a brochure, c1904)

emulated especially by German makers and some Austrian firms. Encouraged by successes in other international exhibitions such as Philadelphia in 1876 and Amsterdam in 1883, the Americans were able by shrewd marketing and vigorous pursuit of export trade to persuade the public that what was widely called the 'American system' was now the norm. It maintained quality and lowered cost by using machinery instead of manual labour, by rationalizing the division of labour and by standardizing parts. Cottage industries had long been employed for the production of some parts, but now the system was extended to all parts, and companies specializing in supplies multiplied. Foundries could cast frames to order, and wood could be properly seasoned and wooden parts supplied to order in many shapes and sizes. Companies specializing in actions had been known since the 1840s, and they certainly saved small makers a great deal of grief and money. The action makers were probably primarily responsible for the final victory of the Erard type of action. By using parts suppliers, even small companies could take advantage of economies of scale, and interchangeable parts meant that many small makers became, in effect, 'compilers' of pianos rather than manufacturers.

The leading companies still boasted that they manufactured everything in their own plants, but their smaller competitors met a large need and a large market. People who could never afford a Steinway could buy an instrument made by Joseph P. Hale in the USA and revel in the status and musical presence of a piano. If Hale's instruments were not as 'good' as Steinway's, they nevertheless served essential musical and social needs.

The piano began to be more than a European instrument. It spread to European colonies, as colonial officials and settlers desired the cultural goods they had known at home. After the Meiji Restoration, when in 1868 Japan first opened itself to the West, the Japanese government began an intensive overhauling of the educational system, including the widespread teaching of the piano and violin in schools. American and European firms provided the instruments, though some Japanese makers such as Nishikawa of Tokyo began work even before the end of the 19th century. The American successes of 1867 also contributed to the extension of exports to all the world. Many firms did not participate, partly by choice, but the Germans and Americans were especially active, the Germans simply taking the Australian market away from

31. *Baby grand piano (the 'Elfin')*
by Broadwood, London,
manufactured in 1924–30 (private
collection)

English makers and having large positions in South American markets. Steinway's expansion into Germany in 1880 gave the company a strong place in European and English markets, and Steinway was the export leader in the USA.

By the onset of World War I, as well as being an international instrument, the piano had become universal as well; no longer found mostly in the drawing-rooms of the wealthy, it was now a nearly ubiquitous furnishing and a source of pride and pleasure in even extremely modest homes. It had also become a modern instrument, manufactured by the latest technological means, designed to withstand climates of all sorts, and marketed by the most up-to-date methods. Some strains were to be found in the industry. The problems of labour unionization had yet to be solved, and the beginning of the 20th century saw some consolidations among firms, such as the purchase of several piano companies, including the proud

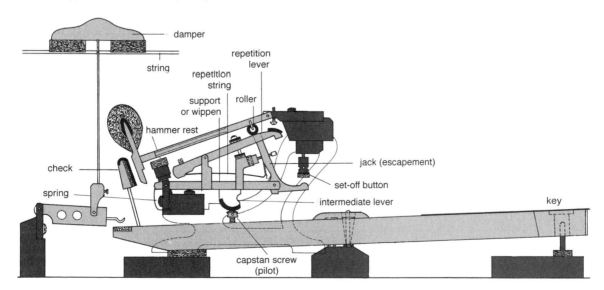

32. *Action of a modern grand piano: on pressing the key the movement is transmitted via the pilot to the intermediate lever; the jack then acts on the roller of the hammer which rises towards the string. The moment the backward projection of the jack contacts the set-off button the jack moves back permitting the hammer to escape and to continue in free flight to strike the string and then begin its descent; it is then caught and retained by the check and repetition lever as long as the key remains depressed. If the key is partly released the hammer is freed from the check, and the roller is acted on directly by the repetition lever; it is thus possible to strike the key again by depressing the key a second time (the jack will re-engage with the roller only when the key has been fully released so that a full hammer stroke may be made)*

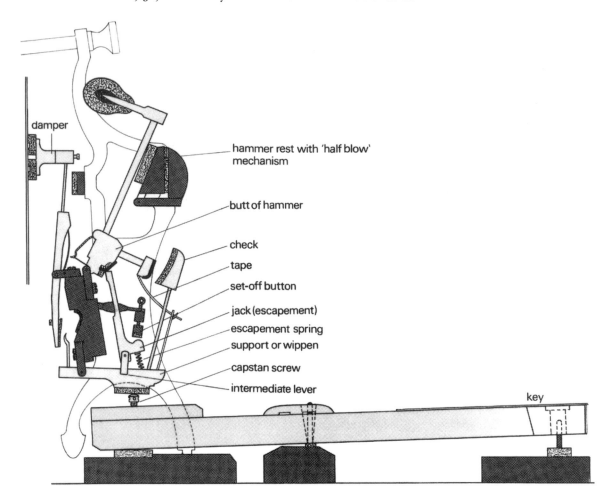

33. Action of a modern upright piano: the movement of the key is transmitted directly to the jack which in rising pushes the hammer forward towards the string until the backward projection of the jack reaches the set-off screw, thus allowing the jack to escape and the hammer to fall back from the string to be caught by the check; the return of the hammer is assisted by the tape which is so adjusted to jerk the hammer away from the string at the moment of impact

old Boston firm of Chickering & Sons, by the American Piano Company. There were new companies, such as D.H. Baldwin in the USA, and rejuvenated old ones, such as Chappell in Britain and Ibach in Germany. Some old ones dropped from sight, notably Streicher in Vienna, and others were bought out, such as Brinsmead in England.

10. FROM 1915.   World War I effectively stopped piano manufacture in countries immediately affected by it, though American production was only restricted. After the war, production soon reached pre-war levels in England, France and the USA, and by 1927 Germany had regained its prior capacity. Public demand for pianos increased mightily during the boom years of the 1920s, when there was also an astounding rise in the production of automatic pianos, especially in the USA. Already in 1919 their production was greater than that of ordinary pianos; in 1923 it reached a peak of 56% of the entire American output of pianos. These mechanisms, invented before the war, came to their flower afterwards (*see* PLAYER PIANO). Earliest in general production was the Pianola of the Aeolian (later Aeolian American) Corporation, first a 'piano player' set in front of the keyboard

that actually depressed the keys, and later a 'player piano' with the mechanism inside the piano's case. In Germany the Welte-Mignon was first brought out in 1904 and the Hupfeld company's DEA REPRODUCING PIANO in 1905. The major American 'reproducing' mechanisms were Aeolian's Duo-Art and the Ampico of the American Piano Company, both released in 1913.

If the rise of automatic pianos tended to diminish the level of active piano playing, other advancing modes of entertainment and recreation may have accelerated decline. During the 1920s the radio was becoming ever more popular as a source of musical and other entertainment – and it was, if anything, even easier to play than the player piano. Competition from the cinema and the automobile for recreational time and money was becoming formidable. Piano playing still attracted many people: the number of music teachers in the USA, where these competing modes of entertainment flourished to the highest degree, actually rose during the 1920s and 30s. Nonetheless, during this period the piano's status as a domestic instrument receded and has never been quite regular.

34. Grand piano ('model 290, Imperial') by Bösendorfer, Vienna, first manufactured c1900 (Musikverein, Vienna)

With the Depression piano manufacture underwent a drastic decline. American production fell to 10% of its pre-Depression level by 1932, German production to about 6% and English to about 30%. Various more or less drastic remedies were tried. Very small grands, well under 1·5 m in length and sometimes in odd shapes, including symmetrical ones, were designed to appeal to families with aspirations to status but straitened finances. As sounding instruments they were 'babies' but not grand. The Mathushek Company in New York attempted unsuccessfully to reinstate the square, in sizes considerably smaller than those familiar in the late 19th century. Beginning in England, very small uprights (the Americans called them 'spinets'), barely higher than keyboard level, were made; they had small soundboards, short strings and 'drop' actions, all of which contributed to technological and tonal inadequacies. Many of them were virtually untunable, their touch was spongy and uncontrollable, their tone an assault on the ear. They were handsomely designed and took up little wall space and even less floor space, but they were probably responsible for a great many children's complete loss of interest in playing the piano. However admirable these attempts to overcome the financial difficulties of the 1930s, their musical contributions were, if anything, negative, and they have been discontinued by almost all manufacturers.

World War II brought an already badly depressed piano industry to a halt. Every country involved required piano companies to stop using valuable steel, iron and other materials for such frivolities as musical entertainment. Steinway manufactured gliders and was permitted to produce a few hundred small uprights for military use. German factories, almost entirely converted to war production, were mostly bombed out of existence (including Steinway's Hamburg factory). English and Japanese companies likewise contributed to the war effort. Some technological improvements came out of the war. The most important in materials were resin glues, less susceptible to temperature and humidity changes than hide glues, and plastics of various kinds, used for key coverings (ivory becoming unusable as elephants were endangered), for bushings, and more recently for cases, allowing considerable freedom in modifying if not completely altering external shapes. Manufacture has benefited from the efficiency of automation technologies. Otherwise there have been few advances in piano design or materials since World War II. There were experiments with microtonal pianos (see MICROTONAL INSTRUMENTS), especially in the 1920s, and various methods of modifying the sound by 'preparing' the piano, most famously by John Cage beginning in the 1930s (see PREPARED PIANO). The actions that became standard in the late 19th century have remained so: the Erard action for grands and the tape-check for uprights, though small uprights use drop actions. Overstringing is universal, and European makers have given up their antipathy to the sostenuto pedal. Hammers and dampers are still made of felt, actions of wood, frames of cast iron, soundboards of spruce. The range of all models has been standardized at seven and a third octaves except for a few larger sizes (e.g. Bösendorfer's Imperial Grand with eight octaves, fig.34). Sizes have also been to some extent standardized. The concert grand is about 275 cm long. Bösendorfer's Imperial is about 15 cm longer; the Challen company in England celebrated King George V's silver jubilee in 1935 with a grand 356 cm long; and Fazioli made the largest grand in production in the late 20th century, 308 cm long. Upright sizes have been standardized to 'full' about 122 to 132 cm; 'studio', about 114 cm; 'console', about 107 cm; and 'spinet', about 91 cm (the latter almost entirely abandoned).

After World War II North American and European industries saw serious compressions: formerly vigorous companies disappeared, various others combined (sometimes ending in dissolution), and there was general retrenchment, though tone quality was not seriously affected. Some successful American firms acquired famous European ones: Baldwin bought Bechstein in 1963, selling it again during hard times in 1987; Kimball, itself part of the Jasper Corporation from 1959, bought Bösendorfer in 1966 and the English action manufacturer Herrburger-Brooks. Steinway has had several owners not named Steinway since 1972, and the company's stock is now traded on the New York Stock Exchange. Only a few notable new enterprises emerged in Western countries. The firm of Alfred Knight, which made impressive uprights in England from 1935 and successfully exported them after World War II, was bought by Bentley Piano Co., which was in turn bought by Whelpdale, Maxwell & Codd in 1993. The ambitious Italian firm of Fazioli, founded in 1981, concentrates on the high end of the trade; its concert grand has received some enthusiastic reports. In the USA the Walter Piano Company (founded 1975) in Elkhart, Indiana, has produced excellent uprights and introduced grands; Fandrich & Sons (founded 1993) in Hoquiam, Washington, impressed many technicians in the mid-1990s with a redesigned upright action, but their marketing has not been aggressive. The great story of the postwar period was the expansion of and dominance by the Japanese piano industry, followed closely by that of South Korea. The vigour with which Asian countries rebounded from the devastations of the 1940s and 50s was exemplified in the piano industry. By 1948 the leading Japanese companies, Yamaha (which had begun making uprights in 1900) and Kawai (established 1925), were again producing pianos, and by 1969, owing in part to extensive and systematic automation technologies, Japanese production of pianos outstripped that of all other countries. In the late 1970s, Yamaha alone was making more pianos than all American companies combined, with an output of about 200,000 annually, sold mostly in Japan. Production has recently slowed somewhat, though it remains the largest of any company. Two South Korean manufacturers, Young Chang (founded 1956) and Samick (founded 1958) have increased production and expanded their facilities. The economic difficulties experienced in 1997–8 apparently damaged the East Asian piano industry only temporarily. The Chinese industry has been less forward, though it has profited by technical advice from elsewhere, and Chinese pianos are being exported as well as sold domestically in increasing numbers. Though early exports of Asian instruments often had structural and tonal problems, considerable improvement has taken place.

A striking trend of the late 20th century was the spread of electronic keyboards and their offspring (*see* ELECTRIC PIANO and ELECTRONIC PIANO). Indeed, the term 'keyboard' has come in the USA to mean an electronic instrument, as distinct from a piano. Synthesizers and MIDI controllers now use the keyboard format almost exclusively, and it is a mild irony that these instruments on their stands look much like little 18th-century square pianos. Several companies have introduced computer-driven reproducing systems attached to conventional pianos, whereby the pianist can record a performance to disk and play it back on the piano itself, or play a pre-recorded performance from computer disk or compact disc. Yamaha has been in the forefront of this development, but Music Research Systems in the USA, which owns the Mason & Hamlin, Knabe and Sohmer piano brands names, pioneered a digital instrument, and both Baldwin and Bösendorfer have produced similar systems.

BIBLIOGRAPHY

A General literature. B Collections. C General history. D Up to 1800. E After 1800. F Local studies. G Other studies.

A: GENERAL LITERATURE

ClinkscaleMP
D. Spillane: *History of the American Pianoforte* (New York, 1890/R)
R.E.M. Harding: *The Piano-Forte: its History Traced to the Great Exhibition of 1851* (Cambridge, 1933/R, 2/1978/R)
E. Closson: *Histoire du piano* (Brussels, 1944; Eng. trans., 1947, rev. 2/1974 by R. Golding)
A. Loesser: *Men, Women and Pianos: a Social History* (New York, 1954/R)
D. Wainwright: *The Piano Makers* (London, 1975)
C. Ehrlich: *The Piano: a History* (London, 1976, 2/1990)
M. Bilson: 'The Viennese Fortepiano of the Late 18th Century', *EMc*, viii (1980), 158–62
E.M. Good: *Giraffes, Black Dragons, and other Pianos: a Technological History from Cristofori to the Modern Concert Grand* (Stanford, CA, 1982, 2/2000)
H. Schott: 'From Harpsichord to Piano: a Chronology and Commentary', *EMc*, xiii (1985), 28–38
E. Ripin and others: *Piano* (New York and London, 1988)

R. Palmieri: *Piano Information Guide: an Aid to Research* (New York and London, 1989)
R. Palmieri, ed.: *Encyclopedia of Keyboard Instruments*, i: *The Piano* (New York, 1994)

B: COLLECTIONS

W. Pole: *Musical Instruments in the Great Industrial Exhibition of 1851* (London, 1851)
'Reports on Musical Instruments', *Exhibition of the Works of Industry of All Nations 1851: Reports by the Juries*, i (London, 1852), 705–30
E. Schelle: 'Musikalische Instrumente', *Officieller Ausstellungs-Bericht*, xv (Vienna, 1873) [report of the Vienna Universal Exhibition, 1873]
G. Kinsky: *Musikhistorische Museum von Wilhelm Heyer in Cöln: Katalog*, i (Cologne, 1910)
V. Luithlen and K. Wegerer: *Katalog der Sammlung alter Musikinstrumente*, i: *Saitenklaviere* (Vienna, 1966)
H. Schott: *Victoria and Albert Museum: Catalogue of Musical Instruments*, i: *Keyboard Instruments* (London, 1985)
C. Ahrens, ed.: *Clavichord und Fortepiano: eine Musikinstrumentenausstellung der Stadt Herne* (Herne, 1989)
H. Henkel: *Besaitete Tasteninstrumente: Deutsches Museum von Meisterwerken der Naturwissenschaft und Technik* (Frankfurt, 1994)
J. Koster and others: *Keyboard Musical Instruments in the Museum of Fine Arts, Boston* (Boston, 1994)
M. Cole: 'Tafelklaviere in the Germanisches Nationalmuseum: some Preliminary Observations', *GSJ*, l (1997), 180–207

C: GENERAL HISTORY

BoalchM
J. Fischhof: *Versuch einer Geschichte des Clavierbaues* (Vienna, 1853)
H. Welcker von Gontershausen: *Der Flügel* (Frankfurt, 1856)
E.F. Rimbault: *The Pianoforte: its Origin, Progress and Construction* (London, 1860)
C. Ponsicchi: *Il pianoforte: sua origine e sviluppo* (Florence, 1867)
G.F. Sievers: *Il pianoforte* (Naples, 1868)
O. Comettant: *La musique, les musicien, et les instruments de musique* (Paris, 1869)
E. Brinsmead: *The History of the Pianoforte* (London, 1870, enlarged 3/1879/R)
H. Welcker von Gontershausen: *Der Clavierbau in seiner Theorie, Technik und Geschichte* (Frankfurt, 1870)
A. Marmontel: *Histoire du piano et de ses origines* (Paris, 1885)
F.M. Smith: *A Noble Art: three Lectures on the Evolution and Construction of the Piano* (New York, 1892)
W.B. White: *Theory and Practice of Pianoforte Building* (New York, 1906)
H.E. Krehbiel: *The Pianoforte and its Music* (New York, 1911/R)
A. Dolge: *Pianos and their Makers* (Covina, CA, 1911–13/R)
S. Wolfenden: *A Treatise on the Art of Pianoforte Construction* (London, 1916, suppl. 1927, repr. together 1975)
M. de Guchtenaere: *Le piano: son origine, son histoire, sa facture* (Ghent, c1923)
C. Sachs: *Das Klavier* (Berlin, 1923)
H. Neupert: *Vom Musikstab zum modernen Klavier* (Bamberg, 1925, 3/1952)
M.A. Blondel: 'Le piano et sa facture', *EMDC*, II/iii (1927), 2061–72
E. Blom: *The Romance of the Piano* (London, 1928/R)
A. Casella: *Il pianoforte* (Rome, 1937, 4/1967)
A.E. Wier: *The Piano: its History, Makers, Players and Music* (London, 1940)
P. Locard: *Le piano* (Paris, 1948, rev. 5/1974 by R. Stricker)
W. Pfeiffer: *Vom Hammer: Untersuchungen aus einem Teilgebiet des Flügel- und Klavierbaus* (Stuttgart, 1948/R; Eng. trans., 1978)
N.E. Michel: *Michel's Piano Atlas* (Rivera, CA, 1953, rev. 10/1997 as *Pierce Piano Atlas*)
F.J. Hirt: *Meisterwerke des Klavierbaus: Geschichte der Saitenklaviere von 1440 bis 1880* (Olten, 1955; Eng. trans., 1968/R as *Stringed Keyboard Instruments, 1440–1880*)
C. Clutton: 'The Pianoforte', *Musical Instruments through the Ages*, ed. A. Baines (Harmondsworth, 1961/R, 2/1966/R), 88–102
W.L. Sumner: *The Pianoforte* (London, 1966, 3/1971)
D.S. Grover: *The Piano: its Story from Zither to Grand* (London, 1976/R)
F. Schulz: *Pianographie* (Recklinghausen, 1978, 2/1982)
J.R. Gaines, ed.: *The Lives of the Piano* (New York, 1981)
D. Gill, ed.: *The Book of the Piano* (Oxford, 1981)

S.K. Taylor, ed.: *The Musician's Piano Atlas* (Macclesfield, 1981)
M. Pizzi: *Histoire du Piano: de 1700 à 1950* (Chambéry, 1983)
D. Crombie: *Piano* (San Francisco, 1995)
J. Parakilas, ed.: *Piano Roles: Three Hundred Years of the Piano* (New Haven and London, 2000)

D: UP TO 1800

BurneyFI; BurneyGN; BurneyH
S. Maffei: 'Nuova invenzione d'un gravecembalo col piano, e forte, aggiunte alcune considerazioni sopra gl'instrumenti musicali', *Giornale de' letterati d'Italia*, v (Venice, 1711), 144–59; Ger. trans. in J. Mattheson: *Critica musica*, ii (Hamburg, 1725/R), 335–42
C.P.E. Bach: *Versuch über die wahre Art das Clavier zu spielen*, i (Berlin, 1753/R, 3/1787/R); ii (1762/R, 2/1797/R); Eng. trans. of pts i–ii (New York, 1949, 2/1951)
Ancelet: *Observations sur la musique, les musiciens et les instrumens* (Amsterdam, 1757/R)
K.C. Krause: 'Nachricht über eine wesentliche Verbesserung der Klaviaturen der Tasteninstrumente', *AMZ*, xii (1809–10), 649–52
C.F.G. Thon: *Ueber Klavierinstrumente: deren Ankauf, Behandlung und Stimmung* (Sondershausen, 1817)
F. de Bricqueville: *Le piano de Mme. DuBarry et le clavecin de la reine Marie-Antoinette* (Versailles, 1892)
A.J. Hipkins: *A Description and History of the Pianoforte and of the Older Keyboard Stringed Instruments* (London, 1896/R, 3/1929/R)
E. de Bricqueville: 'Le piano à Versailles sous Marie-Antoinette', *Revue de l'histoire de Versailles et de Seine-et-Oise*, viii (1906), 193–7
E. de Bricqueville: *Les ventes d'instruments de musique au XVIIIe siècle* (Paris, 1908)
W.H.G. Flood: 'Dublin Harpsichord and Pianoforte Makers of the Eighteenth Century', *Journal of the Royal Society of Antiquaries of Ireland*, xxxix (1909), 137–45
P. James: *Early Keyboard Instruments from their Beginnings to the Year 1820* (London, 1930/R)
H. Brunner: *Das Klavierklangideal Mozarts und die Klaviere seiner Zeit* (Augsburg, 1933)
N. Broder: 'Mozart and the "Clavier"', *MQ*, xxvii (1941), 422–32
C. Parrish: 'Criticisms of the Piano when it was New', *MQ*, xxx (1944), 428–40
H. Gough: 'The Classical Grand Pianoforte, 1700–1830', *PRMA*, lxxvii (1950–51), 41–50
U. Rück: 'Mozarts Hammerflügel erbaute Anton Walter Wien', *MJb 1955*, 246–62
H. Haupt: 'Wiener Instrumentenbauer von 1791 bis 1815', *SMw*, xxiv (1960), 12–84
R. Benton: 'The Early Piano in the United States', *HMYB*, xi (1961), 179–89
C.F. Colt: 'Early Pianos: their History and Character', *EMc*, i (1973), 27–33
E. Badura-Skoda: 'Prolegomena to a History of the Viennese Fortepiano', *Israel Studies in Musicology*, ii (1980), 77–99
C.F. Colt and A. Miall: *The Early Piano* (London, 1981)
B. Kenyon de Pascual: 'English Square Pianos in Eighteenth-Century Madrid', *ML*, lxiv (1983), 212–17
V. Vitale: *Il pianoforte a Napoli nell'ottocento* (Naples, 1983)
S. Pollens: 'The Pianos of Bartolomeo Cristofori', *JAMIS*, x (1984), 32–68
V. Pleasants: 'The Early Piano in Britain (c1760–1800)', *EMc*, xiii (1985), 39–44
S. Pollens: 'The Early Portuguese Piano', *EMc*, xiii (1985), 18–27
W.H. Cole: 'The Early Piano in Britain Reconsidered', *EMc*, xiv (1986), 563–6
M. Hood: 'Nannette Streicher and her Pianos', *Continuo*, x (1986), no.9, pp.2–5; no.10, pp.2–7
A. Huber: 'Mensurierung, Besaitung und Stimmtonhöhen bei Hammerklavieren des 18. Jhdts', *Das Musikinstrument*, xxxv (1986), no.7, pp.58–62; no.9, pp.25–9
B. Kenyon de Pascual: 'Francisco Pérez Mirabal's Harpsichords and the Early Spanish Piano', *EMc*, xv (1987), 508–14
E. Badura-Skoda: 'Zur Frühgeschichte des Hammerklaviers', *Florilegium musicologicum: Helmut Federhofer zum 75. Geburstag*, ed. C.-H. Mahling (Tutzing, 1988), 37–44
A. Huber: 'Were the Early Italian and Portugese Pianofortes Strung Entirely with Brass?', *Das Musikinstrument*, xxxvii/1–2 (1988), 184–94
S. Klima, G. Bowers and K.S. Grant, eds.: *Memoirs of Dr. Charles Burney* (Lincoln, NE, 1988)

P. Everett: *The Manchester Concerto Partbooks* (New York, 1989)
A. Huber: 'Der österreichische Klavierbau im 18. Jahrhundert', *Die Klangwelt Mozarts*, Kunsthistorisches Museum, 28 April – 27 Oct 1991 (Vienna, 1991), 47–72 [exhibition catalogue]
J. Koster: 'Foreign Influences in French Eighteenth-Century Piano Making', *Early Keyboard Journal*, xi (1993), 7–38
M. Latcham: 'The Check in some Early Pianos and the Development of Piano Technique Around the Turn of the Eighteenth Century', *EMc*, xxi (1993), 28–43
M. Latcham: 'The Pianos of Johann Andreas Stein', *Zur Geschichte des Hammerklaviers: Blankenburg, Harz, 1993*, 15–49
K. Komlós: *Fortepianos and their Music: Germany, Austria, and England, 1760–1800* (Oxford, 1995)
C. Leli: *Van piano tot forte* (Kampen, 1995)
S. Pollens: *The Early Pianoforte* (Cambridge, 1995)
S. Rampe: *Mozarts Claviermusik, Klangwelt und Aufführungspraxis: ein Handbuch* (Kassel, 1995)
J. Koster: 'The Divided Bridge, due Tension, and Rational Striking Point on Early English Grand Pianos', *JAMIS*, xxiii (1997), 5–55
M. Latcham: 'Mozart and the Pianos of Gabriel Anton Walter', *EMc*, xxv (1997), 382–400
M. Cole: *The Pianoforte in the Classical Era* (Oxford, 1998)
S.K. Klaus: 'German Square Pianos with *Prellmechanik* in Major American Museum Collections: Distinguishing Characteristics of Regional Schools in the Late Eighteenth and Early Nineteenth Centuries', *JAMIS*, xxiv (1998), 27–80
M. Latcham: 'Mozart and the Pianos of Johann Andreas Stein', *GSJ*, li (1998), 114–53
R. Angermüller and A. Huber, eds.: *Mozarts Hammerflügel* (Salzburg, 2000)

E: AFTER 1800

'Harpsichord', *Rees's Cyclopaedia* (London, 1819–20)
"Felix": 'Piano Fortes', *The Euterpeiad*, iii (1823), 179
C. Kützing: *Das Wissenschaftliche der Fortepiano-Baukunst* (Berne, 1844)
C.A. André: *Der Clavierbau in seiner Geschichte, seiner technischen und musikalischen Bedeutung* (Offenbach, 1855)
F.-J. Fétis: 'Instruments de musique', *Exposition universelle de 1867 à Paris: Rapports du jury international*, ed. M. Chevalier, ii/10 (Paris, 1868), 237–318
A. Le D. de Pontécoulant: *La musique à l'Exposition universelle de 1867* (Paris, 1868)
O. Paul: *Geschichte des Claviers vom Ursprunge bis zu den modernsten Formen dieses Instruments* (Leipzig, 1868/R)
P. Stevens: 'Reports upon Musical Instruments', *Reports of the United States Commissioners to the Paris Universal Exposition, 1867*, ed. W.P. Blake (Washington, DC, 1870)
J. Blüthner and H. Gretschel: *Lehrbuch des Pianofortebaues in seiner Geschichte, Theorie und Technik* (Weimar, 1872/R, rev. 3/1909 by R. Hannemann as *Der Pianofortebau*, 4/1921)
L. Nalder: *The Modern Piano* (London, 1927)
V.A. Bradley: *Music for the Millions: the Kimball Piano and Organ Story* (Chicago, 1957)
W.S. Newman: 'Beethoven's Pianos versus his Piano Ideals', *JAMS*, xxiii (1970), 484–504
D. Melville: 'Beethoven's Pianos', *The Beethoven Companion*, ed. D. Arnold and N. Fortune (London, 1971; New York, 1971 as *The Beethoven Reader*), 41–67
C.I. Walsh: *An Economic and Social History of the Pianoforte in Mid- and Late-Victorian Britain* (diss., U. of London, 1973)
M. Bilson: 'Schubert's Piano Music and the Pianos of his Time', *Piano Quarterly*, xxvii/104 (1978–9), 56–61
C.A. Hoover: 'The Steinways and their Pianos in the Nineteenth Century', *JAMIS*, vii (1981), 47–89
M. Bilson: 'Beethoven and the Piano', *Clavier*, xxii/8 (1983), 18–21
R. Winter: 'The Emperor's New Clothes: Nineteenth-century Instruments Revisited', *19CM*, vii (1983–4), 251–65
D. Wythe: 'The Pianos of Conrad Graf', *EMc*, xii (1984), 447–60
R. Winter: 'Striking it Rich: the Significance of Striking Points in the Evolution of the Romantic Piano', *JM*, vi (1988), 267–92
S. Pollens: 'Early Nineteenth-Century German Language Works on Piano Maintenance', *Early Keyboard Journal*, viii (1990), 91–109

F: LOCAL STUDIES

C. Schafhäutl: *Die Pianofortebaukunst der Deutschen* (Berlin, 1854)
J.L. Bishop: *A History of American Manufactures from 1608 to 1860* (Philadelphia, 1861–6, enlarged 3/1868/R)
J. Parton: 'The Piano in the United States', *Atlantic Monthly*, xx (1867), 82–98

T. Appleton and others: 'The American Pianoforte Manufacture', *Musical and Sewing Machine Gazette* (21 Feb 1880)

Die Pianoforte von Schweighofer (Vienna, 1892) [catalogue]

W. Steinway: 'American Musical Instruments', *One Hundred Years of American Commerce 1795–1895*, ed. C.M. Depew (New York, 1895), 509–15

L. Bösendorfer: 'Das Wiener Klavier', *Die Grossindustrie Österreichs* (Vienna, 1898)

A. Kraus: 'Italian Inventions for Instruments with a Keyboard', *SIMG*, xiii (1911–12), 441–3

R.S. Clay: 'The British Pianoforte Industry', *Journal of the Royal Society of Arts*, lxvi (1917–18), 154–61 [see also general discussion, 161–3]

T.E. Steinway: *People and Pianos: a Century of Service to Music* (New York, 1953, 2/1961)

V. Luithlen: 'Der Eisenstädter Walterflügel', *MJb 1954*, 206–8

O. Rindlisbacher: *Der Klavierbau in der Schweiz* (Berne, 1972)

H. Ottner: *Der Wiener Instrumentenbau 1815–1833* (Tutzing, 1977)

N.J. Groce: *Musical Instrument Making in New York City during the Eighteenth and Nineteenth Centuries* (diss., U. of Michigan, 1982)

D. Wainwright: *Broadwood by Appointment: a History* (London, 1982)

O. Barli: *La facture française du piano de 1849 à nos jours* (Paris, 1983)

R. Burnett: 'English Pianos at Finchcocks', *EMc*, xiii (1985), 45–51

L. Libin: *American Musical Instruments in The Metropolitan Museum of Art* (New York, 1985)

S. Pollens: 'The Early Portuguese Piano', *Emc*, xiii (1985), 18–27

W.H. Cole: 'Americus Backers: Original Forte Piano Maker', *English Harpsichord Magazine*, iv/4 (1987), 79–86

C. Bordas Ibáñez: 'Dos constructores de pianos en Madrid: Francisco Flórez y Francisco Fernández', *RdMc*, xi (1988), 807–51

A. Huber: 'Saitendrahtsysteme im Wiener Klavierbau zwischen 1780 und 1880', *Das Musikinstrument*, xxxvii/9 (1988), 84–94; also in *Saiten und ihre Herstellung in Vergangenheit und Gegenwart: Blankenburg, Harz, 1988*, 79–106

C. Bordas Ibáñez: *Hazen y el piano en España: 175 años* (Madrid, 1989)

C.H. Roehl: *The Piano in America, 1890–1940* (Chapel Hill, NC, 1989)

J. Horowitz: *The Ivory Trade* (New York, 1990)

R. Hopfner: *Wiener Musikinstrumentenmacher 1766–1900* (Vienna, 1999)

G: OTHER STUDIES

D. Spillane: *The Piano: Scientific, Technical, and Practical Instructions relating to Tuning, Regulating, and Toning* (New York, 1893)

W.B. White: *The Player-Piano Up-To-Date* (New York, 1914)

E.J. Dent: 'The Pianoforte and its Influence on Modern Music', *MQ*, ii (1916), 271–94

W. Pfeiffer: *Taste und Hebeglied des Klaviers: eine Untersuchung ihrer Beziehungen im unmittelbaren Angriff* (Leipzig, 1920; Eng. trans., 1967)

W. Pfeiffer: *Über Dämpfer, Federn und Spielart* (Frankfurt, 1962)

E.D. Blackham: 'The Physics of the Piano', *Scientific American*, ccxiii/6 (1965), 88–99

Der klangliche Aspekt beim Restaurieren von Saitenklavieren: Graz 1971

K. Ford: 'The Pedal Piano: a New Look', *The Diapason*, lxxv (1984), no.10, pp.10–11; no.11, p.6 only; no.12, pp.14–15

A.W.J.G. Ord-Hume: *Pianola: the History of the Self-Playing Piano* (London, 1984)

A. Huber: 'Deckelstützen und Schalldeckel in Hammerklavieren', *Studia Organologica: Festschrift für John Henry van der Meer*, ed. F. Hellwig (Tutzing, 1987), 229–52

I. Blüthner-Haessler: *Pianofortebau: Elementar und umfassend dargestellt von einem Klavierbauer* (Frankfurt, 1991)

R. Dunhill: *Handel and the Harris Circle* (Hampshire, 1995)

R. Maunder: *Keyboard Instrument in Eighteenth-Century Vienna* (Oxford, 1998)

II. Piano playing

The history of piano playing is tied to a great many factors: the development of the instrument, the evolution of musical styles, shifts in the relationship of the performer to the score, the rise of virtuosity, the idiosyncrasies of individual artists, changes in audience tastes and values, and even socio-economic developments. On a more practical level piano playing is concerned primarily with matters of touch, fingering, pedalling, phrasing and interpretation. Even a discussion limited primarily to these can point out only the major signposts along the three centuries of the instrument's existence. Much of the lore surrounding the history of piano playing belongs more properly to the realm of anecdote or even myth than to scholarship; much work in this area remains to be done.

1. Classical period. 2. Romantic period. 3. 20th century. 4. Jazz piano playing.

1. CLASSICAL PERIOD.   The earliest performers brought with them well-established techniques for playing the harpsichord and clavichord, both of which were essentially domestic instruments in spite of their cultivation at leading courts throughout Europe. The best international keyboard repertory required considerable agility, dexterity and coordination, but minimal strength. With a maximum range of five octaves, coupled with long-standing resistance on the part of composers to the fully chromatic use of the keyboard (embraced only by J.S. Bach), there were inherent limits to the musical and technical demands a composer might make upon a player.

Much emphasis has been placed upon the similarity of the early fortepiano to both the clavichord and the harpsichord. There exist parallels in case and in soundboard construction; but as far as the performer was concerned the piano imposed a set of new demands. The various escapements introduced as early as Cristofori allowed the pianist to exert more downward pressure than was feasible on a clavichord. The fortepiano, however, was without the resistance encountered in pressing a plectrum past a string; its dip was correspondingly shallower. While the dynamic range of the new instrument was greater than that of a clavichord, it could not achieve the clavichord's various gradations of *piano*, and its maximum volume was still less than that of a well-quilled harpsichord. The special skills required for playing the piano are acknowledged obliquely in C.P.E. Bach's *Versuch*, i (1753): 'The more recent fortepiano, which is sturdy and well built, has many fine qualities, although its touch must be carefully worked out, a task that is not without its difficulties'. It is known that both Carl Philipp Emanuel and his father had access to the Silbermann pianos at the court of Frederick the Great in Potsdam, where the former was employed, but apart from Johann Sebastian's suggestions for improving the action on his visit in 1747 there is no documentation of his performances on the new instrument. Hence for the first six decades or so after its invention the piano co-existed with its more established rivals. Marpurg's *Anleitung* (1755) treats keyboard instruments as a family with broad performance skills in common. Even Türk's *Clavierschule* (1789) – cited by Beethoven in a conversation book as late as March 1819 – is directed as much at clavichordists as pianists. Until one instrument came to be preferred by composers and players alike, it was not economically feasible to aim a method book at a specialized audience. It is probably safe to assume that a still hand and an even touch remained the primary objectives of keyboard players until well after the death of J.S. Bach.

The persistence of these virtues is displayed in a letter Mozart wrote to his father from Augsburg in October 1777, wherein he criticized in biting fashion the playing of Stein's little daughter, Nannette, presumably on one of the maker's new fortepianos:

When a passage is being played, the arm must be raised as high as possible, and according as the notes in the passage are stressed, the arm, not the fingers, must do this, and that too with great emphasis in a heavy and clumsy manner. ... When she comes to a passage that ought to flow like oil and which necessitates a change of finger ... she just leaves out the notes, raises her hand, and starts off again quite comfortably. ... She will not make progress by this method ... since she definitely does all she can to make her hands heavy.

Mozart's rival Clementi still admonished his pupils in his treatise of 1801 to hold 'the hand and arm ... in an horizontal position; neither depressing nor raising the wrist. ... All unnecessary motion must be avoided'. Similarly, Dussek (1796) counselled the student 'never [to] displace the natural position of the hand'. Although Beethoven told Ries that he had never heard Mozart play, Czerny reported otherwise, attributing to Beethoven the observation that Mozart 'had a fine but choppy [*zerhacktes*] way of playing, no ligato'. This remark must be understood against the background of the gradual shift from non-legato to legato that had its beginnings in the high Classical period. Nevertheless, the keyboard music of Beethoven supplies the most imaginative examples of non-legato in the first quarter of the 19th century. In spite of his own legendary virtuosity and gift for improvisation, it is hard to form a coherent picture of Beethoven's performing style from contemporary reports. According to one of the best-known accounts, that by Carl Czerny, 'his bearing while playing was masterfully quiet, noble and beautiful, without the slightest grimace. ... In teaching he laid great stress on a correct position of the fingers (after the school of Emanuel Bach)'. But Czerny appears to contradict himself in reporting further that Beethoven's 'playing, like his compositions, was far ahead of his time; the pianofortes of the period (until 1810), still extremely weak and imperfect, could not endure his gigantic style of performance'. And, according to Beethoven's biographer Schindler, 'Cherubini, disposed to be curt, characterized Beethoven's pianoforte playing in a single word: "rough"'.

Whether Beethoven performed it himself or not, it is certain that works like the 'Hammerklavier' Sonata op.106 demanded far greater technical resourcefulness (including participation of the full arm) than anything written before 1818. The last articulate spokesman for the conservative Viennese tradition was Hummel, whose *Anweisung* (1828) emphasized 'ease, quiet and security' of performance. In order to realize these goals, 'every sharp motion of the elbows and hands must be avoided'. Nevertheless, Hummel consolidated many of the innovations in fingering that had been adopted by Beethoven and others. Almost two-thirds of his method is devoted to this subject, with great stress on the pivotal importance of the thumb. Along with his own music Hummel advocated serious study of J.B. Cramer's *Studio per il pianoforte* (1804–10) and Clementi's *Gradus ad Parnassum* (1817–26), two of the first systematic surveys of keyboard technique. Although Cramer's goal of the absolute equality of the ten fingers was eventually abandoned, his studies were recommended enthusiastically by composers with aims as diverse as Beethoven, Schumann and Chopin. The heavier, more resonant (and less clear) English instruments preferred (and, in Clementi's case, manufactured) by English and French performers are compared without prejudice by Hummel with the lighter, transparent Viennese instruments. The

gradual domination of the English type, including the eventual adoption of the repetition patented by Erard in 1821, exercised a profound influence on the development of piano playing in the second half of the century.

2. ROMANTIC PERIOD. The dawn of Romanticism in the 1830s brought with it the specialization that produced a breed of pianists who were to dominate the salons and concert halls of Europe for the next 80 years. Although the number of amateur pianists continued to grow, the keyboard became increasingly the realm of the virtuoso who performed music written by and for other virtuosos. It is no accident that two composers on the threshold of the new movement, Weber and Schubert, each wrote a great deal of highly original piano music but were also highly original orchestrators, while two full-blooded Romantics of the next generation, Chopin and Schumann, have their achievements more clearly bounded by the capabilities and limitations of the piano. Weber was an accomplished pianist, but both he and Schubert dreamt of success in opera; Chopin became a highly polished virtuoso, while Schumann tried to become one. Among Romantic composers, some shunned or showed little interest in the piano (Berlioz, Verdi, Wagner), and others lived from its extraordinary powers, both as performers and teachers (Chopin, Liszt, Thalberg). This division helps to explain the intense interest after Beethoven's death in developing a range of sonorities for the solo piano that could be compared to an orchestra. Perhaps the most colourful example of this concern is the account by Charles Hallé of a concert he attended in Paris in 1836:

At an orchestral concert given by him and conducted by Berlioz, the 'Marche au supplice', from the latter's *Symphonie fantastique*, that most gorgeously orchestrated piece, was performed, at the conclusion of which Liszt sat down and played his own arrangement, for the piano alone, of the same movement, with an effect even surpassing that of the full orchestra, and creating an indescribable furore.

The problems of studying piano playing are even more formidable over the Romantic era than over its beginnings. There are several reasons for this. In spite of the proliferation of method books by such artists as Moscheles, Herz and Kalkbrenner, none of the most innovatory contributors to 19th-century pianism (Schumann, Mendelssohn, Chopin, Tausig, Liszt, Brahms and Leschetizky) compiled similar guides. Chopin left behind the barest torso of a method book, apparently prompted largely by financial considerations and perfunctory in all but two respects. The closest testimonial in the case of Liszt is the largely neglected *Liszt-Pedagogium* (Leipzig, 1902), assembled by Lina Ramann with fellow pupils including August Göllerich.

Even more exasperating than the lack of guidance from the major performers themselves is the imprecision of the accounts in an age that worshipped flights of poetic fancy. From a novelist like George Sand one might expect the following description of Liszt at the keyboard:

I adore the broken phrases he strikes from his piano so that they seem to stay suspended, one foot in the air, dancing in space like limping will-o'-the-wisps. The leaves on the lime trees take on themselves the duty of completing the melody in a hushed, mysterious whisper, as though they were murmuring nature's secrets to one another.

But the description of a professional musician like Hallé is scarcely of greater value:

One of the transcendent merits of his playing was the crystal-like clearness which never failed him for a moment, even in the most complicated and, for anybody else, impossible passages ... The power he drew from the instrument was such as I have never heard since, but never harsh, never suggesting 'thumping'. Nor is Schumann's comment to Clara: 'How extraordinarily he plays, boldly and wildly, and then again tenderly and ethereally!'.

Mendelssohn is only slightly more helpful:

[Liszt] plays the piano with more technique than all the others ... a degree of velocity and complete finger independence, and a thoroughly musical feeling which can scarcely be equalled. In a word, I have heard no performer whose musical perceptions so extend to the very tips of his fingers.

In the case of Chopin, the other revolutionary of Romantic piano playing, the ground is slightly firmer. It seems astonishing that, even as a fresh arrival in Paris, he could make the following remark:

If Paganini is perfection itself, Kalkbrenner is his equal, but in a quite different sphere. It is difficult to describe to you his 'calm' – his enchanting touch, the incomparable evenness of his playing and that mastery which is obvious in every note.

Certain characteristics of Kalkbrenner's conservative style lingered, as in Chopin's advice to his young niece Ludwika to keep the 'elbow level with the white keys. Hand neither towards the right nor the left'. Chopin staked out a more individual position in the tantalizing fragment of a piano method, owned and transcribed by Alfred Cortot (now in *US-NYpm*; see J.J. Eigeldinger: *Chopin, vu par ses élèves*, Neuchâtel, 1970, 3/1988; Eng. trans., 1986 as *Chopin: Pianist and Teacher*):

Provided that it is played in time, no one will notice inequality of sound in a rapid scale. Flying in the face of nature it has become customary to attempt to acquire equality of strength in the fingers. It is more desirable that the student acquire the ability to produce finely graded qualities of sound ... The ability to play everything at a level tone is not our object. ... There are as many different sounds as there

are fingers. Everything hangs on knowing how to finger correctly. ... It is important to make use of the shape of the fingers and no less so to employ the rest of the hand, wrist, forearm and arm. To attempt to play entirely from the wrist, as Kalkbrenner advocates, is incorrect.

Chopin recommended beginning with the scale of B major, 'one that places the long fingers comfortably over the black keys. ... While [the scale of C major] is the easiest to read, it is the most difficult for the hands, since it contains no purchase points'. Although Hummel is cited by Chopin as the best source for advice on fingering, his own contributions to this area were bold and innovatory. The 27 studies composed in the decade between 1829 and 1839 (including three for Fétis and Moscheles's *Méthode des méthodes*) are a manifesto for techniques still in widespread use. While Cramer, Clementi and Hummel all include exercises based on arpeggios, Chopin extended their comfortable broken octaves to 10ths and even 11ths in his op.10 no.1; in spite of the easily imagined difficulties of high-speed execution he wrote to the strength of the hand, avoiding, for example, the weak link between the third and fourth fingers. The 'Black-Key' Etude op.10 no.5 teaches the thumb to be equally at home on black or white keys (ex.1). The study in octaves, op.25 no.10, demands the participation (forbidden by Kalkbrenner) of the entire arm. Chopin provided fingering more frequently than almost any other 19th-century composer, adding them not only to autographs and copies but into editions used by students such as Jane Stirling.

Although Liszt's earliest efforts at technical studies were contemporary with those of Chopin, his own 'transcendental' studies, not published in their final form until after the latter's death, are repeatedly influenced by

35. *Liszt playing a grand piano by Ludwig Bösendorfer before Franz Josef in Budapest: painting (1872) by an unknown artist (private collection)*

Ex.1 Chopin: Study in G♭, op.10 no.5

Ex.2 Liszt: Paganini Study no.6

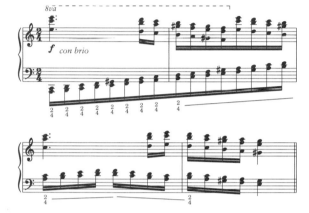

Ex.3 Brahms: Rhapsody in E♭, op.119 no.4

instruments will be possible. In the second half of the 19th century the only constant in this area was probably variety.

The single most important development in the sound of the Romantic piano was doubtless the new emphasis on the sustaining (or damper) pedal. Although Czerny claimed that Beethoven 'made frequent use of the pedals, much more frequent than is indicated in his works', the sustaining pedal was almost universally regarded, up to the first quarter of the 19th century, as a special effect. Writers from Dussek (1796) to Adam (1802) and Hummel (1828) condemned the indiscriminate use of the sustaining pedal, reserving it for passages where an unusual sound was desired (as in the recitative added at the recapitulation of Beethoven's D minor Sonata op.31 no.2; ex.4). Directions for raising the dampers were transmitted in very individual ways by Romantic composers; Schumann was among the first to specify simply 'Pedal' at the head of a passage or movement, while Chopin generally supplied precise and detailed instructions (frequently

Ex.4 Beethoven: Sonata in D minor, op.31 no.2, 1st movt

Chopin's example. The necessity for full involvement of the arm is readily evident from Liszt's fingerings in passages such as ex.2, from the sixth of the Paganini Studies. Brahms, who wrote two sets of variations on the theme of Paganini's A minor Caprice, favoured extensive cross-rhythms and metric shifts in his keyboard music. His specific contributions to piano technique are summarized in the 51 *Übungen* (1893), which feature large leaps, sudden extensions and equally sudden contractions, and the passing of the fifth finger (i.e. the whole hand) over the thumb. This last device is employed freely in both hands of his last piano piece, the Rhapsody op.119 no.4 (ex.3). Because of the lesser leverage available in the actions of the Viennese pianos that Brahms preferred, much of this technical expansion was accomplished on instruments with markedly greater resistance than that of present-day grands. Although data has been published purporting to show a steady increase in resistance through the 1870s, followed by a fall in the 20th century, much more extensive and reliable information will be needed before generalization about the relative touch of differing ignored or suppressed by his 19th-century editors). It is seldom clear whether Chopin intended those passages not marked (such as all but the first three bars of the opening section of the F major Ballade op.38) to be played without the sustaining pedal, or whether it was to be added as general colouring at the performer's discretion.

Liszt's teacher Czerny was one of the first to exchange public performing for full-time instruction, but a dominant specialist teacher did not emerge until after mid-century in the person of Theodor Leschetizky, who numbered among his pupils Paderewski, Gabrilovich, Schnabel, Friedman, Brailowsky, Horszowski, Moiseiwitsch and many more who achieved international fame. Although it became fashionable to speak of the 'Leschetizky method', Leschetizky himself steadfastly refused to freeze his views into print. In searching for the kernel his student Moiseiwitsch observed that 'above all there was his tone. No-one had a tone like his. He never taught us any "secret" there; one just picked up something of the lustre from him'. Perhaps an even greater contribution was Leschetizky's detailed and painstaking approach to the study of repertory, a tradition still pursued in countless masterclasses. Although his English successor Tobias Matthay (of German parentage) produced many books on piano playing, their tortuous language required explications by students (e.g. A. Coviello: *What Matthay meant*, 1948). Matthay's emphasis on muscular relaxation and forearm rotation was valuable as far as it went but has needed modification in the face of more detailed physiological investigations such as those of Otto Ortmann (1929). Ortmann's research led him to the not surprising conclusion that the most efficient playing requires a judicious balance between muscular relaxation and tension.

Few editors of piano music before 1930 approached their task with the reverence for the composer's intentions found in Schenker's 'Erläuterungsausgaben' (1913–21) of the late Beethoven sonatas. It was not only customary but expected that an editor would add his interpretative suggestions to those provided by the composer, rarely bothering to distinguish between the two. Since most 19th-century editors were themselves active performers who frequently claimed direct association with the composer of the repertory being edited, an interventionist attitude was inevitable. The most frequent text changes were the addition of articulation slurs in the music of Bach and Handel – then considered a regular part of the piano repertory – or the exchanging of articulation slurs (especially in the Viennese repertory from Haydn to Schubert) for longer phrase markings. The wholesale addition of dynamic and pedal indications was equally acceptable. In performance the pianist reserved the right to introduce further changes, perhaps restricted to a few discreet octave doublings but perhaps also extending to the interpolation of embellishments and cadenzas. Although it is known that both Beethoven and Chopin objected to such practices, the practices flourished. The most gifted practitioner may have been Liszt, who did not regard even Chopin's music (as the latter bitterly noted) as sacrosanct. Nevertheless, Chopin himself occasionally interpolated embellishments and cadenzas into his music, as shown in an annotated version of op.9 no.2, which shows a variant of the cadenza and an added flourish to the final bar. In later years Liszt renounced his earlier habits, crusading relentlessly over the tinkling of salon music for the acceptance of works by Beethoven, Schubert, Berlioz and others.

The recent vogue for 'Urtext' editions has reaffirmed the importance of the composer in the chain leading to actual performance, but an enthusiasm for textual purity can prove dangerous when accompanied by naivety about the performing conventions and traditions known to contemporary players. In general, variety in articulation persisted much longer than is usually acknowledged, proving essential not only in the music of Haydn and Mozart but also in that of Schubert and Chopin. Romantic composers handled the issues of phrasing and articulation in highly individual ways, frequently alternating between the two types of notation within the same movement, section or even phrase. Because of the complex relationships among primary sources it is rarely a simple matter to establish an 'Urtext', as the comparison of two such editions of almost any work will prove. The realization that not only Mozart and Beethoven but also Chopin and Liszt played on instruments quite different from our own raises the nagging question of whether a modern performer on a modern instrument should attempt to adapt his playing style to that of the earlier piano or should feel free to make changes he feels are necessitated by intervening developments. Indeed, until a significant number of 19th-century instruments by such makers as Graf, Streicher, Broadwood, Bösendorfer, Pleyel, Erard and Steinway are restored to concert condition, there can be little more than speculation as to how they actually sounded, or even whether it would be desirable to include them as a regular part of concert life. Who would advocate playing keyboard music before Dussek (supposed to have been the first to turn his right profile to the audience) with his back to his listeners? Should music before Liszt (the first to perform regularly in public from memory) be played with the music and a page-turner? The renewed interest in historical performance will not make the performer's task less complex; it both increases the number of options and the obligation to become fully informed.

3. 20TH CENTURY.   The development of piano playing in the 20th century received its major impetus from Claude Debussy, who took up where Chopin had left off five decades earlier. Unlike most 19th-century piano composers, Debussy was no virtuoso (few accounts of his playing, and only a fragmentary recording accompanying Mary Garden in a scene from *Pelléas*, survive), but he was on intimate terms with the instrument to which he returned again and again. His piano music is an eclectic blend of Couperin and Chopin (the keyboard composers he admired most) combined with daring new harmonies and textures. The *Suite pour le piano* (1901) proved a landmark in 20th-century pianism, skilfully blending three centuries of keyboard tradition. It should be noted that Debussy achieved his finely graded pedal effects (never specified but always an integral part of the texture) without the benefit of the middle 'sostenuto' pedal found on most modern concert instruments. The capstone to Debussy's piano writing is the set of twelve *Etudes* (1915), fittingly dedicated to Chopin. Beginning with the spoof on 'five-finger exercises' through a chord study, these essays prepare the performer not only for the rest of Debussy's piano music but for much of the keyboard music that followed. Unlike the Romantic composers who cultivated a homogeneous blend, Debussy revelled in

'opposed sonorities', as in his *Etude* of that name (ex.5). In spite of notational fastidiousness in matters of dynamics and phrasing, he elected in the preface of the *Etudes* to grant the performer complete freedom in another important area:

> To impose a fingering cannot logically meet the different conformations of our hands. ... Our old Masters ... never indicated fingerings, relying, probably, on the ingenuity of their contemporaries. To doubt that of the modern virtuosos would be ill-mannered. To conclude: the absence of fingerings is an excellent exercise, suppresses the spirit of contradiction which induces us to choose to ignore the fingerings of the composer, and proves those eternal words: 'One is never better served than by oneself'. Let us seek our fingerings!

The cross influences between Debussy and Ravel may never be entirely sorted out, but it is at least clear that Ravel remained more drawn to the cascades of virtuosity inherited from Liszt. His special fondness for rapid repeated notes (as in *Gaspard de la nuit*) presupposes a crystalline control of touch and nuance essential to all of his music. Although also influenced by Debussy, Bartók travelled an increasingly individual path, beginning with the *Allegro barbaro* of 1911. He is noted for the spiky dissonance that punctuates his keyboard music, but it is too often forgotten that his own playing – both from the recollections of contemporaries and the evidence of numerous sound recordings – was infused with great elegance and rhythmic subtlety. Nevertheless, his frank exploitation of the percussive capabilities of the piano helped pave the way for the experiments with 'prepared' pianos first introduced in Cage's *Bacchanale* (1940) and embraced by many composers since. The placing of small wedges of india-rubber or other materials between the strings to modify the sound is curiously analogous to the mechanical means used in the harpsichord of two centuries

earlier. Other means of tone production, such as tapping the case or the soundboard, have also been added. No standardized notation for transmitting these directions has evolved, varying not only from composer to composer but from work to work by the same composer. These idiosyncratic developments, along with the new interest in historical performance, have helped mitigate the increasing postwar homogenization in the interpretation of the standard repertory.

See also KEYBOARD MUSIC, §III, 6–7.

4. JAZZ PIANO PLAYING.   As an improvised art which is often highly complex, jazz places special demands on piano technique, and jazz pianists have evolved a brand of virtuosity quite distinct from that of the classical tradition. Jazz and blues pianists have not generally set out to acquire an all-embracing technique capable of handling a wide-ranging body of literature; each has concentrated instead on mastering a few technical problems which pertain to his or her individual style, personality and interests. Within these deliberately narrow confines their technical attainments have been quite remarkable, for example the perfect rhythmic separation of the hands required by the boogie-woogie style, the rapid negotiation of wide left-hand leaps in the stride style, or such individual traits as Teddy Wilson's gentle emphasis of inner counterpoints with the left thumb; even classical pianists have difficulty handling these technical problems without sacrificing jazz propulsion or 'swing'. Thus pianists of quite limited technique such as Jimmy Yancey, Thelonious Monk and Horace Silver have developed distinctive and inventive jazz styles, whereas virtuosos such as Friedrich Gulda, André Previn or Peter Nero have not been as successful.

Jazz piano playing evolved early in the 20th century from several separate strands, the most important being ragtime, which was easily within the grasp of the amateur pianist. Its characteristic features – a march-like accompaniment pattern in the left hand against syncopated broken chords in the right – became more technically complex in the 1920s with the Harlem stride school. In a spirit of keen competition its members deliberately set out to dazzle listeners, and especially colleagues, with the speed and daring of their technique. One feature that became almost a fetish was the 'solid left hand', where three-octave leaps at rapid tempo were not uncommon and octaves were regularly replaced by 10ths. By contrast, the right hand played light and feathery passage-work with rapid irregular 3rds, 4ths and pentatonic runs (fingered 3–2–1–2–1). The finest jazz technician, Art Tatum, was especially adept at integrating the hands in rapid passage-work and commanded the admiration of Horowitz; few jazz pianists have been able to match his virtuosity, the only exception perhaps being Oscar Peterson.

A contrasting style arose in the late 1920s with the work of Earl Hines. His 'trumpet style' translated many of the inflections of jazz trumpeting to the right hand of the piano in the form of irregular tremolandos, clusters and punched chords and a thin texture with abrupt *sforzati* and cross-accents. Another development was the boogie-woogie blues style of the 1930s. Here an unwavering rhythmic pattern in the left hand was offset by irregular cross-rhythms and superimposed quintuplet and sextuplet subdivisions in the right, necessitating an absolutely secure rhythmic separation of the hands.

Ex.5 Debussy: Etude X (*Pour les sonorités opposées*)

Animando poco a poco

p expressif et profond

Though crude and homespun by the standards of Tatum and Hines, boogie-woogie nevertheless left its mark on later rhythm-and-blues and rock pianists.

In the 1940s, the 'bebop' style represented a radical rethinking and simplification of previous jazz piano playing. The rhythmic function of the left hand was taken over by the drums and bass of an ensemble and the pianist was left to spin out long lines of 'single-note' melodies (i.e. with one note played at a time) while outlining the harmonic progressions and 'kicking' the beat with sparse chords in the left hand. The emphasis was on a precise and mobile right-hand technique capable of sudden cross-accents, which were generally accomplished by a quick wrist staccato. The inevitable outcome of this approach was an extremely restrained sonority (the pedals were virtually ignored), yet the best bop pianists such as Bud Powell, Thelonious Monk and Horace Silver cultivated a readily recognizable and inimitable touch.

Key figures of the late 1950s to rediscover the different timbres of the instrument were Bill Evans and Cecil Taylor. Evans cultivated an understated technique consisting of blurred pedal effects, careful spacing of notes in a chord ('voicing'), a fondness for low dynamic levels and implied rather than explicitly stated rhythms. Taylor, who had conservatory training, chose avant-garde art music as his starting-point and pursued an extrovert and physically demanding style such clusters, glissandos and palm- and elbow-effects such as those found in Stockhausen's later piano pieces. Both pianists made use of the full tonal range of the instrument, but to completely different ends.

By the later 20th century, emerging jazz pianists were usually trained in a sound classical technique and had a historical grasp of earlier jazz piano playing. This has led to interesting hybrids of classical and jazz technique, especially apparent in the work of Keith Jarrett and Chick Corea. The technical expertise of the players is considerable and almost encyclopedic in scope. The advent of the electric piano has brought a new array of technical problems, such as the handling of the bend bar and the manipulation of volume, wah-wah and other pedals; these have been particularly well mastered by Herbie Hancock and Josef Zawinul. Present-day jazz pianists, however generally prefer the acoustic to the electronic instrument and continue to probe new styles, whether the intricate rhythmic procedures of JoAnne Brackeen and Brad Mehldau, or the virtuoso effusions of Simon Nabatov.

BIBLIOGRAPHY

C.P.E. Bach: *Versuch über die wahre Art das Clavier zu spielen*, i (Berlin, 1753/*R*, 3/1787/*R*); ii (1762/*R*, 2/1797/*R*); Eng. trans. of pts i–ii (New York, 1949, 2/1951)

F.W. Marpurg: *Anleitung zum Clavierspielen* (Berlin, 1755, repr. Amsterdam, 1760/*R*, 2/1765)

D.G. Türk: *Clavierschule* (Leipzig and Halle, 1789/*R*; Eng. trans., 1982)

J.L. Dussek: *Instructions on the Art of Playing the Piano-Forte or Harpsichord* (London, 1796)

M. Clementi: *Introduction to the Art of Playing on the Piano Forte* (London, 1801/*R*)

L. Adam: *Méthode de piano* (Paris, 1802, 2/1805/*R*)

A. Streicher: *Kurze Bemerkungen über das Spielen, Stimmen und Erhalten der Forte-piano* (Vienna, 1802)

J.N. Hummel: *Ausführliche theoretisch-practische Anweisung zum Piano-Forte-Spiel* (Vienna, 1828, 2/1838; Eng. trans., 1829)

C. Montal: *L'art d'accorder soi-même son piano* (Paris, 1836/*R*)

C. Czerny: *Letters to a Young Lady on the Art of Playing the Pianoforte*, ed. and trans. J.A. Hamilton (New York, ?1837–41)

W. von Lenz: *Die grossen Pianoforte-Virtuosen unserer Zeit aus persönlicher Bekanntschaft: Liszt, Chopin, Tausig, Henselt* (Berlin, 1872; Eng. trans., 1899/*R*)

A. Marmontel: *L'art classique et moderne du piano* (Paris, 1876)

A. Fay: *Music-Study in Germany*, ed. M. Fay Pierce (Chicago, 1880/*R*)

F. Kullak: *Aesthetics of Piano-Forte Playing* (New York, 1893)

E. Pauer: *A Dictionary of Pianists and Composers for the Pianoforte* (London, 1895)

C.E. Hallé and M. Hallé, eds.: *Life and Letters of Sir Charles Hallé* (London, 1896/*R*), 57

M. Jaëll: *Le mécanisme du toucher* (Paris, 1897)

C. Weitzman: *A History of Pianoforte-Playing and Pianoforte Literature* (New York, 1897/*R*)

F. Kullak: *Beethoven's Piano-Playing* (New York, 1901)

M. Brée: *Die Grundlage der Methode Leschetizky* (Mainz, 1902, 4/1914; Eng. trans., 1902/*R*)

T. Matthay: *The Act of Touch* (London, 1903)

M. Prentner: *The Leschetizky Method* (London, 1903) [Eng. and Ger.]; also pubd as *The Modern Pianist* (Philadelphia, 1903)

R.M. Breithaupt: *Die natürliche Klaviertechnik* (Leipzig, 1905–6, enlarged 3/1912–22)

J. Hofmann: *Piano Playing* (New York, 1908/*R*)

J. Hofmann: *Piano Questions Answered* (New York, 1909/*R*)

E. Newcomb: *Leschetizky as I Knew him* (New York, 1921/*R*)

J. Lhevinne: *Basic Principles in Pianoforte Playing* (Philadelphia, 1924/*R*1972 with preface by R. Lhevinne)

A. Cortot: *Principes rationnels de la technique pianistique* (Paris, 1928; Eng. trans., 1937)

O. Ortmann: *The Physiological Mechanics of Piano Technique* (London and New York, 1929/*R*)

W. Gieseking and K. Leimer: *Modernes Klavierspiel nach Leimer-Gieseking* (Mainz, 1930, 3/1938 with suppl.; Eng. trans., 1932/*R* as *The Shortest Way to Pianistic Perfection*, *R*1972 with suppl. as *Piano Technique* pts.i and ii)

E. Bodky: *Der Vortrag alter Klaviermusik* (Berlin, 1932)

T. Matthay: *The Visible and Invisible in Pianoforte Technique* (London, 1932, 2/1947/*R*)

A. Cortot: *Cours d'interprétation* (Paris, 1937)

E.J. Hipkins: *How Chopin Played* (London, 1937)

D. Ferguson: *Piano Interpretation: Studies in the Music of Six Great Composers* (New York, 1947)

A. Coviello: *What Matthay Meant* (London, 1948)

A. Foldes: *Keys to the Keyboard* (New York, 1948)

L. Bonpensiere: *New Pathways to Piano Technique* (New York, 1953)

J. Gát: *A zongorajáték technikája* (Budapest, 1954; Eng. trans., 1958, 2/1965, as *The Technique of Piano Playing*)

E. Badura-Skoda and P. Badura-Skoda: *Mozart-Interpretation* (Vienna and Stuttgart, 1957; Eng. trans., 1962, as *Interpreting Mozart on the Keyboard*)

G.G. Neigauz [H. Neuhaus]: *Ob iskusstve fortepiannoy igrī* (Moscow, 1958, 3/1967; Eng. trans., 1973, as *The Art of Piano Playing*)

M. Harrison: 'Boogie Woogie', *Jazz*, ed. N. Hentoff and A. McCarthy (New York, 1959/*R*), 105–35

P. Badura-Skoda, ed.: *Carl Czerny: Über den richtigen Vortrag der sämtlichen Beethoven'schen Klavierwerke* (Vienna, 1963) [annotated reprints from Czerny's *Erinnerungen an Beethoven* and *Vollständigen theoretisch-practischen Pianoforte-Schule* op.500]

H.C. Schonberg: *The Great Pianists* (New York, 1963, 2/1987)

J.F. Mehegan: *Contemporary Styles for the Jazz Pianist* (New York, 1964–70)

J. Kaiser: *Grosse Pianisten in unserer Zeit* (Munich, 1965, 2/1972; Eng. trans., 1971)

H. Grundmann and P. Mies: *Studien zum Klavierspiel Beethovens und seiner Zeitgenossen* (Bonn, 1966)

D. Barnett: *The Performance of Music: a Study in Terms of the Pianoforte* (London, 1972)

K. Wolff: *The Teaching of Artur Schnabel* (London, 1972, 2/1979 as *Schnabel's Interpretation of Piano Music*)

R.R. Gerig: *Famous Pianists and their Technique* (Washington, DC, 1974)

L. Kentner: *Piano* (London, 1976)

J.M. Wildmen: 'The Function of the Left Hand in the Evolution of the Jazz Piano', *Journal of Jazz Studies*, v/2 (1979), 23–39

U. Molsen: *Die Geschichte des Klavierspiels in historischen Zitaten* (Balingen, 1982)

W. Taylor: *Jazz Piano* (Dubuque, IA, 1982)

M. Weiss: *Jazz Styles and Analysis: Piano* (Chicago, c1982)

J. Last: *Interpretation in Piano Study* (Oxford, 1983)

L. Lyons: *The Great Jazz Pianists* (New York, 1983)

H. Neuhaus: *The Art of Piano Playing* (London, 1983)

V. Vitale: *Il pianoforte a Napoli nell' ottocento* (Naples, 1983)

P. Badura-Skoda: 'Playing the Early Piano', *EMc*, xii (1984), 477–80

R.A. Fuller: 'Andreas Streicher's Notes on the Fortepiano', *EMc*, xii (1984), 461–70

P. Loyonnet: *Les gestes et la pensée du pianiste* (Montreal, 1985)

L. Nicholson, C. Kite and M. Tan: 'Playing the Early Piano', *EMc*, xiii (1985), 52–8

J. Ekier: 'Jak grał Chopin?', *Rocznik chopinowski*, xx (1988), 13–25; Eng. trans., as 'Frederick Chopin: How did he Play?', *Chopin Studies*, iv (1994), 9–21

P. Rattalino: *Le grandi scuole pianistiche* (Milan, 1992)

M. Schoenmehl: *Modern-Jazz-Piano: die musikalischen Grundlagen in Theorie und Praxis* (Mainz, 1992)

C. Timbrell: *French Pianism* (White Plains, NY, and London, 1992, 2/1999)

D.E. Rowland: *A History of Pianoforte Pedalling* (Cambridge, 1993)

EDWIN M. RIPIN/STEWART POLLENS (I, 1–2), PHILIP R. BELT, MARIBEL MEISEL/ALFONS HUBER (I, 3), MICHAEL COLE (I, 4, 6), PHILIP R. BELT, MARIBEL MEISEL/GERT HECHER (I, 5), BERYL KENYON DE PASCUAL (I, 7), CYNTHIA ADAMS HOOVER (I, 8), CYRIL EHRLICH/EDWIN M. GOOD (I, 9–10), ROBERT WINTER (II, 1–3), J. BRADFORD ROBINSON (II, 4)

Pianola. A PLAYER PIANO invented in 1895 by E.S. Votey and subsequently made by AEOLIAN (ii). The trademark 'Pianola' (registered in the USA, Great Britain, Canada, South Africa, Australia, Japan and other countries) has become widely known and is frequently misapplied to other makes of player pianos.

FRANK W. HOLLAND

Piano-luthéal. *See* LUTHÉAL.

Piano music. *See* KEYBOARD MUSIC, §III.

Piano orchestrion. A variation of the ORCHESTRION, being a self-playing piano with organ pipes and other devices (such as percussion) added. *See also* MECHANICAL INSTRUMENT.

Piano player [cabinet player, push-up player]. An automatic piano-playing attachment consisting of a self-contained cabinet pushed in front of an ordinary piano and having a row of felt-covered wooden 'fingers' projecting over the keyboard. The cabinet contains a pinned barrel, perforated paper roll or other medium containing the musical programme, which, when set in motion by means of a foot pedal or other mechanism, causes the wooden fingers to depress the keys of the piano keyboard. The piano player developed from the BARREL PIANO, and was the forerunner of the self-contained PLAYER PIANO. *See also* MECHANICAL INSTRUMENTS.

Piano quartet. A composition for piano and three other instruments, usually violin, viola and cello. The form grew out of the accompanied keyboard divertimentos of the 1750s to 80s (*see* ACCOMPANIED KEYBOARD MUSIC) and is loosely related to the early keyboard concerto; many concertos were published for keyboard with two violins and bass instrument (cello). Before about 1780 that scoring was preferred in many quartets; works with viola started to appear in significant numbers from 1780 to 1800, during which time the two-violin scoring was especially common in arranged quartets published in Paris. From 1800 onwards the scoring for viola was more common, although a separate tradition developed of quartets for keyboard with miscellaneous (including wind) instruments.

In England and France, the accompanied sonata tradition (with the keyboard part as the central focus and the strings lightly accompanying) held sway during the early period (works by Tommaso Giordani, Charles Avison, Garth and Pugnani in England; Gaetano Boni, Bonjour and J.A. Bauer in France; Giardini, J.-F. Edelmann, J.S. Schröter, Venanzio Rauzzini in both), while in Vienna and elsewhere concerto-like works by Vanhal and G.C. Wagenseil were widely disseminated. Most works from before 1790 were entitled 'sonata', but 'quartet' in various forms gained favour by 1800. The viola scoring and quartet designation seems to have become standardized first in Vienna during the 1780s in parallel with the increasing use of the piano and the growth there in music publishing.

During the 1780s and 90s, Vienna exhibited something of a flowering of piano quartets. After Mozart's two of 1785 and 1787 (K478 and 493), Hoffmeister followed with a set of six in 1788 and E.A. Förster with six in 1794–6. During the same period large numbers of arrangements of works by Haydn and Pleyel were published in Paris and quickly picked up by other publishers across Europe. The Viennese outpouring continued with works by Paul Wranitzky in 1798, and grew further between 1800 and 1805, with quartets by Beethoven, Eberl, Kauer, Franz Clement, Struck, Tomašek and several others.

Beethoven's three earliest piano quartets date from his youth in Bonn (WOO36, 1785). His op.16 arrangement of his piano and wind quintet is one of many widely disseminated arrangements. Music dealers' catalogues published in 1799 and 1817 listed arrangements of works by Haydn, Mozart and Pleyel amounting to 18 and 51 respectively, many of them originating in Paris and perhaps motivated by a desire to provide new materials for dilettante keyboard players (especially women). Andréin Offenbach produced two different periodical series of keyboard music and chamber music intended for female audiences that included both original and arranged piano quartets (*Journal de musique pour les dames* and *Etrennes pour les dames*).

With changes in musical style, the piano quartet developed and came to have much in common with the PIANO QUINTET. Keyboard style and the disposition of the musical materials among the instruments has generally reflected the overall musical style of the composers writing the pieces. The quartets of Prince Louis Ferdinand of Prussia, who studied the piano with Beethoven, were especially popular. His F minor quartet op.6 was cited by Schumann as one of many influences that shaped his 1829 C minor quartet, along with quartets by Ferdinand Ries, Weber, Dussek, J.B. Cramer and others, and exposure to these works no doubt helped shape his later op.47 quartet. Mendelssohn's three quartets (opp.1–3) exhibit a disposition of the instruments not often found in earlier works (where the basic principle was juxtaposition and alternation of the string body with the piano, as well as of solo with accompanimental textures), wherein the piano sometimes provides only a single line: the musical substance is conveyed by the strings, so that the piano is deployed as just another instrument within the chamber texture, not as one instrument equal in importance to the strings as a group. Brahms also avoids excessive emphasis on a soloistic role for the piano in his opp.25 and 26 quartets, where the string instruments are almost never presented as soloists accompanied by the piano, another texture quite common in earlier works.

By the late 19th century, the piano quartet was established as a genre of serious chamber music, in marked contrast to its beginnings in a tradition originally destined for dilettantes. There are works from this period by Chausson, Dvořák, Fauré, Foote, d'Indy, Raff, Reger, Rheinberger, Saint-Saëns and Richard Strauss. From the 20th century there are works by Bax, Copland, Feldman, Foss, Martinů, Milhaud, Piston, Schnittke and Walton among others, as well as works by Hindemith and Messiaen with clarinet rather than viola. Whereas quartets from 1800 to 1900 generally exhibit a unified conception of style and instrumentation, those of the 20th century exhibit a mixture of styles and approaches to texture and instrumentation almost as various as the number of composers who have turned their attention to the genre. In this move to a more flexible conception of the piano quartet, the 20th century represents something of a return to the state of affairs before 1800, when norms of form, style and instrumentation had yet to be established.

BIBLIOGRAPHY

J. Saam: *Zur Geschichte des Klavierquartetts bis in die Romantik* (Munich, 1933)

W. Altmann: *Handbuch für Klavierquartettspieler* (Wolfenbüttel, 1937)

M.M. Fillion: *The Accompanied Keyboard Divertimenti of Haydn and his Viennese Contemporaries (c1750–1780)* (diss., Cornell U., 1982)

K.H. Stahmer: 'Drei Klavierquartette aus den Jahren 1875/76: Brahms, Mahler und Dvořák im Vergleich', *Brahms und seine Zeit: Hamburg 1983* [HJbMw, vii (1984)], 113–23

B. Smallman: *The Piano Quartet and Quintet: Style, Structure and Scoring* (New York, 1994)

J. Michaels: 'Die ungewöhnliche Entwicklungsgeschichte des Klavierquartetts', *Das Orchester*, xlvi (1998), 10–15

DAVID FENTON

Piano-quatuor. *See* SOSTENENTE PIANO, §3.

Piano quintet. A composition for piano and four other instruments, usually, after 1800, string quartet. Along with the PIANO QUARTET, the form was one of a handful of standardized instrumentations that grew out of the accompanied keyboard sonatas or divertimentos during the second half of the 18th century (*see* ACCOMPANIED KEYBOARD MUSIC) and is loosely related to the keyboard concerto. Some early concertos (such as the three of Mozart's dating from 1782–3) can be performed 'a quattro', which is usually taken to mean by piano and string quartet, but have important formal differences from quintets proper; some quintets however show concerto-derived characteristics. The standard scoring emerged later than for the piano quartet, but some time after the rise of the string quartet in the 1770s and 80s, and it was not until the second quarter of the 19th century that the scoring with string quartet came to eclipse all others.

In all periods, piano quintets were less common than keyboard chamber music for smaller ensembles. Publishers' catalogues issued in the first half of the 19th century list more than twice as many piano quartets as quintets and larger ensembles, and many more piano trios than quartets and quintets combined. The composers of quintets were usually those who also wrote other keyboard chamber music. In the 1770s and 80s piano quintets by J.C. Bach, Tommaso Giordani, Pugnani, Wainwright, Storace and Tindal were published in England; by Tapray

and Hemberger in France; and by Giardini and J.S. Schroeter in both. Many of these works, part of the accompanied sonata tradition, were conceived for amateur players and had relatively simple piano parts. As a more elaborate chamber music style emerged and as the piano emerged as the preferred keyboard instrument, the piano quintet increased in difficulty and complexity. Keyboard parts become more demanding in the period from 1780 onwards. Boccherini's two sets, from the late 1790s, show a well integrated style and the standard instrumentation. But instrumentation varied: J.C. Bach called for flute and oboe in one work, oboe and viola da gamba in another; Giardini used no viola, but a double bass; Hoffmeister used two violas; and among the later composers to use wind instruments are Mederitsch and Bachmann (flute), Triebensee and Eberl (oboe) and Brandl (bassoon). Some composers wrote works exclusively with winds, notably Mozart (K452) and Beethoven (op.16) as well as Grund and Danzi. After 1800, a double bass was sometimes used rather than a second violin, most famously in Schubert's 'Trout' Quintet D667 but also by J.L. Dussek, J.B. Cramer, Hummel and Kalkbrenner. Fewere than half the piano quintets in this period used the scoring of piano with string quartet; most of the composers writing piano quintets were successful as pianists.

By the middle of the 19th century, however, works by Schumann, Spohr and Berwald followed what is now the conventional instrumentation, and the genre took on some of the seriousness of the more prestigious chamber music genres as composers who were not necessarily pianists themselves contributed to the genre. These included works by Borodin, Brahms, Rimsky-Korsakov (for piano and wind instruments), Dvořák, Anton Rubinstein, Saint-Saëns, Franck, Chadwick, Sibelius, Bruch, Stanford, Fibich, Suk, Dohnányi, Vierne, Arthur Foote, Granados and Reger. During this period the model exemplified by Schumann's op.44 or Brahms's op.34, substantial four-movement works, came to be the norm. The perennial challenge of the genre was the relationship between piano and strings, even more so than in the case of the piano quartet with its smaller group of strings. In Brahms's op.34, which had originated as a string quintet and was then arranged as a two-piano sonata before it found its ultimate form, all the instruments are treated as equals, with constant exchange of material and roles, and the piano part has equal weight with that of the string group. Extended solo passages are seldom found, either for strings or for piano.

The Brahmsian, post-Wagnerian style predominated into the early years of the 20th century, with works from Reger, Bartók, Fauré (two), Rheinberger, Webern, Pfitzner, Amy Beach, Dohnányi, Bax and Elgar. Out of the welter of styles that emerged from the experimentation after World War I, a new kind of style divorced from the traditional piano quartet emerged. This is exemplified by Ruth Crawford Seeger's 1929 Suite for Piano and String Quartet, a post-tonal work spare in its writing both for strings and piano, often integrating the piano as just another instrument within the ensemble by using it to declaim only a single line.

More traditional quintets continued to be written, as exemplified in works by Frank Martin, Bloch, Korngold, Goossens, Martinů, Roy Harris and Shostakovich, and after World War II by Piston, Medtner, Bacewicz (two),

Leighton, Milhaud (two), Persichetti, Ginastera, Tcherepnin and others. Most of these works departed from the late 19th-century norm in some way, especially in harmonic language, but in some cases also in the adoption of modernist instrumental techniques such as the incorporation of quarter-tone scales and harmonies and an increase in rhythmic complexity.

In the last quarter of the 20th century, the piano quintet was fertile ground for individual artistic expression, ranging from Rochberg's 1975 quintet, notable for its inclusion of a movement for piano alone (an extreme rarely seen elsewhere in the repertory), to Schnittke's 1976 quintet, which makes significant departures in its harmonic language. The extensive use of quarter tones and closely spaced chords in the strings serves to heighten the contrast between the softer sounds of the strings and the clarity of tone and fixed pitch of the piano. Further still from 19th-century norms is Morton Feldman's 1985 quintet, explicitly identified as for 'Piano and String Quartet', which stretches out over more than an hour, consisting entirely of sustained chords in the strings (often with harmonics), juxtaposed with crystalline rolled chords on the upper two-thirds of the piano keyboard. The musical motion unfolds over so long a time-frame that even the smallest alterations of the harmony and rhythm take on great significance.

BIBLIOGRAPHY

W. Altmann: *Handbuch für Klavierquintettspieler* (Wolfenbüttel, 1937)

M.M. Fillion: *The Accompanied Keyboard Divertimenti of Haydn and his Viennese Contemporaries (c.1750–1780)* (diss., Cornell U., 1982)

N. Simonova: *Fortepiannïy kvintet: voprosï stanovleniya zhanra* [The piano quintet: questions on the formation of the genre] (diss., Gosudarstvennaya Konservatoriya, Kyiv, 1990)

B. Smallman: *The Piano Quartet and Quintet: Style, Structure and Scoring* (London, 1994)

D.W. Fenton: *The Piano Quartet and Quintet in Vienna, 1780–1810* (diss., New York U., in preparation)

DAVID FENTON

Piano roll [music roll]. Perforated paper roll used in the operation of a PLAYER PIANO.

Piano scandé. *See* SOSTENENTE PIANO, §5.

Piano score. *See* SCORE, §1.

Piano trémolophone (Fr.: 'tremolo piano'). *See* SOSTENENTE PIANO, §4.

Piano trio. A composition for piano and two other instruments, usually violin and cello; standard variants include piano with flute and cello (Weber J259), clarinet and viola (Mozart K498, Schumann op.88), clarinet and cello (Beethoven op.11 and Brahms op.114), and violin and horn (Brahms op.40). The genre emerged in the mid-18th century from the Baroque duo and trio sonatas and the keyboard sonata through a shift of emphasis from the string parts to the keyboard (*see* SONATA, §§II and III; ACCOMPANIED KEYBOARD MUSIC).

Obbligato writing (as opposed to continuo parts) for keyboard instruments occasionally appeared in late Baroque chamber music. In a number of J.S. Bach's sonatas, for example (including those for violin, flute or viola da gamba and harpsichord), the texture is predominantly one of three equally important parts, two of them carried by the harpsichord. In his sonatas for harpsichord and violin op.3 (1734) Mondonville shifted the balance in favour of the harpsichord, often reducing the violin to an accompanying role; the change of emphasis was pursued in Rameau's *Pièces de clavecin en concerts* (1741), where the accompanying parts are merely optional. A cello part, often *colla parte* with the keyboard bass line, was sometimes added, particularly by German composers; such accompanied sonatas are the immediate antecedents of the Classical piano trio. In the piano or harpsichord trios of such composers as Johann Schobert (see DDT, xxxix) the harpsichord style of the French school gives way to a keyboard adaptation of the Mannheim style; the keyboard parts no longer relapse periodically into figured bass but are fully written out and dominate the accompanying strings, which, the cello in particular, are rarely genuinely obligatory. Many sets were published with string parts specified 'ad libitum'; sometimes cello parts were not even printed.

In some of Haydn's early piano trios (e.g. HXV:1 in G minor) the musical language recalls Baroque features, but his later examples of the form are as rich in musical substance as the late symphonies and quartets and share their musical language. The relationship between violin and piano is fruitfully exploited in the kind of dialogue anticipated by Mondonville's op.3 or Giardini's op.3 sonatas (c1751), although the cello is rarely emancipated. Haydn's formal and tonal schemes in the piano trios are often boldly imaginative: an example is the B major slow movement in the E♭ trio (HXV:29), which eventually turns to the dominant of the home key and leads directly into the finale.

Trios of this kind were written primarily for pianists, often amateurs. Textural richness could more readily be achieved by the addition of further accompanying parts without prejudicing the simplicity of the piano part with elaborate part-writing. Mozart's early B♭ trio K254, for example, is fundamentally an accompanied sonata. But in his later trios, such as K542 in E, the string parts attain a real measure of independence.

The gradual freeing of the cello part from its historical role as harmonic support continued in the piano trios of Beethoven and culminated in Schubert's trios D898 and 929. Both composers adopted a four-movement scheme for the piano trio, lending their works a scale and importance previously associated with the quartet and the symphony. Single-movement pieces such as Beethoven's 'Kakadu' Variations op.121a for piano trio also began to appear; this work's inclusion of variations for solo piano and for string duo shows how far Beethoven had moved away from the earlier concept of the accompanied sonata. The piano trio became an increasingly popular medium in the early 19th century, and many larger works were arranged for it; Beethoven himself so arranged his Second Symphony.

The piano virtuoso composers of the 19th century, such as Hummel and Chopin, tended to favour their own instrument with a part of great brilliance; the same might be said of Mendelssohn, although his string parts also contribute vitally to the musical substance. Important trios were written by Schumann, Brahms, Smetana, Dvořák and Franck, but even in Brahms's there is sometimes a feeling of striving after effects that might better have been achieved with a larger body of strings – an imbalance resulting partly from the change of musical vocabulary in the 19th century and partly from a development of the capabilities of the piano which quite eclipsed analogous developments in string instruments during the same period. Perhaps it was to compensate for this that composers wrote for all three instruments in an increasingly brilliant style. In the piano trios of Tchaikovsky and Arensky virtuosity is required of all three players, resulting in a kind of composition far removed from the amateur-orientated trios of the 18th century.

In the 20th century the range of trios for the standard ensemble was enlarged, most notably, by Ives (1904–11), Ravel (1914), Rebecca Clarke (1921), Fauré (1922–3), Copland (*Vitebsk*, 1928), Bridge (1929), Martinů (1930, 1950 and 1951), Shostakovich (1944), Alexander Goehr (1966) and Isang Yun (1972–5). There are examples of works which incorporate a single wind instrument by Bartók (*Contrasts*, 1938, clarinet and violin), Lennox Berkeley (1954, violin and horn), Hans Zender (*Trifolium*, 1966, flute and cello), Klaus Huber (*Ascensus*, 1969, flute and cello), and Ligeti (1982, violin and horn). Major technical innovations, applied to a fundamentally conservative medium, included skeletal writing for the piano (with a resultant curtailment of its traditionally dominant role), the provision of lengthy solo sections for strings and piano separately, and the use of string devices such as scordatura tuning, microtones, *col legno* and snap pizzicato. Several piano trios from Germany reveal unusual sources of inspiration, literary and historical: these include Zimmermann's *Présence* (1961), a type of chamber ballet with a speaker, dancers, and three characters (Don Quixote, Joyce's Molly Bloom, and the farcical King Ubu) represented by the trio instrumentalists; Killmayer's *Brahms-Bildnis* (1976), a one-movement work with a 'psycho-programme' which seeks to explore 'the secret inner life-chaos of Brahms'; Wolfgang Rihm's *Fremde Szenen* I–III (1st series, 1982–3), an 'anachronistic' setting prompted by titles in Schumann's diaries; and York Höller's *Tagträume* (1994), comprising seven chamber-style 'tone-poems', based on verses by the Dutch author Ces Nooteboom.

BIBLIOGRAPHY

W. Altmann: *Handbuch für Klaviertriospieler* (Wolfenbüttel, 1934)
G. Cesari: 'Origini del trio con pianoforte', *Scritti inediti a cura di Franco Abbiati* (Milan, 1937), 183–98 [also in *Storia della musica*, iii (Milan, 1941), 465ff]
A. Karsch: *Untersuchungen zur Frühgeschichte des Klaviertrios in Deutschland* (diss., U. of Cologne, 1941)
W. Fischer: 'Mozarts Weg von der begleiteten Klaviersonate zur Kammermusik mit Klavier', *MJb 1956*, 16–34
N. Renner: *Reclams Kammermusikführer* (Stuttgart, 1956, 10/1990, ed. A. Werner-Jensen)
K. Marguerre: 'Mozarts Klaviertrios', *MJb 1960–61*, 182–94
G. Feder: 'Haydns frühe Klaviertrios', *Haydn-Studien*, ii (1969–70), 289–316
H. Hering: 'Das Klavier in der Kammermusik des 18. Jahrhundert', *Mf*, xxiii (1970), 22–37
C. Rosen: *The Classical Style* (London, 1971, enlarged 3/1997), 351ff
R.R. Kidd: 'The Emergence of Chamber Music with Obbligato Keyboard in England', *AcM*, xliv (1972), 122–44
D. Fuller: 'Accompanied Keyboard Music', *MQ*, lx (1974), 222–45
M. Fillion: *The Accompanied Keyboard Divertimenti of Haydn and his Viennese Contemporaries, c.1750–1780* (diss., Cornell U., 1982)
K. Komlós: *The Viennese Keyboard Trio in the 1780s: Studies in Texture and Instrumentation* (diss., Cornell U., 1986)
J.H. Baron: *Chamber Music: a Research and Information Guide* (New York, 1987)
K. Komlós: 'The Viennese Keyboard Trio in the 1780s: Sociological Background and Contemporary Reception', *ML*, lxviii (1987), 222–34
B. Smallman: *The Piano Trio: its History, Technique, and Repertoire* (Oxford, 1990)

MICHAEL TILMOUTH/BASIL SMALLMAN

Piano-violon. *See* SOSTENENTE PIANO, §3.

Piano-vocal score. *See* SCORE, §1.

Piantanida, Giovanni (Gualberto Maria) (*b* Livorno, 11 July 1706; *d* Bologna, on or before 28 Oct 1773). Italian violinist and composer. His father, Giuseppe Maria, was from Livorno and his mother, Maria Maddelena Cavalli, from Florence. In 1735, in the service of the Tsarina Anna Ivanovna, he travelled to St Petersburg with a company of singers to which his wife Costanza (called 'La Pasterla') belonged. He remained there until 1737 as a virtuoso violinist and teacher. During the winter of 1737–8 he performed successfully in Hamburg. With his wife he then went to Holland and in 1739 to London, where, until 1742, he gave numerous concerts, including some with Handel, and published his *VI sonate a tre, due violini e basso e cembalo* op.1 (1742). In 1743 he played at the Concert Spirituel in Paris and in 1744 went to Geneva. He finally settled in Bologna, where, on 10 March 1752, he was appointed *primo violino* of the musical chapel of S Petronio, succeeding Girolamo Nicolò Laurenti, with a monthly stipend of 8 lire.

In 1758 he was nominated to the Accademia Filarmonica. From 1762 until 1764, while still holding the post at S Petronio, he was absent, and his place taken by Antonio Villani. Because of this absence, since he had taken up service elsewhere, Piantanida was dismissed from S Petronio on 16 April the following year, immediately after the election of Giovanni Salpietro to the position. Five years later, on 30 August 1770, Piantanida appeared as a soloist in the closing sinfonia of a solemn mass at S Giovanni in Monte, Bologna. Burney heard him and reported that he played with 'all the fire of youth, with a good tone, and modern taste'. On 10 September of the same year a competition took place for the unusual position of 'capo orchestra of the chapel and *maestro di violino* of this city of Bologna, to continue in this position over the next six years'. Piantanida, having competed with Antonio Palmini from Rome and Gaetano Mattioli from Venice, was announced the winner, with a monthly stipend of 30 lire. This time, however, the trustees, to safeguard themselves from an expected possible repeat of the newly elected maestro's absence, stipulated in the contract that he would receive only 20 lire of his agreed salary, and the other 10 lire would be placed in a special fund that would only be paid out to him at the end of the contract. On 9 October 1770 he was a judge of Mozart's application for entry in the Accademia Filarmonica. On 13 November 1772, apparently in view of his serious health problems, the trustees appointed an assistant, one Cristoforo Babbi, a 'deputy with right to succession'. Less than a year later, on 28 October 1773, the Bologna chronicler Baldassare Carrati, listed him among the dead in the church of S Giorgio in Poggiale, noting that he 'died suddenly in S Petronio on the orchestra steps. He was the famous player'.

Quantz compared Piantanida to Tartini. Opinions on his qualities as a composer, however, are conflicting: Torchi admired the compositional skill of his sonatas while Scheibe and others accused him of plagiarism. A *sonata da camera* for violin and cello exists in manuscript

(*A-Wgm*); six violin concertos, mentioned in the Breitkopf catalogue of 1762, are lost.

His son, Gaetano B. Piantanida (*b* before 1752; *d* Milan, Nov 1835), a pianist and composer, studied music first with his father and then with Mattei at the Liceo Musicale in Bologna. He performed as a pianist in Germany and in Copenhagen, where he published the *Sei ariette italiane* and the *Six romances françaises* sometimes attributed to his father. From 1810 he lived in Milan, where, at the Istituto Musicale, he taught harmony, theory (after 1814) and composition (after 1826); in 1827 he was elected *vice-censore*. He published a set of piano studies, *32 preparazioni alla cadenza combinate in tanti piccoli esercizi* (*c*1823) and a *Salve regina* (*c*1825).

BIBLIOGRAPHY

MooserA

J.A. Scheibe: *Der critische Musikus* (Hamburg, 1738–40, 2/1745/R), ii, 638

J.J. Quantz: 'Labenslauf', in F.W. Marpurg: *Historisch-kritische Beyträge zur Aufnahme der Musik*, i (Berlin, 1754–5/R), 197–250, esp. 221

L. Torchi: 'La musica istrumentale in Italia nei secoli XVI, XVII e XVIII', *RMI*, vi (1899), 693–726; pubd separately (Turin, 1901/R), 199–200

O. Gambassi: *La capella musicale di S. Petronio: maestri, organisti, cantori e strumentisti dal 1436 al 1920* (Florence, 1987), 187–99

O. Gambassi: *L'Accademia filarmonica di Bologna: fondazione, statuti e aggregazioni* (Florence, 1992), 280, 450

GUIDO SALVETTI/OSVALDO GAMBASSI

Pianto (It.). *See* PLANCTUS.

Piatigorsky, Gregor (*b* Yekaterinoslav [now in Dnepropetrovsk], 17 April 1903; *d* Los Angeles, 6 Aug 1976). American cellist and composer of Ukrainian birth. He began to play the cello when he was seven and two years later was admitted to the Moscow Conservatory as a scholarship student of Alfred von Glehn; later he had some private lessons with Brandukov. In 1919 he was invited to join Moscow's foremost string quartet, the Lenin Quartet, led by Lev Tseytlin, and the same year he was appointed principal cellist of the Bol'shoy Theatre orchestra. He left the USSR surreptitiously in 1921, going first to Warsaw, then to Leipzig where he studied with Julius Klengel. In 1924 Furtwängler engaged him as principal cellist of the Berlin PO, a post he left in 1928 to devote himself to a solo career. In Berlin he formed a distinguished sonata partnership with Schnabel, and a trio with Schnabel and Flesch. His American début with the New York PO in December 1929 was the triumphant beginning of an international career. In 1930 he was heard in trios with Horowitz and Milstein, and he formed another trio in 1949 with Heifetz and Rubinstein. Having settled in California, in 1961 Piatigorsky joined Heifetz in establishing a chamber music series in Los Angeles, known as the Heifetz-Piatigorsky Concerts; some of their programmes were heard in New York in 1964 and 1966 and were also recorded. For a number of years he was director of chamber music at the Berkshire Music Center, Tanglewood, and from 1962 until his death was a professor at the University of Southern California, Los Angeles, where his cello classes were renowned; in 1975 a Piatigorsky chair of music was established there. Piatigorsky performed until late in his life, playing at several concerts given for his 70th birthday in 1973, and in London in 1974.

At the height of his career Piatigorsky was acclaimed as a leading cellist of his generation, combining an innate flair for virtuosity with an exquisite taste in style and phrasing; technical perfection was never a goal in itself. His vibrant tone had infinite shadings and his sweeping eloquence and aristocratic grandeur created an instant rapport with his audience. He was at his best in emotional Romantic music, and Strauss commented after hearing him play *Don Quixote*: 'I have heard the "Don" as I thought him to be'. He gave the premières of concertos by Castelnuovo-Tedesco (1935, with Toscanini), Hindemith (1941) and Walton (1957), and the first American performance of Prokofiev's Concerto op.58 (1940). Besides original works for cello (including *Pliaska, Scherzo, Variations on a Theme of Paganini* for cello and piano or orchestra), he published some skilful transcriptions and collaborated with Stravinsky on the cello version of the 'Suite italienne' from *Pulcinella*. There is a rich legacy of Piatigorsky recordings in the solo and chamber music repertory. His autobiography *Cellist* (New York, 1965) has been translated into several languages. Among his numerous awards were several honorary doctorates and membership of the Légion d'Honneur. Piatigorsky owned two magnificent Stradivari cellos, the 'Batta' (1714) and the 'Baudiot' (1725).

BIBLIOGRAPHY

CampbellGC

M. Campbell: 'Professor and Populariser', *The Strad*, civ (1993), 354–7

J.-M. Molkhou: Discography, ibid., 881–4

BORIS SCHWARZ/R

Piatti (It.). *See* CYMBALS.

Piatti, Alfredo (Carlo) (*b* Bergamo, 8 Jan 1822; *d* Crocetto di Mozzo, 18 July 1901). Italian cellist and composer. The son of Antonio Piatti, leader of the Bergamo orchestra, he studied the violin with his father and the cello with his great-uncle, Gaetano Zanetti, whom he succeeded in the theatre orchestra at the age of eight. Recognizing his talent, Mayr allowed Piatti to play a solo at a local festival. After five years at the Milan Conservatory as a pupil of Merighi, he made his début on 21 September 1837, playing his own concerto at a public conservatory concert. In 1838 he made his first tour of Europe. His concerts were artistically successful but financially disastrous, and in 1843, falling ill in Pest, he was forced to sell his cello. In Munich on his way home, he was invited by Liszt to share a concert, which (given on a borrowed cello) proved a great success. Much impressed, Liszt encouraged Piatti to go to Paris; he did so in 1844, making his début on another borrowed instrument. During this visit he was presented by Liszt with a Nicolò Amati cello.

On 31 May 1844 Piatti made his London début and was immediately welcomed as an exceptional artist. Six more concerts were subsequently rapturously received. On 24 June he played in a Philharmonic concert; Mendelssohn (who was conductor and principal soloist) was so impressed that in 1847 he wrote at least part of a cello concerto for him. E. van der Straeten implied that the work was completed, but also stated: 'The manuscript was lost in transit and Mendelssohn never attempted to write it again. Piatti, who knew the manuscript, told the writer that the work did not come up to the violin concerto by a long way'.

In 1844–5 Piatti toured Great Britain, revisited Milan, and spent nearly a year in Russia. In 1846 he settled in London, rejoined the Italian Opera (in which he had first played in 1844), and established his long, influential

Alfredo Piatti

As a result of his distinguished playing and his teaching, Piatti had a profound influence on cello history, especially in England. Playing in the old style, without an endpin, he is said to have had a spectacularly agile technique, superb bow control, perfect intonation and a bright, singing, flexible tone, his interpretations being invariably free from the sentimentality into which so many of his contemporaries were lured.

WORKS
(*selective list*)

2 concs., op.24 (Berlin, 1874), op.26 (Leipzig, 1877)
Concertino, vc, orch, op.18 (Offenbach, 1863)
4 sonatas, vc, pf (Mainz, 1894–6); 2 others unpubd
12 caprices, vc, op.25 (Berlin, 1875)
Arrs. for vc of works by Ariosti, Boccherini, Brahms, Porpora, C. Simpson, Valentini, Veracini, pubd 1881–98

BIBLIOGRAPHY

J.W. von Wasielewski: *Das Violoncell und seine Geschichte* (Leipzig, 1889, enlarged 3/1925/*R*; Eng. trans., 1894/*R*), 110
M. Latham: *Alfredo Piatti* (London, 1901)
W.H., A.F. and A.E. Hill: *Antonio Stradivari: his Life and Work (1644–1737)* (London, 1902/*R*, 2/1909), 127, 137–40, 150
L. Forino: *Il violoncello, il violoncellista ed i violoncellisti* (Milan, 1905, 2/1930/*R*)
B. Weigl: *Handbuch der Violoncell-Literatur* (Vienna, 1911, 3/1929)
E. van der Straeten: *History of the Violoncello, the Viol da Gamba, their Precursors and Collateral Instruments* (London, 1915/*R*), 582–6
F. Niecks: 'Recollections of Violoncellists: Alfred Piatti', *MMR*, xlix (1919), 170–72, 194–6, 317–20

LYNDA MacGREGOR

career in England as performer and teacher. In 1847 he played at a concert given by the Beethoven Quartet Society in Mendelssohn's honour; during 1859 he appeared with Ernst, Joachim and Wieniawski in the society's quartet. That year the Popular Concerts were inaugurated; Piatti was engaged as soloist and as cellist of the quartet led by Joachim, and played regularly at the 'Pops' until his retirement in 1898. On 24 November 1886 he gave the première of Sullivan's concerto at Crystal Palace. He taught privately and as a professor at the RAM; Hausmann, Stern, Becker, Whitehouse and Squire were among his many distinguished pupils. He died at his daughter's home, near Bergamo; his funeral was a public occasion.

An acknowledged connoisseur of instruments, for many years Piatti played on a fine cello by Pietro Giacomo Rogeri, dated 1717; but in 1867 he was given the instrument he had coveted for nearly 25 years – one of Stradivari's finest cellos, made in 1720, and now known as 'The Piatti'. After his death it was bought by Mendelssohn's nephew. It has now been made available on loan to the winner of the Violoncello Society of New York's triennial Gregor Piatigorsky Award.

A composition pupil of Molique (who wrote a concerto for him), Piatti composed a number of works which enjoyed considerable popularity during his lifetime. He also published a good method (London, 1878), and editions of many previously neglected 18th-century works which have now become part of the standard repertory.

Piave, Francesco Maria (*b* Murano, 18 May 1810; *d* Milan, 5 March 1876). Italian librettist. The son of a glassmaker, he studied for the church before obtaining employment as a proofreader. On the failure of his father's business he went to Rome, where he joined a literary circle that included the librettist Jacopo Ferretti, with whom he remained on close terms. He returned to his old position in Venice in 1838, and in 1842 wrote a libretto, *Don Marzio*, for Samuel Levi, but it was not performed. He also provided the third act of Pacini's *Il duca d'Alba*, which Giovanni Peruzzini had been prevented by illness from completing. The autograph survives, heavily corrected by the composer. Piave was recommended to Verdi by Count Mocenigo, and there began a long and successful collaboration from *Ernani* (1844) to *La forza del destino* (1862). During these years Piave supplied Verdi with the texts for *I due Foscari* (1844), *Macbeth* (1847), *Il corsaro* (1848), *Stiffelio* (1850), *Rigoletto* (1851), *La traviata* (1853), *Simon Boccanegra* (1857) and *Aroldo* (1857). Following a period as poet and stage director at La Fenice, Piave moved in 1859 to Milan, where on Verdi's recommendation he obtained the corresponding position at La Scala. On 5 December 1867, on the way to La Scala for a rehearsal, he suffered a stroke which deprived him of speech and movement; he lingered on for nearly nine years in this condition, leaving unfinished a libretto (*Vico Bentivoglio*) for Ponchielli.

Verdi was initially unsure of Piave's abilities and always harried him unmercifully, often having his work revised by others; Piave rewarded him with doglike devotion, and the two remained on terms of sincere friendship. He was frequently summoned to Verdi's side, and they worked together on librettos. Both Verdi and his wife came generously to Piave's aid in his last years.

Throughout his career Piave wrote for many other composers, some well known like Pacini, but most of them insignificant. There is, however, a wide gulf between

Piave's Verdian and non-Verdian librettos. Most of the latter are of poor quality and, with the possible exception of *Elisabetta di Valois* (Antonio Buzzola, 1850; a precursor of *Don Carlos*) and the extraordinary black comedy *Crispino e la comare* (Luigi and Federico Ricci, 1850), might almost have come from another hand: both dramatic tension and crispness of versification are absent. Verdi, however, used to give Piave explicit instructions on what he wanted, and often wrote out in prose the passages he needed to have versified. Piave had a wide vocabulary and a facile pen, and an uncanny ability for turning Verdi's drafts into verse with an economy of words that satisfied Verdi's insistence on brevity and provided him with the striking, illuminating expressions he sought. It was Piave's willingness to meet Verdi's detailed requirements which provided the basis of their work together, and it is on this partnership that his reputation as a librettist must rest.

BIBLIOGRAPHY

GroveO (J. Black) [with full list of works]

G. Pacini: *Le mie memorie artistiche* (Florence, 1875)

E. Checchi: 'Librettisti e libretti di Giuseppe Verdi', *Nuova antologia*, ccli (1913), 529–40

L. Miragoli: *Il melodramma italiano nell'Ottocento* (Rome, 1924)

D. Rosen and A. Porter, eds.: *Verdi's Macbeth* (Cambridge, 1984)

B. Cagli: '"Questo povero poeta esordiente": Piave a Roma: un carteggio con Ferretti, la genesi di Ernani', *Bollettino dell'Istituto di studi verdiani*, x (1987), 1–18

JOHN BLACK

Piazza, Giovanni Battista ['L'Ongaretto'] (*b* Rome; *fl* 1628–33). Italian composer and possibly instrumentalist. According to Pitoni he was a pupil of Vincenzo Ugolini, and he probably continued to live in Rome, though he may have moved to northern Italy, possibly to Venice. His sobriquet is unexplained, though it may mean that he had connections with the Ongaro family, which included the poet Antonio Ongaro. He published at least three books of instrumental music, but of these only *Balletti e correnti … libro terzo*, for viol and continuo (Venice, 1628), survives. Two small books of *Canzonette* by him for solo voice and continuo (both Venice, 1633; facs. of bk2 in ISS, vii) also survive; they contain a total of 20 short pieces (1 ed. in Carter), most of them strophic. The music is unambitious for its date and not very skilful, but it does seem to have been influenced by Venetian songs, which were the most progressive of the time; this suggests that Piazza did have connections with Venice.

BIBLIOGRAPHY

PitoniN

J. Racek: *Stilprobleme der italienischen Monodie* (Prague, 1965)

T. Carter: 'Possente spirto: on Taming the Power of Music', *EMc*, xxi (1993), 517–23

NIGEL FORTUNE

Piazzolla, Astor (*b* Mar del Plata, 11 March 1921; *d* Buenos Aires, 5 July 1992). Argentine composer, bandleader and *bandoneón* player. A child prodigy on the *bandoneón*, Piazzolla and his family emigrated to New York in 1924; in his teens he became acquainted with Gardel, for whom he worked as a tour guide, translator and occasional performer. Piazzolla returned to Buenos Aires in 1937 where he gave concerts and made tango arrangements for Aníbal Troilo, a leading bandleader; he also studied classical music with Ginastera. In 1944 Piazzolla left Troilo's band to form the Orquesta del 46 as a vehicle for his own compositions. A symphony composed in 1954 for the Buenos Aires PO won him a scholarship to study in Paris with Boulanger, who encouraged him in the composition of tangos; the following year he resettled in Argentina and formed the Octeto Buenos Aires and, later, the Quinteto Nuevo Tango, which performed at his own club, Jamaica. Piazzolla left Argentina in 1974, settling in Paris, where he composed a concerto for *bandoneón* and a cello sonata for Rostropovich, among other works.

Piazzolla's distinctive brand of tango, later called 'nuevo tango', initially met with resistance. Including fugue, extreme chromaticism, dissonance, elements of jazz and, at times, expanded instrumentation, it was condemned by the old-guard, including not only most tango composers and bandleaders but also Borges, whose short story *El hombre de la Esquina Rosada* was the basis for Piazzolla's *El tango* (1969); like tango itself, Piazzolla's work first found general approval outside Argentina, principally in France and the USA. By the 1980s, however, Piazzolla's music was widely accepted even in his native country, where he was now seen as the saviour of tango, which during the 1950s and 60s had declined in popularity and appeal. In the late 1980s Piazzolla's works began to be taken up by classical performers, in particular the Kronos Quartet, who commissioned *Five Tango Sensations* (1989). In all he composed about 750 works, including film scores for *Tangos: the Exile of Gardel* (1985) and *Sur* (1987). Shortly before his death, he was commissioned to write an opera on the life of Gardel.

BIBLIOGRAPHY

B. Matamoro: 'Tango: Piazzolla, la vanguardia y después', *Crisis*, i/7 (1973), 21–3

A. Piazzolla: *Astor Piazzolla: a manera de memorias* (Buenos Aires, 1990) [incl. discography]

R. Prince: 'Two to Tango', *Folk Roots*, xi/11 (1990), 31–5

C. Bach: 'A New-Age Score for the Tango', *Américas*, xliii/5–6 (1991), 14–21

CLIFF EISEN

Pibcorn. *See* PIBGORN.

Pibernik, Zlatko (*b* Zagreb, 26 Dec 1926). Croatian composer. After completing his composition studies with Krsto Odak in 1953, he became a professor at the Osijek Music School (1954–60) and then at the Jordanovac experimental elementary school in Zagreb (1960–61), and from 1961 a music editor in the drama studio of Radio-Television Zagreb. He was the artistic director of the Croatian Music Days festival from 1970 to 1979. In 1983 he became editor for *Ars Croatica* and for the complete edition of the works of Josip Slavenski.

Pibernik's music originally had its roots in folksong, especially the partisan songs of World War II. Having written a number of neo-classical and folk-influenced pieces, such as the early piano works and the *Varijacije na narodnu temu iz Slavonije* for orchestra, he developed a strong expressionistic style that showed its full stature in the cantata *Trijumfi, kantata borbe i slave* ('Triumphs, a Cantata of Struggle and Glory', 1959). An imaginative series of five works with the title *Koncertantna muzika* shows his ability to develop his style in new directions. In these pieces the model of the modern chamber concerto is enlarged to include the use of reciters and tape, and the adoption and assimilation of many new techniques. Pibernik has been at the forefront of new music in Croatia, particularly since the late 1960s. He has made extensive use of electronic techniques, mostly in combination with live instrumental resources, and produced a number of dramatic works that cover the borders between music theatre and dramatic oratorio.

WORKS
(*selective list*)

Dramatic: Oni koji ne vide [Those who Do Not See] (musical puppet play), 1963; Sretni leptir [The Happy Butterfly] (musical play), 1964; Veliko modro nebo [The Big Blue Sky] (musical tale), 1964; Kineska priča [Chinese Story] (musical tale), 1965; Nezadovoljina Buba Mara [Dissatisfied Buba Mara] (choreog. musical story), 1965; Legenda o Amoru (ballet), 1972; Igre 'Sfere' [Dances 'Surrounding'] (ballet), 1975; Praznik Ustanka [Revolution Holiday] (staged orat), 1985

Orch: Preludij, passacaglia i fuga, str, 1950; Dječji prizori [Children's Scenes], divertimento, 1951; Simfonijska trilogija, 1952; Capriccio, vn, orch, 1952; Divertimento, chbr orch, 1954; Koncertantna muzika, fl, sax, hp, str, 1956; Na pragu života [On the Threshold of Life], str, 1956; Simfonija mladosti, 1957; Varijacije na narodnu temu iz Slavonije, 1958; Slavonska raspodija, 1958; Simfonijska apoteoza, 1958; Simfonijske metamorfoze, 2 trbn, perc, tambura orch, 1960; Koncertantna muzika no.2, 2 tpt, pf, str, 1961; Ratna priča [Wartime Story], 1964; Conc. for 3 orch, 1968; Simfonija prostora [Space Sym.], 1977; Tri ugodaja [3 Moods], fl, vib, hpd, str, 1991; Album životinja 1 i 2 [Animal Albums 1 and 2], 1992–5; Jednostavna glazba [Primitive Music], pf, orch, 1994; Tranformacije, brass band, orch, 1995

Vocal: Ponoćne ispovijesti [Midnight Confession], A, pf, 1948; Strepnja [Fear], S, pf, 1951; Kantata Osijeku, 1955; Žuti ljiljan [The Yellow Lily], Mez, fl, hp, 1957; Trijumfi, kantata borbe i slave [Triumphs, a Cantata of Struggle and Glory], 10 spkrs, 2 choruses, orch, 1959; Koncertantna muzika no.3, reciter, 12 insts, 1965; Koncertantna muzika no.5 (Conclusa), solo vv, chbr orch, 1970; Kantata o krvi i kamenu [Cantata on Guilt and Stone], 1969; Hvarska madrigaleske [Madrigals from Hvar], 1v, ens, 1986; Preludij za marševe smrti [Prelude for a Funeral March], reciter, chorus, timp, pf, perc, 1995; Molitva [Prayer], S, Mez, org, 1995; partisan and war songs

Chbr: Str Qt, D, 1951, rev. 1983; Tema s varijacijama, str qt, 1954; Divertimento-trio, 1956; Koncepti 2, vn, db, 1974; Slučajnosti [Coincidences], model for improvisation, 1976; Koncepti 4, vc, perc, 1979; Istarske skice [Istrian Sketches], ob, cl, bn, gui, 1991; 4 madrigaleske za kameratu, wind qnt, vn, vc, pf, 1994

Solo inst: Tema s varijacijama, pf, 1948; Sonata eroica, pf, 1950; Sanjarenja [Reverie], pf, 1950; Minijature, pf, 1951; Koncepti 3, db, 1974; Skulpture, pf, 1972

El-ac: Vijesti [Information], reciter, S, ens, tape, 1967; Koncertantna musika no.4, soloists, 4 loudspeakers, 1970–72; Igre u prostoru [Dances in Space], 4-track tape, 1975; Koncepti 5 (Istarski), db, elect, 1982; Elektronske studije, 1987; Post festum, musico-poetic radio play, 1989

Incid music, film scores

Principal publishers: Ars Croatica, Društvo hrvatske kompozitora

BIBLIOGRAPHY

T. Reich: *Susreti sa suvremenim kompozitorima Jugoslavije* [Meetings with contemporary Yugoslav composers] (Zagreb, 1972), 249–50

J. Andreis: *Music in Croatia* (Zagreb, 1974, 2/1982)

A. Koci and others: *Jugoslovanska glasbena dela* [Yugoslav musical works] (Ljubljana, 1980), 399–402

NIALL O'LOUGHLIN

Pibgorn [pibcorn]. A single hornpipe with mouth horn, of Wales. The name is formed from *pib*, meaning pipe, and *corn*, one of many Celtic synonyms for horn or trumpet. The three 18th-century specimens in the Museum of Welsh Life at St Fagans (Cardiff) consist of an elderwood or bone pipe with six finger-holes and one thumb-hole, to which is attached an upcurved bell horn carved with serrated edges and sometimes in an open-jawed shape; a mouth horn is fixed around the reed socket at the top of the pipe. The instruments are between 41 and 52 cm in length. The original reeds of the three extant pibgorns have been replaced; however it is likely (according to W.M. Morris, *British Violin Makers*, London, 1904, 2/1920) that the instruments were fitted with single reeds of cane or quill, like those used in comparable instruments elsewhere.

The importance of the pibgorn in Wales is evident in the earliest writings. The laws of Hywel Dda (codified 940–50) specify that every master employing a *pencerdd* (chief musician) should give him the necessary harp, crwth and pibgorn. However, the instrument was not described in writing until 1775, the date of Daines Barrington's account; the extant specimens also date from that time. References in literary and manuscript sources mention the pibgorn as a pastoral instrument used in the Berwyn Hills (Meirionethshire), in North Pembrokeshire and in the rural communities of mid-South Wales, where farm hands, cattle drovers and shepherds carried their pibgorns to fairs, markets and wakes. By the late 18th century it appears to have been exclusively a rustic instrument, though perhaps more functional than was realized by Edward Jones, who wrote in *Musical and Poetical Relicks of the Welsh Bards* (1794, p.116):

Its tone is medium between the flute and the clarinet, and is remarkable for its melody… it is now peculiar to the Isle of Anglesey, where it is

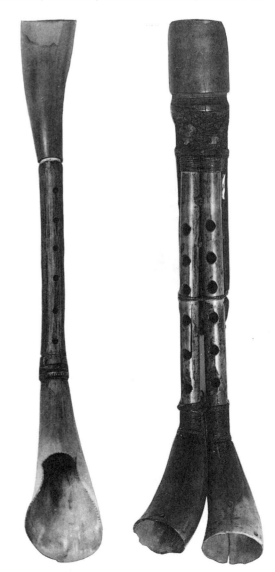

Pibgorn from Anglesey, 18th century (National Museum of Wales, Cardiff)

played by shepherds and tends greatly to enhance the innocent delight of pastoral life.

At that time some pibgorns had a wooden reed-cap instead of a mouth horn, as do surviving specimens of the equivalent Scottish instrument, the STOCK-AND-HORN. The ideal material for the middle section was thought to be bone – particularly the thigh bone (tibia) of a deer. (In lowland Scotland a rustic pipe was made from the thigh bone (stock) of a sheep: it would be reasonable to suggest that the Anglo-Saxon *swegel-horn* (shin-horn) was similar to the pibgorn.) No comparable instruments survive in Ireland, though F.W. Galpin considered that a deer bone now in the National Museum of Ireland may have been the tube of a hornpipe.

In the British Isles there is iconographic evidence from the 15th and 14th centuries. In the Beauchamp window (1447) of St Mary's Church, Warwick, one angel plays a single hornpipe while another holds an identical instrument (see HORNPIPE (i), fig. 1). They resemble surviving pibgorns, apart from having apparently five rather than six finger-holes and straight-cut instead of serrated and jawed bell horns. An illuminated initial in the Beauchamp Psalter (1372) contains the figure of a shepherd outside the walls of Bath, playing what seems to be a single hornpipe with mouth horn. Stone carvings in the roof of the 15th-century parish church of St Eilian, Llaneilian (Anglesey) depict angels playing bagpipes with pipes that end in bells like that of the pibgorn. An early western European depiction is in one manuscript of the late 13th-century *Cantigas de Santa María* (E-E b.I.2), where a double hornpipe similar to the Basque *alboka* is shown. Actual hornpipe fragments survive from a still earlier time. During the latter half of the 20th century, the pibgorn has been revived for use in Welsh folk music.

BIBLIOGRAPHY

D. Barrington: 'Some Account of Two Musical Instruments used in Wales', *Archaeologia*, iii (1775), 30–34

H. Balfour: 'The Old British 'Pibcorn' or 'Hornpipe' and its Affinities', *Journal of the Anthropological Institute*, xx (1890), 142–54

F.W. Galpin: *Old English Instruments of Music* (London, 1910/R, rev. 4/1965/R by T. Dart)

F. Crane: *Extant Medieval Musical Instruments* (Iowa City, 1972), 46

M.S. Defus: 'The Pibgorn', *Welsh Music*, iv/1 (1972–5), 5–10

J. Shoreland: 'The Pibgorn', *Taplas*, no.17 (1986), 15

T. Schuurmans and D.R. Saer: 'The Bagpipe', *Taplas*, 21 (1987), 12–15

JOAN RIMMER/WYN THOMAS

Pibrac [Pybrac], **Guy du Faur de** (*b* Château de Pibrac, nr Toulouse, 1529; *d* Paris, May 1584). French poet, orator and magistrate. He followed a family tradition in pursuing a judicial and diplomatic career: he was *juge mage* at Toulouse in 1557, representative and orator for Gallicanism at the Council of Trent in 1562, *avocat-général* to the Paris parliament in 1565, chancellor to Henri d'Anjou in Poland in 1573, to Marguerite of Navarre in 1578 and to François d'Anjou in 1582. In the mid-1570s he organized the meetings of the Académie du Palais at the request of Henri III. Its meetings seem to have been less concerned with the union of music and poetry (which had been the chief preoccupation of Baïf's Académie a few years earlier) and more with philosophical, rhetorical and ethical subjects.

Pibrac is remembered today for his 126 *Quatrains*, printed between 1574 and 1576. These elevating maxims, taken from Greek and Latin poets or from the books of *Psalms* or *Proverbs*, provided a code for wisdom and virtue which remained an essential part of a moral education right up to the 19th century. They reappeared in innumerable editions during the 17th century, not only in French but in many other languages – English, German, Latin, Greek, even Turkish, Arabic and Persian. During the years of the Counter-Reformation and religious strife they provided French Catholics with a popular rival to the Huguenot Psalter. A single melody was provided for all 126 quatrains when they were published in the *Nouveau recueil et élite de plusieurs belles chansons* (Rouen, *c*1580 RISM *c*1580[8]). It is possible that Pibrac met both Lassus and Boni in Paris in the 1570s (he may have known Boni even earlier, as they were both resident in Toulouse in the 1560s). Lassus's seven four-voice settings of texts by Pibrac were published by Le Roy & Ballard first in 1581 (lost) and reprinted in 1583 (RISM 1583[7]); Boni's settings of all 126 *Quatrains* appeared in 1582. Another complete setting of the *Quatrains*, for two to six voices, that of Paschal de L'Estocart, also appeared in 1582, but this time in Geneva. The musical style is simpler than that of Boni and uses the same melody for several different quatrains. 19 quatrain settings were also published by Jean Planson (1583) and 50 by Jean de Bournonville (1622).

Pibrac's cousin, Jacques du Faur de Pibrac, more commonly called simply 'Du Faur' (*b* Toulouse, *c*1545; *d* after 1574), was an amateur lutenist and composer who collaborated with Baïf and Courville in the early experiments in *musique mesurée*. By 1568 he had graduated in law at the University of Paris and become prior of Saint-Germier, near Muret. All his music is lost.

BIBLIOGRAPHY

J. Claretie, ed.: *Les quatrains de Pibrac, suivis de ses autres poésies* (Paris, 1874)

S. Macary: *Généalogie de la maison du Faur* (Toulouse, 1907)

M. Augé-Chiquet: *La vie, les idées et l'oeuvre de Jean-Antoine de Baïf* (Paris, 1909/R)

A. Cabos: *Guy du Faur de Pibrac: un magistrat poète au XVIe siècle (1529–1584)* (Paris, 1922)

R.J. Sealy: *The Palace Academy of Henry III* (Geneva, 1981)

M.-A. Colin, ed.: *G.Boni: Quatrains du sieur de Pibrac (1582)* (Tours, 2000)

MARIE-ALEXIS COLIN, FRANK DOBBINS

Pibroch [pibrach, pibrugh] (from Scots Gael. *piobaireachd*: 'piping'). A term used since the 18th century to denote that part of the Highland bagpipe repertory known otherwise as *ceòl mór* ('great music') or a single item of that repertory. Daniel Dow in his *Collection of Ancient Scots Music* (1776) refers to 'ports, salutations, marches or pibrachs' and includes the tune *Pibrach Chlann Raonailt*. Devotees of the Highland bagpipe often use the Gaelic spelling *piobaireachd* even when writing in English, as in the dual name adopted in 1903 by a society set up to further the preservation and performance of the repertory: Commun na Pìobaireachd/The Piobaireachd Society. Pibroch is often described as the 'classical' music of the Highland bagpipe to distinguish it from the rest of the piping repertory which consists of dance music, airs and military music (such as 2/4 and 6/8 quick marches).

Its early history is obscure and clouded by many legends of doubtful origin, but it apparently evolved as a form of ceremonial music played at Highland courts, for clan gatherings and as battle music. Hence the main classes of pibroch are the *failte* (salute), *cumha* (lament), *spaidsearachd* (march) and *cruineachadh* (gathering). The last named type usually consists of easily recognized repeated signal motifs. Pibrochs are all in theme and variation form.

Although in earlier times, possibly until the middle of the 18th century, the content and order of the variations were probably somewhat flexible (for example, some early manuscripts indicate frequent restatements of the theme or *urlar*), the variations are now stereotyped and played in a fixed order. This resulted from two important changes: the first was in the mode of transmission (from oral to literary), though, as with other classical traditions, the repertory had always been rigorously taught in a master-pupil situation, often at special 'colleges'; the second was a change in the social function of the pibroch following the effective demise of the clan system during the 18th century. Since 1820 the efforts of individual collectors and organizations, notably the Piobaireachd Society, have resulted in an expansion of the pibroch repertory, not only as a result of the publication and teaching of rare items from manuscript sources, but also by encouraging the composition of new pibrochs through occasional competitions. Beginning in the 1990s, there have been attempts to re-evaluate the received style of playing commonly heard in competitions, the principal platform for the performance of pibroch. This has involved experiments in reviving earlier playing styles as far as can be deduced from manuscripts and oral tradition.

For music examples, further discussion and bibliography *see* SCOTLAND, §II, 6(i).

PETER COOKE

Picada (Sp.: 'pricking' or 'biting'). A kind of staccato bowing. *See* BOW, §II, 2(iv).

Picander. *See* HENRICI, CHRISTIAN FRIEDRICH.

Picañol [Picanyol], **José** (*d* Madrid, ?1769). Catalan composer. In 1734 he was an assistant *maestro de capilla* to Francisco Valls at Barcelona Cathedral. In 1744 he was *maestro* of the Carmelite church in Tarazona and by 17 August 1747 he was *maestro* of the Descalzas Reales convent at Madrid. Musically he was overshadowed by the chief organist of the convent from 1725, José Elías, a fellow Catalan. His comments on the examination music of Juan Nogués (1763, *E-Bc*) show his severe and uncompromising contrapuntal standards. His *Missa 'Ave regina coelorum'* blends a slow cantus firmus with other voices moving in fast functional harmony. He composed eight oratorios for performance by the cathedral chapel at S Felipe Neri, Barcelona; the four works which are dated range from 1720 to 1732. The music preserved at Puebla Cathedral features unbowed violin parts, in which ascending demisemiquaver runs are not uncommon, intermittent organ parts which duplicate the harp continuo, and extended instrumental introductions.

WORKS

Missa 'Ave regina coelorum', D, 8vv, str, hp, org, clarinos, ob; Dixit Dominus, 8vv, str, brass; Laudate Dominum, 8vv, str, brass: all Mexico City Cathedral

Stabat mater, 8vv, vn; Miserere, 4–8vv; Miserere, 12vv, orch, copied 1734; El Sacramento de amor con gloria y pasmo (orat), 11vv, obs, str, org; 5 villancicos, 4–8vv; various motets, cants., orats, 1720–32: all *E-Bc*

8 villancicos, 8–12vv, insts, 1744–7, Puebla Cathedral, Mexico

BIBLIOGRAPHY

SmitherHO, iii; *StevensonRB*
F. Pedrell: *Catàlech de la Biblioteca musical de la Diputació de Barcelona* (Barcelona, 1908–9)

R. Stevenson: 'Sixteenth- through Eighteenth-Century Resources in Mexico', *FAM*, xxv (1978), 156–87, esp. 179–80

ROBERT STEVENSON

Picard. A name held, in one form or another, by many musicians in the 15th century, among them at least three composers. It was sometimes a family name, more often a regional suffix indicating that the holder was from Picardy, in northern France.

(1) Pycard [Picart]   (*fl c*1410). English composer. The lack of an initial for the forename renders identification uncertain, though a possible candidate is a Thomas Pycharde who witnessed a charter together with Thomas Damett, probably the composer, in 1420. One Jehan Pycard alias Vaux was recruited for the chapel of John of Gaunt in 1390/91 and appears to have served until the late 1390s, as he was noted as a principal singing-man in 1392/3 and 1397/8. This may or may not have been the John Vaux resident in the Close of Lincoln Cathedral in 1382 and 1394 (Wathey; Bowers).

After Leonel Power, he is the most fully represented composer in the original layer of the Old Hall Manuscript, and the only English composer in that layer other than Leonel to be ascribed a work other than a concordance outside this source. He is remarkable for the ingenuity and resource of his compositional techniques and has many distinctive features of style. Of his eight surviving works at least four are canons, one of them a double canon. Four canons are ascribed to him in Old Hall, one more to Byttering, and the two remaining canonic works in this source (both Credos) might well be by Pycard. Anselm Hughes first suggested that he might have written the Credo Old Hall no.75, a triple mensuration canon and proportional exercise of truly doctoral complexity, which survives anonymously. The triple canon no.71, copied anonymously, is consistent with the style of Pycard's other canons. His authorship may also be suspected in the case of some canonic compositions with English features preserved in continental manuscripts. Harrison was the first scholar to publish a solution to the Sanctus, no.123, in which the plainchant itself is presented in canon (*NOHM*, iii, pp.103–4). If the canon is two in one, complete consonance results. If a third canonic part is added, as Harrison recommended, this consonance is undermined, and is not much worsened by the addition of further canonic derivations. It is no coincidence that these supernumerary parts fit as well as they do, since the harmonic framework is static and repetitive, and the plainchant has been rhythmicized to fit it. The thin texture of a canon two in one with tenor cannot stand alone, but the missing parts (probably a contratenor and an upper part, which might have been pseudo-canonic) must have been written on the facing page which is now lost. (For a discussion of the incomplete canonic Sanctus see Bent, 1969, pp.87–95, where the possibility is raised of a five-part canonically related cycle by this composer.) The remaining canons by Pycard are indicated either by an explicit Latin directive or simply by a double row of text underlay requiring telescoped performance. No.26 is unusual in applying canon for part of the composition only, and at the interval of a 4th. The Stratford Credo, *GB-STb* 1744, starts with two repeated notes followed by a rest: two of Pycard's Old Hall Glorias open with a descending 5th, each note of which is repeated. It has several melodic and rhythmic features consistent with Pycard's style, but the two surviving parts are not sufficiently legible to determine whether this piece too was canonic, though canon can be made to work for short sections, and the recurrent harmonic pattern of the tenor commends the possibility.

None of Pycard's mass sections can be conclusively related to each other, though technical and stylistic relationships are often evident. (Andrew Hughes, for example, has discussed those of nos.26 and 76.) All Pycard's known works open in C or Ȼ time, often using exceptionally short note values and placing single text syllables on abnormally short notes. His use of *musica ficta*, explicit and implicit, is very bold, often arising from the canonic writing.

All the works that survive intact are in four or five parts, two of them having a solus tenor as an alternative to two of the lower parts. Of the non-canonic pieces only one, no.28, is isorhythmic, and it sets up some complex cross-rhythms between lower and upper parts. The Credo, no.76, uses a unique device, the placing of subsidiary red clefs to indicate 'mental transposition' of the middle section in a manner related to the technique of sights (see Bent, 1969, pp.266–76). Imitation is present in the remaining non-canonic piece, no.78, with some striking involvement of all four parts.

On the Stratford leaf, in the space between discantus and tenor parts, appears the rebus 'long joy long dolour' (with the note form of the long in place of the word 'long' in each case) which calls to mind the appearance of 'long joy bref langour' in the English source of the anonymous and rather later Mass *Quem malignus spiritus*.

WORKS

Edition: *The Old Hall Manuscript*, ed. A. Hughes and M. Bent, CMM, xlvi (1969–72) [OH]

Gloria, 4vv, OH no.26 (except at beginning, 2 middle voices in canon at 4th)
Gloria, 5(4)vv, OH no.27 (upper and lower pairs of voices in canon; alternative solus T provided)
Gloria, 5(4)vv, OH no.28 (isorhythmic, on 'Johannes Jesu care'; alternative solus T provided)
Gloria, 5vv, OH no.35 (2 upper voices in canon)
Credo, 4vv, OH no.76
Credo, 4vv, OH no.78
Credo, inc., *GB-STm* 1744
Sanctus, inc., OH no.123 (2 or more upper voices in canon)

ANONYMOUS WORKS POSSIBLY BY PYCARD

Credo, 5vv, OH no.71 (3 upper voices in canon)
Credo, 5vv, OH no.75 (3 upper voices in complex mensuration canon, including use of blue notation)

BIBLIOGRAPHY

The Picards or Pychards of Stradewy (now Tretower) Castle, and Scethrog, Brecknockshire (London, 1878)
M. Bent: *The Old Hall Manuscript: a Paleographical Study* (diss., U. of Cambridge, 1969)
M.Bent: 'Pycard's Double Canon: Evidence of Revision?', *Sundry Sorts of Music Books: Essays on the British Library Collection presented to O.W. Neighbour*, ed. C. Banks, A. Searle and M. Turner (London, 1993), 10–26
R.Bowers: 'Music and Worship to 1640', *A History of Lincoln Minster*, ed. D. Owen (Cambridge, 1994), 47–76
A.Wathey: 'John of Gaunt, John Pycard and the Negotiations at Amiens, 1392', *England and the Low Countries in the Late Middle Ages*, ed. C. Barron and N. Saul (Stroud, 1995), 29–42
M. Bent: 'A New Canonic Gloria and the Changing Profile of Dunstaple', *PMM*, v (1996), 45–67
For further bibliography *see* OLD HALL MANUSCRIPT.

(2) Biquardus [Wiquardus]   (*fl c*1440–50). Composer of the three-voice hymn settings *In excelsis te laudant* and *Ave stella matutina* in the St Emmeram Choirbook (*D-Mbs* Clm.14274). They may be contrafact songs. On another piece in the same manuscript the ascription 'Biquardus' is erased but still visible. The work is an arrangement of an English song in which the original text *Love woll I* is replaced by *Resurexit victor mortis*. It has no stylistic similarity to the other two pieces. Despite the unison imitation and masterly textural control of these hymns, they can hardly be by the English composer Pycard (1). It is far more likely that Biquardus is Arnold Pickar or Pickhart, a cleric of the diocese of Liège who was in the Kantorei of Emperor Friedrich III from 1444–80, because the pieces appear in the manuscript close to those of another musician working in Vienna, Hermann Edlerawer.

BIBLIOGRAPHY

K. Dèzes: 'Der Mensuralcodex des Benediktinerklosters *Sancti Emmerami* zu Regensburg', *ZMw*, x (1927–8), 65–105
G. Pietzsch: *Fürsten und fürstliche Musiker im mittelalterlichen Köln* (Cologne, 1966)
I. Rumbold: 'The Compilation and Ownership of the "St Emmeram" Codex', *EMH*, iii (1983), 161–235, esp. 176–7

(3) Anthonius Picardus [Picchardo]   (*fl c*1460–70). Composer of the three-voice hymn setting *Phebus astris cum omnibus* in *I-MC* 871 for the feast of St Justina. By comparison with the Biquardus pieces this one is fussy and stumbling, and can scarcely come from the same composer. An 'Ant. Picchardo' sang contrabassus at S Pietro, Rome, in 1507.

Other musicians with the same name include: Andreas Picardi, alias Druet, a singer at the ducal chapel of Savoy from 1 May 1449 to 1 October 1455, who died on 30 October 1455 and whose *exécution testamentaire* was signed by Dufay on 8 November (see Bouquet); Johannes Piccardo [Comitus], who was soprano at the papal chapel in 1478, and was at SS Annunziata, Florence, in 1482, at Florence Cathedral in 1485, and at the chapel of Philip the Fair, 1492–1501 (as Picquet, Picavet); Filippo Pichardo, at SS Annunziata, Florence, in 1482; PIETREQUIN BONNEL 'di Piccardia', at Florence Cathedral, in 1490–92; Jacopo Picchardo, in the papal chapel in 1500; Clyment Thiebault dit Pickart, who sang at the funeral of Philip the Fair, 1507, and whose son Adrien Thiebault dit Pickart (1496–10 March 1546) was in Charles V's chapel, as was Joannes Robert dit Piquart.

BIBLIOGRAPHY

F.X. Haberl: 'Die römische "Schola Cantorum" und die päpstlichen Kapellsänger bis zur Mitte des 16. Jahrhunderts', *VMw*, iii (1887), 189–296
G. van Doorslaer: 'La chapelle musicale de Philippe le Beau', *Revue belge d'archéologie et d'histoire de l'art*, iv (1934), 21–57, 139–61
J. Schmidt-Görg: *Nicolas Gombert, Kapellmeister Kaiser Karls V.: Leben und Werk* (Bonn, 1938)
F. D'Accone: 'The Singers of San Giovanni in Florence during the 15th Century', *JAMS*, xiv (1961), 307–58
R. Gerber: *Zur Geschichte des mehrstimmigen Hymnus* (Kassel, 1965)
M.-T. Bouquet: 'La cappella musicale dei duchi di Savoia dal 1450 al 1500', *RIM*, iii (1968), 233–85
I. Pope and M. Kanazawa, eds.: *The Musical Manuscript Montecassino 871* (Oxford, 1978)

MARGARET BENT (1), DAVID FALLOWS (2, 3)

Picard, Le. *See* LE PICARD family.

Picardia, Petrus de. *See* PETRUS DE PICARDIA.

Picardy third. *See* TIERCE DE PICARDIE.

Picart (i). *See* PICARD, (1).

Picart (ii). *See* L'EPINE family.

Picart [Pickard, Pickart], Nicolas (*b* Paris, 1589/90; *d* after 1648). French violinist, dancing-master and composer. He seems to have been the son of Guillaume Picart, master mat-maker, who had him apprenticed in Paris on 13 August 1602 for six years to the royal violinist Henri Picot; Picart was 12 at the time, and is recorded in Paris on his own account from 1608 to 1618. He is listed as Henrietta Maria's 'mr a danser des filles d h' (dancing-master to the Queen's maids of honour) in 1625, and may have been a member of her household before she came to England as Charles I's bride. He was given a place in the court violin band by a patent dated 22 November 1628, back-dated to Michaelmas 1627, and appears as a treble violin player in lists of the group from 1631 and 1634. He served until the beginning of the Civil War in 1642, when he apparently returned to France and joined the court violin band there. He lived in the Paris parish of St Merri in 1644. In 1646 he was recruited for a violin band at the Swedish court, where he remained until 1649. His only known composition is a rather poor suite of branles in five parts (*S-Uu*, ed. in MMS, viii, 1976).

BIBLIOGRAPHY

AshbeeR, i, iii, viii

J. Ecorcheville: *Vingt suites d'orchestre du XVIIe siècle français* (Paris, 1906/R)

Y. de Brossard, ed.: *Musiciens de Paris 1535–1792: Actes d'état-civil d'après le fichier Laborde de la Bibliothèque Nationale* (Paris, 1965)

M. Jurgens: *Documents du minutier central concernant l'histoire de la musique (1600–1650)*, i (Paris, 1967); ii (Paris, 1974)

P. Holman: *Four and Twenty Fiddlers: the Violin at the English Court 1540–1690* (Oxford, 1993, 2/1995)

P. Walls: *Music in the English Courtly Masque 1604–1640* (Oxford, 1996)

PETER HOLMAN

Piccaver [Peckover], Alfred (*b* Long Sutton, Lincs., 24 Feb 1884; *d* Vienna, 23 Sept 1958). English tenor. He was brought up in New York, where he studied at the American Institute of Applied Music. In 1907 he went to Europe and was engaged for the Neues Deutsches Theater, Prague, where he made his début as Romeo. He continued his studies with Rosario in Milan and Prohaska-Neumann in Prague. In 1910 he joined the Vienna Hofoper, remaining a favourite there until his retirement in 1937. He sang in the first Austrian performances of *La fanciulla del West* and *Il tabarro*. His repertory included Andrea Chénier, Radames, Lohengrin, Walther, Faust, Des Grieux, Don José, Canio, Werther, Florestan and Lensky. He sang with the Chicago Opera from 1923 to 1925 and at Covent Garden in 1924. Piccaver made many recordings, both acoustic and electric, which well convey the velvety yet voluminous character of his voice.

BIBLIOGRAPHY

N. Douglas: *Legendary Voices* (London, 1992), 157–77

HAROLD ROSENTHAL/ALAN BLYTH

Picchardo, Antonio. *See* PICARD, (3).

Picchi, Giovanni (*fl* 1600–25). Italian composer, organist and lutenist. He is depicted playing the lute among three other instrumentalists on the title-page of Fabritio Caroso's *Nobiltà di dame* (Venice, 1600, 2/1605). He was organist of the Cà Grande, Venice, by 1615 according to Romano Micheli (*Musica vaga et artificiosa*, Venice, 1615, p.42), and the title-page of his own *Canzoni da sonar* states that he was still there in 1625. On 5 March

1623 he was also appointed organist of the Scuola di San Rocco, Venice. In 1624 he applied unsuccessfully for the post of second organist at St Marco and was passed over in favour of Giovanni Pietro Berti.

Of Picchi's keyboard works the improvisatory toccata is probably the earliest: it must have been written well before the 1620s, for it appears (in somewhat garbled form) in the *Fitzwilliam Virginal Book*, whose copyist, the younger Francis Tregian, died in 1617. The remaining pieces are dances, eight of which appear in the *Intavolatura di balli d'arpicordo*. In the dedication to the reader Picchi promised 'four books of dances which I shall have printed when I see that this first book proves pleasing to the public'. As no more than the one book has survived, the public's response can only be guessed. Besides a paduana and a large-scale passamezzo paired with a saltarello, it includes several more unusual dances such as a *ballo alla polacha* and a *ballo ongaro*. The keyboard layout consists mainly of a melodic line in the right hand, at times florid and with occasional cadential chords, plus a fuller left-hand accompaniment. But whereas the left-hand part in the earlier dances of Marco Facoli rarely contains more than plain chords, Picchi followed the example of his immediate predecessor Giovanni Maria Radino in occasionally enlivening the texture with simple counterpoint, particularly in the slower movements. His remaining keyboard pieces (in MS at *I-Tn*) are also on a large scale; since two of the three passamezzos have the simpler type of left-hand accompaniment, they at least are probably earlier than the *Intavolatura di balli* (but later than the toccata). Though Picchi was no more than a minor composer, his keyboard works competently met a demand for agreeable and not too difficult music suitable for performing in the home.

Picchi's *Canzoni da sonar*, published in partbook form, consist of 16 canzonas and three sonatas for various combinations of wind and strings: for example one of the two-part works is for two violins or cornetts; another is for violin or cornett with bassoon; and there are two for trombone with violin and two for two violins or horns.

WORKS

Edition: *Keyboard Compositions*, ed. E. Kreider, CEKM, xxxviii (1974)

Intavolatura di balli, hpd (Venice, 2/1621/R)

[19] Canzoni da sonar, a 2–4, 6, 8, bc (Venice, 1625)

Toccata, kbd, *GB-Cfm*; ed. W. Barclay Squire and J.A. Fuller Maitland, *Fitzwilliam Virginal Book* (London and Leipzig, 1894–9/R) i

3 passamezzos (2 with saltarellos), kbd, *I-Tn*

Salve Christe, 1v, bc, in 1625²

BIBLIOGRAPHY

ApelG

D. Arnold: 'Music at the Scuola di San Rocco', *ML*, xl (1959), 229–41

E. Selfridge-Field: *Venetian Instrumental Music from Gabrieli to Vivaldi* (Oxford, 1975, 3/1994)

A. Dell'Antonio: *Syntax, Form and Genre in Sonatas and Canzonas, 1621–1635* (diss., U. of California, Berkeley, 1991)

HOWARD FERGUSON

Picchi, Mirto (*b* San Mauro a Signa, nr Florence, 15 March 1915; *d* Florence, 25 Sept 1980). Italian tenor. He studied in Florence with Giuseppe Armani and Giulia Tess. He made his début as Radames in the season organized by La Scala at the Milan Palazzo del Sport in 1946. At first he sang Verdi and Puccini roles in Italy and abroad, appearing at the Cambridge Theatre, London (1947–8), as the Duke of Mantua, Rodolfo and Cavaradossi, and at the 1949

Edinburgh Festival as Riccardo in *Un ballo in maschera*. In 1952 he sang Pollione at Covent Garden at Callas's London début as Norma. From the early 1950s he specialized in contemporary music, creating roles in Juan José Castro's *Proserpina y el extranjero* (1952, La Scala), Pizzetti's *Cagliostro* (1953, La Scala) and *La figlia di Iorio* (1954, Naples), and Testi's *La celestina* (1963, Florence), and took part in the Italian première of *War and Peace* (1953, Florence). He scored notable successes as Peter Grimes and as Captain Vere (*Billy Budd*), and his large repertory included the Drum Major (*Wozzeck*), Tom Rakewell, Tiresias (*The Bassarids*) and Stravinsky's Oedipus. His last appearance was as Mozart's Don Basilio at La Scala in 1974. Picchi's recordings of Riccardo (Edinburgh), Don Carlos (1951), Pollione (1952) and Jason to Callas's Medea at La Scala (1957) disclose his virtues as a singer of style and subtle artistry seldom found among Italian tenors, compensating for a voice somewhat lacking in native warmth.

ALAN BLYTH

Picchi, Silvano (*b* Pisa, 15 Jan 1922). Argentine composer and music critic of Italian birth. His family emigrated to Córdoba, Argentina, in 1926, then moved to Buenos Aires in 1938. He studied the violin and theory at the National Conservatory in Buenos Aires with (among others) Carlos María Ramos Mejía, Erwin Leuchter and Alberto Ginastera. He has written over 140 symphonic, chamber, choral and solo vocal works, which have won numerous awards in Argentina and elsewhere, including the prestigious National Prize of Argentina. Between 1962 and 1990 he was the music critic for *La prensa* in Buenos Aires. He has also been a professor at the Municipal Conservatory of Music Manuel de Falla in Buenos Aires. Picchi describes himself as a self-taught composer who pursues an independent course. For over ten years, beginning in 1982, he was a member of the Comisión de Música Sinfónica y de Cámara de la Sociedad Argentina de Autores y Compositores de Música (SA-DAIC), which awarded him its Grand Prize in 1991.

WORKS
(selective list)

Orch: Suite irreverente, ballet, 1949; Mozartiana 71, 1971; Serie Argentina, 1974; Sym. no.2, 1977; Sym. no.3, 1979; Segunda serie Argentina, 1983 (rev. 1985); Sym. no.4, 1986; Sym. no.7, 1991; Ates, 1993, Caecilia, 1994
Concs.: Vn Conc., 1952–65; Pf Conc., 1965; Canto a la memoria del soldado muerto, vn, orch, 1982; Velvetpiece, pf, orch, 1992; Invención einsteiniana, vn, orch, 1992
Choral: Ruth (Escena bíblica), solo vv, chorus, orch, 1963; Missa pro populo, chorus, orch, 1971; Invención copernicana, chorus, 1983–4; Mag, choir, 1983; Lamentationes Jeremiae, S chorus, str, 1987
Vocal: Canción de una madre, C solo, fl, pf, 1950; Reminiscencias, 1961; Buenos Aires, 1961; Canciones infantiles, 1962; Solo de muerte, v, gui, 1979; Madrigales, v, gui, 1988
Chbr: Divertimento, 2 gui, chbr orch., 1951; Corda XXII, gui, str qt, 1968; Str Qts nos.2–4, 1979–89; Str Qt no.5, 1984; Conc., vib, 6 aerophones, 1987; Str Qt no.6, 1990; Brass Qnt, 1990; Fractal (Sonatina), vn, pf, 1995
Pf: 3 microdanzas, 1948; Aire popular, 1963; Sonatas nos.1–3 (1980); Pieza para piano en los 12 tonos (Homenaje a Juan Carlos Paz), 1982; Sonata no.4, 1984
Gui: 20 estudios, 1971; Guitangos (2 gui), 1972; Invenciones, 2 gui, 1977

BIBLIOGRAPHY
E. Kay, ed.: *International Who's Who in Music and Musicians' Directory* (Cambridge, 7/1975)

M. Ficher, M. Furman Schleifer and J.M. Furman, eds: *Latin American Classical Composers: a Biographical Dictionary* (Lanham, MD, and London, 1996)

WALTER AARON CLARK

Piccinini, Alessandro (*b* Bologna, 30 Dec 1566; *d* probably at Bologna, *c*1638). Italian lutenist, composer and writer on music. His father, Leonardo Maria Piccinini, his brothers Girolamo and Filippo (see below) and his son Leonardo Maria were all lutenists too. Duke Guglielmo Gonzaga summoned him to his court at Mantua in 1582, but, because of commitments that his father had entered into, he went instead with his family to the Este court at Ferrara, where he and his brothers remained until the death of Duke Alfonso II on 27 October 1597. He then entered the service of Cardinal Pietro Aldobrandini, papal legate at Bologna and Ferrara, who died in 1621. He was a member of the Accademia dei Filomusi, Bologna. Three autograph letters from him survive (in *I-MOs*), one of 31 January 1595 to the Duke of Ferrara and two, of 2 June 1622 and 1 January 1623, to the Duke of Modena.

Piccinini published two volumes, *Intavolatura di liuto, et di chitarrone, libro primo, nel quale si contengano dell'uno, & dell'altro stromento arie, baletti, correnti, gagliarde, canzoni, & ricercate musicali, & altre à dui, e trè liuti concertati insieme; et una inscrittione d'avertimenti, che insegna la maniera, & il modo di ben sonare con facilità i sudetti stromenti* (Bologna, 1623: facs and edn. in AntMI, *Monumenta bononiensis*, ii, 1962) and *Intavolatura di liuto, nel quale si contengano toccate, ricercate musicali, corrente, gagliarde, chiaccone, e passacagli alla vera spagnola, un bergamasco, con varie partite, una battaglia, & altri capricci* (Bologna, 1639), which was seen through the press after his death by his son. The first of these volumes has a particularly important preface in which he described a type of archlute that he claimed to have developed and had made in Padua in 1594. While these claims have aroused scholarly controversy (see in particular Kinsky, and *MGG1*), Piccinini's claim to have invented the archlute – the first extended-neck lute – in the 1590s is plausible, although the extended-neck chitarrone (as a restrung and retuned bass lute) predated his invention. Piccinini also made significant modifications to the chitarrone and according to Giustiniani invented an instrument 'similar to the kithara of Apollo', which he called a pandora and which was perhaps akin to the English *poliphant* (see BANDORA). His preface also includes a short but detailed manual on performance, which advances several interesting ideas: in imitative writing the theme must be played louder so that it stands out; a technique of playing *forte* and *piano* ('ondeggiato') should be adopted in pieces rich in dissonances, which should be highlighted (as, according to him, they were at Naples); embellishments should be left to the taste of the player, but the cadential *gruppo* should always be pronounced, its notes being given equal value, and it should be completed as quickly as possible. Piccinini was a talented composer. His toccatas, which are very varied in form and style, are specially rewarding. The dances have attractive melodies and varied, piquant rhythms; some of them are arranged in suites. Piccinini wrote the music (apparently lost) to *La selva sin amor* (libretto by Lope de Vega Capio), the first opera performed in Spain.

After working with him at the Ferrara court, Piccinini's brothers both went abroad: Girolamo (*b* Bologna; *d*

Flanders, 1615) entered the service of Cardinal Guido Bentivoglio and accompanied him when he was appointed papal nuncio in Flanders, and Filippo (*b* Bologna; *d* Bologna, 1648) worked at the Spanish court until about 1645, when he returned to Bologna; a two-part madrigal by Filippo survives (RISM 1610[17]).

See also ARCHLUTE; CHITARRONE; LUTE, §§5, 6

BIBLIOGRAPHY

MGG1 (O. Mischiati, L.F. Tagliarini)

A. Banchieri: *Discorso di Camillo Scaliggeri della Fratta* (Bologna, 1626), 107f

V. Giustiniani: *Discorso sopra la musica de' suoi tempi* (MS, 1628, *I-La*); pr. in A. Solerti: *Le origini del melodramma* (Turin, 1903/*R*), 111, 124; Eng. trans., MSD, ix (1962), 63–80

A. Masini: *Bologna perlustrata* (Bologna, 1650/*R*), 687

P. Canal: *Della musica in Mantova* (Venice, 1881/*R*), 37, 71

L.F. Valdrighi: *Nomocheliurgografía antica e moderna* (Modena, 1884/*R*), 174, 272

L. Frati: 'Liutisti e liutai a Bologna', *RMI*, xxvi (1919), 94–111

G. Kinsky: 'Alessandro Piccinini und sein Arciliuto', *AcM*, x (1938), 103–18

F. Vatielli: 'L'ultimo liutista', *RMI*, xlii (1938), 469–91

N. Fortune: 'Giustiniani on Instruments', *GSJ*, v (1952), 48

L. de Grandis: 'Famiglie di musicisti del '500. I Piccinini: vita col Liuto', *NRMI*, xvi (1982), 226–32

O. Cristoforetti: 'Les Piccinini et l'évolution organologique du luth à la fin du XVIe siècle', *Musique Ancienne*, no.19 (1985), 4–20

J. Dugot and M. Horvat, eds.: 'Piccinini: Avertimenti, 1623: Les "Avertimenti", ou instructions précédent l'Intavolatura de liuto et di chitarrone, libro primo', *Musique Ancienne*, no.19 (1985), 21–39

PIER PAOLO SCATTOLIN

Piccinni. Italian, later French, family of composers.

(1) (Vito) Niccolò [Nicola] (Marcello Antonio Giacomo) Piccinni [Piccini] (*b* Bari, 16 Jan 1728; *d* Passy, nr Paris, 7 May 1800). He was one of the central figures in Italian and French opera in the second half of the 18th century.

1. LIFE.   Although his father was a musician and his mother the sister of the composer Latilla, he was destined originally for the church. His precocious musical talent, however, would not be suppressed. Most of the information about his early years comes from La Borde. This, the first substantial notice, was incorporated in Ginguené's memorial biography (1800–01); Ginguené claimed to have written the notice for La Borde, in which case it originated from a person close to Piccinni at a time when he could have consulted his subject directly, a possibility strengthened by the precision of some of its details. Thus Piccinni is said to have entered the S Onofrio Conservatory in Naples in May 1742 and to have studied there until 1754, under Leo (*d* 1744), and then under Durante, who had a special affection for him. Prota-Giurleo published documents (1954) that throw doubt on this by indicating that Piccinni became a resident of Naples only in 1753. But Piccinni himself called Durante his teacher in a letter published in Alessandro Manfredi's translation of Fux's *Gradus ad Parnassum* (Carpi, 1761). Further, Villarosa (*RosaM*), using manuscript material left by Giuseppe Sigismondo, wrote that Piccinni was so devoted to his old conservatory that after leaving it he visited it frequently and even acted with some of his old companions in carnival time, as he did in Sigismondo's *I figliastri*.

In 1754 Piccinni embarked on a career of almost exclusively operatic composition. Beginning with comic works, as was the custom, he quickly gained a following in Naples, where the public had formerly been devoted to the *opere buffe* of Logroscino. It was the first of several

1. *Niccolò Piccinni: engraving by J.F. Schröter*

competitive situations that were later to overshadow the career of this amiable and generous man. The extent of his early success and recognition of his promise are reflected in his soon being invited to compose an *opera seria*, his first, for the Teatro S Carlo. This work, *Zenobia* (1756), was also a success and was followed by others, so that in the next few years his output was balanced almost evenly between the serious and comic genres. In 1756 he married one of his singing pupils, the 14-year-old Vincenza Sibilla, who sang his music exquisitely in private but never appeared on the stage. The extent of Piccinni's labours in Italy, his resistance to Burney's inducements to visit England, and his subsequent reluctant move to Paris, were dictated by his desire to obtain the best conditions possible to support seven children (two more died in infancy).

The rapid growth of Piccinni's reputation is indicated by the commission from Rome in 1758 for *Alessandro nelle Indie*. His second Rome opera, *La buona figliuola* (1760), created a furore and began a period in which he remained the undisputed favourite of the reputedly fickle Roman public. Goldoni's rather crude adaptation of Richardson's *Pamela* had already been set by Duni in 1756, with scant success. The charm and vitality of Piccinni's music, which according to Ginguené was composed in only 18 days, conquered Europe; it also won the approval of Jommelli: 'Questo è inventore'. Piccinni produced new works in Rome at every Carnival up to 1773 except that of 1767. His fertility became legendary in a period when prolific operatic composition was by no means unusual. Burney reported Sacchini's assertion that Piccinni had written 300 operas. More sober commentators, like La Borde (or Ginguené), gave a figure of 130 that is not much exaggerated. Piccinni remained in Naples, where Burney met him in 1770 and called him 'a lively agreeable little man, rather grave for an Italian so full of fire and genius'. He was second *maestro di cappella* under Manna at Naples Cathedral, taught singing and on 16 February 1771 was appointed second organist of the royal chapel. Yet from 1758 to 1773 he produced over 30 operas in Naples, over 20 in Rome and others in all the main Italian cities. This period represents the first peak in his achievement.

Piccinni's position in Rome was suddenly undermined by a craze, which began in 1773, for Anfossi, an inferior composer who, although a year Piccinni's senior, had been his pupil in Naples and at first his protégé in Rome. Piccinni's fall was sudden and cruel; a cabal hissed his last Rome opera and he returned to Naples and fell seriously ill. The date of this event is somewhat in doubt. Ginguené placed it in 1775, but Piccinni did not visit Rome in either 1774 or 1775 (1775 was a jubilee year and the theatres were closed). He did go in Carnival 1776, when his *La capricciosa* (also known as *L'incostanza*) followed Anfossi's *La vera costanza* at the Teatro delle Dame, and that seems the most likely occasion for his defeat. However, he maintained his reputation in Naples with a second *Alessandro nelle Indie* and the successful comedy *I viaggiatori*, and by 1776 a superficially more alluring prospect had already arisen in Paris. In 1774 the Neapolitan ambassador there, Caraccioli, had commended Piccinni to the court, and negotiations began. A delay was imposed by the death of Louis XV, but in 1776, with the promise of an annual 'gratification', revenue from his operas and employment by the court and nobility, Piccinni left Naples (16 November). He reached Paris on the last day of the year, suffering cruelly from the cold, knowing no French and with little idea of what was in store. In the subsequent squabbles of the 'Gluckists' and the 'Piccinnists' he almost alone emerged with dignity and credit; his ability to adapt to the needs of the French stage, a far greater adjustment than Gluck had had to make, demonstrates both courage and versatility.

The italophile party was large and influential, and Piccinni soon found friends. Marmontel undertook to adapt the librettos of Quinault and reconcile them to a modern, italianate musical idiom. He had also to coach Piccinni daily in French; if his account is to be trusted, he may be considered as much an accessory to Piccinni's music as Calzabigi was to Gluck's. In 1777 Gluck, who claimed to have discarded his *Roland* on hearing that Piccinni was at work on one, produced *Armide*. Battle was joined over La Harpe's review of it, the performance in Paris of Sacchini's *Olimpiade* and Marmontel's polemical *Essai*. Isolated at the centre of controversy, Piccinni became depressed and expected failure; but *Roland*, performed early in 1778, won both respect and affection from the public. Among the cast even the devout Gluckist Larrivée was won over and performed the title role magnificently.

In 1778–9 Piccinni was engaged to direct a troupe of Italians, giving performances of *opere buffe* at the Académie Royale. The repertory included works by Anfossi, Paisiello, Sacchini and Traetta, as well as Piccinni himself (*Le finte gemelle*, *La sposa collerica*, *La buona figliuola*, *La buona figliuola maritata*, *Il vago disprezzato*). *La buona figliuola* was also known in Paris as *La bonne fille* (Comédie-Italienne, 1771). Later in his Paris sojourn Piccinni was in charge of singing instruction at the Ecole Royale de Musique et de Déclamation, and he undertook

private teaching, including well-paid visits to the country home of La Borde, where he seems to have composed *Didon*. He was evidently used unscrupulously by the court, however, and although from 1783 he was granted a pension, the chief promise of Paris – that he would be better off while writing fewer operas – was hardly fulfilled. He also suffered from the chicanery of the Opéra management. He was promised that his *Iphigénie en Tauride* would be staged before Gluck's; in the event it came two years later and was preceded by the composer's nervous disclaimer of any intention to rival Gluck (*Journal de Paris*, 22 January 1781). Nevertheless it survived the problems of a poor libretto (Dubreuil resisted Ginguené's attempts to improve it) and the drunkenness of Marie-Josephine Laguerre at the second performance. Only when juxtaposed with a revival of Gluck's work was its undoubted inferiority to that masterpiece demonstrated, albeit crudely, by lower receipts. It was favourably received when revived in 1785. In 1783 Piccinni reached his second peak with a highly successful revival of *Atys* and the introduction of *Didon*, which momentarily eclipsed the rising star of Sacchini. The triumph of *Didon* was partly due to the exceptional performance of Mme de Saint-Huberty in the title role; without her at rehearsal it had seemed doomed to failure. Piccinni followed it with two charming and successful comic operas, of which *Le faux lord* would stand revival as well as any of his works.

In 1784 the rival attraction of Sacchini became serious, and Salieri's *Les Danaïdes* diverted attention further from Piccinni. He was no longer a novelty; not only did the dramatically weak *Diane et Endymion* fail to please but he suffered a quite unmerited failure with *Pénélope* in 1785 (it was revived briefly in 1787). A projected revival of *Adèle de Ponthieu*, an inept work which Piccinni had nevertheless revised, came to nothing (1786), and *Clytemnestre*, although rehearsed in 1789, was never performed. Saddened rather than embittered, Piccinni remained generous; he spoke at Sacchini's funeral and proposed an annual concert in memory of Gluck. With the Revolution and the withdrawal of his pension, his position became precarious, and in 1791 he left for Naples, where he was warmly welcomed. In 1792 his daughter indiscreetly married a Frenchman of Jacobin leanings. Deemed guilty by association in the tense and reactionary atmosphere of Naples in those years, Piccinni, on returning from Venice where he had staged two new works, was quite unjustifiably placed under house arrest in 1794. He remained there in indigence and misery for four years, composing psalms, until political changes enabled him to return to France; his family followed as soon as they could. Financially he fared little better; his pension was only partly restored and he was forced to appeal to Bonaparte. By the time he was granted the post of sixth inspector at the Conservatoire he was too ill to benefit from it.

2. WORKS. It has become customary to describe Piccinni in his Italian operas as a composer whose vein was primarily 'the tender, the intimate, the sad and the higher comic', in the words of Abert, who considered him to have been 'made of far finer and more delicate stuff than most of his predecessors and contemporaries'. The same attitude was sometimes expressed at the time; J.A. Hiller wrote (1768) that Piccinni's forte was 'the naive and the tender'. The sentimental role of Cecchina in his most famous opera, *La buona figliuola*, encouraged this view. Contemporary manuscript collections of his arias often

2. Scene from a production of Niccolò Piccinni's 'Atys', by the Stockholm Opera 1784: painting by Pehr Hilleström

show a preference for pieces of this sort, and there seems to be a higher proportion of them in his operas than in most others of the time. While his contemporaries had a special affection for this aspect of his work and prized the elegance and grace of his style in general, most of them also stressed its vigour and variety. Burney called him 'among the most fertile, spirited and original' composers then working, while La Borde (or Ginguené) distinguished in his music 'a vigour, a variety, and especially a new grace, a brilliant and animated style'. Piccinni's style in his Italian operas is in fact a rather complex one in the number and variety of its elements and the sources on which it drew. Its originality, also mentioned by most writers of the time, should probably be seen in the way it brings together, balances and plays off against each other elements of simplicity and complexity in vocal lines, accompanying textures and the relationship between the two. The style (if not the form) of many of Piccinni's pieces from the 1750s would not have seemed out of date even in the 1780s. This is most remarkable in the harmonic layout, the way in which accompaniment motifs are used to clarify and articulate it, and the textures that they result in; all were to remain typical of the Classical style.

Piccinni's gifts included his dramatic imagination and his ability to adapt his music to the situation at hand. While *La buona figliuola* is a masterpiece of sentimental comedy, his intermezzo *La canterina* (1760) is noteworthy for its straightforward comic vigour, particularly in comparison with Haydn's setting of the same text. His French operas, while retaining many italianate characteristics, nevertheless include colourful orchestration, harmonic diversity and an occasional terseness of style that reflect the practices of his adopted country. Although Anfossi's setting of *L'incognita perseguitata* (1773) contains numbers that are more immediately beautiful than anything in Piccinni's setting of 1764 (the heroine Giannetta's aria 'Come figlia ubbidiente' is a case in point), Piccinni avoided the saccharine quality of Anfossi's music by using a wide variety of aria forms and types, and by occasionally introducing rather short arias to punctuate the action. Anfossi's characters are more obviously differentiated than Piccinni's; but Anfossi's attempt to distinguish between them results in rigid stereotypes, whereas Piccinni's characters display much greater flexibility.

Piccinni's music grew over the years in fineness of detail and elegance of craftsmanship, if sometimes falling into the perfunctory. That can be seen in his accompanying techniques, which, starting from the standard mid-century texture in which the first violins doubled the vocal line, developed increasing brilliance of orchestral sound and independence and subtlety of interplay between voice and orchestra. The variety of Piccinni's style found freest play in comic opera, which made rapid shifts of dramatic tone (the sentimental, the mock serious or heroic, the farcical) a basic part of its manner. These were reflected in a tendency to sectionalism in the music, marked by changes of metre, tempo and expressive character. The comic arias fall into many formal patterns, of which the most frequent consists of two complete statements of the whole text in a binary tonal scheme. Piccinni is traditionally said to have introduced the musically and dramatically expansive multi-sectional finale – already found in the operas of Galuppi and other northern composers – into Neapolitan comic opera. His earliest use of it is in his first Roman comic opera, *La buona figliuola*, and he is said to have brought it to Naples in *La furba burlata* (1760), which is lost. Kretzschmar identified Piccinni with what he called the 'rondo-finale', by which he meant not the return of whole sections within the finale (a technique Piccinni was also to use, but which was certainly known before him), but a departure from and return to significant material within a section, linked to characters or dramatic relationships. The layout of the text in some surviving librettos of earlier Neapolitan operas suggests, however, that something of the sort may have been done earlier. In practice his finales, like his comic arias, took many forms.

Although his comic operas have received more attention, Piccinni was also a central figure in *opera seria*, and most of his works in that genre have some remarkable songs. In the first of them, for example, *Zenobia* (1756), the aria 'Ch'io parta?' begins like an accompanied recitative (and away from the tonic of the key) and retains a fluid, declamatory character, although the form remains that of the da capo aria. The duet 'Va, ti consola' does not, as usually happens, have the second singer enter by repeating the first's solo with different words; rather, he makes a strong expressive contrast, changing to the minor, a favourite device of Piccinni's. In the form of his *opera seria* arias Piccinni mostly followed the general trends of the time. In the earliest ones the full da capo predominates, giving way in the course of the 1760s to the dal segno form. In the last to be written before his move to Paris, the dal segno form was replaced by one close to that of sonata form. A few cavatinas appear (arias of one stanza set like the first part of a da capo), and in the 1770s he also used a somewhat related, but more expansive, form (not called cavatina) in which not just one stanza but the complete poem of two stanzas is set straight through and then repeated in a binary tonal layout (a form perhaps taken over from the comic opera).

In his French operas Piccinni used a wide variety of aria forms, including arias in several movements (Dido, 'Vaines frayeurs') and with contrasting middle sections (Sangaride, 'Malheureuse, hélas', *Atys*). He also used arioso and open-ended and incomplete forms. His melodies were much admired, but he was inferior to Sacchini as a lyricist and his line lacks the tautness of Gluck's; too often his cantabile arias seem emotionally uncommitted. Often more effective are arias of that Neapolitan type which, over a motivic continuum, builds a melodic line of short, declamatory phrases (Roland, 'Je me reconnais';

Orestes, 'Cruel et tu dis que tu m'aimes', *Iphigénie*; Diana, 'Cesse d'agiter mon âme', which Grimm called 'the finest aria M. Piccinni has produced in France'). Piccinni's own ideas on proper aria composition are given by Ginguené and are reflected in the writings of N.E. Framery.

In his Italian works Piccinni was already unusually lavish in his orchestration; in France, where a fuller orchestra was normal, he scored more elaborately still and – the opinions of admirers such as Marmontel notwithstanding – more heavily than Gluck. While it is generally true that in Piccinni's French recitatives the orchestral interjections reflect the sense of the words, the effect is often weakened by a rather too regular rhythm of alternation between voice and orchestra and by a certain predictability in the orchestral figures. Piccinni's alternation between short chords and long notes played simultaneously with the voice is often quite dramatic, however, and his occasional use of tremolo accompaniments is effective.

As well as flexible forms and the insertion of ariosos in recitatives, the French heritage in the use of chorus and ballet makes his operas the natural outcome of Encyclopedist principles, embodied particularly in Marmontel's *Essai*: Italian music shorn of its unreasonable excesses, and French forms. In *Roland* the blend is still uncomfortable. The arias and duets are too long for their contexts; but the best recitatives and ariosos, and a few arias, lend

3. Mme de Saint-Huberty in the title role of Niccolò Piccinni's 'Didon', which she created in Paris, 1783: engraving after Dutertre from 'Costumes et annales des grands théâtres de Paris' (1786)

the title role, at least, great dramatic force. The monologue 'O nuit, favorisez mes désirs amoureux' and the subsequent mad scene, in which Piccinni boldly juxtaposed a chord of C major, a dominant ending to an 'open-ended' F minor Allegro, with a Grave in Eb minor, were immediately admired and remain impressive even beside Lully's noble setting. In *Atys* Piccinni achieved a more integrated style, which set the pattern for French opera in the next decade. There are perhaps too many arias (seven for Atys alone), but the interest is better distributed among the roles, as it is in *Iphigénie*. In *Atys* Piccinni rose particularly well to the most French features, such as the dream sequence of song, chorus and dance and the choral lament at the death of Sangaride. He was able, however, to include without incongruity an italianate quartet, in C minor, some 200 bars long; this forms the dramatic crux. The memoirs of André Morellet assert that Piccinni, like Gluck before him, adapted material from his Italian operas in *Atys*. Although his contemporaries favoured *Didon*, *Atys* and *Pénélope* are its equals, and Act 1 of *Pénélope* is perhaps the finest fruit of Piccinni's collaboration with Marmontel.

Piccinni's French operas are not, as has been suggested, an attempt to oppose Gluck's 'reforms' with the methods of Italian *opera seria*. The 'rivalry' is over different musical styles; in dramatic organization both composers represent various possibilities of synthesis between a modern musical language and the traditional French forms. Piccinni was doubtless indebted to Gluck, and his French operas are at least as dramatically engaged as Gluck's. There is, however, more emphasis on musical colour and musical expansion for its own sake. Gluck, belonging to an older generation and inimitable through the very qualities for which he is now most admired, had no very substantial following, although aspects of his works, particularly *Alceste* and the *Iphigénie* operas, contributed to the genre one may term 'Piccinniste opera'. When Piccinni went to France, Italian music was already familiar in concert programmes and had influenced the establishment of a sophisticated *opéra comique* to which, with his skill in handling ensembles and his ability, under-used in the serious operas, to write succinct lyrical numbers, Piccinni contributed as to the manner born. At the Opéra he succeeded where the Frenchman Philidor had not in establishing this synthesis of France and Italy by using the lingua franca of the day in the main national theatre. Thereafter French and German composers increasingly adopted an italianate style. Piccinni prepared the way for Sacchini and ultimately for Spontini, who with his omnipresent lyricism, rich orchestration and dramatic vehemence, is more exactly a Piccinnist than a Gluckist.

WORKS

OPERAS

NC – *Naples, Teatro di S Carlo*
NFI – *Naples, Teatro dei Fiorentini*
NN – *Naples, Teatro Nuovo*
PO – *Paris, Opéra*
RA – *Rome, Teatro Argentina*
RC – *Rome, Teatro Capranica*
RV – *Rome, Teatro Valle*

Le donne dispettose (ob, A. Palomba), NFI, aut. 1754; also as Le trame per amore; La massara spiritosa [not La marchesa spiritosa]
Il curioso del suo proprio danno (ob, 3, Palomba, after M. de Cervantes: *Don Quixote*), NN, carn. ?1755–6, *I-Nc**; rev., with A. Sacchini, as Il curioso imprudente, NFI, aut. 1761
Le gelosie (ob, G. Lorenzi), NFI, spr. 1755; also as Le gelosie, o Le nozze in confusione; *Nc* [mistitled La sponsale di D. Pomponio]
Zenobia (os, P. Metastasio), NC, 18 Dec 1756, *Nc**, *P-La*

Nitteti (os, Metastasio), NC, 4 Nov 1757, *La*
L'amante ridicolo (int, 2, Pioli), NN, 1757, *D-MÜs*; Rome, 1762, *Hs*; also as L'amante ridicolo deluso, *GB-Lbl* (Act 1) [mistitled Il servo padrone], *P-La*; L'amante deluso, *I-Gl*; L'amante ridicolo e deluso, *S-Uu*
La schiava seria (int), Naples, 1757, *D-Bsb*, *Dl*, *F-Pn*, *I-Nc* (? autograph); also as Die Sklavinn, *A-Wn*
Caio Mario (os, G. Roccaforte), NC, ?1757, *I-Nc**, *P-La*
Alessandro nelle Indie [1st version] (os, Metastasio), RA, 21 Jan 1758, *GB-Cfm*, *Lbl*, *I-Nc** *P-La*; also as Alessandro e Poro, *D-ROu*
Madama Arrighetta (ob, 3, Palomba, after Goldoni: *Monsieur Petiton*), NN, aut. or wint. 1758; also as Petiton (int), *I-Nc**; Monsieur Petiton, *P-La* (Act 1)
La scaltra letterata (ob, 3, Palomba), NN, wint. 1758; *I-Nc**, *P-La*; also as La scaltra spiritosa
Gli uccellatori (ob, ? after C. Goldoni), Naples or Venice, 1758
Ciro riconosciuto (os, Metastasio), NC, Nov or 26 Dec 1759, *I-Nc**, *P-La*
Siroe re di Persia (os, Metastasio), Naples, 1759
La buona figliuola [La Cecchina] (dg, 3, Goldoni), Rome, Dame, 6 Feb 1760, *A-KR*, *Wn*, *B-Bc*, *CH-Zz*, *MÜs*, *Rtt* (in Ger.), *F-Pn*, *Po*, *I-Fc* (facs. in IOB, lxxx, 1983), *Gl*, *Mc*, *MOe*, *Nc*, *Rdp*, *Rsc*, *P-La*, *US-Wc*; vs, ed. G. Benvenuti (Milan, 1942); also as La buona figliuola; Cecchina zitella, o La buona figliuola; La buona figliuola zitella; La buona figliuola puta; La baronessa riconosciuta; Cecchina nubile, o La buona figliuola; Das gute Mädchen; The Accomplish'd Maid; Der fromme Pige; La bonne fille
L'Origille (ob, 3, Palomba), NFI, spr. 1760, *I-Nc**, *P-La*
La canterina (int), NFI, spr. 1760, *I-Nc*, *P-La*; perf. with L'Origille
La furba burlata (ob, 3, ?P. di Napoli, after Palomba), NFI, aut. 1760, collab. N. Logroscino; NN, sum. 1762, addns by G. Insanguine; also as I furbi burlati, Naples, 1773, *F-Pn*, *I-Nc**
Il re pastore (os, Metastasio), Florence, Pergola, aut. 1760, *Nc**; Naples, 1765, *P-La*
Le beffe giovevoli (ob, ? after Goldoni), NFI, wint. 1760, aria *I-Nc*
Le vicende della sorte (int, 3, G. Petrosellini, after Goldoni: *I portentosi effetti della madre natura*), RV, 3 Jan 1761, *D-Bsb*, *Dl* (pt. 2), *I-Gl*, *Mc*, *Nc**; also as Le vicende del caso ossia della sorte; Der Glueckswechsel
La schiavitù per amore (int), RC, carn. 1761
Olimpiade [1st version] (os, Metastasio), Rome, Dame, carn. 1761, *Nc**
Tigrane (os, 3, ?after Goldoni's rev. of F. Silvani), Turin, Regio, carn. 1761, *CMbc*, *Nc**, *P-La*; also as Farnaspe, *La*
Demofoonte (os, Metastasio), Reggio nell'Emilia, Pubblico, Fiera (May) 1761, *I-Nc**, *P-La*
La buona figliuola maritata (ob, 3, Goldoni), Bologna, Formagliari, May 1761, *A-Wn*, *D-Dl*, *Mbs*, *F-Pn*, *Po*, *I-Fc*, *MOe*, *Nc*, *P-La*; also as La baronessa riconosciuta e maritata; La Cecchina maritata; La buona moglie
Lo stravagante (ob, 3, A. Villani), NFI, aut. 1761
L'astuto balordo (ob, ?G.B. Fagiuoli), NFI, wint. 1761, *La*; addns by Insanguine
L'astrologa (ob, 3, P. Chiari), Venice, S Moisè, carn. 1761–2, *D-Dl*, *Rtt*, *F-Pn*, *P-La*
Le avventure di Ridolfo (int), Bologna, Marsigli-Rossi, carn. 1762
Artaserse (os, Metastasio), RA, 3 Feb 1762, *D-Hs*, *Mbs*, *F-Pn*, *I-Fc*, *Nc**, *La*, Naples, 1768 *P-La US-Wc*
La bella verità (ob, 3, Goldoni), Bologna, Marsigli-Rossi, 12 June 1762, *I-Nc**
Antigono (os, Metastasio), NC, 4 Nov 1762, *Nc**, *P-La*; rev. RA, carn. 1771
Il cavalier parigino (ob, Palomba), NN, wint. 1762, ? collab. Sacchini
Il cavaliere per amore (ob, 2, Petrosellini), NN, wint. 1762, or RV, carn. 1763, *A-Wn*, *D-Dl*, *I-Nc**, *Rc*, *Tf*, *P-La*(pt 1); also as Il fumo villano
Amor senza malizia (ob), Nuremberg, Thurn und Taxis, 1762
Le donne vendicate (int, 3, after Goldoni), RV, carn. 1763, *A-Wn*, *D-Dl*, *F-Pn* (2 copies), *Po*, *I-Gl*, *Nc**, *US-Bp*, *Wc*; also as Il vago disprezzato [Le fat méprisé]
Le contadine bizzarre (ob, 3, Petrosellini), RC, Feb 1763, or Venice, S Samuele, aut. 1763, *A-Wn*, *D-Dl*, *DS*, *F-Pn*, *I-Fc*, *Nc*, *Rdp*, *P-La** [some MSS ? of 1774 setting], rev. as La contadina bizzarra, Naples, 1774, *I-Nc**; also as La sciocchezza in amore; Le contadine astute; Le villanelle astute
Gli stravaganti, ossia La schiava riconosciuta (int, 2), RV, 1 Jan 1764, *D-Bsb*, *F-Pn*, *GB-Lbl*, *H-Bn* [with addns by Haydn], *I-Nc**,

P-La; also as La schiava, *A-Wn*, *I-Nc*; Gli stravaganti, ossia I matrimoni alla moda; L'esclave, ou Le marin généreux; Die Ausschweifenden

La villeggiatura (ob, 3, ? after Goldoni), Bologna, Formagliari, carn. 1764, qt *Gl*; ? rev. of Le donne vendicate, 1763

Il parrucchiere (int), RV, carn. 1764, *Gl*

L'incognita perseguitata (ob, 3, Petrosellini), Venice, S Samuele, carn. 1764, *A-Wn*, *D-Dl*, *H-Bn* [with addns by Haydn], *I-Gl*, *P-La*

L'equivoco (ob, 3, L. Lantino [A. Villani]), NFI, sum. 1764, *La*(Act 3)

La donna vana (ob, 3, Palomba), NF, Nov 1764, *GB-Lbl*, *P-La*; NF, 1772, *I-Mc*

Il nuovo Orlando (ob, after L. Ariosto), Modena, Rangoni, 26 Dec 1764

Il barone di Toreforte (int, 2), RC, 10 Jan 1765, *B-Bc* (Act 2), *Br*, *D-Dl*, *I-Fc*, *Gl*, *MOo*, *Nc**, *Rdp*, *Tf*, *P-La*

Il finto astrologo (int, ? after Goldoni), RV, 7 Feb or wint. 1765, aria *I-MAc*

L'orfana insidiata (ob), NFI, sum. 1765, addns by G. Astarita

La pescatrice, ovvero L'erede riconosciuta (int, 2, ? after Goldoni), RC, 9 Jan 1766, *A-Wn*, *D-Bsb* (in Ger.), *Dl*, *DS*, *Rtt*, *F-Pn*, *H-Bn*, *I-Fc*, *Gl*, *Nc**, *P-La*, *US-Bp*, *Wc*; also as L'erede riconosciuta; La pescatrice innocente

La baronessa di Montecupo (int), RC, 27 Jan 1766

L'incostante (int, 2, Palomba), RC, Feb 1766, *I-Gl*, *Nc*, *Rdp*, *P-La* (pt 1); also as Il volubile, *D-Dl*, *I-Nc**

La fiammetta generosa [Act 1] (ob), NFI, carn. 1766 [Acts 2 and 3 by Anfossi]

La molinarella (ob, 3), NN, aut. 1766, *F-Pn*, *I-Nc**; also as Il cavaliere Ergasto; La molinara

Il gran Cid (os, G. Pizzi), NC, 4 Nov 1766, *D-Wa*, *I-Nc**, *P-La*, *US-Wc*; also as Il Cid

La francese maligna, Naples, 1766–7, or Rome, 1769

La notte critica (ob, 3, Goldoni), Lisbon, Salvaterra, carn. 1767, *I-Nc*, *P-La*; also as Die Nacht, *D-Bsb*

La finta baronessa (ob, F. Livigni), NFI, sum. 1767, *I-Nc**

La direttrice prudente (ob, 3), NFI, aut. 1767; also as La prudente ingegnosa, aria *Nc*

Mazzina, Acetone e Dindimento (ob), ?Naples, ?c1767

Olimpiade [2nd version] (os, Metastasio), Rome, 1768, *Nc**, *Rdp*, *Rvat*, *P-La*; rev. Naples, 1774, *I-Nc*, *Rsc*

Li napoletani in America (ob, 3, F. Cerlone), NF, 10 June 1768, *B-Bc*, *F-Pn*

La locandiera di spirito (ob, 3), NN, aut. 1768, *I-Nc*

Lo sposo burlato (int, 2, G.B. Casti), RV, 3 Jan 1769, *A-Wn*, *D-Dl*, *F-Pc*, *I-Fn*, *Gl*, *Nc**, *Rdp*, *US-Bp*

L'innocenza riconosciuta (ob), Senigallia, 11 Jan 1769

La finta ciarlatana, ossia Il vecchio credulo (ob), NN, carn. 1769

Demetrio (os, Metastasio), NC, 30 May 1769, *I-Nc**, *P-La*

Gli sposi perseguitati (ob, 3, P. Mililotti), NN, 1769, *I-Nc**, *P-La*, *US-Wc*

Didone abbandonata (os, Metastasio), RA, 8 Jan 1770, *I-Nc**, *Rvat*, *P-La*, *US-Wc*; as La Didone, *I-Mc*

Cesare in Egitto (os, G.F. Bussani), Milan, Ducale, Jan 1770, *F-Pn*, *I-Nc**; also as Cesare e Cleopatra, *P-La*

La donna di spirito (ob), RC, 13 Feb 1770, *F-Pn*

Il regno della luna (ob, not by Goldoni), Milan, Ducale, spr. 1770, *D-Dl*; also as Il mondo della luna, *I-Nc*

Gelosia per gelosia (ob, G.B. Lorenzi), NFI, sum. 1770, *Nc**

L'olandese in Italia (ob, N. Tassi), Milan, Ducale, aut. 1770

Catone in Utica (dm, 3, Metastasio), Mannheim, Hof, 5 Nov 1770, *D-Mbs**, *Rp*, *GB-Lbl* (facs. in IOB, l, 1978), *I-Nc*

Don Chisciotte (ob, Lorenzi, after Cervantes), ? Naples, 1770

Il finto pazzo per amore (ob), ? Naples, 1770

Le finte gemelle (int, 2 or 3, Petrosellini), RV, 2 Jan 1771, *A-Wn*, *D-Dl*, *F-Pn*, *Po*, *GB-Er*, *I-Bc*, *Bsf* (pt 1), *Fc*, *Nc**, *Tf*, *Vc*); also as Le due finte gemelle; Le germane in equivoco

La donna di bell'umore (ob), NFI, 15 May 1771, *Nc**

La Corsara (ob, 3, Lorenzi), NFI, aut. 1771, *Nc**, *US-Wc*

L'americano (int, 2), RC, 22 Feb 1772, *A-Wn*, *D-Dl*, *F-Pn* (1786), *H-Bn*, *I-Fc*; Ratisbana 1776, *D-Rtt* also as L'americano incivilito; L'americano ingentilito

L'astratto, ovvero Il giocator fortunato (ob, 3, Petrosellini), Venice, S Samuele, carn. 1772, *A-Wn*, *D-Dl*, *H-Bn*[with addns by Haydn]; also as Il giocator fanatico per il lotto

Gli amanti dispersi (farsa in prosa and int), NFI, spr. 1772

Le trame zingaresche (ob, Lorenzi), NFI, sum. 1772, *I-Nc**

Ipermestra (os, Metastasio), NC, 4 Nov 1772, *Nc**

Scipione in Cartagena (os, A. Giusti), Modena, Corte, ?26 Dec 1772

La sposa collerica (int), RV, 9 Jan 1773, *D-Dl*, *F-Po*, *I-Nc**

Il vagabondo fortunato (ob, 3, Mililotti), NF, aut. 1773

Le quattro nazioni, o La vedova scaltra (ob, after Goldoni's spoken comedy), ? Rome, 1773

Alessandro nelle Indie [2nd version] (os, 3, Metastasio), NC, 12 Jan 1774, *Nc*, *P-La*

Gli amanti mascherati (ob), NFI, 1774, *I-Nc**

L'ignorante astuto (ob, 3, Mililotti), NFI, carn. 1775, *US-Wc*

Enea in Cuma (parody, Mililotti), NFI, ?spr. 1775, *A-Wn*, *H-Bn*, *I-Nc**

I viaggiatori (ob, Mililotti, ? after Goldoni), NFI, aut. 1775, *Nc*

Il sordo (int), Naples, 1775, *Nc**

La contessina (ob, 3, Coltellini, after Goldoni), Verona, Filarmonico, aut. 1775

La capricciosa [L'incostanza] (ob, 3), RD, carn. 1776, *D-Dl*, *I-Nc*

Radamisto (os, A. Marchi), ? Naples, 1776

Vittorina (ob, Goldoni), London, King's, 16 Dec 1777, *Nc* (Acts 1, 3)

Roland (tragédie lyrique, 3, J.F. Marmontel, after P. Quinault), PO, 27 Jan 1778 (Paris, 1778), vs (Paris, 1883)

Phaon (drame lyrique, 2, C.H. Watelet), Choisy, Court, Sept 1778

Il vago disprezzato (ob), PO, 16 May 1779

Atys (tragédie lyrique, 3, Marmontel, after Quinault), PO, 22 Feb 1780, *D-Ds*, *F-Pn*, *Po*, *I-BGc* (Paris, ?1780, 2/c1783/R1991 in FO, lxv)

Iphigénie en Tauride (tragédie lyrique, 4, A. du Congé Dubreuil), PO, 23 Jan 1781, *D-Mbs*, *F-Po*, *I-Fc*, *Nc* (Paris, 1781/R1973)

Adèle de Ponthieu (tragédie lyrique, J.-P.-A. des Rasins de Saint-Marc), PO, 27 Oct 1781, *F-Lm*, *Pn*, *Po*; rev. or reset, Paris, 1785, unperf.

Didon (tragédie lyrique, 3, Marmontel), Fontainebleau, 16 Oct 1783, *D-Mbs*, *F-Pn*, *Po*, *I-Nc* (Paris, 1783), vs (Paris, 1881/R1970)

Le dormeur éveillé (oc, Marmontel), Paris, Comédie-Italienne, 14 Nov 1783, excerpts pubd separately

Le faux lord (oc, 2, G.M. Piccinni), Versailles, 5 Dec 1783 (Paris, ?1783); also as Der verstellte Lord, *D-Bsb*

Diane et Endymion (os, J.F. Espic Chevalier de Lirou), PO, 7 Sept 1784, collab. Espic, *F-Po* (Paris, 1784)

Lucette (oc, G.M. Piccinni), Paris, Comédie-Italienne (Favart), 30 Dec 1784

Pénélope (tragédie lyrique, Marmontel), Fontainebleau, 2 Nov 1785, *F-Pn*, *Po* (Paris, ?1786)

Clytemnestre (tragédie lyrique, ? L.G. Pitra), Paris, comp. 1787; rehearsed but unperf.

La serva onorata (ob, Lorenzi, after L. da Ponte: *Le nozze di Figaro*), NFI, ?carn. 1792

Le trame in maschera (ob), NFI, carn. 1793

Ercole al Termedonte (os, 2), NC, 12 Jan 1793, *I-Nc*; also as La disfatta delle Amazzoni

La Griselda (eroicomico, 2, ? A. Anelli), Venice, S Samuele, 8 Oct 1793, ?*D-Bsb*, *I-Fc*, *Mc*

Il servo padrone, ossia L'amor perfetto (ob, 2, C. Mazzolà), Venice, S Samuele, 17 Jan 1794

I Decemviri (os), *I-Nc**

Il finto turco (ob), *Nc*

Il conclave del MDCCLXXIV (literary satire, after P. Metastasio), Rome, Dame, carn. 1775

Arias in: Farnace, 1757

Doubtful: Berenice (os, B. Pasqualigo), Naples, c1764; Il conte bagiano (int), RV, carn. 1770; La lavandara astuta (ob), Lucca, Pubblico, aut. 1772; L'enlèvement des Sabines, comp. ? Paris, 1787; Der Schlosser (ob), 1793; Sermiculo (int), *F-Pn*; La pie voleuse, ou La servante de Valaiseau [Die Elster] (ob), *D-Bsb*; Les mensonges officieux (oc, G. Piccinni), Paris; Les fourberies de marine (oc), Paris; I portenosi effetti (ob), *Dl*; Le donne di teatro, arias in *I-Mc* and *Nc*; Amante in campagna (int), *Tf*; Le Cigisbé (oc, 2) (Paris, 1804)

ORATORIOS

Gioas, rè di Giuda, Naples, 1752, *A-Wn**

La morte di Abele (P. Metastasio), Naples, Oratorio de' RR. PP. della Congregazione del Oratorio, ?Lent, 1758, *D-Dhm*, *Dl*, *GB-Lcm*

Sara, ?Rome, ?1769

Gionata (C. Sernicola), Naples, S Carlo, 4 March 1792, *Lcm* (mostly autograph), *I-Fc*, *Nc**

OTHER WORKS

Sacred: Mass, G, 5vv, orch, *I-Nc*; Mass, D, 3vv, *Ac*; Magnificat, c, 3vv, *Ac*; Da te solo, psalm, *Nc*; E quando adempirai, psalm, *Nc*;

Eripe me, psalm, *Nc*; ? La tranquilità, psalm, *Nc*; Beatus vir, *GB-Lbl*; Dixit Dominus, 4vv, *A-Wgm*, ?*GB-Lbl*; Psalm lxxxvii, 1v, vv, orch, 1798, *Lcm**; Pange lingua, *A-Wn*; Tantum ergo, *Wn*; arr. of C.-H. Plantade: Regina coeli laetere, *F-Lm*

Other vocal: La pace fra Giunone ed Alcide (cant.), 3vv, Naples, S Carlo, 1765; Cant. [Pallade, Teseo, Alcide], 3vv, Naples, S Carlo, 1767; Cant. [Giove, Diane, Mercurio], ?Naples, end 1769, *I-Nc*; Giove piacevole nella regia di Partenope, ?Naples, 1771, *Nc*; Prologo e cantata [Giove, L'Aurora, La dea del piacere] (? S. Zini), ?Naples, 1776, *Nc*; Giove revotato (cant.), 3vv, Naples, S Carlino, 1790; Arco di amore (cant., D. Piccinni), 3vv, 1797; Cantata per gala per Ferdinando IV, Naples, *Nc*; 6 canzonets, 2vv (London, n.d.); Il gran re perdona (licenza), S, orch, *Bc*; Hymene e l'I Iymen (coro), for wedding celebrations, *US-Bp*; Solfeggi, S, bc, ?*I-Nc*; frags. of vocal music, *A-Wn**

Inst: Fl conc., D, ed. in Diletto musicale, dcccvii (*c*1981); 3 sonatas, 1 toccata, hpd, *F-Pc*; Sonata a tre motivi, hpd, *GB-Cfm*; Pièce, E, hpd, *F-Pn*; Sinfonia, B♭, hpd/org, *I-Bsf*; sinfonie, ovs. in many libraries, incl. *CH-Bu, Zz, D-Bsb, SWl, E-Mn, Mp, I-Fc, S-Uu*

(2) Luigi [Lodovico] **Piccinni**   (*b* ? Rome or Naples, 1764; *d* Passy, nr Paris, 31 July 1827). He was the third son (the second to survive) of (1) Niccolò Piccinni, who was his teacher. When his father moved to Paris in 1776, Luigi remained in Naples, joining his parents about 1782; he published a set of piano sonatas with a toccata (Paris, 1782). In 1784 his first *opéra comique* was performed in Paris, followed by several others until 1790. In 1791 he returned with his father to Naples and had comic operas performed in several Italian cities during the period 1793–5. From 1796 to 1801 he was Kapellmeister at the Swedish court in Stockholm. He returned to Paris in 1801 and had several *opéras comiques* performed there, 1804–9; in 1810 he suffered a failure at the Opéra with *Hippomène et Atalante*. He thereafter confined his activities to the teaching of singing, except for one last unsuccessful *opéra comique* in 1819.

Luigi Piccinni seems to have been generally regarded as a mediocre composer. Fétis wrote that he was 'devoid of genius and even of that elegant taste that in the theatre sometimes takes its place'. None of his operas was a great success, although some were published, along with songs and piano pieces.

For list of stage works see *GroveO*.

(3) Louis Alexandre [Luigi Alessandro; Lodovico Alessandro] **Piccinni**   (*b* Paris, 10 Sept 1779; *d* Paris, 24 April 1850). He was the illegitimate son of Giuseppe Piccinni (*b* 1758), (1) Niccolò Piccinni's eldest child, who wrote the librettos of two *opéras comiques* composed by his father. Louis studied composition with Le Sueur and had advice from his grandfather on his return to France (1799). He became a skilful accompanist and rehearsal pianist, serving in that capacity first at the Théâtre Feydeau and from 1802 at the Opéra. He was also conductor at the Théâtre de la Porte-St-Martin (1803–7, 1810–16), second accompanist of the imperial chapel from 1804 (in a letter to the editor of the *Courier des Spectacles*, published on 20 Feb 1804, he signed himself 'Accompagnateur du Théâtre des Arts'), and from 1814 chief accompanist of the royal chapel and accompanist of the dauphine's private music from 1818. In 1816 he became third chorus master at the Opéra, later second and finally chief. He was accompanist at the Théâtre du Gymnase from 1820 to 1824, when he was put in charge of stage design at the Opéra, but he was dismissed from there in 1826. In 1827 he managed an unsuccessful theatre season in Boulogne and then was a teacher in Paris (to 1836), Boulogne, Toulouse and Strasbourg. In 1849 he returned to Paris.

A highly prolific composer, Piccinni was best known for his music for a large number of melodramas and ballets at the Porte-St-Martin and other popular Paris theatres.

For list of stage works see *GroveO*.

BIBLIOGRAPHY

BurneyFI; FétisB; La BordeE; RosaM

J.A. Hiller: 'Sechste Fortsetzung des Entwurfs einer musikalischen Bibliothek', *Wöchentliche Nachrichten und Anmerkungen*, iii (1768), 57–64

J.F. Marmontel: *Essai sur les révolutions de la musique en France* (Paris, 1777)

G.M. Leblond: *Mémoires pour servir à l'histoire de la révolution opérée dans la musique par M. le Chevalier Gluck* (Naples and Paris, 1781)

P.L. Ginguené: 'Dessein', 'France', *Encyclopédie méthodique: musique*, ed. N.E. Framery and P.L. Ginguené, i (Paris, 1791)

P.L. Ginguené: *Notice sur la vie et les ouvrages de Nicolas Piccinni* (Paris [1800–01])

J.F. Marmontel: *Mémoires* (Paris, 1804)

G. le Brisoys Desnoiresterres: *La musique française au XVIIIe siècle: Gluck et Piccinni 1774–1800* (Paris, 1872)

M. Tourneux, ed.: *Correspondance littéraire, philosophique et critique par Grimm, Diderot, Raynal, Meister, etc.* (Paris, 1877–82)

A. Jullien: *La cour et l'Opéra sous Louis XVI* (Paris, 1878)

E. Thoinan: *Notes bibliographiques sur la guerre musicale des Gluckistes et Piccinnistes* (Paris, 1878)

A. Jullien: *L'Opéra secret au XVIIIe siècle* (Paris,1880)

H. de Curzon: *Les dernières années de Piccinni à Paris* (Paris, 1890)

A. Cametti: 'Saggio cronologico delle opere teatrali (1754–1794) di Niccolò Piccinni', *RMI*, viii (1901), 75–100

H. Abert: 'Piccinni als Buffokomponist', *JbMP 1913*, 29–42; repr. in *Gesammelte Schriften und Vorträge* (Halle,1929), 346–64

H. Abert: *W.A. Mozart*, i (Leipzig, 1919), 250ff

J.D. Popovici: *La buona figliuola von Nicola Piccinni* (Vienna, 1920)

A. Della Corte: *L'opera comica italiana nel Settecento* (Bari, 1923)

E. Blom: 'A Misjudged Composer', *Stepchildren of Music* (London, 1925), 57–66

A. Della Corte: *Piccinni: Settecento italiano* (Bari, 1928)

P. La Rotella: *N. Piccinni: commemorato nel II centenario della nascita* (Bari,1928)

A. Parisi: 'Intorno al soggiorno di N. Piccinni in Francia', *RMI*, xxx (1928), 219–25

M. Bellucci la Salandra: 'Opere teatrali serie e buffe di Nicolò Piccinni dal 1754 al 1794', *NA*, xii (1935), 43–54, 114–25, 235–48; see also xiii (1936), 55

A. Gastoué: 'Nicolò Piccinni et ses opéras à Paris',*NA*, xiii (1936), 52–8

W. Bollert: 'L'opera Griselda de Piccinni', *Musica d'oggi*, xix (1937), 43–50

C.D. Brenner: *A Bibliographical List of Plays in the French Language 1700–1789* (Berkeley, 1947, 2/1979)

N. Pascazio: *L'uomo Piccinni e la 'Querelle célèbre'* (Bari, 1951)

W.C. Holmes: 'Pamela Transformed', *MQ*, xxxviii (1952), 581–94

U. Prota-Giurleo: 'La biografia di Nicola Piccinni alla luce di nuovi documenti', *Il fuidoro*, i (1954), 27

U. Prota-Giurleo: 'Sacchini fra Piccinnisti e Gluckisti', *Gazzetta musicale di Napoli*, iii (1957), 57–63, 76–80

U. Prota-Giurleo: 'Una sconosciuta cantata di N. Piccinni e il suo ritorno a Parigi nel 1798', *Gazzetta musicale di Napoli*, iv (1958), 8

J.G. Rushton: *Music and Drama at the Académie Royale de Musique, Paris, 1774–1789* (diss., U. of Oxford, 1970)

J.G. Rushton: 'The Theory and Practice of Piccinnisme', *PRMA*, xcviii (1971–2), 31–46

M.F. Robinson: *Naples and Neapolitan Opera* (London, 1972)

J.G. Rushton: '"Iphigénie en Tauride": the Operas of Gluck and Piccinni', *ML*, liii (1972), 411–30

G. Allroggen: 'Piccinnis Origille', *AnMc*, no.15 (1975), 258–97

M. Liggett: *A Biography of Piccinni and a Critical Study of his 'La Didone' and 'Didon'* (diss., Washington U., St Louis, 1977)

F. Degrada: 'Due volti d'Ifigenia', *Il palazzo incantato: studi sulla tradizione del melodramma dal Barocco al Romanticismo* (Fiesole, 1979), i, 155–208

R. Strohm: *Die italienische Oper im 18. Jahrhundert* (Wilhelmshaven, 1979)

F. Lippmann: 'Haydn und die Opera buffa: Vergleiche mit
    italienischen Werken gleichen Textes', *Joseph Haydn: Cologne
    1982*, 113–40
G. Hardie: 'Neapolitan Comic Opera, 1707–1750: some Addenda
    and Corrigenda for The New Grove', *JAMS*, xxxvi (1983), 125–7
M. Hunter: '"Pamela": the Offspring of Richardson's Heroine in
    Eighteenth-Century Opera', *Mosaic: a Journal for the
    Interdisciplinary Study of Literature*, viii (1985), 61–76
M. Hunter: 'The Fusion and Juxtaposition of Genres in Opera Buffa
    1770–1800: Anelli and Piccinni's "Griselda"', *ML*, lxviii (1986),
    363–80
J. Rushton: Introduction to N. Piccinni: *Atys*, FO, lxv (1991)
E. Schmierer: 'Piccinni's *Iphigénie en Tauride*: "Chant périodique"
    and Dramatic Structure', *COJ*, iv (1992), 91–118
M. Calella: 'Un italiano a Parigi: contributo alla biografia di Niccolò
    Piccinni', *RIM*, xxx (1995), 3–49
W. Ensslin: *Niccolò Piccinni, 'Catone in Utica':
    Quellenüberlieferung, Aufführungsgeschichte und Analyse*
    (Frankfurt, 1996)

DENNIS LIBBY (1 with JULIAN RUSHTON), MARY HUNTER (work-
list with JAMES L. JACKMAN, MARITA P. McCLYMONDS,
DAVID CHARLTON)

Piccioli, Giacomo [Jacomo] **Antonio** (*b* Corvaro, nr Rieti;
fl 1587–8). Italian composer. He was a pupil of Costanzo
Porta and, according to the title-page of his *Missa, cantica
Mariae verginis ac sacrae cantiones octo vocibus concinendae* (Milan, 1587, inc.), a Franciscan conventual and
maestro di cappella at Vercelli Cathedral. Dedicated to
Constanzo Sarriano, Bishop of Vercelli, whose coat of
arms appears on the title-page, this volume contains the
Missa 'Factum est silentium' together with three settings
of the *Magnificat* and a number of motets. Piccioli was
still at Vercelli in the following year, when his *Canzonette
a tre voci* (Venice, 1588) were published. He contributed
one mass each to two anthologies: *Missarum quinque
vocum* (RISM 1588¹), which also contains four masses
by Orfeo Vecchi, and *Missae quatuor, & quinque vocibus
decantandae* (1588⁴), edited by Giulio Bonagiunta and
including works by Hauville, Lhéritier and Lassus.

IAIN FENLON

Piccioni [Pizzoni, Pisoni], **Giovanni** (*b* Rimini, 1548/9; *d*
Orvieto, after 17 June 1619). Italian composer and
organist. He was organist at the cathedral of Rimini from
1569 probably until shortly before 15 November 1577
when, according to the dedication of his first book of five-
voice madrigals, he moved from Rimini to Conegliano,
Veneto, where he became *maestro di musica* to the
'Magnifici Signori Desiosi', who formed an academy
there. His books of canzoni of 1580 and 1582 bear
dedications testifying to connections in the Romagna, and
he may once again have been active there during these
years. In the years 1583–6 he may have been in Dalmatia
with Marc'Antonio Venier, as he later claimed (in his
seventh book of madrigals). From August 1586 until 31
December 1591 he was organist at the cathedral of
Gubbio. He held the same post at Orvieto Cathedral from
8 January 1592 until 1617; in 1615 he became *maestro
di cappella* there as well. In 1616 he held the additional
posts of organist and *maestro di cappella* at nearby Monte
Fiascone. He was recalled to Orvieto as organist in 1619,
and the last notice of his activity there is found in the
dedication of his *Concertus ecclesiastici* on 17 June 1619.

Piccioni's extensive output falls into two categories,
distinguishable not only by genre but also generally by
date and style; all his extant earlier prints, up to 1602, are
polyphonic music, except one secular work, while his
surviving later publications are all sacred works that show
the influence of the *seconda pratica*. In the preface to his

Concerti ecclesiastici (1610) he claimed to have taken the
music of Andrea and Giovanni Gabrieli as the model for
his own compositions. He also gave some useful advice
to the less expert performer. First, the organist must
transpose the music to the octave below when playing it
on 'small organs with 3½′ stops such as are to be found in
many Italian towns', because the actual sound they
produce is an octave higher than the human voice; he
particularly recommended this practice for the solo
concertos. He next explained that he had indicated neither
accidentals nor figures as they 'would only confuse the
less expert organist', and more skilled players could in
any case manage without them. Finally, he advised
organists unused to playing from a basso continuo to
score and intabulate the music. The *Salmi intieri concertati*
(1616), which depart from the spezzati style, are an
important example of the use of the new style of the
contrast of solo and tutti.

WORKS
all published in Venice

SECULAR VOCAL

Il primo libro de madrigali, 5vv (1577)
Il primo libro delle canzoni, 5vv (1578)
Il secondo libro delle canzoni, 5vv (1580)
Il terzo libro delle canzoni, 5vv (1582¹³)
Il quarto libro delle canzoni, 5vv (1582¹⁴)
Il quarto libro de madrigali, 5vv (1596)
Il primo libro de madrigali, 6vv (1598)
Il pastor fido musicale: il sesto libro di madrigali, 5vv (1602)
Gli affettuosi madrigali il settimo libro, 5vv (1605)
L'ottavo libro de madrigali, 5vv, lost (cited *PitoniN*)
6 secular works, 5vv, 1600⁶, 1609¹⁷, 1616¹⁰

SACRED VOCAL

Il primo libro delle messe, 5vv (1589)
Concerti ecclesiastici, 1–8vv, bc (org), op.17 (1610)
Psalmi sex, 3vv, et aliae cantiones, 2, 3vv, op.18 (Rome, 1612)
Salmi intieri concertati, 4vv, org, op.19 (1616)
Concertus ecclesiastici, sex cum psalmis in fine, 2–4vv, bc (org),
    op.21 (Rome, 1619)
4 motets, 3vv, bc, 6, 8vv, 1612³, 1616², 1622²
O Jesu mi dulcissime, 6vv; Elegi et sanctificavi cum istum, 8vv, both
    in *PL-Wn*

BIBLIOGRAPHY

EitnerQ; FétisB; PitoniN; SchmidlD; SchmidlDS; WaltherML
A. Banchieri: *Conclusioni nel suono dell'organo* (Bologna, 1609/
    R1934; 2/1626)
F. Piperno: *Gli eccellentissimi musici della città di Bologna: con uno
    studio sull'antologia madrigalistica del Cinquecento* (Florence,
    1985), 19
M. Caraci Vela: 'Lamento polifonico e lamento monodico da camera
    all'inizio del Seicento: affinità stilistiche e reciporcità di influssi',
    Seicento inesplorato: Lenno, nr Como 1989, 339–83, esp. 342
M. Gemmani and P. Righini: *Giovanni Piccioni da Rimini, un
    musicista da scoprire* (Rimini, 1995)

PIER PAOLO SCATTOLIN

Piccola Pasta, La. *See* TACCHINARDI-PERSIANI, FANNY.

Piccolo (It.: 'small'). (1) (Fr. *petite flûte*; Ger. *kleine Flöte,
Pickelflöte, Pikkoloflöte, Oktavflöte*; It. *ottavino, flauto
piccolo*). A small flute sounding an octave higher than the
ordinary or concert flute; *see* FLUTE, §II, 3(i).

(2) Used as an adjective – i.e. in its correct Italian
grammatical form – 'piccolo' describes various instruments, the smallest and highest in pitch of their type, e.g.
the VIOLINO PICCOLO, VIOLONCELLO piccolo, piccolo
clarinet, piccolo timpani and so on. Occasionally the
sopranino cornet in the 19th century was called simply
'piccolo'. The term 'piccolo bass' refers to a rare small
double bass used in jazz; it is fitted with thin strings and

tuned an octave higher than the standard instrument. There is also a piccolo bass guitar, which bears a similar relationship to the electric bass guitar.

(3) An ORGAN STOP.

Piccolo bass. A rare, small DOUBLE BASS used in jazz. It is fitted with thin strings and tuned up to an octave higher than the standard instruments. The player best known for using it is RON CARTER.

Piccolomini, Marietta (*b* Siena, 15 March 1834; *d* Poggio Imperiale, Florence, 23 Dec 1899). Italian soprano. She made her début in February 1852 at the Teatro della Pergola, Florence, in *Lucrezia Borgia* and later that year sang at the Teatro Apollo, Rome, in *Poliuto* and *Don Pasquale*. In 1853 she sang Gilda in *Rigoletto* at Pisa, and at Turin in 1855 she sang Violetta in *La traviata*, a role for which she became famous; she was the first Violetta in London (1856, Her Majesty's Theatre) and Paris (1856, Théâtre Italien). At Her Majesty's in 1858 she sang Arline in *La zingara*, the Italian version of Balfe's *The Bohemian Girl*, and the title role of *Luisa Miller*. She was also heard as Serpina in *La serva padrona*, Zerlina in *Don Giovanni*, Lucia, Adina in *L'elisir d'amore*, Marie in *La fille du régiment*, Amina in *La sonnambula*, Elvira in *I puritani* and Leonora in *Il trovatore*. In 1863 she married the Marchese Gaetani della Fargia and retired from the stage. Her popularity, especially as Violetta, rested more in her youthful, attractive appearance and her acting ability than in her vocal accomplishment. According to Henry Chorley, 'her voice was weak and limited … hardly one octave and a half in compass. She was not sure in her intonation: she had no execution'.

BIBLIOGRAPHY

H.F. Chorley: *Thirty Years' Musical Recollections* (London, 1862/*R*, abridged 2/1926/*R* by E. Newman)
E. Creathorne Clayton: *Queens of Song* (London, 1863/*R*)

ELIZABETH FORBES

Piccolomini, Niccolò (*fl* first half of 16th century). Sienese priest, canon of the Cathedral, professor of canon law at Siena's university, poet and composer. A member of the important Sienese family that had included two popes, Piccolomini was provost of the Cathedral from 1521 to 1532. He is the author of two pieces in Pietro Sambonetto's *Canzone sonetti strambotti et frottole libro primo*, published in Siena (1515²): *Mentre lo sdegno*, ascribed there to 'Nico[lò] Pic[colomini] Pre[te] Sen[ese]', and *S'io fui servo*, ascribed to 'Nicholaus Pre. Se.'

BIBLIOGRAPHY

L. Cellesi: 'Ricerche intorno ai compositori dello "Zibaldoncino Musicale" marucelliano', *Bullettino senese di storia patria*, xxxviii (1931), 307–09
L. Cellesi: 'Il lirismo musicale religioso in Siena nel Trecento e quello profano nel Cinquecento', *Bullettino senese di storia patria*, xli (1934), 93–112
K. Jeppesen: *La Frottola*, i–iii (Århus, 1968–70)
D. Fusi: *Le frottole nell'edizione di Pietro Sambonetto (Siena 1515)* (thesis, U. of Siena, 1976–7)
F. Luisi: *La musica vocale nel Rinascimento* (Turin, 1977)
F.A. D'Accone: 'Instrumental Resonances in a Sienese Vocal Print of 1515', *Le concert des voix et des instruments à la Renaissance: Tours 1991*, 333–59
F.A. D'Accone: *The Civic Muse: Music and Musicians in Siena during the Middle Ages and Renaissance* (Chicago, 1997)

WILLIAM F. PRIZER

Picco pipe. A small DUCT FLUTE 8·5 cm long, named after the instrument used by the Italian musician Joseph Picco [Angelo Picchi] (*b* Robbio, 1830) called the 'Sardinian Minstrel', who in 1854–7 enjoyed massive acclaim in Italy, France and England. The son of a poor shepherd and born blind, he was inspired by the sounds of the village organ. Apparently self-taught, he was heard playing in the Apennine mountains by a huntsman and brought to Milan. After successful concerts in Italy he was awarded a diploma by the Academia di S Cecilia in Rome in 1855 for his performing and extemporizing skills. His debut in London on 21 February 1856 was at Covent Garden. According to press reports, the 'tibia pastorale' he played was nothing more than a three-holed whistle, 2·5 to 3 inches (6·35 to 7·62 cm) in length and made of common white wood which was dyed yellow, a type of child's toy then commonly found at the smallest country fair (*see* ZUFFOLO). With a range of three octaves, he was praised for 'difficult variations, those double notes, those flying octaves, those chromatic runs performed with so much precision and an accent so marked . . . he makes use of all his fingers, using particularly the forefinger of the left hand to close more or less the end of the whistle, in the way that a performer on the horn employs his hand'.

Such were his successes that London flute makers sold an instrument similar to his, made in boxwood or other hardwood, for some years. Like many earlier pipes from the Bronze Age onwards, it is a flute with two finger-holes and a thumb-hole above them, played with one hand. The bore is cylindrical but widely flared at the lower end. When this end is closed with the palm of the other hand

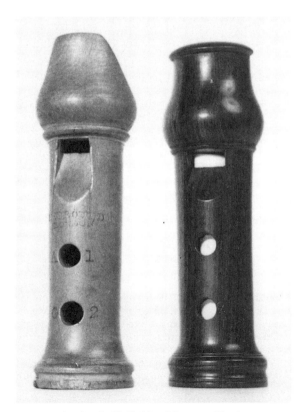

Picco pipe, London, 2nd half of the 19th century (Horniman Museum, London)

the pipe behaves like an ocarina, sounding c''; opening the holes gives the notes g'' to b'', and partially uncovering the end produces all the semitones of this octave. The scale is continued upwards in open harmonics with the end uncovered, and further in stopped harmonics. The English maker A.W. Simpson has recently marketed a modified version in plastic to serve as an introduction to the recorder. However, none of these models appear ever to have equalled Picco's original pipe in range and response.

BIBLIOGRAPHY
Gay, ed.: *Picco, the Blind-Born Sardinian Minstrel* (London, 1856)
C. Welch: *Six Lectures on the Recorder and other Flutes in Relation to Literature* (London, 1911)
A.W. Simpson: *The Picco Pipe Tutor* (Lewes, n.d.)
WILLIAM H. STONE, ANTHONY C. BAINES/
WILLIAM WATERHOUSE

Picerli, Silverio (*b* Ricti; *fl* Naples, 1629–31). Italian music theorist and theologian. He was a friar belonging to a strict order of Franciscans. According to the dedication to the reader in his *Specchio primo di musica* he was forbidden by his order to make music his profession. The same publication reveals that in 1629 he was superior of the convent of S Maria Maddalena at Naples, and the dedication of his *Specchio secondo di musica* shows that in 1631 he was living at another monastery there, S Chiara.

Picerli wrote three treatises, the first two of which are *Specchio primo di musica* (Naples, 1630) and *Specchio secondo di musica* (Naples, 1631). The *Specchio terzo* was announced by Picerli in the *Specchio primo*, but no copy now exists; it dealt with 'theory and the numbers on which music is based'. The *Specchio secondo* reveals that the superiors of Picerli's order gave their approval to the manuscript of the *Specchio terzo* on the same date, 17 January 1631, as the *Specchio secondo*. A copy of the *Specchio terzo* is listed among the books belonging to Girolamo Chiti, who also left a collection of annotations on Picerli's writings (in *I-Bc*).

In the *Specchio primo* Picerli formulated a new system of solmization made necessary by the increasingly widespread use of accidentals; in it he tabulated three 'orders' of music. The *Specchio secondo*, which is concerned almost exclusively with counterpoint, is less original, but its subject matter is presented in a notably clear, well-ordered way, and it was the principal source for the fifth book of Kircher's *Musurgia universalis* (1650). Picerli gave much useful practical advice on consonances, dissonances and 'the way to move from one to the other and to treat them in counterpoint', cadences, canon and various other kinds of counterpoint. Chapter 22 is specially interesting; it deals with 'the particular considerations concerning composition for two, three, four and more voices and for two or more choirs, together with other important matters'. Picerli also paid attention to the art of composing for interchangeable voices, advising on the construction of such compositions so that they are practical for singing (p.189), and to the handling of the basso continuo (pp.166, 184–5 and 191). He appeared too to accept the principles of the *seconda prattica* when he stressed the need to compose 'according to the nature and demands of the subject or text to be set to music' (p.181), using 'consonance and dissonance according to the meaning [of the words], their joy, sadness, grief, failure, mistaken opinion or other emotion, expressing

their significance in the music as well' (p.190). Chapter 18 is noteworthy for its discussion of the number of modes. Systems of three, four, seven and 14 modes are rejected. Picerli concludes that plainchant employs the traditional eight modes, while polyphony uses four more 'irregular' modes. The difference with traditional 12-mode theory is only a terminological one. In addition to Kircher, Picerli's writings influenced Penna, Bononcini, Berardi and Pitoni.

WRITINGS
Specchio primo di musica, nel quale si vede chiaro non sol'il vero, facile, e breve modo d'imparar di cantare di canto figurato, e fermo; ma . . . scoperti nuovi segreti nella medesima circa il cantare, comporre, e sonar di tasti, nascosti (Naples, 1630)
Specchio secondo di musica, nel quale si vede chiaro il vero, e facil modo di comporre di canto figurato, e fermo, di fare con nuove regole ogni sorte di contrapunti, e canoni, di formar li toni di tutt'i generi di musica reale, e finta, con le loro cadenze à proprij luoghi e di porre in prattica quanto si vuole, e può desiderare di detti canto figurato, e fermo (Naples, 1631)
Specchio terzo di musica, written in or before 1631, announced in *Specchio primo*, lost

BIBLIOGRAPHY
EitnerQ; *GaspariC*; *MGG1* (O. Mischiati)
S. Gmeinwieser: *Girolamo Chiti, 1679–1759: eine Untersuchung zur Kirchenmusik in S. Giovanni in Laterano* (Regensburg, 1968), 113
U. Scharlau: *Athanasius Kircher (1601–1680) als Musikschriftsteller* (Marburg, 1969)
R. Groth: 'Italienische musiktheorie im 17. Jahrhundert', *Italienische musiktheorie im 16. und 17. Jahrhundert: Antikenrezeption und Satzlehre*, ed. F. Zaminer (Darmstadt, 1989), 307–79
F. Wiering: *The Language of the Modes: Studies in the History of Polyphonic Modality* (diss., U. of Amsterdam, 1995), 236, 288
AGOSTINO ZIINO/R

Pichl [Pichel], **Václav** [Venceslaus; Wenzel] (*b* Bechyně, nr Tábor, 25 Sept 1741; *d* Vienna, 23 Jan 1805). Czech composer, violinist, music director and writer. He first studied music at Bechyně with the cantor Jan Pokorny. From 1752 to 1758 he attended the Jesuit college at Březnice, where he served as a singer. In Prague he was a violinist at the Jesuit seminary of St Václav and studied philosophy, theology and law at the university. In 1762 he was appointed first violinist of the Týn Church, where he studied counterpoint with the organist J.N. Seger. In 1765 he was engaged by Dittersdorf as a violinist and assistant director for the private orchestra of Bishop Adam Patachich at Nagyvárad (Grosswardein, now Oradea, Romania). After the dissolution of the orchestra in 1769 Pichl became the music director for Count Ludwig Hartig at Prague; in about 1770 he was appointed first violinist of the Vienna court theatre. On the recommendation of the Empress Maria Theresa, who preferred him to Mozart, he became the music director and *Kammerdiener* (valet) for the Austrian governor of Lombardy at Milan, Archduke Ferdinando d'Este; he went to Italy in 1777 (not 1775). The French invasion of Lombardy (1796) caused him to return to Vienna, where he remained in the service of the archduke until his death.

While in Italy Pichl visited all the important music centres, Gyrowetz's autobiography indicates that he was appreciated as one of the foremost European composers of that time. He was in contact with Padre Martini (correspondence of 1778–84, see Straková, 1962), Cherubini, probably also with J.F. Reichardt and others, being a member of the Filarmonici at Mantua (from 1779) and Bologna (from 1782), and for a time music director of the theatre at Monza, near Milan. He is reported to have been Prince Nicolaus Esterházy's musical trustee at Milan; his compositions were performed at Eszterháza by Haydn (e.g. 11 February 1778), who copied his quartets to be performed there in 1780, and who remained in contact with him (see Haydn's letter to Pleyel of 6 December 1802).

Pichl was a man of broad knowledge and manifold interests. At Nagyvárad he wrote Latin librettos which were set to music by both himself and Dittersdorf. Later he compiled a history of Czech musicians in Italy (the manuscript of which was destroyed at Milan during the French occupation) and translated the libretto of Mozart's *Die Zauberflöte* into Czech (lost). He supplied information for numerous entries in Dlabač's *Künstler-Lexikon* and visited him at Prague in December 1802.

Pichl's music stands between the early and high Classical styles. A detailed list of works that he prepared for Dlabač's *Künstler-Lexikon* shows about 900 pieces, the greater number of which are extant. His numerous symphonies, written from about 1769 to 1803, are stylistically close to those of Dittersdorf and of Haydn's middle period (some were confused with works of these composers). They consist of three or four movements, sometimes with a slow introduction; his use of sonata form in both orchestral and chamber works shows a marked contrast between the energetic primary and melodious secondary themes, and some have elaborate development sections. His chromaticism and expressive harmony bear Mozartian traits. In his later years Pichl was appreciated more for his sacred works and violin concertos. He was one of the founders of the Viennese violin school. Dlabač's statement (1794) that Pichl was a violin student of Dittersdorf is not supported by the latter's autobiography: Pichl had already completed his training before Dittersdorf enlisted him for Patachich's orchestra (1765). In Italy he is reported to have studied the violin with Pietro Nardini, to whom he dedicated his *Cento variazioni* op.11. His compositions for solo violin, employing all the current technical devices, are still valued as excellent pedagogical works, particularly the fugues as preparatory studies for works by J.S. Bach. There is no documentary evidence for Gyrowetz's allegation that Pichl was one of Paganini's teachers.

WORKS

MSS mostly in A-Wgm, Wn; CZ-Bm, K, KRa, Pnm; D-Bsb, Dl, SWl; GB-Lbl; H-Bn; I-Bca, Mc, MOe; list in DlabačžKL

ORCHESTRAL

Syms., symphonic concertantes: over 20 pubd as opp.1, 5–6, 8, 15, 17, 24–6, without op. nos. (1778–c1805); c70 in MS (1764–1803); 2 ed. A. Zakin (1977, 1979), 3 ed. in The Symphony 1720–1840, ser. B, vii (New York, 1984) [incl. thematic index]
Over 30 concs., concertinos: 16 for vn, incl. 3 as op.3 (Berlin, 1779) [1 ed. J. Čermák and J. Maštalíř (Prague, 1957)], 1 in A-Wgm and 1 in I-Gl; 1 for db, D-SWl, ed. M. Říha and E. Pošta (Prague, 1972); 1 for bn/db, SWl, ed. H. Herrmann and M. Schlenker for db (Leipzig, 1957); 1 for bn, CZ-Bm; others, mostly lost
c20 serenatas (partitas, notturnos), incl. 3 as op.9 (Berlin, 1784); minuets, German dances

CHAMBER

Qnts: c20 divertimentos, str/(str, wind insts), incl. 6 as op.3 (Paris, ?c1778), 6 as op.5 (Berlin, 1781); 3 as op.30 (Offenbach, 1797)
Qts: 18 str qts, incl. 6 as op.2 (Berlin, 1779), 3 as op.13 (Berlin, 1788); 3 for fl, vn, va, vc, op.12 (Berlin, 1787); 3 for cl, vn, va, vc, op.16 (Berlin, 1790)
Trios: 45 str trios, incl. 6 as op.4 (Paris, ?c1785), 6 as op.7 (Berlin, 1783); 12 for fl, vn, vc, incl. 6 as op.1 (Lyons, n.d.), 2 ed. in MVH, xxiv (1969); 3 sonatas, hpd/pf, vn/fl, vc, op.26 (Vienna, 1795)
Duets: 15 for 2 vn, incl. 6 as op.4 (Berlin, 1780), 3 as op.34 (Offenbach, 1797), 3 as op.38 (Vienna, c1799); 18 for vn, va, incl.

6 as op.10 (Berlin, 1784), 6 as op.18 (Berlin, 1793), 3 for va, vc, op.14 (Berlin, 1789), also as op.16 (Paris, 1793)
Vn solo: 100 variazioni sulla scala del basso fermo per esercizio del violino, op.11 (Florence and Naples, c1787); 100 variations, 1776–96, lost; 12 variations, 1798–1803, lost; 60 capriccios, incl. 12 as op.19 [21] (Berlin, 1796), 12 as op.46 (Vienna, c1801); 6 fughe con un preludio fugato, op.41 (Vienna, 1800), also as op.22 (Berlin and Amsterdam, 1801), as op.35 (Leipzig, 1811), ed. in MAB, vii (1951, 3/1989), 1 ed. in DČHP, no.145; 18 sonatas, b acc., incl. 6 as op.20 (Brunswick and Hamburg, ?c1796); 3 sonatas, vn/va acc., op.23 (Berlin, 1804)
c180 works, 4–8 insts, baryton, lost; c15 partitas, wind insts, CZ-Pnm; 9 sonatas, 6 sonatinas, hpd/pf, lost

STAGE
music all lost

3 Lat. ops (Pichl): Olympia Jovi sacra, Grosswardein, 1765; Pythia, seu Ludi Apolloni, Grosswardein, 1766; Certamen deorum, Grosswardein, 1767
Lat. op 'per Klosterbrack', Vienna, 1770–76
Das Schnupftuch (Spl), Pest, 1774
Der Krieg (Ger. op), Vienna, c1775
Raol de Crequi (ballet), Monza, 1795, collab. P. Winter, lib pubd
4 opere buffe, 3 opere serie
It. arrs. of 8 Fr. ops, 1776–96, incl. A.-E.-M. Grétry: La caravana del Cairo (with addl nos.), Monza, 1795, lib pubd

OTHER VOCAL
Over 100 sacred works, incl. over 30 masses
Mag, Gloria pastorale, I-Bca*
6 It. ariettas (P. Metastasio), 1v, hpd, op.42 (Vienna, 1801), incl. Tu mi chiedi, ed. M. Poštolka, Songs, ii (Prague, 1962)

BIBLIOGRAPHY

DlabačžKL [incl. list of works]; *EitnerQ*; *GerberL*; *GerberNL*
G.J. Dlabacž: 'Versuch eines Verzeichnisses der vorzüglichern Tonkünstler in oder aus Böhmen', *Materialien zur alten und neuen Statistik von Böhmen*, ed. J.A. Riegger, xii (Leipzig and Prague, 1794), 225–98, esp. 268
AMZ, ii–xvi (1799–1814)
R. Kolisko: *W. Pichl's Kammermusik* (diss., U. of Vienna, 1918)
F. Bartoš, ed. and trans.: *Vlastní životopis Vojtěcha Jírovce* (Prague, 1940) [Gyrowetz's autobiography]
M. Poštolka: *Joseph Haydn a naše hudba 18. století* [Haydn and Czech music in the 18th century] (Prague, 1961), 121ff
T. Straková: 'V. Pichl a jeho vztah k G.B. Martinimu' [Pichl's relationship with Martini], *Acta musei moraviae*, xlvii (1962), 163–88 [with edn of Pichl's 18 letters to Martini]
G. Staud: *Magyar kastélyszinházak* [Hungarian castle theatres], ii (Budapest, 1963), 67, 69
D. Bartha, ed.: *Joseph Haydn: gesammelte Briefe und Aufzeichnungen* (Kassel, 1965), 95, 415–16
J. Hárich: 'Das Opernensemble zu Eszterháza im Jahr 1780', *Haydn Yearbook* 1970, 5–46, esp. 26
R. Pečman: 'Böhmen und Italien', *Musica bohemica et europaea: Brno V 1970*, 289–97
J. Pešková: 'Václav Pichl: žák březnické jesuitské koleje' [Pichl: pupil of the Jesuit college at Březnice], *HV*, ix (1972), 160–61
A. Myslík: 'Repertoire und Besetzung der Harmoniemusiken an den Höfen Schwarzenberg, Pachta und Clams-Gallas', *Haydn Yearbook 1978*, 110–19
Z. Pilková: 'Doba osvícenského absolutismu (1740–1810)' [The age of enlightened absolutism], *Hudba v českých dějinách: od středověku do nové doby* [Music in Czech history: from the Middle Ages to the modern era] (Prague, 1983, 2/1989), 211–84, esp. 266, 272
M. Poštolka: *Mladý Josef Haydn* [The young Haydn] (Prague, 1988)

MILAN POŠTOLKA

Pick. *See* PLECTRUM.

Pickel, Conrad. *See* CELTIS, CONRADUS PROTUCIUS.

Pickelflöte (Ger.). Piccolo. *See* FLUTE, §II, 3(i).

Picken, Laurence (Ernest Rowland) (*b* Nottingham, 16 July 1909). English musicologist. He studied natural sciences at Cambridge as a scholar of Trinity College (BA 1931, MA 1935, PhD 1935, DSc 1952), becoming a Fellow of

Jesus College in 1944. He became assistant director of research in zoology at the university (1946–66). His research into Asian music dates from 1944 when as a member of the British Council Scientific Mission to China he had the opportunity of studying the *ch'in* (board zither) with Hsü Yuan-pai and Cha Fu-hsi. From 1951 he frequently visited Turkey, collecting instruments and related data on Turkish art and folk music. He studied the *kanun* (board zither) with Nejdet Senvarol (1951) and the *baglama* (lute) with Saz Evi (1953), both in Istanbul. After acting as Walter Ames Visiting Professor of Zoology at Washington University, Seattle (1959), Picken was appointed assistant director of research at the Faculty of Oriental Studies at Cambridge (1966–76). During this time he was also an editor of the *Journal of the International Folk Music Council* (1961–3) and founder-editor of *Musica asiatica* (1977–84). He was elected Fellow of the British Academy (1973), Docteur Honoris Causa of the Université de Paris X, Nanterre (1988), and Honorary Fellow of Jesus College (1989) and Trinity College (1991), Cambridge, and of the School of Oriental and African Studies, University of London (1991). He received the Trail Medal and Award of the Linnean Society in 1960 and the Curt Sachs Award of the American Musical Instrument Society in 1995; he has also been honoured with two Festschriften, the first one on the occasion of his 60th birthday (*Asian Music*, vi/1–2, 1975, ed. F.A. Kuttner and F. Lieberman) and the second one honouring his 70th birthday (*Music and Tradition: Essays on Asian and other Musics presented to Laurence Picken*, ed. D.R. Widdess and R.F. Wolpert, Cambridge, 1981; for a list of his publications on music see *CHIME: Journal of the European Foundation for Chinese Music Research*, iv, 1991, pp.63–5).

Picken's particular areas of musical research are China and Turkey, though he has also directed attention to other regions of Asia, including Central Asia, South-east Asia, Korea and Japan. The main emphases of his work are historical and organological. The latter is characterized by a scientific approach which embraces a range of aspects such as terminology and taxonomy, manufacturing processes, regional distribution, historical relationships, acoustic properties, ritual connotations or functions, repertory and technique. This work culminated in *The Folk Musical Instruments of Turkey* (1975), the most comprehensive study of Turkish instruments (and perhaps of any folk instrumentarium); it is organized according to the Sachs–Hornbostel system of classification, and includes a defence of that system with reference to scientific taxonomy. Smaller studies of organological problems have appeared in the pages of *Musica asiatica*.

Picken's early studies of Chinese music concentrate on the music of the Tang and Song dynasties, and particularly on the transcription, analysis and cultural history of notated repertories in Tang and Song sources. The search for further records of the secular court repertory of Tang dynasty China led him to investigate the Tōgaku ('Tang music') repertory of Japan. Recognizing similarities between the historical scores of Tōgaku (from the 9th century onwards), Chinese notations of Tang and Song date, Chinese song lyrics from the Tang period, and musical idoms of Central Asia (where much of the Tang court repertory originated), he concluded that the Japanese belief that the Tōgaku repertory was imported from Tang China to Japan is correct; however, transformations

in performing practice – including a substantial retardation of tempo – occurred after its arrival in Japan. From 1972 he established a 'Tang Music Project' to undertake the elaboration of this hypothesis and the analysis of the earliest Tōgaku scores; transcriptions of the latter, analyses of the music, and evidence for the history of the music from Chinese and Japanese sources, are brought together in the multi-volume *Music from the Tang Court* (1981–). The first volume of this series contains a full statement of the objectives and methods of this project, perhaps the most extensive yet undertaken in the historical musicology of Asia. In October 1990, Picken and N.J. Nickson were guests of the Shanghai Conservatory of Music, where they supervised a performance of his transcriptions of Tang and song music.

WRITINGS

'Bach Quotations from the Eighteenth Century', *MR*, v (1944), 83–95

'A Fugue by "Bach"', *PRMA*, lxxvi (1949–50), 47–57

'Instrumental Polyphonic Folk Music in Asia Minor', *PRMA*, lxxx (1953–4), 73–86

'The Origin of the Short Lute', *GSJ*, viii (1955), 32–42

'Twelve Ritual Melodies of the T'ang Dynasty', *Studia memoriae Belae Bartók sacra*, ed. B. Rajeczky and L. Vargyas (Budapest, 1956; Eng. trans., 1959), 147–73

'Chiang K'uei's *Nine Songs of Yüeh*', *MQ*, xliii (1957), 201–19

'The Music of Far Eastern Asia', *NOHM*, i (1957), 83–194; repr. as 'Chinese Music', *Readings in Ethnomusicology*, ed. D.P. McAllester (New York, 1971), 336

'A Note on Ethiopic Church Music', *AcM*, xxix (1957), 41–2

'Three-Note Instruments in the Chinese People's Republic', *JIFMC*, xii (1960), 28–30

'Musical Terms in a Chinese Dictionary of the First Century', *JIFMC*, xiv (1962), 40–43

'Early Chinese Friction-Chordophones', *GSJ*, xviii (1965), 82–9

'Secular Chinese Songs of the Twelfth Century', *SMH*, viii (1966), 125–71

ed., with E. Dal and E. Stockmann: *A Select Bibliography of European Folk Music* (Prague, 1966)

'Central Asian Tunes in the Gagaku Tradition', *Festschrift für Walter Wiora*, ed. L. Finscher and C.-H. Mahling (Kassel, 1967), 545–51

'The Musical Implications of Line-Sharing in the Book of Songs (Shih Ching)', *Journal of the American Oriental Society*, lxxxix (1969), 408

'Music and Musical Sources of the Sonq Dynasty', *Journal of the American Oriental Society*, lxxxix (1969), 21

'T'ang Music and Musical Instruments', *T'oung pao*, lv/1–3 (1969), 74–122

'Tunes Apt for T'ang Lyrics from the *shō* Part-books of *Tōgaku*', *Umakhak ronch'ong: Yi Hye-Gu paksa song'su kinyom* (Seoul, 1969), 401

'Some Chinese Terms for the Musical Repeats, Sections, and Forms, Common to T'ang, Yüan, and *Tōgaku* Scores', *Bulletin of the School of Oriental and African Studies*, xxxiv (1971), 113–18

'A Twelfth-century Secular Chinese Song in Zither Tablature', *Asia Major*, xvi (1971), 102

with K. Pont: *Ancient Chinese Tunes* (London, 1973)

with R.F. Wolpert, A. Marrett and J. Condit: '"The Waves of Kokonor": a Dance-tune of the T'ang Dynasty', *AsM*, v/1 (1973–4), 3

'An Afghan Quail-lure of Typological and Acoustic Interest', *Festschrift to Ernst Emsheimer*, ed. G. Hilleström (Stockholm, 1974), 172–5

Folk Musical Instruments of Turkey (London, 1975)

'The Shapes of the *Shi Jing* Song-texts and their Musical Implications', *Musica asiatica*, i (1977), 85

'Some Children's Sound-Producing Toys and other "Primitive" Musical Instruments from Afghanistan', *Neue ethnomusikologische Forschungen: Festschrift Felix Hoerburger*, ed. P. Baumann, R.M. Brandl and K. Reinhard (Laaber, 1977), 177–90

'Medieval Musics of Asia', *PRMA*, civ (1977–8), 57–66

with Y. Mitani: 'Finger-Techniques for the Zithers *sō-no-koto* and *kin* in Heian Times', *Musica asiatica*, ii (1979), 89 ed., with others: *Music from the Tang Court* (Cambridge, 1981–) [7 vols., 1981–2000]

'Tang Music and its Fate in Japan', *Source Materials and the Interpretation of Music: a Memorial Volume to Thurston Dart*, ed. I. Bent (London, 1981), 191–206

with R. Wolpert: 'Mouth-Organ and Lute Parts of Togaku and their Interrelationships', *Musica asiatica*, iii (1983), 79–95

'String/Table Angles for Harps, from the Third Millenium B.C. to the Present', *Musica asiatica*, iii (1983), 35–51

'T'ang Music and its Fate in Japan', *Source Materials and the Interpretation of Music: a Memorial Volume to Thurston Dart*, ed. I. Bent (London, 1981), 191–206

'The Sound Producing Instrumentarium of a Village in North-East Thailand', *Musica asiatica*, no.4 (1984), 245–70

with E. Markham and R. Wolpert: 'Pieces for Biwa in Calendrically Correct Tunings, from a Manuscript in the Heian Museum, Kyoto', *Musica asiatica*, no.5 (1988), 191–209

with N.J. Nickson and M. Wells: '"West River Moon": a Song-Melody Predicted by a Lute-Piece in Piba Tablature', *CHIME*, x–xi (1997), 172–85

'A Preliminary Note on Didactic Modal Expositions in the Late T'ang', *Essays in Ethnomusicology: an Offering in Celebration of Lee Hye-ku on his Ninetieth Birthday* (Seoul, 1999), 567–81

BIBLIOGRAPHY

'Perspectives on Asian Music: Essays in Honor of Dr. Laurence E.R. Picken', *AsM*, vi (1975) [incl. list of writings]

LUCY DURÁN/RICHARD WIDDESS

Picker, Martin (*b* Chicago, 3 April 1929). American musicologist. He received the PhB (1947) and the MA (1951) from the University of Chicago, where he worked with Gombosi. At the University of California at Berkeley he studied under Lowinsky and Kerman and took the doctorate in 1960. He taught at the University of Illinois from 1959, and in 1961 he joined the faculty of Rutgers University, where he was appointed professor in 1968 and became professor emeritus in 1997. He chaired the department of music from 1973 to 1979. He was editor of the *Journal of the American Musicological Society*, 1969–71. Picker's field of interest is Renaissance music, and his main work has been his critical edition of the chanson albums of Marguerite of Austria (1965; originally submitted as his dissertation); in addition to providing reliable transcriptions, he discusses the cultural background and history of the manuscripts and analyses the texts and music. His later contributions include detailed research guides to Renaissance composers and articles on Isaac.

WRITINGS

'The Chanson Albums of Marguerite of Austria: mss.228 and 11239 of the Bibliothèque Royale de Belgique, Brussels', *AnnM*, vi (1958–63), 145–285

The Chanson Albums of Marguerite of Austria: Manuscripts 228 and 11239 of the Bibliothèque Royale de Belgique, Bruxelles (diss., U. of California, Berkeley, 1960; Berkeley, 1965) [incl. transcrs., 169–505]

'Three Unidentified Chansons by Pierre de la Rue in the *Album de Marguerite d'Autriche*', *MQ*, xlvi (1960), 329–43

'Newly Discovered Sources for *In minen sin*', *JAMS*, xvii (1964), 133–43

with M. Bernstein: *An Introduction to Music* (Englewood Cliffs, NJ, 3/1966, 4/1972)

'A Letter of Charles VIII of France Concerning Alexander Agricola', *Aspects of Medieval and Renaissance Music: a Birthday Offering to Gustave Reese*, ed. J. LaRue and others (New York, 1966/R), 665–72

'Josquiniana in some Manuscripts at Piacenza', *Josquin des Prez: New York 1971*, 247–60

'The Motet Anthologies of Petrucci and Antico Published between 1514–1521: a Comparative Study', *Formen und Probleme der Überlieferung mehrstimmiger Musik im Zeitalter Josquins Desprez: Wolfenbüttel 1976*, 181–99

'The Motet Anthologies of Andrea Antico', *A Musical Offering: Essays in Honor of Martin Bernstein*, ed. E.H. Clinkscale and C. Brook (New York, 1977), 211–37

'Josquin and Jean Lemaire: Four Chansons Re-Examined', *Essays Presented to Myron P. Gilmore*, ed. S. Bertelli and G. Ramakus, ii (Florence, 1978), 447–56

'More *Regret* Chansons for Marguerite d'Autriche', *Musique naturelle et musique artificielle*, ed. M.B. Winn (Montreal, 1979), 81–101

Johannes Ockeghem and Jacob Obrecht: a Guide to Research (New York, 1988)

'The Career of Marbriano de Orto (ca.1450–1529)', *Studien zur Geschichte der päpstlichen Kapelle: Heidelberg 1989*, 529–57

'The Habsburg Courts in the Netherlands and Austria, 1477–1530', *The Renaissance: from the 1470s to the End of the 16th Century*, ed. I. Fenlon (Basingstoke, 1989), 216–42

Henricus Isaac: a Guide to Research (New York, 1991)

'Henricus Isaac and *Fortuna desparata*', *Antoine Busnoys: Notre Dame, IN, 1992* (forthcoming)

'Isaac in Flanders: the Early Works of Henricus Isaac', *From Ciconia to Sweelinck: donum natalicium Willem Elders*, ed. A. Clement and E. Jas (Amsterdam, 1994), 153–65

'Margaret of Austria (1480–1530)', *Women Composers: Music Through the Ages*, ed. M. Schleifer and S. Glickman, i (New York, 1996), 88–97

EDITIONS

Josquin des Prez: Parody Chansons (Hackensack, NJ, 1980)

Fors seulement: Thirty Compositions for Three to Five Voices or Instruments from the Fifteenth and Sixteenth Centuries, RRMMA, xiv (1981)

The Motet Books of Andrea Antico, MRM, viii (1987)

PAULA MORGAN

Picker, Tobias (*b* New York, 18 July 1954). American composer and pianist. He studied with Charles Wuorinen (Manhatten School, 1972–6), Elliott Carter (Juilliard, 1976–8) and Milton Babbitt (Princeton, 1978–80). He quickly attracted critical attention, being characterized at age 24 by Andrew Porter as 'a genuine creator with a fertile, unforced vein of invention' (A. Porter: 'Musical Events', *New Yorker*, 20 Nov 1978). At the age of 18, Picker was an improvising pianist for the Martha Graham School of Contemporary Dance, an experience that encouraged his intuitive, pulse-based musicality. His professed affinity for two composers, one romantic and one modern, also catalyzed his compositional style. He has met the challenge to reconcile the warm, earnest, arching continuity of Brahms and the cool, playful, fractured energy of Stravinsky with music distinctive for its emotional immediacy and impulsive, visceral rhythm.

Picker's early compositions, through to the age of 25, are exclusively chamber works that usually involve searching astringent harmonies, exclamatory gestures and motoric drive; his serialized pitches are often used in a manner that implies a transient tonality within a succession of striking moments. In succeeding works involving full orchestra, these moments are protracted, often into textures of even more sharply defined character. Breadth and grandure is achieved through the slow, pulsed interlocking of theme and pedal point. Melodically elaborated and colorfully scored ostinato passages continually propel the music forward. Picker imbues romantic conventions with a modern spirit which rejects nostalgia, but retains considerable expressive freedom.

One work tends to engender the next, usually with a shift in focus. The unremitting bravura and textural invention of the Violin Concerto (1981) is followed by the weighty, more integrated Symphony No.1 (1982). Piano Concerto No.2, 'Keys to the City', commissioned for the centennial of New York City's Brooklyn Bridge, effectively absorbs American vernacular elements, most conspicuously in a driving boogie woogie passage. Picker's imagination responds particularly well to extramusical subjects. Based on a text by Hermann Melville, *The Encantadas* (1983), a concerto for actor and orchestra, which is distinctive for a wide variety of musical tableaux, has enjoyed internationally successful productions in seven languages. Another work which quickly gained popularity, especially in its orchestrated form, is *Old and Lost Rivers* (1986), a short, serene Texan pastorale for piano which Picker wrote while Composer-in-Residence for the Houston SO (1985–90). Its homogeneous polyphonic texture anticipates more extended works in which faster movements are balanced by those of slow, cursive chromatic lines stretched across sustained harmonies. Representative is the string quartet, *New Memories* (1987), commissioned by the Santa Fe Chamber Music Festival to commemorate the 100th birthday of the local artist Georgia O'Keefe, who died during the writing of the work. Her painting reinforced Picker's awareness of an American southwest geologic time frame that informed his slowly unfolding works of this period. In the hybrid *Romances and Interludes* (1989), Picker confronts the 19th century directly by composing a prelude and two interludes around his orchestration of Schumann's *Three Ramanzen* op.94 for oboe and piano. Thematic allusion and mediating orchestration convincingly bind the otherwise disparate musics in a complementary relationship. *Two Fantasies* (1989) for orchestra revisits favoured textures: a slow, expansive, though somewhat restive movement followed by a kaleidoscopic etude in motoric frenzy.

Between 1978 and 1992, Picker wrote eight songs for soprano and piano, one of which, *Aussohnung*, he orchestrated to become the culminating moment in his Symphony No.2 (1986–7). *The Rain in the Trees* (1993), for soprano, flute and orchestra, based on a text by W.S. Merwin, represents at this time his most expanded use of the voice. In this work, purely instrumental blocks of stratified polyphony alternate between Ivesian vigour and Javanese serenity. It is, however, the rapturous vocal movements which make the lasting effect and anticipate the composer's most ambitious completed project to date, *Emmeline* (1994–6), commissioned by the Santa Fe Opera. The story of a 19th century New England woman's unwitting marriage to a son she bore at 14 and abandonned entails a pathos appropriately met by primarily tonal music which is emotionally charged and theatrically effective. The opera's initial success was exceeded in a second production two years later by the New York City Opera, prompting international commitments and further opera commissions. Written for the Los Angeles Opera, *Fantastic Mr. Fox* (1998) is based on a children's story well served by pulsing, playfully angular counterpoint and tunes which drift in and out of tonality.

WORKS
(selective list)

Ops: Emmeline (2, J.D. McClatchy, after J. Rossner), 1994–6, Sante Fe Op, 27 July 1996; Fantastic Mr Fox (3, D. Sturrock, after R. Dahl), 1998, Los Angeles Op, 9 Dec 1998

Orch: Pf Conc. no.1, 1980; Vn Conc., 1981; Sym. no.1, 1982; The Encantadas (H. Melville), nar, orch, 1983, arr. nar, chbr orch, 1986; Pf Conc. no.2, 'Keys to the City', 1983; Pf Conc. no.3, 'Kilauea', 1986; Old and Lost Rivers, 1986 [arr. of pf work]; Sym. no.2 'Aussöhnung', S, orch, 1986–7; Sym. no.3, str, 1988 [based on Str Qt with Bass]; Romances and Interludes, ob, orch, 1989 [from Schumann: Three Romances, op.94]; 2 Fantasies, 1989; Séance 'Homage a Sibelius', 1991; Bang!, 1992 [2nd movt of 2

Fantasies]; Va Conc., 1990, rev. 1993; And Suddenly It's Evening, 1994

Chbr: Trio, ob, vc, pf, 1974, unpubd; Flute Farm, 4 fl, 1975; Septet, fl, bn, tpt, trbn, vn, pf, vib/glock, 1976; Sextet no.2, ob, cl, pf, vn, vc, vib/glock, 1976; Sextet no.3, fl, vn, vc, db, perc, 1976; Rhapsody, vn, pf, 1978; Octet, ob, b cl, hn, vn, vc, db, hp, vib/mar, 1978; Romance, vn, pf, 1979; Nova, vn, va, vc, db, pf, 1979; The Blue Hula (Sextet no.4), fl, cl, vn, vc, pf, vib/glock, 1981; Serenade, pf, ww qnt, 1983 [based on Nova]; Keys to the City, pf, 8 insts, 1986 [arr. of Pf Conc. no.2]; Str Qt, 'New Memories', 1987; Str Qt with Bass, 1988, orchd; Invisible Lilacs, vn, pf, 1991; Suite, vc, pf, 1998

Pf: Duo, pf 4 hands, 1972, unpubd; When Soft Voices Die, 1977; Old and Lost Rivers, 1986; Pianorama, 2 pf, 1988; 3 Pieces, 1988; 4 Etudes for Ursula, 1995–6

Songs (S, pf unless otherwise stated): Dayton (Picker), 1978; Alicante (Picker), 1978; Aussöhnung (J. Goethe), 1984, arr. as last movt of Sym. no.2; When We Meet Again (E. St Vincent Millay), 1985; Half a Year Together (R. Howard), 1987; Remembering (E. St Vincent Millay), 1987; Native Trees (W.S. Merwin), 1992; To the Insects (Merwin), 1992; The Rain in the Trees (Merwin), S, fl, orch, 1993

BIBLIOGRAPHY

K.R. Schwarz: 'Tobias Picker', *Music and Musicians*, ix (1985), 10–11

JOHN VAN DER SLICE

Pickett, Philip (*b* London, 17 Nov 1950). English recorder player and conductor. His development as a player of the recorder, crumhorn, racket and shawm was inspired by contact with Anthony Baines and David Munrow. As professor of the recorder at the GSMD from 1972 to 1997 he also contributed significantly to the school's pioneering early music department. While noted as a flexible and colourful solo recorder player, his more recent successes have occurred as director of the New London Consort, with whom he has travelled and recorded widely. Clear if often speculative scholarship informs his enterprising programming which ranges from medieval music to mainstream 18th-century repertory. In 1988 he was appointed artistic director of the South Bank Summerscope Festival of Medieval and Renaissance Music, following successes in the City of London Festival. His recordings display a strong sense of communication, consistently accomplished solo singing and astute characterization, as demonstrated in several landmark recordings, including a majestic rendering of Praetorius's Terpsichore dances in 1985 and rhetorically sensitive performances of Monteverdi's *Orfeo* and Blow's *Venus and Adonis*. In 1994 Pickett became director of the Musicians of the Globe, with whom he has recorded music with Shakespearean associations.

JONATHAN FREEMAN-ATTWOOD

Pickett, Wilson (*b* Prattville, AL, 18 March 1941). American soul singer. He moved to Detroit with his family at the age of 14. He first recorded in 1957 as part of the gospel quartet, the Violinaires. Having decided to sing secular music, Pickett replaced Joe Stubbs as lead singer of another Detroit-based vocal group, the Falcons, whose members included future soul stars Eddie Floyd and Mack Rice. In 1962 Pickett composed and sang lead on the Falcons' second hit, *I found a love*, following which he began a solo career.

After brief stints with the Correctone and Double L labels, in 1964 he signed with Atlantic Records. After an undistinguished session in New York, Atlantic co-owner Jerry Wexler suggested that Pickett should record in Memphis at Stax records. Wexler believed that the Southern musicians and approach to recording would be better suited to Pickett's gospel-based style. In 1965 Pickett recorded three sessions at Stax where he was backed by the house band, Booker T. and the MGs (without Jones, who was away at college) and the Memphis Horns. Four hits resulted, *In the Midnight Hour*, *Don't fight it*, *634-5789 (Soulsville U.S.A.)* and *Ninety-Nine and a Half (won't do)*. After Stax closed its doors to outside sessions, Wexler took Pickett to record in Muscle Shoals, Alabama. Possessing perhaps the harshest voice in soul music, by the mid-1970s Pickett had had over 40 records in the rhythm and blues and pop charts.

BIBLIOGRAPHY

G. Hirshey: *Nowhere to Run: the Story of Soul Music* (New York, 1984)
P. Guralnick: *Sweet Soul Music* (New York, 1986)
J. Wexler and D. Ritz: *Rhythm and the Blues: a Life in American Music* (New York, 1993)
R. Bowman: *Soulsville U.S.A.: the Story of Stax Records* (New York, 1997)

ROB BOWMAN

Pick-Mangiagalli, Riccardo (*b* Strakonice, Bohemia, 10 July 1882; *d* Milan, 8 July 1949). Italian composer of Czech birth. The family settled in 1884 in Milan, where he studied at the conservatory (1896–1903). Until 1914 he was active as a pianist, spending some time in Vienna; subsequently he concentrated on teaching and composition, and from 1936 to 1949 was director of the Milan Conservatory. As a composer he excelled in light ballet music: already in *Il salice d'oro* there is a pleasing if facile tunefulness, combined with Viennese dance rhythms and spiced with harmonies and orchestration reminiscent of Strauss and Ravel. In *Il carillon magico*, Pick-Mangiagalli's most successful stage work, this promise reached fulfilment: though slight, the style is recognizably personal, with frequent unrelated triads, chromatic slithers, unusually placed augmented triads and diminished 7th chords and so on. Musical means are perfectly matched to dramatic context. The later stage pieces rarely explore fresh territory: in the *commedia dell'arte* opera *Basi e bote* the basic idiom is still that of *Il carillon*, proving less adequate for a full-length work, but the ballet *Casanova a Venezia* develops the style more positively, with appropriate touches of local and period colour. When in *Notturno romantico* Pick-Mangiagalli attempted a more tragic manner, the result sounds merely second-hand from Puccini and others. His best music, whether for the theatre or not, tends to alternate between the basic moods of gentle nocturnal contemplation and sparkling mercurial exuberance. These two aspects are already evident in the early String Quartet; later they are sometimes deliberately juxtaposed in pairs of contrasted pieces, such as the *Deux lunaires* for piano and the orchestral *Notturno e rondò fantastico*.

WORKS
(*selective list*)

Stage: Il salice d'oro (ballet, Pick-Mangiagalli), op.25, 1911–12, Milan, 1914; Il carillon magico (commedia mimo-sinfonico, Pick-Mangiagalli), op.30, 1915, Milan, 1918; Sumitra (leggenda monomimica, G. Clausetti), op.38, 1917, Frankfurt, 1923; Basi e bote (commedia, 3, A. Boito), op.43, 1919–20, Rome, Argentina, 3 March 1927; Mahit (ballet, Pick-Mangiagalli), op.44, Milan, 1923; Casanova a Venezia (ballet, G. Adami), op.48, Milan, 1929; Notturno romantico (op, 1, A. Rossato), op.60, Rome, Opera, 25 April 1936; 5 other works
Orch: Notturno e rondò fantastico, op.28, 1914; Humoresque, op.35, pf, orch, 1916; Sortilegi, op.39, pf, orch, 1917; 4 poemi, op.45, 1923–5; Piccola suite, 1926; Preludio e scherzo sinfonico,

op.61, 1938; Burlesca, op.34, 1941; Pf Conc., op.72, 1944; other works
Chbr and solo inst: Str Qt, op.18, 1909; 2 lunaires, op.33, pf, 1915; La pendule harmonieuse, op.51, cel/pf, 5 insts, 1929; several works, vn, pf; many other pf pieces, hp music
Small choral pieces, songs, film music, arrs. of Bach, Chopin etc.
Principal publishers: Carisch, Ricordi, Universal, Suvini Zerboni

BIBLIOGRAPHY

G.M. Gatti: *Musicisti moderni d'Italia e di fuori* (Bologna, 1920, 2/1925), 101–10
G.M. Gatti: 'Some Italian Composers of Today, 4: Pick-Mangiagalli', *MT*, lxii (1921), 323–6 [incl. list of works]; repr. with changes in *MQ*, xii (1926), 460–66
D. de' Paoli: 'Riccardo Pick-Mangiagalli', *Bollettino bibliografico musicale*, iii/7 (1928), 1–6 [incl. list of works]
F. Abbiati: 'Musicisti contemporanei: Riccardo Pick-Mangiagalli', *Emporium* [Bergamo], lxxiii (1931), 34–9
J.C.G. Waterhouse: *The Emergence of Modern Italian Music (up to 1940)* (diss., U. of Oxford, 1968), 628ff

JOHN C.G. WATERHOUSE/R

Pickup [pick-up] (Fr. *capteur*, *transducteur*; Ger. *Tonabnehmes*; It. *transduttore*, *pickup*). A transducer that converts sound vibrations received directly from a musical instrument or other source (rather than from the air, as in a microphone) into variations of electrical current. The two most common types are the magnetic pickup, best known in the electric guitar, in which an object (such as a string) containing sufficient iron or steel vibrates in close proximity (typically 2–4 mm) to an electromagnetic coil, and the contact microphone, in which a piezoelectric crystal element is fixed to the source in such a way that it vibrates as if it were part of it. The term 'pickup arm' describes the tone-arm of an LP record player, at one end of which the cartridge is mounted.

See also ELECTRONIC INSTRUMENTS §I, 2(iv).

HUGH DAVIES

Pico, Foriano (*b* Florence; *fl* 1628). Italian ?guitarist, ?composer and ?editor whose name appears on the *Nuova scelta di sonate per la chittara spagnola* (?1628), containing works attributed to PIETRO MILLIONI.

Picon, Molly (*b* New York, 1 June 1898; *d* Lancaster, PA, 6 April 1992). American singer and actress. In Philadelphia, where she grew up, she performed with vaudeville acts (from 1904) and Yiddish repertory companies. She married Jacob (Yonkel) Kalich (1881–1975), the manager of the Grand Opera House in Boston; he subsequently wrote over 40 musicals for her, including *Shmendrick* (1924), *The Little Devil* (1926), *Hello Molly* (1929), the biographical *Oy is dus a Leben*, *Abi gezunt* (1949), *Mazel tov, Molly* (1950) and *Farblondjete Honeymoon* (1955). Their first tour to Europe, in 1921, marked a change of style in European Yiddish theatre from music dramas to musical comedy, and also enhanced Picon's reputation in the USA. On her return she became the leading performer at the Second Avenue Theatre in New York. She first sang on Broadway in 1929, and from 1940 performed in dramatic productions; she also performed on radio and in films. Kalich and Picon appeared together in the play *The World of Sholem Aleichem* (1957) and the film of *Fiddler on the Roof* (1971), and she created the role of Clara Weiss in Jerry Herman's *Milk and Honey* (1961). In collaboration with Joseph Rumshinsky, Picon wrote songs and lyrics for Kalich's works; the most famous were *East Side Symphony*, *Song of the Tenement*, *The Story of Grandma's Shawl*, *Working Goil* and *Hands*. Known as an exuberant actress whose performances often included acrobatics and tap dances, the diminutive Picon coupled a natural comic flair with ingratiating warmth that made her a much-loved performer with both English- and Yiddish-speaking audiences. She wrote two memoirs, *So Laugh a Little* (1962, with E.C. Rosenberg) and *Molly!* (1980, with J.B. Grillo).

BIBLIOGRAPHY
'Picon, Molly', *CBY 1951*; *CBY 1992*
Obituary, *New York Times* (7 April 1992)

SUSAN FEDER

Picot, Eustache (*b* diocese of Evreux, *c*1575; *d* Paris, 26 June 1651). French composer and priest. He was a choirboy and then a *clerc de maîtrise* at the cathedral at Evreux, where in 1592 he became a member of the *puy de musique* in honour of St Cecilia. From 9 May 1601 to the beginning of 1604 he was *maître de musique* at Rouen Cathedral. He then became *sous-maître de musique* at the royal chapel for the January quarter: he appears as such in the records for 1613, together with Formé, who held the post in the July quarter. After Formé's death in 1638 Gobert succeeded him as *sous-maître*, and Picot, while continuing in his own post of *sous-maître*, assumed Formé's other position of composer to the chapel. Veillot, who was to inherit both his posts after his death, became his assistant on 4 May 1643.

According to Gantez, Picot 'cared only for amassing wealth', and indeed livings and prebends were showered on him. In 1613 he requested two permanent livings at the Ste Chapelle du Palais; he did not receive them but repeated his request successfully in May 1620. In the same year the king granted him a prebend as canon at St Hilaire-le-Grand, Poitiers, and in 1626 accorded him the benefice of the abbey of Cercamp, near Arras. This nomination was contested by the Archduchess Isabella, who had granted the same benefice to someone else, and was cancelled after a lawsuit; however, by way of compensation, Picot received on 21 January 1627 the benefice of the abbey of Chalivoy, in the diocese of Bourges. Finally, in 1639 he received the benefice of the abbey of St Bertault de Chaumont, near Reims. His will (reproduced by Brenet) bears witness to the opulence that he enjoyed as a result of these various incomes. He used his money carefully: in 1642 he established an annual Easter Day procession at the Ste Chapelle, stipulating that during it only his own music be performed, and in 1650 made a similar endowment, for the peace of his own soul, at Evreux Cathedral. He also made handsome donations to the Hôtel-Dieu for the benefit of poor patients.

In his will Picot left all his music to Eustache Guéhennault, *maître de musique* at the Ste Chapelle. None of it remains but he listed and described it in the articles of his endowment; it consisted of psalms, responds, antiphons and motets, all with organ interludes. They were probably in a simple contrapuntal or fauxbourdon style, with accompaniment for organ alone. Picot's output included works performed at the coronation of Louis XIII and also at his funeral in 1643, when 'all those present were greatly moved by the plaintive accents of a funeral dirge'.

BIBLIOGRAPHY
BrenetM
A. Gantez: *L'entretien des musiciens* (Auxerre, 1643); ed. with commentary by E. Thoinan (Paris, 1878/*R*)

T. Bonnin and A. Chassant: *Puy de musique, érigé à Evreux, en l'honneur de madame Sainte Cécile* (Evreux, 1837)
A. Collette and A. Bourdon: *Histoire de la maîtrise de Rouen* (Rouen, 1892/*R*)
M. le Moël: *Recherches sur les musiciens du Roy, 1600–1650* (diss., Ecole des Chartes, Paris, 1954)
D. Launay: *La musique religieuse en France du concile de Trente à 1804* (Paris, 1993)

DENISE LAUNAY/JAMES R. ANTHONY

Picqué (Fr.). *Staccato*. See BOW, §II, 2(vii) and 3(vi).

Pidhorets'ky [Podgoretsky], **Borys Volodymyrovych** (*b* Lubny, nr Poltava, 25 March/6 April 1873; *d* Moscow, 19 Feb 1919). Ukrainian composer. He studied at Warsaw Conservatory and then in Moscow under Aleksandr Il'yinsky. In 1912 he was sent by the Music-Ethnographic Commission of the Russian Geographic Society to collect folksongs in Ukraine. He joined the faculty of the Moscow Conservatory in 1915 and was music critic for *Golos Moskvi* and from 1917 for *Izvestiya*. Besides much choral and piano music, he wrote two operas. *Kupal'na iskra* ('The Spark of Kupalo'; 2, L. Yanovs'ka; 1901, Kiev; rev. version, 1907, Lubny) is based on Ukrainian lore regarding the flame of Kupalo (St John's Eve). The principal dramatic element lies in the contrast of the real and the fantastic; in Act 1 the 'real' rests heavily on the use of folk genres in arias and choruses, while in Act 2 the 'fantastic' is expressed through recitative, arioso and a richer harmonic and instrumental fabric. The true protagonist is the chorus, which Pidhorets'ky handles with great skill. *Bidna Liza* ('Poor Lisa'; 4, M. Vashkevych, after a novel by M. Karamzin; 1916, Moscow; rediscovered only in 1968) deals with everyday life and emotions where an individual is the victim of difficult social circumstances; here Pidhorets'ky uses a sharper harmonic language and relies more on orchestral episodes.

BIBLIOGRAPHY
K. Cherpukhova, ed.: *Borys Pidhorets'ky: vybrani retsenzii ta statti* [Selected Reviews and Articles] (Kiev, 1970)
K. Cherpukhova: 'Deyaki pytannya muzychnoï dramaturhii oper B. Pidhorets'koho' [Certain Questions regarding the Musical Dramaturgy of the Operas of B. Pidhorets'ky], *Ukraïns'ke muzykoznavstvo*, no.14 (1979), 23–42
K. Cherpukhova: *Borys Pidhorets'ky* (Kiev, 1990)

VIRKO BALEY

Pidoux, Pierre (*b* Neuchâtel, 4 March 1905). Swiss organist and musicologist. He graduated in 1933 from the theology faculty of the Eglise Libre in Lausanne and studied the organ in Geneva with Montillet from 1933 to 1936. In 1929 he founded the Choeur J.S. Bach in Lausanne, which he directed until 1948, holding at the same time an organ post in Lausanne. In 1948 he was appointed organist at the Montreux Temple. From 1946 to 1965 he was in charge of the hymnology course at the theology faculty of the Eglise Libre in Lausanne; in 1964 he was given the honorary doctorate in theology by the university.

Pidoux's activities have been devoted mostly to hymnology, musicology and teaching. Though he has edited many volumes of other early music, he is known as a specialist in the history of the Huguenot Psalter and has sought especially to promote the music of the Protestant church, for instance with his editorship of the series Collection de Musique Protestante (from 1935). He was co-founder (in 1954) and general editor of the sacred music series Cantate Domino, and in 1967 he became co-director with Luther Dittmer of the complete works of Goudimel, to which he has contributed several volumes.

He has also composed many works for mixed choir and organ.

WRITINGS

'Les psaumes d'Antoine de Mornable, Guillaume Morlaye et Pierre Certon (1546, 1554, 1555): étude comparative', *AnnM*, v (1957), 179–98

'Notes sur quelques éditions des psaumes de Claude Goudimel', *RdM*, xlii (1958), 184–92

Der Psalmengesang in der Liturgie der reformierten Kirche (Lemgo, 1959)

Psaumes des saisons (Yverdon, 1962)

ed.: *Le psautier huguenot du XVIe siècle*, i: *Les mélodies* (Basle, 1962); ii: *Documents et bibliographie* (Basle, 1962)

'Le chant des psaumes dans le culte réformé', *Maison-Dieu*, no.92 (1967), 102–14

'Polyphonic Settings of the Genevan Psalter: are they Church Music?', *Cantors at the Crossroads: Essays on Church Music in Honor of Walter E. Buszin*, ed. J. Riedel (St Louis, 1967), 65–74

'Loys Bourgeois' Anteil am Hugenotten-Psalter', *JbLH*, xv (1970), 123–32

'Der Kirchengesang im Waadtland (Schweiz) im 18. und 19. Jahrhundert: eine Skizze', *Traditionen und Reformen in der Kirchenmusik: Festschrift für Konrad Ameln*, ed. G. Schuhmacher (Kassel, 1974), 41–8

Vom Ursprung der Genfer Psalmweisen (Zürich, 1984)

'Luther, Zwingli, Calvin et le chant d'église', *Cahiers Protestants*, new ser., i (1986), 5–10

'Die Enstehung des Genfer Psalter', *Bulletin der Internationalen Arbeitsgemeinschaft für Hymnologie*, xix (1991), 15–36

'La Genève de Calvin et le chant des psaumes', *Revue musicale de Suisse romande*, xliv (1991), 139–59

Franc, Bourgeois, Davantès: leur contribution à la création des mélodies du psautier de Genève (Geneva, 1993)

EDITIONS

Les Pseaumes mis en rime francoise, par Clément Marot et Théodore de Bèze (Genève, 1565) (Kassel, 1935) [facs. with commentary]

Girolamo Frescobaldi: Orgel- und Klavierwerke (Kassel, 1948–79)

Georg Friedrich Kauffmann: Harmonische Seelenlust, i: *Praeludien über die bekanntesten Choral Lieder für Orgel de David*; ii: *62 Choräle mit beziffertem Bass für Orgel* (Kassel, 1951)

Andrea Gabrieli: Orgelwerke (Kassel, 1941–63)

Claudio Merulo: Canzonen, 1592 (Kassel, 1954)

with H. Hollinger: *Paschal de L'Estocart: Cent cinquante pseaumes de David*, DM, 1st ser., vii (1954)

Anthoni van Noordt: Psalmbearbeitungen für Orgel, 1659 (Kassel, 1954)

La Forme des prières et chants ecclésiastiques, Geneve, 1542 (Kassel, 1959)

Claude Goudimel: Oeuvres complètes, ix: *Les 150 psaumes d'après les éditions de 1564 et 1565* (Brooklyn, NY, 1967)

Théodore de Bèze: Psaumes mis en vers français (1551–1562): accompagnés de la version en prose de Loïs Budé (Geneva, 1984) [facs. with commentary]

Clément Marot et Théodore de Bèze: Les Psaumes en vers français avec leurs mélodies (Genève 1562) (Geneva, 1986) [facs. with commentary]

BIBLIOGRAPHY

SML

P.-A. Gaillard: 'Pour les cinquante ans de Pierre Pidoux', *SMz*, xcv (1955), 503 only

Reviews of *Le psautier huguenot du XVIe siècle*: M. Honegger, *RdM*, xlix (1963), 237–43; F. Lesure, *RdM*, xlix (1963), 243–4; K. Tóth, *SMH*, vi (1964), 390–401

Melanges d'histoire et de bibliographie offerts à Pierre Pidoux: à l'occasion de son nonantième anniversaire, 4 mars 1995, ed. A. Gaucher (Pessac, 1995)

ETIENNE DARBELLAY/DOROTHEA BAUMANN

Piece (Fr. *pièce*, *morceau*; Ger. *Stück*; It. *pezzo*). A non-technical term applied mainly to instrumental compositions from the 17th century onwards. The term was first used to describe a completed work of art or literature (as distinct from a separate portion of a larger mass or substance) in the 16th century. Its earliest use with reference to music, as recorded by the *Oxford English Dictionary*, was in 1601, in Shakespeare's *Twelfth Night* ('that piece of song'; Act 2 scene iv, line 2). The term gained a wider currency in the French genres of *pièce de clavecin* and *pièce de viole* in the later 17th century and the 18th. It is unusual to speak of movements of larger works such as symphonies or sonatas as 'pieces', but there are exceptions: Beethoven used the Italian *pezzo* to refer to the first movement of his C♯ minor Piano Sonata op.27 no.2 in his directions for performance. From the 19th century onwards, German and French composers took to using various compound forms as titles of compositions: *Konzertstück*, *Fantasiestück*, *Klavierstück* and *Orchesterstück* are common, together with more specific titles such as *Nachtstück* and *Blumenstück*. In French, *Pièce de concours* and *Morceau de concert* are found, as well as such exotic designations as *Pièce en forme de habañera*.

Attempts to pin down a more precise definition of a 'piece of music' are beset by philosophical and semantic problems, which were highlighted in the work of certain avant-garde composers of the 1950s and 60s and in subsequent musicological literature. The issues involved include how the concept of a 'piece' has been culturally constructed within Western musical tradition, and what music is thereby excluded from this category. The ontology, or mode of existence, of a piece of music, is also highly problematic. Finally, there is the question of how the concept of 'piece' relates to those of 'composition' and 'work'.

It has been suggested that no definition of 'piece' is general enough to cover every form of composition: even such basic criteria as the Aristotelian requirement of a beginning, a middle and an end have demonstrable exceptions (Crocker). Alternatively, the idea of the piece may be regarded as a way of conceiving musical form that arose during musical history and may be dated tentatively from about 1420–30 to about 1910 (Carpenter). A piece of music is conceived as an object, the qualities and structure of which are fixed by the composer, and which comprises a 'single unified gesture or motion'. The listener remains outside the musical object, and does not participate in it. Carpenter's chronological limits thus exclude medieval sacred polyphony, which was conceived as an element of the liturgy, rather than as an entity in its own right, and, at the other extreme, aleatory music which was not completely determined by the composer. (With less obvious justification, 14th-century secular polyphony is also implicitly excluded.) A number of factors contributed to the 'objectification' of music in the 15th and 16th centuries, including the humanistic understanding of the artist as a creator and the development of printing. After the Renaissance musical history shows an increasing objectification of the piece, supported by factors including Kant's concept of the aesthetic, and composers' striving for ever greater musical unification.

This conception of the musical piece has profound implications for the understanding of musical perception, of music as a temporal entity, and of musical unity. Carpenter also touches on the problem of how a musical piece may be said to exist: it does not have a material presence and is dependent on the composer and upon individual performances for its existence, but it continues to exist beyond these. Ingarden has explored the same theme at greater length (though with reference to the term 'work'). He considers the hypotheses that the identity of a musical work or piece is located first in its performances, then in conscious experiences of it, and finally in its score, but argues that it goes beyond all of these. He concludes that musical works exist as heteronomous objects (that is, they depend for their existence on acts of the composer and listeners) and as intentional, as distinct from real, objects (that is, they have no material presence, but constitute an 'ideal boundary' at which all real performances and experiences of the work aim). The semiologists Jean Molino and Jean-Jacques Nattiez have adopted Ingarden's position, with subtle modifications: rather than viewing the material manifestations of the work as imperfect embodiments of the intentional object, as Ingarden does, Nattiez advocates a de-centred concept of the 'total musical fact', the ontology of which is located in the totality of all the acts of composition that engendered it, the musical score, and all the acts of perception to which it gives rise.

The foregoing theoretical issues are relevant equally to the concepts of 'work' and 'composition' as to 'piece'. However, the three categories differ slightly in ways that go beyond mere usage. A folk melody is a 'piece' of music, but it cannot be said to be a composition. A rudimentary student exercise is a 'composition', but does not possess the stature required to be considered a work. A composition or work must be capable of repetition; however, a skilful improvisation may be perceived as a 'piece' of music, in the sense of a finished product of artistic imagination. Moreover, if an improvisation is recorded, would it then be a composition? If jazz, pop, folk music and non-Western music are considered, the answer to what constitutes a 'piece' becomes even more elusive.

BIBLIOGRAPHY
R. Crocker: 'Some Reflections on the Shape of Music', *CMc*, no.5 (1967), 50–56
P. Carpenter: 'The Musical Object', *CMc*, no.5 (1967), 56–87
R. Ingarden: *Utwór muzyczny i sprawa jego tożsamości* (Kraków, 1973; Eng. trans., 1986, as *The Work of Music and the Problem of its Identity*)
J.J. Nattiez: *Musicologie générale et sémiologie* (Paris, 1987; Eng. trans., 1990, as *Music and Discourse: towards a Semiology of Music*)
PETER FOSTER

Pièce croisée. A term used by François Couperin (*Troisième livre de pièces de clavecin*, 1722) and revived by modern writers to designate a harpsichord piece in which two parts, one for each hand, cross and re-cross one another in the same range, often sounding the same note simultaneously. Such pieces must be performed on a two-manual harpsichord with independent unison registers, one for each manual. The first such instruments seem to have been made in France in the 1640s, and two *pièces croisées* are included among the surviving works of Louis Couperin (*d* 1661).

EDWIN M. RIPIN

Piechteler von Greiffenthal, Matthias Siegmund. *See* BIECHTELER VON GREIFFENTHAL, MATTHIAS SIEGMUND.

Piede (It.). The second formal unit of the Italian 14th-century BALLATA.

Pié de Dieu, Pierre (*fl* early 17th century). French printer, successor to Corneille [?Camille] Hertman in the firm formerly owned by PIERRE HAULTIN.

Pieltain, Dieudonné-Pascal (*b* Liège, bap. 4 March 1754; *d* Liège, 10 Dec 1833). Flemish violinist and composer. He seems to have studied in Liège, and from 1761 to 1763

was a choirboy at the church of St Pierre. He probably remained there until 1765, when he left Liège and went to Italy, no doubt with his friend Henri Hamal. He took lessons from Giornovichi, and probably followed him to Paris: Giornovichi first performed at the Concert Spirituel in 1773, and the *Spectacles de Paris* for that year mentions, among the four tenor violins of the orchestra, a certain Pieltain resident at the Hôtel de Soubise. From 1778 Pieltain regularly played as a soloist with the Concert Spirituel. He also attracted comment for his brawling lifestyle. On 21 March 1779, Pieltain performed one of his own compositions with the Concert Spirituel. Giornovichi left Paris that year, and Pieltain took his place in the Prince de Guéméné's orchestra. His brother, Jacques-Joseph-Toussaint (bap. 24 Jan 1757), a well-known horn player and a pupil of Punto, joined him there. The two musicians returned to Liège with the prince's orchestra, and gave concerts at Spa with Carl Stamitz in September 1780. In 1782 the brothers went to London; Dieudonné-Pascal gave concerts at Drury Lane Theatre, the Lent Oratorios and the New Rooms, and the following year became leader of the orchestra of the Hanover Square Concerts. He also played violin solos at Vauxhall Gardens from 1783, and in 1785 became leader of the Professional Concert. In 1786 he married Marie Chanu, a soprano who performed at the Pantheon and the Salomon concerts.

Pieltain continued his career as a soloist on the Continent while pursuing his activities in London. He was apparently on friendly terms with either Leopold or Wolfgang Amadeus Mozart. The death of Marie Chanu in 1793 caused Pieltain to leave London for good. He played in Germany, Poland and Russia, and seems to have returned to Paris and Liège at regular intervals. It was to Liège that he finally retired, when he turned to teaching and had a number of future violin virtuosos among his pupils, who included Hubert Léonard. Pieltain died in 1833, a wealthy patron of music.

Pieltain's own compositions were mostly for his own instrument: 13 of his violin concertos, six sonatas, 12 quartets, six duets and 12 *petits airs* for violin were engraved. According to Fétis and Vannes, he left some 30 concertos, 167 quartets, six sonatas for violin and cello, and 50 violin studies, all in manuscript, but these are now lost. His works reflect the various contacts he made during his career; his first concertos, for example, are in the direct line of descent from Italian concertos, but his later works reflect the Mannheim style. In his quartets, which show the characteristics of Viennese classicism, Pieltain cultivates a certain melodic elegance without neglecting virtuosity.

WORKS

Vn concs.: 30 incl. 13 pubd, mentioned by Vannes
Str qts: 167 mentioned by Vannes, incl. 6 quatuors concertants, bk 1 (Paris, n.d.); 6 quartettos, op.2*d* (London, n.d.) [nos.1–3, 6 are identical with nos.1–4 of 6 quatuors concertants]; 6 quatuors, op.4, bks 1, 2 (Paris, n.d.); nos.24, 41, 52, 92, 103, 115, *B-Bc*; others, lost
Other works: 6 sonates, vn, op. 1*a* (Paris, n.d.), lost; 6 solos, vn (London, n.d.); Etude, solo vn, str qt, *Bc*

BIBLIOGRAPHY
AudaM; BrenetC; FétisB; PierreH; VannesD
G. De Tiège and P. Vendrix: 'Dieudonné-Paschal Pieltain (1754–1833): étude bio-bibliographie', *Revue de la Société liégeoise de musicologie* (forthcoming)
PHILIPPE VENDRIX

Pieno (It.). Full, as in *organo pieno* (FULL ORGAN), *coro pieno* (full choir), and a *voce piena* (with full voice).

Pierce, Edward. *See* PEARCE, EDWARD.

Pierement. A term widely used since about 1912 in the Low Countries to designate the book-playing street organs of Amsterdam. It is not applied to any other type of mechanical organ. *See* FAIRGROUND ORGAN.

Pierlot, Denis (*fl* Paris, 1784–92). French violinist and composer. According to Fétis, the source for Pierlot's first name, he was a violinist in the orchestra of the Concert Spirituel in 1786. There is no mention of him as soloist, nor does his name appear in connection with any other Parisian orchestra. Gerber wrote of him as still living in 1792. The only other contemporary references to him are all publication announcements by Imbault between 1784 and 1789 concerning his *Deux symphonies concertantes* (the first for two violins, the second for two violins and viola), his *Trois symphonies* op.1, and arrangements by P. Sehnal (*c*1786) of the latter for keyboard with optional violin and cello parts. Only the *symphonies concertantes*, published in 1784, are extant. These show him to be a product of his time; he used a simple harmonic structure, clear-cut four- and eight-bar phrases and an effective but uncomplicated orchestration. Their principal feature is their attractive melodic line, which shows an undeniable lyric gift. Incipits of the three lost symphonies, which also appeared by 1784, are in Imbault's thematic catalogue (Paris, 1790). (*BrookSF*; *Choron-FayolleD*; *FétisB*; *GerberL*)

BARRY S. BROOK, JAIME GONZALEZ

Pierné, (Henri Constant) Gabriel (*b* Metz, 16 Aug 1863; *d* Ploujean, Finistère, 17 July 1937). French composer and conductor. His parents were musicians: his baritone father introduced him to singing and his mother to the piano. When Lorraine was annexed by Germany following the Franco-Prussian War of 1870, the family moved to Paris where Pierné became a student at the Conservatoire. He won *premiers prix* for organ (at 16, Marmontel's class), harmony (at 17, Durand's class), counterpoint (at 18) and *second prix* for organ (Franck's class). He was also in Massenet's composition class, and at 19 he won the Prix de Rome for his cantata *Edith*. After three years in Rome at the Villa Medici, he returned to Paris, to teach at his parents' private school of piano and singing; one of his pupils for piano, Louise Bergon, became his wife in 1890. In that year he succeeded Franck as organist at Ste Clotilde, a post he retained until 1898.

In 1903 he became deputy conductor of the Concerts Colonne. When Edouard Colonne died in 1910 Pierné was appointed principal conductor, remaining president and director of the orchestra until 1933. At the Concerts Colonne he conducted the symphonic repertory of Mozart, Beethoven and Berlioz, he made Franck's works better known, and he conducted first performances of works by leading composers of the time, notably Debussy (*Ibéria*, *Images*, *Jeux*, *Chansons de Bilitis* and *Khamma*), Ravel (*Une barque sur l'océan*, *Tzigane*, and the first suite from *Daphnis et Chloé* over a year before the première of the complete ballet) and Roussel (*Pour une fête de printemps*). For Diaghilev's Ballets Russes he conducted the première of Stravinsky's *Firebird*. From March 1928 to May 1931 he recorded extensively with the Concerts Colonne orchestra for the French Odéon company, including some interesting Berlioz performances (reissued on CD) and works by Ravel.

While Pierné's principal activity was conducting during the musical season in Paris, entailing at least 48 different programmes a year, he was able to devote himself to composition during the summer months, which he spent with his wife and their three children at their house at Ploujean in Brittany. The period of Pierné's compositional activity (1880–1936) falls into three distinct periods. The first was dominated by the piano works, *mélodies*, incidental music and the light early operas. At the threshold of the 20th century he embarked on the ten years of vocal-orchestral frescos, the triptych of oratorios (*La croisade des enfants*, *Les enfants à Bethléem*, *Saint François d'Assise*) which were followed by the Piano Quintet, a work typical of the manner of the second period, on the one hand, and on the other some solid concertante works and other orchestral pieces. The final period, 1916–36, was dominated by the chamber music, the best of the ballet scores (above all *Cydalise et le chèvre-pied*), the comic opera *Fragonard* and the *Divertissements sur un thème pastoral* for orchestra.

Pierné forged a very personal language, classical in form and modern in spirit, balancing technique and individuality, discipline and instinct. From Massenet he learnt the art of melody, and a lightness of touch that is evident in such works as the operatic comedy *On ne badine pas avec l'amour*, staged in 1910. Meanwhile Franck imbued him with the high consciousness of art, the sense of vast architectural structures and the taste for religiously inspired music, which yielded not only the oratorios, but also instrumental works such as the *Paysages franciscains* (1919). Pierné was influenced by Saint-Saëns's notion of 'ars gallica'; he composed a number of works inspired by early French dance forms. He was also open to the style of his contemporaries and was attracted to the exoticism that was much in vogue at the time: oriental scales, pentatonic modes and Spanish-Basque rhythms (for instance, in the second movement of the Quintet). His rostrum at the Concerts Colonne was like an observation post from which he surveyed contemporary musical trends, freely absorbing many of them into his own personal style. That style is pure and refined, incorporating gentle humour and a palpable charm, as well as intermittent gravity and mystical depth. While there is abundant melodic invention, thematic designs tend towards brevity. In terms of form, Pierné shared a preference for cyclical structure and chromatic development. His later style owed something to Debussy's harmonies, to Ravel's luxuriant orchestration, and to Roussel's dynamism.

Pierné was elected a member of the Académie des Beaux-Arts in 1925 and was also made a Commandeur of the Légion d'Honneur in 1935. His cousin Paul Pierné (1874–1952) was also a composer.

WORKS
(selective list)

DRAMATIC

Ops: Le chemin d'amour (oc, 1), 1883, unperf.; Les elfes (légende dramatique, E. Guinand), 1884; Don Luis (oc, 3, Beaumont), 1886, unperf.; Bouton d'or (fantaisie lyrique, 4, M. Carré), Paris, Nouveau, 3 Jan 1893; Lizarda (oc, 3, A. Silvestre), 1893–4; La coupe enchantée (oc, 3, F. Matrat, after J. de La Fontaine), Royan, Casino, 24 Aug 1895 [1 act version perf. Paris, OC, 26 Dec 1905]; Vendée (op, 3, 4 tableaux, C. Foley and A. Brisson), Lyon, Grand, 11 March 1897; La fille de Tabarin (comédie lyrique, 3, V. Sardou and P. Ferrier), Paris, OC, 8 Feb 1901; On ne badine pas avec l'amour (comédie lyrique, 3, G. Nigond and L. Leloir after A. de Musset), Paris, OC, 30 May 1910; Sophie Arnould (comédie lyrique, 1, G. Nigond), Paris, OC, 21 Feb 1927; Fragonard (comédie musicale, 3, A. Rivoire and R. Coolus), 1930, Paris, Porte Saint-Martin, 17 Oct 1934

Ballets: Le collier de saphir (pantomime, 1, 2 tableaux, C. Mendès), perf. 1891; Les joyeuses commères de Paris (ballet-féerie, 5, C. Mendès and G. Courteline), perf. 1892; Le docteur Blanc (mimodrame fantastique, 4, C. Mendès), perf. 1893; Salomé (pantomime lyrique, 1, 5 tableaux, A. Silvestre and Meltzner), perf. 1895; Cydalise et le chèvre-pied (ballet, 2, 3 tableaux, R. de Flers and G.-A. de Caillavet), perf. 1923; Impressions de music-hall (ballet, 4 scenes), perf. 1927; Giration (divertissement chorégraphique, R. Bizet and J. Barreyre), perf. 1934; Images (divertissement chorégraphique, 1, L. Staats and A. Hellé), perf. 1935

Incid music: Izeyl (A. Silvestre and E. Morand), perf. 1894; Yanthis (J. Lorrain), perf. 1894; La princesse lointaine (E. Rostand), perf. 1895; La samaritaine (Rostand), perf. 1897; Francesca de Rimini (M. Crawford, transl. M. Schwob), perf. 1902; Ramuntcho (P. Loti), perf. 1908; Hamlet (Morand and Schwob, after W. Shakespeare), 1910; Les cathédrales (Morand), 1915

VOCAL

With orch: Edith (cant., E. Guinand), 1882; Pandore (scène lyrique, P. Collin), S, spkr, chorus, orch, 1888; La nuit de Noël de 1870 (épisode lyrique, E. Morand), solo vv, chorus, orch, org, 1895; L'an mil, sym. poem, chorus, orch, 1895; La croisade des enfants (légende musicale, after M. Schwob, chorus/children's chorus, orch, org, 1902; Les enfants à Bethléem (mystère, G. Nigond), solo vv, children's chorus, orch, org, 1907; Saint François d'Assise (orat., Nigond, after St Francis of Assisi: Fioretti), 1912

Songs (1v, pf unless otherwise stated): A nous deux (Mme Blanchecotte), 1879; A Saint Blaise (A. de Musset), 1879; Découragement (J. Chailley), 1879; Dernier voeu (Blanchecotte), 1879; L'oeillet rouge (T. Gautier), 1v, pf/orch, 1880; Les trois chansons (V. Hugo), 1880; Mimi Pinson (de Musset), 1881; Le moulin (E. Guinand), 1881; Le sais-tu bien (Blanchecotte), 1882; L'adieu suprême (Blanchecotte), 1883; A Lucette (H. Gauthier-Villars), 1883; Bonsoir (A. Silvestre), 1883; La brise (H. Passerieu), 1883; Chanson de berger (Gauthier-Villars), 1v, pf/orch, 1883; Connaissez-vous mon hirondelle (A. Capon), 1883; Le coup de l'étrier (L. Durocher), 1v, pf/orch, 1883; Les deux roses (J. Soulary), 1v, pf/orch, 1883; En barque (Guinand), 1883; Les filles de Cadix (de Musset), 1883, also orch; Hymne d'amour (C. Grandmougin), 1883; Mignonne (A. Labitte), 1883; Provence (Guinand), 1883; Tristesse (Guinand), 1883; Villanelle (P. Desportes), 1883; Bergerie (Capon), 1v, chorus ad lib, pf, 1884; Ritournelle (F. Coppée), 1884; Le voyageur (A. Silvestre), 1884; Le réveil de Galatée, scène (P. Collin), 1v, pf/orch, 1885; La rieuse, conte en prose (C. Mendès), 1885; Souvenir triste (Gauthier-Villars), 1888; Les petits lapins (J. Aicard), 1890; Tes yeux bleus (L. Solvay), 1892; Ton rire est si doux (P. Collin), 1892; Les trois petits oiseaux (J. Richepin), 1892; Vous souviendrez-vous? (Labitte), 1892; Sur la route (R. Launay), 1896; Contes (J. Lorrain), 5 songs, 1897 [no.2, 1v, chorus, pf/orch]; Soirs de jadis (Lorrain), 3 songs, 1898 [no.3, 1v, spkr, pf]; Boutique japonaise (L. Gallet), 1899; 3 adaptations musicales (Lorrain, Samain, Rosemonde Rostand), 1902; 3 mélodies (T. Klingsor), 3 songs, 1904; 6 ballades françaises (P. Fort), 1921 [no.5, 1v, pf/orch]

INSTRUMENTAL

Orch: Suite d'orchestre no.1, op.11, 1883; Fantaisie-ballet, op.6, pf, orch, 1885; Ouverture symphonique, op.10, 1885; Pf Conc., op.12, 1887; Marche solennelle, op.23, 1889; Pantomime, op.24, 1889; Scherzo-caprice, op.25, pf, orch, 1890; Poème symphonique, op.37, pf, orch, 1901; Ballet de cour, 6 airs à danser, 1901; Concertstück, op.39, hp, orch, 1903; Paysages franciscains, 1919; Divertissement sur un thème pastoral, op.49, 1932; Gulliver au pays de Lilliput, 1935; Viennoise, op.49bis, 1935

Chbr: Fantaisie-impromptu, op.4, vn, pf, 1883; Pièce, g, op.5, ob, pf, 1883; Berceuse, op.8, vn, pf, 1884; Caprice, op.16, vc, pf, 1887; Canzonetta, op.19, cl, pf, 1888; Expansion, op.21, vc, pf, 1888; Pastorale variée, op.30, fl, ob, cl, 2 bn, hn, tpt, c1893; Solo de concert, op.35, bn, pf, 1898; Sonata, op.36, vn, pf, 1900, also arr. fl, pf; Pf Qnt, op.41, 1917; Sonate en une partie, op.46, vc, pf, 1919; Pf Trio, op.45, 1922; Sonata da camera, op.48, fl, vc, pf, 1927; Prélude de concert sur un thème de Purcell, bn, pf, 1933;

Variations libres et final, op.51, fl, vn, va, vc, hp, 1934; Introduction et variations sur une ronde populaire, sax qt, 1936; Trois pieces intim, vn, va, vc, 1938; Voyages au pays du Tendres, fl, vn, vc, hp, 1938

Pf: Intermezzo, c1880; 15 pièces, op.3, 1883, nos.2, 3 and 13 orchd; Album pour mes petits amis, op.14, 1887; Etude de concert, op.13, 1887; Valse, op.15, 1887; Almée, op.18, 1888; Humoresque, op.17, 1888; Rêverie, op.20, 1888; Improvisata, op.22, 1889; Barcarolle, op.26, pf 4 hands, 1890; Ariette dans le style ancien, op.28, 1892; Mazurka, op.28 bis, 1892; Valse impromptu, op.27, pf 4 hands, 1892; Pastorale variée, op.30, 1894; Sérénade à Colombine, op.32, 1894; Bagatelle, op.33, 1898; Sérénade vénitienne, op.34, 1898; 3 pièces formant suite de concert, op.40, 1903, Variations en ab mineur, 1919; Passacaille, op.52, 1932; Prélude sur le nom de Paul Dukas, 1936

Other solo inst: Fugue, G, org, 1882; Impromptu caprice, op.9, hp, 1885; 3 pièces, op.29, org, 1893; Entréc, org, c1900; Scène féerique, harm, cel, 1902

Principal publishers: Choudens, Costallat, Durand, Enoch, Eschig, Hamelle, Heugel, Leduc, Ricordi, Salabert

BIBLIOGRAPHY

O. Séré: Musiciens français d'aujourd'hui (Paris, 1912, rev. 2/1921) [incl. list of works]

D. Sordet: Douze chefs d'orchestre (Paris, 1924)

R. Kemp: 'Gabriel Pierné', Le théâtre lyrique en France (Paris, 1937–9) [pubn of Poste National/Radio Paris], iii, 100–110

H. Busser: Notice sur la vie et les oeuvres de Gabriel Pierné (Paris, 1938)

P. Landormy: La musique française après Debussy (Paris, 1943)

R. Dumesnil: La musique en France entre les deux guerres 1919–1939 (Geneva, 1946)

L. Davies: César Franck and His Circle (London, 1970)

G. Masson: Gabriel Pierné: musicien lorrain (Nancy and Metz, 1987)

GEORGES MASSON

Piero [M(agister) Piero] (fl northern Italy, 1340–50). Italian composer. He was one of the earliest generation of Trecento musicians. Since he was not of Florentine origin he is not mentioned in Villani's Florentine chronicle. It is possible that Piero is the 'Magister Petrus Andreutii' who came from Assisi and who stayed in Perugia in 1335 where he was employed as a 'doctor comunis Perusii in arte cantus'. Piero certainly spent some time in the 1340s and early 1350s with Giovanni da Cascia and Jacopo da Bologna at the courts of the Visconti family in Milan and of the della Scala family in Verona. This is indicated by the texts of his madrigals and cacce. The caccia Con brachi assai, also set to music by Giovanni, was composed at the court of the Visconti: the text mentions the river Adda, which flowed through territory at that time under Milanese rule. All'ombra and Sovra un fiume sing the praises of 'Anna', who also appears in the madrigals of Giovanni and Jacopo and who was presumably associated with the court of the della Scala family. The name 'Margherita' occurs in Sì com'al canto, a madrigal that was also set to music by Jacopo.

Piero was evidently older than Jacopo. He presumably died shortly after 1350. In a legal manuscript from Bologna apparently dating from the first half of the 14th century (D-FUl D23) there is a miniature with musical representation: among other figures, an old man with a beard and tonsure is depicted and named as 'Ser Piero'; despite the very conventional style of the miniature he may be identifiable with the composer (see illustration; also von Fischer, 1973).

Only eight works by Piero are known, all in the Biblioteca Nazionale in Florence (I-Fn Pan.26), although two occur in an older manuscript (I-Rvat Rossi 215) presumably of Paduan or Veronese origin, where they are entered as anonymous pieces. In addition, there are two

Marginal illustration from an Italian legal document, 14th century; the bearded figure on the right may be identifiable with Piero (D-FUl D23, f.302)

further cacce, suspected by Pirrotta (1959) to be works of Piero (in *I-Rvat* 215 and *I-Fn* 26 – with concordance in *GB-Lbl* 29987). None of the pieces seems to have been widely known.

The most striking feature of Piero's work is the canonic technique. He may with certainty be regarded as the composer of the earliest surviving two- and three-part canonic madrigals and cacce. The eight works can be divided into four distinct groups, each of which represents one stage of development from the simple two-voice madrigal to the three-voice caccia. The madrigals *Quando l'àire* and *Sovra un fiume* are written in the style of the oldest and simplest madrigals of the manuscript *I-Rvat* 215. In *All'ombra* and *Sì com'al canto* there are ritornellos with imitative free voice-exchange technique (similar to some anonymous pieces in *I-Rvat* 215). *Cavalcando* and *Ogni diletto* are set to music as two-voice canonic caccia-madrigals (with non-canonic ritornellos), whereas *Con brachi assai* and *Con dolce brama* represent the fully developed Italian caccia genre with canon in the upper voices and a textless tenor. The works of the two last-named groups by Piero had an enduring effect on the younger Jacopo da Bologna and perhaps also on his approximate contemporary, Giovanni da Cascia.

WORKS

Editions: *The Music of Fourteenth-Century Italy*, ed. N. Pirrotta, CMM, viii/2 (1960) [P]
  Italian Secular Music, ed. W.T. Marrocco, PMFC, vi (1967) [M vi]; viii (1972) [M viii]

MADRIGALS

All'ombra d'un perlaro, 2vv, P, M vi (Senhal: 'Anna')
Cavalcando con un giòvine, 2vv, P, M vi (caccia-madrigal)
Ogni diletto, 2vv, P, M vi (It.-Fr. text; caccia-madrigal)
Quando l'àire comença, P, M vi
Sì com'al canto, 2vv, P, M vi
Sovra un fiume regale, 2vv, P, M vi (text inc.)

CACCE

Con brachi assai, 3vv, P, M vi
Con dolce brama, 3vv, P, M vi

DOUBTFUL WORKS

2 cacce: Or qua, compagni, 3vv, P, M viii; Segugi a corda, 3vv, P, M viii (see Pirrotta, 1959)

BIBLIOGRAPHY

N. Pirrotta: 'Per l'origine e la storia della "caccia" e del "madrigale" trecentesco', *RMI*, xlviii (1946), 305–23; xlix (1947), 121–42
N. Pirrotta: 'Marchettus de Padua and the Italian Ars Nova', *MD*, ix (1955), 57–71; repr. in *Musica tra Medioevo e Rinascimento* (Turin, 1984), 63–79
K. von Fischer: *Studien zur italienischen Musik des Trecento und frühen Quattrocento* (Berne, 1956)
N. Pirrotta: 'Piero e l'impressionismo musicale del secolo XIV', *L'Ars Nova italiana del Trecento I: Certaldo 1959*, 57–74; repr. in *Musica tra Medioevo e Rinascimento* (Turin, 1984), 104–14
G. Corsi, ed.: *Poesie musicali del Trecento* (Bologna, 1970), pp.xxxiv ff, 3–10
K. von Fischer: '"Portraits" von Piero, Giovanni da Firenze und Jacopo da Bologna in einer Bologneser Handschrift des 14. Jahrhunderts?', *MD*, xxvii (1973), 61–4
M.T. Brasolin: 'Proposta per una classificazione metrica delle cacce trecentesche', *La musica al tempo del Boccaccio e i suoi rapporti con la letteratura: Siena and Certaldo 1975* [*L'Ars Nova italiana del Trecento*, iv (Certaldo, 1978)], 83–105
E. Paganuzzi: 'Medioevo e Rinascimento', *La musica a Verona*, ed. P.P. Brugnoli (Verona, 1976), 33–70
J. Nádas: 'The Structure of MS Panciatichi 26 and the Transmission of Trecento Polyphony', *JAMS*, xxxiv (1981), 393–427
K. von Fischer: 'Das Madrigal "Sì come al canto" von Magister Piero und Jacopo da Bologna', *Analysen: Beiträge zu einer Problemgeschichte des Komponierens: Festschrift für Hans Heinrich Eggebrecht*, ed. W. Breig, R. Brinkmann and E. Budde (Wiesbaden, 1984), 45–56
N. Pirrotta: ' "Arte" e "non arte" nel frammento Greggiati', *L'Ars Nova italiana del Trecento*, v, ed. A. Ziino (Palermo, 1985), 200–17
V. Newes: 'Chace, Caccia, Fuga: the Convergence of French and Italian Traditions', *MD*, xli (1987), 27–57
E. Paganuzzi: 'La musica alla corte scaligera', *Gli Scaligeri 1277–1387*, Museo di Castelvecchio, June–November 1988 (Verona, 1988), 527–32 [exhibition catalogue]
N. Pirrotta, ed.: *Il codice Rossi 215* (Lucca, 1992) [esp. Preface; facs. edn]
B. Toliver: 'Improvisation in the Madrigals of the Rossi Codex', *AcM*, lxiv (1992), 165–76
E. Paganuzzi: 'Nota sul madrigale "Suso quel monte che fiorise l'erba"', *NRMI*, xxxi (1997), 337–42

KURT VON FISCHER/GIANLUCA D'AGOSTINO

Piero degli Organi [Pierino Fiorentino]. Italian musician, son of BARTOLOMEO DEGLI ORGANI.

Pierray, Claude (*d* Paris, 28 Dec 1729). French violin maker. The finest of the early French makers, his instruments often pass as Italian. He worked in the rue des Fossés-St-Germain-des-Prés; his shop was situated 'proche la Comédie française'. He was a contemporary of JACQUES BOQUAY, whose instruments are similar in appearance, but Pierray on the whole had a better choice of wood for his fronts and achieved a certain extra elegance in the details of his workmanship. Even so, his instruments were not so highly valued at the time as those of Boquay. In addition to the violins, which are now much appreciated by players, Pierray made a number of fine cellos, though some would criticize their rather small dimensions. He also built viols and repaired harpsichords.

BIBLIOGRAPHY

R. Vannes: *Essai d'un dictionnaire universel des luthiers* (Paris, 1932, 2/1951/R as *Dictionnaire universel des luthiers*, suppl. 1959)
S. Milliot: *Les luthiers parisiens du XVIIIe siècle* (Spa, 1997)

CHARLES BEARE/SYLVETTE MILLIOT

Pierre, Constant(-Victor-Désiré) (*b* Passy, nr Paris, 24 Aug 1855; *d* Paris, 12 Feb 1918). French musicologist. He entered the Paris Conservatoire in 1878 and won a prize for bassoon in 1881. Between 1877 and 1882 he played the bassoon in various Paris theatres. He then took a variety of administrative posts, including clerk at the war ministry from 1876 to 1880, and at the Conservatoire in 1881, where he became assistant secretary from 1900 to 1910. He wrote for a number of journals including *Le monde musical* (1891–1900) which he also edited, and won awards from the Société des Compositeurs (1889) and from the Institut de France (Bordin prize, 1900, 1905). His studies on the music of the French Revolution and on the Conservatoire from its founding until 1900 are still the basic source of any research into these subjects, because of their fullness and scientific precision.

WRITINGS

La 'Marseillaise': comparaison des différentes versions (Paris, 1887)
Histoire de l'orchestre de l'Opéra (MS, F-Po, 1889)
La facture instrumentale à l'Exposition universelle de 1889 (Paris, 1890)
Les facteurs d'instruments de musique, les luthiers et la facture instrumentale (Paris, 1893/R)
Le magasin de décors de l'Opéra rue Richer: son histoire (1781–1894) (Paris, 1894)
'La musique à la fête du 14 juillet 1794', *Revue dramatique et musicale*, ii (1894), 608–13
B. Sarrette et les origines du Conservatoire national de musique et de déclamation (Paris, 1895)
L'école de chant de l'Opéra, 1672–1807 (Paris, 1895/R)
Le Magasin de musique à l'usage des fêtes nationales et du Conservatoire (Paris, 1895/R)
Sur quelques hymnes et faits de la Révolution (Paris, 1898)
'L'Hymne à l'Etre suprême enseigné au peuple par l'Institut national de musique', *La Révolution française: revue d'histoire moderne et contemporaine*, xliii (1899), 54–64
Notes inédites sur la musique de la Chapelle Royale (1532–1790) (Paris, 1899)
Le Conservatoire national de musique et de déclamation: documents historiques et administratifs (Paris, 1900)
'Le Conservatoire National de Musique', *RHCM*, iii (1903), 313–34
Les hymnes et chansons de la Révolution: aperçu général et catalogue avec notices (Paris, 1904/R)
'Notes sur les chansons de la période révolutionnaire', *RHCM*, iv (1904), 179–86
Histoire du Concert spirituel 1725–1790 (Paris, 1975) [written 1899]

EDITIONS

Musique exécutée aux fêtes nationales de la Révolution française (Paris, 1894)
Quatre hymnes et chants composés pour les fêtes nationales de la Révolution, transcrits pour piano (Paris, 1897)
Musique des fêtes et cérémonies de la Révolution française (Paris, 1899) [incl. transcrs. of works by Gossec, Cherubini, Le Sueur, Méhul, Catel and others]
Basses et chants donnés aux examens et concours des classes d'harmonie et d'accompagnement [du Conservatoire, 1827–1900] (Paris, 1900)
Sujets de fugue et thèmes d'improvisation donnés aux concours d'essai pour le Grand Prix de Rome (1804–1900) (Paris, 1900)
Hymne à l'Etre Suprême: strophe supprimée reconstituée (Paris, 1904) [works by Gossec]

FRÉDÉRIC ROBERT/JEAN GRIBENSKI

Pierre, Francis (*b* Amiens, 9 March 1931). French harpist. He entered Lily Laskine's class at the Paris Conservatoire, gaining a *premier prix* in 1950, and then continued his studies with Pierre Jamet. He has been particularly active in contemporary and experimental music, having worked closely with Boulez and Maderna in the late 1960s and 1970s, and has given the first performances of many solo and ensemble works by such composers as Berio (*Circles, Sequenza II, Chemins I*, Rands (*Formants I – Les gestes*), Jolas (*Tranche*) and Miroglio (*Réseaux*). Pierre was appointed solo harpist Of the Orchestre de Paris on its formation in 1967. In 1972 he formed the Trio Debussy, to play the repertory for flute, viola and harp.

ANN GRIFFITHS

Pierre, Paul de la. *See* LA PIERRE, PAUL DE.

Pierre Bonnel. *See* PIETREQUIN BONNEL.

Pierre de Corbeil (*d* Sens, 1222). French theologian and prelate. He was a master of theology at the University of Paris; his best-known pupil later became Pope Innocent III. Pierre received ecclesiastical preferment, becoming a canon of Notre Dame in Paris, Archdeacon of York (1198), Bishop of Cambrai (1199) and Archbishop of Sens (1200). He led the council at Paris in 1210 which forbade the public teaching and private reading of Aristotle's works on natural history. As archbishop Pierre was a respected familiar of King Philip Augustus. Of his works, including sermons and commentaries, very few have survived. An Office of the Assumption, used at Sens until the 17th century, and the Office for Circumcision are attributed to him.

It is on the latter that his musical reputation is founded. In 1198 Cardinal Peter of Capua, papal legate for France, addressed a letter to the Bishop and cathedral chapter of Paris concerning the Feast of Fools which traditionally took place on the Feast of Circumcision and which had become the focus for much abuse. This document, an attempt to regulate the celebration of the feast, sets guidelines including prescriptions for processions and the performance of liturgical items 'in organo, vel triplo, vel quadruplo'. Reference to 'quadruplo' at once suggests the four-voice compositions of Parisian composers associated with Notre Dame. Other works of the Notre Dame repertory are, furthermore, associated with Sens; it seems possible that Pierre, who is named among the other members of the chapter, responded to the cardinal's letter by writing an Office for the Feast of Circumcision, and by taking the decrees on musical practice with him to Sens.

The Office for Circumcision (ed. H. Villetard, Paris, 1907) was first attributed to Pierre in 1524 and thereafter in various notes referring to documents no longer traceable, but his association with the Office is circumstantially acceptable. His role in creating it would, however, be rather that of a compiler than author, since the majority of items are of standard liturgical use, or are drawn from the Christmas cycle. Of the 57 pieces not in the normal Circumcision Office, about half have not been traced to other sources: the additions consist mainly of tropes, to versicles such as *Deus in adjutorium*, to *Benedicamus Domino*, to the Ordinary and Proper of the Mass including the Credo, and to responsories and the like. As well as tropes, the Office includes seven conductus, the most famous of which is *Orientis partibus*, a *conductus ad tabulam* from one line of which derives the common but false title of the Office, the 'Feast of the Ass'. Other interesting features are the presence of invitatory and hymn in each of the three nocturns of Matins, and the rubrics, which refer to performance 'in falso' or 'cum organo'.

BIBLIOGRAPHY

J.W. Baldwin: *Masters, Princes, and Merchants: the Social Views of Peter the Chanter and his Circle*, i (Princeton, NJ, 1970), 46, 105
J.W. Baldwin: *The Government of Philip Augustus: Foundations of French Royal Power in the Middle Ages* (Berkeley, 1986)
M.-C. Gasnault: 'Corbeil, Pierre de', *Lexikon des Mittelalters*, ed. R. Auty and others (Munich, 1977–98)
C.M. Wright: *Music and Ceremony at Notre Dame of Paris, 500–1500* (Cambridge, 1989)

ANDREW HUGHES/RANDALL ROSENFELD

Pierre de Corbie (*d* after 1195). French trouvère. He came from the region of the Ile de France, and is probably identifiable with the 'Magister Petrus de Corbeia' who was canon of Notre Dame d'Arras in the late 12th century. He is mentioned as such in contemporary documents from 1188 to 1195, and is thus a member of the older generation of trouvères. Seven songs including one jeu-parti are attributed to him in a very small group of sources. Metrically, all are of the very common bar form type, and several survive with more than one melody.

WORKS

Edition: *Trouvère Lyrics with Melodies: Complete Comparative Edition*, ed. H. Tischler, CMM, cvii (1997) [T]

Amis Guillaume, ainc si sage ne vi, R.1085, T vii, no.625 (jeu-parti; several melodies)
Dame, ne vous doit desplaire, R.158, T ii, no.93
En aventure ai chante, R.408, T iii, no.234 (several melodies)
Esbahis en lonc voiage, R.46, T i, no.34
Limounier, du mariage, R.29, T i, no.20 (two melodies)
Par un ajournant, R.291, T iii, no.171/1
Pensis com fins amourous, R.2041, T xiii, no.1165

For bibliography *see* TROUBADOURS, TROUVÈRES.

ROBERT FALCK

Pierre de la Croix. *See* PETRUS DE CRUCE.

Pierre de Molins [Molaines] (*fl* ?1190–1220). French trouvère. He was probably a member either of a family with estates in the region of Epernay (Marne), or (less likely) of a family residing in the region of Noyon (Oise). A 'Pierre II' appears in archival sources between 1210 and 1224. Pierre de Molins was acquainted with one or more of the oldest generation of trouvères, probably with either Gace Brulé or the Chastelain de Couci. Four works are ascribed to Pierre in the Manuscrit du Roi (*F-Pn* fr.844) and the Noailles manuscript (*F-Pn* fr.12615), all with conflicting ascriptions in other sources. They are in bar form, with no evidence of regular rhythmic organization. Somewhat unusual is the introduction of the outline of a melodic tritone in *Fine amours* through the use of written accidentals in two sources, and the suggestion of the sharpened 4th in *Chanter me fet*.

WORKS

(V) etc. MS (using Schwan sigla: *see* SOURCES, MS) containing a late setting of a poem

Chanter me fet ce dont je crien morir, R.1429 [model for: Anon., 'Destroiz d'amours et pensis sans deport', R.1932; music used in two readings of Gautier de Coincy, 'Pour la pucele en chantant me deport', R.1930 = 1600] (V, a); ed. in CMM, cvii (1997)
Quant foillissent li boscage, R.14 (V); ed. in CMM, cvii (1997)
Tant sai d'amours con cil qui plus l'emprent, R.661 = 715 (R); ed. in CMM, cvii (1997)

Fine amours et bone esperance, R.221 [model for: Anon., 'Fine amours et bone esperance/Me fait', R.222; Anon., 'L'autrier par une matinee', R.530a = 528; Anon., 'Douce dame, vierge Marie', R.1179] (R) (doubtful); ed. in CMM, cvii (1997)

BIBLIOGRAPHY

H. Petersen Dyggve: 'Personnages historiques figurant dans la poésie lyrique française des XIIe et XIIIe siècles, xv: Messire Pierre de Molins', *Neuphilologische Mitteilungen*, xliii (1942), 62–100

For further bibliography *see* TROUBADOURS, TROUVÈRES.

THEODORE KARP

Pierrekin de la Coupele (*fl* 1240–60). French trouvère. Probably a native of the Pas-de-Calais area now designated Coupelle-Vieille and Coupelle-Neuve, Pierrekin addressed *Je chant en aventure* to a count of Soissons, probably Jehan ('le Bon et le Bègue') of Nesle, brother of the trouvère Raoul de Soissons. A poor poet, Pierrekin is credited with six works, three of which survive with music. The most interesting of the melodies is the non-strophic setting of *A mon pooir ai servi*, one of the late additions to the main corpus of the Manuscrit du Roi (*F-Pn* fr.844). Mensurally notated, the work documents various exceptions to strict modal usage, and shows that equivalent line lengths do not always receive the same rhythmic treatment.

WORKS

Edition: *Trouvère Lyrics with Melodies: Complete and Comparative Edition*, ed. H. Tischler, CMM, cvii (1997)

(nm) – *no music*

A mon pooir ai servi, R.1081 (M [Schwan siglum: *see* SOURCES, MS])
Cançon faz non pas vilaine, R.145
J'ai la meillor qui soit en vie, R.1219 (nm)
Je chant en aventure, R.2089
Quant ivers et frois depart, R.374 (nm)
Quant li tens jolis revient, R.1244 (nm)

BIBLIOGRAPHY

F. Gennrich: *Grundriss einer Formenlehre des mittelalterlichen Liedes als Grundlage einer musikalischen Formenlehre des Liedes* (Halle, 1932/R)
A. Långfors: 'Mélanges de poésie lyrique française, VII', *Romania*, lxiii (1937), 470–93

For further bibliography *see* TROUBADOURS, TROUVÈRES.

THEODORE KARP

Pierrequin de Thérache. *See* THÉRACHE, PIERREQUIN DE.

Pierreson Cambio. *See* PERISSONE CAMBIO.

Piersanti, Franco (*b* Rome, 12 Jan 1950). Italian composer. He graduated from the Conservatorio di S Cecilia in double bass and composition, studying with Armando Renzi, director of music at the Cappella Giulia. He also took classes in conducting there with Franco Ferrara and became assistant to Rota. His first incidental music for the theatre came in 1976 and the following year he made his film début with the score to *Io sono un autarchico* directed by Nanni Moretti. He has since composed more than 60 film scores (working with, among others, Carlo Lizzani, Margarethe von Trotta, Ermanno Olmi and Roberto Faenza) and incidental music to more than 30 plays (with such directors as Carlo Cecchi, Giancarlo Cobelli and Luigi Squarzina). Piersanti's melancholy, introspective streak, punctuated by fleeting bursts of lyricism made him the ideal composer for Moretti's *Ecce Bombo* (1977), *Sogni d'oro* (1981) and *Bianca* (1984) and particularly for Gianni Amelio's work including *Colpire al cuore* (1982), *Porte aperte* (1990) and *Lamerica* (1994). However it is in the theatre, for example in a production of Aristophanes's *Acharnians* (Teatro Greco, Siracusa, 1994), in which he has been able to experiment most fruitfully, arriving at a personal style in which the moods and colours of Mediteranean culture, ancient and contemporary, are merged. He has won two David di Donatello awards.

WORKS

(*selective list*)

Stage: Notte con ospiti (op, P. Weiss), 1975; incid music incl. Acharnians (Aristophanes, dir. E. Marcucci), 1994
Film scores: Ecce Bombo (dir. N. Moretti), 1977; Io sono un autarchico (dir. Moretti), 1977; Sogni d'oro (dir. Moretti), 1981; Colpire al cuore (dir. G. Amelio), 1982; I velieri (dir. Amelio), 1983; Bianca (dir. Moretti), 1984; Porte aperte (dir. Amelio), 1990; Il ladro di bambini (dir. Amelio), 1992; Il segreto del bosco vecchio (dir. E. Olmi), 1993; Lamerica (dir. Amelio), 1994; Marianna Ucrìa (dir. R. Faenza), 1997

Other works: Rorate coeli, solo vv, vv, orch, 1975; Last Blues to be Read Someday (various authors, 19th-century Italian text), vv, orch, 1977; Tenso, va, pf, 1979; Adonai, orch, 1994; 3 anagrammi su Nino Rota, fl, 10 insts, 1997; Litania della violenza, (G. Ungazetti, Ho Chi Minh), vv, orch; 2 salmi, vv, orch

BIBLIOGRAPHY

E. Comuzio: Colonna sonora (Rome, 1992)
S. Miceli: 'Presenze musicali in un secolo di cinema italiano', Biennale di Venezia (Venice, 1996)

SERGIO MICELI

Pierson [Pearson], Henry Hugo [Hugh] (b Oxford, 12 April 1815; d Leipzig, 28 Jan 1873). German composer of English origin. Educated at Harrow School, he spent two years in London preparing himself for the medical profession, but also studying music with Attwood and Corfe despite his father's opposition. He entered Trinity College, Cambridge, in October 1836; while there he composed two sets of songs, with words by Byron and Shelley. From 1839 to 1844 he lived in Germany, where he studied under Rinck and Reissiger, and also under Tomášek at Prague; he continued to compose, and his op.7 songs were reviewed by Schumann in 1842. Dresden appears to have been his main centre. In July 1842 he joined Mary Shelley, the poet's widow, on a trip that took him from Dresden to Florence, which he left in November. He also took up with the poet J.P. Lyser, became involved with his wife Caroline (née Leonhardt, 1811–99), an 'improvisatrice', and married her in 1844 after she had secured a divorce. During this period he adopted the nom de plume of Edgar Mannsfeldt, from his wife's family; in about 1853 he decided on Henry Hugo Pierson as the final form of his name (he rarely used the form 'Heinrich').

On 1 June 1844 he was elected to the Reid Professorship of Music at Edinburgh University in succession to Bishop (and in preference to S.S. Wesley and Sterndale Bennett, among others) but he resigned eight months later, having settled in Germany with his wife. His reputation in that country increased with the production of Leila (1848, Hamburg), with a libretto by Caroline, and reached its greatest height when his incidental music to the second part of Goethe's Faust was performed (1854, Hamburg). So popular was this work that for a time it was played in many of the leading German towns annually on Goethe's birthday. His songs were published in Germany and acclaimed by German critics. Meanwhile he tried to improve his hitherto negligible reputation in England. In collaboration with W. Sancroft Holmes, he prepared an oratorio, Jerusalem, which was performed at the Norwich Festival of 1852. A kind of contest was worked up by the press between this work and Bexfield's Israel Restored; although the audience at Norwich seemed to prefer Pierson's oratorio, the London press, led by Davison in The Times, attacked it with extraordinary energy. Davison associated Pierson with the 'aesthetic' school of Schumann, and, less plausibly, with Wagner; this was enough to condemn him out of hand. Chorley in The Athenaeum wrote of 'the crude and fierce noises', 'the high pretensions, fantastic and unauthorized method of construction', and the 'desperate intervals' for the voices. Not unnaturally Pierson was deeply wounded. He did not feel inclined to try his luck in England for some time after this episode. Instead he developed his character as a German composer, publishing a long series of lieder and male-voice partsongs. In 1863 he settled at Stuttgart, where Parry, who studied with him in summer 1867, found him 'kind and jolly', 'a wonderfully well-read man', and knowledgeable about

orchestration. According to Frehn, he composed in 1869 an opera based on Byron's 'Childe Harold', to a libretto by his son-in-law C.L. Bauer. Pierson visited Norwich again in 1869 for the performance of his unfinished oratorio Hezekiah, but this too met with a hostile reception from the press.

In contrast, Meyerbeer said 'H.H. Pearson is in truth a genius; and promises accordingly, as far as I know him, great things for the German opera'. Pierson's reputation in Germany remained at a high level for some time after his death, and his music continued to be performed there. A Leipzig obituary called him a 'great artist, whose strivings were after the noblest ends … highly educated, but after the fashion of true genius somewhat of a recluse'. He adapted the music of his partsong Ye Mariners of England for a German nationalistic hymn O Deutschland hoch in Ehren, which was a hit throughout World War I. In England too Pierson was known by a patriotic song, Hurrah for Merry England.

His larger works are of great interest, for in place of the slavish conventionality that constrained most English music of the time, he set up the opposite ideal of unfettered originality. His melodies, his forms, his harmonies, are quite as unpredictable as those of Berlioz – so much so that when he did occasionally bring a phrase to its normal cadence, even this comes as a surprise. It must be admitted that such methods can quickly exhaust the listener and almost preclude the possibility of cumulative musical structure such as a full-length opera or oratorio requires. Pierson's operas have not been located. Of his extant larger works, the most successful are the Faust music and the symphonic poem Macbeth. Programmatic and episodic, they are well suited to Pierson's gift for short-term

Ex.1 All my heart's thine own

interest and surprise; their scoring is colourful, after the manner of Berlioz; they hold closely to detailed programmes which are linked to short motifs. It is not surprising that their success was confined to German-speaking countries.

It was in his songs that Pierson made his most remarkable contribution. German critics were aware of him as a secondary, but by no means negligible, figure in the history of the lied; in England his songs have hardly been known. Nevertheless he did not adopt entirely the German manner, though Schumann was certainly a strong influence. His English background is noticeable chiefly in his choice and treatment of texts. Throughout his life he returned to great English poets, and above all to Shakespeare, who also inspired much of his orchestral music. He frequently published his songs with both German and English texts, but his minute attention to the verbal stresses of the English texts shows that his native language remained a major force in his art. His melodies are complex, sometimes pretentious: Schumann found them too cumbersome for the simple Burns verses. Often they take a surprising turn, as if in rejection of the English ballad style that he had learnt in his youth (ex.1). The eccentricity of Pierson's musical thought is like a spice: in his most successful songs, such as *Heimweh*, *Ruhe* and *Die weisse Eul'*, it is applied in just sufficient quantity to enhance interest; in his worst, of which *Der Malteser Ritter* may serve as an example, it overwhelms and destroys the lyrical essence. Every one of his songs has points of interest and surprise, if only because of his avoidance of the sentimental clichés of his era.

Pierson also mastered the selfconsciously 'manly' style of the German *Männerchor*, here relying perhaps more obviously on Weber, Schumann and Liszt as models. In his English choral music, including *Jerusalem*, he was less successful, never reaching an understanding with his audience. Of his Anglican church music, commissioned near the end of his life by a London publisher, one beautiful Agnus Dei stands out from a dull and perfunctory collection. His only important work for piano, the three *Musical Meditations*, dedicated to Meyerbeer, is a rare and early example of English programme music.

Pierson translated into English Seyfried's *Beethovens Studien*, Schumann's *Musikalische Haus- und Lebens-Regeln* and several German song lyrics.

WORKS
published in Leipzig unless otherwise stated

STAGE

Der Elfensieg, oder Die Macht des Glaubens (Feenoper, 3, C. Pierson), Brno, 7 May 1845, unpubd
Lelia (romantische Oper, 3, C. Pierson, after her *Schneewittchen*), Hamburg, 22 Feb 1848, unpubd
Contarini, oder Die Verschwörung zu Padua (grosse Oper, 5, M.E. Lindau), 1853, Hamburg, 16 April 1872, unpubd; revived as Fenice, Dessau, 1883
Musik zu Goethe's Faust, zweiter Theil (incid music), 1854, Hamburg, Stadt, 25 March 1854 (Mainz, 1858)

CHORAL

op.
9   6 Gesänge, chorus, pf ad lib (Dresden, c1843): Grablied, Die Heimath, An den Tod, Das Vaterland, Lied des Trostes, Nacht
—   Now the bright morning star (J. Milton), ode, chorus, pf (London, c1850)
—   Salve eternum (B. Lytton), int, S, B, chorus, orch, 1850, vs (London, 1853), GB-Lcm

—   Jerusalem, orat, solo, vv, chorus, orch (London, 1852), as op.100 (c1877)
30   O Deutschland hoch in Ehren (Beharrlich!) (L. Bauer), Volkshymne, male vv (c1860)
31   2 Männerchöre (c1860): Kein schön'rer Tod, Der Liedertafeln Ständchen
32   3 Gesänge (c1860): Die Stimme der Zeit, Wie schlummert sanft, Sag' mir, du vielgeliebtes Herz
35   2 Männerchöre (1862): Reiterlied vor der Schlacht (Bauer), Des Helden Braut (C. Pierson, after V. Alfieri)
—   Germania (Bauer), male vv (1862)
37   Der deutsche Männergesang (c1862)
42   Zu den Waffen, male vv, pf (c1864)
43   Einladung in den Wald, male vv (1864)
—   Des Waldes Wiegenlied (Vienna, c1864)
—   4 Männerchöre (in Tauwitz's Deutsches Liederbuch, Prague, 1865): Erklang dein traulich Wiegenlied, Liedergruss, Ein deutscher Kaufherr, An die Todten
—   Hezekiah, orat, solo vv, chorus, orch, unfinished, perf. Norwich Festival, 1869
73   2 Männerchöre (c1869): Süss und leis (Der Fischerin Wiegenlied) (after A. Tennyson), Vertraue nur der reichen Gnade (Beruhigung) (F. Dahn)
—   Communion Service, F, chorus, org (London, 1870)
—   Te Deum, Benedictus, F, chorus, org (London, 1870)
—   60 hymn tunes (London, 1870–72)
—   Te Deum, B♭, 3 vv, org (London, 1872)
—   Hurrah for Merry England (B. Cornwall), 1v, chorus, pf (London, 1880)

SONGS
for solo voice with piano unless otherwise stated

Editions: H. Hugo Pierson Album (Leipzig, c1875) [P]
   English Songs 1800–1860, ed. G. Bush and N. Temperley, MB, xliii (1979) [B]

op.
—   Thoughts of Melody: 10 Canzonetts (London, 1839, 2/1852): There be none of beauty's daughters (Byron); Beware of the black friar (Byron); Maid of Athens, ere we part (Byron); The isles of Greece (Byron); When we two parted (Byron); Under the greenwood tree (W. Shakespeare); Go, you may call it madness (S. Rogers); Had I a cave on some far distant shore (R. Burns); Maiden, weep, thy mantle round thee (H. Kirke White); When lovely woman stoops to folly, cavatina (O. Goldsmith)
—   [5] Characteristic Songs of Shelley (London, 1840): The odour from the flower is gone (On a Faded Violet); Arethusa arose; Swiftly walk over the western wave (Invocation to Night); Sacred goddess, mother earth (Hymn to Proserpine); False friend, wilt thou smile or weep? (Song of Beatrice Cenci)
—   Rheinlied (N. Becker), Leipzig, 2 Dec 1840
—   2 Lieder (Wahl, after Shelley) (1841): Dein Bild im Traum erweckt (Indisches Ständchen); Windsbraut, du Klägerin (Herbstgrablied); Eng. trans. as Serenade, An Autumn Dirge (London, 1852)
7   6 Lieder (F. Freiligrath, after Burns) (1842): Die finstre Nacht (Die Ayren-Ufer); Nun holt mir eine Kanne Wein (Soldatenlied); Mein Herz ist im Hochland (Des Jägers Heimweh), later pubd with hn (obbl); John Anderson, mein Lieb, B; O säh' ich auf der Heide (Liebe), P; Die süsse Dirn (Die Maid von Inverness)
12   2 Lieder (Dresden, c1843): Wohl glücklich ist (Sängers Glück); Die alten bösen Lieder (Romanze) (? H. Heine)
—   All my heart's thine own (London, 1844), later pubd as All mein Herz, op.22 no.2, P, B
—   O fairy child (Wilson), cavatina (London, 1844)
—   O listen while I sing to thee (M. Shelley), canzonet (London, 1844)
22/1   Verrathene Liebe (A. von Chamisso) (c1845)
—   Durch alle Auen ist's gedrungen (Elegie, den Manen F. Mendelssohn Bartholdys) (C. Pierson) (Hamburg, 1847)
—   Ein Blick (Schlönbach), dramatic romance (Hamburg, c1847)
—   Erscheinung (Schlönbach) (Hamburg, c1847)
—   Liebesübermuth (L. Tieck) (Dresden, c1847)
—   Mondlied (J.W. von Goethe) (Dresden, c1847)

—	Der Heimat fern mit nassem Blick (Heimweh) (C. Beck) (Vienna, c1848), later pubd as op.41, P
—	Es war dein erster Kuss (Marie) (E. Janinski) (Hamburg, c1848)
—	O meine schönste Hoffnung (An Madonna Consolatrice) (Vienna, c1848)
—	Wenn der kalte Schnee zergangen (Der Schnee) (J. Eichendorff) (Vienna, c1848)
—	Wenn in Lenz die Berge grünen (Weinlied) (C. Pierson) (Vienna, c1848)
—	Ave Maria (Offertorium), 1v, orch/pf (Vienna, c1850)
—	Schlachtgetös' ist meine Lust (Vor der Schlacht) (Vienna, c1850)
23	4 Lieder (c1851): Es schlafen rings die Haine (Ruhe), P; Wiegenlied; Nähe der Geliebten; Ach, wenn du wär'st mein Eigen (An die Geliebte), P
26	4 Lieder (c1852), P: Kehrt mir die Lieblichkeit (Erste Liebe); Sie schwuren sich kein Liebeseide (Die Liebenden) (Beck); Bleibt, o bleibt ihr Lippen ferne (Lieb und Leid) (after Shakespeare), B; Willst kommen zur Laube?
27	2 Lieder (1853), P: O weine nicht, du holdes Kind (An Henriette); Tief wohnt in mir (Treue Liebe) (after Byron)
28	2 Lieder (c1854); P: O Abendglocken, Abendhall (C. Pierson, after T. Moore), B; Wo die Myrthen ewig blüh'n (Sehnsucht nach Italien)
—	Viribus unitis (Oestreichs Wahlspruch) (Vienna, c1855)
29	2 Lieder (1859), P: Ich hatt' einen Cameraden (Der gute Camerad) (L. Uhland); Nun schmückt die Rosse (Der Malteser Ritter) (Freiligrath)
33	6 Concert-Lieder (c1861): Sie gleicht der wundervollen Nacht (Das Portrait) (after Byron), P; Wo Claribel tief lieget (Claribel) (C. Pierson, after Tennyson), P; Du tratest in mein dunkles Leben (Mein Glück) (after Lamartine), P; Wenn durch die Piazzetta (Ninetta) (Freiligrath, after Moore), P; Der Eichwald brauset (Thekla's Klage) (F. von Schiller), P; Die Zauberin
34	2 Lieder (c1861): Ständchen; Elegie
—	Der beste Schütz (H. Marggraf), ballad (c1862)
40	2 Gesänge für tiefe Stimme (1863), P: Lass die Rose schlummern (An der Nachtwind) (R. Hamerling); Es war die Zeit der Rosen (C. Held)
44	4 Lieder (c1864): In Venedig, barcarolle; O komm zu mir (E. Geibel, after Moore), serenade, P; Roland der Held! (Freiligrath, after T. Campbell), ballade, P; Mein Lieb ist eine rothe Ros' (Freiligrath, after Burns), P
—	Geh, wo Ruhm dir zuwinkt (Vienna, c1864)
—	Holkisches Reiterlied (Vienna, c1864)
—	4 songs in Tauwitz's Deutsches Liederbuch (Prague, 1865): Gebet für das Reich; Von der Koppe; Die Dorfglocke; Beim Friedhof
60	2 Gesänge (c1865): Rastlos Herz will Ruhm erjagen (F. Seebach, after Cornwall); Sängers Vorüberziehen (Uhland)
61	Über fremde Gräber (Der Friedhof) (F. Dingelstedt), aria, B solo, pf (c1865)
62	Der Burgwall glänzt (Das Hifthorn) (Bauer, after Tennyson), romance (c1865)
63	3 Gedichte von Shakespeare (c1865): Sagt, woher stammt Liebeslust?; Wer ist Sylvia?; Fürchte nicht meine Sonnengluth, B
64	O du, mein alles auf der Welt (F. Oser) (c1865)
65	2 religiöse Gesänge (c1865): Birg mich unter deinen Flügeln (Gebet) (Oser); Der Himmel bringt die Ruhe nur (Freiligrath, after Moore)
66	Mein Herz ist schwer (F. Kohlhauer, after Burns), concert aria, 1v, orch (c1865)
89	2 zweistimmige Lieder, 2vv, pf (c1867): Über allen Gipfeln ist Ruh' (Goethe); Frühling im Herbst (Bauer)
95	3 Gesänge (1868): Hörst du nicht die Quellen gehen (Nachtzauber) (Eichendorff); Das macht das dunkelgrüne Laub' (Herbst); Wenn's Kätzchen heimkehrt (Die weisse Eul') (C. Pierson, after Tennyson), P, B
81	O lieb', so lang' du lieben kannst (Freiligrath) (c1869)
69	Zu Ross, zu Ross (Sturmritt) (F. Löwe), 1v, pf/orch (c1870)
90	2 Lieder (after I. Hill) (c1870): Wie gern ich doch (Liebesträumen); Im hellen, klaren Mondenschein (Ständchen), P
—	Das schlafende Kind (c1875)
—	Die Rose wendet ihr (Traum und Liebe) (A. Bube), 1871, OO. Neighbour's private collection, London

OTHER WORKS

Musical Meditations, 3 romances, pf (London, 1844); ed. in LPS, xvi (1985)
Romantische Ouvertüre, D, orch (Vienna, c1850)
Hamlet, marche funèbre, pf (1850)
Macbeth, sym. poem, op.54, orch (1859)
La Dame de vos pensées, grande nocturne, vc, pf (c1870)
Die Jungfrau von Orleans, ov., orch, op.101, 1867 (1872)
Romeo and Juliet, ov., orch, op.86 (1874)
As you Like it, ov., orch, London, Crystal Palace, 17 Jan 1874

BIBLIOGRAPHY

ADB ('Pierson, Karoline'; F. Brümmer); DNB (R. Newmarch); MGG1 (R. Sietz); SmitherHO, iv
Review of 2 Lieder (1841), AMZ, xliii (1841), 1124 only
R. Schumann: Review of Sechs Lieder op.7, NZM, viii (1842), 32; repr. in R. Schumann: Schriften über Musik und Musiker (Leipzig, 1888), iii, 113–14
M. Shelley: Rambles in Germany and Italy in 1840, 1842 and 1843 (London, 1844)
Testimonials [privately printed in support of Pierson's candidacy for the Edinburgh professorship, 1844], GB-Er
C.F. Whistling and A. Hofmeister: Handbuch der musikalischen Literatur (Leipzig, 3/1844–87)
Review of Leila, AMZ, l (1848), 230–31
G.A. Macfarren: 'Jerusalem, an Oratorio by Henry Hugh Pierson', Musical World, xxvii (1852), 568–71
The Athenaeum (25 Sept 1852), (2 Oct 1852)
H. Zopff: 'Henry Hugo Pierson und seine Musik zum zweiten Theile von Goethes Faust', NZM, lxix (1869), 529–32; lxx (1870), 2–3, 14–15
R.H. Legge and W.E. Hansell: Annals of the Norfolk Music Festival, 1834–93 (London, 1896)
J.A. Fuller Maitland: English Music in the XIXth Century (London, 1902), 110–14
E. Newman: Musical Studies (London, 1905), 88–91
E. Walker: A History of Music in England (Oxford, 1907, rev. 3/1952 by J.A. Westrup), 304–5, 310
F. Hirth: Johann Peter Lyser (Munich, 1911)
J.W. Davison: Music during the Victorian Era: from Mendelssohn to Wagner, ed. H. Davison (London, 1912), 142–6
K. Reisert: O Deutschland hoch in Ehren: … sein Dichter und Komponist, seine Entstehung und Überlieferung (Würzburg, 1917)
P. Frehn: Der Einfluss der englischen Literatur auf Deutschlands Musiker und Musik im XIX. Jahrhundert (Düsseldorf, 1937), 119
P.A. Scholes, ed.: The Mirror of Music 1844–1944 (London, 1947/R), i, 85–7
H.G. Sear: 'Faust and Henry Hugo Pierson', MR, x (1949), 183–90
N. Temperley: 'Domestic Music in England, 1800–1860', PRMA, lxxxv (1958–9), 31–47
P. Hartnoll, ed.: Shakespeare and Music (London, 1964), 216–17
A. and B. Pollin: 'In Pursuit of Pearson's Shelley Songs', ML, xlvi (1965), 322–31
N. Temperley: 'Henry Hugo Pierson, 1815–73', MT, cxiv (1973), 1217–20; cxv (1974), 30–34 [with music examples]
N. Temperley, ed.: Music in Britain: the Romantic Age 1800–1914 (London, 1981/R)
B. Pelker: Die deutsche Konzertouvertüre (1825–1865) (Frankfurt, 1993)
H.E. Smither, ed.: A History of the Oratorio, iv: Oratorio in the Nineteenth Century (Chapel Hill, NC, forthcoming)

NICHOLAS TEMPERLEY

Pietersen, David. See PETERSEN, DAVID.

Pieterszoon, Adriaan (b Delft, ?c1400; d Delft, 1480). Netherlandish organ builder. He may have learnt his trade from the Delft organ builders Godschalk and Jannes. In 1446 he was granted, as an organ builder, the freedom of the city of Bruges. In 1472 he was in Tournai, and was also in Lille as a surveyor. He was patron of a prebend at St Pancraskerk, Leiden, and in 1476 named a Franco Wilhelmi as his deputy. He lived to a great age and died in a Delft home for the aged.

In 1448 Pieterszoon built a new organ in St Niklaaskerk, Veurne, and in 1449–50 enlarged the organ in Antwerp Cathedral. In 1450 or 1451 he returned to Delft, where in 1451 he built a new organ in the Nieuwe Kerk for the Fellowship of the Cross. He built a large organ for the same church in 1454–5 (which during his lifetime was replaced by another) and in 1458–60 began a large organ for the Oude Kerk in Delft (this was given to another builder in 1461 for completion). Apart from the unusually extended keyboard (beyond the normal *f″*, to *a″*), the Oude Kerk organ was generally old-fashioned in design: it was in the medieval 'steep' scale rather than the new diapason scale; the Mixtur stop on the second manual could not be played separately, although the builders Vastart in 1454 and Van Bilsteyn in 1455 had Mixturs which could be used alone; and the Mixtur of the *Blockwerk* had no repetitions (a device which had recently achieved the aim of 'sweetness', i.e. brilliance).

BIBLIOGRAPHY

D. van Bleyswijck: *Beschryvinge der stadt Delft* (Delft, 1667)

M.A. Vente: *Bouwstoffen tot de geschiedenis van het Nederlandse orgel in de 16de eeuw* (Amsterdam, 1942)

M.A. Vente: 'Figuren uit Vlaanderens orgelhistorie: Adriaan Pieterszoon uit Delft', *De schalmei*, ii (1947), 50

M.A. Vente: *Proeve van een repertorium van de archivalia betrekking hebbende op het Nederlandse orgel en zijn makers tot omstreeks 1630* (Brussels, 1956)

HANS KLOTZ

Pietkin, Lambert (*b* Liège, bap. 22 June 1613; *d* Liège, 16 Sept 1696). Flemish composer and organist. He was probably trained at the cathedral of St Lambert, Liège; he then entered holy orders and became second organist in 1630. In 1632 he became first organist and the following year served temporarily as *maître de chapelle* (in place of Léonard de Hodemont, who was his godfather). He was appointed permanently to the post in 1644, and he also held prebends as canon of St Materne and as imperial canon of the cathedral. He retired in 1674.

The ten early motets in the *Grand livre de choeur de Saint Lambert*, several of them based on Marian antiphons and chants from the liturgy for Corpus Christi, show Pietkin's contrapuntal skill but are close in style to music by his immediate predecessors, much of which is in the same collection. His surviving mature works, two sonatas for four instruments and continuo and the 32 motets for voices and instruments published as op.3, are all in a more modern style, with freer contrapuntal textures, italianate melodic lines, expressive chromaticism, and (in the vocal works) rhythms derived from the declamation of the Latin poetry. Sébastien de Brossard, who owned a copy of the *Sacri concentus*, remarked in his famous catalogue that 'all that one might ask or desire for good and solid music is found in this op.3'.

WORKS

Grand livre de choeur de Saint Lambert, 1645, 11 motets (incl. 1 motet for which only the bc part survives), 5–8vv, bc, *B-Lc* Fonds Terry 1325, 520

2 sonatas, 4 insts (3 tr, b), bc, *GB-Ob* Mus.Sch.C.44

Sacri concentus, op.3 (Liège, 1668), 32 motets, 2–5vv, insts, bc

Opp.1–2 and various masses and motets mentioned in church records at Ghent, Oudenaarde and Tongeren are lost

BIBLIOGRAPHY

AudaM; *Vander StraetenMPB*, i

J. Quitin: 'Lambert Pietkin', *RBM*, vi (1952), 31–51

J.M. Anthony: *The Vocal Music of Lambert Pietkin for the Cathedral of Liège* (diss., U. of Michigan, 1977)

JAMES MUSE ANTHONY

Piéton, Loyset [Aloysis, Louys, Loys] (*fl c*1530–45). Composer. His works were widely disseminated in both manuscript and printed sources between 1532 and 1574; the greatest concentration of his works appeared during the 1530s and 40s. Much of his music survives in Italian sources (in Gardane's motet books, in a group of Vatican manuscripts and in such sources of Florentine provenance as the Vallicelliana Manuscript and *I-Fn* Magl.XIX. 125bis), suggesting that he lived in Italy. But his ties to Lyons would appear to be equally strong: Moderne printed seven eight motets by Piéton as well as the *Davidici Poenitentiales Psalmi septem*, published in about 1532; a lost Lyonnaise book of *Psalmi penitentiales* exclusively by him was purchased by Ferdinand Colombus in Lyons in summer 1535.

Florence, Rome, Venice and Lyons represent by no means, however, the only cities in which Piéton's works were known. German printers in Augsburg, Nuremberg and Wittenberg published his works, as did their Flemish counterparts in Antwerp and Leuven. Only a few of Piéton's pieces were printed in Paris; even his one surviving chanson did not appear there, having been printed in the first book of Susato's main series of chansonniers in the company of works by such thoroughly Flemish masters as Josquin Baston, Cornelius Canis and Thomas Crecquillon. Another sign both of Piéton's links with Flemish musicians and of the broad dissemination his music attained may be seen in a reference to his *Magnificat* in the inventory of the music library at the Spanish court of Felipe II, prepared by Géry de Ghersem late in 1602.

The musical style of *Par faulte d'une je suis seulle* reflects, in its pervasive imitation, meandering melody, marked independence of line, and paucity of chordal writing and cadences, the Flemish approach to the chanson. The same is true of such motets as *Salve crux digna* and *Vive Deo semper* and of the *Magnificat quarti toni*, underscoring all the more Piéton's affinity with the Flemish school of composition. A number of the motets use unusual combinations of voices and 'modulations' as far as A♭ or D♭ (as in the six-voice setting of the antiphon *O beata infantia*).

Loyset Piéton should not be confused with Loyset Compère, Luiset Patin, Jean Louys or any of the Loysets attached to the court of Philip the Fair.

WORKS

Davidici Poenitentiales Psalmi septem, 4vv (Lyons, *c*1532)

Missa 'In te Domine speravi', 5vv, *I-Rvat* C.S.19

Ave Maria, 5vv, 1547[25] (intabulation); Beati omnes qui timent Dominum, 4vv (attrib. Lhéritier in 1539[12], 1564[6]; attrib. Piéton in 1532[10], 1542[6], 1545[4], 1569[1]), ed. in SCMot, ix (1998); Benedicta es celorum regina, 6vv, ed. in SCMot, xiii (1993) [intabulation ed. in DTÖ, xxxvii, Jg.xviii/2 (1911/R), 74]; Inviolata integra et casta, 6vv, *I-Fn* Magl.XIX.125bis; Jesum queritis, 5vv, 1547[25] (intabulation); Laudem dicite deo nostro, 4vv, 1542[7]; Magnificat quarti toni, 4vv, ed. P. Bunjes: Georg Rhaw: *Postremum vespertini officii opus … Magnificat octo modorum seu tonorum, 1544* (Kassel, 1970), 123

Nativitas tua, 4vv, 1539[10]; O admirabile commercium, 4vv, ed. in SCMot, ix (1998); O beata infantia, 6vv, ed. A. Smijers: *Treize livres de motets parus chez Pierre Attaingnant en 1534 et 1535*, iii (Paris, 1938), 1 and CMM, iii/4 (1952), 97; Pax vobis, 4vv, 1542[7]; Quae est ista que progreditur, 4vv, ed. in SCMot, xiii (1993); Regina caeli, 4vv, 1539[10]; Salve crux digna, 4vv, 1539[10]; Si acuero ut fulgur, 3vv, 1565[3]; Si ascendero in coelum, 3vv, 1565[3]; Si dormiero dicam quando, 3vv, 1565[3]; Sponsa Christi Cecilia, 4vv, ed. in SCMot, ix (1998); Veni sancte spiritu, 6vv, 1549[3]; Verbum bonum et suave, 6vv, ed. in SCMot, xiii (1993); Virgo prudentissima, 4vv, 1547²⁵ (intabulation); Vive Deo semper, 4vv, 1553⁹

Par faulte d'une je suis seulle, 4vv, ed. in SCC, xxx (1994)

BIBLIOGRAPHY

MGG1 (L. Finscher); *Vander StraetenMPB*

E. Lowinsky: 'A Newly Discovered Sixteenth-Century Motet Manuscript at the Biblioteca Vallicelliana in Rome', *JAMS*, iii (1950), 173–232

C.W. Chapman: 'Printed Collections of Polyphonic Music Owned by Ferdinand Columbus', *JAMS*, xxi (1968), 34–84

L. Bernstein: 'The Bibliography of Music in Conrad Gesner's *Pandectae* (1548)', *AcM*, xlv (1973), 119–63

L. Guillo: 'Les motets de Layolle et les psaumes de Piéton: deux nouvelles éditions lyonnaises du seizième siècle', *FAM*, xxxii (1984), 186–91

R. Clark: *The Penitential Psalms of Loyset Piéton* (thesis, U. of London, 1986)

L. Guillo: *Les éditions musicales de la Renaissance lyonnaise (1525–1615)* (Paris, 1991)

F. Dobbins: *Music in Renaissance Lyons* (Oxford, 1992)

LAWRENCE F. BERNSTEIN/RELF CLARK

Pietoso (It.: 'pitiful', 'piteous'; in non-musical contexts 'compassionate', 'merciful'). An expression mark. Brossard (*Dictionaire*, 1703) defined the term as 'd'une manière capable d'exciter de la pitié ou de la compassion', but the word is of limited usefulness.

For bibliography see TEMPO AND EXPRESSION MARKS.

DAVID FALLOWS

Pietragrua [Grua]. Family of Italian and German musicians.

(1) **Gasparo Pietragrua** [Cranesteyn] (*b* Milan, late 16th century; *d* ?Monza, nr Milan, after 1651). Italian composer and organist. He was an uncle of (2) Carlo Luigi Pietragrua. In 1629 he was organist at the collegiate church of S Leonardo, Pallanza. Fétis stated that he was organist at the collegiate church of nearby Canobio at this time; it is possible that he held the two posts simultaneously or that both statements refer to the same post. He held the same post at the collegiate church of Giovanni Battista at Monza, near Milan, in 1651. He published *Concerti et canzoni francesi* for one to four voices, op.1 (Milan, 1629), and *Musica spedita, cioè Messa, salmi alla romana per cantarsi alli vesperi di tutto l'anno con dio Magnificat, le quattro antifone, & falsibordoni otto, con il Gloria intiero libro 5*, op.9 (Venice, 1651). Fétis also mentioned *Canzonette* for three voices, op.2, and *Motetti* for solo voice, op.3. Settings of *Beatus vir* and *Laetatus sum* for four voices and instruments are now lost (fomerly in *D-Dkh*).

(2) **Carlo Luigi Pietragrua** (*b* Florence, *c*1665; *d* Venice, 27 March 1726). Italian composer, active in Germany. He was an alto in the Hofkapelle of the Elector of Saxony in Dresden from 1687. By a decree of 20 February 1693 he was made vice-Kapellmeister, and during Carnival 1693 his opera *Camillo generoso* was given in Dresden. He left in the following year for Düsseldorf, the residence of the Elector Palatine Johann Wilhelm, where he served under J.H. Wilderer as vice-Kapellmeister of the Hofkapelle; his opera *Telegono* was performed there during Carnival 1697. He served in Düsseldorf until the death of Johann Wilhelm in 1716, when the court moved to Heidelberg and merged with the Innsbruck Kapelle of the new Elector Carl Philipp in 1718; his brother, Vinzenz Paul, also went with the court and was an organist until his death in 1732. A serenade given in Heidelberg in 1718 by 'Carl Peter Grua, Kapellmeister to his Highness, the Elector Palatine'

(according to the libretto) has been attributed to (3) Carlo (Luigi) Grua but is probably the work of Carlo Luigi Pietragrua. In 1719 he was appointed *maestro di coro* at the Ospedale della Pietà, Venice. Three of his operas were performed there in 1721 and 1722; the librettos give the composer as 'Carlo Luigi Pietragrua, Florentino'. Among Steffani's literary remains (in the archive of the Propaganda Fide, Rome) are letters from Pietragrua to Steffani, whom he knew from Düsseldorf, which reveal that while in Italy he recruited singers on behalf of Steffani for the Schönborn Kapelle at Würzburg. In manuscript collections numerous chamber duets by Pietragrua are wrongly attributed to Steffani.

WORKS

music lost unless otherwise stated

DRAMATIC

Camillo generoso (dramma [per musica]), Dresden, carn. 1693, 12 arias, *D-Dl*, aria in *Bsb*

Telegono (tragedia in musica, 5, S.B. Pallavicino), Düsseldorf, carn. 1697, *A-Wn*

Il pastor fido (tragicommedia pastorale, 5, B. Pasquaglio, after G.B. Guarini), Venice, S Angelo, carn. 1721, *Wgm*

La fede ne'tradimenti (dramma per musica, 3, G. Gigli), Venice, S Angelo, aut. 1721

Romolo e Tazio (dramma per musica, 3, V. Cassani), Venice, S Giovanni Grisostomo, aut. 1722

Das fünfte Element der Welt (serenata, ?G.M. Rapparini), Heidelberg, Nov 1718, lib *D-HEu*

Doubtful: Arsinöe, Dresden, 1693; Aleramo ed Adelaide, Dresden, 1694; Festa boschereccia (serenata), Düsseldorf, 9 July 1697

OTHER WORKS

Chamber duets, *D-Dl*, *WD*; *GB-Cfm*, *Lbbc*, *Lcm*; *I-Bc*

Mass (Ky, Gl), 5vv, insts; Beatus vir (motet), 4vv, insts, *D-Dl*; Alleluja (Easter cant.), 5vv, insts, *Bsb*, *GB-Lbl*

(3) **Carlo (Luigi) Grua** [Pietragrua] (*b* ?Milan, *c*1700; *d* Mannheim, 11 April 1773). Italian composer, active in Germany, a nephew of Carlo Luigi Pietragrua. Fétis stated that he was born in Milan. The first printed court calendar of the Elector Palatine's establishment at Mannheim in 1734 names him as Kapellmeister; he accompanied his father, Vinzenz Paul, an organist, from Düsseldorf, and became a member of the orchestra between 1723 and 1728. He held the position of Kapellmeister from 1734 until his death, though after the arrival of Ignaz Holzbauer in Mannheim in 1753 he directed only church music. His most important contributions to Mannheim's music history were the festival opera *Meride*, produced both for the marriage of the future elector, Carl Theodor, and the opening of the new court opera on 17 January 1742, and *La clemenza di Tito*, performed on the birthday of the elector's wife on 17 January 1748. Besides these two operas several oratorios by Grua are known to have been performed in Mannheim between 1740 and 1750. In style his music is typical of the first-generation Mannheim School.

WORKS

music lost, performed in Mannheim, unless otherwise stated

OPERAS

Meride (dramma per musica, 3, G.C. Pasquini), Jan 1742, lib *US-Wc*

La clemenza di Tito (dramma per musica, 3, P. Metastasio), 1748, lib *D-MHrm*

ORATORIOS

La conversione di S Ignazio (2, L. Santorini), 1740, lib *DHEu*

Bersabea, ovvero il pentimento di David (azione tragico-sacra per musica), 1741, lib *HEu*

Jaele (2, Santorini), 1741, lib *HEu*

Il figliuol prodigo (azione sacra, 2, Pasquini), 1742; revived 1749, lib
    HEu
La missione sacerdotale (Santorini), 1746
S Elena al Calvario (azione sacra, 2, Metastasio), 1750, lib *HEu*
La passione di Giesù Christo nostro Signore (Metastasio), Bamberg,
    1754

OTHER SACRED WORKS

Mass, 4vv, insts, 1733, ed. in DTB, new ser., ii/1 (1982); Missa
    brevis, D, 4vv, insts, 1751; Missa brevis, d, 4vv, insts, 1751, *Mbs*;
    Mass, Eb, 4vv, insts, 1757, *Mbs*; Missa brevis, F, 4vv, insts, 1766,
    Mbs
Litanie della Beata Vergine, 5vv, insts, 1737, ed. in DTB, new ser.,
    ii/1 (1982)

(4) Paul [Paolo] **(Joseph) Grua** (*b* Mannheim, 1 Feb
1753; *d* Munich, 5 July 1833). German composer of
Italian descent, son of (3) Carlo (Luigi) Grua. He studied
composition under Ignaz Holzbauer and the violin under
Ignaz Fränzl. In 1776 he is named as a deputy violinist in
the court calendar of the electoral court at Mannheim. A
year later he received a grant of 350 florins from Elector
Palatine Carl Theodor for study in Italy with Padre
Martini in Bologna and probably also with Traetta. In
November 1778 he went with the Mannheim orchestra
to Munich, where in 1779 (according to the court calendar
of 1780) he was named vice-Kapellmeister under Andrea
Bernasconi, whom he succeeded in 1784 as Hofkapellmeister with a salary of 1200 florins. His only opera,
Telemaco, introduced him to the Munich public during
Carnival 1780 (with ballet music by C.J. Toeschi). After
Peter Winter became vice-Kapellmeister in Munich in
1787, Grua confined his activity to church music, as his
father had done. Mozart wrote to his father from Munich
on 13 November 1780 concerning one of Grua's 31
masses: 'one can easily compose half a dozen of this sort
of thing a day'. This judgment relates not only to the
quality of Grua's church music but also to his prolific
output of it.

WORKS

Telemaco (os, 3, Count Serimann), Munich, Jan 1780, *D-Mbs*
28 masses, 4vv, orch, *Mbs*; 2 masses, 4vv, Frauenkirche, Munich; 1
    mass, Eb, 1786, *WEY*; 4 Requiem, 4vv, orch, *Mbs*
29 offs, some with insts; 4 grads, 4vv, org; 6 Miserere, 4vv, orch; 3
    Stabat mater, 4vv, orch; 138 smaller sacred works incl. settings of
    Beatus vir, Dixit Dominus, Laudate Dominum, Laudate pueri,
    Magnificat, Regina coeli, Ave regina, Salve regina, hymns: all *Mbs*
Sym. movt, *AB*; several solo concs. for cl, fl, kbd and ob, *Mbs*

BIBLIOGRAPHY

EitnerQ; FétisB; FürstenauG, i; *GerberL; GerberNL; LipowskyBL;*
    WalterG
C.F.D. Schubart: *Leben und Gesinnungen* (Stuttgart, 1791–3/R)
H. Riemann: Preface to DTB, iv, Jg.iii/1 (1902)
F.W. Stein: *Geschichte des Musikwesens in Heidelberg bis zum Ende*
    des 18. Jahrhunderts (Heidelberg, 1921), 139–40
M. Zenger: *Geschichte der Münchener Oper*, ed. T. Kroyer (Munich,
    1923), 42, 59
F. Lau: 'Die Regierungskollegien zu Düsseldorf und der Düsseldorfer
    Hof zur Zeit Johann Wilhelms, II', *Düsseldorfer Jb*, xl (1938),
    257–88
J. Loschelder: 'Agostino Steffani und das Musikleben seiner Zeit',
    106. *Niederrheinisches Musikfest: Jb*, cvi (1951), 33–48
G. Croll: 'Musikgeschichtliches aus Rapparanis Johann-Wilhelm-MS
    (1709)', *Mf*, xi (1958), 257–64
D. Arnold: 'Orphans and Ladies: the Venetian Conservatoires
    (1680–1790)', *PRMA*, lxxxix (1962–3), 31–47
E. Schmitt, ed.: Preface to *Kirchenmusik der Mannheimer Schule*,
    DTB, new ser., ii/1 (1982)
K.-H. Nagel: 'Die Familie Grua: italienische Musiker in
    Karpfälzischen Diensten', *Mannheim und Italien: zur*
    Vorgeschichte der Mannheimer, ed. R. Würtz (Mainz, 1984),
    32–40

A. Freitäger: 'Carlo Luigi Pietragrua D.Ä. (ca. 1665–1726)', *Musik in*
    Bayern, xliv (1992), 7–41
P. Corneilson: 'Reconstructing the Mannheim Court Theatre', *EMc*,
    xxv (1997), 63–81
K. Böhmer: *W.A. Mozarts Idomeneo und die Tradition der*
    Karnevalsopern in München (Tutzing, 1999)

    NONA PYRON (1), ROLAND WÜRTZ/PAUL CORNEILSON (2–4)

Pietrequin [Pierre] **Bonnel** (*b* Picardy; *fl* late 15th century).
French singer and composer. It is just possible that he is
identifiable with the 'Pierre Donnell' or 'Donelli' reported
at the court of King René of Anjou from 1462 to 1472
and again in 1479. But he certainly worked at the court
of Savoy in 1488–9 and at both the cathedral and the
convent church of the SS Annunziata in Florence in 1490–
91 and 1492–3; later in the decade – perhaps from 1496
to 1499 – he sang in the chapel of Anne of Brittany,
Queen of France. He had probably worked at the French
court before, for he copied one of his chansons, *Qu'en*
dictez vous, and added attributions for three others in *I-*
Fr 2794, a manuscript almost certainly written at the
court during the 1480s. In this source as elsewhere his
works appear under his first name alone, which has led
some writers to ascribe them to Pierre de La Rue or to
Guillaume Pietrequin, a musician by whom no compositions survive.

Pietrequin's chansons – all rondeaux except *Adieu*
florens – vary widely in quality. The pieces in *I-Fr* 2794
observe the contrapuntal and formal conventions of their
genre without notable imagination or technical polish;
Mais que ce fust, however, achieves much greater success
and merits the popularity suggested by its appearance in
nine sources. *Adieu florens* also shows inventiveness in
Pietrequin's varied treatment of repetition within the
tenor melody – perhaps a popular tune – that serves as its
foundation.

WORKS

Adieu florens la yolye, 4vv; ed. in Brown
En desirant ce que ne puis avoir, 3vv; ed. in Jones
Mais que ce fust secretement, 3vv; ed. H. Hewitt, *Harmonice musices*
    odhecaton A (Cambridge, MA, 1942/R)
Mes douleurs sont incomparables, 3vv; ed. in Jones
Qu'en dictez vous suis je en danger, 3vv; ed. in Jones
Sans y penser a l'aventure, 3vv; ed. in Jones

BIBLIOGRAPHY

M.-T. Bouquet: 'La cappella musicale dei duchi di Savoia dal 1450 al
    1500', *RIM*, iii (1968), 233–85
F.A. D'Accone: 'Some Neglected Composers in the Florentine
    Chapels, ca. 1475–1525', *Viator*, i (1970), 263–88
M. Staehelin: 'Pierre de la Rue in Italien', *AMw*, xxvii (1970),
    128–37
G.M. Jones: *The 'First' Chansonnier of the Biblioteca Riccardiana,*
    Codex 2794 (diss., New York U., 1972)
S. Bonime: *Anne de Bretagne (1477–1514) and Music: an Archival*
    Study (diss., Bryn Mawr College, 1975)
L. Litterick: *The Manuscript Royal 20.A.XVI of the British Library*
    (diss., New York U., 1976)
J. Rifkin: 'Pietrequin Bonnel and Ms. 2794 of the Biblioteca
    Riccardiana', *JAMS*, xxix (1976), 284–96
Y. Esquieu: 'La musique à la cour provençale du roi René', *Provence*
    historique, xxxi (1981), 299–312
H.M. Brown, ed.: *A Florentine Chansonnier from the Time of*
    Lorenzo the Magnificent, MRM, vii (1983)
D. Fallows: *A Catalogue of Polyphonic Songs, 1415–1480* (Oxford,
    1999)

    JOSHUA RIFKIN/DAVID FALLOWS

Pietrobelli, Francesco. *See* PETROBELLI, FRANCESCO.

Pietrobono [Petrus Bonus] **de Burzellis** [de Bruzellis, del
Chitarino] (*b* Ferrara, ?1417; *d* Ferrara, 20 Sept 1497).
Italian lutenist and singer, one of the most important

musicians in Italy in the 15th century. He spent most of his career at the Este court in Ferrara, with periods of service at Milan, Naples, Mantua and the Hungarian court. He is first documented in 1441 as a member of the household of Leonello d'Este, marquis of Ferrara, who gave him the considerable sum of 20 gold ducats (the same amount Du Fay had received in 1437). His reputation grew during his service with Leonello in the 1440s and his successor Borso d'Este in the 1450s and 1460s, by which time he was reported to be earning 1000 ducats a year (chiefly in gifts). The first of several portrait medals of him was struck in 1447. He was in close contact with Francesco Sforza, duke of Milan, in the mid-1450s and early 1460s, visiting Milan in 1456. He accompanied Borso to Rome for his investiture as duke of Ferrara in 1471.

Pietrobono remained in Ferrarese service when Borso's brother Ercole I became duke later in 1471, and was a member of the retinue sent to Naples in 1473 to bring back Ercole's bride Eleonora d'Aragona. Tinctoris, who praised him highly in *De inventione et usu musicae*, may have heard him at this time or perhaps on a visit to Ferrara in 1479. He made a strong impression at Naples: King Ferrante I requested the loan of his services in 1476, and he later entered the service of Beatrice d'Aragona, daughter of Ferrante and sister-in-law of Ercole. Plague and a war between Ferrara and Venice drove Pietrobono to Mantua in 1482; he returned between 1484 and 1486. In 1487 he was sent to Hungary in the train of Ippolito I d'Este, the eight-year-old archbishop of Esztergom. He had been particularly requested by Beatrice d'Aragona, wife of Matthias Corvinus, king of Hungary, and he probably remained in her service for several years, as he is not recorded again in the Ferrarese salary rolls until 1493. In 1488 he had written to Francesco Gonzaga, marquis of Mantua, recommending his grandson to Francesco's patronage. He died at an advanced age in 1497.

Pietrobono played the lute as a melodic instrument in ensembles of various sorts. From 1449 onwards he was regularly accompanied by a *tenorista* (perhaps a tenor-viol player), he was said in 1484 to excel in 'soprano' playing, and in 1486 Beatrice d'Aragona asked Ercole d'Este to send her 'Pietrobono and his viols'. He also accompanied his own singing, either alone (as attested by Antonio Cornazzano) or with other instruments. He is frequently recorded as a teacher of both playing and singing. Besides Tinctoris and Cornazzano, his music was extolled by a number of prominent humanists, including Aurelio Brandolino Lippi, Battista Guarini, Filippo Beroaldo, Paolo Cortese and Raffaello Maffei. Although not a note of his music survives, no other musician in 15th-century Italy made such a profound impression on such a wide range of his contemporaries.

BIBLIOGRAPHY

MGG1 ('Bono, Pietro'; E. Haraszti); *LockwoodMRF*; *Vander StraetenMPB*, vi

L.N. Cittadella: *Notizie amministrative, storiche, artistiche relative a Ferrara*, ii (Ferrara, 1868/R)

E. Motta: 'Musici alla corte degli Sforza', *Archivio storico lombardo*, xiv (1887), 29–64, esp. 53–4

A. Bertolotti: *Musici alla corte dei Gonzaga in Mantova* (Milan, 1890), esp. 12–13

E. Haraszti: 'Pierre Bono, luthiste de Mathias Corvin', *RdM*, xxviii (1949), 73–85

E. Haraszti: 'Les musiciens de Mathias Corvin et de Béatrice d'Aragon', *La musique instrumentale de la renaissance: Paris 1954*, 35–59

G. Barblan: 'Vita musicale alla corte sforzesca', *Storia di Milano*, ix (Milan, 1961), 787–852, esp. 803

N. Pirrotta: 'Music and Cultural Tendencies in 15th-Century Italy', *JAMS*, xix (1966), 127–61

L. Lockwood: 'Pietrobono and the Instrumental Tradition at Ferrara in the Fifteenth Century', *RIM*, x (1975), 115–33

A. Bollini: 'L'attività liutistica a Milano dal 1450 al 1550: nuovi documenti', *RIM* xxi (1986), 31–60, esp. 37–9

LEWIS LOCKWOOD/R

Pietrowski, Karol (*fl* c1790–1800). Polish composer. There is no extant biographical information about him, but like other 18th-century Polish composers he was a local musician who composed for chapel orchestras. The manuscript material of one of his two symphonies, both in D, was found with other Polish symphonies among the music at the parish church of Grodzisk near Poznań, together with a *Veni Creator* for soprano, alto and bass, two violins, two horns and organ continuo. The other symphony and an offertorium, *Benedictus sit Deus*, for soprano, alto, tenor and bass, two violins and organ continuo, came to light in the archives of the collegiate church at Poznań itself, where the Benedictus remains. The three other works are now in *PL-Pu*. The symphonies, edited by Jacek Berwaldt in the series Symfonie Polskie, are remarkable chiefly for having been modelled on specific Viennese Classics: the first movement of the 'Grodzisk' Symphony on the *Zauberflöte* overture, the first movement of the 'Poznań' on Haydn's no.70 in the same key and its finale on Haydn's finale (both in D minor and in the same free and peculiar form). Both of Pietrowski's symphonies are scored for two flutes, two horns, two trumpets, timpani and strings, the first consisting of Grave–Allegro, Andante, Minuetto and Presto, the second of Allegro, Andante ma non troppo, Minuetto and Prestissimo. In style and form they represent an advanced stage in the development of the 18th-century symphony in Poland. The two religious works have been edited by Jacek Berwaldt and Jan Prosnak in the series Źródła do Historii Muzyki Polskiej. These are Pietrowski's only known compositions; an offertorium, *Jesu corona virginum*, formerly attributed to him, is the work of F. Piotrowski, director of the cathedral choir of Płock in the early 19th century.

BIBLIOGRAPHY

T. Strumiłło: 'Do dziejów symfonii polskiej' [The history of the Polish symphony], *Muzyka*, iv/5–6 (1953), 26–45

J. Berwaldt: Introduction to *Karol Pietrowski: Symfonie*, Symfonie polskie, ii (Kraków, 1965)

G. Abraham: 'Some Eighteenth-Century Polish Symphonies', *Studies in Eighteenth-Century Music: a Tribute to Karl Geiringer*, ed. H.C. Robbins Landon and R.E. Chapman (New York and London, 1970), 13–22

J. Berwaldt: Introduction to *Karol Pietrowski: Veni Creator, Benedictus*, ZHMP, xxii (1973)

W. Smialek: Introduction to *The Symphony in Poland*, The Symphony 1720–1840, ser. F, vii (New York, 1982)

GERALD ABRAHAM

Pietruszyńska, Jadwiga. See SOBIESKA, JADWIGA.

Pifait. See PIFFET family.

Pífano (Sp.). An ORGAN STOP.

Pifaro, Marc'Antonio [del] (*b* ?Bologna, c1500). Italian composer. Although a native of Bologna, he probably lived too early to be the Marc'Antonio Pifaro mentioned in a Bolognese catalogue as *maestro di cappella* at Carpi Cathedral in 1575. His *Intabolatura de lauto … Libro I* (Venice, 1546) contains a repertory of dances (pavans or chiarenzanas paired with saltarellos having the same tune in triple metre); three are related to vocal pieces. Two of these are modelled on Janequin and Passereau, and the third is based on an unknown Italian work.

BIBLIOGRAPHY

O. Chilesotti: 'Note circa alcuni liutisti italiani della prima metà del Cinquecento', *RMI*, ix (1902), 36–61, 233–63; pubd separately (Turin, 1902) [incl. edns of 5 pieces]
L.H. Moe: *Dance Music in Printed Italian Lute Tablatures from 1507 to 1611* (diss., Harvard U., 1956) [incl. edns of 3 pieces]

JANE ILLINGWORTH PIERCE

Pifaro, Nicolo. *See* NICCOLÒ PIFFARO.

Pifay. *See* PIFFET family.

Piffaro (i) [piffero] (It.). A woodwind instrument. The use of the term (an Italian cognate of fife and *Pfeife*) goes back at least to the 15th century. In the 16th century the term denoted a SHAWM; the closely related term *fiffaro* was used to indicate a transverse flute. 17th-century documents, however, imply that the term *piffaro* could also be used for a flute, and this ambiguity has been the source of some confusion. In present-day Italy the name is still applied to the small shawms that peasants from the Abruzzi (*pifferari*) play at the Christmas season in the streets of Italian cities, accompanied by *zampogne* (bagpipes), but it is also used as a generic name for woodwind instruments. In the 16th century and the early 17th the term also indicated an instrumentalist who played in a wind band.

BIBLIOGRAPHY

H. Geller: '*I pifferari*': *musizierende Hirten in Rom* (Leipzig,1954)
F. Puglisi: 'The Renaissance Flutes of the Biblioteca Capitolare of Verona: the Structure of a "Pifaro"', *GSJ*, xxxii (1979), 24–37
W. Prizer: 'Bernardo piffaro e i pifferi e tromboni di Mantova: strumenti a fiato in una corte italiana', *RIM*, xvi (1981), 151–84
G.M. Ongaro: '16th-Century Venetian Wind Instrument Makers and their Clients', *EMc*, xiii (1985), 391–7

HOWARD MAYER BROWN/GIULIO ONGARO

Piffaro (ii). *See under* ORGAN STOP.

Piffet [Pifet, Pifay, Pifait]. French family of violinists and composers. The activities of the various members are difficult to document because most of the 18th-century references lack forenames.

(1) Pierre Piffet (*b* late 17th century; *d* after 1760). Violinist. He was probably the Piffet who on 17 October 1728 played at a funeral (the earliest known reference to the family's musical activity). On 7 August 1729 he became a member of the 24 Violons du Roi.

(2) Pierre-Louis Piffet (*b* 1706 or 1707; *d* Blois, 26 Sept 1773). Violinist, son of (1) Pierre Piffet. From 1733 he was resident in Amiens. He gained the reversion of his father's position in the 24 Violons on 20 March 1734, and retained membership to at least 1754 and probably into the early 1760s. Of his four children only (4) Louis-François-Barthélemy became a professional musician.

(3) Joseph-Antoine Piffet (*b* ?*c*1710; *d* late 18th century). Violinist and composer, son of (1) Pierre Piffet. A teacher whose pupils included La Houssaye, he joined the Opéra orchestra in 1739, where he remained until 1751. It is reported that he had been a member of the Musique de la Chambre du Roi from 1734. He was possibly a member of the Concert Spirituel orchestra from 1751 and was probably the Piffet who frequently performed solos there from 1756 to 1761, often his own violin concertos. His last documented performance was in 1761. It is also likely that he was the Piffet *le cadet* who published a collection of six violin sonatas with continuo and another of violin duos in about 1750. These pieces, in three or four movements, are mostly bithematic, with both contrapuntal passages and accompanied melody, and, though conventional, they show a mastery of violin technique, especially that involving double stops.

(4) Louis-François-Barthélemy Piffet [*le fils* or *le neveu*] (*b* Amiens, 22 April 1734; *d* Port-au-Prince, Haiti, 19 Aug 1779). Violinist and composer, son of (2) Pierre-Louis Piffet. In 1751 he (or (3) Joseph-Antoine, whom Louis replaced in the Opéra orchestra that year) joined the Concert Spirituel orchestra. The membership of a Piffet in both organizations, though not continuous, can be traced to 1761. On 23 April 1753 he played a solo at the Concert Spirituel, and on 5 September 1754 he became a member of the 24 Violons. A Piffet *le fils* is also listed among the retired members of the Comédie-Française after 1765 (a Piffet was a member of this organization from 1749 to 1758). Louis was apparently the composer of three cantatas for solo voice and instruments – *Les travaux d'Hercule*, *La nouvelle nimphe* and *Le départ de Roquette*; the first two were written and published by 1747, when he was only 13.

Other musicians named Piffet, whose relation (if any) to this family remains uncertain, include Antoine-Joseph Piffet (possibly identical with (3) Joseph-Antoine Piffet), who joined the 24 Violons on 5 February 1734, and Etienne Piffet, called 'Le grand nez'. The latter has frequently been equated with Piffet *le cadet*; it is possible that he was identical with either (3) Joseph-Antoine Piffet or (4) Louis-François-Barthélemy Piffet. He composed two songs published in the *Mercure de France* (November 1751 and March 1752; the first was also published separately in 1763) and may have been the Piffet who performed in London in 1762. A Piffet was praised by the *Mercure de France* (1738); various musicians called Piffet gave concerts in London (1750), competed unsuccessfully for the post of Opéra director (1757), and published a trio called *Petits soupers* (1760).

BIBLIOGRAPHY

La LaurencieEF; *MGG1* (E. Borrel)
C. Pierre: *Histoire du Concert spirituel 1725–1790* (Paris, 1975)

JEFFREY COOPER

Piggott, Patrick (Edward Smerdon) (*b* Dover, 15 June 1915; *d* Bristol, 9 May 1990). English composer, pianist and writer. He studied at the RAM in London (1932–8) with Harold Craxton and Benjamin Dale, and won the coveted Mendelssohn Scholarship, which allowed him to study with Nadia Boulanger in Paris. He performed and broadcast widely, taught at the RAM and later at the Welsh College of Music and Drama, also lecturing at the University of Wales at Cardiff. Between 1965 and 1970 he was head of music at the Midland Region of the BBC. From 1972 he concentrated increasingly on composition, and also completed a pioneering study of John Field.

Piggott's early works show an excellent craftsmanship, as well as the extent of his debt to Ireland, Bridge and Bax. His fastidious approach led him later to destroy or withdraw many compositions, especially those written before 1963. After 1972 he developed an ever more personal style in which, while still paying tribute to the traditional forms of his youth, he found an expressive use of dissonance to match his already strongly marked lyricism. This is particularly apparent in two of his extended last works, *The Quest* for piano and orchestra (1987) and the song-cycle *Rosanes Lieder* (1987–9), commissioned by the BBC and completed only months before his death. His writing for piano reflects his own polished, virtuoso and highly sensitive playing.

WORKS
(selective list)

unpublished unless otherwise stated

Orch: Nocturne, tone poem, vn, orch, 1960; The Quest, pt, orch, 1987; Rosanes Lieder, Mez, orch, 1987–9
Choral: Samplers, female vv, hp, 1986
Solo vocal: Sonnets of the Wingless Hours (E.L. Hamilton), Bar, pf, 1977; Patterns (A. Lowell), S, pf, 1982; A Nocturne (W.S. Blunt), Bar, pf, 1981; St. Valentine's Day (Blunt), Bar, pf, 1981; The Wizard's Funeral (R.W. Dixon), Bar, pf, 1981; The Heart's Journey (S. Sassoon), T, pf, 1984; Candles (C.P. Cavafy), T, fl/pic, vc, pf, 1985; The Two Highwaymen (Blunt), Bar, pf, 1985
Inst: Fantasia quasi una sonata, pf, 1961, rev. 1975; 8 Preludes, pf, c1963; Essay, str qt, c1966; 3 Concert Pieces, pf, 1972; Trio serio, ob, cl, bn, 1972–3; 4 Invocations, pf, 1974; Fantasy Str Qt, 1974–5; Music at Night, pf, 1976; 8 Preludes, pf, 1976–7; Sonata no.2, pf, ?1978; Ballade, vc, pf, 1978; Momenti musicali, pf, 1979–80; Duo concertante, ob, pf, 1983; Str Qt no.3, 1983; 2 Rhapsodies, vc, 1985–7; 8 Preludes and a Postlude, pf, c1989; Sonata, hp

WRITINGS

The Life and Music of John Field, 1782–1837, Creator of the Nocturne (London, 1973)
Rachmaninov: Orchestral Music (London, 1973)
Rachmaninov (London, 1978)

BIBLIOGRAPHY

'Patrick Piggott', *MO*, lxxix (1956), 519
'Patrick Piggott', *Music Teacher*, xliv (1965), 326
L. Foreman: 'Patrick Piggott', *Independent* (25 May 1990) [obituary]

THOMAS COOPER

Pigmy music. *See* PYGMY MUSIC.

Pignatta [Pignati], Pietro Romulo (*b* Rome; *d* after 1699). Italian composer and librettist. In 1683 he was *maestro di cappella* of S Apollinare, Rome. He may have lived in Venice, at least between 1695 and 1700, when five operas by him (whose librettos describe him as an abbot) were given there; three were to his own librettos.

WORKS

OPERAS
known only from librettos; all first performed in Venice

Asmiro re di Corinto (Pignatta), SS Giovanni e Paolo, 15 Feb 1695; revivals as Inganno senza danno, Chi non sa finzere non sa vincere
La costanza vince il destino (Pignatta), SS Giovanni e Paolo, 15 Oct 1695; revivals as L'Oronta d'Egitto
Sigismondo Primo al diadema (G. Grimani), SS Giovanni e Paolo, 1696
Il Paolo Emilio (F. Rossi), Canal Regio, aut. 1699; attrib. Pignatta by Bonlini
Il vanto d'Amore (Pignatta), S Moisè, 1700

OTHER WORKS
2 cants. (3 others doubtful), 1v, bc, D-Dl
Vesper ps, 4vv, bc, 1683[1]
Sonata, C, ob [?tpt], 2 vn, org, b, ?1693, A-Wn (see Smithers)

BIBLIOGRAPHY

EitnerQ; FétisB; SchmidlD
C. Bonlini: *Le glorie della poesia e della musica* (Venice, 1730/R)

D.L. Smithers: *The Music and History of the Baroque Trumpet before 1721* (London, 1973, 2/1988), 274

Pignoni, Zanobi di Francesco (*fl* 1607–41). Italian bookseller and printer, active in Florence. He matriculated in the *Arte dei medici e speziali* on 15 November 1607 and by 1614 had become head of the printing firm founded by Giorgio Marescotti and continued by his son Cristofano. He was also a singer trained in the choir of Florence Cathedral. Pignoni made an auspicious entry into music printing in 1614–15 with no fewer than six editions, including masses and motets by Marco da Gagliano, madrigals by Giovanni del Turco, and Giulio Caccini's *Nuove musiche e nuova maniera di scriverle*. This initiative was prompted by a generous, if shortlived, financial investment in the firm (in June 1614) by three prominent Florentine patrons, Giovanni del Turco, Lodovico Arrighetti and (for Cosimo del Sera) Giovanni Battista da Gagliano: hence the imprint 'Zanobi Pignoni, e Compagni'.

Thereafter Pignoni diversified his interests, printing poetry, occasional items and *descrizioni* of court festivities, while publishing music less frequently: three titles survive from 1617, one from 1618 and two from 1619, including music by Francesco Caccini, Jacopo Peri and Filippo Vitali. All these music editions are closely related in format, typography and content to the earlier ones of Cristofano Marescotti.

By the 1620s Pignoni was in competition with Pietro Cecconcelli, and he produced very few new music editions. The printing quality in Marco da Gagliano's opera *La Flora* (1628) is poor, and Pignoni's later editions of music by Antonio Guelfi (1631), Gregorio Veneri (1631) and Bartolomeo Spighi (1641) are provincial in content, while a reprint (1637) of Giovanni Abatessa's *Cespuglio di varii fiori* (Orvieto, 1635), a set of guitar intabulations, suggests an attempt to reach a popular market. No music editions bearing the Pignoni imprint survive from after 1641, although the C. Marescotti/Pignoni music fount appears in Vitali's *Musiche a tre voci … libro quinto* (Florence, 1647), printed by Lando Landi and Giovanni Antonio Bonardi.

BIBLIOGRAPHY

SartoriD
T. Carter: 'Music-Printing in Late Sixteenth- and Early Seventeenth-Century Florence: Giorgio Marescotti, Cristofano Marescotti and Zanobi Pignoni', *EMH*, ix (1989), 27–72

TIM CARTER

Pigott [Pickett, Pigot], Francis (*b* 1665–6; *d* London, 15 May 1704). English organist and composer. He was perhaps related to Francis and George Piggot, members of the Old Jewry music society in the 1660s; a George Pigot was also appointed clerk of the Corporation of Musick in February 1672. He was a Chapel Royal choirboy from at least August 1678 to Michaelmas 1683. Soon after leaving the chapel he became organist of St John's College, Oxford, and in January 1686 succeeded Benjamin Rogers as organist of Magdalen College. On 27 May 1688 he became the first organist of the Temple Church, London, and on 5 December he married Anne Pelling at St Benet Paul's Wharf. Despite promising the Temple authorities not to be 'organist in any other church or chapel whatsoever', he became organist-extraordinary of the Chapel Royal on 11 December 1695 and succeeded William Child as organist on 24 March 1697. In 1698 he took the MusB at Cambridge. He was succeeded at the Temple Church by his son John (*d* 24 Nov 1762), who also held appointments at St George's Chapel, Windsor (1719), and Eton College (1733) before inheriting a fortune in 1756. Only a few pieces by Pigott survive, but they are good quality. The duet, *The Consort of the Sprinkling Lute*, was apparently 'Sung at St. Ce[ci]lia's Feast'; it may come from an ode written for the 1694 celebrations.

WORKS

I was glad, ? for Queen Anne's coronation, 1703, full anthem, 4vv, *GB-Ob*, *US-AUS* (facs. in *The Gostling Manuscript*, Y. Austin, 1977)
2 songs, 1688[7]
The Consort of the Sprinkling Lute, 2vv, 1695[12]
3 dialogues, frags., *GB-Och*, by 'Picket' and 'Pigot'
Suite, C, kbd, 1700[10]; Jig, kbd, *Och*: both ed. J.A. Fuller-Maitland, *The Contemporaries of Purcell*, viii (London, 1921/*R*)

BIBLIOGRAPHY

AshbeeR, i, ii, v; *BDA*; *BDECM*
W.H. Husk: *An Account of the Musical Celebrations on St Cecilia's Day* (London, 1857)
E.F. Rimbault, ed.: *The Old Cheque-Book, or Book of Remembrance of the Chapel Royal* (London, 1872/*R*)
I. Spink: 'The Old Jewry "Musick-Society": a Seventeenth-Century Catch Club', *Musicology*, ii (1967), 35–41
D. Dawe: *Organists of the City of London 1666–1850* (Padstow, 1983)
H.W. Shaw: *The Succession of Organists of the Chapel Royal and the Cathedrals of England and Wales from c.1538* (Oxford, 1991)
J. Harley: *British Harpsichord Music* (Aldershot, 1992–4)
I. Spink: *Restoration Cathedral Music 1660–1714* (Oxford, 1995)

PETER HOLMAN

Piguet, Michel (*b* Geneva, 30 April 1932). Swiss oboist, recorder player and teacher. One of the first professional musicians to devote his attention to the Baroque oboe, he studied with Roland Lamorlette at the Paris Conservatoire and played first oboe in the Zürich Tonhalle Orchestra from 1956. In 1964 he resigned his orchestral post to concentrate on Renaissance, Baroque and Classical repertory and the revival of the playing techniques of the shawm, early oboe and recorder. In 1972 he opened the first professional class for recorder at the Schola Cantorum Basiliensis, and in 1974 inaugurated a class there for the historical oboe. Piguet assembled an important collection of wind instruments, much of which he sold in 1997, and his research has contributed significantly to the history of the technique of the oboe and the reassessment of the importance of original recorder fingerings. Outstanding among his many recordings are Mozart's Oboe Quartet and Oboe Concerto – both first recordings using historical instruments – and performances of Renaissance music by the Ricercare Ensemble, of which he is director.

WRITINGS

'The Baroque Oboe', *Recorder and Music Magazine*, ii/6 (1962), 171–2
with M. Kirkpatrick: 'Die Oboe im 18. Jahrhundert: Versuch einer Chronologie verschiedener Oboentypen anhand von Messungen und Betrachtungen von neunzehn Instrumenten aus der Sammlung M. Piguet', *Basler Jb für historische Musikpraxis*, xii (1988), 81–107
'Historical Oboes: Sound and Fingering', *A Time of Questioning: Proceedings of the International Double-Reed Symposium* [Utrecht 1994] (Utrecht, 1998)

GEOFFREY BURGESS

Pijper, Willem [Frederik Johannes] (*b* Zeist, 8 Sept 1894; *d* Leidschendam, 18 March 1947). Dutch composer and teacher.

1. LIFE.   He was, with Vermeulen, the most important composer in the Netherlands in the first half of the 20th century; his teaching and writing also made a significant impact. He grew up in a working-class Calvinist milieu in a village outside Utrecht. Due to recurring bronchitis and asthma, he was educated at home until the age of 14 but then attended Gymnasium in Utrecht. Already studying the organ, he left school in 1911 to enroll in the Utrecht Toonkunst Muziekschool, where he studied composition with Johan Wagenaar and the piano with Helena van Lunteren-Hansen. His final examination, in 1915, was in theory, and he continued composition lessons privately for three more years.

The family of his first wife, Annie Werker (they married in 1918), brought him social and musical opportunities in Utrecht, and he came under the influence of two older, Francophile colleagues: Diepenbrock and the critic J.S. Brandts Buys. It was Mengelberg's Concertgebouw première (April 1918) of the Mahler-like First Symphony which brought him national recognition. During 1918–21 he taught theory at the Amsterdam Muziek lyceum and from 1917 to 1923 he wrote for the *Utrechtsch Dagblad*. His long, pithy reviews crusaded against complacency and amateurishness; one victim was the conductor Jan van Gilse, who resigned his post with the Utrecht orchestra in 1922 as a result of Pijper's criticisms. This incident created a nationwide furore, and his reputation as a musical essayist was assured.

A radical new compositional style, confirmed in 1920 with *Heer Halewijn* and the Septet, made Pijper leader of the Dutch musical avant garde. He represented the Netherlands at the founding of the ISCM in Salzburg, 1922; soon after, backed by Sem Dresden, he established the Dutch ISCM section. In 1923 he met the playwright Balthazar Verhagen, and new co-productions of Greek dramas resulted, beginning with *De bacchanten*. Otherwise this was a difficult period. An anticipated critic's post in Amsterdam failed, and he was left almost without work. An affair with his student Iet Stants ended unhappily in spring 1925, and in July he attempted suicide. He then separated from his wife and moved to Amsterdam. His prospects improved when, in September of that year, Dresden appointed him head of composition and orchestration at the Amsterdam Conservatory. Monteux, now second conductor in Amsterdam, was also in search of new compositions; and after two major successes, the Symphony no.3 and the Piano Concerto, he was to champion Pijper's music internationally, performing it in France, Belgium, the UK and the USA. ISCM contacts led to concert tours in France, Belgium, England and Germany, through which his chamber and vocal music gained admirers. Dent and Edward Clark recommended him to Oxford University Press, which now began to publish his piano and chamber works. In 1926 he became co-editor (with Sanders) of *De Muziek*, an outstanding professional journal which they ran for seven years. In the meantime he began a relationship with the author Emmy van Lokhorst; they married in 1927.

Following an earlier, unsuccessful attempt, Pijper in 1930 became head of the Rotterdam Conservatory, a position he held until his death. Several of his former students joined the teaching staff, and together with the local conductor, Flipse, they made Rotterdam a centre for contemporary music. In 1932, supported by his wife, he moved to a luxurious house in Wassenaar, and two years later, following the triumphant Amsterdam première of the opera *Halewijn*, he was knighted. But in 1935, personal troubles again erupted, as another process of separation and divorce began, with subsequent moves to Rotterdam and Leidschendam.

Pijper joined a masonic lodge in 1938 and simultaneously began to practise astrology. From then and throughout World War II, he was preoccupied with *gematris* (a kind of numerological thinking in music which dates back to the Netherlandish polyphonists and also to Bach) and other symbolic thought. In May 1940, following the German bombardment of Rotterdam, fire destroyed his house and most of his possessions; yet copies of nearly all his compositions survived in safekeeping. He kept his conservatory alive during wartime, under very meagre conditions, and served briefly on artistic reconstruction panels after liberation in 1945. Falling ill in the summer of 1946, after the London ISCM Festival, he was diagnosed with cancer in November and died four months later.

His students, including Karel Mengelberg, Stants, van Lier, van Hemel, Bosmans, Guillaume Landré, Piet Ketting, Badings, Henkemans, van Baaren, Escher, Jan van Dijk and Masséus, were prominent in Dutch musical life throughout the 1960s. For a time younger composers attacked this Pijper group (de Leeuw, 1966), but in the mid-1980s a counter-reaction occurred, and since then there have been numerous performances, and recordings, of the orchestral and chamber works and the operas *Halewijn* and *Merlijn*.

2. WORKS.   Pijper's compositions before 1919 are juvenilia reflecting Wagenaar's insistence on learning from older models. However, the *Tema con 5 variazioni* (1913), the *Passepied* for carillon (1916) and especially the String Quartet no.1 (1914), cyclic in structure, deserve to be played, as do the succinct, atonal *3 Aphorismen* (1915), which foreshadow his mature style. For a time his music echoed Mahler (e.g. Symphony no.1) and Debussy (e.g. *Fêtes galantes*, *Romance sans paroles*), but with the first sonatas for violin and for cello and *Maumariée I* (1919), the style became personal and Mediterranean in flavour. Here, as later in life, he wrote for fine performers sympathetic to his work.

A radical departure is the *a cappella* double choir composition *Heer Halewijn* (1920), based on a Bluebeard-like ballad which Pijper knew from his school days in Utrecht. He identified with its opening line: 'Heer Halewijn sang a song; all who heard it had to go to him'. The complex, atonal idiom cost Dresden and his chamber choir, the Madrigaal-vereniging, 35 rehearsals before the première in 1922. Similar *a cappella* pieces were to follow: *Heer Daniëlken* in 1925, *Van den coninc van Castilien* in 1936.

The press typified him as a composer who worked in 'germ cells', a term borrowed from d'Indy and reflecting Pijper's youthful interest in biology. The earliest of these cells (beginning with the Septet in 1920) consist of four notes, which recur throughout a movement or an entire work. The Piano Trio no.2 (1921), Symphony no.2 (1921) and Sextet (1923) are all formed this way, while the Violin Sonata no.2 (1922) uses one mirror-chord as its cell. Traditional thematic development and chord relations are replaced by linear counterpoint (Septet) and occasional heterophony (Trio no.2, Symphony no.2). The Symphony no.2 is remarkable for its lavish instrumentation, which

recalls Mahler's Seventh Symphony, including a solo tenor horn, organ, 4 harps, 3 pianos, 6 mandolins and a large steel plate. It created a break with Mengelberg, who could not understand the score; the Amsterdam première in November 1922 under Pijper's direction was a failure.

Starting with the employment of germ cells, Pijper's music from the 1920s consists of an eclectic mix of devices. The habanera rhythm introduced in the second of the *Fêtes galantes* progressively becomes a fixation in later works. Polymetre apparently stems from Ravel's Piano Trio; it is used widely in Pijper's solo and chamber pieces (briefly in *Merlijn*). Bitonality and polytonality were acquired, soon after World War I, from the music of Milhaud. These 'poly' formations yield a music in which two or more distinct actions, loosely coordinated, appear to be taking place at once. Yet the compositional style also becomes strikingly original. Terseness, abrupt changes and conclusions, thunderous climaxes, restless rhythmic motion and truncated, varied reprises are common to his mature works. The bitonal harmonies, used hauntingly in the *Twee liederen* on old Dutch texts (1923), provide a special flavour. In the incidental music to *De Bacchanten* he superimposes triads of B, D and F major (he had stumbled upon octatonic scales of alternating tones and semitones and their asscociated harmonies, apparently without knowledge of Stravinsky's octatonic writing). In the Cello Sonata no.2 (1923–4), cello and piano parts are mostly autonomous, chordally and rhythmically; polymetre is widespread, and microtones appear in the finale.

Pijper's foreign reputation arose from pieces written in the late twenties: not only the Monteux commissions, but also the fresh and individual Flute Sonata (1925). In three movements, it uses a germ cell based on an altered overtone series. Like the Second Cello Sonata, it has entered the standard repertory. Over time the habanera figures grew more complex and were combined with other Caribbean rhythms; one such formation creates a violent climax near the end of the Piano Concerto (1927). The ragtime-filled Second and Third Piano Sonatinas and the Third Symphony are strongly octatonic, and all have met with success internationally (the latter through Monteux's efforts). This octatonic trend, which Pijper described in his writings as 'pluritonality', continued through the blues-laden Piano Concerto and the *Marialied* (1929). The String Quartet no.4 (1928), based on an octatonic germ cell, attains polymetric extremes; during moments in the finale, none of the players share a common downbeat.

The octatonic focus in Pijper's music diminished after the opera *Halewijn* (1932–3), where one phrase of the Halewijn ballad, used as a germ motif, fits octatonic pitches. In this psychological drama, to Emmy van Lokhorst's libretto, Halewijn's magical song predestines a tragic encounter between himself, symbol of nature (a sung role), and the king's daughter, symbol of reason (in Sprechgesang). Recalling Debussy's *Pelléas et Mélisande*, its exotically perfumed octatonic harmony continues an air of decadence. After *Halewijn* there is a growing preoccupation with counterpoint and a reversion to simpler forms of tonality. In the Sonata for two pianos (1935), written for Bartlett and Robertson, the slow movement is an invention, the finale a fugue. The Violin Concerto (1938–9) employs updated Baroque ritornello forms. The Cello Concerto (1936), however, is a work of

Bergian darkness; in six short sections, it emphasizes the lowest registers of the solo instrument. Like most of his later compositions, it gained public acceptance slowly.

Pijper's accession to freemasonry and astrology led to intense numerical calculations in his compositions (as in the 6 *Adagios,* largely in C major, written in 1940 for a masonic initiation) and occasional use of *soggetti cavati.* In the unfinished Arthurian opera *Merlijn* (1939–45), a rigorous system of proportion and key relations is based on numerology and astrology (Van Dijk and Vestdijk 1992, 147–77). New chord combinations, learned counterpoint, and brilliant, Wagnerian brass scoring suggest an overall renovation of style. The last major composition after *Merlijn* is the nostalgic String Quartet no.5 (1946), of which two movements and a fragment of a third were completed.

Pijper made numerous arrangements, among which the collections of Dutch and French songs show a keen feeling for the old texts and tunes, tastefully enhanced by simple piano accompaniments. By contrast, the *Wachterliederen* and *Old Dutch Songs* series no.2 (1934–5) display his devotion at the time to counterpoint. Pijper's vocal music, including several of these arrangements, is among his best work but remains largely negelcted.

WORKS
STAGE

Ops: Halewijn (sym. drama, 9 scenes, E. van Lokhorst), 1932–3, Amsterdam, Stadsschouwburg, 13 June 1933, rev. 1933–5, Rotterdam, Grote Schouwburg, 6 July 1935 [with archaicized text by E. Jurgens]; Merlijn (sym. drama, 3, S. Vestdijk), 1939–45, unfinished; concert perf., Rotterdam, 7 June 1952
Incid music: Antigone (Sophocles), 1991–20, rev. and expanded, 1922, rev. with new trans. 1925–6; De getemde feeks [The Taming of the Shrew] arrangement (W. Shakespeare), 1923; De Bacchanten (Euripides), 1924; De Cycloop (Euripides), 1925; The Tempest (Shakespeare), 1929–30; Faëton (J. Van den Vondel), 1937

INSTRUMENTAL

Orch: March, perc, str, 1913; Orkeststuk met piano, 1915; Divertimento, pf, str, 1916, lost; 3 Syms.: 1917, 1921, 1926, Pf Conc., 1927; 6 symphonische epigrammen, 1927–8; Vc Conc., 1936, rev. 1947; Vn Conc., 1938–9; 6 Adagios, 1940, arr. pf qnt
Chbr: Serenade, wind, pf, 1913; Pf Trio no.1, e, 1913–14; Str Qt no.1, 1914; Sonata no.1, vn, pf, 1919; Sonata no.1, vc, pf, 1919; Havanaïse, 2vn, 1920; Septet, ww qnt, pf, db, 1920; Str Qt no.2, 1920; Pf Trio no.2, 1921; Sonata no.2, vn, pf, 1922; Str Qt no.3, 1923; Sonata no.2, vc, pf, 1923–4; Sextet, ww qnt, pf, 1923; Sonata, fl, pf, 1925; Trio, fl, cl, bn, 1927; Str Qt no.4, 1928; Ww Qnt, 1928–9; Sonata, vn, 1931; 6 Adagios, pf, qnt, 1940, inc.; Str Qt no.5, 1946, unfinished
Kbd (pf unless otherwise stated): Sonata, E, 1912, inc.; Tema con 5 variazioni, 1913; Berceuse, 1913; Cadenza: Beethoven: Pf Conc. no.1, 1915; 3 Aphorismen, 1915; Passepied, carillon, 1916; Sonatina no.1, 1917; Sonatina no.2, no.3, 1925; Sonata, 1930; Sonata, 2 pf, 1934–5

VOCAL

Choral: Het jagertje (J. Goeverneur), children's chorus, 1913; De lenbe komt (R de Clercq), TTBB, 1917; Op den weefstoel [At the Loom] (de Clercq), SATB, wind, pf 4 hands, 1918; Heer Halewijn (trad.), SSAATTBB, 1920; 2 Ballades de Paul Fort, SSA, pf, 1921, orchd 1933–4; Heer Daniëlken (trad.), SSAATTBB, 1925; Chanson 'Réveillez-vous, Piccars', TTBB, wind, vc, db, timp, 1932, rev. 1944; Van den coninc van Castilien (trad.), TTBB, 1935–6
Solo vocal (1v, pf unless otherwise stated): 7 early songs (A. Fitger, E. Koster, N. Lenau, H von Gilm), 1912–14; 4 liederen (de Bruyn), 1914–16; Douwdeuntje [Lullaby] (R. de Clercq), 1916; 3 Fêtes galantes (P. Verlaine), Mez, orch, 1916; Romance sans paroles (Verlaine), Mez, orch, 1919, rev. 1921; La Maumariée I, II (trad.), 1919–20; 2 liederen (Old Dutch texts), 1923; 16e eeuwsch marialied, 1929; 2 sinterklaas liederen (S. Bessem), 1938–9;

Hymne (P. Boutens), B, orch, 1941–3, Canon ad infinitum, vv, insts, 1942, rev. 1944

ARRANGEMENTS

[8] Vieilles chansons de France, 1v, pf, 1918 [rev. new no. added 1942]; [8] Noëls de France, 1v, pf, 1919 (3 orchd, lost); [8] Oud-hollandsche minneliederen, 1v, pf, 1920 [rev. new no. added 1942]; Die nächtliche Heerschau (C. Loewe), Bar, orch, 1922, rev. 1943; Haydn: Pf Conc., D, reorchd 1921–3; 4 pezzi antichi (It., c1600), 3 vn, vc, 1923 [for incid music De getemde feeks]; 8 Oud-hollandsche liederen, 1st ser., 1v, pf, 1924; 3 Old Dutch Dances, pf, 1926; W.A. Mozart: Phantasie für eine Spieluhr, K608, pf, ww qnt, 1927; P. Hellendaal: Sonata, op.5 no.3, vc, pf, 1927; 2 Wachterliederen, vv, insts, 1934 [from *Souterliedekens*, 1540]; 8 Oud-hollandsche liederen, 2nd ser., 1v, pf, 1935

MSS in *NL-DHk*

Principal publishers: Broekmans & van Poppel, Donemus, Lengnick, OUP, Sénart, JAH Wagenaar

WRITINGS

Around 650 articles and reviews in: *Utrechtsch Stedelijk en Provinciaal Dagblad* (1917–23); *De nieuwe kroniek* (1922–3); *De vrije bladen* (1925–6); *Rotterdamsch Nieuwsblad* (1926–?8); *i10* (1927); *De muziek* (1926–32); *De groene Amsterdammer* (1934–46); *Mensch en melodie* (1946)
De quintencirkel (Amsterdam, 1929, 4/1964)
De stemvork [The Tuning Fork] (Amsterdam, 1930)
'Van Debussy tot Heden', *Algemeene muziekgeschiedenis*, ed. A. Smijers (Utrecht, 1938, 4/1948), 421–75

BIBLIOGRAPHY

S. Dresden: *Het muziekleven in Nederland sinds 1880*, i: *De componisten* (Amsterdam, 1923), 119–25
'De dagtaak [day's work] van de componist Willem Pijper', *Nieuwe Rotterdamsche Courant* (4 and 11 Feb 1928)
P.F. Sanders: ' Willem Pijper', *Moderne Nederlandsche componisten* (The Hague, 1930), 72–110
H.E. Reeser: ' De pianosonate van Willem Pijper', *Caecilia en De muziek*, xci (1934), 186–92
H.E. Reeser: 'De derde Symphonie van Willem Pijper', *Caecilia en De muziek*, xcii/9 (1935), 138–46
Mensch en melodie, ii/nos.6–7 (1947) [Pijper issue]
S. Dresden: 'Willem Pijper (1894–1947): in memoriam', *Tijdschrift voor muziekwetenschap*, xvii (1948), 18–20
K.P. Bernet Kempers: *Inleiding tot de opera Halewijn van Willem Pijper* (Rotterdam, 1949)
K. Mengelberg: 'Willem Pijper 1894–1947', *Music Today,* ed. R. Myers (London, 1949), 36–45
J. Daniskas: ' Het onvoltooid nagelaten symphonisch drama "Merlijn" van Willem Pijper', *Mens en melodie*, vii (1952), 131–6
Thot, iv/3 (1953) [Pijper issue, ed. J. Huibregtsen]
A. Ringer: ' William Pijper and the Netherlands School of the Twentieth Century', *MQ*, xli (1955), 427–45
W.H. Thijsse: ' Willem Pijper en Beethoven', *Opstellen door vrienden en collega's aangeboden aan Dr. F.K.H. Kossmann* (The Hague, 1958), 237–45
W.C.M. Kloppenburg: *Thematisch-bibliografische catalogus van de werken van Willem Pijper* (Assen, 1960)
S. Vestdijk: ' Willem Pijper', *Gestalten tegenover mij* [Shapes before me] (The Hague, 1962), 129–74
A. van Gilse-Hooijer: *Pijper contra van Gilse* (Utrecht, 1963)
R. de Leeuw: ' Het einde van een mythe', *De Gids*, lxxix/1 (1966), 171–3
B. van Lier: ' The Moment which does not Return', *Sonorum speculum*, no.30 (1967), 39–44
H. Ryker: *The Symphonic Music of Willem Pijper 1894–1947* (diss., U. of Washington, 1971)
J. Wouters: ' Willem Pijper', *Dutch Composers' Gallery* (Amsterdam, 1971), 104–35
W. Paap: *Muziekleven in Utrecht tussen de beide wereldoorlogen* (Utrecht, 1972)
Thot, xxiii/4 (1972) [Pijper issue]
F. Hoogerwerf: *The Chamber Music of Willem Pijper* (diss., U. of Michigan, 1974)
M. Flothuis: ' An Unharmonious Figure in an Unharmonious Age', *Key Notes*, no.3 (1976), 26–33
F. Hoogerwerf: 'Willem Pijper as Dutch Nationalist', *MQ*, lxii (1976), 358–74

F. Hoogerwerf: 'The String Quartets of Willem Pijper', *MR*, xxxviii/1 (1977), 44–64

M. Vermeulen: *De stem van levenden* (Arnhem, 1981), 8–15, 127–9

J. Kasander: ' Zonder agressiviteit is creatie ondenkbaar: al pratend met Willem Pijper', *Mens en melodie*, xlii (1987), 222–9

R.P.M.Rhoen: ' Willem Pijper', *Markante Zeistenaren*, ed. J. Meerdink (Zeist, 1991), 134–47

A. van Dijk and M.Vestdijk, eds.: *Merlijn: het ontstaan van een opera* (Amsterdam, 1992)

M. Flothuis: *Denken over muziek* (Kampen, 1993), 92–104

H. Ryker: 'Closing the Circle: Willem Pijper's Music for the Theatre', *TVNM*, xliii (1993), 42–75

Mens en melodie, xlix/9 (1994) [Pijper issue]

H. Pennarts: ' Willem Pijper als vrijmetselaar [Freemason]', *Thot*, xlv (1994), 164–78

H. Ryker: 'i10 en de muziek', *i10, sporen van de avant-garde*, ed. I. van Helmond (Heerlen, 1994), 165–78

K. Thomassen, ed.: *Koninklijke Bibliotheek: Inventaris van de collectie Willem Pijper* (The Hague, 1994)

HARRISON RYKER

Pikayzen, Viktor Aleksandrovich (*b* Kiev, 15 Feb 1933). Ukrainian violinist. After graduating from David Oistrakh's class at the Moscow Conservatory in 1957, he completed postgraduate studies under his direction in 1960. He was a prizewinner at international violin competitions in Prague (1949), Paris (1957), Moscow (1958) and Genoa (1965). In 1960 he became a soloist with the Moscow PO. He is an outstanding virtuoso whose playing is distinguished by exceptional technique and nobility of style, and is noted for his performances of the Bach and Paganini works for violin solo. He tours in many countries and has also served on the juries of many international competitions. In 1966 he began teaching at the Moscow Conservatory.

BIBLIOGRAPHY

J. Creighton: *Discopaedia of the Violin, 1889–1971* (Toronto, 1974)

E. Sainati: 'Picking the Winners', *The Strad*, c (1989), 758–61

I.M. YAMPOL'SKY/R

Pilati, Mario (*b* Naples, 16 Oct 1903; *d* Naples, 10 Dec 1938). Italian composer and critic. He studied composition with A. Savasta at the Naples Conservatory before teaching at the Liceo Musicale in Cagliari (1924–6) and at the Milan Conservatory (1926–30). He returned to Naples, where he held the professorship of counterpoint at the conservatory there (1930–33) and then, that of composition in Palermo, before returning to Naples Conservatory at the end of his life. He was active as a critic for various newspapers and journals, including Rassegna Musicale, and published guides to two operas by Pizzetti, *Orséolo* and *Fra Gherardo*. Pilati shared with many other early 20th-century Italian composers an interest in reviving instrumental music of the past, both Italian and European (his Suite for piano and strings and Piano Quintet are clearly neo-classical and reminiscent of Ravel, while later works assume the characteristics of sonatas of the Romantic era). The influence of Pizzetti is significant, especially in his assimilation of linguistic and formal models (*Il battesimo di Cristo* for soloists, chorus and orchestra) and in a structural rigour, tempered in Pilati's case by a rich vein of folksong inspiration which finds full expression in his last works.

WORKS
(selective list)

Vocal: 2 canciones espanolas, 1v, pf, 1921; Dialogo di marionette (S. Corazzini), 1v, pf, 1921, arr. female vv, chbr orch, 1922; Nanna nanna (14th-century popular poems), 1v, pf, 1924; 3 canti napoletani, 1v, pf, 1925, arr. 1v, chbr orch, 1926; Ps cxxxiii, double chorus, 1925; La sera di A. Fogazzaro, female chorus,

orch, 1926; Il battesimo di Cristo (orat), solo vv, chorus, orch, 1927; Sonetto XV (A. Dante: *Vita nova*), 1v, pf, 1927; 2 madrigali (G. Guarini), 1v, pf, 1932; Echi di Napoli (popular texts), 8 songs, 1v, pf, 1933, arr. 1v, orch, 1935; Amore (V. Cardarelli), 1v, pf, 1934, arr. 1v, 2 va, 2 vc, 1937; La tartaruga (C.A. Trilussa), 1v, pf, 1934

Orch: Notturno, 1922; Suite, pf, str, 1925; 3 pezzi, 1929; 4 canzoni popolari italiane, small orch, 1931; Bagatelle, 1933, arr. pf, 1935; Conc., C, pf obbl, orch, 1933; Alla culla, lullaby, 5 wind, hp, triangle, str, 1938

Chbr and solo inst: 2 pezzi pf 4 hands, 1924; Sonata, fl, pf, 1925; Pf Qnt, D, 1927; 6 bagatelle, pf, 1929; Canzone a ballo, pf, 1929; Sonata, F, vn, pf, 1929; Sonata, A, vc, pf, 1929; Inquiétude, étude mélodique, cl/va/vc, pf, 1930; Preludio, aria e tarantella, vn, pf, 1930, orchd 1932; Str Qt, A, 1931; Caccia, vn, pf, 1932; Divertimento, 3 tpt, 4 hn, 2 trbn, 1932; 2 pezzi facili, pf, 1932; 3 studi, pf, 1932; Tammurriata, vn, pf, 1936 [from Echi di Napoli, 1v, pf]

Principal publishers: Curci, Ricordi

WRITINGS

'"Fra Gherardo" di I. Pizzetti', *Bollettino bibliografico musicale*, iii/5 (1928) 5, 11

'*L'Orséolo' di Ildebrando Pizzetti: guida attraverso il dramma e la musica* (Milan, 1935)

BIBLIOGRAPHY

G.M. Gatti: 'Aspetti della situazione musicale in Italia', *RaM*, v (1932), 38–47

I. Pizzetti: 'La morte del musicista Pilati', *La tribuna* (13 Dec 1938) [obituary]

G. Gavazzeni: 'Disegno di Mario Pilati', *RaM*, xii (1939), 57–70; repr. in *Il suono è stanco* (Bergamo, 1950), 299–306

R. Zanetti: *La musica italiana nel Novecento* (Busto Arsizio, 1985), 952–4

ANTONIO TRUDU

Pilcher. American firm of organ builders. It was founded by Henry Pilcher (1798–1880), a native of Dover who emigrated to the USA about 1832. He set up a business in Newark, New Jersey, in 1833, moving to New Haven, Connecticut, in 1839 and back to Newark in 1844. In 1856 he was joined by his sons Henry jr (1828–90) and William Pilcher (*b* 1830), the firm becoming known as Henry Pilcher & Sons; it moved to St Louis about 1858. There some notable organs were built, including a large instrument for St Paul's Church (1859). In 1863 the firm moved to Chicago, where it remained until 1871 when its factory was destroyed in the great fire. The following year Henry Pilcher senior retired, and the firm, under the directorship of Henry jr and his sons R.E., William E., Paul B. and J.V. Pilcher opened a new factory in Louisville, where it grew and prospered. In 1893 one of its largest organs was built for the St Louis World's Fair (Louisiana Purchase Exhibition). The firm carried on an English tonal tradition and was noted for its complex but reliable wind-chest design, patented early in the 20th century by William E. Pilcher. His sons, Gerard W. and William E. jr, succeeded to the firm, the latter continuing until shortly after his brother's death in 1941; in 1944 the company and its assets were sold to the M.P. Möller Co.

BIBLIOGRAPHY

M. Lippincott: 'Henry Pilcher, Organ Builder', *Quarterly Bulletin* [New York Historical Society], xxxvii/4 (1943), 87–90

O. Ochse: *The History of the Organ in the United States* (Bloomington, IN, 1975)

E.T. Schmitt: 'The English Background of the Pilchers', *The Tracker*, xxxvi/1 (1993), 4–11

BARBARA OWEN

Pilgrimage. Pilgrimage provides a metaphor for life's sacred journey for religions throughout the world. Music is used not only to contextualize and to articulate the different stages of the pilgrim's journey – departure from the quotidian world, the formation of a new community of fellow travellers and arrival at a shrine – but to facilitate the spiritual and physical transformation of the pilgrim's life. The sacred is interpreted through the music of pilgrimage, and it has been argued that in certain cultures, notably Buddhism and Islam, the understanding of music itself may be rooted in pilgrimage practices.

Pilgrimage music metaphorically traces the passage of a human being through life and, upon completing the sacred journey, pilgrims re-experience the event through subsequent performance of pilgrimage repertories (for example, in *talbiyyah*, the song genre associated with the Muslim *hajj*). In most religions pilgrimage repertories are distinct from other sacred repertories and, when they are performed, are especially powerful forms of remembering the genealogies of those who have passed along the path.

Pilgrimage repertories depend on mass participation and therefore they use familiar forms (e.g. hymns) and repetitive structures (e.g. Buddhist mantras). Mass participation, moreover, involves the entire body, not only in the passage along the sacred journey and in processions at the shrine, but also in dance and other forms of ritualized expression. The metaphors of pilgrimage also lend themselves, through stylization and dissemination, to popular and art musics. Metaphors of the sacred journey in the African diaspora pervade blues, gospel and reggae repertories. In addition music representing pilgrimage spills from sacred to secular genres, accompanying processes of sacralization.

Pilgrimage becomes a spatial template by which people map human experience, through music, the landscapes of religious community, nation and politics. Music enables the crossing of political and linguistic borders often required in sacred journey, further inculcating pilgrimage repertories with political significance, such as the return to Jerusalem in songs of the Passover *seder*. The sacred landscapes embedded in pilgrimage repertories often conflict with secular geographies, thereby heightening music's potential to be used in the making of history.

The musical practices of pilgrimage yield genealogies in which music and history intersect. In Buddhism, for example, the sacred journey undertaken by devout Buddhists retraces the journey of the Buddha himself. The musical narratives of Buddhist mantras are therefore individual only in so far as they connect to the larger chain of Buddhist history. Pilgrimage is immanent in Buddhist musical practice with chant and song metaphorically reproducing transitions that have cut across regional and stylistic differences in the musics of Asia during the course of Buddhist history.

The historical tension of diaspora is present in Jewish pilgrimage repertories. The holidays most explicitly associated with exodus and return, Passover, Shavuot and Succot, are collectively known as the 'Three Pilgrimage Festivals', and the songs performed during them bear witness to the exigencies of survival away from the sacred site, Israel, and more specifically, Jerusalem. Jewish repertories are also localized, coalescing around the shrines of saints specific to individual communities. Among Iraqi Jews, for example, women's songs in Judeo-Arabic were performed as part of the trips to shrines of saints whose role in Iraqi-Jewish history was particularly significant.

Western music history owes many aspects of its genealogical and geographical construction to the music of pilgrims of different historical moments, especially during the early Middle Ages and the Early Modern Era. For medieval Christians the known world comprised a cosmos of pilgrimage sites, with Jerusalem at the centre and marginal sites such as Santiago de Compostela on the periphery. Within Europe itself pilgrimage sites often took shape in areas that were sacred to pre-Christian religions, with Christian musical genealogies and histories supplanting those of pre-literate cultures. When the Christian world expanded so too did the sacred landscapes of pilgrimage practices, particularly in Central and South America. The appearance of the Virgin Mary at Guadalupe in Mexico occurred in 1530, only 11 years after the Conquest of Mexico. In the 20th century the music of the Guadalupe pilgrimage is essential to the fabric of Mexican national identity and diaspora.

The pilgrimage practices of Islam give rise to distinctive repertories on local, regional and global levels (*see* ISLAMIC RELIGIOUS MUSIC, §I, 5(i)). The repertories on all these levels express distinctive genealogies and histories ranging from the local to the global. Local music practices emanate from the shrine of an individual Sufi saint and they interact stylistically with regional musics. *Qawwālī* in North India and Pakistan, for example, responds to the canon of Hindustani music. However, the saints celebrated by *qawwāl* at Sufi shrines, such as Amir Khusrau, have themselves been active participants in the shaping of Hindustani music history.

The texts of pilgrimage songs express subjectivities constructed from five primary themes: a specific saint or individual; a miracle; a sacred geography; a genealogy of previous pilgrims; and a political or historical event revisited by pilgrims. Specific musical genres incorporate these themes in different ways according to both religious and musical practice. The most common genre of pilgrimage song in Catholicism, Marian song, is profoundly eponymous. However, individual songs and repertories may also express special connections to space, such as the multilingual Marian songs of the Italian Tyrol, which refer to the political strife that has historically characterized the border region. Hindu *bhajans* may also be used as pilgrimage songs, evoking a spatial dimension by tracing the paths, ancient and modern, taken by Hindu pilgrims to holy sites. *Bhajans* nonetheless may retain a strong sense of authorship and the names of specific poet-composers may be inscribed in the texts themselves.

The musical texts of pilgrimage both specify and generalize the sacred geographies to which they are connected. Many songs accumulate around a single place and bear witness to the significance of that place. The 'Medjugorje song' appeared soon after Marian appearances in Herzegovina in 1981 and during the Bosnian civil war (1992–5) it spread throughout Europe. The melody of the 'Medjugorje song', however, is a contrafact from the so-called 'Fatima song' which musically connects the song to the most important pilgrimage site in Portugal, which has its own musical practices.

Although pilgrimage songs circulate widely in oral tradition, undergoing extensive variation, numerous other media participate in the production and distribution of texts. Passover songs are frequently inscribed in elaborately decorated *haggadot*, the books used in the *seder* services. With the explosion of print technology in the

Early Modern Era, Christian pilgrimage songs quickly appeared on broadsides, on votive paintings and cards, and in printed songbooks intended for lay use. Recording technology in the 20th century has been no less profound in the ways it has expanded the mass dissemination of pilgrimage music. With the advent of inexpensive cassettes in the late 20th century, pilgrimage songs became available on an almost universal scale. Because of the widespread distribution of pilgrimage songs, extensive trade networks developed, with musical artefacts sold at sacred sites, in markets and at other stations along the pilgrimage route itself.

As pilgrimage underwent a global revival in the late 20th century, music contributed fundamentally to the representation of the religious, social and political issues revitalized through late-modern and postmodern religious movements. In the late decades of the 20th century, for example, more than 100 million Europeans embarked on pilgrimages every year, with most evidence suggesting that these numbers would increase even more sharply with the return of officially sanctioned religion to Eastern Europe. Sacred shrines in contested areas – the Middle East, Sri Lanka, national borders in Europe and the Andes – were the sites of a proliferation of traditional repertories and the creation of new musical practices that made the experience of pilgrimage available to a broader population. CD, videotape and the internet have provided new media for pilgrims helping them to interact musically with the public religious practices of pilgrimage.

The music of modern and postmodern pilgrimage often historicized the political response to rising nationalism, racism and political repression. Just as pilgrims cross national borders, so too do they join with co-religionists from other nations and linguistic regions. The miracles and healing that 20th-century pilgrims sought assumed the forms of metaphors, in which spiritual and physical healing often represented the healing of national strife or the extension of resources to those lacking sufficient resources for survival. The music of 20th-century pilgrimages often gave voice to the powerless and used religious faith as a means of empowering subaltern resistance. In doing so it mapped music histories on the political and sacred histories of modernity.

BIBLIOGRAPHY

Catholisch Gesangbuechlein (Munich, 1613); ed. O. Holzapfel (Amsterdam, 1979)

N. Wallner: *Deutsche Marienlieder der Enneberger Ladiner: Südtirol* (Vienna, 1970)

M. Banzai: *A Pilgrimage to the 88 Temples in Shikoku Island* (Tokyo, 1973)

G.R. Schroubek: 'Das Wallfahrts- und Prozessionslied', *Handbuch des Volksliedes*, i (Munich, 1973), 445–62

I. Baumer: *Wallfahrt als Handlungsspiel: ein Beitrag zum Verständnis religiösen Handelns* (Frankfurt, 1977)

V.W. and E. Turner: *Image and Pilgrimage in Christian Culture: Anthropological Perspectives* (New York, 1978)

T. Ellingson: *The Mandala of Sound: Concepts and Sound Structures in Tibetan Ritual Music* (diss., U. of Wisconsin-Madison, 1979)

Marienlob: Lieder- und Gebetbuch für das pilgernde Volk (Abensberg, 1979)

F. Johnston: *The Wonder of Guadalupe* (Chulmleigh, 1981)

T.A. Kochmutton: *A Buddhist Doctrine of Experience: a New Translation and Interpretation of the Works of Vaubandhu, the Yogacarin* (Delhi, 1982)

O. Statler: *Japanese Pilgrimage* (New York, 1983)

E.A. Morinis: *Pilgrimage in the Hindu Tradition: a Case Study of West Bengal* (Delhi, 1984)

W. Radspieler: *Pilgerwege Lourdes* (Bamberg, 1984)

W. Braungart, ed.: *Bänkelsang: Texte – Bilder – Kommentare* (Stuttgart, 1985)

Y. Avishur: *Shirat ha-nashim: shire 'am be-'aravit-yehudit shel yehude 'Irak*[Women's songs: folk songs in Judeo-Arabic of the Iraqi Jews] (Or Yehudah, 1986)

N. Ohler: *Reisen im Mittelalter* (Zürich, 1986)

J. Chélini and H. Branthomme: *Histoire des pèlerinages non chrétiens: entre magique et sacré, le chemin des dieux* (Paris, 1987)

R.B. Qureshi: *Sufi Music of India and Pakistan: Sound, Context and Meaning in Qawwali* (Cambridge, 1987)

M.J. Sallnow: *Pilgrims of the Andes: Regional Cults in Cusco* (Washington DC, 1987)

S.M. Bhardwaj and G. Rinschade, eds.: *Pilgrimage in World Religions* (Berlin, 1988)

A.G. Gold: *Fruitful Journeys: the Ways of Rajasthani Pilgrims* (Berkeley, 1988)

J. Wilkinson, J. Hill and W.F. Ryan: *Jerusalem Pilgrimage: 1099–1185* (London, 1988)

L. al-Faruqi: 'The Shariah on Music and Musicians', *Al-'Ilm: Journal of the Centre for Research in Islamic Studies*, vii (1989), 33–53

M.L. and S. Nolan: *Christian Pilgrimage in Modern Western Europe* (Chapel Hill, 1989)

L. Rupčić: *Erscheinungen unserer lieben Frau zu Medjugorje* (Jestetten, 1989)

U. Tworschka: *Sucher, Pilger, Himmelsstürmer: Reisen im Diesseits und Jenseits* (Stuttgart,1991)

D.F. Eickelman and J. Piscatori, eds.: *Muslim Travellers: Pilgrimage, Migration and the Religious Imagination* (Berkeley, 1990)

Wallfahrt und Alltag in Mittelalter und Früher Neuzeit: Krems an der Donau 1990

J. Eade and M.J. Sallnow, eds.: *Contesting the Sacred: the Anthropology of Christian Pilgrimage* (New York, 1991)

G. Herberich-Marz: *Evolution d'une sensibilité religieuse: témoignages scripturaires et iconographiques de pèlerinages alsaciens* (Strasbourg, 1991)

W.A. Christian: *Moving Crucifixes in Modern Spain* (Princeton, 1992)

T. Karp: *The Polyphony of Saint Martial and Santiago de Compostela* (Berkeley, 1992)

S. Naquin and Yü Chün-fang, eds.: *Pilgrims and Sacred Sites in China* (Berkeley, 1992)

T. Asad: *Genealogies of Religion: Discipline and Reasons of Power in Christianity and Islam* (Baltimore, 1993)

I. Benčiková: 'Príspevok k štúdiu jarmočných piesní na Slovensku' [Contributions to the study of market songs in Slovakia], *Slovenský národopis*, xl (1993), 44–54

F.E. Peters: *The Hajj: the Muslim Pilgrimage to Mecca and the Holy Places* (Princeton, 1994)

P.V. Bohlman: 'Pilgrimage, Politics and the Musical Remapping of the New Europe',*EthM*, xl (1996), 375–412

P.V. Bohlman: 'The Final Borderpost', *JM*, xiv (1996), 427–52

A. Castillo: *Goddess of the Americas/La Diosa de las Américas: Writings on the Virgin of Guadalupe* (New York, 1996)

PHILIP V. BOHLMAN

Piliński, Stanisław (*b* Paris, 5 April 1839; *d* Paris, 20 Jan 1905). Polish pianist and composer, active in France. He was the son of the well-known lithographer Adam Piliński (1810–87), who emigrated in 1831. He spent his childhood in Clermont-Ferrand, singing in the cathedral choir. From 1855 he lived in Paris, attended the Polish school and for five years studied music at Niedermeyer's Ecole de Musique Religieuse et Classique. He then became organist at the church of Ste Marguerite, gave piano lessons and worked with his father on the engraving of old manuscripts. In this work they achieved considerable artistic success, winning a number of prizes at exhibitions in Clermont-Ferrand and Paris (including one at the Exposition Universel of 1878). His popularity as a musician and composer came largely from the Polish community, particularly during the 1880s when he was conductor of the Polish Philharmonic Society. He was a member of the Société des Auteurs, Compositeurs et Editeurs de Musique; the Société des Etudes Japonaises, Chinoises, Tartares et Indo-chinoises; the Académie des

Sciences, Belles-Lettres et Arts de Clermont-Ferrand; and an honorary member of the Association des Anciens Elèves d'Ecole Polonaise in Paris. In the 1890s financial difficulties compelled him to accept the post of librarian at the Centre de l'Union Artistique. He wrote mostly piano pieces and solo songs with piano accompaniment; he was extremely prolific, his works showing strong links with Romantic and national themes, as well as an interest in oriental thematic themes.

WORKS

MSS of unpublished works and of works published in arrangements in F-Pc, Pn, PL-KO; not all works with opus numbers were published.

STAGE

Żmija (Zmiya) [The Viper] (op, 5, W. Gasztowtt, after J. Słowacki), op.50, 1881
Balladyna (ov. and incid music, 5, Słowacki, trans. Gasztowtt), op.162, 1893, orchd 1895

VOCAL

12 accompanied choral works, incl. Hymne à Bouddha, solo vv, chorus, pf, op.51 (Paris, 1873); Ode aux montagnes d'Auvergne, chorus, orch, op.65, pf score (Paris, 1880)
c75 solo songs, pf acc., incl. Le pêcheur de Venise (P. Fauré), op.10 (Paris, 1875); Au rossignol, harmonie poétique (A. de Lamartine), op.17 (Paris, 1875); Menuet and Le printemps (F. Coppée), opp.60, 61 (Paris, 1877); [5] Mélodies (P. Blanchemain, Lamartine), opp.63, 64, 109, 129, 154 (Paris, n.d.); Chants de l'exil (Gasztowtt), pubd as 3 mélodies (Paris, 1906); Les danaïdes (S. Prudhomme), op.120 (Paris, 1907); Présent et avenir (Martin), op.122 (Paris, 1907)
Arrs. of Pol. folktunes

INSTRUMENTAL

Orch: Souvenir de Mazovie, polka-mazurka, op.1, 1857; Polka de puces, op.2, 1857; Sibilla: souvenirs de Pulawy, elegy, op.21, 1863; Souvenir d'Edgar Poë, sym., op.42, ?1869; Fantasia on 'Pije Kuba do Jakuba', op.47, 1869; Ouverture fantastique, op.49, 1870; Polka de quatre pattes, op.133, 1887; Sym., f, op.24, 1896; Fantasia, f, op.12, 1899; Ouverture symphonique … sur la mélodie japonaise, op.68, 1899
Chbr: Qnt, F, fl, 2 vn, vc, pf, hmn ad lib, op.14, 1862; Mao-li-hoa, fantasia on a Chin. air, fl, vn, va, vc, pf, op.58, 1874; Pf Trio, E, op.34, 1880; Souvenirs de l'Ukraine, fantasia, pf, vn, op.3, 1857; Notturno, pf, vn, op.39, ?1868; Fudjiyou, pf, vn, op.67, 1878; Ouverture sur deux chants de Noël, fl, pf, op.192, 1900
Kbd (pf unless otherwise stated): Fantasia, g, org/hmn, op.23, 1862; 2 rêveries, op.4, 1857, 1860; Grande valse fantaisie, op.6, 1858; Valse romantique, op.9, 1858 (Paris, 1905); Elégie sur l'hymne nationale 'Boże coś Polskę', pf/org/hmn (Paris, 1864); Fantaisie ouverture, op.28, 1865; Fantasia, g, op.33bis, 1867; Marche funêbre sur le carillon des morts, org/hmn, op.37, 1867; Praga, marche funêbre, op.38, 1868; Fantasia, B, org/hmn, op.48, 1869; Ov. for an orat, op.41, 1869; Fantasia, Eb, op.45, 1869; Ov. for an oc, op.46, 1869
[8] Scènes polonaises, opp.58, 89, 92, 161, 164, 180, 190, 191, 1876–1900; Intermède entr'acte, op.115, 1884; Intermède-introduction alla pastorale, for an orat or os, op.123, 1886; Fantaisie-ballet, op.144, 1889; [10] Fantaisies alpestres, opp.156, 166, 172, 174, 181, 184–6, 190 and without op. no., 1892–1904; Idéalas harmonies, les cloches des jours de fête à la campagne, op.163, 1894; Offertoire pour l'inauguration de l'orgue de Beaumont-le-Roger, org/hmn, op.168, 1895; Nuit devant la mer, fantaisie nocturne, op.173, 1897; Ouverture de fête, op.179, 1898; Souvenir de Beaumont-le-Roger 'Dans les ruines', fantasia, 1903; many other pieces, incl. barcarolles, fantasias, farandoles, marches, mazurkas, minuets, nocturnes, polonaises, rondos, waltzes; arrs. of orch works, Pol. songs etc.

BIBLIOGRAPHY

PSB; SMP

A. Sowiński: *Słownik muzyków polskich dawnych i nowoczesnych* [Dictionary of Polish musicians past and present] (Paris, 1874/R)
Obituary, *Bulletin polonais littéraire scientifique et artistique*, cxcix (1905), 52
I. Pilińska: *Adam Piliński 1810–1887, Stanisław Piliński 1839–1905* (MS, F-Pn)
I. Poniatowska: 'Autografy Stanisława Pilińskiego w Bibliothèque Nationale w Paryżu', *Sesja muzykologiczna polsko-włoska VII: Warsaw 1975* [Pagine, iv (1980)], 195–232 [with It. summary]

IRENA PONIATOWSKA

Pilkington, Francis (*b* c1570; *d* Chester, 1638). English composer. Other musical members of this Lancashire family included Zacharias and Thomas Pilkington (i), both probably sons of Francis. The former was a chorister at Chester Cathedral until 1612, the latter from 1612 to 1618; by 1625 he was the sixth conduct (or lay clerk), holding this position for at least two more years. Thomas Pilkington (ii), probably Francis's grandchild, was a later chorister at Chester Cathedral. Fellowes stated that Thomas (i) died at Wolverhampton, but it was probably Thomas (ii) of whom Hawkins wrote '[he] died about 1660, at Wolverhampton, aged 35'. It was this Pilkington who, Hawkins asserted, invented an instrument called the orphion, and who was a musician to Queen Henrietta Maria, wife of Charles I.

In 1595 Francis took the BMus at Lincoln College, Oxford, stating that he had been a student of music for 16 years. His father and brother were under the patronage of the Earl of Derby, and Pilkington himself was indebted to the family. By midsummer 1602 he was a conduct at Chester Cathedral, and in 1612 he was made a minor canon, although still a layman. Subsequently he took holy orders, being made a 'full minister' on 18 December 1614. He held a number of curacies in Chester: at Holy Trinity (in 1614), St Bridget's (by 1616; this, as Jeffery has shown, was his main charge), and at St Martin's (by 1622). By 1631 he had added the rectory of Aldford, near Chester, to these, though he relinquished this between 1634 and 1636. Notwithstanding all this, Pilkington maintained his position in the cathedral choir, and from 1623 until his death was precentor, or 'chaunter'. In the preface to his second collection of madrigals (1624) he wrote of his 'now aged Muse', yet suggested that he intended to compile another collection. This did not materialize. On his death his place as a minor canon was filled by John Pilkington – possibly a son or grandson – who had previously been a conduct.

Pilkington's volume of lute-songs (1605) contains much poetry of real quality. Though showing less variety of musical style than Morley's volume of songs (1600), Pilkington's also has the marks of a transitional volume in which the exploration of the powerful new expression that Dowland had introduced into English music in his second volume (1600) is still timid and unsure, despite the predominant seriousness of his choice of verse. Most of Pilkington's songs come closer to the ayres of Campion and Rosseter, though the substantial, long-lined stanzas of his lyrics foster more extensive structures than are typical of the ayres of these two composers. Pilkington lacked their gifts for fresh melodic invention and for devising clearcut, integrated structures. His harmonic movement is sometimes uncomfortable, prone to loss of direction and stagnation. Of the more extensive songs, *Down a down thus Phillis sung* is one of the most attractive. *Beautie sate bathing* shows a lightly humorous touch, but the best pieces in the collection are among the shortest, notably *Diaphenia*, and especially the exquisite *Rest sweet nimphes*. The lyric of *Thanks gentle moone* appears to be from a play, and *With fragrant flowers* is an adaptation for James I of a text used for Elizabeth's entertainment at Elvetham in her progress of 1591 (there is, however, no evidence that Pilkington set the verse on that earlier occasion). There are several occasional pieces, including *Come, come all you*, an elegy to Pilkington's friend Thomas Leighton, probably a relative of Sir William Leighton to whose *Teares or Lamentacions* (RISM 1614[7]) Pilkington contributed two pieces. All Pilkington's ayres were issued in an alternative form for four voices.

The lyrics in Pilkington's first collection of madrigals (1613/14) show a surprising reversion to the light type of verse which Morley had set in the 1590s, and Pilkington's musical style is equally rooted in that period. Pilkington shows little invention or defined character in this first set, and his technique is limited. In the three-voice madrigals he made no attempt to go beyond the simplest canzonet manner used by Morley, but in the four- and five-voice works he essayed a wider range of expression, and his weaknesses are more apparent; his counterpoint is in places feeble and faltering, and his harmonic thrust tends to weaken suddenly (as in his ayres) or be lost completely. A comparison of Pilkington's settings of *Have I found her?* and the Oriana text, *When Oriana walkt*, with those of his Chester Cathedral colleague, Thomas Bateson, is not to Pilkington's advantage (in the latter madrigal the final line is altered, as in Bateson's 'Orianaes farewell' (1604), to 'In heaven lives Oriana').

The prefatory material of Pilkington's second madrigal collection reveals an aggressive provincialism, and it was doubtless his remoteness from London that accounts for his continuing retention of outmoded poetic and musical manners. In general quality, however, the volume shows a marked improvement over its predecessor. In addition to madrigals, it includes two viol-accompanied works, a fantasia for six viols, and a sonorous psalm setting, *O praise the Lord*, which contains a remarkably high level of dissonance. The viol-accompanied *Weepe sad Urania* is an elegy on Pilkington's friend Thomas Purcell (who may have belonged to the same family as Henry Purcell). The best piece in the volume is *Care, for thy soule*, in which Pilkington reset a text which Byrd had treated and published 36 years earlier. In this piece Pilkington combined something of the 'gravitie' of an earlier English tradition with a more emotional expression characteristic of his own times; indeed he borrowed a passage from Weelkes's deeply affective *O my son, Absalom* to begin *Care, for thy soule*, and later employed extended chromaticism in what is expressively the most advanced passage in all his work. In general Pilkington's technique is more secure throughout this volume, and his handling of five and six voices is more assured, with the textures at times taking on a massiveness redolent of Weelkes.

On the title-page of each of his three printed collections Pilkington described himself as a lutenist, and a small quantity of lute music by him survives. Jeffery has suggested that most, if not all of it, is early work. Though well written for the instrument, none is of much musical importance.

WORKS

SACRED

2 pieces, 4, 5vv, 1614[7]; ed. in EECM, xi (1970)
Sacred madrigal, 6vv, in The Second Set of Madrigals (London, 1624[17]); ed. in EM, xxv (1923, 2/1959)

SECULAR

The First Booke of Songs or Ayres, 4vv, lute/orphorion, b viol (London, 1605/R); the versions for 4vv, lute pubd in The Old English Edition, xviii–xx (London, 1897–8/R); the versions for v, lute ed. in EL, 1st ser., vii (1922, 2/1971), xv (1925, 2/1971)

The First Set of Madrigals and Pastorals, 3–5vv (London, 1613/14); ed. in EM, xxv (1923, 2/1959)
The Second Set of Madrigals, and Pastorals, 3–6vv/viols (London, 1624); ed. in EM, xxvi (1923, 2/1958)

INSTRUMENTAL

A Fancie for the Violls in The Second Set of Madrigals (London, 1624[17]); ed. in EM, xxv (2/1959)
Lute music (all ed. in Jeffery): 6 galliards, including Mrs Anne Harccourts Galliarde, Mrs Elizabeth Murcots, Mrs E. Murcots Delight, Mrs Marie Oldfields Galliard and Mr Ti. Wagstaffs Content of Desier; 6 pavanes, including Georg Pilkingtons Funerall, Pavin for the lute and base violl and The Spanish paven; Curranta for Mrs E. Murcott; Goe from my windowe; The L Hastins god morow

BIBLIOGRAPHY

HawkinsH
J.C. Bridge: 'The Organists of Chester Cathedral', *Journal of the Chester and North Wales Architectural … Society*, xix/2 (1913), 63–124
E.H. Fellowes: *English Madrigal Verse, 1588–1632* (Oxford, 1920, enlarged 3/1967 by F.W. Sternfeld and D. Greer)
E.H. Fellowes: *The English Madrigal Composers* (Oxford, 1921, 2/1948/R)
R. Newton: 'The Lute Music of Francis Pilkington', *LSJ*, i (1959), 31–7
B. Jeffery: Introductionto *Francis Pilkington: Complete Works for Solo Lute* (London, 1970) [incl. facs.]

DAVID BROWN

Pilková [née Volbrachtová], **Zdeňka** (*b* Prague, 15 June 1931; *d* Prague, 13 April 1999). Czech musicologist. She studied musicology and ethnography at Prague University (1951–5) graduating in 1955 with a study of the melodramas and Singspiele of Jiří Benda; she took the doctorate in Prague (1968) with a study of the music section of the Prague Artistic Society. After working in the music division of Czechoslovak Radio, Prague (1955–64), she joined the Musicology Institute of the Czechoslovak Academy of Sciences (1964–91). Her special field was Czech 18th-century music, and in particular those Czech musicians who worked abroad, including the Benda family, Kammel, Mysliveček, J.L. Dussek, Antoine Reicha and J.B.G. Neruda. Her preferred medium was the small, fact-based article, solving well-defined questions rather than addressing larger speculative issues. A good linguist, she was one of the few Czech musicologists allowed to travel abroad freely during the communist era and was a frequent participant at international conferences. With her numerous foreign contacts she helped coordinate the Garland series The Symphony 1720–1840, to which she contributed editions of symphonies by Neruda, Kammel and Mysliveček. With Sonja Gerlach she also edited a two-volume edition of Czech violin sonatas (1982–5).

WRITINGS

Dramatická tvorba Jiřího Bendy [The dramatic works of Georg Benda] (Prague, 1960)
Hudební odbor Umělecké besedy 1863–1963: jeho význam a funkce v českém hudebním životě [The music section of the Prague Artistic Society, 1863–1963: its significance and function in Czech musical life] (diss., U. of Prague, 1968)
'Hudební úterky Umělecké besedy v letech 1935–1951' [The Artistic Society's Musical Tuesdays, 1935–51], *Příspěvky k dějinám české hudby*, ii (Prague, 1971), 67–172
'On the Periodization of Czech Music', *Musica antiqua III: Bydgoszcz 1972*, 95–105 [with Pol. summary]
'Der Einfluss von volkstümlichen Elementen in der tschechischen Kirchenmusik der zweiten Hälfte des 18. Jahrhunderts', *Idea národnosti a novodobá hudba: Brno VIII 1973*, 478–86g
'Einige Bemerkungen zur Historiographie der tschechischen Musikeremigration des 18. Jahrhunderts', *Česká hudba: problémy a metody hudební historiografie: Brno IX 1974*, 193–201

'Příspěvek k biografii J.L. Dusíka 1800–1806' [A contribution to the biography of J.L. Dussek, 1800–1806], *HV*, xi (1974), 36–54
'Die Instrumentation der geistlichen Kantaten der böhmischen Komponisten in der ersten Hälfte des 18. Jahrhunderts', *Zu Fragen des Instrumentariums, der Besetzung und Improvisation in der ersten Hälfte des 18. Jahrhunderts: Blankenburg, Harz, 1975*, 49–55; Cz. orig. in *HV*, xiv (1977), 146–59
'Joseph Haydn and his Czech Contemporary Antonín Kammel', *Haydn Studies: Washington DC 1975*, 171–7
'Klavírní sonáty J.L. Dusíka z let 1800–1811' [The piano sonatas of J.L. Dussek, 1800–1811], *Muzyka fortepianowa*, i (1976), 267–82
'Die Widerspiegelung der Französischen Revolution in den Ansichten und im Schaffen der Komponisten tschechischer Herkunft vom Ende des 18. Jahrhunderts', *Vztah hudby a slova z teoretického a historického hlediska; Hudba a revoluce: Brno XII 1977*, 506–20
'Musikzentren in Böhmen: die grösseren und kleineren Musikzentren in Böhmen vom Standpunkt des Instrumentariums', *Musikzentren in der ersten Hälfte des 18. Jahrhunderts und ihre Ausstrahlung: Blankenburg, Harz, 1978*, 30–41
'Theoretische Ansichten Antonín Rejchas über die Oper (unter dem Gesichtspunkt ihrer Beziehung zur Klassik und Romantik)', *The Musical Theatre: Brno XV 1980*, 159–68
'Das Horn in den böhmischen Schriften des 18. Jahrhunderts', *Das Waldhorn in der Geschichte und Gegenwart der tschechischen Musik: Brno 1981*, 66–72
'Doba osvícenského absolutismu (1740–1810)' [The age of enlightened absolutism, 1740–1810], in J. Černý and others: *Hudba v českých dějinách* (Prague, 1983, 2/1989), 217–93
'Jiří Bendas Berliner Jahre und ihr Einfluss auf seine Melodramen', *Neue Aspekte zur Musikästhetik und Musikgeschichte im 18. Jahrhundert: Potsdam 1983*, 67–75
'Die Violinsonaten der böhmischen Komponisten in den Jahren 1730–1770', *Zur Entwicklung der instrumentalen Kammermusik in der 1. Hälfte des 18. Jahrhunderts: Blankenburg, Harz, 1983*, 53–61
'Hudební tisky a cesty jejich šíření v 18. století' [Musical prints and the paths of their distribution in the 18th century], *Muzikologické dialogy: Chrudim 1984*, 69–78
'Praha – Wrocław – Warszawa – Dresden: zur Frage der Musikeremigration im 18. Jahrhundert', *Musica antiqua VII: Bydgoszcz 1985*, 151–65
'Die Sonaten für Tasteninstrument und Violine der böhmischen Komponisten in den Jahren 1770–1810', *Zur Entwicklung der Kammermusik in der zweiten Hälfte des 18. Jahrhunderts: Blankenburg, Harz, 1985*, 36–49; Cz. orig. in *HV*, xxiii (1986), 291–311
'První pokusy o novodobé hudební festivaly v Čechách na přelomu 19. a 20. století' [The first attempts at new types of music festivals in Bohemia at the turn of the 19th and 20th centuries], *OM*, xviii (1986), 257–61
'Die Melodramen Jiří Bendas und die Anfänge dieser Gattung', *Untersuchungen zu Musikbeziehungen zwischen Mannheim, Böhmen und Mähren im späten 18. und frühen 19. Jahrhundert: Mannheim 1987*, 163–77
'18th Century Folk Music in the Czech Lands', *Janáček and Czech Music: St Louis 1988*, 155–63
'Česká hudební historiografie po roce 1945' [Czech musical historiography since 1945], *Hudební věda*, ed. V. Lébl and I. Poledňák (Prague, 1988), 740–56
'Jan Jiří Neruda (ca 1711–1776)', *HV*, xxvi (1989), 99–126
'Josephinische Reformen und ihr Einfluss auf das Musikleben der böhmischen Lände', *Europa im Zeitalter Mozarts: Vienna 1992*, 331–6
'Probleme der Musikgeschichtsschreibung am Beispiel der böhmischen Musik der 2. Hälfte des 18. Jahrhunderts', *Musik Mitteleuropas in der 2. Hälfte des 18. Jahrhunderts: Bratislava 1992*, 29–37
with S. Šimsová: 'Nález závěti Antonína Kammela (1730–1784)' [The discovery of Antonín Kammel's will], *HV*, xxx (1993), 382–8; Eng. trans. in *Czech Music*, xix (1995–6), 87–94
'Prager Mozart-Sänger in Dresdner Quellen', *Festschrift Christoph-Hellmut Mahling*, ed. A. Beer, K. Pfarr and W. Ruf (Tutzing, 1997), 1095–1101
Böhmische Musiker am Dresdner Hof 1710–1845 (forthcoming)

BIBLIOGRAPHY
M. Rutová: 'Jubileum Zdeňky Pilkové', *HV*, xxviii (1991), 387–8
'Výběrová bibliografie PhDr. Zdeňky Pilkové', *HV*, xxx (1993), 187–90; see also *HV*, xxxiv (1997), 362–3
M. Kuna: 'Zdeňka Pilková zemřela' [Zdeňka Pilková had died], *HRo*, lii/6 (1999), 30 only

JOHN TYRRELL

Pillai, T(iruvaduthurai) N. Rajarathnam [Balasubramaniam] (*b* Tirumarugal, Tamil Nadu, 27 Aug 1898; *d* Madras, 12 Dec 1956). South Indian *nāgasvaram* player. During his lifetime T.N. Rajarathnam was hailed as the 'emperor of *nāgasvaram* music', a testament to his skill as a performer. Although interested in technique (he exchanged a shorter instrument for a longer, less strident, *nāgasvaram*) his great strength was his musical imagination. Required to explore and develop *rāga* over a long period of time during night-long processions of temple deities, he revelled in the challenge of unfolding and expanding a *rāga* without repetition, often at the expense of the initial song and its associated text. He was closely identified with a number of *rāga*, in particular *Tōdi*. Disdainful of authority during a period when feudal elements were strong in the patronage system, he had a larger-than-life image. He married more than once – reportedly as many as five times – and spent his large earnings on a lavish lifestyle. However, when he died his admirers had to raise funds to conduct his funeral.

BIBLIOGRAPHY
Y. Terada: *Multiple Interpretations of a Charismatic Individual: the Case of the Great Nagasvaram Musician, T.N. Rajarattinam Pillai* (diss., U. of Washington, 1992)

N. PATTABHI RAMAN

Pillays [Pilloys], **Johannes**. *See* PULLOIS, JOHANNES.

Pilotti-Schiavonetti, Elisabetta (*d* Hanover, 5 May 1742). Italian soprano. A virtuoso of the Hanover royal house, she was a member of the Queen's (later King's) Theatre company in London from 1710 to 1717, making her début in Mancini's *Idaspe fedele*. She sang in the first performances of Handel's *Rinaldo* (Armida), *Il pastor fido* (Amarillis), *Teseo* (Medea) and *Amadigi* (Melissa), in Francesco Gasparini's *Antioco* and *Ambleto*, Giovanni Bononcini's *Etearco*, the pasticcios *Ercole*, *Dorinda*, *Ernelinda*, *Lucio Vero* and *Clearte*, and probably in Handel's *Silla* (Metella). She was the only singer who appeared in all 47 performances of *Rinaldo* between 1711 and 1717. The four parts Handel composed for her, three of them sorceresses, show that she was an exceptional artist with technical agility, dramatic fire and a compass of two octaves (c' to c'''). In 1726 she sang at Stuttgart in a comic opera, *Pyramus und Thisbe*, directed by her husband Giovanni Schiavonetti (*d* 19 March 1730), a Venetian cellist. (*SartoriL*)

WINTON DEAN

Pilsen (Ger.). *See* PLZEŇ.

Pinacci, Giovanni Battista (*b* Florence, 1694–5; *d* Florence, 1750). Italian tenor. For many years he was in the service of the Prince of Darmstadt. He sang in Rome in 1717 (Francesco Gasparini's *Il Trace in Catena*), 1721–3, 1727, 1728 (Vinci's *Catone in Utica* and Feo's *Ipermestra*) and 1731 (including Vinci's *Artaserse*), Milan in 1718–22, 1727 and 1729–30, Florence in 1718 and many later seasons (at least 16 operas), Bologna in 1719 and 1722 (Orlandini's *Ormisda*), Genoa in 1720 and 1723–5, Naples in 1721 (A.M. Bononcini's *Rosiclea in Dania* and Porpora's *Gli orti esperidi*) and Venice in 1723–4 (operas by Giacomelli and Francesco and Michelangelo Gasparini) and 1728. He also appeared in Mantua, Reggio nell'Emilia, Alessandria, Turin and Pistoia. Engaged by Handel for London in 1731–2, he probably made his debut as Bajazet in *Tamerlano*, sang in the revivals of *Poro*, *Admeto*, *Giulio Cesare* and *Flavio*, in the new operas *Ezio* (Maximus) and *Sosarme* (Haliate), and in Ariosti's *Coriolano* and Handel's pasticcio *Lucio Papirio dittatore*. Handel adapted and recomposed Hercules and Lotario in *Admeto* and *Flavio* for him. His wife, Anna Maria Antonia Bagnolesi, was in Handel's company at the same time.

After leaving London, Pinacci sang in Florence in 1732–3, 1739, 1743–4 (when he managed the carnival season) and 1748–9, Naples in 1733–4 (three operas, including Hasse's *Cajo Fabricio* and Pergolesi's *Il prigionier superbo*) and 1747 (Jommelli's *Eumene*), Rome in 1735 (Pergolesi's *L'olimpiade* and two other operas), 1740 and 1742, Venice in 1740–43 (seven operas, including Galuppi's *Oronte re de' sciti*, Hasse's *Alessandro nell'Indie* and Jommelli's *Semiramide*), 1746 (Jommelli's *Tito Manlio*) and 1747 (Hasse's *Demetrio* and Pescetti's *Ezio*) and Livorno in 1738 and 1746. He also appeared in Milan, Padua and Pisa. He was one of the leading tenors of his generation, a dramatic singer with powerful low notes, to judge by the parts Handel composed for him; the compass is *c* to *a'*. He was often criticized for bellowing. (*SartoriL*)

WINTON DEAN

Pinaire [first name unknown] (*fl* Paris, 1748–52). French composer. His name appeared three times in the Paris press between 1748 and 1752 (*Affiches*, 11 March 1748; *Annonces*, 19 Nov 1751; *Mercure de France*, Feb 1752), twice in publication announcements and once as composer of a symphony played at the Concert Spirituel. His 12 known works all appeared in this same period and mark him as one of the earliest French Classical symphonists. Along with his Parisian contemporaries Guillemain, L'Abbé *le fils*, François Martin and others, he explored pre-Classical symphonic trends coming mainly from Italy. His op.1, *Six symphonies en trio* (Paris, 1748), combines elements of the Baroque trio sonata with *galant* traits, and follows the structure of the three-movement Italian sinfonia. The *Six symphonies à quatre* op.2 (Paris, 1751), also in three movements, are more varied in expression; the middle movements bear affective tempo markings and the allegros show a greater awareness of dynamics, orchestral sonority and balanced phrasing. Pinaire's rather advanced writing for the violin suggests that he was a violinist.

BIBLIOGRAPHY

BrookSF
G. de St-Foix and L.de La Laurencie: 'Contribution à l'histoire de la symphonie française vers 1750', *Année musicale*, i (1911), 1–123, esp. 62

BARRY S. BROOK, BARBARA S. KAFKA

Pinarol, Johannes de (*fl* late 15th century). Composer. He is one of a number of composers whose few works are extant only in Petrucci prints (and manuscripts derived from them). His four-voice motet *Surge propera* (*I-Fn* Panc.27, ed. in SCMot, i, 1991) was published in Petrucci's *Motetti A* of 1502. Most of the motets in this collection were written in a manner which combined homophony and imitative four-voice sections with occasionally imitative duets; this style has been associated with late 15th-century Milan and the works of Compère and Weerbeke. As Drake notes, Pinarol's motet fits squarely within this style: the text, from the *Song of Songs*, is divided more or less according to its syntax among four-voice sections that begin in imitation and with imitative duets; straight four-voice homophony is reserved for the affective words 'columba mea' and 'vox enim tua dulcis' (where a strongly implied false relation between B♭ and B♮ emphasizes 'dulcis'). His style of composition may indicate that Pinarol worked at some time in northern Italy. His one extant secular work is a four-voice setting of *Fortuna desperata* (1504³, *D-Mbs* 1516) in which three contrapuntal voices are added to the superius of the chanson, now in the bass.

BIBLIOGRAPHY

G. Drake: *The First Printed Books of Motets, Petrucci's Motetti A Numero Trentatre A (Venice 1502) and Motetti de Passione, de Cruce, de Sacramento, De Beata Virgine et Huiusmodi B (Venice, 1503): a Critical Study and Complete Edition* (diss., U. of Illinois, 1972)

RICHARD SHERR

Pin block. *See* WREST PLANK.

Pincé (i) (Fr.). Plucked, as in plucked instruments, and hence a word for PIZZICATO. *See also* PUNTEADO.

Pincé (ii). An ornament (*see* ORNAMENTS, §7(ii)), variously a mordent, a trill (*pincé renversé*), or an acciaccatura (*pincé étouffé*), and sometimes the word for 'vibrato'.

Pincement (Fr.). A type of mordent. *See* ORNAMENTS, §7.

Pincherle, Marc (*b* Constantine, Algeria, 13 June 1888; *d* Paris, 20 June 1974). French musicologist. He studied musicology at the Sorbonne with Rolland, Laloy and Pirro. After World War I, he taught the history of the violin at the Ecole Normale de Musique in Paris; he also worked as editor-in-chief of *Le monde musical* (1925–7) and *Musique* (1927–30) and as music critic of several newspapers. He was artistic director of the Société Pleyel (1927–55), founding president of the Académie Charles Cros (from 1948), vice-president (1945–8), president (1948–56) and honorary president (from 1956) of the Société Française de Musicologie, a member of the Académie Royale de Belgique and an honorary member of the Royal Musical Association, London.

Pincherle's research was mainly concerned with French and Italian music of the 17th and 18th centuries. His outstanding achievement was his first book on Vivaldi (1948), a pioneer study in which he considered Vivaldi's life, musical environment, instrumental and vocal works and influence with thorough scholarship and imaginative insight, fully supported by musical and pictorial illustrations and documentary evidence. Throughout his work he concentrated on instrumental music, producing books on the quartet and the chamber orchestra, showing particular interest in performance. His library, containing books on the violin, music for strings, autograph compositions and letters, was sold by auction in Paris in 1975.

WRITINGS

'La technique du violon chez les premiers sonatistes français (1695–1723)', *BSIM*, vii (1911), no.8–9, pp.1–32; no.10, pp.19–35
Les violonistes compositeurs et virtuoses (Paris, 1922/R)
'L'Europe musicale aux approches de 1789', *Revue Pleyel*, no.42 (1927), 378–85
Feuillets d'histoire du violon (Paris, 1927)
'Antonio Vivaldi: essai biographique', *RdM*, xi (1930), 161–70, 265–81
'L'opéra et les mécontents au XVIIIe siècle', *ReM*, no.119 (1931), 209–20

'Sur Georges Enesco', *ReM*, no.130 (1932), 271–7
Corelli (Paris, 1933, rev. 2/1954 as *Corelli et son temps*; Eng. trans., 1956/*R*1979 as *Corelli, his Life, his Works*)
'De la piraterie dans l'édition musicale aux environs de 1700', *RdM*, xiv (1933), 136–40
'Sur François Barthélémon', *Mélanges de musicologie offerts à M. Lionel de La Laurencie* (Paris, 1933), 235–45
ed.: *Musiciens peints par eux-mêmes: lettres de compositeurs écrites en français (1771–1910)* (Paris, 1939) [letters from Pincherle's own collection]
'La propagande allemande et la musique', *Contrepoints*, no.1 (1946), 82–97
Antonio Vivaldi et la musique instrumentale (Paris, 1948/*R*) [incl. thematic catalogue of symphonies and concertos]
'Elementary Musical Instruction in the 18th Century: an Unknown Treatise by Montéclair', *MQ*, xxxiv (1948), 61–7
Les instruments du quatuor (Paris, 1948, 3/1970)
L'orchestre de chambre (Paris, 1948)
'De l'enseignement de la composition', *Congresso internazionale di musica VI: Florence 1949*, 130–37
'J.S. Bach et Vivaldi', *Revue internationale de musique*, no.8 (1950), 36–51
'Jean-Sébastien Bach et le violon', *Contrepoints*, no.7 (1951), 47–62
Jean-Marie Leclair l'aîné (Paris, 1952/*R*)
'Aspects de Schoenberg', *SMz*, xciii (1953), 158–60
'L'edizione delle opere di Antonio Vivaldi', *RaM*, xxi (1953), 134–8
Petit lexique des termes musicaux français et étrangers d'usage courant (Paris, 1953, 2/1973)
'L'interpretazione orchestrale di Lulli', *L'orchestra* (Florence, 1954), 139–52
'La musique dans l'éducation des enfants au XVIIIe siècle', *Mélanges d'histoire et d'esthétique musicales offerts à Paul-Marie Masson*, ii (Paris, 1955), 115–21
Vivaldi (Paris, 1955; Eng. trans., 1957 as *Vivaldi: 'Genius of the Baroque*)
Fritz Kreisler (Geneva, 1956)
Albert Roussel (Geneva, 1957) [in Ger. and Fr.]
'On the Rights of the Interpreter in the Performance of 17th- and 18th-century Music', *MQ*, xliv (1958), 145–66
Histoire illustrée de la musique (Paris, 1959; Eng. trans., 1960)
Aux XVIIe et XVIIIe siècles instruments á archet, *IMSCR VIII: New York 1961*, i, 220–31
Le monde des virtuoses (Paris, 1961; Eng. trans., 1963)
Musical Creation (Washington, 1961); repr. in *Lectures on the History of Art and Music*, ed. I. Lowens (New York, 1968), 187–211 [lecture given at Library of Congress, 4 Oct 1960]
'Le malentendu des concerts', *Liber amicorum Charles van den Borren* (Antwerp, 1964), 135–43
Le violon (Paris, 1966, 2/1974)
'Corelli et la France', *Studi corelliani [I]: Fusignano 1968*, 13–18
'François Couperin et la conciliation des "goûts" français et italien', *Chigiana*, xxv, new ser. v (1968), 69–80
'L'orchestre de l'Opéra aux approches de la Révolution de 1789', *Journal musical français musica-disques*, no.179 (1969), 44–6

EDITIONS

J.-J.C. de Mondonville: *Pièces de clavecin en sonates*, PSFM, 1st ser., ix (1935)
J.-J.C. de Mondonville: *Pièces de clavecin avec voix ou violon* (London, 1966) [facs. edn]
J. Bodin de Boismortier: *Sonates pour flûte et clavecin*, Le pupitre, xx (Paris, 1970)

BIBLIOGRAPHY

E. Ader and others, eds.: *Collection musicale Marc Pincherle* (Paris, 1975) [auction catalogue]
'In memoriam Marc Pincherle', *RdM*, lxi (1975) [special issue; incl. G. Thibault: 'Marc Pincherle (1888–1974)', 169–77; J. Gribenski: 'Bibliographie des travaux de Marc Pincherle', 178–96]
M. Talbot: 'The Fortunes of Vivaldi Biography, from Pincherle to the Present', *Chigiana*, xli, new ser. xxi (1989), 113–35

JEAN GRIBENSKI

Pindar [Pindaros] (*b* 522–518 BCE; *d* 442–436 BCE). Theban lyric poet. As a young man Pindar went to study in Athens, which had become an unequalled centre of musical and poetic influences from Ionia and the Peloponnesus. Tradition credits him with having had eminent teachers of choral lyric, chief among them LASUS OF HERMIONE and Agathocles. Lasus developed the dithyramb into a mature art form and supposedly wrote the first prose treatise on music; Plato (*Laches*, 180d1) mentioned Agathocles as Damon's music teacher.

Although Pindar's compositions include all the various types of choral lyric, only the *epinikion*, or victory ode, is well represented by complete surviving examples. The four substantial books of Pindar's *epinikia* are among the great monuments of Greek lyric: each corresponds to one of the four festivals – the Olympia, Pythia, Isthmia and Nemea – and a number of the *epinikia* can be assigned to particular festivals and victors (for example, *Pythian*, xii, written in honour of Midas of Acragas, the prize-winning aulete at the 24th and 25th Pythian festivals in 490 and 486 BCE). His works were for the most part religious; even the secular victory odes show a strength of religious feeling and exaltation that only Aeschylus could match. The literary handling goes far beyond the immediate occasion, usually that of a triumph in the national games. Myth receives special prominence, together with a gnomic element, and the victor is shown in the transfiguring moment of supreme achievement.

All but seven of the 45 extant odes have a triadic metrical scheme of stanza groups: strophe, matching antistrophe and dissimilar epode. Where multiple triadic groups appear, the epodes correspond in metric structure. Pindar's *epinikia* make use of three basic rhythmic patterns: the paeonic, the dactylo-epitritic and the logaoedic. One dactylo-epitritic *epinikion* is described by the poet as Dorian (*Olympian*, iii.5) and one logaoedic *epinikion* as Aeolian (*Olympian*, i.102), but there are also references to the Lydian aulos, *harmonia* and mode (*tropos*) in both rhythmic types (*Olympian*, v.19 and xiv.17; *Nemean*, iv.45 and viii.15). The references to Dorian and Aeolian would seen to pertain more to the overall style of the *epinikia* than to any specific *tonos* or *harmonia*.

The poet refers freely to musical details, displaying a wholly professional pride in his skill. He speaks most often of the kithara, usually calling it 'phorminx' rather than 'lyra' and describing it variously: it was Dorian, seven-stringed and had a deep, ringing tone. The double aulos is virtually always mentioned in any ode that also mentions the lyra, and often the two are in close conjunction; the sole exception (*Olympian*, v) has been thought suspect. This repeated and often explicit evidence for a concerted accompaniment of lyras and auloi serves as a safeguard against creating false antitheses between the two types of instrument. Attempts to parallel metre with mode and strophic response with melody have not succeeded. Pindar mentions in passing the NOMOS, a stylized melodic pattern (*Olympian*, i.101; *Pythian*, xii.23), and the *tropos*, literally 'turning' (*Olympian*, xiv.17) – a term that at this period quite possibly described the contour of a melody, especially when taken in a given mode. The supposedly Pindaric melody of *Pythian*, i, printed by Athanasius Kircher in his *Musurgia universalis* (Rome, 1650), is spurious.

The fragments of Pindar's other works contain a number of noteworthy musical references. 'The Dorian melody is [?the] most dignified', he declares (Bowra, frag.56), seeming to anticipate the later development of doctrines of modal ethos; elsewhere (frag.288), as reported by Plutarch, he confesses his own inattention to the melodic *tropos* and continues by referring strangely to the unjust nature of destructive change in skills and capacities produced by certain kinds of modulations (*metabolai*). The first of these statements is not easily credited to Pindar; the second shows a direct concern with ethos and sounds remarkably like the later complaints of a Phrynichus or a Plato. He also credits TERPANDER with having discovered the BARBITOS (frag.110a), and speaks cryptically of an Aeolian double aulos entering upon 'a Dorian pathway of hymns' (frag.180). Music had ultimate significance for Pindar, however, not as an aggregate of technical details but as the power to which he paid tribute in the opening strophes of *Pythian*, i: a cosmic force capable of instilling order and peace into the communal life of men.

WRITINGS

J. Sandys, ed. and trans.: *The Odes of Pindar, Including the Principal Fragments* (London and Cambridge, MA, 1915, 3/1937/R)

C.M. Bowra, ed.: *Pindari carmina cum fragmentis* (Oxford, 1935, 2/1947/R)

B. Snell, ed.: *Pindari carmina cum fragmentis*, pts i–ii (Leipzig, 1953, rev. 5/1971–5 by H. Maehler)

C.M. Bowra, trans.: *The Odes of Pindar* (Harmondsworth, 1969)

BIBLIOGRAPHY

A. Rome: 'L'origine de la prétendue mélodie de Pindare', *Etudes classiques*, i (1932), 3–11

H. Gundert: *Pindar und sein Dichterberuf* (Frankfurt, 1935/R)

A. Rome: 'Pindare ou Kircher', *Etudes classiques*, iv (1935), 337–50

R. Wagner: 'Zum Wiederaufleben der antiken Musikschriftsteller seit dem 16. Jahrhundert, ein Beitrag zur Frage Kircher oder Pindar', *Philologus*, xci (1936), 161–73

J. Irigoin: *Histoire du texte de Pindare* (Paris, 1952)

R.W.B. Burton: *Pindar's Pythian Odes* (Oxford, 1962)

C.M. Bowra: *Pindar* (Oxford, 1964)

L. Pearson: 'The Dynamics of Pindar's Music: Ninth Nemean and Third Olympian', *Illinois Classical Studies*, ii (1977), 54–69

A. Barker, ed.: *Greek Musical Writings*, i: *The Musician and his Art* (Cambridge, 1984), 54–61 [translated excerpts referring to musical subjects]

M. Heath: 'Receiving the Kōmos: the Context and Performance of Epinician', *American Journal of Philology*, cix (1988), 180–95

A. Burnett: 'Performing Pindar's Odes', *Classical Philology*, lxxxiv (1989), 283–93

C. Carey: 'The Victory Ode in Performance: the Case for the Chorus', *Classical Philology*, lxxxvi (1991), 192–200

M. Heath and M.Lefkowitz: 'Epinician Performance', *Classical Philology*, lxxxvi (1991), 173–91

K. Morgan: 'Pindar the Professional and the Rhetoric of the Kōmos', *Classical Philology*, lxxxviii (1993), 1–15

W.D. Anderson: *Music and Musicians in Ancient Greece* (Ithaca, NY, 1994), 94–109

T.J. Mathiesen: *Apollo's Lyre: Greek Music and Music Theory in Antiquity and the Middle Ages*(Lincoln, NE, 1999), 135–41

WARREN ANDERSON/THOMAS J. MATHIESEN

Pineda, Francisco de Atienza y. See ATIENZA Y PINEDA, FRANCISCO DE.

Pinel, Germain (*b* early 1600s; *d* Paris, early Oct 1661). French lutenist and composer. From a well-to-do Parisian family, he is first mentioned as master lutenist in 1630. In 1645 he entered the service of Marguerite de Lorraine, Duchess of Orléans. In 1647 he was appointed lute teacher to Louis XIV, then nine years old, a post he held until 1656 when he became lutenist and theorbo player of the *chambre*, with a salary that put him among the highest-paid members of the royal music. In the same year he took part in Lully's *Ballet de Psyché* with his younger brother François and youngest son Séraphin, as well as Louis Couperin and others. He is listed among participants

in further Lully ballets in 1657 and 1659. In 1658 he is described as composer and ordinary of the king's music.

Pinel wrote 78 dances and eight *préludes non mesurés* for lute, and one *prélude non mesuré* for theorbo (ed. M. Rollin and J.-M. Vaccaro, Paris, 1982). The exceptionally wide diffusion of his works in manuscript points to his stature as one of the greatest lute composers of the century (for sources see edition and Ledbetter). In their technical resourcefulness and broad paragraphing his *préludes non mesurés* provide the nearest lute equivalent to the harpsichord preludes of Louis Couperin.

BIBLIOGRAPHY

F. Lesure: 'Trois instrumentistes français du XVIIe siècle', *RdM*, xxxvii (1955), 186–7

C. Massip: *La vie des musiciens de Paris au temps de Mazarin* (Paris, 1976)

D. Ledbetter: *Harpsichord and Lute Music in Seventeenth-Century France* (diss., U. of Oxford, 1985)

DAVID LEDBETTER

Pinelli, Ettore (*b* Rome, 18 Oct 1843; *d* Rome, 17 Sept 1915). Italian violinist, conductor, teacher and composer. He studied the violin with his uncle Tullio Ramacciotti and at 13 was giving concerts. In 1864 he studied with Joachim at Hanover. At Rome again, he joined his uncle's ensemble, the original Quartetto Romano, which in 1866, when Ramacciotti left it, became a quintet with the addition of Tito Monachesi, violin, and Giovanni Sgambati, piano. For almost half a century Pinelli and Sgambati, both individually and jointly, made important contributions to Rome's musical life. In 1869 they established a free school of violin and piano for poor children; this was the nucleus of the Liceo Musicale of the Accademia di S Cecilia, founded in 1877, where Pinelli and Sgambati taught for the rest of their lives. Pinelli excelled as a teacher, and many of his pupils had distinguished careers. With Sgambati he founded the Chamber Music Society of Rome; they also alternated as directors of the Royal Court Concerts. In 1874 Pinelli founded the Società Orchestrale Romana which he directed for 25 years. He composed a symphony, a string quartet, an Italian Rhapsody and a number of songs. His editions of works by Bach and Corelli and of études by Campagnoli, Kreutzer and Rolla are no longer in print. His brothers, the pianist Oreste and cellist Decio, also became professional musicians.

FERRUCCIO BONAVIA/ALBERT MELL

Pinello di Ghirardi [Pinello di Gherardi; Pinellus de Gerardis], **Giovanni Battista** (*b* Genoa, *c*1544; *d* Prague, 15 June 1587). Italian composer and singer, active in Germany. Born into a noble Genovese family, he served at a number of important institutions, rising to the position of Kapellmeister at the electoral court in Dresden. In a letter written in 1580 as an application for this post, he stated that he had been 'in der Sangerey' for about 30 years. The exact nature of his education, beyond this suggestion of choirboy training, remains unknown, but coming from an established noble family he may have had some form of private musical training.

His earliest known professional activity dates from 1569, when he was appointed to the chapel of Duke Wilhelm V in Landshut. This experience no doubt exposed him to the works of the already legendary Lassus. Unfortunately, debt was beginning to have an adverse effect on Bavarian court music, and the Landshut chapel was disbanded in 1570. Pinello subsequently moved to Vicenza, where he served as *maestro di cappella* in the cathedral. His earliest extant collection, three books of *canzoni napolitane*, were published in Venice during this period. He returned to Germany no later than 1576, serving as a singer in the Habsburg chapel in Innsbruck. Exactly how long he remained in imperial service is unclear, but it is most probable that he was at the Prague court of Emperor Rudolf II by 1580. On the death of Antonio Scandello in 1580, Elector August of Saxony seemed determined to appoint a foreigner to the post of Kapellmeister in his court. It was offered to Lassus and to Jacob Regnart, but both declined the post. Pinello's name was submitted to August by the Emperor, and the Italian was appointed in November 1580.

Pinello's tenure as Kapellmeister in the Saxon court was one of considerable compositional activity, comprising lieder, German *Magnificat* settings and motets. In other respects, however, it seems as though his employment in Dresden was a failure: he experienced trouble with the choirboys, with his Vice-Kapellmeister, Georg Forster (who had served as interim Kapellmeister before Pinello was appointed) and with the court in general. All this culminated in his release from his duties in 1584. Although these issues probably played a part in his dismissal, Pinello's ties with Rudolf suggest that the composer might also have been a spy. He subsequently returned to Prague, where he assumed the duties of *Knabenpräceptor*, and he served the imperial court until his death in 1587. A collection of five-voice motets was published one year later.

Pinello's output includes settings of Italian, Latin and German texts. His early canzoni are typical of the three-voice Neapolitan style, as exemplified by the works of Nola. His motets and German works, however, reveal a relatively daring use of chromaticism and dissonance. Ranging from dense polyphonic and complex polychoral textures to relatively brief chordal works, some of his Latin and German settings are intensely emotional. Additional collections of masses and madrigals, attributed to Pinello by Walther, are no longer extant. Pinello's first book of three-voice canzoni is also lost. A collection of five-voice *napolitane*, listed by Walther as missing, has apparently survived, in German translation, as the 1584 collection of lieder.

In terms of total impact, however, it seems that Pinello's reputation was limited. None of his collections was ever republished, and just two works were included in printed anthologies. One of these, *When I would thee embrace*, is in Nicholas Yonge's *Musica transalpina* (RISM 1588²⁹). This work is an English translation of *Quand'io voleva*, which as *Wenn ich habe gewolt* was included in the 1584 publication of lieder. Copies of his works in manuscript sources are also relatively infrequent; a six-voice setting of *Veni in hortum meum*, attributed to Pinello in *D-Bsb* 40039, is concordant with a copy ascribed to Caspar Speiser in *D-Dl* Glashütte 5.

WORKS
extant works ed. in Heuchemer

SACRED

Deutsche Magnificat auff die 8 Tonos musicales . . . sampt etlichen newen Benedicamus, 4, 5vv (Dresden, 1583)
Durarumque mutetarum adiunctarum, 8, 10 and more vv (Dresden, 1584)
[18] Muteta, 5vv (Prague, 1588)
Motet, 8vv, 1621²
Motet, *D-Bsb, Dl*, doubtful

SECULAR

Il secondo libro delle canzone napolitane, 3vv (Venice, 1571)
Il terzo libro delle canzone napolitane, 3vv (Venice, 1572)
El quarto libro delle canzone napolitane, 3vv (Venice, 1575)
Nawe kurtzweilige deutsche Lieder, 5vv (Dresden, 1584)

LOST WORKS

Il primo libro delle canzone napolitane, 3vv
6 Messen, 4vv (Dresden, 1582)
Madrigali a più voci (Dresden, 1584)
Libro primo de napolitane, 5vv (Dresden, 1585) [probably Italian-language version of Nawe kurtzweilige deutsche Lieder]

BIBLIOGRAPHY
BoetticherOL; SennMT; WaltherML
E.F. Schmid: *Musik an den schwäbischen Zollernhöfen der Renaissance* (Kassel, 1962), 585
M. Ruhnke: *Beiträge zu einer Geschichte der deutschen Hofmusikkollegien im 16. Jahrhundert* (Berlin, 1963), 217, 254–5
S. Köhler: *Musikstadt Dresden* (Leipzig, 1976, 3/1981)
M.R. Moretti: 'Giovanni Battista Pinello', *Musica & costume a Genova: tra Cinquecento & Seicento* (Genoa, 1990), 170–76
D.O. Heuchemer: *Italian Musicians in Dresden in the Second Half of the Sixteenth Century, with an Emphasis on the Lives and Works of Antonio Scandello and Giovanni Battista Pinello di Ghirardi* (diss., U. of Cincinnati, 1997)
E. Steindorf: *Die sächsische Staatskapelle Dresden* (Berlin, 1997)

DANE O. HEUCHEMER

Piñera (Infante), Juan (Manuel) (*b* Havana, 18 Jan 1949). Cuban composer and pianist. He studied the piano with César Pérez Sentenat, Silvio Rodríguez Cárdenas, Margot Rojas and Ninowska Fernández-Britto, and composition with Enrique Bellver. When the Instituto Superior de Arte was established (1976) he studied composition with Ardévol, as his last pupil. He has won numerous prizes for composition, the most outstanding of which include La Edad de Oro, for music for children, the Unión de Escritores y Artistas de Cuba awards for both symphonic and electro-acoustic music, the 12th International Electro-acoustic Music Competition in Bourges (France) in 1984, and the 3rd TRIMALACA in Rio de Janeiro (1985). As the composer himself affirms, his music can be both profoundly lyrical and an obvious joke at the expense of conventionality. His earliest composition, *La 'cosa' no está en el título* for piano (1972–3), is in sonata form and exploits the rich effects produced by the pianistic treatment of avant-garde concepts. His songs are based on complex poetic texts, especially the work of poets such as José Martí, Mirta Aguirre, Nicolás Guillén and Virgilio Piñera. Associated with theatre music from an early age, his recent theatre pieces have included reworkings of music originally from zarzuelas or musical comedies to create highly contemporary versions for original productions (*Las hijas de Bernarda Alba*, 1992, *El tío Francisco y las Leandras*, 1991), and operas such as *Amor con amor se paga* (1987–97) and *La taza de café* (1989–93).

WORKS
(selective list)

Ops: Amor con amor se paga (J. Martí), 1987–97; La taza de café (J.R. Amán), 1989–93
Orch: Como naufragios, 1988; Entre mi muerte y tu delirio, habanera cycle, str orch, 1993; La travesía secreta, 1996
Chbr: La 'cosa' no está en el título, pf, 1972–3; Passoyaglia, pf, 1983; Residuos, str qt, 1984; El impromptu en Fa de F. Chopin, pf, vn, vc, 1990; Diurno y Postludio, para la mano derecha, pf, 1992; El último viaje del buque fantasma, 1996
El-ac: Tres de dos, 1984; Del espectro nocturno, gui, tape, 1986; Imago (ballet), gui, tape, 1988; Germinal (dance theatre), tape, 1988; Cuando el aura es aúrea o la muy triste historia de los 8'38", s sax, tape; Las pequeñas muertes de la despedida, gui, tape, 1995; La Bals . . . , tape, 1996–97

Vocal: Elogio del cartero, song cycle, 1v, pf, (A.O. Rodríguez), 1988; Arpa y sol, vocalise, 1988; Lejos ya de la inquietud, S, hp, str, 1989; Llueve cada domingo, 1v, pf, (N. Guillén), 1996

Principal publisher: Editora Musical de Cuba

VICTORIA ELI RODRÍGUEZ

Pinet. Variant of the HOMMEL (box zither) of the Low Countries.

Pingirolo, Gabriele (*b* Lodi; *fl* 1589–91). Italian composer. His *Vespertina concentus quatuor concinendi vocibus* (Venice, 1589) was dedicated from Alessandria to Ottavio Saraceno, Bishop of that city, suggesting that Pingirolo was living and working there at the time. Further indications of contacts in the area are offered by the contents of the book, which include a sequence of Vespers psalms together with a setting of the *Magnificat* by Flaminio Tresti who is known to have been in nearby Casale Monferrato in the following year. Another work, the *Missarum quinque vocum liber priumus* (Venice, 1591) survives incomplete. This may be the book of masses that Eitner attributed to an otherwise unknown Paolo Pingirolo (*EitnerQ*).

IAIN FENLON

Pingirolo, Paolo. *See* PINGIROLO, GABRIELE.

Pingoud, Ernest (*b* St Petersburg, 14 Oct 1888; *d* Helsinki, 1 June 1942). Finnish composer of Russian birth and Huguenot origin. He studied privately with Siloti and at the St Petersburg Conservatory with Anton Rubinstein, Rimsky-Korsakov and Glazunov. He studied in Germany until 1906 with Hugo Riemann and spent three years with Reger. As a student he began his remarkable activity on the *St Petersburger Zeitung*, to which he sent articles on music from Berlin (1910–11) and wrote concert and opera reviews (1911–14). In 1918 he emigrated to Finland, where he worked initially as a music teacher. He was director of the Fazer concert agency (1924–31, 1935–7), and ran his own agency from 1931 to 1933. In 1924 he also became manager of the Helsinki City Orchestra, and continued in that role until his death.

The first concert of Pingoud's work, in Helsinki in 1918, marked the arrival of modernism in Finnish music. Works showing the influence of Strauss, Debussy and Skryabin were the boldest that had been heard in Finland, and Pingoud was dubbed a futurist, cubist, ultra-modernist and even a musical bolshevik. He was praised for his brilliant command of orchestration but censured for aspiring to extremes. His feverish productivity was reflected in the rapid succession of premières throughout the early 1920s. His music, conducted by himself, was also performed in Berlin (1923) and in Viipuri, Finland (now Vyborg, Russia), in 1936. Pingoud was above all an orchestral composer, and his work concentrated on the Skryabin-inspired idealist-symbolist symphonic poem. His three piano concertos, however, are in a more traditional style redolent of Liszt and Rachmaninoff. He is at his most modern in the *Fünf Sonette*, which approach the aphoristic early style of the Second Viennese School. His works, however, remained tonal. His *La face d'une grande ville*, heard in Helsinki at the end of the 1930s, was the first Finnish composition to belong to the sphere of urban machine-poetry. In the interwar period when almost all composers drew on nationalist themes and texts, Pingoud was an isolated phenomenon. He was a cosmopolitan, sternly opposed to national aspirations, and for this reason he was to some extent shunned.

WORKS
(*selective list*)

Syms: op.18, 1920, op.20, 1920, op.27, 1923–7
Other orch: Prologue, op.4, 1915; Confessions, op.5, 1916; La dernière aventure de Pierrot, op.6, 1916; Diableries galantes 'Le fétiche', op.7, 1917; Pf Conc., op.8, 1917; Hymnejä yölle [Hymns to the Night], op.9, 1917; Danse macabre, op.10, chorus, orch, 1918; 5 Sonette, op.11, chbr orch, 1918; *Un chevalier sans peur et sans reproche*, op.12, adventure, 1918; Mysterium, op.13, 1919; Flambeaux éteints, op.14, 1919; Chantecler, op.15, 1919; Le sacrifice, op.17, 1919; Profeeta [The prophet], op.21, 1921; Pf concs., op.22, 1921, op.23, 1922; Cor ardens, 1927; Narcissos, 1930; Le chant de l'espace, 1931, rev. 1938; La face d'une grande ville, pf, orch, 1937; La flamme éternelle, 1938–9; Epäjumala [The idol], 1939
Vocal: Nuori Psykhe [The Young Psyche], S, orch, 1923; songs
Chbr: 2 str qts, 2 sonatas, vn, pf, 2 sonatas, vc, pf, Pf Sonata

BIBLIOGRAPHY

E. Salmenhaara: 'Ernest Pingoud: kosmopoliitti Suomen musiikkielämässä' [Ernest Pingoud: a cosmopolitan in Finnish musical life], *Synteesi*, iv (1988), 32–65 [incl. list of works; abridged Eng. version in *Finnish Music Quarterly*, iii (1989), 17–25]
E. Pingoud: *Taiteen edistys* [Progress in Art], ed. K. Aho (Jyväskylä, 1995)

ERKKI SALMENHAARA

Pinheiro, António (*b* ? Montemór-o-Novo, *c*1550; *d* Évora, 19 June 1617). Portuguese composer. According to Barbosa Machado he was a pupil of Guerrero. However, Alegria (1983, p.156) suggests that Pinheiro studied at Évora, probably with Francisco Velez or Matheo de Aranda. The *Reitor do Colégio dos moços do coro* at Évora from 1579 was Vicente Guerreiro but he is not known to have been a musician (see Alegria 1997, p.75). According to Manuel Joaquim, Pinheiro was appointed *mestre de capela* to the Duke of Bragança from 12 March 1576, the first Portuguese known to have held the position. In the *Mercês de D. Teodósio II* (MS, P-VV), Pinheiro is recorded as receiving regular payments from 4 January 1584 which amounted to a modest annual salary of around 10,000 reis plus extras. He was, for example, paid an additional 6000 reis for the *chançonetas* for Christmas of 1593. For the year 1605 his salary was increased to 20,000 reis and he was given two further payments, 3000 reis in 1606 and 4000 reis in 1609. However, by this time, he had already been appointed to and dismissed, on 4 October 1608, from the position of *mestre da crasta* at Évora Cathedral, where his salary had been 40,000 reis. The reasons for the dismissal are not recorded, but both Pinheiro and Miguel Bravo, a bass and rebec player, were dismissed on the same day. Four days later, Domingos Martins was appointed to replace Pinheiro with the much lower salary of 16,000 reis. Pinheiro made an appeal on 11 October and was granted his salary but not reinstated. Bravo was reinstated as an instrumentalist at the cathedral from January 1609 and Domingos's salary was raised to 40,000 reis from February 1610.

Pinheiro's settings of the even-numbered verses of five psalms survive at Vila Viçosa, three in a manuscript probably dating from the early 18th century and two in a volume copied by Julião Ferreira da Crus in 1735. In most verses, the psalm tone is presented in one of the parts with the others providing contrapuntal elaboration. His verses are, on average, slightly longer than those of Juan Navarro (i) (copies of whose psalms also survive at Vila Viçosa) though his doxologies, usually in triple metre, tend to be shorter.

The library of João IV included Pinheiro's four-part settings of *Ave Regina caelorum*, and *Inter natus mulierum* and a five-part *Tollite jungum meum*. The *Biblioteca Lusitana* also lists a book of *Magnificat* settings. All this music is lost.

BIBLIOGRAPHY

JoãoIL

D. Barbosa Machado: *Biblioteca Lusitana* (Lisbon, 1741–59/R)

M. Joaquim: *Vinte livros de música polifónica do Paço ducal de Vila Viçosa* (Lisbon, 1953)

J.A. Alegria: *História da escola de música da sé de Évora* (Lisbon, 1973)

R. Stevenson and others, eds.: *Antologia de polifónia portuguesa, 1419–1680*, PM, ser.A, xxxvii (Lisbon, 1982)

J.A. Alegria: *História da capela e colégio dos Santos Reis de Vila Viçosa* (Lisbon, 1983)

R.V. Nery: *A música no ciclo da 'Biblioteca lusitano'* (Lisbon, 1984)

J.A. Alegria: *Biblioteca do Palácio real de Vila Viçosa: catálogo dos fundos musicais* (Lisbon, 1989)

J.A. Alegria: *O Colégio dos moços do coro da sé de Évora* (Lisbon, 1997)

MICHAEL RYAN

Pinho Vargas (Silva), António (Manuel Faria) (*b* Vila Nova de Gaia, 15 Aug 1951). Portuguese composer and jazz pianist. He studied piano at the Oporto Conservatory and took a degree in history at the University of Oporto. As a jazz pianist he has performed in many countries with his group as well as making six CDs (1974–96), for which he has three times won the Prémio de Imprensa Sete de Ouro for the best instrumental record of the year. His interest in contemporary classical composition came a little later, and he went to study with Klaas de Vries at the Rotterdam Conservatory (graduated 1990). In 1991 he was appointed a teacher at the Escola Superior de Música in Lisbon. He has been musical advisor to the Casa Serralves, Oporto (since 1994), and the Centro Cultural de Belém, Lisbon (1996–9). He was awarded the Comenda da Ordem do Infante D. Henrique in 1995.

Showing many influences, his music ranges from an unequivocal atonal language to neo-tonal passages. The structural starting-points in his music are usually of great simplicity and clarity. Recently, his rhythmic language has become more audibly striated and his harmony more tonally orientated. His second opera, *Os dias levantados*, written for the 25th anniversary of the 1974 revolution, is typical of the present more eclectic phase.

WORKS
(selective list)

Dramatic: Hamlet (incid music, W. Shakespeare), 1987; Tempos difíceis (film score), 1990; A bailarina do mar (dance score), 1990; Aqui na terra (film score), 1993; Edipo, tragédia do saber (chbr op, after P. Paixão), 1995–6; Richard II (incid music, Shakespeare), 1995; Cinco dias, cinco noites (film score), 1996; Os dias levantados (op, 2, M. Gusmão), 1997–8

Orch: Geometral, 22 insts, 1988; Mechanical String Toys, str, 1992; Acting Out, pf, perc, orch, 1998; A impaciência de Mahler, 1999

Vocal: 9 Songs (A.R. Rosa), 1v, pf, 1995

Chbr and solo inst: 3 Fragments, cl, 1987; Mirrors, pf, 1989; Estudo/Figura, 8 insts, 1990; Poetica dell'estinsione, fl, str qt, 1992; Monodia – quasi un requiem, str qt, 1993; Nocturno/Diurno, str sextet, 1994; 3 quadros para Almada, 10 insts, 1994; La luna – quatro fases, gui, 1996; 3 versos de Caeiro, 12 insts, 1997

Selected jazz recordings: Outros lugares (1983); Cores e aromas (1985); As folhas novas mudam de cor (1987); Os jogos do mundo (1989); Selos e borboletas (1991); A luz e a escuridão (1996); As mãos (1998) [collection]

CHRISTOPHER BOCHMANN

Pini, Anthony [Carlos Antonio] (*b* Buenos Aires, 15 April 1902; *d* Barcombe, Sussex, 1 Jan 1989). British cellist of French and Scottish parentage. As a soloist, orchestral leader and chamber musician he had a long and distinguished career. For 13 years he was a soloist at the London Promenade Concerts and also played concertos, particularly Elgar's, with Beecham, Sargent and van Beinum in England and the USA. Pini gave the first performance of Rawsthorne's Cello Sonata (1949), dedicated to him. He was principal cellist of the LPO (1932–9), the BBC SO (1939–43), the Liverpool PO (1943–5), the RPO (1947–63) and the Royal Opera House orchestra (1964–76). He was a member of the Brosa and Philharmonia string quartets; the latter's recordings of Schubert's 'Death and the Maiden' and Mozart's 'Hunt' are classics, as are Pini's recordings of Elgar's Concerto, with the LPO under van Beinum, and Beethoven's 'Archduke' Trio with Solomon and Henry Holst. He taught at the RCM and the GSM (1948–76). His tone was remarkably pure and he played a Grancino cello of 1696. He was awarded the OBE in 1976. His son, Carl Pini (*b* London, 2 Jan 1934), a violinist, is a soloist and was leader of several major British orchestras.

BIBLIOGRAPHY

M. Campbell: 'Pini Remembered', *The Strad*, c (1989), 187–9

WATSON FORBES/MARGARET CAMPBELL

Pini-Corsi, Antonio (*b* Zara [now Zadar], Dalmatia, June 1858; *d* Milan, 22 April 1918). Italian baritone. He made his début in 1878 at Cremona as Dandini in *La Cenerentola*, and for 15 years appeared throughout Italy, specializing in the comic operas of Rossini and Donizetti. Having made his first appearance at La Scala in January 1893, as Rigoletto, he created the role of Ford in Verdi's *Falstaff* on 9 February. That year he also sang Ford at Genoa, Rome, Venice and Brescia, and on 19 May 1894 he repeated the part at Covent Garden, where he had made his début five days before as Puccini's Lescaut. He sang Schaunard in the first performance of Puccini's *La bohème* at Turin (1896), appeared in Franchetti's *Signor di Pourceaugnac* at Genoa and Rome (1898), and made his début at the Metropolitan, New York, in 1899 as Masetto. At La Scala he took part in the first performances of Giordano's *Siberia* (1903) and Franchetti's *La figlia di Iorio* (1906), and appeared in Catalani's *La Wally* (1905) and in *Der Freischütz* (1906). At the Metropolitan, between 1909 and 1914, he sang many character roles, and he created the miner Happy in *La fanciulla del West* (1910) and the Innkeeper in Humperdinck's *Königskinder* (1910). His last appearance was in 1917 in Rossini's *Signor Bruschino* at the Teatro Dal Verme, Milan, when his voice, if not as powerful as it had been 40 years previously, was still as agile as ever and used with the same keen intelligence that had distinguished his performances throughout his long career. His brother, Gaetano Pini-Corsi, a character tenor, sang at La Scala as David in *Die Meistersinger* (1898), Mime in *Siegfried* (1899) and Goro in the first performance of *Madama Butterfly* (1904).

BIBLIOGRAPHY

I. Kolodin: *The Story of the Metropolitan Opera* (New York, 1931)

H. Rosenthal: *Two Centuries of Opera at Covent Garden* (London, 1958)

C. Gatti: *Il Teatro alla Scala nella storia e nell'arte, 1778–1963* (Milan, 1964)

ELIZABETH FORBES

Pinilla, Enrique (*b* Lima, 3 Aug 1927; *d* Lima, 22 Sept 1989). Peruvian composer. He studied in Lima with

Antonio Pini-Corsi as Falstaff

Carlos Sánchez Málaga at the Bach Institute, with Andrés Sas at the Sas-Rosay Academy and with Rodolfo Holzmann at the National Conservatory. Holzmann introduced him to various 20th-century compositional techniques, principally those of Hindemith. At the age of 20 he went to Spain where he studied with del Campo, and then to Paris where he studied with Koechlin. Between 1950 and 1958 he lived in Madrid, studying music with Francisco Calés Otero and taking a degree in composition at the Royal Conservatory. A scholarship from the Deutscher Akademischer Auslandsdienst took him to the Berlin Hochschule für Musik to study for two years with Blacher, who opened wide perspectives in the field of rhythm; particularly important to Pinilla was Blacher's concept of 'variable metres'. This lengthy European training freed Pinilla from the marked nationalist tendency of most Latin American composers, though this did not prevent him from often using elements of Peruvian popular traditions as starting material. He particularly favoured the rhythmic motifs of coastal music (e.g. in *Estudio sobre el ritmo de la marinera*, where he employs 'variable metres', or in *Cinco piezas* for percussion), pentatonic scales (e.g. in *Tema y variaciones*) and Amazonian melodies (e.g. in *Suite peruana*). He returned to Lima in

1961 to teach music history and ethnomusicology at the National Conservatory, and he also held musicological and administrative posts in the National Cultural Institute (1967–73). In 1966–7 he spent a year studying electronic music with Ussachevsky and Alcides Lanza at Columbia University on a Fulbright grant. Pinilla received the Dunker Lavalle Prize in 1966 and a composition award from San Marcos University in 1967. He believed in making use of all available procedures and means, including serial, polytonal or atonal writing and electronic composition (only in *Prisma* for tape), but his stated aim was to widen expressive possibilities rather than to search out unusual sounds. *Evoluciones 1* is probably the best example of his explorations of timbral variation and orchestral writing. In his final years he became interested in a new approach to tonality. Parallel to his activity as a composer, Pinilla was active in literature, cinema and television. He was also the first person to carry out a comprehensive musicological study of 20th-century Peruvian music and is the author of an important account of the history of academic and popular music in Peru.

WORKS
(selective list)

Orch: 4 Pieces, 1960–61; Festejo, 1965; Evoluciones I, 1967; Canción, 1968; Pf Conc., 1970; Suite peruana, 1972; Ayacucho 1824, 1974; Evoluciones II, perc, orch, 1976

Vocal: Cant. (Peruvian trad.), reciter, solo, vv, choir, wind, perc, 1954; 3 canciones (Pinilla), S, orch, 1955; 3 canciones (X. Abril), 1v, pf, 1945; Canciones (M. Adán, C. Vallejo), 1v, pf, 1977; La niña de la lamparaza azul (J.N. Eguren), 1v, 1982; Eventail (J. Sologuren), 1v, pf, 1982; Aloysius Acker (Adán), choir, 1983; He dejado descansar tristemente mi cabeza (E.A. Westphalen), 1v, pf, 1984

Chbr and solo inst: Sonatina, fl, 1950; Sonata, pf, 1952; Suite peruana, pf, 1953; Tema y variaciones sobre un tema pentafónico, pf, 1954; Estudio sobre el ritmo de la marinera, no.2, pf, 1959; Wind Trio, 1959; 3 Movts, pf, perc, 1960; Str Qt no.1, 1960; Coral, pf, 1963; Collages I, II, pf, 1966; Prisma, tape, 1967; 3 Pieces, str, 1968; 5 Pieces, perc, 1977; Variaciones a un coral, pf, 1984; Str Qt no.2, 1989, unfinished

Ballets, film scores, incid music

WRITINGS

'La música contemporánea en el Perú', *Fanal*, no.79 (1966)
'Informe sobre la música en el Perú', *Historia del Perú*, ix, ed. J. Mejía Baca (Lima, 1980)
'La música en el siglo XX', *La música en el Perú* (Lima, 1985)

BIBLIOGRAPHY

Compositores de América/Composers of the Americas, ed. Pan American Union, xi (Washington DC, 1965), 83–90
G. Béhage: *La música en América Latina* (Caracas, 1983)

CÉSAR ARRÓSPIDE DE LA FLOR/J. CARLOS ESTENSSORO

Pink Floyd. English rock group. It was formed in London in 1965 by architecture students Syd Barrett (Roger Keith Barrett; *b* Cambridge, 6 Jan 1946; guitar and vocals), Nick Mason (Nicholas Berkeley Mason; *b* Birmingham, 27 Jan 1945; drums), Roger Waters (George Roger Waters; *b* Great Bookham, Surrey, 9 Sept 1944; bass guitar and vocals) and Rick Wright (Richard William Wright; *b* London, 28 July 1945; keyboards). They began by playing covers of rhythm and blues standards, but combined these with a highly innovatory light show, promising a 'total environment of light and sound'. They thus became the most visible initial exponents of 'psychedelia' and by 1966 were headlining the new UFO club in central London. They deftly exploited media horror at the psychedelic movement, dispassionately denying any use of drugs. In late 1966 they played at the launch of the radical publication *International Times*, an important counter-cultural event. The early style was typified both by the song *Interstellar Overdrive*, which consisted of an opening and closing chromatic riff, enclosing an improvisation structured through a gradual loss and recovery of consistent metre, texture and registral spacing, and also by *Bike*, a childlike song full of metrical shifts and unsuspected timbres. By 1968 Barrett had become impossible to work with (a situation normally credited to psychiatric problems brought on by drug abuse) and his childhood friend Dave Gilmour (David Jon Gilmour; *b* Cambridge, 6 March 1947) was drafted in first to supplement his work on stage, then by mid-1968 to replace him. In this guise they began to move away from the spaced-out, freely improvised material on *Piper at the Gates of Dawn* (Col., 1967) and *A Saucerful of Secrets* (Col., 1968), although in live performance they still employed vivid light shows and back projections.

Up until this time Barrett had been their chief songwriter, a role subsequently taken by Waters. *Atom Heart Mother* (an eclectic mix of acoustic songs and richly orchestrated choral textures) reached number one in the UK in 1970, and a mature style was finally achieved by the long-awaited *The Dark Side of the Moon* (Harvest, 1973). This album brought them to the awareness of a US public, staying in the US album charts for 15 years; it sold more than 19 million copies worldwide and still proved immensely popular when re-released in 1993. Their music had become slow, with resonant, uncluttered guitar work and lyrics concerning various aspects of alienation (lunacy, despair and death). This theme was becoming ever more present in Waters's writing, particularly on the 1979 double album *The Wall* (Harvest). The intervening years had seen two important albums, *Wish You Were Here* (Harvest, 1975), which was previewed at their much praised performance at the Knebworth Festival some months earlier, and *Animals* (Harvest, 1977).

Waters's growing megalomania, much in evidence on *The Wall*, became harder to handle; Wright left in 1980 and after the poorly received, though high selling, *The Final Cut* (Harvest, 1983), Waters also departed. Mason and Gilmour recruited various others (including Wright from the mid-1980s) for the occasional album, most notably *A Momentary Lapse of Reason* (EMI, 1987) and *The Division Bell* (EMI, 1994), in addition to undertaking two international tours and individual projects. Although Gilmour's ringing guitar and their songs' generally slow pace help their style retain its identity, it has long since lost its psychedelic and experimental edge, acting as a voice for a middle-aged, financially successful British audience for whom it evokes exciting memories.

BIBLIOGRAPHY

R. Sanders: *The Pink Floyd* (London, 1976)

B. Miles: *Pink Floyd* (London, 1981)

C. Salewicz: 'Over the Wall', *Q*, no.11 (1987), 38–46

M. Snow: 'The Rightful Heir', *Q*, no.48 (1990), 62–71

N. Schaffner: *A Saucerful of Secrets: the Pink Floyd Odyssey* (London, 1991)

R. Scott: 'Pink Floyd: the Dark Side of the Moon', *Classic Albums*, ed. J. Pidgeon (London, 1991), 105–23 [interview]

A. Mabbutt: '25 Million Gloomy Punters Can't be Wrong', *Q*, no.79 (1993), 52–9

B. McDonald, ed.: *Pink Floyd: through the Eyes of . . .* (London, 1995)

ALLAN F. MOORE

Pinkham, Daniel (Rogers) (*b* Lynn, MA, 5 June 1923). American composer. He started playing the piano and composing at the age of five, and received organ and harmony lessons from C. Pfatteicher at Phillips Academy, Andover, MA (1937–40). Subsequently he studied composition with A.T. Merritt, A.T. Davison, Piston and Copland at Harvard University (1940–44) and with Hindemith, Honegger and Barber at the Berkshire Music Center at Tanglewood. He took private lessons with Nadia Boulanger in composition (1941–7), with Jean Chiasson, P.C. Aldrich and Landowska on the harpsichord and with E. Power Biggs on the organ. He has held teaching positions at the Boston Conservatory of Music, Simmons College in Boston, the University of Boston, Dartington Hall and Harvard (1946–58); he became music director of King's Chapel, Boston (1958). In 1959 he joined the faculty of the New England Conservatory as a lecturer in music history, theory, composition and the harpsichord, later establishing and chairing there the department of early music performance. He performed extensively on the harpsichord in a duo with the violinist Robert Brink, with the Boston SO and in solo recitals. Among his numerous awards are a Fulbright scholarship (1950), a Ford Foundation grant (1962), an American Academy of Arts and Sciences Prize and five honorary doctorates. His works have been commissioned by major institutions and have been widely performed.

Pinkham is a versatile composer whose prolific output covers a great variety of genres. His early involvement with church music as a student organist at Christ Church, Boston, and his attraction to biblical stories and liturgy led to a large body of work for organ, short choral pieces, songs and extended sacred compositions for choir and instruments. Attracted to bell-like sonorities since his time as a school carillonneur at Andover, he incorporated the evocation of bells into many of his instrumental compositions. Reflecting the influence of Stravinsky and Hindemith and his commitment to the early music revival, Pinkham's music of the 1930s and 40s embraces church modes, 16th-century contrapuntal techniques and 17th-century forms and instruments. Though in the 1950s and 60s he employed chromaticism and dodecaphonic techniques and investigated new tonal and intervallic relationships, he never used serial techniques dogmatically, instead combining 12-note rows with tonal elements. In 1970 he began to explore electronic music, creating tapes in his own studio. In many of his numerous works for tape and live musicians, especially organ and voices, he allows the performer rhythmic flexibility and free choice in the order of events to avoid rigid synchronization. With his strong interest in theatre and drama, Pinkham provides theatrical instructions for some of his cantatas, while other works, such as *The Passion of Judas* (1976), can be performed either in concert or as a theatre piece. He has written articles for journals on music.

WORKS
(*selective list*)

Stage: Passion of Judas (cant./op), 1976; Garden Party (op, Pinkham, N. Farber), S, Bar, 2 actors, chorus, 5 insts, tape, 1976; The Dreadful Dining Car (comic melodrama, Pinkham, after M. Twain, N. Farber), Mez, actors, solo vv, 7 insts, 1982; The Left-Behind Beasts (music play for children, Pinkham), actors, chorus, chbr ens, perc, 1985

Choral: Wedding Cant., opt. solo vv, chorus, insts, 1956; Christmas Cant., chorus, insts, 1957; Easter Cant., chorus, insts, 1961; Requiem, solo vv, chorus, insts, 1963; Stabat mater, S, chorus, orch, 1964; St Mark Passion, solo vv, chorus, orch, 1965; Jonah, spkr, solo vv, chorus, orch, 1967; Ascension Cant., chorus, orch, 1970; To Troubled Friends (J. Wright), chorus, str, tape, 1972; Daniel in the Lions' Den, nar, solo vv, chorus, insts, tape, 1972; Fanfares (Bible), T, chorus, insts, tape, 1975; Descent into Hell

(Pinkham), solo vv, chorus, insts, tape, 1979; Hezekiah, solo vv, chorus, tpt, org, 1979; When God Arose, solo vv, chorus, insts, 1979; Before the Dust Returns, chorus, insts, 1981; Lauds, 2vv, insts, 1983; Dallas Anthem Book, chorus, org, 1984; Advent Cant., chorus, insts, 1991; Christmas Syms., solo vv, chorus, insts, 1992; The Dryden Te Deum (J. Dryden), chorus, insts, 1992; The Creation of the World, nar, chorus, insts, 1994; many Psalm motets and works for choir with acc.

Solo vocal: The Song of Jephtha's Daughter (R. Hillyer), S, pf, 1963; 8 Poems of Gerard Manley Hopkins, Bar, va, 1964; Letters from St Paul, S/T, org, 1965; Safe in their Alabaster Chambers (E. Dickinson), Mez, tape, 1972; Charm me Asleep, Bar/Mez, gui, 1977; Transitions, Mez, bn/pf, 1979; Manger Scenes (N. Farber), S, pf, 1980; The Death of the Witch of Endor, A, hpd, perc, 1981; Music in the Manger (Farber), S, hpd/pf, 1981; The Wellesley Hills Psalm Book, medium v, org, 1983; Called Home (Dickinson), Mez, pf, 1996

Orch: Vn Conc., 1956; Sym. no.1, 1961; Catacoustical Measures, 1962; Sym. no.2, 1962; Signs of the Zodiac, opt. nar, orch, 1964; Org. Conc. no.1, 1970; Serenades, tpt, wind orch, 1979; Sym. no.3, 1985–6; Sym. no.4, 1990; Ov. Concertante, org solo, orch, 1992; Org. Conc. no.2, 1995; Org. Conc. no.3, 1996; works for band, music for TV and film

Chbr and solo inst: Sonata no.1, org, str, 1943; Conc., cel, hpd, 1955; Concertante no.3, org, cel, perc, 1962; Partita, hpd, 1962; Sonata no.3, org, str, 1968; Lessons, hpd, 1971; Toccatas for the Vault of Heaven, org, tape, 1971; Blessings, org, 1977; Epiphanies, org, 1978; Masks, hpd, chbr ens, 1978; Miracles, fl, org, 1978; Vigils, hp, 1982; Brass Qnt, 1983; Psalms, tpt, org, 1983; Str Qt, 1990; Organbook nos.1 and 2, 1991; Nocturnes, fl, gui, 1992; Preludes, pf, 1995–6; Divertimento, tpt, hp, 1997; Str Trio, 1998; works for carillon

Arrs., many vocal, of works by Handel, Purcell, Schubert, Selby

Principal publishers: Peters, E.C. Schirmer

BIBLIOGRAPHY

M.W. Johnson: *The Choral Works of Daniel Pinkham* (diss., U. of Iowa,1968)

J. McCray: 'Pinkham: On Composing: an Interview with Daniel Pinkham', *Choral Journal*, xvii/2 (1976), 15–17

D.K. Cox: *Aspects of Compositional Styles of Three Selected Twentieth-Century American Composers of Choral Music: Alan Hovhaness, Ron Nelson, and Daniel Pinkham* (diss., U. of Missouri, Kansas City, 1978)

M.L. Corzine: *The Organ Works of Daniel Pinkham* (diss., U. of Rochester, Eastman School, 1979)

L. Raver: 'The Solo Organ Music of Daniel Pinkham', *American Organist*, xvii/6 (1983), 35–7

M.E. Stallings: *Representative Works for Mixed Chorus by Daniel Pinkham: 1968–1983* (diss., U. of Miami, 1984)

K. DeBoer and J.B. Ahouse: *Daniel Pinkham: a Bio-Bibliography* (Westport, CT, 1988)

H. Pollack: 'A Heritage Upheld: Daniel Pinkham', *Harvard Composers: Walter Piston and his Students, from Elliott Carter to Frederic Rzewski* (Metuchen, NJ, 1992), 189–207

M.A. Radice: 'An Interview with Daniel Pinkham', *American Organist*, xxxi/8 (1997), 56–61

SABINE FEISST

Pinkullu [pinkillu, pincullo, pincollo, pincuyllu, pingullo, pinkayllu]. A generic term for 'flute', in the Andean languages Quechua and Aymara. Today, the many variants of this name apply principally to end-blown DUCT FLUTES, made from cane, wood or bone, of which numerous types are played throughout the Andean regions of Ecuador, Peru, Bolivia, northern Chile and north-west Argentina. The name applies equally to the three-hole pipe, played with a drum by a single player, or to five-, six- or seven-hole duct flutes which are typically played in consort. In a few isolated cases this name is also used to refer to transverse and notch flutes. Due to the paucity of archaeological evidence of pre-Hispanic duct flutes in the region, it is unclear whether the *pincollo* of Inca times, played widely as a courtship instrument, was a duct or notch flute (*see* KENA).

In today's Bolivian and Peruvian Andes, *pinkullu* or *pinkillu* duct flute performance is exclusively male, strongly associated with courtship and usually restricted to the rainy growing season between All Saints (November) and Carnival (February or March). The instrument's sound is widely claimed to attract rain and to cause the crops to grow. On the Bolivian high plateau the clear, high-pitched sound of cane *pinkillu* flutes, played to attract the rain and prevent frosts, is alternated with the harsher and vibrant sound of wooden *tarka* duct flutes, which herald the harvest season and are believed to reduce rainfall.

In central Bolivia, wooden *pinkillu* flutes with six fingerholes, but otherwise closely resembling Renaissance recorders in sizes and voicing, are played in consorts of four to six sizes. They are made by scraping and burning out the pithy centre of, for example, elder (*sauco*) branches. Exceptionally, these flutes are played using interlocking technique (like many Andean panpipes) between paired *tara* and *q'iwa* instruments, pitched a 5th apart.

In parts of northern and southern Bolivia and southern Peru, many types and sizes of wooden *pinkullu* or *pinkillu* duct flute are constructed by splitting curved branches (e.g. acacia) lengthwise. A central channel is gouged from each half, fingerholes and voicing cut, and the two halves bound back together using ox or llama sinews. Complex cross-fingerings are typical in performance and players often favour notes with a rich, vibrant timbre (*tara*).

In contrast to the above rainy-season flutes, three-hole pipes, played by single players as PIPE AND TABOR tend to be associated with festivals of the dry winter months. These include the Ecuadorian *pingullo* and the cane *waka pinkullu* (bull flute) of the Bolivian high plateau, played at Corpus Christi to accompany a dance which parodies the Spanish bullfight. In central Bolivia, the three-hole *kuntur pinkillu* (condor flute) or *quri pinkillu* (golden flute), made from the wingbone of a condor, is occasionally played beside the church door during patronal festivals to accompany the exit of the congregation.

BIBLIOGRAPHY

R. Stevenson: *Music in Aztec and Inca Territory* (Berkeley, 1968)

J.R. Pineda and others: *Mapa de los instrumentos musicales de uso popular en el Peru, Lima* (Lima, 1978)

Música Andina de Bolivia, various pfmrs, LPLI/S–062 [incl. notes by M.P. Baumann]

C.A. Coba Andrade: 'Instrumentos musicales ecuatorianos', *Sarance*, vii (1979), 70

H.C. Buechler: *The Masked Media: Aymara Fiestas and Social Interaction in the Bolivian Highlands* (The Hague, 1980)

M.P. Baumann: 'Music of the Indios in Bolivia's Andean Highlands (Survey)', *World of Music*, xxv/2 (1982), 80

H. Stobart: 'The Llama's Flute', *EMc*, xxiv/3 (1996), 471–82

H. Stobart: 'Flourishing Horns and Enchanted Tubers: Music and Potatoes in Highland Bolivia', *British Journal of Ethnomusicology*, iii (1994), 35–48

HENRY STOBART

Pinnock, Trevor (*b* Canterbury, 16 Dec 1946). English harpsichordist and conductor. He received his musical education as a chorister at Canterbury Cathedral and keyboard player at the RCM in London. His professional début was as a solo harpsichordist, and he has sustained this aspect of his performing career, with many admired recordings of music from the Baroque and Classical periods, including Scarlatti sonatas, Handel's harpsichord suites, and Bach's partitas and Goldberg Variations. Among his recorded performances as a concerto soloist are Poulenc's *Concert champêtre* with the Boston SO, and Bach and Haydn keyboard concertos with the ENGLISH CONCERT, the chamber orchestra which he founded in 1973. He directs it from the keyboard with a characteristic energy and enthusiasm which are readily communicated to audiences. Here, as in his solo career, he has remained almost exclusively within his chosen field of the Italian and German Baroque and some later 18th-century repertory. After their début appearance at the English Bach Festival in 1973, Pinnock and the orchestra recorded keyboard concertos by C.P.E. Bach in 1974 and the following year made a highly acclaimed recording of Vivaldi's *Four Seasons* with Simon Standage. Since then, their numerous recordings have included the major orchestral works of Handel and Bach, symphonies by C.P.E. Bach and Haydn and a notably vital, stylish Mozart symphony cycle. Pinnock has often added the English Concert Choir to his forces, first for a performance of Handel's *Ode to St Cecilia* at the Proms and subsequently for performances and recordings of works including *Messiah*, *Belshazzar* and Haydn masses.

Pinnock has also appeared as a guest conductor with many leading orchestras, including the Boston, San Francisco and Detroit symphony orchestras and with the St Paul and Los Angeles chamber orchestras. He made his Metropolitan Opera début in 1988 with Handel's *Giulio Cesare*. From 1991 to 1996 he was artistic director and principal conductor of the National Arts Centre Orchestra, Ottawa. He was made a CBE in 1992.

GEORGE PRATT

Pinnosa (probably corruption of *vinnosa*, from late Lat. *vinnus*: 'lock of hair'). In Western chant notations a neume signifying three notes, the second higher than the others, the third being semi-vocalized. The *pinnosa* is the LIQUESCENT form of the TORCULUS. Liquescence arises on certain diphthongs and consonants to provide for a semi-vocalized passing note to the next pitch. The *pinnosa* is one of the rarer ornamental neumes, and does not appear on most neume tables, medieval or modern.

BIBLIOGRAPHY

H.M. Bannister: *Monumenti vaticani di paleografia musicale latina* (Leipzig, 1913/*R*)

H. Freistedt: *Die liqueszierenden Noten des gregorianischen Chorals: ein Beitrag zur Notationskunde* (Fribourg, 1929), 33

M. Huglo: 'Les noms des neumes et leur origine', *EG*, i (1954), 53–67

DAVID HILEY

Piňos, Alois (Simandl) (*b* Vyškov, Moravia, 2 Oct 1925). Czech composer and theorist. While qualifying as a forestry engineer in Brno, he was a private composition pupil of Blažek; later he studied under Petrželka (1948–9) at the Brno Conservatory and under Kvapil (1949–53) at the Brno Academy, where he joined the teaching staff in 1953. He was appointed professor of composition at the academy in 1990 and for the next two years was head of composition and conducting. He has taught at the Darmstadt summer courses (1984–94), at international masterclasses run by the Vienna Hochschule für Musik, and at foreign universities, among them Malmö, Freiburg and Riga. In 1994 he was awarded the Czech Critics' Prize for his third string quartet.

In the late 1950s Piňos, with his colleagues Ištvan and Kohoutek, thoroughly applied principles taken from the 20th-century classics. At first they were influenced by Bartók and, in part, Prokofiev, Honegger and Janáček; in the 1960s they drew increasingly on the Second Viennese School and the postwar avant garde. Piňos's detailed study of 12-note serialism, and his contact with aleatory writing and other new developments at the Darmstadt summer courses of 1965 and 1966, contributed greatly to the formation of his technique. His new understanding of dodecaphony, summarized in his theoretical work *Tónové skupiny* ('Note groups'; Prague, 1971), has been used compositionally in his works after the mid-1960s, particularly fine examples being *Konflikty* ('Conflicts') and the concertos. In the late 1960s these detailed miniatures gave way to more complicated forms generated principally by tone-colour. Piňos has sometimes applied his theory of note groups to other parameters than pitch, and his use of chance is generally restricted to a choice in the ordering of controlled structures. Some of his music displays an ironic humour. In 1967 he founded a composers' group with Parsch, Růžička and Miloš Štědroň; during the period 1967–73 they produced ten collaborative works, including *Teamworks peripatie* for soprano, baritone, orchestra and tape (1968–9), and in the 1990s Ivo Medek joined original members Piňos and Štědroň for the collective composition of two chamber operas.

WORKS
(*selective list*)

Chbr ops, collab. I. Medek and M. Štědroň: Věc Cage aneb Anály avantgardy dokořán [The Cage Affair, or the Annal of the Avant Garde Thrown Open], perf. Brno, 1995; Anály předchůdců avantgardy aneb Setkání slovanských velikánů [Annals of the Predecessors of the Avant Garde, or the Meeting of Slavonic Giants]

Orch: Zkratky [Abbreviations], 1963; Conc., orch, tape, 1964; Double Conc., vc, pf, ww, tape, 1966; Chbr Conc., str, 1967; Conc. on BACH, b cl, pf, vc, orch, 1968; Apollo XI, sym., 1970; Serenáda pro BBB [Brno Brass Band], 1983; Org Conc., 1985; Lyrická předehra [Lyric Ov.], orch, 1994; Concertino (Hommage à Leoš Janáček), brass, orch, 1995

Vocal: 2 lyrické skici (J. Skácel), spkr, fl, va, 1964; 4 lyrické skici (Skácel), reciter, fl, b cl, pf, 1965; Ludus floralis (J. Novák), B-Bar, female chorus, tape, 1966; Dicta antiquorum, B-Bar, 1966; Ars amatoria (cant., Ovid), B-Bar, male chorus, orch, 1967; Gesta machabeorum, chorus, tape, 1967; Vyvolavači [Market Criers] (cant., J. Berg], 1969; Síla a moc lásky [Power of Love] (3 songs, B-Bar, str qt, 1982; Pastorela (cant., Moravian folk), chorus, brass ens, perc, 1984; Obžalovaný [The Accused] (F. Kafka), Bar, cl, vn, vc, pf, perc, tape, 1993; Carmina Lauretana, Bar, 1997; Carmina psalmisona, bar, 1998

Chbr: Wind Qnt, 1959; Sonata, va, vc, 1960; Pf Trio, 1960; Suite, str trio, 1961; Karikatury, fl, b cl/bn, pf, 1962; Str Qt, 1962; Konflikty, vn, b cl, pf, perc, 1964; '16.1.1969', pf qnt, timp, 1969; Sonata Concertante, vc, pf, 1974; Composition for 3, fl, cl, mar, marimbaphone, 1975; Wind Qnt, t sax, 2 tpt, 2 trbn, 1980; Für Königstein, vn, perc, 1981; Euphoria I–V, 2–6 players, 1983–98; Nonet, 1983; Cantilena, vn, vc, chbr str, 1988; Dolce far niente, basset-hn/cl, va, vc, db, pf, 1992; Str Qt no.3, 1993; Přiblížení [Approach], elec vn, perc, 1994; Musica affabilis, pf, 1994; 5 vět [5 Movts], fl, ob, cl, hn, bn, 1994; Mortonografie, fl, cl, bn, vn, va, vc, pf, vib, 1996; Sonnenschein für Mondschein Ensemble, fl, cl, vn, va, vc, pf, 1997; Thanks for Every Day, 4 sax/str qt/(fl, ob, cl, bn), 1998

Solo inst: Monology, b cl, 1962; Pulsus intermissi, 1 inst, tape, 1965; Paradoxy, pf, 1965; Paradoxy II, pf, tape, 1966; Hyperboly, hp, 1966; Dialog s Josefem Horákem, b cl, 1969; 231, pf, 1968–9; Kasematy [Casemates], pf, 1982; Sursum corda, org, 1988; Laudatio, org, 1992; Serenade, fl, 1992

El-ac: Statická hudba [Static Music], tape, 1969; Korespondence, 1971; Hudba pro dva, 1972; Nekonečná melodie [Endless Melody], 1973; Panta rhei?, triptych: Antiphon, Metamorphosis, Catharsis, 1985; Lux in tenebris, 1990; Advent, tpt, tape, 1991

Principal publishers: Český Hudební Fond, Modern, Panton, Supraphon

WRITINGS
'K dnešním možnostem tymových komposicí', *OM*, i (1969), 81–2
'Zpráva o týmových skladbách', *HV*, vii (1970), 61–6

'Slovo i fónické struktury v hudbě nestorů Nové hudby v Brně', *HRo*, xxiii (1970), 490–97 [M. Štědroň, J. Berg, A. Piňos, A. Parsch, J. Bulis]
'Musica ex machina contra musicam vivam? Einige Bemerkungen zu Relationen zwischen live-interpretierter und elektroakustischer Musik', *Glasba v tehničnem svetu: Musica ex machina/Die Musik in der technischen Welt: Musica ex machina* (Ljubljana, 1994), 191–6
'Mikrointervaly v české soudobé hudbě: dedictví Aloise Háby?' [Microtones in contemporary Czech music: the heritage of Alois Hába?], *OM*, xxv (1993), 277–84
'Hudba jako provokace' [Music as provocation], *OM*, xxvii (1995)
'Prvky banality a jejich ironizace v soudobé hudbe' [Commonplace elements and their ironic treatment in contemporary music], *OM*, iii (1971), 49–54

BIBLIOGRAPHY
M. Štědroň: 'Brněnská musica nova (1961–1964)', *ČMm*, li (1966), 325
M. Štědroň: 'Paradoxy řízené kompozice: nad profilem Aloise Piňose', *HRo*, xxi (1968), 730–34
M. Štědroň: 'Alois Piňos: k profilu skladatele', *Zprávy muzea vyškovska* (1969), no.77, p.27
M. Štědroň: 'Morava a musica nova', *Slovenská hudba*, xiii (1969), 221–7
D. Gojowy: 'Komponieren im Kollektiv: zur Arbeit des Brünner Komponistenteams', *Musik und Bildung*, iii (1971), 302–3
D. Gojowy: 'Musik, in der es vorwärts geht … : ein Gespräch mit dem tschechischen Komponisten Alois Piňos', *NZM*, Jg.151, no.4 (1990), 18–23

MILOŠ ŠTĚDROŇ

Pin Peat. Cambodian ensemble which accompanies court dance, masked plays, shadow plays and ceremonies, in addition to performing outside these contexts. The large ensemble consists of *korng tauch* and *korng thom*, (circular gong-chimes); *sralai tauch* and *sralai thom* (quadruple reed aerophones); *roneat daik* (metallophone); *roneat aik* and *roneat thung* (xylophones); *ching* (a pair of small cymbals); *skor thom* and *sampho* (drums); and vocalists (*neak chrieng*). The reduced ensemble often comprises *korng thom*, *sralai thom*, *roneat aik*, *sampho*, *ching* and vocalists (*see* CAMBODIA, §2).

TRẦN QUANG HẢI

Pinsuti, Ciro (*b* Sinalunga, 9 May 1829; *d* Florence, 10 March 1888). Italian composer and singing teacher. He made his début as a pianist at the age of nine, and two years later was made an honorary member of the Accademia Filarmonica, Rome. In 1840 he was taken to London, where he studied the piano, composition and the violin. He returned to Italy in 1845 and took lessons with Rossini in Bologna, while teaching the piano at the Liceo Musicale. In 1848 he settled in London as a singing teacher and coached many Italian opera singers, among them Grisi, Mario and Ronconi. From 1856 he was on the staff of the RAM; he was also greatly in demand as an accompanist. A prolific composer, he had three operas produced in Italy: *Il mercante di Venezia* (4, G.T. Cimino; Bologna, 8 Nov 1873), *Mattia Corvino* (3, C. D'Ormeville; Milan, Scala, 24 March 1877) and *Margherita* (2, A. Zanardini; Venice, Fenice, 8 March 1882). He also composed occasional vocal works, piano pieces and nearly 250 songs, many of which were extremely popular.

ELIZABETH FORBES

Pintarić, Fortunat (Josip) (*b* Čakovec, 3 March 1798; *d* Koprivnica, 25 Feb 1867). Croatian composer and organist. He studied music in Varaždin and Zagreb with F. Langer and J.K. Wisner-Morgenstern, and in 1821 was ordained into the Franciscan Order. Besides his other monastic duties he served as cantor and organist, and taught singing and organ in Franciscan monasteries in Zagreb (1821–9, 1832–5, 1857–60), Varaždin (1830–31, 1836–56), Virovitica (1860–65) and Koprivnica (1866–7). Pintarić was a very prolific composer of religious and secular music. As an enthusiastic advocate and supporter of the Croatian national movement of the 1830s and 40s, he attempted to imitate in his compositions the idiom of traditional Croatian music. However, because of his training in the Viennese Classical style he rarely succeeded in this. His best compositions are piano miniatures, particularly genre pieces such as his several *Dudaš*, and organ movements which involve elaborate polyphony. In 1849 he published in Vienna *Knjiga bogoljubnosti karstjanske*, an anthology of 45 religious hymns in Croatian, and in 1860 finished an anthology of church music (revised in 1867), *Crkvena lira*, with 378 instrumental and vocal movements to Latin and Croatian texts, to be used by the congregation and church choirs. Both anthologies were largely based on his own compositions. Pintarić also wrote about 30 masses in Croatian and Latin, many other liturgical works, organ and piano pieces, as well as patriotic songs (MSS in *HR-Zh*, *Zu*, *Zhk*, *Zs*).

BIBLIOGRAPHY
F.Ks. Kuhač: *Ilirski glazbenici* [Illyrian musicians] (Zagreb, 1893, 2/1994), 68–93 [incl. complete worklist]
K. Kupres: 'Prigodom sedamdesetogodišnjice smrti skladatelja O. Fortunata Pintarića reda sv. Franje' [On the 70th anniversary of the death of Rev. Fortunat Pintarić of the Franciscan Order], *Sv. Cecilija*, xxxi/4 (1937), 113–14
K. Filić: *Glazbeni život Varaždina* [Musical life of Varaždin] (Varaždin, 1972), 334–53
V. Prvčić, ed.: 'Znanstveni kolokvij o Fortunatu Pintariću' [Scholarly colloquium on Fortunat Pintarić], *Podravski zbornik*, xviii (1992), 148–205

ZDRAVKO BLAŽEKOVIĆ

Pintelli, Johannes (*b* ?Avignon, *c*1460; *d* Rome, before 26 May 1505). Singer and composer. He was employed at various Florentine musical institutions in the late 15th century, as was his brother Thomas. Johannes was a singer at Siena Cathedral between 1481 and 1484, when he moved to Florence where he is recorded as a singer at the Baptistry, SS Annunziata and the cathedral until 1491. In July 1504 he is described in documents as a member of the papal chapel and he died in Rome shortly before 26 May 1505. D'Accone has suggested that the Pintellis, despite their Italian name, came originally from France and this is confirmed by Vatican documents in which Johannes is consistently called a cleric of the diocese of Avignon (Avignon was, of course, a papal territory at that time and they could have come from an Italian family resident in the area).

Pintelli's extant works consist of one mass and one setting of an Italian text. His *Missa 'Gentils gallans de France'* (*I-Rvat* C.S.41) is based on a monophonic melody found in the collection *F-Pn* f. fr.12744, but also makes reference to two polyphonic settings, both in Florentine sources: an anonymous setting in *I-Fn* Magl.xix.164–7, no.63, and a setting of a different 'Gentils gallans' ascribed to Agricola in *I-Fn* B.R.229. Both his Gloria and Credo are extremely homophonic. His setting of a ballata, *Questo mostrarsi adirata di fiore* (ed. D'Accone, 1970), shows his familiarity with the style of Italian-texted music popular in Florence in the late 15th century.

BIBLIOGRAPHY
F.A. D'Accone: 'Some Neglected Composers in the Florentine Chapels, ca. 1475–1525', *Viator*, i (1970), 263–88

F.A. D'Accone: *The Civic Muse: Music and Musicians in Siena During the Middle Ages and the Renaissance* (Chicago, 1997)

RICHARD SHERR

Pinto, Mrs. *See* SIBILLA.

Pinto, Francisco António Norberto dos Santos (*b* Lisbon, 6 June 1815; *d* Lisbon, 30 Jan 1860). Portuguese composer. A boy soprano, he studied solfège with a singer in the royal chapel of Bemposta, then the horn with the royal cavalry bandmaster Justino José Garcia. At 15 he became a member of the same band and, on 30 September 1830, of the Brotherhood of St Cecilia, not being required to take the usual tests because of his already recognized ability. Two years later he became cornettist in the royal police guard band and in 1833 first horn player of the S Carlos Theatre orchestra. During the next five years he studied composition and orchestration with Manuel Joaquim Botelho, second flautist of that orchestra from 1825 to 1865. In 1854 he won the competition to succeed Franz Kuckembuk as professor of brass instruments at the National Conservatory and in 1857 he was promoted to director of the S Carlos orchestra.

Pinto made his début as a composer with music for the ballet *Adoração do sol* (S Carlos, 19 October 1838), which was danced by Huguet Vestris both that season and the next. During the next 15 years he composed 18 more ballets and, between 1841 and 1859, incidental music for 33 plays by such leading dramatists as Mendes Leal, Augusto Lacerda, José Romano and Silva Leal. His 46 sacred works composed between 1833 and 1859 culminated in the ambitious *Te Deum* given its posthumous première on 17 October 1863 in the church of Loreto in Lisbon in honour of D. Fernando. Although italianate, Pinto's prolific output of theatre and church music competed with Casimiro's for first honours in mid-19th-century Lisbon. Both his eighth orchestral overture (1845), dedicated to Liszt, and his Symphonia in D major in one movement with slow introduction (MS, *P-Em* 147) extracted maximum brilliance from a reduced theatre orchestra.

WORKS
(selective list)

for fuller list see DBP

Stage: 19 ballets, incl. contradanças from Dionisio tirano de Syracusa, 1841, in *Semario harmonico*, 3rd ser., no.63; incid music for 33 plays, incl. ballet from O tributo das cem donzellas (Mendes Leal), 1845, arr. pf in *Semario harmonico*, 3rd ser., nos.126–7

Sacred: 46 works, incl. 3 solemn masses, solo vv, 4vv, orch; 6 masses, 2–4vv, orch; 2 Gloria, 3–4vv, orch; 4 Cr, 3–4vv, orch; 5 matins, 3–4vv, orch; 8 Tantum ergo, 1–4vv, orch; 3 novenas, 1 for 4vv, org, 2 for 3–4vv, orch; 2 TeD, 3vv, orch; 3 Litanies of Our Lady, 3–4vv, orch; 2 Lamentations, 4vv, orch; other pieces for Holy Week

Other vocal: 1 modinha, 1v, pf, in *Semario harmonico*, 3rd ser., no.71; Romance, sung by Clara Novello, S Carlos, 18 June 1851 (Lisbon, n.d.); 2 romances (J. Romano) (Lisbon, n.d.); A pomba e a saudade (Romano), melodia, in memory of Queen Maria II (Lisbon, n.d.)

ROBERT STEVENSON

Pinto, George Frederick (*b* Lambeth, 25 Sept 1785; *d* Chelsea [now in London], 23 March 1806). English composer. His father's name was Samuel Saunders or Sanders, but he took his surname from his mother Julia Pinto, daughter of Thomas Pinto and herself the composer of a published vocal duet, *The Morning* (*c*1788). He began studying the violin very early, and at eight became a pupil of Salomon, who soon presented him as a prodigy.

His first public appearance was at Signora Salvini's benefit on 4 May 1796, when he played a violin concerto. Between 1798 and 1803 he played frequently at concerts in London and the provinces, and is said to have made two excursions to Paris. At Salomon's benefit on 10 March 1800 he played a violin and piano sonata with John Field. He also learnt the piano, which became his favourite instrument. At Corri's Edinburgh concerts in January 1803 he 'presided at the pianoforte', though only 17 years old, when Corri was incapacitated by an accident. Pinto was particularly idolized in Edinburgh; Campbell wrote prophetically in 1802:

Young Pinto is not only an admirable violin player, but also a first-rate performer on the grand piano forte: to excel on two instruments so widely different from each other, is a proof of genius and unwearied application very seldom to be met with. If dissipation, and consequent idleness, do not impede him in his career, what may not the musical world expect in his riper manhood . . . ?

But 'riper manhood' did not await Pinto. After the 1804 season he became increasingly ill; in November 1805 he was engaged for a series of concerts at Oxford, but was able to play in only one, his last public performance. A few months later he was dead, 'a martyr to dissipation'. The symptoms described by eyewitnesses suggest that in fact he died of tuberculosis.

Pinto was a remarkably handsome youth, and was intelligent and well informed on many subjects. He was apparently a tender-hearted person: he loved animals and birds, and he visited prisons to distribute money to the inmates. As a musician he excited an extraordinary degree of admiration from well-qualified critics. Samuel Wesley said that 'a greater musical Genius has not been known'; Salomon remarked that 'if he had lived and been able to resist the allurements of society, England would have had the honour of producing a second Mozart'; J.B. Cramer, William Ayrton and others joined the chorus of enthusiasm. The chief source of their admiration seems to have been Pinto's compositions. Yet within a few years of his death his name was almost forgotten by the public. There was a brief revival of interest in the 1840s and 1850s led by Sterndale Bennett, Davison and Hallé, then oblivion for a century. Only in the early 1960s did Pinto's importance as a composer begin to be recognized once again.

The most remarkable group of works comprises the sonatas for piano solo, more particularly the two sonatas op.3 and the Grand Sonata in C minor 'Inscribed to his Friend John Field' (1803); a Fantasia and Sonata in C minor, left unfinished and completed by Wesley and Wölfl; and three sets of Variations, one of which (in E minor, on 'Je crains de lui parler la nuit' from Grétry's *Richard Coeur-de-lion*) comes up to Pinto's best standards. These works are lavishly endowed with beautiful and original ideas; although the influences of Mozart, Dussek and Cramer are clearly discernible, there are many original touches to give freshness to a well-known idiom, and there are astonishing anticipations of Beethoven, Schubert and even Chopin. Indeed Ringer suggested a direct influence on Beethoven, and remarked, 'as a "prophet" of keyboard things to come Pinto is virtually without peer'. Some of the piano music is comparatively trivial, but in the Rondo and Minuetto printed by Ayrton in *The Harmonicon* the true Pinto is evident on a smaller scale. 'Either would do credit to the name of the greatest composer that ever lived', as Ayrton commented.

Pinto also wrote for his other instrument, the violin. At least one violin concerto is known to have existed (Davison described the manuscript in 1850), but it is lost, and we cannot know how Pinto would have written for orchestra. The violin duets are models of their kind (it was a very popular genre in Pinto's day), comparing favourably with Viotti's. Of the four sonatas for violin and piano, all are genuine duos rather than 'accompanied sonatas', and one (in G minor) is fully up to the standard of the best solo sonatas. Its first movement is 'passionate in mood, cogent in argument, and full of splendid thematic invention' (Geoffrey Bush; see Temperley, 1981).

The third group of compositions, the songs (or canzonets, as Pinto modishly called them), displays a vast range of expression, from the despair of *The Galley Slave* and *Eloisa to Abelard*, through the charming coyness of *Little Warbler* and the nostalgia of *Absence* and *Dear is my Little Native Vale*, to the classic repose of *Invocation to Nature*. The text and music are not always balanced, for this was not Pinto's own performing medium; some are embarrassingly naive in sentiment. But their promise is quite as tantalizing as that of the instrumental music. Only Schubert himself wrote more striking songs before the age of 20.

The speed and intensity with which Pinto produced all this remarkable music in a space of little more than three years, while at the same time pursuing an active career as a performer, seems to give the lie to the stories of his idleness and dissipation. He must have been an extraordinarily fast worker. The one autograph that survives, of an unfinished *Sonata for Scotland*, does show some evidence of haste and impatience; and Wesley, in his preface to the music he edited after Pinto's death, complained of his carelessness. The frequency of errors in his published music is unusually high for the time and place.

One other aspect of Pinto's musicianship has earned him frequent mention in books of music history: his place in the English Bach Revival. In about 1800 a small group of musicians in England, as well as in Germany, began to circulate and discuss the hitherto unknown music of J.S. Bach, and more particularly the preludes and fugues of *Das wohltemperirte Clavier*. No one has conclusively shown that A.F.C. Kollmann was the originator of this movement in England, though his claim would seem to be a strong one. But Samuel Wesley unequivocally stated in his *Memoirs* that it was Pinto who first showed him a copy of Bach's fugues. Other evidence connecting Pinto with Bach is slight, but suggestive; no Bach influence however can be detected in Pinto's music, except perhaps in the fugue of the posthumous Fantasia and Sonata in C minor.

WORKS
printed works published in London unless otherwise stated

Editions: *Four Canzonets and a Sonata . . . by the Late George Frederick Pinto*, ed. S. Wesley and J. Woelfl (Edinburgh, 1808) [W]

English Songs 1800–1860, ed. G. Bush and N. Temperley, MB, xliii (1979) [B]

George Frederick Pinto (1785–1806): Complete Works for Piano Solo, The London Pianoforte School 1766–1860, ed. N. Temperley, xiv (1985) [T]

PIANO
Waltz, G (c1800), T

3 Divertimentos, op.1 (1801), lost, advertised in *Morning Post* (5 Nov 1801)

'Cory Owen' as a Rondo, G (?1801), T

3 Favorite Airs with Variations, op.2 (?1802), T

2 Grand Sonatas, e♭, A, op.3 (1803), T; no.1 ed. N. Temperley (London, 1963)

A Grand Sonata, c (1803), T

Sonata for Scotland, G, 1803, unfinished, *D-Bsb*

3 Sonatas (Sonatinas), G, B♭, C, op.4 (1804–5), T

Fantasia and Sonata, c, ed. J. Woelfl, W, T

Minuetto, A♭, in *The Harmonicon*, ii (1824), 21–3, T

Rondo, E♭, in *The Harmonicon*, v (1827), 209–15, T

INSTRUMENTAL
3 Duetts, F, E♭, A, 2 vn, op.5 (1805)

3 Duetts, G, A, E, 2 vn (?1805)

3 Sonatas, g, A, B♭, pf, vn (?1806), ed. in RRMNETC, xxvii (1999)

Sonata, A, pf, vn/fl, ed. J. Woelfl, W

Concerto, vn, lost, MS described in *Musical World*, xxv (1850), 2

March, C, in 24 Short Pieces, org, transcr. W.J. Westbrook (1885)

Edns/arrs.: III Classical Duets, 2 vn (?1799); J. Haydn: Fugue, f, org/pf (?1804) [from Divertimento op.20/5]

SONGS
6 Canzonets (Birmingham, ?1803): It was a winter's evening (The Distress'd Mother); A shepherd lov'd a nymph so fair; The smiling plains; Nature! sweet mistress (Invocation to Nature), B; Little warbler, chearful be; From thee, Eliza, I must go, B

4 songs pubd singly (1804): Mine be a cot (The Wish); Say, lovely youth (Sapho to Phaon); Dear is my little native vale; Within that heart so good (L'amour timide)

4 canzonets, ed. S. Wesley, W: Oh! think on my fate (The Galley Slave); Alas! what pains (Absence); Soon as the letters (A Canzonett . . . from Pope's Abelard & Eloisa), B; Oh! he was almost speechless (A Canzonett on the Death of a Friend)

3 songs pubd singly (?1810): Oh Phyllyda fair is the morn; Say Celia why that harsh decree; Sweet blended with the smiles of hope

3 songs pubd singly (?1804), lost, mentioned in Gordon (1807): I live alone for love; In vain to forget the dear maid; No longer now I seek delight

The Tear (1805), lost, advertised in op.5

BIBLIOGRAPHY
NewmanSSB; SainsburyD

A. Campbell: *A Journey from Edinburgh through Parts of North Britain*, ii (London, 1802), 189–90

Caledonian Mercury (22 Jan 1803)

M. Gordon: *Authentic Memoirs of the late celebrated Geo. Frederick Pinto collected by a Friend to Genius and Merit* (Edinburgh, 1807); repr. (with alterations) in *The Harmonicon*, vi (1828), 215–16; *Musical World*, xiv (1840), 271–3

S. Wesley: 'Advertisement', *Four Canzonets and a Sonata . . . by the Late George Frederick Pinto* (Edinburgh, 1808)

Gentleman's Magazine, lxxxv/2 (1815), 569–70 [Obituary with memoir of J.P. Salomon]

S. Wesley: *Memoirs* (MS, c1836, GB-Lbl Add.27593), ff.42, 154

Musical World, xxii (1847), 266; xxv (1850), 2

N. Temperley: 'George Frederick Pinto, 1785–1806', *MT*, cvi (1965), 265–70

A.L. Ringer: 'Beethoven and the London Pianoforte School', *MQ*, lvi (1970), 742–58, esp. 754–7

N. Temperley, ed.: *Music in Britain: the Romantic Age 1800–1914* (London, 1981/R), 269, 382–3, 409–11

NICHOLAS TEMPERLEY

Pinto, Guiomar. *See* NOVAËS, GUIOMAR.

Pinto, Julia. Singer, daughter of SIBILLA.

Pinto, Luiz Álvares (*b* Recife, 1719; *d* Recife, ?1789). Brazilian composer, poet and teacher. Diniz discovered two of his works and substantial archival documentation of his activity in 1967; 19th- and early 20th-century Brazilian biographical dictionaries had reported his middle name as Alves, creating confusion with another musician active in the area in the early 19th century, Luiz Alves Pinto.

After elementary studies in Latin, rhetoric, philosophy and music Álvares Pinto went to Portugal about 1740 and studied theory and composition in Lisbon under Henrique da Silva Esteves Negrão (*d* 1787). According to de Mello he taught in 'some noble houses' in the Portuguese capital and was a cellist in the royal chapel ensemble. By 1762 he had returned to Pernambuco, married and become a member of the Irmandade de Nossa Senhora do Livramento. He then devoted himself to music and teaching; among his pupils were several composers and chapelmasters active until the mid-19th century. On the inauguration in 1782 of S Pedro dos Clérigos at Recife he was appointed its first *mestre de capela*. His last achievement for the city's musical life was the founding in about 1787 of the Irmandade de S Cecília dos Músicos, a sort of musicians' union in the Portuguese tradition.

Of the several compositions by Álvares Pinto mentioned in the biographical literature (liturgical works, hymns, Passion music and masses) only two are now known: a *Te Deum* (*c*1760) and a *Salve regina*, both in a private collection. Other works that may be attributed to him on stylistic grounds include two four-voice *Mandatum*, one of them a cappella, a *Miserere* and seven motets. The *Te Deum*, of which only the voice parts, continuo and one horn part remain, reveals in Diniz's edition (Recife, 1968) good technical command of counterpoint (the 'In te Domine' is a double fugue) and fine melodic invention. A manuscript *Arte de solfejar* bearing Álvares Pinto's name was completed at Recife in 1761 (*P-Ln*; facs. (Recife, 1977), ed. J.C. Diniz), and his three-act comedy *Amor mal correspondido*, written in verses and containing a sung chorus, was produced at the Recife Casa da Opera in 1780.

BIBLIOGRAPHY

A.J. de Mello: *Biografias de Joaquim Inácio de Lima, Luiz Alves Pinto e José Correia Picanço* (Recife, 1895)

J.A. Alegría, ed.: J. Mazza: *Dicionário biográfico de músicos portugueses* (Lisbon, 1945) [orig. pubd in *Ocidente*, xxiii–xxvi (1944–5)]

J.C. Diniz: 'Revelação de um compositor brasileiro do século XVIII', *YIAMR*, iv (1968), 82–97

J.C. Diniz: *Músicos pernambucanos do passado*, i (Recife, 1969)

M. Marcondes, ed.: *Enciclopédia da música brasileira: erudita, folclórica, popular* (São Paulo, 1977, 2/1998)

G. Béhague: *Music in Latin American: an Introduction* (Englewood Cliffs, NJ, 1979)

V. Mariz: *História da música no Brasil* (Rio de Janeiro, 1981, 4/1994)

GERARD BÉHAGUE

Pinto, Thomas (bap. Cripplegate, London, 2 Feb 1727; *d* ?Dublin, Dec 1782/Jan 1783). English violinist. His father, William (Guglielmo) Pinto, was a civil servant of Naples who fled to England for political reasons. It is not known who taught Thomas the violin; as a child he played in Corelli's concertos, and led the band at concerts in Edinburgh. He soon became one of the most prominent violinists in Britain, playing both as soloist and leader in many London and provincial concerts and theatres. He replaced Giardini in 1757 as principal violinist at the King's Theatre, London. Having lost £2000 in a joint speculation with Samuel Arnold (they had bought shares in Marylebone Gardens) he withdrew to Ireland, where he was leader of the band at Smock Alley Theatre, Dublin, from 1773 to 1779. He then seems to have retired to Edinburgh, possibly returning to Dublin later still. About 1770 he published a set of six sonatas for violin and bass.

Pinto married first Anna Maria Sibylla Catharina Groneman (b.1721), a German soprano resident in London, and second (16 October 1766) Charlotte Brent, the well-known soprano. His daughter by the first marriage, Julia Pinto, married Samuel Sanders and was the mother of George Frederick Pinto.

BIBLIOGRAPHY

M. Gordon: *Authentic Memoirs of the late celebrated Geo. Frederick Pinto collected by a Friend to Genius and Merit* (Edinburgh, 1807); repr. (with alterations) in *The Harmonicon*, vi (1828), 215–16; repr. in *Musical World*, xiv (1840), 271–3

S. Sadie: 'Music in the Home II', *The Eighteenth Century*, ed. H. Diack Johnstone and R. Fiske (Oxford, 1990), 313–54

A. Bos-Bliek and J. Wentz: 'De trompet en het rad: de lotgevallen van de 18de-eeuwse musicus Albertus Gronemen', *Jaarboek die Haghe* (1997), 145

NICHOLAS TEMPERLEY

Pintscher, Matthias (*b* Marl, 29 Jan 1971). German composer. While still at school, he acquired experience as an instrumentalist and as an occasional conductor of the youth orchestra in his native city. His first compositions, written as an adolescent, resulted from his fascination with the symphony orchestra. He began studying composition with Klebe in 1989 and continued his studies with Trojahn in Düsseldorf (1992–3); Henze also gave him support and encouragement. His early success is reflected in his many honours, which include composition prizes, stipends and commissions from famous opera houses, orchestras, conductors and soloists. He established his reputation as a conductor with the Berlin Staatsoper's première of his ballet *Gesprungene Glocken* in 1994.

Pintscher's music, with its attention to tone colour and its response to compositional impulse, relies on poetic force. Ideas from the visual arts (as in *Figura I–II*) and literature suggest associative structures and dimensions that he translates into music, transforming the intensity gradient of objects or metaphors into atmospheric densities of sound. He has described many of his poetry-inspired works (such as *Monumento I–V*, after Rimbaud) as 'speech-music'; these compositions seek a way through the colour of poetic language into the heart of the poetic scene, while acknowledging that such an ideal cannot be achieved. This sense of imaginary drama led him to compose his first opera, *Thomas Chatterton* (1994–7), on a subject who is, in the words of the composer, 'a creative figure destroyed by his own ordinary nature'.

WORKS
(*selective list*)

Stage: Gesprungene Glocken (ballet, V.G. Büchner, J. Paul, A. Rimbaud), 1993–4, Berlin, 25 April 1994, orch suite, 1996; Thomas Chatterton (op, 2, C.H. Henneberg and Pintscher, after H.H. Jahnn), 1994–7, Dresden, 25 May 1998

Orch: Invocazioni, 1991, rev. 1993; La metamorfosi di Narciso, vc, chbr orch, 1992; Devant une neige (Monumento II), 1993; Dunkles Feld – Berückung, 1993, rev. 1998; Choc (Monumento IV), 1996; 5 Orchesterstücke, 1997

Vocal: a twilight's song (e.e. cummings), S, 7 insts, 1997; Monumento V (Rimbaud), 8 female vv, 3 vc, ens, 1998; Hérodiade-Fragmente (St. Mallarmé), dramatic scene, S, orch, 1999

Chbr and solo inst: Str Qt no.2, 1990; Monumento I, pf, 1991; Omaggio a Giovanni Paisiello, vn, 1991, rev. 1995; Partita, vc, 1991; Str Qt no.4 'Ritratto di Gesualdo', 1992; Tableau/Miroir, pf, 1992; 7 Bagatellen, b cl, 1993; Départ (Monumento III), b cl, trbn, vn, vc, pf, 2 perc, 1993; dernier espace avec introspecteur, accdn, vc, 1994; Nacht. Mondschein, pf, 1994 [from ballet Gesprungene Glocken]; Figura II/Frammento, str qt, 1997; Figura I, accdn, str qt, 1998; In nomine, va, 1999

Principal publisher: Bärenreiter

BIBLIOGRAPHY

M. Töpel: 'Matthias Pintscher: Zweiundzwanzig und schon drei Sinfonien', *Musica*, xlvii (1993), 163–4

R. Kager: 'Theatralik im Blut: der Komponist Matthias Pintscher', *NZM*, Jg.159 (1998), 42–4

M. Töpel: 'Confidence in the Power of the Poetic: the Composer Matthias Pintscher', *Tempo*, no.205 (1998), 12–14

MICHAEL TÖPEL

Pinza, Ezio (Fortunato) (*b* Rome, 18 May 1892; *d* Stamford, CT, 9 May 1957). Italian bass. Having studied at the Bologna Conservatory, he made his début in 1914 in Soncino, near Crema, as Oroveso in *Norma*. After World War I he began to sing in the principal Italian houses: at Rome in 1920 as King Mark in *Tristan und Isolde*, and at La Scala, under Toscanini, from 1922 to 1924 in various roles, including Pogner, Ramfis, Colline, Raimondo (in *Lucia di Lammermoor*) and Tigellino in the première of Boito's *Nerone*. His appearance at the Metropolitan Opera as the Pontifex Maximus in Spontini's *La vestale* in 1926 began a period of 22 consecutive years as a leading bass in New York, where he sang 50 roles and became a great favourite of the public, as much for his handsome presence, engaging personality and spirited acting as for his beautiful and cultivated *basso cantante*. Besides all the main Italian bass roles (among which his Padre Guardiano in *La forza del destino* and Fiesco in *Simon Boccanegra* deserve special mention), he was outstandingly successful as Don Giovanni and as Figaro; he sang also in many French operas, occasionally essayed Wagner in German, and undertook the title role of *Boris Godunov* in Italian. Between 1930 and 1939 he sang in five Covent Garden seasons, and during the same decade he gave numerous performances as Don Giovanni and Figaro at the Salzburg Festival. After leaving the Metropolitan, at the age of 56, he began a second career in musical comedy, operetta and musical films, scoring an enormous success on Broadway in *South Pacific* (1949, Rodgers and Hammerstein). Pinza was unquestionably the most richly gifted and most accomplished Italian bass of his day, as is demonstrated by his numerous recordings, especially those made for Victor (1927–30), when his voice was in its prime.

BIBLIOGRAPHY

GV (J.B. Richards; J.P. Kenyon)

E. Pinza and R. Magidoff: *Ezio Pinza: an Autobiography* (New York, 1958/R)

J.B. Richards, J.P. Kenyon and J. McPherson: 'Ezio Pinza', *Record Collector*, xxvi (1980–81), 51–95, 101–37 [incl. discography]

J.B. Steane: Singers of the Century (London, 1996), 56–60

DESMOND SHAWE-TAYLOR/R

Pinzauti, Leonardo (*b* Florence, 17 Nov 1926). Italian music critic. He studied the violin first at the Florence Conservatory with V. Papini (diploma 1944), and continued studying the violin with Sandro Materassi and harmony and counterpoint with Roberto Lupi (1944–50). In 1950 he took an arts degree from the University of Florence in music history with Torrefranca, and then became Torrefranca's assistant (1950–53). He began his career as a music critic with the *Giornale del mattino* (1949–57), of which he became managing editor (1960–63). He became music critic of *La nazione* in 1965 and *Il resto del Carlino* in 1967; the same year he joined the editorial board of the newly founded *Nuova rivista musicale italiana*, to which he contributed a series of sympathetic interviews with contemporary composers, including Berio, Boulez and Dallapiccola. He taught history of music at the Florence Conservatory (1970–93) and was a member of the government central commission for theatre and tourism; he also acted as musical consultant for RAI television (1965–83). His main areas of interest are Italian Renaissance lute music, the restoration of instruments, Puccini, and Italian 18th-century and contemporary composers. He has received awards from the National Academy and the governments of Italy and Salzburg.

WRITINGS

Da tamburo a tamburo: breve storia degli strumenti musicali (Florence, 1954)

Gli arnesi della musica (Florence, 1965, 2/1973)

'Il critico musicale e giornalista', 'Cronologia della vita', 'Elenco delle opere', 'Bibliografia', *Approdo musicale*, no.21 (1966), 115–57 [Pizzetti issue]

'Prospetto cronologico della vita di F. Busoni', 'Catalogo delle composizioni generali', 'Bibliografia essenziale', *Approdo musicale*, no.22 (1966), 137–51 [Busoni issue]

Il Maggio musicale fiorentino dalla prima alla trentesima edizione (Florence, 1967)

'Prospettive per uno studio sulla musica a Firenze nell'Ottocento', *NRMI*, ii (1968), 255–73

'Un critico dell'Ottocento: G. Alessandro Biaggi', *NRMI*, vii (1973), 388–401

Puccini: una vita (Florence, 1974, 2/1975 as *Giacomo Puccini*)

'Un inedito di Dallapiccola', *NRMI*, ix (1975), 248–56

'Conservazione de restauro degli antichi strumenti', *NRMI*, x (1976), 617–22

'Vittorio Gui a Firenze', *NRMI*, x (1976), 204–10

La musica e le cose (Florence, 1977) [diary of musical activities 1962–75]

Musicisti d'oggi: venti colloqui (Turin, 1978)

'Torrefranca a Firenze', *Musica italiana del primo Novecento: Florence 1980*, 205–17

L'Accademia musicale chigiana da Boito a Boulez (Milan, 1982)

'Mahler e Puccini', *NRMI*, xvi (1982), 330–39

'Le due "stupende lettere" del Petrarca e il romanticismo di Giuseppe Verdi', *Quadrivium*, xxvii (1986), 115–21

'Salisburgo dopo Karajan', *NRMI*, xxiv (1990), 293–7

Variazioni su tema: ritratti di musicisti dal vivo e a memoria (Florence, 1991)

Ezio Pinza in the title role of Mozart's 'Don Giovanni'

'Giacomo Puccini's Trittico and the Twentieth Century', *The Puccini Companion*, ed. W. Weaver and S. Puccini (New York, 1994), 228–43

Storia del maggio: dalla nascita della 'Stabile Orchestrale Fiorentina' (1928) al festival del 1993 (Lucca, 1994)

BIBLIOGRAPHY

D. Spini, ed.: *Studi e fantasie per i settant'anni di Leonardo Pinzauti* (Florence, 1996) [incl. D. Spini: 'A Leonardo', xi–xii]

CAROLYN GIANTURCO/TERESA M. GIALDRONI

Pinzón (Urrea), Jesús (*b* Bucaramanga, 10 Aug 1928). Colombian composer. He came from a musical family and received his first degree in composition and conducting at the National University of Colombia in 1967. He was head of the music department at the University of America, Bogotá (1968–71), and directed the music department of the National Pedagogical University (1972–82). He has taught composition at the National University of Colombia (1967–91) and conducted the Bogotá PO from its foundation in 1967. An active member of the Centro de Estudios Folklóricos y Musicales of the National University (1967–70), his study of vernacular music of the Andean region is one of the first serious writings about traditional music in Colombia. His interest in indigenous music and ritual has been a constant inspiration throughout his life, as is his preference for 'endogenous' music, by which he means music composed for players who know nothing about music theory, often performed on native instruments like the marimba and bombo. He uses modern graphic notation and has created the concept of 'sonoptics', i.e. music to be seen and heard as an extension of conventional notational and improvisatory practices, a concept he discussed at an international symposium held in Rome in 1972. His multi-faceted production has been acclaimed in Sweden, Tokyo, London, Baltimore, Cuba and throughout Latin America.

WORKS
(selective list)

Orch: Sym. no.1, 1966; Estudio, 1970; Estructuras, 1971; Grafico 1, 1974; Disertación filarmonica, 1982; Conc., timp, orch, 1984; Movimiento, 1987; Pf Conc., 1990; The Orchestra, 1992 [didactic work]; Vn Conc., 1995; Creación vallenata, 1996

Vocal: Ñee Iñati, SATB, 1971; Sym. no.2 'Eucaristía', chorus, orch, 1971; 3 creaciones endógenas, female vv, ww, 1972; Pasión y Resurrección de Cristo, B, A, SATB, orch, 1977; La revolución de los comuneros (incid music, Pinzón), S, 6 actors, orch, 1977; Bico anamo, S, SATB, ww qnt, perc, 1979; Cant. por la paz, S, SATB, orch, 1981; Salve Regina, children's vv, org, 1981; Goé Payarí, SATB, orch, 1982; Relato de Sergio Stepansky, B solo, str, 1982; Toccata, chorus, 1989; Evocación huitota, SATB, 1995; Ha nacido el Niño, villancico, SATB, 1995; Las voces silenciosas de los muertos (J. Asunción Silva), S, 4 perc, 1996

Chbr and solo inst: Rítmica 1, fl, db, pf, 1971; Exploraciones, cl, str, 1972; Test psicológico-musica, 3 perfs., 1972; Juego de rondó, perc, 1973 [for children]; Tripartita, str, 1979; Fantasía, pf, 1980; Invención dórica, pf, 1980; Rito cubeo, ww, perc, 1983; Estilos, pf, 1989; Ritmología, perc, 1990; Expresión latina, vn, vc, pf, 1992; Variaciones sin tema, va, vc, db, 1994; Todo está cumplido, str, 1996; Rítmica no.5, 5 perc, 1996

WRITINGS

with A. Pardo Tovar: *Rítmica y melódica del folclor chocoano* (Bogotá, 1961)

'La musica vernácula del Altiplano de Bogotá', *Boletín interamericano de música*, no.77 (1970), 15–30

BIBLIOGRAPHY

C. Barreiro: *Música sin hibiciones* (Bogotá, 1991)

E.A. Duque: 'Jesús Pinzón Urrea: músico', *Revista escala*, no.12 (1986)

E.A. Duque: 'La cultura musical en Colombia, siglos diecinueve y veinte', *Gran enciclopedia de Colombia*, ed. J.E. Melo, vi (Bogotá, 1993), 232–3

Compositores de América/Composers of the Americas, ed. Pan American Union, xvii (Washington DC, 1971)

J.I. Perdomo Escobar: *Historia de la música en Colombia* (Bogotá, 5/1980), 178

SUSANA FRIEDMANN

Pio [Pius], Francesco (*b* Parma, probably *c*1590; *d* Parma, *c*1660). Italian composer. He was a priest. In 1621 he was a teacher at the Collegio di S Caterina, Parma, and from 1655 until his death held an ecclesiastical position at Parma Cathedral (see N. Pelicelli: 'Musicisti in Parma nel secolo XVII [part 4]', *NA*, x, 1933, pp.233–48, esp. 237–8). Much of his small output, which is entirely of church music, consists of double-choir works in the Venetian manner.

WORKS

Il primo libro de salmi concertati, 9vv, et non concertati, 8vv, con una messa concertata, 9vv, bc (Venice, 1621)
Liber primus motectorum, 2–5vv, bc (org) (Venice, 1624)
Liber secundus et secunda pars psalmorum, 8–9vv, bc (org) (Venice, 1625)
1 work, 1628[3]

ARGIA BERTINI

Piobaireachd (Scots Gael.: 'piping'; from *piobair*: 'piper', *eachd*: suffix of function). The term, or its anglicized form 'pibroch', is used in English to denote a specific category of music for the Scottish Highland bagpipes. *See* PIBROCH and SCOTLAND, §II, 6(i).

Piochi, Cristofano [Cristoforo] (*b* Foligno; *d* Siena, in or after 1675). Italian composer and teacher. In 1612 (April–August) he was organist of S Maria in Trastevere, Rome. He was *maestro di cappella* at Amelia from 6 November 1619 to 15 September 1623, and later held similar posts at Faenza and Orvieto. He was *maestro di cappella* of Siena Cathedral from 1668 to at least 1675, and during these years he ran a school for counterpoint at Siena. His three volumes of ricercares and his theoretical writing all no doubt stemmed from his teaching. His six earlier collections of music consist mainly of motets, all of them in the concertato style for small forces with continuo.

WORKS

Cantiones sacrae … liber I, 2–4vv, bc (Orvieto, 1623); Fontes et omnia and Ave rex noster in Catalucci
Il primo libro delli madrigali concertati … con alcune arie nel fine, 2–4vv, bc (Venice, 1626)
Sacrae cantiones … liber II, 2–3vv, bc (Rome, 1637)
Sacrae cantiones … liber III, 2–3vv, bc (Rome, 1651)
Motecta, liber IV, 2–4vv, bc (Bologna, 1668)
Responsoria feria quarta, quinta, & sexta hebdomadae sanctae decantenda, 4vv, bc ad lib (Bologna, 1669)
Ricercari … utilissimi a chi desidera imparare presto a cantare e sonare, libro I, 2–3vv (Bologna, 1671)
Ricercari, libro II, 2vv, op.8 (Bologna, 1673)
Il terzo libro dei ricercari, 3vv, op.9 (Bologna, 1675)

WRITINGS

Compendio in pratica et in teorica delle principali regole da sapersi per un musico, utile sì nel cantare come nel comporre, da diversi autori raccolto, I-Bc, dated 1703 [by G. Chiti, partly based on writings by Piochi]

BIBLIOGRAPHY

EitnerQ
R. Morrocchi: *La musica in Siena* (Siena, 1886/R)
G. Catalucci: 'Cristoforo Piochi maestro di cappella della cattedrale di Amelia (1619–1623)', *Esercizi: musica e spettacolo*, vii (1984), 47–61

NIGEL FORTUNE/RODOBALDO TIBALDI

Pionne (Fr.). A type of bird organ. *See* BIRD INSTRUMENTS.

Pionnier [Pyonnier, Pionerio], **Joannes** (*d* Loreto, 17 Nov 1573). French composer, active in Italy. After holding a singer's post at the Santa Casa, Loreto, for several years, Pionnier became director of the choir on 1 March 1541 and *maestro di cappella* in 1564. He retained this position until his death and was succeeded by Costanzo Porta (G. Tebaldini, *L'archivio musicale della Cappella lauretana*, Loreto, 1921).

Antonio Gardano published three books of Pionnier's motets in 1548, 1561 and 1564, of which only the first, containing 19 motets in five parts, survives. Six motets for five voices, probably duplicating Gardano's prints, and two for six voices appeared in collections between 1539 and 1558 (RISM 1539³; ed. in SCMot, xiii, 1993, 1550², 1554¹⁰, 1555¹⁰, 1556⁸ and 1558⁴). Additional motets are found in manuscripts at *CZ-HKm, D-Rp, I-Bc, TVd, PL-WRu* and *S-Sk*. A single madrigal was included in two of Vincenzo Ruffo's madrigal books (1554²⁹, 1555³¹). Although Pionnier dealt competently with the problems of an imitative style in musical construction, he lacked complete compositional mastery. (There is a modern edition of *Quem dicunt homines* in Cw, xciv, 1963.)

BARTON HUDSON

Piovani, Nicola (*b* Rome, 26 May 1946). Italian composer. He studied privately and after graduating in the piano at the Milan Conservatory (1967) became a pupil of Manos Hadjidakis (1969). Of his more than 80 film scores, the first was for Silvano Agosti. A spare, personal idiom – contemporary but also suffused with archaic traces – is to be found in his work with Marco Bellochio (*Nel nome del Padre*, 1970; *Sbatti il mostro in prima pagina*, 1973; *Marcia trionfale*, 1975) and the Taviani brothers (*La notte di San Lorenzo*, 1982; *Kaos*, 1984; *Good Morning Babylon*, 1987; *Il sole anche di notte*, 1990). His scores for Fellini (*Ginger and Fred*, 1985; *L'intervista*, 1987; *La voce della luna*, 1990), however, are memorable more for the prestige they brought than for their expressive qualities. As well as other film collaborations with Sergio Citti, Mario Monicelli, Giuseppe Bertolucci, Luigi Magni, Nanni Moretti and Bigas Luna, Piovani has written a considerable amount of incidental music (for Carlo Cecchi, Luca De Filippo, Maurizio Scaparro and Vittorio Gassman) and has had great theatrical success with his *racconti musicali* on texts by Vincenzo Cerami (*La Cantata del Fiore*, 1988; *La Cantata del Buffo*, 1989). Other works include a musical, *I setti re di Roma* (1989), to a libretto by Luigi Magni, a ballet, *Fellini* (1995), further *racconti musicali*, *Il signor Novecento* (1992) and *Canti di scena* (1993), and chamber music, including an octet (*Quattro canti senza parole*), a piano trio (*Il demone meschino*), a flute and piano duo (*Ballata epica*) and a saxophone quartet (*L'assassino*). He has been awarded a Nastro d'argento.

BIBLIOGRAPHY
G. Zaccagnini, ed.: 'Intervista a Nicola Piovani', *Piano Time*, no.95 (1991), 23–6

SERGIO MICELI

Piozzi, Gabriele Mario (*b* Quinzano, Venice, 8 June 1740; *d* Dymerchion [Tremerchion], N. Wales, 26 March 1809). Italian tenor, composer and harpsichordist. Escaping from a large family, he found a patron in the wealthy Marquis D'Araciel at Milan. After travelling on the Continent he went to England, about 1776–7, where he made a great impression as a concert singer. Burney reported (*Rees's Cyclopaedia*, 1819–20) that his singing was not sufficiently strong for the theatre but that his 'exquisite' voice and style were modelled on the famous Pacchierotti (who had not yet arrived in London). For several years he was active in England as a singer, teacher and pianist, publishing during that period six collections, mostly for keyboard with accompaniments. Through his friendship with Burney, Piozzi gained access to Dr Johnson's circle where he met the family of Henry Thrale, a wealthy brewer. Piozzi then taught singing to Thrale's daughters and became a regular at social events. After Thrale's death in 1781 Piozzi became increasingly intimate with Mrs Thrale, a woman not only of wealth but also of literary accomplishments; eventually, in 1784, despite resistance from both family and friends, the two were married. Piozzi had amassed a substantial fortune in England, and with this advantageous marriage he was able to discontinue his career as a professional musician, though he occasionally performed in private concerts. After an extended wedding trip (1784–7) that included a visit to Italy, the happy couple settled in London and then at the Thrale mansion at Streatham. In 1795 they retired to their new villa 'Brynbella' in Wales. Piozzi relished his life as a country gentleman, but his last years were marred by severe attacks of gout. Both Piozzi and later his wife were buried beneath the medieval church at Dymerchion.

Piozzi's instrumental works are of only moderate interest. The sonatas are improvisatory and prolix. On the one hand, the basic ideas are highly conventional; on the other, Piozzi strained after novelty in expression, exploiting chromaticism and the dynamic nuance made possible by the piano. In the sonatas the violin is usually dispensable, especially in op.5. The quartets op.1 are essentially harpsichord concertos with alternation of tutti and solo sections.

WORKS

printed works published in London, unless otherwise stated

op.
1   6 quatuor, hpd, 2 vn, vc (*c*1778)
2   6 Sonatas, hpd/pf, vn acc. (*c*1778)
3   A Second Sett of 6 Sonatas, hpd/pf, vn acc. (*c*1779)
4   6 quatuor, 2 vn, va, vc (*c*1780)
5   6 Sonatas, hpd/pf, vn acc. (1781)
6   3 Duets and 3 Canzonets, 1–2vv, kbd (1783)
I vescovi per patria bresciani (cant.), Brescia, 1764, ?lost
Fremia l'inverno (serenata, L. Pignotti), in *Florence Miscellany* (Florence, 1785), 218
La contraddizione (canzonet), in *Musical Library*, iv (1837/*R*)

BIBLIOGRAPHY
BurneyH; EitnerQ; FétisB; GerberL
ABC Dario Musico (Bath, 1780)
H.L. Piozzi: *Observations and Reflections made in the Course of a Journey through France, Italy and Germany* (London, 1789), ed. H. Barrows (Ann Arbor, 1967)
J.L. Clifford: *Hester Lynch Piozzi (Mrs. Thrale)* (Oxford, 1941, 2/1952/*R*)
P.A. Scholes: *The Great Dr Burney* (Oxford, 1948/*R*)
R.R. Kidd: *The Sonata for Keyboard with Violin Accompaniment in England (1750–1790)* (diss., Yale U., 1967), 299
W. McCarthy: *Hester Thrale Piozzi: Portrait of a Literary Woman* (Chapel Hill, NC, 1985)
E.A. and L.D. Bloom: *The Piozzi Letters* (London, 1989) [incl. portrait of Piozzi]
V. Rumbold: 'Music Aspires to Letters: Charles Burney, Queeny Thrale and the Streatham Circle', *ML*, lxxiv (1993), 24

RONALD R. KIDD

Pipa. Pear-shaped plucked lute of China and Korea. It corresponds to the Japanese BIWA and is related to the Vietnamese *đàn tỳ ba*.

1. The Chinese *pipa*. 2. The Korean *pip'a*.

1. THE CHINESE 'PIPA'.   There are two different theories on the origin of the term *pipa*. Some Han dynasty sources state that '*pipa*' originally referred to two different plucking techniques of the right hand: *pi* meant 'to play forward' (to the player's left) with the right hand, while *pa* meant 'to play backward' (to the player's right), equivalent to the modern terms *tan* and *tiao*. But since these etymologies have not been found in any other context, and it is believed that this kind of instrument was introduced into China from a foreign country, some other scholars think *pipa* may be a transliteration of a foreign term for the instrument's name.

Pipa was a general name for various types of plucked lutes from the Han to the Tang dynasties (roughly from the 2nd century BCE to the 9th century CE), including plucked lutes with long or short neck and round or pear-shaped soundbox. According to historical literature, a long straight-necked lute called *pipa* appeared in the Han dynasty (206 BCE–220 CE). It had a round soundbox with four strings and 12 frets. Later, it was called *Han pipa*, or *ruanxian* after the name of an outstanding performer in the 3rd century BCE. The earliest image of a musician playing this straight-necked lute is on a miniature ceramic vessel dated 260 CE. The modern *ruan* is basically the same in shape.

According to a legend described in the poem *Pipa fu* by Fu Xuan (217–78 CE), another type of *pipa* called *xiantao* with a long straight neck and small round soundbox appeared even earlier. Also called *Qin pipa*, the *xiantao* ('string *tao*') was said to have been developed under the Qin dynasty (221–207 BCE) by fixing strings on to a small drum called *tao*, struck by two beads attached by strings to either side of the drum and moved by means of a long handle. But the source was written over 400 years after the Qin dynasty, and there is no supporting archaeological or iconographical evidence for the *xiantao*. Another type called the *Qin-Han pipa* or *Qin-Hanzi*, which appeared in the Sui dynasty (581–618 CE), may be seen as a variation on the straight-necked *Han-pipa*, with a smaller round soundbox and a longer neck. This is considered the ancestor of the modern *qinqin* ('Qin instrument').

The archetype of the modern *pipa*, which has a pear-shaped soundbox, was introduced into China from India in 346–53 CE, but its origin was in ancient Persia. In China this type of *pipa* was known as the *quxiang pipa* ('*pipa* with a crooked neck' – actually a short-necked lute with reversed pegbox). This instrument had four strings and four frets, and was held transversely and plucked with a plectrum. It appears in much early iconography in China, such as the celestial deva-musician playing the *pipa* in a fresco of the Northern Wei dynasty (386–534 CE) in cave no.435 at Dunhuang. During the Sui and Tang dynasties, the *quxiang pipa* was used in various courtly ensembles to accompany singing and dancing, as well as for solo music. Another similar instrument popular in courtly ensembles of the Sui and Tang dynasties was the *wuxian pipa* ('five-string pipa'), also known as *wuxian*. It was similar in shape to the *quxiang pipa*, but smaller. It is thought to have been developed in India (rather than Persia: see Lin, 1962), and was introduced to China from there in the 4th century CE. Some early iconographical

representations may also been seen, such as the celestial deva-musician in a Northern Wei fresco from Dunhuang (Liu and Yuan, 1988, p.62). It disappeared gradually after the Tang dynasty. Versions of the *ruanxian*, *quxiang pipa* and *wuxian pipa* were introduced to Japan during the Tang dynasty.

After the Tang dynasty the instrument commonly known as *pipa* was the four-string *quxiang pipa*. Gradual changes occurred throughout the succeeding millennium: the playing position changed from horizontal to vertical; fingernails, real or false, replaced the plectrum; the number of frets increased from 4 to 14 or 16, and in the 20th century to 17, 24, 29 or 30. Contexts, too, changed: since the Song dynasty, the *pipa* was extensively used among folk musicians and the common people to accompany emerging genres of narrative singing and regional opera. (For living traditions *see* CHINA, §IV, 4(ii)(c).)

The back body of the modern *pipa* is made of teak and the soundboard of *wutong* wood (*Firmiana platanifolia*). The upper frets (on the neck) and the tuning pegs are of ivory, buffalo horn or wood; the lower frets (on the body) are usually of bamboo. The head of the *pipa* is slanted slightly: its middle part is always bent backwards and its top part can be bent either forwards or backwards. The head is usually in the form of a symbolic object (such as a dragon's head, a phoenix's tail or a bat's head) and its middle part is sometimes inlaid with a piece of jade for decoration. The strings were traditionally made of twisted silk and now often of metal or nylon.

A series of manuscripts dated 933 CE, found in Dunhuang at the beginning of the 20th century and now

1. Pipa (four-string lute) of China played by Tsun-Yuen Lui

TABLE 1: Pitches used in *Chengtiiao* tuning

strings				
4th	3rd	2nd	1st	(open-string pitches)
5	1	2	5	
6	2	3	6	
7b	3b	4#	7b	
7	3	4	7	
1	4	5	1	
2	5	6	2	
3b	6b	7b	3b	
3	6	7	3	
4	7b	1	4	16 frcts
5	1	2	5	
6	2	3	6	
7	3	4#	7	
1	4	5	1	
2	5	6	2	
3	6	7	3	
		1	4	
		2	5	

in the Bibliothèque Nationale in Paris, is considered to contain 25 melodies in *pipa* tablature, although their interpretation remains controversial. Most traditional *pipa* scores surviving today use the standard *gongche* notation. Since the 1920s *pipa* music has also been notated in the cipher notation widely adopted in China since then.

Traditionally, the range of the *pipa* is about three octaves (normally from A to f#″ or a″) with 14 or 16 frets. The 16-fret *pipa* has two more high-pitch frets than the 14-fret one. Most of these frets produce intervals approximately equal to Western whole tones (W) and semitones (S), although two frets, the 11th and the 15th (or the 7th and the 11th lower frets), produce ¾ tones or 'neutral tones'. The scheme from the open string upwards is: W S S S W S S S W W ¾ ¾ W W ¾ ¾. Traditionally, there are several different tunings for the four open strings of the *pipa*. The most common is called *zhengdiao* or *xiaogong diao*. The intervals between the four strings are a 4th, 2nd and 4th; today the four strings are normally tuned as A, d, e, a. In this tuning, the strings on the 16-fret *pipa* have the series of pitches shown in Table 1. Although the fretting and tuning systems represent the basic pitches available on the instruments, microtonal changes of pitch of up to a semitone are often effected by pulling or pushing the string sideways. In the 1920s and 30s some musicians rearranged the frets of the *pipa* based on the 12-tone equal temperament, making a 24-fret *pipa*. Since the 1950s this kind of *pipa* has become popular, and the number of the frets increased to 29 or 30, with a range from A to d‴ or e‴. Intervals between all frets are semitones, except that between the 29th and 30th which

is a whole tone. Although factory-made forms are increasingly common, traditional regional forms are still played, such as the *pipa* of *nanguan* in Fujian and that of balladeers in northern Shaanxi.

BIBLIOGRAPHY

S. Kishibe: 'The Origin of the P'i-p'a', *Transactions of the Asiatic Society of Japan*, 2nd ser., xix (1941), 260–304

L.E.R. Picken: 'The Origin of the Short Lute', *GSJ*, viii (1955), 32–42

Chang Renxia: 'Han-Tang shiqi xiyu pipa de shuru he fazhan' [The introduction and development of the *pipa* of the western regions in the Han and Tang periods], *Minzu yinyue yanjiu lunwenji*, i (Beijing, 1956), 14–20

[Lin Qiansan] K. Hayashi: *Dongya yueqi kao* [Study of musical instruments in East Asia] (Beijing, 1962/R)

Yang Yinliu: *Zhongguo gudai yinyue shigao* [Draft history of ancient Chinese music] (Beijing, 1981)

R. Wolpert: 'The Five-Stringed Lute in East Asia', *Musica asiatica*, iii, ed. L. Picken (1981), 97–106

Wu Ben: 'Chuantong pipa de teshu pinwei jiqi dui yuequ de yingxiang' [The special frets of the traditional *pipa* and their influence on its music], *Zhongguo yinyue* (1986), no.2, pp.50–52

Liu Dongsheng and Yuan Quanyou, eds.: *Zhongguo yinyue shi tujian* [Pictorial guide to the history of Chinese music] (Beijing, 1988) [YYS pubn]

Liu Dongsheng, ed.: *Zhongguo yueqi tujian* [Pictorial guide to Chinese instruments] (Ji'nan, 1992) [YYS pubn]

Zheng Zurang: 'Handai pipa'qiyuan shiliao jiqi fenxi yanjiu kaozheng' [Analysis and textual criticism of sources on the origin of the Han dynasty *pipa*], *Zhongguo yinyuexue* (1993), no.4, pp.43–8

2. THE KOREAN 'PIP'A'. There were two types of *pip'a* in Korea, both now obsolete: the four-string *tang-pip'a* ('Chinese *pip'a*') and the five-string *hyang-pip'a* ('native *pip'a*', also known as *ohyŏn*: 'five strings'). According to the treatise *Akhak kwebŏm* (1493), the *tang-pip'a* was about 128 cm long and had a neck which bent backwards at the pegbox; there were four large convex frets on the neck and eight thin ones on the soundtable (fig.2). In performances of *tangak* ('Chinese music') the player used a fan-shaped wooden plectrum and only the four frets on the neck; in *hyangak* ('native music') he used finger-picks and the frets on the soundtable as well as those on the neck. Tunings were various, but an example of a *tangak* tuning is A–d–G–g and of a *hyangak* tuning Bb–eb–eb–bb.

The *tang-pip'a* was used only for *tangak* during the Koryŏ period (918–1392), but in the 15th century it was adapted for *hyangak* as well. The *Akhak kwebŏm* demonstrates various tunings and modes, plus a certain number of tablature symbols; pieces notated in *pip'a* tablature occur as early as the *An Sang kŭmbo* ('An Sang's zither book') of 1572. Surviving instruments differ in a few details from the description in the *Akhak kwebŏm*.

The *hyang pip'a*, according to the *Akhak kwebŏm*, was 104 cm long and had a straight neck tapering gradually from the body. There were ten frets. Players used a pencil-shaped plectrum (*sultae*), as on the zither *kŏmun'go*, and nearly all the frets. As with the *tang-pip'a*, various tunings were used, a typical one being A–e–e–a–c#′. The *hyang-pip'a* was one of the three main string instruments (together with *kŏmun'go* and *kayagŭm*) of the Unified Silla period (668–935). The Chinese *Sui shu* ('History of the Sui dynasty') indicates that the Korean ensemble at the Sui court in the late 6th century included a five-string instrument. A five-string *biwa* (*gogenbiwa*) of the 8th century, in the Shōsōin repository in Nara, Japan, fits the description of the *hyang-pip'a* in the *Akhak kwebŏm*.

The *hyang-pip'a* tradition was marginally preserved by *kŏmun'go* players until 1930, but the instrument subsequently fell into disuse.

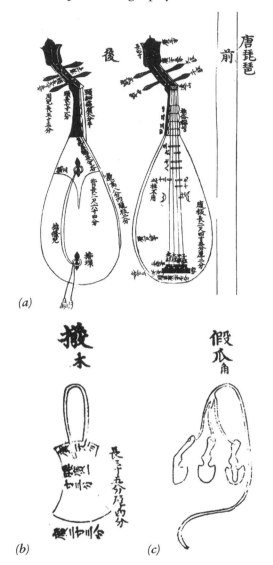

2. Tang-pip'a (four-string lute) of Korea, as depicted in 'Akhak kwebŏm' (1493): (a) back and front views; (b) fan-shaped wooden plectrum; (c) finger-picks

BIBLIOGRAPHY

Sŏng Hyŏn, ed.: *Akhak kwebŏm* [Guide to the study of music] (Seoul, 1493/R), 7.4b–7b and 7.21a–23b

S. Kishibe: 'On the Origin of the P'i-p'a', *Transactions of the Asiatic Society of Japan*, 2nd ser., xix (1940), 259–304

L.E.R. Picken: 'The Origin of the Short Lute', *GSJ*, viii (1955), 32–42

Chang Sahun: *Han'guk akki taegwan* [Korean musical instruments] (Seoul, 1969), 91ff

Song Bang-song: 'The Korean *Pip'a* and its Notation', *EthM*, xvii (1973), 460–93

Cheung Sai-bung: *Zhongguo yinyue shilun shugao* [Draft examinations into Chinese music history] (Hong Kong, 1974–5), 246ff

TSUN-YUEN LUI/WU BEN (1), ROBERT C. PROVINE (2)

Pipe (i) (Ger. *Pfeife*). (1) Generic term for a tube, open or stopped, of wood, metal, cane or other material and with or without finger-holes. Pipes are classified as aerophones in the Sachs–Hornbostel system and subdivided according to whether the sound is generated by an 'air reed' in which the air itself vibrates, set in motion by the player's breath (either confined air reeds as with recorders, or free air reeds as with flutes, depending on whether the player's breath is directed through a rigid channel and against a sharp edge, or not); 'lip reeds' in which the player's lips vibrate to set in motion the column of air and hence to produce a sound (as with brass instruments); or cane reeds in which a tongue of wood, cane or metal vibrates (double as with the oboe, single as with the clarinet or free as with the harmonium). Stopped pipes – those with their lower ends completely closed – sound an octave below open pipes of the same length. Open pipes overblow the 2nd harmonic, an octave above the fundamental; stopped pipes overblow the 3rd harmonic, a 12th above the fundamental. Pipes as musical instruments are of course known in all cultures from prehistoric times to the present day.

(2) Specifically, a small duct flute, usually with three holes, played with a small drum. *See* PIPE AND TABOR.

BIBLIOGRAPHY

SachsH

A. Carse: *Musical Wind Instruments* (London, 1939/R)

A. Baines, ed.: *Musical Instruments Through the Ages* (Harmondsworth, 1961/R, 2/1966/R)

HOWARD MAYER BROWN

Pipe (ii). For pipes in organs, *see under* ORGAN STOP.

Pipe and tabor. A pair of musical instruments consisting usually of a three-hole DUCT FLUTE and a snared drum played together by one person chiefly to provide music for dancing (fig.1).

1. Description. 2. History.

1. DESCRIPTION.   The pipe (Fr. *flute à trois trous*; Provençal *galoubet*; Ger. *Schwegel, Tamerlinpfeife, Tämmerinpfeife*, etc.) is a duct flute with three (occasionally four) holes, played with one hand. In England it is about 30 cm long, pitched in D, usually with a range of an 11th or 12th (in some instruments up to two octaves or more). The three holes allow for fingering four notes. The fundamental tones of the instrument can be sounded by blowing gently, but are not required; hence the first four degrees of the scale are produced as 2nd partial tones an octave above the fundamentals. Overblowing causes a rise of a 5th, making available the upper tetrachord of the scale (the eighth note can also be sounded as a fourth partial) and so on to complete the compass, using whichever partials speak best. The pipe is played with the left hand (the right hand holds the drumstick). The highest hole (at the rear of the instrument) is for the thumb; the other two are for the first and second fingers. The last two fingers grip the pipe at its lower extremity; the little finger can in most cases be extended to half cover the bell and thus supply the lower leading note. (Fingering charts are given in Mersenne, and Gehot.)

The bore of most modern pipes is narrow (in English pipes about 8·5 mm) to facilitate overblowing, and is usually cylindrical, though sometimes tapered to the bottom end. One example, possibly 17th-century in date, has a sophisticated bore shape of inverse conical design (17mm to 5·7mm; see Waterhouse). The scale varies in tuning but usually includes a 'neutral' 3rd (intermediate between a major and minor 3rd) and often a 'neutral' 4th that can be lowered to a perfect 4th by cross-fingering. Emission of the high notes is often improved by making the lip of the instrument of metal, and damaged or worn wooden lips are frequently replaced with metal. Larger

1. Pipe and tabor used to accompany a round dance: miniature from the anonymous Freydal MS, German, 16th century (A-Wkm PS 5073, f.112r)

and deeper pipes have existed. Vidal (1864) mentioned several sizes. Spanish tabor pipes generally have a wider bore and a more powerful tone than English and French pipes. The common Basque *txistu* (Sp. *chistu*), in G, is about 42 cm long with a 13 mm bore; its lip is a long metal plate let into the wood.

English tabor pipes, when not home-made or supplied by regular instrument makers in London, were often imported from France, the English size matching a common size for the GALOUBET of Provence. Boxwood was the usual material, but some 18th-century English-made pipes were of ivory. The manufacture of tabor pipes continues in such centres as Marseilles and San Sebastián; it was revived in England before World War II by Dolmetsch and by Louis Musical Instrument Co. Ltd (London). (Other types of three-holed pipe include ZUFFOLO and the PICCO PIPE.)

The tabor (Fr. *tambourin*) is usually a small side drum with a gut snare (*see* DRUM, §II, 3, but also TAMBOURIN DE BÉARN). The snare crosses the head that is struck, or snares may be provided on both heads. The tabor varies in shape; it may be shallow (like the English tabor in fig.2), or about as deep as it is wide (e.g. the Basque *atabal*), or very deep, with the shell twice as long as the heads are wide (the Provençal model; for illustration *see* TAMBOURIN (ii)). The first two types have existed since the Middle Ages, the last from the 15th century. The tabor is slung from the wrist or shoulder of the player's left arm and is beaten by a stick held in the right hand. In Provence it is regarded as important to strike the snare

itself, to produce a continuous droning sound underlying the beaten rhythm.

2. HISTORY. A reference in the *Ars musica* of Egidius de Zamora (*c*1270), added to a discussion of the tympanum, may be an early mention of the pipe and tabor: 'If a pipe [*fistula*] is joined thereto, it renders the melody sweeter'. Iconography of this period shows a short, fat pipe, in

2. Pipe and tabor, English, 19th century (Victoria and Albert Museum, London)

contrast to its later elongated form. It has been postulated that this resembled the later *flabiol* of Catalonia (Montagu). A poem by Colin Muset (13th century) mentions the 'flaihutel' played 'avec le tabor', while the 13th-century *Roman de Cléomadés* mentions 'flauteors a II dois', presumably referring to the two fingers used in playing. The term 'flageol' was also used from the 13th to 15th centuries; at the wedding of Charles the Bold in 1468, one of the musicians took up 'un tabourin et un flagol' in the course of a comic pantomime. The English expression 'taborer' may have frequently denoted a player of the pipe and tabor, as it later did in, for example, William Kemp's *Nine Daies Wonder* (1600), an account of how the famous actor morris-danced to Norwich accompanied by his 'taborer' Thomas Slye, who is shown in a woodcut (fig.3) with a long tabor pipe (a type also illustrated in Arbeau, 1588).

Dance music was always the pipe and tabor's principal function, as is shown by many old miniatures. Two particularly good medieval scenes of people dancing to it are reproduced by Gérold (*Histoire de la musique*, Paris, 1936, pp.288, 328). It is also shown being used to provide music for jugglers and performing animals, and being played in the military bands of noblemen at tournaments and other occasions; the tabor is often clearly shown being beaten on the snare. In the 16th and 17th centuries the pipe and tabor remained popular and widespread, economically providing a one-man band for dances. Arbeau gave some tunes with their correct tabor beatings. Both the main sources of information about instruments at that time – Praetorius and Mersenne – suggest that the pipe and tabor was then specially well handled in England. Three examples of tabor pipes were found in the excavations of Henry VIII's battleship, the *Mary Rose* (Palmer). Praetorius described the three-hole pipe and

said that it is played in conjunction with a tabor 'by some Englishmen'; it seems that in Germany the pipe and tabor had by that time been replaced by fifes and drums at weddings and other occasions. Mersenne declared that he had heard John Price get a range of three octaves out of the pipe.

The pipe did not escape the 16th-century habit of making treble-to-bass sets for every instrument, as recorded in several German court inventories of the time. In 1596, for example, the Archduke Ferdinand possessed at Schloss Ambras (Innsbruck) 'Flauti mit clainen drümblen zu gebrauchen. 1 pasz. 3 tenor. 1 discant'. Praetorius listed a descant (47 cm long, range *d'* to *e'''*), tenor (61 cm, *g* to *a''*) and bass (70 cm, with a brass crook as in a bass recorder, range not shown), and included scale drawings of the descant and bass, and of a shallow tabor. A bass pipe in the museum of the Brussels Conservatory is about 75 cm long with a 17·5 mm bore and pitched in C, a 9th below the usual pipe. Mersenne said that consorts of three-hole flutes were not much used, and after his time they seem to have vanished altogether.

For the rest of its history the pipe and tabor was relegated to the rural environment where it may still occasionally be heard. In Oxfordshire, where it was known as 'whittle and dubb', it was the normal accompaniment to the Whitsuntide morris dancing until superseded by the violin or the concertina at the end of the 19th century. The Oxfordshire instruments resembled the set in fig.2. When George Butterworth combed the area for morris dances in 1912 he found only one pipe and tabor, in the possession of an elderly man of Bicester who was able to play *The Maid of the Mill* and *Shepherd's Hey* on it. In the second half of the 20th century, as a result of a renewal of interest in morris dancing and the resumption of the manufacture of the metal three-hole pipe, the pipe and tabor also saw a revival.

In France the pipe and tabor is still used in Provence and in Gascogne. In the Basses-Pyrénées a local substitute for the tabor is the *tambourin de Béarn*, also called *tambourin à cordes*, an oblong wooden box with six gut strings which are beaten with a stick as if they were a drumhead. The strings are said to be tuned alternately to the tonic and the dominant of the key of the pipe. In Basque cities, dances such as the aurresku are often accompanied by a band of pipe (*txistu*) and tabor (*tamboril* – small drum, or *atabal* – bass drum) players supported by a side-drum player. In some arrangements the *txistu* harmonizes tunes in 3rds and a bass line is supplied by the *silbote* ('big whistle'; an instrument known only from the beginning of the 19th century), which is pitched a 5th below the *txistu*. The *silbote* player does not have a drum; the other pipers mark the main rhythm on their tabors while the independent side-drum player beats more subtle rhythms. The effect recalls that of a drum and fife band (see BASQUE MUSIC). The simple pipe and tabor, with a pipe about 40 cm long, is found throughout western Spain (as the *pito* or *gaita*, the latter not to be confused with a bagpipe of the same name in north-west Spain, and *tambor*; see SPAIN, fig.5), and Portugal (as the *flauta*) from Salamanca and Miranda do Douro as far south as Huelva and the southern border of Alentejo. The instruments are used in fiesta dances and processions to shrines. In Catalonia (as *flabiol*), and sometimes in the Balearic Islands, in Castile and in the Minho, the pipe is considerably shorter than a normal

3. Pipe and tabor: title-page of William Kemp's 'Nine Daies Wonder' (1600)

tabor pipe (about 20 cm long) and has four or five holes in front and two behind. It is played by shepherds and boys, often without a drum, using both hands. If a tabor is used, the left hand covers three holes in front and the upper thumb-hole, while the upper surface of the little finger covers the lower thumb-hole. The first six or seven notes of the scale are made as fundamentals with the help of cross-fingering, which is feasible since the pipe is so short. For the *sardana* bands (or *coblas*) the *flabiol* is provided with three keys, to assist in playing in different tonalities, and is accompanied by a small *tamboret* attached to the player's arm.

Varieties of pipe and tabor are also found in Latin America. The Colombian *conjunto de gaitas* is an ensemble of two *gaitas* (duct flutes), a *tambor mayor* and a *llamador* (single-headed drums) and a maraca (*see* COLOMBIA, fig.3). The player of the *gaita macho*, which has only two finger-holes, also shakes the maraca. The Tucano Indians of the Colombian Amazon region play an instrument in the form of a turtle-shell; the shell is grasped by the calf and thigh under the bent knee and is rubbed at the waxed end with the palm of the hand. Often one man plays both the turtle-shell and a panpipe together. Musicians in the Altiplano of Bolivia play several pipe and tabor combinations; an example is the use of a small drum with the *waka-pinkillo* (a pipe with two holes at the front and one at the back) played for the *waka-waka*, a Spanish dance miming bull-fighting. The *los sonajeros* Conquest dance of Mexico may also be accompanied by pipes and tabors (*see* MEXICO, fig.6).

In eastern Europe some three-hole pipes are used in traditional music, for example in Slovakia (with the three holes in front) and in Russia (with two holes in front, one behind) where they are made as a pair tuned a 4th apart, to be played by one person. But these pipes are never combined with a drum and it is unlikely that they have any historical connection with the tabor pipe.

BIBLIOGRAPHY

MersenneHU; PraetoriusSM

I. Ansorena: *Txistu ots gozoa 'nola'* (San Sebastián, n.d.) [tutor]
T. Arbeau: *Orchésographie* (Langres, 1588/R1965, 2/1589)
J. Gehot: *Treatise on the Theory and Practice of Music* (London, 1786)
F. Vidal: *Lou tambourin* (Avignon, 1864/R)
R. Stevenson: 'Ancient Peruvian Instruments', *GSJ*, xii (1959), 17–43
C.L. Boilès: 'The Pipe and Tabor in Mesoamerica', *YIAMR*, ii (1966), 43–74
C. Marcel-Dubois: 'Le tambour-bourdon: son signal et sa tradition', *Arts et traditions populaires*, xiv (1966), 3–16
J. Rimmer: 'Tabor Pipes from Aardenburg and Goedereede: some Musical Implications', *Berichten van de Rijksdienst voor het oudheidkundig bodemonderzoek*, xxix (1979), 527–35
F. Palmer: 'Musical Instruments from the Mary Rose', *EMc*, xi (1983), 53–60
J. Ayats, ed.: *En Quirze Perich, Flabiolaire* (Barcelona, 1987)
A. Jambrina Leal and J.R. Cid Cebrián: *La gaita y el tamboril* (Salamanca, 1989)
M. Guys and others: *Le galoubet-tambourin* (Aix en Provence, 1993)
R. Mitjans and T. Soler: *Músics de flabiol* (Barcelona,1993)
A. Vergara Miravete: *Instrumentos y tañedores: música da tradición popular en Aragón* (Saragossa, 1994)
H. Moeck: 'Einhandflöte mit Trommel', *Tibia*, xxi (1996), 168–75
J. Montagu: 'Was the Tabor Pipe Always as we Know It?', *GSJ*, l (1997), 16–30
W. Waterhouse: 'A Rare English Tabor Pipe', *Sine musica nulla vita: Festschrift Herman Moeck*, ed. N. Delius (Celle, 1997), 73–7

ANTHONY C. BAINES/HÉLÈNE LA RUE

Pipegrop [Pipgrop, Pipgroppe], **Heinrich.** *See* BARY-PHONUS, HENRICUS.

Pipelare, Matthaeus (*b c*1450; *d c*1515). South Netherlandish composer. He was active in Antwerp but left there to become Master of the Choristers for the Confraternity of Our Lady at 's-Hertogenbosch, remaining there from the spring of 1498 until about 1 May 1500. His name indicates that either he or a forebear played woodwind instruments, perhaps as a town piper. In the words of Ornithoparchus, as translated by John Dowland in 1609, Pipelare was one of several composers whose works 'flow from the very fountaine of Art'.

Pipelare wrote in almost all the forms of his day, and his style is characterized by its wide diversity, ranging from a dense polyphony, as in the first section of the St John Credo, to a homophonic style, as in *Vray dieu d'amours*. He approached the style of Pierre de La Rue in the sombre melancholy of some of his works, such as parts of the *Missa 'Mi mi'*, but such other compositions as the chanson *Morkin ic hebbe* are gay and light. Two characteristics of his style are the frequent use of syncopation and sequence.

The *Missa 'Floruit egregius infans Livinus'* is in an early style. The cantus firmus, which migrates freely from voice to voice, employs altogether 20 chants for St Livinus. All movements except the Kyrie conclude with the same musical section in triple metre to produce a final 'refrain' reminiscent of Faugues. The third Agnus Dei of the second *Missa sine nomine* is noteworthy for an altus part consisting only of the note A, which is symbolically notated. The *Missa 'L'homme armé'* contains some of his most exciting writing, building up to the grandiose final Agnus Dei. The *Missa 'Dicit Dominus'* is a study in the complexity of rhythmic structure: the cantus firmus appears in various mensurations conflicting with those of the other parts.

The *Missa 'Fors seulement'*, with its rich sonorities, is primarily a cantus firmus mass with the famous melody from Pipelare's own chanson (second setting) rhythmically differentiated from the other parts. On the other hand, all the parts of the first *Missa sine nomine* are so permeated with the pre-existing material that it can be called an example of 'saturation' technique. Sequence and unpretentious singable lines characterize the *Missa 'Johannes Christe care'/'Ecce puer meus'*; the texture of this mass is *a* 3 since the cantus firmus is absent much of the time. This work and the St John Credo were probably written in 1498 or 1499. Pipelare was a master of large complex structures, but that he did not need complicated organization to bring out his finest writing is nowhere more obvious than in his *Missa de feria*, which though simple in style contains some of his most memorable music.

Pipelare's motets show the same diversity of style as his masses. The *Salve regina* and *Ave Maria ... virgo serena* display an early style in their use of short notes in syncopated rhythms. There is a more careful declamation of the text in *Memorare mater Christi* (closely modelled on Josquin's *Stabat mater*) and the *Magnificat*, in which the composer allowed the voices to move within carefully considered vertical sonorities. Here, especially in the *Magnificat*, he looked to the future, not only in his careful treatment of dissonance but also in his sense of balance both among the voice parts and in the phrase structures.

Among his Flemish chansons, *Een vrolic wesen* seems intended as a solo with instrumental accompaniment, as was an earlier setting by Barbireau. Of the three or possibly four French chansons, there are two settings of

Fors seulement, one version based on Ockeghem's famous chanson and a second on a new tenor melody. The second version was extremely popular, to judge both by the many manuscripts and prints that contain it and by the many compositions that in turn were based on it.

WORKS

Edition: *M. Pipelare: Opera omnia*, ed. R. Cross, CMM, xxxiv (1966–7) [C]

MASSES

Missa de feria, 4vv, C ii (paraphrase and c.f. from Gregorian masses XV and XVIII)
Missa 'Dicit Dominus', 4vv, C ii (c.f. ?T from polyphonic composition in *A-Wn* 11883)
Missa 'Floruit egregius infans Livinus', 4vv, C ii (c.f.: text in honour of Livinus, patron saint of Ghent)
Missa 'Fors seulement', 5vv, C ii (c.f. T of his own chanson, second setting)
Missa 'Johannes Christe care'/'Ecce puer meus', 4vv, C iii (c.f. seq 'Johannes Christe care' and ant 'Ecce puer meus' in honour of St John the Evangelist; Gl partly reconstructed in modern edn)
Missa 'L'homme armé', 4vv, C iii (c.f. popular tune)
Missa 'Mi mi', 4vv, C iii (Ag has material from Gregorian Ag, Mass X)
Missa omnium carminum, 4vv, MS lost in World War II
Missa sine nomine (i), 4vv, C iii (c.f. and paraphrase)
Missa sine nomine (ii), 4vv, C iii (c.f.)
Missa, 8vv, MS lost in World War II
Credo de Sancto Johanne evangelista, 5vv, C ii (c.f. ant 'Occurit beato Johanni ab exilio')

MOTETS

Ave castissima, 4vv, C i (text: incipit only)
Ave Maria … virgo serena, 5vv, C i (paraphrase of seq melody; Ct ii reconstructed in modern edn)
Exortum est in tenebris (Ps cxi.4) [= Fors seulement], 4vv, C i
Hic est vere martyr, 4vv, C i (survives only in kbd intabulation)
Laudate, pueri, Dominum, 4vv, 1538⁸, ed. H. Albrecht (Kassel, 1959) [= Hosanna of Missa sine nomine (i)]
Magnificat, 4vv, C i (alternatim with piainsong, 3rd tone)
Memorare mater Christi, 7vv, C i (for the feast of the Seven Sorrows of the BVM; c.f. T of Urreda's Nunca fué pena mayor)
Salve regini, 5vv, C i (alternatim with plainsong)
Sensus carnis mors est [= Ag II of Missa 'Mi mi'], 3vv, C i (text: paraphrase of Romans viii.6)
Virga et baculus tuus (Ps xii.4), 2vv, C i

SECULAR

Een vrolic wesen, 4vv, C i (Barbireau's Sup in Sup)
Fors seulement (i), 4vv, C i (Ockeghem's Sup in the A)
Fors seulement (ii), 4vv, C i (the basis for Pipelare's mass)
Ic weedt een molenarinne, 4vv, C i (paraphrase; based on a folksong)
Mijns liefskins bruyn ooghen, 4vv, C i (survives in 3 transpositions)
Morkin ic hebbe, 4vv, C i (text: incipit only)
Vray dieu d'amours, 4vv, C i (survives in 2 versions)
Vray dieu que pene m'esse, 4vv, C i (also attrib. Compère and Gaspart; probably not by Pipelare)

BIBLIOGRAPHY

R. Cross: *Matthaeus Pipelare: a Historical and Stylistic Study of his Works* (diss., New York U., 1961)
R. Cross: 'The Life and Works of Matthaeus Pipelare', *MD*, xvii (1963), 97–114
R. Cross: 'The Chansons of Matthaeus Pipelare', *MQ*, lv (1969), 500–20
M.J. Bloxam: 'In Praise of Spurious Saints: the *Missae Floruit egregiis* by Pipelare and La Rue', *JAMS*, xliv (1991), 163–220

RONALD CROSS

Piperinus [Pfaefferli], **Christoph** (*b* Berne; *d* Basle, 1565). Swiss clergyman and music teacher. In 1541 he served as a minister's assistant in Interlaken. On 5 November 1543 he enrolled at Basle University where, between November 1546 and summer 1547, he gave private music lessons to Basilius Amerbach, son of the Basle humanist Bonifacius Amerbach. By 1547, Piperinus left Basle for Burgdorf, and from 1552 to 1555 he served as a clergyman in Bueren an der Aare. He apparently returned to Basle for a brief visit in 1559 and died of the plague in 1565.

Piperinus's activities as a music teacher are documented in extraordinary detail in four manuscripts, housed today in the University Library of Basle (*CH-Bu* F IX 32–5, F X 5–9, F X 22–4 and kk IV 23–7). They were compiled by Piperinus solely for the purpose of teaching the 'art of singing' to Basilius Amerbach. Collectively, they document Piperinus's teaching methods, reveal the repertory that he felt appropriate for the 13-year-old to learn and show the musical progress that Basilius would have made over a six-month period. Piperinus's teaching methods encompassed reading and copying music as well as singing music to solmization syllables. His pedagogical repertory included international as well as local polyphony; lieder, chansons, motets, *Magnificat* settings, hymns and secular Latin pieces by such composers as Sermisy, Janequin, Willaert, Senfl and Johannes Wannenmacher. Piperinus also worked as a music copyist; the two surviving manuscripts of Hans Buchner's *Fundamentum* and most of Buchner's organ compositions were copied by him.

BIBLIOGRAPHY

K. Nef: 'Musikunterricht in Basel im 16. Jahrhundert', *ZIMG*, vii (1905–6), 23 only
A. Geering: 'Die Vokalmusik in der Schweiz zur Zeit der Reformation', *Schweizerisches Jb für Musikwissenschaft*, vi (1933), 1–260, esp. 86
A. Geering: 'Von der Berner Stadtpfeifern', *Schweizer Beiträger zur Musikwissenschaft*, i (1972), 105–8
J. Kmetz: *Die Handschriften der Universitätsbibliothek Basel: Katalog der Musikhandschriften des 16. Jahrhunderts: quellenkritische und historische Untersuchung* (Basle, 1988)
J. Kmetz: 'The Piperinus-Amerbach Partbooks: Six Months of Music Lessons in Renaissance Basel', *Music in the German Renaissance: Sources, Styles and Contexts*, ed. J. Kmetz (Cambridge, 1994), 215–34

JOHN KMETZ

Pī phāt. Classical instrumental ensemble of THAILAND, consisting of both melodic and rhythmic percussion instruments and an aerophone (oboe or flute). Functionally, the *pī phāt* performs the highest classes of compositions, such as extended suites and virtuoso pieces, for serious occasions such as the 'teacher-greeting' ceremony *wai khrū*, funerals and Buddhist rituals. The *pī phāt* also accompanies *khōn* (masked theatre), *lakhōn* (dance theatre) and *nang yai* (large shadow theatre).

The essential *pī phāt* ensemble consists of the higher-pitched xylophone *ranāt ēk*, the lower-pitched circular gong-chime *khǫng wong yai*, *pī* (the quadruple-reed oboe that gives its name to the ensemble) plus *ching* (a pair of small cymbals) and one or two drums: *taphōn*, *klǫng sǫng nā*, or *klǫng khāek*. This basic group, called *khrūang hā* ('five instruments'), may be expanded through the addition of the lower-pitched xylophone *ranāt thum*, circular gong-chime *khǫng wong lek* and one or both of the metallophones *ranāt ēk lek* and *ranāt thum lek*, as well as various rhythmic percussion. There are principally three kinds of *pī phāt* in use today: the loud, hard-mallet ensemble *pī phāt mai khāeng* including the quadruple-reed oboe *pī*, the soft-mallet ensemble *pī phāt mai nuam* which includes both the two-string fiddle *sǫ ū* and *khlui* (flute) instead of oboe, and the 'Mon' ensemble *pī phāt mǭn*, which is distinct from the others. Whereas the *pī phāt mai khāeng* plays the highest class of repertory, the *pī phāt mai nuam* plays lighter, more tuneful compositions. The *pī phāt mǭn*, while allegedly of Mon origin, is actually played by Thai musicians primarily for funerals.

Whereas the usual circular gong-chimes are laid out horizontally, those of the Mon ensemble are U-shaped and stand vertically (for illustration *see* GONG-CHIME, Table 1). In addition the Mon ensemble has an oboe distinguished by its deep pitch and large, loosely-attached bell (*pī mǭn*) similar to the *hnè* of Myanmar and may add a set of seven tuned drums (*pōeng māng khǭk*) which has a melodic function and is hung on the inner wall of a circular frame. Other kinds of *pī phāt* ensembles formerly in use are now either extinct or rarely encountered.

The music of the *pī phāt* is perhaps the most challenging to listen to in Thailand's classical repertory owing to its predominantly motivic character. Though the most basic form of the composition is played by the larger circular gong chime, listeners tend to focus on the more active higher-pitched xylophone and oboe parts; the former plays continuous octaves without evidence of phrasing. Even though general listeners in Thailand may have difficulty relating to the music, the sound of the *pī phāt* is associated with the country's most sacred rituals, and most acknowledge that the *pī phāt* represents Thai classical music in its highest form.

BIBLIOGRAPHY

GEWM, [iv] ('Thailand'; T. Miller)
D. Yupho: *Khrǔang dontri Thai* [Thai musical instruments] (Bangkok,1957, 2/1967; Eng. trans., 1960, 3/1987)
D. Morton: *The Traditional Music of Thailand* (Berkeley, 1976)

TERRY E. MILLER

Pipkov, Lyubomir (Panayotov) (*b* Lovech, 6/19 Sept 1904; *d* Sofia, 9 May 1974). Bulgarian composer and conductor; son of Panayot Pipkov. He studied at the Sofia State Music Academy, graduating in 1926, and then in Paris at the Ecole Normale (1926–32) under Dukas (composition), Léfébure (piano) and Boulanger (music history). After graduating he returned to Sofia and worked at the National Opera, first as répétiteur, then as chorus master and finally as director (1944–7). In 1948 he was appointed professor of vocal ensemble and opera at the Sofia State Academy. He co-founded the society Contemporary Music in 1933, was founder of its successor, the Union of Bulgarian Composers, and from 1945 to 1952 he served as secretary of the Bulgarian Choral Union. He was director of the festival March Musical Days in Russe, and of Lilac Musical Days in Lovech. From the mid-1960s he was a member of the ISME.

The author of celebrated works of the 1920s and 30s, Pipkov was one of the most important representatives of the second generation of Bulgarian composers; as such he was a founder of a national style. His musical language evolved naturally through successive stages. In the early 1920s he made his début with chamber pieces in the style of Chopin, Schumann, Debussy and Ravel, while in the First String Quartet (1928, the first also in Bulgaria), having mastered the principles and forms of the European tradition, he moved to embrace Bulgarian folk music. During the remaining Paris years he took on board new genres while endorsing a typically Bulgarian epic sense of drama, an example being *Yaninite devet bratya* ('Jana's Nine Brothers', 1919–32), a work that was in effect the first Bulgarian classical opera. Upon his return to Sofia, Pipkov quickly established himself as a writer, critic (his article 'Za Balgarskiyat muzikalen stil' was something of a manifesto for the society Contemporary Music) and conductor, as well as composer. His vocal-orchestral *Svadba* ('Wedding'), completed in 1935, marks the

beginning of the cantata in Bulgarian music, while the equally innovative First Symphony served to summarize the achievements of his first period.

The second phase in his output spans the 1940s and the first half of the 50s. His epic dramatic style is developed and perfected, particularly in the opera *Momchil* (1939–43), and in Symphony no.2 this gives rise to his most accomplished orchestral writing yet. At this juncture in his career Pipkov extended his teaching activities and assumed a higher public profile, and as an adjudicator and representative of the Union of Bulgarian Composers he travelled extensively throughout Europe.

In addition to their expressiveness and strong sense of drama, the works from the mid-1950s onwards convey the spirit of optimism. This is particularly true of *Oratoriya za nasheto vreme* ('Oratorio for our Time') and *Priglusheni pesni* ('Muted Songs'). The Fourth Symphony (1968–70) is highly individual, while the piano piece *Proletni priumitsi* ('Spring Caprices', 1971–2) revisits compositional ideas from earlier works.

As a whole, the operas and orchestral works have qualities which are akin to the realism of Shostakovich, Bartók and Britten.

WORKS
(selective list)

DRAMATIC

Yaninite devet bratya [Yana's Nine Brothers] (op, N. Veselinov and Pipkov), op.17, 1929–32, Sofia, National, 1937
Momchil (op, K. Radevski, after S. Zagorchinov: *Den Posleden, Den Gospoden* [The Last Day, the Day of Our Lord]), 1939–43, Sofia, National, 1948
Antigona '43 (op, V. Bashev and P. Panchev, after Sophocles), op.63, 1961–2, Ruse Opera, 1963
Film scores: Trevoga [Trouble], op.29, 1948–50; Septemvriitsi [The Septembrists], op.35, 1952–4; Zemya [The Earth], op.41, 1956; Komandirat na otryada [Group Commander], op.45, 1958–59; Stublenskite lipi [The Linden Trees of Stublena], op.58, 1960; Tsarska milost [The Mercy of the Tsar], op.55, 1961–2; Legenda za Paisii [A Legend of Paisii], op.62, before 1973
Incid music

VOCAL

Choral: Svatba [Wedding] (cant., N. Furnadzhiyev), op.10, mixed chorus, orch, 1931–5; Oratoriya za nasheto vreme [Orat for our Time] (V. Bashev), op.61, B, spkr, mixed chorus, children's chorus, 1959; Cant. (P. de Ronsard, F. García Lorca, R. Alberti and others), op.64, S, B, chbr orch, 1963–4; 4 Madrigals (Bulg. poets), op.67, mixed chorus, 1963–4; Dyavolsko darvo [The Devil's Tree] 3 folksongs, op.76, mixed chorus, 1971; Priglusheni pesni [Muted Songs] (M. Tsvetayeva) 4 songs, op.80, female chorus, 1972
Choral songs: Na nivata [In the Field], 1937; Proleten vyatar [A Spring Breeze], 1938; Zhalta peperuda [Yellow Butterfly], 1940; Shumete debri i balkani [Make the Mountain Trees Whisper], 1944; Nani mi nani Damyancho [Sleep Damyancho Sleep], 1948; Tsarevitsa ranna [An Early Corn], 1948; Pesen za malkiya chirak [Song for the Little Apprentice], 1959
1v, ens: 4 Folksongs, op.5, 1v, fl, vc, pf, 1928; Haydushka Planina [The Haidouk Mountain] (after 5 folk songs, op.13, 1v, fl, 2 vn, 2 va, vc, db, pf, perc, 1937; 5 narodni pesni [5 Folksongs], op.18, high v, chbr orch, 1938
Solo songs (1v, pf): 5 pesni, op.4, 1928–9; 7 narodni pesni, op.36, 1948–49; 7 pesni, opp.46 and 51, 1950–60

INSTRUMENTAL

Orch: Sym. no.1, op.22, 1937–40; Prolet nad Trakiya [Spring in Thrace], op.16, chbr orch, 1938; Vn Conc., op.43, 1948–50; Geroichna uvertyura [Heroic Ov.], op.37, 1949; Patuvane iz Albaniya [Journey though Albania], op.38, str, 1949–52; Pf Conc., op.48, 1952–4; Sym no. 2, op.47, 1953–5; Sym.-Conc., op.56, vc, orch, 1953–63; Sym. no. 3, op.65, tpt, str, perc, 2 pf, 1965; Cl Conc., op.70, 1966; Sym. no. 4, op.74, str, 1968–70
Chbr and solo: Str Qt no.1, op.3, 1928; Conc., wind, perc, pf, 1929; Sonata, op.7, vn, pf, 1929; Pf Trio, op.8, 1930; Pf Qt, op.20,

1938; Str Qt no.2, op.31, 1948; Str Qt no.3, op.66, str qt, timp, 1965; Sonata, op.73, vn, 1969

Pf: Pogrebeniye [Funeral], 1921; Sonata, a, 1921–3; Septemvriiska prelyudiya 1923 [Prelude for September 1923]; Pesni bez dumi [Songs without Words], 1926; Poyema, 1926; Balgarska syuita, op.2, 1928; Yunosheski sbornik [Works for Young People], op.14, 1936–7; Pastoral, op.24, 1944; Starinen tants [Dance of Old], op.26, 1946; Metroritmichni kartini i studii [Metrorythmical Parts and Pieces], opp.69 and 77, 1966–72; Proletni priumitsi [Spring Caprices], op.78, 1971–2; Ot yedno do petnadeset [1 to 15], op.81, 1973; Detski radosti [The Children's Joy], 1973–4

WRITINGS

Za balgarskiyat muzikalen stil [On the Bulgarian musical style] (Sofia, 1934)

Nashata muzikologiya na chisti pozitsii [Our musicology from a clear perspective] (Sofia, 1955)

Muzika i savremennost [Music and the contemporary age] (Sofia, 1974)

K. Angeloved.: *Izbrani statii* [Selected articles] (Sofia, 1977)

BIBLIOGRAPHY

I. Kamburov: 'Uspekhite na yedin mlad komponist' [The success of a young composer], *Literaturen glas* (21 Oct 1928)

K. Iliyev: *Lyubomir Pipkov* (Sofia, 1958)

L. Koyen: *Lyubomir Pipkov* (Sofia, 1968)

V. Krustev: 'Lyubomir Pipkov', *Profili* (1976–86)

K.D. Drumeva, M. Kostakeva and I. Khlebarov: *Lyubomir Pipkov* (Moscow, 1976)

G. Tsanev, ed.: 'Lyubomir Pipkov', *Sreshti s minaloto* [Meetings with the past] (Sofia, 1977)

I. Hlebarov: *Tvorcheskata evolyutsiya na Lyubomir Pipkov* [Pipkov's creative evolution] (Sofia, 1996), vol.1

IVAN HLEBAROV

Pipkov, Panayot (*b* Plovdiv, 21 Nov 1871; *d* Sofia, 25 Aug 1942). Bulgarian composer. As a child he studied the violin and sang in Baidanov's choir. In 1893 a scholarship enabled him to study for two years at the Milan Conservatory. Thereafter he returned to Bulgaria to work as a choral and orchestral conductor in Ruse, and from 1905 until his death he was active in Sofia as a teacher, actor, bandmaster, composer, chorus master of the Sofia National Opera, collaborator on a humorous newspaper and writer of poetry and plays.

Pipkov left a large number of choral songs, many for children, but he is notable above all for his small piano pieces, the first Bulgarian contributions to the genre. His very popular choral hymn *Varvi, narode vasrodeni* ('Go, Enlightened People') is sung throughout Bulgaria each 24 May, Slavonic Literature Day.

WORKS
(*selective list*)

22 učilisni pesni [Lieder für die Schule], 1902; 20 Lieder, chorus, 1902; 10 Pf Pieces, 1908–18; Detsa i ptichki [Children and Birds] (children's operetta, Pipkov), 1909; Shturets i mravki [Cricket and Ant] (children's operetta, Pipkov), 1910; Parvi radosti na nac inayushtiya violinist [First Joy of the Young Player], vn, pf, 1932; Varvi, narode vasrodeni [Go, Enlightened People], chorus; Balgarska rapsodiya, pf (1954); folksongs arrs. for brass band, incid music

Principal publishers: Hemus

BIBLIOGRAPHY

A. Andreyev: *Panayot Pipkov* (Sofia, 1952) [with Fr. summary]

Ye. Toncheva: *Panayot Pipkov* (Sofia, 1962)

V. Krastev: *Orchesti po istoriya na balgarskata muzika* [Essays on the history of Bulgarian music] (Sofia, 1970, 2/1977)

LADA BRASHOVANOVA, MARIA KOSTAKEVA
(work-list, bibliography)

Pippo del Violoncello. *See* AMADEI, FILIPPO.

Pique (Fr.). *See* ENDPIN.

Pique, François-Louis (*b* Roret, nr Mirecourt, 1757; *d* Charenton St Maurice, nr Paris, 26 Oct 1822). French violin maker. He was an exact contemporary of Nicolas Lupot; the two were friends and business associates, and such is the similarity of their work that it is often confused. After serving an apprenticeship with Saunier at Mirecourt, Pique moved to Paris where he settled first in the rue Coquillière, near St Eustache; he moved to the rue de Grenelle-St-Honoré in 1798, and finally to the rue des Deux-Ecus. In 1794 Lupot left Orléans to join him, staying four years before opening his own business. The pattern of Pique's violins differs slightly from Lupot's and tends to be a little oversized. He had a liking for fronts of broad grain, and his scrolls are comparatively unimpressive. How much he influenced Lupot and how much it was the other way round is a matter for speculation, but the history of violin making in France probably owes more to Pique than is usually acknowledged. (*VannesE*)

CHARLES BEARE/SYLVETTE MILLIOT

Piquer (Fr.). A term meaning 'to dot' in the sense of NOTES INÉGALES or, as a type of bowing, to detach or separate. According to Loulié (*Elements*, Paris, 1696), *piquer* or *pointer*, applied to a passage of quavers written as equal ('in any time signature, but especially in triple time'), meant that the first quaver was to be played much longer than the second so that the first quaver 'ought to have a dot'. The result is evidently patterns of dotted quavers followed by semiquavers. On the other hand, Brossard (*Dictionaire*, 1703) wrote that *picqué* or *pointé* meant about the same as spiccato or staccato, which to Brossard meant to play the notes detached or separated. He did not mention Loulié's dotted quaver–semiquaver pattern in this connection. *See* BOW, §II, 2(vii); and POINTER.

DAVID D. BOYDEN

Piquigny, Nicholas. *See* PYKINI.

Pirchner, Werner (*b* Hallitirol, 13 Feb 1940). Austrian composer and jazz musician. Self-taught as a composer and vibraphone player, he followed the latest trends in jazz music as a youth. Later influences included the theories of Schoenberg, and the music of composers from Bach, Schubert and Bartók to Thelonious Monk and John Cage. After arranging music for the Austrian armed forces' dance band, he became a freelance composer and performer. Co-founder of the Pirchner-Pepl-JazzZwio (1975–85) with the guitarist Harry Pepl, he has also appeared with the Oscar Klein Quartet, Mumelter's Concertodrom, Austria Dei, the Vienna Art Orchestra, Eisenbahner-Musik Innsbruck, the Lauren Newton Quartet and other performers and ensembles. He began to compose music for classical musicians in 1981. His sound design for Austrian Radio/Ö 1 was completed in 1994.

Pirchner's music projects a state of uncertainty. Mourning and melancholy never appear unambiguously and a suggestion of subversive sadness lingers even when there is a pretence of happiness. His work represents a fragment of culture not only against the apparent culture of the bourgeoisie, but also against the smugness of a provincial, patriotic, pseudo-popularism. Unlike many contemporary composers, Pirchner has not asked himself whether what he has done is new; instead, in the interest of self-criticism, he has taken what was already in existence, subjected it to a process of alienation in a highly original, oddly bizarre fashion and thereby held a mirror up to his country and his region. In his music, seriousness and entertainment are not incompatible opposites. As Harry Larcher noted in a radio broadcast: 'Rarely has a musician, a composer so self-consciously positioned himself between every category of music, the only place where the spirit can still move freely and unsupported by dogmatic allegiance'.

WORKS
(selective list)

Orch: Klänge, PWV 9b, 1977; Präludium und Fiasko, PWV 10, wind, vib, gui, 1977; Chbr Sym. 'Soiree tyrolienne', PWV 16, 1980; Zwentendorf – Wackersdorf. Ein Spaziergang! ... Nach Tschernobyl!, conc., PWV 32, chorus, fl, orch, 1988; Paradiso, PWV 59, 1992; Birthday-Musik, PWV 80, 1996

Chbr and solo inst: Str Qt 'Variations on a Tyrolean Slave Song', PWV 15, wind qnt, 1974; Von der gewöhnlichen Traurigkeit. Zum Kotzen, PWV 17, str qt, 1978; Adrette Duette und Kloanhäusler-Tänze, PWV 11, solo inst, pf; Good News from the Ziller Valley, PWV 12, vn, 1981; Do You Know Emperor Joe?, PWV 13, wind qnt, 1982–3; Kleine Messe 'für den lieben Gott', C, PWV 14, org, 1982; Wem gehört der Mensch ... ?, PWV 31, pf trio, 1988; Die Bewässerung von Mitteleuropa, PWV 39, brass qnt; Mit FaGottes Hilfe, PWV 40, bn; Ein Trompeten-Künstler spielt eine freundliche Weise, wird von einem Spitzel denunziert und erhält eine Verwarnung nebst Androhung eines Disziplinarverfahrens im Widerholungsfalle, PWV 42 wind octet, 1990; Der Strich des Radierers (Trbn Conc.), PWV 79, brass qnt, 1996

Incid music: Kaiser Joseph und die Bahnwärterstochter (F. von Herzmanovsky-Orlando), PWV 25, 1982; Emigranten-Symphonie (B. Brecht: *Arturo Ui*), PWV 23, 1987; Geschichten aus dem Wienerwald (Ö. von Hovath), PWV 26, 1987; Gespenstersonate (A. Strindberg) PWV 35, 1988; Kein schöner Land (F. Mitterer), PWV 28, 1988; Der Sturm (W. Shakespeare), PWV 27, 1988; Ein Jedermann (Mitterer), PWV 47, 1991; Der Weibsteufel (ballet, K. Schönherr), PWV 54, 1991; Die wilde Frau (Mitterer), PWV 51, 1991; Das wunderbare Schicksal (Mitterer), PWV 58, 1992; Jedermann (H. von Hoffmannsthal), PWVElino 70, 1995; film scores

MSS in *A-Wgm*

Principal publishers: Doblinger, Schott, Eigenverlag

Principal recording companies: Extraplatte, ECM, Mood-Records, WEA

BIBLIOGRAPHY

LZMÖ [incl. further bibliography]
O. Costa: 'Geboren in finsterer Zeit: der Komponist und Musiker Werner Pircher', *Das Fenster* [Tyrol], no.41 (1986)
G. Cerha: 'Neue Musik aus Wien 1945–1990', *ÖMz*, xlv (1990), 539–60
H. Christoph: 'In dein Baunzerl drin', *Profil* (16 Dec 1996)

SIGRID WIESMANN

Pirck [Birk, Birckh, Birck, Pirckh, Pürk, Pürck], **Wenzel Raimund (Johann)** (*b* Leopoldstadt, Vienna, bap. 27 June 1718; *d* Leopoldstadt, 17 July 1763). Austrian composer, organist and teacher. He spent his entire career at the Viennese court. From 1726 to 1739 he was a *Hofscholar*; his teachers included Matteo Palotta. On 6 February 1739 he succeeded Georg Reutter (i) as court organist, and he held this position until his death. He also taught music – in particular, keyboard playing – to the archdukes; Christoph Sonnleithner was another of his pupils. In his upbringing and in the style of his music he was a typical product of the imperial court, but copies he made of keyboard works by Handel show the breadth of his musical interests. As Kirkendale has shown, the solid learning that informs his more austere pieces, as well as his predilection for fugues in multi-movement instrumental works, may have influenced the musical tastes of Emperor Joseph II. His output has clearly not survived complete and it has not yet been systematically studied,

especially as regards its importance for the Viennese pre-Classical style.

WORKS

Trattenimenti per clavicembalo (Vienna, 1757)
12 sonatas, str, *A-Wgm*; Sonata con trombe e timpani, C, *Wn*; 17 untitled works (incl. partitas, ballet music), str, *Wgm*; 25 sinfonias, a 4, *Wn*, *H-Gc*; Sinfonia o ouverture della pantomina, G, 1758, *A-Wn*; Sinfonia con corni di caccia, E♭, *Wn*; 16 str qts, *Wn*; Partia, C, a 3, Partia, F, a 4, *KR*; Partitta, a 3, Partitta, A, a 4, *H-Gc*
2 partitas, kbd, *Bn*; other kbd works, *A-Wn*

BIBLIOGRAPHY

KöchelKHM; *MGG1* (O. Biba) [incl. further bibliography]
L. Stollbrock: 'Leben und Wirken des k. k. Hofkapellmeisters und Hofkompositors Johann Georg Reuter jun.', *VMw*, viii (1892), 161–203, esp. 184, 191
W. Kirkendale: *Fuge und Fugato in der Kammermusik des Rokoko und der Klassik* (Tutzing, 1966; Eng. trans., enlarged, 1979)
K. Wagner, ed.: *Abbé Maximilian Stadler: seine 'Materialen zur Geschichte der Musik unter den österreichischen Regenten'* (Kassel, 1974), 94, 115, 183

OTTO BIBA

Pires, (Luís) Filipe (*b* Lisbon, 26 June 1934). Portuguese composer and pianist. From 1946 to 1953 he studied the piano with Lúcio Mendes and composition with Artur Santos and Jorge Croner de Vasconcelos at the Lisbon Conservatory. From 1950 he has pursued a prominent career as a pianist in Portugal and later abroad. From 1957–60 he studied in Hanover, on a government grant, with Winifried Wolf (piano) and Ernst-Lothar von Knorr (composition). He then taught composition at the Oporto Conservatory (1960–70). Meanwhile, he worked as a critic and gave conferences and courses on analysis. During the 1960s he attended the Darmstadt summer courses and studied 12-note composition in Berlin with Kroellreuter (1964) and electronic music in Paris with Pierre Schaeffer (1970–72). From 1972–5 he taught composition, analysis and electronic music at the Lisbon Conservatory, of which he was also director. From 1975–9 he worked as a music specialist for the International Secretariat of UNESCO in Paris, and also in various private and state institutions. Since 1993 he has been professor of composition at Oporto Conservatory. He has received numerous composition prizes in Portugal and abroad.

The music of Pires's early period combines traditional formal structures with modal, 12-note and, since 1954, atonal elements arrived at through a progressive use of chromaticism. From 1958 onwards his music gradually evolved towards a 12-note style. In the 1960s he strove to extend his serialism to duration and dynamics, and explored combinations of timbre, permutations and variable and aleatory elements in relation to the form. In the 1970s he began to compose taped music using natural sources of sound. His interest in non-European cultures is evident in his use of hybrid scales and modes, heterophony and diverse musical quotations. From the 1980s onwards, his music has also had minimalist tendencies.

WORKS
(selective list)

Stage: Instantâneo (ballet), orch, 1962–4; Namban (ballet), tape, 1970; Os persas (incid music, Aeschylus), tape, 1970; O judeu (incid music, B. Santareno), tape, 1980, concert version, 1982; Tordesyalta (musical theatre), multimedia, 1982–3; Zoocratas (musical theatre), 4vv, pf, 1984–7

Orch: Akronos, str, 1964; Perspectivas, 3 groups, 1965; Mobiles, chbr orch, pf, 1968–9; Sintra: música para uma curta metragem imaginária, 1969; Variantes, 1979–80; Evocações, 1988; Epos, 1989–91

Vocal: 2 cantigas de amigo (King Dinis, King Sancho I), 1v, pf, 1949; 4 canções populares portuguesas (folksongs), female chorus, 1951–3, arr. chorus, 1975; 2 redondilhas de Camões, 1v, pf, 1953; 3 poemas de Fernando Pessoa, 1v, pf, 1954, orchd, 1985; 6 poemas de Eduardo Mörike, chorus, 1958; Regresso eterno (R. Cinatti), Bar/spkr, orch, 1961; Portugaliae genesis (old Portuguese and Latin Texts), Bar, chorus, orch, 1968; Canção IV de Camões, 12vv, 1980; 20 canções, chorus, 1981

Chbr: Sonatina, vn, pf, 1952; Sonatina, vc, pf, 1954; Str Qt, 1958; Str Trio, 1959; Pf Trio, 1959–60; Metronomie, fl, hp, va, 1966; Figurações III, 2 pf, 1969; In memoriam Béla Bartók, str qt, 1970; Ostinati, 6 perc, 1970; Diálogos, 8 insts, tape, 1975; Monólogos, 8 insts, 1983; Septet, brass insts, 1985; Stretto, 2 pf, 1987; Miniaturas, b cl, mar, 1994

Solo inst: 3 bagatelas, pf, 1949–52; Partita, pf, 1953, orchd, 1966; Pf Sonata, 1953–4; Estudo, perc, 1966; Figurações I, fl, 1968; Figurações II, pf, 1969; Figurações IV, hp, 1970; Cantiga variada, pf, 1977; Figurações V, a sax, 1984; Figurações VI, mar, 1984; Figurações VII, gui, 1986; Zoocratas, pf [after musical theatre]; Estudos de sonoridades, pf, 1993; Figurações VIII, bn, 1995; Disimulación, gui, 1996

Tape: Estudo electrónico, 1972; Homo sapiens, 1972; Litania, 1972; Reportagem, 1974; Canto ecuménico, 1979

Principal publishers: Are, Curci, Musicoteca, Oficina Musical, Zimmermann

BIBLIOGRAPHY

Catálogo geral da música portuguesa: repertório contemporâneo (Lisbon, 1978–80)

R.V. Nery and P.F. Castro: Sínteses da cultura portuguesa: História da música (Lisbon, 1991)

P. Figueiredo: 'Entrevista com o compositor Luís Filipe Pires', Arte musical, iii (1996), 101–17

ADRIANA LATINO

Pires, Maria-João (*b* Lisbon, 23 July 1944). Portuguese pianist. She first appeared in public at the age of four, and between 1953 and 1960 studied at the Conservatório Nacional in Lisbon with Campos Coelho and Francine Benoit. At 18 she won a scholarship to study in Germany, first at the Musikhochschule in Munich with Rosl Schid and then in Hanover with Karl Engel. In 1970 she won the Beethoven Bicentennial Competition in Brussels and commenced an international career. She made highly acclaimed recital débuts at the Queen Elizabeth Hall in London in 1986 and Carnegie Hall, New York, in 1989. But long periods of silence (notably between 1978 and 1982) have reflected her need for stocktaking and her dislike of the exigencies of a modern concert pianist's life. An avid chamber music player, Pires has toured extensively with the French violinist Augustin Dumay, and in 1994 formed a trio with him and the cellist Jian Wang. Her numerous recordings include two complete sets of Mozart piano sonatas and many of his piano concertos, much Chopin (for whom she shows a special affinity) and discs of Bach, Schubert and Schumann. With Dumay she has recorded chamber music by Mozart, Beethoven, Brahms, Grieg, Franck, Debussy and Ravel. All Pires's performances are distinguished by her crystalline technique, spontaneous poetry and profound, impassioned musicianship.

BIBLIOGRAPHY

H. Smith: 'In Love with Chopin', Gramophone, lxxiv (1996), 14–17

BRYCE MORRISON

Pires, Vasco (*fl* Coimbra, 1481–1509). Portuguese composer. He was appointed a singer at Coimbra Cathedral on 1 April 1481. In 1509 he was described as 'the bishop's singer' and held a prebend at S João d'Almedina. In the sale of some cathedral property on 20 December 1547 he is mentioned as a deceased *mestre de capela*. There are two extant works by him, a four-part *Magnificat quarti toni*, even-numbered verses only (*P-Cug*, choirbooks 12 and 32) and a three-part alleluia, also in the fourth tone (*P-Cug*, choirbooks 9 and 12; ed. in PM, ser.A, xxxvii, 1982). The textless alleluia was the first of a long series of similar pieces written in Portugal: these all lack text but were therefore adaptable to any feast.

BIBLIOGRAPHY

Livros dos acordos do Cabido (MS, P-Cs)

Livro 6° dos emprazamentos (MS, P-Cs), i, ff.82v–83r

M. de Sampayo Ribeiro: Os manuscritos musicais nos. 6 e 12 da Biblioteca geral da Universidade de Coimbra (Coimbra, 1941), 43, 98

R.V. Nery and P. Ferreira de Castro: Sínteses da cultura portuguesa: história da música (Lisbon, 1991), 35

ROBERT STEVENSON

P'iri. Small, cylindrical double-reed pipe of Korea. There are three main types: *hyang-p'iri* ('native *p'iri*'), *se-p'iri* ('thin *p'iri*') and *tang-p'iri* ('Chinese *p'iri*'); the *hyang-p'iri* is sometimes called *sagwan* or *tae-p'iri*. All three types are made of bamboo, use oversize bamboo reeds and have eight finger-holes; they are distinguished by size, timbre, tessitura and repertory. In addition to these three types, there are countless folk instruments with great differences in size, numbers of holes, and playing techniques.

The *hyang-p'iri* is about 27 cm long with a shaved bamboo double reed, itself over 7 cm long and more than 1 cm wide. The first finger-hole is in the rear, and the instrument has a range of less than two octaves, overblowing not being used. The *hyang-p'iri* has a loud, rough and nasal timbre, and in ensembles it is always the lead instrument. It is used both in court music (such as the ensemble piece *Sujech'ŏn*) and in folk music (shaman instrumental ensembles and the virtuoso solo genre *sanjo*). There is a system of onomatopoeic notation using the nasal consonant *n* with various vowels (*na*, *nu*, *nŏ* etc).

The *se-p'iri* is somewhat shorter and more slender than the *hyang-p'iri* but similar in range and construction. Its tone is much gentler than either of the other two *p'iri*, and it is therefore reserved for ensembles which accompany singing (e.g., lyrical *kagok* or *sijo* poetry chanting) or which use the soft Korean string instruments (as in the 'string version' of the suite *Yŏngsan hoesang*). Its use is limited to aristocratic genres.

The *tang-p'iri* is the same length as the *se-p'iri* but is considerably thicker, being made of dark and aged bamboo with prominent nodes. Its bore is the largest of the three types of *p'iri*, and the thumb-hole is the second (not the first) of the eight holes. The *tang-p'iri* is considered the hardest to play and overblowing at the 11th is used to obtain three notes in the high register. Its tone is more strident than that of the *hyang-p'iri*, and it is restricted to court music, both *tangak* ('Chinese music') and *hyangak* ('native music').

All three *p'iri* have a wide dynamic range and are highly expressive. Subtle gradations of pitch, as well as the wide vibrato characteristic of Korean music, may be obtained by varying the lip pressure on the reed, the air pressure and the position of the reed in the mouth.

The *p'iri*, which bears a close relationship to the Japanese HICHIRIKI and the Chinese *guan*, is considered Central Asian in origin, from the ancient state of Kucha, now in western China. The name *p'iri* is used to describe instruments in a Korean ensemble at the court of the

Chinese Sui dynasty (581–618 CE). Korean sources indicate that the *p'iri* was in use at the Korean court by 1076, and 20 *p'iri* were included in a gift of instruments from the Song Chinese emperor in 1114.

The Chinese treatise *Yueshu* (1103) indicates that the *p'iri* (Chin.: *bili*) had nine finger-holes, but the *Akhak kwebŏm* (1493) observes that all the necessary pitches may be obtained with only eight. The Korean instruments have subsequently retained the eight-hole configuration, while the Japanese *hichiriki* still has nine.

BIBLIOGRAPHY

Sŏng Hyŏn, ed.: *Akhak kwebŏm* [Guide to the study of music] (Seoul, 1493/R), 7.12*a* and 7.31*b*–32*a*

Chang Sahun: *Han'guk akkı taegwan* [Korean musical instruments] (Seoul, 1969), 36–43

Pak Pŏmhun: *P'iri sanjo yŏn'gu* [P'iri sanjo research] (Seoul, 1985)

K. Howard: *Korean Musical Instruments: a Practical Guide* (Seoul, 1988), 49–77

ROBERT C. PROVINE

Piriou, Adolphe (*b* Morlaix, 7 Sept 1878; *d* Paris, 3 Feb 1964). French composer. The son of a pharmacist of Scottish origin, he studied for five years at the Ecole Supérieure de Pharmacie in Paris before leaving in order to devote himself to music. He studied the violin with Joseph Debroux and Lucien Capet, and then composition with his brothers-in-law Pierre and Aymé Kunc in Toulouse, where the latter was director of the Conservatoire. On returning to Paris he completed his studies with D'Indy and Sérieyx, and was advised by Florent Schmitt. His compositions won several prizes, and he was active as a music critic and writer (he contributed to *Cobbett's Cyclopedic Survey of Chamber Music*), and as a researcher and producer for French Radio.

Piriou derived his chief inspiration from his native Brittany, which he celebrated in several of his works. Trained in the school of D'Indy, he did not always avoid a longwindedness which sometimes stifled poetic and melodic inspiration. The most original part of his work is in his symphonic compositions and his remarkable ballet with choruses, *Le rouet d'Armor* (1922–3), which skilfully integrates many traditional Breton songs and dances into its colourful language.

WORKS
(selective list)

Stage: Le rouet d'Armor (légende chorégraphique, 2, M. Geistdorfer), op.20, 1922–3, Paris, 1936; Court-circuits . . . lumière (comédie lyrique, 3, A. Henry and J. Wanerdo), op.53, 1939–47, unperf; La Charlezenn (légende lyrique, 3, Piriou and Henry), op.55, 1939–47, unperf; Les esprits de Garonne (poème musical et chorégraphique, 2, A. Berry), op.63, 1951–4, unperf; Dionysos et la mer (sym. lyrique et chorégraphique, A. Moralès Nadler), op.64, 1952, Antigua, 1957

Orch: 3 contes, op.6, 1911; Au pied d'un vieux calvaire, op.11, 1912; Au pays de Komor, orch suite, op.18a, 1920 [see Vocal and Choral: Komor]; Sinfoniale (Sym. no.1), op.32, 1932–3; Par les landes fleuries (Sym. no.2), op.46, 1944–6; Sym. no.3, op.65, 1943

Inst: Sonate, a, op.4, vn, pf, 1908–31; A la belle saison, op.19, pf, 1910–32; 3 contes, op.6, pf, 1911; Jeux d'enfants petits et grands, op.14, pf, 1913; Str Qt, g, op.21, 1923–30; Pavane pour Mélisande, op.22, pf, 1928; Scherzo-danse, op.23, pf, 1928; 3 pièces, op.37, 4 sax, 1935; Divertissement, op.47, 4 cl/4 sax, 1938; Aria et final, op.48, ob, cl, bn, 1938

Vocal and Choral: Cornouailles (grande fresque musicale), op.12, solo vv, chorus, orch, 1912–32; La nativité de la très sainte Vierge (petit orat.), op.16, S, chorus, wind, 1919; Komor (conte musical, C. Leconte de Lisle), op.18, solo vv, chorus, orch, 1920; Neiges et flammes (G.L. Garnier), op.33, 1v, orch, 1933–4

Songs (1v, pf): Heures d'été (A. Samain), op.1, 1905–6; Dans l'ombre des légendes (F. Ménez), op.10, 1912; Chansons marines (C.

Dervenn), op.49, 1937; Efflorescences (L. Marschutz), op.51, 1940–41; La danse (J. de Lassus), op.68, 1955–6

Principal publishers: Lemoine, Salabert

BIBLIOGRAPHY

P. Lespinasse: 'Piriou, Adolphe', *Cobett's Cyclopedic Survey of Chamber Music* (London, 1929, enlarged 2/1963/R by C. Mason)

R. Marot: *Les compositeurs bretons: les sources de leur inspiration* (Nantes, 1988)

V. de Bellaing: *Dictionnaire des compositeurs de musique en Bretagne* (Nantes, 1992)

M.-C. Mussat: 'Le rouet d'Armor', *La Bretagne à l'opéra* (Quimper, 1994), 88–9

JACQUES TCHAMKERTEN

Piron, (Charles) Alexis (*b* Dijon, 9 July 1689; *d* Paris, 21 Jan 1773). French dramatist. After studying law at Besançon, in 1719 he came to Paris where he began a long and successful association with the Fair Theatres. His first work produced there, the monologue *Arlequin Deucalion* (1722), brilliantly flouted the ban on spoken dialogue imposed by the official theatres and immediately established his reputation. In several *opéras comiques* of the 1720s he collaborated with composers of the stature of Rameau (*L'Endriague*, 1723; *L'enrôlement d'Arlequin*, 1726; *La P[ucelage], ou La rose*, 1726; *La robe de dissension*, 1726) and Royer (*Le fâcheux veuvage*, 1725; *Crédit est mort*, 1726). Their newly composed music not only relieved the staple diet of traditional melodies that was still the norm at the Fairs but also, in its 'operatic' style, acted as a clever foil to the *doubles entendres* and the farcical, episodic nature of the plays themselves. Other plays included music by L'abbé (*l'aîne*) (*Le mariage de Momus*, 1722; *Tirésias*, 1722; *L'âne d'or*, 1725) and Voisin (*L'âne d'or*; *Les chimères*, 1725). The playwright probably introduced Rameau to several of his future librettists, among them Fuzelier, who also worked at the Fair Theatres.

Piron's plays for the Comédie-Française – one of which, *Les courses de Tempé* (1734), involved a further collaboration with Rameau – were more coolly received, though the comedy *La métromanie* (1738) was an outright and enduring success.

BIBLIOGRAPHY

R. de Juvigny, ed.: *Oeuvres complètes d'Alexis Piron* (Paris, 1776)

P. Chaponnière: *Piron: sa vie et son oeuvre* (Paris, 1910)

G. Sadler: 'Rameau, Piron and the Parisian Fair Theatres', *Soundings*, iv (1974), 13–29

G. von Proschwitz, ed.: *Alexis Piron, épistolier: choix de ses lettres* (Göteborg, 1982)

GRAHAM SADLER

Pironkov, Simeon (Angelov) (*b* Lom, 18 June 1927). Bulgarian composer. He studied composition with Hadjiev and Stoyanov at the State Music Academy, Sofia, graduating in 1953. Before becoming a freelance composer (1962), he worked as a violinist and conductor. He was later appointed associate professor at the Higher Institute of Theatrical Arts and in 1980 became vice-president of the Union of Bulgarian Composers. In 1985 he was awarded the Herder Prize. His marked intellectual background has led him to adopt ideas found in avant-garde music, though with restraint and always from a philosophical perspective. His writing for films and the theatre has helped shape a laconic and structurally clear musical expression. The orchestral *Noshtna muzika* ('Night Music', 1968) is representative of the so-called Bulgarian neo-romanticism, which began with Nenov and continued in the work of Aleksandar Kandov. The

Bulgarian folk influences in *Night Music* signify a way of combining the experience of the individual with that of the contemporary age. Moral and philosophical questions are preferred subjects in his stage works.

WORKS
(selective list)

STAGE
librettos by the composer

Istinskata apologiya na Sokrat [Socrates' Real Apology] (op, 1, after K. Varnalis), concert perf., 1967; staged Sofia, National, 16 June 1982

Dobriyat chovek ot Sechuan [The Good Person of Szechwan] (op, after B. Brecht), 1969, Stara Zagora Opera, 24 June 1972

Zhitiye i stradaniye greshnago Sofroniya [The Life and Suffering of Sinful Sophronius] (op, 1), 1976; concert perf., 1977

Pustrata ptitsa [The Motley Bird] (comic op, 2 parts), 1979, Ruse Opera, 28 Sept 1980

O, moya mechta [Oh, My Dream] (lyrical comedy, 2 parts), 1985, Ruse Opera, 19 May 1987

OTHER WORKS

Orch: Sym., str, 1960; Dvizheniya [Movements], 1967; Noshtna muzika [Nightmusic], 1968; Rekviyem za ydin neizvesten mlad chovek [Requiem for an Unknown Young Person], 1968; Baletna muzika v pamet na Stravinski [Ballet Music in memoriam Stravinsky], 1972; Music for 2 Pf, Orch, 1973; Conc. rustico, vc, orch, 1982; Lirichna syuita [Lyric Suite], 1983; Fl Conc., 1987; Vn Conc., 1989; Passacaglia, 1991

Vocal: Posveshteniye [Dedication], female v, fl, vc, gui, vib, 1962, rev. 1997; Songs (B. Brecht), 1977; Bosnenska prispivna [Bosnian Lullaby], 1993; Zeleniyat dazhd [Green Rain], chorus, 1994; Fantaziya (H. Heine), Bar, vc, pf, 1997

Chbr and solo inst: Str Qt no.2, 1966; Detski albom [Children's Album], pf, 1983; Str Qt no.3, 1985; Variations, vn, pf, 1985; Ecological Trio, vn, cl, db, 1987; Pesni za smarta [Songs about Death], 1988; Pesni za zhivota [Songs about Life], 1988; Kamerna simfoniya [Chbr Sym.], 11 insts, 1990; Pametta na pianoto [The Memory of Piano], pf, 1995

BIBLIOGRAPHY

R. Biks: 'Kogato sredstvata ne predreshavat' [When media do not predetermine], *Balgarska muzika* (1968), no.6, pp.8–17

A. Palieva: 'Za slovoto i muzikata na Zhitiye i stradaniye greshnago Sofroniya' [Poetry and music in *The Life and Suffering of Sinful Sophronius*], *Balgarska muzika* (1989), no.4, pp.3–7

MAGDALENA MANOLOVA

Pirot, André. See PIRRO, ANDRÉ.

Pirouette. The term used by Mersenne in *Harmonie universelle* for the turned wooden component mounted on a conical brass tube which is inserted into the upper end of a shawm and receives the double reed (*see* SHAWM, §1). It functions as a support for the lips, allowing the reed to vibrate freely inside the player's mouth, facilitating embouchure technique. It was also used on the earlier type of RACKET and on the 18th-century *bason d'amour* (*see* HAUTBOIS D'ÉGLISE. The French term, which Mersenne claimed was used by makers, became universally adopted by modern historians before a 17th-century English term 'fliew' (flue) came to notice in James Talbot's MS treatise of *c*1695 (*GB-Och*). In modern Catalonia, where shawms are still played, the corresponding term is *tudél*, also meaning a bassoon crook.

ANTHONY C. BAINES

Piroye, Charles (*b* ?Paris, 1668–72; *d* ?Paris, 1717–30). French composer, organist and harpsichordist. A pupil of Lully and Lambert, he served from 1690 to 1712 as organist of the Jacobins and from 1708 to 1717 at St Honoré. After leaving St Honoré he seems to have spent the remainder of his life as a harpsichord teacher. In 1732 he was mentioned by Titon du Tillet as one of the 'most

able organists recently deceased', so the claim in the publisher's preface to his *Pièces choisies* that 'his compositions have acquired for him a well established reputation and his learned and delicate way of playing the organ and harpsichord bring each day renewed applause' is not without corroboration. Yet in the *capitation* lists of 1695 Piroye is taxed in the second of three classes, a step below such masters as Couperin, Marchand, d'Anglebert and Grigny. He was among the organists and harpsichordists who had to defend their profession against the onerous claims of the corporation of dance musicians in a dispute which dragged on from 1692 to 1773.

Piroye's works, though not numerous, cover a much broader range than is usual with French organists. His *Pièces choisies* are quite unlike other French organ music of the period, being clearly theatrical in nature. The titles – *La paix, L'allegresse* etc. – suggest divertissements, and the musical styles are those of the dance, with rhythms of the chaconne, gavotte, gigue and so forth. The textures, however, are closer to organ music than to typical harpsichord style. They are all in the form of multisectional 'dialogues' between different choirs of the instrument. According to Jean Bonfils (*MGG1*), the chromaticism and unconventional approach to form in *Jephté* suggest the influence of M.-A. Charpentier more than that of Lully and Lambert.

WORKS

Jephté (tragedy, 3), 1703, *F-Pn*

Messe de M. Biroat ('plain-chant musical'), *Pn*

Cantique pour le temps de noël, S, bc (Paris, 1703); ed. E. Borrel (Paris, 1922)

Le retour d'Eurydice aux enfers, S, 2 vn/fl, bc, intended as an afterpiece to Clérambault's cant. 'Orphée'

3 livres d'airs sérieux et à boire (Paris, 1695–7)

9 airs in Recueil d'airs sérieux et à boire de différents auteurs (Paris, 1695³–1724)

Pièces choisies … tant pour l'orgue et le clavecin, que pour toutes sortes d'instruments de musique (Paris, 1712/R); La béatitude (inc.), ed. F. Raugel, *Les maîtres français de l'orgue aux XVIIe et XVIIIe siècles*, ii (Paris, ?1951)

Premier livre de clavecin, lost (cited in catalogues, 1742 and 1751; facs. of the first piece, La Royale, in *Un Livre d'orgue d'Entrevaux*, Alpes-Maritime, 1984)

BIBLIOGRAPHY

C. Bouvet: 'Un musicien oublié: Charles Piroye', *RdM*, ix (1928), 225–34; also printed as 'Charles Piroye; les Fouquet', *Musiciens oubliés, musique retrouvée* (Paris, 1932), i, 7 [containing a detailed list of works]

R. Delosme: 'La Royale, de Charles Piroye', *Bulletin de l'Atelier d'études sur la musique française de XVIIe & XVIIIe siècles*, vii (1997), 16–17

DAVID FULLER

Pirro, André(-Gabriel-Edme) (*b* St Dizier, Haute-Marne, 12 Feb 1869; *d* Paris, 11 Nov 1943). French musicologist and organist. After studying with his father Jean Pirro, the local organist, he attended Franck's and Widor's organ classes at the Paris Conservatoire as a listener (1889–91); at this time he was organist and *maître de chapelle* at the Collège Stanislas. He also studied law at the Sorbonne while making a private study of music technique, and later attended the arts faculty at Nancy (1898–9). Subsequently he took the doctorat ès lettres at the Sorbonne in 1907 with an important dissertation on Bach's aesthetic. On the foundation of the Schola Cantorum (1896) he became a member of the directorial committee and professor of music history and the organ; after a period as organist at St Jean-Baptiste-de-Belleville (1900–04) he taught at the Ecole des Hautes Etudes

(1904–14). His career reached its climax with his appointment as Rolland's successor as professor of music history at the Sorbonne (1912–37), where in 1920 he established the first practical music university course in France. His pupils included Bridgman, Fédorov, Hertzmann, Machabey, Pincherle, Plamenac, Rokseth and Thibault.

Pirro's early interest in organ playing led him naturally to Bach as the subject of his first book, *L'orgue de Jean-Sébastien Bach*, which provides a valuable examination of Bach's output in relation to that of his precursors. His outstanding *L'esthétique de Jean-Sébastien Bach* attempted to define the symbolism of the music and earned him commendation from Schweitzer.

With three other books Pirro became established as a pioneer of modern French musicology: *Les clavecinistes*, *Schütz* and *Dietrich Buxtehude*, a figure that had attracted his interest during his work on Bach's predecessors. Pirro's numerous articles on early music include studies of the notation and performance of 15th- and 16th-century music, the frottola, Frescobaldi, 17th- and early 18th-century German music and several accounts of French organists; these show his awareness of the necessity for precise documentation of what was then largely uncharted material. His last and greatest work, *Histoire de la musique de la fin du XVIe siècle à la fin du XIVe* is an object lesson in scholarship, being packed with material gained at first hand or checked from reliable sources, and informed by keen critical insight.

WRITINGS

Prefaces in A. Guilmant: *Archives des maîtres de l'orgue des XVIe, XVIIe et XVIIIe siècles* (Paris, 1894–1911/R)
'De la notation proportionelle (XVe et XVIe siècles)', *Tribune de Saint-Gervais*, i (1895), 1, 4, 8
L'orgue de Jean-Sébastien Bach (Paris, 1895; Eng. trans., 1902/R)
'Les organistes français du XVIIe siècle: Jean Titelouze (1563–1633)', *Tribune de Saint-Gervais*, iv (1898), 132–5, 180–4, 207–11, 231–5 [lecture given at Salle de la Société St Jean, Paris, 24 March 1898]
'Heinrich Schütz (1585–1672)', 'Les formes d'expression dans la musique de Heinrich Schütz', *Tribune de Saint-Gervais*, vi (1900), 97–106, 314–21
'François Roberday', *Tribune de Saint-Gervais*, vii (1901), 3–4, 65–71, 110–8
'Un organiste au XVIIe s.: Nicolas Gigault', *RHCM*, iii (1903), 302–7, 550–57
'Louis Marchand', *SIMG*, vi (1904–5), 136–59
'Nicolas de Grigny (1671–1703)', *Tribune de Saint-Gervais*, xi (1905), 14–21
J.-S. Bach (Paris, 1906, rev. 1949; Eng. trans., 1957)
Descartes et la musique (supplementary diss., U. of Paris, 1907; Paris, 1907/R)
L'esthétique de Jean-Sébastien Bach (diss., U. of Paris, 1907; Paris, 1907/R)
'Frescobaldi et les musiciens de la France et des Pays-Bas', *BSIM*, iv (1908), 1127–53
'Remarques de quelques voyageurs sur la musique en Allemagne et dans les pays du Nord, de 1634 à 1700', *Riemann-Festschrift* (Leipzig, 1909/R), 325–40
Dietrich Buxtehude (Paris, 1913/R)
'La musique des Italiens d'après les remarques triennales de Jean-Baptiste Duval, 1607–1609', *Mélanges offerts à M. Henri Lemonnier* (Paris, 1913), 175–85
Schütz (Paris, 1913/R)
'La musique religieuse allemande depuis les psaumes de Schütz (1619) jusqu'à la mort de Bach (1750)', 'La musique en Allemagne pendant le XVIIe siècle et la première moitié du XVIIIe siècle', *EMDC*, I/ii (1914), 929–71, 971–1013
Jean Sébastien Bach auteur comique (Madrid, 1915) [lecture given at Residencia de Estudiantes, Madrid, 26 April 1914]
'Franz Liszt et la Divine Comédie', *Dante: mélanges de critique et d'érudition françaises* (Paris, 1921), 165–84

'Les "frottole" et la musique instrumentale', *RdM*, iii (1922), 3–12
Les clavecinistes: étude critique (Paris, 1924/R)
'Deux danses anciennes (XVIe–XVIIe siècles)', *RdM*, v (1924), 7–16
'Notes pour servir éventuellement à la biographie de Reincken', *Gedenkboek aangeboden aan Dr. D.F. Scheurleer* (The Hague, 1925), 251–64
'Une requête des joueurs de violon de Bitche (XVIIIe s.)', *RdM*, vi (1925), 97–104
'L'art des organistes', *EMDC*, II/ii (1926), 1181–374
'Jean Cornuel, vicaire à Cambrai', *RdM*, vii (1926), 190–203
'Orgues et organistes de Hagenau, de 1491 à 1525 environ', *RdM*, vii (1926), 11–17
'Remarques de quelques voyageurs sur la musique d'Italie entre 1720 et 1730', *Etudes italiennes*, x–xi (1928–9), 131–46
'Gilles Mureau, chanoine de Chartres', *Musikwissenschaftliche Beiträge· Festschrift für Johannes Wolf*, ed. W. Lott, H. Osthoff and W. Wolffheim (Berlin, 1929/R), 163–7
'L'enseignement de la musique aux universités françaises', *Bulletin de la Société internationale de musicologie*, ii (1930), 26–32, 45–56
La musique à Paris sous le règne de Charles VI (1380–1422) (Strasbourg, 1930/R)
'Remarques sur l'exécution musicale de la fin du XIVe au milieu du XVe siècles', *IMSCR I: Liège 1930*, 55–65
'Comment jouer Bach sur l'orgue', *ReM*, xiii/131 (1932), 20–26
'Robinet de la Magdalaine', *Mélanges de musicologie offerts à M. Lionel de La Laurencie* (Paris, 1933), 15–18
'Léon X et la musique', *Mélanges de philologie, d'histoire et de littérature offerts à Henri Hauvette* (Paris, 1934), 221–34
ed., with A. Gastoué and others: *La musique française du Moyen-Age à la Révolution*, Galerie Mazarine of the Bibliothèque nationale, Paris, 1933 (Paris, 1934) [exhibition catalogue]
Histoire de la musique de la fin du XIVe siècle à la fin du XVIe (Paris, 1940)
Mélanges André Pirro: recueil d'articles publié sous le patronage de la Société française de musicologie (Geneva, 1972) [reprint of 13 articles from 1909 to 1935; incl. preface by F. Lesure and index]

BIBLIOGRAPHY

R. Rolland and others: 'Hommage à André Pirro', *Information musicale* (3 Dec 1943)
Y. Rokseth: 'André Pirro', *RdM*, xxiii (1944), 25–42
C. van den Borren: 'André Pirro (1869–1943)', *RBM*, i (1946–7), 177–9
V. Fédorov: 'André Pirro (1869–1943) und Yvonne Rokseth (1890–1948)', *Mf*, iii (1950), 106–19 [incl. list of writings]
S. Baron: 'Bach's Text Settings: Schweitzer and Pirro Revisited', *A Bach Tribute: Essays in Honor of William H. Scheide*, ed. P. Brainard and R. Robinson (Kassel and Chapel Hill, NC, 1993), 17–26

G.B. SHARP/JEAN GRIBENSKI

Pirrotta, Nino [Antonino] (*b* Palermo, 13 June 1908; *d* Palermo, 23 Jan 1998). Italian musicologist. He studied music first at Palermo Conservatory and then from 1927 at Florence Conservatory (organ and organ composition diploma, 1930), and took a liberal arts degree with a thesis in art history at the University of Florence (1931). After a brief period as a radio organist he taught music history and worked as librarian at the Palermo Conservatory (1936–48), later becoming chief librarian of the Conservatorio di S Cecilia, Rome (1948–56); he was a founder (1951) and vice-president of the IAML (1951–4). In 1954–5 he was visiting professor at Princeton University and also lectured at UCLA (summer 1955) and Columbia University (1955); from 1956 to 1972 he was professor at Harvard University, where he was also chairman of the department (1965–8). He returned to Italy in 1972 to take up an appointment as professor of music history at Rome University. He was a member of the American Academy of Arts and Sciences (from 1967), the Accademia Nazionale di S Cecilia and the Accademia Nazionale dei Lincei, as well as honorary member of the AMS, the IMS, the Royal Musical Association and corresponding fellow of the British Academy. A council member for Harvard Publications in Music (1968–72), he received honorary doctorates from Holy Cross College (1970), Chicago University (1975), the University of Cambridge (1985), Princeton University (1987) and the University of Urbino (1996). He was awarded the Feltrinelli prize from the Accademia di Lincei in 1983.

Pirrotta's interest in musicology was stimulated by a request from Ettore Li Gotti, professor of philology at the University of Palermo, to collaborate with him on a study of Sacchetti and the music of his period; for this research (published 1935) Pirrotta taught himself the notation, theory, forms and various other aspects of 14th-century Italian music. His next significant publications (delayed by the war) included an examination of French influence on Italian music of about the same period, and a study of the 14th-century madrigal and caccia. With Li Gotti he examined the newly discovered Lucca manuscript; this led him to an important account of Ciconia (then little known) and his style in relation to his Italian contemporaries. Paolo da Firenze, another composer represented in the manuscript, also became the subject of an independent study. As a result of these investigations he began to edit *The Music of Fourteenth-Century Italy* (1954–64). His writings on the music of the Ars Nova exhibit a patient logic and clarity of thought that characterize all his work: while never refusing to admit the existence of other points of view, his intellectual and musical honesty often led him to adopt a conservative (and thus often wholly independent) position. In many of his studies (e.g. 'Music and Cultural Tendencies in 15th-Century Italy', 1966) Pirrotta used his wide cultural knowledge and informed understanding of humanist sources to illustrate his analysis of the texts and his account of music's place in society. Breadth of understanding and freshness of approach also characterized his study of 17th-century opera; 'Early Opera and Aria' (1968) is an excellent disentanglement of the many interrelated applications of early monodic style. His work on the connections between *commedia dell'arte* and opera further demonstrated his ability to recognize relationships between the various traditions he examined. His articles have been reprinted in four different collections (see 1984, 1987 and 1994).

Pirrotta's thorough knowledge of so many periods (not only of Italian music but other areas of Italian culture as well) made him highly influential in the formation of several prominent American musicologists, and in Italy his careful, methodical approach greatly benefited young scholars. He was honoured with three Festschriften: *In cantu et in sermone: for Nino Pirrotta on his 80th Birthday*, ed. F. Della Seta and F. Piperno (Florence, 1989); *Ceciliana per Nino Pirrotta*, ed. M.A. Balsano and G. Collisani (Palermo, 1994); and 'A Memorial Gathering for Nino Pirrotta', *Studi Musicali*, xxviii (1999). Five issues of periodicals were dedicated to him: *RIM*, x (1975); *MD*, xlix (1975); *Ricercare*, x (1998); *Avidi lumi*, i (1998); and a section of *Studi musicali*, xxviii (1999), 43–63.

WRITINGS

with E. Li Gotti: *Il Sacchetti e la tecnica musicale del Trecento italiano* (Florence, 1935)

Il codice estense lat.568 e la musica francese in Italia al principio del '400 (Palermo, 1946)

'Per l'origine e la storia della "caccia" e del "madrigale" trecentesco', *RMI*, xlviii (1946), 305–23; xlix (1947), 121–42

'"Dulcedo" e "subtilitas" nella pratica polifonica franco-italiana al principio del '400', *RBM*, ii (1947–8), 125–32

with E. Li Gotti: 'Il codice di Lucca', *MD*, iii (1949), 119–38; iv (1950), 111–52; v (1951), 115–42

with E. Li Gotti: 'Paolo tenorista, fiorentino extra moenia', *Estudios dedicados a Menéndez Pidal*, iii (Madrid, 1952), 577–606

'Tre capitoli su Cesti', *La scuola romana: G. Carissimi – A. Cesti – M. Marazzoli*, Chigiana, x (1953), 27–79

'Compiti regionali, nazionali, ed internazionali delle biblioteche musicali', *Musiche popolari mediterranee; Convegno dei bibliotecari musicali: Palermo 1954*, 331–8

'Note su un codice di antiche musiche per tastiera', *RMI*, lvi (1954), 333–9

'Commedia dell'arte and Opera', *MQ*, xli (1955), 305–24

'Marchettus da Padua and the Italian Ars Nova', *MD*, ix (1955), 57–71

'Paolo da Firenze in un nuovo frammento dell'Ars Nova', *MD*, x (1956), 61–6

'Due sonetti musicali del secolo XIV', *Miscelánea en homenaje a Monseñor Higinio Anglés* (Barcelona, 1958–61), 651–62

'Piero e l'impressionismo musicale del secolo XIV', *L'Ars Nova italiana del Trecento I: Certaldo 1959*, 57–74

'Una arcaica descrizione trecentesca del madrigale', *Festschrift Heinrich Besseler*, ed. E. Klemm (Leipzig, 1961), 155–61

'Ballate e "soni" secondo un grammatico del Trecento', *Saggi e ricerche in memoria di Ettore Li Gotti*, iii (Palermo, 1962), 42–54

'Ars nova e stil novo', *RIM*, i (1966), 3–19

'Music and Cultural Tendencies in 15th-Century Italy', *JAMS*, xix (1966), 127–61

'On Text Forms from Ciconia to Dufay', *Aspects of Medieval and Renaissance Music: a Birthday Offering to Gustave Reese*, ed. J. LaRue and others (New York, 1966), 673–82

'Church Polyphony Apropos of a New Fragment at Foligno', *Studies in Music History: Essays for Oliver Strunk* (Princeton, NJ, 1968), 113–26

'Dante "musicus": Gothicism, Scholasticism and Music', *Speculum*, xliii (1968), 245–57

'Early Opera and Aria', *New Looks at Italian Opera: Essays in Honor of Donald J. Grout*, ed. W.W. Austin (Ithaca, NY, 1968), 39–107

'Musica polifonica per un testo attribuito a Federico II', *L'Ars Nova italiana del Trecento: convegni di studio 1961–67*, ed. F.A. Gallo (Certaldo, 1968), 97–112

'Teatro, scene e musica nelle opere di Monteverdi', *Claudio Monteverdi e il suo tempo: Venice, Mantua and Cremona 1968*, 45–64

'Early Venetian Libretti at Los Angeles', *Essays in Musicology in Honor of Dragan Plamenac*, ed. G. Reese and R.J. Snow (Pittsburgh, 1969/R), 233–43

with E. Povoledo: *Li due Orfei: da Poliziano a Monteverdi* (Turin, 1969, enlarged 2/1975; Eng. trans., 1982 as *Music and Theatre from Poliziano to Monteverdi*)

'Tradizione orale e tradizione scritta nella musica', *L'Ars Nova italiana del Trecento: Convegno II: Certaldo and Florence 1969* [*L'Ars Nova italiana del Trecento*, iii (Certaldo, 1971)], 431–41

'Two Anglo-Italian Pieces in the Manuscript Porto 714', *Speculum musicae artis: Festgabe für Heinrich Husmann*, ed. H. Becker and R. Gerlach (Munich, 1970), 253–61

'Gesualdo, Ferrara e Venezia', 'Monteverdi e i problemi dell'opera', *Studi sul teatro veneto fra Rinascimento ed età barocca*, ed. M.T. Muraro (Florence, 1971), 305–19, 321–43

'"Zacharus musicus"', *Quadrivium*, xii/1 (1971), 153–75

'New Glimpses of an Unwritten Tradition', *Words and Music: the Scholar's View … in Honor of A. Tillman Merritt*, ed. L. Berman (Cambridge, MA, 1972), 271–91

'Ricercare e variazioni su "O rosa bella"', *Studi musicali*, i (1972), 59–77

'Note su Marenzio e il Tasso', *Scritti in onore di Luigi Ronga* (Milan and Naples, 1973), 557–72

'Novelty and Renewal in Italy: 1300–1600', *Studien zur Tradition in der Musik: Kurt von Fischer zum 60. Geburtstag*, ed. H.H. Eggebrecht and M. Lütolf (Munich, 1973), 49–63

'Le tre corone e la musica', *La musica al tempo di Boccaccio e i suoi rapporti con la letteratura: Siena and Certaldo 1975*, 9–20 [*L'Ars Nova italiana del Trecento*, iv (Certaldo, 1978)]

'"Musica de sono humano" and the Musical Poetics of Guido of Arezzo', *Medieval Poetic s*, ed. P.M. Clogan (Cambridge, 1976), 13–27

'Semiramis e Amneris, un anagramma o quasi', *Il melodramma italiano dell'Ottocento: studi e ricerche per Massimo Mila*, ed. G. Pestelli (Turin, 1977), 5–12

'Istituzioni musicali nella Firenze dei Medici', *Firenze e la Toscana dei Medici nell'Europa del Quinquecento: Florence 1980*, 37–54

'Willaert e la canzone villanesca', *Studi musicali*, ix (1980), 191–217
'The Tradition of Don Juan Plays and Comic Opera', *PRMA*, cvii (1981), 60–70
'Metastasio e i teatri romani', *Le muse galanti: la musica a Roma nel Settocento: Rome 1982*, 23–34
'I musicisti nell'epistolario di Metastasio', *Il centenario della morte di Metastasio: Rome 1983*, 245–55
'Rhapsodic Elements in North-Italian Polyphony', *MD*, xxxvii (1983), 83–99; It. trans. in *Recercare*, i (1989), 7–21
'Malipiero e il filo d'Arianna', *Malipiero: scrittura e critica*, ed. M.T. Muraro (Florence, 1984), 5–19
'Maniera e riforme nella musica italiana del '500', *Cultura e società nel Rinascimento tra riforme e manierismi*, ed. V. Branca and C. Ossola (Florence, 1984), 463–86
Music and Culture in Italy from the Middle Ages to the Baroque (Cambridge, MA, 1984) [reprs. of selected essays, some rev.; incl. Eng. trans.]
Musica tra Medioevo e Rinascimento (Turin, 1984) [reprs. of selected essays]
'"Arte" e "non arte" nel frammento Greggiati', *L'Ars Nova italiana del Trecento*, v, ed. A. Ziino (Palermo, 1985), 200–17
'Back to Ars Nova Themes', *Music and Context: Essays for John M. Ward*, ed. A.D. Shapiro and P. Benjamin (Cambridge, MA, 1985), 166–82
'I cori per l'"Edipo tiranno"', *Andrea Gabrieli e il suo tempo: Venice 1985*, 273–92
'"Dolci affetti": i musici di Roma e il madrigale', *Studi musicali*, xiv (1985), 59–104
ed., with A. Ziino: *Händel e gli Scarlatti a Roma: Rome 1985*
'Musica e umanesimo', *Lettere italiane*, xxxvii (1985), 453–70
'Poesia e musica', *Letture classensi*, xvi (1987), 153–62
Scelte poetiche di musicisti: teatro, poesia e musica da Willaert a Malipiero (Venice, 1987) [reprs. of articles and papers, 1953–85]
'Note su Minato', *L'opera italiana a Vienna prima di Metastasio*, ed. M.T. Muraro (Florence, 1990), 127–63
Don Giovanni in musica: dall'"Empio punito" a Mozart (Venice, 1991; Eng. trans., 1994)
'Forse Nerone cantò da tenore', *Musica senza aggettivi: studi per Fedele d'Amico*, ed. A. Ziino (Florence, 1991), 47–60
'Rileggendo il "Pirata" di Bellini', *Napoli e il teatro musicale in Europa tra Sette e Ottocento: studi in onore di Friedrich Lippmann*, ed. B.M. Antolini and W. Witzenmann (Florence, 1993), 407–16
'Rossini eseguito ieri e oggi', *La recezione di Rossini ieri e oggi: Rome 1993*, 3–13
'Before the Madrigal', *JM*, xxii (1994), 237–52
'On Landini and Ser Lorenzo', *MD*, xlviii (1994), 5–13
Poesia e musica e altri saggi (Florence, 1994) [reprs. of selected essays]
'"Maniera" polifonica e immediatezza recitativa', *Monteverdi, recitativo in monodia e polifonia: Rome 1995*, 9–20
'Pier Jacopo Martello: "Et in Arcadia ego" ma "cum modo"', *Le parole della musica*, ii, ed. M.T. Muraro (Florence, 1995), 33–46
'Florence from Barzelletta to Madrigal', *Musica Franca: Essays in Honor of Frank A. D'Accone*, ed. I. Alm, A. McLamore and C. Reardon (New York, 1996), 7–18
La notazione del Codice Rossi (Florence, forthcoming)

EDITIONS

The Music of Fourteenth-Century Italy, CMM, viii/1–5 (1954–64)
Paolo Tenorista in a New Fragment of the Italian Ars Nova (Palm Springs, CA, 1961) [facs.]
Il codice Rossi 215: Roma, Biblioteca Apostolica Vaticana (Lucca, 1992) [facs.; incl. introduction, catalogue of works and transcr. of texts]
with G. Gialdroni: *I Musici di Roma e il madrigale: 'Dolci affetti' (1582) e 'Le Gioie' (1589)* (Lucca, 1993) [two madrigal collections]
Chori in musica composti sopra li chori della tragedia di Edippo Tiranno, Andrea Gabrieli: Edizione nazionale dell opere, xii (Milan, 1995)

BIBLIOGRAPHY

M.A. Balsano and G. Collisani, eds.: *Ceciliana per Nino Pirrotta* (Palermo, 1994)
T.M. Gialdroni: 'Bibliografia di Nino Pirrotta', *Studi musicali*, xxviii (1999), 43–63

CAROLYN GIANTURCO/TERESA M. GIALDRONI

Pirumov, Aleksandr Ivanovich (*b* Tbilisi, 6 Feb 1930; *d* Moscow, 20 July 1995). Russian composer. He studied the piano with Vissarion Shiukashvili at the Music School in Tbilisi. From the 1950s he lived in Moscow; he graduated from the class of Kabalevsky at the Moscow Conservatory (1956) and completed his postgraduate studies in 1960. From 1962 he taught composition and counterpoint at the Moscow Conservatory. He was made Honoured Representative of the Arts of Russia in 1983.

Initially Pirumov worked principally with instrumental genres and quickly established himself as a composer with a refined technique and an original style based on the unique synthesis of Armenian folk idiom and contemporary European concert music. He composed several set pieces for the International Tchaikovsky Competition – Prelude and Toccata for the second competition (1962) and Scherzo for the fifth (1974) – and for the All-Union Competition of Young Performers he composed *Kontsertvariatsii* (1972). Shostakovich had a high regard for Pirumov's String Quartet no.2, which was presented as his diploma work on graduation from the Conservatory.

Echoes of Armenian choral songs can be discerned as early as the cantata *Dvadtsat' shest'* ('Twenty-Six', 1956); later, the oriental theme manifests itself in the composer's frequent use of poetry from the East (Rabindranath Tagore, Abulkosim Lakhuti, Avetik Isaakian, Ashot Grashi, Rasul Gamzatov) and in the liberal sprinkling of national tunes and rhythms (e.g. the *Lezghinka* as thematic material). The Second String Quartet and the Third Symphony in particular quote traditional melodies, the latter from the *Sayat'-Nova* collection of songs. Other characteristics include the use of exotic instruments such as the *Duduk*, *Saz* and *Tār*, and choruses based on the verse-refrain form more commonly associated with folksong. The colourfulness, the picturesqueness and the reliance on folk dance genres in his symphonies suggest a link with the music of Khachaturian. But, as distinct from the latter, Pirumov is predisposed towards epic profundity, and towards lucid, lyrical meditation.

WORKS
(selective list)

INSTRUMENTAL

Orch: Sym. no.1, 1956; Sym. no.2, 1963; Sym., str, perc, 1964–5; Sym. no.3, str, 1980; Kontsert-variatsii, pf, orch, 1972; Scherzo, 1974; Conc., ob, str, 1986
Chbr: 4 str qts: no.1, 1954, no.2, 1955, no.3, 1959, no.4, 1967; Sonata, vn, pf, 1979; P'yesï dlya ansambley goboyev [Pieces for Ensemble of Oboes]: Invention, 2 ob, Fugue, 3 ob, Prelude and Fugue on a Russ. Folksong, 3 ob
Pf: Prelude and Toccata, 1960; Sonatina no.1, 1960; Detskiy al'bom [Children's Album], 1966; Sonatina no.2, 1966; Studies, 1966; Variatsii na temu Belï Bartoka [Variations on a Theme by Belá Bartók], 1968; Voinstvennïy tanets [Martial Dance], 1968; Prelude, 1969; 24 Little Fugues, 1986
Other solo inst: 5 Preludes, org, 1967; Partita, ob, 1979
Film scores, incid music for radio plays

VOCAL

Choral: Dvadtsat' shest' [Twenty-Six] (Cant, 2, N. Aseev, A. Grashi), chorus, orch, 1956; Pis'mena [Runes] (6 poems, R. Gamzatov, trans. N. Grebnyov); a cappella chorus, 1966; 4 stikhotvoreniya [4 Poems] (A.S. Pushkin, M. Lermontov, V. Mayakovsky, Gamzatov, chorus, 1973; Dni Oktyabrya [Days of October], (orat, fragments from J. Reed: *Ten Days that Shook the World*, chorus, brass, org, perc, 1976; V pamyat' voina-brata [In Memory of a Warrior, my Brother] (Requiem, 7, A. Tvardovsky), chorus, pf, 1980
1v, pf: Ey, chelovek! [Hey, you!] (R. Gamzatov), song cycle, Bar, pf, 1967; 2 romanca (Pushkin), 1979; 2 soneta (Shakespeare: Sonnets no.25, 71, trans. S. Marshak), 1979

Principal publishers: Sovetskiy kompozitor, Muzïka (Moscow)

BIBLIOGRAPHY

V. Berkov: 'Kamernaya muzïka Pirumova' [The chamber music of Pirumov], *Muzïka i sovremennost'*, ii (1963), 177–98

E. Zakharov: 'Realizuya interesnïy zamïsel' [Bringing to life an interesting conception], *Sovetskaya kul'tura* (26 March 1966) [Sym., str, perc]

P. Vasil'yev: 'Yarkoye sochineniye' [A vivid composition], *Sovetskaya kul'tura*, (5 Dec 1980 [Sonata, vn, pf]

O. Kuzina: 'Aleksandr Pirumov', *Kompozitorï Rossiyskoy Federatsii*, ed. V. Kazenin, iv (Moscow, 1987), 3–33

JURY IVANOVICH PAISOV

Pisa. City in Italy, in Tuscany. Settled by the Romans in 89 BCE, it was one of the four medieval Sea Republics and was conquered by the Medici in 1494. Its oldest musical documents are three *Exultet* settings, two from the 11th century (*campo aperto*, almost completely diastematic) and one from the 13th (in central Italian notation). By the 11th century, the cathedral had a *canonico cantor* (later called *magister schola*), who directed the clerics in liturgical singing, and there is evidence that it had an organ by the 16th century (its bellows were restored in 1571). On 7 February 1556 the clerics' *schola cantorum* was replaced by a new *cappella* based on Flemish models. The cathedral was closed in 1595 because of a fire which apparently destroyed its library; the 17th-century inventories of the library show that during the 16th century the *cappella* repertory had included works by Willaert, Palestrina, Lassus, Marenzio and Vincenzo Galilei. The building was reopened in 1605. The cathedral organ was rebuilt, according to Banchieri (*Conclusioni del suono dell'organo*, 1609), by a 'Flemish' builder in consultation with the cathedral organist Antonio Buonavita, and Emilio de' Cavalieri. Among the *maestri di cappella* of the 17th century were Pompeo Signorucci, Vincenzo Mercanti and Teofilo Macchetti, whose musical manuscripts were acquired in 1715 by the Opera del Duomo (the administrative body of the cathedral) and whose liturgical services (mostly lost) were regularly performed. In the 18th century G.C.M. Clari and G.G. Brunetti were *maestri di cappella*; they performed works by Haydn, Cimarosa and Cherubini and their own four-part compositions with string or organ accompaniment. In the late 20th century the cathedral had a choir of 16 singers, an organist and a music director.

The Cavalieri di S Stefano, a lay order of knights, was founded by Cosimo I de' Medici in 1561. In 1571 their church (S Stefano dei Cavalieri) was consecrated and a *cappella musicale* founded; it had only voices at first but from the 17th century instruments as well. Notable *maestri* include Antonio Brunelli, G.L. Cattani and F.M. Gherardeschi. 311 volumes of music dating from the 17th century to the 19th are extant, as well as 65 volumes of chant (the earliest dated 1561). The order was suppressed in 1859 and the *cappella* disbanded, leaving only an organist. A large organ was built in 1571 by Onofrio Zefferini of Cortona, and a second and smaller one in 1618 by Cosimo Ravani. In 1733–7 A.B. della Ciaia supervised the construction of a new, grand instrument, built by the best Italian makers of the period, with 60 stops and four manuals (a fifth keyboard was a harpsichord), which became one of the most famous organs in Europe. It was modified several times (1839, 1870, 1913–14), and finally connected to the Zeffirini organ and furnished with pneumatic and electric action.

Other centres of sacred music were the church of S Caterina and S Nicola, the church of the Medici grand dukes, who spent Carnival to Holy Week in Pisa regularly from 1601 to 1625 and occasionally until 1684. They brought their Florentine musicians to participate in services at S Nicola, where until 1614 Caccini was *maestro di cappella* and his family performed; works by Peri were also heard there. The first record of secular music dates from 1588, when two 20-part madrigals by Buonavita, then organist at S Stefano, were performed for the arrival of Grand Duke Ferdinand I. The next year, for the arrival of Ferdinand's bride Christina of Lorena, there were mock battles with three pieces by Buonavita interspersed. In 1605 the grand dukes offered *giostre, abbattimenti d'armi, casi armigeri* and a *ballo martiale* to celebrate the marriage of Enea Piccolomini and Caterina Adimari, and in 1606 an *Abatimento di Diario et il finto Alessandro* with words and music by Duke Ferdinand Gonzaga was performed. Further court performances included an opera by Gonzaga (1607, in the hall of the Consoli di Mare, later the Teatro Pubblico) and C. Galletti's *L'Orindo* (1608). Antonio Pisani's cantata *Alfea reverente* (1639) was composed for the arrival of Vittoria della Rovere, wife of Grand Duke Ferdinand II. A number of court opera performances are documented from 1671 until 1701, after which there seems to have been a hiatus until Carnival 1732. The oratorio *Il martirio di San Giovanni Nepomuceno* was given in the cathedral in 1737, and another in 1761 at S Francesco; in 1790 *Debora e Sisara*, an *azione sacra* by P.A. Guglielmi, was given in the Teatro dei Nobili Fratelli Prini (opened 1771). On the whole, however, secular works seem to have dominated, many in honour of the ruling family, notably works by Brunetti in 1761 and 1766. The Teatro dei Nobili continued to operate until the last years of the century, offering two seasons of opera a year (Carnival and spring). It was later administered by the Accademia dei Costanti (1798) and the Accademia dei Ravvivati (1822); in 1878 it became the Teatro Ernesto Rossi. Operas were given up to 1900; it closed in 1930.

In 1807 an outdoor arena was built, the Teatro Diurno (the Arena Garibaldi from 1882). It was originally intended to be a racecourse, but from 1873 it also presented opera (the first being Verdi's *Il trovatore*); it closed in 1895. The Politeama, another outdoor opera theatre, opened in 1865 with Ricci's *Crespino e la Comare*; it was destroyed during World War II. The Regio Teatro Nuovo (now the Teatro Comunale Giuseppe Verdi) opened in 1867 with Rossini's *Guillaume Tell*. It has excellent acoustics, and mounts a short but popular autumn opera season. It was restored from 1985 to 1989 and reopened with the world première of Roberto De Simone's *Mistero e processo di Giovanna d'Arco*.

A Banda dei Cacciatori was founded by the Cavalieri and other Pisan noblemen in 1765; it played at ceremonies all over Tuscany. In 1803 it was reorganized as the Corpo Filarmonico degli Urbani, in 1819 as the Società Filarmonica degli Alfei, and in 1849 (as part of the Guardia Civica) as the Società Filarmonica Militare degli Alfei. From 1868 it was called the Società Filarmonica Pisana. It was still active in the late 20th century.

The first choral society, the Vincenzo Galilei Male-Voice Choir (founded 1881), was a product of the Scuola Corale. In the early 20th century it began to participate in local opera productions; it was reorganized in 1910 as the Società Corale Pisana, and in 1958, under B. Pizzi, it won first prize in the Arezzo International Choral Competition. In 1976 it became a mixed choir. At S Nicola a children's choir, Pueri Cantores, was established in 1963, followed by a young people's choir, Coro Polifonico, in 1991. In 1973 P. Farulli organized a chorus and orchestra to perform Bach; only the choir is still active.

The first concert society, the Società Amici della Musica (1920–60), was succeeded by a section of the Gioventù Musicale (from 1959), the Goethe Institute (1961–6), the Scuola Normale (from 1967), the Associazione Pisana Amici della Lirica (from 1972) and the International Federation of Business and Professional Women (from 1978). This organization also holds a national piano competition each year. Organ concerts are given in the cathedral, where a new organ by Mascioni was inaugurated in 1981; at S Stefano; and at S Nicola, which has a three manual Tamburini organ. The Teatro Verdi organizes an annual opera and concert season. Concerts are also given in the Aula Magna of the university, the Sala degli Stemmi of the Scuola Normale, the church of S Paolo all'Orto (restored as a concert hall in 1992) and, in summer, in Giardino Scotto, in the 'Sapienza' quadrangle of the university and in the gardens of villas on the outskirts of the city.

As early as the 11th century music was taught at the cathedral school, and from the 16th century at the church of the Cavalieri as well. The Scuola Corale was founded by the Società Filarmonica degli Alfei (1855). Because of the proximity of Pisa to the conservatory at Florence and the municipal music schools at Lucca and Livorno, there are no such establishments in the city. There are, however, two private music schools: the Scuola di Musica Giuseppe Bonamici and the Scuola della Società Filarmonica. The International Society for Music Education has a branch in Pisa. The holdings of the Biblioteca Universitaria include 323 librettos and 334 music and music-related manuscripts, several including medieval treatises. In 1987 the Associazione Toscana per la Ricerca delle Fonti Musicali was founded in Pisa; the university series Studi Musicali Toscani was founded by Carolyn Gianturco in 1993.

BIBLIOGRAPHY

G. Cervoni: Descrizzione [sic] de la felicissima entrata del Serenis. D. Ferdinando de' Medici cardinale, Gran Duca di Toscana nella città di Pisa (Florence, 1588)
E. Micheli: Sull'organo della Conventuale di S Stefano (Pisa, 1871)
A. Segrè: Il teatro pubblico di Pisa nel '600 e nel '700 (Pisa, 1902)
A. Gentili: Cinquant'anni dopo . . . il Teatro Verdi ne' suoi ricordi (Pisa, 1915)
F. Baggiani: L'organo di Azzolino B. Della Ciaia nella Chiesa Conventuale dei Cavalieri di S. Stefano in Pisa (Pisa, 1974)
F. Baggiani: Giovanni Carlo Maria Clari (Pisa, 1977)
P. Radicchi: Giovanni Lorenzo Cattani, musicista carrarese al servizio dei Medici (Pisa, 1980)
A.R. Calderoni Masetti: L'Exultet 'beneventano' del duomo di Pisa (Galatina-Lecce, 1989)
P. Raffaelli: I manoscritti liturgico-musicali della Biblioteca Cateriniana e del Fondo Seminario Santa Caterina dell'Archivio arcivescovile di Pisa: storia e catalogo (Lucca, 1993)
S. Barandoni and P.Raffaelli: L'archivio musicale della Chiesa Conventuale dei Cavalieri di Santo Stefano di Pisa: storia e catalogo (Lucca, 1994)
C. Gianturco and L.Pierotti Boccaccio: 'Teofilo Macchetti and Sacred Music in Pisa, 1694–1713', Musicologia humana: Studies in Honor of Warren and Ursula Kirkendale, ed. S. Gmeinwieser, D. Hiley and J. Riedlbauer (Florence, 1994), 393–415
I. Zolesi: I manoscritti musicali della Biblioteca Universitaria di Pisa: storia e catalogo (Lucca, 1998)

STEFANO BARANDONI, CAROLYN GIANTURCO

Pisa, Agostino (fl Rome, 1611). Italian music theorist. In Rome in 1611 he published Breve dichiaratione della battuta musicale, opera non solo utile ma necessaria a quelli che desiderano fare profitto nella musica. Later that year a revised and enlarged version appeared there, as Battuta della musica … opera nova utile e necessaria alli professori della musica (1611/R), as did a sonnet from the latter as Brevissima dichiaratione della battuta della musica. He was a priest and styled himself a 'doctor of canon and civil law, and theoretical and practising musician' on the title-page of Battuta della musica. Since the dedication was signed in Rome it appears that he lived there at the time.

In his manuscript Trattato della battuta musicale (1643), P.F. Valentini stated that 'during the year 1611 differences of opinion arose among certain virtuosos in Rome about musical beat, and books and sonnets about it were published'; Pisa's three publications were among them, and the aura of controversy no doubt accounts for the polemical tone of the two main ones. Of fundamental importance in Pisa's writings is the structure of the musical beat, in particular the establishment of its beginning and end. He cited many authors to support his point of view but his principal authority was Zarlino (Le istitutioni harmoniche, iii, Venice, 1558/R), who maintained that the beat, like the human pulse, had two movements (falling and rising) and two rests, one at the end of each movement. The beat thus begins with a falling movement and ends with the rest after the rising movement. In the introduction to Battuta della musica Pisa described six common erroneous views of the musical beat, which he blamed on the 'new practitioners' attempts to make the beat coincide with the rhythmic and musical accent. He could not accept that the beat should be regulated by the music but maintained exactly the opposite, that it should provide an abstract measurement to which the music must conform.

Pisa's books and ideas were widely circulated and achieved remarkable notoriety up to the end of the 17th century. Valentini explicitly criticized Pisa – whom he called Asip – on many points. Pisa is further quoted by, among others, Banchieri, G.M. Bononcini, Andrea da Modena, Zaccaria Tevo, Zacconi and even Mattheson.

BIBLIOGRAPHY

EitnerQ; GaspariC; MGG1 (O. Mischiati)
R. Schwartz: 'Zur Geschichte des Taktschlagens', JbMP 1907, 59–70
G. Schünemann: Geschichte des Dirigierens (Leipzig, 1913/R), 94–6, 115, 121
M.B. Collins: 'The Performance of Sesquialtera and Hemiola in the 16th Century', JAMS, xvii (1964), 5–28, esp. 10
W. Dürr: 'Auftakt und Taktschlag in der Musik um 1600', Festschrift Walter Gerstenberg, ed. G. von Dadelsen and A. Holschneider (Wolfenbüttel, 1964), 26–36
P. Aldrich: Rhythm in Seventeenth-Century Italian Monody (London, 1966), 25
G. Houle: Meter in Music, 1600–1800: Performance, Perception, and Notation (Bloomington, IN, 1987), 5–8
D. Damschroder and D.R.Williams: Music Theory from Zarlino to Schenker: a Bibliography and Guide (Stuyvesant, NY, 1990), 234

AGOSTINO ZIINO (with FRANS WIERING)

Pisador, Diego (b Salamanca, 1509/10; d ?Salamanca, after 1557). Spanish vihuelist and composer. He was the eldest son of Alonso Pisador and Isabel Ortiz, whose father, Alfonso III de Fonseca, had been an enthusiastic patron of music. Diego took minor orders in 1526 but did not become a priest. In 1532 his father took a position as administrator for the count of Monterrey in Galicia: Diego remained in Salamanca, taking his father's place as major-domo of the city as well as administering the family estate and looking after his mother and younger brother. After his mother's death in September 1550, Diego inherited the bulk of her estate. His brother contested the will; in a letter dated 13 October 1550 his father sided with Diego against his brother, urged him to marry, to sell the office of major-domo and to abandon work on his vihuela tablature. Returning to Salamanca shortly thereafter the father reversed his original position, forced Diego to leave the family home and supported the brother in his attempt to break the will. Diego obtained 30,000 maravedís from the estate on 3 August 1553, and father and son were still unreconciled in 1557.

Pisador's anthology *Libro de música de vihuela* (Salamanca, 1552/R1973) reveals a mediocre musician, but an educated amateur well versed in the principal musical currents of the era. The book, compiled over a 15-year period, contains 95 works including eight masses by Josquin. Also included are motets by Josquin, Gombert, Basurto, Morales, Mouton and Willaert, 22 Spanish songs and *romances*, and madrigals and *villanesche* by Arcadelt, Willaert, Fontana, Nola and Sebastiano Festa. 13 of Pisador's 26 fantasias are monothematic, while the remainder are imitative polythematic works. The best of them show considerable deftness; many are flawed by defective counterpoint and harmonic blandness, though they are elegant in form. Other original works include variations on *Conde claros* and *Guárdame las vacas*, a pavan, contrapuntal hymn settings and psalms set in *fabordón* style. The book is printed in conventional Spanish tablature using either red tablature figures or a separate staff to notate the voices to be sung by the vihuelist.

BIBLIOGRAPHY

BrownI

N.A. Cortés: 'Diego Pisador: algunos datos biográficos', *Boletín de la Biblioteca Menéndez y Pelayo*, iii (1921), 331–5

J.M. Ward: *The Vihuela de Mano and its Music (1536–1576)* (diss., New York U., 1953)

M. Honegger: 'La tablature de Diego Pisador et le problème des altérations au XVIe siècle', *RdM*, lix (1973), 38–59, 191–230; lx (1974), 3–32

G. Simpson and B. Mason: 'The Sixteenth-Century Spanish Romance: a Survey of the Spanish Ballad as Found in the Music of the Vihuelistas', *EMc*, v (1977), 51–8

J. Griffiths: *The Vihuela Fantasia: a Comparative Study of Forms and Styles* (diss., Monash U., 1983)

C. Jacobs: *A Spanish Renaissance Songbook* (University Park, PA, 1988)

F. Roa and F. Gértrudix: *Diego Pisador: Libro de Música de vihuela* (diss., Real Conservatorio Superior de Madrid, 1995)

JOHN GRIFFITHS

Pisanelli, Pompilio (*b* Bologna; *d* after 1606). Italian composer. He is first recorded at the seminary of S Petronio, Bologna, where he was taught by Cimatore, the *maestro di cappella* there. The title-page of his only surviving work *Madrigali a cinque voci* (Ferrara, 1586) describes him as *maestro di cappella* at Pisa Cathedral, and in January 1599 he was appointed to a similar post at S Petronio which he retained until 31 August 1604. The records of Reggio nell'Emilia Cathedral refer to him as *maestro di cappella* from 6 August 1604, when the chapter decided to engage him while he was still in

Bologna. His work at Reggio nell'Emilia met with disapproval, he was dismissed on 6 October 1606 and there is no mention of him after 17 October 1606. Eitner's claim that Pisanelli died in May 1617 aged 80 is based on an incorrect interpretation of a passage in Gaspari's *Catalogo*. Gaspari also cited another work by Pisanelli, *Himnodia totius anni* (1603), for four voices.

BIBLIOGRAPHY

EitnerQ; GaspariC

G. Gaspari: *Miscellanea musicale* (MS, *I-Bc* UU.12), iv, 111*bis*, 116ff

L. Frati: 'Per la storia della musica in Bologna nel secolo XVII', *RMI*, xxxii (1925), 544–65

G. Casali: 'La cappella musicale del duomo di Reggio Emilia all'epoca di Aurelio Signoretti', *RIM*, ii (1973), 181–224

F. Piperno: *Gli eccellentissimi musici della città di Bologna: con uno studio sull'antologia madrigalistica del Cinquecento* (Florence, 1985), 43, 46, 62–4

PIER PAOLO SCATTOLIN

Pisano [Pagoli], Bernardo (*b* Florence, 12 Oct 1490; *d* Rome, 23 Jan 1548). Italian composer, singer and classical scholar. He may have acquired the name 'Pisano' as a result of having spent some time in Pisa. Trained at the cathedral school in Florence, he also sang in the chapel of the church of the SS Annunziata as a student. In 1511, after being ordained a priest, he was appointed master of the choristers at the cathedral school and a singer in the chapels at the cathedral and the baptistry. He became master of the cathedral chapel less than a year later. Evidently he obtained the post through the good offices of Cardinal Giovanni de' Medici, whose family had recently been restored to power in Florence.

Shortly after the cardinal's election to the papacy as Leo X, Pisano went to Rome, where on 20 August 1514 he was appointed a singer in the papal chapel – a position he retained until his death. Leo also gave him several ecclesiastical benefices, among them canonries in the cathedrals of Segovia and Lerida and a chaplaincy in the Medici family church of S Lorenzo in Florence. From 1515 to 1519 he divided his duties between the papal and Florentine chapels, but settled permanently in Rome after the spring of 1520. During the course of a visit to Florence in 1529, while the city was in revolt against another Medici pope, Clement VII, Pisano was accused of being a papal spy. He was imprisoned and tortured before being expelled by the republican government. The incident illustrates how aware his contemporaries were of his close ties with the Medici. He also enjoyed the favour of Clement's successor, Paul III, and in 1546 served as master of his private chapel, a group of six singers including Arcadelt. He was buried in S Maria sopra Minerva, Rome.

Pisano's wide range of interests brought him into contact with some of the leading intellectual and artistic figures of the age. He was a friend of Michelangelo, the painters Bugiardini and Rustici, the poet Annibale Caro and the poet-historian Benedetto Varchi. His edition of the works of Apuleius, *Quae in toto opere continentur L. Apuleij* (Florence, 1522), was dedicated to Filippo Strozzi, husband of Leo X's niece and liberal patron of the arts. Several of his secular works are settings of poems by Filippo's brother, Lorenzo, who was also a playwright and prominent man of letters.

Pisano's settings of the responsories for Tenebrae services in Holy Week are in a simple chordal style, occasionally varied by short contrapuntal passages for two or three voices. Slow rhythms in even semibreve motion and low tessituras are used throughout in all parts and serve to emphasize the solemn, penitential character. According to Pisano's pupil Francesco Corteccia, these works were composed during Pisano's tenure as master of the cathedral chapel. The secular pieces display two distinct styles. The earlier of these is illustrated by the strophic ballatas and canzonettas (composed before 1515), modelled on similar pieces by elder Florentine composers such as Alessandro Coppini and Bartolomeo degli Organi, with whom Pisano may have studied. The principal characteristics are a light homophonic texture, sprightly rhythms, clearly articulated phrases and some repetition of material within the fixed formal structure.

17 pieces in his later style were published by Petrucci in *Musica di messer Bernardo Pisano sopra le canzone del Petrarcha* (Venice, 1520), the first printed collection of secular music containing the works of a single composer and the first to be issued in separate, fully-texted partbooks. These works help to establish his position as a leading figure in the early history of the 16th-century madrigal. In addition to seven canzoni by Petrarch (of which only the first stanza is set), Pisano's *Musica* includes settings of the same kinds of texts favoured by the earliest madrigalists, among them single-stanza ballatas, dialogue-ballatas and madrigals. Features generally associated with the contemporary madrigal are also evident: each is vocally conceived and correct text accentuation is observed. There are a few examples of specific word-painting: Pisano was more often content with conveying the general mood of the text. He accomplished this by contrasting chordal sections with passages in imitation, by alternating short duos or trios within the four-part texture, by repeating individual words or lines of the text with or without new music and by juxtaposing and overlapping musical phrases of different length. Repetition of the last line of the text or a large part of it, a prominent feature of the early madrigal, is also found in several of these settings. Pisano's *Musica* is important because it shows that by 1520 he was writing what may properly be called madrigals. It is impossible to assess what specific influence it had on the works of the genre's earliest masters, notably Festa, Verdelot and Arcadelt, but clearly these composers, with whom Pisano was associated in the papal and Florentine chapels, were aware of his musical achievements.

WORKS

Edition: *Music of the Florentine Renaissance*, ed. F.A. D'Accone, CMM, xxxii/1 (1966) [incl. edn of all except inc. pieces and responds 1–8 for Feria V]

SACRED

Feria V in Coena Domini, responds 1–9, 4vv, *I-Fl* N: In monte Oliveti, Tristis est anima mea, Ecce vidimus eum, Amicus meus, Judas mercator pessimus, Unus est discipulis meis, Eram quasi agnus innocens, Una hora non potuisti, Seniores populi; responds 1–3, *Bc* Q 132
Feria VI in Parasceve, responds 1–9, 4vv: Omnes amici mei, Velum templi scissum est, Vinea mea electa, Tanquam ad latronem, Tenebrae factae sunt, Animam meam, Tradiderunt me, Jesum tradidit, Caligaverunt oculi mei
Sabbato Sancto, responds 1–9, 4vv: Sicut ovis, Jerusalem surge, Plange quasi virgo, Recessit pastor noster, O vos omnes, Ecce quomodo moritur justus, Astiterunt reges terrae, Aestimatus sum, Sepulto Domino

SECULAR
for 4vv unless otherwise stated

Musica ... sopra le canzone del Petrarcha (Venice, 1520), inc. [1520]
Amore, quando io speravo; Amor, se vuoi ch'i' torni; Amor sia ringratiato, 3vv; Cantiano, horsù, cantiano! (anon. in source); Che debb'io far?; Chiare, fresche e dolci acque; Chi della fede altui (anon. in source); Cosi nel mio parlare (anon. in source); De', perchè in odio m'hai; Donna, benchè di rado
El ridir, ciò che tu fai; Fondo le mie speranze, 1520, inc.; Già mai non vider gli occhi (anon. in source); Lasso me ch'i' non so, 1520, inc.; Lasso a me, donna (anon. in source); Lieto non hebbi mai, 3vv (anon. in source); Madonna, se depende (anon. in source); Ne la stagion; Non la lassar, 1520, inc.; Nova angeletta (anon. in source); Or vedi, Amor (anon. in source); Perchè, donna, non vuoi; Poi ch'io parti' (anon. in source)
Quando e begli occhi, 3vv (anon. in source); Quanto più desiar (anon. in source); Questo mostrarsi lieta, 3vv; S'amor lega un gentil cor; Se mai provasti, 1520, inc.; Si è debile il filo; Si 'l dissi mai, 1520, inc.; Son io, donna (3 settings; 1 anon. in source); Tanta pietà; Una donna l'altrier, 3vv (also attrib. incorrectly to C. Festa)

BIBLIOGRAPHY

EinsteinIM
K. Jeppesen: 'Die neuentdeckten Bücher der Lauden des Ottaviano dei Petrucci und andere musikalische Seltenheiten der Biblioteca Colombina zu Sevilla', *ZMw*, xii (1929–30), 73–89, esp. 86
A. Einstein: 'Dante, on the Way to the Madrigal', *MQ*, xxv (1939), 141–55
W.H. Rubsamen: 'From Frottola to Madrigal', *Chanson & Madrigal, 1480–1530: Cambridge, MA, 1961*, ed. J. Haar (Cambridge, MA, 1964), 51–87; music exx, nos.22, 30
F.A. D'Accone: 'Bernardo Pisano: an Introduction to his Life and Works', *MD*, xvii (1963), 115–35
F.A. D'Accone: 'Bernardo Pisano and the Early Madrigal', *IMSCR X: Ljubljana 1967*, 96
F.A. D'Accone: 'Singolarità di alcuni aspetti della musica sacra fiorentina del Cinquecento', *Firenze e la Toscana dei Medici nell'Europa del '500*, ed. N. Pirotta (Florence, 1983), ii, 513–37
FRANK A. D'ACCONE

Pisano [Pisani], **Nicola** (*fl* Naples, 1720–38). Italian composer. He was second harpsichordist at the Teatro S Bartolomeo during the 1720s. Viviani reproduced passages from his dedication letter for the Neapolitan dialect comedy *Le mbroglie de la notte* (1720) in which, in effect, he pleaded indulgence from the cabal of critics who had recently forced the librettist A. Piscopo to retire from working for the Teatro dei Fiorentini. Besides *Le mbroglie* (N. Corvò; Collegio de' Nobili, November 1720), Pisano wrote two other *opere buffe*: *La Rina* (B. Saddumene, in dialect; Fiorentini, spring 1731) and *Climene* (C. de Palma; Nuovo, autumn 1738). A recitative and aria survive (*D-W*); works of a 'Pisani' are in the Archivio del Duomo, Rieti.

BIBLIOGRAPHY

EitnerQ; SartoriL
M. Scherillo: *L'opera buffa napoletana durante il Settecento; storia letteraria* (Naples, 1883, 2/1916/R), 168ff
A. Sacchetti-Sassetti: 'La cappella musicale del duomo di Rieti', *NA*, xvii (1940), 89–104, 121–70
V. Viviani: *Storia del teatro napoletano* (Naples, 1969), 279
F. Cotticelli and P. Maione: *Le istituzioni musicali a Napoli durante il viceregno austriaco (1707–1734): materiali inediti sulla Real Cappella ed il Teatro di San Bartolomeo* (Naples, 1993)
JAMES L. JACKMAN

Pisari [Piseri], **Pasquale** (*b* Rome, *c*1725; *d* Rome, 27 March 1778). Italian composer. The son of a bricklayer, he had a beautiful voice and (according to Baini) was given singing lessons by Francesco Gasparino. His excessive shyness prevented him from taking full advantage of this gift, and he turned to composition, taking lessons from Giovanni Biordi, who trained him in the style of Palestrina. From 1752 he sang bass in the Cappella Sistina, but for a long time only as a poorly paid supernumerary. Baini relates several anecdotes illustrating his extreme poverty. In 1777 a *Dixit* for four choruses (in

D-MÜs), commissioned by the King of Portugal, was performed at SS Apostoli in Rome. The king also commissioned a cycle of Proper settings for four voices and organ for the whole year. Pisari completed this large undertaking in a few months, but, perhaps worn out by it, died before receiving his payment. The settings have not survived.

Pisari closely followed the stylistic principles of Palestrina with such success that Martini called him the 'Palestrina of the 18th century'. Burney, visiting Rome in 1770, expressed great admiration for a 'mass in 16 real parts, which was full of canons, fugues, and imitations: I never saw a more learned or ingenious composition of the kind'. His psalm settings incorporate elements of *falso-bordone*, but motet-like textures predominate. Effective use is made of the contrast between homophony and polyphony, and of the interaction of different choral groups. At times Pisari wrote in a more modern style, and even juxtaposed the old manner with the new. The greater part of his output is polyphonic, however, and modern features such as formal symmetry and greater emphasis on expression are completely fused with the *stile antico*.

WORKS
principal sources: D-Bsb, Mbs, MÜs, Rp; GB-Ob; I-Bc, Pca, Rc, Rvat

Masses: Missa detta Pio VI, 8vv; Missa detta Clemente XIV, 6vv; 5 other masses 6vv, 8vv, ?16vv (see Burney)
Psalms: Dixit Dominus, 16vv, 1775, ed. L. Feininger (Trent, 1961); Miserere, 9vv; other psalms, 4vv, 5vv, 8vv
O Salutaris hostia, 3vv, ed. in *Sammlung ausgezeichneter Compositionen für die Kirche*, ii (Trier, 1859)
Other works: Mag; 3 TeD, 4vv–9vv; Stabat mater; motets, 6–8vv

BIBLIOGRAPHY
BurneyFI; FellererP
G. Baini: *Memorie storico-critiche della vita e delle opere di Giovanni Pierluigi da Palestrina*, ii (Rome, 1828/R)
A. de La Fage: *Essais de diphthérographie musicale* (Paris, 1864/R)
J. Killing: *Kirchenmusikalische Schätze der Bibliothek des Abbate Fortunato Santini* (Düsseldorf, 1910)

SIEGFRIED GMEINWIESER

Pisaroni, Benedetta Rosmunda (*b* Piacenza, 16 May 1793; *d* Piacenza, 6 Aug 1872). Italian soprano, later contralto. She studied in Milan and made her début in Bergamo in 1811 in Mayr's *La rosa bianca e la rosa rossa*. After appearances in Padua, Bologna and Venice, she sang in the première of Meyerbeer's *Romilda e Costanza* (1817, Padua) and was subsequently engaged in Naples, where she created major roles in three of Rossini's operas: Zomira in *Ricciardo e Zoraide* (1818), Andromache in *Ermione* (1819) and Malcolm in *La donna del lago* (1819), repeating Malcolm in Rome (1823) and at La Scala (1824). She also sang in the première of Meyerbeer's *L'esule di Granata* (1821, Milan) and added Arsace in *Semiramide* (1824) and Tancredi (1825) to her repertory. She made her Paris début as Arsace at the Théâtre Italien (1827), and during the next three seasons sang Malcolm, Tancredi and Isabella (*L'italiana in Algeri*) there. In 1829 she appeared in the première of Carafa's *Le nozze di Lammermoor* and sang in London at the King's Theatre. She returned to La Scala in 1831, in Generali's *Romito di Provenza* and Rossini's *Bianca e Falliero*, and then retired.

She had a range of nearly three octaves but a serious illness in 1813 resulted in the loss of her top notes, and she subsequently cultivated her lower register, which increased greatly in volume.

ELIZABETH FORBES

Pisarri, Alessandro (*fl* Bologna, 1660–62). Italian publisher. He was the son of Antonio Pisarri (*d* 1650), who founded the family publishing firm in the early 1600s. Alessandro was the first to publish music, issuing ten volumes of compositions by Maurizio Cazzati between 1660 and 1662 (opp.21–30). After his death, the firm continued under the direction of the Pisarri heirs, publishing in 1689 a set of rules for members of the Accademia Filarmonica (*Ricordi per li signori compositori e per i cantori e sonatori dell'Accademia dei Filarmonici*) and in 1691 Benedetto Bacchini's treatise *De sistrorum figuris ac diferentis*.

BIBLIOGRAPHY
SartoriD
F. Vatielli: 'Editori musicali dei secoli XVII e XVIII', *Arte e vita musicale a Bologna* (Bologna, 1927/R), 239–56

ANNE SCHNOEBELEN

Piscator [Fischer], Georg (*fl c*1610–after 1643). Austrian composer and organist. He was a son-in-law of Reimundo Ballestra. He probably began his career as a choirboy in the chapel of Archduke Leopold of Tyrol at Alsace and Innsbruck. By 1622 he was an organist to the archduke, in whose service he travelled to Italy in 1625 and at whose expense he studied further in Venice and Rome between 1626 and 1628. He returned to Innsbruck and in 1630 was promoted to the position of first organist under Stadlmayr. Italian influences continued to surround him, since several composers from both the Venetian and Roman schools were employed at Innsbruck, and Archduke Leopold maintained close links with Italy. The size of the Innsbruck music chapel was gradually reduced following the death of Archduke Leopold in 1632, and in 1635 Piscator succeeded Georg Holzner as organist at the court of Maximilian I in Munich. He still held that post in 1637, when he received a gift from Ferdinand III for a composition presented to the newly crowned emperor. By 1643 he was chapel master and organist at the Schottenkirche in Vienna and a member of the city's Rosenkranz Brotherhood.

The only complete surviving collection of Piscator's music is the *Quadriga musica* (Innsbruck, 1632), a book of motets for one to four voices dedicated to Archduke Leopold. This collection includes the contents of the earlier *Concerti*, of which only a single partbook without title-page survives. Piscator's solo motets often contrast slow-moving, syllabic sections with cadential passages dominated by elaborate, written-out passaggi. While the music is thoroughly italianate, the restricted harmonic palette, asymmetrical phrases and active continuo lines recall the generation of composers after Viadana rather than more forward-looking contemporaries such as Grandi and Rovetta. The motets for two to four voices, like his two Marian antiphons (in RISM 1629[1]) display a concertato idiom, with short syllabic ideas often combined to create Monteverdian multiple-subject points of imitation. Three organ works are also preserved in an organ book from Neresheim (now in D-Mbs); a number of lost works are listed in a 1656 Munich inventory.

WORKS
[Concerti], 1–4vv (n.p., n.d.)
Quadriga musica, 1–4vv (Innsbruck, 1632) [incl. some works from Concerti]
2 Marian antiphons, 1629[1]
3 organ works [incl. 2 fugues], D-Mbs Mus. Mss. 5368
numerous lost sacred works

BIBLIOGRAPHY

SennT

O. Ursprung: *Münchens musikalische Vergangenheit* (Munich, 1927), 70, 73, 121

H. Schmid: 'Una nuova fonte di musica organistica', *L'organo*, i (1960), 107–13

A. Kirwan-Mort: *The Small-Scale Sacred Concertato in the Early Seventeenth Century* (Ann Arbor, 1981)

A. Beer: *Die Annahme des 'stile nuovo' in der katholischen Kirchenmusik Süddeutschlands* (Tutzing, 1989), 224–5

S. Saunders: *Cross, Sword and Lyre: Sacred Music at the Imperial Court of Ferdinand II of Habsburg (1619–37)* (Oxford, 1995), 4

A. LINDSEY KIRWAN/STEVEN SAUNDERS

Pischek, Jan Křtitel. *See* PIŠEK, JAN KŘTITEL.

Pischner, Hans (*b* Breslau [now Wrocław], 20 Feb 1914). German musicologist, harpsichordist and administrator. In Breslau he studied keyboard instruments with Bronisław von Pozniak and musicology at the university, and worked as a music teacher and concert soloist (1933–9). After war service he joined the staff of the Musikhochschule in Weimar (1946–50), directed the music department of East German radio (1950–54) and held a leading post in the East German Ministry of Culture (1954–62). He took the doctorate at the Humboldt University in 1961 (*Die Harmonielehre Jean-Philippe Rameaus*, Leipzig, 1963/R), before becoming Intendant of the Staatsoper in East Berlin (1963). His publications include *Musik und Musikerziehung in der Geschichte Weimars* (Weimar, 1954), *Musik in China* (Berlin, 1955) and articles (mainly in programmes and daily papers) on J.S. Bach, Wagner, Brecht, Paul Dessau and the political role of culture. As a harpsichordist he played in many European musical capitals and recorded much of Bach's keyboard music, including the violin sonatas with David Oistrakh. His writings and lectures have been published in the collection, *Musik–Theater–Wirklichkeit: ausgewählte Schriften und Reden* (ed. W. Rösler, Berlin, 1979), and he has written an autobiography, *Premieren eines Lebens* (Berlin, 1986).

HORST SEEGER/R

Pišek [Pischek], Jan Křtitel [Johann Baptist] (*b* Mšeno, 13 Oct 1814 [not 14 Oct, which is the baptismal date]; *d* Sigmaringen, 16 Feb 1873). Bohemian baritone. He forsook the study of law for a career as a singer, making his stage début at Prague in 1835 as Oroveso in *Norma*, but was not appreciated. After appearances at Brno, Vienna and Frankfurt, he was engaged in 1884 as Court singer in Stuttgart, where he remained until 1863.

Pišek appeared in London for the first time in 1845, and took part in four concerts given by the Philharmonic Society in that season. He made further appearances with the Society in 1846, 1847, 1849 and 1853. He was very popular as a concert performer, and sang before Queen Victoria and Prince Albert in 1849. In the same year, he sang in Mendelssohn's *Elijah* at the Birmingham Festival, and also appeared in operas by C. Kreutzer and Mozart during the German opera season at the Drury Lane Theatre. His sensitive portrayal of the title role in *Don Giovanni* was highly praised. In 1865 he returned to Prague after 30 years, as Rigoletto. His wide repertory also included Mozart's and Rossini's Figaro, Don Pizarro, Spohr's Faust, Count Luna (*Il trovatore*), Enrico (*Lucia di Lammermoor*), Giorgio (*I puritani*) and the title roles of Herold's *Zampa* and Marschner's *Hans Heiling*, as well as many concert pieces and lieder.

Pišek's voice was rich and expressive over a range of two octaves, and his use of the *mezza voce* and falsetto was particularly admired. Some critics considered his singing mannered and his acting artificial and exaggerated. Berlioz (*Mémoires*), however, had a very high opinion of his talents, and considered him 'perhaps the greatest dramatic singer of the age'. He was also a talented pianist and a composer of songs.

BIBLIOGRAPHY

ČSHS [incl. further bibliography]

JENNIFER SPENCER/ELIZABETH FORBES

Pisendel, Johann Georg (*b* Cadolzburg, 26 Dec 1687; *d* Dresden, 25 Nov 1755). German violinist and composer. His family came from Markneukirchen, but in 1680 Pisendel's father settled in Cadolzburg as a Kantor. Pisendel entered the Ansbach court chapel as a chorister in 1697, and six years later became a violinist in the court orchestra. While at Ansbach he studied singing with Pistocchi and the violin with Torelli. In 1709 he travelled to Leipzig, breaking the journey at Weimar where he met Bach. Pisendel studied at Leipzig University for some time and was soon accepted in musical circles there. In 1709 he performed a concerto by Albinoni (not Torelli) with the collegium musicum, and when Melchior Hoffmann embarked on a concert tour in 1710, Pisendel deputized for him both in the collegium and in the opera orchestra. The following year Pisendel visited Darmstadt; there he took part in a performance of Graupner's opera *Telemach*, but declined the offer of a permanent post at court.

From January 1712, Pisendel was employed as a violinist with the Dresden court orchestra. He took over the Konzertmeister's duties when Volumier died in 1728, the official title being conferred upon him in 1730. During the early years of his employment Pisendel made several tours in the entourage of the electoral prince, visiting France (1714), Berlin (1715) and Italy (1716–17). The Italian visit influenced Pisendel profoundly: a nine-month stay in Venice (from April 1716) enabled him to study with Vivaldi and a close friendship developed between the two musicians. In 1717 Pisendel moved on to Rome (where he took lessons from Montanari), Naples and other Italian cities before returning to Dresden that autumn. After a visit to Vienna in 1718 his tours became less frequent, but he accompanied his royal patron to Berlin (1728, 1744) and Warsaw (1734).

Pisendel was the foremost German violinist of his day. Quantz praised his interpretation of adagio movements and Hasse commented on his assured grasp of tempo. Several leading composers (Vivaldi, Albinoni and Telemann) dedicated works to him. Pisendel was also admired for his success as an orchestral director, in which his precision and thoroughness played a major part. It was said that, before the performance of a new work, he would go through every orchestral part adding detailed bowing and expression marks. Although Pisendel's duties left little time for composition his small output of instrumental music is of the highest quality. A pupil of Heinichen in composition, he also came, through his travels, into direct contact with the French and Italian styles. Italian influence predominates in the violin concertos, which are written in Vivaldian manner but with occasional traces of a more overtly *galant* idiom. The solo violin sonata (dated ?1716 by Jung), is a fine work in the German tradition and may have influenced Bach's music for unaccompanied violin. Manuscript collections in

Dresden show Pisendel to have been among the most important collectors of music in central Germany; many of the scores he owned were later added to those of the Dresden Kapelle and catalogued along with them. The most famous of Pisendel's pupils were J.G. Graun and Franz Benda.

WORKS
MSS in D-Dl

7 vn concs.: g, E♭, E♭, G, D, G, D
4 concerti grossi, 1-movt works: E♭, G, D, D; 1–3 arr. from other concs. by Pisendel, 4 an arr. of the first movt of a conc. by J.F. Fasch (Küntzel no.38)
Sinfonia, B♭; orch piece, c (a 4, but described as trio)
Sonatas, vn, bc, e, D; Sonata, vn, a
Gigue, vn, a, in Telemann: Der getreue Music-Meister (Hamburg, 1728–9)

BIBLIOGRAPHY

F.W. Marpurg: *Historisch-kritische Beyträge zur Aufnahme der Musik*, i (Berlin, 1754–78/R), 206, 210–11, 245–6
A. Schering: 'Zur instrumentalen Verzierungskunst im 18. Jahrhundert', *SIMG*, vii (1905–6), 365–85
H.R. Jung: 'Johann Georg Pisendel: zur 200. Wiederkehr seines Todestages am 25. November', *Musica*, ix (1955), 543–7
H.R. Jung: *Johann Georg Pisendel (1687–1755): Leben und Werk* (diss., U. of Jena, 1956)
'Pisendel-Gedenkfeiern', *Musica*, x (1956), 215–16
K. Heller: *Die deutsche Vivaldi-Überlieferung: Untersuchungen über die in deutschen Bibliotheken handschriftlich überlieferten Konzerte und Sinfonien Antonio Vivaldis* (diss., U. of Rostock, 1965)
P. Ahnsehl: 'Bemerkungen zur Rezeption der Vivaldischen Konzertform durch die mittel- und norddeutschen Komponisten im Umkreis Bachs', *Vivaldi-Studien: Dresden 1978*, 59–72
M. Fechner: 'Improvisationsskizzen und ausnotierte Diminutionen von Johann Georg Pisendel, dargestellt an in Dresden handschriftlich überlieferten Konzerten von Johann Friedrich Fasch uns Johann Gottlieb Graun', *Zu Fragen der Verzierungskunst in der Instrumentalmusik der ersten Hälfte des 18. Jahrhunderts: Blankenburg, Harz, 1979*, 35–55
O. Landmann: 'Dresden, Johann Georg Pisendel und der "deutsche Geschmack"', *Einflüsse einzelner Interpreten und Komponisten des 18. Jahrhunderts auf das Musikleben ihrer Zeit: Blankenburg, Harz, 1980*, 20–34
H.-J. Schulze: 'Telemann–Pisendel–Bach: zu einem unbekannten Bach-Autograph', *Die Bedeutung Georg Philipp Telemanns für die Entwicklung der europäischen Musikkultur im 18. Jahrhundert: Magdeburg 1981*, 73–7
M. Fechner: 'Einige Anmerkungen zu einem Berliner Violonkonzert von Johann Gottlieb Graun und seiner Dresden Realisierung durch Johann Georg Pisendel', *Die Entwicklung des Solokonzerts im 18. Jahrhunderts: Blankenburg, Harz, 1982*, 59–70
A. Treuheit: *Johann Georg Pisendel (1687–1755), Geiger, Konzertmeister, Komponist: Dokumentation seines Lebens, seines Wirkens und Umgangs und seines Werks* (Markt Erlbach, 1987)
R. Lorber: 'Johann Georg Pisendels Concerto D-Dur: die Quellen und deren Einrichtung für eine Rundfunkproduction', *Festschrift Ulrich Siegele zum 60. Geburtstag*, ed. R. Fabor and others (Kassel, 1991), 117–34
M. Fechner: *Studien zur Dresdner Überlieferung der Instrumentalkonzerte von G.Ph. Telemann, J.D. Heinichen, J.G. Pisendel, J.F. Fasch, G.H. Stölzel, J.J. Quantz und J.G. Graun: Untersuchungen an den Quellen und Thematischer Katalog* (diss., U. of Rostock, 1992)
M. Fechner: 'Johann Georg Pisendel und die Dresdner Hofkapelle', *Die Entwicklung der Ouvertüren-Suite im 17. und 18. Jahrhundert: Blankenburg, Harz, 1993*, 116–29

PIPPA DRUMMOND

Piseri, Pasquale. *See* PISARI, PASQUALE.

Pising [Pisinge], William. *See* PYSING, WILLIAM.

Pisk, Paul A(madeus) (*b* Vienna, 16 May 1893; *d* Los Angeles, 12 Jan 1990). American composer and musicologist of Austrian birth. His teachers included Schreker

(counterpoint) and Schoenberg (composition). After receiving the doctorate in musicology from the University of Vienna (1916) and a diploma in conducting from the Vienna Conservatory (1919), he served as secretary of Schoenberg's Society for Private Musical Performances (1918–21). He went on to champion contemporary music as co-editor (with Alban Berg and Paul Stefan) of the *Musikblätter des Anbruch* (1920–28), and as a founding member and secretary of the Austrian section of ISCM (1922). He was music editor of the *Wiener Arbeiter-Zeitung* (1921–34) and active in the ACA (founded in 1927). He also served as director of the music department of the Volkshochschule, Vienna (1922–34), and taught theory at the New Vienna Conservatory (1925–6) and the Austro-American Conservatory near Salzburg (1931–3).

Pisk's connections with ISCM led to acquaintances with American composers such as Cowell and Sessions. Through Frederick Jacobi, he was invited to New York to play Austrian music on CBS and hear performances, sponsored by the League of Composers, of his own works. He emigrated to the USA in 1936, where he renewed contact with Schoenberg, Milhaud and Hindemith. In 1937 he joined the faculty of the University of Redlands, California, becoming head of the music department in 1948. He was later appointed professor at the University of Texas, Austin (1951–63), and Washington University in St Louis (1963–72).

Pisk's compositions tend towards atonality, but do not employ 12-note techniques. His thematic and motivic construction reveals a concern for linear relationships that develop contrapuntally within traditional forms and procedures. Harmonies are based on intervallic structures derived from the melodic contour. Many of his works, while chromatic, employ folk melodies.

WORKS
(selective list)

STAGE
Der grosse Regenmacher (ballet-pantomime), 1927; Schattenseite (monodrama, 1, A. Paquet), op.25, 2 solo vv, chorus, orch, 1930–31; Ballet Music, op.32, 1934

INSTRUMENTAL
Orch: Sym. Ov., op.1, 1914; Partita, op.10, 1924; Little Suite, chbr orch, op.11a, 1932; Divertimento, op.31, 1933–5; Music for Str, op.49, 1936; Passacaglia, op.50, 1944; Buccolic Suite, str orch, op.55, 1946; Adagio and Fugue, op.63, 1948–54; Canzona, chbr orch, op.84, 1954; 3 Ceremonial Rites, op.90, 1957–8; Elegy, str orch, op.93, 1958; Sonnet, chbr orch, op.98, 1960
Chbr: Sonata no.1, op.5, vn, pf, 1921; Str Qt, op.8, 1924; Phantasy, op.13, cl, pf, 1925; Trio no.1, op.18, ob, cl, bn, 1926; Sonata no.2, op.22, vn, pf, 1927; Pf Trio, op.30, 1933–5; Sonata no.3, op.43, vn, pf, 1938–9; Little Ww Music, op.53a, ob, 2 cl, bn, 1943–5; Cortège, op.53b, brass choir, 1945; Sonata, op.59, cl, pf, 1947; Suite, op.60, ob, pf, 1947; Introduction and Rondo, op.61, fl, pf, 1948; Qt, op.72, hn, 2 tpt, trbn, 1951; Suite, ob, cl, pf, 1954–5; Ww Qnt, op.96, 1958; Trio no.2, op.100, ob, cl, bn, 1960; Envoi, op.104, ob, cl, bn, str trio, 1964; 13 Variations on an 8-bar Theme, op.107, pf, 1967; Perpetuum mobile, op.109, brass, org, 1968; Discussions, op.116, ob, cl, bn, va, vc, 1974; Brass Qnt, 1976; many other chbr works
Pf: 4 Pf Pieces, op.3, 1920; 6 Concert Pieces, op.7, 1922; Little Suite, op.11, 1922; Second Suite (Speculum), op.17, 1927; Dance Suite, op.24, 1930; Ballet Music, op.32, 1934, arr. pf, chbr orch, 1954; 5 Sketches, op.39, 1936; Death Valley Sonatina, op.49, 1942; 5 2-Part Studies on Semitone Progressions, op.65, 1949; Sesquitone Sonata, op.66, 1949; Rondo Scherzoso, op.74/1, 1951; Essay, op.74/2, 1952; Sonatina, E, op.94, 1958

VOCAL
Choral: 2 Choruses, women's chorus, orch, op.2, 1918; 3 Choruses (J.P. Jacobsen), op.19, men's chorus, 1927; Die neue Stadt, solo vv, chorus, orch, 1926; 2 Pss, op.45, men's chorus, 1939–40; 2

Choruses, op.52, solo vv, women's chorus, pf, 1944; 4 Choruses, op.71, 1950–51; 3 Mixed Choruses, op.67, chorus, pf, 1950; Sunset (E. Dickinson), chorus cycle, op.81, 1954; The Trail of Life (cant., after Amerindian poems), op.88, 2 solo vv, spkr, chorus, orch, 1956; The Prophecy of Zacharia (Bible: *Zech*), op.89, chorus, org, 1957; God's Omnipotence (Bible: *Job*), op.99, chorus, org, 1960; 2 Shakespeare Sonnets, op.103, 1964

Solo: Gesänge eines fahrenden Spielmanns (S. George), op.6, 1v, pf, 1920–21; 4 Orch Songs (G. Falke, E. Lasker-Schüler, George, A. Platen), op.4, S, orch, 1920; Der Tod (cant., C. Morgenstern, A. Adij, J. Galsworthy), op.14, Bar, orch, 1923–34; Concert Aria 'Ach, Liebe' (Byron: *Childe Harold*), op.20, Bar, orch, 1928–9; Gesang vom Rundfunk (H. Infield), 2 solo vv, chbr orch, 1929; Zwischendeck (J. Ringelnatz, B. Traven), op.23c, 1v, cl, chbr orch/ pf, 1930; Campanella (cant., after 11 poems of the Monk [Tommaso]), op.28, 1v, orch, 1932; A Toccata of Galuppi (R. Browning), op.58, spkr, orch, 1947; The Labyrinth (J.L. Borges, J. Updike), 1v, pf, 1969; over 150 other songs

Principal publishers: Universal, Composers Facsimilie Edition

WRITINGS

Die Messen des Jacobus Gallus (diss., U. of Vienna, 1916; extracts in *SMw*, v (1918), 35–48

'Die Moderne seit 1880: Deutsche', *Handbuch der Musikgeschichte*, ed. G. Adler (Frankfurt, 1924, 2/1930/R), 1002–38

'End of the Tonal Era', *MM*, iii/3 (1925–6), 3–7

'Schoenberg's Twelve-Tone Opera', *MM*, vii/3 (1929–30), 18–21; repr. in *Schoenberg*, ed. M. Armitage (New York, 1937/R), 187–94

'Alban Berg's Leven en Werken', *De Muziek* (7 Oct 1930)

'Ernst Toch', *MQ*, xxiv (1938), 438–50

'Lazare Saminsky: a Musical Portrait', *The Chesterian*, xx (1938–9), 74–83

'Die Folklore in der modernen Musik', *AMz*, Jg.58 (1939), 655–8

'Schoenberg: the Influence on My Musical Youth', *The Canon: Australian Journal of Music*, iii/2 (1949), 94–6

'Anton Webern's Early Orchestral Works', *Anton von Webern: Perspectives: Seattle 1966*, 43–52

'Die melodische Struktur der unstilisierten Tanzsätze in der Klaviermusik des deutschen Spätbarock', *SMw*, xxv (1962), 397–405

with H. Ulrich: *A History of Music and Musical Style* (New York and London, 1963)

'Arnold Schoenberg as Teacher', *Proceedings of the American Society of University Composers*, ii (1967), 51–3

'Elements of Impressionism and Atonality in Liszt's Last Piano Pieces', *Radford Review*, xxiii (1969), 170–76

'Boiled-Down Music for Schoenberg's Private Audience', *St Louis Post-Dispatch* (11 Dec 1983)

EDITIONS

Jacob Handl: Sechs Messen, DTÖ, lxxviii, Jg.xlii/1 (Vienna, 1935/R); *Fünf Messen zu acht und sieben Stimmen*, DTÖ, xciv–xcv (1959); *Drei Messen zu sechs Stimmen*, DTÖ, cxvii (1967); *Fünf Messen zu vier bis sechs Stimmen*, DTÖ, cxix (1969)

Guillaume Costelay: Three French Chansons (New York, 1958)

BIBLIOGRAPHY

J. Glowacki, ed.: *Paul A. Pisk: Essays in his Honor* (Austin, 1966) [incl. H. Moldenhauer: 'Paul Amadeus Pisk and the Viennese Triumvirate', 208–16; K. Kennan: 'Paul A. Pisk', 217–26; W. Reich: 'Paul A. Pisk on Alban Berg', 227 only; and L.P. Farrar: 'The Scholarly Writings and Compositions of Paul Amadeus Pisk', 279–94]

T.W. Collins: *The Instrumental Music of Paul A. Pisk* (diss., U. of Missouri,1972)

E. Antokoletz: 'A Survivor of the Vienna Schoenberg Circle: an Interview with Paul A. Pisk', *Tempo*, no.154 (1985), 15–21

H.-B. Dietz: 'Paul A. Pisk: Eulogy', *Newsletter: the American Musicological Society*, xx/11 (1990), 8

ELLIOTT ANTOKOLETZ

Piskáček, Rudolf (*b* Prague, 15 March 1884; *d* Prague, 24 Oct 1940). Czech composer. He studied composition and the organ at the Prague Conservatory (1903–6). At first he was a composer of serious music, such as the symphonic poem *Sardanapal* (1906), his graduation piece and his only extensive essay in this vein, and the Violin Sonata in A minor, which won the prize of the Czech Academy of Arts and Sciences. Shortly after graduating, however, he began to devote himself to operetta. He also worked in this genre as a conductor at theatres in Prague – the Pištěkova Aréna (1907), the Vinohradské Divadlo (1908–18 and 1921–5) and the Akropolis (1937) – and České Budějovice (1925–6). Of his 40 operettas those that have survived in the repertory are *Slovácká princeska* ('The Moravian-Slovak Princess', 1917), *Tulák* ('The Tramp, 1924) and *Perly panny Serafínky* ('Miss Serafínká's Pearls', 1928). In the first of these he used stylized Moravian folksongs and dances; folk music was also the subject of his non-dramatic works, which include the Fantasia for piano on Czech and Moravian songs, the piano miscellany *Květy Tater* ('Flowers of the Tatras') and miscellanies of Czech folksongs from Bechyňsko and Blaťácko for male chorus. Pieces of this type reveal Piskáček as a deft stylist. His music was published by J.K. Barvitius and F.A. Urbánek. Piskáček's brother Adolf (1873–1919) was a composer and choirmaster. (L. Pacák: *Opereta*, Prague, 1946)

OLDŘICH PUKL

Pisoni, Giovanni. *See* PICCIONI, GIOVANNI.

Pistoia. City in Italy, in Tuscany, to the west of Florence. Music was performed in the cathedral from the 12th century and a singing school for the priests was established soon afterwards. The *cappella* of 1565 had a *maestro*, six singers and two instrumentalists. A bull issued in 1669 by the Pistoiese Pope Clement IX redirected income there from a suppressed convent; from then on, the number of singers averaged about 14, with one or two organists, and a trombone player was added at the end of the 17th century. Freelance instrumentalists were employed for important occasions and some of the chapel singers doubled as string players. The Basilica di S Maria dell'Umiltà also had a *maestro di cappella* and a salaried choir who sang *laudi* on Saturdays during Lent and before Christmas.

Fetonte Cancellieri, a cathedral chorister, was first responsible for the opulent musical festival of S Cecilia in 1611, which was held for almost two centuries. His nephew Felice Cancellieri, an ex-Habsburg singer, founded the Congregazione dei Trentatrè, active by 1644, to finance music for the Oratorians at S Prospero (later renamed S Filippo Neri). Early in the 18th century up to seven oratorios were mounted each carnival season; the number had declined by mid-century, but occasional performances were given until the final suppression of 1808. Many of the city's numerous confraternities included music making and an occasional oratorio among their activities. Conspicuous sums of money went to provide secular and sacred music for the feasts of St James and St Bartholomew. The Jesuit Collegio dei Nobili, 1635–1773, attached to the church of S Ignazio (later Spirito Santo), was patronized by the Rospigliosi family; music, including music drama in honour of the patrons, was performed by the scholars.

Passion plays with music were performed in the cathedral on Good Friday from the 14th century until 1476, when they were moved to the Loggia del Giuramento in the main city square. This served as the city's only theatre until the great hall of the Palazzo del Comune opened its doors, despite much opposition from the Church, at the end of the 16th century. It was used around 1700 for musical events held for the Medici and for the feast of St Agatha, and in the 1800s for celebratory cantatas.

The Accademia dei Risvegliati was founded in 1642 by Felice Cancellieri, who included music in their weekly meetings. The Teatro Risvegliati opened in 1694 with regular seasons of opera for the carnival and the feast of St James on 24 July; late spring and autumn seasons were added later. Concerts were held there, many given by the Accademia degli Armonici (founded in 1787), as well as occasional oratorio performances. It was renamed the Teatro Manzoni in 1864. The 50-year period from 1871 saw lively operatic activity under Vittorio Bellini. After World War II, with easy travel to Florence, few productions were mounted.

The private theatres of the nobility housed music drama in the 17th century, while the popular Teatrino del Corso was active in the 18th. The Arena Matteini (later called the Politeama and Politeama Mabellini) was first used as an open-air venue in 1855. Rebuilt as an opera house a few years later, it staged both opera and operetta until destroyed by fire in 1943.

The city has spawned many famous performers and composers, most of whom made their reputations outside Pistoia. The cathedral music school was important in the training of singers, especially the early 17th-century castratos. The Accademia degli Armonici helped start a music school (now the Scuola di Musica Mabellini) in 1858 to provide members for the chorus and orchestra of the theatre; the school was active throughout the 20th century.

The city was home to the Tronci family of organ builders, active from about 1750 until well into the 20th century. They worked alone and in collaboration with the Agati. A school of organ builders and an organ school, the Accademia dell'Organo, still flourish. Although the city is now culturally dependent on Florence, the open-air jazz festival held each summer in the Piazza del Duomo is of international standing.

BIBLIOGRAPHY

A. Chiappelli: *Storia del teatro de Pistoia* (Pistoia, 1913/*R*)

U. Pineschi: 'Organi ed organari in Pistoia e diocesi', *L'organo*, xi (1973), 99–126

U. Pineschi: 'L'uso dei registri dell'organo pistoiese nei secoli XVIII e XIX', *L'organo*, xii (1974), 3–24

F. Baggiani: *Gli organi nella cattedrale di Pistoia* (Pisa, 1984)

F. Baggiani: 'I maestri di cappella nella cattedrale di Pistoia', *Bullettino storico pistoiese*, lxxxviii (1986), 41–81

J. Grundy Fanelli: 'Un animatore della vita musicale pistoiese del Seicento: Monsignor Felice Cancellieri, sopranista', *Bullettino storico pistoiese*, xci (1989), 53–62

J. Grundy Fanelli: 'La musica per la chiesa e l'oratorio di San Filippo Neri nel Seicento e nel Settecento', *Bullettino storico pistoiese*, xcii (1990), 55–76

J. Grundy Fanelli: 'Il patrocinio musicale e la condizione economica dei musicisti a Pistoia nella prima metà del Settecento', *RIM*, xxviii (1993), 227–53

J. Grundy Fanelli: 'Patronage as a Joint Enterprise: the Risvegliati Theatre in Pistoia', *Il melodramma italiano in Italia e in Germania nell'età barocca: Como 1993*, ed. A. Colzani and others (Como, 1995), 245–53

J. Grundy Fanelli: 'La musica patrocinato dai Rospigliosi: il Collegio dei Nobili', *Bullettino storico pistoiese*, xcviii (1996), 113–28

J. Grundy Fanelli: 'Il Teatro Risvegliati-Manzoni nell'Ottocento', *Fare storia*(Pistoia, 1996), 17–27

J. Grundy Fanelli: 'The Manfredini Family of Musicians of Pistoia', *Studi musicali*, xxvi (1997), 187–232

J. Grundy Fanelli: *A Chronology of Operas, Oratorios, Operettas, Cantatas and Miscellaneous Stage Works performed in Pistoia 1606–1943* (Bologna, 1998)

J. Grundy Fanelli: *The Oratorios of Giovanni Carlo Maria Clari* (Bologna, 1998)

JEAN GRUNDY FANELLI

Pistocchi, Francesco Antonio Mamiliano ['Il Pistocchino'] (*b* Palermo, 1659; *d* Bologna, 13 May 1726). Italian composer and singer. He was a child prodigy, singing in public at the age of three and publishing his first work, *Capricci puerili*, at the age of eight. His father Giovanni was a violinist in the *cappella musicale* at S Petronio, Bologna, from 9 September 1661. In May 1670 Francesco was employed there occasionally as a singer and in 1674 he was given a regular position as a soprano. However, because of their frequent absences both he and his father were dismissed in May 1675. Within ten years he had embarked on a brilliant career as a contralto, performing on various Italian and German stages. From 1 May 1686 to 15 February 1695 he was in the service of the court at Parma. In 1696 he became Kapellmeister at Ansbach to the Margrave of Brandenburg-Ansbach (some of his letters to whom are in *D-BAa* 2006). In May 1697 he went with Giuseppe Torelli to Berlin at the request of the Electress Sophia Charlotte but returned to Ansbach early in 1698. At the end of 1699 he and Torelli moved to Vienna, and in the autumn of 1700 he was in Bologna, where he performed in several churches. Between 1701 and 1708 he was occasionally engaged to sing at S Petronio, Bologna, in the newly reconstituted *cappella musicale*. In 1702 he was named *virtuoso di camera e di cappella* to Prince Ferdinando de' Medici of Tuscany. As a contralto Pistocchi was active in the principal Italian theatres. In 1675 he was the subject of a sonnet, *Ai numi dell'Adria*, published in Ferrara.

Although Pistocchi's operatic career ended about 1705, he continued to sing for several years at functions in various Bolognese churches. He was famous as a singing teacher, and Antonio Bernacchi, A.P. Fabri, Antonio Pasi, Gaetano Berenstadt and G.B. Martini were among his pupils. In 1708 and 1710 he served as *principe* of the Accademia Filarmonica, of which he had been a member since 1687. In 1709 he took holy orders and in 1714 was named honorary chaplain to the Elector Palatine Johann Wilhelm. In November 1715 he became a member of the Congregation of the Oratory at Forlì.

Pistocchi's art of singing probably centred on his ability to ornament, both melodically and rhythmically. Tosi thought him the best singer of all time, with impeccable taste and the ability to teach the beauties of the art of singing without departing from the established tempo. Burney related the story (perhaps legendary) that he ruined his soprano voice by dissolute living, was reduced to being a copyist and while thus employed learnt counterpoint and became a proficient composer. Several years later, according to Burney and others, he recovered his voice, which had by then changed to contralto.

As a composer Pistocchi is notable for melodic elegance and colourful harmony, especially in his treatment of chromaticism. Burney singled out his dramatic recitative in the oratorio *Maria Vergine addolorata* and noted his use of a wide dynamic range in which 'all degrees of the diminution of sound' are used. His letters to Perti (*I-Bc* K.44, P.143–6) also reveal him as an astute critic of music.

WORKS

DRAMATIC
music lost unless otherwise stated

Il Leandro (op, C. Badovero), Venice, Riva delle Zattere, 15 May 1679 [probably by Pistocchi; another version as Gli amori fatali, Venice, S Moisè, Jan 1682, definitely by Pistocchi]

Sant'Adriano (orat), Modena, 1692, *I-MOe*

Il Narciso (pastorale, A. Zeno), Ansbach, Hoftheater, March 1697

Maria Vergine addolorata (orat), Ansbach, 1698; 1 aria ed. in *BurneyH*, ii, 589

Le pazzie d'amore e dell'interesse (op), Ansbach, Hoftheater, 16 June 1699

Le risa di Democrito (op, N. Minato), Vienna, Hoftheater, 17 Feb 1700; part of Act 2, *A-Wn*

La pace tra l'armi, sorpresa notturna nel campo del Piacere (cant.), Ansbach, 5 Sept 1700

I rivali generosi [Act 2] (op, Zeno), Reggio nell'Emilia, Pubblico, April 1710 [collab. C. Monari and G.M. Cappelli]

Il sacrificio di Gefte (orat), Bologna, Madonna di Galliera, 1720

I pastori al Presepe (orat), Bologna, Oratorio di S Filippo Neri, 25 Dec 1721

Davide (orat), Bologna, Madonna di Galliera, 19 March 1721

Duet from Bertoldo, *D-Bsb*

OTHER WORKS

Duetti e terzetti, op.3 (Bologna, 1707)

Scherzi musicali, 1v, bc; 2 in *35 arie . . . del secolo XVII*, ed. G. Benvenuti (Milan, 1922)

Cants. and arias, 1–3vv, bc: *B-Br, D-Bsb, Dl, F-Pn, GB-Cfm, Lbl, I-Ac, Bc, Bsp, Fc, MOe, Nc, PAc, Pca*

Lauda Jerusalem, 3vv, insts, bc (org); Lauda Jerusalem, 5vv, bc (org); Gloria in excelsis, 3vv, 2 vn, bc: *D-Bsb*

Capricci puerili ... in 40 modi sopra un basso d'un balletto, vn, hpd, hp, other insts, op.1 (Bologna, 1667)

Letters: 121 to G.A. Perti, *I-Bc*, and Margrave Georg Friedrich of Brandenburg-Ansbach, *D-BAa*

BIBLIOGRAPHY

BurneyH

G.B. Martini: *Indice ossia Nota degli oratorij posti in musica da diversi autori* (MS, *I-Bc* H.6)

G.B. Martini: *Scrittori di musica: notizie storiche e loro opere* (MS, *I-Bsf*)

P.F. Tosi: *Opinioni de' cantori antichi e moderni* (Bologna, 1723/*R*; Eng. trans., 1742, 2/1743/*R* as *Observations on the Florid Song*)

O. Penna: *Catalogo degli aggregati dell'Accademia filarmonica di Bologna* (MS, *I-Bc*), facs. (Bologna, 1973); sometimes attrib. G.B. Martini

G. Gaspari: *Miscellanea musicale* (MS, *I-Bc* UU.12), iv

V. Martinelli: *Lettere familiari e critiche* (London, 1758), 357

A. Ademollo: *La storia del 'Girello'* (Milan, 1890)

A. Einstein: 'Italienische Musiker am Hofe der Neuburger Wittelsbacher 1614–1716', *SIMG*, ix (1907–8), 336–424

E. Schmitz: *Geschichte der weltlichen Solokantate* (Leipzig, 1914, rev. 2/1955)

H. Mersmann: *Beiträge zur Ansbacher Musikgeschichte bis zum Tode des Markgrafen Georg Friedrich, 1703* (Leipzig, 1916)

N. Pelicelli: 'Musicisti in Parma nel secolo XVII', *NA*, x (1933), 233–48, esp. 245

F. Vatielli: 'L'oratorio a Bologna negli ultimi decenni del Seicento', *NA*, xv (1938), 26–35, 77–87, esp. 85

M. Fabbri: *Alessandro Scarlatti e il Principe Ferdinando de' Medici* (Florence, 1961)

O. Termini: 'Singers at San Marco in Venice: the Competition between Church and Theatre (c1675–1725)', *RMARC*, no.17 (1981), 65–95

F. Della Seta: 'I Borghese (1691–1731): la musica di una generazione', *NA*, new ser., i (1983), 139–208, esp. 165

ANNE SCHNOEBELEN

Piston (i). In brass instruments, the moving component in the many types of valve described generically as 'piston valves' (*see* VALVE (i)). In French the term designates the entire piston valve, hence *cor à pistons* (valved horn), *cornet à pistons* etc. After 1850 the cornet itself became commonly known among musicians in France, Germany and eastern Europe as 'piston' and was so named in scores, even though in the last two areas the cornet usually had rotary valves, which have no pistons. A later term, 'jazz-piston', was used in central Europe to denote the B♭ trumpet when built with piston (Périnet) valves. 'Piston' has also been used in connection with certain duct flutes

on which the note is changed by means of a sliding plunger instead of by finger-holes, for example, the SWANEE WHISTLE. This principle is widely known in Europe and Asia.

ANTHONY C. BAINES/EDWARD H. TARR

Piston (ii). In organs, a button placed above or below the manuals or above the pedal-board, controlling pre-set combinations of stops. The mechanism facilitates rapid changes in registration.

ANTHONY C. BAINES/EDWARD H. TARR

Piston, Walter (Hamor) (*b* Rockland, ME, 20 Jan 1894; *d* Belmont, MA, 12 Nov 1976). American composer and teacher. His family was largely of English origin, though his paternal grandfather, Antonio Pistone, an Italian seaman, arrived in Maine from Genoa. In 1905 the family moved from Rockland, Maine, to Boston, where Piston, after concentrating on engineering in high school, studied art at the Massachusetts Normal Art School (1912–16). It was there that he met his future wife, the painter Kathryn Nason. Largely self-taught as a musician, he earned money playing the piano and violin in dance bands. From 1917 to 1921 he also played the violin in orchestras and chamber ensembles under the direction of Georges Longy. When the USA entered World War I, he quickly learnt to play the saxophone so that he could join the Navy Band. During his service in the Navy, he learnt to play other band instruments as well.

Piston entered Harvard in 1919 as a special music student; he enrolled formally in 1920 and graduated with honours in 1924. His teachers included A.T. Davison and Edward Burlingame Hill, among others. From 1921 to 1924 he conducted the Pierian Sodality, Harvard's student orchestra. He pursued further studies with Dukas, Boulanger and Enescu at the Ecole Normale de Musique (1924–6), where he played the viola in the school orchestra. His two earliest extant works, Three Pieces for the flute, clarinet and bassoon (1925) and the Piano Sonata (1926), reveal the influences of Boulanger and Dukas, respectively. The lean counterpoint of the former reveals a neo-classical elegance related to the styles of Stravinsky and Hindemith, while the romantic grandeur of the latter suggests an affinity with Brahms and Franck. In subsequent scores, such as the Flute Sonata (1930), Piston merged these two aesthetics, forging a conservative modernist style of his own.

Upon his return to Boston in 1926, Piston joined the music department at Harvard, a position he held until his retirement in 1960. He did most of his composing during the summer months, which he spent on a dairy farm in Woodstock, Vermont. His occasional attempts at descriptive music, such as *Tunbridge Fair* for symphonic band (1950) and *Three New England Sketches* for orchestra (1959), took rural New England as their subject. Even in his more abstract works, his syncopated rhythms, austere textures and clipped forms bespoke a special attachment to that part of the country. 'Is the Dust Bowl more American than, say, a corner in the Boston Athenaeum?' he asked. 'Would not a Vermont village furnish as American a background for a composition as the Great Plains?'

Finding an early advocate in Koussevitzky, Piston's first works for orchestra were commissioned by the Boston SO (although Koussevitzky handed over the baton to the composer for their premières). Piston eventually wrote 11

Walter Piston

works for that ensemble, as well as fulfilling commissions from the major orchestras of New York, Philadelphia, Cleveland, Dallas, Louisville, Minneapolis and Cincinnati, among others. Copland also helped to bring him to national attention by featuring his music at Yaddo and the New School for Social Research, and by declaring him in 1936 'one of the most expert craftsmen American music can boast'. He also earned the admiration of numerous other composers, including Igor Stravinsky, Ernst Krenek, Roger Sessions, Howard Hanson, Virgil Thomson and Elliott Carter, for whom in 1946 Piston offered 'hope that the qualities of integrity and reason are still with us'.

Piston's mastery took many forms, including a meticulous hand that allowed his publisher, AMP, to publish his scores in facsimile. (He penned all but one of the illustrations to his *Orchestration* text as well.) Intimately familiar with instruments and possessing a phenomenal ear, he worked primarily at a desk, scoring his music as he composed it, rather than beginning with a piano reduction. His masterful orchestrations emphasize clarity and brilliance as opposed to novelty and effect. Along with a compelling sense of form, he also displayed a dazzling handling of canon, invertible counterpoint, melodic retrograde and inversion, and other contrapuntal techniques. The traditional forms of sonata, rondo, variation, fugue and passacaglia acquired a distinctive lucidity and compression in his hands. One can readily discern in his music an engineer's concern for formal precision, a painter's care for colouristic detail and a violist's attention to inner voices. 'Melody and tonality are extended to allow for all sorts of new sounds and new rhythms', observed William Austin of the Fourth Symphony, 'but melody and tonality organize the whole in essentially the same way they do in Mozart's world, as they rarely do in ours.' While some thought the reserved

quality of his music a limitation, his admirers extolled not only his impressive technical skills, but the 'longing tenderness' of his slow movements and the 'sparkling gaiety' of his scherzos.

Having absorbed Schoenberg's 12-note method as early as the Flute Sonata (1930) and having composed a strict (albeit tonal) 12-note work as early as the *Chromatic Study on the Name of Bach* for the organ (1940), Piston initially established a reputation as a composer's composer. Some of his more accessible efforts in the late 1930s and early 40s, notably *Carnival Song* for chorus (1938), the ballet suite from *The Incredible Flutist* (1938) and the *Second Symphony* (1943), however, found favour among the concert-going public. The Symphony no.4 (1950) and the Symphony no.6 (1955) became particular favourites. As he made more extensive use of the 12-note method in the 1950s and especially the 1960s, his music became more chromatic and dense. These late works were also more adventurous formally, featuring complex one-movement designs, rather than his more traditional three- and four-movement forms.

A relatively slow worker, Piston joked that it took him an hour to decide upon a note and another hour to decide to erase it. He produced about one work a year, the eight symphonies and five string quartets representing the heart of his achievement. During his last two decades he produced a series of concertos (although not necessarily titled as such) for the viola (1957), two pianos (1959), the violin (1960), the harp (1963), the cello (1966), the clarinet (1967), the flute (1971) and string quartet (1976). He often composed with the capabilities and traits of particular players, ensembles and even halls in mind, and these works are no exception. Some of them were written for such celebrated virtuosi as Accardo, Zabaleta and Rostropovich; others were undertaken for distinguished members of the Boston SO, such as the flautist Doriot Anthony Dwyer and other friends. All attest to his great knowledge of instrumental technique.

As a teacher, Piston was the acclaimed author of a series of texts: *Principles of Harmonic Analysis* (Boston, 1933), *Harmony* (New York, 1941), *Counterpoint* (New York, 1947) and *Orchestration* (New York, 1955). Translated into numerous languages, the latter three were among the most esteemed and widely used books of their kind. The harmony texts in particular initiated a modern era of music theory, in which theoretical principles derived 'from the observation of musical practice', as David Thompson has noted. These texts also shed new light on the relationship between harmonic root movement and rhythmic structure, and between orchestration and form. In his occasional critical essays, Piston wrote thoughtfully on subjects such as the music of Roy Harris and the limitations of the 12-note method. Elliott Carter, Leroy Anderson, Arthur Berger, Gail Kubik, Irving Fine, Gordon Binkerd, Ellis Kohs, Leonard Bernstein, Robert Middleton, Robert Moevs, Harold Shapero, Allen Sapp, Daniel Pinkham, Noël Lee, Billy Jim Layton, Claudio Spies, Samuel Adler, Frederic Rzewski and John Harbison, who numbered among his students at Harvard, benefited not only from, in Bernstein's words, his 'non-pedantic approach to such academic subjects as fugue', but from close familiarity with his finely crafted music. Although he encouraged them to find their own way, many of these composers show his stylistic influence, especially in matters of contrapuntal finesse and textural clarity.

Piston's achievements were recognized by Pulitzer prizes for the symphonies nos.3 and 7, a Naumburg Award for the Symphony no.4 and New York Music Critics' Circle awards for the Symphony no.2, the Viola Concerto and the Fifth String Quartet. He was elected to the National Institute of Arts and Letters in 1938, the American Academy of Arts and Sciences in 1940, and the American Academy of Arts and Letters in 1955. He also received a Guggenheim Fellowship, the Coolidge Medal and numerous honorary doctorates. In addition, the French government bestowed upon him the decoration Officier of the Ordre des Arts et des Lettres.

WORKS

ORCHESTRAL

Orch Piece, 1925, unpubd; Sym. Piece, 1927, unpubd; Suite no.1, 1929; Conc. for Orch, 1933; Prelude and Fugue, 1934; Concertino, pf, chbr orch, 1937; Sym. no.1, 1937; The Incredible Flutist (ballet), 1938; Vn Conc. no.1, 1939; Sinfonietta, chbr orch, 1941; Fanfare for the Fighting French, brass, perc, 1942; Prelude and Allegro, org, str, 1943; Sym. no.2, 1943; Fugue on a Victory Tune, 1944, unpubd; Variation on a Theme by Eugène Goossens, 1944 [1 of 10 Jubilee Variations]; Suite no.2, 1947; Sym. no.3, 1947; Toccata, 1948; Sym. no.4, 1950; Tunbridge Fair (Intermezzo), wind. band, 1950; Fantasy, eng hn, hp, str, 1953; Sym. no.5, 1954; Sym. no.6, 1955; Serenata, 1956; Va Conc., 1957; Conc., 2 pf, orch, 1959; 3 New England Sketches, 1959; Sym. no.7, 1960; Vn Conc. no.2, 1960; Sym. Prelude, 1961; Lincoln Center Festival Ov., 1962; Capriccio, hp, str, 1963; Variations on a Theme by Edward Burlingame Hill, 1963; Pine Tree Fantasy, 1965; Sym. no.8, 1965; Variations, vc, orch, 1966; Cl Conc., 1967; Ricercare, 1967; Ceremonial Fanfare, brass perc, 1969; Fantasia, vn, orch, 1970; Fl Conc., 1971; Bicentennial Fanfare, 1975; Conc., str qt, wind, perc, 1976
Arrs. (all unpubd): Debussy: Clair de lune, 1936; Fauré: Prométhée, Act II, scene i, 1945; Beethoven: Pf Sonata 'Moonlight', op.14/2, 1st movt

CHORAL

Carnival Song (L. de Medici), TBB, brass, 1938; March, 1940; Psalm and Prayer of David, SATB, fl, cl, bn, vn, va, vc, db, 1958: O Sing unto the Lord a New Song (Ps xcvi); Bow Down thine Ear, O Lord (Ps xxcvi)

CHAMBER

3 Pieces, fl, cl, bn, 1925; Minuetto in stile vecchio, str qt, 1927, unpubd, withdrawn; Sonata, fl, pf, 1930; Suite, ob, pf, 1931; Str Qt no.1, 1933; Pf Trio no.1, 1935; Str Qt no.2, 1935; Sonata, vn, pf, 1939; Interlude, va, pf, 1942; Qnt, fl, str qt, 1942; Partita, vn, va, org, 1944; Sonatina, vn, hpd, 1945; Divertimento, fl, ob, cl, bn, str qt, db, 1946; Str Qt no.3, 1947; Duo, va, vc, 1949; Pf Qnt, 1949; Str Qt no.4, 1951; Wind Qnt, 1956; Str Qt no.5, 1962; Pf Qt, 1964; Str Sextet, 1964; Pf Trio no.2, 1966; Souvenir, fl, va, hp, 1967; Duo, vc, pf, 1972; 3 Counterpoints, vn, va, vc, 1973; Fugue . . . sur un sujet de Fenaroli, str qt, n.d., unpubd

KEYBOARD

Sonata, pf, 1926, unpubd, withdrawn; Chromatic Study on the Name of Bach, org, 1940; Passacaglia, pf, 1943; Improvisation, pf, 1945; Variation on Happy Birthday, pf, 1970, unpubd

MSS in US-Bp

Principal publishers: Associated, Boosey & Hawkes, E.C. Schirmer, G. Schirmer

WRITINGS
for list of articles see Pollack (1981)

Principles of Harmonic Analysis (Boston, 1933)
Harmony (New York, 1941, 5/1987 with M. DeVoto)
Counterpoint (New York, 1947)
Orchestration (New York, 1955)

BIBLIOGRAPHY

T. Chanler: 'New York, 1934', MM, xi (1933–4), 142–7
A. Berger: 'Walter Piston', Trend (1935), Jan–Feb, 210–22
I. Citkowitz: 'Walter Piston: Classicist', MM, xiii/Jan–Feb (1935–6), 3–11
R.L. Finney: 'Piston's Violin Sonata', MM, xvii (1939–40), 210–13
W.W. Austin: 'Piston's Fourth Symphony: an Analysis', MR, xvi (1955), 120–37
A. Copland: 'Sessions and Piston', Our New Music (New York, 1941, 2/1968), 176–86
E. Carter: 'Walter Piston', MQ, xxxii (1946), 354–75
O. Daniel and others: Walter Piston (New York, 1964)
C. Taylor: 'Walter Piston: for his Seventieth Birthday', PNM, iii/1 (1964–5), 102–14
P. Westergaard: 'Conversation with Walter Piston', PNM, vii/1 (1968–9), 3–17
W.D. Curtis: 'Walter Piston (1894–1976): a Discography', Journal of the Association for Recorded Sound Collections, xiii/2 (1981), 76–95
H. Pollack: Walter Piston (Ann Arbor, 1981) [incl. work-list, further bibliography, discography]
H. Pollack: Harvard Composers: Walter Piston and his Students, from Elliott Carter to Frederic Rzewski (Metuchen, NJ, 1992) [incl. list of writings]
                                        HOWARD POLLACK

Piston flute [pipe]. See SWANEE WHISTLE.

Pitanus, Friedrich. See PITTANUS, FRIEDRICH.

Pitch. The particular quality of a sound (e.g. an individual musical note) that fixes its position in the scale. Certain sounds used in music that occupy no particular scale position, such as those produced by cymbals or the side drum, can be said to be of indefinite pitch. Pitch is determined by what the ear judges to be the most fundamental wave-frequency of the sound (even when, as for example with difference tones, this is an aural illusion, not actually present in the physical sound wave). Experimental studies, in which listeners have been tested for their perception and memory of pitch differences among sounds with wave-frequencies known to the experimenter, have shown that marked differences of timbre, loudness and musical context affect pitch, albeit in relatively small degree. But long-term memory, called ABSOLUTE PITCH, enables some people to identify the pitch of sounds quite apart from their contextual relation to other sounds. Such aspects of pitch are discussed in PSYCHOLOGY OF MUSIC, §II, 1.

Pitch is expressed by combining a frequency value (such as 440 Hz) with a note name. $a' = 440$ Hz is a pitch, as is $g' = 440$. If g' is 440, in equal temperament, then a' will be 494 Hz; if $a' = 440$, g' will be 392 Hz. Frequencies and pitches by themselves are simply natural phenomena; it is only when they are connected to pitch standards that they take on a musical dimension. A pitch standard is a convention of uniform pitch that is understood, prescribed and generally used by musicians at a given time or place. The statement 'Cammerton was at $a' = 415$', for example, combines the name of a pitch standard (Cammerton or 'chamber pitch') with a note-name (a') and a frequency (415 Hz). Over the last 400 years in Europe, the point that has been considered optimal for pitch standards has varied by about six semitones, depending on time and place.

This article discusses the pitch standards that have been used in various places and periods in Europe. The concept of pitch standards and attempts to measure pitch systems in non-Western music are also discussed.

I. Western pitch standards. II. Non-Western and traditional concepts.

I. Western pitch standards

1. Introduction: historical pitch standards. 2. History of European pitch standards since the late 16th century: (i) Italy (ii) France (iii) Germany (iv) J.S. Bach (v) The Habsburg lands (vi) England (vii) Classical pitches, 1765–1830 (viii) Pitch standards since c1830.

1. INTRODUCTION: HISTORICAL PITCH STANDARDS. Pitch standards were not an issue until voices and instruments began playing together. Singers performing *a cappella* found their pitch according to the compass of a given piece and the range of their voices. Consorts of instruments were tuned together, but only in reference to themselves. Until the second half of the 16th century, the only instrument that was played in church music was the organ (which even then played only *alternatim* passages). When secular instruments such as the violin and cornett finally entered the church, pitch standards had to be agreed upon. But the universal standard that we now take for granted was not yet necessary, and different standards operated side by side. In effect this practice survives today in so-called TRANSPOSING INSTRUMENTS such as horns, saxophones and clarinets. An 18th-century hautboy at Cammerton was a whole tone or minor 3rd below the organ at Cornet-Ton, just as a modern clarinet in B♭ or A is a whole tone or minor 3rd below $a' = 440$. The only difference is that today the existence of a single standard ($a' = 440$) is assumed, so some instruments are thought of as 'transposing' and others 'in concert pitch'.

As instruments (particularly wind instruments) travelled, they took their pitches with them. In the 16th and early 17th centuries wind instrument making was highly centralized: the best woodwinds came from Venice, the best brass from Nuremberg. The resulting consistency in pitch over large parts of Europe compared strikingly to the fragmentation that occurred during the Baroque and Classical periods. Since about 1830, with the standardization of the Industrial Revolution, deviations in pitch standards have again become relatively small (which is probably why it was possible eventually to agree on a universal standard at the International Standardizing Organization (ISO) meeting in London in May 1939, confirmed in 1953. There had been international meetings in 1834, 1858, 1862 and 1885, and laws fixing pitch have been passed in Italy in 1887, 1936 and 1888). The present level is about the same as it was in Beethoven's day.

There is little evidence to support the theory that differing pitches were the result of local length standards. Organ builders speak of '5 ⅓′ pitch' and so on as if pitch and length were almost synonymous, but such terms are not always meant literally. The known length standards of a number of European cities bear no obvious relation to their pitch standards, and some cities, like Nuremberg, show an almost continuous range of pitches, depending on the period. Many makers also copied instruments from other places.

It is rarely possible to generalize about pitch standards. Even when the exact period and location are known, different kinds of music often had their own standards (reflected in names such as 'opera pitch', 'chamber pitch' and 'choir pitch'). Although the levels shifted with time, the breaks are rarely clean, so older standards overlapped with newer ones.

Among the most important early writings on pitch history were those by the 19th-century English philologist and mathematician Alexander Ellis. He provided a great quantity of raw data but, lacking a body of practical knowledge of how music had been performed in the past, he was able to give little indication of how it had been used by musicians. Many of Ellis's pitches, calculated to a tenth of Hertz, appear to be more accurate than a careful reading of his text allows, and most later writers

have accepted them too literally. It was the 20th-century American musicologist Arthur Mendel who clarified the way musicians thought about pitch, as a series of standards that sometimes related to each other in transposable intervals (Chorton was a major 2nd above Cammerton, for instance). He also emphasized the importance of both place and date in discussing standards. Despite Mendel's rigorous approach to the subject, however, he gave few absolute values for the relative standards he discussed, and those that he gave were usually conditional. Thus, between the extremes of Ellis's pitch frequencies without names and Mendel's pitch standards without values, performing musicians found little practical guidance.

Until the latter part of the 20th century, in fact, there was no great urgency to know the absolute Hertz values of historical pitches. As a practical matter they affected only singers, who whenever they sang with instruments either accepted the standard $a' = 440$ or persuaded the instrumentalists to transpose for them. The increase of performances on period instruments led to wider acceptance of the possibility of using pitches different to the modern standard, and to a realization that the sonorities and playing techniques of period instruments depended on their pitch levels. It thus became vital to know the performing pitches of works such as the cantatas of J.S. Bach, in which the original parts to the same piece were sometimes written in different keys (see §3(iv) below).

As the techniques of playing, making and restoring early instruments have become better understood, they have provided an important new source of empirical information on pitch that, if carefully approached, enables us to make plausible reconstructions of pitch levels as far back as the late Renaissance. The instruments that yield the most reliable historical pitch data are those that are hardest to alter: cornetts, early flutes, recorders, clarinets and organs. Other instruments are too flexible to be used as direct evidence: pitch estimates based on vocal ranges and string tension, for example, have proven unreliable except as corroboration of other kinds of evidence (written descriptions, musical notation, records of travelling musicians, etc.). Some early pitchpipes and tuning-forks survive, but it is difficult to know whether, when and how most of them were used. A few individual instruments (often organs) still exist whose pitches not only survive but were described at the time they were built. Other instruments can plausibly be associated with named pitch standards (for instance, recorders made in Leipzig with Bach's Cammerton). However, a number of factors can distort pitch evidence, such as the context in which each instrument was used, temperature (which is important for organs but is solved by a warm-up period on woodwinds), physical alterations, wood shrinkage, nominal pitch (e.g. whether the instrument is in F at $a' = 440$ or in G at $a' = 392$), location and date of manufacture, temperament, quality of information and modern assumptions about technique. The sections that follow are based on a study of the pitches of 1,194 original instruments that give plausible information, reported in Haynes, 1995.

Musicians today, playing music from a vast range of times and places, normally identify pitch standards by Hertz values. This convention breaks down when $a' = 415$, for instance, is used in a generic sense to mean all pitch frequencies from, say, $a' = 410$ to 420 Hz. A pitch standard is a musical rather than an acoustical unit, however; in terms of single cycles per second pitch changes radically during concerts, but is nevertheless acceptable to those listening. Hertz values are too specific to represent pitch standards; in fact, our vocabulary lacks a terminology appropriate to this subject. In this article pitches are identified by note names: $a' = 440$ (or thereabouts) is given as A+0; a semitone lower as A–1; a major 2nd above as A+2, and so on. This system helps to visualize transpositions, which are an integral factor in the discussion of pitch, and accommodates the physical reality that although they start by tuning in the same frequency, most instruments are not tuned to an exact Hertz value but rather to a pitch standard. These standards are identified by semitones, a tolerance of half that size (i.e. plus or minus a quarter-tone, or 50 cents) being understood.

2. HISTORY OF EUROPEAN PITCH STANDARDS SINCE THE LATE 16TH CENTURY.

(i) Italy. Mezzo punto and tutto punto were the names of pitch standards associated with the cornett, violin and organ in northern Italy from about 1580 to the end of the 17th century. Mezzo punto, clearly the more common level, was at $a' \approx 464$ (A+1), tutto punto was at $a' \approx 440$ (A+0). Church choirs of the period usually performed at A–1, a pitch known as tuono corista. Certain soft-voiced instruments such as transverse flutes and mute cornetts were also associated with this pitch. Organs were most often tuned at mezzo punto for playing with instruments, and organists transposed down a major 2nd when accompanying singers. Because temperaments and fingering technique made semitone transpositions impractical, wind players may have owned several instruments pitched in consecutive semitones, allowing whole-tone transpositions in various combinations to produce any required scale.

String players probably tuned up or down in order to play in reasonable keys. Most string instruments made in Cremona were probably designed to be played at mezzo punto or tutto punto. Antonio Barcotto (1652) wrote: 'Organs that are high work well with lower voices and violins, which are for this reason more spirited. The lower-pitched organs . . . do not work as well with violins as the high organs'. The gut strings used on the larger sizes of violin could probably have been tuned at least as high as A+1; smaller violins (which were especially popular in the 17th century) could go a semitone higher. Instrumental music was thus performed at A+1 or, less commonly, A+0; music involving choirs was at A–1 or, less commonly, at A+0.

By the 18th century, mezzo punto at A+1 was generally being called corista di Lombardia; it was the normal pitch of church organs in Venice until about 1740, when the organ maker Pietro Nachini began using A+0 (tutto punto), which then became known as corista Veneto. Although A–1 was used in Venetian opera in the early part of the century, it was A+0, apparently regarded as a compromise, that was to remain the principal pitch in Venice throughout the century, and which was adopted as the standard instrumental pitch, firstly in Vienna, and then all over Europe by the end of the 18th century. San Petronio in Bologna, which had been at mezzo punto since 1531, moved down to corista Veneto in 1708. Thus, the 20th-century pitch standard of $a' = 440$ may ultimately be descended from corista Veneto.

Tuono corista at A–1 still had currency in northern Italy during the 18th century; surviving Italian woodwinds were made at this level (as well as A+0). J.M. Anciuti and Carlo Palanca, who were among the important makers, made flutes with alternate joints at both levels, as well as individual recorders at each. Naples and Florence were generally associated with a pitch at A–1 during much of the 18th century.

In Rome, organs were generally at A–1 in Palestrina's time. But about 1600, evidently for the sake of the new castratos, church organs were lowered to A–2 (about $a' = 384$). One source called this pitch corista di S Pietro. Some Roman organs stayed at this level until late in the 19th century. Evidently, strings also played at this low pitch. Hautboy parts written by Handel and Antonio Caldara in Rome are notated a major 2nd lower than those for the rest of the orchestra, indicating that the hautboys involved were pitched a major 2nd higher. The principal hautboist for most or all these pieces was Ignazio Rion, who had come from Venice (where he had taught at the Ospedale della Pietà along with Vivaldi). Rion was evidently playing an hautboy at corista Veneto, while the other instruments (led by Arcangelo Corelli) were at A–2.

(ii) France. Mersenne wrote that a normal pitchpipe was tuned to ton de chapelle, presumably the pitch associated with church organs and choirs. The known pitches of most large organs built in France before 1680 range from $a' = 388$ to $a' = 396$ (A–2); this was the principal level associated with organs in France right into the 19th century. According to Mersenne's dimensions and illustrations of the 1630s, French wind instruments (which in this period never played in church) were at a level similar to the Italian mezzo punto (A+1). In France it was called Ton d'écurie, and woodwinds continued to be made to it until the 18th century (hence the C-hautboys that appear to be 'in D' and the F-recorders 'in G'). But most woodwinds were played at two other pitch standards: Ton de l'Opéra and Ton de la chambre. The orchestra of the new Opéra, created in the second half of the 17th century, adopted the singer's Ton de chapelle at A–2, and called it Ton de l'Opéra. To include winds in the new orchestra required that they be fundamentally redesigned, since (among other reasons) up to that time they had functioned separately in consorts at A+1. Pitch at the Opéra was fixed by the repertory: as long as works by Lully continued to be performed, a change in Ton de l'Opéra would have affected voice ranges and was therefore out of the question. The Opéra may have owned its own instruments and lent them to its players.

Several authors described two separate instrumental pitches in France from the late 17th century. In 1698, Georg Muffat reported one called 'ordinaire' and another approximately a semitone lower that he associated with 'Teatralischen Sachen'. Guillaume-Gabriel Nivers in 1683 also distinguished 'Ton de la Chambre du Roy' from Ton de chapelle a semitone lower. This Ton de la chambre, or 'court' pitch, seems to have been $a' \approx 404$ (A–1½); it is the pitch of many surviving French woodwinds of the period, of some organs, and of many French folk instruments. The name Ton de la chambre was used by other writers, including Loulié (1696) and Brossard (1703). Joseph Sauveur measured the pitches of harpsichords in 1700 and 1713 at $a' \approx 404$. This level is observable in France from about 1680 to 1800, although its period of importance was the reign of Louis XIV. The same frequency was dominant in England in the same period, and was known there as 'consort-pitch'.

There is evidence that all the royal organs (and some others as well) were raised from *Ton de chapelle* (A−2) to *Ton de la chambre* at A−1½ in the 1680s. This may have occurred because court musicians regularly performed in the royal chapels. Organs in other churches did not need to be changed in pitch to accomodate other instrumentalists, since there was a general interdiction on 'symphonists' playing in church (and when on special occasions they did, they usually came from the Opéra). Later in the 18th century the royal organs (like the one in the chapel at Versailles) were tuned back down to A−2. The organ at St Gervais, for example, where François Couperin was organist, was built in 1601 at A−2, and was raised a semitone in 1676 by Alexandre Thierry, organ maker to the King. In 1768 it was lowered to its original pitch of A−2. Thus all of Couperin's music, written either for St Gervais or the royal organs, and all his chamber music written for the court, was probably conceived at *Ton de la chambre* (A−1½).

Many woodwinds from Couperin's period survive at A−2 as well, and not all of them could have been used in the Opéra orchestra. Both A−1½ and A−2 were evidently current. Starting in the second decade of the 18th century French woodwinds began to be made at another somewhat higher pitch: $a' = 410\text{--}415$, or A−1. The term *Ton de la chambre* is not mentioned in later French sources. In 1737, Jacques Hotteterre was using *Ton ordinaire* for instrumental pitch (presumably A−1).

Pitch standards, like other aspects of French music making, changed rapidly after the death of Louis XIV in 1715. A−1 apparently became the predominant woodwind pitch until the 1740s, but this was the period when Italian style overwhelmed the traditional French, and *corista Veneto* came in at the same time; flutes were already appearing at A+0. In 1752, Quantz reported that Parisian pitch was 'beginning almost to equal that of Venice', and in 1757 J.F. Agricola spoke of 'französischen Stimmung' (by which he meant $a' \approx 390$) as a thing of the past. French flutes at A−2 no longer appeared after about 1770. From the time woodwinds at A+0 became common, they may have been used as transposing instruments at the Opéra (within the prevailing standard of A−2. Although this is mere speculation, that would explain the extreme sharp keys and difficult high notes in the woodwind parts to Rameau's operas starting in the 1740s.). The Concert Spirituel was also known for its high pitch. A number of well-known wind soloists from abroad played there starting in the 1730s, and may have influenced pitch through the instruments they brought with them.

By the 1760s *Ton de chapelle*, which had been ambiguous during Louis XIV's reign, was again fixed at its old level of A−2. But both Dom Bedos de Celles and Rousseau reported that *Ton de l'Opéra* was no longer stable, being raised and lowered a quarter-tone or more, depending on the ranges of voices. Repertory also played a part: Lully's works now began to undergo major revisions and additions which may have affected the ranges required from the singers and thus influenced their pitch preferences. The works of Lully and Rameau were still being performed in the early 1770s, but Gluck's 'reform operas' began in 1774, and from 1778 new and old operas were performed alternately. It was probably this state of affairs that the first bassoonist at the Opéra, Pierre Cugnier, described in 1780:

Bassoons that are made in the proportion of eight feet reduced to four, according to the old system of manufacture, are appropriate for playing in cathedrals, where ordinarily the pitch of the organ is very low, as was that of the *Eglise des Innocents* and is still *Ste Chapelle* at Paris and the *Chapelle du Roi* in Versailles. These bassoons can still be used in the Paris *Opéra*, where one changes pitch when the solo voice parts are lower or less high; so that there are of necessity some problems with intonation caused by the difficulty (one can even say the impossibility) of playing in tune with an instrument that is too high or too low.

In the same year that Cugnier's comments were published, an anonymous tract gave the pitch of the Opéra as $a' \approx 404$, or A−1½, which was probably preferred for the newer repertory.

(iii) Germany. The detailed pitch information in Praetorius's *De organographia* of 1618 is pivotal, looking back on the practices of the end of the 16th century and forward to the situation of German musicians confronted with the arrival of the new French orchestral instruments in the later 17th. But (although Praetorius was not confused) his terminology is confusing. He called his reference pitch *CammerThon* (which he used to mean 'secular instrumental pitch' at A+1), but its frequency was quite different from that of 18th-century *Cammerton*. Praetorius used *ChorThon* to mean 'church organ pitch'. Earlier this pitch had been a tone lower than his *CammerThon*, thus A−1, and in certain places, he said, it still was. But *ChorThon* was in process of changing in Praetorius's day. He explained that organs had gradually risen in pitch 'about a tone' until they too were at *CammerThon*. This is why Praetorius was inconsistent in his meaning of the term *ChorThon*, sometimes equating it to *CammerThon* and sometimes making it a major 2nd below it. (Fortunately, he reserved *CammerThon* as his unmoving reference, although he gave it other names as well, like *rechte Thon* and *Cornettenthon*.) Praetorius described with approval the situation in Prague:

Normal modern pitch, to which nearly all of our organs are now tuned, is there called *CammerThon* . . . *ChorThon*, however, which is a whole tone lower, is used only in the churches, primarily for the sake of the singers . . . as it allows their voices to bear up longer, and saves them from becoming husky from working at high pitch.

Evidence from the Habsburg lands confirms his description, *ChorThon* being the usual term for a pitch a 2nd below A+1 (*Zinck-Thon* or *Cornet-Ton*) until at least the time of Janowka (Prague, 1701; see §I, 2(v) below). Praetorius also appears to have been describing a corollary to the system used in northern Italy, in which the organist transposed down a whole step (to *tuono corista* or A−1) from a high instrumental pitch (A+1) for the sake of the singers. The parallel is underlined by Praetorius's use of the phrase '*Chöristen- oder Chor*Thon'.

Another aspect of Praetorius's pitch information that has led to confusion is his scale diagram of a set of organ pipes, or *Pfeifflin zur Chormass*, whose principal purpose, he explained, was to indicate the pitch level of his *CammerThon*. This diagram has been the subject of considerable debate, but it is now generally agreed that it, like other indications (including extant original wind instruments of the period), shows a level at A+1 (Myers, A1997, and Koster, D forthcoming). Praetorius's *CammerThon* was thus parallel to the most common pitch in Italy at the same time, *mezzo punto*.

In the latter part of the 17th century developments in France inspired a revolution in the instrumentarium in Germany. The new designs of woodwinds were tuned a tone or more below most German organs. For various practical reasons, neither the organs nor the woodwinds could adapt to each other's pitch for a period of several generations. As secular instrumental music gradually came to dominate music making, however, so did its pitch. Thus Praetorius's *CammerThon* effectively swapped its meaning with that of *Chorton* (which continued to mean 'church organ pitch'). Jakob Adlung in 1768 referred to this confusion, writing that 'organs are tuned to *Chorton*, as it is now called, which is 1 or 1½ tones higher than *Cammerton*. Formerly it was the reverse, and *Cammerton* was higher than *Chorton*; organs were tuned to what was then called *Cammerton*'. Thus the approximate frequencies of established German pitch standards (A+1 and A 1) were not altered by the musical revolution caused by the arrival of French orchestral instruments, but their names were interchanged.

In the new configuration, transposition became necessary when organs played with other instruments. Vocal parts could be notated at either standard. In some cases, it was simpler (as for Bach at Weimar) to notate the voices with the organ, since the strings were still tuned high. As time went on, it became more common to write voice and string parts at the new low *Cammerton* (as Bach did at Leipzig), leaving only the organ and the brass (the latter representing a stronghold of tradition) at *Chorton*.

The older instruments in the German 17th-century tradition did not vanish immediately. The *chorist-Fagott* or *deutsche Fagott* (i.e. the curtal) long continued its traditional role in providing discrete accompaniment to choirs, and traditional shawms were played well into the 18th century. These instruments were pitched at Praetorius's old high *CammerThon* at A+1. But since the word *Cammerton* was now associated with a low pitch, 'deutsche' (e.g. *deutsche Schalmey*) gradually developed a secondary connotation as an indication of instruments at high pitch. Just as the term 'French' before an instrument's name (*französische Schalmei*), or the use of the French name itself (*Hautbois*) was a sign of an instrument in *Cammerton*, the word 'deutsche' was used to indicate an instrument at A+1 (*see* SHAWM, §4).

We are fortunate in having the original frequencies of at least 36 German organs whose pitch standard was also identified by name:

There are 13 examples of *Cornet-Ton* within a narrow and specific range, averaging *a'* = 463. This level agrees well with the pitch of surviving cornetts.

There are 11 examples of *Chorton*, as high as *a'* = 487 and as low as *a'* = 437 (i.e. A+0, A+1, A+2). They average, however, *a'* = 467.

There are two examples of *Chormass* at *a'* = 489 and *a'* = 466. (*Chormass* is a term frequently encountered in the 17th century and less in the 18th; it was evidently synonymous with *Chorton*).

Cammerton (ten examples) is also consistent and averages *a'* = 416. This level compares well with woodwind pitch between 1680 and 1770.

From this it can be seen that *Chorton* in the 18th century could have been any pitch from A+0 to A+2. 18th-century *Cornet-Ton*, by contrast, was relatively specific and consistent in frequency. Cornetts were commonly used as a reference for pitch frequency in Italy, Germany and the Habsburg lands. Cornetts made in Germany in the 16th and 17th centuries range in pitch from *a'* = 450 to *a'* = 480, but most are close to *a'* = 465.

Praetorius used *CammerThon* and *Cornettenthon* synonymously in the early 17th century. But while the names *CammerThon* and *ChorThon* traded places between the 17th and 18th centuries, *Cornet-Ton* (*Cornettenthon*) remained at the same level, since cornetts did not change in pitch from the 16th to the 18th centuries. *Cornet-Ton*, then, was equivalent to the early 17th-century *CammerThon*, but by the 18th century it had become a specific kind of *Chorton*.

The words *Cornet-Ton* and *Chorton* sounded so similar, and the concepts they denoted overlapped so closely, that it would be surprising if they had not sometimes been confused. *Chorton* was variously described as different from, lower than, and equal to *Cornet-ton*. Because *Chorton* was a general concept rather than a specific frequency, there are a number of references to a 'gewöhnlichen (ordinairen) Chortone' and 'hohe Chortone'. The 'gewöhnlichen' was a whole-tone above *Cammerton* (which was A–1). *Hohe Chorton* was found in the extreme north of Germany: Buxtehude's organ at the Marienkirche, Lübeck, was in *hoch-Chorton* and pitched at A+2. About a third of the surviving organs by Arp Schnitger are at A+2 (the others are at A+1). Organs at A+2 were used to accompany congregational singing in churches that did not use other instruments.

There were those who preferred the sound of organs at *Chorton* (in its general sense) over *Cammerton*. But the most important reason for making high-pitched organs was the expense: a lower pitch required extra pipes at the bottom of each stop, and being the longest pipes they used the most tin. The new organ built in Bach's Thomaskirche in Leipzig in 1773 was still at *Chorton*. By the beginning of the 19th century most organs were built in *Kammerton* (as it was then usually called), although in Saxony in the early 19th century an organ pitch of A+1 was still common.

Cammerton was associated with secular music; in the 18th century it was the usual pitch of instruments other than the organ and brass. Eventually many organs adopted *Cammerton*, which was more convenient when playing with other instruments. As noted above, nine 18th-century German organs at *Cammerton* survive, all at A–1 (which we can assume represented its normal frequency). There were other, lower species of *Cammerton*: the family of *tief-Cammertons*, including *Opera-Ton* and *französischer Thon*. These levels were all approximately a minor 3rd below A+1 and are thus difficult to keep distinct. The existence of *ton de la chambre* in France at A–1½ was probably the root cause of the confusion, since this frequency fell between the levels at A–1 and A–2 that were transposable on most German organ keyboards. The *Cammerton* levels at A–2 and A–1½, being common French pitches, probably came in when the first French woodwinds arrived in the 1680s. But A–1 must also have been current by the 1690s, as a stop in the Jacobikirche organ, Hamburg (Schnitger, 1693), was at *a'* = 408, a minor 3rd below the rest of the organ at *a'* = 489.

Praetorius documented the use of a pitch a minor 3rd below his *CammerThon* (at A+1) that was used, he said, 'a great deal in different Catholic chapels in Germany'. So the level at A–2 was not a complete innovation in Germany with the arrival of French instruments. Indications for *tief-Cammerton* in wind parts disappear after the mid-1720s, though German woodwinds were still made at A–2 until at least 1770.

The parts and occasionally the scores to German music of the early 18th century (such as works for organ and other instruments) that involved the simultaneous use of two and sometimes three different pitch standards were normally notated in different keys. In transposing, composers were obliged to consider a number of interrelated practical factors: the technical effects on different kinds of performers, changes of sonority, key and its relation to affect, and temperament. The effect of transposition on voices was a primary consideration. The tone qualities of the different vocal registers were consciously distinguished until the Classical period, and breaks from chest to head voice, which generally occur at specific frequencies, were avoided. Register placement is obviously shifted by transposition. Transposition could also turn a high tenor part into one for falsettist (countertenor) by changing its range.

Although string instruments were also sensitive to changes of pitch and key, some or all the individual strings were regularly retuned as much as a whole step up and down in the 18th century; examples are found in works by Biber, Kuhnau, Bach and Mozart. Many string instruments then in use had been made in an earlier period when standard instrumental pitch was A+1; they were often tuned up to *Cornet-ton* in the early 18th century.

When parts were not in the appropriate key, organists were expected to transpose at sight. Woodwinds were less flexible. Their fingering system limited them to keys with no more than four sharps or flats, and each tonality had an associated character, technique and intonation. Some woodwinds like the traverso and hautbois d'amour were specialists in sharp keys, while others like the recorder and bassoon tended towards flats.

Temperament was a consideration for the fixed-pitch instruments such as keyboards and lute; melody instruments made ad hoc tuning adjustments as needed. Transpositions of a semitone were impractical in meantone, but when the intervals involved were the major 2nd and minor 3rd, and a so-called 'regular' meantone was used (i.e. one in which all the 5ths but one were tuned the same), intervals were virtually identical in standard tonalities.

(iv) J.S. Bach. Throughout his career, Bach worked with instruments at *Cornet-ton* (A+1) and various levels of *Cammerton*, although his method of notating their parts was different in each of the places he worked. The most complex situation was at Weimar. The organ in the court chapel where Bach was Konzertmeister was documented as in 'Cornet Thon'. During the first year he wrote cantatas, Bach wrote parts for a single 'Oboe' notated a major 2nd above the other parts (organ, voices and strings). The strings must therefore have been tuned up to *Cornet-ton*, and the 'Oboe' must have sounded a tone below the organ (and therefore at the higher level of *Cammerton*, A-1). But the 'Oboe' disappeared at the end of 1714, to be replaced by an instrument Bach consistently called an 'Hautbois', whose parts now differed a minor 3rd from the organ and strings. From this time, Bach also notated certain other instruments at the interval of a minor 3rd, like the 'Basson' and 'Flaut' (recorder). Since the organ stayed at A+1, these instruments must have been at *tief-Cammerton*, or A-2. All the remaining works written for the Weimar chapel show this relationship.

The parts to Bach's music written at Cöthen, on the other hand, are in a single key; presumably all the instruments were at the same pitch. But there is reason to think the prevailing pitch at Cöthen was a form of *tief-Cammerton*, either A-1½ or A-2. The voice ranges of cantatas written there are unusually high, and when he used material from Cöthen later at Leipzig, Bach sometimes performed it at 'tief-Cammerthon'. The problematic trumpet part to the second Brandenburg concerto would be significantly easier on an instrument at *tief-Cammerton* instead of A-1.

At Leipzig, the performing materials for most of Bach's vocal works indicate that the strings, voices and woodwinds were at *Cammerton* and the organ and brass were a major 2nd higher. Bach's predecessor, Johann Kuhnau, had specified in 1717 that the pitch of the organs at the Thomas- and Nicolaikirchen was *Cornet-ton*. But Kuhnau had used figural instruments at intervals of both a 2nd and a minor 3rd below *Cornet-ton*, 'depending', he said, 'on which is most convenient' (i.e. which pitch would yield mutually satisfying keys). He had woodwinds available, in other words, at both normal *Cammerton* and at *tief-Cammerton*. Since tonalities with open strings were preferable on the string instruments, and appropriate tonalities were critical for the unkeyed woodwinds, the presence of woodwinds tuned a semitone apart was extremely practical: it offered Kuhnau a choice of more combinations of keys in which to compose.

During Bach's first year and a half at Leipzig, he took advantage of this option by writing several cantatas at *tief-Cammerton*: nos.22, 23, 63 and 194, and also the first version of the *Magnificat*. (Cantatas nos.22 and 23 were his trial pieces and were performed together; Cantata no.63 had been conceived some years earlier, probably for performance at *tief-Cammerton*, and in Leipzig was performed on the same day as the *Magnificat* – which, with Cantata no.194, had antecedents in Cöthen.) The last known date that Bach used the *tief-Cammerton* option with his regular winds was 4 June 1724. He revised the *Magnificat* for a performance in the 1730s, transposing it from Eb to D, probably because *tief-Cammerton* woodwinds were no longer available. Questions of notation and transposition caused by pitch differences affect the following works by Bach: BWV12, 18, 21, 22, 23, 31, 63, 70a, 71, 80a, 106, 131, 132, 147a, 150, 152, 155, 161, 162, 172, 182, 185, 186a, 194, 199, 208 and 243a. Most but not all these questions are addressed by the *Neue Bach-Ausgabe* (for a detailed discussion, see Haynes, A1995).

(v) The Habsburg lands. The description Praetorius gave of pitch relations in Prague (see §I, 2(iii), above) applied to Vienna as well. There, *ChorThon* (at A-1) was the pitch of church music and was a tone lower than *CammerThon/Cornettenthon* (at A+1). 70 years later Muffat, writing in 1698 for the Habsburg emperors, used the same concepts to describe French pitch:

> The pitch to which the French usually tune their instruments is a whole tone lower than our German one (called *Cornet-Ton*), and in operas, even one and a half tones lower. They find the German pitch too high, too screechy, and too forced. If it were up to me to choose a pitch, and there were no other considerations, I would choose the former [of the French pitches], called in Germany old *Chorton*, using somewhat thicker strings. This pitch lacks nothing in liveliness along with its sweetness.

Writing in Prague in 1701, T.B. Janowka still used Praetorius's terminology; he called the higher pitch *Zinck-thon* and associated the lower one, *Chor-Thon*, with the new French and Italian wind instruments (which he considered to be 'ex B', i.e. in B♭). The older Praetorius-style pitch names persisted well into the 18th century in the Habsburg lands, though by mid-century the terminology began to reverse itself as it had done 50 years earlier in northern Germany. The nomenclature, though not the musical practice, was in direct opposition to the usage in northern Germany at the same time.

The Habsburg court was strongly influenced by northern Italy, and many of its important musicians were Italian. Since instrumental pitch in Venice was normally A+0, it is not surprising to observe *Cammerton* move up a semitone already in Fux's time. By the period 1740–70, if not before, woodwinds being made in Vienna were at $a' \approx 430$–435. In the same period, there are steady reports of organs being tuned down a semitone to A+0, and a number of new ones were also built at this level. In both cases, the influence of Venice was probably responsible (see §I, 2(i), above).

(vi) England.   Various kinds of evidence suggest that at the beginning of the 17th century the primary English church standard was known as 'Quire-pitch', and that its level was $a' \approx 473$, i.e. between A+1 and A+2. Instruments like recorders, cornetts and sackbuts were generally pitched a semitone lower than Quire-pitch (Q–1, $a' \approx 448$; cf. Praetorius: 'The English pitch, however, is a very little lower [than *CammerThon* at $a' \approx 464$], as the instruments made in that country show, for instance cornetts and shawms'). Viol consorts, at Consort-pitch, were another whole-step lower at Q-3, or $a' \approx 400$.

Very few church organs escaped destruction during the Civil War and subsequent Commonwealth (1642–60). At the Restoration the instruments and pitches from before 1642 were temporarily re-established and a number of new organs were built. The newer French woodwinds that came into fashion in the 1670s and their pitch of A–1½ (*Ton de la chambre*; it was conveniently compatible with Consort-pitch at Q-3) eventually became important enough that organs had to be rebuilt or replaced at lower pitches in order to play with other instruments. English organs whose pitches have survived are thus almost always at Quire-pitch, a semitone, or a whole tone below it ($a' \approx 473$, $a' \approx 448$ or $a' \approx 423$). The lowest of these levels, $a' \approx 423$ or Q–2, became the dominant organ pitch in England in the 18th century and into the 19th, identified at least once as 'Chappell-pitch'; when it was later adopted by orchestral instruments in about the 1730s, it was called 'new Consort-pitch'. The other two higher levels vanished during the course of the 18th century. Handel often played an organ built in 1708 by Bernard Smith at the chapel of St James's Palace; this instrument was at $a' = 466$ (A+1).

Old consort pitch at Q–3 or $a' \approx 400$ is represented by woodwinds made by Peter Bressan, Joseph Bradbury, Thomas Cahusac and Thomas Stanesby jr, and by at least one chamber organ attributed to Smith. That it probably extended backwards to the early 17th century is indicated by Praetorius ('Formerly in England . . . most instruments were made to sound a minor 3rd lower than our present-day *CammerThon*') and suggested by the fact that chamber and house music actually flourished during the Interregnum (its pitch therefore remaining unchanged). It is also likely that this was the pitch used by Blow and Purcell when they wrote for wind instruments. It is known that the pitch of the opera orchestra at the Queen's Theatre where Handel produced his first operas was a

quarter-tone higher than *Ton d'Opéra* in France; this would put it at Q–3/A–1½. By the early 1720s, Handel was probably using A–1, which was standard opera pitch on the Continent. His later oratorios were probably performed at 'new Consort-pitch', or Q–2 ($a' \approx 423$); the famous tuning fork left by Handel in 1751 at the Foundling Hospital is at $a' = 422\frac{1}{2}$.

Not all instruments fit into the Quire-pitch grid. The consorts of foreign musicians maintained by Henry VIII played as separate units, for instance, and had no need to conform to organ pitch standards. The organ and cornetts at Christ Church, Oxford, were at A+2 and A+0 respectively. While the quire pitch system was generally valid for all instruments until the first quarter of the 18th century, it began losing importance with the influx of Italians like Giuseppe Sammartini and their instruments at A–1 and A+0. In the period 1730–70 both new Consort-pitch at Q–2 ($a' \approx 423$) and A+0 ($a' \approx 435$) began to appear in woodwinds. By 1770 there were almost no woodwinds at the older Consort-pitch (Q–3); Q–2 was still present but most woodwinds were at A+0 (which was by then common in Venice, Paris, Vienna and much of Germany). Only organs retained the last vestige of the Quire-pitch grid, the majority being tuned to Q–2.

(vii) Classical pitches, 1765–1830.   By the last part of the 18th century church organs throughout Europe tended to be in different pitches than orchestral instruments. Organs were generally pitched as they had been a century before, which, in relation to other instruments, made them too high in Germany and too low in France and England.

The two principal orchestral pitches were A–1 and A+0, and in the course of the Classical period the latter (more accurately $a' = 430$–440) become predominant, although the process of change was gradual and not universal. A+0 was already the predominant instrumental pitch in Venice at the beginning of the 18th century, in Vienna and Prague about 1740, in London and Rome by about 1770, in France about 1780 (officially in the 1790s) and in northern Germany at the beginning of the 19th century.

The Classical period was characterized by minor pitch differences of about a comma (a ninth of a whole-tone or about 21 cents) that could be accommodated on woodwinds by using alternate joints or tuning slides. Each theatre in Vienna and Paris, for instance, had its own slightly different pitch until the 1820s. Multiple joints were usually numbered from lowest to highest, and today often only one joint with a higher number remains; this is an indication that pitch was generally on the rise, since the lower-pitched joints were probably laid aside and eventually separated from the instruments.

In northern Italy at the end of the 18th century wind players were evidently getting their instruments from abroad; many woodwinds by Augustin and Heinrich Grenser are found now in Italian collections. Grensers are normally at about $a' = 433$, a pitch observed in Venice throughout the century. Although the *corista di S Pietro* at A–2 was maintained on organs at the Vatican until late in the 19th century, at the end of the 18th there were reports of woodwinds in Rome at about the same level as Venice. By this time, A+0 had come to be called *coristo Lombardo* and was considered normal in most parts of Italy, including Naples.

In France *Ton d'Opéra*, which had been at A–2 in mid-century (since the traditional repertory, including Lully's works, was still on the boards), began fluctuating between A–2 and A–1½ in the 1770s as a result of reforms and changing repertory. Harpsichords and woodwinds in France varied between A–1 and A+0, the latter predominating by the 1780s. They were sometimes classified according to their pitches as 'modern' (i.e. at A+0) or 'ancien' (A–1). The Concert Spirituel regularly featured soloists from abroad and had a reputation for a high pitch, probably A+0 (*a′* ≈ 435). At the end of the century this pitch, called *Ton d'orchestre*, was officially adopted in Paris by the new Conservatoire. Many of the best woodwinds were shortened at this period, in the hope that they could be retained. The rationalist mentality of the age did not eliminate small variations in pitch standard, as the multiple joints of instruments made at the time testify. Even the *Opéra* was eventually forced to adopt *Ton d'orchestre*, though the poor showing of the singers of the time who attempted the earlier repertory was blamed on the raised pitch level. Charles Delezenne (1854) reported pitches at various theatres in Paris in 1823 as *a′* = 424, 428, 432 and, in 1834, 440.

The Italian influence on pitch throughout Europe was reinforced by the dynamism of the so-called 'Wiener Klassik'. By the second third of the century performances in Vienna were generally at *a′* ≈ 430–435. Pitch remained at this level in Viennese instrumental, dramatic and much church music until the end of the century. Prague and other cities in the Habsburg empire were probably at the same pitch, since the court and many musicians circulated frequently. The latter part of the century saw much coming and going of wind players between Vienna and other places, suggesting a general agreement on pitch: famous soloists would not have switched instruments or set-ups merely for the sake of fluctuating pitch standards.

Reports in the 1770s compared Berlin's low pitch with the high one in Vienna. In some parts of northern Germany A–1 remained the standard until at least 1832. In Dresden, the famous *Cammerton* organs by Silbermann were probably responsible. It may also be that when A+0 became the general European standard, A–1 survived in many places because it had become a church pitch. Not only had organs been made to it in the mid-18th century, but being a whole tone below A+1, it remained more practical than A+0 for transpositions with older organs. Dresden was also a principal woodwind-making centre, and surviving instruments from there are at both A–1 and A+0 (the latter apparently for export). Berlin may have remained low as a result of the lingering influence of Frederick the Great's court (being a flautist, Frederick favoured a low pitch). A general pitch reference in Saxony at this time was the organ at the Nicolaikirche Leipzig, at A–1 (although flutes were made there at both A–1 and A+0).

(viii) Pitch standards since c1830. Since the early 19th century orchestral instruments have evolved through small adaptations rather than revolutionary new designs. As a result, fluctuations in pitch standards have been relatively minor. The mean pitch in Europe in 1858, when the *diapason normal* (*a′* = 435) was promulgated in France, was about *a′* = 446, just as it is today. The universal standard *a′* = 440 established in 1939 was no less artificial and unrealistic.

Historically, as we have seen, pitch has fluctuated both up and down. Present-day pitch is noticeably lower than Victorian England's 'sharp pitch' of *a′* = 452. Pitch at La Scala was at that same level in 1867, up from *a′* = 450 in 1856. In Vienna a generation after Mozart's death pitch seems to have been somewhat lower, at *a′* = 440–445. Thus almost from the beginning singers have been obliged to perform the music of Mozart and Verdi at a level several Hertz higher than the composers intended. At present pitch appears once again to be on the rise from a theoretical (and rarely used in orchestras) *a′* = 440 to as high as *a′* = 450. From a broader perspective these vacillations can be seen as temporary departures from a remarkably stable norm.

BIBLIOGRAPHY

A General. B Italy. C France. D Germany. E Johann Sebastian Bach. F The Habsburg lands. G England. H Classical. I Since *c*1830.

A: GENERAL

PraetoriusSM, ii; PraetoriusTI; Waterhouse-LangwillI
J.J. Quantz: *Versuch einer Anweisung die Flöte traversiere zu spielen* (Berlin, 1752/R, 3/1789/R; Eng. trans., 1966, 2/1985, as *On Playing the Flute*)
J.F. Agricola: *Anleitung zur Singkunst* (Berlin, 1757/R) [trans., with addns, of P.F. Tosi: *Opinioni de' cantori antichi e moderni*, Bologna, 1723/R]; Eng. trans., ed. J.C. Baird (Cambridge, 1995)
A. de la Fage: *De l'unité tonique et de la fixation d'un diapason universel* (Paris, 1859)
A.J. Ellis: 'On the History of Musical Pitch', *Journal of the Society of Arts*, xxviii (1880), 293–336; repr. in A.J. Ellis and A. Mendel: *Studies in the History of Musical Pitch* (Amsterdam, 1969/R)
A.J. Ellis: 'The History of Musical Pitch in Europe', *On the Sensations of Tone* (London, 2/1885/R) [Eng. trans. of H. von Helmholtz: *Die Lehre von den Tonempfindung*, Brunswick, 1863, 4/1877], appx XX, H–N
A. Mendel: 'Pitch in the 16th and Early 17th Centuries', *MQ*, xxxiv (1948), 28–45, 199–221, 336–57, 575–93
A. Mendel: 'On the Pitches in Use in Bach's Time', *MQ*, xli (1955), 332–54, 466–80
A. Mendel: 'Pitch in Western Music since 1500: a Re-Examination', *AcM*, l (1978), 1–93; pubd separately (Kassel, 1979)
C. Karp: 'Pitch', *Performance Practice: Music after 1600*, ed. H.M. Brown and S. Sadie (London, 1989), 147–68
H.W. Myers: 'Pitch and Transposition in the Renaissance and Early Baroque', *A Practical Guide to Historical Performance: the Renaissance*, ed. J.T. Kite-Powell (New York, 1989)
G. Stradner: 'Stimmtonhöhe: Tonarten- und Klangcharacter', *Die Klangwelt Mozarts*, Kunsthistorisches Museum, 28 April – 27 Oct 1991 (Vienna, 1991), 109–20 [exhibition catalogue]
R. Weber: 'Was Sagen die Holzblasinstrumente zu Mozarts Kammerton?', *Tibia*, xviii (1992), 291–8
P.T. Young: *4900 Historical Woodwind Instruments: an Inventory of 200 Makers in International Collections* (London, 1993)
B. Haynes: *Pitch Standards in the Baroque and Classical Periods* (diss., U. of Montreal, 1995)
H.W. Myers: 'Pitch and Transposition', *A Performer's Guide to Seventeenth-Century Music*, ed. S. Carter (New York, 1997), 325–40
D. Wraight: *The Stringing of Italian Keyboard Instruments c.1500–c.1650* (diss., Queen's U. of Belfast, 1997)

B: ITALY

G.B. Doni: *Annotazioni sopra il Compendio de' generi e de' modi della musica* (Rome, 1640); extracts ed. C. Gallico as 'Discorso sesto sopra il recitare in scena con l'accompagnamento d'instrumenti musicali', *RIM*, iii (1968), 286–302
A. Barcotto: *Regola e breve raccordo* (MS, 1652, *I-Bl*); Eng. trans. in *Organ Yearbook*, xvi (1985), 47–70
P.F. Tosi: *Opinioni de' cantori antichi e moderni* (Bologna, 1723/R; Eng. trans, ed. J.E. Galliard, 1742, 2/1743/R as *Observations on the Florid Song*)
G. Paolucci: *Arte pratica di contrappunto* (Venice, 1765–72)
C. Gervasoni: *La scuola della musica* (Piacenza, 1800)
G. Cesari and G. Pannain: *La musica in Cremona nella secondo metà del secolo XVI: e i primordi dell'arte monteverdiana* (Milan, 1939), pp.xv–xxii

R. Lunelli: *Der Orgelbau in Italien in seinen Meisterwerken vom 14. Jahrhundert bis zur Gegenwart* (Mainz, 1956)

L.F. Tagliavini: 'Considerazioni sulle vicende storiche del "corista"', *L'organo*, xii (1974), 119–32

P. Barbieri: 'Il corista bolognese, secondo il rilevamento di V.F. Stancari', *L'organo*, xviii (1980), 18, 25

A. Parrott: 'Transposition in Monteverdi's Vespers of 1610, an "Aberration" Defended', *EMc*, xii (1984), 490–516

P. Barbieri: *Acustica, accordatura e temperamento nell'illuminismo veneto* (Rome, 1987)

P. Barbieri: 'Chiavette and Modal Transposition in Italian Practice (c.1500–1837)', *Recercare*, iii (1991), 5–79

K. Kreitner: 'Renaissance Pitch', *Companion to Medieval and Renaissance Music*, ed. T. Knighton and D. Fallows (London, and New York, 1992), 275–83

P. van Heyghen: 'The Recorder in Italian Music, 1600–1670', *The Recorder in the 17th Century: Utrecht 1993*, 3–64

J.G. Kurtzman: 'Tones, Modes, Clefs and Pitch in Roman Cyclic Magnificats of the 16th Century', *EMc*, xxii (1994), 641–64

D. Lasocki and R. Prior: *The Bassanos: Venetian Musicians and Instrument Makers in England, 1531–1665* (Aldershot, 1995)

C: FRANCE

*La Borde*E; *Mersenne*HU

E. Loulié: *Eléments ou principes de musique* (Paris, 1696, 2/1698; Eng. trans., 1965)

G. Muffat: *Florilegium secundum* (Passau, 1698; ed. in DTÖ, iv, Jg.2/ii, 1895/R)

Traité de la musique moderne, avec quelques remarques sur la musique ancienne (MS, 1702, *GB-Lbl*, c.12r-v)

S. de Brossard: *Dictionaire de musique* (Paris, 1703/R, 3/c1708/R); Eng. trans., ed. A. Gruber (Henryville, PA, 1982)

J.M. Hotteterre: *Méthode pour la musette* (Paris, 1737/R)

J.-J. Rousseau: *Dictionnaire de musique* (Paris, 1768/R; Eng. trans., 1771, 2/1779/R)

F.-J. Fétis: 'Sur le diapason', *Revue musicale*, i/2 (1828)

C. Delezenne: 'Sur le ton des orchestres et des orgues', *Mémoires de la Société des sciences à Lille, 1826–1857* (1854)

C. Pierre: *Les facteurs d'instruments de musique* (Paris, 1893/R)

P.-J. Hardouin: 'Les flottements du diapason', *Musique de tous les temps*, no.23 (1963)

M. Benoit: *Versailles et les musiciens du roi, 1661–1733* (Paris, 1971)

R. Rasch, ed.: *J. Sauveur: Collected Writings on Musical Acoustics* (Utrecht, 1984)

D: GERMANY

*Fürstenau*G, i

J. Mattheson: *Das neu-eröffnete Orchestre* (Hamburg, 1713/R)

J. Mattheson: *Das forschende Orchestre* (Hamburg, 1721/R)

J. Kuhnau: Letter to Johann Mattheson, 8 Dec 1717, J. Mattheson: *Critica musica*, i (1722), 229–39

G.P. Telemann: Preface to *Harmonische Gottes-Dienst*, i (Hamburg, 1725–6)

J.D. Heinichen: *Der General-Bass in der Composition, oder Neue und gründliche Anweisung* (Dresden, 1728/R)

J. Adlung: *Anleitung zu der musikalischen Gelahrtheit* (Erfurt, 1758/R, 2/1783)

J. Adlung: *Musica mechanica organoedi*, ed. J.L. Albrecht (Berlin, 1768/R); ed. C. Mahrenholz (Kassel, 1931)

A.A. Hülphers: *Historisk afhandling om musik och instrumenter* (Västerås, 1773/R)

J. van Heurn: *De orgelmaaker* (Dordrecht, 1804–5/R)

F. Bösken: *Quellen und Forschungen zur Orgelgeschichte des Mittelrheins* (Mainz, 1967–88)

A. Hohn: 'Die Orgeln Johann Andreas Silbermanns', *Acta organologica*, iv (1970), 11–58

E. Nickel: *Der Holzblasinstrumentenbau in der Freien Reichsstadt Nürnberg* (Munich, 1971)

W.R. Thomas and J.J.K. Rhodes: 'Schlick, Praetorius and the History of Organ-Pitch', *Organ Yearbook*, ii (1971), 58–76

U. Dähnert: *Historische Orgeln in Sachsen: ein Orgelinventar* (Frankfurt, 1980)

W. Müller: *Gottfried Silbermann: Persönlichkeit und Werk* (Frankfurt, 1982)

A. Smith: 'Belege zur Frage der Stimmtonhöhe bei Michael Praetorius', *Alte Musik: Praxis und Reflexion*, ed. P. Reidemeister and V. Gutmann (Winterthur, 1983), 340–45

H.W. Myers: 'Praetorius's Pitch', *EMc*, xii (1984), 369–71

E. Segerman: 'Praetorius's pitch?', *EMc*, xiii (1985), 261–3

M. Spielmann: 'Der Zink im Instrumentarium des süddeutsch-österreichischen Raumes 1650 bis 1750', *Johann Joseph Fux und die barocke Bläsertradition: Graz 1985*, 121–55

E. Segerman: 'Eighteenth-Century German and French Pitches', *FoMRHI Quarterly*, no.42 (1986), 62–8

H. Vogel: 'North German Organ Building of the Late Seventeenth Century: Registration and Tuning,', *J.S. Bach as Organist: his Instruments, Music, and Performance Practice*, ed. G. Stauffer and E. May (Bloomington, IN, 1986), 31–40

G. Stradner: 'The Evolution of the Pitch of Cornetts and Trombones at the Time of Scheidt and Buxtehude', *Dietrich Buxtehude and Samuel Scheidt: Saskatoon, SK, 1987*, 106–16

F.-H. Gress: *Die Klanggestalt der Orgeln Gottfried Silbermanns* (Frankfurt, 1989)

E. Segerman: 'The Sizes and Pitches of Praetorius's Sackbuts', *FoMRHI Quarterly*, no.73 (1993), 50–51

M. Schaefer, ed.: *J.A. Silbermann: Das Silbermann-Archiv: der handschriftliche Nachlass des Orgelmachers Johann Andreas Silbermann (1712–1783)* (Winterthur, 1994)

H.W. Myers: 'Praetorius's Pitch: some Revelations of the Theatrum Instrumentorum', *Perspectives in Early Brass Scholarship: Amherst, MA, 1995*, 29–45

H.W. Myers: 'Praetorius's Pitch Standard', *GSJ*, li (1998), 247–67

J. Koster: 'Praetorius's "Pfeifflin zur Chormass"', *Stimmton und Transposition* (Bremen, forthcoming)

E: JOHANN SEBASTIAN BACH

A. Werner: *Städtische und fürstliche Musikpflege in Weissenfels bis zum Ende des 18. Jahrhunderts* (Leipzig, 1911/R)

A. Schering: *Musikgeschichte Leipzigs*, ii: *Von 1650 bis 1723* (Leipzig, 1926/R)

A. Dürr: *Studien über die frühen Kantaten J.S. Bachs* (Leipzig, 1951, 2/1977)

A. Dürr: *Kritischer Bericht*, Johann Sebastian Bach: Neue Ausgabe Sämtlicher Werke, II/iii (Kassel, 1955)

L.D. Dreyfus: *Basso Continuo Practice in the Vocal Works of J.S. Bach: a Study of the Original Performance Parts* (diss., Columbia U., 1980)

U. Prinz: 'Zur Bezeichnung "Bassono" und "Fagotto" bei J.S. Bach', *BJb 1981*, 107–22

P. Brainard: *Kritischer Bericht*, Johann Sebastian Bach: Neue Ausgabe Sämtlicher Werke, I/xvi (Kassel, 1984)

A. Dürr: 'Neue Erkenntnisse zur Kantate BWV 31', *BJb 1985*, 155–9

B. Haynes: 'Johann Sebastian Bach's Pitch Standards: the Woodwind Perspective', *JAMIS*, xi (1985), 55–114

H. Heyde: 'Blasinstrumente und Bläser der Dresdner Hofkapelle in der Zeit des Fux-Schülers Johann Dismas Zelenka (1710–1745)', *Johann Joseph Fux und die barocke Bläsertradition: Graz 1985*, 39–65

H. Heyde: 'Der Instrumentenbau in Leipzig zur Zeit Johann Sebastian Bachs', *300 Jahre Johann Sebastian Bach*, Staatsgalerie Stuttgart, 14 Sept – 27 Oct 1985 (Tutzing, 1985), 73–88 [exhibition catalogue]

W. Schrammek: 'Orgel, Positiv, Clavicymbel und Glocken der Schlosskirche zu Weimar 1658 bis 1774', *Johann Sebastian Bach: Leipzig 1985*, 99–111

A. Dürr: *Kritischer Bericht*, Johann Sebastian Bach: Neue Ausgabe Sämtlicher Werke, I/ix (Kassel, 1986)

W. Cowdery: *The Early Vocal Works of Johann Sebastian Bach: Studies in Style, Scoring, and Chronology* (diss., Cornell U., 1989)

M. Marissen: 'Organological Questions and their Significance in J.S. Bach's Fourth Brandenburg Concerto', *JAMIS*, xvii (1991), 5–52

R. Dahlqvist: 'Pitches of German, French, and English Trumpets in the 17th and 18th Centuries', *HBSJ*, v (1993), 29–41

K. Hofmann: 'Neue Überlegungen zu Bachs Weimarer Kantaten-Kalender', *BJb 1993*, 9–29

F: THE HABSBURG LANDS

T.B. Janowka: *Clavis ad thesaurum magnae artis musicae* (Prague, 1701/R)

P.M. Vogt: *Conclave thesauri magnae artis musicae* (Prague, 1719)

A. Kellner: *Musikgeschichte des Stiftes Kremsmünster* (Kassel, 1956)

A. Mandorfer: 'Musikerziehung in Kremsmünster', *Studien und Mitteilungen zur Geschichte des Benediktinerordens und seiner Zweige*, lxxxviii (1977) 9–52

G. Stradner: 'Zur Stimmtonhöhe der Blasinstrumente zur Zeit Joseph Haydns', *Joseph Haydn: Vienna 1982*, 81–6

E. Selfridge-Field: 'The Viennese Court Orchestra in the Time of Caldara', *Antonio Caldara: Essays on his Life and Times*, ed. B.W. Pritchard, (Aldershot, 1987), 115–52

K. Hubmann: 'Vom rechten Ton am Fagott: zur Frage von Stimmton-Verhültnissen im Barock', *'Musik muss Man machen': eine Festgabe für Josef Mertin*, ed. M. Nagy (Vienna, 1994), 377–84

G: ENGLAND

Hopkins-RimbaultO
R. North: *The Musicall Grammarian being a Scientific Essay upon the Practise of Musick* (MS, 1728, GB-H R.11.xliii); repr. in J. Wilson, ed.: *Roger North on Music* (London, 1959); ed. M. Chan and J.C. Kassler (Cambridge, 1990)
R. North: *Theory of sounds Shewing, the Genesis, Propagation, Effects and Augmentation and Applications of them* (MS, 1728, GB-LB1 Add.3253); repr. in J. Wilson, ed.: *Roger North on Music* (London, 1961)
W. Tans'ur: *A New Musical Grammar, or The Harmonical Spectator* (London, 1746, 5/1772 as *The Elements of Musick Display'd*, 7/1829 as *A Musical Grammar*)
A. Baines and others: 'James Talbot's Manscript', *GSJ*, i (1948), 9–26; iii (1950), 27–45; v (1952), 44 only; xiv (1961), 52–68; xv (1962), 60–69; xvi (1963), 63–72; xxi (1968), 40–51
J.B. Clark: *Transposition in Seventeenth Century English Organ Accompaniments and the Transposing Organ* (Detroit, 1974)
I. Harwood: 'A Case of Double Standards? Instrumental Pitch in England *c*.1600', *EMc*, ix (1981), 470–81 [see also xi (1983), 76–7]
H.W. Myers: 'Instrumental Pitch in England, *c*1600', *EMc*, (1982), 519–22
D. Lasocki: *Professional Recorder Players in England, 1540–1740* (diss., U. of Iowa, 1983)
P.E. Daub: *Music at the Court of George II (c.1727–1760)* (diss., Cornell U., 1985)
D. Gwynn: 'Organ Pitch in Seventeenth Century England', *JBIOS*, ix (1985), 65–78
E. Segerman: 'English Viol Sizes and Pitches', *FoMRHI Quarterly*, no.38 (1985), 55–62
E. Segerman: 'English Pitch Standards, mostly *c*.1600', *FoMRHI Quarterly*, no.65 (1991), 13–16
E. Segerman: 'Early 18th-Century English Pitches, Especially "Consort Flute Pitch" and "Church Pitch of F"', *FoMRHI Quarterly*, no.67 (1992), 54–6
P. Holman: *Four and Twenty Fiddlers: the Violin at the English Court, 1540–1690* (Oxford, 1993, 2/1995)
E. Segerman: 'On Early 17th Century English Vocal and Organ Pitches', *FoMRHI Quarterly*, no.76 (1994), 86–8
M. Goetze: 'Transposing Organs and Pitch in England', *FoMRHI Quarterly*, no.78 (1995), 61–7

H: CLASSICAL

J.H. Lambert: 'Observations sur les flûtes', *Nouveaux mémoires de l'Académie royale des sciences et belles-lettres de Berlin* (Berlin, 1775), 13–48
J.F. Reichardt: *Ueber die Pflichten des Ripien-Violinisten* (Berlin and Leipzig, 1776)
J.J.H. R[ibock]: *Bemerkungen über die Flöte, und Versuch einer kurzen Anleitung zur bessern Einrichtung und Behandlung derselben* (Stendal, 1782/R)
D.G. Türk: *Von den wichtigsten Pflichten eines Organisten* (Halle, 1787/R, rev. 2/1838 by F. Naue)
H.C. Koch: *Musikalisches Lexikon* (Frankfurt, 1802/R)
C.F. Michaelis: 'Auffoderung zur Festsetzung und gemeinschaftlichen Annahme eines gleichen Grundtones der Stimmung der Orchester', *AMZ*, xvi (1814), 772–6
R.G. Kiesewetter: 'Über den Umfang der Singstimmen in den Werken der alten Meister, in Absicht auf deren Aufführung in unserer Zeit: gelegentlich auch Etwas über die mit dem Stimmtone auf den Orgeln und in den Orchestern nach und nach vorgegangenen Veränderungen', *AMZ*, (1820), 154ff, 193ff, 201ff, 321ff, 329ff, 337ff, 345ff, 353ff, 361ff
P. Lichtenthal: *Dizionario e bibliografia della musica* (Milan, 1826/R)
[F. Kandler]: 'Wiens musikalische Kunst-Schätze, in Briefen eines Reisenden', *AMZ*, xxix (1827), 817–24
A. Schindler: 'Die gegenwärtige hohe Orchesterstimmung und ihr Ausgang', *Niederrheinische Musik-Zeitung*, iii/8–9 (1855)
C. Näke: *Über Orchesterstimmung* (Dresden, 1862)
H. Heyde: 'Die Werkstatt von Augustin Grenser d. Ä. und Heinrich Grenser in Dresden', *Tibia*, iv (1993), 593–602

I: SINCE C1830

Grove5 (L.S. Lloyd)
E. Leipp and M. Castellengo: 'Du diapason et de sa relativité', *ReM*, no.294 (1977) [whole issue]
B. Holland: 'Singers Join in a Lament about Rising Pitch', *New York Times* (Jan 1989)

II. Non-Western and traditional concepts

1. Pitch standards. 2. Pitch systems.

1. PITCH STANDARDS.   The earliest information of interest regarding musical pitch is the discovery of 65 clapperless two-tone bells unearthed among 7000 items of funerary goods from the tomb of Marquis Yi, of the Zeng state (*d c*433 BCE) at Zuizhou in China (*see* ZHONG, §2). Bell chimes were apparently restricted to the highest ranks of nobility and could apparently be used to play pentatonic music in a variety of keys. Though bronze bells, stone chimes and ocarinas have been found dating from as early as the second millennium BCE, the importance of the Zeng bells lies in the inscriptions on many of them, for they document the names of standard pitches (*lü*) belonging to each of the different states throughout the domain, that is the pitch to which instruments in offical ensembles would be tuned (*see* CHINA, §II, 4). Subsequently standard pitch in China came to acquire a symbolic and cosmological importance and to be related to other official standards of measurement for length, capacity and weight as manifested in the length and diameter of official pitch pipes. Other traditions may, like the Chinese, have inspired a considerable body of theory concerned with intervals, tunings and temperaments but seem to have shown less concern for absolute pitch standards.

Attention to pitch standards is not confined to literate societies and a standard is likely to be required for any ensemble which includes one or more instruments which are difficult to retune. Clearly ideal vocal ranges will have an impact on the choice of pitch for fixed pitch instruments in ensembles that incorporate the voice. This is still the case, for example, in the performance of Indian classical music where the system tonic pitch *sa* will be selected by the singer to suit his or her own preferred vocal range and other instrumentalists involved in the performance will tune their instruments up or down accordingly or select the most appropriate instrument from a range (flute players, for instance, will carry with them a number of differently pitched flutes). The introduction of factory-made harmoniums has had less effect on South Asian pitch standards than might have been expected, though all harmoniums are assumed to be of the same pitch. Harmonium players also learn to perform in different 'keys' when accompanying the voice so as to suit the preferred choice of pitch for *sa*. This is often centred on or around C for male singers and A or A♭ for female singers. A common way of referring to pitch levels is by specifying the corresponding black or white key on a harmonium. Thus in North India a *tablā* (whose pitch range is limited to a minor 3rd) may be described as *kāli pānc* ('black five', i.e. the fifth black key from the left hand side of the harmonium) which means it is suitable for use at or near the pitch level of D♯.

Apart from harmoniums made for the Indian market, since the mid-19th century other Western instruments and ensembles (accordions, pianos and wind bands, for example) have found a place in the musical practice of other nations and peoples and, as a result, Western pitch standards have come to be adopted. In Japan, where issues of pitch as well as interval structures dominated the work of early scholars, even traditional ensembles have accommodated to a Western pitch norm during the 20th century. The most traditional of instruments, the *shaku-hachi* flute, which was formerly of a standard pitch resulting from a standard length of 54·5 cm, is now made in 12 different sizes equivalent to the pitch of the 12 Western semitones so that any one flute can be chosen to suit the 'key' of a modern ensemble, obviating the need to shade tones which could conflict with the desired tonal effect. Modern European pitch pipes were introduced in Japan around 1920.

In the Arab world European pitch standards are also used. In Cairo, for example, classical musicians in the present day use $a' = 440$ as a standard, though a respected Egyptian musician writing at the beginning of the 20th century indicated that the standard was $a' = 435$ (al-Khula'ī in his 1904 *Kitāb al mūsīqi al-sharqi*). Classical ensembles in Cairo today recognize two tunings, the lower of which gives b' as 440 and which involves violinists and *'ud* players in tuning down a whole step while *nāy* (flute) players select a larger flute. However, as they get older, singers often prefer ensembles to tune down, sometimes as much as a minor 3rd.

2. PITCH SYSTEMS.   Towards the end of the 19th century European comparative musicologists became keenly interested in the pitch systems of non-Western peoples, believing that research in this area would help them with their theories on the origins and development of music. Stumpf and his younger colleague Hornbostel wrestled with related concepts such as *Tondistanz* (interval, see Abraham and Hornbostel, 1926), *Helligkeit* (brightness) and *Tonigkeit* (tone quality or chroma). Stumpf made use of tuning measurements supplied by Alexander Ellis who published mathematical descriptions of various non-Western scales such as the roughly equidistant five-tone Javanese *sléndro* and the Thai equidistant seven-tone scale. For this Ellis had invented the cents system which divided the equal-tempered semitone interval into 100 cents for purposes of accurate comparison of interval size. His essay 'On the Musical Scales of Various Nations' has long been considered a landmark in the development of comparative musicology because it was first to show that a great variety of pitch systems have evolved throughout the world including equal-tempered five- and seven-note scales. The usefulness of his detailed measurements, however, which were derived from work with museum instruments, including gongs and xylophones of doubtful quality and condition, has since been questioned (Schneider, 1990).

Benjamin Ives Gilman pioneered similar work in the USA, making recordings during expeditions among Zuñi and Hopi Indians to understand their pitch systems; he also recorded a Javanese gamelan and other musical traditions that were featured in the World's Columbian Exposition in Chicago in 1893.

The early researchers depended on subjective pitch matching of instrumental and vocal tones with sounds produced from devices such as tuning forks and monochords and faced different problems from those confronting later researchers who used electronic equipment such as the strobocom (Jones) and the melograph (Seeger and Hood). Electronic instruments work by isolating and measuring the lowest pitch (or fundamental) of any musical sound and the problem here is that psychologists

have shown that fundamental frequency cannot be assumed to equate with perceived pitch. Schneider has pointed out that this especially applies to measurements taken from 'inharmonic' instruments such as gongs and xylophones rich in partials that do not bear a simple frequency relationship to the supposed fundamental. He further augues that a complex of tones (timbre) influences the experience of pitch and this seriously complicates the investigation of pitch systems, especially those where the indigenous musicians and theorists (if any) have not articulated their knowledge of the system other than through performance or tuning of instruments.

So-called equidistant or near equidistant scales have presented special problems to researchers since scales of fixed pitch instruments frequently did not achieve theoretically equidistant standards when measured and researchers were left with the problem of deciding if deviations from the norm were musically significant to the musicians and what degree of tolerance in tuning one should allow for. There is some evidence for suggesting that there is a greater degree of tolerance of pitch deviation in the case of musical systems employing large scale steps (such as an anhemitonic equipentatonic scale with steps of 240 cents) than in those traditions using semitones. For instance a Ganda harp or xylophone (Uganda) might be assumed to be tuned to a theoretically equidistant pentatonic scale, yet when measured incorporates steps as small as 200 cents or as large as 280. The problem then remains to discover if these larger and smaller intervals are an essential part of the scalic system or if they are to be disregarded because they are not conceived as different from other intervals which come closer to the equidistant norm (Cooke). Ellis was perhaps the first to face such a problem when a Thai xylophone, whose pitches he had measured, did not turn out to be equidistant. He simply constructed an equidistant seven-note scale on his bichord and asked Thai musicians to compare this scale with the scale derived from the xylophone. The musicians unanimously declared the first (exactly equidistant) scale to be good and the scale derived from the xylophone to be out of tune. He was able to conclude that 'The ideal Siamese scale is, consequently, an equal division of an Octave into seven parts, so that there are no Semitones and no Tones, when the instrument is properly tuned' (p.1105).

Even supposedly well-tuned musical instruments do not necessarily provide all the information one needs about a pitch system, for like the scale of the pianoforte, the tunings may be a compromise and the 'ideal' pitches are more likely to be found from variable pitch instruments or from the singing voice. Futhermore, instruments may provide more pitches than are actually utilized in performance: for instance the *khene* (mouth organ) of Laos is tuned to a diatonic scale but is used to produce basic pentatonic systems.

One cannot assume that pitch systems do not change through time. Berliner, for example (1978, pp.60–61), observed that *mbira* players of Zimbabwe changed the tunings of their instruments and cited the example of the musician Mude who over a period of several years used five different tunings with his group and how he liked to sing with different *chunings* 'for a change'. Berliner added, 'While I would have liked to have been able to posit a theory of Shona *mbira* tuning ... the complexity of the matter makes it premature at this time'. With the increasing globalization of musical culture the Western pitch system is impacting on many non-Western systems. Keeler (*GEWM*, p.390) reported that when the piano was first introduced to Myanmar (Burma) in the 19th century, the white keys were retuned to a Burmese scale for accompanying singers and other instrumentalists, but that this practice has since been abandoned. There are many other examples of the increasing acceptance of Western scales: much has been written about the problems of the *pélog* and *sléndro* scales of Indonesian gamelans over the past century, yet it has also been noted that 'the Indonesian National Anthem, all patriotic school songs and virtually all popular music use the Western Diatonic Scale' (Perlman and Krumhansl, 100). A similar situation exists in many other cultures.

At the end of the 20th century acoustical measurement of vocal and instrumental scales and melodies has been aided by the use of computer programs which can sample frequency over a period of several seconds or more which allows the averaging of frequencies to ascertain the most significant in determining the pitch areas of a musical system. Such work is being supplemented with intra-cultural and cross-cultural tests of musical cognition and perception in the effort to better comprehend the pitch systems. Awareness of issues such as categorical perception of pitch classes and tuning tolerance are being built into experiments and careful observations of tuning processes seek to understand better the ideal scale or most 'comfortable' temperament that an instrument tuner may be aiming at. Nevertheless, the exploration of non-Western musical pitch systems continues to pose challenging problems.

For more information on individual pitch systems refer to individual country articles.

BIBLIOGRAPHY

GEWM, iv ('Burma', W. Keeler; 'Thailand', T. Miller)
A.J. Ellis: 'On the Musical Scales of Various Nations', *Journal of the Royal Society of Arts*, xxxiii (1885), 485–527; appx, 1102–11
B.I. Gilman: 'Hopi Songs', *Journal of American Archaeology and Ethnology*, v (1908) [whole issue]
O. Abraham and E.M. von Hornbostel: 'Zur Psychologie der Tondistanz', *Zeitschrift für Psychologie und Psychologie der Sinnersorgane*, no.98 (1926), 233–49
K.P. Wachsmann: 'Pen-equidistance and Accurate Pitch, a Problem from the Source of the Nile', *Festschrift für Walter Wiora*, ed. L. Finscher and C.-H. Mahling (Kassel, 1967), 583–92
E.M. Burns and W.D. Ward: 'Categorical Perception of Musical Intervals', *JASA*, lv (1974), 456; lviii (1975), 132; lxiii (1978), 456–8
P.A. Berliner: *The Soul of Mbira: Music and Traditions of the Shona People of Zimbabwe* (Berkeley, 1978, 2/1993)
R. Vetter: 'A Retrospect on a Century of Gamelan Tone Measurements', *EthM*, xxxiii (1989), 217–28
P.R. Cooke: 'Report on Pitch Perception Experiments carried out in Buganda and Busoga (Uganda)', *AfM*, vii/2 (1992), 119–25
A. Schneider: '"Okutuusa Amadinda" Zür Frage aquidistanter Tonsysteme und Stummungen in Afrika', *Musikkulturgeschichte: Festschrift für Constantin Floros*, ed. P. Petersen (Wiesbaden, 1990), 493–526
K. Vaughan: 'Pitch Measurement', *Ethnomusicology, an Introduction*, ed. H. Myers (London, 1992), 462–8
M. Perlman and C. Krumhansl: 'An Experimental Study of Internal Interval Standards in Javanese and Western Musicians', *Music Perception*, xiv (1996), 96–116

BRUCE HAYNES (I), PETER R. COOKE (II)

Pitch class. The type of a pitch. Pitches belong to the same class if they have some relation – for example, the octave relation – of compositional or analytical interest. This relation is called an 'equivalence' because, in the context of a particular description of musical structure, pitches in the same class are interchangeable, or equivalent.

Different equivalence relations, each associated with a distinct theory of music, give rise to different kinds of pitch class. Where pitches related by octave transposition are considered equivalent, as in chords described by the theory of harmonic inversion, one may speak of an 'octave-equivalence pitch class'. Thus letter-names, possibly modified by accidentals, such as C, C♯, D♭, D and E♭♭, all denote different classes of pitch. 12-note equal temperament, commonly used to model highly chromatic music, induces another equivalence relation, the enharmonic, and an 'enharmonic-equivalence pitch class' includes all the pitches played on the same key of an equal-tempered keyboard.

In SET theory, pitch classes are defined by both these equivalence relations, so that there are just 12 pitch classes, corresponding to the notes of the chromatic scale, often numbered from 0 to 11. The choice of which pitch class to call 0 is a matter of convention or expedience. The commonest conventional choice is C, in which case C♯ is 1, D is 2 and so on. Or, if the music under consideration is a 12-note serial piece, 0 could stand for the first pitch of the row in its prime or initial statement. Thus each pitch class in a 12-note row denotes one of many possible pitches, related by octave or enharmonic equivalence, all of which are equally appropriate as far as the identity of the row is concerned.

Other kinds of equivalence relations are possible. Division of the octave into more or fewer than 12 equal parts, as in some microtonal and diatonic systems, will yield more or fewer than 12 pitch classes. Compositions – especially of electronic music – can also be made to project an equivalence among pitches related by intervals other than the octave, an equivalence that can be reinforced by the way in which harmonic spectra are constructed.

JOHN ROEDER

Pitch nomenclature. The naming and definition of a particular pitch or class of note. In Western tonal music 12 classes of note are distinguished and may be further defined by their octave. The following discussion describes the systems of pitch nomenclature currently used in Western music and traces their historical development. For systems used by non-Western cultures, *see* NOTATION, §II, 2–4; *see also* GREECE, §I, 6.

The names most commonly used today are those based on the seven notes of the octave, further modified by the addition of accidentals. In English and German practice the letters of the alphabet form the basis of the nomenclature, A–G being used in the former and A–H in the latter. In French, Italian and Spanish the names are ultimately derived from the Guidonian hexachord (see below). In German, suffixes are added to the letter to denote sharp, double sharp, flat and double flat, whereas English, French, Italian and Spanish add the usual words for sharp, flat and so on to the basic name (Table 1).

The origins of modern pitch nomenclature lie in the scale or gamut of Guido of Arezzo (*c*991–2; *d* after 1033), which is set out conveniently in a diagram in the first lesson of Thomas Morley's *Plaine and Easie Introduction to Practicall Musicke* of 1597 (see illustration; *see also* HEXACHORD; SOLMIZATION). In this system notes of different octaves are in many cases distinguished by different names: for example D *sol re* and d *la sol re*. This terminology occurs not only in musical writings but (in

TABLE 1

		A	B	C	D	E	F	G
♭♭	Eng.	A double flat	B double flat	C double flat	D double flat	E double flat	F double flat	G double flat
	Fr.	La double bémol	Si double bémol	Ut double bémol	Re double bémol	Mi double bémol	Fa double bémol	Sol double bémol
	Ger.	Asas	Bes (Heses)	Ceses	Deses	Eses	Feses	Geses
	It.	La doppio bemolle	Si doppio bemolle	Do doppio bemolle	Re doppio bemolle	Mi doppio bemolle	Fa doppio bemolle	Sol doppio bemolle
	Sp.	La doble bemol	Si doble bemol	Do doble bemol	Re doble bemol	Mi doble bemol	Fa doble bemol	Sol doble bemol
♭	Eng.	A flat	B flat	C flat	D flat	E flat	F flat	G flat
	Fr.	La bémol	Si bémol	Ut bémol	Re bémol	Mi bémol	Fa bémol	Sol bémol
	Ger.	As	B	Ces	Des	Es	Fes	Ges
	It.	La bemolle	Si bemolle	Do bemolle	Re bemolle	Mi bemolle	Fa bemolle	Sol bemolle
	Sp.	La bemol	Si bemol	Do bemol	Re bemol	Mi bemol	Fa bemol	Sol bemol
♮	Eng.	A	B	C	D	E	F	G
	Fr.	La	Si	Ut	Re	Mi	Fa	Sol
	Ger.	A	H	C	D	E	F	G
	It.	La	Si	Do	Re	Mi	Fa	Sol
	Sp.	La	Si	Do	Re	Mi	Fa	Sol
♯	Eng.	A sharp	B sharp	C sharp	D sharp	E sharp	F sharp	G sharp
	Fr.	La dièse	Si dièse	Ut dièse	Re dièse	Mi dièse	Fa dièse	Sol dièse
	Ger.	Ais	His	Cis	Dis	Eis	Fis	Gis
	It.	La diesis	Si diesis	Do diesis	Re diesis	Mi diesis	Fa diesis	Sol diesis
	Sp.	La sostenido	Si sostenido	Do sostenido	Re sostenido	Mi sostenido	Fa sostenido	Sol sostenido
𝄪	Eng.	A double sharp	B double sharp	C double sharp	D double sharp	E double sharp	F double sharp	G double sharp
	Fr.	La double dièse	Si double dièse	Ut double dièse	Re double dièse	Mi double dièse	Fa double dièse	Sol double dièse
	Ger.	Aisis	Hisis	Cisis	Disis	Eisis	Fisis	Grisis
	It.	La doppio diesis	Si doppio diesis	Do doppio diesis	Re doppio diesis	Mi doppio diesis	Fa doppio diesis	Sol doppio diesis
	Sp.	La doble sostenido	Si doble sostenido	Do doble sostenido	Re doble sostenido	Mi doble sostenido	Fa doble sostenido	Sol doble sostenido

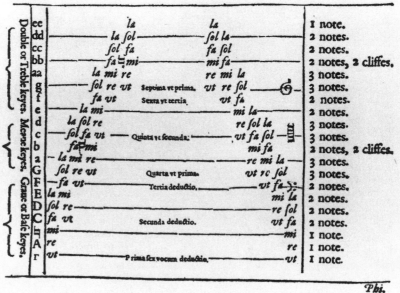

Guido of Arezzo's scale, or gamut, as set out by Morley in his 'Plaine and Easie Introduction to Practicall Musicke' (1597)

the 17th and 18th centuries) also in the writings of the 'natural philosophers' who were Fellows of the Royal Society, such as John Wallis and Robert Smith (iii). In it may be sought the origin of the distinctions between notes of different octaves through the use of upper- and lower-case letters, duplicated letters and so forth, which occur in later, more extended pitch nomenclatures.

In this article (and this dictionary as a whole) *italic* letters are used exclusively with application to pitches as shown in ex.1 line (1). Except in the discussion of other pitch nomenclatures, non-italic capital letters denote pitch classes, not specific pitches.

In Morley's diagram the letters in the left-hand column run by octaves from A to G and from a to g, and continue from aa. In this particular diagram they differ from the letters used in later systems, which run upwards by octaves from each C; yet the terminology of the gamut is the key to such systems of nomenclature, of which the seven most generally encountered in the 20th century are shown in ex.1. (There is one partial exception to this rule of octaves starting with C, in the bass notes of line (2) of ex.1 as applied to the earlier organs.) The first two have been the most important in Britain; the last two are technical methods of designating pitches for instruments tuned in equal temperament. The figures standing above or below each C on the staves at the head of the table in ex.1 give an approximate value, in vibration cycles per second (or Hertz: Hz), for the vibration frequency corresponding to each. More exactly they are the frequencies of each C of the so-called 'philosophical pitch', built up by octaves from an initial frequency of 1 Hz, which makes middle C correspond to 256 Hz (*see* PITCH).

No attempt will be made here to catalogue all the systems of pitch nomenclature used by different writers, most of which are for specialist use or variants of established systems. The apparent confusion is clarified by some acquaintance with their history and by their relationship to the nomenclature of the gamut.

The following explanatory comments on the various schemes set out in ex.1 are numbered to correspond with the lines of the table.

(1) The pitch designation on which this is based is often called the Helmholtz system because its use by Hermann von Helmholtz in his *Tonempfindungen* (1863) made it familiar in Britain. As in three if not four of the systems that follow, the notes are named in octave groups extending from C to the B above. As it is the most widely used pitch nomenclature it is used throughout this dictionary when such a designation is wanted: the usage here prefers C′ (etc.) to Helmholtz's original C′.

(2) This line of ex.1 really groups together, because they are in general consistent, three more or less separate English systems.

The middle portion of the nomenclature in this line was used by Robert Smith (iii) in his *Harmonics* (1748). By this date a pitch classification using C, c, c′, c″ and so on had come into use in England, though its use may not have been at all general. This scheme used C for the note called C *fa ut* in the gamut, and c for middle C, which was called c *sol fa ut* in the gamut. Logically there is much to be said for this system. For since very high and very low notes are the natural extremes in music there would be some advantage in taking middle C as a starting point, and using capital letters for all notes below it and lower-case for all above. On the other hand, the Helmholtz system, not used for organs in Britain, would seem to be more logical for organs, for it would be based on C as the bottom note of an 8′ stop on the manuals. This indeed was its origin in Germany, as is indicated by Helmholtz. The reason why the Helmholtz designations differ from those of this English system, which had a less technical origin, is to be found in that fact.

The use of repeated letters in the left-hand part of line (2) extending downwards through three octaves from the C in the bass staff, is now commonly employed by English organ builders for specifications. Like the names C and c in the middle of the line, the capital C used here is evidently derived from the names given to C in the gamut. Interesting light is thrown on the development of the nomenclature used by English organ builders by the historical section of Hopkins's article 'Organ' in the first edition of this dictionary. If two things are remembered, there is no difficulty in fixing the pitches intended by Hopkins by the designations he used or quoted. First, the number of notes in each organ stop gives a definite indication of its compass. Thus an interval of two octaves and a 5th, say from 'fiddle G to D in alt', the compass Hopkins gave for the Swell in the organ of St Mary Redcliffe, Bristol, 1726, would contain 32 notes (for 'in alt', see below). Secondly, an open pipe of 8′ nominal length would sound CC, one of 16′ nominal length would sound CCC, and one of 12′ nominal length would sound FFF a 4th higher.

The earliest English organ specification recorded by Hopkins is that for a 'payer of organs' for the parish 'of Alhalowe, Barking, next ye Tower of London', 1519. The compass was to be from 'dowble C*e fa ut*', which shows why CC would be two leger lines below the bass staff. From the specifications as a whole it is clear that, for some three centuries, the sequence in this organ nomen-

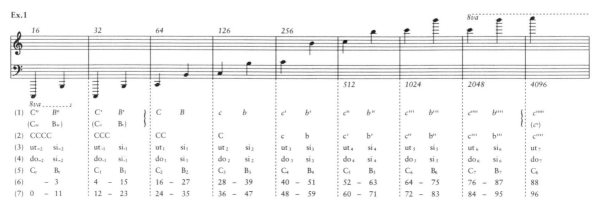

Ex.1

clature was CC, DD, EE, FF, G, A, B, C and so on, and in it the point of change from capital to lower-case letters as shown in Morley's diagram of the gamut is shifted down by a whole tone. The reason is evident. It was inconvenient to use GG for *Gam ut* which originally used the Greek capital gamma. So G was used instead. The specification for the Swell in the organ for St James's, Bermondsey, 1829 (see *Grove 1*), ran from 'Gamut G', which is an octave higher than GG on the Great, as is shown by the number of notes in the two organs, 47 and 59 respectively, both rising to F in alt (*f‴*). Also GGG on the pedals of this organ used a pipe of nominal length 21⅓′, a 4th below the 16′ CCC. To take the change of lettering between FFF♯ and GG was important in the older organs, in which the manuals usually ran down to GG, a note between CCC and CC, and not, as we might expect, above CC. Today, when the manuals always run down to CC, the old point of change loses its significance. The modern English organ-builder commonly speaks of the succession of C's in the keyboard of full compass, with 61 notes (five octaves), as Bottom C (CC), Tenor C (C), Middle C, Treble C, High C (C in alt) and Top C (C in altissimo) and the necessity to distinguish in lettering between FFF♯ and GG does not arise. (Another system calls them respectively Great C, Small C, One-line C, Two-line C and so on; an octave below Great C is Contra C.)

Were a writer on organs today to use the upper part of the nomenclature in line (2), they would (or should) denote the pitches shown. This upper portion of the system was used in the 20th century by some carillon makers and bell-founders. Its immediate source is probably a modern authority, but its ultimate source may be the older English pitch designations used by Robert Smith. It is consistent with the English organ builders' method of naming pitches, though the scale of a carillon seldom goes below G of the organ builder's system (G *sol re ut*, Fiddle G, or *g*). This appears to be an isolated example of the use of Robert Smith's nomenclature today. There is no system of pitch definition in use among English makers of wind instruments; no need for one arises in practice.

(3) This line is the pitch nomenclature in use in France. Its origin lies in the gamut, and the names for notes between *ut* and *si* will be clear from the octave shown in ex.2. With the development of the leading-note in

Ex.2

ut₁ re₁ mi₁ fa₁ sol₁ la₁ si₁ ut₄

European music a name was needed for it, and *si* was adapted from the initials of Sancte Ioannes in the Latin hymn from which Guido took his names for the notes of the hexachord. As in the corresponding German system, shown in line (1) of ex.1, this scheme begins with the bottom C of the organ manual – as *ut*. The rather clumsy *ut*-₁ and *ut*-₂ are therefore used for the notes one and two octaves lower respectively. Some academic musicians and physicists have tended to replace *ut* -₁ by *ut* ₀, and *ut* -₂ by *ut* ₀₁.

(4) This line of ex.1 gives the pitch nomenclature in use in Italy. It differs from the French system only in substituting for *ut* the more singable name *do*, which appears to have replaced *ut* in countries other than France.

(5) This is a pitch nomenclature that has been adopted in the USA for scientific work. It starts with C₀ as the lowest C that the human ear can perceive as a musical

tone. The deepest audible tone normally has a frequency of about 20 Hz. An instrument tuned in equal temperament with *a′* at 440 Hz would theoretically produce for the deepest sound of a 32′ stop a frequency of 16·352 Hz. This is less than a major 3rd below the sound produced by 20 Hz; no human ear will ever hear a deeper C. Many people cannot hear a pure tone corresponding to 16 Hz; what they hear in the deepest note of the 32′ stop in the organ is the effect of its upper partials. This system reckons frequencies in octaves and uses 16·352 Hz as a reference frequency.

(6) and (7). These are American technical methods of defining the notes of keyboard instruments tuned in equal temperament. They are pitch designations only in a narrow sense. In (6) the black and white keys of the piano are numbered consecutively, upwards, the bottom note A being numbered 1. (7) also numbers by the semitones of equal temperament, beginning with the C of the extreme left of the table in ex.1 as 0. In this system, the pitch class C is consequently numbered in multiples of 12, and so *c′* becomes 48. Other notes which are known by the same letter add constant numbers to these multiples of 12, for example, G always adding 7 and A always adding 9. Thus *a′* is 48 + 9 = 57. This system of numbering is called 'semitone count' (SC). These nomenclatures, like so many others, are confusing in their similarity.

'In alt' is a term used to describe notes in the octave immediately above the top line of the treble staff – those running from *g″* to *f‴*. Notes in the next octave (*g‴* to *f‴′*) are called 'in altissimo'. The term is derived from the Italian *in alto*, 'high'. It was used by Thomas Morley in his *Plaine and Easie Introduction*, but not in its precise modern sense: he used 'in alt' to mean 'an octave higher' (and 'in base' to mean an octave lower).

Later the term was limited to notes which lay above the gamut. Morley had explained that when Guido enlarged the scale from 15 to 20 notes the result was to 'fill up … the reach of most voices'. And while he taught Philomathes that 'there can be no note given so high, but you may give a higher, and none so lowe, but that you may give a lower', he added that his scale consisted of but 20 notes 'because that compasse was the reach of most voyces, so that under *Gam ut* the voice seemed as a kind of *humming*, and above *E la* a kinde of constrained skricking'.

It is therefore a reasonable inference that when notes were required to describe the high pitches reached by good sopranos the term 'in alt' was employed to describe notes an octave higher than the top seven notes of the gamut, f *fa ut* to ee *la*. The note on the top line of the treble staff which had no name in Guido's hexachords would thus become 'f *fa ut* in alt'. That very note was called 'F in alt' in the specification for the organ in St James's, Bermondsey, 1829, already quoted. This doubtless explains an ambiguity that writers have noted in the use of 'in alt'. In the usage just indicated it would refer to an octave of notes beginning with F on the top line of the treble staff, *f″*, and running up to E on the third leger line, *e‴*. But in the 19th century, as musicians forgot the old nomenclature of the gamut, there would be an increasing tendency to use 'in alt' with the meaning we began with, for the octave above the treble staff.

BIBLIOGRAPHY

E. Regener: *Pitch Notation and Equal Temperament: a Formal Study* (Berkeley and Los Angeles, 1973)

LLEWELYN S. LLOYD/RICHARD RASTALL

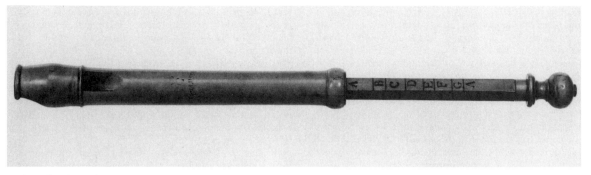

Pitchpipe by Christophe Delusse, Paris, 1772 (Musée de la Musique Paris, no.E.308, C.742)

Pitchpipe (Fr. *flûte d'accord, diapason*; Ger. *Stimmpfeife*; It. *corista a fiato*). A term used for various aerophones designed to give standard pitches to singers or to aid tuning an instrument. Originally it referred to a 'piston flute' (*see* SWANEE WHISTLE, consisting of a recorder head fitted with a movable wooden plunger or piston on which a scale of notes with a range of about one octave was marked. Bédos de Celles (1766–78, p.35) described 'Un Tuyau de ton' as 'a small flute used to give the pitch to the organ and other instruments. It is made of hardwood, such as boxwood, green or black ebony, ivory . . .. Along the plunger, pitches are marked that correspond to a well-tuned organ at the proper pitch'.

Pitchpipes operate on the same level of accuracy as recorders, with a pitch tolerance of about 15 cents. They are important sources of information on earlier pitch standards, since they give names for each of the notes they produce, they are often stamped by the maker, and they sometimes include a date. The spacing of their scales also indicates what kinds of tuning systems were used in practical, everyday music-making. Numerous sources indicate that pitchpipes rather than tuning-forks were normally used as tuning devices for vocal and instrumental ensembles and keyboard instruments until the beginning of the 19th century. Pitchpipes were described by Mersenne (1636–7, p.169), William Turner (i) (1697), Mattheson (1721, p.428), Tans'ur (1746, p.57) and others. Mendel (p.82) cities a pitchpipe which Handel 'constantly carried with him'.

Pitchpipes were often used to fix the pitch of keyboard instruments. Couchet provided his customers with a 'fluijtien' ('little flute') with which to tune his harpsichords. J.C. Petit advised that for tuning the harpsichord the first note should be 'true to the Flute. It should be a small, square Pipe, with which Organ-builders take the fixed Tone to tune the Organ' (*Apologie de l'excellence de la musique*, London, *c*1740). Pitchpipes were described as commonplace for tuning pianos in the *Clavier-Stimmbuch* by Gall (first name unknown) published in Vienna in 1805, but by 1827 they had been replaced by tuning-forks, according to Kiesewetter (*AMZ*, xxix, cols.145–56).

A number of early pitchpipes have survived. Three that are preserved at the Musée de la Musique, Paris, are especially interesting. One, probably made after 1711, gives 'Ton de l'opera' as *a′* = 394 and 'Plus haut de la chapelle a versaille' as *a′* = 407. Another is believed to be by the maker Dupuis (*fl* 1682) and is pitched at about *a′* = 391. The third, made in the late 18th century by Christophe Delusse (no.E.244, C.743), gives two sets of pitches, neither named, at *a′* = 395 and *a′* = 419. Such small 'pocket' pitchpipes should not be confused with the *Stimmpfeife* used by organ makers and described by Adlung (1758; see also Barbour, pp.85–7). The latter were usually larger metal affairs and were blown through the organ's wind-channel. Modern free-reed pitchpipes made of metal (often cased in plastic), which give a series of discrete pitches, are still much-used by students and amateurs.

BIBLIOGRAPHY
J.M. Barbour: *Tuning and Temperament: a Historical Survey* (East Lansing, MI, 1951/R, 2/1953)
A. Mendel: 'Pitch in Western Music Since 1500: a Re-Examination', *AcM*, l (1978), 1–93
B. Haynes: *Pitch Standards in the Baroque and Classical Periods* (diss., U. of Montreal, 1995) [appendixes 1 and 8]

BRUCE HAYNES

Pitfield, Thomas B(aron) (*b* Bolton, 5 April 1903; *d* Bowden, Cheshire, 11 Nov 1999). English composer, teacher, poet and visual artist. He left school unwillingly at the age of 14 to work as an apprentice in an engineering factory. During this period he took private harmony, piano and cello lessons, before abandoning a career in engineering to enrol at the RNCM (1924). Among his earliest published compositions were *Prelude Minuet and Reel* for piano (1931) and a Piano Trio (1931–2), both published by Oxford University Press. On the recommendation of Hubert J. Foss, OUP commissioned Pitfield to produce book illustrations, including a cover for the first edition of Britten's *Simple Symphony*. In 1931 he obtained a scholarship to study at the Bolton School of Art as a teacher of art and cabinet-work, and after qualifying took various teaching posts in the Midlands. During World War II he was a conscientious objector and composed a song for the Peace Pledge Union. From 1947 to 1973 he taught composition at the RMCM, where his students included McCabe, Ogdon, David Ellis, John Golland and Ronald Stevenson. Pitfield's writings on music include *Musicianship for Guitarists* and *Musicianly Scale Practice* (London, 1959 and 1962, respectively).

As a composer Pitfield was self-taught, though he was given early advice by Eric Fogg. He writes in a melodically fresh and delicate diatonic style, with Gallic wit, baroque figuration and tinges of Delian harmony. Though most pieces in his substantial output are miniatures, he has successfully maintained a larger span in works such as the Piano Concerto no.1 and the sonatas for violin and oboe. His music is predominantly light – many works exhibit a sense of humour – but a deeper vein is explored in some of his songs and chamber works. A stylistic trait is the use of irregular time signatures, particularly 7/8, while his melodies make frequent use of folk material.

WORKS
(*selective list*)

Stage (librettos by Pitfield unless otherwise stated): The Elm-Spirit (ballet), perf. 1934; The Rejected Pieman (ballet), perf. 1936; Maid of Hearts (ballet), perf. 1937; The Hallowed Manger (nativity play, 1), 1950–51; The Barnyard Singers (children's op, 2, R. Foster) (1954); Adam and the Creatures (morality play, 1), 1967; Coney Warren (children's comic operetta, 1), 1971; St Columba in Iona (morality play, 1), 1981–82

Orch: Pf Conc. no.1, 1946–7; Sinfonietta, perf. 1947; Theme and Variations, str, 1948; Fantasia, vn, orch, 1953; Ov. on North Country Tunes, 1953; Concert Ov., perf. 1957; Concerto Lirico, vn, orch, 1956–58; Pf Conc. no.2 'The Student', 1958; Concertino, perc, orch, 1961; Ruminations, pf, str, perf. 1970; Conversations, cl, hp, str (1970); Fl/Rec Conc., str, 1985–6; Bucolics, perf. 1991

Choral: Night Music, SATB, 1933, rev. 1947; The Rhyming Shopman, Bar, SATB, orch/str, pf/pf, 1940; A Sketchbook of Women, female chorus, str, perc, pf, 1951; A Sketchbook of Men, B, male chorus, str, perc, pf, 1953; A Sketchbook of Animals, SATB, perc, pf, 1954; The Hills, SATB, orch/org, 1960; many partsongs

Solo vocal: 3 Miniatures, s, vn, 1958; By the Dee (song cycle), Mez/Bar, vn, va, vc (opt. db), pf, perf. 1962; A Shropshire Lass, Mez, orch, 1987; many songs

Other inst: Prelude Minuet and Reel, pf, 1931; Pf Trio, c, 1931–2; Sonatina, a, pf, perf. 1932; The Circle Suite, pf, 1932; Sonata, d, vc, pf, 1937–8; Sonata no.1, A, vn, pf, 1939; Sonatina, va, pf, perf. 1945; Sonata, a, ob, pf (1948); Sonatina, fl, pf, 1948; 2 Russian Tunes, pf (1948); Pf Trio 'Lyric', f, 1948–9; Trio, fl, ob, pf, 1948; Sonatina, F, vn, pf, 1949; Trio, ob, bn, pf, 1952; Sonatina, vc, pf, 1953; Sonatina, hp, 1956; Diversions on a Russian Air, pf (1959); Sonata, accdn, 1963; Studies on an English Dance Tune, pf, 1960; Sonatina no.1, cl, pf, 1964; Sonata, xyl, 1965; Divertimento, ob, vn, va, vc, 1966–7; Sonatina, perc, 1969; Danserye, rec, pf, 1973; Sonatina, db, pf (1974); Sonata no.2, vn, pf, 1979; 3 Nautical Sketches, rec, pf, 1982; Sonatina Pastorale, rec, 1985; Sonata, timp (1985)

MSS in RNCM, S.E. Wimberly Library, Florida Atlantic University, Boca Raton

Principal publishers: Augener, Bardic, Cramer, Elkin, Forsyth, Hinrichsen, Lengnick, OUP, Thames

BIBLIOGRAPHY

T. Pitfield: *The Poetry of Trees* (London, 1944)
T. Pitfield: *No Song, No Supper: an Autobiography* (London, 1986)
T. Pitfield: *Song after Supper* (London, 1990) [autobiography, pt ii]
T. Pitfield: *A Cotton Town Boyhood* (Altrincham, 1995) [autobiography, pt iii]

JOHN B. TURNER

Piticchio, Francesco (*b* ?Palermo; *fl* 1760–1800). Italian composer. He is sometimes said to have been born in Rome, but this seems to result from the confusion of him with the contemporary Roman composer Pietro Paolo Piticchio, some of whose music has also been attributed to Francesco. About 1760 he was a *maestro di cappella* in Palermo. In 1778 he collaborated with Giuseppe Gazzaniga on a comic opera in Rome. His opera *Didone* was performed in Palermo in 1780, followed by a comic opera in Rome in Carnival 1781 and an oratorio in Venice later that year. He then went to Germany as *maestro al cembalo* of an Italian opera company. For about two years, probably from 1782, he was at Brunswick, in 1784–5 at Dresden and in 1785 at Madrid. He spent the years 1786–91 in Vienna and then apparently returned to Italy. In Naples in 1798 he had an opera performed at the S Carlo, the libretto of which describes him as *maestro di cappella* to the hereditary princess. He probably accompanied the royal family when it fled to Palermo to escape the Revolution of 1799, since he composed there an occasional cantata, *La concordia*

felice, to celebrate the return of the king and Nelson from their visit to Naples after the revolution had been put down.

Gerber thought highly of Piticchio's operas, calling him a 'passionate and highly expressive' composer, a judgment that has been echoed by later lexicographers. However, to Da Ponte, who collaborated with him on an opera in Vienna, he was a 'maestro bestia' and 'a man of very little intellect and of the most limited musical gifts'. According to Da Ponte, Joseph II held a similar opinion.

WORKS
OPERAS

Il ciarlatano accusato (dg), Florence, Pallacorda, aut. 1777
Il marchese di Verde Antico (int), Rome, Capranica, Jan 1778, collab. G. Gazzaniga
Didone abbandonata (os, P. Metastasio), Palermo, S Cecilia, carn. 1780; rev. Brunswick, wint. 1784, *D-Wa*
Il militare amante (dg), Rome, Dame, carn. 1781
Gli amanti alla prova [Die Liebhaber auf der Probe] (dg, G. Bertati), Dresden, Hof, 4 Jan 1785, *D-Dl*
Il Bertoldo (dg, 2, L. da Ponte, after Brunati), Vienna, Hof, 22 June 1787, *F-Pn*
La vendetta di Medea (os, O. Balsamo), Naples, S Carlo, 13 Aug 1798

OTHER WORKS

Orats: Samson, Venice, 1781; Pharisei conversio ad sepulchrum, Venice, 1782, *D-Dl*; La Betulia liberata, 1786, *A-Wgm*
Cants.: Il Parnaso (serenata), Madrid, 5 July 1785; Tirsi e Clori, 2 S, insts, Vienna, 27 Feb 1788, *D-Dl*; I voti della nazione napolitana (Da Ponte), 4vv, orch, Vienna, 12 Jan 1791, *Dl*, *I-Mc*; La concordia felice, Palermo, 1799
Songs: 12 petites chansons italiennes (Vienna, 1793); 12 italianische Canzonetten op.3 (Vienna, n.d.); songs, arias, *A-Wn*
Inst: 6 qnts, 2 vn, 2 va, vc (Offenbach, *c*1785); contredanses, vn, b, *I-Mc*; Sym., D, *D-W*

BIBLIOGRAPHY

EitnerQ; *GerberL*; *GerberNL*; *ScheringGO*
L. da Ponte: *Memorie* (New York, 1823–7, enlarged 2/1829–30; Eng. trans., 1929/*R*)
O. Tiby: *Il Real Teatro Carolino e l'Ottocento musicale palermitano* (Florence, 1957), 271
M. Hunter: '"Se vuol ballare" Quoted: an Early Moment in the Reception History of "Figaro"', *MT*, cxxx (1989), 464–7

RON RABIN

Pitoni, Giuseppe Ottavio (*b* Rieti, 18 March 1657; *d* Rome, 1 Feb 1743). Italian composer and writer on music. According to Chiti he was taken to Rome by his parents at the age of 11 months, attended Pompeo Natali's music school at the age of five and sang at S Giovanni dei Fiorentini when he was eight and soon afterwards at SS Apostoli. When he was still very young he became a pupil of Francesco Foggia. In 1673 he became *maestro di cappella* at Monterotondo, near Rome. The following year he went to Assisi Cathedral, where he devoted himself to studying the works of Palestrina. In 1676 he became *maestro di cappella* of Rieti Cathedral and from 1677 until his death he held a similar post at the collegiate church of S Marco in the Palazzo Venezia, Rome (during this time he also held several other appointments in Rome). From 1686 until his death he lived at the Collegio Germanico and directed its church music, which at that time was performed at S Apollinare. From 1694 to 1721 he worked for the chapter of S Lorenzo in Damaso, where from at least 1696 to 1731 he was also responsible for the performances promoted by the music-loving Cardinal Pietro Ottoboni. In 1709 he declined to succeed Alessandro Scarlatti as *maestro di cappella* of S Maria Maggiore, but he was *maestro di cappella* of S Giovanni in Laterano from the previous year until 1719, when he took up a similar post at the Cappella Giulia at S Pietro. He was also employed as a musician at other churches. He was several times first guardian of the Congregazione di S Cecilia, Rome.

Pitoni was an exceedingly prolific composer of church music and was greatly respected in Rome. His music is fundamentally in the Palestrina tradition but contains elements of the concertato and polychoral styles (even four-part works by him were sung by two separated choirs). He frequently distinguished in his titles between the *stile concertato* and the *stile pieno*, the latter denoting the *stile antico*. Organ accompaniments are optional only in a number of four-part *stile pieno* compositions. The pure counterpoint that informed his early works gradually disappeared until, by about 1720, his music was predominantly chordal, with only vestiges of counterpoint. The *stile pieno*, used primarily for penitential liturgical works, reappeared, however, after 1730. In the four-part concertato works solo sections are clearly contrasted with choral sections that include parlando tuttis. After about 1720 solos also appeared in the masses in place of concertato sections for several voices. Concertante instrumental parts were sometimes added. Notable features of Pitoni's polychoral music are its brilliant counterpoint, the exchange of melodic material between voices, and the use of alternating choirs. From 1724 this style is less important in his output, though Chiti reported that at the end of his life he was working on, but was unable to complete, a mass for 12 choirs. Most of his numerous Office hymns are simple monodic or four-part settings, but the psalm settings include works for 16 voices; in many of the psalms a solo voice is contrasted with the ripieno choir.

Pitoni was also a writer on music theory and history. His *Notitia de contrapuntisti*, an important early landmark in music lexicography, provides much useful and otherwise unobtainable information (not always accurate) about, in particular, earlier practitioners in the traditions of church music which he cultivated so assiduously himself.

WORKS

almost all with continuo

SACRED

1 ps in 1683[1]

1 motet, 2vv (Rome, 1697)

The MSS of the following works can be found in *A-Wn, KR; D-Bsb, BG, Dkh, Dl, LEm, Mbm, Mbs, Mf, Mk, Mm, MÜs, Po, Rp, TRb; DK-Kk; F-Pn; GB-Cfm, Lbl, Lcm; I-Ac, Bc, Ls, Nc, Nf, Pca, PS, Rc, Rf, Rli, Rn, Rsc, Rsg, Rsm, Rsmt, Rvat* (incl. many dated autographs)

270 masses and mass parts, 4–6, 8vv, some with insts, most with titles, 2 masses ed. in Musica divina, i/1 (Regensburg, 1853), 2 masses ed. in Monumenta liturgiae polychoralis Sanctae Ecclesiae Romanae, i/5, 7 (Rome, 1955, 1960), 5 masses ed. in Documenta maiora liturgiae polychoralis Sanctae Ecclesiae Romanae, i–v (Rome, 1958–9); 14 ints and Kys, 4, 8vv, 1 ed. in Documenta, ix (1959)

Over 205 ints, 4vv, 1 ed. in Documenta, vi (1959); over 230 grads, 1 ed. in Musica divina, i/4 (Regensburg, 1862); all settings with tracts, 1–5, 8vv, 1 with insts; 15 seqs, 2, 4, 6, 8, 10vv; over 210 offs, 1–2, 4–5, 8vv, 2 ed. in Documenta, vii, viii (1959); 16 comms, 4vv

Mag verses; 1 Mag, ed. in Musica divina, i/3 (Regensburg, 1859); 37 lits, 4–5, 8vv; improperia, Passions and response cycles, 1, 4, 9vv; *c*780 pss, 3–5, 8, 16vv, 1–4 solo vv, some with insts, 2 ed. in Musica divina, i/3 (Regensburg, 1859), 3 ed. in Monumenta, iv/5–7 (1959–60); *c*220 canticles, 4–5vv; 25 Lamentations; *c*640 ants, 1–4vv

Over 250 hymns, 1, 4–5, 8vv, 1 with insts, 1 ed. in Musica divina, i/3 (Regensburg, 1859)

Over 235 motets, 1–4, 6, 8–9vv, some with insts, 6 ed. in Musica divina, i/2 (Regensburg, 1854)

SECULAR

1 madrigal; 3 canons, *D-Bsb, D-MÜs*

Orats, music lost: S Ranieri, Rome, Chiesa de' padri della congregazione dell'Oratorio di S Filippo Neri di Firenze, 1693; Hungaria in libertatem and Hungariae triumphus in Quirinali, Rome, S Ignazio, 1695

WRITINGS

Guida armonica . . . libro primo (Rome, *c*1690); ed. F. Luisi (Bologna, 1989); MSS, *c*1685–1743, *I-Rvat*

Notitia de contrapuntisti e de compositori di musica (MS *c*1725); ed. C. Ruini (Florence, 1988)

Regole di contrappunto (MS, *I-Rsc*)

Aggiunte alle Regole di contrappunto di Giulio Belli (MS, *I-Bc*)

BIBLIOGRAPHY

FellererP

H. Hucke: 'G.O. Pitoni und seine Messen im Archiv der Cappella Giulia', *KJb*, xxxix (1955), 70–94

S. Gmeinwieser: 'Die Musikkapellen Roms und ihre Aufführungspraxis unter G.O. Pitoni', *KJb*, lvii (1973), 69–78

S. Gmeinwieser: 'Giuseppe Ottavio Pitoni (1657–1743)', *AMw*, xxxii (1975), 298–309

S. Gmeinwieser: *Giuseppe Ottavio Pitoni: Thematisches Werkverzeichnis* (Wilhelmshaven, 1976)

S. Gmeinwieser: 'Stil und Kompositionspraxis in der Kirchenmusik Roms im 18. Jahrhundert, dargestellt am Werk des G.O. Pitoni', *Festschrift Erich Valentin* (Regensburg, 1976), 31–40

S. Durante: 'La *Guida armonica* di Giuseppe Ottavio Pitoni: un documento sugli stili musicali in uso a Roma al tempo di Corelli', *Nuovissimi studi Corelliani: Fusignano 1980*, 285–326

M. di Pasquale: '"Vita et opere del molto eccellente Signor Giuseppe Ottavio Pitoni . . . di Cappella nella testimonianza di Girolamo Chiti', *Musica e musicisti nel Lazio*, ed. R. Lefevre and A. Morelli (Rome, 1985), 397–420

S. Gmeinwieser: 'Aspetti della policoralità nelle opere di G.O. Pitoni e di G. Chiti', *La policoralità Romana: Trent 1996*

S. Gmeinwieser: 'Die Guida armonica von G.O. Pitoni', *Festschrift Karl-Heinz Schlager* (Tutzing, 1998), 245–81

SIEGFRIED GMEINWIESER

Pitra, Jean Baptiste (*b* Champforgueil, nr Autun, 1, 12 or 31 Aug 1812; *d* Rome, 9 Feb 1889). French Benedictine scholar. Ordained in 1836, he joined the Solesmes brotherhood in 1841 under Abbé Guéranger, and after his profession of faith in 1843 was appointed prior of St Germain-des-Prés in Paris; while there he assisted Migne with the Latin and Greek patrologies. Between 1845 and 1850 he travelled extensively, seeking in particular Greek and Latin manuscripts for the Solesmes library; many of the texts were later published in *Spicilegium solesmense* (1852–8/R). During a visit to St Petersburg (1860) he rediscovered the metric and strophic structure of medieval Greek liturgical poetry; the results, announced in 1863, were published in his now celebrated study *Hymnographie de l'église grecque* (Rome, 1867). He was made a cardinal in 1863 and appointed librarian of the Vatican libraries in 1869. An authority on the canon law of the Eastern Churches, he published *Juris ecclesiastici Graecorum historia et monumenta* (Rome, 1864–8/R) and collections of early Christian literature (*Analecta sacra spicilegio solesmensi parata*, Paris, 1876–91/R). While it is true that FRANZ JOSEPH MONE was already aware of the principles of structure of Greek verses, it is not proven that Pitra knew these results and claimed the discovery for himself. Pitra's explanation is much more methodical and clearer than Mone's, and his findings were better disseminated.

MILOŠ VELIMIROVIĆ

Pitschner, Gregor. *See* PESCHIN, GREGOR.

Pitt, Percy (*b* London, 4 Jan 1869; *d* London, 23 Nov 1932). English conductor, composer and manager. He studied with Reinecke and Jadassohn in Leipzig and with Rheinberger in Munich. In 1896 he became accompanist, organist and celesta player for the Queen's Hall concerts conducted by Henry Wood, but in 1902 made a decisive switch to opera with an appointment as musical adviser to the Grand Opera Syndicate which ran Covent Garden. The title of musical director, to which he was advanced in 1907, in fact gave him little more than the function of coach, assistant conductor and consultant, but it placed him centrally in the politics of opera. Pitt was the close ally of Hans Richter in the latter's performances of the *Ring* in English at Covent Garden (1908–9) and shared Richter's disappointment that the further establishment of an English repertory was frustrated by the management. On Richter's nomination, Pitt had already become the first English conductor at Covent Garden during the 'grand season' with Poldini's one-act *Der Vagabund und die Prinzessin* (1907). He also conducted *Don Giovanni* in 1909 (with McCormack as Ottavio) and Sullivan's *Ivanhoe* (1910). In Beecham's 1919–20 season at Covent Garden, Pitt conducted *Khovanshchina*, *Pelléas et Mélisande* and other works, and on the subsequent financial collapse of Beecham's operatic enterprise it was Pitt who became artistic director of the succeeding British National Opera Company from 1922 until 1924. From 1922 he was also musical adviser to the newly formed BBC, a post which became a full-time musical directorship from 1924 until he was succeeded by Boult on his retirement in 1930. He conducted the first of the BBC's public symphony concerts at the Central Hall, Westminster, in February 1924, having previously conducted the broadcast of parts of *Die Zauberflöte* from Covent Garden on 8 January 1923. Under Pitt's leadership, the future tone of the BBC's musical enterprise was established.

In earlier years Pitt had a good reputation as a composer. Tetrazzini sang a song he wrote for her, *Sérénade du passant*, at her first Queen's Hall appearance in 1917. His other works include a *Ballade* for violin and orchestra (composed for Ysaÿe), a clarinet concerto and a variety of stage music.

BIBLIOGRAPHY
J.D. Chamier: *Percy Pitt of Covent Garden and the BBC* (London,1938)
ARTHUR JACOBS

Pittanus [Pitanus, Pittach], **Friedrich** (*b* Frankfurt an der Oder, *c*1568; *d* in or after 1606). German composer and clergyman. He attended the local school, where he was taught by Gregor Lange, and in the winter term of 1578 he matriculated at the local university, where he later studied music and theology. On 8 February 1591 he was appointed Kantor of the Marienkirche, Frankfurt an der Oder, but he carried out his duties less satisfactorily than had been hoped, and as early as the beginning of March 1593 he was replaced by the more substantial figure of Bartholomäus Gesius. According to the title-page of a wedding song by him of 1595, he was then a musician at Bernau, near Berlin, and he appears still to have been there in 1599. Shortly afterwards he became a preacher not far away at Grimnitz, near Eberswalde. Most of his music is either lost or inaccessible. He published *Sacrae cantiones* (Frankfurt an der Oder, 1590), for five and six voices, a volume that possibly helped him to his first appointment as Kantor. It seems to have been followed by only a few isolated occasional pieces including the five-voice *Ein Hochzeit gesang ... dem Friedrich Hartmann* (Frankfurt an der Oder, 1595) and *Epithalamium in honorem nuptiarum ... Caspari Ottonis medicinae doctoris* (Frankfurt an der Oder, 1606), for six voices, while in manuscript there is an organ tablature version of a five-part motet, *Quare tristis*, which may be from his 1590 print (in *PL-PE* 305; facs. in AMP, iii, 1965, pp.58–9; extended incipit in AMP, i, 1963, p.97); a few sacred songs by him were formerly in the Stadtbibliothek, Elbing (new Elbląg).

BIBLIOGRAPHY
EitnerQ; *MGG1* (A. Forchert)
H. Grimm: *Meister der Renaissancemusik an der Viadrina* (Frankfurt an der Oder, 1942)
NIGEL FORTUNE/CLYTUS GOTTWALD

Pittar, Fanny Krumpholtz. English composer. Daughter of Anne-Marie Krumpholtz (*see* KRUMPHOLTZ family, (3)).

Pittel, Harvey (*b* Great Falls, MT, 22 June 1943). American saxophonist. He studied with Kalman Bloch and Franklyn Stokes and from 1961 to 1965 attended the University of Southern California, where he obtained his doctorate in music education. Further studies were with Frederick Hemke at Northwestern University (1965–6) and with Joseph Allard (1966–9) while he was in the US Military Academy Band. In 1970 he won a silver medal at the Concours International in Geneva. He made his solo début with the Boston SO in Ingolf Dahl's Saxophone Concerto (1971); his recital début was in 1973 at Carnegie Recital Hall. He has performed with major orchestras in the USA and Europe. In 1972 he formed a saxophone quartet; he has also performed in a trio consisting of saxophone, piano and cello. Among the premières he has presented are those of Berio's *Chemins II b/c*, Babbitt's *Images* and Chihara's Saxophone Concerto. Pittel has taught at the University of Southern California, California State University (Fullerton and Long Beach campuses), Boston University, the Mannes College and, from 1980, the University of Texas, Austin. He has also held workshops at the Aspen Music School and the Berkshire Music Center.

SORAB MODI/R

Pittman, Josiah (*b* London, 3 Sept 1816; *d* London, 23 April 1886). English organist and church musician. The son of a musician, Pittman learnt music from an early age, later studying the organ with S.S. Wesley and the piano with Moscheles. Appointed organist of Christ Church, Spitalfields, at the age of 15, he held similar posts at Tooting (1833) and Sydenham (1835). In 1852, when the Benchers of Lincoln's Inn first elected to introduce a choral form of service in their chapel, Pittman was appointed organist with the task of forming a professional choir of men and boys. Under his leadership a new tradition was created, and Pittman composed many services and anthems for use there; the choir soon earned for the chapel a high position in the ranks of London's 'musical' churches. At a time when the movement to introduce surpliced choirs was arousing wide controversy, Pittman published *The People in Church* (1858), a treatise on the musical privileges and duties of a congregation. The book reflected the seriousness and enthusiasm with which he regarded his own duties; but that high-mindedness was to bring about his downfall. Called upon to include the tune 'Helmsley' in the chapel service during Advent, 1864, Pittman objected to its secular origin. When his objection was overruled, he rashly parodied the tune at the organ during the service and was promptly dismissed. Thereafter he held the post of accompanist at Her Majesty's Theatre (1865–8) and at the Royal Italian Opera, Covent Garden (1868–80).

Pittman was among the first to introduce Bach's 'pedal' fugues to English audiences; and he achieved note as a lecturer on music at the London Institution. His other publications include *The People in the Cathedral: a Letter to the Very Revd Henry Hart Milman* (1859), *Songs of Scotland* and *Songs from the Operas*. He was co-editor with Sullivan of the Royal Edition of Operas, and made an edition of Callcott's *Grammar of Music*.

BIBLIOGRAPHY

B. Rainbow: *The Choral Revival in the Anglican Church, 1839–1872* (London, 1970)

BERNARR RAINBOW

Pittsburgh. City in western Pennsylvania, USA. It was founded in 1758 as a military settlement. The earliest musical heritage was English, but from the start of the 19th century important contributions were made by Welsh and German immigrants. The Welsh brought their singing festivals, known as *cymanfa ganu*, and in 1807 the American artist Samuel H. Dearborn founded the Apollonian Society, devoted to performing popular songs and marches of the day, as well as the music of Mozart and his contemporaries. From 1820 Handel's choruses were regularly performed, and most musical instruments were available after 1830. Choral singing became quite popular, although in Presbyterian churches the presence of choirs and instruments was a matter of controversy through much of the 19th century.

The best-known native composer of the 19th century was Stephen C. Foster (1826–64). An active musician after the Civil War was P.L.C. Tetedoux, a singing teacher and former pupil of Rossini, who organized a Cantata Society that performed sacred works. In the 1890s the industrialist Andrew Carnegie presented Allegheny (which became part of Pittsburgh in 1906) with a library and a music hall containing a large Roosevelt organ. The renovated Carnegie Music Hall (cap. 1972), part of Carnegie Institute in the city's Oakland district, remains the chief venue for chamber music and recitals. The music division of Carnegie Library (founded 1938) is a rich collection that is still the city's major resource for these materials. Among the other wealthy families who have contributed significantly to Pittsburgh's cultural life in the 20th century are the Fricks, the Heinzes, the Mellons and the Scaifes.

1. Orchestras. 2. Opera. 3. Chamber and choral music. 4. Music education. 5. Broadcasting.

1. ORCHESTRAS.   The first ensemble in the city that endured for more than a couple of concerts was the Pittsburgh Orchestral Society, organized and conducted by Gottlieb A. Anton (1854–6). Ad hoc ensembles and visiting orchestras performed during the following decades, until the city's first permanent professional orchestra, the Pittsburgh Orchestra, was established in 1895. Conducted by a local organist named Frederick Archer, the Pittsburgh Orchestra – which developed into the present Pittsburgh SO – gave its first concert in the new Carnegie Music Hall on 28 February 1896. Victor Herbert (1859–1924) was the first to be named music director, a post he held from 1898 to 1904. Herbert was succeeded by Emil Paul until 1910, when financial problems arose and the board disbanded the orchestra. It was not until 1926 that the orchestra was reorganized as the Pittsburgh SO, performing in the 3750-seat Syria Mosque (built 1916), and not until 1930 that a new music director was named: the Pittsburgher Antonio Modarelli (1927–37). Subsequent music directors have been Fritz Reiner (1938–48), William Steinberg (1952–76), André Previn (1976–85), Lorin Maazel (1988–96) and Mariss Jansons, who took over in 1997. In September 1971 the orchestra moved to the 2856-seat Heinz Hall, an elegantly converted 1920s cinema which it owns. Under Maazel's leadership the orchestra achieved international status, with numerous recordings, successful tours to several continents and an ever-growing endowment. Its regular season in Heinz Hall is 22 weeks long, plus seven weekends of Pops concerts. Marvin Hamlisch, composer of *A Chorus Line*, was appointed principal Pops conductor in 1995.

In 1945 Marie Maazel (mother of the conductor) founded the Pittsburgh Youth Symphony, which is conducted by one of the Pittsburgh SO's resident or associate conductors. A second professional orchestra, composed of local union members, now plays for the Pittsburgh Opera, Pittsburgh Ballet and the Civic Light Opera Association (which presents Broadway musicals) as well as several smaller local ensembles.

The Pittsburgh New Music Ensemble, founded by the composer and conductor David Stock in 1976, performs a wide range of contemporary repertory, commissions new works and has been enormously successful in increasing awareness of contemporary music among conservative Pittsburgh audiences. Stock resigned as music director at the end of the 1998–9 season and was succeeded by Pittsburgh-born Gil Rose in August 1999.

2. OPERA.   The first opera given in Pittsburgh was an English version of Rossini's *Il barbiere di Siviglia* by the visiting Francis Courtney Weymyss Troupe on 16 April 1838, but opera did not flourish in Pittsburgh until 1873, when the Frohsinn Society gave Flotow's *Alessandro Stradella* (in German) to much acclaim. In 1874 the Gounod Club performed another of Flotow's operas, *Martha*, in its first operatic series. While famous opera companies (including the New York Metropolitan Opera) visited the city regularly on their tours in the early 20th century, the first permanent professional organization, Pittsburgh Opera, was not established until 1939. Richard Karp, a German viola player who came to the USA to escape Nazi oppression and played in the Pittsburgh SO under Reiner, directed the opera company from 1942 to 1975, when illness forced him to step down in favour of his daughter, Barbara. Cincinnati Opera director James DeBlasis became artistic adviser after Karp resigned following a disagreement with the board in 1979, remaining in that position until Tito Capobianco was appointed general director in 1983. Capobianco increased the budget and production values, especially after the company moved into the state-of-the-art Benedum Center – another renovated cinema – in October 1987. A reorganization took place in 1997, when Capobianco's title was changed to artistic director and Mark Weinstein was brought in for the newly created post of executive

director, to take up the administrative responsibilities Capobianco had relinquished. Capobianco retired from Pittsburgh Opera at the end of the 1999–2000 season. Weinstein was appointed general director.

With few exceptions, Pittsburgh Opera sticks stubbornly to the most familiar repertory. Contemporary operas, American works, even most of the German repertory, have been ignored. *Der Rosenkavalier* did not reach Pittsburgh until 1995. The gap has partly been filled by the Opera Theater of Pittsburgh, an enterprising small company operated on a shoestring budget by former Metropolitan Opera mezzo-soprano Mildred Miller Posvar, who founded the troupe in 1978. It was known until 1987 as Pittsburgh Chamber Opera. Dedicated to promoting young professional singers in standard and modern repertory, the company tours with educational projects in addition to its performances at home. Jonathan Eaton succeeded Posvar as director in August 1999.

3. CHAMBER AND CHORAL MUSIC.   Jenny Lind gave concerts in Pittsburgh in 1851. Today the Y Music Society has the city's oldest recital series, which since 1926 has brought in first-rank artists, from Nathan Milstein and Marian Anderson to Vladimir Feltsman and Itzhak Perlman. The Pittsburgh Chamber Music Society, founded in 1961, offers six concerts each year by well-known ensembles. The Tuesday Musical Club presents free recitals by entry-level performers in the élite, exclusive spaces of the Frick Art Museum. Early music is well served by the Renaissance and Baroque Society, which has developed one of the area's most faithful and enthusiastic followings.

One of the earliest choral societies in the area was the Teutonia Männerchor, formed in 1854. Numerous other singing societies soon arose. The Mozart Club (1879–1919), founded and directed by James Knox Polk McCollum, presented oratorios and other large-scale choral works. The oldest choral society still functioning in Pittsburgh is the Mendelssohn Choir, founded in 1908. Under its music director Robert Page it is the official choir of the Pittsburgh SO, but also gives a three-event subscription series of its own. Other thriving choral groups include the Bach Choir (founded 1934) and the Pittsburgh Camerata, an *a cappella* chamber choir.

4. MUSIC EDUCATION.   The earliest music teachers and performers in Pittsburgh were trained in England. Peter Declary, who arrived in Pittsburgh in 1799, was the city's first teacher of music, while William Evens, a native of Sussex who came to Pittsburgh from Philadelphia in 1811, opened a singing school soon afterwards. He also amassed Pittsburgh's first collection of music scores, histories, theory books and biographies, but was a reluctant lender who allowed few people access. His collection eventually went to the Carnegie Library.

Pittsburgh was one of the first American cities to introduce music into schools (in 1844). Will Earhart, who became music director for the Pittsburgh Public Schools in 1912, produced a widely read report, 'Music in the Public Schools', that strongly influenced music education at this level.

The city's three universities all offer strong undergraduate and graduate courses in music. The state-related University of Pittsburgh is strongest in musicology and composition, while Carnegie Mellon University and Duquesne University (affiliated with the Roman Catholic Church) have extensive courses for performance and music education. All have faculty and student recital series, chamber music, orchestral and choral ensembles, opera workshops and contemporary music groups that perform regularly on their respective campuses and explore repertory more adventurous than do the area's commercial organizations.

5. BROADCASTING.   Pittsburgh was an early centre in the development of radio and the home of KDKA, one of the first commercial radio stations in the USA. KDKA was the first to produce a choral broadcast (by the Westinghouse Community Chorus, in 1922) and the first to have its own orchestra, also in 1922. Pittsburgh's arts radio station, WQED-FM, broadcasts classical music for a large part of every day. Some of its programmes are locally produced and feature local performers. It is associated with the public television station WQED-TV.

BIBLIOGRAPHY

G.M. Rohrer: *Music and Musicians of Pennsylvania* (Philadelphia, 1940)
E.G. Baynham: *A History of Pittsburgh Music 1758–1958* (MS, 1970, *US-Pc*)
Carnegie Magazine, xlix (1975) [whole issue]
F. Dorian and J. Meibach: *A History of the Pittsburgh Symphony Orchestra* (Pittsburgh, 1986)

IDA REED/ROBERT CROAN

Pitz, Wilhelm (*b* Breinig, 25 Aug 1897; *d* Aachen, 21 Nov 1973). German chorus master and conductor. He served as a violinist in the Städtisches Orchester at Aachen from 1913, then in 1933 became chorus master of the Aachen Städtische Oper (with Karajan as musical director) and director of the municipal choir. From 1947 to 1960 he was first conductor of the opera. Karajan's recommendation led to Pitz's appointment as chorus master of the Bayreuth Festival on its postwar reopening in 1951. The remarkable standards he achieved there led Walter Legge to invite him to London in 1957 to build a chorus to partner the Philharmonia Orchestra. The Philharmonia Chorus, a predominantly amateur organization, supported by a few professionals, soon acquired a first-class reputation. After the Philharmonia Orchestra ceased operations and the New Philharmonia Orchestra was established in 1964 the chorus was similarly renamed the New Philharmonia Chorus. Pitz continued as its director until retiring through ill-health in 1971. He occasionally appeared as conductor in his own right, but his special fame arose from the quality of his choral preparation for the concerts and recordings of Klemperer, Giulini and others, and for Bayreuth, from which he also retired in 1971. He was made an honorary OBE in 1969 and held the Grosses Verdienstkreuz of the German Federal Republic.

ARTHUR JACOBS

Più (It.: 'more'). An adverb used in music particularly for tempo adjustments: *più mosso*, 'faster'; *più animato*, 'more animated'; etc.

Pius, Francesco. *See* PIO, FRANCESCO.

Piuttosto (It.: 'rather', 'somewhat'). An adverb used in music in such contexts as *allegro piuttosto presto*, 'lively and fairly fast'.

Piva (i) (It.: 'bagpipe'). An Italian dance of the 15th and 16th centuries. Perhaps originally a peasant dance to the accompaniment of bagpipes, it is described in 15th-century dance manuals as the fastest variety of the courtly

Ex.1 Dalza: *Piva* (for lute) (Suite no.6); Petrucci: *Intabulatura de lauto* (Venice, 1508)

bassadanza. Its steps were twice as quick as those of the bassadanza proper and were enlivened by leaps and turns. By about 1450 it had gone somewhat out of fashion, though occasionally a few bars of it were included in ballo melodies as a contrast to their more sedate sections (*see* BALLO and BASSE DANSE).

The term reappears in early 16th-century sources as the title of a lute dance in quick triple time. The first seven of the nine suites in Dalza's *Intabulatura de lauto* (Venice, 1508) consist of a pavan, saltarello and piva. These dances are very repetitive but have no clearly defined sectional form. The piva is the fastest of the three, usually being notated in *proportio tripla*. In the last two suites the final dance is called 'spingardo': nevertheless these two spingardos and the pivas of the sixth and seventh suites all begin with the same tune (ex.1). Dalza's book also contains a saltarello and piva for two lutes, in which, bagpipe-like, the second lute is restricted to a tonic chord ostinato. What is probably the earliest source of Italian keyboard dances (*I-Vnm* ital.iv.1227, dating from *c*1520) opens with a *Padovana in piva* ('Padoana in the style of a bagpipe dance'). An isolated piva occurs in the *Intabolatura di lauto libro nono il Bembo* of Melchiore de Barberiis (Venice, 1549).

BIBLIOGRAPHY

BrownI
O. Gombosi: 'About Dance and Dance Music in the Late Middle Ages', *MQ*, xxvii (1941), 289–305
O. Kinkeldey: 'Dance Tunes of the Fifteenth Century', *Instrumental Music: Cambridge, MA, 1957*, 3–30, 89–152
R. Chiesea: 'Storia della letteratura del liuto e della chitarra: il Cinquecento, V', *Il Fronimo*, i/5 (1973), 15–20
C. Celi: 'La danza aulica italiana nel XV secolo', *NRMI*, xvi (1982), 218–25
B. Sparti: 'The 15th-Century *balli* Tunes: a New Look', *EMc*, xiv (1986), 346–57

ALAN BROWN

Piva (ii). *See* BASSANO family.

Piva torta (It.). *See* CRUMHORN.

Pivoda, František (*b* Žeravice, nr Hodonín, 19 Oct 1824; *d* Prague, 4 Jan 1898). Czech singing teacher and composer. He was first taught music by his elder brother in Bučovice, and continued his education in Brno (1839). In 1844 he moved to Vienna, completing his musical studies and establishing himself as a teacher of singing, piano and theory. He began to compose and publish songs, and acquired a knowledge of Italian singing methods from Giovanni Basadonna. He also developed an interest in politics and Czech nationalism; he participated in and organized soirées (including amateur theatre productions and concerts) involving Czech artists, and was active in the 1848 uprisings. After settling in Prague in 1860, Pivoda directed his energies towards the development of Czech musical culture. He became popular as a singing teacher and song composer, and was a prolific writer and critic. He was co-founder of several musical institutions, including the Umělecká Beseda (1863) and the Prague choral society Hlahol (1861). In 1869 he established a successful singing school, where many prominent Czech singers were taught. He published many locally influential Czech songbooks and textbooks, in particular his *Nová nauka zpěvu* ('New singing manual', Prague, 1879).

Despite his many positive contributions to the development of Czech music, Pivoda was primarily responsible for the vitriolic disputes over aesthetics which affected Czech musical life in the 1870s. A staunch conservative, he was implacably opposed both to the music of Wagner and to the basic principles of Wagner's reforms. This drew him into conflict with Smetana, as he failed to understand that his contemporary was not striving to write in an openly Germanic, Wagnerian style, but in a patriotic Czech spirit inspired by Wagnerian precepts. He vigorously criticized many of Smetana's later works, especially *Dalibor*, and succeeded in splitting Prague musical circles into two irreconcilable camps. In later years his opposition became irrelevant and, except for his teaching works, his influence and importance diminished. His own compositional output (see complete list in Horák) included many slight piano works, choruses, and over 150 German and Czech songs. The latter, predominantly cast in a simple, folk-like style, remained popular well into the 1880s.

BIBLIOGRAPHY

O. Hostinský: *Bedřich Smetana a jeho boj o moderni českou hudbu* [Smetana and his struggle for modern Czech music] (Prague, 1901, 2/1941)
J. Heyer: *Česká hudební viennensia* (Vienna, 1941)
V. Horák: *František Pivoda, pěvecký pedagog* [Pivoda, singing teacher] (Brno, 1970)
J. Clapham: 'The Smetana–Pivoda Controversy', *ML*, lii (1971), 353–64

KARL STAPLETON

Pivot. A chord (or a note) having different harmonic (or melodic) functions in two different keys, this property being used to effect a smooth transition from one key to the other. Pivot chords are therefore fundamental to the concept of modulation (*see* MODULATION (i)). In moving from F major to C major, for instance, a D minor chord can be used as a pivot, since it functions as VI of F major and II of C major (Beethoven, Pastoral Symphony, bars 53–66 of first movement). More distant modulations may be effected by the use of such chords as the diminished 7th or the Neapolitan 6th. Another type of chord frequently used as a pivot is the APPLIED DOMINANT. 'Pivot' can also describe a note that belongs, either literally or enharmonically (*see* ENHARMONIC), to the tonic triads of two juxtaposed keys and is exploited melodically in such a way that this relationship is made clear. In Chopin's Second Scherzo op.31, F is the fifth scale degree of B♭ minor (bars 1–48) and third of D♭ major (bars 49–132). D♭, in turn, serves not only as the key note of D♭ major but also – spelt as C♯ – as the third degree of A major (bars 265ff).

WILLIAM DRABKIN

Pixell, John Pryn Parkes (*b* Birmingham, bap. 12 Nov 1725; *d* Edgbaston, bur. 4 Aug 1784). English song composer. He was educated at the King Edward School, Birmingham, and Queen's College, Oxford, where he probably developed his interest in music from the weekly concerts presented by William Hayes. In 1750 he was appointed vicar of St Bartholomew's, Edgbaston, where he remained for the rest of his life. He printed two books of songs: *A Collection of Songs with their Recitatives and Symphonies for the German Flute, Violins, etc., with a Thorough Bass for the Harpsichord* (Birmingham, 1759) and *Odes, Cantatas, Songs, etc., divine, moral, entertaining*, op.2 (Birmingham, 1775). The first has the distinction of having its title-page and list of subscribers (342) printed by the eminent John Baskerville. The books contain 44 songs for high voice, with a range of obbligato instruments including horns, oboes, flutes, organ, bassoon and even pipe and tabor, which probably reflects the instruments available at the various local music societies that subscribed to Pixell's work (Lichfield, Oxford, Coventry, Gloucester, Stourbridge and three in Birmingham). The songs, ranging from strophic ballads to psalms and to cantatas with chorus, display competence though no particular originality. A manuscript song, 'Seek ye not these paths to view' (in *GB-Bp*), although tentatively dated ?1820, is thought to have been by Pixell and may in fact be an autograph.

BIBLIOGRAPHY

C.S. James, ed.: *The Registers of Edgbaston Parish Church*, ii (London, 1936), pp.x–xi

P. Gaskell: *John Baskerville: a Bibliography* (Cambridge, 1959), 27–8

ROBERT SPENCER

Pixérécourt, René Charles Guilbert de (*b* Nancy, 22 Jan 1773; *d* Nancy, 25 July 1844). French librettist and dramatist. Son of a nobleman, he intended to become a lawyer, but his plans were interrupted by the French Revolution and he fled to Germany in 1789. By 1793 he had returned to Nancy, then moved on to Paris, where he began writing plays and librettos. Not until 1797 did one of his works reach the public: *Les petits auvergnats*, at the Théâtre de l'Ambigu-Comique which, along with the Porte-St-Martin and Gaîté theatres, was always eager to produce his melodramas once their appeal was clear.

Throughout the 1820s and into the 30s Pixérécourt continued to write melodramas, *opéras comiques* and other stage works; at the same time, he held government posts and was director of the Opéra-Comique (1822–7). He took over the administration of the Gaîté, but in 1835 fire destroyed this house, along with many of his manuscripts, and he was forced to sell his country estate and his considerable library in order to survive financially. He retired and returned to Nancy later that year. His total output for the stage, including the works that were not performed, reached 120 pieces.

Dubbed 'the Corneille of the Boulevards', Pixérécourt was practically the inventor, and certainly the codifier, of the popular French stage form *mélodrame*. Noted for its stock characters, complex plots, sensationalism, startling *coups de théâtre*, scenic virtuosity and a strongly moral outlook, the *mélodrame* flourished in the early decades of the 19th century. Pixérécourt built a catalogue of nearly 60 such plays, beginning in 1798 with *Victor, ou L'enfant de la forêt* (originally intended as an *opéra comique*), developing an international reputation. He also wrote comedies, tragedies, vaudevilles, *féeries*, pantomimes and the librettos of some 21 *opéras comiques*. However, he did not emerge in the front rank of librettists for two reasons: his *opéras comiques*, though skilfully written, are quite conventional; and he seldom had the opportunity to collaborate with a really first-rate musician. Yet he certainly was not ignorant of the dramatic potential of music, for he worked a great deal of it into his melodramas. His most frequent collaborators in that genre were Louis Alexandre Piccinni and Adrien Quaisain. In both dramas and librettos he saw himself as a successor of Sedaine.

Though Pixérécourt's melodramas are best known for the influence they exercised on Romantic drama, they were no less influential on the genre that came to be known as French grand opera. Pixérécourt planned innovatory *mises en scène* and more modern approaches to staging than had been used at the Opéra, and called for ballets with authentic period and national dress. Along with these features, the melodramas' frequent historical associations, their use of tableau-like scenes (especially at the ends of acts) and their lavish, highly contrasting sets clearly affected the character of the new style of opera. Also, like French grand opera, Pixérécourt's dramas were ensemble pieces requiring careful preparation and well-rehearsed stage business. Though he was often accused of treating his actors like slaves, his precise, finely honed productions won praise even from those who were not fond of their crowd-pleasing qualities. In addition, many of the Opéra's finest designers, choreographers and dancers in the 19th century first worked with Pixérécourt at the boulevard theatres, where they were encouraged to develop ideas that were to become the hallmarks of French grand opera.

WORKS SET TO MUSIC

OPÉRA COMIQUE LIBRETTOS

Jacques et Georgette, 1793, not set; *Marat Mauger*, comp. unknown, 1794; *Le mannequin vivant*, Gaveaux, 1796; *Les petits auvergnats*, Morange, 1797; *Les trois tantes*, Solié, 1797; *Victor, ou L'enfant de la forêt*, Solié, 1797 (planned as oc, but perf. the following year as spoken melodrama); *La forêt de Sicile*, Gresnick, 1798; *Léonidas*, Persuis and Gresnick, 1799; *La musicomanie*, Quaisain, 1800 (It., Carafa, 1806); *Le petit page* (with L. T. Lambert), R. Kreutzer and Isouard, 1800; *Le chansonnier de la paix*, 1801; *Flaminius à Corinthe* (with Lambert), Kreutzer and Isouard, 1801; *Marcel, ou L'héritier supposé*, Persuis, 1801; *Quatre maris pour un*, Solié, 1801; *Raymond de Toulouse*, C. G. Foignet and F. Foignet, 1802; *Avis aux femmes*, Gaveaux, 1804; *Koulouf, ou Les chinois*, Dalayrac, 1806; *La rose blanche et la rose rouge*, Gaveaux, 1809 (It., Mayr, 1813); *Ovide en exil*, Hérold, 1818; *L'amant sans maîtresse*, García, 1821; *Le pavillon des fleurs*, Dalayrac, 1822

PLAYS ON WHICH OPERAS HAVE BEEN BASED

L'homme à trois visages (1801): T. S. Cooke, *c*1813, as Rugantino, or The Bravo of Venice

Tékéli, ou Le siège de Montgatz (1803): Hook, 1806, as Tekeli, or The Siege of Montgatz

La forteresse du Danube (1805): Hook, 1807, as The Fortress

Les mines de Pologne (1805): Hook, 1808, as The Siege of St Quintin, or Spanish Heroism

La cisterne (1809): Donizetti, 1822, as Chiara e Serafina

Marguerite d'Anjou (1810): Meyerbeer, 1820, as Margherita d'Anjou

La fille de l'exilé (1819): Donizetti, 1827, as Otto mesi in due ore, ossia Gli esiliati in Siberia

BIBLIOGRAPHY

R.C.G. de Pixérécourt: *Théâtre choisi* (Paris and Nancy, 1841–3)

P. Ginisty: *Le mélodrame* (Paris, 1910)

W. Hartog: *Guilbert de Pixérécourt* (Paris, 1913)

K. Pendle: 'Boulevard Theatres and Continuity in French Opera of the Nineteenth Century', *Music in Paris in the 1830s*, ed. P. Bloom (Stuyvesant, NY, 1987), 509–35

N. Wild: 'La musique dans le mélodrame des théâtres parisiens', ibid., 589–610

KARIN PENDLE

Pixérécourt Chansonnier (*F-Pn* fr.15123). *See* SOURCES, MS, §IX, 8.

Pixies, the. American rock band. It was formed in 1986 in Boston by Black Francis (Charles Michael Kittridge Thompson IV; *b* Long Beach, CA, 1965; vocals and rhythm guitar), Joey Santiago (*b* Manila, Philippines, 10 June 1965; lead guitar), Kim Deal (Mrs John Murphy; *b* Dayton, OH; bass and vocals) and Dave Lovering (*b* 6 Dec 1961; drums). Although they never attained widespread commercial acceptability, their importance, like that of the Velvet Underground 20 years before, lies in the succession of American bands formed in their wake. The Pixies played a blend of uncompromising minimalist rock interwoven with surprising and memorable surf-guitar figures. Francis's hoarse, screaming vocal style was instantly recognizable, and by the release of *Doolittle* (4 AD, 1989), which contained *Debaser* and the minor UK hit single *Monkey Gone to Heaven*, they had emerged as one of the most important bands of their day. Their music played heavily with distortion, dynamics and tempo, and can best be described as 'proto-grunge'. In Francis, the Pixies possessed a songwriter who, with his sense of the absurd, captured perfectly the disenfranchisement of American youth of the 'pre-slacker' generation. The huge success of Nirvana's Seattle sound of the early 1990s was a direct consequence of the Pixies' work in the 1980s. The Pixies disbanded in 1992, with Black Francis (now under the pseudonym of Frank Black) embarking on a solo career and Kim Deal continuing her work with the Breeders. A Pixies retrospective, *Death to the Pixies* (1997), reaffirmed their enduring influence.

DAVID BUCKLEY

Pixinguinha [Vianna Filho, Alfredo da Rocha] (*b* Rio de Janeiro, 23 April 1897/8; *d* Rio de Janeiro, 17 Feb 1973). Brazilian composer, flautist, saxophonist, arranger and bandleader. His father was an amateur flute player and cultivator of the old *choro*. Around the age of ten Pixinguinha played the *cavaquinho* and accompanied his father, who also taught him the flute. He participated in carnival band parades (1911–12), played in night clubs and in the orchestra of the Rio Branco cinema, specializing in musical comedies and operettas. His talents as a flautist were widely recognized and through this he formed his first significant group, Os Oito Batutas, with other important musicians of the period, such as Donga, China and Nelson Alves. Originally including flute, three guitars, singer, *cavaquinho*, mandoline, tambourine, *reco-reco* and *ganzá*, they were presented at the Cinema Palais in 1919 with a typically national repertory that included waltzes, polkas, tangos, *maxixes*, *choros*, *modinhas* and sambas. Within three years the group toured the major cities of southern and north-eastern Brazil, and finally abroad in Paris (1922) and Buenos Aires, also recording works by Pixinguinha, Donga and others.

In 1928 he co-organized the Orquestra Típica Pixinguinha-Donga, mostly for studio work, recording the famous *samba-choro*, *Carinhoso*. After working as an arranger for the Victor Talking Machine of Brazil (1929), he organized the Guarda Velha (1931) from leading Brazilian instrumentalists, and with whom he achieved his best work as a band leader, providing a coherent and effective ensemble structure while allowing room for solo virtuoso display. The band recorded dozens of albums and backed major popular stars of the period, such as Carmen Miranda, Mário Reis and Sílvio Caldas.

Pixinguinha's own compositions number about 140 pieces, mostly *choros*, *polcas-choro*, sambas and a few carnival marches and waltzes, some of which won widespread popularity from the 1920s to 50s. He contributed substantially to the development of a genuinely national popular music and to an increased instrumental sophistication in orchestration and band arrangement.

BIBLIOGRAPHY
L. Rangel: *Sambistas e chorões* (Rio de Janeiro, 1962)
J.R. Tinhorão: *O samba agora vai* (Rio de Janeiro, 1969)
S. Cabral: *Pixinguinha: vida e obra* (Rio de Janeiro, 1978)
E. de Alencar: *O fabuloso e harmonioso Pixinguinha* (Rio de Janeiro, 1979)

GERARD BÉHAGUE

Pixis. German family of musicians.

(1) **Friedrich Wilhelm Pixis (i)** (*b* Lambrecht, 17 May 1755; *d* Vienna, 28 Feb 1820). Organist and composer. He moved to Mannheim in 1771, where he probably studied with Georg Joseph Vogler. In 1790 he was appointed church organist and teacher, following his father, Johann Friedrich Pixis (1735–1805), and between 1790 and 1795 he is also believed to have taught at the Mannheim court. From about 1797 he undertook extensive concert tours with his family, throughout Germany and to Scandinavia, St Petersburg and Warsaw, where his two child prodigy sons, (2) Friedrich Wilhelm (ii) and (3) Johann Peter, attracted much attention and became known in musical circles as 'the Pixis brothers'. Towards the end of 1806 he settled in Vienna. Of his compositions, only a small number of piano trios, two sonatinas for piano and two volumes of organ preludes are extant.

(2) **Friedrich Wilhelm Pixis (ii)** (*b* Mannheim, 12 March 1785; *d* Prague, 20 Oct 1842). Violinist and composer, elder son of (1) Friedrich Wilhelm Pixis (i). He studied first with his father, and by the age of seven had attracted attention as a pianist. He soon concentrated on the violin, however, and studied with Heinrich Ritter and Fränzl-Schüler Luci, before his rapid progress led to study with Ignaz Fränzl. After the successful début of both sons at Mannheim, Friedrich playing the violin and his brother the piano, their father took them on tour in 1796. They travelled first to Karlsruhe and Stuttgart, then to Göttingen, Cassel, Brunswick, Celle, Bremen and Hamburg. During their two-month stay in Hamburg in 1798 Friedrich studied with Viotti, who was so impressed that he wrote duets for him. During their tours Friedrich also performed four-hand piano works with his brother. They subsequently visited Hanover, Leipzig, Berlin and Dresden, and then travelled in Poland, Russia and Denmark. After his return to Mannheim Friedrich was a member of the electoral chapel orchestra until 1806, when the family moved to Vienna so that the brothers could finish their musical training and meet the composers who lived there. Pixis gave concerts in Vienna and further studied music theory and compositions with Albrechtsberger. In 1807 he gave acclaimed performances with his brother in Carlsbad and Prague, and became increasingly drawn to the musical life of Prague. In 1808 he directed quartet programmes there, based on the model of Schuppanzigh in Vienna. In 1810 he became professor at the Prague

conservatory, succeeding Heinrich Dionys Weber, and conductor of the theatre orchestra. Pixis was a renowned teacher and is credited as the founder of the Prague violin school. His pupils included Josef Slavík, Raimund Dreyschock, Kalliwoda, Carl Maria von Bocklet, Moritz Mildner, Johann Kra'l and Michael Kolesvovsky. As a composer he was little known except for one violin sonata; he also wrote a violin concerto and variations for violin and orchestra on *War's vielleicht um eins*. Anna, the elder daughter of his first marriage, was a successful pianist in Prague.

(3) **Johann Peter Pixis** (*b* Mannheim, 10 Feb 1788; *d* Baden-Baden, 22 Dec 1874). Pianist and composer, younger son of (1) Friedrich Wilhelm Pixis (i). Like his brother, (2) Friedrich Wilhelm (ii), he was first taught by his father. He became famous as a pianist at a very early age through his concert tour with his brother and the favourable publicity it received. In addition to being an excellent pianist he accompanied his brother on the cello and played the violin. When the brothers returned to Mannheim after their tour Johann Peter also studied composition. During the summer of 1807 in Carlsbad, he began to perform his own compositions, as his brother had done before him. In 1808 he joined his family in Vienna, where both brothers studied with Albrechtsberger and Johann Peter met Beethoven, Meyerbeer and Schubert. Apart from the war years of 1809–12, he lived in Vienna until 1823. In Vienna he was active as a pianist, teacher and composer; he appeared in concert with various violinists, including his brother in 1816 in Prague, Franz Pechatschek in 1817, and Joseph Boehm in 1818 during a tour to Italy. His attempts to establish himself in Vienna as an opera composer (*Almazinde* and *Der Zauberspruch* were performed in the Theater an der Wien in 1820 and 1822 respectively) proved unsuccessful. His greatest success as a pianist and composer came during his second tour with Boehm in 1823, and his reception in Paris in particular persuaded him to move there permanently in October 1824.

In Paris Pixis met Alexander von Humboldt, Heine, Cherubini, Moscheles, Liszt, Halévy, Berlioz and Rossini. He was regarded there as one of the best piano virtuosos and teachers; many of his works were published in Paris. In 1828 he travelled to England with Henriette Sontag, whom he had met in Vienna. By 1834 his career as a composer and virtuoso was coming to an end, and he devoted himself principally to the career of his foster-daughter (4) Francilla Pixis; they went on concert tours together throughout Europe. In 1840 he moved to Baden-Baden, where he had inherited a house in 1834. In Baden-Baden he taught the piano and, from 1846, promoted the career of his nephew (5) Theodor. He remained there for the rest of his life.

At the height of his career (*c*1818 to the early 1830s) Pixis was a pianist of the first rank. Like Moscheles, Czerny and Kalkbrenner, he exploited the increasing technical resources of the instrument, with subtle differentiation of tone colour, a variety of attack and articulation, with contrasts between lyrical *cantabile* and boldly dramatic playing, and between delicacy of touch and fuller orchestral textures. Pixis was commercially aware, and published many works in popular genres of the time, often utilizing a style of piano writing that was brilliant but technically accessible. His works on a larger scale embody some Romantic characteristics, including tonal

flexibility and variety of colour, within a generally conservative formal outline. His Piano Concerto in C op.100 shows the influence of Weber in its instrumentation and of Hummel in its pianistic figuration. Pixis wrote several sets of variations on operatic themes; with Liszt, Thalberg, Henri Herz, Czerny and Chopin he contributed one variation to the *Hexaméron*, a set of variations on a theme from Bellini's *I puritani*. In the 19th century one of Pixis's most frequently performed compositions was the concert rondo op.120, *Les trois clochettes*.

WORKS
for complete list see Pazdírek

OPERAS
Almazinde oder Die Höhle Sesam (3, H. Schmidt), Vienna, April 1820
Der Zauberspruch, Vienna, 1822
Bibiana oder Die Kapelle im Walde (3, L. Lax), Aachen, 8 Oct 1829
Die Sprache des Herzens (J. Lyser), Berlin-Königstadt, 1836

OTHER WORKS
Orch: Sym., C, op.5 (1812); Ov., F (*c*1815); Pf Concertino, E♭, op.68 (*c*1830); Pf Conc., C, op.100 (*c*1830); Fantasie-militaire, E, pf, orch, op.121 (1833); other works, pf, orch
Chbr: Pf Qt, op.4 (1812); 3 Str Qts, A, d, f♯ op.7 (1814); Sovenir de Paris, vn, pf, op.12; Sonata, vn, pf, op.14; Sonata, fl/vn, pf, op.17; Str Qnt, C, op.23 (1817); 8Sonata, G, fl/ob, pf, op.35 (1823), ed. T. Wye (Frankfurt, 1980); 3 Str Qts, F, c, G, op.69 (1824); Grande Sonata concertante, f♯, vn, pf, op.62 (1825); Pf Qnt, d, pf, vn, va, vc, db, op.99 (?1827); Introduction and Rondo, A, fl, pf, op.102 (1829); 8 pf trios, opp.75, 76, 86, 95, 118, 129, 139, 147; other works
2 pf: Rondo hongrois, E, op.33 (?1819); Variations militaire, op.66 [also for 2 pf, orch/str qt]; Variations brillant, D, op.112 (1829) [also for pf 4 hands]
Pf 4 hands: marches, polonaises, waltzes, variations, other works
Pf solo: 4 sonatas: e♭, op.2, E♭, op.3 (1811), c, op.10 (1815), E♭, op.85 (1826); many variation sets on opera themes, folksongs etc.; 1 variation in Hexaméron [with Liszt and others]; rondos, incl. Les trois clochettes, E, op.120 [also for pf, vn/str qt/orch]; polonaises, fantasias, waltzes, écossais, caprices, other dances and character-pieces
1v, pf: German folksongs, other songs

(4) **Francilla Pixis** [Franziska Helma Göhringer] (*b* Lichtenthal in Baden, 15 May 1816; *d* ?1888). Contralto, foster-daughter of (3) Johann Peter Pixis. At the age of 15 she was placed by her family in the care of Johann Peter Pixis, who had recognized her vocal gifts. Pixis was her principal teacher, although she studied further with Josephine Fodor-Mainville, Henriette Sontag, Rossini and Paer. She made her concert début in London in 1833 and her stage début in Karlsruhe the following year, and she undertook extensive concert tours with her foster-father. She received exuberant praise from the *Neue Zeitschrift* and was particularly successful in Naples and Palermo. After her marriage to a Sicilian Count in 1843 she continued to give concerts, but after the birth of her son in 1844 and poor performances during the carnival operas of 1846 in Cremona, she withdrew from the stage. Her voice was powerful and sonorous, free from strain at louder dynamics and, when required, softly beautiful. Among her most renowned roles were Amina (*La sonnambula*), Romeo (*I Capuleti e i Montecchi*), Norma, Rosina (*Il barbiere di Siviglia*) and Gabriella (Mercadante's *Gabriella di Vergy*). Pixis conceived his operetta *Die Sprache des Herzens* for her, and Pacini wrote for her the leading role in his *Saffo* (1840).

(5) **Theodor Pixis** (*b* Prague, 15 April 1831; *d* Cologne, 1 Aug 1856). Violinist, son of (2) Friedrich Wilhelm Pixis (ii) from his second marriage. He studied

the violin first with his father and then at the Prague Conservatory with Moritz Mildner. In 1846–7, while giving concerts in Paris, he met Vieuxtemps, with whom he studied further. He continued to tour successfully, and from 1850 taught at the Rheinische Musikschule in Cologne. According to Ludwig Bischoff, his playing had a pure, noble and full tone, with astonishing confidence in double stopping and grace and tenderness in ornamentation. He was renowned for his memory and sight-reading ability. Always physically weak, he died of a heart attack at the age of 25. His few compositions, including fantasies for violin and piano on opera themes and other popular melodies, remain unpublished.

BIBLIOGRAPHY

FétisB; GerberNL; PadzírekH; SchillingE

'Memoir of John Peter Pixis', *The Harmonicon*, iv (1826), 65–6

Obituary for (2) Friedrich Wilhelm Pixis (ii), *AMZ*, xliv (1842), 969–72

L. Bischoff: 'Theodor Pixis', *Niederrheinische Musik-Zeitung*, iv (1856), 285–7

R. Batka: 'Aus Joh. Peter Pixis Memoiren', *Kranz: gesammelte Blätter über Musik* (Leipzig, 1903), 86–110

H. Engel: *Die Entwicklung des deutschen Klavierkonzertes* (Leipzig, 1927/R)

W. Stoll: 'Die Brüder Pixis', *Mannheimer Geschichtsblätter*, xxix (1928), 82–94

J. Cvermák: *Friedrich Wilhelm Pixis und seine Konzertreisen durch Europa* (diss., U. of Prague, 1950)

R. Sietz, ed.: *Aus Ferdinand Hillers Briefwechsel* (Cologne, 1958–70)

H. Becker, ed.: *Giacomo Meyerbeer: Briefwechsel und Tagebücher* (Berlin, 1960)

C. Suttoni: *Piano and Opera: a Study of the Piano Fantasies Written on Operatic Themes in the Romantic Era* (diss., New York U., 1973)

L. Schiwietz: *Johann Peter Pixis: Beiträge zu seiner Biographie, zur Rezeptionshistoriographie seiner Werke und Analyse seiner Sonatenformung* (Frankfurt, 1994)

L. Schiwietz: 'Die schaurig-schöne Geschichte von den Räubern bei Maria Kulm und die musikdramatischen Ambitionen eines Nicht-nur-Klaviervirtuosen: Johann Peter Pixis's romantische Oper *Bibiana oder Die Kapelle im Walde*', *Die Oper in Böhmen, Mähren und Sudetenschleisen: Regensburg, 1996*, 80–84

GAYNOR G. JONES/LUCIAN SCHIWIETZ,
STEPHAN D. LINDEMAN

Pizarro, Artur (*b* Lisbon, 17 Aug 1968). American pianist of Portuguese birth. He studied with Sequeira Costa in both Lisbon and America and triumphed in the International Vianna da Motta Competition (Lisbon, 1987), the Greater Palm Beach International Competition (Florida, 1988) and in the Leeds International Piano Competition (1990), where his fine tone and effortless command were revealed notably in Chopin's op.25 Etudes. Since making his London début at the Wigmore Hall in 1988, he has given recitals in Japan, Australia and the USA, appeared with many of the world's leading orchestras and conductors and performed a wide variety of chamber music. His enterprising recorded repertory ranges from music by Liszt and Rachmaninoff to Skryabin (the complete mazurkas as well as the Piano Concerto and 24 Preludes op.11), Kabalevsky, Shostakovich, Milhaud, Rodrigo and Voříšek. He has also recorded a two-piano recital of Spanish music with Sequeira Costa.

BRYCE MORRISON

Pizzetti, Ildebrando [Parma, Ildebrando da] (*b* Parma, 20 Sept 1880; *d* Rome, 13 Feb 1968). Italian composer, conductor and critic. He was the most respected and influential of the more conservative Italian musicians of his generation.

1. LIFE.   The son of a piano teacher, Pizzetti spent most of his childhood (from 1884) in Reggio Emilia. While at school there he showed less inclination towards music than towards the theatre, writing plays for casual performance among his schoolmates. In 1895, however, he entered the Parma Conservatory, where he studied under Telesforo Righi, a modest but outstanding teacher of harmony and counterpoint, and gained his composition diploma in 1901. Meanwhile he became conversant with 15th- and 16th-century Italian instrumental and choral music performed and expounded by Giovanni Tebaldini, one of the pioneers of Italian musicology, who directed the conservatory from 1897 and took a personal interest his development. Pizzetti's leanings towards the theatre by no means diminished, and he grew more and more anxious to compose an opera. Various early attempts, mostly unfinished, already showed his preference for heroic subjects, exalted romantic characters and large-scale construction.

In 1905, having read part of the prologue to D'Annunzio's *La nave* (then a work in progress), Pizzetti formed a close friendship with the poet, who invited him to write incidental music for the play as it was completed, and nicknamed him 'Ildebrando da Parma' (a pseudonym which appears on the covers of several of Pizzetti's early published compositions). Their collaboration culminated, in 1909–12, in *Fedra*: D'Annunzio wrote the original spoken version of this tragedy with the idea already in mind of adapting it as a libretto for Pizzetti. Meanwhile the composer, who had lived by giving private lessons and by acting as assistant conductor (1902–4) at the Teatro Regio di Parma, was appointed to teach harmony and counterpoint at the Parma Conservatory (1907) and then at the Istituto Musicale (later Conservatory) of Florence (1908). During this period he published an article in the *Rivista musicale italiana* on his music for *La nave* (xiv, 1907, pp.855–62) and another on Dukas's *Ariane et Barbe-bleue* (xv, 1908, pp.73–111). His years in Florence, where he lived from 1908 until 1924 (becoming the conservatory's director in 1917), were decisive: the city's keen intellectual and cultural life contributed much to his artistic ripening. This was the time of the famous Florentine periodical *La voce* (1908–16), round which gathered many influential Italian philosophers, writers and other artists: Pizzetti became personally associated with De Robertis, Prezzolini, Papini, Soffici, Bastianelli and others, and himself wrote for *La voce*, *Il marzocco* and the newspapers *Il secolo* (Milan) and *La nazione* (Florence). That he was by nature more conservative than some other 'vocians' is, however, shown by his perplexity and disorientation when he attended the première of *The Rite of Spring* in 1913, by the speedy break-up of his collaboration with Bastianelli in editing the anthology–periodical *Dissonanza* (founded in 1914 and discontinued after only three numbers), and by his largely nominal links with Casella's Società Italiana di Musica Moderna (1917–19).

In later life Pizzetti increasingly withdrew from 'advanced' musical circles, until 1932 he joined with Respighi, Zandonai and other reactionaries in signing a notorious manifesto, published in several Italian newspapers, attacking the more forward-looking trends of the time and recommending a return to tradition (he later, at least partly, recanted). Meanwhile he had become director (1924) of the Milan Conservatory, whence he moved in

1. Ildebrando Pizzetti

1936 to Rome to take the advanced composition course at the Accademia di S Cecilia (president, 1947 to 1952; retired 1958). He conducted more often from about 1930 onwards, in the Americas as well as in Europe, and continued also to write music criticism – notably in *La rassegna musicale* (1932–47) and the *Corriere della sera* (from 1953). He remained active well into the 1960s.

2. WORKS.   In Italy critical attention has tended to focus especially on Pizzetti's operas, and it was certainly in that direction that his greatest ambitions lay, although he also wrote much insturmental music and some fine choral works and songs. After the preliminary gropings of his unpublished juvenilia he formulated, about 1908, a basic set of musico-dramatic principles (first alluded to in his article on Dukas' *Ariane et Barbe-bleue* which thereafter, to a greater or lesser degree, conditioned his entire operatic output. The exception is *La sacra rappresentazione di Abram e d'Isaac*, whose uncharacteristically self-contained lyrical 'numbers' reflect the work's origin in incidental music to a play. Otherwise (obviously in extreme reaction against the melodic indulgences of Mascagni and Puccini) all Pizzetti's operas, from *Fedra* to *Clitennestra*, systematically set out to avoid self-sufficient lyricism, except (as in the beautiful 'Trenodia per Ippolito morto' in *Fedra* or Mara's song near the end of Act 1 in *Debora e Jaele*) when choral groups or individuals are actually depicted as singing songs.

The bulk of Pizzetti's operatic vocal writing consists, rather, of a continuous flexible arioso, sensitive to every nuance of the text and governed by the natural rhythms of the Italian language – the 'Pizzettian declamation' which has been the subject of so much Italian critical discussion, favourable and unfavourable. Although the shade of Wagner can sometimes be perceived in the background, the main models for this arioso are non-Germanic: on the one hand Pizzetti was obviously far from indifferent to the methods of *Pelléas et Mélisande*, and, on the other, there are recurrent signs of his sympathy with the Florentine monodists and the recitatives of Monteverdi. The result has a distinctive physiognomy

and can be intensely expressive, despite a serious risk of monotony in the less inspired scenes, notably those where Pizzetti's characters show a weakness for prolonged ethical discussion.

An outstanding feature of most Pizzetti operas (and the main saving grace of some of the weaker ones) is his richly imaginative, often highly dramatic choral writing. The first act of *Debora e Jaele* in particular – taking more than a hint from *Boris Godunov* – brings the chorus right into the foreground as a complex multiple protagonist whose powerful presence tends to dwarf the individual characters. This probably remains the most intense and moving act in any Pizzetti opera, even if the elegiac last act of *Fedra* is of comparable stature in its more restrained, contemplative way. *Fedra* was written to a libretto by D'Annunzio, a shortened version of his play of the same name. The intricate verbosity of the text undeniably gives rise to occasional longueurs. Moreover Pizzetti's orchestral fabric may at times seem grey. Yet it fuses linear chromaticism and modality into an individual synthesis; while the volatile heroine, and her impact on the other characters are powerfully embodied inthe subtly moulded freely declamatory writing.

None of the later dramatic works can quite equal *Debora e Jaele* and *Fedra*, the two major achievements of Pizzetti's early maturity, although the austere, intermittent intense *Lo straniero* is still worthy of attention. So is the more colourful and theatrical effective *Fra Gherado* – though parts of it show clear signs that his operatic methods were degenerating into routine. By the 1930s

2. Sacrifice of the beautiful slave girl from Pizzetti's 'Fedra', finale of Act 1, La Scala, Milan, 1915, with Salomea Krusceniski as Phaedra: design by I. Bompard from 'L'illustrazione italiana' (28 March 1915)

Pizzetti had become so hidebound by his own theories and his lack of stylistic self-renewal that the imaginative tension of his operas was being seriously undermined. Only after the war did the situation show signs of improving again, notably in the better – especially (once again) choral – parts of *Ifigeuia*, *Assassinio nella cattedrale* and to a lesser extent *La figlia di Iorio*. This partial recovery was undoubtedly helped by happy choices of subjects and texts. Nowhere is this more the case than in *Assassinio* for T.S. Eliot's great play, upon which the work is based, contained several elements that were likely to bring out the best in Pizzetti: plentiful choruses; a central character tormented by moral dilemmas; ethical discourses controlled by a literary talent greater than the composer's own elevated atmosphere in a religious context. The opera has been highly successful in Italy, and has had some currency abroad.

Immediately after Pizzetti's operas in order of importance stand his choral works and other vocal compositions, which may, indeed, in the long run prove more durable, though obviously less ambitious. His studies of Renaissance polyphony had made him conscious, from his student days, of the rich expressive possibilities inherent in pure vocal counterpoint; these he explored in an important series of pieces for unaccompanied voices, ranging from the beautiful choruses in the music for *La nave* to the *Due composizioni corali* of 1961. The free re-creation of Renaissance styles in 20th-century terms, seen in these pieces, sometimes shows striking parallels with the more archaic aspects of Vaughan Williams; it is significant that the fine *Messa di requiem* is almost exactly contemporary with the English composer's G minor Mass, which it in some ways resembles. In Pizzetti's songs, too, it is possible to detect archaic influences, interacting with others of later origin (here too Musorgsky and Debussy were among his main recent models). The structures, without being strophic, are nevertheless unified, in many of the best songs, by a recurrent germinal phrase round which the music has taken shape. Good examples of the kind range from the early *I pastori*, one of Pizzetti's freshest and most justly popular creations, to the *Due poesie di Ungaretti* and the best of the *Altre cinque liriche*.

As he grew towards maturity, a more dramatic conception became discernible in some of his more elaborate songs, a culminating point being reached in the *Due liriche drammatiche napolitane*, in which the operatic methods of *Debora* are foreshadowed in miniature. Moreover, a similar evolution is evident even in his instrumental music, from the frankly lyrical outlook of the First String Quartet and the *Tre pezzi* for piano (closely akin, in their expressive worlds, to *I pastori*) to the far more dramatically conceived Violin and Cello Sonatas, with a return to a more lyrico-dramatic manner in the Trio in A and the Second String Quartet. Noteworthy in these instrumental works is the vocal nature of many of the themes, some of which seem to suggest a sung text: this is strikingly the case in the slow movement ('Preghiera per gl'innocenti') of the Violin Sonata, one of the most nobly expressive movements in the violin and piano literature. Despite the promise of the three early preludes *Per l'Edipo re di Sofocle*, in which the composer's personal voice is already clearly audible, Pizzetti's orchestral music does not, on the whole, reveal him at his best. Nevertheless the colourful incidental music for D'Annunzio's *La pisanelle* (best known now

through the popular concert suite) reveals that the rather grey, drab orchestral palette of so many of his other works, including most of the operas, was the result of deliberate choice rather than inability to do otherwise.

WORKS

OPERAS

Sabina (1, A. Beggi), 1897, unperf., destroyed
Romeo e Giulietta (1, Pizzetti, after W. Shakespeare), 1899–1900, unperf., destroyed apart from 3rd orch int
Il Cid (2, Beggi, after P. Corneille and G. de Castro y Bellvis), unpef., destroyed
Lena (Beggi), 1904 [unrealized project]
Aeneas (prol., 3, Beggi), 1904–7 [sketches only]
Fedra (1, Pizzetti and M. Silvani, after Euripides), 1907–8, inc., unpubd

DRAMATIC

Fedra (3, G. D'Annunzio, after Euripides and Senera), 1909–12, Milan, Scala, 20 March 1915
Gigliola (3, after D'Annunzio: *La fiaccola sotto il moggio*), 1914–15, inc., unpubd
Debora e Jaele (3, Pizzetti, after Bible: *Judges*), 1915–21; Milan, Scala, 16 Dec 1922
La sacra rappresentazione di Abram e d'Isaac (1, O. Castellino, after F. Belcare), 1917–28, Perugia, Morlacchi, 2 Oct 1937 [based on incid music, 1915–17]
Lo straniero (2, Pizzetti), 1922–5, Rome, Opera, 29 April 1930
Fra Gherardo (3, Pizzetti), 1925–7, Milan, Scala, 16 May 1928
Orsèolo (3, Pizzetti), 1928–3; Florence, Comunale, 4 May 1935
L'oro (3, Pizzetti), 1937–42, Milan, Scala, 2 Jan 1947
Vanna Lupa (3, Pizzetti), 1943–7, Florence, Comunale, 4 May 1949, unpubd
Ifigenia (op, 1, Pizzetti and A. Perrini), 1950, RAI, 3 Oct 1950; staged Florence, Comunale, 19 May 1951
Cagliostro (radio op, 1, Pizzetti), RAI, 5 Nov 1952; staged Milan, Scala, 24 Jan 1953, unpubd
La figlia di Iorio (3, D'Annunzio, abridged Pizzetti), 1953–4, Naples, S Carlo, 4 Dec 1954
Povere gente (1, Pizzetti), 1955–6, inc., unpubd
Assassinio nella cattedrale (int, T.S. Eliot, trans. A. Castaldi, abridged Pizzetti), 1957, Milan, Scala, 1 March 1958
Il calzare d'argento (2, R. Bacchelli), Milan, Scala, 23 March 1961
Clitennestra (2, Pizzetti), 1961–4, Milan, Scala, 1 March 1965

INCIDENTAL MUSIC

La nave (G. D'Annunzio), 1905–7, Rome, Teatro Argentina, March 1908
La pisanelle (D'Annunzio), Paris, Châtelet, 11 June 1913
La sacra rappresentazione di Abram e d'Isaac (F. Belcare), 1915–17, Florence, Politeama, June 1917; 2nd version 1926, Turin, Nuovo, 11 March 1926
Agamennone (Aeschylus); Syracuse, Teatro greco, 28 April 1930, unpubd except for Introduzione
Le trachinie (Sophocles), 1932, Syracuse, Teatro greco, 26 April 1933, unpubd
La rappresentazione di S Uliva (C. d'Errico); Florence, cloisters of S Croce, 5 June 1933
Edipo a Colono (Sophocles), Syracuse, Teatro Greco, 24 April 1936, unpubd
La festa delle Panatenee (Homer, Sophocles, and others), 1935, Paestum, among temples, June 1936, pubd only in part
Film scores

ORCHESTRAL

Some juvenilia, unpubd
Per l'Edipo re di Sofocle, 3 orch preludes, 1903; Ouverture per una farsa tragica, 1911, unpubd; Poema emiliano, vn, orch, 1914, unpubd; La pisanelle, suite, 1917 [from incid music, 1913]; Conc. dell'estate, 1928; Rondò veneziano, 1929; L'ultima caccia di S Uberto, orch, opt. chorus, 1930; Canti della stagione alta, pf, orch, 1930; Vc Conc., C, 1933–4; Sym., A, 1940; Vn Conc., A, 1944; Canzone dei beni perduti, 1948; Preludio a un altro giorno, 1952; Hp Conc., Bb, 1958–60; Aria, augurio nuziale, unison vns, orch (1960), arr. vn, pf

VOCAL-ORCHESTRAL

2 liriche drammatiche napolitane (S. Giacomo), T, orch, 1916–18 [only vs pubd]; Introduzione all'Agamennonoe, chorus, orch, 1931 [from incid music, 1930]; 2 inni greci (Homer, Sophocles), S,

chorus, orch (1937) [from incid music La festa delle Panatenee, 1935]; Epithalamium (cant., Catullus), solo vv, chorus, orch, 1939; Oritur sol et occidit, cant., B, orch, 1943, unpubd; Cantico di gloria 'Attollite portas', 3 choruses, 22 wind, 2 pf, pec, 1948; Vanitas vanitatum (cant., Bible: *Ecclesiastes*), solo vv, male chorus, 1959; Filiae Jerusalem, adjoro vos (cant., Song of Songs), S, female chorus, orch (1966); see also ORCHESTRAL [L'ultima caccia di S Uberto]

OTHER VOCAL WORKS

Juvenilia, unpubd except for 3 small choral pieces (1897)
Choral: 2 canzoni corali (Gk. trad., trans. N. Tommaseo), chorus, 1913; Canto d'amore (Gk. trad., trans. Tommaseo), male vv, 1914, pubd in *Almanacco della 'Voce'* (Florence, 1915), 146f; Lamento (P. Shelley), T, chorus, 1920, unpubd; Messa di requiem, chorus, 1922; De profundis, chorus, 1937; 3 composizioni corali, chorus, 1942–3; 2 composizioni corali (Sappho, trans. M. Valgimiglia), chorus, 1961
1v, pf: Epitaphe (V. Hugo), 1903; 3 liriche (I. Cocconi), 1904; Sera d'inverno (M. Silvani), 1906; 5 liriche: I pastori (D'Annunzio), 1908, orchd, La madre al figlio lontano (R. Pantini), 1910, S Basilio (Gk. trad., trans. Tommaseo), 1912, Il clefta prigione (Gk.trad., trans.Tommaseo), 1912, Passeggiata (G. Papini), 1915; Erotica (D'Annunzio), 1911; 2 liriche drammatiche napolitane (di Giacomo), 1916–18 [version of vocal-orch work]; 2 Antiphons (Song of Songs), 1918, unpubd; My Cry (G. Dalliba), 1919, unpubd; 3 sonetti del Petrarca, 1922; Vocalise-étude (1929); Altre 5 liriche, 1932–3: Adjuro vos, Oscuro è il ciel [also orchd], 3 canti greci; E il mio dolore io canto (J. Bocchialini), 1940; 3 liriche, 1944, arr. 1v, small orch; Vocalizzo, Mez, pf, 1957, rev. Mez, orch (1960); 3 canti d'amore, 1960
Other works: 3 canzoni (It. trad.), 1v, str qt/str orch, 1926; 2 poesie di Ungaretti, Bar, pf trio, 1935–6

CHAMBER

Juvenilia, almost all unpubd
Aria, D, vn, pf, 1906; Str Qt, A, 1906; Sonata, A, vn, pf, 1918–19; Sonata, F, vc, pf, 1921; 3 canti, vc/vn, pf, 1924; Pf Trio, A, 1925; Str Qt, D, 1932–3; Colloquio, vn, pf (1949)
Pf: Foglio d'album, 1906; Poemetto romantico, 1909; 3 pezzi 'Da un autunno già lontano', 1911; Sonata, 1942; Canti di ricordanza, 1943 [variations on a theme from op Fra Gherardo]
Principal publishers: Chester, Curci, Forlivesi, Pizzi, Ricordi, Sonzogno, Suvini Zerboni

WRITINGS

'La musica per *La nave* di Gabriele d'Annunzio', *RMI*, xiv (1907), 855–62
'Ariane et Barbebleue', *RMI*, xv (1908), 73–112
La musica dei greci (Rome, 1914)
Musicisti contemporanei: saggi critici (Milan, 1914)
Intermezzi critici (Florence, 1921)
'Questa nostra musica', *Pan*, i (1933–4), 321
Niccolò Paganini (Turin, 1940)
Musica e dramma (Rome, 1945)
La musica italiana dell'Ottocento (Turin, 1947)

BIBLIOGRAPHY
MONOGRAPHS AND COLLECTIONS OF ESSAYS

Thompson9
R. Fondi: *Ildebrando Pizzetti e il dramma musicale italiano d'oggi* (Rome, 1919)

Il pianoforte, ii (1921), 225–53 [special Pizzetti number]
G.M. Gatti: '*Débora e Jaèle* di I. Pizzetti: guida attraverso il poema e la musica*(Milan, 1922)
M. Pilati: *Fra Gherardo di Ildebrando Pizzetti* (Milan, 1928) [incl. work-list and bibliography, both repr. in *Bollettino bibliografico musicale*, iii/5 (Milan, 1928), 5, 11]
M. Rinaldi: *L'arte di Ildebrando Pizzetti e 'Lo straniero'* (Rome, 1930)
G. Tebaldini: *Ildebrando Pizzetti nelle memorie* (Parma, 1931)
A. Damerini and others: *Parma a Ildebrando Pizzetti* (Parma, 1932)
G.M. Gatti: *Ildebrando Pizzetti* (Turin, 1934, 2/1955; Eng. trans., 1951/R)
M. Pilati: *L'Orséolo di Ildebrando Pizzetti* (Milan, 1935)
G. Gavazzeni: *Tre studi su Pizzetti* (Como, 1937)
Rassegna dorica, xi (1939–40), 133–72 [Pizzetti number]
RaM, xiii (1940) [Pizzetti number]
M. Rinaldi: '*Lo straniero di Ildebrando Pizzetti* (Florence, 1943)

G. Gavazzeni: *Ildebrando Pizzetti: 'L'oro, guida dell'opera con due saggi critici*(Milan, 1946)
V. Bucchi, L. Dallapiccola and others: *Firenze a Ildebrando Pizzetti* (Florence, 1947)
Fiera letteraria, v/40 (1950) [Pizzettj number]
G. Gavazzeni: *Altri studi pizzettiani* (Bergamo, 1956)
M. la Morgia, ed.: *La città dannunziana a Ildebrando Pizzetti* (Pescara, 1958)
Approdo musicale, no.21 (1966) [Pizzetti number]
Musica moderna, i (1967) [Pizzetti number]
B. Pizzetti, ed.: *Ildebrando Pizzetti: cronologia e bibliografia* (Parma, 1980)
G.N. Vetro, ed.: *Omaggio a Ildebrando Pizzetti nel centenario della nascità* (Parma, 1980)

SPECIFIC WORKS
operas

A. della Corte: 'Ildebrando Pizzetti e la *Fedra*', *Rivista d'Italia*, xviii/i (1915), 558–70
G. Barini: *Fedra di Gabriele d'Annunzio e Ildebrando Pizzetti*', *Nuova antologia*, cclx (1915), 652 61, 664
D. Sincero: 'La première di Fedra alla Scala', *RMI*, xxii (1915), 319–26
L. Pagano: '*Debora e Jaele* di Ildebrando Pizzetti',*RMI*, xxx (1923), 47–108; repr. in L. Pagano, *La fionda di David* (Turin, 1928), 79–155
G.M. Gatti: 'L'opera drammatica di Ildebrando Pizzetti', *Il pianoforte*, vii (1926), 227–41
F. Brusa: '*Fra Gherardo* di Ildebrando Pizzetti', *RMI*, xxxv (1928), 386–441
A. Lualdi: '*Débora e Jaèle* di I. Pizzetti alla Scala', '*Abramo e Isacco* di Feo Belcari con musiche di I. Pizzetti al Teatro di Torino', *Serate musicali* (Milan, 1928), 3–12, 222–30
A. Bonaccorsi: '*Lo straniero* di Ildebrando Pizzetti', *RMI*, xxxviii (1931), 429–36
M. Rinaldi: 'Il valore della *Fedra* di d'Annunzio nel dramma di Pizzetti', *Rassegna dorica*, viii (1936–7), 2–17
L. Tomelleri: 'Fedra: D'Annunzio e Pizzetti', in A. Casella and others: *Gabriele d'Annunzio e la musica* (Milan, 1939), 47–53; repr. in *RMI*, xliii (1939), 207–13
G. Confalonieri: '*Orséolo* di Ildebrando Pizzetti', *Bruciar le ali alla musica* (Milan, 1945), 153–8
G. Barblan: '*L'oro*, ultima opera di Pizzetti alla Scala',*RMI*, xlix (1947), 57–68
G. Gavazzeni: 'Commenti alla *Debora e Jaele* di Pizzetti', *La musica e il teatro*(Pisa, 1954), 83–135
M. Mila: 'Ascoltando *La figlia di Iorio* di Pizzetti', *RaM*, xxv (1955), 103–7; repr. in *RaM*, xxxii (1962), 264–9
M. Mila: 'L'assassinio nella cattedrale', *Cronache musicali 1955–1959* (Turin, 1959), 163–6
M. Mila: 'L'*Ifigenia* di Pizzetti', *Cronache musicali 1955–1959* (Turin, 1959), 167–9
A. Porter: 'Coventry and London: Murder in the Cathedral', *MT*, ciii (1962), 544–5
P. Santi: 'Il mondo della *Debora*', *RaM*, xxxii (1962), 151–68
E. Paratore: 'Introduzione a *La figlia di Iorio* di Pizzetti', *Studi dannunziani* (Naples, 1966), 331–7
J. Maehder: 'Die Italienische Oper des 'Fin de siécle' als Spiegel politischer Strömungen im Ubertinischen Italien', *Der schöne Abglanz: Stationen der Operngeschichte*, ed. U. Bermbach and W. Konold (Berlin, 1992), 181–210

other works

G.M. Gatti: 'Le liriche di Ildebrando Pizzetti', *RMI*, xxvi (1919), 192–206
M. Castelnuovo-Tedesco: '*La pisanella* d'Ildebrando Pizzetti', *Critica musicale*, ii (1919), 15–7
M. Castelnuovo-Tedesco: 'La sonata per violino e pianoforte di Ildebrando Pizzetti', *Il pianoforte*, i/7 (1920), 1–5
H. Antcliffe: 'Pizzetti as Song-Writer', *The Chesterian*, no.20 (1922), 108–11
H. Antcliffe: 'Pizzetti's Sonata for 'Cello', *MO*, xlvi (1922–3), 147–54
L. Tomelleri: 'La pisanelle ou de la mort parfumèe: D'Annunzio e Pizzetti', in A. Casella and others: *Gabriele d'Annunzio e la musica*(Milan, 1939), 63; also in *RMI*, xliii (1939), 223–33
M. Rinaldi: 'L'*Epithalamium* d'Ildebrando Pizzetti', *Musica d'oggi*, xxii (1940), 221

G. Gavazzeni: 'La sinfonia di Pizzetti', *Musica d'oggi*, xxiii (1941), 291

G. Gavazzeni: 'Tre recenti pagine corali di Pizzetti', *RaM*, xvii (1947), 53–74

B. Rondi: 'I cori di Pizzetti', *La musica contemporanea*, ed. D. de Pauli (Rome, 1952), 80

G. Gavazzeni: 'La musica di scena di Pizzetti', *La musica e il teatro* (Pisa, 1954), 139–86

M. Mila: 'La messa di Pizzetti', *Cronache musicali 1955–1959* (Turin, 1959), 160

OTHER STUDIES

R. Giani: 'Note marginali agli *Intermezzi critici* di Ildebrando Pizzetti', *RMI*, xxviii (1921), 677–90

G.M. Gatti: 'Ildebrando Pizzetti', *MQ*, ix (1923), 96–121, 271–86

G. Rossi-Doria: 'Ildebrando Pizzetti', *Musikblätter des Anbruch*, vii (1925), 413

G.M. Gatti: 'Portrait spirituel de Pizzetti', *ReM*, viii/3–5 (1926–7), 26–35

M. Rinaldi: 'Ildebrando Pizzetti, poeta', *Musica d'oggi*, xiv (1932), 245–57, 293–8

M. Rinaldi: 'Una profetica esaltazione dannunziana dell'arte di Ildebrando Pizzetti', *Rivista nazionale di musica*, xv (Rome, 1934), 2043–9

M. Castelnuovo-Tedesco: 'Ildebrando Pizzetti', *The Book of Modern Composers*, ed. D. Ewen (New York, 1942; 2/1950, 3/1961 as *The New Book of Modern Composers*)

M. Rinaldi: 'Pizzetti, direttore d'orchestra', *Mondo musicale*, i/9 (1945), 1

G. Gavazzeni: 'Pizzetti e i "vociani"', *La Scala*, no.8 (1950), 15–18

G. Gavazzeni: *Musicisti d'Europa* (Milan, 1954), 130ff

F. D'Amico: 'I due Ildebrandi', *I casi della musica* (Milan, 1962), 71

G. Gavazzeni: 'Pizzetti dopo la morte', *NRMI*, ii (1968), 701–9

J.C.G. Waterhouse: *The Emergence of Modern Italian Music (up to 1940)* (diss., U. of Oxford, 1968), esp. 251–307

L. Gherardi: 'Riscoperta del Medio Evo negli studi letterari e ricerca musicale, tre esiti: Respighi, Pizzetti, Dallapiccola', *Chigiana*, new ser., xvii (1980), 35–50

P. Santi: 'La funzione idealogica del modalismo Pizzettiano', ibid., 81–104

C. Orselli: 'Primo incontro di Pizzetti con l'estetismo dannunziano: le musiche per La nave', *Chigiana*, new ser., xvii (1980), 51–62

M.G. Accorsi: 'Fra Bacchelli e Pizzetti: "Devriansi i giullari molto amare, bramo gioia ed amano il cantare"', *RIM*, xxiv (1989), 131–52

J.C.G. Waterhouse: 'Pizzetti in Perspective', *Musica senza aggettivi: studi per Fedele D'Amico*, ii (Florence, 1991), 663–74

C. Piccardi: 'Ildebrando Pizzetti et le néo-madrigalisme italien', *Dissonanz*, no.32 (1992), 17–25

GUIDO M. GATTI, JOHN C.G. WATERHOUSE

Pizzi, Emilio (*b* Verona, 1 Feb 1861; *d* Milan, between 19 and 28 Nov 1940). Italian composer. Some sources state that he was born in February 1862. He began his studies in 1869 at the Istituto Musicale in Bergamo; he then studied at the Milan Conservatory (1881–4) under Bazzini and Ponchielli before working in London (1884–97, and from 1900). From 1897 to 1900 he was in Bergamo as *maestro di cappella* at S Maria Maggiore and director of the Istituto; in later life he returned to Italy, eventually retiring to a rest home in Milan.

Pizzi's operas were performed throughout Europe, and one, *Gabriella* (1893), commissioned for Adelina Patti, opened in Boston. His musical style was excessively eclectic. *The Bric-a-brac Will* (1895, London) was a comedy-drama in the popular Gilbert and Sullivan manner; *La Rosalba* (1899, Turin), to a libretto of Luigi Illica, had Puccini-like melodies; and *La vendetta* (1906, Cologne) was a Corsican tragedy of the *verismo* type, with musical rhetoric to match. His chamber music was very popular, particularly the *romanze*; the style is simple and clear, almost trivial. The sacred works are less important; his *Ultimo canto* won sixth prize at the Steiner contest in Vienna (1896).

MARVIN TARTAK

Pizzicato (It.). A direction to pluck the string(s) of a (generally bowed) instrument with the fingers. It is normally abbreviated 'pizz.'. In Tobias Hume's *The First Part of Ayres* (1605) instruction is given in 'The Souldiers Song' to 'Play three letters with your Fingers', and in 'Harke, Harke' to 'Play nine letters with your finger'. Another early indication is found in Monteverdi's *Combattimento di Tancredi e Clorinda* (1624), in which the players are asked to put the bow aside and 'pluck the strings with two finger'. Heinrich Biber, in the string accompaniment to the 'Nightwatchman's Call' (1673), writes 'Testudine: ohne Bogen'. 'Testudine' (It. *testuggine*: 'tortoise') can also mean the shields used by soldiers in battle: perhaps Biber wanted to imitate the sounds of clashing shields. He also called for what can be interpreted as a snap pizzicato in the violone part of the Battalia. He says that the string must not be struck by the bow but plucked strongly by the right hand, probably imitating a cannon shot. Other early examples require that, for example, the violin be put under the right arm and plucked like a guitar (Carlo Farina: *Capriccio stravagante*, 1627) or that the player play 'senz'arco' with 'the tip of the finger' (J.J. Walther: 'Capriccio X', *Hortulus chelicus*, 1688). In *Musick's Recreation on the Viol, Lyra-Way* (3/1669) John Playford said that plucking with the left hand is called the THUMP. Leopold Mozart (*Versuch einer gründlichen Violinschule*, 1756) devoted a long paragraph to defining pizzicato and explaining how it is to be played, and wrote that 'the strings are plucked with the index-finger or with the thumb of the right hand'; the thumb should be used only when 'whole chords are to be taken in one'.

In orchestral music, pizzicato was relatively uncommon before the Classical era, though Bach frequently used it to accompany the voice or to accompany a solo instrument in concerto slow movements. There are many examples of it in Haydn's symphonies and other music of the Classical era, and composers naturally came to use it in operas to imitate a plucked instrument, for example Mozart in *Die Entführung aus dem Serail* (Pedrillo's 'Im Mohrenland', to imitate his guitar) or in *Don Giovanni* to represent the serenade ('Deh vieni alla finestra'). Its truly dramatic use in orchestral music, however, had to await the age of Beethoven; notable examples are the passage linking the third and fourth movements of his Symphony no.5 or the concluding pages of the Allegretto of his Symphony no.7. Particularly striking later uses of pizzicato in orchestral music must include the Scherzo of Tchaikovsky's Fourth Symphony, where the strings are exclusively pizzicato, and the thrummed pizzicato accompaniment to the cadenza in Elgar's Violin Concerto.

Paganini was the first composer to make extensive use of left-hand pizzicato (usually indicated by a +); he asked for it either simultaneously or in alternation with bowed notes (e.g. in the 24th Caprice). In their cello and violin methods, Jean-Louis Duport (*Essai sur le doigté du violoncelle*, 1806) and Baillot (*L'art du violon*, 1834) wrote of both left- and right-hand pizzicato, as did Galamian in his method (*Contemporary Violin Technique*, 1962). Extensive use was made of both in early 20th-century music, including Bartók's striking use of pizzicato slides and a hard pizzicato in which a string is snapped back onto the fingerboard, a device indicated by the sign: ↿

Brahms, in his Cello Sonata op.99 (4th movement, bars 128ff) asked for a slurred pizzicato, which is achieved by stopping a string firmly with the left-hand finger (or leaving it open), plucking that string with the right hand and then removing or putting down another finger on the same string. The two notes are thus successively produced, but both must be within the compass of the player's hand or a slide effect would result. Multiple stop pizzicatos are normally played from the bottom string to the top, though in some cases, for example where there are repeated chords (as in Bartók's *Music for Strings, Percussion and Celesta*), alternate bottom-to-top and top-to-bottom may be indicated, usually by upward and downward arrows (though the signs for up- and down-bow have occasionally been used for this).

In jazz and dance-band music of the 20th century, the double bass part is often pizzicato throughout, sometimes requiring such techniques as 'slapping' the string. Other special pizzicato effects used in 20th-century music include plucking with the fingernail, to produce a rather sharp sound, or plucking close to the bridge which produces a dry sound lacking in resonance.

See also VIOLIN, §I, 5(iii)(f) and, for the use of the term as applied to guitar playing, PUNTEADO.

SONYA MONOSOFF/R

Pizzini, Carlo Alberto (*b* Rome, 22 March 1905; *d* Rome, 9 Sept 1981). Italian composer and conductor. He studied in Rome with Dobici and Respighi, and took his diploma in composition at the Bologna Conservatory in 1929. In 1931 he took the postgraduate course in composition at the Accademia di S Cecilia in Rome with Respighi, and won the prize of the Ministero della Pubblica Istruzione as his best pupil. He worked as a musical administrator and was musical inspector at the Società Italiana degli Autori ed Editori; from 1938 onwards, he was employed by the RAI, where he was involved in exchanges with foreign countries and was head of the inspectorate of orchestras and choruses. At the same time he pursued an active career as a conductor both in Italy and abroad. He was a member of the Accademia Filarmonica di Bologna.

As a composer, Pizzini demonstrates a clear dependence on the stylistic model of Respighi, revealed in his harmonic language, a propensity for descriptive and richly coloured instrumental forms, and a broad, fluid melodic manner. The symphonic poem inspired by nature is the genre he found most congenial, and the one he turned to most frequently after an initial interest in neo-classical chamber works. He also wrote incidental music, and music for radio, television and film.

WORKS
(selective list)

Stage: Dardanio (fiaba teatrale, 3, E. Curto), Rome, 1928
Orch: Sarabanda, omaggio a Corelli, str, 1930; Sinfonia, c, 1930; Il poema delle Dolomiti, sym. poem, 1931; Strapaese, impressioni dal vero, 1932; Al Piemonte, sym. triptych, 1940; Grotte di Postumia, variations, 1941; Ouverture tascabile, 1959; In Te, Domine, speravi, sym. fresco, 1962; Concierto para tres hermanas, gui, orch, 1969
Other inst: Sonata, c, pf, 1927; Sonata, a, vc, pf, 1928; Sarabanda e fuga, str qt, 1929
Pf works, choral works, songs

ANTONIO TRUDU

Pizzoni, Giovanni. See PICCIONI, GIOVANNI.

Pizzuto, Filippo (*b* Valletta, Malta, 29 Jan 1704; *d* ?Italy, after 1740). Maltese composer and singer. At the age of nine his singing and musical ability won him the salaried position of 'diacono di mezza tavola' at the conventual church of the Order of St John, Valletta. Seven years later he was in Naples studying at the Conservatorio di S Onofrio with Porpora, Ignazio Prota and Francesco Feo. When Pizzuto returned to Malta in April 1728 he joined St John's prestigious *cappella di musica* as a tenor and composed at least three Calendimaggio cantatas: *Il promoteo*, 1734, *La virtù in gara*, 1735, and *Dialogo musicale*, 1737. These are his only known works, and although only the texts survive (in Valletta, National Library of Malta) they indicate a significant talent since only leading composers were selected to compose the annual cantata for performance on the eve of Mayday, solemnly ritualized by the Order throughout the 18th century. Around 1740 Pizzuto left Malta, probably for Italy, but nothing more is known about him.

BIBLIOGRAPHY
V. Laurenza: 'Calendimaggio settecentesco a Malta', *Archivum melitense*, ii (1913–14), 187-203
J. Vella Bondin: 'Maltese Composers of Calendimaggio Cantatas: Fra Filippo Pizzuto', *Sunday Times*, [Malta, 15 May 1994], 28–9

JOSEPH VELLA BONDIN

Pla (Agustín). Spanish or Catalan family of oboists and composers. There is some confusion about the precise authorship of their works, as in the sources the first name is rarely specified. About 70 works survive, but if lost works (mentioned in concert notices and catalogues) are taken into account the total would probably surpass 100. Works that were published include five sets of sonatas (1 for 2 fl/vn/ob, hpd/vc (London, 1754); 1 for 2 vn/ob/fl/p-ardessus de viole, b (Paris, 1759); 1 for 2 ob/vn/fl, b (London, ?1770); 1 for 2 fl/vn, b (London, ?1770); 1 for 2 fl/vn (London, ?1770)), a set of six duets (2 vn (London, ?1773)), and a concerto (2 fl/ob, orch (London, n.d.)); manuscript works are to be found in various European locations (*CH-E, Zz; D-KA, Rtt; E-Mm, Mn*, Aránzazu Monastery; *H-KE; I-CDO, Gl, Mc, PS, TRa*, Udine, Count Federico Ricardi's private collection; *S-Skma*). Almost all the extant instrumental works found outside Spain are in sources attributed, with spelling variants, to 'Sig.ʳ Pla' or 'Sig.ʳˢ Pla's'; in the latter cases (1) Juan Bautista Pla and (3) José Pla may have been joint composers. 19th-century attribution of some manuscript works specifically to Juan or José is probably hypothetical. Attributing and dating of the works is further complicated by Juan and José's frequent re-use of material: they would insert old movements into new sonatas, combine movements from existing works to form new pieces, rework old themes, and adapt concertos for performance as sonatas and vice versa. They may also have borrowed from (2) Manuel Pla's compositions. As regards orchestral and vocal music by 'Pla' in Spanish manuscript sources, other than those cited above, attribution is even more hazardous, as other 18th-century musicians with this surname are recorded in Spain.

Generally the Plas' instrumental works are in the italianate *galant* style of the period, with transitional elements. Structural weaknesses are offset by melodic charm and vivacity. A solo sonata and various concertos preserved in manuscript were obviously written for virtuoso players, whereas most of the printed works are suitable for amateurs. Performances, reprints and manuscripts dating from the 1770s, 80s and even as late as the early 19th century, particularly in England and Germany, testify to the music's continued popularity.

(1) **Juan Bautista** [Joan Baptista] **Pla** (*fl* 1747–73). Probably the eldest of the three Pla brothers, he was a member of the Royal Guards band and played in Madrid court opera productions before travelling abroad. He was at the Portuguese court between 1747 and 1751, in Paris from 1751 to 1752, and in London from 1753 to 1754. From 1754 to 1767 he is recorded as being at the Duke of Württemberg's court, with visits to Italy and Paris in 1762–3. By 1769 he was back in London, and from 1769 to 1773 he was bassoonist at the Portuguese court. He was greatly attached to his younger brother (3) José Pla, who accompanied him abroad and played in concerts with him. The sweetness and brilliance of their playing, their precision and empathy, were highly praised wherever they went. Juan was also a virtuoso salterio player. His compositions include five sonatas (in *I-Gl*), two concertos and at least one Italian aria (mentioned in *Mercure* de France, May 1752 and Dec 1763).

(2) **Manuel Pla** (*b* Torquemada; *d* ?Madrid, 13 Sept 1766). Brother of (1) Juan Bautista Pla. He appears to have spent all his life in Spain. He was an instrumentalist in the Royal Halberdiers band and at Descalzas Reales, Madrid. He played in some court opera performances and deputized in the royal chapel. José Teixidor considered that Manuel, who was also an excellent keyboard player, was more proficient than his brothers as an oboist and composer. He listed among his works 'sinfonías, conciertos, tríos, duetos; salmos, misas, Salve Regina, Stabat Mater; zarzuelas, serenatas, oratorios sacros, villancicos, tonadillas, arias, cantadas y tríos en español', and stated that he set the main scenes of Metastasio's operas and wrote some complete stage works, both serious and comic. Manuscript music survives (in *E-Mn*) for religious plays and for entr'acte pieces composed by M. Pla or Sr Plà. These works, dated between 1757 and 1762, may all be safely attributed to Manuel. The vocal material is workmanlike and typical of its milieu. His six violin duets enjoyed popularity beyond his native country; sources survive in Switzerland, Italy, England and Spain.

(3) **José Pla** (*b* 1728; *d* Stuttgart, 14 Dec 1762). Brother of (1) Juan Bautista Pla. He was younger than Juan, contrary to information published by and reproduced in later biographies. When only 16 years of age he played in a Madrid court opera production. He performed in 1751–2 with Juan at the Concert Spirituel and at court in Paris, where he also played the violin, and in 1753–4 in London. He then returned to Spain for a few years during which he occasionally deputized in the royal chapel. In 1759 he rejoined Juan in Germany, where he died three years later after returning from a visit to Italy. He composed both instrumental and vocal works, and a *Stabat mater* (1756) that can be attributed to him is still extant (in Aránzazu Monastery, Spain).

BIBLIOGRAPHY

GerberL
J. Sittard: *Zur Geschichte der Musik und des Theaters am Württembergischen Hofe*, ii (Stuttgart, 1891/R)
J. Subirá: 'Les produccions teatrals del compositor català Manuel Pla', *Revista musical catalana*, xxx (1933), 353–61

E. Moreno: 'La primera, hasta ahora desconocida, sonata para oboe y bajo continuo española? La sonata de Pla', *RdMc*, ix (1986), 561–75
J. Dolcet: 'L'obra dels germans Pla. Bases per a una catalogació', *AnM*, xlii (1987), 131–88
B. Kenyon de Pascual: *Dos tríos de Pla* (Madrid, 1987) [Introduction and transcr.]
B. Kenyon de Pascual: 'Juan Bautista Pla and José Pla: Two Neglected Oboe Virtuosi of the 18th Century', *EMc*, xviii (1990), 109–10
J. Dolcet: 'Katalonische Oboenvirtuosen am Hof Karl Eugens von Württemberg: Die Brüder Pla', *Tibia*, xvii/1 (1992), 32–7

BERYL KENYON DE PASCUAL

Placker, Christiaan de (*b* Poperinge, nr Ypres, 19 June 1613; *d* Antwerp, 20 Jan 1691). Flemish poet and composer. He entered the Jesuit order as a novice at Mechelen on 27 September 1639. For some time he taught humanities and from 1649 until 1690 was a missionary in the Reformed north Netherlands. In support of his missionary work he published *Evangelische leeuwerck, ofte Historie-liedekens, op de evangelien der Sondagen, evangelische levens der heyligen, Passie ons Heeren Jesu Christi, ende sommige evangelische deughden* (Antwerp, 1667, rev. 2/1682–3), a book of spiritual songs to Dutch texts, of which he himself was the author. In the first edition he referred the reader for the sources of the melodies to well-known songs from the Dutch, Italian, Latin and French repertory. This was common practice at that time, but in the two-volume second edition the music of the borrowed melodies is added; there are also two of his own melodies, for the songs *Den mensch zijnd'in ervelicke zonde* and *Zaligh die weet hier den tijdt van zijn leven*.

BIBLIOGRAPHY

BNB (L. Willems)
F. van Duyse: *Het oude Nederlandsche lied* (The Hague, 1903–22, incl. index and suppl.)
C. Janssens-Aerts: 'Het geestelijke liedboek in de Zuidelijke Nederlanden (1650–1675)', *Ons geestelijk erf*, xxxviii (1964), 337–92, esp. 340, 368–9
G.J. Helmer: *Den gheestelijcken nachtegael: een liedboek uit de zeventiende eeuw* (Nijmegen, 1966), i, 11, 15, 72, 80; ii, 2ff

GODELIEVE SPIESSENS

Placuzzi, Gioseffo Maria (*b* Forlì; *fl* 1667–82). Italian composer and organist. His op.1 identifies him as a native of Forlì, a university graduate in minor orders, and a member of an unspecified academy; op.2 states that before 1682 he was organist at Forlì Cathedral. Two dedications in op.1 to violinists from S Petronio in Bologna suggest possible connections there. This set includes the only Bolognese trio sonatas before Corelli to begin consistently with a slow introduction, but the number of movements remains unstandardized. The presence of *arie* is another conspicuous Bolognese trait. Op.2 retains the old-fashioned format, consisting mainly of single dances and balletto–corrente pairings.

WORKS

Suonate a 2–5, 8, op.1 (Bologna, 1667)
Il numero sonoro modolato in modi armonici et aritmetici di balletti, correnti, gighe, allemane, sarabande e capricci, 2 vn, b (spinetta/violone)/1 vn, con una sinfonia, 2 vn, op.2 (Bologna, 1682)

PETER ALLSOP

Plagal cadence [Amen cadence] (Fr. *cadence plagale*; Ger. *plagale Kadenz*, *unvollkommene Kadenz*; It. *cadenza plagale*). A CADENCE consisting of a subdominant chord followed by a tonic chord (IV–I), normally both in root position.

Plagal mode (from Gk. *plagios*, Lat. *plagalis* or *plagis*). Any of the church modes whose AMBITUS, or range, includes the octave lying between the 4th below and the 5th above its FINAL. The term is thus applied to the four even-numbered modes of Gregorian chant (2, 4, 6 and 8), each of which takes its name from the corresponding odd-numbered mode, with the addition of the prefix 'hypo-': HYPODORIAN, HYPOPHRYGIAN, HYPOLYDIAN and HYPOMIXOLYDIAN; the ambitus of each of these is about a 4th lower than that of its corresponding AUTHENTIC MODE, the term with which 'plagal mode' is contrasted.

The earliest definition of the term is given in Hucbald's *De harmonica* (?*c*880; *GerbertS*, i, 116): 'The plagal, however, descends to the 4th [below its final] and rises as far as the 5th [above]'. In later modal definitions this general rule was extended to include the 6th above the final and the 5th below, except for the Hypolydian mode, where the 5th below the final *f* is not perfect and the 4th below, *c*, remained the lower limit.

The word 'plagalis' has a precise equivalent in the term 'plagios', which refers to the four lower-lying *echoi* in Byzantine modal theory.

HAROLD S. POWERS

Plagge, Wolfgang (*b* Oslo, 23 Aug 1960). Norwegian composer and pianist. A child prodigy, he won the Norwegian national championship for young pianists in 1971 and made his début as a pianist one year later. He started to compose at the age of five and first had his work published aged 12. He studied the piano with Robert Riefling and Jens Harald Bratlie in Norway and with Yevgeny Koroliev at the Hochschule für Musik und Theater in Hamburg, from which he graduated in 1983. He later studied composition with Øistein Sommerfeldt and Johan Kvandal in Norway and in Hamburg with Ligeti and Werner Krutzfeldt. Through his teachers in Hamburg, Plagge came into direct contact with the East European musical traditions of the 20th century, which have considerably influenced his music. He is especially inspired by neo-classical composers such as Prokofiev and Stravinsky, his musical style being characterized by an expanded tonal harmony and brisk, complex rhythms. Plagge has toured continental Europe as pianist and as composer a number of times, and he receives commissions regularly from Norway and abroad.

WORKS
(*selective list*)

Orch: Hn Conc., op.49, 1990; Sinfonietta, op.50, 1990; Vn Conc., op.55, 1991; Pf Conc. no.2, op.60, 1992; Festival Music, the 1994 Version, op.46b, 1994; Hogge i stein [Hewn in Stone], op.77, nar, 3 solo vv, chorus, orch, 1994; Tpt Conc., op.80, 1994; Accdn Conc., op.81, 1995; Conc. grosso, op.85, bn, pf, orch, 1997

Other works: Elevazione, op.21, fl, org/vn, pf, 1994 [2 versions]; 2 Episodes, op.25, vn, va, 1985; Pf Sonata no.5, op.23, 1986; Qnt, op.26, hn, 2 vc, 2 pf, 1986; Asteroids, op.32, cl, bn, pf, 1987; Asteroid Suite, op.33, vc, pf, 1988; Fanfare, op.36, brass, perc, 1988; Music for Two Pianos, op.17, 1989; Sonata I 'A Litany', op.39, hn, pf, 1989; Sonata, op.43, bn, pf, 1990; Monoceros, op.51, hn, 1990; Canzona, op.53, brass qnt, pf, 1990; Pf Sonata no.6, op.34, 1991; Facsimiles, op.66, accdn, 1993; Summa: Chapters from the Tao Ching, op.83, S, T, vn, pf, 1996; Conc. grosso, op.87, 2 pf, timp, brass qnt, 1996; Sonata III, op.88, hn, pf, 1995; Rhapsody, op.89, vn, 1996; Gloria victis, op.91, nar, chorus, hp, 1996; Trio, op.92, 2 bn, pf, 1996; Mare, op.93, 2 pf (4 players), 1997; Sonata, op.94, vn, pf, 1997; Trio, op.95, trbn, tuba, pf, 1997

Principal publishers: Musikkhuset, Norwegian Music Information Centre

HALLGJERD AKSNES

Plagiarism. *See* BORROWING, §9.

Plainchant [plainsong] (from Lat. *cantus planus*; Fr. *plainchant*; Ger. *Choral*; It. *canto plano*). The official monophonic unison chant (originally unaccompanied) of the Christian liturgies. The term, though general, is used to refer particularly to the chant repertories with Latin texts – that is, those of the five major Western Christian liturgies – or in a more restricted sense to the repertory of Franco-Roman chant (GREGORIAN CHANT). A third meaning refers to a style of measured ecclesiastical music, often accompanied by a bassoon, serpent or organ, cultivated in Roman Catholic France during the 17th to 19th centuries (*see* PLAIN-CHANT MUSICAL). This article is concerned with the chant of the Roman and derived rites considered historically, including its place within Christian chant as a whole and its relationship to the liturgy that it serves.

1. Introduction: chant in East and West. 2. History to the 10th century: (i) The early centuries (ii) The origins of Gregorian chant (iii) The origins of plainchant notation. 3. Sources: (i) Common types of liturgical book (ii) Manuscripts: dating, origin and distribution. 4. Basic repertory. 5. Style: (i) Melody (ii) Form (iii) Modality (iv) Performance. 6. Expansion of the repertory: (i) Trope (ii) Prosula (iii) Melisma (iv) Sequence (v) Conductus, *versus*, cantio (vi) *Rorate* chants (vii) Liturgical dramas, laments (viii) The medieval Office. 7. Chant in the religious orders: (i) Cluny (ii) Other orders. 8. Chant in northern and central Europe: (i) General (ii) Denmark, Norway, Sweden, Finland (iii) Poland (iv) Bohemia and Moravia (v) Hungary (vi) Slovenia and Croatia. 9. Chant in Latin America. 10. Developments from 1500 to 1800: (i) Tridentine reforms (ii) Neo-Gallican reforms. 11. Restoration and reform in the 19th century: (i) Early reform in France (ii) Germany and the Cecilian movement (iii) England and Ireland (iv) The reformed editions of Solesmes. 12. 20th-century developments.

1. INTRODUCTION: CHANT IN EAST AND WEST. The roots of the liturgical chant of the Christian Churches lie partly in established Jewish Synagogue practice of the apostolic period, partly in new developments within early Christianity itself and partly in pagan music at the diverse centres where the first churches were established (*see* CHRISTIAN CHURCH, MUSIC OF THE EARLY, and JEWISH MUSIC, §II). Three centres exercised primary influence, Jerusalem, Antioch and Rome, and Constantinople, established as the eastern capital of the Roman Empire in the 4th century, became a fourth. In the centuries after the Edict of Milan (313), when freedom of Christian worship was sanctioned, there developed distinct families of Eastern and Western (Latin) rites, each local rite having its own liturgy and music. The music can be studied, however, only where notation permits: notation appears nowhere before the 9th century, and precise representation of pitch is not found in liturgical books until the 11th century.

The chief representative of the Eastern liturgies is the Greek rite of Constantinople (*see* BYZANTINE CHANT). This seems to have developed from Antiochean and Palestinian elements; it may have been subject also to Roman influence, since it was due to Rome that the ancient site of Byzantium was endowed with a new imperial status. From the 10th century, many manuscripts provide evidence of the Byzantine rite and its music; by the 13th century, the full repertory of Byzantine chant had been copied in a notation as unambiguous as the notation for Western Gregorian chant of the same period. The repertories of other Eastern rites, however, can be studied only through literary and liturgical documents and from modern practice (on the assumption that some aspects of early practice have filtered down through oral tradition). This is true of the historically influential Syrian rites and the old Palestinian (Melkite), Nestorian and Chaldean rites (see SYRIAN CHURCH MUSIC) as well as the Coptic rite (see COPTIC CHURCH MUSIC). The Georgian rite is in some respects the best evidence of early liturgical and musical practice at Jerusalem; noted Georgian hymn collections survive from the 10th century, but their notation is incomplete and transcription is problematic (see GEORGIA, §II). The Armenian rite has similar noted manuscripts from the 13th and 14th centuries, and the Ethiopian rite from the 14th century (see ARMENIA, §II, and ETHIOPIA, §II). The Constantinopolitan liturgy and its music were taken over en bloc by the Slavs in the late 9th century; very full noted traditions survive from the 11th, 12th and 13th centuries, and for a time these reflected the Byzantine tradition quite faithfully. After the 13th-century Mongol invasions the Slavonic tradition became less dependent on the Byzantine Church (see RUSSIAN AND SLAVONIC CHURCH MUSIC).

In the Latin liturgies it became common to preserve the chant through notation. Of the medieval chant repertories of Italy, three survive complete: the Gregorian (still the official chant of the Roman Catholic Church), Old Roman and Ambrosian (see AMBROSIAN CHANT; GREGORIAN CHANT; and OLD ROMAN CHANT). The origins of the Gregorian are obscure; although it bears the name of GREGORY THE GREAT (590–604), it is no longer thought that this repertory represents Roman chant at the time of his papacy. It may represent a Roman recension of chant of the late 7th century or early 8th, or a Frankish recension of a Roman repertory carried out in the late 8th and early 9th centuries with the addition of some local obsolescent Gallican elements (see GALLICAN CHANT). The Old Roman chant poses a related problem. It survives only in five manuscripts from the 11th century to the early 13th from Rome and its environs. No other chant dialect appears in Roman manuscripts before the 13th century. Old Roman is variously viewed as the stylistic forerunner, in part, of the Gregorian repertory; or, in a refinement of this view, as the normal, older usage of Rome that survived in the region of Rome even after the newer Gregorian usage had spread throughout Western Europe; or, on the contrary, as a chant dialect reserved for papal ceremonial while the Gregorian was used in ordinary celebration; or as a late, stylistically degraded outgrowth of the Gregorian repertory. The complex history of the Roman rite and its music, and the problematic relationship between the Gregorian and Old Roman repertories are discussed below (§2(ii)).

The third substantially surviving medieval Italian repertory is the chant of the region of Milan, called Ambrosian after the 4th-century bishop of that city (see AMBROSIAN CHANT). Ambrosian chant is in use at Milan to the present. There are fragmentary remains of two other Italian repertories. The more substantial of these, dating from the 10th, 11th and 12th centuries, comes from the Beneventan zone of south Italy, which stretches across the peninsula from Naples and Monte Cassino in the west to Bari in the east and even reaches across the Adriatic to the coast of Dalmatia (see BENEVENTAN CHANT). From north-east Italy there are isolated 11th- and 12th-century survivals of a chant repertory that may have had considerable importance, since what is preserved comes from Ravenna (see RAVENNA CHANT). A centre for similar developments may also have been the influential patriarchate of Aquileia-Grado further to the north-east (see AQUILEIA). All these five medieval Italian dialects, but particularly the amply preserved Gregorian, Old Roman and Ambrosian, share some basic musical material. Corresponding chants in the various liturgies are melodically related. Thus in some instances an 'old-Italian' chant layer can be discerned behind the stylized regional variants. The recovery of this layer constitutes one of the major challenges in plainchant study.

As part of the movement towards political and liturgical unification begun in regions ruled by the Carolingians in the mid-8th century, all the local musical rites except the Ambrosian were progressively suppressed in favour of the Gregorian. Of the once-flourishing Gallican chant sung throughout Merovingian Gaul and elsewhere in the Frankish kingdoms, only isolated traces survive in manuscripts dating from the 9th to the 12th centuries. Some Gallican material, however, may have been perpetuated in the Gregorian tradition, particularly among its alleluia verses, offertories, processional antiphons (see LITANY, §I, 3(iii), and PROCESSIONAL) and Ordinary chants. The Mozarabic (Old Spanish) rite developed in the Visigothic kingdom in early medieval Spain from the end of the 5th century and continued to flourish in Christian communities during the period of Arab dominance from 711 until its suppression in favour of the Gregorian liturgy in 1085 (see MOZARABIC CHANT).

Table 1 presents a comparative synopsis of the principal chants of the Mozarabic, Roman and Ambrosian Masses (items in parentheses are sung infrequently).

TABLE 1: Principal chants of the Mozarabic, Roman and Ambrosian Masses

Mozarabic rite	Roman rite	Ambrosian rite
(a) LITURGY OF THE WORD		
Praelegendum (Gloria)	Introit	Ingressa
Trisagion	Kyrie	
Benedictiones	Gloria	Gloria (Laus missae)
Prophecy		Prophecy
Psalmo: Clamor		Psalmellus
Epistle	Epistle	Epistle
	Gradual	
	Alleluia	Hallelujah
Threnos (Lent)	Tract (Lent)	Cantus (Lent)
Preces	Sequence	
		(Antiphona ante evangelium)
Gospel	Gospel	Gospel
		(Antiphona post evangelium)
Laudes (Alleluia)		
	Credo	Symbolum
(b) MASS OF THE FAITHFUL		
Sacrificium	Offertory	Offertorium
	Sanctus	Sanctus
	Agnus Dei	
Antiphona ad pacem		
Antiphona ad confractorium		Confractorium
Antiphona ad accendentes		
	Communion	Transitorium
	Ite missa est	Benedicat

The music of one other main Western rite, the Celtic, is almost completely lost. This rite developed principally in Ireland after the missionary work of St Patrick in the 5th century. Its early liturgy was very similar to that of the Gallican Church, and like the Gallican rite it varied from centre to centre. The Visigothic Church is also thought to have influenced the character of the Celtic liturgy. From the second half of the 7th century, however, the Church of Rome began to exert considerable influence in Ireland, as it did in Anglo-Saxon England at the same time, and the liturgy became increasingly romanized. By the time Irish notation first appeared, at the beginning of the 11th century, Roman plainchant had extinguished the native Celtic music (see CELTIC CHANT).

2. HISTORY TO THE 10TH CENTURY.

(i) The early centuries. Consolidation of liturgical practices and the systematic compilation of lists of prayer formularies (*libelli missarum*) for local use in the Western Church began during the 4th, 5th and 6th centuries. This process is manifest in the oldest surviving Mass book of the Western liturgies, the so-called Leonine Sacramentary (also known as the Verona Collection: *I-VEcap* LXXXV (80); ed. Mohlberg, D1956), composed during the first quarter of the 7th century. As far as is known, this fragment containing 1331 collects and other prayers is a composite collection of Roman *libelli missarum* assembled for use at Verona some time between about 560 and 600. Most of its material is attributed to the work of earlier popes: Damasus (pontificate 366–84), Leo I (440–61), Gelasius I (492–6) and Vigilius (537–55). Although the prayers collected in the Leonine Sacramentary were clearly composed for specific feasts, there is no evidence to suggest that they were used as a Proper of the Mass, that is, specific formularies created for and permanently assigned to individual dates in the liturgical year; rather, the celebrant could choose from a *libellus* a variety of prayers relevant to each feast or he could compose his own. There is also some evidence that the texts of non-biblical chants were composed on a similarly ad hoc basis. Consequently, in the absence of any Proper for the texts of the Eucharist there could be no Proper for the music. References in medieval literature to the institution by various popes of 'chants for the liturgical year' probably refer to the collection and arrangement of *libelli* and should not be interpreted as evidence for the development of a musical Proper. McKinnon (F1995, pp.201–02) has argued that a Proper repertory could have been created only by a group of cantors devoted to the cultivation and preservation of chant; the single group of this kind known to have existed in the Western Church before the Carolingian era was the Roman Schola Cantorum, founded probably in the second half of the 7th century. According to McKinnon, the chants of the other major Western liturgies were performed by soloists who largely improvised the melodies they sang, although the simple chants sung by the congregation must have had fixed melodies.

Most of what is known about the early history of the music of the Divine Office comes from the surviving Latin monastic *regulae* ('Rules'), which began to appear in the late 4th century and usually contain descriptions of the cursus – the division of the Psalter throughout the week. Among the most important pre-Carolingian *regulae* were the 5th-century *Instituta* of Cassian, used at Lérins; the early 6th-century *Regula magistri*, written for an unknown monastery near Rome; the Rule of Benedict of Nursia, composed sometime between c530 and c560 for the abbey of Monte Cassino (see Forman and Sullivan, F1997); the *regulae* of Caesarius, bishop of Arles (c470–542); and those of Columbanus (d 615), the Irish monk and founder of Luxeuil and Bobbio. Before the 9th century, monasteries in Francia were free to choose or compile their own Rule and the singing of the cursus varied from community to community. During the reign of Louis the Pious (814–40), however, a series of decrees were issued, imposing on Frankish communities the Rule of Benedict and the canonical Rule of Chrodegang. Although none of these *regulae* describes the actual sound of monastic chanting, they reveal that all full members of the community were expected to know the entire Psalter by heart and to participate in the singing of the Office, which included both choral and solo chanting. However, some Rules, notably the *Regula Benedicti*, state that the solo psalmody should not proceed by order of seniority of the monks, as was the case in many monasteries, but that only those who were able to edify the listeners should be permitted to chant.

Before the the mid-8th century, when the Carolingians assumed political power in the Frankish lands, the liturgical practices of the Western Churches were very diverse. Although the pope held authority over doctrinal matters, he exercised no jurisdiction over the manner in which worship was conducted outside the Roman Church. Even within separate kingdoms liturgical uniformity was unusual; the Gallican rite, in particular, embraced many local traditions. Only in the Visigothic Church in the second half of the 7th century did the bishops of Toledo assume authority over the Old Spanish liturgy and demanded uniformity of worship throughout the kingdom. The Anglo-Saxon Church established by Augustine of Canterbury in 597 is thought to have used a mixture of rites derived mainly from the Irish, Gallican and Roman Churches (Cubitt, F1996), but by the mid-8th century uniformity of liturgy was demanded by the archbishop of Canterbury. At the Council of Clovesho in 747 it was declared that the Anglo-Saxon Church should follow the same liturgy as practised in Rome. In particular, the Anglo-Saxons revered Gregory the Great as the founder of their Church, and by the 8th century they also regarded him as the source of their liturgy. The emulation of the Roman rite by the Anglo-Saxons is particularly significant for the history of Western plainchant, for it is clear that their desire for conformity with Rome was not limited to the texts of the rite but also extended to its music, although it is impossible to judge the extent to which such ideals were enforced in practice. Furthermore, it is likely that the legend of Gregory the Great as the author of the chant repertory which bears his name may have its origins in the English Church (Hiley, C1993, pp.506–07).

(ii) The origins of Gregorian chant. A fundamental policy of the early Carolingian monarchy, one that began under Pippin the Short (751–68) and continued first under Pippin's son Charlemagne (768–814) then under Charlemagne's son Louis the Pious and his grandsons Lothar, Pippin and Charles, was the reform of ecclesiastical discipline and the imposition of religious unity among the Franks and their subject peoples. An important means by which the Carolingians pursued their ideal of religious unity was through the promotion of uniformity in worship. They aimed to replace the diverse Gallican

traditions by a single rite – that of the Roman Church (see Vogel, F1965 and 1966).

The first attempt to standardize the liturgy of the Frankish Church occurred during the reign of Pippin the Short and was probably implemented under his direction. A new sacramentary was issued that had been created from a mixture of Gallican and Roman elements; this type of Mass book is known as the '8th-century Gelasian' or the 'Frankish–Gelasian' Sacramentary. One of its earliest surviving examplars is the Gellone Sacramentary (*F-Pn* lat.12048; ed. Dumas, D1981), probably copied between 790 and 800 at Meaux for Cambrai Cathedral, but given to the abbey of Gellone in 807 (see Gamber, D1963, 2/1968, no.855; and Moreton, D1976). Although copies of the 8th-century Gelasian Sacramentary were disseminated widely and rapidly, their presence only exacerbated the liturgical confusion in the Carolingian Church. Under Charlemagne, therefore, a second sacramentary was declared the standard Mass book of the Frankish Church. In order to give his liturgical reforms more authority Charlemagne asked the pope for a pure ('inmixtum') copy of the sacramentary of Pope Gregory. The book sent by Pope Hadrian I (772–95), which arrived in Francia some time between 784 and 791, was deposited in the palace library as an exemplar from which further copies could be made. Although the original manuscript of the sacramentary, known as the 'Hadrianum', is no longer extant, a single early copy of it survives in the sacramentary of Cambrai (*F-CA* 164), written in 811 or 812 under the direction of Hildoard of Cambrai (see Gamber, op. cit., no.720). This manuscript carries the title: 'In nomine Domini. Hic sacramentorum de circulo anni exposito a sancto Gregorio papa Romano editum ex authentico libro bibliothecae cubiculi scriptum' ('In the name of the Lord. This copy of the sacramentary for the liturgical year composed by Saint Gregory, the Pope of Rome, was written using the exemplar of the authentic book of the palace library').

The Hadrianum, however, proved to be unsatisfactory in two respects. First, it was clearly not the 'pure', authentic text of Gregory the Great that Charlemagne had requested, for it included a number of formularies added since the death of Gregory I in 604, of which the latest were added during the pontificate of Gregory III (731–41). Secondly, the Hadrianum was a papal sacramentary, that is, a book containing the prayers recited by the pope at stational masses, and as such it gave no formularies for the Sundays after Epiphany, Easter and Pentecost, neither did it provide prayers for the special liturgies for funerals, votive masses etc. These apparent lacunae in the sacramentary decreed to be the Frankish standard were filled only during the reign of Charlemagne's son, Louis the Pious (814–40), when Benedict of Aniane (*c*750–821), an Aquitanian monk and architect of many of Louis' church reforms, completed his supplement to the Hadrianum (see Wallace-Hadrill, F1983, pp.258–303; Vogel, B1966, Eng. trans., pp.79–92), with the missing material compiled from other sacramentary texts; some uniquely Gallican feasts and services were also included. Benedict not only carefully distinguished his own work from the text of the original Hadrianum but also distinguished between the prayers he thought were composed by Gregory the Great and those that were later Roman additions. Several Carolingian manuscripts of the

supplemented Hadrianum are extant, notably *F-AUT* 19 copied around 845 in Marmoutier near Tours.

The Hadrianum and its supplement did not immediately replace the other sacramentaries still circulating in Francia in the early 9th century, but it eventually supplanted the other texts to become the standard Mass book of the Frankish Church and was the sacramentary known to the most important liturgical commentators of the 9th century, including Amalarius of Metz (*c*775–*c*850) and Walahfrid Strabo (*c*805–49). (For an edition of the Hadrianum and its supplement, see Deshusses, F1971–82.)

Although most of the documentary sources for the Carolingian Church reforms concern the romanization of the sacramentary and the other liturgical texts, there is also evidence that the same ideals shaped the development of plainchant under the early Carolingians. The earliest descriptions of the reform of chant were written during the reign of Charlemagne, but several of them date the beginnings of the policy of replacing Gallican melodies with those of Rome to the reign of Pippin, in particular to the visit of Pope Stephen II to Francia in 752–4. According to Paul the Deacon (*c*783) Bishop Chrodegang of Metz (742–66), who had escorted Pope Stephen to Francia in 752, began to instruct his clergy at Metz in the Roman manner of chanting (*PL*, xcv, 709). Chrodegang also established a stational liturgy based on the papal rite and formed a schola cantorum to perform the chant (Andrieu, F1930); this was probably the first such choir to be introduced into Francia (see McKinnon, F1995). Pippin's brother, Bishop Remedius of Rouen, also taught his clergy Roman chant. A letter from Pope Paul I (MGH, *Epistolae*, iii, 1892, pp.553–4) written in 761/2 describes how Remedius's monks were unable to learn Roman chant fully from Simeon, a member of the Roman Schola Cantorum, before he was recalled to Rome, and how Remedius then sent his monks to Rome to continue their instruction in the Schola itself. Pope Paul also sent Pippin two Roman chant books, an 'antiphonale' and a 'responsale' (see MGH, *Epistolae*, iii, 1892, p.529); neither one is extant.

Under Charlemagne a number of royal decrees promoted and enforced the Roman rite and its chant throughout Francia. The most important was the *Admonitio generalis* issued in 789 which stated that all the clergy should learn and practise the Roman chant correctly in conformity with Pippin's attempt to abolish the Gallican chant for the sake of unanimity with the Roman Church (MGH, *Capitularia*, i, 1883, p.61). In order to further knowledge of Roman chant scholae cantorum were established in several cathedrals and monasteries and royal envoys (*missi*) were sent to churches to ensure that the liturgy and its chant were correctly performed.

While the texts of the Roman liturgy could be introduced into Frankish churches by the dissemination of manuscripts, the learning of Roman chant must have been a much more difficult process, for without notation music could only have been transmitted orally. This raises several important questions about the success of Frankish attempts to introduce Roman chant and the nature of the relationship between the music sung in Rome in the late 8th and early 9th centuries and that sung in Francia at the same time.

The Carolingian belief that Gregory was the source of their chant was stated at the head of the earliest extant

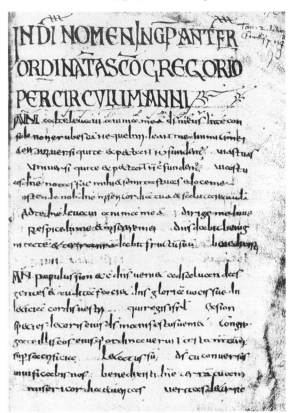

1. 8th- or 9th-century gradual without melodies, Codex Blandiniensis from the region of Ghent (B-Br lat.10127–44, f.90r)

Frankish chant book, the Mont Blandin Antiphoner (*B-Br* lat.10127–44, ff.90–115; see Gamber, D1963, 2/1968, nos.1320, 856), a gradual copied in about 800, later owned by the abbey of Mont Blandin near Ghent (fig.1). The same belief was also enshrined in the hexameter verses that prefaced many medieval chant books, among the earliest of which is the Monza Cantatorium (*I-MZ* CIX; ed. Hesbert, D1935/R, p.2), probably copied in about 800 in north-east France: 'Gregorius praesul meritis et nomine dignus … composuit hunc libellum musicae artis scholae cantorum in nomine Dei summi' ('Bishop Gregory, worthy in his merits and name … composed this little book of the art of music for the Schola Cantorum in the name of the highest God'; see Stäblein, F1968). By the middle of the 9th century the legend of Gregory I's composition of the Roman chant repertory had spread from Francia to Rome itself: a letter from Pope Leo IV written in the 850s threatened an abbot with excommunication if he and his monks did not perform the chant handed down by Pope Gregory I (MGH, *Epistolae*, v, 603). Later in the 9th century John the Deacon (*b* c824; *d* before 882), a monk of Monte Cassino, wrote a *Vita sancti Gregorii* (c873–5; *PL*, lxxv, 60–242) at the request of Pope John VIII (872–82) in which Gregory I was presented as the composer of Roman chant. By the time the Hartker Antiphoner was copied (c980–1011) the legend had developed into the story that the melodies of plainchant were dictated to the Pope by the Holy Spirit in the form of a dove (fig.2; on the development of the legend see Treitler, I1974, and Hiley, C1993, pp.503–13).

Present-day scholars have rejected this image of Gregory as composer of plainchant. Van Dijk (G1961) proposed that the reform of the Roman liturgy by Pope Gregory II (715–31) had been mistakenly attributed to Gregory I by his Carolingian apologists, a theory also explored by Stäblein (F1968). There is no evidence contemporary with Gregory I to suggest that his contribution to the liturgy amounted to much more than the writing of some prayers and perhaps the compilation of a *libellus missarum*, and none of the accounts of Gregory's life written before the Carolingian era mentions any particular interest in music. Schmidt (F1980), however, concluded that it was possible that Pope Gregory's involvement was greater than current scholarship gives him credit for.

Contemporary with the belief that Gregory the Great was the source of Carolingian chant are a number of writings indicating that the repertory performed in Francia during the 9th century was not the same as that sung in Rome. When Amalarius of Metz revised the antiphoner in the 830s he found that there were differences between the texts and *ordo* sung in Rome and those performed in Metz; Walahfrid Strabo (*d* 849) accepted that elements of the Gallican chant were still present in the so-called Roman rite of the Frankish Church. John the Deacon, the Roman author of the *Vita* of Pope Gregory the Great noticed differences between the music of the Franks and that sung in Rome and accused the 'barbaric' Gauls and Germans of being incapable of learning Roman chant. Notker Balbulus (c840–912) of St Gallen responded in an account written some time between 883 and 885: he accused the Romans of deliberate attempts to sabotage the reform of Frankish chant during the reign of Charlemagne by teaching the northern cantors incorrect melodies (see Van Dijk, 'Papal Schola', F1963).

2. The legend of Pope Gregory the Great depicted in the Hartker Antiphoner, c980–1011 (CH-SGs 390–391, f.X; from PalMus, 2nd ser., i, 1970)

Unfortunately there is no means of directly comparing the music sung in Rome with that sung in Francia during the Carolingian era. Notation developed in Francia in the 9th century and fully-notated chant books are known only from the end of that century; notated books from Rome, however, survive only from the 11th century onwards. The repertory notated in the Frankish chant manuscripts is known as GREGORIAN CHANT and is clearly closely related to that preserved in the Roman manuscripts, but there are sufficient differences between the two for the Roman repertory to be recognized as a variant tradition, commonly known as OLD ROMAN CHANT. Stäblein (G1950) was the first to emphasize the importance of this music, although it was already known to Mocquereau (PalMus, 1st ser., ii, 1891/R) and Andoyer (G1911–12, pp.69, 107). Since the 1950s several theories have been advanced to explain the relationship between the Gregorian and Old Roman chants and to address the question of how successful the Franks were in importing Roman music.

Some scholars have argued that both repertories were sung in Rome. Stäblein thought that the Old Roman chant was that sung in Rome at the time of Gregory the Great and that the Gregorian chant developed from it during the papacy of Vitalian (657–72), the probable founder of the Schola Cantorum. The liturgist Van Dijk, however, suggested that the differences in the Gregorian and Old Roman music reflected the existence of two different rites in Rome from the time of Vitalian: the Gregorian repertory being the chant of the papal rite and the Old Roman that of the urban churches ('Gregory the Great', F1963). Smits van Waesberghe offered a variant of this theme: the Old Roman chant was the original repertory of the Roman Church and the papal chapel and the Gregorian was a development of it that emerged during the 7th century in the basilical monasteries. The theories of Van Dijk and Smits van Waesberghe make several assumptions: that the music of these repertories changed little between their creation and the date they were first notated; that the Frankish adoption of Roman chant was limited to only one of the co-existent repertories in Rome; and that the Carolingians were on the whole successful in reproducing the original melodies. Hucke, on the other hand, pointed to the accounts of contemporary writers such as John and Deacon and Notker and argued that the Gregorian chant resulted from the imperfect transmission of the music sung in Rome to Frankish cantors at the end of the 8th century and the virtual separation of the two repertories from around 800 when Charlemagne decreed that all Frankish cantors were to learn the 'Roman' rite from the schola cantorum at Metz (MGH, Capitularia, i, 1881, p.121). (For further details of the theories see OLD ROMAN CHANT, §2).

These widely differing theories concerning the origins of Gregorian chant reveal just how little is known about plainchant during the early Middle Ages. The relationships between different chant traditions are obscure, and very little is understood about the processes involved in the creation of melodies, how and by whom they were performed, and how they were transmitted. Of particular importance is the question of the degree to which melodies were fixed. Many of the arguments have centred on the nature of the Roman Schola Cantorum and the role it played in the creation and maintenance of Roman chant. Its precise origins are obscure; traditionally, its foundation

was ascribed to Gregory the Great, a view maintained by Van Dijk ('Gregory the Great', F1963), but this theory is now generally rejected. The earliest clear evidence for its existence appears only at the end of the 7th century, in the biography of Pope Sergius I (d 701) in the Liber pontificalis (ed. Duchesne, F1886–92), which describes how the young Sergius was handed over to the prior cantorum for training. The Schola Cantorum is now generally thought to have been established some time in the second half of the 7th century (McKinnon, 'The Eighth-Century Frankish-Roman Communion Cycle', F1992; Dyer, F1993). By the time Ordo romanus I (ed. Andrieu, F1931–61/R, ii, 67–108) was composed, probably at the beginning of the 8th century, the structure of the Schola was firmly established. According to this Ordo it was led by the primicerius (or prior), whose duties included beginning and ending the chants of the liturgy, and three other sub-deacons known as the secundus, tertius and quartus (also called the archiparaphonista); the other adult members of the Schola, probably clerics in minor orders, were called paraphonistae, and the young pupils the paraphonistae infantes. The exact size of the Schola Cantorum is not known. (See also SCHOLA CANTORUM (i)).

The Roman Schola Cantorum is the only institution dedicated to the teaching and performance of chant known to have been formed in the West before the Carolingian era. Research by McKinnon ('The Eighth-Century Frankish-Roman Communion Cycle', F1992) suggests that it was largely responsible for the formation of the musical Proper in the Roman rite and the development of a high degree of melodic fixity in the Roman repertory. According to McKinnon the Roman musical Proper emerged quickly over a few generations beginning sometime in the second half of the 7th century and continuing into the early 8th, the reign of Pope Gregory II (715–31) being particularly significant. The idea of a fixed melodic repertory, therefore, developed in Rome and was later adopted by the Carolingians when they began to replace the Gallican chant with the chant of the Roman Schola Cantorum. The earliest fully notated chant books, all of which were written in Francia, display a remarkable uniformity in the plainchant melodies sung throughout the Frankish Church. The variants that these manuscripts contain, though persistent, are not significant enough to detract from the overall impression of a high degree of melodic fixity in the Gregorian repertory.

A peculiar feature of Gregorian chant is its adherence to a system of classification by which chants are categorized within eight modes according to musical characteristics irrespective of their liturgical function. Although the theory of the eight modes, as it developed from the 9th century onwards, classifies melodies by their cadence note (final), ambitus and reciting note, mode also carries implications of melodic idiom, characteristic turns of phrase, which defy easy theoretical definition. Such melodic characteristics were sometimes represented in theoretical writings and in tonaries by a set of eight short melodic phrases associated with syllables such as noeanne, noeagis etc., probably borrowed from Byzantine chant (see Bailey, L1974). While the word 'tonus' was at first preferred for this complex of meanings, 'modus' gradually became more usual ('tonus' referring to the harmonic interval, especially in polyphony) (see Atkinson, L1987 and 1995). A distinction is still commonly made between the theoretical concept of 'mode' and the formulas for singing psalm verses or responsory verses, usually called 'tones'.

The first concrete evidence for the classification of Gregorian chants in eight tones or modes is the fragmentary Tonary of St Riquier, *F-Pn* lat.13159, ff.167–167*v* (see Gamber, D1963, 2/1968, no.1367; and Huglo, D1971, pp.25–6), dating from just before 800 and contained in the Psalter of Charlemagne copied at the abbey of St Riquier in northern France. The modal system already existed at an earlier date, however, in the Eastern Churches. It was taken up by the Franks at the time of the establishment of Gregorian chant in Francia, presumably from Byzantine practice. Apart from the earlier evidence for the *oktōēchos*, Aurelian of Réôme (*fl* 840s) says that it was adapted from the Greeks, as are also the Latin names given to the modes (*protus authentus/plagalis* etc.). (*See* MODE, §II; OKTŌĒCHOS; and PSALM, §II, 6–7.)

It is probable that the classification of the repertory according to melodic type aided the efforts of Frankish cantors to learn and perform the new repertory, particularly the psalmodic chants in which the mode of the antiphon determined the tone of the psalm verse. The composition of tonaries (liturgical books listing chant incipits classified according to the eight modes; *see* TONARY) containing a large number of chants indicates that such books served as a reference tool for cantors, for example the Carolingian Tonary of Metz compiled in the first half of the 9th century (*F-ME* 351; ed. Lipphardt, L1965). However, it is clear that the development of the system of the eight modes also served a theoretical purpose as early as the reign of Charlemagne. The Tonary of St Riquier was probably designed as a didactic or theoretical text, for only a few chants are classified according to their modes and not all of the chant types listed (introits, graduals, alleluias, offertories and communions) contain psalm verses. It is likely that this tonary was written to demonstrate that the whole of the repertory conformed to the system. The same belief is found in many of the early medieval treatises on music theory, beginning with the anonymous work known as the *De octo tonis* which formed the basis of part of Aurelian of Réôme's *Musica disciplina* (*c*840–50). With the composition of the anonymous treatise *Alia musica* in the second half of the 9th century the eight modes were identified (erroneously) with the seven octave species of ancient Greek theory. The authentic modes were the Dorian, Phrygian, Lydian and Mixolydian; and the plagal the Hypodorian, Hypophrygian, Hypolydian and the Hypomixolydian.

Although the Carolingians were convinced that their so-called Roman chant conformed to the system of the eight modes, the evidence of the notated melodies and several theorists shows that the Gregorian repertory was not originally composed in accordance with such a system. There is no evidence that the eight modes were recognized in Rome until Gregorian chant was introduced there. A significant number of Gregorian melodies are classified differently in different places and at different times, and some chants display a kind of modal ambiguity that was frequently a problem for medieval theorists. The conviction that this system encapsulated an ideal state of the repertory, however, was so strong that theorists often 'corrected' chants or sections of chants to bring the 'corrupt' melodies into line with the appropriate mode; in fact, most such melodies probably belonged to a stratum

of Gregorian chant that was in use before the establishment of modal theory. This process of 'correction' may account for some of the differences between the Gregorian and Old Roman repertories.

(iii) The origins of plainchant notation. Few present-day scholars of medieval music would disagree with the premise that early chant melodies dating from before the time of Pippin (751–68) were transmitted from generation to generation by oral methods alone. Isidore of Seville, writing in the first half of the 7th century, said that music had to be memorized because there was no means of writing the sound, and there is no evidence that music notation existed in the medieval West before the Carolingian era. The melody for the prosula *Psalle modulamina* in *D-Mbs* Clm 9543 (see ex.2 below) is possibly the earliest datable example of medieval notation (see Levy, F1995, esp.172, n.5). The chant is followed in the manuscript by the colophon of the scribe Engyldeo, known to have been a cleric at St Emmeram in Regensburg between 817 and 834 (see Möller, *La tradizione dei tropi liturgici*, M1985 and 1987, pp.279–96), and Bischoff (F1940) believes the notated piece to be in his hand, although this has not been universally accepted.

The earliest unambiguous evidence of the use of notation occurs in the *Musica disciplina*, a treatise written in the 840s by Aurelian of Réôme. Examples of neumes are rare before the appearance of fully notated chant books for the Mass at the very end of the 9th century (for a checklist of 9th-century notated manuscripts *see* NOTATION, §III, 1, Table 2). Fully notated antiphoners containing the music for the Office did not appear until a century later. Some have argued that a large number of 9th-century notated sources have been lost and that the writing of music was therefore much more widespread than the surviving evidence suggests. Levy, in particular, has suggested that fully notated chant books existed as early as the reign of Charlemagne and that these were kept in the palace library, together with the Hadrianum and other liturgical texts, as the authoritative exemplars for the teaching of chant (I1987). In Levy's view this exemplar was central to Charlemagne's policy of transmitting Roman chant accurately throughout Francia. However, no direct evidence for such a manuscript survives, and most scholars believe that the scarcity of notation before the turn of the 10th century is a true reflection of how little notation was used during the 9th century (Corbin, J.i 1977; Hughes, I1993, pp.65–6).

The notation found in the early chant books is neumatic, that is, it represents the outline of a melody without specifying the intervals or pitches. Cantors had first to learn a melody by oral methods before they could read it in the notation. The main purpose of such notation was to serve as a reminder of the melody, and the earliest notated chant books were probably used for reference rather than performance. Although specific pitch notations were developed by theorists in the second half of the 9th century, the notation of exact pitch in chant books was not used until the 11th century when several different methods appeared. Heighted point neumes are found in notated chant books from Aquitaine in the early 11th century, and an alphabetic system of defining pitch is found in the Dijon Tonary (*F-MOf* H 159) and some manuscripts from Normandy and England. At the same time Guido of Arezzo propagated the use of the staff with coloured lines or clefs to designate F and C. The development of notations that specified pitch should not be regarded as an 'improvement' on the earlier neumes but as evidence of the changing relationship between the performance and notation of liturgical music and the methods used in teaching and learning plainchant.

Attempts to recover the rhythmical traditions of the 8th, 9th and 10th centuries remain highly speculative. A few neume systems contain special signs thought to be indications of rhythm: St Gallen neumes and those from Laon contain significative (or 'Romanus') letters and supplementary signs (*episemata*), some of which concern the rhythm of the melody, but the exact interpretation of these signs is unclear. Some scholars have suggested that Gregorian chant was performed according to the quantities employed, for example in Latin metrical verse; others, including the monks of Solesmes, believe that the chant was more basically sung in equal notes but with rhythmic nuances.

As with many other aspects of early chant history, the origins of plainchant notation are obscure. A number of different explanations concern the shape of the neumes. Some scholars maintain that neumes are graphic representations of cheironomic gestures – the movement of the precentor's hands as he directed the singers (see Mocquereau, PalMus, 1st ser., i, 1889/R; Huglo 'La chironomie médiévale', I1963). Others believe that Western notation was derived from Byzantine ekphonetic notation, a system used to direct the recitation of lections. Another group has suggested that the neumes owe their form to the accents of classical prosody, whether directly from manuals of Latin grammar or indirectly via Byzantium (see Atkinson, I1995). Treitler (I1982; 'Reading and Singing' and 'Die Entstehung', I1984) has proposed that neumes developed from the various punctuation signs – question marks, points, commas etc. – employed by Carolingian scribes to aid readers in the delivery of texts. However, it may be that none of these theories alone can adequately account for the shape of the neumes and that Carolingian notation evolved independently of any pre-existent source (*see* NOTATION, §III, 1).

Most scholars would hold that the extant varieties of Carolingian notation all derive from a common origin, but they disagree as to the exact nature of this origin. Some argue in favour of a single primitive system of neumes as the source of all the later notations; others consider it more likely that the diversity evident in the extant neumatic systems arose from a set of commonly held concepts about the function of notation and how musical sounds should be represented (Hughes, I1987; Arlt, *Musicologie médiévale: Paris 1982*, J.i 1982). It is certain, however, that neumes were subject to considerable change and adaptation in different Frankish centres throughout the 9th century. The three earliest extant notated graduals, all written around 900 (CH-SGs 339 from St Gallen, F-CHRm 47 from Brittany; LA 239 from Laon), display neumes of different shapes, and several other notational types appear in 10th-century manuscripts. Early notations are generally defined according to their geographical origin: Lotharingian, Breton, Aquitanian, central French, German, Anglo-Saxon, Beneventan and north Italian. The St Gallen and French notations are sometimes called 'accent' or 'stroke' notations, in which one pen-stroke may represent several notes; Aquitanian, Breton and Lorraine notations are termed 'point' neumes, because almost every note is indicated by a separate dot or dash.

Despite the different origins of early notated chant books and the variation in the styles of neumation, the most remarkable feature of the melodic repertory is its uniformity. Variants in the melodies are generally minor and were probably caused by differing opinions about how the melodies were to be sung rather than by scribal error (see Hughes, I1987; I1993). The same variants are often found in groups of manuscripts copied in the same region.

The transition from an oral tradition to the earliest types of written plainchant notation and the role of notation in maintaining the uniformity of the tradition during the 9th century are the subject of considerable debate. Levy's argument for the existence of a notated exemplar during the reign of Charlemagne assumes that the melodic repertory was largely fixed by the end of the 8th century. This assumption is supported by Hughes (I1987, esp. 377), but whereas Levy argues that the uniformity in the manuscripts resulted from the use and copying of notated chant books, Hughes maintains that the chant had acquired a fixed melodic form well before the appearance of the earliest surviving notated manuscripts and that cantors were capable of performing almost all their chants from memory with very little variation. Treitler and Hucke, however, have argued that performance of the Gregorian repertory was not necessarily frozen into uniformity by the advent of notation. In the era of oral transmission cantors would have 'reconstructed' chants at each performance according to their knowledge of traditional forms and melodic materials. To some extent this would continue to be true when notated books were available for reference (see Hucke, I1980, p.466).

3. SOURCES.

(i) Common types of liturgical book. The determined efforts by medieval scribes to make records of the liturgy according to some kind of orderly plan paradoxically led to an almost endless diversity. Balboni's attempts (see D1961 and 1985) to classify liturgical books by general type, though admirable, failed to deal adequately with the books' internal differences. Diversity among the original medieval sources, however, does not necessarily imply disorder (a confusion that can easily occur when such a multiformity is viewed from the perspective of modern liturgical books): it is rare to find an unsystematic anthology of liturgical music (see Huglo, D1988).

Four general categories of plainchant book may be distinguished: the Mass book, the Office book, books containing 'paraliturgical' chants and didactic books. The principal types of chant book for the Mass are the gradual and the noted missal. Office chants are found in the antiphoner and in the noted breviary with psalter and hymnal. Chants to be performed during liturgical processions were commonly included in Mass books at the appropriate place in the liturgical year. In the Later Middle Ages they were frequently collected in a book of their own, the processional. Later medieval forms, which have largely fallen from use, are the paraliturgical chants (various chants consisting of musical and/or textual additions to the established liturgy: tropes, sequences, prosulas, *sequentiae* and *versus*. These occur in several configurations: in separate volumes (e.g. troparia, sequentiaria, versaria); in distinct sections within medieval Mass books; or inserted either singly or in groups within individual Mass Propers. The tonary and certain kinds of abbreviated gradual and antiphoner are pedagogical directories that assisted the cantor in the proper selection and performance of chants.

Other types of liturgical directory prominent during the Middle Ages were the ordinal (*Liber ordinarius*) and the *Consuetudines monasticae* (for modern editions of the latter see Hallinger, Q1963–). The ordinal was a code of rubrics and incipits of formularies, chants and readings, and indicated the order for celebrating the services in a particular church or monastery. The *Ordines romani* (ed. Andrieu, F1931–61/R), a collection of 50 formerly independent *ordines*, the earliest of which dates from the early 8th century, are a particularly valuable source of evidence for the development of the Romano-Frankish rite. The monastic customaries include regulations concerning chanting by monks in both liturgical and non-liturgical contexts. Such ordinals and customaries have come to play an increasingly important role in plainchant research (see Angerer, Q1977; Fassler, Q1985; Foley, Q1988; Vellekoop, D1996).

See also LITURGY AND LITURGICAL BOOKS, §II, and articles on individual books.

(ii) Manuscripts: dating, origin and distribution. Only a small proportion of the medieval sources that once existed are extant today; many manuscripts have been lost to war, fire, water and, in some cases, deliberate destruction. Books containing the texts or music for liturgies that were no longer practised were often neglected, which explains why so few books of the Gallican rite survived the imposition of the Gregorian liturgy. The books of some ecclesiastical centres have been preserved in greater numbers than others. St Gallen, Limoges, Rouen and Benevento, for example, are still represented relatively fully by manuscript sources, but only a handful of early musical sources has survived from such major medieval religious establishments as Cluny, Camaldoli, Nevers, Tegernsee, Metz, Corbie, St Albans, Gorze and Nonantola. The survival of pre-Albigensian musical treasures from churches in southern France, such as Arles, Narbonne, Carcassonne, Albi, Toulouse, Rodez, Aurillac, Béziers, Moissac, Bordeaux and Tulle, can be attributed more to their luxuriant decoration than to their musical and liturgical content. In England and Scandinavia the systematic destruction of 'popish' books during the Reformation is well known.

Establishing an uncontested origin or date for some medieval liturgical manuscripts is, on occasion, virtually impossible. One of the most important advances relating to these problems was the realization that the series of alleluias used at Mass for the 23 Sundays after Pentecost frequently adhered to established local traditions that had persisted for decades or even centuries (Frere, D1894, p.l; Beyssac, D1921). For example, a given set of post-Pentecostal alleluias in manuscript 'x' of known origin may closely match a series in manuscript 'y', thus strongly suggesting that both sources were copied for a specific church, although the manuscripts may have been copied decades apart.

Three 11th-century series of post-Pentecostal alleluias are shown in Table 2. The St Denis (Paris) series was firmly implanted by the mid-11th century (see the eight manuscripts cited by Robertson, D1991, p.106). That used by the Augustinians (Canons Regular) at the abbey of St Victor in Paris is based on the gradual *F-Pa* 197,

ff.80*v*–104*v*, dating from 1270–97, and the St Victor ordinal, *Pn* lat.14452, ff.64–83*v*, dating from about 1200 (see the manuscript descriptions in Fassler, Q1993). The Cluniac series is taken from the 11th-century Cluniac gradual *F-Pn* lat.1087, f.87ff.

Even after centuries of obscurity, chant books in private possession have continued to come to light, including the Cadouin collection (see Corbin, D1954), the gradual of St Cecilia di Trastevere (Hourlier and Huglo, G1952), the Weingarten Troper (Irtenkauf, D1954), the Nevers Troper (Huglo, M1957), the Wolffheim Antiphoner (Emerson, D1958–63), the St Albans Miscellany (Hartzell, D1975), the Mont-Renaud Antiphoner (PalMus, 1st ser., xvi, 1955–6) and the Feininger collection (Gozzi, D1994).

4. BASIC REPERTORY. Hesbert's *Antiphonale missarum sextuplex* (D1935/R), an edition of the Monza, Rheinau, Mont-Blandin, Compiègne, Corbie and Senlis graduals, is the principal documentary means of determining the size and content of the Gregorian Mass repertory performed in the Carolingian Church. In these late 8th- to early 10th-century sources the number of chant texts (any instances of musical notation are additions) agrees closely with the contents of the 11th-century noted gradual from St Gallen, Switzerland, *CH-SGs* 339 (facs. in PalMus, 1st ser., i, 1889/R), which was surveyed by Peter Wagner (C2/1901, i, 205) (Table 3).

Comparable statistics for the size and nature of the Gregorian Office repertory are not yet available. The documentary basis of all Office studies is the earliest source *F-Pn* lat.17346, ff.31*v*–107, a complete Office antiphoner from Compiègne in France, dating almost certainly from 877 (see Huglo, D1993); this unique antiphoner contains a hybrid collection of older liturgical formularies plus newly composed Offices from northern France. From that time to the 16th century a huge number of special Offices were composed in honour of local saints, such as St Thomas of Canterbury, St Louis IX, king of France, or St David, patron of Wales (see Hughes, O1983).

TABLE 2: Post-Pentecostal alleluia cycle

	St Denis	St Victor	Cluny
1.	In te Domine	Deus judex	Deus judex
2.	Diligam te	Diligam te	Diligam te
3.	Venite exultemus	Domine in virtute	Domine in virtute
4.	Confitemini Domino	In te Domine	In te Domine
5.	Qui timent Dominum	Eripe me	Omnes gentes
6.	Domine refugium	Te decet hymnus	Te decet
7.	Omnes gentes	Attendite popule	Attendite
8.	Quoniam Deus magus	Exultate Deo	Exultate Deo
9.	Qui sanat	Domine Deus salutis	Domine Deus
10.	Letatus sum	Domine refugium	Domine refugium
11.	Paratum cor meum	Venite exultemus	Venite exultemus
12.	Exultate Deo	Quoniam Deus	Quoniam Deus
13.	Dominus regnavit	Dominus regnavit	Confitemini
14.	Jubilate Deo	Confitemini	Paratum cor
15.	Domine deus	Paratum cor	Redemptionem
16.	Laudate Dominum	Redemptionem	Qui timent
17.	Deus judex	Qui timent Dominum	Laudate Dominum
18.	Qui posuit fines	Laudate Dominum	De profundis
19.	Adorabo ad templum	Dextera Dei	Confitebor tibi
20.	Attendite popule	De profundis	Lauda anima mea
21.	Te decet hymnus	Lauda anima mea	Qui sanat
22.	De profundis	Qui sanat contritos	Lauda Jerusalem
23.	Dextera Dei	Qui posuit fines	Qui posuit fines

Biblical texts, particularly the Psalter, formed the basis of worship in the Western Churches, although some liturgies admitted a greater number of non-biblical texts than others. Various Latin translations of the psalms existed during the early Middle Ages, producing variations in the texts of chants. The Roman Psalter remained the version used in the Roman Church until the 16th century. The Gallican Psalter, one of the several translations produced by St Jerome, was favoured by the Gallican Church and declared to be the official version of the Frankish Church by Charlemagne. It forms the principal source of Gregorian psalmody, but many Gregorian psalmic texts also derive from the Roman Psalter, thereby proving their Roman rather than Frankish origin. (For a study of these early psalters and the readings of chant texts, see Dyer, F1984; *see also* PSALTER, LITURGICAL).

Most biblical chant texts are rather brief excerpts taken directly from the scriptures; others, such as the communion *Videns Dominus flentes sorores Lazari* for Friday of the fourth week in Lent (*John* xi.33, 35, 43–4, 39), are made up from several passages; and some are paraphrases of the scriptures. The predominance of biblical texts in the basic repertory of Mass chant Propers (about 630 melodies in *CH-SGs* 339) is shown in Table 4 (after Wagner, C2/1901, i, 205).

Chants not normally using biblical texts include many Office antiphons, processional antiphons, Ordinary chants, creeds, acclamations, *preces*, litanies, *historiae* or special Offices for local saints, hymns, sequences and most tropes. Accounting for the textual variants between chant books is a problem sometimes encountered in plainchant research; some of the variation can undoubtedly be attributed to the transmission of distinctive biblical readings belonging to local traditions (for examples *see* GALLICAN CHANT, §5).

The oldest stratum of Gregorian chant may have consisted of a nucleus of about 630 melodies, but so far it has been virtually impossible to estimate the total number of chants used in conjunction with all the medieval Western liturgies. However, it is possible to draw some general conclusions from data collected from a variety of repertorial surveys (the figures cited below should nevertheless be treated with caution).

An extensive index listing about 11,000 chant incipits of the Gregorian repertory based on 19 sources, including modern published chant books, five manuscripts and several scholarly studies, was compiled by Bryden and Hughes (B1969). Scholars collecting and studying the Ordinary chants of the Mass have identified (discounting variants and transpositions) 226 Kyrie melodies (Landwehr-Melnicki, K1955/R), 56 Gloria melodies (Bosse, K1955), 230 Sanctus melodies (Thannabaur, K1962) and 226 Agnus Dei melodies (Schildbach, K1967). Comparable melodic surveys have been made of other classes of

TABLE 4: Sources of texts of the early Gregorian chant repertory in *CH-SGs* 339

	Book of Psalms	Elsewhere in the Bible	Non-biblical
Introits	102	41	6
Graduals	104	13	1
Alleluias	70	14	11
Tracts	17	3	0
Offertories	82	16	4
Communions	64	80	3
Total	439	167	25

chant: 410 alleluia melodies to about the year 1100 (Schlager, K1965), 110 offertory verses (Ott, K1935) and 732 prosulas to Office responsories (Hofmann-Brandt, M1973).

A vast number of Latin versified texts were set to a repertory of well-known hymn tunes; Stäblein (K1956/R) published 557 melodies from ten medieval hymnals and other sources. As for the paraliturgical genres, Van Deusen (M1986) drew attention to over 1400 sequence melodies and 3000 sequence texts in 1400 major extant sources – the sheer quantity of manuscripts containing the sequence is itself testimony to the genre's importance and longevity; Blume published the texts of 495 tropes to the Ordinary of the Mass (AH, xlvii, 1905/R) and 786 tropes to Proper chants of the Mass (AH, xlix, 1906/R); Weiss (M1970) edited 352 introit trope melodies from twelve 10th- and 11th-century manuscripts from southern France.

Hesbert's monumental comparison of 12 secular and monastic antiphoners from the central Middle Ages (CAO, vii–xii, 1963–79) emphasizes the complexity of the sung Office liturgy. The manuscripts that he collated contain about 185 invitatories, 4300 antiphons, 1900 responsories and 325 versicles. It must be kept in mind, however, that these numbers would increase dramatically if all the known metrical and non-metrical chants from special Offices for local saints venerated throughout

Ex.1 Melodic style in Gregorian chant

(a) *Syllabic*

Pa-ter nos-ter qui es in cae-lis san-cti-fi-ce-tur no-men tu-

-um ad-ve-ni-at reg-num tu-um

(b) *Neumatic*

Ve- ni et os-ten-de no- bis fa-ci-em tu- am

(c) *Melismatic*

...lau-da-te   e - - - - - - - - -

- - - - - - - - - - - - - um

TABLE 3: Numbers of chants in the original Gregorian repertory

	Hesbert (texts only)	CH-SGs 339 (with melodies)
Introits	152	149
Graduals	128	118
Alleluias	100	95
Tracts	18	20
Offertories	108	102
Communions	151	147
Total	657	631

TABLE 5: The 11th-century Gregorian eight-mode system

No. of mode	Name in authentic-plagal terminology	Greek name	Final note	Ambitus	Reciting-note
1	Authenticus protus	Dorian	d	d–d'	a
2	Plagalis protus	Hypodorian	d	A–a	f
3	Authenticus deuterus	Phrygian	e	e–e'	b or c'
4	Plagalis deuterus	Hypophrygian	e	B–b'	a
5	Authenticus tritus	Lydian	f	f–f'	c'
6	Plagalis tritus	Hypolydian	f	c–c'	a
7	Authenticus tetrardus	Mixolydian	g	g–g'	d'
8	Plagalis tetrardus	Hypomixolydian	g	d–d'	c'

Western Europe were taken into consideration. In addition, a series of antiphoners frequently containing items not found in CAO have been edited in the CANTUS series (see Collamore and Metzinger, *The Bamberg Antiphoner*, D1990; Olexy, D1992; Steiner, D1996). Randel (H1973) indexed approximately 5000 musical items of the Mozarabic rite, including many hymns that presumably had sung texts but for which the manuscripts do not provide notation.

5. STYLE.

(i) Melody. From a purely formalistic and stylistic standpoint, plainchant melodies of all types, both liturgical and paraliturgical, may conveniently be separated into three classes according to the ornateness of their melodies: syllabic, neumatic and melismatic. In the first group each individual syllable of the text is normally set to one note; in the second, small clusters of two to ten or so notes may accompany a syllable; chants in the third group are essentially neumatic in style, but with florid passages embedded in them (in rare cases a single syllable may be sung to several hundred notes) (see ex.1).

Each liturgical category of chant is in general characterized by a specific melodic type. Scriptural readings, prayers, litanies, Glorias, sequences, creeds, psalms, antiphons, short responsories (*responsoria brevia*), most hymns, salutations and doxologies are normally syllabic. The principal neumatic categories are tropes, introits, Sanctus and Agnus Dei melodies and communions. Graduals, Kyries, alleluias, tracts, offertories, the Great Responsories (*responsoria prolixa*) and *preces* are neumatic types that often contain extensive melismas.

It would be quite wrong, however, to suppose that the relatively simple syllabic chants invariably belong to a stratum of music historically older than the neumatic and melismatic melodies. The degree of melodic complexity is determined much more by the musical competence of the performer(s) involved: priest, congregation, trained schola or soloist(s).

(ii) Form. Another common means of distinguishing plainchant melodies is by their internal musical structure. Three main forms are usually cited: chants sung to reciting notes or recitation formulae; repetitive and strophic forms; and a wide variety of 'free' forms.

Collects, Epistles, Gospels, prefaces, short chapters, doxologies and a variety of blessings and salutations are generally chanted isosyllabically on a monotone, their total length and phrase structure being determined by the text. More elaborate varieties of these liturgical recitatives are introit verses, communion verses, psalms and canticles, which are also sung to a monotone but with the beginning, middle and end of each verse punctuated by brief intonation, flex, mediant and cadential formulae in the manner of simple psalmody.

Two classes of chant, the hymn and the sequence, are well known for their distinctive formal structure and repetitive types of melody. The hymn is a strophic form in which, for example, each four-line stanza of the traditional iambic dimeter or octosyllabic text is sung to the same melody. Sequences are characterized by a striking form of coupled melodic phrases (strophes), frequently, but not always, paired in series (*ABBCCDD* etc.).

Peter Wagner (*Einführung*, iii, C1921/R) and, following him, Apel (C1958) made a distinction between 'gebundene' and 'freie Formen'. By 'gebunden' ('bound', 'tied') Wagner meant a type of delivery that remained constant whatever text was being sung, as for prayer, lesson and psalm tones (Apel: 'liturgical recitative'). The 'freie Formen' (Apel: 'free forms') were those where the melody would differ substantially from piece to piece (as in introits, graduals, alleluias, tracts, offertories and communions). The currency that the word 'free' thus gained may have contributed to an impression that the chants lack shape and sense, which is far from being the case. Their internal structure is largely determined by the syntactical structure of the text, reflected, for example, in the deployment of cadences. Many within a particular type are linked to each other by common melodic formulae. Many alleluias contain internal repetition.

(iii) Modality. From the standpoint of musical analysis, modality is probably the single most homogeneous feature of Gregorian plainchant. This sense of uniformity has been greatly enhanced through the assignation of mode numbers to melodies in modern chant books published since 1905, even though some of the designations conflict with the testimony of early treatises and tonaries. Melodies are classified according to their final cadence notes and the range or ambitus of their melodies. (The reciting note or tenor of simple psalmody could also be added to the classification.) When this system reached its maturity in the 11th century, medieval theorists normally assigned an ambitus of an octave to each mode, whose position was determined by the final cadence note of the mode. Among the four authentic modes the lowest note of the ambitus was the final note; among the plagal modes the ambitus began five semitones below the final note (Table 5). Some chants, particularly if they are in a plagal mode, do not cadence regularly but are considered to be transposed and to end on an alternative final note. This transposition was done 'not in order to bring them into a more convenient range, but because of the intervallic structure of the melody' (Apel, C1958), particularly if, for example, both B♭ and B♮ were required by the same chant.

See above §2(ii); *see also* MODE, §II.

(iv) Performance. The plainchant repertory is frequently divided into three general families according to the manner of performance: antiphonal chants, sung by two

alternating groups of singers; responsorial chants, sung by a soloist (or soloists) in alternation with the choir; chants sung entirely by the celebrant, the soloist or the choir. According to present practice, the psalms, antiphons, invitatories, introits and communions are sung antiphonally by two semichoruses; the Great and short responsories, gradual, alleluia and offertory are sung responsorially; the collects, prefaces, Pater noster, various salutations and doxologies etc. are among the solo chants sung or intoned directly by the Mass celebrant. Considered more closely from a historical perspective and not simply from the basis of modern usage, this seemingly orderly classification is subject to many exceptions and conjectures. For example, some scholars consider the offertory an antiphonal chant; others believe it was responsorial. Hucke (K1970, pp.193–4) admitted three forms: an antiphonal type, a responsorial type and a middle or 'mixed' type. Later, Dyer (K1982, p.30) concluded that there is no evidence whatsoever to support the commonly held view that the offertory's mode of performance changed from responsorial to antiphonal: 'Neither the *Ordines romani*, the medieval liturgists and music theorists (with the possible exception of Aurelian), nor the Gregorian tonaries imply anything other than a responsorial refrain with a few verses. None of them regard the offertory the way they do the antiphonal chants of the Mass, the Introit and Communion'.

It is almost axiomatic that over the centuries performing practice was to some extent modified. Originally, choral antiphons appear to have been sung as a refrain between the verses of the Office psalms, but they have now disappeared. The introit, formerly a processional psalm, was sung antiphonally either by two semichoruses or by a lector and cantor. During the reign of Pope Leo I (440–61) the gradual was still a full psalm, but by the 6th century the text had probably been reduced to a single verse with an elaborate melody sung by a soloist. Even the grand counter-movement of 10th- and 11th-century liturgical expansion, the age of troping and Cluniac prolixity, was short-lived. By the mid-13th century the ornate melismatic verses of the offertory and the psalm verses of the communion had virtually disappeared, except in most German sources.

The performance of the principal Mozarabic chants – the antiphons, responsories, *psalmi*, *clamores*, *threni*, *laudes* and *vespertini* – has been reviewed at length by Randel ('Responsorial Psalmody', H1969), and some of his interpretations differ from those advanced by Brou and by Brockett. There is disagreement, for example, over whether the responsory was sung by one, two or three soloists, by three choirs, or by a combination of soloists and choir (see Brockett, H1968, p.141); on the other hand, a passage in the second prologue of the 10th-century León Antiphoner (*E-L* 8; see Brou and Vives, H1953–9) provides almost indisputable evidence that the Mozarabic antiphon was sung by two alternating choirs (see Randel, op. cit., 87).

The performance of Ambrosian chant in Milan towards the beginning of the 12th century is well documented (see Weakland, H1966/*R*; and Borella, H1964, pp.141ff). The duties of singers at the Ambrosian Mass and at Vespers and the manner of performing various chants are described in the ordinal of Beroldus (ed. Magistretti, H1894/*R*) written shortly after 1125 and in the chronicle of Landulphus senior (*c*1085).

See also PERFORMING PRACTICE, §1, 2(i). For more detailed discussion of the various Mass and Office chants see their individual articles.

6. EXPANSION OF THE REPERTORY.

(i) Trope. In its common generic sense, troping designates the intercalation or addition of music or texts, or both, to pre-existing chants. Specific musical forms associated, correctly or mistakenly, with troping are the trope, prosula and sequence. It is advisable, however, to distinguish them according to clear liturgical and compositional criteria. In particular, not all can be regarded as additions to already existing chants. The notion of 'a single, clear explanation … for the confusing wealth of musical forms introduced in the 9th- and 10th-centuries … a ruling idea of a process whereby all medieval music was necessarily and intimately tied to preexisting materials' is illusory (Crocker, M1966).

The group of scholars at Stockholm University working on the Corpus Troporum project proposed that tropes added to the Gregorian repertory be divided into three categories: 'logogene', in which a verse (or 'element') of chant was inserted before or between the phrases of a pre-existing chant; 'melogene', in which a newly composed text was set to the notes of a previously vocalized melody, one syllable per note; and 'meloform', or pure, wordless melismas, attached to the cadences of chants (usually the introit and Gloria). Logogene tropes are most commonly found with the introit and Gloria, but also with the offertory and communion; their texts frequently point up the the theme of the feast day, to which the texts of the parent chants often bear a less tangible relationship, and the added verses generally respect the melodic style and tonality of the parent chant. Melogene tropes are most commonly found with the alleluias and offertory, frequently also with the Office responsory.

The survey by Odelmann (M1975), while revealing much variety in medieval practice, makes it clear that the term 'tropus' was used primarily to refer to the logogene category, and this nomenclature is retained here. An added text of the melogene type was usually referred to as a 'prosa' or 'prosula' (see §6(ii) below). The *sequentia* sequence (also sometimes called 'prosa') is a largely self-contained liturgical genre with its own independent musical form (for separate discussion see §6(iv)).

The texts of trope verses for introit, offertory and communion that have been edited in the series Corpus Troporum (by 1999 only those for Christmas, Easter and Marian feasts had appeared), from manuscripts mostly of the 10th to 12th centuries from all over Europe, already number many hundreds. Since the manuscript sources are highly variable in their selection of verses and in variant readings, musical editions have tended to concentrate on small groups of sources from particular areas (Aquitaine: Weiss and Evans; Benevento: Planchart; Nonantola: Borders). Gloria tropes have been studied by Rönnau, Falconer and others, but are not yet available in substantial numbers in modern editions.

After the 12th century, the logogene type of trope rapidly fell out of use, but a late and rather special example of it lived on: the famous Marian trope 'Spiritus et alme' to the Mass Gloria (see Schmid, M1988). Literary devices such as simple rhyme ('Christe'/'Paraclete', 'Patris'/'Matris') and the matching of syllables helped bind its six lines to the older Mass text. The melody of the parent Gloria text is still in use as Vatican/Solesmes Gloria IX (*GR* A.i 1908). The oldest known copy is found in *F-R*

U.158, ff.40–40*v*, which is noted with 11th-century Norman neumes (see Hesbert, D1954, p.64 and pls.lxiv–lxv) (fig.3):

> Domine Fili unigenite, Jesu Christe,
> (1) 'Spiritus et alme orphanorum Paraclete',
> Domine Deus, Agnus Dei, Filius Patris,
> (2) 'Primogenitus Marie, virginis matris',
> ... suscipe deprecationem nostram
> (3) 'Ad Marie gloriam',
> ... Quoniam tu solus sanctus,
> (4) 'Mariam sanctificans',
> Tu solus Dominus,
> (5) 'Mariam gubernans',
> Tu solus altissimus
> (6) 'Mariam coronans',
> Jesu Christe

The duality of thought in the trope, acclaiming the Trinity and the Blessed Virgin Mary, was imitated by subsequent medieval and Renaissance composers. For example, the fourth, fifth and sixth phrases were joined to a troped Sanctus (from Marxer, R1908, p.105):

> Sanctus, Pater omnipotens, 'Mariam coronans',
> Sanctus, Filius unigenitus, 'Mariam gubernans',
> Sanctus, Spiritus Paraclitus, 'Mariam sanctificans',
> Dominus Deus Sabaoth [etc.]

In yet another adaptation, the 'Spiritus' lines were taken apart and interlaced into another poetic text (from Bukofzer, M1942, 165–6):

> 'Mariam' matrem gratie,
> Rex regis regni glorie,
> Matrem pie 'sanctificans'.
> 'Mariam' sine crimine,
> Omni pleni dulcedine,
> Virgo matrem semper verans
> Matrem Filio 'gubernans' [etc.]

3. Perhaps the oldest version of the Gloria trope 'Spiritus et alme', noted with 11th-century Norman neumes (F-R U.158, f.40r)

In an anonymous three-part doubly troped polyphonic Gloria from Italy, the 'Spiritus' trope appears to have gained the status of an accepted Gregorian text, for it is combined with the tetrameter trope 'Clementie pax baiula' (PMFC, xii, 1976, no.9, pp.30–37):

> Domine Fili unigenite, Jesu Christe.
> 'Spiritus et alme orphanorum Paraclete'
>   Ex Patre semper genitus,
>   Per flamen dulcis halitus,
>   Ut flos novus est editus,
>   Virga Jesse fecundata.
> Domine Deus, Agnus Dei, Filius Patris.
> 'Primogenitus Marie, virginis matris'
>   Agnus Dei pacificus,
>   Ysaac risus celitus [etc.]

On 8 August 1562 bishops at the Council of Trent declared that references to the Virgin Mary in the Trinitarian Gloria in excelsis were particularly inappropriate (*Concilium tridentinum*, viii: *Actorum*, ed. S. Ehses, Freiburg, 1919, p.917, lines 28–30), and the trope, in any form or context, was deleted from the liturgy.

The oldest reference to Kyrie tropes was once thought to be that by Amalarius of Metz in the third edition (*c*832) of his *Liber officialis* (iii; see Hanssens, F1948–50, ii, 283):

> Ac ideo dicant cantores:
> Kyrie eleison, Domine pater, miserere.
> Christe eleison, miserere, qui nos redemisti sanguine tuo, et iterum:
> Kyrie eleison, Domine, Spiritus Sancte, miserere.

However, Jonsson (M1973) has shown convincingly that these interpolations have nothing to do with tropes but are exegetical comments by Amalarius on the Trinity.

Although a number of logogene-type trope verses were composed for the Kyrie, principally in the area of southern Germany (see Bjork, M1980), the genesis of many other Kyries with Latin verses presents special difficulties. These are the Kyries where the Latin verses have the same melodies as the Greek acclamations, and, moreover, where they seem to add text to the melody on the principle of one syllable per note. In other words, they look like melogene-type prosulas. Since the earliest sources (mainly Aquitanian) of these pieces already contain the Latin verses, it cannot be proved that the melody existed before the Latin verses were composed, that is, they may well have been conceived simultaneously (see Crocker, M1966, p.196; and Bjork, K1976). The designations 'trope' and 'prosula' are, therefore, both misleading from a historical point of view; the compositions are a special festal type of Kyrie with Latin verses. (*See also* KYRIE ELEISON and TROPE (i).)

According to the *Liber pontificalis*, a biographical history of the popes in Rome (see Noble, F1985), the Agnus Dei was introduced into the Mass as a separate chant, unconnected with the Gloria in excelsis, by Pope Sergius I (687–701), and was sung by both clergy and congregation at the rite of the Fraction (breaking of the bread). Later 8th- and 9th-century accounts state that it was sung by the Schola Cantorum and performed during the Kiss of Peace.

In his study of this Ordinary chant, Atkinson (M1975) regarded the earliest verses as distinctive tropes added to the ancient text: 'one can, without hesitation, speak of the Agnus Dei *and* its tropes, even with regard to its earliest settings'. His chronological categories take into consideration a hypothesis advanced by Huglo (M1975).

According to this theory, which has since become central to many early chant studies, the regionalization of the early trope repertory reflects the political division of the Carolingian Empire from about 843 (the Treaty of Verdun) to shortly after 870 (the Colloquy of Meersen). Agnus tropes found in both East and West Frankish manuscripts, which display few variant melodic readings, represent the oldest layer (before 850); a second group of trope texts found in both regions but set to different melodies was written between 850 and 875; a third class was written after 875, and these tropes are restricted to one of the two geographical zones. The appearance of poetic and symmetrical texts is characteristic of 10th-century troping techniques.

The terms 'farsing' and 'glossing' have also been used as synonyms for troping (see FARSE). 'Farsa' often occurred in connection with a special type of troping used in the Epistle in some of the festal liturgies of the Christmas season (New Year, Epiphany etc.; see §6(v) below). Here verses of the lesson alternated with phrases borrowed from pre-existing chants (sequences, hymns etc.). The terms were also employed for certain 'troped' devotional songs popular especially in Bohemia during the 14th and 15th centuries (see Göllner, S1988).

See also TROPE (i).

(ii) Prosula. A prosula is a text added syllabically to a pre-existing melisma. One of the oldest recorded examples is *Psalle modulamina*, in *D-Mbs* Clm 9543, f.119v, for the alleluia with verse *Christus resurgens*; this alleluia is not to be found in the earliest graduals (see Hesbert's *Antiphonale missarum sextuplex*, D1935/R, 102–03) or in the late 9th-century full gradual-antiphoner *F-AI* 44, but is now assigned to the fourth Sunday after Easter. The manuscript *D-Mbs* Clm 9543 may be the oldest datable source of neumatic notation. For each note of the original melody a syllable of new text is provided, the complete alleluia text being itself incorporated, syllable by syllable, in the new prosula. A transcription (by Richard Crocker) of *Psalle modulamina* is given in ex.2 (the words in capitals represent the text of the original verse).

More common than the texting of a complete melody in this fashion was the texting of individual melismas within a chant, particularly those of the alleluia, offertory verse and the Great Responsories (*responsoria prolixa*) of the Office. (See, respectively, Marcusson, M1976; Hankeln, O1998; Hofmann-Brandt, M1973.) Since many such melismas display an internal repeat structure (e.g. *AABBC*), the result may resemble a miniature sequence. In many cases these small sequence-like compositions may have been newly composed as a unit, rather than having originated in the texting of a pre-existing melisma.

A substantial collection of 91 alleluia, offertory and responsory prosulas is found in *F-Pn* lat.1118, ff.115–31, an Aquitanian troper dating from 985–96 (see Steiner, M1969). In prosulation the neume forms of the original melismatic notation, particularly such integral binary and ternary combinations as the *quilisma, podatus, cephalicus* and *epiphonus*, were often separated, in a somewhat unorthodox manner, into individual notes, and each component note of the neume was assigned a text syllable. Evidence of this splitting can be observed in the alleluia prosula *Laudetur omnis tibi caterva* (ex.3) from *F-Pn* lat.903, the gradual-troper-proser of St Yrieix-la-Perche, near Limoges (see PalMus, 1st ser., xiii, 1925/R, p.173, lines 6, 8–10).

The dual notation (melismatic/texted) of prosulas has raised many questions about the method of performance: simultaneous or alternatim (see, for example, Hofmann-Brandt, M1973, pp.148–9; Kelly, M1974; More, P1965–6, pp.121–2). The same question has been raised in connection with sequences, which in most early sources were also set out in both melismatic and texted form.

See also PROSULA.

(iii) Melisma. Since the presence or absence of responsory melismas is somewhat variable in the manuscript tradition, it is not always clear whether they were there from the beginning (whatever that may mean) or additions to a parent responsory. Some appear to have led a semi-independent life, as in the case of the famous 'threefold melisma' (the 'neuma triplex' or 'trifarium neuma') described by Amalarius of Metz in his *Liber de ordine antiphonarii* (18; see Hanssens, F1948–50, iii, 56). According to Amalarius this neumed melisma (see Kelly, M1988) originally belonged to the Christmas responsory *In medio ecclesiae* (CAO, iv, 1970, no.6913) for the feast of St John the Evangelist (28 December), but singers of his day, the 'moderni cantores', transferred it to the Christmas responsory *Descendit de caelis* (ibid., no.6411), which ended with the phrase 'lux et decus universae fabricae mundi'. Prosulation of the last two words of the triple melisma, 'fabrice mundi', and one of its associate texts, *Facinora nostra relaxari mundi gloriam*, that is, the addition of words to the interpolated neumed melodic melisma, may already have begun in the late 9th century.

Added melismas of a different sort are to be found as embellishments of numerous introits and Glorias, above all in early manuscripts from St Gallen (*CH-SGs* 484 and 381; see Huglo, M1978; and Haug, *Cantus planus IV*, M1990). Many of these, too, were texted by the customary method, one syllable for each note of the melisma.

(iv) Sequence. The term 'sequentia' is used here to refer to the textless melismas of varying length and melodic complexity designed to replace the repetition of the liturgical JUBILUS of the alleluia of the Mass with a more extended melody: alleluia–jubilus–verse–*sequentia*. There is controversy as to whether such melodies were actually performed as textless melismas, or whether they were texted from the beginning – the state in which they are known from the late 9th century onwards. The earliest references to such melodies do indeed imply a textless state. The oldest record occurs in the Codex Blandiniensis of the end of the 8th century (ff.114v–115; for manuscript details see §2(ii) above; see also Hesbert, D1935/R, 198), where six alleluia incipits – *Jubilate Deo; Dominus regnavit; Beatus vir; Te decet hymnus; Cantate Domino canticum novum; Confitemini Domino* – are followed by the rubric 'cum sequentia'. Writing between two and four decades later, Amalarius of Metz (*Liber officialis*, iii, 16; see Hanssens, F1948–50, ii, 304) alluded to the *sequentia* as 'jubilatio quam cantores sequentiam vocant' ('this jubilatio which the singers call a sequentia'). The term also appears in the late 9th-century *Ordo romanus V* (see Andrieu, F1931–61/R, ii, 215). Again, Amalarius (*Liber de ordine antiphonarii*, 18; see Hanssens, op. cit., iii, 56) related that when the pope celebrated Easter Vespers the alleluia was adorned with verses and *sequentiae*; such melodies do indeed survive in sources of Old Roman chant, and much longer ones in Ambrosian alleluias (see Bailey, H1983). Most interesting are the canons of the Synod of Meaux in 845, which not only mention the

Ex.2 *Psalle modulamina laudis canora* (D-Mbs Clm 9543. f.119v)

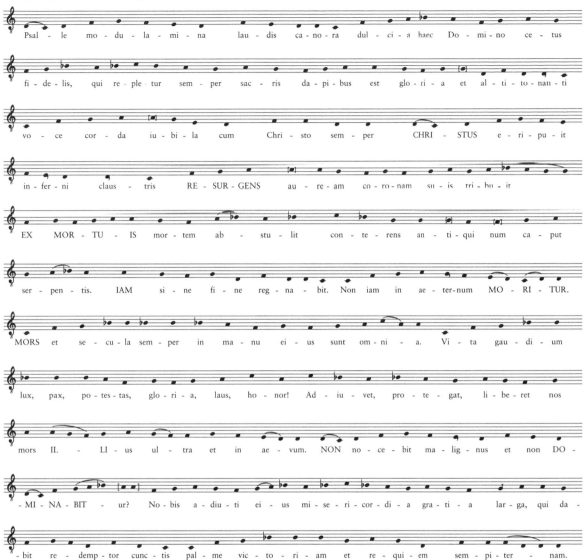

sequentia as a solemn part of the alleluia but also forbid the addition of texts ('quaslibet compositiones, quas prosas vocant') (see *Liturgische Tropen*, M1983–4, p.vii).

Only one surviving manuscript of the 9th century, *F-AUT* S28 (24), transmits *sequentiae* in musical notation, but the texts that Notker of St Gallen composed to sequence melodies – some 40 texts to 33 different melodies – afford at least partial evidence of what melodies were known in the late 9th century (Notker's work was completed in 884). Exactly which melodies were known to Amalarius or the delegates to the Synod of Meaux has not been determined; those cited in the Blandiniensis can be identified with reasonable certainty. But the balance of the evidence seems to favour the existence of at least a moderate number of untexted *sequentiae* early in the 9th century, the practice of texting them already being known by the middle of the century. (*See also* SEQUENTIA.)

The sequences found in manuscripts from the early 10th century onwards are usually transmitted in both melismatic and texted forms. It is, however, difficult to say exactly how many of the melodies thus recorded date back to the early 9th century. Some may have been relatively recently composed as a unity, that is, text and music being conceived simultaneously. Crocker in particular (M1973) has stressed this view of the genre; indeed, he would argue that most if not all of the sequences that

Ex.3 *Laudetur omnis tibi caterva* (F-Pn lat.903)

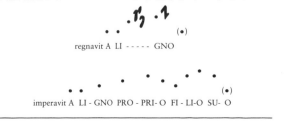

have come down to us were texted from the start. At the same time, a few notated collections of sequence melodies survive without any texts. For example, *F-CHRm* 47, dating from about 900, is the oldest; *CH-SGs* 484 is a St Gallen melody collection, copied in the second quarter of the 10th century; and in the late 11th century, most sequences at Cluny (among other places) were still sung without texts. The fact that very many sequence melodies were texted more than once also shows that to some extent the melodies were regarded as independent musical entities. A famous account of the composition of texts for sequence melodies is to be found in the 'proemium' that Notker of St Gallen wrote for his sequence collection. In early French and English sources it was customary to copy sequence melodies in one part of a manuscript, their texts in another. A peculiarity of many early sources is the names given to the melodies (different names in different areas). Some relate to alleluia verses, others (in French sources) to sequence texts, while many are colourful appellatives whose meanings seem quite obscure, such as *Metensis*, *Aurea*, *Planctus cigni* and *Ploratum* (fig.4).

Planchart (*Recherches nouvelles sur les tropes liturgiques*, M1993, pp.371–2, n.5) has underlined the confusion in terminology that exists between the terms *sequentia* and *prosa*:

The problems are as old as the repertory itself in that, west of the Rhine, the purely melodic addition to the alleluia was called *sequentia*, and the text to the *sequentia* – and by extension the entire piece – was called *prosa*. East of the Rhine, *sequentiae* were virtually never copied as separate pieces, instead they were entered in the margin of the texts to which they were sung, which were provided with no music other than the marginal *sequentiae*. The singer had thus the possibility of singing the melody with or without words. East Franks used the term *sequentia* for the entire combination of words and music. Independent *sequentiae* were all but unknown in Italy, where virtually all manuscripts transmit the text with the music set directly above it. Yet, the Italians adopted the West Frankish terminology, where the text with its music was called *prosa* or prose, and the purely melodic work was called *sequentia*.

The sequence was the single most important genre with an independent musical structure to emerge during the 9th century. Its normal position within the Mass was between the alleluia verse and the reading of the Gospel. In its standard form it is a syllabic chant consisting of a series of paired verses (e.g. *ABBCCDD* etc.), each line of a pair usually having the same number of syllables and the same musical phrase. The strophes vary in length, long ones being frequently placed in immediate contrast next to shorter ones. A distinct modal relationship often exists between the final note of the composition and its many internal cadences. The origin of the sequence's distinctive double-verse structure is not clear. De Goede (M1965, pp.lix–lx), Stäblein (M1978) and other scholars have discussed a small group of topical songs dating from between approximately 840 and 880 in a similar double-versicle form, but the verse structure of these pieces is quite different from that of the sequence and they are not liturgical compositions. As Huglo and Phillips (M1982) assert:

There is no need to insist further that the identification of these texts as 'archaic sequences' rests on questionable grounds. Aspects of their text structure, content, and early manuscript tradition simply do not support a ninth- and tenth-century function as sequences of the mass. It is our twentieth-century approach to the music of that era which is

the principal difficulty here. We know nothing of the early use of these texts, and most seem to have been of very limited dispersion.

The parallel structure characteristic of normal sequences occurs in a Gallican preface for the Easter Vigil, the *contestatio Quam mirabilis sit*, which is made up of 25 double and triple strophes. This *contestatio* is found in a 7th- or 8th-century leaf in the Escorial Library (*E-E*). According to Levy (M1971, p.59), however, the piece was probably sung to a flexible recitative and not to an already existing melisma. A small number of sequences in the early sources are much shorter than the majority and lack the parallel versicle structure. These short 'a-parallel' sequences (surveyed by Kohrs, M1978) appear to be associated with less important feasts.

From the 11th century, other styles were cultivated based on a new approach to rhyme and accent. By the end of the 12th century fully rhymed sequences in regular accentual verse were already entering the repertory in large numbers. The regularity of the texts made it possible to use different pre-existing melodies for the same text, while the usual process of contrafacture, providing new texts for established melodies, continued as before. Many texts composed by the Parisian canon Adam of St Victor (*fl* first half of the 12th century) gained special popularity. (For a discussion of the Victorine sequences used in Paris, see Fassler, M1993).

See also SEQUENCE (i).

(v) Conductus, versus, cantio. A number of 12th- and early 13th-century sources contain Latin songs, variously named conductus or *versus*, mostly in accentual, rhyming verse, which exhibit strophic and refrain forms of the utmost variety and inventiveness. The manuscripts fall into two groups. Song collections with relatively little indication of the liturgical function of the songs are *F-Pn* lat.1139, 3719 and 3549 (from Aquitaine; many songs set polyphonically), *GB-Lbl* Add.36881 (from ?France; many polyphonic), *Cu* Ff.i.17 (from ?England; many polyphonic), and *E-Mn* 288, 289 and 19421 (from Norman Sicily). Many of the same songs and others like them are also found in sources of the special festal liturgies of the Christmas season associated with the 'Feast of Fools' on New Year's Day, the Feast of the Circumcision. These are the New Year's Day Office of Sens (*F-SEm* 46; ed. Villetard, O1907), the New Year's Day Office of Beauvais (*GB-Lbl* Egerton 2615; ed. Arlt, O1970), the Epiphany Office of Laon (*F-LA* 263), and the St James Office of Santiago de Compostela (*E-SC*, ed. Wagner, O1931; many polyphonic songs). The picture that emerges is one where the songs are used as substitutes for traditional chants, especially for the versicle *Benedicamus Domino: Deo gratias*, and for accompanying liturgical actions (entrances and exits, the procession of the reader to the lectern, etc.). Such songs subsequently take their place in an extensive literature of rhymed prayers and devotional verse poetry cultivated in southern Germany, Switzerland, Austria, Bohemia and Poland from the late 13th century to the 17th. Many of these Latin poems were published by Mone (K1853–5/R) and Dreves (AH, D1886–1922/R, i, xx, xxi, xxxviii, xlvb).

Among the favourite objects of this pious devotion were the Trinity, Corpus Christi, the Holy Cross, patron saints, the angels and, above all, the Virgin Mary. A few of the earlier songs reveal Hussite sympathies, such as the Corpus Christi chant *Jesus Christus nostra salus* (AH, xlvb, 1904/R, no.105), which contains as an acrostic the

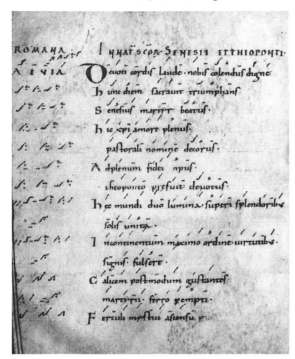

4. Sequence melody 'Romana' and text 'Devoti cordis laude' for Sts Sensius and Theopontus from the troper-proser from Reichenau, 1001 (D-BAs Liturg.5 (Ed.V.9), f.160v)

name I–O–H–A–N–N–E–S, the Latinized first name of Jan Hus (see H. Kaminsky: *A History of the Hussite Revolution*, Berkeley, 1967; and David, S1995). It is often difficult to determine the function of these pieces because the sources provide few helpful titles or rubrics; they may have been sung generally at Vespers, during processions and for private devotions. A clue pointing to some formal use in a service is the frequent inclusion of the terminal abbreviation EVOVAE of the doxology. It is also interesting to note that many of these moderately short poems are in trochaic metre, popular for marches or processions.

The texts of these poems and songs are deeply imbued with stylized symbolism expressed in botanical, astronomical, musical and biblical metaphors. Many are constructed on an acrostic scheme or contain glosses from the Lord's Prayer, *Ave Maria* or *Salve regina*. Among the lengthy metrical Marian psalters, some of which have musical prologues, each of the 150 verses may begin with stock acclamations, such as 'Ave', 'Salve', 'Vale' or 'Eia'. The musical forms are highly variable. Strict poetic forms tend to follow regular patterns such as *aab*, *aabbc* or similar arrangements. Macaronic texts and musical refrains are used, but not to the same extent as in the contemporary English carol. On the other hand, through-composed melodies, which contain at most a few brief internal repeats, are associated with poems lacking end-lines, free poetic metre, or artificial constructions such as the alphabetic acrostic in ex.4.

A CANTIONAL is a collection of these devotional songs and other chants brought together either as a separate section within a gradual, antiphoner or processional, or as an independent book. Most of the music is monophonic with Latin texts, but polyphonic pieces and vernacular translations often appear. The principal manuscript cantionals are *CZ-HK* II.A.6 (olim 43) (16th century);

Pnm XIII.A.2 (16th century); *Pu* III.D.10 (15th century), V.H.11 (14th century), VI.B.24 (16th century), VI.C.20a (15th or 16th century), X.E.2 (15th or 16th century); *VB* 42 (dated 1410); *D-Bsb* germ.8° 180 (15th century) and 280 (15th or 16th century); *EN* 314 (14th century); *Mbs* Cgm 716 (probably from Tegernsee, *c*1430), Clm 5539 (15th century); *Mu* 2° 156, the Moosburg Gradual (14th century); *TRs* 322 (1994); *PL-WRk* 58 (15th century).

(vi) Rorate chants.   Another group of Bohemian liturgical songs with Latin and Czech texts are the RORATE CHANTS, a repertory of Masses and cantiones linked with the introit for the fourth Sunday in Advent, *Rorate coeli*. These votive chants, which were used during the season of Advent, probably originated in Prague in about the mid 14th century and enjoyed wide circulation from the 16th century onwards (see Mráček, M1978).

(vii) Liturgical dramas, laments.   There has been much discussion about the time and place of origin of the famous dialogue between the Marys and angel(s) at the tomb of Christ, *Quem queritis in sepulchro*, which is generally seen as marking the beginning of the so-called 'liturgical drama'. The earliest sources are roughly contemporaneous, *F-Pn* lat.1240 from Limoges and *CH-SGs* 484 from St Gallen, both from the 930s, and this suggests a date of composition around the beginning of the century, perhaps earlier. By the end of the 10th century *Quem queritis* was quite widely known, but the centre of diffusion remains unclear. Whatever its original purpose, it came to occupy one of three standard places in the liturgy: (1) as part of the procession before Mass on Easter Day, the procession making a station by a 'sepulchre'; (2) as an introduction to the introit at Mass on Easter Day; (3) at the end of the Night Office on Easter morning, following the final responsory. (For a discussion of origins see Rankin, N1983–4, and Davril, N1995; on liturgical function see McGee, N1976, and Bjork, N1980.)

At its simplest *Quem queritis in sepulchro* is no more than the question of the angel(s), the reply of the Marys

Ex.4 *Antiphona alphabetaria de Beata Virgine (D-Mbs Cgm 716, f.101v)*

and the assertion of Christ's resurrection by the angel(s), but supplementary verses were usually added. The dialogue was also adapted to the Christmas season, as an exchange between the midwives at the stable and the shepherds seeking the infant Christ, and for Ascension, where angels ask the apostles whom they believe to have risen into heaven. From the 11th century onwards extra scenes from the Easter story were also given a dramatic form. Particularly interesting is the way in which pre-existing Office antiphons and responsories with biblical texts might be drafted in as part of a new ceremony. Sometimes they retained their original liturgical melody, which might cause changes of mode from one item to another; sometimes they received a new setting, with unified musical material (see Rankin, N1981).

Another important development of the 11th century was a revision of the old dialogue *Quem queritis in sepulchro*, with new text and music (the central verses in E mode instead of D). The new version was made in south Germany, although the actual place is not definitely known. The incipits of the central chants are as follows:

Quem queritis in sepulchro (9th–10th century)	Quem queritis O tremule mulieres (11th century)
	Quis revolvet nobis ab hostio lapidem
Quem queritis in sepulchro	Quem queritis O tremule mulieres
Iesum Nazarenum ... O celicole	Iesum Nazarenum ... querimus
Non est hic surrexit	Non est hic quem queritis
	Ab monumentum venimus
	Currebant duo simul
	Cernitis O socii

Already further scenes are indicated here, with the participation of Mary Magdalen (*Ad monumentum venimus*). *Currevant duo simul* is a liturgical antiphon, sung by the choir to explain that Peter and John run to the tomb. The sequence *Victime paschali laudes*, which includes elements of dialogue, and the German hymn *Christ ist erstanden*, after the triumphal announcement of Christ's resurrection, were often worked into the ceremony.

From the 12th century, texts in accentual, rhyming verse become increasingly common, sometimes replacing earlier prose chants, more often as part of new scenes or whole new plays. In many cases the connection with the liturgy appears tenuous, and a distinction seems appropriate between the older type of liturgical ceremony with a representational element, and the newer dramatic play, although such a distinction is difficult to define precisely or to apply in individual cases. Some of the earliest representations of the Epiphany story (the Magi seeking Jesus, Herod, the Slaughter of the Innocents) seem to go well beyond reasonable liturgical bounds (see Drumbl, N1981) and suggest non-liturgical origins. Other plays on sacred matter but with no obvious liturgical connection are the *Sponsus* play, about the wise and foolish virgins awaiting the 'sponsus' (bridegroom), in *F-Pn* 1139 (early 12th century, from Limoges) and the verse plays about the miracles of St Nicholas, in *F-O* 201 (early 13th century, known as the 'Fleury Playbook', perhaps from the cathedral school at Orléans). These plays are linked by the use of strophic verse, where the same music may be used for several strophes (in the case of one of the Nicholas plays, for all strophes). By contrast, the *Ludus Danielis* composed by students of the cathedral school of Beauvais (in *GB-Lbl* Egerton 2615, early 13th century) is astoundingly rich and varied in musical material, mixing the occasional reference to liturgical melodies and conductus

from the Circumcision repertory with a large number of original compositions. The episode of the Slaughter of the Innocents inspired a number of laments of the mother Rachel. Far more numerous, at least in Italian and German sources, are laments sung by the Virgin Mary beneath the cross. Although both types connect loosely with a large repertory of non-liturgical laments (or *planctus*; see Yearley, N1981), the Marian laments, at least, had a place in the regular liturgy, often being sung after the Reproaches during the Adoration of the Cross on Good Friday. (The many German examples are known in the secondary literature as 'Marienklagen'.)

(viii) The medieval Office. The most ambitious compound musical form that flourished in the central Middle Ages was the Office in honour of local saints. Such Offices frequently contained more than 40 separate chants and a plethora of recited prayers: invitatories, antiphons, responsories, versicles, hymns, canticles, collects, psalms, lessons etc. The three nocturns of the night Office, MATINS (*Ad matutinum*), generally followed one of two main schemes. Among the monastic ('regular') orders, who lived according to the Rule of St Benedict (ed. A. de Vogüé, *La Règle de Saint Benoît*, Paris, 1971–7), the Office adhered to the 'monastic cursus'. Matins was made up of 13 antiphons and psalms, 12 lessons and 12 responsories, the 1st and 2nd nocturns each consisting of 6 antiphons and psalms, 4 lessons and 4 responsories, and the 3rd ('Ad cantica') of 1 antiphon with its canticles, 4 lessons and 4 responsories. At diocesan ('secular') establishments, where the Office was said according to the 'canonical' or 'Roman' cursus, Matins consisted of 9 antiphons and psalms, 9 lessons and 9 responsories, equally distributed among the three nocturns. Not all medieval Offices followed these schemes rigidly, however; Hesbert (CAO, ii, 1965, p.vii) demonstrated that some Offices in the early 11th-century Hartker Antiphoner from St Gallen (PalMus, 2nd ser., i, 1970), display a 'mixed' cursus. Taken together, the antiphon, lesson, and responsory texts in both the canonical and monastic Offices were called the 'historia', a term that can be traced back to the early 9th century (see P.J.G. Lehmann: *Erforschung des Mittelalters,* v, Stuttgart, 1962, pp.1–93). Among the oldest Gregorian Offices the *historiae* texts were derived primarily from the scriptures and the writings of the Church Fathers, but the texts of later patronal Offices were based on hagiographical sources, such as the lives (*vitae*) of the saints, stories of sufferings (*passiones*), stories pertaining to the recovery or the transfer (*translationes*) of relics, and stories of miracles, sermons etc. In these patronal Offices the narrative continuity of the saint's biography was carried on at some length in the lessons, while the normally brief antiphon and responsory texts provided a pious commentary.

The creation of a single liturgical formulary from an older *vita* is shown in the following example. Here, an antiphon from the oldest surviving Office of St Valeria of Limoges (in *F-Pn* lat.1085, ff.79–81*v*) is derived from the *Vita antiquior* of St Martial, the first bishop of Limoges, which dates from before 846 (see Emerson, O1965):

'Mariam' matrem gratie,
Rex regis regni glorie,
Matrem pie 'sanctificans',
'Mariam' sine crimine,
Omni pleni dulcedine,
Virgo matrem semper verans
Matrem Filio 'gubernans' [etc]

At the basilica of St Salvatoris Mundi in Limoges, eight feasts commemorating St Martial were introduced into the local liturgy at various times between 930 and 1550. These included his 'Natalis' (30 June and its Octave, 7 July), the first Translation of his relics to Solignac (10 and 17 October), the second Translation to Mons Gaudii (12 and 19 November), the 'Apparitio Martialis' (16 June) and an Office said on certain Thursdays. For purposes of identification the principal 'Natalis' Office of Martial (30 June) is referred to as the 'Venerandam', a name tag taken from its first distinctive patronal formula, the antiphon *Venerandam beatissimi patroni nostri domni Martialis*. In fact, the 'Venerandam' Office in a truncated form (dating from before 932 in *F-Pn* lat.1240, f.68) served as a 'mother' Office: as these various feasts entered the basilical liturgy over the decades, this prototype Office was reformatted, frequently with new patronal material, to create Offices for the new 'offspring' feasts. The two examples that follow indicate the manner by which patronal Offices were often assembled using the practice of shifting pre-existing liturgical formulae from one source to another.

The first concerns the 'Apparitio' feast of St Martial on 16 June; dating from shortly before 1200, it commemorated the miraculous manifestation of Christ to Martial 15 days before the saint's death (i.e. his 'natalis' or 'birth' into heaven – 30 June – according to the *Vita prolixior*, a lengthy and highly imaginative recension of the *Vita antiquior*). In this particular case, some of the original 'Venerandam' responsories for Matins (first column) were transferred to the later monastic rhymed Office of Martial, *Martialis festum recolens Aquitania plaude* (second column) found in *F-Pn* lat.5240, ff.116v–119v:

'Domine Fili unigenite, Jesu Christe.
'Spiritus et alme orphanorum Paraclete'
    Ex Patre semper genitus,
    Per flamen dulcis halitus,
    Ut flos novus est editus,
    Virga Jesse fecundata.
Dominie Deus, Agnus Dei, Filius Patris.
'Primogenitus Marie, virginis matris'
    Agnus Dei pacificus,
    Ysaac risus celitus [etc]

The second example is a feast unique to Notre Dame in Paris (4 December), the canonical Office *In susceptione reliquiarum*, probably composed between 1180 and 1200 (see Wright, O1985; and Baltzer, O1988), commemorating the reception of five relics into the newly built gothic cathedral. Based on *F-Pn* lat.15181, f.361v, this was a composite Office, 'cut wholecloth from pre-existing liturgical materials' (see Wright, op. cit., 7); its nine Matins responsories, for example, were borrowed from five different feasts:

[*In primo nocturno*]

1 Missus es Gabriel (Blessed Virgin Mary)
2. Ave Maria gratia plena (Blessed Virgin Mary)
3. Suscipe verbum virgo (Blessed Virgin Mary)

[*In secundo nocturno*]

    4. Inter natos (John the Baptist)
    5. Vir iste in populo (Andrew)
    6. Ecce iam coram (Stephen)

[*In tertio nocturno*]

7. In hoc ergo loco (Denis, first bishop of Paris)
8. Per beatum Dyonisium (Denis)
9. Vir inclitus Dyonisium (Denis)

These local saints' Offices were initially composed in the Frankish empire.

The dating of the Compiègne gradual–antiphoner (*F-Pn* lat.17436) to 877 (Huglo, D1993) indicates that the Offices for such northern French saints as Medardus, bishop of Noyon (8 June), Crispinus and Crispinianus, martyrs of Soissons (25 October), Vedastus, bishop of Arras (6 February), Quintinus, martyr of St Quentin (31 October), and Germanus, bishop of Paris (28 May), were in circulation before 877.

As new patronal feast-days entered the liturgy, especially after the 11th century, hundreds of new Offices were composed, frequently with texts in alliterative prose, and, from the 12th century, in accentual, rhymed verse. The tunes of the chants accompanying these texts were frequently arranged in modal order, as found in the first nocturn of the monastic Valeria Office cited above:

In primo Nocturno

Formula	Incipit	Mode no.
Antiphon 1	Beata Christi virgo Valeria	1
Antiphon 2	Erat enim gentilibus	2
Antiphon 3	Hanc discipulis Die	3
Antiphon 4	Sollicita pro salute	4
Antiphon 5	Dux Stephanus furore	5
Antiphon 6	Dum spernit Valeria	6

For basic studies of rhymed and versified Offices, see Hughes, O1983 and O1994–6; *see also* VERSIFIED OFFICE.

7. CHANT IN THE RELIGIOUS ORDERS.

(i) Cluny. From an examination of the extensive literature about Cluny, it is clear that the monastery, exempt from episcopal and lay control since its foundation in 910, was the dominant monastic institution in Western Europe at least until 1175. Under the direction of a remarkable succession of abbots, Berno (910–27), Odo (927–42), Aymard (942–54), Majolus (954–93), Odilo (994–1049) and Hugh (1049–1109), the monastery set patterns of reform that influenced the entire Church. The Rule of St Benedict was followed fervently; there was a marked tendency towards uniformity, since Cluny's many provincial dependencies were administered directly from the monastery; and there was a strong emphasis on contemplative spirituality.

An elaborate liturgy occupied most of the monks' daily life at Cluny, yet there are few substantial modern studies of the Cluniac liturgy (see Rosenwein, Q1971). It has been suggested that Cluny was not creative in its liturgy – 'the monastery borrowed and did not create' (Hunt, Q1967, p.109) – and that there were few unprecedented customs (see Rosenwein, op. cit., 132). Plainchant practice at the monastery is also poorly documented (but see Steiner, Q1984). Liturgical books with musical notation that are known to have been used at Cluny itself are rare (see Hourlier, Q1951, pp.231–2); they were probably destroyed when the monastery was pillaged in the 16th, 17th and 18th centuries. The major 11th-century source *F-Pn* lat.1087 (a gradual, proser, kyriale and sequentiary; *see* SOURCES, MS, §I) may not, in fact, be from the monastery at all, even though it contains the Office of St Odilo, the patron saint of Cluny (fig.5). Research into Cluniac plainchant is of necessity based primarily on documents from the monasteries dependent on Cluny (see Huglo, Q1957, pp.81–2; and Hourlier, Q1959).

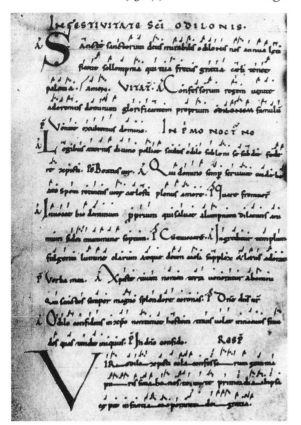

5. Office of St Odilo 'Sancte sanctorum Deus' from an 11th-century gradual from ?Cluny (F-Pn lat.1087, f.112v)

During the abbacy of Hugh of Cluny, an obscure monk named Bernard was directed to codify the traditional liturgical and administrative practices of the monastery. The resulting institutionalized customary of Bernard (ed. M. Herrgott, *Vetus disciplina monastica*, Paris, 1726, pp.134–364) was probably compiled between 1078 and 1082 (see Bishko, Q1961, pp.53–4), or compiled about 1075 and revised between 1084 and 1086 (see Hallinger, Q1970, pp.212–13). Less than a decade later (1083–5) Ulrich of Cluny prepared another customary, heavily indebted to Bernard's work, for Wilhelm of Hirsau (*PL*, cxlix, 635–778).

The liturgical usage of Cluny is also reflected in the order of chanted services adopted by houses dependent on Cluny. The basilica of St Salvatoris Mundi at the monastery of St Martial in Limoges is a good example. In September 1062 this monastery was forcibly reformed by a contingent of Cluniac monks and placed under the ecclesiastical province of Bourges; Adémar de Chabannes was installed as abbot, and the basilica remained under Cluniac rule for 472 years, until 1535. Soon after the reform, the Cluniac alleluia cycle (see above, §4) was used in a gradual and two prosers from the basilica (*F-Pn* lat.1132, 1134 and 1137). Later sources from the basilica that date from the 12th to the 16th centuries adhere closely to the Cluniac order of service codified by Bernard; these include *F-Pn* lat.1320 and 1042 (editions of Bernard's *Ordo officii* and *Ordo missae*), lat.741 (a capitulary and collectarium), lat.810 (a lectionary) and *LG* 4 (a breviary copied in 1491).

See also CLUNIAC MONKS, and BENEDICTINE MONKS.

(ii) Other orders. The development of the other major religious orders took place in two stages. Three monastic orders were founded in the 11th and 12th centuries: the Carthusians in 1084, the Cistercians in 1098 and the Premonstratensians in 1120 (see CARTHUSIAN MONKS; CISTERCIAN MONKS; PREMONSTRATENSIAN CANONS). The two mendicant orders followed later: the Franciscans in 1209 and Dominicans in 1217 (see FRANCISCAN FRIARS and DOMINICAN FRIARS).

Much of this type of monasticism, with a zealous emphasis on poverty, simplicity, solitude and a return to strict conformity to the Rule of St Benedict, had its roots in such 11th-century centres as Camaldoli, Fonte Avellana and Vallombrosa. Even though the formal establishment of the Augustinians took place in 1256 with the 'Great Union', a loose federation of canons already existed in Italy and southern France as early as 1039 (see AUGUSTINIAN CANONS). Monastic reforms of a localized nature occurred about 1100 at Savigny, Fontévrault, and Grandmont, near Limoges.

Several studies of plainchant in the various monastic orders have appeared, including those by Lambres (Q1970) and Becker (Q1971) on Carthusian chant, Marosszéki (Q1952) on Cistercian, Lefèvre (Q1957) and Weyns (Q1973) on Premonstratensian, Hüschen ('Franziskaner', *MGG1*) on Franciscan, and Delalande (Q1949) on Dominican, but for a number of reasons no adequate overview of this music has so far been possible. Firstly, there has been a tendency to neglect the monastic repertory because it is thought to represent the beginnings of a 'decadent' or 'debased' chant, one that deteriorated progressively until the restoration reforms of the late 19th century. Secondly, research in this field has often lacked objectivity and breadth of perspective because it has been carried out by ardent apologists for particular religious orders. Thirdly, and more seriously, there are no substantial studies of Cluniac chant, the precursor of all these monastic chant repertories; undue emphasis is placed on the Cistercian reforms as the 'crest of a wave', the implication being that the liturgy of Cluny was simply a ponderous forerunner of a more enlightened use that evolved at Cîteaux.

(a) Carthusians. Over 40 years separate the foundation of the Carthusian order in 1084 by St Bruno and the first *Consuetudines cartusiae* (*PL*, cliii, 635–760) in 1127 by Guigo, fifth prior of the Grande Chartreuse. No music manuscripts have been identified from this formative period, but it is now generally conceded that the early Carthusians, despite their severe ascetic and solitary life, did use plainchant. Later investigations have concentrated on two underlying problems: the nature of the primitive liturgy and the origins of Carthusian chant.

Becker's work (Q1971) seems to confirm what had long been suspected: that the original Carthusian breviary and antiphoner followed the Roman (secular) cursus, with nine lessons and nine responsories prescribed for Matins; and that by the time of Guigo, the Carthusian Office had become 'monasticized', with 12 antiphons, 12 lessons and 12 responsories as the norm. Concerning the origins of this chant, Becker postulated that the prototype of the Carthusian antiphoner was compiled during the abbacy of Landuin, prior from 1090 to 1100, but it is not known who prepared this redaction or precisely when it was undertaken.

The first Carthusian books may well have drawn on the practice of such religious establishments as Reims, St Ruf, Sèche-Fontaine, Vienne, Grenoble and Lyons, which were associated with St Bruno and his companions. The categorical statement that the 'predominant and exclusive influence in the formation of the Carthusian liturgy was the rite of the primatial See of Lyons' (*New Catholic Encyclopedia*, iii, New York, 1967, p.167) is not acceptable. Lambres (Q1970) pointed out that the Carthusian series of graduals and alleluias for the Pentecost season agrees very closely with that of Grenoble. Later, Becker (Q1975, pp.151–2) produced evidence that the canonical liturgy of Grandmont exerted an important influence on the formation of the Carthusian Office.

The prologue to the Carthusian antiphoner, *Institutionis heremitice gravitas*, written before 1132, is usually attributed to Guigo (but see the conflicting views of Becker, Q1971, pp.183–4, and Lambres, Q1973, pp.216–17, concerning its authorship). Though very brief and unspecific, it is unlike Bernard's *Prologus* to the Cistercian antiphoner (*c*1147) in that it sets forth the general principles of Carthusian plainchant reform. Firstly, 'since the gravity of eremitical life does not permit much time to be spent in the study of the chant', the compilers drastically reduced and simplified the entire repertory. This simplification assisted the hermits in memorizing the rules and melodies of plainchant. Secondly, texts that were not authentically biblical, such as those taken from the Apocrypha, those based on lives of the saints, or texts of private poetic inspiration, were suppressed. Thirdly, lengthy melodic melismas were discouraged, ornamental neumes that required special performance, such as the *quilisma*, were abandoned, and vertical bars were added to the melodies to assist the singers (see Lambres, Q1970, pp.23–4). Use or exclusion of the B♭ in Carthusian chant was not uniform (*see* CARTHUSIAN MONKS).

(b) Cistercians.   There are understandable reasons for the interest of scholars in 12th-century Cistercian chant reforms. The stylistic changes initiated at Cîteaux are historically important; the modifications to the melodies can be readily observed in the sources; the principles of melodic and modal revision are supported by the evidence of a group of early Cistercian musical treatises; and traditional Cluniac liturgical and musical practice can usefully be studied in the light of Cistercian reforms.

The basic Cistercian treatises (*PL*, clxxxii, 1121–66) have been reviewed by Sweeney (Q1972, pp.48–9). According to the *Exordium parvum* (compiled *c*1111), one of the early documents of Cistercian history, Robert, abbot of Molesme, together with 21 monks broke away from the monastery because of 'hindering circumstances' and founded a community at Cîteaux, near Dijon. For the next 40 years, during the tenures of Alberic (1099–1109) and Stephen Harding (1109–32), practically nothing is known of musical practice, except that the *Carta carita prior* of 1119 called for uniformity in all liturgical books and chanting. After 1140 the picture begins to change. Two unique musical statements – a prologue, *Bernardus humilis Abbas Clarevallis*, and a preface, *Cantum quem Cisterciensis ordinis* (ed. Guentner, Q1974) – were included in the Cistercian antiphoner of about 1147.

The author of the prologue, undoubtedly BERNARD OF CLAIRVAUX (1090–1153), described the origins of Cistercian chant. The founding fathers of the order were dissatisfied with their chant books and dispatched several men (scribes) to Metz to transcribe and bring back a copy of the cathedral's antiphoner, which was considered to be authentically Gregorian. Although the newly acquired books were found to be corrupt, they were used for many years. Eventually a committee of brethren deemed to be well instructed in the practice and theory of chant authorized Bernard to supervise the books' revision. Waddell ('The Origin and Early Evolution of the Cistercian Antiphonary', Q1970) expressed his conviction that this pre-Bernardine Messine chant survives in two 13th-century manuscripts, *F-ME 83* (from the Benedictine monastery of St Arnould) and *ME 461* (from Metz Cathedral).

Guy d'Eu, a monk at Clairvaux, is generally regarded as the author of the preface (*see* GUIDO OF EU and TONARY, §6(iv)). This treatise contains the rudiments of Cistercian chant theory. Those responsible for correcting the antiphoner deliberately pursued a course that they considered 'natural': 'chant melodies should conform with certain natural laws rather than perpetuate corrupt usage'. Chant books from Reims, Beauvais, Amiens, Soissons and Metz were singled out as particularly objectionable. A number of fundamental principles were set out in the preface: the unity of the mode must be maintained and cadence notes should belong to their proper *maneria* (the four modes of D, E, F and G); melodies should be modified so that their normal range would lie within the octave and their outer limits would never exceed a ten-note ambitus; B♭ in the musical notation should be excluded wherever possible; long melismas should be shortened; textual repetitions should be avoided; the scribes (notators) should preserve the integrity of proper neumatic structures and not separate them or join them together at will; and Guy insisted that the *neumae*, the *enēchēmata* (intonation formulae), should be corrected so that the *maneria* of each mode was clearly recognizable. As a result of the implementation of these 'natural' laws, the Cistercian sources contain many transposed and truncated melodies. One of the most easily detected stylistic adjustments made in Cistercian chant is the abbreviated melisma, as occurs, for example, in the alleluia *Dominus dixit ad me* for the first Mass of Christmas Day (ex.5).

Another well-known text commonly found appended to Cistercian chant sources is the *Tonale sancti Bernardi* (*PL*, clxxxii, 1153–4), a musical treatise that also sets out

Ex.5 Comparison of Roman and Cistercian versions of part of the verse
    Dominus dixit ad me from the alleluia for the first Mass of Christmas Day

(a) *Graduale romanum . . . editio Schwann P* (Düsseldorf, 1953), 34

(b) *Graduale cisterciense* (Westmalle, 1934), 28–9

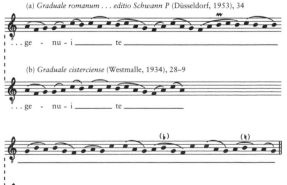

the reform principles of the Cistercians. Huglo (*Les tonaires*, L1971, pp.357–8) identified three versions, some conforming to the original and others abridged. The complex history of the Cistercian hymnal was reviewed by Kaul (see Q1948: xiii, 1951, p.257), Stäblein edited 86 melodies from *A-HE* 20 (12th- or 13th-century) and other manuscripts (K1956/R), and Waddell later edited the Cistercian hymnary anew (Q1984). Most sections of the prototype manuscript used to correct the copies (*correctorium, Normalkodex*), a collection of 15 liturgical books compiled in 1179 and 1191 to ensure uniformity of Cistercian liturgical texts and melodies, are now lost (*F-Dm* 114; see Leroquais, D1934, pp.333–4).

8. CHANT IN NORTHERN AND CENTRAL EUROPE.

(i) General. A significant phase in the history of the Western Church from about 950 to 1350 was the conversion of Scandinavia and central Europe. This expansion of Latin Christianity into Iceland and Norway in the north and to Croatia and Dalmatia in the south began with the decisive defeat of the Magyars and Slavs by Otto I at the Lech river near Augsburg in the summer of 955. Evangelization under the Ottonian emperors followed, leading first to the formation of national kingdoms and then to modern states. The consolidation of Christianity among the Slavs, Bulgar-Turks, Magyars, Uzhs, Pechenegs and Kumans adhered to a general pattern (see Falvy, S1987). At first, influential ruling families were accepted into the Church, then networks of dioceses were formed, among them Magdeburg (955), Poznań (968), Prague (973), Esztergom (1000), Lund (then part of Denmark, 1060) and Zagreb (1094). At the same time Benedictine monasteries were founded and by the 13th century the influx of other monastic and mendicant orders was well under way.

From a musical standpoint this process of Christianization raises several fundamental questions concerning the types of liturgical book that were brought into these lands by missionaries, the types of musical notation they contained, and the types of plainchant that were transmitted to the new dioceses.

As the conversion proceeded, cults of local saints grew up, and by the late 11th century these confessors and martyrs were beginning to be recognized officially in local liturgies; for example, Thorlac of Skálholt in Iceland; Magnus in the Orkney Islands; Olaf II Haraldsson, Hallvard and Sunniva in Norway; Anskar and Canute in Denmark; Eric, Bridget (Birgitta) and Sigfrid in Sweden; Henry in Finland; Stanislas, Adalbert (Wojciech), Hedwig (Jadwiga), Hyacinth (Jacek) and Florian in Poland; Stephen (István), Emeric (Imre) and Ladislas (László) in Hungary; and Ludmilla and Wenceslas (Václav) in Bohemia.

When the construction of monasteries, cathedrals and churches was well under way, scriptoria were set up in ecclesiastical schools. Locally produced liturgical books copied after the late 12th century tended increasingly to conform to newly codified orders of service. Specific diocesan uses became well entrenched from Nidaros (Trondheim) and Linköping to Esztergom and Zagreb. Study of the ordinals and customaries reflecting these uses is valuable for the light they cast on the tradition of the imported liturgies and music, and for the means they provide for determining the nature of later reforms, which, in some cases, lasted well into the 18th century.

A good deal of research has been carried out into Polish, Czech, Hungarian and Croatian plainchant, particularly in the area of manuscript studies; extensive work has also been done on the national sequence collections of Hungary (Rajeczky), Norway (Eggen), Sweden (Moberg) and Poland (Kowalewicz and Pikulik).

(ii) Denmark, Norway, Sweden, Finland. The conversion of the three Scandinavian kingdoms of Denmark, Norway and Sweden can be traced back to the founding of the German archbishopric of Bremen-Hamburg in 864. In Denmark, during the tenure of Bishop Adaldag (937–88), dioceses were set up in Schleswig, Ribe and Århus (all in 948), Odense (956) and Oldenburg (967/8). Although the Christianization of Denmark had been undertaken from Germany, the conversion of Norway during the Viking age came chiefly from England and Ireland in the reigns of King Håkon the Good (935–96) and King Olaf I Tryggvessøn (995–1000). In Sweden missionary efforts during the 9th and 10th centuries were largely unsuccessful; the new faith slowly replaced pagan religions after the baptism of Olof Skötkonung in about 1000 and his sons Anund Jakob (*c*1022–50) and Edmund (*c*1050–60). In Iceland Irish hermits settled as early as the 8th century, but it was not until 1000 that the national parliament, the Althing, accepted Christianity as the national faith. During the 11th century, three northern sees came under the administration of the Bremen-Hamburg archbishopric, then at the peak of its influence: Nidaros in Norway (*c*1029–1103), Skálholt in Iceland (1060) and the Danish province of Skänke (1060).

During this period of conversion and the establishment of bishoprics, the liturgies and music that were introduced into Scandinavia emanated from Germany, France and England. However, the scarcity of manuscript sources resulting from the widespread destruction of medieval liturgical books during the early Reformation in the wake of strong anti-papal sentiment has created special problems for the study of early Scandinavian liturgy and chant. Practically all the surviving original sources are strips of parchment that were used to reinforce the spines of 16th- and 17th-century tax records and books. Danish sources are exceptionally rare; 12 notated manuscripts dating from the 12th to the 16th centuries have been listed by Asketorp (S1984). Over 2300 Norwegian fragments recovered from old tax lists are retained by the Norwegian State Archives (Record Office) in Oslo, and there are many fragments in several Swedish libraries, particularly the University Library in Stockholm. The Icelandic fragments are now chiefly in the Reykjavik National Museum and the Arnamagnaena Collection at the University Library in Copenhagen (see Gjerløw, S1980). In Finland about 10,000 leaves are housed in the Helsinki University Library. While many of the earliest Finnish musical fragments are notated in German or Messine (Lorraine) neumes and appear to have been copied from, or at least based on, models from the diocese of Cologne (Haapanen, S1924), a surprising number of fragments are English or derive from English traditions (Taitto, S1992). Similarly, while the scattered melodies in the 12th-century *Manuale norvegicum* (ed. Faehn, S1962, with musical commentary by Stäblein), a priest's handbook of the Norwegian rite of Nidaros, are essentially Messine forms from north-west Europe (the Low Countries and northern France), Gjerløw has shown that the roots of the Nidaros liturgy are English (S1961, 1968, 1979; see also Attinger, S1998).

Several studies of early Scandinavian liturgy and chant have therefore been devoted to the earliest printed books containing complete liturgies, including the *Breviarium nidrosiense* (Paris, 1519) and *Missale nidrosiense* (Copenhagen, 1519); the *Missale aboense* (Lübeck, 1488); the *Missale lundense* (Paris, 1514) and *Breviarium lundense* (Paris, 1517); the *Breviarium arosiense* (Basle, 1513); the *Missale upsalense vetus* (Lübeck, 1484), *Missale upsalense novum* (Basle, 1513), *Breviarium upsalense* (Stockholm, 1496) and *Breviarium strengense* (Stockholm, 1496).

A definitive discussion of compositional techniques is difficult until further studies are made, but generally speaking most of the new chants were adaptations. The hymnographers set their new texts to well-known melodies, a representative example being the great, late 12th-century Olaf sequence *Lux illuxit laetabunda*, which honours the major patron and King of Norway, St Olaf II Haraldsson (ex.6). At least seven of its melodic phrases ('timbres') have been identified as direct borrowings from the repertory of Adam of St Victor (*fl* first half of the 12th century). Both Reiss (S1912) and Sandvik (S1941) believed that the anonymous author studied in Paris, but Eggen (S1968, p.221) was probably correct when he concluded 'that the composer … probably was a Norwegian, well versed in the international style of sequence

Ex.6 Sequence in honour of St Olaf II, after E. Eggen: *The Sequences of the Archbishopric of Nidaros* (Copenhagen, 1968), 213–14

melodies, [and] that he mainly leaned upon Anglo-French patterns instead of German ones'.

(iii) Poland.   The evangelization of Poland began in 966 with the conversion of Duke Mieszko I, founder of the Piast dynasty that ruled the nation until 1386. With the erection of the first bishoprics in Poznań, Wrocław, Kraków, Gniezno and Kołobrzeg between 968 and about 1000, the Latin rite was introduced into Poland, particularly through Bohemia (see Schenk, S1969, 2/1987, pp.145ff).

A wide variety of chant sources survives in Polish libraries (lists of these manuscripts have appeared from time to time in the journal *Musica medii aevi*). Feicht (S1965), in his survey of early Polish music, divided the development of chant into three historical periods: a Benedictine phase (968–1150), a Cistercian phase (1175–1230) and a Franciscan-Roman phase (after 1240). Węcowski (S1968) showed that south-German musical practice strongly influenced the early Benedictine books. German neumatic notation is found in the sacramentary of Tyniec (*PL-Wn* 302) copied in Cologne in about 1060; the *Ordinarius pontificalis antiquus* copied in the archdiocese of Salzburg at about the end of the 11th century (*WRk* 149); the Evangelarium of Płock (*Kz* 1207) of about 1130; and the *Missale plenarium* (*GNd* 149; facs. in Biegański and Woronczak, S1970–72) from Niederaltaich, dating from between 1070 and 1131. Among the oldest known Polish chants are those for St Adalbert (Wojciech), consecrated Bishop of Prague in 982. These include his metrical Office *Benedic regem cunctorum*, the antiphon *Magna vox laude sonora*, and the sequence *Annua recolamus sancti Adalberti gaudia* commemorating the translation of his relics to Rome in 1000. The edition by Kowalewicz, Morawski and Reginek (S1991) of hymns in Polish sources contains 71 breviary hymn tunes set to 159 texts, including the important *Gaude mater Polonia*, dedicated to St Stanislas, bishop of Kraków (inaugurated 1072), martyr, and the first Pole to be canonized (1253).

The first Cistercian monasteries in Poland were founded in about 1149 at Brzeźnica-Jędrzejów, Ląd and Lekno, but their reformed liturgy and chant seems to have had little impact on established diocesan use and remained confined to the order. Several important 13th- and 14th-century music manuscripts (*PL-Pa* 69; *PE* 118–19, 156–204, *L* 13, *L* 21, *L* 35; *WRu* I.F.411–18) survive from the abbeys of Lubiąz (founded 1175), Henryków (1227), Paradyż (1234), Kamieniec Ząbkowicki (1239) and Pelplin (1258). A study by Morawski (*Polska liryka muzyczna*, S1973) of a set of 49 Cistercian sequences, found in seven graduals, indicates that they originated at St Gallen and other Benedictine monasteries in southern Germany.

At Kraków the Franciscans founded a house in 1237; at least six others followed during the next 20 years. The oldest surviving book in Poland used by the friars is the gradual of the Poor Clares covent in Kraków, copied in the period between approximately 1234 and 1260 (*PL-Kklar* 205). A companion manuscript is the Franciscan gradual of Płock dating from about 1280 (*PLd* VI.3.5). Other significant noted manuscripts are in libraries in Stary Sącz, Gniezno and Kraków.

The pervasive influence of German and French elements in medieval Polish liturgy and music has been demonstrated by Pikulik in his general survey of 475 sequences from 26 diocesan and 23 monastic manuscripts (S1973). In addition to the Cistercian group, the Imbramowice and Kraków Premonstratensian sequences and the Franciscan repertory were formed in Bavaria and Switzerland. But among the Premonstratensian graduals from Wrocław and Czerwinsk and the Dominican books, French types dominate, especially those of Adam of St Victor. The writing of native sequences occurred mainly at the Jagellonian University in Kraków, founded in 1364. Most of the new metrical texts were set to well-known foreign melodies.

Active composition of patronal liturgies in Poland continued into the 17th century. In addition to the Office of St Adalbert, several *historiae* were composed commemorating the major patrons of Poland. The Office of St Stanislas, *Dies adest celebres* (AH, v, 1889/R, p.223), was written by a Dominican friar, Wincenty of Kielce (c1253–5); the Office of St Hedwig (Jadwiga), *Fulget in orbe dies* (AH, xxvi, 1897/R, p.86), dates from the end of the 13th century; and the Office of St Hyacinth (Jacek), *Adest dies celebres* (AH, xlva, 1904/R, p.115), was written by three Dominicans, Ezjasz of Lipnica (d 1609) and the friars Adam and Andrzej.

(iv) Bohemia and Moravia. The evangelization of Moravia began in 863, by SS Cyril and Methodius of the Byzantine Church, but the destruction caused by the Magyar invasions halted the progress of this Christianization. It was rather from Bavaria that Roman Christianity with its liturgy and music became established, the bishopric of Prague in Bohemia being created in 973 (archbishopric 1344), that of Olomouc in Moravia in 1063. Important monastic foundations also date back to the 10th century, for example, the Benedictine convent of St George (Jiří) in Prague in 967, followed later by the houses of the Premonstratensians (Strahov, Prague, 1140) and Cistercians (Sedlec, 1143). German chant traditions are, not surprisingly, evident in early sources of chant from Bohemia. German neumatic notation is found as late as the 14th century, although staff notation (Messine) was introduced by Vitus, dean of St Vitus's (Wojtěch's) cathedral, Prague, in the mid-13th century (examples in Hutter, S1930, 1931; Plocek, S1973).

Proper Offices for the national saints Adalbert, Procopius, Wenceslas and Ludmila have survived (Patier, S1970, S1986). Bohemia was strongly involved in the production of new Ordinary of Mass melodies, votive antiphons, and especially cantiones (see §6(v) above; see also Orel, S1922) in the 14th and 15th centuries, although from the surviving sources it is not always clear in some individual cases whether a piece originated in Bohemia or in south Germany or Austria. During the Hussite period large numbers of Latin chants were translated into the national language (surviving in *CZ-Pnm* II.C.7, the Jistebnice Cantional, from the 1420s). Another individual development is associated with the Utraquists from the 1540s, in whose books liturgical melodies are treated on the one hand to revision in syllabic style, on the other also to the addition of new melismas.

(v) Hungary. The Christianization of the Magyars reached a critical stage in 955 with the baptism of Géza (reigned 972–97), prince of the Árpád dynasty, and his son and successor Prince Vajk, later St Stephen (István), king of Hungary (997–1038, canonized 1083). King Stephen founded ten bishoprics at Esztergom (Lat. Strigonium; Ger. Gran), Győr (Raab), Székesfehérvár

(Stuhlweissenburg), Veszprém (Wesprim), Kalocsa, Bihar, Pécs (Fünfkirchen), Nyitra (Neutra), Vác (Waitzen) and Csanád. During the same period Benedictine monasteries were founded at Pannonhalma (Martinsberg), Bakonybél, and Pécsvárad (see Dobszay, 'Plainchant in Medieval Hungary', S1990). After tribal revolts in 1047 and 1063, Christianity was firmly established by St Ladislas (László; reigned 1077–95); Croatia and Dalmatia were brought under Hungarian control by his nephew Coloman (Kálmán) I (1095–1116). In an effort to retain a uniform Roman liturgy, the Hungarian bishops in about 1100 prescribed the order of service in Bernold of Constance's *Micrologus de ecclesiasticis officiis.* Until 1630 two diocesan rites dominated the Hungarian liturgy: the primatial use at Esztergom and the archbishopric use at Kalocsa. The origins of these liturgies are believed to go back to about 1094.

The earliest surviving plainchant manuscripts in Hungary are notated in German neumes (see Szendrei, S1983, esp. 56–70, and 'Die Geschichte der Graner Choralnotation, S1988). They include a group of manuscripts copied shortly before 1092 and taken to Zagreb at about the time the diocese was founded in 1094 (see (*vi*) below). The oldest fully notated chant book from Hungary is a secular antiphoner, *A-Gu* 211 (Codex Albensis; facs. edn by Falvy and Mezey, S1963), from Székesfehérvár; dating from the first half of the 12th century, it shows strong south German influences, particularly of the Bavarian regions (Passau and Niederaltaich). The order of service seems to follow the Esztergom use.

Descriptive studies of other Hungarian chant sources have been made by Rajeczky and Radó (S1956, 2/1982), Szigeti (S1963), Radó (S1973), Szendrei (S1981) and Dobszay (S1985). Radó's *Libri liturgici manuscripti bibliothecarum Hungariae* (S1973) includes studies of the Pray Manuscript, a sacramentary dating from 1192–5 in Messine notation (no.2); nine missals from Pozsony (Pressburg, Bratislava) (nos.11–14, 27–9, 45–6); the 13th-century Missal of Hungary (no.6); the Vác Manuscript of 1423 (no.40); the missal of George Pálóczi, 1423–39 (no.41); the *Liber variarum cantionum* of 1516 (no.72); the Esztergom pontifical and antiphoner (nos.145 and 180); the Kaschau gradual (no.173); the graduals of Cardinal Bakócz and King Ladislas II (nos.171–2); and an antiphoner from Győr Cathedral (no.181). Facsimiles of the principal Hungarian chant books have been published: the Esztergom noted missal (ed. Szendrei and Ribarič, D1982) and the Esztergom noted breviary (ed. Szendrei, D1998); and Szendrei has transcribed the Esztergom gradual (D1990–93). The complete Hungarian antiphon repertory has been edited by Dobszay and Szendrei (D1999).

The earliest chants produced in Hungary by local poets and composers include an Office for St Stephen, *Ave beate Stephane*, for 20 August, in the Székesfehérvár Antiphoner (ff.114–114v); and three other Offices (ed. Falvy, *Drei Reimoffizien*, S1968): *Confessor Christi Stephane*, for St Stephen; *Laetare, Pannonia*, for Emeric, his son (d 1031); and *Fons eternae pietatis*, for St Ladislas (canonized 1192). Two Offices for St Elizabeth of Hungary (canonized 1253), *Gaudeat Hungaria* and *Laetare Germania*, have also been edited (Haggh, O1995), but these did not originate in Hungary.

(vi) Slovenia and Croatia. In medieval Slovenia and Croatia, two Christian liturgies co-existed. The rural

Slavonic rite was written in Greek-derived Glagolitic script dating from the 9th century and used particularly in northern Dalmatia (see Gamber, S1957; and Martinić, S1981). In the metropolitan cities a modern Cyrillic alphabet was frequently used with the Roman rite. The reconstruction of Slavonic chant has been largely based on chant sung today in the dioceses of Krk, Senj, Zadar and Šibenik. (*See also* GLAGOLITIC MASS, GLAGOLITIC CHANT.)

The Roman rite in Croatia, according to Grgić (S1970, pp.125–6), can be separated into two distinct zones each characterized by a distinct palaeographical tradition. Among the monasteries founded in the 11th century along the Adriatic coast, such as Kotor, Zadar, Šibenik, Trogir, Split and Dubrovnik, there is a strong south-Italian tradition emanating from Monte Cassino and Bari. The liturgy, musical notation and script are distinctly Beneventan (*see* BENEVENTAN CHANT). On the other hand, Carolingian minuscule, German neumatic notation and their later Gothic counterparts dominated in Slovenia and other areas controlled by the German empire and Hungarian monarchy.

A considerable number of medieval liturgical manuscripts survive from this region; pioneer work in identifying them was carried out by Morin and Kniewald, but of special importance is the work of Vidaković (S1960), which shows how deeply Latin medieval notation penetrated into south-east Europe. The earliest manuscripts containing German neumatic notation are associated with the 'Zagreb' liturgy. These books were brought to Croatia from Hungary when the diocese of Zagreb was established in 1094, during the period when Ladislas I and Coloman (reigned 1095–1116) placed Croatia and Slovenia under Hungarian rule in 1096–7. The *Agenda pontificalis* of Bishop Hartwick (*HR-Zu* MR 165) originated at Győr in north-west Hungary; Hudovský (S1971) has shown that the musical notation was added at several stages during the 11th, 12th and 13th centuries. A benedictional (*Zu* MR 89) was copied at Esztergom before 1083 (see Hudovský, S1967) and a sacramentary (*Zu* MR 126) was taken to Zagreb from Hungary by Bishop Duh in the late 11th century.

Among the early Beneventan manuscripts, part of the 11th-century *Missale plenum* was copied at Monte Cassino and part in Dalmatia (see Hudovský, S1965). Specimens of Beneventan notation occur among the Exultet chants in three Gospel books: the St Mary's Evangeliary (*GB-Ob* Can lat.61), the Osar ('St Nicholas') Evangeliary (*I-Rvat* Borg.lat.339) and the St Simeon Evangeliary (*D-Bsb* theol.lat. 4° 278).

9. CHANT IN LATIN AMERICA. After the conquest of the ancient Amerindian nations of Peru, Mexico and the south-western part of the North America by the Spanish colonists, networks of administrative jurisdiction were set up by early 16th- and 17th-century missionary fathers. In many respects the ecclesiastical history of New Spain resembles the evangelization of Scandinavia and eastern Europe some five centuries earlier. At first liturgies and sacred music imported from the Old World were used, but these were rapidly supplemented and modified to harmonize with local native languages and customs. Despite the survival of much evidence, both direct and indirect, knowledge of this chant repertory is still superficial, no doubt largely because it has been regarded as one of the 'corrupt' post-Tridentine versions. Neverthe-

less, when viewed in its own historical and social setting, this chant has an interest of its own.

Plainchant sources used in the New World can be separated into three general categories: liturgical books with musical notation issued by well-known publishing houses in Italy, Germany, France, Spain and Portugal and introduced by the missionaries; chant books printed in the Americas, especially in Mexico; and manuscripts produced locally. About a dozen extant Mexican incunabula with plainchant melodies were printed before 1600, the earliest being the Augustinian ordinary of 1556 (see Spell, T1929; and Stevenson, T1966). In archival surveys of South American libraries, Spiess and Stanford (T1969) and Stevenson (T1970) have recorded no fewer than 350 extant plainchant manuscripts. However, since the primary interest of these scholars has been directed towards polyphonic music, their descriptions of chant books rarely go beyond brief notices. For example, in the Bogotá Cathedral archive there are '32 atlas-size plainchant choirbooks expensively copied on vellum between 1606 and 1608 by the professional music scribe and miniaturist, Francisco de Páramo' (Stevenson, T1970, p.3); and in the cathedral library at Puebla (Mexico) there are about 128 plainchant tomes with illuminations mainly by Lagarto (see Spiess and Stanford, op. cit., 27). Plainchant manuscripts are also found in other Latin American cities, including Mexico City, Quito, and Cuzco (Peru).

Even as late as the early 19th century, manuscript choirbooks were being produced in the Californian missions (see Ray and Engbeck, T1974). From 1769 until 1834, when they were secularized, a chain of 21 Franciscan missions flourished along the central coast of California (see Koegel, T1993). Among these interesting late sources, for example, is a Mass book compiled in 1831 by Padre Narciso Durán (1776–1846) for the church of St Joseph at the Mission of S José (extract in fig.6). In his solicitous *Prologo* (Eng. trans. in da Silva, T1941, p.29), Durán explained his need to simplify plainchant melodies for the Amerindian neophytes. Graduals and offertories were considered too complicated and were not sung; most introits were derived from the melody of *Gaudeamus omnes*, the introit for the feast of the Assumption; and alleluias and communions were chanted to several melodies of the 6th tone. In order to assist the singers, he laid down the rule that chant was to be accompanied in unison by instruments. With all the practical instincts of a good choir director, Durán recommended that the older, married, trained musicians be provided with 'domestic employment, such as weaving, shoemaking or smithying, in order to have them always on hand when there is singing or playing to be done'.

10. DEVELOPMENTS FROM 1500 TO 1800.

(i) Tridentine reforms. In 1536 a bull of convocation was issued by Pope Paul III (pontificate 1534–49) convening the 19th Ecumenical Council of the Western Church, the Council of Trent (1545–63). The purpose of this Council, held in Trent (at that time Austrian), was to clarify doctrinal beliefs and legislate for disciplinary reforms within the Church as a reaction to the Protestant Reformation, in particular to combat the religious reforms of Luther, Zwingli and Calvin. Over a period of 18 years, 25 sessions were held in three separate sittings. Decrees relating specifically to church music were issued on 17 September 1562. The most important pronouncements appeared in the proceedings of session XXII, chapter IX,

6. Mass of Our Lady of Guadalupe (12 December) from the Durán Mass Book, compiled 1831 (US-BEm C.C.59, p.40)

canon IX, which confirmed the sacrificial character of the Mass and Eucharist: *Decretum de observandis et evitandis in celebratione missarum* ('Decree concerning the things to be observed and to be avoided in the celebration of Mass'; see *Concilium tridentinum*, ix: *Actorum*, ed. S. Ehses, Freiburg, 1924, pp.962–3).

The bishops unanimously agreed in the September session: (1) that any simony, irreverence and superstition be banished from Mass; (2) that any unknown priest be forbidden to celebrate Mass; (3) that music be uplifting for the faithful; (4) that spoken words or sung liturgy be clearly intelligible; (5) that all music, whether for the organ or voices, which contained things deemed lascivious or impure ('lascivum aut impurum') be excluded; and (5) that all conversations, walking about, or distracting noise be repudiated during Mass. In Session XXIV (11 November 1563), Canon XII: *Decretum de reformatione lectum* (see *Concilium tridentinum*, ix: *Actorum*, ed. S. Ehses, Freiburg, 1924, p.984), rather vague instructions were issued that provincial synods could establish musical practices according to the local needs and customs of the people. The decrees relating to music that were adopted at the Council of Trent set out broad principles and instructions and were generally couched in negative language; they were not directly implemented by the Council itself, but were put into practice by a series of papal actions during the next 70 years up to 1634.

The initial attempts to introduce a uniform and universal recitation of the Office and Mass in accordance with the mandates of the Council were completed during the pontificates of Pius IV (1559–65) and Pius V (1566–72). In October 1563 a commission was established to reform the breviary and missal. Publication of the reformed Roman breviary was announced on 9 July 1568, and of the corrected Roman missal in a bull dated 14 July 1570. All dioceses were obliged to use the missal. (For a review of the impact of the 1570 missal on south-German dioceses, see Opraem, U1995.)

It is generally accepted that the large repertory of medieval sequences was suppressed from the liturgy at this time. Only four were included in the Faletti-Variscum edition of the 1570 missal: *Victimae Paschali laudes* (written by Wipo, c995–c1050) for Easter and Easter week; *Veni Sancte Spiritus* (by Innocent III, pontificate 1198–1216) for Pentecost and Pentecost week; *Lauda Sion* (by Thomas Aquinas, c1225–74) for Corpus Christi; and *Dies irae* (by Thomas of Celano, d c1250) for the Commemoration of the Dead. Given this missal's chaotic publishing history (see A. Ward, *Ephemerides liturgicae*, cxi, 1997, pp.49–54), it is possible that different editions contain the sequence *Stabat mater* (by Jacopone da Todi, d 1306). Two important revisions of the 1570 Pian missal were issued: one in 1604 under Clement VIII (1592–1605), and the other in 1634 during the pontificate of Urban VIII (1623–44).

Once the new official liturgical texts had been proclaimed, efforts were begun to adapt standard chant melodies to them. On 25 October 1577 Palestrina and Annibale Zoilo were commissioned by Gregory XIII 'to purge, correct, and reform Gregorian chant', but their work was never completed (see Molitor, U1901–2/R, 297). In 1582 Giovanni Guidetti, a student and friend of Palestrina, published in Rome the first complete post-Tridentine chant book, the *Directorium chori ad usum sacrosanctae basilicae vaticanae et aliarum cathedralium et collegiatarum ecclesiarum*. It continued to be republished until 1750 and contained the basic elements for singing the Divine Office: cadence formulae, the principal psalms, hymns, versicles, short responsories, reciting notes for psalms, lessons, Gospels and prayers. A unique feature of the *Directorium* was Guidetti's use of proportional notation: the *semibrevis*, or diamond-shaped note, had the value of a half-*tempus*, the *brevis*, or square note, equalled one *tempus*, and the dotted *brevis cum semicirculo*, or square note surmounted by a pause sign, was equivalent to two *tempi* (fig.7).

These rhythmic notes were frequently explained in later treatises and singing manuals on plainchant, such as G.C. Marinelli's *Via retta della voce corale* (Bologna, 1671/R); Lorenzo Penna's *Direttorio del canto fermo* (Modena, 1689); Andrea di Modena's *Canto harmonico* (Modena, 1690/R); Giuseppe Frezza dalle Grotte's *Il cantore ecclesiastico* (Padua, 1698); O. Rosa de Cairano's *Regole del canto fermo detto gregoriano* (Naples, 1788); and J.G. Mettenleiter's *Enchiridion chorale* (Regensburg, 1853). (On the instrumental accompaniment of plainchant from the 16th century, see §11 below.)

The most important chant book conforming to the reforms of the Council of Trent was the new Roman gradual. On 31 May 1608 Paul V (pontificate 1605–21) granted G.B. Raimondi printing rights, and six musicians were commissioned as editors – Felice Anerio, Pietro Felini, Ruggiero Giovannelli, Curzio Mancini, Giovanni Maria Nanino and Francesco Soriano. By 1611 the membership had dwindled to two members, Anerio and Soriano, both of whom, like Guidetti, had been closely associated with Palestrina. When Raimondi died on 13 February 1614 publication was transferred to the Medici

7. Proportional notation in G.D. Guidetti's 'Directorium chori' (Rome, 1582), p.5

Press in Rome; the *Graduale … iuxta ritum sacrosanctae romanae ecclesiae cum cantu, Pauli V. pontificis maximi iussu reformatio … ex typographica Medicaea* appeared in two volumes, in 1614 (the *Temporale*) and 1615 (the *Sanctorale*).

The Anerio-Soriano Medicean edition of the gradual strongly reflected 16th-and 17th-century humanist interest in the relationship between text and melody. The liturgical texts were revised to 'improve' the quality and character of the Latin, cadential patterns were reshaped, certain stereotyped melodic figures were associated with certain words, melodic clichés were introduced to 'explain' words, melodies were made more tonal by the introduction of the B♭, melismas were abbreviated, and accentual declamation was introduced to improve the intelligibility of the chanted text. For example, some typical melodic and tonal variants may be observed in the Medicean version of the first responsory for Easter Matins (ex.7).

During the interim period between the papal commission to Palestrina and the appearance of the Medicean gradual, various 'reformed' graduals were brought out by Venetian publishers, the first, by Gardano, in 1591, followed by a new version, by Giunta, in 1596. The latter became the basis of a Venetian chant tradition that continued into the late 18th century through successive editions by Giunta, Cieras, Baba, Baglioni and Pezzana. The texts were the standard ones of earlier centuries, although some were slightly revised in accordance with

the new missal. By 1618 an independent 'reformed' gradual was issued in Ingolstadt, and a further one appeared in 1620 in Antwerp. By 1627 the first of a series of editions constituting a Parisian tradition had been published. Minor similarities are evident between certain traditions, but borrowings on a wider scale are generally rare. The importance of the Medicean gradual derived from Rome's position as an ecclesiastical centre, but its readings had little if any influence elsewhere. Various religious orders also created their own versions, in some cases much earlier than the date the reworkings were first documented. The different readings existed side by side with more traditional ones almost wholly rooted in 15th-and 16th-century chant practice.

In general, Giunta and his Venetian successors pruned the medieval melodies most heavily, while greater floridity is evident in the sources from further north. Despite the appearance of many chant treatises describing a range of rhythmic values, only a few values are used in the practical manuals. The most frequent, apart from the standard square shape, is the diamond-shaped *semibrevis*; representing half the normal value, it was associated with weak syllables following accented antepenultimate or even earlier syllables.

The modern Roman breviary in use before the Second Vatican Council is substantially the *Pianum* of 1568 with the revisions it underwent under Clement VIII (1602) and Urban VIII (1631). The latter reform is particularly important in the history of plainchant, because it introduced significant recasting of the traditional Office hymns. Under the direction of four classically trained Jesuits, Famiano Strada, Tarquinio Galuzzi, Girolamo Petrucci and Matthias Sarbiewski, 952 corrections were made to the 98 hymns included in the breviary (see Lenti, U1993, p.31). In their zeal to restore classical metre and prose to the Latin texts, the revisers recast some hymns and in so doing created almost unrecognizable substitutes. These changes in the hymn texts were sanctioned by the Congregation of Rites on 29 March 1629, and the newly revised *Breviarium romanum* was approved by Urban VIII (1623–44) on 25 January 1631 (see Lenti, op.cit.,

Ex.7 Comparison of Roman (Solesmes) and Medicean versions of an Easter responsory

(a) *Liber responsorialis* (Solesmes, 1894), 83

An - ge - lus Do - mi — - ni   de - scen -

(b) *Antiphonarium romanum* (Venice: Giunta, 1614), p.81v

An - ge - lus Do - mi — - ni   de - scen -

- dit de cae — lo   et ac - ce - dens re - vol -

- dit de cae — lo   et ac - ce - dens re   vol -

- vit la - pi — dem   etc

- vit la - pi — dem   etc

32). The following example shows a single hymn in its original and revised versions (from Daniel, M1841–56/R, i, 239).

Original	Reformed
Urbs beata Hierusalem	Coelestic urbs Ierusalem
Dicta pacis visio	Beata pacis visio
Quae construitur in coelis	Quae celsa de viventibus
Vivis ex lapidibus	Saxis ad astra tolleris
Et angelis coronata	Sponsaeque ritu cingeris
Ut sponsata comite	Mille angelorum millibus
Nova veniens e coelo	O sorte nupta prospera
Nuptiali thalamo	Dotata patris gloria
Praeparata ut sponsata	Respersa sponsi gratia
Copulatur Domino	Regina formosissima
Plateae et muri ejus	Christo iugata principi
Ex auro purissimo	Coelo coruscas civitas
Portae nitent margaritis	Hic margaritis emicant
Adytis patentibus	Patentque cunctis ostia
Et virtute meritorum	Virtute namque praevia
Illuc introducitur	Mortalis illuc ducitur
Omnis, qui pro Christi nomine	Amore Christi percitus
Hic in mundo premitur	Tormenta quiquis sustinet
Tunsionibus, pressuris	Scalpri salubris ictibus
Expoiliti lapides	Et tunsione plurima
Suis coaptantur locis	Fabri polita malleo
Per manum artificis	Hanc saxa molem construunt
Disponuntur permansuri	Aptisque juncta nexibus
Sacris aedificiis.	Locantur in fastigio.

In defence of these revised Jesuit hymns, now often considered 'decadent', Pocknee (U1954, p.2) observed that 'the later hymns have a rugged sincerity, a biblical tone, and a clear presentment of the facts of belief which more than atoned for the change of literary style'. Although the revised hymns were made obligatory for the Church at large, most of the monastic orders – the Dominicans, Benedictines, Cistercians, Carthusians and the Papal Chapel itself – rejected Urban's revised hymnal and maintained the earlier forms.

The process of standardization that began at Trent has, unfortunately, often been misunderstood. The Council was, in fact, a truly conservative movement. No new liturgy was set forth (the terms 'Tridentine Mass' and 'Tridentine Office' are misleading); religious establishments throughout Europe were required to follow prescribed customs and normative usage as well as to use 'corrected' liturgical books. Furthermore, the intended musical reforms were not realized, for despite the official imprimatur affixed to most chant books – *Ex decreto Sacrosancti Concilii Tridentini restituti* – a bewildering variety of chant melodies continued to flourish for another 300 years.

(ii) Neo-Gallican reforms. The French nationalistic tradition of relative independence from Rome in both political and ecclesiastical affairs has its roots in the early Middle Ages. During the 17th and 18th centuries a particularly strong surge of anti-papal feeling caused a widespread theological schism within the ranks of the French national church. The *Declaratio cleri gallicani* (19 March 1682), known as the 'Four Gallican Articles', was issued by the dissenting bishop Jacques Bossuet (1627–1704) and resulted in major changes in the liturgy and church music. In the diocese of Paris under Archbishop François de Harlay de Champvallon (1625–95), a revised 'neo-Gallican' breviary was published in 1680, followed by the antiphoner in 1681, the missal in 1684 and the gradual in 1689 (see Launay, U1993, p.292). In these

books many of the standard liturgical formularies were suppressed and replaced with substitutes.

Even more radical editions appeared under Charles de Vintimille du Lac (archbishop of Paris, 1729–46), and these were adopted by more than 50 French dioceses. In the Vintimille edition only 21 original hymns were retained, although new hymns by contemporary hymnographers abounded: 85 by Jean-Baptiste de Santeüil (*d* 1697), nearly 100 by Charles Coffin (*d* 1742; fig.8) and 97 by lesser-known French authors.

Closely associated with these neo-Gallican reforms was the introduction of a distinctive type of music known as the 'chant figuré', sung in a measured and ornamented style. The most important treatises explaining the performance of this measured chant were written by Guillaume-Gabriel Nivers, Léonard Poisson, Jean Lebeuf and François de La Feillée. In his *Méthode nouvelle pour apprendre parfaitement les règles du plain-chant et de la psalmodie, avec des messes et autres ouvrages en plainchant figuré et musical* (Poitiers, 3/1775, pp.96–116), La

8. Hymn 'Te laeta, mundi Conditor' by Charles Coffin from the 'Antiphonaire parisien suivant le nouveau breviare' (pt 11, 1737), p.101

Feillée provided a detailed explanation of the types of notes and principles of performance. In addition to elision, tremolo, accidentals and prolongation signs, the basic note values were as follows: the *quarrées ordinaires à queue* (large square notes with a descending stem to the right); the *quarrées sans queues* (large square notes); the *demi-quarrées à queue* (small square notes with a descending stem to the left); the *demi-quarrées sans queue* (small square notes); the *grandes brèves* (large diamond-shaped notes); and the *petites brèves* (small diamond-shaped notes) (see Launay, op. cit., esp. 413–31, and pls.45–7).

Despite the outward simplicity of this metrical system, performance of *chant figuré* required sophisticated improvisatory skills, including tremolo, vibrato, portamento and ornaments. In order to maintain measure, the choirs were frequently accompanied in unison by a bass instrument, such as a serpent, ophicleide, bassoon, trombone, double bass etc. (see Lebeuf, U1741/R, p.177; and C. Burney: *The Present State of Music in France and Italy*, London, 1771, 2/1773/R, 10ff). Performance of this chant was highly expressive. Verses in the *Messe musicale* of La Feillée, which were sung by a soloist and a choir in alternation, indicate frequent shifts in tempo from *lent*, *lentement* or *gravement* to *gai* or *gracieusement* (fig.9).

Another type of metrical plainchant was commonly practised in the neo-Gallican liturgy, 'l'art du fleuretis ou Chant sur le livre' (Lebeuf, U1741, p.110). *Chant sur le livre* (also termed 'contrapunctum', 'descant' or 'fleuretis') was counterpoint improvised at sight by trained singers to the melodies of the regular service books (see Prim,

U1961). Responsories, antiphons and introits in particular were subject to this type of accompaniment. The plainchant melody was usually sung in strict measured cantus firmus style by strong bass voices accompanied in unison by a bassoon or serpent, while the florid descant melodies were improvised above it. Harmonic and metrical rules were set out in at least ten treatises, especially by Etienne Loulié, Sébastien de Brossard, René Ouvrard and Pierre-Louis Pollio (see Montagnier, 'Les sources manuscrites', U1995).

The Gallican plainchant practised between the mid-17th century to the second Restoration of the monarchy in France (1815–30) has been dismissed with hostility and ridicule, especially by 19th- and 20th-century Roman Catholic clerics and writers. Gallican hymnody, *chant figuré*, *chant sur le livre* and the reformation of the liturgy by humanists during the *ancien régime* have generally been epitomized as insipid, decadent and barbarous – 'un chant étriqué, mesquin, pauvre, horriblement mutilé, une sorte d'habit d'arlequin composé de pièces décousues' (N. Cloet: *Mémoire sur le choix des livres de chant liturgique*, Paris, 1856). In reality neo-Gallican plainchant is a large, self-contained corpus of music with its own historical and liturgical setting, deserving further detailed research.

See also NEO-GALLICAN CHANT and PLAIN-CHANT MUSICAL.

11. RESTORATION AND REFORM IN THE 19TH CENTURY.

(i) Early reform in France. With the Concordat of 7 October 1801 between Napoleon I and Pius VII (pontificate 1800–23) and later concordats of reconciliation (see Gaudemet and others, U1987, 17–29), the forces of

9. 'Messe musicale' from François de La Feillée's 'Méthode nouvelle pour apprendre parfaitement les règles du plain-chant' (3/1775), pp.214–15

separatism and secularism and the confiscation of Church property, onslaughts to which the Roman Church had been subjected during the Enlightenment, gradually subsided. The decline of such political and religious theories as Febronianism, Gallicanism, Josephinism, Jansenism and monarchical absolutism led to spiritual renewal and a golden epoch of ecclesiology during the 19th century. The 40 years between the publication of Félix Danjou's *De l'état et de l'avenir du chant ecclésiastique en France* (Paris, 1844) and the *Liber gradualis* (Tournai, 1883) prepared by Dom Joseph Pothier marked a significant period of chant reform. With the success of the Ultramontane movement in France (see Moulinet, U1997), by the 1840s it was generally recognized that the Harlay and Vintimille chant books were unsuitable and needed to be replaced by books that once again conformed to the Roman liturgy. This need had been expressed three decades earlier by Choron in his *Considérations sur la nécessité de rétablir le chant de l'église de Rome dans toutes les églises de l'Empire français* (Paris, 1811). Despite repeated calls for unity, return to the old Tridentine use proceeded very slowly, diocese by diocese (see especially E.-G. Jouve: *Du mouvement liturgique en France durant le XIXe siècle*, Paris, 1860). Ecclesiastical officials and music scholars were sharply divided as to which chant melodies should be used. Many favoured a return to the early Medicean chant books; others considered that the chants in these books were debased in comparison with the ones in 11th-, 12th- and 13th-century sources in Guidonian notation. A third group defended the authenticity of the early neumatic manuscripts even though the latter were practically indecipherable at the time. Scholars and dilettantes of widely differing persuasions entered the debate, including Pietro Alfieri, Adrien de La Fage, Félix Danjou, Théodore Nisard (né Normand), Nicholas Cloet, Félix Clément, Nicholas Janssen, C.C. Bogaerts, Edmond Duval, Jules Tardif, Louis Lambillotte, Anselm Schubiger, Padre J. Dufour, Stephen Morelot, Augustin Gontier, Louis Vitet, Charles Vervoitte and Alexandre Vincent.

In 1847 Danjou discovered the important 11th-century tonary of St Bénigne de Dijon, F-MOf H 159 (facs. in PalMus, 1st ser., vii–viii, 1901–5/R; fig.10), a manuscript with unique, doubly notated melodies in French neumatic and alphabetical notations. A hand-copied transcription of the manuscript by Nisard (completed 1851; F-Pn lat.8881, formerly suppl. lat.1307) was used as the basis of the Reims-Cambrai *Graduale romanum complectens missas* (Paris, 1851), which represents the first serious attempt to restore medieval chant to modern books. The editors, P.C.C. Bogaerts and E. Duval, defended their work in *Etudes sur les livres choraux qui ont servi de base dans la publication des livres de chant grégorien édités à Malines* (Mechelen, 1855), but reactions to the Reims-Cambrai editions were frequently sour. La Fage's *De la reproduction des livres du plain-chant romain* (Paris, 1853) is a thinly disguised polemic against the Reims-Cambrai gradual. Louis Vitet (*Journal des savants*, 1854, p.92) was astonished that a group of four notes in the Paris gradual of 1826 had been replaced in the Reims-Cambrai edition by a melisma of 48 notes. And Nisard ('Du rythme dans le plain-chant', U1856), defending his own conservative, post-Tridentine-style *Gradual et vesperal romains* (Rennes, 1855), considered impossible the 'radical and revolutionary' attempt to replace current chant melodies by a literal return to the 'chants of St Gregory', as the Reims-Cambrai edition proposed.

During the middle decades of the 19th century two terms, already in favour, were widely adopted by liturgical commentators: 'decadent', to describe any form, style or era of plainchant that ran counter to self-established theories of what constituted 'authentic' chant melodies and/or chant performance; and 'restoration' (Fr. 'restauration'), used to characterize efforts to restore plainchant to its proper place in the Roman liturgy, as for example, Michel Couturier in his *Décadence et restauration de la musique religieuse* (Paris, 1862), or Anselm Schubiger in *Die Restauration des Kirchengesangs und der Kirchenmusik durch das künftige allgemeine Concilium* (Zürich, 1869).

Another effort to restore Gregorian chant resulted in the publication by Louis Lambillotte of a facsimile of the late 9th-century cantatorium of St Gallen, CH-SGs 359. Although it was claimed that the engraved plates were authentic reproductions of the original neumes, they soon proved to be completely unreliable, and Lambillotte's posthumous *Graduale romanum* (Paris, 1857), ostensibly based on this manuscript, contained truncated melodies. As regards the printing of plainchant, it was a monk of the Cistercian abbey of Notre-Dame de Réconfort, Geoffroy de Marnef, who, according to La Fage (*Plainchant*, ii, 1861, p.80), was the first French printer to make a special font of plainchant musical characters.

Three other pioneering works appeared in the mid-19th century: Coussemaker's *Histoire de l'harmonie au Moyen-Age* (Paris, 1852/R), the first comprehensive review of medieval notations based on modern critical methods, which set a standard for subsequent serious palaeographical investigations of chant neumes and rhythm; Joseph d'Ortigue's *Dictionnaire liturgique, historique et théorique de plain-chant* (Paris, 1853/R), the first major dictionary of terms relating to plainchant, containing lengthy excerpts from the works of a wide variety of contemporary scholars, among them Nisard, Lebeuf, Fétis, Rousseau, Coussemaker, Jumilhac, Danjou, Baini, Poisson, Forkel, Lambillotte, Brossard, Du Cange and Kiesewetter; and La Fage's *Cours complet de plain-chant* (Paris, 1855–6), containing the first substantial bibliography of plainchant sources – 282 items are classified according to printed liturgical books, music treatises and practical performance manuals.

An article in D'Ortigue's dictionary on the instrumental accompaniment of plainchant is particularly illuminating and holds a special place in the extensive literature on the subject (see Söhner, U1931; and Wagener, U1964). This practice was well known even at the time of Adriano Banchieri's *L'organo suonarino* (Venice, 1605, 2/1611, 3/1638/R) and assumed a major role in the performance of plainchant after the development of the thoroughbass in *stile nuovo* church music. A veritable deluge of practical manuals were published from the 17th century instructing the organist on the problems of rhythm, the choice and placement of chords, the use of homophonic and contrapuntal accompaniments, the rules for harmonizing each mode, the roles of intonation and cadential formulae, the use of embellishments and how to transpose (ex.8).

In May 1860 over 50 people interested in plainchant reform attended a congress held at Erard's in Paris concerned with the restoration of plainchant and religious music (see *De la musique religieuse: Paris 1860* and

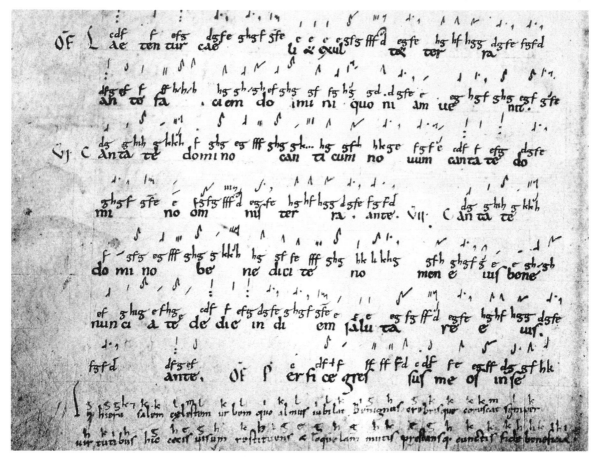

10. Offertory 'Laetentur caeli', notated in French neumatic and alphabetical notations, in the 11th-century tonary of St Bénigne de Dijon (F-MOf H 159, f.112v); from PalMus, 1st ser., viii, 1901–5/R, p.218.

Mechelen 1863 and *1864*, ed. T.J. de Vroye, Paris, 1866). 80 different chant books and manuals published mostly between 1854 to 1860 were presented for consideration, and topics under discussion included the true character of church music, plainchant accompaniment, the place of

Ex.8 Accompanied version of the introit *Requiem aeternam* from the Requiem Mass, from E. Duval: *L'organiste grégorien, ou Accompagnement d'orgue* (Mechelen, 1845), p.34, based on the rules of accompaniment in N.A. Janssen: *Les vrais principes du chant grégorien* (Mechelen, 1845)

6ᶜ Ton: Le prélude doit finir en Fa maj.

choral societies, the performance of church music in certain dioceses and the proper performance of liturgical chant.

In France the performance methods promoted by Louis Niedermeyer at his Institut de Musique d'Eglise (founded 1835) were printed in *La maîtrise: journal de musique religieuse* (1857–61) and in his *Traité théorique et pratique de l'accompagnement du plain-chant* (Paris, 1857, 2/1878; Eng. trans., 1905). These publications exerted considerable influence for over a century (see M. Galerne: *L'Ecole Niedermeyer*, Paris, 1928). Among the better-known 19th-century chant treatises are those by Bogler (1808), Schiedermayer (1828), Stehlin (U1842), Toepler (1848), Benz (1850), Stein (1853), Clément (1854), Nisard (1854, 1860), Gevaert (1856), Miné (1863), Labat (1864) and Hermesdorff (1865–7).

(ii) Germany and the Cecilian movement. During much of the 19th century the emphasis on church music in Germany was confined largely to the development of church choirs and the revival of Renaissance and Baroque polyphonic music; it was at this time that the Palestrina cult began to flourish under such advocates as A.F.J. Thibaut, Giuseppe Baini and Carl von Winterfeld (see Comes, W1974–5; and W. Kirsch and others, eds.: *Palestrina und die Kirchenmusik im 19. Jahrhundert*, Regensburg, 1989). With the appointment in 1830 of Karl Proske as a canon of the Alte Kapelle in Regensburg, that city soon became the centre of this revival activity in

Germany. Important editions of the polyphonic masters appeared in Proske's Musica Divina (Regensburg, 1853–76/R) and Selectus Novus Missarum (Regensburg, 1855–61/R), and in Franz Commer's Collectio Operum Musicorum Batavorum Saeculi XVI (Berlin, 1844–58), Musica Sacra (Berlin, 1839–42, continuing as Selectio Modorum, 1860–87) and Cantica Sacra (Berlin, 1870).

Further reforms took place in the last third of the century with the rise of the CECILIAN MOVEMENT, which had its roots in the scholarship of Proske and Commer (see W. Kirsch: 'Caecilianismus', MGG2). In 1868 the Bavarian priest F.X. Witt founded the Allgemeine Cäcilien-Verein für Katholische Kirchenmusik; based initially in the German cathedral town of Regensburg, this organization, dedicated to the improvement of church music not only in Germany but throughout Europe and the Americas, advocated the performance of 16th-century polyphony, the Palestrina vocal style, and the reform of plainchant and organ playing. Witt propagated his theories in two music periodicals, the Fliegende Blätter für katholische Kirchenmusik (1866–) and Musica sacra (1868–), both of which he founded (see Lickleder, U1988). Cecilian societies were also founded in America, of which the most important centre was that in Milwaukee, Wisconsin, influenced by John Martin Henni (1805–81), first archbishop of Milwaukee, and John Baptist Singenberger (1848–1924), editor of Caecilia: Vereinsorgan des Amerikanischen Caecilien-Vereins (founded in 1874). (For a review of the Cecilian movement in Italy, see Moneta Caglio, U1983.)

Reform of the German plainchant books was carried out in publications by the firm of Friedrich Pustet in Regensburg, which had been granted a privilege (1 October 1868) by the Sacred Congregation of Rites in Rome to publish all the official chant books of the Church according to the Medicean edition. Accordingly, the new Regensburg gradual of 1871, edited by F.X. Haberl, was largely a reprint of the Medicean edition of 1614–15; the Pustet antiphoner of 1878 was based on two editions (Venice, 1585, and Antwerp, 1611). On 4 August 1871 Pius IX officially sanctioned the Pustet editions as the authentic form of Gregorian chant, a decree that was reaffirmed in papal letters (30 May 1873, 15 November 1878) and by decrees of the Sacred Congregation of Rites (26 April 1883, 7 July 1894).

(iii) England and Ireland.   The revival of plainchant in England had begun during the 18th century with the Roman Catholic scribe and publisher John Francis Wade (1711/12–86). His manuscripts and printed books circulated widely throughout the London embassy chapels and among many aristocratic Catholic families. Wade's earliest works consist of hand-copied manuscripts and books with pre-printed staves and text onto and above which plainchant was notated by hand. Manuscripts dating from 1737 to the 1770s cover most liturgical functions. Wade's first printed books without plainchant were English–Latin vesperals. Other plainchant scribes and publishers were active during Wade's lifetime, but those manuscripts that have survived from private aristocratic and embassy chapels are generally considered of inferior quality to Wade's. Printed sources include *The Art of Singing* (London, 1748) published by Thomas Meighan and *The True Method to Learn the Church Plain-Song* (London, 1748) published by James Marmaduke. James Coghlan introduced movable Gregorian type (previous

publications were engraved) with *An Essay on the Church Plain Chant* (London, 1782), a work indebted to Wade and perhaps wrongly attributed to Samuel Webbe the elder.

In the 19th century the revival continued unabated with the works of the Catholic publisher Vincent Novello, the earliest of which, *A Collection of Sacred Music* (London, 1811), included Gregorian arrangements of Samuel Wesley's texts. An abortive Wesley-Novello project to publish comprehensive Gregorian books is evidenced in letters, which also prove that Novello's arrangements were based partly on Wade. Novello's publications were superseded in the late 1840s by those of John Lambert.

In the Anglican Church, the plainchant revival was spawned by the Oxford Movement and the Cambridge Ecclesiological Society. The first significant publication was Alexander Reinagle's *A Collection of Psalm & Hymn Tunes* (London, 1839). Richard Redhead's *Laudes diurnae* (London, 1843) enjoyed brief popularity but was criticized for retaining Latin prosody at the expense of English accentuation. William Dyce's version of Merbecke's *The Book of Common Prayer Noted*, which was published in London in 1843, provides rules for good English prosody, although these are not always easy to apply in *The Psalter* (London, 1849), where notes are provided for each syllable of text only for examples of each tone, not for the complete Psalter.

The 19th-century English plainchant revival produced many aesthetic controversies. Anglican plainchant apologetics surfaced in music magazines such as *The Choir and Musical Record*, *The Musical Times*, *The Musical World* and *The Quarterly Musical Magazine*, and in religious periodicals such as *The British Critic*, *The Christian Remembrancer*, *The Ecclesiologist* and *The Parish Choir*. Concerns included English versus Latin rules of prosody, the nature of accompaniment, the social/moral role of Gregorian chant, and the use of English versus Roman sources. Catholic apologetics are found in *The Tablet* and *The Dublin Review* and receive a Christological context in the writings of Henry Formby.

The late 19th century saw an expansion of the English plainchant revival. In 1888 moves were made to found an English branch of the Cecilians out of the old Catholic Gregorian Association, and in the same year the Plainsong and Mediaeval Music Society met for the first time. In 1929 the Society of St Gregory was also founded to address issues relating to the Catholic liturgy. Owing in part to problems of applicability, 20th-century Anglican publications are varied in their reliance on Solesmes and other Continental scholarship. Catholic publications of the same period, unlike many of their 19th-century antecedents, derive from sources formally approved by Rome.

In Ireland, the Irish Society of St Cecilia was founded by Nicholas Donnelly in 1878. His ideas on reform, as well as those of Witt, were circulated by means of his periodical *Lyra ecclesiastica* (1878–93) (see Daly, U1993). Early plainchant books published in Ireland included an *Officium defunctorum cum suo cantu* by Patrick Wogan (Dublin, 1793) and *A Plain and Concise Method of Learning the Gregorian Note: also a Collection of Church Music, Selected from the Roman Antiphonary and Gradual* by Patrick Hoey (Dublin, 1800). Patrick Wogan also published *High Mass and Sunday Vespers as Sung in Most of the Different Roman Catholic Chapels throughout* the United Kingdom (1818) (see Zon, U1996; and also White and Lawrence, U1993).

(iv) The reformed editions of Solesmes. The major editions of chant books issued in the second half of the 19th century, the Reims-Cambrai gradual and antiphoner (1851 and 1852), the Nisard gradual (1857), the two editions of the gradual edited by Michael Hermesdorff (Trier, 1863 and 1876) and Haberl's Regensburg gradual and antiphoner (1871 and 1878), represent scholarly, 'Romantic' attempts to restore the pre-eminence of plainchant in the Roman liturgy. These books were, however, outflanked by a vigorous campaign to restore the melodies of the earliest chant manuscripts, a far more radical restoration than that so far attempted, and rejecting the outright revival of the Medicean gradual by Haberl. The restoration culminated in the editions issued by the Benedictine monks of SOLESMES between 1883 and the end of World War I. From the time of the monastery's reconstitution in 1833 by Dom Prosper Guéranger (see Johnson, U1984), the monastic and liturgical renewal there reflected Ultramontane ideas – the centralization of Church government in Rome, the independence of the Church from secular authority and the infallibility of the Pope even in administrative decisions. Guéranger rejected neo-Gallicanism, and his views on 17th- and 18th-century liturgy and music, expressed in particularly negative terms in the *Institutions liturgiques* (Paris, 1840–51, 2/1878–85), formed the theoretical and philosophical basis of all subsequent chant reform by the Solesmes Benedictines.

Rousseau (U1945) and Combe (U1969), two historians of Solesmes, traced the beginnings of serious chant studies at the abbey to about 1856, when Dom Paul Jausions began transcribing the Rollington Processional, a 13th- or 14th-century English manuscript. This was nearly 20 years after the re-establishment of the monastery, at a time when the Reims-Cambrai editions were already in use. In 1860 Jausions was joined by Dom Joseph Pothier, destined to become the most respected figure in the restoration movement, and they began a laborious 20-year project of preparing completely new chant books for the Solesmes Congregation based on early neumatic sources.

Like the other chant book editors (Bogaerts, Clément, Nivers, Hermesdorff and Haberl), Pothier published his own treatise (*Les mélodies grégoriennes d'après la tradition*, Tournai, 1880/R), in which he defined his general editorial policies and theories of restoration, explained the rudiments of neumatic and staff notation, and at the same time put forward an oratorical interpretation of rhythm. Gregorian notation had no fixed and absolute note values; therefore the chant was sung in a natural, non-metrical style. Organization of the melody was controlled by two oratorical determinants: the tonic accent of the Latin text and the natural divisions of the text into words and phrases. Pothier's ideas were influenced by the *Méthode raisonnée de plainchant: le plainchant considéré dans son rythme, sa tonalité et ses modes* of Abbé Augustin Gontier (Paris, 1859).

A striking feature of Pothier's *Liber gradualis* of 1883, apart from its typically romantic preface referring to Pope Gregory the Great as author of the Roman gradual, is its distinctive musical notation. Under Pothier's direction new musical type was engraved by Desclée, Lefebvre & Cie in Tournai, Belgium. The hybrid design of these typographical neume characters was modelled on the

notation of 13th- and 14th-century French manuscripts. Special ornamental signs representing the *quilisma*, *cephalicus* and *epiphonus* were adapted from pre-13th-century Guidonian practice (see Schmidt, U1895–6). An explanation of how to perform these neumes has been frequently included in introductions to the Solesmes chant books, such as the modern *Liber usualis*. The Pothier-Desclée-Solesmes font, which is noted for its diversity of type characters and its ability to depict liquescent neumes (fig.11), is still used by some scholars for contemporary transcriptions of early plainchant notations. But there is also a tendency to move away from the Solesmes font to the use of isolated black note heads without stems (see Hiley, C1993).

The modern era of plainchant palaeography began in 1889 with another Solesmes enterprise, the series Paléographie Musicale: les Principaux Manuscrits de Chant … Publiés en Fac-Similés Phototypiques (PalMus; *see* Solesmes, §4). This was the first significant attempt to adapt the new technology of photography to the study of plainchant notation. The manuscripts were not always reproduced in their entirety; paraliturgical sections, for example, were omitted.

A century before the Paléographie Musicale began to appear, engraved specimens of neumes were used as illustrations, some on polychromatic plates, by Gerbert, Jumilhac, Martini, Hawkins, Forkel, Burney and others; like the unusable Lambillotte 'facsimile' of *CH-SGs* 359, however, these hand-made imitations could not match the accuracy of the later photographic reproductions.

11. Mass of St Benedict from J. Pothier's 'Liber gradualis' (1883), p.185

The final decree by the Sacred Congregation of Rites supporting Haberl's Regensburg edition of the chant books, the *Quod sanctus Augustinus*, appeared on 7 July 1894, and by 1901 Pustet's privilege to publish the official chant books had been withdrawn. Among the last Pustet publications was the Regensburg-New York-Cincinnati missal of 1889 whose title publicized the earlier reforms of the Council of Trent and those made under Pius V (pontificate 1566–72), Clement VIII (1592–1605), Urban VIII (1623–44) and Leo XIII (1877–1903). The revocation came at the culmination of a complex and often bitter struggle between factions supporting the Allgemeine Cäcilien-Verein on the one side and the Benedictines of Solesmes on the other. The dispute seen from the Solesmes position was chronicled in detail by Combe (U1969), and Haberl's lengthy first-hand account (U1902) remains an invaluable source for understanding the other point of view.

12. 20TH-CENTURY DEVELOPMENTS.   Leo XIII had long maintained a benevolent attitude towards Haberl and Pustet, but even before the pope's death in 1903 there was a move to replace the Pustet chant books with those of Solesmes, and his successor Pius X (pontificate 1903–14), almost immediately after being elected, took decisive action. In his famous *motu proprio* of 22 November 1903, *Tra le sollecitudini*, Pius X defined the nature and kinds of sacred music, the role of singers, the use of instruments in worship and the length and performance of church music. The highest type of sacred music was the ancient chant of the liturgical manuscripts 'which the most recent studies [i.e. those of Solesmes] have so happily restored to their integrity and purity'. He also encouraged the use of classical polyphony and permitted 'figured music' and *falsobordoni* on certain occasions.

Within two months of the appearance of the *motu proprio*, on 8 January 1904, the Congregation urged that the traditional chant be introduced as quickly as possible; the Vatican edition was officially announced during a general congress held between 4 and 9 April 1904. A second *motu proprio* of implementation was issued on 25 April 1904 stating that publishing rights for the new books would remain with the Vatican; that the restored melodies should conform to the ancient codices; that a special commission of ten members (with Pothier as president) and ten consultants should be appointed to supervise the new editions; and that the monks of Solesmes were to be entrusted with the editing of the music. Despite repeated clashes within the commission over editorial policies and the loss of editorship by Solesmes, three major Vatican chant books were published: the *Kyriale seu ordinarium missae* (1905), the *Graduale sacrosanctae romanae ecclesiae* (1908) and the *Antiphonale sacrosanctae romanae ecclesiae* (1912).

Once the kyriale had been published (see Grospellier, U1905–06), the differences of opinion that divided the commission reached public notice. Dispute centered largely on the antiquity of the manuscripts used to prepare the editions. The 'archaeological school' (Solesmes) insisted that the readings be taken from the oldest accessible sources, whereas the 'traditionalists' (such as Pothier, Gastoué and Peter Wagner), considered it important that the choral tradition of the late Middle Ages also be represented. Since the criteria adopted by the commission favoured the traditionalist position and inclined more to practical wisdom than to abstract theory,

manuscripts representing various national practices were used, some dating from as late as the 14th and 15th centuries. The diversity allowed in the Vatican edition exposed the commission to criticism on the most fundamental aesthetic level.

Besides the problems of determining the authenticity of the restored melodies, there was the difficulty of the restoration of the melodies' original rhythmic structure. By the mid-19th century many scholars, including Fétis, Coussemaker, Danjou, Nisard, Vitet, La Fage, Cloet, Lambillotte, Vincent, Jumilhac and Baini, had faced this problem. And even at this time opinion was divided as to whether chant should be performed in a free oratorical manner without measured note values, or according to some metrical scheme. Between 1895 and 1914, just as the Vatican editions were being prepared, argument among scholars on this matter was at its most intense.

The early mensuralists, among whom were Hugo Riemann, Antoine Dechevrens, Ludwig Bonvin, Georges Houdard, Oskar Fleischer, Eduard Bernoulli and Peter Wagner, conjectured that chant was sung to notes of unequal value that usually bore a proportional 2:1 relationship. The results of their rhythmic interpretations, however, were widely divergent. In the editions of Dechevrens a large number of notes are reduced to the status of rapid ornaments (U1902/R). Many of the rhythmic interpretations rely to a greater or lesser extent on the sophisticated detail in the notation of the early manuscripts from St Gallen (*CH-SGs* 359, 339), Einsiedeln (*E* 121) and Laon (*F-LA* 239), which indicate rhythmic, dynamic or agogic aspects of performance. This was also one of the principal sources of disagreement between Pothier and Mocquereau, Pothier regarding the notation as a local, passing phenomenon, Mocquereau arguing that it was an essential element of the earliest recoverable state of Gregorian chant. In accordance with Pothier's views, the Sacred Congregation of Rites authorized the use of one uniform musical notation in the Vatican editions (11 and 14 August 1905, 14 February 1906, 7 August 1907, 8 April 1908); the addition of certain rhythmic signs was tolerated only under exceptional circumstances.

In 1905, the same year that the Vatican kyriale appeared, the firm of Desclée published a *Kyriale seu ordinarium missae cum cantu gregoriano ad exemplar editionis vaticanae concinnatum et rhythmicis signis a solesmensibus monachis diligenter ornatum*, which reflected the rhythmic theories of Dom André Mocquereau. The basis of the 'méthode bénédictine' advocated by Solesmes, which stood in direct opposition to mensuralist theories, was set out by Mocquereau in *Le nombre musical grégorien* (1908–27). While retaining Pothier's basic ideas of free rhythm, Mocquereau developed an intricate theory of rhythmic motion deriving from the free binary and ternary metres of Greek and Latin rhetoric, although he was careful to point out that Gregorian rhythm was specifically musical and independent of speech rhythm. He denied a distinction between the *punctum* or *virga*, either in terms of their duration or their intensity: the *punctum* represented a low-pitched sound, not a quaver, and the *virga* was a higher-pitched note, not equivalent to a crotchet. Two types of pulse, basic and composite, comprising one, two or three notes, were the constituent members of the melodic phrase. In the Solesmes editions these pulses were indicated by special notational signs – the vertical and horizontal strokes and bars, the rhythmic point (*punctum mora*), and the comma (a short breath mark). The rhythmic movement of these pulses was affected by dynamic modifications, the contrasts of 'élan' and 'repos', which can be compared roughly to upbeat (*arsis*) and downbeat (*thesis*). As a practical aid, Mocquereau devised cheironomic gestures in the form of undulating lines that were sometimes superimposed on the melodies to depict the ebb and flow of the *arsis* and *thesis* movement (fig.12).

Although much labour and 'Romantic' scholarship went into the preparation of the Pothier, Vatican and Solesmes chant books, the latter cannot be considered critical editions in any sense, because they lack commentaries and do not specify the manuscript sources of each melody. Special collections, such as the Solesmes *Variae preces* (1896) and Carl Ott's *Offertoriale* (1935) (see Steiner, K1966, p.164), provide some clues to the sources. However, the modern chant books are by and large functional compilations. To the inexperienced student, these books can easily seem to possess an absolute authority, both musically and liturgically, and can stand as formidable barriers to a true understanding and appreciation of the immense diversity of medieval chant. Such an understanding may be further impeded by the widespread use of textbooks based almost entirely on these publications (for example, Apel's *Gregorian Chant*, C1958).

In the later decades of the 20th century an offshoot of the Solesmes school emerged whose adherents associated themselves with the palaeographic theories of the Solesmes Benedictine monk Dom Eugène Cardine (1905–88). This is the field of Gregorian semiology ('Sémiologie grégorienne'), which extends and modifies the earlier work at Solesmes on the rhythmic detail of the early neumed manuscripts. The principal features of this detail reside in the use of supplementary strokes (*episemata*) attached to the St Gallen neumes, letters ('significative' or 'Romanus' letters) complementing the neumes, the modification of normal neume shapes to indicate peculiarities of delivery, and the way in which notes are grouped (reflected in the 'coupure neumatique', or 'neumatic break'). The wealth of detail is indeed impressive. For example, Smits van Waesberghe (J.i 1936–42, ii, p.250) reported that over 32,300 rhythmic letters occur in *CH-E* 121 (facs. in PalMus, 1st ser., iv, 1894/*R*), over 4100 in *SGs* 359 (PalMus, 2nd ser., ii, 1924/*R*) and over 12,900 in *SGs* 390 and 391 (PalMus, 2nd ser., i, 1900/*R*).

The new investigation of these rhythmic signs is important in two respects: firstly, it has stimulated considerable interest in close reading of primary sources; second, and perhaps more fundamentally, it may contribute to a better historical and musicological understanding of early chant. Semiotics has gained widespread popularity in other fields of music (see J.-J. Nattiez: 'Reflections on the Development of Semiology in Music', *MAn*, viii, 1989, pp.21–75; and J.M. Joncas: 'Musical Semiotics and Liturgical Musicology: Theoretical Foundations and Analytic Techniques', *Ecclesia orans*, viii, 1991–2, pp.181–206); but despite the extraordinary claims made for Gregorian semiology, not least by Cardine himself – 'semiology is the entrance necessary for all knowledge of Gregorian chant' – it is probably still too early to assess its practical implications. Most semiological chant research is published in *Etudes grégoriennes*, *Rivista internazionale di musica sacra*, *Beiträge zur Gregorianik* and *Studi gregoriani*.

A development of great importance in the history of Western plainchant began on 4 December 1963 when the Second Vatican Council (11 October 1962 to 8 December 1965) promulgated its first official document 'The Constitution on the Sacred Liturgy' (*Acta apostolicae sedis*, lvi, 1964, pp.128–9). Outwardly, the article in chapter 5, 'Of Sacred Music', seems very similar to earlier 20th-century legislation on church music, such as Pius X's *Tra le sollecitudini* of 22 November 1903 (*Acta sanctae sedis*, xxxvi, 1903–04, pp.329–39); the *Divini cultus sanctitatem* of 20 December 1928 (*Acta apostolicae sedis*, xxi, 1929, pp.33–41); the *Mediator Dei et hominum* of 20 November 1947 (ibid., xxxix, 1947, pp.588–91); the *Musica sacra disciplina* of 25 December 1955 (ibid., xlviii, 1956, pp.5–25); and the *Instructio de musica sacra et sacra liturgia* of 3 December 1958 (ibid., l, 1958, pp.630–63). Gregorian chant is extolled in fashionable 19th-century jargon, and acknowledgment is given in the manner expected to sacred polyphony, the typical editions, the use of the organ and the role of the modern composer (Articles 113, 116, 117, 120, 121).

Nevertheless, the true intent of liturgical renewal expressed elsewhere in the Constitution is scarcely traditional. Faced with an increasingly secularized society, the Council sought to retain the allegiance of the faithful by endorsing a new pastoral theology of 'active participation' ('actuosa participatio'; see Articles 14, 21, 30 etc.). Unlike the reforms brought about by the Council of Trent, which were conservative in that they sought to standardize and retain existing liturgical practice throughout Europe, the reforms of the Second Council have been regarded by many as essentially contrary to any form of liturgical development known in the past. Fundamental changes have taken place that have profoundly affected the nature and function of traditional Gregorian chant: vernacular languages have largely replaced Latin (Articles 36, 54), completely new liturgical formularies have been introduced, and the structures of the Mass, Office and the liturgical year have been revised (Articles 50, 107 etc.). (*See also* LITURGY OF THE HOURS, and ORDO CANTUS MISSAE.)

Despite the *Instructio de musica in sacra liturgia* (*Acta apostolicae sedis*, lix, 1967, pp.300–20) issued by the Sacred Congregation of Rites on 5 March 1967 to implement the articles of chapter 6, a widespread debate over the democratization of church music continues. Some regard the juridical documents on sacred music published since 1900, the Vatican and Solesmes chant books and later liturgical publications (such as the Roman gradual of 1974, the *Graduale triplex* of 1979 and the *Psalterium, cum cantu gregoriano* of 1981) as out of touch with the

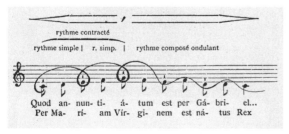

12. *Cheironomic notation from A. Mocquereau's 'Le nombre musical grégorien', ii (1927), p.710*

realities of the post-Conciliar period. Others regard the widespread promotion of the type of 'liturgical' music exemplified by songs in popular idiom, often with a strong socio-political message, slender theological content and variable musical and literary merit, as utterly alien to the Church's heritage; in terms of its melodic and harmonic style, its circumstances of performance (generally young, untrained voices against an accompaniment of guitars, percussion, electronic keyboards etc.) and its secular ethos, much of this music is barely distinguishable from certain genres of pop music.

Given the periodic nature of liturgical reform – approximately every 60 years since the Council of Trent – one might predict that in about the year 2025 another Council will have to be called to deal with, among other things, the liturgical and musical chaos resulting from too liberal an interpretation of 'actuosa participatio' and from the virtual abandonment by the Church of its traditional musical patrimony. At that time it might be well to return some semblance of orthodoxy to the celebration of the liturgy and to restore *cantus planus* to its central place within the Roman rite.

See also ROMAN CATHOLIC CHURCH MUSIC and NOTATION, §III, 1.

BIBLIOGRAPHY

A Modern editions and related literature: (i) Plainchant books (selective list) (ii) Studies. B Bibliographies, discographies. C Surveys of chant and liturgy; methodology. D Sources: manuscripts, facsimiles, incunabula, history of liturgical books, catalogues. E Computer programs and databases. F Early history. G Old Roman chant; relationship with Gregorian chant. H Other chant traditions: Ambrosian, Beneventan, Celtic, Gallican, Mozarabic. I Oral transmission; beginnings of notation. J Notation: (i) Studies of different notations. (ii) Semiology. K The Proper and Ordinary chants of Mass and Office, hymnody, processional chants: studies of history and style. L Theory. M Paraliturgical categories: tropes, sequences, conductus, *versus*, cantiones. N Liturgical dramas, *planctus*, *Marienklagen*. O Studies of specific medieval masses, Offices, feasts, hagiography. P Performance. Q Plainchant and liturgy in the religious orders. R Chant dialects, regional variants, institutions, personalities. S Scandinavia and Central Europe. T Latin America. U. From the Council of Trent to the present.

A: MODERN EDITIONS AND RELATED LITERATURE
(i) Plainchant books (selective list)

D = no. in lists of Société de St Jean l'Évangéliste, Desclée & Cie, Tournai, printers to the Holy See and the Sacred Congregation of Rites.

Antiphonale missarum juxta ritum sanctae ecclesiae mediolanensis, ed. G.M. Suñol (Rome, 1935), D 816 [Ambrosian]
Antiphonale monasticum pro diurnis horis (Tournai, 1934), D 818 [AM]
Antiphonale romanum-seraphicum pro horis diurnis (Paris, 1928), D 834 [Franciscan]
Antiphonale sacrosanctae romanae ecclesiae (Rome, 1912), D 820 [AR]
Antiphonarii cisterciensis ... auctoritate Gabrielis Sortais editi (Westmalle, 1954–5)
Antiphonarium cisterciense auctoritate Dominici Rogues editum (Westmalle, 1947)
Compendium gradualis et antiphonalis romani pro dominicis et festis (Paris, 1924), D 790c
Delectus missarum e graduali romano: a Selection of Masses from the Roman Gradual, Vatican Version. Modern Notation with Rhythmical Signs, Fischer edition, 4370 (New York, 1919) [chants notated in quavers and crotchets]
Dominicale romanum cantus ad missam, vesperas, completorium et benedictionem SS. Sacramenti in dominicis et festis praecipuis (Tournai, 1949), D 865
Graduale cisterciense auctoritate R.D. Hermanni Josephi Smets (Westmalle, 1934)

Graduale juxta ritum sacri Ordinis Praedicatorum auctoritate ... Emmanuelis Suarez (Rome, 1950) [Dominican]
Graduale juxta ritum sacri Ordinis Praedicatorum auctoritate Hyacinthi M. Cormier (Rome, 1923) [Dominican]
Graduale romanum ... editio Schwann P (Düsseldorf, 1953)
Graduale romanum ... restitutum et editum Pauli VI (Solesmes, 1974) [follows liturgical reforms of Vatican II]
Graduale sacrosanctae romanae ecclesiae (Rome, 1908), D 696 [GR]
Graduale sacrosanctae romanae ecclesiae (Burnham, 1930) [Plainsong and Mediaeval Music Society pubn]
Graduale triplex, seu Graduale romanum Pauli PP. VI cura recognitum & rhythmicis signis a Solesmensibus monachis ornatum, neumis laudunensibus (cod. 239) et sangallensibus (codicum San Gallensis 359 et Einsidlensis 121) nunc auctum (Solesmes, 1979)
Hymnarium cisterciense auctoritate Gabrielis Sortais editum (Westmalle, 1952)
Hymni de tempore et de sanctis in textu antiquo et novo cum tonis usitatis in congregatione gallica O.S.B. (Solesmes, 1885)
Liber hymnarius cum invitatoriis & aliquibus responsoriis (Solesmes, 1982)
Liber responsorialis pro festis I. classis et communi sanctorum juxta ritum monasticum (Solesmes, 1894), D 831
Liber usualis missae et officii pro dominicis et festis I vel II. classis (Rome, 1921), D 780
The Liber Usualis with Introduction and Rubrics in English Edited by the Benedictines of Solesmes (Tournai, 1934), D 801 [LU]
Liber vesperalis juxta ritum sanctae ecclesiae mediolanensis, ed. G. M. Suñol (Rome, 1939), D 811 [Ambrosian]
Mass and Vespers with Gregorian Chant for Sundays and Holy Days: Latin and English Text Edited by the Benedictines of the Solesmes Congregation (Tournai, 1957), D 805
Missale romanum auctoritate Pauli PP. VI promulgatum: Ordo missae in cantu (Solesmes, 1975)
Offertoriale, sive Versus offertoriorum cantus gregoriani (Paris, 1935), D 837
Praefationes in cantu missale romanum auctoritate Pauli P. VI promulgatum (Solesmes, 1972)
Processionale monasticum ad usum congregationis gallicae Ordinis Sancti Benedicti (Solesmes, 1893), D 830
Processionarium juxta ritum sacri Ordinis Praedicatorum auctoritate ... Emmanuelis Suarez (Rome, 1949) [Dominican]
Processionarium juxta ritum s. Ordinis Praedicatorum auctoritate ... Hyacinthe Marie Cormier (Rome, 1913) [Dominican]
Proprium de tempore pro partibus Gradualis romani ... cantum gregorianum harmonice modulavit ad normam editionis rhythmicae a Solesmensibus monachis exaratae, ed. J. Baas (Paris, 1925), D 761H [org accomp. to part of the 1908 Solesmes GR]
Psalterium monasticum (Solesmes, 1981)
Variae preces ex liturgia, tum hodierna tum antiqua (Solesmes, 1896), D 808
Vesperale romanum, cum cantu gregoriano (Tournai, 1924), D 840

(ii) Studies

H. Vinck: 'Quelques documents inédits concernant l'édition du Graduale romanum 1908', *Ephemerides liturgicae*, lxxxvi (1972), 290–98
F. Haberl: *Das Kyriale romanum: liturgische und musikalische Aspekte* (Bonn, 1975)
F. Haberl: *Das Graduale romanum: liturgische und musikalische Aspekte*, i: *Die antiphonalen Gesänge, Introitus und Communio* (Bonn, 1976)
L. Kunz: 'Die Editio Vaticana', *Geschichte der katholischen Kirchenmusik*, ed. K.G. Fellerer, ii (Kassel, 1976), 287–93
J. Froger: 'The Critical Edition of the Roman Gradual by the Monks of Solesmes', *JPMMS*, i (1978), 81–97
T. Schnitker and W.A. Slaby, eds.: *Concordantia verbalia missalis romani* (Münster, 1983)
D.M. Fournier: 'Sources scripturaires et provenance liturgique des pièces de chant du graduel de Paul VI', *EG*, xxi (1986), 49–96 [Old Testament]; xxii (1988), 109–75 [Psalms]; xxiii (1989), 27–70 [conclusion]
R.F. Hayburn: 'Printed Editions of the Chant Books', *Sacred Music*, cxv/2 (1988), 19–25 [selective list of sources pubd between 1476–1987]
J.A. Emerson: 'Desclée', *Music Printing and Publishing*, ed. D.W. Krummel and S. Sadie (London and New York, 1990)
J.M. Guilmard: *Tonaire des pièces de la messe selon le Graduale triplex et l'Offertoriale triplex* (Solesmes, 1991)

P. Jeffery: 'The New Chantbooks from Solesmes', *Notes*, xlvii (1991), 1039–63

D.M. Fournier: *Concordance textuelle du Graduale romanum triplex et des versets de l'Offertoriale triplex* (Solesmes, 1996)

L. Agustoni and others: 'Vorschläge zur Restitution von Melodien des Graduale romanum', *Beiträge zur Gregorianik*, xxi– (1996–)

B: BIBLIOGRAPHIES, DISCOGRAPHIES

C. Marbach, ed.: *Carmina scripturarum, scilicet antiphonas et responsoria ex sacro scripturae fonte in libros liturgicos sanctae ecclesiae romanae derivata* (Strasbourg, 1907/R)

G.M. Suñol: *Introducció a la paleografía musical gregoriana* (Montserrat, 1925; Fr. trans., enlarged, 1935) [with extensive bibliography up to the 1920s]

U. Bomm: 'Gregorianischer Gesang', *Archiv für Liturgiewissenschaft*, i (1950), 397–443, iv (1955), 184–222; vi (1959), 256–90; vii (1962), 470–511; ix (1965), 232–77; xiv (1972), 283–328 [annotated bibliography]

J. Smits van Waesberghe: 'L'état actuel des recherches scientifiques dans le domaine du chant grégorien (jusqu'au 1er avril 1957)', *Congrès de musique sacrée III: Paris 1957*, 206–17

H. Walther, ed.: *Initia carminum ac versuum medii aevi posterioris latinorum/Alphabetisches Verzeichnis der Versänfange mittellateinischer Dichtungen* (Göttingen, 1959, 2/1969)

W. Lipphardt: 'Der gegenwärtige Stand der Gregorianik-Forschung', *IMSCR IX: Salzburg 1964*, ii, 156–66

C. Vogel: *Introduction aux sources de l'histoire du culte chrétien au Moyen Age* (Turin, 1966/R; Eng. trans., rev., 1986, as *Medieval Liturgy: an Introduction to the Sources*)

J.R. Bryden and D.G. Hughes: *An Index of Gregorian Chant* (Cambridge, MA, 1969)

A. Hughes: *Medieval Music: the Sixth Liberal Art* (Toronto, 1974, 2/1980) [over 2000 bibliographical entries]

M. Huglo: 'Etat des recherches sur le chant grégorien de 1964 à 1975', *Congrès grégorien international: Strasbourg 1975*, 36–46

D. Schaller and E. Könsgen, eds.: *Initia carminum latinorum saeculo undecimo antiquiorum: bibliographisches Repertorium für die lateinische Dichtung der Antike und des frühen Mittelalters* (Göttingen, 1977)

Revue des sciences philosophiques et théologiques, lxiii– (1979–) [incl. 'Bulletin de liturgie', ed. P.-M Gy: a regular series of bibliographical reports incl. plainchant reviews]

R.W. Pfaff: *Medieval Latin Liturgy: a Select Bibliography* (Toronto, 1982)

R. Steiner: 'Directions for Chant Research in the 1980s', *JM*, i (1982), 34–8

W. Heckenbach: 'Gregorianik-Forschung zwischen 1972–1983', *KJb*, lxvii (1983), 105–14

J. Viret: 'Dix années de recherche grégorienne: 1975–1985', *Congrès de chant grégorien: Paris 1985* [*ReM*, nos.379–80 (1985)], 159–69

B. Rajeczky: 'Trends der heutigen Choralforschung', *Cantus planus III: Tihány 1988*, 93–8 [a survey of 20th-century scholarly pubns on plainchant]

E.C. Hansen: *Nineteenth-Century European Catholicism: an Annotated Bibliography of Secondary Works in English* (New York, 1989)

T. Kohlhase and G.M. Paucker: *Bibliographie gregorianischer Choral*, Beiträge zur Gregorianik, ix–x (1990); xv–xvi (1993) [comprehensive chant bibliography of secondary sources, with more than 4250 entries]

J.F. Weber: *A Gregorian Chant Discography* (Utica, NY, 1990)

Plainsong and Medieval Music [PMM], i– (1992–) [incl. 'Liturgical Chant Bibliography', ed. P. Jeffery; 'Recordings: Recent Releases of Plainchant', ed. J.F. Weber: important and wide-ranging compilations, regularly updated, of published studies/lists of recordings with commentary]

D. Hiley: *Western Plainchant: a Handbook* (Oxford, 1993) [detailed survey of plainchant, incl. extensive retrospective bibliography, pp.xxxi–xcvii]

Ephemerides liturgicae, cvii– (1993–) [incl. 'Studia recentiora de sacra liturgia', ed. A. Ward: a regular series of bibliographical reports incl. plainchant studies]

I. Fernández de la Cuesta: 'Libros de música litúrgica impresos en España ante de 1900, II: siglos XV y XVI', *Música*, iii (1996), 11–29 [approximately 145 printed liturgical books dating from 1485–1600 in 170 different libraries]

M. Huglo: 'La recherche en musicologie médiévale au XXe siècle', *Cahiers de civilisation médiévale*, xxxix (1996), 67–84

D. Hiley: 'Writings on Western Plainchant in the 1980s and 1990s', *AcM*, lxix (1997), 53–93 [with bibliography, pp.70–93]

G.R. Hill and N.L. Stephens, eds.: *Collected Editions, Historical Series & Sets, & Monuments of Music: a Bibliography* (Berkeley, 1997) [see esp. under 'Catholic Church']

C: SURVEYS OF CHANT AND LITURGY; METHODOLOGY

PL; MGG2

E. Martène, ed.: *De antiquis ecclesiae ritibus* (Antwerp, 2/1736–8/R)

M. Gerbert: *De cantu et musica sacra a prima ecclesiae aetate usque ad praesens tempus* (St Blasien, 1774/R)

P. Batiffol: *Histoire du bréviaire romain* (Paris, 1893, 3/1911; Eng. trans., 1912)

S. Bäumer: *Geschichte des Breviers* (Freiburg, 1895; Fr. trans., 1905)

F.E. Brightman: *Liturgies Eastern and Western, being the Texts, Original or Translated of the Principal Liturgies of the Church* (Oxford, 1896/R)

A. Ebner: *Quellen und Forschungen zur Geschichte und Kunstgeschichte des Missale romanum im Mittelalter: Iter italicum* (Freiburg, 1896/R)

P. Wagner: *Einführung in die gregorianischen Melodien: ein Handbuch der Choralwissenschaft*, i: *Ursprung und Entwicklung der liturgischen Gesangsformen bis zum Ausgang des Mittelalters* (Leipzig, 2/1901, 3/1911/R; Eng. trans., 1901/R); ii: *Neumenkunde: Paläographie des liturgischen Gesanges* (Leipzig, 1905, 2/1912/R); iii: *Gregorianische Formenlehre: eine choralische Stilkunde* (Leipzig, 1921/R)

F. Cabrol and H. Leclercq, eds.: *Dictionnaire d'archéologie chrétienne et de liturgie* (Paris, 1903–53)

A. Gastoué: *L'art grégorien* (Paris, 1911, 3/1920/R)

A. Gastoué: *Musique et liturgie: le graduel et l'antiphonaire romains: histoire et description* (Lyons, 1913/R)

E. Bishop: *Liturgica historica: Papers on the Liturgy and Religious Life of the Western Church* (Oxford, 1918/R)

L. Duchesne: *Origines du culte chrétien: étude sur la liturgie latine avant Charlemagne* (Paris, 5/1920, Eng. trans., 1927/R)

L. Eisenhofer: *Katholische Liturgik* (Freiburg, 1924, 4/1937 as *Grundriss des katholischen Liturgik*, rev. 5/1950 by J. Lechner as *Grundriss der Liturgik des römischen Ritus*, 6/1953 as *Liturgik des römischen Ritus*; Eng. trans., 1961)

M. Buchberger, ed.: *Lexikon für Theologie und Kirche* (Freiburg, 1930–38, 3/1993–7)

P. Ferretti: *Estetica gregoriana ossia Trattato delle forme musicali del canto gregoriano*, i (Rome, 1934/R; Fr. trans., 1938); ii ed. and completed P.M. Ernetti as *Estetica gregoriana dei recitativi liturgici* (Venice, 1964)

M. Andrieu, ed. *Le pontifical romain du Moyen-Age* (Vatican City, 1938–41)

G. Dix: *The Shape of the Liturgy* (London, 1945, 2/1947/R)

J.A. Jungmann: *Missarum sollemnia: eine genetische Erklärung der römischen Messe* (Vienna, 1948, 5/1962; Eng. trans., 1951–5/R as *The Mass of the Roman Rite*)

W. Apel: *Gregorian Chant* (Bloomington, IN, 1958, 2/1990)

F.Ll. Harrison: 'The Liturgy and its Plainsong', *Music in Medieval Britain* (London, 1958, 4/1980), 46–103

S. Corbin: *L'église à la conquête de sa musique* (Paris, 1960)

F. Tack: *Der gregorianische Choral*, Mw, xviii (1960; Eng. trans., 1960)

G. Nocilli: *La messa romana: suo sviluppo nella liturgia e nel canto* (Venice, 1961)

G.G. Willis: *Essays in Early Roman Liturgy* (London, 1964)

C. Vogel: *Introduction aux sources de l'histoire du culte chrétien au Moyen Age* (1966/R; Eng. trans., rev., 1986, as *Medieval Liturgy: an Introduction to the Sources*)

G.G. Willis: *Further Essays in Early Roman Liturgy* (London, 1968)

J. Porte, ed.: *Encyclopédie des musiques sacrées* (Paris, 1968–70)

D. Nicholson, ed.: *A Dictionary of Plainsong* (Mount Angel Abbey, OR, 1971)

A.J. Bescond: *Le chant grégorien* (Paris, 1972)

K.G. Fellerer, ed.: *Geschichte der katholischen Kirchenmusik* (Kassel, 1972–6)

B. Stäblein: *Schriftbild der einstimmigen Musik*, Musikgeschichte in Bildern, iii/4 (Leipzig, 1975)

G. Cattin: *Il Medioevo, I*, Storia della musica, i/2 (Turin, 1979, enlarged 2/1991 as *La monodia nel Medioevo*; Eng. trans., 1984, as *Music of the Middle Ages, I*)

R.F. Hayburn: *Papal Legislation on Sacred Music 95AD to 1977AD* (Collegeville, MN, 1979)

D. Hiley: 'Recent Research on the Origins of Western Chant', *EMc*, xvi (1988), 203–13

H. Hucke: 'Choralforschung und Musikwissenschaft', *Das musikalische Kunstwerk: Festschrift Carl Dahlhaus*, ed. H Danuser and others (Laaber, 1988), 131–41

A. Hughes: *Style and Symbol: Medieval Music, 800–1453* (Ottawa, 1989)

R. Crocker and D. Hiley, eds.: *The Early Middle Ages to 1300*, NOHM, ii (1990) [incl. K. Levy: 'Latin Chant Outside the Roman Tradition', 69–110, 733–43; R. Crocker: 'Liturgical Materials of Roman Chant', 111–45, 743–51; R. Crocker: Chants of the Roman Office', 146–73; R. Crocker: 'Chants of the Roman Mass', 174–222; R. Crocker: 'Medieval Chant', 225–309; S. Rankin: 'Liturgical Drama', 310–56, 751–7]

P.-M. Gy: *La liturgie dans l'histoire* (Paris, 1990)

J.W. McKinnon, ed.: *Antiquity and the Middle Ages: from Ancient Greece to the 15th Century* (London, 1990) [incl 'Christian Antiquity', 68–87; 'The Emergence of Gregorian Chant in the Carolingian Era', 89–119; D. Hiley: 'Plainchant Transfigured: Innovation and Reformation through the Ages', 120–42]

J. Harper: *The Forms and Orders of Western Liturgy from the Tenth to the Eighteenth Century: a Historical Introduction and Guide for Students and Musicians* (Oxford, 1991)

H. Möller and R. Stephan, eds.: *Die Musik des Mittelalters* (Laaber, 1991) [incl. R. Steiner: 'Einfuhrung und Verbreitung der lateinischen liturgischen Gesänge in der Karolingerzeit', 33–53; L. Treitler: 'Mündliche und schriftliche Überlieferung: Anfänge der musikalischen Notation', 54–93; A. Haug: 'Neue Ansatze im 9. Jahrhundert', 94–128; H. Möller: 'Institutionen, Musikleben, Musiktheorie', 129–99]

L. Treitler: 'The Politics of Reception: Tailoring the Present as Fulfillment of a Desired Past', *JRMA*, cxvi (1991), 280–98

P. Jeffery: *Re-envisioning Past Musical Cultures: Ethnomusicology in the Study of Gregorian Chant* (Chicago, 1992)

D. Hiley: *Western Plainchant: a Handbook* (Oxford, 1993)

M. Walter: *Grundlagen der Musik des Mittelalters: Schrift – Zeit – Raum* (Stuttgart, 1994) [incl. an extensive bibliography of the secondary literature, 323–65]

R. Flotzinger and G. Gruber, eds.: *Musikgeschichte Österreichs*, i: *Von den Anfängen zum Barock* (Vienna, 2/1995), esp. chaps.3–4

C. Johnson and A. Ward: 'Edmund Bishop's *The Genius of the Roman Rite*: its Context, Import, and Promotion', *Ephemerides liturgicae*, cx (1996), 401–44

D: SOURCES

manuscripts, facsimiles, incunabula, history of liturgical books, catalogues

PalMus [*see* SOLESMES, §4]

G.M. Dreves, C. Blume and H.M. Bannister, eds.: Analecta hymnica medii aevi (Leipzig, 1886–1922/R)

U. Chevalier: *Repertorium hymnologicum* (Leuven and Brussels, 1892–1921)

W.H. Frere, ed.: *Graduale sarisburiense* [GS] (London, 1894/R) [facs.]

W.H. Frere: *Bibliotheca musico-liturgica: a Descriptive Handlist of the Musical and Latin-Liturgical MSS of the Middle Ages Preserved in the Libraries of Great Britain and Ireland* (London, 1894–1932/R)

W.H. Frere, ed.: *Antiphonale sarisburiense* [AS] (London, 1901–25/R) [facs.]

H. Loriquet, J. Pothier and A. Collette, eds.: *Le graduel de l'église cathédrale de Rouen au XIIIe siècle* (Rouen, 1907) [facs. of *F-Pn* lat.904]

H.M. Bannister: *Monumenti vaticani di paleografia musicale latina* (Leipzig, 1913/R)

G. Beyssac: 'Notes sur un graduel-sacramentaire de St Pierre de Bantz du XIIe siècle', *Revue bénédictine*, xxxiii (1921), 190–200

V.M. Leroquais: *Les sacramentaires et les missels manuscrits des bibliothèques publiques de France* (Paris, 1924)

P. Wagner, ed.: *Das Graduale der St. Thomaskirche zu Leipzig (14. Jahrhundert)* (Leipzig, 1930–32/R) [facs.]

M. Andrieu, ed.: *Les Ordines romani du haut Moyen-Age* (Leuven, 1931–56/R)

V. Leroquais: *Les bréviaires manuscrits des bibliothèques publiques de France* (Paris, 1934)

R.-J. Hesbert, ed.: *Antiphonale missarum sextuplex* [AMS] (Brussels, 1935/R)

M. Andrieu: *Le pontifical romain au Moyen-Age* (Rome, 1938–41)

J.M. Hanssens, ed.: *Amalarii episcopi opera liturgica omnia* (Vatican City, 1948–50)

P. Siffrin: 'Eine Schwesterhandschrift des Graduale von Monza: Reste zu Berlin, Cleveland und Trier', *Ephemerides liturgicae*, lxiv (1950), 53–80 [a 9th-century fragment of 4 bifolia from north-east France]

S. Corbin: 'Le fonds manuscrit de Cadouin', *Bulletin de la Société historique et archéologique du Périgord*, lxxxi, suppl. (1954), 1–34

R.-J. Hesbert: *Les manuscrits musicaux de Jumièges*, Monumenta musicae sacrae, ii (Mâcon, 1954)

W. Irtenkauf: Das neuerworbene Weingartner Troper der Stuttgarter Landesbibliothek (Cod. brev. 160)', *AMw*, xi (1954), 280–95

G. Vecchi, ed.: *Troparium sequentiarium nonantulanum: Cod. Casanat. 1741*, MLMI, 1st ser., *Latina*, i (1955) [facs.]

F. Bussi: *L'antifonario graduale della basilica di S. Antonino in Piacenza (sec. XII)* (Piacenza, 1956)

L.C. Mohlberg, ed.: *Sacramentarium veronese* (Rome, 1956, 3/1978) [edn of Leonine Sacramentary]

Le graduel romain: édition critique par les moines de Solesmes (Solesmes, 1957–)

J. Emerson: 'The Recovery of the Wolffheim Antiphoner', *AnnM*, vi (1958–63), 69–97

P.-M. Gy: 'Collectaire, rituel, processional', *Revue des sciences philosophiques et théologiques*, xliv (1960), 441–69

L.C. Mohlberg and P. Siffrin: *Liber sacramentorum romanae ecclesiae ordinis anni circuli* (Rome, 1960)

D. Balboni: 'Nomenclatura per la catalogazione dei liturgici', *Ephemerides liturgicae*, lxxv (1961), 223–36; xcix (1985), 517–24

K. Meyer-Baer: *Liturgical Music Incunabula: a Descriptive Catalogue* (London, 1962)

K. Gamber: *Codices liturgici latini antiquiores* (Fribourg, 1963, 2/1968; suppl., ed. B. Baroffio and others, 1988)

C. Vogel and R. Elze: *Le pontifical romano-germanique du Xe siècle* (Rome, 1963–72)

R.-J. Hesbert, ed.: *Corpus antiphonalium officii* [CAO], vii–xii (1963–79)

H. Husmann, ed.: *Tropen- und Sequenzenhandschriften*, RISM, B/V/1 (1964)

R.-J. Hesbert: *Le tropaire-prosaire de Dublin: manuscrit Add. 710 de l'Université de Cambridge (vers 1360)* (Rouen, 1966) [facs.]

C. Vogel: *Introduction aux sources de l'histoire du culte chrétien au Moyen Age* (1966/R; Eng. trans., rev., 1986, as *Medieval Liturgy: an Introduction to the Sources*)

L. Feininger: *Repertorium cantus plani* (Trent, 1969–71)

W. Heckenbach: *Das Antiphonar von Ahrweiler* (Cologne, 1971)

M. Huglo: *Les tonaires: inventaire, analyse, comparaison* (Paris, 1971)

J. Stenzl: *Repertorium der liturgischen Musikhandschriften der Diözesen Sitten, Lausanne und Genf* (Fribourg, 1972)

F.E. Hansen: *H 159 Montpellier: Tonary of St. Bénigne of Dijon* (Copenhagen, 1974)

K.D. Hartzell: 'A St. Albans Miscellany in New York', *Mittellateinisches Jb*, x (1975), 20–61

B. Moreton: *The Eighth-Century Gelasian Sacramentary: a Study in Tradition* (Oxford, 1976)

N. Stuart: 'Melodic Corrections in an Eleventh-Century Gradual (Paris, B.N., lat. 903)', *JPMMS*, ii (1979), 2–10

R. Pynson: *Processionale ad usum Sarum: 1502*, i (Clarabricken, Co. Kilkenny, 1980) [facs.]

A. Dumas, ed.: *Liber sacramentorum Gellonensis* (Turnhout, 1981)

R.-J. Hesbert, ed.: *Le graduel de Saint-Denis: manuscrit 384 de la Bibliothèque Mazarine de Paris* (Paris 1981) [facs.]

A. Hughes: 'Medieval Liturgical Books in Twenty-Three Spanish Libraries: Provisional Inventories', *Traditio*, xxxviii (1982), 365–94

A. Hughes: *Medieval Manuscripts for Mass and Office* (Toronto, 1982)

K.H. Staub, P. Ulveling and F. Unterkircher, eds.: *Echternacher Sakramentar und Antiphonar: vollstandige Faksimile-Ausgabe im Originalformat der Handschrift 1946 aus dem Besitz der Hessischen Landes- und Hochschulbibliothek Darmstadt* (Graz, 1982)

J. Szendrei and R. Ribarič, eds.: *Missale notatum strigoniense ante 1341 in Posonio* (Budapest, 1982)

L. Treitler: 'Paleography and Semiotics', *Musicologie médiévale: Paris 1982*, 17–27

M.C. Peñas García: *La música en los evangeliarios españoles* (Madrid, 1983) [comparative study of chant tunes]

Die Handschrift St. Gallen, Stiftsbibliothek 359: Cantatorium, Monumenta palaeographica gregoriana, iii (Münsterschwarzach, 1984) [facs.]

I. Fernández de la Cuesta, ed.: *Antiphonale silense: British Library Mss. Add.30850: introducción, indices y edición* (Madrid, 1985) [facs.]

H. Gneuss: 'Liturgical Books in Anglo-Saxon England and their Old English Terminology', *Learning and Literature in Anglo-Saxon England: Studies Presented to Peter Clemoes*, ed. M. Lapidge and H. Gneuss (Cambridge, 1985), 91–142

G. Björkvall: *Les deux tropaires d'Apt, mss. 17 et 18: inventaire analytique des mss. et édition des textes uniques* (Stockholm, 1986)

Die Handschrift Bamberg, Staatsbibliothek, Lit. 6, Monumenta palaeographica gregoriana, ii (Münsterschwarzach, 1986) [facs.]

G.M. Paucker: *Das Graduale Msc. lit. 6 der Staatsbibliothek Bamberg: eine Handschriften-Monographie unter besonderer Berücksichtigung des Repertoires und der Notation* (Regensburg, 1986)

Tradizione manoscritta e pratica musicale: i codici di Puglia: Bari 1986

M. Lütolf, ed.: *Das Graduale von Santa Cecilia in Trastevere (Cod. Bodmer 74)* (Cologny-Geneva, 1987) [facs.]

B.G. Baroffio: 'I manoscritti liturgici italiani: ricerche, studi, catalogazione (1980–1987)', *I.e fonti musicali in Italia*, i (1987), 65–126; ii (1988), 89–134; iii (1989), 91–118; v (1991), 7–129

M. Huglo: *Les livres de chant liturgique* (Turnhout, 1988)

C. Lamagat: *Le fonds des manuscripts médiévaux de la Bibliothèque d'Albi: étude paléographique et approche musicale* (diss., U. of Toulouse II, 1988)

A.E. Planchart: 'Fragments, Palimpsests, and Marginalia', *JM*, lxv (1988), 293–339

O.T. Edwards: 'How Many Sarum Antiphonals were there in England and Wales in the Middle of the Sixteenth Century?', *Revue bénédictine*, xcix (1989), 155–80

Die Handschrift St. Gallen, Stiftsbibliothek 390[–391]: Antiphonarium Hartkeri, Monumenta palaeographica gregoriana, iv (Münsterschwarzach, 1989) [facs.]

M. Kreuels: *Indizes der Handschriften zu Graduale Triplex und Offertoriale Triplex* (Regensburg, 1989) [CH-SGs 359, 339, 376, 390/91, E 121; D-BAs lit.6; F-LA239,CHRm 47, Mont-Renaud (Noyon), MOf H 159, Pn lat.776 (Albi), lat.903 (St. Yrieix); I-BV 33, 34, Rvat 10673, Ra 123 ; A-Gu 807 (Klosterneuburg)]

M.P. Bezuidenhout: *An Italian Office Book of the Late Thirteenth Century* (Cape Town, 1990) [transcr. of a MS in the Grey Collection of SA-Csa]

L. Collamore and J.P. Metzinger, eds.: *The Bamberg Antiphoner, Staatsbibliothek, lit. 25* (Washington DC, 1990) [printout from CANTUS index in machine-readable form]

L. Collamore and J.P. Metzinger, eds.: *Frere's Index to the Antiphons of the Sarum Antiphoner: an Expanded Version* (London, 1990)

L. Dobszay, ed.: *Corpus Antiphonalium Officii – Ecclesiarium Centralis Europae, I/A: Salzburg (Temporale)* (Budapest, 1990) [pubn derived from CAO–ECE database]

H. Möller, ed.: *Das Quedlinburger Antiphonar (Berlin, Staatsbibliothek Preussischer Kulturbesitz, Mus. ms. 40047)* (Tutzing, 1990) [incl. facs.]

J. Szendrei, ed.: *Graduale strigoniense (s. XV/XVI)* (Budapest, 1990–93)

R. Flotzinger: *Choralhandschriften österreichischer Provenienz in der Bodleian Library, Oxford* (Vienna, 1991)

E. Lagnier: *Corpus musica hymnorum augustanum* (Aosta, 1991)

O. Lang, ed.: *Codex 121 Einsiedeln: Graduale und Sequenzen Notkers von St. Gallen* (Weinheim, 1991) [facs.]

A.W. Robertson: *The Service-Books of the Royal Abbey of Saint-Denis: Images of Ritual and Music in the Middle Ages* (Oxford, 1991)

M.K. Duggan: *Italian Music Incunabula: Printers and Type* (Berkeley, 1992) [a history of printed musical notation in Italy, a list of libraries holding incunabula and a chronological index of printed Italian liturgical books to 1500]

D. Hiley, ed.: *Missale carnotense: Chartres, Codex 520*, MMMA, iv/1–2 (1992) [facs.]

R.T. Olexy, ed.: *An Aquitanian Antiphoner: Toledo, Biblioteca capitular, 44.2* (Ottawa, 1992) [printout from CANTUS index in machine-readable form]

M. Huglo: 'Observations codicologiques sur l'antiphonaire de Compiègne (Paris, B.N. lat. 17436)', *De musica et cantu: Helmut Hucke zum 60. Geburtstag*, ed. P. Cahn and A.-K. Heimer (Hildesheim, 1993), 117–30

T. Karp: 'The Cataloging of Chant Manuscripts as an Aid to Critical Editions and Chant History', *Music Reference Services Quarterly*, ii/3–4 (1993), 241–69

E. Palazzo: *Histoire des livres liturgiques: le Moyen Age: des origines au XIIIe siècle* (Paris, 1993)

C. Rodriguez Suso: *La monodía litúrgica en el pais Vasco: fragmentos con notación musical de los siglos XII al XVIII* (Bilbao, 1993)

Z. Czagány, ed.: *Corpus Antiphonalium Officii – Ecclesiarium Centralis Europae, II/A: Bamberg (Temporale)* (Budapest, 1994) [pubn derived from CAO–ECE database]

M. Gozzi, ed.: *Le fonti liturgiche a stampa della Biblioteca musicale L. Feininger* (Trent, 1994)

A. Hänggi and P. Ladner, eds.: *Missale basileense saec. XI (Codex Gressly)* (Fribourg, 1994) [facs.]

B.G. Baroffio and S.J. Kim, eds.: *Bibliotheca apostolica vaticana, Archivio S. Pietro B 79: Antifonario della Basilica di S. Pietro (sec. XII)* (Rome, 1995) [facs.]

W. Arlt and S. Rankin, eds.: *Stiftsbibliothek Sankt Gallen Codices 484 & 381* (Winterthur, 1996) [facs.]

R. Crosatti, ed.: *Il codice Brescia biblioteca capitolare 13, 'Liber antiphonarius divinorum officiorum' cum notis musicis scriptus circa saeculum XIII: studio codicologico-liturgico-musicale del più antico antifonario della cattedrale de Brescia* (Cremona, 1996)

Z. Czagány, ed.: *Corpus Antiphonalium Officii – Ecclesiarium Centralis Europae, III/A: Praha (Temporale)* (Budapest, 1996) [pubn derived from CAO–ECE database]

I. Fernández de la Cuesta: 'Libros de música litúrgica impresos en España ante de 1900, II: siglos XV y XVI', *Música*, iii (1996), 11–29 [approximately 145 printed liturgical books dating between 1485–1600 in 170 different libraries]

D. Hiley, ed.: *Moosburger Graduale: München, Universitätsbibliothek, 2⁰ Cod. ms. 156* (Tutzing, 1996) [facs.]

R. Steiner, ed.: *The Zwiefalten Antiphoner: Karlsruhe, Badische Landesbibliothek, Aug. perg. LX.* (Ottawa, 1996) [printout from CANTUS index in machine-readable form]

K. Vellekoop, ed.: *Liber ordinarius Sancte Marie Traiectensis: the Ordinal of St Mary's Church, Utrecht (Ms. London, British Library, Add.9769)* (Amsterdam, 1996)

R. Camilot-Oswald: *Die liturgischen Musikhandschriften aus dem mittelalterlichen Patriarchat Aquileia*, MMMA, *Subsidia*, ii (1997)

O.T. Edwards, ed.: *National Library of Wales MS. 20541 E: the Penpont Antiphonal* (Ottawa, 1997) [facs.]

R. Steiner, ed.: *Utrecht Bibliotheek der Rijksuniversiteit MS 406 (3.J.7)* (Ottawa, 1997) [facs.]

J. Szendrei, ed.: *Breviarium notatum strigoniense (s. XIII)* (Budapest, 1998) [facs. of CZ-Pst DE. I. 7]

L. Dobszay and J. Szendrei, eds.: *Antiphonen*, MMMA, v (1999)

E: COMPUTER PROGRAMS AND DATABASES

K. Ottosen: 'The Latin Office of the Dead: a Computer Analysis of Two Thousand Texts', *Computer Applications to Medieval Studies*, ed. A. Gilmour-Bryson (Kalamazoo, MI, 1984), 81–7

D. Crawford: 'Surveying Renaissance Liturgical Materials: Methodology and the Computer', *SM*, xxx (1988), 345–54

L. Dobszay: 'The Program CAO-ECE', *SM*, xxx (1988), 355–60

L. Dobszay and G. Proszeky: *CAO–ECE: a Preliminary Report* (Budapest, 1988)

J. Grier: 'Lachmann, Bedier and the Bipartite Stemma: towards a Responsible Application of the Common-Error Method', *Revue d'histoire des textes*, xviii (1988), 263–78

F. Tirro: 'Melody and the Markoff-Chain Model: a Gregorian Hymn Repertory', *Explorations in Music, the Arts, and Ideas: Essays in Honor of Leonard B. Meyer*, ed. E. Narmour and R.A. Solie (Stuyvesant, NY, 1988), 229–60

W.B. Hewlett and E. Selfridge-Field: 'Encoding Neumes and Mensural Notation', and an 'Optical Recognition of Musical Data', *Computing in Musicology*, vi (1990), 23–45

W. McGee and P. Merkley: 'The Optical Scanning of Medieval Music', *Computers and the Humanities*, xxv (1991), 47–53

R. Steiner: 'Directions for Chant Research in the 1990s: the Impact of Chant Data Bases', *IMSCR XV: Madrid 1992*, 695–705

P.R. Cook: 'SPASM, a Real-Time Vocal Tract Physical Model Controller; and Singer, the Companion Softward Synthesis System', *Computer Music Journal*, xvii (1993), 30–44

E. Häkli: 'From Neumes to Network: Music in the Helsinki University Library', *FAM*, xl (1993), 11–16

T.J. Mathiesen: 'Transmitting Text and Graphics in Online Databases: the *Thesaurus Musicarum Latinarum* Model', *Computing in Musicology*, ix (1993–4), 33–58 [*TML*: a database designed to contain the entire corpus of Latin music theory written during the Middle Ages and early Renaissance]

M. Haas: 'Über einige Möglichkeiten der computergestützen Erforschung liturgischer Einstimmigkeit', *Max Lütolf zum 60. Geburtstag: Festschrift*, ed. B. Hangartner and U. Fischer (Basel, 1994), 75–97

R. Steiner: 'CANTUS: a Data Base for Gregorian Chant', *Archiv für Liturgiewissenschaft*, xxxvii (1995), 87–8

F: EARLY HISTORY

L. Duchesne, ed.: *Le Liber pontificalis: texte, introduction et commentaire* (Paris, 1886–92, enlarged 2/1955–7 by C. Vogel)

F.A. Gevaert: *Les origines du chant liturgique de l'église latine* (Ghent, 1890/R)

G. Morin: *Les véritables origines du chant grégorien* (St Gérard, 1890, 2/1904)

V. Krause, ed.: *Walahfrid Strabo: De exordiis et incrementis*, MGH, *Capitularia*, ii (1892), 473–516; repr. with commentary and trans. by A. Harting-Corrêa (Leiden, 1996)

A. Gastoué: *Les origines du chant romain: l'antiphonaire grégorien* (Paris, 1907/R)

H. Netzer: *L'introduction de la messe romain en France sous les Carolingiens* (Paris, 1910/R)

C. Silva-Tarouca: 'Giovanni "archicantor" di S. Pietro a Roma e l'Ordo romanus da lui composta', *Atti della Pontificia accademia romana di archeologia*, 3rd ser., *Memorie*, i (1923), 159–219

M. Andrieu: 'Règlement d'Angilramne de Metz (768–91), fixant les honoraires de quelques fonctions liturgiques', *Revue des sciences religieuses*, x (1930), 349–69

J. Quasten: *Musik und Gesang in den Kulten der heidnischen Antike und christlichen Frühzeit* (Münster, 1930, 2/1973; Eng. trans., 1983)

W.H. Frere: *Studies in Early Roman Liturgy* (London, 1930–35)

M. Andrieu, ed.: *Les Ordines romani du haut Moyen-Age* (Leuven, 1931–61)

T. Klauser: 'Die liturgischen Austauschbeziehungen zwischen der römischen und der fränkisch-deutschen Kirche vom 8.–11. Jh.', *Historisches Jb der Görresgesellschaft*, liii (1933), 169–89

J.-B. Pelt: *Etudes sur la cathédrale de Metz: la liturgie* (Metz, 1937)

B. Bischoff: *Die süddeutschen Schreibschulen und Bibliotheken in der Karolingerzeit* (Leipzig, 1940, 2/1960)

C.W. Dugmore: *The Influence of the Synagogue upon the Divine Office* (Oxford, 1944, 2/1964)

E. Wellesz: *Eastern Elements in Western Chant: Studies in the Early History of Ecclesiastical Music*, MMB, *Subsidia*, ii (1947/R)

J.M. Hanssens, ed.: *Amalarii episcopi opera liturgica omnia* (Vatican City, 1948–50)

A. Chavasse: 'Les plus anciens types du lectionnaire et de l'antiphonaire romains de la messe', *Revue bénédictine*, lxii (1952), 3–94

A. Baumstark: *Liturgie comparée: principes et méthodes pour l'étude historique des liturgies chrétiennes* (Chevetogne, 3/1953; Eng. trans., 1958)

C. Hohler: 'The Type of Sacramentary Used by St. Boniface', *Sankt Bonifatius: Gedenkgabe zum zwölfhundertsten Todestag* (Fulda, 1954), 89–93

H. Hucke: 'Die Einführung des gregorianischen Gesangs im Frankenreich', *Römische Quartalschrift*, xlix (1954), 172–87

H. Hucke: 'Die Tradition des gregorianischen Gesanges in der römischen Schola cantorum', *Katholische Kirchenmusik II: Vienna 1954*, 120–23

J. Smits van Waesberghe: 'Neues über die Schola cantorum zu Rom', *Katholische Kirchenmusik II: Vienna 1954*, 111–19

H. Hucke: 'Die Entstehung der Überlieferung von einer musikalischen Tätigkeit Gregors des Grossen', *Mf*, viii (1955), 259–64

G. Ellard: *Master Alcuin, Liturgist: a Partner of our Piety* (Chicago, 1956)

K. Gamber: *Wege zum Urgregorianum* (Beuron, 1956)

G. Ferrari: *Early Roman Monasteries: Notes for the History of the Monasteries and Convents at Rome from the V through the X Century* (Vatican City, 1957)

H. Ashworth: 'Did St. Augustine Bring the Gregorianum to England?', *Ephemerides liturgicae*, lxxii (1958), 39–43

C.-A. Moberg: 'Gregorianische Reflexionen', *Miscelánea en homenaje a Monseñor Higinio Anglés* (Barcelona, 1958–61), 559–83

C. Vogel: 'Les échanges liturgiques entre Rome et les pays francs jusqu'à l'époque de Charlemagne', *Le chiese nei regni dell'Europa occidentale: Spoleto 1959* [*Settimane di studio del Centro italiano di studi sull'alto Medioevo*, vii (1960)], 185–95

L. Wallach: *Alcuin and Charlemagne: Studies in Carolingian History and Literature* (Ithaca, NY, 1959/R)

E. Werner: *The Sacred Bridge: the Interdependence of Liturgy and Music in Synagogue and Church during the First Millennium* (London and New York, 1959–84/R)

S. Corbin: 'La cantillation des rituels chrétiens', *RdM*, xlvii (1961), 3–36

S.J.P. Van Dijk: 'Gregory the Great, Founder of the Urban Schola Cantorum', *Ephemerides liturgicae*, lxxvii (1963), 335–56

S.J.P. Van Dijk: 'Papal Schola "versus" Charlemagne', *Organicae voces: Festschrift Joseph Smits van Waesberghe*, ed. P. Fischer (Amsterdam, 1963), 21–30

C. Vogel and R. Elze, eds.: *Le pontifical romano-germanique du dixième siècle* (Vatican City, 1963–72)

A. Burda: 'Gregor der Grosse als Musiker', *Mf*, xvii (1964), 388–93

A. de Vogüé, ed.: *Regula magistri* (Paris, 1964)

H. Hucke: 'War Gregor der Grosse doch Musiker?', *Mf*, xviii (1965), 390–93

C. Vogel: 'La réforme cultuelle sous Pepin le Bref et sous Charlemagne', *Die karolingische Renaissance*, ed. E. Patzelt (Graz, 1965), 171–242

H. Anglès: 'Sakraler Gesang und Musik in den Schriften Gregors des Grossen', *Essays Presented to Egon Wellesz*, ed. J. Westrup (Oxford, 1966), 33–42

C. Vogel: 'La réforme liturgique sous Charlemagne', *Karl der Grosse: Lebenswerk und Nachleben*, ed. W. Braunfels, ii (Düsseldorf, 1966), 217–32

A. Burda: 'Nochmals Gregor der Grosse als Musiker', *Mf*, xx (1967), 154–66

B. Stäblein: 'Gregorius praesul, der Prolog zum römischen Antiphonale', *Musik und Verlag: Karl Vötterle zum 65. Geburtstag*, ed. R. Baum and W. Rehm (Kassel, 1968), 537–61

N. Mitchell: '*Ordo psallendi* in the *Rule*: Historical Perspectives', *American Benedictine Review*, xx (1969), 505–27

M. Schuler: 'Die Musik an den Höfen der Karolinger', *AMw*, xxvii (1970), 23–40

B. Stäblein: 'Nochmals zur angeblichen Entstehung des gregorianischen Chorals im Frankenreich', *AMw*, xxvii (1970), 110–21

D.M. Hope: *The Leonine Sacramentary: a Reassessment of its Nature and Purpose* (London, 1971)

J. Deshusses: *Le sacramentaire grégorien: ses principales formes d'après les plus anciens manuscrits* (Fribourg, 1971–82)

J. Deshusses: 'Les messes d'Alcuin', *Archiv für Liturgiewissenschaft*, xiv (1972), 7–41

M. Huglo: 'Römische-frankische Liturgie', *Geschichte der katholischen Kirchenmusik*, ed. K.G. Fellerer, i (Kassel, 1972), 233–44

P.A.B. Llewellyn: 'The Roman Church in the Seventh Century: the Legacy of Gregory I', *Journal of Ecclesiastical History*, xxv (1974), 363–80

B. Stäblein: 'Die Entstehung des gregorianischen Chorals', *Mf*, xxvii (1974), 5–17

C.E. Hohler: 'Some Service-Books of the Later Saxon Church', *Tenth-Century Studies: Essays in Commemoration of the Millennium of the Council of Winchester and Regularis concordia*, ed. D. Parsons (London, 1975)

H. Hucke: 'Karolingische Renaissance und Gregorianischer Gesang', *Mf*, xxviii (1975), 4–18

J. Stenzl: 'Bewahrende und verändernde musikalische Überlieferung', *AMz*, xxxii (1975), 117–23

R. McKitterick: *The Frankish Church and the Carolingian Reforms, 798–895* (London, 1977)

E. Ewig: 'Saint Chrodegang et la reforme de l'èglise franque', *Spätantikes und fränkisches Gallien*, ii, ed. H. Atsma (Munich, 1979), 232–59

M. Huglo: 'Les remaniements de l'antiphonaire grégorien au IXe siècle: Hélisachar, Agobard, Amalaire', *Culto cristiano, politica imperiale carolingia: Todi 1977* (Todi, 1979), 87–120

R.-J. Hesbert: 'L'antiphonaire d'Amalaire', *Ephemerides liturgicae*, xciv (1980), 176–94

H. Hucke: 'Toward a New Historical View of Gregorian Chant', *JAMS*, xxxiii (1980), 437–67

H. Schmidt: 'Gregorianik: Legende oder Wahrheit?', *Ars musica, musica scientia: Festschrift Heinrich Hüschen*, ed. D. Altenburg (Cologne, 1980), 400–11

J. Dyer: 'Augustine and the "Hymni ante oblationem": the Earliest Offertory Chants?', *Revue des études augustiniennes*, xxvii (1981), 85–99

E. Foley: 'The Cantor in Historical Perspective', *Worship*, lvi (1982), 194–213

J.M. Wallace-Hadrill: *The Frankish Church* (Oxford, 1983)

J. Dyer: 'Latin Psalters, Old Roman and Gregorian Chants', *KJb*, lxviii (1984), 11–30

P. Jeffery: 'The Introduction of Psalmody into the Roman Church by Pope Celestine I', *Archiv für Liturgiewissenschaft*, xxvi (1984), 147–55

J.A. Smith: 'The Ancient Synagogue, the Early Church and Singing', *ML* (1984), 1–16

J. Dyer: 'Psalmody and the Roman Mass', *Studies in Music from the University of Western Ontario*, x (1985), 1–24

T.F.X. Noble: 'A New Look at the *Liber Pontificalis*', *Archivum historiae pontificiae*, xxiii (1985), 347–58

J.W. McKinnon: 'On the Question of Psalmody in the Ancient Synagogue', *EMH*, vi (1986), 159–91

J.W. McKinnon: 'The Fourth-Century Origin of the Gradual', *EMH*, vii (1987), 91–106

H. Hucke: 'Choralforschung und Musikwissenschaft', *Das musikalische Kunstwerk: Festschrift Carl Dahlhaus*, ed. H. Danuser and others. (Laaber, 1988), 131–4

H. Hucke: 'Gregorianische Fragen', *Mf*, xli (1988), 304–30

B.G. Baroffio: 'Il canto gregoriano nel secolo VIII', *Lateinische Kultur im VIII. Jahrhundert: Traube-Gedenkschrift*, ed. A. Lehner and W. Berschin (St Ottilien, 1989), 9–23

J. Dyer: 'The Singing of Psalms in the Early-Medieval Office', *Speculum*, lxiv (1989), 535–78

M. Huglo: 'Trois livres manuscrits présentés par Helisachar', *Revue bénédictine*, cv (1989), 272–85

H. Hucke: 'Die Entstehung des gregorianischen Gesangs', *Neue Musik und Tradition: Festschrift Rudolf Stephan zum 65. Geburtstag*, ed. J. Kuckertz and others (Laaber, 1990), 11–23

P. Jeffery: 'Jerusalem and Rome (and Constantinople): the Musical Heritage of Two Great Cities in the Formation of the Medieval Chant Traditions', *Cantus planus IV: Pécs 1990*, 163–74

P. Bernard: 'Les alleluia mélismatiques dans le chant romain: recherches sur la genèse de l'alleluia de la messe romaine', *Rivista internazionale di musica sacra*, xii (1991), 286–362

O. Cullin: 'De la psalmodie sans refrain à la psalmodie responsoriale: transformation et conservation dans les répertoires liturgiques latins', *RdM*, lxxvii (1991), 5–24

P.F. Bradshaw: *The Search for the Origins of Christian Worship: Sources and Methods for the Study of Early Liturgy* (London and New York, 1992)

P. Jeffery: 'The Lost Tradition of Early Christian Jerusalem: some Possible Melodic Survivals in the Byzantine and Latin Chant Traditions', *EMH*, xi (1992), 151–90

J.W. McKinnon: 'Antoine Chavasse and the Dating of Early Chant', *PMM*, i (1992), 123–47

J.W. McKinnon: 'The Eighth-Century Frankish-Roman Communion Cycle', *JAMS*, xlv (1992), 179–227

D. Praet: 'Explaining the Christianization of the Roman Empire: Older Theories and Recent Developments', *Sacris erudiri*, xxxiii (1992–3), 5–119

J. Dyer: 'The Schola Cantorum and its Roman Milieu in the Early Middle Ages', *De musica et cantu: Helmut Hucke zum 60. Geburtstag*, ed. P. Cahn and A.-K. Heimer (Hildesheim, 1993), 19–40

A. Haug: 'Zur Interpretation der Liqueszenzneumen', *AMw*, l (1993), 85–100

M. Huglo: 'D'Helisachar à Abbon de Fleury', *Revue bénédictine*, civ (1994), 204–30

P. Jeffery: 'The Earliest Christian Chant Repertory Recovered: the Gregorian Witness to Jerusalem Chant', *JAMS*, xlvii (1994), 1–38

S. Rankin: 'Carolingian Music', *Carolingian Culture: Emulation and Innovation*, ed. R. McKitterick (Cambridge, 1994), 274–316

J. Dyer: 'Prolegomena to a History of Music and Liturgy at Rome in the Middle Ages', *Essays on Medieval Music: in Honor of David G. Hughes*, ed. G.M. Boone (Cambridge, MA, 1995), 87–115

P. Jeffery: 'Rome and Jerusalem: From Oral Tradition to Written Repertory in Two Ancient Liturgical Centers', ibid., 207–47

K. Levy: 'Abbot Hélisachar's Antiphoner', *JAMS*, xlviii (1995), 171–86

J. McKinnon: 'Lector Chant versus Schola Chant: a Question of Historical Plausibility', *Laborare fratres in unum: Festschrift László Dobszay zum 60. Geburtstag*, ed. J. Szendrei and D. Hiley (Hildesheim, 1995), 201–11

E. Nowacki: 'Antiphonal Psalmody in Christian Antiquity and Early Middle Ages', *Essays on Medieval Music: in Honor of David G. Hughes*, ed. G.M. Boone (Cambridge, MA, 1995), 287–315

P. Bernard: '*David mutatus in melius*, L'origine et la signification de la centonisation des chants liturgiques au VIe siècle par la Schola cantorum romaine', *Musica e storia*, iv (1996), 5–66

C. Cubitt: 'Unity and Diversity in the Early Anglo-Saxon Liturgy', *Unity and Diversity in the Church: Nottingham 1994*, ed. R.N. Swanson (Oxford, 1996), 45–57

R. McKitterick: 'Unity and Diversity in the Carolingian Church', ibid., 59–82

B. Scharf: 'Le origini della monodia sacra in volgare in Francia e in Germania', *Rivista internazionale di musica sacra*, xv (1994), 18–70

J.A. Smith: 'First-Century Christian Singing and its Relationship to Contemporary Jewish Religious Song', *ML*, lxxv (1994), 1–15

M. Forman and T. Sullivan: 'The Latin Cenobitic Rules: A.D. 400–700: Editions and Translations', *American Benedictine Review*, xlviii (1997), 52–68

G: OLD ROMAN CHANT; RELATIONSHIP WITH GREGORIAN CHANT

R. Andoyer: 'Le chant romain antégrégorien', *Revue du chant grégorien*, xx (1911–12), 69–75, 107–114

B. Stäblein: 'Alt- und neurömischer Choral', *GfMKB: Lüneburg 1950*, 53–6

B. Stäblein: 'Zur Frühgeschichte des römischen Chorals', *Congresso di musica sacra [I]: Rome 1950*, 271–5

J. Hourlier and M. Huglo: 'Un important témoin du chant "vieux–romain": le graduel de Sainte-Cécile du Trastevère', *Revue grégorienne*, xxxi (1952), 26–37

M. Huglo: 'Le chant "vieux–romain": liste des manuscrits et témoins indirects', *Sacris erudiri*, vi (1954), 96–124

H. Hucke: 'Gregorianischer Gesang in altrömischer und fränkischer Überlieferung', *AMw*, xii (1955), 74–87

S.J.P. Van Dijk: 'The Urban and Papal Rites in Seventh and Eighth-Century Rome', *Sacris erudiri*, xii (1961), 411–87

S.J.P. Van Dijk: 'The Old-Roman Rite', *Papers Presented to the 3rd International Conference on Patristic Studies: Oxford 1959*, ed. F.L. Cross [*Studia patristica*, v (1962)], 185–205

J. Smits van Waesberghe: '"De glorioso officio ... dignitate apostolica" (Amalarius): zum Aufbau der Gross-Alleluia in den Päpstlichen Ostervespern', *Essays Presented to Egon Wellesz*, ed. J. Westrup (Oxford, 1966), 48–73

S.J.P. Van Dijk: 'Recent Developments in the Study of the Old-Roman Rite', *Papers Presented to the 4th International Conference on Patristic Studies: Oxford 1963*, ed. F.L. Cross [*Studia patristica*, viii (1966)], 299–319

P.F. Cutter: 'The Old-Roman Chant Tradition: Oral or Written?', *JAMS*, xx (1967), 167–81

M. Huglo: 'Les diverses mélodies du *Te decet laus*: à propos du vieux–romain', *JbLH*, xii (1967), 111–16

B. Stäblein: 'Kann der gregorianische Choral im Frankenreich entstanden sein?', *AMw*, xxiv (1967), 153–69

S.J.P. Van Dijk: 'The Medieval Easter Vespers of the Roman Clergy', *Sacris erudiri*, xix (1969–70), 261–363

P.F. Cutter: 'Die altrömischen und gregorianischen Responsorien im zweiten Modus', *KJb*, liv (1970), 33–40

M. Landwehr-Melnicki, ed.: *Die Gesänge des altrömischen Graduale Vat. lat. 5319*, MMMA, ii (1970) [with introduction by B. Stäblein; incl. edn of Old Roman Gradual]

N.M. Van Deusen: *An Historical and Stylistic Comparison of the Graduals of Gregorian and Old Roman Chant* (diss., Indiana U., 1972)

H. Wagenaar-Nolthenius: 'Ein Münchener Mixtum: gregorianische Melodien zu altrömischen Texten', *AcM*, xlv (1973), 249–55

T.H. Connolly: 'The Graduale of S. Cecilia in Trastevere and the Old Roman Tradition', *JAMS*, xxviii (1975), 413–58

H. van der Werf: *The Emergence of Gregorian Chant: a Comparative Study of Ambrosian, Roman, and Gregorian Chant* (Rochester, NY, 1983)

S. Klöckner: *Analytische Untersuchungen an 16 Introiten im 1. Ton des altrömischen und des fränkisch-gregorianischen Repertoires hinsichtlich einer bewussten melodischen Abhängigkeit*, Beiträge zur Gregorianik, v (1988) [whole issue]

P. Bernard: 'Sur un aspect controversé de la réforme carolingienne: vieux–romain et grégorien', *Ecclesia orans*, vii (1990), 163–89

P. Bernard: 'Bilan historiographique de la question des rapports entre les chants vieux–romains et grégoriens', *Ecclesia orans*, xi (1994), 323–53

P. Bernard: 'Les verses des alléluias et des offertoires: témoins de l'histoire de la culture à Rome entre 560–742', *Musica e storia*, iii (1995), 5–40

M.-N. Colette: 'Grégorien et vieux–romain: deux méthodes différentes de collectage de mélodies traditionelles?', *Laborare fratres in unum: Festschrift László Dobszay zum 60. Geburtstag*, ed. J. Szendrei and D. Hiley (Hildesheim, 1995), 37–52

P. Bernard: *Du chant romain au chant grégorien (IVe-XIIIe siècle)* (Paris, 1996)

P. Bernard: 'Les chants propres de la messe dans les répertoires grégorien et romain ancien: essai d'édition pratique des variantes textuelles', *Ephemerides liturgicae*, cx (1996), 210–51

P. Bernard: 'Les variantes textuelles des chant du propre de la messe dans les répertoires grégorien et romain ancien: index des pièces', *Ephemerides liturgicae*, cx (1996), 445–50

H: OTHER CHANT TRADITIONS

Ambrosian, Beneventan, Celtic, Gallican, Mozarabic

F.E. Warren: *The Liturgy and Ritual of the Celtic Church* (Oxford, 1881/R, rev. 2/1987 by J. Stevenson)

M. Magistretti, ed.: *Beroldus, sive Ecclesiae ambrosianae mediolanensis kalendarium et ordines saec. XII* (Milan, 1894/R)

P. Cagin: 'L'antiphonaire ambrosien', *Antiphonarium ambrosianum du Musée britannique*, PalMus, 1st ser., v (1896/R), 1–200

A. Gatard and P. Lejay: 'Ambrosien (chant, rite)', *Dictionnaire d'archéologie chrétienne et de liturgie*, ed. F. Cabrol and H. Leclercq, i (Paris, 1903), 1353–442

R. Andoyer: 'L'ancienne liturgie de Bénévent', *Revue du chant grégorien*, xx (1911–12), 176–83; xxi (1912–13), 14–20, 44–51, 81–5, 112–15, 144–8, 169–74; xxii (1913–14), 8–11, 41–4, 80–83, 106–11, 141–5, 170–72; xxiii (1919–20), 42–4, 116–18, 182–3; xxiv (1920–21), 48–50, 87–9, 146–8, 182–5

W.C. Bishop: *The Mozarabic and Ambrosian Rites: Four Essays in Comparative Liturgiology*, ed. C.L. Feltoe (London, 1924)

P. Wagner: 'Über den altspanischen, mozarabischen Kirchengesang', *Musikhistorischer Kongress: Vienna 1927*, 234–6

G. Prado: 'Mozarabic Melodics', *Speculum*, iii (1928), 218–38

P. Wagner: 'Der mozarabische Kirchengesang und seine Überlieferung', *Spanische Forschungen der Görresgesellschaft*, 1st ser.: *Gesammelte Aufsätze zur Kulturgeschichte Spaniens*, i (1928), 102–41

C. Rojo and G. Prado: *El canto mozárabe* (Barcelona, 1929)

C. Rojo: 'The Gregorian Antiphonary of Silos and the Spanish Melody of the Lamentations', *Speculum*, v (1930), 306–24

P. Wagner: 'Untersuchungen zu den Gesangstexten und zur responsorialen Psalmodie der altspanischen Liturgie', *Spanische Forschungen der Görregesellschaft*, 1st ser.: *Gesammelte Aufsätze zur Kulturgeschichte Spaniens*, ii (1930), 67–113

R.-J. Hesbert: 'La tradition bénéventaine', *Le codex 10673 de la Bibliothèque vaticane*, PalMus, 1st ser., xiv (1931–6), 60–479

W.S. Porter: 'Studies in the Mozarabic Office, I: the Verona Orationale and the Leon Antiphoner', *Journal of Theological Studies*, xxxv (1934), 266–86

F. Cabrol: 'Mozarabe (la liturgie)', *Dictionnaire d'archéologie chrétienne et de liturgie*, ed. F. Cabrol and H. Leclercq, xii (Paris, 1935), 390–491

W.S. Porter: 'Cantica mozarabici officii', *Ephemerides liturgicae*, xlix (1935), 126–55

R.-J. Hesbert: 'Etude sur la notation bénéventaine', *Le codex VI.34 de la Bibliothèque capitulaire de Bénévent*, PalMus, 1st ser., xv (1937/R), 71–161

R.-J. Hesbert: 'L'*Antiphonale missarum* de l'ancien rite bénéventain', *Ephemerides liturgicae*, lii (1938), 28–66, 141–58; liii (1939), 168–90; lix (1945), 69–95; lx (1946), 103–41; lxi (1947), 153–210

G.M. Suñol: 'La restaurazione ambrosiana', *Ambrosius*, xiv (1938), 145–50, 174–6, 196–200, 296–304; xv (1939), 113–16; xvi (1940), 12–16, 108–12

A. Gastoué: *Le chant gallican* (Grenoble, 1939)

M. Avery: 'The Beneventan Lections for the Vigil of Easter and the Ambrosian Chant Banned by Pope Stephen IX at Montecassino', *Studi gregoriani*, i (1947), 433–58

L. Brou: 'Etudes sur la liturgie mozarabe: le trisagion de la messe d'après les sources manuscrites', *Ephemerides liturgicae*, lxi (1947), 309–34

L. Brou: 'Le psallendum de la messe mozarabe et les chants connexes', *Ephemerides liturgicae*, lxi (1947), 13–54

E. Cattaneo: *Note storiche sul canto ambrosiano* (Milan, 1950)

L. Brou: 'L'alleluia dans la liturgie mozarabe: étude liturgico-musicale d'après les manuscrits de chant', *AnM*, vi (1951), 3–90

L. Brou: 'Séquences et tropes dans la liturgie mozarabe', *Hispania sacra*, iv (1951), 27–41

L. Brou and J. Vives, eds.: *Antifonario visigótico mozárabe de la Catedral de León* (Barcelona, 1953–9)

L. Brou: 'Le joyau des antiphonaires latins', *Archivos leoneses*, viii (1954), 7–114

L. Brou: 'Le psautier liturgique wisigothique et les éditions critiques des psautiers latins', *Hispania sacra*, viii (1955), 337–60

E. Cattaneo: 'Il canto ambrosiano: istituzioni ecclesiastiche milanesi', *Storia di Milano*, iv (Milan, 1955), 580–724

M. Huglo: 'Les preces des graduels aquitains empruntées à la liturgie hispanique', *Hispania sacra*, viii (1955), 361–83

M. Huglo and others, eds.: *Fonti e paleografia del canto ambrosiano* (Milan, 1956)

H. Husmann: 'Zum Grossaufbau der ambrosianischen Alleluia', *AnM*, xii (1957), 17–33

R. Jesson: 'Ambrosian Chant', in W. Apel: *Gregorian Chant* (Bloomington, IN, 1958, 2/1990), 465–83

W.S. Porter: *The Gallican Rite* (London, 1958)

G.B. Baroffio: *Die Offertorien der ambrosianischen Kirche: Vorstudie zur kritischen Ausgaben der mailändischen Gesänge* (Cologne, 1964)

P. Borella: *Il rito ambrosiano* (Brescia, 1964)

M. Huglo: 'Liste complémentaire de manuscrits bénéventains', *Scriptorium*, xviii (1964), 89–91

R.G. Weakland: 'The Performance of Ambrosian Chant in the Twelfth Century', *Aspects of Medieval and Renaissance Music: a Birthday Offering to Gustave Reese*, ed. J. LaRue and others (New York, 1966/R), 856–66

G.B. Baroffio: 'Die mailändische Überlieferung des Offertoriums Sanctificavit', *Festschrift Bruno Stäblein zum 70. Geburtstag*, ed. M. Ruhnke (Kassel, 1967), 1–8

J. Quasten: 'Gallican Rites', *New Catholic Encyclopedia*, vi (New York, 1967)

H. Sanden: 'Le déchiffrement des neumes latins et visigothiques mozarabes', *AnM*, xxii (1967), 65–87

C.W. Brockett: *Antiphons, Responsories and Other Chants of the Mozarabic Rite* (Brooklyn, NY, 1968)

D.M. Randel: 'Responsorial Psalmody in the Mozarabic Rite', *EG*, x (1969), 87–116

D.M. Randel: *The Responsorial Psalm Tones for the Mozarabic Office* (Princeton, NJ, 1969)

K. Levy: 'The Italian Neophytes' Chants', *JAMS*, xxiii (1970), 181–227

K. Gamber: 'Der Ordo Romanus IV: ein Dokument der ravennatischen Liturgie des 8. Jh.', *Römische Quartalschrift*, lxvi (1971), 154–70

T. Connolly: 'Introits and Archetypes: some Archaisms of the Old Roman Chant', *JAMS*, xxv (1972), 157–74

T. Connolly: *The Introits of the Old Roman Chant* (diss., Harvard U., 1972)

K.G. Fellerer, ed.: *Geschichte der katholischen Kirchenmusik*, i (Kassel, 1972) [incl. B. Baroffio: 'Ambrosianische Liturgie', 191–204; H. Anglès: 'Spanisch-mozarabische Liturgie', 208–19; M. Huglo: 'Altgallikanische Liturgie', 219–33; M. Huglo: 'Römisch-fränkische Liturgie', 233–44]

P. Ernetti, ed.: *Tradizione musicale aquileiense-patriarchina* (Venice, 1973)

D.M. Randel: *An Index to the Chant of the Mozarabic Rite* (Princeton, NJ, 1973)

A. van der Mensbrugghe: 'The "Trecanum" of the *Expositio missae gallicanae* of S. Germanus of Paris (VI c.): its Identification and Tradition', *Papers Presented to the 6th International Conference on Patristic Studies: Oxford 1971*, ed. E.A. Livingstone [*Studia patristica*, xiii (1975)], 430–33

D.M. Randel: 'Antiphonal Psalmody in the Mozarabic Rite', *IMSCR XII: Berkeley 1977*, 414–22

T. Bailey: 'Ambrosian Psalmody: an Introduction', *Rivista internazionale di musica sacra*, i (1980), 82–99

J. Boe: 'A New Source for Old Beneventan Chant: the Santa Sophia Maundy in MS Ottoboni lat. 145', *AcM*, lii (1980), 122–33

A. Turco: 'Il repertorio dell'ufficio ambrosiano', *Rivista internazionale di musica sacra*, iii (1982), 127–224

T. Bailey: *The Ambrosian Alleluias* (Egham, 1983)

T. Bailey: 'Ambrosian Chant in Southern Italy', *JPMMS*, vi (1983), 1–7

T.F. Kelly: 'Palimpsest Evidence of an Old-Beneventan Gradual', *KJb*, lxvii (1983), 5–23

Die Handschrift Benevento, Biblioteca capitolare 33, Monumenta palaeographica gregoriana, i (Münsterschwarzach, 1984) [facs.]

K. Levy: 'Toledo, Rome, and the Legacy of Gaul', *EMH*, iv (1984), 49–99

M. Huglo: 'L'ancien chant bénéventain', *Ecclesia orans*, ii (1985), 265–93; also pubd in *SM*, xxvii (1985), 83–95; [incl. a table of chants in the Old Beneventan gradual]

T.F. Kelly: 'Montecassino and the Old-Beneventan Chant', *EMH*, v (1985), 53–83

D.M. Randel: 'El antiguo rito hispánico y la salmodia primitiva en occidente', *RdMc*, viii (1985), 229–38

A.E. Planchart: 'The Interaction between Montecassino and Benevento', *La tradizione dei tropi liturgici: Paris 1985 and Perugia 1987*, 385–407

G. Barracane: 'Il rito beneventano dell'Exultet', *Tradizione manoscritta e pratica musicale: i codici di Puglia: Bari 1986*, 63–82

T. Bailey: *The Ambrosian Cantus* (Ottawa, 1987)

B.G. Baroffio: 'La liturgia e il canto ambrosiano: prospettive di ricerca', *IMSCR XIV: Bologna 1987*, ii, 65–8

T.F. Kelly: 'Non-Gregorian Music in an Antiphoner of Benevento', *JM*, v (1987), 478–97 [study of *I-BV* V.21]

T.F. Kelly: 'Beneventan and Milanese chant', *JRMA*, cxii (1987–8), 173–95

T. Bailey: 'Milanese Melodic Tropes', *JPMMS*, xi (1988), 1–12

J. Borders: 'The Northern Italian Antiphons Ante evangelium and the Gallican Connection', *JMR*, viii (1988), 1–53

K.-W. Gümpel: 'El canto melódico de Toledo: alqunas reflexiones sobre su origen y estilo', *Recerca musicològica*, viii (1988), 25–46

T.F. Kelly: 'Une nouvelle source pour l'office vieux–bénéventain', *EG*, xxii (1988), 5–23

O. Cullin: 'La repertoire de la psalmodie in directum dans les traditions liturgiques latines, I:. La tradition hispanique', *EG*, xxiii (1989), 99–139

T.F. Kelly: *The Beneventan Chant* (Cambridge, 1989)

T. Bailey and P. Merkley: *The Melodic Tradition of the Ambrosian Office Antiphons* (Ottawa, 1990)

B. Ferretti: 'La messa di pasqua nell'antica liturgia musicale beneventana', *Bénédictina*, xxxvii (1990), 461–82

J. Pinell: 'Los cantos variables de las misas del proprio de santos en el rito hispánico', *Ecclesia orans*, vii (1990), 245–308

J. Claire: 'Le cantatorium romain et le cantatorium gallican: étude comparée des premières formes musicales de la psalmodie', *Orbis musicae*, x (1990–91), 50–86

N. Albarosa and A. Turco, eds: *Benevento, Biblioteca capitolare 40* (Padua, 1991) [facs.]

I. Fernández de la Cuesta: 'El canto viejo-hispánico y el canto viejo-galicano', *IMSCR XV: Madrid 1992* [*RdMc*, xvi (1993)], 438–56

M.P. Ferreira: 'Three Fragments from Lamego', ibid., 457–76

M. Huglo: 'Recherches sur les tons psalmodiques de l'ancienne liturgie hispanique', ibid., 477–90

T.F. Kelly, ed.: *Les témoins manuscrits du chant bénéventain*, PalMus, 1st ser., xxi (1992) [330 pls from 91 MSS]

D.M. Randel: 'The Old Hispanic Rite as Evidence for the Earliest Forms of the Western Christian Liturgies', *IMSCR XV: Madrid 1992* [*RdMc*, xvi (1993)], 491–6

C. Rodrígues Suso: 'El manuscrito 9 del monasterio de Silos y algunos problemas relativos a la adopción de la liturgia romana en la Península Ibérica', *RdMc*, xv (1992), 474–510

A. Turco: *Il canto antico di Milano: la salmodia alleluiatica e antifonata nelle fonti manoscritte* (Rome, 1992)

A.E. Planchart: 'Old Wine in New Bottles', *De musica et cantu: Helmut Hucke zum 60. Geburtstag*, ed. P. Cahn and A.-K. Heimer (Hildesheim, 1993), 41–64

T. Bailey: *Antiphon and Psalm in the Ambrosian Office* (Ottawa, 1994)

B.G. Baroffio and S.J. Kim: 'Una nuova testimonianza beneventana: frammenti di graduale-tropario-sequenziario a Macerata', *Musica e storia*, ii (1994), 5–15

T.F. Kelly: 'A Beneventan Borrowing in the Saint Cecilia Gradual', *Max Lütolf zum 60. Geburtstag: Festschrift*, ed. B. Hangartner and U. Fischer (Basel, 1994), 11–20

T. Bailey: 'Ambrosian Double Antiphons', *Laborare fratres in unum: Festschrift László Dobszay zum 60. Geburtstag*, ed. J. Szendrei and D. Hiley (Hildesheim, 1995), 11–24

T.F. Kelly: 'The Liturgical Rotulus at Benevento', ibid., 167–186

T.F. Kelly: 'Structure and Ornament in Chant: the Case of the Beneventan Exultet', *Essays on Medieval Music: in Honor of David G. Hughes*, ed. G.M. Boone (Cambridge, MA, 1995), 249–76

J. Borders and L. Brunner, eds.: *Early Medieval Chants from Nonantola*, RRMMA, xxx–xxxiii (1996)

D.N. Power: 'Affirmed from under: Celtic Liturgy and Spirituality', *Studia liturgica*, xxvii (1997), 1–32

I: ORAL TRANSMISSION; BEGINNINGS OF NOTATION

E. Jammers: *Musik in Byzanz, im päpstlichen Rom und im Frankenreich: der Choral als Musik der Textaussprache* (Heidelberg, 1962)

M. Huglo: 'La chironomie médiévale', *RdM*, xlix (1963), 155–71

M. Huglo: 'Tradition orale et tradition écrite dans la transmission des mélodies grégoriennes', *Studien zur Tradition in der Musik: Kurt von Fischer zum 60. Geburtstag*, ed. H.H. Eggebrecht and M. Lütolf (Munich, 1973), 31–42

B. Rajeczky: 'Choralforschung und Volksmusik des Mittelalters?' *AcM*, xlvi (1974), 181–92

L. Treitler: 'Homer and Gregory: the Transmission of Epic Poetry and Plainchant', *MQ*, lx (1974), 333–72

L. Treitler: '"Centonate" Chant: *Übles Flickwerk* or *E pluribus unus*?', *JAMS*, xxviii (1975), 1–23

K. Levy: 'Mediterranean Musical Liturgies: the Quest for Origins', *IMSCR XII: Berkeley 1977*, 413–14

E.J. Revell: 'Hebrew Accents and Greek Ekphonetic Neumes', *Studies in Eastern Chant*, iv, ed. M. Velimirovi (Crestwood, NY, 1979), 140–70

R.-J. Hesbert: 'L'antiphonaire d'Amalaire', *Ephemerides liturgicae*, xciv (1980), 176–94

R.-J. Hesbert: 'L'antiphonaire de la Curie', ibid., 431–59

R.-J. Hesbert: 'The Sarum Antiphoner: its Sources and Influence', *JPMMS*, iii (1980), 49–55

H. Hucke: 'Toward a New Historical View of Gregorian Chant', *JAMS*, xxxiii (1980), 437–67

H. Schmidt: 'Gregorianik – Legende oder Wahrheit?', *Ars musica, musica scientia: Festschrift Heinrich Hüschen*, ed. D. Altenburg (Cologne, 1980), 400–11

A.E. Planchart: 'The Transmission of Medieval Chant', *Music in Medieval and Early Modern Europe: Patronage, Sources and Texts*, ed. I. Fenlon (Cambridge, 1981), 347–63

L. Treitler: 'Oral, Written, and Literate Process in the Transmission of Medieval Music', *Speculum*, lvi (1981), 471–91

D. Hughes: 'Variants in Antiphon Families: Notation and Tradition', *IMSCR XIII: Strasbourg 1982c*, ii, 29–47

D. Jourdan-Hemmerdinger: 'Aspects méconnus des théories et notations antiques et de leur transmission', *Musicologie médiévale: Paris 1982*, 67–99

L. Treitler: 'The Early History of Music Writing in the West', *JAMS*, xxxv (1982), 237–79

L. Treitler: 'Die Entstehung der abendländischen Notenschrift', *Mf*, xxxvii (1984), 259–67

L. Treitler: 'Reading and Singing: on the Genesis of Occidental Music-Writing', *EMH*, iv (1984), 135–208

D.G. Hughes: 'Evidence for the Traditional View of the Transmission of Gregorian Chant', *JAMS*, xl (1987), 377–404

K. Levy: 'Charlemagne's Archetype of Gregorian chant', *JAMS*, xl (1987) 1–30

K. Levy: 'On the Origin of Neumes', *EMH*, vii (1987), 59–90

K. Levy: 'The Two Carolingian Archetypes of Gregorian Chant', *IMSCR XIV: Bologna 1987*, iii, 501–04

L. Treitler: 'The Early History of Music Writing', *JAMS*, xxxv (1987), 238–79

J.A. Caldwell: 'From Cantor to Parchment: Linguistic Aspects of Early Western Notation', *Musica antiqua VIII: Bydgoszcz 1988*, 219–32

A. Haug: 'Zum Wechselspiel von Schrift und Gedächtnis im Zeitalter der Neumen', *Cantus planus III: Tihány 1988*, 33–47

K. Schlager: 'Zur Überlieferung von Melismen im gregorianischen Choral', *SM*, xxx (1988), 431–6

K. Levy: 'On Gregorian Orality', *JAMS*, xliii (1990), 185–227

M.M. Alonso: 'Música de tradicion oral y romanticismo', *RdMc*, xiv (1991), 325–53

L. Treitler: 'Medieval Improvisation', *World of Music*, xxx/3 (1991), 66–91

L. Treitler: 'Mündliche und schriftliche Überlieferung: Anfänge der musikalischen Notation', *Die Musik des Mittelalters*, ed. H. Möller and R. Stephan (Laaber, 1991), 54–93

L. Dobszay: 'The Debate about the Oral and Written Transmission of Chant', *IMSCR XV: Madrid 1992* [*RdMc*, xvi (1993)], 706–29

P. Jeffery: *Re-envisioning Past Musical Cultures: Ethnomusicology in the Study of Gregorian Chant* (Chicago, 1992)

L. Treitler: 'The Unwritten and Written Transmission of Medieval Chant and the Start-up of Musical Notation', *JM*, x (1992), 131–91

D.G. Hughes: 'The Implications of Variants for Chant Transmission', *De musica et cantu: Helmut Hucke zum 60. Geburtstag*, ed. P. Cahn and A.-K. Heimer (Hildesheim, 1993), 65–73

C. Atkinson: '*De accentibus toni oritur nota quae dicitur neuma*: Prosodic Accents, the Accent Theory, and the Paleofrankish Script', *Essays on Medieval Music: in Honor of David G. Hughes*, ed. G.M. Boone (Cambridge, MA, 1995), 17–42

K. Levy: 'Gregorian Chant and Oral Transmission', ibid., 277–86

J: NOTATION

(i) Studies of different notations

E. Bernoulli: *Die Choralnotenschrift bei Hymnen und Sequenzen* (Leipzig, 1898/R)

J.B. Thibaut: *Monuments de la notation ekphonétique et neumatique de l'église latine* (St Petersburg, 1912/R)

P. Ferretti: 'Etude sur la notation aquitaine', *Le codex 903 de la Bibliothèque nationale*, PalMus, 1st ser., xiii (1925/R), 54–211

G.M. Suñol: *Introducció a la paleografía musical gregoriana* (Montserrat, 1925; Fr. trans., enlarged, 1935) [with extensive bibliography up to the 1920s]

P. Wagner: 'Aus der Frühzeit des Liniensystems', *AMw*, viii (1926), 259–76

J. Smits van Waesberghe: *Muziekgeschiedenis der Middeleeuwen* (Tilburg, 1936–42)

J. Hourlier: 'Le domaine de la notation messine', *Revue grégorienne*, xxx (1951), 96–113, 150–58

J. Smits van Waesberghe: 'The Musical Notation of Guido of Arezzo', *MD*, v (1951), 15–53

S. Corbin: 'Les notations neumatiques en France à l'époque carolingienne', *Revue d'histoire de l'église de France*, xxxviii (1952), 225–32

E. Jammers: 'Die paleofränkische Neumenschrift', *Scriptorium*, vii (1953), 235–59

S. Corbin: 'Valeur et sens de la notation alphabétique à Jumièges et en Normandie', *Jumièges … XIIIe centenaire: Rouen 1954*, 913–24

M. Huglo: 'Les noms des neumes et leur origine', *EG*, i (1954), 53–67

J. Hourlier and M. Huglo: 'La notation paléofranque', *EG*, ii (1957), 212–19

J.W.A. Vollaerts: *Rhythmic Proportions in Early Medieval Ecclesiastical Chant* (Leiden, 1958, 2/1960)

M. Huglo: 'Le domaine de la notation bretonne', *AcM*, xxxv (1963), 54–84

J. Rayburn: *Gregorian Chant: a History of the Controversy concerning its Rhythm* (New York, 1964)

E. Jammers: *Tafeln zur Neumenschrift* (Tutzing, 1965)

M. Huglo: 'Règlements du XIIIe siècle pour la transcription des livres notés', *Festschrift Bruno Stäblein zum 70. Geburtstag*, ed. M. Ruhnke (Kassel, 1967), 121–33

E. Cardine: 'Neume', *EG*, x (1969), 13–28

C. Floros: *Universale Neumenkunde* (Kassel, 1970)

A. Moderini: *La notazione neumatica di Nonantola* (Cremona, 1970)

J. Boe: 'Rhythmical Notation in the Beneventan Gloria Trope *Aureas arces*', *MD*, xxix (1975), 5–42

M. Haas: 'Probleme einer *Universalen Neumenkunde*', *Forum musicologicum*, i (1975), 305–22 [concerns Floros, 1970]

B. Stäblein: *Schriftbild der einstimmigen Musik*, Musikgeschichte in Bildern, iii/4 (Leipzig, 1975)

S. Corbin: *Die Neumen* (Cologne, 1977)

M.-C. Billecocq: 'Lettres ajoutées à la notation neumatique du Codex 239 de Laon', *EG*, xvii (1978), 7–144

M.T.R. Barezzani: *La notazione neumatica di un codice bresciano (secolo XI)* (Cremona, 1981)

M. Huglo: 'La tradition musicale aquitaine: répertoire et notation', *Liturgie et musique (IX–XIV s.)*, Cahiers de Fanjeaux, xvii (Toulouse, 1982), 253–68

Musicologie médiévale: Paris 1982[incl. W. Arlt: 'Anschaulichkeit und analytischer Charakter: Kriterien der Beschreibung und Analyse früher Neumenschriften', 29–55; L. Treitler: 'Paleography and Semiotics', 17–27; M.-E. Duchez: 'Des neumes à la portée', 57–60; D. Jourdan-Hemmerdinger: 'Aspects méconnus des théories et notations antiques et de leur transmission', 67–99; D. Escudier: 'La notation musicale de Saint-Vaast d'Arras: étude d'une particularité graphique', 107–20; S. Rankin: 'Neumatic Notations in Anglo-Saxon England', 129–44; Y. Chartier: 'Hucbald de Saint-Amand et la notation musicale', 145–55; N. Phillips: 'The Dasia Notation and its Manuscript Tradition', 157–73; J. Mas: 'La notation catalane', 183–6]

J. Boe: 'The Beneventan Apostrophus in South Italian Chant A.D. 1000–1100', *EMH*, iii (1983), 43–66

M.-N. Colette: 'La notation du demi-ton dans le manuscrit Paris, B.N. lat. 1139 et dans quelques manuscrits du sud de la France', *La tradizione dei tropi liturgici: Paris 1985 and Perugia 1987*, 297–311

H. González Barrionuevo: 'Présence de signes additionnels de type mélodique dans la notation "mozarabe" du nord de l'Espagne', *RdMc*, ix (1986), 11–27

A.C. Santosuosso: *Letter Notations in the Middle Ages* (Ottawa, 1989)

B.G. Baroffio: 'Le grafie musicali nei manoscritti liturgici del secolo XII nell'Italia settentrionale: avvio a una ricerca', *Cantus planus IV: Pécs 1990*, 1–16

M. Huglo: 'Bilan de 50 années de recherches (1939–1989) sur les notations musicales de 850 à 1300', *AcM*, lxii (1990), 224–59

K. Levy: 'On Gregorian Orality', *JAMS*, xliii (1990), 185–227

F.C. Lochner: 'La notation d'Echternach reconsidérée', *RBM*, xliv (1990), 41–58

J. Szendrei: 'Linienschriften des zwölften Jahrhunderts auf süddeutschem Gebiet', *Cantus planus IV: Pécs 1990*, 17–30

M.-N. Colette: 'Indications rythmiques dans les neumes et direction melodique', *RdM*, lxxviii (1992), 201–35

J. Szendrei: 'Die Gültigkeit der heutigen Notationskarten', *IMSCR XV: Madrid 1992*, 744–57 [with maps]

W. Arlt: 'Die Intervallnotationen des Hermannus Contractus in Gradualien des 11. und 12. Jahrhunderts: das Basler Fragment N I 6 Nr. 63 und der Engelberger Codex 1003', *De musica et cantu: Helmut Hucke zum 60. Geburtstag*, ed. P. Cahn and A.-K. Heimer (Hildesheim, 1993), 243–56

H. Möller: 'Deutsche Neumenschriften ausserhalb St. Gallens', ibid., 225–42

A. Odenkirchen: '13 Neumentafeln in tabellarischer Übersicht', ibid., 257–62

K. Schlager: 'Aenigmata in campo aperto: Marginalien zum Umgang mit Neumen', *KJb*, lxxvii (1993), 7–15

J. Boe: 'Chant Notation in Eleventh-Century Roman Manuscripts', *Essays on Medieval Music in Honor of David G. Hughes*, ed. G.M. Boone (Cambridge, MA, 1995), 43–57

B. Hebborn: *Die Dasia-Notation* (Bonn, 1995)

J. Szendrei: 'Quilisma und Diastematie', *Laborare fratres in unum: Festschrift László Dobszay zum 60. Geburtstag*, ed. J. Szendrei and D. Hiley (Hildesheim, 1995), 317–40

T.J. McGee: 'Ornamental Neumes and Early Notation', *Performance Practice Review*, ix (1996), 39–65

C.R. Suso: 'La notation aquitaine au Pays Basque', *EG*, xxv (1997), 37–44

(ii) Semiology

P.M. Arbogast: 'The Small Punctum as Isolated Note in Codex Laon 239', *EG*, iii (1959), 83–133

L. Agustoni: *Gregorianischer Choral: Elemente und Vortragslehre mit besonderer Berücksichtigung der Neumenkunde* (Freiburg, 1963)

C. Kelly: *The Cursive Torculus Design in the Codex St. Gall 359 and its Rhythmical Significance: a Paleographical and Semiological Study* (St Meinrad, IN, 1964)

W. Wiesli: *Das Quilisma im Codex 359 der Stiftsbibliothek St. Gallen: eine paläographisch-semiologische Studie* (Immensee, 1966)

E. Cardine: *Semiologia gregoriana* (Rome, 1968; Eng. trans., 1982); Fr. trans. in *EG*, xi (1970), 1–158

E. Cardine: 'Neume', *EG*, x (1969), 13–28

J. Dabrowski: 'Le signe ST dans le codex 121 d'Einsiedeln', *EG*, xii (1971), 65–86, appx 1–12

A.M.W.J. Kurris: 'Les coupures expressives dans la notation du manuscrit Angelica 123', *EG*, xii (1971), 13–63

N. Albarosa: 'Comportamento delle virghe nei gruppi subbipunctes resupini seguiti da clivis finale nel Codice Laon 239', *EG*, xiii (1972), 15–52

L.F. Heiman: 'The Rhythmic Value of the Final Descending Note after a Punctum in Neumes of Codex 239 of the Library of Laon: a Paleographic-Semiological Study', *EG*, xiii (1972), 151–224

N. Albarosa: 'La scuola gregoriana de Eugène Cardine', *RIM*, ix (1974), 269–97; xii (1977), 136–52

N. Albarosa: 'La notazione neumatica de Nonantola: critica di una lettura', *RIM*, xiv (1979), 225–310

S. Balducci: 'L'interpretazione dei gruppi strofici alla luce delle notazioni antiche', *EG*, xviii (1979), 5–96

L. Agustoni: 'Valore delle note gregoriane', *Rivista internazionale di musica sacra*, i (1980), 49–60, 129–70, 275–89

J.B. Göschl: *Semiologische Untersuchungen zum Phänomen der gregorianischen Liqueszenz: der isolierte dreistufige Epiphonus Praepunctis, ein Sonderproblem der Liqueszenzforschung* (Vienna, 1980)

J.B. Göschl, ed.: *Ut mens concordet voci: Festschrift Eugène Cardine* (St Ottilien, 1980) [incl. bibliography of E. Cardine's writings and a list of semiology theses presented at the Pontificio Istituto di Musica Sacra, Rome]

H. Rumphorst: 'Untersuchung zu zwei Formen des isolierten Pes Subbipunctis in den Handschriften E, C und L: Beitrag zur Frage des Zusammenhangs zwischen Text und Melodie', *EG*, xix (1980), 25–88

N. Albarosa: 'Paleografi non semiologi?', *Musicologie médiévale: Paris 1982*, 101–05

N. Albarosa: 'The Pontificio Istituto de Musica Sacra in Rome and the Semiological School of Dom Eugène Cardine', *JPMMS*, vi (1983), 26–33

L. Agustoni: 'Die gregorianische Semiologie und Eugène Cardine: eine neue Seite in der Geschichte der Restauration des gregorianischen Chorals', *Beiträge zur Gregorianik*, i (1985), 9–22

H. González Barrionuevo: 'El pes initio debilis en las principales familias neumáticas gregorianas', *España en la música de occidente: Salamanca 1985*, i, 69–74

G. Joppich: 'Der Torculus specialis als musikalischer Interpunktionsneume: Vorbereitete Endartikulation als Mittel zur Interpretation des Textes', *Beiträge zur Gregorianik*, ii (1986), 74–113

G. Joppich: 'Die Bivirga auf der Endsilbe eines Wortes: ein Beitrag zur Frage des Wort–Ton–Verhältnisses im gregorianischen Choral', *Beiträge zur Gregorianik*, iii (1986), 73–95

L. Agustoni: 'Die Frage der Tonstufen Si und Mi', *Beiträge zur Gregorianik*, iv (1987), 47–102

R. Fischer: 'Die Ausführung der reperkutierten Noten, ein wesentliches Kennzeichen der Interpretation des gregorianischen Chorals', *Rivista internazionale di musica sacra*, viii (1987), 5–75

L. Agustoni and J.B. Göschl, eds.: *Einführung in die Interpretation des gregorianischen Chorals* (Regensburg, 1987–92)

H. Kersken: *Der dreitönige isolierte Salicus (3tiS) und seine Beziehung zum Text: ein Beitrag zum Wort-Ton-Verhältnis im gregorianischen Choral*, Beiträge zur Gregorianik, vi (1988) [whole issue]

EG, xxiii (1989) [contains 9 articles generally about chant semiology, incl. E. Cardine: 'Les limites de la sémiologie en chant grégorien', 5–10; N. Albarosa: 'Le torculus en fin de neume cadentiel', 71–98; J. Claire: 'La notation musicale de l'Antiphonale romanum', 153–61]

R. Fischer: 'Epiphonus oder Cephalicus?', *Beiträge zur Gregorianik*, viii (1989), 101–05

H. González Barrionuevo: 'Dos grafías especiales del "scandicus" en la notación "mozarabe" del norte de España', *AnM*, xliv (1989), 5–21

H. González Barrionuevo: 'La grafia del "salicus" en la notación "mozarabe" de tipo vertical', *RdMc*, xii (1989), 397–411

A. Turco: 'Semiologia e notazione estetico-modale del pes quassus', *Studi gregoriana*, v (1989), 71–102, vi (1990), 157–89

S. Amoruso and M.G. Cavuoto: 'Cilium, elemento segnico beneventano', *Studi gregoriana*, vi (1990), 123–55

D. Fournier: *Sémio-esthétique du chant grégorien d'après le Graduel neumé de Dom Cardine* (Solesmes, 1990)

J. Claire: 'Dom Eugène Cardine (1905–1988)', *Beiträge zur Gregorianik*, xii (1992), 11–26

M.-N. Colette: 'Indications rythmiques dans les neumes et direction melodique', *RdM*, lxxviii (1992), 201–35

H. González Barrionuevo: 'Los codices "mozarabes" del archivo de Silos: aspectos paleográficos y semiológicos de su notación neumática', *RdMc*, xv (1992), 403–72

R. Sassenscheidt: *Die Neumengruppe Distropha und Climacus: eine paläographisch-semiologische Untersuchung*, Beiträge zur Gregorianik, xii (1992) [whole issue]

K: THE PROPER AND ORDINARY CHANTS OF MASS AND OFFICE, HYMNODY, PROCESSIONAL CHANTS

studies of history and style

F.J. Mone, ed.: *Lateinische Hymnen des Mittelalters* (Freiburg, 1853–5/R)

A. Mocquereau: 'De l'influence de l'accent tonique latin et du cursus sur la structure mélodique et rythmique de la phrase grégorienne', *Le répons-graduel Justus ut palma, deuxième partie*, PalMus, 1st ser., iii (1892/R), 7–77; *Le codex 121 de la Bibliothèque d'Einsiedeln*, PalMus, 1st ser., iv (1894/R), 25–204

F.A. Gevaert: *La mélopée antique dans le chant de l'église latine* (Ghent, 1895–6/R)

A. Mocquereau: 'Du rôle et de la place de l'accent tonique latin dans le rythme grégorien', *Antiphonarium tonale missarum*, PalMus, 1st ser., vii (1901/R), 19–377

J. Jeannin: *Etudes sur le rythme grégorien* (Lyons, 1926)

H. Potiron: *La modalité grégorienne* (Tournai, 1928)

U. Bomm: *Der Wechsel der Modalitätsbestimmung in der Tradition der Messegesänge im IX.–XIII. Jahrhundert* (Einsiedeln, 1929/R)

R.-J. Hesbert: 'La messe *Omnes gentes* du 7e dimanche après Pentecôte et "l'Antiphonal missarum" romain', *Revue grégorienne*, xvii (1932), 81–9, 170–79; xviii (1933), 1–14

P. Ferretti: *Estetica gregoriana, ossia trattato delle forme musicali del canto gregoriano*, (Rome, 1934/R; Fr. trans., 1938)

C. Ott, ed.: *Offertoriale, sive Versus offertoriorum cantus gregoriani* (Paris, 1935)

H. Sowa: *Quellen zur Transformation der Antiphonen: Tonar- und Rhythmusstudien* (Kassel, 1935)

E. Jammers: *Der gregorianische Rhythmus: antiphonale Studien mit einer Übertragung der Introitus- und Offiziumsantiphonen des 1. Tones* (Strasbourg, 1937, 2/1981)

D. Johner: *Wort und Ton im Choral: ein Beitrag zur Aesthetik des gregorianischen Gesanges* (Leipzig, 1940)

L. Brou: 'Les chants en langue grecque dans les liturgies latines', *Sacris erudiri*, i (1948), 165–80; iv (1952), 226–38

L. Brou: 'Marie "Destructrice de toutes les hérésies" et la belle légende du répons *Gaude Maria virgo*', *Ephemerides liturgicae*, lxii (1948), 321–53; lxv (1951), 28–33

J. Froger: 'L'alleluia dans l'usage romain et la réforme de Saint Grégoire', *Ephemerides liturgicae*, lxii (1948), 6–48

H. Potiron: *L'analyse modale du chant grégorien* (Tournai, 1948)

J. Froger: *Les chants de la messe au VIIIe et IXe siècles* (Tournai, 1950)

G. Benoît-Castelli: 'Le "Praeconium paschale"', *Ephemerides liturgicae*, lxvii (1953), 309–34

H. Hucke: 'Musikalische Formen der Offiziumsantiphonen', *KJb*, xxxvii (1953), 7–33

J. Gajard: 'Les recitations modales des 3e et 4e modes et les manuscrits bénéventains et aquitains', *EG*, i (1954), 9–45

D. Bosse: *Untersuchung einstimmiger mittelalterlicher Melodien zum 'Gloria in excelsis Deo'* (Regensburg, 1955)

M. Landwehr-Melnicki: *Das einstimmige Kyrie des lateinischen Mittelalters* (Regensburg, 1955/R)

B. Stäblein, ed.: *Hymnen I: die mittelalterlichen Hymnenmelodien des Abendlandes*, MMMA, i (1956/R)

H. Hucke: 'Zum Probleme des Rhythmus im gregorianischen Gesang', *IMSCR VII: Cologne 1958*, 141–2

C.-A. Moberg: 'Zur Melodiegeschichte des *Pange lingua* Hymnus', *Jb für Liturgik und Hymnologie*, v (1960), 46–74

P.J. Thannabaur: *Das einstimmige Sanctus der römischen Messe in der handschriftlichen Überlieferung des 11. bis 16. Jahrhunderts* (Munich, 1962)

J. Claire: 'L'évolution modale dans les répertoires liturgiques occidentaux', *Revue grégorienne*, xl (1962), 196–211, 229–48; xli (1963), 49–62, 77–102, 127–51

J. Claire: 'La psalmodie responsoriale antique', *Revue grégorienne*, xli (1963), 8–29, 49–62, 77–102

R.-J. Hesbert: 'Un antique offertoire de la Pentecôte: *Factus est repente*', *Organicae voces: Festschrift Joseph Smits van Waesberghe*, ed. P. Fischer (Amsterdam, 1963), 59–69

L. Robert: 'Les chants du célébrant: les oraisons', *Revue grégorienne*, xli (1963), 113–26

J. Szövérffy: *Die Annalen der lateinischen Hymnendichtung* (Berlin, 1964–5)

P. Mittler: *Melodieuntersuchung zu den dorischen Hymnen der lateinischen Liturgie im Mittelalter* (Siegburg, 1965)

K. Schlager: *Thematischer Katalog der ältesten Alleluia-Melodien aus Handschriften des 10. und 11. Jahrhunderts, ausgenommen das ambrosianische, alt-spanische und alt-römische Repertoire* (Munich, 1965)

D.G. Hughes: 'The Sources of *Christus manens*', *Aspects of Medieval and Renaissance Music: a Birthday Offering to Gustave Reese*, ed. J. LaRue and others (New York, 1966/R), 423–34

R. Steiner: 'Some Questions about the Gregorian Offertories and their Verses', *JAMS*, xix (1966), 162–81

H. Hucke: 'Tractusstudien', *Festschrift Bruno Stäblein zum 70. Geburtstag*, ed. M. Ruhnke (Kassel, 1967), 116–20

E. Jammers: 'Rhythmen und Hymnen in einer St. Galler Handschrift des 9. Jahrhunderts', *Festschrift Bruno Stäblein zum 70. Geburtstag*, ed. M. Ruhnke (Kassel, 1967), 134–42

S. Kojima: 'Die Ostergradualien *Haec dies* und ihr Verhältnis zu den Tractus des II. und VIII. Tons', *Colloquium amicorum: Joseph Schmidt-Görg zum 70. Geburtstag*, ed. S. Kross and H. Schmidt (Bonn, 1967), 146–78

M. Robert: 'Les adieux à l'alleluia', *EG*, vii (1967), 41–51

H. Potiron: 'Théoriciens de la modalité', *EG*, viii (1967), 29–37

B. Rajeczky: 'Le chant grégorien, est-il mesuré?', *EG*, viii (1967), 21–8

M. Schildbach: *Das einstimmige Agnus Dei und seine handschriftliche Überlieferung vom 10. bis zum 16. Jahrhundert* (Erlangen, 1967)

K. Schlager: 'Anmerkungen zu den zweiten Alleluia-Versen', *AMw*, xxiv (1967), 199–219

H. Darré: 'De l'usage des hymnes dans l'église des origines à Saint Grégoire-le-Grand', *EG*, ix (1968), 25–36

H. Gneuss: *Hymnar und Hymnen im englischen Mittelalter* (Tübingen, 1968)

L. Treitler: 'On the Structure of the Alleluia Melisma: a Western Tendency in Western Chant', *Studies in Music History: Essays for Oliver Strunk*, ed. H.S. Powers (Princeton, 1968), 59–72

K. Schlager: *Alleluia-Melodien*, MMMA, vii, viii (1968–87)

B. Rajeczky: 'Zur Frage der Verzierung im Choral', *SM*, xi (1969), 34–54

J. Chailley: 'Une nouvelle méthode d'approche pour l'analyse modale du chant grégorien', *Speculum musicae artis: Festgabe für Heinrich Husmann*, ed. H. Becker and R. Gerlach (Munich, 1970), 85–92

H. Hucke: 'Die Texte der Offertorien', *Speculum musicae artis: Festgabe für Heinrich Husmann*, ed. H. Becker and R. Gerlach (Munich, 1970), 193–203

M. Huglo: 'Les listes alléluiatiques dans les témoins du graduel grégorien', ibid., 219–27

K. Levy: 'The Italian Neophytes' Chants', *JAMS*, xxiii (1970), 181–227

T. Bailey: *The Processions of Sarum and the Western Church* (Toronto, 1971)

R. Erbacher: '*Tonus peregrinus*: aus der Geschichte eines Psalmtons' (Münsterschwarzach, 1971)

I. Müller: 'Zu hochmittelalterlichen Hymnensammlungen süddeutscher Klöster', *Ephemerides liturgicae*, lxxxv (1971), 121–49

C.W. Brockett: 'Unpublished Antiphons and Antiphon Series in the Gradual of St-Yrieix', *MD*, xxvi (1972), 5–35

R.-J. Hesbert: 'La théologie du répertoire grégorien', *Musica e arte figurativa nei secoli X–XII: Todi 1972*, 103–32

J. Drumbl: 'Die Improperien der lateinischen Liturgie', *Archiv für Liturgiewissenschaft*, xv (1973), 68–100

J. Hourlier: 'Notes sur l'antiphonie', *Gattungen der Musik in Einzeldarstellungen: Gedenkschrift für Leo Schrade*, ed. W. Arlt and others (Berne, 1973), 116–43

H. Hucke: 'Das Responsorium', ibid., 144–91

E. Jammers: *Das Alleluia in der gregorianischen Messe: eine Studie über seine Entstehung und Entwicklung* (Münster, 1973)

R. Steiner: 'Some Melismas for Office Responsories', *JAMS*, xxvi (1973), 108–31

E. Jammers: 'Gregorianischer Rhythmus, was ist das?', *AMw*, xxxi (1974), 290–311

T.F. Kelly: 'Melodic Elaboration in Responsory Melismas', *JAMS* xxvii (1974), 461–74

C.D. Roederer: 'Can We Identify an Aquitanian Chant Style?', *JAMS*, xxvii (1974), 75–99

J. Claire: 'Les répertoires liturgiques latins avant l'octoéchos, I: L'office férial romano-franc', *EG*, xv (1975), 5–192

E. Ferrari–Barassi: 'I modi ecclesiastici nei trattati musicale dell'età carolingia: nascita e crescita di una teoria', *Studi musicali*, iv (1975) 3–56

T. Bailey: 'Accentual and Cursive Cadences in Gregorian Psalmody', *JAMS*, xxix (1976), 463–71

D.A. Bjork: *The Kyrie Repertory in Aquitanian Manuscripts of the Tenth and Eleventh Centuries* (diss., U. of California, Berkeley, 1976)

T. Miazga: *Die Melodien des einstimmigen Credo der römisch-katholischen lateinischen Kirche* (Graz, 1976)

E.T. Moneta Caglio: *Lo jubilus e le origini della salmodia responsoriale* (Milan, 1977)

H. Avenary: 'Reflections on the Origins of the Alleluia-Jubilus', *Orbis musicae*, vi (1978) 34–42

R. Le Roux: 'Répons du triduo sacro et de Pâques', *EG*, xviii (1979), 157–76

T. Miazga: *Die Gesänge zur Osterprozession in den handschriftlichen Überlieferungen vom 10. bis zum 19. Jahrhundert* (Graz, 1979)

D.A. Bjork: 'Early Repertories of the Kyrie eleison', *KJb*, lxiii–lxiv (1980), 9–43

W. Heckenbach: 'Reponsoriale Communio-Antiphonen', *Ars musica, musica scientia, Festschrift Heinrich Hüschen*, ed. D. Altenburg (Cologne, 1980), 224–32

C. Schmidt: 'Modus und Melodiegestalt: Untersuchungen zu Offiziumsantiphonen', *Forum musicologicum*, ii (1980), 13–43

J. Udovich: 'The Magnificat Antiphons for the Ferial Office', *JPMMS*, iii (1980), 1–15

C.M. Atkinson: '*O amnos tu theu*: the Greek Agnus Dei in the Roman Liturgy from the Eighth to the Eleventh Century', *KJb*, lxv (1981), 7–31

A. Madrignac: 'Les formules centons des alleluias anciens', *EG*, xx (1981), 3–4; xxi (1986), 27–45

C.M. Atkinson: 'Zur Entstehung und Überlieferung der "Missa graeca"', *AMw*, xxxix (1982), 113–45

J. Boe: 'Gloria A and the Roman Easter Vigil Ordinary', *MD*, xxxvi (1982), 5–37

J. Dyer: 'The Offertory Chant of the Roman Liturgy and its Musical Form', *Studi musicali*, xi (1982), 3–30

IMSCR XIII: Strasbourg 1982a [*Schweizer Jb für Musikwissenschaft*, new ser., ii (1982)] [incl. W. Arlt: 'Funktion, Gattung und Form im liturgischen Gesang des frühen und hohen Mittelalters: eine Einführung', 13–26; M. Huglo: 'Le réponsgraduel de la messe: évolution de la forme: permanence de la fonction', 53–73, 74–7; R. Steiner: 'The Canticle of the Three Children as a Chant of the Roman Mass', 81–90; K. Levy: 'A Gregorian Processional Antiphon', 91–102; L. Treitler: 'From Ritual through Language to Music', 109–23]

R. Steiner: 'Reconstructing the Repertory of Invitatory Tones and their Uses at Cluny in the Late 11th Century', *Musicologie médiévale: Paris 1982*, 175–82

R. Jonsson and L. Treitler: *Medieval Music and Language: a Reconsideration of the Relationship* (New York, 1983)

K. Levy: 'Toledo, Rome, and the Legacy of Gaul', *EMH*, iv (1984), 49–99 [discusses a distinctive class of over two dozen Offertory texts]

J.W. McKinnon: 'The Fifteen Temple Steps and the Gradual Psalms', *Imago musicae*, i (1984), 29–49

K. Ottosen: 'The Latin Office of the Dead: a Computer Analysis of Two Thousand Texts', *Computer Applications to Medieval Studies*, ed. A. Gilmour-Bryson (Kalamazoo, MI, 1984), 81–7

R. Steiner: 'Antiphons for the Benedicite at Lauds', *JPMMS*, vii (1984), 1–17

J. Jeanneteau: *Los modos gregorianos: historia – analisis – estética* (Silos, 1985)

S. Rankin: 'The Liturgical Background of the Old English Advent Lyrics: a Reappraisal', *Learning and Literature in Anglo-Saxon England: Studies Presented to Peter Clemoes*, ed. M. Lapidge and H. Gneuss (Cambridge, 1985), 317–40 [discusses the Advent 'O' antiphons]

B. Ribay: 'La modalité grégorienne', *Musica e liturgia nella cultura mediterranea: Venice 1985*, 221–52

J. Boe: 'Italian and Roman Verses for Kyrie eleyson in the MSS Cologny-Genève, Bibliotheca Bodmeriana 74 and Vaticanus latinus 5319', *La tradizione dei tropi liturgici: Paris 1985 and Perugia 1987*, 337–84

J. Claire: 'Les psaumes graduels au coeur de la liturgie quadragésimale', *EG*, xxi (1986), 5–12

R.L. Crocker: 'Matins Antiphons at St. Denis', *JAMS*, xxxix (1986), 441–90

D. Hiley: 'Ordinary of Mass Chants in English, North French and Sicilian Manuscripts', *JPMMS*, ix (1986), 1–128

J. Stevens: *Words and Music in the Middle Ages: Song, Narrative, Dance and Drama, 1050–1350* (Cambridge, 1986)

K.-W. Gümpel: 'Gregorian Chant and *musica ficta*: New Observations from Spanish Theory of the Early Renaissance', *Recerca musicològica*, vi–vii (1986–7), 5–27; rev. version, in Ger., in *AMw*, xlvii (1990), 120–47

L. Agustoni: 'Die Frage der Tonstufen SI und MI', *Beiträge zur Gregorianik*, iv (1987), 47–102 [whole issue]

J. Boe: 'Hymns and Poems at Mass in Eleventh-Century Southern Italy (Other than Sequences)', *IMSCR XIV: Bologna 1987*, iii, 515–41

H. Hucke: 'Musik und Sprache im gregorianischen Gesang', *Musica antiqua VIII: Bydgoszcz 1988*, 449–56

A. Hughes: 'Antiphons and Acclamations: the Politics of Music in the Coronation Service of Edward II, 1308', *JM*, vi (1988), 150–68 [discusses the antiphon *Unxerunt Salomonem*]

J.W. McKinnon: 'The Patristic Jubilus and the Alleluia of the Mass', *Cantus planus III: Tihány 1988*, 61–70

J.W. McKinnon: 'The Roman Post–Pentecostal Communion Series', ibid., 175–86

B. Ribay: 'Les graduels en IIA', *EG*, xxii (1988), 443–107

A.W. Robertson: '*Benedicamus Domino*: the Unwritten Tradition, *JAMS*, xli (1988), 1–62

K. Schlager: 'Zur Überlieferung von Melismen im gregorianischen Choral', *SM*, xxx (1988), 431–6

S. Žak: '*Sollemnis oblatio*: Studien zum Offertorium im Mittelalter', *KJb*, lxxii (1988), 27–51

C.M. Atkinson: 'The *Doxa*, the *Pisteuo*, and the *Ellenici fratres*: some Anomalies in the Transmission of the Chants of the "Missa graeca"', *JM*, vii (1989), 81–106

F. Buttner: 'Zur Geschichte der Marienantiphon *Salve regina*', *AMw*, xlvi (1989), 257–70

J.G. Davies: 'A Fourteenth Century Processional for Pilgrims in the Holy Land', *Hispania sacra*, xli (1989), 421–9

J. Dyer: 'Monastic Psalmody of the Middle Ages', *Revue bénédictine*, xcix (1989), 41–74

J. Dyer: 'The Singing of Psalms in the Early Medieval Office', *Speculum*, lxiv (1989), 535–78

G. Mele: 'Una sconosciuta antifona mariana in B.A.V. Ottob. Lat. 527 e in A.C.O., P. Xlll (Sardegna)', *Studi gregoriani*, v (1989), 59–70

A. Traub: *Hucbald von Saint-Amand 'De harmonico institutione'*, Beiträge zur Gregorianik, vii (1989) [whole issue]

T. Bailey: 'Word-Painting and the Romantic Interpretation of Chant', *Beyond the Moon: Festschrift Luther Dittmer*, ed. B. Gillingham and P. Merkley (Ottawa, 1990), 1–15

M.-N. Colette: 'Le Salve Regina en Aquitaine au XIIème siècle: l'auteur du Salve', *Cantus planus IV: Pécs 1990*, 521–47

M. Floyd: 'Processional Chants in English Monastic Sources', *JPMMS*, xiii (1990), 1–45

T.C. Karp: 'Interrelationships among Gregorian Chants: an Alternative View of Creativity in Early Chant', *Studies in Musical Sources and Style: Essays in Honor of Jan LaRue*, ed. E.K. Wolf and E.H. Roesner (Madison, WI, 1990), 1–40

R. Steiner: 'The Parable of the Talents in Liturgy and Chant', *Essays in Musicology: a Tribute to Alvin Johnson*, ed. L. Lockwood and E.H. Roesner (Philadelphia, 1990), 1–15

A.B. Yardley: 'The Marriage of Heaven and Earth: a Late Medieval Source of the *Consecratio virginum*', *CMc*, nos.45–7 (1990), 305–24 [Sanders Fs issue, ed. P.M. Lefferts and L.L. Perkins]

T.J. Knoblach: 'The O Antiphons', *Ephemerides liturgicae*, cvi (1992), 177–204

J. McKinnon: 'The Eighth-Century Frankish-Roman Communion Cycle', *JAMS*, xlv (1992), 179–227

C.M. Atkinson: 'Further Thoughts on the Origin of the Missa graeca', *De musica et cantu: Helmut Hucke zum 60. Geburtstag*, ed. P. Cahn and A.-K. Heimer (Hildesheim, 1993), 75–93

E. Nowacki: 'Constantinople – Aachen – Rome: the Transmission of *Veterem hominem*', ibid., 95–115 [concerns the antiphons for the Octave of Epiphany]

R. Steiner: '*Holocausta medullata*: an Offertory for St. Saturninus', ibid., 263–74

N. Sevestre: 'La liturgie de la Dédicace et ses hymnes', *Max Lütolf zum 60. Geburtstag: Festschrift*, ed. B. Hangartner and U. Fischer (Basel, 1994), 59–64

G.M. Boone, ed,: *Essays on Medieval Music: in Honor of David G. Hughes* (Cambridge, MA, 1995 [incl. T.H. Connolly: 'The Antiphon *Cantantibus organis* and Dante's *Organi Dei mondo*', 59–75; R.L. Crocker: 'Thoughts on Responsories', 77–85; E. Nowacki: 'Antiphonal Psalmody in Christian Antiquity and Early Middle Ages', 287–315; L. Treitler: 'Once More, Music and Language in Medieval Song', 441–69]

S. Dieudonné: 'Introït de la fête de la Présentation *Suscepimus*', *Requirentes modos musicos: mélanges offerts à Dom Jean Claire*, ed. D. Saulnier (Solesmes, 1995), 275–94

J. Halmo: *Hymns for the Paschal-Triduum in the Medieval Office* (Ottawa, 1995); see also *Worship*, lv (1981), 137–59

T. Karp: The Offertory *In die solemnitatis*', *Laborare fratres in unum: Festschrift László Dobszay zum 60. Geburtstag*, ed. J. Szendrei and D. Hiley (Hildesheim, 1995), 151–65

G. Kiss: 'Die Beziehung zwischen Ungebundenheit und Traditionalismus im Messordinarium', ibid., 187–200

C. Maître: 'La modalité archaïque dans le répertoire d'Autun', *Requirentes modos musicos: mélanges offerts à Dom Jean Claire*, ed. D. Saulnier (Solesmes, 1995), 179–91

R. Steiner: 'Antiphons for Lauds on the Octave of Christmas', *Laborare fratres in unum: Festschrift László Dobszay zum 60. Geburtstag*, ed. J. Szendrei and D. Hiley (Hildesheim, 1995), 307–15

J.W. McKinnon: 'Preface to the Study of the Alleluia', *EMH*, xv (1996), 213–49

I.B. Milfull: *The Hymns of the Anglo-Saxon Church: a Study and Edition of the Durham Hymnal* (Cambridge, 1996)

D. Saulnier: 'Modes orientaux et modes grégoriens', *EG*, xxv (1997), 45–61

L. Treitler: 'Language and the Interpretation of Music', *Music and Meaning*, ed. J. Robinson (Ithaca, NY, 1997), 23–56

L: THEORY

GerbertS, i, 26–7 [Pseudo-Alcuin: De octo tonis]

E. Omlin: *Die Sankt-Gallischen Tonarbuchstaben* (Engelberg, 1934)

J. Smits van Waesberghe, ed.: Johannes Afflighemensis: *De musica cum tonario*, CSM, i (1950)

J. Smits van Waesberghe, ed.: Aribonis: *De musica*, CSM, ii (1951)

J. Smits van Waesberghe: 'The Musical Notation of Guido of Arezzo', *MD*, v (1951), 15–53 [Eng. trans. of pp.47–85 of *De musico-paedagogico et theoretico Guidone Aretino*, Florence, 1953]

M. Huglo: 'Un tonaire du graduel de la fin du XIIIe siècle (Paris, B.N. lat.13,159)', *Revue grégorienne*, xxxi (1952), 176–86, 224–33

K. Meyer: 'The Eight Gregorian Modes on the Cluny Capitals', *Art Bulletin*, xxxiv (1952), 75–94

J. Smits van Waesberghe, ed.: *Guidonis Aretini: Micrologus*, CSM, iv (1955)

M. Huglo: 'Le tonaire de Saint-Bénigne de Dijon (Montpellier H. 159)', *AnnM*, iv (1956), 7–18

R. Weakland: 'Hucbald as Musician and Theorist', *MQ*, xlii (1956), 66–84

P. Fischer and J. Smits van Waesberghe, eds.: *The Theory of Music from the Carolingian Era up to 1400*, i: *Descriptive Catalogue of Manuscripts*, RISM, B/III/1 (1961)

Z. Falvy: 'Zur Frage von Differenzen der Psalmodie', *SMw*, xxv (1962), 160–73

F.J. Léon Tello: *Estudios de historia de la teoría musical* (Madrid, 1962)

J. Chailley, ed.: *Alia musica: traité de musique du IXe siècle* (Paris, 1965)

W. Lipphardt, ed.: *Der karolingische Tonar von Metz* (Münster, 1965)

M. Huglo: 'Un théoricien du XIe siècle: Henri d'Augsbourg', *RdM*, liii (1967), 53–9

H. Potiron: 'Théoriciens de la modalité', *EG*, viii (1967), 29–37

P. Fischer, ed.: *The Theory of Music from the Carolingian Era up to 1400*, ii: *Italy*, RISM, B/III/2 (1968)

M. Huglo: 'Un troisième témoin du "tonaire carolingien"', *AcM*, xl (1968), 22–8

J. Ponte, ed. and trans.: *Aurelianus Reomensis: the Discipline of Music (Musica disciplina)* (Colorado Springs, CO, 1968)

M. Huglo: 'L'auteur du "Dialogue sur la musique" attribué à Odon', *RdM*, lv (1969), 119–71

J. Smits van Waesberghe: *Musikerziehung: Lehre und Theorie der Musik im Mittelalter* (Leipzig, 1969)

M. Huglo: 'Der Prolog des Odo zugeschriebenen "Dialogus de musica"', *AMw*, xxviii (1971), 134–46

M. Huglo: *Les tonaires: inventaire, analyse, comparaison* (Paris, 1971)

L.A. Gushee: 'Questions of Genre in Medieval Treatises on Music', *Gattungen der Musik in Einzeldarstellungen: Gedenkschrift Leo Schrade*, ed. W. Arlt and others (Berne, 1973), 365–433

T. Seebass: *Musikdarstellung und Psalterillustration im frühen Mittelalter: Studien, ausgehend von einer Ikonologie der Handschrift Paris, Bibliothèque nationale, fonds latin 1118* (Berne, 1973)

T. Bailey: *The Intonation Formulas of Western Chant: Studies and Texts* (Toronto, 1974)

L. Gushee, ed.: *Aureliani Reomensis Musica disciplina*, CSM, xxi (1975)

R.A. Skeris: '*Chroma theou*': on the Origins and Theological Interpretation of the Musical Imagery Used by the Ecclesiastical Writers (Altötting, 1976)

M. Bielitz: *Musik und Grammatik: Studien zur mittelalterlichen Musiktheorie* (Munich, 1977)

T. Bailey: 'De modis musicis: a New Edition and Explanation', *KJb*, lxi–lxii (1977–8), 47–60

W. Babb, C.V. Palisca and A.E. Planchart, eds.: *Hucbald, Guido, and John on Music: Three Medieval Treatises* (New Haven, CT, 1978)

T. Bailey, ed.: *'Commemoratio brevis et tonis et psalmis modulandis': Introduction, Critical Edition, Translation* (Ottawa, 1979)

M. Bernhard: *Wortkonkordanz zu Anicius Manlius Severinus Boethius 'De institutione musica'* (Munich, 1979)

A. Seay, ed.: G. Martinez de Biscargui: *Arte de canto llano* [1538] (Colorado Springs, CO, 1979)

J. Snyder: 'Non-Diatonic Tones in Plainsong: Theinred of Dover versus Guido d'Arezzo', *IMSCR XIII: Strasbourg 1982c*, ii, 49–67

N.C. Phillips: '*Musica et Scolica enchiriadis*': its Literary, Theoretical, and Musical Sources (diss., New York U., 1984)

M.A. Ester-Sala: 'Difusió en català de l'obra de J. Bermudo a l'*Ordinarium barcinonense* de 1569', *Recerca musicològica*, v (1985), 13–43

P.A. Merkley: *Conflicting Assignments of Antiphons in Italian Tonaries* (diss., Harvard U., 1985)

P. Merkley: 'The Transmission of Tonaries in Italy', *Studies in Music from the University of Western Ontario*, x (1985), 51–74

M. Huglo and C. Meyer, eds.: *The Theory of Music, iii: Manuscripts from the Carolingian Era to c. 1500 in the Federal Republic of Germany (D-brd)*, RISM, B/III/3 (1986)

K.-W. Gümpel: 'Gregorian Chant and *Musica ficta*: New Observations from Spanish Theory of the Early Renaissance', *Recerca musicològica*, vi–vii (1986–7), 5–27; rev. version, in Ger., in *AMw*, xlvii (1990), 120–47

M. Huglo: 'Les formules d'intonations *noeane noeagis* en Orient et en Occident', *Aspects de la musique liturgique au Moyen Age: Royaumont de 1986, 1987 and 1988*, 43–53

J. Raasted: 'The *laetantis adverbia* of Aurelian's Greek Informant', ibid., 55–66

N. Sevestre: 'Quelques documents d'iconographie musicale médiévale: l'image et l'école autour de l'an mil', *Imago musicae*, iv (1987), 23–34 [concerns illustrations in the tonary of *F-Pn* lat.1118]

C.M. Atkinson: '*Harmonia* and the *Modi, quos abusive tonos dicimus*', *IMSCR XIV: Bologna 1987*, iii, 485–500

M. Bernhard, ed.: *Anonymi saeculi decimi vel undecimi tractatus de musica 'Dulce ingenium musicae'* (Munich, 1987)

Music Theory and its Sources: Antiquity and the Middle Ages: South Bend, IN, 1987 [incl. M. Bernhard: 'Glosses on Boethius', 136–49; M. Huglo: 'The Study of Ancient Sources of Music Theory in the Medieval University', 150–72; J.W. McKinnon: 'Music Theory and its Sources: Antiquity and the Middle Ages', 258–64]

Cantus planus III: Tihány 1988 [incl. C.M. Atkinson: 'From *Vitium* to *Tonus acquisitus*: on the Evolution of the Notation Matrix of Medieval Chant', 181–97; J. Dyer: 'The Monastic Origins of Western Music Theory', 199–225; M. Bernhard: 'Didaktische Verse zur Musiktheorie des Mittelalters', 227–36; Z. Czagány: 'Fragment eines Anonymen Musik traktats des XV. Jahrhunderts aus Leutschau', 237–44; C. Maître: 'Etude lexicologique d'un traité dit de Saint Martial', 257–65]

J. Chailley and J. Viret: 'Le symbolisme de la gamme', *ReM*, nos.408–9 (1988), 1–150

M. Huglo: 'Bibliographie des éditions et études relatives à la théorie musicale du Moyen Age (1972–1987)', *AcM*, lx (1988), 229–72

M. Huglo: 'Notice sur deux nouveaux manuscrits d'Aristote en latin (Munich, Bayerische Staatsbibliothek, Clm 14272, Baltimore MD, the George Peabody Library, Inv. 159413)', *Scriptorium*, xlii (1988), 183–90

R. Killam: 'Solmization with the Guidonian Hand: an Historical Introduction to Modal Counterpoint', *Journal of Music Theory Pedagogy*, ii (1988), 251–73

P. Merkley: 'Tonaries and Melodic Families of Antiphons', *JPMMS*, xi (1988), 13–24

W. Sayers: 'Irish Evidence for the *De harmonia tonorum* of Wulfstan of Winchester', *Mediaevalia*, xiv (1988), 23–38

M. Bernhard: '*Clavis Gerberti*: eine Revision von Martin Gerberts '*Scriptores ecclesiastici de musica sacra potissimum*' (St. Blasien, 1784) (Munich, 1989)

C.M. Bower and C.V. Palisca, ed. and trans.: Anicius Manlius Severinus Boethius: *Fundamentals of Music* (New Haven, CT, 1989)

B. Sullivan: 'Interpretive Models of Guido of Arezzo's Micrologus', *Comitatus*, xx (1989), 20–42

M. Bernhard: 'The *Lexicon musicum latinum* of the Bavarian Academy of Sciences', *JPMMS*, xiii (1990), 79–82

M. Bernhard, ed.: *Quellen und Studien zur Musiktheorie des Mittelalters*, i (Munich, 1990)

M. Bernhard: 'Überlieferung und Fortleben der antiken lateinischen Musiktheorie im Mittelalter', 'Das musikalische Fachschriften im lateinischen Mittelalter', *Geschichte der Musiktheorie*, ed. F. Zaminer, iii: *Rezeption des antiken Fachs im Mittelalter* (Darmstadt, 1990), 7–35, 37–103

Cantus planus IV: Pécs 1990 [incl. H. Möller: 'Der *Tonarius Bernonis*: Rätsel um Gerberts Ausgabe', 69–86; J. Dyer: 'Chant Theory and Philosophy in the Late Thirteenth Century', 99–117; E. Witkowska-Zaremba: 'Music between *Quadrivium* and *Ars canendi*: *Musica speculativa* by Johannes de Muris and its Reception in Central and East-Central Europe', 119–26; Z. Czagány: 'Ein *Diffinitorium musicum* aus dem späten 15. Jahrhundert', 127–39; L. Vikarius: '*Pro cognicione cantus*: a Theoretical Compilation', 141–61]

M. Huglo: 'La réception de Calcidius et des Commentarii de Macrobe à l'époque carolingienne', *Scriptorium*, xliv (1990), 3–20

R.P. Maddox: '*Spatium* and *intervallum*: the Development of Technical Terms for "Interval" in Medieval Treatises', *Musicology Australia*, xiii (1990), 23–7

G. Marzi, ed.: *Anicius Manlius Severinus Boethius: De Institutione Musica* (Rome, 1990)

P. Merkley: 'Tonaries, Differentiae, Termination Formulas, and the Reception of Chant', *Beyond the Moon: Festschrift Luther Dittmer*, ed. B. Gillingham and P. Merkley (Ottawa, 1990), 183–94

K.-J. Sachs: 'Musikalische Elementarlehre im Mittelalter', *Geschichte der Musiktheorie*, ed. F. Zaminer, iii: *Rezeption des antiken Fachs im Mittelalter* (Darmstadt, 1990), 105–61

C. Page, ed.: *The 'Summa musice': a Thirteenth-Century Manual for Singers* (Cambridge, 1991)

K. Slocum: '*Musica coelestis*: a Fourteenth Century Image of Cosmic Music', *Studia mystica*, xiv/2–3 (1991), 3–12

M. Bernhard, ed.: '*Lexicon musicum latinum medii aevi*': *Wörterbuch der lateinischen Musikterminologie des Mittelalters bis zum Ausgang des 15. Jahrhunderts*, i: *Quellenverzeichnis* (Munich, 1992) [a bibliography of secondary sources and a list of published treatises concerning medieval theory]

C. Meyer, M. Huglo and N.C. Phillips, eds.: *The Theory of Music, iv: Manuscripts from the Carolingian Era up to c. 1500 in Great Britain and in the United States: a Descriptive Catalogue*, RISM, B/III/1 (1992)

C. Page: 'A Treatise on Musicians from ?c. 1400: the *Tractatulus de differentiis et gradibus cantorum* by Arnulf de St Ghislain', *JRMA*, cxvii (1992), 1–21

W. Arlt: 'Die Intervallnotationen des Hermannus Contractus in Gradualien des 11. und 12. Jahrhunderts: das Basler Fragment N I 6 Nr. 63 und der Engelberger Codex 1003', *De musica et cantu: Helmut Hucke zum 60. Geburtstag*, ed. P. Cahn and A.-K. Heimer (Hildesheim, 1993), 243–56

M. Bernhard and C.M. Bower, eds.: *Glossa maior in institutionem musicam Boethii* (Munich, 1993)

M. Huglo: 'Les diagrammes d'harmonique interpolés dans les manuscrits hispaniques de la *Musica Isidori*', *Scriptorium*, xlviii (1994), 171–86

C.M. Atkinson: 'Johannes Afflighemensis as a Historian of Mode', *Laborare fratres in unum: Festschrift László Dobszay zum 60. Geburtstag*, ed. J. Szendrei and D. Hiley (Hildesheim, 1995), 1–10

M. Bernhard: 'Traditionen im mittelalterlichen Tonsystem', *Altes im Neuen: Festschrift Theodor Göllner zum 65. Geburtstag*, ed. B. Edelmann and M.H. Schmid (Tutzing, 1995), 11–23

M. Huglo: '*Exercitia vocum*', *Laborare fratres in unum: Festschrift László Dobszay zum 60. Geburtstag*, ed. J. Szendrei and D. Hiley (Hildesheim, 1995), 117–23 [concerns early vocal exercises used at various churches]

E. Witkowska-Zaremba: '*Mi contra fa* and *Divisio toni*', ibid., 331–340

C. Meyer: '*Mensura monochordi*': *la division du monocorde (IXe–XVe siècles)* (Paris, 1996)

J.M.H. Smith: 'A Hagiographer at Work: Hucbald and the Library at Saint-Amand', *Revue bénédictine*, cvi (1996), 151–71

C.W. Brockett: ed.: *Anonymi 'De modorum formulis et tonarius'*, CSM, xxxvii (1997)

C. Meyer, E. Witkowska-Zaremba and K.-W. Gümpel, eds.: *The Theory of Music*, v: *Manuscripts from the Carolingian Era up to c. 1500 in the Czech Republic, Poland, Portugal and Spain: a Descriptive Catalogue*, RISM B/III/5 (1997)

M: PARALITURGICAL CATEGORIES

tropes, sequences, conductus, versus, cantiones

MGG2 ('Cantio'; J. Cerny)

F.J. Wolf: *Über die Lais, Sequenzen und Leiche* (Heidelberg, 1841/R)

H.A. Daniel: *Thesaurus hymnologicus sive hymnorum canticorum sequentiarum circa annum MD usitarum collectio amplessima* (Leipzig, 1841–56/R)

K. Bartsch, ed.: *Die lateinischen Sequenzen des Mittelalters in musikalischer und rhythmischer Beziehung* (Rostock, 1868/R)

J. Kehrein: *Lateinische Sequenzen des Mittelalters aus Handschriften und Drucken* (Mainz, 1873/R)

A. Reiners: *Die Tropen-, Prosen-, und Präfations-Gesängen des feierlichen Hochamtes im Mittelalter* (Luxembourg, 1884)

L. Gautier: *Histoire de la poésie liturgique au Moyen Age*, i: *Les tropes* (Paris, 1886/R)

W.H. Frere, ed.: *The Winchester Troper from MSS of the Xth and XIth Centuries* (London, 1894/R)

E. Misset and P. Aubry: *Les proses d'Adam de Saint-Victor: texte et musique* (Paris, 1900/R)

O. Drinkwelder: *Ein deutsches Sequentiar aus dem Ende des 12. Jahrhunderts* (Graz, 1914)

J. Handschin: 'Über Estampie und Sequenz', *ZMw*, xii (1929–30), 1–20; xiii (1930–31), 113–32

H. Spanke: 'Rhythmen- und Sequenzstudien', *Studi medievali*, new ser., iv (1931), 286–320

F. Gennrich: *Grundriss einer Formenlehre des mittelalterlichen Liedes als Grundlage einer musikalischen Formenlehre des Liedes* (Halle, 1932/R)

H. Spanke: 'Zur Geschichte der lateinischen nichtliturgischen Sequenz', *Speculum*, vii (1932), 367–82

A. Hughes, ed.: *Anglo-French Sequelae Edited from the Papers of the Late Dr. Henry Marriott Bannister* (London, 1934/R)

A. Schmitz: 'Ein schlesisches Cantional aus dem 15. Jahrhundert (Hs. Graz 756)', *AMf*, i (1936), 385–423

H. Spanke: 'Die Kompositionskunst der Sequenzen Adams von St. Victor', *Studi medievali*, new ser., xiv (1941), 1–30

M. Bukofzer: 'Speculative Thinking in Mediaeval Music', *Speculum*, xvii (1942), 165–80

W. von den Steinen: 'Die Anfänge der Sequenzdichtung', *Zeitschrift für schweizerische Kirchengeschichte*, xl (1946), 190–212, 241–68; xli (1947), 19–48, 122–62

W. von den Steinen: *Notker der Dichter und seine geistige Welt* (Berne, 1948/R)

L. Brou: 'Séquences et tropes dans la liturgie mozarabe', *Hispania sacra*, iv (1951), 1–15

R.-J. Hesbert: *Le prosaire de la Sainte-Chapelle* (Mâcon, 1952) [facs.]

J. Handschin: 'Trope, Sequence and Conductus', *NOHM*, ii (1954), 128–74

H. Husmann: 'Die Sankt Galler Sequenztradition bei Notker und Ekkehard', *AcM*, xxvi (1954), 6–18

H. Husmann: 'Sequenz und Prosa', *AnnM*, ii (1954), 61–91

E. Jammers: *Der mittelalterliche Choral: Art und Herkunft* (Mainz, 1954)

L. Kunz: 'Textrhythmus und Zahlenkomposition in frühen Sequenzen', *Mf*, viii (1955), 403–11

G. Vecchi, ed.: *Troparium sequentiarum nonantulanum: Cod. Casanat. 1741*, MLMI, 1st ser., *Latina*, i (1955) [facs.]

H. Husmann: 'Die Alleluia und Sequenzen der Mater-Gruppe', *Musikwissenschaftlicher Kongress: Vienna 1956*, 276–84

H. Husmann: 'Alleluia, Vers und Sequenz', *AnnM*, iv (1956), 19–53

H. Husmann: 'Die älteste erreichbare Gestalt des St. Galler Tropariums', *AMw*, xiii (1956), 25–41

W. Irtenkauf: 'Das Seckauer Cantionarium vom Jahre 1345 (Hs. Graz 756)', *AMw*, xiii (1956), 116–41

M. Huglo: 'Un nouveau prosaire nivernais', *Ephemerides liturgicae*, lxxi (1957), 3–30

J. Smits van Waesberghe: 'Over het ontstaan van sequens en prosula en beider oorsprenckelijke uitvoeringswijze', *Orgaan K.N.T.V.*, xii/Sept (1957), 1–57

R.L. Crocker: 'The Repertory of Proses at Saint Martial de Limoges in the 10th Century', *JAMS*, xi (1958), 149–64

J. Smits van Waesberghe: 'Zur ursprünglichen Vortragsweisen der Prosulen, Sequenzen und Organa', *IMSCR VII: Cologne 1958*, 251–4

R. Weakland: 'The Beginnings of Troping', *MQ*, xliv (1958), 477–88

H. Husmann: 'Alleluia, Sequenz und Prosa im altspanischen Choral', *Miscelánea en homenaje a Monseñor Higinio Anglés* (Barcelona, 1958–61), 407–15

H. Husmann: 'Sinn und Wesen der Tropen, veranschaulicht an den Introitus-Tropen des Weihnachtsfestes', *AMw*, xvi (1959), 135–47

F. Labhardt: *Das Sequentiar Cod. 546 der Stiftsbibliothek von St. Gallen und seine Quellen* (Berne, 1959–63)

P. Evans: 'Some Reflections on the Origin of the Trope', *JAMS*, xiv (1961), 119–30

R.-J. Hesbert: *Le prosaire d'Aix–la–Chapelle: manuscrit 13 du chapitre d'Aix-la-Chapelle (XIIIe siècle, début)* (Rouen, 1961) [facs.]

L. Elfving: *Etude lexicographique sur les séquences limousines* (Stockholm, 1962)

H. Husmann: 'Die Sequenz *Duo tres*', *In memoriam Jacques Handschin*, ed. H. Anglés and others (Strasbourg, 1962), 66–72

J. Smits van Waesberghe: 'Die Imitation der Sequenztechnik in den Hosanna-Prosulen', *Festschrift Karl Gustav Fellerer zum 60. Geburtstag*, ed. H. Hüschen (Regensburg, 1962/R), 485–90

B. Stäblein: 'Der Tropus *Dies sanctificatus* zum Alleluia *Dies sanctificatus*', *SMw*, xxv (1962), 504–15

P. Damilano: 'Laudi latine in un antifonario bobbiese del Trecento', *CHM*, iii (1962–3), 15–57

B. Stäblein: 'Notkeriana', *AMw*, xix–xx (1962–3), 84–99

H.J. Holman: 'Melismatic Tropes in the Responsories for Matins', *JAMS*, xvi (1963), 36–46

B. Stäblein: 'Zum Verständnis des "klassischen" Tropus', *AcM*, xxxv (1963), 84–95

B. Stäblein: 'Zwei Texturen des *Alleluia Christus resurgens* in St. Emmeram, Regensburg', *Organicae voces: Festschrift Joseph Smits van Waesberghe*, ed. P. Fischer (Amsterdam 1963), 157–67

J.A. Emerson: 'Über Entstehung und Inhalt von MüD (München, Bayer. Staatsbibl., Cgm. 716)', *KJb*, xlviii (1964), 33–60

H. Husmann, ed.: *Tropen-und Sequenzenhandschriften*, RISM, B/V/1 (1964)

B. Stäblein: 'Die Sequenzmelodie "Concordia" und ihr geschichtlicher Hintergrund', *Festschrift Hans Engel*, ed. H. Heussner (Kassel, 1964), 364–92

G. Weiss: 'Zum Problem der Gruppierung südfranzösischer Tropare', *AMw*, xxi (1964), 163–71

P. Dronke: 'The Beginnings of the Sequence', *Beiträge zur Geschichte der deutschen Sprache und Literatur*, lxxxvii (1965), 43–73

N. de Goede, ed.: *The Utrecht Prosarium*, MMN, vi (1965)

R.L. Crocker: 'The Troping Hypothesis', *MQ*, lii (1966), 183–203

D. Hughes: 'Further Notes on the Grouping of the Aquitanian Tropers', *JAMS*, xix (1966), 3–12

R.L. Crocker: 'Some Ninth-Century Sequences', *JAMS*, xx (1967), 367–402

P. Damilano: 'Sequenze bobbiesi', *RMI*, ii (1967), 3–35

K. Rönnau: '*Regnum tuum solidum*', *Festschrift Bruno Stäblein zum 70. Geburtstag*, ed. M. Ruhnke (Kassel, 1967), 195–205

K. Rönnau: *Die Tropen zum 'Gloria in excelsis Deo', unter besonderer Berücksichtigung des Repertoires der St. Martial-Handschriften* (Wiesbaden, 1967)

B. Stäblein: '"Psalle symphonizando"', *Festschrift für Walter Wiora*, ed. L. Finscher and C.-H. Mahling (Kassel, 1967), 221–8

P.J. Thannabaur: 'Anmerkungen zur Verbreitung und Struktur der Hosanna-Tropen im deutschsprachigen Raum und den Ostländern', *Festschrift Bruno Stäblein zum 70. Geburtstag*, ed. M. Ruhnke (Kassel, 1967), 250–59

G. Weiss: 'Zur Rolle Italiens im frühen Tropenschaffen: Beobachtungen zu den Vertonungen der Introitus-Tropen *Quem nasci mundo* und *Quod prisco vates*', ibid., 287–92

P. Evans: 'The *Tropi ad sequentiam*', *Studies in Music History: Essays for Oliver Strunk*, ed. H.S. Powers (Princeton, 1968), 73–82

R. Steiner: 'The Prosulae of the MS Paris, Bibliothèque Nationale, f. lat. 1118', *JAMS*, xxii (1969), 367–93

H. Anglès: 'Eine Sequenzensammlung mit Mensuralnotation und volkstümlichen Melodien (Paris, B.N. lat. 1343)', *Speculum musicae artis: Festgabe für Heinrich Husmann*, ed. H. Becker and R. Gerlach (Munich, 1970), 9–18

P. Evans: *The Early Trope Repertory of Saint Martial de Limoges* (Princeton, NJ, 1970)

P. Evans: 'Northern French Elements in an Early Aquitanian Troper', *Speculum musicae artis: Festgabe für Heinrich Husmann*, ed. H. Becker and R. Gerlach (Munich, 1970), 103–10

R.-J. Hesbert: *Le tropaire-prosaire de Dublin: manuscrit Add. 710 de l'Université de Cambridge (vers 1360)* (Rouen, 1970) [facs.]

R. Steiner: 'The Responsories and Prosa for St. Stephen's Day at Salisbury', *MQ*, lvi (1970), 162–82

G. Weiss, ed.: *Introitus-Tropen*, i: *Das Repertoire der südfranzösischen Tropare des 10. und 11. Jahrhunderts*, MMMA, iii (1970)

K. Levy: '*Lux de luce*: the Origin of an Italian Sequence', *MQ*, lxxii (1971), 40–61

D.G. Hughes: 'Music for St. Stephen at Laon', *Words and Music: the Scholar's View: a Medley of Problems and Solutions Compiled in Honor of A. Tillman Merritt*, ed. L. Berman (Cambridge, MA, 1972), 137–59

H. Vogt: *Die Sequenzen der Graduale Abdinghof aus Paderborn* (Münster, 1972)

R.L. Crocker: 'The Sequence', *Gattungen der Musik in Einzeldarstellungen: Gedenkschrift für Leo Schrade*, ed. W. Arlt and others (Berne, 1973), 269–322

H. Hofmann-Brandt: *Die Tropen zu den Responsorien des Offiziums* (Kassel, 1973)

R. Jonsson: 'Amalaire de Metz et les tropes du Kyrie eleison', *Classica et mediaevalia: Francisco Blatt septuagenario dedicata* (Copenhagen, 1973), 510–40

W. Lipphardt: '*Magnum nomen Domini Emanuel*: zur Frühgeschichte der Cantio *Resonet in laudibus*', *Jb für Liturgik und Hymnologie*, xvii (1973), 194–204

J.D. Anderson: 'Tropes: a Reappraisal', *American Benedictine Review*, xxv (1974), 364–76

T.F. Kelly: 'Melodic Elaboration in Responsory Melismas', *JAMS*, xxvii (1974), 461–74

C.M. Atkinson: *The Earliest Settings of the Agnus Dei and its Tropes* (diss., U. of North Carolina, 1975)

A. Holschneider: 'Instrumental Titles to the Sequentiae of the Winchester Tropers', *Essays on Opera and English Music in Honour of Sir Jack Westrup*, ed. F.W. Sterfeld, N. Fortune and E. Olleson (Oxford, 1975), 8–18

M. Huglo: 'De monodiska handskrifternas fördelning i två grupper, öst och väst', *Nordiskt kollokvium III i latinsk liturgiforskning: Esbo 1975* (Helsinki, 1975), 47–65

R. Jonsson: *Corpus troporum*, i: *Tropes du propre de la messe*, pt 1: *Cycle de noël* (Stockholm, 1975)

E. Odelman: 'Comment a-t-on appelé les tropes? Observations sur les rubriques des tropes des Xe et XIe siècles', *Cahiers de civilisation médiévale*, xviii (1975), 15–36

O. Marcusson: *Corpus troporum*, ii: *Prosules de la messe*, pt 1: *Tropes de l'alleluia* (Stockholm, 1976)

L. Brunner: *The Sequences of Verona, Biblioteca Capitolare, CVII and the Italian Sequence Tradition* (diss., U. of North Carolina, 1977)

R.L. Crocker: *The Early Medieval Sequence* (Berkeley, 1977)

J. Mráček: 'Sources of Rorate chants in Bohemia', *Hudební veda*, xiv (1977), 230–41

A.E. Planchart: *The Repertory of Tropes at Winchester* (Princeton, NJ, 1977)

H. Spanke: *Studien zu Sequenz, Lai und Leich*, ed. U. Aarburg (Darmstadt, 1977) [repr. of eight articles pubd 1931–41]

B. Stäblein: '*Pater noster*-Tropen', *Sacerdos et cantus gregoriani magister: Festschrift Ferdinand Haberl*, ed. F.A. Stein (Regensburg, 1977), 247–78

M. Huglo: 'Aux origines des tropes d'interpolation: le trope méloforme d'introït', *RdM*, lxiv (1978), 5–54

K.H. Kohrs: *Die apparallelen Sequenzen* (Munich, 1978)

J.S. Mráček: 'Some Observations on the Manuscript Prague, Státní Knihovna, XVII F 45 as a Source for the Study of Czech Rorate Chants', *Musica antiqua V: Bydgoszcz 1978*, 483–92

B. Stäblein: 'Einiges Neues zum Thema "archaische Sequenz"', *Festschrift Georg von Dadelsen*, ed. T. Kohlhase and V. Scherliess (Neuhausen-Stuttgart, 1978), 352–83

K. Vellekoop: '*Dies ire dies illa*': *Studien zur Frühgeschichte einer Sequenz* (Bilthoven, 1978)

H. Vogt: 'Die Sequenzen des Paderborner Graduale Abdinghof und die Sequenzen der Bursfelder Kongregation', *Musica antiqua V: Bydgoszcz 1978*, 403–14

M. Huglo: 'On the Origins of the Troper-Proser', *JPMMS*, ii (1979), 11–18

D.A. Bjork: 'Early Settings of the Kyrie eleison and the Problem of Genre Definition', *JPMMS*, iii (1980), 40–48

D.A. Bjork: 'The Kyrie Trope', *JAMS*, xxxiii (1980), 1–41

G.M. Hair: 'Editorial Problems and Solutions Concerning the Offertory Tropes for Christmas Day from Ms Paris BN fonds latin 903', *MMA*, xi (1980), 226–57

G. Iversen: *Corpus troporum*, iv: *Tropes de l'Agnus Dei* (Stockholm, 1980)

N. Silvestre: 'The Aquitanian Tropes of the Easter Introit: a Musical Analysis', *JPMMS*, iii (1980), 26–39

N. Van Deusen: 'The Sequence Repertory of Nevers Cathedral', *Forum musicologicum*, ii (1980), 44–59

L.W. Brunner: 'A Perspective on the Southern Italian Sequence: the Second Tonary of the Manuscript Monte Cassino 318', *EMH*, i (1981), 117–64

P. Dronke: '*Virgines caste*', *Lateinische Dichtungen des X. und XI. Jahrhunderts: Festgabe für Walther Bulst*, ed. W. Berschin and R. Düchting (Heidelberg, 1981), 93–117

D. Hiley: 'The Ordinary of Mass Chants and the Sequences [in W1]', *JPMMS*, iv (1981), 67–81

E. Reier: *The Introit Trope Repertory at Nevers: MSS Paris B. N. lat. 9449 and Paris B. N. n. a. lat. 1235* (diss., U. of California, Berkeley, 1981)

D. Schaller: 'Die Paulus-Sequenz Ekkeharts I. von St. Gallen', *Lateinische Dichtungen des X. und XI. Jahrhunderts: Festgabe für Walther Bulst*, ed. W. Berschin and R. Düchting (Heidelberg, 1981), 186–220

W. Arlt: 'Zur Interpretation der Tropen', *Forum musicologicum*, iii (1982), 61–90

G. Björkvall and R. Steiner: 'Some Prosulas for Offertory Antiphons', *JPMMS*, v (1982), 13–35

D. Hiley: 'The Rhymed Sequence in England: a Preliminary Survey', *Musicologie médiévale: Paris 1982*, 227–46

M. Huglo: 'Origine et diffusion de la séquence parisienne: introduction', ibid., 209–12

M. Huglo and N. Phillips: 'The Versus *Rex caeli*: Another Look at the So-Called Archaic Sequence', *JPMMS*, v (1982), 36–43

A.E. Planchart: 'About Tropes', *IMSCR XIII: Strasbourg 1982a* [*Schweizer Jb für Musikwissenschaft*, new ser., ii (1982)], 125–35

N. Van Deusen: 'The Medieval Latin Sequence: a Complete Catalogue of the Sources and Editions of the Texts and Melodies', *JPMMS*, v (1982), 56–61

N. Van Deusen: 'Polymelodic Sequences and a Second Epoch of Sequence Composition', *Musicologie médiévale: Paris 1982*, 213–25

G. Björkvall, R. Jonsson and G. Iversen: 'Le *Corpus troporum*: une équipe de recherche sur les tropes liturgiques du Moyen Age', *Studi medievali*, xxiv (1983), 907–34

J.G. Johnstone: 'Beyond a Chant: *Tui sunt caeli* and its Tropes', *Music and Language*, ed. E.S. Beebe and others (New York, 1983), 24–37

K. Schlager: '*Trinitas, unitas, deitas*: a Trope for the Sanctus of Mass', *JPMMS*, vi (1983), 8–14

Liturgische Tropen: Munich 1983 and Canterbury 1984[incl. H. Hucke: 'Zur melodischen Überlieferung der Tropen', 107–24; S. Rankin: 'Musical and Ritual Aspects of *Quem queritis*', 181–92]

K. Falconer: 'Early Versions of the Gloria Trope *Pax sempiterna Christus*', *JPMMS*, vii (1984), 18–27

M. Fassler: 'Who was Adam of St. Victor? The Evidence of the Sequence Manuscripts', *JAMS*, xxxvii (1984), 233–69

T.F. Kelly: 'Introducing the Gloria in excelsis', *JAMS*, xxxviii (1984), 479–506

La sequenza medievale: Milan 1984, iii [L. Brunner: 'The Italian Sequence and Stylistic Pluralism: Observations about the Music of the Sequences for Easter Season from Southern Italy', 19–44; M.-N. Colette: 'Transcription rhythmique de séquences dans les manuscrits de Saint-Gall', 59–70; G. Cattin: 'Sequenza nell'area ravennate: abbozzo di analisi testuale', 45–57; P. Damilano: 'La sequenza musicale a Bobbio: dipendenze e analogie con la produzione sangallese e limosina', 71–9; B. Gillingham: 'Atavism and Innovation in a Late Medieval Proser', 87–104; D. Hiley: 'The Sequentiary of Chartres, Bibliothèque municipale, Ms 47', 105–17; M. Huglo: 'Les séquences instrumentales', 119–27; A. Roncaglia: 'Sequenza adamiana e strofa zagialesca', 141–54; A. Ziino: 'Sequenza in una fonte sconosciuta dell'Italia centrale', 155–71]

C. Waddell, ed.: *The Twelfth-Century Cistercian Hymnal* (Kalamazoo, MI, 1984) [i: Introduction and Commentary; ii: Edition]

B. Gillingham: 'Atavism and Innovation in a Late Medieval Proser', *Studies in Music from the University of Western Ontario*, x (1985), 79–103 [concerns *F-Pn* lat.5247]

A.E. Planchart: 'Italian Tropes', *Mosaic*, xviii/4 (1985), 11–58

V. Plocek and A. Traub: *Zwei Studien zur ältesten geistlichen Musik in Böhmen* (Cologne and Giessen, 1985)

L. Treitler: 'Oral and Literate Style in the Regional Transmission of Tropes', *SM*, xxvii (1985), 171–83

La tradizione dei tropi liturgici: Paris 1985 and Perugia 1987 [incl. P.-M. Gy: 'La géographie des tropes dans la géographie liturgique du Moyen Age carolingien et postcarolingien', 13–24; G. Cremascoli: 'Les tropes: théologie et invocation', 25–38; G. Iversen: 'Sur la géographie des tropes du Sanctus', 39–62; A. Dennery: 'Le chant des tropes et des séquences et des prosules dans l'ouest, aux XIe–XIIIe siècles', 63–77; C. Leonardi: 'La tematica del Cristo re nei tropi dell'alleluia e dell'Agnus Dei', 79–86; B.M. Jensen: 'Maria visits St. Gallen', 87–93; E. Palazzo: 'Confrontation du répertoire des tropes et du cycle iconographique du tropaire d'Autun', 95–123 + 17 pls.; D. Hiley: 'Cluny, Sequences and Tropes', 125–38; M. Huglo: 'Centres de composition des tropes et cercles de diffusion', 139–44; R. Jacobsson: 'Contribution à la géographie des saints', 145–82; G. Orlandi: 'Metrical Problems in Tropes', 183–96; E. Odelman: 'Les prosules limousines de Wolfenbüttel (ms Cod. Guelf. 79 Gud. lat)', 197–205; G. Björkvall: 'La relation entre les deux tropaires d'Apt', 207–25; E. Castro: 'Le long chemin de Moissac à S. Millan (Le troparium de la Real Acad. Hist., Aemil. 51)', 243–63; N. Sevestre: 'La diffusion de certains tropes en l'honneur de Saint Jean-Baptiste du sud de l'Aquitaine au Languedoc', 265–78; H. Möller: 'Die Prosula *Psalle modulamina* (Mü 9543) und ihre musikhistorische Bedeutung', 279–96; P. Rutter: 'The Epiphany Trope Cycle in Paris, Bibliothèque Nationale, fonds latin 1240', 313–24; J. Boe: 'Italian and Roman Verses for Kyrie leyson in the MSS Cologny-Genève, Bibliotheca Bodmerian a 74 and Vaticanus latinus 5319', 337–84; A.E. Planchart: 'The Interaction between Montecassino and Benevent', 385–407; W. Arlt: 'Von den einzelnen Aufzeichnungen der Tropen zur Rekonstruktion der Geschichte', 439–79]

G. Björkvall: 'Les deux tropaires d'Apt, mss. 17 et 18', *Corpus troporum*, v: *Inventaire analytique des manuscrits et édition des textes uniques* (Stockholm, 1986), 13–22

M. Huglo: 'Les *libelli* de tropes et les premiers tropaires-prosaires', *Pax et sapientia: Studies in Text and Music of Liturgical Tropes and Sequences in Memory of Gordon Anderson*, ed. R. Jacobsson (Stockholm, 1986), 13–22

G. Iversen: '*Pax et sapientia*: a Thematic Study on Tropes from Different Traditions', ibid., 23–58

R. Jacobsson and L. Treitler: 'Tropes and the Concept of Genre', ibid., 59–89

E. Nowacki: 'Text Declamation as a Determinant of Melodic Form in the Old Roman Eighth-Mode Tracts', *EMH*, vi (1986), 193–226

N. Van Deusen: 'The Use and Significance of the Sequence', *MD*, xl (1986), 5–47

J.M. Borders: 'The Northern and Central Italian Trope Repertoire and its Transmission', *IMSCR XIV: Bologna 1987*, iii, 543–53

A. Haug: *Gesungene und schriftlich dargestellte Sequenz: Beobachtungen zum Schriftbild der ältesten ostfränkischen Sequenzenhandschriften* (Neuhausen-Stuttgart, 1987)

H. Becker: 'Theologie in Hymnen. Die Himmelfahrtssequenz *Omnes gentes plaudite*', *Capella antiqua München: Festschrift zum 25jährigen Bestehen*, ed. T. Drescher (Tutzing, 1988), 11–121

Cantus planus III: Tihány 1988 [incl. L.W. Brunner: 'Two Missing Fascicles of Pistoia C.121 Recovered', 1–20; D. Hiley: 'Editing the Winchester Sequence Repertory of ca. 1000', 99–113; H. Binford-Walsh: 'The Ordering of Melody in Aquitanian Chant: a Study of Mode One Introit Tropes', 327–39; B. Déri: 'Zu den Tropen des Introitus *In medio ecclesiae*: die Introitus-Tropen im Kontext der Messe und des Offiziums', 341–53; G. Björkvall: 'Offertory Prosulas for Advent in Italian and Aquitanian Manuscripts', 377–400; C. Hospenthal: 'Tropen in Handschriften aus dem Kloster Rheinau', 401–14; C.E. Brewer: '*Regina celi letare…Alle-Domine*: from Medieval Trope to Renaissance Tune', 431–48]

M.L. Göllner: 'Migrant Tropes in the Late Middle Ages', *Capella antiqua München: Festschrift zum 25jährigen Bestehen*, ed. T. Drescher (Tutzing, 1988), 175–87

J. Grier: 'The Stemma of the Aquitanian Versaria', *JAMS*, xli (1988), 250–88

T.F. Kelly: 'Neuma triplex', *AcM*, lx (1988), 1–30

A.E. Planchart: 'On the Nature of Transmission and Change in Trope Repertories', *JAMS*, xli (1988), 215–49

B. Schmid, ed.: *Der Gloria-Tropus Spiritus et alme bis zur Mitte des 15. Jahrhunderts* (Tutzing, 1988)

A. Dennery: *Le chant postgrégorien: tropes, séquences et prosules* (Paris, 1989)

D. Hiley: 'Rouen, Bibliotheque Municipale, MS 249 (A. 280) and the Early Paris Repertory of Ordinary of Mass Chants and Sequences', *ML*, lxx (1989), 467–82

C. Roederer: *Festive Troped Masses from the Eleventh Century: Christmas and Easter in the Aquitaine* (Madison, WI, 1989)

J. Boe and A.E. Planchart, eds.: *Beneventanum troporum corpus*, RRMMA, xvi–xxviii (1989–97)

B. Baroffio: 'I tropi d'introito e i canti pasquali in un graduale italiano del sec. XIII (Monza, Bibl. Capit., K11)', *Studi in onore di Giulio Cattin*, ed. F. Luisi (Rome, 1990), 3–14

Cantus planus IV: Pécs 1990 [incl. M. Fassler: 'The Disappearance of the Proper Tropes and the Rise of the Late Sequence: New Evidence from Chartres', 319–35; D. Hiley: 'Some Observations on the Repertory of Tropes at St. Emmeram, Regensburg', 337–57; G. Björkvall: 'The Continuity of a Genre: Offertory Prosulas in Cambrai B.M. 172 (167) from the Twelfth Century', 359–70; B. Asketorp: 'Beobachtungen zu einigen späteren Introitustropen', 371–92; J. Borders: 'Tropes and the New Philology', 393–406; E.C. Teviotdale: 'Some Thoughts on the Place of Origin of the Cotton Troper', 407–12; A. Haug: 'Das ostfränkische Repertoire der meloformen Introituotropen', 413–26; G. Iversen: '*Splendor Patris*: on Influence and Genre Definition. Victorine Proses Reflected in the Sanctus', 427–44; H. Binford-Walsh: 'The Internal Stability of Aquitanian Introit Tropes', 445–56; B. Déri: 'Die Teile und das Ganze: die Struktur von *Ales diei nuntius* (Prudentius, Cathemerion 1)', 469–84]

E. Castro: 'Los tropos de la misa en los costumarios catalanes más antiguos', *De musica hispana et aliis: miscelánea en honor al Prof. Dr. José López-Calo*, ed. E. Casares and C. Villanueva (Santiago de Compostela, 1990), 55–75

J. Grier: '*Ecce sanctum quem Deus elegit Marcialem apostolum*: Adémar de Chabannes and the Tropes for the Feast of Saint Martial', *Beyond the Moon: Festschrift Luther Dittmer*, ed. B. Gillingham and P. Merkley (Ottawa, 1990), 28–99

C. Hospenthal: 'Beobachtungen zu den *Ite missa est* im Tropenbestand der Handschriften aus dem Kloster Rheinau', *Schweizer Jb für Musikwissenschaft*, new ser., x (1990), 11–18

C. Hospenthal: 'Tropen im Rheinauer Handschriftenbestand der Zentralbibliothek Zurich nach Gattungen', *Schweizer Jb für Musikwissenschaft*, new ser., x (1990), 19–31

G. Iversen: *Corpus troporum*, vii: *Tropus du Sanctus: introduction et édition critique* (Stockholm, 1990)

J.A. Diamond: *A Tradition of Three Tropes* (Ottawa, 1991)

A. Haug: 'Neue Ansätze im 9. Jahrhundert', *Die Musik des Mittelalters*, ed. H. Möller and R. Stephan (Laaber, 1991), 94–128

B.M. Jensen: 'An Interpretation of the Tropes of the *Inventio Sanctae Crucis* in London, British Library, Cotton MS Caligula A XIV', *Ecclesia orans*, viii (1991), 305–25

S. Rankin: 'The Earliest Sources of Notker's Sequences: St. Gallen, Vadiana 317, and Paris, Bibliothèque Nationale lat. 10587', *EMH*, x (1991), 201–33

S. Rankin: 'Notker und Tuotilo: schöpferische Gestalter in einer neuen Zeit', *Schweizer Jb für Musikwissenschaft*, new ser., xi (1991), 17–42

G. Björkvall and A. Haug: '*Primus init Stephanus*: eine Sankt Galler Prudentius-Vertonung aus dem zehnten Jahrhundert', *AMw*, xlix (1992), 57–78

F. Büttner: 'Welche Bedeutung hat die Uberschrift *Cignea* für Notkers Sequenz *Gaude maria virgo*?', *Mf*, xlv (1992), 162–3

IMSCR XV: Madrid 1992, ii [incl. G. Iversen: 'The Mirror of Music: Symbol and Reality in the text of *Clangat hodie*', 771–89; C.M. Atkinson: 'Music and Meaning in *Clangat hodie*', 790–806; G. Björkvall and A. Haug: 'Texting Melismas: Criteria for and Problems in Analyzing Melogene Tropes', 807–31; B. Møller-Jensen: 'Arthemius, Candida and Paulina in Piacenza: an Interpretation of the Sequence *Adeste hodie festum*', 832–47; E. Teviotdale: 'The Affair of John Marshal', 848–55]

V. Schier: 'Propriumstropen in der Würzburger Domliturgie: ein Beitrag zu Form und Funktion der Tropen im späten Mittelalter', *KJb*, lxxvi (1992), 3–43

J. Stevens: '*Samson dux fortissime*: an International Latin Song', *PMM*, i (1992), 1–40

G. Björkvall: 'Prosody, Metre and Rhetorical Devices in the Unique Tropes of Apt 17', *De musica et cantu: Helmut Hucke zum 60. Geburtstag*, ed. P. Cahn and A.-K. Heimer (Hildesheim, 1993), 203–23

J. Emerson: 'Neglected Aspects of the Oldest Full Troper (Paris, Bibliothèque nationale, lat. 1240)', ibid., 193–217

K. Falconer: *Some Early Tropes to the Gloria* (Modena, 1993)

M. Fassler: *Gothic Song: Victorine Sequences and Augustinian Reform in Twelfth-Century Paris* (Cambridge, 1993)

G. Iversen: 'On the Iconography of Praise in the Sanctus and its Tropes', *De musica et cantu: Helmut Hucke zum 60. Geburtstag*, ed. P. Cahn and A.-K. Heimer (Hildesheim, 1993), 271–308

R. Jacobsson and L. Treitler: 'Sketching Liturgical Archetypes: *Hodie surrexit leo fortis*', ibid., 157–202

R. Jacobsson: 'Unica in the Cotton Caligula Troper', *Music in the Medieval English Liturgy*, ed. S. Rankin and D. Hiley (Oxford, 1993), 11–45

M.A. Leach: 'On Re-Creation in Medieval Music: some Melodic and Textual Relationships among Gloria Tropes', *Ars lyrica*, vii (1993), 25–46

Recherches nouvelles sur les tropes liturgiques [Huglo Fs], ed. W. Arlt and G. Björkvall (Stockholm, 1993) [incl. W. Arlt: 'Schichten und Wege in der Überlieferung der älteren Tropen zum Introitus *Nunc scio vere* des Petrus-Festes', 13–93; C.M. Atkinson: 'Text, Music, and the Persistence of Memory in *Dulcis est cantica*', 95–117; G. Björkvall and A. Haug: 'Tropentypen in Sankt Gallen', 119–74; M.-N. Colette: 'Jubilus et trope dans le Gloria in excelsis Deo', 175–91; M.S. Gros i Pujol: 'Les tropes d'introït du graduel de Saint-Félix de Gérone: Gérone Bib. Sem., Ms. 4', 219–29; P.-M. Gy: 'L'hypothèse lotharingienne et la diffusion des tropes [in Metz, MS 452, destroyed in 1944]', 231–7; D. Hiley: 'Provins Bibliothèque Municipale 12 (24): a 13th-Century Gradual with Tropes from Chartres Cathedral', 239–69; G. Iversen: 'Continuité et renouvellement à Nevers: réflexions sur le répertoire du prosaire-tropaire nivernais, Paris B.N. n.a. lat. 3126', 271–308; R.M. Jacobsson: 'Poésie liturgique et fond biblique: essai sur quatre complexes de tropes en l'honneur de Saint Pierre apôtre et sur leur transmission', 309–41; C. Maître: 'A propos de quelques tropes dans un manuscrit cistercien', 343–59; D. Norberg: 'Problèmes métriques dans les séquences, les offices, et les tropes', 361–9; A.E. Planchart: 'An Aquitanian Sequentia in Italian Sources', 371–93; S. Rankin: 'From Tuotilo to the First Manuscripts: the Shaping of a Trope Repertory at Saint Gall', 395–413; N. Sevestre: 'Prose ou vers?', 429–39; R. Steiner: 'Non-Psalm Verses for Introits and Communions', 441–7]

J. Grier: 'A New Voice in the Monastery: Tropes and Versus from Eleventh- and Twelfth-Century Aquitaine', *Speculum*, lxix (1994), 1023–69

B. Scharf: 'Le origini della monodia sacra in volgare in Francia e in Germania', *Rivista internazionale di musica sacra*, xv (1994), 18–70

W. Arlt: 'Komponieren im Galluskloster um 900: Tuotilos Tropen *Hodie cantandus est* zur Weihnacht und *Quoniam Dominus Iesus Christus* zum Fest des Iohannes evangelista', *Schweizerisches Jb für Musikwissenschaft*, new ser., xv (1995), 41–70

A. Haug: *Troparia tardiva: Repertorium später Tropenquellen aus dem deutschsprachigen Raum*, MMMA, *Subsidia*, i (1995)

D. Hiley: 'The Repertory of Sequences at Winchester', *Essays on Medieval Music: in Honor of David G. Hughes*, ed. G.M. Boone (Cambridge, MA, 1995), 153–93

G. Iversen: '*Cantans – orans – exultans*: Interpretations of Chants of the Introit Liturgy', *Laborare fratres in unum: Festschrift László Dobszay zum 60. Geburtstag*, ed. J. Szendrei and D. Hiley (Hildesheim, 1995), 125–50

A.E. Planchart: 'Notes on the Tropes in Manuscripts of the Rite of Aquileia', *Essays on Medieval Music: in Honor of David G. Hughes*, ed. G.M. Boone (Cambridge, MA, 1995), 333–69

N. Sevestre: 'Fragments d'un prosaire aquitain inédit', *Laborare fratres in unum: Festschrift László Dobszay zum 60. Geburtstag*, ed. J. Szendrei and D. Hiley (Hildesheim, 1995), 285–95 [late 12th-century frags. from *F-MON*]

J. Borders and L. Brunner, eds.: *Early Medieval Chants from Nonantola*, RRMMA, xxx–xxxiii (1996)

B. Møller-Jensen: 'Written in St. Gallen for Minden: the Introit Tropes to *Festivitas omnium sanctorum*', in Berlin, Preussische Staatsbibl. Theol. Lat. IV MS. 11', *Ecclesia orans*, xiii (1996), 43–64

V. Schier: *Tropen zum Fest der Erscheinung des Herrn* (Paderborn, 1996) [incl. extensive bibliography, pp.267–86]

M.-N. Colette: '*Modus, tropus, tonus*: tropes d'introïts et théories modales', *EG*, xxv (1997), 63–95

R. Crocker: *Studies in Medieval Music Theory and the Early Sequence* (Aldershot, 1997) [collection of essays pubd 1958–75]

N: LITURGICAL DRAMAS, PLANCTUS, MARIENKLAGEN

K. Young: *The Drama of the Medieval Church* (Oxford, 1933/R)

H. Eggers and W. Irtenkauf: 'Die Donaueschinger Marienklage', *Carinthia*, cxlviii (1958), 359–82

M. Bernard: 'L'officium stellae nivernalis', *RdM*, li (1965), 52–65

C.C. Flanigan: 'The Roman Rite and the Origins of the Liturgical Drama', *University of Toronto Quarterly*, xliii (1974), 263–84

C.C. Flanigan: 'The Liturgical Drama and its Tradition: a Review of Scholarship, 1965–1975', *Research Opportunities in Renaissance Drama*, xviii (1975), 86–96

V. Saxer: *Le culte de Marie Madeleine en Occident des origines à la fin du Moyen Age* (Paris, 1975)

T. McGee: 'The Liturgical Placement of the *Quem quaeritis* Dialogue, *JAMS*, xxix (1976), 1–29

C.W. Brockett: 'Easter Monday Antiphons and the Peregrinus Play', *KJb*, lxi–lxii (1977–8), 29–46

D.A. Bjork: 'On the Dissemination of *Quem quaeritis* and the *Visitatio sepulchri* and the Chronology of their Early Sources', *Comparative Drama*, xiv (1980), 46–69

C.W. Brockett: 'The Role of the Office Antiphon in Tenth-Century Liturgical Drama', *MD*, xxxiv (1980), 5–27

J. Drumbl: *Quem quaeritis : teatro sacro dell'alto Medioevo* (Rome, 1981)

S.K. Rankin: 'The Mary Magdalene Scene in the *Visitatio sepulchri* Ceremonies', *EMH*, i (1981), 117–64

S.K. Rankin: 'A New English Source of the *Visitatio sepulchri*', *JPMMS*, iv (1981), 1–11

J. Yearley: 'A Bibliography of Planctus in Latin, Provençal, French, German, English, Italian, Catalan, and Galician-Portuguese, from the Time of Bede to the Early Fifteenth Century', *JPMMS*, iv (1981), 12–52

M.L. Norton: The Type II *Visitatio sepulchri*: a Repertorial Study, (diss., Ohio State U., 1983)

S. Rankin: 'Musical and Ritual Aspects of *Quem queritis*', *Liturgische Tropen: Munich 1983 and Canterbury 1984*, 181–92

W. Bulst, M.L. Bulst-Thiele and M. Bielitz, eds.: *Hilarii Aurelianensis versus et ludi, epistolae: Ludus Danielis Belouacensis* (Leiden, 1989), 97–119

E.C. Caridad: 'El texto y la función litúrgica del *Quem quaeritis* pascual en el catedral de Vic', *Hispania sacra*, xli (1989), 399–420

S. Rankin: *The Music of the Medieval Liturgical Drama in France and England* (New York, 1989) [concerns the *Visitatio sepulchri*, *Officium pastor* and *Officium peregrinus*]

M.A. Gómez Pintor: 'El estudio de un drama litúrgico de Santiago de Compostela: análisis, fuentes y documentación', *De musica hispana et aliis: miscelánea en honor al Prof. Dr. José López-Calo*, ed. E. Casares and C. Villanueva (Santiago de Compostela, 1990), 91–110

U. Hennig and A. Traub, eds.: *Trierer Marienklage und Osterspiel: Codex 1973/63 der Stadtbibliothek Trier* (Goppingen, 1990)

C. Bernardi: *La drammaturgia della Settimana Santa in Italia* (Milan, 1991)

C. Davidson and J.H. Stroupe, eds.: *Drama in the Middle Ages: Comparative and Critical Essays, Second Series* (New York, 1991) [contains 22 articles, incl. M.L. Norton: 'Of Stages and Types in *Visitatione sepulchri*', 61–105; J.M. Gibson: '*Quem queritis in presepe*: Christmas Drama or Christmas Liturgy?', 106–28]

E.L. Risden: 'Medieval Drama and the Sacred Experience', *Studia mystica*, xiv/2–3 (1991), 74–83

M. Fassler: 'The Feast of Fools and *Danielis ludus*: Popular Tradition in a Medieval Cathedral Play', *Plainsong in the Age of Polyphony*, ed. T.F. Kelly (Cambridge, 1992), 65–99 [concerns *GB-Ob* lat.c.36, dated *c* 1200]

F. Collins: 'Ten Years of Medieval Music-Drama: a Retrospective', *Early Drama, Art, and Music Review*, xv (1992–3), 12–18

C. Davidson and J.H. Stroupe, eds.: *Medieval Drama on the Continent of Europe* (Kalamazoo, MI, 1993) [incl. H. Linke: 'A Survey of Medieval Drama and Theater in Germany', 17–53; M.L. Norton. 'Of Stages and Types in *Visitatione sepulchri*', 61–102, T.P. Campbell: 'Cathedral Chapter and Town Council: Cooperative Ceremony and Drama in Medieval Rouen', 103–13]

G. Cattin: 'Tra Padova e Cividale: nuova fonte per la drammaturgia sacra nel medioevo', *Saggiatore musicale*, i (1994), 7–112

D.H. Ogden: 'The *Visitatio sepulchri*: Public Enactment and Hidden Rite', *Early Drama, Art, and Music Review*, xvi (1994), 95–102

A. Davril: 'L'origine du *Quem quaeritis*', *Requirentes modos musicos: mélanges offerts à Dom Jean Claire*, ed. D. Saulnier (Solesmes, 1995), 119–36

O: STUDIES OF SPECIFIC MEDIEVAL MASSES, OFFICES, FEASTS, HAGIOGRAPHY

G.M. Dreves, C. Blume and H.M. Bannister, eds.: Analecta hymnica medii aevi [AH] (Leipzig, 1886–1922/R) [edns of 865 poetic Offices in vols. v, xiii, xvii, xviii, xxiv–xxvi, xxviii, xlia, xlv]

H. Felder: *Die liturgischen Reimofficien auf die Heiligen Franciscus und Antonius, gedichtet und componiert durch Fr. Julian von Speier* (Freiburg, 1901)

H. Villetard: *Office de Pierre de Corbeil (Office de la Circoncision) improprement appelé 'Office des fous': text et chant publiés d'après le manuscrit de Sens (XIIIe siècle)* (Paris, 1907)

P. Wagner: 'Zur mittelalterlichen Offiziumskomposition', *KJb*, xxi (1908), 13–32

P. Wagner: 'Die Offizien in poetischer Form', *Einführung in die gregorianischen Melodien, i: Ursprung und Entwicklung der liturgischen Gesangsformen* (Leipzig, 3/1911/R), 300

P. Bayart: *Les offices de Saint Winnoc et de Saint Oswald d'après le manuscrit 14 de la Bibliothèque de Bergues* (Lille, 1926)

J. Gmelch: 'Unbekannte Reimgebetkompositionen aus Rebdorfer Handschriften', *Festschrift Peter Wagner zum 60. Geburtstag*, ed. K. Weinmann (Leipzig, 1926/R), 69–80

E. Jammers: 'Die Antiphonen der rheinischen Reimoffizien', *Ephemerides liturgicae*, xliii (1929), 199–219, 425–51; xliv (1930), 84–99, 342–68

P. Wagner: *Die Gesänge der Jakobsliturgie zu Santiago de Compostela aus dem sogennanten Codex Calixtinus* (Fribourg, 1931)

E. Jammers: *Das Karlsoffizium 'Regali natus': Einführung, Text und Übertragung in moderne Notenschrift* (Strasbourg, 1934/R)

C. Lambot: 'L'office de la Fête-Dieu: aperçus nouveaux sur ses origines', *Revue bénédictine*, liv (1942), 61–123

S. Corbin: 'Les offices de Sainte-Face', *Bulletin des études portugaises*, xii (1947), 1–65

M. Huglo: 'L'office du dimanche de Pâques dans les monastères bénédictins', *Revue grégorienne*, xxx (1951), 191–203

F. Wellner: *Drei liturgische Reimoffizien aus dem Kreis der minderen Brüder* (Munich, 1951)

L. Brou and A. Wilmart: 'Un office monastique pour le 2 novembre dans le nord de la France au XIe siècle', *Sacris erudiri*, v (1953), 247–330

R.-J. Hesbert: 'La composition musicale à Jumièges: les offices de St. Philibert et de St. Aycadre', *Jumièges … XIIIe centenaire: Rouen 1954*, 977–90

C. Hohler: 'The Durham Services in Honour of St. Cuthbert', *The Relics of Saint Cuthbert*, ed. C.F. Battiscombe (Oxford, 1956), 155–91

J. Schmidt-Görg: 'Die Sequenzen der heiligen Hildegard', *Studien zur Musikgeschichte des Rheinlands: Festschrift zum 80. Geburtstag von Ludwig Schiedermair*, ed. W. Kahl, H. Lemacher and J. Schmidt-Görg (Cologne, 1956), 109–17

H. Villetard: *Office de Saint Savinien et de Saint Potentien, premiers évêques de Sens: texte et chant* (Paris, 1956)

Y. Delaporte: 'L'office fécampois de Saint Taurin', *L'abbaye bénédictine de Fécamp: ouvrage scientifique du XIIIe centenaire, 658–1958*, ii (Fécamp, 1960), 171–89, 377

L. Brou: 'L'ancien office de saint Vaast, évêque d'Arras', *EG*, iv (1961), 7–42

C.W. Jones: *The Saint Nicholas Liturgy and its Literary Relationships (Ninth to Twelfth Centuries)* (Berkeley, 1963) [incl. essay by G. Reaney on the music]

R.-J. Hesbert, ed.: Corpus antiphonalium officii [CAO], vii–xii (1963–79)

J.A. Emerson: 'Two Newly Identified Offices for Saints Valeria and Austriclinianus by Adémar de Chabannes (MS Paris, Bibl. Nat., Latin 909, fols.79–85v)', *Speculum*, xl (1965), 31–46

S. Corbin: 'Miracula beatae Mariae semper virginis', *Cahiers de civilisation médiévale*, x (1967), 409–33

C. Hohler: 'The Proper Office of St. Nicholas and Related Matters with Reference to a Recent Book', *Medium aevum*, xxxvi (1967), 40–48

G.M. Oury: 'Formulaires anciens pour la messe de Saint Martin', *EG*, vii (1967), 21–40

M. Ritscher: 'Zur Musik der heiligen Hildegard', *Colloquium amicorum: Joseph Schmidt-Görg zum 70. Geburtstag*, ed. S. Kross and H. Schmidt (Bonn, 1967), 309–26

R. Jonsson: *Historia: études sur la genèse des offices versifiés* (Stockholm, 1968)

D. Misonne: 'Office liturgique neumé de la bienheureuse Marie d'Oignies à l'abbaye de Villers au 13e siècle', *Album J. Balon* (Namur, 1968), 171–89

L. Weinrich: '*Dolorum solatium*: Text und Musik von Abelards Planctus David', *Mittellateinisches Jb*, v (1968), 59–78

P. Barth, I. Ritscher and J. Schmidt-Görg, eds.: Hildegard von Bingen: *Lieder* (Salzburg, 1969)

D. Grémont: 'Le culte de Ste.-Foi et de Ste.-Marie-Madeleine à Conques au XIe siècle, d'après le manuscrits de la *Chanson de Ste.-Foi*', *Revue du Rouergue*, xxiii (1969), 165–75

P. Dronke: 'The Composition of Hildegard of Bingen's *Symphonia*', *Sacris erudiri*, xix (1969–70), 381–93

W. Arlt: *Ein Festoffizium des Mittelalters aus Beauvais in seiner liturgischen und musikalischen Bedeutung* (Cologne, 1970)

P. Dronke: *Poetic Individuality in the Middle Ages: New Departures in Poetry, 1000–1150* (Oxford, 1970, 2/1986)

D. Stevens: 'Music in Honor of St. Thomas of Canterbury', *MQ*, lvi (1970), 311–48

S. Corbin: 'L'apparition du lyrisme dans la monodie médiévale: le chant grégorien', *Studi musicali*, ii (1973), 73–88

G.M. Oury: 'La structure cérémonielle des vêpres solennelles dans quelques anciennes liturgies françaises', *Ephemerides liturgicae*, lxxxviii (1974), 336–52

W. Berschin: 'Historia S. Konradi', *Freiburger Diözesan-Archiv*, xcv (1975), 107

W. Lipphardt, ed.: *Lateinische Osterfeiern und Osterspiele* [LOO] (Berlin, 1975–90)

J. Dubois: *Un sanctuaire monastique au Moyen-Age: Saint-Fiacre-en Brie* (Paris, 1976) [incl. edn of the Offices of St Fiacre]

T. Lundén, ed.: *Officium parvum beate Marie Virginis: Vår Frus tidegärd/Den heliga Birgitta och den helige Petrus av Skänninge* (Stockholm, 1976) [Brigittine breviary]

M. Bernard: 'Un recueil inédit du XIIe siècle et la copie aquitaine de l'office versifié de Saint-Grégoire', *EG*, xvi (1977), 145–59

D. Sicard: *La liturgie de la mort dans l'église latine des origines à la réforme carolingienne* (Münster, 1978)

M. Bernard: 'Les offices versifiés atribués à Léon IX (1002–1054)', *EG*, xix (1980), 89–121

W. Berschin: 'Sanktgallische Offiziendichtung aus ottonischer Zeit', *Lateinische Dichtungen des X. und XI. Jahrhunderts: Festgabe für Walther Bulst*, ed. W. Berschin and R. Düchting (Heidelberg, 1981), 13–48

A. Hughes: 'Chants in the Offices of Thomas of Canterbury and Stanislaus of Poland', *Musica antiqua VI: Bydgoszcz 1982*, 267–77

K. Schlager and T. Wohnhaas: 'Ein Ulrichsoffizium aus Mailand', *Jb des Vereins für Augsburger Bistumsgeschichte*, xvi (1982), 122–58

A. Hughes: 'Modal Order and Disorder in the Rhymed Office', *MD*, xxxvii (1983), 29–51

D. Altenburg: 'Die Musik in der Fronleichnamsprozession des 14. und 15. Jahrhunderts', *MD*, xxxviii (1984), 5–25

P. Damilano: 'Un antico ufficio ritmico della Visitazione nella Biblioteca capitolare di Fossano (Cuneo)', *Rivista internazionale di musica sacra*, v (1984), 133–63

K. Ottosen: 'The Latin Office of the Dead: a Computer Analysis of Two Thousand Texts', *Computer Applications to Medieval Studies*, ed. A. Gilmour-Bryson (Kalamazoo, MI, 1984), 81–7

R.M. Thomson: 'The Music for the Office of St. Edmund, King and Martyr', *ML*, lxv (1984), 189–93

C. Wright: 'The Feast of the Reception of the Relics at Notre Dame of Paris', *Music and Context: Essays for John M. Ward*, ed. A.D. Shapiro and P. Benjamin (Cambridge, MA., 1985), 1–13

J. Blezzard, S. Ryle and J. Alexander: 'New Perspectives on the Feast of the Crown of Thorns', *JPMMS*, x (1987), 23–47

B.H. Haggh: 'The Celebration of the *Recollectio festorum Beatae Mariae Virginis*, 1457–1987', *IMSCR XIV: Bologna 1987*, iii, 559–71

R.A. Baltzer: 'Another Look at a Composite Office and its History: the Feast of *Susceptio reliquiarum* in Medieval Paris', *JRMA*, cxiii (1988), 1–27

J.J. Boyce: 'The Office of St. Mary of Salome', *JPMMS*, xi (1988), 25–47

N. Bux: 'La liturgia de San Nicola', *Ephemerides liturgicae*, c (1988), 562–608 [incl. edns of the Offices and Masses]

D.F.L. Chadd: 'The Transmission of *historiae* for the Offices of Saints: Some Preliminary Considerations', *Medieval Studies: Skara 1988*, 87–106

A. Hughes: 'Chants in the Rhymed Office of St. Thomas of Canterbury', *EMc*, xvi (1988), 185–201

A. Hughes: 'Rhymed Offices', *Dictionary of the Middle Ages*, ed. J.R. Strayer, x (New York, 1988), 366–77 [with extensive bibliography]

K. Schlager: 'Beobachtungen zum Otto-Offizium', *Cantus planus III: Tihány 1988*, 115–26

K. Schlager and T. Wohnhaas: 'Historia Sancti Corbiniani rediviva: die Überlieferung der mittelalterlichen Melodien zum Offizum und der Messe am Corbiniansfest', *Beiträge zur altbayerischen Kirchengeschichte*, xxxvii (1988), 21–42

J.J. Boyce: 'The Office of the Three Marys in the Carmelite Liturgy, after the Manuscripts Mainz, Dom- und Diozesanmuseum, Codex E and Florence, Carmine, Ms. 0', *JPMMS*, xii (1989), 1–38

J. Marquardt-Cherry: 'Ottonian Saints in the Prüm Troper', *Manuscripta*, xxxiii (1989), 129–36

W. Berschin, P. Ochsenbein and H. Möller, eds.: 'Das älteste Gallusoffizium in Lateinische Kultur im X. Jahrhunderts', *Mittellateinisches Jb*, xxiv–xxv (1989–90), 11–37

O.T. Edwards: 'Chant Transference in Rhymed Offices', *Cantus planus IV: Pécs 1990*, 503–19

O.T. Edwards: *Matins, Lauds and Vespers for St David's Day: the Medieval Office of the Welsh Patron Saint in the National Library of Wales MS 20541 E* (Cambridge, 1990)

A. Hughes: 'Word Painting in a Twelfth-Century Office', *Beyond the Moon: Festschrift Luther Dittmer*, ed. B. Gillingham and P. Merkley (Ottawa, 1990), 16–27

H. van der Werf: 'The Composition *Alleluya vocavit Jesus* in the Book named *Jacobus*', *De musica hispana et aliis: miscélanea en honor al Prof. Dr. José López-Calo*, ed. E. Casares and C. Villanueva (Santiago de Compostela, 1990), 197–207

A.B. Yardley: 'The Marriage of Heaven and Earth: a Late Medieval Source of the *Consecratio virginum*', *CMc*, nos.45–7 (1990), 305–24 [Sanders Fs issue, ed. P.M. Lefferts and L.L. Perkins]

G. Cattin: 'The Texts of the Offices of Sts. Hylarion and Anne in the Cypriot Manuscript Torino J.II.9', *The Cypriot-French Repertory of the Manuscript Torino J.II.9: Paphos 1992*, 249–301

A.E. Davidson, ed.: *The 'Ordo virtutum' of Hildegard of Bingen* (Kalamazoo, MI, 1992) [incl. A.E. Davidson: 'Music and Performance: Hildegard of Bingen's *Ordo virtutum*', 1–29; R. Potter: 'The *Ordo virtutum*: Ancestor of the English Moralities?', 31–41; P. Sheingorn: 'The Virtues of Hildegard's *Ordo virtutum*; or, It Was a Woman's World', 43–62; J.B. Holloway: 'The Monastic Context of Hildegard's *Ordo virtutum*', 63–77; G. Iversen: '*Ego humilitatis, regina virtutum*: Poetic Language and Literary Structure in Hildegard of Bingen's Vision of the Virtues', 79–110; 'The *Ordo virtutum*: a Note on Production', 111–22 and 12 MS facs.]

M. Huglo: 'Les pièces notées du *Codex Calixtinus*', *The 'Codex Calixtinus' and the Shrine of St. James*, ed. J. Williams and A. Stones (Tübingen, 1992), 106–24

W.D. Jordan: 'An Assessment of a Fifteenth-Century Manuscript Fragment in the Hone Collection Containing Part of a Rhymed Office for St. Vincent Ferrer', *SMA*, xxvi (1992), 1–33

J. Boyce: 'Das Offizium der Darstellung Mariens von Philippe de Mézières: die Handschriften und der Überlieferungsprozess', *KJb*, lxxvii (1993), 17–38

A. Hughes: 'British Rhymed Offices: a Catalogue and Commentary', *Music in the Medieval English Liturgy*, ed. S. Rankin and D. Hiley (Oxford, 1993), 239–84

S.E. Roper: *Medieval English Benedictine Liturgy: Studies in the Formation, Structure, and Content of the Monastic Votive Office, c. 950–1540* (New York, 1993)

K. Schlager: '*Digne laude nunc melodya*: ein Text zu Ehren der heiligen Elisabeth aus der Handschrift clm 7919 der Bayerischen Staatsbibliothek in München', *Recherches nouvelles sur les tropes liturgiques: recueil d'études*[Huglo Fs], ed. W. Arlt and G. Björkvall (Stockholm, 1993), 415–28

M.J. Bloxam: 'Plainsong and Polyphony for the Blessed Virgin: Notes on Two Masses by Jacob Obrecht', *JM*, xii (1994), 51–75

F. Lifshitz: 'Beyond Positivism and Genre: Hagiographical Texts as Historical Narrative', *Viator*, xxv (1994), 95–113

S. Rankin: 'The Divine Truth of Scripture: Chant in the *Roman de Fauvel*', *JAMS*, xlvii (1994), 203–43

M.J. Zijlstra: 'The Office of St. Adalbert: carte de visite of a Late Medieval Dutch Abbey?', *PMM*, iii (1994), 169–83

A. Hughes: *Late Medieval Liturgical Offices: Resources for Electronic Research* (Toronto, 1994–6) [i: Texts; ii: Sources and Chants]

B. Haggh, ed.: *Two Offices for St Elizabeth of Hungary: 'Gaudeat hungaria' and 'Letare germania'* (Ottawa, 1995)

J. Halmo: *Antiphons for Paschal Triduum-Easter in the Medieval Office* (Ottawa, 1995)

D. Hiley: 'What St. Dunstan Heard the Angels Sing: Notes on a Pre-Conquest Historia', *Laborare fratres in unum: Festschrift László Dobszay zum 60. Geburtstag*, ed. J. Szendrei and D. Hiley (Hildesheim, 1995), 105–15

M. Huglo: 'The Origin of the Monodic Chants in the Codex Calixtinus', *Essays on Medieval Music: in Honor of David G. Hughes*, ed. G.M. Boone (Cambridge, MA, 1995), 195–205

D. Hiley: *Historia sancti Emmerammi Arnoldi Vohburgensis, circa 1030* (Ottawa, 1996)

M. McGrade: 'Gottschalk of Aachen, the Investiture Controversy, and Music for the Feast of the *Divisio apostolorum*', *JAMS*, xlix (1996), 351–408

C. Page: 'Marian Texts and Themes in an English Manuscript: a Miscellany in Two Parts', *PMM*, v (1996), 23–44 [concerns *GB-Cssc 95*, dating from 1409]

T. Scandaletti: 'Una ricognizione sull'ufficio ritmico per S. Francesco', *Musica e storia*, iv (1996), 67–101

R. Hankeln: *Historiae sancti Dionysii Areopagitae: St Emmeram, Regensburg, ca. 1050/16 Jh.* (Ottawa, 1998)

P: PERFORMANCE

A. Kienle: 'Notizen über das Dirigieren mittelalterlicher Gesangschöre', *VMw*, i (1885), 158–69

S.J.P. Van Dijk: 'Medieval Terminology and Methods of Psalm Singing', *MD*, vi (1952), 7–26

C. Gindele: 'Doppelchor und Psalmvortrag im Frühmittelalter', *Mf*, vi (1953), 296–300

H. Hucke: 'Improvisation im gregorianischen Gesang', *KJb*, xxxviii (1954), 5–8

Mother Thomas More [M. Berry]: 'The Performance of Plainsong in the Late Middle Ages and the Sixteenth Century', *PRMA*, xcii (1965–6), 121–34

J.A. Caldwell: 'The Organ in the Medieval Latin Liturgy … 800–1500', *PRMA*, xciii (1966–7), 11–24

W. Suppan: 'Gedanken des europäischen Musikethnologen zur Aufführungspraxis, vor allem des gregorianischen Chorals', *Musica sacra*, xci (1971), 173–83

M. Berry: 'L'exécution du plain-chant à la fin du Moyen Age: l'Intonario Çaragoçano', *Musique, littérature et société au Moyen Age: Paris 1980*, 379–85

W. Hillsman: 'Instrumental Accompaniment of Plain-Chant in France from the Late 18th Century', *GSJ*, xxxiii (1980), 8–16

L.W. Brunner: 'The Performance of Plainchant: some Preliminary Observations of the New Era', *EMc*, x (1982), 316–28

M.E. Fassler: 'The Office of the Cantor in Early Western Monastic Rules and Customaries: a Preliminary Investigation', *EMH*, v (1985), 29–51

L. Agustoni and J.B. Göschl: *Einführung in die Interpretation des gregorianischen Chorals*, i: *Grundlagen* (Regensburg, 1987)

R. Jackson: *Performance Practice, Medieval to Contemporary: a Bibliographic Guide* (New York, 1988), esp. 35–59

E. Nowacki: 'The Performance of Office Antiphons in Twelfth-Century Rome', *Cantus planus III: Tihány 1988*, 79–91

H.M. Brown and S. Sadie, eds.: *Performance Practice: Music Before 1600* (London, 1989)

P. Gizzi: 'Gli Instituta patrum de modo psallendi sive cantandi', *Studi gregoriani*, v (1989), 39–58

H. Copeman: *Singing in Latin, or Pronunciation Explor'd* (Oxford, 1990), esp. appx 8, 301–10

N. Sandon: 'Some Thoughts on Making Liturgical Reconstructions', *Musicology in Ireland*, ed. G. Gillen and H. White (Dublin, 1990), 169–80

J.F. Weber: 'The Phonograph as Witness to Performance Practice of Chant', *Cantus planus IV: Pécs 1990*, 607–14

J.F. Weber: 'Liturgical Reconstruction as Reflected in Recordings', *Historical Performance*, iv (1991), 29–37

T.F. Kelly, ed.: *Plainsong in the Age of Polyphony* (Cambridge, 1992) [incl. J. A. Caldwell: 'Plainsong and Polyphony, 1250–1550', 6–31; M. Huglo: 'Notated Performance Practices in Parisian Chant Manuscripts of the Thirteenth Century', 32–44; R. Sherr: 'The Performance of Chant in the Renaissance and its Interactions with Polyphony', 178–208; I. Fenlon: 'Patronage, Music, and Liturgy in Renaissance Mantua', 209–35]

T.J. McGee, A.G. Rigg and D.N. Klausner: *Singing Early Music: the Pronunciation of European Languages in the Late Middle Ages and Renaissance* (Bloomington, IN, 1996)

R. Lightbourne: 'A Roman Procession (1583)', *Liber amicorum John Steele: a Musicological Tribute*, ed. W. Drake (Stuyvesant, NY, 1997), 117–38

Q: PLAINCHANT AND LITURGY IN THE RELIGIOUS ORDERS

E. Sackur: *Die Cluniacenser in ihrer kirchlichen und allgemeingeschichtlichen Wirksamkeit bis zur Mitte des elften Jahrhunderts* (Halle, 1892–4/R)

B. Albers, ed.: *Consuetudines monasticae* (Stuttgart and Monte Cassino, 1900–12)

A. Degand: 'Chartreux (liturgie des)', *Dictionnaire d'archéologie et de liturgie*, ed. F. Cabrol and H. Leclercq, iii/1 (Paris, 1913), 1045–71

A. Wilmard: 'Cluny (manuscrits liturgiques de)', *Dictionnaire d'archéologie et de liturgie*, ed. F. Cabrol and H. Leclercq, iii/2 (Paris, 1914), 2074–92

A. Malet: *La liturgie cistercienne: sa constitution, sa transformation, sa restauration* (Westmalle, 1921)

D. Knowles: 'The Monastic Horarium 970–1120', *Downside Review*, li (1933), 706–25

P.F. Lefèvre: *L'ordinaire de Prémontré d'après des manuscrits du XIIe et du XIIIe siècle* (Leuven, 1941)

B. Kaul: 'Le psautier cistercien', *Collectanea Ordinis Cisterciensium Reformatorum*, x (1948), 83–106; xii (1950), 118–51; xiii (1951), 257–72

D. Delalande: *Vers la version authentique du graduel grégorien: le graduel des Prêcheurs* (Paris, 1949)

P. Thomas: 'Saint Odon de Cluny et son oeuvre musicale', *A Cluny: Congrès scientifique: fêtes et cérémonies liturgiques en l'honneur des saints abbés Odon et Odilon: Cluny 1949*, 171–80

K. Hallinger: *Gorze-Kluny: Studien zu den monastischen Lebensformen und Gegensätzen im Hochmittelalter* (Rome, 1950–51/R)

J. Hourlier: 'Remarques sur la notation clunisienne', *Revue grégorienne*, xxx (1951), 231–40

R. Duvernay: 'Cîteaux, Vallombreuse et Etienne Harding', *Analecta sacri Ordinis Cisterciensis*, viii (1952), 379–495

S.R. Marosszéki: *Les origines du chant cistercien: recherches sur les réformes du plain-chant cistercien au XIIe siècle*, Analecta sacri Ordinis Cisterciensis, viii (1952), 1–179

U. Franca: 'Antiphonale-lectionarium monasterii Fontis Avellanae', *Katholische Kirchenmusik II:* (Vienna, 1954), 129–37

G. de Valous: 'Cluny', *Dictionnaire d'histoire et de géographie ecclésiastique*, xiii (Paris, 1956), 35–174

M. Huglo: 'Trois anciens manuscrits liturgiques d'Auvergne', *Bulletin historique et scientifique de l'Auvergne*, lxxvii (1957), 81–104

P.F. Lefèvre: *La liturgie de Prémontré: histoire, formulaire, chant et cérémonial* (Leuven, 1957)

K.W. Gümpel: 'Zur Interpretation der Tonus-Definition des Tonale Sancti Bernardi', *Akademie der Wissenschaften und der Literatur in Mainz*, no.2 (1959), 25–51

K. Hallinger: 'Kluny's Bräuche zur Zeit Hugos des Grossen (1049–1109): Prolegomena zur Neuherausgabe des Bernhard und Udalrich von Kluny', *Zeitschrift der Savigny-Stiftung für Rechtsgeschichte, Kanonistische Abt.*, xlv (1959), 99–140

J. Hourlier: 'Le bréviaire de Saint-Taurin: un livre liturgique clunisien à l'usage de l'Echelle-Saint-Aurin (Paris, B.N. lat. 12601)', *EG*, iii (1959), 163–73

P. Schmitz: 'La liturgie de Cluny', *Spiritualità cluniacense: Todi 1958*, (Todi, 1960), 83–99

S.J.P. Van Dijk and J.H. Walker: *The Origins of the Modern Roman Liturgy: the Liturgy of the Papal Court and the Franciscan Order in the Thirteenth Century* (London, 1960)

C.J. Bishko: 'Liturgical Intercession at Cluny for the King-Emperors of Leon', *Studia monastica*, iii (1961), 53–76

B. Hamilton: 'The Monastic Revival in Tenth Century Rome', *Studia monastica*, iv (1962), 35–68

R. Monterosso: 'Canto gregoriano e riforma tra cluniacensi e cistercensi', *Chiesa e riforma: Todi 1963*, 191–220

K. Hallinger, ed.: *Corpus consuetudinum monasticarum* (Siegburg, 1963–)

J. Hourlier: *Saint Odilon abbé de Cluny* (Leuven, 1964)

J. Becquet: 'Le coutumier clunisien de Maillezais', *Revue Mabillon*, no.119 (1965), 1–44

N. Hunt: *Cluny under Saint Hugh 1049–1109* (London, 1967)

N.I. Weyns: 'Le missel prémontré', *Analecta praemonstratensia*, xliii (1967), 203–25

R. Cortese-Esposito: 'Analogie e contrasti fra Cîteaux e Cluny', *Cîteaux*, xix (1968), 5–39

H.G. Hammer: *Die Allelujagesänge in der Choralüberlieferung der Abtei Altenberg: Beitrag zur Geschichte des Zisterzienserchorals* (Cologne, 1968)

D. Meade: 'From Turmoil to Solidarity: the Emergence of the Vallumbrosan Monastic Congregation', *American Benedictine Review*, xix (1968), 323–57

W. Kurze: 'Zur Geschichte Camaldolis im Zeitalter der Reform', *Miscellanea del Centro di studi medioevali*, v (1969), 399–415

S.J.P. Van Dijk: 'Ursprung und Inhalt der franziskanischen Liturgie des 13. Jahrhunderts', *Franziskanische Studien*, li (1969), 86–116, 192–217

H.E.J. Cowdrey: *The Cluniacs and the Gregorian Reform* (Oxford, 1970)

K. Hallinger: 'Herkunft und Überlieferung der Consuetudo Sigiberti', *Zeitschrift der Savigny-Stiftung für Rechtsgeschichte, Kanonistische Abt.*, lvi (1970), 194–242, esp. 212

B.M. Lambres: 'Le chant des Chartreux', *RBM*, xxiv (1970), 17–41

J. Patricia: 'Un processional cistercien du XVe siècle', *EG*, xi (1970), 193–205

G. de Valous: *Le monachisme clunisien des origines au XVe siècle* (Paris, 2/1970)

C. Waddell: 'Monastic Liturgy: Prologue to the Cistercian Antiphonary', *The Works of Bernard of Clairvaux*, i (Spencer, MA, 1970), 153–62

C. Waddell: 'The Origin and Early Evolution of the Cistercian Antiphonary: Reflections on Two Cistercian Chant Reforms', *The Cistercian Spirit: a Symposium*, ed. M.B. Pennington (Spencer, MA, 1970), 190–223

H.J. Becker: *Die Responsorien des Kartäuserbreviers: Untersuchungen zur Urform und Herkunft das Antiphonars der Kartäuse* (Munich, 1971)

B.H. Rosenwein: 'Feudal War and Monastic Peace: Cluniac Liturgy as Ritual Aggression', *Viator*, ii (1971), 129–57

C. Waddell: 'The Early Cistercian Experience of Liturgy', *Rule and Life: an Interdisciplinary Symposium*, ed. M.B. Pennington (Spencer, MA, 1971), 77–116

B.K. Lackner: *The Eleventh-Century Background of Cîteaux* (Washington DC, 1972)

P.F. Lefèvre: 'Les répons prolixes aux heures diurnes du "triduum sacrum" dans la liturgie canoniale', *Analecta praemonstratensia*, xlviii (1972), 5–19

F.J. Smith: 'Some Aspects of Mediaeval Music Theory and Praxis: the Ordo Minorum and its Place in Cultural History', *Franciscan Studies*, xxxii (1972), 187–202

C.P. Sweeney: *The Musical Treatise Formerly Attributed to John Wylde and the Cistercian Reform* (diss., U. of California, Los Angeles, 1972)

B.M. Lambres: 'L'antiphonaire des Chartreux', *EG*, xiv (1973), 213–18

N.I. Weyns, ed.: *Antiphonale missarum praemonstratense* (Averbode, 1973)

F.J. Guentner, ed.: *Epistola S. Bernardi de revisione cantus cisterciense, et Tractatus scriptus ab auctore incerto cisterciense*, CSM, xxiv (1974)

O. d'Angers: 'Le chant liturgique dans l'Ordre de Saint-François aux origines', *Etudes franciscaines*, xxv (1975), 157–306

H.J. Becker: *Das Tonale Guigos I: ein Beitrag zur Geschichte des liturgischen Gesanges und der Ars Musica im Mittelalter* (Munich, 1975)

G. Constable: *Medieval Monasticism: a Select Bibliography* (Toronto, 1976)

J.F. Angerer: 'Die *Consuetudines monasticae* als Quelle für die Musikwissenschaft', *Sacerdos et cantus gregoriani Magister: Festschrift Ferdinand Haberl*, ed. F.A. Stein (Regensburg, 1977), 23–37

M. Huglo: 'Les livres liturgiques de la Chaise-Dieu', *Revue bénédictine*, lxxxvii (1977), 289–348

P. Tirot: 'Un Ordo missae monastique: Cluny, Cîteaux, la Chartreuse', *Ephemerides liturgicae*, xcv (1981), 44–120, 220–51

R. Steiner: 'The Music for a Cluny Office of Saint Benedict', *Monasticism and the Arts*, ed. T.G. Verdon (Syracuse, NY, 1984), 81–114

C. Waddell, ed.: *The Twelfth-Century Cistercian Hymnal* (Kalamazoo, MI, 1984)

M.E. Fassler: 'The Office of the Cantor in Early Western Monastic Rules and Customaries: a Preliminary Investigation', *EMH*, v (1985), 29–51

B. Jessberger: *Ein dominikanisches Graduale aus dem Anfang des 14. Jahrhunderts: Cod. 173 d. Diözesanbibliothek Köln* (Berlin, 1986)

J.J. Boyce: 'Two Antiphonals of Pisa: their Place in the Carmelite Liturgy', *Manuscripta*, xxxi (1987), 147–65

M. Tarrini and A. de Floriani: 'Codici musicali dei secoli XII–XIII negli archivi e nella Biblioteca civica di Savona', *NA*, new ser., v (1987), 7–34 [discusses a Carthusian gradual and a Franciscan gradual from the 13th century]

E. Foley: 'The "Libri ordinarii": an Introduction', *Ephemerides liturgicae*, cii (1988), 129–37

J.J. Boyce: 'The Medieval Carmelite Office Tradition', *AcM*, lxii (1990), 119–51

C. Steyn: 'Manuscript Grey 7 a 27 in the South African Library, Cape Town: the Identity of a Liturgical Book', *South African Journal of Musicology*, xi (1991), 107–25 [study of a 13th-century Premonstratensian gradual, kyriale, sacramentary and calendar from Roggenburg in the Augsburg diocese]

C. Veroli: 'La revisione musicale bernardina e il graduale cisterciense', *Analecta cisterciensia*, xlvii (1991), 3–141; xlviii (1992), 3–104; xlix (1993), 147–256

M. Bezuidenhout: 'The Old and New Historical Views of Gregorian Chant: Papal and Franciscan Plainchant in Thirteenth-Century Rome', *IMSCR XV: Madrid 1992* [*RdMc*, xvi (1993)], 883–900

G. Dubois: 'Liturgie cistercienne', *Bulletin de littérature ecclésiastique*, xciii (1992), 71–84

C. Dumont and M. Coune: 'L'hymne *Dulcis Iesu memoria*: le jubilus serait-il d'Aelred de Rievaulx?', *Collectanea cisterciensia*, lv (1993), 233–42

M. Fassler: *Gothic Song: Victorine Sequences and Augustinian Reform in Twelfth-Century Paris* (Cambridge, 1993)

W.D. Jordan: 'An Introductory Description and Commentary Concerning the Identification of Four Twelfth Century Musico-Liturgical Manuscripts from the Cistercian Monastery of Las Huelgas, Burgos', *Cîteaux*, xliv (1993), 152–236

L. Prensa: 'Hacia una recuperación de la liturgia de la Orden del Santo Sepulcro', *Nassarre: revista aragonesa de musicología*, ix (1993), 181–210

R. Steiner: 'Marian Antiphons at Cluny and Lewes', *Music in the Medieval English Liturgy*, ed. S. Rankin and D. Hiley (Oxford, 1993), 175–204

J.J. Boyce: 'From Rule to Rubric: the Impact of Carmelite Liturgical Legislation upon the Order's Office Tradition', *Ephemerides liturgicae*, cviii (1994), 262–98

C. Veroli: 'La revisione cisterciense del canto liturgico; un compromesso tra rinnovamento e conservazione', *Rivista internazionale di musica sacra*, xv (1994), 88–155

R: CHANT DIALECTS, REGIONAL VARIANTS, INSTITUTIONS, PERSONALITIES

A. Schubiger: *Die Sängerschule St. Gallens von achten bis zwölften Jahrhundert* (Einsiedeln and New York, 1858/R)

O. Marxer: *Zur spätmittelalterlichen Choralgeschichte St. Gallens: der Codex 546 der St. Galler Stiftsbibliothek* (St Gallen, 1908)

R. van Doren: *Etude sur l'influence musicale de l'abbaye de Saint-Gall (VIIIe au XIe siècle* (Brussels, 1925)

H. Anglès: *La música a Catalunya fins al segle XIII* (Barcelona, 1935/R)

S. Corbin: *Essai sur la musique religieuse portugaise au Moyen-Age 1100–1385* (Paris, 1952)

G. Benoît-Castelli and M. Huglo: 'L'origine bretonne du graduel no.47 de la bibliothèque de Chartres', *EG*, i (1954), 173–8

J. Gajard: 'Les récitations modales des 3e et 4e modes et les manuscrits bénéventains et aquitains', *EG*, i (1954), 9–45

Y. Delaporte: 'Fulbert de Chartres et l'école chartraine de chant liturgique au XIe siècle', *EG*, ii (1957), 51–81

J. Chailley: *L'école musicale de Saint Martial de Limoges jusqu'à la fin du XIe siècle* (Paris, 1960)

H. Husmann: 'Studien zur geschichtlichen Stellung der Liturgie Kopenhagens (unter Zugrundelegung des Missale von 1510)', *DAM*, ii (1962), 3–58

P. Dronke, ed.: 'Hildegard of Bingen as Poetess and Dramatist', *Poetic Individuality in the Middle Ages: New Departures in Poetry, 1000–1150* (Oxford, 1970), 150–92

G. Ropa: 'Liturgia, cultura e tradizione in Padania nei secoli XI–XIII', *Quadrivium*, xiii (1972), 17–176

K. Schlager: 'Über den Choralgesang in Mainz', *Archiv für mittelrheinische Kirchengeschichte*, xxvii (1975), 19–26

W. Lipphardt: 'Musik in den österreichischen Klöstern der Babenbergerzeit', *Musicologica austriaca*, ii (1979), 48–68

R.-J. Hesbert: 'Les antiphonaires monastiques insulaires', *Revue bénédictine*, xcii (1982), 358–75

M. Huglo: 'La tradition musicale aquitaine: répertoire et notation', *Liturgie et musique (IX–XIV s.)*, Cahiers de Fanjeaux, xvii (Toulouse, 1982), 253–68

A. Tomasello: *Music and Ritual at Papal Avignon, 1309–1403* (Ann Arbor, 1983)

J. Oberhuber: *Kirchenmusikalische Praxis in Südtirol* (Innsbruck, 1984)

N. Sandon, ed.: *The Use of Salisbury* (Moreton Hampstead, 1984–)

Musica e liturgia nella cultura mediterranea: Venice 1985

D. Hiley: 'Thurston of Caen and Plainchant at Glastonbury: Musicological Reflections on the Norman Conquest', *Proceedings of the British Academy*, lxxii (1986), 57–90

M. Huglo: 'L'antiphonaire: archétype ou répertoire originel?', *Grégoire le Grand: Chantilly 1982*, ed. J. Fontaine, R. Gillet and S. Pellistrandi (Paris, 1986), 661–9

K. Ottosen: *L'antiphonaire latin au Moyen-Age: réorganisation des séries de répons de l'Avent classés par R.-J. Hesbert* (Rome, 1986)

S. Engels: 'Einige Beobachtungen zur Liturgie und den liturgischen Gesängen im mittelalterlichen Salzburg', *Musicologica austriaca*, vii (1987), 37–57

IMSCR XIV: Bologna 1987, i [incl. M. Huglo: 'L'enseignement de la musique dans les universités médiévales', 30–37]; ii [incl. P. Besutti: 'Testi e melodie per la liturgia della Capella di Santa Barbara in Mantova', 68–77; E. Lagnier: 'Il rito e il canto della Valle d'Aosta', 114–19; G. Mele: 'Primo sondaggio sulle fonti liturgiche musicali della Sardegna', 114–19; G. Pressacco: 'La tradizione liturgico-musicale di Aquileia', 119–29; C. Ruini: 'Caratteri peculiari del canto liturgico a Reggio Emilia?', 130–49; D. Hiley: 'The Chant of Norman Sicily: Interaction between the Norman and Italian Traditions', 379–91]; iii [incl. A.W. Robertson: 'The Transmission of Music and Liturgy from Saint-Denis to Saint-Corneille of Compiègne', 505–14]

H. Möller: 'Zur Reichenauer Offiziumstradition der Jahrtausendwende', *SM*, xxix (1987), 35–61

D. Hiley: 'The Chant of Norman Sicily: Interaction Between the Norman and Italian Traditions', *SM*, xxx (1988), 379–9

D. Hiley: 'Editing the Winchester Sequence Repertory of ca. 1000', *Cantus planus III: Tihány 1988*, 99–113.

A. Hughes: 'Antiphons and Acclamations: the Politics of Music in the Coronation Service of Edward II, 1308', *JM*, vi (1988), 150–68

E. Lipsmeier: 'The *Liber Ordinarius* by Konrad von Mure and Palm Sunday Observance in Thirteenth Century Zurich', *Manuscripta*, xxxii (1988), 139–45

J. Morawski: 'Recherches sur les variantes régionales dans le chant grégorien', *SM*, xxx (1988), 403–14

B. Newman: *Saint Hildegard of Bingen: 'Symphonia': a Critical Edition of the 'Symphonia armonie celestium revelationum' (Symphony of the Harmony of Celestial Revelations), with Introduction, Translations, and Commentary* (Ithaca, NY, 1988)

P. Ullmann: 'Die Offiziumstrukturen in der Fastenzeit und die Bestimmung von Diözesanriten', *Cantus planus III: Tihány 1988*, 21–31

I. Woods: 'The Scottish Medieval Church: Sources and Information', *Medieval Studies: Skara 1988*, 107–16

D. Hiley: 'Rouen, Bibliotheque Municipale, MS 249 (A. 280) and the Early Paris Repertory of Ordinary of Mass Chants and Sequences', *ML*, lxx (1989), 467–82

R. Termolen: *Hildegard von Bingen: Biographie* (Augsburg, 1989)

C.M. Wright: *Music and Ceremony at Notre Dame of Paris, 500–1550* (Cambridge, 1989), csp. 3–139

J.A. Barbosa: 'A musica na liturgia bracarense nos seculos XII e XIII: o repertorio musical da missa nos fragmentos de codices do Arquivo Distrital de Braga', *Modus*, iii (1989–92), 81–260 and 11 pls

R. Cogan: 'Hildegard's Fractal Antiphon', *Sonus*, xi (1990), 1–19

S. Flanagan: 'Hildegard and the Global Possibilities of Music', *Sonus*, xi (1990), 20–32

M. Floyd: 'Processional Chants in English Monastic Sources', *JPMMS*, xiii (1990), 1–48

X. Frisque: 'Un reflet de l'école liégeoise de chant grégorien à travers les manuscrits de l'ancienne collégiale Sainte-Croix à Liège', *Bulletin de la Société liégeoise de musicologie*, lxviii (1990), 1–30

J.M. Llorens: 'Prestancia del canto gregoriano en la Capilla palatina de los papas', *De musica hispana et aliis: miscelánea en honor al Prof. Dr. José López-Calo*, ed. E. Casares and C. Villanueva (Santiago de Compostela, 1990), 145–61

M.R. Pfau: 'Mode and Melody Types in Hildegard von Bingen's *Symphonia*', *Sonus*, xi (1990), 53–71

M.T. Levy: *Migration of the Liturgy of the Divine Office of the Roman Rite into Portugal Using as Example Codex 4* of Arouca* (North Sydney, 1991)

P. van Poucke, ed.: *Hildegard of Bingen: 'Symphonia harmoniae caelestium revelationum': Dendermonde, St.-Pieters & Paulusabdij, ms. Cod. 9* (Peer, 1991) [facs. edn]

F.K. Prassl: 'Choral in Kärntner Quellen: Beobachtungen zur Überlieferung von Messgesängen in zwei Missalien des 12. Jahrhunderts', *Musicologica austriaca*, x (1991), 53–102

A.W. Robertson: *The Service-Books of the Royal Abbey of Saint-Denis: Images of Ritual and Music in the Middle Ages* (Oxford, 1991)

R.A. Baltzer: 'The Geography of the Liturgy at Notre-Dame of Paris', *Plainsong in the Age of Polyphony*, ed. T.F. Kelly (Cambridge, 1992), 45–64

A.E. Davidson, ed.: *The 'Ordo virtutum' of Hildegard of Bingen* (Kalamazoo, MI, 1992)

I. Fenlon: 'Patronage, Music and Liturgy in Renaissance Mantua', *Plainsong in the Age of Polyphony*, ed. T.F. Kelly (Cambridge, 1992), 209–35

S. Rankin: 'Notker und Tuotilo: schöpferische Gestalter in einer neuen Zeit', *Schweizer Jb für Musikwissenschaft*, new ser., xi (1992), 17–42

B. Haggh: 'Reconstructing the Plainchant Repertory of Brussels and its Chronology', *Musicology and Archival Research: Brussels 1993*, 177–212

K. Ottosen: *The Responsories and Versicles of the Latin Office of the Dead* (Århus, 1993)

S. Rankin and D. Hiley, eds.: *Music in the Medieval English Liturgy* (Oxford, 1993) [incl. M. Huglo: 'Remarks on the Alleluia and Responsory Series in the Winchester Troper', 47–58; D. Hiley: 'Post-Pentecost Alleluias in Medieval British Liturgies', 145–74

K. Schlager: 'Hildegard von Bingen im Spiegel der Choralforschung: Ruckschau und Ausblick', *Recherches nouvelles sur les tropes liturgiques: recueil d'études*[Huglo Fs], ed. W. Arlt and G. Björkvall (Stockholm, 1993), 309–23

R. Sherr: 'Music and the Renaissance Papacy: the Papal Choir and the Fondo Cappella Sistina', *Rome Reborn: the Vatican Library and Renaissance Culture*, ed. A. Grafton (Washington DC, 1993), 199–223

D. Hiley: 'Chant Composition at Canterbury after the Norman Conquest', *Max Lütolf zum 60. Geburtstag: Festschrift*, ed. B. Hangartner and U. Fischer (Basel, 1994), 31–46

B. Scharf: 'Le origini della monodia sacra in volgare in Francia e in Germania', *Rivista internazionale di musica sacra*, xv (1994), 18–70

B. Haggh: 'The Late-Medieval Liturgical Books of Cambrai Cathedral: a Brief Survey of the Evidence', *Laborare fratres in unum: Festschrift László Dobszay zum 60. Geburtstag*, ed. J. Szendrei and D. Hiley (Hildesheim, 1995), 79–85

J.M.H. Smith: 'A Hagiographer at Work: Hucbald and the Library of Saint-Amand', *Revue bénédictine*, cvi (1996), 151–71

R. Le Roux: 'Les répons de Noël et son octave', *EG*, xxv (1997), 13–36

S: SCANDINAVIA AND CENTRAL EUROPE
Scandinavia

G. Reiss: *Musiken ved den middelalderlige Olavsdyrkelse i Norden* (Christiania, 1912)

A. Maliniemi: *Zur Überlieferung der lateinischen Olavus-Legende* (Helsinki, 1920)

T. Haapanen: *Verzeichnis der mittelalterlichen Handschriftenfragmente in der Universitätsbibliothek zu Helsingfors* (Helsinki, 1922–32) [concerns missals, graduals, lectionaries and breviaries]

T. Haapanen: *Die Neumenfragmente der Universitätsbibliothek Helsingfors: eine Studie zur ältesten nordischen Musikgeschichte* (Helsinki, 1924)

C.-A. Moberg: *Über die schwedischen Sequenzen: eine musikgeschichtliche Studie* (Uppsala, 1927)

C.-A. Moberg: 'Kleine Bemerkungen zum Codex Upsal. C. 23', *STMf*, xi (1930), 37–52

T. Schmid: 'Franziskanische Elemente im mittelalterlichen Kult Schwedens', *Franziskanische Studien*, xxiv (1937), 59–86

B. Dickins: 'The Cult of S. Olave in the British Isles', *Saga-Book of the Viking Society for Northern Research*, xii/2 (1940), 53–80

E. Sandvik: '*Lux illuxit letabunda*', *Symbolae osloenses*, xxi (1941), 117–22

B. Stromberg, ed.: *Missale lundense av år 1514* (Malmö, 1946) [facs.]

T. Schmid: 'Svenska sekvenser', *Fornvännen*, xlix (1954), 211–24

H. Johansson: *Den medeltida liturgien i Skara stift* (Lund, 1956)

S. Helander: *Ordinarius Lincopensis ca. 1400 och dess liturgiska förebilder* (Lund, 1957)

R.A. Ottósson, ed.: *Sancti Thorlaci episcopi officia rhythmica et proprium missae in AM 241 A folio* (Copenhagen, 1959)

T. Schmid, ed.: *Graduale arosiense impressum* (Malmö, 1959–65)

C.G. Undhagen, ed.: *Birger Gregerssons Birgitta-officium* (Uppsala, 1960)

L. Gjerløw: '*Adoratio crucis*: the Regularis concordia and the Decreta Lanfranci: Manuscript Studies in the Early Medieval Church of Norway' (Oslo, 1961)

N.L. Wallin: 'Hymnus in honorem sancti Magni comitis Orchadiae: Codex Upsaliensis C. 233', *STMf*, xliii (1961), 339–54

H. Faehn, ed.: *Manuale norvegicum* (Oslo, 1962)

Breviaria ad usum ritu[m]q[ue] sacros[an]cte[m] nidrosien[sis] eccl[es]ie (Oslo, 1964) [facs. edn of *Breviarium nidrosiense* (Paris, 1519)]

A. Önnerfors: 'Zur Offiziendichtung im schwedischen Mittelalter mit einer Edition des Birger Gregersson zugeschriebenen "Officium S. Botuida"', *Mittellateinisches Jb*, iii (1966), 55–93

E. Eggen: *The Sequences of the Archbishopric of Nidaros* (Copenhagen, 1968)

L. Gjerløw, ed.: *Ordo nidrosiensis ecclesiae (ordubók)* (Oslo, 1968)

L. Gjerløw: 'Votive Masses Found in Oslo', *Ephemerides liturgicae*, lxxxiv (1970), 113–28

F. Birkeli: 'The Earliest Missionary Activities from England to Norway', *Nottingham Mediaeval Studies*, xv (1971), 27–37

J. Bergsagel: 'Anglo-Scandinavian Musical Relations before 1700', *IMSCR XI: Copenhagen 1972*, 263–70

I. Milveden: 'Neue Funde zur Brynolphus-Kritik', *STMf*, liv (1972), 5–51

T. Lundén, ed.: *Officium parvum beate Marie Virginis: Vår Frus tidegärd/Den heliga Birgitta och den helige Petrus av Skänninge* (Stockholm, 1976) [Brigittine breviary]

L. Gjerløw, ed.: *Antiphonarium nidrosiensis ecclesiae* (Oslo, 1979)

L. Gjerløw, ed.: *Liturgica islandica* (Copenhagen, 1980)

B. Asketorp: 'The Musical Contents of Two Danish Pontificals from the Late Middle Ages', *JPMMS*, vii (1984), 28–46

K. Falconer: 'A Kyrie and Three Gloria Tropes in a Norwegian Manuscript Fragment', *STMf*, lxvii (1985), 77–88

A.E. Davidson, ed.: *Holy Week and Easter Ceremonies and Dramas from Medieval Sweden*, (Kalamazoo, MI, 1990)

V. Servatius: *Cantus sororum: Musik- und liturgiegeschichtliche Studien zu den Antiphonen des birgittinischen Eigenrepertoires* (Uppsala, 1990)

C.-A. Moberg and A.-M. Nilsson: *Die liturgischen Hymnen in Schweden, II* (Uppsala, 1991)

N.H. Petersen: 'Another *Visitatio sepulchri* from Scandinavia', *Early Drama, Art, and Music Review*, xiv (1991–2), 10–21

I. Taitto, ed.: *Documenta gregoriana: latinalasien kirkkolaulun lähteitä Suomessa* [Source documents of Latin church music in Finland] (Helsinki, 1992)

G. Attinger: *A Comparative Study of Chant Melodies from Fragments of the Lost Nidaros Antiphoner* (diss., U. of Oslo, 1998)

Central Europe

D. Orel, V. Hornof and V. Vosyka: *Český Kancionál* [A Czech hymnbook] (Prague, 1921, 5/1936)

D. Orel: *Kancionál Franusův z roku* [The Franus hymnbook from 1505] (Prague, 1922)

J. Hutter: *Česká notace* [Czech notation], ii: *Nota choralis* (Prague, 1930)

J. Hutter: *Notationis bohemicae antiquae specimina selecta e codicibus bohemicis, II: Nota choralis* (Prague, 1931)

D. Orel: *Hudební prvky svatováclavske* [St Wenceslas elements in music] (Prague, 1937–9)

B. Rajeczky and P. Radó, eds.: *Melodiarum hungariae medii aevi*, i: *Hymnen und Sequenzen/Himnuszok és sequentiák* (Budapest, 1956, 2/1982)

K. Gamber: 'Das Glagolitische Sakramentar der Slavenapostel Cyrill und Method und seine lateinische Vorlage', *Ostkirchliche Studien*, vi (1957), 165–7

P. Spunar: 'Das Troparium des Prager Dekans Vit (Prag Kapitelbibliothek, Cim 4)', *Scriptorium*, ix (1957), 50–62

C. Kniewald: 'Officium et Missa de Conceptione et Nativitate BMV secundum consuetudinem veterem Zagrabiensem', *Ephemerides liturgicae*, lxxiii (1959), 3–21

A. Vidakovič: 'I nuovi confini della scrittura neumatica musicale nell'Europa sud-est', *SMw*, xxiv (1960), 5–12

G. Birkner: 'Eine "Sequentia sancti Johannis confessoris" in Trogir (Dalmatien)', *Musik des Ostens*, ii (1963), 91–7

Z. Falvy and L. Mezey, eds.: *Codex albensis: ein Antiphonar aus dem 12. Jahrhundert* (Graz, 1963) [facs. edn]

K. Szigeti: 'Denkmäler des gregorianischen Chorals aus dem ungarischen Mittelalter, *SM*, iv (1963), 129–72

H. Kowalewica, ed.: *Cantica medii aevi polono-latina*, i: *Sequentiae* (Warsaw, 1964)

H. Feicht: 'Muzyka liturgiczna w polskim ś'redniowieczu' [Liturgical music in the Polish Middle Ages], *Musica medii aevi*, i (1965), 9–52

Z. Hudovský: 'Missale beneventanum MR 166 della Biblioteca metropolitana a Zagrabia', *Jucunda laudatio*, iii (1965), 306

H. Feicht, ed.: *Muzyka staropolska/Old Polish Music* (Kraków, 1966)

K. Biegański: 'Fragment jednego z najstarszych zabytków diastematycznych w Polsce (dodatek do ms. 149 Bibl. kapit. gnieźnieńskiej – fr. 149)' [A fragment of one of the oldest diastematic sources in Poland (the supplement to Gniezno, Bibl. kapit., MS 149, frag.149)], *Studia Hieronymo Feicht septuagenario dedicata*, ed. Z. Lissa (Kraków, 1967), 96–119

J. Höfler: 'Rekonstrukcija srednjeveškega sekvenciarija v osrednji Sloveniji' [Reconstruction of the medieval sequencer in central Slovenia], *MZ*, iii (1967), 5–15 [with Eng. summary]

J. Höfler and I. Klemenčič: *Glasbeni rokopisi in tiski na Slovenskem do leta 1800: katalog* [Music MSS and printed music in Slovenia before 1800] (Ljubljana, 1967)

Z. Hudovský: 'Benedictionale MR 89 of the Metropolitan Library in Zagreb', *SM*, ix (1967), 55–75

B. Bujić: 'Zadarski neumatski fragmenti v Oxfordu' [Neumatic fragments of Zadar in Oxford], *MZ*, iv (1968), 28–33

Z. Falvy, ed.: *Drei Reimoffizien aus Ungarn und ihre Musik* (Budapest, 1968)

J. Węcowski: 'Początki chorału benedyktyńskiego w Polsce (968–1150)' [The beginnings of Benedictine chant in Poland], *Musica medii aevi*, ii (1968), 40–51

B. Bartkowski: 'Graduał kaników regularnych z Czerwińska' [The gradual of the canons regular of Czerwińsk], *Musica medii aevi*, iii (1969), 130–51

Z. Bernat: 'Pontyfikał wrocławski z XII wieku jako zabytek muzyczny' [A 12th-century Wroclaw pontifical as a musical source], *Musica medii aevi*, iii (1969), 7–29

H. Feicht: 'An Outline of the History of Polish Religious Music', *Poland's Millennium of Catholicism*, ed. M. Rechowicz (Lublin, 1969), 499–553

E. Hinz: 'Notacja muzyczna graduału Rkp. 118/119 z Biblioteki Seminarium Duchownego w Pelplinie' [The musical notation of the gradual MS 118–19 from the Seminary Library at Pelplin], *Musica medii aevi*, iii (1969), 43–58

H. Kowalewicz and J. Pikulik: 'Najstarsza sekwencja o św. Wojciechu: *Annua recolamus*' [The oldest sequence of St Adalbert: *Annua recolamus*], *Musica medii aevi*, iii (1969), 30–42

T. Maciejewski: 'Kyriale cysterskie w najstarszych rękopisach polskich (XIII i XIV wiek)' [The Cistercian kyriale in the oldest Polish manuscripts, 13th and 14th century], *Musica medii aevi*, iii (1969), 59–89

J. Pikulik: 'Sekwencje Notkera Balbulusa w polskich rękopisach muzycznych' [The sequences of Notker Balbulus in Polish musical MSS], *Archiwa, biblioteki i muzea kościelne*, xviii (1969), 65–80

W. Schenk: 'Aus der Geschichte der Liturgie in Polen', *Poland's Millennium of Catholicism*, ed. M. Rechowicz (Lublin, 1969, 2/1987), 145–221

M. Grgić: 'Glazbena djelatnost u Hrvatskoj u 11. stoljeću' [Musical activity in Croatia in the 11th century], *Zadarska revija*, xix (1970), 125–32

D. Patier: 'Un office rythmique tchèque du XIVème siècle: étude comparative avec quelques offices hongrois', *SM*, xii (1970), 41–129 [Procopius]

K. Biegański and J. Woronczak, eds.: *Missale plenarium: Bibl. capit. gnesnensis, MS. 149*, AMP, xi–xii (1970–72) [facs.]

Z. Hudovský: 'Neumatski rukopis *Agenda pontificalis* MR 165 Metropolitanske knjizince u Zagrebu' [The MS *Agenda pontificalis* with neumes, MR 165 of the Zagreb Metropolitan Library], *Arti musices: musikološki zbornik*, ii (1971), 17–30

J. Pikulik: 'Franciszkańskie *Ordinarium missae* w średniowiecznej Polsce' [The Franciscan Mass Ordinary in medieval Poland], *Studia theologica varsaviensia*, ix (1971), 111–30

J. Pikulik: 'Polskie oficja rymowane o św. Wojciechu' [The Polish rhymed Offices for St Adalbert], *Stan badán nad muzyka religijną w kulturze polskiej: Warsaw 1971*, 306–72 [also in Fr.]

J. Morawski, ed.: *Średniowiecze/The Middle Ages*, MAP, i/1–2 (1972)

V. Plocek: 'Eine neu aufgefundene Sequenz von der heiligen Dorothea und ihre Beziehung zu Jenštejns *Decet huius*', *De musica disputationes pragenses*, i (1972), 120–48

J. Szendrei: 'Die Tedeum-Melodie im Kodex Peer', *SM*, xiv (1972), 169–201

B. Bartkowski: '*Visitatio sepulchri* w polskich przekazach średniowiecznych', [*Visitatio sepulchri* in Polish medieval MSS], *Musica medii aevi*, iv (1973), 129–63

T. Maciejewski: 'Graduał z Chełmna' [The Chełmno Gradual], *Musica medii aevi*, iv (1973), 164–245

J. Morawski: *Polska liryka muzyczna w średniowieczu: repertuar sekwencyjny cystersów (XIII–XVI w.)* [Polish musical lyric in the Middle Ages: the Cistercians' sequence repertory (13th–16th centuries)] (Warsaw, 1973),

J. Pikulik: *Sekwencje polskie*, Musica medii aevi, iv (1973); v (1976) [whole issues]

V. Plocek: *Catalogus codicum notis musicis instructorum qui in Bibliotheca publica rei publicae bohemicae socialisticae in Bibliotheca universitatis Pragensis servantur* (Prague, 1973) [describes 243 MS sources with musical notation in CZ-Pu]

P. Radó: *Libri liturgici manuscripti bibliothecarum Hungariae et limitropharum regionum* (Budapest, 1973)

J. Szendrei: 'Te deum als ungarischer Volksgesang im Mittelalter', *SM*, xv (1973), 303–34

J. Andreis: *Music in Croatia* (Zagreb, 1974, enlarged 2/1982)

H. Feicht: *Studia nad muzyką polskiego średniowiecza* [Studies in the music of the Polish Middle Ages] (Kraków, 1975)

H. Ostrzolek: 'Spiewy gregorianskie w "Pontificale" biskupów krakowskich z XI-XII w.' [Gregorian chant in the pontifical of the Kraków bishops from the 11th and 12th centuries], *Studia gdanskie*, ii (1976), 185–210

F. Zagiba: *Musikgeschichte Mitteleuropas*, i: *Von den Anfängen bis zum Ende des 10. Jahrhunderts* (Vienna, 1976), esp. 62–106 [incl. extensive bibliography]

K. Dola: 'Liturgia wielkiego tygodnia w katedrze wrocławskiej w XV wieku' [The Holy Week liturgy in Wrocław cathedral in the 15th century], *Studia teologiczno-historyczne śląska opolskiego*, vii (1979) 179–215

J. Pikulik: 'Śpiewy ordinarium *Ungaricum* w polskich rękopisach przedtrydenckich', [*Ungaricum* chants from the Ordinary in pre-Tridentine Polish MSS], *Muzyka*, xxv/3 (1980), 37–52

F. Pokorný: 'Mährens Musik im Mittelalter', *Hudební veda* (1980), no.1, 36–52

J. Martinić: *Glagolitische Gesänge Mitteldalmatiens* (Regensburg, 1981)

J. Szendrei: *A magyar középkor hangjegyes forrásai* [Notated manuscripts in medieval Hungary] (Budapest, 1981) [with a catalogue of 1098 facs.]

J. Szendrei and R. Rybarič, eds.: *Missale notatum strigoniense ante 1341 in Posonio*, (Budapest, 1982) [facs. edn and critical study]

J. Snoj: 'Fragmenti srednjeveških koralnih rokopisov v ljubljanski Semeniški knjižnici', [Frags. of medieval chant MSS in the Ljubljana Seminary Library], *MZ*, xix (1983), 5–16

J. Szendrei: *Középkori hangjegyírások magyarországon* [Medieval notation in Hungary] (Budapest, 1983) [with Ger. summary]

Nové poznatky o dějinách staršš české a slovenské hudby: Prague 1984 [with Ger. summaries; 22 articles on Bohemian music and Czech-texted Gregorian chant of the 16th-century]

L. Dobszay: 'The System of the Hungarian Plainsong Sources', *SM*, xxvii (1985), 37–65

V. Plocek and A. Traub: *Zwei Studien zur ältesten geistlichen Musik in Böhmen* (Cologne and Giessen, 1985)

B. Rajeczky: 'Gregorianische Gesänge in der ungarischen Volkstradition', *SM*, xxvii (1985), 5–22

P. Ullmann: 'Bericht über die vergleichende Repertoire-Analyse der Brevaire aus Ungarn', *SM*, xxvii (1985), 185–92

R.F. Gyug: 'Tropes and Prosulas in Dalmatian Sources of the Twelfth and Thirteenth Centuries', *La tradizione dei tropi liturgici: Paris 1985 and Perugia 1987*, 409–38

J. Pikulik: 'Les tropes du kyrie et du sanctus dans les graduels polonais médiévaux', ibid., 325–35

W. Domanski: 'Der accentus des gregorianischen Gesangs im Musiktraktat *De accentuum ecclesiasticorum exquisita ratione* von Georg Liban aus Liegnitz/Legnica', *Musik des Ostens*, x (1986), 9–18

W. Domanski: 'Teoria muzyki w traktatach chorało-wych Sebastiana z Felsztyn' [Theory of music in the plainsong treatises of Sebastian of Feleztyna], *Musica medii aevi*, vii (1986) 184–249

T. Miazga: *Wielkanocne śpiewy procesyjne* [Polish Easter processional chants] (Graz, 1986)

D. Patier: 'L'office rythmique de sainte Ludmila', *EG*, xxi (1986) 49–96

A. Reginek: 'Śpiewy pasji chorałowej w Polsce w XV i XVI wieku' [The plainsong Passion chant in Poland in the 15th and 16th centuries], *Musica medii aevi*, vii (1986), 55–116

E. Witkowska-Zaremba: '*Ars musica' w krakowskich traktatach muzycznych XVI wieku*[The ars musica in Kraków plainchant treatises of the 16th century] (Kraków, 1986)

Z. Falvy: 'Middle-East European Court Music (11–16th Centuries): a Preliminary Survey', *SM*, xxix (1987), 63–105

I. Babioch: 'Liber generationis w polskich zródłach Średniowiecznych' [The Liber generationis in Polish medieval sources], *Muzyka*, xxxiii/1 (1987), 3–30

Cantus planus III: Tihány 1988 [incl. J. Mezei: 'Zur Problematik des "germanischen" Choraldialekts', 49–60; K. Schlager: 'Beobachtungen zum Otto-Offizium', 115–25; P. Halász: 'Offices of the Magdalene in Central Europe', 127–42; L. Dobszay: 'Experiences in the Musical Classification of Antiphons', 143–56; A.-M. Nilsson: 'A Hymn in *Historie* of Swedish Saints', 165–80; J. Török: 'Officium rhythmicum des Sancto Paulo', 267–74; J. Szendrei: 'Tropenbestand der ungarischen Handschriften', 297–325; C.E. Brewer: '*Regina celi letare … Alle-Domine*: from Medieval Trope to Renaissance Tune', 431–48]

M. Demović: 'Neumatski fragment dubrovačkog beneventanskog pontifikala' [A neumatic fragment of the Dubrovnik Beneventan pontifical], *Rad Jugoslavenske akademije znanosti i umjetnosti*, cccix (1988), 225–53

I. Ferenczi, ed.: *Graduale ecclesiae hungaricae epperiensis 1635* (Budapest, 1988)

M.L. Göllner: 'Migrant Tropes in the Late Middle Ages', *Capella antiqua München: Festschrift zum 25jährigen Bestehen*, ed. T. Drescher (Tutzing, 1988), 175–87

Medieval Studies: Skara 1988 [incl: A.-M. Nilsson and M. Hedlund: 'Some Music Manuscripts from Medieval Sweden', 17–30; A.-M. Nilsson and J. Ling: 'The Medieval Music of the Monastery, the Cathedral, the Palace and the Pauper's Dwelling', 37–56; V. Servatius: 'Some Remarks on Rhythmical Interpretation of *Missale scarense*', 57–66; A.-M. Nilsson: '*Adest dies leticie*: Studies on Hymn Melodies in Medieval Sweden', 67–85; I. Woods: 'The Scottish Medieval Church: Sources and Information', 107–16]

J. Mezei: 'Közép-európai dallamvariánsok az adventi responzóriumokban' [Melodic variants of the Advent responsories in Central Europe], *Zenetudományi dolgozatok*, (1988), 43–60

J. Morawski: 'Recherches sur les variantes régionales dans le chant grégorien', *SM*, xxx (1988), 403–14

I. Pawlak: *Graduały piotrkowskie jako przekaz chorału gregoriańskiego w Polsce po Soborze Trydenckim* [The Piotrków graduals as transmitters of Gregorian chant in Poland after the Council of Trent] (Lublin, 1988)

R. Rybaric: 'Die Musik im Krönungsritual der Königen von Ungarn', *Musica antiqua VIII: Bydgoszcz 1988*, 877–8

J. Szendrei: 'Choralnotationen in Mitteleuropa', *SM*, xxx (1988), 437–46

J. Szendrei: 'Die Geschichte der Graner Choralnotation', *SM*, xxx (1988), 5–234

P. Ullmann 'Inhalt und Redaktionweisen im Adventsteil der Graner Offiziumsquellen', *SM*, xxx (1988) 447–54

I. Ferenczi: 'Die ungarische Gregorianik im 16. und 17. Jahrhundert', *JbLH*, xxxii (1989), 158–65

J. Snoj: 'Fragmenti srednjeveških koralnih rokopisov s poznogotsko notacijo v Ljubljani', [Frags. of medieval chant MSS in late gothic notation in Ljubljana], *MZ*, xxv (1989), 143–60

Cantus planus IV: Pécs 1990 [incl. J. Szendrei: 'Linienschriften des zwölften Jahrhunderts auf suddeutschem Gebiet', 17–30; C.E. Brewer: 'The Mensural Significance of Bohemian Chant Notation and its Origins', 55–68; E. Witkowska-Zaremba: 'Music between *Quadrivium* and *Ars canendi: musica speculativa* by Johannes de Muris and its Reception in Central and East-Central Europe', 119–26; J. Novotná: 'Die Offertorienverse mit Tropen im Repertoire des Prager Metropolitankapitels', 455–62; H. Vlhová: 'Das Repertorium der Sequenzen in Böhmen bis 1400', 463–8; A.-M. Nilsson: 'The Liturgical Hymns in Sweden: an Edition', 485–502; D. Eben: 'Die Bedeutung des Arnestus von Pardubitz in der Entwicklung des Prager Offiziums', 571–7; I. Ferenczi: 'Das Psalterium strigoniense (1515) als eine Quelle der ungarischsprachigen Graduale', 579–85]

L. Dobszay: 'Plainchant in Medieval Hungary', *JPMMS*, xiii (1990), 49–78 [with extensive bibliography on Hung. chant]

R.F. Gyug, ed.: *Missale ragusinum: the Missal of Dubrovnik (Oxford, Bodleian Library, Canon. Liturg. 342) with an Introductory Study* (Toronto, 1990)

D.R. Holeton: 'The Office of Jan Hus: an Unrecorded Antiphonary in the Metropolitican Library of Estergom', *Time and Community: in Honor of Thomas J. Talley*, ed. J.N. Alexander (Washington DC, 1990), 137–52

J. Szendrei, ed.: *Graduale strigoniense (s. XV/XVI)* (Budapest, 1990–93)

G. Doliner: 'Traditional Church Singing in Kraljevica (Croatia): the Work of Lujza Kozinović', *World of Music*, xxxiii/2 (1991), 50–62

W. Gončarowa: 'Do zagadnienia lokalnych tradycji w chorale (na podstawie wybranych rękopisów Średniowiecznych z Leningradu) [The problem of local tradition in plainchant (on the basis of selected medieval MSS from Leningrad)]', *Muzyka*, xxxvi/1 (1991), 3–43

H. Kowalewicz, J. Morawski and A. Reginek, eds.: *Hymny polskie*, Musica medii aevi, viii (1991) [whole issue, incl. edn of Polish hymns, pp.7–141; and the hymn repertory of the Kraków diocese, pp.142–392 and 43 pls]

D.R. Holeton: 'Two Hussite Latin Antiphonaries', *Ephemerides liturgicae*, cvi (1992), 75–80

R.S. Miller: *The Repertory of MS MR 8: a Medieval Pauline Antiphoner* (diss., U. of California, Santa Barbara, 1992)

J. Morawski: 'Versiculus: z badań nad recytatywem liturgicznym w Polsce'[The versiculus: research into liturgical recitative in Poland], *Muzyka*, xxxvii/4 (1992), 3–59

H. Vlhová: 'Die Ordinarium-Tropen im Troparium des Prager Dekans Vit', *Cantus Planus V: Éger 1993*, 763–79

L. Dobszay: 'Local Compositions in the Office Temporale', *Max Lütolf zum 60. Geburtstag: Festschrift*, ed. B. Hangartner and U. Fischer (Basel, 1994), 65–74

J. Snoj: 'Aleluje velikonocnega casa v ljubljanskih srednjeveskih rokopisih' [Alleluias of Paschal Time in the medieval MSS of Ljubljana], *MZ*, xxx (1994), 19–37

Z.V. David: 'The Strange Fate of Czech Utraquism: the Second Century, 1517–1621', *Journal of Ecclesiatical History*, xlvi (1995), 641–8

D.R. Holeton: 'The Evolution of Utraquist Liturgy: a Precursor of Western Liturgical Reform', *Studia liturgica*, xxv (1995), 1–31

Z. Czagány, ed.: *Corpus Antiphonalium Officii – Ecclesiarium Centralis Europae, III/A: Praha (Temporale)* (Budapest, 1996) [pubn derived from CAO–ECE database]

T.M.M. Czepiel: *Music at the Royal Court and Chapel in Poland, c. 1543–1600* (New York and London, 1996), esp. chap.2

Z. Czagány: 'Egy 13. századi graduále két töredéke' [Two frags. of a 13th-century gradual], *Magyar könyvszemle*, cxii (1996), 145–55 [*H-Bn* E 76, frag. containing an early 13th-century ex. of Graner (Hung.) notation]

H. Vlhová: 'Die Fronleichnamsmesse in Böhmen: ein Beitrag zur spätmittelalterichen Choraltradition', *Schweizer Jb für Musikwissenschaft*, new ser., xvi (1996), 13–36 [concerns, in part, the Hussite liturgy]

T: LATIN AMERICA

L.M. Spell: 'The First Music-Books Printed in America', *MQ*, xv (1929), 50–54

A.B. McGill: 'Old Mission Music', *MQ*, xxiv (1938), 186–93

O.F. da Silva, ed.: *Mission Music of California: a Collection of Old California Mission Hymns and Masses* (Los Angeles, 1941/R)

J.B. Rael: 'New Mexican Spanish Feasts', *California Folklore Quarterly*, i (1942), 83–90

G. Chase: *A Guide to Latin American Music* (Washington DC, 1945, enlarged 2/1962/R as *A Guide to the Music of Latin America*)

R. Stevenson: *Music in Mexico: a Historical Survey* (New York, 1952/R)

R. Stevenson: 'Sixteenth- and Eighteenth-Century Resources in Mexico, pts I–III', *FAM*, i (1954), 69–78; ii (1955), 10–15; xxv (1978), 156–87

R. Stevenson: *The Music of Peru: Aboriginal and Viceroyal Epochs* (Washington DC, 1960), 56–112

R. Stevenson: 'A Newly Discovered Mexican Sixteenth-Century Musical Imprint', *Yearbook, Inter-American Institute for Musical Research*, ii (1966), 91–100

R. Stevenson: 'Latin America, Music in', *New Catholic Encyclopedia*, viii (New York, 1967)

N.A. Benson: 'Music in the California Missions: 1602–1848', *Student Musicologists at Minnesota*, iii (1968–9), 128–67; (1969–70), 104–25

L.B. Spiess and E.T. Stanford: *An Introduction to Certain Mexican Musical Archives* (Detroit, 1969)

R. Stevenson: *Renaissance and Baroque Musical Sources in the Americas* (Washington DC, 1970)

M.D. Ray and J.H. Engbeck: *Gloria Dei: the Story of California Mission Music* (Sacramento, CA, 1974)

M. Crouch and W.J. Summers: 'An Annotated Bibliography and Commentary Concerning Mission Music of Alta California, 1769–1836', *CMc*, no.22 (1976), 88–99

W.J. Summers: 'Spanish Music in California, 1769–1840: a Reassessment', *IMSCR XII: Berkeley 1977*, 360–80

R.M. Gormley: *The Liturgical Music of the California Missions, 1769–1833*, (diss., Catholic U. of America, Washington DC, 1992)

A.E. Lemmon: 'Toward an International Inventory of Colonial Spanish American Cathedral Music Archives', *IMSCR XV: Madrid 1992* [*RdMc*, xvi (1993)], 92–8

L. Waisman: 'Viva Maria! La música para la Virgen en las misiones de Chiquitos', *LAMR*, xiii (1992), 213–25

J. Koegel: 'Spanish Mission Music from California: Past, Present, and Future Research', *American Music Research Center Journal*, iii (1993), 78–111 [with an extensive bibliography]

U: FROM THE COUNCIL OF TRENT TO THE PRESENT

MGG2 ('Caecilianismus'; W. Kirsch)

G. Nivers: *Dissertation sur le chant grégorien* (Paris, 1683)

G. Nivers: *Méthode certaine pour apprendre le plein-chant de l'église* (Paris, 1699, 3/1745)

J. Lebeuf: *Traité historique et pratique sur le chant ecclésiastique* (Paris, 1741/R)

L. Poisson: *Nouvelle méthode, ou Traité théorique et pratique du plain-chant* (Paris, 1745)

F. de La Feillée: *Méthode nouvelle pour apprendre parfaitement les règles du plain-chant et de la psalmodie* (Poitiers, 1748, 4/1784)

Abbé Oudoux: *Méthode nouvelle pour apprendre facilement le plain-chant* (Paris, 1772, 2/1776)

Imbert: *Nouvelle méthode, ou Principes raisonnés du plain-chant* (Paris, 1780)

A. Choron: *Considérations sur la nécessité de rétablir le chant de l'église de Rome dans toutes les églises de l'Empire français* (Paris, 1811)

J.B. Schiedermayr: *Theoretisch-praktische Chorallehre zum Gebrauche beym katholischen Kirchen-Ritus* (Linz, 1828)

J. Antony: *Archäologisch-liturgisches Lehrbuch des gregorianischen Kirchengesangs* (Münster, 1829)

P. Alfieri: *Saggio storico teorico pratico del canto gregoriano o romano per istruzione degli ecclesiastici* (Rome, 1835)

P. Guéranger: *Institutions liturgiques* (Paris, 1840–51, 2/1878–85)

S. Stehlin: *Tonarten des Choralgesanges, nach alten Urkunden durch beigefügte Übersetzungen in Figuralnoten erklärt* (Vienna, 1842)

F. Danjou: *De l'état et de l'avenir du chant ecclésiastique en France* (Paris, 1844)

E. Duval: *L'organiste grégorien, ou Accompagnement d'orgue d'après les vrais principes du chant grégorien* (Mechelen, 1845)

N.A. Janssen: *Les vrais principes du chant grégorien* (Mechelen, 1845)

S. Morelot: 'Du vandalisme musical dans les églises', *Revue de la musique religieuse, populaire et classique* (1845), 129

P.B. de Jumilhac: *La science et la pratique du plain-chant, où tout ce qui appartient à la pratique est établi par les principes de la science* (Paris, 2/1847)

L. Lambillotte: *Antiphonaire de Saint Grégoire: facsimilé du manuscrit de Saint-Gall* (Brussels, 1851, 2/1867)

N. Cloet: *De la restauration du chant liturgique, ou Ce qui est à faire pour arriver à posséder le meilleur chant romain possible* (Plancy, 1852)

C.-E.-H. de Coussemaker: *Histoire de l'harmonie au Moyen-Age* (Paris, 1852/R)

F. Raillard: *Explication des neumes ou anciens signes de notation musicale pour servir à la restauration complète du chant grégorien* (Paris, 1852)

A. de La Fage: *De la reproduction des livres de plain-chant romain* (Paris, 1853)

J. d'Ortigue: *Dictionnaire liturgique, historique et théorique de plain-chant et de musique d'église* (Paris, 1853/R)

J. Tardif: 'Essai sur les neumes', *Bibliothèque de l'Ecole des Chartes*, 3rd ser., iv (1853), 4–28

E.-G. Jouve: *Du chant liturgique, état actuel de la question: quelle serait la meilleure manière de la résoudre?* (Avignon, 1854)

P.C.C. Bogaerts and E. Duval: *Etudes sur les livres choraux qui ont servi de base dans la publication des livres de chant grégorien édités à Malines* (Mechelen, 1855)

A. de La Fage: *Cours complet de plain-chant, ou Nouveau traité méthodique et raisonné du chant liturgique de l'église latine* (Paris, 1855)

E.-G. Jouve: *Dictionnaire d'esthétique chrétienne, ou Théorie du beau dans l'art chrétien, l'architecture, la musique, la peinture, la sculpture et leurs dérivés* (Paris, 1856)

T. Nisard [Normand]: *Etudes sur la restauration du chant grégorien au XIXe siècle* (Rennes, 1856)

P. Alfieri: *Prodromo sulla restaurazione de' libri di canto ecclesiastico detto gregoriano* (Rome, 1857)

J. Dufour: *Mémoire sur les chants liturgiques restaurés par le R. P. Lambillotte* (Paris, 1857)

L. Niedermeyer and J. d'Ortigue: *Traité théorique et pratique de l'accompagnement du plain-chant* (Paris, 1857, 2/1878; Eng trans, 1905)

T. Nisard [Normand]: *Du rythme dans le plain-chant* (Rennes, 1857)

C.J. Vervoitte: 'Considérations sur le chant ecclésiastique à propos du retour à la liturgie romaine', *Précis analytique des travaux de l'Académie impériale des sciences, belles-lettres et arts de Rouen* (1857), 406–55

A. de La Fage: *Routine pour accompagner le plain-chant* (Paris, 1858)

A.M. Gontier: *Méthode raisonnée de plain-chant: le plain-chant considéré dans son rythme, sa tonalité et ses modes* (Paris, 1859)

F. Clément: *Histoire générale de la musique religieuse* (Paris, 1860)

E.-G. Jouve: *Du mouvement liturgique en France durant le XIXe siècle* (Paris, 1860)

F. Raillard: *Mémoire sur la restauration du chant grégorien* (Paris, 1862)

J. Pothier: *Les mélodies grégoriennes d'après la tradition* (Tournai, 1880/R)

P. Schmetz: *Dom Pothiers Liber gradualis, Tournayer Ausgabe: seine historische und praktische Bedeutung* (Mainz, 1884)

P. Schmetz: *Die Harmonisierung des gregorianischen Choralgesanges: ein Handbuch zur Erlernung der Choralbegleitung* (Düsseldorf, 1885, 2/1894)

T. Nisard [Normand]: *L'archéologie musicale et le vrai chant grégorien: ouvrage posthume publié par les soins de M. Aloys Kunc* (Paris, 1890)

Schmidt: 'La typographie et le plain-chant', *Revue du chant grégorien*, iv (1895–6), 36–9, 59–62

F. Mantel: 'M. Danjou et le manuscrit bilingue de Montpellier', *Revue du chant grégorien*, v (1896–7), 10–13, 30–32, 61–2, 90–93

R. Molitor: *Die nach-tridentinische Choral-Reform zu Rom: ein Beitrag zur Musikgeschichte des XVI. und XVII. Jahrhunderts* (Leipzig, 1901–2/R)

Concilium Tridentinum: diariorum, actorum, epistolarum, tractatuum nova collectio (Freiburg, 1901–38/R)

A. Dechevrens: *Les vraies mélodies grégoriennes* (Paris, 1902/R)

F.X. Haberl: 'Geschichte und Wert der offiziellen Choralbücher', *KJb*, xxvii (1902), 134–92

A. Grospellier: 'Bibliographie grégorienne: les éditions du kyriale ou de l'ordinaire de la messe', *Revue du chant grégorien*, xiv (1905–06), 73–83, 115–19

H. Bewerunge: 'The Vatican Edition of Plain-Chant', *Irish Ecclesiastical Record*, 4th ser., xix (1906), 44–63; xx (1906), 414–28; repr. in *Caecilia* [New York], lxxxvi (1959), 44

T. Burge: 'The Vatican Edition of the "Kyriale" and its Critics', *Irish Ecclesiastical Record*, 4th ser., xix (1906), 324–45; repr. in *Caecilia* [New York], lxxxvi (1959), 324

L. David: 'L'édition vaticane du graduel romain', *Revue du chant grégorien*, xvi (1907–8), 125–30

A. Grospellier: 'Le graduel romain de l'édition vaticane', ibid., 115–25

A. Mocquereau: *Le nombre musical grégorienne, ou Rhythmique grégorienne*, i (Tournai, 1908; Eng trans., 1932); ii (Tournai, 1927)

G. Molitor: *Die diatonisch-rhythmische Harmonisation der gregorianischen Choralmelodien* (Leipzig, 1913)

A. Gastoué: 'Les livres de plain-chant en France, de 1583 à 1634', *Tribune de Saint-Gervais*, xx/1 (1914), 1–4; xx/2 (1914), 29–33

K. Weinmann: *Das Konzil von Trient und die Kirchenmusik* (Leipzig, 1919/R)

J.H. Arnold: *Plainsong Accompaniment* (London, 1927, 2/1964)

H. Potiron: *Cours d'accompagnement du chant grégorien* (Paris, 1928; Eng. trans., 1933)

A.L. Mayer: 'Liturgie, Aufklärung, und Klassizismus', *Jb für Liturgiewissenschaft*, ix (1929), 67–127

A.L. Mayer: 'Liturgie, Romantik, und Restauration', *Jb für Liturgiewissenschaft*, x (1930), 77–141

L. Söhner: *Die Geschichte der Begleitung des gregorianischen Chorals in Deutschland vornehmlich im 18. Jahrhundert* (Augsburg, 1931)

F. Peeters: *Practische methode voor gregoriaansche begleiding/Méthodie pratique pour l'accompagnement du chant grégorien* (Mechelen, 1943)

H. Jedin: 'Das Konzil von Trient und die Reform der liturgischen Bücher', *Ephemerides liturgicae*, lix (1945), 5–37

O. Rousseau: *Histoire du mouvement liturgique: esquisse historique depuis le début du XIXe siècle jusqu'au pontificat de Pie X* (Paris, 1945)

J.V. Higginson: *Revival of Gregorian Chant: its Influence on English Hymnody* (New York, 1949)

J. Gajard: *La méthode de Solesmes, ses principes constitutifs, ses règles pratiques d'interprétation* (Tournai, 1951)

C.E. Pocknee: *The French Diocesan Hymns and their Melodies* (London, 1954)

K.G. Fellerer: 'Zur Choralbewegung im 19. Jahrhundert', *KJb*, xli (1957), 136–46

P. Kirchhoffer: 'Exercices progressifs préparatoires à l'accompagnement du chant grégorien', *Revue grégorienne*, xxxix (1960), 174–241

K.G. Fellerer: 'Der semifigurato-Vortrag der Hymnen und Sequenzen im 18. Jahrhundert', *STMf*, xliii (1961), 135–43

J. Prim: '*Chant sur le Livre* in French Churches in the 18th Century', *JAMS*, xiv (1961), 37–49

U. Bomm: 'Von Sinne und Wert der Editio vaticana', *Musicus – Magister: Festgabe für Theobald Schrems zur Vollendung des 70. Lebensjahres*, ed. G.P. Köllner (Regensburg, 1963), 63–75

K.G. Fellerer: 'Gregorianischer Choral und Orgelspiel im 18. Jahrhundert', *Organicae voces: Festschrift Joseph Smits van Waesberghe*, ed. P. Fischer (Amsterdam, 1963), 31–7

J. Pruett: 'The Breviary Reform of 1632: its Effect on the Hymns', *Caecilia* [New York], xc (1963), 23

H. Beck: 'Das Konzil von Trient und die Probleme der Kirchenmusik', *KJb*, xlviii (1964), 108–17

H. Wagener: *Die Begleitung des gregorianischen Chorals im neunzehnten Jahrhundert* (Regensburg, 1964)

A. Milner: 'Music in a Vernacular Catholic Liturgy', *PRMA*, xci (1964–5), 21–32

Die Kirchenmusik und das II. Vatikanische Konzil: Graz 1964 (Graz, 1965)

E. Keller: *Die Konstanzer Liturgiereform unter Ignaz Heinrich von Wessenberg* (Freiburg, 1965)

F. Grasemann: 'Die Franziskanermesse des 17. und 18. Jahrhundert', *SMw*, xxvii (1966), 72–124

'Die Kirchenmusik nach dem II. vatikanischen Konzil', *ÖMz*, xxi (1966), 665–719 [special issue]

C.S. Phillips: *The Church in France 1789–1848: a Study in Revival* (New York, 1966)

Sacred Music and Liturgy Reform after Vatican II: Chicago-Milwaukee 1966

K.G. Fellerer: 'Zur Melodik der Officiums-Psalmen im 19. Jahrhundert', *Essays in Musicology: a Birthday Offering for Willi Apel*, ed. H. Tischler (Bloomington, IN, 1968), 19–24

P. Combe: *Histoire de la restauration du chant grégorien d'après des documents inédits: Solesmes et l'édition vaticane* (Solesmes 1969)

K.G. Fellerer: 'Melchior Hittorps *De divinis officiis*, Köln 1568 als kirchenmusikalische Quelle', *Musa – mens – musici: im Gedenken an Walther Vetter* (Leipzig, 1969), 45–50

V. Vajta: 'Worship in a Secularized Age', *Studia liturgica*, vii (1970), 72–95

L. Soltner: 'Les anciens Bénédictins français et la restauration de Solesmes par Dom Guéranger', *Revue Mabillon*, nos.240–62 (1970–75), 401–41

M. Pfaff: 'Die liturgische Einstimmigkeit in ihren Editionen nach 1600', *Musikalische Edition im Wandel des historischen Bewusstseins*, ed. T.G. Georgiades (Kassel, 1971), 50–61

H. Wagener: 'Zur Choralbegleitung im 19./20. Jahrhundert', *KJb*, lv (1971) 61–78

K.G. Fellerer: 'Zu Choralpflege und Chorallehre im 17./18 Jahrhundert', *KJb*, lvi (1972), 51–72

J. Schuh: *Johann Michael Sailer und die Erneuerung der Kirchenmusik: zur Vorgeschichte der cäcilianischen Reformbewegung in der ersten Hälfte des 19. Jahrhunderts* (diss., U. of Cologne, 1972)

K.G. Fellerer: 'Zur kirchlichen Monodie nach dem Tridentium', *KJb*, lvii (1973), 45–55

W. Pruitt: 'Bibliographies des oeuvres de Guillaume Gabriel Nivers', *RMFC*, xiii (1973), 133–56 [a list of Niver's edns of Gregorian chant, plainchant compositions and books on Gregorian chant]

J. Angerer: *Die liturgisch-musikalische Erneuerung der Melker Reform: Studien zur Erforschung der Musikpraxis in den Benediktinerklöstern des 15 Jh.* (Vienna, 1974)

G. Bereths: *Beiträge zur Geschichte der Trierer Dommusik* (Mainz, 1974)

C. Brinkmann: *Albert Gereon Stein (1808–1881): Kirchenmusik und Musikerziehung* (Cologne, 1974)

P. Harnoncourt: 'Katholische Kirchenmusik vom Cäcilianismus bis zur Gegenwart', *Traditionen und Reformen in der Kirchenmusik: Festschrift für Konrad Ameln*, ed. G. Schuhmacher (Kassel, 1974), 78–133

B. Van Wye: 'Gregorian Influences in French Organ Music before the *Motu proprio*', *JAMS*, xxvii (1974), 1–24

L. Comes: *La melodia palestriniana e il canto gregoriano* (Venice, 1974–5)

K.G. Fellerer: 'Zur Choral-Restauration in Frankreich um die Mitte des 19. Jahrhunderts', *KJb*, lviii–ix (1974–5), 135–47

T. Bailey: 'The Intervention of Scholarship in Gregorian Chant', *Journal of the Canadian Association of University Schools of Music*, v (1975), 1–9

G. Stefani: *Musica e religione nell'Italia barocca* (Palermo, 1975)

M.-N. Colette: *Le répertoire des rogations d'après un processionnal de Poitiers (XVIème siècle)* (Paris, 1976)

F.A. Stein, ed: *Sacerdos et cantus gregoriani magister: Festschrift Ferdinand Haberl* (Regensburg, 1977) [articles generally concerning 19th-century chant, incl. H. Beck: 'Aufgaben für die Musikwissenschaft bei der Erforschung des Cäcilianismus', 51–9; A. Scharnagl: 'Franz Xaver Haberl (1840–1910): Musiker und Musikforscher', 233–45]

G.M. Steinschulte: *Die Ward-Bewegung: Studien zur Realisierung der Kirchenmusikreform Papst Pius X. in der ersten Hälfte des 20. Jahrhunderts* (Regensburg, 1979)

J. Claire: 'Dom André Mocquereau: cinquante ans après sa mort', *EG*, xix (1980), 3–23

W. Hillsman: 'Instrumental Accompaniment of Plain-Chant in France from the Late 18th Century', *GSJ*, xxxiii (1980), 8–16

D. Launay: 'Un esprit critique au temps de Jumilhac: Dom Jacques Le Clerc, bénédictin de la congrégation de Saint Maur', *EG*, xix (1980), 197–219

F. Brovelli: 'Per uno studio de l'*Année liturgique* di P. Guéranger: contributo alla storia nel movimento liturgico', *Ephemerides liturgicae*, xcv (1981), 145–219

A. Scharnagl: 'Regensburger Notendrucker und Musikverlage', *Festgabe Hans Schneider*, ed. H. Leuchtmann (Tutzing, 1981), 99–116

E.J. Traversaro: 'Un manuale di cantus firmus in un manoscritto della Biblioteca civica Berio', *Berio*, xxi/2 (1981), 5–21

K.G. Fellerer: 'Kirchenmusikalische Reformbestrebungen um 1800', *AnMc*, no.21 (1982), 393–409

E. Weber: *Le Concile de Trente et la musique: de la Réforme à la Contre-réforme* (Paris, 1982)

J. Roche: 'Musica diversa di Compietà: Compline and its Music in Seventeenth-Century Italy', *PRMA*, cix (1982–3), 60–79

A. Bugnini: *La riforma liturgica, 1948–1975* (Rome, 1983; Eng. trans., 1990)

E. Moneta Caglio: 'Il movimento Ceciliano e la musica corale da chiesa', *Marco Enrico Bossi e il movimento ceciliano: Como 1983* [*Rivista internazionale di musica sacra*, v/3–4 (1984)], 273–97

H. Hucke: 'Das Dekret *Docta sanctorum patrum* Papst Johannes XXII', *MD*, xxxviii (1984), 119–31

C. Johnson: *Prosper Guéranger (1805–1875): a Liturgical Theologian: an Introduction to his Liturgical Writings and Work* (Rome, 1984)

J. Roche: *North Italian Church Music in the Age of Monteverdi* (Oxford, 1984), esp. chaps.1–3

Der Caecilianismus: Eichstätt 1985 [incl. H. Unverricht: 'Die Choralreformbemühungen unter den Caecilanern', 109–23]

J. da Costa Rodrigues: 'Les répercussions humanistes sur le plain-chant, I', *Chant choral*, xlvii (1985), 273–97

D. Nicholson: *Liturgical Music in Benedictine Monasticism: a Post-Vatican II Survey*, i: *The Monasteries of Monks* (Mount Angel Abbey, OR, 1986)

J. Gaudemet and others: *Administration et église: du concordat a la séparation de l'église et de l'état* (Geneva, 1987)

T. Minagawa: 'Oratio christianorum occultorum in Japonia (16th Cent.)', *IMSCR XIV: Bologna 1987*, iii, 39–43

E. Cardine: 'La notation du chant grégorien aux XVIIe–XIXe siècles', *AnM*, xliii (1988), 9–33

C. Lickleder: *Choral und figurierte Kirchenmusik in der Sicht Franz Xaver Witts anhand der 'Fliegenden Blätter' und der 'Musica Sacra'* (Regensburg, 1988)

C. Lickleder: 'Franz Xaver Witts reformatorischer Ansatz', *Musik in Bayern*, xxxvii (1988), 69–92

H. Schröder: 'Anmerkungen zur Geschichte und zum Funktionswandel katholischer Kirchenmusik im dritten Reich', *KJb*, lxxii (1988), 137–65

H.E. Smither: 'The Function of Music in the Forty Hours Devotion of 17th- and 18th-Century Italy', *Music from the Middle Ages through the Twentieth Century: Essays in Honor of Gwynn McPeek*, ed. C.P. Comberiati and M.C. Steel (New York, 1988), 149–74

G.M. Steinschulte: 'Ecriture oder *Nombre musical*?: zur Kommunikationspotenz des gregorianischen Chorals jenseits von Notation und Text', *Die Sprache der Musik: Festschrift Klaus Wolfgang Niemöller zum 60. Geburtstag*, ed. J.P. Fricke and others (Regensburg, 1989), 527–42

J.A. Svoboda: 'In psalmum *Venite* antiphonae seu invitatoria breviarii Vitoniani (1777) et breviarii Maurini (1787)', *Ephemerides liturgicae*, ciii (1989), 462–500

T. Bailey: 'Word-Painting and the Romantic Interpretation of Chant', *Beyond the Moon: Festschrift Luther Dittmer*, ed. B. Gillingham and P. Merkley (Ottawa, 1990), 1–15

B.E. Ford: 'Charles Winfred Douglas and Adaption of Plainsong to English Words in the United States', *The Hymnal: 1982 Companion*, ed. R.F. Glover (New York, 1990), 194–214

R.A. Weaver: 'Plainchant Adaption in England', ibid., 177–93

H. White and N. Lawrence: 'Towards a History of the Cecilian Movement in Ireland: an Assessment of the Writings of Heinrich Bewerunge (1862–1923), with a Catalogue of his Publications and Manuscripts', *Music and the Church*, ed. G. Gillen and H. White (Dublin, 1990), 78–107

V. Donella: 'La musica sacro-liturgica negli insegnamenti di Paolo VI e di Giovanni Paolo II', *Rivista internazionale di musica sacra*, xii (1991), 42–62 [with references to legislative decrees regarding chant, 1963–85]

I. Fernández de la Cuesta: 'La restauración del canto gregoriano en la España del siglo XIX', *RdMc*, xiv (1991), 481–8

J. Harper: *The Forms and Orders of Western Liturgy from the Tenth to the Eighteenth Century: an Historical Introduction and Guide for Students and Musicians* (Oxford, 1991), 166–87 [esp. chap.11: 'The Reformed Liturgy of the Church of England (1549–1662)']

M. Olarte: 'Evolución de la forma lamentación en la música española del siglo XIX', *RdMc*, xiv (1991), 497–9

J. Claire: 'Dom Eugène Cardine (1905–1988)', *Beiträge zur Gregorianik*, xii (1992), 11–26

E. Weber: 'L'intelligibilité du texte dans la crise religieuse et musicale du XVIe siècle: incidences du Concile de Trente', *EG*, xxiv (1992), 195–202

J. Bettley: 'L'ultima hora canonica del giorno: Music for the Office of Compline in Northern Italy in the Second Half of the Sixteenth Century', *ML*, lxxiv (1993), 163–214

K.A. Daly: 'The Irish Society of Saint Cecilia', *Sacred Music*, cxx/2 (1993), 15–25

D. Launay: *La musique religieuse en France du Concile de Trente à 1804* (Paris, 1993)

V.A. Lenti: 'Urban VIII and the Latin Hymnal', *Sacred Music*, cxx/3 (1993), 30–33

H. White and N. Lawrence: 'Towards a History of the Cecilian Movement in Ireland ... the Writings of Heinrich Bewerunge 1862–1923', *Irish Musical Studies*, ii, ed. G. Gillen and H. White (Blackrock, 1993), 78–107

J. Bettley: 'The Office of Holy Week at St Mark's, Venice, in the Late 16th Century, and the Musical Contributions of Giovanni Croce', *EMc*, xxii (1994), 45–60

V. Donella: 'Le vie della musica sacra dopo il Concilio di Trento', *Rivista internazionale di musica sacra*, xv (1994), 299–310

A. Luppi: 'La musica sacra e il valore teologico della musica in G.W. Leibniz', *Rivista internazionale di musica sacra*, xv (1994), 25–52

C.-H. Mahling, ed.: *Studien zur Kirchenmusik im 19. Jahrhundert: Friedrich Wilhelm Riedel zum 60. Geburtstag* (Tutzing, 1994) [10 essays on 19th-century German chant, incl. M. Mathy: 'Aspekte katholischer Kirchen- und Musikgeschichte im 19. Jahrhundert', 1–12; J. Stenzl: 'Zum gregorianischen Choral im 19. Jahrhundert anhand peripherer Quellen', 88–104]

R. Arnold: *The English Hymn: Studies in a Genre* (New York, 1995)

L. Bianchi: *Palestrina nella vita nelle opere nel suo tempo* (Rome, 1995) [incl. 'Il Concilio Trento e Palestrina', 87–142; 'Palestrina e la riforma del canto gregoriano', 163–85]

K.A. Daly: *Catholic Church Music in Ireland, 1878–1903: the Cecilian Reform Movement* (Blackrock, and Portland, OR, 1995)

J.-P. Montagnier: 'Le chant sur le livre au XVIIIe siècle: les traités de Louis-Joseph Marchand et Henry Madin', *RdM*, lxxxi (1995), 37–63 [lists 12 printed theoretical sources and a résumé of rules]

J.-P. Montagnier: 'Les sources manuscrites françaises du *Chant sur le livre* aux XVIIe et XVIIIe siécles', *RBM*, xlix (1995), 79–100

D.D. Opraem: 'Vom Diözesanmessbuch zum Missale Romanum Pius' V (1570)', *Archiv für Liturgiewissenschaft*, xxxvii (1995), 304–46 [concerns published Mass books in southern Germany *c*1570]

R.M. Wilson: *Anglican Chant and Chanting in England, Scotland, and America, 1660–1820* (Oxford, 1996) [incl. extensive bibliography, pp.307–23]

B.M. Zon: 'The Origin of "Adeste fideles"', *EMc*, xxiv (1996), 279–88 [contains a list of 18th-century Eng. plainchant pubns and MSS]

B.M. Zon: 'The Revival of Plainchant in the Roman Catholic Church in Ireland, 1777–1858: Some Sources and their Commerce with England', *Irish Musical Studies*, v, ed. P.F. Devine and H. White (Blackrock, 1996), 251–61

K. Bergeron: *Decadent Enchantments: the Revival of Gregorian Chant at Solesmes* (Berkeley, 1997)

D. Moulinet: 'Un réseau ultramontain en France au milieu du 19e siècle', *Revue d'histoire ecclésiastique*, xcii (1997), 70–125

B. Zon: 'Plainchant in Nineteenth-Century England: a Review of Some Major Publications of the Period', *PMM*, vi (1997), 53–74

B. Zon: *The English Plainchant Revival* (Oxford, 1999)

KENNETH LEVY/R (1), JOHN A. EMERSON (2–11, with JANE BELLINGHAM and DAVID HILEY; 11(iii) with BENNETT ZON)

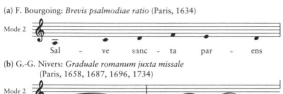

Ex.1 Introit *Salve sancta parens* (transcr. M. Wood)

(a) F. Bourgoing: *Brevis psalmodiae ratio* (Paris, 1634)

(b) G.-G. Nivers: *Graduale romanum juxta missale* (Paris, 1658, 1687, 1696, 1734)

(c) G.-G. Nivers, ed. *Graduale romanum* (Paris, 1697)

Plain-chant musical (Fr.). The reformed or newly composed chant of the 17th to 19th centuries in France, related to the Italian *canto fratto*. The decisive impetus came in the early 1630s from the Oratorians of the rue St Honoré, whose church was designated the royal chapel of the Louvre by Louis XIII, and whose superior conceived the idea of attracting the courtiers by introducing a new kind of chant combining features of the ecclesiastical and modern styles. This initiative resulted in the first collection of such chants – the *Brevis psalmodiae ratio* (Paris, 1634) by François Bourgoing, a member of the Oratory congregation. It was published with an approbation by Mersenne and contains new chants and simplified versions of known melodies; with rare exceptions, all the chants are syllabic. Resembling this work in its simplicity is Nivers' *Graduale romanum juxta missale*, the most extensive collection of *plain-chant musical*, published by Ballard in 1658. Originally intended for use by Benedictine nuns, it was subsequently reprinted several times for Benedictine and Augustinian nuns. Both the gradual and the alleluia for any given liturgical day are composed in the same mode, probably to ease the transition between these two consecutive chants and to impose a general sense of modal and tonal order on the Mass Propers. In 1665 Ballard published a set of *Leçons de Ténèbres en plein-chant musical composé dans le goût de M. Nivers* (Nivers may have coined the term). Four years later, Henry Du Mont brought out *Cinq messes en plain-chant* (Paris, 1669), of which the *Messe royale* kept its popularity throughout France well into the 20th century.

The first theoretical formulations appeared in *L'antiphonaire de Paris* (1681) and in Nivers' *Dissertation sur le chant grégorien* (Paris, 1683), although Nivers' work is more useful for understanding his philosophy of editing traditional melodies (*Graduale romanum*, 1697) than for divining his style of chant composition. Superfluous neumes and note-shapes were eliminated and durations assigned to the remaining ones, false intervals and abuses of prosody, such as neumes on short syllables, were corrected, melismas eliminated, accidentals (including the sharp) introduced, and rules for ornamentation and tempo established; in short, everything possible was done to bring what were understood to be corrupt melodies into conformity with the rules of quantity, pronunciation, expression and good taste. New melodies were freely invented in the same vein. Nivers justified his changes by detailed criticism of traditional melodies, and his attitude was reflected over half a century later in the title of a *Traité critique du plain-chant contenant les principes qui en montrent les défauts et qui peuvent conduire à le rendre meilleur* (Paris, 1749) by Cousin de Contamine.

The opening phrases of two introits, *Salve sancta parens* and *Nos autem*, illustrate some of the more intriguing aspects of *plain-chant musical*. Ex.1a is a simplified version, stripped of all but structural notes, of the more elaborate 'Gregorian' melody in ex.1c; Nivers' version in ex.1b retains much of the Gregorian melody, but a leading note has been added on the second syllable of 'sancta' and there are half the number of notes on the first syllable of 'parens'. In ex.2a occasional structural notes are borrowed from the Gregorian melody in ex.2c, but the complete introit ends on *d'*, thus transforming it into a mode 1 chant; Nivers' version in ex.2b confines itself to mode 4, but it bears little resemblance to the Gregorian melody, and its continuation is replete with raised leading notes and melodic ornaments. Many of Nivers' chants, in fact, are unlike any other known versions. Innovations were to continue into the 18th century, and in later neo-Gallican graduals, for example, both melody and text were abandoned.

The chant was accompanied by the organ in harmony (examples of such accompaniments survive in *F-Pc* Rés.476, *c*1690, printed in *Livre d'orgue attribué à J.N. Geoffroy*, ed. J. Bonfils, Paris, 1974; and *F-V* 1055 (60), compiled by Luc Marchand in 1772) or doubled by the serpent; it served as the melodic basis for organ versets with which it alternated (e.g. *La messe de 2. classe* in *Livre d'orgue de Marguerite Thiery*, ed. J. Bonfils, L'organiste liturgique, xxv, Paris, 1956, based on an original mass by Nivers). Chants were adapted and composed for the principal religious congregations, the tunes varying among places and dioceses. Nivers himself was charged with preparing Office collections for the

Ex.2 Introit *Nos autem gloria* (transcr. M. Wood)

(a) F. Bourgoing: *Brevis psalmodia ratio* (Paris, 1634)

(b) G.-G. Nivers: *Graduale romanum juxta missale* (Paris, 1658, 1687, 1696, 1734)

(c) G.-G. Nivers, ed. *Graduale romanum* (Paris, 1697)

Augustinians, Benedictines, and priests of the communities of St Sulpice and St Cyr. The French chants spread to dioceses in the southern Netherlands and Germany. As its popularity grew in the 18th century, the quality of *plain-chant musical* declined; by 1750 Léonard Poisson was complaining of 'un plain-chant baroque', and even Rousseau (*Dictionnaire*) preferred the traditional kind, in which he detected vestiges of the music of the Greeks. Nevertheless, the *Méthode nouvelle pour apprendre parfaitement les règles du plain-chant* (Poitiers, 1748) by F. de La Feillée went through edition after edition well into the 19th century, inspiring hostile polemics like that of D'Ortigue in his *Dictionnaire* (1853). The circle was closed when the new reformers, the Benedictines of Solesmes, with the zeal of a Viollet-le-Duc, 'gregorianized' original 17th-century chants by undoing the rhythm, removing accidentals and adding melismas.

See also NEO–GALLICAN CHANT and PLAINCHANT, §10(ii).

BIBLIOGRAPHY

FasquelleE ('Plain-chant (mesuré)'; M. Cocheril); *MGG1* ('Choralreform'; K.G. Fellerer)

J. d'Ortigue: *Dictionnaire liturgique, historique et théorique de plainchant et de musique d'église* (Paris, 1853/R)

A. Gastoué: 'Un coin de la musique d'église au XVIIe siècle: le chant des Oratoriens: Louis XIII maître de chapelle', *Variations sur la musique d'église* (Paris, 1912), 62–72

A. Gastoué: 'Le chant des Oratoriens: Louis XII maître de chapelle', *Tribune de Saint-Gervais*, xix (1913), 121–6, 149–54

A. Gastoué: *Musique et liturgie: le graduel et l'antiphonaire romains: histoire et description* (Lyons, 1913/R)

K.G. Fellerer: 'Zur Neukomposition und Vortrag des Gregorianischen Chorals im 18. Jahrhundert', *AcM*, vi (1934), 145–52

C. Pineau: *Le plain-chant musical en France au XVIIe siècle* (n.p., 1955)

C. Pineau: 'A propos d'une messe du quatrième ton d'Henry du Mont', *Musique sacrée*, lxxxi (1963), 51–2

J.-Y. Hameline: 'Les messes de Henry Du Mont', *Henry Du Mont à Versailles* [programme booklet] (Versailles, 1992), 69–82; repr. in *Le concert des muses: promenade musicale dans le baroque français*, ed. J. Lionnet (Paris, 1997), 221–31

D. Launay: *La musique religieuse en France du Concile de Trente à 1804* (Paris, 1993)

J. Duron, ed.: *Plainchant et liturgie en France au XVIIe siècle* (Paris, 1997)

DAVID FULLER/ROBERT GALLAGHER

Plainsong. See PLAINCHANT.

Plainsong and Mediaeval Music Society. English musical society. Its foundation in November 1888 (reported in the *Musical Times*, March 1889) marked an important stage in the revival in England of plainsong as music for use in the Anglican Church. Its declared aims were to form a centre for the dissemination of information, to publish facsimiles and translations of foreign works, and to form a catalogue of all plainsong and measured music in England dating from before the Reformation. H.B. Briggs was honorary secretary until 1901; Anselm Hughes became secretary in 1926, and was until his death in 1974 a leading figure in the society. More recently, the chair has been held by Derek Turner, Frank Llewelyn Harrison, John Stevens, Christopher Page and John Harper.

The society maintained a choir for several decades, but has laid chief stress on the scientific study of plainsong and medieval music. Its numerous publications have been its chief claim to importance. By 1959, when a list was published in Anselm Hughes's book of reminiscences, *Septuagesima*, nearly 70 had appeared. About half were either didactic essays on plainsong, including a translation of the first part of Peter Wagner's *Einführung in die gregorianischen Melodien*, or editions of plainsong with English text for modern use. Facsimiles were notably represented in W.H. Frere's *Graduale Sarisburiense* (1892–4), *Antiphonale Sarisburiense* (1901–24; with an important introduction) and the catalogue *Bibliotheca Musico-Liturgica* (1894–1901). Other early and important publications were *Early English Harmony* by H. Wooldridge and Anselm Hughes, an edition of the Old Hall Manuscript, Hughes's *Worcester Mediaeval Harmony* and Van den Borren's *Polyphonia Sacra*. A scholarly journal has been published annually since 1978, the *Journal of the Plainsong & Mediaeval Music Society*, since 1992 entitled *Plainsong and Medieval Music*.

BIBLIOGRAPHY

A. Hughes: *Septuagesima: Reminiscences of the Plainsong & Mediaeval Music Society, and of other Things, Personal and Musical* (London, 1959)

D. Hiley: 'The Plainsong & Mediaeval Music Society, 1888–1988', *Music in the Medieval English Liturgy: Plainsong & Mediaeval Music Society Centennial Essays*, ed. S. Rankin and D. Hiley (Oxford, 1993), 1–7

DAVID HILEY

Plaint (Fr.). See PLANCTUS.

Plainte [plaint] (Fr.: 'moan', 'groan', 'complaint'). (1) A term used mainly in French music of the 17th and 18th centuries, or in music of that period in the French style, for a slow, expressive piece of lamenting character; unlike the TOMBEAU, however, it was not necessarily associated with death. The most celebrated example is perhaps Froberger's *Plainte faite à Londres pour passer la melancholi* for harpsichord (c1662), which is marked to be played *lentement avec discretion*, i.e. with a sensitive and expressive rubato such as was also appropriate in the *tombeau*. Plaintes occur in J.C.F. Fischer's *Journal du printems* (1695) and *Pièces de clavessin* (1696), both of which are markedly French in style. The plainte in the former (in DDT, x, 1902/R) occurs in the second suite and makes a feature of passages for three solo instruments alternating with full five-part orchestral writing: this almost gives the impression of an operatic scene in which the chorus intensifies the grief expressed by a group of soloists. François Couperin's *Dixième concert* (1724) contains a 'Plainte pour les violes ou autres instrumens' marked *lentement et douloureusement*: its effect is achieved largely through slowly reiterated pedal notes in the bass coupled with a languid melody. Pieces with the title *Les tendres plaintes* occur in Rameau (a rondeau for harpsichord in *Pièces de clavecin*, 1724) and his contemporary J.-B. Dupuits (for hurdy-gurdy and bass). That by Rameau was used again in his *Zoroastre* (1749), where it is intended to convey not the gentle pathos which this and other plaintes perhaps now suggest but something much more positive – the mood of Amélite 'overwhelmed with sadness'. The plaint in Purcell's *The Fairy Queen* (1692), 'O let me ever, ever weep', is introduced by Oberon's words

Sing me the Plaint that did so Nobly move,
When *Laura* Mourn'd for her departed Love.

In its use of a chromatic ground bass it borrows a common feature of the Italian lament. These examples show that the term 'plainte' is associated not with any specific form but rather with pieces employing particular techniques expressing sadness.

(2) Term used to denote particular ornaments; *see* ORNAMENTS, §7.

MICHAEL TILMOUTH (1)

Plaja, Alonso de (*fl* 1500). Spanish composer. Only a single composition, *Regina coeli* (*E-Bo* 5; reproduced in H. Anglès: *La música española desde la edad media hasta nuestros días*, Barcelona, 1941, facs.21), is known. Its style and its appearance in a manuscript containing works by Isaac and Peñalosa, among others, suggest that Plaja was their contemporary. Each phrase opens with imitation, strongly marked rhythmic motifs with syncopations give the piece a popular air. The Kyrie and Gloria on the preceding folios attributed to 'Alonso' may also be by Plaja.

BIBLIOGRAPHY

StevensonSM
E. Ros-Fábregas: *The Manuscript Barcelona, Biblioteca de Catalunya, M.454: Study and Edition in the Context of the Iberian and Continental Manuscript Traditions* (diss., CUNY, 1992), i, 179–85

ISABEL POPE

Plakidis, Pēteris (*b* Riga, 4 March 1947). Latvian composer. He graduated from Valentins Utkins's composition class (1970) at the Latvian State Conservatory and worked as music director for the Latvian National Theatre (1969–74). Since 1974 he has taught composition and theory at the Latvian State Conservatory, where from 1991 he has been a professor. His favourite genre is the concerto for orchestra with solo group, and he has made free use of modernized forms of Baroque music such as the concerto grosso and other forms of instrumental dialogue. Purely musical ideas predominate over extra-musical ones, lending his work a neo-Classical and, in his early period, anti-Romantic disposition. Plakidis's stylistic base expanded in the 1980s, and the logic of Classically rational forms in his works conveniently balances the presentation of diverse musical ideas, Romantic ones included. His solo songs have gained attention for respecting the structure of modern Latvian poetry.

WORKS
(selective list)

Orch: Music for pf, str, timp, 1969; Pf Conc., 1975; Legenda, 1976; Sasauksanās [Calling to Each Other], pic + fl, ob, b cl, hn, orch, 1977; Conc., 2 ob, str, 1982; Conc.-ballade, 2 vn, pf, str; Dziedājums (Canto) [The Singing] (A. Ivaska), 1986; Atskatīsanās [Glance Back], 1990; Conc. da camera, 1992; Intrada, cl, orch, 1992; Vēl viena Vēbera opera [One More Weber Opera], cl, orch, 1993; Variations, orch, 1996

Chbr and solo inst: Improvisācija un burleska [Improvisation and Burlesque], vn, vc, pf, 1966; Prelūdija un pulsācija [Prelude and Pulsation], wind qnt, 1975; Romantiska mūzika [Romantic Music], vn, vc, pf, 1980; Veltījums Haidnam [Dedication to Haydn], fl, vc, pf, 1982; Meditācija [Meditation], hp, 1990; Mazs koncerts [Little conc.], 2 vn, 1991; Night Conversations, cl, pf, 1992

Vocal: Fatamorgāna (cycle, J. Rainis), mixed chorus, 1980; Nolemtība [Destiny] (choral sym., O. Vācietis), unacc. chorus, 1986; Dziesmas vējam un asinīm [Songs for the Wind and the Blood], cycle, Mez, str, 1991; c 10 solo song cycles; cants.; choral songs

Other: film scores; incid music

Principal publishers: Muzīka, Liesma, Sovetskiy Kompozitor, Musica Baltica

BIBLIOGRAPHY

J. Torgāns: 'Par Pēteri Plakidi' [On Pēteris Plakidis], *Latviešu mūzika*, xiii (1978), 68–86

L. Mūrniece, ed.: *Muzīka sovetskoy Latvii* [The music of Soviet Latvia] (Rīga, 1988), 97–102

ARNOLDS KLOTIŅŠ

Plamenac, Dragan (*b* Zagreb, 8 Feb 1895; *d* Ede, the Netherlands, 15 March 1983). American musicologist of Yugoslav origin. He developed an interest in music at an early age but took a degree in law at Zagreb before studying composition with Schreker in Vienna (1912) and Vitězslav Novák in Prague (1919), and musicology with Pirro at the Sorbonne and Adler in Vienna, where he took the doctorate in 1925 with a dissertation on Ockeghem's motets and chansons. At first he worked as a répétiteur and assistant conductor at the Städtische Oper in Berlin (1926–7); he then taught musicology at the University of Zagreb (1928), and became a corresponding member of the Yugoslav Academy of Sciences (1936). In 1939 he went to the USA as the Yugoslav representative to the IMS Congress in New York, and remained there after the outbreak of war. He became an American citizen in 1946. He was professor of music at the University of Illinois (1954–63) and visiting professor of music at the University of Pittsburgh (1964–5) and the University of California, Santa Barbara (1967). He was awarded fellowships by the Guggenheim Foundation and the National Endowment for the Humanities, and also held several offices in the American Musicological Society. He received the honorary doctorate of music from the University of Illinois in 1976.

Plamenac's research and publications centred on music of the 14th to 16th centuries and that of the Adriatic coastal areas in the Renaissance and the early Baroque period. His edition of the works of Ockeghem made possible for the first time a serious evaluation of this composer's position in the development of musical style in the second half of the 15th century; the thoroughness that characterized his work is shown by his continual revisions and enlargements of this edition.

Plamenac's research in the Burgundian chanson repertory is marked by an understanding both of the sources and of the music itself: in particular his important manuscript studies in this field helped to clarify problems about late 15th-century sources. The articles on and the edition of the Faenza Codex provided important insights into the practice of early 15th-century instrumental music.

WRITINGS

Johannes Ockeghem als Motetten- und Chansonkomponist (diss., U. of Vienna, 1925)
'La chanson de L'homme armé et MS.VI.E. 40 de la Bibl. Nationale de Naples', *Fédération archéologique et historique de Belgique: Congrès jubilaire: Bruges 1925*, 229–30
'Autour d'Ockeghem', *ReM*, ix/4–6 (1927–8), 26–47
'Zur "L'homme armé"-Frage', *ZMw*, xi (1928–9), 378–83
'Toma Cecchini, kapelnik stolnih crkava u Splitu i Hvaru u prvoj polovini XVII stoljeća' [Tomaso Cecchini, maestro di cappella of the Split and Hvar cathedrals in the first half of the 17th century], *Rad JAZU*, no.262 (1938), 77–125
'Music in the Adriatic Coastal Areas of the Southern Slavs', *PAMS 1939*, 21–51; abridged and rev. in G. Reese: *Music in the Renaissance* (New York, 1954, 2/1959), 757–62
'An Unknown Violin Tablature of the Early 17th Century', *PAMS 1941*, 144–57
'New Light on the Last Years of Carl Philipp Emanuel Bach', *MQ*, xxxv (1949), 565–87
'A Postscript to Volume II of the *Collected Works* of Johannes Ockeghem', *JAMS*, iii (1950), 33–40
'Keyboard Music of the Fourteenth Century in Codex Faenza 117', *JAMS*, iv (1951), 179–201

'A Reconstruction of the French Chansonnier in the Biblioteca Colombina, Seville', *MQ*, xxxvii (1951), 501–42; xxxviii (1952), 85–117, 245–77

'Deux pièces de la Renaissance française tirées de fonds florentins', *RBM*, vi (1952), 12–23

'New Light on Codex Faenza 117', *IMSCR V: Utrecht 1952*, 310–26

'An Unknown Composition by Dufay?', *MQ*, xl (1954), 190–200; Fr. trans. in *RBM*, viii (1954), 75–83

'The "Second" Chansonnier of the Biblioteca Riccardiana (Codex 2356)', *AnnM*, ii (1954), 105–87; iv (1956), 261–5

'Another Paduan Fragment of Trecento Music', *JAMS*, viii (1955), 165–81

'*Excerpta Colombiniana*: Items of Musical Interest in Fernando Colón's *Regestrum*', *Miscelánea en homenaje a Monseñor Higinio Anglés* (Barcelona, 1958–61), 663–87

'Browsing through a Little-Known Manuscript (Prague, Strahov Monastery, D.G.IV.47)', *JAMS*, xiii (1960), 102–11

'A Note on the Rearrangement of Faenza Codex 117', *JAMS*, xvii (1964), 78–81

'Faventina', *Liber amicorum Charles van den Borren* (Antwerp, 1964), 145–64

'The Two-Part Quodlibets in the Seville Chansonnier', *The Commonwealth of Music, in Honor of Curt Sachs*, ed. G. Reese and R. Brandel (New York, 1965), 163–81

'The Recently Discovered Complete Copy of A. Antico's *Frottole Intabulate* (1517)', *Aspects of Medieval and Renaissance Music: a Birthday Offering to Gustave Reese*, ed. J. LaRue and others (New York, 1966), 683–92

'Tragom Ivana Lukačića i nekih njegovih suvremenika' [On the trail of Lukačić and some of his contemporaries], *Rad JAZU*, no.351 (1969), 63–90

'Rimska opera 17. stoljeća, rodenje Luja XIV i Rafael Levaković' [Roman opera of the 17th century, the birth of Louis XIV and Rafael Levaković], *Arti musices*, iii (1972), 51–62

EDITIONS

Johannes Ockeghem: Sämtliche Werke (Messen I–VIII), Publikationen älterer Musik, Jg.i/2 (Leipzig, 1927); rev. 2/1959 as *Masses I–VIII, Collected Works*, i; *Masses and Mass Sections IX–XVI*, ibid, ii (New York, 1947, 2/1966); *Motets and Chansons* (Philadelphia, 1992) [with R. Wexler]

Ivan Lukačić: Odabrani moteti (Zagreb, 1935)

Facsimile Reproduction of the Manuscripts Sevilla 5-1-43 & Paris N.A.Fr.4379 (Pt. 1), Publications of Mediaeval Musical Manuscripts, viii (Brooklyn, NY, 1962)

Dijon, Bibliothèque publique, manuscrit 517, Publications of Mediaeval Musical Manuscripts, xii (Brooklyn, NY, 1970)

Keyboard Music of the Late Middle Ages in Codex Faenza 117, CMM, lvii (1972)

Julije Skjavetić [Giulio Schiavetto]: Četiri moteta . . . (Venezia, 1564) (Zagreb, 1974)

BIBLIOGRAPHY

G. Reese and R.J. Snow, eds.: *Essays in Musicology in Honor of Dragan Plamenac* (Pittsburgh, 1969) [incl. list of pubns]

K. Kos: 'Dragan Plamenac, istraživač i objavljivač rane glazbe' [Plamenac, rescher and editor of early music], *Arti musices: musikološki zbornik*, xvii (1986), 159–73 [summaries in Eng., Ger.]

C.E. Steinzor: *American Musicologists, c1890–1945: a Bio-Bibliographical Sourcebook to the Formative Period* (New York, 1989), 195–200

TOM R. WARD/R

Planck, Stephan (*b* Passau, *c*1457; *d* Rome, 17 Feb 1501). German printer, active in Italy. He apparently worked with Ulrich Han in Rome; he came into possession of Han's business in 1478, issuing the first of 325 books in 1479 from 'the house of the former Udalricus'. Between 1482 and 1497 he used the earliest Roman plainchant type (that in Han's 1476 *Missale*) for eight music books – five missals (1482, 1488, 1492, 1494, 1496), two pontificals (1485, 1497) and a baptismal (1494). In addition he introduced 12 text types, some as early as 1479; he retained only the music type of his predecessor, adding a few characters of his own. Planck's ability as type designer and cutter, and his skill in setting the type

for complicated melismatic chant, suggests he participated in creating the first music type in Italy.

BIBLIOGRAPHY

DugganIMI

M.K. Duggan: 'A System for Describing Fifteenth-Century Music Type', *Gutenberg-Jb 1984*, 67–76

M.K. DUGGAN

Plancken, Corneille Vander (*b* Brussels, 25 Oct 1772; *d* Brussels, 9 Feb 1849). Belgian violinist, clarinettist and composer. He studied the violin with Eugène Godecharles and Jean Pauwels and was admired as a virtuoso by Viotti, who also became his close friend. From 1797 until about 1817 he was solo violinist of the orchestra at the Grand Théâtre de la Monnaie in Brussels, and in 1820 the king, Willem I of Orange, appointed him first solo violin of the royal chapel, a position he held until the Revolution of 1830. He was also the conductor of the Société du Grand Concerts and the Société Philharmonique, as well as an excellent clarinettist. Known as the founder of the violin school made famous in the 19th century by De Beriot and Vieuxtemps, his pupils included L.-J. Meerts, André Robberechts and J.F. Snel. He composed several violin concertos and a clarinet concerto, none of which has survived.

BIBLIOGRAPHY

EitnerQ; FétisB; VannesD

E.G.J. Gregoir: *Panthéon musical populaire*, iii (Brussels, 1876), 203

GUY BOURLIGUEUX

Planckenmüller, Georg. *See* BLANCKENMÜLLER, GEORG.

Plançon, Jean [Jehan]. *See* PLANSON, JEAN.

Plançon, Pol [Paul-Henri] (*b* Fumay, Ardennes, 12 June 1851; *d* Paris, 11 Aug 1914). French bass. A pupil of Duprez and Sbriglia, he made his début at Lyons in 1877. He first sang at the Paris Opéra in 1883 as Gounod's Méphistophélès, and remained there for ten seasons, taking part in the premières of Massenet's *Le Cid* (Count of Gormas) and Saint-Saëns's for 14 consecutive seasons (1891–1904), singing, besides his French and Italian roles, occasionally in German and even in English (as Friar Francis in the première of Stanford's *Much Ado About Nothing*). In 1893 he appeared for the first time at the Metropolitan Opera, returning as leading bass for 12 of the subsequent seasons there until his farewell to the house in 1908.

Judging by the recordings that survive, Plançon was the most polished singer of his time. His beautiful *basse chantante* had been admirably schooled, and his style was extremely elegant; his many recordings (1902–8) embody standards otherwise outside the experience of a present-day listener. Not only his flawless trills and rapid scales but his cantabile and pure legato, as in 'Voici des roses' (*Faust*) and 'Vi ravviso' (*La sonnambula*), are exemplary.

BIBLIOGRAPHY

J. Dennis: 'Paul Henri Plançon', *Record Collector*, viii (1953), 149–91 [incl. discography and commentary by L. Hevingham-Root]

DESMOND SHAWE-TAYLOR/R

Planctus (Fr. *plaint, complainte*; Ger. *Klage*; It. *pianto, lamento*; Provençal *planh*). A song of lamentation. As a literary and musical genre it was widespread in the Middle Ages, both in Latin and in the vernaculars. There is evidence of the following types of planctus from the 9th century (classification from Dronke, 1970): (*a*) vernacular

Pol Plançon as Méphistophélès in Gounod's 'Faust'

planctus to be sung by women; (*b*) dirges for the dead, especially for royal and heroic personages; (*c*) 'Germanic complaints of exile and voyaging'; (*d*) fictional, as distinct from real-life, planctus on classical or biblical themes. From the 12th century onwards, (*e*) dramatic or semi-dramatic laments of the Virgin Mary and (*f*) *complaintes d'amour* are common.

The earliest planctus for which music survives are in the manuscripts associated with the abbey of ST MARTIAL at Limoges: they include *A solis ortu usque ad occidua* (type *b*) on the death of Charlemagne in 814, written in staffless neumes without mensural indications (*F-Pn* lat.1154; 10th century); and in *F-Pn* lat.1139 (11th–12th centuries) there is a 'Lamentatio Rachelis' (see Cousse-maker), which is a dramatic trope to the liturgical responsory *Sub altare Dei* (type *d*).

Pre-eminent among the 12th-century planctus are six by PETER ABELARD: the principal manuscript for them, *I-Rvat* Reg.lat.288, contains staffless neumes; his poetic subjects are laments of type *d*. Formally his planctus are related to the sequence (see SEQUENCE (i)), two to the 'classical', four to the 'archaic' type. There is a close relation between the earlier planctus and sequences; indeed sequence melodies are sometimes named for planctus. From this relation arises another, between the planctus and the north French LAI of the 12th and 13th centuries: whichever came first, the 'Lai des pucelles' is sung to the same melody as Abelard's 'Planctus virginum Israel'; and the 13th-century (?)English *Samson, dux fortissime*, a dramatic lament with singing roles for Delilah and for a chorus (*GB-Lbl* Harl.978), is both

formally and in melodic idiom related to the lai. (For more details of the planctus–sequence–lai complex, see Spanke, 1931 etc., and Stäblein, 1962.)

The principle of contrafactum, or writing words to a pre-existing melody, extends also to the Provençal planh: the planh is, then, a variety of the sirventes, with topical subject and with borrowed form and melody. The most famous troubadour planh, Gaucelm Faidit's lament on the death of Richard the Lionheart (*d* 1199), is, however, thought to have an original melody. Literary texts in this genre are assembled and classified in Springer (1895); surviving music is available in the standard editions and anthologies (see TROUBADOURS, TROUVÈRES).

The most important type of planctus in the 12th and 13th centuries is the *planctus Beatae Virginis Mariae*; it appears in all European countries (Wechssler, 1893, contains examples in Latin and seven vernaculars, not including English, for which see Taylor, 1906–7). The texts most commonly found are *Planctus ante nescia* and *Flete, fideles animae* (see Young, 1933, i, 496ff). The genre is non-liturgical; but planctus were certainly sung in church. At Palma (Mallorca), perhaps in the 13th century, laments were sung 'by three good singers ('a tribus bonis cantoribus'); later, in about 1440, at least six people took part, and their laments were sung 'before the crucifix set up in the middle of the church' (Donovan, 1958). Whether these ceremonies constituted a 'play' is not certain; but the importance of the planctus in liturgical drama is demonstrated by the centrality of the 'complaints' of the three Marys in plays of the Resurrection (see VISITATIO SEPULCHRI), of the Virgin Mary in the rarer Passion plays, of Rachel in plays of the Holy Innocents, and of Daniel in the Daniel plays. Earlier scholars (Chambers, Young) were inclined to see the origins of the Passion play in the *planctus Mariae*. This view is now questioned; the discovery of the extensive Monte Cassino Passion play from the 12th century with only the briefest planctus (Sticca, 1970) has increased doubt. *See also* MEDIEVAL DRAMA, §§III, 2(i); III, 3(iv).

The Waldensians, a Protestant minority originally from France, developed their own practice of singing *complaintes*, that were narrative songs on Biblical themes (see REFORMED AND PRESBYTERIAN CHURCH MUSIC, § 1, 4(i).

The music of the dramatic or quasi-dramatic planctus was not taken directly from, or composed in imitation of, Gregorian chant. Its emotionalism often contrasts with the restraint of the chant and may derive rather from the *Totenklage* (dirge for the dead) tradition.

The term 'planctus' has also been applied to the emotional utterances typical of domestic laments, where they are often used as choral refrains. *See* LAMENT.

BIBLIOGRAPHY

C.-E.-H. de Coussemaker: *Histoire de l'harmonie au Moyen Age* (Paris, 1852/R)

E. Wechssler: *Die romanischen Marienklagen* (Halle, 1893)

H.W. Springer: *Das altprovenzalische Klagelied mit Berücksichtigung der verwandten Litteratur*, Berliner Beiträge zur germanischen und romanischen Philologie, vii (Berlin, 1895)

E.K. Chambers: *The Mediaeval Stage* (Oxford, 1903/R)

G.C. Taylor: 'The English *Planctus Mariae*', *Modern Philology*, iv (1906–7), 605–37

H. Spanke: 'Über das Fortleben der Sequenzenform in den romanischen Sprachen', *Zeitschrift für romanische Philologie*, li (1931), 309–34

K. Young: *The Drama of the Medieval Church* (Oxford, 1933/R)

H. Spanke: 'Aus der Vorgeschichte und Frühgeschichte der Sequenz', *ZDADL*, lxxi (1934), 1–39

H. Spanke: *Beziehungen zwischen romanischer und mittellateinischer Lyrik mit besonderer Berücksichtigung der Metrik und Musik* (Berlin, 1936/R)

H. Spanke: 'Ein lateinisches Liederbuch des 11. Jahrhunderts', *Studı medievali*, new ser., xv (1942), 111–42

G. Vecchi, ed.: *I 'Planctus' di Pietro Abelardo* (Modena, 1951)

G. Vecchi: 'Il "planctus" di Gudino di Luxeuil: un ambiente scolastico, un ritmo, una melodia', *Quadrivium*, i (1956), 19–40

R.B. Donovan: *The Liturgical Drama in Medieval Spain* (Toronto, 1958)

B. Stäblein: 'Die Schwanenklage: zum Problem Lai-Planctus-Sequenz', *Festschrift Karl Gustav Fellerer zum sechzigsten Gerburstag*, ed. H. Hüschen (Regensburg, 1962), 491–502

H. Wagenaar-Nolthenius: 'Der *Planctus Iudei* und der Gesang jüdischer Märtyrer in Blois anno 1171', *Mélanges offerts à René Crozet*, ed. P. Gallais and Y.-J. Riou (Poitiers, 1966), 881–5

L. Weinrich: '*Dolorum solatium*: Text und Musik von Abaelards Planctus David', *Mittellateinisches Jb*, v (1968), 59–78

L. Weinrich: 'Peter Abaelard as Musician', *MQ*, lv (1969), 295–312, 464–86

P. Dronke: *Poetic Individuality in the Middle Ages: New Departures in Poetry 1000–1150* (Oxford, 1970)

S. Sticca: *The Latin Passion Play: its Origins and Development* (Albany, NY, 1970)

W.L. Smoldon: *The Music of the Medieval Church Dramas* (London, 1980)

S. Sticca: *Il Planctus Mariae nella tradizione drammatica del Medio Evo* (Sulmona, 1984; Eng. trans., 1988)

J. Stevens: *Words and Music in the Middle Ages* (Cambridge, 1986)

R. Crocker and D. Hiley, eds.: *NOHM*, ii: *The Early Middle Ages to 1300* (Oxford, 2/1990)

D. Hiley: *Western Plainchant: a Handbook* (Oxford, 1993)

JOHN STEVENS

Plánický [Planitzky, Planiczky, Planiciczky], **Josef Antonín** [Joseph Anton] (*b* Manětín, Bohemia, 27 Nov 1691, or Pilsen, *c*1690; *d* Freising, Bavaria, 17 Sept 1732). Czech composer. He may be identified with the son Jiří Josef born to Jaroslav Plánický, teacher and organist in Manětín, on 27 November 1691; but in a later document from Countess Maria Gabriela Lažanska (15 October 1720) he is called 'königlicher Kreys-Stadt Pilssen im Königreich Böhmen Patritius'. Countess Lažanska employed him as private tutor for her children and at her small court he met the composers Mauritius Vogt and Gunther Jacob. Probably he was a pupil of Vogt, who was a theorist. With high recommendations from the countess, Plánický travelled in October 1720 in Bohemia, Moravia and Austria. The presence of one of his compositions (a movement from a motet) in Göttweig Abbey suggests that he proceeded from Vienna to Germany, where in 1722 he seems to have been in Freising (now married; he arrived with his brother-in-law, the court musician Ferdinand Notrupp, from Nuremberg). In the same year he applied for a post as tenor in the duke-bishop's musical establishment, and was engaged as both singer and instrumentalist, with the duty of teaching the boys in the seminary. His capabilities must have been considerable as in 1724 he was commissioned to write the opera celebrating a 1000th anniversary (although the establishment included the prominent composer J.J. Pez). The opera, *Zelus divi corbiniani ecclesiae frisingensis fundamentum*, performed on 7 October 1724, is now lost. Apart from documents regarding Plánický's finances nothing further is known of him except the date of his death, and most of his works were lost when the church archive was auctioned in 1803. In his only surviving work, a collection of 12 solo motets, *Opella ecclesiastica seu Ariae duodecim nova idea exornatae* (Augsburg, 1723; ed. in MAB, ii/3 (1968, 2/1988)), he emerges as a composer of considerable dramatic gifts skilled in writing for the voice.

BIBLIOGRAPHY

E. Trolda: 'Josef Ant. Plánický', *Česká hudba*, xx (1913–13), 21–3

K.G. Fellerer: *Beiträge zur Musikgeschichte Freisings* (Freising, 1926)

E. Trolda: 'Josef Antonín Plánický', *Cyril*, lix (1933), 100–13

C. Schoenbaum: *Beiträge zur solistischen katholischen Kirchenmusik des Hochbarocks* (diss., U. of Vienna, 1951)

C. Schoenbaum: 'Die "Opella ecclesiastica" des Josef Antonín Plánický', *AcM*, xxv (1953), 39–79

Z. Pilková: 'Instrumentace kantát autorů z Čech v první polovině 18. stoleti [Instrumentation in sacred Czech cantatas from the first half of the 18th century], *Hudební věda*, xiv/2 (1977), 146–59

CAMILLO SCHOENBAUM

Planquette, (Jean) Robert (*b* Paris, 31 July 1848; *d* Paris, 28 Jan 1903). French composer. He studied briefly at the Paris Conservatoire, gaining a *premier prix* for solfège in 1867 and a *second prix* for piano in 1868; he studied harmony under Duprato. His early works include piano reductions of operas and some songs, among them a set of 12 military songs, *Refrains du régiment*. Planquette sold these outright and thus failed to benefit financially when an instrumental arrangement by François Rauski of one of them, *Le régiment de Sambre-et-Meuse*, became one of France's most popular military marches. For the most part Planquette was forced to make such living as he could from playing the piano and composing songs for *cafés-concerts*. He had great success with a musical monologue, *On demande une femme de chambre*, sung by a leading entertainer of the day, Anna Judic.

His first one-act operettas were performed at the Eldorado music hall and the Délassements-Comiques, and it was while working as a *café-concert* pianist that he had the opportunity to write the operetta that was to bring him fame. *Les cloches de Corneville*, whose book was originally offered to Hervé, had over 400 consecutive performances after being produced at the Folies-Dramatiques in 1877 and reached 1000 performances within a decade. Its 'Legend of the Bells' was especially popular, and its success was repeated abroad, notably in London, bringing Planquette into considerable demand. He was commissioned to write the one-act *Le chevalier Gaston* for the opening of the Monte Carlo Opera House in 1879; while for London he composed *Rip van Winkle* (1882), based on Washington Irving's novel. It has remained his second most popular work and is considered by some to be superior to *Les cloches*, though lacking its melodic quality. For London, too, he wrote *Nell Gwynne* (1884), and adapted *Les voltigeurs de la 32ᶜᵐᵉ* (1880) and *Surcouf* (1887) into *The Old Guard* (1887) and *Paul Jones* (1889) respectively.

The most notable of his later operettas was *Mam'zelle Quat'sous* (1897), but in France his new works after *Les cloches* were less well received and failed to rival the successes of Audran. Planquette was less prolific than other operetta composers of his time, but a more conscientious craftsman. This occasionally results in a lack of spontaneity and a tendency towards stereotyped patterns, but at his best Planquette had an attractive gift for rhythmic élan and melodic refinement. Far from finding the success of *Les cloches* oppressive, he was very fond of Normandy, where it was set. He had a villa, which he called 'Les cloches', built on the Normandy coast at Merville near Cabourg, where he became a municipal councillor. He was also a Chevalier de la Légion d'Honneur.

WORKS
(selective list)

STAGE
*operettas unless otherwise stated; first produced, and vocal scores
published, in Paris unless otherwise stated*

Méfie-toi de Pharaon (1, J. Villemer and L. Delormel), Eldorado, 12
    Oct 1872 (n.d.)
Paille d'avoine (1, A. Jaime, J. Rozale and A. Lemonnier),
    Délassements-Comiques, 12 March 1874 (?1895)
Le serment de Mme Grégoire (1, L.J. Péricaud and Delormel),
    Eldorado, 12 Oct 1874 (n.d.)
Le Zénith (1, A. Perreau), Eldorado, 24 April 1875
Le valet de coeur (saynète, 1, Péricaud and Delormel), Alcazar d'Eté,
    1 Aug 1875 (n.d.)
Le péage (E. André), Théâtre de la Porte Saint Martin, 21 Oct 1876
Les cloches de Corneville (oc, 3, Clairville and C. Gabet), Folies-
    Dramatiques, 19 April 1877 (1877)
Le chevalier Gaston (1, P. Véron), Monte Carlo, Opéra, 3 March
    1879 (1880)
Les voltigeurs de la 32ème (3, E. Gondinet and G. Duval),
    Renaissance, 7 Jan 1880 (1880); rev. as The Old Guard (H.B.
    Farnie), London, Avenue, 26 Oct 1887 (London, 1887)
La cantinière (3, P. Burani and F. Rybère), Nouveautés, 1880 (1881)
Les chevaux légers (1, Péricaud and Delormel), Eldorado, 15 Dec
    1881 (1882)
Rip van Winkle (3, Farnie, after W. Irving), London, Comedy, 14
    Oct 1882 (London, 1882); rev. as Rip! (H. Meilhac and P. Gille),
    Folies-Dramatiques, 11 Nov 1884 (1884)
Nell Gwynne (3, Farnie), London, Avenue, 7 Feb 1884 (London,
    1884); rev. as La princesse Colombine (M. Ordonneau and
    André), Nouveautés, 7 Dec 1886 (1887)
La crémaillère (3, Burani and A. Brasseur), Nouveautés, 28 Nov
    1885 (? only 2 songs pubd, 1886)
Surcouf (prol., 3, Chivot and A. Duru), Folies-Dramatiques, 6 Oct
    1887 (1887); rev. as Paul Jones (Farnie), London, Prince of Wales,
    12 Jan 1889 (London, 1889)
Captain Thérèse (3, G. a'Beckett, A. Bisson and F.C. Burnand),
    London, Prince of Wales, 25 Aug 1890 (London, 1891); Gaîté, 1
    April 1901 (1901)
La cocarde tricolore (3, Ordonneau, after Cogniard brothers), Folies-
    Dramatiques, 12 Feb 1892 (1892)
Le talisman (3, A.P. d'Ennery and Burani), Gaîté, 20 Jan 1893 (1893)
Les vingt-huit jours de Champignolette (Burani), République, 17 Sept
    1895
Panurge (3, Meilhac and A. de Saint-Albin), Gaîté, 22 Nov 1895
    (Paris, 1895)
Mam'zelle Quat'sous (4, A. Mars and M. Desvallières), Gaîté, 5 Nov
    1897 (1897)
Le fiancé de Margot (1, Bisson) (1900)
Le paradis de Mahomet (3, H. Blondeau), Variétés, 15 May 1906
    (1906), completed by L. Ganne

OTHER WORKS

Some dramatic monologues, incl. On demande une femme de
    chambre (Véron) and La confession de Rosette: both 1876 (Paris,
    1878)
Songs, incl. Refrains du régiment (Paris, c1870); dances
Several vocal scores of operas by various composers

BIBLIOGRAPHY
FétisB; GänzlBMT; GänzlEMT
J. Brindejont-Offenbach: 'Cinquante ans de l'opérette française',
    Cinquante ans de musique française, ed. L. Rohozhinsky (Paris,
    1925), 199–232
L'Aubert: 'Audran, Planquette, Varney, etc.', *Le théâtre lyrique en
    France*, ii (Paris, 1937–9), 316–25 [pubd Poste National/Radio
    Paris]
'Histoire de l'opérette française au XIXe siècle', *Le théâtre lyrique en
    France*, ii (Paris, ?1938), 265–325
F. Bruyas: *Histoire de l'opérette en France, 1855–1965* (Lyons, 1974)
R. Traubner: *Operetta: a Theatrical History* (New York, 1983)
See also OPERETTA.
                                            ANDREW LAMB

Planson [Plançon], Jean [Jehan] (*b* ?Paris, *c*1559; *d* after
1611). French composer and organist. On 8 July 1575 he
was appointed organist at the collegiate church of St
Germain-l'Auxerrois, Paris; although Jean Lesecq is
known to have replaced him in the following December,
he was recorded as still holding the post when he won the
harp prize for his five-voice motet *Aspice Domine* and the
triomphe prize for his seven-voice setting of the sonnet
Ha, Dieu que de filetz in the St Cecilia competition at
Evreux in 1578. From 1586 to 1588 he was organist at St
Sauveur, Paris. In 1612 a 'Jehan Pinson' was described as
'marchant bourgeois de Paris et musicien' and about 53
years old.

Planson's prize-winning motet and sonnet were published in his *Quatrains du Sieur de Pybrac, ensemble
quelques sonetz et motetz* (Paris, 1583) for three, four,
five and seven voices; the collection is devoted mainly to
19 settings of Pibrac's moralistic *quatrains*, but also
includes eight sonnets (five to texts by Belleau) and six
motets. Four years later his four-voice *Airs mis en musique
par Jean Planson parisien tant de son invention que
d'autres musitiens* (Paris, 1587; ed. H. Expert and A.
Verchaly, Paris, 1966) appeared; the collection proved so
popular that further editions appeared in 1588, 1593 and
1595. In his dedication to the amateur musician Jean
Louvet, for his 'relaxation and pleasure during these
troubled times', Planson promised a sequel of settings of
more serious texts. Both his collections reflect the influence
of the musicians of the Académie de Poésie et de Musique,
Joachim Thibault de Courville, Beaulieu, Fabrice Marin
Caietain and Le Jeune, but he preferred poems in a
pastoral, folklike vein (such as those by Belleau, La Roque
and Jean Bertaut, the only poet named in the *Airs*)
to the *vers mesurés* of Baïf and his followers. The texts of
32 of the 37 *airs* were published without music at Paris in
1597, and were reprinted several times in the early 17th
century. Although the *airs* were printed in the conventional four partbooks the settings are strictly syllabic and
homophonic, with the melodies (sometimes borrowed
and often folklike) in the top voice. The musical phrases
are short and well-defined, with each line of text marked
off by a bar-line; the poetic metres are often dance-like (a
number have typical branle structure) but of irregular
lengths. Three of the *airs* were set for voice and lute in
Emanuel Adriaenssen's *Novum pratum musicum* (RISM
1592²²) and another for lute solo in Jean-Baptiste Besard's
Thesaurus harmonicus (RISM 1603¹⁵); a sacred contrafactum of *Puis que le ciel* appeared in *La pieuse alouette*
(RISM 1619⁹). Planson also contributed two, more old-
fashioned, four-voice chansons, *En m'oyant chanter
quelquefois* and *Soyons joyeulx*, to one of Le Roy &
Ballard's anthologies (RISM 1583⁹); both were inspired
by settings of the same texts by Lassus. He is reported to
have harmonized seven dance melodies (by the violinist
Michel Henry) for a feast of the Confrérie de St Julien in
Paris in 1587 (see F. Lesure: 'Le recueil des ballets de
Michel Henry (vers 1620)', *Les fêtes de la Renaissance*
[*I*]: *Royaumont 1955*, pp.205–19, esp. 206–7). (For
further discussion see *MGG1*, F. Lesure; Y. de Brossard:
Musiciens de Paris, 1535–1792 (Paris, 1965); and A.
Verchaly: Introduction to *Jehan Planson: Airs mis en
musique à quatre parties (1587)*, Paris, 1966.)
                                          FRANK DOBBINS

Plantade, Charles-Henri (*b* Pontoise, 14/19 Oct 1764; *d*
Paris, 18/19 Dec 1839). French composer, cellist and
teacher. As a youth he studied the cello, probably with J.-
L. Duport; after his arrival in Paris he studied singing and
composition with Langlé, the piano with Hüllmandel and
the harp with Petrini. His first published works were

sonatas for harp and collections of romances. These gained him recognition, and by 1797 he was music master at the Institut de St Denis. From 1799 to 1807 (and later, 1815–16 and 1818–28) he taught singing at the Paris Conservatoire; his most celebrated pupil there was Laure Cinti-Damoreau. Having become music master to Hortense de Beauharnais, who later became Queen of the Kingdom of Holland through her marriage to Louis Napoleon, Plantade was appointed *maître de chapelle* at the Dutch court from 1806 to 1810. The apparent overlap between his activities at the Conservatoire and at court has been accounted for by a leave of absence from either the Conservatoire (Pierre) or from the court (Favre). Plantade was both singing master and stage director at the Paris Opéra from 1812 to 1815.

Until 1815 Plantade composed mostly stage works, but in 1816 he succeeded Persuis as music master to the royal chapel, a position he held throughout the reign of Charles X. In this capacity he wrote a number of religious works. With Cherubini and Lesueur, he supervised the musical events at the coronation of Charles X in 1825; these included performances of his *Te Deum* and *Regina coeli*, both of which were composed for the occasion. Plantade's music is consistent with French style at the turn of the 19th century. His formal background as a singing teacher is reflected both in the preponderance of vocal works in his output and the sympathetic quality of his melodies, which are pleasant, if undistinguished. Plantade's orchestral writing employs woodwind and brass with imagination. His instrumental passage-work is generally simple and scalar, but his overtures and arias often contain unexpected modulations. Although he favoured foursquare phrasing, only occasionally writing an irregular melodic phrase, he handled metre changes with skill.

Plantade's son Charles-François Plantade (*b* Paris, 14 April 1787; *d* Paris, 26 May 1870) studied at the Paris Conservatoire and became a civil servant in the Ministry of Fine Arts. He was involved with the founding of the Société des Concerts du Conservatoire in 1828, and later with that of the Société des Auteurs, Compositeurs et Editeurs de Musique. His compositions include romances, chansons and chansonnettes.

WORKS

STAGE
first performed in Paris
PFE – *Théâtre Feydeau*

Les deux soeurs (oc, 1, [?P.G.] Pariseau), PFE, 22 May 1792
Les souliers mordorés (oc, 2, A. de Ferrières), PFE, 18 May 1793
Au plus brave la plus belle (oc, 1, L. Philippon de La Madelaine), Amis de la Patrie, 6 Oct 1794
Palma, ou Le voyage en Grèce (opéra, 2, P.E. Lemontey), PFE, 22 Aug 1797 (Paris, ?1798)
Romagnesi (opéra, 1, Lemontey), PFE, 3 Sept 1799
Lisez Plutarque (oc, 1), Montansier, spr. 1800
Zoé, ou La pauvre petite (oc, 1, J.N. Bouilly), PFE, 3 July 1800
Le roman (opéra, 1, E. Gosse), PFE, 12 Nov 1800
Bayard à la ferté, ou Le siège de Mézières (oc, 2, M.-A.-M. Désaugiers and [?M.-J.] Gentil), PFE, 13 Oct 1811
Le mari de circonstance (oc, 2, F.A.E. Planard), PFE, 18 March 1813 (Paris, ?1813)

OTHER WORKS
Sacred (many MSS in *F-Pc*): Messe de requiem (Paris, n.d.); 9 other masses; TeD, ?1825; several motets and other works, incl. at least 1 cant.
Other vocal: Recueil de romances et chansons, kbd acc., op.6 (Paris, 1796); 3 duos, hp/kbd acc., op.8 (Paris, 1796); Romances, kbd acc., bks 1–4 (Paris, 1796); Recueil de romances kbd acc., op.13

(Paris, 1802); other collections of romances; at least 3 collections of nocturnes, 2vv
Inst: Sonate, hp, op.1, and others

BIBLIOGRAPHY
Choron-FayolleD; EitnerQ; FétisB; GerberNL
C. Pierre: *Le Conservatoire national de musique et de déclamation: documents historiques et administratifs* (Paris, 1900)
H. Gougelot: *Catalogue des romances françaises parues sous la Révolution et l'Empire* (Melun, 1937)
J. Mongrédien: 'La musique aux fêtes du sacre de Charles X', *RMFC*, x (1970), 87–100
A. Caswell: 'Mme Cinti-Damoreau and the Embellishment of Italian Opera in Paris: 1820–1845', *JAMS*, xxviii (1975), 459–92
LAURIE SHULMAN

Planté, Francis [François] (*b* Orthez, Basses-Pyrénées, 2 March 1839; *d* Saint-Avit, nr Mont-de-Marsan, Landes, 19 Dec 1934). French pianist. He made his début at the age of seven and won a *premier prix* in A.-F. Marmontel's class at the Paris Conservatoire in 1850. Several years later he returned there to study harmony with Bazin, winning a *second prix* in 1855. For a time he was an active performer in Parisian salons as a protégé of Liszt and Rossini and in chamber music concerts with Alard and Franchomme. After playing Beethoven's Concerto no.5 at the Société des Concerts du Conservatoire in 1861, he retired to the Pyrénées for ten years. He resumed his career in 1872, appearing regularly throughout Europe and Russia as soloist, concerto performer and chamber musician. From then on he was recognized as one of the greatest French pianists of the century. In 1886 he played Liszt's Concerto no.2 in A and Hungarian Rhapsody no.2 in Paris in the presence of the composer, who complimented him highly. His concerts could last from three to six hours, and he would sometimes discuss the music with members of the audience seated nearest to him. His only recordings, made in 1928, include seven Chopin études and works by Mendelssohn and Schumann. Despite his advanced age, they reveal an assured and spontaneous style, as well as the 'floating tone' for which he was famous.

BIBLIOGRAPHY
A.F. Marmontel: *Virtuoses contemporains* (Paris, 1882)
A. Dandelot: *Francis Planté: une belle vie d'artiste* (Paris, 1920)
I. Schwerké: 'Francis Planté, Patriarch of the Piano (1839–1934)', *Recorded Sound*, no.35 (1969), 474–94
M. Fabre: 'Liszt et Planté: le premier amour et le dernier concert', *Revue internationale de musique française*, no.2 (1980), 107–14
CHARLES TIMBRELL

Plantin [Plantijn], **Christoffel** [Christofle, Christoph, Christophle] [Platinus, Christophorus] (*b* ?nr Tours, *c*1520; *d* Antwerp, 1 July 1589). Flemish printer of French birth. By 1549 he was in Antwerp, becoming a citizen and a member of the Guild of St Luke the following year. At first he worked as a bookbinder, but after an accident he became a printer in 1555. His combination of scholarship with business acumen made him the most prolific and important publisher of Antwerp during the 16th century. He published learned books of all kinds, including ones in specialized fields such as linguistics and science; many of the latter were illustrated with fine copper-plate engravings. At one time he employed 160 men and had 22 presses in operation. He sent books all over Europe and visited the Frankfurt fairs regularly.

In 1564 Plantin printed a French psalter with music, for which he had a royal privilege, but this book was later placed on the Index of prohibited books, as the religious

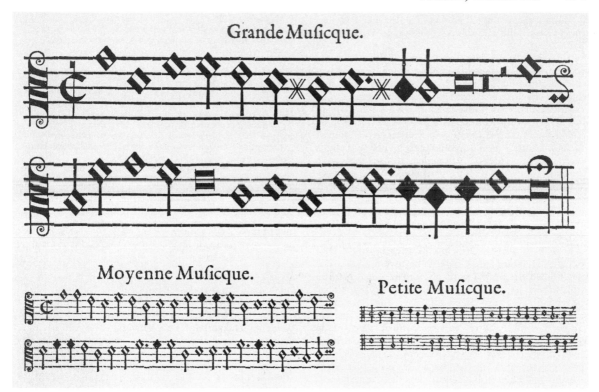

Three sizes of music type cut by Hendrik van den Keere and offered by Christopher Plantin in his type specimen of c1579 (68% of actual size)

troubles in the Low Countries intensified. As official printer to King Philip II of Spain, Plantin acquired a monopoly in printing missals and breviaries for Philip's dominions. During the years 1570–76 he printed more than 50,000 service books, the majority of which were sent to Spain. Although he was outwardly a fervent Catholic, and on good terms with the authorities, there is evidence that Plantin secretly belonged to heretical sects of Anabaptists, and printed for them also. From 1576, the year of the 'Spanish Fury', Plantin experienced severe trading and financial difficulties, and in 1583 he moved to Leiden, leaving the Antwerp business in the hands of his two eldest sons-in-law and returning to Antwerp only when the city's siege was lifted in 1585. He died there four years later.

Apart from the liturgical books, printed with plainsong music types, Plantin originally had no plans to print music, which he considered a risky business. However, when Philip withheld the promised subsidy for a sumptuous antiphoner (planned as a companion volume to the polyglot Bible he had, printed between 1568 and 1573), Plantin began to print music to use the 1800 reams of royal format paper ordered specially for the project. The first volume that he printed, *Octo missae* by George de La Hèle (1578), also uses the large woodcut initials designed for the antiphoner and was sold at 18 florins, a high price for the time. Plantin guarded himself against financial loss by requiring composers whose music he printed to pay for some copies themselves – sometimes for as many as 100 or 150 copies. It is noteworthy that the composers whose music Plantin published were musicians of high standing either in Antwerp or in Philip's chapel in Spain.

At Leiden, Plantin had acquired the title of university printer, and when he returned to Antwerp in 1585, this title passed to his second son-in-law, Frans Raphelengius (*b* Lille, 17 February 1539; *d* Leiden, July 1597), who took over the Leiden office. He printed no music, but as professor of Hebrew established Leiden as a centre of oriental printing. After his death, his two sons Christophe (*d* 1600) and Frans (*d* 1643) took over the business, though the title of university printer lapsed after 1600. The elder Frans and Christophe had become Calvinists, but the younger Frans remained a Catholic, journeyed to Italy, and after his brother's death published several books of madrigals by Cornelius Schuyt, town organist of Leiden (who had also travelled to Italy), and lent music type for an anthology of Italian madrigals (87 pieces by 37 composers) published in 1605 by H.L. de Haestens. Its final music publication was a volume of songs by Sweenlinck (1612) and the Leiden office closed in 1619. The Plantin types were also used in Haarlem for Sweelinck's last book of psalms, printed by H. Kranepoel in 1621, for Valerius's *Nederlandtsche gedenck-clanck* (1626) and for Padbrué's *Nederlandse madrigalen* (1631).

At Antwerp, Plantin's eldest son-in-law Joannes Moretus (Jan Moerentorf) (*b* Antwerp, 22 May 1543; *d* Antwerp, 26 September 1610) inherited the business. He completed the printing of Andreas Pevernage's chansons in four books, Plantin having died while the first was in the press. He printed some books of scholarship and a number of devotional books, and also published two volumes of music by Duarte Lobo. Moretus's sons, Balthasar (1574–1641) and Joannes (1576–1618), who succeeded him, published two books of masses by Lobo. In 1644 Balthasar Moretus the younger (1615–74), son of Joannes the younger, published Palestrina's *Hymni sacri*, a large folio choirbook dedicated to Pope Urban VIII.

Although the music output of Plantin and his successors was small in relation to their other printing, their careful documentation of all their business affairs, including music publication, is of great historical importance. The records at Plantin's house (now the Museum Plantin-Moretus, Antwerp) include lists of books and music he took to the Frankfurt fairs, records of all books bought and sold, founts of type commissioned by him and all his business correspondence. Although his music books were expensive compared with those of his Antwerp contemporary Phalèse, the records show that his publications sold regularly into the 17th century. The high quality of paper, ink and presswork which characterize all Plantin publications ensured his high reputation throughout Europe.

Throughout his life Plantin was a keen collector of typefaces, including music type. In his inventories, music type is listed from 1575 (when he had seven sorts), and on his folio type specimen from about 1579 three music types by H. Van den Keere of Ghent are illustrated: 'grande, moyenne et petite musicque' (see illustration). Plantin also owned three founts of music type cut by ROBERT GRANJON, including one with round notes which, however, he appears not to have used. In 1565, he bought Susato's printing materials, including 'notte petite & notte grosse' and he also received some type from the firm of Phalèse in settlement of debt. There are 28 sets of matrices for music type in the museum. These comprise 12 double-impression plainsong types (including eight cut by Van den Keere and one by Granjon) and 16 single-impression types, of which two are plainsong, two cut by Granjon, three cut by Van den Keere, and nine others.

PUBLICATIONS OF PLANTIN AND HIS SUCCESSORS
excluding liturgical books

ANTWERP

Les pseaumes de David (1564); G. de La Hèle: Octo missae, 5–7vv (1578); P. de Monte: Missa ... 'Benedicta es', 6vv (1579); J. de Brouck: Cantiones, 5, 6, 8vv (1579); C. de Navières: Les cantiques saints (1579); A. du Gaucquier: Quatuor missae, 5, 6, 8vv (1581); S. Cornet: Cantiones musicae, 5–8vv (1581); S. Cornet: Madrigali, 5–8vv (1581); S. Cornet: Chansons françoyses, 5, 6, 8vv (1581); A. de Pape: De consonantiis (1581); J. de Kerle: Quatuor missae, 5vv (1582); C. Le Jeune: Livre de mélanges (1585); P. de Monte: Liber I missarum (1587); D. Petri: Missa (1589), ?lost, listed in Plantin archive; A. Pevernage: Chansons, livre I [–IV] (1589–91); D. Lobo: Opuscula natalitiae noctis (1602); D. Lobo: Magnificat, 4vv (1605); D. Lobo: Liber missarum, 4, 5, 6, 8vv (1621); A. Chyliński: Canones XVI (1634); D. Lobo: Liber II missarum, 4–6vv (1639); G.P. da Palestrina: Hymni sacri (1644)
2 motets, 1 anon. (1595), 1 by C. Verdonck (1602), in historical works by J. Bochius

LEIDEN

A.M.S. Boethius: Vande vertroosting der wysheyd (1585); C. Schuyt: Il primo libro di madrigali, 5vv (1600); C. Schuyt: Hollandsche madrigalen (1603); C. Schuyt: Hymeneo, 6vv (1611); C. Schuyt: Dodici padovane (1611); J.P. Sweelinck: Rimes françoises et italiennes (1612)
Nervi d'Orfeo (1605⁹), printed by H.L. de Haestens 'con gli caratteri Plantiniani de Raphelengii'

BIBLIOGRAPHY

GoovaertsH
J.A. Stellfeld: 'Het muziekhistorisch belang der catalogi en inventarissen van het Plantijnsch archief', *Vlaams jaarboek voor muziekgeschiedenis*, ii–iii (1940–41), 5–50
J.A. Stellfeld: *Bibliographie des éditions musicales plantiniennes* (Brussels, 1949)
C. Clair: *Christopher Plantin* (London, 1960)
M. Parker, K. Melis and H.D.L. Vervliet: 'Early Inventories of Punches, Matrices and Moulds in the Plantin-Moretus Archives', *Gulden passer*, xxxviii (1960), 1–139
E. van Gulik and H.D.L. Vervliet: *Een gedenksteen voor Plantijn en Van Raphelingen te Leiden* (Leiden, 1967)
H. Slenk: 'Christopher Plantin and the Genevan Psalter', *TVNM*, xx/4 (1967), 226–48
H.D.L. Vervliet: *Sixteenth Century Printing Types of the Low Countries* (Amsterdam, 1968)
L. Voet: *The Golden Compasses: a History and Evaluation of the Printing and Publishing Activities of the Officina Plantiniana at Antwerp* (Amsterdam and New York, 1969–72)
R. Rasch: 'Noord-Nederlandse muziekuitgaven met de Plantijnse notentypen', *Gulden passer*, li (1973), 9–18 [with Eng. summary]
S. Bain: *Music Printing in the Low Countries in the Sixteenth Century* (diss., U. of Cambridge, 1974)
A. Rouzet: *Dictionnaire des imprimeurs, libraires et éditeurs des XVe et XVIe siècles dans les limites géographiques de la Belgique actuelle* (Nieuwkoop, 1975)
L. Voet and J. Voet-Grisolle: *The Plantin Press (1555–1589): a Bibliography* (Amsterdam, 1980–83)

SUSAN BAIN

Plantinga, Leon B(rooks) (*b* Ann Arbor, 25 March 1935). American musicologist. He took an MMus, with a major in piano, at Michigan State University. Continuing his graduate education at Yale University, he studied under Palisca and received the PhD in 1964. In 1963 he was appointed to the faculty at Yale, where he became professor of music (1974) and director of the humanities division (1994); he was a Fellow of University College, Oxford (1971–2). He is primarily concerned with musical style, genre and music criticism in the late 18th and early 19th centuries. His book *Schumann as Critic* is a careful study of this aspect of the composer; in it he describes the founding and goals of the *Neue Zeitschrift für Musik*, discusses Schumann's knowledge of music history and aesthetics and elucidates the critical outlook of his reviews. His study of Clementi (1977) quickly became a standard work on that composer and his book *Romantic Music* (1984), with accompanying music anthology, has come to be used as a customary teaching text.

WRITINGS

'Philippe de Vitry's Ars Nova: a Translation', *JMT*, ii (1961), 204–23
'Berlioz' Use of Shakespearian Themes', *Shakespeare in France*, ed. J.H. McMahon (New Haven, CT, 1964), 72
The Musical Criticism of Robert Schumann in the 'Neue Zeitschrift für Musik' (diss., Yale U., 1964)
'Schumann's View of "Romance"', *MQ*, lii (1966), 221–32; repr. in ibid., lxxv (1991), 176–87
Schumann as Critic (New Haven, CT, 1967/R)
'Clementi, Virtuosity, and the "German Manner"', *JAMS*, xxv (1972), 303–30
'Schumann's *Neue Zeitschrift für Musik*, its Origins and Influence', *Robert Schumann: the Man and his Music*, ed. A. Walker (London, 1972, 2/1976), 162–78
Clementi: his Life and Music (London, 1977/R)
Romantic Music: a History of Musical Style in Nineteenth-Century Europe (New York, 1984)
'Theorie und Praxis der Liedkomposition bei Robert Schumann', *Literature und Musik: ein Hanbuch zur Theorie und Praxis eines komparistischen Grenzgebietes*, ed. S.P. Scherr (Berlin, 1984), 117–37
'When did Beethoven Compose his Third Piano Concerto?', *JM*, vii (1989), 275–307
'The Piano and the Nineteenth Century', *Nineteenth-Century Piano Music*, ed. R.L. Todd (New York, 1990), 1–15
with G.P. Johnson: 'Haydn's Andante con Variazioni: Compositional Process, Text, and Genre', *The Creative Process* (New York, 1992), 129–67
'Poetry and Music: Two Episodes in a Durable Relationship', *Musical Humanism and its Legacy: Essays in Honour of Claude*

Palisca, ed. N.K. Baker and B.R. Hanning (New York, 1992), 321–53
Beethoven's Concertos: History, Style, Performance (New York, 1998)

PAULA MORGAN

Planxty. Irish folk-rock group. In 1970 the Irish singer-songwriter Christy Moore assembled a group of Irish musicians for his album *Prosperous*, including Donal Lunny (bazouki), Andy Irvine (mandolin) and the uillean piper Liam O'Flynn. Under the name Planxty (an expression of goodwill), the group revived traditional Irish songs, many of which had previously been performed unaccompanied, often with delicate and exquisite arrangements. Despite their serious intent, there was a contagious sense of good-humour and enjoyment in their performances which invited audience participation. They had a distinctive sound through their instrumental line-up, the witty and enthusiastic Moore, and an adventurous repertory that moved between folksongs and instrumental dance tunes. They found almost immediate commercial success with their single *Cliffs of Doneen*, which preceded their first album *Planxty* (Pol., 1972). Lunny left after the release of *The Well Below the Valley* (Pol., 1972), another album of traditional songs, his place taken by Johnny Moynihan. Moore left after the next album, *Cold Blow and Rainy Night* (Pol., 1974); he was replaced by Paul Brady, but this group made no recordings.

Planxty played mostly traditional music, but their repertory did include the angry political ballad *Only Our Rivers Run Free*, a forerunner of the songs Moore later performed both as a soloist and in the political folk-rock band Moving Hearts. A revival album in 1982 by the band's original members included songs by Bob Dylan, Moore, Irvine and Lunny.

ROBIN DENSELOW

Planyavsky, Alfred (*b* Vienna, 22 Jan 1924). Austrian double bass player and writer on music. He was a member of the Vienna Boys' Choir, 1933–8, and studied, as a tenor and as a double bass player, at the Akademie für Musik in Vienna, 1946–53. He joined the Vienna SO in 1954, and the next year the Vienna Staatsoper Orchestra and the Vienna PO. In 1967 he became a member of the Vienna Hofmusikkapelle. He has written many articles, especially for the *Österreichische Musikzeitschrift* and *Das Orchester* (for which he has been music critic), on his instrument and on Viennese musical traditions. His most important contribution is his book *Geschichte des Kontrabasses* (Tutzing, 1970, enlarged 2/1984).

His son, Peter Felix Planyavsky (*b* Vienna, 9 May 1947), is an organist and composer; he studied at the Akademie in Vienna (with Heiller, Uhl and others), and was appointed organist of the Stephansdom in 1969. He has recorded the complete organ works of Mendelssohn and is also known as a composer of sacred music.

RODNEY SLATFORD

Plaschke, Friedrich [Plaške, Bedřich] (*b* Jaroměř, 7 Jan 1875; *d* Prague, 4 Feb 1952). Czech bass-baritone. He studied in Prague, and in Dresden with Karl Scheidemantel. He made his début at the Dresden Hofoper in 1900 as the Herald in *Lohengrin* and remained a member of that company until 1937, creating Pöschel (*Feuersnot*), the First Nazarene (*Salome*), Arcesius (d'Albert's *Die toten Augen*), Altair (*Die ägyptische Helena*), Count Waldner (*Arabella*) and Morosus (*Die schweigsame Frau*); he was also the first Dresden Barak, Gérard (*Andrea Chénier*)

and Amfortas. He sang Pogner at Bayreuth in 1911 and Kurwenal, Hans Sachs and Amfortas at Covent Garden in 1914. Plaschke toured the USA with the German Opera Company, 1922–4. In Germany he was considered one of the best singing actors of his day. He left a few acoustic recordings, most notably extracts from his Hans Sachs. He was married to the soprano Eva von der Osten.

HAROLD ROSENTHAL/ALAN BLYTH

Plasson, Michel (*b* Paris, 2 Oct 1933). French conductor. He studied at the Paris Conservatoire and in the USA with Leinsdorf, Monteux and Stokowski, winning the Besançon International Competition in 1962. An appointment as music director at Metz, 1966–8, was followed by a long association at Toulouse, where he was director of the Théâtre du Capitole from 1968 to 1983; in 1983 he was appointed music director of the Toulouse Capitole Orchestra. He gave the Théâtre du Capitole a high reputation, conducting a wide repertory that included the première of Landowski's *Montségur* (1985). He has also conducted operas at the Metropolitan, Chicago and San Francisco, and made his Covent Garden début in 1979 with *Werther*; he returned to Covent Garden in 1990–91 for *Guillaume Tell* and *Tosca*. Plasson was appointed principal guest conductor of the Zürich Tonhalle Orchestra in 1987 and music director of the Dresden PO in 1994. A sensitive and elegant conductor, his recordings include operas by Bizet, Gounod, Massenet and Offenbach, much French orchestral music, Magnard's symphonies and *Guercoeur*, and Roussel's *Padmâvati*.

NOËL GOODWIN

Plastische Form (Ger.). A form which relies on proportion and symmetry. *See* ANALYSIS, §I, 3.

Platagē (Gk.). *See* SISTRUM. *See also* CYBELE.

Platania, Pietro (*b* Catania, 5 April 1828; *d* Naples, 26 April 1907). Italian composer and teacher. He studied in Catania and then at the Palermo Conservatory with the great contrapuntist Pietro Raimondi, whose favourite pupil he became. In 1852 his opera *Matilde Bentivoglio* was given in Palermo, so successfully that the city government awarded him 300 ducats. Later that year, when Raimondi resigned as director and counterpoint teacher at the conservatory, he suggested Platania as his successor. The nomination was made, but was unsuccessful because of bureaucratic rivalries. In 1863, under the new government, he won the still-vacant post by competition. In 1882 he became *maestro di cappella* at Milan Cathedral and from 1885 to 1902 was director of the Naples Conservatory. Recognized as the greatest Italian contrapuntist of his day, Platania was admired by Rossini and by Verdi, who invited him to contribute to the abortive Rossini requiem. He was the last illustrious practitioner of the old strict tradition of Italian church music, carrying on its occasional tendency to the colossal, as in his setting of Psalm lxvii, *Exurgat Deus*, for six four-part choruses and orchestra. He also continued to write operas, most notably *Spartaco* (1891), and was one of the first Italian composers of the period to devote himself significantly to instrumental music, particularly to orchestral pieces of an occasional or festive character, like those in memory of Meyerbeer, Pacini and Rossini and the choral symphony for the ceremonial coronation tour of Umberto I (1878). In 1889 he was among the supporters of Mascagni's *Cavalleria rusticana* in Sonzogno's second competition for a new opera.

WORKS

OPERAS

Matilde Bentivoglio (tragedia lirica, 3, G. Bonfiglio), Palermo, Carolino, March 1852, *I-Mr**; vs (Milan, ?1855)

Piccarda Donati (tragedia, 3, L. Spince), Palermo, Carolino, 3 March 1857

La vendetta slava (dramma serio, 2, F. de Beaumont), Palermo, Bellini, 4 Feb 1865, excerpts, vs (Milan, n.d.)

Spartaco (tragedia lirica, 4, A. Ghislanzoni), Naples, S Carlo, 29 March 1891, vs (Milan, 1891)

Unperf.: I misteri di Parigi, c1843; Francesca Soranzo; Giulio Sabino; La corte di Enrico III; Lamma

VOCAL

Sacred: Requiem, 4 solo vv, vv, org, for Vittorio Emanuele II, Palermo, 1878 (Milan, n.d.); 2 missa solemnis: 1 for solo vv, 2 choruses, 2 org, 1883 (Leipzig, 1889); Cr, 2 choruses, org, 1882 (Leipzig, n.d.); San et Bs, 2 choruses, org (Leipzig, n.d.); Exurgat Deus, Ps lxvii, 6 choruses, orch (Leipzig, n.d.); Laudate pueri, Ps cxii, S, vv, pf (Milan, 1880); Ave Maria, filio orbata, double chorus (Leipzig, n.d.); Tota pulchra es, Maria, solo vv, 4vv, org (Leipzig, 1898); Ave Maria, 8 solo vv (Milan, n.d.); Pater noster, 5vv, insts (Leipzig, n.d.)

Other sacred, *I-Mcap*, mostly autograph: Gl, 2 choruses, 2 org, 1883; San, 2 choruses, 2 org; Ecce sacerdos magnus, 4vv, org; Iste est verus sacerdos, 4vv, org; Laetamur omnes, 4vv, org, 1882; Magnificamus te, 4vv; Litany, 4vv; Resurrexit, 2 choruses, 2 org, 1883; Subacta cedunt Tartara, 4vv, org

Secular: Inno alla regina d'Italia; songs

INSTRUMENTAL

Orch: Immagini sinfoniche; Fête valaque; Contemplazione; Italia, sinfonia caratteristica, arr. pf 4 hands (Milan, n.d.); Sinfonia Meyerbeer; Sinfonia, in memory of Pacini (Milan, ?1868); Sinfonia funebre per la morte di Rossini, 1868; Sinfonia festiva, vv, orch, for coronation tour of Umberto I, 1878; Pensiero sinfonico, for inauguration of Bellini monument, Naples, 1886

Chbr: 2 str qts, e, a, 1 pubd (Palermo, 1868)

WRITINGS AND PEDAGOGICAL WORKS

Corso completo di fughe e canoni d'ogni genere dall'antico al moderno: opera pratico-scolastica (Milan, 1871)

Trattato d'armonia seguito da un corso completo di contrappunto dal corale al fugato e partimenti analoghi (Milan, 1872, 2/1883)

Progetto di riforma musicale per la città di Palermo (Palermo, 1874)

Guida teorica al corso pratico-scolastico di fughe e canoni (Palermo, 1879)

Sulla musica in Sicilia nel presente secolo (Palermo, n.d.)

BIBLIOGRAPHY

M.: 'Pietro Platania', *Musica e musicisti: gazzetta musicale di Milano*, lx (1905), 49–51

F. Guardione: *Pietro Platania* (Milan, 1908)

G. De Napoli: 'Pietro Platania', *Musica d'oggi*, x (1928), 248–51

G. Pannain: 'Saggio su la musica a Napoli nel sec. XIX, da Mercadante a Martucci', *RMI*, xxxviii (1931), 193–206; repr. in *Ottocento musicale italiano: saggi e note* (Milan, 1952), 109–72, esp.148

F. Mompellio: 'La cappella del duomo dal 1714 ai primi decenni del '900', *Storia di Milano*, xvi (Milan, 1962), 553–88, esp. 569 [pubn of the Fondazione Treccani degli Alfieri per la Storia di Milano]

ANDREA LANZA

Platel, Nicolas-Joseph (*b* Versailles, 1777; *d* Brussels, 25 Aug 1835). French cellist, teacher and composer. The son of a musician at the French court, he was among the *pages de la musique* to Louis XVI. His first teachers were Louis Richer (singing) and Jean-Louis Duport (cello); later he studied the cello with J.M. de La Marre. He began his career as a cellist at the Théâtre Feydeau, Paris, in 1796. From 1797 to 1801 he lived in Lyons, but he returned to the capital in 1801 and soon made his name as a cello virtuoso. In 1805 he embarked on an extensive tour through France, but on reaching Quimper, in Brittany, he stayed for two years. Next he went to Brest, Nantes and finally to the southern Netherlands, intending to visit the Netherlands and Germany. However, he stayed for several years in Ghent and then in Antwerp (from 1813), where he was principal cellist at the theatre. He was in Brussels from 1820, and in 1824 he became principal cellist at the Théâtre de la Monnaie. When the Royal School of Music in Brussels was founded in 1826, Platel's name was put forward for the post of cello professor. At first it was feared that his cantankerous nature might be prejudicial to his teaching, but the administrative board, while acknowledging that Platel was 'not the pleasantest of men', pointed out that his talent was so superior to that of any other cellist in Brussels that the post could not be offered to anyone else 'without doing him a real injustice'. He was therefore appointed professor by royal decree on 16 January 1827. There is every reason to believe that Platel's conduct was irreproachable, since he was reappointed when the Royal School of Music became a conservatory in 1832. He had a high reputation as a teacher; his many pupils included A.F. Servais, Alexandre Batta and François de Munck. He composed cello solos, concertos, sonatas, other chamber pieces and *romances*, which were published in Paris and Brussels.

WORKS

Vc concs.: nos.1–4 (Paris, n.d.); no.5, Le quart d'heure (Brussels, n.d.)

Chbr: sonatas, opp.2–4, vc, bc (Paris, n.d.); 6 duos, vn, vc (Paris, n.d.); 3 trios, vn, va, vc (Brussels, n.d.)

Solo vc: 8 airs variés (Paris, n.d.); Caprices ou préludes (Brussels, n.d.)

Vocal: 6 romances, 1v, pf (Paris, c1796); Le prisonnier, in Album des dames, ii (Brussels, n.d.); Strophes pour le rétablissement de la santé de S.M. la Reine, in Album des dames, iv (Brussels, n.d.)

BIBLIOGRAPHY

BNB (F. Van Duyse); *Choron-FayolleD*; *FétisB*; *GerberNL*; *VannesD*

E.G.J. Gregoir: *Panthéon musical populaire*, vi (Brussels, 1877), 49, 56, 64, 67

E. Mailly: *Les origines du Conservatoire royal de musique de Bruxelles* (Brussels, 1879)

PAUL RASPÉ/PHILIPPE VENDRIX

Platerspiel (Ger.). *See* BLADDER PIPE.

Plath, Wolfgang (*b* Riga, Latvia, 27 Dec 1930; *d* Augsburg, 18 March 1995). German musicologist. From 1949 to 1951 he studied musicology with Gerstenberg at the Free University, Berlin, and continued with him at Tübingen University, taking the doctorate in 1958 with a dissertation on Bach's *Klavierbüchlein*. After a year (1959–60) as E.F. Schmid's assistant, Plath was appointed by the Internationale Stiftung Mozarteum in Salzburg to become, with Rehm, co-editor of the new collected edition of Mozart's works. He is a member of the Zentralinstitut für Mozartforschung. His research on Mozart's autographs has had far-reaching results on chronology and authenticity.

WRITINGS

Das Klavierbüchlein für Wilhelm Friedemann Bach (diss., U. of Tübingen, 1958; Neue Bach-Ausgabe, v/5, Kassel, 1962–3)

'Das Skizzenblatt KV 467ᵃ', *MJb 1959*, 114–26

'Beiträge zur Mozart-Autographie I: Die Handschrift Leopold Mozarts', *MJb 1960–61*, 82–117

'Der Ballo des "Ascanio" und die Klavierstücke KV Anh.207', *MJb 1964*, 111–29

'Überliefert die dubiose Klavierromanze in As KV Anh.205 das verschollene Quintett-Fragment KV Anh.54 (452ᵃ)?', *MJb 1965–66*, 71–86

'Mozartiana in Fulda und Frankfurt', *MJb 1968–70*, 333–87

'Leopold Mozarts Notenbuch für Wolfgang (1762): eine Fälschung?',
    MJb 1971–2, 337–41
'Typus und Modell [in Mozarts Kompositionsweise]', *MJb 1973–4*,
    145–57
'Beiträge zur Mozart-Autographie II: Schriftchronologie 1770–1780',
    MJb 1976–7, 131–73
'Requiem-Briefe: aus der Korrespondenz Joh. Anton Andrés
    1825–1831', *MJb 1976–7*, 174–203
'Gefälschte Mozart-Autographs: der Fall Nicotra', *Acta mozartiana*,
    xxvi (1979), 2–10; see also ibid., 72–80
'Bericht über Schreiber und Schriftchronologie der Mozart-
    Überlieferung', *Neue Mozart-Ausgabe Mitarbeitertagung: Kassel
    1981*, 69–72
'Chronologie als Problem der Mozart-Forschung', *GfMKB: Bayreuth
    1981*, 371–8
'Ein Gutachten Otto Jahns über die Andrésche Mozart Sammlung',
    Augsburger Jb für Musikwissenschaft, v (1988), 83–101
ed., with others: *Opera incerta: Echtheitsfragen als Problem
    musikwissenschaftlicher Gesamtausgaben: Mainz 1988*[incl.
    'Echtheitsfragen bei Mozart', pts i ii, 207 14, 237 70; 'Literatur
    zu Echtheitsfragen bei Wolfgang Amadeus Mozart', 285–300]
'Zur Überleiferung von Mozarts Szene KV 369:.Augsburger Aspekte
    einer "Münchner" Komposition', *Quaestiones in musica:
    Festschrift Franz Krautwurst*, ed. F. Brusniak and H. Leuchtmann
    (Tutzing, 1989), 479–94
Mozart-Schriften: ausgewählte Aufsätze, ed. M. Danckwardt (Kassel,
    1991) [reprs. of selected essays; incl. list of pubns, 391–5]
'Die "sechste" Fuge aus Mozarts Bach-Transkriptionen KV 405', *De
    editione musices: Festschrift Gerhard Croll*, ed. W. Gratzer and A.
    Lindmayr (Laaber, 1992), 293–303
ed., with J. Mancal: *Leopold Mozart: auf dem Weg zu einem
    Verständnis* (Augsburg, 1994) [incl. 'Zur Echtheitsfrage bei
    Mozart', 97–118; 'Leopold Mozart 1987', 171–82]

EDITIONS

Wolfgang Amadeus Mozart: Neue Ausgabe sämtlicher Werke,
    VIII:20/1/i: *Streichquartette* (Kassel, 1966) [with W. Rehm];
    VIII:22/2: *Klaviertrios* (Kassel, 1966); II:5: *Don Giovanni* (Kassel,
    1968) [with W. Rehm]; IV:12/i: *Kassationen, Serenaden und
    Divertimenti* (Kassel, 1970) [with G. Hausswald]; IV:11/x:
    Einzelstücke (Kassel, 1978) [syms.]; IV:13/1/ii: *Märsche* (Kassel,
    1978); X:29/1: *Werke zweifelhafter Echtheit* (Kassel, 1980) [with
    C.-H. Mahling]; IX:27/1–2: *Klavierstücke*(Kassel, 1982); IX:25/
    1–2: *Klaviersonaten* (Kassel, 1986) [with W. Rehm].

HANS HEINRICH EGGEBRECHT/KONRAD KISTER

Platillos (Sp.). *See* CYMBALS.

Plato [Platōn] (*b* Athens, *c*429 BCE; *d* Athens, 347 BCE).
Greek philosopher. His comments on music are of unusual
interest, not only because his works provide much varied
evidence but also because he was a transitional figure.
During his lifetime the traditional PAIDEIA (meaning both
'education' and 'culture'), built upon unquestioned aristocratic standards of behaviour, had already fallen into
decay; the conservative Aristophanes had lamented its
neglect. Plato was no less conservative in his different way
and was disquieted by the signs of things to come. The
meeting of past and future in his writings lends his
remarks on music a special interest, even when he was
manifestly out of touch with his own times.

1. Attitude to musical instruments. 2. Number theory, ethos,*harmonia*.
3. *Harmonia* and rhythm. 4. Music and legislation. 5. Paideia. 6.
Melodic mimesis. 7. Characteristics of Platonic thought. 8. Influence
on his successors.

1. ATTITUDE TO MUSICAL INSTRUMENTS. Among musical
instruments, only the aulos and kithara commanded
Plato's serious attention. As the *Crito* (54d2–5) shows, he
was aware that auletes could fill the consciousness of
listeners with their playing. The passage refers indirectly
to the buzzing sound of auloi and is probably Plato's
nearest approach to a concern with tonal characteristics.
Such questions, however, had little importance for him; it

was because of its tonal flexibility, not its sound, that he
banned the aulos from his ideal city-states projected in
the *Republic* and the *Laws*. He credited it with the most
extensive compass of any instrument and asserted that
other 'polychordic' and 'panharmonic' instruments –
those affording a wide variety of notes and *harmoniai* –
only imitate it (*Republic*, iii, 399d4–5).

Plato's concern was not with the technical capacities of
the instrument: he wished, rather, to eradicate what he
considered an alien element in Greek religion. The aulos,
said Socrates, is associated with the satyr MARSYAS; we
must follow the MUSES in preferring kithara and lyra, the
instruments of APOLLO (*Republic*, iii, 399e1–3). Their
acceptance represents a further part of the plan, evident
in the *Republic* and especially in the *Laws*, to make music
serve the state religion. As an exception herdsmen will be
allowed to retain their traditional SYRINX (*see* GREECE §I,
5(ii)(b)).

2. NUMBER THEORY, ETHOS, HARMONIA.   Plato did not
claim familiarity with technical theory, but in the *Philebus*
he nevertheless referred to discordant elements being
made 'commensurable and harmonious by introducing
the principle of number' (25d11–e2), a notably Pythagorean sentiment. The same idea is put, negatively, later in
the same work: without number and measurement, any
art is at the mercy of guesswork and of an empirical
reliance upon the senses (55e1–56a3). Here, as often, he
was attacking the empirical harmonicists; yet his position
was ambivalent, for he could also criticize the Pythagoreans (*Republic*, vii, 531a–b), whom he admired on many
counts, for their exclusive interest in the numerical
properties of musical consonances (*see* GREECE, §I, 6).

According to Alcibiades in the *Symposium*, the aulos
melodies attributed to Marsyas are incomparably powerful. Whether the performer is skilful or inept, they grip
the soul and show 'the need of gods and mysteries'
(215c1–6). The passage illustrates the exciting and
orgiastic effect so often associated with the aulos. In an
ideal community, where worship must above all be
decorous, such an instrument can have no place. As might
be expected, Socrates considered the power of music from
a distinctly different approach. The qualities of rhythm
and harmony, he explained, sink deep into the soul and
remain there. The result is grace of body and mind,
attainable in practice solely through the traditional system
of literary and musical education known as *mousikē*
(*Republic*, iii, 412a). Thus a man's habits become his
nature and are manifested as ETHOS.

In the *Timaeus*, a dialogue concerned centrally with the
motion of the soul, Plato proposed that *harmonia* has a
comparable motion and helps to restore order and concord
to the soul; similarly, that rhythm remedies our unmodu-
lated condition (47c7–e2). (*Harmonia*, it must be remembered, is a broad philosophical term that has nothing to
do with the modern concept of chord relationships.)
Mousikē and *philosophia* 'provide the soul with motion';
when this motion has been properly regularized, it blends
high and low sounds into a unity that provides intellectual
delight as an 'imitation of the divine harmony revealed in
mortal motions' (80b4–8). In the *Laws* (vii, 802c6–d6)
Plato held that pleasure is nevertheless irrelevant in itself:
a man enjoys the music to which he is accustomed; while
sober and ordered music makes men better, the vulgar
and cloying sort makes them worse. Although the
doctrines of the *Timaeus* seem to be related to Pythagorean

theories of harmonic number, Plato never showed clearly how the soul could be affected by external patterns of motion related to it through *harmonia*. Indeed, this difficulty is part of a larger problem in Platonic philosophy: how the eternal and non-material can participate in the temporal and material realm.

3. HARMONIA AND RHYTHM.   Plato credited rhythm, metre and *harmonia* with a great inherent power to charm (*Republic*, x, 601a–b). Convinced that his ideal of education could be realized through their use, Plato nevertheless warned that they must remain subordinate to the text (*Republic*, iii, 398d). He saw the various rhythmic patterns as developments of impulses expressed through bodily movements; the *harmoniai* are analysed simply and briefly as 'systems' (*Philebus*, 17c11–d6). His own musical and literary training occurred at a period when he can hardly have gained any strong impression of earlier individual, unsystematized *harmoniai*. Moreover, the scale sequences presented in the treatise *On Music* (i.9) of ARISTIDES QUINTILIANUS as 'called to mind' by Plato in the *Republic* bear some resemblance to the 'complete systems' found in Greco-Roman handbooks (*see* GREECE, §I, 6(iii)(e)).

Plato seldom named individual *harmoniai*, except in a noteworthy passage where he rejected all of them except the Dorian and Phrygian. The former serves to imitate the 'tones and accents' of a brave man under stress, the latter to portray moderate behaviour in prosperity, evidently through the same kind of MIMESIS (*Republic*, iii, 399a–c). His choice had a reasoned basis in the religious observances of his own times and the severe limitations to be imposed upon music and poetry in the ideal city-state of his *Republic*. The Phrygian *harmonia* was strongly associated with Dionysiac worship, with the choral hymn to Dionysus known as the DITHYRAMB and also with the AULOS. In Plato's own time, Dionysus was worshipped with sombre decorum.

In the *Laws*, a work of the writer's old age, Plato treated the *harmoniai* less harshly than he did in the *Republic*; several passages seem to suggest that a variety would be permitted. (See notably *Laws* 670a–71a.) Still, he failed to give any satisfactory full account of the relation between the *harmoniai* and morals. Thus, in a well-known passage (*Laws*, ii, 669b–70b), Plato warned that a wrong handling of music could make the hearer liable to fall into evil habits. He further objected to the lack of taste and the meaningless virtuosity of solo instrumental performances, which seemed to him to have hardly any meaning or mimetic worth. Here the view of music as fostering evil is extreme, even for Plato. Elsewhere in the *Laws* (ii, 654b–d) he suggested that technical finish has secondary importance, a view far more in keeping with his general approach; yet even here his approach is as ambiguous as ever. His attitudes and theories, as expressed in isolated passages, still fail to combine satisfactorily into a philosophical system, however valuable they may be in isolation.

In these circumstances even the views of the musical expert DAMON may well fail to provide a means of unifying Plato's thought; in a significant number of respects Plato showed a critical and independent spirit where music was concerned.

4. MUSIC AND LEGISLATION.   As might be expected, the connection between music and legislation is established almost entirely in the *Laws*, although it is occasionally anticipated in earlier works. When he wrote the *Republic* Plato did not trust the power of written laws to maintain a wholesome culture. In the *Republic*, the musical topic of special interest had been paideutic ethos; it is now *paideia* itself, and, in particular, the place that music should have within it. Egypt, Crete, Sparta and the Athens of earlier days provided Plato with precedents for legislative controls over music. Probably the most striking result is his seemingly paradoxical claim that 'our songs are our laws' (*Laws*, vii, 799e). Earlier, Socrates had observed (*Republic*, iv, 424b–c) that 'the modes [*tropoi*] of music are never moved without movement of the greatest constitutional laws'. The interpretation of these passages has been a matter of controversy, and there is certainly a play on the word *nomos*, which has both a general meaning of 'law', 'custom' or 'convention', as well as a specific musical meaning (*see* NOMOS). Nevertheless, it is reasonable to suppose Plato regarded the influence of music on behaviour (for whatever reason) as so profound as to be a virtual 'law'. Thus, in a literal sense, 'song' and 'law' were inseparable.

'Rightness' (*orthotēs*) has many aspects in the *Laws* and is perhaps the most important single concept bearing upon music in that vast work. Poets, Plato said, are in themselves unable adequately to recognize good and evil. They have unwittingly created the impression that rightness is not even a characteristic of music, let alone the true criterion; and that the true criterion is pleasure (*Laws*, iii, 700d–e).

In the ideal city of the *Laws*, no such debased standard could exist. Free choice of rhythms and melodies would be forbidden, and Plato would allow only those appropriate to texts equating virtue with the good (*Laws*, ii, 661c). None but the civic poet may express himself freely. He must be elderly and also distinguished for his noble deeds, but he need not be talented in poetry or music (*Laws*, viii, 829c–d). Power must be in the hands of the state. Musical contests will be judged by mature citizens (*Laws*, vi, 764d–e), and aged choristers must know *harmoniai* and rhythms in order to distinguish the rightness of a melody (*Laws*, ii, 670a–b). Evidently they will have to be more technically competent than the civic poet, and this fact serves as a reminder of Plato's indecisiveness in choosing criteria. Elsewhere he seems to have been attempting to combine both kinds of prerequisites for music, for he conceded that music may indeed be judged by the pleasure it gives, providing it appeals to a listener of outstandingly noble character and *paideia*. This sort of man, he continued, must judge public performances (*Laws*, ii, 658e–59a). In this passage, as often elsewhere when he approached a musical topic in varying ways, his inconsistency has no final resolution.

5. PAIDEIA.   In the *Laws* Plato proposed that musical and literary training should ensure that 'the whole community may come to voice always one and the same sentiment in song, story and speech' (*Laws*, ii, 664a). Plato pursued such uniformity relentlessly, and it is easy to ignore the admirable earnestness and idealism of his views concerning *paideia*. Education which is not uplifting is not education; men must constantly be exposed to an ethical code higher than their own (*Laws*, ii, 659c). In this process music has a vital role. From the civic point of view, for example, *paideia* is said to be a man's training as a singer and dancer in the public chorus (*Laws*, ii,

654a). But Plato extended the meaning of *paideia* beyond mere dexterity: in the same context he claimed that true *paideia* is loving good and hating evil, and that technique matters little (*Laws*, ii, 654b–d). In the education of young children, as yet incapable of dealing maturely with moral issues, ideals of excellence will be conveyed through terms that can be understood, those of play and song (*Laws*, ii, 659d–e).

The comment is remarkable for the conscious grasp that it shows of the connection between *paideia* and play (*paidia*). Once again, much later in the *Laws*, Plato connected play with song and with dance as well. Man is 'the plaything [*paignion*] of God', he declared; this is the best thing about him, and he should therefore spend his life in 'the noblest kinds of play', sacrificing, singing and dancing (*Laws*, vii, 803c–04b). The central idea of *orthotēs* reappears here: these activities are cited to show rightness in practice. The religious emphasis is noteworthy and typical of Plato, as is the omission of any reference to solo instrumental music. (A musical accompaniment was taken for granted.)

The older, 5th-century education was designed primarily to produce seemly behaviour during the early years of schooling, according to the Platonic Protagoras (*Protagoras*, 325d–e; cf 326a–b for the actual system). In the *Laws* Plato himself made careful provision for elementary schooling; although he always considered *paideia* as a lifelong activity, he was aware that in this instance the beginning was indeed 'half of all'.

Besides his general remarks on education, he dealt with lyre lessons in a remarkable passage (*Laws*, vii, 812d–e): the lyre must sound clearly and in unison with the voice, he declared; heterophony and ornamentation are forbidden, as are various types of exaggerated contrast. These comments are incomparably more technical than any others in the entire range of the dialogues. Plato excluded any kind of variation, rhythmic or melodic, in the accompaniment and any use of countermelody because he believed these interfere with the young pupils' ability to grasp 'within three years the useful elements of music' (*en trisin etesi to tēs mousikēs chrēsimon*).

6. MELODIC MIMESIS.   Although Plato never developed an explicit theory of melodic mimesis, some of its constituent elements can be seen in his work. In his doctrine of habituation he taught that mimetic practices, if begun early in life, grow eventually into habits and become second nature (*Republic*, iii, 395d). He related this to music through his reference in the *Laws* (ii, 655a–b) to the separate melodies that characterize the brave man and the coward; and the two principles are combined in his description of rhythm and of music generally as 'imitations of the characters of better and worse men' (*Laws*, vii, 798d). Since music is thus mimetic, we must judge it not by the degree to which it pleases, but by its rightness, the essential quality of successful mimesis (*Laws*, ii, 668a–b). Rhythms as well as *harmoniai* express these mimetic qualities, and in good music they take their pattern from the natural rhythm of a good man's life (*Republic*, iii, 399a–e).

One might have expected the parallel statement that in such music the *harmonia* expresses the inner *harmonia* of a good man, but he never stated this. The two acceptable *harmoniai*, Dorian and Phrygian, imitate (in a manner never explained) the 'notes and songs' (*phthongous te kai prosōdias*) of brave and moderate men; there is no analogy

with any inner *harmonia*. He seems to have reasoned that *harmonia* must resemble rhythm in imitating certain human activities.

7. CHARACTERISTICS OF PLATONIC THOUGHT.   It was natural for Plato to associate music with spoken language, for he always championed the pre-eminence of the word; yet this combination involved him in a contradiction. He suggested that education is achieved, first by the two main musical elements, *harmonia* and rhythm, which impart a rhythmic and harmonious nature through habituation, and, secondly by the literary content, which produces traits of character closely related to the habits implanted by *harmonia* and rhythm but differing from them (*Republic*, vii, 522a). The contradiction lies in the fact that such character traits are ethical, whereas moral value is irrelevant to *harmonia* and rhythm. Plato generally recognized this, but he linked by association the ethical and non-ethical factors and even used ethical terms to describe the *harmoniai*.

In the dialogues Plato took a narrow view of the pleasure-giving function of music, for example, and his general understanding of musical developments was distinctly old-fashioned. On points of detail his presentation is often vague or incomplete; at times he contradicted himself. Yet he combined a singularly noble vision of the moral function of music with concern for its practical aspects. The ambivalence of his position between the old music and the new itself enabled him to draw upon the heritage of Pythagorean, Sophistic and Damonian thought and also to contribute profoundly, through his own remarkable powers, to the thought of the future. Severe but majestic, he was the last mourner of the traditional Hellenic musical ideals.

8. INFLUENCE ON HIS SUCCESSORS.   The passing of these ideals was also deplored by later critics, including Aristotle's brilliant pupil ARISTOXENUS. Like Plato, he saw the music of his own time as proof of an ethical decline; yet even here Aristoxenus's view is not that of the zealous reformer, and elsewhere there are manifest differences. One of these concerns the Aristoxenian doctrine of rhythm. It certainly involves formal principles that essentially resemble Plato's ideal paradigms; the dialogues nevertheless treat rhythm either as a divine gift or as a mimetic refining of the impulse towards decisive movement.

Hellenistic and Greco-Roman authors were increasingly concerned with cosmic number-relationships, derived from Pythagoras, rather than the aspects of Plato's approach to *mousikē* derived from the observation of society or the physical nature of man. Plato's doctrines of mimesis and ethos were preserved and reinterpreted by Neoplatonic theorists such as Aristides Quintilianus. Plotinus's pupil Porphyry followed Neoplatonic tradition in insisting that the motion of the soul is vitally important for music; the soul itself he held to be a composite tuned to diatonic intervals, a view derived from the *Timaeus* and *Phaedo*.

The Church Fathers' attitudes to music were principally based on Neoplatonic views; they sought persistently to press music into ecclesiastical service as an aid to individual salvation or a way of praising God. They nevertheless credited it with a power for evil and rejected secular music on moral grounds. Likewise, Philo conceptualized Jewish religious traditions in terms of Platonic philosophy, especially in his account of the formation of the world, while Islamic scholars attempted to harmonize their own theology with both Neoplatonism and Aristotelianism. In the hands of Western commentators such as MACROBIUS AMBROSIUS THEODOSIUS and CALCIDIUS and authors such as BOETHIUS, CASSIODORUS and ISIDORE OF SEVILLE, fragments of Platonic theory were passed on to the Middle Ages, where they continued to exert an influence, especially on *musica speculativa*.

WRITINGS

J. Burnet, ed.: *Platonis opera* (Oxford, 1900–07/R)
H.N. Fowler and others, trans.: *Plato in Twelve Volumes* (Cambridge, MA, 1914–37/R)
F.M. Cornford, ed. and trans.: *Plato's Cosmology: the Timaeus of Plato* (London, 1937/R)

BIBLIOGRAPHY

K. von Jan: 'Die Tonarten bei Platon in dritten Buche der Republik', *Jahrbücher für Philologie und Pädagogik*, xcv (1867), 815–26
R. Westphal: 'Platos Beziehungen zur Musik', *Berliner philologische Wochenschrift*, iv (1884), 513–18, 545–9, 609–11, 641–5, 673–7
A.F. Walter: 'Die ethisch-pädagogische Würdigung der Musik durch Plato und Aristoteles', *VMw*, vi (1890), 388–415
K.J. Belling: 'Plato's Position with Reference to Art, and in Particular to Music', *Music*, i (1891–2), 197–203, 317–20
E. Frank: *Plato und die sogenannten Pythagoreer: ein Kapitel aus die Geschichte des griechischen Geistes* (Halle, 1923)
J.F. Mountford: 'The Musical Scales of Plato's Republic', *Classical Quarterly*, xvii (1923), 125–36
J. Regner: *Platos Musiktheorie: eine Studie zur griechischen Musikgeschichte* (diss., U. of Halle, 1924)
A.E. Taylor: *Plato: the Man and his Work* (London, 1926, 7/1960)
A. Rivaud: 'Etudes platoniciennes, II: Plato et la musique', *Revue d'histoire de la philosophie*, iii (1929), 1–30
R. Schaerer: *Epistēmē et technē: étude sur les notions de connaissance et d'art d'Homère à Platon* (Mâcon, 1930)
H. Perls: 'Mousa: étude sur l'esthétique de Platon', *Revue philosophique*, cxvii (1934), 259–84, 441–71
W. Vetter: 'Die Musik im platonischen Staate', *Neue Jahrbücher*, xi (1935), 306–20
G. Junge: 'Die Sphärenharmonie und die pythagoreisch-platonische Zahlenlehre', *Classica et mediaevalia*, ix (1947), 183–94
O. Tiby: 'Note musicologiche al Timeo di Platone', *Dioniso*, xii (1949), 33–55
G. Müller: *Studien zu den platonischen Nomoi* (Munich, 1951, 2/1968)
F.A. Ahlvers: *Zahl und Klang bei Platon* (Berne, 1952)
N.I. Boussoulas: *L'être et la composition des mixtes dans le 'Philèbe' de Platon* (Paris, 1952)
P. Boyancé: 'La religion astrale de Platon à Cicéron', *Revue des études grecques*, lxv (1952), 312–49
W.D. Anderson: 'The Importance of Damonian Theory in Plato's Thought', *Transactions of the American Philological Association*, lxxxvi (1955), 88–102
L. Richter: 'Platons Stellung zur praktischen und spekulativen Musiktheorie seiner Zeit', *GfMKB: Hamburg 1956*, 196–202
B. Kytzler: 'Die Weltseele und der musikalische Raum (Platons Timaios 35a ff.)', *Hermes*, lxxxvii (1959), 393–414
E. Moutsopoulos: *La musique dans l'oeuvre de Platon* (Paris, 1959)
E. Sack: *Platons Musikaesthetik* (Stuttgart, 1959)
G. Arnoux: *Musique platonicienne: âme du monde* (Paris, 1960)
H. Potiron: 'Les notations d'Aristide Quintilien et les harmonies dites platoniciennes', *RdM*, xlvii (1961), 159–76
L. Richter: *Zur Wissenschaftslehre von der Musik bei Platon und Aristoteles* (Berlin, 1961), 27–97
W. Burkert: *Weisheit und Wissenschaft: Studien zu Pythagoras, Philolaos und Platon* (Nuremberg, 1962)
W.D. Anderson: *Ethos and Education in Greek Music* (Cambridge, MA, 1966), 64–110
H. Goergemanns and A.J.Neubecker: 'Heterophonie bei Platon', *AMw*, xxiii (1966), 151–69
P. Boyancé: 'Note sur l'éther chez les Pythagoriciens Platon et Aristote', *Revue des études grecques*, lxxx (1967), 202–9
R. Haase: 'Ein Beitrag Platons zur Tetraktys', *Antaios*, x (1969), 85–91
H.A. Koch: 'Protagoras bei Platon, Aristoteles, und Sextus Empiricus', *Hermes*, xcix (1971), 278–82
Y. Dechavanne: 'L'éducation musicale en Grèce des origines à Platon', *Archeologia: tresors des âges*, lvi (1972), 46–9
E.G. McClain: 'Musical "Marriages" in Plato's Republic', *JMT*, xviii (1974), 242–72
A. Giannarás: 'Das Wachthaus im Bezirk der Musen: zum Verhältnis von Musik und Politik bei Platon', *AMw*, xxxii (1975), 165–83
E.G. McClain: 'A New Look at Plato's Timaeus', *Music and Man*, i (1975), 341–60
E.G. McClain: *The Pythagorean Plato: Prelude to the Song Itself* (Stony Brook, NY, 1978)
A. Barbera: 'Republic 530C–531C: Another Look at Plato and the Pythagoreans', *American Journal of Philology*, cii (1981), 395–410
G.M. Turchetto: 'Plato's Musical Imagination' (diss., SUNY, Stony Brook, 1982)
K. Ioannides: 'L'éthos musical chez Platon', *Philosophia*, xv–xvi (1985–6), 254–65
T.J. Mathiesen: 'Music, Aesthetics, and Cosmology in Early Neo-Platonism', *Paradigms in Medieval Thought: Applications in Medieval Disciplines: Northridge, CA, 1987*, ed. N. van Deusen and A.E. Ford (Lewiston, NY, 1990), 37–64
A. Barker: 'Ptolemy's Pythagoreans, Archytas, and Plato's Conception of Mathematics', *Phronesis*, xxxix (1994), 113–35

For further bibliography *see* GREECE, §I.

WARREN ANDERSON/THOMAS J. MATHIESEN

Platt, Sir Peter (*b* Sheffield, 6 July 1924; *d* Sydney, 3 Aug 2000). English and Australian musicologist and teacher. He studied at the RCM in 1941–2 and again in 1946 after war service, and at Oxford (1946–52), where he took the BLitt with a thesis on the life and music of Richard Dering. His teachers included R.O. Morris, H.K. Andrews, Donald Peart and J.A. Westrup. His professional career was spent in Australia and New Zealand; he was lecturer and senior lecturer in music at the University of Sydney (1952–7), then professor and chair of the music department at the University of Otago, Dunedin; in 1975 he was appointed chair of the music department at the University of Sydney. He also lectured in Europe, the USA and Hong Kong, and in 1990 he was awarded the honorary MMus at the University of Sydney, having become professor emeritus in 1989. From 1990 to 1994 he was editor of *Musicology Australia*, and he was a member of the contemporary music ensemble The Seymour Group.

Platt's concern for the integration of musical educational disciplines had an important effect in Australia and New Zealand and stemmed from his conviction that this region, with its European-based musical culture alongside living indigenous traditions and immigrant music, offers special insights into the nature of music and opportunities for the confluence of Western musicology and ethnomusicology. Under the influence of Donald Peart, Platt became convinced that all music studies – compositional, practical, historical, analytical or sociological – flow from a central definition of music as 'what may be done by humankind with pitches, rhythms and timbres'. Through composition exercises based on classical harmony and the techniques of Debussy and Stravinsky the student may compare the musical traditions of diverse cultures (Indian, Western medieval or Australian Aboriginal) to create an awareness of the rich complex of relationships whose central reference point remains the sounding phenomenon of music. Platt was made member of the Order of Australia a few months before his death.

WRITINGS

'Melodic Patterns in Bach's Counterpoint', *ML*, xxix (1948), 48–56
Dering's Life and Music (diss., U. of Oxford, 1952)
Music as a Living Study (Dunedin, 1957)

'Perspectives of Richard Dering's Vocal Music', *SMA*, i (1967), 56–66

'A Foundation Course in Musical Materials for First Year University Students at the University of Otago', *Challenges in Music Education: Perth 1974*, ed. F. Callaway (Perth, 1976), 179–86

'A Common Attitude to the Pursuit of Music: an Australian opportunity', *Musicology Australia*, xi–xii (1988–9), 2–13

The Poetic Strength of Medieval Thought: a Tribute to the Work of Gordon Athol Anderson (Armidale, 1993) [lecture delivered at U. of New England, 29 Aug 1991]

A Form of Infinity: Music and the Human Spirit (Perth, 1995)

'Debussy and the Harmonic Series', *Essays in Honour of David Evatt Tunley*, ed. F. Callaway (Perth, 1995), 35–60

'Aspects of Dering's Tonality', *Liber amicorum John Steele*, ed. W. Drake (Stuyvesant, NY, 1996), 233–306

EDITIONS
Richard Dering: Secular Vocal Music, MB, xxv (1969); *Cantica Sacra, 1618*, EECM, xv (1974)

J.M. THOMSON

Platter, Felix (*b* Basle, Oct 1536; *d* Basle, 1614). Swiss doctor, professor of medicine and musician. He was the son of the Basle printer and school master Thomas Platter. In 1551 he matriculated at Basle University under the rectorship of Bonifacius Amerbach. He was awarded the baccalaureate of medicine from Montpellier University on 28 May 1556. In 1557 he joined the medical faculty at Basle and in 1571 was promoted to professor of practical medicine.

Platter's abilities as a physician brought him wealth and fame. Yet it was his lifelong interest in music that apparently brought him daily enjoyment. According to his own testimony, he began taking lute lessons at the age of eight from Peter Dorn and Johannes von Scahallen. He also learnt to play the clavichord and harp. As a student in Montpellier he composed and intabulated his own lute pieces, and by 1557 he was performing lute duets with the well-known lutenist Hans Jacob Wecker. He apparently also played with the Strasbourg lutenist Wolff Heckel. Platter bequeathed to his brother an extraordinary collection of musical instruments including ten keyboard instruments, seven viols and six lutes. While none of the music books mentioned in Platter's will have survived, a collection of song text manuscripts copied by Platter is extant (*CH-Bu* AG V 30). These song text sheets consist of about 60 German translations and contrafacta of chansons, madrigals and motets and enable German-texted versions of vocal music by Sermisy, Arcadelt and Lassus to be reconstructed for the first time.

BIBLIOGRAPHY
W. Merian: 'Felix Platter als Musiker', *SIMG*, xiii (1911–12), 272–85

J. Kmetz: 'Singing Texted Songs from Untexted Songbooks: the Evidence of the Basler Liederhandschriften', *Le concert des voix et des instruments à la Renaissance: Tours 1991*, 121–43

M. Staehelin: 'Felix Platter und die Musik', *Felix Platter (1536–1614) in seiner Zeit*, ed. U. Trohler (Basle, 1991), 74–81

J. Kmetz: *The Sixteenth-Century Basel Songbooks: Origins, Content, and Contexts* (Berne, 1995), 127–40, 187–224

JOHN KMETZ

Platters, the. American male popular vocal group. Its principal members were Tony Williams (lead tenor; *b* New Rochelle, NJ, 15 April 1928; *d* New York, 14 Aug 1992), David Lynch (second tenor; *b* St Louis, 1929; *d* 2 Jan 1981), Zola Taylor (soprano; *b* Los Angeles, 1934; Herb Reed (bass; *b* Kansas City, MO, 1931) and Paul Robi (baritone; *b* New Orleans, 1931; *d* 2 Jan 1989). During the second half of the 1950s they applied vocal harmonies derived from the black doo-wop genre to mainstream popular ballads with considerable commercial success. The purity and precision of Williams's singing were the principal features of the Platters' recordings of *Only You* (1955) and *The Great Pretender* (1956), both composed by the group's manager Buck Ram. Other hit records in the USA and abroad included versions of Jimmy Kennedy's *My Prayer* (1956), Kern's *Smoke gets in your eyes* (1959) and Ram's *Twilight Time* (1958). Williams left the group in 1960, later forming his own Platters group. His replacement was Sonny Turner, but by 1970 a series of personnel changes had led to a proliferation of units calling themselves the Platters; Ram, a trained lawyer, expended much money and energy on suing these groups for trademark infringement.

DAVE LAING

Platti, Giovanni Benedetto (*b* Padua or Venice, ?before 1692; *d* Würzburg, 11 Jan 1763). Italian composer. His death certificate gives his age as 64, which would indicate that he was born in about 1698, but information in a letter of 7 October 1764 from Domenico Palafuti to G.B. Martini suggests that the real date of birth could be 9 July 1697; however, Michael Talbot's discovery in Venice (*I-Vas* Milizia da Mar, Bosta 626, Sonardori) of a document mentioning Platti as belonging to the *arte dei sonadori* at the beginning of 1711 means that he cannot have been born later than 1692. Little is known about him before 1722, but in Venice his teachers might have included Francesco Gasparini, Albinoni, Vivaldi, Lotti, Alessandro Marcello or Benedetto Marcello. His father Carlo (*b* c1661; *d* after 1727), a violetta player in the orchestra of the basilica of S Marco, may also have taught him. According to Palafuti in his letter to Martini, Platti travelled to Siena before 1722 and encountered Cristofori's recent invention, the 'cembalo a martelletti', but this is not backed up by any other evidence. It would, however, explain the harmony, style and technique of some of his harpsichord sonatas. In 1722 he went to Würzburg with a group of musicians under the direction of Fortunato Chelleri. There he entered the service of the court of the Prince-Archbishop of Bamberg and Würzburg, Johann Philipp Franz von Schönborn. On 4 February 1723 he married Maria Theresia Lambrucker, a soprano serving at the court. They had eight children, some of whom were musicians, but no music attributable to them has survived. Platti's position at the Würzburg court was as a kind of factotum: he was a singer, he played various instruments, including the violin, the cello, the oboe, the flute and the harpsichord, he performed and he composed. Three letters, only one of which is in Platti's hand, have survived at Würzburg, but they add nothing to our knowledge of his time in Germany. He met the artist Giambattista Tiepolo, who was in Würzburg between 12 December 1750 and 8 November 1753 to decorate the Residenz with frescoes, one of which includes the only known portrait of Platti. Platti continued to work at the Würzburg court until his death.

His surviving output is not very substantial in comparison with that of his contemporaries. It displays two constant characteristics: an exceptional sense of structure and, even in the least inventive pieces, a lively, elegant manner. He made use of both Baroque and pre-Classical forms, almost completely bypassing the *galant* style. Some of his pieces, including the op.1 harpsichord sonatas and the masses, employ the Baroque *fortspinnung* technique, while others, for example the *Miserere*, are more Classical in outlook, with a richer harmonic content. Some of his cello concertos, which can stand beside the best by Boccherini, are also in a more Classical vein, as is the Requiem, which was probably written on the death of one of the Schönborn prince-archbishops (possibly in 1754) and can be considered a masterpiece. The handling of vocal and instrumental resources is remarkable, and Platti's sensitivity is evident in the melodic writing, for example at the beginning of the *Lacrimosa* and in the soprano solo of the *Benedictus*. Some of his harpsichord sonatas and concertos not only constitute contributions to the developing sonata form but also convey a richness and inspiration that looks forward to the pre-Romantic age; rhythmically restless, the music races towards the final chord through ever-changing modulations. Platti seems to have been aware of the possibilities offered by the nascent pianoforte, for some of his pieces include passages in which the range of the keyboard is extended, and some of his adagio movements appear to have been conceived for an instrument that can vary its dynamics or that responds to a sensitive touch. The harpsichord concertos mark the transition from the Baroque to the Classical concerto. In nos.3, 4 and 5 the harpsichord plays a concertante role, and the structure of the Allegro is tutti–solo–tutti–solo–tutti. Nos.6 to 9, however, abandon this form: the strings move from a sustaining role to one where they are in dialogue with the harpsichord, which now has a genuine solo role, taking up and developing the themes announced by the orchestra.

Platti's placement among minor composers such as Vento, G.M. Rutini and Domenico Alberti deserves to be reviewed. Analysis of much of his music has revealed a composer who can be placed among the more important figures of his time.

WORKS
VOCAL
2 masses, 4vv, *D-WD*
Mass, 4vv a cappella, *WD*
Requiem, 4vv, ed. L. Bettarini (Rome, 1985)
Offertorium, 8vv, 2 vn, va, org, *EB*
Stabat mater, B, fl, ob, 2 va, org, *WD*
Miserere, solo vv, chorus, ob, str, org, ed. R. Lupi (Milan, 1967)
2 cantatas, S, str: Sdegni e disprezzi, Già libero già sciolto, *WD*
Corre dal bosco al prato (cant.), S, hpd obbl, 2 vn, va, b, *DB*

INSTRUMENTAL
9 concs., hpd, str, *D-DB*, nos.1 and 2, ed. F. Torrefranca (Milan, 1949–53); nos.5 and 6, ed. in RRMCE, xxxvii (1991)
25 concs., 4 inc., vc obbl, 2 vn, b, *WD*
12 concs., vc concertato, 2 vn, *WD* [9 are from the 25 concs. with vc obbl]
Conc., vn, str, *Dl*
Conc., ob, 2 vn, va, vc, hpd, ed. H. Winschermann (Hamburg, 1964)
6 sonates pour le clavessin sur le goût italien, op.1 (Nuremberg, 1742), ed. G. Pestelli (Milan, 1978)
6 sonate, hpd, op.4 (Nuremberg, 1746), ed. G. Pestelli (Milan, 1986)
6 sonatas, hpd, ed. in IMi, new ser., ii (Milan, 1963)
2 sonatas, hpd, ed. A. Iesuè (Rome, 1982–4)
Arioso, Allegro, hpd, ed. A. Iesuè (Rome, 1984)
Fantasia-gavotta, hpd, ed. A. Iesuè (Rome, 1984)
22 sonatas, a 3, 1 inc., *WD*, most for vn, vc, bc, some incl. ob, 1 incl. bn
12 sonatas, vc, bc, *WD*
4 ricercares, vn, vc, ed. in HM, lxxxvii–lxxxviii (1951/R)
Sonata, vn, b, *WD*
6 sonate, fl, vc/hpd, op.3 (Nuremberg, 1743), no.1, ed. E. Schenck and H. Ruf (Milan, 1955), nos.2 and 3, ed. P. Jarnach (Mainz, 1924/R), no.4, ed. P. Jarnach (Mainz, 1936) and H. Ruf (Baden-Baden, 1954), no.6, ed. H. Ruf (Mainz, 1963)
Trio sonata, fl, ob, bc, ed. H. Kölbel (Wilhelmshaven, 1978)
Solo, ob, b, ed. G. Hausswald (Heidelberg, 1975)

LOST WORKS
Arianna (op), see Torrefranca (1963)
2 orats, formerly *D-WD*: Franchonia cristiana. lib *WÜu*; Sant'Elena a calvario, 1732
Sedecia (azione sacra), formerly *WD*, see Torrefranca (1963)
Serenata, lib *WÜu*
2 concs., hpd, formerly *DS*
Sonata, 2 ob, b formerly *DS*

BIBLIOGRAPHY
GerberL
F. Torrefranca: 'La creazione della sonata drammatica moderna rivendicata all'Italia: Giovanni Platti il grande', *RMI*, xvii (1910), 309–58
F. Torrefranca: 'Poeti minori del clavicembalo', *RMI*, xvii (1910), 763–821
O. Kaul: *Geschichte der Würzburger Hofmusik in 18 Jahrhundert* (Würzburg, 1924)
F. Torrefranca: *Le origini italiane del romanticismo musicale* (Turin, 1930)
F. Torrefranca: 'Prime ricognizioni dello stile violoncellistico Plattiano', *IMSCR IV: Basle 1949*, 203–11
F. Torrefranca: *Giovanni Benedetto Platti e la sonata moderna*, IMi, new ser., ii (Milan, 1963)
M. Fabbri: 'Una nuova fonte per la conoscenza di Giovanni Platti e del suo "Miserere": note integrative in margine alla monografia di F. Torrefranca', *Chigiana*, xxiv, new serv. iv (1967), 181–202
A. Iesuè: 'Le opere a stampa e manoscritte di Giovanni Benedetto Platti', *NRMI*, ix (1975), 541–51
D.E. Freeman: 'The Earliest Italian Keyboard Concertos', *JM*, iv (1985–6), 121–34
A. Iesuè: 'Il concerto con il cembalo solista nel XVIII secolo in Italia', *NRMI*, xx (1986)
A. Iesuè: 'È l'unico ritratto di Platti?', *NRMI*, xxii (1988)
S.H. Hansell: 'Italian Prosody as a Guide to Musical Structure: Accent, Articulation and Accompaniment in the Flute Sonatas of Giovanni Platti', *Fluting and Dancing: Articles and Reminiscences for Betty Bang Mather on her 65th Birthday* (New York, 1992)
F. Dangel-Hofmann: 'Der guthe Houboist von Würtzburg, der platti …', *Halbjahresschrift der Gesellschaft für Bayerische Musikgeschichte*, no.47 (1993)
D.E. Freeman: 'J.C. Bach and the Early Classical Italian Masters', *Eighteenth-Century Keyboard Music*, ed. R.L. Marshall (New York, 1994), 230–69
A. Iesuè: 'Giovanni Benedetto Platti: dal Barocco agli albori del classicismo', *Mantova musica*, no.27 (1994)
A. Iesuè: *Giovanni Benedetto Platti (con il Catalogo delle opere)* (Milan, 1997)
A. Iesuè: 'Giovanni Benedetto Platti: un grande del sonatismo preclassico', *Musicalia*, vi (1997)

ALBERTO IESUÈ

Plattner, Augustin (*fl* 1613–24). German composer and organist. The earliest surviving record is that of Plattner's marriage in the church of St Jakob, Innsbruck, on 17 June 1613. According to the foreword to his *Missae octo vocum cum duplici basso ad organum applicato* (Nuremberg, 1623/4; ed. in Denkmäler der Musik in Baden-Würtemberg, iii, Munich, 1995), Plattner's musical education was financed by Deutscher Orden. From 1621 he worked as organist to the Deutschherrn-Orden in Mergentheim (now Bad Mergentheim in Baden-Würtemberg), where he may have succeeded Andreas Lames. His masses are written for double choir, in the Venetian tradition. Of the eight masses one is a *Missa sexti toni*, one a *Missa pro defunctis* and the other six are parody masses, in which madrigals called *Lieto godea* and *De fortuna*, two motets *Ad te, Domine, levavi* and *Isti sunt triumphatores*, and the German melodies *Christ ist erstanden* and *Joseph, lieber Joseph mein* are used as material.

BIBLIOGRAPHY
EitnerQ; FétisB; GöhlerV; SennMT; WaltherML
P. Wagner: *Geschichte der Messe* (Leipzig, 1913/R)

AUGUST SCHARNAGL/DIETER HABERL

Platz, Robert H(ugo) P(hillip) (*b* Baden-Baden, 16 Aug 1951). German composer and conductor. He studied composition first with Fortner at the Freiburg Conservatory (from 1971), and later with Stockhausen at the Staatliche Hochschule für Musik in Cologne (from 1973), returning to Freiburg to graduate in conducting with Francis Travis in 1977. After studies in the USA, he went back to Cologne in 1980, and in 1983 he founded the Ensemble Köln, which became a leading new music chamber ensemble responsible for many important premières.

Platz is one of the few significant composers of his generation to have been untouched by the neo-Romantic movement that swept through Germany in the late 1970s. Technically, his music is a fastidious, personal continuation of the serial, structuralist path pioneered by Stockhausen; emotionally, however, it often inhabits a hyper-tense, post-Expressionist world more reminiscent of Zimmermann.

Platz's first major work, *Schwelle* (1973–8), a planned 6-part orchestral cycle of which only two parts were completed, already contains significant aspects of his later work: a four-part formal conception related to the seasons and the four elements (perhaps influenced by Stockhausen's *Sirius*), and a clear distinction between 'static' and 'processual' formal components. In *CHLEBNIKOV* (1979) Platz took the first decisive steps towards the 'formal polyphony' (a polyphony not just of parts, but of ensembles and ultimately of independent pieces) that has been a lasting preoccupation of his work; though exactly notated, the piece is conceived in terms of different simultaneous 'musics' (ranging from solos to nonets), regulated at a higher formal level by five different 'levels' of relationship. *Maro & STILLE* (1980) takes the separation of strata further; there are three main components: a song for high soprano and piano, a violin solo (performable separately), and an initially static music for wind instruments and choir. The combination of solo violin and piano with a small wind ensemble foreshadows much of Platz's work from the 1990s.

Chamber works from the 1980s continue to investigate new dimensions of musical form, notably the *Flötenstücke* (1982) and the remarkable *from fear of thunder, dreams. . .* (1987). The latter introduces a static, claustrophobic intensity which also typifies two stage works from the late 1980s, the fragment *VERKOMMENES UFER* and *DUNKLES HAUS*. From the early 1990s, beginning with *SCHREYAHN*, Platz extended 'formal polyphony' to spatial separation of the instrumental forces involved in the various temporally overlapping movements – not only in different parts of the main auditorium, but also outside it. Subsequently, *tôku/NAH* (1994) was composed to overlap with the end of *SCHREYAHN*, and from the mid-1990s on, all of Platz's major works have been conceived as part of an endless chain of interlocking pieces which can also be played independently. However, his intention is not to create an epic cycle of works in the manner of Stockhausen's *LICHT*; any segment of the formal chain is an adequate representation of the underlying idea. At the 1996 Donaueschingener Musiktagen, for example, *ANDERE RÄUME*, *nerv ii* and *Turm/Weiter* were presented as an interlocking sequence, with *Echo II* as an epilogue.

WORKS
(*selective list*)

Ops: VERKOMMENES UFER (scenic composition, 2, H. Müller), 1983–6, unfinished; DUNKLES HAUS (music theatre, 11 stages, C. Litterscheid), 1989–90, Munich, Marstall, 6 June 1991

Orch: Schwelle I and III, orch, tape, 1973–8; tôku/NAH, wind, 1994; Turm/Weiter, 1996

Vocal: Maro & STILLE (T. Brasch), S, 2A, mixed chorus, vn, ob, cl, hn, tpt, trbn, perc, pf, 1980; SCHREYAHN (H. Kattner), S, vc, fl, tpt, 2 pf, 11 wind, 1990; RELAIS (l'oeil) ATILA rounding, B, vn, pf, perc, chbr ens, 1991–2; GRENZGÄNGE STEINE (Kattner), S, 2 pf, orch, 1993

Chbr: CHLEBNIKOV, fl, ob, cl, hn, tpt, trbn, 2 vc, db, tape, 1979; rapport, fl, ob, cl, perc, vn, vc, db, pf, 1979; RAUMFORM, cl, 1981; trail, für einen Pianisten (Klavierstück no.1), pf, 1981; Flötenstucke, a fl, b cl, cl, hn, tpt, hp, va, vc, 1982; Klavierstück no.2, pf, tape, 1984; QUARTETT (Zeitstrahl), str qt, 1986; from fear of thunder, dreams. . ., fl, cl, hn, vn, vc, perc, pf, tape, 1987; Klavierstück no.3, pf, 1988; REZITAL, picc + a fl + b fl + cb fl, tape, 1992; Stein, 2 pf, 1993; dense/Echo I, fl, cl, vn, vc, pf, 1994–6; ANDERE RÄUME, 4 perc, tape, 1994–6; nerv ii, vn, pf, 10 wind, 1995; Echo II, vn, pf, 10 wind, perc, 1995; FLEUR, b cl/t sax, 1996; main FLEUR (Echo III) (1996–98), b cl, t sax, perc, pf, wind ens, live elecs, 1996–8; charm, vn, bass shô + u [mouth organs], 1997; Echo IV, vc, 1997; strange, cl, hp, perc, 1997; down, cl, hn, bn, 2 vn, va, vc, db, 1998; spazio. . . (Echo V), tpt, hn, trbn, 1998; up, pf, 1998

Tape: REQUIEM (B. Rauschenbach), 1983

Principal publishers: Breitkopf & Härtel, Ricordi

BIBLIOGRAPHY

C. von Blumröder: 'Nicht einfach, aber neu. . . zu Robert H.P. Platz', *Neuland*, i (1980), 94–5

E. van den Hoogen: 'Raumform: Formpolyphonie von Robert H.P. Platz', *Neuland*, v (1985), 220–25

R.H.P. Platz: 'Schriften zur Musik 1979–93', *Feedback Papers*, no.39 (1993)

R.H.P. Platz: 'More than Just Notes: Psychoacoustics and Composition', *Leonardo*, v (1995), 23–8

R. Toop: 'Immer weiter', *Musik & Ästhetik*, no.6 (1998), 61–76

RICHARD TOOP

Plautus, Titus Maccius (*b* Sarsina, Umbria, *c*254 BCE; *d c*184 BCE). Roman comic playwright. 20 of his comedies and a portion of another have survived, all *fabulae palliatae* (i.e. plays with Greek settings and costumes). They are free adaptations of Greek originals by MENANDER and other leading authors of the Athenian New Comedy (*c*330–270 BCE), although none of Plautus's prototypes survives.

The abbreviations DV and C in the manuscripts of Plautus indicate the division of scenes into the two main categories of *diverbium*, spoken dialogue, and *canticum*, lines accompanied by a tibia player (*tibicen*). On average, nearly two-thirds of the play is occupied by *canticum*. There were apparently two varieties of *canticum*: the first was recitative, written in iambic, trochaic or anapaestic septenarii or octonarii (seven- or eight-feet lines); the second was lyric song in more intricate and variable metres, chiefly cretics, bacchics and ionics. Although a *canticum* was usually a solo aria, there were sometimes two, three or even four singers, as in the *Mostellaria*, and sometimes the singer danced as well. Like its Greek prototype, Roman comedy dispensed with the chorus as an integral part of the play. Sometimes the tibia player would provide a musical interlude as in the *Pseudolus* (573a).

According to the prefatory remarks, *didascalia*, to Plautus's *Stichus*, a slave musician named Marcipor composed the accompaniment and used *tibiae sarranae* throughout. This is the only direct reference to Plautus's use of the double pipes, although there is some information about his contemporary TERENCE (see Wille, 1977, pp.86–7). However, the diversity and brilliance of his lyric metres show how important was the musical element; his virtuosity, which translations can hardly begin to suggest, rivals that of Aristophanes. In six of his plays lyrics take up about a quarter of the total text, and the entire corpus has slightly more recitative than regular spoken dialogue. The *cantica* of Plautus are often highpoints; in several of his plays they are combined with dancing to provide a joyful concluding scene. The tibia accompaniment must have had extraordinary rhythmic variety, if, as is probable, it corresponded to the intricate variety of the lyric metres. Nothing definite is known about the melodic nature of these settings and the difference between speech and song in performance has itself been questioned (Beare, 1950, pp.219ff), although such scepticism is a minority view. Cicero's remark (*Academica priora*, ii.7.20; cf ii.27.86) that connoisseurs of theatre music could tell from the first notes (*primo inflatu*) of the tibia prelude what work was to be performed might be evidence for fixed musical settings, but this would seem to be inconsistent with what is otherwise known about secular music in antiquity. Possibly the *tibicen* regularly stated and then improvised on a familiar theme.

Within the imagined world of the plays, supposedly Greek but reflecting many Roman characteristics, the female musician, *tibicina* or *fidicina* (from *fides*, 'lyre'), lacks any status, being regularly bought and sold and a butt of jesting. Plautus seldom made technical allusions to music. In *Pseudolus* (1275), he refers to *ionica*, a kind of lascivious dance (cf Aristophanes, *Frogs*, 130) and in *Stichus* (760), to *cantionem … cinaedicam* (from *cinaedus*, 'sodomite').

See also ROME, §I.

WRITINGS

W.M. Lindsay, ed.: *T. Macci Plauti comoediae* (Oxford, 1904–5/R)
P. Nixon, ed. and trans.: *Plautus* (London and Cambridge, MA, 1916–38/R)

BIBLIOGRAPHY

E. Fraenkel: *Plautinisches im Plautus* (Berlin, 1922; It. trans., enlarged, 1960)
W. Beare: 'The Delivery of Cantica on the Roman Stage', *Classical Review*, liv (1940), 70–79
W. Beare: *The Roman Stage* (London, 1950, 3/1964), 45ff, 219ff
G.E. Duckworth: *The Nature of Roman Comedy* (Princeton, NJ, 1952, enlarged 2/1994 by R. Hunter), esp. 361ff
E. Paratore: 'Il flautista nel Duskolos e nello Pseudolus', *Revista di cultura classica e medioevale*, i (1959), 310–25
G. Wille: *Musica romana* (Amsterdam, 1967), 158ff, 308ff
E. Paratore: 'Plaute et la musique', *Maske und Kothurn*, xv (1969), 131–60
F.H. Sandbach: *The Comic Theatre of Greece and Rome* (London, 1977)
G. Wille: *Einführung in das römische Musikleben* (Darmstadt, 1977), 80–82

WARREN ANDERSON/THOMAS J. MATHIESEN

Plautzius [Plautius, Plautz, Blautz, Plavec], **Gabriel** (*b* Carniola; *d* Mainz, 11 Jan 1641). Slovene composer active in Germany. His signature 'Carniolus' implies that he originated from Carniola (Kranjska), today a province of Slovenia. On 10 April 1612 he was appointed Kapellmeister at the electoral court at Mainz of prince elector Johann Schweikardt von Kronberg. Together with his employer, he took part in the imperial coronations, providing 'exquisita et rara musica'. His most important surviving music is the collection of 26 songs *Flosculus vernalis sacras cantiones, missas aliasque laudes B. Mariae conteniens* (Aschaffenburg, 1620–21; ed. T. Faganel, Ljubljana, 1997) for three to eight voices with continuo. It includes three masses, two introits, a communion motet, eight Marian songs and 12 songs on psalmodic and sequence texts. These last are in mostly *stile antiquo* motet style, with frequent use of *proportio tripla*. Some of the pieces also show an early Baroque construction, with solo concertante passages and a tripartite ritornello. There are also three pieces in RISM 1627^2 and four pieces edited in Cvetko (1963).

A letter survives from Plautzius to the abbot of the Benedictine monastery in Munster-Schwarzach (23 April 1622), to whom Plautzius donated a collection of music. After 1626 sources also mention Daniel Bollius in the role of organist and Kapellmeister at Mainz, and from 1631 Bollius appears to have been helping 'the court composer of Mainz in poor health' with his duties. An entry in an obituary book in Mainz (12 January 1641) comments that Plautzius was 'most exquisite in musical instruments and without peer in the art of composition with ten or 12 voices'.

BIBLIOGRAPHY

J.F. Mantenesins: *De parentela, electione et coronatione Ferdinandi* (Cologne, 1621)
A. Gottron: 'Gabriel Plautz, 1612–1641, Kapellmeister des Mainzer Erzbischofs Schweikard von Kronberg', *KJb*, xxxi–xxxiii (1936–8), 58
A. Gottron: *Mainzer Musikgeschichte von 1500 bis 1800* (Mainz, 1959), 43ff, 55–6
H.F. Friedrichs: *Aschaffenburg im Spiegel der Stiftsmatrikel, 1605–1650* (Aschaffenburg, 1962)
D. Cvetko: *Skladatelji Gallus, Plautzius, Dolar in njihovo delo/Les compositeurs Gallus, Plautzius, Dolar et leur oeuvre* (Ljubljana, 1963) [in Slovenian and Fr.]
D. Cvetko: *Histoire de la musique slovène* (Maribor, 1967), 90ff
A. Gottron: 'Gabriel Plautz: dvorni kapelnik v Mainzu', *MZ*, iv (1968), 57–61
K.F. Becker: *Die Tonwerke des XVI. und XVII. Jahrhunderts oder Systematisch-chronologisch Zusammenstellung der in diesen zwei Jahrhundert Gedruckten Musikalien* (Hildesheim, 1969)
A. Rijavec: 'Gabriel Plavec und sein "Flosculus vernalis"', *Musica antiqua III: Bydgoszcz 1972*, 323–30 [with Fr. summary]
W. Steger: *Gabriel Plautz: ein Mainzer Hofkapellmeister im frühen 17. Jahrhundert* (Würzburg, 1991)

TOMAŽ FAGANEL

Plavec, Gabriel. *See* PLAUTZIUS, GABRIEL.

Player organ. An organ, other than a BARREL ORGAN, which may be played either by a keyboard or by perforated paper rolls; it is similar in this respect to a PLAYER PIANO. The earliest player organs were reed instruments and were developed from the small portable automatic REED ORGAN (*see also* ORGANETTE). The first was the Symphony, made by Wilcox & White of Meriden, Connecticut, in 1888. This was little more than an American organ with a paper-roll-playing mechanism. The makers of the VOCALION reed organ produced a small 46-note organette called the Syreno. This became the basis of the first AEOLIAN player organ, built into a piano-type case and working on suction. The compass was extended to 58 notes and the instrument was named the Aeolian Grand (first produced in 1895). The Aeolian Company's most successful player organ was a pressure-operated instrument, the Orchestrelle. A wide range of Orchestrelles was made between 1890 and 1918, all featuring a rich variety of Vocalion-patented ranks of orchestrally voiced reeds.

Although generally retaining a single keyboard, two-manual Orchestrelles were made which used 112-note music rolls arranged to control two separate divisions of stops: these were particularly fine instruments. Manufacture was mostly in America but many were assembled for the British market by Aeolian's piano factory at Hayes, Middlesex. Despite their relatively high cost, Orchestrelles enjoyed great popularity, having a large and varied repertory of music. In Europe the best makers of player reed organs were Schiedmayer in Stuttgart (the Scheola) and Mustel in Paris (the Concertal).

Player organ technology was soon applied to the pipe organ and Aeolian built a number of costly domestic instruments including some which used the Duo-Art system that was developed for the REPRODUCING PIANO. These pipe organs controlled their own stops and swell shutters from the music roll. Some of the finest player pipe organs were built by Estey and by Skinner in America, and by Welte in Germany. These generally were 88-note actions which would play piano rolls, but alternatively 58-note actions could be fitted to play the rich library of Aeolian music rolls.

BIBLIOGRAPHY

J. Fox: 'The Aeolian Orchestrelle', *Music & Automata*, i (1984), 253–62

A.W.J.G. Ord-Hume: *Harmonium*(Newton Abbot, 1986)

A.W.J.G. Ord-Hume: 'Who Invented the Aeolian Orchestrelle? The Story of the Vocalion', *Music & Automata*, iv (1989), 240–57

ARTHUR W.J.G. ORD-HUME

Player piano. A piano fitted with a self-playing mechanism, normally pneumatic, capable of playing from a perforated paper music roll (piano roll). The first automatic piano-playing mechanism was the BARREL PIANO, developed at the end of the 18th century. Later developments dispensed with the cumbersome barrel; for example, A.-F. Debain's Antiphonel (1846) operated the piano through a system of wooden boards or planchettes studded with metal pins to represent the music to be played. Napoleon Fourneaux's barrel-operated Pianista (1863) was the first pneumatic piano-playing machine. These were the prototypes of the piano player (also called a cabinet player or push-up player), the forerunner of the player piano. The piano player consisted of a cabinet containing the pneumatic mechanism. When pushed in front of an ordinary piano, a row of felt-covered wooden fingers at the back rested on the keyboard to play it. Inside the cabinet a music roll or note-sheet would pass over a 'tracker bar', usually of brass, with some 65 (later 88) slots or ports, one for each note. When a perforation in the moving note-sheet uncovered a port in the tracker bar, suction (generated by foot treadles) would draw air through the port to operate a pneumatic striking action, forcing the wooden finger down. This principle is generally known as the 'paper-as-a-valve' system. Levers in the front of the cabinet controlled tempo, the relative loudness of treble and bass, and the operation of the sustaining pedal of the piano; in many cabinets the latter could also be controlled automatically from the music roll. In France, towards the end of the 19th century, some mechanical piano players were still made which played perforated cardboard discs, rolls of heavy waxed paper, or zigzag folded music books.

The player piano was the outcome of a whole series of pioneering piano-playing systems, some of the earliest being mechanical and a few being electrically operated. It signalled a radical improvement on previous player methods, the mechanism being built into the piano itself. The control levers were placed in a panel underneath the keyboard. The pneumatic action, fundamental to the player piano, had been developed and refined first in the small portable automatic reed organ called the ORGANETTE.

Robert W. Pain built a 39-note, mechanically operated player piano for Needham & Sons in 1880, following it with a 65-note electrically operated one in 1888. Wilcox & White of Meriden, Connecticut, successfully combined a piano and reed organ with a roll-playing inner player in 1892. Considerable experimental work was taking place simultaneously in America and Germany: in 1895 Edwin Scott Votey invented the first 'Pianola' piano player (and applied for a patent in 1897), the mechanism of which was later adapted to form his company's first 'inner player', and Hupfeld of Leipzig produced a similar instrument at about the same time. However, the first piano to have a practical pneumatic player mechanism built into it was that patented by Theodore P. Brown of Worcester, Massachusetts, in 1897. Melville Clark built his first 'inner-player' player piano in 1901, and in 1904 he was the first person to fit a player mechanism to a grand piano.

By careful pedalling and judicious use of expression controls, damper pedal control and tempo regulator, musically pleasing effects could be obtained on a player piano. Some music rolls included printed instructions suggesting the dynamics etc., to be used by the person operating the instrument. Since many people to whom the player piano appealed were musically unskilled, however, player piano manufacturers soon attempted to make the expressive effects automatic by incorporating them into the functions that could be controlled automatically from the music roll. This was then played on an 'expression' piano equipped with pneumatic functions to 'interpret' the supplementary perforations controlling pedalling and regulating the force applied to the hammers. For further discussion of the expression system, and of subsequent, more sophisticated forms of fully automatic, self-playing pianos, *see* REPRODUCING PIANO.

The 'key-top' player was a much smaller and with simpler mechanism made to fit on top of the keyboard. A hand-cranked pneumatic model was introduced by 1899, and several electrically-pumped models were introduced in the USA after World War II, but the variety had insufficient suction power to be able to replicate expressive piano performance due to the small size of its air reservoir.

The success of the early player piano brought many manufacturers into the business, each with its own version. The compass of the piano keyboard that could be played by the player system was somewhat abbreviated due to the physical bulk of the early actions. In the beginning, instruments which played on 58 of the keyboard's notes were common. Other models were produced which worked on 61, 65, 70, 73, 82 and 88 notes. The lack of standardization was a major problem to the manufacturers of music rolls, and in 1910, at a convention of player manufacturers held at Buffalo, New York, it was agreed to standardize on two compasses of 65 and 88 notes.

Between 1900 and 1930, 2·5 million instruments were sold in the USA. In London, a 1922 trade directory listed no fewer than 52 makers. In 1900 171,000 'ordinary' pianos were made and 6000 player pianos; by 1925, at the peak of the player piano's vogue, the totals were

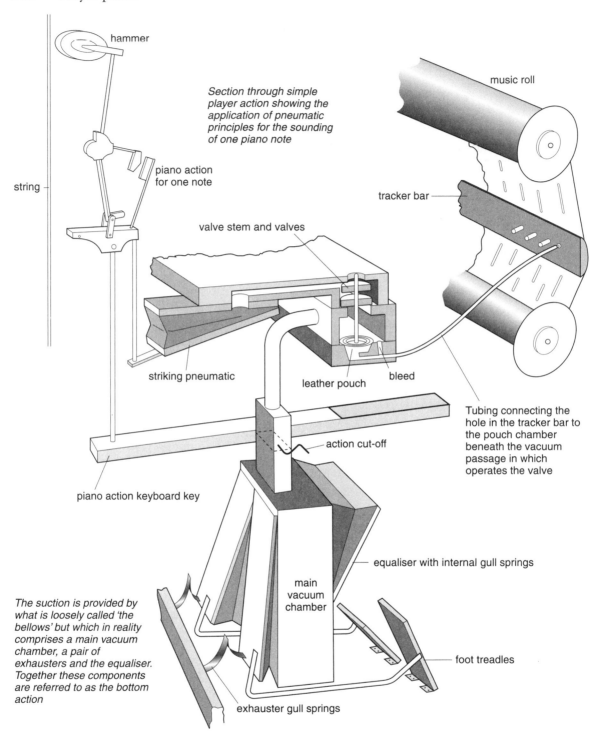

hammer

Section through simple
player action showing the
application of pneumatic
principles for the sounding
of one piano note

music roll

piano action
for one note

string

tracker bar

valve stem and valves

striking pneumatic

leather pouch

bleed

Tubing connecting the
hole in the tracker bar to
the pouch chamber
beneath the vacuum
passage in which
operates the valve

action cut-off

piano action keyboard key

equaliser with internal gull springs

main
vacuum
chamber

The suction is provided by
what is loosely called 'the
bellows' but which in reality
comprises a main vacuum
chamber, a pair of
exhausters and the equaliser.
Together these components
are referred to as the bottom
action

foot treadles

exhauster gull springs

1. Reproducing mechanism diagram

136,000 ordinary pianos and 169,000 player pianos. Important manufacturers included, in the USA, the Aeolian Co., American Piano Co., Auto-Pneumatic Action Co., Melville Clark Piano Co., Standard Player Action Co., and Wilcox & White Co.; in Germany, Hupfeld and Kastner-Autopiano; and in England, Marshall and Sons and the Aeolian Co. Ltd (a branch of the American firm, also known as the Orchestrelle Co.). Many other piano manufacturers purchased player mechanisms for installation in their own pianos. In addition to player pianos for the home, coin-operated machines were produced for use in cafés, restaurants, hotels and other public places. The success of Aeolian's 'Pianola' inspired others to capitalize on sound-alike names: Triumphola, Odeola,

Let the Pianola Piano bring you happiness in 1914.

Do not merely hope for increased happiness in the year that is before you—ensure it by purchasing a Pianola Piano. There is no other investment you can make which will so surely bring pleasure to you and every member of your household, for by its means everyone can play the music they love. Day in, day out, through many a year, the influence of the world's sweetest music will brighten and cheer you through the dull routine of life.

The Pianola Piano is the genuine Pianola combined with the STEINWAY, WEBER, STECK, or STROUD Piano. You are invited to play at Æolian Hall, or to write for Illustrated Catalogue " T."

THE ORCHESTRELLE COMPANY, ÆOLIAN HALL,
135-6-7, New Bond Street, LONDON, W.

2. 'Let the Pianola Piano bring you happiness in 1914'. Advert from 'The Sphere', 17 January 1914.

The Pianola with the London Symphony Orchestra
at Queen's Hall.

A great artistic triumph

At Queen's Hall, London, before a vast audience, the Pianola once and for all vindicated the unique position which it holds in the artistic world. In conjunction with the famous London Symphony Orchestra, conducted by Herr Arthur Nikisch, the Pianola was used to play the well-known Grieg Concerto in A minor and the Liszt Hungarian Fantasie. The Pianola was also used to accompany the well-known vocalist, Miss Elena Gerhardt, in songs by Strauss and Wolff. Immense enthusiasm has been aroused amongst the public and press by this remarkable concert, but none greater than that of Herr Arthur Nikisch himself.

Herr ARTHUR NIKISCH,
who conducted the orchestra
on this occasion, wrote :—

"Before leaving for Germany I feel that I must congratulate you on the great artistic success you achieved with the Pianola at the Orchestral Concert on Friday last. When I was asked to conduct this concert the idea was interesting to me, but it was not until after the rehearsal that I realised with astonishment and admiration that with the Pianola the performer could express every nuance and shade of musical feeling and that he could impart to the instrument his individual reading with absolute clearness and without any trace of mechanical effect.

The performance of the Grieg Concerto, the solo Pianoforte part being played by means of the Pianola, was a revelation to me. Not only was the ensemble perfect, but in the passages where special prominence was given to the solo instrument, such as the cadenza, the result was magnificent. Save for the fact that the instrument supplies the performer with absolutely perfect technique, the Pianola should never again be referred to as a mechanical instrument.

I am convinced that the Pianola is destined to become of great educational value and that its future influence on all that appertains to musical knowledge and enjoyment is incalculable."
(Signed)   ARTHUR NIKISCH.

Call at Æolian Hall and play the Pianola Piano or write for Catalogue "T."

The Orchestrelle Company,
ÆOLIAN HALL,
 135-6-7, New Bond Street, London. W.

3. 'The Pianola with the London Symphony Orchestra'. Advert from 'The Sphere'.

Monola, Pedola, Humanola and so on, while even the controls were given fanciful names such as Phrasiola, Tempola, Automelle and Transposa. The trade mark 'Pianola' itself became synonymous with the player piano, and was commonly adopted as a generic term for any self-playing piano. This form of marketing could not detract from the true value of the instrument, for there is little doubt that the player piano helped to popularize a great deal of music which might otherwise never have been widely known. It was acclaimed as an instrument of musical education by several well-known pianists of the time, who were handsomely paid to write testimonials. Many lending libraries of music rolls were established, and every piano retailer sold players and their rolls.

During the 1929–31 Depression, the market collapsed and sales of player pianos dwindled to almost nothing. In spite of concerted attempts to revive the player-piano market in London, the industry was finished long before the outbreak of World War II. Basic player pianos are still produced in small numbers in America; digitally controlled reproducing pianos have gained a certain popularity for use in public places.

BIBLIOGRAPHY
A. Dolge: *Men who made Piano History* (Covina, CA, 1876/R)
A. Dolge: *Pianos and their Makers* (Covina, CA, 1911–13/R)
W.B. White: *The Player Piano up to Date . . . a Comprehensive Treatise on the Principles, Construction, Adjustment, Regulation and Use of Pneumatic Mechanisms for Piano-Playing* (New York, 1914)
J. McTammany: *The Technical History of the Player* (New York, 1915/R)
E. Newman: *The Piano-Player and its Music* (London, 1920)
H. Ellingham: *How to Use a Player Piano* (London, 1922)
S. Grew: *The Art of the Player Piano: a Text-Book for Student and Teacher* (London, 1922)
W.B. White: *Piano Playing Mechanisms* (New York, 1925)
H.N. Roehl: *Player Piano Treasury* (Vestal, NY, 1961, 2/1973)
Q.D. Bowers: *Encyclopedia of Automatic Instruments* (New York, 1972)
C. Ehrlich: *The Piano: a History* (London, 1976, 2/1990)
A.W.J.G. Ord-Hume: *Pianola: the History of the Self-Playing Piano* (London, 1984)
C.H. Roell: *The Piano in America, 1890–1940* (Chapel Hill, NC, 1989)
ARTHUR W.J.G. ORD-HUME

Playford. English family of music publishers and booksellers.

(1) **John Playford (i)** (*b* Norwich, 1623; *d* London, between 24 Dec 1686 and 7 Feb 1687). Publisher, bookseller, and vicar-choral of St Paul's Cathedral. During the period 1651–84 he dominated the music publishing trade (then virtually confined to London) in a business to which his son (2) Henry Playford succeeded. For the printing of his books he engaged the services of Thomas Harper (successor to Thomas Snodham, who had inherited the business of Thomas East), William Godbid (successor to Harper) and his own nephew (3) John Playford the younger, who, apprenticed to Godbid, entered into business in 1679 with the latter's widow Anne. The format, style and printing of Playford's books, together with evidence from the stationers' registers, suggest with some certainty that they were printed with East's types, although for title-pages, other than those engraved, a less florid style than the earlier borders was preferred. In many instances Playford adopted East's device and its surrounding motto, 'Laetificat cor musica' (fig.1).

1. Device adopted by Playford's printer, Thomas Harper, from Thomas East

1. Life. 2. Publications.

1. LIFE.   A monument at St Michael-at-Plea, Norwich, to his father John, a mercer, and local records show that he was one of a large family many of whom were scriveners or stationers. Since there is no record of his entry at the grammar school his brother Matthew attended, he was probably educated at the almonry or choir school attached to the cathedral, where he acquired a knowledge of music and the 'love of Divine Service' to which he later referred. Shortly after the death of his father (22 March 1639) he was apprenticed to John Benson, a London publisher of St Dunstan's Churchyard, Fleet Street (23 March 1639/40), for seven years, achieving his freedom on 5 April 1647, when he became a member of the Yeomanry of the Stationers' Company. This entitled him to trade as a publisher.

He lost no time in securing the tenancy of the shop in the porch of the Temple Church from which all his publications were issued until his retirement. It was one of the addresses of Henry Playford until 1690, when the stock was auctioned. Royalist by family and by personal inclination, Playford began publishing political tracts culminating in *The Perfect Narrative of the Tryal of the King* and others relating to the executions of royalist nobility (reprinted in 1660 as *England's Black Tribunal*). In November 1649 a warrant was issued for the arrest of Playford and his associates. Nothing more is known of him until a year later, when on 7 November 1650 he entered in the stationers' registers 'A booke entituled The English Dancing Master'. Although registration before publishing was theoretically obligatory he entered so few of his music books that it is impossible to tell if this, subsequently published in 1651 (fig.2), was his first.

In 1653 he was admitted clerk to the Temple Church, an office he held with some distinction to the end of his life, devoting himself to the repair and maintenance of the building and to promoting the seemly ordering of the

2. Title-page of 'The English Dancing Master' (London, 1651), printed by Thomas Harper and published by John Playford

services. At about this time he married. When his wife Hannah inherited from her father, Benjamin Allen, publisher of Cornhill, the Playfords moved (1655) from the neighbourhood of the Temple to Islington, where she established a boarding-school for girls, which she maintained until her death in 1679. Playford then moved back to London, taking a house in Arundel Street, Strand, which later passed to his son.

The court books of the Stationers' Company show that Playford was called to the Livery in 1661. In 1681 a letter from the king to the master and wardens required that he and others named be admitted to the court of assistants. Soon afterwards he was allotted a share in the English Stock which managed the company's lucrative monopoly in psalms, primers and almanacks. In the successive purges of the court in 1684 and 1685 he survived unscathed, no doubt through royal protection. In 1684 he retired from active business in favour of his son Henry and another young man, Robert Carr. A number of books, however, retained his imprint until 1686. In his will of that year, which names Henry Purcell and John Blow as beneficiaries, he desired to be buried in the Temple Church, or in St Faith's, the stationers' chapel in the undercroft of St Paul's, but no record of the burial is known in either place. Playford was also deeply involved with the Company of Parish Clerks of London; he presented them with several copies of his 1671 *Psalms and Hymns*, which had psalm tunes arranged for four male voices. He was credited with the invention of a stringed instrument called the 'psalmody' for accompanying metrical psalms (*see* PSALTERER).

Though unloved in the competitive world of publishers, Playford was highly esteemed by poets and musicians. Nahum Tate, the poet laureate, wrote a 'Pastoral Elegy' on his death which was movingly set to music by Henry Purcell. The dedications and prefaces to his publications reflect his commercial acumen, his xenophobia, and his devotion to the monarchy and to the divine service decently ordered.

2. PUBLICATIONS.   Playford's publications, apart from the political tracts and miscellaneous non-musical works, fall into three categories: theory of music and lesson books for various instruments, which usually contain brief instructions followed by 'lessons' or short pieces derived from popular airs; collections of songs and instrumental pieces; and psalms, psalm paraphrases and hymns. He began to publish music in 1651; new books succeeded one another rapidly in the early years, becoming more sparse later. Examination of the contents, however, shows that often a 'new edition' differs little from its predecessor although new 'lessons' may have been added and some others subtracted, and the later songbooks may be selections or rearrangements of earlier titles under new names. It is generally assumed that *The English Dancing Master*, addressed to the 'Gentlemen of the Innes of Court', came first, but *A Musicall Banquet* (also 1651) bears, as well as Playford's imprint, that of John Benson, his former master. *The English Dancing Master*, with many enlarged editions (some entitled *The Dancing Master*) until 1728, is probably Playford's best-known work, because of the modern revival of the country dance and because of its status as the largest single source of ballad airs. *A Musicall Banquet* contains the genesis of later books: *Musick's Recreation* (1652), *Catch that Catch Can* (1652; variously entitled *The Musical Com-*

3. *John Playford in 1663 (the two musical phrases indicate his membership of the Catch Club): engraving by Richard Gaywood*

panion and *The Pleasant Musical Companion* in some later editions), *A Breefe Introduction to the Skill of Musick* (1654; later *An Introduction to the Skill of Musick*) and *Court Ayres* (1655). All but the first continued in new and enlarged editions. The *Introduction* was immensely influential for 100 years or more; its theoretical sections were copied or cited in numerous later treatises and in the didactic introductions to psalmody books. *Apollo's Banquet for the Treble Violin* (1669) reflects a new fashion for this 'brisk and airy' instrument that was to last for the next 30 years, but the lessons for the cittern and the virginals, which did not last much beyond the mid-17th century, are evidence of declining sympathy with Playford's nostalgia for these instruments.

The same is true of the hymns, songs and instrumental pieces addressed to the proficient performer. As examples of the creative genius of Henry Purcell, Matthew Locke, William and Henry Lawes, Christopher Simpson and Richard Dering, they afford interest to the scholar, but are without those qualities which enabled the vocal music of the Tudor period eventually to outlast them. The latter had been the property of Thomas East. In 1653 Playford offered them as part of his bookseller's stock in his *Catalogue of All the Musick Bookes Printed in England*. In 1690, when the stock of his shop by the Temple Church was to be sold by auction, they were again catalogued for the benefit of 'those remote from London' and offered to buyers for a few pence.

Playford's numerous editions of the metrical psalm tunes, for one voice (*The Whole Book of Psalmes*, 1661), two voices (*Introduction*, 1658), three voices (*The Whole Book of Psalms*, 1677), four voices (*Psalms and Hymns*, 1671), keyboard (*The Tunes of Psalms*, c1669), and cittern and gittern (*A Booke of New Lessons*, 1652), supplemented his practical work at the Temple Church and the Company of Parish Clerks. They represent an ambitious attempt, quite separate from his books of devotional hymns for domestic use, to raise the standards of music in worship by means of a well-instructed parish clerk and male choir. His aim was to restore the old tunes in correctly harmonized versions rather than to introduce new ones. Success came only after his death, with the burgeoning of voluntary parish choirs in the 1690s; many of his tune harmonizations were used throughout the 18th century in England, Scotland and North America.

PUBLICATIONS
(*selective list*)

all published in London; Playford's printers and partners not cited

A Musicall Banquet in 3 Choice Varieties: The First … New Lessons for the Lira Viol: the Second, Musica Harmonia, New Allmans … for Tr and B Viol, by W. Lawes and other Authors: the Third … New Catches and Rounds: to which is added Rules … for such as learne to Sing or to Play on the Viol (1651[6]) [each part was later expanded into a book]; The English Dancing Master: or, Plaine and Easie Rules for the Dancing of Country Dances, with the Tune to Each Dance (1651/R; numerous rev. edns to 1728) [entitled The Dancing Master in some later edns]; A Booke of New Lessons for Cithern and Gittern (1652; enlarged 3/1666); Musick's Recreation on the Lyra Viol (1652[7], 4/1682[9]); Select Musicall Ayres and Dialogues (1652[8]; enlarged 2/1653[7]; selections 3/1659[5]) [1659 edn entitled Select Ayres and Dialogues]; J. Hilton, ed.: Catch that Catch Can (1652[10]; enlarged 7/1686[4]; other edns to c1720) [entitled The Musical Companion, The Pleasant Musical Companion in some later edns]

A Catalogue of All the Musick Bookes … Printed in England (1653); H. Lawes: Ayres and Dialogues … the First Booke (1653); J. Playford: A Breefe Introduction to the Skill of Musick (1654; other edns to 1730 incl. 1655 [having as pt ii T. Campion's Art of Composing with addns by C. Simpson]; 1657 [omitting Campion, but incl. Directions for Playing the Viol de Gambo and Tr Vn]; 1658 [adding The Tunes of the Psalms as they are Commonly Sung in Parish-Churches]; 1660 [having as bk 3 Campion's Art of Descant with addns by C. Simpson]; 1674 [incl. Order for Performing Divine Service in Cathedrals], [some edns entitled An Introduction to the Skill of Music]; H. Lawes: The Second Book of Ayres and Dialogues (1655); Court Ayres … of 2 Parts, Tr, B, for viols/vns (1655[5]; rev. 2/1662[8] as Courtly Masquing Ayres) [enlarged from Musica Harmonia in A Musicall Banquet]

W. Child: Choise Musick to the Psalmes of David (1656) [variant repr. of First Set of Psalms, 1639, advertised in A Musicall Banquet, but no earlier exemplar known]; M. Locke: His Little Consort (1656); H. Lawes: Ayres and Dialogues … the Third Book (1658); M. Locke and C. Gibbons: Cupid and Death … reprinted with Scenes and Music (1659) [orig. pubd without music, 1653]; J. Playford, ed.: The Whole Book of Psalmes Collected into English Meeter (1661) [orig. pubd 1562; 6 edns to 1687]; R. Dering: Cantica sacra, 2, 3vv, bc (org) (1662) [ded. by Playford to Queen Henrietta Maria]; Musick's Hand-Maide Presenting New and Pleasant Lessons for Virginals or Harpsycon (1663[7])

Musick's Delight on the Cithren, Restored and Refined (1666[4]); The Treasury of Musick (1669[5]) [incl. the 1659 selection of Ayres and Dialogues, bks 2, 1655, and 3, 1658, of Lawes's Ayres and Dialogues]; The Tunes of Psalms to the Virginal or Organ (c1669) [sheet inserted in some copies of Musick's Hand-Maide]; Apollo's Banquet for the Tr Vn (1669; other edns to 1701); J. Playford: Psalms and Hymns in Solemn Musick, 4vv, on the Common Tunes … ; also 6 Hymns, 1v, org (1671) [ded. to the Dean of St Paul's]; T. Greeting: The Pleasant Companion … for the Flageolet (1672, 4/1682); London Triumphant (1672) [Lord Mayor's Show]; Choice Songs and Ayres, 1v, theorbo/b viol: being Most of the Newest Songs sung at Court and at the Publick Theatres (1673[3]; enlarged 3/1676); M. Locke: The Present Practice of Musick

Defended and Vindicated against the Exceptions … laterly published by Thomas Salmon … together with a Letter from John Playford (1673)

T. Jordon: The Goldsmith's Jubilee or London's Triumphs (1674) [Lord Mayor's Show]; Cantica sacra containing Hymns and Anthems, 2vv, org, both Latine and English … the Second Sett (1674[2]) [ded. to the king]; The Triumphs of London (1675) [Lord Mayor's Show]; G. Sandys and H. Lawes, rev. J. Playford: A Paraphrase upon the Psalms (1676) [orig. pubd 1638]; J. Playford, ed.: The Whole Book of Psalmes (1677; 20 edns to 1757) [not identical with the 1661 pubn]; Musick's Hand-Maid: New Lessons and Instructions for the Virginals (1678[6]); Short Rules and Directions for the Tr Vn (1679) [lost]; Choice Ayres and Songs … the Second [–Fifth] Book (1679[7], 1681[4], 1683[5], 1684[3]); T. Jordon: London's Glory (1680) [Lord Mayor's Show]; H. Purcell: Sonnata's of III Parts (1681); G. Diesener: Instrumental Ayres in 3 and 4 Parts … in 3 Books (1682); The Triumphs of London (1683) [Lord Mayor's Show]

(2) Henry Playford (*b* ?Islington, 5 May 1657; *d* London, May–Dec 1709). Publisher, bookseller and dealer, son of (1) John Playford (i). He continued his father's business but was unable, owing to competition from the publishers of engraved music and to his conservatism and training in the old methods of booksell-ing, to maintain the same dominance of the music publishing trade. Nevertheless, during the late 1680s and early 1690s he was probably London's best-known music publisher.

Apprenticed to his father in 1674 and freed in 1681, he initially published in conjunction with John Playford (i), who shortly before his death handed over part of his business to his son and to Robert Carr, son of the music publisher John Carr. Henry worked from the same addresses as his father, a shop in the Temple and a house in Arundel Street. After three publications he parted company with Robert Carr, and thereafter published largely on his own account, occasionally in partnership with other publishers. His early works mainly followed the examples set by his father or were new editions of his father's titles. From 1687 he began to publish large numbers of non-musical works, which were to remain important in his output. He married Anne Baker in 1686; records of one daughter have been located. From 1690 until 1693 Playford was active in promoting sales and auctions of art works and antiquarian music books; from 1692 he was responsible for the publication of most of Purcell's music in association with that composer and later his widow Frances.

Around 1695 Playford found that competition from publishers of engraved music (notably John Walsh, John Hare and Thomas Cross) greatly affected his sales, and so he took action to regain his share of the market. He tried issuing a series of engraved songsheets in 1697 but soon reverted to the older, more familiar methods of printing from type. In 1699 he purchased equal shares in William Pearson's improved music type fount, the 'new London character'. To attract a wider audience he initiated new forms of publication, including the music periodical *Mercurius musicus* (1699–1702) and the cheap collections of popular songs entitled *Wit and Mirth: or, Pills to Purge Melancholy*. Further, he attempted to establish a network of music clubs to promote his publications. These innovations were finally to no avail, as Playford's old-fashioned methods were quickly superseded by those of the new publishers of engraved music.

Playford never reached his father's seniority in the Stationers' Company. He was called to the livery in 1686, and awarded a half-yeomanry share in the English Stock in 1696. Records document five apprentices. His stock was sold by John Cullen from 1706, and also by John Young who probably sold them on Pearson's behalf. After his death, his saleable type-printed works were issued by John and Benjamin Sprint and William Pearson, and the engraved ones by John Walsh and John Hare. In his will he left his estate to his wife Anne.

Henry continued to reissue many of his father's titles, after updating them to suit modern tastes, until his death. The influential treatise *An Introduction to the Skill of Musick* (five editions) was reissued in 1694 with a new section on 'The art of Descant' by Purcell. Among Henry's works modelled on those of his father were the song collections *The Theater of Music* (1685–7), *The Banquet of Music* (1688–92) and *Deliciae musicae* (1695–6).

Playford's most significant publication was perhaps *The Divine Companion* (1701), for which he commissioned eight leading professional composers, including Blow, Jeremiah Clarke (i) and Croft, to provide psalm tunes, hymns and anthems in a simple but up-to-date style. The anthems, as he pointed out in his preface, were the first printed for parish churches, and they would be reprinted, revised and imitated in dozens of books of parochial psalmody during the following century. One of Clarke's best-known hymn tunes, 'Uffingham', originated here (as 'Evening Hymn') while his 'St Magnus' appeared in the expanded second edition (1707).

PUBLICATIONS
(selective list)

all published in London; Playford's printers and partners not cited

Works first pubd by (1) John Playford (i): The Dancing Master (8/1690), 12/1703; other edns to 1728); The Second Book of the Pleasant Musical Companion (2/1694, 5/1707/R); An Introduction to the Skill of Musick (11/1687; 15/1703; other edns to 1730); Apollo's Banquet (5/1687[5], 6/1690[4], bk 2, 1691[5]; other edns to 1701); The Second Part of Musick's Hand-Maid (1689[7]); T. Greeting: The Pleasant Companion … for the Flageolet (5/1683)

Works pubd by Henry Playford: The Theater of Music (1685[5], 1685[6], 1686[3], 1687[5]); Harmonia sacra, or Divine Hymns and Dialogues (1688[1], 1693[1]); The Banquet of Music (1688[6], 1688[7], 1689[5], 1690[5], 1691[6], 1692[8]); Thesaurus musicus … the Second Book (1694[7]) [the 1st pubd 1693 by J. Hudgebut]; Deliciae musicae (1695[7], 1695[8], 1696[5], 1696[6], 1696[7]); The A'Lamode Musician … ingraved from the Originalls (1698[2]) [the 'Originalls' were pubd separately, early examples of sheet music]; H. Hunt: A Collection of Some Verses out of the Psalms … Composed in Two Parts (2/1698); The Tunes of the Psalms (1698); Wit and Mirth (1699[6], 1700[4]); A Book of Directions to Play the Psalmody, an Instrument Invented by John Playford (1699); Mercurius musicus (1699[4]–1702); S.S. and J.H.: Tunes to the Psalms (1700); The Divine Companion (1701; 2/1707; other edns to 1722); H. Purcell: Orpheus Britannicus … the Second Book (1702); The Diverting Post (1706) [house journal]

(3) John Playford (ii)   (*b* Stanmore Magna, *c*1655; *d* ?20 April 1685). Printer, nephew of (1) John Playford (i). He has been confused with other members of the family also named John, and with one, believed to be a bookseller, who spelt his name Playfere, but there is now no doubt that he was the son of the Rev. Matthew Playford (brother or half-brother of John Playford (i)), vicar of Stanmore Magna, who forfeited both livelihood and property because of his royalist sympathies.

At some time, probably in the 1670s, William Godbid, a printer of scientific books and music, took young John Playford as apprentice; at Godbid's death in 1679, his widow, Anne, took John into the partnership and advertised in *The Art of Descant* (refashioned from Campion's *Art of Composing* published by 'Snodham

alias Este') that 'the only Printing-house in England for Variety of Musick and Workmen that understand it, is still kept in Little Britain by A. Godbid and J. Playford Junior'. In 1682 Playford seems to have acquired the ownership of the business and in the same year his name appears in the livery list of the Stationers' Company; in 1683 he attended the company's Court of Assistants. He died between 20 April 1685, when he signed his will, and 29 April when the will was proved, bequeathing the business to his sister Eleanor.

BIBLIOGRAPHY

Day-MurrieESB; KrummelEMP

E. Arber and G.E.B. Eyre: *Archives of the Worshipful Company of Stationers … Transcript of the Registers 1554–1708* (London, 1875–1914)

F.A. Inderwick: *Calendar of the Inner Temple 1505–1714* (London, 1895)

F. Kidson: 'The Petition of Mrs Eleanor Playford', *The Library*, 3rd ser., vii (1916), 346

F. Kidson: 'John Playford and 17th Century Music Publishing', *MQ*, iv (1918), 516–34

E.A. Ebblewhite: *The Parish Clerks' Company and its Charters* (London, 1932)

C.L. Day and E.B. Murrie: 'English Song-Books and their Publishers 1651–1702', *The Library*, 4th ser., xvi (1936), 355

W.C. Smith: 'Some Hitherto Unnoticed Catalogues of Early Music', *MT*, lxxvii (1936), 636–9, 701–704

M. Dean-Smith, ed.: *Playford's English Dancing Master 1651* (London, 1957) [annotated facs.]

M. Tilmouth: 'Some Early London Concerts and Music Clubs 1670–1720', *PRMA*, lxxxiv (1957–8), 13–26

C. Blagden: *The Stationers' Company: A History, 1403–1959* (London, 1960)

M. Tilmouth: 'A Calendar of References to Music in Newspapers Published in London and the Provinces (1660–1719)', *RMARC*, i (1961/R), 1–107

L. Coral: 'A John Playford Advertisement', *RMARC*, no.5 (1965), 1–12

N. Temperley: 'John Playford and the Metrical Psalms', *JAMS*, xxv (1972), 331–78

N. Temperley: 'John Playford and the Stationers' Company', *ML*, liv (1973), 203–12

M.M. Curti: *John Playford's Apollo's Banquet, 1670* (diss., Rutgers U., 1977)

P.A. Munstedt: *John Playford, Music Publisher: a Bibliographical Catalogue* (diss., U. of Kentucky, 1983)

N. Temperley: *The Music of the English Parish Church* (Cambridge, 1979)

D.R. Harvey: *Henry Playford: a Bibliographical Study* (diss., Victoria U. of Wellington, 1985)

J. Barlow, ed.: *The Complete Country Dance Tunes from Playford's Dancing Master* (London, 1985)

G. Beechey: 'Henry Playford's *Harmonia Sacra*', *The Consort*, xlii (1986), 1–14

I. Spink: Introduction to *John Playford: Music for London Entertainment, 1600–1800*, vols. A5a and A5b (London, 1989)

R. Thompson: 'Manuscript Music in Purcell's London', *EMc*, xxiii (1995), 605–98

MARGARET DEAN-SMITH/NICHOLAS TEMPERLEY

Playlist. A selection of popular songs guaranteed air time on a given radio station. It first originated in the 1940s and 50s in American radio broadcasting. The Top 40 playlist included those songs currently in the higher reaches of the chart, a selection of those records climbing the chart but still outside the Top 40 ('bubbling under'), a number of new releases, mostly from major records labels and which were predicted to become hits, and a few older songs considered classics. Some of these records, for example the current number one, were played several times a day ('heavy rotation'), while other playlisted items were guaranteed to be heard only a few times each week. The format was open to corruption as record labels attempted to buy their records air-time ('payola'). In the British Isles the pirate radio stations, independent radio stations and BBC Radio 1 have had playlist policies, particularly during daytime hours. In the 1990s Radio 1 developed the concept of the A, B and C lists, adopting a sliding scale of plays with the most popular songs installed on the A list. However, many big-selling artists from punk, hardcore, metal and new wave in the 1970s to rap, hip hop and jungle artists in the 80s and 90s have been excluded from the playlists altogether, despite their commercial appeal. In 1991, for example, Iron Maiden's *Bring your daughter to the slaughter* was not playlisted by Radio 1 despite being at number one in the UK charts.

BIBLIOGRAPHY

S. Barnard: *On The Radio: Music Radio in Britain* (Milton Keynes, 1989)

M. Cloonan: *Banned! Censorship of Popular Music in Britain: 1967–92* (Aldershot, 1996)

DAVID BUCKLEY

Plaza(-Alfonzo), Juan Bautista (*b* Caracas, 19 July 1898; *d* Caracas, 1 Jan 1965). Venezuelan composer and musicologist. He began music studies at the age of 15 with Jesús María Suárez; within a year he was asked to lead the choir and to teach music to his fellow pupils in the Caracas French School. Thereafter he studied law and medicine at the university while continuing to act as choirmaster at the French School, where he produced his first large work, the zarzuela *Zapatero a tus zapatos*. In 1920 a scholarship took him to the Scuola Superiore di Musica Sacra in Rome; there he was taught by Casimiri, Manari, Ferretti and Dagnino, taking the degree of Master of Sacred Composition (1923). Returning to Caracas in that year, he was appointed choirmaster of the cathedral (1923–47) and professor of harmony at the Escuela Nacional de Música (1924–8), where he later instituted and taught courses in music history (1931–62) and aesthetics (1948–62). From 1936 to 1944 he undertook the study and cataloguing of a large quantity of colonial music that had been discovered in 1935; this work led to the publication of the 12-volume collection *Archivo de Música Colonial Venezolana* (Montevideo, 1943). While serving as director of culture in the Ministry of Education (1944–6) he established the Escuela Preparatoria de Música, which, under his direction (1948–62), became one of the most vital music schools in the country. Throughout these years he also appeared as an organist and as conductor of the Venezuela SO. After retiring in 1962 he gave his attention to further researches in the colonial music archive and to the cataloguing of his own work.

The most productive period of Plaza's life coincided with his tenure as cathedral choirmaster. After 1947 he wrote less, and the later works show an increasing abandonment of traditional tonality and a tendency towards introspection. Most of his compositions are vocal pieces, written for the church or for the choruses at the schools in which he taught; notable within this group are the Requiem (1933) and *Las horas* (1930). The principal influences on his early music were those of Puccini and Perosi; later pieces show his interests in Impressionism and in Stravinsky's music. Throughout his career he was active as a writer and lecturer, giving hundreds of radio talks and writing copiously in daily newspapers and scholarly journals on the subject of music, largely to educate lay readers. In 1990 the Fundación Juan Bautista

Plaza was established to preserve and catalogue not only his musical works but the large mass of writings that have yet to be systematically studied. Most of the archive of the Fundación is now in the Biblioteca Nacional de Venezuela, and its catalogue is nearing completion. The publication of his complete works is being considered.

WORKS
(*selective list*)

Masses: Misa breve, e, TB, orch, org, 1924; Misa en honor de S Inés, unison vv, org, 1925; Misa en honor de Santiago Apóstol, STB, orch, 1926, arr. TTB, org, 1944; Requiem, unison vv, org, 1926; Requiem, TTBB, orch, 1933; Mass, TTB, 1936; Missa 'Popule meus', TTB, orch, 1937; Misa en honor de S Juan de la Cruz, 2vv, org, 1944; Misa litúrgica de la esperanza, TB, org, 1962

Motets, psalms, offertories

Secular vocal: Las horas (F. Paz Castillo), SATB, orch, 1930; Zapatero a tus zapatos (zar); many unacc. choruses

Orch: Elegía, eng hn, str, 1923; El picacho abrupto, sym. poem, 1926; Vigilia, sym. poem, 1928; Campanas de pascua, sym. poem, 1930; Fuga criolla, str, 1931, Fuga romántica venezolana, str, 1950, Elegía, str, timp, 1953; Marcha nupcial, 1959

Songs, 1v, pf: 7 canciones venezolanas (L. Barrios Cruz), S, pf, 1932; many others

Other: chbr works; many works for pf, org, gui; educational music, official arr. of Venezuelan national anthem

Principal publishers: Associated, G. Schirmer, Fundación Vicente Emilio Sojo, Casimiri

WRITINGS

'Music in Caracas during the Colonial Period (1770–1811)', *MQ*, xxix (1943), 198–213

Música colonial venezolana (Caracas, 1958)

El lenguaje de la música (Caracas, 1966, 2/1985)

Temas de música colonial venezolana (Caracas, 1990)

BIBLIOGRAPHY

Compositores de Américas/Composers of the Americas, ed. Pan American Union, ix (Washington DC, 1963), 105–21

E. Plaza-Alfonzo: 'Apuntes sobre la vida, la persona y la obra de Juan Bautista Plaza', *Cultura universitaria*, no.89 (1965), 46–65

M. Castillo Didier: *Juan Bautista Plaza: una vida por la música y por Venezuela* (Caracas, 1985)

M. Labonville: 'Juan Bautista Plaza: a Documented Chronology; Catalogue of his Writings; Plaza and the Press', *Revista musical de Venezuela*, xxxvii (1998), 1–172

M. Labonville: *Musical Nationalism in Venezuela: the Work of Juan Bautista Plaza* (diss., U. of California, Santa Barbara, 1999)

ALEJANDRO ENRIQUE PLANCHART

Plaza (y Manrique), Ramón de la (*b* Caracas, 1831; *d* Caracas, 15 Dec 1886). Venezuelan music historian. He spent two years (*c*1853–5) in north-eastern USA, where he broadened his musical knowledge. A year after his marriage (on 12 March 1869) to the wealthy Mercedes Ponce Valdés he became a deputy to the Venezuelan Congress. In recognition of his services as head of a legislative commission concerned with religious matters he was made a general. By presidential decree he became first director of the newly created Instituto Nacional de Bellas Artes on 3 April 1877. He was an amateur cellist and composer whose sensitivity, practical musicianship, wide reading, extensive American and European travels and informed patriotism made him the ideal interpreter of his nation's artistic past. Although his creative ability is often downplayed, works such as the *Barcarola* in D minor (1872) show him to be a salon composer of charming talent. His luxuriously printed *Ensayos sobre el arte en Venezuela* (Caracas, 1883/R), published to commemorate Bolívar's birth, was not the first Latin American music history – Juan Agustín Guerrero's *La música ecuatoriana desde su origen hasta 1875* (Quito, 1876) preceded it – but it is still one of the best; it has been drawn upon extensively in later writings on the ject, particularly those of L. Cortijo Alahija. It ombines extensive analysis of aboriginal music with a recise and extremely valuable history of European music in Venezuela from the founding of Caracas to Plaza's time; it includes a 56-page musical appendix. He also published *El drama lírico y la lengua castellana como elemento musical* (Caracas, 1884), a study of Spanish as a vehicle for opera.

BIBLIOGRAPHY

J.A. Calcaño: 'Nuestro primer libro sobre arte', introduction to facs. of R. de la Plaza: *Ensayos sobre el arte en Venezuela* (Caracas, 1977), pp.xiii–xix

R. Stevenson: 'Ensayos sobre el arte en Venezuela', *RMC*, no.141 (1978), 53–5

A.R. Villasana: *Ensayo de un repertorio bibliográfico venezolano: años 1808–1950* (Caracas, 1979), vi, 583–4

M. Milanca Guzmán: 'Ramón de la Plaza Manrique (1831?–1886): autor de la primera historia musical publicada en el continente latinoamericana', *RMC*, no.162 (1984), 86–109

V.E. Guevara: '*Barcarola* de Ramón de la Plaza Manrique el compositor', *Revista musical de Venezuela*, no.37 (1998), 235–42

ROBERT STEVENSON

Pleasants, Henry (*b* Wayne, PA, 12 May 1910; *d* London, 4 Jan 2000). American author and critic. He trained as a singer and pianist at the Philadelphia Musical Academy and Curtis Institute of Music, with subsequent private studies in singing, piano and composition. In 1930 he became music critic for the *Philadelphia Evening Bulletin*, and music editor from 1934. After army service (1942–50), mostly in North Africa and Europe, he joined the US Foreign Service and was based successively in Munich, Berne and Bonn (1950–64). During this time (1945–55) he was also central European music correspondent for the *New York Times*. He settled in London and was London music critic for the *International Herald Tribune* (1967–97) and an editor for *Stereo Review*, as well as a frequent contributor to the musical press in Britain and the USA. The Curtis Institute awarded him an honorary doctorate in 1977. He is married to the harpsichordist and fortepianist Virginia Pleasants.

Pleasants's writings extend and elaborate a critical principle which accords serious attention to the popular musical vernacular of the 20th century (jazz, theatre music, rock and pop), in the belief that these styles have gained a dominant position in world music not only as commercial entertainment, but also as art. His study of great singers is related to this in suggesting that the art of singing reached its zenith in the Baroque period; since then it has been in conflict with the demands of emotional expression and compositional techniques and cannot survive if lyrical grace is not the chief element of its style.

WRITINGS

ed. and trans.: E. Hanslick: *Vienna's Golden Years of Music, 1850–1900* (New York, 1950, rev. 2/1963/R as *Music Criticism 1846–99*)

The Agony of Modern Music (New York, 1955)

Death of a Music? The Decline of the European Tradition and the Rise of Jazz (London, 1961)

ed. and trans.: *The Musical Journeys of Louis Spohr* (Norman, OK, 1961)

ed. and trans.: *The Musical World of Robert Schumann: a Selection from his own Writings* (London, 1965/R 1988 as *Schumann on Music*)

The Great Singers: from the Dawn of Opera to our own Time (New York, 1966)

Serious Music – and All That Jazz! (New York and London, 1969)

The Great American Popular Singers (New York, 1974)

ed. and trans.: *The Music Criticism of Hugo Wolf* (New York, 1978)

ed. and trans.: F. Wieck: *Piano and Song* (New York, 1988)

Opera in Crisis (London, 1989)

The Great Tenor Tragedy: the Last Days of Adolphe Nourrit as Told (mostly) by Himself (Portland, OR, 1995)

NOËL GOODWIN

Plectrum [pick, flat-pick] (Fr. *médiator, plectre*; Ger. *Dorn, Kiel, Plektrum, Schlagfeder*; It. *plettro*). A general term for a piece of material with which the strings of an instrument are plucked. Tinctoris called the plectrum of antiquity 'pecten' and that of the Middle Ages 'penna' (quill). Ancient Greek sources used the terms 'plectron' and 'pecten'. Plucked instruments with stopped strings and more specifically lute-type instruments – such as the *biwa* of Japan and the Western lute itself up to the late 15th century – have often been played with a plectrum, in some instances a rather large one (*see* JAPAN, fig.17), in others a more delicate type (*see* LUTE, fig.7).

Sources since the Middle Ages describe plectra made from eagles' talons as well as ones of wood, metal (*see* SITĀR, fig.1c), ivory, bone, tortoiseshell, parchment and quill. The use of synthetic material, such as nylon or plastic, for plectra is now almost universal. Medieval Arabic writings describe the use of plectra on the lute. In muslim Spain the musician ZIRYĀB (*d* 852) was accredited with replacing the traditional wooden plectrum with one made from an eagle's talon. This material was said to be successful because of its subtle tip, its purity, and its flexibility between the fingers; the strings also lasted longer. Eagle's talon or tortoiseshell plectra are still somtimes used by 'ūd players, although synthetic materials are now more common.

Iconographical evidence shows the use of a bird's feather quill by European lute players, but that the transition to thumb-and-index-finger technique took place between about 1460 and 1500, although the two techniques must have co-existed over a long period. The duets in various 16th-century publications of lute music (e.g. F. Spinacino: *Intabulatura de lauto*, Venice, 1507/R), while specifying the use of thumb-and-finger technique, preserve a style of single-note lines and chordal playing that in many cases could be played with a plectrum, and is clearly descended from the extemporary playing technique of the previous century. This style is evident in some of the pieces in the 'Pesaro Manuscript' (*c*1500, I-PESo 1144).

The initial sound of a string set into vibration by a plectrum is naturally more akin to that of a string plucked by a fingernail than by the flesh of the finger. A plectrum facilitates tremolando effects (as on the mandolin) and vigorous strumming, but does not favour the kind of polyphonic texture that was cultivated on the high-Renaissance lute and vihuela. Psaltery-type instruments, such as the zither and the Middle Eastern *qānūn*, are likely to be played with a plectrum (*see* QĀNŪN), but harps virtually never are, as the player often has a relatively unclear view of the strings and so tends to rely on the sense of touch to help distinguish them. The term also refers to the small tongue which plucks the string of a harpsichord (it may be of leather or plastic instead of quill). A modern technique of virtuoso melodic playing with a 'pick' or 'flat-pick' (plectrum) on a (normally steel-strung) guitar is often referred to as 'flat-picking'.

BIBLIOGRAPHY

J. Tinctoris: *De inventione et usu musicae* (Naples, *c*1481)

W. Bachmann: *Die Anfänge des Streichinstrumentenspiels* (Leipzig, 1964, 2/1966; Eng. trans., 1969)

V. Ivanoff: 'Das Lautenduo im 15. Jahrhundert', *Basler Jb für historische Musikpraxis*, viii (1984), 147–62

V. Ivanoff: *Das Pesaro-Manuskript: ein Beitrag zur Frühgeschichte der Lautentabulatur*(Tutzing, 1988)

E. Neubauer: 'Der Bau der Laute und ihre Besaitung nach arabischen, persischen und türkischen Quellen des 9. bis 15. Jahrhunderts', *Zeitschrift für Geschichte der Arabisch-Islamischen Wissenschaften*, viii (1993), 279–378

VLADIMIR IVANOFF

Pleeth, William (*b* London, 12 Jan 1916; *d* London, 6 April 1999). English cellist. He studied at the London Academy of Music (1924–8), with Herbert Walenn at the London School of Violoncello (1928–9) and with Julius Klengel at the Leipzig Conservatory (1930–32). He made his début in Leipzig in 1931 and in London in 1933. As a soloist he gave the premières of several works dedicated to him including Rubbra's *Soliloquy* (1943) and Franz Reizenstein's Cello Concerto (1948). As a chamber music player he appeared with the Blech Quartet (1936–41), the Allegri Quartet (1952–67), the Rubbra-Brainin-Pleeth Trio (1946) and in many quintet performances with the Amadeus String Quartet. He also played sonatas with his wife, the pianist Margaret Good (*b* 27 April 1906; *d* 25 July 2000), with whom he made some notable recordings. His playing was distinguished by an exuberant, extrovert style, combined with a passionate conviction which was embodied in the full and colourful tone he produced from his 1732 Stradivari. He was professor of cello and chamber music at the GSMD (1948–78) and visiting professor at the RCM (1987–95). Among his pupils were his son Anthony and Jacqueline du Pré. He published *Cello* (with Nona Pyron, London, 1982). He was made an OBE in 1988.

BIBLIOGRAPHY

CampbellGC

M. Campbell: 'William Pleeth: a Profile', *The Strad*, lxxxviii (1977–8), 6–15

F. Shelton: 'William Pleeth and the Teacher's View', *The Strad*, xcii (1981–2), 31–3

M. Campbell: 'One of a Kind', *The Strad*, cvii (1996), 610–13

M. Campbell: Obituary, *The Independent* (7 April 1999)

WATSON FORBES/MARGARET CAMPBELL

Plein jeu (Fr.: 'full registration'; pl. *pleins jeux*). The most common generic French term for a MIXTURE STOP or the Diapason chorus. Possibly derived from *plain jeu*, 'integrated registration', the phrase seems to have arisen in the 16th century to designate the combination of stops yeilding the tonal result of the heretofore undivided, stopless BLOCKWERK. At Notre Dame, Alençon (1537–40), the term *principal du corps* was still used, corresponding to the Dutch, German and probably English term 'principal', i.e. not a single rank but the Diapason chorus as a whole. At Chartres in 1542, the contract refers to a more extensive *plain jeu*, complete with the eight 32′ pedal pipes and the doubled and tripled 8′ and 4′ ranks. For Mersenne (*Harmonie universelle*, 1636–7), *plain jeu* included a Tierce but not the highest Cymbale mixture. Bédos de Celles (*L'art du facteur d'orgues*, 1766–78) codified a concept which had been perfected decades earlier: the *grand plein jeu* was based on the *Grand Orgue* mixture chorus to which was invariably coupled the higher-pitched *petit plein jeu* of the *Positif*; the latter could be played alone in brisk movement or in alternation with the *grand plein jeu*. (To facilitate tuning, larger *pleins jeux* were usually divided into Fourniture and Cymbale registers with elegantly interlocking breaking schemes.) Thus the *plein jeu* formed one of the systematic registration recipes of the Classical French organ, in contrast, for instance, to the GRAND JEU or the *jeu de tierce*. Evoking divine majesty in its stately radiance, it was commonly featured in the opening versets of mass movements (Kyrie, 'Et in terra pax', Sanctus), and it became particularly associated with a sustained four- or five-voice texture with constant and slowly resolving suspensions. It was rarely used, however, for fugal textures, these rather played on the *grand jeu*.

In the 19th century the Chorus structures of the French Classical organ were progressively broken down as horizontal writing gave way to more operatic, orchestral or pianistic gesture. Consequently, the *plein jeu*, while retaining secondary and residual use in *alternatim* practice, was conceived primarily as a tonally reinforcing element of the GRAND CHOEUR or FULL ORGAN, being included with the reeds rather than with the foundation stops on the divided windchests. The French builders often adopted the concept of the German *Progressivharmonika* (*plein jeu harmonique*) which, by suppressing the high-pitched ranks in the bass and progressively adding ranks in the upper range, favoured homophonic texture and helped strengthen the naturally weaker trebles. In 1913 Alexandre Cellier (in *L'orgue moderne*) could still write that 'nowadays the *pleins jeux* are scarcely ever used except in combination with the combined choruses of reeds and foundation stops'.

After World War I French builders gradually returned to earlier concepts of the Diapason chorus and its functions, subsequently integrating certain German Baroque designs such as the Terzzimbel in order to favour the corresponding repertory. (To be sure, there has never been the same amount of experimentation with mixture compositions in France as there was in the *Orgelbewegung* period in Germany.) To describe the new sounds, words such as 'luminous' and 'scintillating' appeared. Composers have made clever use of the colouristic possibilities thus offered. Ultimately, however, the most far-reaching conceptual change resulted from expecting the *plein jeu* convincingly to render both the massive Classical French texture and the vigorous, transparent fugal writing epitomized by Bach. The validity of this nearly unattainable goal has been questioned and *plein jeu* design at the end of the 20th century tended increasingly to fall back on specific historical models, chosen case by case.

See also ORGAN, §V, 7, and REGISTRATION, §I, 5.

BIBLIOGRAPHY

J. Fellot: *L'orgue classique français* (Paris, 1962, 2/1993)

G. Lhôte: 'Remarques sur l'orgue français', *ISO Information*, no.1 (1969), 66–7

P. Hardouin: 'Les pleins-jeux classiques français', *L'orgue français classique: Souvigny 1983*, 83–136

C.-W. Lindow: *Jeux de mutation: pleins-jeux*, L'orgue: cahiers et mémoires, no.31 (Paris, 1984)

J. Saint-Arroman: *L'interprétation de la musique française, 1661–1789*, ii (Paris, 1988), 412–25

PETER WILLIAMS, KURT LUEDERS

Plena. A song genre of Puerto Rico. It is believed to have originated in the early 20th century, with a binary form consisting of solo or duet melodies followed by choral refrains. Narrative texts, often humorous, contain social commentary. The *plena* is characterized by extensive syncopation, while the use of triplet figures in vocal lines creates rhythmic contrast with the duple metre accompaniment of guitars, *panderetas* (tambourines) and *conga* drums and, more recently, orchestras with extended percussion sections.

WILLIAM GRADANTE/R

Plenary mass. A setting of both the Ordinary and the Proper of the Roman Catholic Mass. Examples are rare: they include Du Fay's early *Missa Sancti Jacopi* and the mass of Reginaldus Libert, both probably from the 1420s, as well as the mass for St Anthony Abbot ascribed to a certain Piret (*I-TRmp* 89) and perhaps Du Fay's mass for St Anthony of Padua, both evidently from the 1440s. But the priniciple became common only in the requiem (*see* REQUIEM MASS, §2).

Pleno (It.; Lat. *plenum*). Full, as in *organo pleno. See* FULL ORGAN.

Plessas, Mimis (*b* Athens, 12 Oct 1924). Greek composer and pianist. Performing in live bands and for the radio since his teens, his early musical influences were predominantly Western, mainly jazz and ragtime. In the late 1940s he went to the USA to continue his studies in chemistry, and also to work as a musician. Returning to Greece in 1951, he soon started winning critical acclaim and success as a composer of light songs. During the 1960s he became established as a composer for the cinema, working predominantly with the production company Finos Films and with director Giannis Dalianidis. While his dramatic scores for films like *Iligos* ('Vertigo', 1963) and *To Choma Vaftike Kokino* ('The Earth became Red', 1965) won him prizes and critical acclaim, his songs for such comedies and musicals as *Koritsia gia Filima* ('Girls for Kissing', 1965), *I Thalassies i Chandres* ('The Blue Beads', 1967), *Mia Kyria sta Bouzoukia* ('A Lady at the Bouzouki-Club', 1968) and *Gorgones ke Manges* ('Mermaids and Lads', 1969) significantly increased his popularity.

Until the late 1960s his musical style was predominantly Western, following contemporary trends of light song. Towards the end of the decade his work integrated more elements of traditional popular Greek music (*laiki*), becoming part of a trend of artistic popular music: typical of this is the use of the *bouzouki*. The collection of songs *O Dromos* ('The Road'), with lyrics by Lefteris Papadopoulos, is characteristic of his work during this period. More recently Plessas has composed instrumental pieces for orchestra, and experimented with electronic music. However, his main contribution to Greek music remains tied to his songs which enjoyed renewed popularity among Greek youth in the 1990s.

LYDIA PAPADIMITRIOU

Plessis. *See* DUPLESSIS family.

Plessis, Hubert du. *See* DU PLESSIS, HUBERT.

Pletnev [Pletnyov], Mikhail (Vasil'yevich) (*b* Arkhangel'sk, 14 April 1957). Russian pianist and conductor. His father was an accordion teacher, his mother a pianist, accompanist and teacher. When the family moved to Kazan', Pletnev learned to play several instruments, including the piano, which he went on to study at the Central Music School in Moscow from the age of 13 under Yevgeny Timakin, then from 1974 at the Conservatory with Yakov Fliyer, and, after Fliyer's death, with Lev Vlasenko. In 1978 he won first prize in the Tchaikovsky International Piano Competition. His subsequent recording of his own arrangements from Tchaikovsky's *Nutcracker* suite and

Shchedrin's *Anna Karenina* created a sensation. Pletnev's pianism is characterized by consummate clarity of fingerwork, self-awareness (sometimes to the point of mannerism) and cool intelligence. His recordings of Rachmaninoff and Scarlatti are outstanding.

In 1990 Pletnev founded the Russian National Orchestra, the first self-financing orchestra in Russia, drawn largely from the best players in former state-subsidised ensembles such as the Bol'shoy Opera. Their recordings, starting with a highly praised Tchaikovsky 'Pathétique' Symphony, reflect Pletnev's own temperament in their highly polished intensity. His interest in the art of transcription has continued with an arrangement of Beethoven's Violin Concerto for clarinet and orchestra (1995). He is also the composer of orchestral works and has worked as choreographer with the Bol'shoy Ballet School.

BIBLIOGRAPHY

A. Kandinsky-Rïbnikov: 'Zametki ob iskusstve Mikhaila Pletneva' [Observations on the art of Mikhail Pletnev], *SovM* (1982), no.11, pp.61–70

M. Zilberquit: *Russia's Great Modern Pianists* (Neptune, NJ, 1983), 397–439 [interview with Pletnev]

G. Tsïpin: *Portretï sovetskikh pianistov* (Moscow, 1990), 308–19

R. Cowan: 'In a Russian Winter', *Gramophone*, lxxii/Dec (1994), 14–16

DAVID FANNING

Pleyel (i). Austro-French family of composers, musicians, publishers and piano makers, active in France. (For the firm of piano makers, *see* PLEYEL (ii).)

(1) Ignace Joseph [Ignaz Josef] Pleyel (*b* Ruppersthal, 18 June 1757; *d* Paris, 14 Nov 1831). Composer, music publisher and piano maker. He founded a major publishing house and a piano factory and his compositions achieved widespread popularity in Europe and North America.

1. LIFE. Pleyel's baptismal certificate in the parish office names his father Martin, a schoolteacher, and his mother Anna Theresia (Maria Christina Theresa in *MGG1*). He is said to have studied with Vanhal while very young, and in about 1772 he became Haydn's pupil and lodger in Eisenstadt, his annual pension being paid by Count Ladislaus Erdődy, whose family at Pressburg was related to Haydn's patrons, the Esterházys. The count showed his pleasure at the progress of his protégé by offering Haydn a carriage and two horses, for which Prince Esterházy agreed to provide a coachman and fodder.

Little is known of the daily activities of Haydn's several pupils. A few incidents concerning Pleyel's apprenticeship are recounted in Framery's *Notice sur Joseph Haydn*, in which the author claimed that 'these various anecdotes were furnished me by a person who spent his entire youth with him and who guarantees their authenticity'. That person is generally identified as Pleyel, living in Paris when the *Notice* appeared there in 1810. The assumption is strengthened by the manner in which the narrative favours Pleyel, always emphasizing the closeness of his relationship with Haydn and the master's affection and esteem for him.

During this period Pleyel's puppet opera *Die Fee Urgele* was first performed at Eszterháza (November 1776), and at the Vienna Nationaltheater. Haydn's puppet opera *Das abgebrannte Haus*, or *Die Feuerbrunst*, was also first performed in 1776 or 1777, with an overture (or at least its first two movements) now generally accepted as being by Pleyel.

Pleyel's first position seems to have been as Kapellmeister to Count Erdődy, but again that period of his career is undocumented. He and the count were members of the masonic Lodge 'Zum goldenen Hirschen', founded by the count's brother Ludwig, and located from 1778 in the town of Fidisch, near Eberau in Burgenland. The musical importance of the count's chapel is affirmed in the notice published after his death on 13 July 1786: a variety of instruments as well as several hundred symphonies, concertos, quintets, operas, masses and other works were to be sold two years later in Vienna for the benefit of the poor (*Wiener Zeitung*, 9 Aug 1788). Pleyel's String Quartets op.1 (1782–3, B 301–6) are dedicated to Count Erdődy for his 'generosity, paternal solicitude and encouragement'.

During the early 1780s Pleyel travelled in Italy. Through Norbert Hadrava, an ardent music lover and part-time composer attached to the Austrian embassy in Naples, Pleyel was asked to compose lyra (hurdy-gurdy) pieces for performance by Ferdinand IV, the 'Lazzarone' King of Naples; Hadrava had instructed the king in an elaborate version of the instrument, and also procured commissions for Haydn and Sterkel. Two of Pleyel's works for the hurdy-gurdy survive in autographs (B 202 and 202.5). In 1784 Hadrava engineered the commissioning of an opera: Pleyel's *Ifigenia in Aulide* had its première at the S Carlo theatre on the king's nameday, 30 May 1785, and there were 18 further performances that summer.

Meanwhile (probably in 1784) Pleyel had become assistant to F.X. Richter, Kapellmeister of Strasbourg Cathedral, and he succeeded to the post when Richter died in 1789. From 1786 he also conducted and organized a series of public concerts in collaboration with J.P. Schönfeld, Kapellmeister of the Strasbourg Temple Neuf. On 22 January 1788 he married (Franziska) Gabrielle (Ignatia) Lefebvre, daughter of the *tapissier* Stephen Laurence Lefebvre, with whom Pleyel was later involved in a variety of business investments. Four children survived the union, the eldest of whom was (2) Camille Pleyel. The Strasbourg period was Pleyel's most productive musically (fig.1); most of his compositions date from the years 1787–95. His pupils of that time included Ferdinand Fränzl, who dedicated his op.1 to Pleyel, and P.-J. Pfeffinger.

The Revolution having abolished the cathedral's religious functions and the city's secular concerts, Pleyel accepted an invitation to conduct the Professional Concert in London, and stayed there from December 1791 until May 1792 (thus, contrary to some sources, he cannot have composed the *Marseillaise*, which had been written in Strasbourg by Rouget de Lisle in April). There is no evidence for the assertion that Pleyel let himself be used by the entrepreneur Wilhelm Cramer of the Professional Concerto to draw listeners away from Haydn's concurrent series with the impresario Salomon, nor even that he was aware of Haydn's plans when he accepted the invitation. The composers remained unaffected by the rival publicity, expressing mutual affection, dining together, performing each other's music and attending each other's concerts. Haydn generally received more critical and popular acclaim, but Pleyel's concerts were also well attended; and his compositions, especially the *symphonies concertantes* and quartets, were highly praised in the press.

1. *Ignace Joseph Pleyel: stipple engraving by William Nutter after Thomas Hardy, 1793*

During Pleyel's London stay, George Thomson of Edinburgh asked him to compose the introduction and accompaniments for a series of Scottish airs and to write a set of piano trios. Thomson's remarks in a letter to Kozeluch about having been 'juggled, disappointed and grossly deceived by an eminent musical composer with whom I entered into an agreement some years ago' and his decision to use Kozeluch's settings for the second volume of Scottish songs have been construed to mean that Pleyel had in some way behaved dishonourably. But Thomson evidently retained no animosity, for during a trip to Paris in 1819 he paid a friendly visit to Pleyel's shop and in a letter home praised his publications extravagantly.

After returning to the Continent, Pleyel bought the large Château d'Itenwiller at St Pierre, near Strasbourg, probably with the considerable earnings of his London concerts (the last, on May 14, had been the usual 'benefit'). According to a dramatic story (which remains undocumented despite searches in Strasbourg archives, and varies in each telling) Pleyel was repeatedly arrested during 1793 by Revolutionary authorities who suspected him of pro-Austrian or aristocratic sympathies; he was released only after writing (while under guard) the rather banal patriotic hymn *La révolution du 10 août 1792, ou Le tocsin allégorique* (B 706). This includes references to the popular *Ça ira* and to several works by Grétry, and requires a large ensemble of voices and instruments, including church bells and cannons. The première in Strasbourg Cathedral (on 10 August 1793) used bells chosen by Pleyel from those requisitioned from churches of the region no longer holding services. The last of subsequent performances occurred in 1799 at the inauguration of the concert hall of the city's Réunion des Arts.

Early in 1795 Pleyel settled in Paris, opened a music shop and founded a publishing house, which issued some 4000 works during the 39 years it existed, including many by Boccherini, Beethoven, Clementi, Cramer, J.L. Dussek, Haydn and other friends of Pleyel and his son. Some of them (e.g. Dizi, Kalkbrenner, Méhul, Rossini) were involved in the firm by financial investment. Pleyel established agents for the sale of his publications all over France, and maintained an active exchange of letters and music with some of the foremost European music publishers (e.g. Artaria of Vienna, Böhme of Hamburg, Breitkopf of Leipzig, Hoffmeister of Vienna, Hummel of Amsterdam and Simrock of Bonn), sometimes arranging for reciprocal engraving of their issues.

The most important achievement of the Maison Pleyel was probably its issue of the first miniature scores, a series entitled Bibliothèque Musicale. It began in 1802 with four of Haydn's symphonies, and continued with ten volumes of his string quartets, followed by chamber works by Beethoven, Hummel and Onslow (the last in 1830). In 1801 Pleyel also issued a *Collection complette des quatuors d'Haydn, dédiée au Premier Consul Bonaparte*, the title-page beautifully engraved by Aubert (fig.2), the separate parts engraved by Richomme and probably edited by the violinist Baillot. The prefatory material includes a handsome portrait of Haydn by J. Guérin and a thematic catalogue 'of all Haydn's quartets, sanctioned by the author and arranged in the order in which they appeared'. This statement and Haydn's earlier relationship with Pleyel have involved the edition in the debate concerning the authenticity and order of certain quartets

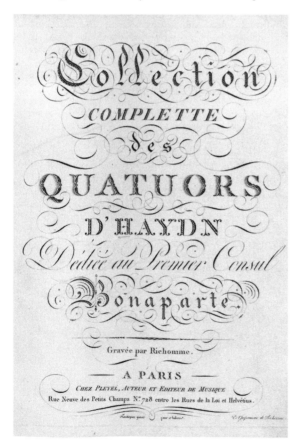

2. Title-page, engraved by Aubert, of Pleyel's 'Collection complette des quatuors d'Haydn, dédiée au Premier Consul Bonaparte' (Paris: Pleyel, 1801)

generally attributed to Haydn. The edition also includes two pages of subscribers' names, many of them notable musicians (e.g. Cherubini, Dussek, Grétry, Kreutzer, Méhul, Salomon, Viotti) or aristocracy centred on Vienna (e.g. Erdődy, Esterházy, Golitsïn, Harrach, Lobkowitz, Rasumovsky, Swieten, and Thurn and Taxis). The first edition contained 80 quartets, subsequent editions adding two, then one, as Haydn composed them.

In 1805 Pleyel travelled with his son (2) Camille to Vienna, where his string quartets were warmly received. They also paid several visits to the aging Haydn; they heard Beethoven play the piano and were greatly impressed by his brilliant improvisational technique. But one of the primary reasons for the visit, the establishment of a branch publishing office, failed despite the support of local friends. The firm had been plagued since its inception by a series of legal contests that were not exceptional but sapped Pleyel's energy and financial resources. In 1813 he made a determined effort to sell the publishing enterprise, describing his stock in a letter to a prospective buyer as 48,000 plates of pewter (*fin étain*) or copper, printed music he had published or for which he was agent, instruments (violins, violas, double basses, trumpets, trombones, bows, strings etc.), manuscripts not yet engraved and unused paper. 'In the last two years I have published more than 200 new works, of which 29% to 30% have not yet been put on sale ... Most of my editions have been engraved by Richault, Lobry, Petit and Marquerie, the best engravers in Paris'.

During the 1820s Pleyel indulged his love of rural life by spending increasing amounts of time on a large farm about 50 km from Paris. During the same period the firm's output became more predominantly popular, as symphonies, sonatas and quartets were replaced by *romances*, *chansonnettes* and similar genres by Bayle, Bizot, Georgeon, Panseron and (especially) Pauline Duchambge, whose songs were always issued with alternative piano and guitar accompaniments. The firm also issued many fantasias, variations, rondos and potpourris of operatic *airs* by Adolphe Adam, Carulli, Duvernoy, Mayseder, Pixis and others. In 1834 the Maison Pleyel ceased its publishing activities entirely, selling its stock of plates and printed works to various Paris publishers, among whom were Lemoine, Prilipp, Delloy, Richault and Schlesinger.

2. WORKS.   The enormous popularity of Pleyel's music during his lifetime is reflected in the testimony of contemporary journals and of early writers like Gerber and Fétis. The small town of Nantucket, Massachusetts, then still a whaling port, formed a Pleyel Society in 1822 'to chasten the taste of auditors', according to a newspaper announcement. The most telling evidence of the appeal of his music lies in the thousands of manuscript copies that filled the shelves of archives, libraries, churches, castles and private homes and in the thousands of editions produced in Europe and North America (fig.3). In quality the works vary greatly, although most show considerable facility and a thorough technical grounding. The earlier works in particular display thematic originality and ingenious developments that make them fresh and attractive. After about 1792 his talent seems to have diminished; his inventiveness waned and he occasionally succumbed to routine procedures.

An insufficiently recognized aspect of Pleyel's production is the extent to which whole works, movements or

3. Title-page of Pleyel's 'Six Grand Lessons for the Harpsichord or Piano-forte' (London: Preston, between 1787 and 1810)

parts of movements were re-used. Some of the borrowing was obviously by the composer, but much was perpetrated by publishers, probably without his knowledge or consent. Most of the songs with keyboard accompaniment, for example, which were highly popular around the turn of the 19th century especially in English-speaking countries, are settings of movements from symphonies or quartets (e.g. *Henry's Cottage Maid*, from B 137; *Time a Favorite Sonnet*, from B 327A; *Fanny's Worth*, from B 350; and the ubiquitous *German Hymn*, from B 349). Nevertheless many of the songs have considerable charm. Certain categories of the instrumental works consist entirely of arrangements: the quartets for keyboard and strings, the four-hand keyboard works and all ensembles that include guitar or harp. Working in an age when music was considered a commodity to be put to the widest possible use, Pleyel did not hesitate to issue a concerto with alternative solo parts for flute, clarinet or cello (B 106), or to transform a set of piano trios (B 465–70) into flute quartets (B 387–92) or string trios (B 410–15) by 'scrambling' the original 18 movements into an almost entirely new juxtaposition of movements in transposed keys. Such procedures reflect Pleyel's total acceptance of the tastes and values of contemporary music lovers, which may explain his widespread popularity. The duets for violins, flutes or other combinations have never lost their appeal as teaching pieces. Many works of other genres merit resuscitation for study and performance.

WORKS

Most printed works appeared in multiple editions and in arrangements for various combinations of instruments. Dates in parentheses indicate the earliest editions. Letters appended to B numbers indicate works in which some movements are different from those in the preceding work. For a complete concordance of prints and thematic catalogue, see R. Benton: *Ignace Pleyel: a Thematic Catalogue of his Compositions* (New York, 1977) [B]

SYMPHONIES
nos. refer to Benton, 1977

121, c, 1778, *F-Pn** (inc.) (1787), ed. A. Badley (Wellington, 1998); 122, A, 1778, *A-Wgm** (inc.) (1786); 123, F, 1782–4 (1788); 124, D, 1782–4 (1790); 125, B♭, 1782–4 (1787), ed. A. Badley (Wellington, 1998); 126, D (1785), ed. H. Riessberger (Vienna, 1990) and in RRMCE, viii (1978); 127, B♭ (1785–6); 128, C (1786), ed. A. Badley (Wellington, 1998); 129, C (1786); 130, G (1786), ed. A. Badley (Wellington, 1998); 131, C (1786); 131A, C, ?1786–93, *A-R, ST, CZ-OP, D-HR, Mbs, Rtt, TEG, I-CRg, Mc, MOe, US-Wc*; 131B, C, 1786 or after, *A-ST, D-HR, Mbs, I-Mc, MOe*; 132, B♭ (1786), ed. in RRMCE, viii (1978); 132A, B♭, ?1786–90, *CH-Zz, D-DO, HR, Rtt, I-MOe, Vnm*; 133, D, 1786 (1787); 134, E♭, 1786 (1787), ed. J.L. Petit (Paris, 1973); 135, B♭, 1786 (1787); 136, F, 1786 (1787), ed. in The Symphony 1720–1840, ser. D, vi (New York, 1981); 136A, F, 1786 (1787); 137, A, 1786 (1787), ed. A. Badley (Wellington, 1998); 139, E♭ (1789); 140, F (1789), ed. F. Oubradous (Paris, 1957); 140A, F (1791–2); 141, G (1789); 142, c (1790); 143, C (1790), ed. in The Symphony 1720–1840, ser. D, vi (New York, 1981); 144, E♭ (1790); 145, D (1790); 146, G (1790); 147, d (1791), ed. in The Symphony 1720–1840, ser. D, vi (New York, 1981); 147A, D, 1791 or after, *F-Pn** (inc.); 148, E♭ (1793); 149, B♭ (1794); 150, B♭ (1799); 150A, B♭, 1799–1800, *Pn**, *GB-Lbl**; 151, C, by 1800, *Lbl**; 152, E♭, ?1801, *F-Pn**, *GB-Lbl**; 153, f, ?1801, *F-Pn** (inc.); 154, C, *Pn** (inc.) (1803), ed. in The Symphony 1720–1840, ser. D, vi (New York, 1981); 155, a, ?1803, *Pn**, *GB-Lbl**; 156, G (1804); 157, C (?1804–5); 158, C, *A-Wn, D-AB, HR, GB-Lbl, I-Fc*; 159, F, *D-Rtt*; 160, d, *I-MOe*; 161, D, *D-DO, I-MOe*

CONCERTOS, SYMPHONIES CONCERTANTES

B	
101	Vc conc., C, *F-Pn*, 1782–4
102	Vc conc., D, 1782–4, lost
111	Symphonie concertante, E♭, solo vn, va, vc, ob, perf. 1786
103	Vn conc., D, 1785–7 (1788)
103A	Vn conc., D (1788)
104	Vc conc., C (1788)
105	Va/Vc conc., D (1790); ed. C. Hermann (Frankfurt, 1951)
112	Symphonie concertante, B♭, solo vn, va (1791); ed. in The Symphony 1720–1840, ser. D, vi (New York, 1981)
113	Symphonie concertante, F, 2 solo vn, va, vc, fl, ob, bn, perf. 1792
106	Cl/Fl/Vc conc., C (1797); ed. A. Pejtsik (Zürich, 1985)
114	Symphonie concertante, A, 2 solo vn/solo pf, vn, perf. 1792
115	Symphonie concertante, F, solo (fl, ob, bn, hn)/(pf, vn) (1802 or 1805); ed. F. Oubradous (Paris, 1959)
107	Bn conc., B♭, *CZ-Pnm*
108	Vc conc., C, *A-Wgm**
116	Symphonie concertante, F, solo pf, vn, *I-Gl*

MISCELLANEOUS ORCHESTRAL AND CHAMBER

201	Nocturne, D, ob, 2 hn, vn, va, vc, vle, 1780, *F-Pn**
201A	Nocturne [Serenade], D, solo vn, solo vc, 2 hn, vn, va, b, 1780–90 (1790)
202	[Untitled work], C, 2 hn, 2 vn, va, b, 2 hurdy-gurdies, c1785, *Pn** (inc.)
202.5	Nocturne, 2 cl, 2 hn, 2 va, b, 2 hurdy-gurdies, 1785, *D-Bsb**
203–14	Twelve Minuets (6 with trios), 2 ob, 2 hn, 2 vn, b, 1785–7 (1787)
215	Nocturne [Serenade], C, ob, 2 hn, vn, 2 va, vc, b (1787)
216	Serenade, F, ob, 2 hn, 2 vn, va, b (1790)
217	Nocturne, B♭, ob, 2 hn, 2 va, b; ed. B. Pauler (Winterthur, 1989)
218	Adagio, a, solo vn, 2 ob, 2 bn, hn, 2 vn, va, b, *F-Pn**
219	Serenade [Parthia], 2 cl, 2 bn, 2 hn [transcr. from recording, source unknown]
220	Divertimento, G, 2 hn, 2 vn, va, vc, *A-Wgm**, *F-Pn** (inc.)

QUINTETS, SEXTETS, SEPTETS

271–2	Str Qnts, E♭, g, 2 vn, 2 va, vc (1785)
273	Str Qnt, C, 2 vn, 2 va, vc (1786)
276	Str Qnt, a, 2 vn, 2 va, vc (1786)
277	Str Qnt, f, 2 vn, 2 va, vc, perf. 1786; ed. in RRMCE, liii (1998)

251	Septet, E♭, 2 vn, va, vc, db, 2 hn (1787)
274–5	Str Qnts, D, B♭, 2 vn, 2 va, vc (1787)
280–82	Qnts, G, C, E♭, fl, ob, vn, va, vc (1788); no.282 ed. H.Steinbeck (Vienna, 1968)
283–4	Str Qnts, F, D, 2 vn, 2 va, vc (1788)
278–9	Str Qnts, B♭, G, 2 vn, 2 va, vc (1789)
285	Str Qnt, F, 2 vn, 2 va, vc (1789)
261	Sextet, F, 2 vn, 2 va, vc, b (1791); ed. W. Sawodny (Munich, 1993)
286	Qnt, g, hpd, fl, vn, va, b, A-Wgm*
287	Str Qnt, g, 2 vn, 2 va, vc, F-Pn*

QUARTETS

301–6	Str Qts, C, E♭, A, B♭, G, D, op.1, RUS-SPsc* (1782–3, nos.303–4, inc.)
307–12	Str Qts, A, C, g, E♭, B♭, D (1784)
313–18	Str Qts, B♭, A, e, C, E♭, D, 1785 (1786)
319–24	Str Qts, C, G, F, A, B♭, D, 1786 (1786)
325–30	Str Qts, E♭, B♭, A, C, G, F, 1786 (1787); 326A, 327A, 329A (1787); 325A, 328A, 330A (1788)
331–3	Str Qts, B♭, G, d, 1786 (1787), ded. King of Prussia
334–6	Str Qts, C, A, E♭, 1786 (1787), ded. King of Prussia
337–9	Str Qts, D, F, g, 1786 (1787), ded. King of Prussia
340–42	Str Qts, G, c, D, 1786 (1787), ded. King of Prussia
343–5	Str Qts, F, A, F (1788)
346–51	Str Qts, C, F, E♭, G, B♭, A (1788), ded. Prince of Wales: 348A, 350A (1788)
352	Qt, E♭, vn, 2 va, vc (1788); ed. U. Drüner (Zürich, 1976)
381–6	Qts, D, F, A, G, B♭, C, fl/vn, vn, va, vc (1789)
353–8	Str Qts, C, B♭, e, G, A, f (1791), ded. King of Naples
359–64	Str Qts, F, B♭, D, E♭, G, E (1792)
387–92	Qts, D, F, A, C, G, A, fl, vn, va, vc (1797); nos.387–9 ed. J.-P. Rampal (New York, 1977)
393–4	Qts, D, G, fl, vn, va, vc (1799)
365–7	Str Qts, C, B♭, f (1803), ded. Boccherini
367A	Str Qt, f, F-Pn*
367B	Str Qt, f, Pn
368–9	Str Qts, E♭, D (?1810), ded. Viotti, Pn* (no.368, inc.)
369A	Str Qt, D, Pn*
369B	Str Qt, D, Pn*
370	Str Qt, g, Pn*
395	Qt, E♭, fl, 2 cl, bn, D-ASh; ed. G. Meerwein (London, 1970)

TRIOS

Kbd Trio = Trio [Sonata] for keyboard, flute/violin, cello

428–30	Kbd Trios, C, F, G, 1783–4 (1785); nos.428–9 ed. W. Stockmeier (Munich, 1976);B 430 is by Haydn:H XV:5
401–3	Str Trios, E♭, D, F, vn, va, vc (1787); ed. B. Päuler (Zürich, 1971)
404–9	Str Trios, C, E♭, D, e, B♭, G, 2 vn, vc (1788 or 1789); nos.404–6 ed. W. Thomas-Mifune (Lottstetten, 1987)
431–6	Kbd Trios, C, G, B♭, A, e, D (1788), ded. Queen of Great Britain
437–9	Kbd Trio, F, G, E♭ (1790), ded. Elizabeth Wynne
440–42	Kbd Trio, B♭, C, f (1791), ded. Mme de Marclésy
443–5	Kbd Trios, C, F, D (1793) (Scottish Airs, bk 1)
446–8	Kbd Trios, G, B♭, A (1794) (Scottish Airs, bk 2)
449–51	Kbd Trios, C, G, B♭ (1794) (Scottish Airs, bk 1)
452–4	Kbd Trios, D, B♭, A (1794–5) (Scottish Airs, bk 2)
455–7	Kbd Trios, G, C, B♭ (1795–6) (Scottish Airs, bk 3)
461	Kbd Trio, D (1795–6)
458–60	Kbd Trios, G, D, C (1796–8) (Scottish Airs, bk 4)
462–4	Kbd Trios, F, D, B♭ (1796) (with favourite airs)
465–7	Kbd Trios, F, C, E♭ (1796), ded. Eugénie Beaumarchais
468–70	Kbd Trios, B♭, A, C (1796–7), ded. Mme de Gramont
410–15	Str Trios, D, F, G, B♭, G, A, 2 vn, vc (1797); ed. B. Päuler (Adliswil, 1992)
471–3	Kbd Trios, B♭, D, E♭ (1798), ded. Mme Martilière
474–6	Kbd Trios, F, B♭, E♭ (1803), ded. Empress of Russia
416	Str Trio, B♭, 2 vn, va, F-Pn*

DUOS

571–2	Duos, B♭, G, kbd (1787)
573	Duo, B♭, kbd, vn (1788)
501–6	Duos, C, D, F, G, A, B♭, vn, vc (1788); ed. A. Pejtsik (Adliswil, 1990)
507–12	Duos, B♭, F, C, G, D, A, 2 vn/fl, or fl, vn (1788)
513–18	Duos, B♭, D, A, F, C, e, 2 vn (1789)
519–24	Duos, C, g, A, B♭, G, d, 2 vn (1789)
525	Duo, C, va, vc (1792)
526–8	Duos, C, F, E♭, vn, va (1795); ed. U. Drüner (Winterthur, 1987)
529–31	Duos, G, B♭, c, vn, va, or 2 vn (1796)
531A	Duo, d, 2 fl (1796)
574–9	Duos, C, F, G, B♭, D, E♭, kbd, fl/vn (1796)
575A	Duo, F, 2 vn (1796–7)
580–85	Duos, F, D, B♭, e, C, A, kbd, fl/vn (1798)
532–4	Duos, C, g, D, 2 vc (1799/R); ed. W. Thomas-Mifune (Lottstetten, 1984)
532–7	Duos, C, g, E♭, G, B♭, D, 2 vn, F-Ppincherle* (no.536) (1799)
538–43	Duos, C, G, a, F, D, e, 2 vn (1806); ed. G. Maglioni (Milan, 1954)
544–9	Duos, D, E♭, C, B♭, f, G, vn, va (1808–12)

KEYBOARD, HARP SOLOS

601–12	12 German dances, kbd (1792)
613	Rondo, E♭, hp/kbd (1796)
614	Swiss Air with Variations, B♭, kbd/hp (1796)
615	Air with Variations, B♭, pf (1798)
616–17	Pieces, c, B♭, hp/hpd (1798)
618–24	7 Pieces, pf (?1799)
625–7	Sonatas, a, F, G, kbd (1800)
628–63	36 Ecossaises, pf (1803)
664–9	6 Ecossaises, pf (?c1810)
670	Sonata, B♭, kbd, A-Wn, B-Bc, D-WRl, I-OS
801–27	27 instructional exercises pubd in a pf method (1796), incl. 3 for pf 4 hands, also attrib. Dussek

STAGE, VOCAL

701	Die Fee Urgele (marionette op, 4, K. von Pauersbach, after C.-S. Favart), Eszterháza, Nov 1776, A-Wn*
702	Overture to J. Haydn: Die Feuersbrunst, H XXIXb:A, ?1775–8, US-NH
703	Ifigenia in Aulide (op, 3, ? A. Zeno), Naples, S Carlo, 30 May 1785, F-Pn* (Act 3), I-Nc, P-La
704	Deutsche Aria, E♭, v, pf (1790)
705	Hymne à la liberté (Rouget de Lisle), Revolutionary song, v, pf (1791)
706	La révolution du 10 août 1792, ou Le tocsin allégorique, Revolutionary hymn, vv, orch, 1793, F-Pn
707–38	32 Scottish songs, arr. 1–2vv, pf, vc, 1792–3, Pn*, GB-Lbl* (1793–9)
739	Hymne du temple de la raison, v, pf, ?1792–4
740	Hymne à la nuit (Viscount de Parny), v, pf (1795)
741	Mass, G, 1796–7, CZ-Pnm, D-BAR, I-Fc
742–53	Winter-Unterhaltung (12 songs), v, pf (c1798)
754	Requiem, E♭, F-Pn*
755	Cum Sancto Spiritu, fugue, D, chorus, orch, A-Wgm*
756	Mass, D, Wn*, I-Fc

(2) (Joseph Stephen) Camille Pleyel (*b* Strasbourg, 18 Dec 1788; *d* Paris, 4 May 1855). Composer, pianist and business associate of his father (1) Ignace Pleyel. He studied with his parents and with Desormery (probably Jean-Baptiste, the son), Dussek and Steibelt. In 1813–14 he toured southern France, giving piano recitals and arranging for the sale of music and pianos, sometimes in exchange for wood, wine or other materials, in Montpellier, Bordeaux and Toulouse. On 1 January 1815 he became a legal partner of the firm, after which it used the trade name 'Ignace Pleyel et fils aîné'. Nevertheless he spent the period from 16 March to 21 July of that year in London, perhaps to avoid the danger of conscription created by Napoleon's return to power for 100 days (the period corresponded almost exactly with his stay abroad).

In London Pleyel was introduced by the elderly Salomon to the Prince Regent, and on the queen's 71st birthday, 19 May, he performed for a company that included the prince, Queen Charlotte and Princess Charlotte. He also gave several public performances, including one at the Philharmonic Society on 1 May and a two-piano recital with Kalkbrenner. In addition he gave piano lessons, examined pianos and reported to his father on their construction, arranged for the purchase and delivery of mahogany, looked without success for an able piano builder to work for the firm and tried to collect various debts due to the firm. His frequent companions were the pianists Cramer, Kalkbrenner and Ries and the piano makers Broadwood and Tomkison.

After his return to Paris Pleyel gradually assumed more responsibility for the running of the firm, especially the piano-building side of its activities. On 5 April 1831 he married the pianist (3) Marie Moke; they separated after four years.

Pleyel was a close friend of Chopin, who made his Paris début on 26 February 1832 (and gave his final Paris concert on 16 February 1848) in the Salle Pleyel, opened by the firm in 1830. After Camille's death the firm was taken over by Auguste Wolff. (For its later history *see* PLEYEL (ii).) In the summer of 1837 Pleyel accompanied Chopin to London in an unsuccessful effort to cheer the pianist, who was suffering from his unrequited love for Marie Wodzińska. According to Legouvé, who admired Pleyel for his generous nature as well as his exceptional capacity for administration, Chopin was often heard to say, 'There is only one man left today who knows how to play Mozart; it is Pleyel, and when he is willing to play a four-hand sonata with me, I take a lesson'.

Before devoting himself entirely to commercial activities, Pleyel wrote a number of compositions for the piano (the last being op.51). They were issued by the Pleyel firm and in London; apart from a few sonatas and trios they are chiefly fantasias, potpourris of opera airs, rondos, nocturnes, airs, caprices and *mélanges*.

(3) (Camille) Marie (Denise) Moke Pleyel

(*b* Paris, 4 Sept 1811; *d* St Josse-ten-Noode, nr Brussels, 30 March 1875). French pianist, teacher and composer, wife of (2) Camille Pleyel. At an early age she displayed talent for the piano. She studied successively with Jacques Herz, Ignaz Moscheles and Frédéric Kalkbrenner and at the age of 14 performed Kalkbrenner's first concerto at the Théâtre de la Monnaie, Brussels. By 1830 she was teaching the piano at a girls' school (the Institut Ortho-pédique in the Marais section of Paris), where her colleagues and admirers included Ferdinand Hiller and Berlioz (who taught the piano and the guitar respectively). She became engaged to Berlioz after her mother's objections to him were weakened by his having finally won the Prix de Rome. Three months after his departure for Rome in December 1830, however, she married (2) Camille Pleyel. She continued her piano teaching, writing to a friend in July of her fond husband, who 'has willingly consented to my continuing to give lessons; you know that I am very attached to my independence'. Chopin dedicated to her his three Nocturnes op.9 in 1833, the same year that Kalkbrenner did the same with his *Fantaisie et variations sur une mazourka de Chopin* op.120.

After legal separation from her husband (1835) Mme Pleyel resumed her performing career, reaping enormous successes in Bonn, Dresden, Leipzig, Vienna, St Petersburg, Paris and London; one of her English performances prompted De Quincey to write of her as 'the celestial pianofortist. Heaven nor earth has yet heard her equal'.

In 1842 she requested and received permission to establish her domicile in Belgium. From 1848 until 1872 she was a piano teacher at the Brussels Conservatory, of which the director was F.-J. Fétis. Fétis wrote that she was responsible for the establishment of a true school of piano playing in Belgium; that her playing was notable for astonishing technical facility, but also for strength, tonal modifications, charm and poetry; and that among the many famous pianists heard by him, no other gave the feeling of perfection that her playing created. She was also appreciated by Mendelssohn and Liszt and the latter, a personal friend with whom she performed four-hand works, dedicated to her his *Réminiscences de Norma* (1841) and the *Tarantelle di bravura d'après la Tarantelle de 'La muette de Portici' d'Auber* (1846). Pleyel composed several works for the piano, including a *Rondo parisien pour piano* op.1, a Fantasia on motifs from Weber's *Preciosa* and an Andante.

BIBLIOGRAPHY

BrookSF

N.E. Framery: *Notice sur Joseph Haydn* (Paris, 1810)

J.F. Lobstein: *Beiträge zur Geschichte der Musik im Elsass und besonders in Strassburg* (Strasbourg,1840), 33ff

J.-B. Weckerlin: *Musiciana* (Paris, 1877) [incl. several letters to Pleyel]

O. Comettant, ed.: *Un nid d'autographes* (Paris, 1885, 2/1886) [incl. letters to Pleyel]

C. Pierre: *Les hymnes et chansons de la Révolution* (Paris, 1904/R)

M. Vogeleis: *Quellen und Bausteine zu einer Geschichte der Musik und des Theaters im Elsass* (Strasbourg, 1911/R)

M. Pincherle: 'L'édition musicale au dix-huitième siècle', *Musique*, i (1927–8), 493–8 [incl. letter from George Thomson to Pleyel]

A. Hedley: *Chopin* (London, 1947, rev. 2/1974 by M.J.E. Brown)

A. Carse: 'A Symphony by Pleyel', *MMR*, lxxix (1949), 231–6

H.C.R. Landon, ed.: *The Collected Correspondence and London Notebooks of Joseph Haydn* (London, 1959)

J. Klingenbeck: 'Ignaz Pleyel und die Marseillaise', *SMw*, xxiv (1960), 106–19

A. Tyson: 'Haydn and Two Stolen Trios', *MR*, xxii (1961), 21–7

J. Klingenbeck: 'Ignaz Pleyel: sein Streichquartett im Rahmen der Wiener Klassik', *SMw*, xxv (1962), 276–97

G. de Rothschild: *Luigi Boccherini: sa vie, son oeuvre* (Paris, 1962; Eng. trans., rev., 1965)

R. Benton: 'Ignace Pleyel, Disputant', *FAM*, xiii (1966), 21–4

R. Benton: 'London Music in 1815, as seen by Camille Pleyel', *ML*, xlvii (1966), 34–47

R.R. Smith: *The Periodical Symphonies of Ignaz Pleyel* (diss., U. of Rochester, NY, 1968) [incl. scores of syms. B 126, 132, 136, 143, 147]

R. Benton: 'A la recherche de Pleyel perdu, or Perils, Problems and Procedures of Pleyel Research', *FAM*, xvii (1970), 8–15

J. Zsako: 'Bibliographical Sandtraps: the Klavierschule, Pleyel or Dussek?', *CMc*, no.12 (1971), 75–9

R. Benton: 'Pleyel's *Bibliothèque musicale*', *MR*, xxxvi (1975), 1–4

R. Benton: 'Bemerkungen zu einem Pleyel-Werkverzeichnis', *Mf*, xxix (1976), 280–87

R. Benton: *Ignace Pleyel: a Thematic Catalogue of his Compositions* (New York, 1977)

R. Benton: 'A Résumé of the Haydn–Pleyel Trio Controversy, with some Added Contributions', *Haydn-Studien*, iv/2 (1978), 114–17

R. Benton: 'Pleyel as Music Publisher', *JAMS*, xxxii (1979), 125–40

E. Radant: 'Ignaz Pleyel's Correspondence with Hoffmeister & Co.', *Haydn Yearbook 1981*, 122–74

R. Benton: *Pleyel as Music Publisher: a Documentary Sourcebook of Early 19th-Century Music* (Stuyvesant, NY, 1990)

RITA BENTON

Pleyel (ii). French firm of piano makers. It was founded in 1807 at Paris by the composer Ignace Pleyel (*see* PLEYEL (i)). The firm quickly adopted and improved the best features of English piano making; JEAN HENRI PAPE helped Pleyel from 1811 to 1815 with the building of cottage pianos or 'pianinos', small vertically strung uprights

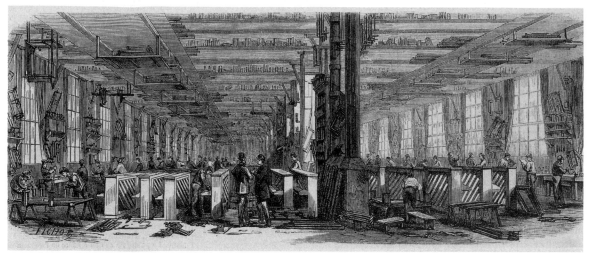

The manufacturing of upright pianos at the Pleyel factory, France (L'illustration, 2 April 1887)

invented by the English maker Robert Wornum (ii) which were new to France. In 1815 Ignace's son Camille Pleyel joined the firm; 14 years later the pianist Frédéric Kalkbrenner joined too and did much to publicize Pleyel pianos. Chopin became closely associated with the firm; he made his début in Paris (26 February 1832) at the Salle Pleyel and later owned a Pleyel grand of 1839 (no.7267) with a single escapement and a light touch. Chopin said 'when I feel in good form and strong enough to find my own individual sound, then I need a Pleyel piano'. The soundboard introduced by Pleyel in 1830 consisted of mahogany veneer running across pine boards and is thought to have encouraged a bright, silvery sound. Cramer, Moscheles and Steibelt were also friends of the firm. Business increased so much that the firm claimed 250 employees and, probably with exaggeration, an annual production of 1000 pianos in 1834. By the 1870s the annual output had increased to 2500, a level that was maintained for the rest of the century.

In 1855 Camille died and was succeeded by his son-in-law, Auguste Wolff (*b* Paris, 3 May 1821; *d* Paris, 9 Feb 1887), the firm becoming Pleyel, Wolff & Cie. After Wolff's death his son-in-law Gustave Lyon (*b* Paris, 19 Nov 1857; *d* Paris, 12 Jan 1936) assumed control of 'Pleyel, Lyon et Cie'. Lyon developed a *harpe éolienne* (*see* AEOLIAN HARP), but is more famous for his development of the chromatic harp (*see* HARP, §V, 7(ii), esp. fig.34) at the end of the 19th century. It dispensed with pedals, substituting a string for each semitone of the octave. Debussy wrote for it, but it has never achieved the popularity of the double-action harp, as the number of strings is nearly double and it requires a totally different finger technique. Under Lyon the firm also made chromatic timpani, chimes, practice keyboards, the 'Duoclave' (in 1895), which consisted of two grand pianos built into a single case, and the two-manual EMANUEL MOÓR PIANOFORTE with a steel coupler designed by Lyon himself (see Shead). Lyon's action was subsequently used by Bösendorfer in their own double-keyboard instruments. Under the trade name 'Pleyela' the firm brought out a reproducing piano-player mechanism.

At the turn of the century Pleyel began making two-manual harpsichords, with $2 \times 8'$ and $1 \times 4'$, six pedals and classical casework (*see* HARPSICHORD, §5(i)). Wanda

Landowska suggested a new design in 1912, a modern departure having little in common with the classical instrument, with a heavy case including a cast-iron frame, a special tuning system, seven pedals and a 16' register (*see* HARPSICHORD, fig.15). About two such instruments were made annually. It was this instrument that Landowska played throughout her career. In 1961 the firm was merged with Gaveau-Erard, but it continued to make pianos under the name of Pleyel. In 1976 the merged firm was bought out by Schimmel of Brunswick, who produced instruments under a licence agreement until 1994, when the French piano firm Rameau took over.

BIBLIOGRAPHY

J. Turgan: *Les grandes usines de France: la manufacture de pianos de MM. Pleyel, Wolf* [sic]*et Cie* (Paris, 1862)

J.P.O. Comettant: *Histoire de cent mille pianos et d'une salle de concert* (Paris, 1890)

T. de Fourcaud: *La Salle Pleyel* (Paris, 1893)

R.E.M. Harding: *The Piano-Forte: its History Traced to the Great Exhibition of 1851* (Cambridge, 1933/R, 2/1978/R)

B. Dahl: 'The Ehlers' Pleyel', *The Harpsichord*, vi (1973), 3 only

J.A. Richard: 'The Pleyel Harpsichord', *The English Harpsichord Magazine and Early Keyboard Instrument Review*, ii/5 (1977–81), 110–13

H.A. Shead: *The History of the Emanuel Moór Double Keyboard Piano* (Old Woking, 1978)

O. Barli: *La facture française du piano de 1849 à nos jours* (Paris, 1983)

N. Schimmel: *La facture du piano: un artisanat d'art* (Brunswick, 1990–91)

MARGARET CRANMER

Plica (Lat.: 'fold'). In Western chant notations the name used in the 13th and 14th centuries for liquescent neumes. It describes their usual shape: a single stroke doubling back on itself to make a 'U' or inverted 'U', thicker at the curve. The *plica* is a two-note neume, containing the pitch where the *plica* was placed on the staff plus a higher ('U' shape) or lower (inverted 'U') note. The second note was semi-vocalized to provide a passing or anticipatory note before the next pitch. The semi-vocalization was most commonly practised on the consonants '*l*', '*m*', '*n*' and '*r*', before another consonant (2452 out of 3500 cases in the study in PalMus, 1st ser., ii, 1891), sometimes when they were the only consonant between vowels; on the second vowel of diphthongs; on the consonant pair '*gn*'; sometimes on '*d*' and '*t*' at the ends of words (particularly *et*,

Ex.1

1st-mode ligature pattern

1st-mode with plicas

2nd-mode ligature pattern

2nd-mode with plicas

TABLE 1

	long	▪ or ▪	plica longa ascendens
			plica longa descendens
	breve	▪	plica brevis ascendens
			plica brevis descendens

sed, *ut*); sometimes on soft '*c*' and soft '*g*' (before '*e*' and '*i*'); sometimes also on '*d*', '*s*', '*t*' and '*x*', before other consonants; and on '*i*' or '*j*' when used as a consonant.

While early writers on neume shapes and names (see Huglo) called the ascending form *epiphonus* and the descending form *cephalicus*, 13th-century theorists used the term 'plica'. Thus Jehan des Murs (*GerbertS*, iii, 202):

> Clives, plicae, virga, quilismata, puncta, podati,
> Nomina sunt harum; sint pressi consociati.

The *plica* retained its basic function of indicating liquescence in all plainchant manuscripts and in most sources containing polyphony and non-mensural secular monophony until the 14th century. The situations in which Mocquereau found liquescent neumes used in 10th- and 11th-century manuscripts (see PalMus, 1st ser., ii, 1891) are distinguished in the same way in later sources (with minor differences resulting from different pronunciation practice, to which, in fact, liquescent neumes are a guide). Of later theorists only Lambertus (Pseudo-Aristotle) attempted a description of the method of voice production involved (*CoussemakerS*, i, 273): 'The plica is sung by narrowing or closing the epiglottis while subtly including a vibration of the throat'; this seems to be a picturesque way of saying that the forethroat is formed as for consonants while the vocal chords are still vibrating.

In Parisian repertories of polyphony of the early 13th century, however, the *plica* was also used in melismatic music, without liquescent function. Five of the rhythmic modes, which were the basis of the method of indicating rhythm in this music, did not provide for a note on at least one beat of a ternary measure (i.e. one quaver out of every three in 3/8 transcription; or two out of six in 6/8 transcription). Ex.1 shows how *plica* strokes added to patterns of 1st- and 2nd-mode ligatures provide these

notes (see Apel, pp.228–9, for more complex examples). The *plica* most often implies an added note at the interval of a 2nd. Definite instances of larger intervals are rare, one such being found in the conductus *Deduc Syon uberrimas*: in *E-Mn* 20486 on the syllable '-tas' of 'gravitas' there is a two-note descending ligature *d–G* (f.84*r*, staff 4); in *D-W* 677 there is a *plica* on *d* with a slight thickening at the end of the stroke on *G* (f.160*r* [151*r*], staff 10); while *I-Fl* 29.1 and *D-W* 1206 have a *plica* with stylized square note head and a long descending tail to the right (f.336*v*, staff 4, f.94*r*, staff 6, respectively).

In the second half of the 13th century discrete note shapes were evolved for *plica longa* and *plica brevis*, to complement the standard long and breve shapes; Table 1 gives the commonest forms. The Parisian repertories of the second half of the 13th century are, however, largely of syllabic music (i.e. motets), and the *plica* retained its basic function of denoting liquescence. Walter Odington, who called it 'semitonus et semivocalis' (*CoussemakerS*, i, 236), preferred to use the longer method of writing 6th-mode passages (continuous breves): 'certior est et acceptior' (*CoussemakerS*, i, 245), presumably to avoid confusion between the two functions.

The *plica* was frequently preceded by another note of the same pitch; the reason for this is not always clear. The group can usually be confidently transcribed as equivalent to a long (crotchet or dotted crotchet) rather than a breve (quaver), but this is by no means a universal rule (see Tischler). It was to some extent interchangeable with the simple *plica*, with a two-note ligature or with a three-note group in which the first two notes were of the same pitch. A comparison of the notation of *D-W* 677, 1028, *E-Mn* 20486 and *I-Fl* 29.1 for the tenor parts of the 17 polyphonic conductus they have in common shows 50 or so simple *plicae* found alone above a single syllable, 100 or so 'compound' *plicae*, and 170 or so binaria or single note + binaria, in any one manuscript: 12–15% are found in an alternative form in one or more of the other three manuscripts. *E-Mn* 20486 shows a preference for simple *plicae*, *D-W* 1028 for binaria or single note + binaria; sometimes *D-W* 677 and *E-Mn* 20486 use a binaria with elongated first element where the other manuscripts have a compound *plica* or single note + binaria. More detailed statistics both depend on and help investigation of the layering of the repertory as a whole.

The single note + binaria is the usual form in square staff notation of the *pressus* (descending) and *pes quassus* (ascending) compound neumes. Although these neumes originally entailed a special manner of performance (Jehan des Murs said the *pressus* should be performed evenly and swiftly; *GerbertS*, iii, 202), they have no special shape in, for instance, Parisian 13th-century chant manuscripts, to draw attention to this characteristic. Kuhlmann (p.111) suggested that in Parisian polyphony the note-group denoted a vibrato, being what Jerome of Moravia called *flores* (*CoussemakerS*, i, 91–2). At any rate the compound *plica* was usually used in situations where liquescence was appropriate.

The Fathers of Solesmes (PalMus, 1st ser., ii, 1891) said that not every such situation was matched by a liquescent neume, but did not give figures to show how often. Table 2 gives statistics for the tenor parts of the three- and two-part conductus in *I-Fl* 29.1; it shows the number of times a syllable ending '*l*', '*m*', '*n*' or '*r*' and followed by another consonant (words such as *salve*,

TABLE 2

I-Fl 29.1	∩	¶∩	⌐	¶⌐	Total
total number of occurrences on liquescent consonant	165 38.6%	164 38.4%	85 19.9%	13 3%	427
in conductus also found in other sources	143 41.7%	138 40.2%	53 15.5%	9 2.6%	343
in unica	22 26.2%	26 31%	32 38.1%	4 4.8%	84

omnes, cantat, virgo) is matched by a simple *plica*, a compound *plica*, a binaria or a single note + binaria (ascending or descending forms). The use of binaria may possibly be a tendency in later pieces or in those that are more certainly Parisian; separate figures are therefore given for pieces that are also found in other sources and for unica, to show approximately how the repertory of the manuscript is divided (for further evidence see Hiley). The polyphonic pieces of the Roman de Fauvel (*F-Pn* fr.146), the last source in mensural music to use plicas to any great extent, still used the plica for liquescence.

BIBLIOGRAPHY

A. Mocquereau: 'Neumes-accents liquescents ou semi-vocaux', *Le répons-graduel Justus et palma*, PalMus, 1st ser., ii (1891), 37–86

J. Pothier: 'De la plique dans le plain-chant', *Revue du chant grégorien*, iii (1895), 55–9 [summarized by P. Bohn, *MMg*, xxvii, 1895, p.47]

G.M. Suñol: *Introducció a la paleografia musical gregoriana* (Montserrat, 1925; Fr. trans., rev. and enlarged 2/1935)

H. Freistedt: *Die liqueszierenden Noten des gregorianischen Chorals* (Fribourg, 1929)

G. Kuhlmann: *Die zweistimmigen französischen Motetten des Kodex Montpellier, Faculté de médecine H 196* (Würzburg, 1938)

W. Apel: *The Notation of Polyphonic Music 900–1600* (Cambridge, MA, 1942, rev. 5/1961)

M. Huglo: 'Les noms des neumes et leur origine', *EG*, i (1954), 53–67

H. Tischler: 'Ligatures, Plicae and Vertical Bars in Premensural Notation', *RBM*, xi (1957), 83–92

H. Anglès: 'Die Bedeutung der Plika in der mittelalterlichen Musik', *Festschrift Karl Gustav Fellerer* (Regensburg, 1962), 28–39

D. Hiley: 'The Plica and Liquescence', *Gordon Athol Anderson (1929–1981): in memoriam* (Henryville, PA, 1984), 379–91

DAVID HILEY

Plishka, Paul (*b* Old Forge, PA, 28 Aug 1941). American bass. He studied at Montclair State College, and received his initial stage experience with Paterson Lyric Opera, New Jersey. In 1965 he joined the Metropolitan Opera National Company, singing Mozart's Bartolo and Puccini's Colline. When the touring company was disbanded, he was invited to join the Metropolitan Opera at Lincoln Center, where he made his début in *La Gioconda* (1967). He has remained a member of the company throughout his career, singing leading roles in both the serious and *buffo* repertories, among them Leporello, Oroveso (*Norma*), King Mark, Fiesco (*Simon Boccanegra*), Philip II, Falstaff, Varlaam, Pimen and Boris Godunov. He made his La Scala début in *La damnation de Faust* in 1974, and in 1991 sang Kutuzov (*War and Peace*) at San Francisco. His mellow, voluminous bass can be heard in recordings of *Anna Bolena*, *I puritani*, *Norma*, *Faust*, *Le Cid* and *Falstaff*.

MARTIN BERNHEIMER/R

Pliyeva, Zhanna Vasil'yevna (*b* Tskhinvali, Southern Ossetia, 10 Feb 1949). Ossetian composer and pianist. She graduated from the Rimsky-Korsakov State Conservatory, Leningrad, in 1972 having studied the piano with D. Svetozarov and composition with Orest Yevlakhov and A. Mnatsakanian (with whom she studied as a graduate); in 1979 she worked there for a probationary period as assistant to Sergey Slonimsky. She became a member of the Composers' Union in 1976. She was a prize-winner in the All-Union Composers' Competition in 1977 and in the Tokyo International Composers' Competition, 1993. She is an honoured artist of Republic of Northern Ossetia-Alania, 1993. After having various posts as orchestral musician, teacher and researcher (including director of Tskhinvali School of Music, 1979–85, and president of the Praesidium of the Georgian Music Society, 1989–90), since 1990 she has devoted herself to full-time composition.

Pliyeva's works combine the mythology and musical dialects of the mountain peoples of the northern Caucasus with a contemporary idiom which is notable for its passion of utterance and natural ease of fantasy. This fusion of the latest techniques with the imagery of epic poetry is evident in the First Symphony (soprano, strings and percussion) and in the one-movement Third Symphony. The specific links between Pliyeva's music and Ossetian culture form part of a broader, non-explicit connection with the ancient art of the northern Caucasus. These links are expressed not in the musical language but in the way of thinking and in faithfulness to the spirit of her native culture.

Pliyeva's orchestral writing is notable for the rich contrasts between instrumental groups which result in a kind of new heterophony; other tendencies include powerful dynamic climaxes, structural breaks and textural movement. In the aesthetic plan of the musical wholes, separate component parts are logically reliant on each other. By the 1980s she was employing less conventional forces such as tape and prepared piano.

WORKS

Stage: Deti solntsa [Children of the Sun] (children's op, 2, G. Dzugayev), 1981; Fatima (ballet, 3), 1982–4; Strasti po Ėdamu [The Passion of Adam] (passion play, 2), 1993

Orch: Sym. no.1, S, perc, str; Sym. no.2, 1976; Sym. no.3, 1978; Sym. no.4, 1990–91; Sym. no.5, 1994; Muzïka dlya strunnïkh [Music for Strings], 1996

Choral: O rodine [About my Homeland] (G. Dzugayev), chorus, pf, 1979; Shutochnaya [Comic Song], 1979; Solovey poyot [A Nightingale Sings], female vv, 1979; Sospeso (nyedoskazannoye) [Sospeso (Understated)] female vv, 2 prep pfs; Chenena (trad.), genre scene, 1987; Slïshu . . . Umolklo . . . [I'm Listening . . . It's Gone Quiet . . .] (trad.), 4 choruses for children

Chbr: 3 p'yesï, 2 vns, 1972; P'yesï, cl, pf, 1972; P'yesï, tpt, pf, 1972; Pf Trio, 1973; Stsena, pf, vn, 2 vcs, dömbra, 1990; Pesn' pesney [Song of Songs], brass qt, 1991; Mirazh, 2 pfs, tape, 1992; Sonata, vc, 1992; Pesni [songs], 2 vcs, 1993; Sonata, vn, 1993

Pf: Prelyudii 1970–72; Poema, Tokkata, 5 sarkazmov, 4 fugov, 1963–75; Minatyurï, for children, 1978, 2 bks; Ritual'nïy [Ritual], 1978; Trezvuchiya [Triads], 1978; Tokkatina, 1979; Puteshestviye v zoopark [A Trip to the Zoo], for children, 1980; 4 Sonatas: 1982, 1984, 1990, 1995

Vocal (1v, pf): Iz osetinskogo ėposa [From Ossetian Epos] (trad.), song cycle, S, T, pf, 1977; Monolog Tsezarya [Caesar's Monologue] (G. Bestauti), 1988; Osenniye gryozï [Autumn Reveries] (L. Kotsta), S, pf, 1989

Incid music, el-ac works, music-hall songs

WRITINGS

'K voprosu genezisa osetinskoy geroicheskoy pesni' [The problem of the origin of Ossetian heroic song], *Fidiuag* (1989), no.7

'Iz glubinï vekov' [From the depths of the centuries], *Sovetskaya Ossetiya* (1985)

BIBLIOGRAPHY

M. Yakubov: *Zhanna Pliyeva* (Moscow, 1982)

T. Kopïlova: 'O tvorcheskom vechere osetinskikh kompozitorov' [An evening of the work of Ossetian composers], *SovM* (1983), no.9

A. Degtyarev: 'Yarkaya individual'nost'' [Outstanding individuality], *Muzïkal'naya zhizn'* (1996), nos.5–6, pp.27–8

ALLA VLADIMIROVNA GRIGOR'YEVA

Plocek, Václav (*b* Prague, 28 Aug 1923). Czech musicologist. He studied composition with Otakar Šín and Miroslav Krejčí at the Prague Conservatory (1942–7), the piano with Jan Heřman (1942–5) and musicology and aesthetics at Prague University (1945–8), where he took the doctorate under Hutter in 1948 with a dissertation containing an analysis of the St Vít troper of 1235. Subsequently he joined the music section of the Prague State Library, taking a diploma in librarianship there in 1950. In 1964 he moved to the Musicology Institute of the Czechoslovak Academy of Sciences, where he devoted himself to the systematic study of Czech medieval music, analysing and editing sources, and Czech musical palaeography. In 1967 he obtained the CSc with a catalogue of music manuscripts in Prague University library. He retired in 1988. Plocek was the leading and almost the only Czech musical medievalist of his generation, maintaining a demanding discipline despite official discouragement in the 1950s and later, and thus providing a valuable link with the achievements of Czech pre-war medieval studies. His lasting achievement is the catalogue of musical manuscripts in the State Library in Prague (1973) and the three-volume edition of music for the Easter liturgical plays (1989).

WRITINGS

Versus super offerta (diss., U. of Prague, 1948; extracts pubd as 'Původ svatováclavského responsoria "Laudemus Dominum"' [The origin of the St Vít responsory *Laudemus Dominum*], *Ročenka Universitní knihovny v Praze 1957*, 130–37 [summaries in Eng., Ger., Russ.])

'Nově nalezená sekvence o svaté Dorotě a její poměr k Jenštejnově "Decet huius"' [A newly discovered sequence on St Dorothy and its relation to Jenštejn's *Decet huius*], *Ročenka Universitní knihovny v Praze 1956*, 67–95; Ger. trans. in *De musica disputationes Pragenses*, i (1972), 120–48

'Zpracování nejstarších hudebních rukopisů v Universitní knihovně' [Working on the oldest manuscripts in the University library], *Ročenka Universitní knihovny v Praze 1958*, 12–20

'Nejstarší dvojhlasy v rukopisech Universitní knihovny' [The oldest two-part manuscripts in Prague University library], *Ročenka Universitní knihovny v Praze 1960–1961*, 129–48; Ger. trans. in J. Fukač, V. Plocek and M.K. Černý: *Bydgoszcz 1966: Beiträge zur Geschichte der tschechischen Musik* (Prague, 1966), 65–109

Catalogus codicum notis musicis instructorum qui in Bibliotheca publica rei publicae Bohemicae socialisticae in Bibliotheca universitatis Pragensis servantur (CSc diss., Czechoslovak Academy of Sciences, 1967; Prague, 1973)

'Zásady popisu rukopisů psaných ve starých notačních systémech' [Principles in the description of manuscripts written in early systems of notation], *HV*, v (1968), 230–63 [summaries in Eng., Ger., Russ.]

'K problematice našich nejstarších tanečních skladeb' [Some questions concerning the oldest Czech dance compositions], *HV*, vi (1969), 3–25 [summaries in Eng., Ger.; abridged Ger. trans. in *SMH*, xiii (1971), 242–7]

'Ještě k problematice Czaldy waldy' [More about the Czaldy waldy problem], *HV*, vii (1970), 46–57 [summaries in Eng., Ger., Russ.]

'Středověký zpěv v rukopisech Státní knihovny ČSR' [Medieval song in manuscripts of the Czech State Library], *Ročenka Universitní knihovny v Praze 1974*, 1–21

'Nejstarší doklad velikonočních slavností v Čechách' [The oldest document of Easter ceremonies in Bohemia], *Uměnovědné studie*, i (1978), 77–152

'Repetitio a responsio ve středověkých zpěvech' [Repetitio and responsio in medieval songs], *HV*, xviii (1981), 35–48

'Metody a cíle analýzy středověkých monodií' [The methods and aims of analysing medieval monodies], *Uměnovědné studie*, iv (1983), 7–49

'Pracovní problematika středověkých jednohlasých rukopisů' [Problems of working with medieval monophonic manuscripts], *Studie o rukopisech*, xxiii (1984), 77–84

Zwei Studien zur ältesten geistlichen Musik in Böhmen (Giessen and Cologne, 1985)

Melodie velikonočních slavností a her ze středověkých pramenů v Čechách I–III [The melodies of Easter ceremonies and plays from medieval sources in Bohemia] (Prague, 1989)

BIBLIOGRAPHY

J. Novotná: 'Sedmdesátiny Václava Plocka' [Plocek's 70th birthday], *HV*, xxx (1993), 185–7 [incl. selective bibliography]

JOSEF BEK/JOHN TYRRELL

Płocka, Marek z. *See* MAREK Z PŁOCKA.

Plomer [Plourmel], **John.** *See* PLUMMER, JOHN.

Plousiadenos, Joannes [Joseph of Methone] (*b* Crete, ?1429; *d* Methone, 9 Aug 1500). Composer of Byzantine chant, theologian, music theorist, *domestikos* and scribe. He lived for over 20 years in Italy, mostly in Venice (1472–*c*1492, 1497–8), and became bishop of Methone, taking the name of Joseph. He died in Methone during the Turkish massacre and was subsequently recognized as a Christian martyr. His musical achievements have often been overshadowed by his literary and political activities, particularly his involvement with the Union of Florence and his service as a political envoy for the Vatican, which led to accusations of heresy and of being a philocatholic.

Plousiadenos is one of two 15th-century Byzantine musicians (the other is Manuel Gazes) to have composed and notated a Byzantine *koinōnikon* (*GR-AOdo* 315, ff.66*v*–67*r*) in two-part polyphony; his associations with Venice may have opened him to the influence of the Quattrocento practice of *cantus planus binatim*. This communion chant, *Ainete ton Kyrion* ('Praise the Lord'), has been seen as evidence that *cantare super librum diaphonia* was applied to the Byzantine practice of *isokratēma* – the improvised *ison* singing first documented in the 13th century. His many other compositions, notated in Late Byzantine neumes (*see* BYZANTINE CHANT, §3(iii)) though not in polyphony, include settings of the Divine Liturgies, the Cherubic Hymn and *Magnificat*; psalms, including the *polyeleos* (Psalm cxxxiv) and the *amomos* (Psalm cxviii, for funerals); *allēlouiaria* in all eight modes; *theotokia*, *koinōnika* and *katanyktika* (laments for the dead); and *stichēra* for various liturgical feasts (in *ET-MSsc* gr.1234).

Plousiadenos's music treatise *Ermeneia tēs parallagēs* ('Interpretation of the *parallagē*') discusses most of the difficult aspects of Byzantine music theory, including PARALLAGĒ (in this context, the modulation or transition and relationship and interrelationship between the eight modes). The *Ermeneia* is also famous for its illustration, in *GR-AOd* 570, of a geometric figure with a concentric cross and diamond that is derived from the Koukouzelian wheel (a circle depicting the modulation of modes; *see* KOUKOUZELES).

BIBLIOGRAPHY

M. Manoussakas: 'Recherches sur la vie de Jean Plousiadenos (Joseph de Méthone) (1429?–1500)', *Revue des études byzantines*, xvii (1959), 29–49

M. Adamis: 'An Example of Polyphony in Byzantine Music of the Late Middle Ages', *IMSCR XI: Copenhagen 1971*, ii, 737–47

G. Stathēs: *Ta cheirographa byzantinēs mousikēs: Hagion Oros* [Byzantine music MSS: Mt Athos], i (Athens, 1975); iii (Athens, 1993)

D. Conomos: 'Experimental Polyphony "According to the ... Latins" in Late Byzantine Psalmody', *EMH*, ii (1982), 1–16

B. Schartau: 'A Checklist of the Settings of George and John Plousiadenos in the Kalophonic Sticherarion Sinai gr. 1234', *Cahiers de l'Institut du Moyen Age grec et latin*, no.63 (1993), 297–308

D. Touliatos: 'Ioannes Plousiadenos and his Treatise on Music' *Liturgiya, arkhitektura i iskusstvo vizantiyskogo mira: Moscow 1991* [Liturgy, architecture and art of the Byzantine world], ed. K.K. Akent'yev, iii (St Petersburg, 1996), 532–45

D. Touliatos: 'Ioannes Plousiadenos: the Man, his Music, and his Musical Treatise', *Thesaurismata*, xxviii (1998), 1–12

D. Touliatos: *Ioannes Plousiadenos and his Treatise 'Interpretation on the Parallagē'*, MMB, *Corpus scriptorum* (forthcoming)

DIANE TOULIATOS

Plovdiv. Town in Bulgaria. It became an important cultural centre soon after the country's liberation from Ottoman domination in 1878. Interest in visiting Italian troupes led to the foundation of a local singers' society in 1896. The earliest attempts to create an opera theatre date from 1910. Ten years later a privately owned Khudozhestvena Opera (Artistic Opera) was organized, and in 1922 the Plovdivska Gradska Opera (Plovdiv City Opera) was formed by Russian immigrants; by 1944 the Plovdivska Oblastna Opera (Plovdiv District Opera) had been established. On 15 November 1953 the Plovdivska Narodna Opera (Plovdiv National Opera) had its official opening in the Naroden Teatar (National Theatre) with *The Bartered Bride*. From the very beginning the company's profile was determined by its ensemble, which included the paired soloists Penka Koyeva and Aleksey Milkovski, Valentina Aleksandrova and Georgi Velchev, and by its varied repertory, from *Die Zauberflöte, Les contes d'Hoffmann, L'heure espagnole* and *Adriana Lecouvreur* to *Kát'a Kabanová* and Pipkov's *Antigona '43*. The conductors Russlan Raychev, Krasto Marev and Dimitar Manolov have also contributed to the company's success. Opera performances alternate with drama, and are given chiefly on the stage of the Trade Union Culture House; there are three performances weekly, with three to four premières a year. The season lasts from September until July.

MAGDALENA MANOLOVA

Plowright, Rosalind (Anne) (*b* Worksop, 21 May 1949). English soprano. She studied in Manchester and at the London Opera Centre, making her début in 1975 as the Page in *Salome* with the ENO. In 1976–7 she sang Countess Almaviva and Donna Elvira with Glyndebourne Touring Opera. Her later roles with the ENO have included Miss Jessel, Elizabeth I (*Maria Stuarda*), Hélène (*Les vêpres siciliennes*), Elisabeth de Valois and Tosca. Plowright made her Covent Garden début in 1980 as Ortlinde, returning as Donna Anna, Maddalena (*Andrea Chénier*), Leonora (*Il trovatore*), Ariadne, Senta and Desdemona. In 1982 she made her US début at San Diego as Medora (*Il corsaro*), followed by Violetta and Chabrier's Gwendoline. She first sang at La Scala in 1983 as Suor Angelica, returning as Gluck's Alcestis (1987). After singing Cherubini's Medea (in French) at Buxton in 1984, she repeated the role at Covent Garden and (in Italian) at Lausanne. Her repertory has also included Norma, Butterfly, Lady Macbeth, Tatyana and Gioconda.

Among Plowright's recordings are Spontini's *La vestale* and impassioned interpretations of Leonora in both *Il trovatore* and *La forza del destino*. A versatile, highly dramatic artist, she has a full-toned, dark-coloured voice particularly rich in the middle register. She experienced vocal problems at the height of her career, but returned to sing Santuzza at the Berlin Staatsoper in 1996, and Giorgetta (*Il tabarro*) at the ENO in 1997.

BIBLIOGRAPHY

H. Matheopoulos: *Diva* (London, 1991), 133–44

ELIZABETH FORBES

Plucked drum. A term used by Hornbostel and Sachs (*see* MEMBRANOPHONE) for a type of instrument, popular in South Asia, in which the vibrations of a plucked string are transmitted to a membrane. The *gopīyantra* and *ānandalaharī* have been classified as plucked drums, but research on their acoustical properties suggests that this category may more properly be regarded as that of a VARIABLE TENSION CHORDOPHONE.

Plucked dulcimer. *See* APPALACHIAN DULCIMER.

Plüddemann, Martin (*b* Kolberg, Pomerania [now Kołobrzeg, Poland], 29 Sept 1854; *d* Berlin, 8 Oct 1897). German composer and singer. As a child, Plüddemann heard chamber and operatic music in his home, which stimulated an early love of music. He studied at the Leipzig Conservatory (1871–6) under Ernst Friedrich Richter. After a brief service as Kapellmeister in St Gallen (1878), Plüddemann left for Munich to study singing with Julius Hey and Friedrich Schmitt. There he also began a writing career with the publication of several polemical articles on music. The loss of his voice in 1880 forced him to give up singing. At first he turned to music criticism in Munich. After years of travel, including a stay in Berlin, he conducted the Singakademie in Ratibor (1887), taught singing at the Steiermärkische Musikschule in Graz, and on his return (1894) to Berlin, where he remained until his death, he wrote music criticism for the *Deutsche Zeitung*.

Plüddemann's lifelong ambition was to rekindle interest in a neglected area of German song: the ballad. He established 'ballad schools', first in Berlin (1886) and later in Graz (1890), where he strove to realize his ideal in collaboration with young singers and composers. Although his efforts prompted numerous ballad-evenings, he laboured on behalf of the declining genre without accomplishing any lasting success.

Plüddemann classified the ballad as a genre distinct from the lied for three general reasons: that delineation of character dominates the ballad, but not the lied; that the lied is characterized by sensuous lyricism, the ballad by a blend of melody that helps in the narration of dramatic action; and that while one mood often pervades an entire lied, mood in the ballad changes with each dramatic action. Taking his revered Loewe as a model, Plüddemann developed a vocal style suitable for narration, which he termed his 'parlando-ballad style'. His ballads achieve unity through the modified recurrence of musical sections and with leitmotifs. Their declamation is lively and faithful to the verses, and the dramatic characterization (influenced by Wagner) is, at its best, vividly etched and gripping. The piano parts are symphonically complex and rich in imagery – some look like piano reductions of orchestral scores. Plüddemann explored the early German Romantic poetry based on sagas, fairy tales and medieval historical subjects to find ballad texts. Outstanding examples of his settings include *Siegfrieds Schwert* (J.L. Uhland), *Der alte Barbarossa* (F. Rückert) and *Der Taucher* (F. von Schiller), all in volume i of his *Balladen und Gesänge*. He also wrote lieder and arranged folksongs for chorus.

WORKS

published in Nuremberg unless otherwise stated

[48] Balladen und Gesänge, 8 vols. (1891–9); [8] Lieder und Gesänge (1893)
Works for chorus incl. [8] Altdeutsche Liebeslieder, 4 male vv (Berlin, 1879); 6 Lieder (J. Eichendorff), 4 male vv (1901)

WRITINGS

Die Bühnenfestspiele in Bayreuth (Colberg, 1877, 2/1881)
Aus der Zeit, für die Zeit (Leipzig, 1880)
'Karl Loewe', *Bayreuther Blätter*, xv (1892), 318–37
Introduction to *Balladen und Gesänge* (Nuremberg, 1891–9)

BIBLIOGRAPHY

R. Batka: *Martin Plüddemann und seine Balladen* (Prague, 1896)
L. Schemann: 'Über die Bedeutung der Ballade für unsere Zeit und unsere Zukunft: ein Brief an Martin Plüddemann', *Bayreuther Blätter*, xx (1897), 34–41
R. Bilke: 'Martin Plüddemann', *Die Musik*, vii/1 (1907–8), 89–97
L. Schemann: *Martin Plüddemann und die deutsche Ballade* (Regensburg, 1930) [with portrait, selected writings and letters]
W. Suppan: *Die Romantische Ballade als Abbild des Wagnerischen Musikdramas, GfMKB: Kassel 1962, 233–5
E. Kravitt: 'The Ballad as Conceived by Germanic Composers of the Late Romantic Period', *Studies in Romanticism*, xii (1973), 499–515
S. Youens: 'Martin Plüddemann and the Ballad Revival', *Hugo Wolf: the Vocal Music* (Princeton, NJ, 1992), 147–61
E. Kravitt: 'The Ballad and the Kinderlied', *The Lied: Mirror of Late Romanticism* (New Haven, CT, 1996), 124–32

EDWARD F. KRAVITT

Pludermacher, Georges (*b* Guéret, 26 July 1944). French pianist. He started piano lessons at the age of four and at 11 entered the Paris Conservatoire where he studied with Lucette Descaves and Jacques Février and was awarded many honours. He continued his studies with Géza Anda in Lucerne in 1963–4, and won second prize in the Leeds International Pianoforte Competition in 1969 and first prize in the Géza Anda Competition in 1979. Pludermacher has toured widely in France and throughout Europe, both as soloist and in chamber music, becoming particularly well known as an interpreter of contemporary music: he played in the first performance of Boucourechliev's *Archipel 1* at Royan in 1967 and has appeared frequently with the Domaine Musical and with Musique Vivante, directed by Diego Masson. He was appointed professor of piano at the Paris Conservatoire in 1993. His recordings include an outstanding account of Mozart's complete sonatas and evocative renditions of many of Debussy's works, especially the *Estampes* and *Images*.

RONALD KINLOCH ANDERSON/CHARLES TIMBRELL

Plummer [Plomer, Plourmel, Plumere, Polmier, Polumier], **John** (*b* ?*c*1410; *d c*1484). English composer. By 1441 he was a member of Henry VI's Chapel Royal; he is traceable in Windsor in 1442 and from 1444 to 1455 he was the first to hold the title (though not to perform the duties) of Warden or Master of the Chapel Children. By 1449 he had joined the London Gild of Parish Clerks. As late as 1467 he was still nominally a Gentleman of the Chapel Royal under Edward IV; but he settled in Windsor in the early 1450s and by 1454–5, perhaps earlier, he had become verger of the Royal Free Chapel of St George in Windsor Castle, remaining in that position until 1483–4. Until 1967 only four works by Plummer were known,

three votive antiphons and a motet. These showed him as a suave but progressively-minded composer who experimented with invertible counterpoint and imitation: *Anna mater*, for three tenors and an optional triplex, is particularly remarkable in the latter respect. His Kyrie and Gloria pair in *GB-Lbl* Add.54324 is evidence that he also wrote large-scale isomelic masses; this in turn suggests that the anonymous mass on ff.107*v*–16 of *I-TRmp* 1376 (olim 89), which resembles *Anna mater* both in its general style and in its very unusual disposition for three equal tenors, may also be by Plummer.

Further to these works, the Mass 'Omnipotens Pater' in the opening 'English fascicle' of *B-Br* 5557 bore an ascription 'Plourmel' until the mid-19th century (Staehelin). This ascription is now replaced by an unacceptable one to 'G. Binchois' in what is clearly a 19th-century hand; the cycle is stylistically compatible with, although tonally more adventurous than, the more securely ascribed works of Plummer (Curtis). The Sanctus and Agnus Dei have also been identified in a fragmentary English source.

WORKS

Edition: *Four Motets by John Plummer*, ed. B. Trowell (Banbury, 1968) [T]
Mass with Kyrie trope 'Omnipotens Pater', 3vv, *B-Br* 5557 (ed. in EECM, xxxiv, 1989)
Kyrie 'Nesciens mater', Gloria 'Nesciens mater', 4vv, *GB-Lbl* Add.54324 (fragmentary, chant in iv; Ky with trope 'Deus creator omnium'; Gl anon., but paired with Ky)
Anna mater matris Christi, 4vv; T 24, ed. in EECM, viii (1968), 34 (text from responds, rhymed office of St Anne)
Descendi in hortum meum, 3vv; T 13 (also in *GB-Olc* Latin 89, *D-Mbs* Mus.Ms.3725; cancelled fragment in *I-TRmp* 1377, olim 90; fragmentary kbd arr. in Buxheim Organbook, ed. in EDM, xxxviii, 1958, p.216)
Tota pulcra es, 3vv; T 16 (also in *CZ-HKm* II A 7; *I-Las* 238, frag.)
Tota pulcra es, 3vv; T 20, ed. in EECM, viii (1968), 28

DOUBTFUL WORKS

Kyrie 'Deus creator omnium', Gl, Cr, San, Ag, 3vv, *I-TRmp* 89 (anon. but scoring and style suggest Plummer's authorship)
Ibo michi ad montem mirre, 3vv, *TRmp* 1377 (olim 90) (anon., attrib. Plummer by Scott and Burstyn, 1972, on stylistic grounds, questioned by Strohm; for edn see Scott)
O pulcherrima mulierum, 3vv (attrib. Frye by Bukofzer, *MGG1*; attrib. Plummer and ed. in *StrohmM*)
Qualis est dilectus tuus, 3vv; ed. in CMM, xlvi/2 (1969), 74 (also attrib. Forest; probably by Forest)

BIBLIOGRAPHY

StrohmM
C. Johnson: 'John Plummer, Master of the Children', *Antiquaries Journal*, i (1921), 52–3, 94–5
A. Seay: 'The *Dialogus Johannis Ottobi in arte musica*', *JAMS*, viii (1955), 86–100, esp. 93 [Hothby's praise of 'Plumere']
B.L. Trowell: *Music under the Later Plantagenets* (diss., U. of Cambridge, 1960), i, 62, 68; ii, 185, 289
M. and I. Bent: 'Dufay, Dunstable, Plummer: a New Source', *JAMS*, xxii (1969), 394–424
S. Burstyn: *Fifteenth-Century Polyphonic Settings of Verses from the Song of Songs* (diss., Columbia U., 1972), 192–205, 220ff
A.B. Scott: '*Ibo michi ad montem mirre*: a New Motet by Plummer', *MQ*, lviii (1972), 543–56
M. Staehelin: 'Möglichkeiten und praktische Anwendung der Verfasserbestimmung in anonym überlieferten Kompositionen der Josquin-Zeit', *TVNM*, xxiii/2 (1973), 79–91
A.-M. Seaman and R. Rastall: 'The Music of Oxford, Bodleian Library, MS Lincoln Latin 98', *RMARC*, no.13 (1976), 95–101 [see also A.-M. Seaman, *RMARC*, no.14 (1978), 139–40]
G.R.K. Curtis: *The English Masses of Brussels, Bibliothèque Royale, MS. 5557* (diss., U. of Manchester, 1979)
A. Wathey: *Music in the Royal and Noble Households in Late Medieval England: Studies of Sources and Patronage* (New York, 1989)

BRIAN TROWELL

Pluriarc. A term coined by George Montandon (1919) and adopted by André Schaeffner (1936) to refer to the Central African instrument also known as a bow lute (Hornbostel and Sachs, 1914; Wegner, 1984) of which there are two types. A pluriarc consists of a hollowed wooden resonator with strings running either parallel or slightly inclined to the soundboard. In contrast to harps and lutes, however, pluriarcs are not held by one string-bearer, but each string has its own flexible carrier. For this purpose, in the first type of pluriarc short arcs are inserted into a series of holes bored into the top wall of the resonator or, in the second type, they are attached to the back of the resonator and/or partly inserted. These differences affect the method of tuning.

The term 'pluriarc' for this class of instruments has been contested, as has the term 'bow lute', mainly due to the fact that both terms suggest an evolutionary sequence from musical bows consisting of 'one arc' to an instrument of 'several arcs'. Jean Sebastien Laurenty was also reluctant but opted for the term 'pluriarc' (1960, p.117). Ulrich Wegner has maintained the term 'bow lute', while acknowledging that the French term 'pluriarc' represents an appropriate description of the instrument's most salient feature (1984, p.82). Any such evolutionary relationships between musical bows in Africa have not been confirmed.

Our earliest sources for pluriarcs include three Benin bronze plaques (Dark and Hill, 1972) and an illustration by Michael Praetorius (1620) of the front and back of a five-string specimen belonging to the second type, probably acquired in Gabon or the Congo from a Teke musician or from an adjacent ethnic group. The earliest source from the historic Kongo kingdom is Girolamo Merolla's 1692 illustration of a *nsambi*. For south-western Angola, the earliest illustration comes from Brazil: a detailed drawing by Alexandre Rodrigues Ferreira who, on his 'philosophical journey' of 1783–92 in northern Brazil, met a slave who played a seven-string pluriarc of the first type called *cihumba* in the related languages of Angola's Huíla province.

The contemporary geographic distribution of pluriarcs is largely confined to three areas that are now distinct:

1. South-western Angola: a representative is the *cihumba*, still popular in Huíla province. This area expands into northern Namibia where somewhat different varieties have been played by Khoisan language-speakers. Among the !Ko of eastern Namibia and Botswana a five-string variety has become an instrument associated with women.

2. West-central Africa from the ancient Kongo and Kuba states across the equatorial zone to the Teke in the Republic of Congo and into Gabon (see GABON, fig.5); it is an area dominated by the second type of pluriarc, however, with great internal variety. Laurenty distinguishes no less than ten organological varieties for the area of the Democratic Republic of the Congo alone (1960, p.117). Among the Nkundo in western Congo and among the Ekonda, very large five-string *lokombi* (or Teke: *lukombe*) were used, while the Fang (Faŋ) of Gabon developed types entirely manufactured with materials from the raffia palm.

3. Benin in south-western Nigeria: an area where the tradition has survived since the days of ancient Benin. Music and poetry accompanied by the *akpata* (see illustration) have been documented in great detail by Dan Ben-Amos (1975). The *akpata* is characterized by a specific triangular shape of the cross-cut of its resonator,

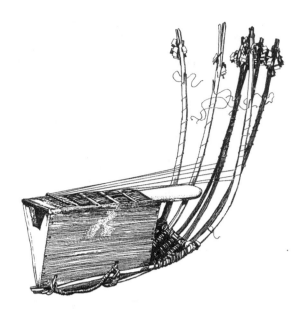

The akpata pluriarc of the Edo-speaking people of Benin, South-western Nigeria (drawing reproduced from Ben-Amos, 1975)

but the attachment of the arcs follows the system of the second type of pluriarc.

It is not possible to know where and when the African pluriarc was invented. But, since it was well established in all three separate areas outlined above during the earliest periods of European contact, its invention most likely occurred several centuries earlier. Invention in one location and diffusion to other places is the most likely scenario for the pluriarc's remote history. The Benin type shows relatively close organological links to the west-central African cluster, while the south-western Angolan types stand apart. Either the pluriarc was invented in Central Africa and spread with coastal contacts from Gabon or the Republic of Congo to ancient Benin, as well as south into Angola, or it was an invention of the ancestors of Edo (Ẹdo)-speaking peoples of Nigeria and spread the other way.

BIBLIOGRAPHY

PraetoriusSM

G. Merolla: *Breve e svccinta Relatione del viaggio nel regno di Congo nell'Africa Meridionale . . .* (Naples, 1692)

E.M. von Hornbostel and C. Sachs: 'Systematik der Musikinstrumente: ein Versuch', *Zeitschrift für Ethnologie*, xlvi/4–5 (1914), 553–90

G. Montandon: 'La génealogie des instruments de musique et les cycles de civilisation', *Archives Suisses d'Anthropologie Générale*, iii (1919), 1–71

A. Schaeffner: *Origine des instruments de musique* (Paris, 1936)

J.S. Laurenty: *Les cordophones du Congo Belge et du Ruanda-Urundi* (Tervuren, 1960)

P. Dark and M. Hill: 'Musical Instruments on Benin Plaques', *Essays on Music and History in Africa*, ed. K. Wachsmann (Evanston, IL, 1972), 67–78

G.T. Nurse: 'Musical Instrumentation among the San (Bushmen) of the Central Kalahari', *AfM*, v/2 (1972), 23–7

D. Ben-Amos: *Sweet Words: Story Telling Events in Benin* (Philadelphia, 1975)

G. Kubik: *Angolan Traits in Black Music, Games and Dances of Brazil* (Lisbon, 1979)

U. Wegner: *Afrikanische Saiteninstrumente* (Berlin, 1984)

E.W. Müller: 'Die Musikinstrumente der Ekonda in der Sammlung des Mainzer Instituts für Ethnologie und Afrika-Studien', . . . *und der Jazz is nicht von Dauer: Aspekte afro-amerikanischer Musik:*

Festschrift für Alfons Michael Dauer, ed. B. Hoffmann and H. Rösing (Karben, 1998), 135–44

GERHARD KUBIK

Plutarch of Chaeronea [Ploutarchos Chairōneus] (*fl c*50–*c*120 CE). Greek philosopher and writer. A descendant of an old and respected family in Boeotia, he was one of the most important Greek authors of his time. He wrote more than 200 separate works, of which some 50 biographies, 78 other works comprising the so-called *Moralia*, and a few extant fragments reflect his interests in biography, rhetoric, logic, philosophy and antiquities. He studied with Ammonius and later travelled widely, visiting Athens, Egypt and Rome. For the last three decades of his life he was a priest at Delphi and participated in the revival of the shrine under the emperors Hadrian and Trajan, the latter granting him consular privileges (according to the *Suda*).

The dialogue *On Music* (*Peri mousikēs*) was included among the *Moralia* by tradition, but current scholarship regards it as almost certainly not the work of Plutarch. Nevertheless, it contains a wealth of information on ancient Greek musical life, including important historical material pertaining to Pythagorean music theory, the 'invention' of various musical forms and the development of early musical scales. Some of this material is attributed to works (now lost) by Alexander of Aetolia, ARISTOXENUS, GLAUCUS OF RHEGIUM and Heraclides Ponticus. The dialogue, set in the form of a SYMPOSIUM on the second day of the Saturnalia, is in a sense the earliest 'history' of Greek music. The two primary speakers in the dialogue, Lysias and Soterichus (the precentor, Onesicrates, appears mainly at the beginning and the end), represent respectively the practical and theoretical viewpoints of music and its development. After describing various musico-poetic forms (*see* GREECE, §I, 4) and attributing them to early 'inventors' (including Amphion, Archilochus, Linus, Marsyas, Olympus the Mysian, Orpheus, Phrynis of Mytilene, Pindar, Polymnestus of Colophon, Sacadas of Argos, Stesichorus, Terpander and many others; see individual entries and *see also* NOMOS), Lysias explains the construction of the enharmonic genus, its relationship to the other genera, and a special *spondeion* scale (*see* GREECE, §I, 6(iii)(e)), the precise structure of which remains obscure. As the second speaker, Soterichus begins by observing that the gods themselves, especially APOLLO, must be given credit for the invention of music. He then expands on Lysias's practical presentation, correcting and augmenting his descriptions of the musico-poetic forms and the *spondeion* scale. He subsequently turns his attention to the realm of Pythagorean mathematics and music, especially as preserved in Plato's *Timaeus* (35b–36b), Aristotle's *Physics* (iii.4, 203a4–16) and *Metaphysics* (i.5, 985b23–987a28), Euclid's *Elements* (vii), Nicomachus's *Introduction to Arithmetic* (i.7–10) and Theon of Smyrna's *On Mathematics Useful for the Understanding of Plato*. This material leads Soterichus to conclude that music should be elevating, instructive and useful; as such, it should form an essential part of PAIDEIA. Modern musical innovations, including some of those already mentioned by Lysias, have in his view led music to its present low estate, aptly represented by the famous fragment from the *Cheiron* of PHERECRATES. In order to restore music to its proper place, the ancient style must be copied and the proper use of music must be determined by philosophy. This observation leads Soterichus to review the principles of harmonics and rhythmics, the knowledge of which is insufficient alone for the creation or judgment of musical art. After Soterichus draws his speech to a close with a quotation from the Hymn to Apollo (*Iliad*, i.472–4), the precentor Onesicrates provides the philosophical capstone of the dialogue: as Pythagoras, Plato and Archytas have revealed, music is of value because the revolution of the universe is based on music (*mousikē*) and god has arranged everything to accord with *harmonia* (*kath' harmonian*).

In addition to the pseudepigraphous dialogue *On Music*, a number of authentic treatises within the *Moralia* contain important information on Pythagorean mathematics and music (*On the Generation of the Soul in the Timaeus*; *see* ARISTIDES QUINTILIANUS), the ethical effect and value of music in society (*Table-Talk*), and the history of musical instruments (*Ancient Customs of the Spartans*; *Life of Crassus*; *On Progress in Virtue*; *On the Control of Anger*). Both the *Lives* and the *Moralia* of Plutarch were popular in the Byzantine empire, and the organization and preservation of his writings, including the pseudepigrapha, was largely due to the Byzantine scholar Maximus Planudes. *On Music* is preserved alone in the late 12th-century *I-Vnm* gr.app.cl.VI/10 (RISM, B/XI, 273), one of the most important codices containing texts on ancient Greek music. Two codices of the late 13th or very early 14th century preserve the complete texts of the *Lives* and the *Moralia*: *F-Pn* gr.1671 and 1672 (RISM, B/XI, 66–7). Three others of the same general age preserve the whole of the *Moralia*: *I-Ma* gr.859 (C 126 inf.; RISM, B/XI, 186), presumed to have been copied for Planudes; *Rvat* gr.139 (RISM, B/XI, 207); and *Fl* gr.80.5 (RISM, B/XI, 165), copied from the Vatican codex. The first published translation of the dialogue *On Music*, by Carlo Valgulio (based on *Rvat* gr.186: RISM, B/XI, 210), appeared in 1507, and the treatise had a considerable impact on musical humanism in the Renaissance and on later writers.

WRITINGS

C. Valgulio: *Prooemium in musicam Plutarchi ad Titum Pyrrhinum* (Brescia, 1507), ff.a2r–b2v [trans. on ff.b3r–d5v]; corrected text in *Plutarchi Caeronei, philosophi, historicique clarissimi opuscula (quae quidem extant) omnia* (Basle, 1530), ff.25v–32v and 244v–247v

G. Xylander, trans.: 'De musica', *Plutarchi Chaeronensis Moralia ... omnes de graeca in latinam linguam transcripti* (Paris, 1570), 564–75

P.J. Burette, ed. and trans.: *Dialogue de Plutarque sur la musique* (Paris, 1735/R); also pubd in *Mémoires de littérature tirés des registres de l'Académie des inscriptions et belles lettres*, x (1736), 111–310 [commentaries, ibid., xiii (1740), 173–316; xv (1743), 293–394; xvii (1751), 31–60]

J.H. Bromby, trans.: *The Peri mousikēs of Plutarch* (Chiswick, 1822)

R. Volkmann, ed.: *Plutarchi De musica* (Leipzig, 1856)

R. Westphal, ed. and trans.: *Plutarch über die Musik* (Breslau, 1866)

J. Philips, trans.: 'Concerning Music', *Plutarch's Morals Translated from the Greek by Several Hands*, ed. W.W. Goodwin (Boston, 1870), i, 102–35

H. Weil and T.Reinach, eds. and trans.: *Plutarque: De la musique, Peri mousikēs* (Paris, 1900)

G. Skjerne, ed. and trans.: *Plutarks Dialog om Musiken* (Copenhagen, 1909)

F. Lasserre, ed. and trans.: *Plutarque: De la musique* (Olten, 1954)

K. Ziegler, ed.: *Plutarchi Moralia*, vi/3 (Leipzig, 1966)

B. Einarson and P.H.De Lacy, eds. and trans.: 'On Music', *Plutarch's Moralia*, xiv (London and Cambridge, MA, 1967), 343–455

L. Gamberini, trans.: *Plutarco 'Della musica'* (Florence, 1979)

BIBLIOGRAPHY

L. Laloy: 'Quels sont les accords cités dans le ch. xix du *Peri mousikēs*?', *Revue de philologie*, xxii (1899), 132–40

L. Laloy: 'Anciennes gammes enharmoniques', *Revue de philologie*, xxiii (1899), 238–48; xxiv (1900), 31–43

R.P. Winnington-Ingram: 'The Spondeion Scale', *Classical Quarterly*, xxii (1928), 83–91

K. Ziegler: 'Plutarchea, I: Zu *De musica*', *Studi in onore di Luigi Castiglioni* (Florence, 1960), 1107–35

E.K. Borthwick: 'Notes on the Plutarch *De Musica* and the *Cheiron* of Pherecrates', *Hermes*, xcvi (1968), 60–73

J.P.H.M. Smits: *Plutarchus en de grieske muziek: de mentaliteit van de intellectueel in de tweede eeuw na Christus* (Bilthoven, 1970)

J. Dillon: *The Middle Platonists, 80 B.C. to A.D. 220* (Ithaca, NY, 1977)

E. Werner: 'Pseudo-Plutarch's Views on the Theory of Rhythm', *Orbis musicae*, vii (1979–80), 27–36

T.J. Mathiesen: *Ancient Greek Music Theory: a Catalogue Raisonné of Manuscripts*, RISM, B/XI (1988)

C.V. Palisca: *The Florentine Camerata: Documentary Studies and Translations* (New Haven, CT, 1989) [incl. trans. of C. Valgulio's Proem to *On Music*]

T.J. Mathiesen: *Apollo's Lyre: Greek Music and Music Theory in Antiquity and the Middle Ages* (Lincoln, NE, 1999), 355–66

THOMAS J. MATHIESEN

Plzeň (Ger. Pilsen). City in the Czech Republic. It is the industrial and cultural centre of West Bohemia and shares with Brno the richest Czech theatre tradition after Prague. The first permanent theatre was constructed in 1832. Operas were staged only sporadically; a permanent Czech opera ensemble, the first outside Prague, started to perform there in 1869, the year that Smetana's *The Bartered Bride* was conducted there by Mořic Anger (1844–1905). Since then there has been a tradition of dressing the characters in that opera in folk costumes of the Plzeň region. A number of Czech premières of foreign works were produced in Plzeň around that time, including *Tannhäuser* in 1888, three years before it was staged in Prague. The Velké Divadlo (Great Theatre) opened in 1902 with Smetana's *Libuše*; it was reconstructed between 1980 and 1987 (550 seats). Since 1955 it has been called Divadlo J.K. Tyla. Small-scale operas were performed between 1945 and 1965 in the Malé Divadlo (Small Theatre), a former German theatre built in 1869. In 1966 the Komorní Divadlo (Chamber Theatre) was opened. Of several notable conductors (including Karel Kovařovic, 1886–7, and Václav Talich, 1912–15), it was Bohumír Liška (1955–67) who presided over the city's most remarkable operatic era, with a repertory of both Czech and foreign operas, especially the modern ones. The most important productions included Hanuš's *Flames* (1956 première), Prokofiev's *The Gambler* (1957), Britten's *Albert Herring* (1958), Nejedlý's *The Weavers* (1961 première), Jeremiáš's *Enšpígl* (1962) and the première of Hurník's *The Lady and the Robbers* (1966). Thanks to the long-term activities of the opera scene and the systematic work of the municipal musical school (founded in 1920) a large body of listeners formed in Plzeň and a number of composers, musicians and theorists lived there.

In 1909 the Sdružení pro Komorní Hudbu (Chamber Music Association) was founded; during its 40 years of existence it organized 249 concerts, featuring 27 orchestras, with guests including Rubinstein, Casals, Ansorge and Ada Sari. The Hudební Odbor Osvětového Svazu (Musical Section of the Educational Association) was formed in 1908; under its aegis Václav Talich founded the first symphony orchestra in Plzeň. In 1934 it became the Plzeňská Filharmonie; from 1984 it was called the Komorní Orchestr (Chamber Orchestra). In 1946 the Plzeňský Rozhlasový Orchestr (Plzeň RO) was formed.

The Plzeň conservatory (founded 1961) has its own symphony orchestra.

The mixed choir Hlahol was founded in 1862. It became a centre of the Dvořák cult, performing his *Stabat mater* in 1884; in 1900 it made tours to Paris, Brussels and elsewhere. Part of the Hlahol choir separated to form the Smetana choir in 1901. Other choral groups include the Pěvecké Sdružení Učitelů Plzeňska (Teachers' Choir of the Plzeň Region, 1907–15), Pěvecké Sdružení Západočeských Učitelů (West Bohemian Teachers' Choir, 1929–51), Česká Píseň (Czech Song), Ženský Akademický Sbor (Women's Academic Choir, 1962–92) and children's choirs.

BIBLIOGRAPHY

IV. pěvecká župa plzeňská 1898–1948: 50 let spolupráce západočeských pěveckých spolků [Fourth Singers' Association in Plzeň 1898–1948: 50 years of cooperation between West Bohemian choirs] (Plzeň, 1949)

A. Špelda: *Průvodce hudební Plzní* [A guide to musical Plzeň] (Plzeň, 1960)

100 let českého divadla v Plzni [100 years of the Czech theatre in Plzeň] (Plzeň, 1965)

A. Špelda: 'Organizace hudebního života v Plzni 1900–68' [Organization of musical life in Plzeň], 'Plzeňská zpěvohra ve čtyřletí 1918–22' [Opera in Plzeň between 1918 and 1922], *Padesátiletí západočeské kultury* (Plzeň, 1969), 163–81, 187–200

J. Fiala: *Západočeská vlastivěda* [History and geography of West Bohemia] (Plzeň, 1995)

EVA HERRMANNOVÁ

Pneuma (Gk.: 'spirit'; pl. *pneumata*). A category of neume in Byzantine chant. See BYZANTINE CHANT, §3(ii); *see also* NEUMA.

Pocci, Franz, Graf von (*b* Munich, 7 March 1807; *d* Munich, 7 May 1876). German composer and writer on music. In childhood he showed talent for drawing, painting and music, and although he studied law at the universities of Landshut and Munich, he continued his artistic activities, composed and performed at the piano. From 1847 to 1863 he was Hofmusikintendant at the Bavarian court. As a composer, Pocci excelled at writing miniatures, and was at his most characteristic in children's songs, for which he showed a special gift. His plays with musical settings for the Munich Marionette Theatre added new vitality to puppet opera; he also designed the scenery for these productions. He was less successful in composing in larger forms. Pocci was extremely versatile not only as a musician but also as a writer; he wrote independent literary works and song texts, in addition to writing on music.

WORKS
most MSS in Pocci family archives, Ammerland am Starnbergersee

STAGE

Undine, 1829 (inc.)
Der Liebe als Alchymist (Spl, 2, L. Koch), Munich, 1840
Der artesische Brunnen (incid music, L. Feldman), 1845
Der Roaga (incid music, F. von Kobell), 1847
45 puppet operas, for the Munich Marionette Theatre

OTHER WORKS

Vocal: 23 choruses, 53 qts, 25 trios, 29 duets, 137 solo songs, 71 children's songs, 18 sacred songs; Mass, d
Pf: Sonate fantastique; Frühlingssonate; Bildertöne, 6 Stücke für Klavier; Sechs Klavierstücke; 9 ländler; 8 Steirische Tänze; works for 4 hands; other works
Chbr: Nokturn, vc, pf; Str Qt; Zum Zeitvertreib, 6 ländler, 2 zithers; Phantasiestück, harp; Sonate, fl, pf; Soldatenmarsch, 2 fl, pf; Morgenlied, hn, pf; other works

WRITINGS

'Über die Romantik der modernen Musik', *Deutsche Blätter für Literatur und Leben*, ed. F. von Elsholtz, A. von Maltitz and F.A. von Zu-Rhein (Munich, 1840), 93–4
'Über Ouverturen', ibid, 158–9
'Musikalischer Sonnenaufgang', ibid, 205–7
Many articles in *Münchner allgemeine Zeitung*, 1853–69

BIBLIOGRAPHY

ADB (H. Holland); *ES* (H.R. Purschke)
H. Holland: *Franz Graf Pocci: ein Dichter- und Künstlerleben* (Bamberg, 1890)
L. Hirschberg: 'Franz Pocci der Musiker', *ZMw*, i (1918–19), 40–70 [with list of pubd works]
F. Pocci: *Franz Poccis lustiges Komödienbüchlein* (Munich, 1921)
F. Pocci: *Das Werk des Künstlers Franz Pocci* (Munich, 1926)
K. Pastor: *Franz Pocci als Musiker* (Munich, 1932) [with complete list of works]
G. Goepfert: *Franz von Pocci: Zeremonienmeister – Künstler – 'Kasperlgraf'* (Weilheim, 1988)

GAYNOR G. JONES

Poche [pochette, pochette d'amour] (Fr.; It. *pochetto*). *See* KIT.

Pochettino [pochissimo]. *See under* POCO.

Pociej, Bohdan (*b* Warsaw, 17 Jan 1933). Polish music critic. He studied musicology with Zofia Lissa, Chomiński and Feicht at Warsaw University (1953–9). From 1959 to 1994 he was a member of the editorial board of the bi-weekly *Ruch muzyczny*. He has also written for *Tygodnik powszechny*, *Polska* and *Polnische Perspektive*. Possessing one of the keenest minds in contemporary Polish music criticism, Pociej combines in his analyses both a technical and an aesthetic approach. His writings have been strongly influenced by the philosopher Roman Ingarden.

WRITINGS

'O twórczości Bogusława Schäffera' [The works of Bogusław Schäffer], *Muzyka*, ix/3–4 (1964), 44–58
Klawesyniści francuscy [French harpsichord composers] (Kraków, 1968)
'Opis – analiza – interpretacja' [Description, analysis, interpretation], *Res facta*, no.4 (1970), 151–65 [on Górecki's *Elementi* and *Canti strumentali*]
Bach: muzyka i wielkość [Bach: music and greatness] (Kraków, 1972)
Idea – dźwięk – forma [Idea, sound, form] (Kraków, 1972)
'Uwagi o wartościach w muzyce' [Considerations on values in music], *Res facta*, no.6 (1972), 140–60
Lutosławski a wartość muzyki [Lutosławski and value in music] (Kraków, 1976)
Szkice z późniego romantyzmu [Sketches of the late Renaissance] (Kraków, 1978)
Mahler (Kraków, 1990)

ZYGMUNT M. SZWEYKOWSKI

Pockorny, Franz Xaver. *See* POKORNY, FRANZ XAVER.

Poco (It.: 'little', 'somewhat'). A direction that modifies many tempo, expression and dynamic marks in music. In strict Italian, *poco forte* and *poco allegro* would mean the opposite of *forte* and *allegro*; and *Grove5* drew attention to the slovenliness of that usage, pointing out that *un poco forte* and *un poco allegro* were correct. But *poco allegro* is current, for better or worse, and must be considered part of 'musicians' Italian' (*see* TEMPO AND EXPRESSION MARKS, §3). *Pochettino*, the diminutive, and *pochissimo*, the superlative, are also current in musical scores.   □

Podatus (from Gk. *pous, podos*: 'foot'). *See* PES (ii).

Podéš, Ludvík (*b* Dubňany u Hodonína, 19 Dec 1921; *d* Prague, 27 Feb 1968). Czech composer and administrator. In 1941 he changed from language studies in Brno to enter the conservatory of that city, but his musical education was interrupted by World War II. He returned to study composition with Kvapil at the conservatory (1945–8) and musicology with Bohumir Štědroň and Jau Racek at Brno University (1945–9), taking the doctorate for his thesis on socialist realist music, *Hudba v pojetí socialistického realismu*. Podéšť worked for Czech radio (1947–51), was artistic director of the V. Nejedlý Army Arts Ensemble in Prague (1953–6) and then directed music for Czech television from 1958. He contributed to the journal *Hudební rozhledy*, and as an administrator was involved with the Union of Czechoslovak Composers. Towards the end of his life he spent much of his time in Casablanca and concerned himself intensively with theory.

The source of his music's spontaneity may be found in the folk music of Moravian Slovakia, his native region. In his music of the 1940s he followed the post-Janáček tradition. In about 1950 he began to respond to the new policy of socialist realism, writing orchestral works (such as the symphonic poem *Raymonda Dienová*) that were melodically conventional and readily comprehensible in general; during this period he was closely associated with youth and army ensembles. His suites and dances for orchestra were influenced by Czech and Moravian folk music, as were the early operettas, while works from his latter years – cut short by his premature death at the age of 46 – draw on studies he made in Morocco of exotic musical cultures; this is true of *Hamada* for orchestra and particularly the Partita for strings, guitar and percussion, both composed in 1967.

WORKS
(*selective list*)

STAGE

Hrátky s čertem [Gossip with the Devil] (fairy-tale op, 7, Podéšť, after J. Drda), 1957–60, Liberec, 12 Oct 1963
Apokryfy (trilogy of TV ops, Podéšť, after K. Čapek), 1957–8, Brno, 17 Dec 1959
Staré zlaté časy [The Good Old Days] (1)

Svatá noc [Holy Night] (1), Brno, 5 June 1959

Romeo a Julie (1)

Emílek a dynamit [Emílek and the Dynamite] (operetta, 2, V. Dubský and J. Bachánek), Prague, Na Fidlovacce, 12 May 1960
Filmová hvězda [The Film Star] (operetta, 3, K.M. Walló), Ostrava, J. Myron, 2 June 1960
Noci na seně [A Night on the Hay] (operetta, 3, Z. Endris and Z. Borovec), unperf.

OTHER WORKS

Orch: Hudba ve starém slohu [Music in Olden Style], str, pf, 1948; Sym., 1948; Raymonda Dienová, sym. poem, 1950; Pf Conc. no.1, 1952–3; Jarní serenáda [Spring Serenade], vn, orch, 1953; Suite, 1956; Siciliana, variations, 1957; Pf Conc. no.2, 1958; Concertino, 2 dulcimer, orch, 1962; Azurové moře [Azure Sea], 1967; Hamada, 1967
Vocal: Maminčiny písně [Mummy's Songs] (J. Seifert), S, pf, 1943; Smrt [Death] (O. Scheinpflugová), A, pf, 1943, rev. as cant.; Legendy o panně Marii [Legends of the Virgin Mary], A, 1947; Písně na staré motivy [Songs on Ancient Themes], B-Bar, chbr orch, 1956; Maminka [Mummy] (Seifert), children's chorus, orch, 1963
Chbr and solo inst: Písně smutné paní [Songs of a Sorrowful Lady], 4 fantasias, pf, 1941; Str Qt no.1, 1942; Wind Qnt, 1946; Sonata, vn, pf, 1947; Str Qt no.2, 1948; Suite, va, pf, 1956; Sonata, 2 vc, pf, 1957; Partita, str, gui, perc, 1967
Principal publishers: Český hudební fond

BIBLIOGRAPHY

ČSHS

P. Novák: 'Podéšťova symfonická báseň Raymonda Dienova', *HR*, v (1952), 7–8

A. Martínková, ed.: *Čeští skladatelé současnosti* [Czech composers of today] (Prague, 1985)

JIŘÍ FUKAČ/KAREL STEINMETZ

Podešva, Jaromír (*b* Brno, 8 March 1927). Czech composer. He was born into an artistically talented family; his father, a leading Brno violin maker, took charge of his early musical studies. He studied composition under Kvapil, from 1946 at the Brno Conservatory and then at the Janáček Academy of Music in Brno (1947–51), where he continued as a postgraduate assistant. He served as secretary of the Union of Czechoslovak Composers in Prague (1956–9) and later as chairman of the Brno branch for some years. A UNESCO scholarship took him on an eight months' trip to France, the USA and England (1960–61) to study with Dutilleux and Copland. From 1969 until the late 1980s he taught composition at the Ostrava Conservatory. Towards the end of this appointment he wrote the textbook *Úvod do studia skladby* (Introduction to the Study of Composition), though it has yet to be published.

Podešva's early music was greatly influenced by that of Novák and Janáček. In the 1950s he was involved with the popular music and mass political songs that were being developed, but his concert music was becoming more subjective, more concerned with a personal response to poetry. For example, his Third Symphony (1966) was based on the verse of M. Kundera and B. Hrabal, while the Fifth is a setting of František Halas and Yevgeny Yevtushenko. His music has changed from a free tonality to a simultaneous use of tonality and dodecaphony; the procedures are discussed in his treatise (1973). Podešva has also produced some popular educational works, though his greatest achievement are the symphonic pieces, quartets and quintets.

WORKS
(selective list)

STAGE AND VOCAL

Opustíš-li mne [If You Leave Me] (op, Podešva, after Z. Pluhař), 1962–3, rev. 1965–6; Bambini di Praga (ballet-op buffa, after B. Hrabal), 1968

Sonata (F. Halas), S, pf, 1968; Symfonietta přírody [Sinfonietta of Nature] (M. Holub), chorus, 1962; Nevídáno, neslycháno [Unseen, Unheard] (J. Kainar), children's chorus, 1965; Hodiny [Hours] (K. Kapoun), chorus, 1977; Listy A. Dvořáka z Ameriky do vlasti [Dvořák's Letters from America to his Homeland], Bar, orch, 1991

ORCHESTRAL

Syms.: no.2, fl, str, 1961; no.3 'Kulminace-Perla na dně' [Culmination-Pearl Deep Down], after M. Kundera and B. Hrabal, 1966; no.4 'Hudba Soláně' [Solán Music], fl, hpd, str, 1967; no.5 '3 zlomky padesátiletí' [3 Fragments of the Quinquennium] (F. Halas, Ye. Yevtushenko), Bar, orch, 1967; no.6, 1970; no.7 'In memoriam J.P. jun', after K.H. Mácha and L. Stehlík, 1982–3; no.8 'Ostravská', 1986; no.9, 1989; no.10, 1993

Other: Kounicovy koleje, sym. poem, 1952; Fl Conc., 1965; Conc., str qt, orch, 1971; Beskydská svita [Beskydy Suite], 1974; Tpt Conc., 1975; Vn Conc., 1975; Pocta L. Jančkovi [Homage to Janáček], 1977; Conc., str, 1978; Slavnosti sněženek [Snowdrops' Parties], 1980; Cl Conc., 1981; Sinfonietta festiva, chbr orch, 1983; Va Conc., 1986

CHAMBER AND SOLO INSTRUMENTAL

Str qts nos.1–3, 1948, 1950, 1951; Nonet no.1 'O sťastných dětech' [Happy Children], 1954–5; Str Qt no.4, 1955; Wind Qnt, 1961; Str Qt no.5, 1965; Pařížské vteřiny [Paris Seconds], suite, pf, 1969; Hledání úsměvu [Looking for a Smile], suite, va, pf, 1969; Nonet

no.2, 1972; Str Qt no.6, 1976; Qt, cl, vn, vc, pf, 1977; Kruh [Circle], va, 1982; Cl Qnt, 1984; Neslavné přídavky [Infamous Encores], 5 pieces, str, 1994

Principal publishers: Český hudební fond, Panton, Supraphon

WRITINGS

Současná hudba na západě [Contemporary music in the west] (Prague, 1963)

Možnost kadence v dvanáctitónovém poli [The possibility of cadence in the dodecaphonic field] (Prague, 1973)

BIBLIOGRAPHY

J. Trojan: 'Tvůrčí profil J. Podešvy' *HRo*, xviii (1965), 936–40

J. Trojan: 'Symfonické paralely J. Podešvy', *HRo*, xxi (1968) 149–51

K. Steinmetz: 'Malé zamyšlení nad kompozičními postupy J. Podešvy v díle Pocta Leoši Janáčkovi' [Thoughts on Podešva's compositional approach in *Homage to Janáček*], *HRo*, xxii (1979), 421–5

V. Gregor, K. Steinmetz, eds.: *Hudební kultura na Ostravsku po roce 1945* [Music life of the Ostrava region after 1945] (Ostrava, 1984), 163–5

A. Martínková: *Čeští skladatelé současnosti* [Czech composers of today] (Prague, 1985), 117

M. Navrátil: 'Jaromír Podešva: čas syntézy' [Podešva: A time of synthesis], *HRo*, xxxix (1986), 515–19

J. Havlik: *Česká symfonie 1945–1980* (Prague, 1989)

JIŘÍ FUKAČ/KAREL STEINMETZ

Podgaits, Yefrem Iosifovich (*b* Vinnitsa, 6 Oct 1949). Russian composer. He began to study the violin at the age of nine at the Children's Music School No. 30 in Moscow where he also received his first composition lessons from Nadezhda Markovna Gol'denberg, a student of Yavorsky. At the Moscow Conservatory he studied composition with Butsko and then with Sidel'nikov; he also studied orchestration with Yury Aleksandrovich Fortunatov. He was employed by and worked as the editor of *Soyuzkontsert* until 1981, when he was appointed accompanist to the children's choir *Vesna* [Spring]. This was a turning point in his career: he started writing extensively for children of various ages and created a new genre – the miniature for children's choir (ages 6–10), writing more than 70 works in this genre. In 1993 and 1994 the *Vesna* children's choir was awarded prizes in Italy and France for their performance of his *Vremena goda* ('The Seasons'). During the 1980s he became interested in musical theatre for children, writing his first opera *Alisa v zazerkal'ye* ('Alice Through the Looking Glass'); from 1989 he has been the music director of the Children's Theatre of Opera and Ballet in Moscow.

Podgaits has a subtle and colourful style of choral writing; the cantata *Kak narisovat' ptitsu* ('How to Draw a Bird') is marked by humour and inventive shading. In his concertos – which are often scored for an unconventional combination of instruments and orchestra – he developed new resources from the baroque concerto model. Although toccata episodes and sharp accentuation of the material provide the main basis for the rhythmic energy, many of his compositions are characterized by their melodic *cantabile*.

WORKS
CHILDREN'S WORKS

Choral: Poéziya zemli [The Poetry of the Earth] (a cappella cant., J. Keats and others), op.34, children's chorus, 1982; Kolïbel'nïye pesni [Lullabies], op.54, children's chorus, org, 1985; Lunnaya svirel' [Lunar Reed-Pipes] (cant., S. Kozlov), op.51, children's chorus, fl, vn, pf, perc, 1985; Vremena goda [The Seasons] (conc., Kozlov), op.63, children's chorus, pf, 1987; Missa veris, op.127, children's chorus, org, 1996; also over 70 choral miniatures for young children

Inst: Detskiy al'bom [An Album for Children], op.19, pf, 1978; Syuita, op.64, vc, pf, 1987; Syuita, op.69, pf, 1987; 12 duètov, op.133, 2 tpt, 1988; Pf Conc. no.2 'Samarskiy' [The Samara], op.79, 1989; Mozaika, op.81, 2 bn, 1990; Detskiye istorii [Stories of Children], op.100, 2 pf, 1993; 6 p'yes dlya malen'kogo Paganini [6 Pieces for the Little Paganini], op.103, vn, pf, 1993

OTHER WORKS

Stage: Alisa v zazerkal'ye [Alice Through the Looking Glass] (op, V. Oryol, after L. Carroll) op.29, 1981; Chyornïy omut [The Black Slough] (op-cant., after Kozlov), op.62, children's chorus, orch, 1987; Mï bïli vorob'yami [We were Sparrows] (children's op, L. Yakovlev), op.77, 1989; Moydodïr (children's ballet, G. Malkhasyants, after K. Chukovsky), op.95, 1992; O, Barbi (comic op, V. Ryabov and R. Sats, after C. Gozzi: *The Green Bird*), op.97, 1992; Posledniy muzïkant [The Last Musician] (children's fantastic op, V. Pavlova, after N. Nielsen), op.96, 1992; Dyuymovochka [Thumbalina] (op, Ryabov and Sats, after H.C. Andersen), op.122, 1995; Povelitel' mukh [The Lord of the Flies] (rock op, Yakovlev, after W. Golding), op.117, 1995

Orch: Vc Conc., op.9, 1973; Sym. no.1, op.14, 1977; Ironicheskoye pa-de-de [An Ironic Pas de Deux], op.35, 1982, arr. vn, pf, 1990; Hpd Conc., op.42, 1983; Sym. no.2, op.40, 1983; Vn Conc. no.1, op.43, 1983, red. vn, pf, 1988; Sym. no.3 'Budet laskovïy dozhd'' [There Shall be Gentle Rain] (S. Tïsdale), op.48, S, org, strs, perc, 1984; Concertino, op.55, fl, chbr orch, 1986; 2 Vn Conc., op.59, 1986; Adagio, op.74, children's chorus, chbr orch, 1988; Triple Conc., op.75, vn, vc, pf, orch, 1988; Concerto-Lambada, op.82, ob, perc, pf, strs, 1990; Vn Conc. no.2 'Concordanza', op.101, 1993; Sarafan dlya Mishelya [A Sarafan for Michelle] op.112, cl, str, 1994]

Vocal: Iz Uol'ta Uitmena [From W. Whitman] (cant.), op.10, mixed chorus, orch, 1973; Kak narisovat' ptitsu [How to Draw a Bird] (cant., Oryol, after J. Prévert), op.27, S, children's chorus, orch, 1980; Ritm i noch' [Rhythm and the Night] (I. Bunin), op.26, 1v, vib, pf, 1980; Veshchaya pechal' [Prophetic Sorrow] (O. Mandelstam), op.87, 1v, pf, 1990; Psalmï tsarya Davida [The Psalms of King David] (a cappella conc.), op.113, mixed chorus, 1994; Nemotrya ni na chto [Despite Everything] (chbr cant., R. Chernavina), op.116, 1v, a sax, pf, 1995; Ave Maria, op.128, mixed chorus, 1996

Chbr: Sonata no.1, bn, pf, 1966; Sonata, op.17, va, pf, 1978; Qnt, op.24, 2 bn, vn, db, pf, 1980; Sonata, op.33, vn, pf, 1982; Sonata, op.45, vc, pf, 1984; Obrazï Ril'ke [Images of Rilke], op.16b, vn, pf, 1985; Richerkar, op.53, perc ens, 1985; Concerto brevis, op.66, perc, inst ens, 1987; Pieta, op.65, vn, org, 1988; Sonata no.2, op.30, bn, pf, 1989; 7 pesen odinochestva [7 Songs of Loneliness], op.46b, a sax, pf, 1990; Iyul'skoye intermetstso [A July Intermezzo], op.91, fl, cl, vn, vc, hpd, 1991; Ozhidaniye nezhnosti [The Anticipation of Tenderness], op.94, viola d'amore, vib, hpd, 1991; Sonnet, op.93, perc, pf, synth, 1991; Vozvrashcheniye [Home-Coming], sonata, op.109, ob, pf, 1994; Bakhchiyev-kontsert, op.115, 2 pf, 1995; Agnus Dei and Ludus humanis, op.126, sax qt, 1996

Solo inst: Polifonicheskiye ètyudï [Polyphonic Studies], op.44, pf, 1983; Sonata-Partita, op.57, hpd, 1986; Dialog s Shopenom [A Dialogue with Chopin], op.90, fl, 1991; 6 nastroyeniy [6 Moods] op.104, pf, 1993; 5 inventsiy [5 Inventions], op.106, pf, 1993

Principal publishers: Muzïka, Sovetskiy kompozitor

BIBLIOGRAPHY

P. Merkur'yev: 'Alisa v Zazerkal'ye [Alice through the looking glass], *Muzïka v SSSR* (1985), no.4, 93
Ye. Podgaits: 'Otvetï na anketu zhurnala' [Replies to a questionnaire in the journal], *SovM* (1988), no.3, pp.6–7
N. Shantïr': 'O ptitse' [About a bird], *Melodiya* (1990), no.2, pp.19–20
Yu. Druzhkin: 'Glyadya iz 90-kh' [Looking from the 90s], *MAk* (1993), no.3, pp.35–9

INNA BARSOVA

Podgoretsky, Boris Vladimirovich. See PIDHORET'SKY, BORYS VOLODYMYROVYCH.

Podio, Francesco. See DEL POMO, FRANCESCO.

Podio [Puig], Guillermo de [Despuig, Guillermo] (*fl* late 15th century). Spanish priest and music theorist. Born possibly in Valencia or Tortosa, he is usually identified with the Guillermo de Puig who was curate of S Catalina, Alzira, from 1479 to 1488. A Guillermo Molins de Podio held a benefice at Barcelona Cathedral, and was a chaplain to John II of Aragon in 1474. The relationship between these two clergymen has not been established. The theorist wrote *Ars musicorum* (Valencia, 1495/R; ed. A. Seay, Colorado Springs, 1978) and *In enchiridion de principiis musicae* (MS, I-Bc; ed. Anglès); the latter, apparently intended for Spanish students at Bologna, may be evidence that Podio visited that city. The first treatise comprises eight books and sets out to be exhaustive; an expanded treatment of part of it appears anonymously in *In enchiridion*. Podio's musical aesthetic was based on the ideas expounded by Boethius; thus, he regarded music as a mathematical and physical science, integrated into the Quadrivium according to the Pythagorean system. He classified musicians as theoretical or practising exponents, the former, as was customary, being regarded as superior. On several important points he opposed Ramis de Pareia's innovations, particularly in his discussion of the sizes of intervals, where he adhered to Pythagorean arithmetic. In the same way, he retained and discussed the use of Guidonian solmization, rather than adopt Ramis's syllabic notation. Podio attributed the growth of Roman chant and its relationship to polyphony to Pope Vitalian. *Ars musicorum*, with its traditional bias, is an important source of information on the mensural notation of the 15th century. In it Podio drew attention to certain 'errors' in Gaffurius, thereby highlighting the differences between contemporary Italian and Spanish notational practice. In many ways Podio was the most influential Spanish theorist of his time. Ramis was barely known or mentioned by Iberian writers, whereas Podio was regularly cited and commended even in the 18th century. In particular, he influenced Gonzalo Martínez de Bizcargui, the other leading Spanish theorist active in the period.

BIBLIOGRAPHY

StevensonSM
J. Ruiz de Lihory, Barón de Alcahalí: *La música in Valencia* (Valencia, 1903)
H. Anglès: 'La notación musical española de la segunda mitad del siglo XV: un tratado desconocido de Guillermo de Podio', *AnM*, ii (1947), 151–73
F.J. León Tello: *Estudios de historia de la teoría musical* (Madrid, 1962/R)

F.J. LEÓN TELLO

Podius, Franciscus. See DEL POMO, FRANCESCO.

Podles, Ewa (*b* Warsaw, 26 April 1952). American mezzo-soprano of Polish birth. She studied at Warsaw State Music High School and won prizes at competitions in Moscow, Toulouse, Barcelona and Rio de Janeiro. Engaged at the Wielki Theatre, Warsaw, she sang roles ranging from Cenerentola to Konchakovna (*Prince Igor*). In 1984 she sang Rosina at Aix-en-Provence and made her Metropolitan début as Handel's Rinaldo. Between 1985 and 1989 she sang Cornelia in *Giulio Cesare* in Rome, Malcolm (*La donna del lago*) in Trieste and Adalgisa in Vancouver. She made her Covent Garden début in 1990 as Hedwige (*Guillaume Tell*) and her début at La Scala as Ragonde (*Le comte Ory*) in 1991, the year she also sang Delilah at the Opéra Bastille and Arsace (*Semiramide*) at La Fenice. In 1997 she performed and recorded the title role of Handel's *Ariodante* with Les Musiciens du Louvre. Her flexible, rich-toned voice, very individual in timbre, is ideal for the Rossini coloratura contralto roles, notably Tancredi, which she has sung at

La Scala (1993) and recorded to acclaim. Podles is also admired as a concert singer, in works such as Verdi's Requiem and *Das Lied von der Erde*, and is an accomplished recitalist, as can be heard on a vivid recording of Russian songs.

ELIZABETH FORBES

Podprocký, Jozef (*b* Žakarovce, 10 June 1944). Slovak composer. After attending secondary school in Gelnica he studied the piano and composition at the Košice Conservatory (1961–5). He then continued his composition studies with Cikker and Alexander Moyzes at the Academy of Performing Arts, Bratislava, and after graduating in 1970 returned to Košice, where he was appointed theory and composition lecturer at the conservatory.

Initially, his sources of inspiration were home-grown. This was clear from his adherence to the traditions of the Slovak school and in his attempting to find a new, creative approach to folklore. These beginnings were later transformed, effected by an interest in Bartókian technique and the rational principles of the Second Viennese School. His ideal is homogenous composition based on traditional processes, employing a musical vocabulary that builds upon the achievements of the avant garde of the inter-war period. His work also reflects a developing interest in east Slovakian folklore and the classical music tradition of his region. Among his best works are a series of string quartets inspired by Bartók.

WORKS
(selective list)

Orch: Dialóg, op.2, hn, hp, str, 1964; Dramatická štúdia, op.9/1, 1967, rev. 1978; Concertino, op.11, vn, str, 1970; . . . aere perennius momentum . . . , ov., op.16, 1973; Koncertantná partita, op.19, org, orch, 1975; Symfónia v 2 častiach [Sym. in 2 movts], op.30, 1987; Zvony [Bells], op.31, 1991; Conc. piccolo, op.32, accdn, timp, str, 1991

Vocal: Ave Maria, op.7/2, 1v, org/str, 1966, rev. 1990; Vesper dominicae (I. Krasko), op.7/1, Bar, fl, hp, 2 vn, va, vc, 1966; Reverzie 'Hommage à Schönberg', op.12, Bar, accdn, 1972; 2 kavatíny (R. Thákur), op.22, B, fl, cl, va, vc, 1980; Ave verum corpus, op.34/4, SATB, 1992; Missa slovaca, op.35, 1v, org, 1993; Fire, Fire (madrigal paraphrase), op.26/2, S, cl, str, 1994 [after T. Morley]

Chbr and solo inst: Variations, op.3, str qt, 1964; Fugue and 4 Inventions, pf, 1965; Pf Sonata, C, op.4, 1965; Expresie, op.6, vn, va, 1966; Sempre solo, sonata, op.5, fl, 1966; Divertimento, op.10, wind qnt, 1969; Str Qt no.1, op.15, 1972; Rébusy [Puzzles], op.20, accdn, 1975; Str Qt no.2, op.21, 1976; Reminiscentio sopra F.X. Zomb, op.24, org, 1979; Str Qt no.3 'Hommage à Bartók', op.27, 1981; Str Qt no.4, op.37, 1994

Principal publisher: OPUS

VLADIMÍR GODÁR

Poe, Edgar Allan (*b* Boston, MA, 19 Jan 1809; *d* Baltimore, 7 Oct 1849). American writer. Beyond its bizarre and macabre surface, his work consistently reveals a concern with neurotic states, with frequent hints of interpretation in Freudian terms. This, and his technique of symbol and suggestion, recommended his writings to many composers at the turn of the century. Debussy and Ravel claimed that they were more influenced by Poe than by any music or composer. Debussy, who was fascinated by the tales in Baudelaire's translation, planned a work based on *The Fall of the House of Usher* at least as early as 1890; 18 years later he was projecting this (with *The Devil in the Belfry*) as a double bill for the New York Metropolitan. Poe's influence involves not just vocal settings of texts but a literary philosophy shaping a musical one, something far more intricate and mysterious. His advocacy of

technical refinement and unity of atmosphere, as well as uncompromising anti-didacticism, attracted a variety of composers, including Rachmaninoff, Schmitt, Ireland, Milhaud, Messiaen and Rouders. Poe's view of music as 'suggestive and indefinite' – 'sensations which bewilder while they enthral' – bears comparison with that of the symbolists. The sympathy he found between musical sounds and mental states is most fully expounded in *The Bells*, which inspired Rachmaninoff's choral symphony of the same name; a similar link is also found in the linking of the sensitive and troubled Roderick Usher with the vibrating strings of a guitar. The most European of American writers, Poe magnetized first European composers, but in the later 20th century he inspired settings by numerous Americans, including Bernstein, Charles Sanford Skilton, George Crumb, Leonard Slatkin, Philip Glass and Deborah Drattell.

BIBLIOGRAPHY
GroveO (B.R. Pollin)
M.G. Evans: *Music and Edgar Allan Poe* (Baltimore, 1939/R)
E. Lockspeiser: *Debussy et Edgar Poe: manuscrits et documents inédits* (Monaco, 1962) [incl. lib, scenario and sketches by Debussy for Poe operas]
B.R. Pollin: 'More Music to Poe', *ML*, liv (1973), 391–404
R. Orledge: *Debussy and the Theater* (Cambridge, MA, 1982)
B.R. Pollin: 'Music and Poe: a Second Annotated Check List', *Poe Studies*, xv (1982), 7–13, 42
J. Sullivan: 'New Worlds of Terror: the Legacy of Poe', *New World Symphonies* (New Haven, CT, 1999), 61–94

PAUL GRIFFITHS/JACK SULLIVAN

Poelchau, Georg Johann Daniel (*b* Kremon, nr Riga, 23 June 1773; *d* Berlin, 12 Aug 1836). German music collector. He studied at Jena University (1792–6) and from 1798 worked as a solo tenor, concert organizer and singing teacher in Hamburg. After his marriage with Amalie Manicke, the daughter of a rich Hamburg aristocrat (1811), he devoted himself to his music collection. In 1813 he moved to Berlin; from 1814 he was a member of the Sing-Akademie. He travelled extensively to enlarge his collection and corresponded with other collectors, especially Aloys Fuchs and R.G. Kiesewetter, and he was director of the library of the Sing-Akademie from 1833.

Poelchau started a general collection of manuscripts in his youth. Later he concentrated on music, dividing his collection into four sections: books on music from the 15th–17th centuries; printed music from the 16th–17th and the 18th–19th centuries; and music manuscripts. He also collected letters by and portraits of musicians. As the owner of many Bach manuscripts he played an important role in the emerging Bach renaissance; he also possessed autographs by Handel, Haydn, Mozart and Beethoven and many manuscripts of works by Keiser, J.H. Rolle, Telemann and others. A series of editions from his collection was begun in 1811 with Bach's *Magnificat* BWV243a. Poelchau offered his collection to the Prussian government in 1823, but it was only in 1841, after his death, that his son Hermann sold it to the Königliche Bibliothek, Berlin (now in *D-Bsb*; some items, including many early prints, in *PL-Kj*).

BIBLIOGRAPHY
MGG1 (W. Virneisel)
P. Kast: *Die Bach-Handschriften der Berliner Staatsbibliothek* (Trossingen, 1958)
K. Engler: 'Georg Poelchau in Göttingen', *GfMKB: Berlin 1974*, 376–9

K. Engler: *Georg Poelchau und seine Musikaliensammlung: ein Beitrag zur Überlieferung Bachscher Musik in der ersten Hälfte des 19. Jahrhunderts* (Tübingen, 1984)

J. Vyšohlídová: 'Bohemika ve sbírce autografu Státní Knihovny v Berlíne' [Bohemian sources in the autograph collection of the Staatsbibliothek in Berlin], *MMC*, no.32 (1988), 93–149 [with Ger. summary]

KONRAD KÜSTER

Poenicke, Johann Peter. *See* PENIGK, JOHANN PETER.

Poggi, Ansaldo (*b* Villa Fontana di Medicina, nr Bologna, 1893; *d* Bologna, 1984). Italian violin maker. He was taught to make instruments by his father, a woodworker and amateur violin maker. During World War I he served in a military band, and afterwards he returned home and resumed making violins and playing. He received a diploma from the Accademia Filarmonica in Bologna in 1920. His work as a maker came to the attention of Giuseppe Fiorini, then living in Zürich, who accepted him as a pupil. Poggi spent a month in Zürich in 1921, after which he returned to Bologna; he made his famous 12 violins for Fiorini in 1921–2. Poggi himself later divided his career into three periods: self-taught to 1921; study and preparation until 1927; and professional maturity after 1927.

Poggi's workmanship was precise and carefully planned. Most of his instruments were based on the Stradivari model, but some followed Guarneri and some were made to his own pattern. The scrolls are very well cut and usually edged with blacking. The varnish, usually orange-yellow to light orange-red, but sometimes golden yellow, is always bright and shiny. After World War II his instruments have slightly different features. While Poggi was clearly a consummate craftsman, the most noteworthy feature of his violins is their unusually responsive and full tone which makes his instruments much sought after. His instruments were awarded first prizes at the 1925, 1927 and 1929 Rome competitions. Poggi also exhibited a quartet as well as several other individual instruments in the Cremona Exhibition of 1937. He retired officially in 1972, but continued to make instruments until his death.

BIBLIOGRAPHY

VannesE

R. Regazzi: *Ricordo di Ansaldo Poggi* (Bologna, 1994)

G. Carletti: *Ansaldo Poggi, liutaio/Ansaldo Poggi, Violin-Maker* (San Giovanni in Persiceto, 1995)

JAAK LIIVOJA-LORIUS, ROBERTO REGAZZI

Poggi, Francesco (*fl* 1586; *d* 1634). Italian harpsichord and virginal maker. Originally from Venice, he worked in Florence. 19 of his known surviving instruments are virginals, many of them unsigned; two harpsichords have also been identified as his work. His early instruments, dating from 1586 to 1603, are polygonal, thin-cased instruments; thereafter he preferred a thick-cased, rectangular design. Poggi's work is of organological interest because of the large number of instruments, which permits a detailed study of instrument making practices. Four of his surviving unsigned virginals have split sharps (*see* ENHARMONIC KEYBOARD), a feature which enjoyed some popularity in the early 17th century in Florence and Rome.

BIBLIOGRAPHY

BoalchM

D. Wraight and C. Stembridge: 'Italian Split-Keyed Instruments with Fewer than Nineteen Divisions to the Octave', *Performance Practice Review*, vii/2 (1994), 150–81

R.D. Wraight: *The Stringing of Italian Keyboard Instruments c1500–c1650* (diss., Queen's U. of Belfast, 1997), esp. 229–37

DENZIL WRAIGHT

Poggioli, Antonio (*b* Samarugio, Rome, *c*1580; *d* Rome, 10 March 1673). Italian music publisher and book dealer. Described in documents of the period as a 'cartulario' and 'librarius', he built up his publishing concern from a bookdealer's business that he had probably founded himself. It was situated in central Rome (Parione), and his sign, which appears in his publications, was a hammer. Following his marriage in 1607 he had at least four children of whom one, Giovanni (*b* 17 July 1612; *d* 30 Sept 1675), followed his father's occupation. Both father and son were buried at S Maria in Vallicella (the Chiesa Nuova) in Rome.

Antonio Poggioli published most types of instrumental and sacred and secular vocal music, including reprints of Arcadelt, Lupacchino and Tasso, a complete edition of Cifra's motets and important anthologies of motets. His publications date from 1620 to 1668 and represent the work of seven Roman printers, among them Robletti, Masotti, Grignani and Mascardi. Giovanni Poggioli is known only as the editor of the later of the two, slightly different, editions of the *Scelta di motetti* that appear to have been published within days of each other in 1647. The earlier edition, which is not included in RISM, was dedicated by Antonio on 29 July to a 'senatore' and 'consiliario' of Messina and includes motets by composers associated with that city. These are replaced by Roman motets in the later edition, dedicated by Giovanni on 31 July to Paolo Coccia, 'Signore del Poggio Sommavilla'. The *Scelta* was also published, with further changes, at Antwerp by Phalèse in 1652, as *Delectus sacrarum cantionum* (in *GB-Och*; not in RISM). It provides a representative selection of Roman *concertato* motets for two to five voices from the mid-17th century.

BIBLIOGRAPHY

EitnerQ; *GaspariC*, ii, 356; *MGG1* (P. Kast); *SartoriD*

H. Leichtentritt: *Geschichte der Motette* (Leipzig, 1908/R)

P. Kast: 'Biographische Notizen zu römischen Musikern des 17. Jahrhunderts', *AnMc*, no.1 (1963), 38–69, esp. 58

COLIN TIMMS

Pögl, Peregrinus (*b* Sandau, nr Magdeburg, 1 March 1711; *d* Neustadt am Main, 15 Nov 1788). German composer. He entered the Benedictine monastery at Neustadt am Main in 1735. He was a prolific composer of church music, but only two of his many publications appear to have survived. He was regarded by his contemporaries as a leading church composer, but his surviving publications suggest that this reputation was exaggerated. In his *Antiphonale marianum* (1763) the vocal solos are heavily decorated in an instrumental rather than a vocal idiom, and the quality of musical invention is not commensurate with their technical difficulty. The choral writing in this volume is repetitive and dull in texture. In general, Pögl's music lacks rhythmic life and his attempts to use chromatic harmony are rarely successful.

WORKS

Obiectum pinnarum tactilium, op.1 (Neustadt am Main, 1746), 6 trio sonatas

Sacrificium Deo vespertinum, 4vv, 2 vn, org, op.3 (Bamberg, 1747), 4 vespers

Incensum dignum in odorum, 4vv, 2 vn, org, op.5 (Neustadt, 1754), 19 offs

Antiphonale marianum, 4vv, 2 vn, 2 clarinos, org, vc, op.7 (Neustadt, 1763), 32 ants

6 masses: the title-page of the only extant volume in *D-Mbs* is missing; perhaps these form op.2, 4 or 6

ELIZABETH ROCHE

Poglietti, Alessandro [Boglietti, Alexander de] (*b* ?Tuscany, early 17th century; *d* Vienna, July 1683). Austrian composer and organist of Italian birth. He may have received his musical training in either Rome or Bologna. He later settled in Vienna. At the beginning of 1661 he is known to have been organist and Kapellmeister to the Jesuits at the church 'Zu den neun Engelschören'. On 1 July of the same year he was appointed court and chamber organist in the Kapelle of the Emperor Leopold I. He was very highly regarded as a teacher of keyboard playing and composition, and monks came from all over Austria to be taught by him. He formed particularly close ties with the Benedictine abbey at Göttweig, Lower Austria, where he occasionally stayed as a guest, and it was there in 1677 that his only known opera, *Endimione festeggiante*, was performed, on the occasion of a visit by the emperor. He also enjoyed the friendship of Count Anton Franz von Collalto and the Prince-bishop of Olomouc; in 1672 he inherited large estates near their residences at Brtnice and Kroměříž. He was held in such esteem that the emperor raised him to the ranks of the aristocracy, and the pope created him a Knight of the Golden Spur. He lost his life during the siege of Vienna by the Turks.

Poglietti is primarily important for his keyboard music. After Froberger and together with Kerll he represents one of the most vital links between Frescobaldi and composers of the late Baroque era such as J.S. Bach, Handel, Fux and Gottlieb Muffat. His sketchbook (see Riedel, 1968), and his *Compendium oder kurtzer Begriff, und Einführung zur Musica* (1676) offer guidance to students of 17th-century keyboard playing and an introduction to the art of composition. The 12 ricercares, many copies of which have survived, belong to the series of significant contrapuntal compositions that started with Frescobaldi's *Fiori musicali* (1635) and ended with Bach's *Die Kunst der Fuge* and were regarded as models of the strict style. Poglietti was particularly interested in musical imitations. In his *Compendium* he noted down many themes for 'all manner of capriccios, variously imitating on an instrument the songs of birds and other sounds'. They occur in the section in which he is concerned with the imitation of natural sounds (e.g. nightingale, canary, cuckoo, cock and hen) and of the sounds of bells, work and war. Many pieces by him on such themes have survived, for example *Über das Henner-und Hannergeschrei, Teutsch Trommel und Franzoik Trommel* and battle music such as the *Toccatina sopra la ribellione di Ungheria* (1671) and the *Toccata fatta sopra l'assedio di Filippsburgo* (1676). *Rossignolo*, a cycle dedicated to the Emperor Leopold I in 1677 on the occasion of his marriage to his third wife, Eleonora, is specially rich in programmatic movements. It is mainly musical instruments that Poglietti imitated here, though he also used elements from the folk music of particular countries and regions, often cleverly stylized, as in *Böhmisch Dudlsack, Hollandisch Flagolett, Französische Baiselements, Pollnischer Sablschertz, Soldaten Schwebelpfeif, Ungarische Geigen* and *Steyermarckher Horn*. The keyboard writing in these pieces is unusually full and brilliant. By virtue of its overall structure, symbolic content and skilful handling of form and variation technique, *Rossignolo* must rank as one of the most important cycles in the literature of keyboard music.

WORKS

VOCAL
in CZ-KRa, unless otherwise stated

Endimione festeggiante (op, J. Dizent), Göttweig, 12 Jan 1677
Missa, 4vv; Missa, 5vv, insts; Missa, 3vv, vn, bc, 1680
Requiem aeternam
Magnificat, 3vv, vn, org
Litaniae Lauretanae, 8vv, insts
Ave regina coelorum, 5vv
2 motets, 5, 8vv, insts

INSTRUMENTAL
Toccatina sopra la ribellione di Ungheria, kbd, 1671 [with dance movts]; ed. in DTÖ, xxvii, Jg.xiii/2 (1906/R)
Toccata fatta sopra l'assedio di Filippsburgo, kbd, 1676
Rossignolo, kbd, 1677; ed. in DTÖ, xxvii, Jg.xiii/2 (1906/R); facs. in 17th Century Keyboard Music, vi (1987)
Toccata del 7. tono, kbd [with canzon and dance movts]
12 ricercares, kbd; ed. in Die Orgel, ii/5–6 (Lippstadt, 1957)
Many suites, canzonas, capriccios, short preludes and fugues, kbd; 2 suites, facs. in 17th Century Keyboard Music, xvii (1987), xxiii (1988); some ed. W.E. Nettles, *Alessandro Poglietti: Harpsichord Music* (University Park, PA, and London, 1966); ed. E. Fadini, *Alessandro Poglietti: composizioni per il cembalo* (Milan, 1984); 3 pieces ed. S. Wollenberg in Faber Early Organ Series, xv (1989)
8 sonatas, many balletti, str insts; selections in DTÖ, lxvi, Jg. xxviii/2 (1921/R)
For sources see Riedel, 1960

THEORETICAL WORKS
only those on music

Compendium oder kurtzer Begriff, und Einführung zur Musica, 1676, *A-KR*
Regulae compositionis (for sources see Federhofer)

BIBLIOGRAPHY

A. Koczirz: 'Zur Lebensgeschichte Alexander de Pogliettis', *SMw*, iv (1916), 116–27
P. Nettl: 'Die Wiener Tanzkomposition in der zweiten Hälfte des 17. Jahrhunderts', *SMw*, viii (1921), 45–175
G. Frotscher: *Geschichte des Orgelspiels und der Orgelkomposition* (Berlin, 1935–6/R, mus. suppl. 1966), 479ff
A. Kellner: *Musikgeschichte des Stiftes Kremsmünster* (Kassel, 1956), 245
H. Federhofer: 'Zur handschriftlichen Überlieferung der Musiktheorie in Österreich in der zweiten Hälfte des 17. Jahrhunderts', *Mf*, xi (1958), 264–79
R. Pečman: 'Lidové taneční motivy v Pogliettiho suitě *Rossignolo*', *Sborník prací filosofické fakulty brněnské university*, ix, F4 (1960), 47–60
F.W. Riedel: *Quellenkundliche Beiträge zur Geschichte der Musik für Tasteninstrumente in der zweiten Hälfte des 17. Jahrhunderts* (Kassel, 1960, 2/1990), 80ff, 142ff
F.W. Riedel: 'Neue Mitteilungen zur Lebensgeschichte von Alessandro Poglietti und Johann Kaspar Kerll', *AMw*, xix–xx (1962–3), 124–42
F.W. Riedel: 'Alessandro Pogliettis Oper *Endimione*', *Festschrift Hans Engel*, ed. H. Heussner (Kassel, 1964), 298–313
W. Apel: *Geschichte der Orgel- und Klaviermusik bis 1700* (Kassel, 1967), 551ff; (Eng. trans., rev., 1972), 566ff
C.D. Harris: *Keyboard Music in Vienna during the Reign of Leopold I, 1658–1705* (diss., U. of Michigan, 1967)
J. Sehnal: 'Die Musikkapelle des Olmützer Bischofs Karl Liechtenstein-Castelcorn in Kremsier', *KJb*, li (1967), 79–123
C.D. Harris: 'Viennese Keyboard Music at Mid-Baroque', *The Diapason*, lx/6 (1968), 18–21
H. Knaus: *Die Musiker im Archivbestand des kaiserlichen Obersthofmeisteramtes (1637–1705)* (Vienna, 1968)
F.W. Riedel: 'Ein Skizzenbuch von Alessandro Poglietti', *Essays in Musicology: a Birthday Offering for Willi Apel*, ed. H. Tischler (Bloomington, IN, 1968), 145–52
S. Wollenberg: *Viennese Keyboard Music in the Reign of Karl VI* (diss., U. of Oxford, 1975)
C. Lunelli: 'Una raccolta manoscritta seicentesca di danze e partite per cembalo nella Biblioteca Comunale di Trento', *L'Organo*, xvi (1978), 55–75
J.R. Shannon: *Organ Literature of the 17th Century* (Raleigh, 1978)

R. R. Pečman: 'Volkstanzmotive in Pogliettis Suite *Rossignolo*', *Tanz und Musik im ausgehenden 17. und im 18. Jahrhundert: Blankenburg, Harz, 1991*, 112–18

FRIEDRICH W. RIEDEL/SUSAN WOLLENBERG

Pogorelich, Ivo (*b* Belgrade, 20 Oct 1958). Croatian pianist. He studied at the Tchaikovsky Conservatory in Moscow (1975–8), where his most influential teacher was Aliza Kezeradze, whom he subsequently married. Pogorelich first came to wide public notice when Martha Argerich resigned from the jury of the 1980 Warsaw International Chopin Competition in protest at his elimination. He gave a notable début recital in New York's Carnegie Hall in 1981 and settled in Britain in 1982. Pogorelich is a virtuoso performer, capable of producing a vast tonal palette, although his interpretations can sometimes be marred by eccentricities of tempo and rubato. His wide repertory ranges from Bach and Scarlatti to Prokofiev, while his many recordings include exceptionally refined and brilliant readings of Ravel's *Gaspard de la nuit* and Prokofiev's Sixth Piano Sonata. Active in fundraising for charitable causes and in creating opportunities for young musicians, he was named an Ambassador of Goodwill at UNESCO in 1988. The same year he inaugurated the Bad Wörishofen Festival in Germany, which offers a platform to talented young performers; two years earlier he had established a Young Musicians' Fellowship in Croatia. In 1993 he founded the Ivo Pogorelich International Solo Piano Competition at Pasadena, California.

JESSICA DUCHEN

Ivo Pogorelich, 1982

Pogues, the. Irish folk-rock band. Their leader Shane MacGowan (*b* Kent, 25 Dec 1957) was first in the punk band the Nipple Erectors; as former Irish folk musicians joined the name was changed to Pogue Mahone, later shortened to the Pogues. In London in the early 1980s they became notorious for their excessive drinking and bad manners; they performed at breakneck speed with lyrics yelled out with the ferocity of a punk band, horrifying the folk scene with their treatment of traditional Irish songs. They toured with the Clash and recorded their first album *Red Roses for Me* (Stiff, 1984) which, along with frantic traditional material, included songs such as the 'Dark Streets of London' by MacGowan, who developed into an unexpectedly remarkable lyricist and songwriter; a collection of his lyrics was later published as *Poguetry* (London, 1989). A second album, *Rum, Sodomy and the Lash* (Stiff, 1985), included a rousing but poignant reworking of Ewan MacColl's 'Dirty Old Town', along with MacGowan's brutal but fetching 'A Pair of Brown Eyes', which became a minor hit.

By 1988 the band included Terry Woods from Steeleye Span. They joined with the producer Steve Lillywhite for *If I Should Fall from Grace with God* (EMI), which included the hit single 'Fairytale of New York' by MacGowan and in which he performed with Kirsty MacColl, the daughter of Ewan and wife of Lillywhite. By now MacGowan's drinking was damaging his work; he was unable to appear with the band when they toured with Bob Dylan, and subsequent albums (*Peace and Love*, WEA, 1989, and *Hell's Ditch*, WEA, 1990) were a disappointment. MacGowan left the Pogues in 1991, his place taken first by Joe Strummer from the Clash, and then by the band member Peter 'Spider' Stacy, who sang on the Pogues' album, *Waiting for Herb* (WEA, 1993). MacGowan continued with a new group, the Popes.

ROBIN DENSELOW

Pohanka, Jaroslav (*b* Olešnice, Moravia, 29 June 1924; *d* Brno, 28 April 1964). Czech musicologist. He studied composition, flute and piano at Brno Conservatory (1940–43, 1946–7) and after teaching music at a gymnasium in Brno (1948–50), he became director of a music school in Šlapanice, near Brno (1951–60), and then a research assistant in the music history department of the Moravian Museum (1960–64). He was able to put to use his interest in early Czech music and his extensive knowledge of its sources both in his transcriptions for the ensemble Collegium Musicum Brunense, of which he was co-founder and artistic director, and in his *Dějiny české hudby v příkladech* (1958). This major Czech compilation is a critical edition of basic Czech sources from the earliest times to the first half of the 19th century. In it, just as in the 13 volumes of Musica Antiqua Bohemica which he prepared for publication, Pohanka was responsible for revealing many new sources and bringing to notice a number of neglected composers of worth, such as J.A. Losy, J.K. Tolar and P.J. Vejvanovský. Pohanka's edition of Vejvanovský was intended to supplement a projected monograph on this composer. In his last years his energy was concentrated principally on amassing and working on material for his book *Loutna a její podíl na vývoji instrmentální hudby v Čechách* [The lute and its part in the development of instrumental music in Bohemia], which he left incomplete at his death.

WRITINGS

'Loutnové tabulatury z rajhradského kláštera' [Lute tablatures from the Rajhrad monastery], *ČMm*, xl (1955), 193–203 [with Fr. summary]

'O nejstarších českých skladbách pro loutnu' [The oldest Czech works for lute], *HRo*, viii (1955), 245 only

'Výkonní hudebníci v Brně: příspěvek k sociálnímu postavení hudebníků ve 14. století' [Performing artists in Brno: a note on the social status of musicians in the 14th century], *HRo*, xi (1958), 387 only

'Lidové tance z pozůstalosti Kristiána Hirschmentzla' [Folkdances from the estate of Kristián Hirschmentzl], *Radostná země*, x (1960), 105–11 [with Ger. summary]

'Neznámá kantáta L. van Beethoven?' [An unknown cantata by Beethoven?], *ČMm*, xlvi (1961), 137–44 [also in Ger.]

'Bohemika v zámecké hudební sbírce z Náměště n. Osl.' [Bohemica in the music collection of the castle of Náměšť nad Oslavou], *ČMm*, xlviii (1963), 235–60 [with Ger. summary]

'Historické kořeny české kramářské písně' [The historical roots of Czech fairground songs], *Sborník Václovkova Olomouc 1961* (Prague, 1963), 89–96

EDITIONS

Václav Jan Tomášek: Tre ditirambi op.65, MAB, xxix (1956)

Dějiny české hudby v příkladech [The history of Czech music in examples], DHM, vi (1958)

Jan Antonín Losy: Pièces de guitarre, MAB, xxxviii (1958)

Pavel Josef Vejvanovský: Serenata e sonate per orchestra, MAB, xxxvi (1958); *Composizioni per orchestra*, MAB, xlvii–xlix (1960–61)

Jan Křtitel Tolar: Balletti e sonate, MAB, xl (1959)

Franz Krommer: II quartetti per oboe, MAB, xlii (1959)

Jan Zach: Cinque sinfonie d'archi, MAB, xliii (1960)

Anton Filtz: Sei sinfonie per orchestra op.2, MAB, xliv (1960) [Symphony no.3 is by J.C. Bach]

Georg Benda: Sinfonie, MAB, lviii; lxii; lxvi (1962–5)

Wolfgang Amadeus Mozart: Quartette mit einem Blasinstrument, Neue Ausgabe sämtlicher Werke, viii/20/2 (Kassel, 1962) [K285, 285a, 285b, 298, 370/368b]

BIBLIOGRAPHY

'In memoriam Jaroslava Pohanky', *ČMm*, xlix (1964), 285 only

R[udolf] P[ečman]: 'In memoriam Jaroslava Pohanky', *HRo*, xvii (1964), 468 only

ALENA NĚMCOVÁ

Pohjannoro, Hannu (Einari) (*b* Savonlinna, 4 July 1963). Finnish composer. He studied composition at the Sibelius Academy in Finland with Rautavaara, Aho and Heininen, graduating in 1996. He supplemented his studies in the winter of 1993–4 in Berlin with Schnebel. He was one of the most promising of young Finnish composers to come before the public in the 1990s. His music has most often a post-serial basis. His output is still small and consists mainly of chamber music and works for tape. His earliest compositions of the 1990s avoid any kind of pomposity, achieving powerful effects by the most delicate means. In particular, the sensitivity of his chamber music – for example in the nonet *eilisen linnut* ('the birds of yesterday', 1994) and *kuvia, heijastuksia* ('images, reflections', 1992) for piano – is as though traced with a silken thread; the influence of Kurtág and Morton Feldman is considerable. Pohjannoro's musical mobility has increased in more recent works, and has become more classical and linear, as in the orchestral work *korkeina aamujen kaaret* ('lofty the arches of morning', 1996). His imagination springs at its most free in the work for bass clarinet and tape *saari, rannaton* ('island, shoreless', 1994).

WORKS

matkalla [travelling], nocturno, fl, 1991; välähdyksiä [glimpses], 7 miniatures, vc, 1992; kuvia, heijastuksia [images, reflections], pf, 1992; röyhkeinä nousevat hiljaisuudesta, varjot jäävät [haughtily they rise from silence, only the shadows remain], tape, 1992, rev. 1994; viides vuodenaika [fifth season], accdn, pf, 1993; Berlin Experiment, any ens, 1993; eilisen linnut [the birds of yesterday],

chbr ens, 1993–4; saari, rannaton [island, shoreless], b cl, tape, 1994; valo jäätynyt, kaukana tuuli [frozen the light, far away the wind], fl, vc, pf, 1994–5; korkeina aamujen kaaret [lofty the arches of morning], orch, 1995–6; valon jälkiä äänet [sounds, traces of light], fl, cl, gui, vc, 1996; maan väreiksi taipuu valo [into the colours of earth bends the light], kantele, perc, 1997; Str Qt 'syksyn huoneet' [the rooms of autumn], 1997

OSMO TAPIO RÄIHÄLÄ

Pohjola, Seppo (*b* Espoo, nr Helsinki, 4 May 1965). Finnish composer. He belongs to one of the most celebrated musical families in Finland: his father is the choral conductor Erkki Pohjola, his aunt is the pianist Liisa Pohjola and his cousin the conductor Sakari Oramo. Seppo Pohjola is, however, the family's only composer of any repute. He studied composition at the Sibelius Academy in Helsinki with Heininen and Jokinen. He came before the public at the beginning of the 1990s and quickly gained a foothold in Finnish musical life. Like many of his contemporaries he has concentrated on instrumental and chamber music, moving with each work into various stylistic spheres. His two string quartets, for example, are very different: the first (1991) reveals the influence of Ligeti; the second (1995), with its hammering rhythmic motifs, could be described as an Expressionist work. In his recent compositions, Pohjola has moved away from a post-serial style, aiming at more of a Romantic and Impressionist sound. The text that he wrote to accompany *Game Over* (1996) stresses that there is no question of modernist composition in this chamber work, and that its sound ideal is, rather, one of Mendelssohnian Romanticism. In his largest composition to date, *Vae Victis* (1997) for orchestra, Pohjola consciously draws near to the sound-world of Debussy.

WORKS

3 Pieces for Str Trio, 1987; Str Qt no.1, 1989–91; Splendori, pf, 1991; Pixilated, 1992; Gimla, accdn, pf, 1993; Daimonion, chbr orch, 1994; Balletto per 10, chbr orch, 1994; Str Qt no.2, 1995; Pf Qt, 1996; Game Over, fl/pic, cl/b cl, pf, perc, vn, va, vc, 1996; Vae Victis, orch, 1997; Taika, orch, 1999; Vinha, orch, 1999

OSMO TAPIO RÄIHÄLÄ

Pohl, Carl Ferdinand (*b* Darmstadt, 6 Sept 1819; *d* Vienna, 28 April 1887). German music historian, organist and composer. He came from a musical family, his grandfather having been a maker of glass harmonicas, his father (*d* 1869) chamber musician to the Duke of Hesse-Darmstadt, and his mother a daughter of the composer Bečvařovský. He was trained as an engraver, but in 1841 he settled in Vienna and after studying under Sechter became in 1849 organist of the new Protestant church in the Gumpendorf suburb. His compositions, of which at least 14 collections of songs and keyboard pieces were printed, date mostly from these years. In 1855 he resigned his post for reasons of health and devoted himself thereafter to teaching and writing.

In 1862 he published a pamphlet on the history of the glass harmonica. From 1863 to 1866 he lived in London, occupied in research at the British Museum on Haydn and Mozart; the result was *Mozart und Haydn in London*, a work whose accurate detail makes it still very useful. In 1866, through the influence of Jahn, Köchel and others, Pohl was appointed archivist and librarian to the Gesellschaft der Musikfreunde in Vienna. As custodian of the society's large collections he produced monographs describing their history and extent, and collaborated with Haberl and A. Lagerberg in Eitner's *Bibliographie der Musik-Sammelwerke* (1877). Pohl was also an active music critic and opposed many of Hanslick's views. By far his most important work was the biography of Haydn, which he undertook at the instigation of Jahn, and whose final volume was completed after his death. Although it contains errors and omissions, Pohl's work has nevertheless remained the basis for all serious Haydn biographies since its publication.

WRITINGS

Zur Geschichte der Glas-Harmonica (Vienna, 1862; Eng. trans., 1862)

Mozart und Haydn in London (Vienna, 1867/R)

Die Gesellschaft der Musikfreunde des österreichischen Kaiserstaates und ihr Conservatorium (Vienna, 1871)

Denkschrift aus Anlass des hundertjährigen Bestehens der Tonkünstler-Societät ... in Wien (Vienna, 1871)

Gebäude und Kunstsammlungen der Gesellschaft der Musikfreunde (Vienna, 1872)

Joseph Haydn, i (Berlin, 1875); ii (Leipzig, 1882); iii (Leipzig, 1927/R) [completed by H. Botstiber]

Denkschrift aus Anlass des fünfundzwanzigjährigen Bestehens des Singvereines der Gesellschaft der Musikfreunde (Vienna, 1883)

Festschrift aus Anlass der Feier des 25jährigen ununterbrochenen Bestandes der im Jahre 1842 gegründeten Philharmonischen Concerte in Wien (Vienna, 1885)

Articles and reviews in *AMZ, MMR, Jb des Conservatoriums der Gesellschaft der Musikfreunde, ADB, Grove1* and many others

BIBLIOGRAPHY

ADB (E. Mandyczewski)

P. Spitta: 'Joseph Haydn in der Darstellung C.F. Pohl's', *Zur Musik: Sechzehn Aufsätze* (Berlin, 1892/R), 151–76

K. Geiringer: 'Der Brahms-Freund C.F. Pohl: unbekannte Briefe ... an Johannes Brahms', *ZfM*, Jg.102 (1935), 397–9

J.P. Larsen: *Die Haydn-Überlieferung* (Copenhagen, 1939)

F. Krautwurst: 'Aus der Frühgeschichte der Schubert-Forschung: Briefe von Carl Ferdinand Pohl und Max Friedlaender', *Neues musikwissenschaftliches Jb*, ii (1993), 91–111

FRANZ GEHRING/BRUCE CARR

Pohl, David. *See* POHLE, DAVID.

Pohl, Richard (*b* Leipzig, 12 Sept 1826; *d* Baden-Baden, 17 Dec 1896). German critic and translator. He studied philosophy, chemistry and physics in Karlsruhe, Göttingen and Leipzig, and was given basic musical training by E.F. Wenzel in Leipzig. There he made friends with Schumann; he later planned an oratorio on Luther with Schumann, wrote for him the linking text for the concert version of *Manfred* and helped with other texts. In 1852 he moved to Dresden, where he worked as a private teacher and wrote for Brendel's *Neue Zeitschrift für Musik* under the pseudonym 'Hoplit' (a reference to the heavily armed infantry of ancient Greece). Already a committed Wagnerian (he prided himself in being called 'der älteste Wagnerianer' by Wagner himself), he became the declared voice of Wagner, Liszt, Berlioz and other progressive musicians of the New German School; all three composers were his friends. During his years in Weimar (1854–63), Pohl helped Brendel edit the *Neue Zeitschrift für Musik* and the *Angregungen für Kunst, Leben und Wissenschaft* (1856–61). Pohl actually came to Weimar as a result of the appointment to the court orchestra of his first wife, the harp virtuoso Johanna Eyth (*b* Karlsruhe, 19 March 1824; *d* Baden-Baden, 25 Nov 1870). Liszt later expressed his gratitude for Pohl's 'faithful and noble devotion ... to the Weimar Progressive Period in the years 1849–58' (letter of 12 September 1884). Wagner was appreciative of Pohl's championship; later, however, coolness arose over Pohl's published view that Wagner had derived his chromatic harmony in *Tristan* from Liszt. Though not a particularly insightful

critic (he was accused of being a 'scribbler'), Pohl worked hard and proved himself to be a reliable partisan, doing much to arouse interest in his chosen composers. Particularly valuable were his German translations of Berlioz's prose writings and some of Liszt's articles from the 1850s. He also wrote some poetry, a novel (*Richard Wiegand*) based on Wagner, some songs and instrumental pieces. In 1864 he retired to Baden-Baden.

WRITINGS

Akustische Briefe (Leipzig, 1853)

Das Karlsruher Musikfest (Leipzig, 1853)

Die Tonkünstler-Versammlung zu Leipzig (Leipzig, 1859)

Bayreuther Erinnerungen (Leipzig, 1877)

'Erinnerungen an Robert Schumann', *Deutsche Revue*, ii (1878), 169–81, 306–17

'Autobiographisches', *Musikalisches Wochenblatt*, xii (1881), 3, 15–17, 26–7, 39–40, 56, 67–8

Gesammelte Schriften über Musik und Musiker (Leipzig, 1883–4/R) [3 vols.: Wagner, Liszt, Berlioz]

Die Höhenzüge der musikalischen Entwickelung (Leipzig, 1888)

'Bülows Briefe', *Neue deutsche Rundschau*, v (1894), 446–76, 578–94, 783–801

ed. L. Pohl: *Hector Berlioz' Leben und Werke* (Leipzig, 1900) [based on material by R. Pohl]

Texts for Schumann (*Manfred*) and Liszt (*Prometheus*); Ger. trans. of Berlioz's collected writings (Leipzig, 1864) and Saint-Saëns (*Samson et Dalila*)

ed. L. Pohl: *Richard Wiegand: Episoden aus dem Leben eines grossen Musikers* (Braunschweig, 1904)

BIBLIOGRAPHY

H.R. Schäfer: 'Der älteste Wagnerianer', *Neue Musik-Zeitung*, xiv (1893), 211–12

A. Seidl: 'Richard Pohl', *Bayreuther Blätter*, xx (1897), 116–21

O. Kitzler: *Musikalische Erinnerungen mit Briefen von Wagner, Brahms, Bruckner und Richard Pohl* (Brno, 1904)

H. Schorn: 'Richard Pohl', *NZM*, Jg83 (1916), 393–5

S. Hartlaub-Pohl: *Richard Pohl (1826–1896): ein Lebensbild* (Baden-Baden, 1967)

J. Thym: 'Schumann in Brendel's *Neue Zeitschrift für Musik* from 1845 to 1856', *Mendelssohn and Schumann*, ed. J.W. Finson and R.L. Todd (Durham, NC, 1984), 21–36

JOHN WARRACK/JAMES DEAVILLE

Pohle [Pohl, Pohlen, Pole, Pol, Bohle], **David** (*b* Marienberg, nr Chemnitz, 1624; *d* Merseburg, 20 Dec 1695). German composer and instrumentalist. He received his musical training from Schütz at Dresden. He worked for short periods at the courts at Dresden, Merseburg (as an instrumentalist between 1648 and 1649), Kassel (about 1650), Weissenfels, Zeitz and Merseburg again (all during the 1650s) before settling at Halle, where he became Kapellmeister in 1660. At Halle he composed and directed many large masses and sacred concertos at the cathedral and wrote at least seven Singspiels, most of them to texts by the court secretary, David Elias Heidenreich. Between 1674 and 1677 he also worked at the related courts at Weissenfels and Zeitz. He was Kapellmeister at Zeitz from 1678, and when the Halle court was transferred to Weissenfels in 1680 he was replaced as its Kapellmeister by J.P. Krieger, who in 1678 had been appointed his assistant. He remained at Zeitz until 1682, when he moved to a similar position at Merseburg; he remained there until his death. He published none of his music, and much of it is lost. The earliest surviving pieces are the arias to strophic poems by Paul Fleming composed at Kassel in 1650. Most of his other extant vocal music is sacred; it shows his strong preference for Latin texts, both biblical and non-biblical, which he set as concertos for few voices. Between 1663 and 1664 he composed cantatas for the entire church year, each consisting of a concerto based on a biblical verse combined with an aria to a strophic ode by Heidenreich. The one extant work from this cycle, *Siehe, es hat überwunden der Löwe*, offers an early example – although not the first – of a concerto-aria cantata (see Frandsen). Pohle's sonatas are distinguished by cantabile melody, rich harmony and a dark sound resulting from scoring that favours the middle and lower instruments.

WORKS

SACRED LATIN VOCAL

Amo te Deus, 3vv, 3 insts, bc, *D-Dl*, *S-Uu*
Benedicam Dominum (2 versions), 2vv, 3 insts, bc, *Uu*
Bonum est, 3vv, bc, *Uu*
Diligam te Domine, 1v, 2 insts, bc, *D-Kl*
Domine ostende, 5vv, 5 insts, bc, *S-Uu*; ed. B. Grusnick (Neuhausen-Stuttgart, 1976)
Domine quis, 4vv, 5 insts, bc, *Uu*
In te Domine speravi, 3vv, 3 insts, bc, *Uu*
Jesus auctor, 3vv, 2 insts, bc, *Uu*
Jesu care, 1v, 2 insts, bc, *Uu*
Miserere mei Deus, 5vv, 5 insts, bc, *D-Kl*
Nascitur Immanuel, 5vv, 5 insts, bc, *Dl*
Oculi mei, 3vv, 2 insts, bc, *S-Uu*
Paratum cor, 1v, 2 insts, bc, *Uu*
Te sanctum, 5vv, 7 insts, bc, *Uu*
Tulerunt Dominum, dialogue, 6vv, 6 insts, bc, *Uu*
Verbum caro factum est, 3vv, 2 insts, bc, *Uu* (anon.)
Vox Domini, 1v, 2 insts, bc, *Uu*

SACRED GERMAN VOCAL

Der Engel des Herrn, 4vv, 4 insts, bc, *Uu*
Es wird ein Stern aus Jacob aufgehen, 4vv, 3 insts, bc, *D-Bsb*
Herr, wenn ich nur dich habe, 1v, 5 insts, bc, *Bsb*
Herr, wenn ich nur dich habe, 3vv, 3 insts, bc, *S-Uu*; ed. H.J. Moser (Stuttgart, 1964)
Ihr Völker bringet her, 3vv, 3 insts, bc, *D-Bsb*
Jesu, meine Freude, 4vv, 3 insts, bc, *Bsb*, *Kll*
Nur in meines Jesu Wunden, 6vv, 6 insts, bc, *S-Uu*
Siehe, es hat überwunden der Löwe, 5vv, 7 insts, bc, *D-Bsb*, *Kll*
Wie der Hirsch schreiet, 1v, 3 insts, bc, *S-Uu*; ed. U. Herrmann (Neuhausen-Stuttgart, 1982)

For lost works see Serauky

SECULAR VOCAL

13 arias (P. Fleming), 2vv, 2 vn, bc, 1650, *D-Kl*; 12 ed. W. Gurlitt, *David Pohle: Zwölf Liebesgesänge nach Paul Flemming* (Kassel, 1938)
Kein Augenblick vergeht, madrigal, 3vv, bc, *S-Uu*
Marindchen, du siehst hold und schöne, aria, 2vv, 5 insts, bc, *Uu*
Weiss und Schwarz, 2vv, 2 insts, bc, *Uu*

SINGSPIELS

all lost; most librettos by D.E. Heidenreich

Liebe krönt Eintracht, 1669; Der singende Hof-Mann Daniel, 1671; Aspasia, 1672; Der glückselige Liebes-Fehl Prinz Walrams aus Sachsen, 1673; Der verliebte Mörder Herodes, 1673; Die verwechselte Braut, 1675; Das ungereimte Paar Venus und Vulcanus, 1679

INSTRUMENTAL

25 sonatas, a 4–8, bc, *D-Kl*, *S-Uu*; Sonata a 8, C, ed. H. Winter (Hamburg, 1965); Sonata a 6, F, ed. H. Winter (Hamburg, 1968)
2 suites, a 4, *D-Kl*; 1 ed. J. Ecorcheville, *Vingt suites d'orchestre du dix-septième siècle français* (Paris and Berlin, 1906/R)
Ballet, *PL-GD* (lute tablature)

BIBLIOGRAPHY

MeyerMS
W. Serauky: *Musikgeschichte der Stadt Halle*, ii/1 (Halle and Berlin, 1939/R)
C. Engelbrecht: *Die Kasseler Hofkapelle im 17. Jahrhundert* (Kassel, 1958)
F. Krummacher: *Die Überlieferung der Choralbearbeitungen in der frühen evangelischen Kantate* (Berlin, 1965)
G. Gille: *Der Schützschüler David Pohle (1624–1695): seine Bedeutung für die deutsche Musikgeschichte des 17. Jahrhunderts* (diss., U. of Halle, 1973)
G. Gille: 'Die geistliche Vokalmusik David Pohles (1624–1695)', *Musik und Kirche*, xlv (1975), 64–74
G. Gille: 'Der Kantaten-Textdruck von David Elias Heidenreich, Halle 1665, in den Vertonungen David Pohles, Sebastian Knüpfers, Johann Schelles und anderer: Zur Frühgeschichte der Concerto-Aria-Kantate', *Mf*, xxxviii (1985), 81–94
M. Märker: 'David Pohles Weihnachtskantate "Nascitur Immanuel" und die Frühgeschichte der Concerto-Aria-Kantate', *Schütz-Jb*, xvii (1995), 81–96
M.E. Frandsen: 'Albrici, Peranda und die Ursprünge der Concerto-Aria-Kantate in Dresden', *Schütz-Jb*, xviii (1996), 123–39

KERALA J. SNYDER